Indonesia

written and researched by

Stephen Backshall, David Leffman, Lesley Reader and Henry Stedman

with additional contributions from

Arnold Barkhordarian, David Jardine, Lucy Ridout and Graeme Steel

www.roughguides.com

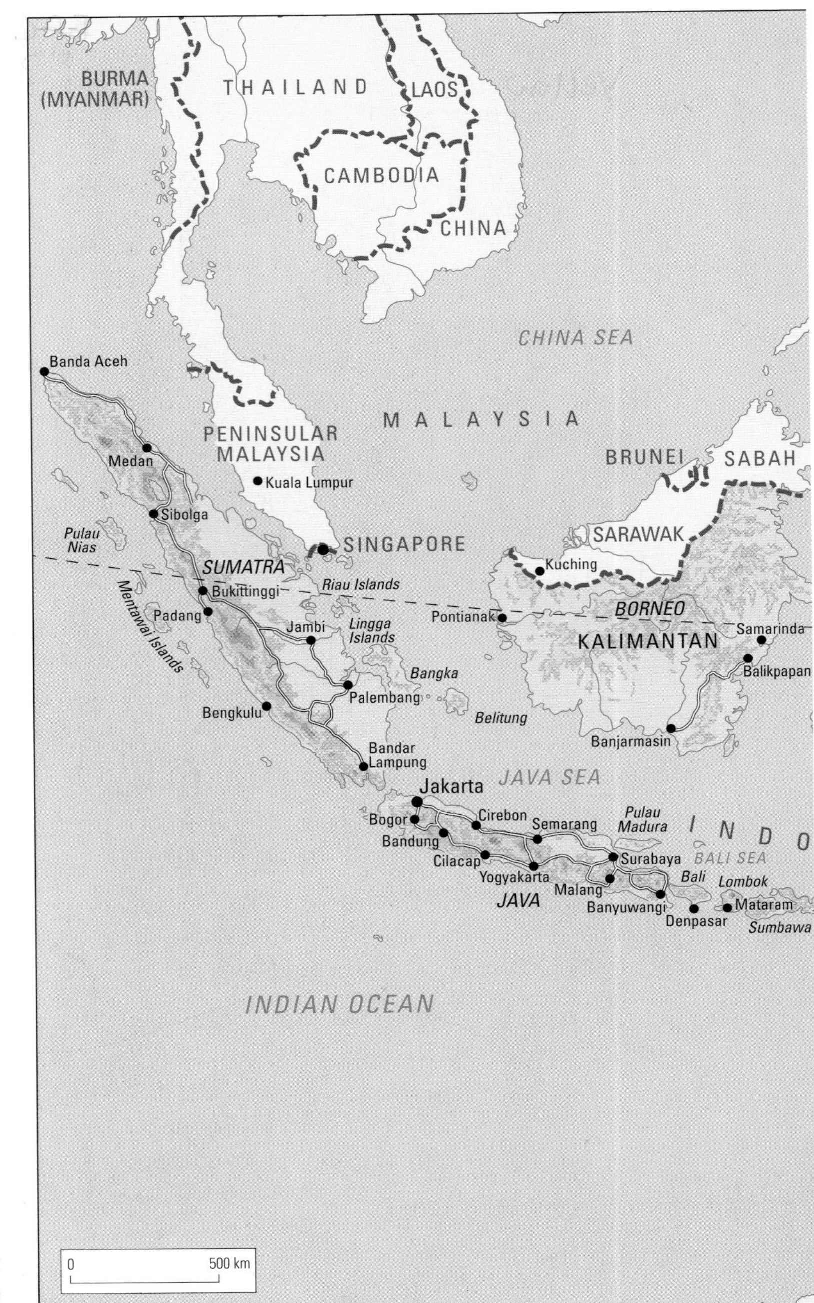
BURMA (MYANMAR)
THAILAND
LAOS
CAMBODIA
CHINA
CHINA SEA
Banda Aceh
MALAYSIA
PENINSULAR MALAYSIA
Medan
BRUNEI
SABAH
Kuala Lumpur
Sibolga
Pulau Nias
SARAWAK
SINGAPORE
SUMATRA
Kuching
Riau Islands
Mentawai Islands
Bukittinggi
Padang
Pontianak
BORNEO
Jambi
Lingga Islands
Samarinda
KALIMANTAN
Balikpapan
Bangka
Palembang
Bengkulu
Belitung
Banjarmasin
Bandar Lampung
JAVA SEA
Jakarta
Bogor
Cirebon
Pulau Madura
Semarang
INDO
Bandung
Surabaya
BALI SEA
Cilacap
Yogyakarta
Malang
Bali
Lombok
JAVA
Banyuwangi
Mataram
Denpasar
Sumbawa
INDIAN OCEAN
0
500 km

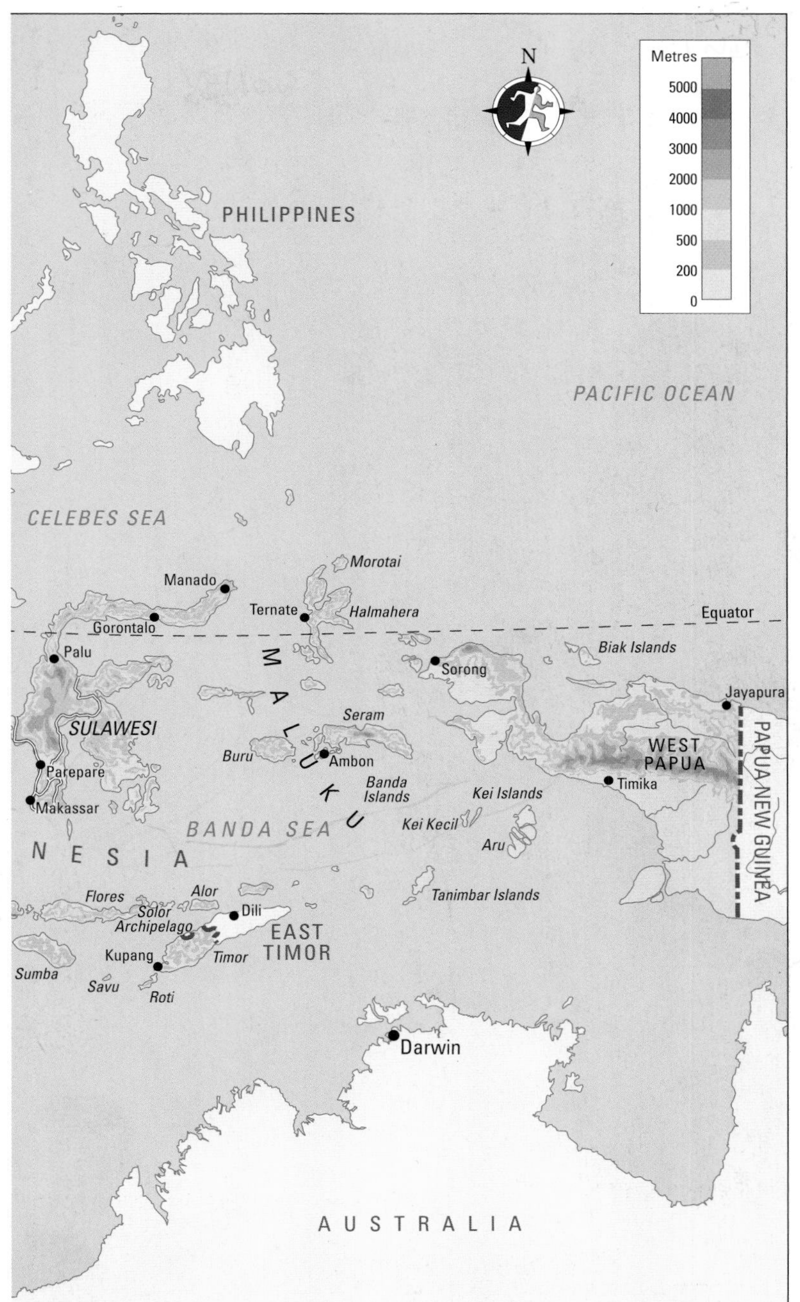

N
Metres
5000
4000
3000
2000
1000
500
200
0
PHILIPPINES
PACIFIC OCEAN
CELEBES SEA
Morotai
Manado
Ternate
Halmahera
Equator
Gorontalo
Palu
MALUKU
Biak Islands
Sorong
Jayapura
Seram
SULAWESI
WEST PAPUA
PAPUA NEW GUINEA
Buru
Ambon
Parepare
Banda Islands
Timika
Kei Islands
Makassar
BANDA SEA
Kei Kecil
Aru
NESIA
Flores
Alor
Tanimbar Islands
Solor Archipelago
Dili
EAST TIMOR
Kupang
Timor
Sumba
Savu
Roti
Darwin
AUSTRALIA

Introduction to

Indonesia

For sheer size, scale and variety, Indonesia is pretty much unbeatable. The country is so enormous that nobody is really sure quite how big it is; there are between 13,000 and 17,000 islands. It's certainly the largest archipelago in the world, spreading over 5200km between the Asian mainland and Australia, all of it within the tropics and with huge areas of ocean separating the landmasses. Not surprisingly, Indonesia's ethnic, cultural and linguistic diversity is correspondingly great – the best estimate is of 500 languages and dialects spoken by around 200 million people.

The largely volcanic nature of the islands has created tall cloud-swept mountains swathed in the green of rice terraces or rainforest, dropping to blindingly bright beaches and vivid blue seas, the backdrop for Southeast Asia's biggest wilderness areas and wildlife sanctuaries. All of this provides an endless resource for adventurous trekking, surfing, scuba diving, or just lounging by a pool in a five-star resort. You'll find that the Indonesians themselves are one of the best reasons to visit the country – despite recent troubles, people are generally very open and welcoming, whether they're sophisticated city dwellers or remote island villagers. The ethnic mix is overwhelming: this is the world's largest Muslim country, but with a distinct local flavour, and there are also substantial populations of Christians, Hindus and animists, whose forms of worship, customs and lifestyles have been influencing each other for centuries.

Worryingly, it is this very religious and racial diversity that in recent years has threatened to unravel the very fabric of Indonesian society. Riots in many parts of the country have pitched Muslims against their Christian neighbours, with two of these battles – in the Maluku Islands and in Poso

Fact file

- Covering more than 1,904,000 square kilometres, including over 13,000 islands, Indonesia is the world's biggest archipelago, its fourth largest country and the largest Muslim nation.
- The population stands at over 225,000,000, with over half living on the island of Java. Highly diverse ethnically, there are more than 350 local languages spoken throughout the islands.
- Draped across the equator between the Indian and Pacific islands, set entirely within the tropics and right on the volcanic ring of fire, Indonesia has a hugely varied landscape, from desert and coral reef to rainforest and snow-capped mountains. Its highest peak, Puncak Jaya in West Papua, stands at 5050m.
- Indonesia's main exports are oil and gas, plywood, textiles, rubber and palm oil.
- Indonesia is a democratic republic. The highest political institution is the People's Consultative Assembly, headed by the president, who is elected by the assembly to serve a term of five years. The 500-strong House of Representatives is made up largely of democratically elected politicians, each representing at least 400,000 citizens.

in Central Sulawesi – developing into full-scale civil wars. On Java and other islands, deep-rooted anti-Chinese sentiment surfaced in particularly bloody fashion in 1998 and continues to smoulder to this day. More localized **ethnic violence** has its source in the transmigration policies of the Indonesian government, whose aim was to settle far-flung areas such as Kalimantan with migrants from overpopulated regions including Java and Madura, often without local consultation and with little heed given to traditional land rights. Unsurprisingly, resentment and violence have sometimes boiled over. However, with a new and popular president, Megawati Sukarnoputri, in power, and the economy finally showing signs of recovery, it is hoped that – while further bloodshed is perhaps inevitable – the fury and frequency of these internecine battles may start to subside.

Indonesia has also been badly battered in recent years by the **separatist struggles** of a couple of its provinces. Despite wide-ranging democratic reforms introduced by Megawati and her predecessor, Gus Dur, two disaffected provinces, Aceh in North Sumatra and West Papua (formerly Irian Jaya), tired of years of repression and corruption, unhappy that the new democratic reforms do not go far enough for their liking, and emboldened by East Timor's successful secession (the former Indonesian province became the world's newest country in 2001), began to clamour for their own **autonomy**, launching bloody uprisings that continue to this day. Whether their respective struggles prove successful – and what will happen to Indonesia if they are – remains to be seen, though with these two provinces lying at the geographical extremes of the archipelago, it's tempting to think that any break from Indonesia will have little adverse effect on the rest of the country.

The terrorist bomb attack in Kuta on Bali in October 2002, while seen by most observers as a tragic one-off, has shown that upheaval and tragedy can strike anywhere in the archipelago. Until this awful event, the targeting of foreigners in Indonesia was extremely rare, and while a few places have been virtually off-limits for a few years now, most of the country remains safe, and the vast majority of the Indonesian people extremely welcoming to visitors. However, it pays to keep abreast of the latest develoments within the country and take heed of any travel warnings issued by your own government. Keeping an ear to the ground for developments and acting with a degree of common sense and sensitivity should be enough to ensure that your own trip to the contry is a safe and enjoyable one.

Give yourself plenty of time to cover the large distances, and allow yourself more than the rock-bottom budget

Travel across the archipelago is pretty unforgettable, in tiny fragile planes, rusty ferries and careering buses. Give yourself plenty of time to cover the large distances; if you only have a couple of weeks, you'll have a better time if you restrict yourself to exploring a small area properly rather than hopping across 3000km to see your top ten sights. If you do have longer, try to plan a trip that doesn't involve too much doubling back, consider an open-jaw international plane ticket, and try to intersperse lengthy journeys with a few days of relaxation in peaceful surroundings. Also, leave yourself some leeway – if you're in a hurry with a vital plane to catch, something is bound to go wrong. Having said all this, the places which are hardest to

Safety in Indonesia

Despite its troubles, there are very few places in Indonesia that are truly off-limits to tourists, the main ones being **Maluku**, the legendary Spice Islands to the east of Sulawesi, and the province of **Aceh** in North Sumatra. For this reason, these two places have been excluded from this edition of the book, though we do provide brief rundowns of their recent troubled histories, and the current situation. Poso, in **Central Sulawesi**, was also out of bounds at the time of research, though a recent peace plan was beginning to show encouraging signs of holding, suggesting that the province may soon open up again. For this reason, Poso and its neighbouring lake have been included in the book, although the accounts have not been updated since the last edition. Other trouble hotspots, such as **West Papua** and **West Timor**, have occasionally been out of bounds to travellers over the past few years, though at the time of research they had reopened and were welcoming foreigners again, and have therefore been thoroughly updated and covered in this book.

reach are often well worth the effort, and some of the most rewarding experiences come when you least expect them. An enforced day's malinger between transport in an apparently dull town might end with an invitation to watch an exorcism, or to examine a collection of ancestor skulls over coffee and cigarettes.

Just as you should give yourself more time than you think you'll need, allow yourself more than the rock-bottom **budget** – even if it means a shorter trip. Indonesia can be very economical, but there's plenty to spend your money on: watching every last rupiah will detract from the enjoyment.

Where to go

Java, with the country's largest cities, industries and highest concentration of people – over sixty percent of the population live here – is the epicentre of modern Indonesia, but also a place of great beauty, its lush volcanic landscape harbouring stately old settlements and splendid temples. Towards the western end of the island is **Jakarta**, the country's overgrown and polluted capital, home to over ten million people and some of Indonesia's finest museums. Outside Jakarta, **West Java** features upmarket beach resorts giving access to the infamous Krakatau volcano; rolling tea plantations around the Puncak Pass; the cultural centre of Bandung; and the popular coastal haven of Pangandaran. Moving

Betel nut

One habit that you're bound to notice in rural Indonesia is the chewing of pinang, or betel. These small pellets are made up of three essential ingredients – sliced areca palm nut, wrapped in a pepper leaf smeared with chalky lime – lodged inside the cheek. The resultant juice works as a mild stimulant, also producing bright-red saliva which eventually stains the lips and teeth red. Other ingredients can be added according to taste, including tobacco, cloves, cinnamon, cardamom, turmeric and nutmeg. You'll see mainly the older folk indulging in this pastime, and may come across decorated *sireh* boxes, used to store the ingredients, in museums. To some Indonesians, the betel nut is more than just a mild narcotic. In the islands of Nusa Tenggara, and in particular the island of Sumba, the betel nut is also a symbol of peace and unity. It is customary, when visiting Sumbanese villages, to bring some betel and share it with the kepala desa (village chief). The act of spitting the resulting red saliva on the ground has important religious connotations on the island, the saliva representing blood being returned to the earth – a central part of the Sumbanese belief sytem.

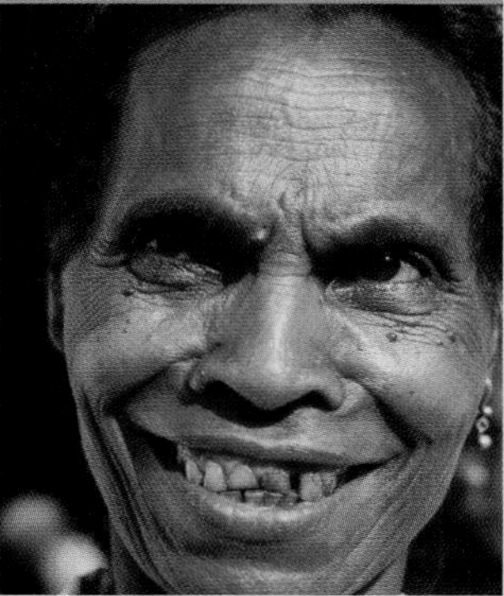

across the island, **Central Java** is the heartland of ethnic Javanese art, education and language. Surakarta and Yogyakarta (more often known as Solo and Yogya) are the ancient capital cities of Central Java's royal families – both fabulously evocative. The province also boasts the finest classical ruins in the archipelago, from the huge Borobodur (Buddhist) and Prambanan (Hindu) temples, to the enigmatic ruins of the Dieng plateau. Most tourists head to **East Java** for the awesome volcanic scenery around smoking Gunung Bromo, while the marvellous rolling uplands of the Ijen Plateau and the idiosyncratic backwater of Pulau Madura are luring increasing numbers of visitors.

The sixth largest island in the world, over 1800km long, **Sumatra** has everything in abundance and nothing in miniature: its mountain ranges, lakes and national parks are vast, its cities overwhelming, and its roads long and arduous. While there is little appeal to Medan, the main city of the island, the rest of the province of **North Sumatra** is becoming a popular tourist destination, thanks to attractions such as the wonderful orang-utan sanctuary at Bukit Lawang, the resorts of Danau Toba, the surfers' mecca of Nias and the chilly little hill resort of Berastagi. North Sumatra is also one of the gateways to the Gunung Leuser national park – the largest park in Southeast Asia, with such exotic inhabitants as the clouded leopard, marbled cat and sun bear. Further south in **Central Sumatra**, the area around Bukittinggi is best known as the homeland of the Minangkabau people, with their distinctive matrilineal culture,

flamboyant architecture, costume and dances. Danau Maninjau is developing as a laid-back resort, and many people use the west-coast port of Padang as a jumping-off point to the richly forested Mentawai Islands, where the inhabitants still maintain their subsistence economy, living in communal longhouses. Many travellers hurtle through **South Sumatra**, and miss the highlights of the strange megaliths of the upland Pagaralam area; the remote and idyllic coast around Krui; and the mountains of the Bukit Barisan Selatan national park, which shelter rhinos and tigers – although a few visitors do make it to the remarkable elephant training school in the Way Kambas national park.

Just east of Java, the Hindi island of **Bali** has long been the jewel in the crown of Indonesian tourism, albeit a jewel that has struggled to retain its sparkle in the wake of the 2002 Kuta bombing, with plummeting tourist numbers leaving many local people in dire financial straits. Bali's charms remain intact, however, and the welcome for visitors is guaranteed to be especially warm as the island endeavors to re-establish its main industry. While some of Bali is undeniably concrete jungle, its appeal is very evident – in pristine beaches, elegant temples studding the fabulous verdant landscape of the interior, and some of the loveliest hotels in Indonesia. The most popular areas are the hectic and happening coastal resorts of Kuta and Legian in the south, Lovina in the north, where you can snorkel, dive and dolphin-watch from the black-sand beach, and the cultural centre of Ubud, where painting, carving, dancing and music-making are the lifeblood of the area. Further afield, the central volcanoes provide great hiking away from the crowds, whilst the main temple and spiritual heart of the island, Besakih, is firmly on the tourist trail but dramatically located on the slopes of Gunung Agung, Bali's highest mountain.

The up-and-coming region for visitors is the arcs of islands which comprise **Nusa Tenggara**. The beautiful beaches and temples of Lombok have provided an overflow for Bali for over a decade, but visitors who brave an erratic ferry service are discovering the delights of remote and intriguing islands such as Sumba, where grand funeral ceremonies punctuate the religious calendar. Nusa Tenggara's main attraction is its immense variety: neighbouring islands can be as different as if they were on separate continents. Star attractions, in addition to great surfing, include the coloured crater lakes of Kelimutu on Flores and the world's largest lizards – Komodo dragons. However, Nusa Tenggara's most lasting impression comes from the traditional festivals and animist lifestyles of its peoples.

The peak tourist season is between mid-June and mid-September and again over Christmas and New Year

Kalimantan is Indonesia's lion share of the island of Borneo, and there are still some wild corners left to explore. The pick of these are at Tanjung Puting, a southwestern fragment of protected riverine forest offering guaranteed close contact with orang-utans; and – much harder to reach – traditional Dayak villages in Kalimantan's unspoilt central mountains and jungles. Kalimantan's cities are generally functional, purpose-built places, though the Muslim port of Banjarmasin, complete with floating markets, has at least some character.

The geography of **Sulawesi** has divided the island into three distinct areas. The southern third is split between the coastal Bugis – famous seafarers and infamous pirates, with excellent shipbuilding skills – and highland Torajans, one of Indonesia's most self-confident ethnic groups. Central Sulawesi's attractions range from the easy scenery of the Togian Islands to hard-core hiking in the mountainous fringes in search of elusive megalithic cultures. Meanwhile, the north of the island contains untouched rainforest, with Indonesia's best scuba diving to be found around Pulau Bunaken, out from the easygoing city of Manado.

In the far east of Indonesia, **West Papua** (formerly Irian Jaya), located to the west of Papua New Guinea on one of the world's largest islands, is a Holy Grail for explorers: great areas of its rainforests, mountains and valleys remain untouched by Western incursion. Most visitors will plan their trips around this inhospitable but fascinating region from the capital city Jayapura, or from Pulau Biak, which has fabulous birds and coral reefs. Planes penetrate to the Baliem Valley, the highland home of the Dani people, who hunt with bows and arrows and wear penis gourds and feathered headdresses. In the south, the Asmat region has a rich artistic tradition, while to the north, the Bird's Head Peninsula features stunning ancient cave paintings, gorgeous lakes and delicate reefs. There are a multitude of other exciting destinations in Irian, but they are the preserve of modern-day Marco Polos and occasional missionaries.

When to go

Indonesia's **climate** is highly complex. The whole archipelago is tropical, with temperatures at sea level always between 21°C and 33°C, although cooler in the mountains. In theory, the year divides into a wet and a dry season depending on the effects of the two major winds, the **monsoons**, that drive wet or dry air towards the islands. However, in many places it's pretty hard to tell the difference between wet and dry, and the heat and humidity can be extremely oppressive at any time of the year. Very roughly, in much of the country November to April are the wet months (January and February the wettest) and May through to October are dry. However, in northern Sumatra and central and northern Maluku, this pattern is effectively reversed. The whole picture becomes even more difficult when you

Average daily temperatures (°C, max and min) and monthly rainfall (mm)

	Jan	Feb	Mar	Apr	May	Jun	Jul	Aug	Sep	Oct	Nov	Dec
Balikpapan (Kalimantan)												
max (°C)	29	30	30	29	29	29	28	29	29	29	29	29
min (°C)	23	23	23	23	23	23	23	23	23	23	23	23
rainfall (mm)	201	175	231	208	231	193	180	163	140	132	168	206
Jakarta (Java)												
max (°C)	29	29	30	31	31	31	31	31	31	31	30	29
min (°C)	23	23	23	24	24	23	23	23	23	23	23	23
rainfall (mm)	300	300	211	147	114	97	64	43	66	112	142	203
Makassar (Sulawesi)												
max (°C)	29	29	29	30	31	30	30	31	31	31	30	29
min (°C)	23	24	23	23	23	22	21	21	21	22	23	23
rainfall (mm)	686	536	424	150	89	74	36	10	15	43	178	610
Padang (Sumatra)												
max (°C)	31	31	31	31	31	31	31	31	30	30	30	30
min (°C)	23	23	23	24	24	23	23	23	23	23	23	23
rainfall (mm)	351	259	307	363	315	307	277	348	152	495	518	480

take into account the local **microclimates** that pattern the islands. Generally, in purely practical terms, the best time to visit is outside the rainy season; during the rains, you can expect transport, especially ferries and small planes, to be disrupted, roads and rivers to flood, and mountain-climbing to become both dangerous and unrewarding. In the gaps between downpours, though, the newly washed landscape is at its most dazzlingly beautiful.

Another factor to take into account is the wealth of **local festivals** (see p.59), many of which are moveable against the Western calendar. The **peak tourist season** across the islands is between mid-June and mid-September and again over the Christmas and New Year season for Western visitors. This is particularly relevant in the major resorts, where prices rocket and rooms can be fully booked for days, and sometimes weeks, on end. Bear in mind also that there is a large domestic tourist market; major Indonesian holidays see everyone moving to their favourite spot, and the end of Ramadan brings national chaos, with many people travelling to visit their families.

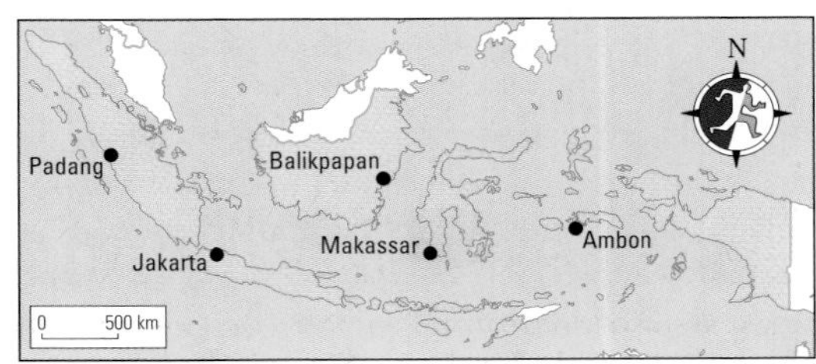

things not to miss

It's not possible to see everything Indonesia has to offer in one trip – and we don't suggest you try. What follows is a selective taste of the country's highlights: spectacular temples, great beaches, outstanding festivals and unforgettable hikes. They're arranged in five colour-coded categories, which you can browse through to find the very best things to see and experience. All highlights have a page reference to take you straight into the guide, where you can find out more.

ACTIVITIES | CONSUME | EVENTS | NATURE | SIGHTS

01 **Gamelan music** Page **1062** • The frenetic syncopations of the Balinese xylophone provide the island's national soundtrack.

02 South coast beaches of Prigi Page **306** • Roaring surf and golden beaches make the south coast of East Java one of the island's best-kept secrets.

03 Orang-utans in Bukit Lawang Page **356** • Conveniently close to the Sumatran capital, Medan, Bukit Lawang is your best chance to see orang-utans in their natural habitat, and a good base for exploring Gunung Leuser national park – Indonesia's largest.

04 Minangkabau houses Page **406** • The spectacular, soaring roofs of the traditional houses of central Sumatra represent the horns of a buffalo.

05 **Pura Luhur Batukau** Page **654** • Secluded high in the foothills of a sacred mountain, this is one of Bali's most beautiful and atmospheric temples.

06 **Traditional villages** Pages **737 & 792** • From the layout of the houses to the architecture of the buildings, in Nusa Tenggara ancient beliefs and customs inform every part of a traditional village's design.

07 **Food** Page **48** • From succulent fruits to volcanic curries, with local specialities including roast bat, dog and jungle rat, Indonesia's cuisine is never bland.

08 Tarsiers at Tangkoko Reserve Page **962** • The world's smallest primate is fairly easy to spot in its natural habitat in northern Sulawesi.

09 Pulau Nias Page **381** • Teenage boys leap over two-metre tall "jumping stones" to prove their agility and bravery on Pulau Nias, home to a rich tribal culture.

10 Banjarmasin floating market Page **838** • Photogenic Kuin market is Indonesia's largest.

11 Climbing Gunung Rinjani Page **701** • The most challenging and rewarding climb on Lombok takes in forest, rocky peaks and a dramatic crater lake.

12 Baliem festival Page **1002** • This spectacular August festival is the best time to see the tribesmen of Papua in all their befeathered glory.

13 Candi Borobudur Page **218** • The world's largest Buddhist stupa and the biggest single monument in the southern hemisphere stands coveniently close to the cultural capital of Yogyakarta.

14 Gili Islands Page **690** • Pure white sand, crystal-clear turquoise waters and a laid-back atmosphere make these perennial favourites well worth a visit.

15 Yogyakarta Page **208** • Dance and other classical Javanese arts still thrive in Yogya, the centre of art and culture in Java.

16 Sunda Kelapa Page **105** • Colourful and majestic, the world's last wooden trading schooners dock at this picturesque old harbour on Jakarta's north shore.

17 Gunung Agung Page **599** • A perfectly conical summit, impressively visable from much of central and eastern Bali.

18 Shopping for arts and crafts Page **68** • From pottery to penis gourds, fabrics to furniture, Indonesia is a shopper's paradise. The cultural capitals of Yogya on Java and Ubud on Bali are great places to begin.

19 Ubud Page **566** • Set within stunning, lush scenery, the village of Ubud is Bali's top inland destination.

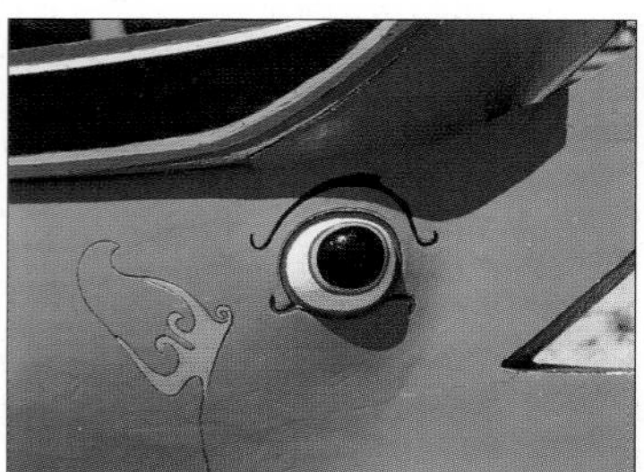

20 **Pemuteran** Page **661** • Traditional fishing boats are a common sight at this inviting little beach haven on the northwest coast of Bali.

21 **Krakatau** Page **138** • Smouldering angrily, the world's most famous volcano is visible and visitable from the shores of West Java.

22 **Pasola** Page **797** • This annual pageant of horseback spear-throwing is the most spectacular festival in Nusa Tenggara, possibly in Indonesia.

23 **Surfing at "G-Land"** Page **337** • One of many legendary Indonesian surf-spots, attracting the world's best surfers at the Quiksilver World Tour Circuit each year.

24 **Komodo dragons** Page **730** • The largest lizard in the world, a prehistoric throwback, exists on just a few, mostly uninhabited islands off the west coast of Flores.

25 Tanah Toraja funeral ceremony Page **918** • Processions, animal sacrifices and intriguing rituals – all destined to send the deceased to Puya, the Torajan afterlife.

26 Bogor Botanical Gardens Page **141** • Founded by Sir Stamford Raffles, these world-famous gardens stand in a mountain town famous for its thunderstorms.

27 Padang Bai Page **614** • This bustling port also offers pretty beaches, attractive temples, excellent diving and snorkelling and a laid-back travellers' scene.

ACTIVITIES | CONSUME | EVENTS | NATURE | SIGHTS

28 Pulau Belitung

Page **485** • A former pirate's hideout with great beaches and intriguing offshore islands, Belitung is connected by ferry to Singapore but remains quiet and unexplored.

29 Snorkelling and diving

Page **62** • Stretched between the Indian and Pacific oceans, Indonesia has some of the world's best dive sites, including many that are almost completely unexplored.

30 Gunung Bromo

Page **324** • Atmospheric, photogenic and chilly, Bromo volcano sits smoking in a region of awesome scenery.

Contents

Using this Rough Guide

We've tried to make this Rough Guide a good read and easy to use. The book is divided into six main sections, and you should be able to find whatever you want in one of them.

Colour section

The front colour section offers a quick tour of Indonesia. The **introduction** aims to give you a feel for the place, with suggestions on where to go. We also tell you what the weather is like and include a basic country fact file. Next, our authors round up their favourite aspects of Indonesia in the **things not to miss** section – whether it's great food, amazing sights or a fantastic festival. Right after this comes the Rough Guides' full **contents** list.

Basics

The basics section covers all the **pre-departure** nitty-gritty to help you plan your trip, and the practicalities you'll want to know once you're there. This is where to find out how to get there, what paperwork you'll need, what to do about money and insurance, how to get around – in fact just about every piece of **general practical information** you might need.

Guide

This is the heart of the Rough Guide, divided into user-friendly chapters, each of which covers a specific region. Every chapter starts with a list of **highlights** and an **introduction** that helps you to decide where to go, depending on your time and budget. Likewise, introductions to the various towns and smaller regions within each chapter should help you plan your itinerary. We start most town accounts with information on arrival and accommodation, followed by a tour of the sights, and finally reviews of places to eat and drink, and details of nightlife. Longer accounts also have a directory of practical listings. Each chapter concludes with **public transport** details for that region.

Contexts

Read Contexts to get a deeper understanding of what makes Indonesia tick. We include a brief **history**, articles about **religion**, **music** and the **environment**, and a detailed further reading section that reviews dozens of **books**.

Language

The **language** section offers useful guidance for speaking Bahasa Indonesia and pulls together all the vocabulary you might need on your trip, including a comprehensive **menu reader**. Here you'll also find a **glossary** of words and terms peculiar to the country.

Index + small print

Apart from a **full index**, which includes maps as well as places, this section covers publishing information, credits and acknowledgements, and also has our contact details in case you want to send in updates, corrections or suggestions for improving the book.

Chapter list and map

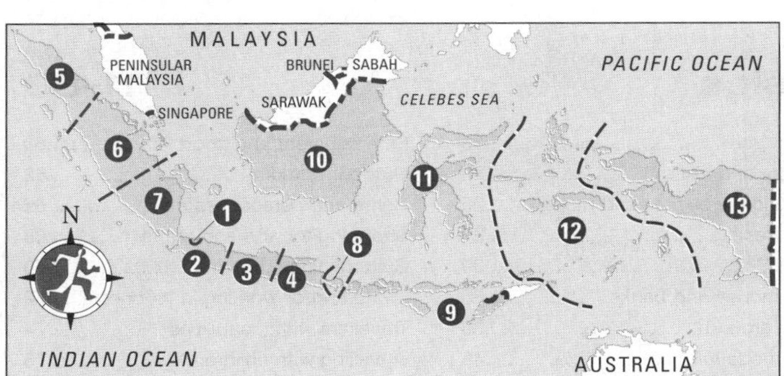

Contents

Colour section i–xxiv

Basics 11–80

Guide 81–1029

Contexts 1031–1083

Language 1085–1096

Index + small print 1097–1113

Map symbols

maps are listed in the full index using coloured text

Main road
Road
Minor road
One way street (town maps)
Pedestrian street
Steps
Path
Railway
River
Ferry/hydrofoil route
International boundary
Provincial boundary
Chapter division boundary
Airport
Bus/bemo stop
Accommodation
Restaurant
Campsite
Market
Mosque
Temple
Museum
Fort
Point of interest
Ruins
Lighthouse
Arch
Waterfall
Crater
Rocks
Hill
Mountains
Mountain peak
Viewpoint
Cave
Marsh
Spring
Surf area
Parking
Hospital
Clinic
Information office
Telephone
Post office
Bank
Petrol Station
Statue
Golf Course
Gate
Wall
Building
Church
Cemetery
Muslim cemetery
Park
Beach
Swamp

Basics

Basics

Getting there

As you'd expect for such a vast country, Indonesia has plenty of international airports and seaports, and there are many different ways of getting to them. Java's Sukarno-Hatta airport in Jakarta, and Bali's Ngurah Rai airport, just outside of Kuta, are the major international gateways to Indonesia. Air fares always depend on the season, with the highest running from the beginning of July through to the end of August, when the weather is best in most of the archipelago; fares drop during the "shoulder" seasons – April to June and September – and you'll get the best prices during the low season, October to March (excluding Christmas and New Year, when prices are hiked up and seats are at a premium).

You can often cut costs by going through a **specialist flight agent** – either a consolidator, who buys up blocks of tickets from the airlines and sells them at a discount, or a **discount agent**, who in addition to dealing with discounted flights may also offer special student and youth fares and a range of other travel-related services such as travel insurance, rail passes, car rentals, tours and the like. Some agents specialize in **charter flights**, which may be cheaper than anything available on a scheduled flight; however, departure dates are fixed and withdrawal penalties are high. For some destinations, particularly Bali, you may even find it cheaper to pick up a bargain **package deal** from a tour operator and then find your own accommodation when you get there.

If Indonesia is only one stop on a longer journey, you might want to consider buying a round-the-world (RTW) ticket. Some travel agents can sell you an "off-the-shelf" RTW ticket that will have you touching down in about half a dozen cities (Bali and – to a lesser extent – Jakarta are on many itineraries); others will have to assemble one for you, which can be tailored to your needs but is likely to be more expensive. Figure on at least £650/$900 for a RTW ticket including Indonesia, or £900/US$1300 for a tailor-made trip.

Booking flights online

Many airlines and discount travel websites offer you the opportunity to book your tickets online, cutting out the costs of agents and middlemen. Good deals can often be found through discount or auction sites, as well as through the airlines' own websites.

Ⓦ**www.etn.nl/discount.htm** A hub of consolidator and discount agent web links, maintained by the non-profit European Travel Network.

Ⓦ**www.geocities.com/Thavery2000** Has an extensive list of airline toll-free numbers and websites.

Ⓦ**www.flyaow.com** Online air travel information and reservations site.

Ⓦ**www.smilinjack.com/airlines.htm** An up-to-date list of airline website addresses.

Ⓦ**http://travel.yahoo.com** Incorporates a lot of Rough Guide material in its coverage of destination countries and cities across the world, with information about places to eat and sleep etc.

Ⓦ**www.cheaptickets.com** Discount flight specialists.

Ⓦ**www.cheapflights.com** Bookings from the UK and Ireland only. Flight deals, travel agents, plus links to other travel sites.

Ⓦ**www.lastminute.com** Bookings from the UK only. Offers good last-minute holiday package and flight-only deals.

Ⓦ**www.expedia.com** Discount air fares, all-airline search engine and daily deals.

Ⓦ**www.travelocity.com** Destination guides, hot web fares and the best deals for car hire and accommodation. Provides access to the travel agent system SABRE, the most comprehensive central reservations system in the US.

Ⓦ**www.hotwire.com** Bookings from the US only. Last-minute savings of up to forty percent on regular published fares. Travellers must be at least 18, and there are no refunds, transfers or changes allowed.

Ⓦ **www.priceline.com** Name-your-own-price website that has deals at around forty percent off standard fares. You can't specify flight times (although you do specify dates), and the tickets are non-refundable, non-transferable and non-changeable.
Ⓦ **www.skyauction.com** Bookings from the US only. Auctions tickets and travel packages using a "second bid" scheme. The best strategy is to bid the maximum you're willing to pay, since if you win, you'll pay just enough to beat the runner-up regardless of your maximum bid.
Ⓦ **www.travelshop.com.au** Australian website offering discounted flights, online bookings, packages and insurance.
Ⓦ **www.gaytravel.com** Gay online travel agent, concentrating mostly on accommodation.

Flights from the UK and Ireland

During the high season, a discounted flight to Indonesia is likely to cost you around £650; flights get booked solid, and should be reserved several weeks in advance. Prices drop considerably at other times of the year, when you should be able to find a fare under £500.

From London, there are direct flights to **Bali** with Garuda; otherwise, the fastest and most comfortable way of reaching Java or Bali from Britain is with either Singapore Airlines, Malaysia Airlines or Qantas, all of which make the journey in around eighteen hours, including a wait of an hour or two in either Singapore or Kuala Lumpur. Other airlines (see opposite) have longer connection times in either Europe or Asia, though they do sometimes slice a fair bit off the price. Currently, Lauda Air and Royal Brunei are quoting the cheapest **fares**, at around £460 low season and £580 during high season.

For destinations other than Jakarta or Denpasar or Bali, if you're prepared to change planes along the way you can take a Garuda flight from London to Bali, and then on via Jakarta to Medan (**Sumatra** £570 low season/£700 high season return) or anywhere else that Garuda fly to in Indonesia. Singapore Airlines subsidiary Silk Air fly direct from Singapore to Mataram (**Lombok** £530/720), Manado (**Sulawesi** £510/635), Padang, Palembang or Medan (**Sumatra**, for around £510/640 each) or Balikpapan in **East Kalimantan** (£530/660); Malaysia Airlines also fly to Medan as well as Pontianak in **West Kalimantan** (£545/660) and Surabaya on **Java**, while Royal Brunei flies to both Surabaya and Balikpapan.

Stopovers, open jaws and round-the-world tickets

If you want to make full use of all that flying time and **stop over** on the way there or back, you'll probably have to go with the associated national airline – for example, Malaysia Airlines for stops in Kuala Lumpur or Thai International for a break in Bangkok – for which service there should be no extra charge. Garuda offer free stopovers in either Bangkok or Singapore (depending on the routeing) and, for a nominal supplement, will allow an extra stop within Indonesia, at Jakarta or Medan.

Open-jaw tickets are return fares where you make your own way between different arrival and departure points – an ideal option if you want to avoid retracing your steps. Because many airlines "common-rate" all fares within the region, the cost of an open-jaw ticket may also not be appreciably higher than a return fare.

Those continuing on to Australia should consider investing in a **round-the-world ticket**, which allows you several stops in Asia or elsewhere. For example, a one-year open ticket from London taking in Bangkok, Bali, Brunei, Brisbane/Melbourne, Auckland and New York starts for as little as £650 rising to around £1100 if you add stops in India and the South Pacific.

Organized tours and package holidays

Inevitably more expensive than if you travelled independently, **package tours** to Indonesia are nonetheless worth investigating if you have limited time or a specialist interest. Several companies offer **overland trips**, ranging from travelling by bus between Java and Bali via the main sights, to hard-core hiking through West Papua or Kalimantan. The range of **cruises** on offer is huge, from two- or three-day tasters to much longer voyages taking in a wider area of Asia; be sure to check how long you have ashore at specific stops if you plan to explore any particular area. Sold as the ultimate in romantic destinations, several companies, including Thomas Cook Holidays, Kuoni Worldwide and Airwaves, offer packages catering for those intending to **get married on Bali**. You will have to complete certain formalities at the British Embassy in Jakarta and be resident in Indonesia for ten working days before the marriage. Men must be at least 23 years old and women 21, and they must be of the same religion; deals vary slightly, so it's important to check exactly what is and is not included.

Airlines

Air France UK ⓣ0845/0845 111, Republic of Ireland ⓣ01/605 0383, ⓦwww.airfrance.co.uk.
Air New Zealand UK ⓣ020/8741 2299, ⓦwww.airnz.co.uk.
All Nippon Airways (ANA) UK ⓣ020/7224 8866, ⓦwww.ana.co.jp.
British Airways UK ⓣ0845/77 333 77, Republic of Ireland ⓣ1800/626 747, ⓦwww.britishairways.com.
Canadian Airlines UK ⓣ08705/247 226, Republic of Ireland ⓣ01/679 3958, ⓦwww.cdnair.ca.
Cathay Pacific UK ⓣ020/7747 8888, ⓦwww.cathaypacific.com.
China Airlines UK ⓣ020/7436 9001, ⓦwww.china-airlines.com.
Emirates Airlines UK ⓣ0870/243 2222, ⓦwww.emirates.com.
Garuda Indonesia UK ⓣ020/7467 8600, ⓦwww.garuda-indonesia.co.uk.
Gulf Air UK ⓣ0870/777 1717, ⓦwww.gulfairco.com.
Japan Airlines UK ⓣ0845/774 7700, ⓦwww.jal.co.jp.
KLM UK ⓣ08705/074 074, ⓦwww.klmuk.com.
Korean Air UK ⓣ0800/0656 2001, Republic of Ireland ⓣ01/799 7990, ⓦwww.koreanair.com.
Kuwait Airways UK ⓣ020/7412 0006, ⓦwww.kuwait-airways.com.
Lauda Air UK ⓣ020/7630 5924, ⓦwww.laudaair.co.uk.
Lufthansa UK ⓣ0845/7737 747, Republic of Ireland ⓣ01/844 5544, ⓦwww.lufthansa.com.
Malaysia Airlines (MAS) UK ⓣ020/7341 2020, Republic of Ireland ⓣ01/676 1561 or 676 2131, ⓦwww.mas.com.my.
Qantas UK ⓣ0845/774 7767, ⓦwww.qantas.com.au.
Royal Brunei Airlines UK ⓣ020/7584 6660, ⓦwww.bruneiair.com.
SAS Scandinavian Airlines UK ⓣ0845/607 2772, Republic of Ireland ⓣ01/844 5440, ⓦwww.scandinavian.net.
Saudia UK ⓣ020/8995 7777, ⓦwww.saudiairlines.com.
Singapore Airlines UK ⓣ0870/608 8886, Republic of Ireland ⓣ01/671 0722, ⓦwww.singaporeair.com.
Silk Airlines UK ⓣ0870/608 8886, Republic of Ireland ⓣ01/671 0722, ⓦwww.singaporeair.com.
Thai International UK ⓣ0870/606 0911, ⓦwww.thaiair.com.
United Airlines UK ⓣ0845/8444 777, ⓦwww.ual.com.

Flight and travel agents

In Britain

Bridge the World UK ⓣ020/7911 0900, ⓦwww.bridgetheworld.com. Specializing in round-the-world tickets, with good deals aimed at the backpacker market.
Destination Group UK ⓣ020/7400 7045, ⓦwww.destination-group.com. Good discount air fares, as well as Southeast Asian inclusive packages.
Flightbookers UK ⓣ0870/010 7000, ⓦwww.ebookers.com. Low fares on an extensive selection of scheduled flights.
Flynow UK ⓣ0870/444 0045, ⓦwww.flynow.com. Large range of discounted tickets.
North South Travel UK ⓣ & ⓕ01245/608 291, ⓦwww.northsouthtravel.co.uk. Friendly, competitive travel agency, offering discounted fares worldwide – profits are used to support projects in the developing world, especially the promotion of sustainable tourism.
Quest Worldwide UK ⓣ020/8547 3322, ⓦwww.questtravel.com. Specialists in round-the-world discount fares.
STA Travel UK ⓣ08701/600 599, ⓦwww.statravel.co.uk. Worldwide specialists in low-cost flights and tours for students and under-26s, though other customers are welcome.
Top Deck UK ⓣ020/7370 4555, ⓦwww.topdecktravel.co.uk. Long-established agent dealing in discount flights.
Trailfinders UK ⓣ020/7628 7628, ⓦwww.trailfinders.com. One of the best-informed and most efficient agents for independent travellers; produces a very useful quarterly

magazine worth scrutinizing for round-the-world routes.

Travel Bag UK ⓣ0870/900 1350, ⓦwww.travelbag.co.uk. Discount flights to Indonesia and the rest of the Far East; official Qantas agent.

Travel Cuts UK ⓣ020/7255 2082, ⓦwww.travelcuts.co.uk. Canadian company specializing in budget, student and youth travel and round-the-world tickets.

In Ireland

Apex Travel Dublin ⓣ01/241 8000, wwww.apextravel.ie. Specialists in flights to Southeast Asia.

Aran Travel International Galway ⓣ091/562 595, ⓦwww.homepages.iol.ie/~arantvl/aranmain.htm. Good-value flights to all parts of the world.

CIE Tours International Dublin ⓣ01/703 1888, ⓦwww.cietours.ie. General flight and tour agent.

Co-op Travel Care Belfast ⓣ028/9047 1717. Flights and holidays around the world.

Go Holidays Dublin ⓣ01/874 4126, ⓦwww.goholidays.ie. Package tour specialists.

Joe Walsh Tours Dublin ⓣ01/872 2555 or 676 3053, Cork ⓣ021/427 7959, ⓦwww.joewalshtours.ie. General budget fares agent.

Lee Travel Cork ⓣ021/277 111, ⓦwww.leetravel.ie. Flights and holidays worldwide.

McCarthy's Travel Cork ⓣ021/427 0127, ⓦwww.mccarthystravel.ie. General flight agent.

Neenan Travel Dublin ⓣ01/607 9900, ⓦwww.neenantrav.ie.

Premier Travel Derry ⓣ028/7126 3333, ⓦwww.premiertravel.uk.com. Discount flight specialists.

Rosetta Travel Belfast ⓣ028/9064 4996, ⓦwww.rosettatravel.com. Flight and holiday agent.

Student & Group Travel Dublin ⓣ01/677 7834. Student and group specialists.

Trailfinders Dublin ⓣ01/677 7888, ⓦwww.trailfinders.ie. (see UK entry for details).

Tour operators

Arc Journeys 102 Stanley Rd, Cambridge CB5 8LB ⓣ01223 779200, ⓕ779090, ⓔarcjourney@aol.com. Tailor-made specialists with a large portfolio of suggestions for trips to Indonesia. They also have "The Spice Islands", a series of seven-day tours of Bali, Maluku, Sulawesi and Flores.

Earthwatch Institute Belsyre Court, 57 Woodstock Rd, Oxford OX2 6HU ⓣ01865/311600, ⓕ311383, ⓔinfo@uk.earthwatch.org. Volunteer work on ever-changing Indonesia-wide projects, including assisting locally based archeologists or biologists, or helping in community programmes. Groups are small and you tend to stay with local people rather than in hotels; costs – excluding flights – start at around £800 for two weeks.

Explore 1 Frederick St, Aldershot GU11 1LQ ⓣ01252/319448, ⓕ343170, ⓦwww.explore.co.uk, ⓔinfor@explore.co.uk. A variety of adventure holidays are available, including a fifteen-day East Indies *Seatrek* sailing from Bali to Flores (from £995 without flights, £1395 with flights).

Footprint Adventures 5 Malham Drive, Lincoln LN6 0XD ⓣ01522 690852, ⓕ501392, ⓦwww.footventure.co.uk, ⓔsales@footventure.co.uk. This company is a trekking and wildlife specialist. The trips include the eighteen-day Sumatra Explorer, taking in Bukit Lawang and the Kerinci-Seblat national park (£640), and the five-day "Rinjani Adventure", including the climb to the summit (ten days from £545). All prices exclude flights.

Hayes and Jarvis Hayes House, 152 King St, London W6 0QU ⓣ0208/748 5050, ⓦwww.hayes-jarvis.com. A range of south Bali and Lombok (Senggigi) holidays, from £819 for one island and £908 if you combine Bali and Lombok.

Imaginative Traveller 14 Barley Mow Passage, London W4 4PH ⓣ0208/742 8612, ⓕ742 3045, ⓦwww.imaginative-traveller.com, ⓔinfo@imaginative-traveller.com. Thirteen-day Bali and Lombok tour, including a visit to the Gili Islands and a climb of Mount Rinjani. Price £460 excluding air fares.

Kuoni Travel UK ⓣ01306/742 888, ⓦwww.kuoni.co.uk. Flexible package holidays to long-haul destinations, including a ten-night Balinese tour and good family deals.

Magic of the Orient UK ⓣ01293/537 700, ⓦwww.magic-of-the-orient.com. Tailor-made holidays, rather than packages, to destinations including Java, Bali, Ubud, Lombok, Sulawesi and Sanur; these very well-informed consultants can lead you off the beaten track.

Silverbird 4 Northfields Prospect, Putney Bridge Rd, London SW18 1PE ⓣ0208/875 9090, ⓕ875 1874. ⓦwww.silverbird.co.uk. Far East specialist offering tailor-made holidays including Bali and/or Lombok. They occasionally advertise "Golden Opportunities", which are extremely good-value special deals for a limited period – for example, ten days in Sanur from £719 (flights and room only).

Steppes East Castle Eaton, Cricklade SN6 6JU ⓣ01285/810267, ⓕ810693, ⓦwww.steppeseast.co.uk, ⓔsales@steppeseast.co.uk. A top-of-the-range company, specializing in tailor-made trips throughout Indonesia which are available all year, but also offering small-group trips such as "Soul ships and Coral Reefs", a seventeen-day trip in Sulawesi (from £2120).

Travelbag Adventures 15 Turk St, Alton GU34 1AG ⓣ0207/287 7744, ⓕ01420/541022, ⓦwww.travelbag-adventures.co.uk. Offers a small-group trip (maximum twelve people) around Bali and Lombok, taking fifteen days and costing from £999 with flights. There is also an option without flights for £499.

Flights from the USA and Canada

The Indonesian national airline, Garuda, no longer fly to the States or Canada. However, from the US and Canada there's a choice of flights on other carriers, either flying across the Pacific or the Atlantic. Prices quoted are round-trip, assume midweek travel (where there's a difference in price), exclude taxes (roughly US$65/CAN$40) and are subject to availability and change.

From the US

A number of airlines (see below) will fly you **from the US** to Jakarta (on Java) or Denpasar (on Bali). However, if your destination is one of the other islands, you'll probably find it most convenient to take Singapore Airlines, whose subsidiary, Silk Air, operates connections to Sumatra, Lombok, Kalimantan and Sulawesi. You might also want to bear in mind that most of the Asian national airlines allow one free stopover each way (additional stopovers cost extra). On Malaysia Airlines flying westward, for example, you could spend a few days in Tokyo, Taipei or Kuala Lumpur.

Singapore Airlines currently offer the best value on published fares to **Jakarta** or **Denpasar**. Their round-trip APEX fares from LA to Denpasar, for example, are US$1183 (low season)/US$1395 (high season). However, you should first shop around for a better price from **discount agents** (see p.18) or your local travel agent. At the time of writing, for example, low-season fares to Bali were available for as little as US$750 (New York–Denpasar) or US$925 (LA–Denpasar). As with all long-haul flights involving a possible change of planes, complex scheduling and big time differences, you'd be well advised to double-check the details of any stopovers involved in the various routeings.

From Canada

From Canada, your best option is a flight on one of the Asian airlines. Cathay Pacific's published APEX fares from Toronto to either Jakarta or Denpasar are currently CAN$2867 (low season)/CAN$3107 (high). Once again, you'll most likely get better deals from a discount outfit or even your local travel agent. At the time of writing, there were return fares to Jakarta from Toronto for around CAN$1310 (low season)/CAN$1660 (high) and from Vancouver for CAN$1420 (low)/CAN$1990 (high).

Circle Pacific and round-the-world tickets

If Indonesia is only one stop on a longer journey, you might want to consider buying a **round-the-world** (RTW) or **Circle Pacific** ticket. Some travel agents can sell you an "off-the-shelf" RTW/Circle Pacific ticket that will have you touching down in about half a dozen cities (Denpasar and/or Jakarta are on several itineraries); other agents will assemble one for you, which can be tailored to your needs but is likely to be more expensive.

Airlines

Air Canada ⓣ1-888/247-2262, ⓦwww.aircanada.ca.

Air China East Coast ⓣ1-800/982-8802, West Coast ⓣ1-800/986-1985, Toronto ⓣ416/581-8833.

Air France US ⓣ1-800/237-2747, Canada ⓣ1-800/667-2747, ⓦwww.airfrance.com.

Air New Zealand US ⓣ1-800/262-1234, Canada ⓣ1-800/663-5494, ⓦwww.airnz.com.

British Airways US ⓣ1-800/247-9297, ⓦwww.british-airways.com.

Cathay Pacific US ⓣ1-800/233-2742, ⓦwww.cathay-usa.com.

China Airlines US ⓣ1-800/227-5118, ⓦwww.china-airlines.com.
Emirates Air US ⓣ1-800/777-3999, ⓦwww.emirates.com.
Garuda Indonesia US ⓣ1-800/342-7832, ⓦwww.garuda-indonesia.com.
N.B. Garuda has currently suspended all North American services – check the current situation before use.
Gulf Air US ⓣ1-800/553-2824, ⓦwww.gulfairco.com.
Japan Air Lines US ⓣ1-800/525-3663, ⓦwww.japanair.com.
KLM/Northwest US ⓣ1-800/447-4747, ⓦwww.klm.com.
Korean Airlines US ⓣ1-800/438-5000, ⓦwww.koreanair.com.
Kuwait Airways US ⓣ1-800/458-9248, ⓦwww.kuwait-airways.com.
Lufthansa US ⓣ1-800/645-3880, Canada ⓣ1-800/563-5954, ⓦwww.lufthansa-usa.com.
Malaysia Airlines US ⓣ1-800/552-9264, ⓦwww.mas.com.my.
Philippine Airlines US ⓣ1-800/435-9725, ⓦwww.philippineair.com.
Qantas Airways US ⓣ1-800/227-4500, ⓦwww.qantas.com.
Singapore Airlines US ⓣ1-800/742-3333, Canada ⓣ1-800/6688103, ⓦwww.singaporeair.com.
Thai Airways International US ⓣ1-800/426-5204, Canada ⓣ1-800/668-8103, ⓦwww.thaiairways.com.
United Airlines US ⓣ1-800/538-2929, ⓦwww.ual.com.

Discount travel companies

Air Brokers International US ⓣ1-800/883-3273 or 415/397-1383, ⓦwww.airbrokers.com. Consolidator and specialist in round-the-world and Circle Pacific tickets.
Airtech US ⓣ1-877-247-8324 or 212/219-7000, ⓦwww.airtech.com. Standby seat broker; also deals in consolidator fares and courier flights.
Council Travel US ⓣ1-800/226-8624, ⓕ617/528-2091, ⓦwww.counciltravel.com. Nationwide organization that mostly, but by no means exclusively, specializes in student/budget travel. Flights from the US only.
Educational Travel Center US ⓣ1-800/747-5551 or 608/256-5551, ⓦwww.edtrav.com. Student/youth discount agent.
High Adventure Travel US ⓣ1-800/350-0612 or 415/912-5600, ⓦwww.airtreks.com. Round-the-world and Circle Pacific tickets. The website features an interactive database that lets you build and price your own round-the-world itinerary; also offers Asian overland connections
Skylink US ⓣ1-800/247-6659 or 212/573-8980, Canada ⓣ1-800/759-5465, ⓦwww.skylinkus.com. Consolidator.
STA Travel ⓣ1-800/777-0112 or 800/781-4040, ⓦwww.sta-travel.com. Worldwide specialists in independent travel; also student IDs, travel insurance, car rental, rail passes, etc.
Student Flights ⓣ1-800/255-8000 or 480/951-1177, ⓦwww.isecard.com. Student/youth fares and student IDs.
TFI Tours International US ⓣ1-800/745-8000 or 212/736-1140, ⓦwww.lowestairprice.com. Consolidator.
Travac US ⓣ1-800/872-8800, ⓦwww.thetravelsite.com. Consolidator and charter broker with offices in New York City and Orlando.
Travelers Advantage ⓣ1-877/259-2691, ⓦwww.travelersadvantage.com. Discount travel club; annual membership fee required (currently $1 for 3 months' trial).
Travel Avenue ⓣ1-800/333-3335, ⓦwww.travelavenue.com. Full-service travel agent that offers discounts in the form of rebates.
Travel Cuts Canada ⓣ1-800/667-2887, US ⓣ1-866/246-9762, ⓦwww.travelcuts.com. Canadian student-travel organization.
Worldtek Travel US ⓣ1-800/243-1723, ⓦwww.worldtek.com. Discount travel agency for worldwide travel.

Tour operators

Abercrombie & Kent ⓣ1-800/323-7308 or 630/954-2944, ⓦwww.abercrombiekent.com. Offer expensive tours around Southeast Asia, including stops in Bali.
Absolute Asia ⓣ1-800/736-8187 or 212/627-1950, ⓦwww.absoluteasia.com. Huge number of private, tailor-made tours covering the entire archipelago.
Adventure Center ⓣ1-800/228-8747 or 510/654-1879, ⓦwww.adventure-center.com. Hiking and "soft adventure" specialists. Run eighteen different tours through Indonesia, from 8 to 29 days' duration, including less-travelled destinations such as Sumba and Papua.
Adventures Abroad ⓣ1-800/665-3998 or 604/303-1099, ⓦwww.adventures-abroad.com. Adventure specialists running six tours to Indonesia from 11 to 29 days.
Asian Pacific Adventures ⓣ1-800/825-1680 or

818/886-5190, ⓦwww.asianpacificadventures.com. Run a number of tours to Indonesia, with destinations including Bali, West Papua, Sulawesi, Nusa Tenggara, and an unusual five-day trip to the Mentawai islands.
Asia Trans Pacific Journeys ⓣ1-800/642-2742, ⓦwww.southeastasia.com. Run a number of tours including a nineteen-day cruise in a huge wooden vessel around the islands of Nusa Tenggara.
Goway Travel ⓣ1-800/387-8850 or 416/322-1034, ⓦwww.goway.com. Umbrella site listing various flight and package deals to Indonesia.
Japan & Orient Tours ⓣ1-800/377-1080, ⓦwww.jot.com. Run the occasional short 3–4 day tour to Bali, with optional add-on trips to Sulawesi's Toraja land and the orangutans of southern Kalimantan.
Journeys International ⓣ1-800/255-8735, ⓦwww.journeys-intl.com. Tours take in Bali, the orang-utans of Camp Leakey and the Baliem Valley.
Nature Expeditions International ⓣ1-800/869-0639, ⓦwww.naturexp.com. Run twelve-day "Treasures of Bali and Java" tour, including trips to Borobudur and the temples of the Prambanan plain.
Pacific Delight Tours ⓣ1-800/221-7179, ⓦwww.pacificdelighttours.com. Run short tours to Bali, usually combined, bizarrely, with a trip to Hong Kong.
Vacationland ⓣ1-800/245-0050, ⓦwww.vacation-land.com. Run nine- to ten-day tours and packages to Bali.
Wilderness Travel ⓣ1-800/368-2794, ⓦwww.wildernesstravel.com. Specialists in hiking, cultural and wildlife adventures; they also run a sailing tour from Bali to Komodo and Rinca.

Flights from Australia and New Zealand

Despite continual rumours of imminent ferry services, flying is at present the only scheduled way to reach Indonesia from Australia and New Zealand. Low-season fares operate February to March, and October 16 to November 30; the shoulder season is January 16–31, April to June and July 1 to October 15; and high season is December 1 to January 15. When buying your ticket, the agents listed on p.20 can fill you in on the latest deals, and usually give up to ten percent discount on student and under-26s fares.

From Australia

Garuda and Qantas both have direct, similarly priced flights several times a week **to Denpasar** and **Jakarta**. Fares to Denpasar from Sydney, Melbourne, Brisbane, Cairns or Adelaide are common-rated at A$1196 (low season) and A$1300 (high season). From Perth it will cost you A$799/999, and from Darwin A$649/799. For Jakarta, prices from all starting points are around A$100 lower.

Unfortunately, Merpati's weekly flight from **Darwin to Kupang** in West Timor has not been operating for the past two years, though hopefully the service will be revived when tourists return in large numbers again.

Royal Brunei offers the cheapest **indirect flights** from Australia to Indonesia, flying to Jakarta or Balikpapan from Brisbane (A$899/1099 either), Darwin (A$675/A$919), or Perth (A$750/999), via a night in Brunei's capital, Bandar Seri Begawan. Other Southeast Asian airlines stop in Indonesia en route to their home cities; while this is more expensive than a direct return to Indonesia, it's worth considering if you're planning a long trip which will involve leaving Indonesia briefly to renew your visa (see p.23). Singapore Airlines and Malaysia Airlines, for example, offer returns via Denpasar and Jakarta to Singapore and Kuala Lumpur respectively for around A$1399/1499 from eastern Australian cities, and A$1199/1299 from Perth.

From New Zealand

From **Auckland**, there are direct flights to Denpasar and Jakarta with Garuda for NZ$1349 (low season) and NZ$1499 (high season) and Air New Zealand (NZ$1599/1699). Add on NZ$300 return from **Christchurch** and **Wellington**, or you can fly indirectly via Australia with Qantas, Ansett or Air New Zealand at the added cost of the domestic fare from New Zealand (NZ$450/690 to Sydney or Brisbane).

Round-the-world tickets

Qantas, Ansett and Air New Zealand combine with a variety of carriers to offer tailored, unlimited stopover **round-the-world** (RTW) fares from A$4500/NZ$4800, as well as more restrictive global packages that take you via Denpasar and Jakarta. Air New Zealand-KLM-Northwest's "World Navigator", Malaysia Airlines' "Global Experience" and Qantas-BA's "Global Explorer" all start from A$2599/NZ$3089, including limited backtracking and six stopovers worldwide, with additional stopovers for A$100/NZ$120 each.

Package holidays

Garuda, Qantas and Air New Zealand, in conjunction with several wholesalers, offer flight/accommodation **packages** – mostly to Bali – costing little more than the air fare, with airport transfers thrown in. Other operators (see below) might also offer car or 4WD rental at around A$50/NZ$60 a day, including insurance. Bookings can be made from most travel agents, but before you book ask about any special conditions or hidden costs that may apply.

There is also a wide range of **surfing** and **diving** packages. Pro Dive Travel is one of the biggest diving operators; they offer seven nights and six dives in Bali departing from Sydney for A$1585.

Airlines

Air Canada Australia ⓣ1300/655 767 or 02/9286 8900, New Zealand ⓣ09/379 3371, ⓦwww.aircanada.ca.
Air China Australia ⓣ02/9232 7277, New Zealand ⓣ09/979 7251.
Air France Australia ⓣ1300/361 400 or 02/9244 2100, ⓦwww.airfrance.com.
Air New Zealand Australia ⓣ13 24 76, New Zealand ⓣ0800/737 000, ⓦwww.airnz.com.
British Airways Australia ⓣ02/8904 8800, New Zealand ⓣ09/356 8690, ⓦwww.britishairways.com.
Cathay Pacific Australia ⓣ13 17 47, New Zealand ⓣ09/379 0861 or 0508/800 454, ⓦwww.cathaypacific.com.
China Airlines Australia ⓣ02/9244 2121, New Zealand ⓣ09/308 3371, ⓦwww.china-airlines.com.
Continental Airlines Australia ⓣ02/9244 2242, New Zealand ⓣ09/308 3350, ⓦwww.flycontinental.com.
Emirates Australia ⓣ02/9290 9700 or 1300/303 777, New Zealand ⓣ09/377 6004, ⓦwww.emirates.com.
Eva Air Australia ⓣ02/9221 0407, New Zealand ⓣ09/358 8300, ⓦwww.evaair.com.
Garuda Australia ⓣ02/9334 9970, New Zealand ⓣ09/366 1862, ⓦwww.garuda-indonesia.com.
Gulf Air Australia ⓣ02/9244 2199, New Zealand ⓣ09/308 3366, ⓦwww.gulfairco.com.
Japan Airlines Australia ⓣ02/9272 1111, New Zealand ⓣ09/379 9906, ⓦwww.japanair.com.
KLM Australia ⓣ1300/303 747, New Zealand ⓣ09/309 1782, ⓦwww.klm.com.
Korean Air Australia ⓣ02/9262 6000, New Zealand ⓣ09/914 2000, ⓦwww.koreanair.com.
Lufthansa Australia ⓣ1300/655 727 or 02/9367 3887, New Zealand ⓣ09/303 1529 or 008/945 220, ⓦwww.lufthansa.com.
Malaysia Airlines Australia ⓣ13 26 27, New Zealand ⓣ0800/657 472, ⓦwww.mas.com.my.
Philippine Airlines Australia ⓣ02/9279 2020, ⓦwww.philippineair.com.
Qantas Australia ⓣ13 13 13, New Zealand ⓣ09/357 8900, ⓦwww.qantas.com.au.
Royal Brunei Airlines Australia ⓣ07/3017 5000, ⓦwww.bruneiair.com.
Singapore Airlines Australia ⓣ13 10 11, New Zealand ⓣ09/303 2129 or 0800/808 909, ⓦwww.singaporeair.com.
Tap Air Portugal Australia ⓣ02/9244 2344, New Zealand ⓣ09/308 3373, ⓦwww.tap-airportugal.pt.
Thai Airways Australia ⓣ1300/651 960, New Zealand ⓣ09/377 3886, ⓦwww.thaiair.com.
United Airlines Australia ⓣ13 17 77, New Zealand ⓣ09/379 3800 or 0800/508 648, ⓦwww.ual.com.

Travel agents

Anywhere Travel Australia ⓣ02/9663 0411 or 018/401 014, ⓔanywhere@ozemail.com.au.
Asean Travel Australia ⓣ02/9868 5199. Southeast Asian air fares, hotel accommodation in capital cities, and tours.
Asian Travel Centre Australia ⓣ03/9245 0747, ⓦwww.planit.com.au. Discounted air fares and accommodation packages in Southeast Asia.
Budget Travel New Zealand ⓣ09/366 0061 or 0800/808 040, ⓦwww.budgettravel.co.nz.
Destinations Unlimited New Zealand ⓣ09/373 4033.
Flight Centres Australia ⓣ02/9235 3522 or 13 16 00, New Zealand ⓣ09/358 4310, ⓦwww.flightcentre.com.au.

Northern Gateway Australia ⓣ08/8941 1394, ⓦwww.northerngateway.com.au.
STA Travel Australia ⓣ1300/360 960, ⓦwww.statravel.com.au, New Zealand ⓣ0508/782 872, ⓦwww.statravel.co.nz.
Student Uni Travel Australia ⓣ02/9232 8444, ⓔaustralia@backpackers.net.
Thomas Cook Australia ⓣ13 17 71 or 1800/801 002, ⓦwww.thomascook.com.au, New Zealand ⓣ09/379 3920, ⓦwww.thomascook.co.nz.
Trailfinders Australia ⓣ02/9247 7666.
Travel.com Australia ⓣ02/9249 5232 or 1300/130 482, ⓦwww.travel.com.au, New Zealand ⓣ09/359 3860, ⓦwww.travel.co.nz.
Travel and Tour Specialists Australia ⓣ07/3221 4599, ⓦwww.allaboutasia.com.au. Discount air fares, plus hotel and resort packages in Bali and the rest of Southeast Asia.

Tour operators

Adventure Specialists Australia ⓣ02/9261 2927. Overland and adventure tour agent.
The Adventure Travel Company New Zealand ⓣ09/379 9755, ⓔadvakl@hot.co.nz. NZ agent for Peregrine (see below).
Adventure World Australia ⓣ02/9956 7766 or 1300/363 055, ⓦwww.adventureworld.com.au, New Zealand ⓣ09/524 5118, ⓦwww.adventureworld.co.nz. Agents for a vast array of international adventure travel companies that operate trips to every continent.
Allways PADI Travel Australia ⓣ1800/338 239, ⓦwww.allwaysdive.com.au. All-inclusive dive packages to prime locations throughout Southeast Asia.
Asian Explorer Holidays Australia ⓣ03/9245 0777, ⓦwww.asianexplorer.com.au. Holidays to Bali, Lombok, Yogya, Jakarta and Bintan Island in the Riau Archipelago.
Birding Worldwide Australia ⓣ03/9899 9303, ⓦwww.birdingworldwide.com.au. Organizes birdwatching trips around the globe.
Golden Bali Travel Australia ⓣ08/8227 1522, ⓦwww.goldenbali.com. All aspects of travel to Bali and the rest of Indonesia, including accommodation, tours and transport.
Intrepid Adventure Travel Australia ⓣ1300 360 667 or 03/9473 2626, New Zealand ⓣ0800/174 043, ⓦwww.intrepidtravel.com.au. Small-group tours to Southeast Asia, with the emphasis on cross-cultural contact and low-impact tourism; run a variety of tours to Indonesia from four days to one month in duration, and cover Sumba and West Papua among more popular destinations.
Peregrine Adventures Australia ⓣ03/9662 2700 or 02/9290 2770, ⓦwww.peregrine.net.au. In New Zealand, see Adventure Travel Company (see above). Adventure tours including eight days on Lombok and fifteen days on Java and Bali.
Pro-Dive Travel Australia ⓣ02/9281 6166 or 1800/820 820, ⓦwww.prodive.com.au. Dive packages to Southeast Asia and worldwide.
San Michele Travel Australia ⓣ02/9299 1111 or 1800/22 22 44, ⓦwww.asiatravel.com.au. Long-established Southeast Asia specialist, with emphasis on Indonesia.
Silke's Travel Australia ⓣ1800 807 860 or 02/8347 2000, ⓦwww.silkes.com.au. Gay and lesbian specialist travel agent.
The Surf Travel Co Australia ⓣ02/9527 4722 or 1800/687 873, New Zealand ⓣ09/473 8388, ⓦwww.surftravel.com.au. Packages and advice for catching waves through the whole Pacific region.

Getting there from Southeast Asia

If you've the time, there are numerous ways to reach Indonesia through adjacent countries. When planning such a route, bear in mind that if you don't already have an Indonesian visa, you must enter the country through an **official gateway** – see p.24. Coming from the US or Europe, one advantage is that flights to Indonesia's neighbours are often cheaper than services direct to Jakarta or Bali. Generally, however, you'll rarely save once additional accommodation and overland transport is added in; however, the routes allow a broader taste of the region, as well as taking you to some less-travelled parts of Indonesia.

From Thailand via the Malay Peninsula

If your time is not too limited, it can work out cheaper to buy a ticket to **Bangkok** or another Southeast Asian city, and take an onward flight to Bali or Lombok from there. Discounted return flights to Bangkok cost from about £400 from London and US$800 from Los Angeles. Many Bangkok travel agents are able to offer particularly good deals because of lax government control on fares. This may also come in handy if you're planning to stay in Indonesia longer than sixty days and will therefore need to leave the country to renew your visa (see p.23). If you want to see more en route, you could fly to Bangkok, and then continue your journey overland.

Silk Air, a subsidiary of Singapore Airlines, currently operates direct **flights** from Singapore to Mataram on Lombok, Manado and Makassar on Sulawesi, Balikpapan in East Kalimantan, and Padang and Palembang on Sumatra, each for around US$230/400 one-way/return. Singapore Airlines also flies Singapore–Denpasar and Singapore–Jakarta several times a day. From Malaysia, there are direct flights from **Kuala Lumpur** to Jakarta, Denpasar, and Makassar in southern Sulawesi.

Buses and **trains** connect Bangkok with Malaysia and Singapore, from where you can travel by **boat** to Indonesia. There's a choice of routes between Bangkok and Singapore, going via Penang or Kuala Lumpur; visit the Malaysian Railways website (ⓦwww.ktmb.com.my) for details. One Malaysia-bound train leaves Bangkok's Hualamphong station every day (book at least one day in advance from the station ticket office or designated agencies), arriving at Butterworth (for Penang) 21 hours later; second/first class sleeper tickets cost about US$53. If continuing to Singapore, you'll need to change trains here for the remaining fifteen-hour journey (a through ticket costs about US$124 first class. Alternatively, you could take one of the four daily trains from Bangkok to Thailand's main southern terminal at Hat Yai (16hr) and change on to the daily Hat Yai–Kuala Lumpur train (14hr). Through fares to Kuala Lumpur are approximately US$71 first-class sleeper; from here, you can travel on to Singapore for around US$90.

Buses and **taxis** from Hat Yai to Penang run throughout the day and take six hours; buses from Hat Yai take eighteen hours to Singapore. There are also long-distance buses and minibuses from the tourist centres of Krabi, Phuket and Surat Thani to Penang, Kuala Lumpur and Singapore.

A number of **sea routes** connect Indonesia with southern Malaysia and Singapore. A variety of slow ferries and high-speed boats depart Penang for Medan in northern Sumatra daily (4–14hr), and daily services run between Melaka and Dumai, south of Medan (2hr 30min). You can also reach Batam, Bintan and Karimun islands, in Indonesia's Riau archipelago, from Johor Bahru in southern Malaysia or from Singapore.

From Borneo

The island of **Borneo** is split between the tiny Sultanate of Brunei and the Malaysian states of Sabah and Sarawak in the north, and Indonesian Kalimantan in the south.

You can fly directly to **Bandar Seri Begawan**, the capital of Brunei, on Royal Brunei from London or Australia (£521/A$925 low season), and on Malaysia Airways via Kuala Lumpur to **Kuching** in Sarawak (£475/US$975/A$1150) or Sabah's **Kota Kinabalu** (£535/US$1050/A$1250). These three cities are linked by road, so all make a viable starting point for a crossing into Indonesia.

Indonesia's only official open **land border** is 40km southwest of Kuching at **Etikong**. Buses from Kuching regularly run over the border into Kalimantan and across to the city of Pontianak. Alternatively, you can cross from Sabah by catching a ferry from **Tewau**, a full two days' bus ride southeast of Kota Kinabalu, to Tarakan or Pulau Nunukan in northeastern Kalimantan – see p.875 for more details. With about a month to spare, you could even use these crossings to make a complete circuit of Borneo.

From the Philippines and Papua New Guinea

Discounted return fares to the Philippine capital, **Manila**, start at around £550/US$1000/A$900.

From Manila, it's possible to island-hop through the Philippine archipelago to **General Santos**, port for the southern island of Mindanao. Occasional cargo ports ply the route between here and Bitung in northeast Sulawesi.

The crossing **from Vanimo in Papua New Guinea** to Jayapura in West Papua is open at the time of writing, though it is not as yet an official gateway; you can pick up an Indonesian visa in Vanimo. Details of this crossing can be found on p.990.

Red tape and visas

Currently, citizens of Britain, Ireland, most of Europe, Australia, New Zealand, Canada and the USA do not need a visa to enter Indonesia if intending to stay for less than sixty days, and if entering and exiting via one of the designated gateways. There are currently around thirty of these ports in the Indonesian archipelago – sixteen major airports, thirteen seaports and one land border – at which you can get a free, non-extendable sixty-day visa on arrival (see p.24 for the full list). Note that "sixty days" includes the date of entry. It's best not to overstay your visa.

There have been news reports recently indicating that this system is about to change slightly. The number of countries whose nationals can pick up a visa at a designated gateway will rise (currently there are 48 countries on this list). However, according to the rumours, there will in the near future be a charge for the visa, and the length of the visa will be cut from sixty to thirty days. The rumours go on to say that a visa may be extendable for another thirty days at one of the immigration offices in Indonesia. How much tourists will have to pay to get one of these new visas (and in what currency), and how much it will cost for an extension, have yet to be announced. It's worth contacting your local embassy for details; a list of embassies and consulates is given on p.24.

In addition, your passport must be valid for at least six months and you must be able to show **proof of onward travel** or sufficient funds to buy a ticket. Over the past couple of years the Indonesian authorities have become a lot more thorough in enforcing these rules, and some international airlines may ask to be shown proof of onward travel before letting you board a flight into Indonesia. They may also request to see relevant documents such as visas (for Australia, for example) – if you don't have the right documents, you'll probably have to sign a form waiving the airline's responsibility.

If you need to stay more than two months, or are entering via a non-designated gateway, then you'll need to obtain a visa through the nearest Indonesian consulate or embassy before entering Indonesia. The simplest to obtain are **tourist visas**; initially valid for four weeks, they cost £10 in the UK, US$25 in the USA, CAN$50 in Canada, A$125 in Australia and NZ$150 in New Zealand. **Business visas** (also called **single visit** visas) involve a fair amount of paperwork, including supporting letters from your current employer and a sponsor in Indonesia, and are valid for five weeks; they cost £22 in the UK and the same price as a tourist visa elsewhere. Both tourist and business visas can be extended for up to six months at immigration offices in Indonesia, if you can convince the authorities that your need is legitimate – this is not necessarily easy.

However, it's quite simple, if expensive, to get yourself a **new sixty-day visa** by leaving the country for a few hours and then coming straight back in through a designated port of entry. Most people choose to go to Singapore; numerous unofficial expat "residents" do the Singapore hop on a regular basis and immigration officials don't seem too bothered by this. Penalties for **overstaying your visa** are quite severe: on departure, you'll be fined US$20 for every day that you've exceeded the limit, up to a maximum of fourteen days. If you've exceeded the fourteen-day overtime limit, you'll get blacklisted from Indonesia for two years.

Should you need to contact the government **immigration offices** (*kantor immigrasi*), you'll find them listed in the "Listings" sections of the large city entries.

Indonesian embassies and consulates abroad

A full list of all Indonesian diplomatic missions worldwide can be found at ®www.dfa-deplu.go.id/diplomatic/diplmission.htm.

Australia 8 Darwin Ave, Yarralumla, Canberra, ACT 2600 ⓣ02/6250 8600, ®www.welcome.to.kbri-canberra.org.au; Level 2, 45 King William Street, Adelaide, SA 5000 ⓣ08/8217 8282; Level 20, Riverside Centre, 123 Eagle Street, Brisbane QLD 4000 ⓣ07/3309 0888; 20 Harry Chan Ave, Darwin, NT 5784 ⓣ089/41 0048; 72 Queen Rd, Melbourne, VIC 3004 ⓣ03/9525 2755; 134 Adelaide Terrace, East Perth, WA 6004 ⓣ08/9221 5858; 236–238 Maroubra Rd, Maroubra, Sydney, NSW 2035 ⓣ02/9344 9933, ®www.indosyd.org.au.

Canada 55 Parkdale Av, Ottawa, ON K1Y 1E5 ⓣ613/721 41100, ®www.indonesia-ottawa.org; 129 Jarvis St, Toronto, ON M56 QH6 ⓣ416/360-4020); 1630 Alberni St, Vancouver, BC V6G 1A6 ⓣ604/682-8855.

Ireland see UK and Ireland.

Malaysia 233 Jl Tun Razak, 50400 Kuala Lumpur ⓣ03/245984 2011; 723 Jl Anyer Molek, 8000 Johor Bahru ⓣ07/221 2000; Jl Kemajuan, Karamunsing, 88817 Kota Kinabulu, Sabah ⓣ088/218 600; 467 Jl Burma, 10350 Penang ⓣ04/374 686.

New Zealand 70 Glen Rd, Kelburn, Wellington, PO Box 3543 ⓣ04/475 8697; 2nd Floor, Beca Carter Hollings Femer Ltd, 132 Vincent St, Auckland ⓣ09/300-9000.

Singapore 7 Chatsworth Rd, Singapore 1024 ⓣ737 7422.

Thailand 600–602 Petchaburi Rd, Bangkok 10400 ⓣ02/252 3135–40.

UK and Ireland ®www.indonesianembassy.org.uk. For recorded information about visa requirements call ⓣ0906/550 8962. For postal applications, contact The Embassy of the Republic of Indonesia, 38 Grosvenor Square, London W1X 9AD, or call in at Consular Section, 38A Adams Row, London W1K 2HW ⓣ020/7499-7661.

USA 2020 Massachusetts Ave NW, Washington, DC 20036 ⓣ202/775-5200, ®www.embassyofindonesia.org; 5 E 68th St, New York, NY 10021 ⓣ212/879-0600, ®www.indony.org; Two Illinois Center, 233 North Michigan Avenue, Suite 1422, Chicago, IL 60601 ⓣ312/9380101; 3457 Wilshire Blvd, Los Angeles, CA 90010 ⓣ213/383-5126; 1111 Columbus Av, San Francisco, CA 94133 ⓣ415/4749571; 10900 Richmond Av, Houston, Texas TX77042 ⓣ713/7851691.

Official immigration gateways into Indonesia

When planning your overland trip, check that your proposed ports of entry *and exit* are officially recognized **immigration gateways** where tourist visas can be issued; if not, you'll need to buy an **Indonesian visa** before you arrive in the country. The most recent development on this front is the decision to make Nunukan and Tarakan (both in northeast Kalimantan) official gateways; in addition, the border Mota Ain between West and East Timor, while not an official gateway, is currently allowing foreigners to leave Indonesia even if they have only the regular "short stay" tourist pass. Once in East Timor, a new Indonesian visa can be acquired in the capital, Dili (see p.783). It is also rumoured that the border near Jayapura between West Papua and Papua New Guinea will become a visa-free gateway soon.

Airports

Bali Ngurah Rai, Denpasar.
Java Sukarno-Hatta, Jakarta; Adi Sumarmo, Solo; Juanda, Surabaya.
Kalimantan Sepinggan, Balikpapan; Soepadio, Pontianak.
Lombok Selaparang, Mataram.
Maluku Pattimura, Ambon.
Riau Hang Nadim, Pulau Batam.
Sulawesi Sam Ratulangi, Manado; Hasanuddin, Makassar.
Sumatra Polonia, Medan; Simpang Tiga, Pekanbaru; Tabing, Padang.
Timor El Tari, Kupang.
West Papua Frans Kaisiepo, Biak.

Seaports

Bali Benoa, Sanur; Padang Bai.
Java Tanjung Priok, Jakarta; Tanjung Perak, Surabaya; Tanjung Mas, Semarang.
Kalimantan Nunukan; Tarakan
Maluku Yos Sudarso, Ambon.
Riau Batu Ampar, Pulau Batam; Sekupang, Pulau Batam; Tanjung Pinang, Pulau Bintan.
Sulawesi Bitung, Manado.
Sumatra Belawan, Medan.

Land borders

Kalimantan Etikong.

Information, websites and maps

After the economic crisis of the late 1990s, the government decided to close most of its tourism promotion offices abroad in order to save money (a short-sighted policy, since the closure of these offices will lead inevitably to a smaller number of tourists, and a consequent loss of revenue).

The few offices that are still open offer general information on the islands, an outline of transport between the islands, and listings for upmarket accommodation and restaurants. Alternatively, contact your nearest Indonesian embassy or consulate, as listed opposite. Their resources are limited, but you'll probably get a glossy brochure or two. In Australia, it's also worth contacting DWI Tour Australia in Sydney (☎02/9211 3383), as they also send out tourist literature on Indonesia.

You'll find a better range of information about Indonesia on the **internet**, from sites sponsored by commercial businesses to travellers' bulletin boards and newsgroups. The latter can be particularly useful if you want to canvass opinions on a particular destination or guesthouse, or if you want other travellers' advice on your proposed itinerary. A selection of the best websites is given below.

There's a range of **tourist offices** within Indonesia, including **government-run organizations**, such as Kanwil Depparpostel offices, operated by the Jakarta-based directorate general of tourism, and the province-oriented **Dinas Pariwisata** (Diparda). You'll find their offices in larger urban areas and major tourist sites. Though they often lack hard information, staff often speak some English, and may be able to provide useful maps and lists of services, advise about local transport or arrange guides. **Opening hours** are roughly Monday to Thursday 8am to 2pm and Friday 8am to 11am.

An increasingly common alternative to government services is **private operators**, which range from roving freelances operating out of tourist hotels or restaurants, to established organizations with their own offices. Many are excellent and offer free advice, though they make money through steering you towards their friends and business associates, from whom they receive a commission. Word of mouth and your own judgement is the best way to avoid con artists.

While getting involved with the local **police** is sometimes more trouble than it's worth, in remote locations where there are no other sources of information, they may be able to provide advice and even maps of the surrounding region. Don't expect any English to be spoken, but if you're willing to spend some time in pleasantries, they can go out of their way to help you – just remember that they're not obliged to do so.

Indonesian tourist offices abroad

Australia Public Relations Agency, Garuda Indonesia Office, 4 Bligh St, PO Box 3836, Sydney ☎232-6044.
Germany Indonesia Tourist Promotion Office, Wiessenhuttenplatz 17, Frankfurt ☎0611/235681.
Singapore Indonesia Tourist Promotion Office, 10 Collyer Quay, 15-07 Ocean Building, Singapore 0104 ☎5345731.
UK Indonesian Promotion Office ☎0906/550 8959 (brochure order only).
USA Indonesia Tourist Promotion Office, 3457 Wilshire Blvd, Los Angeles, CA 90010 ☎231/387 2078.

Useful websites

In addition to those sites listed below, many of the provincial tourist authorities have their own websites. Simply type in the name of the province into a search engine and these sites should appear in the list.

The arts

Agung Rai Museum of Art
ⓦwww.nusantara.com/arma. A good chance to

see some of Bali's most famous paintings, including works by Walter Spies, I Gusti Nyoman Lempad, Rudolph Bonnet and Anak Agung Gede Sobrat.

Bali Echo ⓦwww.baliwww.com/baliechomagazine. Bali's bimonthly cultural journal and visitors' guide is reproduced almost in full online. It's well worth a browse for its features on subjects as diverse as Kuta nightlife and black magic in Bali.

Indonesian Art Net ⓦwww.indonesianart.net. Good coverage of the arts in Indonesia, including reviews and listings of events.

Indonesian Heritage ⓦwww.indonesianheritage.com. A very comprehensive site, linked to an encyclopedia of Indonesia. Covers virtually all aspects of Indonesian history, society, arts.

Seniwati Gallery ⓦwww.seniwatigallery.com. Recommended site sponsored by the Seniwati Gallery of Women's Art in Ubud. View a selection from the gallery's permanent collection, and browse a catalogue of paintings for sale.

News

Antara – Indonesian News Service ⓦwww.antara-online.com/english.asp. English-language site of the official Indonesian news service.

Asiaweek ⓦwww.asiaweek.com. Good range of articles taken from this weekly print magazine that specializes in Asian affairs, plus headline snippets from the archives. Accessible without subscription.

Far Eastern Economic Review ⓦwww.feer.com. Condensed articles taken from the printed version of this Asia-oriented news magazine. Accessible without subscription.

Indo Exchange.com ⓦwww.indoexchange.com. Indonesian business news, exchange rates.

Inside Indonesia ⓦwww.insideindonesia.org. Web version of the hard-hitting bimonthly magazine that's full of insightful and thought-provoking articles about political, social and environmental issues across the archipelago.

Jakarta News Net ⓦhttp://jakartanews.net. Politics, economics and business.

Jakarta Post ⓦwww.thejakartapost.com. Domestic Indonesian news hot off the press; subscription unnecessary.

Jakarta Web.com ⓦwww.jakweb.com. News from the capital, plus business coverage and national news.

Tempo Interactive ⓦwww.tempointeractive.com. Online version of Indonesia's respected weekly news magazine (English-language edition), with the day's headline stories.

Van Zorge Report ⓦwww.vanzorgereport.com. Highly respected detailed analysis of the political scene in Indonesia; some reports can only be accessed by subscription. Updated daily.

Yahoo! News Indonesia ⓦhttp://dailynews.yahoo.com/fc/Asia/Indonesia. Reasonable news service using press agency releases from Reuters, Associated Press etc.

Travel

Archipelago ⓦwww.archipelago-emag.com. E-magazine devoted to Indonesian travel and environmental news.

ASDP Perum ⓦwww.asdp.co.id/english. Website of the second largest ferry company in Indonesia, with timetables – not always up-to-date – of the basic ferry services, though as yet no information on the new fast ferry services.

Australian Department of Foreign Affairs ⓦwww.dfat.gov.au. Advice and reports on unstable countries and regions.

Bali and Lombok Hotels and Accommodation Travel Forum ⓦwww.travelforum.org/bali/index.html. Very good travellers' forum, with lots of regular contributors who make frequent tips to Bali; especially useful for getting first-hand recommendations on drivers, tailors and particular room numbers. It also has a hotel reservation site.

Bali Online ⓦwww.baliwww.com/bali. One of the best umbrella sites for Bali, offering a wide variety of different tourist-oriented links and services, including a room-finder, tour-planner, web directory with 2000 links, the latest tourism news, and a travellers' forum.

Bali Paradise Online ⓦwww.bali-paradise.com. Another excellent wide-ranging umbrella site, with dozens of categories, alphabetically sorted and ranging from architecture, airline information, banks and car rental to the lowdown on nightlife, real estate, weather, and also has a travellers' forum.

Bali Travel Guide ⓦwww.balitravelguide.com. The official site of the Bali Tourism and Development Centre.

Bali Villas Travel Forum ⓦwww.balitravelforum.com. The most helpful forum offering masses of travellers' advice and recommendations from recent travellers to Bali. It gets a lot of traffic, nearly all of it good-humoured, and also includes polls on the best and worst of Bali.

British Foreign and Commonwealth Office ⓦwww.fco.gov.uk. Constantly updated advice for travellers on circumstances affecting safety in over 130 countries.

Canadian Foreign Affairs Department ⓦwww.dfait-maeci.gc.ca/menu-e.asp. Country-by-country travel advisories.

Destination Indonesia ®www.destination-indonesia.net. A serious site devoted to Indo politics, economics, social issues and *Inside Indonesia* journal articles.

Expat Forum ®www.expat.or.id/info/sitemap.html or ®http://expatforum.digitaldevelopment.com. An excellent site for expats living in Indonesia, offering message boards, jobs, listings for social clubs and events, book lists, places to visit, garage sales, personal, wanted, household staff, house search and etiquette etc.

Indonesia Tourism ®www.indonesia-tourism.com.The official website of Indonesian tourism; it reads like a glossy brochure, but contains some useful information on places to go, cultural hints, transport and general information about the country. Also has a hotel booking facility.

Kereta api Indonesia – Indonesian railways ®http://members.tripod.com/~keretapi. Site devoted to the history and current situation of Indonesia's trains and rail system.

Lombok Island ®www.lombokisland.com. A small, all-purpose Lombok site, featuring a general introduction to tourist spots, plus some links to Lombok hotels, airlines and ferry companies.

Lonely Planet Thorn Tree ®http://thorntree.lonelyplanet.com/thorn. A very popular travellers' bulletin board, divided into regions (eg islands of Southeast Asia). Ideal for exchanging information with other travellers and for starting a debate, though it does attract an annoying number of regular posters just itching for an argument.

Pelni ®www.pelni.co.id. Website of Pelni, the national passenger ship company, in both English and Indonesian; currently very well maintained, with details of timetables, which ferries are currently in dock, details of each ship's age and capacity and the facilities on board.

Peter Loud's maps of Indonesia ®http://users.powernet.co.uk/mkmarina/indonesia/indonesia.html. Reasonably detailed maps of various regions of Indonesia, Including the remoter regions of Nusa Tenggara and West Papua's Baliem Valley. Includes dive site maps.

Petra East Java ®www.petra.ac.id/english/eastjava. Surabaya's Petra University travel information site, good for destinations in East Java.

Tourism Indonesia ®www.tourismindonesia.com. Rival website to Indonesia tourism, offering much the same information, though examining the country in rather more depth. Also offers a hotel booking facility.

Travel Helpers ®www.geocities.com/TheTropics/2442/indonesi.html. Interesting site where travellers with experience of particular countries offer to answer other peoples' queries.

Underwater Indonesia ®www.underwaterindonesia.com. Great site on diving, PADI sites.

US State Department Travel Advisories ®http://travel.state.gov/travel_warnings.html Website providing "consular information sheets", detailing the dangers of travelling in most countries of the world.

Maps

While there's no shortage of **maps** of Indonesia available abroad, none is absolutely accurate. Good all-rounders, suitable for general travel or for navigation in your own transport, include GeoCentre's 1:2,000,000 series, which covers Indonesia in two sections and fine detail, with clearly defined topography and road surfaces. Another longtime standby, the Nelles Indonesia series includes a more convenient single-sheet spread of the country, as well as larger-scale maps of individual regions and provinces, sometimes including basic plans of major cities. Most popular of all, however, are the ever-growing range of provincial maps and town plans provided by Periplus; though not always accurate, they are very user-friendly and the most up-to-date maps available. All of the above mark locations of major tourist sights and services.

In Indonesia, bookshops and tourist organizations stock home-produced maps of provinces and localities. Some list every road, village, river tributary and mountain, while others are more useful for wallpaper than for orienteering. A blend of both, Travel Treasure Maps have annotated sketches of popular regions such as Bali and Tanah Toraja, and make a good supplement to a decent road map.

Map outlets

In the UK and Ireland

Blackwell's Map and Travel Shop 50 Broad St, Oxford OX1 3BQ ®01865/793 550, ®http://maps.blackwell.co.uk/index.html.

Easons Bookshop 40 O'Connell St, Dublin 1 ®01/873 3811, ®www.eason.ie.

Heffers Map and Travel 20 Trinity St, Cambridge CB2 1TJ ®01223/568 568, ®www.heffers.co.uk.

Hodges Figgis Bookshop 56–58 Dawson St,

Dublin 2 ⓣ01/677 4754, ⓦwww.hodgesfiggis.com.

John Smith & Son 100 Cathedral St, Glasgow G4 0RD ⓣ0141/552 3377, ⓦwww.johnsmith.co.uk.

James Thin Booksellers 53–59 South Bridge Edinburgh EH1 1YS ⓣ0131/622 8222, ⓦwww.jthin.co.uk.

The Map Shop 30a Belvoir St, Leicester LE1 6QH ⓣ0116/247 1400, ⓦwww.mapshopleicester.co.uk.

National Map Centre 22–24 Caxton St, London SW1H 0QU ⓣ020/7222 2466, ⓦwww.mapsnmc.co.uk.

Newcastle Map Centre 55 Grey St, Newcastle-upon-Tyne, NE1 6EF ⓣ0191/261 5622, ⓦwww.newtraveller.com.

Ordnance Survey Ireland Phoenix Park, Dublin 8 ⓣ01/8025 349, ⓦwww.irlgov.ie/osi.

Ordnance Survey of Northern Ireland Colby House, Stranmillis Ct, Belfast BT9 5BJ ⓣ028/9025 5761, ⓦwww.osni.gov.uk.

Stanfords 12–14 Long Acre, WC2E 9LP ⓣ020/7836 1321, ⓦwww.stanfords.co.uk, ⓔsales@stanfords.co.uk. Maps available by mail, phone order or email. Other branches within British Airways offices at 156 Regent St, London W1R 5TA ⓣ020/7434 4744, and 29 Corn St, Bristol BS1 1HT ⓣ0117/929 9966.

The Travel Bookshop 13–15 Blenheim Crescent, W11 2EE ⓣ020/7229 5260, ⓦwww.thetravelbookshop.co.uk.

In the USA and Canada

Adventurous Traveler Bookstore 102 Lake Street, Burlington, VT 05401 ⓣ1-800/282-3963, ⓦwww.adventuroustraveler.com.

Book Passage 51 Tamal Vista Blvd, Corte Madera, CA 94925 ⓣ1-800/999-7909, ⓦwww.bookpassage.com.

Distant Lands 56 S Raymond Ave, Pasadena, CA 91105 ⓣ1-800/310-3220, ⓦwww.distantlands.com.

Elliot Bay Book Company 101 S Main St, Seattle, WA 98104 ⓣ1-800/962-5311, ⓦwww.elliotbaybook.com.

Forsyth Travel Library 226 Westchester Ave, White Plains, NY 10604 ⓣ1-800/367-7984, ⓦwww.forsyth.com.

Globe Corner Bookstore 28 Church St, Cambridge, MA 02138 ⓣ1-800/358-6013, ⓦwww.globecorner.com.

GORP Books & Maps ⓣ1-877/440-4677, ⓦwww.gorp.com/gorp/books/main.htm.

Map Link 30 S La Patera Lane, Unit 5, Santa Barbara, CA 93117 ⓣ805/692-6777, ⓦwww.maplink.com.

Rand McNally ⓣ1-800/333-0136, ⓦwww.randmcnally.com. Around thirty stores across the US; dial ext 2111 or check the website for the nearest location.

Travel Books and Language Center 4437 Wisconsin Ave NW, Washington, DC 20016 ⓣ1-800/220-2665, ⓦwww.bookweb.org/bookstore/travelbks.

The Travel Bug Bookstore 2667 W Broadway, Vancouver V6K 2G2 ⓣ604/737-1122, ⓦwww.swifty.com/tbug.

World of Maps 1235 Wellington St, Ottawa, Ontario K1Y 3A3 ⓣ1-800/214-8524, ⓦwww.worldofmaps.com.

In Australia and New Zealand

The Map Shop 6–10 Peel St, Adelaide, SA 5000 ⓣ08/8231 2033, ⓦwww.mapshop.net.au.

Specialty Maps 46 Albert St, Auckland 1001 ⓣ09/307 2217, ⓦwww.ubdonline.co.nz/maps.

MapWorld 173 Gloucester St, Christchurch, New Zealand ⓣ0800/627 967 or 03/374 5399, ⓦwww.mapworld.co.nz.

Mapland 372 Little Bourke St, Melbourne, Victoria 3000, ⓣ03/9670 4383, ⓦwww.mapland.com.au.

Perth Map Centre 1/884 Hay St, Perth, WA 6000, ⓣ08/9322 5733, ⓦwww.perthmap.com.au.

Insurance

Before travelling to Indonesia, you'd do well to take out an **insurance policy** to cover against theft, loss, and illness or injury. Before paying for a new policy, however, it's worth checking whether you are already covered: some all-risks home insurance policies may cover your possessions when overseas, and many private medical schemes include cover when abroad. In Canada, provincial health plans usually provide partial cover for medical mishaps overseas, while holders of official student/teacher/youth cards in Canada and the US are entitled to meagre accident coverage and hospital inpatient benefits. Students will often find that their student health coverage extends during the vacations and for one term beyond the date of last enrolment.

After exhausting the possibilities above, you might want to contact a specialist travel insurance company, or consider the travel insurance deal we offer (see box). A typical travel insurance policy usually provides cover for the loss of baggage, tickets and – up to a certain limit – cash or cheques, as well as cancellation or curtailment of your journey. Most of them exclude so-called dangerous sports unless an extra premium is paid: in Indonesia, this can mean scuba diving, whitewater rafting, windsurfing and trekking. Many policies can be chopped and changed to exclude coverage you don't need – for example, sickness and accident benefits can often be excluded or included at will. If you do take medical coverage, ascertain whether benefits will be paid as treatment proceeds or only after return home, and whether there is a 24-hour medical emergency number. When securing baggage cover, make sure that the per-article limit – typically under £500 – will cover your most valuable possession. If you need to make a claim, you should keep receipts for medicines and medical treatment, and in the event you have anything stolen, you must obtain an official statement from the police.

Rough Guides travel insurance

Rough Guides offers its own travel insurance, customized for our readers by a leading UK broker and backed by a Lloyd's underwriter. It's available for anyone, of any nationality and any age, travelling anywhere in the world.

There are two main Rough Guide insurance plans: **Essential**, for basic, no-frills cover; and **Premier** – with more generous and extensive benefits. Alternatively, you can take out **annual multi-trip insurance**, which covers you for any number of trips throughout the year (with a maximum of 60 days for any one trip). Unlike many policies, the Rough Guides schemes are calculated by the day, so if you're travelling for 27 days rather than a month, that's all you pay for. If you intend to be away for the whole year, the Adventurer policy will cover you for 365 days. Each plan can be supplemented with a "Hazardous Activities Premium" if you plan to indulge in sports considered dangerous, such as skiing, scuba diving or trekking.

For a policy quote, call the Rough Guides Insurance Line on UK freefone ⓣ0800/015 0906; US toll-free ⓣ1-866/220 5588; or, if you're calling from elsewhere, ⓣ+44 1243/621 046. Alternatively, get an online quote or buy online at ⓦwww.roughguidesinsurance.com.

Health

The vast majority of travellers to Indonesia suffer nothing more than an upset stomach; generally, hygiene and health standards are improving. If you have a minor ailment, it's usually best to head to a pharmacy (*apotik*); most have a decent idea of how to treat common ailments and can provide many medicines without prescription.

Otherwise, ask for the nearest *doktor*, *doktor gigi* (dentist) or *rumah sakit* (hospital). If you have a serious accident or illness then you will need to be evacuated home or to Singapore, which has the best medical provision in Asia. It is, therefore, vital to arrange **health insurance** before you leave home (see p.29).

Before you go

Immunizations are not required for visitors to Indonesia, but several are strongly recommended. Typhus, hepatitis A, tetanus and polio are the most important ones, and rabies, hepatitis B, Japanese encephalitis, diphtheria and TB are all worth considering if you're planning trips outside of Java or Bali.

For up-to-the-minute **information**, make an appointment at a travel clinic (see p.34), although immunizations can be costly, as these clinics are private. They also sell travel accessories, including mosquito nets and first-aid kits.

A doctor should be consulted at least two months in advance of your departure date, as not all immunizations can be given at the same time, and some take a while to become effective (hepatitis B, for example, can take six months to provide full protection).

In the UK, pick up the Department of Health's free publication, *Health Advice for Travellers*, a comprehensive **booklet** available at the post office, or by calling the Health Literature Line on ☎0800/555777. The content of the booklet, which contains immunization advice, is constantly updated on pages 460–464 of CEEFAX. Most general practitioners in the UK can give advice and certain vaccines on prescription, though only some immunizations are free under the NHS.

Precautions

Prevention is always better than cure. Remember that most **water** that comes out of taps has had very little treatment, and can contain a whole range of bacteria and viruses. These micro-organisms cause diseases such as diarrhoea, gastroenteritis, typhus, cholera, dysentery, poliomyelitis, hepatitis A and giardiasis, and can be present no matter how clean and safe the water looks. The only water you should ever put in your mouth – and that includes brushing your teeth – should be bottled, boiled or sterilized. Fortunately, except in the furthest-flung corners of the archipelago, **bottled water** is on sale everywhere. You should be careful about cutlery, plates, salads and vegetables that have been washed in tap water and are still wet. Bear in mind that while **ice** is made in government-run plants from sterilized water, its methods of transport are not the most hygienic – it's best avoided.

If you're planning to head off the beaten track or don't fancy shelling out daily for bottled water, you should consider taking a **water purifier** with you. While boiling water for ten minutes kills most micro-organisms, it's not the most convenient method. Sterilization with **iodine tablets** is effective, but the resulting liquid doesn't taste very pleasant – though flavouring with cordial can mask this slightly – and you'll probably want to filter the water as well. Iodine is unsafe for pregnant women, babies and people with thyroid complaints. Portable water purifiers, which sterilize and filter the water, give the most complete treatment.

An estimated eighty percent of the indigenous population of rural Indonesia carry **intestinal parasites**, flukes and worms, contracted either through water, poorly

First-aid kit

Some of the items listed below can be purchased more easily and cheaply in an Indonesian **apotik**; Imodium and dental/sterile surgical kits will need to be bought before you leave home.

Antiseptic cream
Insect repellent
Antihistamine
Plasters/band aids
Water sterilization tablets or water purifier
Lint and sealed bandages
A course of flagyl antibiotics (for giardia) and norfloxacin (for bacterial diarrhoea)
Antifungal/athletes foot cream
Imodium (Lomotil) for emergency diarrhoea treatment
Paracetamol/aspirin
Anti-inflammatory/Ibuprofen
Multivitamin and mineral tablets
Rehydration salts
Emergency dental kit with temporary fillings
Hypodermic and intravenous needles, sutures and sterilized skin wipes
Condoms and other contraceptives

cooked fish, pork or beef, or from walking around barefoot. Wearing sandals or thongs in the shower, and making sure all food is cooked thoroughly are the best precautions to take. Should you pick up flukes or worms, they may be very difficult to diagnose. Your best bet is to have a full checkup at your home country's tropical diseases hospital on your return; parasites can usually be killed off quickly and easily with a short course of tablets.

Though the Indonesian government would have the international community believe that **AIDS** is not yet a problem, this could not be further from the truth. Using latex **condoms** during sex reduces the risks. Bring a supply of them with you, take special care with expiry dates and bear in mind that condoms don't last as long when kept in the heat. Blood transfusions, intravenous drug use, acupuncture, dentistry, tattooing and body piercing are high-risk. Get a dental checkup before you leave home, and carry a sterile needles kit for medical emergencies.

Pharmacies and doctors

You'll find **pharmacies** (*apotik*) in towns and cities selling a wide range of medicines, many of which you would need a prescription to buy back home. Only in the main tourist areas will assistants speak English; in the village health posts, staff are generally interested and well meaning, but ill-equipped to cope with serious illness.

If you need an English-speaking **doctor**, seek advice at your hotel (some of the luxury ones have an in-house doctor) or at the local tourist office. For more serious problems, you'll find a public **hospital** in major cities and towns, and in some places these are supplemented by private hospitals, many of which operate an accident and emergency department.

Stomach upsets and viruses

If you travel in Asia for an extended period of time, you are likely to come down with some kind of stomach bug. Usually this is just a case of **diarrhoea**, caught through bad hygiene, unfamiliar or affected food, and is generally over in a couple of days if treated properly. Dehydration is one of the main concerns if you have diarrhoea, so **rehydration salts** dissolved in clean water provide the best treatment. **Gastroenteritis** is a more extreme version, but can still be cured with the same blend of rest and rehydration. Oralit is the most frequently available brand in pharmacies, but you can make up your own by mixing three teaspoons of sugar and one of salt to a litre of water. You will need to drink as much as three litres a day to stave off dehydration. Eat non-spicy, non-greasy foods such as **young coconut**, unbuttered toast, rice, **bananas** and noodles, and avoid alcohol, coffee, milk and most fruits. Charcoal tablets work wonders for some people, and there are blocking medicines, Lomotil and Imodium. Since diarrhoea purges the body of the bugs, taking them is not recommended unless you have some urgent reason to be mobile. Antibiotics are a worse idea, as they can wipe out friendly bacteria in the bowel and render you far more susceptible to future attacks.

The next step up from gastroenteritis is **dysentery**, diagnosable from blood and mucus in the (often blackened) stool. Dysentery is either amoebic or bacillary. The latter is caused by a bacteria causing a high fever and vomiting, and serious attacks will require antibiotics. Amoebic dysentery shares the above symptoms except for the fever and vomiting. It can last for weeks and recur, and therefore must always be treated, preferably in hospital.

Giardiasis can be diagnosed by foul-smelling farts and burps, abdominal distension, evil-smelling stools that float, and diarrhoea without blood or pus. Don't be over eager with your diagnosis though, and treat it as normal diarrhoea for at least 24 hours before seeking out some Flagyl antibiotics. (Note that drinking alcohol while on these could result in serious liver damage).

Hepatitis A or E is a waterborne viral infection spread through water and food. It causes jaundice, loss of appetite and nausea and can leave you feeling wiped out for months. Seek immediate medical help if you think you may have contracted hepatitis. The new Havrix vaccination lasts for several years, provided you have a booster the year after your first jabs. Hepatitis B is transmitted by bodily fluids, during unprotected sex or by intravenous drug use.

Cholera and **typhus** both occur in Indonesia, though you are unlikely to come into contact with them. They are infectious diseases, generally spread when communities rely on sparse water supplies. It's worth getting vaccinated against typhus, but the World Health Organization now reckons the cholera vaccine is only about fifty percent effective.

Malaria and dengue fever

Indonesia is within a **malarial zone**, although in the developed tourist resorts, for example, in Bali, there is little risk. If you are visiting any other areas, even in transit, you should take full precautions and, in any case, check the advice of your doctor before you travel, as information regarding malaria is constantly being updated. The latest information shows an increase in infections of the most serious form of the illness and there are reports of resistance to certain drug treatments by some strains. Pregnant women and children need particular advice on dosage and the different drugs available.

Malaria is caused by a parasite in the saliva of the anopheles mosquito which is passed into the human when bitten. There are various prophylactic drug regimes available, depending on your destination, all of which must be taken according to a strict timetable, beginning one week before you go and continuing four weeks after leaving the area. If you don't do this, you are in danger of developing the illness once you have returned home. One drug, **Mefloquine** (sold as Larium) has received some very critical media coverage; in some people it appears to produce disorientation, depression and sleep disturbance, although it suits other people very well. If you're intending to use Larium you should begin to take it two weeks before you depart to see whether it will agree with your metabolism. Because of the side effects of Larium a new drug, **doxycycline**, has become the malaria prophylactic of choice amongst the majority of Indonesian travellers. The usual dosage Is one tablet per day, with a maximum usage of six months (with Larium it is one year). Anyone planning to scuba dive should discuss the use of both doxycycline and Larium very carefully with their medical advisers as there has been some indication of an increased risk of the "bends".

None of the drugs is one hundred per cent effective and it is equally important to the prevention of malaria to stop the mosquitoes biting you: sleep under a net, burn mosquito coils and use repellent on exposed skin when the mosquitoes are around, mostly after dark.

The **symptoms** of malaria are fever, headache and shivering, similar to a severe dose of flu and often coming in cycles, but a lot of people have additional symptoms.

Don't delay in seeking help fast: malaria can be fatal. You will need a blood test to confirm the illness and the doctor will prescribe the most effective treatment locally. If you develop flu-like symptoms any time up to a year after returning home, you should inform a doctor of the areas you have been travelling in and ask for a blood test.

Another important reason to avoid getting bitten is **dengue fever**, a virus carried by a different species of mosquito, which bites during the day. There is no vaccine or tablet available to prevent the illness, which causes fever, headache and joint and muscle pains among the least serious symptoms, and internal bleeding and circulatory-system failure among the most serious, and there is no specific drug to cure it. It is vital to get an early medical diagnosis and get treatment. Reports indicate that the disease is on the increase across Asia. According to experts, epidemics of the disease tend to occur in five-year cycles; while malaria can occur at any time, travellers visiting Indonesia in 2003 should be especially careful.

Other things that bite or sting

The most common irritations for travellers come from tiny pests which can wreck a good night's sleep. **Fleas**, **lice** and **bed bugs** thrive in run-down guesthouses, and adore grimy sheets. Examine your bedding carefully, air and beat the offending articles and then coat yourself liberally in insect repellent.

Ticks are nasty pea-shaped bloodsuckers which usually attach themselves to you if you walk through long grass. A dab of petrol, alcohol, tiger balm or insect repellent, or a lit cigarette, should convince them to leave. **Leeches** are generally only a problem in the jungle and in fresh water. These relatives of the earthworm attach themselves to the skin, apply an anticoagulant and anaesthetic and then proceed to ingest blood. They will eventually fall off when replete, but you won't want to leave them that long. Salt, applied directly, is the best remedy, but all the anti-tick treatments also work. **DEET** is an effective deterrent, and applying it at the tops of your boots and around the lace-holes is a good idea. Always wear shoes, and, for trekking, boots with socks tucked into your trousers. With all of these irritants, there is a danger of infection to or through the bitten area, so keep bites clean and wash with antiseptic soap.

Indonesia has many species of both land and sea **snakes**, and encounters in wilder places are fairly common. Contrary to popular belief, however, most snakes do their best to avoid people, and will generally get out of your way long before you know they are there. Not all are venomous, but three to watch out for are: **cobras**, fast, nervous snakes who become aggressive if startled; boldly striped **kraits**, which are sluggish and slow to move at your approach; and **pit vipers**, whose cryptic coloration and habitual immobility make them a potentially dangerous inhabitant of thick undergrowth. If confronted, back off; if **bitten**, apply a pressure bandage as tightly as you would for a sprain, splint the affected limb, keep it below the level of the heart and try to stay still – the idea is to slow the venom's entry into the bloodstream – and get to hospital as soon as possible. Tourniquets, cutting open the bite and trying to suck the venom out have long been discredited.

Indonesia's other venomous beasts – which include in West Papua the world's only poisonous bird, the New Guinea Pitohi – are mostly on the small side. **Scorpions** are found in a range of habitats and range from large, black varieties capable of painful but otherwise harmless stings, to smaller and more dangerous species. If stung, avoid the temptation to cool the stung area (as this intensifies the pain), avoid rubbing, keep the wound warm and get to hospital quickly.

Crocodiles and **sharks** occupy far more time in travellers' nightmares than their realities. You will see sharks if you spend any amount of time snorkelling or diving on Asia's reefs: they are inquisitive but rarely aggressive. The most dangerous species such as the tiger and mako are rare sights for snorkellers, the former liking muddy estuaries and the latter the open sea.

Rabies is transmitted to humans by the bite of carrier animals, who have the disease in their saliva; **tetanus** is an additional danger from such bites. All animals should be treated with caution, but particularly monkeys, cats and dogs. Be extremely cautious with wild animals that seem inexplicably tame, as this can be a symptom. If you do get bitten, scrub the wound with a strong antiseptic and then alcohol – whisky will do – and get to a hospital as soon as possible. Do not attempt to close the wound. The incubation period for the disease can be as much as a year or as little as a few days; once the disease has taken hold it will be fatal.

Heat problems

Travellers who are unused to tropical climates regularly suffer from **sunburn** and **dehydration**. Limit your exposure to the sun in the hours around midday, use high-factor sunscreen and wear dark glasses and a sunhat. You'll be sweating a great deal in the heat, so the important thing is to make sure that you drink enough (see p.30 for advice on water). If you are urinating very little, or your urine turns dark (this can also indicate hepatitis), increase your fluid intake. When you sweat you lose salt, so make sure your intake covers this: add some extra to your food, or take oral rehydration salts (see p.31). A more serious result of the heat is **heatstroke**, indicated by high temperature, dry red skin and a fast erratic pulse. As an emergency measure, try to cool the patient off by covering them in sheets or sarongs soaked in cold water and turn the fan on them; they may still need to go to hospital, though. **Heat rashes**, **prickly heat** and **fungal infections** are also common: wear loose cotton clothing, dry yourself carefully after bathing and use medicated talcum powder or antifungal powder if you fall victim.

Medical resources for travellers

The following helplines and clinics will be able to advise you on the latest health news in Indonesia, which vaccinations you will require and which course of malaria prophylactics are the most appropriate for your trip.

Websites

ⓦhttp://health.yahoo.com Information on specific diseases and conditions, drugs and herbal remedies, as well as advice from health experts.
ⓦwww.tmvc.com.au Contains a list of all Travellers Medical and Vaccination Centres throughout Australia, New Zealand and Southeast Asia, plus general information on travel health.
ⓦwww.istm.org The website of the International Society for Travel Medicine, with a full list of clinics specializing in international travel health.
ⓦwww.tripprep.com Travel Health Online provides an online-only comprehensive database of necessary vaccinations for most countries, as well as destination and medical service provider information.
ⓦwww.fitfortravel.scot.nhs.uk UK NHS website carrying information about travel-related diseases and how to avoid them.

In the UK and Ireland

British Airways Travel Clinics 28 regional clinics (call ⓣ01276/685 040 for the nearest, or consult ⓦwww.britishairways.com), with several in London (Mon–Fri 9.30am–5.15pm, Sat 10am–4pm), including 156 Regent St, London W1 ⓣ020/7439 9584: no appointment necessary. There are appointment-only branches at 101 Cheapside, London EC2 (ⓣ020/7606 2977); and at the BA terminal in London's Victoria Station (ⓣ020/7233 6661). All clinics offer vaccinations, tailored advice from an online database and a complete range of travel health-care products.
Communicable Diseases Unit Brownlee Centre, Glasgow G12 0YN ⓣ0141/211 1074. Travel vaccinations.
Dun Laoghaire Medical Centre 5 Northumberland Ave, Dun Laoghaire, Co. Dublin ⓣ01/280 4996, ⓕ280 5603. Advice on medical matters abroad.
Hospital for Tropical Diseases Travel Clinic 2nd floor, Mortimer Market Centre, off Capper St, London WC1E 6AU (Mon–Fri 9am–5pm by appointment only; ⓣ020/7388 9600; a consultation costs £15, which is waived if you have your injections here). A recorded Health Line (ⓣ09061/337 733; 50p per min) gives hints on hygiene and illness prevention, as well as listing appropriate immunizations.
Liverpool School of Tropical Medicine Pembroke Place, Liverpool L3 5QA ⓣ0151/708 9393. Walk-in clinic (Mon–Fri 1–4pm).
Malaria Helpline 24-hour recorded message ⓣ0891/600 350; 60p per minute.
MASTA (Medical Advisory Service for Travellers Abroad) London School of Hygiene and Tropical Medicine. Operates a prerecorded 24-hour Travellers' Health Line (UK ⓣ0906/822 4100, 60p per min; Republic of Ireland ⓣ01560/147 000, 75p per minute), giving written information tailored

to your journey by return of post.

Nomad Pharmacy 40 Bernard St, London, WC1; and 3–4 Wellington Terrace, Turnpike Lane, London N8 (Mon–Fri 9.30am–6pm, ⓣ020/7833 4114 to book vaccination appointment). They give advice free if you go in person, or their telephone helpline is ⓣ09068/633 414 (60p per min). They can give information tailored to your travel needs.

Trailfinders Immunization clinics (no appointments necessary) at 194 Kensington High St, London (Mon–Fri 9am–5pm, except Thurs to 6pm, Sat 9.30am–4pm; ⓣ020/7938 3999).

Travel Health Centre Department of International Health and Tropical Medicine, Royal College of Surgeons in Ireland, Mercers Medical Centre, Stephen's St Lower, Dublin ⓣ01/402 2337. Expert pre-trip advice and inoculations.

Travel Medicine Services PO Box 254, 16 College St, Belfast 1 ⓣ028/9031 5220. Offers medical advice before a trip and help afterwards in the event of a tropical disease.

Tropical Medical Bureau Grafton Buildings, 34 Grafton St, Dublin 2 ⓣ01/671 9200

In the USA and Canada

Canadian Society for International Health 1 Nicholas St, Suite 1105, Ottawa, ON K1N 7B7 ⓣ613/241-5785, ⓦwww.csih.org. Distributes a free pamphlet, "Health Information for Canadian Travellers", containing an extensive list of travel health centres in Canada.

Centers for Disease Control 1600 Clifton Rd NE, Atlanta, GA 30333 ⓣ1-800/311-3435 or 404/639-3534, ⓕ1-888/232-3299, ⓦwww.cdc.gov. Publishes outbreak warnings, suggested inoculations, precautions and other background information for travellers. Useful website plus International Travellers Hotline on ⓣ1-877/FYI-TRIP.

International Association for Medical Assistance to Travellers (IAMAT) 417 Center St, Lewiston, NY 14092 ⓣ716/754-4883, ⓦwww.sentex.net/~iamat, and 40 Regal Rd, Guelph, ON N1K 1B5 ⓣ519/836-0102. A non-profit organization supported by donations, it can provide a list of English-speaking doctors in Indonesia, climate charts and leaflets on various diseases and inoculations.

International SOS Assistance Eight Neshaminy Interplex Suite 207, Trevose, USA 19053-6956 ⓣ1-800/523-8930, ⓦwww.intsos.com. Members receive pre-trip medical referral information, as well as overseas emergency services designed to complement travel insurance coverage.

Travel Medicine ⓣ1-800/872-8633, ⓕ1-413/584-6656, ⓦwww.travmed.com. Sells first-aid kits, mosquito netting, water filters, reference books and other health-related travel products.

Travelers Medical Center 31 Washington Square West, New York, NY 10011 ⓣ212/982-1600. Consultation service on immunizations and treatment of diseases for people travelling to developing countries.

In Australia and New Zealand

Travellers' Medical and Vaccination Centres The Travellers' Medical and Vaccination centres offer vaccinations, visa-application health checks, medical kits for sale, a list of English-speaking doctors abroad and, via their website, a virtual doctor to address your health concerns whilst abroad. They have clinics at the following locations:

27–29 Gilbert Place, Adelaide, SA 5000 ⓣ08/8212 7522.

1/170 Queen St, Auckland ⓣ09/373 3531.

5/247 Adelaide St, Brisbane, Qld 4000 ⓣ07/3221 9066.

5/8–10 Hobart Place, Canberra, ACT 2600 ⓣ02/6257 7156.

147 Armagh St, Christchurch ⓣ03/379 4000.

5 Westralia St, Darwin, NT 0800 ⓣ08/8981 2907.

270 Sandy Bay Rd, Sandy Bay, Hobart, Tas 7000 ⓣ03/6223 7577.

2/393 Little Bourke St, Melbourne, Vic 3000 ⓣ03/9602 5788.

5 Mill St, Perth, WA 6000 ⓣ08/9321 1977, plus branch in Fremantle.

7/428 George St, Sydney, NSW 2000 ⓣ02/9221 7133, plus branches in Chatswood and Parramatta.

Shop 15, Grand Arcade, 14–16 Willis St, Wellington ⓣ04/473 0991.

Costs, money and banks

After three years of economic turmoil, fluctuating prices and tumbling rupiahs, during which the Indonesian currency tumbled from Rp3000 to Rp10,000 to the US dollar (and at one point, immediately following the fall of Suharto, stood at an incredible Rp20,000 to one dollar), the Indonesian economy – and the rupiah with it – does at last seem to have found some sort of stability. However, it's too early to say with any confidence that the crisis is over; as a result, it's also very difficult to say with any degree of accuracy how much it costs to travel in Indonesia.

Currency

The Indonesian currency is the rupiah (abbreviated to "Rp"), for which there are no smaller units. Notes are the main form of exchange and come in denominations of Rp100, Rp500, Rp1000, Rp5000, Rp10,000, Rp20,000 and Rp50,000, increasing in size according to value. Be warned that most people won't accept ripped or badly worn banknotes, so *you* shouldn't either. Coins, mainly used for public telephones and bemo rides, come in Rp25, Rp50, Rp100, Rp500 and Rp1000 denominations, though you'll very rarely see the lower values nowadays.

Officially, rupiah are available outside of Indonesia, but its volatile value means that very few banks carry it at present. You can check the latest exchange rate through a bank, or with Oanda, an online currency converter at ⓦwww.oanda.com/cgi-bin/ncc, which gives you the day's rate for 164 currencies and compiles free, wallet-sized conversion tables for travellers to print out and use on the ground.

Due to Indonesia's fluctuating financial situation, all accommodation prices in this guide are given in their more stable US dollar equivalents, even for places where you are not required to pay in this currency. Prices quoted in rupiah for transport and other services were correct at the time of research and have been retained to give a relative idea of costs – though in practice, the prices of many of these things will be higher than those quoted in the guide.

Costs

How much you spend in Indonesia will depend on where you visit, how much you move around and how much discomfort you're prepared to endure. You'll keep all **costs** to a minimum if you concentrate on Java, Sumatra, Bali, Lombok and Nusa Tenggara, where it's possible to travel fairly cheaply. On all except Nusa Tenggara, there's usually a good range of services too – though you'll find that there's also plenty to spend money on. In the outer regions, such as Kalimantan, Sulawesi, Maluku and West Papua, severe geography and a lack of infrastructure may mean flying or cruising between places are the only options for travel, while the cost of goods imported from elsewhere in Indonesia will be that much higher.

Taking all this into account, if you're happy to eat where the locals do, use the cheapest forms of public transport and stay in simple accommodation, you could manage on a **daily budget** of £6.50/US$10 per person. For around £10/US$14 a day (less if you share a room), you'll get a few extra comforts, like hot water and air-con in your accommodation, bigger meals, a few beers, and the ability to travel in better style from time to time. Staying in luxury hotels and eating at the flashiest restaurants, expect to spend upwards of £70/US$110 per day.

There's generally a **fee** to enter museums, archeological sites and – in Bali – temples, which can range from a small donation (before which you're often shown a register recording grossly inflated amounts given by previous visitors) to several thousand rupiah.

Bargaining

One of the most obvious ways of lowering your everyday costs, **bargaining** is an art which requires not only a sense of humour but also a fair amount of tact – it's easy to forget that you're quibbling over amounts which mean a lot more to an Indonesian than to you. Pretty much everything is negotiable, from cigarettes and woodcarvings to car-rental and accommodation rates. The first price given is rarely the real one, and most stall-holders and shopkeepers engage in some financial banter before finalizing the sale. Have a look at what others are paying first, but expect to pay more than locals, and to make a few blunders before getting a feel for the game. On average, buyers will start their counterbid at about 25 percent of the vendor's opening price, and the bartering continues from there.

Places that are geared towards the upmarket tourist trade usually don't like to bargain, and many such hotels and shops display "fixed price" notices on their walls. Even here it's worth asking about "low-season discounts", however, and there are some tourist-oriented services – such as diving – where negotiating will still net you substantial savings.

Banks and exchange

You'll find **banks** capable of handling foreign exchange in provincial capitals and bigger cities throughout Indonesia, with privately run **moneychangers** in major tourist centres. Where there's a choice, it's always worth shopping around: moneychangers sometimes offer better rates than banks, and you'll often find big differences not just between separate institutions, but also individual branches of the same bank. As a rule of thumb, Indonesian **banking hours** are Monday to Friday 8am to 3pm and Saturday 8am to 1pm, but these can vary, with restricted hours for foreign-exchange transactions. Where available, moneychangers open early and close late.

Always time-consuming, the **exchange process** is straightforward enough in banks, though there may be minimum or maximum **limits** to transactions. You may also be asked to supply a **photocopy** of your passport, or the **receipt** (or proof of purchase) that you get when you buy your travellers' cheques. With moneychangers, always establish any **commissions** before signing cheques; many display promising rates, but charge a hefty fee or only give that rate for big transactions. Always count your money carefully, as it's not unknown for unscrupulous dealers to rip you off, either by folding notes over to make it look as if you're getting twice as much as you actually are, or by distracting you and then whipping away a few notes from your pile.

Travellers' cheques and cash

Travellers' cheques are the best way to carry the bulk of your funds around. Though you get a slightly poorer rate than for cash, they can be replaced if lost or stolen (keep a list of the serial numbers separate from the cheques). Stick to major brands, such as **American Express** and **Visa** – outside Bali and Java, you'll have trouble cashing anything else. Dollar travellers' cheques are the most acceptable form of currency, followed by sterling, though euro travellers' cheques will probably become widely acceptable in time too. Larger denominations are preferable, as you tend to get better rates. If you're planning a trip to less-travelled regions of Indonesia, US dollars are just about the only kind of travellers' cheques acceptable, and many banks will refuse to accept even them – if they accept anything at all, it will be **US dollars cash**. In emergencies, it's not unknown for small-town businesses or even village stores (generally Chinese-run) to exchange dollars, though at poor rates. Notes do need to be in perfect condition, however.

Credit and debit cards

Credit cards are a very handy back-up source of funds, and can be used either in ATMs or over the counter. Mastercard, Visa and American Express are accepted just about everywhere, but other cards may not be recognized in Indonesia. Remember that all cash advances are treated as loans, with interest accruing daily from the date of withdrawal; there may be a transaction fee on top of this. However, you can use Cirrus/Maestro debit cards to make withdrawals from many ATMs in Indonesia, which is not liable to interest payments, and the flat transaction fee is usually quite small

– your bank will be able to advise on this. Make sure you have a personal identification number (PIN) that's designed to work overseas.

A compromise between travellers' cheques and plastic is **Visa TravelMoney**, a disposable prepaid debit card with a PIN which works in all ATMs that take Visa cards. The card is available in most countries from branches of Thomas Cook and Citicorp.

Wiring money

Having money wired from home using one of the companies listed below is never convenient or cheap, and should be considered a last resort. It's also possible to have money wired directly from a bank in your home country to a bank in Indonesia, although this is somewhat less reliable, because it involves two separate institutions. If you go this route, your home bank will need the address of the branch bank where you want to pick up the money, and the address and telex number of the Jakarta head office, which acts as the clearing house; money wired this way normally takes two working days to arrive, and costs around £30/$45 per transaction.

Money-wiring companies

American Express Moneygram
UK and Republic of Ireland ⓣ0800/6663 9472, US and Canada ⓣ1-800/926-9400, Australia ⓣ1800/230 100, New Zealand ⓣ09/379 8243 or 0800/262 263, ⓦwww.moneygram.com.
Thomas Cook UK ⓣ01733/318 922, Belfast ⓣ028/9055 0030, Dublin ⓣ01/677 172, US ⓣ1-800/287-7362, Canada ⓣ1-888/823-4732, ⓦwww.us.thomascook.com.
Western Union UK ⓣ0800/833 833, Republic of Ireland ⓣ1800/395 395, US and Canada ⓣ1-800/325-6000, Australia ⓣ1800/649 565, New Zealand ⓣ09/270 0050, ⓦwww.westernunion.com.

Getting around

Comprising well over 10,000 widely scattered islands, it's likely that, unless you concentrate on a single region, simply getting around Indonesia will occupy a fair amount of your time here. At first, things look simple, with plenty of flights, boats, buses, and even trains waiting to ferry you around the archipelago. But, in practice, getting a ticket – which can be hard enough in itself – is no guarantee that the vehicle or vessel will even leave, at least at the advertised time or on any particular day.

While travel isn't always difficult, you'll save yourself a good deal of stress if you keep your schedule as flexible as possible, and are prepared for an inevitable number of frustrations. Delays are common to all forms of transport – including major flights – caused by weather, mechanical failure, or simply not enough passengers turning up. While this won't be a problem with destinations which are covered by multiple transport options, in some places there may be no choice except to travel in discomfort, or to spend days waiting for a plane or boat to materialize.

Buses and minibuses

Outside of West Papua, there are few regions of Indonesia where roads have yet to reach, and **bus travel** is the most frequently used way of getting about the archipelago's islands. On the plus side, buses are cheap and easy to book, leave roughly on time, and give you a good look at the country. The down side is that they're slow, cramped and often plain terrifying: drivers manage incredibly well given the state of the roads and their vehicles, but, as they leave no margin for error, **accidents** can be devastating. Consequently, where there's a choice of operators on any particular route, it pays to ask local people which bus company they recommend.

Tickets are sold a day or more in advance from the point of departure or bus company offices – which are not necessarily near the relevant **bus station** (*terminal* in Indonesian). Where services are infrequent, it's a good idea to buy tickets as early as possible, while on other routes it's seldom necessary to turn up more than an hour in advance. Buses might stop along the way to pick up passengers, though usually they don't leave until they're full. Tell the driver your exact destination, as it may be possible to get delivered right to the door of your hotel, although just as many buses terminate at their company offices, again leaving you some distance from the nearest terminal or city centre.

The average **long-distance bus** has padded seats but little leg- or headroom. Indonesians dislike draughts, so don't expect open windows, however hot or smoky conditions inside become. **Luggage** gets stored on the roof (where you can't keep an eye on it), in the aisle or on your lap. Sometimes films are shown, and there's always a sound system blasting out *dangdut* or Western pop. Very occasionally on the luxury services you'll get a **snack** of some sort as you board, and there are regular **meal stops** at roadhouses along the way. **Air-con** alone is not worth paying any extra for – vents are often disconnected or blocked – but on long journeys, it's worth forking out for a **luxury bus**, if available, which will have reclining seats. These cost twice as much as the standard buses.

On shorter routes, you'll use **minibuses**, widely known by their Balinese tag, **bemo**, along with **Kijang**, a 4WD lookalike with only two-wheel-drive capability. Though cramped and annoyingly prone to circle their starting points endlessly, looking for customers and fuel, once on their way they're faster than buses and, if you use a series of them to hop long distances, cheaper. Fares are handed over on board, and rarely advertised – keep an eye on what others are paying to avoid being overcharged. You may also have to pay for any space your luggage occupies. In resort areas such as Bali, a more pleasant option are **tourist shuttle buses** specifically for Westerners – though far more expensive than local services, these will take you between points as quickly and smoothly as possible.

Planes

In some areas, **flying** may be the only practical way to get around. The **cost** of air travel may seem high compared with your living expenses in Indonesia, but tickets are reasonably priced considering the distances involved, and the alternative to a three-hour flight may well be a hellish, forty-hour bus ride, or a ten-day sea voyage.

The main airlines are state-operated **Garuda**, which handles international flights (though you might use them for transport within Indonesia), and **Merpati**, the main domestic operator.

Provincial services are supplemented by smaller outfits such as **Mandala** and **Bouraq**, **Pelita**, **Lion Air** and others, and you'll even find remote communities serviced by **missionary aircraft**. The quantity and quality of services is very uncertain at present, however. Garuda's fleet is decent enough, and Pelita, formerly part of the Pertamina oil company, have the newest planes and the best service, but don't expect much from other airlines. Though all the airlines charge much the same fares, Merpati used to offer discounts for students under 25 regardless of nationality, and although this seems to be being phased out, it's worth enquiring.

As long as you do so in advance, **buying a ticket** is usually straightforward on main routes, with airline offices and agents in any town with an airport – whether the flight actually takes off is another matter. **Agents** may even offer discounts, and are often more conveniently located than airline offices. Avoid having to change international air tickets in Indonesia – usually there's no trouble, but you may find yourself stung for unofficial fees.

It's essential to **reconfirm** your seat, as waiting lists can be huge, and the temptation for airline staff to bump you off at the slightest pretext in favour of a benefactor is enormous; if possible, get a computer printout of the reconfirmation. **Check-in times** are an hour before departure for domestic flights, two hours for international, but you need to get to the airport **early**, as seats on overbooked flights are allocated on a first-come, first-served basis. At other times, "fully booked" planes are almost empty, the result of customers not appearing at the last minute, and if you really have to get somewhere, it's always worth going to the airport to check. **Baggage allowance** is twenty kilos, though smaller aircraft serving provincial routes often have a ten-kilo limit, with heavy excesses. On remoter routes, small craft, grass runways and a lack of radar means weather conditions can cause flight cancellations at short notice. **Departure taxes** are currently between Rp9000 and Rp30,000 for internal flights and Rp100,000 for international ones.

Boats and ferries

Indonesia is a land of water, and **boats** are how most of the population – and an increasing number of foreigners – choose to travel between islands, either on the state shipping line, **Pelni**, or on anything from cargo freighters to tiny fishing vessels. Some regions also have extensive **river networks**, with local ferries and speedboats connecting coastal cities with the villages of the interior; see individual chapters for details of these. Slow, occasionally relaxing, but often as fraught as other forms of transport, going by water at least offers a complete change of style from buses or planes, and there's an unparalleled level of contact with local people.

Pelni

Pelni currently operates 29 **passenger liners**, most of which run on two-week or monthly circuits and link Java with ports on all the main island groups between Sumatra and West Papua; see p.42–43 for a chart of the Pelni routes. The vessels are European built, carry 500 to 1600 passengers each, are well maintained if a bit grubby, as safe and punctual as any form of transport in Indonesia can be, and the only widespread form of public transport that offers any luxury. They are usually named after mountains in Indonesia. Their comprehensive website (®www.pelni.co.id) contains details, in English, of timetables and prices.

Booking a ticket can take some planning, especially if you're hoping to link up with specific services. Comprehensive **timetables** for the whole country are hard to find, though don't pass up on the chance to grab one if you have the chance. Pelni offices rarely have anything to give away, though they should have complete timetables on the wall which you might be allowed to photocopy, and they will at least know local schedules. If you're planning an extensive tour around Indonesia, it's worth calling in at Pelni's head office in Jakarta (see p.95), the only place where you're almost guaranteed to find a country-wide timetable, which, incidentally, is usually surprisingly accurate. **Tickets** are available from Pelni offices three days before departure, but as there's a big demand for cabin berths, it's best to pay an **agent** to reserve these for you as early as possible. Note that you can only buy tickets for services which depart locally – you can't, for example, book passage in Makassar for a vessel that leaves from Bitung.

There are several levels of comfort to choose from, not all of them available on every vessel; it's always possible to **upgrade** after boarding, assuming that berths are available. **First class** consists of a private cabin with a double bed, washroom, TV and air-con – about US$40 a day is standard. **Second class** is similar, but with four bunks and no TV (US$30); **third class** is a six-bunk cabin without the washroom (US$20); and **fourth class** is just a bed in a dormitory (US$15). All are good value for money, and include **meals** (eaten in a dining room), which tend to be plentiful rather than interesting; cabins also have large **lockers** to store your luggage.

The alternative is to travel **ekonomi class** (Rp100,000/US$10.50); the experience is noisy, cramped and thick with cigarette smoke, though it's bearable for short trips and not always awful on long ones. You need to buy a rattan mat to sit on, get to the port early (timetables give expected arrival times as well as departures), go aboard and get down into the ekonomi decks to stake out your spot on the floor – all of which you'll be doing with hundreds of others. Don't leave luggage unattended in ekonomi: lock it shut and chain it to something immovable, or lose it. Food is doled out from a hatch and is edible at best, so stock up in advance with instant noodles and biscuits.

Most Pelni ferries follow the same routes on their outward and return legs, calling in at the same ports on both journeys. The map on pp.42–43 shows the exact route for most of the ferries, except for those with simple routes such as number 2, and numbers 25 to 29.

ASDP fast ferries

A new and very welcome introduction has been the arrival of the three **ASDP fast ferries** (*Kapal Ferry Cepat* in Indonesian, or KFC for short), two of which connect Surabaya with Bali and Nusa Tenggara, and one of which sails north from Surabaya to Kalimantan. In a strange way, the experience is similar to taking a flight: baggage is weighed, taken from you and stored in the hold; while on board, the seats are reclinable, a film is shown and stewards come round serving (not very tasty) food. While not cheap (a seven-hour journey, for example, costs about Rp175,000/US$18 in the cheapest (Bisnis) class, the service is very good, and they take less than a third of the time of Pelni vessels.

Perintis and car ferries

Where Pelni and the fast ferries don't venture, you'll find that **Perintis** (Pioneer) freighters do, along with numerous local craft. While these are always willing to rent deck space to passengers for next to nothing – say US$3 for 24 hours – comfort and privacy aboard will be nonexistent. Boats are typically in poor condition and jammed to the gunwales with people, their possessions and livestock; if you're lucky, there'll be an awning to protect you from the elements. On larger vessels, you may find that the crew will rent their beds at about US$5 a person a day. Otherwise, you'll need your own sleeping mat, drinking water and snacks – though on Perintis vessels, there's usually a galley where you can buy rice and fish heads for a few thousand rupiah. Guard your gear and don't flash anything around, especially when the boat pulls in to ports en route. Schedules for these services will be posted at ports, and while you may be able to buy tickets in advance through local agents, you can always pay for your passage on board.

ASDP also run car ferries around Nusa Tenggara. In general, they're cheap and uncomfortable, but they do provide an essential service, and save you having to wait two weeks for the next Pelni ferry. Their website (ⓦwww.ferry-asdp.co.id/english) is rather out of date (they still claim to stop in Komodo, something they haven't actually done for at least two years), but gives some indication of the routes they serve.

Trains

Inevitably slow, not always cheap or comfortable, and restricted to Java and Sumatra, Indonesia's **railways** are nonetheless worth trying out for relief from the rigours of bus travel. You'll find a range of service and comfort between different routes.

Java has a pretty comprehensive rail network stretching right across the island, and linking many important ports and bigger cities. Conditions range from fairly dire **ekonomi** class (horrendously overcrowded open carriages with bare wooden benches as the only furnishings) to comfortable **eksecutif** compartments complete with air-con, sleeper berths and karaoke – and even a man who comes round offering cushions for rent and meals for sale. **Tickets** for ekonomi can be bought at the time of travel, but anything more upmarket is best booked through an agent a few days in advance.

Sumatra's railways are pretty fragmentary, limited to disconnected services at either end of the island. In southern Sumatra, a limited but useful service links Palembang, Bandar Lampung and Lubuklinggau.

Cars and bikes

In some parts of Indonesia, it's possible to **rent vehicles** and drive yourself around. Bali's compact scale makes **car rental** a good alternative to public transport for touring the island, for example, and in many places you'll find **motorbikes** and **bicycles** available for short-range exploration. However, bad roads, hectic traffic and bizarre road rules might make **chartering** a vehicle and driver a more attractive proposition – one that Indonesians themselves often take advantage of.

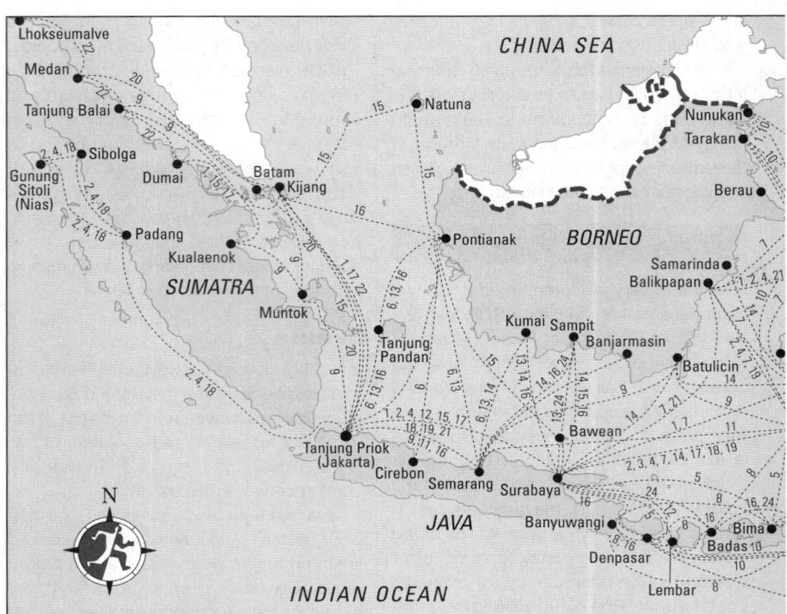

	Name of Ferry	Frequency	Departure Port
1	*KM Kerinci*	fortnightly	Dumai (S. Kalimantan)
2	*KM Kambuna*	every five days	Belawan (Medan)
3	*KM Rinjani*	fortnightly	Surabaya
4	*KM Umsini*	fortnightly	Bitung (N. Sulawesi)
5	*KM Kelimutu*	monthly	Surabaya
6	*KM Lawit*	fortnightly	Kumai (S. Kalimantan)
7	*KM Tidar*	fortnightly	Balikpapan
8	*KM Tatamailau*	monthly	Banyuwangi
9	*KM Sirimau*	fortnightly	Kupang
10	*KM Awu*	fortnightly	Denpasar
11	*KM Ciremai*	fortnightly	Tanjung Priok
12	*KM Dobonsolo*	fortnightly	Tanjung Priok
13	*KM Leuser*	fortnightly	Tanjung Priok
14	*KM Binaiya*	fortnightly	Surabaya
15	*KM Bukit Raya*	fortnightly	Tanjung Priok
16	*KM Tilongkabila*	monthly	Surabaya
17	*KM Bukit Siguntang*	fortnightly	Dumai
18	*KM Lambelu*	fortnightly	Bitung (N. Sulawesi)
19	*KM Sinabung*	fortnightly	Tanjung Priok
20	*KM Kelud*	every four days	Tanjung Priok
21	*KM Doro Londa*	monthly	Tanjung Priok
22	*KM Pangrango*	fortnightly	Tanjung Priok
23	*KM Sangiang*	fortnightly	Tahuna & Lirung
24	*KM Wilis*	fortnightly	Surabaya
25	*KM Fudi*	every four days	Balikpapan
26	*KM Ganda Dewata*	every two/four days	Makassar
27	*KM Agoa Mas*	fortnightly	W. Sulawesi
28	*KM Egon*	every two days	Banjarmasin
29	*KFC Jet Liner*	every three days	Tanjung Priok

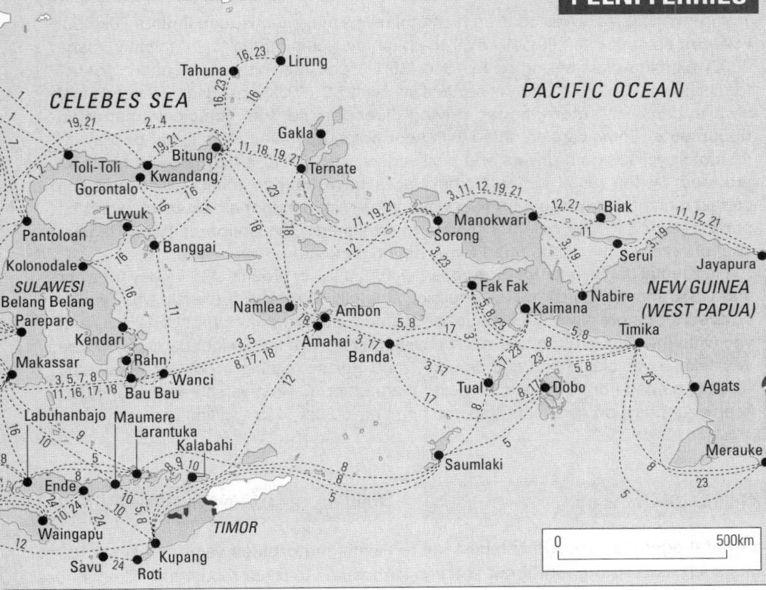

Destination	Via	Name of Ferry
Nunukan (E. Kalimantan)	N. Java, W/S. Sulawesi	*KM Kerinci*
Tanjung Priok (Jakarta)	Tanjung Balai	*KM Kambuna*
Jayapura	Makassar, Ambon, Banda, N. Papua	*KM Rinjani*
Nias	Balikpapan, W. Sulawesi, Makassar, Surabaya, Tanjung Priok, Padang	*KM Umsini*
W. Papua	Flores, W. Timor, southern W. Papua, return to Surabaya, S. Sulawesi, Fak Fak	*KM Kelimutu*
Java	Pontianak, Tanjung Priok	*KM Lawit*
Nunakan (E. Kalimantan)	W. Sulawesi, Makassar, Surabaya	*KM Tidar*
W. Papua	Sumbawa, Flores, W. Timor, Bali, Makassar	*KM Tatamailau*
Tanjung Balai (Riau)	Flores, Makassar, E. Kalimantan, N. Java	*KM Sirimau*
Nunukan (E. Kalimantan)	Sumba, Flores, Kupang, Alor, Makassar, W. Sulawesi	*KM Awu*
Jayapura	Semarang, Makassar, Sulawesi, Ternate, N. Papua	*KM Ciremai*
Jayapura	Surabaya, Bali, Kupang, Ambon, N. Papua	*KM Dobonsolo*
W/S. Kalimantan	N. Java	*KM Leuser*
S/E. Kalimantan	W. Sulawesi	*KM Binaiya*
Pontianak	S. Kalimantan, Natuna	*KM Bukit Raya*
Pontianak, Tahuna	N. Java, E/S. Sulawesi, W. Flores, Sumbawa, Lombok, Bali, S. Kalimantan	*KM Tilongkabila*
W. Papua/Tual (Maluku)	Sumatra, Kijang, N. Java, Makassar, Ambon, Banda, Tual	*KM Bukit Siguntang*
Nias	Maluku, Makassar, Surabaya, Tanjung Priok, Padang	*KM Lambelu*
Jayapura	Surabaya, Makassar, Balikpapan, N.Sulawesi, Ternate, N. Papua	*KM Sinabung*
Medan	Batam	*KM Kelud*
Jayapura	Surabaya, Makassar, Kupang, Ambon, Balikpapan, Sulawesi, Ternate, N. Papua	*KM Doro Londa*
Malahayati (Aceh)	Medan	*KM Pangrango*
Merauke (S. Papua)	Bitung (Sulawesi), W/S. Papua, Tual (Maluku)	*KM Sangiang*
Kupang	Sampit (S. Kalimantan), Sumbawa, Flores, Sumba, Sabu, Rote	*KM Wilis*
Makassar	Surabaya/Tanjung Priok	*KM Fudi*
Surabaya/Jakarta	—	*KM Ganda Dewata*
E. Kalimantan	—	*KM Agoa Mas*
Semarang/Surabaya	—	*KM Egon*
Batam	—	*KFC Jet Liner*

Road rules and insurance

Traffic in Indonesia drives on the left and there is a maximum **speed limit** of 70kmph. **Fuel prices** have risen steadily over the past few years; at the time of writing (June 2002) premium was selling at Rp1600 ($0.17) per litre, premix, a superior petrol formula, was Rp2200, and diesel fuel at Rp1250 ($0.13) per litre. Drivers must always carry an **international driving licence** and the **vehicle registration documents**. Some cars are fitted with **seat belts**, but using them is not obligatory. All motorcyclists, both drivers and passengers, must wear a **helmet**, which will be provided by the rental outlet. Some places have strange traffic rules, including certain roads that change from two-way to one-way during the day, which won't be publicized in any way comprehensible to foreigners. The **police** carry out regular spot checks, and you'll be **fined** for any infringements.

A few rental outfits offer **insurance** for an added fee of around US$5 a day for a car and US$3 for a motorbike. Read policies carefully to establish exactly what you're covered for before signing. Some fix a maximum payment of around US$25, even if you write the vehicle off; others don't cover you for more than minor damage. Before you take a vehicle, check it thoroughly, and get something in writing about any existing damage or you'll end up being blamed for it. Most vehicle rental agencies keep your passport as security, so you don't have a lot of bargaining power.

Renting a car

Car-rental agencies abound in tourist hot spots such as Bali. A good, if not entirely comprehensive list of agencies can be found at ⓦwww.ezyhotel.com/car_rentals.

Hertz have branches in both Jakarta (ⓣ021/8307460) and Bali (ⓣ0361/768375), though you'd need nerves of steel to drive in the capital. Costs are around US$50–60 per day. Avis have also reopened a branch in Jakarta, at Jalan Diponegoro 25 (ⓣ021/31429000).

Local operators offer a range of vehicles, most frequently 800cc Suzuki Jimneys, which can seat about six (around US$40 per day), and larger, more comfortable 1600cc Toyota Kijangs (US$50 per day). The rates drop if you rent for a week or more; one day means twelve hours, and the above prices exclude fuel. You'll need to produce an **international driving licence** before you rent, and be warned that vehicles may be in short supply on major public holidays. The main (and most reliable) local operator is TRAC, operated by Toyota-Astra, with branches all over Java, Bali, Lombok and Medan and Pekanbaru in Sumatra. A full list of their branches can be found on their website (ⓦwww.trac.astra.co.id).

Renting motorbikes and bicycles

Rental **motorbikes** vary from small 100cc Yamahas to more robust trail bikes. Prices start at US$5 per day without insurance, with discounts for longer rentals. If you don't have a valid international motorbike **licence**, it may be possible to obtain a local one by taking a test and paying a fee of Rp100,000. Conditions are not suitable for inexperienced drivers, with heavy traffic on major routes, steep hills and difficult driving once you get off the beaten track. There are increasing numbers of accidents involving tourists, so don't take risks.

In most tourist areas, it's possible to rent a **bicycle** for around US$2 a day; check its condition before you set off, and carry plenty of water, as it's hot and thirsty work. Bear in mind that bemos are extremely reluctant to pick you and your bike up if you get tired or stranded somewhere.

Chartering vehicles

You can **charter** cars and motorbikes – meaning you rent the vehicle and driver – just about anywhere in Indonesia. In tourist areas, you'll find operators who specialize in renting to foreigners; elsewhere, **taxis**, **ojek** (motorbike taxis) and even public **minibuses** are all available for charter by the hour or day – just approach the driver and bargain directly for a rate. You're expected to pay for the driver's meals and accommodation if the trip takes more than a day, and you must be very clear about who is paying for fuel, where you want to go and stop, and how many people will be travelling. With somebody else taking care of the roads, you will have plenty of time to look around, but it's impossible to predict the quality of the driving. Count on up to US$5 per day for the driver, in addition to the cost of the vehicle rental.

Urban transport

Indonesian cities all have comprehensive public transport, most of it congregating around transit points and marketplaces. Colour-coded or numbered, and bulging with passengers, minibus **bemos** are ubiquitous; they might run fixed circuits, or adapt their routes according to where their customers want to go. Rides usually cost Rp1000, but **fares** are never displayed, and you'll get overcharged at first – watch what others are paying and hand over the exact amount.

Taxis range from clapped-out rattletraps to shiny new Toyota Kijangs, and can usually be found at airports and outside bigger hotels. Airport taxis are very expensive, and you have to buy a fixed-price ticket from a booth in the terminal building. Elsewhere, make sure the **meter** is on and insist on its use, or **fix a fare** for your trip before setting off.

Other standbys include **ojek** (single-passenger motorbikes) and, in villages, towns and city suburbs, **becak** (cycle-rickshaws), which take two passengers in a covered seat in front of the driver. Jakarta and Banjarmasin also have motorized becak, called **bajaj**. Negotiating **fares** for these vehicles requires a balance of firmness and tact that can only be picked up with practice; try for around US$0.20 per kilometre for ojek and about the same for bajaj or becak, though you'll have to pay more for the latter if there are any hills along the way. Other drawbacks to becak are that drivers are often not locals and may have no idea of your where your destination is. They are also notoriously tough customers – never lose your temper with one unless you want a serious fight.

In a few places – particularly on Lombok and parts of northern Sulawesi – you'll also find **horse-drawn traps** known variously as **dokar**, **bendi**, **andong**, **cidomo** and even Ben Hur. These are often nicely decorated, complete with jingling bells, which you'll hear long before the cart trundles into view, and are used to carry both goods and people. As always, negotiate the fare before getting aboard – US$0.30 would be about the minimum fare.

Accommodation

Indonesia boasts an enormous range of places to stay, most of which offer extremely good value, and finding a bed for the night to suit your budget is rarely a problem. In cities and larger towns, along with popular tourist locations, the choice includes basic hostels, family homestays and topnotch hotels, while even in the wilder reaches of the country you'll find villagers willing to put you up for the night.

Finding a room often begins immediately on reaching a new place, when **touts** who hang around the transport terminals approach new arrivals. It's worth listening to them, especially during peak season in resort areas, when vacancies can be scarce; sometimes touts charge for their services, but the place they'll take you to may give them a commission instead (and often add it to your bill). **Prices** for the simplest double room start at around US$1, with luxury resort hotels topping US$300, and even up to US$1000 for a presidential suite. However, there's a good deal of **seasonal price variation** in resort areas: in the **peak season** (mid-June through to August, and from December to January), you'll find room rates in these places at a premium. During the **low season** (February through to May, and September through to November), you can do some serious **bargaining**, saving up to forty percent of the published rate in hotels, or at the very least getting the service tax (which the better hotels tend to charge) deducted. **Single rooms** (*kamar untuk satu orang*) are a rarity, so lone travellers will get put in a double at about 75 percent of the full price. **Check-out time** is usually noon. Many places are also happy to rent out rooms **long-term** at monthly rates, with more salubrious long-term rental properties available in areas well patronized by foreigners.

The cheapest accommodation has shared **bathrooms**, where you wash using a scoop-and-slosh **mandi**. This entails dipping a scoop into a huge basin of water (often built into the bathroom wall) and then sloshing the water over yourself. The basin functions as a water supply only and not a bath, so never get in it; all washing is done outside it and the basin should not be contaminated by soap or shampoo. **Toilets** in these places will be Indonesian-style squat affairs, flushed manually with water scooped from the pail that stands alongside, so you'll have to provide **toilet paper** yourself. More upmarket places will have en-suite rooms, with Western-style facilities such as sit-down toilets, showers, hot water, and bathtubs.

Accommodation price codes

All the **accommodation** listed in this book has been given one of the following price codes. The rates quoted here are for the **cheapest double room** in high season, except for places with dorms, where the code represents the price of a single bed. Where there's a significant spread of prices indicated (❹–❼, for example), the text will explain what extra facilities you get for more money. The 11–21 percent tax charged by most hotels is not included in these price codes.

Because of the current instability of the rupiah, accommodation prices are given throughout in their more stable **US dollar equivalents**, even for places which accept payment in rupiah.

❶ under $2
❷ $2–5
❸ $5–10
❹ $10–15
❺ $15–35
❻ $35–60
❼ $60–100
❽ $100 and over

Hotels

Almost any place calling itself a **hotel** in Indonesia will include at least a basic breakfast in the price of a room. All but the cheapest add a service-and-tax **surcharge** of up to 22 percent to your bill, and upmarket establishments quote **prices** – and prefer foreigners to pay – in dollars, though they accept plastic or a rupiah equivalent. In popular areas such as Bali or Tanah Toraja, it's worth **booking ahead** during the peak seasons; some hotels will also provide transport to and from transit points if requested in advance.

Bland and anonymous, **cheap urban hotels** (❶–❹) are perhaps the least attractive lodgings in Indonesia, designed for local businesspeople rather than tourists. Rooms will be tiny, and facilities limited to desk fans and shared, Indonesian-style toilets and mandi. Nonetheless, they are clean enough for short stays and tend to be conveniently located near transport terminals.

Moderately priced hotels (❺–❼) are larger and more formal operations. There may be a choice of fan or air-con rooms, almost certainly with hot water. Fridges, phones and TVs feature in the more costly ones, along with swimming pools and "cottage" or "bungalow"-style accommodation.

Expensive hotels (❽–❾) can be very stylish indeed – Bali has some beauties, complete with spacious ornamental gardens. Facilities are top-class, probably incorporating tennis courts and a gym, as well as several restaurants and a stage for nightly culture shows. The rooms themselves, however, though luxuriously equipped, often lack any local colour or flair. **Super-luxury category hotels** (❾) are places where you'll certainly be treated to indulgent and tasteful accommodation, the furnishings occasionally inspired by traditional palace designs. With the vast drop in the number of tourists visiting Indonesia over the last few years, and the instability of the rupiah, there are now some terrific **bargains** to be had at the more luxurious end of the accommodation market.

Homestays and hostels

The bottom end of Indonesia's accommodation market is provided by **homestays and hostels**, which come in several forms, with an emphasis on friendly service and simple, inexpensive lodgings. Breakfast, or at least a snack and a cup of coffee, is usually included, and **meals** are generally available for an extra charge and with advance warning.

Penginapan, or homestays, are most often simply spare bedrooms that a family rents out to supplement their income, though there's often not much difference between these and **losmen**, **pondok** and **wisma**, which are also family-run operations, though organized more along hostel lines. Rooms vary from whitewashed concrete cubes to artful rattan and bamboo structures built to resemble traditional buildings – some are even embellished with woodcarvings and set in their own walled gardens. Furnishings tend to be fairly stark: hard beds and bolsters are the norm, and you may or may not be provided with a light blanket. Most losmen rooms come with netted windows and fans, and nearly all have cold-water bathrooms.

Staying in villages and camping

If you spend much time roaming rural Indonesia, it's possible at some point that you'll end up staying overnight in **villages** without formal lodgings, where your only option is to seek a bed in a family house. It's certainly an experience to sleep over in a Dayak longhouse in Kalimantan, a Torajan *tongkonan* in Sulawesi, or a village hut in the West Papua highlands, but even in more prosaic regions you're guaranteed close contact with local people – and where foreigners are rare, come prepared to be the centre of attention. In all events, first seek out the nearest person in authority, either the local police in larger villages, or the **kepala desa** (village head), to ask permission to stay. While this is seldom a problem, don't take people's hospitality for granted; some communities may be hardly able to spare what they feed you, and your presence may well disturb village life. In exchange for accommodation and meals, you should offer cash or useful **gifts**, such as rice, salt, cigarettes or food, to the value of about US$1–2. The only bathroom might be the nearest river, with all bodily functions performed in the open – in these circumstances, avoid onlookers by waiting until after dark. Standard rations of rice and fish become monotonous on extended stays, but it's sometimes possible to buy fresh food and ask your hosts to prepare it for you, giving you the opportunity to try some local delicacies.

With such readily available and inexpensive alternatives, **camping** is something you'll only need to do if you undertake extensive trekking through Indonesia's wilderness areas. If you prefer to camp, however, note that there are few, if any, officially designated campsites, though villagers and farmers will probably be happy to let you camp on their land for a small fee. Tents and cooking equipment should all be brought from home, as you'll have difficulty finding such things in Indonesia. Some national parks don't allow camping at all, while in others it's common practice, so always check first. In well-established hiking areas, such as Lombok's Gunung Rinjani, all camping gear, from tents to sleeping bags and cooking equipment, may be available from local villages; in other places you'll have to be entirely self-sufficient.

Eating and drinking

If you come to Indonesia expecting the depth and exuberance of cooking found elsewhere in Southeast Asia, you'll be disappointed. It's not that Indonesian food is bad – far from it – just that meals lack variety. At first, coconut milk and aromatic spices add intriguing tastes to the meats, vegetables and fruits, but after a while everything starts to taste the same – spiced, fried and served with rice. However, there are a number of regional cooking styles and local specialities in Indonesia, and with a little determination you'll be able to track them down amongst the higher-profile Chinese food, pizzas, hamburgers and French fries on offer.

For a food glossary, see p.1092

Indonesian food

Rice (*nasi*) is the favoured **staple** across much of the country, eaten two or three times a day. A few places, however, are either unable to afford this luxury or have yet to grow tired of local alternatives. Many regions with poor soil or low rainfall grow **cassava** (manioc), a tuber native to South America which was introduced during colonial times. In the highlands of West Papua they favour **yams** (sweet potatoes), and in rural Maluku the crop is **sago** (tapioca), the starchy pith of a spiky, swamp-dwelling palm. **Noodles**, a Chinese import, are also widely popular, though they tend to supplement rice rather than replace it.

As you would expect of an island nation, the **seafood** is often superb, and some markets regularly display excellent tuna, mackerel, reef fish, octopus, squid, lobster and shellfish. **Chicken**, **goat** and **beef** are the main meats in this predominantly Muslim country, but non-Islamic areas offer the chance to try other **game** – deer and pig are favourites, but you may also find dog, rat and even cassowary and fruit bat on local menus.

Vegetarians can eat well in Indonesia: bitter starfruit leaves, aubergines, water spinach (*kangkung*), plus various beans, green peppers, assorted kales, cabbages, Oriental lettuces, carrots, tomatoes and pumpkins are all available in markets, though restaurant selections can be limited to **cap cay** – fried mixed vegetables. There's also plenty of **tofu** and the popular **tempeh**, a fermented soya-bean cake, thought to have originated in Java about a century ago.

There's a wide assortment of **fruit** available across the country. You'll see banana, coconut and papaya growing in back gardens, with markets often loaded with pineapple, watermelon, citrus fruit including **pomelo** (a sweet, thick-skinned grapefruit), guava, avocado, passion fruit, mango, soursop and its close relative, the custard apple. Then there are the seasonal, purple-skinned **mangosteen**, whose sweet white flesh is one of the best of all tropical fruits; hairy, perfumed **rambutan**, closely related to the lychee; dry **salak** or snakefruit, named after its brown scaly skin; and the **starfruit** (*carambola*), whose taste and texture resembles a watery, crunchy apple. **Jackfruit**, which can weigh 20kg, has bobbly skin and flesh, and can be eaten ripe as a fruit or cooked green in curries as a vegetable. Venerated by connoisseurs, you won't forget an encounter with **durian**: oval, football-sized, encased in a spiky armour, and emitting a stench which has seen it banned from airlines and hotels. Ripening towards the end of the year, the durian splits into segments, each revealing a seed surrounded by pasty yellow pulp, the taste of which is acrid, rich, acidic and savoury all at once. Indonesians adore durian and pay high prices for quality fruit, but many Westerners find the smell, let alone the taste, utterly foul.

The backbone of all Indonesian cooking, **spices** are ground and chopped together, then fried in copious oil to form a **paste**, which is either used as the flavour base for **curries**, or rubbed over ingredients prior to **frying** or **grilling**. While all pastes are broadly similar, their composition varies from place to place, and with whichever meat or vegetable is being cooked. **Chillies** always feature, along with **terasi** (also known as *belacan*), a fermented shrimp paste whose raw odour is mitigated by cooking. Ginger, onion and garlic add background flavour; more subtle scents derive from lime leaves, lemon grass, pandanus leaves, lime juice, cinnamon and turmeric. Another vital ingredient is *gulah merah*, a dark **palm sugar** sold in cakes. Some regions also use **cloves** and **nutmegs**, two spices native to Maluku which have been exported overseas for two thousand years.

Cooking and styles

Cooking methods tend to be uncomplicated. **Chargrilling** adds a nicely smoky flavour to sate, chicken, and especially seafood, but **frying** is by far the most common way of preparing food – deep-fried chicken is so popular it could claim to be Indonesia's national dish. Vegetables may be plain boiled, but the other main cooking method is **stewing**, often in coconut milk. This results in either a soupy, **wet curry** (*gulai*), or continues until all the liquid is evaporated, producing a **dry curry** (rendang), with the ingredients left in a rich, spicy coat.

Meals are served with a number of **relishes** such as **soy sauce** – available in thick and sweet (*kecap manis*), or thin and salty (*kecap asin*) forms – and **sambal**, a blisteringly hot blend of chillies and spices, to be used with caution until your taste buds adjust.

Light meals and **snacks** include various rice dishes such as **nasi goreng**, a plate of fried rice with shreds of meat and vegetables and topped with a fried egg, and **nasi campur**, boiled rice served with a small range of side dishes. **Noodle** equivalents are also commonly available, as are **gado-gado**, steamed vegetables dressed in a peanut sauce, and **sate**, small kebabs of meat or fish, barbecued over a fire and again served with spicy peanut sauce. Indonesian **soups** tend to be watery but filling affairs, stacked with noodles, vegetables, meatballs, or unidentifiable bits and pieces.

Indonesian **bread** (*roti*) is made from sweetened dough, and usually accompanies a morning cup of coffee. **Cakes** (*kueh*) are a big afternoon institution in parts of the country; the Muslim city of Banjarmasin in Kalimantan is renowned for the special evening selection prepared during Ramadan for the faithful to break their daytime fast. Indonesians actually have a notoriously **sweet tooth**, relishing snacks such as **es kacang**, a mound of shaved ice piled over cooked soya beans, lovingly drenched in brightly coloured syrup and condensed milk, which is surprisingly refreshing. You'll also come across all sorts of fruit-flavoured **ice cream**, including durian.

Regional cooking tends to differ most in emphasis and ingredients used rather than the method of cooking. **Balinese** cuisine is one of the most accomplished, sweet and not overly hot, and well worth tracking down if you visit the island. Sumatran **Padang restaurants** are found right across Indonesia, the typically fiery food precooked – not the healthiest way to eat – and displayed cold on platters piled up in a pyramid shape inside a glass-fronted cabinet. There are no menus; you either select your composite meal by pointing to the dishes on display, or just sit down, the staff bring you a selection, and you pay for what you eat. The range of options is variable: you may encounter boiled *kangkung* (water spinach); *tempeh*; egg, vegetable, meat or seafood curry; fried whole fish; potato cakes; and fried cow's lung.

Asian and Western food

Indonesia's substantial ethnic Chinese population means that **Chinese food** is widely available, and you'll probably be familiar already with the range of southern- and Straits-style dishes. In the biggest cities and tourist spots, you'll also find other **Asian and Western restaurants**, offering everything from Indian through to Mexican and Italian cuisine – sometimes very good, but often mediocre. Multinational **fast-food** chains have really taken the country by storm over the past few years, with *McDonald's*, *Burger King*, *KFC* and *Dunkin' Donuts* all well-established in towns and cities.

Places to eat, etiquette and prices

The cheapest places to eat in Indonesia are at the **mobile stalls** which ply their wares around the streets and bus stations during the day, and congregate at night markets after dark. Known as **kaki lima** – five legs – individual carts specialize in one or two dishes, and have their own cooking apparatus, ingredients and even plates, cutlery and stools for their customers. Vendors call out their selection; you simply place your order and they cook it up on the spot. In big cities, you could spend weeks eating out at these carts and never be served the same thing twice; those in Sulawesi's Makassar are famous, forming a kilometre-long string along the seafront in the afternoon.

Slightly more upmarket – often only because the fixtures and location are more permanent – **warung** are the bottom line in Indonesian restaurants, usually just a few tables and chairs in a kitchen offering much the same food as *kaki lima*. **Rumah makan** (literally "eating house") are bigger, offer a wider range of dishes and comfort, and may even have a menu. Anything labelled as a **restaurant** will probably be catering to foreigners, with fully fledged service and possibly international food. Don't count on everyone's meal arriving together in smaller establishments, as there may be just one gas burner in the kitchen.

Indonesian **meal times** are vague, with many people snacking throughout the day rather than sitting down at fixed times for a major feed – if they do, it will most likely be in the evening. Coffee shops and market and transit-station snack stalls are open from dawn until after dark, but more substantial places generally open mid-morning and close by 8 or 9pm, possibly shutting down through the afternoon as well.

Eating out, it's usual to order and eat individual dishes, though each diner may receive a bowl of rice and a range of smaller dishes which everyone shares – the origin of the **rijstaffel** (rice-table), a Dutch version of this style of serving food. **Food etiquette** is pretty much the same as in the West, though in cheaper places and at home Indonesians generally eat with their right hands instead of using cutlery, mashing a ball of rice in their fingers and using it to scoop up a mouthful of food. Most warung and restaurants will have a basin in a corner so you can wash before and after eating.

Prices vary dramatically depending on the location rather than the quality of the meals. Stalls or warung serve dishes for as little as US$0.50, while tourist restaurants will charge from three times as much for the same dish. For non-Indonesian food such as pizza, pasta and steak, prices start at around US$3.50. Where restaurants are reviewed in the guide, **inexpensive** means you will get a satisfying main dish for less than US$2, **moderate** means it'll be

US$2.50–5, and **expensive** is US$5.50 and over. In addition, many of the moderate and all of the expensive establishments will add up to 21 percent **service tax** to the bill.

Drinks

Alcohol can be a touchy subject in parts of Indonesia, where public drunkenness is, on the whole, at least frowned upon, and in Muslim areas may incur serious trouble. There's no need to be overly paranoid about this in cities, however, and the locally produced **beers**, Anker and Bintang Pilsners, are good, and widely available in 320ml and 620ml bottles at Chinese restaurants and bigger hotels. In non-Islamic regions, even small warung sell beer.

Spirits are less publicly consumed, and, depending on local rules, may be technically **illegal**, so indulge with caution. Nonetheless, home-produced brews are often sold openly in villages, discreetly supplied by local sources, or specially prepared for festivals. **Tuak** (also known as **balok**) or **palm wine** is made by tapping a suitable tree for its alcoholic sap, comes in plain milky-white or pale red varieties, and varies in strength depending on how long it has been left to ferment – you can either walk away from a litre of the stuff, or else need two days to recover. Far more potent are rice wine (variously known as **arak** or **brem**), and **sopi**, a distillation of *tuak*, either of which can leave you incapacitated after a heavy session. **Imported spirits** are only available in major tourist areas and at expensive hotels.

Indonesian **coffee** is amongst the best in the world, and Indonesians are great coffee and **tea** drinkers. Coffee is prepared by putting ground coffee in a glass, adding boiling water, and waiting for the grounds to settle before drinking. Indonesians then ladle in copious amounts of sugar, or occasionally condensed milk, and gape in disbelieving horror at Westerners who dare to drink their coffee unsweetened. Instant coffee is available in tourist restaurants.

Don't drink **tap water** in Indonesia. **Boiled water** (*air putih*) can be requested at accommodation and restaurants, and dozens of brands of **bottled water** (*air minum*) are sold throughout the islands, as are imported **soft drinks**. It's also tempting to try the masses of delicious, freshly made **fruit drinks** available, but be cautious, as in many places you can't be sure of the purity of the water or ice used in their manufacture (see "Health" on p.30).

Communications

Although the communications network in Indonesia is improving all the time, and the phone and postal services in the big cities are often very efficient, in smaller towns and villages you may still find the whole process very time-consuming and frustrating.

Mail

The **postal system** in Indonesia is reasonably reliable, at least in the cities. Most **post offices** (*Kantor pos*) in Indonesia follow standard government office hours (Mon–Thurs 8am–2pm, Fri 8–11am, Sat 8am–1pm), though those in the larger cities often stay open longer, and some even open on Sunday. Stamps (*perangko*) and aerogrammes (*surat udara*) can be bought, letters (*surat*) and parcels (*paket*) can be sent, and in some cases, email, fax and poste restante facilities are available at these offices. Supplementing the government offices are the privately owned **warpostels**, which are a little more expensive but often more conveniently located, and stay open longer.

Letters

Postage is phenomenally expensive, with the current rates for airmail postcards and letters under 200g as follows: Australia Rp4000, Canada Rp6500, Europe Rp6000, USA Rp7500 and New Zealand Rp5000. Airmail post takes about a week, and a local letter to anywhere in Indonesia takes three to seven days.

Parcels

In the larger cities in Indonesia, the **parcels** section is usually in a separate part of the building to the rest of the post office (and sometimes even in a separate building altogether). Sending parcels overseas from Indonesia is expensive and time consuming. From Indonesia, parcels can be sent by surface mail (under 10kg only) – the cheapest way of sending mail home – or airmail, and you can register (*tercatat*) and insure the contents too. Don't seal the parcel before staff at the post office have checked what's inside. In the larger towns and cities, there's usually somebody outside the post office who offers a parcel-wrapping service. A parcel weighing up to 1kg airmailed to Europe takes about three weeks and costs around Rp100,000; a 2kg parcel costs Rp220,000 (by sea it will cost Rp120,000 and take three months). *Kantor pos* won't handle anything over 10kg, so if you want to send anything particularly large, you're better off using the services offered by the major galleries and craft shops, who pack everything carefully and also insure it.

Poste restante

Mail can be sent to Indonesia via **poste restante**. The system in Indonesia is fairly efficient, though stick to the cities – post offices in small towns and villages often don't have a poste restante service. Most post offices hold letters for a maximum of one month. To ensure that your mail doesn't get filed under your first name, ask the sender to write your surname in block capitals and underline it. The address should consist of: poste restante (preferably also in capitals), Kantor pos, city, province, Indonesia. When picking up mail, be sure that the staff check under your first name too, as misfilings are common.

Telephones

There are two types of telephone office in Indonesia: the government-run **Telkom** (and, occasionally, **wartel Telkom**) offices, which you'll find in every town and city, and privately owned **wartels**, which, like the warpostels above, tend to be slightly more expensive (and occasionally very much more expensive, so always check their tariff first), but

Useful codes and numbers

For the time difference, see p.79

Phoning Indonesia from abroad

From the UK Dial ☎0062 + area code minus the first 0 + number.
From Ireland Dial ☎01062 + area code minus the first 0 + number.
From the USA Dial ☎01162 + area code minus the first 0 + number.
From Canada Dial ☎01162 + area code minus the first 0 + number.
From Australia Dial ☎001162 + area code minus the first 0 + number.
From New Zealand Dial ☎0062 + area code minus the first 0 + number.

Phoning from Indonesia

Dial ☎00 + IDD country code (see below) + area code (minus the first 0) + number.

DD codes

UK ☎44, Ireland ☎353, USA ☎1, Canada ☎1, Australia ☎61, New Zealand ☎64

Useful numbers

International directory enquiries ☎102
Local and long-distance directory enquiries ☎106
Local and long-distance operator ☎100
International operator ☎101

are often conveniently located. Both offer similar services, including fax, telex and telegraph services, though the wartels rarely have a **collect-call service** and if they do they tend to charge a premium for you to use it.

The government telephone offices are often open all the time; some of the wartels are also open 24 hours a day, though most close at midnight and open again at 7am. In addition to these offices, large towns and cities also have public **payphones**, which are useful for local calls and which take Rp100 and Rp500 coins. Put the coins in only after the person you're calling has picked up the phone and started speaking. These phones are slowly being phased out in favour of phones that take telephone cards (*kartu telepon*). Telephone cards are sold in units of 20 (Rp2000), 60 (Rp6000), 80 (Rp8000), 100 (Rp10,000), 280 (Rp28,000), 400 (Rp40,000) and 680 (Rp68,000). *Kartu telepon* are sold at kantor telkom and in some wartel, postal agents and money exchange booths. There are now several types of phone card – and two types of card phone, which can make using them very frustrating. If possible, check out the phone before buying the card. If you get stuck with mismatching card and phone, head for the nearest large hotel, as these usually have both types of card phone in the lobby.

Local and long-distance calls

As Telkom moves towards privatization, the cost of phoning will probably continue to rise. A **local call** (*panggilan lokal*) is a call to any destination that shares the same area code. These calls can be made from coin-operated phones, card phones, or at Telkom and wartel offices. The cost is around Rp500 per minute.

Long-distance domestic calls (*panggilan inter-lokal*) – to anywhere in Indonesia with a different area code – are charged according to a **zone system**. For example, if you're ringing from Jakarta, Sumatra, Java and Bali are in Zone 1, Kalimantan in Zone 2 and so on, to West Papua in Zone 5. The cost varies between Rp1135 to Rp3000 per minute. These rates are subject to a discount for calls made between 9pm and 6am. To confuse matters further, in addition to the zone system there is also a two-tier system of charges depending on whether you want to make a normal (*biasa*) call or an express (*segara*) call that connects you much faster, but costs twice as much.

International calls

Two phone companies provide IDD services: **Indosat**, for which you dial ☎001, and **Satelindo**, which uses ☎008. Both phone

Charge cards

One of the most convenient ways of phoning home from abroad is via a **telephone charge card** from your phone company back home. Using a PIN number, you can make calls from most hotel, public and private phones that will be charged to your account. Since most major charge cards are free to obtain, it's certainly worth getting one at least for emergencies; enquire first though whether your destination is covered, and bear in mind that rates aren't necessarily cheaper than calling from a public phone.

In **the UK and Ireland**, British Telecom (☎0800/345 144, ⓦwww.chargecard.bt.com) will issue free to all BT customers the BT Charge Card, which can be used in 116 countries including Indonesia; AT&T (dial ☎0800/890 011, then 888/641-6123 when you hear the AT&T prompt, to be transferred to the Florida Call Centre; free 24hr) have a similar card called the Global Calling Card, as does NTL (☎0500/100 505), which can be used in more than sixty countries abroad, though the fees cannot be charged to a normal phone bill.

In the **USA and Canada**, AT&T, MCI, Sprint, Canada Direct and other North American long-distance companies all enable their customers to make credit-card calls while overseas, billed to your home number. Call your company's customer service line to find out if they provide service from Indonesia, and if so, what the toll-free access code is.

To call **Australia and New Zealand** from overseas, telephone charge cards such as Telstra Telecard or Optus Calling Card in Australia and Telecom NZ's Calling Card can be used to make calls abroad, which are charged back to a domestic account or credit card. Apply to Telstra (☎1800/038 000), Optus (☎1300/300 937), or Telecom NZ (☎04/801 9000).

companies charge identical rates, fixed by the government, and use identical time bands for identical discounts, so it doesn't matter which you choose. There are three price bands according to when you phone, but the time bands alter slightly according to which country you are phoning. All calls at weekends and on national holidays are discounted by 25 percent. IDD rates (per min) are as follows: UK Rp9400 and Ireland Rp7150 (both plus 20 percent 2–5pm, minus 25 percent 3–11am); USA and Canada Rp8300 (plus 20 percent 9am–noon, minus 25 percent 11pm–7am); Australia Rp8300 (plus 20 percent 9am–noon, minus 25 percent 10pm–6am); New Zealand Rp8300 (plus 20 percent 9am–noon, minus 25 percent 11pm–7am).

The cheapest place to make an international call is at the Kantor Telkom or on a card phone, where you are guaranteed to be charged at the basic rate; privately run wartel always add ten percent tax, and may add quite a bit extra too, so check first. Wartel Telkom IDD rates are fixed and nearly always cheaper than those charged by the privately run wartel. Prices are quoted in a variety of ways, either per minute or for an initial three-minute call and then per additional minute. Most places quote their rates without the obligatory ten percent tax. Official /Telkom prices per minute (minus tax) are: UK and Ireland Rp9500; USA Rp8300; Canada Rp7200; Australia Rp7500; New Zealand Rp7500; Germany Rp10,700. You get a 25 percent discount on these rates after 9pm, and at weekends. Note also that substantial savings can be made by purchasing a **Telkom Save Card** (available from **wartels**, hotels, shops, supermarkets and airports), which allows for calls at up to seventy percent discount on wartel prices. The card comes with a password, and you dial a toll-free number.

In addition to IDD, a few of the big hotels, Telkom offices and airports also have **home-country direct** phones. With these, you simply press the appropriate button for the country you're ringing, and you'll be put through to the international switchboard of that country. With these phones you can **call collect** (reverse-charge calls), or the operator will debit you and you can settle with the cashier after the call. Home-country direct phones are also useful if you have a BT or AT&T chargecard. They do, however, cost more than IDD phones. To reach your home-country operator on an IDD phone, dial ⓣ001-801 – and then the special HCD country code: UK ⓣ44; Ireland ⓣ08; USA ⓣ10; Canada ⓣ16; Australia ⓣ61; New Zealand ⓣ64.

Mobile phones

If you want to use your **mobile phone** in Indonesia, you'll need to check with your phone provider whether it will work abroad, and what the call charges are. For details of which mobiles will work in Indonesia, contact your mobile service provider. Most mobiles in Australia and New Zealand use GSM, which works well in Southeast Asia – check with your provider. In the UK, for all but the very top-of-the-range packages, you'll have to inform your phone provider before going abroad to get international access switched on. You may get charged extra for this depending on your existing package and where you are travelling to. You are also likely to be charged extra for incoming calls when abroad, as the people calling you will be paying the usual rate. If you want to retrieve messages while you're away, you'll have to ask your provider for a new access code, as your home one is unlikely to work abroad. Most UK mobiles use GSM too, which gives access to most places worldwide. For further information about using your phone abroad, check out ⓦwww.telecomsadvice.org.uk/features/using_your_mobile_abroad.htm.

Email and the internet

Internet access is becoming increasingly widespread in Indonesia, and there are now tourist-friendly internet offices and cybercafés in many towns and cities on Bali, Java, Lombok, Sumatra, and the main cities of Sumbawa, Sulawesi and West Papua (though in Nusa Tenggara Timor, only Kupang In West Timor and Ende and Maumere on Flores are as yet connected). All these places offer internet access as well as email services, and most charge around Rp10,000 per hour online, though in some places with poor connections – such as Tanah Toraja in Sulawesi – costs can be much higher. There's usually an extra charge for printing out emails, and a small charge for receiving emails at the cybercafé's email address.

If you're going to be passing through cyber-friendly tourist centres on a fairly regular basis, **email** can make a good alternative to post office postes restantes – even if you're not on the internet at home. For details of Indonesia websites, see pp.25–27.

One of the best ways to keep in touch while travelling is to sign up for a free internet **email address**, for example YahooMail or Hotmail – accessible through ⓦwww.yahoo.com and ⓦwww.hotmail.com. Any cybercafé will have these sites bookmarked for easy access, and will help you set up a new account. Give friends and family your email address and they can send you email any time – it will stack up in a nice pile in your in-box, ready for you to access at any internet café, or hotel with internet access.

If you plan to email from your **laptop** in Bali and Lombok, be advised that very few losmen have telephone sockets in the room, and that many upmarket hotels charge astronomical rates for international calls. The usual phone plug in Indonesia is the American standard RJ11 phone jack. See the Help for World Travellers website (ⓦwww.kropla.com) for detailed advice on how to set up your modem before you go, and how to hardwire phone plugs where necessary. One potentially useful way round the cost issue is to become a temporary subscriber to a local ISP: visit ⓦwww.balivillas.com/net.html for reviews, prices and links to relevant Indonesian ISPs. This site also links to the public ISP Telkom at ⓦhttp://plasa.com/instan/eindex.html, which requires no registration or monthly fee to dial up: you simply dial ⓣ0809 8 9999 from your laptop, then enter the username "telkomnet@instan" and the password "telkom". This service should cost R150/minute, but check with the hotel first, as some add surcharges or bar ⓣ0809 numbers.

The media

Since Suharto was toppled in May 1998, Indonesia's newspapers, after years of suppression and enforced self-censorship, have become increasingly bold in their criticism of the government and their coverage of Indonesia's politics in general. It appears that these days newspapers are allowed to voice their own political opinions and, unsurprisingly, nearly all have sided with the pro-reform movement in its attempt to introduce democracy to the country. Occasionally, the newspapers go too far and slip from reporting into polemic – but even this is a welcome change after thirty years of turgid, criticism-free reporting of the Suharto regime.

Newspapers and magazines

Indonesia has a number of large-circulation dailies, including the Catholic mouthpiece, *Kompas*, the Denpasar-based *Bali Post*, the Jakartan *Sianr Harapan*, and *Suara Karya*, the newspaper of Golkar. There are currently just two **English-language** dailies, the broadsheet *Jakarta Post* (ⓦwww.thejakartapost.com), which is published daily except Sundays and the hard-to-get-hold-of *Indonesian Observer*. Both are published in Jakarta and appear daily. Most of the stuff they publish is pretty dull, though they do print international news agency pieces and sports results from Europe, America and Australia. If you can get hold of it, you'll find the best domestic and international news coverage in the weekly **magazine** Tempo (ⓦwww.tempointeractive.com), published in both Indonesian and English versions, but not widely distributed outside of Java. The best cultural read is the locally produced *Latitudes* (Rp20,000), a glossy and well-written English-language monthly magazine which looks at contemporary Indonesian society and is not particualrly aimed at tourists. For a truly balanced and thought-provoking account of Indonesian current affairs, *Inside Indonesia* magazine, published six times a year from offices in Australia, is superb. Subscriptions can be taken out by writing to them at PO Box 1326, Collingwood, VIC 3066, Australia, ⓦwww.insideindonesia.org.

The foreign news section in the *Jakarta Post* is fairly slight, and for in-depth coverage of international events you're better off buying the Western weeklies like *Time*, *Newsweek* or the *Economist* – though the latter is hard to find in Indonesia. The much-respected *Far Eastern Economic Review* provides a more in-depth coverage of events in Indonesia, though it's almost impossible to find outside the big cities.

Indonesia's English-language magazines

For a list of **Indonesian language** newspapers still publishing in Indonesia, visit: ⓦwww.iit.edu/~indonesia/jendela.

Djakarta! The City Life Magazine ⓦwww.djakartamag.com. A monthly English-language magazine covering all that's going on in Jkt, especially social and entertainment with listings of events.

Jakarta Kini and Javi Kini ⓦwww.tempointeractive.com. Free glossy English monthly published on behalf of the Indonesian Tourism Promotion Board running to 40 pages, highlighting what's on in Indonesia, travel articles, restaurant film reviews. Available through most 4 and 5 star hotels and some bookshops.

Indonesia Tatler A monthly English edition for Indonesia of the London-based magazine. Mostly society gossip, profiles, interviews and syndicated features.

Island Life ⓦwww.islandlifemag.com. A glossy Jakarta-based monthly travel/lifestyle magazine covering the whole of Indonesia.

Latitudes ⓦwww.latitudesmagazine.com. A Bali-based monthly magazine covering sociological, anthropological, political issues in Indonesia.

Kem Chick's World A free monthly English-language magazine, published in Jakarta and of interest to expats. It is available from Kem Chicks supermarket, Jl Kemang Raya 3–5.

Krakatau ⓦhttp://krakatau.inilho.com. A quarterly bilingual Indonesian/English adventure and leisure magazine covering Indonesia.

Tempo Now has a weekly English edition. This magazine offers serious political, economic and business news and analysis, and investigative journalism.

Wine & Dine Indonesia A new monthly English-language magazine covering food, wine and some travel.

Bali's English-language magazines

Bali and Lombok have numerous free publications aimed at tourists, including several large-format glossy magazines, published monthly and mostly available in the bigger hotels.

Bali and Beyond ⓦwww.baliandbeyond.co.id. Free, full-colour, tabloid monthly newspaper, less glamorous looking than the above, but packed with similarly thought-provoking pieces.

Bali Echo ⓦwww.baliwww.com/baliechomagazine. The best read of all, a locally produced, glossy but informative and well-written English-language magazine, which comes out about every two months. The magazine runs features on contemporary and cultural issues in Bali and Lombok, does interviews with local personalities and reviews new restaurants, clubs and shops. Distribution is a bit erratic, but some Kuta and Ubud bookstores stock it.

Bali Travel News ⓦwww.bali-travelnews.com. Fortnightly glossy newspaper listing upcoming temple festivals and films showing at Denpasar's cinema, as well as running features on tourist attractions.

Bali Tribune Similar in style and content to *Hello Bali*, and just as recommended.

The Beat Free what's-on magazine, focusing on Bali's nightlife and carrying listings for gigs, parties and clubs.

Hello Bali Well-written pieces on the culture of Bali and Lombok and includes travel articles, restaurant reviews, inspirational photographs plus tourist-oriented advertisements.

Television and radio

Thanks to the introduction of **satellite television**, almost everywhere in Indonesia can receive a TV signal, and even the smallest villages in the most remote corners of the archipelago have a satellite dish. Although almost everything is in Indonesian, original English-language films and TV series are not dubbed, but are broadcast in English and subtitled in Indonesian. Furthermore, RCTI, a private station available in most regions, has an English-language news broadcast every day at 6.30pm (Western Indonesian Time). **Televisi Republik Indonesia** (**TVRI**) and **TPI** are the two state-run channels, which supposedly broadcast to every region, as indeed do the private stations RCTI, SCTV, An Teve, Indosiar, Trans, TV7, Lativi and Metro TV. In addition, the satellite dishes can also pick up CNN, MTV and other English-language channels.

Radio Republik Indonesia is the national radio station, broadcasting round the clock from every provincial capital in the country. Most of the programmes are in Indonesian, though they occasionally have English-language news bulletins. You can watch some of the programmes being recorded, such as the wayang performances in Central Java (see p.242 for details). Tickets are free, and details of forthcoming programmes can be found in the reception or lobby areas of radio stations. There are plenty of other, smaller stations in Indonesia that broadcast to the local area only. If you have a shortwave radio, you should be able to pick up English-language stations such as the BBC World Service and the Voice of America. Times and wavelengths can change every three months, so check a recent schedule before you travel. The website ⓦwww.bbc.co.uk/worldservice lists all the World Service frequencies around the world, while the VOA website ⓦwww.voa.gov does the same for the American service.

Opening hours, holidays and festivals

Opening hours are complicated in Indonesia, with government offices, post offices, businesses and shops setting their own timetables.

As a rough outline, **businesses** open Monday to Friday 8am to 4pm and Saturday 8am to noon, with variable arrangements at lunchtime. **Banking hours** are Monday to Friday 8am to 3pm, Saturday 8am to 1pm, although banks may not handle foreign exchange in the afternoons or at weekends. Moneychangers usually keep shop rather than bank hours. **Post offices** operate roughly Monday to Thursday 8am to 2pm, Friday 8 to 11am, Saturday 8am to 12.30pm, though in big cities they often stay open much longer; if they have internet cafés, these will sometimes stay open until late evening. **Markets** start soon after dawn, and the freshest produce will be gone by 10am, though trading continues through the day, firing up again after dark at **night markets**. Be aware, however, that all these times are **flexible**: opening times for **museums** or **temples** are also very flexible, and sometimes boil down to whenever staff or caretakers manage to turn up.

Whatever they actually are, all opening hours also tend to be relatively longer in tourist areas, and much shorter in rural regions. **Muslim businesses** – including **government offices**, which now have a five-day working week – may also close at 11.30am on Fridays, the main day of prayer, and on **national public holidays** all commerce is compulsorily curtailed.

In addition to national public holidays, there are frequent **religious festivals** throughout Indonesia's Muslim, Hindu, Chinese and indigenous communities. Each of Bali's 20,000 **temples** has an anniversary celebration, for example, and other ethnic groups may host elaborate **marriages** or **funerals**, along with more secular holidays. Your visit is almost bound to coincide with a festival of one kind or another, and possibly several.

Muslim festivals

Ramadan, a month of fasting during daylight hours, falls during the ninth Muslim month (which, as the Islamic calendar is a lunar one, changes dates every year, though it usually starts around October to December). Followers of the Wetu Telu branch of Islam on Lombok observe their own three-day festival of *Puasa* rather than

National public holidays

Most of the **public holidays** fall on different dates of the Western calendar each year, as they are calculated according to Muslim or local calendars.

December/January *Idul Fitri*, the celebration of the end of Ramadan.
January 1 New Year's Day (*Tahun Baru*).
March/April *Nyepi*, Balinese *saka* New Year.
March/April Good Friday and Easter Sunday.
May *Idul Adha* (*Hajh*) Muslim Day of Sacrifice.
May *Waisak* Day, anniversary of the birth, death and enlightenment of Buddha.
May/June Ascension Day.
June/July *Muharam*, Muslim New Year.
July/August *Maulud Nabi Muhammad*, the anniversary of the birth of Mohammed.
August 17 Independence Day (*Hari Proklamasi Kemerdekaan*) celebrates the proclamation of Indonesian Independence in 1945 by Dr Sukarno.
December Ascension Day of Mohammed.
December 25 Christmas Day.

the full month, however. Even in non-Islamic areas, Muslim restaurants and businesses shut down during the day, and in staunchly Islamic parts of the country, such as rural Lombok, Sumatra or Kalimantan's Banjarmasin, you should not eat, drink or smoke in public at this time. **Idul Fitri**, also called *Hari Raya* or *Lebaran*, the first day of the tenth month of the Muslim calendar, marks the end of Ramadan and is a two-day national holiday of noisy celebrations.

Al Miraj (February) celebrates Mohammed being led to God through the seven heavens by the archangel and his return to earth with instructions for the faithful, which included observance of the Muslim five-times-a-day prayers. In May or June, the festival of sacrifice, **Idul Adha**, commemorates Abraham's willingness to sacrifice Ishmael at God's command, and is marked by the cleaning and tidying of cemeteries and by animal sacrifice. **Muslim New Year,** *Muharram*, usually falls in June or July, followed by the celebration of the **birthday of Mohammed**, *Maulud Nabi Muhammed*, in August, with festivities lasting throughout the following month.

Local festivals

Many of these festivals change annually against the Western calendar. The *Calendar of Events* booklet, produced annually by the Directorate General of Tourism, should be available in tourist offices in Indonesia and overseas, and is vital if you're planning an itinerary to include a festival anywhere in the archipelago.

Erau Festival, Tenggarong, Kalimantan and Timor. September. A big display of indigenous Dayak skills and dancing.

Tabut, Pariaman, west Sumatra and **Tabot**, Bengkulu, south Sumatra (the same festival by different names). An annual ceremony held in the tenth Muslim month to commemorate the martyrdom of Mohammed's grandchildren, Hassan and Hussein. The festivals involve huge models of the *bouraq*, a winged horse with a woman's head, believed to have rescued the souls of the heroes and carried them to heaven.

Funerals, Tanah Toraja, Sulawesi. Mostly May to September. Buffalo sacrifice, bullfights, and *sisemba* kick-boxing tournaments punctuating days of eating and drinking.

Galungun, Bali. An annual event in the *wuku* calendar (just one of Bali's calendars), which means it takes place every 210 days. The elaborate, ten-day family festival celebrates the victory of good over evil, and all the ancestral gods are thought to come down to earth to take part.

Kasada, Bromo, East Java. Annual festival at Gunung Bromo in which offerings are made to the gods, thrown into the crater following the instructions of the gods to Jaker Serger, from whom the Tenggenese people of the area are descended.

Nyepi, throughout Bali. End of March or beginning of April. The major festival of the *saka* year, another of the Balinese calendars, and the major purification ritual of the year. The days before *nyepi* are full of activity – religious objects are taken in procession from temples to sacred springs or to the sea for purification. Sacrifices are made and displayed at crossroads where evil spirits are thought to linger, to lure them into the open. The night before *nyepi*, the spirits are frightened away with drums, gongs, cymbals, firecrackers and huge papier-mâché monsters. On the day itself, everyone sits quietly at home to persuade any remaining evil spirits that Bali is completely deserted.

Pasola, West Sumba. Four times a year, twice in February, twice in March. The most spectacular festival in Nusa Tenggara, where, following days of religious preliminaries,

Forthcoming festival dates

Ramadan begins October 27, 2003; October 16, 2004; October 5 2005.
Galungun June 18, 2003; January 14 & August 11, 2004; March 9 & October 5, 2005.
Idul Fitri November 25, 2003; November 14, 2004; November 4, 2005.
Kuningan June 28, 2000; January 24 & August 21, 2004; March 19 & October 15, 2005.
Maulud Nabi May 14, 2003; May 2, 2004; April 21, 2005.

two teams of spear-wielding horsemen from neighbouring villages engage each other in battle on the beach.

Sekaten, Central Java. The celebration of the birthday of the prophet Mohammed, held in the royal courts of Central Java, combined with more ancient, mystic rituals that predate Islam. The festivities start with a month-long festival of fairs, gamelan recitals, wayang kulit and wayang orang performances, before culminating in a procession around the royal courts, at the end of which food is offered to Java's fertility god. The date of Sekaten varies from year to year, being linked to the lunar Javanese and Islamic calendars.

Entertainment and sport

Despite the new distractions of discos, cinemas and TV, religious festivals and ceremonies are a major form of entertainment. Encompassing all kinds of events, from Balinese dances and temple festivals to Javanese puppet shows and the traditional funerals of Sulawesi and Kalimantan, these events are still enthusiastically performed across the archipelago. Tourists, as exotic guests, are generally welcome to attend.

Traditional and national sports

Illegal unless performed for religious ceremonies, **cockfighting** can still be seen in Bali and, to a lesser extent, in parts of Kalimantan and Sulawesi, where certain rituals require the shedding of blood. Where it's practised, you'll see men of all ages and incomes caressing their birds in public, often gathering in groups to show them off and weigh up their rivals. When not being pampered, the birds spend their days in individual bell-shaped bamboo baskets, often placed in quite noisy public places, so that the bird won't be scared when it finally makes it to the ring. The best prizefighters can earn their owners sizeable sums of money, and a certain status too, but despite all this the men are unsentimental about their animals – a dead bird is a financial rather than an emotional loss. Traditional **buffalo races** are also held in Bali and Madura, and **bullfights** – bloodless battles of strength between two animals, rather than along the Spanish model – are an integral part of Torajan funeral ceremonies.

As far as competitive sports go, **takrau** is a popular back-yard game, where players pass a rattan ball between them using any part of the body except the hands. Indonesia does well on the international **badminton** scene, with **soccer**, and an indigenous **martial arts** style called **pancak silat**, also enjoying nationwide popularity.

Dance and music

Given the enormous cultural and ethnic mix that makes up Indonesia, it's hardly surprising that the range of traditional **music** and **dance** across the archipelago is so vast. Each group of people has its own traditional forms, and in many cases these are highly accessible to visitors, although for many the most memorable moments will be the unplanned occasions when they stumble across a dance practice or an orchestra rehearsal.

Best known are the highly stylized and mannered **classical performances** in Java and Bali, accompanied by the **gamelan orchestra** (see p.1062 and the box opposite). Every step of these classical dances is minutely orchestrated, and the merest wink of an eye, arch of an eyebrow and angle of a finger has meaning and significance. The tradition remains vibrant, passed down by

Gamelan performances

Yogyakarta (Yogya)

There's lots going on in **Yogya**, much of it geared to the large number of tourists who visit the town each year, so if you're not staying long, you'll find performances more easily than in Solo.

Daily **gamelan** and **dance** performances for tourists are held at the Kraton, and nightly two-hour wayang performances at the Agastiya Institute. Other central venues include the Kepatihan, Taman Budaya, and Pujukusuman, the dance school where the late Romo Sas (one of Yogya's top dance teachers) taught until recently. There are regular tourist performances of dance and gamelan in the hotels; the performers are often students from ISI (Institut Seni Indonesia), the Institute of Indonesian Arts. A live RRI (Radio Republic Indonesia) broadcast takes place at the Pura Pukualaman each month. Further out of town are the Lembaga Studi Jawa, a foundation set up recently for the study and performance of Javanese arts; Bagong Kussiardja's dance foundation, where you may be able to watch rehearsals; and ISI, where exam recitals and performances of new dance and gamelan music are held at certain times of year.

Annual **festivals** to look out for are the Festival Kesenian Yogyakarta (gamelan, dance and wayang), the International Gamelan Festival (including new compositions and groups from abroad), and the Sekaten and Kraton festivals. Sekaten is held each year in both Solo and Yogya. Performances of the **Ramayana** ballet are held regularly at Prambanan Temple (outside Yogya) – pricey, but worth seeing.

Surakarta (Solo)

There are regular live RRI broadcasts of **gamelan** music from the two palaces in **Solo**: the Kraton Hadiningrat and the Mangkunagaran. Listeners are welcome – it's a great opportunity to see the palace gamelans being played. Broadcasts take place at lunchtimes and late evenings (10pm–midnight). Dates are determined by the 35-day month of the Javanese calendar; go to the RRI and check the noticeboard for details of all live broadcasts. STSI (Sekolah Tinggi Seni Indonesia), the "High School of Indonesian Arts", is a bus ride from the centre of town. Exam recitals and performances take place at the end of each semester. **Dance rehearsals** take place at the Mangkunagaran every Wednesday morning. There are all-night **wayang** performances each month at STSI (see p.243), Taman Budaya Surakarta (on the campus of STSI) and the RRI. Nightly **wayang orang** (dance-drama) performances take place at the Sriwedari Amusement Park, and there are regular tourist performances at the larger hotels, such as *Hotel Kusuma Sahid*.

Bali

There is always plenty of activity in **Bali** – the easiest performances to find are those arranged for tourists. The best way to find out what's happening where is to go to the tourist board in Denpasar, buy a Balinese calendar, and get a list of the major **odalan** (village temple ceremonies). The major temple festivals *Galungan* and *Kuningan* are held every 210 days. *Odalan* are held more frequently. **Gamelan** and **dance** is a big feature in Ubud, Peliatan and Teges. Other places to visit if you have more time are Sabah (where there is a *legong* troupe), Sukawati (*gender wayang*), Batur (*gong gede*) and the villages of Sawan and Jagaraga in north Bali.

In Denpasar, the **Bali Arts Festival** is held in July/August each year, and performances are held at STSI throughout the year.

experts to often very young pupils. Ubud on Bali and Yogyakarta on Java are the centres for these dances, with shortened performances staged to cater to the shorter attention spans of Western visitors. Other performances are much more geared to local audiences – the *Ramayana* and *Mahabharata* dance-dramas tend to fall into this category.

It's best to respect local **dress code** if you go to performances in the palaces in Java – avoid sleeveless tops and shorts. In Bali a temple sash must be worn if you visit a temple.

For more on individual dance forms, see pp.582 of the Bali chapter, and to find out about Indonesian shadow puppet plays, **wayang kulit** and **wayang golek**, see p.209 of the Central Java chapter.

Outdoor pursuits

Indonesia is a dream location for those with a passion for the great outdoors. Its seas are home to coral reefs, there are scaleable mountains and volcanoes, wide rivers, rainforest, and endless stretches of beach.

In Java, Bali, Lombok and Sumatra you'll have little trouble finding companies who will set you up with anything from a mountain bike to a mask and snorkel. But it's the remote areas which are often more interesting, and there you'll need a little more imagination. Be aware that your **travel insurance** may not cover you for accidents incurred while participating in high-risk activities, or may require a higher premium.

Scuba diving

The wealth of life beneath Indonesia's seas is amazing, and many of the world's best **diving sites** are found here. The Banda Islands in Maluku, Alor in Nusa Tenggara and Pulau Bunaken off Sulawesi have all been regularly rated in the world's top five, while a lot of diving in more accessible places is still exceptional. The vast diversity of tropical fish and coral is complemented by visibility that can reach over 30m. During the wet season, particularly the monsoon, visibility can be reduced – the best time for diving is between April and October.

The diversity and number of Indonesia's diving sites is virtually unparalleled, but places where you can hire scuba equipment by the day are limited. Most major beach resorts have dive centres, often in the smarter hotels, but further afield you'll probably have to rely on live-aboard cruises or even on having your own gear.

Generally speaking, a day's diving with two tanks, lunch and basic equipment costs $35–100, subject to bargaining. Be aware that it is down to you to **check your equipment**, and that the purity of an air tank can be suspect, and could cause serious injury. Also check your guide's credentials carefully, and bear in mind that you may be a long way from a decompression chamber. Some intrepid divers have managed to hire equipment from pearling operations; again, remember that the equipment may not be safe.

Bali has many good sites including the famous *Liberty* wreck off the north coast, and lots of good tour operators; Lombok's operators are limited to Sengigi and the Gili Islands. There have been reports of dodgy equipment being used by some of the dive boats, so it's best to stick to the bigger, more established companies. Several large dive companies have offices in Jakarta, and there are dive opportunities in Ujong Kulong national park, Krakatau, and several (average to poor) sites along the south coast of Java. Most dive centres charge similar rates for dives and courses. One-day dive trips usually cost around US$50–95 including equipment, and two- to five-day trips cost about US$85 per day, all inclusive. Sample prices for courses include four-day open-water PADI courses for US$300–400, and two-day advanced open-water courses for around US$245–350. Many dive centres do not include the dive manual and exam papers in the price of the four-day open-water course.

Nusa Tenggara is alive with astounding reefs, but dive operators are scarce, apart from in Lombok. To get into the Komodo national park you will need to take the inexpensive live-aboard *Komodo Plus* out of Sape Sumbawa. The park has some breathtaking diving, being particularly noteworthy for the abundance of gargantuan pelagics. Out of **Lahubanbajo Flores**, you can take day-trips to reasonable sites with the Bajo Beach Diving Club at the hotel of the same name. Elsewhere on Flores, **Maumere** was once an important dive site, but after a massive earthquake in 1992, many sites are silted over. There are two good dive operators at Waiara, a short trip east of town. There are several expensive **live-aboards** out of Bali, such as Baruna, Kuta, (Ⓣ0361/753820, Ⓕ753809, Ⓦwww.baruna.com), with prices from $699 for 3 nights inclusive, and Grand Komodo Tours & Dives, Sanur, Bali (Ⓣ0361/287166361, Ⓕ287165, Ⓦwww.komodoalordive.com). These operators all run trips into Nusa Tenggara and further afield, though to count on such a trip, you will need to round up your own group of passengers.

Sumatra is not well known for its diving, though Pulau Weh off the north coast has dive facilities and some fantastic sites. The 99 islands of Pulau Banyak are also full of potential, having burgeoning populations of turtles and stingrays and a couple of relatively new dive setups. The scene off Padang is enticing, as the Indian Ocean laps the coast there – there is one operator in Padang (see p.403).

Kalimantan has just one dive site, northeasterly Pulau Derawan, but it gets consistently good reports from visitors – manta rays and turtle rookeries, rather than coral, are the draw here. **Sulawesi**, on the other hand, pulls in divers from all over the world, most of whom home in on the vertigo-inducing walls at Bunaken Marine Reserve out from the northern city of Manado. Lesser-known sites include the crystal-clear waters around the Togian Islands in central Sulawesi, while the virtually unexplored reefs of the Tukangbesi group off southeastern Sulawesi are attracting more adventurous divers.

Surfing

Indonesia is one of the world's premier **surfing** destinations, with an enormous variety of class waves, and destinations spreading from the tip of Sumatra right down to Timor and beyond. The prime attraction is surfing perfect, uncrowded breaks, with paradisal coastlines laid out before you. The price you'll have to pay for this is that, unless you take expensive all-in surf cruises, you'll have to drag your board hundreds of kilometres on rickety, crowded public transport in sweltering heat. In June and July, during the best and most consistent surf, you can also expect waves to be crowded, especially in Java and Bali. For all-in **surf safaris** on luxury yachts, try STC (Ⓔsurftrav@ozemail.com.au), who offer boat trips around all major destinations.

Details of all the best surf spots in Bali and Lombok are given in the relevant sections of this guide, but serious surfers would do well to consult the book *Indo Surf and Lingo*, available for A$32.95 (US$22.95 outside Australia); you can also buy it from surfshops and bookshops in Bali. Good websites include Ⓦwww.baliwaves.com, which carries an almost daily report on the current state of Bali's waves (updated several times a week), and also features stories, links and details of surfing tours; Ⓦwww.balisurfcam.com, which features tips, wave descriptions, swell and tide charts and a daily report; Ⓦwww.surfermag.com, the *Surfer Mag* website, also carries surf news and tips for Bali and elsewhere; Ⓦwww.surftravelonline, which has a gallery of sensational photos; Ⓦwww.balix.com/surfing, which has a reasonable set of links to relevant surf sites, but doesn't appear to be updated very regularly.

The monthly magazine *Surf Time* is all about the Indonesian surfing scene, and is available free from most surf shops in Kuta.

The bimonthly cultural magazine the *Bali Echo* regularly publishes articles on the Indonesian surf scene, and often features interviews with top local surfers. For up-to-date local wave information, tune into Bali's Hard Rock Radio on 87.6FM, which broadcasts five-minute surf reports on weekdays (8–9am, noon–1pm & 5–6pm).

Equipment

On Bali and in some of the larger surf centres you can rent **boards**, though they may not be up to much – you should try to bring your own board. A padded board-bag is essential, as your pride and joy is going to take a lot of pounding as it gets chucked up onto bus roofs with the trussed-up goats. Most public transport will want to charge your board as an extra seat, and there's not much point arguing, especially in Balinese bemo terminals where things can turn a little ugly if you refuse to pay. Kuta has some great surf shops, but if you're heading further afield you'll need your own kit, plus high-strength sun block and medical supplies (with plenty of iodine for coral cuts). A helmet and thin suit is advisable if you plan to surf over some of Indonesia's scalpel-sharp reefs.

The waves

At its best, **Desert Point** is the best of Indonesia's waves. Situated on Lombok's southwest tip, it's also known for being very unpredictable, and many surfers do little else here than sit around in battered beach huts. It's a long barrelling left-hander, and when it's good it's very good – some say the best in the world.

The next big one is Grajagan in the Alas Purwo national park on Java's southeastern tip. **G' Land** as it's known, is one of the world's better left-handers and a stopoff for the pro tour. It has four sections, of which Speedies is the most consistent, with a perfect long ride, promising endless tubes and walls. Unless you fancy trekking out there alone and camping, then the only way to hit G' Land is via an organized tour from Kuta Bali. Java's other "surfers-only" spot is **Pulau Panaitan** in the Ujong Kulon national park. One Palm Point is a perfect barrelling left, doable in a large swell, and there are more around to ensure you have a little breathing space. Other popular spots on Java include **Batu Keras** near Pangandaran, **Cimaja** near Pelabuhan Ratu and the turtle-breeding grounds of **Genteng**.

Nias off Sumatra is quite the surfing mecca, remote and primitive but playing host to the pro tour. You don't need to take expensive charter yachts to get to its cheap losmen, although you will to get out to the **Mentawai** and **Hinakos** islands, which have awesome empty waves with endless barrels. The outer reef at Nias offers the best rides here, but needs a hefty swell to take off. There is, however, a short right-hander to play around on while you wait. There are also good sites all down the west coast including Meulaboh, Tapaktuan and nearby Pulau Simeulue.

Nusa Tenggara is the fastest growing of surfing locations, partially because of the short flight from Darwin to Kupang, and also because of the plentiful empty waves and minimal cost of living. T' Land at Nemberala beach on **Pulau Roti** is legendary, a long consistent left that's not quite as hollow as its near-namesake on Java. You can often see surf legends supping coconut milk with the locals in Nemberala's laid-back beach bungalows. Rua, Pero and Tarimbang on **Sumba** offer everything from hollow to mellow, and even the remote **Savu** and **Raijua** islands are being explored, particularly as stops on cruising surf safaris. Sumba is becoming particularly popular with surfers and with big-game fishers. Cruises around Nusa Tenggara are likely to stop off at **Sumbawa's Hu'u**, with its multiple breaks, including the long-respected Lakey Peak and Periscopes. The more hardy surfers could trudge down to Sumbawa's **west coast** and live it rough near the excellent breaks of Supersuck, Scar Reef and Yo Yos; don't expect four-star facilities, though. Lombok's south coast offers many reasonable rides for most of the year; **Kuta Beach** is as good a place as any to start looking.

Surf culture and **Bali** have become utterly inseparable. **Kuta** and **Legian** beach breaks are great for beginners, with boards for rent just about everywhere. You can also rent a boat out to the Kuta Reef which is pretty good between mid- and high-tide. Other sites on the west coast include **Padang**, which can be genuinely huge and pretty formidable. **Ulu Watu** is another that regularly leaves surfers in intensive care; don't be tempted unless you're totally up to it. On the east coast, **Nusa Dua** is a fast right-hander with long rides, and **Sanur** offers more of the same but over reef. In the western monsoon from October to March, Nusa Dua and Sanur are excellent, while the other side of the peninsula is better from April to September. Whenever Bali's waves are at their best, they are guaranteed to be jam-packed.

Rafting

Indonesia's best-established location for **white-water rafting** is on **Bali**, with many tour companies in Kuta and Ubud offering tours to shoot the rapids in the rivers in the east of the island. There are also well-established operations in **West Java** near Pangandaran and Pelabuhan Ratu. Outfits offering white-water tours in new locations are gradually springing up in pockets around the archipelago; enquire at local tourist offices.

Some of the best whitewater is to be found in Sumatra's **Gunung Leuser national park**, where extended tours through the jungle offer occasional Grade VIs, and even the odd small waterfall to tumble down. Most tours start from Muarasitulan, but the most intense begin further upriver near Blankergeran. Elsewhere in Sumatra, there are some relatively tame single-day tours out of Bukit Lawang, and popular tubing rides are organized by many of the losmen there.

At most locations around Indonesia, single days on the river generally cost $25–60, extended tours (around $50 per day) including camping out at the riverside, all meals, and a guide to cook them for you.

Trekking and climbing

Indonesia offers endless **trekking** opportunities of varying degrees of difficulty, with terrain ranging from broad, easily followed paths, to exhausting, near-invisible jungle trails which traverse steep mountain ridges and fast-flowing rivers. Some areas take you into the domain of remote tribes, while others are worth the effort for the experience and satisfaction that comes from simply completing the distance. You'll find that hard-core point-to-point hiking is not generally a good way to see **wildlife**, however, and for this you're better off thoroughly exploring a smaller region.

Whatever your motivation and wherever you go, it's worth knowing what you're up against. Thick forest can be a magical environment, especially when animals and birds start up their chorus at dawn and dusk; but weighed down with a pack, covered in leeches and soaked to the skin from sweat and rain it can also be exhausting and claustrophobic. More open country and wider trails means exposure to the sun, and you need to come properly prepared. **Boots** with a firm grip are essential; beware of poor stitching, which can rot within days. For longer treks you'll need a **tent** (or a guide who can build a shelter), and also some warm clothing and a **sleeping bag** for chilly evenings in high country. **Backpacks** leak, so put all your gear in plastic bags. Make sure you carry a knife, butane lighter, torch with spare bulb and batteries, hat, a water canteen, a compass and a first-aid kit. The first-aid kit should contain: antihistamines (for insect bites, or irritating plants); a crepe bandage; two compress bandages; a whistle; a good canteen; a strip of Band-Aid; scissors; antibiotic powder (more effective in the tropics than cream); fungicide cream; eyewash; fine tweezers; needles; candles; and a good penknife. Insect repellent is not much use while you're walking – it washes off within minutes – but you can use it to get rid of leeches at rest stops. You'll obviously have to take your own **food** when trekking, and it's also polite to have something to give to people who might provide meals elsewhere, as villagers may be short of supplies themselves. The standard village rations become monotonous on extended stays, but it's sometimes possible to buy fresh meat, and guides might carry spears or guns in case of an encounter with game along the way.

One way or another, you'll definitely need **guides**, and not just to find the paths: turning up at a remote village unannounced can cause trouble, as people may mistrust outsiders, let alone Westerners. If you have no time, experience or language skills, **tours** (arranged either overseas or within Indonesia) are the most convenient way to organize everything, though they're expensive and, bound to a schedule, the experience can feel rushed. Far better options are either to track down an experienced, English-speaking guide in the nearest city, or – with adequate Indonesian – travel as far as possible on your own, and then engage local help, bearing in mind that locals may have neither the time nor the inclination to assist you. In some regions Indonesian may not be enough, so make sure your guides speak the local dialects. National-park officers will often know suitable people to act as guides.

While the possibilities for mountain trekking and volcano scaling are practically limitless in Indonesia, there is little or no structure for **sport climbing**, though you can bring all your own equipment. The only **mountains** of any serious note are Trikora and Puncak Jaya in West Papua. The latter is the highest mountain between the Himalayas and the Andes, and can be climbed only on extended and expensive tours out of Jayapura or the Baliem Valley. To climb Trikora, special permits are required from government authorities in Jakarta. Gunung Rinjani on Lombok is a popular hike, possible without a guide in two days and one night. Kerinci on Sumatra and Semeru on Java are both serious endeavours for fit trekkers, while easier undertakings are Batur on Bali and Bromo on Java – both hugely rewarding, involving less effort. Straddling the border between North Sumatra and Aceh, the Gunung Leuser national park is Southeast Asia's largest, and offers some of the best trekking opportunities on the archipelago, from simple one-day walks around the Bukit Lawang orang-utan sanctuary near Medan, to two-week hikes to the summit of Gunung Leuser. Sumatra, Kalimantan and West Papua contain some of the largest stands of **tropical forest** left on the planet, despite continued summer fires, clearance for farming and ferocious logging.

Crime and personal safety

Foreign fatalities resulting from the suppression of independence movements in West Papua and Timor, and the urban violence which surrounded the political upheavals of 1998, all undermine the idea that Indonesia is a safe place to travel. However, while it would be misleading to play down these events, it's also true that serious incidents involving Westerners are rare, and most tourists have trouble-free visits to Indonesia.

Petty theft, however, is a fact of life in Indonesia, and without becoming overly paranoid, it's sensible to minimize any risks. Although as a Westerner you're obviously richer than the average Indonesian, most crime is opportunistic: the fewer opportunities you present, the less likely you are to be targeted. Don't flash signs of wealth around, such as expensive jewellery or watches. Carry travellers' cheques, the bulk of your cash and important documents – especially airline tickets, credit cards and passport – under your clothing in a **money belt**. While these can be irritating to wear, the major hassles incurred by losing vital items are considerably worse. Money belts are basically invisible, unlike all-too-obvious **bumbags**, which, besides signalling the location of your valuables, are easy to cut off in a crowd. Ensure that **luggage** is lockable

Emergencies

In an emergency dial the following numbers:
Police ☎110
Ambulance ☎118
Fire ☎113

(gadgets to lock backpacks exist), and never keep anything important in outer pockets, which deft fingers can swiftly open without your knowledge. Don't hesitate to check that doors and windows – including those in the bathroom – are secure before accepting **accommodation**; if the management seems offended by this, you probably don't want to stay there anyway. Some guesthouses and hotels have **safe-deposit boxes** which solve the problem of what to do with your valuables while you go swimming; a surprising number of tourists leave their possessions unattended on beaches and are amazed to find them gone when they return.

Along with a list of travellers' cheque numbers, keep separate **photocopies of your passport** so you can prove who you are if the original goes missing. In many places the availability of exchange services makes carrying large amounts of cash unnecessary. If you have to carry large sums, keep enough hidden away from your main stash so that if your money is stolen you can still get to the police, get in touch with a consulate and pay for phone calls while you sort everything out – US dollar notes are very useful in these circumstances.

If you're unlucky enough to get **mugged**, never resist and, if you disturb a thief, raise the alarm rather than try to take them on – they're after your valuables and are unlikely to harm you if you don't get in their way. More often, however, things will go missing by stealth, either from accommodation or the top of a bus, or from your pocket in a crowd. Be especially aware of **pickpockets** on buses or bemos, who usually operate in pairs: one will distract you while another does the job.

Afterwards, you'll need a **police report** for insurance purposes. Police stations are marked on the maps in the guide; in smaller villages where police are absent, ask for assistance from the headman. Unless your Indonesian is sound, try to take along someone to translate, though police will generally do their best to find an English-speaker. Allow plenty of time for any involvement with the police, whose offices wallow in bureaucracy; you may also be charged "administration fees" for enlisting their help, the cost of which is open to sensitive negotiations. If you are **driving**, the chance of entanglement with the police increases; spot checks are common, and by law drivers must carry their licence and the vehicle registration papers.

Finally, have nothing to do with **drugs** in Indonesia. The penalties are tough, and you won't get any sympathy from consular officials. If you are arrested, or end up on the wrong side of the law for whatever reason, you should ring the consular officer at your embassy immediately.

Shopping for arts and crafts

Indonesians have a strong artistic heritage, and different regions of the country are renowned for their textiles, woodcarving, jewellery or general craftsmanship. Some pieces are only available in the provinces, towns or villages where they are created; others are on sale in tourist shops and marketplaces across the land.

There are various ways of learning about local styles and artistic quality. A trip around the nearest market stalls or shops will furnish a good idea of what's on offer, and perhaps the opportunity to meet artists or craftsmen. Major art galleries and **regional museums** are also a good starting point, illustrating more traditional pieces and quality. In hard-core tourist hot spots such as Bali, you'll find streets crammed with all manner of outlets, from makeshift stalls to sophisticated glass-fronted boutiques, liberally sprinkled with a persistent gang of **hawkers** who will try to sell you local handicrafts at prices that drop in seconds. Traditional covered **markets**, or **pasar**, tend to be much more rewarding places to hone your bargaining skills, and, while necessities are generally their mainstay, many also have sections selling locally crafted trinkets, or even gems and the odd antique coin. Often you'll find areas set aside as the *pasar seni*, or **art market**, which sell everything from sarongs and lengths of printed batik to gold bracelets and rings, all aimed at local consumers.

Remember that any touts, guides and drivers you may engage to help you often get as much as fifty percent **commission** on any item sold – not only at the customer's expense but also the vendor's.

Woodcarving

There's a fine range of **woodwork** in Indonesia. Javanese factories turn out beautifully crafted teak **furniture** of mostly Dutch-inspired design. **Bali** offers an endless range of ornamental wooden fruit and animals as well as superb classical and modern designs from Ubud and the surrounding villages, while Kalimantan's Dayaks and the Asmat of West Papua produce renowned **carvings**. However, you do need to be particularly careful with wood – it's a material which travels badly, and whose exact provenance can have a major effect on the price. **Sandalwood** (*cenana*), for instance, is extremely valuable, but its pungent aroma can be faked by packing lesser timber in sandalwood sawdust for several days, or by scenting the impostor with sandalwood oil – both difficult tricks to detect. **Ebony**, originating from Kalimantan and Sulawesi, is another commonly faked wood – dyed mango wood is similarly heavy, but the genuine article has a pearly lustre rather than being boot-polish black.

Most tropical woods **crack** when taken to a drier climate, or as they lose sap after carving; check any potential purchase carefully for putty-filled flaws. Some places try to minimize the problem by treating finished pieces in polyethylene glycol (PEG), which can prevent cracking in certain circumstances. Conversely, newly carved pieces might deliberately be aged by exposure to the elements for a few months, so that they can be sold as "antiques" – Indonesia has been well combed by collectors over the years, and it's very unlikely that wooden artefacts are particularly old. Check all weathered pieces for rot and termite damage, as well as for shoddy restoration work.

Textiles

Javanese cotton **batik** is the best-known Indonesian **textile**, and you'll find a big selection at any city market. Stylish and boldly patterned, batik is used for everything from sarongs and formal shirts, to tablecloths and surfers' board-bags. Some pieces are **screen-printed**, but more authentic designs still involve a complex process of **waxing**, **dyeing** and **boiling**. Prices will reflect the method used; check whether the colour has authentically percolated through to the reverse side of the cloth.

Weaving is also practised, both for commercial and private use – in villages across Indonesia, you'll see women using hand looms. Cotton is the most widespread fabric employed, though **silk** is often preferred for important pieces, and artificial materials are replacing heavier, home-made plant fibres. Important ceremonial dress may incorporate luxurious materials such as gold-and-silver brocade. The most distinctive weaving style is **ikat**, a demanding technique that involves dyeing the weft threads with the finished pattern before weaving begins, creating a fuzzy edge to the bold designs. Some areas are famed for their distinctive *ikat*: the islands of **Flores** and **Sumba** in Nusa Tenggara produce marvellous patterns incorporating human and animal motifs, while **geringsing** double *ikat* from Bali's Tenganan village uses a painstakingly intricate process to produce stunning designs, and the island's **songket** weave is also renowned.

With such lovely fabrics to work with, it's hardly surprising that Indonesia also produces some great **clothes**. Aside from inexpensive wear available in markets countrywide, tourist centres such as Bali's Kuta swarm with classy and original boutiques, as well as the highest proliferation of stalls selling baggy *ikat* trousers, skimpy batik dresses, and even fine **leather clothing**. Local designers keep an astute eye on **Western fashions** and come up with stylish but unusual collections, many of which are geared as much to Western winters as they are to Asian climes.

Jewellery

Influenced by India and the Arab world, there is some exquisite **jewellery** available in Indonesia. Local smiths produce the ornamental kris and heavy wedding arrays worn by many ethnic groups, and turn out the day-to-day jewellery coveted by wealthier Indonesians. Men prefer heavy rings, sometimes set with semiprecious stones; women sport earrings, bracelets and necklaces. Most island groups have metalworking centres, such as Celuk in Bali, and Java's Yogyakarta.

Some things, such as Balinese imitation brand-name **watches**, are obviously fake, but look good anyway; at other times you'll want to make sure you're buying the real thing. Gold colour can be applied to other metals, or intensified on poor gold, by heating the artefact in nitric acid. Hailing from Maluku, Indonesian **pearls** – black, yellow or white – are reasonably priced because most are **seeded**, the growing process initiated by inserting a tiny plastic bead into the oyster, around which the pearl forms. Beware if someone starts justifying steep prices by claiming a pearl is natural, something you can't prove without an x-ray.

Ethnic art and antiques

Some of Indonesia's myriad **ethnic groups** have discovered that Westerners will pay money for everything from their bows and baby carriers to their kitchen utensils, and have started to produce these objects for the tourist market. For the average tourist, it's best to stick to obviously genuine articles which would be pointless to fake: Lombok **pottery**, or **stone adze blades** or **penis gourds** from West Papua make unusual and inexpensive mementos of your trip.

Other pieces, such as antique **Chinese porcelain** (often looted from tombs), gold heirlooms, clothing and carvings, are another story altogether. Apart from the likelihood of being ripped off – even experienced dealers have been duped by Indonesian forgers – export of old artefacts without a permit is illegal, and the practice of alienating such items from their cultural context is morally hard to justify.

Painting has a long history on Bali and is now a subject for serious study and collection, with exhibitions and sales overseas as well as on the island. For more on this, see p.576.

Cultural hints

The Indonesian people are extremely generous about opening up their homes, places of worship and festivals to the ever-growing crowd of interested tourists. However, while they are long-suffering and rarely show obvious displeasure, they can take great offence at certain aspects of Western behaviour. The most sensitive issues involve Westerners' clothing – or lack of it – and the code of practice that's required for formal situations.

It's worth noting, however, that the degree to which Indonesian etiquette is observed varies from place to place and in certain situations. Overall, Java and Bali have the strongest cultural codes, but this doesn't mean you should automatically drop your standards elsewhere, and it's best to be overly polite until you have assessed the local situation.

Social conventions

Indonesians are generally very sociable people, and dislike doing anything alone. When forced to, it's normal for complete strangers engaged in some common enterprise – catching a bus, for instance – to introduce themselves and start up a friendship. **Sharing cigarettes** between men is in these circumstances a way of establishing a bond, and Westerners who don't smoke should be genuinely apologetic about refusing; it's well worth carrying a packet to share around even if you save your own "for later".

Conversations in Indonesia often open with "*dari mana?*". Though literally meaning "where are you from?", it's often intended as less of a question than simply a greeting – giving your nationality is a good response. Next will be enquiries into your marital status and whether you have children; negative answers often evoke expressions of sympathy as they are seen as essential stages in most Indonesians' lives.

As Indonesians find it difficult to understand the Western obsession with **privacy**, or the need for some Westerners to simply have a few minutes to themselves from time to time, the constant attention – not to mention inevitable cries of "Hello mister" yelled out by children whenever a foreign face appears in less cosmopolitan regions of the country – means that Western tempers tend to fray after a while. Another major source of irritation for foreigners is the vague notion of **timekeeping** that pervades almost every aspect of Indonesian life. Lack of punctuality is such a national institution that there is even a term for it: *jam karet* ("rubber time"). You'll save yourself a lot of stress if you remember this when visiting a bank, or having to wait hours for transport to depart.

However bad things become, keep your temper. As elsewhere in Asia, Indonesians dislike **confrontational behaviour**, and will rarely show anger or irritation of any kind. Tourists who lose their cool and get visibly rattled for whatever reason will be derided, and even baited further, rather than feared.

Displays of affection are also subdued. Indonesians of the same sex often hold hands or hug in public, but heterosexual couples should avoid overt physical contact, which can cause trouble in conservative areas. **Critical opinions** of the state are likewise best kept to oneself, and the same goes for attitudes towards religious beliefs and conventions – people do discuss these things, but seldom with new aquaintances.

The body

For various religious and practical reasons, Indonesians view parts of the body in specific ways. Broadly speaking, a person's **head** is seen as sacred, and should never be touched casually by another – not even to pat a child or to ruffle someone's hair in affection. Conversely, the **feet** are held to be unclean, so never use them to indicate anything, or point them at a person or sacred object. The **left hand** is used for washing after defecating, and Indonesians never eat with it – avoid using it to pass or receive things.

Despite what you'll see around the biggest beach resorts, most Indonesians are extremely offended by topless and nude **bathing**. True, rural Indonesians bathe publicly in rivers and pools, but there's an unspoken rule of invisibility under these circumstances and women generally wear sarongs, and men shorts or underwear, often using segregated areas. If you bathe alongside them, do as they do.

Social etiquette

Dressing neatly is akin to showing **respect** in Indonesia, and away from the biggest resort areas it's best to avoid scruffy clothing or articles which are seen as immodest. These include thongs, shorts, vests, or anything which leaves you with bare shoulders.

When dealing with people in authority – police or government officials, for example – wearing something formal shows that you take their position seriously, and they will be that much more willing to help you. While you should always do your best, this is obviously one area where local standards apply: visiting an immigration department for a visa extension will require more dress sense than greeting a village head (who may himself only be wearing shorts and thongs) after a day's hiking in the jungle.

Language (see p.1085) is also used to express respect in Indonesia. Many Indonesian dialects include a "higher" language for use in formal situations, but even in everyday encounters, an older man than yourself (or even an obviously younger man if he's in a position of authority) should be addressed as ***Bapak*** or ***Pak***, a woman as ***Ibu*** or ***Bu***. **Body language** also comes into play: when walking between people who are talking together, Indonesians apologize for the intrusion by dropping their shoulders in a characteristic stoop; until you pick up this gesture, saying *ma'af* will suffice.

Religious etiquette

In a country where a belief in God is compulsory, Indonesians take their religions very seriously. Anyone entering a **place of worship** should be aware of the necessary etiquette. **Mosques** are generally open to the public, though everyone is required to take their shoes off before entering, and to wear long sleeves and long trousers; women should definitely cover their shoulders and may also be asked to cover their heads as well (bring a scarf or shawl, as there probably won't be any provided). Men and women pray in separate parts of the mosque, though there are unlikely to be signs telling you where to go. Dress regulations also apply when visiting **Balinese temples,** and many religions also prohibit **women** from engaging in certain activities – or even entering a place of worship – during menstruation. If attending a **religious festival**, find out beforehand whether a dress code applies; guests at Torajan funerals, for example, should wear dark clothing.

Living and/or working in Indonesia

Working is forbidden on an Indonesian tourist visa, and cash-in-hand jobs are thin on the ground. A few tourists manage to set themselves up in Bali or Jakarta as foreign-language teachers; otherwise, the most common moneymaking ploy is the exporting of Indonesian goods (fabric, clothes, jewellery and other artefacts). Divemasters have also been known to find short-term work, though sometimes in exchange for food and lodgings instead of wages. On Bali, the fortnightly *Bali Advertiser* carries a "situations vacant" column, and is a good place to look for office and hotel jobs. It's available free from some hotels and tourist offices.

Another pre-planning strategy for working abroad, whether teaching English or otherwise, is to get hold of *Overseas Jobs Express* (Premier House, Shoreham Airport, Sussex BN43 5FF; ⓣ01273/699611, ⓦwww.overseasjobs.com), a fortnightly publication with a range of job vacancies, available by subscription only. Vacation Work also publishes books on summer jobs abroad and how to work your way around the world; call ⓣ01865/241978 or visit ⓦwww.vacationwork.co.uk for their catalogue. In the USA, **HarperCollins** (Perseus Division ⓣ1-800/242-7737) publishes *International Jobs: Where They Are, How to Get Them*, including a listing of vacancies (usually English teachers) in Indonesia.

Travel magazines like the reliable *Wanderlust* (every two months; £2.80) have a Job Shop section which often advertises job opportunities with tour companies. A useful website is ⓦwww.studyabroad.com, with listings and links to study and work programmes worldwide.

Teaching English

There are two options: find or prepare for finding work before you go, or just wing it and see what you come up with while you're out there, particularly if you already have a degree and/or teaching experience. Teaching English – often abbreviated as ELT (English Language Teaching) or TEFL (Teaching English as a Foreign Language) – is the way many people finance their way around the greater part of the world; you can get a CELTA (Certificate in English Language Teaching to Adults) qualification before you leave home or even while you're abroad. International House has branches in many countries which offer the course, and you could even turn it into a proper career. Strictly speaking, you don't need a degree to do the course, but you'll certainly find it easier to get a job with the degree/certificate combination. Certified by the RSA, the course is very demanding and costs about £944 for one month's full-time tuition; you'll be thrown in at the deep end and expected to teach right away. The British Council's website, ⓦwww.britishcouncil.org/work/jobs.htm, has a list of English-teaching vacancies. American citizens may find it useful to contact the American Chamber of Commerce or visit their website at ⓦwww.amcham.or.id, or the American-Indonesian Chamber of Commerce (AICC) at ⓦwww.aiccusa.org.

Study and work programmes

Perhaps the easiest way to work legally in Indonesia is to join a work or study programme. While not cheap – and not very rewarding financially once you are out in Indonesia – the following organizations nevertheless provide an easy way to secure a working visa, and the variety of work and locations offered to participants is often large and exciting.

From the UK and Ireland

British Council 10 Spring Gardens, London SW1A 2BN ⓣ020/7930 8466. Produce a free leaflet which details study opportunities abroad. The

Council's Central Management Direct Teaching (Ⓣ020/7389 4931) recruits TEFL teachers for posts worldwide (check the British Council In Indonesia's website, Ⓦwww.britishcouncil.org/indonesia, for a current list of vacancies), and its Central Bureau for International Educational and Training (Ⓣ020/7389 4004; publications Ⓣ020/7389 4880, Ⓦwww.centralbureau.org.uk) enables those who already work as educators to find out about teacher development programmes abroad. It also publishes a book *Year Between*, aimed principally at gap-year students detailing volunteer programmes, and schemes abroad.

International House 106 Piccadilly, London W1V 9NL Ⓣ020/7491 2598, Ⓦwww.ihlondon.com. Head office for reputable English-teaching organization which offers TEFL training leading to the award of a Certificate in English Language Teaching to Adults (CELTA), and recruits for teaching positions in Britain and abroad, including positions on Java and Bali.

Raleigh International 27 Parsons Green Lane, London SW6 4HZ Ⓣ020/7371 8585, Ⓦwww.raleigh.org.uk. Operating since 1984, this youth development charity organizes community and environmental work projects around the world. Prospective 17- to 25-year-old "Venturers" must first attend a demanding assessment weekend to prove they've got what it takes, but minimum requirements prior to this are the ability to swim and to speak English (participants come from many nations and backgrounds). Ten 10-week expeditions are run every year, where project groups of about 12 people live in basic conditions in remote areas. If you're older than 25 and professionally qualified, you can join as volunteer staff overseeing the younger "Venturers". To take part in the programme, all participants must fundraise on Raleigh's behalf. They have no expeditions to Indonesia at present, though they may well do in the near future, and they are currently running an expedition to Mount Kinabalu in Sabah, East Malaysia, just a short hop across the border from East Kalimantan.

VSO (Voluntary Service Overseas) 317 Putney Bridge Rd, London SW15 2PN Ⓣ020/8780 7200, Ⓦwww.vso.org.uk. Highly respected charity that sends qualified professionals (in the fields of education, health, community and social work, engineering, information technology, law and media) to spend two years or more working for local wages on projects beneficial to developing countries. Some fundraising is involved. English language teaching, accountancy and health professional positions are regularly advertised for Indonesia.

From the USA

Note: most universities have semester abroad programmes to certain countries; the following are independent organizations that run programmes in many countries.

AFS Intercultural Programs 198 Madison Ave, 8th Floor, New York, NY 10016 Ⓣ1-800/876-2377 or 212/299 9000, Ⓦwww.afs.org/usa. Runs summer experiential programmes aimed at fostering international understanding for teenagers and adults, and also a student exchange programme between American and Indonesian (Javanese and Balinese) students.

Bernan Associates 4611-F Assembly Dr, Lanham, MD 20706 Ⓣ1-800/274-4888, Ⓦwww.bernan.com. Distributes UNESCO's encyclopedic *Study Abroad.*

Council on International Educational Exchange (CIEE) 205 E 42nd St, New York, NY 10017 Ⓣ1-800/40-study, Ⓦwww.ciee.org/study. The non-profit parent organization of Council Travel, CIEE runs summer, semester and academic-year programmes in countries which in the past have included Indonesia, and publishes *Work, Study, Travel Abroad and Volunteer! The Comprehensive Guide to Voluntary Service in the US and Abroad.*

Volunteers for Peace 1034 Tiffany Rd, Belmont, VT 05730 Ⓣ802/259-2759, Ⓦwww.vfp.org. Non-profit organization with links to a huge international network of "workcamps", two- to four-week programmes that bring volunteers together from many countries to carry out needed community projects. Most workcamps are in summer, with registration in April–May. Annual membership including directory costs $20. Currently runs three programmes in Indonesia, In Bengkulu on Sumatra, and Yogyakarta and Semarang In Central Java.

World Learning Kipling Road, PO Box 676, Brattleboro, VT 05302 Ⓣ802/257-7751, Ⓦwww.worldlearning.org. Its School for International Training (Ⓣ1-800/336-1616, Ⓦwww.sit.edu) runs accredited college semesters abroad, comprising language and cultural studies, homestay and other academic work. Programmes in 40 countries, including a project to Increase the awareness minority rights in Indonesia.

From Australia and New Zealand

Australian Volunteers International 71 Argyle St, Fitzroy, Melbourne Ⓣ03/9279 1788, Ⓦwww.ozvol.org.au. Postings for up to 2 years in a wide variety of disciplines in developing countries including Indonesia.

Travellers with disabilities

Indonesia makes few provisions for its own disabled citizens, which clearly affects travellers with disabilities. Simply at the physical level, pavements are usually high and often uneven with all sorts of obstacles, and only rarely have slopes for you to get on or off them; access to most public places involves steps and very few have ramps. Public transport is inaccessible to wheelchair users, and the few pedestrian crossings on major roads have no audible signal. On the positive side, however, some accommodation comprises bungalows in extensive grounds, with spacious bathrooms, and the more upmarket hotels are increasingly aware of the requirements of disabled travellers.

For all of these reasons, it may be worth considering an **organized tour** – the contacts below will help you start researching trips to Indonesia. If you want to be more independent, it's important to know where you must be self-reliant and where you may expect help, especially regarding transport and accommodation. It's also vital to be honest – with travel agencies, insurance companies and travel companions. If you don't use a wheelchair all the time but your walking capabilities are limited, remember that you're likely to need to cover greater distances while travelling (often over rougher terrain and in hotter temperatures) than you're used to. If you use a wheelchair, have it serviced before you go and carry a repair kit.

Read your travel **insurance** small print carefully to make sure that people with an existing medical condition are not excluded. Use your travel agent to make your journey simpler: airlines can cope better if they are expecting you, with a wheelchair provided at airports and staff primed to help. A **medical certificate** of your fitness to travel, provided by your doctor, is also very useful; some airlines or insurance companies may insist on it. Take a back-up prescription, including the generic name of any drugs in case of emergency. Carry spares of any clothing or equipment that might be hard to find and, if there's an association representing people with your disability, contact them early in the planning process.

Make sure that you take sufficient supplies of any **medications**, and – if they're essential – carry the complete supply with you whenever you travel (including on buses and planes), in case of loss or theft. It's also a good idea to carry a doctor's letter about your drug prescriptions with you at all times – particularly when passing through airport customs – as this will ensure you don't get hauled up for narcotics transgressions. If your medication has to be kept cool, buy a thermal insulation bag and a couple of freezer blocks before you leave home; that way, you can refreeze one of the two blocks every day while the other is in use. The staff in most hotels, restaurants and bars should be happy to let you use their freezer compartment for a few hours. You may also be able to store your medication in hotel and guest-house refrigerators – though make a considered judgement about security first.

Based in the US, **Access Able Travel** (Ⓦwww.access-able.com) is a first-rate **website** for disabled travellers, with bulletin boards for passing on tips and accounts of accessible attractions, accommodation, guides and resources around the globe. As yet, there's no information posted on Indonesia, but Access Able is fairly new and growing fast – email Ⓔcarol@access-able.com for the latest.

Contacts for travellers with disabilities

In the UK and Ireland

Disability Action Group 2 Annadale Ave, Belfast BT7 3JH, Ⓣ028/9049 1011. Provides information

about access for disabled travellers abroad.
Irish Wheelchair Association Blackheath Drive, Clontarf, Dublin 3 ⓣ01/833 8241, ⓕ833 3873, ⓔiwa@iol.ie. Useful information provided about travelling abroad with a wheelchair.
Tripscope Alexandra House, Albany Rd, Brentford, Middlesex TW8 0NE ⓣ08457/585 641, ⓦwww.justmobility.co.uk/tripscope, ⓔtripscope@cableinet.co.uk. Registered charity providing a national telephone information service offering free advice on international transport for those with a mobility problem.

In the USA and Canada

Access-Able ⓦwww.access-able.com. Online resource for travellers with disabilities.
Mobility International USA 451 Broadway, Eugene, OR 97401, voice and TDD ⓣ541/343-1284, ⓦwww.miusa.org. Information and referral services, access guides, tours and exchange programmes. Annual membership $35 (includes quarterly newsletter).
Society for the Advancement of Travelers with Handicaps (SATH) 347 5th Ave, New York, NY 10016 ⓣ212/447-7284, ⓦwww.sath.org. Non-profit educational organization that has actively represented travellers with disabilities since 1976.
Travel Information Service ⓣ215/456-9600. Telephone-only information and referral service.
Twin Peaks Press Box 129, Vancouver, WA 98661 ⓣ360/694-2462 or 1-800/637-2256, ⓦwww.twinpeak.virtualave.net. Publisher of the *Directory of Travel Agencies for the Disabled* ($19.95), listing more than 370 agencies worldwide; *Travel for the Disabled* ($19.95); the *Directory of Accessible Van Rentals* ($12.95) and *Wheelchair Vagabond* ($19.95), loaded with personal tips.
Wheels Up! ⓣ1-888/389-4335, ⓦwww.wheelsup.com. Provides discounted air fare, tour and cruise prices for disabled travellers, including trips to Bali; also publishes a free monthly newsletter and has a comprehensive website.

In Australia and New Zealand

ACROD (Australian Council for Rehabilitation of the Disabled) PO Box 60, Curtin ACT 2605 ⓣ 02/6282 4333; 24 Cabarita Rd, Cabarita NSW 2137 ⓣ02/9743 2699. Provides lists of travel agencies and tour operators for people with disabilities.
Disabled Persons Assembly 4/173–175 Victoria St, Wellington, New Zealand ⓣ04/801 9100. Resource centre with lists of travel agencies and tour operators for people with disabilities.

Travelling with children

Indonesians love children, make a great fuss of their own and other people's, and permit them to go pretty much anywhere. The country has a great deal to offer children: plenty of beaches and outdoor activities, the colour and dynamism of traditional dance and music, and even a few theme parks in Java and Bali.

Travel itself is particularly exhausting for children, however, and at first it may be best to concentrate on a relatively small part of the country until you gauge how much they can take. You might choose to opt for the comfort and convenience of a **package deal**, where you can rely on having organized transport, air-con, hot water and a swimming pool to hand, plus the use of babysitters if required. If you make your own arrangements, some **upmarket hotels** make significant concessions to couples with children, perhaps offering extra beds for one or two under-12s sharing a room with their parents, but in other accommodation, you may need to rent three- or four-bed rooms if your child is too big to share a bed with you. On the whole, children who occupy their own seats on **buses and bemos** are expected to pay full fare. Most **domestic flight** operators charge two-thirds of the adult fare for children under 14, and ten percent for infants.

Although you can buy disposable **nappies** (diapers) in city supermarkets, prices are somewhat inflated. Bring a **changing mat**, as few public toilets have special baby facilities. Also consider investing in a **child-carrier backpack** for lugging around your smallest offspring (prices start at around US$45/£30 for ones that weigh less than 2kg), as pavements and road surfaces are invariably too bumpy for a comfortable push-chair ride. **Buggies**, however, can come in handy for feeding and even bedding small children, as highchairs and cots/cribs are only provided in a few of the most upmarket hotels; car-rental companies never provide baby seats. A child-sized **mosquito net** might be useful as well. **Powdered milk** is available in major centres, but is otherwise hard to find; sterilizing bottles is also a far more laborious process in Indonesian hotels and restaurants than it is back home.

As long as you avoid the spicier items, **Indonesian food** is quite palatable to children, though, as with adults, you should be careful about unwashed fruit and salads and about dishes that have been left uncovered for a long time (see p.48–51). The other main hazards are dogs (keep your distance), thundering traffic, huge waves and strong currents, and the **sun** – sunhats, sun block and waterproof suntan lotions are essential, and can be bought in the major resorts.

The **Bali for Families** website (Ⓦwww.baliforfamilies.com) is extremely useful, created by parents who have lots of first-hand experience of travelling in Bali with their children. As well as child-friendly hotel recommendations, lists of essential equipment to take, and ideas on how to entertain the family, there's also a travellers' forum. You might also want to canvas other travellers' opinions, which you can do by posting your queries on the Kids To Go Travelling with Children bulletin board (Ⓦwww.thorntree.lonelyplanet.comlonelyplanet.com/thorntree/kiddies/topics.htm). For specific advice about kids' health issues, either contact your doctor, or consult one of the travellers' medical services listed on pp.34–35, or, in the UK, call the Nomad Medical Centre (Ⓣ020/8889 7014), which publishes a special information sheet on keeping kids healthy when abroad.

Useful US contacts for travellers with children include **Rascals in Paradise**, 2107 Van Ness Ave, Suite 403, San Francisco CA 94109 Ⓣ415/921-7000 or 1-800/872-7225, Ⓦwww.rascalsinparadise.com, who can arrange scheduled and customized itineraries built around activities for kids, including a fourteen-day tour of Bali and a second tour to see the orang-utans of South Kalimantan's Camp Leakey. **Travel With Your Children**, 40 Fifth Ave, New York, NY 10011 Ⓣ212/477 5524 or 1-888/822-4388, publish a regular newsletter, *Family Travel Times* (Ⓦwww.familytraveltimes.com), as well as a series of books on travel with children including *Great Adventure Vacations With Your Kids*.

Women travellers

Indonesia does not, overall, present huge difficulties for women travellers, either travelling alone or with friends of either sex. However, an image of Western women as promiscuous and on holiday in search of sex is common throughout the archipelago, having spread outwards from Bali where the gigolo scene is well established. In tourist areas across the country – such as Bukittinggi and the Gili Islands – there are plenty of young men hanging around hoping to strike lucky, although they're more likely to be a nuisance rather than anything more sinister.

Reactions to foreign women vary widely across the country, and in the particularly devout Muslim areas, most obviously Sumatra, it pays to be especially careful about **dress**. Even then, verbal harassment of solo women travellers is not unknown. Observe how local women dress both on the streets and on the beach. While topless sunbathing has become very popular in major tourist areas on Bali and Lombok, and it is unlikely that local people will say anything directly to you when you are there, it's worth being aware how far outside the local dress code such behaviour is. Whatever you do on the beach, you should cover up when you head inshore, and visits to temples, mosques or festivals carry their own obligations regarding dress (see p.70).

There is a large population of young men on Bali and Lombok, and increasingly elsewhere, known variously as Kuta cowboys, guides, mosquitoes (they flit from person to person) or gigolos, whose aim is to secure a **Western girlfriend** for the night, week, month or however long it lasts. They vary considerably in subtlety, and while the transaction is not overtly financial the woman will be expected to pay for everything. You'll see these couples particularly in Bali and Lombok, where local outrage is not as overt as elsewhere in the country. If a Western woman and a local man are seen together, this is the first assumption made about their relationship. Local reaction on Bali and Lombok is variable, from hostility through acceptance to amusement, although outside these areas, most Indonesian people are frankly appalled by such goings-on. **Sex** outside marriage is taboo in both the Hindu and Muslim religions, and young girls throughout Indonesia are expected to conform to a strict code of morality.

However, Indonesian women are much freer with regard to dress, movement and employment than in many other Muslim countries, and you'll encounter women in public and working in the tourist industry pretty much everywhere you go. Many are keen to practise their English, especially if they are students; however, as a woman travelling through the islands, a bit of Indonesian is especially useful for talking to local women of all ages, who generally want to find out as much about life in the West as visitors want to learn about life in Indonesia.

Gay and lesbian travellers

Surprisingly for a society that places so much emphasis on parenthood, homosexuality is broadly accepted in Indonesia, and there is even a place in some of the archipelago's traditional societies for transvestites, who were formerly attached as retainers and dancers at royal courts. Today, the legal age of consent for both gay and heterosexual sex is 16, though homosexuals are often forced through social pressures eventually to marry and become parents. As it's more acceptable in Indonesia to show a modest amount of physical affection to friends of the same sex than to friends or lovers of the opposite sex, gay couples generally encounter less hassle about being seen together in public than they might in the West.

Jakarta and Bali are Indonesia's two main **gay centres**, with the younger scene gravitating towards Kuta, where there are renowned, unproblematic cruising areas and a mixed gay crowd of Indonesians and foreigners. A lot of gay visitors and expatriates do have affairs with Indonesian men, and these liaisons tend to fall somewhere between holiday romances and paid sex. Few gay Indonesians in these circumstances would classify themselves as rent boys – they wouldn't sleep with someone they didn't like, and most don't have sex for money – but they usually expect to be financially cared for by the richer man (food, drinks and entertainment expenses, for example), and some do make their living this way. Outside Java and Bali, you won't find anything resembling a gay scene, and the most visible homosexuals are transvestite prostitutes (sometimes known as "*waria*") who hang out in locally known public spaces.

Contacts for gay and lesbian travellers

The Utopia website (Ⓦwww.utopia-asia.com) is an excellent resource for gay travellers in Bali and the rest of Indonesia. As well as travellers' reports on the local scene, it offers tours of Bali tailor-made for the gay traveller, and provides up-to-date lists of all major Indonesian gay and lesbian organizations. The umbrella organization for gays and lesbians in Bali and Lombok is Gaya Dewata, at Jalan Belimbing, Gang Y 4, Denpasar, Bali 80231 (daily 9.30am–3.30pm; Ⓣ0361/222620, Ⓕ229487; Ⓔycui@denpasar.wasantara.net.id). For more information on the AIDS situation in Indonesia, see p.31.

In the UK

Dream Waves Redcot High St, Child Okeford, Blandford, DT22 8ET Ⓣ01258/861 149, Ⓔdreamwaves@aol.com. Specializes in exclusively gay holidays, including Bali.
Madison Travel 118 Western Rd, Hove, East Sussex NN3 1DB Ⓣ01273/202 532, Ⓦwww.madisontravel.co.uk. Established travel agents specializing in packages to gay- and lesbian-friendly mainstream destinations, and also to gay/lesbian destinations. Can also tailor individual round-the-world itineraries with stopovers In Bali or Jakarta possible.
Also check out **adverts** in the weekly papers *Boyz* and *Pink Paper*, handed out free in gay venues.

In the USA and Canada

Damron Company PO Box 422458, San Francisco CA 94142 Ⓣ1-800/462-6654 or 415/255-0404, Ⓦwww.damron.com. Publisher of the *Men's Travel Guide*, a pocket-sized yearbook full of listings of hotels, bars, clubs and resources for gay men; the *Women's Traveler*, which provides similar listings for lesbians; and *Damron Accommodations*, which provides detailed listings of over 1000 accommodations for gays and lesbians worldwide. All of these titles are offered at a discount on the website. Listings Include Bali, and Yogyakarta in Central Java.
Ferrari Publications PO Box 37887, Phoenix, AZ 85069 Ⓣ1-800/962-2912 or 602/863-2408, Ⓦwww.ferrariguides.com. Publishes *Ferrari Gay Travel A to Z*, a worldwide gay and lesbian guide; *Inn Places*, a worldwide accommodation guide; the guides *Men's Travel in Your Pocket* and *Women's Travel in Your Pocket*, and the quarterly *Ferrari Travel Report*.
International Gay & Lesbian Travel Association 4331 N Federal Hwy, Suite 304, Ft Lauderdale, FL 33308 Ⓣ1-800/448-8550, Ⓦwww.iglta.org. Trade group that can provide a list of gay- and lesbian-owned or -friendly travel agents, accommodation and other travel businesses.

In Australia and New Zealand

Gay and Lesbian Travel Ⓦwww.galta.com.au. Directory and links for gay and lesbian travel worldwide.
Gay Travel Ⓦwww.gaytravel.com. The site for trip planning, bookings, and general information about international travel.
Parkside Travel 70 Glen Osmond Rd, Parkside, SA 5063 Ⓣ08/8274 1222 or 1800/888 501, Ⓔhwtravel@senet.com.au. Gay travel agent associated with local branch of Hervey World Travel; all aspects of gay and lesbian travel worldwide.
Silke's Travel 263 Oxford St, Darlinghurst, NSW 2010 Ⓣ02/9380 6244 or 1800/807 860, Ⓔsilba@magna.com.au. Long-established gay and lesbian specialist, with the emphasis on women's travel.
Tearaway Travel 52 Porter St, Prahan, VIC 3181 Ⓣ03/9510 6344, Ⓔtearaway@bigpond.com. Gay-specific business dealing with international and domestic travel.

Directory

Addresses A recent law banning the use of foreign words for business names, including those for accommodation and restaurants, has caused a few problems. Some hotels have circumvented the new rule by just adding the word "Hotel" in front of their name (this is an Indonesian as well as an English word), but others have had to start over. Street names are another cause of confusion, many having been renamed as historical or political figures fall in and out of fashion. Where relevant, we have included both new and old names for hotels and streets, as many people still refer to them by the old name, though the sign will show the new version.

Airport departure taxes Rp100,000 on international flights, and between Rp10,000 and Rp30,000 for domestic flights.

Contraceptives Birth control is a major issue in Indonesia. The government *Dua Anak-anak Cukup* ("Two Children are Enough") campaign continues to promote restraint to a disbelieving population. Condoms (*kondom*) are available from pharmacists, but don't rely on local suppliers for other contraceptives.

Electricity Usually 220–240 volts AC, but outlying areas may still use 110 volts. Most outlets take plugs with two rounded pins.

Laundry services There are no public laundries, but most hotels and losmen have a laundry service, and tourist centres have plenty of services outside the hotels as well.

Left Luggage Informal services are offered by most losmen and all hotels. Major airports also have left-luggage facilities, charging around Rp5000 per item per day. It's expensive, but there's no time limit.

Time The Indonesian archipelago is divided into three time zones. Sumatra, Java, Kalimantan Barat and Kalimantan Tengah are on Western Indonesian Time (7hr ahead of GMT, 15hr ahead of US Pacific Standard, 12hr ahead of US Eastern Standard, and 3hr behind Sydney); Bali, Lombok, the Nusa Tenggara islands, Sulawesi and South and East Kalimantan are on Central Indonesian Time (8hr ahead of GMT, 16hr ahead of US Pacific Standard Time, 13hr ahead of Eastern Standard Time, and 2hr behind Sydney); West Papua is on Eastern Indonesian Time (9hr ahead of GMT, 17hr ahead of US Pacific Standard, 14hr ahead of US Eastern Standard, and 1hr behind Sydney).

Tipping Tipping is not generally expected; in any case, up to 22 percent service and goods tax is added to accommodation and restaurant bills. However, in the tourist resorts on Bali and Lombok it is becoming increasingly common – generally about ten percent to waiters (if no service charge is added to the bill), drivers and tour guides; a few thousand rupiah to bell boys and chamber-maids in mid-range and upmarket hotels. Exceptions are made for metered taxi drivers, where you may want to round the fare up to the nearest Rp1000, and car drivers, who many people tip at the end of their rental if they have given good service. If someone in authority has gone out of their way to help you, however, a gratuity may be appreciated, though expect some sort of hint to be made first or you may end up causing offence.

Toilets *WC*, pronounced "wey sey" in Indonesian. Classier accommodation may have Western-style plumbing, but most Indonesian toilets are squatting affairs: a hole in the ground with somewhere to place your feet either side. Toilet paper is seldom provided, though paper or tissues are easy to buy across the country; instead, you clean yourself afterwards with your left hand, using the pail and scoop alongside, which are also used to flush the toilet. They tend to be very wet places, so avoid bringing in anything you'll have to place on the floor.

Guide

Guide

1

Jakarta and around

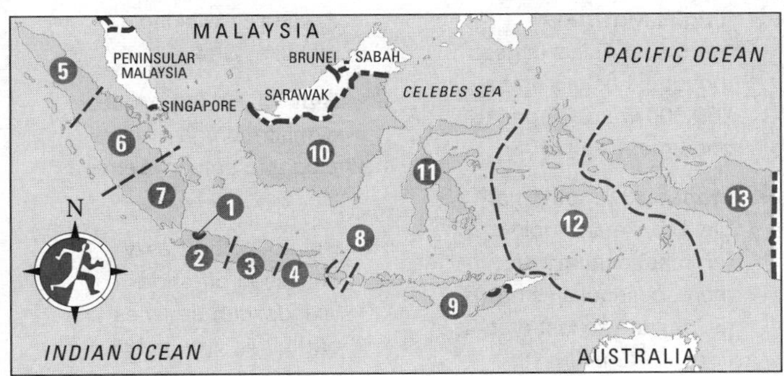

CHAPTER 1
Highlights

* **Sunda Kelapa** Enjoy the romance of the world's last wooden trading schooners. See p.105

* **Taman Fatahillah** Among the last remnants of old Dutch Batavia. Don't miss *Café Batavia,* described by *Newsweek* as one of the world's great bars. See p.104

* **Istiqlal Mosque** Southeast Asia's largest mosque, hosting up to 250,000 worshippers at one time. See p.108

* **Monas** 137-metre marble, bronze and gold torch national monument, colloquially known as "Sukarno's last erection". See p.106

* **Jalan Surabaya** One of Southeast Asia's great flea markets, with antiques old and "new". See p.118

* **Pasar Rawa Bening** A treasure trove of semi-precious stones. See p.119

* **Tanamur Disco** Not to be missed flagship of Jakarta's rollicking nightlife. See p.116

* **Blok M** Jakarta expat nightlife, bargain shopping and colourful street life. See p.117

* **Pulau Seribu** Easily accessed off-shore islands with beaches and birds. See p.122

1

Jakarta and around

Bounded to the north by the Java Sea and the south by the low Bogor Hills, Indonesia's overwhelming capital, **JAKARTA**, is one of the fastest growing cities in the world. The capital currently sprawls over 656 square kilometres of northern Java, and its inexorable expansion continues both east to Tangerang and west towards Bekasi districts, with which it now almost imperceptibly blends. From a mere 900,000 inhabitants in 1945, the current population is well over 10 million. In reality, the number of people living in Greater Jakarta, which is known by the typically Indonesian acronym of **Jabotabek** (Jakarta-Bogor-Tangerang-Bekasi), can never be known accurately, censuses having proved unreliable. Despite a 1971 moratorium that declared the city closed to immigrants, the population continues to grow at a rate of around 200,000 every year, many of the newcomers being unskilled migrants from rural Java. The City Government again launched controversial raids in January 2002 to weed out people without Jakarta ID cards, raids which critics condemned as both unjust and ineffective.

Few foreign visitors find the city as alluring as the local population, and over the years Jakarta has been much derided. Yet those prepared to spend some time in the capital will find that the city, for all its faults, has a certain brash, go-getting charm all of its own. Indeed, once you've adjusted to its frenetic pace and mastered the public transport system (the city is too hot and polluted to walk very far in), you'll discover a number of pockets of interest. Indeed, Jakarta is in many ways a dream for photographers and artists; for example, the endearing suburb of **Kota** in the north – the former heart of the old Dutch city – still retains a number of beautiful historic buildings, as does the neighbouring port of **Sunda Kelapa**.

The capital also has some of the country's finest museums, including the **Maritime Museum** in Sunda Kelapa, the **Wayang Museum** in Kota and, best of all, the **National Museum** in the centre of the city. The latter, having raided many of Indonesia's most famous archeological sights for its exhibits, provides an excellent introduction to the culture and history of the entire archipelago. It's on the western edge of **Medan Merdeka** (Merdeka Square), in the centre of which stands the **Monas Monument**, a concrete and gold column 137m high, which has become a symbol of the city.

Immediately to the south lies the **Golden Triangle**, a square-kilometre cluster of ostentatious skyscrapers, muscular 1960s-style "Heroes of the Revolution" monuments and multistorey shopping plazas, with plenty of markets to trawl through by day and bars to hit in the evening. The Golden Triangle epitomizes the avarice of Suharto's family and cronies; some of the blocks of flats built at the height of the speculators' boom in the early to mid-

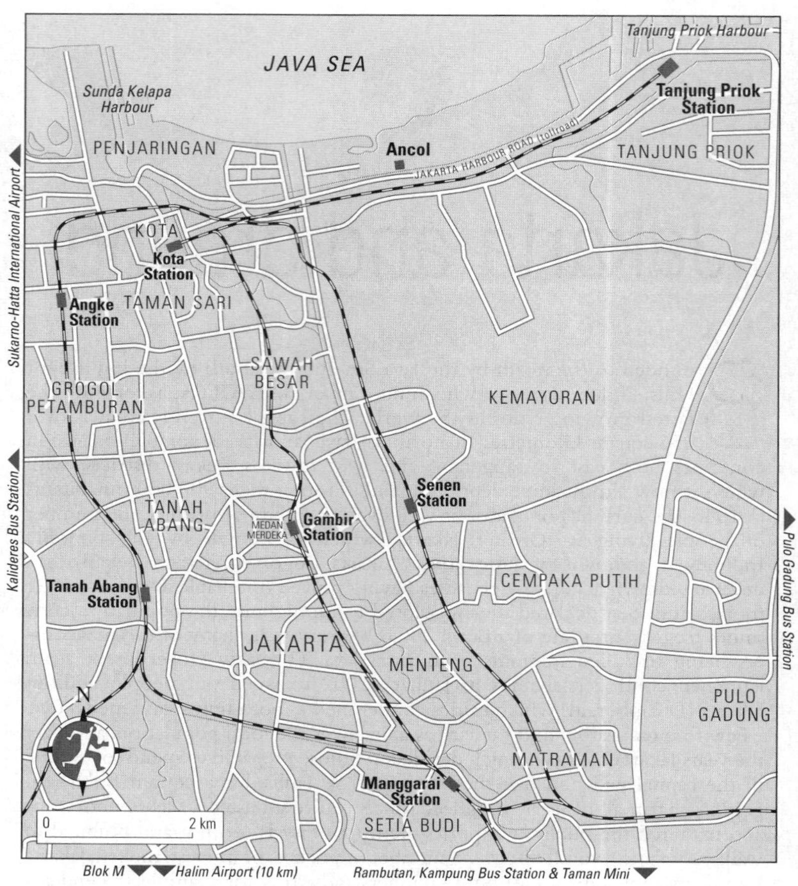

1990s are still largely unoccupied. Perhaps nowhere demonstrates more clearly the ostentation of the New Order elite than the Jakarta Hilton Hotel, the largest Hilton in the world, owned by the Sutowo family.

Even in the most prosperous parts of Jakarta one can still find tiny but numerous kampung, twilight worlds of murky alleyways, open sewers, crying children and scurrying vermin. It is this stupefying juxtaposition of outstanding wealth and appalling poverty that many find so offensive. Large sections of Jakarta remain ugly and inefficient, the vast metropolis ringed by endless crumbling suburbs, traversed and vectored by congested eight-lane expressways and malodorous canals, huge shiny office blocks sharing the roadside with rubble-strewn wasteland and slums. It remains a wonder, especially given the notorious corruption, that Jakarta works at all.

Nevertheless, there is also something inherently fascinating about a city that both leads the country and yet at the same time appears to be growing apart from it. The capital is far richer (over eighty percent of foreign investment into the country flows through Jakarta at some stage), bigger and more cosmopolitan than anywhere else on the archipelago and, despite the waves of immigrants, the native citizens, the **Betawi** (a Malay derivation from the word "Batavia"), still cling to their own dialect and customs. As such, it is worth giving Jakarta at least a day or so, if only to experience a part of the country unique in terms of wealth, size and flavour.

Some history

The site of modern-day Jakarta first entered the history books in the twelfth century, when the **Pajajarans**, a Sundanese kingdom based in West Java, established a major trading port at the mouth of Sungai Cilikung. Before that, this swampy area of land had been home to nothing more than a few small fishing villages, albeit ones that had existed since at least the fifth century AD, according to a stone tablet found near Tanjung Priok.

The Hindu Pajajarans named their port Sunda Kelapa and maintained control over the area for more than three hundred years. By the early sixteenth century, the port was a flourishing trading post receiving ships from all over Southeast Asia. In 1522, the Portuguese dropped by en route to the Spice Islands, pausing long enough to erect a godown (warehouse) and sign a Treaty of Friendship with the Pajajarans. By the time the Portuguese returned some twenty years later, Jakarta had been invaded by the Islamic **Sultanate of Banten** (today a separate province, 50km to the west). The Bantenese successfully beat off a Portuguese counter-attack, and retained control of the port; Sunda Kelapa was renamed **Jayakarta**, "City of Victory", and the date of their invasion, June 22, 1527, is still celebrated as the city's birthday.

The Bantenese enjoyed only a short reign, however, before the **Dutch** arrived. In 1610, the Dutch were allowed by the ruling prince, Fatahillah, to move from Banten, their previous capital in the archipelago, to Jayakarta. Once there they built a large godown, which by 1618 – much to Prince Fatahillah's annoyance – they had converted into a fortress. Fatahillah, in order to counteract this rise in Dutch power, made an alliance with the English, and together they attempted to oust the Dutch from the city. The Dutch barricaded themselves into their new fortress and survived the Bantanese-English onslaught until, in 1619, reinforcements led by **General Jan Pieterszoon Coen** arrived to drive off the attackers and liberate the Dutch held there – but not before the city was heavily damaged during the fighting. The city was rebuilt, renamed **Batavia** after an obscure Germanic tribe of the Netherlands, and became the property of the East India Trading Company, the VOC.

For the rest of the seventeenth century, the Dutch, for whom Batavia had become the administrative centre of a vast trading empire, attempted to transform the city into a tropical version of their beloved Amsterdam. Twice, in 1628 and 1629, they came under attack from the powerful Mataram empire of Central Java (see p.1038). Yet both times they were victorious in the face of enormous odds, and by the end of the century, Batavia, with its network of canals and imposing civic buildings, did indeed resemble the Dutch capital, and was dubbed the "Queen of the East".

However, the eighteenth century witnessed a decline in the city's fortunes. The canals silted in the swampy soil, while the stagnant water became an ideal breeding ground for diseases such as cholera and malaria. The situation became so bad that the city was nicknamed the **White Man's Graveyard**; according to contemporary statistics, a large proportion of the soldiers sent out to Batavia perished there. The city gradually gravitated south to higher ground, where the air was less fetid and the water purer. Then, in 1740, the Chinese, who formed the backbone of the manual workforce in the city, rebelled against

Jakarta's ethnic mix

Just about every ethnic group in Indonesia is represented in Jakarta. This mix is seen in place names such as **Kampung Melayu** and **Kampung Bali**, reflecting Malay and Balinese settler influences of the past. For example, particular kampung (villages) may be noted for their Menadonese influence, or suburbs like Kelapa Gading for their preponderance of Chinese.

The Balinese addition to the gene pool goes back a long way: in the seventeenth century, Balinese female slaves were in great demand for European households and as wives for Chinese migrants. **Taman Suropati** in Menteng is named after a freed Balinese slave. The VOC brought in slaves from all over the archipelago, and as far away as Malacca and the Malabar Coast, as well as Arakan in modern-day Myanmar and Bengal. Inevitably, miscegenation followed: despite the hierarchy of racial types established by the Dutch, by the middle of the nineteenth century the **Betawi** sub-culture had emerged in the capital, incorporating elements of Javanese, Sundanese, Balinese, Dutch, Chinese and Arabic.

The **Chinese** have been a major component of Jakarta's population since the seventeenth century, when they were classified as "*Vreemde Oosterlingen*" ("foreign Asiatics") along with the Arabs, Armenians, Indians, Persians, Ambonese, Timorese and Bugis. Jakarta's Chinatown, which was much damaged in the 1998 May riots, lies in and around **Glodok**, the heart of downtown. There has been considerable recovery and a brand-new **Pasar Glodok**, the centre of the bargain electronics trade, was completed in 2001. Signs of Chinese cultural revival are evident: there are no longer prohibitions on the use of Mandarin characters on signs, Chinese New Year is openly celebrated with lion dances, while various areas are known for their Chinese food.

Old Batavia's **European** population was also very much of a mix, including those of Portuguese German, Swedish, French and Danish origins (Portuguese was still in official use in the city as late as the second half of the eighteenth century). Bahasa Betawi, a distinct dialect emerging from this polyglot influence, is widely used in the capital, but even visitors with good Indonesian or Malay will be confused by this argot.

The **Bataks**, who originate from North Sumatra, especially the Lake Toba region and the Karo Highlands, are very numerous in the city – your taxi driver or bus conductor could well be one. The ethnic **Indians** are not nearly so numerous but are quite influential in business – for example, the sports goods stores around the Pasar Baru district, which has a Sikh temple, are mainly Indian-owned.

A word is in order for perhaps the most unusual addition to Jakarta's ethnic mix, the **Scots,** who stage the annual **Jakarta Highland Gathering**. This event, hosted by the Java St Andrew's Society, is held every year in late May, and is the largest of its kind outside Scotland. Bagpipers, Scottish dancing, caber-tossers – the whole Caledonian works – as well as a superbly organized programme that includes sky-diving, soccer, marching bands and Indonesian cultural shows make this one of the city's best days out in the year and certainly the best occasion on the calendar for relaxed mixing between Indonesians and expatriates.

harsh treatment by the Dutch. The Dutch and Indonesian populations responded by massacring large numbers of the Chinese and destroying the Chinese enclave of Glodok, to the south of Batavia. While this prevented any further trouble, it also seriously depleted the city's workforce and the economy collapsed as a result. By the end of the eighteenth century, VOC corruption had become uncontrollable, and the company was wound up.

A brief tenure by the **British** followed between 1811 and 1816 under the enlightened reformist Governor Sir Thomas Stamford Raffles, whose enormous two-volume *A History of Java* remains an essential reference work. Post-Napoleonic changes in Europe resulted in Jakarta reverting once more to Dutch rule, and the city began to flourish again, earning yet another sobriquet, "The Pearl of the Orient". A new harbour, Tanjung Priok, was built to cope with the rapid increase in trade, and Jakarta became a hub of enterprise and profit. Unfortunately, much of this new wealth was generated by the exploitative Culture System of forced crop cultivation imposed by the Dutch; profits were divided unequally between the city's population, with the native Betawi seeing little of the spoils. This naturally led to resentment, which eventually grew into the nationalist movement of the twentieth century.

On March 5, 1942, the **Japanese** invaded Batavia during their lightning sweep through Southeast Asia. The city was once again renamed, with the old Bantenese name "Jayakarta" being shortened to "Jakarta". Dutch power was destroyed, as was the myth of European supremacy.

At the end of the war, Indonesians quickly took advantage of the Japanese capitulation, resulting in the **Proklamasi** (Declaration of Independence) by **Sukarno** and **Hatta**, the major prewar Independence activists, on August 17, 1945. The Dutch were absent at the declaration, the vast majority having been held under atrocious conditions at various locations by the Japanese. British forces went ashore in the capital and elsewhere in late September, initially to secure the release of Allied POWs and other internees, but were soon engaged by Indonesian groups (see p.1043).

The Dutch began to return in late 1945, many emerging from the horrors of Japanese captivity in camps on Java and Sumatra. Many of those returning assumed a restoration of the *status quo ante* was imminent, but their hold on the country was now untenable. Hysterical anti-Sukarno propaganda on Dutch radio – broadcast from Australia – only inflamed tensions. After four years of often brutal campaigning by Dutch forces attempting to reimpose colonial rule, they were forced to admit defeat and leave. British forces engaged in fierce actions against Nationalist forces in Surabaya, Bandung and Semarang among other cities in 1945–46. This forgotten little war, which was fought ostensibly to secure the POWs and other internees, resulted in many British and Indian casualties before British-led forces were withdrawn mid-December 1946. In December 1949, Sukarno entered Jakarta amid scenes of wild jubilation, to become the first president of the Republic of Indonesia.

Although many welcomed Sukarno's victory, his plans for a new Jakarta had town planners and architects alike shaking their heads in despair. Many of the Dutch civic buildings not destroyed during the Japanese occupation were pulled down by the new administration. In the following two decades, ugly Soviet-style monuments sprouted up across the city, while huge **shantytowns** emerged on the fringes of Jakarta and along its flood-prone riverbanks. Many people drawn to the city in the hope of making their fortune instead found only abject poverty.

Following social unrest in 1965, the newly installed president, Suharto, attempted to address the problem by implementing **welfare programmes** for the city's poorer inhabitants, and other measures designed to secure the capital's long-term economic future. Though these programmes had some beneficial effect, they also led to even further migration to the city. The recession of the 1980s saw oil exports plummet and the government, in an attempt to stave off economic disaster, switched to a programme of rapid industrialization which only drew more workers to the city, where they joined the disaffected masses on the outskirts of Jakarta. The migrants' squalid living conditions contrasted sharply with the air-con lifestyles of the elite in the city, generating enormous resentment against the rich, the successful and the Chinese, who many saw as having benefited unfairly from the government's economic policies.

Despite Suharto's attempts to keep the city's burgeoning middle class happy, they were becoming tired of a government riddled with corruption. Suharto's nepotism caused widespread resentment, with his family getting all the most lucrative business contracts; an example of this is the Grand Hyatt Hotel-Plaza Indonesia complex at the southern end of Jalan Thamrin, which belongs to his second son Bambang. In May 1998, students took to the streets to protest against the old regime and its policies. The **orchestrated violence** that followed included looting of mainly Chinese businesses – the evidence for this is still apparent in the shattered windows around Glodok – and gang rapes of Chinese girls, as the city descended into anarchy until, on May 21, 1998, Suharto stepped down, to be replaced by his vice-president, B.J. Habibie.

The post-Suharto years have been marked both by a lack of direction from the government and further state violence, paradoxical as this may sound. In November 1998, police and army troops fired on students at **Atma Jaya University** in the centre of the capital, killing fourteen; the autopsy on one victim indicated the use of dum-dum bullets. As with the killings in May of the same year, no one in authority has been held to account. Student demonstrations have become less frequent, while Muslim radical groups such as **Laskar Jihad** and the **Islamic Defence Front (FPI)** have made their presence felt; there is some evidence of links to al-Qaeda. The Islamic Defence Front, alleged to have connections with at least one high-ranking army officer, were responsible for city-wide attacks on bars and massage parlours in 2000 and 2001, but pose little real threat to foreign visitors, despite their belligerent rhetoric.

Jakarta safety

Over the years, many travellers have arrived in Jakarta concerned about the capital's alleged dangers. While more dangerous than Singapore, Jakarta is definitely safer than a city like Manila, where the gun laws are quite different. As a rule of thumb, the only people carrying firearms in Jakarta are the police and the military. True, the city has a flourishing underworld, especially around markets such as Tanah Abang, bus and train terminals, and nightlife districts such as Blok M and Mangga Besar, but gangsters tend to be armed with knives. Locally, criminals of this sort are known as **preman** (freeman) and they pay off either the police or the military. These preman elements pose no danger to foreigners except in isolated instances outside nightspots such as the Tanamur disco, where visitors are advised not to retaliate to any provocation from the taxi touts.

Jakarta is, however, notorious for ferocious **street brawls** between rival bands of secondary-schoolboys. These fights can erupt even on main thoroughfares such as Jalan Diponegoro and Jalan Thamrin; youths in school uniform can be seen wielding sticks, rocks and machetes, apparently oblivious to the public. Non-combatants are usually not threatened, but it is advisable to get out of the way quickly.

Pickpockets are a menace on third-class trains, especially those between Kota and Bogor, Jatinegara station being a favourite haunt, and on some bus routes into and out of Pasar Senen. They sometimes work as groups; if operating singly, they are easily dealt with. Shout "Pencuri!" ("Thief!") as a last resort, if you think you are the object of a robbery – but be aware that public retribution against robbery suspects can be bloody. **Sexual assaults** are not unknown but rare. Western women do attract attention, but need only take the care they might take in any large city.

In general, and considering its great size and complex social problems, Jakarta has an unwonted reputation for being dangerous. Of course, visitors should keep their wits about them, but there's no need to treat every situation as threatening.

The potential for widespread unrest remains, especially as President Megawati's government, elected in late 1999, announced large price hikes in January 2001 for domestic fuel and electricity. The crisis brought on by the heavy rains in early 2002 raised fears of disturbances, when the city was hit by arguably the worst flooding in the city's 475-year history. Dozens of people died, and hundreds of thousands were badly affected, with major disruptions to public services and utilities, and great misery brought to many of the marginalized recent immigrants, especially those living along the banks of the Ciliwung River.

Orientation, arrival and information

To head from north to south through the centre of Jakarta is to go forward in time, from the old Dutch city of Batavia and the Chinese quarter of Glodok in the north to the modern golf courses and amusement parks in the south. **Medan Merdeka**, the giant, threadbare patch of grass crowned by the dizzying National Monument, is the spiritual centre of Jakarta, if not exactly its geographical one. The presidential palace lies on the northern rim of the square, and the main commercial district is just a short distance to the south. The major north–south thoroughfare which passes along the western edge of Merdeka forms the central artery of the capital, changing its name a number of times along its route, from **Jalan Gajah Mada** in the north to **Jalan Merdeka Barat** as it passes along the square, then **Jalan M.H.Thamrin** (hereafter just called Jalan Thamrin) and finally, in the south of the city, **Jalan Jend Sudirman**.

The main area for budget accommodation, **Jalan Jaksa**, lies to the south of Medan Merdeka. Running south from the southwestern corner of Medan Merdeka, **Jalan Thamrin** and **Jalan Sudirman** are lined with a number of world-class hotels.

Arrival

As you would expect for one of the world's largest cities, Jakarta has a wealth of international and domestic transport connections. Apart from the impressive **Sukarno-Hatta airport** to the west of the city, and the tiny Halim airport to the south (which, following the drop-off in domestic flights after the riots in 1998, currently does not serve commercial airlines and is being used as a base by the Indonesian air force), there are also four central **train stations** (and dozens of minor suburban ones) and three major **bus stations**, most of which are tucked away in the suburbs, a lengthy bus ride away from the city centre.

By air

Both international and domestic flights into Jakarta land at **Sukarno-Hatta airport**, 13km west of the city centre. Indonesian Immigration is notoriously inefficient and corrupt, and even if three or more flights arrive at the same time they are reluctant to open all the available desks. Beyond the huge queues at passport control, the baggage reclamation area has a number of exchange booths, one or two hotel booking companies and a small **yellow board** with details of how to get from the airport to the city centre, including approximate taxi fares and details of the DAMRI bus service. Through customs, there's a small and not over-helpful **tourist office** and more exchange booths, most of which close at 10pm. Try to change as little money here as possible: the rates

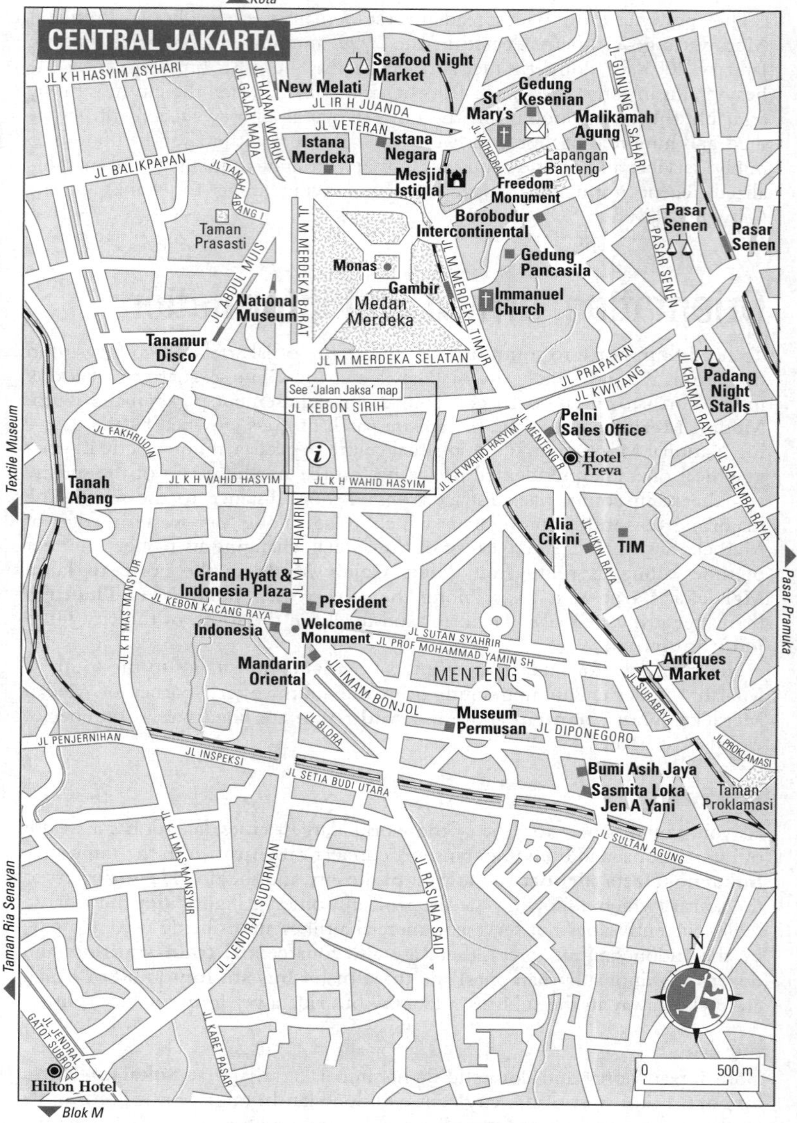

are 25 percent lower than those on offer in the banks in the centre of town. There's a hotel, the *Aspac* (see p.101) at terminal 2E, for those who can't face the trip into town immediately.

If you arrive before 10pm, turn left out of the terminal and walk about 200m to the **DAMRI buses**, the cheapest way to get to the city centre (Rp8000). These single-decker white buses with a navy-blue stripe along the side leave every half-hour between 6am and 9.30pm, taking 45 minutes to reach Gambir station in the heart of the city. Others head towards Blok M in South Jakarta, Rawamangun in East Jakarta and Kemayoran in North Jakarta. It's a fifteen-minute walk from Gambir to Jalan Jaksa and twenty minutes to Jalan Thamrin; a bajaj between the two now costs approximately Rp3000, fuel prices having risen markedly. If you're not carrying heavy luggage, the easiest way to Jaksa is to exit Gambir facing the National Monument, turn left and walk south, following the overhead railway line until you reach Jalan Kebon Sirih where the traffic will be coming from your right. Turn right here and walk another five minutes until you see the "*Kawasan Wisata Malam*" arch at the north end of Jaksa.

Attempts to regulate the **taxis** at the airport have proved short-lived, and visitors are advised to ignore any driver offering services from the car park. With **taxis**, in addition to the metered fare, passengers must also pay the toll fees (approximately Rp7000 in total) plus another Rp2500 guaranteed service fee. Adding all these charges together, the total cost of a taxi ride to Jalan Jaksa is approximately Rp40,000. Recommended taxi firms include Steady Safe, Kosti, Blue Bird Group, Express and Citra from the rank outside arrivals.

By train

Gambir station, characterized by its livid pea-green columns, is the most popular and convenient of all the major transport terminals, being just a fifteen-minute walk away from the travellers' centre of Jalan Jaksa. See above for details of how to get to Jaksa from the station.

Of the other stations, **Kota**, near old Batavia, is the busiest. To reach Jalan Jaksa from Kota, catch bus #P1, #P10, #P11, #AC01, #AC10 or #ACB1, which will drop you by the *Sari Pan Pacific Hotel*, about a ten-minute walk away. From here, head for the *McDonald's* on the corner of Jalan Wahid Hashim and follow this street for about half a kilometre – Jaksa is on your left. From the *Sari Pan Pacific*, buses continue south to the Welcome Monument and other international hotels.

A third train station, **Tanah Abang**, serving Merak (for Sumatra), lies to the west of Jalan Thamrin (bus #P16 to Sarinah department store and Gambir), and a fourth station, **Pasar Senen**, is situated 1km east of Gambir (bus #15 or #P15 to Jalan Jaksa), though you're unlikely to arrive at either of these.

By bus

Jakarta's **bus stations** are uniformly noisy, bewildering and inconveniently situated; it's no wonder so many people choose to enter and leave the capital by train instead. Each of the bus stations serves different destinations, although there are overlaps: buses to and from Sumatra, for example, arrive at both Kalideres and Pulo Gadung stations.

The **Pulo Gadung** station, 12km to the east of the city, is probably the noisiest and least bearable of the lot. It's also notorious for gang rivalries, and occasionally fights erupt there. If you're travelling from Central or East Java or Bali you'll probably arrive here. To get to the centre of town, catch bus #AC 08, which passes the crossroads in Menteng; alight opposite the Indian Cultural Centre (ask the driver) on Jalan Imam Bonjol. From there, cross the road and turn the corner by the Centre; walk for about a minute along Jalan Cokroaminoto until the Batak church, where you'll find the bajaj rank. Take a bajaj for Rp3000–4000 to the *Hotel Cipta* on Jalan Wahid Hasyim; the hotel faces the one-way traffic coming towards you down Jaksa.

Buses from West Java pull in at the **Kampung Rambutan** station, 18km south of the city centre near Taman Mini. Buses #P10, #P11, #P16 and

Moving on from Jakarta

Travel agents in town, as well as many of the hotels, sell bus, ferry and discounted plane tickets (for recommended agencies, see p.122). Bus tickets are sometimes available on the day of departure, but plane and train tickets should be bought a week beforehand. The Pelni agents now sell ferry tickets a fortnight in advance; it's best to buy a ticket as early as possible.

By plane

All scheduled **flights**, both domestic and international, currently leave from Sukarno-Hatta airport. There is a **departure tax** of Rp11,000 on domestic flights, and Rp50,000 for international departures. DAMRI buses depart for Sukarno-Hatta from Gambir station every thirty minutes between 6am and 9.30pm (45–90min, depending on traffic; Rp5000). Ignore the taxi drivers who will insist that the last bus has already left. **Check in** one hour before departure for domestic flights, two hours for international flights. Getting to the airport by taxi (from Rp30,000), you need to be aware of potential bottlenecks along Jalan Sudirman towards the Semanggi cloverleaf, especially in the late afternoon. From Jalan Wahid Hasyim, it's best to direct the driver (elementary directions will do) down Jalan K.S. Tubun and enter the toll road at the Slipi toll gate. Fares rise significantly after the buses have stopped running.

By train

Most of the **trains** travelling to West and Central Java destinations begin their journeys at Gambir station (for destinations and times, see p.124). There are two special offices (daily 7.30am–7pm) selling tickets for the luxury trains, such as the Argo Gede express to Bandung and the Argolawu express to Yogya and Solo. Travellers need to be firm with the notoriously aggressive Madurese ticket touts who work Gambir station and with whom railway officials appear to be in cahoots; don't have dealings with them. Although Kota station is on the same line as Gambir, some of the trains departing from Kota do not stop at Gambir, and many start their journey at Gambir and miss out Kota. The other two stations, Pasar Senen and Tanah Abang, are further out of town, have fewer services and rarely see tourists.

The train from Jakarta to Bandung passes some tremendous scenery, especially on the latter half of the journey. Between Plered and Bandung there are a dozen viaducts, the most spectacular between Cisomang and Cikadongdong. To get the best views, ask for an 'A' seat.

#AC10 to Kota all ply the route from Rambutan to the stop opposite the *Sari Pan Pacific Hotel* (and vice versa), taking ninety minutes (or possibly less outside the rush hour). The third station, **Kalideres**, lies 15km to the west of the city centre; serving destinations west of Jakarta such as Labuan, it rarely sees tourists. Bus #64 provides a means of escape to Jalan Thamrin for those few poor souls who end up at this rat-infested dump.

By ship

All Pelni boats arrive at **Tanjung Priok harbour**, 500m from the bus station of the same name. The port authorities have built a new terminal and tried to regulate the taxis; even so, arrival here can be bewildering, with crowds thronging the exit to welcome their relatives. The nervous or claustrophobic are advised to position themselves as near to the top of the ferry's landing steps as possible to make a quick getaway. To get to Jalan Jaksa, take bus #P125 from the station and alight at the junction of Jalan Kebon Sirih and Jalan Thamrin (ask the conductor) or the *Sari Pan Pacific Hotel*. From there it is a ten-minute walk to the north end of Jalan Jaksa.

By bus

The capital has good **bus** connections to all points in Java, and many cities on neighbouring islands too. There is usually a range of prices for every destination, depending on the type of bus you're travelling in. While you pay a premium for tickets bought from an agency in town, some of the buses leave from outside the agency, saving you a trip to the bus station. If your bus does depart from the station, leave plenty of time (at least 90min) to get from downtown to your terminal, whichever one you're departing from, as traffic is always heavy in Jakarta. Note that bus #78 is the most direct bus between the Jalan Thamrin department store and Kalideres. The best way to get to Bogor – especially in the rainy season, when its railway station may be flooded – is to take #AC10 from the *Sari Pan Pacific Hotel* on Jalan Thamrin to the stop opposite Universitas Kristen Indonesia (ask the driver) at Cawang, and then a local bus (Rp2000) to Bogor terminal. If you're going on to Cibodas (see p.152), cross the road from the terminal, walk about 100m up the left-hand side of the hill and catch any bemo bound for Cianjur via Puncak.

By ferry

Pelni ferries sail from Tanjung Priok harbour. To get there from Jalan Thamrin, bus #125 runs via Jalan Gunung Sahari before continuing on to Tanjung Priok bus station, 500m from the harbour. Board opposite the *Sari Pan Pacific Hotel*, and allow at least 75 minutes for your journey from Jalan Jaksa. A taxi from Jalan Jaksa to the harbour should cost no more than Rp25,000. The most convenient Pelni booking office (Mon–Thurs 8am–noon & 1–2.30pm, Fri 8–11.30am & 1–2.30pm) is on the second floor of the Toptable Plaza on Jalan Menteng Raya, a ten-minute walk from Jaksa. To get there, turn left at the south end of the street and walk through the traffic lights to Jalan Johar, continuing under the railway onto Jalan Cut Meutia, which connects to Menteng Raya – the Plaza is directly in front of you at the intersection. For the latest timetable, call in at Global Travel, Jl Jaksa 49.

The **Kapuas Express ferry** runs twice weekly from Godown 2 at the Sunda Kelapa harbour to Pontianak in Kalimantan Barat. Tickets can be bought in advance from Global Travel, Jl Jaksa 49. For details of other ferries from Sunda Kelapa, contact the harbourmaster's office on the second floor of the Departemen Perhubungan at the end of Baruna III in Sunda Kelapa.

Travelling by ferry from Borneo, the chances are you'll arrive at **Sunda Kelapa harbour**, near the Kota district. Walk fifteen minutes to Kota railway station (ask for directions at the harbour gate), and catch bus #P1, #P10, #P11, #AC01, #AC10 or #ACB1 to the junction of Jl Kebon Sirih and Jl Thamrin or the *Sari Pan Pacific Hotel*.

Information

Jakarta's **tourist office** (Mon–Fri 9.30am–5pm, Sat 9.30am–noon; ⓣ021/3142067) – the "Pelayanan Informasi Parawisata Jakarta" – is tucked away in the Jakarta Theatre building, opposite the Sarinah department store on Jalan Wahid Hasyim. Though their knowledge of specifics (such as bus numbers) is a little sketchy, and they don't yet have a hotel booking facility, they do provide a good free map of the city along with a number of glossy brochures. If you're after something more detailed, consider buying a copy of the Periplus map of Jakarta, the most accurate and user-friendly available (you'll always find map vendors on Jalan Jaksa). A second, smaller tourist office dealing mainly with train enquiries can be found by the southern entrance of Gambir station.

The main tourist office stocks *The Visitor*, a free monthly **guide** to the city which includes brief listings of events and entertainment, and the free *Welcome to Indonesia* brochure, a bimonthly guide to the whole archipelago. Occasionally they have copies of the useful annual Jakarta *Shopping Mall Guide*. Two monthly magazines, the English-language *Jakarta Kini*, available from some hotels, and the bilingual *Djakarta*, which is sold at the Duta Raya Wartel on Jalan Jaksa, include fairly comprehensive entertainment guides; it's also worth checking out the *Jakarta Post*.

City transport

Jakarta is too hot, smoggy and vast to make walking a realistic option, and visitors should try to grasp the basics of its extensive **public transport** options. The bus network is comprehensive, convenient and cheap, although the vast profusion of buses thundering around the city can leave you bewildered, and the derring-do of the Kopaja and Metro-Mini drivers is especially alarming. However, the air-con buses provide a reasonably comfortable mode of travel; alternatively, many people pay a little more and catch a bajaj or taxi. Whatever mode of transport you choose, remember that the volume of traffic in Jakarta is such that jams are inevitable: for a bus journey of 10km, allow at least an hour. For all the apparent indiscipline, with drivers ignoring lanes and cyclists speeding towards you in the dark against the traffic on one-way streets, Jakarta sees very few accidents.

Buses

Where possible, **bus numbers** have been included in the relevant sections of the chapter to help you find your way around the city. Sometimes the tourist office can also help with bus routes; one of the busiest bus stops in Jakarta lies just a few metres away from the tourist office, outside the Sarinah department store.

Buses operate a **set-fare system**, where the same fare is charged regardless of how far you travel. This fare varies, however, according to the type of bus you are travelling on. The cheapest are the small, pale-blue minivans (the city-licensed Mikrolet), which operate out of Kota bus station (the numbers of which are always preceded by the letter "M"), and the **large coaches** that can be found all over the city (both charge just Rp700). However, if the bus number on these large coaches is preceded by the letter "P", the fare rises to Rp1000. The small, battered orange **micro-minibuses** (Metro-Mini) charge Rp700, regardless of whether there is a "P" in front of the number or not. The large, fume-belching **double-deckers** charge Rp750, and, at the top of the scale, **air-con buses** (easily recognizable because the doors are kept shut while in motion) cost Rp3300. On the air-con buses you pay the driver as you board; for all the others a conductor comes round and collects the fare. The fare is usually posted on the inside of the bus, so you should never be overcharged. For all their rough demeanour and reckless driving, bus crews are generally very honest.

Travelling on the city's buses exposes you to a seemingly endless stream of vendors selling pens, belts, newspapers, snacks, sweets and soft drinks, and buskers ranging from urchins with voices that would make stones weep to Batak trios singing the lusty songs of the Lake Toba region – be ready with a

△ Al–Azhar mosque, Jakarta

couple of coins for tips. Pickpockets do operate, but are far less of a danger than is often suggested.

To alight from buses either call out *"kiri"* (left), or rap the overhead rail several times with a coin.

Bajaj

Now that the traditional cycle-rickshaws, or becak, have been banned from Jakarta for being too slow (although a small population survives in the theme park at Ancol), the noisy two-stroke motorized rickshaws, or **bajaj** (pronounced "ba-jais"), have now monopolized Jakarta's backstreets. Before hopping in the back of one, however, be sure to bargain very hard and remember that bajaj are banned from major thoroughfares such as Jalan Thamrin, so you may well end up being dropped off a long way from your destination. A plan is afoot to replace bajaj with something quieter and less polluting, but, like the projected subway, this has little chance of immediate implementation. As a guide to fares, a bajaj ride from the north end of Jalan Jaksa to the main post office should be no more than Rp4000.

Taxis

Jakarta's numerous **taxis** are inexpensive, and the service has improved greatly over the years. Rates are usually around Rp1000 per kilometre, and all cabs are equipped with meters. Since a minumum fare increase in 2000, there have been two categories of taxi fare: *tarif baru* (new fare, flag fall Rp3000) and *tarif lama* (old fare, flag fall Rp2000). If you are especially budget-conscious, look out for the latter, which display a sign to that effect on the windscreen. A useful expression is: "*Tolong pakai meternya*" (please use your meter), as some opportunistic drivers do try to take advantage of tourists. Drivers may expect a tip from foreigners, and are usually reluctant to give you change; if, for example, your fare is Rp9200, and you give the driver Rp10,000, forget the balance.

As Jakarta's many traffic lights are the haunts of beggars, aggressive buskers and opportunists looking for a quick bag snatch, passengers should make sure all doors are locked and windows closed. Groups of youths also congregate at U-turns, offering drivers unofficial police "services", directing traffic; it's best to ignore them completely.

Accommodation

There is an oversupply of business and tourist-class **hotels** scattered throughout Jakarta, the best of which are listed below. Budget hotels, however, are fewer in number and are all situated, with one exception, on and around the traveller's sanctuary of Jalan Jaksa to the south of Medan Merdeka in the heart of the city. Jakarta's **budget accommodation** is more expensive than elsewhere in most of the rest of the archipelago, with no commensurate increase in quality: prices start at Rp7000 for a dormitory bed in the cheapest hostel. In spite of this, most places are constantly full, so try to ring ahead to book a space.

Jalan Jaksa and around

Jalan Jaksa and the adjacent kampung are unique to Jakarta, having become a magnet to travellers and a second home to many expatriates who frequent its watering holes in the evenings, as well as supporting a well-knit Indonesian

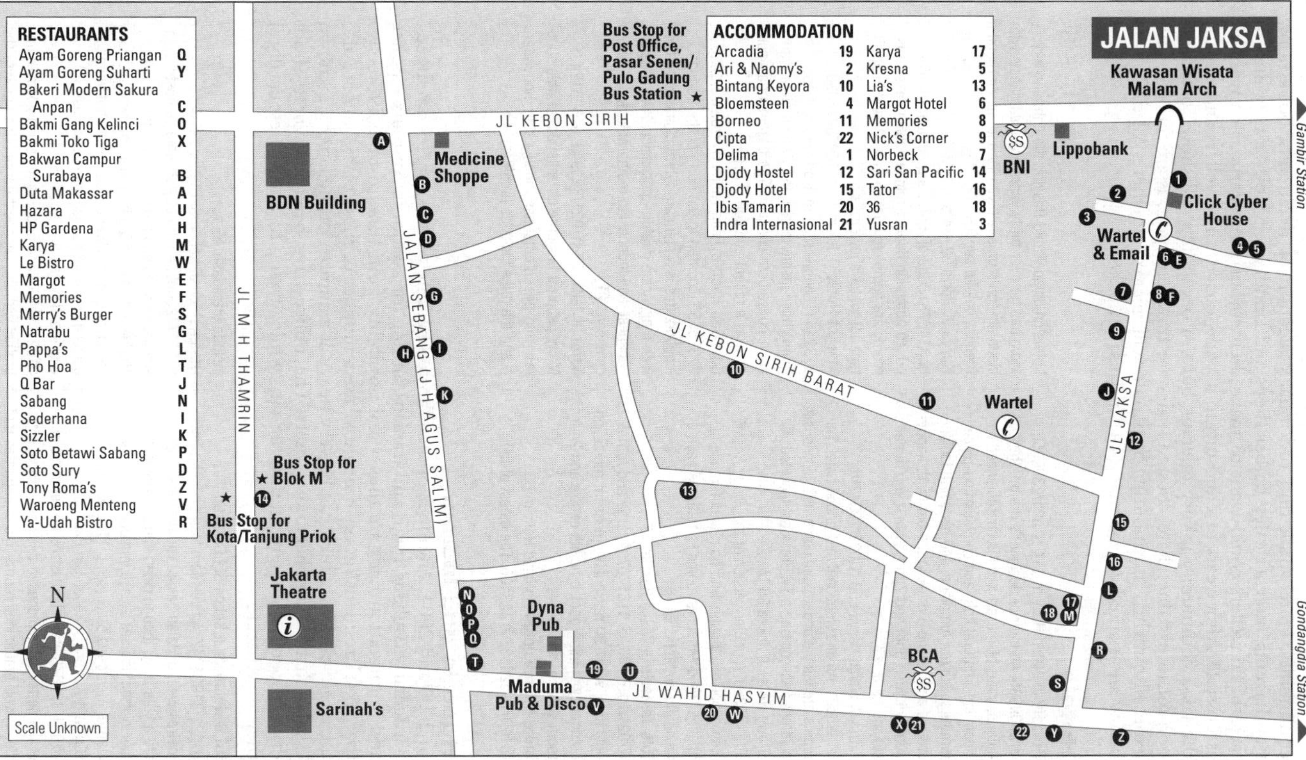
JALAN JAKSA
Kawasan Wisata Malam Arch
Merdeka Square & Kota
Welcome Monument
Gambir Station
Gondangdia Station
RESTAURANTS
Ayam Goreng Priangan Q
Ayam Goreng Suharti Y
Bakeri Modern Sakura Anpan C
Bakmi Gang Kelinci O
Bakmi Toko Tiga X
Bakwan Campur Surabaya B
Duta Makassar A
Hazara U
HP Gardena H
Karya M
Le Bistro W
Margot E
Memories F
Merry's Burger S
Natrabu G
Pappa's L
Pho Hoa T
Q Bar J
Sabang N
Sederhana I
Sizzler K
Soto Betawi Sabang P
Soto Sury D
Tony Roma's Z
Waroeng Menteng V
Ya-Udah Bistro R
ACCOMMODATION
Arcadia 19
Ari & Naomy's 2
Bintang Keyora 10
Bloemsteen 4
Borneo 11
Cipta 22
Delima 1
Djody Hostel 12
Djody Hotel 15
Ibis Tamarin 20
Indra Internasional 21
Karya 17
Kresna 5
Lia's 13
Margot Hotel 6
Memories 8
Nick's Corner 9
Norbeck 7
Sari San Pacific 14
Tator 16
36 18
Yusran 3
Bus Stop for Post Office, Pasar Senen/ Pulo Gadung Bus Station
Bus Stop for Blok M
Bus Stop for Kota/Tanjung Priok
JL KEBON SIRIH
JL KEBON SIRIH BARAT
JALAN SEBANG (J H AGUS SALIM)
JL M H THAMRIN
JL JAKSA
JL WAHID HASYIM
BDN Building
Medicine Shoppe
BNI
Lippobank
Click Cyber House
Wartel & Email
Wartel
Jakarta Theatre
Dyna Pub
Maduma Pub & Disco
BCA
Sarinah's
N
Scale Unknown

community. Here you'll find the usual collection of restaurants, bookshops, travel agents, internet cafés, barber shops and laundry services – everything, in fact, that travellers could want to make their sojourn in Jakarta as convenient as possible. After years of exposure to a wide variety of travellers and expats, the Jaksa community is very tolerant, but visitors should still show consideration for local values: bare-chested males are frowned upon, as are females with exposed midriffs, and shouting at people will get you nowhere. All the places below are marked on the map of Jalan Jaksa on p.99.

Hotels

Arcadia Jl Wahid Hasyim 114 ⓣ021/2300050, ⓕ2300995. An interior designer's dream, this unique, state-of-the-art hotel is characterized by clean lines, natural light and conversation-piece furniture. Quite a fun place, and it's worth looking around and having a drink in the bar (with happy hour between 5pm and 7pm), even if you're not staying here. ❺

Cipta Jl Wahid Hasyim 53 ⓣ021/3904701, ⓕ326531. An unexceptional mid-priced hotel. The rooms are fairly standard, but come with individually controlled air-con and a TV. Breakfast included. ❹

Djody Hotel Jl Jaksa 35 ⓣ021/3151404, ⓕ3142368. A pricier version of the *Djody Hostel* (see opposite), though with no real difference in quality. The downstairs rooms sometimes have a mosquito problem. ❸

Ibis Tamarin Jl Wahid Hasyim 77 ⓣ021/3157706, ⓕ3157707. A large and rather ugly hotel with 130 reasonably pleasant rooms, an outdoor swimming pool, a health centre and 24hr room service. ❺

Indra Internasional Jl Wahid Hasyim 63 ⓣ021/3152858, ⓕ323465. The oldest of the hotels on Jalan Wahid Hasyim, the light and airy *Indra* has for over thirty years provided guests with clean air-con rooms (all with TV and minibar) and a friendly, helpful service. ❹

Karya Jl Jaksa 32–34 ⓣ021/3150519, ⓕ3142781. One of a growing number of mid-priced hotels on budget-minded Jalan Jaksa. All rooms are complete with air-con, TV and intermittent hot-water showers. ❹

Margot Hotel Jl Jaksa 15 ⓣ021/3913830, ⓕ324641. An average mid-priced hotel; the rooms have inside mandi and TV (complete with an in-house porn channel). The basement air-con dorm is a recent addition. ❷–❺

Sari San Pacific Jalan Thamrin ⓣ021/323707, ⓕ323650. Located to the north of the Sarinah junction, this is a standard international-class hotel with a nightclub (featuring occasional live music), Japanese and Indonesian restaurants and a delicatessen. ❽

Tator Jl Jaksa 37 ⓣ021/323940, ⓕ325124. Many people's favourite on Jalan Jaksa, this spotless mid-priced hotel has friendly staff, hot water – and the price includes breakfast. ❹

Hostels and losmen

In 2000 and 2001, a number of these hostels became centres for Asian refugees, particularly Afghans, Iraqis and Iranians, aiming for asylum in Australia – police and immigration raids are thus a real possibility from time to time. Note also that Jaksa's resident "good-time girls" use a number of these places and are also the target of raids, which can be very heavy as a number of the latter are known "shabu-shabu" (amphetamine) users. The police have been known to shoot drug suspects elsewhere around the city while "trying to escape", especially if they are African.

Ari & Naomy's Jl Kebon Siri Barat Gg VII/3 ⓣ021/31904347. A five-room losmen just a few metres west of Jalan Jaksa. The upstairs rooms are a little poky, though clean enough. Downstairs, this losmen doubles as accommodation for the staff of *Memories Café*. (see p.112) ❶

Bintang Keyora Jl Kebon Siri Barat 52 ⓣ021/323878. A medium-sized hostel that's one of the better-value places in this price range, with clean, well-maintained rooms and cheap rates that include breakfast. ❸

Bloemsteen Jl Kebon Siri Timur I/174 ⓣ021/323002. A perfectly acceptable hostel with spacious rooms and a pleasant, sunny balcony. The bathrooms are the cleanest and best in Jalan Jaksa, and the showers even dribble hot water occasionally. There's also internet access. ❶

Borneo Jl Kebon Siri Barat 35–37 ⓣ021/3140095. A large, ramshackle hostel-cum-brothel with the cheapest dormitories in town. The east wing is a little sleazy, though bearable, but the filthy west wing should be avoided. ❶

Delima Jl Jaksa 5 Ⓣ021/337026. The oldest and one of the best value of the city's hostels. Established in 1969, the *Delima* is beginning to rest on its laurels a little: some of the rooms could do with a good spring-clean, and the staff could be friendlier. However, it's still a good spot, especially by Jakarta standards; favoured by asylum-seekers, it's nearly always full in the high season. ❶–❷

Djody Hostel Jl Jaksa 27 Ⓣ021/3151404, Ⓕ3142368. Not to be confused with its slightly more expensive sister down the road, the rather gloomy *Djody Hostel* comprises 24 rooms, all watched over by a 24hr security guard. ❷

Kresna Jl Kebon Siri Timur I/175 Ⓣ021/325403. An acceptable budget hotel; the rooms downstairs are tiny and dank, while those upstairs are brighter, and the showers are powerful and clean. Free tea is available throughout the day. ❷

Lia's Jl Kebon Siri Barat Gg VIII/47 Ⓣ021/3162708. Recommended little hostel with a pleasant front garden, located in an ideal spot behind high fences in a quiet alleyway 200m to the west of Jalan Jaksa. The clean and basic rooms are reasonable value by Jakarta's standards, and there's free tea and coffee throughout the day. ❷

Memories Jl Jaksa 17 (no phone). Secreted away behind the *Memories Café*, reached via the toilets and a spiralling metal staircase, are two beautiful double rooms. Great value, but remember the café has live music until late. ❸

Nick's Corner (aka **Wisma Niki**) Jl Jaksa 16 Ⓣ021/336754, Ⓕ3107814. A large and popular hostel offering a variety of budget and not-so-budget rooms. The two mixed-sex, air-con dormitories are reasonable, though they both lack windows and are a little dark. Another favourite of prostitutes. ❶–❸

Norbeck Jl Jaksa 14 Ⓣ021/330392. Surrounded by barbed wire, this hostel has the external appearance of Stalag 45. Inside, lists of rules are plastered everywhere, and the cell-like rooms are cramped and dark, each lit by a single, naked bulb. Such is the shortage of budget options in the capital, however, that many poor souls still end up here. ❷

36 Jl Jaksa 36b. A small hostel with claustrophobic rooms located down Gang 12, at the southern end of Jalan Jaksa. Rates are reasonable, however, and include breakfast. ❷

Yusran Jl Kebon Siri Barat Dalam VI/9 Ⓣ021/3140373. A surprisingly pleasant budget hostel, tucked away at the end of Gang 6 to the west of Jaksa. The single is cramped, airless and full of mosquitoes, but the doubles are spotless and comfortable. Bargaining is possible. ❶–❷

The rest of the city

Although there are plenty of mid-priced and rather bland hotels all over the city, mainly catering to businesspeople and with boardrooms and conference centres the norm, a couple of areas in the centre of town have a particularly high concentration. The best and most expensive hotels in the city huddle around the Welcome Monument on **Jalan Thamrin** to the southwest of Gambir station, or are strung out along **Jalan Sudirman**. Be warned that most of the rates below are subject to a two percent tax and, although payment in rupiah is acceptable, the exchange rates they offer are often very poor.

Ambhara Jalan Iskandarsyah 1, Blok M. A four-star hotel with fine restaurant and two pubs, including the quasi-British *Stanford Arms*. ❻–❼

Aspac Terminal 2e, Bandara Sukarno-Hatta Ⓣ021/5590008, Ⓕ5590018. Hotel situated in one of the terminals of Jakarta's international airport. Fairly basic and lacking atmosphere, but clean and satisfactory. Rooms can be hired out for 3hr or 6hr during the day, for those who fancy a little comfort and privacy when waiting for their flight. ❺

Borobudur Intercontinental Jalan Lapangan Banteng Selatan Ⓣ021/3805555, Ⓕ3809595. Once the best in the city, this grand hotel has struggled to regain its supremacy after closing briefly in 1998 for refurbishment. The gardens are beautiful, however, and contain an open-air swimming pool, tennis courts and a jogging track. The rooms themselves are equally sumptuous, and come with satellite TV, air-con and a minibar. ❽

Bumi Asih Jaya Jl Solo 4 Ⓣ021/3860839, Ⓕ3900355. A small and relaxing fifteen-room hotel set in a leafy suburb to the south of Jalan Diponegoro. The highlight is the carefully tended garden, a small smog-free haven in the heart of Jakarta. ❹

Bumi Johar Jalan Johar 17 Ⓣ021/3145746. A 5min walk east from Jalan Jaksa, this bijou hotel is good value, with comfortable air-con rooms, hot and cold water and a 16-channel TV service. ❺–❻

Grand Hyatt Jalan Thamrin ⓣ021/3901234, ⓕ334321. A massive Suharto family-owned complex in the centre of town, with luxurious rooms and an entire shopping centre in the basement. Other features include a pool, restaurants, pubs and live entertainment. ❽

Hotel Menteng 1 Jl Gondangdia Lama 30. This medium-priced hotel five minutes from Gambir is better known for the all-night disco *The Hotmen's* attached to it. Large, comfortable air-con rooms with hot and cold water make it attractive to business travellers. ❺

Indonesia Jalan Thamrin ⓣ021/2301008, ⓕ3141508. The cheapest of the hotels clustered around the Welcome Monument roundabout, housing Japanese and Indonesian restaurants, a bar (hosting regular cultural evenings) and some pretty plush rooms. ❽

Mandarin Oriental Jalan Thamrin ⓣ021/3141307, ⓕ3148680. Huge, superior-class hotel with swimming pool, Italian and Chinese restaurants and a nightclub. ❽

New Melati Jl Hayam Wuruk 1 ⓣ021/3841943, ⓕ3813526. An Indonesian-owned hotel struggling to compete with its international rivals. All rooms are fitted with TV, air-con, telephone, mini-bar and bath. Rates include breakfast. ❺

Omni Batavia Jl Kali Besar Barat 46 ⓣ021/6904118, ⓕ6904092. A beautiful place located by a canal in the Kota district. The spectacular stained-glass facade conceals a plush hotel with full facilities, including a swimming pool, cake shop and a number of restaurants. ❽

President Jl Thamrin 59 ⓣ021/2301122, ⓕ3143631. A four-star, Japanese-owned hotel with 315 rooms, Japanese and Chinese restaurants and an outdoor pool. ❽

Treva International Jl Menteng Raya 33 ⓣ021/31900240. A good-quality mid-range hotel with a fine coffee shop, close to Gambir station. ❻

The City

Jakarta's prettiest quarter, and the home of some of its better tourist attractions, lies at the northern end of the city. The quaint old Dutch suburb of **Kota** and the adjoining port of **Sunda Kelapa** contain a number of handsome period buildings, many of which, such as the former **Dutch Town Hall** (now the home of the **Jakarta History Museum** and the highly rated **Museum Wayang**, surround the old **Town Square of Batavia**. Photogenic schooners still dock at the port, which also features the extremely well-presented **Maritime Museum**.

Back in the centre of town, the **National Museum** is worth visiting for its vast and often dazzling collection of Indonesian antiquities; a trip here can be combined with a climb to the top of the 137-metre monument **Monas** for an overview of the city and its ever-present smog.

Some of the suburbs in the immediate vicinity of Monas are surprisingly quiet and leafy (though these are relative terms in Jakarta), including the **Lapangan Banteng** to the east – featuring yet more Dutch architecture – and the embassy enclave of **Menteng** to the south. Both have a number of buildings and sights that are mildly diverting, and are worth a stroll.

Kota (Old Batavia)

Located in the north of the city, the quaint old district of **Batavia** used to serve as the administrative centre of a great trading empire, stretching from South Africa all the way to Japan. The Dutch filled their tropical capital with glorious and imposing examples of colonial architecture, both civic and private, and enclosed the whole within a huge defensive wall. These walls, built in the 1620s by General Coen, the first governor of Batavia, have long since disappeared, and many of the old buildings have suffered a similar fate. A few classic examples of Dutch architecture have survived, however, and give a good idea of how this district must have looked during its heyday. Today, Kota (the district that

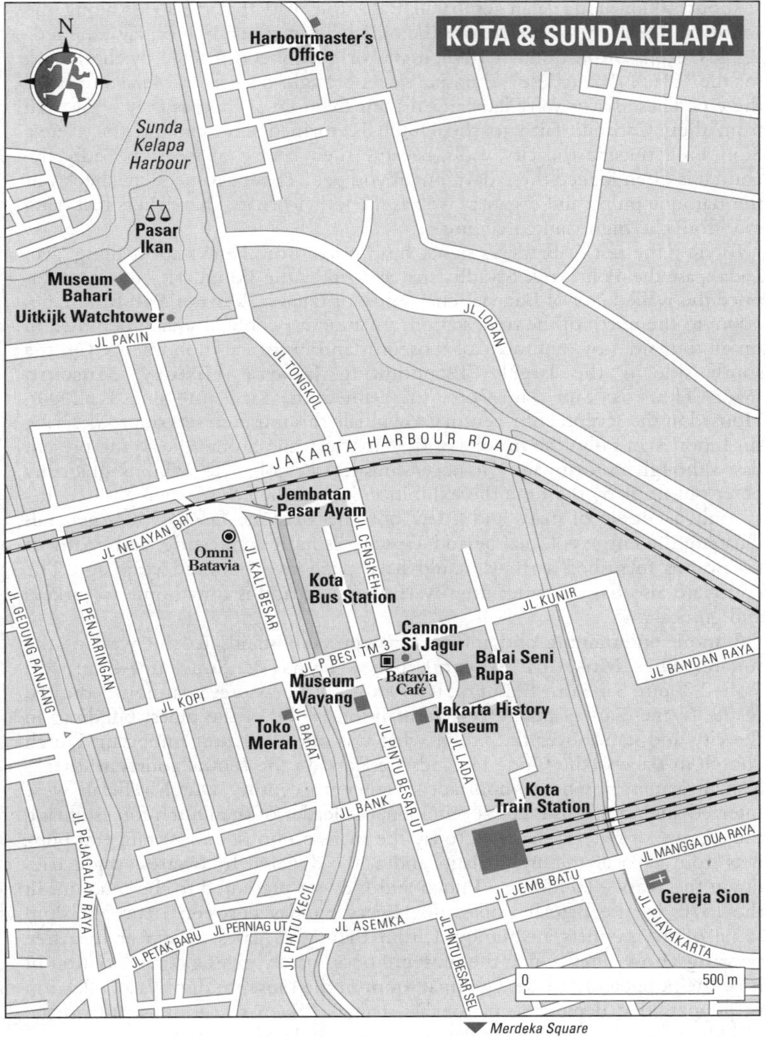

encompasses Batavia) ranks as Jakarta's prettiest quarter, though it has to be said this is partly because of a lack of any real competition.

There are plenty of buses heading north from the stop opposite the *Sari Pan Pacific Hotel* on Jalan Thamrin to Kota: look out for #P1, #P11, air-con #P17, #ACo1, #AC10 and #ACB1. All these buses drive north along Jalan Gajah Mada past the still unrepaired Chinese shophouses of the Glodok district (damaged in the May 1998 disturbances) and the impressive facade of **Kota train station**, which stands to the right of the road. This is a good place to jump out and begin a tour of the city.

About 400m along Jalan Jembatan Batu, the road that runs east along the southern side of the station, stands the oldest surviving church on Java, the red-brick **Gereja Sion**. Built in 1695, it was originally constructed by the Dutch for the "Black Portuguese", Eurasian slaves brought over from Melaka to build the city. These slaves were later given their freedom as long as they converted from their Catholic faith to the Dutch Reformed Church, and the Gereja Sion, built outside the city walls, became their centre of worship. Sadly, the church is often locked these days, but, if you get a chance to peek in, check out the Baroque pulpit and organ, as well as the rather ornate chandeliers that hang low from the high vaulted ceiling.

To view the rest of Batavia's sights, head north from Kota station along Jalan Lada, past the Politeknik Swadharma, and enter the boundaries of what was once the walled city of Batavia. The centre of Batavia, **Taman Fatahillah**, lies 300m to the north of the train station, an attractive cobbled square hemmed in on all four sides by a number of museums and historical monuments. On the south side is the largely disappointing **Jakarta History Museum** (Mon–Thurs & Sun 9am–3pm, Fri 9am–2pm, Sat 9am–1pm; Rp2000). Housed in the seventeenth-century town hall, this museum sets out to describe (in Indonesian only) the history of the city from the Stone Age to the present day, although unfortunately it never finishes the job. The exhibits gradually peter out until, by the time the exhibition has reached the seventeenth century, only a couple of maps and a few portraits of stony-faced Dutch generals illustrate the entire colonial period. Upstairs is more interesting, with many of the rooms furnished as they would have been two hundred years ago. The courtyard also has a distinct time-warp feel to it, and is now home to turkeys and guinea-fowl.

A more entertaining and informative museum stands to the west of the square. The **Museum Wayang** (Tues–Thurs & Sun 9am–3pm, Fri 9am–2.30pm, Sat 9am–12.30pm; Rp1000) is a four-storey mansion dedicated to the Javanese art of puppetry. The mansion is one of the oldest buildings in the city, and stands over the site of what was once the most important Dutch church in Batavia, the Oude Holandsche Kerk. In the central courtyard there's a small cemetery where important seventeenth-century Dutch officials were interred, including Jan Pieterzoon Coen, the leader of the Dutch forces during the capture of Batavia in 1619. Today the mansion houses a vast range of puppets from all over the archipelago, and a few donated by overseas dignitaries down the years – including a Punch and Judy set presented to the museum in the 1970s by the British ambassador. Every Sunday between 10am and 2pm some of the puppets are removed from their glass cases to appear in a free **wayang show**, after which the museum occasionally gives a demonstration of how the puppets are made. The final room in the museum displays a collection of puppets that depict the nationalist struggle, given to the museum on the fiftieth anniversary of Independence by the people of Rotterdam.

Continuing clockwise around the square, on the northern side stands the exquisite *Café Batavia* (see p.115), worth visiting for its stunning interior alone. The brainchild of Australian businessman Graeme James, it is an intelligently refurbished Dutch colonial premises which *Newsweek* has described as one of the world's finest bars. Next door is the ornate **Cannon Si Jagur**, a cannon built by the Portuguese to defend the city of Melaka and taken by the Dutch as booty in 1641. On the side of the cannon is the Latin inscription *Ex me ipsa renata sum* – "Out of myself I was reborn" – and the whole thing is emblazoned with sexual imagery, from the clenched fist (a suggestive gesture in Southeast

Asia, particularly when the thumb, as in this instance, pokes between the second and third fingers) to the barrel itself, a potent phallic symbol in Indonesia.

To the east of the square are the **Balai Seni Rupa** (Tues–Thurs & Sun 9am–3pm, Fri 9am–2pm, Sat 9am–1pm; Rp1000), Jakarta's fine arts museum, and accompanying **Ceramics Museum**. Housed within the former are some works by Indonesia's most illustrious artists, including portraits by Affandi and sketches of the capital by Raden Saleh.

Sunda Kelapa

North of Taman Fatahillah lies the historic harbour of **Sunda Kelapa** (daily 6am–6pm; Rp250) which, established during Pajajaran times, grew to become the most important in the Dutch empire. Although the bulk of the sea traffic docks at Tanjung Priok today, a few of the smaller vessels, particularly some picturesque wooden schooners, still call in at this 800-year-old port.

Sunda Kelapa lies approximately 1km due north of Taman Fatahillah. You can either walk (about 20min) or, if you're lucky, you may be able to hail one of the ojek operating in the area. If you do catch one of these, ask the rider to drop you off by the entrance to the port itself, where, after paying the entry fee, you can wander amongst the beautiful schooners that dock in the harbour. All cargo here is handled manually, and there are no derricks in sight, so excellent photo opportunities abound. Rowing boats are also available for rent, to make the trip around the harbour.

From the port, cross over the bridge to the west of the harbour and turn right at the nineteenth-century watchtower, the **Uitkijk**, originally built to direct shipping traffic to the port. Here, buried in the chaotic **Pasar Ikan** (fish market) that occupies this promontory, you'll find the entrance to the excellent **Museum Bahari**, or Maritime Museum (Tues–Thurs & Sun 9am–3pm, Fri 9am–2.30pm, Sat 9am–12.30pm; Rp1000). This huge, cat-infested place, built in 1652, was once an old warehouse for valuable eighteenth-century merchandise such as spice, pepper, tea, coffee and cotton. The museum it houses today is neatly arranged in chronological order, and charts the relationship between the Indonesian archipelago and the sea that both divides and surrounds it, beginning with the simple early fishing vessels and continuing through the colonial years to the modern age. All kinds of sea craft, from the Buginese *phinisi*, the *kora-kora* war boat from the Moluccas and the tiny *alut pasa* boat from Kalimantan, can be seen here. The exhibits are thoughtfully displayed and the English-language labels are packed with information. Even though most of the items are unspectacular, this place still ranks as one of Indonesia's best and most enjoyable museums.

After you've pottered around the fish market, head south, keeping the Kali Besar canal on your left. On the way you'll pass a number of old VOC shipyards and rather dilapidated warehouses before you come to an ornate wooden drawbridge. This is the 200-year-old **Jembatan Pasar Ayam** (Chicken Market Bridge), the only drawbridge left of the many that traversed the canals of this once-busy commercial district. The streets that flank the canal to the south of here were once the smartest addresses in Batavia, and the grand Dutch terraced houses still stand, the most famous being the Chinese-style **Toko Merah** (Red Shop) at no. 11 Jalan Kali Besar Barat – the former home of the Dutch governor general Van Imhoff. The Batavia bus station lies on the eastern side of the canal, from where you can catch a bus back to Jalan Thamrin (bus #938) or on to Ancol (minivan #M15).

Medan Merdeka and around

The heart and lungs of Jakarta, **Medan Mederka** (Freedom Square) is a square kilometre of sun-scorched grass in the centre of the city; tree-planting is having the desired re-greening effect on the south side of the square. Once a mere cattle field and later a Dutch military training ground, today the square is the symbolic and administrative centre of independent Indonesia. It has also become something of a revolutionary hot spot too: it was here in the 1940s that Sukarno whipped his supporters up into a revolutionary frenzy with impassioned anti-imperialist speeches, and the biggest demonstration of the May 1998 riots took place here, as students confronted the soldiers assigned to protect the presidential palace on the northern side of the square.

It seems fitting, therefore, that standing at the centre of the square today is the most recognizable of all of Jakarta's Independence monuments, the **Monas** (short for "Monumen Nasional"), a soaring 137-metre marble, bronze and gold torch, commissioned by Sukarno in 1962 to symbolize the indomitable spirit of the Indonesian people. Today, it also stands as a potent expression of Sukarno's extravagance. A lift has been incorporated into "Sukarno's last erection" (as it's commonly known, in a wry allusion to the man's famous philandering), allowing sightseers to survey the sprawling capital from the top (daily 8am–5pm; Rp3100, plus Rp1000 camera fee); avoid weekends, when the queues are at their longest. The ticket includes entry into the **National History Museum** (daily 8am–5pm; Rp600) in Monas's basement, a series of 48 dioramas that depict the history of Jakarta. Unfortunately, Indonesia's early history has been rather glossed over, while the twentieth century, which takes up over half of the dioramas, has been given a pro-Suharto reworking. All in all, it's not particularly enlightening.

Looking north from the top of Monas, two neighbouring white buildings on the northern side of the square catch the eye. The one on the right is the back of the **Istana Negara** (National Palace), the front of which faces north onto Jalan Veteran. Formerly the rather sumptuous home of a Dutch businessman, and at one time used as a residence for the Dutch governors-general, it is now used solely for important State functions. The Dutch governor-general moved out of the Istana Negara in 1879, when the more splendid **Istana Merdeka** (Freedom Palace), formerly known as the Koningsplein Palace, was completed. Presidents Sukarno and Abdurrahman Wahid made this palace their official residence during their terms in office, but Suharto seldom used the place, preferring a more secluded and fortified residence on Jalan Cendana in Menteng.

The **Taman Prasasti** (Museum of Inscriptions; daily 9am–2pm; Rp1000), on Jalan Tanah Abang I, lies about 500m west of Medan Merdeka. This "museum" is actually the Kebon Jahe Cemetery, a peaceful, tree-shaded, eighteenth-century graveyard that is the last resting place of a number of notable people, including Olivia Raffles (who died in 1814), the first wife of Sir Stamford, and the nineteenth-century Dutch historian Dr F. Stutterheim. To get here from Monas, take the wide road heading northwest towards the Istana Merdeka, and from there continue west to Jalan Majapahit. About 50m north along Majapahit, a small canal runs west; walk along the path by the side of this canal, then turn left at the end of the path and head south for 300m.

The National Museum

The **National Museum** (Tues–Sun 8.30–11.30am; Rp200), on the western side of Medan Merdeka, is highly recommended as an introduction to Indonesia's history and culture. Unfortunately, many of the exhibits, particularly on the ground floor, are unlabelled, though the Indonesian Heritage Society conducts **tours** in English (Wed–Fri 9.30am). The museum, established in 1778, is the country's oldest and largest, and houses a wide collection from all over the archipelago, grouped into categories such as musical instruments, costumes and so on. Many of the country's top ruins have been plundered for their statues, which now sit unmarked in the courtyard in the centre of the museum. Highlights on the ground floor are a batik made by Raden Kartini, the huge Dongson **kettledrums** and, best of all, the skull and thighbone of **Java Man**, found by Eugene Dubois in 1936 at Sangiran, near Solo (see p.246).

The museum's most precious artefacts lie **upstairs**, however, in two high-security rooms. They include the cache of **treasures** found at the foot of Central Java's Mount Merapi in 1990 by workmen excavating volcanic gravel; the collection is held in the room on the left-hand side at the top of the stairs. Over 16kg of ancient golden artefacts were discovered there, including a beautifully wrought golden water scoop, a gold wallet (decorated with an unusual winged conch motif and fitted with a gold wire strap, so that it resembles a little handbag), and a tiny and exquisite gold bowl, probably used to hold flower petals during religious ceremonies. The second room, opposite, houses a small collection of daggers and necklaces from the fifth-century Hindu Kutai Kingdom of Tenggarong in Kalimantan, possibly Indonesia's first recognized kingdom.

Incidentally, the small bronze statue of an elephant that sits outside the museum was a gift from the king of Thailand in 1871. Thanks to this statue, the museum is often called Gedung Gajah, the "Elephant Building".

There are sometimes cultural performances here such as Betawi theatre and Javanese dance at weekends; for details, check the *Jakarta Post*.

East of Medan Merdeka – the Lapangan Banteng

East of and opposite the Gambir station is the circular, pillared **Immanuel Church**, or Willemskerk as it was christened by the Dutch Protestants who built it in 1835. The church stands on the corner of Jalan Medan Merdeka Timur and Jalan Taman Pejambon, the latter leading, via the **Gedung Pancasila** (Pancasila Building) – a pretty, lawn-fronted mansion dating from 1830 and named after the famous Pancasila Speech, delivered from here by Sukarno in 1945 – to a tree-fringed square marked out with football pitches. This 300-square-metre expanse of grass and mud is **Lapangan Banteng** (Buffalo Field), or Waterlooplein as the Dutch, who designed the square as a centrepiece of their new Weltervreden district in the nineteenth century, used to call it. If you're coming here from Jalan Jaksa, catch bus #15 or #P15 from Jalan Kebon Sirih.

From the centre of the park a huge, grimacing statue of a man looms up, his face contorted by the strain of breaking free from the chains that bind his arms. This is the **Freedom Monument**, erected by Sukarno in 1963 to celebrate the "liberation" of West Papua from the Dutch. Like the majority of Sukarno's monuments, size is everything (it's over 80m tall), while aesthetic considerations take a back seat.

A number of buildings of note surround the square. The enormous white edifice to the east of the *Borobodur Intercontinental* is the **Department of Finance Building**. It was originally designed to be the residence of the Dutch Governor Daendals, but was not completed by the time he had to leave the country in 1811 when Napoleon's armies occupied the Low Countries. The building has been used as a government office almost continuously since then. The **Mahkamah Agung**, Jakarta's Supreme Court, dominates the square's eastern end, and the Catholic **St Mary's Cathedral**, a Neo-Gothic structure dating from 1830, stands over the western end. With its black-topped spires and large circular window above the front entrance, the church looks rather like Notre Dame.

Directly opposite the Cathedral is the largest mosque in Southeast Asia, the dazzling white **Mesjid Istiqlal**, opened in 1978 on the site of the former Dutch fort of Noordwijk. The mosque and its grounds are so huge that it actually connects the northwestern corner of the Lapangan Banteng with the northeastern corner of the Medan Merdeka, about 350m away. The sheer scale of the mosque is impressive: it can hold up to 250,000 people, although it's only on the Muslim holy days of Idul Fitri and Idul Adha that it is likely to reach this capacity. It's not very prepossessing and, approaching from the east, the mosque resembles a giant multistorey car park, with its five open-sided floors visible through the dull-grey concrete exterior framework. For a small donation, and providing you're not too skimpily dressed (don't wear shorts), the security guards will take you on a brief, informal tour. The main *qibla* room inside the mosque is the most interesting part, its floors decked with carpets from Arabia and Persia, while the twelve pillars that support the dome are made of steel imported from Germany. Heading back towards the main courtyard, in one corner the minaret towers, at its foot a 2.5-tonne wooden drum from east Kalimantan – the only traditional feature in this otherwise state-of-the-art mosque.

Menteng

Menteng, the prosperous and leafy suburb to the east of Jalan Thamrin, was just farmland a century ago. Bought and developed by the city council in 1908, it quickly became an exclusive enclave for ambassadors, politicians and top government officials. It's a pleasant area to walk through, although the sights are few and far between, so you should be prepared for a fair bit of walking.

From the Welcome Monument on Jalan Thamrin, catch one of the buses heading southeast along Jalan Imam Bonjol. Fifteen hundred metres along the road (bus #AC08 runs the entire length of Jalan Imam Bonjol), on the right-hand side is the **Museum Permusan** (Mon–Thurs 8.30am–2.30pm, Fri 8.30–11am, Sat 8.30am–1.30pm; free). The building was once the home of Tadashi Maeda, a Japanese naval commander sympathetic to the Indonesian struggle for Independence, and houses his private collection from the occupation days. It was here that Sukarno and Hatta were brought following their kidnapping by the hardline Menteng 31 Asrama, a youth group dedicated to fighting for Independence. In the boardroom at the back the two leaders were forced to write their Proclamation of Pancasila speech, aided by Admiral Maeda (see p.1042).

Students of modern Indonesian politics may wish to head south down Jalan Ditiro to the canal, then west for two blocks to the **Sasmita Loka Jen A. Yani** (The House of General A. Yani; Tues–Sun 8am–3pm; free). Jen A. Yani, a man whose name lives on in hundreds of street names throughout the country, was Chief of Staff during the latter years of the Sukarno era, and was responsible for the West Papuan campaign in 1961 (see p000). This house, parts of which have been left virtually untouched since Yani's murder during the so-called Communist coup of 1965, contains a hagiographic exhibition about his life and works, mainly told through old black-and-white photographs.

Like the Museum Permusan, this is just one of many museums dedicated to Indonesia's military heroes and its fight for Independence that lie scattered throughout the city, all of which are of minimal interest to the average tourist. Most sightseers would probably find it more worthwhile continuing east along Jalan Diponegoro to the **antiques market** of Jalan Surabaya (see p.118). This fascinating half-mile-long flea market is one of the best places to buy souvenirs in the capital, most of which can be had fairly cheaply if you're good at bargaining. Five minutes walk to the east is the **Cikini train station**, on the ground floor of which there is a big trade in basketware.

There are a couple of sights further east of here under the train tracks, though again they are of minority interest only. South along Jalan Panataran is the **Taman Proklamasi**. As the name suggests, it was on this spot – the former site of Sukarno's house – that the Independent Republic of Indonesia was proclaimed on August 17, 1945. In 2001, a permanent exhibition "100 Years of Bung Karno" opened, which is dedicated to the "Father of Indonesia", President Sukarno; the free open-air exhibition can be visited at any time of the day. The house has now disappeared, to be replaced by a pleasant and very neat garden, in the middle of which are statues of Sukarno and Hatta. It's another 1.5km east of here – take the #AC08 from Jl Diponegoro – to **Pasar Pramuka**, one of Jakarta's large bird markets where, as is typical with markets of this kind in Indonesia – birds, reptiles and rodents are kept in cruel, cramped conditions. The same bus runs westbound from Pasar Pramuka back to just south of the *Mandarin Oriental Hotel*.

One of Jakarta's rare secluded quiet spots is **The Commonwealth War Graves Commission Cemetery** in the suburb of **Menteng Pulo**. Here lie 1179 men and women of the British Commonwealth and British Imperial forces who died in Indonesia between February 1942 and December 1946. Most senior of those buried here is Brigadier A. Mallaby, killed in Surabaya in October 1945 when British forces confronted the infant Republic of Indonesia, a neglected episode in Britain's colonial history. Anyone wishing to visit this beautifully maintained spot behind Gereja Belanda, the handsome Dutch church next to the *Park Lane Hotel* on Jalan Casablanca, should first ask the church warden for the keys. There is a second **Dutch cemetery** at Ancol, which also honours British dead, including several dozen men of the Royal Artillery who were executed at Subang, West Java in February 1942.

Tanah Abang: the Textile Museum

Jakarta's **Textile Museum** (Tues–Thurs & Sun 9am–4pm, Fri 9am–3pm; Rp1000) stands to the west of the Tanah Abang train station at Jalan Aipda K.S. Tubun 4. Catch bus #P16 heading north from Thamrin to the Tanah Abang market, then walk west for five minutes over the bridge. Housed in a spacious old Dutch villa, once owned by a Turkish consul, the collection displays over three hundred **indigenous textiles** from every part of the archipelago. The exhibits are well presented and the house is cool and spacious, though it's really only for those with a special interest in the subject. Exhibits include a rare set of **rattan armour** from West Papua, an explanation of the batik-making process and examples of the different types of traditional batik patterns.

The outskirts

The **funfairs** at Ancol and Taman Mini (the extraordinary "Disney-esque" theme park in the southern suburbs) provide both locals and visitors with a perfect escape from the noise and smog of Jakarta's city centre, while the one at Taman Ria, Senayan on Jalan Gerbang Pintu beside the National Stadium complex, also offers a boating lake and Ferris wheel. A trip to Taman Mini can be combined with a visit to the neighbouring **Museum Purna Bhakti Pertiwi**, a breathtaking collection of gifts presented to Suharto and his wife that has to be seen to be believed.

Taman Ria Senayan

The newest fairground attraction, **Taman Ria Senayan** (daily 8am to 8pm) has a Ferris wheel, carousels and a boating lake. Situated on Jl Gerbang Senayan close to the National Assembly building, it's a good place to go when you are travelling with children; you can also relax at the lakeside here with a beer at *Bugil's Dutch Café*. To get here from Jalan Jaksa, a taxi should cost around Rp10,000, or take any bus going south from the *Sari Pan Pacific Hotel* towards Cimone via Semanggi.

Taman Impian Jaya Ancol

The oldest and nearest of Jakarta's two theme parks, **Taman Impian Jaya Ancol** (daily 8am–midnight; Rp2500, Rp3000 on Sun) lies 10km to the north of Medan Merdeka, 3km east of Kota. To get here from Thamrin, catch bus #AC01, #ACB1, #AC10, #P1, #P11 or #P17 heading north to Kota station, then minibus #M15 from Kota to Ancol – or you can wait for bus #125, which passes along Jalan Merdeka Barat on its way to Ancol. The entry fee gets you into the park, although many of the main attractions have a separate entrance charge. The centrepiece of Ancol is the **Dunia Fantasi** (Fantasy World; Mon–Fri Rp11,000, Sat & Sun Rp12,000), an Indonesian take on Disneyland featuring a fairly extensive collection of roller coasters and water chutes (Rp5000–6000 per ride). If you're going to try more than a couple of them, it's worth buying the **all-inclusive ticket**, which covers the cost of all the rides (Mon–Fri Rp21,000, Sat Rp23,000, Sun Rp25,000).

Other attractions include **Seaworld** (Rp10,000 per show) where freshwater dolphins and sea lions perform, an excellent aquarium, the Gelanggang Samudra (Rp10,000), a **golf course**, souvenir market (Pasar Seni) and a rather busy **swimming pool complex** (Mon–Sat 8am–8pm, Sun & hols 8am–8pm; Mon–Fri Rp7000, Sat, Sun & hols Rp11,000), which includes a wave pool, water slides and a river run. At night, and especially at the weekends, the park plays host to local bands, and there's also a drive-in cinema. All in all, it's a rather expensive day out, but the best place to go in Jakarta if you have kids to entertain.

Taman Mini Indonesia Indah (TMII)

The **Taman Mini Indonesia Indah** (daily 8am–5pm; Rp2500), a huge theme park celebrating the rich ethnic and cultural diversity of the archipelago, was the brainchild and obsession of the late Madame Suharto. The park lies 18km south of Medan Merdeka: catch bus #P10, #P11 or #P16 to Kampung Rambutan bus station, then minibus #T19 or #M55 to the entrance, and allow an hour for the journey. Alternatively, a taxi from Jalan Jaksa to TMII costs Rp22,000. There is so much to see and do at Taman Mini that it's possible to spend all day here, although most of it can be seen in a frenetic three or four hours if you're really pushed for time.

The exorbitant cost of building the park (US$27million) and the enforced removal of the villagers on whose land it was built (the Suhartos used Jakarta underworld figures to intimidate opponents of the scheme) drew strong criticism from both home and abroad. However, ever since it opened in 1975, the park has been a roaring success, and visitors tend to be pleasantly surprised that it isn't as tacky as could be expected.

At the centre of the park is a huge man-made lake, around which are 27 houses, each representing one of the 27 provinces of Indonesia, built in the traditional style of that region: cultural performances often take place outside these houses. It is possible to rent a motorized "**swan-boat**" from the western side of the lake (Rp1500) to take you to the scale model of the archipelago that has been sculpted in the centre.

The park also contains a number of **museums**, all of which charge an entry fee of around Rp500. The best of these is the **Science Museum**, on the eastern side of the lake, which features many interactive exhibits. The Asmat Museum, housing woodcarvings from the Asmat tribe of West Papua, and the Museum Indonesia, with displays on the county's people, geography, flora and fauna, are also worth visiting. Other attractions include the **Sports Museum** – which includes photos of President Suharto in a tracksuit doing aerobics – a **Telecommunications Museum**, the **Komodo Museum** (a natural history museum housed within a giant replica of a Komodo dragon), and an **insectarium**. Add to this two **aviaries** (Rp3000), a large **aquarium** (closed Mon; Rp3000) an **orchid garden** (Rp500), a **swimming pool** (Rp2000) and a **children's park**, and you have the makings of a fun day out. There's also a **cinema** (Rp4000, Rp8000 for "VIP seats"), built in the shape of a giant snail and housing what is said to be the world's largest cinema screen (29.3m by 21.5m) on which a whirlwind travelogue of the archipelago is shown daily (noon & 3pm).

There are plenty of ways of getting around the park. Next to the swan-boat port is the main station for the **sky-train** (Rp2000), which circles the lake and provides excellent views over it. There's also a **mini train** (Rp1000) which rings the park at ground level, a **cable car** (Rp5000 for the 10min trip) which runs east–west above the lake, and a **car and open trailer** that ferries passengers around the park for free. These last three modes of transport can be picked up at the western end of the lake, near the **information kiosk** and the Pancasila Monument.

Museum Purna Bhakti Pertiwi

Although it's easily possible to spend all day at Taman Mini, try and put aside a little time to visit the neighbouring **Museum Purna Bhakti Pertiwi** (daily 9am–4pm; Rp2500) – you'll be amazed at what you find here. The luxurious marble building, spacious and deliciously air-con, has four floors, each containing a jaw-dropping array of treasures. This collection is, in the main, made up of gifts presented to President Suharto and his wife by foreign ambassadors, fellow heads of state and local dignitaries. While many of the exhibits are rather kitsch – and the very idea of such an outrageous display of opulence may seem obscene in one of Asia's poorest countries – the artistry involved in some of the exhibits cannot fail to impress. Intricately carved elephant tusks, welcoming statues (*pembrana*), and even an entire gamelan orchestra made entirely of old Balinese coins threaded together, plus enough gold and jewellery to wipe out the national debt, are all gathering dust here. But it is the huge and intricately detailed woodcarvings that are astounding; a series of panels depicts the life story of Suharto on the walls of the lobby, in the centre of which stands a ten-metre tree trunk carved with the story of the *Rama Tambak*, an episode of the *Ramayana* tales where the force of good, represented by Sri Rama Wijaya, successfully builds a dam to reach his wife, Dewi Shinta, who is being held captive on Alengka by Rahwana, king of Alengka. Also on the ground floor, look out for the enormous rubber-tree root decorated with the gods of the *langlang buana*, the nine gods of Balinese Hinduism who control the nine points of the Balinese compass; it took fifteen craftsmen sixteen months to complete. The artistry displayed throughout the museum is amongst the best in Indonesia, and, when combined with the fierce air-con and the clear and concise English-language labels, more than justifies the effort it takes to get here.

Eating

Food is more expensive in the capital than anywhere else in Indonesia, and prices rose again in early 2002 due to government-dictated hikes. It can come as a bit of a shock to find that staples such as *cap cay* and nasi goreng cost twice as much as they do elsewhere in the archipelago. That said, there is twice as much choice here too, and the different types of **cuisine** that can be found in the city centre, from French to Mexican to Japanese to Italian, lend Jakarta a truly international flavour. Over the last decade, the capital has been swamped by **fast-food** restaurants, with all the big names from the West appearing, as well as their home-grown imitators such as *California Fried Chicken*. The extremely busy *McDonald's* in the Sarinah department store is the one most frequented by travellers, mainly because it's open 24hr and thus catches the post-nightclub crowd. There's also a *Pizza Hut* in the Jakarta Theatre building on Jalan Wahid Hasyim, and branches of *Dunkin' Donuts*, *Sizzler* and *Baskin & Robbins* on Jalan H.A. Salim (aka Jalan Sabang). Recommended food courts include the basement of Pasaraya in Blok M, the basement of the Sarinah department store and the top floor and basement of Plaza Indonesia.

Jalan Jaksa

The budget restaurants on **Jalan Jaksa** have become havens of peace and comfort; it's not surprising that travellers can spend much of their time in the capital sheltering inside one of them. In the evenings the street is a magnet for Jakarta's younger expat crowd, many of them in the TEFL business. These places look fairly similar: a bamboo-wall facade facing the street, with a map of Indonesia on the wall alongside pictures of Western rock stars; ornate aquariums also feature prominently. For a map of eating places in and around Jalan Jaksa, see p.99.

Karya Jl Jaksa 32–34. A surprisingly inexpensive café in the courtyard of the distinctly non-budget *Hotel Karya*. The rather bland all-you-can-eat breakfast is reasonable value (Rp15,000), and the café is also one of the few places on Jaksa to serve draught beers (Rp8000 per glass).

Margot Jl Jaksa 15. The service can be somewhat slow, but this is a reasonable spot for simple breakfasts of the toast and jam and coffee variety.

Memories Jl Jaksa 17. A restaurant on two floors with a small bookshop built into one corner of the ground floor. The large menu of Western and local dishes is somewhat overpriced – though some of the dishes, including the Sichuan chicken (Rp9000), are terrific, and this place remains one of the most popular on the street. Live local music and reggae in the evenings make the joint jump.

Merry's Burger Jl Jaksa 40. The cheapest place on the street, no-frills *Merry's* offers burgers starting at Rp6000 (Bintang Rp8500); inexpensive, but not especially good value, although the upstairs balcony is a haven of peace and quiet.

Pappa's Jl Jaksa 41. A good place for lunch at the quieter southern end of Jaksa, *Pappa's* specializes in Indian-style curries (Rp16,000–20,000), with "paper dums" (Rp500) optional. Open more or less 24hr, this café is a popular nocturnal haunt for expat journalists, with a large Bintang costing Rp12,000. The service is sometimes surly.

Q Bar Jl Jaksa 18. A popular hang-out for a mix of expats, Indonesian gays, good-time girls and tourists. Does very good wood-fired pizzas.

Ya-Udah Bistro Jl Jaksa 49. By far the best-value place to eat on Jalan Jaksa and among the best anywhere around Jakarta, Swiss-run *Ya-Udah's* 80+ item menu includes excellent Hungarian goulash (Rp9500), bockwurst (Rp13,500) and an unbeatable Chef's Salad (Rp6500). The American breakfasts are also very popular (Rp12,500), and a large beer costs Rp10,000. Watch for the specials such as international sausage selections; the efficient waitress service puts many other emporia to shame.

Street food

Local street food thrives as much in Jakarta as it does in other parts of the archipelago. **Jalan H.A. Salim**, more commonly known by its former name of **Jalan Sabang**, features a wide variety of warung that line the pavements in the evening, selling some delicious snacks including *murtabak* (deep-fried pancakes), both sweet and spicy, *bakso*, terrific sate, and a number of other tasty treats. During shop opening hours, Jalan Sabang can be extremely noisy, especially outside the clothes stores which all seem to have outlandish PA systems.

Other places to look for street food include **Jalan Kendal**, which runs east from Jalan Thamrin, 800m south of the Welcome Monument, which is known for its goat's-head soups; **Jalan Pecenongan**, running north directly opposite the Istana Negara, 1km due north of Monas, which specializes in seafood dishes; the string of warung in the gang next to Duta Suara Music, Jl Sabang 26A, which is also very popular with the locals during the daytime; and the western end of **Jalan Kebon Sirih Barat**, which offers some of the cheapest food in the capital. Exceptionally popular is the nasi goreng *kambing* warung every evening at the north end of Jalan Kebon Sirih Barat where it joins Jalan Kebon Sirih. It has few rivals in the city, and Indonesian customers often end up sitting on the walls of neighbouring compounds to enjoy the fare. One of the best – and least-publicized – places to go in the evenings lies just south of the Senen Atrium on **Jalan Kramat Raya**, where from sunset to the small hours a row of excellent *nasi padang* stalls is set up on the side of the southbound lanes (unfortunately, the noise of passing traffic may take some getting used to). On the Monas side of **Gambir station** there is another row of semi-alfresco stalls, where *soto Betawi* (Batavia soup) is among the favourites.

Jalan H.A. Salim (Jalan Sabang)

More commonly known as **Jalan Sabang**, Jalan H.A. Salim, running parallel with and west of Jalan Jaksa, plays host to a string of decent restaurants catering for every budget and taste. The restaurants in this area are marked on the map on p.99.

Ayam Goreng Priangan Jl Sabang 55a. A fairly inexpensive Indonesian fried-chicken restaurant. Try their version of *ayam bakar* – chicken cooked in coconut milk and grilled in a sweet soya sauce – for Rp3300.

Bakeri Modern Sakura Anpan Jl Sabang 25a. A Western-style cake shop with a fine display of multi-tiered wedding cakes in the window. Luxurious and distinctly non-budget fare, but if you feel like treating yourself, try their chocolate cake (Rp4000 per slice).

Bakmi Gang Kelinci Jl Sabang 53. Small food mall which includes a *Baskin & Robbins* ice-cream parlour as well as the *Khong Guan* biscuit-and-cake shop; recommended for *nasi cap cay*.

Bakwan Campur Surabaya Jl Sabang 23. An unpretentious and reasonably cheap Surabayan restaurant serving good-value East Javanese food. Their *tahu isi* (tofu and vegetables in batter) is particularly delicious.

Duta Makassar On the corner of Sabang and Kebon Sirih. This is one of four palm and bamboo Indonesian eating places at this site, specializing in *ikan bakar* South Sulawesi-style. Highly recommended for its *ikan bawal* accompanied by *sop sayur asem*, an excellent astringent soup, mint leaves and rice (Rp14,000) and grilled squid (Rp12,000).

HP Gardena Jalan Sabang. An unusual "hot pot" restaurant, where you choose the ingredients – they're on display in a fridge at the back, and range from fish cakes (Rp4500) to meatballs (Rp4500) along with various salad items – which are then served with spicy sauce dips.

Natrabu Jl Sabang 29a. An excellent mid-priced Minang restaurant (Padang-style food from West Sumatra) with red-liveried waiters serving such delicacies as buffalo lungs and kidneys. There's also live traditional Minang music every evening (7–9.30pm).

Sabang Jl Sabang 51a. A mid-priced restaurant serving an unusual combination of Indonesian and Western dishes alongside a large but unimpressive bakery.

Sederhana Jl Sabang 33. A clean, superior-quality Padang restaurant much patronized by locals. Expect to pay Rp2000–3000 per dish, but be warned: the bananas on the table are Rp500 each.
Sizzler Jl Sabang 39. A Western-style mid-priced restaurant, a cross between a fast-food shack and a steakhouse, with all-you-can-eat salad bar and sundae bar. Much patronized by expats and wealthier locals.
Soto Betawi Sabang Jl Sabang 55. A linoleum-floored budget cafeteria serving mainly soups. Check out their *soto Betawi* special – fish soup – or the rather overpriced but tasty *soto ayam*.
Soto Sury Jl Sabang 27b. A no-nonsense soup kitchen, which has recently expanded its menu to include nasi rawon, gado-gado and nasi campur.

Jalan Wahid Hasyim

Running by the southern end of Jalan Jaksa, **Jalan Wahid Hasyim** has a selection of large restaurants at the moderate to expensive end of the market. The restaurants in this area are marked on the map on p.99.

Ayam Goreng Suharti Jl Wahid Hasyim 51. A fried-chicken restaurant, clean and friendly, but the decor and menu are rather uninspiring and the food is not very good value (Rp15,000 for a whole chicken).
Bakmi Toko Tiga Jl Wahid Hasyim 65. The latest branch of a chain of Indonesian/Chinese restaurants founded in Semarang. Noodles and good value *nasi cap cay* are the speciality here.
Chili's First floor, Sarinah Building. An American bar and restaurant serving Tex-Mex food; a good place to watch TV sports.
Green Pub Jakarta Theatre, Jalan Wahid Hasyim. Tex-Mex food, country and western music, tequila slammers and marguerItas: pricey, but popular with expats.
Hazara Jl Wahid Hasyim 112. This elegantly decorated North Indian restaurant has a big following, but portions are small and prices quite inflated.
Le Bistro Jl Wahid Hasyim 71. A classy French restaurant hidden behind a wealth of foliage and looking totally out of place on this busy road. Vintage wagons parked in the courtyard give a clue to the decor inside: a wealth of old pots and pans, gramophones and other antique ironmongery. The food (French, of course) is terrific, although not cheap, with main courses around Rp30,000.
Marinara Seafood Buffet First floor, Sarinah Building. An all-you-can-eat seafood outlet; the Rp30,000+ lunch buffet includes soft drinks.
Pho Hoa Jl Wahid Hasyim 135. Vietnamese fast food on the corner of Jalan Sabang and Jalan Wahid Hasyim. As you might expect, rice and noodles feature prominently, including excellent vermicelli with spicy chicken and lemon grass (Rp9000), which you can order with extra tripe (Rp1000) if you feel so inclined.
Tony Roma's – A Place for Ribs Jl Wahid Hasyim 49. An expensive restaurant with a lengthy Western menu, specializing in ribs served in a variety of mouthwatering ways (Rp25,000–35,000 for a rack).
Waroeng Menteng Jl Wahid Hasyim 81. An Indonesian restaurant next to the Spanish Embassy, serving truly excellent *ikan mas pepes*, the Sundanese banana leaf-baked fish (Rp19,000+) and a very good *nasi timbel komplit* (Rp18,000). Take a book, as the service is slow.

Jalan Cokroaminoto, Menteng

If you make the walk around Menteng (see p.108), this can be reached in five minutes by bajaj from Jaksa's south end, and has a number of eating places.

Ayam Goreng Waroeng Pojok On the corner of Keris Galeri. A new and home-grown attempt at the fast-food formula; worth a try for local fried chicken.
Mario's Place Ground floor, Menteng Plaza. A nicely appointed restaurant and wine bar with live music in the evenings. Good for steaks and salads.
Saburo Ground floor, Menteng Plaza. A Japanese noodles restaurant recommended for its tasty stocks; try *mie kishi-katsu* with deep-fried chicken in breadcrumbs (Rp 14,500).
Tamnak Thai Jl Cokroaminoto 85. A pleasant Thai restaurant; while it lacks the reputation of *Suan Thai* and *Lan Na Thai*, the fish dishes are good.

The rest of the City

Bugils Taman Ria Senayan. Next to the boating lake, Dutch-owned *Bugils* is a friendly place for a quiet beer and Dutch-style food.

Café Batavia Taman Fatahillah, Kota. One of the best and most popular establishments in Jakarta, the 24hr *Café Batavia* is decorated with photos of Hollywood stars, who look down on you as you tuck into the beautifully cooked food: a mixture of Chinese, Indonesian and Western dishes. This café is the best place to come for cocktails in the city, with over sixty to choose from. An added attraction is the nightly live jazz and soul music. It's pricey, but if you have any reason to celebrate in Jakarta, this is the place to do it.

Domus Jl Veteran 1, 30. Italian restaurant specializing in regional dishes, *Domus* has a good selection of wines, a cigar lounge and the *Cuba Libre Bar* upstairs.

Eastern Promise Jl Kemang Raya 5. A South Jakarta English pub and Indian restaurant popular with expat drinkers, serving the best British pies for hundreds of miles (steak and kidney, chicken and mushroom etc) as well as Balti curries. The happy hour is 4–7pm.

Kelapa Gading Food City Jalan Boulevar Raya. Thirty to forty minutes by taxi from Jalan Jaksa, this large semi-open-air complex in the predominantly Chinese suburb of Kelapa Gading makes for a great evening out. Set next to the huge KG Mall, it has Chinese, Vietnamese, Makassarese and other restaurants laid out around a square. Particularly recommended are *Bangkok 69* for its seafood, *Remaja* for its beef dishes, *Jade Garden* for its all-round Chinese cuisine and *Gurjari*, possibly the best Indian outlet around.

Maharaja Jl Veteran 1, 26. A family-run Indian restaurant that does good *masala dosai*.

Oasis Jl Raden Saleh 47 ⓣ021/3150646. Jakarta's finest, this historic restaurant, housed in a large, 1920s Dutch villa in Cikini, is expensive but worth it. The decor, with its huge teak-beamed ceilings, crystal chandeliers and enormous stained-glass window, is suitably opulent. To the strains of the house band, diners can tuck into Western delicacies such as steak tartare and duckling *bigarade*. For something a little different, try the *rijsttaffel*.

Orleans Jl Adityawarman 67. Friendly *Orleans* is two minutes walk from the east-facing exit to Blok M bus terminal – it's worth the trip for the steaks, Boston clam chowder and prawns Creole; there's also a quiet bar upstairs.

Queens Tandoori Permata Plaza, Jl Thamrin 57. Good North Indian food with solid *naan* breads, a fifteen-minute walk from Jalan Jaksa.

Raden Kuring Jl Raden Saleh Raya 62, Cikini. Possibly the best of the city's *kuring* restaurants, specializing in Sundanese food; the pleasant ambience is enhanced by the little garden in the middle of the restaurant, and also cultural performances in the evenings. Try any of the *pedang*, kebab-style meat dishes (Rp19,000) and the *ikan mas pepes*.

Seulawah Jl Mas Mansyur 9, Karet Tengsin, Central Jakarta. Acehnese restaurant. The Acehnese are famous for their marijuana production – and it's rumoured that some dishes here contain it. Anyhow, try the *plie'u*, a vegetable curry or the biriani-style rice dishes.

Nightlife and entertainment

Many stories have circulated down the years about the city being difficult and dangerous at night. Consequently, most travellers don't even leave **Jalan Jaksa** in the evening, preferring to hang out in one of the many bars that are strung along the road, of which *Ya-Udah Bistro, Memories* and *Ali's Bar* are currently the most popular. However, those prepared to venture further than the end of Jalan Wahid Hasyim will be rewarded with the choice of highly professional cultural performances, some of the sleaziest, wildest nightclubs in Southeast Asia, plus excellent bars. You need to have a destination in mind before you leave your hotel, though – Jakarta is not a city where you can just wander around looking for somewhere to spend the evening.

Cultural shows

Jakarta isn't great for indigenous **cultural performances**, and if you're heading off to Central Java – in particular Yogya and Solo – you're better off waiting. However, you shouldn't have to search too long to find something going on somewhere in the capital. The big international hotels are a good place to begin looking, as they usually hold some form of traditional dancing or musical performance in the evening – though you'll almost certainly have to eat there in order to watch.

The **Gedung Kesenian**, at Jalan Kesenian 1 (Ⓣ021/3808283), just north of the general post office, is the oldest **theatre** in Jakarta – it was originally the Schouwberg Playhouse and dates back to 1821. Following its reopening in 1987 it has become regarded as the main venue in Jakarta for renditions of **classical music**, **ballet**, **wayang orang** and **choral concerts**. The Bharata Theatre at Jalan Kalilio 15, Pasar Senen (bus #15 from Jalan Kebon Sirih), is another venerable – if somewhat stuffy – old venue in Jakarta, and holds traditional wayang orang and **ketoprak** performances every night at 8pm. If you're in Jakarta on a Sunday, check out the Wayang Museum on Fatahillah Square in Kota (see p.104), which holds a free four-hour **wayang kulit** performance at 10am.

TIM (Taman Ismail Marzuki), at Jalan Cikini Raya 73 (Ⓣ021/322606), is the main arts centre in the capital, featuring musical performances, plays, dance, art exhibitions and films – there's even a small planetarium here, although this is currently closed to the public. On Sunday mornings you can watch (for free) classical Indonesian dance instruction being given to young Indonesian girls, while relaxing over a drink in one of the string of outdoor cafés here. Pick up a timetable of forthcoming events from the TIM or the tourist office in the Jakarta Theatre. The **RRI** (Radio Republik Indonesia), the national radio station whose headquarters are on Jalan Medan Merdeka, just to the north of the National Museum, occasionally records **gamelan** performances and wayang shows in the studios there. It's worth calling in to see when the next public performance is and whether there are any tickets available. Other venues that hold occasional cultural performances include the grounds of Ancol, near the Pasar Seni art market (see p.118), and the Taman Mini on Jalan Pondok Gede Raya (see p.110).

Nightclubs

Lacking the reputation abroad of either Bangkok or Manila, Jakarta's **nightclubs** fall into three broad categories. The first category includes clubs that are part of one of the big international hotels, such as the *Music Room* at the *Borobudur Intercontinental*, and the *Pitstop* at the *Sari San Pacific*. These tend to be rather glitzy, expensive and exclusive establishments for the Jakarta nouveau riche, although Westerners are seldom turned away, providing they obey the dress code of no sandals, shorts or T-shirts.

The second and largest group is the innumerable small, sleazy joints found throughout the city, such as the bars along Jalan Mangga Besar in Kota. These are usually inexpensive (around Rp5000 entry), but a little dull unless you're into **karaoke**, which often takes place during the early part of the evening.

Finally, in a class all by itself, there's the **Tanamur Disco** (Rp30,000), at Jalan Tanah Abang Timur 14. What separates this place from the rest is not the music, which is a danceable but fairly mainstream mix of European and American house, nor indeed the decor – a reasonably unexciting combination of neon strip lights and stained wood – but the clientele it attracts: expats, pimps, prostitutes, ladyboys, junkies and the occasional traveller, all gathered together on two floors under one roof to dance the night away. During the week you can expect about five hundred revellers every night, and on Friday and Saturday there can be three times that number; Sunday night is Ladies' Night, when women get in free. Be forewarned, however, that this place has all the appearance of a major firetrap. Next door is *JJ's*, a smaller and quieter disco which survives on the overspill from the *Tanamur*. Entry is free here after 2am, and the place stays open until 5am.

Be warned that there is a considerable trade in ecstasy in some discos including *The Hotmen's* in the *Hotel Menteng 1*, Jalan Gondangdia (see p.102). Users run the real risk of being picked up in police raids; as a useful precaution, carry a copy of your passport, but not the real thing.

Bars and live music

The *Hard Rock Café*, part of the Sarinah building on the corner of Jalan Wahid Hasyim and Jalan Thamrin, is by far and away the most popular **live-music venue**, particularly with Jakarta's wannabees. In amongst the various bits of minor rock memorabilia, the stained-glass window of Elvis Presley is an unexpected delight. The drinks are very expensive (with a coffee at US$3 the cheapest item on the menu), but the place is usually packed, the atmosphere is always lively, and it's within crawling distance of Jalan Jaksa. The most salubrious live-music venue in Jakarta, however, remains the *Café Batavia* on Fatahillah Square in Kota, a mix of Indonesian charm combined with colonial standards of cleanliness and comfort (see p.115 for more details). Jazz and soul groups perform here most evenings.

The *Jaya* pub, on the opposite side of the road from the *Sari San Pacific* hotel at Jalan Thamrin 12, is now in its 22nd year and has become one of Jakarta's oldest and best-loved watering holes. Early in the evening the *Jaya* can be depressingly quiet, with only the occasional expat dropping by, but after 10.30pm the place starts filling up as locals and Westerners alike come to listen to the jazz and soft-rock sounds of the resident band.

BB's, which is upstairs next to Menteng Plaza at Jl Suryo 1, Menteng, has good bands playing blues and reggae, and the music here tends to start late; the best nights are Thursday, Friday, and Saturday.

The **dangdut** scene is worth investigating, and an evening spent in either *Cagar Alam* or *Parahiangan* on Jalan Blora, second left south just beyond the *Mandarin Oriental*, can provide an enjoyable insight into Indonesian nightlife and this hugely popular style of music (see p.1067). The live dangdut band at *Parahiangan* features haunting bamboo flute music (*suling*), and the mixed Indonesian crowd likes to let their hair down to the shuffling steps of **joget**. Occasionally you can see and hear the truly exotic **jaipongan** here too. The first drink includes the cover charge.

The *Hard Rock* corporation is not the only Western company to have branches of its restaurants/cafés/bars in Jakarta: *Planet Hollywood*, on Jalan Jend Gatot Subroto, just southeast of the Semanggi Interchange, *TGI Fridays*, part of the Ascott Centre, west of the Welcome Monument along Jalan Kebon Kacang Raya, and the *Fashion Café*, behind the BNI Tower on Jalan Sudirman, have all been introduced to Jakarta recently. All of these are very popular with expats, as is the small *Dyna Bar*, down an alley just off Jalan Wahid Hasyim to the west of Jalan Jaksa, which has a happy hour in the early evening.

If you're after a huge night out, head for **Blok M**, which has a wealth of bars and English-style pubs. A taxi from Jl Jaksa should be no more than Rp14,000. A good place to start a crawl is Jalan Palatehan, a scruffy rubble-strewn street once mysteriously called "The Street of Dreams". At the north end is the British-owned *D's Place*, which holds two Ladies' lucky draws a night; the jackpot is often much greater than the official monthly minimum wage, and the place is consequently packed out with wayfaring young Indonesian women. *D's Place* also hosts a fortnightly pub quiz, at 6.30pm on Sundays. Next door is *The Sportsman's Bar and Grill*, specializing in televised sports; it is a good place to watch Six-Nations rugby games and American Football, as well as English Premiership soccer. The *Top Gun Bar*, just opposite the *Sportsman's*, is a famous pick-up joint, as is *Oscar's*, which often has good live music after 9pm (closed Sun). Round off your evening by heading off to the all-night *Lintas Melawai* bar and disco next to the *Hotel Melawai* on Jalan Melawai on the south side of Blok M. *The Stanford Arms* is a British-style pub in the four-star *Hotel Ambhara* opposite the Blok M bus terminal exit. Popular with South Jakarta expats, this has Happy Hour from 5–8pm. About 200m away is *The Orleans* at Jl Adityawarman 67, where the upstairs bar attracts a loyal crowd of long-term Jakarta expats and Indonesian eccentrics, and is a good place to sound out the possibilities of work.

Shopping

Jakarta may be a little short on sights, but nobody could complain about the lack of **shops**, **bazaars**, **markets** and **shopping centres** in the capital. These range from the extremely downmarket (the Pasar Senen is the place to come for secondhand clothes and army surplus gear) to the exclusive (the air-con Indonesia Plaza under the *Grand Hyatt Hotel*, for example, plays host to all the top Western designer labels, for which you pay top Western prices). Many of the plazas and arcades are concentrated around Blok M in the south of the city, where you'll find a huge variety of stores and stalls to sift through. Best buys in Jakarta include **compact discs** and **batik clothing**.

Crafts and antiques

While the city has no particular indigenous craft of its own, in the way that Yogya, for example, has puppets and batik and Jepara has teak furniture, the capital isn't a bad place to go souvenir hunting. There are a couple of markets where artefacts from all over the archipelago can be found, and prices are reasonable. The **antiques market** on Jalan Surabaya, one block west of Cikini station in Jakarta's Menteng district, is a good place to begin your trawl. Much of the stuff cannot really be classified as antique, though there's some fine silver jewellery, and traditional Javanese wooden trunks and other pieces of furniture. Collectors of old records, particularly 1970s disco albums, will also find plenty of bargains.

The entire third floor of the **Sarinah** department store is given over to souvenirs, with wayang kulit and wayang goleng puppets, leather bags and woodcarvings a speciality. A similar selection of souvenirs can be found at Ancol's **Pasar Seni**, alongside galleries displaying work from a variety of local artists, most of whom produce paintings of stereotypical Indonesian landscapes and chaotic city scenes in an attempt to cater for tourists. There is also a bewildering array of rather gauche woodcarvings, from full-size models of eagles to scale models of Javanese houses. These carvings may not appeal to everyone, but the obvious skill and patience that goes into producing them is quite impressive. **Hadi Handicraft** in Plaza Indonesia specializes in good-quality, reasonably priced, brightly painted wooden statues and ornaments, mainly from Central Java. Finally, there are three reasonable souvenir shops on Jalan

Pasar Baru, north of the GPO: Toko Bandung at no. 16b, the Ramayana Art Shop at no. 17, and the Irian Art Shop at 16a. Despite their names, each sells souvenirs from all over the archipelago.

Those interested in **precious stones** should visit Pasar Rawa Bening, the gemstones market next to Jatinegara railway station, East Jakarta. Here you can bargain for a variety of items such as moonstone and lapis lazuli. To get there, take the train from Gondangdia, five minutes walk from the south end of Jalan Jaksa, but beware the notorious Jatinegara pickpockets.

Records, compact discs and other bargains

Recorded music, both indigenous and Western, is particularly good value in Indonesia, and in Jakarta you get a wider and more up-to-date selection than anywhere else. Compact discs and tapes are thirty to fifty percent cheaper than in Europe. The ground floor of the Sarinah department store has a reasonable selection, as has Delta Disk at Jalan Sabang 27; Duta Disk nearby; Bulletin Records on the top floor of the Gajah Mada Plaza, 150m north of the Pelni head office on Jalan Gajah Mada; Duta Suara on Jalan Sabang at no. 26, and a number of neon-lit boutiques in the shopping centres around Blok M.

Clothes, **bags** and **watches** are also very cheap in Jakarta, although the quality is often suspect. **Pasar Senen** (bus #15 or #P15 from Jalan Kebon Sirih, at the northern end of Jalan Jaksa) is a good place to browse for these articles. The stalls here also stock a wide selection of Indonesian army-surplus gear, including camping and trekking equipment. The fourth floor of the Sarinah department store is devoted to good-quality **batik** clothes, though not everyone will find the exuberant shirts and full-length skirts to their taste. A similar selection can be found at the branch of Batik Kris in the Indonesia Plaza, the most exclusive store of its kind in the capital. **Keris Galeri** on Jalan Cokroaminoto in the Menteng district has a fine range of batik goods and souvenirs, while perhaps the best bargains are to be found in **Blok M** during Ramadan as the big annual Muslim holiday approaches, when you can pick up a batik shirt for as little as US$2.

Listings

Ambulance ⓣ118.

Airlines International: Aeroflot, *Hotel Sahid Jaya*, Jl Jend Sudirman, Kav 24 ⓣ021/5702184; Air China, ADD Building, Tamara Centre, Suite 802, Jalan Jend Sudirman ⓣ021/5206467; Air France, Summitmas Tower, 9th floor, Jalan Jend Sudirman ⓣ021/5202261; Air Lanka, Wisma Bank Dharmala, 14th floor, Jalan Jend Sudirman ⓣ021/5202101; Balkan Air, Jl K.H. Hasyim Ashari 33b ⓣ021/373341; Bouraq, Jl Angkasa 1–3, Kemayoran ⓣ021/6288815; British Airways, BDN Building, Jalan Thamrin ⓣ021/2300277; Cathay Pacific, Gedung Bursa Efek, Jl Jend Sudirman Kav 52–53 ⓣ021/5151747; China Airlines, Wisma Dharmala Sakti, Jl Jend Sudirman 32 ⓣ021/2510788; Emirates, *Hotel Sahid Jaya*, 2nd floor, Jl Jend Sudirman 86 ⓣ021/5205363; Eva Air, Price Waterhouse Centre, 10th floor, Jl Rasuna Said Kav C3 ⓣ021/5205828; Garuda, Jl Merdeka Selatan 13 (ⓣ021/2311801), includes city check-in, with a second office at the BDN Building, Jl Thamrin 5; Japan Airlines, MID Plaza, Ground floor, Jl Jend Sudirman Kav 28 ⓣ021/5212177; Kuwait Airways, behind the BNI building, Jl Sudirman; Lufthansa, Panin Centre Building, 2nd floor, Jl Jend Sudirman 1 ⓣ021/5702005; Malaysian Airlines, World Trade Centre, Jl Jend Sudirman Kav 29 ⓣ021/5229682; Myanmar Airways, Jl Melawai Raya 7, 3rd floor ⓣ021/7394042; KLM, New Summitmas, 17th floor, Jl Jend Sudirman Kav 61–62 ⓣ021/5212176 or 5212177; Korean Air, Wisma Bank Dharmala, 7th floor, Jl Jend Sudirman

Kav 28 ☎021/5782036; Mandala, Jl Garuda 76 ☎021/4246100, also Jl Veteran I 34 ☎021/4246100; Merpati, Jl Angkasa 7, Blok B15 Kav 2 & 3 ☎021/6548888 and 24hr city check-in at Gambir station; Philippine Airlines, Plaza Mashil, 11th floor suite 1105, Jl Jend Sudirman Kav 25 ☎021/3810949, 3810950 or 5267780; Qantas Airways, BDN Building, Jalan Thamrin ☎021/327707; Royal Brunei Airlines, World Trade Centre, 11th floor, Jl Jend Sudirman Kav 29–31 ☎021/2300277; Sabena, Ground floor, Wisma Bank Dharmala, Jl Jend Sudirman Kav 28; Saudi Arabian Airlines, Wisma Bumiputera, 7th floor, Jl Jend Sudirman Kav 75 ☎021/5710615; Silk Air , Chase Plaza, 4th floor, Jl Jend Sudirman Kav 21 ☎021/5208018; Singapore Airlines, Chase Plaza, 2nd floor, Jl Jend Sudirman Kav 21 ☎021/5206881 or 5206933; Thai International, BDN Building, Ground floor, Jalan Thamrin ☎021/330816 or 3140607.

Airport enquiries ☎021/5505000.

Art galleries Indonesia has a flourishing art scene, and at any time there are exhibitions around the city.

Bentara Budaya, Jl Palmerah Selatan 17 ☎5483008; Cemara 6, Jl Cokroaminoto 117, (Mon–Sat 9am–6pm; ☎ 324505); Duta Fine Arts Foundation, Jl Kemang Utara 55A, (Tues–Sat 10am–7pm, Sun–Mon 11am–4pm; ☎7990226; Galeri Cipta 2&3, Taman Ismail Marzuki, Jalan Cikini Raya; Galeri Mini, Japan Foundation, Summitmas 1, Jl Sudirman, (Mon–Sat 10am–6pm); Galeri Nasional Indonesia, Jl Merdeka Timur 56 ☎34833955. In addition, the World Trade Centre, Jalan Sudirman, holds regular exhibitions on the ground floor next to the Hong Kong and Shanghai Bank.

Banks and exchange Offering a better rate than any bank or moneychanger, the numerous ATMs dotting the city are by far and away the best and most convenient places to buy Indonesian rupiah. Many of the banks, the post office, the Sarinah department store and Gambir all have their own ATM machines. Most banks open 8am to 3.30pm, with an hour for lunch. The majority of the big international banks in Jakarta line the main north–south thoroughfare through the city, Jalan Thamrin. The Bank BNI and Lippobank, however, just west of the northern end of Jalan Jaksa on Jalan Kebon Siri, offer the best rates in town, with the latter also offering credit-card advances. The exchange counters of both open at 10am. The Bank Rama on the ground floor of the Sarinah department store has a reasonable rate for US dollars. The AMEX office is now located at Graha Aktiva, Jalan Rasuna Said, Kuningan; catch bus #11 heading south from Sarinah. Currently, this is the only place that accepts Australian dollar travellers' cheques (AMEX travellers' cheques only). The rates of exchange at the moneychanging booths around Jalan Jaksa offer a worse rate than the banks, but remain open until fairly late in the evening and over the weekend too, when the banks are closed. If you take a bajaj (Rp3000) to Toko Gunung Agung, the bookstore and stationery shop on Jalan Kwitang Raya opposite the *Aryaduta Hyatt Hotel*, PT Ayu on the mezzanine floor usually offers very competitive rates.

Bookshops For new titles, the American chain QB World Books on Jalan Sunda behind the Sarinah department store has the widest selection, including a good collection of works on Indonesia. The fourth floor of Sarinah is also worth a browse. For secondhand books, visit Cynthia's Bookshop on Jalan Jaksa, or the small, well-stocked bookshop in the corner of *Memories Café*. Another worth the diversion is the secondhand bookshop next to the theatre at TIM.

Car rental Avis, Jl Diponegoro 25 (☎021/3142900 or 3150853), is currently the only car-rental organization operating in Jakarta.

Cinemas The following can be contacted for details of showings:

Bentara Budaya Jakarta, Jl Palmerah Selatan 17 ☎5483008; Mega Mall 21, Mega Mall, Jl Pluit Raya ☎6683621; Planet Hollywood 21, Jl Gatot Subroto 16 ☎5256351.

The Jakarta Theatre, opposite the Sarinah department store, shows reasonably up-to-date films for Rp10,500. There's also the GM21 cinema north of the Gajah Mada Plaza on Jalan Gajah Mada, and on the eleventh floor of the British Council there's a screening of a recent British film every Thursday and Saturday afternoon at 3.30pm. TIM (see p.116) is also reasonable, and in September holds the Jakarta International Film Festival, which features films from all over the world, as is the programme at the Umar Ismail Film Institute, Jl Rasuna Said C22. The *Jakarta Post* regularly reviews current showings. *Teater Utan Kayu*, Jl Utan Kayu 68H, East Jakarta (☎8373388), is a centre for innovative film and theatre.

Cultural centres The foreign cultural centres, of which there are many in Jakarta, often organize movie screenings and art exhibitions to show off artistic talent from their country; programmes change regularly, so phone for details. Australian Cultural Centre, Jl H. Rasuna Said Kav C 15–16 ☎021/5227111; the British Council, Jl Jend Sudirman 71 (☎021/5223311), has an excellent library and regular Thursday-afternoon movie screenings; Centre Culturel Française, Jl Salemba

Raya 25 ☎021/4218585; Erasmus Huis, Jl H. Rasuna Said, Kav 5–3 (☎021/5252321), is the Dutch arts centre, one of the oldest cultural institutes in the city; Goethe Institute, Jl Mataram Raya 23 (☎021/8509719), is a German cultural centre renowned for its photographic exhibitions; Italian Cultural Centre, Jl Diponegoro 45 ☎021/337445; Japanese Cultural Centre, Summitmas Building, Jalan Jend Sudirman ☎021/5255201; Jawarharlal Indian Cultural Centre, Jl Diponegoro 25 (no phone), often organizes meditation courses.

Embassies and consulates Australia, Jl H. Rasuna Said Kav 10–11 ☎021/25505555; Britain, Jalan Thamrin ☎021/3156264; Canada, Metropolitan Building 1, Jl Jend Sudirman Kav 29 ☎021/5712507; China, Jl Jend Sudirman Kav 69 Kebayoran Baru ☎021/7243400; Germany, Jl Thamrin 1 ☎021/3901750; India, Jl Rasuna Said S-1, Kuningan ☎021/5204150; Japan, Jl Thamrin 24 ☎021/5212177; Korea, Jl Gatot Subroto 57 ☎021/5201915; Malaysia, Jl Rasuna Said 1–3, Kuningan ☎021/5224947; Netherlands, Jl Rasuna Said S-3, Kuningan ☎021/5251515; New Zealand, Jl Diponegoro 41 ☎021/330680; Singapore, Jl Rasuna Said 2, Kuningan ☎021/5201489; South Africa, Wisma GKBI Jalan Sudirman ☎021/7193304; Thailand, Jl Imam Bonjol 74 ☎021/3904055; US, Jl Medan Mereka Selatan 5 ☎021/360360.

Hospitals and clinics The MMC hospital on Jalan Rasuna Said in Kuningan is widely regarded as the best in town (☎021/5203435). There is also the private SMI (Sentra Medika International) clinic at Jl Cokroaminoto 16 in Menteng (☎021/3157747), run by Australian and Indonesian doctors. If you are really budget-conscious, *Praktek Umum* are public clinics that charge minimally; ask at your hostel for the nearest such available clinic.

Immigration Expert help with immigration queries may be had at Global Travel, Jl Jaksa 49.

Internet access The GPO is the largest (over 25 terminals), cheapest (Rp2000 for 15min, Rp9500 for 65min), and most efficient place to collect and receive email in Jakarta (Mon–Sat 8am–9pm, Sun 9am–3pm). Catch bus #15 or #P15 from Jalan Kebon Sirih. The Wartel at Jl Jaksa 17 has a small email centre on the first floor (daily 8am–9pm; Rp5000 for 30min), while just a few metres north is the slightly more expensive Click Cyber Café (Rp6000 for 30min). A second branch, Click International, can be found at departure terminals D and E at Sukarno Hatta International. NisNet at Jl Kebon Sirih Barat 170 has friendly staff but suffers periodic problems with its server. Jaksa Internet cafés tend to be very inconsistent, and are often shut on Sundays and holidays.

Laundry Try the Angel Laundry service opposite *Ari and Naomy Hostel* on Jl Jaksa Gg 7; clothes are hand-washed and ready in one day for a reasonable charge (around Rp20,000 for a small rucksack full). DeWasz, next to Keris Galeri, Jl Cokroaminoto, Menteng does one-day dry cleaning.

Libraries Most of the cultural centres listed opposite have libraries where you can browse. The best is the very comfortable British Council library, 1st floor, S. Widjojo Centre, Jalan Sudirman 71, which gets generally up-to-date copies of *The Guardian* and *The Times* as well as a wide selection of periodicals. It also has an extensive video library.

Pharmacies The Medicine Shoppe, Jl Kebon Sirih 2 (Mon–Sat 8am–9pm), is the best pharmacy near Jalan Jaksa, and the staff are very helpful. Titimurni, Jl Kramat Raya 28 (catch the #P2 bus from Pasar Senen), is the only 24hr pharmacy in the centre of Jakarta.

Photographic shops There are plenty of good stores on Jalan Agus Salim, or you can try the MM Photo Studio in the Sarinah department store.

Post office Jakarta's huge main post office lies to the north of Lapangan Benteng (Mon–Sat 8am–8pm, Sun 9am–5pm), northeast of Medan Merdeka (catch bus #15 or #P15 from Jalan Kebon Sirih, to the north of Jalan Jaksa). Poste restante is currently at counter no. 55; although this counter is officially closed on Sunday, you can usually find someone who'll check your mail for you. There are also plenty of warpostel dotted around, including a number on Jalan Jaksa and Jalan Thamrin, and all the big international hotels have mail services.

Swimming The *Hotel Indonesia* by the Welcome Monument allows non-residents to use their pool for Rp7000 during the week, rising to a hefty Rp15,000 at weekends; the price includes a soft drink. You can also swim at the Ancol theme park (see p.110).

Teaching English It's currently relatively easy and profitable to earn money teaching English in Jakarta, and more and more expats are turning their backs on the more traditional centres – such as Japan and Singapore – to teach in Indonesia's capital. Although a TEFL certificate opens a few more doors, there are plenty of opportunities for those who do not possess this qualification. A good place to start looking for jobs is the English-language *Jakarta Post*. If you can't find anything there, try ringing around the language schools, most of which are based in the south of the city. They include the American Language Centre, Blok M, Jl Barito 2, Jakarta Selatan ☎021/7226449; the English Education Centre, Jl S Parman 68, Slipi ☎021/5323176; English First, Tamara Bank

Building, 4th floor, Jalan Sudirman, Jakarta Pusat ☎021/5203655; and the Korean Institute, Jl Bina Mirga 56, Jakarta Timur ☎021/8444958. These institutes, while they pay well (typically Rp5 million per month plus other perks), usually require a commitment of at least one school year (Sept–June). Part-time work, both at schools and in private homes, is also fairly easy to come by. Another alternative is to approach regular Jalan Jaksa expats, many of whom are teachers.

Telephone and fax There is no main government-run communications centre in the city. The Indosat building, however, at the southern end of Jalan Medan Merdeka Barat (no. 21), has a small international phone office (including IDD and HCD) on its ground floor (payment by cash only), and the two wartels near Jalan Jaksa – the RTQ warpostel at Jl Jaksa 17 (8am–midnight), and the wartel on Jalan Kebon Sirih Barat – offer a similar service, though the prices are a shade higher in these. IDD calls can be made from *Click Cybercafé* (see p.121), *Pappa's Café* (see p.112) and the lobby of the *Hotel Cipta* (see p.100) on Jalan Wahid Hasyim; the last of these is available 24hrs.

Travel agents and city tours Far and away the best travel agent on Jalan Jaksa is Global at no. 49. There are a few other good travel agencies around, including RQ Tours and Travel at no. 25 (☎021/3904501), PT Robertur Kencana at no. 20b, Jaksa Holiday at no. 11 (☎021/3140431), PT Pangandaran Wisata Indonesia at no. 35 (☎021/3151404) and WAFA at no.7. Another good tour company is Gray Line, Jl Tanjung Selor 17a (☎021/6308105), which runs tours around Jakarta for US$15–20. Most of the international hotels have a Gray Line representative, who can book tours for you.

Around Jakarta

Most excursions from Jakarta are dealt with in Chapter Two, on West Java, but the paradise islands of **Pulau Seribu** are included here as they come under the administrative boundary of Jakarta. The islands make for one of the most popular day-trips from the capital, particularly with expats working in the city.

Pulau Seribu

Called the **Pulau Seribu** (Thousand Islands), the string of coral atolls running south–north off the shores of Jakarta actually number no more than two hundred, and the figure is nearer one hundred at certain times, depending on tidal changes. The Pulau Seribu chain is in fact a **marine park**, although development has been allowed on 37 of the islands, where some fairly high-class resorts have sprung up.

There is no doubt that the islands are beautiful: the sand is white and fine, palm trees stretch all the way from the lush green interior to the water's edge, and the seas surrounding the northernmost islands are a delicious shade of blue. They are not, however, perfect; their proximity to Jakarta ensures that they are swamped by day-trippers every weekend, and the effects on the islands and their surrounding coral is, alas, only too manifest. But if your visit to Indonesia is confined to its capital, and if you want a brief taste of what you're missing by not travelling further afield, then a trip to Pulau Seribu is highly recommended, particularly on a weekday, when the chances are you'll have an island all to yourself.

The islands

Some of the Pulau Seribu are of historic interest, especially those nearest to Jakarta. **Pulau Onrust** was the last stop for General Coen in 1619, where he mustered his troops and prepared them for the onslaught on Jayakarta. The remains of a nineteenth-century shipyard and fort can still be seen here, once the most magnificent in Southeast Asia, according to James Cook, who stopped by in 1770. The foundations of another old Dutch fort, this time dating from the nineteenth century, can be found on nearby **Pulau Kelor**, and a third on **Pulau Bidadari**, once the home of a large leper colony and today the most popular destination for day-trippers from Jakarta. Even though it is just 15km away, Pulau Bidadari is so peaceful during the week that it feels a million miles from the capital – that is, until the raw sewage from Jakarta laps against your shins as you paddle in the sea. For this reason it's a lot more pleasant and hygienic to head to one of the northern islands, which can be reached by boat from Bidadari.

The waters around **Pulau Ayer**, another popular day-trip from the capital, are marginally better, but it's only when you get to **Pulau Panggang Besar**, 40km due north of Jakarta's Sukarno-Hatta international airport, that they really start to improve. **Pulau Kelapa**, another 10km further north, is the liveliest of the islands, and home to almost half of the atoll's 16,500 population, most of whom have yet to share in the benefits of tourism and continue to eke out a living from the ocean. A little further north of Kelapa is **Pulau Panjang**, home to the only airstrip in the area, which is handy for people who wish to go snorkelling around the reefs of **Pulau Kotok**, play golf on **Pulau Bira**, or stay at the most exclusive resort in the atoll, the *Pulau Seribu Marine Resort* on the islands of **Pulau Antuk Timur** and **Pulau Antuk Barat**. North of Bira are some of the most picturesque parts of Seribu: **Pulau Putri**, with some of the best restaurants in the atoll, as well as a transparent underwater tunnel where you can observe the marine life without getting your hair wet; **Pulau Pelangi**, home to some of the best beaches and the *Pelangi Resort*, which has tennis courts; and finally **Pulau Papa Theo**, an exquisite divers' island with simple but well-maintained huts powered by a temperamental generator.

Pulau Rambut, also known as **Pulau Burung**, is a bird sanctuary off the Tangerang shore to the west of the airport, with large breeding colonies of herons, egrets and cormorants as well as rarer species such as milky storks. If you are intending a weekend's bird-watching, take a taxi to the beach at **Tanjung Pasir** west of the airport, and from there the local ferry (Rp2000) takes 20–25 minutes to make the crossing to neighbouring **Pulau Untung Jawa**, where simple accommodation is available with mattresses on the floor (Rp30,000), as well as several excellent warung serving grilled fish and squid. To get to Pulau Burung, hire a boat from a local fisherman for the ten-minute crossing.

Practicalities

There is one daily public **ferry** to Pulau Seribu, leaving from the Ancol Marina (part of the Ancol fun park) and calling in at the islands of Tidung (Rp4000) and Kelapa (Rp6000). However, neither of these islands are "resorts", and you'll need to charter or rent a second boat to take you to the other islands. To rent a speedboat from Ancol for one day costs at least one million rupiah, but as the outermost islands are only a couple of hours away it is possible to cover a lot of the atoll in that time.

The resorts, some of which charge US dollars, also operate their own private speedboats to whisk you to their islands: most boats depart from the Ancol Marina at about 10am. Only return tickets are available, with the costs varying from island to island. The resorts, such as those on Pulau Pelangi and Pulau Putri, generally include lunch on their trips, while others, such as the Pulau Seribu and Bidadari resorts, charge an entry fee. The rates are also a little cheaper (and sometimes free) if you are staying overnight in the resort. Return fares include: Pulau Bidadari (Rp25,000, plus Rp6000 entry fee), Pulau Ayer

(Rp51,000), Pulau Putri (US$55), Pulau Pelangi (US$55) and Pulau Papa Theo (US$50).

Accommodation

Accommodation on all of the islands, though expensive, is not luxurious. Rooms can be booked before you arrive by visiting the resort representatives in Jakarta. Be warned that rates can rise by up to a third at most of these places during the weekends, and be certain to find out exactly what is included in the package – whether there are any trips to the neighbouring islands and so on. Make sure meals are included in the package too, as the resort restaurants are often the only option on the island and tend to be expensive. The following is a selection of the best and most popular resorts, along with their agents in Jakarta, listed – with the exception of *Pulau Seribu Marine Resort* – by island, not by the name of the establishment.

Pulau Ayer PT Sarotama Prima Perkasa, Jl Ir. H. Juanda III/6, Jakarta ⓣ021/342031. Resort consisting of 42 land and floating cottages plus three larger bungalows, along with tennis, volleyball and badminton courts, swimming pools, and a dive shop with diving equipment and jet skis for rent. ❻

Pulau Bidadari PT Seabreez Indonesia, Terminal Pulau Bidadari, Marina Jaya Ancol, Jakarta ⓣ021/680048. Resort positioned at the southern end of the atoll with bar, disco, and both land and floating cottages. ❼

Pulau Kotok Duta Merlin Shopping Arcade, Jakarta ⓣ021/362948. Excellent surfing and diving is available just offshore at this beautiful resort, much favoured by Japanese tourists. ❻

Pulau Papa Theo PT Batemuri Tours, *Wisata International Hotel*, Jalan Thamrin, PO Box 2313 ⓣ021/320807. The most spartan accommodation of all the Pulau Seribu resorts, where the simple thatched bungalows are situated right on the beach. ❺

Pulau Pelangi PT Pulau Seribu Paradise, Jl Wahid Hasyim 69, Jakarta ⓣ021/335535. All rooms on beautiful Pelangi come with air-con, fridge and an outdoor shower. ❼

Pulau Putri PT Pulau Seribu Paradise, Jl Wahid Hasyim 69, Jakarta ⓣ021/335535. Balinese cottages with traditional thatched roofs are the main feature of this exquisite resort in the north of the atoll. ❼

Pulau Seribu Marine Resort PT Pantara Wisata Jaya, Jakarta ⓣ021/3805017. The most exclusive of the resorts, divided between the islands of Pulau Antuk Timur and Barat, which attracts Japanese tourists by the shipload. Facilities are fairly luxurious, and the diving shop is one of the best in the archipelago. ❼

Travel details

Trains

Jakarta Gambir to: Bandung (hourly; 2hr 20min–3hr); Bogor (every 30min; 1hr/Pakuan express, 9 daily; 55 min); Cilacap (1 daily; 7hr 20min); Cirebon (18 daily; 5hr); Malang (1 daily; 18hr 5min); Merak (2 daily; 4hr); Purworketo (9 daily; 4hr 20min–6hr 10min); Semarang (7 daily; 5hr 35min–9hr 15min); Solobapan, Solo (4 daily; 7hr–10hr 25min); Surabaya (5 daily; 9hr–14hr 30min); Yogyakarta (6 daily; 6hr 50min–8hr 40min).

Buses

It is impossible to give the frequency with which bemos and buses run, as timetables change all the time, and are never strictly adhered to at the best of times. Nevertheless, on the most popular and shorter routes you should be able to count on getting a ride within the hour, especially before noon.

Jakarta (Pulo Gadung station, unless otherwise stated) to: Balaraja (1hr); Banda Aceh (60hr); Bandung (from Kampung Rambutan station; 4hr 30min); Bogor (from Kampung Rambutan station; 45min); Bukittinggi (30hr); Cileungi (1hr); Denpasar (24hr); Garut (5hr); Jonggol (1hr 30min); Kotabumi (2hr); Medan (from Pulo Gadung or Kalideres; 2 days); Merak (from Kalideres; 3hr); Padang (from Pulo Gadung or Kalideres; 32hr); Puworketo (8hr); Semarang (8hr 30min); Solo (13hr); Surabaya (15hr); Tegal (6hr); Yogyakarta (12hr).

Special trains from Jakarta

To	From	Name	Departs	Time
Bandung	Gambir	*Argogede*	10am	2hr 20min
			6pm	2hr 20min
	Gambir	*Parahiyangan*	hourly	3hr 30min
Cirebon	Kota	*Cirebon Eksp*	6.45am	2hr 50min
	Kota		10.10am	5hr 21min
	Gambir		4.55pm	3hr 4min
Semarang	Gambir	*Argobromo*	8.35pm	5hr 35min
	Gambir	*Senja Ekseku*	10.50am	6hr 52min
	Gambir	*Fajar Bis*	7.40am	6hr 27min
Solobapan (Solo)	Gambir	*Senja Utama II*	7.40pm	9hr 42min
Surabaya	Gambir	*Argobromo*	8.35pm	9hr
	Kota	*Bima*	6pm	13hr 50min
	Pasar Senen	*Kertajaya*	5pm	11hr 38min
	Gambir	*Jayabaya*	1.45pm	11hr 48min
	Pasar Senen	*GBM Selatan*	noon	14hr 30min
	Pasar Senen	*GBM Utama*	3.40pm	12hr 21min
	Kota	*Parcel Eksp*	6.05pm	12hr 48min
Yogyakarta	Gambir	*Fajar Utama*	6.10am	7hr 50min
	Gambir	*Fajar Utama II*	6.20am	7hr 45min
	Gambir	*Senja Utama*	7.20pm	8hr 21min
	Gambir	*Senja Utama II*	7.40pm	8hr 41min

Pelni ferries

All Pelni ferries leave from Tanjung Priok, where the new terminal building has made the wait for boarding somewhat more agreeable. For a chart of the Pelni routes, see p.42

Jakarta to: Batam (*KM Kelud* every 4 days; 24hr); Belawan, Medan (*KM Kelud* every 4 days; 2 days); Denpasar (*KM Dobonsolo* 2 monthly; 39hr); Kijang (*KM Bukit Raya* 2 monthly; 39hr/*KM Kerinci* 2 monthly; 24hr/*KM Sirimau* 2 monthly; 41hr); Kumai (*KM Lawit* 2 monthly; 3–4 days); Nias (*KM Kambuna* 2 monthly; 52hr; *KM Lambelu* 2 monthly; 2 days); Padang (*KM Kambuna* 2 monthly; 29hr); Pontianak (*KM Lawit* 4 monthly; 31hr/*KM Ambulu* 3 weekly; 37hr/*KM Tilongkabila* monthly; 31hr); Sampit (*KM Tilongkabila* monthly; 44hr); Makassar(*KM Lambelu* 2 monthly; 2 days/*KM Kambuna* 2 monthly; 2 days/*KM Sirimau* 2 monthly; 3 days/*KM Bukit Siguntang* 2 monthly; 2 days).

Other ferries

Jakarta Sunda Kelapa to: Pontianak (*Kapuas Express* 2 weekly; 19hr).

Flights

Jakarta to: Balikpapan (7 daily; 2hr 10min); Banda Aceh (daily; 3hr 45min); Bandung (10 daily; 40min); Banjarmasin (5 daily; 1hr 40min); Batam (8 daily; 1hr 35min); Bengkulu (2 daily; 1hr 15min); Denpasar (16 daily; 1hr 50min); Dili (4 weekly; 4hr 40min); Jambi (3 daily; 1hr 20min); Jayapura; (2 daily; 8hr); Manado (4 daily; 4hr 45min); Mataram (6 weekly; 3hr 15min); Medan (16 daily; 2hr 10min); Merauke (3 weekly; 10hr 20min); Padang (7 daily; 1hr 40min); Palangkaraya (daily; 1hr 45min); Palembang (14 daily; 1hr 5min); Palu (daily; 3hr 15min); Pangkalpinang (3 daily; 1hr 5min); Pekanbaru (7 daily; 1hr 40min); Pontianak (9 daily; 1hr 30min); Semarang (17 daily; 55min); Surabaya (33 daily; 1hr 20min); Surakarta (4 daily; 1hr 5min); Tanjungpandan (daily; 1hr); Ujung Padang (12 daily; 2hr 20min); Yogyakarta (14 daily; 1hr 5min).

2

West Java

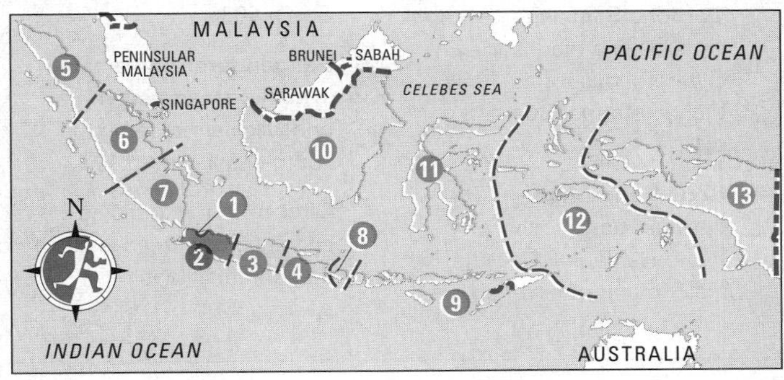
MALAYSIA
PENINSULAR MALAYSIA
SINGAPORE
BRUNEI
SABAH
SARAWAK
CELEBES SEA
PACIFIC OCEAN
INDIAN OCEAN
AUSTRALIA
N
1
2
3
4
5
6
7
8
9
10
11
12
13

CHAPTER 2 Highlights

* **Krakatau** The world's most famous volcano, facing Carita Beach on the Sundra Straits. **See p.138**
* **Ujung Kulon national park** The last refuge of Java rhino in rainforest setting on the Sunda Straits. **See p.139**
* **Bogor Botanical Gardens** Stunning gardens in a mountain city notorious for its thunderstorms. **See p.141**
* **Gede Pangrango national park** A UN World Heritage Site with major stand of bird-rich mountain forest on twin volcanoes. **See p.153**
* **Gunung Patuha** Hike in a little-visited mountain area above the scenic Ciwidey Valley, with a crater lake and dense forests. **See p.166**
* **Garut/Cipanas** Relax in the hot springs of "The Switzerland of Java". **See p.168**
* **Pangandaran** A dramatic surf-washed beach and wildlife refuge on the south coast. **See p.171**
* **Cirebon** An untouristed coastal city with no less than three sultans' palaces. **See p.178**

2

West Java

One of the most populous places in all of Asia, **West Java** might appear to the traveller to be one dense continuum of human settlement. Even so, the region is still characterized by great natural beauty. Its central spine is the most mountainous part of Java; here, and towards the southern coast, the land is dominated by dozens of tightly clustered volcanoes, many of which are still very evidently active. Agriculture of all kinds flourishes among the highlands; the fertile slopes of these peaks and craters are often given over to mammoth tea plantations, which thrive on the province's plentiful rainfall. By contrast, the northern coastal plain of West Java is a flat and fairly drab sweep that was mostly reclaimed from malarial swamps in the nineteenth century.

The well-worn travellers' route from Jakarta to Central Java passes through Bogor, Bandung and Pangandaran, but there are plenty of interesting destinations only slightly off the trail. **Krakatau**, one of the world's most famous and destructive volcanoes, is sandwiched between the west coast of Java and Sumatra; still extremely active, it offers a taste of the unpredictable power of nature. The **Ujong Kulon national park** on the southwest peninsula gives a glimpse of the island's wild inhabitants such as leopards, monkeys, crocodiles, turtles and the Banteng ox. Its most famous occupant, though, is the world's rarest large land mammal, the **Javan rhinoceros** – only an estimated seventy animals exist here and in Vietnam. Inland and east of the west coast beaches, the playground of Jakarta's wealthy, is an insular cluster of tiny villages whose inhabitants are known as the **Badui**. These isolated tribes are thought to be the descendants of the original Sundanese people, who inhabited the highlands before the advent of Islam. Their traditional society has resisted the Indonesian government's attempts to envelop them and erode their way of life, and visitors require a permit to visit the outer villages – the inner villages are completely off-limits to outsiders.

South of Jakarta is the city of **Bogor**, formerly known as Buitenzorg ("without care"), with its famous Botanical Gardens and presidential palace. The gardens have a spectacular extension on the edge of the Gede Pangrango national park at **Cibodas**, which is surrounded by montane forest at high altitude between Bogor and West Java's capital city of **Bandung**. Colonial Dutch architecture, modern shopping centres and the gaudy appeal of "Jeans Street" are the main attractions here, though there is a profusion of waterfalls, hot springs, tea plantations and volcanic craters worth visiting around the city.

Probably the most popular stop for visitors to West Java lies right at its boundary with Central Java – **Pangandaran**, a seaside town with superb seafood, crashing surf and endless expanses of sand. The variety of possible excursions

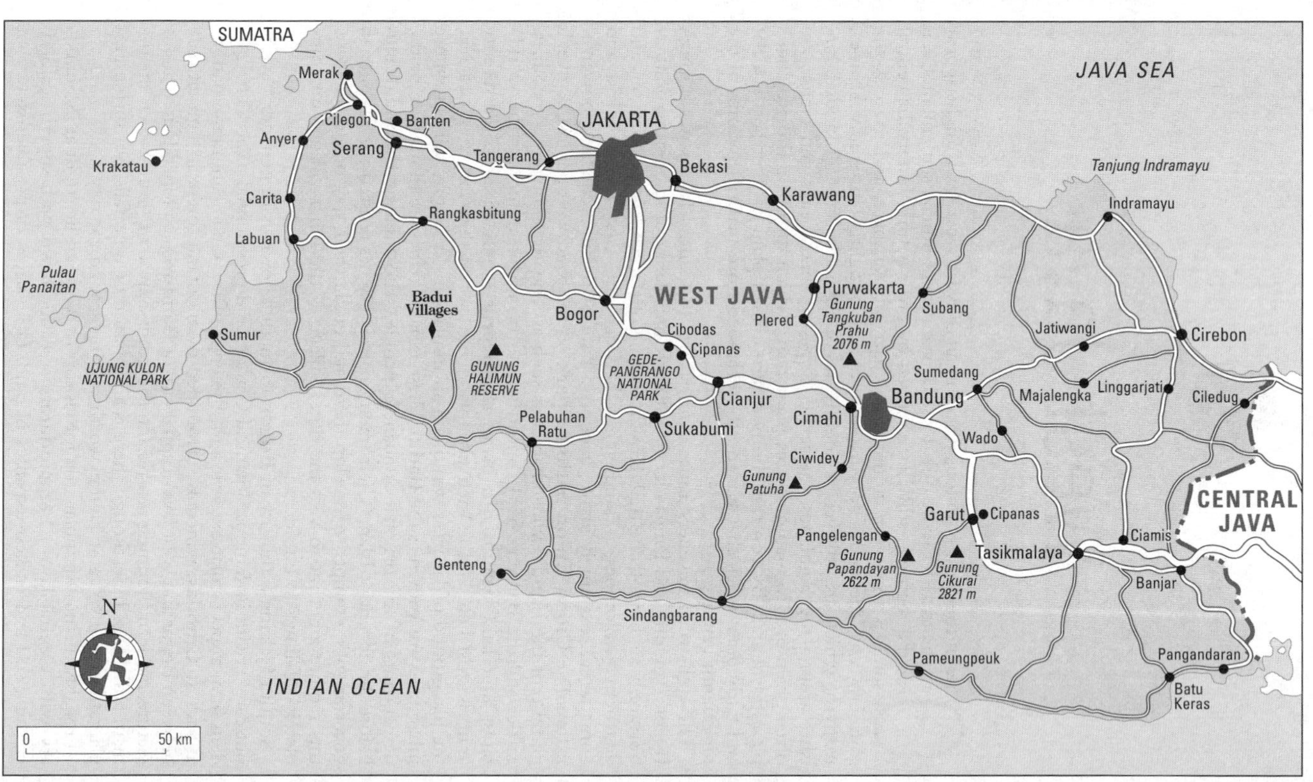
SUMATRA
JAVA SEA
Merak
Cilegon
Banten
Anyer
Serang
JAKARTA
Krakatau
Tangerang
Bekasi
Tanjung Indramayu
Carita
Karawang
Indramayu
Rangkasbitung
Labuan
Pulau Panaitan
Purwakarta
Badui Villages
WEST JAVA
Gunung Tangkuban Prahu 2076 m
Subang
Bogor
Plered
Jatiwangi
Cirebon
Sumur
Cibodas
Cipanas
GUNUNG HALIMUN RESERVE
UJUNG KULON NATIONAL PARK
GEDE-PANGRANGO NATIONAL PARK
Sumedang
Bandung
Majalengka
Linggarjati
Ciledug
Cianjur
Cimahi
Pelabuhan Ratu
Sukabumi
Wado
Ciwidey
Gunung Patuha
CENTRAL JAVA
Garut
Cipanas
Pangelengan
Ciamis
Gunung Papandayan 2622 m
Tasikmalaya
Gunung Cikurai 2821 m
Genteng
Banjar
Sindangbarang
N
Pameungpeuk
Pangandaran
Batu Keras
INDIAN OCEAN
0
50 km

around the town and the friendly atmosphere of some of its travellers' enclaves are a great draw, and some visitors end up staying for weeks. On the north coast, near the boundary with Central Java is the seaport of **Cirebon**, with its ancient kratons and museums, rarely visited but rich in historical interest.

Java's rainy season lasts from January to March, during which time you are guaranteed heavy rain every day and spectacular electrical storms, generally in the afternoons. West Java's tourist attractions are flooded with domestic visitors at weekends and on all national holidays. However, transport around West Java is better than anywhere else in Indonesia; train lines join most of the major cities, and buses and luxury coaches regularly connect destinations within and without the region.

Railway buffs should enjoy the **rail journeys** through the West Java mountains, some of the finest in the country. Between Plered and Bandung there are a dozen viaducts, the most spectacular lying between Cisomang and Cikadongdong. The journey between Bandung and Tasikmalaya also takes you through some dramatic volcanic scenery. For the really hardy, the run from Bogor to Sukabumi around the slopes of Gunung Salak may be worth the discomfort of some of the most run-down rolling stock in Java in order to experience the spectacular mountain views.

Cyclists and **motorcyclists** should also make the most of this province. Cyclists will appreciate the agreeable flat stretches, such as that west from Cirebon across the rice plains towards Jatiwangi, while there are also many hill climbs to draw the adventurous, most through superb scenery. Among these are the run to Subang from Bandung through the pine and bamboo forests around Tanjungsari, from Jatiwangi to Subang, and also the climb from Soreang to the hot springs of Cimanggu on the slopes of Gunung Patuha southwest of Bandung, by way of the market town of Ciwidey.

Some history

The Sundanese who inhabit West Java today – and are Java's second largest ethnic group – are also its indigenous people. The first major power in the region was the Hindu **Tarumanegara empire**, which governed the area as early as the fifth century, whose most famous king, Purnavaraman, has his footprint immortalized in a rock at Ciampea near Bogor (see p.142). It is thought that Hinduism probably came to Java from southern India around the beginning of the first millennium; the Hindus arrived from southern India to trade and passed on to the native Sundanese the legacy of their religion.

Much later, in the fourteenth century, the **Pajajaran empire** was formed, with its base as Bogor. The comparatively short period of Pajajaran's existence is seen as the Sundanese heyday, providing the source of most of the popular heroes and legends of West Javan culture, and constituting the last and pre-eminent period of Sundanese power and autonomy. The Pajajaran people are thought to have been the first to settle what is now Jakarta, but long ago disappeared as a separate ethnic entity.

The history of the Hindu Sundanese came to an end with the defeat of king **Sri Baduga Maharaja** in around the fifteenth century. In the 1500s, the Muslim state of Demak sent prophets from Mecca into Southeast Asia in an attempt to convert the people to Islam; the Muslim army based itself in Banten, extending its influence to conquer Pajajaran and most of West Java. The most important of the prophets sent into Java was Syarif Hidayatullah, who managed to convert the strategic harbour towns of Banten, Cirebon and Kelapa Sunda (modern Jakarta) before his death in 1568. Banten was thereafter to become the most vital port in Southeast Asia, taking over from Portuguese Malacca.

Sundanese culture

The lush valleys of the province were the first places to be settled permanently, around the fifth century AD. The first inhabitants and their descendants are known as the **Sundanese**, who even today make up 75 percent of the province's population. They maintain their own language, although really only as a supplement to Bahasa Indonesia, and distinct forms of dance, theatre and cuisine. The language is similar to Javanese and Balinese in that it has three basic levels, depending on the social rank of the speaker and the addressee.

Followers of the archaic **Sundanese religions** originally worshipped the spirits of their ancestors. Villages were probably arranged, as today's Badui villages, with the elders of sacred and protected inner settlements acting as holy priests, dictating customs to the peasantry who inhabited the outer villages. Apart from the tiny enclaves of the Badui in the Kendeng mountains and Kampung Naga near Tasikmalaya, Sundanese religions have dissolved into mainstream Islam, and most of the people are now staunch Muslim.

Most Sundanese **art forms** have evolved within the strict social divide of the class system, and all of the different styles of dance and music were designed either for the elite or the masses. **Jaipongan**, for example, is a form of popular dance accompanied by weird music; originally performed by prostitutes, it can be quite bawdy and erotic. The style also acquired certain nuances of Indonesia's martial art form, **pencak silat**, when Dutch plantation owners tried to ban its practice. Jaipongan is now danced with the accompaniment of a drummer and a few gamelan players, and members of the audience are often invited on stage to take part. An art form that developed almost entirely for the court and the elite was **gamelan degung**, an ensemble of gongs, metalophones and a flute, the instruments themselves becoming sacred possessions for the Priangan, West Java's hereditary rulers.

The original Sundanese art form, however, is **pantun sunda**. A pantun is a story, recited by a solo, often blind, male performer with supposed supernatural powers, using narration, dialogue and songs to tell stories of ancestor heroes, the storyteller accompanying himself with a *kacapi* (zither). Performances are marathon affairs,

In the late sixteenth century, Western colonial powers first began to take interest in **Banten**. The Portuguese and British had the first trade interests here but they were to be utterly superseded by the Dutch. Under the Dutch, the towns of Bogor, Bandung and Batavia expanded into bustling cities with a European feel, and much of the countryside and its people were put to work growing tea and coffee.

The Dutch East India Company was dissolved in 1799, but Java remained under Dutch protection. This period was remarkable for the creation of the **Great Post Road**, which ran from Anyer on the west coast to Panarukan on the east and which cost the lives of some 30,000 Javanese labourers. However, Java was soon lost to the British, and by 1811 was governed by Sir Thomas Stamford Raffles, who later earned fame as the founder of Singapore. Raffles was an enlightened reformer, albeit paternalistic, who might have brought significant change to Java had he had more time. His monumental two-volume *History of Java* remains a major reference work. There was little or no attempt made by any of the colonialists to bring European education or civilization to West Java; instead, they concentrated their efforts on pacifying the population by disinheriting their leaders. This neglect had far-reaching effects: law and order degenerated until towns such as Banten were considered too dangerous for Westerners to venture into, and the Cirebon area suffered a terrible famine that left hundreds of thousands of Indonesians dead. In response, beginning at 8pm, directly after the Islamic evening prayer, and finishing at 4am, before the morning prayer. These shows are usually commissioned by a family for a *hajat* (ritual feast), circumcision, wedding or rice harvest ceremony, the primary reason being that the storyteller is not just an entertainer but a shaman; the teller is believed to be able to contact the spirits and receive blessings for the *hajat*. Contemporary *pantun sunda* performances are more concerned with entertainment than spirituality, and are likely to poke fun at modern preoccupations such as materialism. Shows are much shorter and often include a bowed-lute player, a female singer and a full gamelan orchestra.

In many ways closely related to *pantun sunda* is the Sundanese puppet drama **Wayang golek**. In contrast to the shadow plays of the rest of Java that use flat leather puppets, wayang golek uses three-dimensional wooden rod puppets. The stories are traditionally taken loosely from the *Mahabharata* and *Ramayana*, and can be a potent satirical weapon. Modern puppeteers often use the wooden characters to make caustic political comment and crude, near-the-knuckle humour that human performers would never get away with. The orchestrator of the wayang golek is the highly-skilled *dalang*, who operates all the characters while singing and reproducing the voices giving sound effects and emphasis by tapping on the wooden puppet's chest and playing a type of xylophone with his feet. He is also considered to be a sort of shaman, and someone with a divine gift. Plays last from 9pm until 5 or 6am, with hundreds of different voices and songs – they're exhausting even for the spectators, particularly as they're accompanied by the constant noise of a nine-man gamelan orchestra. A good *dalang* commands an immense salary, and the profession, far from dying out, is flourishing.

Wayang topeng, or mask dance, is a similar show found almost exclusively in Cirebon. It's generally accepted that the wayang forms were developed to convey Islamic teachings, used to mould audience opinion on political matters and provide information. Wayang was certainly commandeered in the 1960s to publicize government programmes.

the Muslim prince Diponegoro began the "Java War", which lasted from 1825 until 1830. At the beginning of the twentieth century a new nationalist movement began to grow. One branch of the movement was to intensify the passion of its peasant members in their Islamic identity; the other branch went on to become the Indonesian Communist Party (PKI). The PKI became the world's third largest communist party, with many front organisations. Slavishly loyal to Moscow, the PKI staged an adventurist rising at Madiun, East Java in 1948. It became a fundamental component of Sukarno's nation-building politics, but was feared and loathed by the Right, which used the bungled coup d'etat of September 30 1965 as an excuse to murder hundreds of thousands of PKI members and sympathisers. Estimates of the number of victims of this bloodbath, one of the greatest of the twentieth century, run as high as two million, and, although the real figure may be lower, Indonesia still has to come to terms with the slaughter.

Since the fall of Suharto in late May 1998, political changes affecting Indonesia have promoted greater regional consciousness. West Java has been divided, with the creation of the new province of Banten, while moves afoot may lead to Cirebon and its surrounding regencies forming another new province (Indonesia had 27 provinces, including the occupied territory of East Timor, but now has 32).

Krakatau and the west coast

The west coast of Java is not generally included in either package tourist or backpacker itineraries, despite the two exceptional attractions of **Krakatau** and the **Ujong Kulon national park**; permits to both are required, as is a lot of planning if you're travelling independently. Between Jakarta and Merak is the historic pepper-trading port of **Banten**, a minor pilgrimage point for Muslims and a major historical site. Much of the West Java coastline is taken up by the exclusive beach resorts of **Anyer**, **Carita** and **Labuan**, easy weekend escapes from the pollution of Jakarta and almost entirely the haven of the city's rich.

Banten and Pulau Dua

In the fifteenth century, the port of **BANTEN** was probably the largest and most important in all of Southeast Asia. Today, Banten is a tiny cluster of Islamic buildings and ruins, remembered only by Javanese Muslims, who recognize its importance in the history of Indonesian Islam. It's very much a day-trip destination, offering some interesting buildings and an air of faded glory. If you're coming to Banten from Jakarta, take one of the frequent non-AC buses from the Kalideres bus station for the two-hour journey (Rp5000) to **Serang**, a grotty town about 90km to the west. From the Serang bus terminal, it's a ten-kilometre minibus ride (20min, Rp 1000) to Banten. There's no accommodation in town, but there are lots of warung near the square selling soups and rice dishes; there's also lots of tourist tat on sale.

In its heyday, Banten was a huge, bustling city where Ming porcelain was traded with the exotic spices of Maluku, and the Chinese set up trading posts and lived in communities alongside Vietnamese, Thais, Japanese, Arabs and seafarers from Sulawesi. In 1527, Sultan Hasanudin's Muslim army seized Banten and proclaimed him its king, after which Banten became a gateway into Indonesia for Islam, which quickly took root in West Java and has remained the most powerful religion. The thriving port's most important commodity was pepper, with over 1500 tonnes exported each year, but silk, velvet, paper, gold, Chinese fans, ivory, rubies, medicine, olive oil, carpets and perfumes, honey, fruit and rice were also traded here. In ancient Javanese, *banten* means "rebellion" or "refusal", and accordingly Banten's natives resisted Dutch occupation with frequent uprisings, until 1808, when the Dutch tired of this resistance and destroyed most of Banten, blockading the harbour and forcing traders to use their port of Sunda Kelapa in Batavia (Jakarta). After this, Banten was utterly bypassed by trade and fell into ruin, pretty much the state it's in now.

The Town

As you come into Banten, the first sight of note is the **Istana Kaibon**, the palace of Queen Aisayah. It's now a crumbling ruin with an impressive main gateway and thick stone walls and archways, and is undergoing a long-running restoration programme, with limited results. Continuing towards the fortified alun-alun, the town's centre, the roadsides become crowded with gaudy vending carts. On the western side of the square is the **Mesjid Agung**, the mosque built in 1566 by Sultan Hasanuddin (whose name adorns streets all over Indonesia). It's a large building with a five-tiered roof and is the main attraction for domestic tourists. At the north of the mosque lies the royal cemetery, where four former sultans of Banten are buried, and nearby a squat **minaret** with a spiral staircase inside and two circular balconies offering limited views of the surrounding old town. In one corner of the square sits an engraved bronze cannon, and in another are two stone thrones dating from the fifteenth century. Close to the eastern side of the square, the **archeological museum** (Tues–Sat 9am–4pm; Rp1000) contains stacks of weapons, bronze and brass kris blades, ironwork, coins, pieces of terracotta and Ming porcelain. There are also a few examples of iron spikes once used by Banten's **Debus players**, Islamic ascetics who have for centuries specialized in self-mutilation, the effects of which are rendered harmless by meditation. In Banten there are still regular performances of Debus on Saturday nights at Jalan Kebonjati 34 (Rp5000).

Pulau Dua

In Banten Bay lies **Pulau Dua**, a small island with a big reputation for birdlife. Since 1937 it's been a protected national park for migratory birds, but also has a burgeoning population of egrets, cormorants, pelicans, herons and sea eagles. It lies only 1km to the east of Banten and can easily be accessed at low tide, when you can walk all the way over to it across mud flats, although take care not to get cut off by the water. At all other times you will have to charter a boat to reach the island.

Merak

At the extreme northwestern tip of Java, **MERAK** is the port for ferries across the Sunda Straits to Bakauheni on **Sumatra**. The port is extremely busy and there's no reason to stay here, though if you should get stuck the *Hotel Anda* at Jalan Florida 4 offers basic rooms with fan and mandi (☎0254/71041; ❶). **Ferries** to Sumatra from Merak leave about every thirty minutes and take ninety minutes; crowds of buses connect with the ferries to take you on to Bandar Lampung, Palembang or destinations further north in Sumatra. Trains to Merak run from Jakarta's Tanah Abang station, while frequent buses to Merak depart from Kalideres.

Anyer

The most prominent building in **ANYER**, which lies 15km south of Merak, is a delightful forty-metre **lighthouse** built by Queen Wilhelmina of Holland in 1885 as a memorial to the townspeople killed by the eruption of Krakatau. Its gleaming white plaster walls and classic shape offer a rare touch of elegance on this overdeveloped coast, and the views from the top are beautiful (although you may have problems finding the caretaker to let you in). Anyer was also the starting point for the **Great Post Road**, begun by the Dutch in the nineteenth century, running 1000km from here to the eastern tip of Java. Off the coast of Anyer lies Pulau Sangeang, an uninhabited island with vast areas of untouched jungle. Diving companies in town offer tours to the reefs that surround Sangeang, which boasts a sunken wreck and perfect coral formations swarming with tropical fish.

Accommodation

There are no road numbers or exact addresses for any of the buildings along the main coast road, so all **accommodation** is described in the order in which it appears as you head south from the market.

Pondok Sanghiang Close to Anyer village ☎0254/602910. Reasonable rooms with air-con and attached mandi. The restaurant provides decent fried-chicken, squid or prawn dishes for around Rp10,000 per person, and breakfast is included. ❺

Kalimaya Resort, Tours and Travel ☎0254/601266. Eleven rooms and cottages, from simple doubles or triples to detached bungalows with kitchen and living room for up to eight people; most have air-con and all have bathrooms. The tour office specializes in diving tours for certified divers, at around US$60 a day. The restaurant serves European, Chinese and Indonesian food, from nasi goreng (Rp8000) to lobster (Rp80,000). ❻–❽

Ryugu Hotel Putri Duyung ⓣ0254/601239. A Japanese-style resort, built to cater for the small number of Japanese expatriates working in Jakarta. Each room has its own Japanese name, a garden, telephone, fax, hot water, air-con and TV; there's also a profusion of karaoke facilities and Japanese food. ❼–❽

Hotel Sangyang Indah ⓣ & ⓕ0254/601299. This luxury hotel specializes in sports, with tennis, volleyball, badminton, billiards, swimming and watersports available. All rooms have satellite TV, air-con, hot water and telephone. ❼–❽

Eating

The vast majority of people staying in Anyer opt for the hotel restaurants, which almost without exception serve a variety of Chinese dishes, steaks, hamburgers and seafood. There are several small warung opposite the *Pisita Anyer* beach resort, mostly frequented by staff from the local hotels, selling basic, inexpensive food such as nasi campur and nasi goreng. Opposite the *Hotel Sanghiang Indah* lies the *Warung Ikan Bakar*, the building with the thatched roof and the wartel adjoining its restaurant; they offer an excellent range of fresh seafood: shrimps, squid and whatever fish has been caught that day, served as a complete meal with rice and vegetables for around Rp12,000. As with everywhere else around the country, local prices were affected early 2002 by fuel price hikes.

Carita

CARITA's resort strip starts about 20km south of Anyer market and 7km north of Labuan. A profusion of quality hotels line the main road running parallel to the beach, but, unlike Anyer, there are also a few places in the inexpensive and moderate range. Carita can be quite an easy and welcome escape from the city; a bus from Kalideres bus station in Jakarta, usually changing to a colt at Labuan, takes just over three hours. If you do have to change at Labuan terminal, don't get conned into taking transport round to the stop for colts to Carita – just walk two minutes towards the seafront and round to the right.

Though Carita boasts one of the most sheltered stretches of sea in Java, at weekends the bay reverberates with the constant brain-numbing roar of jet skis and powerboats, and it's not a particularly relaxing place for a swim. Carita is, however, the best spot to arrange **organized tours** to Krakatau and Ujong Kulon: the Black Rhino tour company (ⓣ0253/81072) on the opposite side of the road from the marina is recommended. A full four-day and three-night tour to Ujong Kulon costs US$170 per person for a minimum of four people, a day-tour to Krakatau costs US$30–50. Guides who approach you at your hotel or on the street often quote ludicrous prices and can be totally unqualified. If **watersports** are your thing, the Marina Lippo Carita (ⓣ0253/81525) offers everything from jet skiing to parasailing, as well as tours to Krakatau and Putri Gundul for snorkelling. Sample prices include Rp12,000 for fifteen minutes in a speedboat, or Rp80,000 for thirty minutes' water-skiing.

Between Carita and Anyer is the small beach of **Karang Bolong** – a massive boulder was dumped here by the tidal waves that followed the eruption of Krakatau, and it's now a popular attraction for Indonesian tourists. There's a Rp2000 charge to use the beach.

Accommodation

All **accommodation** is on or close to the main seaside road, known as Jalan Carita Raya or Jalan Pantai Carita. There are no building numbers, so all are listed here in the order they appear along this road heading north from Labuan town. All hotels and guesthouses increase their prices dramatically at weekends and as much as triple them during national holidays, when it's advisable to book as much as a month in advance.

Cinde Wulung ⓣ0253/83307. Cheap rooms are available here at off-peak times, and bargaining is advisable. All rooms have either fan or air-con and come with en-suite mandi. Additional services include massage and a seafood restaurant – the spicy grilled fish is recommended. ❹
Pondok Karang Sari (no phone). Large family rooms for four to eight people inside huge, spotless wooden cottages with thatched roofs. ❺
Pondok Bakkara ⓣ0253/81260. One of the cheapest places here, though not especially clean and often full. All rooms have mandi inside but, unusually, no fan. ❶
Sunset View ⓣ0253/81075. Friendly staff, clean rooms and interesting decor make this one of the best-value places on the west coast. They are in the process of building a café, but until it's finished your "full breakfast" will be just a cup of tea. ❷
Yussi Penginapan ⓣ0253/81074. The cheapest rooms have shared facilities and are rather dingy; the upstairs rooms with air-con and mandi are a little better. ❸
Carita Krakatau ⓣ0253/83027. Behind the restaurant of the same name, these spotless tile-floored rooms with mandi, fan and breakfast included are the best deal in town. ❷
New Gogona ⓣ0253/81122. The brand-new block of rooms with air-con are pristine, the older ones with fan are grotty and best avoided. ❷–❸
Naida Beak (no phone). Has a variety of family bungalows and is designed to take large budget-conscious groups, cramming up to ten people into each room. Single and double rooms are also available. ❸–❺
Penginapan Joe ⓣ0253/82887. The rooms here are a little dark, but the proprietors are keen to bargain midweek. ❸
Krakatau Seaside ⓣ0253/81081. Stunning houses on a private stretch of beach, all faithful reproductions of Indonesian *rumah adat*. The facades are beautiful two-storey copies of Acehnese, Torajan, Minahasan and Badui houses, while inside they have air-con, TV and even billiard tables. ❼–❽
Lucia Cottages ⓣ0253/81262. One of the few places in Indonesia that actually offers lower prices for tourists, with detached bungalows or single/double rooms around a swimming pool and some of the comfiest beds in Carita. ❸–❺

Eating

The public parts of the beach are lined with food carts selling *murtabak*, sate and soto. The main road has many **warung** selling cold drinks, and some basic food such as *ikan bakar* and nasi goreng.

Café de Paris At the 14km Anyer marker. A plush air-con place with a variety of European and Chinese dishes and seafood. It's comparatively pricey, at around Rp18,000 for a hamburger.
Carita Krakatau 30m towards Anyer from the marina, on the inland side of the road. The menu offers a limited seafood selection; a good fish steak or prawn dish will cost around Rp10,000.
Diminati Opposite the entrance to the marina. Boasts the cheapest cold beer in town at Rp4500, and does an excellent *kakap* fish steak complete with vegetables and chips for Rp10,000.
Marina Lippo Carita On the beach in the prominent marina complex that is about halfway along Carita's resort strip ⓣ0253/81525. Great food but wildly overpriced; the Thai spring rolls are only Rp9000, but fish and seafood dishes start at Rp30,000.
Pasundan Kusing 100m short of the *Lucia Cottages* on the inland side of the road. A small Sundanese smorgasbord with fried chicken or beef, sweet-and-sour corn soup, fried *tempe* and *tahu*, rice and vegetables costs just Rp5000. A mixed hotplate with beef, prawns, squid and quails' eggs is Rp20,000.

Labuan

LABUAN is a dull and dirty port town serving as a transport crossroads for the glitzy coastal resorts further north. Regular buses come directly here from Jakarta's Kalideres terminal (3hr), while a slow and smoky steam train chugs once a day between Labuan and Merak, taking about twice as long as the bus. The PHPA office in Labuan claims that the trains that run this route are the oldest still in service worldwide, one having been built in Germany in 1899, one in the Netherlands in 1909, and another in Switzerland in 1916.

Although not especially appealing in itself, Labuan does have some cheap (though poor-value) accommodation which is useful at weekends, when everywhere from here to Anyer will be crowded and very expensive. It's also the best place to arrange **independent tours** to Krakatau and the Ujong Kulon national park, and the place to get the essential park **permits** (Rp5000). There's a small information centre inside with photographs, charts and commentary in English to give you a taster of what the parks offer; the people who work here are very friendly and helpful, though they don't speak much English. The BRI **bank** on the south side of the bus terminal will change cash and travellers' cheques; the **post office** is on Jalan Perintis Kemerdekaan heading towards Carita, as is the **PHPA parks office** which is further out, almost opposite the *Rawayan* hotel. There are a few nondescript **warung** around the town, but no restaurants.

Accommodation

Hotel Caringi Jl Perintis Kemerdekaan 20 ☎0253/81388. All of the rooms here have mandi attached, but none have fans, and they're pretty dingy. ❶–❷

Hotel Citra Ayu Jl Perintis Kemerdekaan 27 ☎0253/81229. Basic but clean, and all the rooms have fans. ❶

Rawayan Jl Raya Carita 41 ☎0253/81386. The nicest place in Labuan, on the road towards Carita and away from the noise and grime of town. The quaint bungalows and private rooms all have mandi, and some have air-con. ❸–❹

Telaga Biru Just off Jalan Raya Carita, about 2km from Labuan and on the opposite side of the road from the sea (no phone). The best budget option in and around Labuan; all the quiet rooms have mandi inside. ❶

Krakatau

The makers of the disaster movie *Krakatoa, East of Java* were obviously too busy to consult a map before entitling their film. Clearly visible west of the beaches near Merak and Carita is **Krakatau volcano**, the crumbled caldera of Pulau Rakata and the epicentre of the 1883 explosion whose force was equivalent to 10,000 Hiroshima atomic bombs. Today, **Anak Krakatau**, the child of Krakatau volcano, is a growing infant island surrounded by what remains of the older peaks. Having first reared its head from the seas in 1930, Anak Krakatau's glassy black cone sits angrily smoking amongst a collection of elder relatives, and is the tangible legacy of one of the most destructive events in recorded history.

As you approach Krakatau from Java, you round the northeastern point of Pulau Rakata, its sheer northern cliff face soaring straight out of the sea to nearly 800m. Several small, jagged spurs of black lava jut out of the water and are thought to predate the 1883 eruption. The outer islands are all that remain of Krakatau's original cone, and are now forested and filled with birds, snakes and monitor lizards. Anak Krakatau, however, is the place most visitors want to see – it's a barren wasteland and still very much active. To get here requires a **motorboat trip** (4–6hr) from Labuan or Carita, which on a calm day is delightful, but at all other times should be avoided as the water can be too much for small boats to handle. From the landing point it takes about thirty minutes to walk up to the crater, from where you can see black lava flows, sulphurous fumaroles and smoke, with occasional expulsions of ash and rock. Find out whether you can land or not by checking conditions daily.

The easiest way to visit Krakatau is with the Black Rhino tour company in Carita (p.136), who try to assemble **tour groups** and split the boat cost, and are pretty reliable. Depending on how many people can be gathered, it could cost as little as Rp100,000 per person; prices per person come down the larger the group. If you have your own group, enquire at the PHPA parks office in Labuan (see opposite) and see if they can fix you up with a boat and captain, which should cost around Rp500,000 for the day. Don't forget to bring lots of water and some food (include emergency supplies).

The volcano

Krakatau sits right on the brim of the **Sunda shelf**, a colossal continental plate underlying much of Asia, whose boundary runs just kilometres off the southern coast of Sumatra and Java. The shelf lies alongside one of the most volcanic regions of the world, with Krakatau its most infamous progeny.

In the middle of the nineteenth century, Krakatau was uninhabited, except for the hordes of tropical birds, monkeys and reptiles that filled its thick jungles. The island was dominated by three peaks, Danan, Perbuatan and Rakata (which means "crab" in ancient Javanese), and stood 813m above sea level. In 1620, the Dutch East India Company had set up a small naval station here to harvest timber and sulphur from the island's plentiful stocks. However, people didn't settle, and when Krakatau awoke the island was mercifully free of people.

In May 1883, the first **tremors** were reported in Sumatra and also in First Point Lighthouse, in Ujong Kulon national park. On May 19, after 200 years of inactivity, Krakatau's northern volcano of Perbuatan **erupted**, explosions being heard along both shores of the Sunda Straits. The air-pressure waves stopped clocks and smashed windows in Batavia (Jakarta) and Bogor, and pumice began to fall into the Sunda straits.

However, it was the *tsunamis* or tidal waves that caused the majority of deaths in the region. The first huge wave followed an explosion at 5.45am on August 27, 1883, which was heard in central Australia. This huge wave crashed into Anyer town on the west coast of Java and completely razed it, but was still only a ripple compared with what was to come. At 10am an explosion of unimaginable proportions rent Krakatau island; the boom was heard in Rodrigues in the western Indian Ocean, while tremors were detected as far away as the English Channel and off the coast of Alaska. As the eruption column towered 40km into the atmosphere, a thick mud rain began to fall over the area, and the temperature fell by 5°C. One single *tsunami* as tall as a seven-storey building, raced outwards towards the coasts of Java and Sumatra, demolishing everything in its wake. Three hundred towns and villages were simply erased, and 36,417 people killed as it rushed kilometres inland. The government gunboat *Berouw* was lifted from the middle of Teluk Betung's Chinese quarter, where an earlier wave had stranded it, and carried 3km inland, before being deposited up a hill 10m above sea level. Once into the open sea, the waves travelled at up to 700kph, reaching South Africa and scuttling ships in Auckland harbour.

The **aftermath** of Krakatau's eruption was to circle the globe for the next two years in the form of fine ash particles. These lowered global temperatures, created psychedelic sunsets and seemed to tinge the moon and the sun blue or green. In July 1884, well over a year after the eruption, bones and skulls were washed ashore in Zanzibar in East Africa; they had been borne across the Indian Ocean on pumice stone rafts. Two-thirds of Krakatau had vanished for good, and on those parts that remained, not so much as a seed or an insect survived.

The Ujung Kulon national park

At the extreme southwestern tip of Java lies a small forested peninsula overlooked by the modern world. In the **Ujung Kulon national** park, a World Heritage site, you can glide in a dugout canoe on abundant rivers overhung with dense jungle, and experience the Java that captured the imagination of explorers hundreds of years ago.

Practicalities

Organized tours from Carita are the easiest means of getting to Ujung Kulon (see p.136). Independent visitors to the park should obtain a PHPA **permit** and book accommodation, both of which can be done at the PHPA office in Labuan (see p.138); this step is not needed for visitors on organized tours. One option is then to charter a boat for up to fifteen people from Labuan to one of the islands inside the park (5hr; around US$175). A cheaper alternative is to take a minibus from Labuan to **Sumur** (3hr; Rp5000), about 20km short of the park. In Sumur there are hordes of ojek or motorcycle taxis waiting to ferry trekkers on to **TAMANJAYA** (45min; Rp5000), on the mainland before the isthmus that forms the gateway to the main body of the park. Tamanjaya is a small village with a few basic supply shops, a PHPA office where it's possible to obtain your **permit**, and a losmen. There are guesthouses (❷) within the park on **Pulau Handeleum** and **Pulau Peucang**; the latter also has a restaurant and rather swanky **accommodation** (❺–❻). This accommodation can either be booked at the PHPA office in Labuan, or through organized tour companies in Jakarta or Carita. If you intend staying in the park, you're much better off buying supplies in Labuan, as they're very limited here. A **guide** is required by park law for anyone entering Ujung Kulon. The cheapest guides can be hired at Tamanjaya PHPA office, where there is a flat charge of Rp10,000 a day.

The park

The main body of Ujung Kulon is a bulbous peninsula joined to the mainland by a narrow land bridge. Also part of the park is large Pulau Panaitan, which lies about 5km off the northwestern shore, and a host of tiny islands, including Pulau Handeleum and Pulau Peucang, nestling in bays close to the mainland. The whole park covers around two hundred square kilometres, just over half being land, and the rest coral reef and sea, filled with turtles, sharks and rays.

Ujung Kulon's most famous inhabitant is unfortunately also the most elusive. The park was set up by the Dutch in the early twentieth century to protect the single-horned **Java rhinos**. These animals were once so common that early Batavia was menaced by them; however, they have been on the verge of extinction for over a century, killed by poachers who exported the horn to the Chinese, who value its qualities as an aphrodisiac. The famously myopic rhino has hide with four definite plates like body armour, its mouth hooked into a beak. The rhino's horn is actually a lump of solid hair and has no bone or connection to the animal's skull. Nowadays, although the rhino is the attraction that brings most visitors to the park, some of the guides who have worked here for years have never seen one.

What you are most likely to see are scores of **snakes** and sizeable monitor lizards, monkeys, wild pigs and a cornucopia of **birds** in an environment of swamps, grassy fields, jungle and white-sand beaches. Some of the river mouths and swampy areas are home to the estuarine crocodile and false gharial, which are both shy of human contact. The **panther**, another notoriously elusive beast, dwells here in small numbers, and the **hawksbill turtle** comes annually to the beaches to breed and lay its eggs. The park is also famed for its **primate colonies**, the rare Java silver leaf-monkey, crab-eating macaques and gibbons joining the hornbills and mynah birds in making their presence noisily evident. The thieving macaques can be a real menace, so don't leave your possessions unguarded.

Trekking

There are limitless possibilities for **trekking** inside the park. The best thing to do is consult your guide and decide what best suits your budget and what you most want to see. **Peucang** and **Handeleum islands** are good places to start from. They are both reachable by boat directly from Carita or Labuan, and have bungalow accommodation; Peucang also has its own restaurant, and the waves off the south coast have begun to attract a steady trickle of surfers.

It's possible to walk around the entire north edge of the peninsula in less than a week. There are observation towers – where you can watch the wildlife without your scent and presence scaring them – at Cigenter, Nyiur near Cape Alàng-Alang and also near Mount Bayung at Cibunar in the south. Over a dozen rough wooden shelters are dotted around the park, where five or six people can sleep; bear in mind that you'll have to bring all your own provisions.

One of the most rewarding but well-worn trails starts at the guesthouse on Pulau Handeleum. Just across the water from here at the mouth of **Sungai Cigenter** is the feeding centre of the same name, an open meadow grazed by Banteng oxen and home to a huge colony of brilliantly coloured bee-eaters. A rough walking trail leads from the feeding grounds all the way round the coast back to the Tamanjaya park headquarters, through knotted mangroves and rainforest. The first shelter for trekkers is just past Sungai Cikarang, about a nine-kilometre walk from Cigenter. You could either overnight here, or continue for 6–7km to the next shelter at Tanjung Alang-Alang, a marshy area full of birds and, unfortunately, mosquitoes. From here it's a twenty-kilometre trek to Ciujungkulon feeding ground, which lies across the Peucang straits from Pulau Peucang. From Ciujungkulon you can either continue around the coast or take a short cut over the headland. Either way, it will take you at least a couple of days to get back to Tamanjaya; there are five shelters at roughly ten-kilometre intervals along the trail.

Bogor and around

Jakarta's fast-growing satellite city of **Bogor**, famous for its **Botanic Gardens**, affords a convenient stopover on the way to the West Java Highlands. This volcanic region has stunning scenery, beautiful hill resorts such as **Selabintana** outside Sukabumi and a world-famous national park, **Gede-Pangrango**, as well as the home villages of the animistic Badui people. The south coast affords the quiet beach retreat of **Pelabuhan Ratu**.

Bogor

Just an hour's train journey south of Jakarta and perhaps destined to become one of its suburbs, **BOGOR** is very different from the capital. In contrast with Jakarta's stifling sweatiness, Bogor's cool wet climate has earned it the nickname of "The City of Thunder". Bogor is no longer a serene colonial hill station; its streets are chaotic and crowded, with an oversupply of smoke-chugging bemos, and Western-style shopping centres are springing up along the tree-lined avenues. The best relief from the increasing frenzy of the city is to be found right at its heart: the **Kebun Raya Botanical Gardens**, which have been Bogor's greatest asset since 1817, and provide more greenery than can be found in the whole of the polluted capital. The plants are kept healthy by Bogor's rainstorms, which average nearly one a day, usually in the late afternoon, when the train station forecourt may be knee-deep underwater.

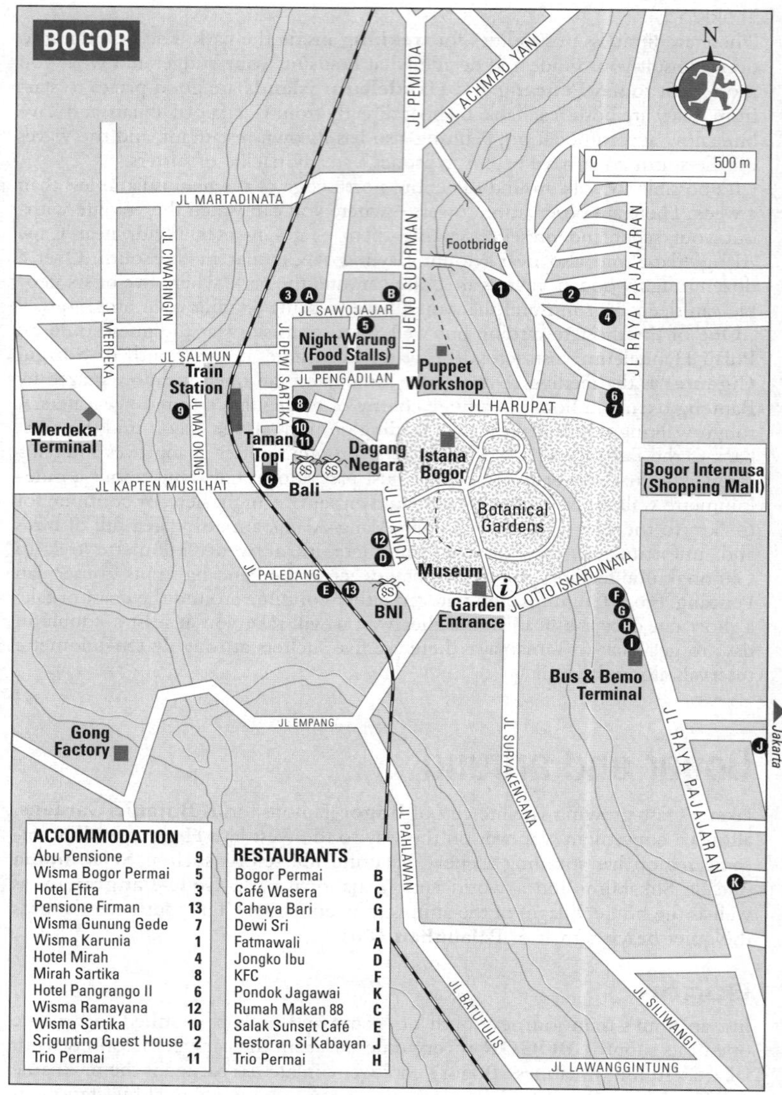

Some history

Several engraved rocks in the vicinity of Bogor suggest its history dates back to long before the well-documented times of colonial occupation. These stones are known as *batu tulis* (rock writings). One such stone at Ciampea has several footprints and an inscription, said to have been left by the Hindu king Purnavaraman, who ruled Java in the fifth century, possibly centring his kingdom here in Bogor. Bogor was certainly the capital of the **Pajararan empire** from the twelfth to the sixteenth centuries. During **colonial** times, the wealthy Dutch grew tired of the heat of Batavia (Jakarta) and sought residences in the cooler highlands; although it stands not quite 300m above sea level, Bogor's climate is appreciably cooler.

In 1745, governor-general Willem van Imhoff passed through Bogor region on a fact-finding mission and decided to make his home here. He started on a large estate named **Buitenzorg**, roughly translated as "free of worries", which was the site of many wild parties, the elite of Batavia flocking to hunt in the grounds. In 1811, Sir Stamford Raffles took up residence and renovated the buildings; it was he who made the first start on the famous botanical gardens, with help from botanists from London's Kew Gardens. From 1870 until 1942, the palace became the official residence of all Dutch governors-general in Indonesia. Briefly occupied by the Japanese during World War II, it was handed over to the Indonesian people in 1949, when it officially became known by its current title: Istana Bogor, or Presidential Palace.

Arrival, city transport and information

The rail journey from Jakarta to Bogor is quick and reliable, with a choice of the non stop Pakuan express (9 daily; Rp6000) from Gambir or the regular stopping train (Rp1500) from Gondangdia, a five-minute walk left from the south end of Jalan Jaksa. Bogor **train station** is about 500m northwest of the Botanical Gardens and within walking distance of most of the popular budget accommodation. Buses leave opposite Jakarta's Christian University (UKI) at Cawang (#AC10 from the *Sari Pan Pacific Hotel*) every ten or fifteen minutes, arriving at the **bus terminal** in Bogor, about 500m southeast of the gardens. The main bemo stop is behind the bus terminal, but the best place to pick up bemos is on the main road that borders the southern edge of the gardens. The bemo system in Bogor is extremely complicated and you'll need to ask a local for precise instructions for every trip. There is a small **tourist information** centre (Mon–Fri 9am–4pm) at the main, southern entrance to the gardens; they have a few maps of the town and gardens. Jalan Kapten Musilhat and Jalan Juanda on the western side of the gardens are lined with **banks**; it's worth shopping around for the best exchange rates.

Accommodation

Whilst Bogor mainly offers flash business hotels, its status as a weekend retreat means it has a reasonably wide range of **accommodation**, and there are a few family hostel-type places for budget travellers.

Abu Pensione Jl Mayur Oking 15 ⓣ0251/322893. With excessively friendly staff, river views, free drinks and excellent breakfasts, *Abu* is probably the best budget losmen in Bogor. The top rooms have hot water and air-con or fan as an option. The cheapest rooms have none of these, but are clean. ❷–❸

Wisma Bogor Permai Jalan Sawajajar/Jend Sudirman 23a ⓣ0251/321115. A delightful new establishment with hot water, large beds and fridges in all the rooms, plus a good Indonesian breakfast. ❹–❺

Hotel Efita Jl Sawajajar 5 ⓣ0251/333400, ⓕ333600. Rather swanky, with air-con, hot water, fridge, TV and telephone in every room. Breakfast is included in the price. ❹–❺

Pensione Firmane Jl Palendang 48 ⓣ0251/323246. Currently the only place in Bogor to offer dorm beds (three people to a room; Rp9000 each), *Firman* has long been the budget travellers' favourite in Bogor. They offer good information and various tours around West Java, though the accommodation is nothing special. ❷

Wisma Gunung Gede Jl Raya Pajajaran 36 ⓣ0251/324148. Situated opposite Bank Niaga, this is a sparkling place with huge suites, hot water, family-sized fridges, and gardens. ❹

Wisma Karunia Jl Serupur 35–37 ⓣ0251/323411. A quiet, friendly, family-run place that's as secluded as you'll get so close to the centre of a Javanese city. All but the most basic rooms have mandi and fan, and breakfast is included. The owners run an efficient door-to-door bus service to Bandung. ❷–❸

Hotel Mirah Jl Pangrango 9a ⓣ0251/328044, ⓕ329423. The hotel has an inviting shaded pool open to non-guests for Rp10,000. All rooms have air-con and hot water, and the price includes a decent breakfast. ❸–❺

Mirah Sartika Jl Dewi Sartika 6a ⓣ0251/312343, ⓕ315188. Quite a flashy place, with TV, telephone and air-con, although there's no hot water, even in its top-class rooms. There's a conference hall for business rental. ❹

Hotel Pangrango II Jl Raya Pajajaran 32 ⓣ0251/312375, ⓕ377750. All the rooms here have knee-deep carpets, TV and video, air-con, hot water, fridge and telephone. In addition, there's a swimming pool, moneychanger, ballroom and laundry service. ❸–❺

Wisma Ramayana Jl Juanda 54. Opposite the west side of the Botanical Gardens, this guest-house has rooms with little verandahs around a courtyard and a quiet, pleasant atmosphere. ❷

Wisma Sartika Jl Gedung Sawa III 19 ⓣ0251/323747. Run by a charming, English-speaking Indonesian woman, *Sartika* is spotlessly clean, and provides endless hot drinks and an American breakfast. This is another candidate for the best Bogor losmen, having the advantage of being well away from traffic, although just a few minutes from the station. Classier rooms have mandi inside; all the rooms have fans. ❷–❸

Srigunting Guest House Jl Heulang 11a ⓣ0251/311243, Jl Merak 14 ⓣ0251/323080 and Jl Bincarung 12 ⓣ0251/333296. This family-run group of guesthouses sport absolutely over-the-top palatial architecture, with crystal chandeliers, gold leaf over everything and cavernous suite rooms with hot water, fridge, TV and air-con. Midweek, prices are subject to huge reductions and you can try additional bargaining. ❺

Trio Permai Dewi Sartika 2 ⓣ0251/329672. The basic rooms here are a little dark and grotty, but have fan and mandi; the more expensive ones are much better with good spring beds. The price includes tea, coffee and breakfast. ❷–❹

The City

The pathways of the **Botanical Gardens** (daily 8am–5pm; Rp1600) wind between towering bamboo stands, climbing bougainvillea, a small tropical rainforest, and ponds full of water lilies and fountains. Perhaps the garden's best-known occupants are the giant rafflesia and *bungu bangkai*, two of the world's hugest (and smelliest) flowers. About 15,000 endemic species have been collected here, as well as thousands of tropical varieties from around the world. Unfortunately, many of these are kept in private greenhouses closed to the public. However, bird-watchers might like to take their time; among the species to be seen here are orange-headed thrushes, hanging parrots and small blue kingfishers, as well as the herons that breed on the small lake.

Near the main entrance to the park is a memorial to Olivia Raffles, wife of the governor-general Sir Stamford Raffles, who died in Bogor in 1814, author of the remarkable *A History of Java*, an outstanding reference to all things Javanese and Sundanese. Also near the entrance to the park is the **Zoological Museum** (daily 8am–4pm; Rp700), one of the foremost botanical research centres in Asia, which houses 30,000 specimens. This immense collection is badly organized and dilapidated, but nonetheless fascinating. It includes Asian insects and reptiles, as well as the complete skeleton of a blue whale, a stuffed Java rhino, a giant Japanese crab, a mammoth Flores rat, a Komodo dragon and a selection of Indonesian mammals.

The **Bogor Presidential Palace** (Istana Bogor) is in the northern corner of the gardens; you can get within a stone's throw of it (across a pond) if you head directly north as soon as you enter the park. To actually enter the palace, however, you'll need to get a **permit** about a week in advance from the tourist office at Jalan Merak 1 (ⓣ0251/325705), and will probably have to join a tour. The palace was built in a mainly European style, the exterior having a distinctly Ionian facade, with pillars and a triangular pediment. It contains President Sukarno's immense art collection, as well as his library and film room. Though Sukarno loved the palace, his successor Suharto scorned it; some say this was because Sukarno's ghost still wanders the buildings. The grounds are patrolled by herds of rather tame roe deer that sometimes forage along the outer fence, hoping for titbits. Sources differ on whether the deer were introduced from mainland Asia or all the way from Holland, but either way it seems certain they were brought here to grace the governor-general's dinner table.

Wayang golek puppets are made at a workshop found to the northwest of the gardens; ask for Pak Dase's place. If you're interested in **gamelan** and **Javanese gongs**, visit Pak Sukarna's factory on Jalan Pancasan to the southwest of the gardens. Here the instruments are forged using traditional methods, and are also for sale.

There is one **batu tulis** in Bogor town, 2km south of the entrance to the gardens at Jalan Batu Tulis – make sure you remove your shoes before entering the shrine that houses the stone. The inscription dates from 1533 and was written in Sundanese Sanskrit, dedicated to King Surawisesa of the Hindu Pajajaran empire. What are said to be the king's footprints are also visible in the stone. Sukarno made his home close to the small shrine that now houses the stone, believing it to possess great magical power. He also asked to be buried near here, but Suharto refused permission. The other *batu tulis* in this area is to be found at **Ciampea**, northwest of Bogor. It's actually quite impressive, a sizeable, shiny black boulder with the footprint of King Purnavaraman and an extremely clear inscription dating back 1500 years. To get there, take a bemo from the train station to Ciampea (30min; Rp1000) and then ask for a colt (20min; Rp600) on to Batutulis.

Eating

Fast food outlets are multiplying in Bogor: the Bogor Plaza opposite the main gates to the Botanical Gardens has *KFC* and *Dunkin' Donuts*; the Bogor Internusa mall has *CFC* and *Dunkin' Donuts*. The green minibus #7 (5min; Rp300) from outside the Bogor Permai food court takes you to the Plaza Jambu Dua, a huge shopping centre with ten-pin bowling and many fast-food joints. Along Jalan Pengadillan, near the Telkom and train station, are bunches of **night stalls**, which set up after 6pm and sell excellent seafood and Chinese snacks; you can get a terrific meal for under Rp10,000, but these stalls sometimes shut very early. Near the gates to the gardens there is a profusion of **gorengan**, street vendors who look like Dutch milkmaids, with their wares dangling from poles across their shoulders. *Gorengan* means "frying" and, true to form, these vendors cover pretty much anything in batter and deep-fry it; favourites here are fried banana, yam and cassava.

Bogor Permai On the corner of Jalan Jend Sudirman and Jalan Sawojajar. A small food complex housing a fine delicatessen, the best bakery in Bogor and a stand selling tasty pizza slices (Rp2000) as well as hot dogs and sandwiches. The *Bogor Permai* restaurant in the back of the building is one of the highest-quality places in Bogor, selling excellent seafood and steaks; most courses start at around Rp15,000. There are also email facilities available here.

Café Wasera One of several cheap eating places in Taman Topi, the little park in front of the station. *Café Wasera* offers various fruit juices and cheap sate dishes.

Cahaya Bari & Trio Permai Near the bus station on Jalan Raya Pajararan. Two of the flashiest, cleanest Padang restaurants you'll ever see, offering an excellent assortment of meats and seafood, cooked in a variety of sauces.

Dewi Sri Jl Pajajaran 3. A clean establishment serving Indonesian food; the ayam goreng (Rp5000) is recommended.

Fatmawali Jl Sawajajar 7. A canteen-style self-service place with cold meats and veggies and excellent fried chicken; a very reasonable full meal costs under Rp5000.

Jongko Ibu Jl Juanda 36. Serves decent, cheap Sundanese food and you can eat outside watching the world go by. *Karedok* – salad with chilli sauce – is good and fiery, while steamed carp in banana leaf is a local favourite.

Pondok Jagawai Jl Raya Pajajaran 3. A variety of

food from around the world is served here; *shabu shabu* (Japanese meat fondue) costs Rp25,000 for three people, Wiener schnitzel is Rp10,500. The chicken steak and Australian lamb chops are also recommended.

Rumah Makan 88 Taman Topi. Inexpensive Chinese and Sundanese dishes.

Salak Sunset Café Jl Paledang 38. Serves a variety of Indonesian and European dishes and has views over the river and valley. Spaghetti costs Rp5000, hamburgers Rp3200.

Restoran Si Kabayan Jl Bina Marga 12. One of the best places to try genuine Sundanese dishes. The tables are arranged under thatched parasols around a small garden, and the food is exquisite. *Ikan mas* is a speciality, and they also do several complete meals if you are a blinded by the choice.

The Badui villages

When Islam conquered Java, very few vestiges of the island's **animist** past were left. However, one of the few places left untouched was a group of isolated communities in the Kendeng mountains in the most western area of Java. Today, around three thousand of their descendants known as the **Badui** still live in protected villages about 50km south of the town of Rankasbitung. One reason they managed to maintain their independence during the spread of Islam may have been because the new Muslim sultans feared tampering with the power of the Badui priests on their "magic mountain". Certainly, the Badui's tenacious retention of tradition in the face of four hundred years of pressure is quite remarkable, and after the Indonesian government had failed to force them to adopt the national language, religion and methods of schooling, the villages were made a sort of national park.

Visitors now require a **permit** to enter and, even with a permit, can only visit the "outer villages". Badui magic and law are centred on three "inner villages" that are closed to visitors. The elders and high priests of Badui religion never leave here, and make the rules that govern all the other villages. Every year in April and May, during the *seba* ceremony, the Badui bring offerings to the *puun*, the high priest of the inner Badui, a sacred talismanic leader who possesses hereditary "magical" powers.

Practicalities

Unless you take an organized trek all the way from Jalan Jaksa or Carita, visiting the Badui is quite an undertaking. It will take you several days out of any of the major tourist centres and a fair bit of organizing. Whether you go alone or in a tour, you'll be staying in makeshift accommodation with strenuous walking between villages.

The first stop for independent travellers intending to visit the Badui is **Rankasbitung**, a large, dull town about 80km west and slightly south of Jakarta. To get there, take a bus either from Labuan (1hr 30min; Rp2000), or from Kalideres in Jakarta (3hr; Rp3500). To visit the outer villages you must first get a **permit** from the PHPA office (Mon–Sat 7.30am–1.30pm) in Rankasbitung, at the Kantor Dinas Parawisata, Jalan Pahlawan 31a. The permit costs Rp8000 and lasts for three days; the office is also the best source of information for the area. Another option is to take a tour from a company such as Black Rhino tours in Carita (see p.136) or one of the tour operators along Jalan Jaksa in Jakarta (see p.122). From Rankasbitung there are three minibuses a day to **Cibolger**, a small village just outside the Badui districts; the last minibus leaves at midday. To charter a minibus there and back will cost about Rp150,000. In Cibolger, Pak Hussein has a small souvenir shop of the same name and warung, and he also takes paying guests, though his house is not a losmen and should not be treated as such. From Cibolger, it's about a one-kilometre walk to **Katu Ketek**, the first outer Badui village.

The villages

KATU KETEK has several traditional houses and the people all wear the blue garb, black sarong and batik headscarves of the outer villages. Priests from the inner villages wear white and do not cut their hair; they are also forbidden from keeping large domestic animals, getting drunk and eating at night. The villagers grow *tangkil*, a variety of nut, on the mountainsides: these are then processed into *emping* crackers. They also grow fruits such as sawo, soursop and durian. From Katu Ketek it's a two-hour walk to **KATU JANGKUNG**, through mountainous territory. The next village is **CIGULA**, three hours' walk away, passing **Dangdong Ageng**, a small lake that marks the gateway to the protected inner villages. Cigula is another charming village: its traditional houses have thatched roofs and open porches where people work shaded from the sun. If you're lucky you might see them making and playing the bamboo *angklung* instrument or weaving baskets out of rattan.

From Cigula, it's another two hours' walk to **GAJEBOK**, probably the nicest village to stay, with exceptionally friendly people and a nearby river that's good for a cooling mandi. The people of Gajebok are known for their traditional textiles and for making bags from beaten tree bark. Ask for Pak Ailin if you are in need of food or shelter, as he often provides for visitors. If you don't want to stay, it's a hard four-hour trek back to Katu Ketek, passing through a few tiny kampung.

Selabintana and Sukabumi

SELABINTANA, a quiet hill resort sitting near to the foot of Gunung Gede, is dominated less by the surrounding volcanoes than by the *Hotel Selabintana*. It's a quiet, peaceful place, with some good walking, and is also an alternative gateway to the Gede Pangrango national park, with a path leading from nearby to the summits of the two mountains. The road uphill to the *Selabintana* is lined with guesthouses, hotels and restaurants, but even so you'll probably have trouble finding a place to stay at the weekends. To get here, first take a bus to nearby **SUKABUMI** from Bogor (3hr; Rp3000) or Bandung (3hr 30min; Rp4000) or the train from Bogor (4 daily; Rp 3000). Sukabumi is a large town 8km south of Selabintana, with lots of hotels, banks and places to eat, but it's noisy and busy with none of the charm of its neighbour. Sukabumi is the transit town for those wishing to reach **Pelabuhan Ratu** (see p.148); otherwise its one claim to fame is that it has had more recorded tremors than any other town in Indonesia, and in 1972 was razed to the ground by a huge quake that killed 2500 people.

To get to Selabintana, catch angkot #10 heading up the mountainside from the Yogya department store in Sukabumi. At the six-kilometre marker is a turning off to the left; occasionally bemos will run down here to the *Pondok Halimua* campsite (3km; Rp300, or Rp5000 for a charter). This riverside field amongst the tea plantations is used at the weekends for guide and scout jamborees, there are no facilities and you are allowed to pitch your tent free of charge. From the campsite, there's a well-trodden path to the main tourist site in the area, the **Ciborum waterfalls**. Here the icy cold water plunges thirty metres or so, and you can take an invigorating mandi underneath – although at weekends you'll have a large audience. From here it's a ten-kilometre walk to the Gede and Pangrango volcanoes – a much more strenuous route than from the Puncak Pass side.

Accommodation

Most of the **hotels** line the road from Sukabumi to the *Hotel Selabintana* and the small bemo terminal at its entrance. There are no street numbers so they're listed here in the order they appear, proceeding uphill from the six-kilometre marker. It gets cool here in the evenings, so accommodation places don't have fans or air-con.

Pondok Asri ⓣ0266/225408. The *Asri* has large bungalows and clean private rooms; guests have access to all of the *Hotel Selabintana*'s facilities. ❺–❻

Wisma Melati Jl Selabintana Wetar 8 ⓣ0266/227905. Down the side road opposite the small bemo terminal, this is a friendly family-run place among the rice paddies. ❸

Hotel Melinda ⓣ0266/224444. Architecturally, the *Melinda* most resembles a multistorey car park, but it has good clean rooms; only the more expensive ones have hot water. ❸–❹

Hotel Pangrango ⓣ0266/211532, ⓕ221520. Most of the rooms are in private cottages; classier rooms have hot water and TV. Other facilities include tennis courts, a swimming pool and a Saturday-night disco. ❸–❺

Hotel Selabintana ⓣ0266/221501 ⓕ223383. If you want to stay here at the weekend, you'll need to book over a month in advance. The hotel is looking a little worn and is in need of refurbishment, but it's still the last word in country-club style. The facilities include tennis courts, volleyball, a swimming pool, golf course and conference centre; the rooms and bungalows have hot water, TV, spring beds and a central video system. ❹–❼

Sukabumi Indah ⓣ0266/224818. The basic rooms are clean and very good value, with hot water and TV, while the cottages are palatial. There are also tennis courts and a pool. ❸–❺

Veteran Jl A Yani 2. If you really have to break your journey at Sukabumi, this modest place offers passable rooms. ❶

Eating

All the hotels have their own **restaurants**, offering Indonesian, Chinese and European foods. However, midweek you'll probably have to settle for nasi goreng. Around the terminal there are several cheap warung and a couple of rumah makan selling standard Indonesian fare such as mie goreng and nasi ayam.

Café Pondok Mendiri Slightly downhill from the *Sukabumi Indah*. Serves European food such as hamburgers for Rp7500, as well as a few Chinese and Indonesian dishes.

Rumah Makan Sate Kelinci 100m down the hill from the *Pangrango*, on the opposite side of the road, and offering good views over the surrounding country. As the name suggests, it specializes in sate, but also serves other Indonesian food; figure on Rp5000 for ten sticks of goat, chicken or beef sate.

Pelabuhan Ratu and around

PELABUHAN RATU, "The Queen's Harbour", is a fishing village on the south coast of the Sukabumi district that has become a thriving weekend retreat. Its bay is filled with colourful fishing platforms and boats, and the nearby coves and stretches of clean, dark sand make this by far the most pleasant quick-fix escape from Jakarta. The queen who gave the harbour its name is the goddess of the South Seas, an unstable female deity who, according to the legend, threw herself into the waves at **Karang Hawu** to the west of here. On April 6 every year, local fishermen sacrifice buffalo and shower flower petals on the surface of the sea to please the goddess and secure themselves a good catch. Feasting, racing in brightly decorated boats and dancing follow the ceremonies. From November 25–27 each year, Pelabuhan Ratu hosts the Indonesian big-game fishing tournament. One look around the **fish market** to the east of the bus terminal will show you why: huge black-striped and blue marlin, swordfish, sailfish and tuna are all on display, as well as shark and barracuda.

During the week, Pelabuhan Ratu is an idyllic, peaceful, sleepy village. At the weekends and on public holidays it gets crowded with rich domestic tourists from all the major cities in West Java, and you have to book everything weeks in advance. There's a host of activities to enjoy around Pelabuhan Ratu, with several waterfalls, caves and rivers to explore, watersports and, of course, lots of beaches.

Heading west from town, over the first hill that cuts off Pelabuhan Ratu's cove, the next beach and village is **CITEPUS**. It has a long stretch of beach with mild surf and a profusion of cheap seafood restaurants and homestays (see below).

Practicalities

Buses from Bandung and Bogor come via Sukabumi; the trans-south coast highway may one day be completed, and traffic will be able to come direct from Carita on the west coast, but this project seems unlikely to get under way any time soon. All of these buses arrive at the bus terminal just inland from the port, in front of which is the tourist information centre and **warpostel**. The majority of hotels are to the west of town and on the coastal road running all the way to Cilangkon.

The **tourist information centre** (daily except Fri 9am–4pm) near the bus terminal is one of the best in all of West Java, offering a good selection of maps, brochures and pamphlets, such as the excellent *All Around Bandung* guidebook; they also run diving, fishing and **white-water rafting** tours in the vicinity. **Diving** usually takes place near Karang Hantu and Sorong Parat down the southeastern peninsula, where you'll find decent coral and lots of brightly coloured fish, though none of the more exciting pelagic (open sea) species. A day's diving with two tanks costs US$75, snorkelling US$48 and a PADI open water course US$285; to book, call Moray Diving (Ⓣ0268/41686). White-water rafting on the nearby grade III Sungai Citakik costs Rp75,000 for a half-day or Rp120,000 for a full day; to book in advance, contact PT Linten Jeram Nusantara (Ⓣ0811/103397, Ⓔharsa@rad.net.id). Student discounts are available, but all rates go up at the weekend.

Accommodation

Just over two kilometres to the west of Pelabuhan Ratu town, the village of **Citepus** is a better place to stay – it's quieter, and with a nicer beach. Practically every house offers rooms for rent; most are well equipped and cost upwards of Rp30,000, but there are also a few really cheap places. There are no road numbers here, so accommodation is listed in the order you'll find it along the coastal road heading west from Pelabauhan Ratu.

Gunung Mulia Ⓣ0268/41129. On the main coastal road above the restaurant of the same name. Has a few rooms with fan and mandi and is a little noisy because of passing motorcycle traffic. The attached wartel has international call facilities. ❷

Handayani Guest House Jalan Sirnagalik. Signposted from the main road, this is down a side street opposite the *Kebyar* disco. The *Handayani*'s rooms are rather dark, but all of them have en-suite mandi. ❷

Pondok Dewata Jalan Sirnagalik Ⓣ0268/41022. Perhaps slightly overpriced, but has en-suite mandi and fan, and breakfast is included. ❸

Simpang Pojok Jalan Sirnagalik Ⓣ0268/41468. Very reasonable prices for quiet and clean rooms, the only drawback being that the lights are situated directly above the ceiling fan. ❷

Karang Sari On the right-hand side of the road up the hill as you head out of Pelabuhan Ratu Ⓣ0268/41078. The basic rooms here are good value, with fan and mandi, while the posher rooms have air-con. ❸–❹

Buana Ayu Ⓣ0268/41111. Well-appointed rooms by a good restaurant, all of them sporting mandi and fan. ❸

Bayu Amrta Ⓣ0268/41031, Ⓕ41344. All rooms have satellite TV, air-con and a water heater, probably a little surplus to requirements in this sweltering town. The restaurant here affords a tremendous view over the bay. ❹

Bukit Indah At the highest elevation of the hotels on the hill west of town ⓣ0268/41331. Great views over the coast, and clean rooms with fan and en-suite mandi. The restaurant specializes in Japanese food – *shabu shabu* and *sukiyaki* – and Korean *yaki niku.* ❸–❹

Penginapan Makessa Indah Citepus village, in an excellent setting amongst the rice paddies. The clean, well-kept rooms have air-con. ❸

Padi Padi About 2.5km west of Pelabauhan Ratu in Citepus ⓣ0268/42124, ⓕ42125. A very well-equipped hotel, with swimming pool, book and film library, tennis courts, games, rafting and fishing. All the beautifully designed rooms have air-con and TV with laser disc. ❺

Cleopatra Hotel and Restaurant Pantai Rekreasi Citepus 114. A resort-type hotel close to the beach, offering air-con rooms with TV. ❹

Samudra Beach Hotel About 5km from Pelabuhan Ratu ⓣ0268/41200, ⓕ41203. Boasts gardens with insipid sculptures of whimsical nude females, and also tennis courts. Superb rates for groups and midweek – the rooms have air-con, phone, TV and hot water. ❺–❻

Eating

The **food** in Pelabuhan Ratu is generally first-rate, fresh seafood being the order of the day. In Citepus, the beach is lined with literally hundreds of identical seaview warung selling *ikan bakar*, squid and prawns. Most shut midweek, but the larger places such as the *Sederhana*, *Mulia* and *Ikan Bakar* always have a full menu. The restaurants below are listed as they appear heading west from the bus station.

Martini Opposite the tourist information centre. This restaurant, with its stripy awning and glass fronting, has a slightly fast-food feel about it, but sells decent seafood.

Masakan Khas Sundalbu M Opposite the tourist information centre, good for the usual Sundanese staples.

Sederhana Opposite the police station. Slightly more rough-and-ready than the majority of its counterparts, but with real quality cooking. The tofu special with shrimps, chicken, veggies and chillies is wonderful (Rp10,000).

Gunung Mulia/Varia Sari These identical places serve good seafood with a few Chinese and Indonesian dishes; it's worth asking what's fresh in that day. The frog fried in chilli is worth a try.

Ratu (Queen) The best place in Pelabuhan Ratu town, set apart by its huge fish tank containing a pair of black-tip reef sharks. They do an American breakfast for Rp8000, lobster for Rp25,000, and take a lot of care in the presentation of the food.

Periangan The standard seafood menu is supplemented with several set menus for two people, usually fish, fried rice and gado-gado for Rp10,000.

Wantilan The first place on the left as the road starts up the hill at the western end of town. The most expensive place here, with excellent seafood and European dishes. Figure on about Rp30,000 for a meal with fish, salad and a beer.

Around Pelabuhan Ratu

In the immediate vicinity of Pelabuhan Ratu, 3km along the coastal road from Citepus is the four-star *Samudra* hotel (❺–❼), which caters for every conceivable beach activity. At the village of **Karang Hawu**, 10km from Pelabuhan Ratu, there's an interesting natural bridge and blowhole cave in the volcanic black rock at the water's edge, as well as a reasonable beach, perhaps a little too crowded with hawkers' stalls to be picturesque. This is the legendary beach where the goddess of the South Seas hurled herself into the waves, and is something of a pilgrimage site; there is a small shrine to her on top of a nearby rock. Angkots from Pelabuhan Ratu usually terminate 14km away at **Cisolok Kota**, from where you can catch an ojek to **Cipanas village**, where four geysers spurt sulphurous jets as high as 7m into the sky. The wind-borne spray provides a pleasant hot shower and you can bathe where two hot and cold streams meet. It's a three- to four-kilometre drive to Cipanas, which shouldn't cost more than Rp1000. From Cipanas there's a hot, steep three-kilometre trail up to a **waterfall**.

Also from Cisolok, you can take an ojek an extra 5km to **Cibangban beach**, probably the best along this stretch of coast. At the extreme west of the long flat strand are some rocky caves, one filled with bats. At the eastern end of the beach, paths lead up over the clifftops to give spectacular panoramas of the coast and secluded coves.

At Rawakalang, 3km to the east of Pelabuhan Ratu, is Goa Lalay, a large smelly **bat cave**. It's not much to see during the day, but at dusk it's the exit point for tens of thousands of bats, leaving en masse for a feed.

About 60km to the southeast of town lies **Ujung Genteng** beach, a good surfing spot but better known as the breeding ground for hundreds of giant leatherback, hawksbill and green turtles. You're particularly likely to see them coming ashore to lay their eggs during a full moon in October and November. To get there from Pelabuhan Ratu, take a bus to Ciwaru (2hr; Rp3000) and then a minibus for the hour-long trip to Ujung Genteng.

Ciawi to Cipanas

The main road that heads east from Bogor through the **Puncak Pass** to Bandung goes first through the suburb of **Ciawi** and on through assorted hill resorts to **Cipanas**, where the tourist strip peters out. Before motor transport, this journey required as many as four pairs of ponies as well as buffalo to pull passenger carriages up the steep inclines. The road is for the most part thronged with holiday villas, bungalows, expensive restaurants and hotels that are a favourite retreat of rich Jakartans. Many of these buildings have been constructed without permission of any kind; this unrestricted development, with all the deforestation of the watersheds that goes with it, has proved a contributory factor in Jakarta's floods. Occasionally, a genuinely attractive panorama appears between the hoardings and motels, most famously from the **mountain road** between Cisarua and Cipanas as it winds its way up through the tea plantations into the Puncak Pass.

Ciawi is not particularly attractive, and the profusion of accommodation is generally fairly empty. **CISARUA**, just before the pass, is slightly better and has a colourful fruit and vegetable market. A favourite side-trip from here is to the **Cilember waterfalls**, seven small falls separated by forest and expanses of rice paddies. The first five are easily visited without a guide; the trip will take around five hours, including a brief stop to cool off at some of the falls. If you want to see all seven, you will need a guide and allow a full day. To get to the first fall, hire an ojek from Cisarua (3km; Rp1500). This waterfall is over-visited, strewn with litter and full of picnicking families, but the falls get better the further up you go; to get there catch an ojek. The *Kopo Hostel* in Cisarua handles tours around here and to destinations in the Cibodas area (see p.152). The hostel is at Jalan Raya Puncak 557 (Ⓣ0251/254296; ❶), near to the Telkom office, and has dormitory beds as well as a variety of private rooms. To get to Cisarua, either get on a Bandung bus and ask to be let off, or take a white bemo uphill from just past the end of the toll road opposite Bogor bus terminal.

About 1km further towards the Puncak Pass from Cisarua is a cheap but often busy public **swimming pool**. About 2km east of Cisarua is a turn-off for **Taman Safari Indonesia**, a wildlife park with species from all around the world. Any transport plying the Bogor–Bandung route can drop you off at the turning, then you will have to flag down an angkot to get to the park. The *Ibu Cirebon Restaurant* (on the right-hand side of the road about 2km towards the pass from the *Kopo Hostel*), which serves Sundanese and Indonesian food, is worth a stop. The *Pinisi Rumah Makan* is a huge galleon in the style of a Makassar schooner, stuck in a pond and serving limited and pricey Indonesian food; they also have a tiny, pathetic amusement park, and at weekends there's a nightclub in the "hold". Across the road, the *Aero Rumah Makan* is unmissable, mainly due to the genuine, rapidly rusting DC6 suspended on tree trunks above the restaurant. Unfortunately, it's now too dangerous to eat in the plane, but it still makes for an interesting setting for a meal – if you're willing to risk the fuselage crashing down through the roof halfway through your fried chicken. In Cipayung, about 2km before Cisarua as you head uphill towards the pass, *Handayani* on the left-hand side serves good Sundanese food.

Almost at the top of the pass, the *Rindu Alam* restaurant, which serves moderately-priced Indonesian staples, has some of the best views over the Bogor area, and at weekends you can watch the paragliders sailing over these heights or keep an eye out for a rare, soaring eagle. It's a perfect place to sit with a cup of tea that could have been picked a stone's throw away, looking over an endless undulating carpet of tea bushes. From here, you can hike downhill 1km or so to the massive **Gunung Mas tea plantation**, which allows visitors to tour some of the site and try their tea.

On the Bandung side of the pass, **CIPANAS** is the first stop, a rather grotty town whose natural hot water is piped into baths in some of its hotels. It's still quite popular with domestic tourists and has a little nightlife, but it's pretty sleazy, with none of the natural beauty of nearby Cibodas. If you're wondering why all the town's names here are prefixed with "Ci", it means "water", and refers to the area's abundant supplies of natural volcanic hot water, or *cipanas*.

Cibodas

Coming from Bogor, 2km before Jalan Raya Puncak enters Cipanas, Jalan Raya Cibodas heads south (uphill) to the main gates of the Botanical Gardens of **Cibodas**. The road is one huge nursery, lined with flowers, bonsai trees and shrubs, all for sale. The beautiful gardens are filled with exotic plants and surrounded by the majestic, soaring mountains and thick forests of the wonderful **Gede Pangrango national park** (Taman Gede Pangrango).

A row of Padang **restaurants** at the turn-off up to Cibodas sell good cheap chicken and vegetable curries with rice. At the bottom of the hill on the right of Jalan Raya Cibodas are two very friendly Sundanese warung. Cibodas itself offers snack food stalls but very little in the way of warung. The only one of note is *Rizkys*, on the left-hand side of Jalan Raya Cibodas about 60m before the park gates. They are renowned for making a terrific fresh sambal to go with their basic rice dishes. The **Cibodas Golf Course**, 300m up the path to the right as the road splits, sells expensive Indonesian food and drinks. The beautifully kept course itself is in an exquisite location on the side of the volcanoes; green fees are Rp40,000–150,000, although the weekends are significantly more expensive.

Going on **to Bandung** from here, take a bemo to the bottom of the hill, cross the road and flag down any air-con bus (Rp16,500) for the 2–3hr journey, allowing more time in the late afternoon. Returning **to Jakarta**, you're best advised to flag down any non-air-con bus bound for Kg. Rambutan (Rp11,000) and take the #AC10 from there as far as the stand opposite the *Sari Pan Pacific Hotel,* if you're heading to Jalan Jaksa.

Accommodation

Most of the **accommodation** is to be found on Jalan Raya Cibodas; the usual problems with weekend overcrowding apply.

Cibodas Guest House and Valleyview Restaurant Jl Raya Cibodas 13–15a ⓣ0255/512051. A quality Balinese-style hotel, with views of the surrounding valley and a swimming pool. All rooms have TV and en-suite mandi. ❸

Freddy's Guest House On the right-hand side of Jalan Raya Cibodas, about 500m from the main park gates ⓣ0255/515473. Run by Freddy and his wife, this friendly B&B offers lovely views over this intensive market gardening area. The rooms are reasonable, with shared mandi. Birdlife International has long had connections with this losmen; you'll find a bird-watchers' log book here. Particularly keen bird-watchers should ask for Adam, who can take you to nesting sites of the endangered Java hawk-eagle. ❷

Pondok 145 Jl Raya Cibodas 145 ⓣ0255/511512. A friendly place with very basic and inexpensive rooms. Has a basic rumah makan next door that provides breakfast for all the guests. ❸

Pondok Pemuda Cibodas Directly after the toll gate into the gardens, but before the gardens themselves, the road splits right to this youth hostel (no phone). The dormitories here are best avoided, with their prison-camp-like rows of mattresses and large rodent population; the private rooms are better, but may also suffer from the rat problem. ❶–❷

Gede Pangrango national park

Established in 1889, **Cibodas** is one of the oldest tropical forest reserves in the world. Twinned with the Botanical Gardens of Bogor, this owes existence to Sir Stamford Raffles. **The Gede Pangrango national park**, backing onto the gardens, covers some 125 square kilometres. Now a UN-designated **World Heritage Site**, the park forms part of the UNESCO Man and the Biosphere Programme. It is particularly well-known for its **primate population**: the Java gibbon, ebony-leaf and rare Java leaf-monkeys and the common long-tailed macaque all breed here. The Java gibbon, known locally as *Owa* on account of its haunting "owa-owa" call, is the rarest gibbon in the world, with only around 100 animals here in the park and fewer than 1000 in total, its numbers having been sorely depleted by the household pet trade. Other rare inhabitants of the park include the blue leopard, leopard cat and even the occasionally heard but seldom seen Asian hunting dogs. Reptiles such as camotes lizards are, however, plentiful. You may also come into close contact with Malay stink badgers, so be prepared for their malodorous effusions. Trees in the park include the magnificent Guardsman-straight *rasamala*, once coveted far and wide for resin but now heavily logged-out in most places.

A **permit** is required to enter the park, and can be obtained at the Cibodas gate (daylight hours only; Rp2000). The excellent information centre near the gate provides information on walks, and shows films on environmental work within the park, and on its flora and fauna. Ask for the superb *Cibodas to Cibeureum* guidebook written by botanist Keith Harris.

Two **volcanoes** dominate the park. Gede, the more easterly of the two, stands 2958m above sea level; its first recorded eruption was in 1747, but the biggest was in the 1840s. It has now been silent since a small event in 1957, although many experts think it's due for a big blast. The taller and older peak, Pangrango, grew on top of the colossal Mandalawangi crater; it stands at 3019m above sea level, and is considered to be long extinct. The two peaks are connected by an extended ridge running at around 2400m; it's possible to walk between the two summits (2hr), along a path tangled with lichen-covered branches.

A three-kilometre walk from the main gate takes you up to the Cibeureum, Cidendeng and Cikundul **waterfalls**. Cibeureum is the largest, at an impressive 53m. On the way there are several shelters to avoid the rain; you'll also pass **Telaga Biru** (Blue Lake), which is really only a pond. Sometimes the water is a wonderfully pure deep blue, and at other times soluble volcanic nitrates in the water encourage algae to grow, forming a green slime across the surface. The lower sub-montane zone is dominated by large oaks, rattans, chestnuts and laurels, with many of the impressive buttressed trees and lianas typical of lowland rainforest.

After the waterfalls, 5km from Cibodas, a **hot-water stream** flows, where temperatures can reach 75°C. From here it's a long hard slog to the **summit of Gede**: in total, it's a ten-kilometre (5hr) trek uphill from Cibodas. It's also possible to follow trails over the mountainside to Selabintana in Sukabumi province, a nine-kilometre (5hr) walk. The summit of Gede offers spectacular views, particularly if you camp nearby the night before and can get here before the clouds roll in, but be warned that temperatures up here are about 9°C lower than in the village, and at night can fall close to 0°C. Near the top of Gede is an amazing **alpine meadow** named Suryakancana, strewn with edelweiss flowers. Pangrango's summit, on the other hand, is more forested, and views are limited. It's essential to be very well prepared for any walk to either summit: you should bring lots of water, food, warm clothes and strong walking boots; an umbrella may also come in handy.

The park's **birdlife** attracts ornithologists from all over the world. Its crowning glory is undoubtedly the emblematic Java hawk-eagle; Adam at *Freddy's Guest House* (see p.153) is an expert on this species, and can lead you to nesting sites. Other things to look for are mixed flocks with scarlet minivets and babblers, as well as Sunda blue robins, Sunda whistling thrushes and the truly lovely indigo flycatcher. Bird-watchers should come well equipped with binoculars and notebooks. *Birding Indonesia* (Periplus) contains a full species list for Indonesia.

Bandung and around

Nestling in a deep bowl 190km southeast of Jakarta and protected by a fortress of sullen volcanoes, **BANDUNG** is the capital of West Java. With a population exceeding 2.5 million, it's also the third largest city in Indonesia. 750m above sea level, Bandung has one of the most **pleasant climates** in the country, enjoying cooler days and slightly fewer rainstorms than Bogor to the west.

The city is primarily known as a centre of industry and education. Sixty percent of Indonesia's textiles are produced here, and the nation's aircraft and food-processing industries are based in the city. Sukarno studied at the Bandung Institute of Technology in the 1920s, and musicians, dancers and artists come here to study traditional art forms.

Bandung is a reasonably lively city, with a lot of restaurants, shops, bars and regular cultural performances, as well as a few good nightclubs. However, the city's few interesting **Art Deco** buildings are now lost in an ocean of smog-blackened plaster, crumbling pavements and chugging bemos, and the old alun-alun (town square) that was a tree-lined, refined social focus in colonial days is hemmed in by gaudy shopping centres and cinemas. The main attraction for visitors is the **surrounding countryside** – Tangkbuhan Prahu volcano to the north, and the tea plantations and waterfalls that separate the crater and the city suburbs. To the south are a profusion of hot springs and crater lakes as well as more tea plantations.

Some history

Bandung stands on a plain that was once a lake, drained away by an earthquake. When the Dutch arrived in the seventeenth century, the majority of the area was still saturated swampland. Before this, only a tiny village stood here, nominally part of the kingdom of Pajararan based in Bogor to the west. The area was almost unknown beyond its forbidding mountain ridges until 1628, when

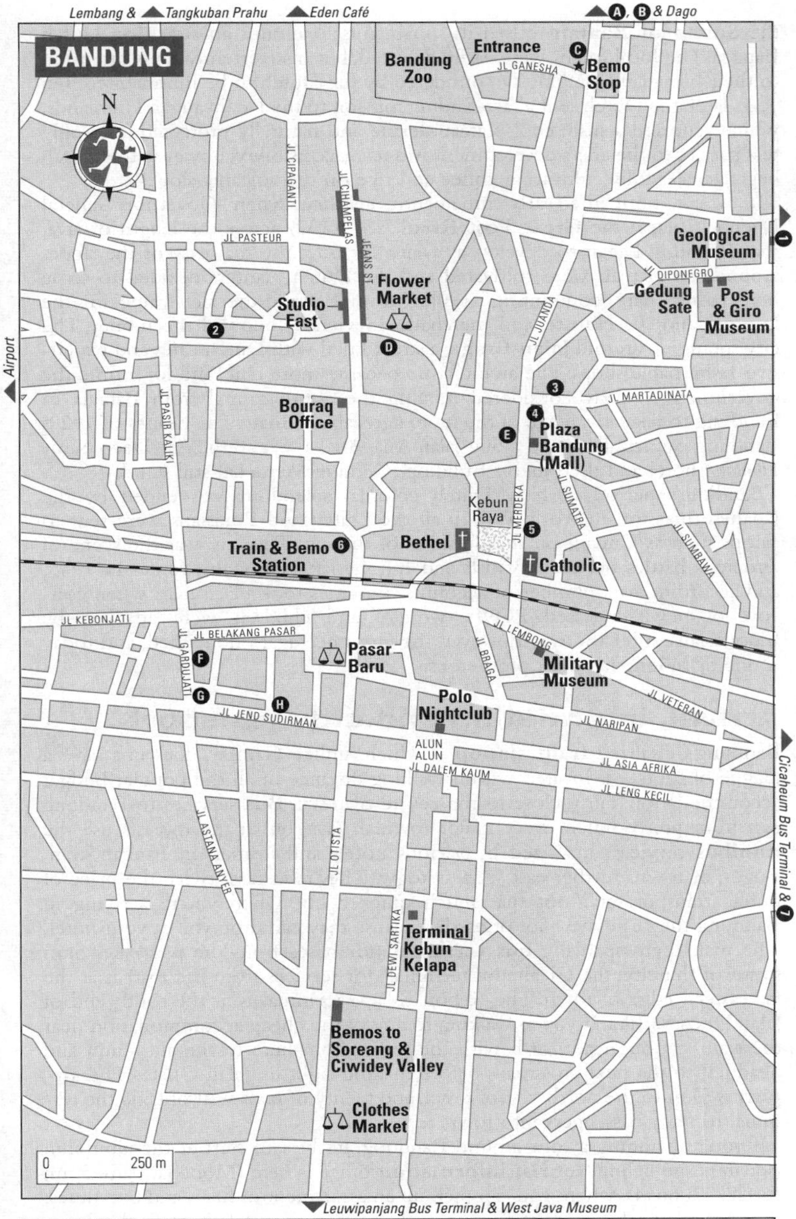

BANDUNG

Lembang & Tangkuban Prahu
Eden Café
A, B & Dago
Entrance
Bandung Zoo
JL GANESHA
C
Bemo Stop
JL CIPAGANTI
JL CIHAMPELAS
JL PASTEUR
JEANS ST
Geological Museum
1
JL DIPONEGRO
Gedung Sate
Post & Giro Museum
Flower Market
Studio East
2
D
JL JUANDA
Airport
3
JL MARTADINATA
Bouraq Office
JL PASIR KALIKI
4
E
Plaza Bandung (Mall)
JL MERDEKA
JL SUMATRA
Kebun Raya
Bethel
5
Catholic
JL SUMBAWA
Train & Bemo Station
6
JL KEBONJATI
JL BELAKANG PASAR
JL LEMBONG
JL GARDUJATI
F
Pasar Baru
JL BRAGA
Military Museum
G
H
Polo Nightclub
JL VETERAN
JL JEND SUDIRMAN
JL NARIPAN
ALUN ALUN
JL DALEM KAUM
JL ASIA AFRIKA
JL LENG KECIL
Cicaheum Bus Terminal & 7
JL ASTANA ANYER
JL OTISTA
JL DEWI SARTIKA
Terminal Kebun Kelapa
Bemos to Soreang & Ciwidey Valley
Clothes Market
0 250 m
Leuwipanjang Bus Terminal & West Java Museum

ACCOMMODATION

Anggrek Golden Hotel	3	Hotel Guntur	6
Wisma Asri	1	Hyatt	5
Catellya International Guest House	2	Pondok Pemuda	4
		Supratman 101 Youth Hostel	7

RESTAURANTS

Restaurant		Restaurant	
Dago Tea House	A	O'Hara's	H
Gardujati	F	RM Pulen 3	B
Hanamasa	E	Tizis	C
Holland Bakery	G	Toyoyo	D

the **Sultan of Banten** roused its inhabitants to mount an attack on Dutch Batavia. The local forces were easily defeated, but inadvertently drew attention to their homeland, previously considered by the Dutch to be uninhabited. Ten years later, the Dutch sent a fact-finding mission to the Parahyangan Highlands, which reported a lush, cool plateau, fertile and naturally protected. The only real barrier to the area's development was its inaccessibility; however, the Dutch began successfully cultivating coffee and rice on the volcanic slopes.

It wasn't until the early nineteenth century, when Governor-General Daendels began the **Great Post Road** (see p.132) across the length of Java, that Bandung began to develop as a city. By now, the majority of the slopes around the plateau were cultivated and the Dutch planters decided to settle here rather than "commuting" 190km from Batavia; the rich came for the hunting and the climate, and merchants inevitably followed the money. The city sprang up around **Jalan Braga**, a street lined with Dutch cafés and expensive, fashionable shops. The architecture became more chic, and for a time the government actually considered moving the entire capital from Batavia to Bandung to take advantage of the more agreeable climate. The beauty of 1920s Bandung can still be tasted along Jalan Asia-Afrika, where the Art-Deco *Savoy Homann* hotel and the Liberty Building (Gedung Merdeka) still stand.

Bandung's period of hazy Dutch colonial splendour was ended by the Japanese invasion in World War II; all the Dutch and Eurasians were sent to camps such as Cimahi on the outskirts of the city. The city was the scene of ferocious battles between British and Indonesian Nationalist forces in 1945, and according to a number of accounts, atrocities took place here when convoys of newly released POWs, women and children were attacked by Indonesians. After the war, however, the city once again flourished, and today is one of Indonesia's most prosperous.

Arrival, information and city transport

Bandung's civilized **train station** – which, unlike Gambir, does not have a plague of touts – is located within walking distance of all the popular budget accommodation, fairly close to the centre of town. **Bus** services to Bandung run from pretty much every major town in Java, but many tourists use the **minibus** services organized by various hotels and losmen in Pangandaran, Bogor, or towns further east such as Yogya. They're at least twice the price of public transport and not that much quicker, but when you're arriving in Bandung they can save a lot of hassle because they can drop you at your hotel. The main Leuwipanjang **bus terminal** (for buses from the west) lies 5km south of the city; the Cicaheum terminal (for services from the east) is at the far eastern edge of town. The Kebon Kelapa terminal is at the south end of Jalan Dewi Sartika. If you're walking to any of the cheap accommodation near the train station, head north with the traffic from here to the alun-alun and head left to the next crossroads before turning right up Jalan Otista. The **airport** is 5km to the northwest of town, and plenty of taxis wait outside the terminal to ferry passengers into town.

If you're planning a tour around Bandung, it's best to start at the alun-alun (square). The helpful **tourist information** office is here (Mon–Sat 9am–5pm; ⓣ022/4206644), where you can pick up an assortment of maps and brochures; the staff all speak excellent English and can give you details of forthcoming events and cultural performances. They also keep copies of the free magazine *Jakarta Kini*, published monthly by IndoMultiMedia and also covering West Java. While you should definitely not believe all the hype, this provides good practi-

cal information on restaurants, clubs and bars, and offers a bonanza of adverts for all of the upmarket hotels in Bandung. The square itself is surrounded by shopping centres, several cinemas, banks and towering tinted-glass high-rises.

Bandung's comprehensive **public transport system** can be confusing for the uninitiated. White and blue DAMRI buses are supercheap, at Rp250 a journey, and ply routes between the bus terminals through the centre of town. They're often very crowded, but if you wait for one to pull into any terminal it's generally easy to get a seat. At weekends, these minibuses are also allowed to use the Puncak Pass to get between Bogor and Bandung, while buses are diverted via Sukabumi to avoid the traffic. Red angkots also run a useful circular route, around and past the train station and square, to the Kebun Kelapa bus terminal, which services Cicaheum bus terminal, Dago and Ledeng. If you're heading to Lembang, take one of the angkots running from Station Hall on the south side of the station. Other angkots are usually named, but rarely with anything related to a destination you might need; it's best to ask a local.

Accommodation

Coming into town from the airport or bus terminals, it's usually best to get dropped off at the train station. The cheap **hostels** are all a stone's throw away, as are a few good mid-range places. If it's quality you're after, then head for the *Savoy Homann*, one of the most elegant hotels in the whole of Indonesia.

Inexpensive

Wisma Asri Jl Merak 5. Near to the Post and Giro Museum, this is a charming, quiet place with comfortable, clean rooms. The large rooms with shared mandi are a little overpriced, but those with air-con, TV, fridge and hot water are very reasonable. ❸–❹

Hotel Astia Graha Jl Dalam Kaum 130 ⓣ022/435202. Although very central, this is a quiet place with a TV in every room and Indonesian breakfast included in the price. ❸–❹

By Moritz Jalan Kebonjati/Luxor Permai 35 ⓣ022/4205788, ⓕ4207495. A popular travellers' hangout, with dormitory beds from Rp8500 a night, as well as singles and doubles with the choice of en-suite or shared mandi. Serves one of the best breakfasts around. ❶

Catellya International Guest House Jl Dr Rum 12 ⓣ022/435306. Located about fifteen minutes' walk uphill from the station, this reasonable place has rooms with en-suite mandi and is conveniently placed for the Lembang bemos that pass the front door. ❷

Hotel Citra Jl Gadujati 93 ⓣ022/6005061. Close to the train station, and one of the best bargains in Bandung. The sparkling rooms have mandi, TV, fan and air-con, although there's no breakfast. ❷

Hotel Guntur Jl Otto Iskandardinata 20 ⓣ022/4203763. An ageing hotel with pleasant, well-kept gardens; the double rooms have hot water and en-suite mandi. ❸

Hotel Palem Jl Belakang Pasar 119. Located behind the market of Pasar Baru, a five-minute walk from the station. The small but pleasant rooms come with TV and air-con. ❷–❸

New Le Yossie Jl Belakang Pasar 112 ⓣ022/4204543. The downstairs café is popular for breakfast, but the hostel itself is not quite as well kept as some of the others here. ❶

Pondok Pemuda Jl Merdeka 64 ⓣ022/4203155. Feels a bit like military barracks, but the prices reflect this. It's well known for its public music studios, where you can pay by the hour to record a masterpiece. ❶

Losmen Sakardana Jl Kebonjati 50/7b ⓣ022/439897. Rooms do not have a fan or breakfast included, but are very cheap; some travellers stay away because of the mournful-looking ebony leaf-monkey kept in a tiny cage by the foyer. ❶

Supratman 101 Youth Hostel Jl Supratman 102 ⓣ022/473204. Cheap and cheerful youth hostel that's a good place to hook up with Indonesian travellers. Dorm rooms are adequate. ❶

Surabaya Jl Kebonjati 73. Five minutes walk to the right of the station's south exit. *Surabaya* has the appearance of an old colonial coaching inn; the rooms here are adequate but long overdue a re-paint. ❶

Hotel Trio Jl Gardujati 55 ⓣ022/615755. Rooms range from basic ones with fan and en-suite mandi to those with hot water and air-con. The restaurant serves European and Japanese food, and every Wednesday they have a draw for a lucky couple to stay free. ❸–❹

Mid-range to expensive

Anggrek Golden Hotel Jl Martadinata 15 ⓣ022/4205537. The immaculate rooms have air-con, phone and hot water, and the prices are quite reasonable for the quality. ❺

Hyatt Jl Sumatra 51 ⓣ022/4211234, ⓕ4204090. Probably the flashiest five-star hotel in Bandung; the facilities include a health and fitness centre, Cantonese restaurant, gardens and a pub. ❼–❽

Hotel Panghegar Jl Merdeka 2 ⓣ022/432286, ⓕ431583. Well-known for its rooftop revolving restaurant, the *Panghegar* has all you would expect from a three-star hotel, with air-con, hot water, swimming pool and health club; it also stages classical dance on Wednesday and Saturday evenings. ❼–❽

Savoy Homann Jl Asia-Afrika 112 ⓣ022/432244, ⓕ436187. If you want colonial flavour then this is the place (see opposite). Sizeable rooms, some with views of the courtyard gardens. The excellent restaurant offers a full *rijsttaffel* for a minimum of six people (Rp20,000). ❽

The City

Heading east from the alun-alun down Jalan Asia-Afrika, you come to the **Gedung Merdeka building** on the opposite side of the road from the square. It was built in 1895 as a union building for Dutch associations, but achieved a degree of fame in 1955 as the site of the first Non-Aligned Movement Conference, where delegates from 29 countries met to discuss issues concerning both continents. Kwame Nkrumah and Nehru were among other luminaries apart from Sukarno attending. Today, the building is known as the Asia-Afrika or Liberty building, and has a small **museum** inside commemorating the founding conference. The auditorium is arranged as it was then, and is decorated with documents and photographs of the delegates.

Another building of interest on Jalan Asia-Afrika is the **Savoy Homann** hotel (see opposite). The first hotel on this site was a rickety bamboo affair raised on stilts, opened in 1871 by the Homann family just before the first rail link from Batavia. The present Art Deco structure with its distinctive curved facade was not opened until 1939, just in time for the invading Japanese to take it over as a hospital and residence for their officers. During the Asia-Afrika Conference, dignitaries such as Nasser, Sukarno and Ho Chi Minh all stayed here, and Sukarno allegedly employed call girls to garner information from prostrate diplomats. Slightly west of here is the beginning of **Jalan Braga**; in the 1920s it was a chic shopping boulevard, and there's still one **bakery** here that's tried to hang on to its history, while a few of the stylish facades remain above the Japanese fast-food and camera shops. The side streets that run off Jalan Braga were notorious before World War II for their raucous bars and brothels – at night a lot of the seediness remains, but without the liveliness. However, during the day it's an essential trip for the many quality bakeries fighting for your custom, with extravagant neon-decorated cakes, and sweet-looking pastries that are actually filled with curry.

Jalan Braga is bisected at its northernmost point by the train tracks, and a little further north is Bandung's biggest park, **Kebun Raya**, with the city hall and two large churches around it. Just east of here – off Jalan Sumatera – is the bizarre Taman Lalu Lintas, the "**Traffic Park**". Designed to educate kids in the way of the highway, it has a system of miniature cars, roads and street signs to introduce youngsters to road rage. A twenty-minute walk to the northeast of here, heading along streets with a few period buildings, is the **Gedung Sate** building at Jalan Diponegoro 22, known as the Sate Building because the regular globules on its gold-leaf spire resemble meat on a skewer. Built in the 1920s by a Dutch architect with Thai influences, it's one of the most impressive buildings in Bandung. Once the governor's office, it now houses local government offices. Next door to the Gedung Sate building is the **Post and Giro Museum** (Mon–Sat 9am–2pm; free), with stamps from around the world and assorted postal paraphernalia.

The excellent **Geographical Museum** (Mon–Thurs 9am–2pm, Fri 9–11am, Sat 9am–1pm; free) is near to the Gedung Sate at Jalan Diponegoro 57. Inside are mountains of fossils, rock and mineral samples, as well as several full dinosaur skeletons, a four-metre mammoth skeleton and a replica of the skull of the famous Java man. It's a huge building, which also houses Indonesia's geological survey offices. Other museums in the city include the **Military Museum** or Museum Wangsit Siliwangi at Jalan Lembong 38 (Mon–Fri 8am–2pm; free), which contains weapons and material from World War II, and celebrates the achievements of the Siliwangi regiment, the Green Berets of Indonesia, based in Bandung. There is also the **Museum of West Java Province** or Museum Negeri Jawa Barat (Tues–Sun 9am–2pm; free), southeast of the Kebon Kelapa terminal at Jalan Otto Iskandardinata 638. This contains a collection of mock-ups, reconstructing West Java's cultural history, including gamelan and angklung, as well as replicas of the *batu tulis* (inscribed stones) of Bogor.

Jeans Street

One of the foremost attractions of modern Bandung is Jalan Cihampelas, a kitsch kaleidoscope known to Westerners as **Jeans Street**, situated 1km to the north of the centre of town. For a stretch of a couple of hundred metres, the street is flanked by shopping centres, fast-food palaces and shops selling cheap T-shirts, bags, shoes and jeans. To attract the floating punter, shopfronts are adorned with colossal plaster giants straddling spaceships and fluffy stucco clouds – a wide-eyed five-metre Rambo with chipped curls and fading head-band glowers down onto cavorting aliens in Makkasar schooners. The full quotient of superheroes soar above signs for supercheap fake Levis (complete with instantly detaching buttons), the whole show played to a soundtrack of the worst bubblegum pop. The jeans that gave the street its name are no longer such a bargain, but there are some excellent cheap T-shirts, bags and trainers to be had, and no shortage of choice. Alternative places to Jalan Cihampelas to shop for bargain jeans are the south ends of Jalan Dewi Sartika and Jalan Otista; the latter has a huge clothes market.

Eating

Bandung offers a varied range of cuisine, with Japanese, Sundanese and Chinese food, plus European-style bakeries and fast food. Most of the huge shopping centres have the multinational chains represented, and some have excellent **food courts** as well. The Plaza Bandung on Jalan Merdeka is the city's best; they have *McDonald's*, *Churches Texas Fried Chicken*, *CFC* and *Dunkin' Donuts*. On the top floor is the Emerald Plaza, which serves a mixture of Indonesian, Japanese and Western fast food such as *teppanyaki*, *nasi rames*, *ayam bakar*, sandwiches and burgers, as well as a bewilderment of brightly coloured drinks. Yogya, near the alun-alun, is Bandung's top department store and has a top-floor food court. Here there's an *A&W* with Sundanese fast food, steaks, sandwiches and *Abra kebabra,* an Australian fast food outlet for palatable lamb, chicken or beef kebabs (Rp15000).

Chinese

Dunia Baru Jl Gardujati 39. The long menu includes chicken in oyster sauce for Rp14,000 and pork hotplate for Rp15,500.

Fung Ling Jl Gardujati 9. One of the best places in Bandung, specializing in dim sum. *Fung Ling* accepts all major credit cards and has a genuinely classy feel, with prices to match.

Gardujati Jl Gardujati 52. Serves Beijing food but specializes in frog and hotplate dishes, most of which cost Rp6000–12,000.

Hoo Reng Jl Kebun Kawang 64. The house speciality is *ayam kulayoak*, chicken fried in a kind of sweet-and-sour sauce at Rp11,000 – *ayam ca jamur* with corn is the same price and also delicious.

Queen Jl Dalam Kaum 79. An extremely popular place serving superb Cantonese food. The set menu is an excellent deal: for Rp15,000 you get crab and corn soup, sweet-and-sour pork, chicken soy, shrimps in a nut sauce, veggies, rice and fruit.

Siang-Siang Jl Gardujati 34. A brassy Chinese restaurant, serving big portions at reasonable prices.

Indonesian

There are **Indonesian warung** all over Bandung; Jalan Gardujati manages to combine some of the most enticing and nauseating odours in Asia. Side streets near the square serve some of the best warung food, with excellent seafood, soto and sate, while the nearby Ramayana department store's ground-floor food hall serves the same food in more sanitized surroundings. Jalan Dalam Kaum has some good **Indonesian restaurants**: *Bu Jin* at no. 124 and *Sari Bundo* at no. 75 are two of the better Padang restaurants in town. *Aneka Sari* at no. 60 specializes in *kangkung* at Rp8500.

Bakmi Ayam Jl Cibadak 52. Serves Indonesian staples such as nasi campur and ayam goreng at reasonable prices.
Happy Seafood Jl Kebon Kawang 26. Very cheap seafood: simply sift through the polystyrene buckets until you find the fish you fancy and they'll barbecue it in front of you.
Toyoyo Jl Pasir Kartiki 32. An Indonesian barbecue with excellent sate and baked chicken, mostly at under Rp8000 a head.

Japanese

Hanamasa Jl Merdeka 39–41. A selection of Japanese *izakaya* favourites such as *ebi furae* and *yakitori* – a little on the expensive side.
Kantin Jepang 88 Jl Braga 88. The The formica decor is a bit of a nightmare, but the food is fine: *ebi tempura* costs Rp8000; beef *yakiniku*, Rp7500; and *teriyaki*, Rp7500.

Sundanese

Dago Tea House At the north end of Jalan Juanda, and the welcome finishing point for the Maribaya to Bandung walk (see p.166). The fine views of Bandung valley and the outside tables are the primary attraction; diners sit on the floor on rattan mats looking down on the city. *Dago* serves good, reasonably priced Sundanese food, plus Western dishes such as steaks and omelettes.
RM Pulen 3 Jl Juanda 260. Up towards the *Dago Tea House* and the Bandung Zoo. Serves inexpensive, typical Sundanese food in a bamboo-rich setting. *Chicken cizzadin herbs* – a delicious piece of chicken with a tasty coating – costs Rp1500; *ikan masis* Rp15,000.
Sari Sunda Jl Sukarno Hatta 479/Jl Jenderal Sudirman 103–107. Two separate places run by the same management, both serving superb Sundanese food in pleasant surroundings. The croquette potatoes and tofu baked with chilli in banana leaves is excellent.
Sindang Raret Jl Naripan 9. More a destination for its Saturday-evening wayang golek performances than for its slightly overpriced food and gaudy interior. *Gurame* fish is a speciality at Rp12,000, and a large *bintang* costs Rp6000.

Western

Western food is available from food courts in the big shopping centres and department stores, as well as in most of the hotel restaurants.

Amsterdam Café Jalan Braga. Popular with expats, this place serves outrageously small beers at large-bottle prices along with steaks and burgers.
Myukebra Jl Kebon Kawang 9. At the bemo terminal on the north side of the train station. Has live music on Saturday nights. Set meals include steak, French fries and a drink for Rp9500.
North Sea Bar Jalan Braga 82. A long-established and slightly sleazy expat hangout serving expensive European fare such as Wiener schnitzel and steak (Rp30,000).
Tizis Jl Kidang Pananjung 3; off Jalan Juanda, just north of the large bemo stop. A real find and an expat haven, *Tizis* home-cook possibly the best bread, sausages and pastries in Java. There's a sit-down restaurant serving steaks, pizzas and ice cream, and the glazed apple pie (Rp2800) is sensational.

Bakeries

Due to the European influence in Bandung, the town has many **bakeries**, particularly along Jalan Braga, while *Tizis* (see above) offers some of the best bread and cakes in Java.

Braga Permai Jl Braga 58. A flashy and expensive bakery out the back of the even flashier restaurant (complete with grand piano). They offer thirty kinds of ice cream and very elaborate cakes.
Holland Bakery Jalan Gardujati. There are a number of these bakeries around Bandung, serving Indonesian-style cakes.
London Bakery Jalan Braga. A modern European-type place serving a range of coffees and teas and with newspapers and books in English.
Sari Sari Jl Sudirman 90. An excellent delicatessen and bakery serving takeaway curries, soups and vegetarian fare as well as imported crisps and snacks.
Sumber Hidangan Jalan Braga. Apparently the same as it was in the 1930s; it certainly hasn't been painted since. Serves pastries, ice cream and Western snacks among yellowing black-and-white photos of the café's heyday.

Nightlife

For such a large city, Saturday nights are surprisingly unpredictable and you can't count on your chosen bar or nightclub being lively. On weekdays, you're best off heading for the **bars**. Most **clubs** start late on Fridays and Saturdays, with places like *Fame Station*, *Polo* and *Studio East* not really kicking off until midnight.

Caesars Palace Jl Braga 129. This aspires to being the most upmarket nightclub in Bandung. Prepare to be stung at the bar – a small beer retails at Rp25,000. Door staff are fussy but unspecific about their dress code, so don't come looking messy. 8pm–3am daily; Rp30,000.

Enhaii Jl Setiabudi 186. A real student hangout bar with pool tables and darts; the live bands have a tendency to perform wailing Beatles numbers.

Fame Station 11th floor, Lipo Building, Jl Gatot Subroto. This club has a generally lively, young crowd and often features live music. It serves Western food, and offers terrific views of the city. 11am–2am daily; Rp15,000.

Laga Pub Jl Junjungan 164. With food and live music every night, this is an expat favourite. A beer costs a reasonable Rp7000, and there's a Rp5000 cover charge.

North Sea Bar Jl Braga 82. An unashamed pick-up joint for the older expat male – others may be a little put off by the seedy atmosphere and hefty prices. Open daily until 2am.

O'Hara's *Hotel Perdana Wisata*, Jl Jenderal Sudirman 66–68. Looks more like a Boston tavern than an Irish pub, with polished wood and American pictures everywhere. The live music is generally covers of mainstream pop; Rp8000.

Polo 15th floor, BRI building, Jalan Asia-Afrika. The expensive nightclub for Bandung's young elite; the music is mainly imported, from house to Euro-techno, which makes it the place for serious partying. 10pm–3am daily; Rp20,000.

Studio East Jl Cihampelas 129. Draws a very young, mostly student crowd to the packed, sizeable dance floors; they play a variety of dance music. You're likely to get completely mobbed by friendly Bandung students. 10pm–2am daily; Rp10,000.

Cultural performances

Bandung is the capital of Sundanese culture, with a high percentage of West Java's artists choosing to live and study here. To find out about special performances, pick up a copy of *Jakarta Kini* magazine from the tourist information office. Worth visiting is Sang Angklung Mang Ujo, a workshop where children study **angklung** and will perform for visitors. To get there, take a Cicaheum colt and ask to be let off at Padsuka near the Cicaheum terminal; from there, it's a five-minute walk north up on the right-hand side of the road.

Most regular cultural performances, however, are held at hotels or restaurants. The *Sindang Reret* restaurant at Jalan Naripan 9 has Saturday-evening **wayang golek** performances at 8pm, which can be enjoyed with a traditional Sundanese meal. At Jalan Merdeka 2, the *Panghegar* hotel has Wednesday- and Saturday-evening cultural performances in its restaurant, which usually consist of Sundanese dance and classical singing; you don't have to pay for the show, but you do have to have a meal. The *Sakadarna* homestay (see p.158) has Saturday-evening shows by Banten's **debus players**, who perform feats of self-mutilation, such as eating glass and setting red-hot coals upon their heads. On Sunday mornings there are often shows at Bandung Zoo in the north of town, usually either the Indonesian martial art **pencak silat**, or **puppet plays**.

In addition, many of the small villages around Bandung have wayang golek performances on Saturday evenings which can go on all night, the puppets often commenting on village gossip in rough, crude dialogue. If you want to go to one of these performances, the tourist information centre doesn't offer much help with details; you'll have to find yourself a contact in one of the kampung, and make sure a camera-wielding tourist will be welcome.

Probably the most spectacular event to be seen in the Bandung area is the local sport of **ram fighting**. To the sound of Sundanese flutes and drums, the rams are set 10m apart and then released. They sprint together, before making a huge rearing lunge till their horns clatter together with a bone-shuddering crack. There's no blood; just flying wool and clouds of dust as the locals wildly speculate on which ram will back off first. These fights begin at 10am every other Sunday near the Ledung terminal on Jalan Setiabudi. It's a 500-metre walk up Jalan Serson Bajuri; ask directions to the *adu domba*.

Shopping

Bandung's biggest **market**, the *pasar baru*, lies between the train station and the square. It's a bit of a fleapit, and offers little to tempt tourists to part with their rupiah. A much more aesthetically pleasing place, however, is the *pasar bunga*, the **flower market** just east of Jeans Street by the river. Kings **department store** near the square is good for clothes and sarongs, while the Sarinah department store at the southern end of Jalan Braga has a range of souvenirs from all over the archipelago (although it's not as extensive as the one in Jakarta). Jalan Sulawangi features a cooperative called Just For You, an organization employing handicapped people to make **batik** and **crafts** for tourist souvenirs. Just north of the train station on Jalan Kebon Kawang is the Cupu Manik wayang golek **puppet-making factory**, where you can buy puppets for upwards of Rp30,000. Jalan Cibaduyut in southwest Bandung has a variety of shops selling bags, leather shoes, sandals and T-shirts at reasonable prices.

Listings

Airline offices Garuda had its main offices in the *Hotel Preangher Aerowista* at Jl Asia-Afrika 181 but the hotel burnt down in May 2002. Merpati is at Jl Asia-Afrika 73, while the Bouraq office is at Jl Cihampelas 27, on the way to Jeans Street.
Banks and exchange There are plenty of banks in Bandung, including the BRI on the alun-alun. The two Golden Megacorp moneychangers on Jalan Lembong opposite the 24hr Telkom building and at Jalan Otista 180 have excellent rates but often long queues.
Bookshops Several places on Jalan Braga sell English-language books and newspapers.
Galleries Galeri 16, Jl Raya Cibeureum 16; Galeri Adira, Jl Kiara Condong 33E; Galeri Café and Spa, Jl Sersan Bajuri Km 4.7; Taman Budaya Jl Bukit Dago Selatan 53 ☎022/2504912.
Hospital There is a 24hr clinic with English-speaking doctors at Jl Cihampelas 161.
Post office The main branch is on Jalan Asia-Afrika at the corner of Jalan Banceuy (Mon–Sat 8am–9pm).
Telkom For international telephone, telex and fax, the main Telkom office is on Jalan Lembang (24hr); there are also numerous wartels around town.

North of Bandung

The mountainous region to the north of Bandung is the heart of the **Parahyangan Highlands** – the "Home of the Gods" – a highly volcanic area considered by the Sundanese to be the nucleus of their spiritual world. The sights of this area can just about all be covered in a day, if you start early. Public transport runs right to the summit of **Tangkuban Prahu volcano**, where you can walk around the craters for a few hours and catch a bemo to **Ciater** to relax in the **hot springs** there, or visit the busy little market town of **Lembang**. Heading back towards Bandung, **Maribaya** offers some more hot springs and also a set of **waterfalls**. From Maribaya, there's an established walk down through the monkey-filled forest to the *Dago Tea House* (see p.161), where you can enjoy Sundanese food and – of course – a cup of locally grown tea, while looking down on Bandung city.

Tangkuban Prahu

One of the most famous – and most visited – volcanoes in West Java, 1830-metre **Tangkuban Prahu** lies 29km to the north of Bandung. The volcano's name translates as "the upturned boat", a tag whose origin is obvious if you get a day clear enough to see the volcano at a distance from Bandung. To get there from Bandung, take a Subang minibus from the train station (30min; Rp2000) and ask to be put down at the turn-off for the volcano. At the turn-off there's a guard post, where you must pay Rp1250 to visit the volcano. An asphalt road runs right to the top of the volcano; from the guard post you can charter an ojek or minibus to the summit (10min; Rp5000) or wait until a number of people arrive and share a minibus. Alternatively you could walk up – it's about 4km up the main road, or there's a good detour via the Domas Crater. Simply walk just over 1km up the road from the guard post, then take the footpath to the right by the first car park.

The **volcano** has not had a serious eruption for many years, though in 1969 there were a series of explosions and expulsions of mud, ash and smoke. Today, the volcano still spews out vast quantities of sulphurous gases, and at least one of its **ten craters** is still considered active. The main crater is called Kawah Ratu (Queen's Crater) – this is the one you can see into from the end of the main road. The car park at the summit is usually filled with vendors come to take advantage of the hundreds of visitors every day. There is also a small **information booth** here, where you can get details about walking around the main crater and down to some of the smaller ones. Kawah Ratu is a huge cauldron of dull greys, with occasional splashes of yellow and black, and sometimes a small coloured crater lake. If you walk around the crater for about 500m, the

The legend of Tangkuban Prahu

The Sundanese have a **fable** to explain the distinctive shape of **Tangkuban Prahu**. Sunda was once ruled by a king and queen with a beautiful but petulant daughter. One day as she sat weaving she dropped her shuttle and vowed she would marry whoever returned it to her. Unfortunately the family's faithful dog came back with the shuttle in his mouth. When the princess married the dog and they had a son, **Sangkuriang**, the princess decided to keep his father's identity secret from her new offspring. One day the young prince and the dog went hunting, but without success; ashamed to return home empty-handed, Sangkuriang killed the dog and had it served to his mother. When eventually the dog was missed, the prince was forced to confess. The princess was so distraught she struck Sangkuriang a fierce blow on the head and then disappeared, to wander the kingdom alone.

Some years later, she met a man and fell in love with him. On their wedding day, however, she discovered a mark on his head and realized it was the scar that he bore from her own blow and that he could only be her son. Desperate to put off the wedding, she set the condition that before sunrise Sangkuriang would have to build a huge dam across Sungai Citarum and build a boat for the two of them to sail away in, or they could not be married. He laboured through the night with the help of friendly spirits, and his mother soon saw that he would accomplish the task. In desperation, she called on the gods to save her and they broke the walls of the mighty lake. As the waters rushed away, Sangkuriang's boat was overturned and he was crushed beneath it. The mother then took her own life. Looking at Tangkuban Prahu from a distance, you can see in silhouette the capsized hull of Sangkuriang's boat.

other craters soon become visible; if you're so inclined, you can trek right down into these hissing, smelly pits and see pools of bubbling mud and clouds of rotten egg gas. From the summit you can also trek down to **Domas Crater**, which has fine views and, still, a small working sulphur mine. Many guides offer their services to aid people on tours around the volcanoes, but they're not really necessary, as it's pretty obvious where you should and shouldn't go – but be sure to wear strong hiking boots, and use common sense.

Ciater hot springs

Any minibus heading northeast from the gates of Tangkuban Prahu will take you the 6km to **CIATER**, a small village nestling among the tea fields. The hot springs here have been tapped into a set of hot falls, showers and pools for the exclusive use of the *Sari Ater Hot Spring Resort* (☎0264/470894; ❼–❽). The resort offers electrotherapy, hydrotherapy, acupuncture, restaurants, tennis courts, horse-riding and, of course, natural hot water; it also has an extensive range of facilities, and all rooms have TV, video, fridge, telephone and most have heaters. Those not staying at the resort can still use the springs, for a price – it costs Rp2500 to enter the complex and a further Rp7000 to use the pools, which is well beyond the pockets of Ciater locals. The pools are, however, some of the best around; you can sit under the steaming waterfalls at night, when the outside air is decidedly chilly – on clear nights it's a sensational place for stargazing. There are plenty of cheap losmen and a few warung on the main road in Ciater, with prices starting at about Rp15,000.

From Ciater, you can take a minibus further north to the **Ciater tea factory**. The road ascends into the mountains, with tea bushes stretching into the distance in every direction. The factory itself offers a tour for visitors, where you can see the tea being processed, taste some of the product and climb a lookout tower for some awesome views.

Lembang

The return journey from Tangkuban Prahu to Bandung passes through **LEMBANG**, a hill town known mainly for its fruit and vegetable market but with a few quality hotels. This bustling little market town lies on the slopes of Tangkuban Prahu, a highly productive agricultural area. The town is the last resting place of the famous German researcher of Java, **Franz Wilhelm Junghuhn**, author of *Topographical and Natural Science Journeys Through Java*, who is honoured in the taman (park) bearing his name.

Three kilometres west of the town is a large and splendid Thai temple, **Visanna Graha**, run by the Thai Dharmaduta Foundation and located just before the village of Cisarua. The temple affords a pleasing profile against the mountains on a clear day. To get there, take a bemo from the left turning just before the arch at the southern end of Lembang. About 4 km further along this road is the Cimahi Waterfalls (Curug Cimahi), which you can get to by ojek from the Cisarua terminal. Weekdays, this spot makes a good place for a quiet toe-dip.

The scenic landscape around Lembang affords some spectacular cycling opportunities with sharp uphill and downhill stretches; Lembang to Curug Cimahi (7km), and the road northeast towards Subang are probably the best. Cyclists may also enjoy the 15km run uphill from Bandung on a sharply winding road, although care should be taken with oncoming buses. All over this area, vistas of the mountain scenery and the lush cultivation open up.

If you are breaking your journey at Lembang, there are a couple of recommended places to stay. *Pondok Bella Vista*, Jl Kol Masturi 3, is a pleasant losmen with clean rooms and outside mandi (❷). To get there, turn left just before the arch at the southern entrance to Lembang. *Pondok Panorama*, Jl Tangkuban Perahu 22 ⓣ022/2786190; ❶), is a reasonable losmen with friendly staff, beside the main road north out of town.

Maribaya to Dago

From Lembang terminal near the market, you can take one of the frequent minibuses (Rp500) 4km to **MARIBAYA** a resort that at weekends is jam-packed with people (Rp2000). The **waterfalls** near to the entrance gate are surrounded by landscaped paths, which have the effect of making even the falls look artificial. Nearby are the **hot springs**, which have been tapped into a public pool. Further down from the main melee of people and vendors is the largest waterfall, which you have to pay an additional fee to see. In an unfortunate piece of Asian tourist site planning, a huge iron bridge painted red has been built right across the lip of the falls. From the bridge itself you can only see the river, as the falls are too close; from below, it completely obscures the view of what is clearly a spectacular waterfall. However, the bridge is the starting point for a wonderful walk down to the **Dago Tea House** (see p.161) on the edge of Bandung. The walk is about 6km and will take under two hours, all of it downhill. The path winds through a gorge and forests; just before the teahouse are tunnels used by the Japanese in World War II and the **Dago waterfall**, surrounded by bamboo thickets. From *Dago's*, plenty of minibuses head back into the centre of town (15min; Rp500).

South of Bandung

The little-visited volcanic region to the south of Bandung ought to receive more visitors than it does. The scenic **Ciwidey Valley** offers good walks and hot springs, and lies only two hours southwest of the city. The other main attraction is the **Cisangkuy Valley**, offering mountain scenery and tea estates. The Ciwidey Valley leads to the forested slopes of **Gunung Patuha**, at 2,434m one of the highest peaks in the Parahyangan Highlands. At its summit lies **Kawah Putih**, a small crater lake that changes colour from white to blue.

The town of **CIWIDEY** forms a good base for exploring this area; it's set in richly productive agricultural land – even strawberries are grown here – and you can still see traditional blacksmiths at work. To get here from Bandung, walk towards the southern end of Jalan Otista until you find a green bemo (every 10min; Rp2000) for the 45-minute journey heading south to Soreang, a market town with many ponies-and-traps. From the market place there, continue 10km uphill for the twenty- to thirty-minute journey to Ciwidey by bemo (every 10min; Rp2000).

For **accommodation**, the *Sindang Reret* on Jalan Ciwidey Raya just before the north end of the town offers comfortable air-con rooms and a traditional Sundanese restaurant set over fishponds (ⓣ022/5928205; ❸). Bemos (Rp1000) run uphill every fifteen minutes or so from the marketplace to **Cimanggu** hot springs (Rp2000) below Gunung Patuha – there are chalets for rent here (❺), as well as the hot springs pool (Rp2000) at Walini, a further 1km away among the tea estates. You can also continue to the little lake at Situ Patengan, where boats can be hired.

Cyclists can put their bikes on top of a Soreang-bound bemo; from Soreang, the eighteen-kilometre climb uphill to Cimanggu sets a challenge for the fittest. Walking is recommended, and if you alight at the gate to Wisata Kawah Putih just before Cimanggu, there's a challenging two-and-a-half-hour trek up the road to the top of Gunung Patuha. A large rock on the left about 1.5km from the gate affords a fantastic early morning view across the Bandung Basin to Tangkuban Prahu, and even to Gunung Ciremai some 70km away to the northeast. The forest further up provides excellent bird-watching opportunities; you may be lucky with sightings of soaring eagles.

Thickly forested Gunung Tilu (2,043m) forms another diversion. To get there, take an ojek from the village of Cisondari, about 2km north of *Sindang Reret*, to the village of Gambung 12km away; haggle with the drivers for a fare out to this cool spot. A little further on is the tea research station at Gambung, where it's possible to hire a guide for a trek on Gunung Tilu, which offers splendid walking through bird-rich forest.

In the neighbouring **Cisangkuy Valley**, the last 15km uphill into the mountain town of Pangelengan are remarkable for the beauty of the cultivated terraces. **PANGELENGAN** itself is an unprepossessing little market centre; opposite the bus terminal here you'll find *Pondok Puri Pangelengan*, a reasonable losmen with non-air-con rooms (❷). Pangelengan is surrounded by the huge Malabar Tea Estates, which afford terrific views of the surrounding mountains, including Gunung Tilu. If you want to spend some time here, the *Malabar Guest House* (❺) on the tea estate of the same name is a cool and peaceful retreat from which a number of invigorating walks and cycle rides can be undertaken. The rooms are comfortable and each comes with a shaded porch. Prior booking is advisable. Contact PTP, Nusantara VIII, Jl Sindangsirna 4, Bandung ⓣ022/2038966 (ask for Conny).

To get to Pangelengan from Bandung, take a non-air-con bus from Kebon Kacang (every 30min; Rp4000) or walk to the south end of Jalan Otista, from where bemos (every 10min; Rp2000) run to the dirty little market town of Banjaran. Change here for buses running up the valley.

Sumedang

The relaxed and prettily located town of **SUMEDANG** lies two hours northeast of Bandung, and is famous throughout Java for *tahu Sumedang* (deep-fried bean curd). Set among volcanic peaks, Sumedang has a fine local museum, and offers a quiet retreat to break the journey from Bandung to Cirebon. To get there, catch a Cirebon-bound bus (every 30min, 1–2 hr; Rp4500) from Bandung's Cicaeheum terminal. You'll cross the most notorious stretch of the historic **Groote Postweg**, the Great Post Road (see p.132); many of the 30,000 Javanese labourers who lost their lives during its construction died on the section around Tanjungsari, halfway between Bandung and Sumedang. If you catch the bus as far as Tanjungsari and ask to be put off at *Patung Kornel* (Kornel Statue), you can absorb something of the history of this scheme. The statue depicts a meeting between **Prince Kornel**, the ruler of Sumedang, and the Dutch governor-general **Marshal Daendals**. Kornel, who had protested the waste of life, can be seen extending his left hand in greeting to Daendals, an unmistakeable sign of contempt.

In town, on Jalan Geusan Ulun stands an excellent little museum, **Praba Geusan Ulun** (daily 8am–noon, Fri 8–10am), which houses a good collection of traditional Sundanese weaponry, as well as the crown jewels and other finery of the Pajajaran kings. If you want to stay in Sumedang, try the *Hanjuang Hegar*, Jalan Mayor Abdurachman 165 (ⓣ0261/201820; ❷–❸). Don't be put off by the rather dark reception area; this is a friendly hotel with some air-con rooms.

For those staying in Sumedang, the 1684m **Gunung Tampomas** north of the town is an added attraction, climbable within a day from the village of

Cimalaka (7km north of Sumedang), and the adventurous are rewarded with terrific views across the peaks and farmlands of the surrounding area. To get there, take a bemo to Cimalaka and ask for "galian pasi", the gravel-mining site from which a comfortable trail winds uphill (2-3hr). It's possible to find a guide in the village.

This volcanic area also offers good opportunities for **cycling** and **motorcycling**. The very scenic route southeast towards Tasikmalaya through Wado and Malangbong takes you through the upper Cimanuk Valley and across the slopes of Gunung Cakrabuwana. The northeasterly route takes you to Subang around the slopes of Gunung Tampomas.

Garut, Cipanas and around

Surrounded on all sides by volcanic mountains, the original Javan spa town of **GARUT** was once known as the "Switzerland of Java". Since the 1920s, it has been a retreat for those coming to laze in natural hot water and wander in the surrounding countryside to waterfalls, rivers and steaming volcano craters. Today, Garut has become a large modern town, rather noisy and grimy, and its popularity has greatly diminished. However, it's easily accessible by bus from Bandung (every 30min, 2hr; Rp2000), and Tasikmalaya (every 30min, 2hr; Rp2000).

The majority of visitors choose instead to head right to the foot of Gunung Guntur and **CIPANAS**, a quiet village 6km from Garut with guesthouses and hotels. The main attraction here is the abundant hot, clean water piped into tiled baths in all the hotels, losmen and private houses. There are many settlements in West Java called Cipanas – it means "hot water" – but this is by far the most appealing. From Garut bus station, walk round to the next-door bemo terminal and take the brown bemo #4 to Cipanas (15min; Rp500).

Cipanas is a delightful place to stay, and its surrounding villages are also a picture-postcard idyll of Javanese rural life. The plentiful rice paddies are punctuated by large, glassy ponds making perfect reflections of the surrounding palm trees and flowering bushes. Often you can see the remarkable sight of scores of villagers, waist deep in the water, herding tens of thousands of tiny fish into pens made out of moss and pondweed. Other villagers sort the fish into rattan baskets to be sold in town. Looming in the background to the village are the sulky volcanic peaks of Gunung Guntur, Galunggung, Papandayan and the perfect cone of Cikurai. You can walk to nearby waterfalls and can climb Gunung Guntur – a hard five-hour trek.

Accommodation and eating

All **accommodation** listed here lies along the road running into Cipanas from the main Bandung–Garut road; every place features piped-in hot-water baths. The larger hotels all have **restaurants**, the *Tirta Merta* probably the most reasonably priced. There is also a row of warung beside the *Tirtagangga* that serve basic fare including reasonably priced sate, as well as cold beer.

Pondok Asri Jl Raya Cipanas 184 ☎0262/231209. The rooms here are nothing special, but have the largest baths in town. ❷–❸

Cipanas Indah Jl Raya Cipanas 113 ☎0262/233736. Prices at this plush place double during holidays and weekends; otherwise, the pristine bungalows and rooms are a good bargain, and have all amenities. The restaurant is not bad, with a few European dishes to supplement the Sundanese cooking. ❺–❼

Cipta Bela Jl Raya Cipanas 111 ☎0262/231494. A very standard place: there are at least ten others around it which are practically identical. All have clean, white-tiled bedrooms and bathrooms whose plaster is in an advanced state of steam decay. ❷

Kurnia Jl Raya Cipanas 131. Arguably the best deal in Cipanas, this place has rooms made from rattan and bamboo and is very cheap. ❷

Pondok Melatim Jl Raya Cipanas 133. A pleasant place with rattan rooms and nice, deep baths. They claim not to raise their prices at weekends. ❷
Putra Lugina Jl Raya Cipanas 711 ⓣ0262/237767. Behind the *Cipta Bela*, a quiet establishment with large rooms and big reductions midweek. ❸
Tirta Merta The first hotel on the left as you pass through the gateway into Cipanas. Reasonably upmarket rooms; the restaurant's speciality is ginseng coffee with a long list of its restorative qualities to supplement the healing waters. ❹–❺
Tirtagganga Hot Springs Jl Raya Cipanas 130 ⓣ0262/231811. The most expensive, and easily the best, place here – Suharto stayed here in the past. Has a large, clean outdoor swimming pool with the novel addition of a poolside bar, where you can order a beer waist deep in steaming water. ❺–❼
Tirta Sari Jl Raya Cipanas 120. Rooms lack natural light, but the place is cheap and has good views across the ponds towards Gunung Cikurai. ❷
Pondok Wulandari Jl Raya Cipanas 99 ⓣ0262/234675. Unusually for this area, the well-kept rooms all come with a fan and TV, and are a good bargain at the price. ❸

Around Garut

Ten kilometres north of Garut, on lily-covered **Situ Cangkuang** is a small island with the only Hindu shrine left in West Java, which possibly dates to the ninth century, older than both Borobudur and Prambanan. It's not particularly big or impressive, but boatmen will take you over to the island on punted bamboo rafts across the flower-tangled waters – an experience which makes the trip worthwhile. Take any bemo or bus heading to Bandung and ask to be let off at Leles; from here it's a fifteen-minute walk to the lake.

The most impressive sight in the area is the active volcano, **Gunung Papandayan**, 25km southwest of Garut town. Catch a minibus to Cisurapan, the turn-off for the volcano road, a small village with a cluster of houses and a few warung. Here hordes of ojek riders wait to ferry tourists the 8km to the summit car park. From the car park, it's a fifteen-minute uphill walk to the centre of the crater, and all around you pools of bubbling mud and enthusiastic steam geysers spew out sulphurous clouds, the vents marked by sparkling yellow deposits, a continual roar and a poisonous stench. Papandayan's biggest eruption was in 1772, but it is still distinctly alive. Trek upwards from the crater for superb views down into the valley and of the surrounding, forested peaks; the path leads upwards to a saddle at the crater rim, between twin summits. From here you can choose to walk upwards to either of the summits, or you can take the path right over the top of the mountain to descend into the valley on the other side. The path heads through beautiful forests full of skinny eucalyptus and fan palms, before suddenly breaking out into an endless unnaturally perfect expanse of tea plantations. Be warned that this is a very isolated area: you will be more than welcome in the villages, but when you need to return to civilization there is only one truck a day, which circles the area for Bandung at 8am. Otherwise, it's a five-hour return trek over the mountain and back to Cisurupan.

From Garut, a road winds for about 35km through tea plantations and pine forests to the **south coast**. **Pameungpeuk** is the main town, and has a couple of losmen. All the way from here to Pelabuhan Ratu is a coastal road with small villages that see very few visitors. The beaches are stunning and usually empty of people, but due to the strong currents you're best advised to stay close to shore when swimming.

Kampung Naga

About halfway between Garut and Tasikmalaya lies **KAMPUNG NAGA**, a tiny village in a steep-sided valley. The village's houses were constructed to ancient Sundanese dictates, with bamboo walls and thatched roofs, arranged facing the rising sun in neat rows. Kampung Naga is extremely picturesque, snug amongst the stepped rice paddies and shaded by abundant palm trees. There are a few souvenir stalls and a mosque, and though there's not really much to do here and locals pay scant attention to tourists zapping through on whistle-stop photo opportunity tours, they are extremely welcoming to (and curious about) those who take the trouble to stop and have a chat. To get to the village, take any bus between Garut and Tasikmalaya and ask to get off at Kampung Naga – you'll probably have to pay the full fare to Tasikmalaya (Rp5000–15,000). It takes about fifteen minutes to walk to the village down steep concrete steps. There is no accommodation here, but a handful of warung line the main road.

Tasikmalaya

Lying 120km southeast of Bandung is the town of **TASIKMALAYA**, famous for its batik cloth and woven rattan goods. There's not a tremendous amount to do in Tasik, but it's a good base for climbing **Gunung Galunggung**, which last erupted in the early 1980s. The crater has a large green and bubbling lake, most of the surrounding area is thick with ash and there are occasional expulsions of ash, smoke and even rocks from numerous vents around the area. The best way to reach the summit is to take a minibus to Pasar Indihiang (30min; Rp700) and then change to another minibus or ojek to get you to Cipanas (45min; Rp2500). From the village it's a two-hour walk to the summit and there's only one trail, so you don't really need a guide. There are some **hot springs** at the beginning of the trail – a good spot to relax after the climb.

The road from Garut to Tasikmalaya passes through some especially beautiful volcanic scenery, the best of which is around **Malangbong**, lying below Gunung Cakrabuwana and Gunung Sedakeling, 15km before Tasikmalaya. The last part of the road into Tasik from Bandung, about 10km before you reach the town, is lined with innumerable stalls selling rattan, wooden and **bamboo handicrafts**: baskets, carvings, lampshades, floor-mats and furniture. The handicrafts-producing village of **Rajapolah**, 12km north of Tasikmalaya, will also turn up some bargains. Hats are the centrepiece here, including *topi pandan*, made from pandanus leaves, the water weed *topi samak*, and *dudukuy cetok*, the farmer's hat made from split bamboo; you can also find decorated umbrellas. Buses between Tasik and from Garut (every 30min) should cost Rp4500 for non-air-con.

Practicalities

Tasikmalaya **train station** is fairly central, 800m northeast of the square, on the main line from Yogya to Jakarta, while the **bus station** is about 3km southwest of town so you'll need to catch a bemo or becak to get between the two. The *Hotel Yudanegara*, at Jalan Yudanegara 19 (Ⓣ0265/324906; ❹–❺), is the plushest in town: all its rooms have hot water, TV and air-con. For a more basic option, try the *Tasik* at Jalan Komala Sari 29 (❶), a friendly family-run hotel, where the rooms come with en-suite mandi but no fan. Most of the other **accommodation** is on the central Jalan Yudanegara, where the mosque and police station are situated; there are also a lot of luxury hotels out on Jalan Martadinata, the road to Bandung. Jalan Mesjid Agung behind the mosque has a line of excellent, flashy Padang **restaurants**, and the *Top Bakery*, on Jalan Yudanegara opposite the *Wisma Gall*, offers pastries and good fried chicken.

The Pangandaran peninsula

Pangandaran is a bulbous peninsula dripping down into the Indian Ocean, its beaches lashed by huge, impressive waves rolling unabated from Antarctica. Kilometres-long sands back onto massive coconut plantations, and the surrounding countryside offers many excursions. The **town** itself runs either side of the narrow isthmus connecting Pangandaran with the mainland, and then abruptly halts, most of the base of the bauble-shaped peninsula being taken up by a forested **national park**. The beach to the west is rent by powerful wind and waves, the eastern cove sheltered and quiet, and both are littered with idle, brightly painted blue prahus – sporadically the seafront comes alive, when almost everyone in town comes down to the waterfront to pull in nets full of writhing fish. Less easy on the eye are the souvenir stalls bordering the seafront; amongst tacky beachwear, shells and coral are countless shells and carcasses from Pangandaran's once-abundant turtle and monitor lizard population, with some stalls displaying as many as twenty turtles, their shells up to 1m across. Pangandaran has one of the best **fish markets** you'll ever see, surrounded by warung where they'll cook up pretty much anything they can catch.

The beaches

The **beaches** to the west are particularly famed for their **sunsets**, providing memorable images of silhouetted locals, cycling along the seafront with baskets and fruit on their heads, in front of crashing swell with the whole horizon stained scarlet. You can also often see huge frigate birds soaring above the waves. At dusk, the skies fill with incredible flocks of mammoth fruit bats, which have the wingspan of a young condor. The locals traditionally farm this natural flying-food extravaganza in a resourceful manner; boys stand on the seafront at dusk with kites, whose lines are intermittently strung with fish hooks. The bats catch their wing membrane on these snags and are drawn in like fishes. It's quite a rare sight now, which is not a bad thing for unsuspecting onlookers, as the high-pitched incessant wail of the bats as their wings rip like cling film is disturbing. The bat's flesh has a gamey flavour like venison, and is said to be an excellent treatment for asthma.

The national park

At present you can only walk in the **national park** on limited routes with guided tours from one of the many operators around town (see p.172). The park was once used by local people for farming, until 1921 when a wealthy landowner introduced Banteng cattle and Indian deer to the peninsula as a

Pangandaran festivals

Kites remain important in Pangandaran; every July and August, with the arrival of the east winds, there is a **kite-flying festival** held at the beach. Competitors come from all over the world for exhibitions and, more importantly, for kite-fighting. The strings of the kites are treated with glue and ground glass so that they become potent weapons: when a flier's string comes in contact with that of an opponent, they pull and release the kite in a swinging motion to try and sever the other's line. The fun is supplemented with beauty pageants and sports competitions, dancing and art exhibitions.

Another festival is that of the **Sea Queen**, held in August, with decorated prahus putting out to sea and offerings made to the goddess to improve the year's fish crop.

source of fresh meat for nearby farms. Just fifteen years later, the area was declared a wildlife reserve, and one reason it remains so is the presence of the **Javanese rafflesia**, a huge reeking flower that reaches the diameter of a car tyre. It's actually a parasite, flowering during the rainy season, and is pollinated not by bees but by a fly. Its relative, the Sumatran rafflesia, is the largest flower in the world and can grow up to 1m in diameter.

About eighty percent of the national park is secondary **rainforest**, with small stands of primary forest and open grasslands. Occupants include Banteng oxen, mouse- and barking deer, armadillos, civets, flying lemurs, several species of primates and hornbills, and the beaches are good places to spot turtles, coming ashore both to lay their eggs and bask in the sun. You can get to some wonderful beaches and sheltered areas offering reasonable **snorkelling**. Get your guide to take you to the magnificent limestone caves and the fifty-metre waterfall tumbling straight into the sea; there's a good pool for swimming at the top. **Surfing** off the park's coast is good to exceptional – there's a reef break on the Western border, though you are not, strictly speaking, supposed to surf there, but a few people still do. The coral the waves break over is razor-sharp, so bring a helmet and plenty of iodine.

Practicalities

Buses into Pangandaran town stop at the terminal just beyond the isthmus on the mainland, and outside the town gates. The nearest train station on the main line is at **Banjar**; regular trains to and from Bandung (4hr) and Yogya (4–5hr) call here. Banjar is two hours away by bus and, depending on whether you get a flash air-con-and-video number or a standard local one, you pay between Rp2000 and Rp10,000. With the expansion of Pangandaran town, most travellers tend to stay out at the beach enclave of **Cikembulan**, a small village 4km to the west. Most buses into Pangandaran continue past Cikembulan; alternatively, catch an ojek from the bus terminal. To get to the main beach area, turn left out of the terminal and on to the ridiculous 1km toll road – a remnant of New Order planning – and either walk or catch a becak.

The tourist information office, situated by the main gates into town, always seems to be closed. Tourist information booths in town are found everywhere, but they're only interested in selling tours. The **information service** between the *Losmen Mini Satu* and *Chez Mama Cilacap* restaurant is an exception, with a friendly and accommodating owner who has maps of the town and some good advice about trips out of Pangandaran and into the national park, has most essentials for tourists, but is short of a bank. The BRI in town has lousy rates for exchanging foreign currency and is only open until lunchtime. Many of the restaurants, hotels and tourist bureaus exchange money, but their rates are also poor. The very efficient **Telkom office** is open 24hr and situated on Jalan Kidang Panunjang as you head from town towards the gates. The **post office** is also on Jalan Kidang Panunjang, closer to the centre of town (Mon–Sat 8am–2pm, Fri & Sun 8–11am). Right by the post office is the local **cinema** (five showings daily), where a few relatively new English-language films are shown with Indonesian subtitles and terrible picture quality.

Accommodation

The Pangandaran peninsula is now filled with **losmen** and **hotels**, having very few residential buildings at all. Prices can triple at weekends and holidays, and you'll need to book in advance. You may well find that you're expected to pay more for your first night in a place, or that you're required to stay more than

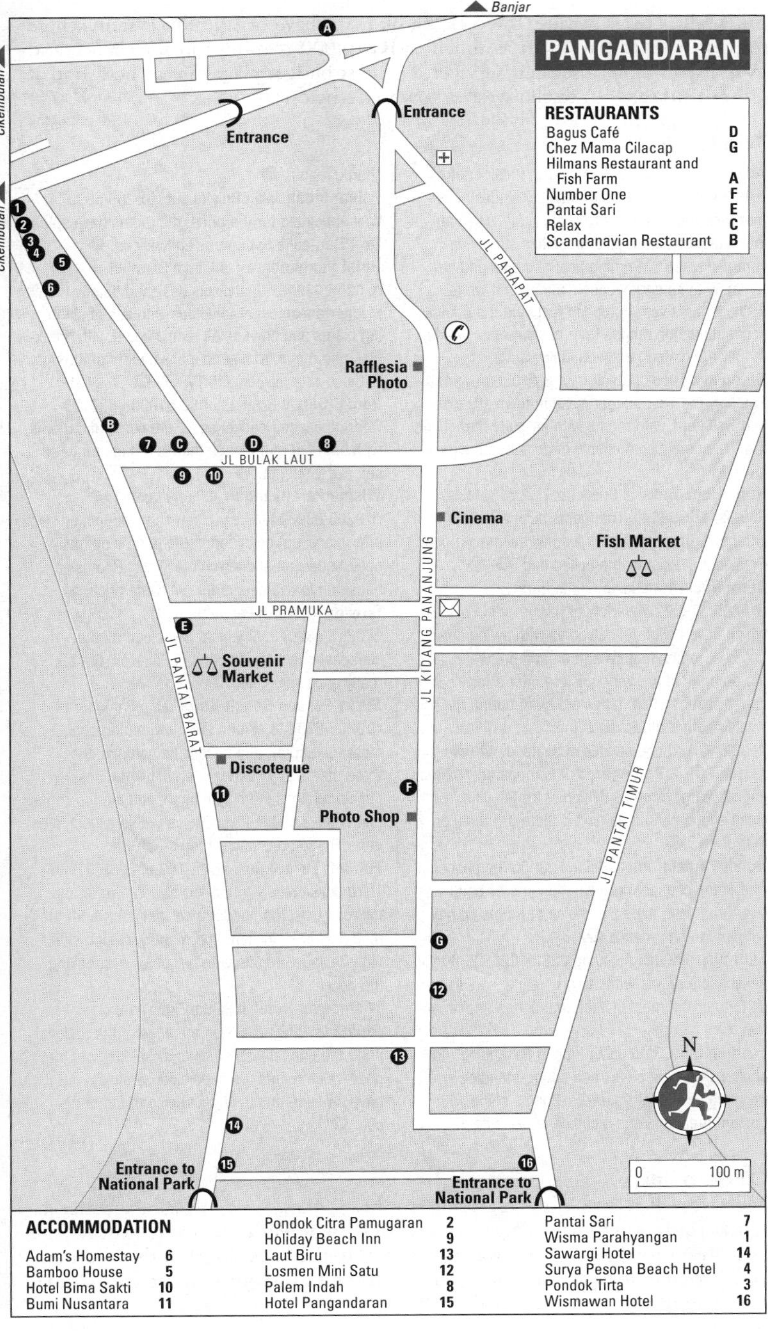

PANGANDARAN
Banjar
Cikembulan
Cikembulan
Entrance
Entrance
RESTAURANTS
Bagus Café D
Chez Mama Cilacap G
Hilmans Restaurant and Fish Farm A
Number One F
Pantai Sari E
Relax C
Scandanavian Restaurant B
JL PARAPAT
Rafflesia Photo
JL BULAK LAUT
Cinema
Fish Market
JL PRAMUKA
JL KIDANG PANANJUNG
Souvenir Market
JL PANTAI BARAT
Discoteque
Photo Shop
JL PANTAI TIMUR
N
0
100 m
Entrance to National Park
Entrance to National Park
ACCOMMODATION
Adam's Homestay 6
Bamboo House 5
Hotel Bima Sakti 10
Bumi Nusantara 11
Pondok Citra Pamugaran 2
Holiday Beach Inn 9
Laut Biru 13
Losmen Mini Satu 12
Palem Indah 8
Hotel Pangandaran 15
Pantai Sari 7
Wisma Parahyangan 1
Sawargi Hotel 14
Surya Pesona Beach Hotel 4
Pondok Tirta 3
Wismawan Hotel 16

one night. This is because the ojek/becak mafia have organized a system where losmen have to pay them as much as Rp10,000 commission for each guest, even if you didn't use their services. The best budget places are to be found at **Cikembulan**, 4km to the west of town (see below).

The town

Adam's Homestay Jl Pamugaran Bulak Laut ⓣ0265/639164. A kind of traveller's guesthouse for those with a little extra cash, *Adam's* has an intimate atmosphere and amenities such as a library, a small swimming pool and bike and car rental. With its dark wooden beams and white walls, it has a very European feel, and the pristine accommodation ranges from basic rooms with fan to fully appointed family bungalows. ❹

Bamboo House Jl Bulak Laut 8 ⓣ0265/679419. Probably the best budget place in town, it's quiet and well kept, with rooms with en-suite mandi and fan. There are also a couple of detached bungalows. ❷

Hotel Bima Sakti Jl Bulak Laut 12 ⓣ0265/639194, ⓕ639640. The rooms have air-con, TV and hot water, and there's a small swimming pool. Breakfast is toast with a boiled egg. ❹–❺

Bumi Nusantara Jalan Pantai Barat ⓣ0265/379032. A variety of rooms, some of which have delightful balconies with swing chairs. The best rooms feature air-con and hot water, and the proprietors are very quick to offer a forty percent discount when things are quiet during the week. Another attraction is their buffet meals – Rp30,000 for huge swaths of seafood. ❺–❼

Pondok Citra Pamugaran Jl Pamugaran 142 (no phone). Largish rooms designed for families – clean enough and a bargain if there are three or four of you. ❸

Holiday Beach Inn Jl Bulak Laut 50 (no phone). One of the cheapest places, though they don't offer breakfast; there's a choice of rooms with or without fan and mandi. ❶

Laut Biru Jl Kidang Panang 228 ⓣ0265/639046. Reasonable rooms with fan and mandi can sleep up to four; the rates include free coffee and breakfast. ❷

Losmen Mini Satu Jalan Kidang Pananjung (no phone). Basic but clean, and a long-standing favourite of budget travellers. Rooms come with fan and breakfast and a choice of en-suite or shared mandi. ❶

Palem Indah Jalan Bulak Laut ⓣ0265/639374. Well appointed for the price; the rooms have satellite TV, en-suite bathrooms and air-con. ❹

Hotel Pangandaran Jl Pantai Barat 95 ⓣ0265/639062. A stylishly designed, faintly Mediterranean set of buildings with lots of climbing plants and flowers. All rooms come with breakfast, and range from simple ones with fan through to those with air-con and TV. ❸–❹

Pantai Sari Jl Bulak Laut 80 ⓣ0265/639175. Offering banana pancakes for breakfast and rooms with both fan and mandi; there's a huge range to suit every budget. ❶–❹

Wisma Parahyangan Jl Pamugaran 144 ⓣ0265/639324. A very clean and well-looked-after place, but considering the price they really need better fan and air-con facilities. Rooms can house up to five people for the same price. ❸

Sawargi Hotel Jl Pantai Barat 47 ⓣ0265/639042. Airy, light and clean rooms – the cheapest only have fan and not air-con, but are really good value. ❸

Surya Pesona Beach Hotel Jalan Pamugaran ⓣ0265/639428. With a large swimming pool, massage parlour and beachside gardens, the three-star *Surya Pesona* is probably the best-appointed hotel in Pangandaran. and the top-range rooms have all the luxuries you would expect, plus there are some cheaper rooms. ❹–❻

Pondok Tirta Jl Bulak Laut 140 ⓣ0265/639265. Third house along on the left as you turn off the toll road from the bus terminal, set back from the road, this is a pleasant and friendly losmen with high-ceilinged rooms with balconies overlooking the beach. ❷

Wismawan Hotel Jl Pantai Timur 262 ⓣ0265/379376. Right on the edge of the national park; the price doesn't include breakfast, but the good-value rooms are superclean, well laid out, have en-suite mandi and a choice of fan or air-con. ❸

Cikembulan

Most travellers are now choosing to head 4km west of Pangandaran to **Cikembulan**, a small village with several **beachside losmen** nearby. The beachfront road runs all the way from town to the back doors of these losmen, and a parallel road inland leads there from the bus station – most public buses continue down this road past the village.

△ Shadow puppets, Java

Delta Gecko Village ☎0265/630286. Probably the best losmen in West Java, with everything a traveller could require. The dormitories and bungalows are beautifully designed around well-kept gardens, a central meeting area and restaurant, and it's a top place to meet people and have a few cold beers. There's a lavish seafood buffet every Wednesday evening with Jaipongan dancing and *pencak silat* displays, vegetarian buffets every night, volleyball, free bike rental, coffee, tea, coconuts and breakfast, motorbike hire, a library, stacks of good information and a generally lively crowd. ❶

Tono Homestay Near to the roundabout on the beach road into town (no phone). A quiet, friendly and family-run establishment; all rooms have en-suite mandi and fan. ❷

Eating

The assorted restaurants near the **fish market** off Jalan Pantai Timur should not be missed. The small square is surrounded by near-identical warung; none are very plush, but they all sell the cheapest, freshest seafood to be found for miles. Simply wander around the warung, looking through the polystyrene ice-boxes outside until you find what you want and then barter for the price, cooked and with accoutrements; you can obtain a meal with enough fish to sink a battleship for around Rp5000. As for the rest, Pangandaran has a surfeit of places, usually constructed out of bamboo, offering hamburgers, omelettes, nasi goreng and seafood.

Bagus Café Jl Bulak Laut 66. This inexpensive and popular café's speciality is roasted rice and garlic with seafood (Rp5500), but they also serve a few European dishes.

Chez Mama Cilacap Jl Kidang Pananjung 187. A popular and well-established place, the specialities include Asian and European desserts such as black-rice pudding, lychees, longon and crêpes suzettes.

Franco's Pizzeria Cikembulan, next to *Delta Gecko* (see above). An Italian-run joint serving magnificent, oven-fired pizza. A large pizza with a few extra toppings will cost about Rp11,000 – considerably more expensive than the pizzerias in town, but well worth it.

Hilmans Restaurant and Fish Farm Jl Merdeka 312. Outside the gates to Pangandaran town, but recommended if you fancy splashing out. The open verandah looks out over fishponds where your lunch has probably been farmed; there's live music every night, and the menu includes lobster tails (Rp40,000), club sandwiches (Rp5000) and a cold Bintang (Rp5000).

Holiday Beach Inn Jl Bulak Laut 50. The cheap restaurant serves great Chinese food such as tofu, beef and shrimps for Rp5000; their pizzas are pretty good too, at around Rp5000.

Number One Jalan Kidang Pananjung. Serves *arak* cocktails, and offers a few Sundanese dishes such as *nasi timbel* for Rp3500, as well as pizzas for Rp5000.

Padang Jaya Jl Pamugaran 37, right on the corner with Jalan Pantai Barat. A typical Padang restaurant serving hot and spicy fish curries, usually under Rp5000.

Pantai Sari Jl Bulak Laut 80. Mainly European dishes, with pretty good pizzas for only Rp5000.

Relax Jl Bulak Laut 74. Probably the swishest café/restaurant in town, *Relax* is well known for its home-baked bread, milkshakes and ice cream, all of which are excellent but expensive. A mixed sandwich with chicken, cheese and salad will cost Rp8000.

Scandanavian Restaurant Jalan Pantai Barat, near the junction with Jalan Bulak Laut. Serves a good selection of European food, including meatballs, hot dogs and burgers; a full meal costs around Rp10,000.

Around Pangandaran

Although Pangandaran is the most popular beach resort in Java, the water in the immediate vicinity of the village is for the most part too rough for swimming. Consequently, the biggest attraction here is the surrounding countryside. The area's prevalent geological feature is raised coral beds and huge tracts of limestone; the relatively high rainfall has transformed these into **gorges**, **caverns** and **waterfalls** of staggering beauty, draped with moss and overhanging forest, with emerald rivers and deep-blue pools.

The most famous site in the Pangandaran area is the not-to-be missed **Green Canyon**. Groups of tourists take boats up Sungai Cijulang, either noisy motor-boats, or rowing boats – slower and harder work, but infinitely more appealing. Upriver, the banks steepen into cliffs towering above you; when the boats can go no further they moor at the entrance to a gorge so narrow it looks like a tunnel, its walls draped with stalactites and water dripping constantly from tree roots high above you. To continue through the pools upriver into the canyon, you have to rely on a combination of careful walking and swimming. Essentials for the trip include a bathing costume and sun block; footwear is optional and you can hire a rubber ring for the up-canyon trek if you're unsure in the water. Boats takes about six people and can be haggled down to about Rp20,000. To get to the jetty, take one of the frequent buses west from Pangandaran and ask to be let off at Green Canyon or Cukang Taneuh, which is right by the turn-off for Batu Keras. Alternatively, losmen and travel agents in town offer packages for upwards of Rp20,000 per person.

The **Cituman Dam** is a place of stunning beauty that is (as yet) still quiet even at weekends. The river here falls over several sets of broad, but low waterfalls with distinctive limestone shapes and caves, surrounded by thick forest. The only means of getting all the way to Cituman is by foot or by motorcycle, as the road is appalling. Either hire a motorbike, or take a minibus 8km (Rp1000) west of town to the easily missed signpost, at the turn-off for Cituman Dam (on the right-hand side of the road), then hire an ojek to take you the remaining 3km (15min; Rp1500).

Difficult to find, but very attractive, is **Gunung Tiga**, a park near the Cituman Dam with great views, a few bat caves and another beautiful river and cavern system. To get there, take the same route as for Cituman, but ask for an ojek to Gunung Tiga. For the waterfalls, walk up the hill at the end of the rough road, and continue for about 500m. Just before the peak of the hill, there's a tiny path to the right down through the coconut palms – follow this all the way downhill to the river. The water has several glorious blue pools and, if you follow it upstream, there's a magnificent cave you can swim into, a vertical slash in the cliff-face.

Another extraordinary trip down the coast to the west of Pangandaran is to **Sindang Kerta**. In front of the beach of Sindang Kerta village is a flat rock bed that is usually above sea level, all except for a deep channel like a river through the rock. Fish swimming into the channel are inevitably trapped and, at the right time of day, **sea turtles** come in to feed. Standing on the rock bed, you can be almost within touching distance of giant-green, hawksbill, loggerhead and brown turtles, their massive heads popping up like bobbing coconuts before they dive in with a splash of flippers and shell. Unfortunately, this extraordinary sight will probably not remain for much longer; the piles of dead turtles in the stalls along Pangandaran's seafront have all come from these seas, and locals see them more as a menace to their fish stocks than as beautiful and rare creatures. The PHPA post in Sindang Kerta is recognizable by the sign outside advertising "Telur Penyu" (Turtle Eggs), which the guards will cheerfully dig up and sell to anyone who's interested; they also keep two adult turtles in minute tanks for tourists to photograph. To get to Sindang Kerta by public transport, catch a minibus to Cijulang (30min; Rp750), then another bus to Cikalong (1hr 30min–2hr; Rp2000), before catching an ojek for the seven-kilometre ride to Sindang Kerta (Rp1500).

Batu Keras

BATU KERAS (Hard Rock) is a popular beach spot and **surfers' enclave** 35km west of Pangandaran. From September to February there's a good right-handed reef break here; the unreliable right-handed point break at the west end of the beach often warms up in the early mornings and late afternoons and is good for beginners. It's worth noting that sharks are regular visitors to this bay, and it's not uncommon to see groups of mussel-collecting locals yelling and hurling rocks at a long black fin as it cruises around the point.

There are several **places to stay** at Batu Keras. The *Dadang* **homestay** on Jalan Genteng Parakan (❶) is a lovely, clean place, run by a young surfie couple who expect guests to be part of the household, sharing fish barbecues and evening singalongs. *Alanas* losmen is at Jalan Legok Pari 336 (Ⓣ0811/230442; ❷) at the end of the beach. An unashamed surfer's hangout, it's easily recognized by the surfboard signpost outside, and you can rent surfboards for Rp20,000 a day.

To get to Batu Keras from Pangandaran, take a bus to Cijulang (Rp1500), from where you can take an ojek, passing through mangrove and coconut plantations. Haggle strongly for the price; Rp6000 seems about maximum, depending on how much you are carrying.

On to Central Java

The journey between Central and West Java is either solely by bus, or can include a memorable riverboat trip through some of the quietest and most picturesque lowland scenery in Java. From Pangandaran, take a bus to the town of **KALIPUCANG** (45min; Rp1000), 15km to the east of the main bus terminal. From this small village there's a regular ferry trip (4hr; Rp1500) through to Cilacap in Central Java, from where there are buses on to Yogya and beyond. The ferry takes you past mangrove swamps and fishing villages, across the Segara Anakan Lagoon. Boats leave at 7am, 9am and 1pm; if you intend making it all the way to Yogya or Wonosobo in one day, you'll need to try and make the first boat. There are many buses advertised in Pangandaran that sell the whole trip as a package. Otherwise, when the ferry stops at Cilacap harbour you'll need to catch a becak, bemo or ojek to the terminal, and then catch a bus on from there.

Cirebon and around

On the northern coast, right on the boundaries of Central and West Java, lies the port of **CIREBON**. The town has a long Islamic history, and is also known as *Kota Udang* (Prawn City), the area being famous for their cultivation. As it lies a good way off the tourist trail, it receives very few Western visitors; it is, however, a very mellow and welcoming place. The town is overlooked by Gunung Ciremai, West Java's tallest mountain (3078m); its last eruption was in 1805.

In contrast with the large elevated towns of West Java, Cirebon's coastal position makes it a sweaty place to tour around. In town, the great Sang Cipta Rasa **mosque** is one of the oldest Islamic structures in Java, completed in 1480, with a two-tier roof similar to those found in Bali and Banten, while the three **kratons** (walled city palaces) have museums filled with fascinating objects. Cirebon's old harbour is usually filled with beautiful **Makkasar schooners**, plying routes between here and Kalimantan with timber, concrete and rice.

Some history

Cirebon has always been a melting pot of Sundanese and Javanese culture, due to its situation right on the border between West and Central Java. It was only a tiny harbour settlement until the fourteenth century, when Hinduism began to spread over Southeast Asia; traders from India came upon the tiny outpost and began to use it as a port. However, when the Hindu Majapahit empire disintegrated, **Islam** began to take root in Java. Its first ambassador to Cirebon was the preacher Hidayatullah, who came here from Mecca and was to become the pre-eminent missionary for Islam in Western Java. As Hidayatullah was based in Cirebon, the town became the centre for West Java's Muslims, and as Banten, Sunda Kelapa, Karawang and Indramayu – Sunda's major towns – converted to Islam, so Cirebon's stature increased. Hidayatullah died in 1568, and was buried on the nearby mountain Gunung Jati, a name that became synonymous with his own and is an oft-used Indonesian street name in his honour. The mountain itself is a site of pilgrimage for Javanese Muslims.

In the seventeenth century, Cirebon's power declined and it became a vassal state of Mataram. In 1678, the opulent Muslim sultans of Cirebon signed contracts with the Dutch East India Company, ceding them sole rights over the area's imports and exports in return for Dutch recognition of the sultan's control and agreements that would secure his wealth. However, the monopoly of trade was greatly abused by the Dutch and led to immense poverty and famine in the Cirebon area. Many of the peasants were sold into slavery, and the colonists also inadvertantly introduced smallpox and venereal disease. In the nineteenth century, the Dutch divided the kingdom of Cirebon into five royal households, before finally paying the sultans off and effectively removing them from power. The sultans kept their palaces and lifestyles but were to have no further part in the political affairs of the region.

Today, the majority of Cirebon's 250,000 inhabitants are Muslim, totalling about eighty percent of the populace, and the rest are Hindu and Christian. Cirebon now prospers, as an important industrial link on the northern coast road and main Bandung road, connecting the first and third largest towns in Indonesia with the rest of Java. However, there is growing pressure to have Cirebon and the adjoining regencies of Majalengka, Sumedang, Kuningan and Indramayu declared a separate province, a move supported by the ruling PDI-P.

Arrival and orientation

Cirebon town is strung northwest to southeast along the coast, with Teluk Penyu (Turtle Bay) off to the east. The main street is Jalan Siliwangi, which runs parallel to the coast; the **train station** is towards the north of town and just off Jalan Siliwangi, with the long-distance **bus station** lying on the outskirts of town in the southeast. When you arrive here you will be assaulted by the cab- and becak-driver mafia who will tell you categorically that there is no public transport in Cirebon. Ignore their rather aggressive demands, and just walk outside the terminal gates and catch a blue minibus into town, asking *"ke stasiun kereta api"* ("to the railway station") if you want to get to the budget hotels near the train station. The real budget places are right outside the station gates, and the majority of **restaurants** and **accommodation** in all categories are within walking distance, most strung along Jalan Siliwangi.

Accommodation

If you're arriving in Cirebon by train, you won't have to go far to find a place to stay; there's **accommodation** for all pockets within walking distance. The

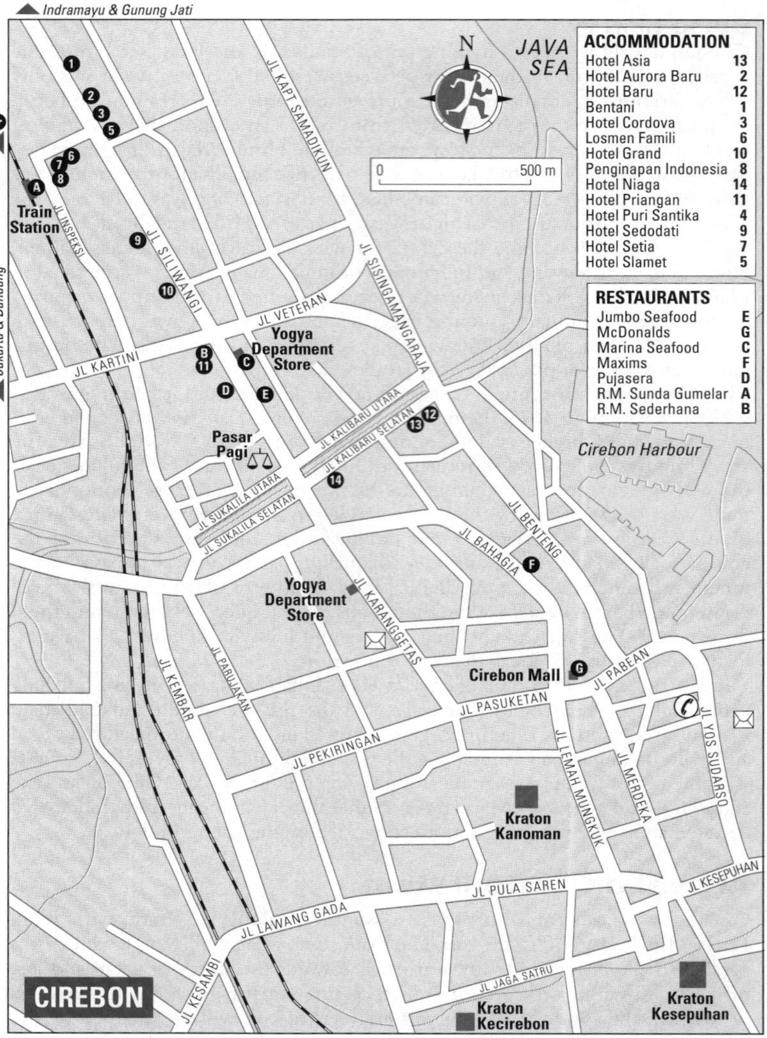

CIREBON

Indramayu & Gunung Jati

Jakarta & Bandung

ACCOMMODATION	
Hotel Asia	13
Hotel Aurora Baru	2
Hotel Baru	12
Bentani	1
Hotel Cordova	3
Losmen Famili	6
Hotel Grand	10
Penginapan Indonesia	8
Hotel Niaga	14
Hotel Priangan	11
Hotel Puri Santika	4
Hotel Sedodati	9
Hotel Setia	7
Hotel Slamet	5

RESTAURANTS	
Jumbo Seafood	E
McDonalds	G
Marina Seafood	C
Maxims	F
Pujasera	D
R.M. Sunda Gumelar	A
R.M. Sederhana	B

few **budget** places to be found in Cirebon tend to be fairly poor quality and many are brothels, though they probably won't cause you any hassle, while **moderate** hotels tend to be much more competitively priced here than in other places in West Java.

Hotel Asia Jl Kali Baru Selatan 15 ☎0231/202183. A quiet and simple place that's kept relatively clean, offering a breakfast of bread, egg and coffee; cheaper rooms have shared mandi, while more expensive ones have en-suite bathrooms and fans. ❷

Hotel Aurora Baru Jl Siliwangi 62 ☎0231/233145. Rooms here have air-con, hot water and TV and are actually quite plush, offering good value for money. ❸

Hotel Baru Jl Kali Baru Selatan 3 ☎0231/201728. The ekonomi rooms here are clean and have some natural light, which is a rarity in Cirebon. They come with a shower, a decent fan and a breakfast of fried rice and bread, and are probably the budget traveller's best option. ❷–❹

Bentani Jl Siliwangi 69 ⓣ0231/203246. Probably the last word in luxury in Cirebon, three-star *Bentani* has a swimming pool, tennis courts, sauna, Japanese, Chinese, Indonesian and European restaurants, plus all facilities in the rooms. ❼

Hotel Cordova Jl Siliwangi 87 ⓣ0231/204677. Essentially a good mid-range hotel with air-con, en-suite rooms, the *Cordova* also has a few reasonable cheap rooms out the back without the amenities. ❶–❹

Losmen Famili Jl Siliwangi 66 ⓣ0231/207935. The most basic rooms have shared mandi and no fan, while others are large and airy, with fan and mandi, but are a little dilapidated. ❶–❷

Hotel Grand Jl Siliwangi 98 ⓣ0231/208867. Quite a charming if faded old place – the sizeable rooms have air-con, TV and hot water. ❸–❹

Hotel Niaga Jl Kali Baru Selatan 47 ⓣ0231/206718. Despite its decrepit facade, this hotel is quite well kept inside, and its rooms have air-con, hot water and TV. ❸–❹

Penginapan Indonesia Jl Inspeksi 11. On the track outside the train station, this place has grotty boxrooms through to newer rooms with en-suite mandi; the latter are twice the price but three times the value. ❶

Hotel Priangan Jl Siliwangi 108 ⓣ0231/202929. A very clean place set around nice internal rock gardens; the basic rooms come with mandi and fan and the top-class ones have air-con, TV and a minibar. A breakfast of eggs and coffee is included. ❷–❸

Hotel Puri Santika Jl Dr Wahidin 32 ⓣ0231/200570. A top-class establishment with a pool, tennis courts and health club. The rooms are large, with hot water, fridge, minibar and air-con. ❼

Hotel Sedodati Jl Siliwangi 72 ⓣ0231/202305. A two-star hotel with air-con, TV and hot water in all the rooms. They have a Chinese restaurant with reasonable prices, parking space for all their guests and offer a fried-rice breakfast free of charge. ❺

Hotel Setia Jl Inspeksi 1222/31 ⓣ0231/207270. Has a good variety of moderately priced rooms, from basic with fan through excellent-value rooms with air-con and TV, to those with hot-water showers. ❷–❸

Hotel Slamet Jl Siliwangi 95 ⓣ0231/203296. An average place, the cheapest rooms here have fan and TV, while for twice the price you get air-con, hot water and a fridge. ❷–❸

The kratons

The three kratons (walled city palaces) that remain in Cirebon are today the city's only real attraction, and even so they are very much overshadowed by those of Yogya and Solo. The two kratons that are open to public viewing are **Kraton Kesapuhan** and **Kraton Kanoman**, both dating back to the sixteenth century. **Kraton Kecirebon** remains the residence of the royal family; although it's closed to the public, you can get a reasonable look at it through the fence. It's smaller and more modern than the other two, having only been built in the early nineteenth century.

Kraton Kesapuhan

Kraton Kesapuhan (daily 8am–4pm; Rp1000) lies about a twenty-minute walk from the centre of town at the southern end of Jalan Lemah Wungkuk. The first building at the site of this most important Cirebon **kraton**, was constructed on the orders of the preacher Hidayatullah in around 1552. It was completely rebuilt at least once, and received a major restoration in 1928. Though an Islamic building, the gate and main pavilions have the form of a Hindu *candi* (temple), with the split gate commonly seen in Balinese shrines. While they are definitely older than the majority of the kraton's buildings, these features were probably only influenced by the thirteenth- and fourteenth-century Hindu styles (that predated the spread of Islam), rather than actually having been built by Hindus. The buildings display a mixture of styles, having clear Dutch, Chinese, Javanese and Sundanese influences. The kraton has a **museum**, containing artefacts such as gamelan instruments and kris, but it's not as good as the museum in the Kraton Kanoman.

Kraton Kanoman

The **Kraton Kanoman** is situated close to the centre of town on Jalan Kanoman (daily 8am–4pm; Rp1000), and features crystal chandeliers from France, tiles from Holland and Ming porcelain, alongside more conventional Sundanese and Islamic embellishments. The **museum** contains such oddities as a Portuguese suit of armour weighing 45kg found at Sunda Kelapa, wooden boxes from Egypt and China that are over 500 years old, and a bamboo cage used for keeping unruly children in. Other novelties include evil-looking spikes used for body piercing during trance by the Debus players from Banten (see p.135), while the star exhibit is a very similar **chariot** to one found in the Kraton Kesapuhan – one of the two is original and one a copy, and both museums claim that theirs is the real thing. Hindu influence is evident in the chariot's elephant face, Chinese-dragon body and Egyptian wings, and the whole vehicle has an efficient suspension, the wings hinged so that, as it drove over rough roads, the bumping would make the wings flap. All in all, it's about as strange a contraption as you'll ever see.

Eating

Cirebon's speciality is **nasi lengko**: rice with sambal, meat, tofu, *tempe*, bean sprouts and fried onions. Handcarts also sell fried chicken and delicious fried spring rolls with green chillies. The Yogya department store to the north of Jalan Siliwangi has a ground-level Indonesian restaurant serving moderately priced staples, while the Yogya further south on the same road features the *Marina* restaurant and a much more varied food court, with Sundanese, Padang, Madura and Yogyakartan food all served by different outlets. The Cirebon Mall Hero has *McDonald's*, *Dunkin' Donuts*, *KFC*, *Pizza Hut* and an Indonesian fast-food court with simple, quick nasi goreng for Rp3000. The Pasar Pagi off Jalan Siliwangi has some pretty cramped little warung where you can get fantastic cheap food; some places offer quarters of chicken, barbecued in a spicy marinade, for under Rp3000-5000.

The neighbouring town of Indramayu is famous for its mangoes, which appear in the Cirebon market in mid-November, while locally grown rambutan arrive around January.

Jumbo Seafood Jl Siliwangi 191. Fantastic seafood barbecues at reasonable prices.

Marina Seafood Yogya department store, Jalan Siliwangi. A flashy and expensive seafood restaurant that takes all major credit cards and serves lobster tails, assorted seafood and fish soups. Meals start at Rp50,000 a head.

Maxims Jl Bahagia 45. Cirebon's best-known restaurant is another seafood affair, as you will see from the huge fish tanks as you enter. Crab and prawns are the speciality, but they have a pretty comprehensive and reasonably priced menu.

Pujasera Next to Bank Jabar and *Dunkin' Donuts*, Jalan Siliwangi. A little eveningtime food court serving Chinese food, *Sop Buntut* at Rp7000 and the local favourite *nasi lengko* for Rp6000.

R.M. Sunda Gumelar Station forecourt. A friendly Sundanese warung, recommended for various tasty *nasi rames*.

R.M. Sederhana Jl Siliwangi 124. Serves mainly Sundanese food; the specialities include goldfish steamed in banana leaves.

Listings

Banks There are plenty of banks along Jalan Yos Sudarso down by the old harbour. Bank Danamon at no. 12 is good for credit-card advances and has an ATM; BNI at no. 3, Bank Bali at no. 1 and Bank Lippo at no. 26 all have good rates for foreign exchange.

Bookshops There is a great bookshop/stationers in the Cirebon shopping centre at the southern end of Jalan Bahagia, with lots of English-language books and maps from around the archipelago.

Internet CentralNet at Ruko Grand Centre, Blok B/9 (Ⓣ0231/209266) offers friendly, cheap service. Also Imagine at Jl Bahagia 65A.

Post office Jalan Yos Sudarso, near the harbour.

Telkom Jalan Yos Sudarso; 24hr international phone and fax.

Around Cirebon

The foremost site of interest in the Cirebon area is **Trusmi**, a **batik-making centre** 6km to the west of town. Other nearby villages such as Weru, Kalitengah and Kaliwuru are also known for their batik, but Trusmi is definitely the best place to go if you want to see the process and buy the finished article. Cirebon's batik is very different from that of Central Java, with its own distinctive designs, influences and colours. Chinese- and Arabic-style designs are commonplace, their use in local batik dating back at least five centuries. The colours are not generally as gaudy and bright as you might see in Yogya, tending towards indigos, dark browns, background whites and muted yellows, but the designs are generally very striking. Ibu Masina's workshop in Trusmi is the best place to start if you want to get a feel for Batik. Take angkot GP from Gunungsari terminal, 400m to the west of the Yogya department store, to Plered (15min; Rp500), and then ask for the Pabrik Batik.

The villages of Tegalwangi, 5km west of Cirebon, and Beber, a further 5km away, are both known for their rattan furniture. Arjawawinangun, 14km west of the town, makes stained-glass ornaments and lampshades. All are good places to bargain, and in the case of rattan, you can arrange shipments home.

Twelve kilometres southeast of Cirebon in the direction of Kuningan, on the slopes of Gunung Ciremai, lies the village of **Linggarjati;** catch a Kuningan-bound bus from the terminal (every 30min; Rp2000). It was the site in 1946 of negotiations that led to a short-lived political agreement between Indonesia and Holland which brought hostilities to an end, commemorated by a very small museum in the village. Set in splendidly fertile countryside, Linggarjati also gives access to moderately taxing treks on the mountain; foreigners are seldom seen here, but enquiries will secure you a guide with whom you can haggle a price, depending on distance.

Cibulan, 3km north of Kuningan, has a large bathing pool that swimmers share with fish locally held to be sacred. To get there, take a Kuningan-bound bus (Rp3000) from Cirebon terminal.

Travel details

Buses

It's almost impossible to give the frequency with which bemos and buses run, as they only depart when they have enough passengers to make the journey worthwhile. Journey times also vary a great deal. The times below are the minimum you can expect these journeys to take. Privately run shuttle, or door-to-door, buses run between the major tourist centres on Java.

Bandung to: Bogor (frequent; 3hr); Cirebon (frequent; 3hr 30min) Jakarta (from Leuwi Panjang terminal, frequent; 4hr 30min–5hr 30min); Pangandaran (twice daily; 5hr); Sukabumi (frequent; 3hr).

Bogor to: Bandung (frequent; 3hr); Jakarta (frequent; 1–2hr); Pelabuhan Ratu (frequent; 2hr 30min); Sukabumi (frequent; 1hr 30min).

Cirebon to: Bandung (frequent; 3hr 30min); Jakarta (frequent; 5hr); Yogya (frequent; 9hr).

Pangandaran to: Bandung (frequent; 5hr); Jakarta (frequent; 12hr); Tasikmalaya (frequent; 3hr).

Trains

Bandung to: Jakarta (hourly; 2hr 20min); Yogya (8 daily; takes from 9hr).

Bogor to: Jakarta (every 20min; 1hr 30min).

Cirebon to: Jakarta (four *ekspres* trains daily; 3hr).

Ferries

The only real option for sea travel is the ferry from Merak to Sumatra, which leaves about every 30min (90min).

Flights

Bandung airport is the only one in West Java that presently runs flights for tourists, with Merpati, Bouraq and Garuda all operating out of its Hussein Sastranegara terminal.

Bandung to: Mataram (daily; 8hr 25min); Palembang (daily; 2hr); Singapore (daily; 3hr); Solo (3 weekly; 1hr 30min); Surabaya (3 daily; 1hr 20min); Ujung Pandang (daily; 4hr 20min); Yogyakarta (4 weekly; 1hr 20min).

Central Java

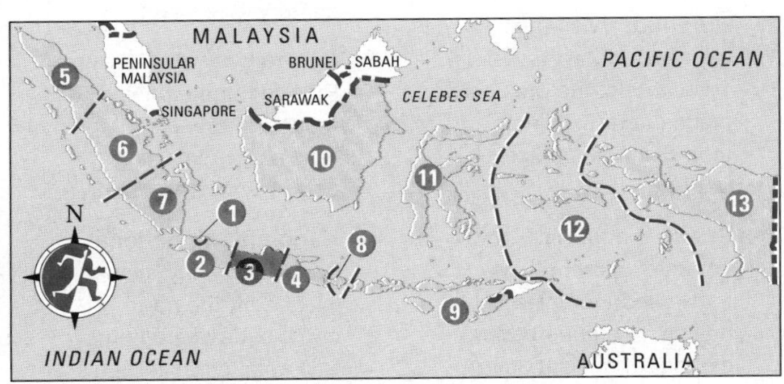

CHAPTER 3 **Highlights**

* **Sultan's Palace, Yogyakarta** Explore palace life in the spiritual and cultural centre of Java. See p.200
* **Gunung Merapi** Indonesia's most volatile volcano offers the adventurous climber awesome views of the lava flow. See p.217
* **Borobudur** Visit the largest Buddhist temple in the world, the greatest piece of classical architecture in the archipelago. See p.218
* **Prambanan Plain** The complex of more than thirty Hindu temples makes for a superb bicycle tour of ancient Java. See p.222
* **Dieng plateau** Set in a rumbling volcanic caldera, and home to the numerous Hindu temples. See p.229
* **Puro Mangkunegoro** The palace of the second royal house of Solo testifies to the sophistication of Javanese court life in the eighteenth century. See p.240
* **Cog railway, Ambarawa** Ride through stunning mountain scenery on Java's last remaining cog railway. See p.262
* **Karimunjawa national park** The 27 idyllic islands off the north coast of Java are home to a unique fragile wilderness. See p.270

3

Central Java

Central Java is the breadbasket of Indonesia, a wide swath of farmland covering almost a third of the island. It's one of the most densely populated rural areas in the world: a 2000 census estimated the population to be nearly 34 million, crammed into an area of some 34,505 square kilometres. Despite this overcrowding, the scenery is remarkably pastoral, the volcanic soil and tropical climate conspiring to produce a landscape of glimmering ricelands dotted with the occasional classical ruin, a few large towns, countless small villages and, running from east to west across the province, a spine of temperamental volcanoes.

This mountainous backbone splits the province into two distinct regions. To the south is the **Kejawen**, homeland of the ethnic Javanese and the epicentre of their arts, culture and language. The Kejawen's boundaries extend well into both West and East Java, but its heart is undoubtedly within Java's two royal cities, **Yogyakarta** and **Solo**. Once the rival capitals of the disintegrating Mataram empire, today the two cities, steeped in culture and history and with first-rate facilities for travellers, are the mainstay of Java's tourist industry. They also provide excellent bases from which to explore the remains which dot the surrounding countryside. A little to the west of Yogyakarta is the world-famous **Borobudur**, a giant Buddhist temple built in the ninth century by the Saliendra dynasty. Midway between Yogya and Solo is the equally fascinating **Prambanan complex**, a series of soaring Shivaite temples constructed by the Saliendras' Hindu contemporaries, the Sanjayas. Continuing east, just before the border with East Java are a couple of enigmatic fifteenth-century Hindu temples, **Sukuh** and **Ceto**, set on a glorious mountainside. Finally, high up in the centre of the chain of volcanoes, there's **Dieng**, a windswept plateau with some of the oldest classical temples in Java, a chilly alternative to the sunbaked ruins of the plain.

North of the volcanoes, the landscape gently melts into a narrow, fertile plain which separates the foothills from the sea. This is the coastal, or **Pasisir** (fringe) region of Central Java. Isolated from the court culture of the interior, the coastline has traditionally been influenced by foreign traders who docked in the port on their way to and from the Spice Islands, and thus has a more cosmopolitan, mercantile atmosphere. It was through these ports that Islam first entered Java, via Arabian and Indian sailors. Indeed, the island's first Islamic empire was founded around the twin ports of **Demak** and **Jepara**, and it is still one of the most emphatically Muslim parts of Indonesia. Today, the Pasisir region is home to some sacred **Islamic sites** (the revered mosques of Demak and Kudus and three of the graves of the Wali Songo), a number of big industries (clove cigarettes in **Kudus** and batik in **Pekalongan**) and a smattering of crumbling colo-

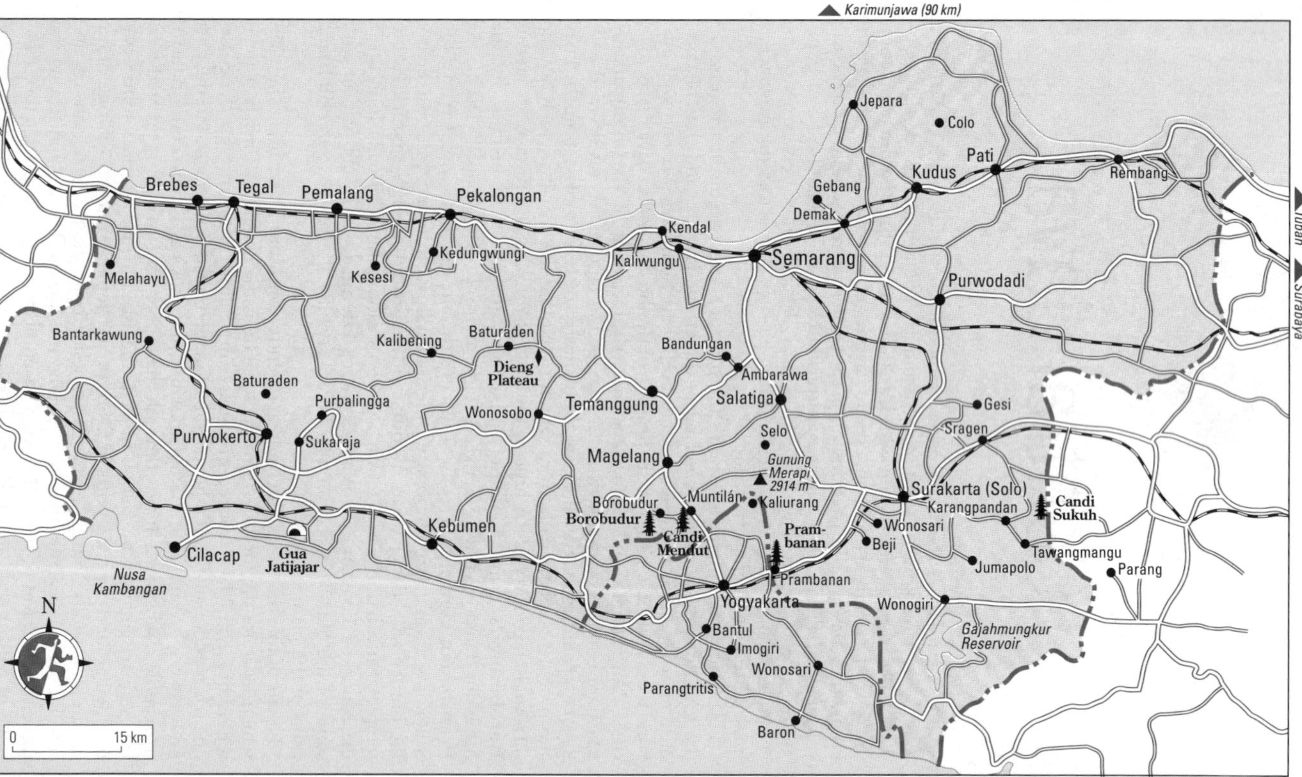
Karimunjawa (90 km)
Jakarta
Bandung
Tuban
Surabaya
Jepara
Colo
Pati
Kudus
Rembang
Gebang
Demak
Brebes
Tegal
Pemalang
Pekalongan
Kendal
Kaliwungu
Semarang
Purwodadi
Melahayu
Kesesi
Kedungwungi
Bantarkawung
Kalibening
Baturaden
Dieng Plateau
Bandungan
Ambarawa
Baturaden
Purbalingga
Wonosobo
Temanggung
Salatiga
Gesi
Purwokerto
Sukaraja
Selo
Sragen
Magelang
Gunung Merapi 2914 m
Surakarta (Solo)
Borobudur
Muntilan
Kaliurang
Karangpandan
Candi Sukuh
Borobudur
Candi Mendut
Pram-banan
Wonosari
Beji
Tawangmangu
Kebumen
Cilacap
Gua Jatijajar
Jumapolo
Parang
Prambanan
Yogyakarta
Wonogiri
Nusa Kambangan
Bantul
Imogiri
Gajahmungkur Reservoir
Wonosari
Parangtritis
Baron
N
0
15 km

nial buildings. Though it's frequently visited by devout Indonesian Muslims and foreign businesspeople, the lack of major tourist attractions and the inhospitable **climate** – the Pasisir is prone to flooding in the rainy season and searingly hot for the rest of the year – puts most tourists off. For those who persevere, however, the area can make a fascinating side tour.

In general, **getting around** Central Java is not a problem; the region is fairly small and is well served by both road and rail. Travelling between the north and the Kejawen is slightly tricky, though, as only three highways (between Purworkerto and Tegal, Semarang and Salatiga, and Purwodadi and Solo), and one train track (Semarang to Solo), link the two regions. There are, nevertheless, a number of smaller, stomach-churning roads winding their way through, up or around the volcanoes.

Moving on from Central Java is fairly straightforward; from Yogya and Solo there are road and rail links with Jakarta, Bogor, Bandung and Surabaya, and direct buses to Bali. Along the coast, the road and railway between Jakarta and Surabaya run through all the major towns in the Pasisir. The Pelni ferry company connects Semarang with Banjarmasin (Kalimantan), and there are airports in Cilacap, Semarang, Yogya and Solo.

Yogyakarta (Jogjakarta) and around

Halfway between volatile Gunung Merapi and the treacherous Southern Seas, **YOGYAKARTA**, a prosperous city of 500,000 inhabitants, stands proudly at the very heart of Javanese culture. It's pronounced "Jogjakarta" but known locally as "Yogja"; to avoid this confusion there are plans under way to officially change the spelling to Jogjakarta. Thanks largely to sponsorship from the city's two royal households, the Hamengkubuwonos and the Paku Alam family, the classical **Javanese arts** – batik, ballet, drama, music, poetry and puppet shows – all thrive in Yogya as nowhere else on the island. Even the city's name is a literary reference, being derived from Ayodya, the peaceful kingdom of King Rama in the *Ramayana* tales. Small wonder, then, that this is the best place to enjoy Javanese performances and exhibitions.

Yogyakarta also ranks as one of the best-preserved and most attractive cities in Java. At its heart is the residence of Yogya's first family, the revered **Hamengkubuwonos**, whose elegant palace lies at the centre of Yogya's quaint old city, the **Kraton**, itself concealed behind high castellated walls. These fortifications, while they have not always been successful in keeping out enemies, have certainly managed to ward off the ravages of time. Wander through at dawn, and the Kraton seems to have been totally forgotten by this century, its meandering alleyways and spacious, high-walled boulevards imbued with a sense of calm.

Yogya, however, is not just a museum piece, but a thriving modern metropolis, as well acquainted with email and MTV as it is with golek and gamelan. The city's forward-looking **Gajah Mada University** stands at the cutting edge of technology, and draws students from all over the archipelago. Tourists flock to Yogya, attracted not only by the city's courtly splendour but also by the nearby temples of **Prambanan** and **Borobudur**. As a consequence, there are more hotels and tourist facilities here than anywhere else in Java and, unfortunately, a correspondingly high number of touts, pickpockets, con artists and other unsavoury characters. Nevertheless, with its handy transport connections, good food and accommodation options and easy-going, friendly nature, Yogya is the perfect base from which to become acquainted with the Javanese people, their history and culture.

Some history

Yogyakarta grew out of the dying embers of the once-great Mataram dynasty. In 1752, the Mataram empire, then based in Solo, was in the throes of the **Third Javanese War of Succession**. The reigning susuhunan, **Pakubuwono II**, had been steadily losing his grasp on power for the past decade in the face of a rebellion by his brothers, **Singasari** and **Mangkubumi**, and the sultan's nephew, **Mas Said**. To try to turn the tide, Pakubuwono persuaded Mangkubumi to swap sides and defend the court, offering him in return control over three thousand households within the city. Mangkubumi agreed, but the sultan, backed by the Dutch (who were worried about Mangkubumi's growing popularity) later reneged on the deal. Enraged, Mangkubumi headed off to establish his own court. He chose his spot carefully, one that was both in the shadow of the sacred mountain, Merapi, and also near to the previous Mataram capitals at **Kota Gede**, **Karta** and **Plered** (the royal towns of sultans Senopati, Agung and Amangkurat I respectively). Thus Yogyakarta was born. Mangkubumi's new court was granted official recognition in the 1755 **Treaty of Giyanti**, with Mangkubumi bestowing on himself the title of **Sultan Hamengkubuwono I** (He Who Holds the World in His Lap).

Hamengkubuwono and his followers spent the next 37 years building the new capital, with the Kraton as the centrepiece and the court at Solo as the blueprint. Hamengkubuwono also set about capturing more land until, by the time he died in 1792, his territory exceeded Solo's. After his death, however, the Yogya sultanate went into freefall. Hamengkubuwono II fell out so badly with the newly arrived British that the latter stormed the palace in 1812, aided by the sultan's brother, **Prince Notokusumo**. It was the last time any of the courts were sacked by a European power. For his part, Notokusumo was rewarded with his own court in the centre of Yogya, with control over four thousand households. A second major altercation occurred in 1825, when a member of the royal house, **Prince Diponegoro**, led the Javanese into a bloody five-year battle against the Dutch, who by this time held most of Java: over ten percent of the population was killed as a result of the fighting. From this moment on, the Dutch were firmly in control and even had the power of veto when appointing sultans.

Drained of power and resources, the palace spent the rest of the nineteenth century convalescing, concentrating less on warmongering and more on its artistic side. **Sultan Hamengkubuwono VIII**, in particular, was a great sponsor of the arts, occasionally putting on epic, four-day spectacles of dance and drama at the Kraton.

Nationalist feeling, however, continued to grow throughout this period. In 1946, the capital of the newly declared Republic of Indonesia was moved to Yogya from Jakarta, and the Kraton became the unofficial headquarters for the republican movement. With the financial and military support of **Sultan Hamengkubuwono IX**, Yogya became the nerve centre for the native forces. The town was rewarded for its efforts by being granted its own province, the **Daerah Istimewa Yogyakarta** (Special Territory of Yogya). Today, more than fifty years on from the War of Independence, the royal household of Yogya continues to enjoy almost slavish devotion from its subjects. Indeed, during the May 1997 riots, it was only through the intervention of the current sultan, Hamengkubuwono X, who addressed an angry crowd of students demonstrating against the regime of President Suharto, that Yogya was saved from the looting and burning that afflicted so many other cities in Java. As one of the most influential politicians in the government, the sultan has received countrywide praise and respect for his position at the forefront of the democratic reform movement.

Arrival, orientation, information

There is no public transport running directly between Yogyakarta's **Adisucipto Airport**, 10km to the east of the city on the way to Prambanan, and the city centre. If you head 200m south out of the airport and on to Jalan Adisucipto, you can flag down a passing bus (Rp1000) heading west to Yogya. Alternatively, a taxi from the airport to Yogya costs around Rp25,000.

The **Tugu train station** lies just one block north of (and an easy 5min walk away from) Jalan Sosro, on Jalan Pasar Kembang. A becak from the station to Jalan Prawirotaman should cost no more than Rp2000; a taxi, Rp7000; or catch southbound bus #2 (Rp1000) from Jalan Mataram, one block east of Jalan Malioboro.

All inter-city buses arrive at the **Umbulharjo bus station**, 3km east of the city centre. From the adjacent **local bus station** there are regular services into town, including bus #2 (30min; Rp1000), which travels via Jalan Prawirotaman. Bus #5 (Rp1000) drives past the western end of Jalan Sosro, although it can take up to an hour. If you're arriving in Yogya from Borobudur, Magelang, Ambarawa or elsewhere in the north, and you plan to stay in Sosro, you can alight at the southern end of Jalan Magelang and walk (or take a becak; Rp5000) 600m south to Sosro.

Yogya is trisected by three parallel rivers – the **Winongo**, **Code** and **Gaja Wong** – running north to south through the city. Most of the interest for visitors is focused on the two-kilometre-wide strip of land between the two westernmost rivers, Kali Winongo and Kali Code – this lies beside the **Kraton**, the historic heart of the city. While most of Yogya follows a more or less orderly grid pattern, the Kraton is a welcome oasis of jumbled streets and capillary alleyways.

Although it clearly lies outside of the walled city, according to official definition the Kraton also includes **Jalan Malioboro**, the main street heading from the old city's northern gates into the heart of Yogya's noisy business district. A kilometre north of the Kraton walls, the budget travellers' mecca of **Jalan Sosrowijayan** (known as Jalan Sosro) runs west off Malioboro to the south of the train station. There's a second, more upmarket cluster of tourist hotels and restaurants on **Jalan Prawirotaman**, in the prosperous southern suburbs to the southeast of the Kraton.

Yogya's English-speaking **tourist office**, the most efficient and informative in Central Java, is located at Jalan Malioboro 14–16 (Mon–Sat 8am–7pm; ⓣ0274/566000). This is the best place to find out about local events and entertainment, language and meditation courses, and they can provide maps, bus timetables and a useful calendar of events. It's also the office of the tourist police (same ⓣ), which is open 24 hours a day.

City transport

Most of Yogya's major attractions can be visited on foot from either Jalan Sosro or Jalan Prawirotaman. However, for many of the city's lesser-known sights away from the city centre, you'll need to use the comprehensive public transport system. The extensive bus network and the city's taxis are ideal for longer journeys, while becak are handy for trips within the city centre.

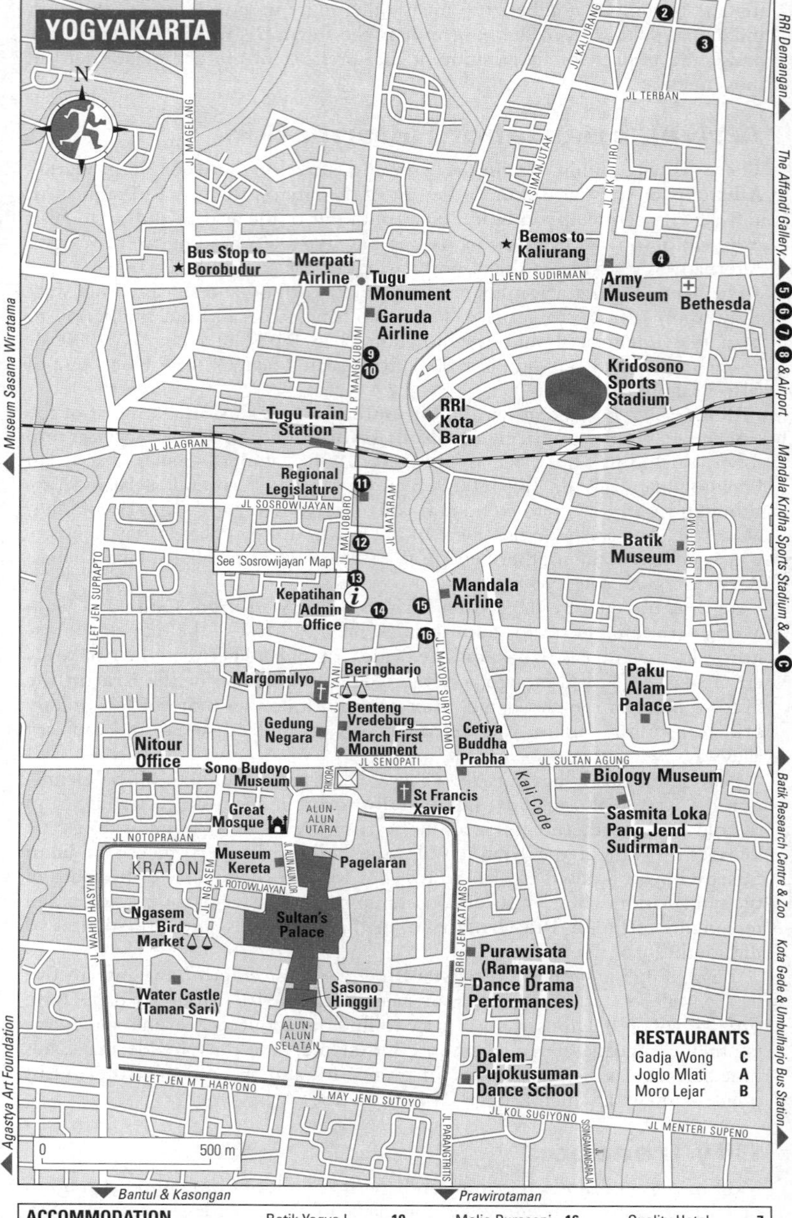

ACCOMMODATION

Akur Hotel	15
Ambarrukmo Palace Hotel	5
Aquila Prambanan	6
Arjuna Plaza	9
Batik Yogya I	10
Gajah Mada	2
Hyatt Regency	1
Ibis	12
Wisma Laras Hati	14
Melia Purosani	16
Mutiara	13
Natour Garuda	11
Novotel	4
Quality Hotel	7
Radisson Yogya Plaza Hotel	3
Sheraton Mustika	8

Useful bus routes

#2 Umbulharjo bus station–Jalan Sisingamangaraja (for Prawirotaman)–Jalan Brig Jen Katamso (along the eastern wall of the Kraton)–Jalan Mataram–Kridono sports centre–Gajah Mada University–Jalan Simanjutak (for minibuses to Prambanan)–Jalan Mataram–Jalan Sisingamangaraja–Umbulharjo.

#4 Umbulharjo–Jalan Sultan Agung–Jalan Mataram–Prambanan minibus station on Jalan Simanjutak–Jalan Malioboro–Jalan Ngeksigondo (Kota Gede)–Umbulharjo.

#5 Umbulharjo–Jalan Parangtritis (western end of Jalan Prawirotaman)–Jalan Wahid Hasyim (along the western wall of the Kraton)–Jalan Sosro (western end)–train station–Jalan Magelang (for buses to Borobudur)–Jalan Pringgokusuman (west of Sosro)–Jalan Let Jen Suprapto–Jalan Ngasem (bird market)–Jalan Parangtritis–Umbulharjo.

#15 Umbulharjo–Jalan Sisingamangaraja (for Prawirotaman)–Jalan Brigjen Katamso–GPO–Gaja Mada University–Umbulharjo.

(Bus #15 is often the only service running after 6pm, when it only runs as far as the GPO before heading straight back to Umbulharjo.)

All **buses** (see above) begin and end their journeys at the Umbulharjo bus station. Always allow plenty of time for your journey, as the routes are circuitous and the traffic heavy. The fare, payable on the bus, is a set Rp1000 regardless of the distance travelled. Most buses stop running at about 6pm, although the #15 runs to the GPO until 8pm. The most useful bus for travellers is the #4, which runs south down Jalan Malioboro before heading to Kota Gede and the Umbulharjo bus station.

There are literally thousands of **becak** in Yogya, mainly around the transport and tourist centres. Though the constant hassle from the drivers can be annoying, becak are the most convenient form of transport, especially as they can take the narrow back roads and bicycle lanes to bypass the circuitous one-way system. It should cost no more than Rp2000 to travel from Jalan Sosro to the GPO (Rp5000 from Jalan Prawirotaman), although hard bargaining is required. The horse-drawn carriages, known as **andog**, which tend to queue along Jalan Malioboro, are a little cheaper. **Taxis** are also good value (Rp2500, plus Rp1500 per km); you can usually find them hanging around the GPO, or ring Jas (ⓣ0274/373737), Setia Kawan (ⓣ0274/522333) or Sumber Rejo (ⓣ0274/514786).

Yogya is a flat city with fairly well-maintained roads, and as such is an enjoyable (if slightly hair-raising) city to cycle in. A number of budget hotels rent out bikes. If yours doesn't, try Bike 33 in Jalan Sosro Gang I: charges are a standard Rp5000 per day. Orange-suited parking attendants throughout the city will look after your bike for Rp500. Self-drive car hire is in its infancy in Yogya, but the better hotels can generally arrange this for you.

Accommodation

There are well over 150 **hotels** and **losmen** in Yogya, ninety percent of them concentrated around just two roads: Jalan Sosrowijayan and Jalan Prawirotaman. **Jalan Sosro**, in the heart of the business district, is a busy, downmarket location whose tempo is dictated by thumping rock music emanating from the restaurants. **Jalan Prawirotaman**, on the other hand, is a lazier, leafier and more affluent street, its pace set by the somnolent tap of the *bakso* sellers who plod up and down the pavement every afternoon. By and large, both streets offer excellent-value accommodation, although the facilities at Jalan Prawirotaman are far superior, with most hotels boasting a swimming pool and air-con as standard. Most budget hotels offer a fan and attached mandi. Discounts can often be had and should always be asked for, even at the more expensive hotels.

Jalan Sosro and around

Budget

Aziatic Jl Sosro 6 (no phone). An asylum-like hotel, its faded grandeur hard to discern, with ancient steel four-poster beds furnishing the otherwise spartan rooms. ❶

Bagus Jl Sosro Wetan GT1/57 ⓣ0274/515087. Guesthouse with small but adequate rooms, free tea and coffee, and bathrooms that are cleaned daily. Inexpensive and very good value. ❷

Beta Jl Sosro GT1/28 ⓣ0274/512756. Losmen consisting of eleven reasonably comfortable though slightly cramped rooms, and four mandi. Guests are often subjected to batik hard sell from the owner. ❷

Bladok Jl Sosro 76 ⓣ0274/560452, ⓔbladok@yogya.wasantara.net.id. A friendly, efficient and impeccably clean hotel built round a central courtyard, with a fish pond in the centre and a swimming pool. The cheaper rooms have a mandi, while the more expensive ones have showers. Highly recommended, although breakfast isn't included. ❷

Citra Anda Jl Sosro Wetan GT1/144 (no phone). While the exterior resembles a maximum-security jail, the interior is much more homely, with some comfortable furnishings and attached mandis. Recommended. ❷

Dewi I Jalan Sosro ⓣ0274/516014. A largish losmen offering decent-sized, spotless – if simple – rooms at reasonable prices. Good value. ❷

Ella Jl Sosrodipuran GT1/487 ⓣ0274/582219, opposite *Hotel Bladok*. Clean fan-cooled rooms, warm showers, free tea and coffee, wonderfully friendly staff and good information on local sights and events. Rates include a decent-sized breakfast. One of the best. ❷

Gembira Jl Sosro 35 ⓣ0274/512605. Sister of *Oryza*, with a high standard of rooms. Free tea and coffee included. ❸

Jaya Jl Sosro GT1/79 ⓣ0274/515055. Inexpensive losmen with free tea and coffee. It resembles a junk shop, with furniture and artefacts scattered everywhere, but not bad value. ❷

Karunia Jl Sosro 78 ⓣ & ⓕ0274/565057. Over-decorated hotel crammed with antiques and souvenirs, with a reasonable rooftop restaurant. Most of the rooms are perfectly acceptable, though some have no windows and are a little gloomy, and the noise from the nearby church can be intrusive. ❷

Lita Jl Sosro Wetan GT1 (no phone). Decorated with paintings and sculptures by local artists, this losmen offers large, spotless rooms at reasonable prices. Very good value indeed. ❷

Lotus Jl Sosro Wetan GT1/167 ⓣ0274/515090. Light, airy and clean losmen, popular with Yogya's adolescents, who congregate in the lounge to watch TV. There's also a fine rooftop balcony. ❷

Monica Jl Sosro GT1/192 ⓣ0274/580602. This dazzlingly clean hotel, built round a garden, is one of the most handsome on Sosro. ❷

Oryza Jl Sosro 49–51 ⓣ0274/512495. Similar decor to the *Gembira*, with huge pictures on the walls and pleasant furnishings. Good value. ❷

Selekta Jl Sosro 150 ⓣ0274/566467. Rivalling *Ella* as the best of the budget bunch. On the whole, a very welcoming losmen with a good atmosphere; the rooms are capacious, clean and cooled by ceiling fans. Rates include breakfast. ❷

Superman and **New Superman** Jl Sosro Gang I/71 & 79 (no phone). *Superman* was once the travellers' favourite, but is less popular than the newly built *New Superman* a little further down the same gang. The latter is in pristine condition and offers good-value accommodation, with fine rooms. ❶

Supriyanto Inn Jl Sosro Wetan GT1/59 (no phone). Another very popular choice, though often full, at a good location in central Sosro, away from the mosque and hubbub of the *gang*. Often full, though. ❶

Suryo Jl Sosro Wetan GT1/145 (no phone). Jauntily decorated little homestay, with bright furnishings and modern furniture, run by an energetic octogenarian. Free tea and coffee. ❷

Utar Jl Sosro Wetan GT1/161 ⓣ0274/560405. A fairly popular losmen, but lacking in atmosphere. A little too much pressure is applied by the managers in trying to persuade residents to visit their batik shop, but otherwise it's not a bad place. ❷

Moderate

Most of these hotels are on **Jalan Pasar Kembang**, one block north of Jalan Sosro opposite the train station.

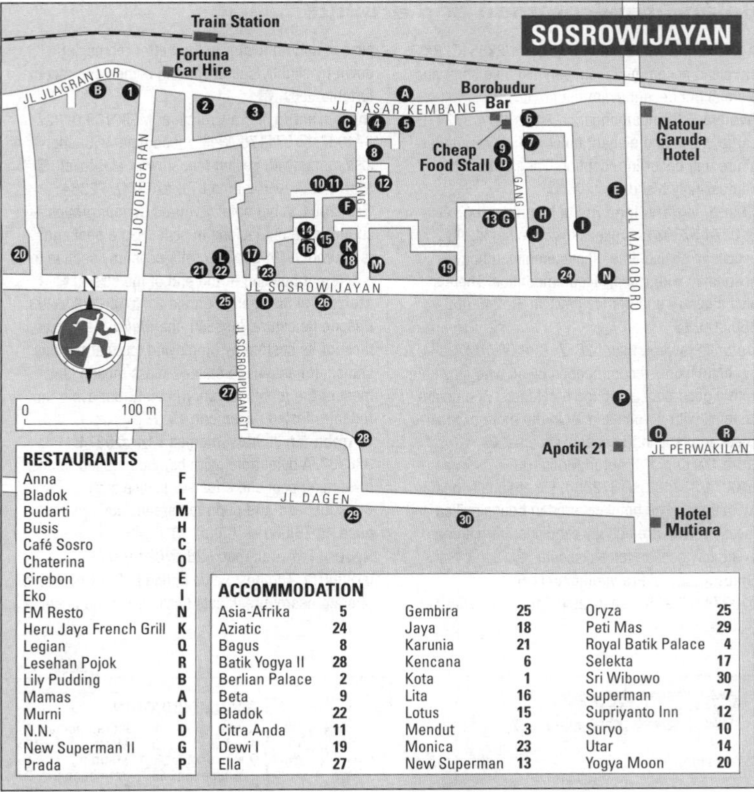

Asia-Afrika Jl Pasar Kembang 21 ☎0274/566219. All the rooms here are en suite, and come with hot water; there's also an attractive lounge/lobby area and an open-air pool. ❸

Batik Yogya II Taman Yuwono complex, Jalan Dagen ☎0274/561828, Ⓕ561823. Cottage-style accommodation in a quiet but convenient location, with a good swimming pool and restaurant attached. ❺

Berlian Palace Jl Pasar Kembang 61 ☎0274/560312. Eighteen rooms with air-con, hot shower, TV and in-house video. ❹

Kencana Jl Pasar Kembang 15 ☎0274/513352. Hotel with double rooms only, either with air-con or fan. Breakfast and tax included. ❶–❹

Kota Jl Jlagran Lor 1 ☎0274/515844. A real colonial feel pervades this lovely hotel, even though it was only established in the 1950s. The best on the street, with fifteen beautiful en-suite rooms, each complete with minibar and hot and cold running water. ❹

Mendut Jl Pasar Kembang 49 ☎0274/563435. Large, clean rooms with air-con, hot water and telephone, built round a large outdoor pool. ❺

Peti Mas Jl Dagen 27 ☎0274/513191. A fine hotel with excellent pool and clean, comfortable rooms. ❹

Royal Batik Palace Jl Pasar Kembang 29 ☎0274/89849. Salubrious, en-suite, air-con rooms, and a good outdoor swimming pool, bar and restaurant. ❺

Sri Wibowo Jl Dagen 23 ☎ & Ⓕ0274/563084. Javanese-style hotel, with lots of parking space, a souvenir shop and even a massage parlour. Rooms, however, are a little soulless. ❸

Yogya Moon Jl Kemetiran 21 ☎0274/582465. Sparkling hotel in a rather run-down area to the west of Sosro. The rooms, all en suite, have air-con, phone and TV; the economy singles are terrific value. ❹–❺

Jalan Prawirotaman and around

Agung Jl Prawirotaman 68 ⓣ0274/375512. Basic but clean accommodation, very likeable staff, and a small but decent swimming pool. ❸

Ayodya Jl Sisingamangaraja 74 ⓣ0274/372475. Large, plush and elegant hotel with Javanese furniture and decor in reception. The rooms are depressingly bland, though. ❹

Dusun Jogja Village Inn Jl Menukan 5 ⓣ & ⓕ0274/373031, ⓔjvigecko@indo.net.id. An excellent, stylish little place combining homely hospitality with classy accommodation. There's also a library and games pavilion. Rp245,000–350,000. ❺

Duta Jl Prawirotaman I 26 ⓣ & ⓕ0274/372064. A big hotel highly recommended by all who stay here, with a good pool and huge breakfasts. Rooms are tasteful, with air-con and TV in the more expensive ones, and fans in the cheaper rooms. ❸

Duta Garden Jl Timuran MGIII/103 ⓣ0274/373482, ⓕ372064. Exceptionally beautiful cottage-style hotel covered in bougainvillea and roses. Rooms are equally exquisite; bargain hard in the low season for a discount. ❺

Galunggung Jl Prawirotaman I 36 ⓣ0274/376915. Reasonable little hotel, with TV, air-con and hot water in the better rooms, let down by slightly dull decor and some very uncomfortable beds. ❸

Indraprastha Jl Prawirotaman MGIII/169 ⓣ0274/374087, ⓕ371175. Well-priced hotel with spotless rooms with ceiling fan, shower and toilet. ❷

Metro Jl Prawirotaman I 71 ⓣ0274/372364, ⓕ372004. A big hotel favoured by tour groups – comfortable but lacking in style. Has a pool and restaurant, with a fairly grotty economy section in a different building at the end of the street. ❷

Metro II Jl Sisingamangaraja 21 ⓣ0274/376993. Despite its central location, the *Metro II*, still grabs most of its custom by employing touts at the bus station. It has a huge stained-glass facade, and most of the rooms are very homely, but avoid the rodent-infested basement. ❸

Prambanan Jl Prawirotaman I 14 ⓣ0274/376167. A quiet hotel with bamboo-walled rooms, swimming pool and eager-to-please staff. Breakfast and afternoon tea are included in the price. Rp76,000–116,000. ❸

Rose Jl Prawirotaman I 28 ⓣ0274/377991, ⓕ380011. The best value option in Prawirotaman, offering hearty breakfasts (included in the price), a

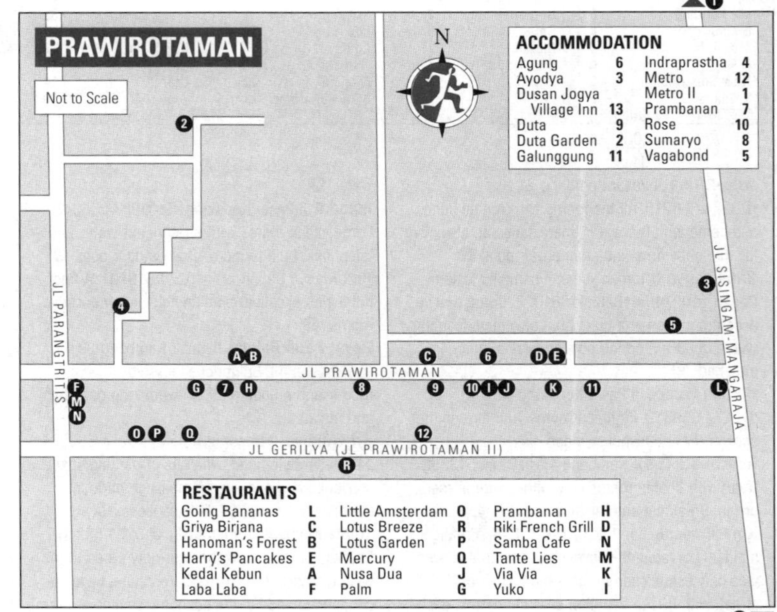

swimming pool and very cheap rooms. Bargain in the low season for an even better deal. ❸

Sumaryo Jl Prawirotaman 22 ⓣ0274/377552, ⓕ373507. Perfectly adequate mid-priced hotel with basic amenities and TV in the better rooms. Handy if the *Rose* next door is full. ❸

Vagabonds (aka **Kelana**) Jl Sisingamangaraja 28b ⓣ0274/371207. A budget hostel to rival the best of Sosro, this is Yogya's International Youth Hostel. Very cheap, offering excellent information, a small library, laser-disc screenings every night, and you can use the pool at the *Dusun Jogja Village Inn* for Rp5000. ❷

The rest of the city

Akur Hotel Jl Mataram 8 ⓣ0274/520527. Half-hotel, half-opticians, this modern, largish and rather bizarre hotel has comfortable rooms with hot-water showers but is a little lacking in atmosphere. ❺

Ambarrukmo Palace Hotel Jl Adisucipto 66 ⓣ0274/566488, ⓕ563283. A four-star international hotel on the way to the airport, comprising 265 air-con, en-suite rooms with TV and minibar. There's also a good restaurant, with nightly wayang and *Ramayana* shows. ❻

Aquila Prambanan Jl Adisucipto 48 ⓣ0274/565005, ⓕ565009. Popular with well-off Indonesians, this hotel on the airport road boasts 191 rooms, many affording views over Prambanan. It also offers Japanese, Chinese and Javanese restaurants, and a pub with billiards and darts. ❺

Arjuna Plaza Jl Mangkubumi 44 ⓣ0274/513063, ⓕ561862. Located near the Tugu Monument, this hotel describes itself as a "hotel with a smile", but actually has quite a formal, businesslike atmosphere. The rooms are smart but unexceptional. ❺

Batik Yogya I Jl Mangkubumi 46 ⓣ0274/562510, ⓕ561823. Sister of Sosro's *Batik Yogya II*, this place is less attractive, but with similar facilities, including hot-water showers and TV. Rp200,000–300,000. ❺

Gajah Mada Bulaksumur, Gajah Mada University campus ⓣ0274/563461. The best option near the university, to the north of the city. Nothing special, but perfectly acceptable for a short-term stay. ❹

Hyatt Regency Jalan Palagan Tentara Pelajar ⓣ0274/ 869123, ⓕ869588, ⓔinfo@hyattyogya.com. The most sumptuous hotel in Yogya, 3km north of the city centre, with an impressive tiered swimming pool, elegant restaurants and manicured golf course. *The* place if you want luxury. ❼

Ibis Jl Malioboro 52–58 ⓣ0274/516974, ⓕ516977, ⓔibisyk@indo.net.id. New, pastel-pink hotel ideally located behind the Malioboro Mall. The rooms are equipped with all the usual facilities (minibar, air-con and TV), and other features include a pool, sauna and gym. ❻

Wisma Laras Hati Jl Sosrokusuman DNI/182 ⓣ0274/514513. One of the better budget options on this small alley to the east of Malioboro, and one of the few to accept foreigners along this *gang*. ❷

Novotel Jl Jend. Sudirman 89 ⓣ0274/580930, ⓕ580931, ⓔnovyog@indo.net.id. A more upmarket sister hotel to the *Ibis*, with well-appointed rooms, good bathrooms and cable TV, located just north of the Sports Stadium. ❼

Melia Purosani Jl Suryotomo 31 ⓣ0274/589521, ⓕ588070. An imposing, peach-coloured resort-style hotel, with a large swimming pool and comfortable rooms with all amenities, in a good location east of Malioboro. ❼

Mutiara Jl Malioboro 16 ⓣ0274/563814, ⓕ561201. Right in the centre of Malioboro.The rather bland rooms have individual air-con, fridge, phones with IDD, and colour TV with in-house videos. ❺

Natour Garuda Jl Malioboro 60 ⓣ0274/566353, ⓕ563074. Established in 1911, this is Yogya's oldest hotel, with 235 standard and suite rooms, with tennis courts, two swimming pools and a shopping arcade. They also host gamelan recitals (see p.209). ❻

Quality Hotel Jl Laksda Adisucipto 48 ⓣ0274/565005. Located on the airport road to the east of the city, with elegantly furnished rooms. ❻

Radisson Yogya Plaza Hotel Jl Gejayan, Complex Colombo ⓣ0274/584222, ⓔradisson@yogyahotel.com. A good business-orientated hotel located to the north of the train station. Rooms are very comfortable and there's a pleasant pool, a bar and two good restaurants offering Western/Asian fare. ❺

Sheraton Mustika Jl Laksda Adisucipto Km.8,7 ⓣ0274 511588, ⓕ511589, ⓔhsmyogya@indo.net.id. A long way from the city centre, but only 2km from the airport. Comes near to the *Hyatt* for luxury, with an impressive swimming pool, spa, good food, and outstanding views of Mount Merapi. ❼

The Kraton

The layout of Yogya reflects its character: modern and brash on the outside, but with an ancient and traditional heart in the **Kraton**, the walled city designed by Yogya's first sultan, Mangkubumi. Derived from the Indonesian word for "king" (*ratu*), *kraton* means "royal residence" and originally referred just to the sultan's palace. Today, however, *kraton* usually denotes the whole of the walled city (plus Jalan Malioboro), which includes not only the palace but also an entire town of some ten thousand people.

The Kraton has changed little in the two hundred years since Mangkubumi's time; both the palace and the 5km of crenellated icing-sugar walls surrounding the Kraton date from his reign. Essentially, the Kraton is little more than a charming, close-knit town overlaid with a veneer of quiet aristocratic pride. Its character changes from one area to the next. Immediately around the palace, there's a reverential hush in the high-walled streets, which are lined with quaint whitewashed cottages. Further west, the atmosphere is as chaotic and intimate as that of any other Javanese kampung: front doors are left open, laundry drips from lines strung between buildings, grandmothers sit gossiping on the doorsteps and children splash around in the mud in the alleyways.

With plenty of time, you could wander through the Kraton for days; for those in a hurry, the main sights – the **Sultan's Palace**, **Sonobudoyo Museum** and the **Taman Sari** – can be visited on foot in a day.

Alun-alun Utara

Most people enter the Kraton through the northern gates by the GPO, beyond which lies the busy town square, **Alun-alun Utara**, a large field of threadbare, yellowing grass. The alun-alun has always been the venue for public entertainments; in the nineteenth century, by far the most popular of these were the fights staged between a tiger, of which there was once a ready supply in the region, and a buffalo. In typically Javanese fashion, these contests took on symbolic meaning: the savage and cruel tiger was naturally identified with the Dutch, while the Javanese were represented by the buffalo, a steadfast, determined and proud beast. Almost invariably, the tiger started off the strongest, only to be defeated in the end by the obduracy of the buffalo. The anti-colonial Yogyans would be doubly delighted at this result if a visiting Dutch dignitary was watching too. The tiger, however, was not always the victim of this entertainment:

> **The emperors sometimes make criminals, condemned to death, fight with tigers. In such cases, the man is rubbed with borri, or tumeric. The tiger, who has for a long time been kept fasting, falls upon the man with the greatest fury, and generally strikes him down at once with his paw. Even if he (the criminal) ultimately succeeds in killing his ferocious antagonist, he must suffer death, by command of the emperor.**
>
> *Island of Java*, John Joseph Stockdale (1811)

Of all the banyan trees growing on and around the alun-alun, the two at the centre are considered the most sacred. It was here, during the eighteenth and nineteenth centuries, that the opposing sides of a dispute would congregate – one at each tree – and put their arguments to the sultan. After some deliberation, the sultan would issue his verdict, which was, of course, irrevocable.

As is traditional in Java, the city's Great Mosque, or **Mesjid Agung** stands on the western side of the alun-alun (visit outside of prayer times: noon, 3pm, 6pm, 7pm & 4.30am). The mesjid was built in 1773 by Mangkubumi, following traditional Javanese lines, with a multi-tiered roof over an airy, open-sided

△ Borobudur, Central Java

prayer hall. The building is rather tatty, however, with a corrugated-iron roof and chipped paintwork sorely in need of repair.

A few minutes' walk north of the mosque, just by the main gates, stands the **Sonobudoyo Museum**, Jl Trikoro 6 (Tues–Thurs 8am–1.30pm, Fri 8–11.15am, Sat & Sun 8am–noon; Rp1000). Opened in 1933 by Hamengkubuwono VIII, the museum houses a fine exhibition of the arts of Java, Madura and Bali. From the outside, the building, with a gamelan pendopo before the entrance, is a mini version of the sultan's palace facing it. Of the exhibits inside, the intricate, damascene-style wooden partitions from Northern Java are particularly eye-catching, as are the many classical gold and stone statues dating back to the eighth century. Just outside the entrance, a shed houses a small puppet workshop that supplies the characters for the museum's evening wayang kulit performances (see p.209).

The Sultan's Palace

On the southern side of the alun-alun lies a masterpiece of understated Javanese architecture, an elegant collection of ornate kiosks and graceful pendopos housed within a series of spacious, interconnecting courtyards. This is the **Sultan's Palace**, or Karaton Ngayogyakarta Hadiningrat (Palace of the Town of Yogyakarta). Distinctly unostentatious, and in places quite spartan, this single-storey palace is nevertheless rich in symbolism; designed as a scale model of the Hindu cosmos, every plant, building and courtyard in the palace represents some element of this mystical universe. The sultans, though professing the Islamic faith, still held on to many of the Hindu and animist superstitions of their forefathers, and believed this particular design would ensure the prosperity of the royal house.

The palace is split into two parts, with two separate entrances (and, unfortunately, two sets of entrance fees too). The first section, the **Pagelaran** (Mon–Thurs, Sat & Sun 8am–1pm, Fri 8–11.30am; Rp1000, plus Rp500 camera fee, Rp1000 for a video camera), lies immediately to the south of the alun-alun. Most tourists bypass it, as there's little to see apart from two large, drab pendopos and an extremely mediocre display of regal costumes. The first and biggest pendopo functioned as the palace's reception, where foreign dignitaries and public officials would await an audience with the sultan. It was also the first home of the Gajah Mada University, founded in the 1940s by Hamengkubuwono IX, and is used today for theatrical and musical performances, particularly during the Sekaten festival (see p.60). The stairs at the back of the pendopo lead up to the **Siti Inggil** (High Ground), a platform on which the sultans of Yogya are crowned.

Forming a backdrop to the Siti Ingill, the massive wooden **Bronjonolo Gate** leads through to the rest of the palace. As it's now permanently closed, to gain entrance you have to walk down Jalan Alun-alun Lor, the road running alongside the western walls of the palace. On the way, you'll pass the small **Museum Kereta** (Mon–Thurs, Sat & Sun 8am–4pm, Fri 8.30am–1pm; Rp1000, plus Rp500 camera fee), housing a dusty collection which includes ten tatty royal chariots. Most impressive is the Kanjeng Kyai Cekatak, the diamond-studded saddle and harness of Hamengkubuwono I.

A hundred metres beyond the museum stands the entrance to the main body of the **palace** (Mon–Thurs, Sat & Sun 8.30am–2pm, Fri 8.30am–1pm; Rp3000 including optional guided tour, Rp500 camera fee, Rp1000 for video). Shorts and revealing clothes are frowned upon in this part of the palace; you will seldom be refused entry, but you may be required to rent a batik shirt from the ticket office (Rp1000).

Loro Kidul

The curious relationship between the sultan of Yogya and **Ratu Loro Kidul**, the Goddess of the South Seas, is one of the most intriguing and enduring themes of court folklore. The tradition began with the founder of the Mataram dynasty, Senopati. Just before his assault on the kingdoms of the north coast, an attack that led to the founding of the Mataram empire, Senopati withdrew to the south coast for a few days to gather his thoughts and contemplate a plan of action. Meditating on the cliffs, he was spotted by Loro Kidul, whose underwater palace lies offshore at Parangtritis. Senopati followed the goddess to her home, where for three days she instructed him in the arts of war and lovemaking. Thanks to her tuition, Senopati went on to conquer the north coast with ease, and soon most of Java came under his control (whether the lovemaking classes were equally effective is not recorded). All the subsequent leaders of Mataram have continued to pay tribute to Loro. In Solo, a tower in the centre of the royal palace has a floor reserved solely for the use of the susuhunan (king) and the goddess, and Mangkubumi's Taman Sari (see p.202) was apparently modelled on Loro's water palace.

The superstitious fixation with Loro Kidul continues to this day. Annual offerings are presented to the goddess at Parangkusumo (see p.216), where Senopati emerged after his crash course in love and war. In Solo, on the anniversary of the coronation of the susuhunan, the sacred *bedoyo ketaweng* dance is performed in tribute to the goddess (who, it is believed, sometimes joins in with the dancing). And many of the congregation who attended the coronation of Sultan Hamengkubuwono X of Yogya in 1989 noted a strong fragrance borne along by a sudden breath of wind halfway through the ceremony – a sure indication that Loro Kidul had come to witness the crowning of her next devotee.

The palace has been the home of the sultans since Mangkubumi arrived here from Solo in 1755. The hushed courtyards, the faint stirrings of the gamelan drifting on the breeze and the elderly palace retainers, still dressed in the traditional style with a kris tucked by the small of their back, all contribute to a remarkable sense of timelessness.

You enter the complex through the palace's outer courtyard or **Keben** (after the keben trees that grow here), where the sultan used to sit on the stone throne, which still stands in the centre of the large pendopo, and pass sentence on lawbreakers. The palace itself lies through the **Sriminganti Gate** to the south of the Keben. Throughout the palace, you'll notice that most gates have a wall immediately behind them, to prevent evil spirits from entering further into the building – it's believed that they can only walk in straight lines.

Two pendopos stand on either side of a central path in the next courtyard – known as the **Sriminganti** (To Wait For the King) courtyard – each sheltering an antique gamelan orchestra under a timber roof. The eastern pendopo, the **Bangsal Trajumas**, also houses a number of royal curios including an early royal playpen, which looks like an oversized birdcage.

Two silver-painted *raksasa* (temple guardian statues) guard the **Donapratopo Gate** to the south and the entrance to the next courtyard, the **Pelataran Kedaton**. Once through, you find yourself in the largest and most important courtyard in the palace. On your left stands a small **Dutch kiosk**, resembling a stained-glass bandstand. On your right, and forming the northwestern corner of the courtyard, is the yellow-painted **Gedung Kuning** (Yellow Building), the offices and living quarters of the sultan. This part of the palace is out of bounds to tourists, as the current sultan (Hamengkubuwono X), his wife and five daughters still spend much of their time here.

A covered corridor joins the Gedung Kuning with the so-called Golden Throne Pavilion, or **Bangsal Kencono**, the centrepiece of the Pelataran Kedaton. In the imagery of the Hindu cosmos, the pavilion represents Mount Meru, the sacred mountain at the very centre of the universe. It's an impressive pendopo, with an intricately carved roof held aloft by some hefty teak pillars. The carvings on these sum up the syncretism of the three main religions of Indonesia, with the lotus leaf of Buddhism supporting a red-and-gold diamond pattern of Hindu origin, while around the pillar's circumference runs the opening lines of the Koran: "There is no God but Allah and Mohammed is his prophet." Adjoining the Bangsal Kencono to the south is a large marble-floored ceremonial dining hall, the **Bangsal Manis**.

The only other rooms open to the public in the Pelataran Kedaton are the small **utility rooms** lining the courtyard's southern wall, which house a collection of tea sets as well as the odd regal spittoon. The royal tea-makers, a group of three elderly ladies, still make the tea three times a day and carry it forth, with all due ceremony, to the sultan's office in the Gedung Kuning.

Running north–south beyond the Pelataran Kedaton's eastern wall is a series of three more courtyards, once the quarters of the royal princes. A large, arched gateway flanked by two huge drums connects the Pelataran Kedaton with the middle of these three courtyards, the **Kesatrian**, home to both another gamelan orchestra and, in galleries along the east and southern wall, a collection of **royal portraits**, some by the esteemed nineteenth-century artist Raden Saleh. Most of the buildings in the **southern courtyard**, including the central glass pavilion, are filled with the photographs and personal effects of the Independence hero Hamengkubuwono IX. The **Gedung Kopo**, the buildings lining the **northern courtyard**, was once the palace hospital and now houses a small palace museum. The exhibits here include replicas of the royal thrones, and gifts given to the sultans by various heads of state.

The Taman Sari and Pasar Ngasem

A five-minute walk to the west of the palace, along Jalan Rotowijayan and down Jalan Ngasem and Jalan Taman, is the unspectacular **Taman Sari** (Water Garden) of Mangkubumi (daily 9am–3pm; Rp1000, plus Rp500 camera fee). This giant complex was designed in the eighteenth century as an amusement park for the royal house, a convenient and luxurious escape from the everyday chores of being sultan. Incorporated into this paradise were a series of swimming pools and fountains, an underground mosque, a large boating lake and a few small groves of coconuts and cloves. A tower was also built, from which the sultan could watch his harem splashing around in the pools below. Having made his selection from the bathers, Mangkubumi would then retire to the tower's bedroom.

Unfortunately, the Taman Sari fell into disrepair soon after the death of Mangkubumi. The elaborate design and multistorey buildings required an enormous amount of maintenance, which proved beyond the means of the cash-strapped sultans. The British invasion in 1812 damaged many of the Taman's buildings, and a serious earthquake in 1867 accelerated its decline, so most of what you see today is a concrete reconstruction. The main entrance gate is the most complete and attractive part of the ruins; you can still wander through the cobwebbed underground passages, where the shell of the sultan's underground mosque is visible. Above ground, however, most of the complex has been lost to the advance of the kampung, which encroaches from every side and which derived much of its building material from the Taman's rubble.

Also within the former grounds of the Taman Sari, Yogya's bird market, the **Pasar Ngasem**, stands on a dusty half-acre lot on what was once part of the boating lake. The market is at its busiest on Sundays, although whatever day you arrive you should see all manner of birds, dogs, lizards and rodents for sale; some may find the confinement of the animals distressing.

Jalan Malioboro

The two-kilometre stretch of road heading north from the alun-alun is as replete with history as it is with batik shops and becak. Originally this panoply of souvenir stalls and batik outlets was designed as a **ceremonial boulevard** by Mangkubumi, along which the royal cavalcade would proceed on its way to Mount Merapi. The road changes name three times along its length, starting as Jalan J.A. Yani in the south, continuing as Jalan Malioboro, and finally becoming Jalan Mangkubumi – and it's one long unbroken stream of diesel-belching traffic heading south. The pavement is where the real action happens; in the very early morning, and especially on Sundays, it becomes an outdoor gymnasium, with many Yogyans congregating to perform t'ai chi. During the day, these same pavements reach bursting point as the souvenir market gets into full swing; in the evening, the food sellers arrive to set up their stalls and create a great long alfresco diner.

At the southern end of the street, at the junction of Jalan J.A. Yani and Jalan Senopati, a number of historical buildings face each other. On the northeast corner, opposite the imposing, colonial-style GPO, the **March First Monument** is a statue of four soldiers on a plinth marching purposefully behind their flag-waving commander, Colonel Suharto. The statue is also known as the Six Hours in Yogyakarta monument, as it commemorates the six-hour recapture of Yogya from the Dutch in 1949.

Behind it are the orderly hedgerows and flowerbeds of the old Dutch fort, the **Benteng Vredeburg**, Jl Ahmad Yani 6 (Tues–Thurs 8.30am–1.30pm, Fri 8.30–11am; Rp750). Thanks to their successful divide-and-rule policies in the mid-eighteenth century, the Dutch had acquired a stranglehold on Central Java, and ordered Mangkubumi to build the fort in 1756. It took over twenty years to complete, however, mainly because Mangkubumi was unwilling to spare men and materials from his own ongoing pet project, the Taman Sari. This relic of Dutch imperialism has been restored to its former glory, and the solid, whitewashed walls form an impressive and austere facade on Jalan J. A. Yani. Inside, the fort houses a series of dioramas split between three barrack rooms which recount – ironically enough, considering their setting – the end of colonialism in Indonesia. The dioramas, particularly of the battles that took place in Yogya itself, are well-made and informative, and the air-con in the fort is probably the best in Yogya.

Another imposing old colonial building lies over the road. The **Gedung Negara** (State Guesthouse) was built in 1823 for the Dutch resident and became the presidential palace in the 1940s, when Yogya was made the capital of the republic during the Revolution. Just across the narrow road that runs along the northern wall of the Gedung Negara stands the small and peaceful Norman-style **Gereja Margomulyo** (1830), Yogya's oldest church, with wooden pews and stained-glass windows.

Opposite the church, by way of contrast, the **Pasar Beringharjo** buzzes noisily throughout the day. Established during the reign of Mangkubumi and named after the bering-tree forest that once grew here, the current building was commissioned by Hamengkubuwono IX in 1925. A multi-level, dimly lit complex dominated by mass-produced batik (with a small, good-quality selection in the southeastern corner on the ground floor), the market is raucous, disorganized and great fun.

Three hundred metres north, on the right behind the tourist office, is a grand collection of pavilions known as the **Kepatihan Administration Office**, formerly the residence of the Patih, or minister of Yogya. Another 300m north, on the same side of the street, are the large lawns of the **Regional Legislature**; a statue of the Independence hero General Sudirman overlooks the road from the front of the lawn.

Malioboro continues for another kilometre north. The end of Mangkubumi's original path is marked by the **Tugu Monument**, a curious obelisk commemorating the founding of Yogya in 1755; it replaced an earlier obelisk on the same spot, which marked the official northern limit of the Kraton.

The rest of the city

Outside the Kraton walls, Yogya develops a split personality. To the **north**, the city is permanently choked with traffic, and appears as rowdy and polluted as most Javan cities. The tourist attractions here are numerous, but cannot compare with the Kraton. To the **south** of the Kraton, the city is far calmer and more affluent; there are no sights as such, but a number of local artists have set up shops and galleries here that merit a look.

Jalan Senopati and Jalan Agung

The busy road heading east from the GPO, which initially goes by the name of **Jalan Senopati**, plays host to a number of sights. Three hundred metres east of the GPO, at the junction where Jalan Senopati transforms into Jalan Agung, your eye will probably be caught by Yogya's foremost Buddhist temple, the **Cetiya Buddha Prabha**, its vivid red paintwork flecked with gold; occasional wayang performances are held here. Four hundred metres further on, on the same side of the road at Jl Sultan Agung 22, is the **Biology Museum** (Mon–Thurs 7.30am–1.30pm, Fri 7.30–11am, Sat 7.30am–12.30pm; Rp500), a collection of long-dead animals, some pickled and some stuffed, the star attraction being a rather sorry-looking orang-utan. Just round the corner to the east of here, on Jalan Bintaran Wetan 3, is the **Jend. Sudirman** (The House of General Sudirman), which has been preserved and turned into an unexciting museum displaying photos and memorabilia associated with the Independence hero (Ⓣ0274/376663, Mon–Fri & Sun 8am–2pm; free).

Yogyakarta's second court, **Paku Alam** (Ⓣ0274/372161, Tues, Thurs & Sun 9.30am–1.30pm; free), lies 50m to the northeast of the museum on the north side of Jalan Agung. As is traditional, the minor court of the city faces south as a mark of subservience to the main palace. The royal household of Paku Alam was created in 1812 by the British for Notokusumo (Paku Alam I), the brother of Sultan Hamengkubuwono II and the Brits' most important ally in the sacking of the Kraton that year. By dividing Yogya between two courts, the British deliberately duplicated the divide-and-rule tactic used so successfully by the Dutch in Solo fifty years earlier.

The octogenarian Paku Alam VIII died in 1998, having been on the throne for over sixty years – by far the longest reign of all Central Java's rulers. The quarters of his successor, Paku Alam IX, are concealed from public gaze at the back of the palace. The part that is open to general view – by the southeastern corner of the courtyard – houses a motley collection of royal artefacts, including a huge family tree and a room filled with the prince's chariots, which appear to be permanently shrouded in white dust sheets.

Two kilometres further east along Jalan Sultan Agung (which changes its name to Jalan Kusumanegara 100m or so after Paku Alam), on the eastern banks of the Kali Gajah Wong, lies the **Gembira Loka Zoo** (daily 8am–6pm;

Rp3000), home to a large selection of African and Asian animals, including the Komodo dragon and orang-utan.

Jalan Sudirman

Jalan Sudirman, which heads east from the Tugu monument towards the airport, and its continuation, **Jalan Adisucipto**, are flanked by a number of minor tourist attractions. These sights are very spread out, so the road is probably best tackled by taxi or, if you can stand the traffic, bicycle. If you just want to see the Affandi Gallery (see below) – the biggest attraction on this road – catch bus #8 (from Umbulharjo) which stops outside.

The **Army Museum**, also known as Museum Dharma Wiratama, lies 1km east of Tugu, on the corner of Jalan Sudirman 75 and Jalan Cik Ditiro (Mon–Fri 8am–1.30pm; free). Housed in the former offices of revolutionary hero **General Sudirman**, the museum traces his rise through the ranks, as well as housing a wide collection of uniforms, medals and other paraphernalia, including Sudirman's old car. Some of the captions are in English, but not enough, unfortunately, to make sense of many of the exhibits.

Thanks to Yogya's one-way system, it's impossible to drive or cycle east for the next kilometre. To bypass this stretch, head north for 400m along Jalan Cik Ditiro, then east for 1km along Jalan Terban, before heading south back along Jalan Gejayan to Jalan Sudirman, which by now has reverted to a two-way road once more. Jalan Sudirman changes its name at this point to Jalan Adisucipto.

Two kilometres east along Jalan Adisucipto, on the west bank of the Kali Gajah Wong, you'll find the **Affandi Gallery** at Jl Solo 167 (Mon–Fri & Sun 8.30am–4pm, Sat 8.30am–1pm; Rp1250, Rp2500 camera fee). Heralded by the *New Statesman* in 1952 as the most important post-war painter in the world, Affandi, the son of a clerk at a Dutch sugar plantation, was born in Cirebon in 1907, but spent most of his life and did most of his paintings in Yogya, in the unusual house-cum-studio that still stands on stilts above the river near the galleries. After dropping out of high school, Affandi spent much of the 1920s and 1930s painting cinema hoardings in order to survive, scraping up the paint remnants at the end of the day to indulge in his own creative passion after work. It was during these formative years that he developed his idiosyncratic style, discarding the paintbrush and palette because they denied him spontaneity, preferring instead to apply the paint to the canvas directly from the tube, forming thick swirls of colour into a style that Sukarno once described simply as "crazy". Many of the paintings were completed in just one hour. The galleries were built after Affandi's death in 1990, and contain over a hundred of his greatest works, including several self-portraits and a number of landscapes and streetscapes painted in America and Holland. His eldest child, Kartika, has since followed in her father's footsteps, and a few of her paintings now hang in the gallery alongside those of her father. Affandi's unusual car – a fish-shaped Colt Galant hot rod – stands in the forecourt by the entrance.

The **Ambarrukmo Palace Hotel** is situated 1km further east, on the same side of the road. Its grounds once belonged to a pleasure palace built for Hamengkubuwono III. There's little to see now of the palace, save for the main pendopo and a floating pavilion (Bale Kambang), which has been converted into a top-class restaurant (see p.208). There's also the odd chariot, and a couple of mannequins looking rather awkward in court dress. From here, cross over the road to the **Ambar Budaya Craft Centre**, a government-owned souvenir superstore specializing in wayang puppets, woodcarvings and earthenware pottery. The goods aren't exceptional, and similar items can be found in town, although the prices are fixed and reasonable.

Continuing east for 1.5km, a major road – Jalan Janti – appears on the right. Head down here for a further kilometre, then turn left to the **Di Museum Pusat Tni-Au Dirgantara Mandala** (Mon, Tues & Sun 8am–1pm; Rp500), dedicated to Indonesia's glorious tradition of aviation. Officially, you're meant to tell the authorities – via the tourist office – at least one day in advance that you wish to visit this museum; in practice, however, if you just turn up and hand over some form of ID they will often let you through. The museum is an unexpected pleasure, with plenty of aircraft on show, from early biplanes to modern jet engines.

Kota Gede and the Museum Wayang Kekayon

The small, wealthy suburb of **Kota Gede** lies 5km southeast of the town centre. To get here, catch bus #4 from Jalan Malioboro and jump off at Tom's Silver, a journey of about forty minutes. The suburb is famous today as the centre of the silver industry (see the shopping section on p.210 for details). For 39 years, however, this was the capital of the Mataram empire. Founded by Senopati in 1575, the court at Kota Gede lasted until Senopati's grandson, Sultan Agung, re-established the court at Karta during the early years of the seventeenth century. The graves of Senopati and his son and heir, Krapyak, form the centrepiece of the **Kota Gede Cemetery** (Mon & Tues 10am–noon, Fri 1–3pm), which lies to the rear of the suburb's **Grand Mosque**. The body of Yogya's second sultan, Hamengkubuwono II (1810–11 & 1812–14), the bane of both the Dutch and British colonialists, also rests here. Traditional court dress must be worn, and can be rented at the ticket office.

One of Yogya's best museums, the **Museum Wayang Kekayon**, lies 7km east of town on Jl Raya Yogyakarta-Wonosari Km 7 no. 277 (daily except Mon 8am–3pm; Rp1000). It takes visitors on a journey through the development of puppeteering and explores the many different forms of wayang today. Fronted by a large pendopo, the displays inside the surrounding buildings include such seldom-seen treasures as a *wayang beber* set, where the action is drawn onto a large scroll of paper which is slowly unfurled as events progress; a set of wooden puppets from a *wayang wahyu* set, used to tell the story of the Nativity; and a *sejati wayang* set, which uses puppets as an educational tool to re-enact various twentieth-century events. If you didn't catch the Wayang Museum in Jakarta, this is the next best thing. To get there, take a Wonosari-bound bus from the bus station for ten minutes.

Eating

Yogya's specialities are ayam goreng and *nasi gudeg* (rice and jackfruit), and many foodstalls serve nothing else. Every evening on Jalan Malioboro, the noise of traffic is replaced by the equally clamorous night-time **food market**. Hundreds of warung set up at about 4pm; by 8pm, the entire street is thronged with diners. Wherever you choose to eat along this street, make sure you know how much everything costs: stallholders are not averse to raising their prices to extortionate levels, and in many of the larger **lesehan** places (where you sit on the floor by low tables), particularly those by the end of Jalan Sosro, diners pay restaurant prices. The stalls by the train station and on the top floor of the Malioboro Mall are cheaper. If all this frenzy is a little too taxing on the nerves, head to the **warung** at the end of Gang I, a regular travellers' haunt serving a wonderfully spicy goat curry for around Rp3000.

Jalan Sosro and Jalan Prawirotaman are chock-full of good-quality restaurants, offering close approximations of Western dishes alongside standard Indonesian fare. Prices are usually very reasonable, too: about Rp5000 for nasi goreng. Most of these restaurants open around midday, and remain open until the last customer has left – usually at about 10pm, although in some cases much later. The restaurants on Prawirotaman are a shade more expensive than those on Sosro, but their food is usually superior.

Jalan Sosro

Anna's Gang I/127. Popular little family-run restaurant proffering some wonderful, genuinely Indonesian food. If you don't like their *nasi gudeg* (Rp7000), they promise to refund your money.

Bladok Jl Sosro 76. Part of a hotel, this open-air mid-priced restaurant serving mainly Indonesian dishes is a little more expensive than the Sosro norm, but definitely worth it.

Budarti Gang II/125. Excellent-value restaurant, especially good for breakfasts and snacks. The pancakes are superb, the fruit juices very cheap, and the ginseng coffee (Rp2000) addictive.

Busis Gang I. Small restaurant with a predictable Western and Indonesian menu. The food itself, however, is inexpensive and tasty.

Café Sosro Gang II. Another family-run place, serving good, filling and reasonably priced Indonesian and Western food, such as chicken sandwiches and spaghetti bolognese. Come here for lunch rather than in the evenings (they close at 9pm), when the service can be very slow and many of the dishes are unavailable.

Chaterina Jalan Sosro 41. Very reasonably priced restaurant with *lesehan* seating at the rear, serving some of the best food in Sosro, but let down a little by hassle from the batik touts.

Cirebon Jalan A. Jani 15. A large, high-ceilinged establishment full of caged birds and fish tanks. The food, in particular the noodle dishes, is tasty (although portions are small), and the drinks are ice-cold. Perfect for afternoon snacks.

Eko Gang I. Unpretentious little place serving hearty breakfasts and run-of-the-mill Indonesian dishes at reasonable prices.

FM Resto Jalan Sosro. Great atmosphere with live music, catering to a mainly Western crowd. The food is good and therefore quite expensive.

Heru Jaya French Grill Gang I/79. Moderately priced restaurant serving tasty Western food of varying degrees of authenticity.

Legian Jl Perwakilan 9. An upstairs restaurant overlooking Malioboro, reached via a grotty entrance to a billiards hall. Serves mid-priced Indonesian, Chinese and Western meals; the service can be very slow, but the food is well presented and good.

Lesehan Pojok Jalan Perwakilan. An inexpensive *lesehan* establishment just along from the *Legian*, serving *nasi gudeg* and other local dishes. A good alternative to eating in Sosro.

Lily Pudding Jalan Jlagran Lor. This place, 50m to the west of the train station on the opposite side of the road, turns out a treasure trove of treacle treats. Try their nine-inch caramel pudding for Rp7000.

Mamas Jl Pasar Kembang 71. Long-established and popular eating place near the train station, serving cheap and generous helpings of Indonesian food.

Murni Gang I. A busy little alcohol-free budget restaurant, serving huge portions of probably the best-value curry in Sosro. Closed in the evenings.

N.N. Gang II. A family-owned place with good service and very cheap, hearty food – particularly the delicious soups.

Prada Jl Malioboro 145. Built above the tasteful souvenir shop, this medium-priced café serves authentic Western dishes and screens movies in the evenings. Try their mouthwatering *calzone* (Rp12,000).

New Superman II JL Sosro Gang I/99. A popular restaurant offering delicious pancakes, ice-cold beer, regular screenings of European football, and Internet facilities.

Jalan Prawirotaman

Going Bananas Jl Prawirotaman 48. Café/souvenir shop at the eastern end of the street. Good coffee, sandwiches and light meals.

Griya Birjana Jalan Prawirotaman. Hugely popular restaurant on the main drag, serving Indonesian and Western fare and ice-cold beer. Lively atmosphere in the evenings, and good value all the time.

Hanoman's Forest Jl Tirtodipura 5. The main reason to come here is to watch the nightly (8pm) cultural entertainments – wayang puppet shows, Javanese ballet and live bands. The food – mid-priced Western, Chinese and Indonesian – is much improved since their move from Jalan Prawirorotman.

Kedai Kebun Jl Titodipura 3 ⓣ0274/76114. Stylish restaurant/art gallery, good (mostly Western) food, and a pretty garden.

Little Amsterdam Jl Prawirotaman II. Large menu of Western dishes, with the emphasis on steaks and freshly baked bread. Medium-priced.

Lotus Breeze Jl Prawirotaman I. The younger and better-looking of the two *Lotus* restaurants, with delicious if slightly overpriced Western/Indonesian food served by occasionally stroppy waiters.

Lotus Garden Jl Prawirotaman MG3/593a. A partner of the *Lotus Breeze*, this mid-priced restaurant specializes in high-quality, healthy local dishes, and with a good vegetarian selection. It also stages puppet shows and classical and modern dance performances throughout the week at 8pm (Rp12,000).

Mercury Jl Parawirotaman II MG3/595. A beautiful, colonial-style restaurant serving surprisingly affordable mid-priced Indonesian and Western dishes.

Nusa Dua Jalan Prawirotaman. A highly recommended and inexpensive restaurant with a large menu of Indonesian, Chinese and Western dishes served by very professional, friendly staff.

Palm Jl Prawirotaman 12. Indonesian, Chinese and some well-prepared Western meals. Cheap.

Prambanan Jl Prawirotaman 14. Mostly Indonesian and Chinese food; good, but sees few customers.

Riki French Grill and **Harrys's** (sic) **Pancakes** Jalan Prawirotaman. Two noisy, popular restaurants in one location. Hardly *haute cuisine*, but passable. Mid-priced.

Samba Café Jalan Parangtritis. A smallish daytime café specializing in Western sandwiches and snacks. **Tante Lies** Jl Parangtritis 61–75. An inexpensive but excellent Indonesian restaurant, just off Jalan Prawirotaman.

Via Via Jl Prawirotaman 24b ⓣ0274/386557, ⓔviavia@yogya.wasantara.net.id. A popular, foreign-run traveller's hangout, serving decent European and Indonesian food, and providing good information on things to do in Yogya.

Yuko Jl Prawirotaman 22. Mid-priced restaurant in the *Rose Hotel*, serving mainly Indonesian dishes. The food is of a high quality, with particularly good chicken dishes.

The rest of the city

Ambarrukmo Jalan Adisucipto ⓣ0274/566488 This former palace (see p.205) has a marvellous floating restaurant where you can sit and watch traditional Javanese dancing or puppet shows. Meals are expensive here, catering for tourists with foreign currency to spend, but the food is stylish.

Gadja Wong Jl Gejayan 79D ⓣ0274/588294. Very popular restaurant on the banks of the River Wong, east of the city centre (20min by becak). Good-value Indonesian, Italian and Indian food.

Joglo Mlati Jl Kebon Agung 170, Sendangadi, Mlati, Sleman ⓣ0274/866700. Just north of town, a restaurant-cum-arts centre, with an Indonesian, Chinese and Italian menu and gazebo dining. Recommended for its great romantic atmosphere, and the Javanese dishes are excellent. Expensive.

Moro Lejar Balangan, Wukiran Sari, Cangkiran, Sleman ⓣ0274/895035. An out-of-town restaurant with a nice setting of lilyponds, waterfalls and greenery, serving mostly seafood, including very good grilled fish.

Nightlife and cultural entertainment

Yogya's **nightlife** stops early; very few places stay open beyond midnight, and most of the action happens between 7pm and 10pm, when the city's **cultural entertainment** is in full swing.

If you're not going to a show, your options for a night out are limited, though a few **bars** are worth checking out. The *Laba Laba*, Jalan Prawirotaman 2, is an overpriced restaurant and bar serving weird cocktails: try the "Laba Laba Special", a potent mixture of Guinness, whisky and shandy. The *Borobudur Bar*, Jalan Pasar Kembang 17, by the northern end of Sosro Gang I, is one of the few places that stays open after midnight. With its carefully cultivated downmarket image attracting locals, expats and tourists alike, this place continues to be a roaring success. Live bands, usually performing unintentionally hilarious covers of Western rock classics, feature most nights from 9.30pm. Attracting a younger, trendier crowd are two new bars. Not far from the Sultan's Palace in Jalan Brigen Katamso, just a few streets east of the Kraton, is the *Etnik Kafe* (ⓣ0274/375705, ⓔetnikkafe@etnikkafe.every1.net), combining a café and outdoor nightclub. Bands from Yogya and other cities regularly perform from 9.30pm–1.00am. Also worth trying is *Java Kafe* at Jl Magelang 163, 2km north of the train station (ⓣ0274/624190), which has live music, a well-stocked bar and an international menu.

If you want to keep on drinking, one of the cheapest and most convenient places is the *Rumah Musik* **disco**, part of the *Hotel Mendut*. Popular with locals, this place has live music every evening (usually Indonesian *dangdut*), and doesn't charge an entrance fee, but it's not a scintillating place. A second disco, with a dress code (which is usually dropped for Westerners), operates in the basement of the *Mutiara* hotel at Jalan Malioboro 16. Once these two have closed (at around 3am), the only place left open is the *Takashimura* karaoke bar in the east of the city at Jalan Solo 35. A taxi here should cost no more than Rp12,000.

Wayang kulit and wayang golek

Wayang kulit is the epitome of Javanese culture, and visitors should try to catch at least a part of one of these shows, although **wayang golek**, where wooden puppets are used, tends to be easier to follow, as the figures are more dynamic and expressive. For a preview of both forms, head to the Sultan's Palace. On Saturday mornings (9am–1pm) there's a practice-cum-performance of wayang kulit in the Sriminganti courtyard, and every Wednesday (9am–noon) a free wayang golek show. On Monday and Wednesday mornings between 10.30am and noon, free **gamelan** (see p.1062) performances are given. The *Natour Garuda Hotel* (see p.197) also holds regular gamelan recitals every evening at 8pm.

With one honourable exception, all of the wayang performances listed below are designed with tourists' attention span in mind, being only two hours long. Hard-core wayang kulit fans, however, may wish to check out the all-nighter at the Alun-alun Selatan (see Sasana Hinggil below). For the latest timings and schedules, ask at the tourist office or your hotel.

Agastya Art Institute Jl Gedongkiwo III/237. Tucked away on the banks of the Kali Winongo in the city's southwestern suburbs, this establishment was founded to train *dalang* and prevent wayang kulit from dying out in Central Java. Wayang kulit performances are held every day at 3pm except Saturday – when a wayang golek performance is staged (Rp5000).

Ambar Budaya (aka **Dewi Sri**) Jl Adisucipto 66. This government craft centre opposite the *Ambarrukmo Palace Hotel* hosts a daily wayang kulit performance (8pm; Rp2500).

Ambarrukmo Palace Hotel Jl Adisucipto 66. A free wayang golek show in the restaurant is put on as an accompaniment to the food (Mon 8pm).

Hanoman's Forest Jl Tirtodipura 5 ⓣ0274/372528. Every Wednesday at 7pm this restaurant presents a 2hr wayang kulit show (Rp7500).

Nitour Jl K.H.A. Dalan 71 ⓣ0274/376450. This centre, outside of the northern walls of the Kraton, puts on a wayang golek performance of the *Ramayana* tales (daily except holidays 11am–1pm; Rp5000).

Sasana Hinggil Alun-alun Selatan. Yogya's only full-length wayang kulit performance runs from 9pm to 5.30am on the second Saturday of every month, and on alternate fourth Saturdays (Rp5000).

Sonobudoyo Museum Jl Trikora 1. The most professional and popular wayang kulit show, performed daily for 2hr (8pm; Rp7500).

Javanese dancing

The **Ramayana** dance drama is a modern extension of the court dances of the nineteenth century, which tended to use that other Indian epic, the *Mahabharata*, as the source of their story lines. These dramas can still be seen in many theatres throughout Yogya today. The biggest crowd-pulling spectacle around Yogya has to be the moonlit performance of the *Ramayana* ballet, which takes place every summer in the open-air theatre at Prambanan temple, and can be booked in Yogya (see p.224 for details). The city also hosts a number of other dance productions based on the *Ramayana* tales.

Ambarrukmo Palace Jl Adisucipto 66. Javanese dance shows are held every evening at 8pm in the *Borobudur Restaurant*, on the seventh floor of the *Ambarrukmo Palace Hotel*, with the *Ramayana* ballet performed three times a week (Mon, Wed & Sat).

Hanoman's Forest Jl Prawirotaman 9. Performances by Hanoman's dancers, combining elements of classical and modern dance, from around 7–9pm (Rp7500).
Lotus Garden Restaurant Jl Prawirotaman II. Selection of dance styles from the archipelago (Tues, Thurs & Sat, 8pm; Rp3000).
Melati Garden Jl Prawirotaman II. Dance shows from Java, Sumatra and Bali (Mon, Wed & Fri 8pm–9.30pm; free).
Ndalem Pujokusirman Jl Brig Jen Katamso 45. A two-hour performance of classical Javanese dance at one of the most illustrious dance schools in Yogya (Mon, Wed & Fri 8pm; Rp15,000).
Purawisata Theatre Jalan Brig Jen Katamso ☎0274/374089. Every night for the last eighteen years, the Puriwisata Theatre has put on a 90min performance of the *Ramayana*. The story is split into two episodes, with each episode performed on alternate nights; on the last day of every month, the whole story is performed. Free transport from your hotel is also provided by the theatre (8–9.30pm; Rp30,000 or Rp42,000).
Sultan's Palace Every Sunday and Thursday, the Kraton Classical Dance School holds public rehearsals (10am–noon). Well worth catching, and there's no cover fee once you've paid to get into the palace.

Shopping

Yogya is Java's souvenir centre, with mementoes from the entire archipelago finding their way into the city's shops and street stalls. **Jalan Malioboro** is the main shopping area; you won't unearth any real treasures in the makeshift markets that hog Malioboro's pavements, but for inexpensive souvenirs (batik pictures, leather bags, woodcarvings and silver rings), this is the place to come.

A recent development on the shopping scene is the establishment of a number of upmarket **souvenir emporiums**, which sell tasteful, individual local craft items rather than the usual mass-produced offerings. Two such places are Sosro's Going Bananas (no. 44) and Something Different in Prawirotaman. Batik Keris, Jl A. Yani 104 (☎0274/512492) and Batik Mirota, Jl A. Yani 9 (☎0274/588524) are both reputable souvenir shops, offering a huge array of souvenirs from Yogya and elsewhere in Indonesia. Another good option – although a little way out of town towards the airport – is the Desa Kerajinan, the government's craft centre opposite the *Ambarrukmo Palace Hotel* at Jalan Adisucipto 66.

Silver

The suburb of Kota Gede is the home of Central Java's **silver industry** in Central Java. It's famous for its fine **filigree** work, although the sort of products created are varied; if you've been hankering after a replica of Borobudur temple in solid silver, or even a scale model of an aircraft carrier, then Kota Gede is the place to come. If you can't find exactly what you want, it's possible to commission the workshops to produce it for you. Some workshops allow you to wander around and watch the smiths at work, such as the huge Tom's Silver at Jalan Ngeksi Gondo 60 (daily 8.30am–7.30pm) and the cheaper MD Silver, Jl Pesegah KG 8/44 (just off Jalan Ngeksi Gondo; same hours). Their prices are high compared to the smaller establishments, so always bargain hard. A few, such as Borobudur Silver on the way to Kota Gede at Jalan Menteri Supeno 41 (daily 8am–8pm) give discounts to HI and ISIC card-holders.

If your budget is limited, it's worth visiting the many stalls along Malioboro, which sell perfectly reasonable silver jewellery, much of it from East Java or Bali. Expect to pay Rp5000 for a ring, and Rp10,000 for earrings.

Batik

With the huge influx of tourists over the last twenty years, Yogya has evolved a **batik** style that increasingly panders to Western tastes. There's still plenty of the traditional indigo-and-brown batik clothing – sarongs, shirts and dresses –

for sale, especially on Jalan Malioboro and the Beringharjo market. Recently, however, Yogya has come to specialize in batik painting, much of it based around psychedelic swirls or chocolate-box Javanese landscapes designed to appeal to tourists.

There are batik galleries everywhere, and touts hang around the tourist centres trying to persuade you to visit their gallery. The **Batik Museum**, north-east of the Kraton at Jl Dr. Sutomo 13 (daily 8am–7pm; Rp500), helps put the craft in its historical context and provides examples of the various techniques and styles.

If your knowledge of batik is shaky, it might be wise to begin your quest at the **Balai Penelitian Kerajinan dan Batik** (Batik and Handicraft Research Centre), east of the Kraton at Jalan Kusumanegara 2 (Mon–Thurs 9–11.30am, Fri 9–10.30am). This government-run centre researches ways of improving production techniques; you can tour the building, and by the entrance there's a small shop selling fixed-price batik paintings from about Rp50,000. From the research centre, head west to the collection of **galleries** in the Kraton, most of them tucked away in the kampung occupying the grounds of the old Taman Sari. Ninety-nine percent of the paintings on offer here are mass-produced, but a thorough search might unearth that elusive one percent of original work. For the best-quality – and most expensive – batiks in town, head to **Jalan Tirtodipuran**, west of Jalan Prawirotaman, home of the renowned artists Tulus Warsito (at no. 19a) and Slamet Riyanto (no. 61a), as well as a number of good-quality galleries. If you still haven't found a piece of batik that you like, you could try and make one yourself by signing up for one of the many batik courses held in Yogya; see p.212 for details.

Leather and pottery

All around Yogya, and particularly in the markets along Jalan Malioboro, hand-stitched, good-quality **leather** bags, suitcases, belts and shoes can be bought extremely cheaply. A number of Malioboro's shops also sell leather goods; check out Kerajinan Indonesia at no. 193 and the Fancy Art Shop at no. 189a. Prices start at Rp45,000 for the simplest satchel – check the strength of the stitching and the quality of the leather before buying. Many of these leather products originate from the village of **Manding**, 12km south of Yogya, where you can find the widest selection of leather goods and the best bargains. By visiting one of the workshops, you can have something made to your own design. To get to Manding, catch a white Jahayu bus from Jalan Parangtritis (every 15min; 25min; Rp1000).

Javanese pottery is widely available throughout Yogya. Again, the markets along Malioboro – and particularly in Pasar Beringharjo – are good sources, as are the souvenir shops along Jalan Tirtodipuran. Bargain hard, and expect to pay about Rp60,000 for a thirty-centimetre-high pot. Much of the pottery comes from tiny **Kasongan** village, 7km south of Yogya, 1km to the west of the main road to Bantul. The town is a riot of ochre pottery, with huge Chinese urns, decorative bowls, erotic statues, whistles, flutes and other pottery instruments – and you can see the potters in action. To get there, take a Jahayu bus from Yogya bus station, or from Jalan Haryono (Rp1000).

Antiques, puppets and curios

In the vicinity of Jalan Prawirotaman, there are a number of cavernous antique shops dealing mainly in **teak furniture** from Jepara and the north. Much of it is very fine quality, but the cost of mailing these bulky items home may be prohibitive. **Antique shops** include Ancient Arts at Jalan Tirtodipuran 50 and

Dieng at no. 30, while good-quality furniture can be found at Mirota Moesson, Jl Parangtritis 107. Many of these outlets sell traditional Javanese wooden trunks, the exteriors beautifully carved with detailed patterns, for which you can expect to pay at least US$50. Fancy Javanese chairs and desks are also very popular, though the prices are high.

Harto is a large company with a number of outlets around Jalan Tirtodipuran, each specializing in a particular sort of souvenir. One shop sells **woodcarvings**, for instance, and another deals in **wayang kulit puppets**; expect to pay at least Rp75,000–150,000 for a reasonable-quality thirty-centimetre puppet. There are also a couple of puppet shops on Jalan Prawirotaman, and two at the northern end of Malioboro.

Other popular souvenirs include personalized **rubber stamps**, made while you wait for about Rp15,000 each on the pavements of Jalan Malioboro, and the traditional Yogyan batik **headscarf** (*iket*), distinguishable from the Solo variety by the large pre-tied knot at the back, costing about Rp5000. Samudra Raya at Jalan Sosro GT1/32 specializes in good-quality models of traditional Indonesian ships; prices start at about Rp250,000.

Listings

Airlines Bouraq, Jl Menteri Supene 58 ☎0274/562664; Garuda, *Ambarrukmo Palace Hotel* ☎0274/565835, and at the airport ☎0274/563706; Merpati, Jl Diponegoro 31 ☎0274/514272; Mandala, *Hotel Melia Purosani*, Jl Mayor Suryotomo 573 ☎0274/520603. All have the same opening hours: Mon–Fri 7.30am–5pm, Sat & Sun 9am–1pm.

Banks and exchange Yogya is one of the few places where the moneychangers offer a better deal than the banks, at least for cash. In particular, PT Gajahmas Mulyosakti, Jl A. Yani 86a, and PT Dua Sisi Jogya Indah, at the southern corner of the Malioboro shopping centre, offer very competitive rates. PT Baruman Abadi in the *Natour Garuda Hotel*, Jl Malioboro 60, offers good rates and stays open longer (Mon–Fri 7am–7pm, Sat 7am–3pm). In Jalan Prawirotaman, the Agung moneychanger at no. 68 and Kresna at no. 18 offer the best rates. Of the banks, go for the BNI, Jl Trikora 1, just in front of the post office, or BCA Jalan Mangkubumi, both of which accept Visa and Mastercard at their ATMs. Banks are closed on Saturdays and Sundays.

Batik courses Lucy's (no phone) in JL Sosrowijayan Gang I runs a very popular one-day course (9am–3pm; Rp10,000–25,000, depending on the size of the finished batik). The *Via Via Café* at Jl Prawirotaman 24b (☎0274/386557, Ⓔviavia@yogya.wasantara.net.id) runs a similar course for Rp15,000, and a one-week course for US$150. Right by the entrance to the Taman Sari is the workshop of Dr Hadjir (☎0274/377835), who runs a 3- to 5-day course (US$25 for three days, plus US$5 for materials). His course is one of the most extensive and includes tutoring on the history of batik and the preparation of both chemical and natural dyes. Gapura Batik, Jl Taman KP III/177 (☎0274/377835) also runs a 3- or 5-day course. The Puriwisata school, at the northern end of Jalan Brig Jen Katamso, runs a rather expensive but comprehensive batik course (Rp50,000 per session). The Batik Research Centre at Jl Kusumanegara 2 (no phone), runs intensive 3-day courses for US$55. For the truly committed, they also run a 3-month course. Booking is often required for courses.

Bookshops The Lucky Boomerang at Jl Sosro Gang I/67 has the best selection of English-language novels, guidebooks and other books on Indonesia. In Prawirotaman, both Bima Books, on Gang II, and Kakadu Books at no. 41, have the odd secondhand gem on their shelves, though neither is particularly cheap. Prawirotaman International Bookstore at Jl Prawirotaman 30 stocks imported books and magazines, while the Gramedia Bookshop in the Malioboro shopping centre also has a fair selection of English-language books on Indonesia.

Bus tickets Most travel agencies and homestays sell bus tickets.

Car and motorbike rental Fortuna 1 and 2 are two branches of the same company near the train station at Jl Jlagran Lor 20–21 and Jl Pasar Kembang 60 (☎0274/564680 or 589550). A Honda Astrea motorbike can be rented for Rp50,000 per day. Jeeps cost Rp100,000, or double that if you wish to hire a driver too. Just down the road, Kurnia Rental at no. 63 (☎0274/520027) offers a similar deal, as does Star Rental at Jl

Adisucipto 22 (☎0274/519603) near the *Ambarrukmo Palace Hotel*.

Cinema The most central is the Indra Cinema at Jl J. A. Yani 13A, behind the Cirebon Restaurant, screening mainly kung fu films. For the biggest choice of Hollywood and Hong Kong films, visit Ratih 21, north of the train tracks on Jl Mangkubumi 26. Empire 21 and Regent, which are side-by-side in Jalan Urip Sumoharjo, have similar showings.

Cookery courses The *Via Via Café*, Jl Prawirotaman 24b, runs afternoon courses (Rp50,000), where they teach you how to make their wonderful version of gado-gado as well as other Indonesian staples. They also hold one-week courses for US$150.

Dance and gamelan courses Several places offer courses in gamelan (the traditional orchestra of Java – see p.1062), mostly concentrating on percussion – xylophones and gongs. The following have introduction sessions and tuition: Gadjah Mada University, Faculty of Cultural Sciences, Jl Nusantara 1, Bulaksumur ☎0274/901137 or 513096 ext 217, ⓔfib@ugm.ac.id; Indonesian Arts Institute, Faculty of Performing arts, Gamelan Studies, Jl Parangtritis Km5.6 ☎0274/384108/375380; Santa Dharma University, ILCIC, Mrican Tromol pos 29, Yogyakarta ☎0274/515352 ext 534, ⓔilcic@usd.ac.id. Mrs Tia of the Ndalem Pujokusirman school at Jl Brig Jen Katamso 45 (☎0274/371271) is a former pupil who invites foreigners to join her 2hr group lessons beginning at 4pm. At the northern end of the same street stands the Puriwisata (☎0274/374089), an open-air theatre and mini theme park which holds Javanese dance courses for Rp50,000 per 3hr session. They also run a school for gamelan (Rp50,000 per session). The *Via Via Café* at Jalan Prawirotaman 246 runs intensive one-week courses for US$150.

Internet access A proliferation of internet places have recently opened in Yogya. Wasantara-Net (Mon–Sat 8am–9pm, Sun 9am–8pm) at the GPO charges Rp4000 for 30min, Rp7000 for 1hr. The *Pujayo Internet Café* at Jl C. Simanjutak 73, east of the Tugu monument, stays open longer and charges just Rp3000 for 15min (daily 8am–10pm). Jl Sosro Gang I also has a number of places, including CMC at GT1/70, next to *Superman II* (Rp3000 for 15min); Whizzkids – reputedly very slow – at GT1/96, opposite *Superman II* (Rp5000 for 15min); *Superman II* itself (Rp5000 for 15min); and the popular Metro Internet in the *Metro Guesthouse*, Jl Prawitotaman II/71. Also around Sosro are Warung Internet at the northern end of Gang II (Rp2000 for 5min), and Internet Rental (Rp1250; for 5min), a few metres north of *Ella's Homestay* on Jl Sosrodipuran Gang 1. In Prawirotaman, the *Metro Hotel* has installed an email terminal (Rp3000 for 15min), and there's the *Café Internet* at Jl Prawirotaman 11.

Hospitals and clinics The Gading Clinic, south of the Alun-alun Selatan at Jl Maj Jen Panjaitan 25, has English-speaking doctors (☎0274/375396), as does the main hospital in Yogya, the Bethesda, Jl Sudirman 70 (☎0274/566300), and the Ludira Husada Tama Hospital, Jl Wiratama 4(☎0274/620091).

Immigration office Jl Adisucipto Km10, on the way to the airport near the *Ambarrukmo Palace Hotel* (Mon–Thurs 8am–2pm, Fri 8–11am, Sat 8am–1pm; ☎0274/514948).

Language courses Puri (☎ & ⓕ0274/583789), just to the east of the RRI auditorium at the Kompleks Kolombo 4 on Jalan Cendrawasih, offers a two-week intensive course for US$390 (payable in dollars only), or a 10hr version for US$30. Realia, Jl Pandega Marta V/6 (☎0274/564969) offers expensive courses (Rp100,000 per hr), which are cheaper for a number of people. Puri Bahasa Indonesia (☎0274/588192) at Jl Bausasran 59, two blocks east of Jalan Malioboro, runs similar language courses ($5 per hour). For a brief introduction, the *Via Via Café* on Jalan Prawirotaman holds a 3hr course for Rp25,000. The *Wisma Bahasa*, Jl Rajawali Gang. Nuri 6 (☎0274/520341), is a new school that has already earned a good reputation for its teaching techniques, where conversation and role-playing forms a large part of the curriculum. As well as their standard "Bahasa Indonesian" courses (90hr over 3 weeks for US$450), they also run a 5-day "traveller's course" (US$100).

Laundry Most hotels offer some sort of laundry service, or visit Bike 33 on Jalan Sosro Gang I, or the AGM laundry near the *Rose Hotel* on Jalan Prawirotaman.

Massage and relaxation Gabriel, a fluent English speaker who works at *Anna's Restaurant* in Sosro Gang II/127, does a full-body massage for Rp50,000 (90min). The Lotus Moon, at the back of the *Lotus Garden Restaurant*, offers a traditional Javanese massage as well as herbal treatments in private rooms.

Pharmacies Kimia Farma 20, Jl Malioboro 179, is open 24hr. The Apotek Ratna, Jl Parangtritis 44, is open daily 8am–10pm.

Photographic shops There are two reputable stores: Kodak Expres and Fuji Film Plaza, both near the eastern end of Sosro on Jalan Malioboro. Fuji and Kodak also have branches near Prawirotaman at Foto Duta (Fuji), Jl Parangtritis 54, and nearby

Foto Super (Kodak). The prices are about the same in all of them: Rp6000 for developing, Rp900 per photo for printing.

Post office Jl Senopati 2, at the southern end of Jalan Malioboro (Mon–Sat 6am–10pm, Sun 6am–8pm). The parcel office is on Jalan Maj Jen Suryotomo (Mon–Sat 8am–3pm, Sun 9am–2pm). Parcel-wrappers loiter outside the office during these times.

Swimming The *Batik Palas Hotel* south of Jalan Sosro allows non-guests to use their pool for Rp7000 (daily 9am–9pm), as does the *Mutiara* (Rp6000). The *Ibis* allows nonresidents to use its health centre including pool, sauna and gym for Rp20,000.

Telephone The main Telkom office at Jl Yos Sudarso 9 is open 24hr and has Home Direct phones too. There's a wartel office at Jl Sosro 30 and another on Jalan Parangtritis, south of Jl Prawirotaman Gang II.

Tour operators Yogya is full of tour companies offering trips to the nearby temples (Rp25,000 for a tour of both Prambanan and Borobudur), as well as further afield. The price generally doesn't include entrance fees, and the only advantage of taking a tour is convenience. Kresna, based at Jl Prawirotaman 18 (☎0274/375502) but with agents all over the city, is one of the largest and most experienced. However, a couple of companies offer something a little different. *Via Via*, the travellers' café at Jl Prawirotaman 246, organizes bicycle and hiking tours around the local area, while Moyasi Alternative Tours at Jl Prawirotaman 20 (☎0274/382863) organizes treks around the major temples. Neither is particularly cheap, however, with an 8hr Borobudur tour costing Rp47,500.

Travel agents Probably the most reputable is Indras Tours and Travel at Jl Malioboro 131 (☎0274/561972), just a few metres south of the eastern end of Jalan Sosro. Or try Cendana Harum, Jl Prawirotaman Gang II 838 ☎0274/374760; Hanoman, Jl Prawirotaman 9 ☎0274/372528; Intan Pelangi, Jl Malioboro 18 ☎0274/562895; Jaya, Jl Sosro 23 ☎0274/586735; Kresna Tours, Jl Prawirotaman 18 ☎0274/375502; Nitour, Jl KHA Dahlan 71 ☎0274/375165; Panin Tour, Jl Sosro 28 ☎0274/515021; or Utama, Jl Dagen 17; ☎0274/518117.

South of Yogya

Yogya lies just 28km from the south coast of Java. Its nearest resort, **Parangtritis**, like most of the beaches on this southern coast, is a rather bleak, melancholy place, and the people of Yogya have always associated the south coast with death. The royal palace in Yogya was deliberately built with its back to the south, and the sultan was forbidden to exit through the palace's southern gate until after his death, when his body would be carried to the royal cemetery at Imogiri. This cemetery lies in the **Gunung Sewu** (Thousand Mountains), a line of limestone cliffs rising unexpectedly from the southern plain, separating Yogya from the coast. The cliffs also contain the cave complex of **Goa Cerme**. All of these sights, whilst not essential, are mildly diverting if you're in Yogya for a while. Buses run regularly, although the road is not straight – due largely to the Gunung Sewu – and journey times are lengthy, considering the short distances involved.

Most of the other beaches on the south coast, such as **Krakal**, **Kukup** and **Baron**, lie in a chain 60km to the southeast of Yogya. Once again, they are somewhat bleak, and – with the exception of Baron – dangerous for swimming. Whilst these beaches are not particularly enticing, for a break from Yogya, it's worth making a trip to the tranquil **Wanagama Park**, established by the Gaja Mada University on the side of once-barren Gunung Kidul, en route to Wonosari and the beaches.

South to Parangtritis

Right in the heart of the Gunung Sewu range, situated in the village of **Imogiri** (Mountain of Mist) 17km from Yogyakarta, lies the most important **royal cemetery** in Java (Mon 10am–1pm, Fri 1.30–4pm; Rp1000, Rp500 camera fee, plus Rp1000 to rent the compulsory full Javanese dress costume).

Regular minibuses from Yogya bus station take 45 minutes (Rp1000) to reach the stop 1km from the site; the village itself is reached by climbing 346 steps up a wooded hill. The cemetery, a terraced, walled-in compound hidden in the hill-top forest, is a delightfully peaceful spot. The deceased of three of Central Java's four royal houses are buried here (only the Mangkunegoros of Solo are excluded, because of the rivalry between the royal houses), with the Pakubuwonos of Solo on the left-hand side of the entrance and the Hamengkubuwonos of Yogya on the right. Most of these graves are rather simple and plain, although the tomb of Mataram's greatest leader, Sultan Agung (who founded the cemetery in 1645), is a touch more lavish. A small brick shelter has been built around Agung's grave, which lies at the top of the hill, where worshippers – usually elderly palace retainers from Yogya – congregate to burn incense, sprinkle rose petals over the coffin and offer prayers to the sultan.

Goa Cerme, an elaborate cave system in the upper reaches of Gunung Sewu, lies 9km southeast of Imogiri. The caves (daily dawn–dusk; Rp1000) are dark, dank and eerie, with stalactites and stalagmites and the occasional bat or swift fluttering overhead. The caves stretch for over 1km, and to walk through them you'll need to bring a torch and clothes suitable for wading, as in some places the water is up to 1m deep. A local guide (around Rp10,000 for 2hr), available from the entrance, is essential, and both the *Ella* homestay (see p.194) and *Vagabonds* in Yogya organize tours (see p.197). To get there independently from Imogiri, catch a bus to the small junction village of **Silok**, 5km to the south (Rp1000 from Imogiri, Rp2000 by Jahayu bus from Yogya), where it's easy to pick up an ojek (Rp5000) for the six-kilometre journey to Goa Cerme. From the point where you'll be dropped off, it's a twenty-minute clamber up to the entrance.

White Jahayu buses drive through Silok on their way to **Parangtritis**, 12km away, a windswept four-kilometre stretch of black sand which, no matter how many people are visiting, always seems a lonely and desolate place. This is the home of Loro Kidul, the Goddess of the Southern Seas (see box on p.201); Senopati, the father of the Mataram dynasty, emerged from her palace at **Parangkusumo**, 1km east along the beach. Don't be tempted to go for a swim to look for her, however, as a vicious undertow will pull even the strongest swimmer under. The white Jahayu buses terminate here (Rp1000 from Silok, Rp2000 from Jalan Parangtritis or the bus station in Yogya). The bus pulls in at the small village separating the main road from the beach, consisting of a number of warung, the odd tired souvenir shop and a few wind-battered losmen. One of the best of these is *Hotel Widodo*, with rooms from Rp20,000, including breakfast, and an adjoining restaurant which serves reasonable food. The best hotel is the unexpectedly luxurious *Queen of the South Hotel* (Ⓣ0274/367196; ❽), situated on a cliff overlooking the beach. Bungalows surround a pool and bar and there is a fine outdoor restaurant and superb views.

Wanagama Park and the southeastern beaches

Forty years ago, the lush forested hills of **Gunung Kidul**, 34km to the east of Yogya, were a barren desertscape: a combination of deforestation and soil degradation had left the area bare and infertile. In 1967, two members of Gajah Mada University's Faculty of Forestry attempted to reforest the hills, sowing only the hardiest plants and watering them using intensive irrigation techniques. The result is a sixty-square-kilometre marvel of rejuvenation that has attracted the attention of ecologists and scientists the world over; even royalty, in the shape of Prince Charles, has paid a visit. More a curiosity than a tourist attraction, **Wanagama Park** is nice for a stroll, and provides a breath of fresh air from Yogya. There's some basic accommodation behind the reception area, which can be used if there are no tour groups staying (ring Professor Oemi Susemo at Gajah Mada to check availability; Ⓣ0274/515480; ❶). It's possible to camp in the forest, though you must bring your own equipment. Wanagama Park lies 9km to the south of the Wonosari road, fifty minutes from Yogya; catch a bus from Yogya's Umbulharjo bus station (Rp1000), then an ojek (Rp5000) from the junction.

The bleak, isolated **beaches** to the southeast of Yogya lie 40km further on from Wanagama. On one side is a raging sea, driven by a vicious undertow which has dragged many an unwary swimmer to their death; on the other are the snagging, sharp limestone cliffs, which plunge vertically down from 50m or more into the rough surf. Beyond these cliffs lies one of the poorest, most barren areas in the whole of Java, where people eke out a living growing peanuts on the poor soil. Even the beaches themselves are gritty, windswept and unwelcoming, far removed from the golden sands of Bali. Nevertheless, there's a melancholy beauty about these beaches, and, if you just want to get away from the crowds, the south coast is the place to come. There are also a few secluded spots where swimming is possible, and even one or two stretches of white sand.

Unfortunately **Baron**, the most accessible of the beaches, is a seedy alcove populated largely by fishermen, gum-chewing malcontents and snarling feral dogs. It is, however, a base for exploring the coast, and you can find rooms right on the beach at the basic *Bintang Beach* (❷), a few of which boast hot water and TV. To get to Baron, catch a bus to the village of Wonosari (75min; Rp5000), then a colt for one hour south (Rp5000); if this colt is not running, catch one to Bintaos (same price), 8km from Baron, and hitch from there. The last bus back from Baron leaves at 4pm (1pm on Fridays).

A ten-minute walk west of Baron lies a small beach where it's safe to swim. On the eastern cliff, and clearly visible from the beach, a stairway leads five minutes over the hill to **Kukup**, a quieter and fractionally less ugly version of Baron. Six kilometres further east (Rp7500 by ojek from Baron) lies the similar-looking **Krakal**. A further 5km east is **Pantai Sundak**, possibly the bleakest, most isolated and, perversely, the most pleasant of the lot, with only a few fishing pagodas on the overshadowing hills to keep you company. Note that buses between Yogya and these beaches are infrequent and – as with trips to Baron – involve a change at Wonosari. The bus service to this part of the coast stops altogether after 3pm.

Gunung Merapi and Kaliurang

Marking the northern limit of the Daerah Istimewa Yogyakarta, symmetrical, smoke-plumed **Gunung Merapi** ("Giving Fire") is an awesome 2911-metre presence in the centre of Java, visible from Yogyakarta, 25km away. This is Indonesia's most volatile volcano, and the sixth most active in the world. The Javanese worship the mountain as a life-giver, its lava enriching the soil and providing Central Java with its agricultural fecundity. However, its ability to annihilate has frequently been demonstrated over the centuries. Thirteen hundred people died following a particularly vicious eruption in 1930, and as recently as 1994, an entire mountain village was incinerated by molten lava, killing 64 people. Every year at the anniversary of the sultan's coronation, an offering is brought from the Sultan's Palace in Yogya and placed on the rim of the crater in an attempt to placate the mountain god.

Nearly a kilometre up on Merapi's southern slopes is the village of **KALIURANG**, a tatty, downmarket but tranquil hill station and an extremely popular weekend retreat for Yogyakartans. A bus from Yogya's Umbulharjo station costs Rp1000, while bemos from behind the Terban terminal on Jalan Simanjutak cost Rp2000. In Kaliurang, you can join a trekking group (see below) to the summit, a fairly arduous five-hour scramble through the snake- and spider-infested forest covering Merapi's lower slopes. The tigers, which terrorized this forest as recently as the 1960s, have now all been killed off. During Merapi's dormant months (usually March to October), it's possible to climb all the way to the top, but at other times, when the volcano is active, you may have to settle for a distant view from the observation platform. All treks begin in the dark at 3am, when the lava, spilling over the top and tracing a searing path down the mountainside, can be seen most clearly. Bring warm clothes, a torch and sturdy boots (sandals offer little protection against poisonous snakes).

Treks, which cost Rp15,000 including breakfast, are organized by *Vogel's Hostel* in Kaliurang, Jalan Astya Mulya 76 (☎0274/895208; ❷), which also happens to be one of the best budget **hostels** in Java. It's split into two parts: the rooms in the new extension are beautiful and good-value, while those in the old building (a former holiday home for a member of Yogya's lesser nobility) are spartan but inexpensive, ranging from Rp5000 in the dormitory to

For details of climbing the northern side of Gunung Merapi, see p.248.

Rp20,000 for a bungalow. The **food**, including Indonesian staples and Western snacks, is truly delicious and there's a large travellers' library. The owner, Christian Awuy – the head of the rescue team in Kaliurang – is a veritable encyclopedia of volcano knowledge. If you're looking for somewhere plusher, try the *Village Taman Eden*, Jalan Astya Mulya (☎0274/895442; ④), a collection of luxurious villas built round a central swimming pool. *Wisma Gadja Mada* (☎0274/895225; ④), Jl Wreksa 447, is a colonial period guesthouse with villa-style accommodation.

Borobudur and around

Forty kilometres west of Yogya on the fertile Kedu Plain, surrounded on three sides by volcanoes and on the fourth by a series of jagged limestone cliffs, lies the largest Buddhist temple in the world. This is **Borobudur**, Java's number one tourist attraction and the greatest single piece of classical architecture in the entire archipelago.

The temple is actually a colossal multi-tiered Buddhist stupa lying at the western end of a four-kilometre chain of temples (two of which, **Candi Mendut** and **Candi Pawon**, have been restored and stand by the road to Borobudur), built in the ninth century by the Saliendra dynasty. At 34.5m tall, however, and covering an area of some 200 square metres, Borobudur is of a different scale altogether, dwarfing all the other *candi* in the chain.

Despite its size, first impressions of Borobudur may leave you feeling a little underwhelmed. It is rather squat – like a collapsed pyramid – and the sheer horizontal massiveness of the structure is somewhat obscured by the trees of the tidy park which surround it. Indeed, the Hindu temples at Prambanan (see p.224), with their soaring vertical lines uncluttered by surrounding foliage, seem more impressive when viewed from a distance. Nevertheless, Borobudur's greater fame is merited. It's bigger than Prambanan, and older by about forty years, and in the silent hours of dawn and dusk it can seem more enchanting.

Some history

The world's largest Buddhist stupa was actually built on **Hindu** foundations. In 775 AD, the Hindu Sanjaya dynasty built a large step pyramid – probably the beginnings of a Shivaite temple – on the plain of Kedu. This site was considered propitious, as it lies near the confluence of two rivers, the **Elo** and the **Progo**, which to the Sanjayas would have evoked the most sacred confluence of all, the Ganges and the Yamuna in northern India. Also, to the northeast towards Magelang, stands **Gunung Tidar**, the so-called "Head of the Nail", which Javanese believe fixes the island, preventing it from drifting on the sea.

Naming Borobudur

One of the greatest mysteries surrounding **Borobudur** is the origin of its name. One theory suggests it's derived from the Sanskrit *Vihara Buddha Uhr* (Buddhist Monastery on a Hill), while others claim that *Budur* is actually a place name, and that *Borobudur* means – "Monastery of Budur". The most likely explanation, however, is found in a stone tablet from 842AD on which is inscribed the word *Bhumisambharabhudara* (Mountain of Virtues of the Ten Stages of the Boddhisattva). It's believed that the name *Borobudur* is derived from *bharabhudara*, the last part of this tongue twister.

Just fifteen years later, however, the construction was abandoned: the Buddhist **Saliendras**, having swept down through the Malay Peninsula and into Java, gradually drove the Sanjayas eastwards, forcing them to leave their building work behind. The Saliendras then appropriated the pyramid as the foundation for their own temple, beginning in around 790 AD and completing the work approximately seventy years later. Over 1.6 million blocks of andesite (a volcanic rock washed down by, and mined from, the nearby rivers) were used in Borobudur's construction, cut and joined together in such a way that no mortar was used. Sculptors then adorned the lower galleries with reliefs, before the whole lot was covered with stucco and painted.

Unfortunately, the pyramid foundation inherited from the Hindus proved inherently unstable; throughout Borobudur's infancy, the structure required constant attention. Though the classical architects had designed an ingenious **drainage system**, channelling water through gullies to collect in a gutter via the mouths of gargoyles, it proved insufficient and the temple began to **subside**. To try to remedy this, a "hidden foot" was added at the base of the temple as a buttress to prevent the whole lot sliding down the hill. (Interestingly, this base is adorned with reliefs every bit as detailed as the rest of the temple, even though it lay buried in the earth and out of view). But not even the hidden foot could solve the problem of drainage. As the temple lurched on its unsteady foundations, cracks appeared in the walls and floors, through which rainwater seeped until the hill became totally waterlogged.

After about a century, the Saliendras abandoned the site. The return of the Hindu Sanjayas as the dominant force in the region, along with earthquakes, and the mysterious migration of the Javanese from Central to East Java, all contributed further to the temple's subsequent decline.

For almost a thousand years Borobudur lay neglected, until it was "rediscovered" by the British in 1815. Plans to restore Borobudur, however, didn't leave the drawing board for the rest of the century. A Dutchman, Theo Van Earp, made cosmetic improvements to the temple's exterior during a five-year project beginning in 1907, but the foundations, which by this time required urgent attention, remained untouched. In 1973, as Borobudur's condition became critical, **UNESCO** began to take the temple apart, block by block, and the waterlogged hill was replaced with a concrete substitute. By its successful completion, the project had taken eleven years and cost US$21 million, but left Borobudur with sound foundations at last.

Practicalities

Most people choose to see the site on a day-trip from Yogya. Plenty of agencies (see p.214) offer all-inclusive tours, or you can catch one of the regular buses from Yogya's Umbulharjo station, which calls in at the southern end of Jalan Magelang (handy for Jalan Sosro) before heading off to Borobudur bus station, ninety minutes away on the eastern edge of Borobudur village (Rp5000). The entrance to the temple grounds lies 500m southwest of the bus stop, to the north of the temple itself.

There's a free museum in the temple grounds, which has a detailed account of the UNESCO restoration, and a small train (Rp2000), which circles the temple every ten minutes. A number of **hotels** have appeared in the village in recent years. At the top of the range, is *Hotel Amanjiwo* (Ⓣ0293/788333, Ⓦwww.99bali.com/hotels/amanjiwo; ❽) situated 3km south of the temple. Reputed to be the most expensive hotel in Java, the luxury of this place has to be seen to be believed. The views are splendid, while the suite-style

Rafting in Central Java

With its wealth of navigable rivers and sumptuous scenery, rafting should be a well-established tourist activity in Central Java. However, there are only two companies offering visitors the chance to ride the rapids. The better of the two is the Lotus River Rafting Company (Ⓣ0293/788281), operating out of the *Lotus Guesthouse* in Borobudur (see below), who arrange four-hour trips down the Progo and Elo (US$40–50). Some of the rapids have been classified as Class III, the highest level of difficulty allowed for untrained rafters. Both trips are exhilarating and, save for the occasional panicking buffalo (which might upset the boat), fairly safe. A slightly shorter trip through calmer water can be arranged through the *Hotel Puri Asri* (see p.228) in Magelang (Ⓣ0293/764115).

rooms are built in magnificent stone, grouped around a rotunda. *Hotel Manohara*, Komplek Taman Wisata Candi Borobudur (Ⓣ & Ⓕ0293/788131; ❺), is the second-best hotel in the village, lying to the east of the temple within the actual grounds. All rooms have air-con, TV and hot water, and the temple fee is included in the price; each evening they put on a free lecture and slide show about Borobudur. The most popular budget choice is the *Lotus Guesthouse* at Jalan Medang Kamulan 2 (Ⓣ0293/788281; ❷), opposite the entrance to Borobudur park. The simple but clean *Losmen Borobudur* stands on the road that runs alongside the eastern edge of the temple grounds, at Jalan Balaputradewa 1 (Ⓣ0293/788258; ❷). Across the street to the north, at Jalan Balaputradewa 10, stands *Losmen Saraswati* (Ⓣ0293/788283; ❷), offering fairly smart rooms with ceiling fans, and a large, shady tree-lined garden. A ten-minute walk east of the temple is *Pondok Tinggal Hostel*, Jl Balaputradewa 32, (Ⓣ0293/788145; ❸), with clean bamboo-decorated rooms and a nice garden.

Most people who stay in Borobudur overnight choose to **eat** in their hotel. The *Losmen Saraswati* has a good, inexpensive restaurant serving simple Chinese and Indonesian dishes, while the classic Western and Japanese food at the *Hotel Amanjiwo* is excellent, though pricey. There are a number of warung in the station, which all close at about 5pm, and one budget restaurant serving good, cheap meals that stays open until about 9pm; it has no name, but stands to the west of the station on the opposite side of the road.

The ruins

Borobudur is precisely orientated so that its four sides face the four points of the compass. The entrance to the grounds (daily 6am–5.30pm; foreigners are charged in dollars at a set rate: $5, $7.50 for optional guided tour) lies to the north, although the traditional place to begin your tour of Borobudur is the eastern side – Buddhist pilgrims would have approached this side of the temple via the sacred path, which once connected Borobudur with Mendut and the other *candi*. Having reached the temple, they would then walk clockwise around its base, before ascending to the next tier via the eastern stairway. This process was repeated on every level, until eventually they arrived at the summit. In this way, not only would they be able to follow the stories of the reliefs adorning each of the terraces, but they would also, by walking clockwise around the stupa, be performing *pradaksina*, a major ceremonial act in Buddhist worship.

Borobudur is pregnant with symbolism. Unlike most temples, it was not built as a dwelling for the gods, but rather as a representation of the Buddhist cosmic mountain, Meru. Accordingly, at the base is the real world, while at the summit lies nirvana. Thus, as you make your way around the temple passages and slowly spiral to the summit, you are symbolically following the path to enlightenment.

Borobudur's first five levels – the square terraces – are covered with three thousand reliefs representing man's earthly existence. As you might expect, the lowest level, the so-called hidden foot, has carvings depicting the basest desires and passions. In Buddhist teaching this level of existence is known as the *kamathadu*. For a taste of these ribald carvings, visit the southeast corner of the temple where UNESCO, during their restoration, left four panels uncovered.

The reliefs on the next four tiers – the first four levels above ground – cover the Rupadhatu, the beginning of man's path to enlightenment. On these levels there are ten series of carvings, four on the first tier and two on each of the subsequent three tiers. Each one tells a story, beginning by the eastern stairway and continuing in a clockwise direction. Follow all ten stories, and you will have circled the temple ten times – a distance of almost 5km. Buddha's own path to enlightenment, the *Lalitavistara*, is told in the upper panels on the inner wall of the first gallery. The reliefs below this series, and indeed both series on the opposite wall, depict scenes from the Jataka tales, the stories of Buddha's former lives before his enlightenment. Climbing the stairs from this first tier, the second, third and fourth galleries recount the story of the *Gandavyuha*, which tells of a merchant, Sudhana, who sets off on the path to enlightenment, encountering Bodhisattvas on the way. The story is concluded on the fourth level. The high gallery walls, or balustrades, on these first four levels effectively reduce the light coming into the gallery and cut visitors off from the outside world – a symbol, perhaps, of the murky spiritual world inhabited by man on these lower terraces. As you enter the fifth level, however, the walls fall away to reveal a breathtaking view of the surrounding fields and volcanoes. You are now in the third and final section of Borobudur; just as levels two, three and four represented the Sphere of Forms, so the upper levels – five, six, seven and eight – constitute the Sphere of Formlessness. Suddenly, all the busy reliefs crowding the walls of the lower levels disappear, as the visitor reaches enlightenment: below is the chaos of the world, above is nirvana, represented by a huge empty stupa almost 10m in diameter. Surrounding this stupa are 72 smaller ones, each occupied by a statue of Buddha. Including those in the niches on the lower levels, there's a total of 432 Buddhas at Borobudur. The stupa at the top, however, is empty. There was once a Buddha here, too, but it seems somehow appropriate that this has disappeared, nirvana signifying, after all, a state of non-being.

Candi Mendut and Candi Pawon

Originally Borobudur was part of a chain of four temples joined by a sacred path. Two of the other three temples have been restored, and at least one, **Candi Mendut** (daily 6.15am–5.15pm; Rp250), 3km east of Borobudur, is worth visiting. The third temple, situated at the village of Bajong, is unfortunately beyond repair. Buses between Yogya and Borobudur drive right past Mendut (Rp5000 from Yogya for the 1hr 20min journey, Rp1000 for the 10min from Borobudur). Built in 800 AD, Mendut was rediscovered in 1834 and restored at the end of the nineteenth century. The exterior, while heavily decorated, is unremarkable. The three giant statues sitting inside, however, are exquisitely carved and marvellously preserved. As Charles Walter Kinloch, the "Bengal Civilian", wrote in his travelogue, *Rambles in Java and the Straits in 1852*, "of the two ruins, the Boro-Bodor are by far the most extensive; but the figures of Mundoot are far more perfect". Originally there were seven statues here; those that remain are the great three-metre Buddha – who, unusually, sits on a throne with his legs in front of him rather than in the lotus position – flanked by the Bodhisattvas Avalokitesvara and Vajrapani. In the early evening the sun dips low enough to shine on all three: try and be here then.

One kilometre west of Mendut on the banks of the river is **Candi Pawon** (open 24hr; free). This small building is dedicated to the Buddhist god of fortune, Kuvera. Unlike both Mendut and Borobudur, the temple does not have Hindu foundations but is wholly Buddhist. From here, it is just 1.5km back to Borobudur bus station; it takes only about thirty minutes to walk, and passing bemos should charge Rp500.

The Prambanan Plain

The sixty-kilometre Yogya–Solo highway is one of the most dangerous routes in Java, with buses and lorries careering down the middle of the road, forcing pedestrians, becak and other traffic to scatter into the neighbouring paddy-fields. In contrast to all this mayhem, 18km outside of Yogya the highway passes through one of the most unhurried and verdant spots in Java. Nourished by the volcanic detritus of Mount Merapi and washed by innumerable small rivers and streams, this is the **Prambanan Plain**, a patchwork blanket of sun-spangled paddy-fields and vast plantations of wheat, maize and cane, sweeping down from the southern slopes of the volcano. As well as being one of the most fertile regions in Java, the plain is home to the largest concentration of ancient ruins on the island. Over thirty **temples** and **palaces**, dating mainly from the eighth and ninth centuries, lie scattered over a thirty-square-kilometre area. Though many of these are little more than heaps of rubble lying forgotten behind thick groves of sugar cane or amongst the lush forest of the hills, a number have been restored to something approaching their original state.

The temples were built at a time when two rival kingdoms, the Buddhist **Saliendra** and the Hindu **Sanjaya** dynasties, both occupied Central Java. Their relationship with each other is unclear, although it is widely believed that their rivalry was political rather than military. In 832 AD, the Hindu Sanjayas gained the upper hand, possibly after their king had married a Saliendran princess. It was soon after this that the greatest of the ruins, the Hindu Prambanan **temple complex**, was built, perhaps in commemoration of their return to power. It seems that some sort of truce followed, with temples of both faiths being constructed on the plain in equal numbers.

Practicalities

Most people visit the Prambanan temples on a day-trip from Yogya, and, unless you're fanatical about ruins – or if you're too tired to cycle back – this is probably the best option. Although you could spend days looking at all the ruins on the plain, the majority of visitors come to examine only the three temples at the Prambanan complex, which takes no more than a couple of hours.

Prambanan village is little more than a small huddle of houses lining the southern side of Jalan Adisucipto, across the road from the Prambanan complex. Most public buses drop passengers off along this road, from where you'll have to walk for five minutes to reach the eastern entrance to the complex.

There are a few **accommodation** options in Prambanan: *Losmen NY Muharti*, Jalan Tampurnas Ngangkruk 2–3 (☎0274/496103; Rp30,000), offers

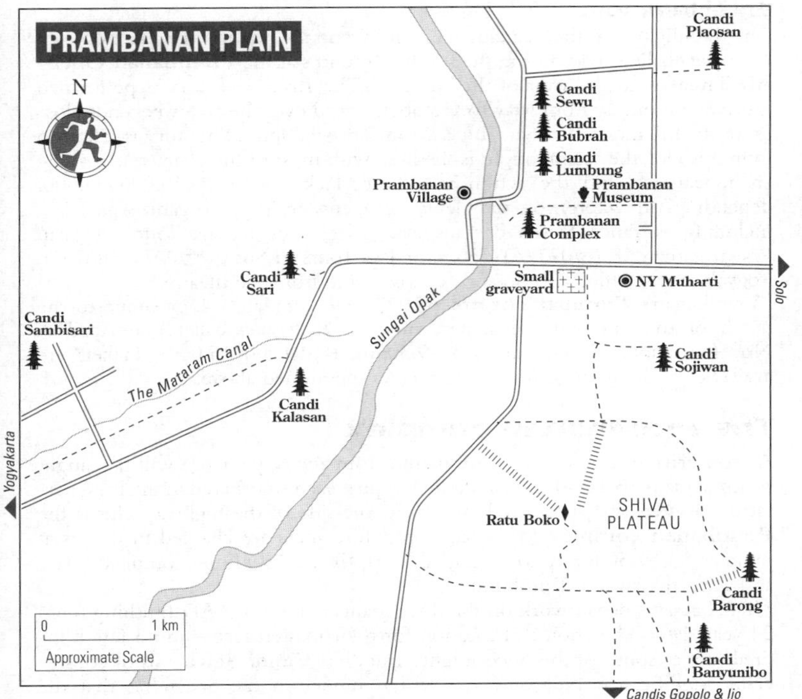

rudimentary rooms and, to the north of the open-air theatre, the *Prambanan Village Hotel* (☎0274/496435; ❺) provides more salubrious accommodation and a fine Japanese restaurant. The *Hotel Prambanan Indah*, Jl Candi Sewu 8 (☎0274/497353; ❷–❹), has a range of rooms, some with hot water and TV, while the ugly *Hotel Galuh*, Jl Manis Renggokom 1 (☎0274/496854; ❸–❹), has basic bunk bed rooms with attached shower, plus more expensive ones with hot water and TV. There are also a couple of cheap **restaurants** near the *Muharti*, though these close in the evening, leaving visitors with no option but to dine in their hotel.

Getting there

Although many tour companies in Yogya offer all-inclusive packages to Prambanan, it's easy enough to get there independently by catching a local bus from Yogya or Solo. Unfortunately, there's no public transport to take you to the other ruins on the plain, which is partly why many visitors choose to rent a bike and cycle here from Yogya. Fume-choked Jalan Adisucipto is the most straightforward route, but there's a quieter and less polluted alternative. Head to the north of Yogya along Jalan Simanjutak and Jalan Kaliurang until you reach the Mataram Canal, just past the main Gajah Mada University compound. Follow the canal east for 12km, which takes about an hour, and you'll come out eventually near Candi Sari on Jalan Adisucipto. This canal path is a little worn in places, and the surface has been seared by the sun into a series of bumps and potholes, but it's by far the most scenic route. Prambanan village lies 4km to the east of Candi Sari, along Jalan Adisucipto.

Entertainment

The highlights of the dancing year in Central Java are the phenomenal *Ramayana* ballets held during the summer months at the **Prambanan Open-Air Theatre**, to the west of the complex. The *Ramayana* story is performed just twice monthly from May to October, spread over the two weekends closest to the full moon (Fri, Sat, Sun & Mon; 7.30–9.30pm). The story is split into four episodes; the second night is the best, with most of the characters making an appearance, and the action is intense. Tickets cost Rp10,000–35,000, depending on where you sit; plenty of agents in Yogya organize packages including entrance fees and transport. Check out Kresna Tours, at Jalan Prawirotaman 18 (Ⓣ0274/375502), or Jaya Tours in Sosro (Ⓣ0274/586735). Yogya's tourist office also organizes taxis to and from the theatre.

Prambanan's **Trimurti Theatre** (Ⓣ0274/496408), an indoor venue to the north of the open-air arena, performs the *Ramayana* ballet (Jan–April & Nov–December, Tues–Thurs 7.30–9.30pm; Rp10,000–15,000). Tickets are available on the door or from the agencies mentioned above.

The Prambanan complex

As you drive east along Jalan Adisucipto from Yogya, your eye will be caught by three giant, rocket-shaped andesite temples, each smothered in intricate narrative carvings that suddenly loom up by the side of the highway. This is the **Prambanan complex** (daily 6am–5pm; foreigners are charged in dollars at set rates: $5, $7.50 for optional guided tour), the largest Hindu complex in Java and a worthy rival to Borobudur.

The Sanjayas began work on the three giants around 832 AD, finishing them 24 years later. The choice of location for their masterpiece – just a few hundred metres south of the once-mighty Buddhist **Candi Sewu** – is of considerable significance. Not only was it a reminder to the Saliendras that the Hindus were now in charge but, by leaving Sewu unharmed, it also gave a clear message to the Buddhists that the Sanjayas intended to be tolerant of their faith. The three Prambanan temples were in service for just fifty years before they were abandoned, following the mysterious migration of the Javanese from Central to East Java. Earthquakes in the seventeenth century compounded the temples' decline, and for the next two centuries they were left in ruins. Restoration work finally began under the Dutch in the 1930s, but it was only in 1994 that the restoration of the inner courtyard was completed.

There are two entrances to the complex: tour buses pull up at the eastern gate, where the souvenir sellers gather, while a second entrance stands by the northwest corner of the complex by the open-air theatre. A **tourist train** (Rp1000) has been added to Prambanan's attractions, which takes passengers on a ten-minute ride around the complex, beginning at the main entrance and continuing up to Sewu. It terminates by the **Prambanan Museum** (daily 7am–6pm), which houses a small cinema, where a thirty-minute **audiovisual** about the complex is screened (Rp2000).

The central courtyard

The temple complex itself consists of six temples in a raised **inner courtyard**, surrounded by **224 minor temples**, which now lie in ruins. The three biggest temples in the courtyard are dedicated to the three main Hindu deities: Shiva, whose 47-metre temple is the tallest of the three, Brahma (to the south of the Shiva temple) and Vishnu (north). Facing these are three smaller temples housing the animal statues – or "chariots" – that would always accompany the gods:

Loro Jonggrang and the unwanted suitor

According to local legend, the statue of Durga in the Shiva Temple is actually the petrified body of **Loro Jonggrang** (Slender Virgin), the daughter of King Ratu Boko. Indeed, it is not uncommon to hear the Javanese refer to the temple as "Candi Loro Jonggrang". The story goes that the princess was once pursued by an unwanted suitor. In her efforts to rid herself of his unwelcome attention, one night she told him that she would marry him only if he built a temple for her before dawn.

Unfortunately for the princess, as the night progressed it became increasingly obvious that the man, aided by a troupe of gnomes, would complete the task. In desperation, the princess ran to the village and ordered the locals to pound the rice logs earlier than usual, this being the traditional way to announce the dawn. She also commanded them to set fire to the fields to the east of the village, in the hope that the blaze would resemble, from a distance, the sun rising. The unwanted suitor, however, recognised her deceit, and in a rage turned the princess to stone and placed her in his temple, where she remains to this day.

Hamsa the swan, Nandi the bull and Garuda the sunbird. The only other buildings in the courtyard are two small kiosks, to the north and south, which were possibly once treasuries or storerooms.

A stone inscription dating from 856 AD, found at Prambanan and now in the National Museum in Jakarta, describes the **Shiva Temple** as a – "beautiful dwelling for the god", and it's hard to disagree with this assessment. The base is decorated with the **Prambanan Motif**, a chaotic collection of creatures gathered around the so-called **Tree of Life**. The exceptional quality of the carving here is maintained on the balustrade of the first terrace, reached via one of the four stairways. A procession of singers and dancers parade on the outer side of the walkway of this first terrace, while the inner wall, beginning at the eastern steps and continuing clockwise around the temple, recounts the first half of the *Ramayana* epic in a series of gloriously intricate scenes.

At the top of the steps is the **inner sanctuary** of the temple, divided into four chambers. The eastern chamber contains a statue of Shiva himself, while the southern one houses a statue of the pot-bellied sage **Agastya**. In the western chamber is Shiva's elephant-headed son, **Ganesh**, and in the north, Shiva's consort, **Durga**. Before heading off to view the other two temples, have a peek inside the temple of Shiva's chariot, **Nandi the Bull**. Inside you will find a large, beautiful sculpture of Nandi impassively facing the temple of his master.

Though smaller than the Shiva Temple, the other two temples are just as painstakingly decorated. The first terrace of the **Brahma Temple** takes up the *Ramayana* epic where the Shiva Temple left off, whilst the carvings on the terrace of Vishnu's temple recount stories of **Krishna**. Statues of the relevant deities are housed in the chambers at the top of the stairways.

Other temples on the Prambanan Plain

The other **ancient sites** on the Prambanan Plain (dawn–dusk; free), although not as spectacular as the Shiva Temple, are nevertheless quite engaging. The fact that you are almost certain to be the only person on site, thanks to the poor transport facilities and a lack of interest amongst tourists, only adds to the attraction. Only the three temples immediately to the north of Prambanan are within easy walking distance of the Shiva Temple, although it's possible to reach most of the others by bicycle. A number are scattered on and around the **Shiva Plateau**, which rises sharply from the plain to the south of Prambanan village.

Temples near the complex

Three temples stand in a row 1km to the north of Prambanan, reached via the children's park next to the museum. All three date from the late eighth century, just predating Borobudur. **Candi Lumbung** consists of sixteen small, crumbling temples surrounding a larger, equally dilapidated central temple. The pile of stones to the north is **Candi Bubrah**. Both of these temples were merely subsidiary buildings to Candi Sewu (Thousand Temples), 200m to the north of Bubrah.

Buddhist **Sewu**, 1km north of Candi Prambanan, once consisted of 240 small shrines surrounding a large, central temple. Despite the presence of a number of Rakasa guards similar to those in the Sultan's Palace in Yogya, the temple has been severely vandalized and looted down the years. Yet the vast amount of building material, Buddhist stupas and some quite elaborately carved andesite stones scattered on the site are testimony to the scale of Sewu.

The two temples of **Candi Plaosan** lie a ten-minute bike ride – or a thirty-minute walk – to the east of Candi Sewu. They were built soon after the power had shifted back to the Hindu Sanjayas in 832 AD; today, like Sewu, they're surrounded by building debris. The only temple at Plaosan currently open is a two-storey building which – thanks to an extra set of windows above the second floor – looks from the outside like three. Inside, there are two stone Bodhisattvas sitting on either side of an empty lotus petal, which once held a bronze statue of Buddha. Circling the temple are the fragmented remains of 116 stupas and 58 smaller temples.

Temples west of Prambanan

The most westerly of all the temples on the plain, **Candi Sambisari**, lies 11km east of Yogya, 2.5km north of the highway and about 1km north of the Mataram Canal. Coming from Yogya, look for the turn-off to the left just past Yogya airport (the temple is not signposted from the Mataram Canal, so if you are travelling along this route be sure to ask directions frequently). Possibly the last of the Sanjayan temples, Sambisari is, like Prambanan, dedicated to Shiva. It was only discovered in 1966, having lain for centuries beneath layers of volcanic ash, and today is set in a large pit, 10m below ground level. The carvings on the exterior wall are of Durga (to the north), Ganesh (east) and Agastya (south). A linga – a symbol of Shiva – stands to attention on the altar inside.

East of Sambisari, the oldest ruin on the plain is **Candi Kalasan**, a fourteen-square-metre Buddhist temple dedicated to the cult of Tara. In fact, it's the oldest Buddhist temple on Java, having been inaugurated in 778 AD. Despite restoration in the early 1920s, the building is in a far from perfect condition. The statues, some of which were solid bronze, have all disappeared, as has the central, crowning stupa and the decorative plasterwork that once shrouded the entire building. Nevertheless, what remains, especially the fierce *kala* carved above the doors and windows, is very fine. To get there from Sambisari, return to the Mataram Canal and continue east once more. After thirty minutes' walk, the canal meets the highway at Kalasan village. **Candi Kalasan** lies on the other side of the road in a small copse of trees, just 200m south of the canal.

Two hundred metres along the highway north of Kalasan, across the road, is the turn-off for **Candi Sari**, an early ninth-century Buddhist temple. Like Candi Plaosan, this seventeen-metre edifice originally had two storeys, but the wooden second floor has long since rotted away. The exterior of the temple is finely carved, and includes many portraits of the female Bodhisattva, Tara, to whom it is dedicated.

Temples south of Prambanan

This set of temples is best tackled by bicycle, as the paths are narrow and the distances fairly large. **Candi Sojiwan** is a plain, square temple, sparingly decorated with *Jataka* scenes; once a Buddhist sanctuary, it was built around and was contemporary with Candi Sewu. To get there from Prambanan village, cycle down the path which begins by the small graveyard for ten minutes until you come across a small village school on the left-hand side. Turn left and cycle for a further five minutes: Sojiwan lies on the right-hand side of the path.

From here, head back onto the main path and south towards the foot of the Shiva Plateau. The path to the summit of the plateau and **Kraton Ratu Boko** is too steep and bumpy for bicycles, so ask to leave them at the house at the bottom. Little is known about this kraton, which today is little more than a widely dispersed set of ruins; some suggest it's a religious building; others that it was a palace for the king, namely Ratu Boko (Eternal Lord). The ruins are in two parts: one section consists of a series of bathing pools, while the other, 400m to the west, includes the ceremonial gate that adorns many tourist posters and postcards.

The views from the kraton are wonderful, as they are from **Candi Barong**, a *candi* to the south of Kraton Ratu Boko. It's possible to walk between the two (over 1km each way), although the path is very indistinct. If you're cycling, head west towards the main road, Jalan Raya Piyungan; from here turn left (south) and continue for 1.5km to a signpost on your left, pointing the way to Barong (a further 1km east). This *candi* is actually two hillside Buddhist temples mounted on a raised platform on the southern slopes of the plateau. A little way back along this path and to the south is **Banyunibo**, a pretty Buddhist shrine dedicated to Tara. From there, head back onto the main road and turn right; Prambanan village lies 2km away.

Yogya to Dieng

The road between Yogya and the Dieng plateau, home of the oldest temples in Indonesia, is punctuated by dozens of small towns and surrounded by some beautiful, bucolic scenery. Most of these towns hold little of interest to the average tourist, though those interested in Indonesian history may wish to visit **Magelang**, where Diponegoro, leader of the Javanese during the five-year war against the Dutch, was arrested and sent into exile. If you don't want to tackle the fairly arduous journey from **Yogya to Dieng** in one day, you could stop at gorgeous **Wonosobo**, a hill-top retreat with a couple of minor tourist attractions in its immediate vicinity.

The main highway heading north from Yogya wriggles through the Kali Progo valley at the foot of Gunung Merapi. After 30km, the road bisects Muntilan, a medium-sized town which suffers more than most when Merapi erupts, due to its unfortunate position at the end of a lava channel which begins at the volcano's crater. The town huddles around the Magelang–Yogya highway at the point where two minor roads branch away, one heading east to the mountain village of **Selo** (see p.248) and the other running southwest in the direction of **Purworejo** and Borobudur.

Magelang

Forty kilometres to the north of Yogya and set right in the heart of a huge amphitheatre of volcanoes, sprawling **MAGELANG**, a conglomeration of wide boulevards and grand colonial architecture, is the starting point for buses to Wonosobo village. Most people catch the next bus out, but it's worth venturing outside of the bus station to see Magelang's only attraction, the one-room **Diponegoro Museum** (open daily on request; free). The museum is located in a wing of what is now a teaching academy, but was once the home of the local Dutch resident. It was in this house that Diponegoro was arrested by the Dutch on March 28, 1830 (see p.1039). Amongst the museum's collection of Diponegoro memorabilia is the chair he sat on when negotiating with Governor De Kock, as well a set of his robes and a couple of paintings of him on horseback. Magelang also makes a good base for visiting Borobudur. The nicest hotel in the town is *Hotel Puri Asri*, Jl Cempaka 9 (Ⓣ0293/64115; ❸), which offers good views, clean rooms and a decent restaurant. A little cheaper is *Hotel Trio*, Jl Jend. Sudirman 68 (Ⓣ0293/65095; ❷–❺), with a good range of rooms, a pool and a pleasant restaurant. Of the few places to eat, *Citrus Café*, Jl Pramudha Wardani 6, offers simple, cheap Indonesian, Chinese and Western fare.

Wonosobo

Magelang is also the transit town between Yogya and **WONOSOBO**, an hour's drive from Magelang. Wonosobo is a sleepy hill-top village, 35km west of Magelang, along a narrow mountain road with splendid panoramic views of Sumbing's grassy foothills. For most visitors, pretty Wonosobo is little more than a gateway to the Dieng plateau. A few travellers, however, prefer to stay in Wonosobo and commute to the plateau, a one-hour bus ride away, since the hotels and restaurants here are superior to those in Dieng and the climate is far more agreeable. There's little to do in Wonosobo itself, although a couple of attractions are located nearby. At **Kalianget**, 3km north of Wonosobo, there's a hot spring and swimming pool (daily 6am–6pm; Rp600), where the waters are believed to be good for eczema. An angkuta (with "Garung" written on the side), leaves from behind the tourist office and takes just ten minutes to get there (Rp2600). Seven kilometres along the same road is **Telaga Menjer**, a pretty little lake set in picturesque foothills where it's possible to swim; take a local bus from Menjer village (Rp1000).

Practicalities

Wonosobo stretches languidly between the bus station in the south, up the hill to the alun-alun, where you'll find the helpful **tourist office** (Mon–Thurs 7am–2pm, Fri 7–11am, Sat 7am–12.30pm; Ⓣ0286/321194). **Buses** from the lowlands pull into the southern terminus; if, however, you wish to travel straight on to Dieng, walk up the hill to the junction with Jalan Kyai Muntang: Dieng buses run past here before calling in at the Dieng terminus to the west of town. An **andong** between the two stations costs Rp1000. A *dokar*, or **horse cart**, is a nice way to tour this town and costs Rp5000.

There is **accommodation** to suit all budgets in Wonosobo. At the top end is the *Gallery Hotel Kresna*, Jl Pasukan Ronggolawe 30 (Ⓣ0286/324111, Ⓔkresna-htl@magelang.wasantara.net.id; ❻), a beautifully renovated colonial resthouse. *Surya Asri Hotel* at Jl A. Yani 137 (Ⓣ0286/322992, Ⓕ23598; ❺) is the next best option; all rooms are en suite, with hot and cold running water, TV and phone. The most popular option for backpackers, however, is the *Duta* at Jl RSU 3, 200m south of the Dieng bus station (Ⓣ0286/321674; ❷). It has a pleasant, family atmosphere – and a couple of pet deer running around the garden – while the en-suite rooms are extremely comfortable. One block east of

Jalan A.Yani is the *Citra Homestay*, Jl Angkatan 29 (☎0286/321880; ❷), a new place with very clean rooms and shared bathrooms. Like the *Duta*, the *Citra* also offer a Rp5000 **tour** around the paddy-fields and local villages.

Anybody who stays in Wonosobo for a night should pay a visit to the *Dieng Restaurant* on Jl Angkatan 45, a popular travellers' hangout serving buffet-style Chinese, Western and Indonesian **food**. Practically next door is the *Asia Restaurant* at no. 47, which offers good Chinese food and steaks.

Dieng

Four hours north of Yogya, and a 26-kilometre bus ride north of Wonosobo, negotiating the creases and folds of Gunung Sindoro, brings you to the damp and isolated village of **DIENG**, nestling on a plateau of the same name. The landscape here is a radical departure from the rest of Java; the vegetation is sparse, the largely denuded hills are terraced not with paddy-fields but with cabbage patches and flowerbeds, and the chilly plain is windswept and misty.

The **Dieng plateau** lies in a volcanic **caldera** formed by the collapse of underground lava reservoirs. This has led to some curious natural phenomena, such as multicoloured **sulphurous lakes** and craters where pungent gas hisses and billows out of crevices in the earth. Dotted among these features are a number of small **temples**, some of the oldest in Java. The name Dieng is a corruption of the Sanskrit *Di-Hyang* (Abode of the Gods), and it is thought that the plateau was considered sacred by the Hindu Sanjaya dynasty. The temples are largely unimpressive when compared to the giants at Prambanan and Borobudur, and the scenery – though a pleasant change from the lowlands – can become a little monotonous after a while. Nevertheless, the combination of the temples with the sheer strangeness of the landscape make Dieng an unusual and rewarding stop for tourists, and a must for geologists, hikers and temple lovers.

Dieng is at its best in the morning before the mist and damp sets in, so try to arrive at the temples early, and bring **warm clothes** and **waterproofs**. Although there are plenty of **tours** from Yogya, they're really not worth considering since it's a four-hour journey each way, with just one hour on the plateau. Instead, try to spend a night or two here, but be prepared to rough it a little: the weather is temperamental, the nights are cold and the food is bland.

It's also possible to reach the plateau from the north coast. Buses leave from Pekalongan, taking four hours to cover the 107km to **Batur**, a tiny village on the western edge of the plateau. This journey often involves a change of buses in Kalibening. From Batur it takes 45 minutes by bus to Dieng (Rp1000).

Dieng village

Tiny **Dieng village** is no more than a string of buildings lining the eastern side of **Jalan Raya Dieng**, the road running along the plateau's eastern edge. Four hundred metres north of the village the road turns sharply left and heads west. The road to Wonosobo (a 1hr bus ride away) ends at Jalan Raya Dieng by the village's two main travellers' hostels. This junction also acts as Dieng's **bus stop**, for buses to Wonosobo as well as other villages on the plateau. The **tourist office** (which seldom sticks to the advertised opening times of 8am–4pm) lies 200m north of the junction. When it's closed, a small kiosk near the two hostels deals with new arrivals and sells tickets to the Arjuna complex, the main set of temples that lies across the road from the village.

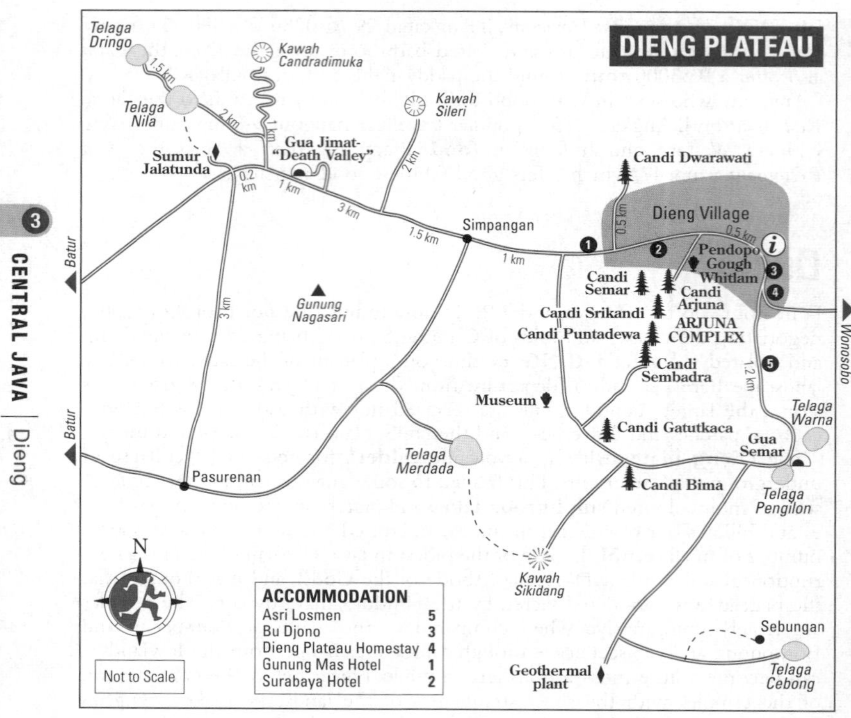

One would expect **accommodation** in the "Abode of the Gods" to be a little more heavenly than Dieng's tawdry bunch of losmen; all overcharge, especially those offering hot-water baths, which only the most hardy can do without here. At the northern end of town, the VIP rooms at the *Gunung Mas Hotel* (❹) have hot water and TV, though the prices charged for the somewhat shabby accommodation are ludicrous. A better option is the *Dieng Plateau Homestay* on Jalan Raya Dieng (❷), which has clean rooms and friendly staff. The rooms at the *Losmen Dieng*, Jalan Raya Dieng 16, are basic and full of flies, and the mandi are excruciatingly cold; however, it's still the best budget option (ⓣ0286/322035; ❶). *Bu Djono*, next door (❷), has shabbier rooms but superior food. Two hundred metres to the south at Jalan Resimin XVIII/9 stands the *Asri Losmen* (ⓣ0286/322476; ❷). The rooms are smarter (those in the new wing are the best value), but the place lacks atmosphere. Finally, the *Surabaya Hotel*, Jl Raya Dieng 52, is simple and clean, with cold-water mandis (ⓣ0286/321181; ❷).

Transport and tours

Other than the temples, many of the plateau's attractions are a bus or car ride away from Dieng, and the bus network on the plateau is limited. All **westbound buses** from Dieng pass through Simpangan village (Rp1000), 2km distant, where the road splits. The buses all take the southern road to Batur, 11km away (Rp2500 from Dieng), annoyingly for those who want to visit the sights, which are all on the northern road. The only way to reach these by public transport is to stay on the bus until **Pasurenan** (Rp1000), 4km before Batur, then take an ojek (Rp2500) up the hill to the northern road and Sumur Jalatunda. Alternatively, hire an ojek from Dieng village to take you directly to the sights (Rp10,000 per day). Most of these tourist attractions are signposted from the main road, although you may still have trouble finding them as the paths are badly maintained. Place-name spellings change frequently on the signposts, but note that Dieng and Tieng are two different places.

The *Dieng Plateau Homestay* offers **tours** around Dieng: their sunrise tour (Rp5000) is very popular. They also run excursions to **Sembungan**, the highest village on Java, at an altitude of 2160m.

The temples

It is believed that the Dieng plateau was once a completely self-contained **retreat** for priests and pilgrims. The ominous rumblings of the volcano beneath their feet, combined with the mist that daily enveloped them, must have convinced the early Hindus that this plateau was indeed sacred. Unfortunately, it was also completely waterlogged, and the architects had to devise a series of **tunnels** to drain the fields. The entire plateau, including the drainage system, was eventually abandoned in the thirteenth century during the unexplained evacuation of Central Java. Dieng sank into swampy obscurity until 1814, when the Dutchman **H.C. Cornelius** visited the area and discovered the ruins of over **two hundred temples** on the plateau. Forty years later, the basin was drained and the ruins fully catalogued. While tunnels once drained the plateau, wooden walkways now bridge the squelchier parts of the caldera.

All of the temples are within easy walking distance of Dieng village; the furthest from the village, Candi Bima, is located just over 1km to the south.

The Arjuna complex

The eight temples left on Dieng today are a tiny fraction of what was once a huge complex built by the Sanjayas in the seventh and eighth centuries. Of these temples, the five that make up the **Arjuna complex** (daily 6.15am–5.15pm) lie in the fields immediately to the west of Dieng village, and are believed to be the oldest. The tourist office at Dieng have imposed a Rp5000 entrance fee, payable at the small kiosk in the village.

The temples have been named after heroes from the *Mahabharata* tales, although these are not the original names. Three of the five were built to the same blueprint: square, with two storeys and a fearsome kala head above the main entrance. The most northerly of these two-storey temples, the **Arjuna temple**, is the oldest on Java (c.680 AD). Dedicated to Shiva, the temple once held a giant **linga** (a phallic-shaped stone) which was washed by worshippers several times a day; the water would then drain through a spout in the temple's north wall. The ugly, dumpy construction opposite, appropriately called **Candi Semar** after Arjuna's unattractive servant in the *Mahabharata*, is thought to have held Shiva's carriage, **Nandi**. Next to Arjuna stands **Candi Srikandi**, the exterior of which is adorned with reliefs of Vishnu (on the north wall), Shiva (east) and Brahma (south). This configuration is unique in Java, suggesting that the Javanese Hindus had not yet established the standard pattern of gods that can be seen at Gedung Songo (see p.261) and Prambanan (see p.224). The next temple south, the fifteen-metre **Candi Puntadewa** is the tallest of the five. It towers above neighbouring **Candi Sembadra**, the smallest and most southerly of the group.

Other temples

Candi Gatutkaca, a contemporary of Candi Arjuna, overlooks the Arjuna complex and lies 300m to the southwest of the village. Nearby, a singularly unimpressive **museum** (no set opening hours; free), acts as a warehouse for the decorations and furnishings of Dieng's unrestored temples, which have been dumped here in a random fashion. The caretaker who has the key to unlock the museum is often absent, so you can't always get in – which is no great loss.

The most peculiar-looking temple on the plateau (and the only one facing east) is **Candi Bima**, named after the brother of Arjuna. The temple is a twenty-minute walk south of Gatutkaca along a rutted path. Rows of faces stare impassively back at passers-by from the temple walls, a design based on the temples of southern India.

The eighth and final restored temple on the plateau lies some way to the north of the rest, 500m beyond the village behind the *Hotel Gunung Mas*. This is **Candi Dvaravati**, a plain, single-storey stone structure, which can be a peaceful place to sit and listen to the noises of the village below. It dates from the middle of the eighth century; the linga found inside proves that it was once dedicated to Shiva.

Natural attractions at Dieng

Dieng perches 2093m above sea level in the crater of a still-active volcano, which occasionally stirs to remind villagers of its presence, as in 1979 when over 150 people died after a cloud of poisonous gas leaked into the atmosphere. For most of the time, however, these sulphurous emissions do little more than provide the plateau with a number of unusual natural phenomena. Amongst these are the **coloured lakes**, where sulphurous deposits shade the water blue, from turquoise to azure. **Telaga Warna** (Coloured Lake), 2km along the main road heading south from the village, contains the best example of these sulphur-tinted waters. The lake laps against the shore of a small peninsula which contains a number of meditational caves. It was in one of these caves, **Gua Semar**, that Suharto and Australian prime minister Gough Whitlam decided the future of Timor in 1974. A visit to the lakes and caves can be combined with a visit to the Arjuna complex and Candi Bima, which makes for an interesting day's hiking.

Of the other lakes on the plateau, **Telaga Nila** and **Telaga Dringo**, 12km west of Dieng village, are the prettiest – but don't be tempted to swim, as the waters are too sulphuric. A trip to these two can be combined with visiting **Sumur Jalatunda**, a vast, vine-clad well just off the main road. The small boys who hang around the well selling small, smooth pebbles will – for a fee – show you the little-used path to the two lakes, although the route is too slippery to use after heavy rain.

Just 250m further along the road is the turn-off to **Kawah Candradimuka**, one of the many *kawah* (mini-craters) dotted around the plateau. The crater is a twenty-minute walk up the hill from the road; five minutes along the path, a small path on the left heads west to Telaga Nila. Take care by the crater, as there's no guard rail on the slippery slope to prevent you from sliding into the crater below. The sulphurous smell can be nauseating, and the steaming vents may obscure your view of the bubbling mud pools. Further east along the road, an overgrown path leads up to **Gua Jimat**, or Death Valley, where the sulphurous emissions are fatal to anyone and anything who stands too close. It is possible to take a view of this eerie site, but stand well back where the fumes are tolerable to avoid being overcome.

Tuk Bima Lukar is a small spring situated a few hundred metres behind the *Dieng Homestay*, which lies on the road to Wonosobo. The spring water, which is said to keep bathers eternally young, trickles from man-made stone spouts over a thousand years old.

Cilacap and around

Isolated from Yogya by the **Menoreh hills**, a slender, low-lying limestone ridge to the west of the city, and from the north coast (Pasisir region) by Java's imposing row of volcanoes, the coastal region to the southwest of Yogya has a distinctive backwater feel. There are few attractions in the area, which comprises the regencies of Kulonprogo, Purworejo, Kebumen and Purwokerto, but it's pleasant to travel through the landscape of gently undulating forested hills. Most foreign travellers who stray down this far have joined the major west–east highway at **Cilacap**, a busy port at the southwestern corner of the province, and don't stop again until they reach Yogya. However, local holiday-makers venture here regularly to enjoy the fresh mountain air of **Baturaden** or view the strange statues at **Gua Jatijajar**.

Cilacap

The biggest city on Central Java's southern coast, friendly **CILACAP** sees plenty of tourists, many passing through on their way to and from Pangandaran. The port at Cilacap, 170km from Yogya, has the only deep-water berthing facilities on Java's south coast, a fact the Dutch were quick to recognize and exploit during their tenancy. They built a large fort overlooking the sea, **Benteng Pendem** (daily 8am–6pm; Rp1000), which has become Cilacap's main tourist attraction. Though neglected and overgrown, the exterior of the fort is in a good state of repair compared to most on the island, with fortifications, barrack-rooms and even the former surgery intact.

The fort stands in the shadow of a huge **oil refinery**, the main source of Cilacap's wealth today. Both occupy the southeastern tip of town by **Pantai Teluk Penyu** (Turtle Bay), an ugly stretch of black sand used by the locals for early-evening fifty-a-side soccer matches. If you have a little time to kill, consider renting a fishing boat (Rp5000 per hour) from **Seleko harbour**, to the west of the oil refineries, and ask the owner to take you to **Nusa Kampangan**, a small island lying a few kilometres off Cilacap's western coast. The island features a wildlife park, although the wildlife isn't much in evidence. There are no facilities of any kind here, but it's a pleasant place to amble around.

Practicalities

The **ferry** from Pangandaran disgorges passengers at **Lomanis port** in the northwest corner of the city; the **bus station** is 1km to the east. **Angkuta #C2** performs a complete loop around the city, beginning at the bus station, heading south to the town square then returning to the station via Lomanis port.

The **hotels** in Cilacap are very good value. The *Wijaya Kusuma*, Jalan J. A. Yani 12, opposite the tourist office and near the town square, is the most comfortable, with all rooms equipped with air-con, hot water and colour TV (Ⓣ0282/534871; ❺). Angkuta #C2 stops right outside the hotel. A close second is the pleasant *Hotel Mutiara*, Jl Gatot Subroto 136, (Ⓣ0282/531545; ❺), which has hot-water, air-con and satellite TV. In the mid-range, try the centrally located *Cilacap Indah*, Jl Jend. Sudirman 1 (ⓣ0282/533543; ❸), or *Teluk Penyu*, Jl Dr. Wahidin 57 (ⓣ0282/534304; ❷–❹). Alternatively, the *Losmen Anggrek*, Jl Anggrek 16 (ⓣ0282/533835; ❷), offers a quiet, side-street location and clean rooms with attached mandi. The *Perapatan*, Jl J. A. Yani 62 is considered the best Chinese **restaurant** in Cilacap.

Purwokerto and Baturaden

PURWOKERTO, one hour by bus from Cilacap and two from Wonosobo, is the main transport junction for the southwestern corner of Central Java. It's a well-organized city that promotes itself with the acronym "BERSERI", the components of which are the Indonesian words for clean, healthy, neat and beautiful. It is all of these things, but this doesn't alter the fact that there's absolutely nothing here to persuade tourists to linger. If you do decide to stay here rather than Baturaden, the best hotel in town is the *Dynasty*, Jl Dr. Angka 71 (ⓣ0281/634321; ❺), with excellent facilities for such a small town, including a pool.

Nineteen kilometres to the north, and 670m up on the southern flanks of **Gunung Slamet**, sits the large mountain village of **BATURADEN**. Regarded by many as the prettiest hill station in Central Java, the village is easily accessible by taking a green bemo from the Puwokerto terminus (Rp1000). The slopes above Baturaden are shaggy with pine and provide the village with the most beautiful backdrop of any hill station in Central Java. It's possible to scale Gunung Slamet from Baturaden, a climb of seven hours, although it's easier and safer to begin the **ascent** from the northern slopes and the village of **Serang**. **Permits** (Rp5000) are required by all climbers, and are available from the permit office at the northern end of the village of Moga, 1km from Serang. To get here, take a bus to Belik, on the eastern slopes of Slamet, from Purwokerto (1hr; Rp1000), then a thirty-minute colt ride (Rp2000) from there to Moga. Guides, which are essential, are available from the office at Moga. The sheer size of the climb necessitates a night out on the mountain, so bring the appropriate gear.

Baturaden itself comprises just one road, Jalan Parawisata, which splits into two at the bus station before reuniting further up the hill at the tawdry fun park **Taman Rekreasi** (daily 6am–6pm; Rp1000). As with most hill stations in Java, the cheapest **accommodation** is located at the lower end of the village. The *Inti Sari* (❷), opposite the *King Karaoke Singing House*, is one of the cheapest options in the village, with large rooms, clean beds and a pleasant manager. Similar in standard and price are the losmen *Puji* (❷) and *Kerta Rahayu* (❷), further down the hill towards the gates of the city. At the top of the hill, the *Hotel Rosenda* on Jalan Parawisata (ⓣ0281/681570; ❺) ranks as the best in town, with a swimming pool, tennis courts and rooms in the comfortable main building or in cheaper, shabbier cottages. Down below the *Rosenda*, the *Pringsewu* **restaurant** serves very tasty Indonesian dishes such as *cap cay*, but note that the prices are higher on the English-language menu.

Gua Jatijajar

The statue and stalactite monstrosity of **Gua Jatijajar** (daily 6am–5.30pm; Rp1500) ranks as the number-one tourist attraction in the tiny regency of **Kebumen**, attracting local sightseers by the thousands every day. The cave itself lies 35km to the south of Purwokerto; if you're coming from that direction, ask the bus driver to drop you off at Ijo (Rp1000), 13km from Jatijajar, then catch a minibus (Rp500) from there. There are four direct buses from Cilacap (Rp1300), with the last one returning to Cilacap at 4pm. If you're coming from the east, alight at Gombong (Rp3300 from Yogya), where you can pick up a direct bus to the cave (Rp1000).

The cave, hollowed out of a series of limestone cliffs running parallel with the coast, was probably quite attractive until the authorities decided to cram the interior with ghastly statues re-creating the history of the mythical **Pahaharan Kingdom**. It has since been defaced with centuries worth of graffiti, which is probably the most interesting thing about it. Outside, dozens of hawkers try to sell all manner of tourist tat. There are two **accommodation** options nearby; the first, right by the entrance, is the adequate *Pondok Jati Diri* (❷), a no-nonsense little family losmen with cramped rooms. A ten-minute walk back towards Ijo brings you to the pristine *Hotel Puspita* on Jalan Raya Gua Jatijajar (❹).

Surakarta (Solo)

Sixty-five kilometres northeast of Yogya, along the same terrifying, high-speed highway bisecting the Prambanan Plain, stands quiet, leafy low-rise **SURAKARTA**, or **SOLO**, as it's more commonly known. This is the older of the two royal cities in Central Java, and its ruling family can lay claim to being the rightful heirs to the Mataram dynasty. For all Yogya's pomp and ceremony, its royal house is merely the younger, brasher sibling of Solo's ancient court.

Like Yogya, Solo has two **royal palaces** and a number of **museums**, evidence of a past culture that's every bit as colourful as those of its rival. Indeed, Solo's traditional court society is widely regarded as the most refined on Java. The dancing performances are considered to be more graceful, the poetry more "highbrow", and the court language more polished and polite. Yet Solo's tourist industry is nowhere near as developed as Yogya's. Instead, the city's main source of income is from textiles, and the biggest **textile market** in Java stands next to the larger of Solo's two royal houses, **Kasunanan Palace**, in the heart of the city. A number of cottage industries have also sprung up around town, producing everything from gamelan sets to tofu.

Because tourism takes a back seat in Solo, many visitors are fooled into believing that the city can be seen on a day-trip from Yogya. But it has enough attractions to keep sightseers occupied for a couple of days, and also makes an ideal base from which to visit the home of Java Man at **Sangiran**, as well as the intriguing **temples** of **Gunung Lawu**, **Candi Ceto** and **Candi Sukuh**.

Some history

Until 1744, Solo was little more than a quiet backwater village, albeit one that lay just 10km east of Kartasura, the former capital of the Mataram kingdom. Exhausted by two destructive **Wars of Succession** in the mid-eighteenth century, the Mataram dynasty then suffered at the hands of the Dutch after the reigning susuhunan (king), **Pakubuwono II**, unwisely chose to back the Chinese in their attempt to avenge the Batavian massacre of 1740 (see p.87). The Dutch, supported by the Madurese, had little trouble overcoming the opposition, and the court at Kartasura was sacked as a result. Convinced that Kartasura was jinxed, Pakubuwono II (which translates as "Nail at the Centre of the Universe") consulted various soothsayers and advisers in his search for a more auspicious location for his capital. In 1745, the entire court was dismantled and transported in a great procession to Surakarta, on the banks of the Kali Solo.

The Mataram's luck, however, did not change, and internecine squabbles within the royal house continued to weaken it. Pakubuwono II died just four years later, and his heir, Pakubuwono III, was powerless to stop his uncle, Mangkubumi, taking half the kingdom for his new court at Yogya following the **Third Javanese War of Succession**. Two years later, in 1757, the power of the Surakarta court was diminished still further by the creation of the **royal house of Mangkunegoro**, right in the centre of Solo. Thereafter, Solo's royal houses wisely avoided fighting, instead throwing their energies into the arts and developing a highly sophisticated court culture. The nobles of the city, particularly those who lived during the rule of the aesthete **Pakubuwono V**, laid down their weapons, and the gamelan pavilions became the new theatres of war, with each city competing to produce the more refined court culture.

This nonaggressive stance has continued into the twentieth century. Although a breeding ground for nationalist sentiment during the 1920s, the town took a back seat to Yogya in the **War of Independence**. In hindsight, this inertia was a mistake; whilst Yogya was rewarded with its own province and is regarded as the epicentre of the Independence movement, Solo was denied any special privileges and was forced to merge with the rest of the Central Javan province.

Taking in the calm, unhurried atmosphere of the city today, it's hard to believe that Solo suffered more permanent damage than any other city on Java (with the possible exception of Jakarta) during the **riots** of May 1997. Yet in just five hours of protests and rioting on the evening of May 14, both of the city's shopping centres – the Singosaran and Gajah Mada plazas – were burnt down, and nineteen people were killed when a shoe shop near the Singosaran Plaza collapsed after looters started fires within the building. Solo has remained in the news: Australia's pronouncements on the Indonesian military-backed carnage in East Timor and its pre-emininence in peace-keeping there (see p.773) led to numerous anti-Australian protests in Solo and Yogya. Late in 2001, the US's actions in Afghanistan in the wake of the September 11 attacks on New York and Washington led to angry demonstrations by student groups and to the "sweeping" of hotels by radical Muslim groups in search of Americans. No tourists were known to have been intimidated or hurt, and the tension has abated for the present, but Solo and Yogya's students are quick to react against what they see as anti-Indonesian or anti-Muslim actions by the US and her allies.

Orientation, arrival and information

Solo sits on the western banks of the Kali Solo, Java's longest river. It doesn't take long to become acquainted with the layout of central Solo, as nearly all of the hotels, sights and facilities are either on, or within walking distance of, the main road through the city, **Jalan Brig Jen Slamet Riyadi** (hereafter called simply Jalan Riyadi), which stretches from **Kartasura** in the west to just beyond the alun-alun (town square) in the east. The centre of the travellers' scene is Jalan Dahlan, a smallish road heading north off Jalan Riyadi. Behind the shops on the south side of Jalan Riyadi are a series of traditional kampung: riddled with winding alleyways flanked by some of the oldest houses in the city, they're fascinating places to explore.

Adisumaryno Airport, Central Java's only international airport, occupies former farmland 10km to the west of Solo and 2km north of Kartasura. There's

SOLO

ACCOMMODATION	
Cakra	13
Cendana	14
Central	7
Dagdan's	17
Dana	16
Happy Homestay	5
Istana Griya	8
Joyokusuman	18
Kota	9
Kusuma Sahid Prince	4
Lor In	11
Mama's	10
Novotel	12
Riyadh Palace	19
Sahid Raya	6
Surya	1
Trihadhi	2
Trio	3
Westerners	15

RESTAURANTS	
Adem Ayam	I
Bima	K
Kafe Gamelan	A
Kafé Solo	J
Kantin Bahagia	G
Kusuma Sari	E
Lumba Lumba	F
Monggo Pinarak	D
Sehat	H
Superman's	C
Warung Baru	B

no public transport direct to Solo from the airport, although a half-hourly **minibus** to Kartasura (Rp1000) drives along the main road alongside the runway, and from Kartasura you can catch a double-decker to Solo (Rp1000). A **taxi** from the airport to Solo (20min) costs approximately Rp18,000, or slightly less in the opposite direction.

All buses to Solo terminate at the **Tirtonadi bus station** in the north of the city. Just across the crossroads by the northeastern corner of Tirtonadi is the **minibus terminal**, Gilingan. From the front of the *Hotel Surya*, overlooking Tirtonadi, orange angkuta #6 departs for the town centre, stopping at **Ngapeman**, the junction of Jalan Gajah Mada and Jalan Riyadi. Heading to the bus station from the town centre, catch a BERSERI bus (Rp1000) from the bus stop on Jalan Riyadi, 100m east of Jalan Dahlan. A becak from the bus station to Jalan Dahlan costs approximately Rp3000. You'll pay the same fare from the **Balapan train station**, 300m south of Tirtonadi.

Solo boasts three **tourist offices**, located at the airport, at Tirtonadi bus station and behind the Radyo Pustoko museum at Jl Riyadi 275. Only the last one (Mon–Sat 8am–4pm; ⓣ0271/711435) is of any real use, offering a reasonable range of brochures and a couple of staff who speak a little English.

City transport

Solo's **double-decker buses** are unique in Central Java. Ignore the numbers on the front of them, as they all travel along the same route: from Kartasura in the west, down Jalan Riyadi, past the post office and on to Palur, where you can catch buses to Tawangmangu. Unable to return on the same route thanks to the one-way system of Jalan Riyadi, they head west along Jalan Veteran instead. The fare is a flat Rp1000, whatever the distance.

The main **taxi** stand is situated by the Mata Hari department store; taxis are metered. The **becak** are more reasonable: unlike those in Yogya, Solo's becak do not charge a higher rate if there's more than one person in the carriage. As always, remember to bargain hard. Solo is flat and, for a Javanese city, relatively free of traffic, so **cycling** is an excellent way to get around. Bikes can be rented from many of the homestays for Rp7500 per day.

Accommodation

Solo is full of **hotels** and **losmen** catering to every pocket, with new ones appearing all the time. Nearly all lie within 100m of the main road, Jalan Riyadi, or near the train station. Most of the **budget hotels** are hidden in the kampung to the south of Jalan Riyadi, and can be difficult to find. The simplest solution is to hire a becak driver to take you to the hostel of your choice, although, as is usual, the hostel owner pays a commission to the driver which comes out of your pocket via a higher room charge. **Breakfast** is included in the price in nearly every hotel.

Cakra Jl Riyadi 201 ⓣ0271/645847, ⓕ648334. With its swimming pool, billiard room, batik shop, parking facilities and air-con rooms, this is one of the best-value hotels in this category, and in a great central location too. ❺

Cendana Gang Empu Panuluh III 4, Kemlayan Kidul ⓣ0271/752821. One of the newer places in town, aimed at the budget market. The owner, Bullet, is eccentric but harmless. His hotel contains some of the nicest rooms in this price range, featuring Javanese furniture and large fans. ❶

Central Jl Dahlan 32 ⓣ0271/742814. A big hotel that's seen better days. The green-tiled floor and cheap, wooden furniture are tatty, and the rooms aren't exactly cosy. Useful, however, if the other places in the city centre are full. ❶

Dagdan's Baluwerti Rt II/7 42 ⓣ0271/754538. The only hotel within the kraton walls, located at the southeast corner of the palace. It's an attractive little place, with roses growing up the walls of the central courtyard and smart rooms sharing a well-scrubbed bathroom. Highly recommended. ❷

Dana Jl Riyadi 286 ⓣ0271/711976, ⓕ713880. A large hotel with 49 air-con rooms, conveniently situated opposite the tourist office and museum. ❺

Happy Homestay Jl Honggowongso, Gang Karagan 12 ⓣ0271/712449. Also known as *Hotel Bahagia*. Basic rooms in the main house – with a mattress on the floor and a small fan as the only furniture – are supplemented by cleaner, more spacious rooms in the main floor annexe; the upstairs rooms are bigger and better. It's one of the friendliest homestays around, and deservedly popular amongst backpackers and long-term residents. ❷

Istana Griya Jl Dahlan 22 ⓣ0271/ 632667. A new and well-run homestay tucked away down a little *gang* behind the *Steak House*, with the smartest and best-value rooms in this price range. Quiet and highly recommended. ❷

Joyokusuman Jl Gajahan 7 Rt II/3 ⓣ0271/654842. Large, beautiful, individually decorated rooms with net-covered four-poster beds and balconies. Most guests are long-term residents, many studying meditation. ❷

Kota Jl Riyadi 125 ⓣ0271/632841. An unexceptional cheap hotel with the usual facilities and a slightly seedy atmosphere, but well situated in the centre of town near Jalan Dahlan. ❷

Kusuma Sahid Prince Jl Sugiopranoto 20 ⓣ0271/746356, ⓕ744788, ⓔhskusuma@indo.net.id. Once the royal court of Susuhunan Pakubuwono X's son, this converted palace is the most stylish place in central Solo. Set in five landscaped acres with a swimming pool at the back and pendopo reception – complete with gamelan orchestra – at the front. Air-con, TV and fridge come as standard in all rooms. ❺

Lor In Jl Adiscucipto 47 ⓣ0271/724500. An ex-Sheraton hotel 5km from the city on the road from the airport. It has a magnificent garden setting with a ruined tropical village theme, and comfortable rooms with traditional Javanese and Dutch colonial furnishings. Highly recommended. ❺

Mama's Kauman Gang III/49, Jalan Yos Sudarso ⓣ0271/652248. One of the best places to come for a batik course. Also provides good local information and runs bicycle tours to nearby villages. The breakfasts (included in price), though sometimes bland, are occasionally excellent (their fruit salads are particularly good, and free tea and coffee is available throughout the day). Upstairs rooms are cheaper and noisier. ❶

Novotel Jl Riyadi 272 ⓣ0271/724555 or 716800, ⓕ724666 ⓔnov-solo@indoi.net.id. A luxury hotel with its own pool, gym, Indonesian, Japanese and Chinese restaurants and plush, air-con rooms. ❺

Riyadh Palace Jl Riyadi 335 ⓣ0271/717181, ⓕ721552. One of Solo's newest hotels, occupying a good central location, but otherwise fairly unexceptional. ❺

Sahid Raya Jl Gajah Mada 82 ⓣ0271/744144, ⓕ744133, ⓔsahid-raya@slo.maga.net.id. A 4-star hotel with 160 rooms; the facilities include a swimming pool, pub, café, and rooms with air-con, fridge and TV. ❺

Surya Jl Setia Budi 17 ⓣ0271/721915. Right next to the bus terminal, so noisy and far from the centre – though handy if you're catching an early-morning bus. Reasonable rooms, but you'll find better-value accommodation in town. ❸

Trihadhi Jl Monginsidi 97 ⓣ0271/637557. One of the better options by the train station, a well-run, homely place with large, cool rooms. ❷

Trio Jl Urip Sumoharjo 25 ⓣ0271/632847. *Trio's* cool, tiled reception opens onto a pleasant courtyard, a wonderful retreat from the bustle of the market outside. The rooms are clean but a little dark; there's no breakfast, but tea and coffee are served throughout the day. ❷

Westerners Jl Kemlayan Kidul 11 ⓣ0271/633106. A cramped, plant-filled hangout that accepts foreign travellers only, offering inexpensive rooms and dormitory beds. ❶

The City

Solo has grown horizontally rather than vertically over the years. There are no skyscrapers in the centre, and nearly all the twentieth-century constructions are just a few storeys high, merging seamlessly with the city's traditional architecture to create a pleasing harmony of ancient and modern. The best examples of Solo's architectural heritage are the royal houses off Jalan Riyadi, namely **Puro Mangkunegoro** to the north of the street and the **Kasunanan Palace** to the south. The latter lies within Solo's **walled city**, an area every bit as pretty as Yogyakarta's Kraton. Unlike Yogya's old quarter, however, Solo's kraton does not dominate the city centre; it's tucked away to the east of the city.

The kraton

The kraton at Solo provided Yogya's first sultan, Mangkubumi, with many ideas for the layout and design of his new city. Anyone who has been to Yogya will doubtless notice many similarities, starting with the **alun-alun**, a large grassy square lying immediately behind the city gates on Jalan Riyadi. Further exploration reveals still more similarities: to the west of the square stands the **royal mosque**, or **Mesjid Agung**, built to a traditional Javanese design by Pakubuwono III in 1750, with a multi-tiered (*joglo*) roof surmounting an enclosed pendopo, and, to the south of the alun-alun, a giant open-sided pendopo announces the austere presence of the city's royal residence, the **Kasunanan Palace**.

Kasunanan Palace

Brought from Kartasura by Pakubuwono II in one huge day-long procession in 1745, the **Kasunanan Palace** (daily except Fri 8.30am–2pm; Rp3500) is Solo's largest and most important royal house. Guides are available free of charge; it's definitely worth using their services, as the charms of the place lie not in spectacular construction or ostentatious furnishings, but in the tiny architectural and ornamental details, many imbued with symbolism, which are easy to overlook.

Behind the *pagelaran* stands a second pendopo, the **Siti Inggil**. This provides shelter for a **sacred cannon**, yet another relic of Kartasura brought here in the 1745 procession. Traditionally, the susuhunan would give speeches from this pendopo, taking advantage of the structure's excellent acoustics.

Continuing south, you pass through one gate and come to a second, which leads through to the main body of the kraton. This gate is saved for ceremonial use only. A smaller gate to the right remains the sole preserve of members of the royal family, and commoners must turn left and enter the main body of the palace by the eastern entrance. This opens onto a large courtyard whose surrounding buildings house the palace's fairly disorganized **kris collection**, as well as silver ornaments and royal paraphernalia. The highlights include three Dutch **chariots** dating from the last century and a huge ceremonial kris, used to protect the palace from evil spirits.

An archway to the west of the courtyard leads into the susuhunan's living quarters; shoes must be removed before you enter this section. The current sultan, the septuagenarian Pakubuwono XII, is still in residence, along with a few of his 35 children and two of his six wives. Many of the buildings in this courtyard are modern reconstructions, the originals having burnt down in 1985 in a fire caused by an electrical fault. The octagonal **watchtower** to the north, however, is original. One of its floors is the sole preserve of the susuhunan for his meetings with Loro Kidul, the Goddess of the South Seas (see p.201). Every year, on the anniversary of his coronation, the susuhunan, in a private ceremony, enters the room to renew his acquaintance with the sea goddess.

Outside the kraton

The rest of Solo's major sights lie to the west of the kraton, on or around Jalan Riyadi. The second royal house in Solo, the **Puro Mangkunegoro** (guided tours only Mon–Thurs 8.30am–2pm, Sun 8.30–1pm; Rp5000), stands 1km west of the kraton and, like Yogya's court of Paku Alam, faces south towards the Kasunanan Palace as a mark of respect. With its fine collection of antiques and curios, in many ways the Puro Mangkunegoro is more interesting than the Kasunanan palace, to which it is subservient.

The palace was built in 1757 to placate the rebellious **Prince Mas Said**

(Mangkunegoro I), a nephew of Pakubuwono II, who had originally joined forces with Mangkubumi against the king during the Third Javanese War of Succession. Relations with Mangkubumi deteriorated, however, after the latter founded Yogya and was recognized as its sultan, and Mas Said was at one stage regarded as an enemy of both royal courts as well as the VOC (Dutch East India Company). Exhausted by fighting wars on three fronts, Mas Said eventually accepted a VOC-brokered peace deal which gave him a royal title, a court in Solo and rulership over four thousand of Solo's households. In return, Mas Said promised peace.

The palace hides behind a high white wall, entered through the gateway to the south. The vast **pendopo** (the largest in Indonesia) which fronts the palace, shields four gamelan orchestras under its rafters. Three of these are sacred and only to be played on very special occasions. Be sure to look up at the vibrantly painted roof of the pendopo, where Javanese zodiac figures form the main centrepiece.

The main body of the palace lies behind the pendopo. A portrait of the current resident, Mangkunegoro IX, hangs in the **Paringgitan** – an area reserved specifically for wayang kulit performances – by the entrance to the **Dalam Agung**, or living quarters. The reception room of the Dalam Agung has been turned into a very good museum, with displays of ancient coins, ballet masks and chastity preservers.

A further kilometre west along Jalan Riyadi is the **Radya Pustaka Museum** (Mon–Thurs & Sun 8am–1pm, Fri & Sat 8–11am; Rp500). Built by the Dutch in 1890, this is one of the oldest and largest museums in Java, housing a large Dutch and Javanese library as well as collections of wayang kulit puppets, kris, and scale models of the mosque at Demak and the cemetery at Imogiri. Just a few metres west lies the **Sriwedari Park** (daily 2–8pm), an amusement park which holds nightly wayang orang performances (see p.242). Another 200m further west, at Jalan Dr Cipto 15, is the **Dullah Museum**, a gallery of paintings and sculptures by Pak Dullah, a prolific artist whose work was collected by, amongst others, President Suharto.

Eating and drinking

Solo has some good-value restaurants, including a couple of very good budget places around Jalan Dahlan, but nothing like the number or variety found in Yogya. Its warung, however, are renowned throughout the island. Local specialities include *nasi liwet* – chicken or vegetables and rice drenched in coconut milk, served on a banana leaf – and *nasi gudeg*, a variation on Yogya's recipe. For dessert, try *kue putu* (coconut cakes) or *srabi*, a combination of pancake and sweet rice served with a variety of fruit toppings. Most of these delicacies can be purchased along Jalan Teuku Umar, one block west of Jalan Dahlan, and on the roads around the Sriwedari Park in the evening.

Solo's sweets and cakes are also irresistible. The *Donat Amerikan*, just round the corner from Jalan Dahlan on Jalan Riyadi, sells plenty of tasty cream-topped, jam-filled goodies. The *New Holland Bakery*, further up Jalan Riyadi, has a similarly saccharine selection, with a pub and restaurant upstairs.

Restaurants

Adem Ayam Jl Riyadi 342. Large, slightly overpriced restaurant split into two sections, serving Javanese and Chinese food.

Bima Jl Riyadi 128. Large and swish ice-cream parlour serving a decent selection of ice cream as well as Indonesian and European dishes at surprisingly low prices. 11am–9.30pm.

Kafe Gamelan Jl Dahlan 28. Quiet place serving good Indonesian food and excellent fruit juces at reasonable prices.

Kafe Solo Jl Secoyadan 201. Stylish mid-priced

restaurant with a good choice of beef and chicken dishes, salads and other Western fare. Great if you fancy a change from rice (although they offer that too).

Kantin Bahagia Pujosari Market, Jl Riyadi 275. Highly recommended tiny bar and restaurant, just to the south of Jalan Riyadi in the Pujosari Market, serving good-value Indonesian staples and cheap beer. Stays open until 1am to catch the post-cinema crowd.

Kusuma Sari Jl Riyadi 111. A popular local hang-out, serving ice cream and grilled dishes. Unusually for Indonesia, it has a no-smoking policy.

Lumba Lumba Pujosari Market, Jl Riyadi 275. A shady, welcoming retreat, serving standard and cheap Indonesian snacks and lunches. It's one of a large number of restaurants/warung to the west of Sriwedari Park, most of which offer a similar, small menu.

Monggo Pinarak Jl Dahlan 22. This mid-priced restaurant/book and batik shop is owned by a well-travelled, woolly-hatted Bangladeshi, and most of its menu is made up of dishes from the Indian subcontinent. The food, apart from the excellent chicken *dopiaza*, is adequate rather than exceptional, but the dishes make a refreshing change from Indonesian food and the service is very good. There's an internet connection at the rear of the restaurant and a good-quality souvenir shop at the front.

Sehat Pujosari Market, Jl Riyadi 275. A snake restaurant/warung near Sriwedari. You choose your meal whilst it's still hissing and tell the chef how you want it done. Rp15,000 for the whole snake, Rp5000 for sate or, if you just want a snack, Rp2000 for the penis.

Superman's Jalan Dahlan. A mid-price travellers' place, this time specializing in steaks. Their nasi goreng special, with the rice wrapped inside an omelette, is a tasty variation on an Indonesian staple.

Warung Baru Jl Dahlan 8. The most popular travellers' restaurant in Solo. Good, inexpensive Western and Indonesian food, with delicious home-made bread. The *Warung Baru* also organizes tours, batik courses, and after 7pm a little old lady often calls round offering massages.

Nightlife and entertainment

The Solonese will try to convince you that this is the "city that never sleeps", but, in spite of the best efforts of the muezzin at 4am, this simply isn't true. There are four **nightclubs** in Solo: the rather dingy *Nirwana* in Pasar Besar, Jalan Urip Sumoharjo; *Legenda*, a slightly better place catering for a youngish crowd on Jalan Honggowongso; *Freedom*, in Jalan A.Yani to the northwest of the city centre in the Manohan district; and *Solo Bilyar & Disco Dangdut* above the Pasar Gede, a disco specializing in *dangdut* music (see p.1067) with an attached pool hall. Only the latter is worth staying up for. All charge a Rp20,000 entrance fee, for which you receive one free beer (except on Saturday). If you just want a drink, head to the *New Holland Pub and Restaurant* on Jalan Slamet Riyadi where a live band performs every evening after 10pm.

As with all big Indonesian cities, Solo has plenty of **cinemas** and **pool halls**. The Sriwedari Park on Jalan Riyadi has a four-screen cinema, Solo 21, which shows recent Hollywood blockbusters alongside the mandatory kung fu flicks, with tickets only Rp5000. A similar programme runs at the huge cinema, Fajar 123, on Jalan Sudirman near the post office.

Performing arts

For the last two centuries, the royal houses of Solo have directed their energies away from the battlefield and towards the stage, with each developing a highly individual style for the traditional Javanese arts of gamelan and wayang. The Puro Mangkunegoro's performances of **wayang orang** (daily 10am–noon) are more rumbustuous and aggressive than the graceful, fluid style of the Kasunanan Palace (Sun 10am–noon). Another option is the three-hour performance at Sriwedari Park (Mon–Sat 8–11pm). Radio Republik Indonesia (RRI) records wayang orang performances every first and third Tuesday of the month (9.30pm–midnight); for tickets to the show, enquire at the RRI, Jl Marconi 51, just to the south of the Balapan train station.

Both court styles were, until recently, fiercely protected from impersonation. It was forbidden to stage a performance of the sacred *bedoyo* (where a troupe of female dancers move in exact unison with each other) and *srimpi* dances (four dancers moving in two pairs) outside of the two courts. Now, however, a third player has arrived on the scene; the STSI – Indonesia's Academy of Performing Arts – in the suburb of Kentingan to the northeast of the city, has invented new, nontraditional forms of wayang. Visit the **academy** (Mon–Thurs & Sat 9–5pm; free) and you can see a variety of dances, diluting traditional Solonese movements with Balinese and other styles.

Gamelan is also something of a Solonese speciality. The small gamelan orchestra at the *Sahid Kusuma Hotel* plays every afternoon and evening in the reception hall (free). Radio RRI records a gamelan performance every second and fourth Thursday of the month (9pm); enquire at the RRI building (see below) for the free tickets and performance times. The Kasunanan Palace also holds a gamelan performance every fifth Monday (on the Javanese day of Malam Selasa Legi), while the Puro Mangkunegoro puts on a free ninety-minute performance on Saturday evenings at 9pm.

Wayang kulit fans are also well catered for. The finest *dalang* in Java, Ki Anom Suroto, lives in Solo; when he's not touring the world, Suroto plays for private functions in the city. Inquire at the tourist office for details of his next performance, and you may be fortunate enough to be invited along. Every 35 days (on the Javanese day of Rebo Legi) Suroto invites a *dalang* to perform at his house off Jalan Riyadi, near the *Cakra Hotel*. The Kasunanan Palace also organizes a performance of wayang kulit in the evening of the fourth Saturday of every month (around 7pm; free), which is then broadcast on radio. On the third Tuesday and Saturday of every month, RRI (the radio station), Jl Marconi 51, allows the public in to watch the recording of their wayang kulit performance from 9pm–5am.

Shopping

Solo has some excellent **markets**, two of which are of particular interest to foreign visitors. The three-storey **Pasar Klewer** (daily 9am–4pm), by the southwest corner of the alun-alun, claims to be Java's largest **batik** market. It's certainly huge and confusing, and trying to locate a particular stall can take forever, especially as so many look alike and sell similar products. You can pick up designs from all over Java, although brown and indigo, the traditional colours of Solo's batik, predominate. Most of the batik is *cap*, although *tulis* and *lurik* homespun are also available. It's possible to have an item of clothing made to measure in just one day, although unless your Indonesian is very good, you may have trouble explaining exactly what you want. For a good range of batik at set prices, try Batik Danar Hadi, Jl Dr. Rajiman 164, Batik Keris, Jl Yos Sudarso 62, or Batik Semar, Jl RM Said 148.

The **Pasar Triwindu** (daily 8am–4pm), off Jalan Diponegoro, just to the south of the Puro Mangkunegoro, is supposedly an antiques market, but you'd be very lucky to find anything of value among the piles of cheap souvenirs. Another place for "antiques" is the **Bali Art Shop** at Jl K.H. Hasyim Asyari 51, between the kraton and Jalan Yos Sudarso. This boutique is crammed to the rafters with all kinds of souvenirs and junk – and possibly the odd genuine antique – making it the most enjoyable place for rummaging around in.

There are two other markets in Solo. The large and buzzy **Pasar Gede**, or Central Market, 300m north of the post and telephone offices, is a mainly Chinese affair, selling fruit and vegetables. The biggest market in Solo is the intoxicating and chaotic **Pasar Legi**, which sells food, especially fruit and vegetables, and household goods. It's on the way to the bus station; catch a BERSERI bus heading east along Jalan Riyadi.

Listings

Airlines Bouraq, Jl Gaja Madah 86 ⓣ0271/634376; Garuda and Merpati, *Cakra Hotel*, Bank Lippo Building, Jl Riyadi 328 ⓣ0271/744955; Silk Air, 3rd floor, BCA Building, Jalan Riyadi ⓣ0271/711369.
Banks and exchange The Bank BCA, in the vast BCA building at the eastern end of Jalan Riyadi, currently offers the best rates in town. The exchange offices are on the second floor, and are open 10am–noon only. The Golden Money Changer at the northern end of Jalan Yos Sudarso, and PT Desmonda, next to the *Bima Restaurant* at Jl Riyadi 128, are both open throughout the day, though their rates are inferior to the banks. Most of the banks, which can be found at and around the eastern end of Jalan Riyadi, have ATMs, as does the *Novotel* hotel at Jl Riyadi 272.
Batik courses For all the hype of Yogya, Solo is the best place to try your hand at batik. The homestays and restaurants organize a number of courses costing Rp10,000–20,000 depending on whether you are making a small wall-hanging or designing a T-shirt: the *Warung Baru* restaurant on Jl Dahlan 8 runs an extremely popular course taught by the amiable Ecoh. His workshop is 2km from the restaurant, but transport is provided. *Mama's Homestay*, Kauman Gang III/49, Jalan Yos Sudarso (ⓣ0271/752248), was once a batik factory, and a few high-quality cloths are still produced here. Those who sign up for the one-day course work alongside the local artists.
Bookshops There's no English-language bookshop in Solo. The *Monggo Pinarak* restaurant has a small selection of books for sale, although it keeps the best ones for itself and its diners.
Bus tickets Most homestays and travellers' restaurants sell door-to-door bus tickets to popular tourist destinations, as does Niki Tours on Jl Yos Sutowijoyo 45 (ⓣ & ⓕ0271/717733) and Sahid Tours and Travels (ⓣ0271/742105). For the complete selection of bus and minibus companies, however, head to the Gilingan minibus terminal, east of the main Tirtonadi bus terminal.
Car rental Star Car Rental, Jl Laksda Adiscupto 22 ⓣ0271/562403. Their agent in town is Niki Tours on Jl Sutowijoyo 45 (ⓣ & ⓕ0271/717733). Jeeps cost Rp150,000 per day, rising to Rp300,000 for a sedan car. Weekly and monthly rates are also available.
Ferries On Jalan Veteran there are a couple of tiny kiosks which have details of the Pelni ferries.
Hospital Rumah Sakit Kasih Ibu, Jl Riyadi 404 and Rumah Sakit Panti Kosala (aka Rumah Sakit Dr Oen), Jl Brig Jen Katamso 55. Both have some English speaking doctors.
Immigration office Jalan Adisucipto, on the way to the airport ⓣ0271/748479.
Internet access *BB-Net*, Beteng Plaza, Jalan Riyadi (Rp8000 for 1hr); *Logikom Internet*, Jl Ronggowarsito (Rp8000 for 1hr); *Monggo Pinarak Restaurant*, Jl Dahlan 22, (Rp15,000 for 1hr).
Meditation courses Solo has become the centre of meditation in Java. The staff at the *Joyokusuman Hotel*, Jl Gajahan 7 Rt II/3 (ⓣ0271/754842), will be able to advise you on the courses available. Some of the most popular teachers are: Pak Soewondo, at the green-doored Jl Madukoro 21, a few hundred metres west of the kraton walls, who holds a free, 2hr Javanese relaxation session every Wednesday evening at 6pm; Pak Ananda Suyono, of Shanti Loka at Jl Ronggowarsito 88 (ⓣ0271/742348), to the north of Jalan Dahlan, who offers New Age meditation five days per week; Pak Hardjanto, who teaches yoga at the statue-filled Global Hinduism centre, opposite the eastern entrance to the Kraton at Jl Sidikoro 10a (ⓣ0271/635210). The most popular teacher with European students is Pak Suprapto Surjodarmo, whose dance/meditation courses (approximately US$700 for a month) are held out of town to the north of Solo in Mojosongo.
Photographic shops There are two reasonable photo stores in Solo: Foto Citi, just a few metres east of Jalan Dahlan on Jalan Riyadi, and Foto Sampurna, further east at Jalan Riyadi 24.
Post office Jalan Jend Sudirman (daily 6am–10pm). The poste restante closes in the evening.
Swimming The pool at the *Kusuma Sahid* hotel is open to nonresidents for a hefty Rp10,000 (daily 7am–8pm), while that at the *Cakra* (7am–7pm) charges a more reasonable Rp7500.
Telephones Just behind the Telkom offices on Jalan Sumoharjo, at Jl Mayor Kusmanto 3, there's a 24hr wartel office. There's also a wartel on Jalan Riyadi to the west of Jalan Yos Sudarso.
Tours Niki Tours, Jalan Sutowijoyo 45 (ⓣ & ⓕ0271/717733), offers a number of trips to nearby attractions, such as Sukuh and the Tawangmangu waterfall, for US$22. Most trav-

△ Gotang puppets

ellers use them for their bus to Bali, which includes a night's accommodation at Mount Bromo (US$39). They also have an office at Jl Yos Sudarso 17. Inta Tours & Travel, Jl Riyadi 96 (ⓣ0271/751142, ⓕ56128), offers a similar deal. Better value, and more rewarding, are the cycling tours organized by many of the homestays and travellers' restaurants – for example, *Mama's*, Kauman Gang III/49, Jalan Yos Sudarso ⓣ0271/652248; *Relax*, Jalan Kemlayan; *Ramayana*, Jl Dr. Wahidin 22; and *Warung Baru*, Jl Ahmad Dahlan 8. They cost around Rp10,000 and usually include a visit to a gamelan factory, bakery, tofu factory and even an arak manufacturer.

Travel agents Try Sahid Gema Wisata, Jl Riyadi 380 (ⓣ0271/742105 or 741916), or Niki Tours at Jl Sutowijoyo 45 (ⓣ & ⓕ0271/717733).

Around Solo

You could happily spend a week making day-trips from Solo, though there's nothing in the vicinity of the city quite as impressive as Yogya's two most famous excursions, Prambanan and Borobudur. Nevertheless, all of the following attractions are accessible by public transport and some, particularly the two *candi* on **Gunung Lawu**, **Sukuh** and **Ceto**, 40km due east of Solo, are well worth visiting. **Kartasura**, the first capital of the Mataram, lies just to the west of downtown Solo and is the nearest of the attractions, though there's actually little to see. The discoveries of the remains of one of mankind's oldest ancestors at **Sangiran**, 18km to the north of Solo, are now housed in a small archeological museum; while they're of vital importance to paleontologists, they're unlikely to captivate the average visitor. Forty-eight kilometres west of Solo, the village of **Selo** provides climbers with an alternative base to overcrowded Kaliurang from which to tackle **Gunung Merapi**, and 16km to the south of Solo is the regency of **Wonogiri** which, as with most of the south coast regencies, remains largely unvisited by tourists.

Kartasura

Ten kilometres to the west of Solo lies the ancient city of **Kartasura**, the former capital of the Mataram kingdom, founded by Amangkurat II in 1677 after his uncle, **Puger**, had appropriated the old court at Plered for himself. Thanks to the complete removal of the court to Solo by Pakubuwono II, there is little to see here except the former kraton's massive old **brick walls** which today encircle a graveyard (daily 4.30am–11pm; donation – Rp5000 seems sufficient). Double-decker buses from the junction of Jalan Wahidin and Jalan Riyadi in central Solo head west to Kartasura every ten minutes (Rp1000). The walls are about 1km to the south of the main Kartasura–Solo road; jump off at the "Kraton" road sign and walk or take a becak the rest of the way.

Two kilometres south of Kartasura lay an even older capital, **Pajang**, home of the embryonic Mataram dynasty in the early sixteenth century, but nothing of it now remains.

Sangiran

The unassuming little village of **SANGIRAN**, 18km north of Solo, ranks as one of the most important archeological sites in Central Java. One million years ago, Sangiran was the home of **Pithecantropus Erectus**, or **Java man** as he's more commonly known. His remains – a few fragments of jawbone – were discovered by the German paleontologist Dr G.H.R. von Koenigswald in 1936, following excavations by Eugene Dubois (see p.1033) in 1891. Until human bones over 2.5 million years old were discovered in Kenya's Rift Valley,

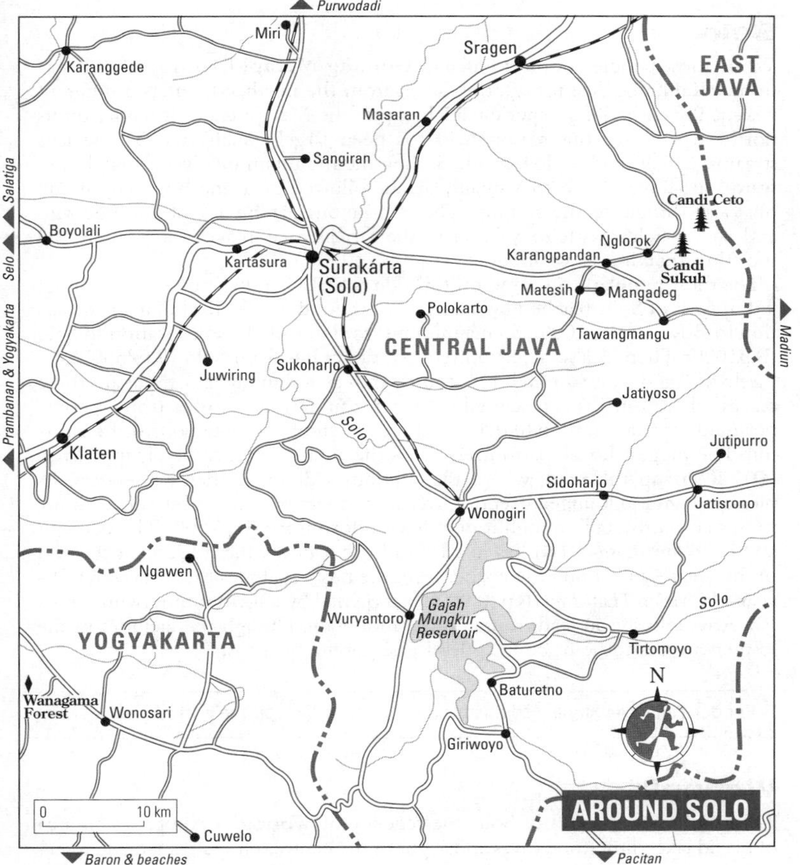

Koenigswald's discoveries were the oldest hominid remains ever found, and the first to support Darwin's theory of evolution. Many scientists of the day even suggested that Java man might have been the so-called "missing link", the creature supposedly providing the evolutionary connection between anthropoid apes and modern man.

Plenty of other fossils were unearthed here, including the four-metre-long tusk of a mastodon. These discoveries, along with replicas of Java man's cranium (the real skulls are in Bandung), are housed in Sangiran's single-room **museum** (daily 8am–5pm; Rp1000), where a life-size diorama tries to bring to life Java man's world. None of the museum's captions is in English, though you can buy an English-language brochure (Rp5000). Another prehistoric site in the area is **Miri**, 10km to the north of Sangiran off the main road to Purwodadi, although the museum is smaller and less informative than Sangiran's.

To get to Sangiran, take a Damri or BERSERI bus from Solo's Jalan Slamet Riyadi to Kalijambe (Rp1000), then either wait for a yellow angkuta (Rp1000) or hire an ojek (Rp5000) to take you to the village.

Selo

While most people choose to ascend **Gunung Merapi** from Yogya's hill station at Kaliurang (see p.217), the ascent from the north side offers a different yet equally enthralling experience. The lip of the Merapi crater is higher on its northern side; for this reason Selo has been largely unaffected by the lava streams, which tend to flow south. Scaling the mountain involves a straightforward four-hour **climb** to a small plateau, followed by a one-hour slog uphill on loose shingle to the summit. The continuous patchwork of volcanic hills and paddy-fields, with Yogyakarta in the far distance, makes for possibly the most breathtaking view on Java.

The most popular base camp on this side is **SELO**, a dusty one-horse village 43km west of Solo, reached by taking a westbound bus from the Tirtonadi station to Boyolali (Rp1000), then a minibus from outside Boyolali station to Selo (Rp1000). There is also a very infrequent direct bus from Solo (Rp2500).

Selo village is not so much of a tourist trap as Kaliurang, but there are three places where tourists can stay, all of which can arrange **guides** (three people per guide maximum; Rp40,000 for the day's climb) to take you to the summit. The biggest **hotel**, patronized by all the tour groups, is the *Agung Merapi* (❷), 200m up the road, where the minibuses disgorge their passengers. Its pleasant bamboo lounge/reception area is let down by some substandard, dingy rooms and surly staff, though it does have a dormitory (Rp7500). The decrepit and basic *Jaya Losmen* (❶) lies just 100m further down the hill, and at the end of the village, just round the corner from the bus stop, hides the marvellous 25-year-old *Melati Homestay* (Rp20,000). It is owned by a former mountain guide, Pak Arto, whose son leads tours up the mountain. Though the facilities in the losmen are basic, the price includes a nasi goreng breakfast.

For details of climbing the southern side of Gunung Merapi, see p.217.

Wonogiri

Thirty kilometres south of Solo, the regency of **Wonogiri** comprises an area of placid lakes, limestone caves and, right in the centre, a huge man-made reservoir. It was originally part of the territory given to Mangkunegoro in 1757 as part of the peace deal with the VOC (see p.241). **WONOGIRI TOWN** is the capital, a hilly, tree-lined place with little to offer the average tourist, though there is an imposing black-stone **heirloom tower** on the road to Solo, 6km west of Wonogiri. The tower was built during Mangkunegoro's reign and holds sacred relics from his court; every year, in the Javanese month of Suro, they are taken out and washed in the **Gajah Mungkur Reservoir** (daily 7am–6pm; Rp600), an 83-square-kilometre freshwater lake formed when the Kali Solo was dammed near its source. To get there, catch one of the frequent minibuses from Wonogiri station (Rp1000). A lot of controversy surrounded the building of this dam, as an estimated sixty thousand villagers were moved to accommodate the project. Today the reservoir serves as a water **fun park** for locals, with jet skis (Rp20,000 for 15min) and motorboats (Rp30,000 for 1hr) for rent. This region is also popular with local hikers and trekkers, who come to take advantage of one of the few wilderness spots in Java. A small information booth by the park's entrance has details of walks in the area.

Gunung Lawu

Pine-crowned **Gunung Lawu** (3265m), a two-hour drive due east of Solo, is one of the largest volcanoes on Java. It's also one of the least active, and its placid nature has tempted a few religions over the years to build temples on its forested slopes. Over ten such sites stand on the mountain's upper reaches, of which two, **Sukuh** and **Ceto**, have been restored to their former glory.

The temples are usually visited on a day-trip from Solo, but the area deserves more time if you can afford it. In particular, the mountain provides perfect conditions for **hiking**; the gradients are mainly undemanding and the air, particularly on the upper slopes, is cool and refreshing. Despite the whine of the cicadas, the chatter of tea-pickers and the distant noise from isolated villages, the whole mountain is imbued with a soothing sense of stillness and peace.

Tawangmangu, a hill resort on Lawu's southwestern slopes, is the best place to stay. The main transport hub in the area is **Karangpandan**, 12km back towards Solo from Tawangmangu, and 45 minutes by bus from Solo on a twisting mountain road, past a large stone statue of Semar, Indonesia's favourite *Mahabharata* character. From Karangpandan, there are frequent buses towards the temples and the other nearby attractions; ojek are also available to all the sites, but their prices are often ridiculously high.

Tawangmangu

The mountain village of **TAWANGMANGU** has a pleasant climate and features a busy fruit market and a forty-metre waterfall, **Grojogan Sewu** (8am–4.30pm; Rp1500), at its northern end. Tawangmangu spreads over one square kilometre, from the bus station in the south up to the waterfall. An **angkuta** (Rp500) from the bus station describes a loop around the town, driving right past the waterfall.

Accommodation is situated mostly along the main road on the ascent up Mount Sewu. Note that room prices double at weekends at most of the hotels. *Wisma Yanti*, Jl Raya Lawu 65 (Ⓣ0271/697056; ❷) is among the cheapest, with a range of rooms. It's rather run down, which is a shame as the old Dutch building could be charming if it was renovated. Further up the hill is the *Wisma Lumayan*, Jl Raya Lawu 10, which is a definite step up from the *Wisma Yanti* with a choice from simple to larger and more comfortable rooms (Ⓣ0271/697481; ❷–❸). *Pondok Indah*, Jl Raya Lawu 22, is a well-run hotel; each room has a sitting area, hot water and TV (Ⓣ0271/697024; ❸). The *Pondok Garuda*, Jalan Raya Tawangmangu, offers panoramic views of the valley below, and all rooms come with bathroom and satellite TV (Ⓣ0271/697294; ❷–❹). The grandest hotel in town is the *Komajaya Komaratih* at Jalan Lawu Kav. 150–151, a few metres from the turning to the waterfall. It offers good rooms, a reasonable restaurant, a swimming pool and tennis courts (Ⓣ0271/697125; ❺).

Directly opposite the *Komajaya* is the *Rumah Makan Bangun Trisno*, which serves simple Indonesian dishes. Otherwise, try the cheap and friendly *Sapto Argo*, opposite the *Wisma Lumayan*.

Candi Sukuh

Situated 910m up the forested western slopes of Gunung Lawu, **Candi Sukuh** (daily 6.15am–4.30pm; Rp1500) is one of the most interesting of Java's classical temples. Catch a bus from Karangpandan bound for Kubening and hop off at **Nglorok** village (Rp1000), where you buy your ticket for the temple. From here, you can rent an ojek (Rp5000) for the steep two-kilometre journey.

Walking on Lawu

It's advisable to start a **trek** on Lawu as early as you can, before the sun becomes too fierce. In the morning there are also more field-workers about, who can help you if you get lost. It's possible to walk all the way from Candi Ceto to Candi Sukuh, and from there to the waterfall at Tawangmangu in around five hours. However, there's not enough time to do this as a day-trip from Solo, as it can take up to four hours just to get to Ceto, and the last bus back to Solo leaves Tawangmangu at 5pm. Day-trippers should thus consider missing out Candi Ceto and joining the trail at Candi Sukuh for the final leg to the waterfall.

The walk **between Ceto and Sukuh** is a pleasant three-hour ramble, passing first through large fields of vegetables and summer fruits, then under the branches of the pine forest shrouding Lawu's summit. The path begins 200m below Ceto, where a small track branches left from the road towards the fields. This path is very difficult to follow, and you will probably need to ask the workers in the field for directions (*Di mana Candi Sukuh?*). After about an hour, you arrive at the **forest**, where again you will probably need help in finding the correct path. From this point on, the trail is straightforward.

The two-hour stroll **from Sukuh to the waterfall** at Tawangmangu, over gently undulating fields and foothills, is the easiest and most rewarding walk on Lawu. The trail is fairly easy to follow, although 1km from Sukuh the road splits; a signpost points the way to **Candi Palanggatan**. The fifteenth-century *candi* itself is nothing more than a collection of mossy boulders under a tree, but the neighbouring village is pretty and the inhabitants can point out a short-cut through fields that leads back onto the main path. After skirting a few hills, crossing the occasional stream and passing through the villages of **Plalar** and neighbouring **Goyong**, you eventually reach the forty-metre waterfall.

Sukuh was built in around 1430, though nobody knows exactly who constructed it, to whom it was dedicated, or why. It is thought that the temple was abandoned about a hundred years later, when the great Islamic conversion of Java occurred. Sukuh was discovered in 1815 and a little restoration work was done in 1917, but it wasn't until 1989 that the temple was returned to something approaching its former splendour.

The west-facing temple is built on three low terraces, and fronted by the remains of a small ceremonial gateway; three large turtles, their backs flattened to form three circular dais, stand on the third terrace, guarding the entrance to the temple proper. A grey stone pyramid with its top lopped off, Sukuh bears a remarkable resemblance to the Mayan temples of Central America. A set of steps leads up from the western side of the temple to the **roof**, from where you can enjoy marvellous views over the valley below.

Although Sukuh is unadorned, lying all around is a veritable orgy of semi-explicit statuary, with a few displaying fairly impressive genitalia – it would appear that Sukuh was linked to some sort of **fertility cult**. There are also plenty of grotesque **bas reliefs** that appear to have been lifted straight from a comic book. Most of these depict scenes from the life of **Bima**, an incarnation of Shiva in the *Mahabharata*, who became the centre of a religious cult in the fifteenth century.

Candi Ceto

Candi Ceto, lying 1400m up the northern flanks of Gunung Lawu, is the youngest classical temple on Java. To get there, catch a bus from Karangpandan to the village of **Kalbening** (Rp1000), from where it's a steep two-hour climb

(5km) up the mountainside. The temple was built around 1740, during the death throes of the Majapahit empire. It might just be the isolated location, or perhaps the mist that frequently shrouds the terraces, but Candi Ceto has a mystical, almost eerie atmosphere, an effect that's heightened when Hindu worshippers from Bali pay a visit and perform their chanting in the main temple.

Ceto stands on ten narrow terraces stretching up the mountainside, beyond a large monumental gateway, similar in style to those found on Bali. The first few terraces beyond the gate lack decoration, although you'll notice a **giant bat** carved on the paving on the fourth level. The **bat** carries on its back a **large turtle**, which in turn carries crabs, lizards and frogs on its shell. The upper levels have been filled with a few open-sided wooden pendopos. On the top three terraces there are also a number of small kiosks sheltering a variety of icons, including one of Bima, as well as yet another large linga. The main temple, with the same pyramidal shape as Sukuh, stands on the very top terrace.

Mangadeg hill

Mangadeg hill, 8km southeast of Karangpandan, is home to two **royal grave** sites, rarely visited by tourists. The first set of graves you come to is the Suharto family mausoleum, **Astana Giribangun** (daily 7am–5pm; free), a large wooden pendopo modelled on the royal graveyard at Imogiri (see p.214); the plots for every member of the family have already been marked out. Crowds still gather round the grave of Mme Suharto, who died in 1995, to pay homage with rose petals and prayers. Just a few hundred metres above the Suhartos, reached by a spiralling path, is the final resting place of the members of the **Mangkunegoro dynasty** (daily 7am–5pm; donations of Rp5000–10,000 compulsory), of which Mme Suharto was a part. The Mangkunegoros are the only royal family of Yogya or Solo not buried at Imogiri. The tombs of the first eight sultans are found here, and attract their own set of devotees.

To get to Mangadeg hill, catch a bus from Karangpandan to Matesih (ask for Makam Suharto; Rp1000), then an ojek (Rp5000) or very infrequent bemo (Rp2000) from there. The drive up affords some stunning views over the rice fields below, with Lawu dominating the background, and on the way souvenir sellers line the road offering visitors the chance to stock up on Suharto memorabilia.

Semarang and around

SEMARANG is the capital of Central Java and, with a population approaching 1.5 million, the country's fifth largest city. It's a typically big and bustling Indonesian metropolis, a **commercial centre** rather than a tourist town. Visually, the city resembles a scaled-down version of Jakarta, with its wide, tree-lined streets and muddy canals, between which a surfeit of ugly shopping centres, unlovely office blocks, imposing international hotels and tacky fast-food shacks have appeared. But the buildings and roads are neither as huge nor as numerous as Jakarta's, and the levels of noise and pollution are similarly reduced – on the whole, the city is more attractive and unhurried than the capital.

Manuscripts from the ninth century refer to a small port called **Pergota**, which seems to correspond to the location of present-day Semarang, and suggest that the city was originally an entrepôt harbour for the Hindu kingdoms of the interior. For centuries, the port remained relatively insignificant while the neighbouring harbours at Jepara and Kudus grew into the centres of the island's first Islamic empire. In the seventeenth century, however, Jepara and Kudus began to slowly clog up with silt washed down from the volcanoes, and Semarang soon became the biggest port on the north coast. It continued to grow under the Dutch, after having been given to the **VOC** in lieu of debts by the Mataram sultan **Amangkurat I** in 1677. The decision by the Dutch to install the **governor** of Java's Northeast Province here was further evidence that the city now enjoyed a pre-eminent status on the north coast.

Today, Semarang stretches all the way from the silted coastline in the north right across the flat coastal plain and into the foothills of **Gunung Ungaran** to the south. As with Jakarta, the city's charms lie not in the modern parts of the town but in the small pockets that have thus far evaded the attentions of the developers. These include the **Chinese quarter**, the largest in Java, which provides the city with some much-needed colour and vibrancy, and the eerily quiet former **Dutch commercial district**. There's also **Gedung Batu**, one of the most important and intriguing Chinese temples on Java, in the south-western suburbs of the city.

Though you can see pretty much all the city has to offer in a day or two, Semarang is the best base for exploring northern Central Java, with excellent train and bus connections to the rest of the Pasisir (the northern coastal region of Java), as well as south to Yogya. The batik town of **Pekalongan**, along with the ancient ports of **Demak**, **Kudus** and **Jepara**, once the most important harbours on Java and still amongst the wealthiest cities on the island, are all within a two-hour bus ride from Semarang, while the countryside to the south of the city holds a number of sights worth exploring, including the delightful Hindu temples of **Gedung Songo** in the foothills of Mount Ungaran.

Orientation, arrival and information

For the most part, Semarang is a flat city, which only begins to rise towards the south as it climbs the first, shallow inclines of Gunung Ungaran. Two canals, the **Banjer Kanal Barat** and **Timur**, demarcate the western and eastern limits respectively of the city centre. Most of the action takes place in a triangular area formed by three major hubs: **Simpang Lima**, the heart of the modern part of Semarang in the south of the city; the **Tugu Muda roundabout**, in the west; and, on the edge of the Chinese quarter in the northeast of downtown, **Johar market** and the nearby **post office**. Once you have grasped the relative positions of these three hubs and the three roads that connect them – **Jalan Pemuda**, which links Tugu Muda with Pasar Johar, **Jalan Pandanaran**, which runs between Simpang Lima and Tugu Muda, and **Gajah Mada**, which heads north from Simpang Lima and bisects Jalan Pemuda a few hundred metres to the west of the post office – finding your way around the city should present few problems.

Arrival

All of Indonesia's major national airlines operate flights into Semarang's **Jend A. Yani Airport**, 5km to the west of central Semarang. There is no direct bus service into town, although if you walk 1km south from the airport you can catch bus #2 which travels east via Tugu Muda and Jalan Imam Bonjol to the bus station (Rp1000). Alternatively, a taxi will set you back about Rp12,000.

Semarang has two **train** stations. Most trains stop at the **Tawang station** in the heart of the old Dutch quarter on Jalan Merak, from where a becak to Jalan Pemuda should cost no more than Rp3000. The *Tawang Mas* and *Tawang Jaya* from Jakarta terminate at the **Poncol station** on Imam Bonjol, which is with-

in walking distance of many inexpensive hotels. A few trains call at both stations, including the *Bangunkarta* (which travels from Jombang via Solo and Semarang to Jakarta), and the *Pandanaran* from Solo.

Arrive in Semarang by public bus and you'll be deposited at the **Terboyo bus terminal**, about 3km to the east of the town centre. Bus #2 (Rp1000) travels from the bus terminal past Pasar Johar and down Jalan Pemuda. Travelling in the opposite direction, catch one of the buses that pass by the *Hotel Oewa Asia*. **Private minibuses** usually drop passengers off by the junction of Jalan Let Jend Haryono and Jalan H. Agus Salim, about 1km east of Pasar Johar. From there, you can walk or take a becak (Rp2000).

Finally, those who arrive by Pelni **ferry** from Banjarmasin, Pontianak or Kumai on Kalimantan, or from Jakarta's Tanjung Priok harbour, should hire a becak to take them from the port into town, a distance of 2km (Rp3000).

Information

There are no fewer than four **tourist offices** in Semarang. By far the most useful is the provincial tourist office, **Dinas Parawisata** (Mon–Thurs 7am–2pm, Fri 7–11am, Sat 7am–1pm; ⓣ024/607184), in what is known as the PRPP zone, an industrial area to the northwest of the city centre. Of the four, this one has the most knowledgeable staff, as well as the widest collection of maps and brochures, covering the whole of the Central Javan province. To get there, catch one of the many PRPP-bound buses from Pasar Bulu, then walk east to the first set of traffic lights; the office is 100m to the south of the junction in Blok BB, Jalan Maduroko.

The most central tourist office in the city is at the ground-floor desk of the **Plaza Simpang Lima**. The third tourist office hides in the former reception of the old zoo at **Raden Saleh Park**, Jl Srivijaya 29 (ⓣ024/311220); nobody here speaks English. Finally, there's a small office at the **airport**. These three have approximately the same opening times as the Dinas Parawisata.

City transport

With the searing heat and the city's attractions so widely dispersed, Semarang is not a place for aimless wandering. Fortunately, the **public transport** network is fairly comprehensive, though the city's one-way system means buses and angkuta often alter their routes on the return journey.

Fares on the big blue-and-white **city buses** are a flat Rp1000; bus #2 is the most useful route, running from the bus station to the Kalibenting roundabout via Jalan Pemuda. For most of your time in Semarang you'll probably be using the orange **angkuta** vans, which buzz around the city beeping their horns at bystanders. Like the city buses, they charge a flat Rp1000. Nearly all Semarang's angkuta begin and end their journeys at Simpang Lima. **Becak** are as common in Semarang as they are in the rest of Central Java. They aren't allowed to use many of the major roads and have to take more circuitous routes, so it may be quicker to walk. **Taxis** mostly congregate around the big hotels on Simpang Lima, and outside the post office; alternatively, call Atlas (ⓣ024/315833) or Puri Kencana (ⓣ024/288291).

Accommodation

Semarang's **hotels**, like the city itself, are geared more towards businesspeople than tourists. Most of the hotels tend to be in the medium or expensive price bracket, although there are a number of cheaper options on Jalan Imam Bonjol, the street to the north of Jalan Pemuda near the train station. A fan is fairly essential in this sweaty city, and it's worth paying a little extra for one. Free tea and coffee, usually left outside your room in a plastic jug, come as standard in virtually every hotel.

Blambangan Jl Pemuda 23 ⓣ024/3541649. A clean hotel, if a little threadbare in places, 300m west of Pasar Johar. The less expensive rooms have fans, the rest have air-con, while the suites also have TV. Parking facilities and a free photocopied map of central Semarang are two of the advantages. A step up from the other budget hotels – but then so is the price. ❷

Ciputra Simpang Lima ⓣ024/8449888, ⓕ8447888, ⓔmailsmg@hotelciputra.com. One of the best hotels in town, overlooking the main square, with all the facilities you'd expect from a four-star hotel, including a good restaurant, cake shop and pool. The buffet breakfasts are excellent, while the bar is popular with expats. ❻

Graha Santika Jl Pandanaran 116–120 ⓣ024/8413115, ⓕ8413113. Four-star hotel just off Simpang Lima. All rooms have minibar, TV and in-house films; there's also a gymnasium, swimming pool and a very good 24hr café. ❻

Grand Candi Jl Sisinamangaraja 16 ⓣ024/8416222, ⓕ8415111 ⓔgchotel@indosat.net.id. A new and luxurious hotel to the southeast of town, located just above the Patra Jasa. Its four-star facilities rival those of the *Ciputra* and *Patra Jasa*. ❻

Jaya Jl M.T. Haryono 87 ⓣ024/3543604. A cavernous, rather run-down hotel, convenient for the minibus station. The rooms are airy with high ceilings, and most have en-suite bathrooms. ❷

Kesambi Hijau Jl Kesambi 7 ⓣ024/8312642. Another excellent mid-range hotel in the foothills of Candi, 2km south of Simpang Lima. The hotel is shaped like a traditional Javanese house from the nineteenth century, but with a 1920s Art Deco interior, and a terrace in the garden affording beautiful views of the valley below. The bungalows, with TV and fridge, are especially good value. ❸–❺

Metro Jl H. Agus Salim 2–4 ⓣ024/3547371, ⓕ3510863. Long-established three-star hotel, once the best in town but now a little faded, opposite Johar market. The Health and Hair Studio in the basement includes a sauna, whirlpool, exercise room and barber, and there's even a department store. ❺

Oewa Asia Jl Kol Soegiono 12 ⓣ024/3542547. A traditional favourite with Western travellers, sited near the post office. The rooms, fan or air-con, are a little basic for the price, although breakfast is included; for Rp5000 more, you can have a TV too. All rooms have an intercom for room service. ❷

Patra Jasa Jalan Sisingamangaraja ⓣ024/8414141 or 831441, ⓕ8314448, ⓔhotelpatra@semarang.wasantara.net.id. A resort-style four-star hotel, older than the *Ciputra* and *Grand Candi*, but very popular in its class, overlooking the town about 15 minutes away. Very good facilities, including a tennis court, swimming pool and spa. ❻

Queen (aka **Quirin** or **Quirien**), Jl Gajah Mada 44–52 ⓣ024/3547063, ⓕ3547341. A rather trendy hotel, with designer lampshades in the lobby and local modern art hanging from the walls of the café. The atmosphere is pleasant and relaxed, and the rooms come with TV, air-con and hot water. ❹

Raden Patah Jl Jend Suprapto 48 ⓣ024/3511328. A very good budget choice, east of the Gereja Blenduk. The fully renovated building is over fifty years old and has a dignified atmosphere. The rooms are light and airy; those in the west wing are newer, more attractive and very good value. ❷

Singapore Jl Imam Bonjol 12 ⓣ024/3543757. A reasonable budget option near the *Oewa Asia*. The staff at this large hotel are very friendly, and there are plenty of sofas and chairs in the sociable lobby area. Unfortunately, the rooms are rudimentary and graffiti-strewn, and the wooden shuttered windows offer little protection against the noise outside. ❷

Surya Jl Imam Bonjol 28 ⓣ024/3540355, ⓕ3544250. An attractive marble-tiled hotel, just 100m down from the *Singapore*. Air-con, hot water and TV come as standard. ❹

The City

Semarang's sights are grouped around the three major hubs of the town centre: Tugu Muda, Pasar Johar and Simpang Lima. **Tugu Muda** has been the administrative centre of Semarang since the eighteenth century, and is still surrounded by some important government buildings from the Dutch era. The area around **Pasar Johar** was the main commercial district and remains one of the liveliest parts. It's also the home of the city's huge Chinese population, and a stroll through the alleyways of the vibrant **Chinese quarter** is one of the most rewarding ways to spend an afternoon here. **Simpang Lima** is the modern centre of town, a large grassy square surrounded by big hotels, shopping centres and, in the northwest corner, the city's biggest mosque, the **Mesjid Baiturahman**.

Travelling by **public transport** between these three hubs is fairly simple, though the one-way system means it's far easier to travel clockwise around the centre of town. Bus #2 travels east along Jalan Pemuda from Tugu Muda to Pasar Johar. To get from Pasar Johar to Simpang Lima, listen for the cry of "Peterongan" or "Tegalwareng" from the angkuta queuing from the northwest corner of the market. (For the return trip, catch angkuta #7 or #16 from outside the Mesjid Baiturahman, which travels straight up Gajah Mada to Jalan Pemuda.) Finally, around the corner to the south of the mesjid, on Jalan Pandanaran, angkuta #8 pulls in to pick up customers wishing to travel west to Tugu Muda and on to Karung Ayu.

Tugu Muda and Jalan Pemuda

The major transport hub of **Tugu Muda** is surrounded by well-preserved, austere Dutch buildings, relics from a time when this was the administrative centre of Semarang. At its centre stands a giant stone **candle-shaped sculpture** dedicated to the memory of the two thousand local youths who died fighting the Japanese in 1945. Locals often refer to this roundabout as **Pasar Bulu**, after the market that stands to the west. This ramshackle, rather dingy two-tier bazaar deals mainly in food and household goods, is always lively, and offers a welcome retreat from the sun. Moving clockwise around the roundabout from here, to the north, facing Pasar Bulu, is the white-painted home of the **Dutch resident** Nicolaas Hartingh, a gleaming eighteenth-century construction that has now been converted into a teachers' academy. To the west of the roundabout is **Lawang Sewu** (Thousand Doors), named for its many doors and windows. Constructed in 1913, it was once the offices of the Dutch train company and was later appropriated by the Japanese army during the war. Opposite, to the southwest of the roundabout, stands the former Dutch law court. Today the building houses Semarang's military museum, the **Museum Perjuangan Mandala Bhakti** (Tues–Thurs 8am–2pm, Fri 8am–11.30am, Sat 8am–12.30pm, Sun 8am–1pm).

From Tugu Muda, heading northeast, is **Jalan Pemuda**, the colonial city's main boulevard. At over 2km long, Jalan Pemuda remains a wide and handsome thoroughfare, with huge government buildings and imposing steel-and-glass offices dominating the western end, while the eastern stretch is flanked by small terraced shops and restaurants. At the northeastern end of Jalan Pemuda stands the impressive **post office**, another colonial building, dating from the beginning of the twentieth century.

The old city and Chinatown

Just across the road from the post office lies **Pasar Johar**, the most atmospheric and boisterous part of Semarang. The **market**, a tangle of claustrophobic covered alleyways punctuated by several wide dirt tracks running north–south, stands over the site of the former alun-alun. The nearby **Mesjid Agung**, occupying the traditional position to the west of the square, was once the city's major mosque; it's still known as the Grand Mosque, even though it has now been eclipsed in size and importance by the modern **Mesjid Baiturahman** on **Simpang Lima**. Non-Muslims are forbidden to enter either mosque.

Sandwiched between two of the city's many canals to the northeast of Pasar Johar lies the former **Dutch commercial district**, once the throbbing heart of the city, but which has long since disintegrated into a dusty, deserted area of crumbling offices and dilapidated warehouses. The canals themselves were once the major arteries transporting goods to the warehouses from the **harbour** – which is a good place to begin a tour of this quarter; you will probably need to catch a becak to get there.

One kilometre due south of the harbour is the solid, white-walled **Gereja Blenduk** (Domed Church), now known as the Gereja Immanuel, on Jalan Jend Suprapto, the only building in this quarter that really shouldn't be missed. Built in 1753, it's the second oldest church in Java (after Jakarta's Gereja Sion), and inside there's a wonderful (but now defunct) Baroque **organ**; a modern organ hides behind the facade.

The large and busy Jalan Let Jend Haryono runs from the north to the south of the city. Walking south down the road, past the junction with Jalan H. Agus Salim, the narrow entrances on the west (left-hand) side lead to the **Chinese quarter**, a suffocating kampung of twisting paths and terraced multi-level shacks festooned with drying laundry and caged songbirds. The most striking building in this area, the eighteenth-century **Tay Kak Sie Temple**, lies tucked away on Gang Lombok on the east bank of the canal. The temple was built in 1772 and is dedicated to both Confucius and the goddess of mercy, **Kuan Yin**. Garish red amongst the dull, grey shantytown buildings of the rest of the area, it contains many bronze and gilt figures, apparently scattered at random.

Out from the centre

Within a five-kilometre radius of the town centre are a number of attractions, many of which are very popular with local tourists. **Gedung Batu**, perhaps the most famous Chinese temple on Java, is the most interesting of these, while the **Nyona Meneer jamu factory** provides visitors with a fascinating insight into Javanese herbal medicine. The **PRPP** complex in the north of the city plays host to an **amusement park**, the **Puri Maerokoco** (a version of Jakarta's Taman Mini), a **beach** (of sorts) and a **Marine Recreation Park**. On the way to the PRPP is the highly recommended **Ronggowarsito Museum**, one of the best in the province.

Gedung Batu

Gedung Batu (daily dawn–dusk; free) lies 5km southwest of the city centre on the west bank of the Banjer Kanal Barat. To get there, catch city bus #2 from Jalan Pemuda to Karung Ayu, then take one of the dilapidated Daihatsus (Rp1000) that run south along the canal. The deep-red Gedung Batu (Stone Building) temple is dedicated to **Zhenghe**, a fifteenth-century envoy of the Chinese Ming dynasty, whose job took him to most of Southeast Asia, India and the East African coast. It consists of four shrines standing roughly shoulder to shoulder at the foot of a steep, wooded hill, and is built around a cave in which Zhenghe supposedly meditated after landing on Java for the first time in 1406. As you approach from the north, a number of buildings partially obscure the temple, including a wayang theatre right outside the main gates, and a large platform nearby for the annual Jaran Sam Po festival. Zhenghe's **cave** lies at the rear of the third shrine from the left as you face the temple. Next door, in the westernmost shrine, a monk offers to read your fortune (in Mandarin only).

Unusually, Muslims also worship at this site – Zhenghe was a follower of Islam, as was his helmsman **Kyai Juru Mudi Dampoawang**, whose grave lies a little to the left of Zhenghe's cave. As two of the first Muslims to visit Java, their trip probably paved the way for the conversion of Java to Islam over a century later. The easternmost shrine, to the left of Kyai's grave, combines elements of both faiths: a red anchor to symbolize the seaborne arrival of the Islamic faith (although the anchor is actually from a Dutch VOC ship), neatly juxtaposed with a statue of Confucius.

The Nyona Meneer jamu factory

The **Nyona Meneer jamu factory** at Jl Kaligawe 4 (Mon–Fri 8am–5pm; free), 500m west of the bus station, provides an excellent introduction to **jamu**, the Javanese version of **herbal medicine**. To get there, catch the station-bound bus from outside the *Oewa Asia* hotel, and get out when you see the large portrait of Nyona Meneer above the front entrance of the factory. The Nyona Meneer Jamu Corporation is one of the biggest manufacturers in Indonesia. What started off as a one-woman operation in the early years of the twentieth century is now a vast international concern employing over two thousand people, with shops in every high street in Java, sending remedies to New Zealand, Holland, Saudi Arabia and Japan. A factory guide will take you upstairs to a **museum** recounting the life and times of Nyona Meneer, using old photographs and a number of her personal effects (including the mixing bowl she used to conjure up many of her potions), as well as large displays of herbs and Nyona Meneer goods. If you ask nicely, you may also be given a tour of the **factory** itself, which is on the ground floor. This is where many of the company's 250 lotions and potions are produced. For men, there are virility pills and impotence cures, while women can choose from a range of remedies designed to counteract the ravages of time, such as *tresanih*, which apparently "keeps wife attractive to husband, to maintain husband and wife intimacy". Whatever your problem or ailment, it's not uncommon for the guide to present visitors with a little box of assorted products at the end of the tour.

Pekan Raya Promosi Pembangunan (PRPP)

Lying right on the coast to the northwest of Semarang, the **PRPP** is a fairly soulless, government-planned commercial district and the site of Semarang's huge annual trade fair. To get to the PRPP, catch one of the frequent buses (Rp1000) from Pasar Bulu. The biggest attraction at the PRPP is the **Puri Maerokoco** (daily 7am–6pm; Sun & holidays Rp1500, all other times Rp1000), which lies 500m to the west of the PRPP bus stop. This is Semarang's version of Jakarta's Taman Mini, a somewhat tatty theme park housing a brief introduction to the cultures and crafts of Central Java. The 35 full-size houses inside the park, one for each regency in Central Java, have been designed and built using the traditional methods of that regency. Each has been placed at the appropriate position on an island shaped to resemble Central Java, in the middle of a small lake. A bridge on the northern side of the lake connects the island to the "mainland".

Signposted to the northeast of the bus stop is the overpriced **Marina Recreation Park** (daily 8am–5pm; Rp7500), boasting a large swimming pool. Another kilometre to the east lies the awful **Tanjung Mas Beach** (dawn–dusk; Rp1000), a wasteland of mud flats, food shacks and coarse heathland by the sea, popular with Sunday day-trippers from the city.

On the way back to Semarang, it's worth hopping off the bus as it rejoins Jalan Sugiyopranoto and catching a #2 bus west to Kalibanteng and the **Ronggowarsito Museum**, Jalan Abdulrachman (Mon–Thurs 8am–2pm, Fri 8–11am, Sat 8am–12.30pm, Sun 8am–1pm; Rp500). This well-organized museum is the largest in Central Java, and presents a chronological history of the province, including a detailed section on the Hindu-Buddhist empires, with a few stone statues and icons, as well as the usual overkill on the

Independence struggle. There are only a few captions in English, but guides are on hand (for a small fee).

Eating and drinking

Evenings in Semarang are considerably enlivened by the presence of **warung**, which set up at dusk around Simpang Lima and Pasar Johar. Semarang has a couple of culinary specialities, including *lumpiah*, a tasty vegetarian spring roll usually dripping with grease. Pasar Johar abounds with stalls where you can sample these for around Rp500 each. Typically for the north coast, *Murtabak* (savoury pancakes) are also popular here; at the southern end of Gajah Mada, right by Simpang Lima, a number of stalls sell these for Rp1500–10,000, depending on size and choice of filling, while another stall can be found in Pasar Johar.

The choice of good-quality restaurants in Semarang is disappointing, although, as you'd expect from a city with such a large Chinese population, there are some decent **Chinese restaurants** in the centre. Those hungering for a fix of Western **fast food** should head to the Simpang Lima, where there's a *Californian Fried Chicken* and a *McDonald's* at the Ciputra Mall and a *Pizza Hut* at the Plaza Simpang Lima. There's also a *Kentucky Fried Chicken*, 500m west of the Simpang Lima, at the junction of Jalan Pandanaran and Jalan M.H. Thamrin. For international cuisine, the restaurants in the *Ciputra* and *Grand Candi* hotels are good, but expensive by Semarang standards.

Gang Gang Sulldi Jalan Sudiharto. Glamorous Korean restaurant by the driveway to the *Green Guesthouse*. Expensive and delicious.
Pringgading Jl Pringgading 54. Tasty Chinese food – a little pricey, but with very good service.
Queen Coffee Shop *Queen Hotel*, Jl Gajah Mada 44–52. An excellent, mid-priced air-con retreat from the midday sun, serving a good range of Western fast food, ice-cold drinks and ice creams. Closes at 4pm.
Sari Medan Jalan Pemuda. At the eastern end of Jalan Pemuda. The best Padang food in Semarang, and reasonably priced too.
Sinar Laut Jalan Gajah Mada. Medium-priced Chinese restaurant next door to the marginally superior *Tio Ciu* (see below), with an extensive menu, including a wide range of seafood.
Tio Ciu Jalan Gajah Mada. A huge menu of Chinese food – much of it exotic – is the main attraction at this large medium-priced restaurant, although dishes are often unavailable.
Toko Oen Jl Pemuda 52. Almost a tourist attraction in its own right, this fifty-year-old Dutch restaurant serves some tasty Western food, including excellent cakes. Trophies from the Cannes food festival – pertinent reminders of its heyday of linen tablecloths and uniformed waiters – are proudly displayed. Mid-priced.

Nightlife and entertainment

For such a big town, **nightlife** in Semarang is fairly quiet. The favourite expat haunt is the bar in the *Hotel Ciputra*, while the *Ritzeky Pub* on Jalan Sinabung Buntu is another place to meet expats and play pool or darts; it also serves some good, filling Western food. The *Restaurant Odrowino* on Jalan J. A. Yani has a live band from 9pm to midnight. The *Metro Hotel*, Jl J.H. Agus Salim 2–4, houses the *Xanadu* disco, which is often rather empty and dull. The *MM* disco on Jalan Gajah Mada is livelier, especially at weekends, and attracts a younger crowd. Other than these options, there's little to do except go to the **movies** (see p.260) or play **billiards** (check out the hall above Pasar Johar.

Though Semarang isn't exactly a cultural hotbed, there are a couple of options if you want to see traditional **Javanese entertainment**. The Raden Saleh Park at Jl Srivijaya 29 (☎024/3311220) hosts a special outdoor **wayang kulit** performance every 35 days, on each Thursday Wage night of the Javanese calendar (from 7pm). The Sobokarti Folk Theatre, next to the Yogya Plaza on Jl Dr Cipto 31–33, also stages a wayang kulit performance every Saturday night (8–11pm). If you're in the vicinity on Saturday morning, pop in to see the local children being taught the basics of puppeteering. A third venue for wayang kulit is the RRI at Jl J. A. Yani 134–136 (☎024/3316330), which holds a lengthy (8pm–4am) performance on the first Saturday of every month. If you'd rather see live action rather than puppets, there's a free performance (8pm–1am) of the popular folk melodrama **ketoprak** every Monday night in the fields of the Raden Saleh Park.

Listings

Airlines Bouraq, Jl Gajah Mada 16 ☎024/3515921, Garuda/Merpati, Jl Gajah Mada 11 ☎024/3517137; Mandala, Bangkok Plaza, Jalan MT Haryono ☎024/3444736.
Airport enquiries ☎024/3608735.
Banks and exchange BCA (Mon–Fri 8am–3.30pm) at Jalan Pemuda offers reasonable rates and an ATM which accepts Visa and Mastercard. The BDN, 50m further down Jalan Pemuda, offers a very competitive rate, but only accepts Citicorps US dollar travellers' cheques.
Bookshops Gramedia in Jalan Pandanaran has a good selection of books in English, including guidebooks and maps. Otherwise, Gunung Agung in the Ciputra Mall, just behind *Hotel Ciputra*, offers a reasonable selection in English.
Buses Most door-to-door bus companies are gathered around the north end of Jalan Let Jend Haryono, including Patas Tours, Jl Let Jend Haryono 47 (☎024/3544654), and Fortuna, Jl Let Jend Haryono 76 (☎024/3544848).
Cinema Studio 21, on the southwest corner of Simpang Lima; Manggala, Jl Gajah Mada 119; Admiral 21 on Jalan Kimangun, 200m north of Jalan J. A. Yani. All show current Hollywood movies.
Ferries The Pelni office is at Jl Mpu Tantular 25 (☎024/3555156), just over the canal from the GPO.
Hospital Saint Elizabeth Hospital, Jalan Kawi (☎024/3315345), is probably the most sophisticated; Tlogorejo Hospital, Jalan Ahmad Dahlan ☎024/8446000; William Booth Hospital, Jl Letjen S. Parman 5. All have staff who can speak some English.
Internet access Cyber Café, Jl Pemuda 4 (next to the main post office), open Mon–Sat 8am–10pm, Sun 8am–8pm.
Permits Research permits for the islands of Karimunjawa are available from the fourth floor of the Office of Nature Conservation (KSDA), Jalan Menteri Supeno, at the end of Gang 1 (Mon–Thurs 7am–2pm, Fri 7–11am; ☎024/3414750).
Film processing The Fuji Image Plaza, Jl Gajah Mada 3, is one of the biggest and most reliable in Semarang.
Post office Jl Pemuda 4. The poste restante counter is a hole in the wall on the eastern side of the building (daily 8am–4pm).
Shopping The best shopping centre is Ciputra Mall just behind *Hotel Ciputra*, which has a reasonable range of shops, including a good supermarket. The Batik Keris branch here offers a selection of batik and other handicrafts.
Swimming The best pool is probably the Marina Recreation Park (daily 8am–5pm; Rp5000). Alternatively, try asking at one of the big hotels; the *Graha Santika* and the *Patra Jasa* are open to non-guests for a charge.
Telephones The 24hr Telkom office is at Jl Jendro Suprapto 7, east of the GPO.
Travel agents Haryono Tours and Travel, Jl Pandanaran 37 ☎024/3444000; Nitour, Jl Indraprastha 97; Nusantara, Simpang Lima Plaza.

South of Semarang

The northern slopes of Gunung Ungaran offer a number of seldom-visited (yet charming) sights, which can be seen either on a day-trip from Semarang or as stopovers on the way to Yogya and the Kejawen region. Thirty kilometres south of the city lies the attractive little hill station of **Bandungan**. Just a few kilometres east of Bandungan, the Hindu temple complex of **Gedung Songo** provides a peaceful alternative to the overcrowded ruins at Prambanan, while 10km further south lies the bustling little market village of **Ambarawa**, the home of Java's train museum.

Bandungan

The small village of **BANDUNGAN**, 1000m up on the northern slopes of Gunung Ungaran, is the closest **hill-top retreat** to Semarang (Rp5000 for the 75min trip from the Terboyo terminal). At weekends, hundreds of city folk head to the hills to escape Semarang's heat – although even in Bandungan the afternoon temperatures are hot enough to melt the village's only tarmac road. As a result, the village tends to cater more for Indonesian holiday-makers than Western visitors. However, a few foreigners do make it here, as the village, with its green-carpeted hills, is one of the prettiest hill retreats in Central Java, and also makes a convenient base for visiting the nearby Gedung Songo temples.

Bandungan is little more than a number of hotels built round a fairly large daily agricultural market. It lies at the junction of three roads: one leads to Semarang, a second plummets down to Ambarawa, while a third heads southwest to the medium-sized town of Temanggung via the Gedung Songo. All the facilities (save for a place to change money) and **restaurants** are clustered around this junction where the buses drop you off. Despite its small size, the town still manages to cram in a recreation park (Rp1500, plus extra for swimming or tennis), massage parlour, tofu factory and flower market.

The best-value **hotel** here is the *Girimulyo* at Jl Gitungan 79a (Ⓣ0298/711175; ❷), a fifteen-minute hike up the very steep hill at the top of the village. The comfortable doubles have stained-glass windows, while the singles are adequate but less pleasant. One of the nicest places to stay is the colonial *Rawa Pening Pratama*, Jalan Bandungan Sumowono Raya (Ⓣ0298/711134; ❸), a few hundred metres west of Bandungan on the way to Gedung Songo. This cool and uncluttered colonial hotel has plenty of character, and the well-trimmed gardens (with pool and tennis courts) are perfect for relaxing in after a day's hiking. Hidden away up a steep road off Jalan Bandungan Sumowono is *Ananda Cottage*, Jalan Golak Kenteng Village (Ⓣ0298/791145; ❺), which offers stunning views towards Salatiga and stylish, if slightly worn accommodation. The most upmarket hotel in the village is *Nugraha Wisata*, Jl Bandungan Sumowono Raya Km 1 (Ⓣ0298/711501; ❺), with modern rooms, swimming pool and an Indonesian/Chinese restaurant. Note that at weekends and holiday times, hotels in Bandungan sometimes charge up to thirty percent more than the standard rates quoted above.

Gedung Songo

One of the finest archeological gems in Central Java, **Gedung Songo** (daily 6.15am–5.15pm; Rp1500) is a series of eighth-century **Hindu temples** on the slopes of **Gunung Ungaran**. To get here from Bandungan, catch a westbound bus (Rp1000) to the turn-off, 4km away, then an ojek for the final, steep 6km (Rp3000 up, Rp1500 on the downhill run). The temples are arranged around the sides of a ravine; it takes about two hours to walk around the entire site, or you can hire a **horse** from behind the ticket office (from Rp10,000). Turn up very early, bring a picnic (officially forbidden, but unpunished as long as you clear up after yourself) and make a day of it. Bring your swimsuit and a towel too, as it is possible to bathe in the hot **sulphurous spring** at the bottom of the ravine. Avoid weekends and you'll have the place pretty much to yourself.

The location of Gedung Songo is stunning. To the west loom the twin mountains Sumbing and Sundoro; to the south, perfectly symmetrical Gunung Merbabu, with the smoke-plumed summit of Gunung Merapi over its left shoulder. In the distance to the southeast, completing the volcanic crescent, towers slate-blue Gunung Lawu.

The name Gedung Songo (Nine Buildings) is a strange one – there are a lot more than nine buildings here. But the Javanese consider nine to be a propitious number, and have divided the temple groups accordingly. Of these nine groups, only five have been restored (groups I, II, III, VI and VII). The other four are still in ruins, and are usually passed unnoticed by sightseers. All except one of the temples were built between 730 and 780 AD, the exception being the **first temple** on the route, which was constructed in the early years of the ninth century. It's also the only temple to stand alone, unaccompanied by any subsidiary buildings. From here, a path, part of the original eighth-century walkway, heads up the hill to temple groups II and III.

Gedung Songo provides a neat link between the first Hindu temples in Java – the seventh-century temples at Dieng (see p.229) – and the magnificent Hindu *candi* built a few years later. They share scale, simplicity of design and dramatic scenery with Dieng, and also provide the prototype for the temples of Prambanan and Sambisari. This is best illustrated at **temple group III**, the last complex before the ravine. The layout of the main temple is, like Dieng's, very simple; it even has a small building facing the main temple similar to Dieng's Candi Semar. However, the layout of the temple and the carvings on the walls follow a pattern that was to be repeated on the Prambanan Plain a few years later. The walls are adorned with pilasters, and have icons of **Ganesh**, **Agastya** and **Durga** carved into the rear, south and north walls respectively. Nearby is a small shrine to **Nandi** and, on the left, a shrine to **Vishnu**.

From here, head down into the ravine and up the other side for the last two restored temple groups, VI and VII. Both of these share many of the same architectural features as group III. At **group VI**, for example, as with temple group III, a small stairway on the western side leads up to a small portico and into a small empty *cella*. The exterior of the temple is once again decorated by pilasters, and a central niche has been carved in each wall, each of which once housed a statue of a Hindu god.

Ambarawa

The busy market town of **AMBARAWA**, in the southern foothills of Ungaran, lies 32km south of Semarang on the main Yogya–Semarang highway. During the Japanese occupation there was a major prison camp here; today, with the prison walls long since demolished, the city is known for its excellent train museum, **Museum Kereta Api** (daily 8am–midnight; Rp1000). Here you'll find 21 turn-of-the-twentieth-century steam locomotives, built mainly in Germany and Switzerland. The museum is also the starting point of Java's only **cog railway**, which runs for just 9.5km, between Ambarawa and **Bedono** via Jambu. Up to eighty people can travel along the line to Bedono and back in the sumptuously restored train dating from 1902 – reckoned to be the oldest functioning cog steam train in the world – a three-hour journey which includes a one-hour stop at Bedono for lunch ($130 for hire of whole train). The spectacular journey takes you through verdant countryside with views of volcanic peaks and crater lakes with a spread of luscious green rice paddy below. For details, contact the PJKA, Jl Thamrin 3, Semarang (☎024/3524500) or Ambarawa station directly (☎0298/591035). Those on a smaller budget will have to content themselves with the **toy train**, the *Lori Wisata*, which runs as far as **Jambu** (10km return trip; Rp20,000), via **Ngampin** (5km return trip; Rp10,000).

It's not worth staying in Ambarawa, as the hotels at Bandungan, 7km away, are better value and offer a much more pleasant setting. However, if you do need to spend a night here, the *Hotel Aman* at Jl Pemuda 13 (☎0298/591791;

Rp20,000–25,000), halfway between the museum and the bus station, has some perfectly adequate rooms, and there are a couple of Padang restaurants in the town centre.

The Pasisir

The **Pasisir region** of Central Java provides an interesting alternative, or indeed supplement, to the usual Yogya–Solo route through Central Java. The word *pasisir* is the Javanese word for "fringe", and is used to refer to the northern coastal region of Java. Most of Pasisir's towns are connected by a single train line which runs alongside the great **Coastal Road** stretching between Anjar and Banyuwangi. This highway was commissioned by the Dutch governor Daendals in 1805 using local labour – 20,000 Javanese perished during its construction. Today, no north-coast town in Central Java is more than a couple of hours' drive from Semarang, and all the most interesting places can be visited as day-trips from the provincial capital.

With one exception – the batik town of **Pekalongan** – the coastal region **west of Semarang** holds little for the average sightseer and sees few tourists. There are a number of attractions to the east, however, which are of particular interest if you want to learn more about Javanese history and the spread of Islam on the island. East of Semarang is a large promontory that was once a separate island, formed by the volcanic thrust of **Gunung Mariah** at its centre and severed from the mainland by a navigable channel. Some of the towns which today lie inland were once major ports serving this channel. These ports were the first to convert to Islam, and in the early 1500s, **Demak** and **Jepara** even became the centre of a short-lived Islamic empire. As the silt from the volcanic hills flowed to the coast, however, these harbours suffocated and the channel separating Gunung Muriah from Java disappeared. Today, these cities retain a strict and, by Java's standards at least, orthodox atmosphere. Some of the former ports have found new ways of making money – **Kudus**, for example, has a thriving *kretek* industry – while others have slipped into an undisturbed sunbaked torpor.

Most people who travel to the Pasisir from the Kejawen do so by taking the Yogya–Semarang route via Magelang and Ambarawa. There is, however, a far more scenic route from Yogya via Dieng to Pekalongan. Be warned that this journey takes well over eight hours to complete – the roads are terrible – and it's advisable to spend at least one night in Dieng (see p.229) or Wonosobo (see p.228) to break the journey.

Pekalongan and around

Eighty-three kilometres west of Semarang is **PEKALONGAN**, an essential stop for anyone interested in **batik**. Everywhere you go in this pretty, relaxing old colonial town, the words *Kota Batik* (Batik City) seem to follow you, painted on public buildings, slapped on the sides of buses and even printed on litter bins. It's an apt description, for Pekalongan runs on batik: babies are swathed in it, kids march to school in it, government officials perspire in it, couples get married in it and the dead are buried in it.

The batik produced in Pekalongan is in marked contrast to that of Yogya and Solo. Unrestricted by tradition and the whims of a sultan, Pekalongan's batik is far more innovative, and the colours more celebratory, with a violent clash of vivid reds, creams and yellows, but also delicate patterns of birds and flowers.

The town was one of the first to embrace the new dyeing technology in the eighteenth century; with so many more colours at its disposal, and a disproportionately large number of master craftsmen setting up in the town, the Pekalongan repertoire expanded to include ever more outrageous, vibrant designs. Despite a serious decline in the traditional batik industry in recent years, as techniques for mass-producing printed cloth improve, Pekalongan's reputation as *Kota Batik* remains unrivalled.

The **Batik Museum** (Mon–Thurs & Sat 7.30am–3.30pm, Fri 7am–noon; free) on Jalan Majapahit in the south of the city (Rp2000 by becak west from the alun-alun) displays a small selection of different batik styles from all over Java. The few accompanying captions are, unfortunately, all in Indonesian, and many find the museum a little dull, although you can combine a visit here with the squawking bedlam of Pekalongan's **bird market**, on the same street.

A good place to shop for batik clothing is **Pasar Banjarsari**, the large and muddy market on Jalan Sultan Agung, 500m north of the alun-alun. Here you'll find cheap, ready-to-wear items such as the exuberant shirts so beloved by Javanese males. If you're after something a little more exclusive, head to one of the boutiques that hide away in the **Arab Quarter** to the east of Jalan Sultan Agung; try Jacky's Batik on Jl Surabaya VA/1, Ridaka at Jl H.A. Salim Gang VI/4, or BL Batik, Jl KH Mansur 87. Jalan Hayam Wuruk, the main east–west road at the southern end of Jalan Sultan Agung, also plays host to a string of batik purveyors, including Ayu Batik, Larissa, Aneka and, best of all, Achmad Yana Batik, down a little *gang* to the west of the bridge on Hayam Wuruk.

Practicalities

Pekalongan's **train station** hides in the southwest corner of the town, about 1km to the west of the alun-alun. **Minibuses** congregate to the north of the alun-alun, while the main **bus station** lies to the southeast of the city. To reach the bus station, catch an angkuta from the junction to the north of the unhelpful **tourist office** on Jl Angkatan 1945 (Mon–Sat 7am–2pm), 1km east of the train station.

The main focus of the town is the large square to the north of Pasar Banjarsari, about 1km north of the alun-alun. Here, housed in a couple of attractive old colonial buildings, are the **GPO** and **Telkom** office. A becak from the train station should cost no more than Rp3000, and most bemos drive by the square too.

Pekalongan has some fairly good **accommodation** options. The *Asia*, Jl KH Wahid Hasyim 49 (Ⓣ0285/422125; ❷), an extremely friendly hotel conveniently close to the minibus station, offers the best-value cheap rooms in town, although these are basic. Despite this, tatty *Gajah Mada*, Jl Gajah Mada 11 (Ⓣ0285/422185; ❷), remains the most popular of the budget hotels, if only because it's opposite the train station and stays open all night to receive late arrivals. The *Hayam Wuruk*, Jl Hayam Wuruk 152–154 (Ⓣ0285/422823 or 424322; ❸), is the best in the mid-range price bracket, a clean hotel with a kindly manager and comfy rooms. The plushest and largest place in town is the *Istana* at Jl Gajah Mada 23–25 (Ⓣ0285/23581; ❹), opposite the train station, with a billiard room and karaoke club (beginning at 8pm), which converts into a nightclub at 10.30pm.

Most of Pekalongan's **eating places** are concentrated around the train station along both sides of Jalan Gajah Mada. Look out for the Pekalongan speciality, *soto kerbau* (water-buffalo soup). The *Purimas Bakery*, Jl Hayam Wuruk 191, sells excellent fresh bread as well as cold drinks, coffee and snacks. The *Remaja*, Jl Dr Cipto 30, offers Indonesian, Chinese and a few Western dishes, while the restaurant at *Hotel Nirwana*, Jl Dr Wahidin 11, serves good Chinese food.

Kedungwungi

The finest batik factory on the north coast – if not the whole of Java – is the **Oey Soe Tjoen factory** (daily except Fri 8am–3.30pm) in **KEDUNG-WUNGI**, a small village 9km to the south of Pekalongan. To get here, catch a bemo from the junction of Jalan Mansyur and Jalan Slamet (Rp1000). The workshop is on the main street at Jl Raya 104 (Ⓣ285/85268); look out for a tiny "Batik Art" sign above the door. It was established in 1923 by the eponymous Oey Soe Tjoen, grandfather of the present owner, Muljadi Widjaya. The latter's wife, Istiyana, is the shop-floor supervisor and will guide you around the workshop, where you can see the painstaking skill of the artists as they carefully apply each dot of wax to the cloth. Only three or four pieces are completed each month, with a top-quality batik taking nine months to finish and costing around $80. Those who are tempted to splash out will have to order and pay in full now, then wait nine months for their purchase to arrive (delivery within Indonesia only).

Demak

Lying halfway between Semarang and Kudus at the southwestern corner of the Gunung Muriah peninsula, **DEMAK** was once both a major port and the capital of Java's first Islamic kingdom. The town is only a thirty-minute bus ride east of Semarang's Terboyo terminal (Rp1000), and is best visited either as a stop on the way to Kudus, or as a day-trip from Semarang. Demak's bus station is located on the southern side of the alun-alun.

Details of Demak's glory days are very sketchy, but it's widely believed that the city was founded around 1500 by either a Chinese Muslim called **Cek Kopo**, or by his son, **Raden Patah**. The town later went on to defeat the last remnants of the ailing Hindu Majapahit empire, although there are few details as to when this occurred. The most popular theory is that Raden Patah's son, **Trenggana** (c. 1505–47), led Demak to a final victory against the Majapahits in around 1527. After expanding the kingdom of Demak to most of north and eastern Java, Trenggana was killed in battle in 1547; his kingdom collapsed soon after.

Whilst Trenggana used his sword to spread the word of Mohammed, one of the members of his court, **Sunan Kalijaga**, enticed the Javanese population to Islam by hosting gamelan and wayang kulit performances in the fifteenth-century **Mesjid Agung** (Grand Mosque). This mosque, the oldest in Central Java and the holiest on the whole island, stands to the west of Demak's alun-alun and is the town's centrepiece. Legend has it that the mosque was built by the Wali Songo; Sunan Kalijaga himself was said to have formed the mosque from wood in one night's effort. Indonesia's Muslims attach such importance to the mosque that seven visits here are believed to be equivalent to a haj to Mecca. For non-Muslims, however, the mosque holds little of interest, except for its combination of incongruous architectural styles: the three-tiered roof is typically Javanese, the **minaret** is a Hindu–Muslim hybrid, and the fairy lights at night are reminiscent of a British seaside resort.

Sharing the mosque's courtyard is a small **museum** (daily 8am–5pm; donation), which traces the fortunes of the building through the centuries, with photos and scale models. The large, overcrowded **cemetery** behind the museum houses the graves of the first two sultans of Demak, Trenggana and Raden Patah.

Kudus and around

If Pekalongan rejoices in the name Kota Batik, then **KUDUS**, a fairly quiet industrial city built around Sungai Serang, can justifiably claim to be Kota Kretek. **Kretek**, the ubiquitous sweet-smelling clove cigarettes, were mass-produced for the first time here in the 1920s, and today over 25 *kretek* manufacturers are based in and around the city, mostly to the east of Sungai Serang in the newest part of Kudus. This is also where most hotels, restaurants and shopping plazas can be found, many of them around the alun-alun in the north of town.

The western part of Kudos is quieter and prettier than the more modern eastern half. Here you can find traces of the city's past, including its most important **mosque**, the **Mesjid Al-Aqsa**, one of the most venerated on Java,

Kretek and Kudus

Many people in **Kudus** will try to convince you that *kretek* was a Kudus invention and the brainchild of a local man, **Almarhum Nitisemito**. In fact, people had been smoking cloves in Java for centuries, wrapping the tobacco and clove compound in dried corn husks. Mr Nitisemito, however, was the first to use cigarette paper rather than corn husks, and this simple innovation led to the establishment of Java's first *kretek* factory, built right in the heart of Kudus.

The name *"kretek"* is onomatopoeic: *kretek* means "to crackle", and describes the sound of the cigarette as it burns. The cigarettes also frequently make a popping sound, and occasionally a husk of clove will fizz out and burn the smoker's clothes; more than one person has gone up in flames in this way.

The **Bal Tiga** (Three Balls) brand Mr Nitisemito founded in the 1920s brought great prosperity to his home town. It also made him a very wealthy man, particularly as he insisted he smoked *kretek* as a way of alleviating the symptoms of asthma. Nitisemito became famous for his tireless promotional work, which included sponsoring sporting occasions, starting up his own radio station and even producing a full-length feature film promoting his cigarettes. Despite all his efforts, ferocious competition and incompetent management brought Nitisemito's company to its knees; by the time he gasped his last, wheezy breath in 1953, he was already bankrupt.

Nonetheless, *kretek* cigarettes continue to go from strength to strength. Today, *kretek* is the preferred choice of 85 percent of Indonesia's smoking population. Over 202 billion cigarettes were smoked in 2000, and the industry now employs over four million people, two percent of the population of Indonesia. Hand-rolled cigarettes incur lower taxes (twenty percent as opposed to forty percent) than machine-rolled cigarettes, and account for thirty percent of the *kretek* market. Despite this avoidance, taxes on *kretek* are still worth about five percent of the national budget to the government – only oil revenue contributes more.

But are *kretek* cigarettes as good for asthma sufferers and smokers in general as Nitisemito claimed? Not surprisingly, the answer is a resounding "no". Tar and nicotine levels in *kretek* are up to four times higher than those of conventional cigarettes, and they are even banned in several countries. The other problem is that eugenol, the clove oil produced in the cigarette, also produces damage to the lungs. The World Health Organisation estimates that 57,000 Indonesians die annually because of smoking, and the Indonesian Health Department reports 200,000 new cancer cases annually – it is not known how many are smoking-related. Indonesia is said to have the highest rate of growth of cigarette smokers in the world, representing four percent of world consumption. Estimates vary, but it's thought that around sixty percent of males and five percent of females smoke – something confirmed by casual observation anywhere in the country.

on Jalan Menara. Kudos is renowned as a centre for Islamic study, its name deriving from the Arabic for "holy", *al-Kuds*. The mosque was founded in 1549 by **Jafar Shodiq**, considered one of the "wali songo", or nine holy saints of Indonesia, credited with the conversion of much of Indonesia to Islam. The building you see today is a twentieth-century construction, though the dumpy-looking **minaret** is an original seventeenth-century design and resembles contemporary Hindu towers found on Bali. It's possible to climb the tower to study the old drum at the top, which is still used to call the faithful to prayer. Sunan Kudus's body lies to the rear of the mosque, in a tomb embellished with intricate latticework.

The minaret (menara) of Al-Aqsa was used as a model for the 27-metre **Tugu Identitas**, the ungainly tower opposite the Matahari department store. Visitors can climb the tower (daily 8am–5pm; Rp750), which affords reasonable views over the rather unprepossessing city.

The oldest and largest *kretek* manufacturer in town is **Djarum**, which, with 25,000 workers located in sixteen factories throughout the town and nearby villages, is also the city's biggest employer. The strong perfume of cloves emanating from their main factory off Jalan J. A. Yani, which runs south from the alun-alun, is likely to remain one of your lasting impressions of the north coast. It's possible to have a **guided tour** around this factory; simply take your passport to their head offices on Jalan J. A. Yani, 1km south of Kudus's alun-alun. You'll be shown around the **blending and rolling room**, where eight hundred women (all the workers are female, and the supervisors nearly all male) produce, on average, 2,400,000 cigarettes per eight-hour day, six days a week. You should also be able to visit the **packing room**, where another three hundred women work feverishly in teams of six, producing 300,000 packs per day.

To find out more about the origins and development of *kretek*, visit the **Kretek Museum** (Mon 8am–2pm, Tues & Thurs 9am–2pm, Sat 9am–1pm; donation), set in a field on the southeastern fringes of town; a becak from the Matahari department store in the centre of town should cost no more than Rp3000. As well as recounting – in Indonesian only – Mr Nitisemito's life (see box opposite), the museum also houses a display of the machinery used in *kretek* production. A collection of promotional merchandise and cigarette packets takes up almost half of the museum.

Practicalities

The **bus station** lies an inconvenient 4km south of the **Matahari department store** at the centre of Kudus. Yellow angkuta travel between the bus station and the Mata Hari junction, costing a standard Rp1000. Kudus' main thoroughfare, Jalan J. A. Yani, runs north from Mata Hari to the alun-alun. The **tourist office** is situated in a children's park to the east of town. There is an entry fee of Rp1000 to the park, although this will be waived if you explain you want to visit the tourist office only. The BCA **bank** on Jalan J. A. Yani has a foreign-exchange counter.

The **accommodation** options are pretty limited. The cheapest, the *Losmen Amin* at Jl Menur 51 (☎0291/438301; ❶), stands one block south of the Pasar Kliwon, an ugly concrete shopping centre to the east of the alun-alun. The *Amin* is less of a hotel than a zoo, with mice in the courtyard, mosquitoes in the bedrooms and even fish in the mandi; on the plus side, its genial manager does provide free tea and a mosquito coil. For something equally bizarre yet a little more upmarket, head to the *Hotel Air Mancur* at Jl Pemuda 70 (☎0291/4332514; ❷), east from the southeastern corner of the alun-alun. This is one of these surreal hotels that the Chinese seem to specialize in, bursting at the seams with caged birds, monkeys, mini-waterfalls and lily ponds. The rooms seem positively bland by comparison, though they're very comfortable and fairly good value. Of the more expensive hotels, *Hotel Notosari* at Jl Kepodang 12, just off the main street, Jalan Jend. A. Yani, is very central and has reasonable rooms, with hot water, air-con and TV (☎0291/437227 or 437245; ❹). *Hotel Grita*, Jalan Agil Kusumadya (☎0291/438449; ❺), is the town's best hotel, with slightly better rooms than the *Notosari*, but it's some way out of the centre. Both hotels have swimming pools.

There are some decent **eating** options in Kudus. The local speciality is *lenthog Kudus*, sticky rice wrapped in banana leaf, which is sold on the street in the evening. A couple of roads leading east off Jalan J. A. Yani come alive at night with food stalls: Jalan Kepodang specializes in *martabak* sellers, while those on Jalan Kutilang provide the usual Indonesian fodder. Also on Jalan Kutilang is the *Rilek's Café*, which serves tasty toasted sandwiches; it's a good place to come for lunch. The *Garuda Restaurant* at the junction of Jalan Jend Sudirman and the alun-alun is one of the top places in town, and their prices are reasonable – check out the *nasi rames*. Otherwise, *RM Hijau Mas*, Jl Jend A. Yani 1 (closed Fri) serves good Indonesian food, as does *Sederhana Restaurant*, Jl Agil Kusumadya 59B, which specializes in seafood.

Colo

Eighteen kilometres to the north of Kudus lies the small village of **COLO**, the starting point for the one-kilometre hike up the side of Gunung Muriah to the **grave of Sunan Muriah**. Sunan Muriah was another member of the Wali Songo, and his grave has become a place of pilgrimage for devout Javanese. Yellow-and-brown angkuta from behind the Matahari shop in Kudus terminate in the centre of Colo (Rp1000). The grave lies at the top of a long set of steps, in the shade of a mosque reputedly built by the Sunan himself. Most of what you see today was built in the last 150 years, and few of the features are original. However, the view over the valley below is quite breathtaking. It's worth visiting the dramatic Air Terjun Monthel **waterfall**, only thirty minutes' walk further on. The only **accommodation** in Colo is the simple government resthouse *Pesanggrahan Colo* (☎0291/435157; ❷–❸).

Jepara

The affluent coastal town of **JEPARA** lies on the western side of the Gunung Muria promontory, 41km northeast of Semarang. Clues as to the source of Jepara's wealth line the roads into the city, where carpenters and **woodcarvers** sit outside their shops producing furniture, reliefs and souvenirs of occasionally stunning quality. So renowned are the craftsmen of Jepara that their town is nicknamed **Kota Ukir** (The City of Woodcarvers).

In contrast to the serene and unassuming little port of today, following the death of Demak's Sultan Trenggana in 1546, Jepara rose to become the most important town on the north coast, first under Trenggana's brother-in-law, **King Yunus**, and then under the leadership of the notorious **Queen Kalinyamat**. Together, these two organized three raids on the Portuguese stronghold of Melaka. The Portuguese managed to repel these attacks, but not before an enormous amount of damage had been caused to the city's defences.

Jepara's strategic position and excellent deep-water berthing facilities also attracted the attention of the early Dutch arrivals. In the early 1600s, Jepara became the coastal headquarters of the **VOC**, whose tenure proved to be an awkward period in the town's history. In 1614, the fragile relationship between

Raden Kartini

As the daughter of the regent of Jepara, **Raden Kartini** had a very privileged upbringing, by Javanese standards. Born in 1879 in Mayong, a small village to the south of Jepara, Kartini was one of the very few Indonesian women allowed to attend the Dutch school in the town. The education she received there led her to question certain fundamental mores of Javanese society: in letters to Dutch friends, written after she left school, she attacked polygamy, which at the time was still widely practised on the island. She also opposed the role of the Dutch colonialists, whom she felt had deliberately deprived the Javanese people of a proper education. After marrying the regent of Rembang, Kartini published a powerful article entitled "Educate the Javanese!", and went on to put her theories into practice, founding a school with her husband in their home. Both the classroom and the house have been preserved, and can be visited by applying to the tourist office in Rembang, a small town 30km east of Kudus. Tragically, Kartini died aged 24, giving birth to her first child. Her letters and articles were collected and in 1911 published under the title *From Darkness to Light*. Her pioneering efforts at social restructuring are still celebrated throughout Indonesia on April 21 every year, a date now known as Kartini Day.

the Mataram ruler **Sultan Agung** and the VOC disintegrated, after the former refused to supply the latter's troops with rice. In retaliation some Dutch soldiers urinated against Jepara's mosque and insulted the sultan, comparing him to a dog. The Javanese took their revenge by killing three soldiers; the Dutch in turn responded by setting fire to all the Javanese ships in the port. Thereafter, the two sides played out a cold war, until eventually, in 1799, the VOC was wound up by the Dutch government and the coastal headquarters were moved to Semarang. Jepara's importance dwindled as a result.

Today, Jepara is a fairly small town centred around the alun-alun, and most things are within walking distance of this square. Surrounding the alun-alun are a number of historical sights, which survive as testimony of the town's colourful past. The former residence of the regent of Jepara, now a faceless collection of government offices, stands on the eastern side of the alun-alun. This was the childhood home of **Raden Kartini**, the social reformer and campaigner for Javanese rights (see box above). A **museum** dedicated to her life and work lies on the north side of the square (Mon–Fri 7am–4pm, Sat & Sun 9am–5pm; Rp750). A guide from the neighbouring tourist office will take you around this reasonably diverting museum for Rp5000 or so, pointing out the **Kartini family tree** and quotes from her book, *From Darkness to Light*. Up the hill behind the museum, a ten-minute walk away, are the remains of the **VOC fort**, now little more than a few foundations set amidst an abandoned graveyard.

Practicalities

Jepara is a very compact little town. The **bus station** is no more than 400m west of the alun-alun, where you'll find the **tourist office** (Mon–Thurs 7am–1.30pm, Fri 7–11am, Sat 7am–12.30pm). **Ferries** to and from Karimunjawa (see p.270) dock at Kartini beach, a rather dismal fun park 1.5km southwest of the bus station; a becak from the town centre to the port will set you back Rp3000.

For **accommodation**, the firm favourite with budget travellers is *Losmen Menno Jaya*, behind Menno Photo at Jl Diponegoro 40b (☎0291/591143; ❷), 200m east of the bus station. The old Lanchester car in the courtyard hints at the state of the rooms surrounding it: old and dilapidated, but comfortable. The

Jeparan woodcarvings

Though the souvenirs and furniture of Jepara can sometimes veer towards the kitsch, there's no denying the skill and patience of the craftsmen who produce them. Genuine antiques, reproductions and modern designs, carved mainly out of locally grown **teak**, can all be purchased here. Before buying, however, remember to include in any calculations the cost of shipping, which often far exceeds the purchase price. A trawl of the wood shops should begin at **Tahunan**, 4km south of Jepara (take a brown angkuta from the bus station; Rp1000), a tiny village with a high concentration of furniture and souvenir stores. About 1km on the road back towards Jepara, a turn-off leads to the village of **Senenan**, where craftsmen specialize in carving exquisitely intricate reliefs, many of which end up as table tops or wall-hangings in Jepara's sitting rooms. Most of the craftsmen here are only too willing to show you around their workshops.

friendly *Hotel Elim*, Jl Dr. Sutomo 13–15 (ⓣ0291/591406; ❸) is popular with foreign tourists, offering reasonable rooms with air-con, hot water and TV, while its restaurant serves tasty Indonesian and Western food. A few minutes' walk down the road is *Hotel Kalingga Star*, Jl Dr. Sutomo 16 (ⓣ0291/591054; ❸), a more modern-looking rival to the *Elim*, while the *Hotel Jepara Indah* at Jl Cokroaminto 12 (ⓣ0291/593549 ⓔjepara.inn@hotmail.com; ❺), two blocks south of the alun-alun, is the newest and best in town; all the rooms have TV, air-con and fridge.

Of the numerous **eating** options, *Bulyo*, at the junction of Jalan Kartini and Jalan Dr Sutono, is a good-value restaurant/souvenir shop serving passable Indonesian food and ice-cold drinks. Further west down Jalan Sutomo, the bamboo-and-wood *Milyo* serves very tasty mid-priced Indonesian food. The *Pondok Makan Maribu* next to the *Hotel Kalingga Star* offers a wide choice of Indonesian, Chinese and Western food. Finally, the *Rumah Makan Citra* in Jalan Ringin Jaya is a good bet for seafood.

The Karimunjawa national park

The coral-ringed islands of the **Karimunjawa national park** are a sleepy, sun-drenched haven where life is conducted in perpetual slow motion. An approximate translation of *Karimunjawa* is "Not clearly visible from Java", and although they lie just 90km off the mainland coast, the islands might as well be a million kilometres away, such is the contrast they provide with the mainland. There is so little traffic on the biggest island, **Pulau Karimunjawa**, that the local cats take their afternoon naps on the sunbaked tarmac of the only road. Karimunjawa doesn't suffer from Java's population problem, either – of the 27 islands, only five are inhabited.

All of this, sadly, may be about to change. While most of Karimunjawa has been declared a **nature reserve**, the parts which haven't have been bought up by developers keen to cash in on the undoubted beauty of the islands, with their golden beaches and excellent snorkelling and diving opportunities. A casino has already been planned for Pulau Tengah, and every second Monday a boat laden with wealthy sunseeking day-trippers from Jakarta arrives at gorgeous Pulau Menjangan Kecil. However, the development boom is still in its infancy and, for the time being, Karimunjawa remains an isolated idyll.

The islands

The main settlement on Karimunjawa lies on the southern tip of **Pulau Karimunjawa**, one of the largest islands in the group. A road from the village heads north along the west side of the island and continues north through adjoining **Pulau Kemujan** via the airport, which serves planes coming from Semarang. About 11km along this road from the village, a set of 616 steps leads off up the hill to the **grave of Nyumpungan**, the islands' only man-made tourist attraction. Nyumpungan, the wayward son of Sunan Muriah (see p.268), introduced Islam to the island after his father had banished him from court and sent him into exile. As with so many other graves on the north coast, the tomb appears to have been made from bathroom tiles.

In an attempt to balance the islands' potential earnings with the need to preserve their unquestionable beauty, the authorities have divided the Karimunjawa islands into several zones. In the first of these, the **utilization zones**, developers are allowed to do pretty much what they want. The most westerly of the Karimunjawa islands (15km from Pulau Karimunjawa) and the cluster of islands to the south of Pulau Karimunjawa have both been placed in this category. Most of the other islands, plus the central hills of Pulau Karimunjawa, have been declared **wilderness zones**, where limited tourist activities, such as snorkelling and hiking, are allowed. Finally, there is the **core sanctuary zone**, consisting of **Pulau Geleang** and neighbouring **Pulau Burung**. Officially, these islands and their splendid coral are off-limits to anybody who doesn't have a research permit (available from the KSDA in Semarang – see p.260); however, the authorities have yet to devise a way of policing the zone properly. While this is good news for snorkellers, who can paddle away unhindered here, it is tragic for the fauna of these islands, and fishing and turtle-egg collecting still continue unhampered on both.

The best **beaches** in Karimunjawa are undoubtedly on **Pulau Menjangan Kecil**, southwest of Karimunjawa. The sand is white, and a paddle around the western side of the island attracts hundreds of small fishes, crabs and rays. If and when Menjangan Kecil is spoiled, the award for best beach will go to the picture-postcard **Pulau Cemara Kecil**, west of Pulau Karimunjawa.

Practicalities

The most comfortable way of getting to Karimunjawa is to catch one of the twice-weekly **flights** from Semarang (see p.273). A very irregular bemo service runs between Karimunjawa airport and the village (Rp3000). The alternative method is to take one of two **ferries** from Jepara, both of which sail twice a week. The larger, modern *KMP Muria* docks at the pier at the eastern end of Karimunjawa village, while the smaller *Kota Ukir* arrives at the western end.

The only way to travel between the islands is to **rent a fishing boat**. A day-trip around pulaus Geleang, Burung, Menjangan Kecil and Menjangan Besar should cost no more than Rp75,000 per boat.

There are eight **homestays** in Karimunjawa village, and the deal is much the same in all of them. The *Arie* homestay (❷), 400m west of the eastern pier, is run by Ipong, an ex-Jeparan woodsmith-turned-prawn-farmer, and ranks as the best. His immaculate homestay serves excellent food (largely fish, of course); they also run tours to the other islands, rent snorkelling gear and can arrange fishing boats to the other islands. The *Kelapa Desa* (Rp30,000), 150m west of *Arie*, offers the best accommodation option for large groups. Two other islands offer accommodation: **Pulau Menjangan Besar**'s only inhabitants have a couple of rooms above their outdoor aquarium (❷), and there are also some "luxury" (a relative term here) cottages on **Pulau Tengah** (❹), one of the less attractive islands lying to the east of Pulau Karimunjawa. These need to be booked in advance: contact PT Satura Tours, at Jl Cendrawasih 4, Semarang (ⓣ0297/3555555).

There is a **GPO** and **Telkom** office in Karimunjawa village, and even a couple of souvenir shops, but no bank. There are a couple of tiny warung, both at the western end of the village near the small pier, which only open for a couple of hours (5–7pm).

Travel details

Buses and bemos

It's almost impossible to give the **frequency** with which bemos and buses run, as they only depart when they have enough passengers to make the journey worthwhile. **Journey times** also vary a great deal; the times below are the minimum you can expect to take. Privately run shuttle, or **door-to-door**, buses run between the major tourist centres on Java.

Borobudur to: Magelang (45min); Yogyakarta (2hr).
Cilacap to: Purwokerto (1hr); Wonosobo (4hr); Yogyakarta (5hr).
Dieng to: Pekalongan (4hr, via Kalibening); Wonosobo (1hr).
Purwokerto to: Cilacap (1hr); Dieng (5hr).
Semarang to: Cirebon (5hr 30min); Demak (30min); Jakarta (9hr 30min); Jepara (1hr 30min); Kudus (1hr); Magelang (2hr); Pekalongan (2hr 30min); Surabaya (8hr); Yogyakarta (3hr 30min).
Solo to: Bogor (11hr); Jakarta (13hr); Malang (7hr); Purwodadi (1hr 30min); Surabaya (6hr); Yogyakarta(2hr).
Wonosobo to: Cilacap (4hr); Dieng (1hr); Magelang (1hr); Purwokerto (2hr 30min).
Yogyakarta to: Bandung (9hr 30min); Bogor (10hr 30min); Borobudur (2hr); Cilacap (5hr); Denpasar (15hr); Jakarta (11hr 30min); Magelang (1hr 30min); Prambanan (45min); Probolinggo (9hr); Semarang (3hr 30min); Solo (2hr); Surabaya (7hr 30min).

Trains

The estimated journey times listed below are for the fastest scheduled trains.

Cilacap to: Jakarta (2 daily; 8hr 10min); Surabaya (daily; 11hr 15min).
Pekalongan to: Cirebon (13 daily; 1hr 50min); Jakarta (13 daily; 4hr 20min); Semarang (14 daily; 1hr 20min); Surabaya (6 daily; 4hr 45min).
Purwokerto to: Cilacap (1hr).
Semarang to: Cirebon (13 daily; 3hr 5min); Jakarta (13 daily; 5hr 40min); Pekalongan (14 daily; 1hr 20min); Solo (2 daily; 3hr 20min); Surabaya (6 daily; 4hr).
Solo to: Bandung (5 daily; 8hr 50min); Jakarta (6 daily; 10hr 30min); Malang (1 daily; 6hr 25min); Purwokerto (6 daily; 3hr 15min); Semarang (2 daily; 3hr 20min); Surabaya (6 daily; 3hr 20min); Yogyakarta (14 daily; 1hr 30min).
Yogyakarta to: Bandung (6 daily; 6hr 30min); Jakarta (14 daily; 8hr 45min); Malang (daily; 7hr 30min); Purwokerto (7 daily; 4hr 15min); Solo (14 daily; 1hr 30min); Surabaya (11 daily; 4hr 50min).

Pelni ferries

For a chart of the Pelni routes, see p.42 of Basics.

Semarang to: Banjarmarsin (*KM Kelimutu* weekly; 24hr); Kumai (*KM Lawit* 2 monthly; 21hr/*KM Binaiya* 2 monthly; 21hr); Pontianak (*KM Lawit* 2 monthly; 33hr/*KM Tilongkabila* 2 monthly; 2–3 days); Sampit (*KM Tilongkabila* monthly; 24hr); Ujung Pandang (*KM Ceremai* 2 monthly; 30hr/*KM Sirimau* 2 monthly; 50hr).

Other ferries

Cilacap to: Pangandaran (4 daily, last at 1pm; 3hr 30min).
Jepara to: Karimunjawa (*KMP Muria* 2 weekly; 4hr; *Kota Ukir*, 1 weekly; 7hr).
Karimunjawa to: Jepara (*KMP Muria*, 2 weekly; 4hr; *Kota Ukir*, 1 weekly; 7hr).
Semarang to: Banjarmasin (1weekly; 26hr); Kumai (1 weekly; 24hr); Pontianak (2 monthly; 33hr); Sampit (2 monthly; 24hr); Tanjung Priok (2 monthly; 20hr).

Flights

Cilacap to: Jakarta (1 daily; 1hr 15min).
Semarang to: Jakarta (17 daily; 55min); Surabaya (4 daily; 50min); Karimunjawa (2 weekly; 1hr); Ujung Pandang (1 daily; 2hr 20min).
Solo to: Jakarta (6 daily; 1hr 5min); Singapore (2 weekly; 2hr 20min); Surabaya (2 daily; 1hr 5min).
Yogyakarta to: Bandung (4 weekly; 1hr 15min); Denpasar (6 daily; 2hr 15min); Jakarta (13 daily; 1hr 5min); Surabaya (6 daily; 1hr).

4

East Java

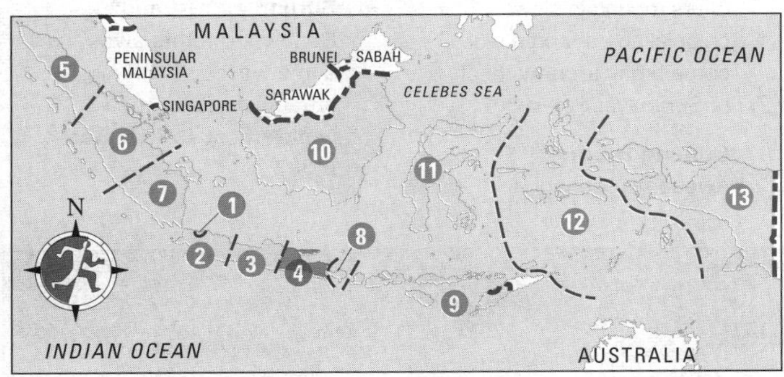
MALAYSIA
PENINSULAR MALAYSIA
SINGAPORE
BRUNEI
SABAH
SARAWAK
CELEBES SEA
PACIFIC OCEAN
N
INDIAN OCEAN
AUSTRALIA
1
2
3
4
5
6
7
8
9
10
11
12
13

CHAPTER 4 Highlights

* **Bull races at Madura** Watch the exciting spectacle of pairs of oxen racing over 100m courses. See p.296

* **Paradise beaches at Prigi** A picture postcard view of the south coast. See p.306

* **Malang** This hill resort offers mountain views, colonial charm and a welcome break from the heat of Surabaya. See p.307

* **Gunung Bromo** Awesome scenery and wonderful sunrises; it's also home to the Tenggerese, perhaps the original inhabitants of Java. See p.324

* **Kawah Ijen** This stunning blue-green crater lake offers fantastic views of Raung and Merapi. See p.331

* **Surfing at "G-Land"** Renowned for its awesome waves, Plenkung attracts some of the world's best surfers. See p.337

4

East Java

The province of East Java (Java Timur) stretches over 350km, from near Solo in the west to the port town of Banyuwangi in the east. The main settlement is Surabaya, the second largest city in Indonesia, with a population of around 3.5 million, which most visitors at least pass through. It's a huge, often overwhelming metropolis, with few sights of interest, but it's a useful base from which to explore the extensive remains of the Majapahit kingdom at Trowulan to the southwest.

The people of the region are predominantly Javan, but around ten percent are from **Pulau Madura**, located just a few kilometres across the water from Surabaya, and have a different ethnic, linguistic and cultural background to the mainland. Known for its fast, furious and colourful annual ox races, the island is a peaceful backwater peppered with interesting historic remains.

The main waterway of East Java, **Sungai Brantas**, which reaches the sea in the Surabaya area, rises northwest of **Malang** and flows 314km through Blitar, Tulungagung, Kediri and Mojokjerto. Malang itself is a cool, attractive colonial city, with a large student population and plenty of worthwhile excursions nearby, including the antiquities of **Singosari** and **Candi Jawi**, the mountain resorts of **Batu** and **Selecta**, and the **beaches** along the southern coast.

The **mountains** that form the spine of Java spread right through the province, from Gunung Lawu (3265m) in the west, with the attractive hill resort of **Sarangan** nestling on its lower slopes, to the more dramatic peaks further east. For most visitors, the major draw is the huge volcanic massif and national park around **Gunung Bromo**. The views from **Gunung Penanjakan** and **Cemoro Lawang** and a dawn hike to the summit of Bromo itself make for a marvellous trip, and well-prepared hikers can tackle **Gunung Semeru** (3676m), the highest peak in Java.

Along the north coast, where slow rivers run into the calm Java Sea, are the ports of **Probolinggo** and **Pasuruan**, both useful access towns for Bromo. Off the **south coast**, the Sunda shelf drops steeply just a few kilometres offshore. Strong currents and dramatic surf characterize this coast, and the **beaches** of Pacitan in the west, those south of Malang, and Sukamade in Meru Betiri national park, are glorious, while scenic **Grajagan Bay** in Alas Purwo national park is a world-class **surfing** spot.

In the far east of the region, the population centres of **Jember** and **Banyuwangi** are essentially transit points (the ferry port for Bali is nearby), offering excellent access to the national parks of **Baluran**, **Alas Purwo** and **Meru Betiri**. Although the Javan tiger is nearly extinct, the area is still rich in bird and animal life. The small town of Bondowoso is a base for the wonderful **Ijen Plateau**, its highlight the stunning crater lake of Kawah Ijen.

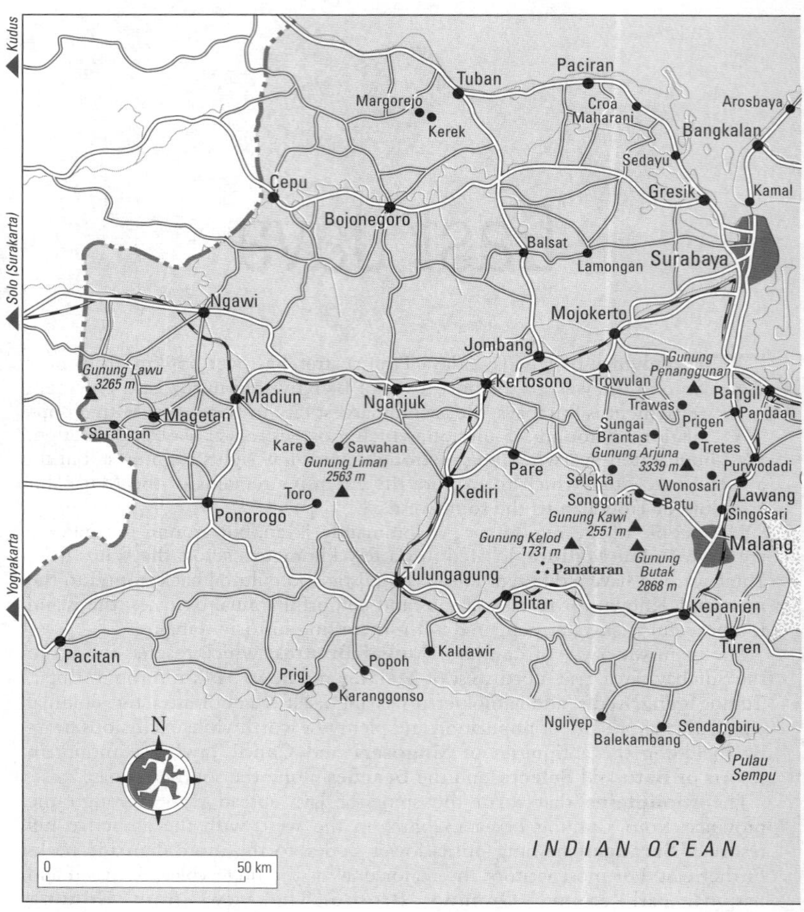

Kalibaru, on the main Jember to Banyuwangi highway, is a cool, pleasant place to stay and enjoy the nearby coffee, cocoa and rubber plantations.

The best time to visit if you're intending to **trek** is from March through to October, outside the **monsoon** period. Many of the major climbs in East Java are impossible in the rains, although the monsoon does bring intermittent showers between periods of startling sunshine, and this is when the area is at its most lush and verdant, the rivers and waterfalls full and dramatic.

Some history

From the fifth to the tenth centuries AD, the recorded history of Java is largely that of central Java, where the ascendant kingdoms of the time were located. After 919 AD, however, the dominant kingdoms shifted to the east. The reason for this is unknown, although possible causes were outside invasion, volcanic eruption (Merapi is thought to have erupted in 928) or an epidemic of

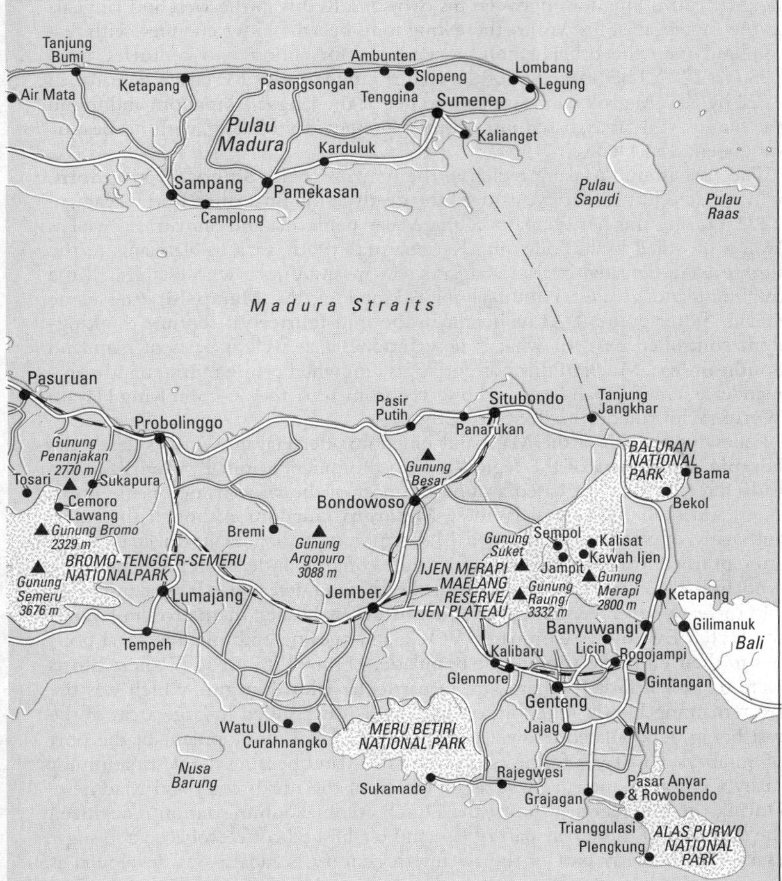

massive proportions. It is known that a ruler called Sindok established a palace of the **Sanjaya kingdom** southwest of Surabaya in 929, and was later succeeded by his daughter. Records indicate that this kingdom was powerful enough to invade Sumatra in the late tenth century.

The most famous early ruler of the region was **Airlangga**, who ruled the Sanjaya kingdom in the eleventh century. In 1016 a rebellion against King Dharmawangsa led to the king's defeat, and the destruction of the capital of the east Javanese kingdom. The 16-year-old crown prince, Airlannga (son of Balinese king Udayana) took refuge in a mountain hermitage, where, it is claimed, he developed magical powers through fasting and meditation. Four years later he became the ruler of a small coastal kingdom near Surabaya; by the age of 30, he was in a position to attempt to regain his ancestral lands; and by the time of his death in 1049, he was not only the supreme ruler, but also had regained the territories over which his ancestors had ruled. On his death he divided his kingdom between his two sons, Kediri in the west and Janggala in the east. Against his wishes, these kingdoms became bitter enemies, with first one and then the other gaining ascendancy for almost two centuries, from 1050 to 1222. The final ruler of the Kediri kingdom was Kertajaya, defeated in 1222 by Ken Angrok, who went on to defeat the Janggala kingdom and found the Singosari dynasty, based just north of present-day Malang, with his beautiful queen, Ken Dedes.

The area around Malang is rich in the remains of the **Singosari kingdom**, which lasted just seventy years until the death of the final ruler, Kertanagara, in 1292. During this period, parts of the Malay peninsula and Sumatra, as well as Java, were ruled by it. Following Kertanagara's death, various claimants to the throne were defeated by Kertanagara's son-in-law, Vijaya, who established the mightiest and greatest Hindu/Javanese kingdom, the **Majapahit** (the name means "bitter gourd"). At its height in the mid-fourteenth century, the kingdom controlled most of what is now Indonesia, as well as parts of mainland Southeast Asia. Much of this was due to its renowned prime minister and commander in chief, Gajah Made, who served from 1331 to 1364, and King Hayam Wuruk, who ruled from 1350 to 1389.

Following the fall of the Majapahit kingdom after Hayam Wuruk's death, the **Islamic kingdoms** of the region rose to prominence, initially Demak in the early fifteenth century, based around the port of the same name on the north coast, and then the central Javanese **Mataram** kingdom. Although the rulers and army of Surabaya challenged Mataram's attack on the north coast in an attempt to control all trade in the area, they could do little against Sultan Agung who, from 1620 to 1625, laid siege to the city and defeated it by starvation.

In the early seventeenth century, the **Dutch** established themselves in Java via the Dutch East Indies Company (VOC), and became embroiled in local politics in their efforts to subdue the population. From 1767 to 1777, their efforts were turned against East Java and in particular **Blambangan**, which was the last remaining Hindu kingdom on Java. Its defeat resulted in large areas of the east being depopulated. However, with the colonial development of the port of Surabaya, East Java's fertile agricultural heartland became the destination for many Central Javanese, as well as settlers from the north coast and Madurese. During the nineteenth century, the Dutch colonial administration recognized the potential of this fertile part of Java and established coffee, tobacco and sugar estates. In the early part of the twentieth century, Surabaya was developed as the region's administrative centre, and a major building programme was undertaken to give it all the trappings of a major city. Today, Surabaya is the main port and manufacturing centre in the region, and is ringed by industrial complexes, their growth accelerating year by year. However, away from the metropolis, extensive rice terraces dominate the valleys between the volcanoes, and fruit orchards, vegetable fields and coffee, rubber and cocoa plantations are the mainstay of the upland economies.

Surabaya and around

Polluted, noisy and sprawling, **SURABAYA** is the second largest city in Indonesia, and the major port of East Java. With time and effort, the city is comprehensible and even enjoyable – but for most tourists, Surabaya is somewhere to head through as fast as possible on the way to more interesting destinations. If you do want to linger, the **Chinese** and **Arab quarters** to the north of the city centre and the **zoo** and **museum** to the south are the most interesting sights, and a trip to one of the enormous shopping centres is a great insight into how more and more local people are spending their leisure time. Outside the city, **Trowulan**, a two-hour bus ride to the southwest, features impressive Majapahit remains in a peaceful, rural setting.

Some history

It's uncertain when Surabaya was actually founded, although May 31, 1293 has been designated for that honour, the supposed date of the founding of the mighty **Majapahit** kingdom. During the era of the Majapahit, the city was less important than the other north-coast ports such as Tuban and Gresik, and it was not until the early nineteenth century that Surabaya overtook Pasuruan in size. Although it was small, it gradually became more influential, and by 1622 had control of Gresik, much of the Brantas valley and even parts of Kalimantan. The kingdom of Mataram was in the ascendant in Central Java, and by the seventeenth century the two kingdoms were at loggerheads. In 1610, Mataram started what would be a long-running **war** against the kingdom of Surabaya, and in 1620 Sultan Agung attacked the town with 80,000 troops, devastating the hinterland and poisoning the city's water supply. By 1625, Surabaya was on its knees; records of the time indicate that no more than 500 of its 50,000–60,000 people were left. However, at the end of the seventeenth century, the **VOC** established a post in the city, and trade in a wide variety of products flourished, including rice, salt and sugar. In 1717, the inhabitants rebelled against the colonizers, although after six years the city was retaken by the Dutch, who developed it into the largest and most important port in Java. By 1900, Surabaya, with its avenues, large imposing bungalows and civic buildings, was the biggest town in the Dutch East Indies, even bigger than Batavia, and until the 1950s, when Tanjung Priok took over, the most important port in Indonesia.

The Dutch development of the nineteenth and early twentieth centuries meant that whole communities were displaced. Conditions in the kampung outside the showcase colonial areas were appalling and a huge police presence protected the Dutch from increasing local dissatisfaction. Following the declaration of Indonesian **Independence** on August 17, 1945, the people of Surabaya were hopeful that colonial rule was over. However, by early September, Dutch officials released from their wartime internment had returned to Surabaya as though nothing had happened. On September 16 the Dutch flag was raised on the roof the *Oranje Hotel* (now the *Hotel Majapahit Mandarin Oriental*) on Jalan Tunjungan; a group of young local people stormed the hotel and tore part of it down, an event now known as the **Flag Incident**.

In the following months, groups of Indonesian youths went on the rampage against foreigners, and the situation became increasingly tense when a British infantry brigade landed in October. At Jembatan Merah, a three-day battle was waged between the British and thousands of Indonesian youths armed only with bamboo spears. Eventually, the British as well as resident foreigners were overwhelmed by the **Indonesian People's Security Army** (Tentara Keamanan Rakyat), and thousands of attached supporters; the death toll on both sides was high. British reinforcements eventually arrived and the **Battle of Surabaya** lasted for three weeks before the eventual defeat of the Indonesians by Allied and Dutch land, sea and air assaults. Thousands of Indonesians died, and most of the population fled the city. The beginning of the battle on November 10 is celebrated throughout Indonesia as **Heroes Day** (Hari Pahlawan), for although the Indonesians lost the battle, it marked a significant point in the fight for Independence.

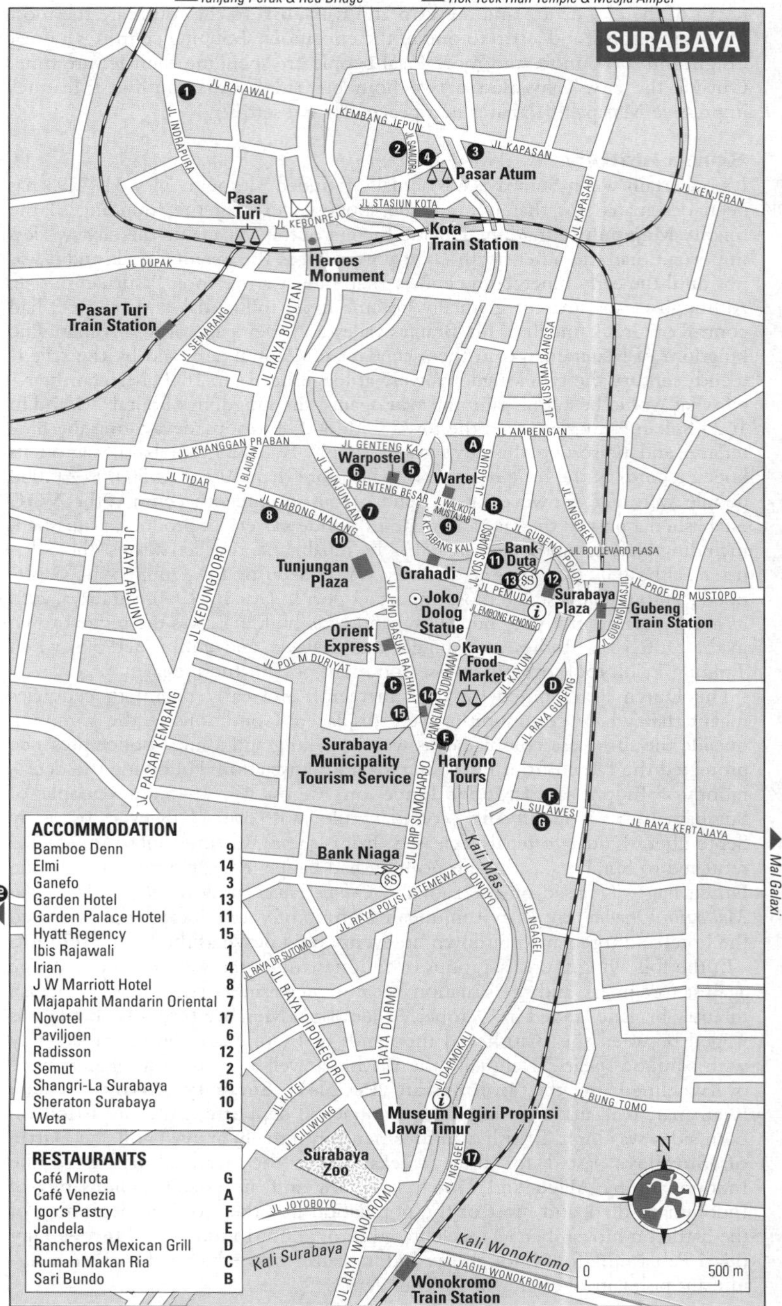
Tanjung Perak & Red Bridge
Hok Teck Hian Temple & Mesjid Ampel
SURABAYA
JL RAJAWALI
JL INDRAPURA
JL KEMBANG JEPUN
JL SAMUDRA
JL KAPASAN
Pasar Atum
JL KENJERAN
JL KAPASARI
Pasar Turi
JL KEBONREJO
JL STASIUN KOTA
Kota Train Station
Heroes Monument
JL DUPAK
Pasar Turi Train Station
JL SEMARANG
JL RAYA BUBUTAN
JL KUSUMA BANGSA
JL AMBENGAN
JL KRANGGAN PRABAN
JL GENTENG KALI
Warpostel
Wartel
JL TIDAR
JL BLAURAN
JL TUNJUNGAN
JL GENTENG BESAR
JL WALIKOTA MUSTAJAB
JL AGUNG
JL EMBONG MALANG
JL KETABANG KALI
JL ANGGREK
JL GUBENG POJOK
JL BOULEVARD PLASA
JL RAYA ARJUNO
JL KEDUNGDORO
Tunjungan Plaza
Grahadi
Bank Duta
JL YOS SUDARSO
JL PEMUDA
Surabaya Plaza
JL PROF DR MUSTOPO
Gubeng Train Station
JL GUBENG MASJID
Joko Dolog Statue
JL EMBONG KENONGO
JL JEND BASUKI RACHMAT
Orient Express
Kayun Food Market
JL KAYUN
JL POL M DURIYAT
JL PANGLIMA SUDIRMAN
JL RAYA GUBENG
JL PASAR KEMBANG
Surabaya Municipality Tourism Service
Haryono Tours
JL SULAWESI
JL RAYA KERTAJAYA
Mal Galaxi
Kali Mas
Bank Niaga
JL URIP SUMOHARJO
JL DINOYO
JL RAYA POLISI ISTEMEWA
JL NGAGEL
JL RAYA DR SUTOMO
JL RAYA DIPONEGORO
JL RAYA DARMO
JL DARMOKALI
JL BUNG TOMO
JL KUTEI
JL CILIWUNG
Museum Negiri Propinsi Jawa Timur
Surabaya Zoo
JL NGAGEL
N
JL JOYOBOYO
Kali Wonokromo
JL RAYA WONOKROMO
Kali Surabaya
JL JAGIH WONOKROMO
0
500 m
Wonokromo Train Station
Bungusarih Bus Station & Airport
Margorejo Indah Sports Centre
ACCOMMODATION
Bamboe Denn 9
Elmi 14
Ganefo 3
Garden Hotel 13
Garden Palace Hotel 11
Hyatt Regency 15
Ibis Rajawali 1
Irian 4
J W Marriott Hotel 8
Majapahit Mandarin Oriental 7
Novotel 17
Paviljoen 6
Radisson 12
Semut 2
Shangri-La Surabaya 16
Sheraton Surabaya 10
Weta 5
RESTAURANTS
Café Mirota G
Café Venezia A
Igor's Pastry F
Jandela E
Rancheros Mexican Grill D
Rumah Makan Ria C
Sari Bundo B

Arrival, information and city transport

All **flights** arrive at Juanda International Airport, 18km south of the city. No public bus service connects with the town centre, but there's a rank for fixed-price **taxis** (Rp26,000). There is a **tourist office** at the airport (Mon–Sat 8am–9pm; ⓣ031/8667513 ext. 538).

If you arrive by **sea** – probably by Pelni ferry – you'll dock at Tanjung Perak port in the far north of the city, which is served by C, P and PAC buses (see p.284).

Surabaya has three main **train stations**. **Gubeng station** is in the east of town: there are entrances on Jalan Gubeng Mesjid and Jalan Sumatera. A hotel reservation desk is located here (daily 8am–8pm), but they only deal with the most expensive places. Gubeng serves Banyuwangi, Malang, Blitar, Yogyakarta, Solo and Jakarta via the southern route across Java – some of these trains also pass through **Kota station**, which lies towards the north of the city centre. The entrance to Kota is at the junction of Jalan Semut Kali and Jalan Stasiun. **Pasar Turi station**, in the west of the city centre on Jalan Semarang, serves destinations along the northern route across the island to Jakarta via Semarang.

Moving on from Surabaya

Surabaya is the main air, sea, rail and road hub for East Java and has excellent **connections** across Indonesia and internationally. It is a visa-free entry point for arrivals by air (see "Basics" on p.23). Some **international flight** destinations are reached direct, whilst others have connections via Jakarta or Denpasar; see p.291 for airline offices in Surabaya. **Domestic flights**, through Bouraq, Garuda and Merpati, are numerous. Taxis from Gubeng station taxi rank to the airport are fixed at Rp26,000.

From **Bungurasih bus station**, there are frequent departures to destinations on Java, and as far east as Flores and up to Banda Aceh on Sumatra. Buses to local destinations operate several times hourly during daylight hours and hourly through the night. For departures within East Java, just buy your ticket on the bus. You will pay Rp200 for a ticket to get into the departure area – the bays are clearly labelled and porters will point you in the right direction for your bus. Be wary, though: the lists detailing fares are not easy to find, and overcharging has been known.

Express **air-con buses** are considerably more expensive than the standard variety (generally double the fare). Long-distance journeys are completed by night buses (departing 2–6pm) from Bay 8; the ticket offices for all the night-bus companies are in the bus station. Booking is advisable at least the day before, but outside holiday time you'll probably be able to buy your ticket on the spot. If you can't bear the slog out to the bus station, central **minibus** companies run more expensive daily trips to the main Javan destinations, leaving from outside their offices. For Yogyakarta, Solo and Semarang, try Tirta Jaya, Jl Jend Basuki Rachmat 64 ⓣ031/5468687.

Surabaya's port, **Tanjung Perak**, is the major port in East Java, and no fewer than thirteen of the fleet of eighteen **Pelni ferries** call here on their routes through the archipelago, making it an excellent place to leave by sea. The Pelni office is at Jl Pahlawan 112 (Mon–Thurs 9am–noon & 1–3pm, Fri–Sat 9am–noon; ⓣ031/339048, ⓕ338958). Staff here speak some English, and can provide information about the Pelni services throughout Indonesia.

Trains depart from all three Surabaya stations. Gubeng station serves Banyuwangi, Malang, Blitar, Solo, Yogyakarta and Jakarta; most of the Gubeng station trains also stop at Kota station. Pasar Turi station serves Jakarta via Semarang and other north-coast towns.

The main **bus terminal** is Bungurasih (also known as Purabaya), 6km south of the city, reputed to be the biggest in Indonesia. All long-distance and inter-island buses start and finish here, plus many of the city buses and bemos. Local buses into the city (15min; Rp1500) leave from the far end of the terminal: follow the signs for "Kota". Many of the C, P and both PAC buses serve Bungurasih. There's also a huge taxi rank here, but you'll hardly ever get a driver to agree to use the meter or fix a reasonable price to the city, and you should expect to pay about Rp15,000, even with hard bargaining, to anywhere in town.

The city centres on a triangle of major roads: **Jalan Jend Basuki Rachmat**, **Jalan Panglima Sudirman** and **Jalan Pemuda**. Government buildings, major shopping centres and facilities such as exchange and tourist offices are found here or nearby. Jalan Jend Basuki Rachmat turns into Jalan Tunjungan to the north and leads eventually, via several more name changes, to the port of Tanjung Perak on the coast. To the south of the centre, Jalan Urip Sumoharjo aloo changes its name several times, and leads eventually to Bungurasih via the zoo and museum. Just to the east of the central area, Sungai Kali Mas winds roughly north–south through the city, although its frequent twists and turns make it a rather unreliable orientation point.

A word of warning: **crossing the road** in Surabaya is hair-raising. Roads are often four or five lanes wide, traffic is fast, traffic lights are regarded as mere suggestions by drivers, and footbridges very few. Look out for long poles with red stop signs on them at some traffic lights – you hold them high towards the traffic to let drivers know you're crossing.

Information

There are two central **tourist offices** in Surabaya, which can provide sketch maps of the city and answer questions: at Jl Pemuda 118 (Mon–Fri 7am–5pm, Sat 7am–3pm; ⓣ031/5478853), which is east of the Surabaya Plaza, across the road and almost at the junction with Jalan Kayun; and at Jalan Darmokali (Mon–Thurs 7am–3pm, Fri 7am–2pm; ⓣ031/575448). The main office is out towards the bus station at Jalan Wisma Menanggal (Mon–Thurs 7am–3pm, Fri 7am–2pm; ⓣ031/8531814, ⓕ8531822), but it's very hard to find, and probably most useful for telephone enquiries. The Surabaya Municipality Tourism Service, Jl Jend Basuki Rachmat 119–121 (Mon–Fri 7am–2pm; ⓣ031/5344710, ⓕ5468717), opposite the *Hyatt Regency Hotel*, has a few leaflets.

In addition to the tourist offices, one of the best places to get **information** is *Bamboe Denn* (see opposite). They give their guests up-to-date details of bus, train and air connections, have a useful sketch map, and are well-informed on local bus and bemo connections in the city.

The free monthly **magazine** *Jakarta Kini* is an excellent resource for visitors. Most of the upmarket hotels stock it; otherwise, you can collect a copy from the magazine office, Indo Multi Media at the *Hyatt Regency*, Jl Jend Basuki Rachmat 106–128 (Mon–Fri 8.30am–5pm; ⓣ & ⓕ5326299). The company has offices throughout Indonesia, and the Surabaya branch also stocks the current issues of *Hello Bali* plus maps of Jakarta, Yogya and Bali.

If you're staying in Surabaya for any length of time, a detailed **city map** is useful; the bookshops Gramedia and Gunung Agung (see p.290) stock them. The best map by far is the *Surabaya Atlas Jalan and Indeks*, published by PT Enrique and available in folded and sheet form.

City transport

City transport in Surabaya is provided by a vast fleet of **buses** and **bemos**. Three types of public buses operate in the city, with routes indicated by letters.

They stop only at designated places, which are often signified by blue bus-stop signs; signal to them to stop, and pay the conductor once you are seated. **Ordinary buses** cost Rp1000 per trip; one useful service is the "C" route, which runs from Bungusarih past Tunjungan Plaza, in through the centre of the city and up to Tanjung Perak, passing conveniently close to the post office on the way. Slightly more luxurious buses cost Rp1500, depending on the route, and are designated by "P"; both P1 and P2 complete the same route as the ordinary-service C. Top of the range are the extremely comfortable **air-con buses** – they cost Rp2000 and are designated PAC1 and PAC2, operating the same routes as P1 and P2.

There are also plenty of **metered taxis**; meters start at Rp2800, and a trip within the city centre will cost Rp7000–10,000. These are supplemented by huge numbers of **becak**, which cover the back roads not served by the main public transport.

Accommodation

The range of **accommodation** in Surabaya isn't great – many of the places in the centre are aimed at top-flight business travellers, although there are a couple of excellent exceptions for budget travellers. The less expensive places are slightly further from the centre, in the area north of Kota station, which is inconvenient both for buses (you'll need to figure out the bemos around here) and the central sights. However, it's better placed for exploring the older parts of the city, and it's near Kota station.

Inexpensive

Bamboe Denn Jl Ketabang Kali 6a ⓣ031/5340333. This is the main backpacker accommodation in the city. It isn't easy to find, and lies a thirty-minute walk from Gubeng station (Rp5000 by becak), but local people will point you in the right direction. Accommodation is very basic in tiny singles, doubles and dorms, all with shared bathrooms, but there's a pleasant sitting room and simple, inexpensive meals and snacks are available. The real plus is the excellent information available – all guests receive a sketch map of the city, and the staff are always keen to help. ❷

Hotel Ganefo Jl Kapasan 169–171 ⓣ031/3711169. This is a large, unrenovated colonial bungalow down an alleyway opposite Bank Umum. There are plenty of high ceilings and original features, although the rooms are fairly basic. The cheaper rooms have fan and outside bathroom; the pricier ones have air-con and bathroom. ❷

Hotel Irian Jl Samudra 16 ⓣ031/3520953. A cool, pleasant old-style bungalow, with a choice of rooms. There are shared bathrooms and fan at the lower end, and attached bathrooms in the more expensive rooms. ❷

Hotel Paviljoen Jl Genteng Besar 94–98 ⓣ031/5343449. Spotlessly clean rooms in an old colonial bungalow; the ones at the back have excellent verandahs around a courtyard, and all have attached cold-water mandi, while top-end rooms have air-con. This is an excellent choice if you want both comfort and a central location. Southbound buses P1 and P2 stop just at the end of the street on Jalan Tunjungan, and guests get a small sketch map of the city. ❸

Hotel Semut Jl Samudra 9–15 ⓣ031/24578, ⓕ332601. In the area north of Kota station. All rooms have air-con and attached bathroom, with cold water in the less expensive rooms and hot water in the pricier ones. In addition, there are deep, cool verandahs looking into the garden, a coffee shop and restaurant. ❸

Mid-range

Hotel Elmi Jl Panglima Sudirman 42–44 ⓣ031/5322571, ⓕ5315615, ⓔelmihtl@indosat.net.id. Rather 1970s in style, this popular mid-range hotel right in the town centre offers nice rooms, a pool, a 24-hour coffeeshop, bar and disco. ❺

Garden Hotel Jl Pemuda 21 ⓣ031/5321001, ⓕ5316111. Showing its age, but comfortable and convenient. Guests can use the *Garden Palace Hotel* facilities, including the pool, to which it is linked by a corridor. ❺

Garden Palace Hotel Jl Yos Sudarso 11 ⓣ031/5321001, ⓕ5316111 ⓔgarden@rad.net.id. Whilst not in the luxury class of some of the newer city-centre hotels, this place, and the attached *Garden Hotel*, are both very popular with Indonesian business people. It has an attractive lobby area with a bustling atmosphere, a business centre, 24-hour coffee shop and small pool. The rooms are comfortable without being outstanding. ❺

Hotel Ibis Rajawali Jl Rajawali 9–11 ⓣ031/3539994, ⓕ3539995, ⓔibisraja@accorsub.co.id. An attractive colonial edifice, with good three-star facilities, situated in the old commercial quarter, just across from the historic Red Bridge. ❺

Hotel Weta Jl Genteng Kali 3–11 ⓣ031/5319494, ⓕ5345512. A central, good-value choice in this price range, with a small but attractive lobby area, friendly and helpful staff, clean, attractive rooms with air-con and hot-water bathrooms. The staff will always discuss discounts. ❺

Expensive

Hyatt Regency Jl Jend Basuki Rachmat 106–128 ⓣ031/5311234, ⓕ5321508, ⓔhrsub@rad.net.id. A recommended and stylish hotel; the rooms are plush and comfortable, and the communal areas extremely grand. There are five restaurants and bars, two pools, squash and tennis courts plus a health and fitness centre. ❼

Hotel Majapahit Mandarin Oriental Jl Tunjungan 65 ⓣ031/5454333, ⓕ5454111, ⓔmandarin@rad.net.id. Originally built in 1910 by the son of the Singapore *Raffles Hotel* founder. In the 1930s, an Art Deco front and foyer were added, and the hotel also played a significant role in the efforts to gain independence (see p.281). It's still the most atmospheric hotel in the city, with a tangible Maughamesque feel, stylish rooms, two restaurants, a health centre and a 25m outdoor pool. ❻

Novotel Jl Ngagel 173–175 ⓣ031/5018900, ⓕ5019117, ⓔnovotel@accorsub.co.id. The sister hotel to the *Ibis*, but in retro-ethnic style. To the south of the city centre, but still only ten minutes away from the centre. The entrance areas are relaxed and stylish, with plenty of wood and bamboo, and the rooms all have hot water and air-con. There's an attractive pool, tennis courts and fitness centre, and apartments for monthly rental. ❻

Radisson Jl Pemuda 31–37 ⓣ031/5316833, ⓕ5316393, ⓔradsub@indosat.net.id. Very centrally located, behind Plaza Surabaya and opposite the World Trade Centre. The rooms are pleasant, the restaurants are good and the staff very helpful. ❻

Shangri-La Surabaya Jl Mayjen Sungkono 120 ⓣ031/5661550, ⓕ5661570, ⓔsur-bc1@shangri-la-sby.co.id. The most popular five-star hotel, located in West Surabaya, about twenty minutes from the town centre. It has a grand lobby lounge, four restaurants, a pool and bakery. ❼

Sheraton Surabaya Jl Embong Malang 25–31 ⓣ031/5468000, ⓕ5467000, ⓔsheraton@rad.net.id. Centrally located, with all the luxury and facilities you'd expect at this price; there's a small outside pool surrounded by foliage, a health club, business centre and excellent restaurants and bars. ❼

Westin Surabaya Jl Embong Malang 85–89 ⓣ031/5458888, ⓕ5193034, ⓔwestinsu@indo.net.id. The only Indonesian *Westin* is centrally located, opulent and comfortable, with a great lobby area two storeys high, an interior waterfall, plus a rooftop pool and fitness centre. ❼

The City

There are enough **sights** in Surabaya to keep most visitors occupied for a day or two: imposing colonial architecture, a lively Chinese quarter, and the harbour, where traditional schooners dock. However, unless your natural habitat is the Asian metropolis, there is little to keep you here long.

The centre

In the **centre** of Surabaya, the main sights are grand buildings from the colonial era. On Jalan Tunjungan, the *Hotel Majapahit Mandarin Oriental*, previously the **Oranje Hotel**, was the site of the "Flag Incident" (see p.281), in which a blow was struck for Indonesian Independence. Its plain exterior belies the opulent interior. Nearby on Jalan Pemuda, **Grahadi** is the graceful and elegant official residence of the governor of East Java; built in the late eighteenth century, it has been extensively renovated. The statue across the road depicts **R.T. Soerjo**, the first Indonesian governor to live in Grahadi after Independence. In a small garden opposite the Grahadi building, the most famous statue in Surabaya, **Joko Dolog** (1289), depicts King Kertanagara, the last ruler of the

Surabaya Sue

Christened **Surabaya Sue** by the Australian press during the Indonesian War for Independence, the woman also known as K'tut Tantri, Vannine Walker and Muriel Pearson, remains a controversial figure. Born of Manx parents in Scotland in 1908, she moved to Hollywood and worked as a journalist, before travelling to Bali in the 1930s, inspired by the film *Bali: The Lost Paradise*. She told her own story in *Revolt in Paradise* (see p.1078), which, although a gripping read, arguably strays from the facts.

By her own account, Surabaya Sue initially lived as a guest of the Rajah of Bangli, and then established one of the first hotels on Kuta Beach. She was imprisoned by the Japanese for two years during their occupation of Surabaya, placed in solitary confinement and tortured. On her release, she gained fame as a fighter for **Indonesian Independence**, and had plenty of hair-raising adventures during her time with the independence movement. She is best known for her broadcasts about the Indonesian cause, which, as a foreign woman reporting from the scene of the conflict, attracted much-needed international attention. After Independence, she lived for many years in a hotel in Jakarta courtesy of the Indonesian government, but eventually died in 1997 in an old people's home in Australia. Her last wish was for her ashes to be taken to Bali for a full *ngaben* ceremony, the Hindu cremation rite. As a non-Hindu, this caused considerable disturbance among the religious authorities on Bali – in death, Surabaya Sue proved as controversial as she had been in life.

Singosari kingdom, in the form of Buddha. Originally erected in the area of Malang, it was brought to Surabaya about three hundred years ago and remains highly revered by local people, as the floral offerings all around testify. At the end of Jalan Pemuda by the river is the **submarine** *Pasopati*; originally Russian, it saw service in the Indonesian navy from 1962 to 1994.

North of the centre

Surabaya's **Chinese quarter** hums with activity, with an abundance of traditional two-storey shophouses lining narrow streets and alleyways, and minuscule red-and-gold altars glinting in shops and houses – an evocative contrast to the highways and massive malls of the city centre. The area centres on Jalan Slompretan, Jalan Bongkaran and the part of Jalan Samudra southwest of the 300-year-old **Hok Teck Hian temple** on Jalan Dukuh. The temple itself is a brilliant and vibrant place with several tiny shrines spread over two floors, Buddhist, Confucian and Hindu effigies, and four splendidly fierce statues guarding the main entrance, just inside the door. The main altar downstairs is the largest in the complex, dedicated to Kong Cow Kong Ting Cun Ong, the "Son of the Angels". Also downstairs, Macho, the "Angel of the Sea", is the focus of prayers for those involved in export and import. Upstairs, at the altar to Kwan Im Poosat, the "Valentine Angel", pregnant women come to pray for the sex of their child.

The oldest and most famous mosque in Surabaya is **Mesjid Ampel**, located in the Arab area, the **kampung Arab** or **Qubah**, to the north of the Chinese quarter. The whole kampung, bounded by Jalan Nyanplungan, Jalan K.H. Mas Mansur, Jalan Sultan Iskandar Muda and Jalan Pabean Pasar, was originally settled by Arab traders and sailors who arrived in Kali Mas harbour: their descendants still live here. It's a maze of tidy, well-kept alleyways crammed with flowers, beggars and shops selling Muslim hats, perfumes, dates and souvenirs. Mesjid Ampel, built in 1421, is the site of the grave of Sunan Ampel, one of the nine *wali* (see p.1035) credited with bringing Islam to Java in the sixteenth century; as such, it remains a site of pilgrimage and reverence. Sunan Ampel is regarded as one of the most important *wali,* guiding and advising the others, two of whom (Sunan Bonang and Sunan Drajat) were his sons. Sunan Ampel's own origins are uncertain: it's thought his father was from Central Asia or the Middle East. He married a princess of Campa, came to East Java in the early fifteenth century and died in 1479. The area isn't particularly tourist-friendly, and women will have to dress extremely conservatively and take a scarf to cover their heads to stand any chance of being allowed in the mosque.

The **Heroes Monument** (Tugu Pahlawan), between Jalan Bubutan and Jalan Pahlawan and to the south of the Arab quarter, is a tall pointed pillar built in the 1950s to celebrate the heroes of the Battle of Surabaya. It's located in a plain open space surrounded by wide, traffic-clogged roads. Below the monument is a museum (daily 7.30am–4.30pm; free), which commemorates the battle. A five-minute drive further north, the **Jembatan Merah** (Red Bridge) is so called because of blood spilt during a legendary fight between the shark (*sura*) and crocodile (*baya*), which now form Surabaya's coat of arms and are the possible origin of the city's name. It was also the site of heavy fighting during the Battle of Surabaya (see p.281); the flaming gold monument in nearby Jembatan Merah Plaza commemorates that battle.

In the far north of the city, timeless **Kalimas harbour** (the name means "river of gold"), a two-kilometre length of wharves and warehouses at the eastern end of the main port, lies just north of the Arab Quarter on Jalan Kalimas Baru. To get there, take bus C, P1 or P2 or either PAC bus to Tanjung Perak and walk around to the east. It's fantastically atmospheric, the traditional Sulawesi schooners (*pinisi*) loading and unloading cargoes which are either unsuitable for containerization, or destined for locations too remote for bigger ships. You need permission to take photographs; ask at the police post by the harbour entrance.

South of the centre

One of the best places to visit in the city, **Surabaya Zoo** (Kebun Binatang Surabaya), Jl Setail 1 (daily 7am–6pm; adults Rp5000, children Rp4000), lies 3km south of the city centre. To get there, buses C, P1, P2 or either PAC bus all pass by on their way between the city centre and Bungusarih. With over 3500 animals, it's surprisingly pleasant and, at least in parts, less distressing for animal-lovers than many Indonesian zoos. The enclosures of the orang-utans, Komodo dragon and giraffes are large and separated from the public by moats, but the big cats, bears and horses are kept in cramped conditions, the birds have pitifully small cages and there's even a bad-taste display of stuffed animals. Still, it's a verdant, peaceful spot, popular with families, a pleasant escape from the lunacy of the city and a good place to take a picnic and relax for a few hours – though beware of pickpockets, especially on Sundays when the zoo is packed.

A few minutes' walk from the zoo is the **Museum Negiri Propinsi Jawa Timur**, MPU Tantular, Jl Taman Mayangkara 6 (Tues–Fri 8am–3pm, Sat & Sun 8am–2pm; Rp500). The entrance features a *thuk-thuk*, an ornately carved wooden drum from Madura, while the galleries are crammed with arts and crafts and assorted archeological objects. There's an especially fine collection of shadow puppets and *topeng* masks, and some of the more outlandish items include a penny-farthing bicycle, a Daimler motorcycle and an ancient gramophone and records. Some attempts have been made to label items in English, although there's little explanation.

Eating and drinking

From the central night market on Jalan Genteng Besar through the popular food courts in the shopping centres to luxurious dining in the top-flight hotels, the city has a wealth of **eating** options. For fast food, there are nine branches of *McDonald's* in Surabaya; the central ones are in Plaza Surabaya, Jalan Pemuda, Plaza Tunjungan, Jalan Basuki Rachmat and in Jalan Raya Darmo. *Pizza Hut*, Jl Raya Darmo 79A, is very popular with well-to-do Indonesians.

Café Mirota Jl Sulawesi 24. Attached to the souvenir shop of the same name, this tiny café serves snacks and light meals of soup, rice and noodles. Cheap.

Cascades At the *Hyatt Regency*, Jl Jend. Basuki Rachmat 106–128. A poolside restaurant on the roof with very good international dishes. The *Primavera* on the same floor offers the best Italian in town. Both are expensive but excellent.

Coffee Garden At the *Shangri-La Hotel*, Jl Mayjen Sungkono 120. Excellent splurge lunchtime and dinner buffet (Asian, Western), also à la carte; very popular with expat residents. The *Portofino* Italian restaurant upstairs has a lovely ambience, but is highly priced, as are the Chinese and Japanese restaurants here.

Igor's Pastry Jl Biliton 55 ⓣ031/5038342. A shop selling high-quality cakes, and sweet and savoury pastries, perfect for snacking in your hotel room.

Indigo At the *Hotel Majapahit Mandarin Oriental*, Jl Tunjungan 65. Just off the lobby of this stylish old-world hotel, this contemporary coffee shop serves excellent Indonesian, Chinese and Western dishes, including great pizzas. Upstairs is the *Sarkies* restaurant, probably the most elegant in town; with an ambience of the tropics circa the 1920s, serving Asian cuisine, with seafood a speciality.

Jendela Resto Gallery, Jl Sonokembang 4. An outdoor restaurant-cum-art gallery, popular with a young crowd, serving Indonesian and Western food. Reasonable prices, and some of the evening bands do very good cover versions.

Kayun Food Market Jalan Kayun. Actually a collection of permanent outdoor eating places along the Kalimas river. Of an evening this is a cheap and atmospheric place to eat local food.

Kafé Excelso This Indonesian chain has branches on the ground floor of Surabaya Plaza and a couple in Tunjungan Plaza, and is very popular with well-heeled Indonesians and expatriates. They have an excellent choice of expensive Indonesian coffees (choose between Bali, Toraja, Sumatra or Java Arabica blends), plus iced coffee, salads, snacks, cakes and ice creams.

Ming Court Restaurant At the *Garden Palace Hotel*, Jl Yos Sudarso 11. This recommended first floor restaurant offers very good, reasonably priced Cantonese style food, something quite rare among Chinese restaurants in Surabaya.

Queen's Mela At the *Sheraton Hotel*, Jl Embong Malang 25–31. Surabaya's only Indian restaurant, with stylish decor and delicious but expensive food.

Rancheros Mexican Grill Jl Sumatra 106. Just along from *Colors Bar* (see p.290), this smart restaurant offers great TexMex style food.

Rumah Makan Ria Jl Kombes Pol M Duryat 7. A recommended and extremely popular Indonesian restaurant, reasonably priced, with fast service and offering an excellent introduction to the cuisine.

Sari Bundo Jl Walikota Mustajab 70. A popular place serving reasonably priced Padang food, considered the best Padang restaurant in town.

Tunjungan Plaza Food Court The largest food court in Surabaya, on the seventh floor of the biggest and brashest of the city's shopping plazas. There is a vast array of fast food available here: *KFC, McDonald's*, Singaporean noodles, Cajun grills, New Zealand ice cream, crepes and kebabs.

Café Venezia Jl Ambengan 16. Located on a busy and noisy corner; you can eat outside or in the high-ceilinged cool interior. There's a comprehensive menu of Indonesian, Chinese, Japanese, Korean and Western food, plus plenty of ice creams and sundaes. Prices are in the moderate to expensive range.

Entertainment

There's no shortage of **entertainment** in Surabaya, although it's a lot easier to find a disco or cinema in the city than a wayang kulit show. **Cinemas** in the city include: Mitra 21, Jl Pemuda 15; Galaxi, Mal Galaxi, Jalan Raya Kertajaya Timur; and Studio, Plaza Tunjungan I, Jalan Basuki Rachmat – all show English-language films, subtitled in Indonesian.

The **discos** (daily 10pm–2am) listed here alternate recorded music with live. They're generally fairly expensive, but admission prices vary – some places like to have expats and let them in free, because they drink more than the locals. However, on a Saturday night and if a well-known band is playing, there's usually an entrance charge ranging from Rp20,000 to Rp60,000. Local beer averages Rp20,000 a glass, and one glass is sometimes included in the admission price – ordering by the pitcher is much cheaper. Popular discos include *Desperadoes* at the *Shangri-La Hotel*, *Station* at the top of Plaza Tunjungan, and *Java Jimmy's* at the *Westin*. With a large student population in the city, there are plenty of **live music** venues (bands start playing from 9:30pm): *Colors* on Jalan Sumatra is very popular.

Traditional music, dance and drama

More traditional entertainment is available at RRI Surabaya, Jl Pemuda 82–90, which has free **wayang kulit** shows every Saturday at 10pm. At Taman Hiburan Rakyat (an amusement park known locally as Tay Ha Air) on Jalan Kusuma Bangsa, regular folk **comedy** performances are held from 6pm to 11pm (ask the tourist office for performance schedules). Slightly further afield, performances of traditional **dance** and **drama** are given during the dry season (July–Nov) at Pandaan (see p.314). Many people travel from Surabaya for all three shows; contact Surabaya travel agents (see p.292) for all-inclusive trips, or the tourist offices for information.

Shopping

What Surabaya lacks in culture, it makes up for in shopping, which is regarded here as a pastime. The city offers the best shopping centres outside of Jakarta; opening times are from 10am to 9.30pm every day. The largest by far is **Plaza Tungungan** on Jalan Basuki Rachmat. In three sections, this offers an incredible array of shops, selling virtually everything local and imported and offering a great array of facilities in addition to the shops: cinemas, a supermarket, pharmacies, cafés and restaurants. A new addition to Plaza Tungungan is the adjoining Sogo Department Store, offering mostly good-quality imported goods. **Plaza Surabaya** on Jalan Pemuda is more local in content, but more manageable in size. **Mal Galaxi** on Jalan Raya Kertajaya Indah Timur, is also smaller than Plaza Tunjungan; it's a twenty-minute taxi ride east of the city centre in a wealthy Chinese residential area, and offers a good range of quality shops with a number of international brands.

For a more traditional shopping experience, try **Pasar Turi** on Jalan Semarang, where most Surabayans shop. The market is very cheap, but overcrowded and hectic – watch out for pickpockets and snatch-and-run thieves. **Pasar Atum** is a two-storey concrete local market, packed with stalls selling pretty much everything and is popular with the Chinese, especially for dressmaking and tailoring (cloth downstairs, dressmakers and tailors upstairs). Bemo M will get you here from the east end of Jalan Genteng Kali in the city centre. For details of supermarkets, see "Listings" on p.292.

Books, magazines and newspapers

There's a reasonable range of English-language **books** available in the city, but don't expect bargain prices, as imported books tend to be expensive.

Gramedia Jl Jend Basuki Rachmat 95, in Plaza Tungungan 1, and at Jl Manyar Kertoarjo 16 (near Mal Galaxi). A range of English-language titles plus some maps, guidebooks and stationery. The *Jakarta Post* usually gets here by the afternoon, and there are some international magazines such

as *The Economist*, *Time* and *Newsweek*.
Gunung Agung In Plaza Surabaya, Plaza Tunjungan and Mal Galaxi. A rival to Gramedia, with a reasonable English section and stationery, including a good guidebook and map section.
Hyatt Regency Newsstand In the *Hyatt Regency Hotel*, near the reception. A good selection of English-language titles, paperback fiction, magazines and newspapers.
Mirota Jl Sulawesi 24. A good secondhand book selection, one of the few in the city. Prices start from Rp8000, and they buy back at half the price.
Sogo Department Store Adjoining Plaza Tungungan, offering mostly English-language books and magazines.

Souvenirs

Shopping for **souvenirs** in Surabaya doesn't give you the number or range of shops or choice of goods that you'll find in Bali or Yogyakarta, but there are a few places well worth checking out.

Batik Keris Tunjungan Plaza and Mal Galaxi. A well-known chain of textile and souvenir shops, offering an extensive range, from tiny batik purses to pure-silk sarong and scarf sets. They have a good choice of sarongs in all styles of Javanese batik, plenty of shirts and other ready-made clothing, plus carvings, puppets and pictures.
Danar Hadi Jl Pemuda 1J and Jl Diponegoro 184. Offers batik cloth and ready-made garments, cushions and pictures.
Oleh Oeh Jl Kupang Indah III/22. Offers an excellent range of Indonesian furniture, souvenirs and gifts; expat-run, with reasonable set prices.
Mirota Jl Sulawesi 24. A brilliant souvenir shop, with plenty of items from across the islands: carvings in modern and classical style, basketware, leatherwork, furniture, paintings, ready-made batik items and material, T-shirts, silk textiles and silver. There's also a good secondhand book selection.
Sarinah Jl Tunjungan 7. Has a souvenir and craft department on the second floor, with a huge range of textiles, woodcarvings and assorted craft items; the range also includes penis sheaths from West Papua. Fitting rooms are available.

Listings

Airline offices The following airlines are found in the Hyatt Graha Bumi Modern, Jl Jend Basuki Rachmat 106–128 (next to the *Hyatt Hotel*): British Airways, 5th floor ⓣ031/5326383; Cathay Pacific, 1st floor ⓣ031/5317421, ⓕ5321582; China Southern, 2nd floor ⓣ031/5326319, ⓕ5311734; Eva Air, 5th floor ⓣ031/5465123, ⓕ5455083; Garuda ⓣ031/5457747, ⓕ5326322; Lufthansa, 5th floor ⓣ031/5316355, ⓕ5322290; Malaysia, 1st floor ⓣ & ⓕ031/5318632; Northwest, 5th floor ⓣ031/5317086, ⓕ5684843; Qantas, 5th floor ⓣ031/5452322, ⓕ5452569; Saudia, 2nd floor ⓣ031/5325802; Thai Air, 5th floor ⓣ031/5340861, ⓕ532638. Elsewhere are: Bouraq, Jl P. Sudirman 70–72 ⓣ031/5452918, ⓕ5321621 and Jl Genteng Kali 63 ⓣ031/5344940; Emirates, Lt Dasar, *Hyatt Regency*, Jl Jend Basuki Rachmat 106–128 ⓣ031/5460000, ⓕ5479520; KLM, World Trade Centre, Jl Pemuda 27–31 ⓣ031/5315096, ⓕ5315097; Mandala, Jl Diponegoro 73 ⓣ031/5687157; Merpati, Jl Raya Darmo 111 ⓣ031/5688111, ⓕ5685400; Singapore Airlines, 10th floor, Menara BBD Tower, Jl Jend Basuki Rachmat 2–6 ⓣ031/5319217, ⓕ5319214; Trans Asia Airways Regency, Jl Jend Basuki Rachmat 106–128 ⓣ031/5463181, ⓕ5467675.
Airport information ⓣ031/8667642 or 8667513.
Banks and exchange All of the main Indonesian banks have huge branches in Surabaya, with exchange facilities. Bank Duta, Jl Pemuda 12, is fast, central and efficient, and offers Visa and Mastercard advances. Bank Niaga, Jl Raya Darmo 26–28 is a good place to change travellers' cheques or foreign currency, and English is spoken. A number of foreign banks have representation: ABN-AMRO, Jl Pemuda 54; Citibank, Jl Basuki Rachmat 86; Deutsche Bank, Jalan Wima Dharmala, Jl Pang. Sudirman 101–103; HSBC, Hyatt Graha Bumi Modern, Jl Basuki Rachmat 106–128; and Standard Chartered, Jl Panglima Sudirman 57.
Car rental There are only a few car rental agencies in Surabaya, but hotels can generally arrange something. An international driver's licence is required for self-drive and the following companies offer self-drive or chauffeur-driven. Trac-Astra Rent-A-Car, Jl Basuki Rachmat 115–117 (ⓣ031/5462500), is recommended and the cars are well maintained. Otherwise, try Avis Rent-A-Car, Jl Mayjen Sungkono 139 (ⓣ031/5623522), or Indorent, Jl Raya Gubeng 17 ⓣ031/5463151.
Consulates Australia (actually a Western Australia

trade office, not a consulate, but they'll help where possible), World Trade Centre, Jl Pemuda 27–31 ⓣ031/5319123; UK, c/o Hong Kong and Shanghai Bank, 3rd floor, Graha Bumi Modern, Jl Jend Basuki Rachmat 106–128 ⓣ031/5326381, ⓕ5326380; US, Jl Dr Sutomo 33 ⓣ031/5676880.

Dentist Dr Olivia, Jl Sedap Malam 16 ⓣ031/5343299. Western-standard, English-speaking dentist; by appointment.

Doctor Dr Paulus Rahardjo, Jl Simpang Darmo Permai Untara 1/5 ⓣ031/7321759 or 08165403233 (mobile). English-speaking, popular with expats; by appointment.

Golf Surabaya has four golf courses open to visitors at very reasonable daily rates. Bukit Darmo Golf ⓣ031/7315555; Ciputra Golf ⓣ031/7412555; Graha Famili Golf ⓣ031/7310396; and Yani Golf ⓣ031/5681321.

Hospitals The following are recommended and have staff and doctors who speak English and Dutch: Rumah Sakit Darmo, Jl Raya Darmo 90 ⓣ031/5676253; Rumah Sakit Mitra Keluarga, Jalan Satelit Indah II, Darmo Satelit ⓣ031/7345333; Rumah Sakit Katolik St. Vincentius A Paulo (known as "RKZ"), Jl Diponegoro 51 ⓣ031/5677562; Rumah Sakit Surabaya Internasional, Jl Nginden Intan Barat B ⓣ031/5993211. For emergencies, the RKZ or RS Darmo are the best, most central options.

Immigration office Jl Jend S. Parman 58a ⓣ031/8531785.

Internet access There are four public internet terminals in the main post office (Mon–Thurs 8am–8pm, Fri & Sat 8am–3pm; Rp3000 for the first 15min and Rp180 per min after that). Internet cafés disappear as fast they spring up, but try Café Fresh, 5th floor, Plaza Tungungan, Jalan Basuki Rachmat, or Planet on the corner of Jalan Bangka and Jalan Biliton. All the big plazas have at least one internet café, and prices vary from Rp3000 to Rp8000 per hour.

Post office The main post office (Mon–Thurs 8am–3pm, Fri & Sat 8am–1pm) is at Jl Kebonrojo 10. To get there from the city centre, take a C, P1, P2, PAC1 or PAC2 bus from outside Tunjungan Plaza to the junction of Jalan Kebonrojo and Jalan Bubutan; to get back to the city, go along to the other end of Jalan Kebonrojo and pick up the same buses on Jalan Pahlawan. Poste restante is at the philatelic counter in the centre of the post office; get mail addressed to you at: Poste Restante, Post Office, Jl Kebonrojo 10, Surabaya 60175, Java Timur. The parcel office (Mon–Thurs 8am–3pm, Fri 8–11am & 12.30–3pm, Sat 8am–1pm) is to the right of the main building. If you're just sending letters, a more central post office is at Jl Taman Apsaril 1 (Mon–Thurs 8am–12.30pm, Fri 8–11am, Sat 8am–noon), just off Jalan Pemuda in the city centre.

Supermarkets Gelael, Jl Basuki Rachmat 16–18 (almost next to Plaza Tunjungan); Hero, ground floor, Plaza Tunjungan; Sogo Supermarket, adjoining Plaza Tunjungan; and Papaya, Jl Raya Darmo Permai Selatan 3, all offer a good selection, including imported groceries, wine and spirits.

Swimming The best pools are Margorejo Indah Sports Centre, Jalan Margorejo, complete with water slides, and Graha Residen Swimming Pool, Jl Darmo Harapan 1 with an Olympic size pool, a children's pool and a separate diving pool. The public Brantas Kolam Renang, Jl Irian Barat 37–39, is central but oversubscribed and not very relaxing. Several of the three- to five-star hotels open their pools to the public for a charge; try the *Elmi* or *Radisson*.

Taxis Blue Bird ⓣ031/3721234; Silver ⓣ031/5600055; Zebra ⓣ031/841111.

Telephone and fax The warpostel at Jl Genteng Besar 49 (daily 5am–11pm) has telephone, fax and letter services. One of the most convenient wartels (daily 24hr) is the one on the ground floor of Tunjungan Plaza. It's a bit tucked away, under the main steps leading down into Tunjungan 2, just behind *Kafé Excelso*. There's another 24-hour wartel at Jl Walikota Mustajab 2–4.

Travel agents Many agents in Surabaya offer all-inclusive tours to the sights of the region, either day-trips or longer, plus international bookings. Try Haryono Tours and Travel, Jl Sulawesi 27–29 ⓣ031/5033000 or 5034000; Orient Express, Jl Panglima Sudirman 62 ⓣ031/5456666; or Pacto, *Hyatt Regency Hotel*, Jl Jend Basuki Rachmat 106–128 ⓣ031/5460628.

Trowulan and around

Almost certainly the capital of the glorious Majapahit kingdom from the late thirteenth century until 1478, **TROWULAN** is situated 35km southwest of Surabaya, en route to Jombang. Trowulan itself is a small sleepy village, with **archeological remains** spread across an area of about a hundred square kilometres around it. The number and impressive size and design of the buildings, plus the range of artefacts found, give a sense of the might and majesty of the kingdom that had such influence on the region and beyond, into Bali. This historical significance, combined with the peaceful setting – a lovely maze of small, quiet lanes leading between cornfields and through small hamlets with tiny house compounds and thatched barns – make it well worth seeing.

While some of the sites are really too far flung from Trowulan unless you have a rental car or motorcycle, the best way to visit most of the places of interest is to get a bus heading for Jombang and ask to be put off in Trowulan (Rp8000); you'll know you're there as all the pillars and gateposts on the main road are painted red. The turning you want is Jalan A. Yani: it's through two large red pillars, a few metres after a small wartel sign, on the left if you are coming from Surabaya. Crowds of **becak** can take you around the sites (Rp20,000–25,000 for about 3hr), or you can do the whole lot on foot, but you'll need the entire day. There is no accommodation in the village but Mojokerto (see p.294) makes a good base if you want to stay in the area.

The sites

The **Trowulan Museum** (daily except Fri 8am–2pm; Rp500) on Jalan A. Yani is a useful and enlightening adjunct to visiting the sites, and is perhaps the best introduction to it: labels are in English. The range of items is huge, including stone statuary, terracotta, earthenware and Chinese porcelain; the most famous artefact, however, is an enormous stone statue of Airlangga as the god Wishnu perched atop a *garuda*. Opposite the museum, the artificial lake of **Kolam Segaran** illustrates the huge disposable wealth of the Majapahit kingdom (see p.1034): it's said that at the end of opulent feasts laid on to impress outsiders, crockery and cutlery from the meal would be thrown into the lake.

Turning right out of the museum, it's almost 1km to the **Pendopo Agung**, the totally rebuilt Grand Reception Hall: only the stone foundations under the pillars supporting the roof are original. There are vivid modern statues of Gajah Made, the famous fourteenth-century commander in chief and prime minister of the Majapahit kingdom, and Raden Wijaya 1, the founder and first ruler of the Majapahit, whose 1293 coronation is depicted in a relief on the back wall of the hall.

Around 200m north of the Pendopo Agung, a turning to the right leads for 2km to one of the most imposing Trowulan sites, **Candi Bajang Ratu**. It's a dramatic red-brick gateway on the left of the road, thought to date from the mid-fourteenth century (originally there were walls running to the left and right of the gateway). Continuing on the same road, which bends around to the right, after 500m you'll come to the village of Dinuk, just beyond which is **Candi Tikus** (Rat Temple), which has been sympathetically renovated and lies in attractive and well-maintained grounds. It is so named because in 1914 it was discovered by farmers looking for a nest of rats that had been plaguing the area. The ancient ritual-bathing area, now dry, is sunk deep into the ground: it has a central platform, on which are the remains of what were the highest structures in the complex, representing the mythical and holy Mount Mahameru, from which Hindus believe the elixir of immortality springs.

Retrace your steps up Jalan A. Yani to the main road: several of the most impressive remains lie to the north of here, including the hugely impressive **Candi Brahu**, a solid, imposing, tower-like rectangular temple, the largest of all the remaining structures from the Majapahit kingdom. Another 500m along the same road, a sign points to **Candi Siti Inggill**, a shady burial ground in a high, walled compound. Turning right out of here it's another 500m back to the main road: you'll then be about a kilometre beyond the main Jalan A. Yani junction towards Jombang. Heading back towards Surabaya, **Gapura Wringin**

Lawang, another great red-brick gateway, lies about 200m to the right off the road, 1.5km from the junction.

Mojokerto

The small town of **MOJOKERTO**, 8km north of Trowulan, provides the closest accommodation to the ruins. There are regular buses to Mojokerto from Surabaya, terminating at Terminal Kertojoyo in the south of the city. To get to the town centre, pick up a bemo (most are yellow) to the centre of town, locally called "pasar". These bemos also head out to Trowulan and end their journey about 200m beyond the Jalan A. Yani junction in Trowulan that leads down to the museum.

Mojokerto's **station** is centrally located on Jalan Bhayangkara, and the post office is a kilometre north of the town centre on Jalan A. Yani, next to the 24-hour telephone office. There are only a few **accommodation** options. *Hotel Slamet*, Jl P.B. Sudirman 51 (☎0321/321400; ❷–❹), offers a huge variety of rooms, with air-con in the more expensive ones. To get there, turn right out of the station, take a left at the next junction and the hotel is 200m down the road on the right – about a ten-minute walk. A budget alternative is *Wisma Tenara*, Jl H.O.S. Cokroaminoto 3 (☎0321/322904; ❷–❸). Go past the *Hotel Slamet* to the next junction, turn right and *Wisma Tenara* is on the left, just before the BCA building; they are used to tourists here, and staff are friendly and welcoming. Two standards of room are available – cheaper ones with fans or newer ones with air-con – and all have attached bathrooms; there's also a pleasant garden in the back and attractive verandahs. At the time of writing there were no **exchange facilities** in town, so be sure to bring enough local currency with you. If you're not too impressed by Mojokerto, only thirty minutes' drive south of the town is a splendid new hotel, *Sativa Sanggraloka*, Jl Raya Pacet Km3, Pacet, Mojokerto (☎0321/690227 or 690228; ❻). Based upon designs from the Majapahit period, this new hotel offers splendid luxury in a natural setting, with a range of cottages and villas. There's a pool and tennis court, and a restaurant serving Indonesian, Chinese and Western meals. It's difficult to get to by local transport, but an ojek could be arranged from Mojokerto; expect to pay around Rp15,000.

Tuban and around

One hundred kilometres northwest of Surabaya, the attractive coastal town of **TUBAN** is not often visited by foreign tourists and makes an interesting side-trip from Surabaya, with a relaxed seaside feel and a few interesting sights. Most visitors will arrive on the main street, Jalan Panglima Sudirman, which runs along the waterfront; the alun-alun, which lies directly opposite the jetty, marks the centre of town.

The foundation of Tuban dates from the twelfth century, when it was an important trading centre with the rest of Asia. The Chinese have long had a presence here and the **Klenteng Kwan Sing Bio** temple, facing the sea on Jalan P. Sudirman, is the largest Chinese temple in Indonesia, with an impressive entrance depicting gigantic dragons and crabs. If you're here on a Sunday afternoon, it's worth catching one of the free **puppetry performances**, which relate Buddhist epics, spiced with social comment. On the alun-alun, the late-nineteeth-century **Masjid Agung**, with three pointed domes and an elegant facade of Mooresque archways, is particularly elegant, and more Arab in style than many mosques in Java. Just behind here is a small lane leading to the **grave of Sunan Bonang**, one of the nine holy men who introduced

Islam into Java before his death in 1525. Pilgrims come from all over Java to pray here. The tomb (open all hours) is surrounded by elegant whitewashed walls and archways, decorated with Chinese and Dutch ceramics set into the walls. Dozens of souvenir shops line the nearby streets, selling images of Sunan Bonang on T-shirts, posters and bottles of holy water.

Practicalities

There are regular **bus** connections to Tuban from Surabaya, departing from Bungarasi bus terminal (2hr 30min; Rp5000), and going via Lamongan and Babat; however, if you have your own transport, a more scenic route takes you via the Gresik toll road and along the coast road via Sedayu. Returning to Surabaya, regular buses leave the Tuban terminal at the intersection of Jalan P. Sudirman and Jalan Teuku Umar. There's a **tourist office** at Jl Sunan Bonang 6 (daily except Sun 8.30am–4pm; ⓣ0356/321321), offering a number of free maps and tourist brochures.

There is a good choice of **accommodation** in Tuban. The *Losmen Jawa Timur*, Jl Veteran 25 (ⓣ0356/322312; ❷), alongside the town square, is a good budget option, basic but clean, but the best hotel is undoubtedly the new *Resor Tuban Tropis*, Jl Basuki Rachmad 3 (ⓣ0356/325800, ⓕ325888; ❸), situated ten minutes' walk southeast of the alun-alun. The hotel is surprisingly sophisticated, with a range of rooms and suites, some self-contained with kitchens; it also has a swimming pool, fitness centre, a restaurant serving Indonesian, Chinese and Western food, a café and a bar.

For places to eat, the restaurant at the *Resor Tuban Tropis* is the most sophisticated in town. Otherwise, the *RM Pangestune*, Jl Semarang 1, next to the *Hotel Purnama*, offers good local seafood dishes (try the squid cooked in its ink). *RM Mahkota*, Jl Dr Wahidin Sudiro Husodo 77 is a popular Chinese restaurant offering mostly seafood. There are many warungs and some simple depots down by the jetty on Jalan Yos Sudarso, which are very lively in the evening.

Around Tuban

Tuban is famous for its style of **batik** (*gedog*), made in the Kerek area, 15km west of Tuban. The batik style is unique, the thick, coarsely woven cloth made entirely on a handloom. The designs depict stylized sea creatures, especially crustacea, and are much more rustic than the refined styles of Solo and Yogyakarta. Most famous for the indigo base, the colours have great depth; several of the dyes are derived from plants and the ink of the cuttlefish. **MARGOREJO**, a picturesque hamlet where every family seems to be making batik, is the best place to buy, and as soon as a visitor arrives, locals will come out with lengths of cloth. It's also a great place to see the various stages of batik production; prices range upwards from Rp20,000 per piece, and ready-made garments are available. To get to the Kerek region, take a bemo from the bus terminal in Tuban to the village of Merakurak (5km; Rp1000) and change there for another bemo (Rp500). If you can't get to the village, visit the batik shop in Tuban town, Lontar Baturetno, Jl WR Supratmasn 7, but expect to pay more.

Pulau Madura

Located just 3km across the Madura Strait, **Pulau Madura** could hardly be more different from the hustle and bustle of Surabaya: it's a restful and totally rural place, where village and small-town life continue in timeless fashion.

Kerapan sapi

Each year in August and September, when the season's ploughing is over, early knockout heats of **kerapan sapi** (ox races) start throughout Madura to find the fastest pair of oxen on the island. In the rural economy, dependent on the strength and expertise of the animals, the races originated as a way of toughening up the oxen – and having some fun. Individual and village pride can be boosted considerably by having a prizewinning pair of these enormous beasts. Each weighing up to 600kg, they are yoked together and adorned with highly decorated bridles, while the rider half-stands and half-sits precariously on a flimsy-looking long pole that is dragged behind, as they charge over a course just over 100m long, reaching speeds of up to 50km per hour.

The stakes are high: the overall island-wide winner can usually count on a motorcycle and/or a TV as their prize, while local loss of face and misery results from a defeat. The owner of a good racing ox will be able to sell it for Rp20,000,000; a promising two- or three-year-old with racing potential changes hands for Rp5–7,000,000.

The oxen are carefully looked after by their owners, exempted from heavy work, fed herbal potions and vast quantities of raw eggs; it's said they're even massaged and sung to in order to lull them to sleep at night. It isn't surprising, therefore, that a favourite Madurese saying tells how local farmers treat their cattle better than their wives. The finals take place in September or October in Pamekasan, accompanied by ceremonies, parades, dancing and gamelan orchestras; check in tourist offices in Surabaya for exact dates (see p.284).

Whilst August and September are the months to visit Madura to see *kerapan sapi*, every Monday throughout the year in the late afternoon at **Bluto**, 12km southwest of Sumenep, there is a practice session when farmers try out their racing bulls. It's all very informal, and without the pomp and ceremony of the big races, but it's a good chance to get a flavour of what it's all about.

There is little commercialization, giving one a view of traditional Indonesian life centuries old. Although a quiet backwater for much of the year, the island bursts into activity during the exciting **kerapan sapi** (ox races), held every August and September. There is plenty of accommodation and public transport, and the roads are not busy, as most locals don't have cars.

Stretching 160km from west to east and around 35km from north to south, Madura is mostly flat, although there is a low range of hills across the centre. The main towns are **Bangkalan** in the west, **Pamekasan** and **Sampang** in the centre and **Sumenep** in the east. The main road on the island links the major settlements along the south coast, and there's a narrower, quieter and well-surfaced road along the north coast. Sumenep is more visitor-friendly than the other larger towns, and makes for a pleasant overnight stay.

Some history

Previously made up of several warring states, Pulau Madura was first unified in the fifteenth century by the prince of Arosbaya. The Wali Songo and their disciples brought Islam to the island in the fifteenth and sixteenth centuries: Sunan Giri from Gresik is considered to have been most involved in Madura's conversion. Arosbaya's son converted to Islam in 1528, and eventually established the whole island as Muslim.

Relations between Java and its much smaller neighbour have always been volatile. In 1624, the Central Javanese kingdom of Mataram conquered Madura as part of the siege of Surabaya; it was recorded as a long and hard battle, the

Madurese women fighting beside their men to try to repel the invaders. In 1670, the famous and much-feted **Prince Tronojoyo** began his takeover of the whole of Madura with the help of Makasar pirates, and then led a revolt against the Mataram and drove them off the island. By 1671, he had control of the island; in 1675, he took Surabaya back from Mataram, and within a couple of years much of East Java was in his hands. However, that same year, the Dutch sided with the Mataram against Trunojoyo, and he was eventually defeated.

In the first half of the eighteenth century, Mataram ceded Madura to the Dutch, who installed princes at Bangkalan, Pamekasan and Sumenep. In exchange for the Dutch accepting and supporting them as rulers, the **Madurese princes** provided goods, workers and soldiers for the Dutch colonial government. Gradually, in the course of the nineteenth century, their power was reduced; by the beginning of the twentieth century they were effectively figureheads.

During World War II, the Japanese occupation was very harsh and, since Independence, conditions on the island have continued to be very difficult. Farming is tough, the soil is stony and the climate dry; as a result throughout Indonesia and beyond there are many Madurese who have left the island to make a living elsewhere. Those who remain behind are mostly involved in **agriculture** – tobacco is a major cash crop – and fishing.

Arrival, information and island transport

Ferries operate from **Tanjung Perak** in Surabaya across the Madura Strait to Kamal in the west of Madura around the clock (every 30min; Rp2500). There are plans for a bridge to span the strait, and the initial work is now in progress. An alternative route to Madura is the ferry (Mon, Tues, Thurs, Fri & Sat 1pm; 4hr; Rp6500) from **Tanjung Jangkar** in the far east of Java, 60km north of Banyuwangi, to **Kalianget** in the east of Madura. If you get stranded at Kalianget, there is one losmen, *Baitul Kamal* (❷).

Madura has no tourist offices, as the offices in Surabaya cover it; you can expect little in the way of hard facts, but you may get some colour brochures. The PT *Karya Pembina Swajaya* **map** of Madura, available from Surabaya bookshops (see p.290), is the most detailed available, and is very useful if you're planning on getting off the beaten track with your own transport.

Minibuses operate on the routes between the major towns on the island: Kamal to Sumenep (3hr 30min–4hr), Kamal to Sampang (1hr 30min–2hr), and Kamal to Pamekasan (2hr 30min). These are supplemented by smaller, local routes within and around the larger towns. From Kalianget, local minibuses operate to Sumenep. There are no official **car or motorcycle rental** outlets, but it's easy to make unofficial arrangements: enquire at your accommodation.

Bangkalan and the west

The town of **BANGKALAN**, 16km north of the port of Kamal, is the main population centre in the west of the island and a busy commercial and administrative hub – though there's little to persuade visitors to linger. The **museum** (Mon–Fri 7.30am–5pm, Sat & Sun 8am–4pm; Rp500) overlooking the main square has some old carriages, cannons, musical instruments and lovely carvings, but only justifies a short visit. The main sight of the west is **Air Mata**, 11km northeast of Bangkalan and 5km southeast of the village of Arosbaya, the cemetery of the Cakraningrat family, who once ruled Sumenep. It's an extensive area, with a vast number of graves, most of which have been attractively restored. The highest grave and a favourite pilgrimage spot is that of Srifar Ambami Tjakraningrat I, popularly known as Ibu Ratu, who ruled from 1545 until 1569. A ten-minute walk down the hillside, there's a **spring** whose water is reputed to guarantee eternal youth – most visitors leave with a bottleful of it. To get there, take a colt to Arosbaya and then change for Air Mata.

Practicalities

Colts from Kamal terminate at the town square on Jalan K.H. Moh. Kholil. The **post office** is at Jl Trunojoyo 2, the **telephone office** nearby at Jl Trunojoyo 11, and, for changing cash and travellers' cheques, BCA **bank** is further along at Jl Trunojoyo 15a. The only decent **accommodation** in Bangkalan is at the *Hotel Ningrat*, Jl K.H. Moh. Kholil 113 (Ⓣ031/3095388; ❹), but if this is outside your price range and you get stranded, you could try the *Melati Hotel*, Jl Maygen Sungkono 48 (Ⓣ031/3096457; ❷), or *Hotel Surya Purnama* at Jl Kartini 19 (Ⓣ031/3096449; ❷). For **places to eat**, *Depot Wirasa*, Jl Trunojoyo 75a, has a good selection of Indonesian and Chinese food and is inexpensive and clean. The tiny *Cipta Rasa* in Jalan Mayjen Sungkono has simple Indonesian food and friendly service.

The centre of the island

The next large town to the east is **SAMPANG**, a small commercial centre built around an alun-alun, with a notable absence of sights. The small market town and beach resort of **CAMPLONG**, 35km east of Sampang, is situated on an attractive river estuary. You'll find one of the best **accommodation** options on Madura here: *Pondok Wisata Camplong* (Ⓣ0324/321586; ❹), comprising attractive bungalows and two-storey cottages, all with verandahs, set in pleasant, well-maintained grounds. There's a reasonable beach, a fair-sized pool, and an inexpensive restaurant serving Indonesian and Chinese food. Cheaper rooms have fans, more expensive ones air-con, and all have attached bathroom. All public transport between Pamekasan and Bangkalan passes the entrance.

The capital of Madura and its largest town, **PAMEKASAN** lies in the middle of the island. Centred on the large, shady alun-alun, with a bold new central mosque on the northern side, the town has little charm and not much to interest visitors. The village of **KARDULUK**, 28km east of Pamekasan, has several furniture workshops where the craftsmen use **jati wood** from the Kangean Islands. It's unlikely that you'll be carrying a four-poster bed or a huge chest home, but it's fun to look at the intricately carved designs. Also on show are the high Bekisar cages, built for the famed local cocks. At Meubel Ricky in the village you can see the **workshop** as well as the product.

Sumenep and the east

SUMENEP in the far east of the island is its most attractive town, with worthwhile sights – an old palace, museum, mosque and beaches – and the best choice of accommodation. It was hugely prosperous in the eighteenth century, which the Dutch claimed was due to local trading outside the VOC monopoly, which was illegal at the time. It's now a quiet, peaceful backwater, but its past glory is still in evidence for visitors to enjoy.

The Town

The centrepiece of the town is the eighteenth-century **Mesjid Agung** (also known as Mesjid Jam'q), a large, cool and white-tiled edifice with a lovely and imposing tiered gateway. The mosque is carefully tended, and has wonderfully carved wooden doors and an attractive interior, with rich gold decoration and blue-and-white Chinese tiles; the two grandfather clocks on the verandah add to the colonial feel of the place. Opposite Mesjid Agung, the **Taman Adipura Kota Sumenep** are attractive, well-laid-out gardens.

Museum Daerah and the neighbouring kraton (both Mon–Fri 7.30am–5pm, Sat & Sun 8am–4pm; Rp500) are two worthwhile sights, located at Jl Dr Sutomo 8, which leads from the east side of Taman Adipura Kota Sumenep directly opposite the mosque. The museum is in two parts: an old carriage house and a building within the kraton grounds. Together, they house an eclectic collection of old photographs of the Madurese royal family, carriages, textiles, furniture, porcelain, masks, weapons, wooden shoes, a tiger skin and a whale skeleton. There are no labels in English, and everything is incredibly jumbled up: the museum staff will show you round and explain things as far as possible, but it's frustrating that such a potentially fascinating collection is lying around in disrepair.

Far better is the **kraton**, the old palace, which dates from 1762, was designed by a Chinese architect, and is the only remaining palace in East Java. The Pendopo Agung (Grand Hall) is an open-sided and especially fine building, with lovely gold-painted woodcarving, old lanterns and a cool tiled floor. Visitors can look into but not enter the other rooms, which include bedrooms with carved Madurese four-poster wooden beds and dressing tables. The entrance to the palace compound is called the "Smiling Gate", apparently because the rajah used to sit up there and smile as he watched the princesses bathing and relaxing in the **Taman Sari** (Water Garden) next door. The pools are now dry, painted in modern colours and poorly maintained, but it is easy to imagine how it must have looked. Every year on October 31 (the anniversary of the founding of Sumenep), a procession through the town starts from the palace.

The local market, **Pasar Anom**, just north of the bus terminal, is wonderfully lively, with textiles, clothes, household goods and food and drink stalls: it bustles with people every day, although the main market days are Monday and Thursday. There's also a small market complex at the top of Jalan Trunojoyo, just north of Mesjid Agung, with a couple of shops selling batik, but the choice is very limited. Other options for **souvenir shopping** are Primitif Antique, Jl Wahid Hasyim 12a, which stocks furniture, carvings and attractive small boxes (from Rp25,000); Prima, at Jl A.Yani 88, which sells boxes and small wooden boats alongside bulkier items; and Madura Art Shop, Jl Brig Jend Abdullah 34, which is also worth a browse.

High on a hill a kilometre or so from Sumenep lies the royal burial ground of **Asta Tinggi**. The major royals are in the central walled area, with the minor relatives off to the sides. The most venerated graves belong to the second and third rajahs, and it's here that the faithful come to recite the Koran. To get there, take a becak to the bottom of the final hill, but you'll then have a thirty-minute walk to the top.

Practicalities

The main **bus terminal**, Wiraraja, lies 1.5km south of the town centre. Jalan Trunojoyo leads from the terminal into the centre, which is just north of Mesjid Agung. All long-distance buses, as well as buses from Pamekasan and points west, arrive at Wiraraja; take a becak or local bemo into the town centre from here. There are two other, smaller, terminals in Sumenep: Giling, for bemos to Lombang, and Kegongagong for bemos to Kalianget. **Leaving Madura**, there are direct hourly buses from Sumenep back to Surabaya (3hr;

Rp5000), departing from Wiraraja and going via Kamal. You can buy a ticket on the bus or at the ticket offices along Jalan Trunojoyo, just north of the terminal.

Sumenep offers several **accommodation** options. *Hotel Wijaya 1*, Jl Trunojoyo 45–47 (ⓣ0328/622433; ❷–❹), is a recommended central choice, a five-minute walk south of the alun-alun, offering rooms with shared bathroom through to VIP en-suite rooms with air-con. *Hotel Wijaya 2*, Jl Wahid Hasyim 3 (ⓣ0328/622532; ❷), about 200m away from its namesake, sits in a quieter road and has rooms of a similar standard, but only three with air-con. *Wisma Sumekar*, Jl Trunojoyo 53 (ⓣ0328/21502; ❷–❸), a block south of *Hotel Wijaya 1* towards the bus station, offers rooms ranging from those with no fan and outside bathroom up to rooms with air-con and TV.

Madurese **food** long ago entered the mainstream Indonesian diet: sate, soto and *rujak* (hot spiced fruit salad) all hail from here. Whilst the local specialities of Madurese sate and soto seem very similar to the varieties found on the mainland, local people insist they are vastly superior, owing to the inclusion of high-quality fish stock in the ingredients. The *Hotel Wijaya 1* has a restaurant with reasonable Indonesian food; it also offers Western breakfasts and cold beer. *Rumah Makan 17 Agustus*, Jl Raya P. Sudirman 34, has a limited rice and noodle menu, with some sate and plenty of good-value drinks, including beer; to get there, turn right at the crossroads just north of the Mesjid Agung. To sample the Madurese speciality *soto Madura* head for the warungs alongside the alun-alun.

The **post office** is at Jl Urip Sumoharjo 5 (Mon–Thurs 8am–2pm, Fri 8–11am, Sat 8am–noon), 1km east of the town centre. The most convenient wartel is at Jl Raya P. Sudirman 55 (daily 24hr), and the 24-hour **telephone office** is 1km east of the post office at Jl Urip Sumoharjo 41. You can **exchange** cash and travellers' cheques at BCA, Jl Trunojoyo 196.

Lombang

The beach at **LOMBANG**, 43km northeast of Sumenep, is long and lovely, with white sand in all directions and a few warung located in the trees behind. There have been attempts to prettify the area – a red-tiled promenade with fancy lamps has been constructed – but it doesn't detract from the spot too badly. There are some direct minibuses from Sumenep at the weekends and on public holidays (Rp3000), when the beach is a favourite excursion spot for local people, but otherwise you'll have to get a minibus from Giling terminal in Sumenep to Legung (Rp2000); it goes through attractive, rolling countryside via the small villages of Gapura, Antulung and Batang Batang. From Legung, it's 3km to the gate where the beach track leaves the road, and then another kilometre to the beach – it may be possible to pick up a becak to the beach or you can negotiate with minibus drivers, although they'll still only drop you at the gate. It's a pleasant walk down to the beach on a track lined with *cemara udang*, the elegant, feathery bush for which the area is famous.

On the track down to the beach, *Lombang Homestay* (❶) offers very simple **accommodation** in the family house, with outside shared mandi. The owners will prepare simple local food by arrangement, but make sure the price is established first.

The islands to the east

Administratively attached to Sumenep, the 66 islands that spread east from here are well off the beaten track: it's over 240km from the mainland to **Sekala**, the furthest island. The islands are hugely varied: some have fabulous white-sand beaches, others thick vegetation right to the water's edge. The largest group is

△ Sulphut mines, Ijen plateau, East Java

4 EAST JAVA

the **Kangean Islands**, a group of thirty, the smallest of which, Bungin, is a mere 50m by 35m. Twice-weekly ferries take cargo and passengers from Kalianget to Kangean Island, the largest of the group. The ferry docks at Batu Guluk, 10km from the main town of Arjasa, where you'll find the *Pasanggrahan* (❷), a government rest house that also accepts travellers. The coral reefs are good for snorkelling on the island, although you'll need to bring your own equipment.

The north coast

The roads along the **north coast** have a few more bends than those along the south, but are well maintained and surfaced and present vehicles with few problems. There are no towns, just small villages beside the river estuaries that dot the coastline. With the dry climate and poor soil, the majority of people here earn their living from fishing. From Sumenep to Kamal along the north coast is 163km (along the south it is 170km, but along much faster roads). There is no direct public transport between these two towns along the north coast, but you can village-hop between them, changing at Pasongsongan, Ketapang, Tanjung Bumi and Bangkalan to get to Kamal.

Located 20km northwest of Sumenep, the pretty beach at **SLOPENG**, several kilometres long and backed by big dunes, spreads away from the small village. The most attractive part lies to the west of the village, where the bays are more sweeping and visitors and inhabitants fewer. The village specializes in **topeng mask** production: there are about ten makers in the area and buyers come from craft shops in Jakarta, Bali and Surabaya. Some are sold as new, while others are "antique" in the usual Indonesian sense of being made to look old. If you have your own transport and want to see the masks being made from local *bintaos* wood (it takes three days from start to finish, and the skill is passed from father to son), then visit the hamlet of Tenggina, 4km south of Slopeng – you'll have to ask for the workshops and will probably be able to buy a mask for Rp50,000 if your bargaining skills are good.

The village of **PASONGSONGAN**, 10km west of Slopeng, has market day on Tuesday, when things get very packed and lively. It's an attractive village with red-roofed houses, and there's a good **place to stay**, the *Coconut Rest House* (❶; ask for Pak Taufik), on the road down from the village to the new fish auction building on the coast. Accommodation is in the family house, which has two bedrooms with a shared bathroom, and a small verandah at the front where you can watch the world go by. There's a 24-hour wartel and a post office in the village. Minibuses operate direct to Pasongsongan from Sumenep.

The largest north-coast settlement is **KETAPANG**, where the road from Sampang on the south coast meets the north coast. The only "sight" is **Air Terjun**, a waterfall on the east side of the village, where you can swim. The only accommodation in the village is at *Pasanggrahan* (❶), on the opposite side of the football field from the police station, in the centre of the village. It's very basic, and more used to government officials than tourists.

One of the island centres of batik is **TANJUNG BUMI**, 25km west of Ketapang, where all the families are involved in the work, the skills passed from mother to daughter. The most time-consuming part of the enterprise is the waxing of cloth using tiny fine-tipped pourers, and you're more likely to see this than the more colourful dyeing operations. The village gets few visitors, and people are generally happy to show you what they do. If you're interested in buying, you should be able to negotiate a sarong for around Rp100,000, which, given that it will have taken a month to make, is pretty reasonable.

From here, it's 60km to Kamal via Bangkalan (see p.297); there are many prawn farms along the coast and a number of distinctive and opulent mosques under construction in the area.

West of Surabaya

The area to the **west of Surabaya** looks fairly enticing on the map: the volcanic masses of Gunung Lawu and Gunung Liman in the middle bounded by the northern plains and the low southern hills leading to the sparsely populated southern coastline. Although it has some spots of interest – most particularly the pretty hill resort of **Sarangan**, the seaside town of **Pacitan**, the **Candi Penataran** temple complex and the idyllic south coast beaches of **Prigi** – the area is dominated by large towns such as Madiun and Kediri, which are really only useful as transit points.

Sarangan and around

Located 40km west of Madiun in the Gunung Lawu area beyond the village of Magetan, the hill resort of **SARANGAN** is a popular destination, attracting visitors from all over Java to enjoy the pretty views of the lake, the upland climate and the clear air. Most local people come up for a weekend, and a couple of days is probably long enough for most visitors. It's easily accessible on public transport: buses (from Bungurasih terminal; every 20min; 3–4hr; Rp8000) and trains (from Gubeng station; 8 daily; 3hr; Rp25,000) connect Surabaya with Madiun; take a bus from Madiun to Magetan (30min; Rp3000) and then a microlet to Sarangan (45min; Rp1500). Alternative access is from Tawangmangu in Central Java (see p.249): regular minibuses ply this route (30min; Rp2000). There is a **payment gate** at the entrance to the resort area (Rp1000 per person, Rp1500 per car, Rp1000 per motorbike).

Sarangan itself covers quite a small area, concentrated on the north and east shores of the small **crater lake**, Telaga Pasir, with a cluster of accommodation, restaurants and market stalls. It's at its liveliest at weekends and holidays: there are motorboats and pedal-boats for rental (Rp15,000 per hour), you can take a horse ride (notice the little bags under their tails to collect the manure for local fields), walk around the lake and visit the local waterfalls of Tirtosari, Sarang Sari and Mojoseni – ask for directions locally.

Practicalities

There's a huge amount of **accommodation** in Sarangan, although there are fewer budget options than at Tawangmangu. A recommended option is *Hotel Abadi* (ⓣ0351/888018; ❺), set above the northern end of Telaga Pasir; all the rooms are large and there are pleasant views of the lake. *Hotel Sarangang* (ⓣ0351/888022, ⓕ888203; ❹), high on the hill overlooking the lake, is a well-established place, popular with tour groups, offering pleasant terraces and good views. The white-tiled and functional *Hotel Nusa Indah*, Jl Raya Telaga 171 (ⓣ0351/888021; ❸), in the centre of town, has a wide variety of rooms (all with hot water) and is close to the lake; some rooms have terraces and views of the surrounding countryside.

The 24-hour **wartel** is at Jl Telaga 65, the **post office** is on Jalan Cemoro Sewu (the main road that heads through the resort and on to Tawangmangu), as is the **tourist office** (Mon–Sat 8am–4.30pm; ⓣ0351/888401). Sarangan has no shortage of **places to eat**, one of the simplest and most pleasant being the *Rumah Makan Rejeki*, with a limited menu of inexpensive local food and a small verandah; it is just opposite the *Telaga Mas Internasional Hotel* on the road to the lake. *Hotel Sarangan* has a colonial era dining room, which serves very affordable set dinners, although they need a few hours' notice to prepare.

Pacitan

The small coastal town of **PACITAN**, with its wonderful nearby beaches, is located 119km southeast of Solo. There are some direct buses from Solo; otherwise, change at Wonogiri. Alternatively, access is from Ponorogo, which typically takes two to three hours on the invariably packed buses.

Pacitan is a quiet and pleasant little town, with an attractive, good-sized alun-alun, with animal statues, well-laid-out flowerbeds and pretty shrubs. Jalan A. Yani runs along the south side, with the bus terminal 1km to the south along Jalan Gatot Subroto, which leads southwest from the eastern end of Jalan A. Yani. The **tourist office** is at Jl Letjen Suprapto 4 (Mon–Thurs 7am–3pm, Fri 7am–noon, Sat 7am–1pm; ⓣ0357/884535), the 24-hour **Telkom** office at Jl A. Yani 65, and there's a 24-hour wartel attached to *Hotel Pacitan*. The **post office** is at Jl Ronggowarsito 11, and you can **exchange** cash at: BRI, Jl A. Yani 12; Bank Danamon, Jl Raya P. Sudirman 143a; and BNI, Jl Raya P. Sudirman 142.

If you want **accommodation** in town rather than by the beach, by far the best option is *Srikandi*, Jl A. Yani 67 (ⓣ0357/881252; ❸), with helpful management and good rooms, located in two buildings; all have TV, attached mandi, either fan or air-con, and fine views in all directions. The attached restaurant, set back from the main road to avoid the traffic noise, has a substantial menu of chicken, seafood, Indonesian, Chinese and Western dishes, and plenty of vegetarian options.

The main **beach**, Pantai Teleng Ria (admission Rp500, car Rp1000, motorbike Rp500), lies 4km southwest of town. To get there, either hire a becak directly from town (Rp3000) or one of the microlets (Rp1000) that ply the route at weekends and on holidays, or take a westbound bus and get off where the beach road joins the main road, about 3km west of the town: it's 1km down to the beach from here. The long and curving white-sand bay has forested headlands at either end and attractive hills rising up behind, and Japanese WWII lookout points are set into the headland. It's a lovely spot, but not always safe for swimming – take local advice, and be careful. *Happy Bay Beach Bungalows* (ⓣ0357/881474; ❷), run by an Australian and the only **accommodation** on the coast, just on the left at the end of the road to the beach, provides rooms or bungalows with a small verandah attached. The attached restaurant provides a limited menu of Western, Indonesian and seafood options. The beach can be very busy at weekends and during holidays when the warung open up for business, but the rest of the time it's totally peaceful. There is a swimming pool on the road down to the beach (daily 8am–5pm; Rp1000), plus a small children's play area.

Blitar and around

Probably founded in the ninth century and with a current population around 120,000, **BLITAR**, southwest of the Arjuna mountains, is rather ignored by Western visitors – it's a small, busy town and nearby **Candi Panataran** is a significant draw, but there's little else to lure tourists. It is, however, much visited by Indonesians, who come to visit the mausoleum of President Sukarno, the country's first president.

The town centres on the **alun-alun**, where the government offices and Mesjid Agung are located. Jalan Merdeka runs along the south side of the square and continues west for about 1km as the main shopping street, until it makes a sharp left and becomes Jalan Mawar. Another smaller turning, Jalan Kerantil, continues straight on at this bend to the market area, Pasar Legi, and then a couple of hundred metres further to the bus terminal. There are no metered taxis, but plenty of becak and ojek; a trip across town will cost Rp3000.

Situated on Jalan Slamet Riyadi, a couple of kilometres northeast of the centre of town on the way to Candi Panataran, **Sukarno's Mausoleum**, Makam Bung Karno (daily 8am–5pm; free), is a huge, imposing monument, with dozens of souvenir shops lining the entrance road. The entrance is through a large, dark grey split gate, and the graves are inside a glass building with a three-tiered roof. Sukarno is in the centre with his parents on either side. Inside it's a very Indonesian scene, with elderly people intoning prayers and young visitors posing for photographs.

Following his overthrow in May 1967, Sukarno retired to Bogor, where he remained until he died in 1970. He was buried on this site, next to his mother, in the (clearly misplaced) hope of the government of the time that such an obscure location would not become a pilgrimage site. With Sukarno's daughter now president, the entire site is now openly venerated and thousands flock here, especially at weekends and at holiday times. Not easy to find even when you are on top of it, **Sukarno's Museum**, Jl Sultan Agung 59 (daily 6.30am–6pm; free), has no sign and is not obviously open: you need to ring for admission. The house was the home of Sukarno's parents and is full of family pictures, photographs of world leaders (including JFK), as well as personal mementos. One of Sukarno's cars is parked in the garage.

Practicalities

Blitar is well connected to other cities in East and Central Java, with regular buses from Malang (2hr; Rp4000), Madiun (3hr; Rp6000), Surabaya (4hr; Rp8000) and Solo (6hr; Rp10,000). Blitar's **bus terminal** lies south of town on Jalan Kerantil; buses and colts (Rp1000–3000) run the 4km along Jalan Veteran to the centre. Trains from Surabaya via Malang (5hr; Rp5000) arrive at the **train station** on Jalan Wijayakusuma, south of *Sri Lestari Hotel*. Moving on, both Rosalia Indah, west of the bus terminal at Jl Mayang 45 (Ⓣ0342/802149), and Ranta, Jl Mayang 47 (Ⓣ0342/802583), provide daily luxury **minibus** services to Surabaya, Solo and Yogyakarta; hotel pick-ups are included in the price.

For foreign **exchange**, BNI, Jl Kenanga 9, can change cash, but not travellers' cheques. The **post office** is at Jl Mastrip 87 (Mon–Thurs 8am–2pm, Fri 8–11am, Sat 8am–1pm), and the **Telkom office** is at Jl Jend A. Yani 10.

The best **accommodation** in Blitar is at *Hotel Sri Lestari*, Jl Merdeka 173 (Ⓣ0342/801766, Ⓕ801763, Ⓔlestari@blitar.wasantara.net.id; ❸–❽), offering a range of rooms to suit all budgets. Rooms in the main colonial era house were recently renovated and have the most character, with antique furnishings, hot water, air-con and TV. To get there, exit the bus terminal to Jalan Kerantil and walk 1km up Jalan Merdeka: the hotel is on the right. Less expensive, *Penginapan Aman*, Jl Merdeka 130 (no phone; ❶), has very basic rooms with shared bathroom and no fans – it stretches back from the road, so some rooms are fairly quiet.

There is a choice of **places to eat** in town, from a pleasant night market at the northern end of Jalan Mawar just near the Jalan Kerantil junction to the more formal *Ramayana*, Jl Merdeka 63–65, with a huge range of Chinese meals and a smaller choice of Indonesian ones. The restaurant at *Sri Lestari* is moderate to expensive with Indonesian, Chinese and Western dishes; portions are large and attractively presented. *Roti Orion*, Jl Merdeka 113, sells sweet breads and muffins.

Candi Panataran

Situated 12km north of Blitar, **Candi Panataran** (daily 7am–5pm; donation) sits on the lower slopes of Gunung Kelod (1731m); bright-yellow bemos ply directly from town. Dedicated to Shiva, it's famous as the largest temple complex in East Java, but it's a pleasant rather than grand historical site, the grounds dotted with attractive statues. Nothing in the complex is complete and, although with a bit of imagination you can get some idea of the original 300m by 100m site, it has nothing in scale or interest to rival great Central Javan monuments.

Dating back to the end of the twelfth century, the temple was continually expanded, and much of what is visible today was built during the Majapahit times, when it was very prominent, visited several times by King Hayam Wuruk and Gajah Made. The area is divided into three major courtyards. The outer courtyard has the bases of what would have been large and imposing assembly halls (pendopo), one carved and the other not. At the back of this courtyard, discernible by red marks on the ground, is the Dated Temple, with the inscription "1369", a worn Ganesh inside and a very eroded Bhoma over the door. The middle courtyard houses the roofless Naga Temple, named because of the snakes carved around it; it is thought that originally this would have supported a Balinese-style multi-tiered, wood-and-thatch *meru*. Built in 1347, the main temple would have been in the third and inner courtyard, although only the lower terraces now remain of what must once have been a very impressive building. There are some very skilfully carved reliefs, including circular tablets with animal carvings and images from the *Ramayana* epic. The highly eroded stone to the side of the main structure carries the earliest inscription on the site, "1197". At the back right-hand corner of the complex, a short path leads about 200m down to an attractive pool dating from 1415.

Prigi and Karaggongso

Set around a beautiful bay, the **Prigi area**, southwest of Blitar and south of the towns of Trenggalek and Tulungagung, offers postcard-perfect palm-fringed beaches, pleasant accommodation and good seafood. To get there from Blitar (1hr; Rp4500) or Tulungagung (30min; Rp3500), take a bus west towards Trenggalek, getting off at Durenam. From Durenam, take a colt to Watulimo, and change here for a bemo to Prigi. To reach Prigi from Pacitan, you'll need to catch a bus to Ponorogo, then another to Tulungagung, alighting at Durenam. At the entrance to Prigi, you'll have to pay an **entrance fee** to the resort (Rp1600 per person, Rp1000 per car).

PRIGI itself is a small fishing port with a nice vista of the bay, dotted with colourful *prahu* fishing boats. There is **accommodation** here at *Hotel Prigi*, Jl Raya Pantai Prigi (ⓣ0355/551180, ⓕ551702; ❸), with simple but adequate rooms, a tennis court and a small restaurant. Prigi has a few very simple eating-places, but the best **food** is at *Hong Seafood Restaurant* (prevoiusly the *Depot Lumintu*), facing the town beach.

Nicer and better-located accommodation can be found around the bay at the remote village of **KARANGGONGSO**. To get there, take a bemo from the entrance to Prigi (Rp1500) – a pleasant twenty-minute run along the coast, skirting a fine swimming beach, and passing through a state forest before finally arriving at Karaggongso. On the right is a sign for *Pondok Prigi I* (Ⓣ0355/551187, Ⓔpondok_prigi@blitar.wasantara.net.id; ❹–❻), which offers a range of good accommodation right on the beach. For a group, the "Induk" suites offer excellent value in self-contained bungalows. Simple food is available if you order in advance, and a motorboat can be hired to take you round the bay (Rp75,000) or to Pantai Damas, a secluded beach on the opposite side of the bay. One kilometre on from the *Pondok Prigi I*, the *Pondok Prigi II* (no phone; ❸) offers simple cottages around a pretty garden, with lovely views of the sea. Breakfast is included in the price.

Malang and around

The second largest city in East Java, **MALANG**, 90km south of Surabaya, is a busy city with a population in excess of 600,000. Situated at an altitude of 450m and circled by attractive volcanoes, it is cool, tree-lined and much more tourist-friendly in all respects than Surabaya. The city has a reputation similar to Bandung in West Java as a centre for higher education and learning, with an enormous number of schools and colleges attracting students from all over Indonesia; it is said that up to half the population is made up of students. Though there are no real rock-bottom places to stay, value for money is far better than in Surabaya.

Outside the city, the temple remains of **Candi Singosari** and **Candi Jawi** offer an insight into the ancient kingdoms of the area, **Taman Candra Wilwatika** at Pandaan stages regular dance performances in the dry season, and the **Bogor Botanic Gardens** at Purwodadi, spreading onto the lower slopes of Gunung Arjuna, are a peaceful escape. Further afield, the **hill resorts** of Batu and Selecta are great escapes from the lowland heat, while the **beaches** along the south coast make for a long trip from Malang, but provide stunning scenery, idyllic offshore islands and a sense of being well off the tourist trail.

Some history

Stone inscriptions found at Dinoyo, a suburb of Malang, suggest the area has been inhabited for over 1200 years. A king called Gajayana ruled the **Kanjuruhan kingdom** from Malang, which is believed to have been founded in 760 AD. It was also the centre of the thirteenth-century **Singosari kingdom**, whose legacy is visible in the temples at Singosari (see p.313) and Prigen (see p.314). It remained significant in Majapahit times, and important ministers were always stationed in the area, a prominence that continued into the time of the Mataram kingdom. Used as a refuge by the defeated Surapati following the Third Javanese War (1746–57), the area around the city suited the rebel purposes, as it was inaccessible and difficult to search. Various VOC campaigns eventually led to the defeat of the final Surapati threat in 1777, but by that time the successive campaigns against the rebels had caused almost the entire population to flee the area.

Malang reached its current prominence only in the last 130 years, following the European efforts to establish rubber, coffee and cocoa **plantations** in the area as well as the government's sugar ones. As the European population grew, Malang developed, with fine, distinctive bungalows on tree-lined avenues and vacation houses in attractive resorts further afield. Merdeka Square, on the south side of Sungai Brantas, was built in 1882, and circular Tugu Park on the north side became an administrative centre in 1914, when a big colonial residential area was also developed to the northwest. Since World War II and Independence, cigarettes have been a major local employer (Bentoel are based here), with education the other main focus of activity.

Arrival, city transport and information

The **Arjosari bus terminal**, 7km northeast of the city centre on Jalan Ratu Intan, serves Surabaya, Probolinggo and Jember. Frequent blue **city bemos** (4am–11pm; flat fare Rp1500) connect it to the centre. City bemo routes run between two of the three Malang bus terminals and are labelled by the two letters of the relevant terminals. "A" refers to Arjosari, "G" is for **Gadang bus**

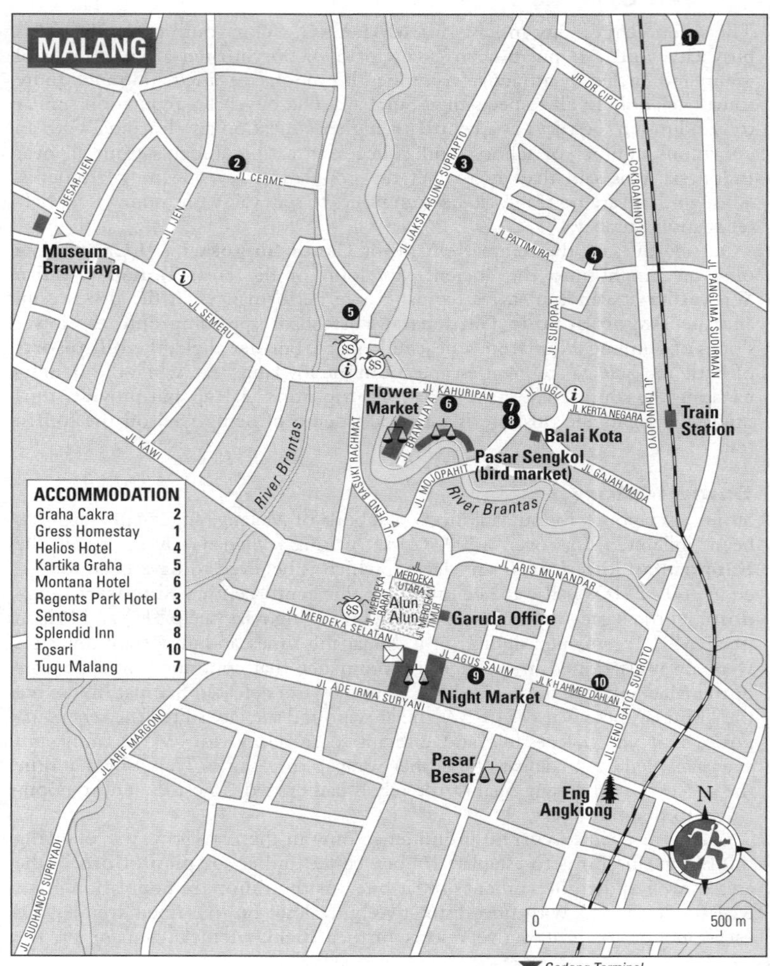

terminal (serving Blitar, Lumajang, Trenggalek and Tulungagung), 5km south of the city centre on Jalan Kolonel Soegiono, and "L" is for **Landung Sari bus terminal** (serving Kediri and Jombang) on Jalan Majen Haryono, 6km northwest of the city centre; for example, LA operates between Landung Sari and Arjosari. It's worth noting that route GA and AG are not the same route – this is not a problem if you're going to the terminals, but it can be if you're heading to an intermediate point.

The city's **commercial centre** is the alun-alun to the south of Sungai Brantas, with the main shopping and market area along or near Jalan Agus Salim, which runs off the south side. Jalan Mojopahit runs across Sungai Brantas and links this commercial sector with the Tugu area to the north, in which most government offices are located; the **train station** is a short walk from here. Also heading north from the alun-alun is Jalan Jend Basuki Rachmat, which, changing its name several times on the way, eventually leads to the Arjosari terminal.

Information

There are several **tourist offices** in Malang. The best is a bit tucked away at Jl Semeru 4 (Mon–Sat 9am–5pm, Sun 9am–1pm; Ⓣ0341/366852, Ⓕ367637) in a small shop next to *Dunkin' Donuts*, operated by the local members of the Indonesian Guides Association. They have plenty of leaflets and reference books on the whole region, and the knowledgeable staff book minibus tickets, operate tours (see "Listings" on p.313), advise on hotels and restaurants, rent out bicycles (Rp5000 a day), motorcycles (Rp50,000) and cars (Rp300,000 including driver and petrol), and can find you a **licensed guide** (Rp50,000 per day). They can also arrange white-water rafting (see p.313 for more details).

Also convenient is the East Java Tourist Office, Jl Jend Basuki Rachmat 6h (Mon–Fri 8am–2pm; Ⓣ0341/323966), which operates out of a wooden kiosk at the top of Jalan Mojopahit and has a few pamphlets about the area and a photocopied map of Malang. Malang Municipality Tourist Office is at Jl Tugu 1a (Mon–Thurs 9am–1pm, Fri 9–11am, Sat 9am–12.30pm; Ⓣ0341/327661); it's in Dewan Perwakilan Rakyat Kotamadya Daerah, Tigat II Malang, the municipal offices just east of the Balai Kota (Town Hall) on the south side of Tugu.

The **national park office** (Taman Nasional Bromo-Tengger-Semeru), Jl Raden Intan 6 (Mon–Thurs 8am–2pm, Fri 8–11am, Sat 8am–1pm; Ⓣ0341/491828), close to Arjosari terminal, has general leaflets about Bromo and a booklet in English on climbing Semeru. You can get a permit here for climbing Semeru, but it's probably more convenient to buy it in Ranu Pane (see p.325).

There are several Malang **maps** available. Most are detailed but don't include a street index, so are of limited use. The most extensive is published by Kariya Pembina Swijaya and available from Gramedia in Malang (see p.312). The *Surabaya Periplus Travel Map*, available inside and outside Indonesia, includes Malang and is useful for the city area, but it doesn't reach as far as the three bus terminals.

Accommodation

There is some excellent **accommodation** in Malang, and, although there are no really cheap places, value is generally good, which (allied to the climate and atmosphere of the city) makes it an attractive place to stay.

Hotel Graha Cakra Jl Cerme 16 ⓣ0341/324989, ⓕ367856, ⓔgrhcakra@indo.net.id. Located to the north in the old Dutch residential area near Jalan Ijen, this recommended hotel is the next best to the *Hotel Tugu Malang* (see below). In a 1930s building, it's a stylish boutique hotel, offering excellent rooms and facilities. All rooms are well appointed and tasteful, and it has an attractive pool. The only negative is the food, which is poorly presented and dull; the rates include breakfast for two. ❻

Gress Homestay Jl Kahayan 6 ⓣ0341/491386, ⓕ474407. A GA or AL bemo will drop you off at Jl Mahakan; get off at Apotik Mahakan. This is a real homestay, with spotless rooms, attached bathroom (some with hot water) and fan in an attractive family house with plenty of greenery. There's a kitchen for guests, and the owner can help you arrange trekking, fishing and local tours. ❸

Helios Hotel Jl Pattimura 37 ⓣ0341/362741, ⓕ353797. The best budget choice in the city, although rather noisy. The clean rooms, all with large verandahs, lead off an attractive, lush courtyard garden; the cheaper rooms have shared mandi, while the more expensive ones have attached mandi. The staff are knowledgeable and helpful, and can arrange tours, car and motorcycle rental, and book bus tickets. ❷

Kartika Graha Jl Jaksa Agung Suprapto 17 ⓣ0341/361900, ⓕ361911. Very modern, somewhat brash hotel; the light, airy lobby area has four storeys of balconies on one side and huge windows on the other, and a 24-hour coffee shop. There are two pools (Rp10,000 for non-guests), and the rooms are very comfortable. ❺

Montana Hotel Jl Kahuripan 9 ⓣ0341/362751, ⓕ327620. Conveniently close to Tugu. All rooms have a hot-water bath; the cheaper ones have a fan, the more expensive ones air-con. The communal areas are light with lots of greenery, and there's a lobby coffee shop. Good value for this location. ❹

Regents Park Hotel Jl Jaksa Agung Suprapto 12–16 ⓣ0341/363388, ⓕ362966, ⓔregent@indo.net.id. A multistorey hotel on the north side of the city. The rooms are comfortable but dull, with hot tub, air-con and good views. The lobby is a bit dark, but there's an attractive coffee shop plus a pleasant pool (non-guests can use this for Rp10,000). ❻

Sentosa Jl K.H. Agus Salim 24 ⓣ0341/366889, ⓕ367098. In the middle of the main shopping area, but surprisingly quiet. The plain but spotless lower-end rooms have outside bathrooms while the top ones have hot water and air-con. ❷

Hotel Splendid Inn Jl Mojopahit 4 ⓣ0341/366860, ⓕ363618. All rooms have hot-water bathrooms and there's a small pool; this is an old-fashioned, pleasant maze of a place, and the best in this price category. Lower-end rooms have fans; the upper-end ones, air-con. ❸

Hotel Tosari Jl K.H. Ahmad Dahlan 31 ⓣ0341/326945, ⓕ367098. In a central location with clean, tiled rooms and seats in the corridors outside the rooms. Cheaper rooms have shared bathroom, while the most expensive ones have an attached bathroom and hot water. ❸

Hotel Tugu Malang Jl Tugu 3 ⓣ0341/363891, ⓕ362747, ⓔmalang@tuguhotels.com. This is the most luxurious hotel in Malang, with a lovely atmosphere; it has won awards and features regularly in the travel pages of newspapers. It has small but attractive, individually furnished rooms (those facing inwards are quieter), a pool in a lush courtyard, antiques and art displays everywhere and a business centre. There's also an excellent, reasonably priced restaurant and a stylish bar. ❻

The City

There's no shortage of things to look at in Malang. The most attractive and evocative **colonial area** is around Jalan Ijen to the northwest of the centre, with renovated bungalows in wide, palm-lined boulevards. It's a rich and refined area, with fabulous iron railings that guard the privacy of the wealthy of the city. To get there, take bemo GL (which goes along Jalan Ijen), or MM (along Jalan Kawi nearby). **Museum Brawijaya**, Jl Ijen 25a (daily 8am–2pm; donation), is a military museum fronted by tanks, guns and amphibious vehicles. Only the enthusiast will find much of interest inside, though it's full of paintings and photographs of military events and past commanders, cases of guns of every type, memorabilia and old maps of Malang. Altogether the museum is a rather chilling celebration of Indonesian military might, including artefacts connected with the suppression of Irian Jaya.

The circular park at Jalan Tugu, fifteen minutes' walk from the city centre on Jalan Mereka, was also laid out by the Dutch, with the Balai Kota (Town Hall) on one side; the **Independence monument** in the centre has replaced the original fountain. It's a ten-minute walk from here along Jalan Mojopahit, across Sungai Brantas (a rather narrow, uninspiring waterway at this point) up to the alun-alun. A fascinating **bird market** can be found in the Pasar Sengkol/Jalan Brawijaya area; head down towards the river from Jalan Mojopahit on the south side of the river. The number and variety of birds is amazing, and there are brilliantly carved wooden cages on sale too. Birds change hands for Rp2–3,000,000 for good singers, and up to Rp7,000,000 for exceptional ones – the black grasshoppers on sale are for feeding them. Local bird-singing competitions are held every two to three months; enquire at the tourist office if you're interested. The **flower market** is slightly further north of the bird market – you can walk to it from Jalan Brawijaya. It ranges down the riverbank of Sungai Brantas and is more like a nursery, with huge amounts of shrubs and garden plants on offer, and some cut flowers in the sheds at the bottom.

A Chinese temple, **Eng Ankiong**, Jl Laksamana Martadinata 3, lies at the junction of that road with Jalan Zainel Zakse, Jalan Pasar Baru and Jalan Jend Gatot Suproto. It's an imposing new temple, with a marble-tiled floor and a splendid gateway, some lovely gold altar-fronts, plenty of detailed and dramatic sculpted dragons curling around columns and a lily pond to the right of the main temple with a dramatic rock island in the centre. Don't miss the temple behind the main shrine, where there are two rows of beautifully and evocatively carved modern wooden statues of ancient Chinese sages.

Eating, drinking and entertainment

There is an excellent **night market** on Medan Merdeka on Saturday evenings and every night during Ramadan, which turns the whole of the square into a bustling tent city with a terrific range of food. For more formal dining there are plenty of choices.

Amsterdam Restaurant Jl Terusan Kawi 2. On a busy corner with tables inside and out, there is a huge moderate to expensive menu, with steak as the speciality – but also many Indonesian staples, sandwiches, hot dogs, salads, French fries, seafood and Chinese food.

Asri Dua Jl Brig Jen Slamet Riadi 14. Has a small menu of good-value Indonesian and Chinese food plus steaks and sandwiches in clean, attractive surroundings.

Café Bunga Bali Jl Bromo 44. Very stylish restaurant offering excellent Western dishes, including their speciality Swiss *rösti*, and a well-stocked bar. Local musicians play pop, rock and jazz most evenings from 9pm.

Dunkin' Donuts At Ramayana Centre, Jalan Merdeka Timur. The usual sweet and savoury choices in this air-con chain.

Hemat Lezat Jl Trunojoyo 19a. Serving traditional Indonesian food, with a big menu of rice, soup and noodle options. This is one of a trio of good-value inexpensive places, convenient if you are staying in *Helios Hotel*.

Kole Kole Jl Jend Basuki Rachmat 97a. Air-con, attractive and clean with pleasant music and no TV, this is a good place for a quiet meal in the moderate to expensive range, with Indonesian, Western and Chinese options.

Melati Pavilion At the *Hotel Tugu Malang*, Jl Tugu 3. Probably the most luxurious dining in Malang: the restaurant is beside the pool in a leafy courtyard. There's a huge menu of steaks, with plenty of other Western, Indonesian, Chinese, Japanese and Dutch dishes. It's a lovely, evocative place, part of an excellent hotel, and the prices are very reasonable. The attached café serves mostly Dutch cakes, biscuits and pastries, and the walls are decorated with Dutch East Indies advertisements.

Rindu Jl K.H. Agus Salim 29. Centrally located Padang restaurant, with a big selection of attractively prepared and displayed food.

Toko Oen Jl Jend Basuki Rachmat 5. This has been a restaurant and ice-cream parlour since 1930 and is a Malang institution, particularly favoured by Dutch visitors, many coming to see where their ancestors ate. The menu is substantial, with sandwiches, salads, steaks, seafood and Chinese food, all at moderate prices, although the standard isn't great. The room has high ceilings, net curtains, plenty of dark-wood and cane chairs, a bay window looking out towards *McDonald's* across the road and some stained glass. The grandeur is decidedly faded, however, and whilst the waiters don uniforms in the evenings, during the day they look pretty ordinary.

Tugu Kafé Dan Roti Jl Kahuripan 3, attached to *Hotel Tugu Malang*. The café is well decorated and furnished and has an excellent range of moderately priced sweet breads, cakes and savouries, and customers can order anything from the *Melati Pavilion* menu (see p.311). The downside is that the road is very noisy – this place looks idyllic, but certainly doesn't sound it.

Entertainment

Performances of **traditional dance** and **gamelan** are held at Senaputra (Sun 11am except during Ramadan; Rp1500). During the week it's possible to see the students practising and you may be lucky enough to see the traditional dances – *basakalan*, a welcoming dance, and the Malangan masked dance, which tells the *Panji* stories. The only **disco** in Malang is at the *Kartika Graha Hotel* (daily 10pm–2am; Rp15,000); on some evenings, women get in free.

Shopping

There are several modern **shopping centres** in Malang, most of them along Jalan K.H. Agus Salim – they're not as glossy as the Surabaya ones, but are well stocked. If you're looking for souvenirs, Sarinah Department Store & Hero Supermarket, Jalan Jend Basuki Rachmat, has a second-floor gift shop selling craft items from both Bali and Java. There's an excellent range of goods, from Rp5000 for small batik items and Rp30,000 for batik cotton sarongs, up to Rp750,000 for silk. There are also woodcarvings in both traditional and modern styles, baskets, boxes, dolls and puppets. Batik Keris, Komplek Pertokoan Ria, Jl Merdeka Timur 2d/e, is just opposite the Mitra Shopping Centre and comprises five floors of textiles and gift items, with sarongs from Rp20,000 to more than Rp1,000,000 for pure silk sarong and scarf sets, a huge range of textiles sold by the metre and many ready-made items of clothing. There are also some wood and leather gift items. **Pasar Besar**, Jalan Kyai Tamin, occupies a whole city block and contains all the stalls, range of goods and excitement usual in excellent Indonesian market areas. Attached to this is the Matahari Department Store, the best in town, with a food court, supermarket and *KFC*.

For **bookshops** Gramedia, Jl Jend Basuki Rachmat 3, has the best choice, with a good range of imported English books, travel guides and maps. An alternative is Toko Sari Agung, Jl Jend Basuki Rachmat 2a, which has three floors but a smaller choice of English books. Jalan Mojopahit, just south of the bridge across Sungai Brantas, is lined with secondhand bookshops. Most are Indonesian and cater for the large local student population, but there are quite a few English books and ageing periodicals if you rummage.

Listings

Airline offices Garuda, Jl Merdeka Timur 4 ⓣ0341/369494, ⓕ369656; Merpati, *Hotel Kartika Graha*, Jl Jaksa Agung Suprapto 17 ⓣ0341/361909, ⓕ354745.

Banks All the big banks have large branches in Malang. The following are convenient for foreign exchange: Bank Bumi Daya, Jl Merdeka Barat 1; BNI, Jl Jend Basuki Rachmat 75–77; and BCA, Jl Jend Basuki Rachmat 70–74 (on the corner of Jl Kahuripan).

Buses Minibuses are available between Malang and Surabaya, Solo, Yogyakarta, and Semarang; expect to pay around three times the express bus price. Several places also sell nightbus tickets, which include a hotel pick-up – you'll pay slightly more than if you book directly, but if you have piles of luggage it can be helpful. Agents are: Harapan Transport, Jl Surapati 42 ⓣ0341/353089, close to *Helios Hotel*; Haryono, Jl Kahuripan 22 ⓣ0341/367500, who can book Pelni and flight

tickets; *Helios Hotel*, Jl Pattimura 37 ⓣ0341/362741, ⓕ353797; Juwita, Jl K.H. Agus Salim 11 ⓣ0341/362008; Toko Oen Travel Service, Jl Jend Basuki Rachmat 5 (next to the restaurant) ⓣ0341/364052, ⓕ369497; and Tuju Transport, Jl Kertanegara 5 ⓣ0341/368363, who also book Pelni and flight tickets.
Car and motorbike rental There are no official agencies, so enquire at your accommodation. *Helios Hotel* has motorcycles for Rp35,000 without insurance. Guests leave a photocopy of their passport as security, and people not staying at the hotel must leave their actual passport. Car rental from *Helios Hotel* is Rp200,000 per day inclusive of driver and petrol.
Hospital Rumah Sakit Umum Daerah Dr Saifal Anwar, Jl Jaksa Agung Suprapto 2 ⓣ0341/366242; Rumah Sakit Umum Lavalette, Jl W.R. Supratman 10 ⓣ0341/362960.
Immigration office Jalan Jend A. Yani Utara ⓣ0341/491039.
Internet access The post office has public internet access via eight terminals (Rp7000 an hour); public internet terminals can also be found at Auka Warung Internet at Jl Surapati 40 (daily 9am–9pm; ⓣ0341/32652; Rp7000 an hour).
National park office Taman Nasional Bromo Tengger Semeru, Jl Raden Intan 6 (Mon–Thurs 8am–2pm, Fri 8–11am, Sat 8am–1pm; ⓣ0341/491828).
Pharmacy Kima Farma 53, Jl Kawi 22a (ⓣ0341/326665), is large, well-stocked and open 24hr.
Post office Jl Merdeka Selatan 5.
Tours There are several places in Malang that can arrange tours. Typically, day-tours will include some sights in Malang and the local temples of Jago, Kidal, Singosari or the southern beaches. *Helios Hotel* offers a large range aimed at backpackers with a considerable reduction in the price per person if more than five people go on the same trip. The tourist office run by local members of the Indonesian Guides Association, Jl Semeru 4 (ⓣ0341/366852, ⓕ367637), has a huge range of guided tours, from a 3hr Malang city tour, through to day tours to Balekambang, Batu, Kawi, Blitar or Bromo. Toko Oen's Tour & Information Service, Jl Basuki Rahmat 5 (ⓣ0341/364052) in the café of the same name, is recommended by travellers.
White-water rafting On the slopes of Mount Semeru, the 15km-long Ireng-Ireng river offers near perfect white-water rafting. The full route is for experienced rafters only, but less experienced rafters can follow the river some of the way. For further information contact PT Alfaria Romea, Jl Kawi 23 (ⓣ0341/369642, ⓕ369643), or Punan Adventure, Lumajang (ⓣ0334/887016, cimel@malang.wasantara.net.id).

Between Malang and Surabaya

There are plenty of local sights that are on or very close to the main Malang–Surabaya road, most of them easily reached from either place. **Candi Singosari** (sometimes known as Ken Dedes Temple after the wife of Ken Angrok, the founder of the Singosari kingdom) is on Jalan Kertanegara, just 300m to the west of the main road in **SINGOSARI**, 12km north of Malang. The bright-green bemo (LA) operates from Arjosari to Lawang via Singosari (Rp3000). The turning to the temple is just on the Malang side of BCA bank in Singosari and is marked by a large black gate – plenty of becak wait here to ferry visitors.

It is almost certain that the area was the capital of the powerful Singosari kingdom from 1222 until 1292. The **temple** was built in the early 1300s in memory of Kertanagara, the last king of Singosari, who died in 1292. His kingdom flourished while Kublai Khan ruled over China; Kublai Khan demanded tribute from all the rulers in Asia and sent a messenger to Kertanagara's court. The king sent his reply back to China, carved in the forehead of the messenger. Just as Kublai Khan was getting ready to send armed retaliation, Kertanagara and much of the court was ambushed and murdered by soldiers of neighbouring kingdoms.

The temple itself is tall and grand, built on a central platform with a soaring roof. It seems that it was never completed: the carving was carried out from the top down and the bottom parts are bare. Niches are carved in the sides of the temple, but most are empty, apart from the statue in the south side, thought to represent Agastya (also known as Bhatara Guru), an ancient sage said to have arrived in Java walking on water. There are plenty of assorted figures in the grounds, but they are very eroded; the most fascinating statues being the ferocious **Arca Dwarapala**, a pair of four-metre-high rotund and goggle-eyed guardians who possibly guarded the entrance to the long-vanished palace of Singosari; they are on either side of the road 200m further west from the crossroads, just beyond the temple entrance.

At **PURWODADI**, 21km north of Malang, **Kebun Raya Purwodadi**, Jalan Raya Purodadi (daily 7am–4pm; Rp3000, car Rp5000, motorcycle Rp5000 – neither form of transport are allowed in the grounds on Sundays), is an outpost of the Bogor Botanic Gardens (see p.141). The entrance is right beside the road – take a Malang-bound bus from Surabaya and get off at the gardens gate 2km south of Lawang (Rp7000). It's a lovely spot: peaceful, quiet and well-maintained, spreading across the lower slopes of Gunung Arjuna. It's worth taking a look at the beautiful **Coban Baung waterfall**, which can be seen just from behind the gardens; take the signposted dirt road just before the gardens entrance and follow to the end. Alternatively, there is a suspension footbridge at the rear of the gardens, which allows for a ten-minute trek over Mount Baung and to the waterfalls below.

A side excursion to the **tea plantation** of **WONOSARI** is possible from here. Carry on past the gardens to the town of Lawang (about 10min) and when you come to the train station on the left, take the signposted turning to "Agro Wisata Kebun Wonosari" on the right. Following a very steep road up the slopes of Mount Arjuna, you will come to the tea plantation after about twenty minutes' drive. Local minibuses go most of the way up from the main Lawang road, but you'll need to take an ojek for the last leg. Wonosari is located at between 950 and 1350 metres and is delightfully cool. Spread over seven square kilometres, the sweeping valleys of tea are quite stunning to look at. Established in 1910, the plantation grows Indian Assam and Chinese Cyrenci tea, some of which is exported to the Middle East and is even found in famous tea brands sold in the UK. Tours of the tea factory and plantations can be arranged on site. **Accommodation** is available within the plantation at *Wisata Agro Kebun Wonosari* (ⓣ0341/426032, ⓔwonosari@telkom.net; ❸–❺), varying from simple rooms to very pleasant cottages.

At **PANDAAN**, midway between Surabaya and Malang, about 45km from each, the open-air amphitheatre, **Taman Candra Wilwatika**, is 2km from the town centre towards Tretes and hosts fortnightly dance-dramas in the dry season (July–Nov). Admission is free; enquire at the tourist offices in Surabaya for a schedule, or at the travel agents there if you want to arrange an all-inclusive tour.

Built in the thirteenth century to commemorate Kertanagara, **Candi Jawi** is located in the village of **PRIGEN**, 4km west of Pandaan on the road to Tretes. It is one of the most complete of the local temples and has been well restored. It soars 17m high; the brick moat surrounding it is still visible, and the backdrop of the mountains, especially Gunung Penanggungan, is lovely. It's thought that the temple once housed statues of both Shiva and Buddha, as the king believed there to be a strong connection between Shivaism and Buddhism. Next to the temple, the Candi Art Shop, Jl Raya Candi Jawi 25, has loads of stuff to browse through, including old money, ceramics, kris, textiles and pictures. Prigen boasts some of the best **accommodation** in East Java: *Finna Golf and Country Club Resort*, Jalan Raya Barsari Prigen (ⓣ0343/634888, ⓔfinnagolf@pasuruan.wasantara.net.id; from $50), offers stunning cottage accommodation, spacious and beautifully designed, each in its own garden and with in-room jacuzzi, built around a beautiful golf course setting, with good restaurants, a lawn tennis court and swimming pool.

In the **TRAWAS** area, the **Seloliman Environmental Education Centre** or PPLH (Ⓣ0321/618752 or 031/5031621, Ⓕ618754, Ⓔpplh@ino.net.id; or via the Surabaya office Ⓣ031/5031621; ❺), makes for a particularly interesting stay and supports a worthwhile cause. A noncommercial, nongovernmental organization, the PPLH opened in 1990 to provide visitors with an opportunity to learn about the fragile ecosystem of the area. Situated on the slopes of Mount Penanggunan, amongst verdant rice terraces and teak forest, the centre provides educational facilities, a restaurant and comfortably rustic **accommodation** in eight beautifully designed bungalows (up to 4 people) and two guesthouses (4–6 people). The grounds are beautiful, and guided walks through the forest can be arranged. Numerous tenth-century temples dot the slopes of the mountain, connected by a pilgrimage path, and it's only a few minutes' walk to the tenth-century **Jolotundo bathing ponds** (open daylight hours; Rp2500). Unfortunately, many carvings have been moved from the site to the National Museum in Jakarta, but it's a pretty site nonetheless, with enormous overhanging trees. Locals bathe here in ancient cubicles separated for either sex, and Hindu pilgrims make regular offerings. To get to the PPLH from Surabaya, take a Malang-bound bus (1hr; Rp4000) to Pandaan. From there, take a colt (Rp3000) to Trawas and get off at the T-junction near the *Restaurant Asri*. Take an ojek here for the last 9km (about Rp10,000).

The Batu area

The twin hill resorts of Batu and Selecta are close together on the southern slopes of Gunung Welirang and Gunung Arjuna, just over 20km west of Malang. Previously favoured **hill resorts** of the Dutch, they are now extremely popular with visitors from Malang and Surabaya, the most wealthy of whom own villas in and around the villages; for a few cool days up in the mountains, out of the noise and heat of the cities, they are well worth a trip. The area is easily accessible on public transport, as pale-purple bemos ply from Landung Sari terminal in Malang to Batu (30min; Rp2000), and plenty of buses pass through the resort. Batu bus station is on Jalan Agus Salim just 1km south of the alun-alun.

The centre of **BATU** is the large alun-alun with an incongruous central statue of a glossy apple perched on top of a cabbage, and all facilities for visitors are close by. The local shopping centre, Plaza Batu, is on the north side opposite Mesjid Besar An Nuur. The post office can be found at Jl Raya P. Sudirman 87, the BCA bank and Telkom office on Jalan A. Yani, and there's a 24-hour wartel to the right of Plaza Batu. *Pelangi Restaurant*, Jl Raya P. Sudirman 7, is a good, clean, inexpensive **eating place**, with an Indonesian, Chinese and East Javan menu and tables and chairs at the front or low sitting areas behind. The more exotic *Warung Bethania* on Jalan Diponegoro has a woodland theme and some Western food.

The small and delightful village of **SONGGORITI** lies down in the valley off the main road 1.5km west of Batu; lime-green bemo route B operates from Batu terminal to Songgoriti. There's a pleasant public swimming pool in the village, Tirta Nirwana (daily 7am–5pm; Rp3000), and nonresidents can pay to use the pool at *Hotel Air Panas Alam Songgoriti* (Rp5000). Jalan Arumdalu has plenty of warung offering inexpensive local food.

Six kilometres north of Batu, **SELECTA** is higher (at 1150m) and slightly quieter than Batu, but has little character. The main attraction in Selecta is **Taman Rekreasi** (daily 7am–5pm; Rp5000), landscaped gardens which were established by the Dutch in 1930, burnt to the ground in 1947 during the fighting for Independence, and since restored. There's a lovely swimming pool here (Rp5000), with an attractive garden, as well as some accommodation (see below). The **wartel** in Selecta is open from 7am until 10pm.

Heading **west from Batu**, the road climbs up, finally through countryside, to a large plain and the neighbouring villages of Pandesari and Pujon, where vegetable fields and nurseries line the road. All of the roads beyond Batu have fine views of the whole area. The small village of Sepalu is marked by a cow monument on the road; take the turning here for the one-kilometre road to the gateway to **Coban Rondo waterfall** (daily 7am–5pm; Rp3000, car Rp1000, motorcycle Rp500), but there's another 4km to the waterfall itself; it's an attractive road, with bamboo stands and some good views of the surrounding countryside across Songgoriti, Batu and Arjuna. There's a **campsite** about 2km from the gate (Rp5000 per tent per night; enquire at the ticket office) and the **Arena Gajah** (Elephant Arena), where three Sumatran elephants (from the elephant training school at Way Kambas national park in Sumatra; see p.511) give displays on Sundays. From the parking area, it's 200m on a tiled pathway to the impressive waterfall, a thirty-metre drop down a horseshoe-shaped cliff. There is also a small children's swimming pool (Rp1000).

Accommodation

Much of the **accommodation** in the area is aimed at well-heeled Indonesians who come up to the hills for a cool weekend or holiday – the value isn't brilliant, but discounts are possible on quiet weekdays. If you're in a group, you could consider renting a **villa**, one of the many grand houses that dot the hillside. Local touts will approach you as soon as you arrive, and you should bargain hard.

Batu

Hotel Kartika Wijaya Jl Panglima Sudirman 127 ⓣ0341/592600, ⓕ591004. Acknowledged as one of the best in the area. Although it looks grand from the outside, the rooms are ordinary and the whole lot is due for renovation. However, any problems are made up for by the excellent pool and its attractive surroundings and the nearby coffee shop. ❺

Hotel Kawi Jl Panglima Sudirman 19 ⓣ0341/591139. A decent travellers' losmen with basic rooms and small verandahs facing across a small garden area. It isn't easy to find; look out for *Depot Kawi* and Salon Kawi about 200m to the north of the town centre. ❷

Hotel Metropole Jl Panglima Sudirman 93 ⓣ0341/591758, ⓕ595456. One of the better-value places towards the top end of the market: the rooms are comfortable, and there's an attractive lobby, coffee shop, pool and children's play area. ❺

Perdana Hotel Jl Panglima Sudirman 101 ⓣ0341/591104, ⓕ591727. Block-built and with no outstanding features, but better value than many similar places in town. ❸

Songgoriti

Hotel Air Panas Alam Songgoriti Jl Raya Songgoriti 51 ⓣ & ⓕ0341/593553. This is the most upmarket option in the village, spread over two sites several hundred metres apart. The hotel is well maintained and attractive, and all rooms have water supplied by the local hot spring believed to have curative value. Those at the main site are adobe-style, and there are cottages at the upper site, where the swimming pool (admission Rp2500 for non-guests) is located. Significant discounts are available outside weekends and holidays. ❹–❺

Hotel Arumdalu Jl Arumdalu 4 ⓣ & ⓕ0341/591266. This is a large setup with a small pool and garden and plenty of accommodation options; the cheaper rooms are very basic and can be noisy, as they are close to the restaurant, but the more expensive rooms are quieter, and offer hot water and TV. It isn't luxurious, but the location is pleasant. ❷

Pondok Rahayu Jl Arumdalu 8 ⓣ0341/593814. A good budget alternative in a family house that has basic rooms with cold-water mandi; there's also a small garden. ❸

Selecta

Hotel Santosa Jl Hotel Santosa 1 ⓣ0341/591066. Signed off the road to the left just below the *Hotel Victory*, several hundred metres through back alleyways, this place is well worth considering at the budget end. The rooms are pleasant, have cold-water mandi, verandahs and good views across town. ❷

Hotel Selecta Taman Rekreasi ⓣ0341/591025, ⓕ592369. The accommodation here is expensive for what you get and rather shabby. The big advantage is proximity to the excellent public pool and the attractive grounds, overrun with people on holidays and at weekends. ❺

Hotel Victory Jl Raya Junggo 107 ⓣ0341/592985, ⓕ593012. Located 200m beyond the turning to the Taman Rekreasi. The cheaper rooms are nothing special, but the big plus is the two-storey-high upper lounge with huge windows; the coffee shop overlooking the pool is particularly pleasant. ❺

Southern beaches

The road **south of Malang** heads along the course of Sungai Brantas for 18km to the small town of **Kepanjen**, where it divides – east to Lumajang around the southern flanks of the Bromo area, and west around the southern side of Gunung Butak and its nearby peaks to Blitar. Due south again, the rolling southern hills are nowhere near as dramatic as the volcanoes around Malang, but the area is peaceful and rural, and the coast has three fine **beaches** (entrance charge for all three: Rp5000 per adult, Rp1000 per car and Rp500 per motorbike). All are popular weekend excursions for local people, and very quiet during the week. With your own transport, any or all are a very easy day-trip from Malang. If you are using public transport, the busy village of Sendangbiru is easily accessible, with Balekambang and Ngliyep easiest to get to at weekends. There is basic accommodation at all of the beaches. Note that both Balekambang and Ngliyep beaches are **dangerous for swimming**, which is in any case prohibited here.

Road access to **Sendangbiru**, the furthest east of the three beaches, is via Turen, 16km east of Kepanjen. The junction to the beach is south of Turen: turn left at the main junction, then right after about 1km and the turn is signposted. Using public transport, there are a few direct microlets from the Gadang terminal in Malang to Sendangbiru. Alternatively, take a Lumajang-bound bus from Gadang terminal, get off in Turen and pick up a minibus to Sendangbiru. The busy 43-kilometre road to Sendangbiru from Turen twists and turns through the rolling coastal hills via the small, cool market town of Sumbermajung Wetan. The best beach is actually at Tambakrejo, 1km before you arrive at Sendangbiru proper. It is the last turning left and if you miss it you can backtrack by foot from Sendangbiru. Sendangbiru beach itself is rather dirty for swimming, but very sheltered, with colourful boats pulled up onto the sand and a jetty 500m to the west. There are lovely views along the coast, especially to the east, where great cliffs line the shore, surf pounding against them. Just 500m off the beach, forested, hilly **Pulau Sempu** has some enticing beaches and rocks lying off the coast. A charter to the island costs Rp50,000–75,000, if you bargain well. The **losmen** (no phone; ❶) at the western end of Sendangbiru beach has no name, and rooms are basic; it's in a good location overlooking the water, though surrounded by an unattractive fence.

The next beach west is **Balekambang**, accessed via Gondanglegi, 6km west of Turen on the road from Kapanjen. There are bemos and buses from Gadang terminal in Malang via Gondanglegi to Bantur, 13km before the beach. From Bantur, there may be minibuses to the beach at the weekends; otherwise, you'll need an ojek (Rp5000). The beach is about 500m long and is incredibly picturesque, with three small offshore islands. Pulau Wusanggeni has a small *bale* (lookout point) and is joined to the beach by a walkway. Next to the west is Pulau Ismoyo, with the Balinese-style Pura Sagara Amritajati overlooking the ocean. Then, another 400m west, forested Pulau Anoman is joined to land by another walkway. Next to the *Depot Asri* warung, near the bridge to Pulau Ismoyo, is a small **losmen** (no phone; ❶) with basic bamboo-and-tile rooms with attached mandi, set close to the beach and with small verandahs. If you want something a bit smarter, walk a few metres further east to *Depot Barokah*, where there's a losmen (❷), also nameless, with white-tiled, red-roofed rooms.

Access to **Ngliyep**, 35km from Gondanglegi, the most westerly of the three beaches, is also via Bantur; there are some bemos from Gadang terminal in Malang to Ngliyep, and more frequent ones from Kepanjen, but during the week it's very quiet. With your own transport, you can take a back road from Balekambang to Ngliyep, but it isn't a straightforward route; check directions on the way. Ngliyep beach is actually two small beaches enclosed by rocky headlands covered by forest with a few enticing paths to explore. The scenery is impressive, with some attractive offshore islands. The closest of these, Gunung Kombang, is linked to the most easterly bay by an unsafe-looking bridge; massive surf pounds the rocks here. There are plenty of warung and two places to stay: the *Pasanggrahan* (❶), on the beach, with small rooms and shared bathroom, and another small losmen (❶) virtually next door.

The Bromo region

The **Bromo region** is best known for its awesome scenery; at its heart is a vast, ancient volcanic crater with sheer walls over 300m high. Within this crater, a host of picturesque mountains, including the dramatic, still-smoking **Gunung Bromo** (2392m), rises up from the "Sea of Sand", the sandy plain at the crater's base. Hundreds of thousands of visitors come to the area each year to climb Bromo for the sunrise – a stunning sight, and far less strenuous than many other Indonesian peaks.

One hypothesis for the formation of the area is that **Gunung Tengger**, then the highest mountain in Java at over 4000m, erupted to form a caldera of between 8km and 10km in diameter with crater walls between 200m and 700m high. This is now the main outer crater rim with the Sea of Sand in the bottom, while further eruptions formed the smaller inner peaks such as Bromo, Batok and Widodoren that rise up from the Sea of Sand.

The Tengger

The Tengger area is home to the **Tengger** people, who are ethnically, culturally and linguistically different to the Javanese. Legend tells that the Tengger people are descended from Rara Anteng, daughter of the last king of Majapahit, and Jaker Serger, a descendant of the god Brahamana. They could not have children and prayed to the gods, promising to sacrifice a child if they were made fertile. Their wish was granted and they went on to produce 25 children, but did not keep their promise. The gods were angered and the area was devastated by disease and death, and eventually the youngest child of the couple, Raden Kusuma, was taken by his father to the Sea of Sand, where a huge eruption took the child and created Gunung Bromo. Jaker Serger was also ordered to donate half the harvest to the Bromo crater every Kasada month (last month) of the Tengger calendar. Today, the **Kasada festival** (moveable against the Western calendar, so enquire at tourist offices for the exact date) is the most important in the area; at midnight, priests begin their prayers on the Sea of Sand to call the gods down to earth and bless the people, who then climb to the Bromo crater at dawn and throw their offerings of vegetables, flowers and money into the caldera.

This unique landscape now comprises the **Bromo-Tengger-Semeru national park**, which ranges in altitude from 750m to 3676m, with mountainous rainforest, casuarina forest and grasslands. It is estimated that around 600 species of flora survive in the park, including 157 species of orchid in the southern areas. The fauna includes monkey, macaque, barking deer, leopard, panther, porcupine and pangolin. The park's boundaries encompass **Gunung Penanjakan**, which is a favourite viewing point in the area, and soaring **Gunung Semeru**, the highest peak in Java and a reasonable objective for trekkers who are fit and prepared.

It's best to visit in the **dry season**, when the clouds are fewer, the views better, and the walking more pleasant. However, whatever time of year you visit, take warm clothes – it gets chilly at night. All the accommodation places will provide you with a blanket. A good **map** of the area is the Periplus *East Java and Surabaya* map, available at city bookshops.

Approaches to Bromo

There are two main **approaches** to the Bromo region. The most popular is to head inland from **Probolinggo** on the north coast via the villages of Sukapura, Wonokerto and Ngadisari, to the crater's edge at Cemoro Lawang. There is accommodation in all of the villages, although most people stay at **Cemoro Lawang** in order to make the dawn trip to Gunung Bromo as easy as possible. Alternative access is from **Pasuruan**, also on the north coast, inland to the villages of **Tosari** and **Wonokitri**. These villages are further west from Cemoro Lawang, but linked by road to Gunung Penanjakan, so they offer an excellent approach for the sunrise from there.

Probolinggo

Visited by King Hayam Wuruk of the Majapahit dynasty in 1359, the area delighted the king so much that it was named Prabu Linggah (The Place the King Was Pleased to Stay), which these days has become **PROBOLINGGO**, a town of around 200,000 people 38km east of Pasuruan. The alun-alun in the centre of town isn't particularly impressive, although the **Mesjid Agung** on the western side is low and elegant. The area around the alun-alun and down Jalan Dr Suroyo is the government and administration centre, whilst Jalan Sutomo and Jalan Raya P. Sudirman form the commercial and shopping hub.

The **station** is on the northern side of the alun-alun, while the **bus terminal** is 6km southwest of town; yellow microlets run to the town centre. There are good road and rail connections from throughout East Java, Bali, Yogyakarta and Jakarta. Minibuses for Cemoro Lawang (every 20min; 8am–4pm) leave from the terminal, and there are two buses daily – they are labelled "Sukapura" and "Ngadisari" on the front but also serve Cemoro Lawang.

The best **accommodation** is *Hotel Bromo Permai*, Jl Raya P. Sudirman 237 (Ⓣ0335/427451, Ⓕ22256; ❸), with six standards of room ranged around a small garden with a little restaurant attached; the prices include a nasi goreng breakfast. They have a map of the town to consult, and staff are helpful and used to travellers. They can arrange chartered transport to Cemoro Lawang and have train information; a warpostel is attached to the hotel. To get here from the bus station take a G or F yellow microlet and, from here to the terminal or station, a G. For eating, *Rumah Makan Sumber Hidup*, Jl Dr Moch Saleh 2, is a big airy place at the junction with Jalan Raya P. Sudirman; you can eat inside or outside from an extensive menu of rice, sate, soup, juices and ices. *Restaurant Malang*, Jl P Sudirman 48, has an extensive menu of well-cooked Indonesian and Chinese dishes in the inexpensive to moderate range, plus plenty of drinks.

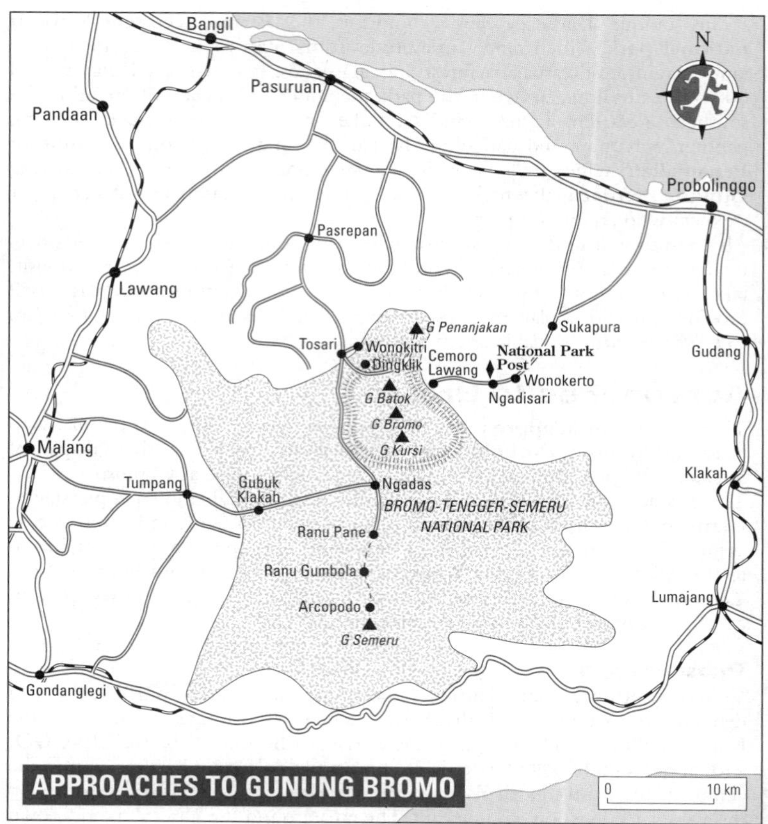

APPROACHES TO GUNUNG BROMO

The banks on Jalan Suroyo do **foreign exchange**: Bank Bumi Daya at no. 23, BCA at no. 28, BRI at no. 30, or BNI at no. 46. The **post office**, Jl Suroyo 33 (daily 7am–8pm), has public internet access. The **wartel** (7am–11pm), next to the main Telkom administration office, is at Jl Suroyo 37. For everyday **shopping**, the Sinar supermarket, Jl Raya P. Sudirman 102, will meet most needs, or try the Sinar Terang department store, Jl Dr Sutomo 125. Gajah Made (or GM), Jl Dr Sutomo 42, is the newest shopping centre, with a department store and supermarket plus some food places.

Cemoro Lawang

The small village of **CEMORO LAWANG**, 46km from Probolinggo, is perched on the crater's edge and has grown up largely to service the tourists who visit the Bromo region; it's the easiest place from which to set off on the pre-dawn excursion to Gunung Bromo itself.

From the crater's edge in Cemoro Lawang there are brilliant **views** of the entire area. Gunung Penanjakan is over to the northwest (far right); you can identify it by the radio and telecommunications masts at the summit. The chopped-off cone in the foreground is Gunung Batok (2440m); looking southwest (left), the two pointed peaks are Gunung Widodoren (2614m) and Watangah; then there is huge smoking Gunung Bromo in the foreground. Gunung Semeru is in the far distance behind and to the left of Bromo. The best lookout spots are at the end of the road from the north coast in Cemoro Lawang and in front of *Lava View Lodge*. Access to Cemoro Lawang is from Probolinggo: minibuses run up to the crater rim from 6am to 5.30pm via the villages of Sukapura, Wonokerto and Ngadisari, all of which also have accommodation.

There is a **national park post** on the Probolinggo–Cemoro Lawang road at Ngadisari, 14km from Probolinggo, where you pay admission to the park (Rp2100, Rp6000 per 4WD, Rp2500 per motorcycle); you'll be issued with a ticket. The **national park office** (Kantor Taman Nasional Bromo Tengger Semeru; daily 7.30am–4pm) in Cemoro Lawang has displays about the area, but little printed material either about the park or local treks. *Hotel Yoschi* (see below) is the best place for local information, especially if you want to trek, and can arrange transport.

There's a **wartel** (daily 3am–10pm) on the left as you reach the top of the road; you can call worldwide from here, although the lines are less reliable than from more accessible areas. If you want **souvenirs**, the shop attached to the wartel in Cemoro Lawang has some good T-shirts. There's a **health centre** in Ngadisari, Jl Raya Bromo 6, just by the checkpoint.

Moving on, minibuses (8am–4pm; Rp4000) and buses (2 daily; Rp5000) operate from Cemoro Lawang to Probolinggo (2hr). Several places advertise minibus and express bus tickets, which are more expensive but more convenient than organizing them yourself in Probolinggo. Touts are numerous here; establish the price in advance.

Accommodation in and around Cemoro Lawang

There is plenty of **accommodation** in Cemoro Lawang, Ngadisari, Wonokerto and Sukapura: Ngadisari is 3km from the rim, Wonokerto 5km and Sukapura about 18km. **Camping** is no problem, as this is a national park; Penanjakan is popular, although the sunrise hordes will disturb you, and there's a good site 200m further along the rim from the *Lava View Lodge* in Cemoro Lawang.

Ngadisari

Hotel Cik Arto ⓣ0335/541014. Just below the terminal in Ngadisari. This is a new place, with smart rooms at the front and less expensive rooms at the back, in a pleasant garden setting. All rooms have attached cold-water mandi. ❸

Wonokerto

Hotel Bromo Jl Wonokerto 5, Wonokerto ⓣ0335/23484. If you're on a very tight budget, this place is worth considering. Small rooms, with cold-water mandi, around a small garden area. There's an attached restaurant. ❷

Hotel Yoschi Jl Wonokerto 1, Wonokerto ⓣ0335/541014. A great place with many options: the cheaper rooms have shared bathroom, while the top-priced ones are actually cottages. The decor is attractive and the garden is a delight. Staff provide plenty of good information on the area and sell maps of local hikes. You can also use the book exchange, book bus tickets, arrange local guides, charter transport and rent warm jackets. ❷–❺

Sukapura

Grand Bromo Hotel ⓣ0335/581061. Located 2km south of Sukapura, a long way from the crater, this is the most upmarket place in the area, with comfortable rooms, all with hot-water bathrooms, and staff who speak excellent English. The more expensive rooms have stunning views north to the coast. There are tennis courts and three pools (non-guests can use the pool for Rp5000). ❺–❼

Cemoro Lawang

Hotel Bromo Permai ⓣ & ⓕ0335/541021. Just on the left at the end of the road as it reaches the crater's edge at Cemoro Lawang. There's a wide choice of rooms; the top-end ones are big and comfortable, but the small cheaper rooms with shared cold-water mandi have little to recommend them. ❷

Café Lava Hostel ⓣ0335/541020. A justly popular travellers' choice, close to the crater rim, on the main road into Cemoro Lawang. There are two standards of room: the less expensive ones are basic with shared cold-water mandi (often a long walk away), while the more expensive ones are spotless, with lovely sitting areas in an attractive garden. ❷

Cemoro Indah ⓣ0335/541197. On the crater's rim around to the right from the *Hotel Bromo Permai*. The main road into Cemoro Lawang forks about 200m before it reaches the crater rim; the left fork goes to the centre of the village, and the right fork to the *Cemoro Indah*. There's a big choice of rooms, from basic ones with cold-water shared mandi to stunningly positioned bungalows with hot water, while the attached restaurant is equally well located. ❸–❺

Lava View Lodge ⓣ0335/541009. About 500m left along the crater's edge from the centre of Cemoro Lawang; go through the concrete area between the row of shops and *Hotel Bromo Permai* and follow the main track. This is a popular and recommended choice, offering comfortable rooms – all have attached bathrooms, very good Indonesian buffet, live music (often blues guitar) and the views are brilliant, especially from the top-end rooms and the restaurant. ❸

Eating

There are plenty of **places to eat** in the vicinity of Cemoro Lawang, and they're well-used to catering to Western tastes. All those listed below offer Western and Indonesian food or, if you fancy cheaper food, you'll see mobile food stalls selling basic soups and noodles throughout the day and evening on the main roads in Cemoro Lawang.

Café Lava Attached to the *Café Lava Hostel*. Moderately priced with plenty of travellers' favourites, including steaks, pancakes, sandwiches and drinks.

Cemoro Indah Restaurant Attached to the *Cemoro Indah Hotel* and located near the crater rim; the views are brilliant, and the moderately priced food is varied.

Hotel Yoschi Restaurant Attached to *Hotel Yoschi* in Wonokerto. A delightful place with lots of wood, bamboo, batik, fresh flowers and a pleasant atmosphere, plus an excellent range of inexpensive to moderately priced food.

Kafé Venus At the Cemoro Lawang terminal. A clean place with attractive bamboo decor and inexpensive to moderately priced food; it's excellently located if you've just arrived and are starving or waiting for transport.

Lava View Lodge Restaurant A la carte Indonesian and Western food, and very good local buffet, set in a great position not far from the crater's edge in Cemoro Lawang, with spectacular views.

Pasuruan

Located 60km southeast of Surabaya, the port town of **PASURUAN** is a convenient stopping-off spot close to Bromo on the way to or from Tosari and Wonokitri; buses run every few minutes throughout the day between Surabaya and Pasuruan (1–2hr), and there are daily trains (1hr 30min) from Gubeng station in Surabaya. There are good **bus and rail services** throughout East Java, as well as east to Bali and west to Yogyakarta. Microlets run direct to Tosari, although there is no sign at the terminal.

The town is famous for the fine examples of Dutch colonial architecture remaining, attesting to its former prominence and prosperity as a major sugar producing centre. Also notable is **Mesjid Agung Ali-Anwar**, on the west side of the main square, a gleaming delight with white-and-green patterning, lovely arches, gleaming domes and a towering minaret. The main north-coast road is Jalan Raya, which runs west–east along the northern edge of the town parallel to the coast. The town centre, the alun-alun, lies several hundred metres south and is reached via Jalan Niaga, which turns into Jalan Nusantara further south. The **bus and bemo terminal** is at the eastern end of Jalan Raya, about 1.5km from the alun-alun, and the **train station** just north of Jalan Raya, on

Jalan Stasiun. The **tourist office**, Jl Hayam Wuruk 14 (Ⓣ0343/429075), is situated in the district government offices, Kantor Kapeputan Pasuran.

For **accommodation**, *Hotel Pasuruan*, Jl Nusantara 46 (Ⓣ0343/424494, Ⓕ421075; ❸), has three standards of room, from cold-water bathroom and fan rooms up to those with air-con and hot-water bathrooms. *Wisma Karya*, Jl Raya 160 (Ⓣ0343/426655; ❷), has a range of rooms behind an old colonial bungalow, although the cheaper ones are often full. The top-end rooms have air-con, but the cheaper ones with fan and attached cold-water mandi are adequate.

There are plenty of **places to eat** in Pasuruan, from the small night market around the alun-alun to *Rumah Makan Savera*, on Jl Raya 92a, a clean and welcoming place with a huge, inexpensive menu of Indonesian and Chinese food.

The **post office** (Mon–Thurs 7.30am–2pm & 3–8pm, Fri 7.30–11.30am & 1–8pm, Sat 7.30am–1pm & 2–8pm), Jl Alun-alun Utara 1, provides public internet access (Rp3000 for 15min). There's a 24-hour **wartel** at Jl Stasiun 11 and **exchange facilities** at BNI, Jl A.Yani 21 and BCA, Jl Periwa 200, 200m west of the terminal.

Tosari and Wonokitri

Just over 40km south from Pasuruan, the small villages of Tosari and Wonokitri sit 2km apart on neighbouring ridges of the Bromo massif foothills. These are excellent choices for early access to **Gunung Penanjakan**, and are less tourist-orientated than Cemoro Lawang. Both villages are quiet, upland communities with a peaceful atmosphere, and a day or so here can easily be combined with a stay at Cemoro Lawang to get the most out of the area. Microlets that go to one also go to the other, and both villages have accommodation. Coming from Pasuruan, the road divides about 500m before Tosari: the right fork leads up to the market area of that village, and the left fork twists up to the next ridge and Wonokitri. Wonokitri is a compact, shabby town with good views, while Tosari is more spread out, with an attractive ridge to the northeast that leads to the *Hotel Bromo Cottages*. Although there is no sign at the bemo station in Pasuruan, there are direct minibuses from there to Tosari, a better option than getting a minibus to **Pasrepan** and having to change there. There are bemos from Pasrepan to Tosari and Wonokitri, and ojek also ply the route – they tend to inflate the price for tourists (Rp10,000 is fair).

In **TOSARI**, the *Hotel Bromo Cottages* (Ⓣ343/571222, Ⓕ571333; ❺) provides adequate, but very overpriced accommodation in furnished cottages, with hot water, bathtubs and stunning views. In the main building there is a comfortable lounge, and the *Dahlia Restaurant* offers moderate to expensive Chinese, Indonesian and Western meals. They can arrange local trips, have karaoke and traditional dance shows and the shop rents out warm jackets. There are often discounts available. If you are coming via Surabaya, it's worth checking Orient Express (see p.292), as they quote competitive prices at the hotel either for accommodation only or as part of a package deal to Bromo. On the same ridge, about 300m before *Hotel Bromo Cottages*, *Penginapan Wulun Aya*, Jl Bromo Cottage 25 (Ⓣ0343/57011; ❷), is small and clean with good views from the balconies. *Mekar Sari*, Jl Raya 1 (no phone; ❶), is a small rumah makan selling inexpensive Indonesian food, and has a few simple rooms with shared cold-water mandi and a good roof terrace.

WONOKITRI offers several places to stay, including the *Pondok Wisata Surya Nuta* (Rp50,000), a concrete, charmless building with little going for it. Far better choices are *Kartiki Sari* (no phone; ❷), with simple rooms, and *Bromo Surya Indah* (Ⓣ0343/571049; ❸), which is just before the Pendopo Agung, the

Balinese-style village meeting hall, about 300m before the national park checkpost at the far end of the village; rooms have attached bathroom, clean bedding and good views, and there's a simple restaurant, in an area where finding a place to eat is difficult.

At the **national park checkpoint** and information centre at the southern end of Wonokitri there are some maps and charts to consult, though their main role is collecting the **admission fee** to the park (Rp5000, Rp7500 per car, Rp5000 per motorcycle).

Bromo and the other peaks

The highlights of the area are **Gunung Bromo**, with its dramatic smoking crater; **Gunung Penanjakan**, on the outside crater's edge and one of the favourite sunrise spots; and **Cemoro Lawang**, with its brilliant panoramic view of the crater, where most visitors stay (see p.320). The park also contains the highest mountain in Java, **Gunung Semeru**, and, while most visitors will be content with admiring its dramatic profile from a distance, it's also possible to climb to the summit. The Bromo area attracts more than 250,000 tourists each year, peak seasons being June to September and again at Christmas and New Year.

Gunung Bromo

There are a variety of excursions possible from Cemoro Lawang (see p.320), the most popular being the wonderfully atmospheric climb to the top of **Gunung Bromo** (2392m). If you are lucky with the clouds, there may be an absolutely spellbinding sunrise. You can walk, get a horse or take a vehicle down the crater's edge and across the Sea of Sand to the base of Gunung Bromo. To walk, either follow the cobbled road or the path from near the *Hotel Bromo Permai* to the Sea of Sand and follow the main track across to the mountain. Allow about an hour to get to the base of the mountain and, if you're going for the sunrise, a torch is useful, as you'll be walking in the dark. If you want a **horse**, the fixed prices are posted on notice boards in the centre of Cemoro Lawang (Rp10,000 one-way between Cemoro Lawang and Bromo, Rp20,000 return; you can also rent horses by the hour (Rp10,000–20,000). It's possible to do it by vehicle, either in a rented car or by ojek (Rp50,000); there is a steep, cobbled but motorable three-kilometre road down to the Sea of Sand from Cemoro Lawang and then the main road is marked across the Sea of Sand by white stones. Vehicles go to just beyond the temple at the bottom of Gunung Bromo, while horses can continue the steepish 500m or so to the base of the steps up the mountain itself. However you get there, you'll still have to manage the 249 concrete stairs (30min) up to the crater rim, from where there are great views down into the smoking crater and back across the Sea of Sand. Just at the top of the steps there are some protective railings, but these don't extend far; you can walk further around to get away from the crowds, but it's very narrow, with long drops on either side.

For a longer trip, you can **charter a 4WD** from Cemoro Lawang to take you to Penanjakan for the sunrise, back to Bromo for the climb and then return to Cemoro Lawang. All prices are negotiable and it's much cheaper if you arrange it yourself with a driver rather than through a hotel, but you'll be looking at around Rp85,000 for the return trip to Bromo and Rp100,000 or more for the longer trip described above. All prices are per jeep, which will hold two or three people.

Gunung Penanjakan

There are three choices for excursions from Wonokitri, which include Gunung Penanjakan (2770m), the best spot for the sunrise across the entire Bromo area; you'll need to charter local transport for any of them. The most straightforward is to go to Gunung Penanjakan for the sunrise and return to Wonokitri or Tosari (Rp75,000 per 4WD, Rp30,000 motorcycle). Alternatively, you can go to Penanjakan for the sunrise, cross the Sea of Sand to Bromo and then return to Wonokitri or Tosari after you've climbed to the top. The longest option is to go to Penanjakan and Bromo and then on to Cemoro Lawang (Rp100,000 per 4WD, Rp50,000 per motorcycle for either of the final two). This last option doesn't seem very popular, but is a good choice if you want to visit both the Tosari/Wonokitri and the Cemoro Lawang areas, avoiding a trip via the north coast. There is no motorable road that links Penanjakan, Tosari or Wonokitri directly with Cemoro Lawang.

The road from Wonokitri and Tosari up to Penanjakan (11km) is steep and attractive with some excellent views, but very twisting. There's a lookout at Dingklik, 6km beyond Wonokitri and 5km before Penanjakan, where one road goes down the crater wall to the Sea of Sand and the other up to Penanjakan. Leave Tosari or Wonokitri at around 4.30am to get to the lookout spot for sunrise; it's about 200m from the car park to the usually crowded lookout itself. The whole crater area lies below, Bromo smoking and Semeru puffing up regular plumes while the sun rises dramatically in the east. This is a national park, so you can camp up here if you wish, but be aware that unless you select your spot carefully, you'll be invaded before dawn by the hordes of visitors.

Gunung Semeru

Essentially a dry-season expedition (from June to September or possibly October), the climb up **Gunung Semeru** (3676m), Java's highest mountain, takes at least three full days. It's for fit, experienced trekkers only, and requires good preparation and equipment. The volcano is still active, with over 20,000 seismic events recorded in a typical year. The last major eruption was in 1909, when 200 people died, and since 1967 it has been constantly active. It's vital to take a local guide and listen to advice about the safety of the area – even the approaches to the main climb can be confusing, as the farmland and forest are extensive. In fact, there are two main routes up the mountain, a newer, more popular trail and an old trail called "Ajek-Ajek", which is shorter but steeper.

The path starts at the village of **RANU PANE**, to the north of the mountain, accessible by microlet and chartered 4WD from Malang or Tumpang, or – if you're in the Bromo area – via a path across the Sea of Sand. In the village, you need to check in at the **PHPA office** and get your **permit** (Rp5000; for an extra charge you can also get a certificate if you complete the climb), unless you already have it from Malang (see p.309). The PHPA office will also recommend porters – one porter is needed for each person climbing (Rp50,000 per porter). It's best to bring your own sleeping bag and tent, and rent a cooking stove in Ranu Pane. In the village, trekkers can stay in the *Forest Guest House* (❶), where you'll need to cook for yourself, or there's a **campsite** near the PHPA office.

The first part of the trek is the three-hour walk from Ranu Pane, along a wide path leading gently uphill through the forest to **Ranu Gumbolo** (2400m). There is a lake here; you can camp or find a place to stay in the village but most people carry on, through the small upland village of Oro Oro Ombo to **Cemoro Kandang** village. Near this path is Sumber Manis, the last water source before the summit, so make sure you get directions to it. At

Cemoro Kandang, it's possible to camp among the *cemoro* trees, or a few of the shelters may be useable. Alternatively, continue for a further thirty minutes or so to **Kalimati** village (2700m), two to three hours from Ranu Gumbolo, along a much steeper path. If you still have time and are fit, you could continue for another one to two hours to the last camping point at **Arcopodo** (3000m). It's through the forest and is tough going, but will make the following day shorter and easier. From here, you'll feel the earth shudder every twenty or thirty minutes as the volcano erupts.

If you camp at Arcopodo and are fairly fit, allow three hours to the **summit** and leave at about 3am to get there for the sunrise, which involves climbing in the pitch dark for much of the time. There are very few trees above Arcopodo, and this is the really tough part, extremely steep, and covered in fine, slippery sand up to ankle height which gets more slippery as the day progresses and it warms up; carry only water and plenty of high-energy food. From the crater's edge on a clear day, you can see as far as Bali. The regular explosions of gas and ash throw debris 100m into the air, and it's especially dangerous if the wind changes direction as the gas is poisonous. In 1997, two climbers were killed by a big eruption which sent boulders flying out of the crater. On the way back, stay the night at Cemoro Kandang and descend the next day to Ranu Pane; don't forget to report back to the PHPA office.

If you don't want to make your own arrangements, a **package trip** for two to four people will cost about Rp1,000,000 excluding transport and porters from Ranu Pane, but including a guide and equipment. To arrange this, contact the *Helios Hotel* in Malang (see p.310).

The far east

The **far east** of Java, between Bromo and Bali, is often overlooked by visitors, who simply want to transit it as quickly as possible. This is unfortunate, as the area not only contains some excellent and accessible **national parks** – Baluran, Alas Purwo and Meru Betiri – but also some lovely **coastline** on the southern side, plus the largely neglected but stunning **Ijen Plateau**, with its rolling upland areas of coffee plantations, dramatic soaring peaks and the spectacular crater lake of **Kawah Ijen**. The east remains largely rural, although communications are good and there is sufficient accommodation.

Jember

The city of **JEMBER** is large, busy and invariably clogged with traffic. However it has good facilities for travellers and is a useful place to get information about the Meru Betiri national park and to book accommodation there. **Buses** from the north arrive at the Arjasa terminal 6km north of Jember; others, including long-distance services, drive in at the Tawang Alun terminal, 6km west of the city centre on Jalan Darmawangsa. From both terminals, there are Damri buses (Rp1000) or yellow microlets (Rp1500) into the town centre: A or B buses marked "Tawang Alun-Arjasa" travel via the alun-alun, a useful orientation point. From Tawang Alun, it's also possible to pick up metered Argo taxis. There's a third bus station at Pakusari, 8km southeast of the city, served by Banyuwangi buses, which also use Tawang Alun. A fourth bus terminal, Ajung, serving Watu Ulo, is 5km from the city centre in the village of Ambulu.

The **train station** is on Jalan Wijaya Kusuma, which runs north from the northwest corner of the alun-alun. Jember is on the main line across Java as well as the branch line to Panarukan on the north coast, and there are plenty of services throughout East Java. Longer-distance services between Jember and Jakarta or Bandung involve a change in Yogyakarta or Surabaya.

The **tourist office**, Jl Gajah Made 345 (Mon–Thurs 7am–2pm, Fri 7–11am, Sat 7am–12.30pm; ⓣ & ⓕ0331/425471), produces a brochure about the area but is otherwise not particularly useful. It's possible to book tours and accommodation on the **Ijen Plateau** at PT Perkebunan Nusantara XII (known as PTP 12), Jl Gajah Made 249 (ⓣ0331/86861, ⓕ85550). The KSDA office, Jl Jawa 36, has responsibility for Pulau Sempu. The **national park office** for **Meru Betiri**, Jl Sriwijaya 40 (Mon–Thurs 7am–2pm, Fri 7–11am, Sat 7am–1pm; ⓣ0331/435535), is 3km southeast of the alun-alun; staff are knowledgeable and keen to help and have literature in English. Some Meru Betiri accommodation needs to be booked here; otherwise, book at Ledokombak, Jl Gajah Made 224 (Mon–Fri 7.30am–noon & 12.30–3pm, Sat 7.30am–12.30pm; ⓣ0331/84814), which is 200m east of the Bank Indonesia building.

There is a 24hour **Telkom office** at Jl Kartini 4–6, at the southwest corner of the alun-alun. For **exchange** there's BCA, Jl Gajah Made 14–18, BNI Jl Raya P. Sudirman 9, or Bank Bali, Jl Trunojoyo 35. The **post office** (Mon–Fri 8am–9pm, Sat 8–11am, Sun 8am–1pm) is on the north side of the alun-alun, at Jl Raya P. Sudirman 5, and offers internet access (Mon–Sat 8am–5pm, Sun 8–11am; Rp7000 per hour), or try Warung Internet, Jl Kalimantan 77, near the university – microlet D passes the door. For **shopping**, the Johor Plaza, Jl Diponegoro 66, has a three-storey Matahari department store.

Catering largely for business travellers, there are several good **accommodation** choices in the city. *Hotel Anda*, Jl Kartini 40 (ⓣ0331/489475; ❷) is a ten-minute walk west of the alun-alun, but it's not easy to find, so take a becak. Very popular with visiting Indonesians, the rooms are clean, tiled, and have balconies and attached mandi, while the more expensive rooms have air-con and hot water. The *Hotel Safari*, Jl K.H.A. Dahlan 7 (ⓣ0331/481882, ⓕ481887; ❸–❹), is a central option, off a small road south of Jl Trunojoyo, with Bank Bali on the corner. It's quiet, and has a huge variety of rooms; the nicest overlook the small garden. About 1km south of the alun-alun, the *Hotel Sulawesi* at Jl Letjen Suprapto 48 (ⓣ0331/433555, ⓕ431343; ❹–❺), is the most luxurious hotel in Jember; it's also popular, so book ahead. All rooms have air-con, hot water and TV, and there's a 24-hour coffee shop in the lobby area.

For **places to eat**, *RM Lestari* at Jl Kartini 16 serves Indonesian food in a pleasant atmosphere, while *Sari Utama* at Jl Gajah Mada 33 is an elaborate Chinese restaurant, offering moderate to expensive food and also karaoke.

Watu Ulo and Papuma Beach

Thirty kilometres south of Jember, the village of **Watu Ulo** stretches along a black sanded beach of no great beauty, but just a kilometre south over the headland is **Papuma Beach**, one of Java's finest. On Sundays, it's packed with tourists from Jember, and with good reason: with its powder white sand, crystal clear water and dramatic rock formations, it's one of the best beaches on the south coast. Stretching along both sides of the Tanjung Papuma peninsula, the beach is set on the fringes of a stunningly wild nature reserve, home to a number of exotic species of bird and animal life, including – so reports go – the Javan tiger. Some basic accommodation was being built at the time of writing, while warungs serve simple food. To get there from Jember, take a colt from the Arjasa terminal to Ambulu (Rp3000) and a bemo (Rp1000) from there to Watu Ulo. An ojek will take you over the very steep road to Papuma Beach (Rp3000) or wait for an infrequent bemo (Rp1000).

Meru Betiri national park

Declared a national park in 1982 to protect the habitat of the fast-declining Javan tiger, **Meru Betiri** lies on the south coast to the east of Jember, and contains some of the last remaining lowland rainforest in Java. The chances of seeing the **Javan tiger** are virtually nil: in two recent censuses, only faeces, marks on trees and footprints were found, and staff reckon there are no more than four of the animals left. Far more common are two varieties of leopard, wild pig, banteng, birds (the hornbill, peacock and kingfisher are the most dramatic, but there are also yellownapes, woodpeckers, pigeons, bulbuls and eleven species of cuckoo) and – the main reason visitors go to the park – the **turtles** that nest on Sukamade beach. Four varieties of turtle have been seen here: green, hawksbill, snapping and leatherback. The best season for spotting them is November to March, although some observers note that, for leatherbacks, April to July and September to December are better. The park is also home to the **Rafflesia** plant (*Rafflesia zollingeriana*), which is visible at the beginning of the rainy season.

Practicalities

Access is much easier with your own transport or on an **organized tour**. Tours can be arranged through the two *Margo Utomo* hotels in Kalibaru (see p.338), or from Surabaya with Nusarisata Tours, Jl Kertajaya Indah Timur 8, Ⓣ031/592 5384, Ⓕ592 3085, Ⓔinfo@nusarisata.com). On public transport, head to Jagag by bus (2hr from Jember or Banyuwangi; Rp3000), take a minibus or microlet to Pasangrahan (1hr; Rp5000), and another microlet to Sarangan via the park post at **RAJEGWESI** (1hr; Rp3000); there's a government guesthouse here if you get stranded (❶), and you can hire a trekking guide at the park post if you want to get off the beaten track (Rp25,000 per day). There's a **beach** near Rajekwesi, called Teluk Hijau (Green Water), which has white sand and, as the name suggests, green water. From Rajegwesi, it's another 18km to **Sukamade beach** – take an ojek or charter a microlet. There is a camping area near the beach and national park **accommodation** (❶), but as there are only four rooms, you need to book at the office in Jember (see p.327); you can either take food to cook in the kitchen, or the staff will supply simple meals. The other accommodation is at the plantation guesthouse (❷) about 5km from the beach, run by Ledokombak, which must be booked in advance at their office in Jember at Jl Gajah Made 224 (Mon–Fri 7.30am–noon & 12.30–3pm, Sat 7.30am–12.30pm; Ⓣ0331/84814). Accommodation is in basic rooms with fan and attached cold-water mandi, and breakfast is included in the price, although simple meals can also be cooked by the staff.

There are even fewer visitors to the **west** of the park; access is from Jember to Ambulu (from Ajung terminal), 25km south of Jember, and from there to **Curahnangko** village. From the market there, arrange an ojek to travel the further 19km to the beach at **Bandialit** via the **park post** at Curahnangko. The campsite at Bandialit is pretty scruffy, and at the time of writing the plantation guesthouse was closed, but it's worth checking in Jember.

During the rainy season – December and January are the most difficult months – the park is very often inaccessible, as the rivers that rise in the coastal hills and flow to the south coast tend to flood. **Permits** (Rp1500) are available in the park office in Jember (see p.327), or at the park posts at Rajekwesi or Curahnangko.

Bondowoso

Attractively situated between Gunung Argopuro to the southwest and Gunung Beser to the north, **BONDOWOSO**, 33km north of Jember, is a small, relaxed town, useful for reaching the Ijen Plateau. There's good **access** by road or rail; the **train station** is 2km southeast of the alun-alun and there are regular trains from Panarukan on the north coast via Situbondo, and from Jember. The **bus station** is 500m beyond the train station and served by direct buses from throughout East Java. Coming from Banyuwangi (see p.332), you'll need to change at Situbondo if you come around the north coast, or Jember if you come on the southern route. **Becak** wait at the bus terminal and station to ferry arrivals around town.

The centre of town is the **alun-alun**, less manicured than many but still attractive, and surrounded by the main administration buildings. The main shopping street, Jalan Raya P. Sudirman, runs from the northeast corner of the square.

There is good **accommodation**: the place most used to travellers is *Hotel Anugerah*, Jl Mayjen Sutoyo 12 (Ⓣ0332/421870; ❶), with lots of options including top-end rooms with air-con – all rooms have attached mandi and outside sitting areas overlooking a small garden. The owner speaks good English, and can advise on things to see and help with chartering transport (Rp120,000 to Ijen, including fuel and driver); there's also a small restaurant attached. The plushest place is the recommended *Hotel Palm*, Jl A. Yani 32 (Ⓣ0332/421201; ❻), with nine standards of room from very small, basic ones with shared bathroom to huge rooms with air-con, TV and hot-water bathrooms. The lounge/coffee bar overlooks the attractive garden and there's a swimming pool (daily 5am–6pm; nonresidents weekdays Rp5000, Sat & Sun Rp7500).

The most atmospheric **place to eat** is the extensive night market along Jalan Martadinata, which heads east off the southeast corner of the alun-alun. The restaurant attached to *Hotel Anugerah* is a good bet for simple Indonesian and Chinese meals, as is *Rumah Makan Lezat*, Jl Raya P. Sudirman 95, which is clean, airy, good value and popular – although the menu is in Indonesian only. On the same street at no. 4, further towards the town square, the *Restaurant Sari Rasa* offers good Indonesian dishes.

The **post office** is at Jl Jaksa Agung Suprapto 9 (Mon–Thurs 7.30am–noon & 1–4pm, Fri 7.30–11.30am, Sat 7.30am–1pm, Sun & holidays 8–11am). There's a 24-hour **Telkom office** at Jl Mayjen Panjaitan 6; the road is left off Jalan A. Yani about 500m south of the alun-alun. You can only **exchange** cash, not travellers' cheques, at BNI, Jl A. Yani 26.

Moving on from Bondowoso, there are direct buses throughout East Java and to Denpasar. There are no direct buses to Banyuwangi, so change at Jember or Situbondo. Bondowoso is on the branch rail line between Panarukan on the north coast 8km west of Situbondo and Jember – change here onto the main east–west railway line from Banyuwangi through to Surabaya and points west.

The Ijen Plateau

The **Ijen Plateau** is a large upland area southeast of Bondowoso, which includes the peaks and foothills of Gunung Ijen (1994m), Gunung Raung (3332m), Gunung Suket (2950m) and Gunung Merapi (2800m), plus several smaller peaks. The entire area is rural, with coffee plantations and vegetable gardens blending into the forested uplands, and a few widely dispersed villages.

The highlight is the dramatic lake, **Kawah Ijen**, in the crater of the dormant volcano from which dozens of miners dig sulphur by hand.

Access and accommodation

From Bondowoso, there are four **buses** daily to the plateau and irregular buses between Sempol and Jampit and Blawan and Pal Tuding (see opposite). Buses tend to leave the Ijen area early in the morning for Bondowoso, and then head back up from about 10am onwards, but it is worth checking at the terminal in Bondowoso. From Sempol to Pal Tuding, it's necessary to hitch or use an ojek (Rp15,000 one way).

From Bondowoso, buses head for the small village of Wonosari, 11km to the northeast; the turning to Ijen is signposted 2km north of here. The road winds through the village of Sukosari and then begins to rise more steeply, the rice giving way to pine forest as the air gets cooler and habitation peters out. At the checkpoint onto the plateau, **Pos Malabar**, the small *Warung Ijen* sells noodles, coffee, soft drinks and cigarettes. The road then descends 7km to the small village of **SEMPOL**, a total of 55km from Wonosari. It's a tiny upland village; the main population centre in the area, superbly located amongst coffee plantations and forested mountains.

The closest **accommodation** to Ijen, 1km from the main road in the hamlet of **KALISAT** is the guesthouses *Jampit II* and *III* (bookings for both can be made via Jember ⓣ0331/486861; ❸), which are signposted "Penginapan Kaliasat" from the centre of Sempol. Located on the edge of a small valley, the accommodation is set in pleasant grounds: cheaper rooms have cold-water attached mandi, while the more expensive ones have hot water. Staff here can arrange riding, fishing, coffee-plantation walks, coffee-factory tours, excursions to Kawah Ijen, local guides, transport and inexpensive food. *Arabica Homestay* (bookings via Jember ⓣ0331/486861; ❸), near to *Jampit II* and *III* guesthouses, is popular with tour groups and is well maintained and friendly, with good local food.

There's a fourteen-kilometre rough road south from Sempol via the hamlet of Kepekan to **JAMPIT**, where you'll find *Jampit I* (no phone; ❷–❹) in an attractive colonial house set in manicured grounds. Cheaper rooms have nearby hot-water bathrooms, and more expensive ones have attached hot-water bathrooms with bathtubs. They get few visitors and even fewer vehicles: the local people get around on horseback. Book at *Jampit II* and *III* (see above), where they will help you arrange transport.

Two kilometres beyond Sempol is another checkpoint, **Pos Plalangan**. There is a junction here with the poorly surfaced, five-kilometre road to **BLAWAN**; ojek run from Sempol (Rp5000 one-way). The village is attractively located in a sheltered valley, with hot springs nearby, as well as a waterfall. The only accommodation is at the *Catimore Homestay* (❷), next to the coffee-processing factory behind an old colonial bungalow. The rooms are clean although basic, with attached hot-water bathrooms and pleasant grounds at the front.

Alternative access to the plateau is from Banyuwangi (see p.332), with a fifteen-kilometre climb initially to Licin, then another 18km to Pal Tuding via Pos Pengamatan at the village of Jambu (4km from Licin), and the villages of Ampel Gading and Sodang (8km from Licin). Without your own transport, take a Lin 3 from Blambangan bemo terminal to Sasak Perot in Banyuwangi, a small microlet terminal in the west of the city. There are microlets to Licin and the 4km on to Jambu, then you can charter an ojek to Sodang, but only occasionally all the way to Pal Tuding (Rp50,000 return). If not, it's a ten-kilometre walk from Sodang to Pal Tuding.

Kawah Ijen

The main road from Pos Plalangan continues another 10km to **Pal Tuding**, the starting point for the three-kilometre (90min) hike to the highlight of the area, **Kawah Ijen**, the crater lake. There is a campsite at Pal Tuding, next to the **national park office**, where you must register and pay the entrance fee (Rp4000, car Rp5000, motorcycle Rp3000). There is also dormitory accommodation at the national park office (Rp15,000); you'll be more comfortable with your own sleeping bag. At the tiny *Café Edelwys* attached to the office, you can buy snacks, drinks and basic meals. From Pal Tuding, the path heads steeply uphill northeast through the forest and is wide and easy to follow. After 45 minutes it passes a monitoring post, and the climb steepens. Just above here the path splits: the right fork, the best route, leads to the crater rim and the left fork to the dam at the end of the lake. After a while the path to the crater rim levels out, continues around the mountain and suddenly arrives on the bare, exposed rock of the mountainside, 200m above the lake in the crater below. It's a dramatic, austere landscape, with folds of almost bare rock sloping down into the crater; the only sign of life is stunted lichen. You can walk along the top of the crater for a fair distance in both directions, or descend to the edge of the lake along the narrow path that the sulphur miners use – allow 30–45 minutes to get down, and twice that to get back up.

The **sulphur miners** come up to Kawah Ijen daily; they set off from the Banyuwangi area before dawn, walk up to the lake from Licin, hack out a full load of sulphur (50–70kg) by hand, which they bring up to the crater rim and back down to Licin where they receive around Rp150 per kilo. It's dangerous work, and sudden eruptions and sulphur fumes have been known to kill miners.

Situbondo

Located 34km north of Bondowoso, the not-quite-coastal town of **SITUBONDO** is spacious, clean and convenient for access to and from Bondowoso and the Ijen Plateau. Situbondo is on the **rail** branch line between Panarukan on the north coast and Jember, and there are regular **buses** from throughout East Java. The town is quite spread out, with the central commercial and administrative area around the bus terminal. Five hundred metres west is the alun-alun, with **Mesjid At-Abror** on the west side, a low, modern mosque with a tall minaret. The train station is 500m southwest from the alun-alun. The main west–east road through town runs along the north side of the alun-alun and north of the bus terminal/market area: it is named Jalan A. Yani to the west of the town centre, and Jalan Basuki Rachmat to the east. The junction with the road south to Bondowoso is on the eastern outskirts of town.

If you want to **stay**, *Hotel Ramayana* at Jl Sepudi 11a (☎0338/671663; ❷) is central; turn right out of the bus terminal, and you'll find it 20m along the road. There's a big choice of rooms, so look at several before you choose. There are plenty of **places to eat** in the market area near the bus station, and also *Rumah Makan Malang*, Jl Basuki Rachmat 207, which is a clean, cool, Chinese place with a huge menu of inexpensive and moderately priced food.

There are a couple of banks which **exchange** cash, but not travellers' cheques: BNI, Jl Basuki Rachmat 235, and BCA, Jl Diponegoro 68. The **post office** is at Jl A. Yani 131 on the north side of the alun-alun, with the 24-hour **Telkom office** next door. Alternatively, there's a wartel at Jl Sepudi 7 (daily 8am–11pm), close to the bus station.

Baluran national park

Located in the far northeast corner of Java, the **Baluran national park** (Ⓦwww.balurannationalpark.com) is one of the driest parts of the island. Forty percent of it is savannah grassland, which surrounds the central mountain, the extinct volcano of **Gunung Baluran** (1275m), although there's also mangrove, coastal forest, swamp forest and monsoon forest.

The park is particularly good for **birds**: over 150 species have been spotted here, including weavers, woodpeckers, kingfishers, peafowl, jungle fowl and the increasingly rare Java sparrow. Monitor lizards up to two metres long also inhabit the park, and larger mammals are common, including banteng, deer, wild pig, monkeys, macaque and leopard. For serious nature-spotting, avoid the weekends, when the park is very crowded.

The **national park post** – where you buy tickets (Rp5000, car Rp4000, motorcycle Rp3000) and can book accommodation at Bekol and Bama – is at **Wongsorejo**, 30km north of Banyuwangi on the main road around the north coast. A couple of hundred metres into the park from the post, there's a **visitor centre** with maps, photographs and other information. From here, a twelve-kilometre poor-quality road leads through forest and grassland to **BEKOL**, a fairly built-up hamlet with basic accommodation (no food available; ❶), offices and several observation towers. One observation tower overlooks the nearby waterhole, while the one on the top of the hill gives great views of the broken crater rim of Gunung Baluran, inland up to Gunung Merapi and across the Bali Strait. There are plenty of well-marked walking trails in the park, most of them around 3km long. If you want to explore the more remote areas, arrange a park guide at the park post. Without your own transport, ojek (Rp10,000) or taxis (Rp35,000) are available from the park entrance to Bekol.

On the coast at **BAMA**, 3km along a rough but motorable track from Bekol, there's a two-hundred-metre beach with mangrove stands at either end and basic accommodation (no food available; ❶) in wooden cottages on stilts, which have verandahs looking seawards and bathrooms nearby. From the beach, there are views across to Bali, as well as various local walks.

Banyuwangi

The town of **BANYUWANGI** (Fragrant Water) is often bypassed by visitors, as the port giving access to **Bali** and **Java** is actually in **Ketapang**, 8km to the north. However, it's a manageable, lively place, built against the stunning backdrop of the Ijen Plateau to the west and with fine views across to Bali to the east. It's a useful base for excursions to the **Alas Purwo** and **Baluran national parks** and, with good-quality accommodation in all price brackets, is a great place to draw breath and plan your route through East Java, or through Bali if you're travelling eastwards – the town has excellent transport links throughout the region.

Historically, Banyuwangi was the capital of Blambangan, the sixteenth-century Hindu kingdom that ruled the eastern tip of Java. Although the rapidly expanding Muslim kingdom of Mataram attacked Blambangan during the early seventeenth century, it managed to survive as the last Hindu kingdom on Java and was mostly ignored by the Dutch until the eighteenth century, when they took it over.

Arrival and information

Arriving from Bali, you'll dock at the **ferry terminal** at **Ketapang**, 8km north of Banyuwangi; there is a helpful East Java **Tourist Office** (daily

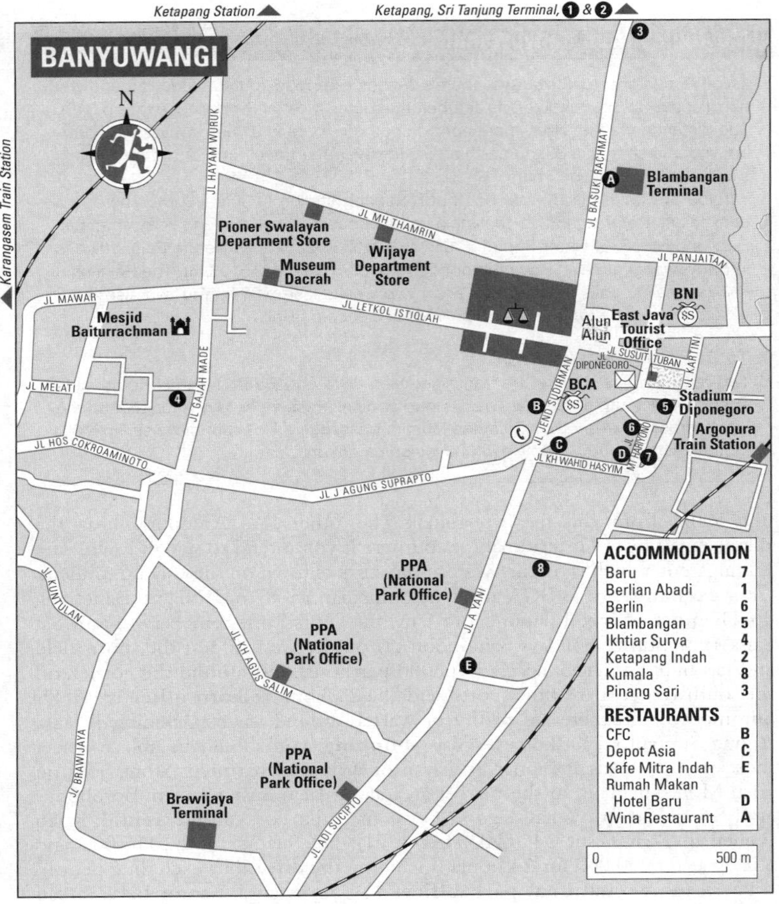

8am–7pm) inside the terminal building, and another tourist office on the road towards the truck terminal 200m south of the passenger terminal, Jalan Gatot Subroto LCM (Mon–Thurs 7am–2pm, Fri 7–11am, Sat 7am–12.30pm); they both have some English leaflets. In Banyuwangi itself, the **East Java Tourist Office**, Jl Diponegoro 2 (Mon–Thurs 8am–2pm, Fri 8–11am, Sat 8am–1pm), is opposite the post office under the stands of the sports ground.

There are several **bus terminals** serving Banyuwangi. The main long-distance terminal is Sri Tanjung, 2km north of Ketapang, from where there are regular buses throughout East Java and beyond. On the northern edge of the town centre is the Blambangan microlet terminal and, 3km from the city centre on the southwestern edge, Brawijaya terminal. Microlets numbered 1, 2, 4 and 5 ply between Brawijaya and Blambangan, and yellow microlets 6 and 12 link Blambangan and Sri Tanjung, as do blue Kijang. They are known locally as Lin 1, Lin 2, and so on.

Arriving by **train**, there are several stations, the main one being Ketapang,

Moving on from Banyuwangi

If you're heading **to Surabaya**, there's a choice of road routes, either around the north coast via Situbondo or via Jember; the routes meet at Probolinggo (see p.319). The distance via the hillier, more scenic southern route is 311km, whilst the northern route is shorter (280km) and flatter. However, the travel time on both routes is similar, at five to seven hours.

If you are travelling by **rail**, book at Ketapang station (9.30am–3pm). There is a convenient **Pelni** agent on the main road opposite the Ketapang ferry terminal: Hariyono NPPS, Jl Gatot Suproto 165 (Ⓣ & Ⓕ0333/22523), while the Pelni office is in Banyuwangi at Jalan Raya Situbondo (Ⓣ0333/510325, Ⓕ510326). The Pelni ship *KM Tatamailou* calls at Ketapang every two weeks (see p.339). You can also book tickets for the *KM Dibonsolo*, which calls at Benoa on Bali.

To Bali from Banyuwangi

Two ferry terminals serve the traffic between Java and **Bali**. The truck terminal is about 200m south of the main passenger terminal. Passenger ferries run around the clock, crossing every thirty minutes (30min; passengers Rp1400, bicycles Rp2000, motorcycles Rp3600, cars Rp18,000 including driver).

just 500m from the ferry terminal. The others are Argopura, near the Blambangan microlet terminal (get off here if you intend to stay in town), and Karangasem, which is on the western outskirts of town on the way up to Licin.

For **exchange**, go to BCA at Jl Jend Sudirman 85–87 or BNI at Jl Banetrang 46. The **post office**, Jl Diponegoro 1 (Mon–Thurs 8am–3pm, Fri 8–11am, Sat 8am–1pm, Sun & holidays 8am–noon), is on the west side of the sports field and has public internet access (Rp6000 per hour). Just around the corner, off the southwest corner of the sports field, the 24-hour **Telkom office** is at Jl Dr Sutomo 63, and there are plenty of wartels around town, including Jl Jaksa Agung Suprapto 130. For everyday **shopping**, you should be able to meet most of your needs at Pioner Swalayan or Wijaya Department Store, both on Jalan M.H. Thamrin. In the market area along Jalan Susuit Tuban, Borobodur at Jl Susuit Tuban 37 has a good range of batik. For **vehicle rental**, Koko Rental, Jl Ikan Pesut 34 (Ⓣ0333/411371), has Suzukis at Rp175,000 and Kijang at Rp250,000 for 24 hours (including the driver but excluding petrol).

There are two **national park offices** in Banyuwangi: Kantor Balai Taman Nasional Baluran, Jl K.H. Agus Salim 132 (Ⓣ0333/24119), and Kantor Balai Taman Nasional Alas Purwo, Jl A. Yani 108 (Ⓣ0333/411587, Ⓕ411857). Both are open Monday to Thursday 7am to 2pm, Friday 7am to 11am, Saturday 7am to 1pm. They have some brochures in English about the parks and will try to answer queries. Accommodation in the parks can be booked at the park posts close to the entrances.

Accommodation

There are plenty of **places to stay** in Banyuwangi and on the way to Ketapang in all price brackets; most are used to tourists, and can help with vehicle charter.

Hotel Baru Jl M.T. Hariyono 82–84 Ⓣ0333/421369. Popular with travellers, in a quiet central location a 10min walk from the post office. All rooms have attached mandi, and the more expensive ones have air-con. ❷–❸

Hotel Berlian Abadi Jl Yos Sudarso 165 Ⓣ0333/427688. 4km north of Blambangan terminal, on the way to Ketapang, this is an excellent place, although it can be a bit noisy as the road is so busy. All rooms are tiled and the pool is very good, although not included in the room charge at the lower end; admission is Rp2500. There's also an attached restaurant. ❷–❺

Hotel Berlin Barat Jl M.T. Hariyono 93 ⓣ0333/421323. With the same owners as *Hotel Baru*, this place is more spacious; rooms are of a similar standard, and all have attached mandi. ❷

Hotel Blambangan Jl Dr Wahidin 4 ⓣ0333/421598. On the south side of the sports field, about 100m from the post office, accommodation is in an old colonial bungalow and a two-storey building behind. All rooms are large with high ceilings, and those upstairs have balconies. ❶

Hotel Ikhtiar Surya Jl Gajah Made 9 ⓣ0333/421063. About 1.5km west of the town centre, reached by Lin 8 from Brawijaya terminal or Lin 4 or 7 from Blambangan. This is a large setup with rooms around a garden, and there are many standards of accommodation on offer. ❷

Hotel Ketapang Indah Jl Gatot Suproto Km6 ⓣ0333/422280, ⓕ423597. The best of the top-end hotels in the area – accommodation is spread throughout attractive grounds, 6km north of Blambangan terminal on the way to Ketapang. All rooms have partially open-air bathrooms, hot-water showers and air-con, and there's a pleasant lounge area and restaurant with great views across to Bali, plus a good-sized swimming pool. Special discounts are often available. ❸

Hotel Kumala Jl A. Yani 21B ⓣ0333/ 423533. A friendly place, with clean quiet rooms, some with hot water, air-con and television. ❸

Hotel Pinang Sari Jl Basuki Rachmat 116–122 ⓣ0333/423266, ⓕ426173. In a garden setting, 500m north of Blambangan terminal, the grounds are attractive and some rooms are furnished in traditional bamboo and wood. ❷

The Town

The main market area is on Jalan Susuit Tuban, which links the alun-alun with the sports stadium, Stadium Diponegoro, 500m to the southeast. In a modern building at Jl Sri Tanjung 3 on the north side of the alun-alun, **Museum Daerah Blambangan** (Mon–Sat 8am–4.30pm; Rp500) has a small collection of furniture and ceramics; the nearby **Mesjid Baiturrachman** is elegant and cool. The **Chinese temple**, Vihara Tan Tin Jin, is dedicated to the Chinese architect responsible for Pura Taman Ayun in Mengwi (see p.650). You can see local **batik production** in Temenggungan, the area north of the museum.

Eating and drinking

Many of the hotels have attached restaurants, and there is a night market along Jalan Pattimura offering warung food.

CFC Jl Sudirman 170. The usual fast-food fried options and blissful air-con.

Depot Asia Jl Dr Sutomo 2, near Jalan Jend Sudirman and Jalan Jend A Yani intersection. Good Indonesian and Chinese food at reasonable prices.

Kafe Mitra Indah Jl A. Yani 93. Offers Indonesian, Chinese and Western food, with an adjoining café for cakes and pastries.

Rumah Makan Hotel Baru Jl M.T. Hariyono 82–84. Just opposite *Hotel Baru*, this place serves up inexpensive rice and noodle dishes in cool, relaxed surroundings.

Wina Restaurant Jl Basuki Rachmat 62, on the street side of Blambangan terminal. It's an excellent place if you're passing through the terminal, serving inexpensive fried chicken, *nasi ramen*, *nasi rawon*, juice and ices.

South of Banyuwangi

There are several spots worth a visit to the **south of Banyuwangi**. Gintangan offers an excellent chance to view rural Javanese life firsthand, whilst the **Alas Purwo national park** is a terrific draw for surfers, and great for wildlife-spotting.

The small, attractive village of **GINTANGAN** is located 30km south of Banyuwangi. There's plenty to see in the locality: it's just 3km to the local beach and 7km to Muncur, the second largest natural harbour in Indonesia. Bamboo items are produced here, including hats, baskets and boxes. To access Gintangan, get off the Banyuwangi–Jember bus at the village of Gladag, a few kilometres south of the large junction town of Rogojampi. Gintangan is 3km east of Gladag: ojek, becak, andong and the occasional microlet ply the route. There is a **homestay** in the village, *Gintangan Homestay* (☎0333/632166; ❶); the owner, Amanu, was previously a guide in Bali and now teaches English, and he can arrange for you to visit the local traditional bone-setter who uses massage to heal. Simple warung provide basic meals.

On the northwestern side of Grajagan Bay, 50km from Banyuwangi, **GRAJAGAN** is a pretty, bustling fishing village, with dozens of multicoloured boats on the water. The **beach**, Pantai Coko, is signposted from the village: it's 300m to the gate (admission Rp2000, car Rp500, motorcycle Rp300), and then another 2km through the forest to the beach. This is a favourite local excursion spot, but during the week it's pleasantly quiet. Due to the surf, take local advice (there's a forestry office at Plengkung – see opposite) about safe swimming spots, be very careful and never swim near the rocks. The black-sand beach is fairly small, with a wooded headland to the south and brilliant views around the bay – to the east, it's possible to see across to Cape Purwo, south of Plengkung. There is **accommodation** at *Wisma Perhutani* (no phone; ❶) in basic rooms (bring your own sheet sleeping bag) with deep verandahs, attached mandi and electricity supplied by a generator in the evening. To get to Plengkung and its surf camp (see opposite), it's possible to charter boats from Grajagan – you'll start bargaining at US$200 for a boat for ten people, so there's little advantage in going from Grajagan rather than overland through Alas Purwo (see below). **Access to Grajagan** is through Srono, a village 11km south of Rogojampi. By public transport, there are minibuses from Brawijaya terminal in Banyuwangi to Purwoharjo, 10km south of Srono, and then microlets for the final 14km to Grajagan.

Alas Purwo national park

Occupying a densely forested peninsula at the far southeastern extremity of Java, the **Alas Purwo national park** offers a good chance to see Asiatic wild dogs, banteng, deer and monkeys. There's also plenty here for birdwatchers, including peafowl, jungle fowl, pitta, kingfishers, waders, and several varieties of migrant birds such as plovers, redshanks, whimbrels, samerlings and pelicans.

To get to Alas Purwo, buses from Brawijaya terminal in Banyuwangi marked for Kalipait actually terminate 1km further on at **Dam Bunting**, a small village with a few shops where you can stock up on food, although you'll get a better choice if you bring supplies from further afield. From here, the road to the beach passes through **Pasar Anyar**, where there's a **visitor centre** with maps, displays and information about the park. It's then another 14km to the beach at Triangulasi via the park post at **Rowobendo**, where you pay for **admission** (Rp2000, car Rp2000, motorcycle Rp1000), and can arrange accommodation. Without your own transport, you'll need to charter an ojek from Dam Bunting to Triangulasi (Rp10,000 one-way, if you bargain).

The beach at **Triangulasi** is stunning: a curving white arc several kilometres long, with huge surf pounding as far as the eye can see across to Plengkung in the distance, and Grajagan and Grajagan Bay to the west with the coastal hills rising behind. It's a fabulous spot, although far too dangerous for swimming. At Triangulasi, there is basic **accommodation** (Rp15,000) 200m from the beach, in simple wooden rooms on stilts with a bathroom at the back, a kitchen with a wood fire and a few simple utensils. There are no warung on the beach; you need to take food with you and be prepared to cook it.

Two kilometres southeast from Rowobendo at **Sadengan**, there's a tower from which to observe the wildlife. At **Ngagelan**, accessed by a motorable road 6km from Rowobendo, turtles (green, leatherback, hawksbill and Oliver

Ridley) come to the beach to lay eggs (November to March is the best time), and there is a hatchery where the eggs are protected. From Triangulasi, it's 3km to **Pancur**, on the coast towards Plengkung – you can walk, or the road is passable – where there's a **campsite**. From Pancur, it's about 3km to Goa Istana, an ancient meditation spot, and 13km from Triangulasi to Plengkung, right on the peninsular tip 14km from the park entrance.

PLENGKUNG, known also as **"G-Land"** (Ⓔ g-land@rad.net.id), is renowned worldwide for its great **surfing**, boasting possibly the longest left breaks in the world. With reef breaks often reaching 5m, this is surfing for the experienced only. Since its inclusion in the Quicksilver World Tour Circuit, Plengkung has gained an international following among surfers. **Tours** can be booked through PT Wadasari Wisata Surf, Jl Pantai Kuta 8b, Denpasar, Bali (Ⓣ 0361/7555588, Ⓕ 755690), or Plengkung Indah Wisata, Andika Plaza Blok A 22/23, Jl Simpang Dutah 38–40, Surabaya (Ⓣ 031/5315320). There are two **camps** for surfers, *Joyo's* (bookings though Plengkung Indah Wisata – see above; ❹) and *Bobby's* (bookings though Wadasari Wisata Surf – see above; ❺), right on the beach. *Joyo's* is the simplest, with traditional bamboo huts, shared bathrooms and electricity. Buffet meals (Indonesian and Western) are available but pricey. Just south is *Bobby's*, which has shared bathrooms, electricity and better food (included in the price). Both camps offer table tennis, volleyball, billiards and evening film showings. The only alternative accommodation is the **PHPA post** (❷), situated between the two camps, offering two basic rooms with shared mandi and no food. Both surfers' camps are **closed** from December to April, when weather conditions are dangerous.

Kalibaru

Located 50km west of Banyuwangi, along twisting roads with dramatic views north to the Ijen area and south to Meru Betiri national park, **KALIBARU** is a cool and pleasant village and a good base from which to explore the surrounding coffee, cocoa and rubber plantations. If you want to see the **plantations** at their best, the coffee season is from April to September; cocoa is dependent on the water supply but the crop is most prolific from June to August, and rubber is produced all year and is most spectacular in the rainy season, when the trees produce most latex. PTP Nusantara XII is a substantial plantation (closed Sun), located 12km south of Glenmore, 10km east of Kalibaru. If you go on Friday, you'll also be able to enjoy the large weekly cattle market in Glenmore.

Other local **excursions** include **Tirto Argo**, a natural spring surrounded by a pool 10km from Kalibaru, and the waterfall, **Air Terjun**, at Wonorejo, 5km north of Kalibaru, which is a popular Sunday excursion for local people and accessible by ojek (Rp10,000 return if you bargain). **White-water rafting** is available from *Margo Utomo* (see p.338) and a small **train** runs to Dresin from Kalibaru (minimum of six people); there's nothing much in Dresin, the pleasure being the leisurely journey through the countryside. If you want to explore further afield, Meru Betiri national park (see p.328) is accessible from Kalibaru, either with *Margo Utomo* on an organized tour or with your own transport.

Practicalities

Access to Kalibaru is straightforward: all **buses** between Banyuwangi and Jember pass through (every 10min during the day); for long-distance destinations, change in Banyuwangi. Kalibaru is on the main east–west **rail** line between Banyuwangi and Surabaya, Malang and Yogyakarta. The **wartel** is about 50m west of the station in Kalibaru, Jl Raya Jember 168 (daily 5am–midnight). Next door is the **post office**, Jl Raya Jember 15 (Mon–Thurs 7.30am–3pm, Fri 7.30–11.30am, Sat 7.30am–1pm).

The best **place to stay** in Kalibaru is the *Margo Utomo Homestay* (sometimes called *Margo Utomo I*), Jl Lapangan 10 (ⓣ0333/897700, ⓕ897124; ❸), which is behind the station; cross to the north side of the tracks on foot, and the homestay is up a small side road. Accommodation is in attractive colonial bungalows with high ceilings, verandahs and hot-water bathrooms set in pleasant grounds. The homestay can organize transport to anywhere in East Java and Bali (Rp225,000 to Surabaya, Rp250,500 to Denpasar on Bali), and have a range of local tours available to plantations and villages, or further afield to Baluran, Sukamade, Alas Purwo and Kawah Ijen. They also arrange local guides (Rp50,000 per day) and jungle trekking, from the area south of Glenmore through to Rajekwesi beach, where you are collected by car. There are minimum numbers, usually two people, for all trips. Next door to *Margo Utomo Homestay*, *Wisma Susan*, Jl Lapangan 12 (ⓣ0333/897289; ❷), has clean, neat, tiled rooms in the garden of a family house. All rooms have attached mandi and there is warm water in the evening; the price includes breakfast. *Margo Utomo Cottages*, Jl Putri Gunung 3 (ⓣ0333/897420) is a modern sister hotel of *Margo Utomo Homestay*, and is nicely situated by a river about two kilometres east of the town (❹).

Travel details

Buses

It's almost impossible to give the **frequency** with which **bemos and buses** run, as they only depart when they have enough passengers to make the journey worthwhile. **Journey times** also vary a great deal. The times below are the minimum you can expect these journeys to take. Privately run shuttle, or **door-to-door**, buses run between the major tourist centres on Java.

Banyuwangi to: Bandung (daily; 24hr); Blitar (hourly; 12min); Jakarta (daily; 20–24hr); Jember (every 20min; 3–4hr); Kalibaru (every 20min; 2hr 30min); Madura (Sumenep; hourly; 12hr); Malang (hourly; 7hr); Pasuruan (5 hourly; 6hr); Probolinggo (5 hourly; 5hr); Semarang (2 daily; 15–17hr); Situbondo (every 20min; 2–3hr); Solo (hourly; 11–13hr); Surabaya via the southern route (every 20min; 5–7hr); Surabaya via the northern route (every 10min; 5–7hr); Yogyakarta (hourly; 12–14hr).

Batu to: Jombang (hourly; 3hr); Kediri (hourly; 3hr); Malang (hourly; 30min).

Blitar to: Banyuwangi (hourly; 12hr); Denpasar (8 daily; 18hr); Jakarta (6 daily; 19hr); Kediri (4 hourly; 2–3hr); Malang (every 10min; 3hr); Pacitan (hourly; 5hr); Solo (5 daily; 6hr); Surabaya (2–6 hourly; 4hr); Yogyakarta (hourly; 7hr).

Bondowoso to: Besuki (every 30min; 1hr); Blawan (4 daily; 3hr); Denpasar (daily; 8–9hr); Jember (every 20min; 1–2hr); Madura (Sumenep; 7 daily; 9hr); Malang (2 daily; 5–6hr); Situbondo (every 20min; 1hr); Surabaya (hourly; 4hr).

Jember to: Banyuwangi (7–12 hourly; 3–4hr); Blitar (2–4 hourly; 6–7hr); Denpasar (1–5 hourly; 7–8hr); Kalibaru (7–12 hourly; 1hr); Madura (Sumenep; every 30min; 9–10hr); Malang (4–6 hourly; 5–7hr); Probolinggo (every 5min; 3–4hr); Surabaya (every 5min; 6–8hr); Yogyakarta (hourly; 12–14hr).

Kalibaru to: Banyuwangi (7–12 hourly; 2hr 30min); Jember (7–12 hourly; 1hr).

Kediri to: Blitar (4 hourly; 2–3hr); Denpasar (daily; 18hr); Jakarta (daily; 18hr); Malang (4 hourly; 3hr); Nganjuk (6 hourly; 1hr); Surabaya via Pare and Malang (5 hourly; 5hr); Surabaya via Kertosono (5 hourly; 4hr); Yogyakarta via Solo (5 daily; 6hr).

Madiun to: Jakarta (daily; 16hr); Solo (hourly; 4hr); Surabaya (every 20min; 3–4hr); Yogyakarta (hourly; 6hr).

Malang to: Bandung (daily; 16hr); Banyuwangi (hourly; 7hr); Bengkulu (daily; 36hr); Blitar (hourly; 3hr); Denpasar (daily; 15hr); Jakarta (daily; 15hr); Jambi (daily; 48hr); Jember (hourly; 4–5hr); Kediri (hourly; 3hr); Medan (daily; 3 days); Palembang (daily; 36hr); Pasuruan (hourly; 1–2hr); Pekanbaru

(daily; 48hr); Probolinggo (hourly; 2–3hr); Situbondo (hourly; 4hr); Surabaya (every 20min; 1hr 30min–2hr 30min); Yogyakarta (hourly; 7–9hr).
Mojokerto to: Surabaya (every 20min; 1hr 30min–2hr).
Pacitan to: Blitar (hourly; 4–5hr); Jakarta (18 daily; 13–15hr); Solo (4 hourly; 4–5hr); Surabaya (daily; 7hr).
Pasuruan to: Banyuwangi (5 hourly; 6hr); Denpasar (daily; 12hr); Jember (hourly; 3hr); Malang (hourly; 2–3hr); Mojokerto (hourly; 2hr); Probolinggo (5 hourly; 1hr); Surabaya (5 hourly; 1–2 hr).
Probolinggo to: Banyuwangi (5 hourly; 5hr); Bondowoso (1–2 hourly; 2–3hr); Denpasar (hourly; 11hr); Jakarta (hourly; 24hr); Jember (4 hourly; 2–3hr); Malang (hourly; 2–3hr); Mataram (Lombok; hourly; 16hr); Pasuruan (5 hourly; 1hr); Situbondo (5 hourly; 2–3hr); Solo (hourly; 7hr); Surabaya (2 hourly; 2hr); Yogyakarta (hourly; 8–9hr).
Situbondo to: Banyuwangi (every 20min; 2–3hr); Bondowoso (every 20min; 1hr); Jember (every 20min; 2hr); Malang (hourly; 5–6hr); Pasuruan (every 20min; 3–4hr); Probolinggo (every 20min; 2–3hr); Surabaya (every 20min; 5–6hr).
Surabaya to: Banyuwangi (every 30min; 5–7hr); Bondowoso (hourly; 4hr); Bukitinggi (daily; 48hr); Denpasar (5 daily; 11hr); Jakarta (20 daily; 14hr); Jember (every 30min; 4hr); Madiun (2 hourly; 3hr); Madura (Sumenep; hourly; 5hr); Malang (every 30min; 2hr 30min); Mataram (2 daily; 20hr); Medan (daily; 3 days); Mojokerto (every 20min; 2hr); Pacitan (2 hourly; 7hr); Padang (daily; 48hr); Palembang (daily; 36hr); Pekanbaru (daily; 48hr); Probolinggo (every 30min; 2hr); Semarang (every 30min; 6hr); Solo (every 30min; 5hr); Situbondo (every 30min; 3hr); Sumbawa Besar (daily; 26hr); Yogyakarta (every 30min; 7hr).

Trains

Banyuwangi to: Jember (daily; 3–4hr); Kalibaru (daily; 2hr 30min); Malang (daily; 5–6hr); Probolinggo (daily; 5–6hr); Surabaya (3 daily; 7hr); Yogyakarta (daily; 15hr).
Blitar to: Bangil (5 daily; 3hr 20min); Kediri (3 daily; 1hr 30min); Kertosono (3 daily; 2hr 30min); Malang (5 daily; 1hr 50min); Surabaya (8 daily; 4–5hr).
Bondowoso to: Jember (2 daily; 2hr); Kalisat (2 daily; 1hr); Panarukan (2 daily; 2hr); Situbondo (2 daily; 1hr 30min).
Jember to: Banyuwangi (6 daily; 3–4hr); Malang (daily; 4hr); Panarukan (2 daily; 4hr); Probolinggo (3 daily; 1–2hr); Surabaya (2 daily; 3hr); Yogyakarta (daily; 12hr).
Kalibaru to: Banyuwangi (7 daily; 1–2hr); Jember (2 daily; 2hr); Malang (daily; 6hr); Probolinggo (daily; 4hr); Surabaya (2 daily; 5hr); Yogyakarta (daily; 14hr).
Madiun to: Bandung (3 daily; 9–11hr); Banyuwangi (daily; 11hr); Jakarta (5 daily; 8–12hr); Jombang (daily; 1hr 30min); Kediri (daily; 2hr); Malang (daily; 5hr); Purwokerto (daily; 5hr); Solo (5 daily; 1hr 20min); Surabaya (8 daily; 2hr 30min–3hr 30min); Yogyakarta (5 daily; 3hr 30min).
Malang to: Banyuwangi (daily; 5–6hr); Blitar (5 daily; 1hr 50min); Jakarta (daily; 12hr 30min–18hr); Surabaya (8 daily; 3hr).
Mojokerto to: Bandung (daily; 18hr); Blitar (3 daily; 3hr); Jakarta (2 daily; 15hr); Madiun (2 daily; 1hr 45min); Malang (3 daily; 4hr 15min); Surabaya (7 daily; 1–2 hr); Yogyakarta (2 daily; 4hr).
Pasuruan to: Banyuwangi (4 daily; 5hr); Blitar (daily; 3hr 30min); Denpasar (daily; 12hr); Kediri (daily; 4hr 40min); Malang (daily; 1hr 40min); Surabaya (daily; 1hr 30min); Yogyakarta (daily; 10hr).
Probolinggo to: Banyuwangi via Jember and Kalibaru (4 daily; 5–6hr); Kediri via Malang and Blitar (daily; 5–6hr); Surabaya (3 daily; 2–4 hr).
Situbondo to: Bondowoso (2 daily; 1hr 30min); Jember (2 daily; 2–3hr); Kalisat (2 daily; 1–2hr); Panarukan (2 daily; 30min).
Surabaya Kota station to: Bandung (2 daily; 16–18hr); Banyuwangi (3 daily; 6–7hr); Blitar via Malang (5 daily; 4–5hr) or Kertosono (4 daily; 4–5hr); Malang (7 daily; 3hr); Jakarta (3 daily; 14–16hr); Kertosono (6 daily; 2hr); Yogyakarta (2 daily; 5–6hr). Pasar Turi station to: Jakarta (6 daily; 12–16hr). Gubeng station to: Bandung (3 daily; 16–18hr); Banyuwangi (2 daily; 6–7hr); Jakarta (3 daily; 14hr); Mojokerto (7 daily 1–2hr); Pasuruan (daily; 1hr 30min); Probolinggo (3 daily; 2–4 hr); Purwokerto (daily; 7hr 50min); Yogyakarta (daily; 5hr 10min).

Pelni ferries

For a chart of the Pelni routes, see p.42 of Basics. Surabaya is the busiest port for Pelni boats; ferries from Surabaya sail to their destination ports every two weeks, unless stated below. The following is a summary of the more popular routes and not a complete listing.
Banyuwangi The *KM Tatamailou* calls in at Banyuwangi every 2 weeks, destination Merauke (5 days). Ports visited include: Amahai (4 days); Ambon (4 days); Badas (22hr); Bau Bau (3 days); Bima (28hr); Dili (3 days); Denpasar (7hr); Dobo (5 days); Fak-Fak (5 days); Kaimana (6 days);

Labuanbajo (35hr); Larantuka (2 days); Makasar (46hr); Merauke (5 days); Saumlaki (4 days); Tual (5 days); Timika (twice fortnightly 6–8hr).
Surabaya Ambon (*KM Bukit Siguntang, KM Dibonsolo, KM Lambelu, KM Rinjani*; 2–3 days); Badas (*KM Pangrango*; 21hr); Balikpapan (*KM Tidar*, 3 times fortnightly; 22hr); Banda (*KM Bukit Siguntang, KM Rinjani*; 3 days); Banjarmasin (*KM Kelimutu*, 5 times fortnightly; 24hr); Batulicin (*KM Binaiya, KM Leuser*, 23hr); Bau-Bau (*KM Bukit Siguntang*; *KM Lambelu, KM Rinjani*; 2 days); Bawean (*KM Pangrango*; 7hr); Biak (*KM Dibonsolo*; 5 days); Bitung (*KM Kambuna, KM Lambelu, KM Umsini*; 3 days); Blinyu (*KM Bukit Raya*; 5 days); Denpasar (*KM Dibonsolo*; 16hr); Dili (*KM Dibonsolo*; 53hr); Dobo (*KM Bukit Siguntang*; monthly; 4 days); Dumai (*KM Bukit Siguntang, KM Kerinci*; 3 days); Ende (*KM Pangrango*; 3 days); Fak-Fak (*KM Rinjani*; 4 days); Jayapura (*KM Dibonsolo, KM Rinjani, KM Umsini*; 6–7 days); Kaimana (*KM Bukit Siguntang*; monthly; 4 days); Ketapang (*KM Pangrango*; 3 days); Kijang (*KM Bukit Siguntang, KM Kerinci*; 2 days); Kumai (*KM Leuser*, 22hr); Kupang (*KM Dibonsolo*; 44hr); Kwandang (*KM Umsini*; 3 days); Labuanbajo (*KM Pangrango*; 2 days); Letung (*KM Bukit Raya*; 4 days); Makasar (*KM Bukit Siguntang, KM Kambuna, KM Kerinci, KM Lambelu, KM Rinjani, KM Tidar, KM Umsini*; 24hr); Manokwari (*KM Dibonsolo, KM Rinjani, KM Umsini*; 4–5 days); Midai (*KM Bukit Raya*; 3 days); Nabire (*KM Rinjani, KM Umsini*; 5 days); Namlea (*KM Lambelu*; 3 days); Natuna (*KM Bukit Raya*; 3 days); Nias (*KM Kambuna, KM Lambelu*; 3 days); Nunukan (*KM Tidar*, 3 days); Padang (*KM Kambuna, KM Lambelu*; 30–42hr); Pantoloan (*KM Tidar*, 43hr); Pare-Pare (*KM Tidar*, 26hr); Pontianak (*KM Bukit Raya*; 39hr); Rote (*KM Pangrango*; 3 days); Sabu (*KM Pangrango*; 3 days); Samarinda (*KM Binaiya, KM Leuser*, 3 days); Sampit (*KM Binaiya, KM Bukit Raya, KM Pangrango*; 21–24hr); Semarang (*KM Binaiya, KM Kelimutu*; weekly; *KM Leuser, KM Pangrango*; 44–50hr); Serasan (*KM Bukit Raya*; 3 days); Serui (*KM Rinjani, KM Umsini*; 6 days); Sibolga (*KM Kambuna, KM Lambelu*; 3 days); Sorong (*KM Dibonsolo, KM Rinjani, KM Umsini*; 4 days); Tambelan (*KM Bukit Raya*; 3 days); Tanjung Priok, Jakarta (*KM Bukit Siguntang, KM Dibonsolo, KM Kambuna, KM Kerinci, KM Lambelu*; 16–21hr); Tarakan (*KM Tidar*, weekly; 3 days); Tarempa (*KM Bukit Raya*; 3 days); Ternate (*KM Lambelu*; *KM Umsini*; 4 days); Toli-Toli (*KM Binaiya, KM Kambuna, KM Kerinci, KM Leuser*, 3–4 days); Tual (*KM Bukit Siguntang, KM Rinjani*; 4 days); Waingapu (*KM Pangrango*; 48hr).

Other ferries

Banyuwangi to: Gilimanuk (Bali; every 30min; 30min).
Kalianget (Madura) to: Tanjung Jangkhar (daily; 4hr).
Kamal (Madura) to: Surabaya (every 30min; 30min).
Surabaya to: Kamal (Madura; every 30min; 30min).
Tanjung Jangkhar to: Kalianget (Madura; daily; 4hr).

Flights

Surabaya to: Ambon (suspended at present, 18 weekly; 4hr); Balikpapan (3 daily; 2hr); Banda Aceh (suspended at present, daily; 10hr); Bandung (4 daily; 1hr–2hr 30min); Banjarmasin (2 daily; 2hr); Batam (3 daily; 3hr 25min); Denpasar (12 daily; 1hr 10min); Dili (10 weekly; 4hr 30min); Gorontalo (4 weekly; 5hr); Jakarta (22 daily; 1hr 20min); Jayapura (5 daily; 9hr); Kendari (2 daily; 5hr); Kupang (3 daily; 6hr 35min); Manado (daily; 4hr); Mataram (5 daily; 1hr 30min); Medan (5 daily; 7hr); Palangkarya (daily; 5hr); Palu (2 daily; 6hr); Pekanbaru (daily; 6hr); Pontianak, via Jakarta (4 daily; 6hr); Samarinda (daily; 7hr); Semarang (6 daily; 50min); Solo (daily; 1hr 10min); Ternate (daily; 8hr 15min); Timika (2 daily; 11hr 40min); Ujung Pandan (11 daily; 1hr 30min); Waingapu (3 weekly; 3hr 20min–5hr 35min); Yogyakarta (8 daily; 50min).

5

North Sumatra and Aceh

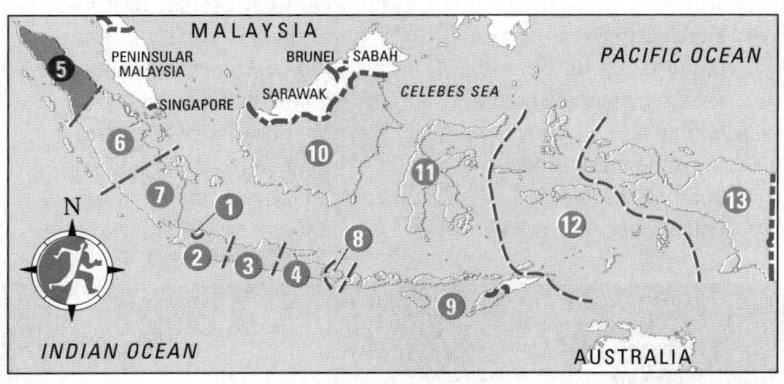

CHAPTER 5

Highlights

* **Mesjid Raya, Medan** Listen to the twilight ezan, sung from the black and pearl domes of Medan's largest mosque, for a poignant insight into Islamic life. See p.352
* **Bukit Lawang** Catch the orphaned apes at the Orang-Utan Rehabilitation Centre as they swing out of the jungle at feeding time. See p.356
* **Berastagi** Set amongst picturesque Karonese villages, sleepy Berastagi is only a few hours' trek from the sulphurous summits of two active volcanoes. See p.364
* **Pulau Samosir, Danau Toba** This stunning green island in the centre of Southeast Asia's largest freshwater lake is the spiritual heartland of the Toba Batak people. See p.374
* **Pulau Nias** Far-flung Pulau Nias boasts Sumatra's best beaches, barrelling surf and ancient megalithic villages. See p.381
* **Gunung Leuser national park** Camping out in the rainforest with a local guide, listening to the chatter of monkeys and the call of jungle birds, is an unforgettable experience. See p.359

5

North Sumatra and Aceh

The landscape of Indonesia's two westernmost provinces, North Sumatra and Aceh, is defined by the Bukit Barisan, a volcanic mountain range that runs along the whole of the western side of Sumatra. The mountains rear almost vertically from the Indian Ocean in the west, before sloping gradually away towards the Malacca Straits in the east. The rivers that run from these central highlands to the plains of the east coast carry vast deposits of extremely fertile volcanic silt, and since colonial times the eastern deltas have featured huge coffee, tea and tobacco plantations. This agricultural richness, combined with some considerable offshore oil reserves, has helped to ensure the prosperity of this far-flung corner of the Indonesian archipelago.

North Sumatra now receives more tourists than any other Indonesian province except Bali and Yogyakarta. Most arrive at the island's bustling capital **Medan** on the east coast, an entry point from Malaysia. Just a couple of hours' drive north from Medan is the hugely popular Orang-Utan Rehabilitation Centre at **Bukit Lawang**.

For many visitors, however, the main interest of North Sumatra lies in its rugged central highlands, whose inhabitants descended from a wave of immigrants who arrived in the North Sumatran hinterland over four thousand years ago. They evolved almost completely in isolation from the rest of the island, developing languages and cultures that owe little to any outside influences. While there are a number of these highland tribes scattered throughout the two provinces, the most famous are the **Batak** of North Sumatra (see box on p.362–4). The Europeans who first discovered the Batak at the end of the eighteenth century reported back tales of cannibalism that engrossed the Western world. The fascination obviously still holds, even though cannibalism here is now a thing of the past: every year visitors flock in their thousands to the Batak homelands. The chilly hill station of **Berastagi**, part of the Karo Batak territory, and the many waterside resorts around beautiful **Danau Toba** – Southeast Asia's largest lake and the spiritual home of the Toba Batak – throng with tourists every summer, as does the surfer's mecca of **Pulau Nias**, home to another indigenous group of ex-cannibals.

Bukit Lawang, Berastagi, Danau Toba and Nias form a perfect diagonal route across the centre of the province. The tourist infrastructure is good, with an excellent transport network – most points of interest are near the Trans-Sumatra Highway – and some first-class hotels, homestays and restaurants. Apart for the remote outpost of Nias and the seldom-visited southern Batak lands, English is widely understood. With such a diverse terrain in North Sumatra, **weather** is fairly localized, though in general the highlands are much less humid than the sweltering eastern plains, and occasionally the nights can be bitterly cold.

Northwest of North Sumatra, the province of **Aceh**, with its breathtaking scenery, picture-perfect beaches and dense primary jungle, has since 1999 been engulfed in a violent separatist struggle that has put a stop to all tourist travel in the province. Although there has been some improvement in recent months, Aceh remains volatile, and travel in the province is not advised; for more information, see the box below.

Safety in Aceh

Ever since the declaration of independence in 1945, Aceh has tried to break away from the Indonesian republic, a struggle sadly characterized by constant **separatist violence**. Over 6000 people have lost their lives since 1990. The **Free Aceh Movement** (GAM) formed in 1976 galvanized Acehnese resistance to what it saw as exploitation by transmigrants, big business and the Jakarta government. In the chaos following the currency crisis of 1997, the GAM once again demanded **autonomy** from the republic of Indonesia. It wasn't hard to see why; not only have there been reports of **torture, rape and murder** of local Acehnese by the Indonesian army, but ever since Suharto's "new order" of foreign investment and big business, the Acehnese claim their natural resources have been plundered to feed the corrupt and distant power brokers of Jakarta. In fact, as much as thirty percent of central government funds in 2000 were said to derive from Acehnese oil alone, little of which was spent locally.

In 1999, the newfound **independence** of East Timor and rumblings of discontent in Irian Jaya (now West Papua) further encouraged the GAM. This prompted a fierce response from the military, as each successive president made sure to underline the policy of "Bhinneka tunggal" (unity in diversity), by stamping down hard on what could be the slippery slope towards Balkanization of the whole country. 2001 was a bloody year, with over 1000 deaths – mostly due to fighting between Indonesian army forces and local rebels – as well as bomb blasts in the capital Banda Aceh, and insurgency in the highlands. **Peace talks** in 2002 led to the signing of an **treaty** on December 9 of that year. In it, the province was promised autonomy, seventy percent of its oil and gas revenues, and an election in 2004 – though not the independence they had hoped for. However, by the end of January 2003 there were already indications that the ceasefire agreement had been broken, with the shooting of an Indonesian policeman at a roadblock just the latest in a series of reported incursions by both sides.

Although tourists have never been targets for either side in the conflict, the employees of western businesses – namely the oil giant Exxon-Mobil – have been attacked, though most likely because of their collusion in "robbing" Aceh of oil rather than their American connections. However, the danger of being caught in the **separatist crossfire** continues: for this reason, **Rough Guides advises against travel in the region**. At the time of writing, many **roadblocks** were in place on the roads leading north into Aceh, and there were reports of soldiers **extorting money** from travellers. The eastern coast road was said to be the safest, while any travel along the central road via Takengon was out of the question; flying in was the safest bet. If you do consider visiting Aceh, be certain to **appraise the situation in advance** via the media, your consulate and by word of mouth in Medan.

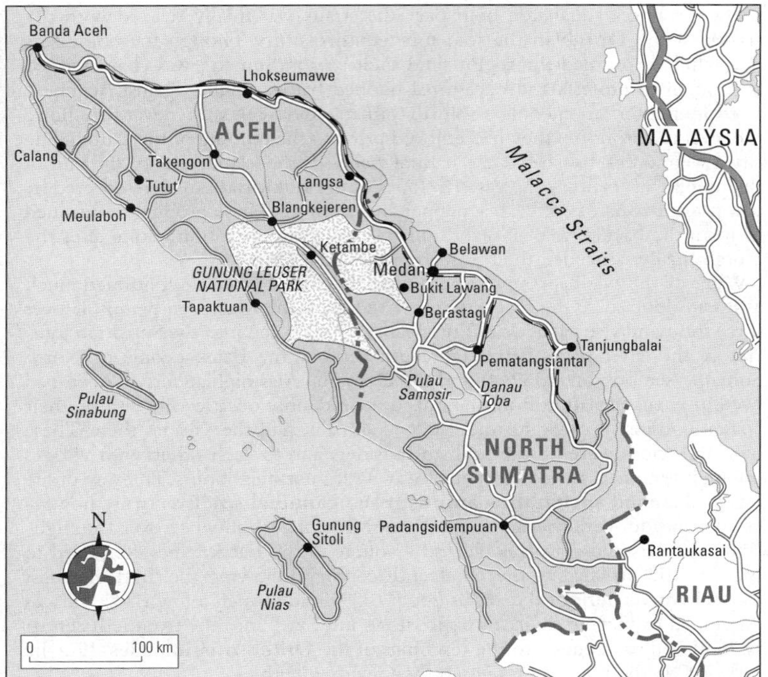

Some history

The coastal towns of North Sumatra and Aceh were amongst the first in Indonesia to convert to **Islam**, brought over by seafaring traders from India and Arabia as early as the eighth century AD. These towns, located at the mouths of the numerous small rivers that empty into the Malacca Straits from the highlands, thrived as trading ports, eventually coalescing into a number of small kingdoms. A visit by the Chinese eunuch and envoy **Cheng Ho** in the fifteenth century persuaded these coastal kingdoms that there was a fortune to be made by fulfilling China's demand for **pepper**. As a result, for the next four hundred years North Sumatra and Aceh were amongst the world's biggest pepper producers, and it became the region's most lucrative export. Consequently, some of the small kingdoms, particularly in Aceh, enjoyed a degree of power out of all proportion to their tiny size.

This wealth attracted the attention of outsiders, keen to appropriate some of the spoils for themselves. The **Portuguese**, following their capture of Malacca in 1511, began to raid the east coast, which by this time had already fallen under the sway of the Sriwijayan empire of southern Sumatra. The Sriwijayan tenure in the Sumatran east coast was brief, partly because of the rise in power of the Acehnese sultanate based on the northern tip of Sumatra at Banda Aceh. This sultanate enjoyed supremacy over much of northern Sumatra, and even over the Malaysian peninsula, under the leadership of **Iskandar Muda** (1607–36).

The Acehnese sultanate's hold over the straits was finally relaxed with the arrival of the **Dutch** in the mid-nineteenth century. Though the colonizers never fully subsumed the region, and their stay in Sumatra was characterized by numerous protests and occasional pitched battles fought against Acehnese freedom fighters, the people of North Sumatra and Aceh were never to achieve the level of autonomy they had enjoyed prior to the coming of the Dutch. The latter were quick to exploit the natural riches of the island, and by the end of the nineteenth century the eastern slopes of the Bukit Barisan were covered by vast **plantations** of coffee, tea, pepper and palm oil. These products continued to form the backbone of North Sumatra's prosperous economy long after the Dutch finally conceded their Sumatran territories in 1946.

While all this was happening on the coast, life in the **interior** continued much as it had done since the first settlers arrived from the Malaysian peninsula over three thousand years ago. Until Europeans first ventured into the Sumatran interior in the latter part of the eighteenth century, the Batak people of North Sumatra (see box on p.362–4) and the Gayo and Alas highlanders of Aceh had lived in virtual isolation from the outside world, only occasionally visiting their coastal cousins in order to trade or, occasionally, raid the villages there. These highland tribes were hostile both to outsiders and to each other, with villages often existing in a state of perpetual war with their neighbours. The way of life revolved around **agriculture**, **animism** and **cannibalism**. Eventually, however, the outside world began to exert an ever stronger influence over the highlands: the Alas and Gayo people and a couple of the Batak tribes converted to Islam in the first half of the nineteenth century, following the fundamentalist **Paderi movement** of the 1830s (see p.1039), and though a few Batak villages continued to practise their animistic rituals until well into the twentieth century, most had succumbed to the teachings of the **Dutch missionaries** – by the early 1900s, the majority professed the Christian faith.

Medan

MEDAN, Indonesia's fourth largest city, has acquired a reputation as a filthy and chaotic metropolis with few charms. This is somewhat unjust: although it's true that Medan is as addicted as any other big Indonesian city to shopping centres and fast-food culture, the capital of North Sumatra also has some glorious examples of turn-of-the-twentieth-century **colonial architecture** and a couple of colourful **temples** from the same period. To the south and west of the city are neat parks and pleasant leafy suburbs – once the home of the Dutch gentry – where the roar of traffic is reduced to a barely audible hum.

The city grew from a small village, Medan Putri, situated at the confluence of the Deli and Babura rivers. *Medan* is Indonesian for "battlefield", and for most of the sixteenth century the fields surrounding the village were the scene of pitched battles between the rival sultanates of Deli Tua, near the modern-day port of Belawan, and Aceh. The Acehnese eventually prevailed and, as peace returned to the region, Medan slipped back into obscurity until an itinerant Dutch entrepreneur, **Jacob Nienhuys**, arrived in 1862. Recognizing the potential of the rich volcanic soil of the Bukit Barisan, Nienhuys began to grow **tobacco** on a small plot of land granted to him by the sultan of Deli. Soon European entrepreneurs were flocking to North Sumatra to ask for similar concessions from the sultan, and the rapid transformation of the region began. During the nineteenth century, the Dutch grew rich from the vast plantations stretching up the slopes of the Bukit Barisan to the west of the city.

Modern Medan is largely a product of these prosperous colonial times. From a sleepy backwater village of fewer than two hundred people in 1823, the city has blossomed into a huge metropolis with a population of 1.2 million. The European entrepreneurs who built sumptuous **mansions** and grand offices brought with them thousands of immigrant labourers from China and India, who in turn established quarters in the booming city, constructing an array of **temples**. Even the local royalty migrated to the city to be nearer the action, and the sultan of Deli's official residence, **Maimoon Palace**, and the nearby **Mesjid Raya**, were added to the cityscape. Though none of these buildings are unmissable, if you fancy the comforts of a large and modern metropolis combined with some faded colonial grandeur, then Medan deserves at least a day of your time.

Arrival, orientation and information

Thanks to a local superstition that noise drives away evil spirits, Medan's **Polonia airport** lies near the town centre at the southern end of Jalan Imam Bonjol. A taxi from the airport to the main square, Lapangan Merdeka, shouldn't cost more than Rp10,000. **Belawan Harbour** lies 25km to the north of the city. A complimentary bus service to the town centre is laid on to meet the hydrofoil ferries from Penang; the yellow "Morina" angkutas #81 or #122 (Rp2000) also ply the route.

Medan has two main **bus stations**. The huge Amplas terminal, 5km south of the city centre, serves buses arriving from points south of Medan, including Java, Bukittinggi and Danau Toba. White "Medan Raya" or "MRX" minibuses (Rp1000) leave from Amplas terminal, travel past Mesjid Raya and on to Lapangan Merdeka via Jalan Brig Jend A. Yani. The Pinang Baris bus station,

Moving on from Medan

Medan's Belawan Harbour serves both passenger **ferries** to Malaysia and local Pelni ferries to other parts of Indonesia. There are currently two ferries sailing to Penang: the *Perdana Expres* and the *Bahagia Expres*. With both, transfer to the port from the agency you buy your ticket from is free, and the cost for both is the same: Rp150,000 one-way and Rp250,000 return, including the departure tax from Indonesia. The **Pelni** ship *KM Bukit Siguntang* calls in every four days at Belawan on its way to Jakarta. Pelni does not offer a complimentary lift from central Medan to Belawan, so you'll have to make your own way; the cheapest method is to catch the yellow angkuta "Morina" #81 or #122 – they leave from Pinang Baris bus station and from the west side of Jalan Pemuda, just south of the intersection with Jalan Perang Merah. See p.355 for ferry agents.

When leaving Medan by **bus**, remember that buses to points north and west of Medan depart from Pinang Baris (reached by DAMRI bus #2 from the tourist office, or angkuta "Koperasi" #64 heading west along Jalan R H Jaunda or north along Jalan Pemuda), while the Amplas terminal (reached by angkuta "Soedarko" #3 or #4 heading south along Jalan Palangka Raya) serves most other destinations with two important exceptions. Travellers to **Berastagi** will find it much quicker to catch an angkuta to Padang Bulan (#60 or #41 from the Istana Plaza heading west on Jalan R.H. Juanda, or #10 heading north along Jalan Pemuda), a lay-by in the southwestern corner of the city, from where buses (named *Sinabung Jaya*, *Sutra* and *Karsima*) leave every ten minutes. Those heading to **Singkil** (for Pulau Banyak) have their own direct minibus service, leaving daily at 1pm (Rp17,000) from the *Singkil Raya Café* at Jl Tobing 81 (aka Jalan Bintang), a few blocks east of the Medan Mall in the heart of the bird market.

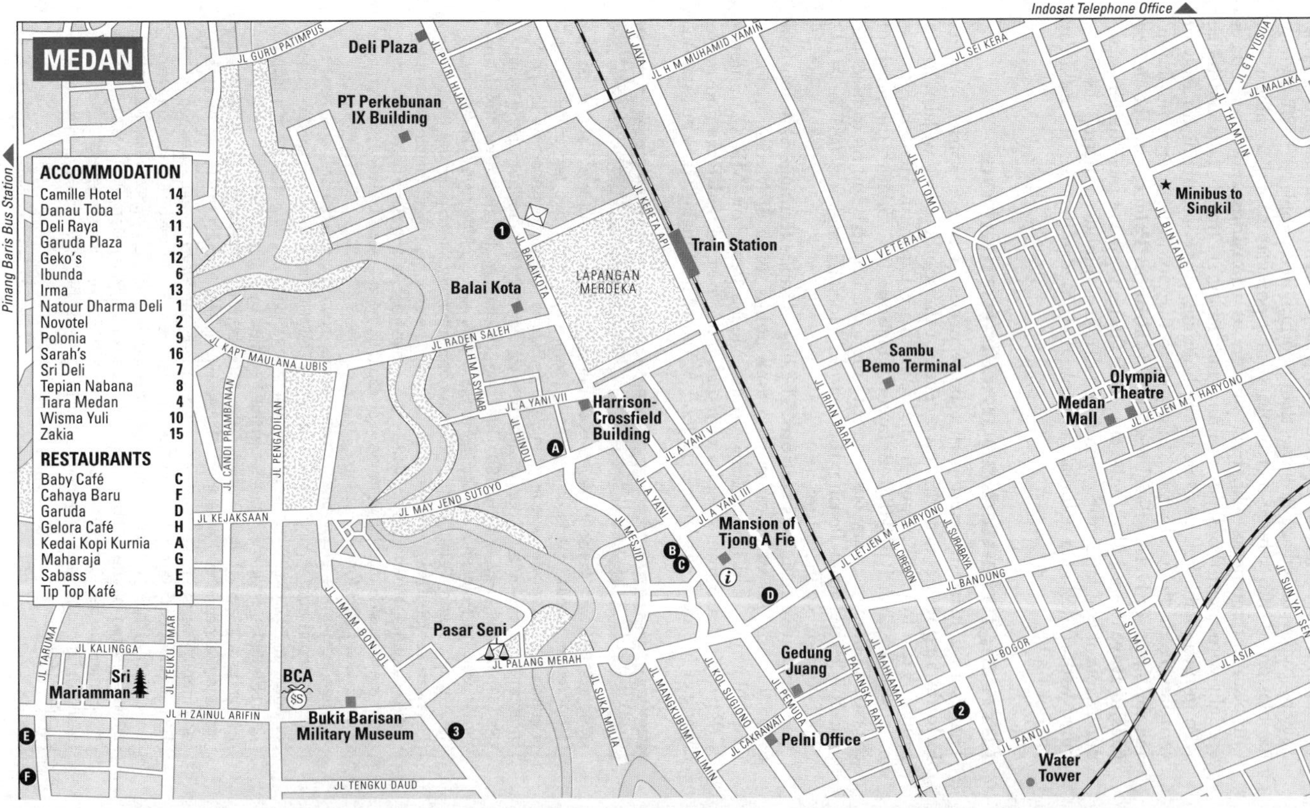
MEDAN
ACCOMMODATION
Camille Hotel 14
Danau Toba 3
Deli Raya 11
Garuda Plaza 5
Geko's 12
Ibunda 6
Irma 13
Natour Dharma Deli 1
Novotel 2
Polonia 9
Sarah's 16
Sri Deli 7
Tepian Nabana 8
Tiara Medan 4
Wisma Yuli 10
Zakia 15
RESTAURANTS
Baby Café C
Cahaya Baru F
Garuda D
Gelora Café H
Kedai Kopi Kurnia A
Maharaja G
Sabass E
Tip Top Kafé B
Indosat Telephone Office
Matahari Plaza
Pinang Baris Bus Station
Deli Plaza
PT Perkebunan IX Building
Balai Kota
LAPANGAN MERDEKA
Train Station
Sambu Bemo Terminal
Olympia Theatre
Medan Mall
Minibus to Singkil
Harrison-Crossfield Building
Mansion of Tjong A Fie
Gedung Juang
Pelni Office
Water Tower
Pasar Seni
BCA
Bukit Barisan Military Museum
Sri Mariamman
JL GURU PATIMPUS
JL PUTRI HIJAU
JL JAVA
JL H M MUHAMID YAMIN
JL SEI KERA
JL G R YUSUA
JL MALAKA
JL THAMRIN
JL BINTANG
JL SUTOMO
JL VETERAN
JL KERETA API
JL BALAIKOTA
JL RADEN SALEH
JL KAPT MAULANA LUBIS
JL H M A SYINAB
JL A YANI VII
JL HINDU
JL A YANI V
JL A YANI
JL A YANI III
JL IRIAN BARAT
JL LETJEN M T HARYONO
JL CIREBON
JL SURABAYA
JL BANDUNG
JL SUMOTO
JL SUN YAT SEN
JL ASIA
JL BOGOR
JL MAHKAMAH
JL PALANGKA RAYA
JL PEMUDA
JL CAKRAWATI
JL KOL SUGIONO
JL MANGKUBUMI ALIMIN
JL SUKA MULIA
JL PALANG MERAH
JL MESJID
JL MAY JEND SUTOYO
JL KEJAKSAAN
JL PENGADILAN
JL CANDI PRAMBANAN
JL IMAM BONJOL
JL TEUKU UMAR
JL KALINGGA
JL TARUMA
JL H ZAINUL ARIFIN
JL TENGKU DAUD
JL PANDU

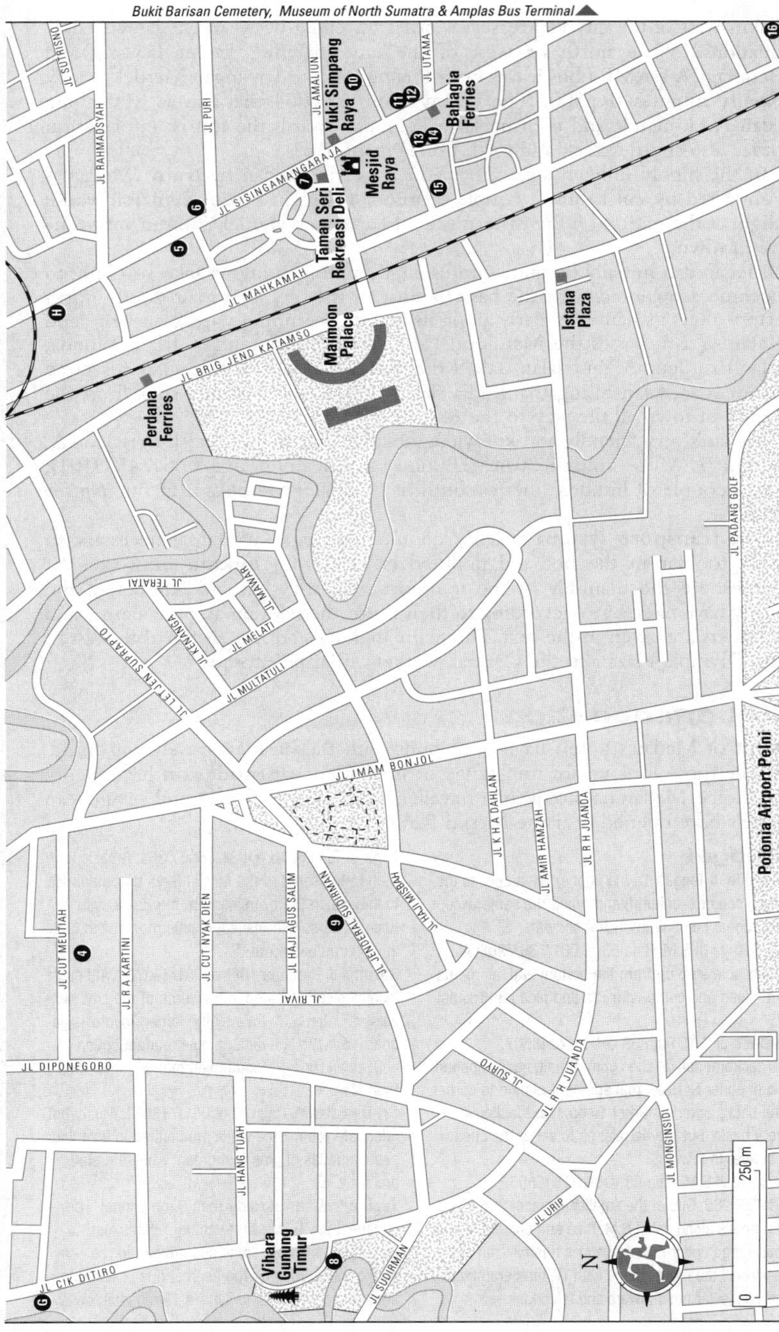

Bukit Barisan Cemetery, Museum of North Sumatra & Amplas Bus Terminal
JL SUTRISNO
JL RAHMADSYAH
JL PURI
JL AMALIUN
JL UTAMA
Yuki Simpang Raya
Bahagia Ferries
JL SISINGAMANGARAJA
Mesjid Raya
Taman Seri Rekreasi Deli
JL MAHKAMAH
Maimoon Palace
Istana Plaza
JL BRIG JEND KATAMSO
Perdana Ferries
JL TERATAI
JL MAWAR
JL KENANGA
JL MELATI
JL MULTATULI
JL LETJEN SUPRAPTO
JL PADANG GOLF
JL IMAM BONJOL
JL K H A DAHLAN
JL AMIR HAMZAH
JL R H JUANDA
Polonia Airport Pelni
JL HAJI MISBAH
JL JENDERAL SUDIRMAN
JL HAJI AGUS SALIM
JL CUT NYAK DIEN
JL CUT MEUTIAH
JL R A KARTINI
JL RIVAI
JL DIPONEGORO
JL SURYO
JL MONGINSIDI
JL HANG TUAH
JL URIP
Vihara Gunung Timur
JL SUDIRMAN
JL CIK DITIRO
250 m
0
N

10km west of the city centre, serves buses travelling between Medan and destinations to the north or west of the city, including Bukit Lawang and Berastagi. A DAMRI bus leaves from Pinang Baris to Lapangan Merdeka every twenty minutes (Rp300). The yellow mini-van #64 that travels west along Jalan R.H. Juanda and then up Jalan Pemuda towards the tourist information office also shuttles back and forth from Pinang Baris.

In the highly unlikely event that you arrive in Medan by **train** (Medan is connected by rail to just a couple of minor towns in North Sumatra), you'll alight at the station on the eastern side of Lapangan Merdeka, in the very centre of town.

Medan can initially be quite confusing, though it shouldn't take you long to become acquainted with the basic **layout** of the city. The main south–north artery alters its name regularly along its length, beginning with Jalan Brig Jend Katamso as it passes the Maimoon Palace, before changing to Jalan Pemuda, Jalan Brig Jend A. Yani, Jalan Balai Kota, and finally Jalan Putri Hijau. A second major road, Jalan Sisingamangaraja (Jalan S.M. Raja for short) runs from the centre of town all the way to the Amplas bus terminal.

Medan's very friendly and knowledgeable **tourist office** is at Jl Brig Jend A. Yani 107 (Mon–Thurs 8.30am–2.30pm, Fri 8.30am–noon; ⓣ061/4538101), just a couple of hundred metres south of Lapangan Merdeka near the *Tip Top Kafé*.

The **transport system** is fairly comprehensive, so it's rarely necessary to walk too far in the hot and polluted city centre. **Angkuta** mini-vans, or bemos, are the mainstay of the transport network; they are numbered, and many have names too, according to their route; the relevant angkuta names and numbers are given in the text. The main angkuta station is at **Sambu**, west of the Olympia Plaza and the Central Market on Jalan Sutomo.

Accommodation

Most of Medan's hotels have been built with the business traveller in mind. While those looking for mid-range or luxury **accommodation** have plenty of choice, Medan has no distinct travellers' centre. However, a number of cheap hotels have opened near the Mesjid Raya.

Budget

Camille Jl Tengah 1a (no phone). Next door to the *Irma* (see next column) and much the same except the rooms come with bucket showers. ❷

Deli Raya Jl S.M. Raja 53 ⓣ061/736 7208. A noticeable step up from the bottom end, all rooms are clean and come with TVs and nice bathrooms. ❷

Geko's Jl S.M. Raja 59 ⓣ061/7343507, ⓔgeckomedan@yahoo.com. Small, newly opened hotel under German management aiming to corner the backpacker's market. Rooms and facilities are very basic, but the bar claims to serve the cheapest beer in town. ❷

Ibunda Jl S.M. Raja 33 ⓣ061/7345555, ⓕ7358989. One of the smaller, cheaper and friendlier hotels along Jalan S.M. Raja and one of the best mid-range options, the *Ibunda* is a family-run place where all the rooms come with TV, temperamental air-con, solar hot showers and telephone. ❸

Irma Jl Tengah 1b ⓣ081/2606 0304. A basic losmen to the south of the Mesjid Raya that manages to survive on the overspill from the *Zakia*, with twenty sparsely furnished, double rooms with fans and shared bathroom. ❷

Sarah's Jl Pertama 10/4 ⓣ061/743783. Although inconveniently located in the south of the city, just west of Jalan S.M. Raja by the large "Toyota" signboard, *Sarah's* is a decent, quiet budget option with clean rooms – some with mandi – and good food. ❷

Sri Deli Jl S.M. Raja 30 ⓣ061/713571. Musty but adequate rooms; the walls are painted in soothing pastel shades of pink and green, while the staff are surly. ❷

Tepian Nabana Jl Hang Tuah 6 (no phone). The cheapest place in town (with dorm beds just Rp3000), it's a little dingy and difficult to reach by public transport, with the nearest bus or angkuta stop outside the *Danau Toba*, a 15min walk away.

Closed for refurbishment at the time of writing. ❷
Wisma Yuli Jalan S.M. Raja, Gang Pagaruyung 79b ⓣ061/736 9704. One of the oldest travellers' places in Medan, with dorms and doubles. It's rather dingy, but all rooms have a fan, and there's a Home Country Direct phone in reception. ❷
Zakia Jl Sipisopiso 10–12 ⓣ061/722413. The best of the budget options, with fine views of the mosque and rooftops, the *Zakia* is attractive and spacious with clean, basic dorms (Rp8000) and rooms with or without plumbing. ❷

Mid-range and expensive

Danau Toba Jl Imam Bonjol 17 ⓣ061/4157000, ⓕ453 0553, ⓔhdti@nusa.net.id. The liveliest of the luxury hotels, with first-class facilities including a health centre and an excellent outdoor pool, as well as the *Tavern Pub* and *Ari Kink Kink* disco in the grounds – two of the busiest nightspots in town. Currently undergoing a much-needed restoration, the *Danau Toba* has dropped its prices drastically and now offers the best-value accommodation in town, persuading even backpackers to splash out and stay here. ❺
Garuda Plaza Jl S.M. Raja 18 ⓣ 061/736 1234, ⓕ736 1111, ⓦwww.garudahotel.com. Despite its kilometres of grey carpet, the 151-room *Garuda Plaza* is the best of a fairly uninspiring bunch strung out along Jalan S.M. Raja. It has helpful staff, a decent-sized swimming pool and some of the fiercest air-con in Sumatra. ❺
Natour Dharma Deli Jl Balai Kota 2 ⓣ061/414 7744, ⓕ4144477. Stately, centrally located hotel built round the former *Hotel De Boer*. All 180 rooms have air-con, TV and minibar; other facilities include a pool, bar, expensive café and a good cake shop. ❺
Novotel Jl Cirebon 76a ⓣ061/456 1234, ⓕ4572222, ⓔnovonet1@indosat.net.id. A large hotel adjoining the Plaza Hong Kong. All the rooms have air-con, TV, IDD telephone, minibar and hair dryer as standard; other features include Chinese and Indonesian restaurants, a pub, tennis courts, a gym and a swimming pool. ❺
Polonia Jl Jend Sudirman 14 ⓣ061/5351111, ⓕ538870, ⓔpolonia@indosat.net.id. Located in the heart of Medan's well-heeled residential district, the 200-room *Polonia* boasts, amongst the usual luxury features, an excellent Chinese restaurant, squash and tennis courts and a small pool. ❺
Tiara Medan Jalan Cut Mutiah ⓣ061/457 4000, ⓕ451 0176, ⓦwww.tiarahotel.com. A peacefully located luxury hotel and conference centre with 204 air-con rooms (complete with IDD, television and minibar), a health centre, restaurant, a number of bars but (strangely for a hotel of this size) no pool. ❼

The City

Many of Medan's attractions lie to the south of Lapangan Merdeka along Jalan S.M. Raja and Jalan Pemuda, where you'll find the diverting **Museum of North Sumatra**, the **Maimoon Palace** and the splendid **Mesjid Raya**. In the Indian quarter to the west are two of the most spectacular and atypical **temples** – one Taoist, one Hindu – in the whole archipelago. In addition, all around Lapangan Merdeka there are wonderful examples of **colonial architecture**, particularly along Jalan Brig Jend A. Yani, which was Medan's high street during the Dutch era.

The Museum of North Sumatra, Mesjid Raya and Maimoon Palace

If you plan to spend only one day in Medan you should restrict your sightseeing to the city's three main attractions, all of which lie in the south of the city on or near Jalan S.M. Raja (named after a Batak king killed by the Dutch in 1907). The first of these is the **Museum of North Sumatra** (Tues–Sun 8.30am–noon & 1.30–5pm; Rp500) at Jl Joni 51, 500m east of Jalan S.M. Raja on the southern side of the Bukit Barisan cemetery. Like most provincial museums in Indonesia, this is a large, informative, well-laid-out and inexplicably deserted place. The concrete reliefs on the museum's facade depict a couple dressed in traditional costume from each of the different ethnic groups of the province (the various Batak tribes, the Niha people of Nias and the Malayu of the east coast). Inside, the museum tells the story of North Sumatra from prehistory to the present day, with the inevitable emphasis on Indonesia's struggle for independence. Highlights include a couple of Arabic gravestones from the eighth century AD – proof that Islam arrived on Sumatra more than a thousand years ago – and a number of ancient stone Buddhist sculptures found buried under Medan's Chinatown district. Most of the exhibits are labelled in English.

Eight hundred metres north of the museum on Jalan S.M. Raja, the black-domed **Mesjid Raya** (9am–5pm, except prayer times; donation) is one of the most recognizable buildings in Sumatra. Built in 1906, the mosque, with its arched windows and blue-tiled walls, seems to have a Turkish or Moroccan influence, though it was actually designed by a Dutch architect in 1906. While obeying the iconoclastic restrictions of Islam in its refusal to depict living creatures, Mesjid Raya manages to be both ornate and colourful, with vivid Chinese stained-glass windows and intricate, flowing patterns painted on the interior walls and carved into the doors.

The mosque was commissioned by Sultan Makmun Al-Rasyid of the royal house of Deli. The family graveyard lies at the back of the mosque, while 200m further west, opposite the end of Jalan Mesjid Raya, stands their royal house, **Maimoon Palace** (daily 8am–5pm; Rp3000), built in 1888. With its yellow-painted walls (yellow is the traditional Malay colour of royalty), black crescent-surmounted roofs, Moorish archways and grassy lawns (which, like the mosque's, are the venue for impromptu thirty-a-side football matches every evening), the palace has many features in common with the mosque, and the two complement each other fairly well. The interior of the palace, however, is rather disappointing: the brother of the current sultan still lives in one wing, and only two rooms are open to the public, neither of which justify the entrance fee. The first room is the **reception hall**, complete with the royal throne (yellow, of course) and pictures of the sultans and their wives; the second room is a showcase for bad batik paintings and souvenirs.

Maimoon Palace lies at the southern end of **Jalan Pemuda**, a busy six-lane highway with few other attractions apart from, perhaps, the **Gedung Juang '45** (daily except Fri 9am–2pm). This is yet another museum devoted to Indonesia's fight for Independence. If you've been to one of these sort of museums before then you'll know what to expect, though this one is slightly different in that it uses oil paintings and storyboards (rather than the usual dioramas) to recount Indonesia's glorious struggle. It isn't really worth visiting, though one bizarre inclusion is a Molotov cocktail, for which the museum thoughtfully provides the full list of ingredients.

Jalan Brig Jend A. Yani and Lapangan Merdeka

At the northern end of Jalan Pemuda, **Jalan Brig Jend A. Yani** was the centre of colonial Medan and, amongst the modern sports and souvenir shops, there are a couple of early-twentieth-century buildings. Of these, the most impressive is the weathered **Mansion of Tjong A Fie** at no. 105. This beautiful, green-shuttered, two-storey house was built for the head of the Chinese community in Medan, who made and lost a fortune investing in the plantations during the turbulent 1920s and 1930s. The mansion is closed to the public, but there's plenty to admire about the exterior – the dragon-topped gateway is magnificent, with the inner walls featuring some faded portraits of Chinese gods and mythological characters.

The mansion stands almost directly opposite one of Medan's oldest and finest eating places, the *Tip Top Kafé* (see p.354), one of a number of uniform but handsome European buildings along this street. The most impressive, the 1920s **Harrison-Crossfield Building** (now labelled "London, Sumatra, Indonesia

TBK", at Jalan Brig Jend A. Yani's northern end, was the former headquarters of a rubber exporter and is now the home of the British Consulate and the British Council library.

Beyond this building, the road, as it passes along the western side of Lapangan Merdeka, changes its name to **Jalan Balai Kota** after the gleaming white **Balai Kota** (Town Hall). The *Natour Dharma Deli Hotel* – formerly the *Hotel De Boer*, the setting for the Ladislao Szekely novel *Tropic Fever* – is next door, while the **Kantor Wali Kota Madya**, the city post office that dates back to 1911, stands nearby on the northwestern corner of the square. In front of the post office is a (now defunct) **fountain** dedicated to the man who brought prosperity to the city, Jacob Nienhuys.

There's little of interest on the rest of Jalan Balai Kota, though the grand headquarters of **PT Perkebunan IX** (a government-run tobacco company) lie just to the west along narrow Jalan Tembakau Deli, 200m north of the *Natour Dharma Deli Hotel*. This dazzlingly white building, the first two storeys of which are faced by a series of small, attached pilasters, was commissioned by Nienhuys in 1869 as the offices of the VDM (Vereenigde Deli Maatschappij), the governing body of Dutch plantation owners. It was the first European building in Medan and remains one of its most impressive and lavish examples of colonial architecture.

The Military Museum and the Indian quarter

Running west from the southern end of Jalan Brig Jend A. Yani, Jalan Palang Merah crosses Sungai Deli before continuing west as Jalan H. Zainul Arifin. The sights along this strip are really of minor interest and include the former **Dutch Assistant Resident's Office**, now a branch of the Standard Chartered Bank, which stands in the grounds of the *Hotel Danau Toba* on the southeastern corner of the junction with Jalan Imam Bonjol. Four hundred metres further on, past the incredibly dull **Bukit Barisan Military Museum** (Mon–Fri 8am–3pm; donation) – home to a few tatty old uniforms and amateurish paintings of Indonesia's struggle for independence – is the **Sri Marriamman Temple**. Built in 1884 and devoted to the goddess Kali, this typically colourful and elaborate temple is Medan's oldest and most venerated Hindu shrine. Visitors are asked to remove their shoes before entering, and remain silent inside the temple grounds.

The Sri Marriamman temple marks the beginning of the **Indian quarter**, the **Kampung Keling**, the largest of its kind in Indonesia. Curiously, this quarter also houses the largest Chinese temple in Sumatra, the Taoist **Vihara Gunung Timur** (Temple of the Eastern Mountain), which, with its multitude of dragons, wizards, warriors and lotus petals, is tucked away on tiny Jalan Hang Tuah, 500m south of Sri Marriamman.

Eating, drinking and entertainment

Medan has a cosmopolitan mix of **eating places**. Chinese food tends to dominate the warung, while there are some fine Indian restaurants in and around Kampung Keling. Medan also has its own style of alfresco eating, where a bunch of stall-owners gather in one place, chairs are put out, and a waitress brings a menu listing the food available from each of the stalls. The best of these is the *Taman Rekreasi Seri Deli*, which encircles the small pond to the north of Mesjid Raya.

The expat community's contribution to Medan's cuisine is pastries and cakes. Amongst the many Western-style **bakeries** in town are the *French Baker* at Jl Pemuda 24c, *Medan Bakers* at Jl-Zainul Arifin 150, and three on Jalan Tuama opposite the northern end of Jalan Cik Ditiro: the *Tahiti*, *Suans* (which does good ice cream) and the *Royal Holland*. **Fast-food** junkies are also well catered for, with a branch of *McDonald's* opposite the Mesjid Raya, a *Wendy's*, *Jolibee*, *Dunkin' Donuts* and *KFC* in the Deli Plaza on Jalan Balai Kota, and a *McDonald's* and *Dunkin' Donuts* in the Medan shopping centre.

The President Theatre **cinema** on Jalan Balai Kota, 100m north of the GPO near the Deli Plaza, shows the latest Hollywood releases. For **bowling**, try Taman Ria (Mon–Fri 5pm–midnight, Sat & Sun 2pm–midnight). Games cost Rp2500 (Rp1500 for students, 5–7pm only), and shoe rental Rp1000. To get there, catch any Pinang Baris-bound bus or bemo and jump off when you see the Taman Ria (on your right as you come from the town centre).

Restaurants and warung

Baby Café Jl Jend A. Yani 98. An overpriced, dimly lit, wood-panelled restaurant, often deserted during the day but rowdy in the evening when the Hash House Harriers (see below) call in.

Cahaya Baru Jl Cik Ditiro 8l. The newest and best of Medan's Indian restaurants, the service at this small place in the heart of the Indian quarter is fast and friendly, the prices very reasonable and the food excellent (including some delicious *masala dosas*).

Garuda Jl Palang Merah 26. A good, cheap, 24hr-restaurant with superb fruit juices and a wide selection of Padang dishes.

Gelora Café Jl S.M. Raja 4. An indoor version of the *Taman Rekreasi Seri Deli* (see p.353), where you sit at a table and a waitress brings you a menu with all the food on offer from the budget-priced stalls: the *murtabak* are particularly good.

Kedai Kopi Kurnia Jl Maj Jend Sutoyo 22. One of the most popular Chinese eating places in Medan, the open-sided *Kedai Kopi Kurnia* serves hearty portions of no-nonsense noodle dishes at very reasonable prices. Try their *kue tiawgoreng* – possibly the best of its kind in Sumatra.

Maharaja Jl Cik Ditiro 8c. This budget Indian restaurant's menu is small, unimaginative and rather overpriced, but the food is tasty and the staff welcoming.

Sabass Jl Cik Ditiro 42. Cheap and cheerful Indian café selling scrumptious *murtabak* and – rare in Indonesia – spicy *roti canai* (Rp750).

Tip Top Kafé Jl Jend A. Yani 92. One of the oldest restaurants in Sumatra and a tourist attraction in its own right, the mid-priced *Tip Top*'s vast menu contains page after page of mouthwatering Western food. Beef sandwiches, frogs legs and, best of all, a wide selection of ice cream, alongside more traditional Indonesian and Chinese dishes. The seats on the verandah are the perfect place to sit and watch the world go by.

Nightlife and entertainment

For such a big city, Medan's **nightlife** is surprisingly subdued. *Lyn's* at Jl Jend A. Yani 98 is one of the few karaoke-free joints in town. With a dartboard, a piano, a well-stocked bar and a well-stained carpet, it's the closest you'll come to a British pub in Medan, and has become the favourite watering hole for that most British of establishments, the Hash House Harriers, an expat club founded in Malaysia in the nineteenth century which dedicates itself to drinking and raising money for charity. The *Tavern Pub*, part of the *Danau Toba* complex, also aims for a pub atmosphere, and its combination of draught beer and live music (usually local rock bands performing Western covers) is currently a hit with well-heeled locals and expats alike. The *Equator Pub*, upstairs in the Hong Kong Plaza, is pretty soulless, though it does have occasional live music (usually local soft-rock bands).

Disco devotees are restricted to just a few choices. The *Ari Kink Kink Disco*, next to the Standard Chartered Bank in the grounds of the *Hotel Danau Toba*, has an excellent sound system and is by far the trendiest and most popular in town. You need to buy a drink at the door (beers cost Rp18,000), though there is no extra entry charge. The same entrance policy is enforced by the *Haus Musik Nightclub* on Jalan Sutoyo, just 50m east of the bridge, which draws a younger crowd, with a mix of Western dance classics and Asian bubblegum pop; this is also the club of choice for Medan's **gay** community. The third – and sleaziest – option is the cavernous *Horas Theatr*, opposite the water tower at the northern end of Jalan S.M. Raja, which does have a certain seedy glamour.

Medan isn't a hotbed of culture, but there is usually some sort of **dance** or **music display** happening somewhere. The tourist office will be able to advise you on what's going on and where. The small stage at the back of the Pasar Seni on Jalan Palang Merah holds regular performances by traditional dance troupes and bands; look on the board by the entrance on Jalan Listrik for details of forthcoming events. The North Sumatra Cultural Centre (also known as the Taman Budaya), on Jalan Perintis Kemerdekaan near the PT Indosat building, also holds music and drama performances.

Shopping

Medan's main shopping centre lies to the east of Lapangan Merdeka on Jalan Letjen M.T. Haryono, where you'll find dozens of small street stalls selling everything from fake Rolex watches to clockwork drumming monkeys. There are also two gigantic shopping centres: the swish Medan Mall, crammed with flashy boutiques and fast-food shacks, and the more run-of-the-mill Mata Hari Plaza. Jalan Brig Jend A. Yani is the centre of Medan's **souvenir** and **antiques** trade: the Rufino Art Shop at no. 56, Asli Souvenirs at no. 62 and the Indonesian Art Shop at no. 30 are all worth investigating. Pasar Seni, the open-air market on Jalan Palang Merah, also has a large selection of souvenir kiosks, though there's little in the way of antiques and the overall quality is not very good. The Yuki Simpang Raya is a department store opposite the Mesjid Raya.

Listings

Airline offices Bouraq, Jl Brig Jend Katamso 411 ⓣ061/4552333; Cathay, Tiara Building, Jalan Cut Mutiah ⓣ061/4537008; Garuda, Jl S Monginsidi 34a ⓣ061/4556777 (includes city check-in), also at the *Hotel Dharma Deli*, Jl Balai Kota ⓣ061/516400, and the Tiara building, Jalan Cut Mutiah ⓣ061/538527; Mandala, Jl Brig Jend Katamso 37e ⓣ061/4579100; MAS, *Hotel Danau Toba*, Jl Imam Bonjol 17 ⓣ061/4519333; Merpati, Jl Brig Jend Katamso 72–122 ⓣ061/4514102; Silk Air, 6th floor, Bank Umum Servitas Building, Jalan Imam Bonjol ⓣ061/4537744; SMAC, Jl Imam Bonjol 59 ⓣ061/564760; Thai, *Hotel Dharma Deli*, Jalan Balai Kota ⓣ061/510541.

Banks The BCA, at the corner of Jalan Pangeran Diponegoro and Jalan H. Zainul Arifin, offers by far the best rates in town, though it only changes money between 10am and noon.

Consulates Australia, Jl Kartini 32 ⓣ061/455780; UK, Jl Kapt Pattimura 450 ⓣ061/8210 5259; Malaysia, Jl P. Diponegoro 43 ⓣ061/453 1342.

Ferries Pelni is at Jl Sugiono 5 (ⓣ061/4518899), opposite the blue BNI building (Mon–Fri 9am–3pm, Sat 8–10.30am). For ferries to Penang, visit the Perdana agent at Jl B.I. Katamso 35 (ⓣ061/545803, ⓕ549325), or the Bahagia agent, Sukma Tours and Travel, at Jl S.M. Raja 92 (ⓣ061/706500), one block south of the Mesjid Raya.

Hospital Dewi Maya Hospital, Jl Surakarta 2 ⓣ061/4574279.

Internet access Indonet, Jl Brig Jend Katamso 32I, is currently the cheapest in town (Rp4000 per hour), though it's usually very busy and can be slow. The *Novonet Café*, on the third floor of the Hong Kong Plaza (9am–midnight), and the new Infosinet, Jl Brig Jend Katamso 45J, on the corner opposite the palace, are a little quicker. The Warposnet at the GPO (Mon–Sat 8am–11pm, Sun 8am–7pm) charges Rp6000 per hour. The Internet centre at the post office is inefficient and expensive.

Pharmacy Apotik Kimia Farma, Jl Palang Merah 32, is open 24hr.

Post office Jalan Balai Kota, on the northwest corner of Lapangan Merdeka (Mon–Fri 7.30am–8pm, Sat 7.30am–3pm). The poste restante is currently at counter 11, while the parcel office is round the north side of the building.

Swimming The *Danau Toba* allows nonresidents to use their pool for Rp8000 per day, for which you also get a soft drink. The public swimming baths, Renang Kolam, at Jl S.M. Raja 6, charge only Rp2000 per day (6am–6pm).

Telephone offices Overseas calls can be made from the futuristic Indosat office (7am–midnight), on Jalan Jati at the intersection with Jalan Thamrin (Rp500 by becak from the GPO). The *Tip Top Kafé*, *Wisma Yuli* and the *Losmen Irama* all have Home Country Direct telephones.

Travel agents Boraspati Express Tours & Travel, Jl Dazam Raya 77 ⓣ061/4567906, ⓕ061/4567906; Lagundri Tours, Jl Pabrik Tenun 54 ⓣ061/415 3891, ⓕ547508; Trophy Tours, Jl Brig Jend Katamso 33 ⓣ061/4155666, ⓕ4510340.

Work The Grand Education Centre, Jalan Kapten Muslim (ⓣ061/852872), invites tourists and travellers to come and teach English to their pupils in exchange for food and accommodation.

Bukit Lawang

Tucked away on the easternmost fringes of the Bukit Barisan range, 78km north of Medan, the **Orang-Utan Rehabilitation Centre** at **BUKIT LAWANG** has become one of North Sumatra's major tourist attractions. The centre has enjoyed great success since its inception in 1973, and travellers and day-trippers turn up in droves to watch the orang-utans during their twice-daily feeding sessions. Whilst the orang-utans never cease to be entertaining, they aren't the only attraction of Bukit Lawang. The setting for the village, on the eastern banks of the roaring Sungai Bohorok opposite the steep, forest-clad slopes of the Gunung Leuser national park, is idyllic. It also contains some of the most charming and inexpensive losmen in Sumatra, with balconies overlooking the river and macaques on the roof looking for food. In between the feeding times there are a number of other **activities** to choose from, ranging from the life-threatening (floating down the Bohorok in an inner tube; see box on p.361) to the leisurely (sitting in one of the many riverside restaurants writing postcards). Bukit Lawang does have its faults: at weekends it's often insufferably packed with day-trippers from Medan, and during the rainy season some of the low-lying losmen can become flooded. But don't let this put you off – most of the time, Bukit Lawang is an enchanting place.

The Orang-Utan Rehabilitation Centre

The **Bukit Lawang Orang-Utan Rehabilitation Centre** was founded in 1973 by two Swiss women, Monica Borner and Regina Frey, with the aim of returning captive and orphaned orang-utans back into the wild. The wild orang-utan population had been pushed to the verge of extinction by the destruction of their natural habitat, and the apes themselves had become extremely popular as pets, particularly in Singapore, where a baby orang-utan can fetch up to US$40,000. The centre's aim was to reintroduce domesticated orang-utan back into the wild, and transfer those apes whose habitat was under threat from the logging companies to the Gunung Leuser national park.

Upon arrival, new inmates are kept in cages for up to six months at the **quarantine station** behind the centre. Here, those who have spent most or all of their life in captivity are re-taught the basics of being a wild orang-utan, such as the art of tree climbing and nest building. Once they've mastered these techniques, the orang-utans are freed into the forest near the centre to gain experience of living in the wild. They are still offered food twice a day at the centre's feeding platform, though the menu – bananas and milk – is deliberately monotonous to encourage the apes to forage for their own food in the forest. Once they have proved that they can successfully fend for themselves, the orang-utans are taken far off into the park and released to begin a new life.

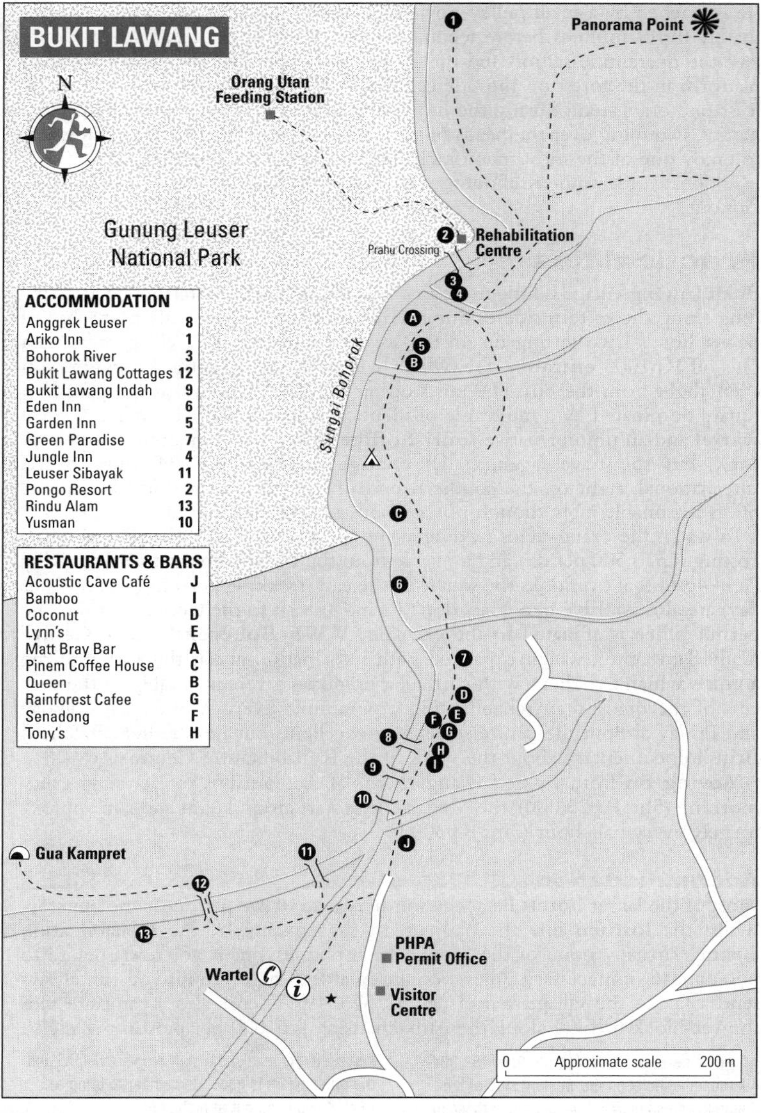

Though the Rehabilitation Centre is normally closed to the public, visitors are allowed to watch the twice-daily (8am & 3pm), hour-long **feeding sessions** that take place on the hill behind the centre. However, you should *never* touch or feed the orang-utans, as this can spread disease and encourage dependency. All visitors must have a **permit** from the PHPA office (see p.358), which should be handed in at the Rehabilitation Centre on arrival. The centre is reached by a small pulley-powered canoe that begins operating approximately thirty minutes before feeding begins. A member of staff leads people past the quarantine station and up the hill to the feeding station – a wooden platform in the forest on the side of the hill. All being well, you should see at least one orang-utan during the hour-long session, and to witness their gymnastics, swooping over the heads of the crowd on their way to the platform, is to enjoy one of the most memorable experiences in Indonesia.

To donate or learn more about the centre, visit the excellent Ⓦwww.orangutans-sos.org.

Practicalities

Bukit Lawang village is little more than a kilometre-long, hotel-lined path running along the eastern side of Sungai Bohorok (though recently a number of newer hotels have sprung up on the western side too). The village charges a one-off Rp1000 **entrance fee**, which will probably be extracted before you even alight from the bus. The bus stops at the southern end of the path in a square dominated by a multitude of identical souvenir stalls, as well as a small **wartel** and an uninformative **tourist office** (Mon–Sat 7am–2pm). There's no bank, but the travel agencies all **change money**; the PT Pura Buana International, right on the southern end of the path just before the square, offers reasonable rates, though not as good as those in Medan.

To watch the orang-utans feeding at the rehab centre you'll need a **permit**, costing Rp20,500 per day and available from the **PHPA Permit Office** (daily 7am–4pm) that overlooks the square to the east. Trekking permits (Rp3500 per day) are also available here; they don't include a visit to the feeding station. The permit office is affiliated to the excellent **WWF Bohorok Visitor Centre** (daily 8am–3pm), which is packed with information about the park and the animals which live there, with particular emphasis given, inevitably, to the success of the orang-utan rehabilitation programme. Every Monday, Wednesday and Friday at 8pm the centre screens an excellent (but now rather scratched) British documentary about the work of the Rehabilitation Centre.

Moving on from Bukit Lawang, there's an 8.30am bus to Berastagi every morning (5hr; Rp25,000); the Medan Buses start around 5am and run approximately every half-hour (3hr; Rp3000).

Accommodation

Most of the larger **hotels** lie at the southern end of the path near the bus stop, whilst the **losmen** line the path up to the crossing by the Rehabilitation Centre. Virtually none of the losmen have phones, but if you're desperate to book ahead (unnecessary, unless you are in a very large group) you can always send a fax to the village wartel (Ⓕ061/575349). There's also a campsite plus shower-block halfway along the path, charging Rp1000 per person per night.

Anggrek Leuser Ⓣ061/414 5559, Ⓕ453 8047. A large, quiet hotel on the western side of the Bohorok with some good-value rooms; those set back from the river are slightly cheaper than the ones on the waterfront. The restaurant, standing on stilts in a fish pond, is recommended. ❷

Ariko Inn Set in a lovely forest clearing a 30min walk north from the bus stop, the *Ariko's* 24 bungalows are clean and pleasant, though the power supply is sometimes unreliable. The restaurant serves hearty meals, the staff are very helpful and the atmosphere is good. Remember to bring a torch if you head out at night. ❶

Bohorok River Ⓣ061/ 457 5227. Well placed on the river, with basic spacious rooms and willing staff. It's a little far from the centre, but all the better value as a result. ❷

Bukit Lawang Cottages North of the Bohorok at the southern end of the village Ⓣ061/456 8908. Each bungalow comes with a shower and fan, and the restaurant is one of the best in Bukit Lawang. The "Jungle bathrooms" – half open to nature – are a nice feature. ❷

Bukit Lawang Indah ⓣ061/4575219. Clean, friendly and informative, this large and dependable guesthouse, with doubles for just Rp7000, is as inexpensive as they come. ❶

Eden Inn ⓣ061/575341. One of the best-value places in Bukit Lawang. The rooms are spacious and clean and have pleasant balconies overlooking the river, plus the staff are friendly and the food is excellent. ❸

Garden Inn ⓣ061/579159. Attractive, friendly losmen with clean rooms, situated on the hill east of the river. ❶–❷

Green Paradise A small bamboo-weave losmen under British management, with clean dorms (Rp6000) and a good balcony café at the back; they also offer lessons in coconut carving. ❶

Jungle Inn About 100m south of the Prahu crossing. A popular losmen, full of carved wooden furniture with some of the most spacious and comfortable rooms in the budget price range; the "honeymoon suite", where the bed has been partitioned off behind curtains, is particularly attractive. The popular restaurant serves some good curries and cakes. ❸

Leuser Sibayak ⓣ & ⓕ061/415 0576. Large, attractive and peaceful, this family-run wisma is very homely and great for kids. The big double rooms with attached bathroom are spotless, while the new luxury rooms by the river have shower and TV. ❶–❷

Pongo Resort ⓣ061/542574. Attractive resort with an unattractive name situated right next to the Rehabilitation Centre. The 21 smart but unexceptional villas are quite expensive by Bukit Lawang's standards, though a permit to watch the feeding sessions is included in the price. ❹

Rindu Alam ⓣ061/545015, ⓕ575370. A vastly overpriced, impersonal hotel to the west of the bus station, popular with tour groups. The gardens are pleasant and the rooms are large and comfortable. ❺

Yusman A large collection of terraced doubles south of the *Bukit Lawang* Indah; clean and simple, with its own restaurant. ❶

Eating and drinking

Most of the losmen have their own **restaurants**. The menus are similar in all of them, but down the years a few have come to specialize in a certain type of food. The *Eden*, for instance, is renowned for its cheap Western food, while the *Bukit Lawang Cottages* is noted for its local fare.

Away from the losmen, there's a proliferation of good traveller-orientated places and many of them screen DVDs in the evening. *Bamboo*, opposite the northernmost bridge, does good pizzas, while *Tony's* a few doors along is popular for pancakes. Continuing north, the mid-priced *Senadong* specializes in fish, while the *Rainforest Café* opposite has a range of Indonesian food supplemented with milkshakes and chips. *Lynn's* has a large Western menu featuring steak and is full of lounging travellers every evening, while *Coconut* next door fills with the same crowd for breakfast. *Pinem Coffee House* is a haven for the caffeine addict and the *Matt Bray Bar* – a Sumatran enclave of Rastafari – has spirits and beer to go along with the thumping reggae. The big *Queen* restaurant serves cheap Western food and, in their own words, "bloody cold beer". Most atmospheric of all, however, is the *Acoustic Cave Café* towards the southern end of town. A walkway leads away from the river and into a cave where the drinks flow and guitars jam every night from 9pm.

Trekking around Bukit Lawang

Bukit Lawang is the most popular base for organizing **treks** into the **Gunung Leuser national park**, with plenty of guides based here, including a number who work part time at the rehabilitation centre. The park around Bukit Lawang is actually a little over-trekked, and in the past most serious walkers preferred to base themselves in Ketambe in southern Aceh, though this is ill advised at present due to violence in the region (see box on p.344). But if you only want a short day-trek, a walk in the forest around Bukit Lawang is fine, and your chance of seeing monkeys, gibbons, macaques and, of course, orang-utans is very high. If you do decide to do a **long trek** from Bukit Lawang, a

Fauna and flora in the Gunung Leuser national park

Tigers are found everywhere in Sumatra and are very numerous in some districts. On the whole they are useful animals, as they keep down the number of boars, which are harmful to cultivated fields. But when the tiger is old and no longer fleet enough to catch wild pigs, deer, and apes, it has to be satisfied with poorly armed human beings. Such a man-eater spreads terror in the neighbourhood and is a hindrance to social intercourse.

Sumatra, Its History and People, Edwin M. Loeb (1935)

The **Sumatran tiger** is no longer the "hindrance to social intercourse" that it once was. There are only about five hundred left in the whole of Sumatra, and about sixty of these live within the Gunung Leuser national park – one of the largest populations left on the island. Your chance of seeing one of these magnificent creatures is extremely slim, and, sadly, they are not the only endangered creature in the park. The **Asian elephant**, **clouded leopard**, **marbled cat** and its cousin the **golden cat**, plus **crocodile** and **sun bear**, live within the confines of the park, and all have dwindled alarmingly in number over the last fifty years. The park also plays host to possibly the most endangered animal in the whole of Indonesia: the **Sumatran rhinoceros**. About forty of these shy creatures are believed to still live in Leuser, mainly near Sungai Mamas in the southwestern corner of the park in an area that is out of bounds to trekkers.

Of all the endangered species in Leuser, the only one that visitors have a reasonable chance of encountering is the **orang-utan**. Thanks largely to the Rehabilitation Centre at Bukit Lawang, over five thousand now live in the park. Other primates that you should see include the white-breasted **Thomas leaf monkey** – easy to spot as it crashes through the forest canopy – **long- and pig-tailed macaques**, the **white-handed gibbon** and the cuddly **black siamang**, which resembles an elongated teddy bear as it hangs from the uppermost branches of the tallest trees.

Back on the ground, Leuser also has four species of **deer** (the muntjac, barking deer and two types of mouse deer), the **ajak** (a wild dog) and, in the upper reaches of the park, a fairly large **mountain goat** population. Flying squirrels, flying foxes, bats, tortoises, turtles, and a number of species of snake are also present in the park, including the **king cobra** and the magnificent **python** – the biggest snake in Indonesia, at over 10m long.

Of Leuser's 325 different bird species, the **hornbills** are probably the most recognizable. There are eight different types in Leuser, including the rhinoceros and helmeted hornbill. Sightings of both types are common. Other species of birds include the **kingfisher**, **babbler**, **argus pheasant** (a dull-brown cousin of the peacock) and the **common drongo**.

There are estimated to be over 8500 plant species in Leuser, and new ones are still being discovered. **Orchids** are common in the park, particularly at the higher altitudes, and they can provide some much-needed colour amongst the muted greens and browns of the forest floor. Indeed, the higher you climb, the more colourful Leuser becomes, with meadows of primrose and wild strawberries dominating the hillsides. The most spectacular flower of all, however, is the lowland **rafflesia**. There are two different types in the park, the *Rafflesia acehensis* and the *Rafflesia zippelni*, and, although neither are as sizeable as the *Rafflesia arnoldi*, the flower can still be as big as a large cabbage. Late October, when the plant is in bloom, is the time to see them.

five- to seven-day walk to Ketambe – assuming Ketambe is safe – passes through some excellent tracts of primary forest, and a three-day hike to Berastagi is also possible.

Tubing

Despite the risks involved, at some stage during your stay in Bukit Lawang you might be tempted to have a go at **tubing** – the art of sitting in the inflated inner tube of a tyre as it hurtles downstream, battered by the wild currents of the Bohorok. The tubes can be rented from almost anywhere for about Rp2000 per day, or your losmen may supply them for free. There is a bridge 12km downstream of the village, where you can get out, dry off and catch a bus back. If you're not a strong swimmer, consider tubing on a Sunday, when lifeguards are dotted along the more dangerous stretches of the river around Bukit Lawang, to cope with the influx of day-trippers from Medan.

First, you must to have a **permit** (see p.358) for every day you plan to spend in the park. You should also be careful when choosing your **guide**. The PHPA office at Bukit Lawang recommends three local guides: Pak Nasib, Pak Mahadi and Pak Arifin. Their fees are higher than average, at approximately US$15 including lunch and permit for a one-day trek, but you can be certain that they know the forest well. Most of the other guides charge about Rp20,000 per day. Whoever you decide to hire, make it plain you are firmly against feeding or touching the apes – both of which puts them under threat. Guides have been known to set up their own feeding stations to ensure you get a sighting each time you trek. It's tempting, but if you participate in this you'll be part of the extinction problem rather than the solution. **Tents** are usually provided by the guides, but check this before setting off. There is no one best time of the year to go trekking, although it's probably best to avoid the rainy seasons (April, May & Oct–Dec), when some rivers are impassable and fewer animals come to the rivers and watering holes to drink. Late July and August are good months, as the fruit is ripe and you'll see lots of primates.

There are a couple of **minor walks** around Bukit Lawang that don't actually cross into the park, so permits and guides are unnecessary. The short, twenty-minute (one-way) walk to the **Gua Kampret** (Black Cave) is the simplest. It begins behind the *Bukit Lawang Cottages* and heads west through the rubber plantations and, though it's easy, you'll still need good walking shoes and a torch if you're going to scramble over the rocks and explore the single-chamber cave. Officially, the cave has an Rp1000 entrance fee, though there's often nobody around to collect it.

By contrast, the path to **Panorama Point** in the hills to the northeast of Bukit Lawang is difficult to follow. Most people take the path that begins behind the now defunct *Back to Nature Guesthouse*, though this heads off through secondary forest and it's very easy to lose your way. A slightly easier route to follow – though much longer – is the path behind the Poliklinik near the visitor centre. Passing through cocoa and rubber plantations, with only the chatter of monkeys and birds to keep you company, it will take you around ninety minutes to reach Panorama Point.

The Karo Highlands

Covering an area of almost five thousand square kilometres, from the northern tip of Danau Toba to the border of Aceh, the **Karo Highlands** comprise an extremely fertile volcanic plateau at the heart of the Bukit Barisan mountains. The plateau is home to over two hundred small farming villages and two main towns: the regional capital, Kabanjahe, and the popular market town and tourist resort of **Berastagi**.

The Batak

Despite two hundred years of fairly intensive study by ethnologists, anthropologists and linguists, the **Batak** people of the North Sumatran highlands remain something of a mystery. Nobody is sure exactly when they arrived (it was probably three to four thousand years ago), where they came from (north Thailand, Burma and Borneo all being possibilities), or why they chose to settle in the remote Sumatran hinterland rather than on the fertile plains of the east coast where they presumably first landed.

Since European missionaries first encountered them in the latter years of the eighteenth century, the Batak have never ceased to fascinate Western observers. Part of their appeal lies in their uniqueness: with a homeland that was almost inaccessible until the twentieth century, and a reputation for belligerence and cannibalism that served to deter would-be explorers from venturing too far into their territory, the Batak lived and evolved in almost total isolation. Batak hostility towards outsiders also extended to their neighbours. Early Batak villages, though traditionally very small, were completely self-contained; communication between one settlement and its neighbour was virtually nonexistent, with no paths or roads running between them, and inter-village feuding was commonplace. Inevitably, this eventually led to more permanent divisions, and today the Batak are divided into six distinct ethno-linguistic groups: the **Pakpak**, whose homeland lies to the northwest of Danau Toba; the **Karo** of Berastagi and Kabanjahe; the **Simalungun** who live in the region around Pematangsiantar; the **Toba** Batak of Danau Toba; and the southern **Mandailing** and **Angkola** groups. Each of these groups has its own language, rituals, architectural style, mode of dress and religious beliefs.

Some history

Apart from a brief mention by the Greek historian Herodotus, Marco Polo's claim that the Batak ate their parents when they were too old to work in the fields, and an account by the fifteenth-century Venetian merchant, Nicolo di Conto, who talked of a "Batech" tribe that practised cannibalism regularly (and used the skulls as a form of currency), there is almost no pre-eighteenth-century record of the existence of the Batak. The first detailed account was in 1772, by a English botanist, **Charles Miller**. According to Miller, these highland people were skilled farmers who lived in heavily fortified villages, worshipped the spirits of their ancestors, and spent most of their spare time waging war with their neighbours.

Following from Miller's reports, in 1783 the British explorer **William Marsden** set off for the Batak lands to carry out the first detailed study of its people. This work eventually resulted in Marsden's seminal book, *The History of Sumatra*. He was fascinated by the dichotomous nature of the Batak: though they practised cannibalism, their culture, with its own distinctive languages and a unique system of writing, was one of the most advanced on the island. Despite the remoteness of the Batak lands, Marsden noticed traces of a southern Indian influence in the various calendars and languages, and he cited over 150 Toba Batak words which had their origins in Sanskrit.

By the mid-nineteenth century, outside influences – particularly religious ones – had begun to make significant incursions into the Batak way of life. The two southernmost Batak groups, the Angkola and Mandailing people, had both converted to Islam following their defeat in the Paderi Wars of 1829–31 (see p.1039). Following the "discovery" of Danau Toba by the eccentric Dutch linguist **H.N. Van der Tuuk** in 1853, the Dutch campaign to convert the Batak people to Protestantism began in earnest. When the **Dutch army** arrived in 1907, the Batak, riven by petty internal disputes, were unable to muster a united force and were quickly subjugated. In the same year the last Batak king, Sisingamangaraja, died in battle, and the highlands of North Sumatra were added to the growing list of territories under Dutch control. In the post-colonial order, the Batak merged into the Indonesian republic, retaining their distinct culture. Benefiting from the schooling they received from Dutch Protestant missionaries, they now fill a disproportionate number of positions as teachers, doctors and other skilled trades.

Batak animist religion

As with most of Indonesia's religions, the traditional beliefs of the various Batak groups have a veneer of Islam or Christianity. However, various **animist religions** are still widely practised by the Batak, particularly in the Karo and Pakpak homelands. Every Batak religion maintains that there is one **supreme god** who created the earth, although the exact method he used (in Batak mythology the supreme god is always male) varies from one Batak group to the next. This deity, whilst all-powerful, is also a remote figure who chooses not to meddle in petty human affairs, preferring instead to spend his time at home with his wife (which, according to the Toba Batak, is a giant blue chicken).

When they require spiritual assistance, the Batak contact their late ancestors; to help them in this they hire the village **shaman**, known as the *guru* in Batak (or *dukun* in Toba), whose job it is to communicate with the deceased. As the Batak traditionally ascribe the onset of sickness to a sign that the soul (*tondi*) has temporarily left the body, so the guru also acts as the local doctor, healing the body by calling back the soul. The village guru is a vital part of village life even today, ranking second only to the village head in the local hierarchy.

Contacting the spirit world, however, is no easy matter. For starters, the *dukun* is all but impotent without his or her (*dukun* are just as likely to be female as male) trusty staff, known as the *tunggal* in Toba Batak. This staff – exquisitely carved from dark wood – was useless unless it had first taken possession of a **magic spirit** and, as with most Batak ceremonies, the method of obtaining this spirit was fairly gruesome. The first step was to catch a child from a nearby hostile village, who would then have molten lead poured down his or her throat. Cutting the body open, the guru would take the deceased child's entrails and, having added a few secret ingredients, mash them into a magic pulp which would then be poured into a hollow in the centre of the staff.

Islam and Christianity

The first major change to the religious make-up of the Batak occurred in the early nineteenth century with the **Paderi movement**. Formed in the Minangkabau Highlands and led by **Imam Bonjol** (who lives in street names all over the country today), the Paderi were a fundamental Islamic force whose "convert or die" approach to proselytizing met with remarkable success in the southern Batak lands, particularly in the Tapanuli region inhabited by the Angkola and Mandailing Batak. The Dutch, distracted by the Diponegoro-led uprising in Java (see p.1039), suffered some heavy defeats at the hands of the Paderi before winning a decisive victory at Daludalu in 1838.

Though flanked to the north (by the Acehnese) and south by Muslims, the four remaining Batak groups – the Toba, Pakpak, Karo and Simalungun tribes – resisted all attempts to convert them to Islam. More surprisingly, where Islam failed, Dutch missionaries succeeded, and soon the majority of the Toba, Pakpak and Simalungun Batak **converted to Protestantism**. The Karo continued to resist, however, and by 1940 there were only five thousand Karo Christians. They were eventually persuaded to convert in 1965 following the suppression of the communist coup when, in a state of McCarthyite paranoia, the Sukarno government considered any member of a minority faith – including animists and atheists – to be communists.

Although the nineteenth-century Dutch missionaries initially met with a lot of

continued overleaf.....

continued from previous page

resentment – due in part to their policies of banning un-Christian festivals, and prohibiting the use of Batak musical instruments – they did expose the Batak to Western **education**. Dutch missionary schools were founded in the Batak lands during the early 1800s, particularly around Danau Toba, and as a result the Toba Batak people are amongst the most educated, powerful and richest minorities in the country today, with senior figures in government, commerce and the military. The Toba Church has also grown to become the largest in Indonesia, with over three million members.

Cannibalism and the Batak

It is unknown what significance, if any, the Batak attached to the eating of human flesh. For five of the six groups, however (the Karo are the exception), **cannibalism** was an established – if infrequent – pastime. Marco Polo, during his time on the island in 1492, was one of the first Europeans to hear about cannibalism in Sumatra. His tales were embellished by a number of Portuguese explorers who followed in his wake, though as neither they nor Marco Polo ever set foot in Batak territory their stories were always secondhand and usually exaggerated.

The first European to give an eyewitness account of cannibalism was the nineteenth-century German geographer Franz Junghun, who reported just three instances during his eighteen-month stay with the Toba Batak in 1840–41. Whilst this would indicate the Batak practised cannibalism far less frequently than the early Europeans imagined, Junghun's account of one such feast shows that the rumoured savagery of such events was no invention:

> **The captive is bound to a stake in an upright position . . . the chief draws his knife, and explains that the victim is an utter scoundrel and not a human being at all. The Raja [chief] then cuts off the first piece, being either a slice of the forearm or the cheek, if this be fat enough. He holds up the flesh and drinks with gusto the blood streaming from it. . . Now all the men fall upon the bloody sacrifice . . . some eat the meat raw . . . the cries of the victim do not spoil their appetites. It is usually eight or ten minutes before the wounded man becomes unconscious, and a quarter of an hour before he dies.**

The nineteenth-century Batak made no secret of their love of human flesh; not only was this an effective deterrent against would-be invaders, but also helped them to gain employment as mercenary soldiers with the coastal Sumatrans. As in other parts of Indonesia, the practice died out early in the twentieth century.

Berastagi

Lying 1330m above sea level, 70km southwest of Medan and 25km due north of the shores of Toba, **BERASTAGI** is a cold and compact little hill station in the centre of the Karo Highlands. Founded by the Dutch in the early 1920s as a retreat from the sweltering heat of Medan, it has been popular with tourists ever since. Though there's little to do in Berastagi apart from savouring the three different **markets** or challenging the locals to a game of chess, the town provides a perfect base for **trekking** and exploring the surrounding highlands. Berastagi is encircled by neatly ploughed fields and tiny, thatched Karo villages, a gorgeous bucolic landscape bookended by two huge but climbable active volcanoes, Gunung Sibayak and Gunung Sinabung (see p.371). Considering the town's plentiful supply of cheap restaurants and hotels, it's easy to see why Berastagi has blossomed into North Sumatra's favourite hill station.

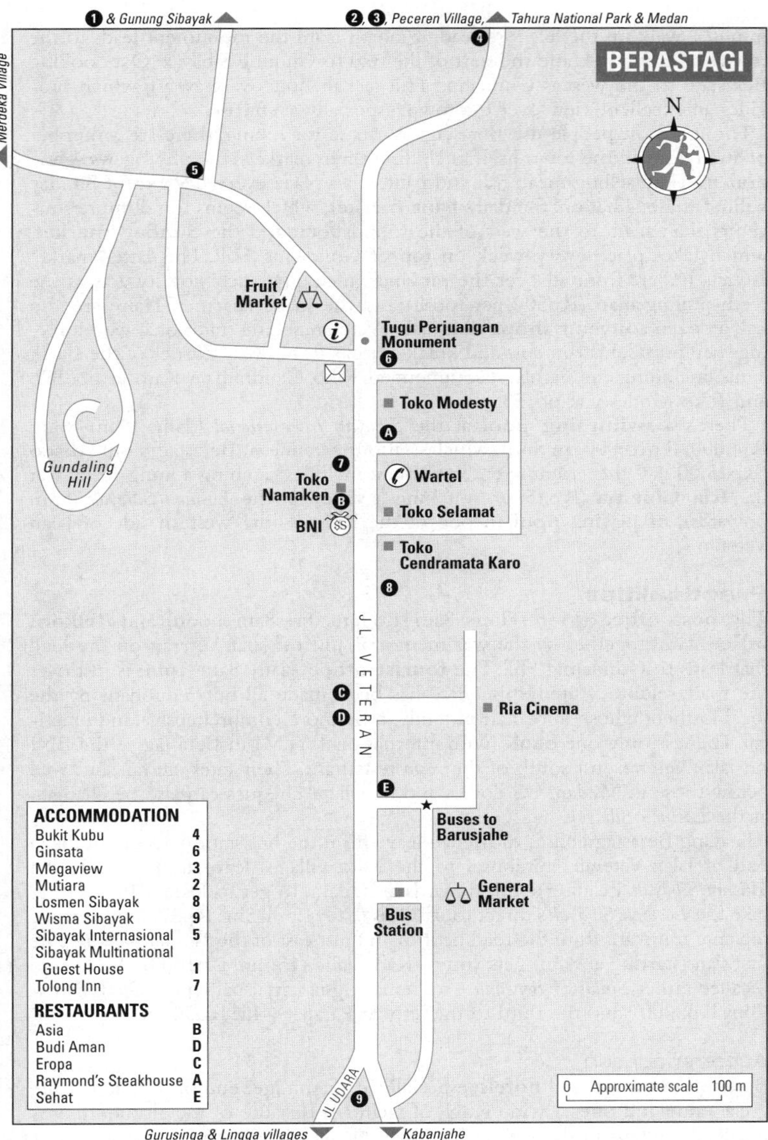

The Town

Berastagi – the town, incidentally, with perhaps the greatest number of alternative spellings in the entire archipelago, with Brastagi and Berestagi being the two most common variants – is little more than an overgrown, one-street village. That street is Jalan Veteran, at the northern end of which stands the **Tugu Perjuangan**, a memorial to those who fell in 1945 against the Dutch. Five minutes' walk up the left fork leading north from the monument leads to the town's luxury hotels and the start of the trail to Gunung Sibayak. Overlooking Berastagi to the west is Gundaling Hill (a half-hour walk away), which provides an excellent view over the town, especially at sunrise.

Though most people use Berastagi as a base for hiking, there are a number of attractions in the town itself, including three markets: the photogenic **general market**, selling meat, fish and fruit, takes place every day except Sunday behind the bus station; the daily **fruit market**, which seems to sell more souvenirs than fruit, to the west of the roundabout; and the **Sunday market**, which takes place every week on top of Gundaling Hill. This latter market attracts traders from all over the province, including such novelty acts as the teeth-pulling man (Rp500 per tooth) and the snake charmer. There are also half a dozen **souvenir shops** along Jalan Veteran, selling traditional woodcarvings, sculptures, instruments and knick-knacks from every corner of the Batak lands, including the highly recommended Toko Cendramata Karo at no. 89b and Toko Modesty at no. 33.

There's a **swimming pool** at the *Sibayak Internasional* (daily 10am–8pm; Rp6000, Rp10,000 on Sun), which is also the venue of Berastagi's only **disco** (Rp25,000). Other evening entertainment includes catching a kung-fu flick at the **Ria Cinema** (Rp2500), watching a **video** at the *Losmen Sibayak* (8pm onwards), or playing **pool** in one of the halls on the western side of Jalan Veteran.

Practicalities

The **post office** (Mon–Thurs 8am–1.30pm, Fri 8am–noon) and **Telkom office** stand together by the war memorial, just off Jalan Veteran on the road that leads to Gundaling Hill. The **tourist office** (daily 8am–7pm) is just over the road; seldom visited, this office has been made all but redundant by the local losmen, whose information tends to be more comprehensive and practical. There is only one **bank** (with international ATM) in Berastagi – the BNI on Jalan Veteran just south of the *Asia* restaurant. Their rates are fair, but well below those in Medan. US dollars and travellers' cheques can also be changed at the *Losmen Sibayak*.

Leaving Berastagi, buses to Medan leave from the bus station at the southern end of Jalan Veteran, minibuses to the Karo villages leave from outside the *Wisma Sibayak*, heading south down Jalan Udara. To get to Danau Toba, either take the *Losmen Sibayak*'s direct tourist bus (daily 2pm; 5hr; Rp37,000) or three separate minivans from the road next to and just east of the *Wisma Sibayak*. The first van (starting at 8am) gets you to Kabanjahe (15min; Rp1000); the second – called either *Simas* or *Sepedan* – to Pematangsiantar, usually just called Siantar (3hr; Rp5000); and the third to the jetty at Parapat (1hr; Rp3000).

Accommodation

Berastagi's **losmen** and **hotels**, especially at the budget end of the market, are great value and offer a wide range of facilities. Because of the altitude there's no need for fans in the rooms, but thick blankets are essential, and most losmen offer hot showers at Rp1000 a time.

Bukit Kubu Jl Sempurna 2 ☎0628/939 3263. The best-looking hotel in Berastagi, built by the Dutch in the 1930s and set in the middle of its own nine-hole golf course. The old part of the hotel, with its polished-wood floors and open fireplaces, is a delight. Book ahead, as it fills up quickly with tour groups from Holland. ❸

Ginsata Jl Veteran 27 ☎0628/91441. A quiet, unfussy hotel overlooking the main roundabout that's good if you want privacy. The rooms are basic and inexpensive with shared hot showers (Rp2000 a time), and there's even cheaper accommodation

△ Entrance to mosque, Medan

available in the cottage behind the hotel. ❷

Megaview Jalan Raya Medan ⓣ0628/91650, ⓕ91652. A huge, luxurious hotel on the road to Medan with a decent-sized swimming pool, bar and karaoke lounge. Rooms have IDD telephones, hot water, satellite TV and a balcony. ❺

Mutiara Jl Peceren 168 ⓣ0628/91555, ⓕ91383. Another enormous luxury hotel to the north of Berastagi with a Chinese restaurant, cocktail lounge and a swimming pool that has its own floating bar. A buffet breakfast is included in the rates. ❺

Losmen Sibayak Jl Veteran 119 ⓣ0628/91122. The younger sister of the *Wisma Sibayak*, under the same management but with a slightly higher standard of rooms and added features such as a book exchange, Pelni ticket office, all sorts of tours and a pizza restaurant that shows videos every evening. One of the best choices in Berastagi. ❷

Wisma Sibayak Jl Udara 1 ⓣ0628/91104. One of Sumatra's best and longest-established hostels: the walls are covered with good information (some a little dated), the travellers' comments books are very useful, and the beds are clean and very cheap. ❶–❷

Sibayak Internasional Jalan Merdeka ⓣ0628/91301, ⓕ91307, ⓔsibayak@indosat.net.id. The oldest of Berastagi's luxury hotels, with 73 rooms and 30 cottages. Facilities include squash and tennis courts, a heated swimming pool, billiards and even a small cinema. ❼

Sibayak Multinational Guest House Jl Pendidikan 93 ⓣ0628/91031. Yet another branch of the Sibayak chain, set in its own gardens 1km north of town on the way to Sibayak. Even the cheapest rooms come with their own terrace and a hot shower; rooms in the old 1930s Dutch section of the house are larger but cost more. ❷–❸

Tolong Inn Jl Veteran 9 ⓣ0628/19966. A friendly but overpriced budget option with a restaurant downstairs. ❷

Eating

For such a small town, Berastagi has a surprisingly wide range of **restaurants**. *Raymond's Steakhouse*, Jl Veteran 49, is one of the best in town: prices compare with the losmen restaurants, yet it provides better service, music and food – New Zealand lamb, T-bone and rump steaks (Rp8000–12,000) – and there's also veggie fare. *Budi Aman* serves Indonesian food including fish curries, but closes after lunch. The *Ginsata Café*, below the hotel of the same name, serves up bitter tamarillo juice, which complements their fiery curries pretty well. *Asia*, Jl Veteran 10, is a very busy mid-range Chinese restaurant with an extensive menu, as is the *Eropa* on the same street at no. 48g, which does an excellent plate of steaming *kue tiaw* for Rp6000, also has chips and is a good place for breakfast. Another good option, the *Sehat* at no. 315, is a no-nonsense, family café selling cheap Indonesian and Chinese food. The restaurants of the *Wisma* and *Losmen Sibayaks* are also recommended, especially the *Wisma*, which offers pizzas – and also "crunchy dog in blood sauce".

The Karo villages

During the Dutch invasion of 1904, most of the larger **villages** and towns in the Karo Highlands were razed to the ground by the Karonese themselves to prevent the Dutch from appropriating them. If you're interested in seeing traditional Karo architecture (see p.370), it's worth making a visit to the few small outlying villages that survived the Dutch period. The most accessible of these traditional villages is **PECEREN** (Rp500 entrance fee), just 2km northeast of Berastagi. Coming from the town, take the road to Medan and turn down the lane on your right after the *Rose Garden* hotel. There are six traditional houses here, but although some are in good condition – the colourful gables on the first house in the village look as if they were made yesterday – the village itself is probably the least picturesque in the region, with modern housing encroaching on every side.

There are three more villages to the south of Berastagi that, when combined, make a pleasant day-trek from town: it takes about three hours to cover all three. The villages tend to be extremely muddy in places, so don't wear sandals,

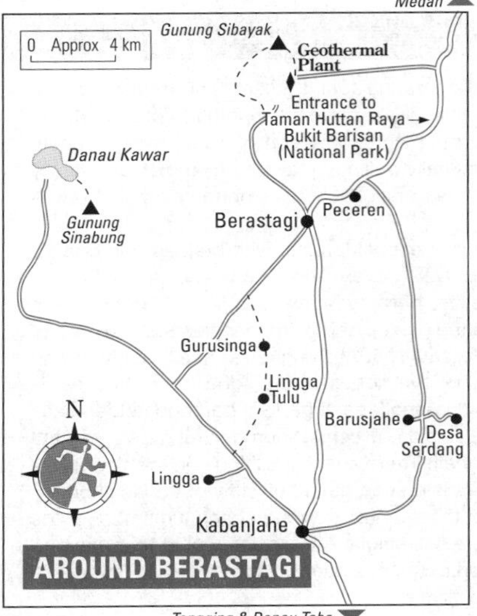

and many of the villagers, especially the women, are very shy, so always ask before pointing your camera at them.

The first of the three villages, **GURUSINGA**, lies about an hour's walk south of Berastagi. From the southern end of Jalan Veteran, take the road running southwest alongside the *Wisma Sibayak*. After about twenty minutes you'll come to a path signposted "Jl ke Koppas", which heads off through neatly sown cabbage and potato fields, many of which are dotted with bathroom-tiled family graves. Gurusinga, home to a number of huge traditional thatched longhouses sandwiched between more modern concrete homes, stands at the far end of these fields. The path continues along the western edge of the Gurusinga to the village of **LINGGA JULU** (which has a few unspectacular longhouses by the pathway), before passing through a bamboo forest. At the end of the path, turn left and head down the well-signposted road to **LINGGA**, the main tourist village in the Karo.

The Karo

According to local legend, the Karo people were the first of the Batak groups to settle in the highlands of North Sumatra – indeed, the name "Karo" means "first arrivals". As with all Batak groups, the strongly patrilineal Karo have their own language, customs and rituals, most of which have survived, at least in a modified form, to this day. These include the **reburial ceremony** held every few years, where deceased relatives are exhumed and their bones washed with a mixture of water and orange juice, and convoluted **wedding** and **funeral ceremonies**, both of which can go on for days.

When the Dutch arrived at the beginning of this century they assumed, mistakenly, that the Karo were cannibals. The now-defunct Karonese tradition of filing teeth, combined with a fondness for chewing betel nut that stained their mouths a deep red, gave the Karo a truly fearsome and bloodthirsty appearance. In fact, the Karo, alone amongst the Batak tribes, abhorred cannibalism, though their traditional **animist religion** was as rich and complex as any of the other Batak faiths. Today the Karo are a religiously pluralist society, over seventy percent of the people being Christian, fifteen percent Muslim and the rest adhering to the traditional Karo religion.

Asserting an even stronger influence than their religious beliefs, however, are their **family ties**. The Karonese society is ordered along strong patrilineal lines, with each member of society belonging to one of the five Karonese clans. Marriage within a clan is forbidden, and every member of Karonese society is bound by obligations to their clan, which are seen as more important than any religious duties. Failure to obey these ties, so the Karo believe, can result in severe misfortune, from drought to disease and even death.

Karo architecture

There are only a few examples of the Karo *rumah adat* (traditional houses) left on the plateau today. Each house takes an entire village up to six months to build and, following the destruction wreaked during the Dutch invasion of 1904, most villagers turned their back on this sort of communal dwelling in favour of simpler, one-family concrete units. As a result, not one of the traditional houses on the plateau today is less than fifty years old.

Rumah adat were made of wood from the local forests, with braided bamboo for the gables and palm for the roofs; nails were never used. The houses are extremely tall and stand on thick, metre-high stilts, but nevertheless look fairly dumpy. The most impressive part of the exterior is the gables, the palm triangles at either end of the house, usually woven into intricate patterns. At the gables' apex, at either end of the roof ridge (which, unlike the concave ridges of the Toba Batak houses, is straight), are a set of buffalo horns, and beneath each gable a bamboo ladder leads up to a verandah and into the house. Inside, a central corridor runs between the entrances, dividing the ground floor in half. There are no partitions on this floor, save for the sleeping quarters, and family life is carried out in full view of the neighbours. Eight to ten families live inside each of these houses, though once a member of the family turned 17 – assuming they were still single – he or she would then have to sleep outside, either in a room attached to the rice barn or in the local *los*, the open-sided meeting hall in the centre of the village.

Three hundred metres before Lingga village you'll come to the one-room **Karo Lingga Museum** (7am–5pm; donation), home to a few wooden cooking utensils, the odd totem and other obsolete Karonese implements. There are English labels, which can be difficult to decipher, although an attendant is usually on hand to provide further explanations. Lingga itself has some of the best *rumah adat* in the area, many of which are over 150 years old. Unfortunately, the village has also become something of a tourist trap: you have to pay Rp500 just to enter and, if you want a guide – necessary if you want to go inside one of the houses – it's another Rp2500. None of this money seems to have gone on restoring the buildings, some of which are in very bad condition. Once you've finished wandering around the village catch a minibus to Kabanjahe (last bus 5pm; Rp1000), from where you can catch a bemo back to Berastagi (last bus 7pm; Rp1000). You shouldn't wait longer than twenty minutes for either bus, and the journeys are less than ten minutes long each.

There are another couple of villages to the southeast of Berastagi within a couple of kilometres of each other – **Barusjahe** and **Desa Serdang**. Very few tourists make it here, so there's not the mercenary atmosphere evident at Lingga – although, as a consequence, there's even less incentive to restore the houses, most of which date from the 1930s and are in a terrible state. Buses to Barus Jahe leave from the north side of Berastagi's general market; from Barus Jahe it's a stiff thirty-minute walk to Desa Serdang.

Volcanoes around Berastagi

There are two active **volcanoes** more than 2000m high in the immediate vicinity around Berastagi. **Sibayak** (2094m), to the north of town, is possibly the most accessible volcano in the whole of Indonesia, and takes just four hours to climb and three hours to descend, while the hike up **Sinabung** (2452m), to the southwest of town, is longer and tougher, and involves an hour by car to the start of the trail. The lists of missing trekkers plastered all around

Berastagi prove that these climbs are not as straightforward as they may at first seem. For both volcanoes, set off early in the morning. It's a good idea to take food and water, particularly bananas and chocolate for energy, and warm clothing. The tourist office urges climbers always to take a guide, which you can hire from them or from your losmen, though for Sibayak a guide is really unnecessary providing you're climbing with someone. The *Losmen Sibayak* offers various guided treks to both peaks.

Gunung Sibayak and the Taman Hutan Raya Bukit Barisan

Before attempting **Sibayak**, pick up one of the *Wisma Sibayak*'s free maps, and read their information books too. To get to the volcano from town, take the left fork after Tugu Perjuangan (but keep the fruit market on your left) and continue under the arch to the *Sibayak International*. Turn right just before the hotel itself and carry on beyond the *Sibayak Multinational Guest House* until you reach a house with a large gate; this is where you pay the hiking fee of Rp1000 and register your name. From here, take the path on the far left (not through the gate) and carry on up. The path is easy to follow – other than a fork to the right downhill which you must not take – until you reach three large stones in the road. Here you climb a few rough, muddy steps onto an embankment on the left, and the path continues up to the crater, where steam roars out of the yellow, sulphurous fissures near the summit. Carry on anticlockwise round the crater until the stone hut in the crater stands between you and the lake. From this point, scramble up and over the top of the crater and with any luck you should see the first few broken steps of the path down. If you walk too far, you'll come to a TV antenna – not a bad thing, really, as you can see the downwards path from its base.

The steps are in a terrible condition and eventually peter out altogether, and the path continuing through the forest to the Sibayak Geothermal plant at the bottom is easy to miss. If there are less than three hours' daylight left and you're uncertain of the way down, walk back down the way you came up. Behind the plant are some **hot springs** (Rp1500), where you can soak your tired calf muscles (take off any silver jewellery before entering the pool, or the sulphurous water will turn it black). From the spring you can catch a bemo back to Berastagi (Rp1500), passing on the way the **Taman Hutan Raya Bukit Barisan** (Rp1000), a small arboretum that keeps a few wild animals in filthy and cramped conditions.

Gunung Sinabung

While the less active **Gunung Sinabung** is only 150m higher than Sibayak, the ascent is a lot harder and takes longer – about six hours to get up and four to come down. A guide is recommended for this trek, as the trail is difficult to follow; once again, the *Wisma Sibayak* have a good photocopied map of the climb.

You'll need to start by taking a taxi to tiny Danau Kawar (1hr, Rp20,000 per car) where the path begins by the side of a restaurant to the north of the lake, and continues through cabbage fields for approximately an hour, before entering thick jungle. The walk becomes relentlessly tough soon after; having left the jungle, you have to scramble up steep and treacherous rocky gullies. It takes around a couple of hours to reach the edge of a cliff looking down into Sinabung's two craters. Take care when walking around up here, as the paths are crumbling and it's a long way down.

Danau Toba

Lying right in the middle of the province, jewel-like **Danau Toba** is Southeast Asia's largest freshwater lake. It was formed about eighty thousand years ago by a colossal volcanic eruption: the caldera which was created eventually buckled under the pressure and collapsed in on itself, the high-sided basin that remained filling with water to form the lake.

A second, smaller volcanic eruption 50,000 years after the first created an island the size of Singapore in the middle of the lake. This island, **Samosir**, is the cultural and spiritual heartland of the **Toba Batak** and the favoured destination for foreign travellers. Ferries leave regularly from **Parapat** – the largest and most convenient gateway for Samosir – and other lakeside towns to the tiny east-coast peninsula of **Tuk Tuk** and neighbouring **Ambarita**, the most popular resorts on Samosir. From these resorts you can go trekking in the deforested hills in the centre of Samosir, or cycle around the coastline, calling in at the tiny **Batak villages** with their flamboyant tombs, distinctive concave-roofed houses and pretty wooden churches on the way.

If you're not into hiking or biking, however, there's very little to do on the island except relax. Luckily, the **resorts**, with their bookshops, bars and magic mushroom omelettes (illegal but ubiquitous), are well equipped to help you do

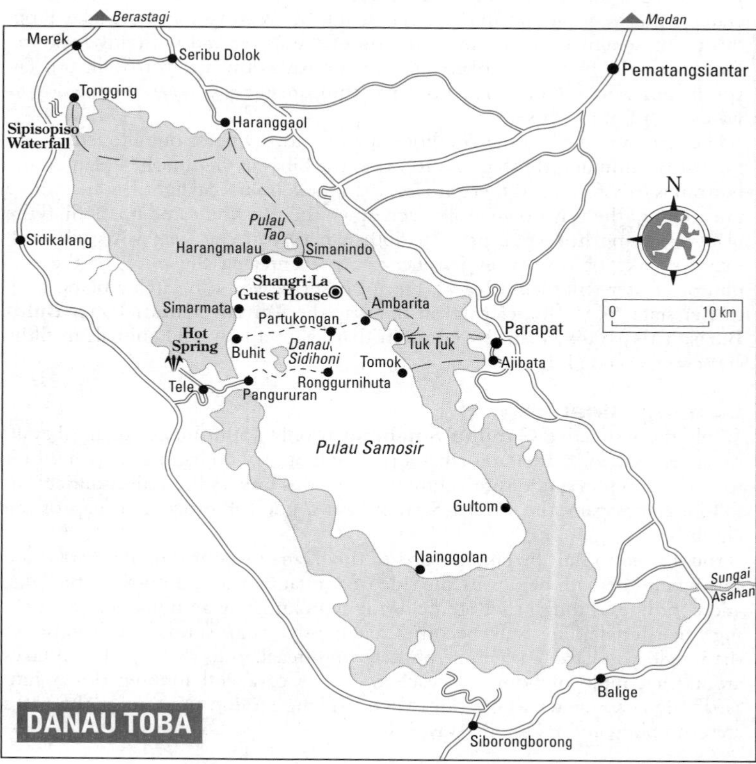

just this, and Danau Toba is the perfect spot to chill out after the rigours of travel in Sumatra.

Getting there

There are five main gateways to Samosir – details of ferry schedules are given on p.390. Most tourists catch a ferry (ask to be dropped at your specific guesthouse from the Tigaraja Harbour in the resort of **Parapat** (see p.374); it's certainly the most convenient jumping-off point, with ferries every hour during the day to Tuk Tuk and Ambarita. If you have your own transport, **Ajibata**, the next cove south of Parapat, operates five car ferries per day to Tomok, the main town on Samosir's east coast.

Though the other two towns with ferry connections to Samosir are more charming than Parapat, frequent bus changes are necessary to get to either of them, and the ferries are far less frequent: the market town of **Haranggaol**, 40km north of Parapat, has a weekly ferry to Samosir departing on Monday mornings, which calls in at Simanindo on its way to Ambarita; there is also a ferry from **TONGGING** (Mon 7.30am), which connects with the service from Haranggaol to Simanindo and Ambarita. The easiest way to get to Tongging from Berastagi is to take *Losmen Sibayak*'s tourist bus, which leaves at 2pm (5hr; Rp37,000) and goes via Kabanjahe. To get to Haranggaol from Berastagi, take the bus to Kabanjahe, and then another towards Pematangsiantir, getting off near Haranggaol. Tongging has a picturesque location on Toba's northern shore near the spectacular 120-metre **Sipisopiso** ("like a knife") **Waterfall**, plunging from the side of the Toba basin to a small stream near the lake. Tongging's *Wisma Sibayak Guesthouse* (Rp15,000–Rp40,000) is a well-run place with some smart rooms – it's best to check it's open before you arrive by contacting the *Losmen Sibayak* in Berastagi (ⓣ0628/91122 or 91104), which is run by the same family.

Finally, there is a way of getting to Samosir overland: buses from the Pakpak Batak town of Sidikalang travel to the east coast of Samosir via the **bridge** connecting the western shores of the island with the mainland. Before tourism in Aceh dried up, this was a popular gateway to Samosir for travellers coming from the west coast of Aceh.

Moving on from Danau Toba

Most travel agents on Tuk Tuk can sell through tickets to your next destination, with the ferry crossing to Parapat included in the price. Ferries leave every hour from Ambarita (6.45am–4.45pm; Rp800) and Tuk Tuk (7.45am–2pm; Rp1000) to Parapat, calling at all the ferry ports on the peninsula before they do so. If your bus leaves early in the morning (for example, the popular 6am bus to Bukittinggi), you may have to spend a night in Parapat. There's also the occasional ferry to Tongging (from Ambarita and Tuk Tuk) and Haranggaol (from Ambarita); details are given on p.390. The trip to **Berastagi** (see p.364) is a complex one, involving two bus changes and a total journey time of four to six hours. Firstly, you'll have to catch a bus to Pematangsiantar from Parapat (1hr; Rp1000), and from there a bus to Kabanjahe (3hr; Rp1700) and then a bemo to Berastagi (15min; Rp300). An alternative is to catch the daily tourist bus (Rp15,000), a four-hour ride that takes in the Sipisopiso Waterfall and the small Pematangpurba King's Palace on the way. Tickets can be bought from any travel agent. The first bus to Pangururan from Tomok (via the Tuk Tuk turn-off and Ambarita) leaves Tomok at 8am. From Pangururan, buses leave every hour up to 2pm for Sidikalang, two hours away.

Parapat

Situated at the point where the Trans-Sumatran Highway touches the eastern shore of Toba, **PARAPAT** is a town split in two. There's the rather tawdry **resort**, crammed with hotels, restaurants, karaoke bars and souvenir shops and, set on the hills away from the lake, a fairly humdrum area where you'll find the bus station, bank and telephone office. Buses arriving in Parapat drive through the resort to the ferry terminal before heading back to the bus station. You can get a minivan to and from the bus station at any time for Rp1000.

Nearly all the hotels in Parapat are geared towards Southeast Asian tourists rather than Westerners, who tend to head straight for the resorts on Samosir. Parapat does, however, have one or two advantages over Samosir's resorts: the rates at Parapat's **Bank BNI**, for example, on Jalan Sisingamangaraja, are far superior to anything offered on Samosir, and the cost of calling home from one of the wartels or Parapat's **Telkom office**, on the back road between the bus station and the quay, is fifty percent cheaper than from Samosir. The twice-weekly (Wed & Sat) **food markets** by the Samosir jetty are lively and diverting.

With over sixty hotels in town, there's plenty of **accommodation** to choose from, though there are only a few budget options. Of these, *Charley's*, right by the ferry terminal and next to the market at Jl Pekan Tiga Raja 7 (Ⓣ0625/41277; ❷), is by far the best. The hotel has some comfortable and spotless en-suite doubles, and Charley is one of the most helpful and entertaining hotel managers in Sumatra. In the mid-price bracket, the *Hotel Wisata Bahari*, Jl Pulau Samosir 3–6 (Ⓣ0625/41302 Ⓕ41309; ❹) near the highway, is the best of a pretty average bunch, while at the upper end of the market the three-star *Natour Parapat*, Jl Marihat 1 (Ⓣ0625/41012, Ⓕ41019; ❺), stands head and shoulders above everything else. Each of the *Natour*'s 97 rooms come equipped with a TV, video and hot water, and the residents can make use of the hotel's private beach.

Pulau Samosir

Pulau Samosir is the spiritual heartland of the Toba Batak people, and one of the most fascinating, pleasant and laid-back holiday resorts in Indonesia. Until 1906, Samosir was not an island at all but a peninsula, connected to the lake's western shore by a narrow sliver of land running between Pangururan, the capital of Samosir, and the mainland hot spring resort of Tele. In 1904, the Dutch carved a hole through this 250-metre-long isthmus to create a canal, simultaneously converting Samosir into an island, connected to the mainland by a bridge.

Few tourists get to see this side of the island, preferring instead to stay on the touristy eastern shores of Toba, where there's a string of enjoyable resorts, from **Tomok** in the south, to **Tuk Tuk**, **Ambarita** and the island's cultural centre, **Simanindo**, on Samosir's northern shore.

Despite the vast number of hotels and restaurants, the tourist infrastructure on Samosir is fairly poor. There's no official **tourist office**, although many of the guesthouses, in particular *Bagus Bay Homestay* and *Tabo*, have their own travel agencies which can book flights, buses and all manner of tours around the island. The Gokhon Library, a small bookshop on Tuk Tuk, has some good maps of the island, and will also refill your water bottle with filtered water for Rp1500. None of the **banks** change money, but guesthouses often will, and there are a handful of moneychanging shops. There are now many **telephone offices** or wartels where you can make international calls – though at inflated rates. Many of the guesthouses have **internet** connections, though once again

Traditional crafts and performing arts on Toba

Step inside any souvenir shop in Toba, and it won't take you long to realize that the Batak are skilled **woodcarvers**. The *tunggal*, the guru's magic staff, is traditionally carved with the faces of ancestors, as well as lizards, geckos and other creatures. Seldom used today, *tunggal* are still produced for the tourist market, cut into three segments to make them easier to fit into a rucksack. The Toba Batak also make the *pustaha*, a concertina-style book made of bark (or sometimes bamboo) and used to record spells and rituals. Another favourite souvenir is the *porhalaan*, bamboo cylinders covered with Batak script that the villagers would use to determine the most propitious time to harvest crops or get married.

The Batak are skilled **weavers**, and on special occasions such as weddings or funerals the women of Toba still wear the traditional full-length woven shawl over their shoulders (Karo women tend to wear the woven cloth as a head covering). These days most of the weaving is done by machine, and using chemically produced dyes, though there are a couple of shops in Parapat where you can pick up a used, hand-woven shawl for as little as Rp15,000, depending on quality and condition.

The Toba Batak pride themselves on their musical prowess: all the men on Toba seem to be able to play the guitar, with which they serenade Western women. Amongst the indigenous **musical instruments** used to accompany the traditional dances are sets of cloth-covered metal gongs called *gondang*, and the two-stringed violin. Batak **dances** tend to be slow and repetitive, with minimum movement; sometimes, during weddings and funerals, the dance can go on all night and the stamina of the performers is incredible. Perhaps the most famous – and certainly the strangest – of the Toba Batak dance forms is the unique *sigale gale* **funeral dance**, where a life-size wooden puppet, its face painted to resemble the deceased, is wheeled around the room to offer comfort to the relatives. Some of the more advanced *sigale gale* puppets even have sponges built in behind the eyes, so that the puppet can cry at the whim of the puppeteer (who operates the mannequin by strings). You can see performances of *sigale gale* at Simanindo on Samosir (Mon–Sat 10.30am & 11.45am, Sun 11.45am).

the rates are much higher than normal with Rp25,000 per hour being the average.

Though sunbathing, reading, shopping and drinking are the most popular activities on Tuk Tuk, there are alternative recreational activities on the peninsula if you look hard enough. The shores here are safe for **swimming**; the most popular place is the roped-off section of the lake by *Carolina's*, complete with pontoons, canoes and a diving board. One or two of the big hotels plan to buy and rent out jet skis. Many of the larger homestays and hotels have **sports equipment**, which they often allow nonresidents to use. *Bagus Bay*, for example, provides facilities for badminton, volleyball, basketball and even a pool table – though the equipment is in poor condition. *Roy's Pub* has a table tennis table, which patrons can use during the day.

Accommodation

In general, the **accommodation** on Samosir is excellent value, especially if you're good at bargaining, particularly in the low season, when the hotels are desperate for custom. You'll usually be set upon by touts way before you even reach the island, such is the fierce competition between the losmen, but it's important that you choose your accommodation carefully, as in most cases the hotel owner will insist that you eat in their restaurant every evening. Accommodation in the homestays often takes the form of quasi-Batak bungalows, made of concrete rather than wood and usually a tad more comfortably furnished. At the budget end, most places charge an extra thirty percent for a room with hot water. If you're in Tuk Tuk in the high season and the hotels are full, try asking in the restaurants, many of which have a couple of rooms for rent out the back.

Tuk Tuk

Over thirty losmen and hotels, numerous restaurants, bars, bookshops, travel agents and souvenir stalls stand cheek by jowl on the **Tuk Tuk** peninsula. If you plan to stay here, tell the ferryman which hotel you plan to go to and he'll drop you off on the nearest quay. In general, the cheapest accommodation is on the northern side of the peninsula, while the more luxurious hotels are found on the long eastern shoreline.

Bagus Bay Homestay ⓣ0625/451 287. Clean and basic bungalows set in large grounds, with excellent facilities including a pool table, internet café, bike-hire, badminton court, board games, bar, videos three times a night and a twice-weekly Batak dancing display. The food is variable. ❷

Carolina's ⓣ0625/41520, ⓕ41521, ⓔCarolina@psiantar.wasantara.net.id. One of the classiest complexes on the peninsula: accommodation comes in the form of huge, Batak-style bungalows, each with a lakeside view and its own little section of beach. The Rp120,000 luxury rooms with fridge, hot water and TV are the best on the island. ❺

Hariara's One of the most charming spots on Tuk Tuk: four spacious, tastefully decorated rooms situated in wonderful, carefully tended gardens. The rooms come with a walk-in wardrobe and Western bathroom; ask at the *Boruna*, 100m along the road, for the key. ❷

Lek Jon's ⓣ0625/41578. A budget, 38-room losmen with possibly the pushiest touts in Parapat. The rooms are plain but pleasant, and the staff are a lot of fun – until, that is, you decide to eat elsewhere. ❶

Linda's A long-established travellers' favourite, run by the indefatigable Linda and family. The old and rather spartan accommodation has recently been augmented by a set of four luxury rooms with hot running water. This is one of the few places that doesn't mind if you eat elsewhere, though the cooking is great and the portions always huge. ❶–❷

Mas ⓣ0625/451051. A combination of draughty, old cottages (over 100 years old in some cases) and newer, more comfortable, concrete homes, located halfway between Tuk Tuk and Ambarita next to an allotment of banana and papaya fruit. Once again, the management gets extremely cross if you don't eat at their restaurant. ❶–❷

Nina's ⓣ0625/451150. An enchanting lakeside place with three beautiful, antique Batak houses, a 10min walk north of Tuk Tuk. It's basic but very clean and you'll get your own bathroom. The vegetarian restaurant at the front makes this out-of-the-way retreat one of the best budget choices on the island. ❶

Romlan's ⓣ0625/41557. Turn right down a track just before the *Sumber Pulomas* hotel to get here. This exquisite little guesthouse has been hugely popular for many years now, despite its unfavourable location behind a rubbish dump. The traditional-style bungalows, with their freshly painted exteriors adorned with hanging baskets, are probably the best of their kind on the island. Some rooms have private mandi. ❶–❷

Samosir Cottages ⓣ0625/41050, ⓕ451 170, ⓔsamosirres@hotmail.com. Possibly the best mid-range accommodation on the peninsula, with prices ranging from basic rooms above the reception to luxury bungalows (complete with hot water and a bathtub) overlooking the lake. It's friendly, with a good restaurant and also internet access. ❶–❷

Sibigo ⓣ0625/451074. A small but expanding guesthouse down a small track near *Carolina's*. The clean, quiet and comfortable rooms, particularly those on the beach overlooking the water, are a bargain. ❷

Silintong I (ⓣ0625/451 242, ⓕ451 225) and **II** (ⓣ0625/451 281, ⓕ451282). Two oversized and overpriced hotels along the eastern stretch of the peninsula. The rooms are pleasant enough, and the hotel's orchid collection in the garden is gorgeous – but the rates are absurdly high by Tuk Tuk standards. ❹

Tabo Cottages ⓣ0625/451 318, ⓕ41614, ⓔtabors@indo.net.id. Mid-range hotel with a large range of facilities, including bike hire, internet access and a bookshop. The rooms are most comfortable, and at the top end come with "Jungle bathroom"; the food conjured up in the restaurant

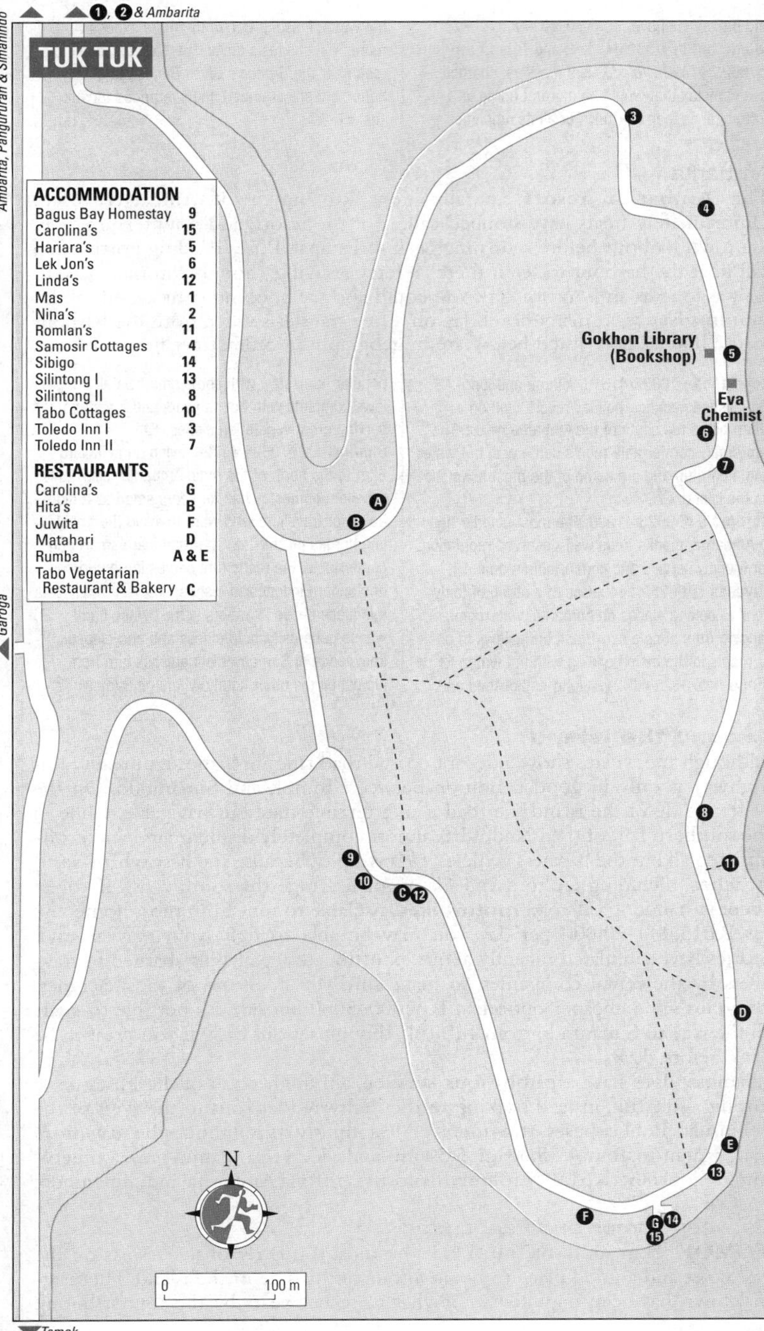
TUK TUK
1, 2 & Ambarita
Ambarita, Pangururan & Simanindo
Garoga
Tomok
ACCOMMODATION
Bagus Bay Homestay 9
Carolina's 15
Hariara's 5
Lek Jon's 6
Linda's 12
Mas 1
Nina's 2
Romlan's 11
Samosir Cottages 4
Sibigo 14
Silintong I 13
Silintong II 8
Tabo Cottages 10
Toledo Inn I 3
Toledo Inn II 7
RESTAURANTS
Carolina's G
Hita's B
Juwita F
Matahari D
Rumba A & E
Tabo Vegetarian Restaurant & Bakery C
Gokhon Library (Bookshop)
Eva Chemist
N
0
100 m

and bakery is above reproach. ❷–❹

Toledo Inn I (☎0625/41181) and **Toledo Inn II** (☎0625/41429). *Toledo I* is a massive, characterless complex that would be more at home in Torremolinos than Tuk Tuk. For all its amenities – hot water, fans, air-con in the more expensive rooms – it still feels tacky. The *Toledo II*, down the road near the *Brando's Blues Bar*, is marginally better, but still cramped and overpriced for Tuk Tuk. ❸–❺

Ambarita

The **Ambarita resort** actually lies 2km north of Ambarita town. Unfortunately, boats have stopped calling at the resort, and now terminate in the town harbour before returning back to Parapat. Buses heading north often call in at the harbour to see if there's a ferry arriving, though you may have to wait as long as an hour for one. You could also try booking your accommodation in advance, as many hotels lay on a free transfer service from the harbour to the hotel. Those listed below are in geographical order, travelling north.

Sopo Toba ☎0625/41616. A large and long-established package-holiday resort, built on a steep hill to the south of the Ambarita resort. The supremely comfortable rooms come with hot water and a bathtub and are some of the most luxurious on the island. ❺

Barbara's ☎0625/41230. The most popular hotel in Ambarita, thanks to its well-deserved reputation for friendly service and comfortable rooms. ❷

Thyesza ☎0625/41443. One of a string of fairly similar-looking places on Ambarita, with rooms ranging from simple neo-Batak bungalows to pricier rooms in the main building with hot water. ❷

Kings II ☎0625/41421. A long-established and popular homestay, with some smart Batak bungalows complete with hot showers and a restaurant serving great vegetarian dishes. ❸

Shangri-La ☎0625/41724. Lying an awkward 6km to the north of the main Ambarita resort, this excellent homestay has for years acted as a hideaway for travellers who want to avoid the travelling hordes on Tuk Tuk. The rooms are smart and comfortable, the restaurant serves large portions of standard Indonesian dishes, but what really sets this place above all others is the owner, Pami, whose generosity, helpfulness and encyclopedic knowledge of Sumatra distinguishes him from almost all the other hotel owners on Samosir. ❸

Around the island

Although most maps show a decent coastal road ringing Samosir, in reality this highway is only in good condition between Tomok and Simanindo. On the western side of the island the road is in a terrible state but navigable, while in the southern half of the island it has almost completely disintegrated and is off-limits to all but the hardiest vehicles. This is a pity, because the best **white-sand beaches**, including Gultom and Nainggolan, fringe the south coast. If you're adept at handling off-road **motorbikes**, available to rent from most homestays for Rp15,000–20,000 per day, you may be able to fight your way around. Stories have circulated recently about extortionate repair bills charged to travellers by the rental companies, so make sure you take care of the machines. **Bicycles** are a cheaper option, at Rp4000–5000 per day; it's possible to cycle all the way to Simanindo from Tuk Tuk, though set out early if you want to be back before dark.

Samosir does have a **public bus service**, although none of the buses drive through Tuk Tuk, instead sticking to the highway that runs to the west of the peninsula. Public buses run more-or-less hourly throughout the day from Pangururan to Tomok (5.30am–5.30pm) and vice versa (8am–9pm), a ninety-minute journey (Rp1500) round the north coast via Ambarita and Simanindo.

Between Tomok and Pangururan

TOMOK, 2km south of Tuk Tuk, is the most southerly of the resorts on the east coast and a good place to begin a tour of this side of the island. The original town has been engulfed somewhat in recent years by the tourist boom,

Trekking across Samosir

The hills in the centre of Samosir tower 700m above the water and, on a clear day, afford superb views over the lake and beyond. At the heart of the island is a large plateau and **Danau Sidihoni**, a body of water about the size of a large village pond. It is possible, just, to walk from one side of the island to the other in one day – it takes ten hours or more – but a stopover in one of the villages on the plateau is usually necessary, so take overnight gear and a torch.

The climb from the eastern shore is very steep, but from the western shore the incline is far more gradual, so many trekkers start by catching the first bus to Pangururan (leaving at 8am from Tomok; Rs4000), arriving at about 10am. This account, however, begins in Ambarita on the eastern shore, and more specifically on the uphill path that starts to the north of the Ambarita petrol station. It's a stiff climb, but if you don't lose your way you should, two hours later, find yourself in the tiny hilltop village of **Partukongan** – aka Dolok or "summit" – the highest point on Samosir. There are two hostels here, *John's* and *Jenny's*, in fierce competition not only with each other, but also with the three losmen in the next village on the trail, **Ronggurnihuta**. The villagers can be a bit vague when giving directions, so take care and check frequently with passers-by that you're on the right trail. All being well, you'll find Ronggurnihuta is a three- or four-hour walk away from Partukongan, with **Pangururan** three to four hours further on at the end of a tortuously long downhill track (18km) that passes **Danau Sidihoni** on the way. Arrive in Pangururan before 5pm and you should be in time to catch the last bus back to the eastern shore; otherwise, you'll have to stay in one of Pangururan's rather soulless hostels, such as the *Wartel Wisata* at Jl Dr T.B. Simatupang 42 by the bus stop (ⓣ0626/20558, ⓕ20559; Rp20,000).

with dozens of virtually identical souvenir stalls lining the main street. This chain of stalls leads all the way up the hill to Tomok's most famous sight, the early nineteenth-century stone **sarcophagus of Raja Sidabutar**, the chief of the first tribe to migrate to the island. The coffin has a Singa face – a part-elephant, part-buffalo creature of Toban legend – carved into one end, and a small stone effigy of the king's wife on top of the lid, sitting with a bowl by her knees and a coconut shell on her head. It's an unusual coffin, and the best surviving example of the ornate stone sarcophagi that once dotted the landscape of Samosir. On the way to the tomb, halfway up the hill on the right, is the small **Museum of King Soribunto Sidabutar** (Mon–Sat 9am–5pm; Rp1500), a small collection of tribal artefacts, stuffed animals and fading photographs relating to Tomok's turn-of-the-twentieth-century king, housed in a one of a row of traditional Batak cottages.

On the way to Ambarita from Tomok, due west of Tuk Tuk, is the tiny village of **Garoga**, from where you can hike to the waterfall of the same name. The falls are only really worth seeing after a heavy downpour, being little more than a dribble at other times, though it's possible to go swimming in the pools at the bottom; ask the locals for directions.

In **AMBARITA** itself there is a curious collection of stone chairs (7am–5pm; Rp1000), one of which is mysteriously occupied by a stone statue. Most of the villagers will tell you that these chairs acted as the local law courts two hundred years ago, where defendants were tried and the guilty executed. Others say that the chairs are actually less than fifty years old, and the work of a local mason who copied drawings of the original.

SIMANINDO lies at the northern end of the island, 15km beyond the town of Ambarita and 9km beyond the *Shangri-La Hotel*. The **Simanindo Museum**

Toba architecture

As with all Batak houses, the cottages of the Toba are made of wooden planks bound together with palm fibre, and stand on two-metre-high pillars (these days made of stone to prevent them rotting away). They have two distinguishing features. The first is the **saddle-shaped roof** sloping down towards the centre of the house, but rising at either end above the front and back entrances. Originally this roof would have been thatched with palm fibres, but corrugated metal is now far more common. The second feature is the highly decorated wooden **gable**, intricately carved into a number of geometric patterns and cosmological designs and painted with the traditional Toba colours of black, white and red. One of the best examples of this kind of work stands by the highway in Ambarita, just north of the Tuk Tuk turn-off. As is customary, the smiling, mythical elephant–buffalo hybrid, Singa, features prominently, looking out above the front entrance made deliberately small so visitors are forced to bow in respect when entering. Though much smaller than the *rumah adat* of Berastagi, Toba houses could still hold up to four families; today, however, there are very few communal houses left.

(daily 12.30–5pm; Rp3000) is housed in the former house of Raja Simalungun, the last Batak king, who was assassinated in 1946 for colluding with the Dutch. The museum has some mildly diverting trappings of village life, including spears, magical charms and a wooden *guri guri* (ashes urn). The large *adat* houses in the **traditional village**, through the stone archway, are unexceptional save for their thatched roofs – a rarity on Samosir. The museum and village also hold traditional Batak dancing performances every morning (10.30–11.10am at the museum, 11.45am–12.30pm in the village), though the performances at the **Gokasi cultural centre** (10–11am & 11.15am–12.15pm; Rp10,000), 1.5km further along the highway, are said to be better.

Continuing round to the western side of the island, **Simarmata**, halfway between Simanindo and Pangururan, is one of the best-preserved Batak villages on Samosir, though sadly all of the houses have lost their thatched roofs. There's little to see in **Pangururan** itself, though there's a **hot spring** (Rp1500) across the bridge in the village of **Tele**. The springs are at their busiest at the weekends and are cleaned out on Mondays, so Tuesday and Wednesday are the best and most hygienic days.

Eating

While many of the hotels try to stop their guests from eating anywhere else except their own restaurants, there are plenty of eating places dotted around Tuk Tuk should you manage to escape. Many of the restaurants try to cook Western food – burgers, pancakes and so on – and down the years they've become quite good at it. Local delicacies include *babi guling* (roast suckling pig) and *anjing* (dog, though the restaurants on Tuk Tuk tend not to advertise this).

Carolina's Widely recognized as the best-quality restaurant on the island, the expensive *Carolina's* – part of the hotel of the same name at the south of the peninsula – has an extensive menu of Indonesian and Chinese food and hosts cultural performances most evenings.

Hita's On the north side of the "neck" of the peninsula, opposite the footpath. The best-value budget restaurant on the whole of Tuk Tuk, a no-nonsense travellers' place that deserves to be more popular. The menu consists mainly of excellent inexpensive tacos and curries. If you're on this side of the peninsula, don't miss out.

Juwita On the southern tip of the peninsula, at the top of the hill, 100m to the west of *Carolina's*. Plain, unpretentious budget café serving dishes that are a little overpriced but occasionally delicious – for example, the *kanghung* (a kind of spinach) with *teras* (fermented shrimp paste). They also offer cooking courses.

Matahari On the east side of the island, 200m south of *Romlan's* guesthouse. An unexceptional mid-price restaurant notable only because they serve roast suckling pig – providing there are at least ten of you willing to pay Rp50,000 each.
Nina's Vegetarian Restaurant Just north of Tuk Tuk and attached to the hotel of the same name, this small, inexpensive place serves mostly local food, but without the meat. The menu is extensive, the service cheery, and it's well worth the trip.
Rumba Swiss-owned budget to mid-priced restaurant with two branches on Tuk Tuk. Most of the food at *Rumba* is of a very high standard, particularly the pizzas, and if you order a day in advance you can try local delicacies such as *ikan mas*.
Tabo Vegetarian Restaurant and Bakery Next door to *Bagus Bay Homestay* on the southern side of the peninsula. Part of the guesthouse of the same name, this mid-priced restaurant has the most imaginative menu on Samosir including gratins, burgers, risottos and salads. Try the *tempe* with lemon for starters, then move on to the vegetable curry before rounding it all off with a milkshake. The portions are small, but their freshly baked bread is the best in North Sumatra.

Nightlife

Toban **nightlife** revolves around videos, rock music and alcohol. In Ambarita you're pretty much confined to your hotel, such is the paucity of restaurants and bars there, but in **Tuk Tuk** you have some choice. Many of the hotels and bars on the peninsula offer free videos, including the *Bagus Bay* (three videos per night) and *Leo's* (two), just north of *Samosir Cottages*. A couple of bars shun videos in favour of loud music, such as the *Brando's Blues Bar*, south of *Leo's*, which has a pool table and a large selection of CDs, and *Roy's Pub*, south of *Linda's* on the opposite side of the road, which has its own disco and sometimes hosts live bands. *Saza's*, near *Leo's* and *Brando's*, has a number of pool tables that are in a fairly good condition – a rarity in Indonesia.

For those who prefer something a bit more cultural, the *Bagus Bay Homestay* has traditional **Batak dancing** (Wed & Sat 8.15pm); they even promise to drop you off back at your hotel at the end of the performance. The dancers are a lacklustre bunch who look like they'd rather be elsewhere, but the band are enthusiastic and good fun. *Anju's*, north of *Samosir Cottages*, has live bands playing traditional Batak tunes (Tues, Thurs & Sat), and most of the big hotels on the peninsula (*Carolina's*, *Silintong*, *Toledo*) put on some sort of cultural entertainment – though you may have to eat in their restaurants if you want to catch the show.

Pulau Nias

Though the journey is long and arduous, and involves passing through the unlovely town of **Sibolga**, most visitors agree that any effort expended to get to Nias is worth it. An island the size of Bali, with a rich tribal culture, wonderful beaches and some of the best surfing in the country, **Pulau Nias** is a microcosm of almost everything that's exciting about Indonesia. Lying 125km southwest of Sibolga, the island's reputation as a land of malarial swamps and bloodthirsty natives kept visitors at bay for centuries, leading to the development of a culture free from the influences of India, Arabia, Europe and, indeed, the rest of Indonesia. The 600,000 Niasans speak a distinct language, one that has more in common with Polynesian than any Indonesian tongue.

Pulau Nias is, culturally at least, split into two distinct regions – north and south. The north of Nias is largely swampland and, save for the capital, **Gunung Sitoli**, contains little appealing to the average tourist. The south, however, has a number of fascinating **hill-top villages**, such as **Orahili**, **Bawomataluo** and the spiritual heartland of **Gomo**, where the last few rem-

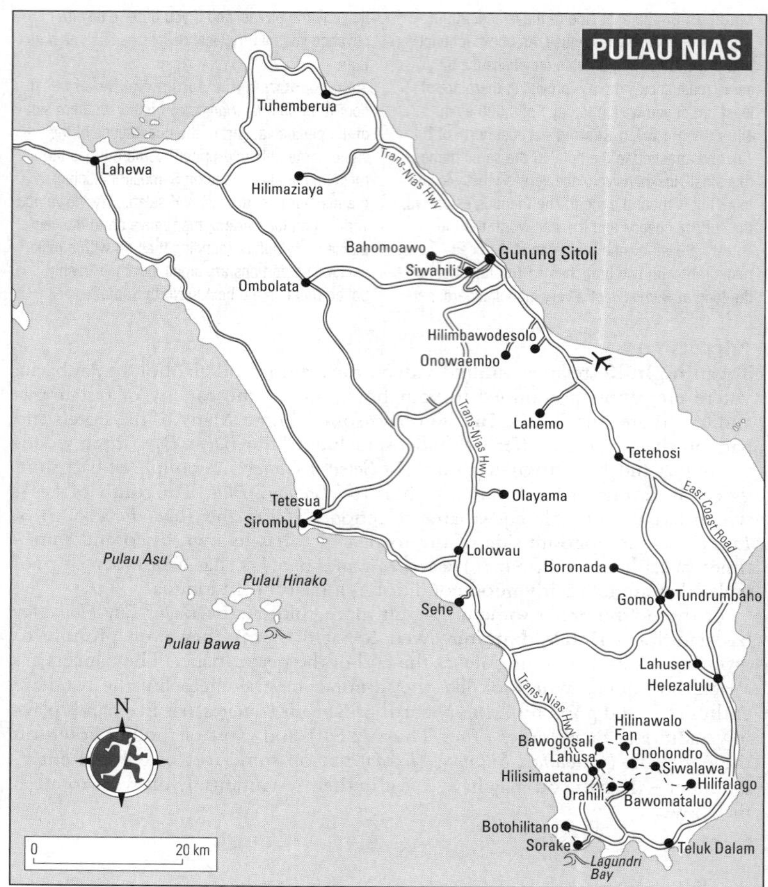

nants of Nias's famed megalithic culture survive. The south also has the best and most popular beaches, such as the **surfer's paradise** at **Lagundri Bay**, invaded every year by hordes of sun-tanned boarders eager to catch some of the best right-handers in the world.

Nias can be a difficult place to travel around. The landscape is rugged and there are very few roads, with only two major highways on the whole island: the **Trans-Nias Highway** between Gunung Sitoli in the northeast and Lagundri in the southwest, and a smaller track running along the island's eastern shore. Both are in an appalling state of disrepair after floods in late 2001, and while some feeble efforts are being made to fix the endless chain of potholes (some a few metres across), the journey from Gunung Sitoli to Teluk Dalam in the south now takes seven hours instead of the usual two.

The Niasans have a reputation for being unfriendly and aggressive – a reputation that isn't entirely undeserved. Nevertheless, most visitors agree that the hardships of Nias are more than outweighed by its beauty and unique culture.

Malaria (see p.32) continues to be a problem on the island, and chloroquine-resistant strains have been reported. Take the correct prophylactics and bring repellent and a mosquito net.

Some history

According to local folklore, the people of Nias are descended from six gods who begat the human population of Gomo, in the centre of the island. Western anthropologists, however, hold different views of early Niha history; though most scholars now agree that the Niha people arrived on Nias in about 3000 BC, where they came from is still a matter for conjecture. A **proto-Malay people** speaking an Austronesian language with traces of Polynesian and Malagasy (the language of Madagascar), whose sculptures resemble closely those of the Nagas in the eastern Himalayas and whose physiognomy shows similarities with the Batak people of North Sumatra, evidence seems to link the Nihas with most of southern Asia and beyond.

For many centuries after their arrival/inception, the people of Nias had almost no contact with the outside world. Thus, like the Batak on the mainland, the Niha people developed a highly idiosyncratic, agrarian way of life; they also showed a similar predilection for waging war with each other. Unlike the Batak, however, the Niha never developed a system of writing. They lived in small villages, each of which functioned according to a strict three-tier **class system**, with the village chief at the top and the slaves – usually people captured from nearby villages in raids – at the bottom. These slaves were important as symbols of prestige and wealth; later, in the 1600s, they also became a valuable source of income, as traders from Aceh began calling in at Nias to buy **slaves**, which they paid for with gold. The precious necklaces and bangles worn during festivals today were probably wrought from the gold of these eighteenth-century slave-runners.

The slave-traders were the first outsiders to pay regular visits to the island, and paved the way for others to follow. The **Dutch** arrived in 1665 to exploit the slave trade for their own ends, and remained on the island for most of the next 250 years, save for a brief five-year interregnum by the British under Stamford Raffles during the 1820s. The Dutch tenure was largely characterized by their increasingly violent attempts to subjugate the island completely. During the 1860s, they destroyed several villages in southern Nias – an act of aggression that rankles with the locals to this day. The Dutch finally gained complete control over the island in 1914, only to be forced to relinquish it again thirty years later by the Japanese army during World War II.

Attempts to convert the Niha to Christianity met with similar resistance. The Dutch and British both failed, and although the German Rhenish missionaries, who first arrived in 1865, managed to convert most of north Nias by the end of the century, the southern half remained resistant. This resilience led to heavy-handed tactics by the missionaries, culminating in a campaign to rid the island of all traces of animism. Nearly all of the Niha's animistic totems were either destroyed or shipped to Europe, where they still reside in the museums of western Germany and Holland, and many of the island's oldest megaliths disappeared at this time. Indeed, so complete was the eradication of the old religion that, of the few remaining stone megaliths, nobody knows who created them, why, or what all their hieroglyphics mean. Today, over 95 per cent of Nias is now, nominally at least, Christian, and the last recorded instance of headhunting, an essential component of Niha animism, occurred way back in 1935.

Approaching Pulau Nias: Sibolga

With its series of pitch-black tunnels cut into the jungle-clad cliffs, its roadside waterfalls and heart-stopping hairpin bends, the last, vertiginous five kilometres of the six-hour drive down to **SIBOLGA** from Parapat is breathtakingly dramatic. Even the town itself looks pretty from this distance, resembling the quaint little seaside settlements found all the way along the western coastline. Unfortunately, the reality is somewhat different: Sibolga is a small drab place with a chronic lack of anything worth seeing, and with little to recommend it other than one or two good hotels and a couple of decent Chinese restaurants. It is, however, the main port for ferries to Nias, and, as such, sees its fair share of travellers.

The most interesting thing about Sibolga is its **racial mix**: though not officially Toba Batak territory, there has been a huge influx of people from the Toba region who came looking for work. Indeed, they now outnumber the original coastal Muslim inhabitants, and, when you add to this the significant ethnic Chinese population who have been here for centuries, you end up not only with a highly cosmopolitan town, but also one that's filled to bursting with mosques, churches and Buddhist temples.

Although there's almost nothing to do in town – except, maybe, visit the Tagor Cinema in the evening – there are a couple of reasonable **beaches** nearby: the white-sand **Pantai Pandan**, 10km south of Sibolga, is quiet and pretty, while **Pantai Kalangan**, 300m further on, is popular with locals and charges an Rp250 entry fee. Oplets (the local term for bemo) to both beaches run from Sibolga bus terminus on Jalan Sisingamangaraja. Recently there have been reports of a few **scams** involving tourists and bogus uniformed "narcotics police" looking for a bribe. Another ruse revolves around finding out a friend's name and then delivering a "message" – usually a request for money – while in a third scenario, a local boy offers you drugs moments before a bona fide but corrupt policeman "discovers" you both. Be on your guard.

Practicalities

All **buses** and bemos call in at the terminus on Jalan Sisingamangaraja, at the back of the town away from the coast, though some long distance tourist minivans (for Medan and Bukit Tingi) leave in the morning from just east of the jetty. The **port** for ferries to Nias – as well as the occasional Pelni boat from Padang – is about 1.5km south of here at the end of Jalan Horas. For full details of passenger ferries to Nias, which run every day except Sunday, see p.390. **Tickets** for the ferry to Nias can be bought from PT Simeulue at Jl S. Bustami Alamsyah 9 (☎0631/21497), near the Bank BNI. Ask about the current situation concerning the unreliable direct ferry to Teluk Dalam (see p.387) at the port. The **Pelni agent**, PT Sarana Bandar Nasional, is near the market by the bus terminus at Jl Patuan Anggi 39 (☎0631/22291).

If you're heading to Nias, it's advisable to **change money** before you go, unless you're using plastic (there's an ATM in Gunung Sitoli). The BNI bank with ATM on Jl S. Parman 3 (Mon–Fri 8am–4.15pm) is your last chance; the cash and travellers' cheques rates are slightly lower than those in Medan, but far superior to anything on Nias.

Budget travellers forced to stay in Sibolga overnight should head to one of the Chinese-run **hotels**, such as the friendly and efficient *Pasar Baru*, on the junction of Jalan Raja Djunjungan and Jalan Imam Bonjol (☎0631/22167; ❸), or the *Indah Sari* at Jl Jend A.Yani 29 (☎0631/21208; ❷), which is a tad scruffier but still acceptable. The best hotel is the stately *Wisata Indah* at Jl Brig Jend

Katamso 51 (Ⓣ0631/23688, Ⓕ23988; ⑤), with air-con rooms and a sea view.

The best **restaurants** are on Imam Bonjol. The *Hebat Baru* at no. 79 and the slightly cheaper *Restoran Restu* opposite at no. 58c both serve excellent Chinese food and are very popular with the locals. The surgically clean *Hidangan Saudara Kita* at Jl Raja Djunjungan 55 also serves excellent Padang food.

Gunung Sitoli

The capital of Nias, **GUNUNG SITOLI**, isn't the sort of place you'd want to spend much time in; most travellers head straight through to the beaches in the south. There's nothing really unpleasant about the place, however, and if it wasn't for the fact that the people here are about 30cm smaller than their mainland neighbours, you could be in any small city on the west coast of Sumatra. As the island's administrative centre, Gunung Sitoli has the best facilities on Nias, and if you want to send a letter, make a phone call or change money, this is the best place to do it.

If you do decide to stay in Gunung Sitoli for a day, consider paying a visit to the **Nias museum** (Tues–Sun 8.30am–5pm; free), halfway between the town and the harbour. This tiny building houses the most complete set of Niha antiquities in Indonesia, most of which are labelled in English. The small armoury by the front entrance contains some of the most impressive items, including leather shields and tunics from the nineteenth century. The centre also shows videos of the traditional dances of Nias.

Practicalities

Gunung Sitoli is little more than a stretch of shops and houses along the shore, with a number of roads running off them up the hills overlooking the town. Coming from the harbour in the north, Jalan Yos Sudarso splits into the parallel Jalan Gomo (right) and Jalan Sirao (left, nearest the sea). They both soon converge again to form Jalan Diponogero. Until the ferries to Teluk Dalam begin sailing regularly again, almost everybody's first sight of Nias is Gunung Sitoli's **harbour**, approximately 2km north of the town; frequent minivans (Rp5000) connect the two, terminating at the **bus station** on Jalan Diponogero near the southern end of town. Those who take advantage of SMAC airlines' reasonably priced flights between Medan and Gunung Sitoli (Mon, Wed & Fri; 7am $55), arrive at the tiny **airstrip** to the southeast of town; the twenty-kilometre 4WD ride to the town centre is included in the flight price.

Two of the ferries to Sibolga – the *Poncan Mo'ale* and *KM Cucut* – share a **ticket office** on the main road by the port, while PT Simeulue is at Jl Sirao 23 right in the centre of town. The ticket office for **Pelni ferries** is at Jl Lagundri 38 (Ⓣ0639/21846), tucked away to the east of Jalan Sirao, one block back from the coast. Nias's only **tourist office** is located south of the bus station on Jalan Diponegoro (Mon–Fri 8am–4pm; Ⓣ0639/21950); the staff are willing, but have little information and no maps. The **post office** stands on the opposite corner of the green at Jl Hatta 1, next to the **Telkom office**. One block further south, at Jl Imam Bonjol 40, is the **Bank BNI**; the rates (US dollar cash and travellers' cheques only) are poor, but there's an international ATM here. Sitoli is also the only place on the island with **internet access**, at the Laser Computer Café 100m south of the bus station.

One of the reasons why so many travellers hurry through Gunung Sitoli is its paucity of decent **accommodation**. The better-value places are on the southern side of town, near the bus station and across the river bisecting

The architecture of Nias

Although the **rumah adat** of north and south Nias look very different, they share some important design features. As with Batak houses, no nails were used in their construction; instead, the Nihas would bind the planks together with palm leaves. Both styles of houses are **earthquake-proof** too: the stilts on which the buildings stand are placed both vertically and obliquely, giving the foundations greater flexibility and allowing them to ride the tremors rather than collapse altogether. Indeed, the number of stilts used to support the house were an indication of how important the resident was in the village hierarchy. A chief would usually own a house that was at least six supporting posts wide, whilst a commoner's would measure only four posts across.

The most obvious difference between the two types of house is the floor plan, which in north Nias is an oval shape and, in the south, a rectangle. The houses of the north are also squatter and tend to stand alone, whilst those of the south are much taller, have soaring, two-sided roofs and stand shoulder to shoulder with each other along the village street.

There is plenty of the traditional housing of southern Nias left in the hill-top villages (see p.388), though only a few examples of the houses of northern Nias remain, and no new ones are being built. One house built in the traditional northern Nias style still stands on the Trans-Nias Highway, about 30km outside Gunung Sitoli. The village of **Siwahili**, 6km uphill from Sitoli, also has a couple of good examples, though there are no buses and little traffic, so be prepared to walk the whole way.

Gunung Sitoli. These include the *Marja* at Jl Diponegoro 128 (☎0639/22812; ❷), and the slightly grimier *Laraga* at no. 135 (☎0639/21760; ❷), both of which offer acceptable but poky rooms. Sitoli's most popular **restaurant**, the excellent Padang food specialist *Rumah Makan Nasional*, is 100m further down Jalan Sirao at no. 87. Back near the *Hawaii*, at Jl Sirao 10, the Chinese restaurant *Bintang Terang* serves that rarest of north Nias luxuries: ice-cold beer.

Gomo and the villages of the central highlands

Both north and south Nias regard the **central highlands** as the cradle of their culture, where, according to local mythology, the six Niha gods descended to earth and begat the island's human population. The main village here is the unprepossessing **GOMO**, which is virtually inaccessible thanks to its location 8km west of the east-coast road on a rutted mud track. There is one bus daily (at 6am) from Teluk Dalam to Gomo; otherwise, you'll have to catch a bus to Lahuser, halfway between Teluk Dalam and Gunung Sitoli on the coastal road, and hope that you can hitch a lift from there.

Gomo has just six **rumah adat** left (the others burnt down in a fire some years ago), built in the style of southern Nias with a rectangular rather than an oval floor plan. The most important is the **Chief's House** which, though nothing like as elaborately decorated as the one in Bawomataluo (see p.388), is still reasonably ornate and has a wealth of lizards and monkeys carved into the woodwork below the rafters. A set of stone tables and chairs, remnants of a much greater collection of stone furniture, stands outside.

Though there's little to do in Gomo itself, the people are quite friendly – certainly when compared to the inhabitants of the villages further south. With its one un-named **losmen** (❶), Gomo is the best base for exploring the central highlands. When trekking to any of the villages here, it's a good idea to hire a guide in Gomo (around Rp20,000 a day), as the paths are often extremely difficult to follow and you may have to ford rivers. Good boots, warm waterproof clothing and a torch are essential.

Tundrumbaho, 4km northeast of Gomo, is perhaps the most interesting of the villages, containing the best examples of Nias's megalithic art, including a number of menhirs (oblong or rectangular standing stones) and stone chairs carved with the heads of Naga (a mythical, snake-like creature).

Six kilometres northwest of Gomo lies **Boronada**, the hill where the gods were supposed to have arrived on earth. It has little in the way of sights, but the atmosphere here is eerie, as befits the most sacred spot on the island. Boronada is a two-hour walk from Gomo, along a very slippery and difficult-to-follow path, beginning on the asphalt road heading down to the river. On the way, after 45 minutes or so, you should pass a small path by a shop that winds its way down for 200m to a deep pool, once the entrance to a nineteenth-century **gold mine**. At the end of the main track, which quickly dwindles into a slippery and indistinct path, is Boronada. There's little here now save for a curious two-metre-tall stone pyramid, which the locals will tell you was once filled with gold, and a couple of unimpressive small statues.

South Nias

South Nias is the home of the island's greatest tourist attractions, including the **surfer's paradise** of Lagundri and the **hill-top villages** around Bawomataluo. Until the direct ferry from Sibolga to **TELUK DALAM**, the largest town in southern Nias, begins sailing more regularly again – at the time of writing, ferry departures are supposed to be on Mondays, Wednesdays and Sundays, but in fact you're lucky if the boat turns up at all – most travellers are being forced to travel down from Gunung Sitoli. There is little to do in undistinguished Teluk Dalam, though you can change money at a painfully bad rate in the shops, and there's a small post office.

The horseshoe bay of **Lagundri** lies 12km west of Teluk Dalam; buses run in the morning between the two (Rp1500), stopping by the small bridge at the Sorake/Botohili junction, where the Trans-Nias highway starts. (This is also the place to wait for buses out of Lagundri.) In practice, it's much more convenient to ask for a motorbike ride from your losmen (Rp5000). Lagundri Bay has been famous amongst **surfers** since the 1970s. There are two beaches in the bay: Lagundri beach itself gives the bay its name, while the waves actually break at neighbouring **SORAKE** (also called Jamborai), on the western edge of the bay. In July and August the waves can reach 5m high and travel for up to 150m – fantastic for experienced surfers, and only Hawaii has more consistent big surf. Because of the size of the waves and the coral reefs hidden underneath the water, this is not a good place for beginners – but in the small wave season (Christmas) you might try your hand at the 1m waves. As this is a reef and not a sandy beach, booties are a very good idea; there's nothing worse than watching the perfect "rights" roll across the bay while you sit in the café nursing cut feet. Other notable breaks (there are many) include "The Machine", one bay east of Lagundra, and Jungle Beach, one bay west of Sorake (a 1km walk). There are also breaks off the secluded islands of **Bawa** and **Asu**, which are reachable by boat (Rp50,000 for a maximum of eight people); there are a few bungalows there which charge about Rp15,000 per person.

Unless you've got your own board, you'll have to **hire** one at Rp20,000 a day (less if you hire it by the week). The boards on offer are a poignant reminder of what sharp coral can do to fibreglass – or flesh. Check the whole board carefully for dings (dents), so you don't get accused of causing them when you return it – repairs cost Rp30,000 per blemish, or Rp500,000 for a new board. It's worth considering buying one if you're going to stick around.

If you're not a surfer and don't fancy trekking in the highlands, there's little to keep you occupied in Sorake, and though in the centre of the bay the water is calm enough to **swim** in, you'd be better off going to Lagundri beach for the sand. **Botohili**, the nearest traditional village, is just a twenty-minute walk away in the hills behind the break.

The **accommodation** at Lagundri and Sorake beach consists almost entirely of simple wooden beachside bungalows. Sorake has the surfing image, with every other building a surf-hire place or a guesthouse, while Lagundri is more laid back. There are over forty losmen stretching out all along the bay, with a particularly high concentration at Sorake. Most are virtually identical, and recommending one above the other is impossible. Most have electricity, cost next to nothing (usually Rp5000 per night, or free if you stay for a fortnight or more), though you'll be expected to eat there too. Watch out for your stuff in Lagundri, as there are many reports of pickpockets and theft. Bear in mind this is a malaria hot spot; you might want to insist on a mosquito net where you're staying, and take extreme care over twilight swims when you won't be wearing long sleeves and trousers. The local authorities plan to tear these cheap losmen down eventually and replace them with sturdier places, such as the luxurious air-con *Sorake Beach Resort* (Ⓣ0630/21195; ❺) at the western end of Sorake. Things are progressing at a snail's pace, however, and it looks as if the cheaper losmen will be here for a few years yet.

The **food** in Lagundri is slightly more expensive than elsewhere in Sumatra, and can be rather bland. To pep up mealtimes, consider buying the lobster, crayfish and other seafood from the fishermen who stroll up and down the bay. If you do manage to escape from your losmen, the *ToHo*, on the road running along the back of Sorake, has an extensive menu of Western food and ice-cold beer. It's a little jazzier than *Dolyn Café* on Sorake beach, but the latter is the surfers' day-time hang out and tends to have more atmosphere. Fifty metres up the road from the *Dolyn* is a no-name **wartel** from which you can make international calls.

Bawomataluo and the south Nias villages

The **villages of south Nias** are fairly small, being little more than two neat rows of rectangular thatched houses separated by a wide paved street lined with stone tables, chairs and sculptures. For defensive purposes, the villages were always built on hill tops and surrounded by a large stone wall, though, almost without exception, these walls have now disappeared. In the centre of every village you'll find a two-metre tall **jumping stone** (*fahombe*), which once would have been topped by sharp sticks and thorns. The custom was for teenage boys to jump over this stone to show their bravery and agility (or, if they didn't jump high enough, their innards); you can see a picture of a *fahombe* ceremony on the back of a Rp1000 note.

BAWOMATALUO (Sun Hill) is the most impressive of these villages. It's an hour's walk uphill from the turn-off on the Teluk Dalam–Lagundri road; taxis from Lagundri to the turn-off charge Rp1000, and ojek cost Rp2000 (or Rp3000 all the way to Bawomataluo). If it's Saturday morning you may be able to catch one of the buses returning from Teluk Dalam market at the turn-off.

Bawomataluo has been exposed to tourism for too many years now, and touts pursue you relentlessly. The old village consists of just two roads: the main one runs east–west, while a shorter but equally wide cul-de-sac branches off due

Trekking around Bawomataluo

Bawomataluo can be seen as part of a larger **trek** around the southern hills; the map on p.382 is designed to help you plan a route around the nearby villages. When trekking, always take waterproof clothing, plenty of food (there aren't many shops en route) and a torch, and aim to reach a main road by mid-afternoon at the latest in order to catch a bus back. Buses from Teluk Dalam to Lagundri along the south coast road stop running at about 4pm, and along the Trans-Nias Highway to Lagundri they stop at about 5pm.

The following account describes a longer walk around all the villages in the immediate vicinity of Bawomataluo, a fifteen-kilometre loop that a fairly fast walker should be able to complete in around five hours, not counting stops. The trek begins one hour uphill from the Bawomataluo turn-off at the pleasant but plain village of **Orahili**, home to a couple of small and unimpressive stone carvings and a number of traditional houses, most of which have swapped the thatch on their roofs for more practical corrugated metal. You can take a minivan here from Lagundri (ask your losmen). At the far end of Orahili, at the end of the cul-de-sac on your left, a series of steps heads uphill to **Bawomataluo** (see opposite and below).

Behind the Chief's House in Bawomataluo, a scenic path leads to **Siwalawa**, one hour away. The village stretches along the path for at least 500m, though the oldest part actually lies at the very end, up some steps to the left of the main path. At the end of this old quarter a path heads downhill and divides: turn right along the obvious path and you eventually arrive at Hilifalago; turn left and you pass through the rather unexciting village of Onohondro – the path descends to a large stream (which can be waist-high in the rainy season) and, twenty minutes further on, leads to the large village of **Hilinawalofau**. The old part of the village has some good examples of traditional housing, though the introduction of a huge satellite dish to the main street somewhat ruins the look of the town. The former chief's house has been converted into a very basic guesthouse, the *Ormoda* (1).

Forty minutes later you'll arrive at **Bawogosali**, a small village with some recent stone carvings lining the path. The village is dominated by the large church, behind which a path leads up to the crest of a hill and along to **Lahuna**. This village lies at an important crossroads: continue past the end of the village and you'll reach, 45 minutes later, Bawomataluo, or turn right, and after a steep descent you arrive at **Hilisimaetano** with it's impressive chief's house. For many visitors, Hilisimaetano is their favourite spot on Nias: the village is an excellent state of preservation, the people seem to be a little friendlier than in other places on Nias and, unusually, many of the paving stones have been carved with reliefs of lizards, ships and signs of the zodiac. At the very end of the path, twenty minutes beyond Hilisimaetano, the Trans-Nias Highway thunders by, from where you can catch an ojek back to Lagundri (Rp8000).

south from opposite the Chief's House. As you'll notice with almost every village, the primary function of these streets seems to be to dry laundry, and Bawomataluo's famous **stone carvings** are usually strewn with various undergarments during daylight hours. This is a pity, as the stonework, particularly on the tables and chairs outside the Chief's House, is exceptional. These chairs once held the corpses of the recently deceased, who were simply left to decay in the street before being buried. The jumping stone here is the largest on Nias; boys charge tourists upwards of Rp10,000 for the privilege of watching them jump over it.

This quality of craftsmanship is continued inside the nineteenth-century **Chief's House** (9am–5pm; donation), where the walls are decorated with carvings of lizards, monkeys, and, in the top right-hand corner of the eastern wall, a depiction of an early European ship – a reference, perhaps, to the arrival of the Dutch in 1665. A pair of carved royal seats for the chief and his wife share the same wall. Other notable features of the house are the plethora of pig's jaws hanging from the rafters, and the huge hearth at the back of the room.

Travel details

North Sumatra has a reasonably large and efficient transport network. Don't despair if the bus times given here don't tie in with your plans: there are dozens of minibuses, bemos and labi-labi also plying the routes.

Buses

Where the bus frequency is not given, buses depart at least once an hour.

Berastagi to: Kutacane (daily 9am; 6hr); Medan (2hr); Parapat (via Kabanjahe and Pematangsiantar; daily 6hr).

Bukit Lawang to: Berastagi (tourist bus, twice daily; 5hr); Medan (every 30min, last at 6pm; 3hr).

Gunung Sitoli to: Teluk Dalam (every 30min, last at 4pm; 6hr).

Medan (Amplas terminal) to: Bukittinggi (half hourly; 18hr); Jakarta (hourly; 48hr); Padang (four daily; 20hr); Parapat (hourly, last at 6pm; 3hr); Sibolga (daily at 6pm; 12hr).

Medan (Padang Bulan) to: Berastagi (every 20min; 2hr).

Medan (Pinang Baris terminal) to: Bukit Lawang (every 30min until 6pm; 3hr).

Parapat to: Berastagi (via Kabanjahe and Siantar; 6hr); Bukittinggi (6 daily; 14hr); Jakarta (3 daily; 43hr); Medan (10 daily, last at 11am; 3hr); Padang (3 daily; 16hr); Sibolga (3 daily at 12pm; 6hr).

Sibolga to: Bukittinggi (3 daily; 12hr); Medan (3 daily; 8hr); Parapat (daily; 6hr).

Trains

Medan to: Balai (3 daily; 4hr); Binjai (3 daily; 30min); Pematangsiantar (3 daily; 3hr 30min).

Pelni ferries

For a chart of the Pelni routes, see p.42.

Gunung Sitoli to: Padang (*KM Umsini*, fortnightly; 12hr/*KM Lambelu*, fortnightly, Sat 9am; 15hr); Sibolga (*Sumber Rezeki*, daily except Sun, 10am; 10hr).

Medan (Belawan harbour) to: Jakarta (Tanjung Priok harbour) (*KM Kelud*, five weekly; 44hr; *KM Kambuna*, fortnightly, 30hr); Penang (*KM Bahagia*, Mon & Tues 2.30pm, Thurs noon, Sat 10am; 4hr/*KM Perdana*, Wed, Fri & Sun 10am; 4hr).

Sibolga to: Gunung Sitoli (*KM Umsini*, fortnightly, Sat 10am; 4hr).

Other ferries

Ajibata to: Tomok (5 daily; 45min).

Ambarita to: Haranggaol (Mon 6.30am; 3hr); Parapat (hourly 6.45am–4.45pm; 45min); Tongging (Tues 9am; 3hr 30min).

Gunung Sitoli to: Sibolga (*KM Cucit/Poncan Mo'ale*, daily except Sun 8pm; 8hr).

Haranggaol to: Ambarita (Mon 1pm; 3hr); Simanindo (Mon 1pm, Thurs 7pm; 1hr 10min).

Parapat to: Ambarita (hourly 8.45am–6.45pm; 45min); Tuk Tuk (roughly every 2hrs 8.30am–9.00pm; 30min).

Pulau Simeleue (Sinabang) to: Meulaboh (Tues, Thurs & Sat 6pm; 12hr).

Pulau Weh (Balohan) to: Banda Aceh (2 daily 10am & 2.30pm; 2hr 30min).

Sibolga to: Gunung Sitoli (*KM Cucit/Poncan Moale*, daily except Sun 8pm; 8hr/*Sumber Rezeki*, daily except Sun 6pm; 10hr).

Simanindo to: Haranggaol (Mon 9am; 1hr 10min).

Tongging to: Ambarita (Mon 9am; 3hr 30min); Tuk Tuk (Mon 9am; 3hr 45min).

Tuk Tuk to: Parapat (hourly 7am–2pm; 30min); Tongging (Tues 10am; 3hr 45min).

Flights

Gunung Sitoli to: Medan (3 weekly, Mon, Wed, Fri 12pm; 1hr 10min); Padang (weekly; 1hr).

Medan to: Batam (3 weekly; 1hr 15min); Dumai (weekly; 1hr 25min); Gunung Sitoli (3 weekly, Mon, Wed, Fri 7am; 1hr 10min); Jakarta (10 daily; 2hr 15min); Kuala Lumpur (1 or 2 daily; 1hr); Padang (2 daily; 1hr 10min); Pekanbaru (daily; 2hr); Penang (2 or 3 weekly; 40min); Sibolga (6 weekly; 1hr); Sinabang (3 weekly; 1hr 20min); Singapore (3 or 4 daily; 1hr 30min).

Meulaboh to: Medan (SMAC, 3 weekly; 1hr 45min).

Sibolga to: Medan (6 weekly; 1hr).

6

Padang and central Sumatra

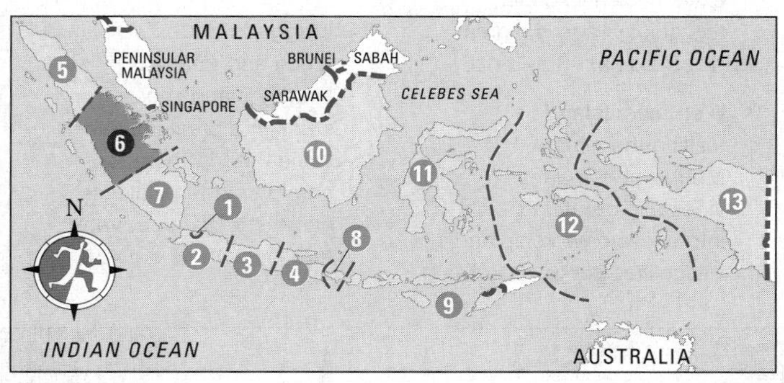

CHAPTER 6

Highlights

* **Padang cuisine** Home to Indonesia's best-loved and most varied cuisine, the sensual overload of Padang's local restaurants are a must. See p.400

* **Bukittinggi** The dramatic Harau canyon and the ancient Minang court ruins are a short hop from Bukittinggi. See p.404

* **Maninjau** Edging a blue lake, at the summit of an extinct volcanic crater, this quiet village is a great place to relax. See p.418

* **Mentawai Islands** Visiting the remote Mentawai Islands provides a fascinating insight into ancestor worship and village life. See p.420

* **Kerinci-Seblat national park** Sumatra's largest national park is home to elephants, tigers and rhinos, as well as the picture-book cone of Mount Kerinci. See p.427

* **Pasar Baru, Tanjung Pinang** An assault of tastes and smells, this traditional covered market makes for one of the richest scenes of local colour in Sumatra. See p.450

* **Lingga Islands** The green and peaceful Lingga Islands seem stuck in a previous age, while the trip there, on an old wooden Chinese cargo ship, is an adventure in itself. See p.456

6

Padang and central Sumatra

Central Sumatra is dominated by the soaring Bukit Barisan mountain range, and characterized by cool upland valleys, mountain lakes and innumerable jungle-covered peaks. The range drops steeply to the Indian Ocean on the west coast and slopes more gently to the eastern plains, providing the source of the huge river systems – the Siak, Kampar, Indragiri and Batanghari – that cross the eastern plains on their meandering way to the Malacca Straits and the South China Sea.

Major **gateways** into Indonesia are provided by the west coast port of **Padang** and the islands of **Batam** and **Bintan** in the Riau Archipelago, between the Sumatran mainland and Singapore: the islands have excellent transport connections to the rest of the country. Travellers entering Sumatra through the Riau Islands can transit in the prosperous city of **Pekanbaru** before heading north to Medan and Danau Toba, south to Bandar Lampung, perhaps via the little-visited city of **Jambi**, or west to Bukittinggi, the main tourist destination in the region.

The heartland of Minang culture, **Bukittinggi** is a cool and relaxed town with a thriving travellers' scene, perched picturesquely on the edge of the Ngarai Sianok Canyon, within sight of Gunung Merapi and Gunung Singgalang. Nearby, **Danau Maninjau** is developing plenty of low-key lakeside guesthouses: what it lacks in scale compared to Danau Toba, it makes up for in atmosphere and tranquillity. Further south lies the **Kerinci-Seblat national park**, one of the largest and most diverse parks in Indonesia, with a rich plant and animal life and a huge number of ecosystems, home to the (possibly mythological) *orang pendek*, the local equivalent of the Himalayan yeti. The second highest peak in Indonesia, Gunung Kerinci (3805m) is, with care and preparation, a feasible summit for fit trekkers, but the park also offers less demanding treks. The **Mentawai Islands** lie 100km off the west coast of Sumatra, separated by the 2000-metre-deep Mentawai Strait, and are inhabited by groups of people who have long been isolated from the Sumatran mainland and who manage to maintain a traditional way of life.

For those with the time and inclination, it's possible to meander through the back roads of central Sumatra, not only to avoid a lengthy haul on major roads, but to visit some pleasant villages and towns and see the glorious scenery on the coastal route **south to Bengkulu**.

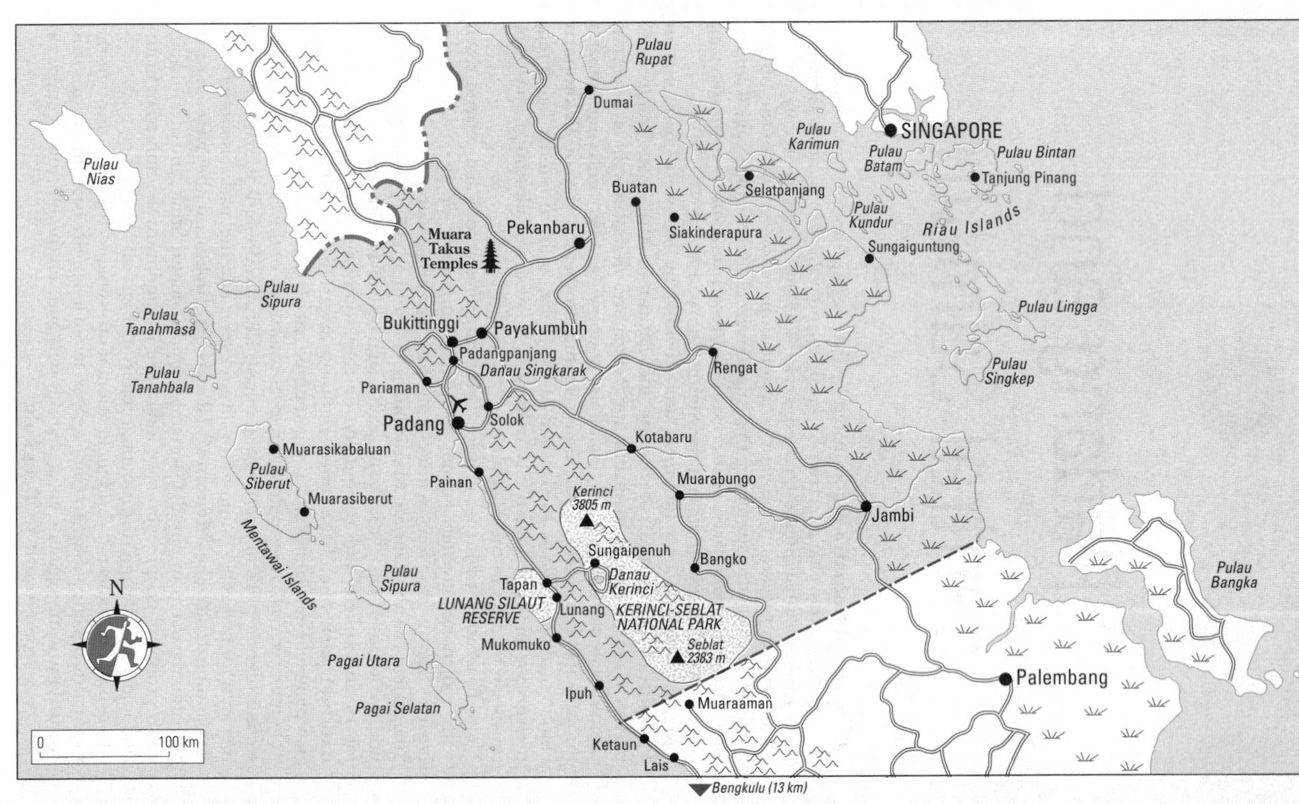

Pulau Rupat
Dumai
Pulau Karimun
SINGAPORE
Pulau Batam
Pulau Bintan
Tanjung Pinang
Buatan
Selatpanjang
Siakinderapura
Pulau Kundur
Riau Islands
Sungaiguntung
Pekanbaru
Muara Takus Temples
Pulau Nias
Pulau Sipura
Pulau Lingga
Pulau Tanahmasa
Bukittinggi
Payakumbuh
Padangpanjang
Danau Singkarak
Rengat
Pulau Singkep
Pulau Tanahbala
Pariaman
Solok
Padang
Kotabaru
Muarasikabaluan
Pulau Siberut
Painan
Muarabungo
Muarasiberut
Kerinci 3805 m
Jambi
Mentawai Islands
Sungaipenuh
Bangko
Pulau Bangka
Pulau Sipura
Tapan
Danau Kerinci
LUNANG SILAUT RESERVE
Lunang
KERINCI-SEBLAT NATIONAL PARK
N
Mukomuko
Seblat 2383 m
Pagai Utara
Palembang
Ipuh
Muaraaman
Pagai Selatan
0
100 km
Ketaun
Lais
Bengkulu (13 km)

Getting around the area on public transport can be gruelling. Whilst long-distance buses are regular and frequent, the distances involved are great. The roads, like those on the rest of Sumatra, are tortuous, and the driving can be hair-raising in the extreme. There are plenty of road connections on to Java from even the smallest towns, but if you intend to use sea or air to make your trip less stressful, you'll need to plan carefully, as only the large cities have airports, and ferry connections are generally irregular, especially on the west coast.

The **climate** of the area is far from temperate. The city of Padang, on the western side of the Bukit Barisan range where the precipitation of the Indian Ocean is dumped as the moisture-laden winds rise over the mountains, is extremely hot and humid and an awful sweaty shock if you're flying in from cooler climes. It has the highest rainfall in Indonesia, with a yearly average of 4508mm – putting it in the top ten of rainiest inhabited spots in the world. Pekanbaru and Jambi on the eastern side of the island can be just as hot, but as they are in the rain shadow they have a drier, more tolerable climate. Throughout the region, the mountains offer a pleasant relief from the heat, and up on the summit of Gunung Kerinci temperatures as low as 5°C are common.

Some history

The history of the Padang hinterland, the Minang highlands (see p.404), and the Kerinci area (see p.427) is traceable back to prehistoric times, but settlement of the west-coast areas took place rather later. Reefs off the west coast made it difficult for ships to negotiate, and until the sixteenth century all trade routes were along the Malacca Straits to the east of Sumatra. The most famous **ancient kingdom** in this area, the Malayu, based on Sungai Batang Hari near Jambi, flourished from the seventh to the thirteenth centuries and was located in the east of the island, open to outside influences from that direction: remains at Muara Takus suggest Buddhism had reached the island as early as the ninth century.

Late in the seventeenth century, the **British**, driven by the Dutch East India Company from their major Indonesian stronghold at Banten in 1682, began to expand their interests in Sumatra; they controlled the port of Padang from 1781 to 1784, and again between 1795 and 1816, shipping coffee to America. However, life and trade was seriously interrupted by war in the Minang highlands, which broke out in 1803 between the traditional long-established Minangkabau rulers and the **Paderi**, fundamental Muslim reformers. In some valleys, the Paderi gained control without a fight, while in others fierce fighting raged for years. The British had operated as arbitrators to some extent, a role which the **Dutch** inherited when they took over the region. (The **conflict** between the colonial powers had been long and intense, and it was only at end of the Napoleonic Wars in 1816 that Britain was forced to return Holland's prewar holdings to them). The Dutch signed a treaty with the Minangkabau nephew of the Raja Alam of Pagarruyung and built a fort at Bukittinggi. Eventually, after years of fierce resistance in the so-called **Paderi Wars**, the Dutch gained control of the entire area in 1837 on the death of Imam Bonjol, the Paderi leader.

The Dutch victory united the Minang highlands and Padang under one administration. Enforced production of **coffee** in the highlands continued, increasingly with conditions that only benefited the Dutch. In 1868, the discovery of a **coalfield** along Sungai Umbilin began years of debate about the best method of exploitation of the resource, eventually resulting in the construction of a **railway** between the highlands and **Padang**, which was completed in 1896. The city began to thrive: ships called at the port to stock up with coal, and Teluk Bayur, the port for Padang, was constructed to cope with the traffic.

Dutch rule was not without its problems, and local Minangkabau, well-educated but unable to find jobs, took part in an armed uprising in 1926. When it was quashed by the Dutch, many of the participants were sent to Boven Digul, the prison camp in what is now West Papua. In modern times **Pekanbaru** has grown rich on the oil and gas fields that have boomed throughout Central Sumatra, providing about sixty percent of the total Indonesian output. The **Riau Islands** are the site of huge tourist and industrial investment and Padang is gradually opening up, with improved international air connections.

Padang and around

A bustling port and university city, attractive **PADANG**, with a population of over one million, is the administrative capital of West Sumatra province and the business and transport hub for the entire region. Situated on the north bank of Sungai Arau and ranging north for 10km between the coast and the Bukit Barisan mountains, the city is famed throughout Indonesia as the home of *Makanan Padang* (Padang food), whose typically spicy dishes feature large amounts of chillies, served on individual small plates from which every diner takes their pick. The city's roads are broad and leafy, and many of the modern buildings show the influence of Minang architecture, usually in their impressive, soaring roofs. Public transport is easy to negotiate and there are excellent air, road and sea connections both throughout the region and on to other islands, with a number of worthwhile **excursions** possible to nearby beaches and islands. However, most tourists pause only briefly in Padang, the majority aiming for the nearby hill town of Bukittinggi, the Mentawai Islands, the Kerinci-Seblat national park, or more distant Bengkulu.

Padang has always been an **ethnically mixed** place, the largest group being the Minangkabau people from the nearby highlands, plus Javanese, Chinese, Tamils and Niasans. The Niasans, from the Nias Islands (see p.381), are descendants of slaves brought to the mainland by the Dutch, while the Javanese are descended from nineteenth-century soldiers sent to help the Dutch in the Paderi Wars and convicts sent as forced labourers, with more recent arrivals coming as workmen and civil servants. The earliest Chinese migrants came in the late seventeenth century, and the Tamils arrived with the British army during their periods in control of the area.

Arrival, information and city transport

Padang is a **visa-free entry point** to Indonesia (see p.23). All flights land at **Tabing Airport**, 9km north of the city centre. The bank and moneychangers are located at the front of the international arrivals building, and there's a taxi ticket office – collect the fixed-price ticket from the office and pay the driver on arrival at your destination (prices within the city are around Rp20,000). Out on the main road (200m walk from the terminal), buses #14a and #14b (Rp700) stop just outside the airport gates: those heading to the left go into

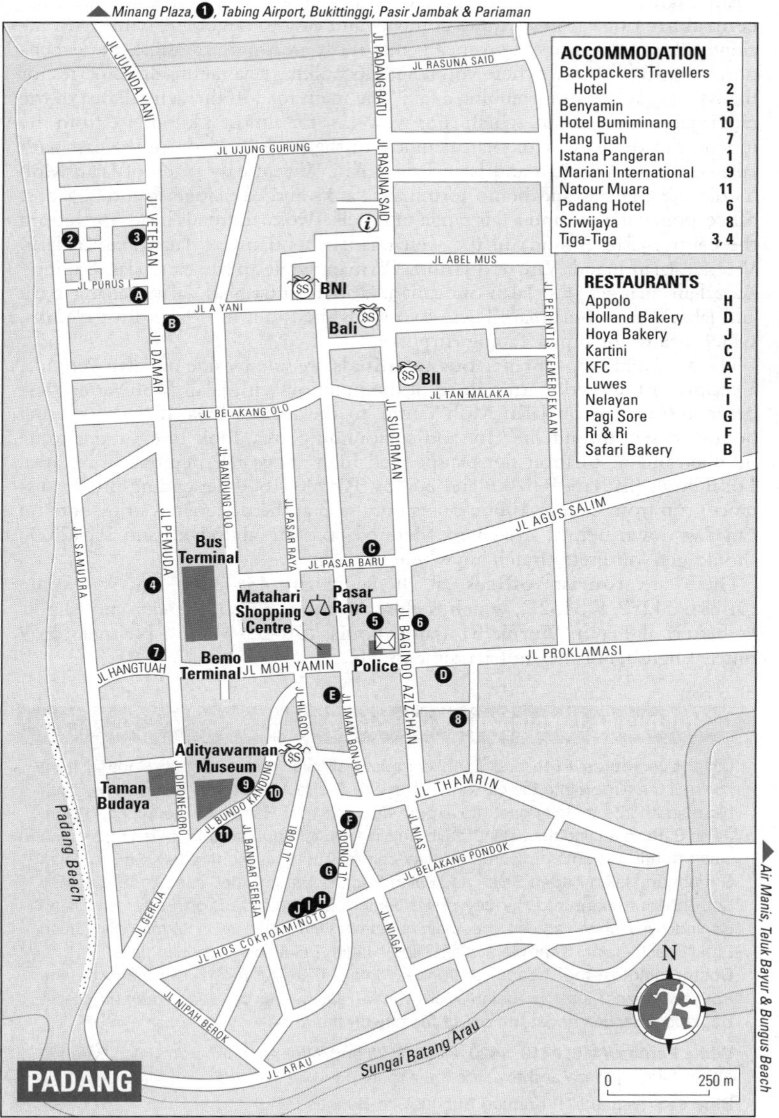

the city. Small white bemos also stop here and will take you to the bemo terminal in town for Rp700, the flat fare within the city. Pelni **boats** arrive at the port of Teluk Bayur, 7km south of town, from where you can take a white bemo to the city centre.

Although it sprawls inland and along the coast for several kilometres, the **central area** of Padang is quite compact and easy to negotiate, while the efficient public transport system means that most areas are accessible, the exception being Batau Arau, where you'll end up walking several hundred metres for the Mentawai boats or grabbing a taxi. The main road in the central area of the city is Jalan Moh Yamin, which runs west–east for almost a kilometre from the junction in the west with Jalan Pemuda, to the large junction in the east with Jalan Bagindo Azizchan and Jalan Proklamasi. Within easy reach of Jalan Moh Yamin are the bus and bemo terminals, banks and exchange facilities, a post office, police station, and a fair range of hotels. Two main roads head north from the centre: Jalan Pemuda in the west changes its name to Jalan Damar, Jalan Veteran, Jalan Juanda Yani and Jalan S. Parman, while in the east, Jalan Bagindo Azizchan changes into Jalan Sudirman, Jalan Rasuna Said, Jalan Padang Baru and Jalan Khatib Sulaiman. These two roads then join into Jalan Prof Hamka, which heads north past Tabing Airport.

The local and long-distance **bus terminals** are side by side on Jalan Pemuda, a couple of hundred metres north of the junction with Jalan Moh Yamin. The bemo terminal is on Jalan Moh Yamin, in the market area. If you are using bemos to get around the city and surrounding area, look out for the route number and destination signs suspended high above the bemo waiting area. Local buses (flat fare Rp700) and bemos (Rp500–1000 depending on the distance) run from 6am to 10pm. Buses only stop at the designated stops, but you can flag down bemos anywhere. Metered taxis are abundant, and Rp12,000 should get you pretty much anywhere in town.

There are **tourist offices** at Jl Sudirman 43 (Mon–Fri 9am–4pm; Ⓣ0751/34232, Ⓕ34321), which is closer to the centre of the city, and (slightly better) Jl Hayan Wuruk 51 (same hours; Ⓣ0751/34186). Neither speak much English, but they're friendly enough.

Useful bus and bemo routes in Padang

Local **bus routes #14a** and **#14b** complete circular routes around Padang from north of the airport into the city and out again. The routes are very similar. They both head south into the city past the airport via Jalan Prof Hamka to the Minang Plaza, Jalan S. Parman and the Jalan Khatib Sulaiman junction. The #14a then heads along Jalan Khatib Sulaiman towards the city centre. The #14b continues south to Jalan S. Parman, Jalan Raden Saleh and Jalan Padang Baru; it then joins #14a and they both head straight into the city down Jalan Rasuna Said, Jalan Sudirman, Jalan Bagindo Azizchan, across the main junction with Jalan Moh Yamin and Jalan Proklamasi, Jalan Thamrin, Jalan Nias, Jalan Belakang Pondok, Jalan H.O.S. Cokroaminoto, the beach entrance, Jalan Gereja, Jalan Diponegoro, the Adityawarman Museum, Jalan Moh Yamin, Jalan Hilgoo, Jalan Thamrin, Jalan Bagindo Azizchan and north out of the city on the route they have come in on.

White bemos #416, **#419**, **#420**, **#422**, **#423** and **#424** run north from Jalan Pemuda out to Minang Plaza and towards the airport.

Blue #437, signed "Tl Kabung Bungus", to Bungus Beach.

White #423 to Pasir Jambak.

Blue #402 to Air Manis.

Blue #432, **#433**, **#434** to Teluk Bayur.

Moving on from Padang

The **long-distance bus terminal** (Rp200 entrance) on Jalan Pemuda is the departure point for all buses, and where you'll find most of the ticket offices; the rest are located on Jalan Pemuda. All bus companies operate their own schedule with their own fares so it's worth shopping around. There are daily departures (6am–7pm) to destinations throughout Sumatra, Java, Bali and Nusa Tenggara.

Pelni **ferries** call at Teluk Bayur, which is on the fortnightly circuit of *KM Lambelu* and *KM Kambuna* (see p.465). The Pelni office is at Jl Tanjung Priok 32 (Ⓣ0751/61624) at Teluk Bayur, 7km south of Padang.

There are plentiful **airline connections**, both domestic and international, from Tabing Airport. If you're heading straight up to Bukittinggi from the airport, cross the road and hail long-distance buses heading in the opposite direction: they pass every twenty minutes or so during the daylight hours. Although there's talk of reinstating them, at present there are no passenger **rail** services in the area.

Accommodation

As with most Sumatran cities, **accommodation** in Padang is aimed largely at domestic business travellers. Mid-range and luxury hotels predominate, with an emphasis on facilities such as air-con and satellite TV rather than ambience. If you don't want to stay in the city itself, see p.403 for accommodation options within easy travelling distance, and remember that Bukittinggi (see p.404) is only two hours' drive away, with very frequent buses plying the route.

Backpackers Travellers Hotel Jl Pursus 2, 13 Ⓣ0751/34261, Ⓕ34265. Dorms and rooms with and without attached mandi in the middle of a residential area and near a beach. It's a little hard to find: travelling north (away from the bus terminal) along Jalan Veteran, take the first left after *KFC* (there's a green "Bukit Barisan" bungalow on the corner) onto Jalan Purus I. Carry on for 100m, passing a side road, turn right along a filthy canal and take the second left. ❷

Benyamin Jl Pasar Baru IV Ⓣ0751/22324. In a small alleyway that runs off Jalan Bagindo Azizchan, served by the #14a and #14b buses. Clean fan rooms with attached bathrooms are in two-storey buildings around a central courtyard. The only down side is the early-morning noise from the nearby market area. ❷

Hotel Bumiminang Jl Bundo Kandung 20–28 Ⓣ0751/37555, Ⓕ37567. The most luxurious and most expensive hotel in Padang, the four-star Bumiminang offers everything that a top-class hotel should, with pool, tennis courts, business centre and tasteful communal areas in a central location. ❼

Hang Tuah Jl Pemuda 1 Ⓣ0751/26556, Ⓕ26558. The best and most popular of the hotels near the bus terminal, on the corner of Jalan Pemuda and Jalan Hang Tuah. There's a range of basic but adequate rooms with fan and attached cold-water mandi, up to those with air-con and satellite TV. ❸

Istana Pangeran Jl Veteran 79 Ⓣ0751/51333, Ⓕ54613. Between the city centre and airport, close to a rather unattractive local beach, this is one of the top Padang hotels, and is very popular with tour groups. There's a good-sized swimming pool (non-guests can use this for Rp10,000) and tennis courts (rackets available at the hotel). Rooms are comfortably furnished, and communal areas are attractive and welcoming. ❺

Mariani International Jl Bundo Kandung 35 Ⓣ0751/25466, Ⓕ25410. Centrally situated opposite the *Bumiminang*, this hotel offers comfortably furnished rooms with attached cold-water mandi and air-con as well as more expensive rooms with hot water. The communal areas are nothing special, but the location is convenient for the city centre, and motorbike rental is available. ❹–❺

Natour Muara Jl Gereja 34 Ⓣ0751/35600, Ⓕ31163. Located near the museum and beach, with a quiet atmosphere and an attractive outdoor dining area. The rooms are pleasant but not outstanding and the cheaper ones overlook the car park. There's no pool. ❺

Padang Hotel Jl Bagindo Azizchan 28 Ⓣ0751/31383, Ⓕ35962. Rather overpriced, but with passable and clean rooms in bizarre semi-roofed corridors; there's air-con and TV at the top end. Served by the #14a and #14b buses in both directions. ❸–❺

Sriwijaya Jalan Alanglawas Ⓣ0751/23577. This

budget option is tucked away in a quiet road that runs south from Jalan Proklamasi, about a ten-minute walk from the #14a and #14b bus routes. The compound is quiet and rooms are basic, but there are small sitting areas outside each. The staff are welcoming, but speak little English. ❷

Tiga-Tiga Jl Pemuda 31 ☎0751/22633. The older of the two hotels in town with this name is opposite the bus terminal, an unprepossessing downstairs giving way to a pleasant upstairs sitting area – the lighter, airier rooms are on the upper floors and a good choice of accommodation is on offer. The cheapest have no fan, and outside mandi, while the most expensive have attached bathroom and air-con. ❷–❸

Tiga-Tiga Jl Veteran 33 ☎0751/22173. The newer *Tiga-Tiga* is further out from the city centre than its namesake, about 3km north, and is pleasant and clean with slightly better and more expensive rooms. ❷–❸

The City

With some shopping, a visit to the museum and trips to nearby beaches, it's possible to pass a pleasant couple of days in Padang; the climate is not particularly conducive to long **walking tours** of the city. The Chinatown area (Kampung Cina), roughly bounded by Jalan H.O.S. Cokroaminoto, Jalan Pondok and Jalan Dobo, features traditional shophouses and herbalists, as well as restaurants and coffee shops (see opposite) in which to cool off. Just south of here, between Jalan H.O.S. Cokroaminoto and Jalan Arau, is the Muara district – now very dilapidated, but still the commercial area serving the port, and with a couple of good examples of faded colonial architecture.

The **Adityawarman Museum** (Tues–Sun 9am–4pm; Rp1500) is housed in a large *rumah gadang*, a traditional Minang house, with some great carved woodwork and an attractive red-tiled roof and traditional rice barns at the front, set in well-maintained grounds. It's one of the most pleasant museums in Sumatra: the rooms are light and airy and the grounds are a popular meeting and picnic place for local people, especially at weekends. There's some attempt to label the exhibits in English, although the usual range of farm implements, musical instruments, carpentry tools, textiles, old banknotes and weapons isn't exactly a revelation, but the displays relating to Minangkabau culture, plus the textiles, kris and finely worked basketware, all make a visit worthwhile.

For a good **local shopping** experience, ignore the large new shopping centres (see "Listings" on p.402) and head instead for Pasar Raya in the city centre, a terrific **market**, awash with fruit and vegetables, cooking ingredients, household goods and clothes.

Padang beach is accessed from the southern end of Jalan Samudra near the junction with Jalan Gereja. Though many local people are quite dismissive of it – the sand is dark and the area is popular and decidedly scruffy – it's lively and sociable around sunset and at weekends, when the warung and the drink carts arrive.

Eating

It makes little sense to come to the homeland of **Padang food** without visiting at least one of the city's **restaurants**, distinguishable by dishes overflowing with curries piled up in their windows. There's no menu: you simply tell staff you want to eat and up to a dozen small plates are placed in front of you (see pp.48–50 for details of the most common dishes on offer). However, it's a cuisine with problems for vegetarians – make sure there are some eggs or tofu on offer before you sit down – and it's usually extremely spicy. Generally, the redder the sauce, the more explosive it is to the taste buds: the yellow, creamy dishes are often milder, but there's also an innocent-looking volcanic green sauce.

At the southern end of Jalan Pondok, due south of the market area towards the river, you'll find a small **night market** of sate stalls, and this street, and nearby Jalan Niaga, has a range of good places. Another night market operates on Jalan Imam Bonjol, a few hundred metres south of the junction with Jalan Moh Yamin. For fast food, try *KFC* at Jalan Bundo Kandung and Jalan Veteran – expensive, but a cool haven on a hot day.

Appolo Jalan Hos Cokroaminoto. A busy Chinese seafood place; it fills up fast with locals at night, so come early.
Holland Bakery and Cake Shop Jl Proklamasi 61b. With a good choice of cakes and sweet breads, this is especially popular at weekends with local people.
Hoya Bakery Jl H.O.S. Cokroaminoto 48. A thriving bakery with a small coffee shop attached.
Kartini Jl Pasar Baru 24. The most popular of the many Padang-style restaurants along this street. They are used to tourists and the food is fresh and well cooked, with all the usual Padang specialities on offer.
Luwes Jalan Imam Bonjol. Very popular with families, this simple fried rice and noodles place is inexpensive, friendly and has great food. Open till late.
Matahari Foodcourt 2nd floor, Matahari Shopping Centre. Air-con, with a wide range of Indonesian options such as soup, gado-gado, sate, *murtabak*, drinks and juices.
Nelayan Jl H.O.S. Cokroaminoto 44a–b. Expensive Chinese and seafood specialist, with an air-con first floor. The food is good, the menu vast (five types of fish alone, cooked in four different ways), but it's the place for an expensive blowout rather than everyday eating.
Pagi Sore Jl Dobi 143. A popular and good-value Padang restaurant with plenty of choice, one of the nicest of the many restaurants on this road.
Ri & Ri Jalan Pondok. Pleasantly decorated, with a relaxed atmosphere, this is both a Padang place (10am–2pm) and a slightly plusher restaurant in the evening, when there's a menu offering frog, chicken, squid and goat dishes, as well as the basic rice and noodle options.
Safari Bakery Jalan Damar, at the corner with Jalan A. Yani. Popular bakery and coffee shop, often crowded with students.

Entertainment

The Taman Budaya **cultural centre** is on Jalan Diponegoro, close to the museum. It hosts the occasional cultural show or concert, but appears to be largely underused, and during the day is almost totally deserted. Look out around town for posters advertising events, or enquire at the tourist offices.

Tabut

Although for much of the year there's little to attract visitors to the coastal town of **Pariaman**, 36km north of Padang, the annual **Tabut festival**, held from the first to the tenth of the Islamic month of Muharam (moveable in the Western calendar, but around June to August), is the highlight of the West Sumatran cultural calendar, also celebrated in Bengkulu as the Tabot festival (see p.59). Access to Pariaman is by bus from either Padang or Bukittinggi.

The festival is staged in honour of Hassan and Hussein, Mohammed's grandsons, who were martyred at the Battle of Karbela defending their religion. A magical *bouraq*, a winged horse with the head of a woman, was believed to have rescued the souls of the heroes and carried them to heaven. Local villages compete to create the grandest *bouraq* effigies, and on the final day they are paraded through the streets accompanied by much music, dancing and festivity. Two *bouraq* meeting on the route indulge in a mock battle with much praise of their own *bouraq* and hurling of insults at others. The procession ends at the coast, where the effigies are flung into the sea followed closely by local people who want to grab mementos – the gold necklaces decorating the effigies are the most prized. Horse races, swimming contests and cultural performances accompany the event. Enquire at the tourist office if you are in the area at this time.

Currently popular **discos** are the *President*, in the cinema complex on the corner of Jalan Khatib Sulaiman and Jalan Joni Anwar, north of the centre, and the *Luky* on Jalan Diponegoro, a few hundred metres south of the museum. Both operate daily (10pm–2am) and the Rp11,000 cover charge includes a drink.

Shopping

Whilst you are unlikely to head to Padang for your main souvenir shopping (Bukittinggi offers a far better choice), you'll find everyday necessities at the **Matahari Shopping Centre** on Jalan Moh Yamin. The gleaming **Minang Plaza**, 7km north of the city centre on Jalan Prof Hamka, houses three floors of shops and fast-food outlets including the Suzuyu Department Store. **Postcards** are elusive: try Gramedia Bookstore on Jalan Damar, but don't hold out too much hope for English-language novels – they are virtually nonexistent between the secondhand bookshops of Bukittinggi and Jakarta. For **souvenirs**, Sartika, Jl Sudirman 5, has a considerable range of stuff; modern handicrafts including purses and baskets start at the Rp5000 mark, and there are textiles plus a range of wooden carvings from the Batak and Nias areas of Sumatra as well as further afield from Lombok and Maluku (up to Rp500,000).

Listings

Airline offices Garuda, Jl Jend. Sudirman 2 ⓣ0751/30737, ⓕ30174; Mandala, Jl Pemuda 29a ⓣ0751/32773, ⓕ33184, and Jl Veteran 20 ⓣ0751/33100; Merpati, in the grounds of the *Panguaran Beach Hotel*, Jl Ir. H. Juanda 79 ⓣ0751/444831, ⓕ444834; Pelangi, Jl Gereja 34, in the grounds of the *Natour Muara Hotel* ⓣ0751/38103, ⓕ38104; Silk Air, in the *Hotel Bumiminang*, Jl Bundo Kandung ⓣ0751/38120, ⓕ38122.
Banks and exchange BCA, Jl H. Agus Salim 10a; Bank Dagang Negara, Jl Bagindo Azizchan 21; BNI, Jl Dobi 1. There are several moneychangers near the bus station offering slightly poorer rates but longer hours and less paperwork: PT Citra Setia Prima, Jl Diponegoro 5 (Mon–Sat 8am–noon & 1–4.30pm); PT Enzet Corindo Perkasa, Jl Pemuda 17c (Mon–Fri 8am–4pm, Sat 8am–2pm).
Courier DHL is at PT Birotika Semesta, Jl Damar 57a ⓣ0751/22769; also at Jl Pemuda 51b ⓣ0751/33076, ⓕ62751.
Hospitals Rumah Sakit Umum Padang, Jalan Perentis Kemerdekan ⓣ0751/26585; Rumah Sakit Selasih, Jl Khatib Sulaiman 72 ⓣ0751/51405.
Immigration office Jalan Khatib Sulaiman ⓣ0751/55113.
Pharmacy There are many in the city; a reliable one is Apotic Bunda, Jl Veteran 4a ⓣ0751/28333.
Post office The main post office is conveniently located at Jl Bagindo Azizchan 7, just north of the junction with Jalan Moh Yamin. Poste restante here is reasonably efficient.
Telephone and fax The main Telkom office is several kilometres north of the city centre on Jalan Khatib Sulaiman, at the junction with Jalan K. Ahmad Dahlan. More convenient 24-hour wartels are found everywhere in the city.
Tour operators PT Bingkuang Mas Tours, Jl Veteran 32c (ⓣ0751/36950), offers Minangkabau tours from US$175 for three days and two nights, Siberut for seven days and six nights (from US$380) and Kerinci (from US$329) – all prices are per person and minimum numbers of two or four are required. They also have charter cars at Rp150,000 per day. Pacto Tours and Travel, Jl Tan Malaka 25 (ⓣ0751/37678, ⓕ33335), offers Minangkabau tours to the Bukittinggi area for three nights and four days (from US$195), and Siberut for seven days and six nights (from US$849), though you're advised to check the prices in Bukittinggi before signing up.

Nearby beaches and islands

The **beaches** and **islands** north and south of the city are easily accessible. Although not outstanding, there are some attractive spots with pleasant accommodation; ideal if you need to recover from long-distance travel.

Diving around Padang

Whilst still in its infancy, **diving** in the waters off Padang is enticing. This coast is the only part of Indonesia that touches the Indian Ocean, and features some species particular to those waters. Other advantages are that the water is generally warm and visibility good. There are several sites within an hour or two by motorboat from Padang, including Pulau Pandan, Pulau Sibuntar, Pulau Laut, and the Kapal Wreck, the remains of a cargo ship. However, the highlight of the area is **Pulau Pieh**, which features a submerged reef and a wreck. The only dive company in town is Padang Diving, Jl Batang Arau 88 B/6 ⓣ0751/25876, ⓕ28121. The prices depend on the number of people in the group, but are typically US$80 per person if there are three people, which includes transport, a diving guide, two full tanks, a weight belt and lunch; other equipment is available for rental.

Bungus beach

If you enquire locally for a good beach, people will direct you unerringly to **Bungus beach**, 20km south of Padang, easily reachable on blue bemo #437 (40min; Rp3000) from the city-centre terminal. The long curving white-sand bay enclosed by lush, jungle-covered headlands, with Pulau Kasik just offshore, is very enticing. Despite the oil depot at the far southern end of the bay and a plywood factory at the northern end, it's a pleasant spot, and you're far enough from both to enjoy the beach. The ocean is full of fishing boats, and you can see the boat-builders at work a few hundred metres to the north of the losmens. There's a range of economical beachside **accommodation**, a good choice being at Km21, where there's a surprisingly local flavour for such a popular spot. The *Knokke Inn* (ⓣ0751/171053; ❷–❸) comprises simple bamboo bungalows with attached bathrooms through to more spacious, attractive bungalows with air-con and bathtubs. All are on the beach, facing the ocean, and the large restaurant offers simple Indo-Chinese and travellers' fare. A five-minute walk north, *Carlos Coffee Shop and Losmen* (ⓣ0751/751153; ❷–❸) offers a lively coffee-shop scene and a range of basic bungalows. Trips to the nearby islands are available here, from Rp75,000 per person for the day. Another two or three minutes' walk north, *Pesona Restaurant* (ⓣ0751/751192) has a new set of clean, tiled bungalows (❸) attached.

The Bungus Islands

The scattered **Bungus Islands** are, as yet, little developed for tourism, and are best explored on a trip from Bungus beach (see above) – if one idyllic, unspoilt spot isn't quite to your liking, you can simply find another. If you want to stay on the islands, *Pusako Island Resort* (ⓣ0751/61777, ⓕ61774, or contact Pusako Sikuai Wisata, Jl Muara 38b, Padang ⓣ0751/37811, ⓕ22895; ❽) is a top-end resort with plenty of facilities on **Pulau Sikuai**, with accommodation in comfortable bungalows with air-con, hot water and TV. Further south, on larger, mountainous **Pulau Cubadak**, where there are opportunities for trekking and wildlife-spotting, *Paradiso Village* (contact INA Tours, *Hotel Dipo International*, Jl Diponegoro 25, Padang ⓣ0751/34261, ⓕ34265; ❽) is a similar development, with accommodation in two-storey wood-and-thatch bungalows. Canoe rental and boat trips are available. **Pulau Pagang**, a relatively unspoilt island, has a few bungalows on it (❹), and can be reached via *Carlos Coffee Shop* (see above).

Pasir Jambak

Pasir Jambak, 15km north of Padang, is a long, black-sand beach which you'll share only with local fisherfolk during the week. Take white bemo #423

(30min; Rp1000) to the entrance gate of the beach area (Sat & Sun Rp350). The sole **accommodation** place is *Uncle Jack's Homestay* (ⓣ0751/39739; ❷); either walk along the beach or head straight through the gateway and stay on the road for 2–3km – this is the shorter and easier route if you're lugging a pack. Accommodation is in basic rooms situated a few metres from the beach, some with mosquito nets and some without. Snorkelling trips to nearby **Pulau Sawo** are possible. It's definitely a very convenient beachside place for your last night if you're flying out from Padang, and staff can arrange a taxi to the airport.

Bukittinggi and the Minang highlands

As far as the eye could distinctly trace was one continued scene of cultivation interspersed with innumerable towns and villages, shaded by coconut and other fruit trees. I may safely say that this view equalled anything I ever saw in Java. The scenery is more majestic and grand, the population equally dense, and the cultivation equally rich.

Almost two hundred years later, Sir Stamford Raffles' description of the **Minang highlands** still rings at least partially true; whilst the area is densely populated and served by hectic roads, the gorgeous mountainous landscape, soaring rice terraces and easily accessible Minang culture make this a deservedly popular stop on any trip through Sumatra.

The Minang highlands consist of three large valleys. The **Agam Valley** runs north–south between the towering masses of Gunung Singgalang to the west and Gunung Merapi to the east, with **BUKITTINGGI**, a bustling hill town, the administrative and commercial centre of the whole district. The craft villages of Koto Gadang and Pandai Sikat are easily accessible in the Agam Valley, as is Batang Palupuh, which features the famous rafflesia flower. The **Limapuluh Valley** lies east of Bukittinggi, and has its commercial centre in the town of **Payakumbuh**. The road between Bukittinggi and Pekanbaru passes through this valley, from where there's a detour for the beautiful **Harau Canyon**, popular with local people and tourists alike. Centred around the town of **Batusangkar**, southeast of both Bukittinggi and soaring Gunung Merapi, the **Tanah Datar Valley** was the site of the **Minang court** for five hundred years from the fourteenth century: the wonderful **palace** at Pagaruyung is the finest surviving example of Minang architecture.

Located to the west of the main highland area, **Danau Maninjau** is rapidly developing as an appealing travellers' destination, though there's little to do but enjoy the cool air and beautiful scenery.

Some history

The origins of the **Minangkabau** people are shrouded in myth. One legend tells that they are descended from Iskander Zulkarnain (in some stories said to be Alexander the Great), who was the product of the union of Adam's youngest son with a fairy. Iskander's third son, Maharaj Diraja or Sri Maharajo Dirajo ("Glorious King of Kings"), reached Gunung Merapi at a time when the remainder of Sumatra was underwater, and he founded the first clan, which settled first in Pariangan on the southern slopes of the mountain.

The name "Minangkabau" has several possible origins. Some sources claim it comes from "*pinang kabhu*" which means "original home". Another legend tells

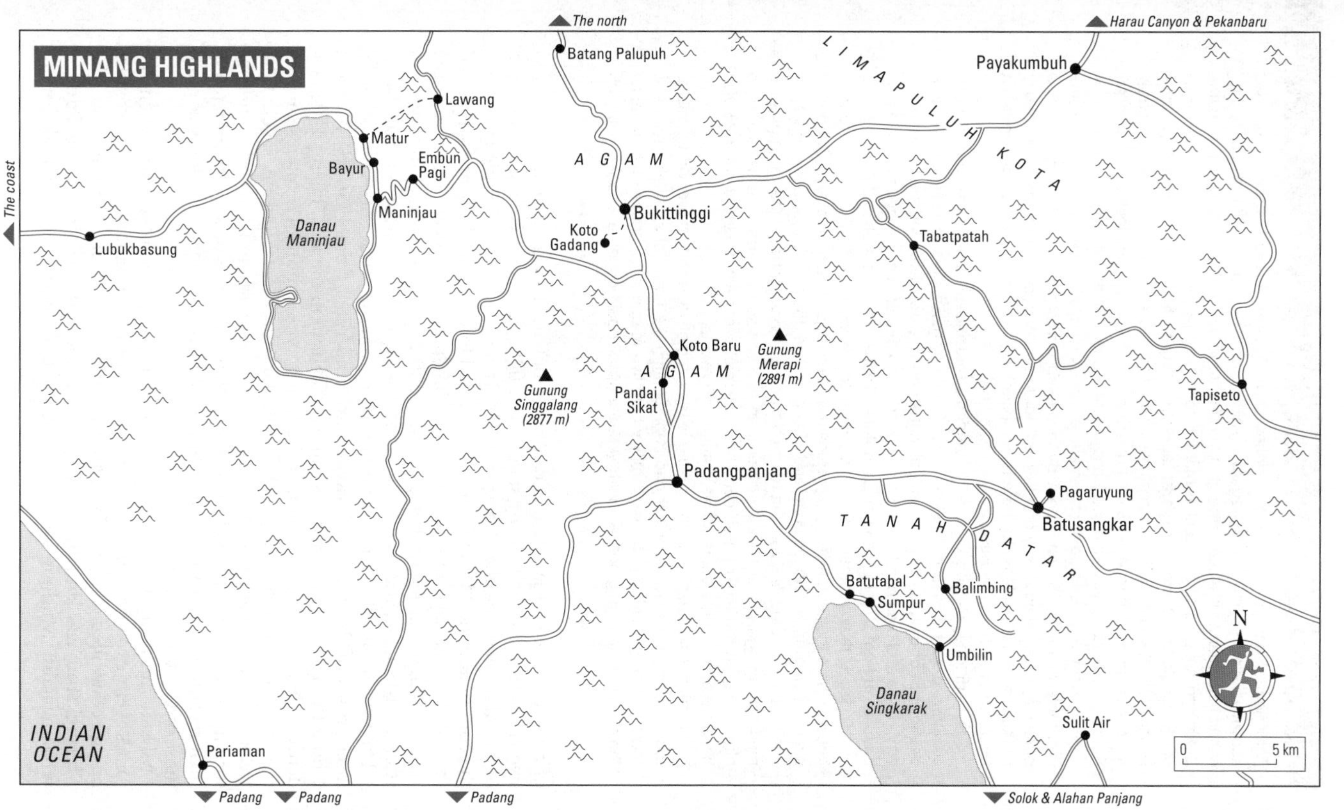
MINANG HIGHLANDS
The north
Harau Canyon & Pekanbaru
The coast
Batang Palupuh
Payakumbuh
Lawang
Matur
Bayur
Embun Pagi
Maninjau
Danau Maninjau
Lubukbasung
LIMAPULUH KOTA
AGAM
Bukittinggi
Koto Gadang
Tabatpatah
Koto Baru
Pandai Sikat
Gunung Merapi (2891 m)
Gunung Singgalang (2877 m)
Tapiseto
Padangpanjang
Pagaruyung
Batusangkar
TANAH DATAR
Batutabal
Sumpur
Balimbing
Umbilin
Danau Singkarak
Sulit Air
N
0
5 km
INDIAN OCEAN
Pariaman
Padang
Padang
Padang
Solok & Alahan Panjang

The Minangkabau

Throughout Sumatra and indeed Indonesia, you'll meet **Minangkabau** people, also known as Minang, who proudly regard the highlands (*darek*), around Bukittinggi as their cultural heartland. It's estimated that around four million Minangkabau live in the Bukittinggi area, but that at least as many, if not more, live outside, examples of the age-old Minangkabau custom of **merantau** – travelling to find one's fortune. Distinctive Minang architecture, colourful costumes and stylized, exuberant dances are easily accessible to visitors to West Sumatra, and across the entire archipelago the popular Padang restaurants serve the spicy and distinctive food of the Minang people.

While many of these traditions remain, especially in the rural area of the *darek*, the inevitable changes brought about by increased population, the shift away from a purely agricultural economy and the drift to urban centres has changed the society to the extent that, at least to the casual observer, there's often little to distinguish a Minang family from any other in West Sumatra.

The traditional Minang culture is staunchly **matrilineal**, one of the largest such societies extant. It's also Muslim, a combination that makes it appealing to academic anthropologists who have studied the people extensively. Inheritance of property, name and membership of the clan is through the female line, houses and fields passed on from a woman to her daughters. Traditionally, the males, often as young as 10, leave their mother's home to live in the *surau* (the men's religious prayer house) where they eat, sleep, pray, study the Koran and learn martial arts. Daughters stay in their mother's house up to and after marriage, their husbands occasional visitors to them in the *bilik* (sleeping room). As one writer described, "the Minangkabau man has no rights over his wife other than demanding that she remains faithful to him... she, on the other hand, can always demand that her husband come to visit her from time to time and fulfil his marital obligations."

The most visible aspect of the culture is the distinctive **architecture**, with massive roofs soaring skywards at either end, representing the horns of a buffalo. Typically, three or four generations of one family would live in one large house built on stilts, the *rumah gadang* (big house) or *rumah adat* (traditional house), a wood-and-thatch

of a fight between a Javanese and Minang buffalo; facing an attack by a massive Javanese army, the Minang suggested a fight between two buffaloes instead of a conflict between the two armies. The Javanese found a gigantic animal for the contest and the Minang a very small calf. However, the Minang had starved the calf for ten days and they tied an iron spike to its head. It mistook the Javanese buffalo for its mother, and savaged its opponent to death in its furious attempts to suckle, and thus became the *minang kerbau* ("victorious buffalo").

The first historical records of the area date from the fourteenth-century stone inscriptions of the ruler **Adityavarman**, who ruled from 1356 to 1375, and who is thought to have created a unified kingdom in the area. There's little evidence of his successors, though, in the seventeenth century, Portuguese envoys reported that three Minang rulers controlled the three highland valleys. The wealth and importance of the area in the fourteenth and fifteenth centuries sprung from the gold which was mined there, and the power accompanying such resources meant that at their height the Minangkabau kingdoms covered most of Central Sumatra.

Minang authority began to decline after the eighteenth century, when the mines were exhausted, the alternative crops of coffee, salt, gambir and textiles being controlled largely by Muslim traders. A frontal assault on the Minangkabau was launched in the early nineteenth century by the **Paderi**, fundamentalist Muslims intent on forcing the matriarchal Minangkabau to structure often decorated with fabulous wooden carvings. Each area of the house is decorated with a range of motifs with a particular significance. For example, one pattern may represent humility, another the difference between good and evil. Each has a row of separate bedrooms for the younger women who sleep with their children and are visited at night by their husbands. Older women and unmarried girls do not have separate bedrooms. In front of the line of sleeping rooms, a large meeting room is the focus of the social life of the house. Outside the big house, small rice barns, also of traditional design, hold the family stores.

Within one house, **authority** for internal matters resides with the oldest woman, advised by the *mamak* (mother's brother), the oldest male family member, who has responsibility for affairs outside the house and is the final authority over the children within it. Male representatives of the village meet together to decide affairs of communal importance, and are a large and diverse group made up of the male head of each clan, *penghulu*, the head of each *surau* and each *mamak*. However, while men have authority over matters in the village such as village land, only the women own the land and can pass it on.

Some authorities believe that this lack of important positions for young men in the villages drove them to *merantau*, from which they would ideally return with stories to tell, and goods with which to attract a wife. However, more recently this shift away has been permanent for many Minangkabau in search of employment or education, many taking wives and young children with them and some young, unmarried women even going on their own. While they may return to the village only rarely, they will invariably regard it as home.

Some of the Minang culture is accessible to visitors via **pencak silat**, the traditional martial art, taught to both men and women. You'll be able to see it, together with traditional dances, accompanied by a variation of a gamelan orchestra, in tourist performances in the Bukittinggi area (see p.411). Textiles and a variety of craft items are Minangkabau specialities – their jewellery and weaving are especially worth seeking out (see p.412).

adopt Islam, and abandon gambling, drinking, taking opium and betel. Violence was precipitated in 1803, and by 1815 the Paderi had control of much of the Minang highlands. In 1821 the Dutch became involved, signing an agreement with the nephew of the Raja Alam of Pagarruyung (who may or may not have had the right to sign it), whereby they were given the Tanah Datar Valley. They built Fort de Kock, in the area now called Bukittinggi, and joined with the remaining Minangkabau leaders to fight the Paderi. It was a long campaign and not until 1837, when they captured the renowned Paderi leader Imam Bonjol in his home in Bonjol, did the tide really turn. The fighting stopped the next year, with the Minang highlands under Dutch control. However the war had a long-term impact, cementing devout Islamic ideas alongside a large number of traditional beliefs and customs or *adat*.

Arrival, orientation and information

Whilst a few long-distance tourist services may drop you at your hotel of choice (check at the time of booking), other **long-distance buses** terminate at the Air Kuning terminal, 3km southeast of the town centre. Buses from Padang stop on the southern outskirts of town on Jalan Sudirman before turning off for the terminal; you can get a red #14 or #19 bemo into the town centre from this junction, and all but one of the accommodation options are within an easy walk of the route.

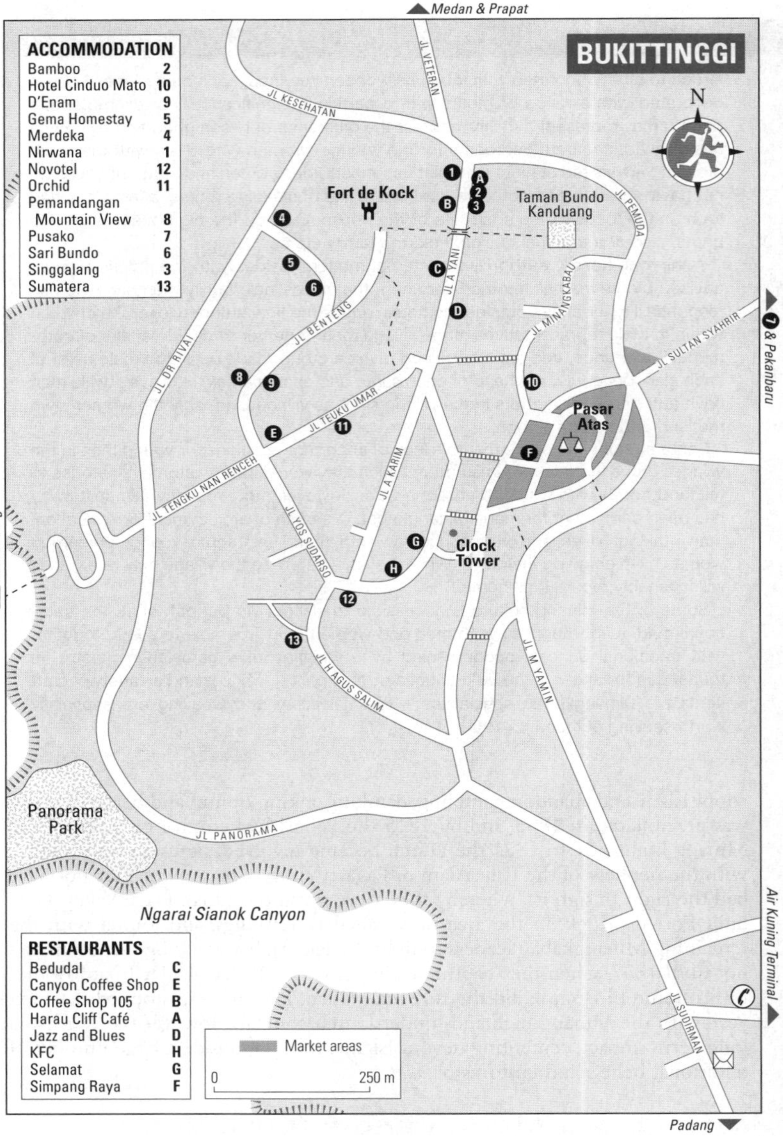

Medan & Prapat
BUKITTINGGI
N
ACCOMMODATION
Bamboo 2
Hotel Cinduo Mato 10
D'Enam 9
Gema Homestay 5
Merdeka 4
Nirwana 1
Novotel 12
Orchid 11
Pemandangan Mountain View 8
Pusako 7
Sari Bundo 6
Singgalang 3
Sumatera 13
JL VETERAN
JL KESEHATAN
Fort de Kock
Taman Bundo Kanduang
JL PEMUDA
JL A YANI
JL MINANGKABAU
JL BENTENG
JL DR RIVAI
JL SULTAN SYAHRIR
7 & Pekanbaru
Pasar Atas
JL TEUKU UMAR
JL A KARIM
JL TENGKU NAN RENCEH
JL YOS SUDARSO
Clock Tower
Koto Gadang
JL H AGUS SALIM
JL M YAMIN
Panorama Park
JL PANORAMA
Ngarai Sianok Canyon
Air Kuning Terminal
RESTAURANTS
Bedudal C
Canyon Coffee Shop E
Coffee Shop 105 B
Harau Cliff Café A
Jazz and Blues D
KFC H
Selamat G
Simpang Raya F
Market areas
0
250 m
JL SUDIRMAN
Padang

Situated on the eastern edge of the Ngarai Sianok Canyon and with the mountains of Merapi and Singgalang rising to the south, Bukittinggi spreads for several kilometres in each direction into adjoining suburbs, before fading into open fields. However, the central part of town, which is of most interest to visitors, is relatively compact and easy to negotiate. The most useful landmark is the clock tower just south of the market area at the junction of Jalan

Moving on from Bukittinggi

All local and long-distance buses leave from the Aur Kuning terminal to the south-east of the town centre, where you'll find the ticket offices. **Local buses** operate from 7am to 5pm although, as usual, frequency tails off in the afternoon. There are departures throughout the day to Padang, Solok, Batusangkar, Payakumbuh, Maninjau, Bukit Palupuh and Bonjol. For **long-distance** destinations, there are several companies (see p.413), but it's worth booking two or three days ahead to get the departure and seat you want. Destinations include Aceh, Sibolga, Parapet, Medan, Jambi, Pekanbaru, Bengkulu, Palembang, Lubuklinggau (for the South Sumatra train service), Jakarta and Bandung.

Tourist buses to Danau Toba are also on offer, through the travel agents in town (see p.413). Travel agents in Bukittinggi can also arrange Pelni and airline tickets from Padang, which is the closest port and airport.

A.Yani (the main thoroughfare) and Jalan Sudirman (the main road leading out of town to the south). Jalan A.Yani, 1km from north to south, is the tourist hub of Bukittinggi, and most of the sights, hotels, restaurants and shops that serve the tourist trade are on this street or close by.

There is no official **tourist office**, but there are a number of private tour operators who are very knowledgeable; East West Tours and Travel, Jl A.Yani 99 (☎0752/21133) is one of the best. **Bemos** scurry around town in a circular route, with a flat fare of Rp700. To get to the bus terminal, stop any red bemo heading north on Jalan A.Yani, which will circle to the east of town and pass the main post office before turning left to Aur Kuning.

Accommodation

Now flourishing as a popular tourist destination, Bukittinggi has **accommodation** at all prices and all levels of sophistication. However, most places are a little disappointing for such a popular spot, especially the many grand-lobbied and grimy-roomed mid-range places. At the budget end of the market, the places on Jalan A.Yani are an option, although many are decidedly grubby and noisy with distant mandi. Fortunately, some better-value places have sprung up nearby. The luxury hotel trade is gradually moving in, and the competition should produce good discounts.

Inexpensive

Bamboo Jl A. Yani 132 ☎0752/23388. The rooms are basic and dark with attached mandi; there's a small sitting area, which makes this better than the average Jalan A. Yani place. ❶

Hotel Cinduo Mato Jl Cinduo Mato 101 ☎0752/32146. Decent, tiled rooms with cold shower in a characterful old house by the market. ❸

D'Enam Jalan Yos Sudarso ☎0752/21333. Not far from the centre on a quiet road, with a variety of dorms and rooms in an airy bungalow. All are good value and there's a lounge for residents and a laundry service next door; the only drawback is the temperamental plumbing. ❶–❷

Gema Homestay Jl Dr A. Rivai ☎0752/22338. A clean, basic and homely place run by a nice family. There are five rooms, all with cold water. ❷

Merdeka Jl Dr A. Rivai 20 ☎0752/23937. On the corner with Jalan Benteng; the #14 bemo passes the door. A small guesthouse in and around a colonial bungalow set in a good-sized garden – the large, cool rooms have high ceilings and cold water mandi. It's slightly more expensive than the other budget places, but is clean and pleasant, and a good choice. ❷

Nirwana Jl A. Yani 113 ☎0752/32032. The most characterful of the rock-bottom places at the northern end of this road. Rooms without attached mandi are in a rambling old bungalow. If you don't fancy this one, it's easy to look at the other places nearby. ❷

Orchid Jl Teuku Umar 11 ☎0752/32634. A good-value place, one step up from the bottom end, with clinically clean though rather stark rooms, many with balconies. The price includes breakfast, and the more expensive rooms have TVs and hot water. ❷

Pemandangan Mountain View Jalan Yos Sudarso ⓣ0752/21621. One of the few places to take advantage of the scenery. However the rooms, all with cold-water mandi, are extremely basic and more than a little run-down. The road is quiet and the small garden has seats from which to admire the great views. ❷

Sari Bundo Jl Yos Sudarso 7a ⓣ0752/22953. Opposite the more prominent *Benteng*, in a quiet, convenient location, the dingy, overpriced but passable rooms are a disappointment after the exterior and lobby. All rooms have hot water; the better ones have tubs. ❸–❹

Singgalang Jl A. Yani 130 ⓣ0752/21576. The rooms, all without mandi, are adequate but very variable, so ask to see several. However, there's a quiet sitting area towards the back of the hotel; for this reason, it's probably the best place on Jl A. Yani. It's also a good place to enquire about Silat classes (see p.407). ❷

Sumatera Jl Dr Setia Budhi 16e ⓣ0752/21309. Centrally located on a quiet road, the rooms have attached bathroom with hot water. The accommodation is adequate for this price, but the real bonus is the balcony with its stunning views. ❷

Mid-range and expensive

Novotel Jalan Laras Datuk Bandaro ⓣ0752/35000, ⓕ23800, ⓔnovotelbkt@padang.wasantara. net.id. Located in the middle of town, this is the newest addition at the luxury end of the market and has a balconied multistorey foyer with a fountain, a heated swimming pool and classy ambience. ❺–❽

Pusako Jl Sukarno-Hatta 7 ⓣ0752/32111, ⓕ32667. Recently knocked off its perch as Bukittinggi's premier establishment by the *Novotel*, this Aerowisata hotel is located on a quiet hillside 7km east of the town centre in lush gardens with an attractive swimming pool. Rooms have balconies with swimming pool or mountain view. ❺

The Town

The most famous landmark in the town is the **Clock Tower** (*Jam Gadang*), built in 1827 by the Dutch when the town was their stronghold during the Paderi Wars. Situated in manicured gardens, it's attractive during the day, despite the traffic hurtling around it, but even more so at night, lit by strings of fairy lights.

A few hundred metres to the north, **Fort de Kock** (daily 8am–7pm; Rp1500) was built by the Dutch in 1825 and is linked to the park, **Taman Bundo Kanduang**, on the hill on the other side of Jalan A. Yani, by a footbridge high above the road; there's little left of the original fort but some old cannons and the obvious remnants of the protective moats. It's a popular place with local people and there are plenty of seats and quiet spots to enjoy the views. Looking south, Gunung Merapi, although the higher, is the less impressive mountain on the left, and Gunung Singgalang the much more dramatic and stereotypically cone-shaped volcano to the right.

The park's **museum** is housed in a traditional *rumah gadang*, and features clothing, musical instruments, textiles, household objects and models of traditional houses. Some of the exhibits have English descriptions and there are attempts to explain aspects of Minangkabau life. Unfortunately, the way to the museum passes through the **zoo** area, which is sadly well stocked and is as inhumane an example of such a place as you'll find anywhere.

Much more pleasant is a trip to **Panorama Park** (daily 7am–7pm; Rp1500), perched on a lip of land overlooking the sheer cliff walls down into Ngarai Sianok Canyon, the best Bukittinggi sight by far. Local people use Panorama Park as a picnic area and general strolling ground, especially in the late afternoon or at weekends. Beneath the park stretch 1400m of Japanese **tunnels** (Rp1500) and rooms built with local slave labour during World War II as a potential fortress. You can venture down into these dank, miserable depths, although there's nothing really to see. The **Ngarai Sianok Canyon** is part of a rift valley that runs the full length of Sumatra – the canyon here is 15km long and around 100m deep with a glistening river wending its way along the bottom. The Dutch named the canyon "Buffalo Hole", as the sides are so steep that animals grazing on the edge would occassionally plunge to their death hundreds of metres below.

Eating and drinking

There are plenty of **restaurants** in town – a good mix of travellers' places and local ones – and a small **night market** each evening near the junction of Jalan A.Yani and Jalan Teuku Umar, serving simple sate, noodles and rice dishes. For fast food, there's a *KFC* at Jl A.Yani 1.

Bedudal Jalan A. Yani. A pleasant place with an extensive, good-quality menu of Western fare including pizzas and steaks.

Canyon Coffee Shop Jl Teuku Umar 18b. An inexpensive and popular travellers' place with a friendly atmosphere in a quiet street just off Jalan A. Yani. They offer seventeen varieties of toast and eight variations on coffee, plus the usual shakes, juices, salads, omelettes, steaks and basic Indonesian dishes.

Harau Cliff Café Jalan A. Yani. Although situated on a particularly noisy section of road, this place is extremely good value (steak is Rp10,000 and sate, gado-gado and *cap cay* under Rp6000), and has attractive furnishings and a relaxed atmosphere.

Jazz and Blues Jalan A. Yani. Somewhere between a bar and a restaurant, this is where the friendly local Rastafarians hang out. The Western and local food is fair, and there's always music on the stereo.

Selamat Jl A. Yani 19. One of the best Padang restaurants in town, they usually have eggs in coconut sauce, which is especially good for vegetarians, and are used to Westerners.

Sianok Restaurant At the *Novotel*, Jalan Laras Datuk Bandaro. Offering the plushest, most expensive dining experience in town, with imported steaks, Western and Indo-Chinese meals, at a price. There are better-value buffets, Italian, Chinese, Indonesian, Minang and Western barbecue nights, special Minang lunches and daily afternoon tea.

Simpang Raya Jalan Muka Jam Gadang. This large, popular restaurant has good-quality Padang food plus a basic Indonesian menu with soup, rice or noodle dishes. The upstairs windows overlook the clock tower.

The Coffee Shop 105 Jl A. Yani 105a. A popular place with a small porch area right on the busy main street, which serves good travellers' fare at reasonable prices. Good for potato salad and people-watching.

Entertainment

Nightly **Minangkabau dance shows** (daily except Tues and Fri 8.30pm; Rp20,000) are put on by a variety of local dance troupes in a hall just behind *Hotel Jogya* on Jalan Moh Yamin; head up the small road on the left of the hotel, and the hall is on the right. The venue is a bit spartan, and out of the tourist season the shows are poorly attended, but the energy and vibrancy of the music and performers makes it a must-see in Bukittinggi. The audience are welcome to take photographs, and if you're a shrinking violet sit near the back, or you'll be hauled up to join in at the end.

Minang dancing is accompanied by *talempong pacik*, traditional Minang music performed by a **gamelan orchestra** similar to those of Java and Bali, with gongs (both on a stand and hand-held), drums and flutes. While the music clearly belongs to the same family as that of Sumatra's eastern neighbours, it's far more vibrant, energetic and catchy. The dances – although equally carefully choreographed and reliant upon stylized foot, hand and even eye movements – are much more exuberant, with expansive movements and even smiles of sheer pleasure on the faces of the performers, a sight rare in the classical Javanese and Balinese performances.

The show, a series of traditional dances, begins with a great **drumming** display on the *tabuah*, a huge drum which traditionally sent messages between villages and later signalled the times of attendance at the mosque, and continues with a welcome dance (*tari pasambahan*), where the male dancers begin with movements from the Minang martial art of *silek* and the female dancers offer betel leaf to the guests. The instruments include the *bansi*, a high-pitched wind instrument, and the *saluang*, a small, reedless bamboo flute, which uses a five-tone minor scale and hence produces a melancholy sound. Most shows include a demonstration of *silek*, the Minang martial art taught to both young men and women, and the *tari piriang*, a dance that originated in the rice fields after harvest time when young people danced with the plates they had just eaten from: piles of extremely sharp crockery shards are trodden, kicked and even rolled in by the dancers as part of the performance.

Shopping

Apart from the shops aimed particularly at tourists, Bukittinggi is a thriving **market town** for the surrounding area every day of the week, but with even more produce and energy on Wednesday and Saturday. Lively **Pasar Atas** (Upper Market) is just south of the clock tower and is an area of alleyways lined with stalls and shops selling everyday goods and souvenirs; the newspaper stalls at the clock tower end usually have the English-language *Jakarta Post* by the afternoon. Across the other side of Jalan Pemuda, **Pasar Bawah** (Lower Market) sells more foodstuffs and produce and is equally vibrant.

Bookshops

Anyone heading into central and southern Sumatra, an English-language book desert, is strongly advised to take full advantage of the **bookshops** in Bukittinggi. Whilst the postcard situation elsewhere in Sumatra isn't quite so dire, you won't encounter the choice that you'll get in Bukittinggi, so it pays to stock up. Javanese batik greetings cards are also on sale for Rp2000; they vary from gaudy to attractive.

Rendezvous On the corner of Jalan A. Yani and Jalan Pemuda. A few classics to supplement the rather airport-like collections elsewhere.
Setia On the corner of Jalan Teuku Umar and Jalan A. Yani. A reasonable choice of secondhand material.
Stylist Jalan A. Yani. Worth a quick look, but mostly stock airport novels.
Tilas Jl Teuku Umar 11a and Jl A. Yani 124. Bookshops that are also postal agents, they offer a good selection of new and secondhand books, including a range of titles about Indonesia and Sumatra.

Souvenirs

Bukittinggi is a good hunting ground for a range of **souvenirs** from across the archipelago, although prices of items from further afield are high. It's generally the case that the closer you get to the place of origin the cheaper the items will be, so bear your itinerary in mind. It's wise to read claims about the antiquity of items with scepticism. There are a couple of unnamed shops on Jalan Teuku Umar, with attractive boxes from Lombok, Batak calendars and West Papuan and Batak woodcarvings.

Minang Art Shop Jl A. Yani 51. The range here is wide, even up to large wooden cupboards, but think about shipping before you indulge.
Sumatera Jl Minangkabau 19. This place is worth searching out in the Pasar Atas market area – the range is extensive, including textiles from Sumba and West Papua (around Rp250,000) and king sticks of various sizes and designs (Rp80,000) from North Sumatra.
Tanjung Raya Art Jl A. Yani 85. Centrally located with friendly staff, this place is a treasure trove of ancient and modern artefacts, all jammed into a few rooms. Javanese puppets rub shoulders with spooky bone figures from Kalimantan, textiles, rifles, cellos, ceramics, bows, old money, telescopes, Chinese compasses and fob watches.

Listings

Banks and exchange BRI, Jl A. Yani 3; BNI, Jalan A. Yani (with international ATM). Several travel agents including Tigo Balai Indah, Jl A. Yani 100 (daily 8am–8pm; ⓣ0752/31996), change travellers' cheques and offer cash advances against Visa and Mastercard.

Car and motorbike rental Enquire at your accommodation or any of the travel agents in town. Typical prices are Rp250,000 for a 12hr car rental with or without driver, and Rp300,000 for 24hr, although these will be prices for local trips – if you're going further afield, they will be higher. Insurance is not available.

Hospital Rumah Sakit Dr Achmad Mochtar is on Jalan Dr A. Rivai ⓣ0752/21013, 33825. The tourist information offices will advise on English-speaking doctors in Bukittinggi.

Post office The main post office is inconveniently far from the town centre on Jalan Sudirman. Poste restante here is reasonably secure and organized. However, there's a convenient postal agent near the clock tower, and Tilas bookshops on Jalan Teuku Umar and Jalan A. Yani are also postal agents.

Telephone The main telephone office is on Jalan M. Syafei towards the southern end of town, around the corner from the post office. There are also many wartels in town.

Tour operators There are a variety of one-day tours (Rp65,000 per person) available: enquire at your accommodation, in the tourist office or in the coffee shops. The Minangkabau tour goes by several names and takes in Baso, the lookout at Tabek Patek, the traditional water-driven coffee mill at Sungai Tarab, Batusangkar, the palace at Pagaruyung, Balimbing, Danau Singkarak and Pandai Sikat. The Maninjau tour includes Koto Gadang, Sungai Landir, Danau Maninjau, Lawang, Embun Pagi and the Ngarai Sianok Canyon. The Harau Valley tour first visits the caves at Ngalau Indah, followed by Payakumbuh and then Andaleh to see rattan crafts, the irrigation system at Payobasung, the traditional water mill at Batu Balang and the waterfalls in the Harau Valley. A wide range of longer tours are on offer from the travel agents in town. Typically, these are three or more days involving trekking, camping and/or staying overnight in local villages. Average costs are US$20 or US$22.50 per person per day. East West Tours and Travel, Jl A. Yani 99 (ⓣ0752/21133), and Travina Tours and Travel Service, Jl A. Yani 107 (ⓣ0752/21281), offer a three-day "Village, Jungle and River" trip, taking in Sungai Hitan, Alahan, Laring Mountain, Jambak, Sungai Masang, Tapian and Maninjau. Puti Bungus, Jl Teuku Umar 7a (ⓣ0752/23026), has something similar, but includes Bonjol and calls it an "Equator Trip". It also offers a five-night/six-day trip to visit the Kubu people in Jambi district. Enquire at the *Harau Cliff Café* on Jalan A. Yani for local rock-climbing trips. You can arrange kayaking or white-water rafting at Minangkabau Rafting, Jl Tengku Nan Renceh 20 (ⓣ & ⓕ0752/22913), either of which cost US$39 per person per day and have minimum requirements of two or three people. The most widely publicized tour is a trip to Siberut in the Mentawai chain of islands, accessed via Padang. Bukittinggi is the best place to arrange such a trip; see p.421 for more details on Siberut and tips on arranging your tour.

Travel agents East West Tours and Travel, Jl A. Yani 99 ⓣ0752/21133; PT Tigo Balai Indah, Jl A. Yani 100 ⓣ0752/31996; Travina Tours and Travel Service, Jl A. Yani 107 ⓣ0752/21281; PT Batours Agung, Jl A. Yani 105 ⓣ0752/34346, ⓕ22306; Puti Bungus, Jl Teuku Umar 7a ⓣ0752/23026. Tourist buses are on offer to Danau Toba. Expect to be quoted Rp27,000 for a thirteen- or fourteen-hour journey. Travel agents can also arrange Pelni and airline tickets from Padang.

Around Bukittinggi

Whilst Bukittinggi is a pleasant place to relax for a couple of days, it's also worth making the effort to get out into the surrounding countryside to get a closer glimpse of highland rural life, enjoy the scenery and visit some of the cultural sights. The Agam Valley area, with Bukittinggi at its centre, features **Koto Gadang** village, famous for silverwork; **Pandai Sikat**, a weaving and woodcarving centre; the Rafflesia Sanctuary at Batang Palupuh, 13km out of town (see the box on p.414); as well as the sights in and around **Padangpanjang**. **Gunung Singgalang** to the west and **Gunung Merapi** to the east of the Agam Valley are enticing climbs for the fit and energetic.

Rafflesia

One of the most accessible places in Sumatra to see the rare **Rafflesia** flower is at Batang Palupuh, 13km north of Bukittinggi; take a local bus (Rp1500) and ask in the village. Enquire at the tourist office in Bukittinggi first as to whether it's worth making the journey: the blooms are irregular, but even in bud the plant is remarkable. *Rafflesia arnoldi* is the largest flower in the world – up to 90cm across, named after Sir Stamford Raffles of Singapore fame and his botanist chum Dr Joseph Arnold, who discovered the plant in southern Sumatra whilst Raffles was based in Bengkulu. It grows in tropical, extremely humid conditions and is actually a parasite on a forest vine, without a stem, leaves or roots of its own. Whilst many writers extol its size and the remarkable red-and-white colouring, most do not wax nearly so lyrical about its appalling smell (resembling rotting meat), which attracts the insects that pollinate the flowers. It generally flowers for a couple of weeks from August to December.

Koto Gadang

KOTO GADANG is a small attractive village situated on the western edge of the Ngarai Sianok Canyon. Though you can get bemos to the village, many people try to find the route from Bukittinggi by foot (an hour's walk) that starts off down Jalan Tengku Nan Renceh, and then heads along a footpath to the footbridge across the river and up the steps on the other side of the canyon. Be aware that there's a well-orchestrated scam, with local people refusing to point the way and hapless tourists being helped by young lads who lead them for a two-hour rough trek through the canyon and then expect payment. The village itself is quiet and attractive with plenty of small **silver workshops** and shops selling various good-value pieces of silver jewellery – much is traditional filigree work, but many places have adapted to more Western tastes.

Gunung Merapi and Gunung Singgalang

Access to 2891-metre **Gunung Merapi** (Fire Mountain) is from **Koto Baru**, 12km south of Bukittinggi. The climb is strenuous rather than gruelling, and takes five hours up and four down if you're reasonably fit. Most people climb at night, to arrive at the top for the sunrise. The first four hours or so are through the forest on the lower slopes of the mountain and then across bare rocks leading to the summit. The top, although you can't tell this from below, is actually a plateau area with the still smoking crater in the middle. You may spot bats, gibbons and squirrels in the forest, but the main reason to go is the view across to Gunung Singgalang. Although easily accessible from Bukittinggi and a popular climb, bear in mind that the mountain did erupt in the 1980s and killed several people. You should engage a local guide (your losmen will find you one), who knows the mountain and has climbed before. Make sure you take enough water, food to keep up your energy, warm clothes for the top and sturdy footwear. Typical prices for the guide and transport are US$15 per person from Bukittinggi.

You'll need to be much fitter if you want to tackle the steeper, longer (allow 5–6hr to get up and 4–5hr to get back down) and tougher climb up **Gunung Singgalang**. At 2880m it's almost as high as Merapi, and from Bukittinggi appears the more enticing of the two, with its almost perfect conical shape. It has a small crater lake, Telaga Dewi, at the summit, from where you'll be treated to fine views of the surrounding area. Access is from Pandai Sikat (see opposite), and the trail begins from the TV relay station 5km up the mountain at 1600m – vehicles can go this far. Take all the precautions advised above for Merapi; prices for a guide are similar.

Buffalo fights

Animal-lovers may balk at the idea of watching **buffalo fights** (*adu kerbau*), a popular local event in several of the villages near Bukittinggi, but the reality is rarely gory, usually good fun and occasionally hilarious. Fights draw huge crowds, and it can be as entertaining watching them as watching the bovine contestants.

There are usually two bouts held every day except Friday and Saturday, starting at around 4pm. The massive buffalo are led towards each other and enticed to lock horns. They are in fact not particularly aggressive beasts, so this can take a while. Once their horns are locked they then push and heave against one another, with spectators urging on their favourite – the loser is the buffalo which turns tail and runs away first. At this point the hilarity begins, the crowding spectators diving for cover.

Regular contests take place in villages near Bukittinggi: currently Pincuran Tujuh on Tuesday and Batagak on Wednesday, but check with the tourist information office in Bukittinggi. Either arrange a Rp25,000 ticket through a travel agent or at the tourist office, who will include transport, or go independently and pay Rp2000 at the gate. The most accessible location is Batagak, 9km south of Bukittinggi on the way to Panangpanjang; the entrance is through a set of white gates just above the road.

Pandai Sikat, Padangpanjang and the Anai Valley

If you're climbing Gunung Merapi, you'll pass through the small village of Koto Baru, 12km south from Bukittinggi. From Koto Baru, take the turning at the *Yus Djamal* sign to reach the nearby village of **PANDAI SIKAT**, famed for **weaving** and **woodcarving**, 2–3km up the road; bemos ply the route if you don't want to walk. The village is full of craftspeople, based in small workshops with shops attached. Weaving is done on a simple foot loom to produce the traditional *songket* cloth for the scarf, *selendang*, and sarong sets; the amount of effort involved will depend on how fine the thread is, but typically it will take a woman, weaving for five hours each day, about three weeks to produce three metres of cloth. However, whilst pretty much everything else is done by hand and the patterns are largely traditional, new patterns based on old motifs can be computer-generated to make the task of fitting the pattern into the thread counts much easier. Whilst you'll see *songket* sets costing up to Rp1,000,000 and huge items of furniture, the shops also sell attractive small souvenirs, with carved wooden boxes from Rp25,000 and purses from Rp20,500.

PADANGPANJANG is situated at the junction of the roads west to Padang (72km), north to Bukittinggi (19km) and east to Batusangkar (20km). It's a long ribbon development that lines the road for several kilometres and has a laid-back atmosphere, an attractively bustling small market area and a couple of **accommodation** options as alternatives to the tourist enclave of Bukittinggi (though be aware that prices are higher here). *Wisma Mutiara* (℡0752/83668; ❸) is on the main road leading north from the town centre, and is adequate, with private, cold-water bathrooms. The main attraction in town is the **Centre for Information and Documentation on Minangkabau Culture** (Pusat Dokumentasi and Informasi Kebudayan Minangkabau; daily 9am–1pm & 2–5pm; ℡0752/82852), which has a fine collection of Minang items housed in a fabulous *rumah gadang*, set in gorgeous grounds with a small cafeteria; for Rp17,000, you can get dressed up in traditional Minangkabau costume. A reproduction Minang village is under development, with different types of buildings, all full size, currently standing in somewhat sterile surroundings. The **tourist office** is in the centre at Jl A. Hamid Hakim 11 (Mon–Fri 8am–3pm, Sat 8am–1pm; ℡0752/82320), but they get very few foreign visitors and have no English material available.

Further southwest, towards Padang, the **Anai Valley** is 10km from Padangpanjang. A small **nature reserve** has been established here (the entrance is between the road markers "Padang 63km" and "Padang 64km") and is home to tapirs, monkeys, a good smattering of Sumatran birds and, at certain times of the year, the gigantic flower *Amorphophallus titanum*. It's a very popular weekend day-trip for Padang locals, when it turns into a hubbub that frightens away anything wild, but you'll see more if you visit during the week. There may be simple **accommodation** available in **Kandung Empat**, the village just south of the entrance to the reserve (towards Padang), but *Uncle Dede's* (no phone; Rp20,000 per person including meals) was closed at the time of writing.

Batusangkar and Tanah Datar

Reached via Padangpanjang, the largest town in the Tanah Datar Valley is **BATUSANGKAR**, 39km southeast of Bukittinggi. The **Minang court** of the fourteenth to nineteenth centuries was based in the valley, the gold and iron mines of ancient times being the source of its riches. The entire area offers many cultural relics, megaliths and places of interest, and to explore it fully takes more than the limited time available on the one-day Minangkabau tours from Bukittinggi (see p.413). Unfortunately, while the town itself is convenient as a base, it isn't particularly attractive.

The **tourist office** is at Jl Pemuda 1 (☎0752/71300), and the **accommodation** all clustered fairly close together on the same street: *Pagaruyung*, Jl Prof Hamka 4 (☎0752/71533; ❷); *Yoherma* at no. 15 (☎0752/71130; ❷); and *Parma*, Jalan Hamka (☎0752/71330; ❷). All have a range of basic but adequate rooms and restaurants attached. If you have time to stay longer, BIEC (Brotherly International English Course) at Jl S. Parman 99 (☎0752/93268) offers accommodation to visitors in exchange for English tuition for their students.

The most worthwhile tourist destination in the area is **Pagaruyung** (daily 7am–6pm; Rp1500), the reconstructed palace of the last raja alam of the Minangkabau, Sultan Arifin Muning Alam Syah. The palace, 5km north of Batusangkar, was destroyed in a devastating fire in 1864, and reconstructed using traditional techniques 25 years ago, the woodcarving alone taking two years to complete by Pandai Sikat carvers. It's an imposing sight and a reminder of the traditional skills that still remain with the fiercely proud Minangkabau. The building comprises the traditional three storeys – the first for official visitors, the second for unmarried daughters and the third for meetings; the rice barn at the front would traditionally have held food to help the poor, and the palace mosque is in the garden, with the kitchen at the back.

Danau Singkarak and beyond

Danau Singkarak, a spectacular crater lake about 20km long, is reached via a turning to the south, 5–6km along the Padangpanjang–Batusangkar road. Alternative access from Padang is via Solok. The lake doesn't have the grandeur of Maninjau (see p.418) and, with the main road hugging the eastern shore, the surroundings can be a bit noisy, but it's still an attractive area.

Buses heading south from Bukittinggi to the Kerinci area pass through here, and with seats on the right-hand side of the bus you'll get good views. There isn't much **accommodation** in the area: at the northern end of the lake the *Singkarak Sumpur Hotel* (☎0752/82103, Ⓕ82529; ❸–❹) is signed from the road as it descends to the lakeside, and is located 6km along a country lane. The more expensive rooms are pleasant with balconies and fine views, the lower price ones poor value; meals are moderately priced. The lake at this end is rather dirty, although the hotel does have a pool.

On the main road at **Batutebal**, 18km south of Pandangpanjang and 45km from Solok, there's a white gateway and road to the lakeside; enquire at *Mutiara*, a small warung, about **boat charter**: you'll start negotiating at Rp200,000 for the day for a boat holding five or six people. One kilometre further south the *Jayakarta*, Jalan Raya Padang Panjang Solok Km19 (☎0752/21279; ❸–❹), is the only other accommodation on the lakeside, with adequate rooms, and a great terrace with chairs where you can relax in between swims in the lake.

Further south, **Umbilin** is a big transit village around the mouth of the river, which is crossed by a large iron bridge. This is the junction for the Batusangkar road via Balimbing, and bemos ply the route irregularly and on south to Singkarak and Solok. Just 14km south of Umbilin, *Tenbok Kachang* is a small restaurant area on the lakeside, from where you can also rent pedal boats (Rp15,000 an hour) to explore the waters. From here, the road continues south via Singkarak and the busy market town of Solok to the town of **Lubuk Selasih**, with Gunung Tabang rising 2599m behind, and then another 10km to the two lakes, **Danau Dibawah** and **Danau Diatas** (Lower Lake and Upper Lake). They're far smaller than the other lakes in the area but still beautiful, and are renowned because they lie just 1m apart, but at different levels. If you want to explore the area, the nearby village of **ALAHANPANJAN** has **accommodation** at *Hillmaya Guest House*, Jl Imam Bonjol 227 (☎0755/60151; ❷), which is 2km beyond the village centre up a very steep road. Public transport plies the route on market days (Thurs & Sat); otherwise you'll have to walk or hitch a lift.

Payakumbuh and the Harau Canyon

PAYAKUMBUH is the main population centre in the **Limapuluh Kota Valley**, a stunningly fertile, densely populated area that's thought to have been the first part of the Minang highlands to be settled. The town, lies 33km to the east of Bukittinggi, at the foot of Gunung Malitang (2262m). There's a small **tourist information office** at Jl Olah Raga 1 (Mon–Thurs 8am–2.30pm, Fri 8–11.30am, Sat 8am–1pm; ☎0752/92907) and **accommodation** at *Rizal's Guest House*, Jl Parit Rantang 71 (no phone; ❷), or at the slightly nicer *Wisma Flamboyant*, Jl Ade Irma Suryani 11 (☎0752/92333; ❷), both just off Jalan Sudirman, the main road into town from Bukittinggi.

Numerous **megalithic remains** pepper the area, most densely around Sungai Sinamar, Guguk (a village 13km from Payakumbuh) and the isolated valley of Mahat – a rough track leads north from Limbanang, 20km from Payakumbuh. Most are simple standing stones or mortars, only a few are inscribed and they lack the beauty of the Pasemah Plateau megaliths (see p.496), although the mystery of their existence is just as intriguing. Skeletons have been found underneath some of the stones, suggesting a role in burial, but local legend tells that they played a part in feasts or in the prediction of the weather.

The Harau Canyon

The most popular excursion in the area is to the **Harau Canyon** (daily 9am–4.30pm), a nature reserve in an area bounded by dramatic towering cliffs. It lies just off the main road 14km northeast of Payakumbuh. **Permits** (Rp1500) are available from the ticket office at the entrance. For rock-climbing expeditions, enquire at the *Harau Cliff Café* in Bukittinggi (see p.411). It's said that tigers, leopards, panthers, deer and honey bear inhabit the nature reserve, which consists of rainforest and has some spectacular waterfalls, best seen in the wet season when they rage 100m down into the forest. But this is much-visited territory, especially at weekends, and realistically you can expect monkeys, butterflies, birds and *Homo sapiens*. Most of the tour operators in Bukittinggi offer a day-trip here, but these generally include the Harau Valley only briefly, and if you want to see the canyon properly you'll need to take two or three days, camping in the valley. Enquire in Bukittinggi for someone who will put a trip together for you, or ask at the tourist office there.

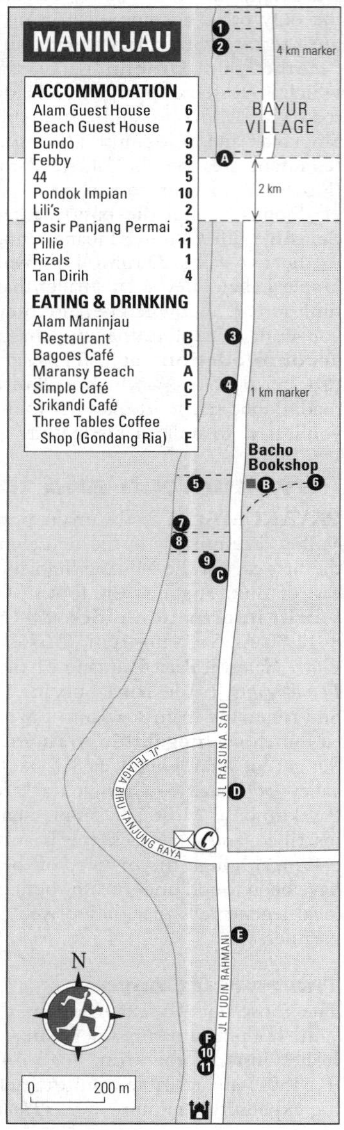

Danau Maninjau

Rapidly developing a reputation as a pleasant and hassle-free area for rest and relaxation on the way to or from Danau Toba, **Danau Maninjau** is situated 15km due west of Bukittinggi, although public transport on the road takes a long-winded 37km (90min) to get there, with the final descent to the lake along a scenic 44-bend road. At an altitude of 500m, the lake is 17km long and 8km wide, and set 600m below the rim of an ancient volcanic crater, with jungle-covered crater walls, almost sheer in places, providing a picturesque backdrop. The area of interest for tourists, and all the facilities, centres on the village of **MANINJAU** (meaning "to look out across"), just where the road from Bukittinggi reaches the lakeside road, and, to a lesser extent, the village of **Bayur** 4km to the north.

Many visitors spend all their time here swimming or chilling out, although a few places have canoes to rent and there are plenty of **excursions** in the area. If you get off the bus at the point where the road from Bukittinggi reaches the crater rim to the east of the lake, **Embun Pagi** (Morning Mist), at almost 1100m, offers stunning views of the lake. Alternatively, get off the bus at the village of Matur, walk the 5km to the village of Lawang and then another 5km to the higher lookout point of **Puncak Lawang**. Halfway down the track from Lawang to Bayur village, the *Anas Homestay* (❶) is a great place to relax. Accommodation is in log cabins in the forest, lit by oil lamps at night, and with monkeys scampering around outside.

Roads and tracks circle the lake, which is about 55km in circumference, and plenty of places rent out bicycles (Rp10,000) and motorcycles (Rp75,000 per day). However, the track on the far side of the lake from Maninjau village has become extremely rough during the road "improvements", so check the current condition before you set off, and be sure to take plenty of water and food for the day. There's a **waterfall** in the forest above Maninjau village, and it takes about 45 minutes to walk there.

After your exertions, **traditional massage** is available from an elderly Javanese lady for Rp25,000 per hour; enquire at the *Alam Maninjau Restaurant*. Most evenings on Danau Maninjau are given over to eating and then an early night, although the *Alam Guest House* hosts **traditional dance shows** when there are enough customers: Rp15,000 including a soft drink, or Rp25,000 including beer.

Practicalities

There is no official **tourist information office**, but there are many private ones, the best of which is Indo Wisata Travel (☎0752/61418), just north of the main junction next to *Bagoes Café*. This is also the best place for **internet access** and changing travellers' cheques (they don't accept plastic). The **post office** isn't far from the main junction on Jalan Telaga Biru Tanjung Raya; the 24-hour **Telkom office** is on the main street near the bank, which unfortunately doesn't change money. There are a couple of secondhand **bookshops**: the best is Bacho Bookshop. **Moving on**, there are regular **buses** back to Bukittinggi. If you want to go to Padang, there are minivans travelling to Lubukbasung on the west of the lake, from where you can pick up Padang buses during the day. There's little time difference between going via Bukittinggi and via Lubukbasung. Enquire at the tourist office about other direct buses in Maninjau: at the time of writing, direct buses run daily to Pekanbaru, and you can also book through to Batam with a few hours' halt in Pekanbaru – allow two days and a night.

Accommodation

Accommodation is ranged along the east side of the lake, from about 500m south of the junction of the lakeside road with the road from Bukittinggi, to just north of the 5km marker. There's a range of accommodation available, most in simple homestays or small guesthouses, although a few places offer more luxurious options, a trend that looks set to increase. Not many rooms have attached mandi: reviews state if they do.

Alam Guest House Up on the hillside away from the lake ☎0752/61069. The views from the balcony are fantastic, but the building is a bit run-down after some fire damage. The rooms, all with mandi, are nice but a little overpriced. ❷

Beach Guest House ☎0752/61082. A bustling and popular place in a great location on the lakeside; turn off the road at the big "Bintang" sign. Offers a wide range of rooms, some with attached mandi and a small verandah and hammocks; there's also a small beach. ❶–❷

Bundo A tiny, central homestay in the middle of the fields (no phone), this is a friendly, family-run place a short walk to the lakeside. ❷

Febby ☎0752/61586. Smaller and quieter than the *Beach Guest House* nearby, this is right on the lakeside but still convenient for the facilities of Maninjau village. ❷

44 ☎0752/61238. Very inexpensive shoreside bungalows with attached mandi and a small restaurant. The rooms are nicer than most budget places twice the price, and the family are very welcoming. Excellent value. ❶

Pondok Impian ☎0752/61288. A serene wooden house in the village itself, backing onto the lake shore. The cold-water bathrooms are shared, but this is still a great choice. ❷

Lili's (no phone). A very attractive, New Zealand-run place with fine, shared-mandi bungalows, some right on the lake, and a tree house. The attached café is good value, making this one of the best beachside places. ❶–❷

Pasir Panjang Permai Ⓣ0752/61111, Ⓕ61255. One of only two large setups on the lake, but the rooms are nothing special and the corridors dark and dingy. Look at several rooms, as they are very variable. ❹–❺

Pillie Towards the southern end of Maninjau village Ⓣ0752/61048. This lakeside place is clean, cool and tiled, with simple rooms and huge mandi nearby plus a pleasant upstairs balcony. ❷

Rizals 4km north of Maninjau village Ⓣ0752/61404. Pleasant bamboo bungalows with mosquito nets, set back from their own white-sand beach and situated in a coconut grove. There are good views of the lake, and the attached restaurant has a stilted area over the water. ❷

Tan Dirih Ⓣ0752/61263. Small, tiled, spotless place with sun loungers on a terrace overlooking the lake. It's the best mid-range place; all rooms have hot water and tubs. ❸

Eating and drinking

Alam Maninjau Restaurant Situated just off the road at the start of the track up to the *Alam Guest House*, this open-sided *bale* is well decorated, has a relaxed atmosphere with easy-listening music, magazines to read and a good range of meals. Main courses are around Rp12,000 for chicken, sirloin and *teriyaki*, while baked potatoes with cauliflower cheese cost Rp7000 and basic Indonesian dishes Rp6000. Reconstruction work after fire damage was under way at the time of writing.

Bagoes Café Good quality Western and Indonesian restaurant specializing in fish from the lake.

Maransy Beach This is the place for a special meal or a sunset beer. The restaurant is set on stilts over the lake and offers an excellent range of drinks, including cocktails (Rp6000 upwards), beer and white wine. The food consists of soups and appetizers such as papaya cocktail and stuffed eggs, and main courses, including goulash and beef escalope, as well as Indonesian, Chinese and Western options. To finish up, you can have Irish coffee (Rp10,000). Moderate to expensive.

Simple Café Situated close to the road but with good views across the rooftops down to the lake. A vast inexpensive menu offering all the usual Western and Indo-Chinese favourites.

Srikandi Café With a small shaded garden at the front containing a tiny waterfall, this place at the southern end of Maninjau village offers a slightly grander dining experience than most of the nearby options. The menu is large and varied: soups cost Rp5000–6000 (pumpkin, curried apple, Thai tom yam), with main courses at around Rp15,000 including stir-fries, sate, fish, steak, pizzas and burgers.

Three Tables Coffee Shop (Gondang Ria) South of the main junction, this is a tiny place with a good upstairs balcony, serving inexpensive Padang food plus the usual travellers' fare.

The Mentawai Islands

The enticing **Mentawai Islands**, 100km off the west Sumatran coast and separated by waters around 2000m deep, are home to an ethnic group who are struggling to retain their identity in the modern world. There are over forty islands in the chain, four main ones plus a host of smaller dots of land. From north to south the main islands are Siberut, Sipura, Pagai Utara (North Pagi) and Pagai Selatan (South Pagi). Only **Siberut**, the largest island, at 110km long by 50km wide, is accessible to tourists. The necessity for visitors' **entry permits** is in a constant state of flux, with control of the islands' natural resources being a contentious issue between independently minded islanders and the Sumatran mainland. At the time of writing, permits were not needed, but check with a tour operator (see p.413) for the current situation.

The breaks off the Mentawai chain are already popular; while not as famous as the Nias wave, the mostly north-facing reefs are less crowded and are something of a "best-kept secret" in the **surfing** world. The best time of year for surfing is mid-April to October, with the big barrel season in July and August. December is the quietest time, but beginners should take advantage of the small January and February swells (and the twenty percent Nov–March discount). In Padang, the excellent Mentawai Surf Sanctuary (Mentawai Wisata Bahari), centrally based at Level 2, *Hotel Bumiminang*, Jl Bundo Kandung 20–28 (Ⓣ & Ⓕ0751/37545, Ⓕ37548, Ⓦwww.mentawai.com), operates live-aboard ten-berth yachts from the city and has "full wave priority permits" in protected surf zones with more than forty breaks; a trip starts at about US$130 per person per night. Diving, snorkelling and river treks are also on offer, and there are plans for accommodation in the isolated west-coast areas of the region.

The islands are covered in primary tropical rainforest, and their traditional **culture** is based on communal dwelling in longhouses (*uma*), shared by between five or ten related families and scattered along the river valleys with all transport on foot or by canoe and, more recently, speedboat. The ages-old culture had, until fairly recent times, been largely unaffected by events on the mainland, and the Hindu, Buddhist and Islamic waves of cultural change that swept Sumatra in the past left the Mentawai chain largely untouched, its people pursuing a lifestyle of subsistence agriculture, growing sago, yams and bananas as the staple crops, with husbandry of chickens and pigs supplemented by hunting and fishing. It's a largely egalitarian society without chiefs or servants, with **religious beliefs** centred on the importance of coexisting with the invisible spirits that inhabit the world and all the objects in it; even the personality and spirit of a person's possessions are important, and they must not be used thoughtlessly. Many traditional ceremonies are carried out to appease the spirits in case the activities of humans accidentally distress them.

With the advent of Christian missionaries and the colonial administration at the beginning of this century, change was forced upon the people and many of their religious practices were banned. Following Independence, when the Indonesian government forbade all indigenous religions, the people were forced to adopt one of the state religions, and most became nominal Christians. Although many traditional rituals were officially banned, ritual objects destroyed and the people moved away from the *uma* into single-family houses, many beliefs and practices have survived and some villages have built new *uma*.

However, there's no doubt that the islands themselves and the people on them remain under considerable **threat** from all sides. The culture is in danger as the Indonesian government seeks to integrate the people into what it perceives as mainstream life. The environment is under immediate threat from a planned 700–square-kilometre **palm-oil plantation** which would cover sixteen percent of the island of Siberut – an oil-palm nursery is already open in the village of Saumanuk. Work on the plantation seems likely to be offered to transmigrants from other parts of Indonesia rather than the islanders themselves, who would soon be outnumbered. At the same time, big business is also interested in the islands for exclusive tourist developments. Overall, the future for the traditional life of Mentawai looks bleak.

Siberut

The island of **Siberut** is the best-known, largest and most northerly of the Mentawai chain and the only one with anything approaching a tourist industry. Access to the island is by **overnight ferry** from Padang and, whilst it's still possible to visit the island independently, the vast majority of visitors go on trips arranged and starting from Bukittinggi, organized and guided by young

Tour tips for Siberut

• You'll be inundated by guides in Bukittinggi touting trips to Siberut; try to get a guide by personal recommendation.
• You may spend some days hanging around in Bukittinggi waiting for the tour to be put together; there are usually minimum numbers required, so it makes sense to start making enquiries as soon as you get to Bukittinggi and spend the waiting days sightseeing.
• Listen carefully to the guide's attitude towards the Mentawai people.
• The people speak a language totally distinct from Indonesian on the mainland and you'll have a better time if you really try to communicate. See below for some phrases.
• Read and obey guidelines about behaviour that are given to you. The people have a complex system of taboo behaviour.
• Be aware that on a five-day trip Day One usually means a 3pm departure from Bukittinggi and two hours hanging around in Padang waiting for the boat. Similarly, the boat docks soon after dawn in Padang, so Day Five may well end at 10am when you get to Bukittinggi.
• Try to keep it small – four to six people is bearable. More than that and you'll inundate the places you visit.
• Meet the people on the trip before you leave and confirm what you've been told about numbers and itinerary.
• Trekking in the jungle will give you very poor views of anything but the jungle: it's muddy, slippery and you have to get across rivers and deal with leeches. Accommodation is extremely basic. Take as little with you as possible; most tours arrange for you to store stuff in Bukittinggi.
• Malaria is endemic on the island. Ideally take your own net or borrow one from the tour company. Follow the advice in Basics (p.32), for entering a malarial area.

Some language

Hello - Ani loita
Thank you - Masura bagata
You're welcome - Sama makerek
What's your name? - Kai see onim?
My name is.. - Onningkku..
Are you married? - Umu daley mo an ekeo?
Not yet - Tabey
Already - Aley pak an
How many children do you have? - Peega togum?
Many - Myget
What is that? - Ponia edah?
Wait a minute - Bola
Go - Mayeeta
Come back - Doilee
Cigarette - Oobey
I don't smoke - Tak maubek aku
Water - Oinan
Today - Gogoy nenek
Tomorrow - Mancheb/sobi
Yesterday - Sokat
Slowly - Moiley moiley
I am hot - Ma ro ket aku
I am hungry - Ma lajei aku
I am thirsty - Ma ongo aku
I am tired - Ma geyla aku
I am sick - Ma bey si aku
Leech - Alu matek
Mosquito - See ngit ngit
Pig - Sakokok
Cat - Mow
Dog - Jojo

men from West Sumatra rather than Mentawai people. The tours are promoted in Bukittinggi as a trip to see the "primitive" people and "stone-age" culture, and photos will be shoved under your nose of tattooed people in loincloths. Generally, Mentawai people welcome tourism, although they get little financial benefit from it; they see it as a way of validating and preserving their own culture and raising awareness of their plight in the outside world.

The long separation from the mainland – Siberut was once joined to Sumatra – has meant that some primitive species of **flora and fauna** have survived on the island, while many species have evolved separately. Siberut is home to monkeys, squirrels, civets, frogs and reptiles as well as a range of birdlife. However, the rare primates are the most famous inhabitants, and the black gibbon, Mentawai macaque, Mentawai leaf-monkey and pig-tailed langur are endemic to the island.

If you go on a **tour**, it will probably centre on the southeast of the island. You'll typically bypass Muarasiberut on the way in and take in Maillepet beach, then the areas of Tateburu, Ugai, Madobag, Rogdog and Bat Rorogot with a speedboat back to Muarasiberut. You'll be able to watch and join in with people going about their everyday activities, such as farming, fishing and hunting. The ceremonies of Siberut are something of a draw for tourists, but many of those that tourists "happen" to see are actually staged for them with replica items; to wear the real clothing and use the real ritual items for such a purpose might offend the spirits

Visiting Siberut independently

Independent visitors may need to get a **permit** in Padang, depending on the current situation; the Mentawai Surf Sanctuary (Mentawi Wisata Bahari) at Level 2, *Hotel Bumiminang*, Jl Bundo Kandung 20–28 (Ⓣ & Ⓕ0751/37545, Ⓕ37548, Ⓦwww.mentawai.com) can give you the details. If you do need a permit, you won't be sold a boat ticket without one. Go to the office at least a day in advance of when you want to travel (for travel on Monday, apply on Friday), with a photocopy of your passport, including the Indonesian entry stamp, and the immigration card you received on arrival in the country. The company has Indonesian government authority to issue permits, but the future is uncertain; they may consider limiting the number of tourists and the areas/times they can visit, and also licensing tour operators from Bukittinggi. Listen out in Bukittinggi, or check the website for developments.

Two companies run **ferries** between Padang and the island: PT Rusco Lines, Jl Bt Arau 88 D/11 (Ⓣ0751/21941), and PT Semeleue, Jl Bt Arau 7h (Ⓣ0751/39312); tickets cost Rp45,000, plus Rp1000 port tax. Currently, sailing days are Monday, Wednesday and Friday to Siberut, with return trips on Tuesday, Thursday and Saturday. Rusco also call at Sikabulan, the small coastal settlement on the east coast further north from Muarasiberut. There are two boats, the government *Barau*, which operates irregularly out of Bungus, and the much better *Sumber Rezike Baru*. The government ferry is a 25-metre motorboat; the lower decks are close to the extremely noisy, exhaust-belching engine with little breeze from outside. There's an open area in the back to sit, but the ship video operates all hours just outside the door. The *Rezike* is a larger, more comfortable affair.

If you are travelling independently, you should approach the Siberut Guide Association (Ⓣ0759/21064) to find a **guide**; once again, the Mentawai Surf Sanctuary (Mentawai Wisata Bahari; see p.421) has good contacts. You could also try Um (Ⓣ081/1665 744) and Yanto (Ⓣ0759/2670 0135), two experienced local guides. The cost depends largely on where you want to go. The major expense is speedboat transport to the start and from the end of the trek. One person in the southeast area will be looking at about Rp1,000,000 for five days, to include transport, accommodation, food, porters and a guide, whilst three people will pay about Rp500,000 each. If you want to go over to the west coast, for example, to Atabai or Sakuddei, trekking across the island to get there and trekking back via the coast, two weeks would cost about Rp1,500,000 per person for a party of three.

Muarasiberut and the beaches

The main town of **MUARASIBERUT** is the administrative and commercial centre of the island, although in reality it's a sleepy little shanty-style village along the coast and around the mouth of the river, with a population of under a thousand people. Many of the inhabitants are from other parts of Indonesia and are here for commercial or business reasons. There's a working beach: the entire population seems to turn out every couple of days to see the ships call in and local owners operate small "speedboats", most of them unstable large canoes with a powerful engine on the back, which ferry passengers and cargo around. The town has electricity and every couple of houses boasts a satellite dish. Whatever is happening to the traditional lifestyles in the interior, the Muarasiberut population is well tuned to CNN news and Hindi movies.

The only **accommodation** in Muarasiberut is *Syahruddin's Homestay* (☎0759/21014; ❶) on the coast at the mouth of the river. The building is wooden, light and airy, but at low tide looks straight onto stinking mud flats which is where the toilets discharge. Rooms have no mosquito nets, and shared mandi. There's an excellent coffee shop across the road serving inexpensive rice, noodles and barbecued fish, plus several other rumah makan and a few small shops with basic supplies. A good landmark is the town mosque with its corrugated iron dome, a couple of hundred metres back from the shore. The **post office** and **Telkom** offices are just behind, but there are no banking or exchange facilities on the island.

It's possible to visit the beaches independently, the main expense being the charter boat from Muarasiberut – take your own snorkelling gear. A basic guesthouse at **Masilo beach** (Rp30,000 per person including meals), provides accommodation in bamboo-and-thatch huts – mattresses and mosquito nets are not supplied. A charter boat will cost about Rp100,000 one-way. The beach is white sand, but the offshore coral isn't brilliant; it's popular with tour groups and domestic tourists, so an idyllic getaway can't be guaranteed. Further away, **Pulau Sibiti** is far quieter and less popular. It's a great white-sand beach with good snorkelling; fishing is a possibility, but it's advisable to take food and a stove. It'll cost about Rp5000 to camp here for the night – pay the family who live on the beach.

The west-coast road

As an alternative to all or part of the Trans-Sumatran Highway journey from the Padang/Bukittinggi area south to Lubuklinggau, about 149km east of Bengkulu, it's possible to travel **south to Bengkulu** on the far pleasanter, quiet coastal road. The great advantage of this is the spectacular scenery, the isolated rural villages and the slow pace of life, far removed from the major cities at either end. Be warned, however, that although there's public transport the full length of this route, it's time-consuming, and much of the accommodation is very simple. Cyclists may find the route appealing as it's quiet and fairly flat, though shadeless for long stretches. There's also an interesting detour possible – east from **Tapan to Sungaipenuh**, into the Kerinci-Seblat national park (see p.427).

△ Bukittinggi, Central Sumatra

Padang to Tapan

The road from Padang to Painan, 77km south of Padang, runs inland through the foothills of the Bukit Barisan range. **PAINAN** is a small fishing town with a long, curving beach littered with fishing boats and their associated paraphernalia. Traces of the fort built in 1664, soon after the Dutch established their first west Sumatran base here, can be seen on Pulau Cingkruk, just offshore at Painan. There's basic accommodation in town; enquire at the **tourist office** at Jalan Ilya Yakub (Mon–Thurs 8am–2pm, Fri 8–11am, Sat 8am–12.30pm; ⓣ0756/21005).

South of Painan, the road leaves the mountains and follows the coastal plain through to Tapan (136km), although from Air Haji it runs inland rather than following the coast as it juts out to Cape Indrapura. The junction market town of **Tapan** is a three-road town: north to Padang (213km), east to Sungaipenuh (64km), and south to Bengkulu. The route to **Sungaipenuh** in the heart of the Kerinci-Seblat national park is convenient; there are regular buses between Tapan and Sungaipenuh. The village of **SUNGAI GAMBIR** offers easy access to national park forests and is a good place to relax; you can swim in the nearby Batang Tapan and walk in the forest. Tigers roam the area during the durian season (Oct–Dec), and you can watch them safely from tree houses built by the villagers. You'll need to stay in family houses or with the kepala desa, but there's a warung that sells snack meals like *mie sop* and gado-gado. Further east on this road, the village of **Sako** offers good birding – look out for the Argus pheasant, hornbills, bulbuls, leafbird, drongo and forktail. Ask at the local rumah makan about accommodation.

Tapan to Bengkulu

From Tapan, the road south heads out towards the coast again. Located 20km south of Tapan, and 1km south of **LUNANG**, the restaurant/losmen *Kasihan Ombak* (no phone; ❶) is the best place to stay along this stretch of road. Just west of the village, the **Lunang Silaut Reserve** is a freshwater swamp forest over which there have been fierce battles in recent years, with big-business interests campaigning to turn it into a palm-oil plantation, while environmentalists are concerned with the area's importance as a fish breeding ground where tapir, tiger, bear and crocodile thrive. The swamp is home to two kinds of parrot, and one of the world's rarest storks (Storm's stork) has been seen here, as well as the threatened white-winged wood duck. Enquire at the village of Tanjung Pondok, just south of Tapan, or at *Kasihan Ombak*, about finding a local boatman for a trip out into the area.

South from here, the road surface is good and the whole area is enticing, with glimpses of glittering ocean just a few hundred metres to the west. Beware though – these beaches have a savage undertow, and not all are safe for swimming, so you must take local advice.

Although **MUKO-MUKO**, 40km south of Lunang, is marked pretty boldly on maps, the reality is somewhat different. It has the only Telkom office between Sungaipenuh and Bengkulu, but, apart from this, boasts only a few remains of an English fort, Fortress Anne, where Sir Stamford Raffles had a garrison in the early nineteenth century. The town beach, lined with spruce trees rather than palms lies between the estuaries of the rivers Manjuto and Selagan, which flow into the Indian Ocean at Muko-Muko.

At the village of **PENARIK**, about 30km south of Muko-Muko, there's basic accommodation in *Losmen Bayung* (❶) in the centre of the village. Further south at **IPUH** there's more of a choice, including *Wisma Damai* (❶). Enquire here about the best local beaches – Air Hitam to the north is pretty good. Further south again, at **Seblat**, there are more local beaches and basic accommodation. The village of **Ketahun**, a few kilometres further on, is spread out along the two banks of a small river; there's a small losmen on the southern side. The larger, bustling town of **Lais** at the junction with the road east to Arga Makmur, lies just 95km north of Bengkulu.

The Kerinci-Seblat national park

Sumatra's largest national park, with elevations varying between sea level and 3800m, the **Kerinci-Seblat national park** is named after its two highest mountains, Gunung Kerinci (3805m), north of Sungaipenuh, and Gunung Seblat (2383m), much further south. It's a brilliant destination for nature-spotting and trekking, and the scenery is particularly lush.

The park was established in the 1990s and comprises a huge variety of ecosystems, including tropical lowland forest, hill forest and mountain forest. Thirty species of mammal roam here, including the Sumatran rhinoceros, Sumatran elephant, Sumatran tiger (there are perhaps seventy or eighty within the park, so a sighting is unlikely), tree leopard, clouded leopard (the least-known of all the cats in Asia), tapir, muntjac deer, Malaysian bear and gibbon. There are also records of 139 bird species and 4000 species of flora, and reported sightings of the *orang pendek* (see the box on p.430).

Around the edges of the park, **encroachment** is a serious issue; local farmers cross park boundaries to clear forest and plant crops, as part of a shifting agriculture system that will move to another area the following year and destroy more. Many of the animals are under constant threat from **poaching**, both for food but also because of the continuing international trade which includes rhino horn and bear's gall bladder. Another threat is from **illegal logging**, which in Kerinci-Seblat is said to account for the loss of thousands of hardwood trees annually. There are several culprits: local pirate operators, the army, and large logging concerns which trespass in the park area. Don't assume that every logging operation you see is illegal: some selected areas are cut legally and then returned to the park, one advantage being that with regrowth the undergrowth gets denser and the leaf-eaters get fatter, attracting both them and their natural hunters into the area. There are also designated permanent logging areas, where the trees are cut and reforestation takes place. The other major threat to the park is that the government simply gives whole areas over for use as rubber, tea, sugar cane, cocoa or palm-oil **plantations**, which support an extremely limited biodiversity. The message from all of this is to get to the park and enjoy it while you can, as there'll probably be less of it in coming years.

There are various **access points**, and it's possible to traverse a considerable length of Sumatra dipping in and out of the park. The most northerly parts are accessible from Painan just below Padang, the southern areas around Curup and Lubuklinggau are accessible from Bengkulu, whilst **Sungaipenuh** (see p.429) is the location of the park headquarters (you can obtain **permits** from here; Rp1500) and the place from which to tackle Gunung Kerinci and the trek to Danau Gunung Tujuh.

Trekking in Kerinci-Seblat national park

Scores of treks are possible, ranging from easy one- and two-day walks along well-used trails between villages, to forest treks of a week or more. National park officers and rangers are happy to advise on the huge number of possibilities, and if you've a special interest in perhaps flowers or birds they will advise.

Trekking in the area isn't only for those with an interest in flora and fauna. **Traditional villages** and longhouses still survive in the heart of the oldest villages in Kerinci: look for them in Siulak Mudik, Lempur and Pondok Tinggi. Ask about traditional **Kerincinese dancing** and **magic ceremonies** in villages such as Seramphas, Lempur, Siulak, Kluru and even, on occasion, Sungaipenuh. These aren't advertised or put on for tourists, but are the real thing, including one, *tarik asiek*, where the spirit of a tiger supposedly enters the dancer.

Enquire at the national park office, *Mitra Kerja*, in Sungaipenuh for national park **guides**; they are often villagers already working as volunteer helpers for the park. Guide fees for non-English-speaking deep-forest village guides are around US$4 per day and for porters US$3 per day, but rates vary from area to area. Trekkers requiring guides who speak English or who have a particular speciality should expect to pay a higher daily rate. Trekkers pay for their guide's food and transport, and it's traditional to also provide a daily packet of cigarettes.

Suggested itineraries

Talang Kemoning (or Lempur)–Sungai Ipuh (Bengkulu) Three days. There are fine views of Gunung Raya (2576m), and a possible detour via Gunung Beliarang for sulphur fountains, geysers and hot springs. You can expect good birding, and you may spot tiger, tapir and siamang. Alternatively, rhino were spotted in the mid-1990s on a trail slightly to the north.

Talang Kemoning–Gunung Beliarang Gunung Beliarang is immediately south of Gunung Raya and north of Gunung Kunyit, an active volcano. You can go there and back in a day, but it's better to make it a two-day trip.

Lempur–Seramphas–Dusun Tuo (Jambi) Two or three days on easy and well-used trails between villages; there's little climbing, but the trail is muddy during the rainy season. Highlights are elephant, tapir and tiger, giant tortoises (which are occasionally seen between Lempur and Seramphas), plus caves and hot springs.

Pungut–Renapermatik–Pelompek A three-day trek, mainly through traditional farms and forest on well-used trails. There are excellent views of Gunung Tujuh and Gunung, with siamang, deer and tiger sometimes reported, good birdwatching – and look out for the Kerinci rabbit, which hasn't been spotted since 1933.

Pungut–Patah Tiga Three to four days of walking through beautiful hill forest, with very fine birding, many animals and superb cloud forest on Bukit Sunting and Gunung Danau. The trek can be extended (five days) to Air Liki, where you can take a raft to Banko.

Tanjung Genting–Gunung Mesjid–Sungaipenuh A stiff walk from the village to the peak of Gunung Mesjid, followed by an easy walk along the peaks fringing the Kerinci valley, with hot springs, waterfalls and good moss forests. An extra day to Air Haji or Sungai Gambir is possible.

Tandai–Gunung Tujuh–Danau Tujuh–Palompek This takes five days, initially on old logging trails in lowland hill forest (400m), with plenty of wildlife and sensational birding, before entering primary hill forest and the climb up to just below Gunung Tujuh (2700m) and down to Danau Gunung Tujuh, and then (one day) to Palompek. Take a local boat across the lake with fishermen.

Danau Tujuh circular Three days' walking the lakeside and ridge trails, with fantastic views and many rare orchids in season (September to November). Sampans can be borrowed from local fishermen.

Padang Aro–Kayu Aro Deep-forest trekking in the hills behind Gunung Kerinci, with fantastic views of the volcano.

Sungaipenuh and Danau Kerinci

Situated in a high fertile valley close to Danau Kerinci and densely farmed with rice, tea, coffee and cloves, the small, attractive town of **SUNGAIPENUH**, 277km southwest of Padang, is the location of the Kerinci-Seblat national park headquarters and, as well as being well worth a couple of days in its own right, is an excellent base for the exploration of the park.

Mesjid Agung in the Pondok Tinggi area of town is a huge and highly unusual mosque, with Roman as well as Arabic features, built in 1874 on the site of an older mosque and constructed without the use of a single nail. The six-metre-long drum (*beduk*) is used to summon the worshippers to prayer, and the whole interior has a wonderfully graceful and devout atmosphere. You'll be asked to make a donation.

Nestling at more than 750m above sea level and surrounded by peaks of about 2000m, the glorious highland lake **Danau Kerinci** lies 5km southeast of Sungaipenuh. The whole area is a rift valley on a geological fault line: Danau Kerinci was the epicentre of an earthquake in October 1995 that registered 7.1 on the Richter scale. There are predictions of more problems, plus a possible eruption of Gunung Kerinci, in the near future. To get good views of the lake, which is invisible from Sungaipenuh, take public transport along the lakeside road to Jujun and then on along the road to Lempur. Alternatively, head up Bukit Tapan to the west of town.

The wealth of **megalithic remains** in the area point to the existence of an ancient civilization which vanished about a thousand years ago and whose disappearance may have been linked to an eruption of Gunung Raya to the southwest of the lake. There's even speculation that at one time the great Sriwijaya kingdom was based here. The most impressive stones are at Muak village, 30km south of Sungaipenuh at the southern end of Danau Kerinci; access is by bus via Jujun and Lempur. The weirdest is **Batu Gong**, a three-metre-long spaceship shape – with circles supposedly representing portholes and stick figures visible. Also worth a look is **Batu Patah** (Broken Stone), a four-metre-long column which local legend claims was part of a column that once reached almost to the moon – a child toppled it and it broke in half, with one part falling to earth near Bukittinggi and one part here. For those who want to explore further, Benik, Lempur, Pendung, Pondok and Kunum, 6km south of Sungaipenuh, all have megaliths. Amateur archeologists may want to root around at Masego, south of Lempur beyond the southern end of the lake, where standing stones have been discovered: the area has been little investigated.

There are plenty of **waterfalls** – the most accessible being Letter W (pronounced "Way"), 10km north of Kersik Tua; the fifty-metre waterfall is 200m from the main road to the right. Birdwatchers should look out for spotted leafbirds and swifts here.

Several villages in the Danau Kerinci area produce distinctive **handicrafts**. At Pendung village, accessed from Semerup, the blades for traditional knives (*parang*) are manufactured; local blacksmiths mourn the demise of the British-made Land-Rover, as the worn-out springs were a good source of metal. The scabbard and handle are added at Jujun at the southern end of the lake. You can see the craftsmen and buy an example, for which you can expect to pay Rp25,000 – the most expensive have a scabbard made from a single piece of durian root, while cheaper ones are made from strips of wood. Rattan baskets are produced at Sungai Tutung.

Orang Pendek

The terrestrial primate **orang pendek** (short man), apparently a little over 1m high, is well known to local people throughout the Bukit Barisan Mountain Range. Workers have seen, heard and found the footprint of this creature, but so far it has eluded photographers – to the extent that many naturalists doubt its existence. Sceptics say it's a sun bear seen in unusual lighting conditions and others believe it to be a folk memory of the orang-utan, which once lived in the area. However, if this was the case, the animal would be arboreal, yet all the signs are that *orang pendek* is terrestrial. The search continues and has international support.

Practicalities

Sungaipenuh is easily accessible, although you may have to change buses in Bangko on the Trans-Sumatran Highway. Buses from Padang may arrive as late as 2am, but the hotels are open to accommodate them. Buses to Padang leave at 9am and 8pm daily. The **bus terminal** itself is in the main market in the southeast of town, though some buses stop just southwest of it. In either case, walk northwest (towards the centre) for two hundred metres until you hit Jalan Imam Bonjol. The sports field in front of you, with a tall monument on the southeastern side, is the town's hub and all **accommodation** is a short walk from here.

Aroma, Jl Imam Bonjol 14 (Ⓣ0748/21142; ❷–❸), is conveniently central, at the southern corner of the sports field. The basic rooms are grimy, but the most expensive are reasonable, with hot-water bathrooms. For the other two options, walk up Jalan Diponegoro (which soon becomes Jalan Marudi when you cross a small bridge), leading northwest from the northern corner of the sports field. *Yani*, Jl Muradi 1 (Ⓣ0748/21409; ❷–❸), is friendly and has clean – if basic – budget rooms and a few cold-water mandi doubles. A little further along the road, turn left up the curving Jalan A. Yani on your left, just past the huge Masjid Baiturrahman, and you'll come to the best choice of all, the *Matahari*, Jalan A. Yani (Ⓣ0748/21061; ❷–❸), which offers large rooms in a big old house, some with attached mandi and tub. This is also the best place to pick up a guide.

For **eating**, *Minang Soto* at Jl Muradi 4 (next to the *Yani* hotel), serves good, inexpensive Padang food, as does its twin restaurant of the same name across the road. *Simpang Tiga*, on Jalan H. Agus Salim in the market area, dishes up excellent Padang food: the brains in coconut sauce are particularly good. Up the hill from the *Matahari*, *Dendeng Batokok Diatas* provides very simple local food. Another good place is the little unnamed rumah makan just downhill from the national parks office, opposite the hospital on Jalan Basukit Rahmet. It's usually full of nurses and park wardens, and the *tempeh sambal* and jackfruit curries are wonderful.

The BNI bank, opposite *Matahari*, has **foreign exchange** facilities and an ATM; the 24-hour **Telkom office** is on Jalan Imam Bonjol next to the *Aroma*, and the **post office** is at Jl Sudirman 1a. The long-distance bus companies have offices near the *Yani* hotel. The excellent **national park office**, Jl Basuki Rahmat 11 (Mon–Thurs 7.30am–4pm; Ⓣ0748/22250, Ⓕ22300), can be found on the edge of town: look for a white gateway with red lettering, and ask for the "TNKS", or you'll get blank looks. They offer information and advice about the park and issue **permits** (Rp15,000 each for Gunung Kerinci or Danau Gunung Tujuh, plus Rp250 insurance), although you can also get these at the park offices closer to each place. Enquire here for national park guides (warden Afnir will direct you), who will charge Rp30,000–40,000 per day, per group of one to four people. Guides will provide cooking pots and can rent you a sleeping bag (Rp15,000) and tent (Rp20,000). The office has some printed material, can give you a topographical map and has excellent photographs of local wildlife on display. Look especially for the image of the black golden cat, a variety of the golden cat with an excess of the pigment melanin – this picture, taken in 1996, was the first ever taken of the creature.

If you stay in town for a day or two, particularly at the *Matahari*, local tour guides will probably find you and offer their services; one of the best is Li, an experienced guide. Several **tours** are on offer, including visits to the Kubu people near Bangko (see p.464) from around US$20 a day; trips to the Ladeh Panjang swamp area, including Gunung Beliarang, lasting two days and one night (from US$75); three-day/two-night trips to the Belibis and Kasah caves (US$75); a one-night/two-day guided climb up Gunung Kerinci (US$75); and a day-trip to the megalithic stones in the area (US$15). Trips to the Gunung Lumut wildlife-spotting area are around US$15 a day. Alternatively, it's possible to charter a car and local driver for upwards of Rp150,000 a day and put together your own trip; be very careful that both parties are clear about what is and isn't included, and clarify the time scale and exact itinerary.

Gunung Kerinci and around

The grandeur of **Gunung Kerinci** (3805m), the highest mountain in Sumatra, can be admired and (for the energetic) scaled from the attractively cool highland village of **KERSIK TUO**, 48km north of Sungaipenuh. The entire region is beautiful, with brilliant green-tea plantations on gently rolling hillsides as far as the eye can see.

To get to Kersik Tuo, catch a local bus from the bus station in Sungaipenuh, or from the *Yani* hotel (the bus conductors yell "Kayuaro", which is the local name for the entire district); it takes between and hour and ninety minutes to get to Kersik Tuo, via the attractive market village of Bendeng. If you're coming from Padang, the long-distance buses to Sungaipenuh pass through Kersik Tuo. There are several homestays in the village, although at the time of writing the Eco-Rural Travel Co-operative office, the coordinating body for homestays and guides in the area, had been closed for some time. *Darmin Homestay* (no phone; ❶) is on the main road, several hundred metres north of the side road to Gunung Kerinci and is clean and welcoming, with an upstairs sitting area and a balcony out the front with views straight towards Gunung Kerinci. The owners will cook basic meals. *Homestay Keluarga Subandi* (no phone; ❶) is also at the southern end of the village, opposite the turning to Gunung Kerinci, and is a great contact for guides and equipment hire.

You can obtain local information and details of possible trips at any of the homestays. Expect to pay Rp30,000 per day for a porter and Rp40,000 for a guide. They will help you plan **excursions** in the area or arrange all-in tours including transport. Tours and per-person prices include: Kerinci (two days; US$54), Danau Gunung Tujuh (one day; US$17), Danau Belibis (one day; US$16), Ladeh Panjang (four days; US$99), Danau Kerinci (one or two days; US$29/44), tea estates (one day; US$9), and the Kasah cave and around (three days; US$60).

Climbing Gunung Kerinci

The highest active volcano in Sumatra, **Gunung Kerinci** (3805m) is a tough climb with uncertain rewards at the top. The views can be stunning early in the morning, but the weather is very changeable, and after a hard slog to get to the top you may be enveloped in fog. The **crater**, over 500m across, is still active and belches poisonous gases, so a great deal of care is necessary: there's no path around the crater's edge. The mountain is famous for the white-flowered Javanese edelweiss (*Anaphalis javanica*), which is found only on volcanoes, can grow to 4m and looks remarkably striking on the bare volcanic soil. It's also incredibly enticing for **birdwatching**, as the scene of recent sightings of Schneider's pitta: the bird was first spotted on this trail in 1988, after forty years during which it was thought to be extinct. Salvador's pheasant is even more elusive, but, like the pitta, is generally seen on the lower slopes, while another rare bird, the red-billed partridge, prefers the higher elevations. Altogether, the Kerinci trail is one of the best birding areas in the park: expect babblers, thrushes, mesias and fantails as well as warblers, woodpeckers, minivets and the rare Sumatran cochea, plus several species of hornbill. You can also hope to spot gibbons, macaques, leaf-monkeys, and there are thought to be tigers in the area.

To tackle the **summit** you need to be properly prepared. Temperatures regularly plummet to 5°C and, although there are "shelters", they are open-sided and often roofless: you will definitely need a sleeping bag and a tent is highly desirable. Enquire at the homestays about rental, but it's far better to have your own. Regardless of the dubious environmental impact of using wood from the forests to cook, the wood is often wet, so it's advisable to take a stove, as well as appropriate rain gear. A spring above Shelter 2 provides fresh drinking water, and there are a few other spots further down, but check this before you set off. Hiring a **guide** is highly recommended, as a number of climbers have come to grief up here – whilst it's relatively straightforward to follow the path going up, it can be easy to miss on the descent.

The route goes from a side road in Kersik Tua, guarded by a statue of a roaring lion, and you walk 5km, following the obviously main route, to the PHPA office, where you'll need to sign in and get a **permit** (Rp15,000), if you don't already have one. From here it takes about two hours' climbing through cultivated fields and then into the forest to Shelter 1; you'll pass a small shelter on the way that has no number. From Shelter 1, it's a further two to three hours to Shelter 2, where most people aim to spend the night. You'll need to get up between 3am and 5am to complete the two hours to the top for dawn. The slippery volcanic rock gets steeper and steeper as you go up above the treeline – in places steps have been cut, but it's very hard going. Most people make it from Shelter 2 to the summit and back down to Kersik Tua in one day.

Danau Gunung Tujuh

The trek to **Danau Gunung Tujuh** (Seven Mountains Lake), the highest volcanic lake in Southeast Asia at an altitude of 1996m, is a much less gruelling excursion than that to Gunung Kerinci. However, it's still extremely picturesque, and as rewarding a one-day hike as you'll find in Sumatra. In addition, you can hope to spot pretty much the same variety of **wildlife** here as you would on the mountain, and the variety of birds is wonderful. Danau Gunung Tujuh is a freshwater lake in the ancient crater of an extinct volcano, 4.5km long and 3km wide. As long as you leave early, it's a relatively straightforward day-trip there and back from Kersik Tua, but really deserves more time and appreciation than this. Lone male travellers should be especially careful, as the lake is said to be home to *dewa*, beautiful female spirits who sing to entice men into a life of eternal slavery.

The walk starts from the village of **Ulujernih** (also known as Pesir Bukit), 2km on from the slightly larger **Pelompek**, which is 7km north of Kersik Tua.

Pelompek, a busy little market town is a good place to buy supplies for the trek, and there are a couple of rumah makan. You can take a direct minibus to Pelompek from the terminal in Sungeipenuh, and take an oplet on to Ulujernih. Should you end up walking from Pelompek, the only major side road to the right (east) leads 2km to Ulujernih. Just under 1km beyond Ulujernih, the national park office is amongst a small huddle of concrete houses at the far end of the valley, and you'll see the national park gateway. There's also a losmen here, the *Pak Edes* (Rp15,000), which sells a few provisions. At the office you can book in, buy a **permit** if you don't already have one (Rp15,000), and, if necessary, arrange a **guide** (around Rp25,000 per day).

The track from the office is wide, cobbled and negotiable on a motorcycle for 1.5km to a clearing in the forest where the park guesthouse, now burnt down, used to stand. The path to the lake passes to the left of the remnants and on into the forest, where it climbs relentlessly to Shelter 2, which is on the crater rim above the lakeside an hour and a half's hike (not counting rests) through the forest from the clearing. It's a large and obvious track, and you don't need a guide. From the shelter, take the main track left, and the steep descent to the lakeside takes about fifteen minutes; you'll catch a few glimpses of the water through the trees on the way down. At the bottom, you'll be treated to the magnificent sight of the **Air Terjun** (waterfall), which is literally a gash in the side of the crater, from which the lake water tumbles down and over the precipice. It's an awesome sight and the peak of Gunung Kerinci is visible from here.

The lake is surrounded by mountains, the seven of the name, and dominated by **Gunung Tujuh** on the far side, with densely forested slopes right down to the water's edge. This scene is particularly lovely in the early morning, when wisps of mist rise off the surface and the siamang gibbons (one of the highest recorded sightings of the species) start to call as the sun comes up. Down on the lakeside there's a fairly sizeable shelter, but you'll be more comfortable in a tent. The duration of your stay is really only determined by how much food you've brought: you should bring a stove. For those with time and inclination there are shelters further around the left-hand side of the lake called **Pos Merah** and **Pos Maliki** – you'll need a guide to help you find these.

The rest of the park

With time and determination, there are huge areas of the park to be explored. Situated in a side-cone of Gunung Kerinci on the southern flanks, **Danau Belibis** is a small crater lake set at 2050m above sea level. It's known for sightings of wild duck and is an easy day-trip from Kersik Tuo. The start of the trail is two hours from Kersik Tuo at the edge of the plantation land (you'll need a guide to locate it), and you'll have to make a two-kilometre leech-infested forest hike to the lake, which has some great views of Gunung Kerinci.

There are two **swamps** within reach of Kersik Tuo. At 1950m, Ladeh Panjang is the highest peat-moss swamp in Sumatra, situated due west of Kerinci and caused by geological blocking of the valley forming two nearby lakes – Sati and Singkarak. The habitat is of dwarf peat-swamp woodland with tussocks of sedge and grass between the trees, which are hung with long lichens. Access is on foot (6hr) from **Kebun Baru** village, 18km from Kersik Tuo. The track starts through cultivated land with most of it in the forest – you'll need camping gear as well as a guide. Danau Bento (Sangir Hulu) is a freshwater swamp forest at 1375m, named after a type of wild rice that used to dominate the swamp.

Pekanbaru and around

The administrative capital of Riau province, an amalgamation of mainland and island districts spreading from the edge of the Bukit Barisan mountains almost to the coast of Borneo, the booming oil town of **PEKANBARU** is a major gateway into Indonesia from Singapore. Most travellers head straight through and, whilst there are few specific sights to detain you, the town is easy to get around, and has a relaxed atmosphere as long as you get away from the bus terminal, which is full of some of Sumatra's most persistent touts.

The historical origins of Pekanbaru date back to a small village called Payung Sekaki which changed its name to Senepelan during the time of the Siak kingdom. Gradually, a commercial centre grew up at the site and a market (*pekan*) was established: in 1784, the name Pekanbaru was coined. Just before World War II, oil was discovered in the area and exploited first by the Japanese, and then by newly independent Indonesia, turning Pekanbaru into a boom city in the process.

Located 130km west of Pekanbaru, roughly equidistant between it and Bukittinggi, **Muara Takus** is home to the remains of a ninth- and tenth-century Buddhist kingdom, and **Siak Sri Indrapura**, 120km towards the coast from Pekanbaru, provides the most tangible evidence of the Siak kingdom, which dominated the area from 1725 to 1945. **Dumai**, around 190km north of Pekanbaru, is the major east-coast Sumatran port – there's no reason to come here except for ferries (see box p.436).

Arrival, information and city transport

Flights land at the Simpang Tiga airport, 9km south of the city centre. The closest public transport is 1km away on the main highway, where you can catch public buses into the Pasar Pusat terminal in the city centre. Otherwise, fixed-price taxis charge Rp20,000 for the trip. **Long-distance buses** arrive at the terminal on Jalan Nangka about 2.5km south of the river, from where you can catch a blue bemo to the city centre. Most express **ferry services** from Batam or Bintan land at Buton, where you can take a bus either to the bus terminal at Jalan Nangka or the express-ferry office at the northern end of Jalan Sudirman. Slow boats arrive at the main port area at the northern end of Jalan Saleh Abbas in the Pasar Bawah market area, a couple of hundred metres west of Jalan Sudirman.

With only a few suburbs to the north, the bulk of Pekanbaru is situated on the south banks of Sungai Siak, extending for 8km out towards the airport. The main street is Jalan Sudirman, which runs north–south right from the river itself through the centre of town to the airport area. Most places of interest to tourists, including hotels, restaurants and shops, are within easy reach of this thoroughfare.

The **tourist information office**, Jl Diponegoro 24 (Mon–Thurs 8am–2pm, Fri 8–11am, Sat 8am–12.30pm; ⓣ0761/31562, ⓕ31565), has plenty of English-language leaflets and will try to help with enquiries – it's a bit out of the way and probably not worth the trek unless you need very specific information.

City transport

Public buses and bemos operate on roughly fixed routes around town. **Buses** (6am–9pm; Rp700) run the length of Jalan Sudirman and beyond, between the Pasar Pusat terminal near the Jalan Imam Bonjol junction with Jalan Sudirman

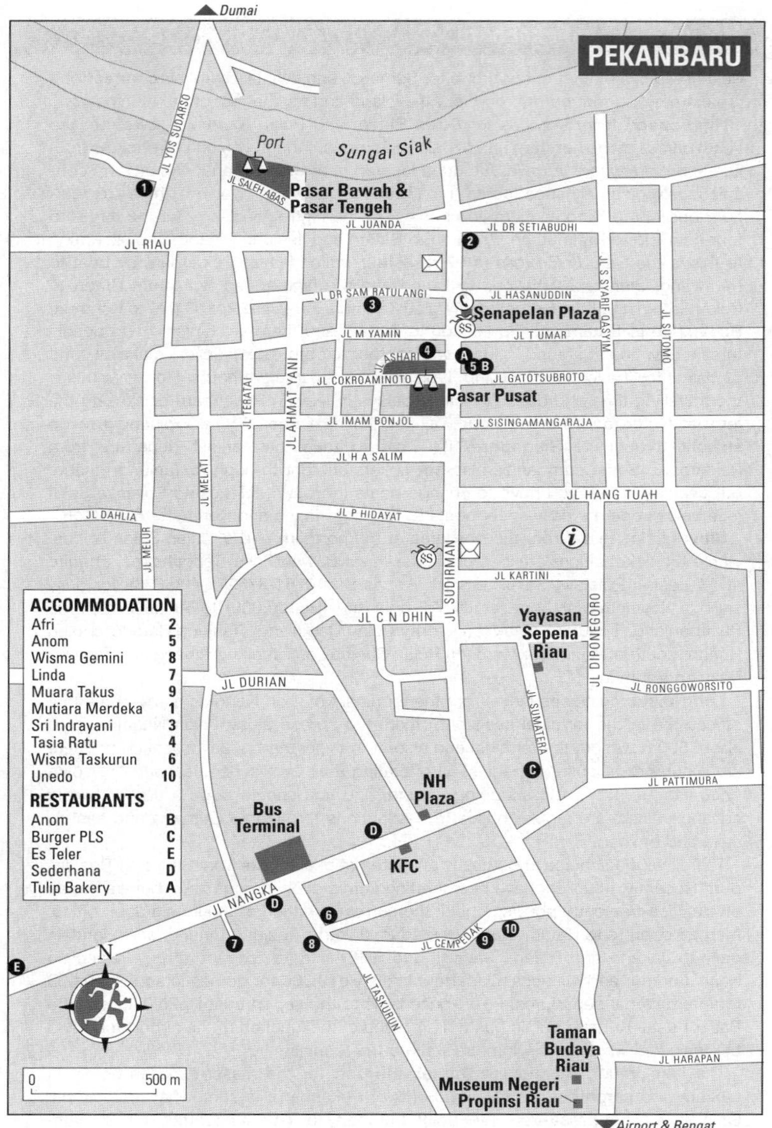

and Kubang terminal, which is 3km beyond the turning to Simpang Tiga airport. **Bemos** (Rp700) operate to and from the main bemo terminal, Sekapelan, which is situated just west of the main market area behind Jalan Sudirman. Bemos are colour-coded and marked with their destination. A couple of useful services are the **blue** bemo (6am–11pm) to Tangkerang, which is the museum area, south of town (they usually pass near the Jalan Nangka bus

Moving on from Pekanbaru

Pekanbaru is a major transport hub for Sumatra, and sea, land and air **connections** are extremely good, both throughout the island and for the rest of the archipelago.

High-speed ferry services for Pulau Batam and Pulau Karimun leave from the ticket offices at the northern end of Jalan Sudirman, though you can buy tickets from just about anywhere in town. Although located near the river and with adverts conspicuously picturing speedboats, most services actually involve a three- to four-hour bus trip to Buton, where you transfer to the high-speed ferry for the three- to four-hour trip to Karimun and then on to Batam and Tanjung Pinang. The exception to this is the *Garuda Express* (Ⓣ0761/42489), which leaves Pekanbaru by boat to Perawang, then takes the bus to Buton and the high-speed ferry from Buton to Pulau Batam and then (sometimes) Pulau Karimun. Fares are Rp100,000 to Karimun, Rp120,000 to Batam and Rp165,000 to Bintan, and there are typically two departures a day, one at around 7.30am and another at 5pm. Ticket sellers make all sorts of claims for the length of the trip, typically from six to eight hours. However, this is the travelling time and doesn't include delays in leaving Pekanbaru or missing the ferry at Buton and the two-hour wait for the next one. If you're planning to go straight through to **Singapore**, it's best to take the earliest departure from Pekanbaru. Some companies also sell tickets straight through to Tanjung Pinang, but check whether you have to change boats in Batam. PT Lestari Polajaya Sakti (see below) operate daily speedboats to Tanjung Pinang and Karimun from Buton.

Slow ferries leave from the port area at the northern end of Jalen Saleh Abbas, where the ticket offices are located, in the Pasar Bawah/Pasar Tengah area. Enquire at PT Lestari Polajaya Sakti, Jl Saleh Abbas 8 (Ⓣ0761/37627, Ⓕ35623), for daily sailings that leave at 5pm for the 25-hour trip (Rp100,000) to Pulau Batam via Selatpanjang, Tanjung Samak (on nearby Pulau Rangsang), Tanjung Batu (on Pulau Kundur south of Karimun), Moro (on Pulau Sugibawah), Tanjung Pinang and Tanjung Balai on Karimun.

Long-distance buses leave from the terminal on Jalan Nangka; many of the bus offices are in the terminal itself but others are spread along Jalan Nangka up to about 500m west of the terminal and also at the very start of Jalan Taskurun. There are a number of bus companies, all operating their own schedules with their own price lists, so it's worth shopping around, and you should book a day or two in advance. There are regular buses to destinations throughout Sumatra and east to Java and beyond.

There's a good choice of domestic and international **flights** from Simpang Tiga airport. Recently, travellers have been getting immigration stamps here, but it's not an official visa-free entry port, so check the current situation at the immigration office. Merpati operate to Batam, Padang, Medan, Jakarta, Tanjung Pinang, and Mandala daily to Jakarta and Batam. Merpati and Silk Air fly to Singapore and Pelangi to Kuala Lumpur and Malacca. Departure tax is Rp10,300 for domestic and Rp20,000 for international departures. Fixed-price taxis to the airport cost Rp20,000, and the Pasar Pusat–Kubang public bus will drop you at the junction of the airport road and the main highway, a one-kilometre walk to the terminal.

The immigration situation at **Dumai**, the port for the massive ocean-going oil tankers and cargo carriers, 189km north of Pekanbaru, is somewhat ambiguous. Officially it is not a visa-free entry point, but many long-term expatriates in Sumatra report that **visas** are issued here and, with the daily high-speed crossing taking between two and three hours to Malacca, it's actually the cheapest and quickest way to exit and re-enter Indonesia by sea. Check the situation locally before you set off. If you get stranded in Dumai there's little accommodation to recommend, but check out the *City Hotel*, Jl Sudirman 445 (Ⓣ0765/21550; ③), or the much less expensive *Wisma Hang Tua* (②) at no 431.

terminal on their way back into town), and the **yellow** service (6am–8pm), which goes to Rumbai, a northeast suburb, via Jalan Riau, passing close to the *Mutiara Merdeka* hotel. Other areas of town that are named on bemos are Sukajadi (the bemo terminal next to the bus terminal on Jalan Nangka), Panam in the southwest suburbs, and Pasar Limapuluh at the north end of Jalan Sutomo on the east side of town.

Accommodation

Accommodation in Pekanbaru is not great; with the town awash with oil money and the majority of trade passing through, there's little charm or hospitality to the hotels. Most places could divide the rates by two before they seemed value for money, especially at the lower end of the scale (which bottoms out at Rp35,000). The essential choice is between the central area – most places are within a short distance of Jalan Sudirman – or the bus terminal area, about 5km south. If you decide on the bus terminal area, you're advised to steer clear of the basic, noisy and poor-value places on Jalan Nangka itself and aim for the quieter roads to the south. Jalan Taskurun and Jalan Cempaka are good hunting grounds.

Afri Jl Dr Setiabudhi 5 ⓣ0761/33190. Conveniently located on the corner of Jalan Sudirman about 200m south of the speedboat ferry dock, this is a clean, multistorey setup with air-con rooms and attached mandi. Extremely convenient if you arrive very late at this end of town. ③

Anom Jl Gatot Subroto 1–3 ⓣ0761/36083, ⓕ37671. Located centrally, about 100m from Jalan Sudirman, this recently renovated place has spotlessly clean rooms opening off a central courtyard, some with hot water. Prices include a small breakfast, and there's a popular Chinese restaurant attached. ③–④

Wisma Gemini Jl Taskurun 44 ⓣ0761/32916. The more expensive rooms are reasonable and have air-con and TVs, but the place needs a clean, and you're better off elsewhere if you're trying to save money. ③–④

Hotel Linda Jl Nangka 145 ⓣ0761/36915. A big white house on a quiet alleyway that leads off Jalan Nangka, opposite the bus terminal, about 50m west of *Penginapan Linda* – don't get these places confused. Offers a big range of rooms, all with bathrooms attached. This is a much better bet than any of the more obvious places on the main road; you'd walk past it in most towns, but here it's not a bad choice. ③–④

Muara Takus Jl Cempaka 17 ⓣ0761/21045. Set back slightly from the road and convenient for the bus terminal, this is one of the best-value places, with rooms ranging from those with outside bathroom and no fan to those with attached bathroom and fan. Better than places twice the price. ②–③

Mutiara Merdeka Jl Yos Sudarso 12a ⓣ0761/31272, ⓕ32959, ⓔmerdeka@indon.net.id. The plushest and most expensive hotel in town, which offers excellent facilities including a travel agent, business centre and small pool (open to nonresidents for Rp5000). This is still the most popular option at this end of the range, and there's an efficiency and buzz missing in the imitators, but you pay for it, and it isn't particularly convenient for public transport. They offer occasional excellent weekend deals. ⑤–⑦

Sri Indrayani Jl Dr Sam Ratulangi ⓣ0761/35600, ⓕ31870, ⓔindrabs@indonet.id. The most pleasant rooms have a small verandah leading out into a garden area. This is more spacious and classier than others in this price range and though it lacks the facilities of the *Mutiara Merdeka*, you get satellite TV and air-con. ③–⑤

Tasia Ratu Jl K.H. Hasyim Ashari 10 ⓣ0761/33431, ⓕ38912. A small, quiet and friendly place in this price range, centrally located just off Jalan Sudirman. It's signed from Jalan Sudirman and has air-con and hot water in all rooms, which are well furnished. ⑤–⑥

Wisma Taskurun Jl Taskurun 37 ⓣ0761/23555. Situated on Jalan Taskurun, which runs south off Jalan Nangka just opposite the bus terminal, this is 200m up on the left. All rooms have an attached mandi – with fans at the lower price range and air-con at the upper. The rooms are basic and reasonably clean. ②–③

Unedo Jl Cempaka 1 ⓣ0761/223396. This has clean fan or air-con rooms with attached cold-water mandi; there's a small garden. It's about 50m from Jalan Sudirman and is convenient for the bus terminal. ③

The City

Pekanbaru is a well-maintained, bustling oil city, with broad, spacious streets and a mixture of Sumatran, Javanese, Chinese and expat inhabitants. The city is rather low on sights, but one definitely worth seeing is **Yayasan Sepena Riau**, Jl Sumatera 7 (Mon–Sat 10am–4pm), a small private museum and souvenir shop. It's an absolute treasure trove that rivals most provincial museums, the artefacts collected by one family over many years. The centrepiece is a collection of artefacts connected with traditional Riau weddings – costumes, furnishings and crockery – surrounded by Chinese ceramics, weapons, European glass, photographs and jewellery; there are no labels, but the owner will show you around and explain things. **Museum Negeri Propinsi Riau** (Mon–Sat 8am–4pm; Rp1000) is a typical Sumatran museum with the prerequisite stuffed animals, traditional-wedding setup, model traditional houses, costumes, weapons, implements, Chinese ceramics and old money, displayed with very little explanation. There are some Western children's games: kites, spinning tops and hoops, and a local game called *pari* with counters and holes in a board. There's also a model of Muara Takus (see p.439), but overall it's a forlorn collection with little entertainment or educational value. Next door, the **Taman Budaya Riau**, the cultural centre, hosts occasional performances of dance and music: enquire at the tourist office.

The **markets** provide a fascinating kaleidoscope of local life: Pasar Pusat is the food and household-goods market, and Pasar Bawah and Pasar Tengeh in the port area have an excellent range of Chinese goods, including ceramics and carpets.

Eating, drinking and entertainment

Pekanbaru has an excellent range of **restaurants** serving Western, Chinese and Indonesian food as well as several small **night markets** – even if you stayed in the city for a month, you could have every meal at the brilliant Pasar Pusat night market (located in the market area near Jalan Bonjol) and not eat the same thing twice. Tables are laid out for diners, protected against the rain by awnings. There are also branches of *KFC* at Senapelan Plaza, Jl Teuku Umar 1 (just off Jalan Sudirman), and Jl Nangka 69–71.

Pekanbaru's **nightlife** isn't particularly thriving. The **bar** at the *Mutiara Merdeka* hotel is the liveliest and most popular with the well-heeled business travellers who abound in the city. The local **disco** scene is very variable: ask at your accommodation for the latest recommendation.

Anom Jl Gatot Subroto 3. Attached to the *Anom Hotel*, this is a popular moderate/expensive Chinese restaurant with a range of seafood, chicken and pork dishes plus the usual Chinese delicacies.

Burger PLS Jalan Sumatera. Senapelan–Gobah bemos run along the street: this place is just outside the *Amie Art Shop*. It's a basic, good-value, fast-food stand and they do fine hot dogs and burgers with dill pickles; ask them to go easy on the chilli sauce, which is extremely hot.

Es Teler 77 Jl Nangka 124b. The usual range of ices, juices and simple Indonesian snacks in the standard fast-food setting that this chain specializes in.

Kuantan Coffee Shop At the *Mutiara Merdeka* hotel. The prices here match the location in the plushest hotel in town, with a huge menu of Japanese, Chinese and Western food (up to imported T-bone steak at Rp45,000), but offering other options such as pizza, sandwiches and ice cream. They have special theme nights and a business lunch, which are good deals. Open 24hr.

Sederhana Jl Nangka 121–123. Two co-owned Padang-style restaurants on opposite sides of the road that offer good value but spicy eating in the area near the bus terminal. This is one of the larger, more popular places and also has *murtabaks*.

Swensen's Jl Teuku Umar 1. In the Senepelan Plaza just off Jalan Sudirman, this international ice-cream-parlour chain offers a standard range of sundaes and soft drinks that are undoubtedly a taste of home, but pricey.

Tulip Bakery Jl Sudirman 153. A two-storey, very popular fast-food place which veers towards the upper end of the price range (steaks for Rp30,000), but also offers burgers, pizza, juices and drinks at moderate prices. With air-con, a relaxed atmosphere and a few tables looking out into the street, it's cool and comfortable.

Shopping

There are a couple of multistorey **shopping centres** in Pekanbaru. **Senapelan Plaza**, Jl Teuku Umar 1, just off Jalan Sudirman, has five floors including a Suzuyu Department Store, *KFC*, *Swensen's* ice-cream parlour and the Gelael Supermarket, plus a variety of clothing, fabric, cassette and CD shops. The newer **NH Plaza**, Jl Husni Thamrin 2, is just off Jalan Nangka east of the bus station, and houses a similar range of shops. The main Pekanbaru market is **Pasar Pusat**, around Jalan Cokroaminoto to the east of Jalan Sudirman. Pasar Bawah and Pasar Tengah, between Jalan M. Yatim and Jalan Saleh Abbas in the port area, is excellent for **souvenirs**, especially ceramic Chinese goods. Guci Indah, Jl M. Yatim 1a, has a very good selection ranging from tiny teapots to 2m vases. The Amie Art Shop, Jl Sumatera 178 (Senapelan–Gobah bemos go up this street), is one of the few souvenir shops in town and also offers some modern art by local painters.

Listings

Airline offices Garuda, *Mutiara Merdeka* hotel, Jl Yos Sudarso 12a ⓣ0761/29115, ⓕ45062; Mandala, Jl Sudirman 308 ⓣ0761/20055, ⓕ23808 & Jl Prof. M. Yamin 49 ⓣ0761/32948, 33759; Merpati, Jl Prof. M. Yamin 49b ⓣ0761/32948, ⓕ33759; Pelangi, Jl Pepaya 64c ⓣ0761/28896, ⓕ29435; Silk Air, *Mutiara Merdeka* hotel, Jl Yos Sudarso 12a ⓣ0761/28175, ⓕ28174.

Banks and exchange All the main banks have branches in the city, including BCA, Jl Sudirman 448, and BNI, Jl Sudirman 63.

Car rental PO Gelara Indah, Jl Sisingamangaraja 1 ⓣ0761/27754; Rumpun Jaya Car Rental, Jl Arengka 57 ⓣ0761/62678, ⓕ37397. Expect to pay about Rp250,000 for a Kijang or similar for a day excluding petrol and driver; a driver would be a further Rp50,000 per day.

Hospitals Rumah Sakit Santa Maria, Jl A. Yani 68 ⓣ0761/20235; Rumah Sakit Umum Pusat Pekanbaru, Jl Diponegoro 2 ⓣ0761/36118.

Immigration office Jalan Singa ⓣ0761/21536.

Pharmacies Several are situated on Jalan Sudirman, and are generally well stocked; Kencana, Jl Sudirman 69; Djaya, Jl Sudirman 185, on the corner with Jalan Gatot Subroto.

Post office The main post office is at Jl Sudirman 229 and poste restante should be sent here; it's reasonably efficient, but there's a more convenient post office for sending mail at Jl Sudirman 78, close to the northern end of Jalan Sudirman.

Telephone and fax The Telkom office is at Jl Sudirman 117 and there are wartels all over town, including Jl Gatot Subroto 6.

Travel agents Mutiara Nusantara Travel at *Mutiara Merdeka* hotel, Jl Yos Sudarso 12a ⓣ0761/32495, ⓕ32959; Prima Travel, Jl Sudirman 25 ⓣ0761/21421; PT Kotapiring Kencana, Jl Sisingamangaraja 3–7 (ⓣ0761/24009, ⓕ34970) is a Pelangi agent, and offers day-tours to Muara Takus, Siak and Ma Lembu for Rp110,000 per person and a half-day city tour for Rp50,000, but you'll need a minimum of two people.

Around Pekanbaru

Muara Takus, the remains of an ancient Buddhist complex which is only part of a far larger collection of ruins spread over several square kilometres, lies 130km west of Pekanbaru. It was probably built between the ninth and eleventh centuries during the time of the Sriwijayan empire. Whilst archeologists may find the rather desolate complex of interest, and there's enough mystery centred around the site to enable plenty of amateur theories, this isn't an unmissable sight in Sumatra.

One local legend tells that the ancient city was so big it would take a cat three months to cross the roofs of the buildings, while another relates that it was the burial ground of an ancient Hindu ruler who was turned into an elephant upon his death – wild elephants are said to congregate here at the full moon to dance in his honour. It seems likely that the temples are royal graves, and the complex features a rare ancient brick stupa, **Candi Maligai**, which has been completely restored; this is a construction rarely seen in Indonesia, associated with the Mahayana Buddhist tradition. The entire complex is surrounded by walls over 70m long on each side, as well as earth ramparts. To get to Muara Takus by public transport, take a westbound bus to Muaramahat and then a bemo to the site via Kototengah (3hr total). The *Arga Sonya* (❷) is the government **guesthouse** in the area.

Far more worthwhile, but almost as far from the city in the opposite direction, is **Siak Sri Indrapura**, the restored palace of the eleventh sultan of Siak, Sultan Abdul Jalil Syafuddin, which lies 120km downriver from Pekanbaru at Siakinderpura. A bus (2–3hr) leaves from the northern end of Jalan Sudirman each morning, and from the terminal at Pasar Lima Puluh; enquire at the port area of Jalan Saleh Abbas if you fancy a river trip (ferry 4hr, speedboat 1–2hr).

The palace was built in 1889 at a time when the sultan controlled a huge area of eastern Sumatra, as his ancestors had done since 1725. The palace was abandoned after Independence and soon began to deteriorate, until Caltex, the petroleum company, contributed to its renovation. It's now brilliant white, with a multitude of minarets, arches and colonnades contributing to the grand effect. There's a small **museum** in the palace with many historical objects and photographs linked to the royal family, especially the last sultan, though the best of them have been removed to the National Museum in Jakarta (see p.106). Royal burial grounds, a mosque and a court building lie in the palace grounds. Enquire locally for the basic **hotels** and **losmen** in town; there are several rumah makan and a small market.

The Riau Islands

The original home of the *orang laut* (sea people), the descendants of pirates and nomadic traders, the **Riau Archipelago** consists of more than a thousand islands spread in a huge arc across the South China Sea between the east coast of Sumatra and the northwestern tip of Kalimantan. These islands can be a brief staging post on the sea journey from Singapore, but are interesting destinations in their own right, meriting at least a few days' exploration – perhaps on the way to further-flung destinations such as the Lingga Islands. Beware though: Singaporean influence is strong here, and prices are high. Some of the islands are off limits to visitors, as they house refugees from mainland Asia.

The largest and most accessible islands, **Karimun**, **Batam** and **Bintan**, are the best known, and are rapidly developing as the industrial and tourist hinterland for their close neighbour Singapore. Sleepy **Pulau Kundur** is the least developed for tourism, the coastal tin mining being something of an eyesore in a few spots around the island. Until 1975, these were forest-covered islands, ringed by mangrove swamps and with a small population living in scattered coastal villages; in the 1980s, however, industrial and tourist development commenced. Batam has the most obvious industrial compounds, alongside golf courses, high-quality holiday accommodation and expensive resort areas, while Karimun and Bintan are still managing to hang onto traditional life to some

Luxury Riau at bargain prices

The **luxury resorts** of Batam and Bintan are expensive compared with most Indonesian accommodation, although good value by Western standards. Whilst facilities are among the best in Sumatra, catering largely for the highly discerning Singaporean holiday market, the walk-in prices are high, anything from US$100 per night plus tax and service. However, you can book a hugely discounted stay through travel agents in Singapore – many trips booked in Singapore include return transport. Batam and Bintan are well advertised in Singapore in the English-language newspaper, the *Straits Times*, and the best current deals are featured there. Singaporeans gravitate to the islands at weekends, so weekday deals are even better value. The resorts are very variable in facilities, atmosphere and location; decide which suits you best and be especially careful in Batam – plenty of the advertised breaks are based in Nagoya rather than on the coast. If you miss the *Straits Times* adverts, try the following Singapore travel agents, who all offer deals to the islands – you could expect to pay less than half the walk-in price – or contact the Singapore offices of the resorts to see what they have on offer. Typical offers are US$240 per person for a three-day/two-night stay during the week, including transport and meals.

For **golf**, you'll be better off booking an all-in deal from Singapore than arranging accommodation and visitors' rates at the golf clubs separately. Many of the clubs arrange deals through offices in Singapore. Tering Bay Development (Ⓣ065/2718823, Ⓕ2718851) offers an all-in deal including accommodation in Nagoya and green fees, from US$144 per person.

Channel Holidays PTE Ltd Ⓣ065/2761332, Ⓕ2769700.
Continental Travel and Tours PTE 3 Coleman St, #02–14 Peninsula Shopping Centre Ⓣ065/3388920.
Fascinating Holidays 333 Orchard Rd, #03–47 Mandarin Shopping Arcade Ⓣ & Ⓕ065/7355511.
Gunung Raya #01–13 Golden Mile Complex Ⓣ065/2947711.
Ken-Air 35 Selegie Rd, #02–25, Parklane Shopping Mall Ⓣ065/3367888.
SIME Travel 100 Beach Road, #02–50/53 Shaw Leisure Gallery Ⓣ065/2977922, Ⓕ2977422.
Sinba Travel #02–56 World Trade Centre Ⓣ065/2707779.

extent. On Bintan this is achieved by the massive tourist enclave in the north of the island, Bintan Resort, separating most of the tourist infrastructure from mainstream island life. For real adventurers, the islands to the east and north, the Anambas, Natuna and Tambelan islands have little infrastructure for visitors, and transport is infrequent.

Pulau Karimun

The most westerly of the accessible Riau Islands is **Pulau Karimun**, which is a smaller version of Batam: there's considerable industrial development, although most of it in quarrying rather than manufacturing, and an embryonic tourist industry that's trying to lure the cash-rich Singaporeans here for their weekend breaks. The main town of **Tanjung Balai** is about 60km west of Batam and easily reached from Pekanbaru (the boats going to Sekupang on Pulau Batam call here), Batam, Bintan or Singapore. The closest **tourist offices** are in Batam and Bintan but they have very little information about Karimun. The most detailed printed maps of the island (which isn't saying much) are Periplus's *Batam* and *Bintan*.

Located at the far west of the Riau group, at the southern end of the Malacca

Straits, Karimun was strategically important during the seafaring centuries, and from the seventh through to the sixteenth century the allegiance of the local *orang laut* was vital to control of the shipping routes through the straits. In more recent times, outsiders sought to take the island from various branches of the Riau sultanate, but in 1824 the Dutch took control and continued their occupation until Independence. Unfortunately, there are absolutely no discernible remains of what must have been a colourful and turbulent history.

Tanjung Balai

The main population centre, the town of **TANJUNG BALAI** on the south coast, is one of the draws of the island, a busy port that spreads for about 2km along the shore, with numerous wooden jetties where a huge variety of craft load and unload their wares to service the bustling market area behind. There's not much to do, and there's no beach, but it's a pleasant spot except for the persistent ojek drivers; there's no need to hire one as all the accommodation in town is an easy walk from the jetty. There are three main streets in the town: as you get off the ferry and walk through the car park inland, the road takes you to a large eagle statue at a junction. Running left (northwest) is Jalan Trikora, the main drag, which continues in a straight line and turns into Jalan Pramuka further along. Jalan Nusantara runs parallel to and about 20m shorewards of Jalan Trikora following the coast. Parallel to these roads again and one further inland from Jalan Trikora is Jalan Teuku Umar. The main shopping street is **Jalan Nusantara**, around 1km of shops selling pretty much anything you could want, from coffee and clothes to gold. To the north of Jalan Nusantara, in and around the three major roads described above, numerous smaller roads and alleyways comprise the commercial heart of the town. Be warned that street numbers seem to have little relevance to position in Tanjung Balai. At the northwestern end, off Jalan Setia, **Pasar Baru** is a typical Indonesian **market**, which is open daily from early morning until mid-afternoon, with stalls piled high with food of all varieties and household goods galore.

The **post office** can be found at Jl Pramuka 43 (Mon–Thurs 7.30am–3pm, Fri 7.30–11.30am, Sat 7.30am–1pm) and, about 200m up the hill further east from the eastern end of Jalan Teuku Umar, the **telephone office** (daily 24hr) is at Jl Teluk Air 2. There are numerous **wartel** around town, including a 24-hour one in the ferry terminal area and others at Jl Ampera 28 (daily 6am–midnight), Jl Nusantara 6 (6.30am–midnight) and Jl Trikora 25 (7am–midnight), all of which have fax facilities. **Internet access** is available from Spider Net on Jalan Trikora, just northwest of the night market. To **change money**, head for BNI (Mon–Fri 7am–3pm, Sat 9am–noon), about 100m from the eastern end of Jalan Trikora. For most people, the **night market** at Jalan Pelabuhan (see opposite) will be entertainment enough; otherwise, all of the plusher hotels have karaoke bars.

Both domestic and international departures leave from the **ferry terminal** at the eastern end of Tanjung Balai; all the ticket offices are located just inside the gates. The Pelni agent is PT Barelang Surya at counter jetty 3 (Ⓣ0777/23157), though you can also buy Pelni tickets from the travel agents on Jalan Trikora. There are no commercial flights from Bandar Sei Bati, the airport 12km north of Tanjung Balai, but you can buy tickets for flights from Batam from any of the travel agents in town. The best place is the helpful and English-speaking PT Balindo Tours and Travel, Jl Trikora 27, on the corner of Jalan Nusantara (Ⓣ0777/326184, Ⓕ326183), who are agents for Merpati, Garuda and Bouraq. You might also try PT Aksa Utama Tours and Travel, Jl Trikora 6 (Ⓣ0777/22060).

Accommodation

Most of the **accommodation** caters for the Singaporean weekenders and tends to emphasize facilities rather than ambience or character. Independent Western travellers are extremely rare on the island, and there are few places that cater specifically for them.

Wisma Gloria Jl Yos Sudarto 46 ⓣ0777/21133, ⓕ21033. Come out of the ferry terminal car park and turn right along the coast past *Wisma Karimun* – it's about 100m walk at the end of the road. Though rather ramshackle and poorly maintained, this place has plenty of character, and has some good views from the balconies. It's the best of only two cheap places in town. ❷–❸

Harmoni Jl Pelabuhan 5 ⓣ0777/21099. This is the alternative budget option and is pretty grimy. This street turns into the night market after dark, so if you stay here you'll be right in the thick of things; rooms are very basic with outside bathroom, but they have fans. ❷

Wisma Indah Jl Nusantara 27 ⓣ0777/21490. Rooms are unexciting and clinically clean, there's air-con and hot water, and an open sitting area on stilts over the water at the back. Fair value in this price bracket. ❸

Wisma Karimun Pantai Taman Wisata ⓣ0777/21088, ⓕ21488. On your right as you get off the ferry. The most economical of the three pricey seafront places, the economy rooms are good value. You pay for the convenient location, air-con and en-suite hot-water bathrooms rather than the ambience. ❸–❹

Paragon Hotel Jalan Trikora & Jl Nusantara 38d ⓣ0777/21688, ⓕ31331. About 200m from the ferry terminal in the heart of the town, this large hotel is a block deep, so has entrances on two roads. It's the most professional place in town, with good-quality rooms, all with air-con and hot-water bathrooms; booking is recommended. ❺

Hotel Pelangi Jl Teuku Umar ⓣ0777/23100, ⓕ23558. This large setup with reasonable-quality rooms is close to the ferry terminal; walk straight ahead (away from the sea) out of the terminal car park up the hill, and the hotel is about 75m up on the left past the eagle statue. All rooms have air-con and hot water, and some have sea views; there's a moderately priced lobby coffee shop and restaurant. ❹–❺

Hotel Taman Bunga Pantai Taman Wisata ⓣ0777/324088, ⓕ324886. Right next to the ferry terminal and painted bright turquoise. It's a bustling, lively place catering for a young Singaporean crowd, and all rooms have air-con and hot-water bathrooms attached. ❸

Wisma Tanjung Balai Jl Nusantara 127b ⓣ0777/21072. Come out of the terminal car park, turn left and left again. Despite an unpromising, tiny doorway, the rooms – with or without a view of the water – are what you'd expect in this price range, and there's a restaurant on stilts over the water at the back. The staff are friendly and speak some English. ❸–❹

Eating

There's an excellent choice of **places to eat** in Tanjung Balai, and prices aren't unduly inflated to take advantage of Singaporean affluence, although if you're going for top-of-the-range seafood options you should find out the prices beforehand. The **night market** on Jalan Pelabuhan, between Jalan Nusantara (just west of BNI) and Jalan Teuku Umar, operates from early until late evening, is extremely popular and great for a whole range of inexpensive Indonesian dishes. There's another good market just southeast of the jetty on the way to the *Wisma Gloria*. If you fancy **Padang food**, head for Jalan Kesatria, which links the eastern end of Jalan Trikora with Jalan Nusantara. There are several places – wander along and see who has the best selection on show.

Do & Me Jl Nusantara 48. One of the few air-con fast-food places in town. They serve moderately priced fried chicken, and Western options such as lamb chops, sausages, sirloin steak, French fries and baked beans, plus a wide range of burgers, ice desserts and drinks.

Pujasera Food Centre At the end of Jalan Nusantara nearest the jetty. A typical Indonesian food court consisting of several inexpensive food and drink stalls, with a sitting area in the middle. The huge bonus here is that the tables at the back overlook the water, so catch the breeze – it's a great place to chill out in the day and watch harbour life.

Siang Malam At the jetty end of Jl Trikora 178. Extremely popular seafood place with tanks outside where you choose your meal – this is one of several seafood stops in this area, not far from the night market. The food is moderate to expensive.

Around the island

Pulau Karimun offers beaches, mountains and a waterfall, all relatively close together and, while none of these features are unmissable on their own, the island is pretty in parts and has largely managed to retain its rural character, despite development. With your own transport or relying on public transport, it's possible to visit Pantai Palawan on the west coast, the inscribed Batu Bersurat stone, and Gunung Jantan and the Pelambung waterfall in the north-east.

As the island is only just over 20km at its longest point, you can cover a fair chunk of it in a day, and the old-style **buses** are a fun way to get around. An alternative is to rent one of the unofficial taxis that hang around in the ferry terminal area; with your own transport and without climbing Gunung Jantan or lingering too long on the beaches, you'll be able to cover the entire island in three to four hours. Bargain hard and you should be able to get car, driver and petrol for Rp100,000–150,000.

There are three main roads from Tanjung Balai and the nearby town of **MERAL**, 10km to the west, to the other points of interest. Minibuses operate from 6am to 10pm between Tanjung Balai and Meral (Rp1000), where they stop in or just outside the small but hectic bus terminal in the centre of town and from where you can catch buses north. The road between Tanjung Balai and Meral is busy and uninteresting – the south of the island is flat and built-up and there's little of interest to stop off for.

The attractive beach of **Pantai Palawan**, a 400-metre-long white-sand curving bay between rocky headlands, is located on the west coast, 20km from Tanjung Balai. The road there isn't particularly attractive: quarries start 5km north of Meral and the coast is dotted with industrial ports. However, from the beach itself the industrial hinterland is invisible and this is a favourite weekend picnic and excursion spot. There are several warung, some open during the week, and there's **accommodation** in one small, nameless, losmen (no phone; ❷), which has wood-and-thatch bungalows with verandahs facing the beach, electricity supplied in the evenings by generator, mosquito wire at the windows and attached cold-water mandi. At the time of writing, a few large touristy hotels were also springing up, eager for the Singapore dollar. To get here by public transport, take a bus from Meral towards the west-coast settlement of Pangke (Rp2000). Tell the driver where you are heading and you'll be dropped off at the junction with the beach road, 2km before Pangke. From here, it's a three-kilometre walk to the beach – you may be able to hitch at the weekends, but during the week the road is totally deserted. The alternative is to get one of the unofficial taxis that wait outside the ferry terminal at Tanjung Balai; expect to pay about Rp60,000 per person each way if you bargain well. Be sure to make the pick-up arrangements when you get there, as there are no phones.

The road to the small settlement of **PASIR PANJANG** at the northern end of the island, 26km from Tanjung Balai, passes to the west of Gunung Jantan, the only real hill on the island. The foothills are attractively forested, and this part of the island feels very distant from the hustle and bustle of the south. The reason to visit the north is the beach, 2km beyond Pasir Panjang, where the **Batu Bersurat** stone bears an ancient Malay inscription. There are various interpretations of the inscription – one theory is that it is graffiti carved by a Buddhist monk. To one side of the inscription, the indentations in the rock are said to be the footsteps of Lord Buddha himself, making it something of a pilgrimage spot, adorned with white cloths and other offerings. The entire area is being quarried and you'll only be able to visit the beach and stone on Sundays, when there's no blasting in the area.

If you want to visit **Gunung Jantan**, the highest point on the island at 439m, and the waterfall, **Air Terjun Pelambung** (also known as Air Terjun Pongkar), you'll need to travel up the east-coast road. There's a bus from Tanjung Balai to Pongkar and a minibus from Tanjung Balai to Pasar PN (also known as Kota PN and Teluk Uma), 12km up the coast, and then another bus on north. About 1km before Pongkar, a small nondescript village, a wide asphalted road leads inland from a spot called Bukit Pongkar, up towards the mountain – this is the road that maintenance vehicles use to access the telecommunications tower at the top. It's 5km to the summit, from where there are good views to Singapore and Malaysia. Alternatively, there's a path to the top from the Air Terjun Pelambung waterfall; you'll need to take someone to show you the way, as it's pretty overgrown and very muddy. To reach Air Terjun Pelambung, follow the main road through Pongkar; it turns into a track after about 1km and there's a flooded tin quarry on the sea side and a small warung and parking spot on the left. The foreground isn't particularly attractive, but there are good views offshore to the northeast to the island of Karimun Kecil (Small Karimun), also known as Karimun Anak (Child of Karimun). From here it's a 700-metre walk along a mostly concreted path to the waterfall where water tumbles about 15m down a jumble of rocks into a concreted pool. There are several stalls, the rubbish is depressing and the humidity and mosquitoes unenticing.

Pulau Kundur

Situated just south of Karimun and southwest of both Singapore and Batam, **Pulau Kundur** is the furthest of the Riau Islands on the tourist trail, a laid-back spot where it's quite easy to get off the beaten track for a few restful days. It isn't a visa-free entry point, however, and arrivals from Singapore must clear immigration in Tanjung Balai on Pulau Karimun.

Tanjung Batu

The main town, **TANJUNG BATU**, is situated on the southeast coast, separated from nearby Pulau Unggar by a narrow strait; it hasn't the charm of Tanjung Balai, but it's a lot quieter and less pushy. Concentrated just behind the port area, it has wide streets, plenty of shops and a relaxed atmosphere. There's little specific to see apart from **Giri Shanti**, one of many Chinese temples, on the coast on the northeast side of town. It's a spectacular spot for catching the breeze, there are tables on the balcony outside, and the temple has fabulous doors, decorated with images of fierce guardian deities, and an intriguing grotto altar guarded by a tiger statue.

The town has several decent **accommodation** options, all an easy walk from the port, but prices here are a little inflated by the proximity of Singapore. Walking out of the ferry terminal and inland (northwest) takes you along Jalan Permuda. Immediately on your left, *Wisata Lipo*, Jl Pemuda 3 (Ⓣ0779/21076; ❸), is a fair mid-range place; it's a bit dark, but the rooms are reasonable. At the other end of Jalan Permuda, away from the waterfront, is the T-junction with Jalan Merdeka. The market is on the right, while on the left, across a yard are the two top spots: the gleamingly new *Hotel Prima* (Ⓣ0779/431308; ❹), and next door the *Hotel Pelangi* (Ⓣ0779/21739; ❸–❹). Both offer clean air-con rooms with satellite TV and hot-water bathrooms, and both can arrange taxis and boat tickets, but the *Prima* is the better of the two. A good budget place is the *Wisma Bintang*, Jalan Amanaf (also called Jalan Pasar Ikan) 10–11 (☎0779/21280; ❷–❸). This is the least expensive place in town, but it's clean and has some attractive balconies overlooking the port, the staff are a friendly lot too. It's very close to the jetty; turn right as soon as you get off, and walk to the end of the road, and it's on the corner.

For informal **eating**, the night market at Jalan Merdeka near the clock tower at the junction with Jalan Sudirman operates from early evening until late. It's large, with a huge variety of food – you could put together a seven-course meal if you had the inclination. For something more formal, Jalan Besar, parallel to Jalan Sudirman towards the northeast side of town, is lined with Chinese restaurants, and Jalan Sudirman itself has plenty of *kedai kopi* for basic breakfasts and daytime snacks. *Gembira Restaurant*, attached to the hotel of the same name, is located right on the water's edge, some tables having good views of the bustle of the wharves and across to Pulau Unggar. You can eat here economically by sticking to fried rice and noodles – the chicken, prawns and seafood are in the moderate to expensive range. It's a little hard to find, but just head right from the ferry terminal and try to get to the waterfront.

There are no **exchange** facilities on the island, so make sure you bring enough cash. The **post office** (Mon–Thurs 8am–2pm, Fri 8–11am, Sat 8am–12.30pm) is at Jl Kartini 44 – this is the street parallel to and left of (as you face inland) Jalan Permuda, while there are many **wartels** (daily 7am–11pm) on Jalan Sudirman. There are no **vehicle rental** companies but enquire at your hotel if you want to rent a motorcycle, for which you can expect to pay around Rp60,000 a day. For car charter, either enquire at your accommodation or negotiate with the unofficial taxis that hang around on Jalan Pemuda, just up from the ferry terminal; bargain very hard and expect to pay Rp150,000 a day with driver. All **ferries** leave from the terminal at the end of Jalan Pemuda in Tanjung Batu, and the ticket offices are found here.

Around the island

The island sights are pretty much limited to **beaches**. Some are attractive with white sand, but much of the island is ringed by mangrove swamp. The other problem is that the tin-dredging platforms, clearly visible off most of the coast, churn up the sea bottom so that the water is essentially dark-brown sludge. Around 3km southwest of town, **Gading** can be reached by ojek (Rp6000): there's no public transport. It's a pleasant enough beach with a forest behind and a grave – a local pilgrimage spot – at the far end. The sweeping white-sand bay of **Lubuk**, 4km from town (Rp1000 by bus from Jalan Merdeka, Rp10,000 by ojek) has a small village and a Chinese temple behind. Inland from the village, a short climb through the forest leads to **Siamban Hill**; you'll need to ask for directions. Take a picnic – there's a shelter at the top and a rock-pool for bathing on the way. Further up the west coast, 18km from Tanjung Batu, **Sawang** (Rp1000 by bus) is another small village with a beach. Further north from here, **Pantai Mata Air** is one of the more attractive beaches, with dramatic rocks in the water and onshore. Heading towards the north of the island, the land is increasingly devastated by the quarry workings for granite and sand, and there's no major forest cover left.

Over on the east coast, the village of **URUNG** has an attractive market area and a large Chinese temple, Vihara Maitri Segara. From here, it's possible to get the local ferry to **Pulau Belat** just across a small strait – you can take an ojek across the island to another ferry on the northeast coast, over to Sungai Utan on Pulau Papan, which has some sulphur springs.

Pulau Batam

Apart from its proximity to Singapore, just 20km at the closest point, and usefulness as a major staging post on to Indonesia, there's little to recommend **Pulau Batam** to travellers, and nothing to make staying here overnight a worthwhile experience, unless you can afford top-class accommodation or can arrange one of the excellent deals available in Singapore.

For much of its **history**, Batam was a jungle-covered island, surrounded by mangrove swamp, its few inhabitants making a living from the sea. Things have changed dramatically in the last decade, as Singapore's labour shortage has caused it to look to the surrounding areas for manufacturing bases. There are now numerous joint ventures between the Singapore government and Indonesian companies, and people from throughout Indonesia are flocking here for work – the population of 100,000 may well increase twentyfold in the next few years.

Just as the move towards industrial development has come from Singapore, so the tourist industry is developing its facilities to cater for stressed Singaporeans seeking weekend breaks in top-class accommodation, or the ministrations of Indonesian prostitutes, now that the AIDS scare has frightened them away from the Thai border towns. The island boasts several excellent **golf courses**, where visitors can play – for a price. **Getting around** the island isn't easy or efficient on public transport. Regardless of what hotels tell you, there are public buses between main centres from the bus terminal in Jodoh (the northern suburb of Nagoya) but they are irregular, and operate only in daylight hours. However, there are more regular services between Batu Ampar and Nagoya and from Sekupang to Bengkong via Nagoya. Most local people share taxis for local hops – they'll pull up if they see you by the road – but for longer trips you'll

Moving on from Pulau Batam by sea

There are four main ferry terminals on Batam, one in a bay at the northwest of the island and the others on three peninsulas on the north coast. All are at least a half-hour taxi ride from the main town. The bayside **Waterfront ferry terminal**, Teluk Senimba, has fourteen daily ferries to the World Trade Centre in Singapore, operating 7.40am–7.40pm from Singapore, and 8.45am–8.30pm from Batam. **Sekupang** in the westernmost peninsula houses the **domestic** – where you'll arrive coming from Sumatra – and **international terminals** (200m apart). The international terminal features a bank and post office, and departures are highly organized. An electronic board announces the time of the next Singapore (World Trade Centre) departure; they operate every thirty minutes from 7.30am to 7pm, with an 8pm final departure in each direction Monday to Wednesday. **Batu Ampar**, further east, has departures to Singapore (World Trade Centre) with nine crossings daily 7.30am to 9pm. **Nongsa**, further east again (Ⓣ0778/761777), operates six crossings a day (8am–7pm) to and from Tanah Merah terminal in Singapore.

The **Pelni boat**, *Kelud*, operates from Batam to Jakarta. You can book at the Sekupang terminal, any travel agent or from the Pelni agent, Andalan Aksa Tour, Komplex New Holiday, Block B, 9 (Ⓣ0778/454181, Ⓕ456443). There's also a Pelni agent at the domestic terminal (Ⓣ0778/325586).

The arrival and departure points for Tanjung Pinang on Pulau Bintan are either Sekupang (hourly) or **Telaga Punggur** on the east coast where ferries operate every fifteen minutes from 8am to 5pm. No bus service operates to Telaga Punggur, so you'll need to use taxis: expect to pay Rp50,000 between the terminal and Nongsa, Rp35,000 to Nagoya and Rp45,000 to Sekupang.

end up taking your own taxi. There are a few reputable companies; KPTDS (Ⓣ0778/325507) has a counter at the domestic ferry terminal at Sekupang and displays fixed prices for its red and white cars: to the airport (Rp40,000), Nongsa (Rp45,000) and Nagoya (Rp25,000). An all-day rental will set you back a whopping Rp250,000. The **Batam Tourist Promotion office**, Jalan R.E. Martadinata (Mon–Thurs 8am–2pm, Fri 8–11am, Sat 8am–12.30pm; Ⓣ0778/322852), is in a row of shops, that also features a travel agent, to the left across the car park as you exit the international terminal at Sekupang. You might also try the Batam Tourist Office at Jalan Pramuka, 2 Sei Harapan (Mon–Thurs 8am–4pm, Sat 8am–12.30pm; Ⓣ & Ⓕ0778/321409). It's worth trying to get a map of the island from one of these, a large hotel, bookshop or travel agent.

Nagoya

Situated in the middle of the north coast of the island, the main town on Batam is **NAGOYA**, also named Lubuk Baja (Pirate's Waterhole). It's just south of the Batu Ampar terminal, and 10km east of Sekupang. Soulless, and inconvenient for all transport points, the town has little to recommend it, although you may find yourself spending an (expensive) night here if you miss ferry connections at some point. Jalan Imam Bonjol is the main thoroughfare, awash with moneychangers, banks and expensive hotels. The lower end places are mostly just west of the stretch that includes the *Hotel Nagoya Plaza*. Designated for commercial and administrative development, **Batam Centre** is a few kilometres southeast of Nagoya. At present it comprises just a couple of shopping centres, not even good ones at that, so there's little reason to come.

Accommodation

Your choice of **accommodation** is mostly between luxury beach resorts and Nagoya's big hotels and grossly overpriced basic losmen, many of which charge by the hour. There are a few bearable places in Nagoya that will overcharge without quite breaking the bank, but they're few and far between. Also, make sure you know what currency you are being quoted because Singapore dollars (S$) are widely used throughout the island, although you can pay in either currency to settle your bill. It's worth repeating that the best rates are available from Singapore (see the box on p.441) and if you do arrive on spec or book independently, especially midweek, then you should seek discounts of up to 40 percent of the walk-in price. Most of the priciest beachfront places are on Nongsa, the peninsula in the far northeast of the island.

Hotel Bahari Kompleks Nagoya Business Centre Block D, No 100 Ⓣ0778/421911, Ⓕ428584. Clean, small air-con rooms with cold water mandi, and a few without plumbing. This is the closest you'll get to a decent mid-range place in Nagoya. ❸–❹

Wisma Batam Indah Kompleks Nagoya Business Centre Block VI No 2 & 3 Ⓣ0778/424531. Grimy and dark, filthy in places but at least it's not a brothel. The cheapest, bearable place in Nagoya that doesn't offer "short time room". ❷

Hotel Harmony Jl Imam Bonjol Ⓣ0778/459308, Ⓕ459306, Ⓔharmony@indosat.net.id. One of the best hotels in town with a third-floor swimming pool, several restaurants, a fitness centre, bar and karaoke lounge. There's a pleasant atmosphere and lots of shops in the huge reception area. ❻–❽

Mandarin Regency Jl Imam Bonjol 1 Ⓣ0778/458899, Ⓕ458057, Ⓦwww.mandarin-regency.com. This is the classiest hotel in Nagoya, with a grand yet relaxed look and feel, extremely comfortable rooms, all the facilities and eating options to be expected at this end of the range, and a good-sized pool in the central courtyard. ❺–❻

Waterfront City On the coast south of Sekupang Ⓣ0778/381888, Ⓕ381142 (booking also through 9th floor, 1 Maritime Square, Singapore, Ⓣ065/276 2295, Ⓕ2765536). Served by its own ferry terminal, this enormous site is set to develop as the premier activity resort on Batam. Water-skiing, jet skiing, paragliding, bungy-jumping, and go-carting – at a price. There are shuttle buses every half-hour between the resort and Sekupang. ❻

Eating

Staying in the resorts pretty much limits you to eating there unless you have your own transport or use taxis. If you are staying in Nagoya, there are plenty of authentic Indonesian **restaurants** and prices are fair – in the evening, a good **night market** sets up at Pujasera Mira, next to the *Mandarin Regency Hotel* on Jalan Imam Bonjol, where good-priced sate, soup, noodles, rice and drinks are available in relaxed surroundings. There's also a *KFC* on Jalan Imam Bonjol, next to the *Hotel Harmony*.

Food centre Komplex New Holiday. With plenty of counters selling seafood, Chinese and Indonesian food, plus coffee and assorted drinks, this place is constantly busy and has a good, buzzy atmosphere.
Gardino Komplex TG Pantun, Block N, 9. A small bakery with cakes and sweet breads and a few tables in case you want to eat in.
Lovely Vegetarian Komplex Bumi Indah Block III No 19. Lovely Chinese vegetarian food: *tahu* (tofu), tempeh, roast potatoes and veggies for all those who've seen one too many chickens go to the chopping block. To get there, take the first turning off Jalan Imam Bonjol, just past (northwest), and on the opposite side of the road from, the *Hotel Nagoya Plaza*. Follow the road past a dogleg for 150m.
Nusantara Coffee House At the *Mandarin Regency Hotel*. Plush surroundings and seamless service with good but expensive food – curries and stir-fries for Rp25,000 up to pepper steak at Rp50,000. Tax and service aren't included in the price.
Saraso Komplex New Holiday, Block E, 6. A small place, popular with local people and serving good-quality, inexpensive Padang food.

Listings

Airline offices Bouraq, Jalan Imam Bonjol, Komplex Bumi Ayu Lestari, Block A/3, Nagoya ⓣ0778/421840, ⓕ452788; Garuda, Jalan Imam Bonjol, Danagraha Building, Levels 1 & 3, Nagoya ⓣ0778/458620, ⓕ452515; Mandala, just east of Jalan Imam Bonjol, near the Lippo bank, at Juyanah Plaza 1 ⓣ0778/424632, ⓕ454657; Merpati, *Hotel Nagoya*, Jalan Imam Bonjol ⓣ0778/456767, ⓕ458133.
Banks and exchange There are many to choose from, including: BCA, Jl Raja Ali Haji 18; BRI, Jl Imam Bonjol 8/9. The gold shops on and behind Jalan Imam Bonjol operate as moneychangers if you have cash; Tanjung, Komplex Bumi Indah, Block I, 9.
Golf Day membership is available at golf clubs, but is expensive. At the Indah Puri Golf Club, for example, green fees are S$90 for eighteen holes on weekdays, S$130 at weekends, plus caddy, trolley, clubs and shoe rental.
Hospitals Rumah Sakit Rita, Jalan Sekupang ⓣ0778/323931; Rumah Sakit Otorita Batam, Jl Dr Cipto Mangunkusumo ⓣ0778/322121.
Immigration office Jl Laki L.R.E. Maradinata ⓣ0778/462069, 462004.
Internet access There are many internet cafés in the main streets. Of the cluster on Jalan Sultan Abdul Rachman (leading east off Jalan Imam Bonjol near the Lippo Bank), the Anggraini is a reliable choice.
Post office The main post office is at Jalan Sudirman at Batam Centre. In Nagoya, the post office is on the second floor of the row of shops after the *Hotel Nagoya Plaza* – the sign points up to Mesjid Arafah.
Telephone Wartels (7.30am–midnight) are numerous all over town: PT Tandiguna Utama, Komplex TG Pantun, Block E, 5; Kelabang Sakti, Komplex New Holiday, Block B, 7/8; and Mahligai Sari, Komplex Nagoya Business Centre, Block IV, 34 (24hr).

Pulau Bintan and beyond

Situated less than 10km from Batam at the closest point, **Pulau Bintan** is about two and a half times the size of Singapore, which seems to have left plenty of room for **traditional culture** to survive alongside the plush tourist development. For this reason, there's much to recommend it: not only is it more attractive than other nearby islands, but there's much more of an Indonesian feel about the place and things are reasonably priced. For independent travellers, especially those on a budget, the delight of Bintan is that

Moving on from Pulau Bintan

The **international and domestic ferry terminals** (Sri Bintan Pura) are on the coast in the heart of Tanjung Pinang, with the ticket offices ranged in the terminal area, along Jalan Merdeka and Jalan Bintan. There are connections throughout southern Sumatra and on to Java. For **Pulau Batam**, ferries operate every fifteen minutes from 8am to 5pm between Tanjung Pinang and Sekapung and Telaga Punggur on Batam. **Bandar Bentan Telani** is the ferry terminal in Bintan Resort, with connections only with Tanah Merah ferry terminal on Singapore.

There are several **Pelni sailings** to and from Pulau Bintan, which give access to the entire archipelago: they operate out of Kijang on the southeast corner of the island and all boats operate on a two-weekly cycle. The Pelni agent in Tanjung Pinang is Kepel Cepat ASDF, Jl Pos 1 (Ⓣ & Ⓕ0771/23483).

Flights leave from Kijang airport, 15km southeast of Tanjung Pinang. The airlines have many offices in town, mostly on Jalan Bintan; try PT Pinang Jaya, Jl Bintan 44 (Ⓣ0771/21267, Ⓕ22046).

Tanjung Pinang, the main town on the island, has been largely untouched by the tourist influx and, with the most aggressive development confined to the massive Bintan Resort enclave on the north coast, low-key guesthouses and the few plusher developments of **Trikora** on the east coast continue to cater for those who want a few days of sun and sand.

Historically, Bintan was far more significant than Batam. In the sixteenth century the ruler of Malacca, defeated by the Portuguese, fled to Bintan with his court. Although the court then moved several times, to Johor and Lingga, a branch of the royal family settled on Pulau Penyengat, a tiny island within sight of Tanjung Pinang.

Tanjung Pinang

Lying on the southeast coast of the island, the traditional capital of the Riau Islands, **TANJUNG PINANG**, is an attractive bustling port town with an excellent market and good tourist facilities. It also has brilliant transport links throughout Indonesia, rather better than those on the island itself – it's often quicker to get to Singapore than to cross the island on a public bus. This is one of the most characterful cities in the Riau archipelago, and you'll see the odd chess hustler or tribal shamen – complete with microphone – squatting on the pavement holding an audience enthralled. There's plenty of accommodation in all price ranges in the town and many of the sea departures leave from the centrally located ferry port.

The **town centre** is compact and everything you're likely to need is within easy walking distance. As you step out of the ferry terminal and turn left, you'll see a large archway at a T-junction. Straight ahead through the arch (southeast) is the main street, Jalan Merdeka. There are a few sights in the town itself, although the colourful and lively **Pasar Baru** is undoubtedly the gem. This is a terrific traditional Indonesian market: tiny alleyways are lined with shops and stalls selling mountains of exotic food, household goods, textiles, tools and religious artefacts. To get there, walk 200m to the end of Jalan Merdeka (southeast or away from the ferry terminal) until you get to a large junction. Immediately to the left is Jalan Pelantir 2 (also known as Jalan Pasar). The covered market is between Jalan Pelantir 2 and Jalan Lorong Gambir, which runs parallel (at right angles to the coast), though there are also many stalls on both these streets. The harbour end of Jalan Pelantir 2 is especially atmospheric, with old wooden Chinese *godowns* and shrines.

The town has a large Chinese trading population and there are plenty of red-and-gold **temples** with smoking incense, fierce dragons and serene statues of Chinese goddesses. One of the most attractively situated and atmospheric temples, **Cetia Bodhi Sasana** – with Kuan Yin, the goddess of mercy, in pride of place – is on the harbourfront looking across the water at the end of the most, easterly jetty on Jalan Pelantir 2. It's a great spot to watch the local boats and fishing eagles. The **Riau Kandil Museum**, Jalan Bakar Batu, is currently closed; ask at the tourist office for the latest information.

The Tanjung Pinang **tourist office** is at Jl S M Amin 7 (ⓣ & ⓕ0771/25373). It's very close to the ferry terminal; coming from the ferry, walk right before the arch, and look for a white villa immediately on your right. The main **post office** is at Jl Brigjenkatamso 122, but there's also a convenient post office on Jl Merdeka 7 near the terminal which has **internet** facilities. All poste restante should be sent here; they don't get many tourists using the service, but staff are helpful and efficient. The **Telkom** office is at Jl Hang Tuah 11 (7am–midnight), but there are many **wartels** in town. The **bus terminal** is Batu Tujuh (Stone Seven) on the outskirts of town; *angutan* minivans ply between the town centre and the terminal (Rp2000) from 6am to 10pm, and public buses operate to Tanjung Uban (2hr; Rp6000) during daylight hours, but are irregular and infrequent. The port of Kijang (1hr) can only be reached by share (or private) taxi from town, you'll pay Rp5000 each for a car of five. There are regular *ankutan* minivans to Trikora (1hr; Rp10,000) from Jalan Gambir but resist being talked into "chartering" the whole van. You can also get a shared taxi to Trikora for the same price from the yard opposite the BNI bank on Jalan Teluk Umar. To get back from Trikora, just wait for an *ankutan* by the roadside – the last one is usually at about 5pm.

Accommodation

There's a good range of **accommodation** in Tanjung Pinang, from luxury operations to much more basic, budget places. The budget mainstays are the **homestays** on Jalan Lorong Bintan II, which connects Jalan Samudera and Jalan Bintan.

Bintan Beach Resort Jl Pantai Impian 1 ⓣ0771/23661, ⓕ23995. This is the only resort conveniently close to Tanjung Pinang, 5km from the ferry terminal. There are great coastal views, a big pool and plenty of activities on offer including island tours. All rooms and public areas are comfortable, the deluxe rooms with verandahs being especially appealing. ❻–❼

Bong's, **Johnny's** (ⓣ0771/311633) and **Rommel's** Jl Lorong Bintan II. These are all basic, clean and pleasant budget homestays with rooms in central family houses – *Johnny's* is the nicest by a shade and is also a good place to get information, especially about the Linnga Islands. They are close together but barely signed at all – you might have to ask your way when you get into the street. To find them from Jalan Merdeka, turn up Jalan Bintang (heading away from the sea); just after the Apotic Kima Farma (a pharmacy), turn right along a narrow, unpromising alley. *Bong's* and *Johnny's* are in a tiny yard at the dogleg, *Rommel's* is a little further on the right. All ❷

Furia Jl Merdeka 6 ⓣ0771/29922, ⓕ29955. A clean, tiled option, just opposite the harbour exit. All rooms have hot water and air-con. ❺

Wisma Gunung Bintan Jaya Jl Samudera 38 (note that the street is signed as Jalan S M Amin) ⓣ0771/29288, ⓕ29388. A three-storey building just at the exit from the harbour area. It's very clean, light and tidy and although the rooms are small, they all have hot water and air-con, and couldn't be any closer to the ferry; good value. ❸–❹

Hotel Laguna Jl Bintan 51 ⓣ0771/311555, ⓕ312555. The most luxurious place in Tanjung Pinang, this has a restaurant with room service, satellite TV, and all the trimmings you'd expect at this price. ❺–❻

Laut Jaya Hotel Jl Pelantar II 98 (the street is also called Jalan Pasar) ⓣ0771/311471, ⓕ311473. Clean, tiled and well located, with some rooms overlooking the water, just round the corner at the sea end of the market, a short walk on from *Riau Holidays Indah*. ❹–❺

Riau Holidays Indah Jl Pelantar II 53 (the street is also called Jalan Pasar) ⓣ & ⓕ0771/22715. The entrance towards the harbour end of Jalan Pelantar II is unpromising, but this characterful place extends far back in various courtyards. The deluxe rooms are comfortable, with lounge chairs and satellite TV, but the real delight are the verandahs at the back and the upstairs terraces overlooking the harbour and across to Senggarang. ❹–❺

Surya Jalan Bintan ⓣ0771/21811. This is a good budget choice with just a few fan rooms, some with and some without attached mandi, set around an attractive garden. Get a room as far from the busy road as you can. ❷–❸

Tanjung Pinang Jl Pos 692 ⓣ0771/21236, ⓕ21379. One of the biggest, most-advertised, mid-range places; it's a bit shoddy, but is conveniently located in the middle of the market area and has a big range of scruffy rooms, all with air-con and TV but little personality. ❹–❺

Eating, drinking and entertainment

There are several **night markets** in town: there's a convenient little one at the entrance to the harbour area on Jalan Hang Tuah, and another, Kedai Harapan Jaya, just outside the entrance to the *Laut Jaya Hotel* at the end of Jalan Pelantar II, but the biggest in town is at **Bintan Mall** (daily 5pm–2am), on the outskirts of town next to the *Paradise Hotel* and near the main post office. Most food here is inexpensive, but check prices of more exotic seafood before you commit yourself. Another large night market is on Jalan Teluk Umar, opposite the BNI, and there's yet another on Jalan Gambir, the left fork at the end of (away from the ferry) Jalan Merdeka.

Stella is a popular **disco** opposite the *Paradise Hotel* on the outskirts of town, but other than this Tanjung Pinang doesn't exactly throb with excitement after dark.

Bintan Indah 99 Bintan Mall, Jalan Pos. There are various stalls in this small, popular food centre at the entrance to Bintan Mall.

Damai Baru Jl Merdeka 69. One of many open-fronted coffee shops that dot the town – great places to watch the world go by, although rather hot and noisy.

Pagi Sore Jl Merdeka 85. A popular local eating place, all the better for offering rotis as well as rice and noodles.

Roti Saiman Perancis Bintan Mall Blok A-7. A well-presented, good-quality range of sweet breads, savouries and cakes at moderate prices, that you can eat in or take away.

Suka Ramai Jl Merdeka 18. On the second floor above a shop, the menu is varied and moderately priced, with Indonesian favourites, fish and steaks, plus plenty of drinks.

Listings

Banks and exchange BCA, Jl Temiang 27–29; BNI, Jl Teuku Umar 630; Mandiri, Jl Teuku Umar 23; Lippo Bank, Jl Merdeka 11. Jalan Merdeka is lined with moneychangers, who will change Singapore and US dollars cash.

Car rental Enquire at your accommodation, but you should be able to get a decent vehicle, such as a Kijang with or without driver, for Rp200,000 a day. You can rent a motorbike for about Rp35,000 a day.

Hospitals Rumah Sakit Umum, Jl Sudirman 795 ⓣ0771/21733 or 21163; Rumah Sakit Angkatan Laut, Jalan Ciptadi ⓣ0771/25805

Immigration Jl Jend A. Yani 31 ⓣ0771/21034; there's also an office on the ferry pier.

Souvenirs There isn't a great choice of souvenirs in town, but Sangga Budaya, Jalan Basukit Rahmet (opposite BRI), is an Aladdin's cave of items both new and old from across the archipelago. Embong Fatimah at the corner of Jalan Samudera and Jalan Merdeka, just at the exit to the ferry terminal area, also stocks a range of new wooden, basketware and textile items.

Supermarket Yupiter, Jl Merdeka 60.

Telephone Jl Hang Tuah 11 (7am–midnight).

Travel agents There are many on Jalan Bintang, but elsewhere you could try PT Pinang Jaya, Jl Bintan 44 ⓣ0771/21267, ⓕ22046; Bintan Panorama, Jl Bakar Baru 50a ⓣ0771/21894, ⓕ22572; New Oriental, Jl Merdeka 61 (ⓣ0771/521614, ⓕ24145) for ferry tickets to Singapore; Osaka, Jl Merdeka 43 (ⓣ0771/21829), also for ferry tickets to Singapore.

Trikora

At **TRIKORA**, on the east coast of Pulau Bintan, the beach area covers around 30km of coastline comprising bay after palm-fringed bay. The disadvantage is that, when the tide goes out, it goes quite a long way, leaving dull-looking flats. To get around, you can hail one of the *ankutans* that ply the road up and down the coast.

The **accommodation** is a little on the expensive side for what you're getting and begins 5km north of the small, attractive village of **KAWAL**, situated at the point where the main trans-island road reaches the east coast, and where many of the houses are built over the river on stilts. Heading north from Kawal, the first accommodation is at the friendly *Bukit Berbunga Cottages* (no phone; ❸), where there's just a hand-painted sign on the road; a hundred-metre track leads down to the wood-and-thatch cottages with attached mandi, mattresses on the floor and electricity at night. Just 200m north, *Yasin's Guest House* (Ⓣ0771/26770; ❸) has three types of wood-and-thatch bungalows on offer, all with verandahs, from small ones without attached mandi to large options with shower and toilet attached; the bungalows are not quite as nice as at the *Bukit Berbunga Cottages*.

Less than 1km north, *Trikora Beach Resort* (Ⓣ0771/24454, Ⓕ24456; ❺) is the most luxurious place on this coast, with attractive gardens, good views to offshore islands, and accommodation in comfortable bungalows with verandah, air-con, satellite TV and hot water. A moderately priced restaurant serves Indonesian and Chinese food, and bicycles are available for rental. One kilometre on, in the next bay, *Restaurant Pantai Trikora* is a series of wooden houses on stilts built over the water and joined by wooden walkways, whose extensive menu offers moderate to expensive prawn, chicken and fish dishes. Out in the bay you'll see numerous *kelong*, the strange fishing boat/platforms where your lunch was probably swimming a few hours ago. Heading 2km further north, *Shady Shack* (no phone; ❸) is a homely spot with a reputation for serving good food; rooms are simple but clean and come with mandi. **Snorkelling** gear and boats are available for rental for trips to the surrounding islands (Rp50,000 for boat and gear) and this is also the place to ask about scuba diving trips (Rp600,000 per person per day). At the time of writing, another losmen – *Travel Lodge* – was springing up next door. Currently, there's no development further north, although one of the best beaches on the coastline, **Trikora Tiga**, is 10km north of *Shady Shack*. It consists of several kilometres of glorious white sand, gently lapped by turquoise waters. At the weekends, several warung open up to cater for day-trippers from around the island, but during the week it's pretty much deserted.

Pulau Mapur

Around 16km off the east coast of Bintan, **Pulau Mapur** has long white beaches, rocky headlands and very few visitors. At the time of writing, a new luxury guesthouse was under construction on the island, but those on a budget can enquire in the villages for homestays near the most popular beaches of Pantai Belakang on the north coast or Pantai Songsing on the east. It takes an hour to get to the island on one of the local boats that ply throughout the day from Kijang, the ferry port on the southeast corner of Bintan.

A huge section of the island, covering the entire northern coastline, an area half the size of Singapore, has been designated as the **Bintan Resort** (central information line Ⓣ0770/691388), known locally as "Lagoi", with over three hundred lots of land ready for development. It's a huge and grand concept, and a massive example of the type of tourist development that aims to separate tourists from local people as securely as possible – for whose protection is never entirely clear. Bintan Resort has its own **ferry terminal** at Bandar Bentan Telani, serving Tanah Merah terminal on Singapore, and its own extremely good road and transport system. However, only one rutted and decaying nine-kilometre road links Bintan Resort to the rest of the island, and it's watched over by several security checkpoints; anyone taking rental cars outside the resort area to the rest of the island pays a premium.

To get to the resort from Tanjung Pinang, take one of the hourly buses (last bus at 4pm) from the terminal at Batu Tujuh to the junction at Batu 66. There are minibuses from here to take you the rest of the way. Within the resort, **car rental** is available from Indorent (ⓣ0771/91931); they have a counter at Bandar Bentan Telani and offer everything from two-hourly rental with or without driver to daily and longer rental of 59-seater coaches. A four-seater jeep costs US$100 per day excluding driver or petrol. If you don't want to rent transport, a **shuttle bus** service operates between the hotels and the ferry terminal (S$3–9), which is convenient for getting to and from your accommodation as well as moving between the hotels for lunch and dinner.

Bintan Resort accommodation

Banyan Tree ⓣ0770/693100, ⓕ693200, or book in Singapore ⓣ065/3254193, ⓕ2266128. This is the most tasteful, stylish and refined establishment, with accommodation in beautifully decorated private villas that have a private outside Jacuzzi or swimming pool. There are several top-class restaurants here, a private health spa, and a sailing boat for charter. ❽

Club Med ⓣ0770/692801, ⓕ692826. Part of the international hotel chain, there are almost three hundred rooms, two pools, a spa and a wide range of sports facilities, including a range of watersports. Good facilities for small children. ❽

Mana Mana ⓣ0770/692555, ⓕ692557. This bustling place is big on watersports and activities, and is the liveliest and least expensive of the resorts. Accommodation is in wood-and-tile cottages, which are comfortable without being plush, and there's a thriving watersports centre (jet skiing Rp200,000 per hour, windsurfing Rp70,000 per hour; dives for qualified divers from Rp100,000), and tennis courts. Surfing is possible in February and March, while diving is best in April. ❻

Mayang Sari ⓣ 0770/692580, ⓕ0778/692576, or book in Singapore ⓣ065/7328515, ⓕ7323959. The most westerly resort offers accommodation right on the beach, in fabulously high-ceilinged, simply but stylishly decorated cottages in cream and dark wood, with a verandah overlooking the gardens. This is a quiet, elegant place, but there's no pool – visitors use the facilities at nearby *Mana Mana*. Meals in the restaurant cost $15–25. ❽

Hotel Sedona ⓣ0770/691388, ⓕ691399, or book in Singapore ⓣ065/2233223, ⓕ2417878. The largest setup, at Bintan Lagoon, with over four hundred rooms in four-storey blocks. Public areas are huge and busy, there are six restaurants and snack bars, a large swimming pool, a health spa and leisure centre. Plenty of other activities are also on offer, including sea sports, table tennis, table football, and there are bicycles for rent. ❽

Sol Elite ⓣ0770/692505, ⓕ692550. With a gym, pool, tennis courts, watersports, sauna, traditional massage, business centre, coffee shop, two restaurants and karaoke, this place caters well for stressed executives. ❼

Senggarang

Just across the bay from Tanjung Pinang, **SENGGARANG** village was originally settled by Bugis people from Sulawesi, with traditional stilted houses over the water. Take a public ferry during daylight hours (10min; Rp2000) from Pelantar II, the jetty leading out from the Pasar Baru market area in Tanjung Pinang. From the end of the Senggarang jetty, you'll walk several hundred metres inland through the village before you get to dry land. It's pretty picturesque, although the humidity, rubbish smell and mosquitoes can be ghastly.

Once on land, turn left along the road and walk for 200m or so to the local volleyball court. The simple **warung** on the coast side are good places for refreshment, and a huge banyan tree nearby has overtaken a two-storey **Chinese temple**, whose walls are suspended in the roots, with a small shrine still at ground level. A further 200m brings you to the modern Chinese temple, Vihara Tirta Maitreya, at the foot of the shipping beacon. There's little reason to linger, because another couple of hundred metres around the coast is **Vihara Darma Sasana**, a complex of three temples facing seawards: the temple compound is very large and clearly affluent, featuring statues, fountains, ponds and artificial waterfalls galore – often gaudy but with an endearing exuberance. The right-hand temple has a 200-year-old dragon statue on the roof, and the central deity in the smallest temple is Toa Pek Kong, god of the earth – people intending to build a house make offerings here for good fortune in the enterprise.

Pulau Penyenget

Out in the bay, clearly visible from Tanjung Pinang, small **Pulau Penyenget** is well worth a trip for its pleasant and peaceful atmosphere, lovely old buildings and lingering sense of ancient glories. The name means "Wasp Island", and is thought to have come about because of the wasp stings inflicted on early sailors who came ashore for fresh water.

During the eighteenth century, the island was united under the sultan of Johor. However, in 1804, Sultan Mahmud gave Penyenget to his wife, Raya Hamidah, an action that split the state of Johor into two rival factions: Penyenget and the surrounding islands went on to be ruled by Raya Hamidah's son, while his half-brother took over Lingga. In 1819, Sir Stamford Raffles persuaded Hamidah's son to give him Singapore in exchange for protection and a stipend from the British. With security and British funds, Penyenget became a major centre for Muslim religion and literature – scholars from Mecca came to teach in the mosque and many works of Malay literature were written here. Many of the ruins date from that time, an era regarded as a "Golden Age" when around nine thousand people lived on the island. Many of the current population of around two thousand are descended from the ancient royal family.

Just 2.5km long by 750m wide, the island is reached by small **ferry** (daylight hours; 15min; Rp2000) from Pelantar I, at the end of Jalan Pos, just around the corner from the small post office in the centre of Tanjung Pinang. There are two jetties on Penyenget, both on the north coast and about 500m apart; boats call at both but it's easiest to orientate yourself if you get dropped at the most westerly near the mosque – you'll see the turrets and creamy paintwork from the water. Allow three or four hours to explore the island, and take plenty of water and some snacks as there are only a few shops. From the jetty, walk through the village built on stilts over the water to dry land. Prior to Dutch colonization, the centre of population was on the southern side of the island, looking away from Tanjung Pinang. However, the people were forced to move to the north, where they could be overseen by the Dutch in Tanjung Pinang.

From the jetty, the road leads straight to **Mesjid Raya Sultan Riau**, which was commissioned by Sultan Abdurrahman in 1832, although not completed until 1844, and is now restored to its turreted and domed glory. The floor is covered with richly patterned prayer mats, fabulously carved old cupboards hold an Islamic library, and in the glass case there's a stunning nineteenth-century Koran. Outside the mosque, a left turning along Jalan Y.D.M.R. Abdurrahman leads past a munitions store, **Gedung Mesiu**, up the hill to the **grave of Raja Abdurrahman**, who lies alongside other royal dignitaries. Follow the path up the left side of the graveyard enclosure, and at the top you'll see the moat walls and a few remaining cannons from the fort of **Bukit Kursi**, built in 1782 at the highest point of the island for defence against Dutch attack during the Riau Wars (1782–1832).

Back on Jalan Y.D.M.R. Abdurrahman, a right turn past the mosque takes you south across the island to **Istana Raja Ali**, the palace of the raja who ruled from 1844 to 1857. It isn't huge by palace standards and is undergoing renovation, but in the grounds there's a map of all the island sights: about a dozen sights are identified, many of them no more than a pile of stones. The path goes through the palace grounds and, continuing out the other side, leads across to the south side of the island. Off to the left of the road across the island are the **graves of Raja Ali** and **Raja Jaafur**, his father, who ruled from 1806 to 1832. Down on the south coast, turn left, and after a couple of hundred metres follow Jalan Nakhoda Ninggal to **Tungku Bilek** (Lady Room), the ruined two-storey house by the sea. It was once inhabited by the sister of one of the sultans and was so named because she was said never to leave her room. Nearby are the remains of other residences and a palace.

On the north side of the island, about 200m east of the mosque, is the **grave of Raja Hamidah**, also known as Engku Puteri, who died in 1844 and is revered as the original owner of the island. This is a place of pilgrimage for Muslims, who believe it to be *keramat*, able to bring about miracles. Of all the graves on the island it's the most lovely, set in a restored yellow-and-green compound with a central mausoleum.

Other ferry excursions

Plenty of other excursions are possible from Tanjung Pinang, if you're willing to charter a boat. On the Senggarang side of the inlet, take a boat from the Pelantar II jetty in Tanjung Pinang for an expedition along **Sungai Ular** (Snake River). The river winds inland through mangroves to a small Buddhist temple, with painted murals of the life of Buddha adorning the walls. Ask directions here for the walk to Senggarang, or negotiate the boat trip as a return.

Another possible excursion from Tanjung Pinang is to uninhabited **Pulau Sore**, which lies about 8km to the southwest of town. There are attractive white-sand beaches where you can spend a pleasant day relaxing, but be sure to take all supplies. Negotiations for the return trip from Pelantar I will start at Rp50,000, and make sure you fix the time you want to be collected. **Pulau Terkulai**, about 20km to the northwest, is also attractive, but the Batam ferries pass very close by.

The Lingga Islands

Ranging about 120km either side of the equator, the **Lingga Islands** are a scattered group of hundreds of dots of land, which feature in few travel itineraries despite their great scenery, easy access from Tanjung Pinang or Jambi, quiet charm and the convenience of regular (if infrequent) ferry connections. The main islands of the group are **Pulau Lingga** and **Pulau Singkep**, both of which get a handful of visitors and have basic, though adequate, facilities. With a bit of Indonesian, though, you can hop off the boat at one of its ports of call throughout the islands and enjoy the slow pace of life. Wherever you are heading, and for however long, take enough cash, as there are no exchange facilities on the islands and no tourist offices.

Pulau Lingga

With a tortuous shape, few roads and a jungle-covered mountainous interior, **Pulau Lingga** is an enticing place for adventurous visitors. The near absence of traffic and especially litter make a welcome change from the Riau Islands; the commercial boom has passed Linnga by and the friendly locals seem unfazed by the occasional traveller. The central towering summit of Gunung Daik (1164m), the highest point in the Riau or Lingga islands, gives the island its name – *linggam* is Sanskrit for "phallus". The island was the base of part of the Riau sultanate in the nineteenth century, when one faction established itself on Pulau Penyenget and the other removed itself here. Many of today's inhabitants are descended from royal families and there are some ancient remains to explore.

The main settlement on the island is **DAIK**, towards the south of the island, a small development on the riverbanks. Outside of monsoon, the daily (except Sun) speedboat from Tanjung Pinang on Pulau Bintan stops here, and this is also the place to embark when you're leaving. In rough seas, the same boat docks at the lovely harbour town of **Pancur** on the east coast, where there is a tiny losmen. From here it's a pleasant thirty minutes by sampan (Rp50,000 per boat, so the fare depends on the number of passengers, usually Rp10,000 each) upriver through the mangroves, to the end of the road at Resun, and then another thirty minutes (Rp10,000) by ojek to Daik, 14km from here. Be quick off the boat at Pancur to avoid missing the sampan; you'll have to charter your own if you're late. Three times a week there's a speedboat direct from Tanjung Pinang to **Tanjung Buton**, on the coast south of Daik, and from here it's an ojek ride (Rp3000) into town. Small ferries from Pulau Penuba, between Pulau Lingga and Pulau Singkep, go directly up the small river to Daik, as does the boat to Dabo (Pulau Singkep) and Jambi (on the mainland), every other day.

There are a couple of basic **losmen** in Daik – enquire locally – but the best place to stay is at the welcoming **homestay** of Maslan, whose house is at the tiny hamlet of Kampung Sempincan, 2km from Daik. It's a twenty-minute walk, or Rp2000 by ojek, and the effervescent Maslan will feed and house you for Rp35,000 a day. The place is full of chickens and dogs, there's a river to swim in, and Maslan is usually in good voice for the karaoke TV shows in the evening. This is also the place to enquire about trekking (see p.458). Daik has a few simple **warung**, a **post office**, some market stalls by the river but no exchange facilities. The only public transport on the island is by ojek, but the road system isn't extensive, heading around 20km southeast of Daik. Otherwise, small local boats circle around the coast.

There's little to do in Daik itself apart from enjoy the unhurried pace. Just to the north of town is the nineteenth-century **Mesjid Jamik**; according to local legend, the carver of the fine pulpit was executed after finishing the job so that no one else could ever own such a beautiful work of art. Outside town itself, you can walk for an hour or so north to **Istana Damnah**, the palace of Sultan Mahmud, who is buried behind Mesjid Jamik; built a considerable distance inland for protection from pirate raids, the palace was taken by the Dutch in 1911. Much of the building was constructed from wood, which was destroyed when the Dutch attacked, or has rotted over time, but some foundations, remnants of a pavilion, a toilet and parts of a staircase are still discernible. Some of the path is very overgrown, so make sure you get clear directions or take a guide. The old fort, **Bukit Cengkeh**, just off the path to the palace, was built on a hill overlooking the river, but a few ancient cannons are all that remain.

At Maslan's homestay (see p.457), you can organize **treks** to Gunung Daik (three days, Rp150,000) or one-day trips (Rp50,000) to one of the waterfalls near Daik or (better) at Resun.

Pulau Penuba

Located in the strait between Pulau Lingga and Pulau Singkep, the small island of **Pulau Penuba**, which features great beaches on both its north and south coasts, is accessible either from Tanjung Buton on Pulau Lingga or Jago on Pulau Singkep: regular public boats run between both destinations during daylight hours. If you're in a rush you can charter, but bargain hard – negotiations will start at around Rp60,000 one-way. There are two small, basic places to stay on Pulau Penuba: *The Mess* near the town square (❷) and *Penginapan Penuba* (❷).

Pulau Singkep

The most southerly of the Lingga chain, **Pulau Singkep** is a large island about 20km south of Pulau Lingga, roughly 35km at its longest and widest points, with the main population centre at **Dabo** in the middle of the east coast. Now a backwater, this once-flourishing island is a terrifically friendly place, great for seeing genuine island life, free from modern industry and the influence of Singapore. Ferry connections to Sumatra leave from here, but the main port for connections north, particularly from Tanjung Pinang, is at **Jago**, on the northern tip of the island, about 25km by road from Dabo (the bus takes 1hr; Rp5000). A ferry to Daik (Pulau Lingga) departs every other day from Dabo harbour, though during the monsoon it sometimes leaves from Jago instead. The same goes for the old Chinese **wooden cargo ships**, which leave Pulau Singkep every other morning or so bound for Jambi, weaving their way en route past hundreds of small islands, many of them uninhabited, before ploughing straight up the Sungai Batang Hari River. The journey itself, though cramped and eighteen hours long, is a great experience.

Singkep lacks the ancient royal links of nearby Lingga, but has a history as a **tin** island akin to that of Bangka and Belitung. It was always a smaller player than the other islands, but became a commercial producer in 1891 when world demand was at a height; production ceased in the 1980s, as demand and prices fell. These days the inhabitants earn a living from farming, rubber and timber, but many have moved elsewhere for work, particularly north to the new industrial and tourist enclaves of the Riau Islands. There's talk of Riau-style luxury tourism developing down here, but (as yet) no concrete plans.

Dabo

DABO has quietened down since the tin company ceased operation, but evidence of its former glory is still apparent in wide, spacious streets and attractive bungalows, and it offers a pleasant, laid-back glimpse of ordinary Indonesian life. If you **arrive** from Jambi or Daik, you'll dock at the main jetty in town from where it's a short walk to any of the accommodation places. Buses from the port of Jago (Rp10,000) will drop you at the accommodation of your choice. The twice-daily boat to and from Tanjung Pinang (Pulau Bintan) docks at the more sheltered Jago in monsoon and Dabo in calm weather.

There isn't a great amount to do in town. **Cetiya Dharma Ratna** is a new, grand Chinese temple well worth a look for its fabulously colourful murals and statues, the wafting incense helping to create a rich atmosphere. Much of the population takes a stroll out here in the late afternoon and there are good views along the sweeping, white-sand, palm-fringed bay, which stretches for several kilometres in each direction.

The main **Telkom office** is about 1km outside town; more convenient is the Singkep Agung 24-hour wartel on Jalan Penuba, one of three in town. Inevitably, there's now a **cybercafe** on Jalan Pasar Lama, and the **post office** (Mon–Thurs 7.30am–3.15pm, Fri & Sat 7.30am–1.30pm) is on Jalan Pahlawan, about 100m west of the junction with Jalan Kartini and the grand Mesjid Azzulfa mosque.

The town offers several **accommodation** options. *Gapura Singkep*, Jl Perusahaan 14 (Ⓣ0776/21136; ❷–❹), is a two-storey building set back from the road and a little hard to spot. It's a good choice, with a wide variety of rooms, ranging from clean economy fan rooms with mandi to large, air-con doubles with hot water and satellite TV. Also recommended is the new, clean *Sri Indah*, Jl Perusahaan 10 (Ⓣ0776/21099; ❷–❸) a little way down across the street.

There are plenty of **places to eat** in town, including many nameless coffee shops and warung: head for Jalan Pramuka and Jalan Merdeka, north of Jalan Pasar Lama that runs across the centre of town. *Gongang Lidah* on Jalan Pelabuhan serves basic, inexpensive Indonesian and Chinese meals.

Around the island

A few buses ply the lanes **around the island**: the nondescript towns of Jago and Raya are the main destinations. If you want to explore independently, enquire at your accommodation or in shops in town; you should be able to pick up a bicycle for about Rp6000 a day, but motorcycle rental is pricey (around Rp5000 an hour, or double that if you want a driver).

If you travel outside Dabo, the beach of **Pantai Batu Berdaun**, 4km southwest of town (Rp5000 by ojek), is narrow but long and sweeping, with good views back to Dabo and across to Pulau Lalang off the coast to the south. It's a popular weekend excursion with local people but very quiet in the week, and big enough so that you can get away from the crowds at any time. Closer to town, 3km to the northeast, **Pantai Jodoh** and **Pantai Indah** (which has warungs on Sunday) are near enough to walk to fairly easily – just keep the water on your right on the way there. Inland, the small Batu Hampar **waterfall**, just off the Raya road about 11km from Dabo, is a pleasant spot, and you can swim in the pool.

Jambi and around

Most travellers bypass the eastern city of **JAMBI**, the capital of the province of the same name, situated on the south bank of **Sungai Batang Hari**, the longest river in Sumatra. Although there's little to detain visitors to Jambi for long, there are some interesting archeological sites nearby and the city might make a passable halt for a day if you're heading east through Sumatra, or are taking the ferry route from/to Pulau Singkep.

Arrival, information and city transport

The **long-distance bus terminal** is at the new Simpang Rimbo terminal several kilometres west of the centre. Yellow bemos run from Simpang Rimbo to Rawasari bemo terminal in the heart of Jambi. **Flights** land at Sultan Taha airport (Ⓣ0741/22244), 6km south of the city centre; red bemos operate between the airport and Rawasari terminal in the town centre, and fixed-price taxis charge Rp10,000.

JAMBI

ACCOMMODATION	
Abadi	1
Adipura	9
Anggrek	4
Dalia	6
88	7
Jambi Raya	5
Mayang Sari	2
Mexicana (MC)	8
Novotel	3

RESTAURANTS	
Christine Bakery	B
Jalan Rami Warung	A
Jumbo	C
Mayang Mangurai Kafé	D

The river and the area around the port are the main **orientation** point in Jambi, with Jalan Sultan Taha and Jalan Raden Pamuk running along the southern bank. Just behind these roads, the maze of lanes and alleyways of the market and commercial centre contain most of the facilities that travellers will need, some of the accommodation options and the Rawasari bemo terminal. From the town centre, several main roads head away from the river, most usefully Jalan Gatot Subroto, which changes into Jalan Sudirman on the way to the airport; Jalan Sultan Agung, which splits into Jalan Prof Dr Sumantri Brojonegoro through the suburb of Telanapura to the southwest of the centre; and Jalan Prof J.M. Yamin, which leads due south.

Moving on from Jambi

There are **bus** connections throughout Sumatra and Java but the difficulty can be finding out about them, as each company operates to different destinations and the offices aren't terribly close together. Either a travel agent in town, or the bus station itself is the best place to start enquiries. Try Tawang Tours and Travel, Jl H.P. Kusama 43 (ⓣ0741/35193), near the bemo station. You might also try the offices around the junction of Jalan Prof J.M. Yamin and Jalan H.O.S. Cokroaminoto opposite. It's worth shopping around a bit to get the departure time you want. ANS, Jl H.O.S. Cokroaminoto 42 (ⓣ0741/64801), operate to Padang and Medan; Indrah Putri, Jl H.O.S. Cokroaminoto 22 (ⓣ0741/65502), to Bandar Lampung and Palembang; Lorena, Jl H.O.S. Cokroaminoto 14 (ⓣ0741/40620), are a big setup with services to Jakarta, plus plenty of other Java destinations including Surabaya, Solo and Probolinggo and on to Bali. At Toko Melan, Jl Prof H.M. Yamin 56 (ⓣ0741/60240), you can book straight through to Batam. For departures to Bengkulu, Pekanbaru, Bangko and Muara Bungo, ask at the ticket offices in the Simpang Rimbo terminal. Conveniently situated in the centre of town, ACC, Jl Dr M. Assaat 60 (ⓣ0741/25593), offer departures to Palembang, Pekanbaru, Muara Bungo, Jakarta and Bandung. A handily located office servicing Palembang, Bengkulu, Padang and Medan is PO. Jaya Bersama, Jalan Prof M. Yamin (ⓣ0741/53660) – just south of the Rawasari bemo terminal off Jalan Halim Perdana Kusuma.

By **air**, Merpati and Mandala operate scheduled flights from Jambi while SMAC have some irregular flights (see "Listings" p.463 for offices in the city). From Jambi, Pelni operate only cargo **ships**, two of which go through to Dabo on Pulau Singkep and Daik on Pulau Linnga. If you're trying to find out about these or other sailings, walk down to the nearby harbour behind Angso Dua and ask there; alternatively, ask at the port administration office, Kantor Administrator Jambi, Jl Sultan Taha 4 (ⓣ0741/22020), or try the Pelni office: Serikat Pekerja Pelni, Jl Sultan Thaha 17 (ⓣ0741/22102).

The **tourist office** on Jl Basuki Rachmat 11 (Mon–Thurs & Sat 7.30am–2pm, Fri 7.30am–11am; ⓣ0741/40330, ⓕ41733) is accessible by a green bemo from the central terminal; ask for "Walikota Madya". They produce a few brochures in English and will try to answer specific questions, but are a bit surprised to see tourists.

City transport

For getting around in the city, small **bemos** operate on fixed routes with a Rp800 flat fare, between the Rawasari terminal in the centre of town and outlying suburbs. They are divided into four main colour-coded routes: red operates to the airport; green to Walikota Madya; blue to Telanapura and Simpang Rimbo bus terminal; and yellow to Simpang Rimbo. Each colour has three or four sub-routes – these are listed above the stands where the bemos terminate at Rawasari.

There are plenty of **taxis**, metered and unmetered (the unmetered ones congregate at the northern end of Jalan Dr M. Assaat), though even those with meters tend to think tourists are fair game for a double fare. A trip from the centre to anywhere in the city should be less than Rp10,000.

Accommodation

As with most Sumatran cities, Jambi's **accommodation** is dominated by hotels catering for business travellers, although it's possible to find reasonable budget options. Most hotels are located in the central area, either on and around Jalan

Jend Gatot Subroto or up Jalan Halim Perdana Kusuma, with some alternatives in the southwestern suburb of Telanapura, where the exterior grandeur and character of some places is unfortunately not reflected in the rooms.

Abadi Jl Jend Gatot Subroto 92–98 ⓣ0741/25600, ⓕ23065. This centrally located place is one of the most comfortable in town, and it's all the quieter for being slightly set back from the road. Rooms have air-con, hot water and TV, and there's also a pool. ❺

Adipura Jl Prof Dr Sumantri Brojonegoro 119 ⓣ0741/60200, ⓕ32869. The bemos running between Simpang Rimbo and Rawasari terminal pass the door; the partly traditional building and attractive entrance hall is alluring but rooms are utilitarian rather than luxurious. Rooms away from the road are quieter. ❸

Anggrek Jalan Iskander Muda, Lorong Camar III 94 ⓣ0741/25545, ⓕ33956. This central, clean place on a quiet alleyway directly behind the *Novotel*/Matahari Plaza complex is excellent value. Less expensive rooms have outside bathroom and fan, while the more costly ones have bathroom and air-con. ❷–❸

Dalia Jl Lorong Camar III 100 ⓣ0741/50863. Right in the middle of town on a quiet alleyway between the Matahari shopping centre and Rawasari terminal. It's a friendly place and the rooms are reasonable but a little dark and musty – budget ones have fan and outside mandi, whilst more expensive options aren't really worth it but have air-con and inside mandi. Ask to see several rooms, as they vary in size. ❷–❸

88 Jl Halim Perdana Kusuma 8 ⓣ0741/33286. Inexpensive and close to the town centre, with helpful staff; there are plenty of rooms on offer, from some with fans and unattached mandi to some with air-con and attached mandi. ❷–❸

Jambi Raya Jl Lorong Camar III ⓣ0741/34971, ⓕ34972. A decent mid-range place in a quiet but central location. The staff speak a little English, and the rooms all come with air-con and bathrooms. Rp110,000–175,000.

Mayang Sari Jalan Iskander Muda, Jl Lorong Camar III 88–90 ⓣ0741/20695, ⓕ20898 Close to the *Anggrek*, this is a large setup offering utilitarian rooms, all with air-con and bathroom. ❸

Mexicana (MC) Jl Halim Perdana Kusuma 10 ⓣ0741/22163. A poorly looked after place with tiled floors, air-con en-suites and mosquitoes. It's best not to check under the beds. ❷–❸

Novotel Jl Gatot Subroto 44 ⓣ0741/27208, ⓕ27209. This four-star, central hotel offers the best and most expensive facilities in town, including swimming pool, fitness and business centres and tennis courts. Rooms are luxurious, and there are good views across the city. ❺–❻

The City

Jambi is a combination of the old prewar seat of the Jambi sultanate on the banks of the river with the new administrative suburb, **Telanapura**, to the southwest. It's a bustling tidal river port, with exports of palm oil, plywood, timber and rubber (the mainstays of the thriving provincial economy) passing through; sad testimony to the destruction of much of Jambi's ancient forests by rubber and palm-oil plantations. The province was also very badly hit by the devastating forest fires of 1997–98. With its position close to the Malacca Straits and prominence as an ancient kingdom, the ethnic mix in the city includes Malays, Arabs, Chinese and Buginese as well as Javanese and Balinese from more recent transmigration initiatives and the mobile Minangkabau from nearby western Sumatra.

One of the best sights in the city, and a fascinating place to wander around, is the daily **Angso Dua market**, located between Jalan Sultan Taha and the river. It's an unmodernized maze of tiny alleyways lined with stalls selling fresh and dried fish, vegetables, fruit, spices and all kinds of meat. About 1km further east, a small public park on the banks of **Sungai Batang Hari** at the eastern end of Jalan Sultan Taha, where it turns into Jalan Raden Pamuk, gives views across the broad expanse of the river and west to the main port area. Towards dark, you may be lucky with a dramatic sunset, and plenty of food stalls cater for local people who come to enjoy the river breeze.

Jambi has its own textile tradition, believed to have been developed at the time of the ancient Malayu kingdom. In traditional **Jambi batik** designs you can see Sungai Batang Hari wending its way through the patterns, which often include old-style sailing ships and swans, although the traditional dark-blue, dark-red and yellow colour range is now being widened to fit modern tastes. At the Sanggar Batik dan Kerajinan **workshop**, Jl Prof Dr Sri Soedewi 18a (Mon–Sat 8am–3pm), you can see the tortuous process of batik production, where designs are sketched out followed by repeated waxing, dyeing and drying: a sarong typically takes twenty days to make. There's a good range of items for sale – cotton scarves cost between Rp20,000 and Rp40,000, while you'll pay around Rp500,000 for a four-metre length of pure silk. An alternative destination to see Jambi batik is **Mudung Laut**, a small village across the Batang Hari – you can reach it by ferry (Rp700) from Jalan Sultan Taha, where Selaras Pinang Masak is also a workshop/showroom.

The **Museum Negeri Propinsi Jambi** (Tues–Thurs & Sun 8am–2pm, Fri 8am–11am, Sat 8am–1pm; Rp1000), Jalan Prof Dr Sri Soedewi, at the junction with Jalan Jend Urip Sumoharjo, is about 4km from the city centre; take a green bemo from Rawasari. It contains a selection of old weapons, local costumes, stuffed animals, traditional wedding ceremony decorations and models of houses: labelling is mostly in Indonesian. There are some beautiful Chinese ceramics found in Sarko regency from the Tang, Sung and Han dynasties and many intricate fish-traps. The **Arca Bhairawa** is a fabulous four-metre, fourteenth-century statue of the half-Sumatran, half-Javanese nobleman Adityavarman who ruled over the area, decorated with human skulls at its base. He is depicted as a Tantric Buddhist deity, standing on a hapless baby – the statue here is a replica, the original being in the National Museum in Jakarta (see p.106).

Eating and drinking

Jambi is filled with **eating places**, from the warung of the Jalan Camar area up to top-quality restaurants in the luxury hotels, and everything in between.

Christine Bakery Jl Dr M. Assaat 40. One of several small bakeries in town serving a good range of sweet breads and cakes; there's some seating.

Jalan Rami Warung Jalan Rami. A covered strip of food stalls with a row of benches inside, this is the most fun place to have lunch or dinner. There's nasi ayam and sate on offer, but the speciality here is the gado-gado. You can also get icy juices freshly squeezed into your glass.

Jumbo Jl Raden Mattaher 116. This is a simple local favourite with an extensive and inexpensive range of sate, *murtabak*, *pempek*, *mie bakso*, ice desserts and juices.

Mayang Mangurai Kafé At the *Novotel*, located on the balcony above the hotel lobby, with some good views onto the bustling road below. The atmosphere is plush and, although there are plenty of expensive options – including burgers, sandwiches, smoked salmon, steaks and lamb chops – there are also much more reasonable dishes such as gado-gado and nasi goreng. Drinks are pricey though: beer is Rp12,000 a glass.

Simpang Raya Jl Jend Gato Subroto 134. A popular, inexpensive place with a wide variety of chicken and fish dishes. It's a cool retreat from the busy street.

Listings

Airline offices Mandala agent, PT Aquavita Jaya Travel Service, Jl Jend Gatot Subroto 86 ⓣ0741/50643; Merpati (also agents for Garuda), *Hotel Abdi*, Jl Jend Gatot Subroto 92–98 ⓣ0741/21370, ⓕ20774; SMAC, Jl Orang Kayo Hitam 26 ⓣ0741/22269.

Banks and exchange BCA, Jl Raden Mattaher 15; BNI, Jl Dr Sutomo 20; BRI, Jl Dr Sutomo 42.

Bookshops Toko Buku Gloria, Jl Raden Mattaher 43–44, stocks the English-language *Jakarta Post* and *Observer* newspapers and a city map of Jambi, and they occasionally sell postcards.

Cinema Sumatera 2, Jalan Halim Perdana Kusuma, is central and has showings of Hollywood blockbusters on four screens.
Golf Lapangan Golf Jambi, Jalan Jend A. Thalip ⓣ0741/62854. Green fees for nine holes are Rp70,000 and Rp90,000 for eighteen holes. There are clubs for rent for additional fees.
Hospitals Rumah Sakit DKT (military hospital), Jl Raden Mattaher 33 ⓣ0741/23164; Rumah Sakit Santa Theresia, Jl Dr Sutomo 19 ⓣ0741/23119; Rumah Sakit Umum Jambi, Jl Letjen Suprapto 2 ⓣ0741/62364.
Immigration office About 15km out of town at Telani Pura ⓣ0741/62033, ⓕ61383.
Port administration office For details of shipping out of Jambi, contact the Kantor Administrator Jambi, Jl Sultan Taha 4 ⓣ0741/22020, ⓕ25280.
Internet access There are a few places in town where you can get online. Try Warnet Sentosa just outside the main entrance to the Matahari Plaza.
Post office Jl Sultan Taha 5; they get few tourists here and it isn't recommended for poste restante.
Shopping Matahari Plaza, Jalan Jend Gatot Subroto, is the newest and best shopping centre in town, with a fast-food plaza, bookstore, department store and supermarket.
Swimming Jalan Slamet Riyadi (daily 7am–6pm; Rp2000).
Telephone and fax The main 24hr Telkom office is at Jl Raden Mattaher 8, but there are wartels all over town.

Around Jambi

The major archeological site within reach of Jambi is the **Muara Jambi** complex (daily 8am–4pm; donation), 26km downstream from the city. If you go on Sunday, when most local people visit, boats ply Sungai Batang Hari (speedboats charge Rp60,000 for ten passengers) leaving from two spots, east of Boom Batu just in front of the governor's office and west of Boom Rakit. Make sure you fix the price before you embark. Alternatively, the taxi fare will cost Rp60,000 each way.

Thought to date from the seventh to the thirteenth century, the complex is testimony to the power of the Malayu kingdom. Chinese histories detail the visit of Malayu emissaries to the court of the Tang dynasty in 644–645 AD, and a Chinese monk, I-Tsing, visited the Malayu court around thirty years later. The site comprises the remains of the ancient port of Malayu, an extensive area of Hindu and Buddhist shrines set amongst canals and large water tanks on the north bank of Sungai Batang Hari. The city is said to have been destroyed in

Visiting the Kubu people

Around 1000 remaining **Kubu** people, the original southern Sumatran inhabitants, still live in the Jambi forests. They traditionally lived as hunter-gatherers in the jungle, and have resisted government efforts to settle them, preferring to maintain their nomadic lifestyle. However, as their environment has been under threat from all sides, they have begun to settle to some extent, taking up agriculture but still resisting integration into mainstream Indonesian life – it remains to be seen what the future holds for them.

Travel agents in Jambi (see p.461) may be able to put a tour together; otherwise, ask in Bukittinggi at Puti Bungus, Jl Teuku Umar 7a (ⓣ0752/23026); guides in Sungaipenuh (see p.431) also offer a trip. In Jambi, try: Jambi Mayang Tour, Jl Raden Mattaher 27 (ⓣ0741/51686, ⓕ32869); Tawang Tours and Travel, Jl H.P. Kusama 43 (ⓣ0741/35193); or PT Aquavita Jaya Travel Service, Jl Jend Gatot Subroto 86 (ⓣ0741/23637).

To go independently, you'll need fairly good Indonesian. From Bangko, take a local bus to Pauh village, where you'll need to report to the *kepala camat* (the district head), and then to Air Hitam, close to the areas where some Kubu people have settled and where you'll need to find a guide to take you on foot the rest of the way. Expect to pay about Rp40,000 a day.

about 1377 by the son of Prince Telanai, the last ruler of the city. A fortune-teller predicted that the son of the prince would bring disaster to the kingdom, so the prince put him in a chest and threw it into the sea. It arrived in Siam, where the child was raised as a member of the royal court, eventually returning to Muara Jambi with a huge Siamese army to kill his father and destroy the city.

So far, three main structures have been restored – Candi Tinggi, Candi Gumpung and Candi Kedaton – and, whilst many of the finds in the area are in a small site **museum**, a lot of artefacts have been taken to Jakarta.

Travel details

Buses

Bukittinggi to: Bandar Lampung (5 daily; 24hr); Bandung (5 daily; 34hr); Batam (daily; 24hr); Batang Palupuh (hourly 7am–5pm; 30min); Batusangkar (hourly 7am–5pm; 1hr 30min); Bengkulu (4 daily; 18hr); Bonjol (hourly 7am–5pm; 1hr); Jakarta (10 daily; 32hr); Jambi (5 daily; 15hr); Lubuk Basang (hourly 7am–5pm; 1hr 30min); Lubuklinggau (4 daily; 12hr); Medan (10 daily; 18hr); Maninjau (hourly 5am–7pm; 2hr); Padang (every 10min 7am–5pm; 2hr 30min); Palembang (1 daily; 20hr); Payakumbuh (hourly 7am–5pm; 1hr); Pekanbaru (10 daily; 6hr); Prapat (2 daily; 14hr); Sibolga (daily; 12hr); Solok (hourly 7am–5pm; 1hr 30min–2hr).
Jambi to: Banda Aceh (daily; 36hr); Bandar Lampung (10 daily; 22hr); Bandung (daily; 34hr); Bangko (hourly; 5hr); Batam (daily; 24hr); Bengkulu (2 daily; 11hr); Denpasar (Bali, 2 daily; 48hr); Jakarta (3 daily; 30hr); Mataram (Lombok, daily; 3 days); Medan (10 daily; 36hr); Muara Bungo (hourly; 5hr); Padang (10 daily; 24hr); Palembang (10 daily; 8hr); Pekanbaru (2 daily; 11hr); Probolinggo (daily; 48hr); Solo (daily; 48hr); Surabaya (daily; 48hr); Yogyakarta (daily; 36hr).
Maninjau to: Bukittinggi (hourly; 1hr 30min); Padang (2 daily; 3hr); Pekanbaru (daily; 8hr).
Padang to: Banda Aceh (4 daily; 28hr); Bandar Lampung (10 daily; 24hr); Bengkulu (4 daily; 18hr); Bukittinggi (every 20min 6am–7pm; 2hr 30min); Jakarta (10 daily; 30–35hr) Jambi (6 daily; 20hr); Medan (10 daily; 20hr); Palembang (4 daily; 22hr); Pekanbaru (10 daily; 9hr); Prapat (10 daily; 20hr); Sibolga (4 daily; 18hr); Solok (every 20min 6am–7pm; 1hr).
Pekanbaru to: Bandar Lampung (10 daily; 24hr); Bengkulu (2 daily; 30hr); Bukittinggi (10 daily; 6hr); Denpasar (daily; 4 days); Dumai (10 daily; 3hr); Jakarta (10 daily; 34hr); Jambi (6 daily; 9hr); Maninjau (daily; 8hr); Mataram (Lombok, daily; 4 days); Medan (daily; 25–35hr); Padang (10 daily; 9hr); Palembang (20 daily; 18hr); Prapat (daily; 22–30hr); Sungaipenuh (daily; 12hr) Yogyakarta (4 daily; 44hr).
Sungaipenuh to: Bangko, transit for Palembang, Bandar Lampung and Jakarta (10 daily; 5hr); Bengkulu (daily; 9hr); Dumai (daily; 14hr); Jambi (daily; 7hr); Muko-Muko (daily; 4hr); Padang (4 daily; 12hr); Painan (2 daily; 7hr); Pekanbaru (daily; 12hr).

Pelni ferries

For a chart of the Pelni routes, see p.42 of Basics.
Batam to: Jakarta (Tanjung Priok) (*KM Kelud*, twice weekly; 16hrs; *KFC Jetliner*, twice weekly; 18hrs)
Pulau Bintan (Kijang) to: Ambon (*KM Bukit Siguntang*, weekly; 2 days); Balikpapan (*KM Kerinci*, fortnightly; 4 days); Banda (*KM Bukit Siguntang*, fortnightly; 4 days); Bau Bau (*KM Bukit Siguntang*, fortnightly; 4 days); Bawean (*KM Bukit Raya*, fortnightly; 4 days); Dobo (*KM Bukit Siguntang*, fortnightly; 8 days); Dumai (*KM Bukit Siguntang*, fortnightly; 14hr/*KM Kerinci*, fortnightly; 15hr); Kaimana (*KM Bukit Siguntang*, fortnightly; 8 days); Letung (*KM Bukit Raya*, weekly; 12hr); Makasar (*KM Bukit Siguntang*, fortnightly; 3 days/*KM Sirimau*, fortnightly; 5 days; Midai (*KM Bukit Raya*, fortnightly; 33hr); Natuna (*KM Bukit Raya*, fortnightly; 27hr); Nunukan (*KM Kerinci*, fortnightly; 6 days); Pantoloan (*KM Kerinci*, fortnightly; 9 days); Pontianak (*KM Bukit Raya*, fortnightly; 3 days); Sampit (*KM Bukit Raya*, fortnightly; 5 days); Semarang (*KM Sirimau*, fortnightly; 3 days); Serasan (*KM Bukit Raya*, fortnightly; 35hr); Surabaya (*KM Bukit Raya*, fortnightly; 4 days/*KM Bukit Siguntang*, fortnightly; 2 days/*KM Kerinci*, fortnightly; 2 days); Tambelan (*KM Bukit Raya*, fortnightly; 44hr); Tanjung Priok (*KM Bukit Raya*, fortnightly; 42hr/*KM Bukit Siguntang*, fortnightly; 26hr/*KM Kerinci*, fortnightly; 26hr/*KM Sirimau*, fort-

nightly; 2 days); Tarakan (*KM Kerinci*, fortnightly; 6 days); Tarempa (*KM Bukit Raya*, fortnightly; 14hr); Toli Toli (*KM Kerinci*, fortnightly; 5 days); Tual (*KM Bukit Siguntang*, fortnightly; 6 days).
Padang to: Ambon (*KM Lambelu*, fortnightly; 5 days); Balikpapan (*KM Umsini*, fortnightly; 4 days); Bau Bau (*KM Lambelu*, fortnightly; 4 days); Bitung (*KM Umsini*, fortnightly; 6 days); Makasar (*KM Umsini*, fortnightly; 3 days/*KM Lambelu*, fortnightly; 3 days); Namlea (*KM Lambelu*, fortnightly; 5 days); Nias (*KM Umsini*, fortnightly; 17hr/*KM Lambelu*, fortnightly; 12hr); Pantoloan (*KM Umsini*, fortnightly; 5 days); Sibolga (*KM Umsini*, fortnightly; 12hr/*KM Lambelu*, fortnightly; 18hr); Surabaya (*KM Umsini*, fortnightly; 2 days/*KM Lambelu*, fortnightly; 2 days); Tanjung Priok (*KM Umsini*, fortnightly; 31hr/*KM Lambelu*, fortnightly; 29hr); Ternate (*KM Lambelu*, fortnightly; 6 days); Toli Toli (*KM Umsini*, fortnightly; 5 days).
Pulau Karimun (Tanjung Balai) to: Belawan (*KM Kambuna*, 3 monthly; 20hr); Muntok (*KM Sirimau*, monthly; 3 days); Tanjung Priok (*KM Kambuna*, 3 monthly; 3 days).

Other ferries

Padang to: Siberut (3/4 weekly; 12hr).
Pekanbaru to: Sekupang (daily; 7–11hr); Selatpanjang (daily; 16hr); Tebingtinggi Island (daily; 6–10hr); Tanjung Balai (Pulau Karimun; daily; 5–9hr and 25hr); Tanjung Pinang (daily; 8–12hr and 22hr); Tanjung Samak (Pulau Rangsang; daily; 18hr); Tanjung Batu (Pulau Kundur; daily; 20hr); Moro (Pulau Sugibawah, daily; 21hr).
Pulau Batam to: Singapore: Batu Ampar (World Trade Centre; 9 daily; 1–2hr), Sekupang (World Trade Centre; 24 daily;1–2hr), Nongsa (Tanah Merah; 6 daily; 1–2hr), Teluk Senimba (World Trade Centre; 14 daily; 1–2hr); Tanjung Pinang (Pulau Bintan; 36 daily; 1–2hr).
Pulau Bintan (Tanjung Pinang) to: Batam (every 30min; 1–2hr); Dabo on Pulau Singkep (2 daily; 5–7hr); Daik or Panchur on Pulau Lingga (daily; 4hr); Johor Baru in Malaysia (3 daily; 6hr); Pangkal Balam (weekly; 8hr); Pekanbaru (daily; 12 hrs); Pulau Lingga (6 weekly; 4–6hr); Singapore (from Tanjung Pinang to Tanah Merah 3 daily; 1hr 30min; from Bandar Bentan to Tanah Merah; 3–7 daily; 45min); Tanjung Balai (daily; 2–3hr); Tanjung Batu (daily; 3–4hr); Tanjung Priok (3 weekly; 24hr).
Pulau Karimun (Tanjung Balai) to: Dabo (via Tanjung Pinang; daily; 7hr); Johor Baru in Malaysia (4 daily; 4–6hr); Pekanbaru (2 daily; 6–7hr); Selat Panjang (for connections to Pekanbaru or Jambi; 4 daily; 5hr); Sekupang on Pulau Batam (8 daily; 3hr); Singapore (10 daily; 1hr); Tanjung Batu (on Pulau Kundur; 7 daily; 1–2hr), Tanjung Pinang (4 daily; 3hr), Kukup in Malaysia (7 daily; 4hr).
Pulau Kundur (Tanjung Batu) to: Dabo (via Tanjung Balai and Tanjung Pinang; daily; 7–8hr); Tanjung Balai (6 daily; 1–2hr); Pekanbaru (daily; 5–6hr); Sekupang, (4 daily; 3hr); Singapore via Tanjung Balai (5 daily; 1–2hr); Sungai Guntung (for connections to Jambi; 2 daily; 3–4hr).
Pulau Lingga to: Dabo on Pulau Singkep (3 weekly; 2hr); Tanjung Pinang (from Pancur; 6 weekly; 4hr); (from Tanjung Buton; 3 weekly; 5hr); Jambi (3 weekly; 18hr).
Pulau Singkep (Jago) to: Daik on Pulau Lingga (3 weekly; 2hr); Tanjung Pinang (2 daily; 5–7hr).
Siberut to: Padang (4 weekly; 12hr).

Flights

Pulau Batam to: Ambon (daily; 9hr); Balikpapan (3 weekly; 5hr); Bandung (3 weekly; 3hr); Banjarmasin (daily; 6hr); Denpasar (daily; 5hr 20min); Jakarta (5 or 6 daily; 1hr 35min); Jambi (2 weekly; 55min); Manado (daily; 7hr); Mataram (2 weekly; 3hr 55min); Medan (3 weekly; 3hr 35min); Padang (4 weekly; 1hr); Palembang (daily; 1hr 10min); Pangkal Pinang (2 weekly; 40min); Pekanbaru (daily; 50min); Pontianak (weekly; 1–2hr); Semarang (2 or 3 daily; 4hr); Surabaya (3 daily; 3hr 30min); Ujung Pandang (9 weekly; 6hr 30min); Yogyakarta (2 daily; 3hr).
Pulau Bintan to: Jakarta (6 weekly; 1hr 45min); Pekanbaru (6 weekly; 55min).
Jambi to: Balikpapan (daily; 6hr 30min); Batam (4 weekly; 1hr 15min); Denpasar (4 daily; 5hr 10min–7hr 20min); Jakarta (3 daily; 1hr 20min); Medan (2 daily; 6hr 40min); Pontianak (daily; 5hr); Semarang (2 daily; 4–6hr); Solo (daily; 5hr); Surabaya (1 or 2 daily; 4hr 20min); Yogyakarta (3 daily; 3hr 35min).
Padang to: Bandung (daily; 2hr–3hr 30min); Batam (4 weekly; 1hr); Jakarta (3 daily; 50min); Medan (daily; 1hr 10min); Palembang (1–2 daily; 1hr 10min–2hr 40min); Pekanbaru (3 weekly; 50min).
Pekanbaru to: Batam (1–2 daily; 50min); Jakarta (5 daily; 1hr–1hr 40min); Kuala Lumpur (4 weekly; 1hr); Malacca (4 weekly; 40min); Medan (daily; 1hr); Padang (3 weekly; 40min); Tanjung Pinang (4 weekly; 50min).

7

Palembang and South Sumatra

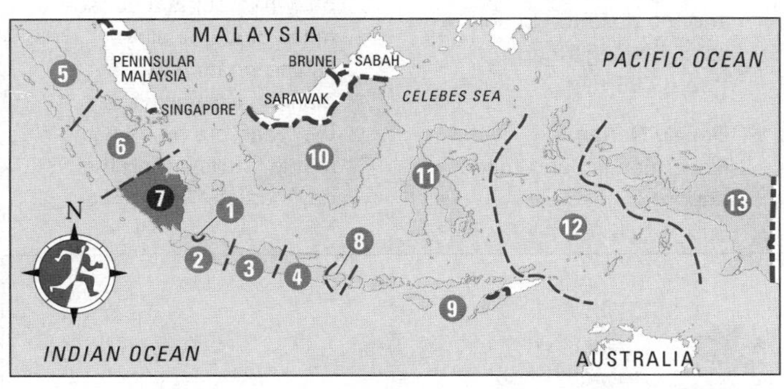

CHAPTER 7 Highlights

* **Palembang weaving shops** Visit one of Palembang's many traditional looms where silk and gold thread have been used for centuries to create *jumputan pelangi* – rainbow cloths. See p.478

* **Pulau Belitung** On little-visited Pulau Belitung, hire a moped and explore the boat-building village of Tanjung Binga and the deserted beaches of Tanjung Tinggi. See p.485

* **Danau Ranau** Fishermen in hand-made dugout canoes ply Danau Ranau, a tranquil lake nestling in the extinct crater of Gunung Seminung. See p.499

* **Krui** Vibrant, small and characterful, the coastal town of Krui is a great place to swim, soak up the local vibe and watch the hauling in of the day's catch. See p.501

* **Bandar Lampung harbour** Bandar Lampung's busy harbour is a dense maze of steps, alleys, fishing boats and plankboard walkways, the wharf crammed with market stalls selling the day's catch. See p.503

7

Palembang and South Sumatra

Despite its soaring mountains, picturesque lakes, areas of historical interest, fascinating offshore islands and dramatic coastline, **South Sumatra** is often passed over by travellers rushing between Bukittinggi and Java. In fact, it has a great deal to offer those willing to get off the beaten track. The geographical division between the western mountains of the Bukit Barisan range and the low-lying plains, swamps and river estuaries of the east continues right down to the south of the island. Seventy kilometres from the east coast, the huge city of **Palembang** straddles the mighty Sungai Musi and, though there's little to entice visitors, it's an important access point for the rarely visited islands of **Bangka** and **Belitung**, both now sleepy backwaters after the death of the lucrative tin trade that was the mainstay of their economies for centuries.

On the west coast, the old British colonial outpost of **Bengkulu** retains plenty of charm, and is also a useful stopping-off point for those heading offshore to remote **Pulau Enggano**, inland to the bustling market town of **Curup** and the mountainous Rejang Lebong area, or to the southeast to explore the mysterious megaliths of the **Pasemah Plateau**.

Although highland **Danau Ranau** lacks the scale and majesty of the more famous Sumatran lakes, its tranquil setting off the main tourist drag makes it an excellent alternative, while the nearby fishing village of **Krui** offers access to the full glory of the totally undeveloped southwest coastline.

In the far south of Sumatra, an almost inevitable stopoff on any journey between Sumatra and Java is **Bandar Lampung**, beautifully located on the shoreline and hills surrounding Lampung Bay. From here, there are good routes to the rarely visited **Bukit Barisan Selatan national park** through the southern town of Kota Agung, and the better-known **Way Kambas national park**, which features a remarkable elephant training school.

The whole region lies south of the equator, with average **temperatures** at sea level hovering around 26–27°C, and a rainy season from October to May. However, the complex geographical features of the island have created microclimates, particularly in the mountains, characterized by unpredictable weather. In the "dry" season, you can still expect rain on about one day in four. In the wet season, torrential downpours are interspersed with hours of bright sunshine; anyone planning a lot of trekking or travelling on back roads would be

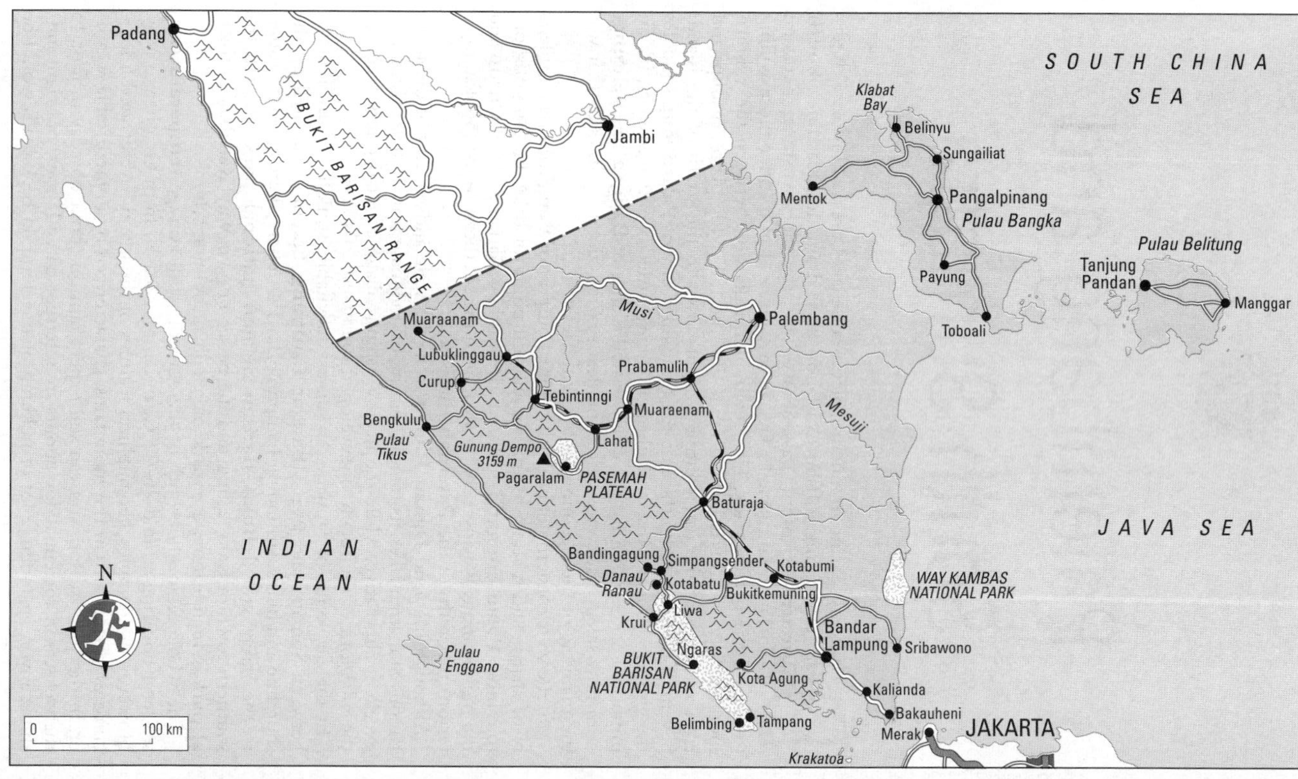
SOUTH CHINA SEA
JAVA SEA
INDIAN OCEAN
Padang
Jambi
BUKIT BARISAN RANGE
Klabat Bay
Belinyu
Sungailiat
Mentok
Pangalpinang
Pulau Bangka
Payung
Toboali
Pulau Belitung
Tanjung Pandan
Manggar
Musi
Palembang
Muaraanam
Lubuklinggau
Curup
Tebintinngi
Prabamulih
Muaraenam
Mesuji
Bengkulu
Pulau Tikus
Lahat
Gunung Dempo 3159 m
Pagaralam
PASEMAH PLATEAU
Baturaja
Bandingagung
Simpangsender
Kotabumi
Danau Ranau
Kotabatu
Bukitkemuning
WAY KAMBAS NATIONAL PARK
Liwa
Krui
Bandar Lampung
Sribawono
Pulau Enggano
Ngaras
BUKIT BARISAN NATIONAL PARK
Kota Agung
Kalianda
Bakauheni
Belimbing
Tampang
Merak
JAKARTA
Krakatoa
N
0
100 km

well advised to avoid this period, as the rain causes landslides and blockages.

Much of southern Sumatra is now developing basic **tourist facilities**, although it's perfectly possible to travel for weeks in the region without meeting more than a handful of other travellers. **Access** into and within the area is excellent: the larger towns have airports and there's a limited but useful passenger rail service between Palembang, Bandar Lampung and Lubuklinggau. Frequent and speedy bus services link Sumatran cities with Java, via a highly efficient 24-hour ferry service between Bakauheni on Sumatra and Merak on Java. As in all of Sumatra, distances are huge, driving can be terrifying and, once you get onto smaller cross-country routes, patience and planning are needed.

Palembang

Useful for travellers on their way to the islands of Bangka and Belitung, or as a stopping point on an easterly route through Sumatra, **PALEMBANG** is the administrative capital of the South Sumatra province, and the second largest city in Sumatra after Medan. With a population nudging 1.6 million, this huge sprawling metropolis has grown up over the last 1200 years. Once one of the world's main trading ports, near shipping lanes that linked Europe and the Far East, the city is situated on the main artery of Sungai Musi, with vast ships docking for access to the industrial and agricultural hinterland.

Palembang's name comes from *limbang* ("to pan for gold"); the early affluence of the city probably came from gold panned from the river. The area first rose to prominence in the late seventh century as the heart of the Buddhist Sriwijaya Kingdom, which dominated Sumatra for the following four centuries and had important trade links throughout Southeast Asia. Even when the Sriwijaya kingdom waned, Palembang remained an important port, with international links to China and the Malay mainland. However, its political history was turbulent, with a succession of Malay, Chinese and Javanese rulers. During Dutch colonial rule, Palembang became a major administrative centre for the nearby plantations and the tin mines on Pulau Bangka. After independence, Palembang reinvented itself as the main depot of oil export in South Sumatra; those taking the ferry to Pulau Bangka cannot fail to notice the gigantic wharves, tankers and filling stations on the way to the open ocean.

Arrival, information and city transport

Flights land at **Sultan Badaruddin II airport**, 12km northwest of the city centre, with fixed-price taxis (Rp20,000) running to the city centre – the only public transport are red Kijang on the main road, almost 2km from the terminal. **Kertapati train station** is 4km southwest of the city centre on a spur of land between Sungai Musi and one of its main tributaries, the Ogan. Taxis (official and unofficial) linger outside the station for all arrivals, and their drivers will try to tell you there's no public transport into town, which isn't true. Turn right out of the main station entrance and buses and bemos (Rp2000 into town) wait on the main road, about a 300-metre walk away.

There are several arrival points for **long-distance buses**, but no main central terminal. Many buses terminate at their offices; the main cluster of offices is on the southern side of the Ampera Bridge on Jalan Pangeran Ratu, near the junction with Jalan K.H.A. Wahid Hasyim and Jalan Jend A. Yani. Pekanbaru buses terminate at Kilometer Lima, a clutch of bus offices 5km north of the city centre; there's plenty of public transport into the city centre from here,

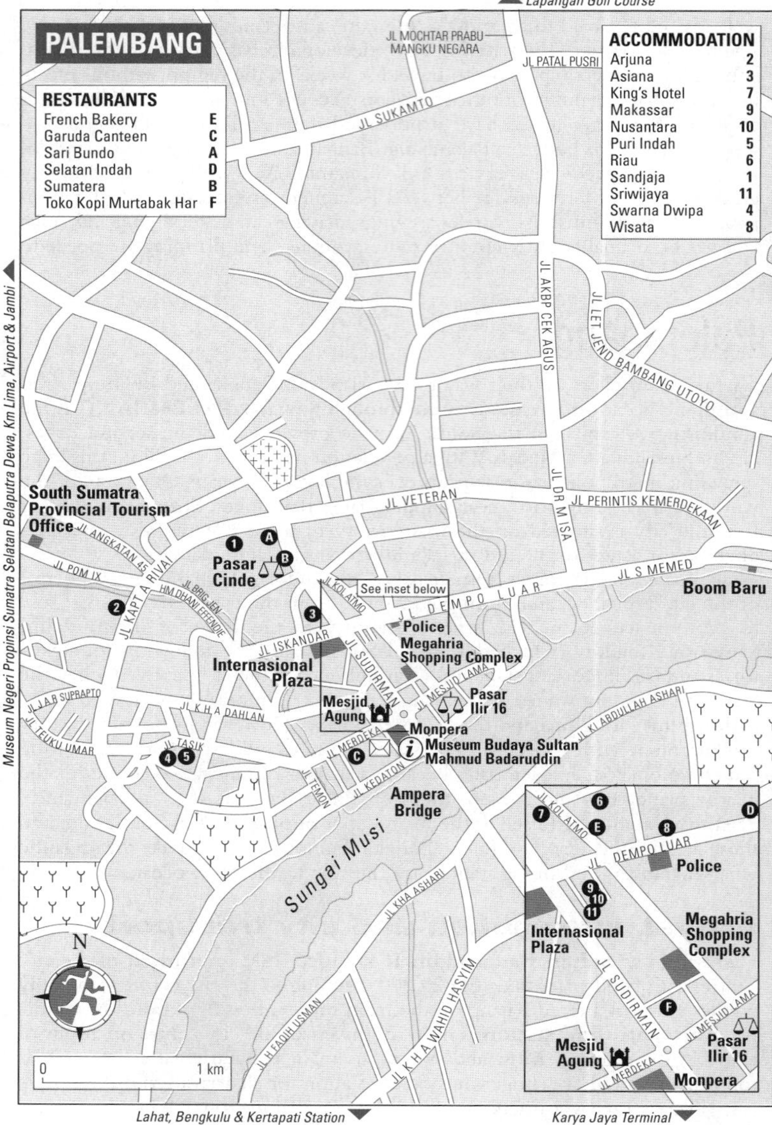

including red Kijang (Rp1000). Arriving by sea from Pulau Bangka, you'll arrive at Boom Baru, the small **ferry port** 2km east of the city centre; cream Kijang operate into the area around Ampera Bridge from here.

The main point of **orientation** in Palembang is gigantic Sungai Musi, which runs southwest–northeast through the city. The north bank is known as the Ilir bank, with the areas numbered from 1 downstream to 36 upstream, while the Ulu bank, the south bank, is divided in districts from 1 upstream to 14 down-

Moving on from Palembang

The departure point for all buses is the Karya Jaya **long-distance bus terminal**, 12km south of the centre, with ticket offices inside the terminal. A number of bus companies operate their own schedules and price lists, so it's worth shopping around to get the most convenient departure time and best price. Yellow *terminal* minivans operate between here and the roundabout at the end of Jalan Mesjid Lama in the centre of town. Buses run throughout the day (6am–7pm) to destinations all over Sumatra, Java and eastwards. You can also pre-book tickets at a travel agent in town (see "Listings" on p.480).

The main concentration of **bus offices** is just south of Ampera Bridge on Jalan Pangeran Ratu, while the Pekanbaru offices and departures are at Kilometre Lima, near the 5km marker on Jalan Sudirman, north of the city centre. There are also several bus offices on Jalan Kol Atmo, on the stretch opposite the *King's Hotel*. Prices vary considerably but make sure you know what you're getting – there are large buses, small buses and minibuses on most routes. Benteng Jaya, Jl Kol Atmo 632a/1230 (ⓣ0711/370730), have daily air-con services to Jakarta. Bintang Mas, Jl Kol Atmo 587 (ⓣ0711/372452), depart three times daily in air-con minibuses to Bandar Lampung and Jakarta. C.S.H. 88, Jl Kol Atmo 621/66 (ⓣ0711/357107), operate daily to Bengkulu. Kramat Djati, Jl Kol Atmo 58c (ⓣ0711/374889), service all Java destinations – in many cases transiting in Jakarta or Bandung. Lorena, Jl Kol Atmo 50 (ⓣ0711/360441), is one of the largest operators, with a huge number of destinations on Sumatra, Java and on to Bali. NPM, Jl Merdeka 317 (ⓣ0711/363319), offer air-con and non-air-con buses to Bukittinggi, Padang, Medan and Jakarta.

Pelni boats leave from Palembang to Padang's Teluk Bayur harbour; Padang is on the fortnightly circuit of *KM Kambuna*, which starts from Bitung and then continues to Toli Toli, Pantoloan, Balikpapan, Makasar (Ujung Pandang), Surabaya, Tanjung Priok, Padang, Sibolga, Nias, Padang, Tanjung Priok, Surabaya, Makasar, Balikpapan, Pantoloan, Toli Toli and back to Bitung. Up-to-date sailing dates are available from the Pelni office at Jl Tanjung Priok 32 east of the centre (ⓣ0751/33624). You can also catch a speedboat to **Pulau Bangka** from Boom Buru, the riverport 2km east of the centre (catch a cream Kijang from Ampera bridge).

There are plentiful **airline connections**, both domestic and international, from Tabing airport. Merpati operate four times daily to Jakarta, daily to Bandung, Batam, Medan and Palembang, and three times weekly to Pekanbaru. International flights are provided by Pelangi to Johor Bahru and Kuala Lumpur, and Silk Air to Singapore. Passenger **train** services in the area have recently been reinstated, but are likely to be unreliable. There are three trains a day to Bandar Lampung via Batu Raja and another three daily to Lahat.

stream. The river is crossed in the centre of the city by the mammoth Ampera Bridge, pretty much unique in Sumatra for scale and ugliness, and the Musi Bridge, several kilometres to the west. On the north bank, the road crossing the Ampera Bridge continues straight as the city's main thoroughfare of Jalan Sudirman; most hotels, shops, banks and offices are within easy reach. Jalan Sudirman changes its name to Jalan Suka Bangkuni and Jalan Kolonel H. Burlian on the northwestern outskirts of the city towards the airport.

As with most Sumatran destinations, the tourist offices are generally helpful, but the quality of information they can provide is often limited. The city **tourism office**, Kantor Dinas Pariwisata Kotamadya, at Jl Sultan Mahmud Badaruddin 1 (Mon–Fri 8am–4pm; ⓣ0711/358450) produces a few English-language brochures, but the staff seem mainly concerned about persuading tourists to take them along as guides for river trips. The Diparda office on Jalan Demang Lebar Daun Kav IX (Mon–Fri 8am–4pm; ⓣ0711/311345, ⓕ311544) also displays some brochures in English, but the building is somewhat inaccessible. If you're staying more than a day or two, a detailed city map is useful; the best map of Palembang is published by Indo Prima Sarana (IPS), available at Toko Buku Diponegoro, Jl Sudirman 27b; the city tourism office can also provide a basic map.

City transport

Palembang is a big bustling concrete jungle of a place, so it's vital to learn to negotiate the relatively straightforward **public transport** system. The main types of vehicles operating are large public buses and smaller Kijang in various colours, supplemented by old-fashioned small twenty-seater buses. The large

Palembang transport

Bus terminals

Karya Jaya 12km south of the centre, reached by yellow minivans from the roundabout at the end of Jalan Mesjid Lama. Note that some yellow minivans go to the train station; for Karya Jaya, the conductors shout out "Terminal".
KM12 (Kilometre Duabelas) is on the main road close to the airport.
Kertapati 4km southwest of the city centre, on the south side of Sungai Musi.
Perumnas Terminal Sako, northeast of the city centre. Buses head here along Jalan Sudirman, east along Jalan Basuki Rachmad and Jalan Sukamto, and north along Jalan Mochtar Prabu Mangku Negara.
Plaju Next to the Pertamina oil complex, southeast of the city centre. Buses arrive via Ampera Bridge, east along Jalan Jend A. Yani and Jalan Di Panjaitan, and south along Jalan Kapten Abdullah.
Pusri The Pusri industrial complex, east of the city on the north bank of the Sungai Musi. Buses go north along Jalan Sudirman, east along Jalan Veteran and Jalan Perintis Kemerdekaan, and north along Jalan Yos Sudarso and Jalan R.E. Martadinata, terminating close to Jalan Mayor Zen.

Kijang routes

Red West along Jalan Tasik to Jalan Kapten A. Rivai, north at Jalan Sudirman to the airport turnoff, then back into town along Jalan Sudirman, down Jalan Kol Atmo into Jalan Mesjid Lama, across the top of Pasir 16, straight across the major roundabout at the north side of Ampera Bridge into Jalan Merdeka and into Jalan Tasik.
Blue Jalan Merdeka, Jalan Tasik, west across Jalan Kapten A. Rivai at Jalan Teuku Umar into Jalan J.A.R. Suprapto to UNSRI (University of Sriwijaya) on Jalan Srijaya Negara, out onto Jalan Demang Lebar Daun, and south along Jalan Sudirman to Jalan Merdeka.
Grey From Ampera Bridge, along Jalan Merdeka, north along Jalan Diponegoro, to Jalan Radial, across Jalan Kapten A. Rivai to Jalan Angkatan 45 to the Pakjo area, returning the same way.
Brown Ampera, Jalan Merdeka, south along Jalan Diponegoro, Jalan Wirosentiko and Jalan Pangeran Sidoing Laut to Pulau Palah (the area roughly opposite Kertapati station but on the north bank); it returns the same way.
Yellow East on Jalan Merdeka and Jalan Sudirman, behind Internasional Plaza on Jalan Candiwalang, then Jalan Sudirman, Jalan Veteran, the area north of Jalan R. Sukamto (Sekip area) and back to Kantor Gubernor on Jalan Kapten A. Rivai, Jalan Tasik and Jalan Merdeka.
Green Ampera, Jalan K.H.A. Dahlan, Jalan Radial, Jalan Kapten A. Rivai, to the golf course via Jalan May Ruslan, to Jalan Let Jend Bambang Utoyo and the terminal at the northern end of Jalan Yos Sudarso.
Cream Ampera, Jalan Sayangan, Jalan Slamet Riady, Jalan Memed, to Boom Baru and along Jalan Yos Sudarso to the terminal at the north end of the road.

public buses run from 6am to 10pm between whatever two terminals (listed in the box on p.474) are labelled on the front window. The smaller buses operate circular routes: the **yellow** bus plies Kertapati, Ampera Bridge, Jalan Merdeka, Jalan Diponegoro, Jalan Letkol Iskander, Jalan Sudirman and back to Kertapati (the train station), while the **red** bus operates between Ampera Bridge and Plaju.

Old-fashioned **Kijang** are the other mainstay of the public transport system, operating on colour-coded routes throughout the city for a flat fare of Rp700; there's sometimes a bell to push in the back when you want to get off. Times are variable: most operate from 4am to 10pm, but the Kertapati service runs 24hr. Many of them pass through the area known as Ampera, at the north end of the bridge around the junction with Jalan Mesjid Lama. The main routes are shown in the box on p.474.

There are plenty of meter **taxis** in the city, which you can simply flag down; you can also charter one for around Rp40,000 per hour in the city, and Rp200,000 for day-trips out of town.

Accommodation

There's a huge amount of **accommodation** in Palembang, much of it lying close to Jalan Sudirman or easily accessible by public transport. Although there's a preponderance at the middle and top end, you can still find budget options.

Inexpensive

Asiana Jl Sudirman 45e ⓣ0711/365016. Central, but difficult to find; look out for a *penginapan* sign and blue-tiled stairway leading up from a small door just north of the junction with Jl Letkol Iskander/Diponegoro, with Internasional Plaza on the corner. All rooms are very simple with unattached mandi, but the place has been tiled throughout and is cleaner than most, with a balcony overlooking the street. The rooms away from the street are quieter. ❷

Makassar Jl Letkol Iskander 17 ⓣ0711/359565. A bit unwholesome and situated up an alley, but friendly. Next door to the *Nusantara*, this place is orientated towards budget travellers; some rooms have attached mandi. ❷

Nusantara Jl Letkol Iskander 17 ⓣ0711/353306. An inexpensive – if somewhat grimy – option down an alleyway right next to the Pasaraya JM department store. The rooms at the bottom end have fan and attached bathroom, while the pricier ones have air-con. ❷–❸

Puri Indah Jl Merdeka 38–40 ⓣ0711/355785. In a quiet location about 1km from the centre opposite a park corner; reached by red Kijang. The rooms are slightly musty and adequate rather than luxurious, but all have air-con. ❸

Riau Jl Dempo Dalam 409 ⓣ0711/352011. A good-value, popular budget place; all rooms have fan and outside bathroom. Situated on a quiet but central road with space out the front to sit and watch the world go by. ❷

Sriwijaya Jl Letkol Iskander 31 ⓣ0711/355555, ⓕ364565. The best of the budget options is just 50m from the junction with Jalan Sudirman, an attractive hotel at the end of an alleyway in a central but quiet location – although it's easy to miss the sign on the main road. It has plenty of rooms with a variety of facilities, with fans at the lower price range and air-con at the top, and pleasant balconies. ❷–❸

Mid-range and expensive

Arjuna Jl Kapten A. Rivai 219 ⓣ0711/356719, ⓕ358505. A pristine place offering a variety of rooms, with a small lobby coffee shop. The only drawback is that the economy rooms have no air-con. Yellow Kijang heading west from the large Jalan Sudirman/Jl Veteran junction pass the door, as do red Kijang from outside the post office, although they go a long way round. ❹

King's Hotel Jl Kol Atmo 623 ⓣ0711/362323, ⓕ310937. A heavily advertised luxury hotel in the centre of town, with grand communal areas and restaurants and plush rooms with individual safes, hair dryers, hot water and air-con. There's a small fitness club, business centre, karaoke bar and nightly live music in the fourth-floor bar until 2am, but no swimming pool. Rooms are variable, so it's worth looking at several. ❺

Sandjaja Jl Kapten A. Rivai 6193 ⓣ0711/310675, ⓕ313693. Central and well furnished, with all the luxury and facilities you'd expect at this end of the range, including a gym, Japanese restaurant and a pleasant swimming pool with a shady sitting area nearby. ❻

Swarna Dwipa Jl Tasik 2 ⓣ0711/313322, ⓕ362992. A good-quality hotel peacefully located about 1km west of the city centre opposite a park, on the route of the red Kijang operating from the town centre. It features a small pool, restaurant and a bar with nightly live music. ❺–❼

Wisata Jl Letkol Iskander 105–7 ⓣ0711/352681, ⓕ313956. Centrally located with helpful staff, with a white tablecloth pizza restaurant on the ground floor; the rooms have all the comfort of the grander places, with air-con, hot-water tub and colour TV. However, it's hard to spot from the road. ❹–❺

The City

Palembang's major landmark, the huge **Ampera Bridge** over Sungai Musi, was built with war reparation money from the Japanese government and opened in 1964. The central section of the bridge originally lifted to allow larger ocean-going vessels to pass; unfortunately, this caused such traffic chaos that when the mechanism broke down in 1970, it wasn't repaired.

Although a trip on **Sungai Musi** is widely touted by the tourist office, an hour or so of observing river life is more than enough for most visitors, especially as the river itself is so polluted it can leave you with itching skin and streaming eyes and nose. However, it's a good way to get to grips with the geography of the city, especially if you head west to the tributaries of the Musi: the Ogan is crossed by the Wilhelmina Bridge near the station and Sungai Kramasan slightly further west. A slow boat (*Ketek*) should cost Rp30,000 for an hour; Abi Sofyan at the city tourism office just north of the bridge is a good guide and source of local information. To bargain on your own, simply head for the waterfronts at Ampera or Pasar Ilir 16. On Independence Day (August 17), *bidar* boat races are held on Sungai Musi, with long canoes shaped like animals, each holding forty rowers dressed in colourful costumes.

Heading east along the river, leafy **Pulau Kemaro** lies just off the north bank, 7km from Ampera Bridge. The island has a Buddhist temple on a spot also sacred to Muslims, and followers of both religions come here to pray. Legend has it that the temple is the burial spot of a Chinese princess who came to the area to marry the king of the Sriwijaya kingdom. Her dowry was sent ashore in huge jars; the king, expecting precious jewels, flung them into the river when he discovered the first one contained only preserved vegetables. In despair, the princess drowned herself in the river, before the king realized that the remaining pots were indeed filled with gold and precious stones.

Monpera (Monumen Perjuagan Rakyat Sumatera Bagian Selatan) is a concrete monstrosity in the city centre adorned with a huge black Garuda, located at the junction of Jalan Sudirman and Jalan Merdeka (Rp1000). It commemorates the "Battle of Five Days and Nights" in 1947, when the Dutch regained control of the oil- and coalfields around Palembang from the nationalist rebels. The modern ugliness stands in stark contrast to the towering minarets and fine lines of the **Mesjid Agung** (Grand Mosque) across the road, built in 1740 by Sultan Mahmud Badaruddin I and sympathetically renovated.

Just behind Monpera in the town centre, the **Museum Budaya Sultan Mahmud Badaruddin** (Mon–Sat 8am–2pm; donation), is on the first floor of a grand nineteenth-century building. The limited collection features predictable displays of textiles, weapons, traditional dress, crafts and coins. However, the gardens of the museum, from which huge numbers of Sriwijayan artefacts were excavated, are pleasant, and house a couple of attractive Ganesh and Buddha statues.

Far more worthwhile is one of the best Sumatran museums, the **Museum Negeri Propinsi Sumatra Selatan (Belaputra Dewa)**, the South Sumatra regional museum, Jl Srijaya 288, Km5.5 (Mon–Thurs & Sat 8am–2pm, Fri 8–11am; Rp1000), which lies 6km north of the city centre. Built about twenty-five years ago, it has several large, airy galleries with huge verandahs, set in pretty, well-kept gardens. The galleries hold geological exhibits, weapons, ceramics, textiles and traditional costumes, supplemented by a collection of *pallawa prasasti*, stones inscribed in the ancient Malay language. In the grounds are impressively carved stone megaliths and troughs, many from the Lahat and Pagaralam area (see p.497), plus an attractive, traditional *limas* house, closed to the public.

Eating and drinking

There are plenty of places to eat in Palembang, ranging from warung in the **night markets** on Jalan Letkol Iskander and Jalan Sayangan to the more formal rumah makan and top-class restaurants. Palembang specialities include *ikan belida* (eel) – thankfully no longer coming from the polluted Musi – served with various hot and spicy sauces, and *pempek*, available throughout Sumatra, but originating in this area. The latter are fried or grilled balls made from sago, fish and seasoning, served with sauce.

French Bakery Jl Kol Atmo 481. One of several small bakeries in town, where you can sit inside and enjoy the variety of sweet bread and cakes on offer. This one also has a small menu of Indonesian soups and basic foods.

Garuda Canteen In the same building as the Garuda supermarket/department store, about 400m west of the main post office. With inexpensive ice concoctions, juices, soups, noodles and local *pempek*, this is a good place for a filling meal.

KFC Next to Gelael supermarket at Internasional Plaza. It serves the usual expensive chicken and French fries, but it's cool and the air-con is free, even if the food and drink has ten percent tax added to displayed prices.

Milano's Pizza In the *Hotel Wisata*, this white tablecloth place is moderately expensive but serves recognizable pizzas (Rp30,000) for the homesick.

Sari Bundo Jl Sudirman 1301, on the corner of Jalan Kapten A. Rivai. A bustling, popular and inexpensive Padang restaurant offering good food in utilitarian but pleasant surroundings.

Selatan Indah Jl Letkol Iskander 434. A moderate to expensive place with an extensive Chinese menu and a good local reputation.

Sumatera Jl Sudirman 906. The substantial menu includes traditional inexpensive Indonesian food plus burgers, sweet breads and juices.

Swenson's In *KFC* at Gelael. Conveniently central branch of the American ice-cream chain, though expensive, at Rp10,000–16,000 for your favourite sundae. However, it has great air-con, and is a good place to rest from the sightseeing.

Toko Kopi Murtabak Har Several of these great *Har* Muslim Indian coffee shops are dotted around town; one of the most central is at Jl Sudirman 23, south of the corner of Jalan T.P. Rustan Effendi. They're especially recommended for their *murtabak* breakfasts; the pancake comes with an egg inside and served with potato curry. If you splash out on a coffee as well, you'll still pay less than Rp5000.

Shopping

From modern shopping centres to old-fashioned markets selling local textiles and lacquerware, Palembang offers plenty of shopping options. The Gramedia **bookshop**, Jl Kol Atmo 1301, close to *King's Hotel*, has postcards and even the occasional English classic novel; Toko Buku Diponegoro, Sudirman 27b, sell the most detailed city map of Palembang, published by Indo Prima Sarana (IPS).

Shopping centres and markets

For a thoroughly modern shopping experience, the four-storey **Internasional Plaza** at the junction of Jalan Sudirman and Jalan Letkol Iskander includes a

Matahari department store, supermarket, food plaza and fast-food outlets. The famous **Pasir Ilir 16 market**, between Jalan Mesjid Lama and Sungai Musi, 150m east of Ampera Bridge sells authentic batik from Java, Palembang *songket*, sets of sarong and *selendang* from around Rp300,000. Further north on Jalan Sudirman, between Jalan Cinde Welan and Jalan Letnam Jamais, the traditional **Pasar Cinde** market features a maze of alleyways lined with stalls selling food, clothes and household items galore. The **Megahria shopping complex** on the corner of Jalan T.P. Rustan Effendi and Jalan Kol Atmo, a covered market with alleyways of tiny shops, sells pretty much anything you could desire; if you're looking for **gold**, try the western end, which is lined with jewellers.

Textiles

The **textile specialities** of Palembang are *songket* and *jumputan pelangi*, silk material with patterns created using tie-dye techniques (*pelangi* means "rainbow" in Indonesian). The centre for the workshops and showrooms is in 32 Ilir, 2km to the west of the city centre along the northern riverbank; a brown Kijang from Ampera or Mesjid Angung will get you there. You can also watch (or buy) *songket* weaving on backstrap looms along Jalan Ki Gede Ing Suro. The cost of the finished product depends partly on the fineness of the thread and the amount of effort needed to create a piece; typically, a sarong and *selendang* set takes a weaver working eight-hour days a month to complete. Prices are from Rp600,000 to Rp900,000 for such sets, and from Rp150,000 for a batik set, skirt, jacket or four-metre silk dress length; for gold thread, you'll pay up to five million rupiah. Whilst the *songket* work is generally rather glittery and showy, much of the *jumputan pelangi* is extremely attractive. Try **Serengam Sentai**, 32 Ilir Serengam, Jl Ki Gede Ing Suro 264, RT 11 (Mon–Sat 9am–5pm), and **Cek Ipah**, Jl Ki Gede Ing Suro 141, which has an excellent range of textiles and helpful staff. Their workshop produces *songket* sets up to Rp35 million, but these are usually not in stock – the Rp400,000 versions are available. *Jumputan pelangi* is available in four-metre lengths from Rp50,000 per metre and both *ikat* and a very unusual *batik prada*, batik cloth with gold paint, are also for sale. *Prada* means "gilded", and the gold in this work is more subtle and less dense than that used in other parts of the archipelago.

Lacquerware

Another Palembang speciality is **lacquerware**, a technique probably introduced to the area by the Chinese, in which wood and basketware items are sealed, painted, decorated with black ink designs and covered in a layer of lacquer produced from ant's nests. Deep red and gold are the traditional colours, and each of the decorations has significance: flowers for beauty, a lion for strength, the golden phoenix for an end to problems, and butterflies to signify the pleasures of the night – good sleep, good dreams and love. Mekar Jaya at Jl Slamat Riady 45a has a variety of bowls and vases up to 1m tall in black and gold, with swirling floral patterns, priced from Rp15,000 to over Rp1,000,000. The Jalan Guru Guru and Serelo areas (see p.480) are also good hunting grounds.

Souvenirs

On **Jalan Faqih Jalahuddin**, a small road heading north of Jalan Merdeka just west of Mesjid Agung, you'll find woodcarving, lacquerware and a range of "antiques". Toko Antik at no. 39 is great fun, a real treasure trove of ceramics, junk and antiques, where you can spend hours rooting around. At no. 103f, Karya Ukir Saria Agung sells lacquerware, with attractive small bowls at

△ Bengkulu

Rp30,000–40,000 and impressive larger plates for Rp60,000. The other main area is **Serelo**, at the far end of Jalan Guru Guru: turn left and first right, and 300m further on you'll be in Jalan AKBP. HM. Amin. Alternative access from the other end is 100m south of Internasional Plaza opposite the BNI bank. There are plenty of small shops and workshops; the most exclusive is Galleri Mir Senen at no. 43, with a huge range of old and new arts and crafts from throughout Indonesia including furniture, carvings, ornaments and jewellery. Everything is displayed in attractive surroundings, and the owners accept credit cards and can arrange shipping. Next door at no. 45 is Batik Palembang, offering gorgeous old textiles from Rp750,000 to over Rp1,000,000. However, there are plenty of less expensive shops around, and it's a great area for browsing. Mahligan Art at no. 442 and Toko Lukman at no. 41a both sell attractive lacquerware.

Entertainment and nightlife

The **bar** of the *King's Hotel* is something of a meeting place for the better-off locals, especially at the weekends. The **discos** at *Darma Agung* at Km6, north of the city on Jalan Sudirman (11pm–2am; Rp20,000) and the less expensive, but also popular nightly discos at the *Princess Hotel* (Jl Letkol. Iskandar Blok D-2 38) and *Puri Indah Hotel* were closed by the district authority at the time of writing, but there are plans to reopen them.

There are also several **cinemas** in town, including Studio on Jalan Sudirman, which is set back off the road just south of the prominent Bank Bumi Daya, Internasional 21, on the fifth floor of Internasional Plaza, and Megahria cinema, in the shopping complex of the same name on Jalan T.P. Rustan Effendi. Much of the diet is sex or kung fu, but Western movies also make it here.

Listings

Airline offices Bouraq, Jl Dempo Luar 31 ⓣ0711/313790; Deraya agent, PT Saung Mas, Jl Kapten A. Rivai 220a ⓣ0711/363421, ⓕ358350; Garuda, *Hotel Sandjaja*, Jl Kapten A. Rivai 35 ⓣ0711/315333, ⓕ352224; Mandala, Jl Letkol Iskander Block D2/66 ⓣ0711/312168, ⓕ310424; Merpati, Jl Kapten A. Rivai 6193 ⓣ0711/372366, ⓕ312131.

Banks and exchange There are many banks just east of the junction of Jalan Mesjid Lama and Jalan Sudirman. These include BNI, Jl Sudirman 132, and BCA Jl Sudirman 185. More banks are on Jalan Kapten A. Rivai, 250m southwest of the *Sandjaja* hotel. BCA is at Jl Kapten A. Rivai 22; BII is at Jl Kapten A. Rivai 1293.

Golf Lapangan golf course, Jl A.K.B. Cep Agus 23, just northwest of the junction of Jl Sukamto and Jl Mochtar Prabu Mangku Negara ⓣ0711/352952. This eighteen-hole course is the largest in South Sumatra. Green fees are Rp60,000 (Mon–Thurs) and Rp90,000 (Fri–Sun & holidays); there's a caddy fee of Rp12,000. Equipment is available for rental: Rp70,000 for a full set of clubs for eighteen holes, and Rp25,000 for shoes.

Hospitals Rumah Sakit Charitas, Jl Sudirman 809 ⓣ0711/353375; Rumah Sakit A.K. Gani, Jalan Benteng, near the main post office ⓣ0711/354691; Rumah Sakit Umum Palembang, Jl Sudirman 890 ⓣ0711/354008.

Immigration office Jl May Memet Sastrawiriya 1, near Boom Baru ⓣ0711/710055.

Internet access At the post office, or at a few places on Jalan Dempo Luar; try *Aldonet* at no. 946 (Rp5000 per hour).

Pharmacies There are plenty of pharmacies in the central areas of town: Apotik Rora, Jl Sudirman 200 (ⓣ0711/350086), is open 24hr.

Post office The main post office is centrally located at Jl Merdeka 3 and has an efficient poste restante system.

Swimming Lumban Kirta, Jalan Pom IX, 1.5km northwest of the centre, features an indoor Olympic-sized pool with separate diving area (daily 8am–7.30pm; Rp2000).

Telephone and fax The main 24hr Telkom office is at Jl Merdeka 5 near the post office, and there are wartels at Jl Sudirman 1004b (daily 7am–midnight) and Jl Letkol Iskander 902a (24hr).

Travel agents The excellent Caremta Tours and Travel, Jl Dempo Luar 29–30, 1km northeast of the centre (☎0711/356653, ℱ312589), is one of the largest and best organized, offering city tours (Rp120,000 for 3hr), Sungai Musi trips (Rp175,000 for 3hr) and tours further afield (Bangka: three nights/two days inclusive of all meals, transport and accommodation for Rp810,000). Try also Wisin Tours and Travel, Jl Taman Siswa 173h (☎0711/366811).

Pulau Bangka and Pulau Belitung

Usually mentioned in the same breath by locals and travellers alike, **Pulau Bangka** and **Pulau Belitung** are located in the South China Sea off the coast of east Sumatra, and have many historical and modern characteristics in common. The islands are pleasant and sleepy backwaters on the way to nowhere, although administratively attached to the South Sumatra province. The lucrative tin trade that fuelled the islands' economies for centuries has virtually died, the pepper trade brought plentiful but unpredictable rewards to Bangka, and the anticipated tourist boom on both islands has so far failed to materialize. Bangka and Belitung remain, for now, ideal destinations for those who want to get a little off the beaten track.

Geologically, the islands are similar: low-lying with no hint of the volcanic origins of mainland Sumatra. Instead, they originated from the ancient, non-volcanic core of the Sunda Shelf, like the Riau and Lingga islands to the north. A rich vein of tin runs through the islands, continuing northwards to Pulau Singkep, Malaysia and Thailand. Originally covered in tropical jungle, mining and tin-smelting have decimated the primary habitat of the islands, which has been replaced by scrubland interspersed with countless *kolong*, artificial lakes most easily visible from the air, created by the open-cast tin-mining and since abandoned.

Some history

Tin was probably discovered on the islands in the early years of the eighteenth century. Like the Europeans, the Chinese had a huge demand for the metal, which they used for joss paper (very thin foil burnt in religious ceremonies), and to mix into alloys to make mirrors, teapots, candlesticks, vases and coins. The tin mined from mainland China could not meet demand, and from the early eighteenth century the Chinese were interested in the deposits on Bangka and Belitung, as were the Dutch, who had failed in their attempt to get a monopoly on the tin trade in the Malacca area after they acquired the city in 1641. Over the following centuries, it was largely **Chinese coolie labour** that worked the mines, initially for the sultan of Palembang and later for the Dutch, and though the islands acquired a worldwide reputation for the tin itself, they also gained notoriety for appalling working conditions, dubious recruiting methods and the poor health of the coolie labour. Generally, conditions on Bangka were worse than on Belitung – coolies sometimes resorted to cutting off their own thumbs so they could not work in the mines near Mentok and could return home. By the mid-nineteenth century, tin was third behind coffee and sugar in export earnings from the Dutch East Indies.

Throughout the history of the tin mines, many Chinese labourers did not return home after the end of their contracts and settled on the islands, raising families of their own. Local-born or *perinakan* Chinese now form about 25 percent of the population of Bangka, the largest settlement of *perinakan* Chinese outside Java, but rather less on Belitung (about ten percent).

Both islands suffered badly during **World War II**. Bangka was occupied by the Japanese two days after the surrender of Singapore on February 15, 1942, and

Belitung was taken two months later. A thousand Japanese soldiers were based on the islands, and malnutrition and disease were rife among the local and Chinese population. Young women were often forced to work as prostitutes, and many people were sent elsewhere as forced labour; for example, in 1943, a thousand people from Belitung were shipped to Palembang to work in the petroleum fields. Many Chinese fled during this period; nowadays only a quarter of the population of Bangka is Chinese and on Belitung this falls to just one tenth. The national mining company, Tambang Timbah, controls the biggest part of production, and though the tin deposits on Belitung are finished, on Bangka mining still rules the economy, employing migrants from all over Indonesia.

Pulau Bangka

Attractive scenery, good beaches, a peaceful and relaxed lifestyle and easy access from the mainland make **Pulau Bangka** an ideal place to rest up for a few days away from the crowds and noise of Palembang. It can also be a peaceful stopoff point on an island-hopping trip between Jakarta and the Riau Islands.

Separated from the Sumatran mainland by the narrow Bangka Strait (which is only 20km wide at the closest point), the island of **Bangka**, with a population of around 650,000, describes the shape of a seahorse's head – a very large seahorse, 180km long from northwest to southeast, roughly a tenth of the size of Java. The origins of its name have produced several theories: *vanga* (tin) in Sanskrit – sometimes spelt *wangka* – features on a Sriwijayan inscription from 686 AD found on the island; a second theory claims that the early settlers discovered *bangkai* (bodies) of previous inhabitants. Another interpretation is that the name comes from *wangkang*, which in Southeast Asia is the name for a Chinese junk. Whichever is true, they point to the two foundations of Bangka's history – tin and seafaring.

By the start of the twentieth century, with the local population increasing but only involved in the tin industry in secondary ways (such as supplying the workers), it became apparent that local income needed a boost. The Dutch encouraged **pepper** as an income crop, which has now largely taken over the Bangka economy. Travellers to Bangka will spot the vines in fields lining the road; they grow to about 3m and produce pepper for around five years. The main problem with pepper production, as with primary goods throughout the world, is the huge fluctuations in price on the world market; local initiatives are currently exploring fruit exports to Palembang and Jakarta, shrimp farming, timber production and the export of granite, in an attempt to create a stable local economy.

Getting to Bangka from Palembang

High-speed ferry departures to **Pulau Bangka** are from Boom Baru, a couple of kilometres east of Palembang city centre; take a cream Kijang or minibus from Ampera or Jalan Mesjid Lama (where the red Kijang can drop you off), and get off at the BNI bank – the terminal lies a 200m walk towards the river. A couple of companies operate boat services and there are up to three departures daily (7–9.30am; 3–4hr) to Mentok, and three ferries back to Palembang from Mentok at 8am, 10am and 2pm. The one-way fare is Rp55,000, plus Rp1500 port tax – be wary of being sold an expensive "VIP" ticket. You can also buy a Mentok–Pangkalpinang bus ticket (Rp8000) when you check in at the terminal – it saves hassle when you arrive, as the bus can drop you at your hotel. There are plenty of agents in Palembang selling tickets but it's just as easy to buy your ticket at the terminal.

Islanders are hopeful that **tourism** is going to develop on Bangka to take the place of tin. The reality is that tourist development remains very low-key, catering largely for the domestic market. Until there's more big money invested to entice the Singaporean tourists who flock to Batam and Bintan to make a much longer trip, this is unlikely to change significantly. In fact, at the time of writing, far more investment was going into Belitung; while the attractive beaches of Bangka make it unlikely the island will be overlooked altogether, it's safe to assume it will remain a quiet, little-known and rather charming destination in the foreseeable future.

Mentok, Sungailiat and the northern beaches

The hydrofoil service from Palembang arrives at **MENTOK** harbour on the northwest coast. Two accommodation options are located near here: the good-quality *Hotel Jati Menumbing* (Ⓣ0716/21388; ❸–❹) at Gunung Menumbing, 15km from Mentok; and the basic *Losmen Mentok* (no phone; ❷) on Jalan A Yani. The bus station is right by the ferry port and buses for Pangalpinang (Rp8000) meet each arrival. Try to tell the driver the name of your accommodation and (if it's in Pangalpinang), he'll probably drop you off at your door.

The easiest option for getting around the island is to charter **transport** – ask at your accommodation – but there is also public transport between the major towns and villages. If you're stuck in Mentok, there's an attractive beach running for a kilometre just west of the port – although it doesn't match the finest beaches to the northeast. It's a little too close to the shipping, but there's a fine lighthouse on the western point.

The best beaches – the main reason to come to Bangka – are located in the north of the island, one on Klabat Bay, but with the main concentration on the northeast coast. On the north coast, *Romodong Seaview Cottages* (book at Jalan Bukit Intan 1 no. 147, Pangalpinang; Ⓣ & Ⓕ0717/21573, or make reservations in Jakarta Ⓣ021/5604150, Ⓕ5670469; ❻) lies 20km north of the small village of Belinyu along a road that's mostly asphalt but in poor condition. It's situated in a great position on a picturesque white-sand bay 4km long, with excellent views to the offshore island of Pulau Lampu and across Klabat Bay, which makes it one of the best places to stay on the island. Accommodation is in wooden bungalows with air-con, cold-water bathrooms and good verandahs, and there's an inexpensive to moderately priced restaurant attached. Other beaches to explore lie nearby, and a ferry service runs across to the other, more remote, side of the bay.

The beaches on the northeast coast of the island range north and south of **SUNGAILIAT**, a small town 32km north of Pangalpinang, which is pleasant enough but really only useful for access to the beaches. Sungailiat is reached by bus from Pangalpinang terminal, with departures roughly hourly (30min; Rp5000). Sungailiat **tourist office** is at Jalan Jend Sudirman (Mon–Thurs & Sat 8am–2pm, Fri 8–11am; Ⓣ0717/92496); the staff are helpful, and have English-language brochures. The **accommodation** options in Sungailiat include *Wisma Flamboyant*, Jl Dr Sam Ratulangi 1 (Ⓣ0717/92076; ❷–❸), which has some rooms with air-con and attached mandi and some without; and the friendly *Pondok Wisata Moeliya Homestay*, Jl Jend Sudirman 154–156 (Ⓣ0717/92157, Ⓕ92111; ❷), a genuine homestay, with accommodation in a family house with a spacious garden, set back from the busy road. There are a variety of rooms on offer, from those with fan to some with air-con and TV, and it's advisable to book. The smartest place in town is *Hotel Citria*, Jl Jend Sudirman 343 (Ⓣ0717/92404, Ⓕ93210; ❹–❺); the rooms have air-con and hot water.

Seven kilometres south from Sungailiat, the first hotel on the beach is *Teluk Uber Hotel*, Jl Pantai Teluk Uber 1 (Ⓣ0717/435564; ❸). It's less publicized and much simpler and cheaper than the other places on this coast. Accommodation is in an attractive block with verandahs looking to the beach and there's a moderately priced restaurant set in the large grounds. Two kilometres further south, and a significant jump in price and quality, is *Tanjung Pesonna Indah*, Jalan Pantai Rebo (Ⓣ0717/435560, Ⓕ435561; ❺). The hotel is situated on a headland, with bays on either side and fine views north to Teluk Uber and south to the Tikus and Rebo beaches. It's a huge establishment, with a large restaurant, coffee shop, disco, karaoke and billiard hall; at weekends the place comes alive, but can be rather soulless during the week. Twelve kilometres north of Sungailiat, the *Sahid Parai Indah*, Jalan Pantai Parai Tenggiri (Ⓣ0717/94888, Ⓕ94000, Ⓦwww.parai.com; reservations can be made in Jakarta Ⓣ021/3511555, Ⓕ5655458; ❻), is the largest and most expensive hotel on the coast, with a grand two-storey entrance lobby. The lower-priced accommodation is in a two-storey block, with the more expensive rooms in cottages in the grounds. Meals are Rp25,000 for breakfast, Rp35,000 for lunch and Rp40,000 for dinner, in an attractive open-sided restaurant near the beach, which is a pretty white-sand cove. There's a large swimming pool and tennis courts with rackets for rent, and the glorious Matras beach is only about 500m to the north.

Pangalpinang

The main town of Pulau Bangka, **PANGALPINANG**, lies on the east coast, 138km away from Mentok (3–4hr), and is a small, pleasant town with wide streets and a laid-back atmosphere. There's an ethnically mixed population of around 120,000, including descendants of early Chinese, Arab and Indian settlers. The town has good tourist facilities but few sights: the Tin Museum was opened in 1932, but is now unfortunately closed (check on its current status with the tourist office).

Local bemos run from the **bus terminal** 2km from town on the southern outskirts into the market area in the town centre, but the bus goes on from the terminal down Jalan Mesjid Lama to the junction of Jalan Sudirman, so you might well get dropped of at your door if you ask. Pangkalan Baru **airport** is 6km south of town. Fixed-price taxis (Rp15,000) operate between here and Jalan Sudirman in town. Alternatively, take a yellow angkot (Rp5000) from the airport to the market area in the centre of town, just east of Jalan Sudirman. From here you can take a red angkot (Rs1000) to anywhere along Jl Sudirman. Belitung hydrofoils and Jakarta jetfoils arrive at **Pangkal Balam port**, 4km north of town, served by red angkots, also from Jalan Sudirman.

The main street in Pangalpinang is Jalan Sudirman, which runs roughly north–south for well over 1km; the centre of town is at the main crossroads with Jalan Mesjid Jamik, and the market area is a couple of hundred metres east of this. Most hotels, restaurants and offices are either on or close to Jalan Sudirman, the vast majority lying north of the junction. The **tourist office**, Jalan Bukit Intan (Mon–Thurs & Sat 8am–2pm, Fri 8–11am; Ⓣ0717/32546), has a good English brochure about the island, but is a bit short on other information; it's probably better to make specific enquiries at hotels or travel agents in town. Of the latter, Carmeta (see opposite) is the most helpful.

The **post office**, which also offers **internet** access, is at Jl Sudirman 18, the 24hr **Telkom** office at Jl Sudirman 6, and there are several **banks**: BNI at Jl Sudirman 1, BCA at Jl Mesjid Jamik 15, and Bank Dagang Negara at Jl Sudirman 7. The **airlines** serving the island have offices here: Merpati, Jl Sudirman 45 (Ⓣ0717/421132); Buraqu, Jl Sudirman 88 (Ⓣ0717/438799);

Pelita, Jl Sudirman 112 (Ⓣ0717/424205) and Mandala, Jl Sudirman 36 (Ⓣ0717/422268), while the Deraya/Merpati/Pelni agent is PT Priaventure, Jl Sudirman 10 (Ⓣ0717/421013). For Jakarta or Pulau Belitung hydrofoils, book at CV Gunawan Wisatajaya, Jl Sudirman 69 (Ⓣ0717/422734), and for Belitung hydrofoils and Palembang ferries, book at Carmeta, Jl Sudirman 35a (Ⓣ0717/424333, Ⓕ431785). Carmeta can also book a through bus and ferry ticket from your accommodation to Palembang. The Pelni office is at Jl Depati Amir 67 (Ⓣ0717/422216). Carmeta is also the place to ask about car hire; a car and driver will cost Rp250,000 a day.

For **souvenirs**, Toko Timah TKF, at the northern end of Jalan Sudirman, has some attractive and unusual tin gifts, ranging from vases and boxes (Rp35,000) up to large and intricate model ships (Rp1,000,000).

Accommodation

Bukit Sofa Hotel Jl Mesjid Jamik 43 Ⓣ0717/421062. Deservedly popular, due to its decent, very inexpensive rooms at the bottom end; there are some air-con ones as well. ❷–❸

Hotel Griya Tirta Jl Semabung Lama 272 Ⓣ0717/433436, Ⓕ433439. A new gleaming place 1.5km from Jalan Sudirman towards the coast. Well-furnished rooms open onto an attractive courtyard with a small coffee shop. ❺

Hotel Jati Wisata Jl Kartini 3 Ⓣ0717/431500, Ⓕ431222. Airy and plush, with clean, comfortable rooms with air-con and hot water, and a restaurant. Take the road opposite the church and follow it along the football field for 150m to a junction – the hotel is opposite on the right. ❸–❹

Hotel Sabrina Jl Diponegoro 73 Ⓣ0717/422424, Ⓕ432900. In a quiet location a short walk from the main street, Jalan Sudirman; take the road by the BRI bank that leads along the football field. The corridors are ominous, but the rooms are nice with hot water, colour TV and air-con; the larger ones have bathtubs. ❹–❺

Srikandi Jl Mesjid Jamik 42 Ⓣ0717/421884. A friendly and lively place featuring decent basic rooms with attached cold-water mandi. Unfortunately, it's often full. ❷

Wisma Jaya 1 Jl Depati Amir 8 Ⓣ0717/421696, Ⓕ432077. Off Jalan Sudirman, at the junction where the post office lies. The clean and pleasant rooms have air-con and hot water, while the courtyard at the back has attractive deep verandahs and houses an open-air restaurant. ❹–❺

Melati Jl Mesjid Jamik 15 Ⓣ0717/424419. Just behind the wartel of the same name, this has clean rooms with attached mandi. Rooms vary in size and quality, so ask to see several; the upstairs ones are quieter. ❷–❸

Sera Indah Jl Imam Bonjol 18 Ⓣ0717/421579. On the street opposite the *French Bakery* on Jalan Sudirman. A strangely eerie, decaying place, run by a friendly family. There's one grand marbled room with a mirrored ceiling and bathtub. ❹

Serrata Hotel On Pantai Pasir Padi, 10km away Ⓣ0717/431574, Ⓕ431573. The closest beach hotel to Pangkalpinang, offering wooden cottages with tiled roofs. There's a good-sized pool, restaurant, boating lake and tennis courts, and you can charter boats out to nearby Pulau Pinang. ❺

Eating

The *French Bakery* at Jl Sudirman 27 and *Holland Bakery*, nearby at no. 25, offer a good choice of sweet breads and cakes. *Bagadangraya*, Jl Sudirman 30, and, across the road, *Saribundo*, Jl Sudirman 77, both serve good-value **Padang food**. *A Sui*, Jalan Kampung Bintang Dalam, is the seafood restaurant recommended by locals, with excellent dishes at moderate prices in simple surroundings. *Pondok Kelapa* on Pantai Pasir Padi, close to *Serrata Hotel*, serves moderately priced seafood and rice dishes and enjoys a sea breeze.

Pulau Belitung

Bangka's neighbour, 80km to the southeast, is **Pulau Belitung**. Despite great beaches and enticing offshore islands, very few tourists make it this far and it remains – for now – an almost undiscovered gem. The island is turning to tourism for income, though there is still no development on the best **beach** on the island, **Tanjung Tinggi**.

According to one local story, the island's name comes from "Bali potong" ("a cut of Bali"): supposedly, Belitung was once part of Hindu Bali but was for some reason cut off and driven away to its present site. For centuries Belitung was at the furthest reaches of the powerful ancient Indonesian kingdoms, and the inlets and offshore islands close to one of the world's most lucrative shipping channels in the Malacca Strait made the island an ideal **pirate hideaway**. In 1822, pirates captured the Dutch ship *Anna Maria* and two members of the crew were sold as slaves to the chief of the village of Sijuk in the northwest, but were eventually freed when a Malay noble paid two balls of opium for their release. Other Dutchmen were known to have been kept as slaves on the east coast of the island in Burung Mandi; when the Dutch gained control over the island, there was already a Dutch-style house in the area.

Tanjung Pandan

The main town on Belitung is **TANJUNG PANDAN**, a pleasant, laid-back port with only its personality and atmosphere to attract and detain visitors. The **museum** at Jl Melati 41 (daily 8am–5pm) is pretty much the only sight in town; housed in a bungalow, it features a small collection of weapons, coins, textiles and craft items. The **beach** is tidal and quite grey, with the added disadvantage of being fairly close to the port. However, some warung here open at dusk, and it's a pleasant place to have a sunset drink looking across to Pulau Kalmoa and other distant islands.

Ferry services arrive at the **port** area of Tanjung Pandan, about 1km from the town centre, while flights arrive at Buluhtumbang **airport**, 14km from town. Fixed-price taxis from the airport are Rp20,000 into the centre; there's a taxi counter at the front of the terminal. Otherwise, it's a one-kilometre walk to the main road between Tanjung Pandan and Manggar, where you can pick up public transport into the **bus terminal**. The bus terminal, reached by blue angkot #20 and #22, is 2km from the centre of Tanjung Pandan on Jalan Sudirman; there are hourly buses to Manggar (2hr; Rp5000), but only in the morning from about 7am to 11am. Although the town is spread out, it's small enough to walk around; if you catch a **bemo** (they run from 7am to 5pm, as do buses around the island), it'll be Rp700 flat rate anywhere in town.

The helpful **tourist office** (Dinas Parwisata), Jl Sekolah 23 (Ⓣ0719/21398), provides a map of the island and the staff speak reasonable English. Carmeta Tours and Travel, 21 Jl Haryono (Ⓣ0719/24887, Ⓕ25133), a sister branch of the shop in Bangka, is a decent source of information and can book tickets for flights, ferries and buses. The **post office** is at Jl Merdeka 12, and there are **wartels** all over town (5am–11pm), and **internet access** at *Warnet Trendy*, Jl Sriwijaya 30. For **money exchange**, use BRI, Jl Merdeka 11, or BNI at Jl Merdeka 13.

Moving on from Belitung, the options are plentiful. A hydrofoil leaves daily at 7am to Pulau Bangka; as ever, be warned against being sold a VIP ticket. Pelni has offices at the harbour at Jl Pabean 119 (Ⓣ0719/21719); the *KM Lawit* calls weekly on its way to Tanjung Priok (Jakarta) and Pontianak, and the *Tilongkabila* plies the same route every month (see p.515). The office in Tanjung Pandan will, for some reason, only sell ekonomi tickets. The only flight option is with Merpati, Jl Sudirman 2 (Ⓣ0719/21677, Ⓕ21422), who fly once a day to Jakarta. *Carmeta Tours*, Jl MT Haryono 22 (Ⓣ0719/24887), on the junction with Jalan Yos Sudharso, is a reliable travel agent and can arrange boat and plane tickets. It's worth knowing that even if you take the first ferry to Bangka in the morning, you'll still miss the last onward connection to Palembang.

Accommodation

Dewi Wisma Jl Sriwijaya 122 ⓣ0719/21134. Attractive, airy and scrupulously clean, with deep verandahs and high-ceilinged rooms opening out onto a small garden. A restaurant is attached, and rooms have air-con and cold-water mandi. ❸

Hotel Makmur Jl Endek 24 ⓣ0719/27566. Centrally located with a variety of rooms. The very inexpensive ekonomi doubles with a fan and outside bathroom are a touch squalid but passable; the pricier rooms are better presented, although there's no hot water. The ground floor rooms open out onto a small garden at the back. ❷–❸

Hotel Martini Jl Yos Sudarso 17 ⓣ0719/21432, ⓕ21433. The grandest and most expensive hotel in town is centrally located and has pleasant, open-sided corridors with plenty of garden areas and fountains. The staff are friendly and helpful, and the rooms are comfortable although not luxurious. ❹–❺

Wisma Pantai Belitung Permai Jalan Pantai Pandan ⓣ0719/21659, ⓕ22310. The only beach accommodation in town is more than a little faded and has an exhausted feel, but the location is good. To get there, head southwest down Jalan Departi Gegedek for 1km and turn left at the monstrous, star-shaped mosque. Accommodation is in large bungalows. ❸

Hotel Surya Jl Endek 808 ⓣ0719/21550. Just along the road from *Hotel Makmur*, on the second floor, with a small entrance on the street. The rooms are basic but clean, with fan or air-con; the slightly more expensive rooms have attached mandi. ❷–❸

Eating and drinking

The friendly **night market** at the end of Jalan Endek has a few stalls that cook up the usual Indonesian specialities quickly, cheaply and well. If you prefer to dine in a **restaurant**, *Pribumi*, Jl M.T. Haryono 21, serves excellent Indonesian food in a neat, open-fronted establishment with friendly staff. It's a touch expensive, but the food is good-quality and they even serve Guinness. The most elegant place to eat in town is the well-located *Restaurant Pandan Laut*, 2km north of the centre on Jalan Patimurah. It's a seafood place built on stilts right over the mangroves by the beach; they also have a good selection of fruit juices. There's very little nightlife in Tanjung Pandan, but the beach can get lively at weekends.

Around the island

The main reason to come to Belitung is to find that magical little white-sand **beach** that you can enjoy in isolation. While it's not particularly easy to get around the island and the chances of somewhere being undiscovered are shrinking fast, there are still deserted little coves to explore. There is public transport around the rest of the island, but it's infrequent, and getting around is much easier with your own transport. To get to the beaches of the west coast (see below), you have two options: you can charter a taxi for a minimum of six hours (Rp100,000), or – much more fun – hire a moped. Rates for mopeds are Rp35,000 for six hours (Rp50,000 for 12hr); enquire at the *Hotel Citra*, Jl Sriwijaya 41 (ⓣ0719/21391), or at your accommodation.

Ten kilometres north of Tanjung Pandan, the small village of **TANJUNG BINGA** lines the road just behind the pretty white beach, with a multitude of attractive wooden jetties protruding into the ocean as mooring for the local fishing boats. If you're lucky, you'll also see the local boat-builders at work. The beach is pleasant, but foreign sunbathers soon draw a crowd of onlookers. However, there are four alluring offshore islands which make an excellent day-trip (take all your supplies): Pulau Kera, Pulau Batu, Pulau Burung and Pulau Babi. All are between five and ten minutes away by chartered speedboat and excellent for a day-trip. There are simple cottages on Pulau Burung; for more information, enquire in Tanjung Binga, either at the shops on the main street or at the police station.

Another 17km north at **TANJUNG KELAYAN**, which has an attractive sandy beach, there are basic thatched cottages with concrete attached mandi at *Kelayan Indah* (no phone; ❷). The cottages have verandahs, with good views of Pulau Kelayan and Tanjung Tinggi off the coast. It gets busy here at weekends, when warung and drinks stalls open up to cater to day-trippers, but weekdays are totally peaceful. A few kilometres northwest, the shore road peters out and there are some lovely tiny beaches looking out onto rocky islands you can reach by swimming – you'll most likely have them all to yourself.

At **TANJUNG TINGGI**, undoubtedly the most gorgeous beach on the island, 4km beyond Tanjung Kelayan, the beauty is due to the purity of the gleaming white sand and the brilliant clarity of the turquoise and azure waters. A little way out to sea, there are numerous boulders jutting out of the water. As you approach the beach you'll see the small and basic rumah makan *Siera*, which serves a few simple dishes. Further along the beach is deserted and serene.

Around on the **east coast** there are some large, isolated, pleasant beaches north of **MANGGAR**, but they have no facilities and access can be difficult. Manggar is the best base for exploring this coast, being a pleasant little town, although rather spread out. It's 3–4km from the bus terminal to the town centre, which has all basic amenities such as a post office and telephone office. There are several inexpensive places to stay, but the best is *Nusa Indah*, Jl Pegadaian 87 (Ⓣ0719/91293; ❷–❸), a small, clean, friendly homestay near Pasar Sayur and the town centre, with fan and air-con rooms with attached mandi.

One of the most popular and attractive beaches on the east coast is at the small village of **BURUNG MANDI**, a few kilometres north of Manggar, a long, curving strand that attracts plenty of day-trippers at the weekends but is otherwise quiet. Thirty kilometres further north, **Pulau Pring**, the town of **Kelapa Kampit** and **Sengaran** beach are well off the beaten track, while **Malang Lepau**, about 15km north of Manggar, is a small working beach with a huge wooden jetty protruding into the sea with enticing views south to other distant and deserted coves. **Pulau Memperak**, off the east coast, has some attractive coral and is a fledgling **scuba diving** site – ask at the tourist office at Tanjung Pandan for diving contacts.

Forty kilometres south of Tanjung Pandan, **Membalung** district is noteworthy only during the April **harvest festival** of *Maras Taun*. If you're lucky enough to be around at this time, ask around about performances of *Beripat*, a traditional martial art related to *Silat* (see p.407), involving rattan sticks. The sticks are smeared with red clay, thus enabling points to be scored on the opponent's back. Competitors have been known to get carried away and draw blood, so think twice before accepting an offer to join in.

Bengkulu and around

Located across the other side of the Bukit Barisan Mountain range from the Trans-Sumatran Highway, the ex-colonial city of **BENGKULU** has long been something of a backwater. The administrative capital of the small province of the same name, it boasts several attractive sights and is a pleasant stopping-off point on trips to remote **Pulau Enggano**, the lively town of **Curup** which is a good base for walkers, and the **Pasemah Plateau**.

The area around Bengkulu is home to several ethnically distinct peoples. The mountain-dwelling Rejang comprise the main groups: the highland Rejang and Rejang Pasisir who inhabit the lower western land, with the remainder the Pasemah people of the Plateau (see p.496) and the Serawai people of the southern area. The people of Enggano (see p.495) are a different ethnic mix, more closely related to Mentawai dwellers than the people of the mainland.

With improved communications, Bengkulu is now relatively **accessible**, although you need a bit of time as it's a hefty 149km from the Trans-Sumatran Highway at Lubuklinggau. However, access to the Pasemah Plateau is straightforward from the city and, with attractive beaches and mountain areas as well as sights to explore, there are plenty of reasons to add Bengkulu to any itinerary.

It's worth bearing in mind that Bengkulu shares the geography and **climate** of Padang on the west side of the Bukit Barisan range. The moisture-laden winds off the Indian Ocean dump their burden of water as they rise up over the mountains; Bengkulu is an attractive, but decidedly humid place.

Some history

The **British** first took Bengkulu (then called Bencoolen) as their Sumatran base in 1685, after they had been driven out of Banten by the Dutch; for 140 years it was Britain's only colony in Southeast Asia. Just as the Dutch had established themselves in Padang in 1663 to form part of their trade network, so the British founded Bengkulu in 1685, initially as an alternative source of pepper. However, it was an extremely isolated outpost of empire, way off the main trade routes; its importance soon declined, and later reports tell of little trade, poor health and desperate boredom.

British control of Bengkulu was not unbroken; in 1719, local people regained the city, and held it for several years; in 1760, the French Admiral Comte d'Estaing took the city for some months, and his compatriot Admiral Linois overran and pillaged Bengkulu in 1803. However, during their sojourn in the city, the British explored far and wide, and the earliest surviving accounts of many parts of Sumatra date from that time. Thomas Stamford Raffles was governor of Bengkulu from 1818 to 1824, completed many of his naval excursions throughout the region from his base in Bengkulu, from where he also visited the Minang highlands in 1818. In 1825, the British handed Bengkulu over to the Dutch, in exchange for authority over the Malay Peninsula and Singapore. Whilst the British had only maintained control of the coastal area, the Dutch launched a series of military expeditions in the 1850s and gained control of the mountainous region inland where, at the end of the century, gold was discovered, and it soon became the major supplier of gold in the Dutch East Indies. When the Japanese army entered Bengkulu in 1942, they wrested power from the retreating Dutch and pressed the province into support of the Japanese war effort. Thousands of people died by forced labour, hunger and disease, a situation which continued until the Japanese retreated at the end of the war and Bengkulu became part of the new Indonesian republic.

Arrival, information and city transport

Flights come into Padang Kemiling **airport**, 14km south of town and a 200-metre walk to the main road from the terminal. Pulau Baai harbour is 15km south of the city centre. There are currently no Pelni passenger services serving Bengkulu, but enquire at the Pelni office, Jl Khadijah 10 (ⓣ0736/21013), to see if they will get reinstated. From both the airport and the harbour, fixed-price **taxis** into the city are Rp20,000, or take a bus either to Sebakul bus terminal (if you're moving straight on) or Pasar Minggu in the city centre; you may need to change at Simpang Lingka Barat terminal. The situation regarding **bus terminals** is confused. Panorama terminal, a few kilometres from the

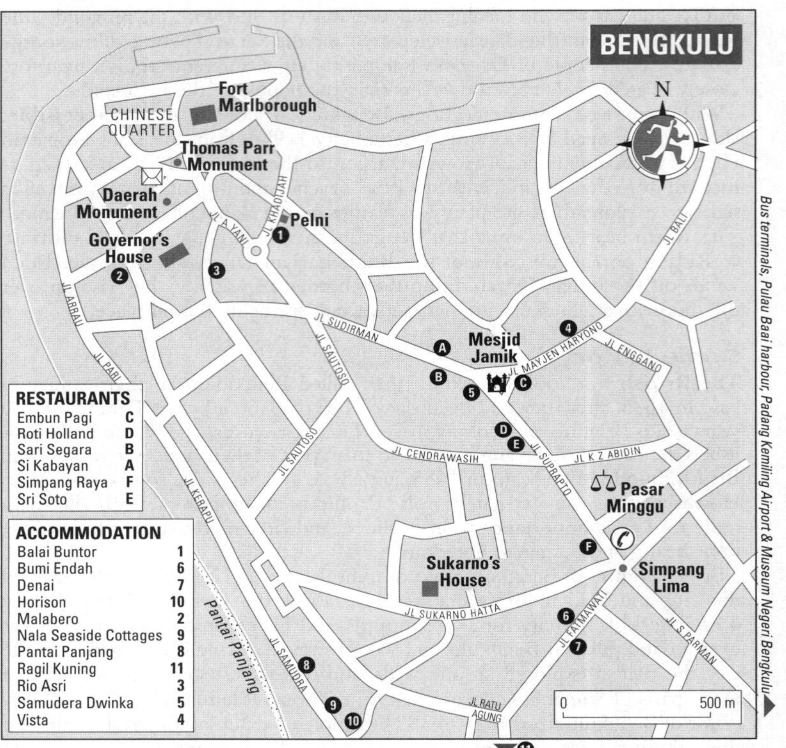

city centre, was formerly the long-distance terminal, but at the time of writing had become a transit hub for bemos. Nearly all long-distance departures are from the new bus terminal at Sebakul, around 12km southeast of the city. For details of bus company offices, see p.494.

Situated on the Indian Ocean, between the estuaries of Sungai Air Bengkulu to the north and Sungai Jenggalu to the south, the oldest part of Bengkulu lies on an attractive headland around Fort Marlborough overlooking the sea. The main bulk of the town spreads south along the coast for about 10km. Its main thoroughfare runs the entire length of town, roughly northwest–southeast, but changing its name from Jalan A. Yani at the top near Fort Marlborough through Jalan Sudirman, Jalan Suprapto, Jalan S. Parman, Jalan Jend Sutoyo, Jalan Kapt Tendean and finally Jalan Pangeran Natadiraj out towards the airport.

City transport

Negotiating Bengkulu's **city transport** is difficult for locals as well as visitors. There are no local buses, but hundreds of yellow, dark-red and green **bemos**, known locally as "taxis", scurry around town. The trouble is that they pretty much go where they want when they want – neither the colour of the vehicle nor the destinations fading on the windscreen seem to bear any relationship to where they are heading. You simply flag one down and tell them your destination; if you're in luck, the driver will nod. There is, however, one reasonably reliable route: a green bemo from the *Punca Dept Store* on Jalan Suprato in the town centre should get you to Panorama, from where a white bemo leaves for Sebakul bus terminal, and vice versa.

Otherwise, the trick is to know what the various areas of town are called. The area around Fort Marlborough is "Kampung", the Pasar Minggu area is known as "Minggu", the bus terminal is "Terminal Sibakul" and the main roads through town known simply by name: "Suprapto", "Sudirman", and so on. The Simpang Lima (Five Ways) junction is a convenient landmark, where Jalan Suprapto changes into Jalan S. Parman at the junction with Jalan Fatmawati and Jalan Sukarno Hatta.

Cycle rickshaws and **horse-drawn carts** are also available to rent, mostly off the main streets, and any bemo will turn itself into a taxi in the wink of an eye. Be sure to establish the price before you get in.

Accommodation

The **accommodation** options in Bengkulu are surprisingly good, and despite the many utilitarian and noisy hotels catering for the Indonesian business market, even the most inexpensive places seem to pass the broom around a little more frequently than the national average.

Balai Buntor Jl Khadijah 122 ⓣ0736/21254. Near the Bank Indonesia, this is a good choice with a quiet location and helpful staff who speak some English. The inexpensive rooms have cold-water mandi; the more expensive ones have air-con and are good value. ❷–❸

Bumi Endah Jl Fatmawati 29 ⓣ0736/21665, ⓕ342451. Conveniently close to Simpang Lima, although on a fairly quiet road; despite having the same street number as the *Denai*, this less expensive but slightly overpriced option is actually across the road. The cheaper rooms have fans, while the more expensive ones have air-con; all are well-maintained. ❸–❹

Denai Jl Fatmawati 29 ⓣ0736/21981, ⓕ22029. Comfortable and friendly, but a bit moth-eaten and dark – all rooms have hot water and air-con. The more expensive rooms have lounge chairs and a fridge. ❹

Horison Jl Pantai Nala 142 ⓣ0736/21722, ⓕ22072. Situated on a small hill just back from the beach, this is the best hotel in town, with a pleasant swimming pool and panoramic views of the ocean. Rooms all have hot water and air-con, and there's even a billiards room. ❺

Malabero Jl Prof Dr Hazairin S.H. 23 ⓣ0736/21004. With a central location near the Governor's House, this is a large old bungalow with high ceilings and huge rooms. A pleasant option in this price range. ❷–❸

Nala Seaside Cottages Jl Pantai Nala 133 ⓣ0736/21855, ⓕ21855. Despite the address, it's actually on Jalan Samudra, just across the road from the beach. The area is busy at weekends and in the evening, but you'll often end up with the beach to yourself on weekdays. Accommodation is in small wooden bungalows with air-con, TV and cold-water mandi. ❸

Pantai Panjang Jl Samudera 40 ⓣ0736/24001. Large and attractive wooden bungalows, with fan or air-con, in a pleasant if slightly ramshackle setting overlooking the beach. ❸

Ragil Kuning Jl Kenanga 99 ⓣ0736/22682. By far the best budget option in the city, situated in a great water garden complete with streams and sitting areas; the area is quiet and hard to locate, but well worth the effort. You need to get a bemo to "Skip Lewat Simpang Pantai", which will go up Jalan Flamboyant, along Jalan Rafflesia and stop at the top of Jalan Kenanga if coming from the centre of town. Rooms have attached mandi and a small verandah; cold drinks are available, and they can rustle up a couple of basic dishes. ❷

Rio Asri Jl Veteran 63 ⓣ0736/21952, ⓕ25728. Situated down a quiet side road, this high-quality hotel is well located. The rooms are very variable, so ask to see several; all have air-con and hot water, and there's a pool. ❺

Samudera Dwinka Jl Sudirman 246 ⓣ0736/21604, ⓕ23234. Clean, friendly and good-value, the cheaper rooms have fan and cold water while the more expensive ones have air-con and hot-water mandi with tubs. ❸–❹

Vista Jl Mt Haryono 67 ⓣ0736/20820. This simple and clean hotel is one of the best central budget places; any bemos going into Pasir Minggu pass along here. There's a range of rooms, including some very inexpensive ones with no fan, though all are sparklingly clean. There's a pleasant garden area at the back, where you'll find the quietest rooms. ❶–❸

The City

The overriding impression of Bengkulu is of a garden city, especially in the area around Fort Marlborough and the Governor's House at the northern end of town. Here in particular, roads are wide and tree-lined, pavements and even trees are painted in gleaming white and blue, and the stately buildings and parks are bedecked with statues and monuments.

Built in 1715, **Fort Marlborough** (Benteng Marlborough; daily 7am–7pm; Rp1000) was constructed to replace the original British fortification at Fort York, 2km away. It has been well restored and almost sparkles in the sunshine, set in pretty gardens and with excellent views out to sea and up the coast. It looks sturdy enough, with cannons positioned to guard against attack from the ocean, solid walls, hefty doors and surrounding ramparts. However, on the two occasions it came under serious attack, from local people in 1719 and the French in 1760, the British failed to defend it effectively. An English gunner writing at the time had little confidence: "It would moulder away every wet season and the guns often fall down into the ditches." The outer wall is surrounded by a further defence, a dry moat, its aim not only to keep the enemy out, but to keep the sentries in – whilst on duty, they developed a habit of wandering off in search of alcohol. It's an evocative spot; at the entrance you walk between old gravestones of soldiers who died in Bengkulu, and it's easy to imagine their sense of isolation if you look westwards from the ramparts across the ocean. The nearest land is thousands of kilometres away, whilst inland from the fort, in the days before roads, the soaring mountains were virtually impenetrable.

Close to Fort Marlborough, at the northern end of Jalan A. Yani, the **Thomas Parr Monument** is prominently marked on maps, but is a fairly insignificant, empty domed building. Parr was a very unpopular governor of the colony who had tried to reduce the power of the "Bugis Corps", used by the British East Indies Company in addition to their own forces. Parr's career ended in 1807, when he was stabbed and beheaded, probably by Bugis mercenaries.

To the west of the fort around Jalan Panjaitan, a recent fire destroyed some of the old **Chinese quarter** of town, with its characteristic two-storey shophouses; it remains to be seen what rebuilding will look like here. Further south, the **Governor's House** is not open to the public, but you can look through the iron railings at the grand classical lines of the white-painted building and carefully manicured grounds. In the park nearby, the **Daerah Monument** is an elegant soaring pinnacle in its own grounds, surrounded by railings. The Christian **cemetery** behind the church on Jalan Veteran is a rather shadeless and sad place, which reflects the savage toll that life in the tropics took on the foreign occupiers. It's said that some of Raffles' family are buried here.

Two kilometres south, at the junction of Jalan Sudirman, Jalan Suprapto and Jalan Mount Haryono, **Mesjid Jamik** was designed by President Sukarno, an architect by profession, while he was exiled in Bengkulu. It has the clean, austere lines of most mosque architecture, but the speeding traffic on all sides is a somewhat distracting counterpoint to prayer. A couple of hundred metres south of the mosque, just to the east of Jalan Suprapto, **Pasar Minggu** is a wonderful old-style Indonesian market that has not yet been transferred into a boring concrete box: it's worth wandering the tiny alleyways crammed with local coffee, songbirds in cages, piles of fruit, rattan and basketware. Out on the back road leading into the market, stalls selling stainless steel for mosque domes are clustered.

Under 1km southwest of here and a short walk from the Simpang Lima junction, **Sukarno's House** (Rumah Kediaman Bung Karno; daily 8am–5pm; Rp500), on Jalan Sukarno Hatta, is the house to which the future first president of Indonesia was exiled from 1938 to 1942, together with his family. It's a large, airy bungalow with high ceilings and deep verandahs, set back from the road in spacious grounds. The rooms have been left largely as they were at the time of his occupation, with books and clothes (now mouldy and faded) behind glass-fronted cupboards; there's even the bicycle that Sukarno used to visit his second wife, who lived locally. Old photographs on display suggest that, even in exile, Sukarno maintained a vigorous political and social life.

Three kilometres south of Simpang Lima, the **Museum Negeri Bengkulu**, Jalan Pembangunan (Mon–Thurs 8am–4.30pm, Fri 8–11am, Sat & Sun 8am–1pm; free), is housed in a grand and impressive traditionally designed building. The inside offers the usual range of poorly labelled items that can be seen in provincial museums all over Sumatra: faded textiles, baskets, models of traditional houses, ceramics, old money and weapons, and artefacts connected with traditional wedding ceremonies. Of slightly more interest is the colourful display of Tabot towers, drums and flags from the annual local Tabot festival (see p.59).

Eating, drinking and entertainment

There's a good range of places to eat in Bengkulu, from simple roadside warung to more expensive and stylish restaurants. The best **night market** is near Pasar Minggu, on Jalan K.Z. Abidin, which leads from the market area out onto Jalan Suprapto. Although it's comparatively small, the stalls are varied and you could easily put together a four-course meal of soup or sate, followed by a main rice or noodle dish, moving onto *murtabak* and then *es campur* and/or coffee.

Embun Pagi A large and conveniently located Padang place, serving fish and chicken dishes; it's a little quieter than the places on the main roads.

Roti Holland Jalan Suprapto. One of several good bakeries in this part of town; they all serve sweet breads and cakes, and have a few tables and chairs if you want to sit and relax.

Sari Segara Jl Sudirman 199a. The best of the clutch of seafood places on Jalan Sudirman, opposite Mesjid Jamik, at the junction with Jalan Suprapto. The menu is huge, and includes crab, squid, fish and lobster in a choice of sauces. Moderately priced, with well-cooked food in basic surroundings.

Si Kabayan Jl Sudirman 51. Pleasant restaurant in a garden setting; the meals are served on low tables in individual bamboo huts. There's a wide range of Indonesian food on offer, most of it reasonable value, although the juices are expensive.

Simpang Raya Jl Suprapto 380a. Almost opposite the Telkom office, this large restaurant is the local branch of the popular chain of Padang restaurants.

Sri Solo Jl Suprapto 118. Sells basic, inexpensive noodle, chicken, rice, soup, sate, ice and juices. Good-value, and popular with locals.

Entertainment

The Bioskop Segar **cinema**, on Jalan Sudirman, shows Hollywood movies, mostly with subtitles. The *Long Beach* **disco**, at the south end of Pasir Panjang Cempaka Gading, attracts the local trendies as well as some holiday-makers staying on the beachfront. Indonesian dance music – which isn't as tacky as you might think – is on the cards (nightly 10pm–2am; Rp15,000).

Shopping

Bengkulu is a good place to buy **textiles** if you're after something a little out of the norm. The local speciality is **batik besurek**. Originally used as a wrap for the dead, it's now made in cotton or silk and consists of batik with hand-painted elements applied afterwards. The best place to see the workshops is Bem Collection, Jl Ciliwung Bawah 2 (☎0736/25420); they also have a showroom. To get there, take any bemo heading south towards the airport. Beyond the Padang Harapan roundabout, a sign points east to Billar Pasir Putih – it's a pleasant, rural stroll along a small lane for 1–2km to the small house and workshop. For more everyday needs, Puncak, at Jl Suprapto 28, is a three-storey **department store** containing a small supermarket.

Listings

Airline offices Mandala, Jl Sukarno Hatta 39 ☎0736/52520; Merpati, Jl Sudirman 246 ☎0736/27111, Ⓕ23105.
Banks and exchange BCA, Jl Suprapto 150, is the only bank in town which will touch anything beyond American dollar travellers' cheques; they also offer advances on Visa and Mastercard. If you have only dollar travellers' cheques, you'll still be welcome at BNI, Jl S. Parman 34. There are ATMs at these branches as well as other locations throughout the centre.
Buses Most of the bus companies have offices on Jalan Bali and Jalan Maygen Haryono. If they don't serve your destination, they'll soon direct you to one that does. Putra Rafflesia, Jl Maygen Haryono 12 (☎0736/20313), is one of the largest companies, and operates to destinations throughout Sumatra, Java and Bali. For more local destinations like Lahat and Curup, try Sriwijaya on Jl Bali 36b (☎0736/21320). They have a fixed price list on the wall that you should double-check, when they quote you the fare.
Car rental Enquire at your hotel or Yudi Rent A Car, Jl Khadijah 95 (☎0736/26726). Expect to pay around Rp250,000 per day, with or without driver.
Hospital Rumah Sakit Daerah, Jalan Hibrida ☎0736/52005.
PHPA Jl Mahoni 11 (☎0736/21697) for local information about Rafflesia. The office for Bukit Barisan national park is at Kota Agung (see p.512).
Post office The central post office is located at Jl S. Parman 111. They get very few tourists, and the poste restante service is not recommended. A more convenient office is near the Parr Monument at Jl R.A. Hadi 3.
Telephone and fax The 24hr Telkom office is centrally located at Jl Suprapto 132. There's another 24hr office at Jl Kolonel Barlian 51, next to the post office near the Parr Monument. Wartels both international and local are dotted all over town.

The coast

Bengkulu's **beaches** are a terrific attraction. The main strand is 7km long and starts as Pasir Nala in the north, changing its name further south to **Pasir Panjang Gading Cempaka**; it runs along the west side of the city, reached by walking along the coastal road from the port. It was supposedly named after a princess of the same name who, according to legend, was as fragrant as frangipani (*cempaka*) and had skin like ivory (*gading*). Just 5km off the coast, **Pulau Tikus** (Rat Island) is, despite its name, an excellent option for a day-trip. It's only about 100m long and is part of a much larger underwater coral reef which still contains some iron anchors from old sailing ships that sheltered in the lee of the reef from the huge Indian Ocean swells. It's rich in sea life, but you'll need to take your own snorkelling gear and supplies for the day. Arrange a boat charter from the beach from Rp90,000.

Curup and around

The scenic 85-kilometre trip from Bengkulu to **CURUP** offers views of interesting pinnacle mountain formations; regular buses run the route throughout the day (2hr; Rp10,000). At Bukit Daun there's a lookout point with views back to Bengkulu, before the road climbs through the forest up to the pass and gate at Puncak, before descending to Kepatiang and the Penanjung area, where you'll spot coffee beans drying by the road.

Curup is a small, bustling market town, in the centre of the region known as the Rejang Lebong. The climate here is cooler than the scorching coastal heat of Bengkulu, and the town is a useful base from which to explore the surrounding mountainous area or to stop over on the trip between Bengkulu and the Trans-Sumatran Highway at Lubuklinggau.

There are a few **accommodation** options. *Griya Anggita*, Jl Iskander Ong 24 (☎0732/23289; ❷–❸), offers a range of rooms and is clean, quiet and friendly, with a 24-hour restaurant serving inexpensive Indonesian food such as nasi goreng, mie goreng and sate. To get there by bemo from town, ask for "Gang Berlian". Further from the town centre, *Hotel Mira* lies in a quiet location at Jl Letjen Suprato 106 (☎0732/21506; ❷). It's a family-run place, offering a range of clean rooms, all with attached cold-water mandi. To get there, ask bemo drivers for "Talang Rimbo Lama".

The main commercial street is Jalan Merdeka, and the BCA and BRI are located here along with several **restaurants**. Excellent Padang food is available at *Bundo Kandung*, Jl Merdeka 175, with especially fine *otak* (brains), *ayam kalio* (chicken in coconut sauce) and *perkadel* (croquettes).

Around Curup

There are several excursions around town, one of the closest being to the **Suban hot springs** (daily 5am–7pm; Rp700, plus Rp1000 for swimming and Rp1000 for a hot shower), but don't expect natural surroundings: huge amounts of concrete were used to construct the pools, water channels, sitting areas and restaurants. Take a bemo for 5km from Curup to the signed gateway on the main road, and you'll then have 1.5km to walk along a leafy lane to the entrance.

Further afield, **Bukit Kaba** lies about 30km from Curup and is an active volcanic area. If you're using public transport, take a local bus or bemo from the terminal along the Lubuklinggau road to Simpang Bukit Kaba, and then a bemo to Sumber Urip, where you can find a **guide** – you shouldn't go alone. From there, the path is wide and obvious, and it takes two hours to walk to Puncak (a four-wheel drive vehicle can get this far), from where it's an hour's walk to Kawah, where you can look down into the smoking crater belching sulphurous fumes. The nearby landscape is volcanic and bleak, with only lichens able to survive the chemical composition of the soil, although the distant forests and mountains are rather more picturesque. This part of the path needs care; although it's well trodden and there are steps cut in the steep parts, it's narrow in places and can be windy. For the best views, start early – leave Curup at 6–7am, as it gets cloudy and rainy later in the day.

Pulau Enggano

Pulau Enggano, 29km long and 14km wide, is situated 114km from the coast of Sumatra and is surrounded by fantastic coral, great beaches, brilliantly coloured oceans and five smaller islands. The name means "mistake" in Portuguese, and probably relates to the time of the Portuguese exploration of the archipelago. With swampy coasts and with no primary forest left, the island is mainly flat (the highest point is 281m), inhabited by wild pigs, cattle and buffalo. The scenery, sea and the chance to get way off the beaten track are the main reasons to come here; there's little in the way of sights.

The origins of the Engganese people are somewhat mysterious. They're thought to be a mix of the Veddoid people of South India and Sumatrans from the mainland, though they resemble the people of the Nicobar Islands in the Bay of Bengal. Other theories suggest they are descended from the original nomadic Sumatrans who fled across the ocean when the Malay people began to arrive; they also share some characteristics with the inhabitants of the Mentawai Islands further north. Their language is related to the Austronesian family of languages, and is radically different from anything on the mainland. These days the indigenous Engganese are greatly outnumbered by Javanese, Sumatrans and Chinese. The local economy is based on fishing, copra and the cultivation of rice, coffee, pepper and cloves.

Reaching **Pulau Enggano** is an adventure in itself. At the time of writing, there was talk of an imminent daily ferry service aboard the *Raja Enggano* between the island and Pulau Baai – not an island, but a riverport 30km from Bengkulu, accessible only by taxi. Enquire at the Pelni office in Bengkulu (see p.489), or at the nascent offices of ASDP in Pulau Baai. There are absolutely no tourist facilities on Pulau Enggano, so to get around the island you'll need to walk or get the boat around the coast. The only **accommodation** is in local houses; you should go first to the **kepala desa** at Malakoni, to let him know of your arrival and to ask advice. You'll need a fair level of Indonesian to make the most of the opportunity to mingle with the local people.

The Pasemah Plateau

Located in a cleft in the Bukit Barisan range of mountains, the seventy-kilometre-long **Pasemah Plateau** is an extensive fertile highland plain surrounded by mountains. The area's main attractions for tourists are the ancient stone **megaliths**, believed to be remnants of a Bronze Age culture, and hiking on **Gunung Dempo**. Getting to the area is straightforward, and visitors can base themselves in the pleasant town of **Pagaralam**, accessible directly from Bengkulu on a highly picturesque bus trip. Coming from the south, you'll most likely transit through **Lahat**, close to the Trans-Sumatran Highway and 67km south east of Pagaralam.

Pagaralam and Gunung Dempo

Situated a cool 710m above sea level, the small upland town of **PAGARALAM** to the east of **Gunung Dempo**, which towers over the area, is an attractive base from which to explore the area, particularly the megaliths. It's a busy market town serving the small villages dotted around the highland area, and it gets enough visitors for people to be unsurprised by Westerners.

Long-distance buses from Bengkulu, Lahat, Palembang, Bandar Lampung and Jakarta serve the **bus terminal**, 2–3km west of the town centre. To get to the central market from the bus terminal, take a red bemo, for a flat fare of Rp500. Some buses, mostly to and from Lahat, terminate at Simpang Mannak, a junction 4km out of town, reached by dark blue bemos from the town centre (Rp1000).

The best **accommodation** for travellers intending either to trek around Gunung Dempo or visit the megaliths is the friendly and helpful *Hotel Mirasa*, Jl May Ruslan 62 (Ⓣ0730/21484; ❷). It offers simple rooms with verandahs and attached cold-water mandi in a garden setting; the cheaper rooms at the back look out across local paddy-fields, and the attached restaurant serves good, inexpensive Indonesian food. Ask here for details of local guides, either for the megaliths in the area, or for the Gunung Dempo climb. To get to the *Mirasa*, take a blue bemo along Jalan May Ruslan from the market area. Alternatively, buses from Bengkulu will pass by the door; ask the driver beforehand to drop you off.

As darkness falls, the market area turns into a **night market**. There are several **restaurants**: in the market, *Toko Tasdik*, Jl Lettu Hamid 104, is a relaxed place serving Indonesian favourites and specializing in *murtabak* and *pempek*; *Singgah Kudai*, Jl Lettnan Penalis 27, offers local and Padang food: try the *sayur nangkha* (jackfruit curry), *sambal tempe* (dry potatoes, nuts and chilli served in a fiery sambal sauce), or *pindang* (beef soup flavoured with saffron, ginger, chilli and onions).

The **post office** is at Jl Kapten Senap 37, on the road south towards *Hotel Mirasa*. The **Telkom office** (24hr) is next door, at Jl Kapten Senap 36, and there's a more central wartel on Jl Vandrik Karim 355 (6am–11pm). Pagaralam has no facilities for changing money.

Climbing Gunung Dempo

Dominating the town and the entire Pasemah Plateau is the 3159-metre **Gunung Dempo**, its summit comprising two peaks separated by a col. It's best climbed during the dry season, from May to August. It's highly recommended that you take a **guide** from Pagaralam who is familiar with the mountain, as the trails are little used, hard to find and it's easy to get lost. Expect to pay US$30–40 for the two days; the guide can also provide all equipment except sleeping bags; ask at the *Hotel Mirasa* for details.

It takes two full days to get up and down the mountain, so it's best to leave Pagaralam at around 6am on the first morning. Your trip will involve a short bemo ride (red) to the village of Pabrik at the base of the mountain, and then a half-day walk to Pembibitan where you'll sleep some of the night at the guide's house. An midnight start from here will see you to the top of the mountain at about 7am for dawn; you return the same day. There are thought to be tigers and several species of monkeys and birds on the forested slopes around the mountain, but you're more likely to hear than see them.

The megaliths

Many of the best **megaliths** from the area have been removed to the National Museum in Jakarta (see p.106) and the Museum Negeri Propinsi Sumatera Selatan in Palembang (see p.477). However, many weird and ancient stone carvings, troughs and graves still remain dotted around fields and villages close to Pagaralam, dating from AD1–500. Some are solitary, others stand in groups, and they depict humans and animals; although most are seriously eroded, they're still strangely evocative. The local belief is that an angry magician called Lidah Pahit ("Bitter Tongue") was responsible for the statues: anyone who displeased him was turned into stone. Most stones have some sort of caretaker, and you'll be expected to sign a visitors' book and pay Rp1000 per person for a look.

There are megaliths all around Pagaralam; either ask for directions locally or negotiate a guide for the day (about Rp25,000). The easiest to locate, in the grounds of **Mesjid Takwar**, 300m from the *Hotel Mirasa* going back towards the town, is a small carving depicting a man subduing an elephant. Others worth visiting include: the group of statues known as Batu Beribu and the relief carving of a warrior (Batu Balai) in **Tegur Wangi**, about 6km from Pagaralam; the one-metre-tall Batu Gajah ("Elephant Stone"), also known as Batu Kerbau, at **Belumai**, 3–4km from Pagaralam; and Batu Gajah and Batu Orang, a mother with long hair and a baby on an elephant in a forest site at **Pulau Panggung**, 10km northeast of Pagaralam. Another easily accessible megalith is Arca Manusia Debelit Ulas ("Stone Megalith Fighting Snake") at **Tanjung Aro**. Simply walk 1km northwest along the highway from the *Hotel*

Mirasa, and take the first left through the village. After about 750m from the turning, just before a fork in the road, you'll see a white "Kompleks Megalitik" (megalith complex) sign on the right. The small compound houses the snake carving as well as some stone dwellings and is well worth the short walk.

Lahat

LAHAT is a useful transport hub for the Pasemah Plateau, with good road and rail links to the rest of Sumatra (the Trans-Sumatra Highway runs to the north of town). However, the town itself has little to detain tourists.

Orientation is pretty straightforward; Lahat is centred around the crossroads of Jalan Mayor Ruslan and Jalan Inspektur Yazid. There's one major street through town: the southwestern end (towards Pagaralam) is Jalan Mayor Ruslan I, which then turns into Jalan Mayor Ruslan II and eventually III as you move northwest. All accommodation and eating places are towards the northwestern end. The **train station** is very central, about 100m off Jalan Mayor Ruslan I, with twice daily services to and from Lubuklinggau and Palembang. There's a small **bus terminal** in town, on Jalan Mayor Ruslan II, with departures to Pagaralam as well as all the major cities in the area. For bus tickets, try Lantra Jaya (Ⓣ0731/322326), which has offices in the terminal itself, but be sure to double-check the quoted departure time against the time written on your ticket – like many Sumatran travel agents, they have an overcautious habit of getting you to the office a couple of hours early. The **tourist office** (Mon–Thurs 7.30am–1.30pm, Fri 7.30–11am, Sat 7.30am–12.30pm; Ⓣ0731/22469) is at Jl Let Amir Hanzah 150 (the road parallel to Jalan Mayor Ruslan II and just behind the bus station). It has little material in English, and no information about how to reach any local sights except by "charter taxi". Just around the corner is the 24-hour **Telkom** office, Jl Serma Yamis 1, but the **wartels** on Jalan Mayor Ruslan II and III (daily 7am–11pm) are more convenient. You'll find the **post office** at Jl Emil Salim 2, next to the tourist information, and there's a BNI **bank** on Jalan Mayor Ruslan III opposite the *Nusantera* hotel.

The **accommodation** options in town are pretty overpriced for what you get, and you won't get a fan because of the "altitude". Best value is the *Losmen Simpang Lahat*, Jl Mayor Ruslan II 19 (Ⓣ0731/321940; ❷–❸), though it's a little musty. Out on the Trans-Sumatran Highway, *Hotel Cendrawasih*, Jl Cemara 185 (Ⓣ0731/321981, Ⓕ324233; ❸–❹), is more upmarket, and has a pleasant garden. *Lantana*, Jl Mayor Ruslan II 69, is the most upmarket and relaxing **place to eat**, with good-value food. There's no menu here: you choose what you fancy from the display. You might also try the night market at Pasar Lematang just off Jalan Mayor Ruslan II.

Danau Ranau and Krui

Nestling in the crater of Gunung Seminung, which rises to 1340m from the western shore, **Danau Ranau**, 16km long and 9km wide, is the most peaceful of all the Sumatran lakes. It offers the cool, mountain scenery of other popular lake destinations such as Toba and Maninjau, but, being a couple of hours off the Trans-Sumatran Highway, takes a bit of effort to reach, and there are no real tourist facilities. However, it's a great place to chill out (literally – it's worth taking a sweater) for a day or two, and is easily combined with a stop at the low-key coastal village of **Krui**, about 70km to the west, an excellent base for exploring the entire coastline.

Danau Ranau

Situated around 100km south of the Trans-Sumatra Highway town of Baturaja and 70km from the west coast at Krui, **Danau Ranau** is surrounded by the attractive mountain scenery of the Bukit Barisan range, with forest-covered mountain slopes and cultivated areas planted with coffee, cloves, tobacco and fruit trees. Several villages dot the lakeside: **SIMPANGSENDER** on the northeast shore is the local transport hub, while **BANDINGAGUNG** on the north side has the largest number of **accommodation** options. The Saturday market is just about the only excitement at Bandingagung, although at holiday times, visitors arrive in droves to rent out boats for lake trips. There are also a few places to stay at **PUSRI** on the eastern shore, and **KOTABATU** at the southern end of the lake. Kotabatu is far livelier than the other settlements around the lake, but it's not possible to walk beside the lake here; with easy transportation between the villages, and only a few other visitors, it's a pleasant place to relax, enjoy the lake and gain a view of small-town upland life.

It's possible to charter a boat from Kotabatu for the hour-long trip across the lake to the **hot springs** on the western shore, where you can bathe in the hot water and then dip in the cold of the lake. Unfortunately, overzealous use of wire and concrete has created a rather ugly setting for this. The wind gets up in the afternoon, making for a colder and choppier trip across, so it's advisable to go early and take a sweater. Boats cost about Rp50,000 for a day-long charter. This can be combined with a trip to the small island of **Pulau Marisa**, located a few hundred metres off Kotabatu's shore. Local people tell how the island appeared one night as a test in a love triangle. A princess called Puteri Aisah was being courted by two undesirable men: Lidah Pahit ("Bitter Tongue") – the fearsome magician responsible for the Pagaralam megaliths (see p.497) – and Simata Empat ("Four Eyes"). Desirous of neither, she nevertheless agreed to marry the one who could build a bridge from the hot springs to the village of Bandingagung in a single night. Both were rejected when small Pulau Marisa was the best either of them could manage.

The most energetic excursion from the lake is to scale **Gunung Seminung**, usually tackled as a long day-trek. The path goes up from near the hot springs, so you start and finish with a boat trip across the lake then climb up through the jungle for about five hours to the summit, from where there are excellent views of the area. It's four or five hours' descent before the trip back across the lake from the hot springs. Enquire at your accommodation for a **guide** (Rp50,000) who is familiar with the path up the mountain, which is little used and likely to be overgrown.

Practicalities

Access to the area from the north is via the Pasar Baru bus terminal in Baturaja, a not unpleasant but otherwise uninteresting town on Sungai Ogan, and the Trans-Sumatra Highway, 272km north of Bandar Lampung. Large minibuses leave irregularly for the three–hour trip to Simpangsender on the lake; the last departure is at 2pm. Unfortunately, most drivers raise the prices for tourists (Baturaja–Simpangsender should cost around Rp10,000), secure bags in their vehicle and then vanish for three or four hours until they fancy making the trip, while other buses have come and gone. The best approach is to hang onto your bag until you board a bus that is clearly about to depart, politely resisting all demands to pay in advance (the locals pay upon arrival; take note of how much they hand over, and do the same). There are plenty of stalls selling tea and snacks in the bus station while you haggle and wait. If you're stuck here for the night, you can stay at the well-kept *Hotel Harison*, Jl HS Simanjuntak 5 (☎0735/321005; ❸–❹).

The road from Baturaja runs via the bustling village of Muaradua, and arrives in the Ranau area at Simpangsender; most buses stop here, so you'll probably have to catch a bemo (Rp2000) to your accommodation. If your bus continues, some will turn west to Bandingagung on the north shore, while others head south along and above the east shore through the Pusri area and on to Kotabatu on the south shore. Coming from Krui or points south, buses pass through Liwa and then arrive at the lakeside at Kotabatu on the southern shore. Regular and frequent **bemos** scurry between Kotabatu, Simpangsender and Bandingagung, and there are long-distance bus connections from all three villages (see p.514). There's a **post office** (Mon–Thurs 7.30am–3pm, Fri 7.30–11.30am, Sat 7.30am–1pm) at Simpangsender, on the road from Muaradua, but currently **no banks** in the area; Bandingagung has a couple of **wartels**, but there are no telephones in the losmens.

Moving on, there are plenty of bus offices in the area, the biggest range being in Simpangsender, where they line the main road out towards Pusri. Twice-daily services leave for Jakarta, Bengkulu and Bandar. In Bandingagung, there are regular departures throughout the day to Simpangsender for onward connections; alternatively, PT Putri Sulung has an office in Jalan Batu Mega, Bandingagung's main street, offering daily departures to Jakarta, Bandar Lampung and Palembang. The same company has an office just as you enter Kotabatu from the north, offering the same departures as Bandingagung. Daily buses to Liwa (change there for Krui) leave each morning at about 8am from all three villages; check at your accommodation or the bus offices for current departure times.

Accommodation

The biggest choice of **accommodation** is in the small, quiet village of **Bandingagung** on the northern shore. The **Pusri** area on the sloping hillside overlooking the eastern shore offers the best views of the lake, although there's almost no habitation nearby so eating options are limited. All the Pusri accommodation requires a steep walk of 1km or so down from the shore road marked by a gateway.

Bandingagung

Losmen Batu Mega Jl Sugiwaras 269. One of the best places on the shore, with good views of the lake from the lounge and a small verandah out front. The family who run it are friendly and informative about the area, offering three very clean rooms, one with attached mandi. To find it, walk down to the lake and – keeping the water on your left – walk to the edge of town, looking for the sign on your right. ❷

Losmen Danau Indah Jl H. Faqih Usman 28. Backs onto the lake road. The rooms are very small and basic, although some have attached mandi, and the lighter garden rooms have a small sitting area out front. There's also a large restaurant area and garden. ❶

Losmen Permata Jl Empu Sepadang 97. Towards the far edge of town, a 200m walk from the market. Walk straight along the first road inland (running parallel to the shore road), keep the lake on your left and continue as the road peters out; you'll see the sign. *Losmen Permata* is simple and pleasant in a quiet location; the rooms have shared mandi. ❶

Hotel Seminung Permai Jl Akmal 89. Just inland from the jetty on the eastern edge of town; the rooms are simple without attached mandi, and the place is a little dark. ❶

Hotel Surya Indah On the road into town close to the local school, offering good rooms, all with attached cold-water mandi. There's a small garden and a verandah, and it's out of the bustle of town but a long walk down to the lake. ❷

Hotel Wisata Jalan Pasar. Situated opposite the market, just up from the lakeshore. The rooms are very clean, without attached mandi; they are variable, so ask to see several, and check at the shop next door if the place is locked. ❷

Pusri

Danau Ranau Cottages The most professionally run place in the area, with attractive, well-maintained grounds sloping down to the lake. There's a pleasant open-sided restaurant, and excursions across the lake can be arranged from here. A variety of accommodation is available, from simple rooms situated a block away from the lake with attached cold-water mandi, to lakeside wood-and-thatch cottages (no hot water). ❷–❸

Wisma Pusri Just past *Danau Ranau Cottages* (it's hard to see where one establishment starts and the other ends); a large setup with a range of decent rooms, some with attached bathrooms. ❷–❸

Kotabatu

Losmen Pantai Indah Jalan Pembangunan II. Situated on the unpaved road down to the lakeside from town, and has small, basic rooms. ❷

Losmen Seminung Jaya Jl Perintis Kemerdekaan 25. *Seminung Jaya* lies 300m towards Liwa from the sharp bend in the middle of town, and about 100m past the mosque on the right – you'll probably need to ask, as there was no sign outside at the time of writing. The downstairs rooms are dark and poky – try to get the upstairs room, which is next to a sitting area overlooking the main street. ❷

Eating

Eating options in Danau Ranau are severely limited, and you're best off asking your losmen to arrange meals – most are run by a family who will be happy to get the extra revenue. However, there is one good, friendly **restaurant**, *Rumah Makan Megawisata*, in Bandingagung, just east of the centre by the jetty; they serve local fish and even understand vegetarianism. The no-name place next door – little more than a stall – serves basic rice, jackfruit and meat dishes.

Krui and around

The small west-coast fishing town of **KRUI**, 40km south of Danau Ranau, is well off the tourist track. It was once the site of a tiny British outpost during their occupation of Bengkulu between 1685 and 1824, although little evidence of this remains. Today, it's simply a pleasant (although very hot) place to spend some time enjoying small-town life and the excellent beaches along the deserted, unspoilt coastline that stretches north and south from the town. To reach the furthest of the beaches, you need to rely on the rather haphazard public transport of the area, or charter your own transport – but even the beaches close to town are worth exploring. **Access** to Krui is either direct from Bandar Lampung or Bengkulu (there are daily buses), from Danau Ranau via **Liwa**, or from Bukitkemuning on the Trans-Sumatra Highway, also via Liwa. Bemos for Krui (45mins; Rp5000) leave from the Liwa bus terminal throughout the day. If you get stuck in Liwa, there's accommodation at, amongst others, *Permata Hotel*, Jl Raden Intan 53 (Rp55,000), which is adequate but has an unpredictable variable water supply. You'll have to get a bemo there, as it's a couple of kilometres north on the high road towards Danau Ranau. Liwa also has an ATM in the centre of town.

The two local **beaches** in Krui, separated by a high, tree-covered headland with a large warning lamp on the top, are both several kilometres long. Adorned by fishing boats and nets, Salalau is the working beach to the north of town. To the southwest of town, Labuhan Jukung is a palm-fringed white-sand beach lapped by turquoise waters, darkening to azure and deep blue further offshore; during weekdays, you can often have several kilometres of deserted sand all to yourself. There are views from both beaches of jungle-covered spurs to the north as well as Pulau Pisang. To get there, walk south out of town for five minutes and take a right (west) at or after the "Garuda Hitam" military post. It's easy to spot, as there's a large, squawking, plastic Garuda (eagle) at the front.

An interesting offshore excursion is to **Pulau Pisang** (Banana Island), just off the coast. You can either charter a boat from Krui (about Rp20,000 each way), or take a bemo (Rp5000) to the village of Tambakak, 14km north of Krui, and catch the local boat service operating from there (Rp3000). There's no accommodation on the island, and you should assume you'll have to walk everywhere, although there's an occasional bemo. The island is especially famous for *kain tapis*, and you should see local women weaving the age-old traditional designs of this intricate cloth.

Further up and down the coast from Krui, there are tiny villages and **beaches** to explore: to the north, as far as Pugung Tanjung, 50km from Krui, and to Mandiri, 10km south of Krui. Local bemos reach both these spots, and in the south they run beyond this to Ngaras. However, they are irregular, tail off early in the afternoon, and you should take plenty of water in case you have a long wait for transport. The coves are all very varied and most visitors will find a favourite, but **Pugung Penengahah**, 30km north of Krui, is particularly attractive, with large rocky outcrops set amongst the pale sand. The beach at **Malaya**, 5km further north, has lovely white sand and picturesque rocks rising from the ocean.

Practicalities

It's easy to find your bearings in Krui, as all buses arrive on Jalan Merdeka, or its southern continuation, Jalan Kesuma. This is the only main road through town, and everything you'll need to find is on it. Krui offers several basic, good-value **accommodation** options. The central *Hotel Sempana Lima*, Jl Kesuma 708 (☎0728/51040; ❷), is the largest place in town, with a variety of rooms. All have bathrooms, and the economy ones are the best budget options in town. Although the Tourist Information Service downstairs seems largely defunct, staff can help with local information. Over the road, *Losmen Gembira*, Jl Kesuma 701 (☎0728/51009; ❶–❷), has rooms with or without attached mandi; it's a bit dark inside, but there are a couple of pleasant garden areas out the back. Further south you'll find the new *Wisma Selawa* (☎0728/51817; ❷), which is spotless and friendly; all rooms have mandi attached. The usual range of Indonesian **food** is on offer in town, with plenty of small rumah makan. Try *Abu Sutarno*, Jl Kesuma 705, opposite *Hotel Sempana Lima* – it's a big, friendly, open-fronted place, and the sate is especially good.

Moving on, there are bus offices on Jalan Kesuma near the *Hotel Sempana Lima*, as well as on the edge of town on the Liwa road. PO Sumber Jaya Indah has daily departures to Bandar Lampung (which everyone calls "Rajabasa", after the bus terminal), and Krui Putri (☎0728/51633) offers daily departures to Bandar Lampung and Bengkulu via the coast road, plus a daily service to Ngaras. The **post office** is at Jalan Tanah Lapang. You can make local and international calls from any of the **wartels** on Jalan Kesuma (daily 7.30am–midnight).

The far south

The **far south** of Sumatra comprises bays and inlets, offshore islands, wild coastline, soaring mountains and extensive plains. As the island narrows towards its southern tip, just 27km from Java, there's easy access between the major sights. As the major transport hub of the region, the city of **Bandar Lampung** is beautifully situated, but lacks decent budget accommodation, though there are plenty of extremely good-quality moderately priced hotels. To the east, many visitors are attracted to the famous birdwatching haunts and elephant training school at the **Way Kambas national park**. Although the **Bukit Barisan Seletan national park** on the southwestern peninsula is much less visited, it's an enticing area with dense forests and a jagged coastline to explore, sustaining a wide range of flora and fauna. At the southern tip of Sumatra, south of Bandar Lampung, the inlets and coves of **Lampung Bay** are peaceful and attractive, and the offshore islands both in and beyond the bay offer exciting excursions, most notably island-hopping and snorkelling. Access to Java is from the port of **Bakauheni** at the southern tip of Sumatra; most travellers between Java and Sumatra pass through the area, although relatively few stop here.

Bandar Lampung and around

Situated in the hills overlooking Lampung Bay, from where you can see as far as Krakatau, **BANDAR LAMPUNG** has the most stunning location of any Sumatran city. It's an amalgamation of the cities of Teluk Betung, the traditional port and trading area down on the shorefront, and Tanjung Karang, the hectic administrative centre on the hills behind. Local people – including bus drivers and conductors – continue to refer to Teluk Betung and Tanjung Karang, and when you're coming to the city from other parts of Sumatra, your destination will usually be referred to as Rajabasa, the name of the bus terminal.

To the southeast of the city, **Pulau Condong** is accessible via Pasir Putih beach, and, also to the southeast, a day-trip to **Padang Cermin** is a pleasant excursion, with some wonderful coastal scenery along the way. East of the city are the ancient remains at **Pugung Raharjo**, with traces of a fortified village and megalithic stones.

Arrival and information

Coming by bus from anywhere north of Bandar Lampung, you'll arrive at the **Rajabasa terminal**, 7km north of the city, and one of the busiest bus terminals in Sumatra. Follow the signs towards the main road for microlet (the local name for bemos); light-blue bemos run into town 24 hours a day (10min; Rp1000), terminating at Pasar Bawah, the market area just south of Jalan Kotoraja. Alternatively, catch the bus (every 20min until 6pm; Rp1000) that goes to Pasar Bawah before continuing its circular route down Jalan Raden Intan, along Jalan A. Yani and up Jalan Kartini before going out to Rajabasa again. Note that if you stay on past Pasar Bawah, it counts as two journeys, so you'll have to pay double.

Coming to the city from Bakauheni or Kalianda, buses arrive at **Panjang terminal**, about 1km east of Panjang market to the east of the city on the coast. Some terminate there, while others go on to Rajabasa. Orange bemos (Rp700) run between Panjang terminal and Sukaraja bemo terminal in the heart of Teluk Betung; from here, you can take a purple bemo into the city (until 10pm; Rp1000) as far as Pasar Bawah, or a large orange bus direct to Rajabasa via the eastern ring-road (every 20min; Rp1000).

Bandar Lampung is part of the triangular **rail network** between Bandar Lampung, Palembang and Lubuklinggau. The train station lies on Jalan Kotoraja, about 100m north from Pasar Bawah. The local **high-speed ferry terminal**, with services running to and from Jakarta, is at Sukaraja, just next to the bemo and bus terminal.

Branti airport lies 25km north of the city; to get to the city from there, walk 200m onto the main road and catch a Branti–Rajabasa bus to Rajabasa (Rp500) and take connections to the centre from there. Fixed-price taxis from

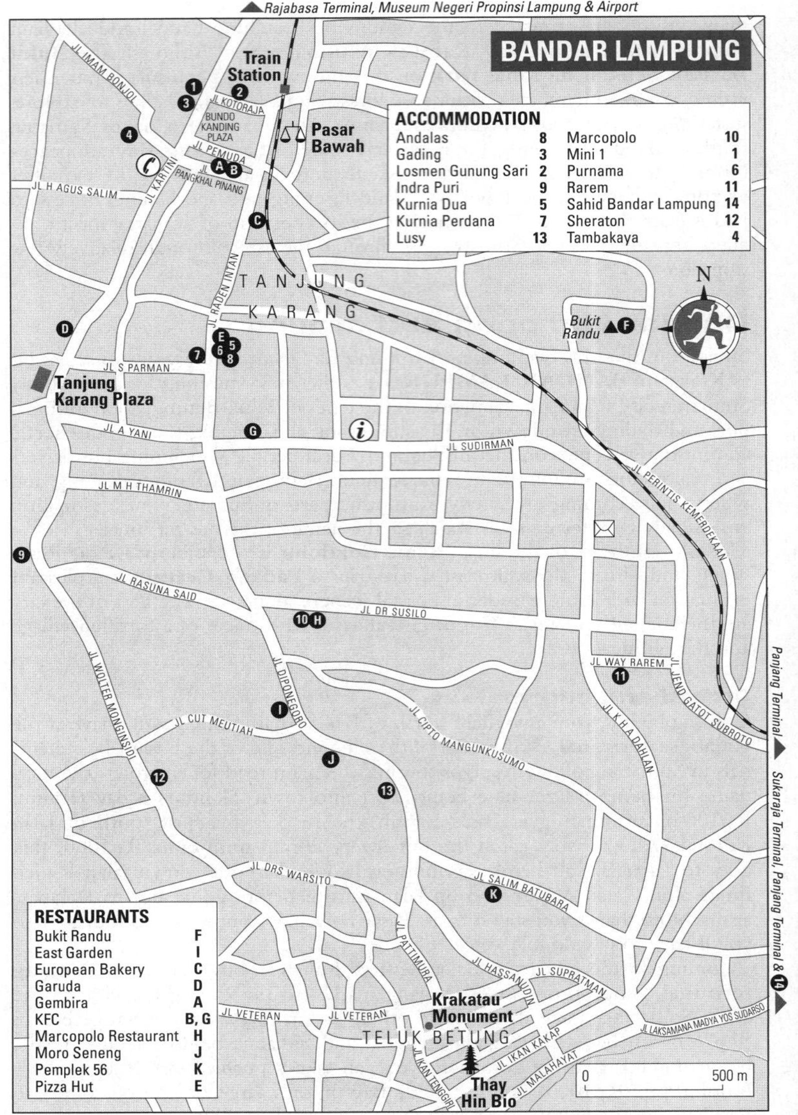

the airport into town cost Rp30,000; you may be able to persuade one on the main road to use a meter, but don't count on it.

The **tourist office** in town, Dinas Investasi Kebudayaan Dan Parwisata (you can just ask for the "Kantor Parwisata") is at Jl Jend Sudirman 29 (Ⓣ0721/261430, Ⓕ266184). The staff are friendly and helpful, especially Sami, a former tour guide, who's very well informed.

Moving on to Java

There are regular **buses** to destinations in **Java** from Bandar Lampung's Rajabasa terminal. Alternatively, buses to Bakauheni (the ferry terminal for departures to Merak on Java) leave from Rajabasa or, more conveniently, **Panjang terminal** on the southeast edge of the city – to get to Panjang terminal, take an orange bemo from Sukaraja terminal (10min; Rp1000).

Charter or **share-taxis** to Jakarta (a 7hr journey) are available from Bandar Lampung taxi firms. Try Dynasty, Jl K.H.A. Dahlan 53 (☎0721/485674), or Taxi 666, Jalan Kartini (☎0721/485769). Expect to pay Rp40,000–55,000 per person.

A high speed **jetfoil** to Merak operates five times daily (6am–4pm) from the ferry terminal just beside the Sukaraja bus terminal. The crossing takes about ninety minutes and costs around Rp30,000.

Ferries from Bakauheni operate around the clock for the two-hour crossing to Merak, every twenty minutes during the day but less frequently at night. There are two classes: it costs Rp5000 in A (with air-con) and Rp3000 in B (no air-con). High-speed ferries also depart approximately hourly, from 7.40am to 5pm (40min; Rp13,000).

City transport

One of the delights of Bandar Lampung is the efficient and straightforward **public transport** system. In any case, the city is so spread out, you'll waste time trudging up and down hills if you don't come to grips with it quickly.

The DAMRI **bus services** operating every ten minutes or so from 6am to 6pm only call at designated stops; they're very useful for getting between the two major terminals, Rajabasa and Sukaraja, or up and down Jalan Randen Intan and Jalan Diponegoro through the heart of the city. Labelled clearly on the front, **Rajabasa–Karang** runs from Rajabasa along Jalan Teuku Umar into the city and left into Jalan Kotoraja, terminating at Pasar Bawah. It returns to Rajabasa down Jalan Raden Intan, along Jalan A. Yani and up Jalan Kartini before heading out to Rajabasa. The bus labelled **Karang–Betung** operates from the Pasar Bawah area down Jalan Raden Intan, Jalan Diponegoro and Jalan Salim Batubara, the southern end of Jalan K.H.A. Dahlan and Jalan Yos Sudarso (also known as Jalan Laksamana Madya Yos Sudarso) to Sukaraja terminal. On the return route, they run along Jalan Yos Sudarso, Jalan Ikan Kakap, up Jalan Ikan Tenggiri, Jalan Pattimura, Jalan Diponegoro, Jalan A. Yani, Jalan Kartini and around to Pasar Bawah. There's also an orange bus (not to be confused with the small orange bemo), which runs from Sukaraja direct to Rajabasa via the eastern ring-road (every 20min; Rp1000).

Buses are supplemented by small **bemos** (flat fare Rp700; 5am–9pm), which are colour-coded (see box on p.506), and have their routes printed on them somewhere – often inconveniently on the back. Like bemos throughout Indonesia, their routes are less fixed than buses, and don't be surprised if you find yourself going a strange way round to drop one of the passengers off at home. If you tell the driver your destination as you enter, they'll drop you off where you're staying. Most stop at about 9pm, but the purple ones carry on for another hour or so, and the light blue service runs 24 hours a day.

In addition, there are plenty of easily identified metered **taxis**; fares across the city rarely run to more than Rp15,000. Be firm with drivers about using the meter before you get in – they prefer to try to negotiate a (high) price with you beforehand.

Useful bemos

Purple Between Pasar Bawah and Sukaraja terminal via Jalan Randen Intan, Jalan Diponegoro, Jalan Salim Batubara (or Jalan Hassanudin), the southern end of Jalan K.H.A. Dahlan and Jalan Yos Sudarso. Coming back up, they run along Jalan Yos Sudarso, Jalan Malahayat, up Jalan Ikan Tenggiri, Jalan Pattimura, Jalan Diponegoro, Jalan A. Yani, Jalan Kartini and around to Pasar Bawah.
Light blue Between Rajabasa terminal and Pasar Bawah.
Orange Between Sukaraja and Panjang terminals.
Green Between Pasar Bawah and Garuntang (Jalan Jend Gatot Subroto), via Jalan Sudirman and Jalan K.H.A. Dahlan, which is useful for the post office, wartel and tourist information. This is one of the most wayward of all bemos, taking just about any route through the area bounded by Jalan Dr. Susilo and Jalan Sudirman.
Dark red Between Tanjung Karang Plaza (at the junction of Jalan Agus Salim and Jalan Kartini) and Kemiling (Langka Pura), on the western edge of the city.
Grey – Parar Bawah and Sukarame on the eastern edge of the city.

Accommodation

Although Bandar Lampung has a range of pleasant mid- to top-range hotels, offering good-value **accommodation**, the situation is grim if you're on a very tight budget. You have the choice of paying mid-range prices and not getting your own bathroom, or – if you pay any less – putting up with absolute squalor. In general, the north of the city offers less amenable surroundings than the south. In particular, the area around Pasar Bawah, while simply noisy during the day, becomes a night-time haunt for pimps. If you're strapped for cash, the best thing to do is to stay at Kalianda (see p.513), coming to the city on day-trips or to make onward connections.

Inexpensive

Andalas Jl Raden Intan 89 ⓣ0721/263432, ⓕ261481. Good-value, centrally located hotel, with a decent range of pleasant rooms, all with air-con and hot water. ❸

Gading Jl Kartini 72 ⓣ0721/255512. Situated on a quiet alleyway in a busy area, conveniently near the market area and a short walk from the bus route from Rajabasa. A large hotel, offering a variety of rooms. ❸

Losmen Gunung Sari Jalan Kotaraja ⓣ0721/240189. Extremely inexpensive and filthy, but you'll survive the night if you bring your own insect repellant – and they do clean the sheets. If they're full and recommend *Renny*, up a nearby alley, it's only worth the trip to satisfy morbid curiosity: the alley itself is more comfortable. ❶

Kurnia Dua Jl Raden Intan 75 ⓣ0721/252905, ⓕ262924. Accessible from Rajabasa terminal on the DAMRI bus, this utilitarian concrete hotel has little character, but is large and popular with Indonesian travellers, offering plenty of options, from basic rooms without mandi through to those with mandi and air-con. ❷–❸

Kurnia Perdana Jl Raden Intan 114 ⓣ0721/262030, ⓕ262924. A small, friendly and pleasant setup, close to *Kurnia Dua*. All rooms have air-con, bathroom and colour TV; the more expensive rooms also have hot water, and the price includes breakfast. ❸

Lusy Jl Diponegoro 186 ⓣ0721/485695. Situated about 1km from the large Jalan Dr Susilo junction; Karang–Betung buses and purple bemos pass the door. The accommodation is very basic, but it's clean, and all rooms have attached mandi, while some have fans or air-con. The ones at the front are noisy, but the generally poor quality of Bandar Lampung's budget places make this a good option – it's the only really inexpensive place that isn't filthy. ❷–❸

Mini 1 Jl Dwi Warna 71 ⓣ0721/2555928. A small hotel in a quiet alley off Jalan Kartini, opposite *Hotel Gading*. The rooms are clean and basic, with attached mandi, but no frills. ❸

Purnama Jl Randen Intan 77–79 ⓣ0721/251447. Hotel built around a dusty courtyard, offering air-con en-suite rooms, some with hot water. Not bad value, considering the competition. ❸

Tambakaya Jalan Imam Bonjol, Gang Beringin 60 (no phone). Tucked away behind Jalan Imam Bonjol. Basic but adequate small rooms with shared bathroom. ❷

Mid-range and expensive

Indra Puri Jl Wolter Moginsidi 70 ⓣ0721/258258, ⓕ262440. A luxury hotel perched high on a hill, it's very comfortable, though without the exclusivity of the *Sheraton*. Look out for the special deals that they offer from time to time. ❼

Marcopolo Jl Dr Susilo 4 ⓣ0721/262511, ⓕ254419. Whilst there's no public transport past the hotel, *Marcopolo* is only 200m from the junction of Jalan Dr Susilo and Jalan Diponegoro, where Karang–Betung buses pass. All rooms have hot water, air-con and TV. The hotel has three swimming pools, including an Olympic-sized main pool and a great terrace restaurant/bar with excellent views across Lampung Bay. The less expensive rooms are extremely good value. ❹–❺

Rarem Jl Way Rarem 23 ⓣ261241, ⓕ262691. Tucked away behind Jalan K.H.A. Dahlan and on the green bemo route (either ask to be dropped off at the door, or get off at the junction of Jalan Dr Susilo and Jalan K.H.A. Dahlan), this small place is super-clean: even the shared bathrooms are pristine, with rooms with shared mandi up to those with private bath and air-con. The small garden is a haven of peace in the bustling city. ❸–❹

Sahid Bandar Lampung Jl Yos Sudarso 294 ⓣ0721/488888, ⓕ486589. One of the best hotels in town, the public areas are comfortable and relaxed and the rooms attractive. There's a 24hr coffee shop, with a range of moderate to expensive Western and Indonesian meals; the hotel has a small pool and is situated on an unremarkable beach 1km east of Sukaraja terminal; the sea-view rooms have a good panorama of Lampung Bay. ❻

Sheraton Jl Wolter Moginsidi 175 ⓣ0721/486666, ⓕ486690. The most luxurious and expensive hotel in town, inconveniently located on the western outskirts; public transport doesn't pass by. There's a small and attractive pool, fitness centre, business centre and tennis courts, while communal areas are luxurious but with a relaxed atmosphere. The rooms are at the standard you'd expect from this international chain. ❼–❽

The City

Perhaps the most thought-provoking (although unimpressive in itself) thing to see in Bandar Lampung is the **Krakatau Monument**, located in a small park on Jalan Veteran, a steep ten-minute climb from the waterfront at Teluk Betung. The monument is a huge metal buoy, washed up here from Lampung Bay in 1883 by the tidal waves following the eruption of Krakatau, which killed over 35,000 people on both sides of the straits (see p.138).

Southeast of the monument on Jalan Ikan Kakap is Thay Hin Bio, a wonderfully atmospheric **Chinese temple**. To get here from the monument, head south along Jalan Ikan Tenggiri, and Jalan Ikan Kakap goes off to the left; buses heading up to Tanjung Karang from Teluk Betung pass along here. Worshippers make offerings and pray here, and the ornate statues and red-and-gold decorations are enclosed in swirls of smoke from burning incense. You're welcome to buy a pack of incense and printed prayers for offerings, and local people will show you where to place each item. A great way to catch a glimpse of local life is to wander the streets just north of the temple; a maze of alleys too narrow for cars extends up the hill, bisected by many sets of stairs. It's also worth walking all the way down Jalan Ikan Tenggiri as it gradually changes from a road, to a track, and finally to a boardwalk. At the end, the fishing boats unload their catch and haggle energetically with the market vendors.

Several kilometres north of the water, Tanjung Karang offers brilliant views of the whole city. One of the easiest vantage points is the top of **Bukit Randu**, about 1km to the east of Jalan Raden Intan, and the view is worth the hike. If you don't want to use the pricey restaurant near the top, just keep walking up between the various buildings to the lookout spot on the summit.

The **Museum Negeri Propinsi Lampung**, Jl Abdin Pagar Alam 64 (Tues–Thurs 8am–1.30pm, Fri 8–10.30am, Sat & Sun 8am–noon; Rp500), lies 1km south of Rajabasa terminal, in a huge traditional building set back from the road behind a car park. There's a good collection of artefacts, including drums, kris, statues, jewellery and masks, plus some megalithic figures, mostly reproductions of items found at Pugung Raharjo (see p.510). Some of the large traditional baskets, up to 1m tall, are very impressive. Unfortunately, only with the textiles has any attempt been made at English labelling, and even that is very cursory. There are some good items here, but, given Lampung's rich textile heritage, it's not a significant or educational collection.

Eating

There's a great variety of places to eat in Bandar Lampung, the highlight being a visit to Pasar Mambo, the **night market**, at the southern end of Jalan Hassanudin, which operates from dusk until about 11pm. The range of food on sale is huge, and each stall has its own set of tables. Chinese and seafood stalls are a speciality; the more exotic fare such as prawns and crabs can be pricey. There are also plenty of stalls in the market selling sweets and ices: *Es John Lenon* is one. For fast food, there's a *KFC* upstairs at Gelael supermarket, Jl Sudirman 11–15 and Jl Pangkhal Pinang 18; the air-con is a life-saver on a hot day.

Bukit Randu Perched on top of the hill of the same name. This place transforms into a restaurant in the evenings, which is so extensive that there's an information booth at the entrance. The main options are a couple of large dining rooms or individual pavilions in the garden, with panoramic views of the city and Lampung Bay. It's about 1km off Jalan Raden Intan, and you'll need transport to get here – unless you want to work up a real appetite.

East Garden Jl Diponegoro 106. An excellent and very wide-ranging Chinese/Indonesian place, with lots of *tauhu* (tofu) and tempeh dishes as well as soups, noodles, seafood and many iced fruit juices. Clean, inexpensive and excellent value – they've even got a takeaway.

European Bakery Jl Raden Intan 35a. This standard bakery offers an extremely good range of moderately priced sweet breads and cakes, which you can either eat in or take away.

Garuda Jl Kartini 31. Just north of Tanjung Karang Plaza, this is a central and convenient branch of a popular chain, serving all the Indonesian staples at moderate prices in relaxed surroundings.

Gembira Jl Pangkhal Pinang 20. Next door to *KFC*, in a street with plenty of good *mie ayam* places, the inexpensive and popular *Gembira* offers a huge range of local dishes, including *pempek*, soups, chicken dishes and ice confections.

Kebun Raya At the *Sheraton Hotel*. This is the place for a real splurge, although you can enjoy the luxurious surroundings and seamless service by ordering nasi goreng at Rp20,000.

Marcopolo Restaurant At the *Marcopolo Hotel*. The room inside is plain and uninspiring, but the outside terrace, with a fantastic view over the entire city and out into Lampung Bay, makes this a great place for a meal or just a drink. Western, Chinese and Indonesian food ranges from rice and noodle dishes at Rp10,000, up to pepper steak at Rp40,000.

Moro Seneng Jl Diponegoro 38. You can eat in basic style at the front or in the garden at the back; they offer good-value Indonesian and Chinese food such as nasi and mie dishes at Rp6000, up to shrimp, *gurame* and squid at Rp20,000.

Pemplek 56 Jl Salim Batubara 56. Just one of a huge range of *pempek* places along this road; they are named by the number on the street, and all serve inexpensive *pempek*, the grilled or fried Palembang speciality of balls made from sago, fish and flavourings, which are dished up with a variety of sauces.

Pizza Hut Jalan Raden Intan, next to *Kurnia Dua* hotel. Part of the popular chain, with all the usual for homesick travellers and anglophile locals.

Nightlife

If you want to join the jet-setters, the **bar** at the *Sheraton Hotel* is fairly lively. At over Rp1,000,000 for a bottle of champagne (plus tax and service), you'll need to be fairly well heeled, although less exotic drinks come at Rp9000–11,000; get there between 5 and 8pm for happy hour. The **disco** area of town is Jalan Yos Sudarso; at the time of writing, *Oya* (9pm–2pm; Rp15,000), about 500m east of the Sukaraja terminal, was the favourite, but check locally for up-to-date information, as the Indonesian disco scene changes fast.

Shopping

While hardly a mecca for shoppers, Bandar Lampung is a good place to stock up on necessities if you're heading off the beaten track in Sumatra. **Pasar Bawah**, at the top end of Jalan Raden Intan, just south of the train station, is a maze of stalls piled high with fruit and vegetables, as well as mountains of household goods. A massive Matahari department store is being developed nearby, so the future of the market is uncertain. At the northern end of Jalan Kartini, **Bundo Kanding Plaza** is a traditional market now housed in a concrete box: this is the place for clothing, bags, make-up, toys and household stuff. There are also some good **textile shops**, both for the local speciality, *kain tapis*, and for imports of batik from Java. If you need postcards, stock up here; the nearest ones to the north are in Bukittinggi. The most extensive **bookshop** is **Gramedia**, Jl Raden Intan 63, which sells postcards, a good range of dictionaries, and the English-language *Jakarta Post* newspaper.

Shopping centres, department stores and supermarkets

The **Gelael supermarket**, Jl Sudirman 11–15, supplies extremely expensive fresh fish, meat, fruit and vegetables and all the items that the affluent Indonesian middle-classes require, such as cheeses, cornflakes, and canned soups. The **King's department stores** (Jl Raden Intan 73, Jl Let Jend Suprapto 138 and Jl Ikan Hiu 1a) have supermarkets attached, selling a small range of souvenirs including *songket* purses and wall hangings and postcards. The newest **shopping centre** is Tanjung Karang Plaza, Jl Kartini 21, with an Artomoro department store, supermarket, and several fast-food places plus a host of small shops.

Textiles and souvenirs

Batik Galeri In the Tanjung Karang Plaza. Offers a range of cotton sarong lengths at Rp75,000, and also some glorious, but pricey, silk.

Batik Indonesia Jl Dwi Warna 1, opposite the main Telkom office. They stock an excellent range of *kain tapis*, but expect to start negotiating at Rp60,000 for a 100cm by 70cm hanging, and also the more demure *tenung Lampung*, an *ikat* weave, at around Rp15,000 per metre. Smaller items such as purses and bags are also on sale from Rp10,000.

Mulya Jl Pemuda 2. A good range of Javanese batik, with prices from Rp18,000.

Mulya Sari Lampung Collection Jl M.H. Thamrin 79. At the Jalan Wolter Moginsidi end of the road, this shop sells top-quality goods and asks high prices for old and new textiles. There's a great selection, but staff think nothing of quoting Rp10 million for a 4m by 50cm panel.

Odi Gallery Jl S. Parman 4b. Not far from Jalan Kartini, this gallery sells fabulous modern, locally made pottery in great contemporary shapes from Rp20,000, and ironwork stands to go with it.

Putra Indonesia Jl S. Parman 37. Midway between Jalan Kartini and Jalan Raden Intan. They have an excellent and extensive selection of textiles and fabric items, including cotton bags and *songket* at about Rp40,000 and small panels of *kain tapis* from Rp35,000.

Ruwajurai Jl Imam Bonjol 34. Opposite Bundo Kanding Plaza, Ruwajurai has a huge range of textiles including *kain tapis*, with negotiations for smaller items (20cm by 30cm) starting at Rp30,000, up to Rp1,000,000 for one-metre panels.

Listings

Airline offices Merpati, Jl Diponegoro 189 ⓣ0721/268486, ⓕ268467.

Banks and exchange BCA, Jl Yos Sudarso 100; BRI, Jalan Raden Intan.

Car rental Enquire at your hotel or at the travel agents in town. Expect to pay Rp250,000 per day for an air-con Kijang with or without driver. If you rent a taxi by the day, you should be able to get a basic saloon without air-con for Rp150,000 per day.

Cinema There are three screens on the top floor of the Tanjung Karang Plaza, Jalan Kartini, showing English language films.

Hospital Rumah Sakit Bumi Waras, Jalan Wolter

Moginsidi ⓣ0721/255032; Rumah Sakit Immanuel Way Halim, Jalan Sukarno Hatta B ⓣ0721/704900; Rumah Sakit Abdul Muluk, Jalan Kapten Rivai ⓣ0721/703312.
Immigration office Jalan Diponegoro 24 ⓣ0721/482607 or 481697.
Internet access There are only a few outlets in town. The warnet at the post office (open until 6pm) is basic but functional; there's another just south of *East Garden* restaurant on Jalan Diponegoro.
Pelni The office is at Panjang harbour (near the terminal) on Jl Sumatera 70 ⓣ0721/31732.
Pharmacies There are plenty of pharmacies on Jalan Raden Intan, one of the larger ones being Enggal, Jl Raden Intan 122, just south of the *Kurnia Perdana Hotel.*
Post office Jl K. H. A. Dahlan 21.
Telephone and fax The main Telkom office is at Jl Kartini 1 and there's also a 24hr wartel at Jl Majapahit 14, one of many in town.
Tour operators Elendra, Jl Sultan Agung 32 ⓣ & ⓕ0721/704737; Krakatoa Lampung Wisata, next to the *Sheraton Hotel* ⓣ & ⓕ0721/263625. Both offer day-trips to Way Kambas (US$61), Way Kanan (US$99), Pugung Raharjo (US$40) and Merak Blantung (US$60), plus a two-day trip to Krakatau (US$150). All prices are per person, and a minimum number of people (usually two) will be required.

Around Bandar Lampung

About 8km from Panjang terminal, on the southeast edge of Bandar Lampung, **Pasir Putih beach** is easily accessible from the city on any of the public transport plying from Panjang towards Bakauheni. It's not the most glorious beach in the world – being within sight and smell of the nearby factories. However, you can arrange a charter from here to some worthwhile offshore islands, and the *bagan* (floating fishing nets) just offshore are picturesque. **Pulau Condong**, about 3km from the beach, is actually three islands. The most attractive of the three is Pulau Bule ("Albino Island") – possibly named after the sands or the foreigners who frolic here – which has excellent white-sand beaches and some offshore coral. It's totally undeveloped, so you'll need to take all your food and water, plus snorkelling gear. Bargain for around Rp35,000 for the return boat trip, fifteen minutes each way, and don't forget to tell the boatman the pick-up time.

An excursion along the western edge of Lampung Bay towards **Padang Cermin** makes for a good day out, with the road clinging to the rocky shoreline along tiny coves, through small villages and with great views of the bay itself across towards Kalianda and back to Bandar Lampung. Bemos and minibuses operate from Jalan Ikan Bawal, near the *Hotel Sriwijaya*. Seven kilometres south from Bandar Lampung, the small village of Lampasing is the scene of daily fish auctions (4–5pm), which you can catch on the return journey. At Gunung Betung there's a forestry office and small **camping** ground with great views of the area, and at Ketapang, a small fishing village 32km from Bandar Lampung, you can charter a boat for a half- or full-day trip to the white beaches of **Pulau Legundi** out to the south on the way to Krakatau. It's a two-hour trip in each direction and you can expect to pay around Rp100,000 for the day. There's little to see once you arrive at Padang Cermin – it's a small town – but you catch return transport here.

The remains at **Pugung Raharjo**, 42km east of the city, are said to date from the twelfth to the seventeenth century, with megalithic standing stones, stepped temple mounds, and ramparts and ditches providing evidence of a fortified village. Local legend claims that water from the spring has magical properties and can restore youth. Set in amongst local crops and spread over quite a large area, there isn't much here for the casual visitor, although enthusiasts may appreciate the small **museum**, which houses inscribed stones and statues found on the site. Explorations only began about 45 years ago, when transmigrants to the area began discovering remains and relics as they cleared their land. It's accessible by public transport from Panjang terminal; take a bus towards Sribawono, and the site is 2km to the north of the main road at Jabung. If you have your own transport, it's worth combining this trip with a visit to Way Kambas national park.

Way Kambas national park

If the southern tip of Sumatra is famous for anything, it's for the **Way Kambas national park**, and in particular the **Elephant Training Centre** there. The park consists entirely of lowland, never rising more than 100m above sea level, but has a variety of ecosystems including freshwater swamp, forest, grassy plains and coastal and riverine systems. It has been designated as a protected area for over 75 years, but has unfortunately been extensively logged, so that only around a fifth of the original forest remains.

The park's inhabitants include Sumatran elephants (there are thought to be about 300 living in the park, including those at the training centre), rhinos, leopards and tapirs, several varieties of primate, honey bears, deer, tree cat and wild pig. Reptiles include monitor lizards and crocodiles, and 286 species of birds have been sighted. Serious birdwatchers visit the park as one of the best places to spot the **white-winged duck** and **Storm's stork**, both of which are endangered species and very rare. There are thought to be only about 250 white-winged duck throughout Southeast Asia, and thirty or so of them in Way Kambas national park; some have favourite spots close to the accommodation at *Way Kanan*. The dry season, from June to November, is the most comfortable visiting time, and you're likely to see kingfishers, fish eagles, adjutants, leafbirds, bulbuls and sunbirds.

Practicalities

The problem for visitors is that Way Kambas is rather difficult to get to, and getting around once you're there is no easier. No vehicles are allowed in the park, so you'll either need your own vehicle (see p.509) or rely on **ojek** that operate (for hefty fees) within the park. Many people choose to visit on a **day-trip** from Bandar Lampung that centres on the Elephant Training Centre; however, this means you lose the opportunity to see the wilder parts of the park. To appreciate the area properly you should stay in the park itself (for tour operators, see "Listings" opposite).

To reach the park from Bandar Lampung, take a minibus from Panjang terminal to Rajabasalama, a small village 10km north of Way Jepara. The access road into the park leads off the main road from the junction here. The national park office (Balai Taman Nasional Way Kambas) itself is in Rajabasalama and you'll need to buy a **permit** (Rp1750 per person per day). Once inside, expect to pay the waiting ojek Rp7500–10,000 for the one-way trip from here to the Elephant Training Centre, and at least fifty percent more to the accommodation at *Way Kanan*. You'll also need to arrange a time to be collected.

There are two main routes from the park entrance, one leading 9km to the Elephant Training Centre at Karang Sari, the other 13km to *Way Kanan Resort* for extremely basic **accommodation** (Rp40,000); you need to take cooked food or food and a stove. From *Way Kanan*, it's possible to arrange trips on Sungai Way Kanan (2hr; Rp25,000) and **jungle treks** (park guides cost about Rp15,000 per day).

The park

The **Elephant Training Centre** (daily 8am–4pm) opened in 1985 and is one of the largest of such operations in Southeast Asia. It was created as the solution to the wild elephant problem of the region; since the 1960s, much of the forest had been cleared for plantations and settlements and the displaced elephants were a constant nuisance and danger to new settlers, attacking crops and, in some cases, homes. As a protected species, the elephants were legally immune from retribution, so, with the help of Thai elephants and their trainers, a programme was set up to train them to operate within the tourist industry rather than become prey to illegal poaching and revenge by angry villagers. You can see the elephants in **training** (Mon–Sat 8–10am & 3–4pm) or see the Sunday **display** put on for tourists (11.30am & 1.30pm), when the elephants demonstrate football, counting and other tricks. Rides are Rp20,000 per half hour, or you can just climb on for a minute for Rp2500.

Way Kambas is currently the site of a controversial and extremely expensive scheme to create a breeding and ecotourism reserve for the **Sumatran rhinoceros.** A few rhinos have been repatriated here from zoos around the world where they have failed to breed, in the hope that in larger numbers and in more natural surroundings they will reproduce successfully. Currently being financed by Indonesian and international funds, the plan is that the centre should become self-financing from tourist income generated by elephant-back safaris through part of the park.

Kota Agung and the Bukit Barisan Selatan national park

The deeply indented coastline to the west of Bandar Lampung is generally ignored by tourists. Yet the areas around Lampung Bay and the more westerly Semanka Bay are hugely attractive, as the Bukit Barisan Mountain range reaches its southern extremity at the Indian Ocean, with rolling, mist-covered hills and forests rising from shimmering waters dotted with myriad tiny islands. Access to the **Bukit Barisan Selatan national park** is from **Kota Agung**, a small coastal town 80km west of Bandar Lampung.

Kota Agung

The quiet, attractive town of **KOTA AGUNG** is a pleasant destination in its own right, even if you don't want to go to the national park. The streets are wide, life is slow and there's little to race around for, although the port area is busy and bustling with fishing boats and ships unloading. The town has all the facilities you need: the **post office** is at Jalan Bhayang Kara, while the 24-hour Telkom office is an inconvenient 3km outside town on the Bandar Lampung road. The wartel at Jl Merdeka 86 (5.30am–11.30pm) is more central, opposite the bus terminal. The Bukit Barisan **national park office** (Mon–Fri 7am–3pm; ⓣ0722/21064) is at Jalan Raya Terbaya (also known as Jalan Juanda).

The best-value **accommodation** option is the *Setia Hotel*, Jl Samudra 294 (ⓣ0722/21065; ❸), which offers basic but clean rooms, some with attached mandi. From the bus terminal, walk down the road that runs along the left side of the wartel; after 200m, *Setia Hotel* will be facing you. Three hundred metres closer to the sea is *KS*, Jl Samudra 90 (no phone; ❷), whose rooms are similar although none has attached mandi.

The Bukit Barisan Selatan national park

Consisting of the entire southwest finger of land pointing into the Indian Ocean, the **Bukit Barisan Selatan national park** (South Bukit Barisan national park) stretches from Cape Rata and Cape Cina in the south to the area northwest of Danau Ranau. Covering 3568 square kilometres, it's home to elephants, tigers, bears, rhinos, crocodiles, the Sumatran mountain goat, the slow loris, hornbills and argus pheasants, among many other species. The floral highlights are orchids, rafflesia and the world's tallest flower, *Amorphophallus titanum*. **Permits** (Rp2500) are available at the national park office in Kota Agung (see above).

Alternative access to the park is from **Sukaraja**, 20km west of Kota Agung, where there's a camping ground – refreshingly cool at 560m above sea level, with some good views of Semanka Bay. Sukaraja is accessible by local bus from Kota Agung to Sedatu and then ojek, and national park guides can advise on treks in that area. It's possible to see rafflesia around here between June and October. The **Danau Suwoh** area is another possible destination, but access is difficult: four hours by ojek from Kota Agung up an atrocious track to a camping ground in an area that is actually made up of four lakes: Asam Besak is the largest, and the others are Lebar, Minyak and Belibis. Access to the **northern parts** of the park is via the PHPA post at Liwa.

Trekking in the park

There are various routes into the park, one of the most interesting being a **four-day trek** across the southern tip. You'll need to contract a **guide** – enquire at the national park office in Kota Agung. Expect to pay a national park guide about Rp40,000 a day, plus expenses; you'll need to discuss with him what supplies to take. Day one involves a five-hour scheduled boat service from Kota Agung to Tampang on the southern edge of Semanka Bay. Day two is an eight- or nine-hour trek through the lowland tropical rainforest, crossing the south-flowing Blambangan and Seleman rivers on the way, over to the west coast at the village of Belimbing, situated on a beautiful bay backed by beach forest including Australian pine. Day three is a walk back to Tampang via the coast. Wild buffalo roam between the mouths of the two rivers, and it's possible to spot turtles here: green turtles, hawksbill turtles and leatherback turtles are all known in the park. You'll also pass Danau Menjukut, a naturally dammed lake of brackish water just behind the coast, and home to various water birds and waders such as wild ducks, egrets and kingfishers. Somewhat perversely, the water level is lower in the rainy season, as the heavy rain breaks the natural dam between the lake and the ocean. The trek from Tampang to the lake takes four hours one-way, so it's a possible destination for a shorter trek if you don't want to do the whole thing. Day four is back from Tampang to Kota Agung. An alternative return route from Belimbing is to head north to Ngaras (there are a lot of river crossings, so this isn't a trip for the rainy season), and from there pick up public transport to Krui (see p.501).

Kalianda

Situated just under 60km southeast of Bandar Lampung, the small coastal town of **KALIANDA** is a great alternative to the hassle and expense of the city, and an excellent stopping-off point whether you're entering or leaving Sumatra. It's served by public transport from the Bakauheni ferry terminal and from the Panjang and Rajabasa terminals in Bandar Lampung. Public transport in Kalianda arrives at Terminal Pasar Impress in front of the main market; wander the alleyways here to enjoy the sights, sounds and smells.

The best travellers' **accommodation** is in the *Beringin Hotel*, Jl Kesuma Bangsa 75 (Ⓣ0727/2008; ❷), in a large, colonial-style bungalow with big rooms, an airy lounge and a garden at the back. You'll get your own mandi, plus nasi goreng in the morning, so it's excellent value. To get here from the terminal, go back onto the main road, turn right and continue for about 400m to a junction where a large road, Jalan Kesuma Bangsa, joins from the right; head down here past the local school, and the hotel is at the far end on the left. Alternatively, engage one of the many ojek that hang around the terminal, and cruise around town.

The **post office** is at Jalan Pratu M. Yusuf and the **telephone office** on the main street is open 7am to midnight. The main shopping street where you'll find most necessities is Jalan Serma Ibnu Hasyim, a short walk from the *Beringin Hotel*. There are several basic local **restaurants** in town.

There's little to do here, although the local **beach** is pleasant and there's a small **Chinese temple** near the post office. The *Beringin Hotel* can advise you on or organize **excursions** further afield, including a two-day trip to **Krakatau** (about Rp85,000 per person), overnighting on Pulau Sebesi. You can also visit Kahai and the nearby islands, as well as Bandar Lampung and local Balinese villages, complete with traditional Balinese house compounds and temples.

Around Kalianda

The small semicircular white-sand beach at **Merak Belantung**, 10km north of Kalianda, lies 2–3km from the main Bandar Lampung–Bakauheni road; there's a huge sign pointing the way, and bus conductors and bemo drivers know it well. Plenty of ojek wait at the turning to take you down there. Entrance to the beach area costs Rp1500 at the weekend and Rp1000 on weekdays, when you'll pretty much have the place to yourself. The beach is a little dirty, but there are good views back to Bandar Lampung and out to Sebesi and Sebuku, and even Krakatau on a clear day. There's basic **accommodation** on the beach in brick-and-thatch cottages with a tiny verandah and small attached mandi at *Merak Blantung Cottages* (no phone; ❸), with electricity from 5pm but no fans. During the week, you'll need to make arrangements about food with the cottages, as there's nothing nearby, but at weekends, hosts of warung set up near the beach for day-trippers.

Around 30km south of Kalianda, the ferry terminal between Sumatra and Java lies at **Bakauheni**. There's no reason to stay in Bakauheni; arriving at any time of the day or night, there are buses to Rajabasa terminal and Panjang terminal in Bandar Lampung, bemos to Kalianda and other local villages, and taxis to Bandar Lampung. There's also a 24hr wartel and a couple of shops. For details of ferries from Bakauheni, see box on p.505.

Travel details

Buses

Bandar Lampung to: Bakauheni (every 30min; 2–3hr); Banda Aceh (3 daily; 3 days); Bengkulu (5 daily; 15hr); Bukittinggi (6 daily; 24hr); Denpasar (4 daily; 48hr); Dumai (4 daily; 25hr); Jakarta (20 daily; 8hr); Jambi (8 daily; 20hr); Kalianda (every 30min; 1–2hr); Kota Agung (every 30min; 2hr); Krui (4 daily; 8hr); Liwa (4 daily; 6hr); Medan (12 daily; 48hr); Padang (6 daily; 24hr); Palembang (10 daily; 8hr); Pekanbaru (6 daily; 24hr); Parapet (10 daily; 48hr); Yogyakarta (20 daily; 24hr).

Banding Agung (Danau Ranau) to: Bandar Lampung (daily; 6hr); Jakarta (daily; 14hr); Palembang (daily; 8–10hr).

Bengkulu to: Bandar Lampung (7 daily; 15hr); Curup (10 daily; 3hr); Denpasar (daily; 3 days); Dumai (5 daily; 20hr); Jakarta (daily; 24hr); Jambi (5 daily; 10hr); Krui (2 daily; 10hr); Lahat (4 daily; 7hr); Lubuklinggau (10 daily; 6hr); Medan via

Parapet and Danau Toba (2 daily; 48hr); Pagaralam (4 daily; 7hr); Palembang (5 daily; 18hr); Pekanbaru (5 daily; 20hr); Probolinggo (daily; 48hr); Solo (daily; 2 days); Yogyakarta (daily; 48hr).
Kotabatu (Danau Ranau) to: Bandar Lampung (daily; 6hr); Jakarta (daily; 14hr); Liwa (every 2hr; 1hr); Palembang (daily; 8–10hr).
Krui to: Bandar Lampung (4 daily; 7hr); Bengkulu (2 daily; 10hr); Bukit Kemuning (hourly; 2–3hr); Liwa (every 30min; 45min); Ngaras (daily; 3hr).
Lahat to: Bandar Lampung (4 daily; 8hr); Baturaja (4 daily; 4hr); Bengkulu (4 daily; 7hr); Jakarta (3 daily; 14hr); Palembang (10 daily; 5hr).
Pagaralam to: Bandar Lampung (2 daily; 8hr); Bengkulu (4 daily; 6hr); Jakarta (2 daily; 20hr); Lahat (10 daily; 2hr); Palembang (6 daily; 5hr).
Palembang to: Bandar Lampung (10 daily; 8hr); Bengkulu (5 daily; 12hr); Bukittinggi (10 daily; 18hr); Denpasar (10 daily; 48hr); Jakarta (12 daily; 18–20hr); Jambi (10 daily; 8hr); Medan (10 daily; 40–55hr); Padang (10 daily; 18hr); Pekanbaru (20 daily; 15–18hr); Simpangsender (daily; 8hr); Yogyakarta (10 daily; 48hr).
Simpangsender (Danau Ranau) to: Bandar Lampung (2 daily; 6hr); Baturaja (hourly; 3–4hr); Jakarta (2 daily; 14hr); Liwa (every 2hr; 1hr); Palembang (daily; 8hr).

Trains

Bandar Lampung to: Palembang via Kotabumi, Martapura, Baturaja and Prabamulih (3 daily; 6–8hr).
Lahat to: Lubuklinggau (3 daily; 4hr); Palembang (2 daily; 5hr).
Lubuklinggau to: Palembang via Tebintinngi, Lahat, Muaraenam and Prabamulih (3 daily; 6–8hr).
Palembang to: Bandar Lampung, via Prabamulih, Baturaja, Martapura and Kotabumi (3 daily; 6–8hr); Lubuklinggau via Prabamulih, Muaraenam, Lahat and Tebintinngi (3 daily; 6–9hr).

Pelni ferries

For a chart of the Pelni routes, see p.42.
Muntok to: Tanjung Balai (*KM Sirimau*, fortnightly; 26hr); Tanjung Priok (*KM Sirimau*, fortnightly; 20hr).
Tanjung Pandan to: Cirebon (*KM Lawit*, fortnightly; 48hr); Kumai (*KM Lawit*, fortnightly; 3 days); Pontianak (*KM Lawit*, weekly; 15hr/*KM Tilongkabila*, fortnightly; 16hr); Semarang (*KM Lawit*, fortnightly; 28hr/*KM Tilongkabila*, fortnightly; 48hr); Tanjung Priok (*KM Lawit*, weekly; 17hr/*KM Tilongkabila*, fortnightly; 14hr).

Other ferries

Bakauheni to: Merak (every 20min; 40min–2hr).
Bandar Lampung (Sukaraja) to: Merak (5 daily; 90min).
Bengkulu to: Enggano (3 weekly; 12hr).
Mentok (Pulau Bangka) to: Palembang (hydrofoil 3 daily; 4hr)
Palembang to: Mentok (Pulau Bangka) (hydrofoil 4 daily; 2–3hr; ferry 3 weekly; 11hr).
Pangkal Pinang to: Tanjung Balai on Pulau Batam (daily; 10hr); Tanjung Pandan on Pulau Belitung (daily; 4hr).
Pangkal Balam to: Tanjung Pandan on Pulau Belitung (jet foil daily; 4hr, Jakarta (weekly; 8hr).
Tanjung Pandan (Pulau Belitung) to: Pangkal Balam (Pulau Bangka) (jet foil daily; 4hr; ferry 2 weekly; 12hr).

Flights

Bandar Lampung to: Jakarta (6 daily; 55min); Palembang (weekly; 1hr 5min).
Bengkulu to: Jakarta (2 daily; 1hr 10min); Palembang (5 weekly; 1hr 15min).
Palembang to: Balikpapan via Jakarta (daily; 5hr); Bandar Lampung (weekly; 1hr 5min); Bandung (3 weekly; 50min); Batam (10 weekly; 1hr 5min–1hr 35min); Bengkulu (5 weekly; 1hr 15min); Denpasar via Jakarta (5 daily; 4hr 30min); Jakarta (12 daily; 1hr 5min); Johor Bahru (4 weekly; 55min); Kuala Lumpur (4 weekly; 2hr 50min); Padang (daily; 1hr); Pangkalpinang (2 daily; 50min); Semarang (3 daily; 2hr 40min); Singapore (3 weekly; 1hr 50min); Surabaya via Jakarta (5 daily; 40min); Tanjung Pandan (daily; 1hr 20min); Ujung Pandang via Jakarta (3 daily; 8hr); Yogyakarta via Jakarta (daily; 4hr 50min).
Pangkalpinang (Pulau Bangka) to: Batam (2 daily; 1hr 30min); Jakarta (2 daily; 1hr); Palembang (daily; 50min).
Tanjung Pandan (Pulau Belitung): Jakarta (5 weekly; 1hr); Palembang (11 weekly; 1hr 20min); Pangkalpinang (daily; 50min).

8

Bali

8
BALI

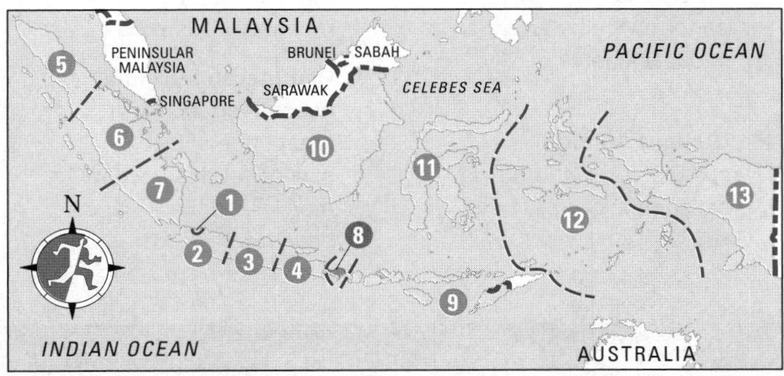
MALAYSIA
PENINSULAR MALAYSIA
BRUNEI
SABAH
SARAWAK
SINGAPORE
CELEBES SEA
PACIFIC OCEAN
N
INDIAN OCEAN
AUSTRALIA
1
2
3
4
5
6
7
8
9
10
11
12
13

CHAPTER 2

Highlights

* **Jimbaran beach barbeques** Fresh fish grilled over coconut husks and served at candlelit tables on the sand. **See p.550**
* **Neka Art Museum, Ubud** The island's most impressive art collection. **See p.575**
* **Kecak dance** Unforgettable torchlit performance by an *a cappella* chorus of fifty men. **See p.582**
* **Gunung Agung** The spiritual heart and physical summit of Bali. **See p.599**
* **Nusa Lembongan** Pretty, relaxed island with great beaches. **See p.601**
* **Lovina** Laid-back beach resort in the north. **See p.640**
* **Pura Luhur Batukau** One of Bali's most beautiful temples, secluded in the foothills of a sacred mountain. **See p.654**
* **Pemuteran** Delightful accommodation and great underwater scenery at this uncommercialized black-sand beach. **See p.661**

Bali

The island of **Bali** has long been the primary focus of Indonesia's flourishing tourist industry. The island is small (it extends less than 150km at its longest point), volcanic, and graced with swaths of extremely fertile land, much of it sculpted into terraced rice paddies. Sandy beaches punctuate the dramatically rugged coastline and world-class surf pounds the shoreline. Culturally, Bali is equally rewarding. It is the only **Hindu** society in Southeast Asia, and exuberant religious observance permeates every aspect of contemporary Balinese life.

The tiny island, with a population of three million, draws in more than one and a half million foreign visitors every year, plus around a million domestic tourists. As a result, it has become very much a mainstream destination, offering all the comforts and facilities expected by better-off tourists, and suffering the predictable problems of congestion, commercialization and breakneck Westernization. However, Bali's original charm is still very much in evidence, its stunning temples and spectacular festivals set off by the gorgeously lush landscape of the interior.

Bali's most famous resort is **Kuta** beach, a six-kilometre sweep of golden sand, whose international reputation as a hangout for weekending Australian surfers is enhanced by its numerous restaurants, bars, clubs and shops. Travellers seeking more relaxed alternatives generally head across the southern peninsula to **Sanur**, eastwards to peaceful **Candi Dasa**, north to the black, volcanic sands of **Lovina** or, increasingly, to the rapidly developing villages in the far east known collectively as **Amed**. Even quieter but more upmarket seaside options can be found at **Jimbaran** in the south and **Pemuteran** in the northwest. All these resorts make comfortable bases for **divers** and **snorkellers**, being within easy reach of the islands' fine reefs; Bali also boasts an unusually accessible wreck-dive. **Surfers** head for the famed south-coast swells, particularly around **Uluwatu**, and the offshore island breaks of **Nusa Lembongan**.

Despite the obvious attractions of the beach resorts, most visitors also venture inland to experience more traditional island life. The once-tiny village of **Ubud** has become a hugely popular cultural centre, a still charming but undeniably commercialized place, where traditional dances are staged every night of the week and the streets are full of arts and crafts galleries. In general, the villages are far more appealing than the towns, but Bali's capital, **Denpasar**, the ancient capital of **Klungkung** and the north-coast city of **Singaraja** are all worth a day-trip for their museums, markets and temples.

The island's other big draw is its proliferation of elegant Hindu **temples** – particularly the spectacular island temple of **Tanah Lot**, the extensive **Besakih**

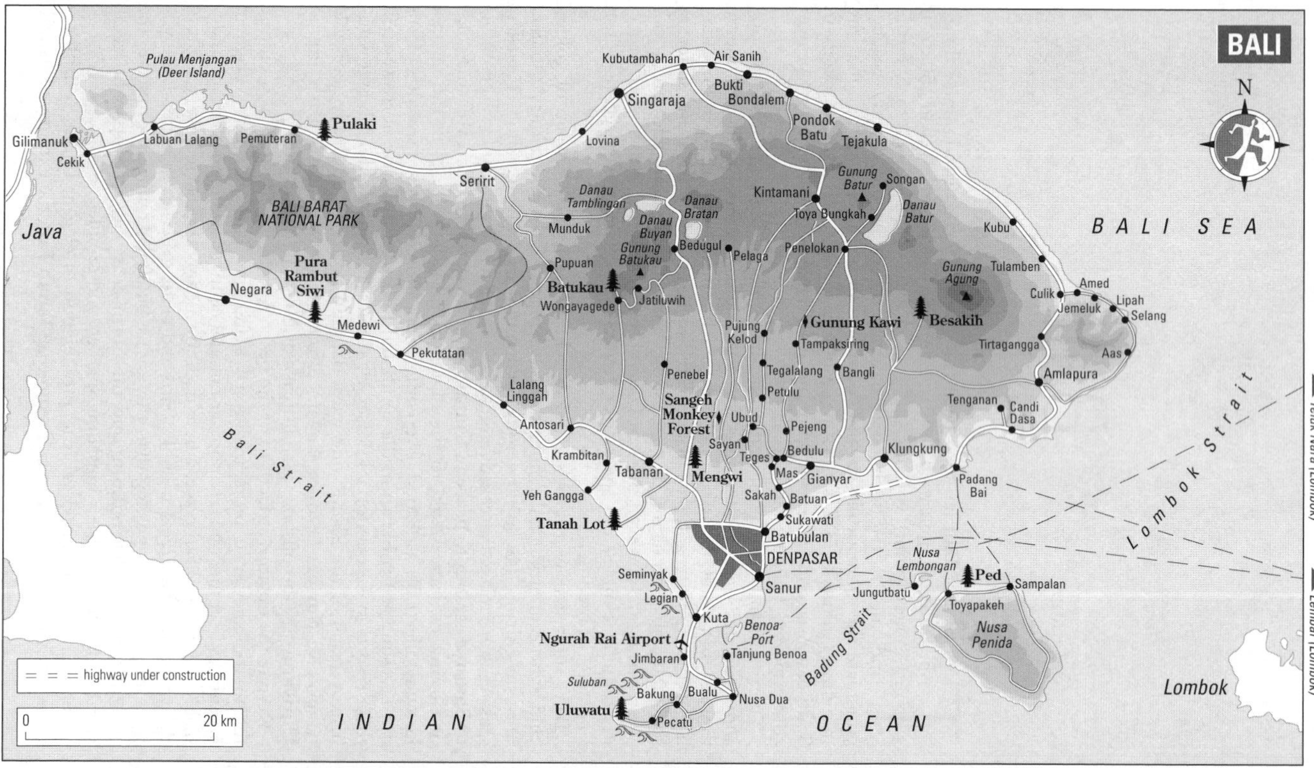
BALI
N
BALI SEA
Java
INDIAN OCEAN
Lombok
Bali Strait
Badung Strait
Lombok Strait
Teluk Nara (Lombok)
Lembar (Lombok)
Pulau Menjangan (Deer Island)
Gilimanuk
Cekik
Labuan Lalang
Pemuteran
Pulaki
BALI BARAT NATIONAL PARK
Negara
Pura Rambut Siwi
Medewi
Pekutatan
Seririt
Lovina
Singaraja
Kubutambahan
Air Sanih
Bukti
Bondalem
Pondok Batu
Tejakula
Kubu
Tulamben
Culik
Amed
Jemeluk
Lipah
Selang
Aas
Tirtagangga
Amlapura
Tenganan
Candi Dasa
Padang Bai
Klungkung
Gunung Agung
Besakih
Gunung Batur
Songan
Danau Batur
Kintamani
Toya Bungkah
Penelokan
Gunung Kawi
Tampaksiring
Bangli
Pujung Kelod
Tegalalang
Petulu
Pejeng
Bedulu
Ubud
Sayan
Teges
Mas
Gianyar
Sakah
Batuan
Sukawati
Batubulan
DENPASAR
Sanur
Danau Tamblingan
Danau Buyan
Danau Bratan
Munduk
Bedugul
Pelaga
Gunung Batukau
Pupuan
Batukau
Wongayagede
Jatiluwih
Penebel
Sangeh Monkey Forest
Mengwi
Lalang Linggah
Antosari
Krambitan
Tabanan
Yeh Gangga
Tanah Lot
Seminyak
Legian
Kuta
Ngurah Rai Airport
Jimbaran
Benoa Port
Tanjung Benoa
Suluban
Bakung
Bualu
Nusa Dua
Uluwatu
Pecatu
Nusa Lembongan
Jungutbatu
Ped
Sampalan
Toyapakeh
Nusa Penida
= = = highway under construction
0
20 km

complex on the slopes of Gunung Agung (if you can stand the hassles), and **Pura Luhur Lempuyang** in the far east. Temple festivals, held throughout the island and at frequent intervals during the year, are also well worth attending; most are open to tourists. There are also a number of hiking possibilities, many of them up **volcanoes**. The ascent to the summit of **Gunung Batur** is extremely popular, while **Gunung Agung** is for the very fit. Bali's sole national park, Bali Barat, has relatively few interesting trails, but it is a rewarding place for **bird-watching**, as is the area around Danau Bratan in the centre of the island.

Visitors to Bali should be aware of the **peak tourist seasons**; resorts get packed out between mid-June and mid-September and again over the Christmas and New Year period, when prices rocket and rooms can be fully booked for days, if not weeks, in advance.

Some history

The earliest written records in Bali, metal inscriptions or *prasasti*, dating from the ninth century AD, reveal Buddhist and Hindu influence from the Indian subcontinent, visible also in the statues, bronzes and rock-cut caves at Gunung Kawi and Goa Gajah. The most famous event in early Balinese history occurred towards the end of the tenth century, when Princess **Mahendratta** of East Java married the Balinese King **Udayana**. Their son, **Erlangga**, born around 991 AD, later succeeded to the throne of the Javanese kingdom and sent his regent to rule over Bali, thus bringing the two realms together until his death in 1049.

In the following centuries, the ties between Bali and Java fluctuated as kingdoms gained and lost power. In 1343, the island was colonized by the powerful Hindu **Majapahit** kingdom of East Java. The Balinese who did not accept these changes established their own villages in remote areas. Their descendants, known as the **Bali Aga** or *Bali Mula*, the "original Balinese", still live in separate villages, such as Tenganan near Candi Dasa and Trunyan on the shores of Danau Batur. Throughout the fifteenth century, the power of the Majapahit empire on Java declined as the influence of Islam expanded. The empire finally fell in 1515 and the priests, craftsmen, soldiers, nobles and artists of the Hindu Majapahit fled east to Bali, flooding the island with Javanese cultural ideas.

The Balinese first came into contact with Europeans – Portuguese and Dutch – during the sixteenth century, though the island was largely ignored, as it produced little of interest to outsiders. The exception was **slaves**, who were shipped through the port of Kuta and had a reputation for being particularly strong and hard-working. However, by the mid-1830s the main Dutch concern was to gain control of the region before the British, and in 1840 the **Dutch** envoy, Huskus Koopman, began a series of visits with the aim of persuading the Balinese to agree to Dutch sovereignty over the island. This ultimately led to violent clashes with the rajahs, and in 1849 the **Third Dutch Military Expedition** of 7000 troops landed in Buleleng, attacked the fortress at Jagaraga and defeated the Balinese, with the loss of only about thirty men to the Balinese thousands.

The Dutch then set up headquarters at Padang Bai and decided to attack Karangasem. On their arrival at the palace, the rajah of Karangasem, his family and followers, all committed **puputan** (ritual suicide). The Dutch troops then headed west towards Klungkung. However, an **agreement** was drawn up in Kuta on July 13, 1849, whereby the Balinese recognized Dutch sovereignty,

Balinese village life

Most Balinese earn their living from agriculture and live in **villages**. People employed in the cities or tourist resorts may well commute from their village homes each day, and even those whose villages are far away still identify with them and return on particular festivals.

Village layout

Orientation in the Balinese world does not correspond to the compass points of north, south, east and west. Gunung Agung, dwelling place of the gods and the highest peak on Bali, is the reference point, and the main directions are **kaja**, towards the mountain, and **kelod**, away from the mountain (which in practice usually means towards the sea). The other directions are *kangin*, from where the sun rises, and its opposite, *kauh*, where the sun sets.

House compounds

Each Balinese household consists of several structures, all built within a confining wall. When a son of the family marries, his wife will usually move into his compound. Most domestic activities take place outside or in the partial shelter of **bale**, raised platforms supported by wooden pillars, with a roof traditionally thatched with local grass (*alang-alang*). Outside the *kelod* wall, families have their garbage tip and pig pens. Prior to calling in the *undagi*, the master builder who understands the rules relating to buildings laid down in ancient texts, an expert in the Balinese calendar is consulted, as an auspicious day must be chosen. Before building starts, a **ceremony** takes place in which an offering, usually a brick wrapped in white cloth, is placed in the foundation of each building so that work will proceed smoothly. When the work is finished, a series of ceremonies must take place before the compound can be occupied. The final ceremony is the **melaspas**, an inauguration ritual which "brings the building to life".

Village organization

The smallest unit of social organization in each village is the **banjar**, or neighbourhood. Each adult male joins the local *banjar* when he marries. The *banjar* gathers in the village meeting house, the **bale banjar**, to discuss land issues, plans for temple ceremonies, the local gamelan orchestra, government projects and any problems. All decisions are reached by consensus. The *banjar* has considerable authority: if members neglect their duties they can be fined or even expelled from the village.

The subak

Much of daily village life revolves around the *sawah*, or **rice-fields**, and numerous complex rituals accompany all the stages of cultivation encapsulated in the worship of Dewi Sri, the goddess of rice and prosperity. The local organization in charge of each irrigation system is the **subak**; these are known to have existed on Bali since the ninth century. The maintenance of the irrigation system, along with detailed planning to ensure that every farmer gets the water he needs, is co-ordinated by the *kliang* (head) of the *subak*. Any *subak* with plans that may influence the irrigation system, such as changing dry fields to wet, has to consult the regional water temples, and ultimately, the **Jero Gede**, chief priest of Pura Ulun Danu Batur.

Life-cycle celebrations

Ceremonies are carried out at important points in an individual's life to purify them, and make sure they have sufficient spiritual energy to remain healthy and calm. Following the **birth** of a baby, the parents and child are regarded as unclean (*sebel*). For the mother and baby this lasts 42 days; for the father it lasts until the baby's umbilical cord drops off, when, in the **kepus pungsed** ritual, the cord is wrapped in cloth, placed in an offering shaped like a dove and suspended over the baby's bed. The child's **first birthday**, *oton*, occurs after 210 days (a Balinese year), and is the first occasion that it is allowed contact with the ground. The **tooth-filing ritual**, *mapandes*, takes place between six and eighteen years of age, and is a hugely important celebration with guests, music and lavish offerings; the elderly, and even the dead, have been known to have their teeth filed. The aim of the ritual is to eliminate any hint of coarse, uncontrolled behaviour by filing down the upper canine teeth or fangs (*caling*) and the four teeth in between: six in total. There are two options for **marriage** (*pawiwahan* or *nganten*). The most correct is *mamadik*, when the marriage is agreed between the two sets of parents. Much more common is *ngerorod* or *malaib*, elopement: the couple run off and spend the night together, with sufficient subterfuge that the girl's parents can pretend to be outraged. The following morning, a private ceremony (*makala-kalaan*) is carried out, and the couple are married. The girl's parents will not be invited as there is supposed to be bad feeling between the two sides. However, three days later both sets of parents meet at the *ketipat bantal* ceremony and are reconciled.

Cremation

The ceremony that visitors to Bali are most likely to witness is **cremation** (*pengabenan* or *palebonan*), the most spectacular manifestation of religious observance on the island. Following death, the body must be returned to the five elements of solid, liquid, energy, radiance and ether to become ready for reincarnation. It is usually buried, sometimes for years, while elaborate **preparations** are made: animals must be slaughtered, holy water acquired, and gamelan, dancers and puppet shows organized. An animal-shaped sarcophagus is built from a solid tree trunk, covered with paper and cloth and decorated with mirrors, tassels and tinsel. The cremation tower has tiers, at the base of which a small *bale* houses an effigy of the dead person and the body itself. The event itself is joyful, accompanied by the soft music of the bamboo **gamelan angklung**. The sarcophagus and cremation tower are carried to the cemetery and twirled around many times to make sure the soul is confused and cannot find its way back home to cause mischief for the family. At the cremation ground, the body is transferred from the tower into the sarcophagus, which is anointed with holy water and set alight. After burning, the ashes are carried to the sea or to a stream which will carry them to the ocean.

Caste and names

Balinese society is structured around a hereditary **caste system** which, while far more relaxed than its Indian counterpart, does nonetheless carry certain restrictions and rules of etiquette, as ordained in the Balinese Hindu scriptures. Of these, the one that travellers are most likely to encounter is the practice of **naming** a person according to their caste. At the top of the tree is the **Brahman** caste, whose men are honoured with the title **Ida Bagus** and whose women are generally named **Ida Ayu** (or **Dayu**). Traditionally revered as the most scholarly members of society, only Brahmans are allowed to become high priests (*pedanda*). **Satriya** (or Ksatriya), the second stratum of Balinese society, are descendants of warriors and rulers and are named accordingly: **Cokorda**, **Anak Agung**, **Ratu** and **Prebagus** for men, and **Anak Agung Isti** or **Dewa Ayu** for women. The merchants or **Wesia** occupy the third most important rank, the men distinguished by the title **I Gusti** or **Pregusti**, the women by the name **I Gusti Ayu**. Finally, at the bottom of the heap comes the **Sudra** caste, that of the common people, which accounts for over ninety percent of the population. Sudra children are named according to their position in the family order, with no distinction between male and female: a first-born Sudra is always known as **Wayan** (or, less commonly, **Putu** or **Gede**), the second-born is **Made** (or **Kadek**), the third **Nyoman** (or **Komang**) and the fourth **Ketut**. Should a fifth child be born, then the naming system begins all over again with Wayan. In order to distinguish between the sexes, Sudra caste names are often prefaced by "**I**" for males and "**Ni**" for females, eg I Wayan. The Sudra are not looked down upon or denied access to specific professions (except that of *pedanda*), and a high-caste background guarantees neither a high income nor a direct line to political power.

and in return the Dutch agreed to leave the rajahs to administer their own kingdoms. From their administrative capital in **Singaraja**, the Dutch made some improvements on the island, particularly in irrigation and by planting coffee as a cash crop. They also brought in new regulations against slavery and the tradition of *suttee*, when widows would throw themselves on the funeral pyres of their dead husbands.

Having taken control of the south of the island, the Dutch decided to assert their monopoly over **opium trading**, traditionally carried on by Chinese and Buginese traders. On the announcement of this on April 1, 1908, there was **rioting** in Klungkung followed by clashes with Dutch troops. When more troops arrived in Klungkung on April 28, 1908, they witnessed another *puputan* in which two hundred members of the royal household committed suicide. In January 1909, the whole of Bali came under Dutch control.

In December 1941, Japan entered **World War II**; their fleet arrived off Sanur on February 18 and landed 500 troops, which moved unopposed to Denpasar and then through the island, which they occupied without a fight. The **occupation** was short-lived, but it had profound political effects as it showed that the Dutch colonialists were vulnerable.

When Indonesia made its declaration of **independence** on August 17, 1945, some Balinese were unhappy: Java was Muslim, and the traditional enmity between the two islands made many people uncertain about joining a republic dominated by Java. Returning to retake their colony in March 1946, the Dutch faced ferocious fighting on Java but initially little opposition on Bali. However, the guerrilla forces, led by **Gusti Ngurah Rai**, a young army officer, attempted to ambush the Dutch, who eventually killed all 97 of the rebels; Ngurah Rai is now remembered as a hero. The status quo returned, local rulers overseen by Dutch administrators. The Dutch, having lost control of the islands to the west, created the Republic of East Indonesia, with the capital in Makassar in Sulawesi, and in 1948 declared Bali to be an autonomous state within that republic.

The early years of independence were not kind to Bali; although Sukarno's mother was Balinese, the Balinese felt neglected by the government in Jakarta. Sukarno visited his palace at Tampaksiring regularly, with a massive entourage that demanded to be fed, entertained and then sent on their way with gifts. During the 1960s, a groundswell of resentment against the government grew in Bali. The Balinese began to believe that a state of spiritual disharmony had been reached, and preparations were made for a traditional island-wide **purification ceremony**, Eka Dasa Rudra, held in 1963 against the backdrop of a fiercely rumbling Gunung Agung that eventually erupted causing great devastation (see box on p.599).

Later events in Jakarta increased the disaster in Bali. Following the **Gestapu** affair during the night of September 30, 1965, a wave of killings spread across Indonesia. Estimates suggest that 100,000 were killed on Bali, with actual or suspected members of the Communist Party, their sympathizers and the Chinese population the main targets.

Since Suharto's downfall the Balinese have grown ever more publicly vocal about their government; following much disillusion during the incumbency of Habibie and Gus Dur, the Balinese joy knew few bounds when **Megawati Sukarnoputri** (known as simply Mega on Bali, where she is generally adored) became president. Among other concerns, they are looking to her to redress the increasing control of the Balinese tourist industry by wealthy entrepreneurs from Jakarta.

When this book went to press in February 2003, Bali had recently been dealt its most devastating blow yet. The **terrorist bomb attack** in the heart of

Kuta's nightlife district left hundreds of local people and foreign visitors dead, and the island's tourism-dominated economy in tatters. How quickly Bali recovers will depend both on the Indonesian government's response to its internal security problems and on tourists' ability to see the attack as a tragic one-off.

South Bali

The triangle of mainly flat land that makes up **the south** is some of the most fertile in Bali, and also the most densely populated, with more than a thousand people resident on every square kilometre. Bali's administrative capital, **Denpasar**, is here, and so too are the island's major tourist resorts, which have sprung up along the spectacular white-sand beaches: at **Kuta** and **Jimbaran** in the west, and **Sanur** and **Nusa Dua** in the east. Furthermore, the combination of large offshore reefs and a peculiarly shaped coastline have made this region a genuine surfers' paradise, with some of the best breaks in the world.

Denpasar

Despite roaring motorbikes and round-the-clock traffic congestion, Bali's capital **DENPASAR** (meaning "next to the market") remains a pleasant city at heart, centred on a grassy square and dominated by family compounds grouped into traditional *banjar* districts, with just a few major shopping streets criss-crossing the centre. It feels nowhere near as hectic as Kuta but, as there's no nightlife, few tourists spend much time here.

Arrival, information and city transport

If you're arriving in Bali by air, you'll land at **Ngurah Rai Airport**, which is not in Denpasar as sometimes implied, but just beyond the southern outskirts

Moving on from Denpasar

Denpasar's four main bemo terminals serve towns right across the island; see the plan on p.529. **Tegal** station serves destinations south of Denpasar, including Kuta, Jimbaran, and Bualu (for Tanjung Benoa). **Kereneng** station serves Sanur. **Batubulan** station in the nearby village of Batubulan (see p.564) serves Ubud and the east coast, including Candi Dasa, Padang Bai and Tampaksiring, and is also the departure point for the Damri bus service to Nusa Dua via Sanur (dropping passengers outside the *Radisson* hotel) and the eastern outskirts of Kuta. **Ubung** station (see p.528) serves north and west Bali, with bemos to and from Tanah Lot, Medewi, Gilimanuk (for Java), Candikuning (Bedugul), Munduk and Singaraja (for Lovina), as well as **buses** to and from Java and Padang Bai (for Lombok). The small bemo terminal near the **Sanglah** hospital serves Benoa Harbour and Suwung. Getting from one terminal to another is fairly easy, but connections can be quite time-consuming.

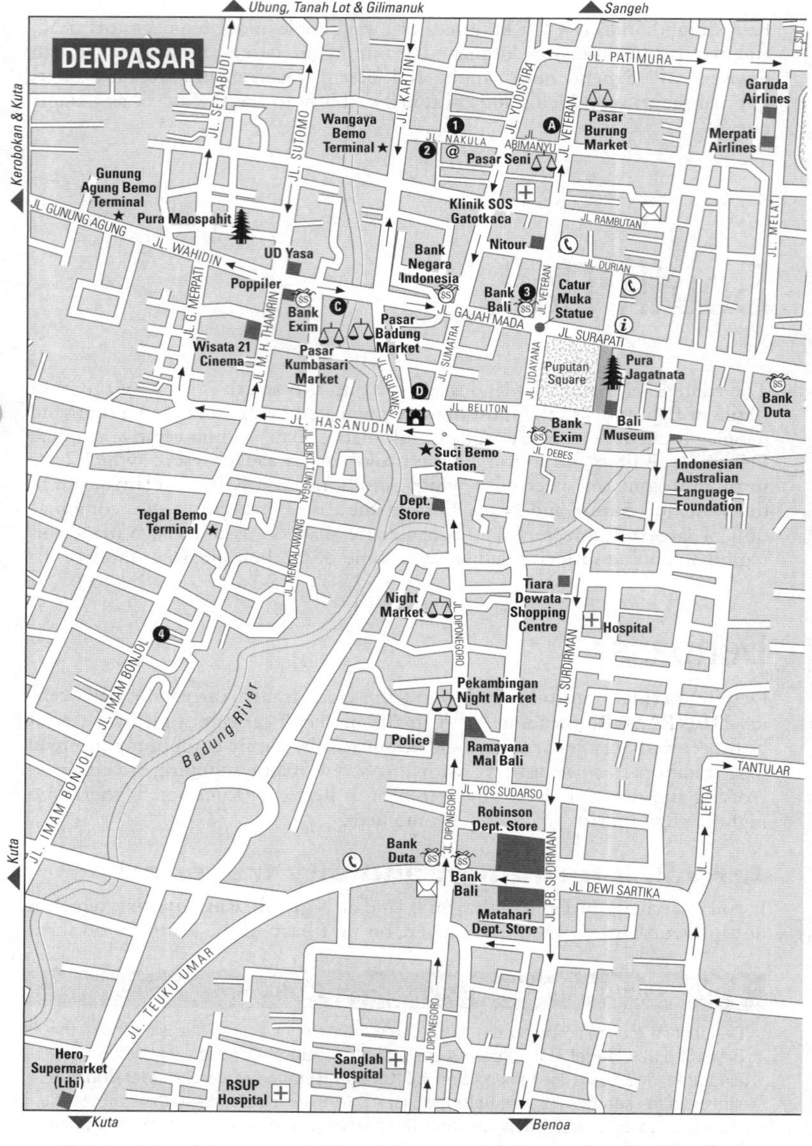

of Kuta in Tuban. For full airport information, see the box on p.538. Arriving by bemo or public bus from another part of the island, you'll almost certainly be dropped at one of the four main **bemo stations**, which lie on the edges of town; see the plan on p.529 for an overview, and the box for full details. Denpasar's **tourist office** is just off Puputan Square, at Jl Surapati 7 (Mon–Thurs 8am–3pm, Fri 8am–1pm; ⓣ0361/234569).

Denpasar's city transport system relies on the fleet of different coloured **pub-**

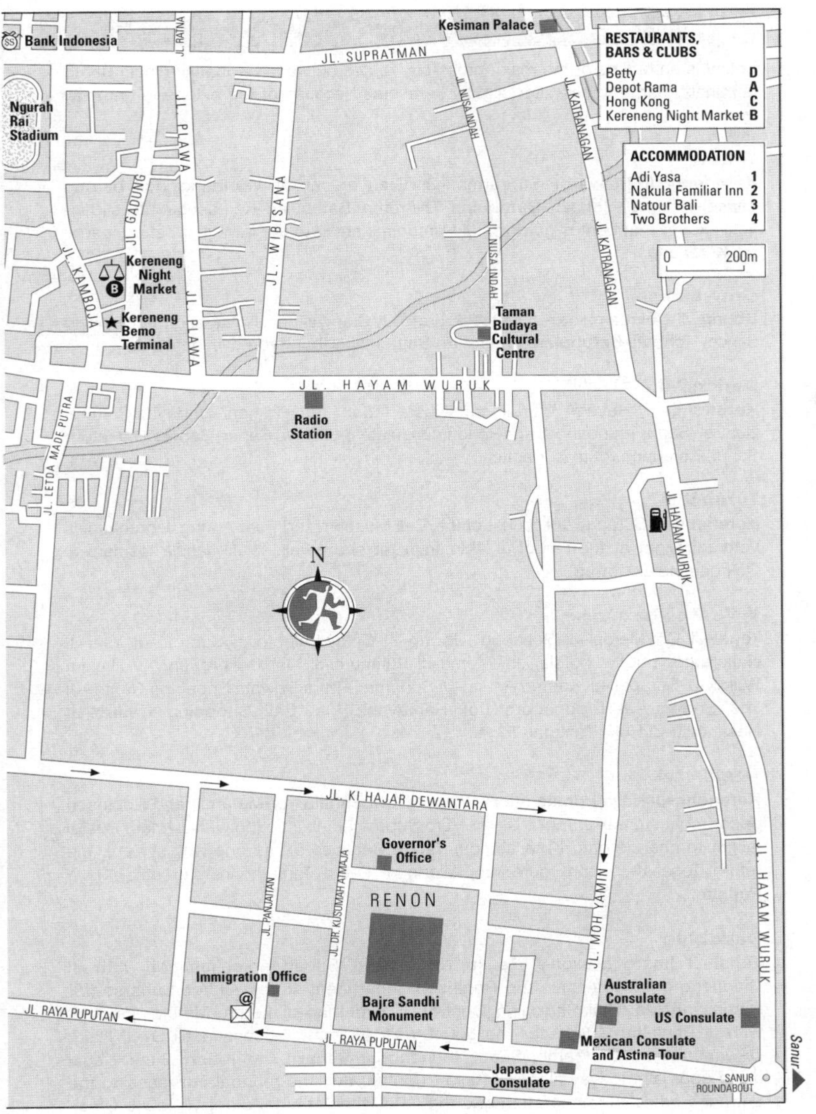

lic bemos that shuttle between the city's bemo terminals; see p.528 for a summary of the main routes. Most Denpasar bemos have at least their first and last stops printed in large letters on the vehicle (for example, Tegal–Ubung–Kereneng–Tegal), and most are colour-coded. Prices are fixed, and a list of rates is displayed in the controller's office at each terminal, but tourists are often obliged to pay more – generally around Rp2000 for a cross-city ride. Metered **taxis** also circulate around the city, as do horse-drawn carts (*dokar*).

City bemo routes

Below is an outline of the major cross-city routes between Denpasar's main **bemo** terminals. Some routes alter slightly in reverse because of the extensive one-way system.

Yellow

Kereneng–Jl Plawa–Jl Supratman–Jl Gianyar–cnr Jl Waribang (for barong dance)–Kesiman–Tohpati–**Batubulan**. The return Batubulan–Kereneng route is identical except that bemos go down Jl Kamboja instead of Jl Plawa just before reaching Kereneng.

Grey-blue

Ubung–Jl Cokroaminoto–Jl Gatot Subroto–Jl Gianyar–cnr Jl Waribang (for barong dance)–Tohpati–**Batubulan**. The return Batubulan–Ubung route is identical.

Dark green

Kereneng–Jl Hayam Wuruk–cnr Nusa Indah (for Taman Budaya Cultural Centre)–Sanur roundabout (for Renon consulates)–Jl Raya Sanur–**Sanur**. The return Sanur–Kereneng route is identical.

Turquoise

Kereneng–Jl Surapati (for tourist office, Bali Museum and Pura Agung Jagatnata)–Jl Veteran (alight at the cnr of Jl Abimanyu for short walk to Jl Nakula losmen)–Jl Cokroaminoto–**Ubung**.

Yellow or turquoise

Tegal–Jl Gn Merapi–Jl Setiabudi–**Ubung**–Jl Cokroaminoto–Jl Subroto–Jl Yani–Jl Nakula (for budget hotels)–Jl Veteran–Jl Patimura–Jl Melati–**Kereneng**–Jl Hayam Wuruk–Jl Surapati–Jl Kapten Agung–Jl Sudirman–Tiara Dewata Shopping Centre–Jl Yos Sudarso–Jl Diponegoro (for Ramayana Mal Bali Shopping Centre)–Jl Hasanudin–Jl Bukit Tunggal–**Tegal**.

Beige

Kereneng–Jl Raya Puputan (for GPO)–Jl Dewi Sartika (for Matahari and Robinson department stores)–Jl Teuku Umar–Hero Supermarket–junction with Jl Imam Bonjol (alight to change onto Kuta bemos)–**Tegal**. Because of the one-way system, the return Tegal–Kereneng route runs along Jl Letda Tantular instead of Jl Raya Puputan.

Dark blue

Tegal–Jl Imam Bonjol–Jl Teuku Umar–Hero Supermarket–junction with Jl Diponegoro (for Matahari and Robinson department stores)–Jl Yos Sudarso (for Ramayana Mal Bali Shopping Centre)–Jl Sudirman–Jl Letda Tantular–junction with Jl Panjaitan (alight for the 500m walk to Immigration and GPO)–Jl Hajar Dewantara–Jl Moh Yamin–Sanur roundabout–**Sanur**. The return Sanur–Tegal route goes all the way along Jl Raya Puputan after the roundabout, passing the entrance gates of Immigration and the GPO, then straight along Jl Teuku Umar, past Hero Supermarket to the junction with Jl Imam Bonjol (where you should alight to pick up Kuta-bound bemos) before heading north up Jl Imam Bonjol to Tegal.

Accommodation

Accommodation is disappointingly shabby, catering more for the quick-stop Indonesian business traveller than for fussier tourists.

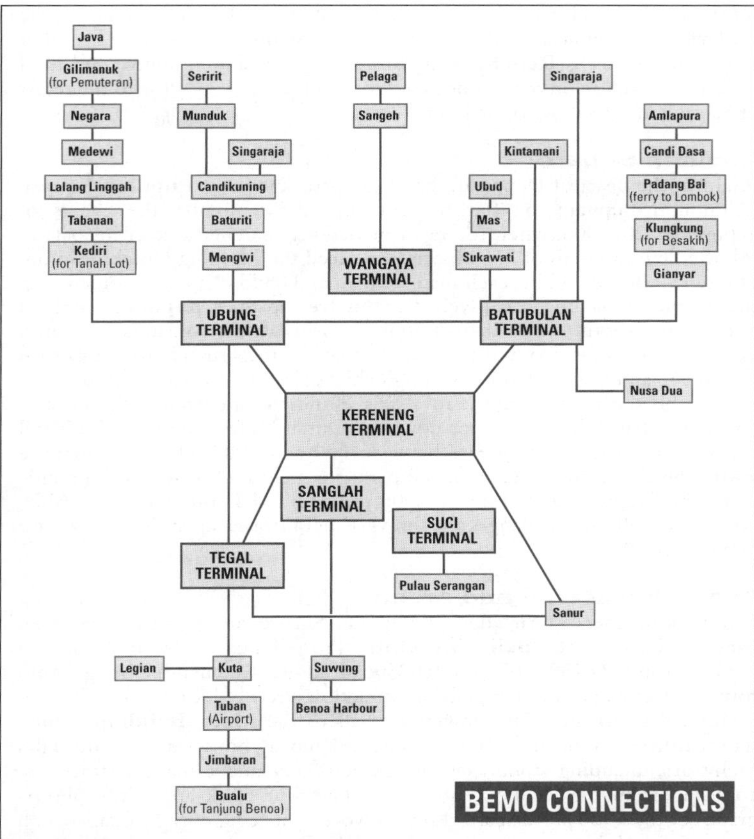

Adi Yasa Jl Nakula 23 ⓣ0361/222679. This long-running losmen, an easy walk from the museum, is most backpackers' first choice. Rooms are cheap and en suite, if slightly run-down and not all that secure. From Kereneng, take an Ubung-bound bemo and walk 300m west from the Pasar Seni art market at the Jl Abimanyu junction with Jl Veteran. The weirdly routed Tegal–Kereneng bemos also pass the front door. ❷

Nakula Familiar Inn Jl Nakula 4 ⓣ0361/226446. Spruce modern place, where every room has a balcony and bathroom. Not as popular as *Adi Yasa* across the road, but more comfortable. ❸

Natour Bali Jl Veteran 3 ⓣ0361/225681, ⓕ235347, ⓔntrbali@denpasar.wasantara.net.id. Denpasar's oldest hotel has a certain quaint appeal and offers reasonable if rather characterless rooms. Has a pool and is central. ❺

Two Brothers (Dua Saudara) Jl Imam Bonjol Gang VII, 5 ⓣ0361/484704. Rooms are spotless if a bit scruffy; none has its own bathroom. Good value singles. A 5-min walk south of Tegal bemo station. ❷

The City

Denpasar's central and most convenient landmark is **Puputan Square**, marking the heart of the downtown area and the crossover point of the city's major north–south and east–west roads. A huge stone statue of **Catur Muka** stands on the traffic island here, the four-faced, eight-armed Hindu guardian of the cardinal points indicating the exact location of the city centre. The other important district is **Renon**, Denpasar's leafy-green administrative and local government centre on the southeastern edge of the city, very close to the resort of Sanur and served by Sanur-bound bemos.

Puputan Square

Right in the heart of Denpasar, the grassy park known as **Puputan Square** (Alun-alun Puputan, or Taman Puputan) commemorates the events of September 20, 1906, when the rajah of Badung marched out of his palace, followed by hundreds of his subjects, and faced the invading Dutch head on. Dressed all in holy white, each man, woman and child clasping a golden kris, the people of Badung had psyched themselves up for a **puputan**, or ritual fight to the death, rather than submit to the Dutch colonialists' demands. Historical accounts vary, but it's thought that the mass suicide took place on this square and was incited by Badung's chief priest who, on a signal from the rajah, stabbed his king with the royal kris. Hundreds of citizens followed suit, and those that didn't were shot down by Dutch bullets; the final death toll was reported to be somewhere between 600 and 2000. The huge **bronze statue** on the northern edge of the park is a memorial to the Badung citizens who fought and died in the 1906 *puputan*, and a commemorative **fair**, with food stalls and wayang kulit shows, is held in the square every year on September 20.

The Bali Museum and around

Overlooking the eastern edge of Puputan Square on pedestrianized Jalan Mayor Wisnu, the **Bali Museum** (Sun–Thurs 7.30am–3pm, Fri 7.30am–1pm; Rp750, children Rp250; turquoise Kereneng–Ubung bemo route) is Denpasar's most significant attraction, prettily located in a series of traditional courtyards. The downstairs hall of the **Main Building**, which stands at the back of the entrance courtyard, mostly houses items from Bali's prehistory, including stone axes, bronze jewellery and a massive stone sarcophagus from the second century BC. The four black-and-white photographs of the 1906 *puputan* are also well worth lingering over. Upstairs, you'll find a fine exhibition of traditional household utensils, many of which are still in common use today. These include the **coconut grater** – here carved into an animal shape, complete with genitalia – and the bizarre, tiny bamboo cages for **fighting crickets**, designed to hold the male insects used in the popular local sport of cricket fighting. The compact **First Pavilion** holds some fine examples of the four major styles of Balinese **textiles**: the ubiquitous *endek* (or *ikat)*, the rarer *geringsing*, or double-*ikat*, which comes from Tenganan (see p.613), *songket* brocades, and gold screenprinted *perada* (or *prada*). For more on Balinese textiles, see p.613. Built to resemble the long, low structure of an eighteenth-century Karangasem-style palace, the **Second Pavilion** contains all manner of **religious** paraphernalia, including a curious bell-shaped bamboo cage that's still used by some villagers in a traditional ceremony to mark the first Balinese year of a baby's life (210 days). The Balinese **calendars** on the right-hand wall are complex compositions arrived at through astrological and religious permutations and are still used to determine auspicious dates for all sorts of events, from temple festivals to house-building. The **Third Pavilion** is given over to **theatrical** masks, costumes and puppets. Most impressive are the costumes for the shaggy-haired

Barong Ket and his archenemy, the witch-like **Rangda** (see p.582 for more on their role in Balinese dance-dramas).

Just over the north wall of the Bali Museum stands the modern state temple of **Pura Agung Jagatnata**, set in a fragrant garden of pomegranate and frangipani trees. As with nearly every temple in Bali, Pura Agung Jagatnata is designed as three courtyards, though in this case the middle courtyard is so compressed as to be little more than a gallery encircled by a moat. **Carvings** of lotus flowers and frogs adorn the tiny stone bridge that spans the moat (access at festival times only) and there are reliefs illustrating scenes from the *Ramayana* and *Mahabharata* carved into the gallery's outer wall. Twice a month, on the occasion of the full moon and of the new moon, **festivals** are held here, with wayang kulit (shadow puppet) shows performed in the outer courtyard (around 9–11pm).

Pasar Badung and Pasar Kumbasari

The biggest and best of Denpasar's traditional **markets** is the chaotic **Pasar Badung**, which stands at the heart of the downtown area, set slightly back off Jalan Gajah Mada. It used to be housed in a traditional three-storey covered stone and brick *pasar* beside the Sungai Badung, but this burnt down in 2000, so the stallholders now conduct their trade in the open air, 24 hours a day, in an impossibly packed warren of overflowing alleyways. Easiest access into the market is from the northern end of Jalan Sulawesi, though many of the most interesting wares, including sarongs and ceremonial paraphernalia, are set out on the stalls that abut the western edge of Jalan Sulawesi and can be perused from the street. Be prepared to find yourself landed with a **guide**: local women hang out around the Jalan Sulawesi entrance and are keen to accompany tourists round the market.

Just west across the narrow Sungai Badung from Pasar Badung, a few metres south of Jalan Gajah Mada, the four-storey **Pasar Kumbasari** is dedicated to art-market goods such as handicrafts and clothes and is a good inexpensive place to shop.

Taman Budaya Cultural Centre

In the eastern part of town, on Jalan Nusa Indah, fifteen minutes' walk from the Kereneng bemo station, or direct on a Sanur-bound bemo, the **Taman Budaya Cultural Centre** (daily 8am–3pm; Rp250) houses a moderately interesting art museum and from mid-June to mid-July hosts the annual **Arts Festival**, a huge programme of drama, dance and art exhibitions.

The main **exhibition hall** is housed in the long, two-storey building towards the back of the compound, and begins with an overview of Balinese **painting**, with a few examples in each of the *wayang*, Ubud, Batuan and Young Artists styles (see p.576 for more). Religious and secular **woodcarvings** fill the next room, together with an assortment of *Ramayana* and *topeng* dance masks. There are more ambitious carvings downstairs, along with a collection of modern non-traditional paintings.

Eating, drinking and entertainment

Eating and **drinking** hardly rate as one of Denpasar's great pleasures, but you won't go hungry here. Most restaurants stop serving by 9pm, after which your best option is a visit to the Kereneng night market.

Denpasar holds little in the way of bars or clubs, but there's a five-screen Wisata 21 **cinema** complex at Jl Thamrin 29 (Ⓣ0361/424023), and a smaller one on nearby Jalan Kartini; soundtracks are usually in the original language, and schedules are listed in the *Bali Post*. All tour agents can arrange transport and tickets for Balinese **dance** performances in the Denpasar and Ubud areas; shows are staged daily in most places. Prices start at Rp100,000 through a tour agent, or about Rp50,000 on the door. The nearest options for going to a show independently are the daily **barong** (9.30–10.30am), at both the Catur Eka Budhi on Jalan Waribang in the Kesiman district on the eastern edge of town (Batubulan-bound bemo from either Ubung or Kereneng) and at the Pura Puseh in Batubulan (bemo from Ubung or Kereneng), and the nightly **kecak** (6.30–7.30pm) at the Stage Uma Dewi, which is also on Jalan Waribang in Denpasar's Kesiman district (bemo as above), about 300m south of the barong dance stage. For some background on Balinese dance, see the box on p.582.

Cafés and restaurants

Betty Jl Sumatra 56. Recommended unpretentious local café with a big, cheap English-language menu that includes an imaginative vegetarian selection. Closes 9pm.

Depot Rama Jl Veteran 55. Inexpensive neighbourhood warung serving nasi campur, nasi goreng, *nasi soto ayam* and lots of noodle dishes. Very convenient for the Jl Nakula losmen.

Hong Kong Jl Gajah Mada 99. Classy, air-conditioned Chinese restaurant offering a huge variety of moderately priced set meals and à la carte choices. Karaoke at night.

Kereneng Night Market Just off Jl Hayam Wuruk, adjacent to Kereneng bemo station. Over fifty vendors convene here from dusk to dawn every night, serving up piping hot soups, noodle and rice dishes, *babi guling*, fresh fruit juices and cold beers. Long trestle tables are set up around the marketplace.

Listings

Airline offices Garuda city check-in at Jl Melati 61 ⓣ0361/254747).

Banks and exchange There are exchange counters at most banks and ATMs for Visa, MasterCard and Cirrus Maestro on all main shopping streets. Visa cash advances are available at Bank Bali, diagonally opposite the Matahari department store at Jl Dewi Sartika 88 ⓣ0361/261678, and at Bank Duta, Jl Hayam Wuruk 165 ⓣ0361/226578. The GPO in Renon (see below) is a Western Union agent.

Embassies and consulates Most foreign embassies are based in Jakarta (see p.121), but there's an Australian consulate at Jl Moh Yamin 4 in Renon, Denpasar ⓣ0361/235092, ⓔausconbali@denpasar.wasantara.net.id; and a US consulate at Jl Hayam Wuruk 188 in Renon, Denpasar ⓣ0361/233605, ⓔamcobali@indo.net.id. The British consulate is in Sanur.

Hospitals and clinics Sanglah Public Hospital at Jl Kesehatan Selatan 1, Sanglah (five lines ⓣ0361/227911–5; bemos from Denpasar's Kereneng bemo station), is Bali's main public hospital, with the most efficient emergency ward and some English-speaking staff. It also has Bali's only divers' decompression chamber. Kasih Ibu, Jl Teuku Umar 120 ⓣ0361/223036, is a 24-hour private hospital and fine for minor ailments; Klinik SOS Gatotkaca, Jl Gatotkaca 21 ⓣ0361/223555, is open 24 hours and staffed by English-speaking medics.

Immigration office Corner of Jl Panjaitan and Jl Raya Puputan, Renon (Mon–Thurs 8am–3pm, Fri 8–11am, Sat 8am–2pm; ⓣ0361/227828; Sanur–Tegal bemo).

Internet access Bali's internet HQ is the very cheap Wasantara Net at the Warposnet (Mon–Sat 8am–8pm), located at the back of the GPO compound in Renon (Sanur–Tegal bemo route); more central email centres are Hello Internet in the Ramayana Mal Bali on Jl Diponegoro, and the place across from the *Adi Yasa* losmen on Jl Veteran.

Pharmacies Inside all the main department stores (see below); also, Apotik Kimia Farma at Jl Diponegoro 125.

Phone offices There are Telkom offices at Jl Teuku Umar 6, and on Jl Durian. IDD phones in the Tara Dewata department store on Jl Sutoyo and dozens of wartels all over the city. Home Country Direct phone at the Bali Museum.

Police There are police stations on Jl Pattimura and Jl Diponegoro.

Post offices Denpasar's poste restante (Mon–Sat 8am–8pm; Sanur–Tegal bemo) is at the GPO on Jl Raya Puputan in Renon. The Jl

Rambutan PO, near Puputan Square, is more convenient.

Shopping Fashions, general necessities and handicrafts at Ramayana Mal Bali shopping centre, Jl Diponegoro 103 (9.30am–9.30pm; Kereneng–Tegal and Tegal–Sanur bemos), Matahari department store, Jl Dewi Sartika 4 (9.30am–9pm; Tegal–Sanur bemo) and Tiara Dewata Shopping Centre, Jl Sutoyo (9am–9pm; Kereneng–Tegal bemo). English-language books at Matahari's basement bookstore; traditional and contemporary fabrics from any shop on Jl Sulawesi; religious and ceremonial paraphernalia from UD Yasa, Gajah Mada 148.

Swimming Public pool at Tiara Dewata Shopping Centre, or use the one at the *Natour Bali* hotel for a small fee.

Travel agents Domestic Garuda and Merpati airline tickets from Nitour next to the *Natour Bali* hotel, Jl Veteran 5 ⓣ0361/234742, ⓔnitourbali@denpasar.wasantara.net.id; international and domestic airline tickets from Puri Astina Putra, Jl Moh Yamin 1a ⓣ0361/223552, ⓔastina@denpasar.wasantara.net.id, opposite the Australian Consulate in Renon. Pelni boat tickets from Jl Diponegoro 165 ⓣ0361/234680. Train tickets (for Java) from Jl Diponegoro 150 Blok B4 ⓣ0361/227131.

Kuta–Legian–Seminyak

The biggest, brashest, least traditional beach resort in Bali, the **KUTA–LEGIAN–SEMINYAK** conurbation continues to expand from its epicentre on the coast 10km southwest of Denpasar. Packed with hundreds of losmen, hotels, restaurants, bars, clubs, souvenir shops, fashion boutiques and tour agencies, the eight-kilometre strip plays host to several hundred thousand visitors a year, many of them regulars and a lot of them surfers – all here to party, shop or, indeed, surf. And yet, for all the hustle, it's a very good-humoured place, almost completely unsleazy, with no strip bars, and arguably the best beach on the island.

Although Kuta, Legian and Seminyak all started out as separate villages, it's now impossible to determine the demarcation lines. We've used the most common perception of the borders. **Kuta** stretches north from the Matahari department store in Kuta Square to Jalan Melasti, while **Tuban** is defined as Kuta's increasingly built-up southern fringes, extending south from Matahari to the airport. **Legian** runs from Jalan Melasti as far north as Jalan Arjuna; and **Seminyak** goes from Jalan Arjuna up to *The Legian* hotel and Pura Petitenget in the north. The resort's main road, **Jalan Legian**, runs north–south through all three districts, a total distance of 6km, and a lot of businesses give their address as nothing more than "Jalan Legian". Kuta's other main landmark is **Bemo Corner**, the tiny roundabout at the southern end of Kuta that stands at the Jalan Legian–Jalan Pantai Kuta intersection. The name's misleading, as the Denpasar bemos don't actually depart from this very spot, but it's a useful point of reference. In recent years many roads in the resort have been **renamed**, which can make life very confusing: the most common alternative road names are given in brackets on the maps.

Arrival, information and transport

For information on **airport arrivals** see the box on p.538. Arriving in Kuta by **shuttle bus**, you could be dropped almost anywhere, depending on your shuttle bus operator. Drivers for the biggest, Perama, drop passengers at their office on Jalan Legian, about 100m north of Bemo Corner, but will sometimes stop at spots en route if asked.

Public bemos have a number of routes through the Kuta area. Coming

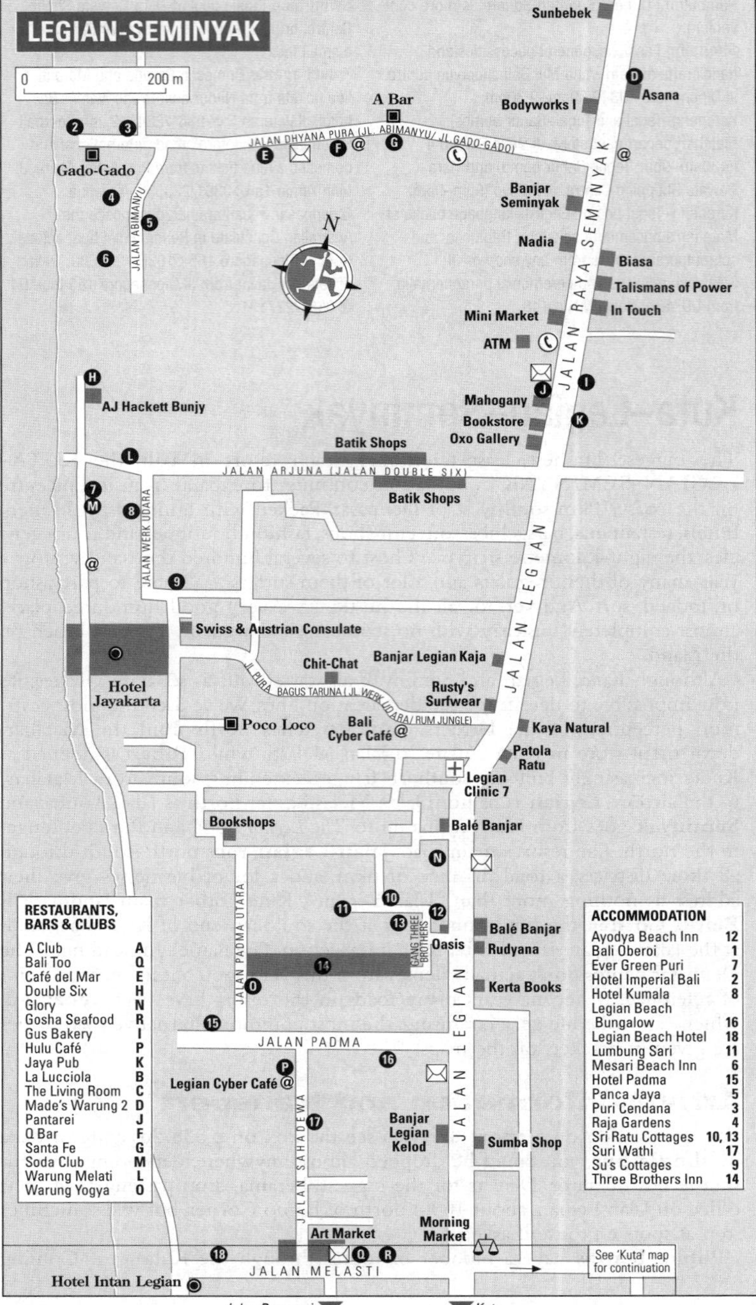

LEGIAN-SEMINYAK
0 200 m
1, A, B, C, Jalan Laksmana, Kerobokan & Canggu
Sunbebek
Asana
Bodyworks I
A Bar
JALAN DHYANA PURA (JL. ABIMANYU/ JL.GADO-GADO)
Gado-Gado
JALAN ABIMANYU
Banjar Seminyak
Nadia
Biasa
Talismans of Power
In Touch
Mini Market
ATM
JALAN RAYA SEMINYAK
N
AJ Hackett Bunjy
Mahogany
Bookstore
Oxo Gallery
Batik Shops
JALAN ARJUNA (JALAN DOUBLE SIX)
Batik Shops
JALAN WERK UDARA
Swiss & Austrian Consulate
Hotel Jayakarta
Chit-Chat
Banjar Legian Kaja
JL PURA BAGUS TARUNA (JL WERK UDARA/ RUM JUNGLE)
Rusty's Surfwear
Poco Loco
Bali Cyber Café
Kaya Natural
Patola Ratu
Legian Clinic 7
JALAN LEGIAN
Bookshops
Balé Banjar
JALAN PADMA UTARA
GANG THREE BROTHERS
Balé Banjar
Oasis
Rudyana
Kerta Books
JALAN PADMA
Legian Cyber Café
JALAN SAHADEWA
Banjar Legian Kelod
Sumba Shop
Art Market
Morning Market
JALAN MELASTI
Hotel Intan Legian
See 'Kuta' map for continuation
Jalan Benesari
Kuta
RESTAURANTS, BARS & CLUBS
A Club A
Bali Too Q
Café del Mar E
Double Six H
Glory N
Gosha Seafood R
Gus Bakery I
Hulu Café P
Jaya Pub K
La Lucciola B
The Living Room C
Made's Warung 2 D
Pantarei J
Q Bar F
Santa Fe G
Soda Club M
Warung Melati L
Warung Yogya O
ACCOMMODATION
Ayodya Beach Inn 12
Bali Oberoi 1
Ever Green Puri 7
Hotel Imperial Bali 2
Hotel Kumala 8
Legian Beach Bungalow 16
Legian Beach Hotel 18
Lumbung Sari 11
Mesari Beach Inn 6
Hotel Padma 15
Panca Jaya 5
Puri Cendana 3
Raja Gardens 4
Sri Ratu Cottages 10, 13
Suri Wathi 17
Su's Cottages 9
Three Brothers Inn 14

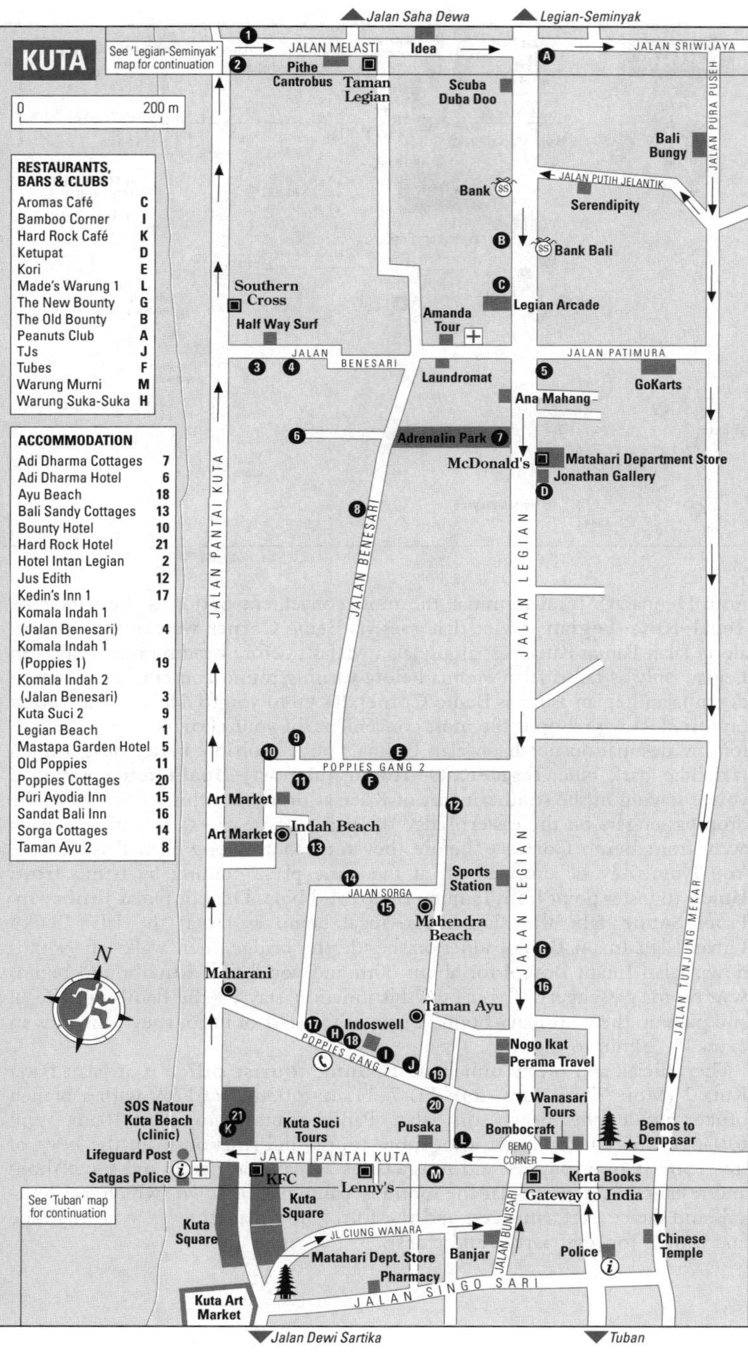
KUTA
See 'Legian-Seminyak' map for continuation
0
200 m
RESTAURANTS, BARS & CLUBS
Aromas Café C
Bamboo Corner I
Hard Rock Café K
Ketupat D
Kori E
Made's Warung 1 L
The New Bounty G
The Old Bounty B
Peanuts Club A
TJs J
Tubes F
Warung Murni M
Warung Suka-Suka H
ACCOMMODATION
Adi Dharma Cottages 7
Adi Dharma Hotel 6
Ayu Beach 18
Bali Sandy Cottages 13
Bounty Hotel 10
Hard Rock Hotel 21
Hotel Intan Legian 2
Jus Edith 12
Kedin's Inn 1 17
Komala Indah 1 (Jalan Benesari) 4
Komala Indah 1 (Poppies 1) 19
Komala Indah 2 (Jalan Benesari) 3
Kuta Suci 2 9
Legian Beach 1
Mastapa Garden Hotel 5
Old Poppies 11
Poppies Cottages 20
Puri Ayodia Inn 15
Sandat Bali Inn 16
Sorga Cottages 14
Taman Ayu 2 8
Jalan Saha Dewa
Legian-Seminyak
JALAN MELASTI
Idea
JALAN SRIWIJAYA
Pithe Cantrobus
Taman Legian
Scuba Duba Doo
Bali Bungy
JALAN PURA PUSEH
JALAN PUTIH JELANTIK
Bank
Serendipity
Bank Bali
Southern Cross
Half Way Surf
Amanda Tour
Legian Arcade
JALAN BENESARI
JALAN PATIMURA
Laundromat
GoKarts
Ana Mahang
Adrenalin Park
McDonald's
Matahari Department Store
Jonathan Gallery
JALAN PANTAI KUTA
JALAN BENESARI
JALAN LEGIAN
POPPIES GANG 2
Art Market
Art Market
Indah Beach
Sports Station
JALAN SORGA
Mahendra Beach
JALAN TUNJUNG MEKAR
N
Maharani
Taman Ayu
Indoswell
POPPIES GANG 1
Nogo Ikat
Perama Travel
SOS Natour Kuta Beach (clinic)
Wanasari Tours
Kuta Suci Tours
Pusaka
Bombocraft
Bemos to Denpasar
Lifeguard Post
JALAN PANTAI KUTA
BEMO CORNER
Satgas Police
KFC
Lenny's
Kerta Books
Gateway to India
See 'Tuban' map for continuation
Kuta Square
Kuta Square
JL CIUNG WANARA
JALAN BUNISARI
Matahari Dept. Store
Banjar
Police
Chinese Temple
Pharmacy
Kuta Art Market
JALAN SINGO SARI
Jalan Dewi Sartika
Tuban

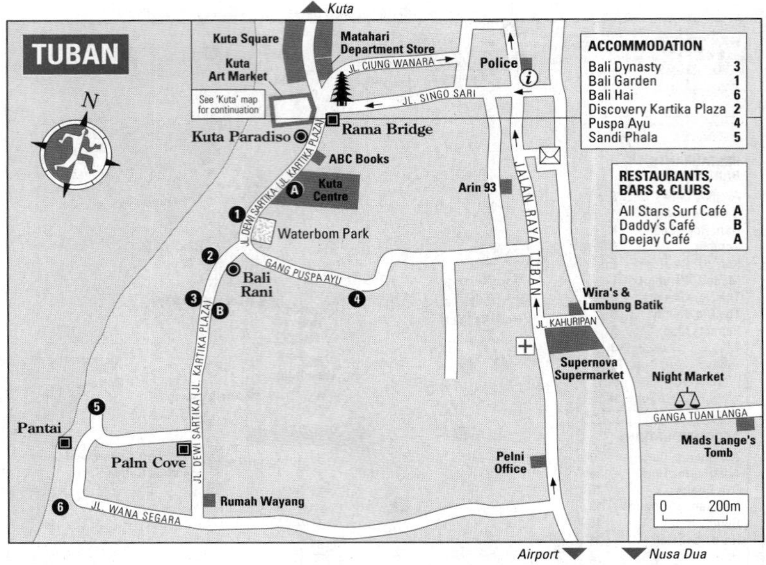

from Denpasar's Tegal terminal, the most convenient option is the dark blue **Tegal–Kuta–Legian** service that goes via Bemo Corner, west and then north along Jalan Pantai Kuta, east along Jalan Melasti before heading north up Jalan Legian only as far as Jalan Padma before turning round and continuing south down Jalan Legian as far as Bemo Corner. It's up to you to decide which point on this clockwise loop is the most convenient for your chosen losmen, though for any destination north of Jalan Padma, you're probably better off getting a taxi. The dark blue **Tegal–Kuta–Tuban (airport)–Bualu** route is fine if you're staying in the southern part of Kuta, as drivers on this service generally drop passengers on the eastern edge of Jalan Singo Sari – a five-minute walk away from Bemo Corner – before they turn south along Jalan Raya Tuban. You'll probably be dropped off at the same place coming by bemo **from Bualu** (transfer point from Tanjung Benoa and Nusa Dua) or **from Jimbaran**. From **Sanur**, take the blue Sanur–Tegal bemo as far as the Jalan Teuku Umar/Jalan Imam Bonjol junction, beside the bridge, then walk left (south) down Jalan Imam Bonjol for about 30m and you'll find Kuta-bound bemos waiting for passengers. If you miss this junction, stay on the bemo until Tegal and pick up the next Kuta-bound bemo at the start of its journey (this adds an extra 10–20min to the trip).

The official, and pretty unhelpful, **Badung tourist office** is at Jalan Raya Kuta 2 (Mon–Thurs 7am–2pm, Fri 7–11am; ⓣ0361/756176), with a branch office beside the beach on Jalan Pantai Kuta (Mon–Sat 10am–5pm; ⓣ0361/755660). You'll get a lot more tourist information from the bevy of free **tourist newspapers** and **magazines** available at hotels and some shops and restaurants, in particular the monthly pamphlet *Bali Plus* (which lists festivals and dance performances) and the fortnightly magazine *the beat* (nightlife and listings for gigs, parties and clubs).

△ Washing the salt off after swimming, Kuta, Bali

Ngurah Rai Airport

All international and domestic flights use **Ngurah Rai Airport**, in Tuban, 3km south of Kuta. For all arrival and departure **enquiries**, call ⓣ0361/751011, extn 1454.

Arrivals

Once through immigration, you'll find several 24-hour **currency exchange** booths and a **hotel reservations desk** (open for all incoming flights). There are Visa, Cirrus and MasterCard **ATMs** inside the baggage claims hall and outside the Arrivals building. The **left-luggage** office (Rp5500/day per item) is located outside, midway between International Arrivals and Departures. The **domestic terminal** is in the adjacent building, where you'll find offices of the domestic airlines Garuda and Merpati.

Most mid-priced and upmarket hotels will pick you up at the airport if asked in advance. Otherwise, the easiest but most expensive mode of transport to anywhere on the island is by **prepaid taxi**, for which you'll find a counter in the Arrivals area beyond the Customs exit doors; you pay at the booth before being shown to the taxi. **Fares** are fixed: currently Rp25,000 to Tuban and south Kuta; Rp25,000 to central Kuta (Poppies 1 and 2); Rp27,500 to Legian (as far as Jl Arjuna); Rp30,000 to Seminyak; and Rp35,000 to the *Bali Oberoi*. Further afield, you'll pay Rp25,000 to Jimbaran; Rp35,000–50,000 to Denpasar; Rp55,000 to Sanur or Nusa Dua; Rp60,000 to Tanjung Benoa; Rp70,000 to Canggu; Rp115,000 to Ubud; or Rp199,000 to Candi Dasa. Bear these prices in mind before you start bargaining with one of the **touts** who gather round both the International and Domestic Arrivals areas.

Alternatively, **metered taxis** ply the road immediately in front of the airport gates (turn right outside Arrivals and walk about 500m – they're not licensed to pick up inside the compound). You'll find their rates for rides into Kuta–Legian–Seminyak at least fifty percent cheaper than the prepaid taxi prices.

Cheaper still are the dark-blue **public bemos** whose route takes in the big main road, Jl Raya Tuban, about 700m beyond the airport gates. Bear in mind, though, that it's difficult to stash large backpacks in bemos. The northbound bemos (heading left up Jl Raya Tuban) go via Kuta's Bemo Corner and Jl Pantai Kuta as far as Jl Melasti, then travel back down Jl Legian, before continuing out to Denpasar's Tegal terminal. You should pay around Rp1500 for a bemo ride to Kuta or Legian or around Rp3000 to Denpasar.

If you want to go straight from the airport to **Ubud**, **Candi Dasa** or **Lovina**, the cheapest way (only feasible during daylight hours) is to take the bemo to Denpasar's Tegal station and then continue your journey by bemo from there; see the plan on p.529 for route outlines. A trip by bemo to Ubud will involve three different bemos and cost around Rp11,000. More convenient, but a little more expensive, is to take a bemo or prepaid taxi from the airport to Kuta's Bemo Corner, then walk 100m north up Jl Legian to Perama shuttle bus office, where you can book yourself onto the next tourist shuttle bus, most of which run every two or three hours (see p.540). The priciest way is by prepaid taxi direct from the airport (see above).

Transport

Public transport in Kuta–Legian–Seminyak is less than ideal, as the dark-blue public **bemos** only cover a clockwise loop around Kuta, leaving out most of Legian and all of Seminyak (see above for details of the route). You can flag them down at any point; the standard fare is Rp1000, but tourists are sometimes obliged to pay up to Rp2000. During the day, bemos usually circulate at five- or ten-minute intervals, but very few run after nightfall and none at all after about 8.30pm. The alternative to bemos is either a **metered taxi** (which charge Rp4000 flagfall and then Rp2000 per km, day or night) or the infor-

Departures

For a small fee, any tour agent in Bali will **reconfirm** your air ticket for you, and most can also change the dates of your ticket. Or see below for a list of international airline office phone numbers and addresses. If you're flying Garuda, you might want to make use of the city check-in offices in Kuta (see p.547), Denpasar (see p.532) and Sanur (see p.562), where you can offload your luggage the day before.

Most hotels in Kuta, Sanur, Nusa Dua and Jimbaran will provide **transport** to the airport for about Rp20,000. **Metered taxis** are cheaper: around Rp16,000 from Kuta. All tour agents offer **shuttle buses** to the airport: shop around for the most convenient schedule (journey times also vary), and reckon on paying about Rp10,000 from Sanur, Rp15,000 from Ubud, Rp25,000 from Candi Dasa and Rp40,000 from Lovina. During daylight hours, you can also take the dark-blue Tegal (Denpasar)–Kuta–Tuban **bemo** from Denpasar, Kuta or Jimbaran, which will drop you just beyond the airport gates for Rp2000–3000.

Airport **departure tax** is Rp100,000 for international departures and Rp20,000 for domestic flights. Airside in the departures area, there's an **internet centre**, international card **phones**, a couple of snack bars, and dozens of souvenir **shops**, but be warned that prices here are hugely inflated.

International airline offices in Bali

Most airline offices open Mon–Fri 8.30am–5pm, Sat 8.30am–noon; some close for an hour's lunch at noon or 12.30pm.

Garuda has offices and city check-ins inside the *Sanur Beach Hotel* in southern Sanur (24-hour ⓣ0361/270535), and at the *Natour Kuta Beach Hotel* in Kuta (ⓣ0361/751179).

Offices of the following carriers are inside the compound of the *Grand Bali Beach Hotel* in Sanur: **Air France** ⓣ0361/288511 extn 1105; **Cathay Pacific** ⓣ0361/286001; **Continental Micronesia** ⓣ0361/287774; **JAL** ⓣ0361/287576; **Northwest Airlines** ⓣ0361/287841; **Qantas** ⓣ0361/288331; **Thai International** ⓣ0361/288141. Offices of the following are in Ngurah Rai Airport itself: **Air New Zealand** ⓣ0361/756170; **ANA** ⓣ0361/761101; **Eva Air** ⓣ0361/759773; **Malaysia Air** ⓣ0361/764995; **Royal Brunei** ⓣ0361/757292; and **Singapore Airlines/Silk Air** ⓣ0361/768388. **Lauda Air** is at Jl Bypass Ngurah Rai 12 (ⓣ0361/758686) and the nearest **British Airways** office is in Jakarta (see p.119).

Domestic airline offices in Bali

Air Mark Ngurah Rai Airport ⓣ0361/759769; **Awair** No walk-in office ⓣ0361/768403, ⓦwww.awairlines.com; **Garuda** Jl Melati 61, Denpasar ⓣ0361/254747, ⓦwww.garuda-indonesia.com; **Merpati** Jl Melati 51, Denpasar ⓣ0361/235358, ⓦwww.merpati.co.id; **Pelita** Book through travel agents, ⓦwww.pelita-airventure.com.

mal taxi service offered by the **transport touts** who hang around on every corner.

Every major road in the resort is packed with tour agents offering **car rental**; most offer 800cc Suzuki Jimnys (Rp100,000 per 24hr) as well as larger, more comfortable 1600cc Toyota Kijangs (Rp150,000); try Kuta Suci at Jalan Pantai Kuta 37c (ⓣ0361/765357, ⓔkutasuci@mail.com). At the most reputable outlets, insurance is included. Most places will also provide a **driver** for the day, for an extra Rp50,000–100,000, including fuel. A recommended freelance English-speaking guide and driver is Wayan Artana (mobile ⓣ0812/396 1296,

ⓔiartana@hotmail.com). You can also rent **motorbikes** (Rp35,000–60,000/day) from many of the same outlets. **Bicycles** (Rp15,000 per 24hr) can also be rented at some car and motorbike rental places, or through your losmen.

Moving on from Kuta

Bemos

To get from Kuta to most other destinations in Bali by bemo almost always entails going via Denpasar, where you'll probably have to make at least one cross-city connection.

Dark-blue bemos to **Denpasar**'s Tegal terminal (around Rp3000; 25min) run regularly throughout the day; the easiest place to catch them is at the Jl Pantai Kuta/Jl Raya Tuban intersection, about 15m east of Bemo Corner, where they wait to collect passengers, although you can also get on anywhere on their loop around Kuta (see p.536 for details).

From Tegal, other bemos run to **Sanur** and to Denpasar's other bemo terminals for onward connections; full details are on p.528 and on the map on p.529. Note that, to get to Batubulan station (departure point for **Ubud**), the white Damri bus service from Nusa Dua is quicker than taking a bemo to Tegal and another to Batubulan; you can pick it up at the fuel station on the intersection of Jl Imam Bonjol and Jl Setia Budi, about ten minutes' walk northeast of Bemo Corner. Dark blue bemos from Tegal to Bualu (for **Nusa Dua** and **Tanjung Benoa**) also pass this intersection, and will pick you up on Jl Setia Budi if you signal. Some Tegal–Bualu bemos serve **Jimbaran** on the way, and there's also a dark-blue Tegal–Jimbaran bemo, which occasionally continues on through the Bukit – possibly as far as **Uluwatu**.

Shuttle buses

If you're going anywhere beyond Denpasar, the quickest and priciest public transport option from Kuta is to take a tourist **shuttle bus**. Every one of the hundred or more tour agencies in Kuta–Legian–Seminyak offers "shuttle bus services", so prices are competitive, and most travellers choose according to convenience of timetable and pick-up points. Drop-offs are unknown on the smaller operations, most of which will drop you only at their offices in your destination.

The island's best-known and biggest shuttle bus operator is **Perama Travel**, whose unobtrusive head office is located 100m north of Bemo Corner at Jl Legian 39 (daily 7am–10pm, ⓣ0361/751551, ⓔperama_tour@hotmail.com). This is the departure point for all Perama buses, although you can pay an extra Rp3000 to be picked up from your hotel and can also buy tickets on the phone and through other agents. Perama buses are non-air-con and run between Kuta and all the obvious tourist destinations on Bali as well as to some major spots on Lombok and Sumbawa (prices include the boat transfer); see Travel Details on p.663 for a full list. Perama also sell through tickets for public buses to Java. Prices are reasonable; for example Rp15,000 to Ubud, Rp40,000 to Lovina, Rp50,000 to Senggigi on Lombok.

Transport to other islands

Many Kuta travel agents will sell **boat tickets** to other islands on a variety of operators, including Bounty Cruise, Mabua, *Osiania 3* and Barito. All boats leave from Benoa Harbour, described on p.563, where you'll also find details of destinations and ticket prices. Details of the local Pelni office (for long-distance boats to other parts of Indonesia) are on p.563. Perama **shuttle-bus** tickets to destinations on Lombok, Sumbawa and Java all include the ferry (see above).

All Kuta agents sell **domestic airline tickets**. Sample one-way fares include Rp235,000 to Mataram on Lombok, Rp430,000 to Yogyakarta, Rp810,000 to Jakarta. Full airport information is on p.538.

Accommodation

The resort's most **inexpensive** losmen are mainly concentrated in the Kuta area, particularly along Poppies 1, Poppies 2 and Jalan Benesari. **Moderately priced** rooms are good value in Legian, often featuring air-con and use of a pool, and the **expensive** places that dominate Tuban and northern Seminyak generally occupy grounds right on the beach. Many mid-priced and expensive hotels offer discounts for online bookings and major savings outside high season.

Kuta and Tuban

Kuta is where the action is, the most congested and hectic part of the resort. The beach gets crowded, but it's a good stretch of sand and deservedly popular; it's also the surfing centre of the resort. Be warned that during the **rainy season** (late October to March), the middle stretches of Jalan Sorga and Poppies 2 can remain flooded for days. South of Jalan Pantai Kuta, Kuta beach officially becomes **Tuban** beach and things quieten down a great deal, though most hotels here are some distance from restaurants and shops.

Inexpensive

Ayu Beach Inn Poppies 1 ⓣ0361/752091, ⓕ752948. Popular, good-value option with two pools, internet access, and a restaurant. Rooms (some air-con) are decent if not exactly spotless. ❸–❹

Jus Edith south off Poppies 2 ⓣ0361/750558. Extremely popular losmen with eleven basic rooms; close to the action and very inexpensive. ❷

Kedin's Inn 1 Poppies 1 ⓣ0361/756771. Twenty-seven large, adequate, fan-cooled rooms, including some very good-value three-person ones, set around a garden. ❸

Komala Indah 1 (Jl Benesari) Jl Benesari ⓣ0361/753185. A range of terraced bungalows (some air-con) set in a pretty garden less than 200m from the beach. ❷–❹

Komala Indah 1 (Poppies 1) Poppies 1 ⓣ0361/751422. These terraced bungalows set around a central courtyard garden are conveniently located and one of the cheapest places to stay in Kuta. ❷

Komala Indah 2 (Jl Benesari) Jl Benesari ⓣ0361/754258. Simply furnished, inexpensive losmen rooms located in a quiet area thirty seconds' walk from the beach. ❷–❸

Kuta Suci 2 Bungalows Gang Mangga, off Poppies 2 ⓣ0361/752617. Eleven very cheap rooms in terraced bungalows in a garden. ❷

Puri Ayodia Inn Jl Sorga ⓣ0361/754245. Exceptionally good-value losmen between Poppies 1 and Poppies 2, with clean well-furnished rooms. Fills up fast. ❷

Puspa Ayu Bungalows Gang Puspa Ayu, Tuban ⓣ0361/756721. The cheapest and most popular accommodation on this residential street has nice enough bungalows (some air-con) 200m off the main road. ❹

Sandat Bali Inn Jl Legian 120 ⓣ0361/753491. Recommended set of clean and well-maintained rooms (some air-con), just a few metres from *The New Bounty*. ❸

Sorga Cottages Jl Sorga ⓣ0361/751897, ⓕ752417; ⓦwww.angelfire.com/id/sorga, ⓔsorga@idola.net.id. Good-value, comfortably furnished rooms (some air-con) in a three-storey block set round a small pool and a restaurant. ❹–❺

Taman Ayu 2 Jl Benesari ⓣ0361/754376, ⓕ754640. A small block of very reasonably priced and unusually well-maintained bamboo-walled fan rooms plus a handful of bungalows. ❸

Mid-range

Bali Sandy Cottages Off Poppies 2 ⓣ0361/753344, ⓕ750791. Attractive, good-value fan and air-con rooms set around a large pool and lawn. A quiet location, but close to the beach and restaurants on Poppies 2. ❺

Bounty Hotel Poppies 2 ⓣ0361/753030, ⓕ752121, ⓦwww.balibountygroup.com. Large, exceptionally well-maintained terraced bungalows (all air-con) set in a garden with two pools. Popular with young Australians. ❻

Mastapa Garden Hotel Jl Legian 139 ⓣ0361/751660, ⓕ755098, ⓦwww.indo.com/hotels/mastapa, ⓔmastapa@denpasar.wasantara.net.id. Secluded and quiet but very central garden haven, with pool. All rooms are air-con, there's internet access and free transport from the airport. ❻

Old Poppies Poppies 2 ⓣ0361/751059, ⓕ752364, ⓦwww.poppies.net. Characterful Bali-style cottages with carved doors, thatched roofs and fans. Beautiful garden, and use of the pool at *Poppies Cottages*. ❻

Sandi Phala Off Jl Dewi Sartika, Tuban ⓣ0361/753780, ⓕ236021. Terraced rooms and smarter wooden chalets set on beachfront land, which makes them exceptional value. Some air-con, and a pool. ❺–❻

Expensive

Adi Dharma Access from both Jl Legian and Jl Benesari: hotel ⓣ0361/754280, cottages ⓣ751527, both ⓕ753803, ⓦwww.indo.com/hotels/adhi_dharma. Nicely furnished air-con "cottage" rooms in a terraced block, plus some more upmarket rooms in a separate building. Pool, and games room. ❼

Bali Garden Hotel Jl Dewi Sartika, Tuban ⓣ0361/752725, ⓕ753851, ⓦwww.baligardenhotel.com. Huge, attractive low-rise hotel complex, with high-standard rooms and a lovely beachfront garden. ❽

Hard Rock Hotel, Jl Pantai Kuta ⓣ0361/761869, ⓕ762162, ⓦwww.hardrockhotelbali.com. Unashamedly un-Balinese hotel, with a rock-music theme throughout. Fantastic series of swimming pools, and a prime location. ❽

Hotel Intan Legian Corner of Jl Pantai Kuta and Jl Melasti ⓣ0361/751770, ⓕ751891, ⓦwww.balihotels.com/legian/intan.htm, ⓔhilegb@indosat.net.id. Huge, comfortable cottages set in terraced gardens, a hop across the road from the beach. Swimming pool. ❽

Poppies Cottages Poppies 1 ⓣ0361/751059, ⓕ752364, ⓦwww.poppies.net. Extremely popular, elegantly designed traditional cottages, with air-con and a swimming pool. Reservations essential. ❼

Legian and Seminyak

Significantly calmer than Kuta, **Legian** has a reputation for attracting the resort's more laid-back travellers as well as long-stay surfers. Many of the smaller, lower-mid-range hotels are better value than in Kuta, with easy access to the shore. Upmarket **Seminyak** is quiet and pleasant and attracts tourists who've been to Bali before and want more peace and seclusion second time around. It's also where many expats choose to live, so the shops and restaurants cater for them. Away from the main drag, Jalan Raya Seminyak, things are quite spread out, so you may end up using a lot of taxis.

Legian

Ayodya Beach Inn Jl Three Brothers ⓣ0361/752169, ⓔayodyabeachinn@yahoo.com. Shabby but inexpensive terraced rooms in a garden. ❷–❸

Ever Green Puri Jl Arjuna ⓣ0361/730386. Amazingly good-value budget fan-cooled rooms and bungalows in a prime spot close to a fine stretch of shore. There's a surf school on the premises. ❸

Hotel Kumala Jl Werk Udara ⓣ0361/732186, ⓕ730407, ⓦwww.kumalahotel.com. Recommended place that offers lots of appealing rooms and cottages, all with air-con, plus two pools. ❺

Legian Beach Bungalow Jl Padma ⓣ0361/751087. Simple but pleasant enough bungalows set in a garden with a pool close to the shops and near the beach. Friendly and well priced. ❸–❹

Legian Beach Hotel Jl Melasti ⓣ0361/751711, ⓕ752651, ⓦwww.legianbeachbali.com. Huge collection of upmarket bungalow accommodation, in an attractive garden with two pools. ❽

Lumbung Sari Jl Three Brothers ⓣ & ⓕ0361/752009, ⓔlumbung_sari@yahoo.com. Huge, two-storey air-con bungalows, with kitchen, plus some cheaper fan rooms in a central block. Swimming pool. ❺

Hotel Padma Jl Padma 1 ⓣ0361/752111, ⓕ752140, ⓦwww.hotelpadma.com. Smart rooms in a hotel wing as well as more attractive bungalow accommodation. Nice garden with two pools and a kids' club. ❼–❽

Sri Ratu Cottages Jl Three Brothers ⓣ0361/751722, ⓕ754468, ⓦsriratu.tripod.com, ⓔsriratuhotel@yahoo.com. Divided into two compounds, with seven attractive bungalows in a garden and nineteen very clean air-con rooms set around a pool across the way. ❹–❺

Suri Wathi Jl Sahadewa 12 ⓣ0361/753162, ⓕ758393, ⓔsuriwati@yahoo.com. Friendly, family-run losmen with good-value bungalows (some air-con) and smaller rooms. Quiet but convenient, with a pool. ❸–❺

Su's Cottages Jl Bagus Taruna/Jl Werk Udara 532 ⓣ0361/730324, ⓕ762202. Spotless, nicely furnished rooms in a small, friendly, family-run losmen. Some air-con and a tiny pool. ❹–❺

Three Brothers Inn Jl Three Brothers ⓣ0361/751566, ⓕ756082, ⓔthreebrothersbungalows@yahoo.com. Variety of large, characterful cottages (the upstairs fan-cooled ones are best) in a rambling garden. ❺–❻

Seminyak

Bali Oberoi Jl Laksmana ⓣ0361/730361, ⓕ730791, ⓦwww.oberoihotels.com. Set beside the beach to the north of the main Seminyak district, the traditional-style coral-rock bungalows here are favoured by the rich and famous. Published rates from $255. ❽

Hotel Imperial Bali Jl Dhyana Pura ⓣ0361/730730, ⓕ730545, ⓦwww.bali-imperial.com. Plush, classy hotel rooms and cottages set in a beachfront garden; two pools and tennis courts. ❽

Mesari Beach Inn Jl Abimanyu, south off Jl Dhyana Pura ⓣ0361/730401. Just three exceptionally cheap no-frills rooms in a plot that gives direct access to the beach. ❸

Panca Jaya Jl Abimanyu, south off Jl Dhyana Pura ⓣ & ⓕ0361/730458. Simple but comfortable enough losmen, offering some of the cheapest rooms in the area. ❸

Puri Cendana Jl Dhyana Pura ⓣ0361/730869, ⓕ730868, ⓦwww.puri-cendana.com. Balinese-style two-storey cottages with air-con in a gorgeous garden just 30m from the beach. Swimming pool. ❼

Raja Gardens Jl Abimanyu, south off Jl Dhyana Pura ⓣ0361/730494, ⓕ732805. Six nicely furnished bungalows plus pool, a minute's walk from the beach. Family-run and good value. ❺

The resort

There's nothing much to see in Kuta–Legian–Seminyak, but there's plenty to do, both in the resort and on day-trips out. The **beach** is quite possibly the most beautiful in Bali, with its gentle curve of clean, golden sand stretching for 8km, its huge breakers, and the much-lauded Kuta sunsets. The most congested swathe is Kuta beach itself, along Jalan Pantai Kuta; the most peaceful is at Seminyak, between Jalan Dhyana Pura and *La Lucciola* restaurant at Petitenget, but the sands around Jalan Arjuna in north Legian make a pleasant alternative. The waves that make Kuta such a great beach for surfers make it less pleasant for **swimming**, with a strong undertow as well as the breakers to contend with. You should always swim between the red- and yellow-striped flags, and take notice of any warning signs. **Lifeguards** are stationed all along the Kuta–Legian stretch and the central lifeguard post is on the beach at the corner of Jalan Pantai Kuta.

Surfing

Because the beach is sandy and there's no coral or rocks to wipe out on, Kuta is the best place in Bali to learn to surf. The resort's four main **breaks** – known as Kuta Beach, Legian Beach, Airport Lefts and Kuta Reef – all offer consistent, almost uniform waves, with lots of tubes, and are best surfed from April to October. Monthly **tide charts** are compiled by *Tubes* bar on Poppies 2 and are available there as well as at most surfwear shops in the resort. Poppies 2, Poppies 1 and Jalan Benesari form the heart of Kuta's surf scene, and these are the best areas to **buy boards** or get them repaired, but you can easily **rent boards** on the beach (Rp35,000). **Surfing lessons** (from $35 per half-day) are offered by the Cheyne Horan School of Surf, based at the *Ever Green Puri* hotel, Jl Arjuna 7a in north Legian (ⓣ0361/735858, ⓦwww.schoolofsurf.com).

Several tour agents in Kuta organize regular **surfing tours** from March to October to the mega-waves off Sumbawa, East Java (including the awesome G-Land; see p.337), West Java, Lombok and West Timor. Prices for these all-inclusive "surfaris" depend on whether you want tent or hut accommodation, and start at US$250 for a week. Established surfari operators include Wanasari Wisata, inside the G-Land surf shop, Jl Pantai Kuta 8b (ⓣ0361/755588, ⓕ755690, ⓦwww.grajagan.com); Indoswell.com on Poppies 1 (ⓣ0361/763892, ⓕ763893, ⓦwww.indoswell.com); and *Tubes* bar on Poppies 2 (ⓣ0361/772870, ⓦwww.g-land.com).

Watersports and other activities

Surfing aside, Kuta is not a great centre for **watersports** and, although the resort is stuffed with tour agencies offering snorkelling, diving, sea-kayaking, whitewater rafting and fishing trips, they will all take you elsewhere to do these things. Internationally certified **diving courses** (see p.560) can also be organized through agents in Kuta–Legian–Seminyak. If you want to go parasailing, jet-skiing, windsurfing or water-skiing, your best option is to make your own way to Tanjung Benoa (see p.551) or Sanur (see p.555). Kuta's **Waterbom Park** on Jalan Dewi Sartika, Tuban (daily 8.30am–6pm; $16.50, 5–12-year-olds $9), is an aquatic adventure park with water slides, helter-skelters, and a lazy river with inner tubes. Another good watery option is the **Hard Rock pool** (daylight hours; adults Rp50,000, kids Rp25,000, two adults plus two kids Rp125,000), inside the *Hard Rock* hotel complex on Jalan Pantai Kuta. It's hundreds of metres long, and includes water chutes, a sandy beach area, volleyball net and poolside food and drink waiters.

Many of Bali's most spectacular sights are easily visited from Kuta as part of a day-trip, and every tour agent offers ten or more fixed-itinerary **organized tours**. Tours generally travel in an air-con eight- to ten-person minibus, last from around 8.30am to 4.30pm, and cost Rp60,000–100,000 per person. Or charter your own car-with-driver (see p.439).

Several companies run more energetic day-trips, for example **whitewater rafting** ($70; kids $45), **kayaking** ($68), and **mountain-biking** ($54; kids $37); contact Bali Adventure Tours (Ⓣ0361/721480, Ⓦwww.baliadventuretours.com) or Sobek (Ⓣ0361/287059, Ⓦwww.sobekbali.com). Perama (Ⓣ0361/751551, Ⓔperama_tour@hotmail.com) lead guided sunrise **mountain climbs** up Gunung Agung ($40).

Massages and **beauty therapies** are becoming increasingly popular in Kuta, especially the traditional Javanese *mandi lulur* treatment, an exfoliating body scrub involving turmeric paste and yoghurt. Recommended beauty centres include Bodyworks 1, Jl Raya Seminyak 63 (Ⓣ0361/730454), and Bodyworks 2 at Jl Kayu Jati 2, near the *Bali Oberoi* in Petitenget (Ⓣ0361/733317).

Eating

There are hundreds of **places to eat** in Kuta–Legian–Seminyak, and the range is phenomenal, from tiny streetside warung to outstanding international restaurants. Kuta's main **night market** (*pasar senggol*) gets going after sundown on Gang Tuan Langa at the southern edge of Kuta. In the mornings, many tourists head for the **buffet breakfasts** (7.30–11.30am) served at Jalan Melasti and Jalan Sahadewa restaurants, where for around Rp13,000 you get as much hot and cold food as you can manage. Unless otherwise stated, all restaurants are open daily from breakfast-time through to at least 10pm.

Kuta and Tuban

Aromas Café Jl Legian. Delicious but pricey, vegetarian Lebanese, Italian, Indian and Indonesian food served in large portions.

Daddy's Café Jl Dewi Sartika, Tuban. Reasonably priced and very authentic Greek restaurant with an unrivalled selection of mezes, seafood platters, plus genuine kebabs, souvlaka and moussaka.

Golden Lotus Inside the *Bali Dynasty Resort*, Jl Dewi Sartika, Tuban. Good upmarket Chinese restaurant; pricey but tasty. All-you-can-eat buffets on Sundays, 10am–2.30pm; dim sum is served from noon to 2.30pm the rest of the week.

Ketupat Behind the Jonathan Gallery jewellery shop at Jl Legian 109. Superb menu of exquisite Indonesian dishes based around fish, goat and chicken, plus some vegetarian options. Upmarket but not overpriced.

Kori Poppies 2. Refined dining in an elegant setting. Delicious if pricey swordfish, lobster mornay, red fish curry and home-made ice creams. Not great for vegetarians, but otherwise worth the money.

Made's Warung 1 Jl Pantai Kuta. Longstanding mid-priced Kuta favourite whose table-sharing policy encourages sociability. Mainly standard Indonesian fare, rijsttafels, plus cappuccino and cakes.

TJs Poppies 1. Popular, long-running Californian/Mexican restaurant with tables set around a water garden. Moderately priced menu covering the full gamut of tortillas, fajitas, margaritas and daiquiris.

Warung Murni Jl Pantai. Exceptionally cheap, old-style travellers' warung where the *nasi goreng* costs a bargain Rp5000 and there are just half-a-dozen formica tables.

Warung Suka-Suka Poppies 1. Popular, extremely cheap'n'cheerful warung with just a few tables and a menu that includes select-your-own Padang food, *nasi campur*, *bakso* (soup) and omelettes. Cheap beer too.

Legian

Bali Too Jl Melasti. Popular inexpensive place serving delicious spicy Thai soup and some less interesting Indonesian and Western standards. Good-value breakfast buffets.

Glory Jl Legian 445, 200m north of Jl Padma ☎0361/751091. Hearty breakfasts and weekly Saturday-night Balinese home-cooking buffets (Rp30,000/kids Rp15,000). Call for free transport to the buffets.

Gosha Seafood Jl Melasti. The most popular seafood restaurant in Legian; reasonably priced lobster a speciality.

Warung Melati Jl Arjuna. A favourite of economy-minded expats, this Masakan Padang-style place is a bargain with a good range of ready-cooked foods from which to assemble your Rp5000 meal.

Warung Yogya Jl Padma Utara 79. Another deservedly popular, unpretentious and very cheap Indonesian eatery. Tasty home-cooked classics, including *nasi campur* (veg or non-veg) and *nasi pecel*.

Seminyak

Gus Bakery Jl Raya Seminyak 16B. French bakery/coffee shop: pastries, fruit tarts and good breads.

Made's Warung 2 About 100m north of Jl Dhyana Pura on Jl Raya Seminyak. Fairly pricey Indo-European menu that looks unadventurous but tastes great and is served in copious portions.

La Lucciola Jl Petitenget, but access only by a footpath from the Pura Petitenget car park, or from the beach ☎0361/730838; reservations advisable. The open-sided beachfront dining room is a favourite spot for sunset cocktails and romantic dinners. Expensive, Mediterranean-inspired menu.

The Living Room Jl Petitenget, about 350m beyond Pura Petitenget ☎0361/735735. Nightly from 7pm; reservations advisable. Delightful, colonial-style eating experience, whose fairly expensive pan-Asian menu includes red-on-red swordfish and honey-glazed roasted Balinese duckling.

Pantarei Jl Raya Seminyak 17. Stylish place with a contemporary ambience and a pricey, mainly Greek menu of mixed meat kebabs, grilled swordfish, and the famously expensive lobster spaghetti.

Soda Club Beachfront, off the west end of Jl Arjuna. Trendy, mid-priced seafront bar-restaurant offering sofas with a sea view, and a menu that runs from seafood to stroganoff, with plenty of veggie options.

Nightlife and entertainment

Kuta boasts the liveliest and most diverse **nightlife** on the island, with most bars and clubs staying open till at least 1am. As most of the action is concentrated in Kuta, it's quite possible to walk from bar to bar and then home again: the main streets are well lit and usually pretty lively till at least 3am, although muggings do occur. As a rule, the clubs and bars of Kuta–Legian–Seminyak are friendly enough towards lone drinkers, male or female. Although women are unlikely to get serious hassle, you'll get seriously chatted up by the resident gaggle of **gigolos** who haunt the bars in search of romance.

Kuta is not exactly renowned for its wealth of cultural entertainment, but most tour agencies organize trips to see **Balinese dancing** at venues outside the resort. In Kuta itself, the *Natour Kuta* hotel on Jalan Pantai puts on a medley show of several Balinese dances every Friday at 7.30pm, with a buffet dinner ($12; kids $6). See the box on p.582 for more about Balinese dance.

Bars and clubs

Kuta's nightlife is very much a younger travellers' scene, with the most popular bars and clubs (*such as The New Bounty*), packed out by 11pm and still raging at 2am. A number of the venues listed below feature **live music** from local bands, as does the restaurant at the *Barong* hotel on Poppies 2 and the one at *Indah Beach* hotel further west along the same road. To avoid the prospect of drinking alone, you could join the twice-weekly Peanuts Pub Crawl (every Tues & Sat from 6.30pm; Rp15,000; call ⓣ0361/754149 for details) which transports punters to the main drinking spots along Jalan Legian, including the *Peanuts* disco-bar.

Up in **Legian–Seminyak**, the scene is more self-consciously fashionable and expensive, and attracts a bigger crowd of expats and well-heeled Indonesians. For a more intimate experience, head for Jalan Dhyana Pura (aka Jalan Abimanyu), where there's a cluster of trendy little dance-bars. All Seminyak clubs keep well abreast of current dance sounds and employ plenty of Western as well as local DJs; the Ecstasy-fuelled rave scene is well established at most of the major venues.

Kuta's **gay scene** is becoming more developed, with a dedicated gay bar in Legian at *Hulu Café*, another one at *Q Bar* on Jalan Dhyana Pura in Seminyak, and a strong presence at other venues on the same road.

Kuta and Tuban

All Stars Surf Café Kuta Centre, Jl Dewi Sartika, Tuban. Surf bar with different bands playing nightly (9pm–2.30am), surfing videos on 15 screens, lots of memorabilia, plus pool tables and dartboards.
Deejay Café Behind the *All Stars Surf Café* in Kuta Centre, Jl Dewi Sartika 8x. Sophisticated club that's part open-air and part air-con, playing mainly trance and tribal underground. Nightly 11pm–6am.
Hard Rock Café Jl Pantai. Despite being part of the international chain, this place attracts a large, youngish crowd from around 11pm when the live music starts. Expensive drinks. Closes 2am (weekends 3am).
The Old Bounty Just north of Jl Benesari on Jl Legian, and **The New Bounty**, between Poppies 1 and Poppies 2 on Jl Legian. These two identical novelty buildings, both built to resemble Captain Bligh's eighteenth-century galleon, play mainly contemporary hits and are especially popular with young Australians. The *New Bounty* runs happy hours nightly (7pm–2am), and doesn't shut down till dawn.
Peanuts Club Just south of the Jl Melasti intersection on Jl Legian. Large disco and bar with low-grade live music in the streetside section, and a classic rock sound system plus glitterball to dance to inside. Pool table and karaoke bar and reasonably priced drinks; closes around 2am.
Tubes Poppies 2. The top surfers' hangout in Kuta, fully kitted out with noticeboards, surfing videos and signed champion boards, plus a bar and pool tables. Live music every Mon, Wed & Fri. Closes around 2am.

Legian and Seminyak

A Club Jl Basangkasa 10a (just before the turn-off to the *Oberoi*), Seminyak. Trendy spot where the resident DJs play mainly house music and host regular one-off parties. Tues–Sat from 10pm.
Café del Mar Jl Dhyana Pura 100x, Seminyak. Fairly cool place, with nightly DJs spinning up-to-date sounds, a fashion-conscious crowd and a bar full of cocktails. Nightly from 9pm.
Double Six ("66") Off the beachfront end of Jl Arjuna, Seminyak. Huge, trendy, upmarket club with a dance floor, international DJs, and several bars. On Saturday nights (2–4am) there's a bungee jump outside. Pricey drinks, and a hefty admission charge (weekdays Rp30,000; Sat Rp50,000), which includes one small beer. Nightly midnight–6am.
Hulu Café Jl Sahadewa, Legian. Kuta's most outré gay venue stages glamorously over-the-top drag shows from 10.30pm. Open Tues–Sun 4pm till late.
Jaya Pub Jl Raya Seminyak 2. Fairly sedate live-music venue and watering-hole for older tourists and expats. Twenty or so tables and no real dance floor.
Q Bar Jl Dhyana Pura, Seminyak. Seminyak's main gay venue stages different nights every day of the week, including drag shows, cabarets and retro theme nights. Nightly 6pm–1.30am.
Santa Fe Jl Abimanyu, Seminyak. Very popular bar and restaurant, larger than many on this road, that gets lively quite soon after dark and has live music from cover bands several nights a week. Shuts about 1.30am.

Shopping

Kuta–Legian–Seminyak is a great place to **shop**, and most stores stay open until at least 9pm. For basic necessities and food, check out **Matahari department store** in Kuta Square, Kuta (the smaller branch on Jalan Legian is not so interesting). There are plenty of secondhand bookstores on Poppies 1, Poppies 2, Jalan Benesari, Jalan Padma Utara, Jalan Legian and the east–west stretch of Jalan Pantai Kuta.

Books and music

Bombocraft Jl Pantai Kuta 8c, Kuta. Handmade musical instruments from around the world.
Bookshop Jl Raya Seminyak. Range of new books in English, mostly on Indonesia, plus some fiction.
Fuji Jaya Poppies 2, Kuta. Reasonable stock of secondhand books in good condition.
Kerta Books Four branches: two on Jl Legian, plus one each on Jl Pantai and Jl Padma Utara. Good stocks of secondhand books.
Mahogany Next to *Pantarei* on Jl Raya Seminyak. Good range of CDs, DVDs and Playstation games.
Matahari department store Kuta Square, Kuta. Keeps a few new English-language books on Bali and Indonesia.
Men at Work Jl Singo Sari, Kuta. Decent selection of CDs and DVDs.

Clothes and jewellery

Kuta Art Market Beach end of Jl Singo Sari. Collection of small shops and stalls selling cheap clothes.
Sports Station Jl Legian, Kuta, 200m north of Perama Travel. Sports shoes, snorkel sets and badminton racquets.
Suarti Legian, near *Mastapa Garden* hotel. Distinctive modern necklaces, bracelets and earrings.
Surfwear shops Bali Barrel, Billabong, Blue Surf, Mambo, Quicksilver, Stussy and Surfer Girl – along Jl Legian and every other shopping street in the resort. Brand-name surf- and skate-wear.
Talismans of Power Jl Raya Seminyak. Dramatic silver jewellery in unusual designs.

Crafts, textiles and homewares

Ana Mahang Jl Legian 159, Kuta. Ikat scarves, bedspreads and hangings from Sumba and Flores.
Arin 93 Gang Kresek 5a, off Jl Singo Sari, Tuban. Batik paintings by master batik artist Heru.
Batik textiles Jl Arjuna, Legian. This road has more than a dozen batik textile shops.
Idea Jl Melasti, Legian. Stylish handicrafts and gifts.
Lombok Pottery Blok C11, Kuta Centre, Jl Dewi Sartika, Tuban. An outlet for the attractive earthenware made under the auspices of the Lombok Pottery Project.
Lumbung Batik Jl Kahuripan, Tuban. Useful fixed-price shop for sarongs, hangings and bedspreads.
Nogo Ikat Jl Legian 47, Kuta. Upmarket *ikat* furnishings and fabric by the metre.
Oxo Just north of Jl Arjuna on Jl Raya Seminyak. Hand-crafted wooden puppets from all over Asia.
Wira's Above Lumbung Batik on Jl Kahuripan, Tuban. Huge range of fabrics by the metre, plus a dressmaking service.

Listings

Airline offices Garuda city check-in is at *Natour Kuta Beach Hotel* on Jl Pantai Kuta, Kuta ⓣ0361/751179.
Banks and exchange There are Visa, MasterCard and Cirrus ATMs on every major street. The Bank Bali opposite *The Bounty* at Jl Legian 118 offers Visa cash advances, as do several banks in Kuta Square. There's a Moneygram agent in Blok E of the Kuta Centre complex on Jl Dewi Sartika in Tuban. Be very careful about being ripped-off at exchange counters in Kuta: many places short-change tourists by rigging calculators or double-folding notes. One chain of recommended moneychangers is PT Central Kuta, which has several branches on Jl Legian plus one on Jl Melasti, many of them inside Kodak film shops. There's another reputable moneychanger just a few metres north up Jl Legian from Bemo Corner, on the east side of the road. If you do get caught in a moneychanging scam, contact the community police (see below).
Batik classes Batik artist Heru gives workshops at Gang Kresek 5a, off Jl Singo Sari, Tuban ⓣ0361/765087, ⓔarin93batik@hotmail.com. Three-day workshops cost Rp350,000.
Hospitals and clinics Bali's efficient chain of tourist-oriented 24hr clinics known as Legian Clinics numbers 1–7, have two branches in

Kuta–Legian–Seminyak. Legian Clinic 1 is on Jl Benesari, north Kuta ⓣ0361/758503; Legian Clinic 7 is on Jl Legian, 100m north of *Glory* restaurant, in Legian ⓣ0361/752376. Both offer consultations with an English-speaking doctor (Rp100,000), emergency call-out (Rp400,000), minor surgery and dental services. A similar service is offered by the SOS Natour Kuta Beach, next to the *Natour Kuta* hotel on Jl Pantai Kuta ⓣ0361/751361, and the Kuta Clinic on Jl Raya Tuban ⓣ0361/753268. Nearly all the large, upmarket hotels have an in-house doctor. A couple of places on the outskirts of Kuta also have good reputations for dealing with expat emergencies: Bali International Medical Centre (BIMC) at Jl Bypass Ngurah Rai ⓣ0361/761263, and International SOS at Jl Bypass Ngurah Rai ⓣ0361/755768. The nearest hospitals are in Denpasar; see p.532.

House Rental Both Krakatoa internet centre at Jl Raya Seminyak 56 (opposite Jl Dhyana Pura) and Bali@Cyber Café on Jl Bagus Taruna have noticeboards full of adverts for long- and short-term house rentals in Legian and Seminyak.

Internet access You're rarely more than 500m away from an internet centre; most places charge Rp300–500/min. Hi-tech centres include: Bali @ Cyber Café and Restaurant, Jl Pura Bagus Taruna 4, Legian (daily 8.30am–11pm); Legian Cyber C@fe, Jl Sahadewa 21, Legian (daily 8am–10.30pm); and Krakatoa, Jl Raya Seminyak 56, opposite Jl Dhyana Pura (Mon–Fri 8am–10pm, Sat & Sun 8am–8pm). The Lazale chain of internet cafés charges a ridiculous Rp1000/min.

Laundry Many losmen and all hotels offer laundry services. There's a coin-operated laundromat at Jl Benesari 19.

Left luggage All hotels and losmen will store your luggage if you reserve a room for your return; some charge a nominal fee. There's also left luggage at the airport (see p.538).

Pharmacies On every major shopping street, as well as Legian Clinic 1, on Jl Benesari, north Kuta; next to Bemo Corner on Jl Legian, south Kuta; inside the Matahari Department Store in Kuta Square; and on Jl Singo Sari.

Phones The government wartel is inconveniently sited down at the airport, but there are dozens of private wartels in the resort, most of them open from 8am–midnight. All the email centres offer fax services.

Police The local community police, Satgas Pantai Desa Adat Kuta, are English-speaking and in 24-hour attendance at their office on the beach in front of *Natour Kuta Beach Hotel* (ⓣ0361/762871). The government police station is at the intersection of Jl Raya Tuban and Jl Singo Sari.

Post offices Kuta's GPO and poste restante is on a *gang* between Jl Raya Tuban and Jl Tanjung Mekar (Mon–Thurs 8am–2pm, Fri 8am–noon, Sat 8am–1pm). Poste/fax restante also at Asthini Yasa Postal Agent, opposite *Glory* restaurant on Jl Legian, Legian (Mon–Sat 8am–8pm; ⓕ0361/752883). Many other shops throughout the resort double as postal agents and keep normal shop hours.

Travel agents Domestic and international airline tickets are available from the following agents, some of which also sell express boat tickets: Kuta Suci, Jl Pantai Kuta 37c ⓣ0361/765357, ⓔkutasuci@mail.com; Lila Tours, inside *Natour Kuta Beach* hotel, Jl Pantai Kuta ⓣ0361/761827, ⓔlilatur@indosat.net.id; Perama Travel, Jl Legian 39 ⓣ0361/751551, ⓔperama_tour@hotmail.com; and Amanda Tour, Century Plaza complex, Jl Benesari 7, ⓣ0361/755660, ⓔamantour@indosat.net.id. Get Pelni boat tickets from the Pelni office, about 250m south of Supernova at Jl Raya Tuban 299 ⓣ0361/763963 or 723689.

The Bukit and Nusa Dua

About 4km south of Kuta, Bali narrows into a sliver of land before bulging out again into the **Bukit**, a harsh, scrubby limestone plateau that dangles off the far southern end of the island. While the inhospitable terrain leaves most Bukit residents in despair, its craggy shoreline is a source of great delight for **surfers** – the Padang Padang and Uluwatu breaks are rated as some of the classiest, and trickiest, in Indonesia, at their best from April to October. The biggest concentrations of accommodation are at the upmarket resorts of **Jimbaran**, on the east coast, and **Nusa Dua** on the west.

Jimbaran

The tiny fishing village of **JIMBARAN**, a couple of kilometres south of Ngurah Rai Airport, has flowered into a pleasant little resort. A dozen developments front the beach here, most of them upmarket chain hotels, but the pace is still unhurried and the sand soft and golden.

Jimbaran is famous throughout Bali for its **fish**, and every morning at dawn the fishermen return to trade their catches at the Kedonganan market at the far northern end of the beach. In the evening, the day's catch is served up at the dozens of beach warung that specialize in barbecued seafood. Most of Jimbaran's villagers live away from the beach, down the *gang* that runs off the main Kuta–Jimbaran–Uluwatu road, which cuts a swathe through the heart of the village. The fruit and vegetable market thrives at the crossroads in the centre of the village and, just across from here, under a huge holy tree, stands the eleventh-century temple, Pura Ulun Siwi.

You can get to Jimbaran on the dark-blue **bemo** service that runs throughout the day from Tegal in Denpasar to Jimbaran, via Kuta's eastern fringes (see p.528). Fares are about Rp2000 from Kuta and around Rp4000 from Denpasar. A **taxi** ride from Kuta is about Rp19,000. No tourist shuttle buses currently run to Jimbaran, but all the mid-range and upmarket Jimbaran hotels have free transport to Kuta. A fleet of dark-blue metered taxis also circulates around Jimbaran day and night.

The beachfront Waterworld **watersports** booth just north of the *Keraton* rents out jet skis, offers windsurfing lessons, and runs PADI dive courses and expeditions; however, they bus most of their customers across to Tanjung Benoa (see p.551). The **surf** break known as Airport Rights is off the coast here, best reached by chartering a *prahu* from an off-duty fisherman (about Rp15,000 one-way).

The SOS Uluwatu **clinic** at Jl Uluwatu 111x (Ⓣ0361/705110) deals with minor ailments, but more serious medical cases will be transferred to Denpasar (see p.532).

Accommodation

Most **hotels** in Jimbaran are upmarket and have grounds that lead down to the beach. Nearly all of them offer significant discounts outside peak season.

Bali Inter-Continental Jl Uluwatu 45 Ⓣ0361/701888, Ⓕ701777, Ⓦwww.interconti.com/bali. Large, luxury beachfront hotel comprising low-rise wings surrounded by lush gardens with three pools. ❽

Four Seasons Resort Ⓣ0361/701010, Ⓕ701020, Ⓦwww.fourseasons.com. One of the finest hotels in Bali. Each villa occupies its own traditional Balinese compound, containing separate living, sleeping and bathroom pavilions. Set high on a hill. Published rates start at $575. ❽

Nelayan Jimbaran Jl Pemelisan Agung Ⓣ & Ⓕ0361/702253. A good range of spacious rooms, including losmen-style accommodation, with fan, plus some air-con rooms. Close to the shore. ❹–❺

Pansea Puri Bali Jl Uluwatu Ⓣ0361/701605, Ⓕ701320, Ⓦwww.pansea.com. Forty-one gorgeously designed individual cottage compounds, plus swimming pools and a kids' play area. Beachfront location. ❽

Puri Bambu Jl Pengeracikan, Kedonganan, north Jimbaran Ⓣ0361/701377, Ⓕ701440, Ⓦwww.puribambu.com. Comfortable, mid-range place where all rooms have air-con and there's a pool. A 3min walk from the beach. ❻

Puri Indra Prasta Jl Uluwatu 28a Ⓣ0361/701552. Clean, simple, but fairly attractive losmen rooms (fan and air-con) set around a swimming pool, about five minutes' walk from the beach. ❹–❺

Eating

The **fresh-fish barbecues** served up by Jimbaran's beachfront warung are so good that people travel here from Kuta, Nusa Dua and Sanur just to sample them. There are over fifty of these beach-shack warung, grouped in three distinct areas along the shorefront between Kedonganan in the north and Jalan Bukit Permai in the south. The setup is similar in every one, with tables set out on the sand, and a menu that sells the day's catch (priced per 100g), grilled in front of you. Though food is served during the day, the warung are at their liveliest from around 7pm. Fish prices usually include various sauces plus a spread of vegetable dishes, so accompanying vegetarians will not starve.

Broadly speaking, the knot of warung up near the fish market in **Kedonganan** offer the cheapest food and the least refined ambience, but beware of **rigged scales** in this area. The most popular Kedonganan warung include *Sharkey's*, *Pudak* and *Ayu Wandira*; do not confuse the copycat *Roma* warung next to *Sharkey's* with the more reputable original, *Roma Café*, further south in central Jimbaran. The warung on the shorefront between Jalan Pemelisan Agung and the *Keraton Bali* hotel in **central Jimbaran** are less basic and have a good atmosphere. Reputable options here include *Bamboo*, *Lia*, *Jimbaran Beach Café* and the recommended *Roma Café*. Further south, at the foot of the road up to the *Four Seasons* on the beach known as **Pantai Muayu**, you'll find the most upmarket of the seafood warung, including *Kalang Anyar* and *Intan Sari*.

Around the Bukit

Just a couple of kilometres south of Jimbaran, the road climbs up onto the limestone plateau, and it's well worth pausing for a look back across the stunning **panorama** of southern Bali. About 2km south of the *Four Seasons* junction, a huge sign points you east off the main Uluwatu road to **Garuda Wisnu Kencana**, or **GWK** (daily 8am–10pm; cars Rp5000, motorbikes Rp1000). This controversial project, which is still being carved out of the hillside, is set to be a cultural park and events centre, centred around a towering 146-metre gold-plated statue of the Hindu god Vishnu astride his sacred vehicle, the half-man, half-bird Garuda. It's due to be completed by 2003, but at the moment all that's open is a restaurant, an art gallery (free), and the partially constructed statue, which you can climb for an extra Rp15,000.

Bukit surfing beaches

About 1km south of the GWK-turn off, the road forks at the village of **BAKUNG**, veering right for Uluwatu via several **surfing beaches**, and left for Nusa Dua. Follow the Uluwatu road for a kilometre and you'll pass a couple of **places to stay**, patronized mainly by surfers: *Bukit Inn* (formerly *Villa Koyo*; Ⓣ0361/702927, Ⓕ703362, Ⓦwww.indo.com/hotels/villakoyo; ❺) has thirty attractive air-con rooms plus a pool and internet access, while across the road, *Mr Ugly's* (Ⓣ0361/702874; ❷) has three basic but perfectly decent rooms.

A few kilometres south of *Bukit Inn*, a large sign announces the turn-off to **DREAMLAND** and **BALANGAN** surf beaches, a stunning stretch of coast with gloriously white sands. The access road runs about 4km through an abandoned condo project before meeting short dirt tracks to the beach; en route you'll be asked for a Rp5000 **toll** per person for use of the beach. About ten warung have been rigged up under the cliff at Dreamland, serving standard travellers' fare; a couple also offer overnight crash pads (❷). The setup at Balangan, accessed via a nearby dirt track, is similar.

Back on the main Bukit road, 2km south of the Dreamland turn-off, there's a right fork signed to **BINGIN, IMPOSSIBLES** and **PADANG PADANG**. Bingin and Impossibles are accessible only via a potholed dirt track which takes you a couple of kilometres off the road, and Padang Padang is visible from the main road. A knot of warung have sprung up along the cliffside at Bingin to cater for visiting surfers. At Padang Padang, the warung have been moved off the beach and onto the east side of the road; some of them offer **beds** (❷), or you could try the more comfortable *Ayu Guna Inn* (Ⓣ082/361 1517; ❸), 300m further north beside the main road.

SULUBAN, location of the famous **Uluwatu surf breaks**, is signed off the road about 2km south of Padang Padang. These breaks are a surf mecca, with five separate left-handers, all of them consistent and surfable at anything from 1–5m. As at Bingin and Padang Padang, there's a tiny surfers' "resort" at Suluban, or more upmarket accommodation at the *Uluwatu Resort* (Ⓣ0361/709648, Ⓕ775319, Ⓦwww.uluwaturesort.com; ❼) which is set on the cliff beside the steps down to the beach and offers, as well as a pool, the most attractive rooms on this entire stretch of coast. *Rocky Bungalows* (Ⓣ0818/351643; ❹) is a short bike ride from the surf, down a side-road off the main Uluwatu road.

Pura Luhur Uluwatu

One of Bali's holiest and most important temples, **Pura Luhur Uluwatu** (Rp3000, including compulsory sarong and sash, plus Rp1000 parking fee) commands a superb position on the tip of a sheer rocky promontory jutting out over the Indian Ocean, 70m above the foaming surf. Views over the serrated coastline to left and right are stunning and, not surprisingly, this is a favourite spot at sunset, when the **kecak and fire dance** (*sanghyang jaran*) are also performed (daily 6–7pm; Rp35,000). Constructed almost entirely from blocks of greyish-white coral, Pura Luhur Uluwatu is one of Bali's sacred directional temples, or *kayangan jagat* (a state temple which has influence over all the people of Bali, not just the local villagers or ancestors), acting as the guardian of the southwest and dedicated to the spirits of the sea. Its festivals are open to all, and during the holy week-long period at Galungan, Balinese from all over the island come here to pay their respects. The temple structure itself, though, lacks magnificence, being relatively small and for the most part unadorned.

Pura Luhur Uluwatu stands at the far southwestern tip of the Bukit, and of Bali – it's 18km south of Kuta and 16km west of Nusa Dua. If you don't have your own **transport**, the easiest way to visit is by joining a tour from Kuta. You'd be lucky to find a **bemo** from Denpasar or Kuta going all the way to Uluwatu, so your cheapest option is to get a dark-blue Tegal (Denpasar)–Kuta–Jimbaran bemo to its Jimbaran terminus and then flag down a metered taxi for the last leg. Coming back from Uluwatu is more of a problem as you're very unlikely to find a taxi here: either ask your taxi to wait for you, try and hitch a ride from the temple car park, or arrange an unofficial motorcycle taxi ride with a local lad.

Nusa Dua and Tanjung Benoa

About 11km southeast of Kuta, Bali's most artfully designed high-class beach resort luxuriates along a coastal stretch of reclaimed mangrove swamp. This is **NUSA DUA**, a sparklingly pristine enclave that was purpose-built to indulge the whims of upmarket tourists. The dozen or so five-star hotels boast expansive grounds running down to one of Bali's prettiest white-sand beaches but, aside

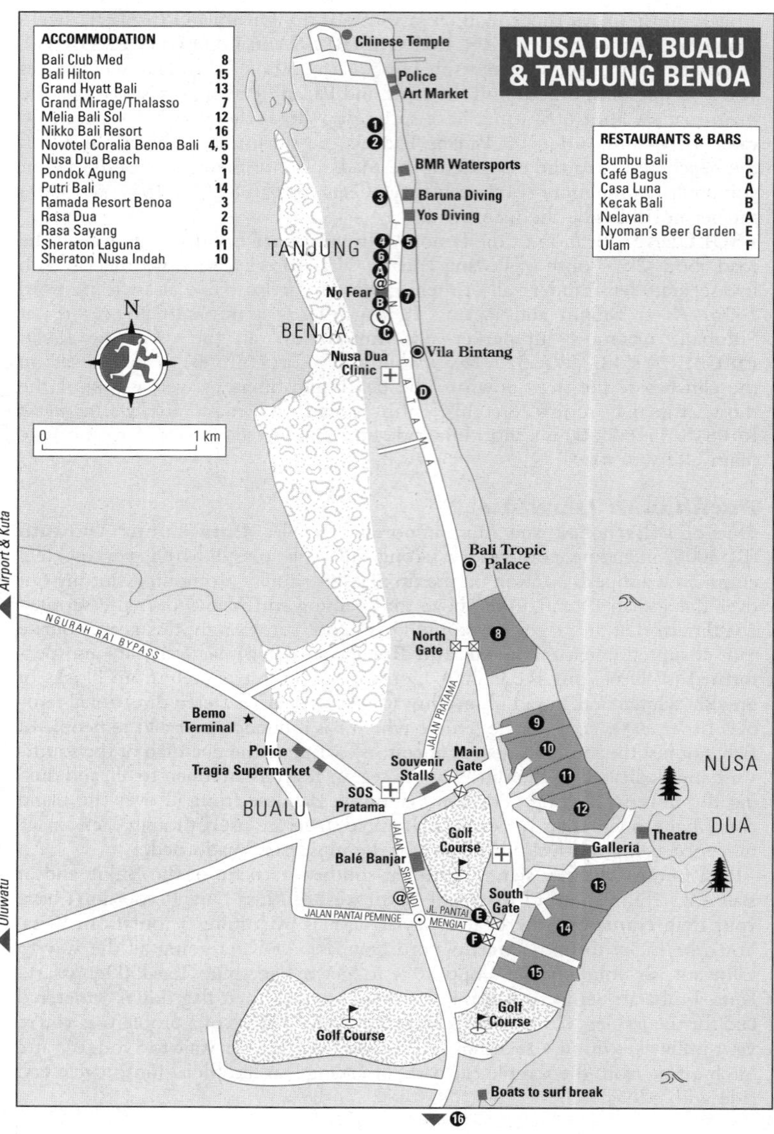

Don't confuse Tanjung Benoa with **Benoa Harbour** (Pelabuhan Benoa; described on p.563) which lies about 1km north across the water from Tanjung Benoa's northern tip, but is only accessible to the public by a circuitous land route. Fast boats to Lombok, Pelni boats to other parts of the Indonesian archipelago, sea planes, and most excursion boats depart from Benoa Harbour, not Tanjung Benoa.

from a central shopping and entertainments complex, there's absolutely nothing else in Nusa Dua: no losmen or mid-range hotels and no markets, *banjar* or noodle stalls. There are, however, a few more signs of real life along the narrow sandbar that extends north from Nusa Dua. **TANJUNG BENOA**, as this finger-like projection is known, still functions as a fishing village, but also boasts a rash of realistically priced tourist accommodation, and lots of watersports facilities; avoid the northern stretch of Tanjung Benoa's beach though, which is scruffy and unappealing. Sandwiched between Nusa Dua and Tanjung Benoa, the village of **BUALU** is where you'll find the *banjar*, temples, warung, family homes and non-tourist-orientated business common to any small Balinese town. A few tourist restaurants have also been established here.

Arrival and transport

The only means of **public transport** to Nusa Dua and Tanjung Benoa are the dark-blue bemos that depart Denpasar's Tegal bemo station (see p.528) and go via the eastern edge of Kuta and then via Jimbaran before racing back down the highway to terminate at **Bualu**, where the main road forks right for Nusa Dua and left for Tanjung Benoa. Bemos are not allowed inside the Nusa Dua gateway, so to get to the beaches and hotels from here you'll either have to walk the one or two kilometres or flag down a taxi. Bemos do serve Tanjung Benoa, though: green ones run about once every thirty minutes between the Bualu bemo terminal and the Chinese temple at the northern end of Tanjung Benoa. Getting outgoing bemos back from Bualu to Kuta or Denpasar is an unreliable business after about 3pm and you may be forced to charter one. A free shuttle bus runs approximately hourly from Kuta Square's Matahari Department Store (the Jalan Ciung Wanara entrance) to the Galleria shopping complex in the heart of Nusa Dua, a five-minute walk from the beach – useful for making a day-trip.

A fleet of multicoloured **free shuttle buses** (hourly 8am–11pm) also operates between the Galleria shopping complex at the heart of Nusa Dua and the big Nusa Dua and Tanjung Benoa hotels. If staying in one of the cheaper Tanjung Benoa hotels, you're limited to the green public bemos, or to the pale-brown Kowinu Bali **metered taxis** (Ⓣ0361/771661; Rp4000 flagfall, then Rp2000 per km) which circulate fairly regularly around both resorts. Alternatively, you can rent **bicycles** and **cars** from most hotels, or from one of the shops in Tanjung Benoa, on the stretch of Jalan Pratama between *Vila Bintang* and *Rasa Sayang*.

Accommodation

All **accommodation** in Nusa Dua is of the highest standard. Published prices start at around US$160 per double room, but most travel agents should be able to get you a decent discount and online deals are plentiful. Tanjung Benoa caters for a wider span of budgets, mainly offering accommodation in the lower- and mid-range price bracket at the north end of the peninsula and more expensive ones as you get closer to Nusa Dua.

Nusa Dua

Bali Hilton Ⓣ0361/771102, Ⓕ771616, Ⓦwww.hiltonindonesia.com. Huge, grandly designed complex with spacious rooms, lush gardens, a free-form pool and five restaurants. Plenty of activities for kids. ⑧

Grand Hyatt Bali Ⓣ0361/771234, Ⓕ772038, Ⓦwww.hyatt.com. Terraced rooms and cottages surrounded by sumptuous grounds, plus an amazing series of free-form swimming pools. ⑧

Sheraton Nusa Indah Ⓣ0361/771906, Ⓕ771908, Ⓦwww.sheraton.com. Upmarket rooms and extensive sports facilities. The family suites, creche and numerous kids' activities make it especially good for families. ⑧

Tanjung Benoa

Novotel Coralia Benoa Bali Jl Pratama ⓣ0361/772239, ⓕ772237, ⓦwww.novotelbali.com. Elegant but comfortable low-rise Balinese-style hotel whose grounds run down to a nice stretch of beach. Three pools, a kids' club and a good babysitting service. ❽

Pondok Agung Jl Pratama 99 ⓣ & ⓕ0361/771143, ⓔroland@eksadata.com. Small, stylish place with the best-value, though not the cheapest, accommodation at this end of Tanjung Benoa. Some air-con. ❹–❺

Ramada Resort Benoa Jl Pratama 97a ⓣ0361/773730, ⓕ773840, ⓦwww.ramadahotels.com. Attractive, low-key hotel complex with good facilities and luxurious but cosy rooms (some are wheelchair-friendly). Good value. ❼

Rasa Dua Jl Pratama 98 ⓣ0361/771922, ⓕ773515, ⓔbaliyacht-service@yahoo.com. Four simple but pleasant losmen-style rooms in a small garden area, with bamboo furniture and partially open-air mandi. ❸

Rasa Sayang Jl Pratama 88 ⓣ0361/771643, ⓕ777268, ⓔrsbind@yahoo.com. Popular and good-value small hotel, offering simple rooms in a terraced block. Some air-con. ❸–❺

Watersports and other activities

Nearly every Nusa Dua hotel rents out some **watersports** equipment; prices are similar, but facilities are more extensive at the Tanjung Benoa end of the beach, where you'll find Yos Marine Adventures, Jl Pratama 10 (ⓣ0361/773774, ⓦwww.yosdive.com), and Baruna (ⓦwww.baruna.com), both of which do parasailing, waterskiing, wakeboarding and jet-skiing, as well as fishing expeditions, plus **diving** trips and courses (see p.560). The Bali Club Med resort (daily 10am–6.30pm; ⓣ0361/771521), just inside Nusa Dua's North Gate, issues a good-value **day pass** to non-guests (Rp165,000; kids Rp82,500), which buys use of all sports facilities and swimming pools, as well as a buffet lunch. Nusa Dua's main **surf break**, known simply as Nusa Dua, is accessible by boat from a signposted point south of the *Bali Hilton*; it's best surfed from September to March.

The eighteen-hole championship Bali Golf and Country Club **golf course** (ⓣ0361/771791; green fees US$142) is spread across three areas of the resort, the main part dominating the southern end of Nusa Dua. Many of the top-notch hotels have **spas**, including the award-winning one at *Nusa Dua Beach* (ⓣ0361/771210), the seawater therapies at the *Grand Mirage* (ⓣ0361/771888) in Tanjung Benoa, and the Mandara spa at *Club Med* (ⓣ0361/771521).

Eating

You'll find the cheapest and most authentic Balinese **food** at the warung along Jalan Srikandi in Bualu village. Some pricier tourist restaurants have emerged on the Bualu side of Nusa Dua's South Gate, where the atmosphere is less stilted than in Nusa Dua and the Galleria, though prices are still pretty high. Many restaurants in Tanjung Benoa and Bualu offer **free transport** from local hotels; where this service is available, we have included the phone number in the review.

Bumbu Bali Next to *Matahari Terbit Bungalows*, Jl Pratama, Tanjung Benoa ⓣ0361/774502. One of the best restaurants in the area, serving exquisite, and expensive, Balinese cuisine.

Café Bagus Jl Pratama, Tanjung Benoa ⓣ0361/772716. The place to come for breakfast with a good range of different, mid-priced set options.

Kecak Bali Jl Pratama, Tanjung Benoa ⓣ0361/775533. Pricey, quality Balinese food including duck sate, a multi-course seafood dinner, and a meat- or fish-based *rijsttafel*.

Nelayan Jl Pratama, Tanjung Benoa. Deservedly popular mid-priced place which serves great Balinese curries and a good range of fresh fish and seafood dishes.

Nyoman's Beer Garden Just outside the South Gate on Jl Pantai Mengiat in Bualu. Cheap draught beer, pool tables, moderately priced bar food and a lively atmosphere.

Ulam Just outside the South Gate at Jl Pantai Mengiat 14 in Bualu ⓣ0361/773776. Fairly pricey seafood restaurant with fresh fish and seafood cooked to order.

Shopping and entertainment

Spread over a huge landscaped area in the middle of the resort, the **Galleria** shopping and entertainments plaza (daily 9am–10pm) is accessible by free shuttle bus from all major hotels and sells everything from coconut carvings to Nikes; there's also a supermarket and a duty-free outlet here plus countless restaurants.

Free **Balinese dance** shows are staged in front of a different restaurant in the Galleria every night from 7.30pm. All the hotels also stage regular **cultural events**; the *Nikko Bali* (☎0361/773377) does a "Desa Bali Night" which includes cock-fighting, Balinese dance and village food stalls (Wed 7–9.30pm; $35, kids $17.50), as well as a cultural dinner that includes a *kecak* dance performance (Mon same hours and prices). At *Club Med* (☎0361/771521), non-guests can buy an **evening pass** for Rp275,000 which gives access to a buffet dinner (with unlimited wine), cultural show (from 7pm), and hotel disco.

Listings

Airline offices Garuda city check-in inside the Galleria (daily 8am–7pm; ☎0361/771444).

Banks and exchange There are ATMs for Visa, MasterCard and Cirrus in the Galleria. You can change money in Tanjung Benoa at several shops on the stretch of Jl Pratama between *Vila Bintang* and *Rasa Sayang*, at the Galleria, and at all Nusa Dua hotels.

Cookery lessons At several Tanjung Benoa restaurants: *Bumbu Bali* (Mon–Fri; ☎0361/774502, $85/65 per day/half-day, book ahead); *Kecak* (☎0361/775533, $55/40); and *Casa Luna* (Mon, Wed & Fri 8.30am–2pm; ☎0361/773845, Rp350,000).

Hospitals and clinics Nusa Dua Clinic, Jl Pratama 81a, Tanjung Benoa (daily 24hr; ☎0361/771324), staffed by English-speaking medics; or SOS Pratama, beside the main junction in Bualu, Jl Pratama 1a (☎0361/773409). All Nusa Dua hotels provide 24hr medical service.

Internet access At all major hotels; also at email centres opposite the *Grand Mirage* hotel in Tanjung Benoa and on Jl Srikandi in Bualu.

Postal services There's a postal agent in the Galleria complex, and another one in Bualu.

Sanur

Stretching down the southeast coast 18km from Ngurah Rai Airport, **SANUR** is an appealing, more peaceful alternative to Kuta, with a long, fairly decent white-sand beach, plenty of attractive accommodation in all price brackets and a distinct village atmosphere. Because it lacks the clubs and all-night party venues of Kuta, Sanur can seem a bit tame to younger travellers, but there are plenty of restaurants and enough bars to keep most visitors entertained. It's also a good place to bring the kids, is one of Bali's main centres for water sports, and works well as a base for exploring other parts of Bali.

Arrival and transport

The fastest and most direct way of getting to Sanur from most other places on Bali is by tourist **shuttle bus**. The biggest operator, Perama, has several ticket agents in Sanur; the main one, which is also the official drop-off point, is Warung Pojok minimarket, Jl Hang Tuah 31 in north Sanur (☎0361/287594); the bus driver may agree to drop you off elsewhere along Jalan Danau Tamblingan, otherwise you'll need to take a bemo or taxi to your hotel from opposite Warung Pojok.

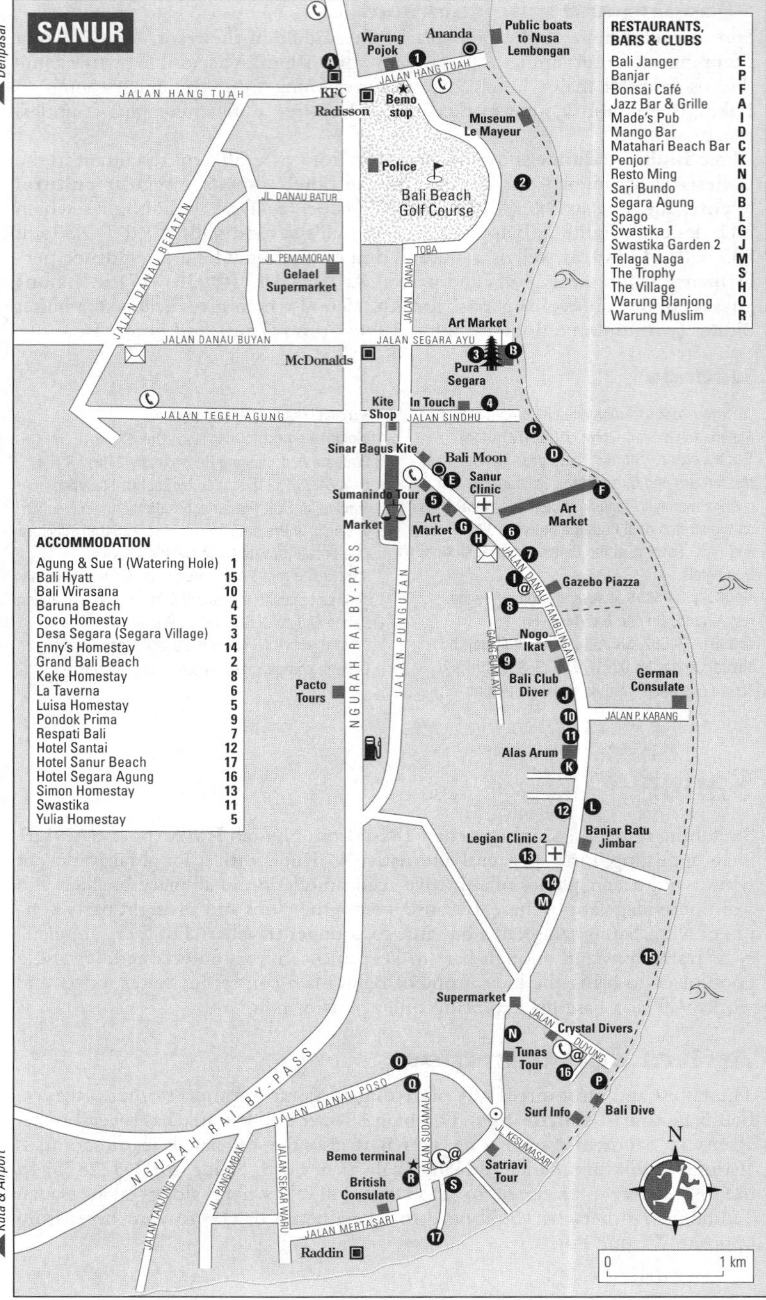
SANUR
Denpasar
Kuta & Airport
RESTAURANTS, BARS & CLUBS
Bali Janger E
Banjar P
Bonsai Café F
Jazz Bar & Grille A
Made's Pub I
Mango Bar D
Matahari Beach Bar C
Penjor K
Resto Ming N
Sari Bundo O
Segara Agung B
Spago L
Swastika 1 G
Swastika Garden 2 J
Telaga Naga M
The Trophy S
The Village H
Warung Blanjong Q
Warung Muslim R
ACCOMMODATION
Agung & Sue 1 (Watering Hole) 1
Bali Hyatt 15
Bali Wirasana 10
Baruna Beach 4
Coco Homestay 5
Desa Segara (Segara Village) 3
Enny's Homestay 14
Grand Bali Beach 2
Keke Homestay 8
La Taverna 6
Luisa Homestay 5
Pondok Prima 9
Respati Bali 7
Hotel Santai 12
Hotel Sanur Beach 17
Hotel Segara Agung 16
Simon Homestay 13
Swastika 11
Yulia Homestay 5
Warung Pojok
Ananda
Public boats to Nusa Lembongan
JALAN HANG TUAH
KFC
Radisson
Bemo stop
Museum Le Mayeur
Police
Bali Beach Golf Course
JL. DANAU BATUR
JL. PEMAMORAN
JALAN DANAU BERATAN
TOBA
JALAN DANAU
Gelael Supermarket
Art Market
JALAN DANAU BUYAN
JALAN SEGARA AYU
McDonalds
Pura Segara
Kite Shop
In Touch
JALAN TEGEH AGUNG
JALAN SINDHU
Sinar Bagus Kite
Bali Moon
Sanur Clinic
Sumanindo Tour
Market
Art Market
Art Market
JALAN DANAU TAMBLINGAN
Gazebo Piazza
GANG BUMI AYU
Nogo Ikat
Bali Club Diver
German Consulate
JALAN P. KARANG
Pacto Tours
NGURAH RAI BY-PASS
JALAN PUNGUTAN
Alas Arum
Banjar Batu Jimbar
Legian Clinic 2
Supermarket
JALAN DUYUNG
Crystal Divers
Tunas Tour
Bali Dive
Surf Info
JALAN DANAU POSO
JALAN SUDAMALA
JL. KESUMASARI
Bemo terminal
British Consulate
Satriavi Tour
JALAN TANJUNG
JL. PANGEMBAK
JALAN SEKAR WARU
JALAN MERTASARI
Raddin
N
0 1 km

The only direct **bemos** to Sanur leave **from Denpasar**. Dark green bemos from Denpasar's Kereneng terminal run to north Sanur (around Rp3000; 15min), where they drop off outside the *Grand Bali Beach* compound at the Ngurah Rai By-Pass/Jalan Hang Tuah junction only if asked; otherwise they usually head down Jalan Danau Beratan and Jalan Danau Buyan, before continuing down Jalan Danau Tamblingan to the *Trophy Pub Centre* in south Sanur. Dark-blue bemos from Denpasar's Tegal terminal run direct via Jalan Teuku Umar and Renon (around Rp3000; 30min) and then follow the same route as the green Kereneng ones, depending on passenger requests. **From Kuta**, you'll need to change at Tegal in Denpasar, though you can save time if you get off the Kuta bemo at the bridge where Jalan Imam Bonjol intersects with Jalan Teuku Umar and hop onto a blue Sanur-bound bemo instead. Coming **from Nusa Dua** you can take the white, Batubulan-bound Damri bus, which drops passengers on the Ngurah Rai By-Pass, near the *Radisson* hotel in north Sanur; you can also use this service if coming **from Ubud**, changing onto the Damri bus at Denpasar's **Batubulan** terminus.

There are no official tourist offices in Sanur, but plenty of tour agents are only too happy to provide **information** about potential day-trips.

Transport

Sanur stretches 5km from its northernmost tip to the far southern end. The public **bemos** which transport people to and from Denpasar's two terminals are quite useful if you're sticking to the main streets (around Rp2000 for any journey within Sanur). Otherwise, flag down a metered **taxi** (Rp4000 flagfall, then Rp2000 per km), or bargain hard with a transport tout.

Moving on from Sanur

Most hotels and losmen will arrange transport to the **airport** from around Rp35,000, or you can hail a metered taxi for slightly less. It costs about the same for private transport to **Benoa Harbour**.

Dozens of tour agents and small shops advertise **shuttle bus** services; the largest operator is Perama. Perama's main ticket agent and pick-up point is Warung Pojok minimarket, Jl Hang Tuah 31 in north Sanur (☎0361/287594); other Perama ticket outlets, where you may also be able to be picked up, include Nagasari Tours (☎0361/288096) opposite *Gazebo* hotel on the central part of Jalan Danau Tamblingan, and Tunas Tour, Jl Danau Tamblingan 102 (☎0361/288581), next to *Resto Ming*. Sample fares include Rp10,000 to Kuta/Ngurah Rai Airport or Ubud, Rp25,000 to Candi Dasa, and Rp75,000 to Kuta in Lombok. See Travel Details, p.662, for more.

Moving on by **bemo** to anywhere on Bali entails going via Denpasar – either the green bemo to Kereneng, or the blue bemo to Tegal. For **Kuta** and **Jimbaran**, it's easiest to go via Tegal (see "Arrival" for a handy short-cut); for most other destinations the Kereneng service is more efficient, though you'll have to make another cross-city bemo connection from Kereneng in order to get to the Batubulan terminal (for **Ubud and the east**) or the Ubung terminal (for **the west and the north**).

Sanur is the main departure point for **boats** to **Nusa Lembongan**, which leave from a jetty at the eastern end of Jalan Hang Tuah in north Sanur. There are currently two public services a day, for which tickets are sold from the beachfront office near the *Ananda Hotel* (daily 8am & 10am; Rp30,000; 1hr 30min); and one Perama shuttle boat, which should be booked the day before at the Perama office (daily 10.30am; Rp40,000; 1hr 30min). See p.663 for more details.

The touts also rent out **cars** and **motorbikes**, as do most of Sanur's tour agencies. Sanur is an ideal place for riding **bicycles**, available from most hotels and from the *Bali Wirasana* minimarket on Jl Danau Tamblingan, for Rp12,000–20,000 a day.

Most tourist businesses in Sanur offer a range of **sightseeing trips** to Bali's most popular sights (Rp60,000–100,000 per person in a group of eight), or you can choose to rent a car with driver for about Rp350,000 per day.

Accommodation

Sanur's budget **accommodation** is nothing like as prolific as Kuta's, but there are a number of reasonable possibilities, none of which is more than ten minutes' walk from the beach. Mid-priced hotels are particularly good in Sanur, the majority of them small, cosy setups with beautiful gardens, a pool and air-conditioning. The best of the beachfront is taken up by upmarket hotels.

Inexpensive

Agung & Sue 1 (Watering Hole) Jl Hang Tuah 37 Ⓣ & Ⓕ0361/288289. The cheapest rooms (some air-con) in this part of Sanur, only 250m from the beach. Internet access. ❸

Coco Homestay Jl Danau Tamblingan 42 Ⓣ0361/287391. Archetypal homestay offering a few budget rooms behind the family art shop. Some of the cheapest accommodation in Sanur. ❷

Enny's Homestay Jl Danau Tamblingan 172 Ⓣ0361/287363, Ⓕ287306. Seven immaculately furnished rooms behind the family shoeshop near a path to the beach. Some air-con. ❸–❹

Keke Homestay Gang Keke 3, off Jl Danau Tamblingan 96 Ⓣ0361/287282. Tiny losmen that's basic but friendly and offers simple fan rooms with cold-water mandi. ❸

Luisa Homestay Jl Danau Tamblingan 40 Ⓣ0361/289673. One of three very similar losmen clustered together behind streetside businesses. Basic but cheerful accommodation. ❷

Simon Homestay Down a tiny *gang* at 164d Jl Danau Tamblingan Ⓣ0361/289158. Small, sparklingly clean family losmen with nicely furnished rooms. Some air-con. ❸–❹

Yulia Homestay Jl Danau Tamblingan 38 Ⓣ0361/288089. Friendly, family-run losmen with nice, cheap bungalows. ❸

Mid-range

Bali Wirasana Jl Danau Tamblingan 138 Ⓣ0361/288632, Ⓕ288561, Ⓔwirasana@indosat.net.id. Though the cheapest rooms here aren't that great, they're large, clean and centrally located, plus there's internet access and use of the pool next door. Some air-con. ❹–❺

Baruna Beach Jl Sindhu Ⓣ0361/288546, Ⓕ289629, Ⓦwww.geocities.com/baruna_hotel. Tiny beachfront complex of six pleasant bungalows, all with air-con. Good value for the location. ❺

Hotel Segara Agung Jl Duyung 43 Ⓣ0361/288446, Ⓕ286113, Ⓦbaliwww.com/bali/roomfinder/segaraagung.htm. Occupying a very quiet spot just a couple of minutes' walk from the beach, with twenty bungalows and a pool in a pretty garden compound. Some air-con. ❺–❻

Pondok Prima Gang Bumi Ayu 23 Ⓣ0361/286369, Ⓕ289153, Ⓔprimacottage@telkom.net. Very quiet, good-value place that's well off the main road and offers some very spacious bungalows in a tropical garden plus rooms in a block. There's a pool and some air-con. ❺

Respati Bali Jl Danau Tamblingan 33 Ⓣ0361/288427, Ⓕ288046, Ⓔbrespati@indo.net.id. A pristine collection of good-value bungalows in a compact seafront compound with a pool. Some air-con. ❻–❼

Swastika Jl Danau Tamblingan 128 Ⓣ0361/288693, Ⓕ287526, Ⓦwww.homestead.com/colb/swastika.html, Ⓔswastika@indosat.net.id. Deservedly popular place, with 78 comfortable fan and air-con rooms in bungalows set around a delightful garden with two swimming pools and a kids' pool. Named after the ancient Buddhist symbol, not the Nazi emblem. ❻

Expensive

Bali Hyatt Jl Danau Tamblingan Ⓣ0361/281234, Ⓕ287693, Ⓦwww.bali.hyatt.com. Enormous, appealingly plush establishment, offering topnotch rooms and facilities plus 36 acres of award-winning tropical gardens stretching down to the beach. ❽

Desa Segara (Segara Village) Jl Segara Ayu ⓣ0361/288407, ⓕ287242, ⓔsegara1@denpasar.wasantara.net.id. Understated elegance pervades the "village", which is made up of six compounds of very attractive traditional-style accommodation in grounds that run down to the sea. ❼–❽

Grand Bali Beach Off Jl Hang Tuah ⓣ0361/288511, ⓕ287917, ⓔgbb@indosat.net.id. Huge establishment with rooms in a central tower block plus some cottages. Lots of water sports and four swimming pools. ❽

Hotel Sanur Beach Semawang ⓣ0361/288011, ⓕ287566, ⓦwww.aerowisata.co.id/sanur. Sprawling complex with landscaped seafront gardens, a fine beach and luxury-grade rooms plus a spa and a watersports centre. ❽

La Taverna Jl Danau Tamblingan 29 ⓣ0361/288497, ⓕ287126, ⓦwww.indo.com/hotels/la_taverna, ⓔlatavern@dps.mega.net.id. Small beachside hotel offering comfortable, cosy bungalows, including some stylish split-level ones. ❽

The resort

A huge expanse of Sanur's five-kilometre shoreline gets exposed at low tide and the reef lies only about 1km offshore at high tide. The currents beyond the reef are dangerously strong, which makes it almost impossible to swim here at low tide, but at other times of day swimming is fine and watersports are popular. You'll find Sanur's best **sand** in front of the *Grand Bali Beach*, where non-guests can rent sun-loungers, and in front of the *Sanur Beach* at the far southern end.

Sanur's two biggest **watersports** operators are associated with hotels but are open to all: the *Grand Bali Beach* watersports centre (ⓣ0361/288511), and the Blue Oasis Beach Club (ⓣ0361/288011) at *Sanur Beach*. Many of the dive centres listed on p.561 also rent out watersports equipment, including kayaks, windsurfers and jet skis, and most offer parasailing as well. The main departure point for fishing expeditions is Tanjung Benoa (see p.551), though some boats do leave from Sanur. Sanur's three main **surf breaks** – Sanur, the Tandjung Sari Reef and the Hyatt Reef – are at their best from September to March. Sanur has its own nine-hole **golf course** in the grounds of the *Grand Bali Beach* (ⓣ0361/288511 ext 1388); green fees are US$50.

Museum Le Mayeur

One of Sanur's earliest expatriate residents was the Belgian artist Adrien Jean Le Mayeur de Merpres (1880–1958), whose home is now open to the public as **Museum Le Mayeur** (Sun–Fri 8am–4pm; donation); access is via the beachfront path that turns right off Jalan Hang Tuah in north Sanur. Le Mayeur arrived in Bali at the age of 52 and soon fell in love with the teenage Ni Pollok, considered by many to be the best *legong* dancer in Bali. She posed for many of his pictures and by 1935 the two were married and living in this house right on Sanur beach. Much of the original structure remains – a typical low-roofed wooden building with sumptuously carved doors, lintels and pediments. Le Mayeur did most of his painting in the courtyard garden, which features in many of the paintings and photographs displayed inside the house.

Diving in south Bali

Sanur is one of south Bali's two main **diving** centres (the other is Tanjung Benoa, see p.555), and many of the outfits that sell dive excursions from shops in Kuta and Nusa Dua have their headquarters in this area. It's a good place to learn to dive, as the local dive sites are close by, but more experienced divers usually prefer the dives off the east and north coast of Bali. There is one **divers' decompression chamber** on Bali, located at Sanglah Public Hospital, Jl Kesehatan Selatan 1 in Denpasar (☎0361/227911).

Dive courses and excursions

All the centres listed below run internationally **certificated diving courses**, including four-day open-water PADI **courses** ($300–400) and two-day advanced open-water courses ($245–350); most also offer half-day introductory dives ($50–75). Prices are competitive, but be sure to check whether equipment rental, insurance and course materials are included. Be wary of any operation offering extremely cheap courses: maintaining diving equipment is an expensive business in Bali so any place offering unusually good rates will probably be cutting corners and compromising your safety.

Despite the proliferation of dive shops, **Sanur's own dive sites**, which lie just a short distance off the coast along the east-facing edge of the reef, are a bit of a disappointment. The coral is not that spectacular, and visibility is only around 6–10m, but the area does teem with fish. Most boats can't access the reef at low tide, so check how long you're likely to have for diving. The average cost of a single dive off Sanur is about $40 ($15 for accompanying snorkellers).

Rates for **one-day dive excursions** to the more interesting reefs elsewhere in Bali (including two tanks but not necessarily all equipment) include: the north-coast reefs and wrecks of Tulamben or Amed (see p.621) for $55–85; the island of Pulau Menjangan (Deer Island, p.660) for $70–105; and the east-coast islands of Nusa Lembongan (p.601) and Nusa Penida (p.605) for $75–105. Overnight **diving safaris** to these sites cost around $85 per person all-inclusive.

Eating

Sanur has plenty of **restaurants**, most of them located either along the main road through the resort, Jalan Danau Tamblingan, or along the beachfront walkway between *La Taverna* and Jalan Sindhu, and between Jalan Kesumasari and Jalan Duyung. The **night market** which sets up at the Jalan Danau Tamblingan/Jalan Sindhu intersection is a good place for cheap Indonesian dishes. The resort closes down quite early at night, and most tourist restaurants are loath to accept orders after 9.30pm.

Bonsai Café Beachfront walkway just north of *La Taverna* hotel, access off Jl Danau Tamblingan. Breezy seafront café, restaurant and bar (open until 2am) with expansive views serving mid-priced pizza, pasta and seafood, plus good-value cocktails.

Kafé Tali Jiwa In front of the *Santai Hotel*, Jl Danau Tamblingan 148. One of Sanur's best vegetarian menus, plus mid-priced traditional Balinese fish and chicken dishes.

Resto Ming Jl Danau Tamblingan 105. Seafood is a speciality here, particularly lobster thermidor and king prawns.

Sari Bundo Jl Danau Poso. Typical cheap *Masakan Padang* place serving spicy Sumatran dishes 24hr a day.

Segara Agung On the beachfront next to *Desa Segara*, north-central Sanur ☎0361/288574. Ideally located restaurant with a huge choice of mid-priced dishes, including lots of seafood. Run as a co-operative with all profits going to local schools and clinics; call for free transport.

Spago Jl Danau Tamblingan 79. Sleek, elegantly styled restaurant with an outstanding, and expensive, menu of Mediterranean-fusion cuisine.

Telaga Naga Opposite the *Bali Hyatt* on Jl Danau Tamblingan. Very upmarket *Hyatt* restaurant comprising a series of garden pavilions. Specializes in

Dive centres

All tour agents in south Bali sell diving trips organized by Bali's major **diving operators**, but for specific queries, you should try to speak directly to one of the dive leaders. Established operators include:

AquaMarine Diving Jl Raya Seminyak 56, Kuta ⓣ0361/730107, ⓕ735368, ⓦwww.aquamarinediving.com. UK-run.

Bali International Diving Professionals Jl Sekarwaru 9, south Sanur ⓣ0361/270759, ⓕ270760, ⓦwww.bidp-balidiving.com. Also offers nitrox dives, underwater weddings, dive courses for 8–11-year-olds, and special dives for disabled divers. UK/Balinese-run.

Bali Pesona Bahari (formerly Bali Marine Sports), Jl Bypass Ngurah Rai, Blanjong, south Sanur ⓣ0361/289308, ⓕ287872, ⓦwww.bmsdivebali.com. One of the first PADI dive shops in Bali and now a PADI Gold Palm Resort.

Baruna Jl Bypass Ngurah Rai 300b, Kuta ⓣ0361/753820, ⓕ753809, ⓦwww.baruna.com. Also in the *Grand Bali Beach* hotel, off Jl Hang Tuah, north Sanur ⓣ0361/288511 extn 1381; and on Jl Pratama in Tanjung Benoa. Long-established operator.

Blue Oasis Beach Club *Sanur Beach* hotel, south Sanur ⓣ0361/288011, ⓦwww.blueoasisbc.com.

Crystal Divers Jl Duyung 25, south-central Sanur ⓣ & ⓕ0361/286737, ⓦwww.crystal-divers.com. One of only a few PADI five-star dive centres in Bali. Run by English and Danish divers.

Scuba Duba Doo Jl Legian 367, Kuta ⓣ & ⓕ0361/761798, ⓦwww.divecenterbali.com. US-run.

Yos Marine Adventures Jl Pratama 106, Tanjung Benoa ⓣ0361/773774, ⓕ752985, ⓦwww.yosdive.com. Large, reliable outfit. Offers diving excursions for children and for disabled divers if arranged in advance.

Cantonese and Szechwan dishes. Nightly 6–11pm.

The Village Opposite *La Taverna* hotel, Jl Danau Tamblingan. Classy, mid-priced menu that includes pumpkin bisque, European breads, plenty of seafood and home-made ice cream.

Warung Blanjong Jl Danau Poso 78. Recommended, cheap restaurant that serves only Balinese dishes, both veggie and non-veggie specialities.

Warung Muslim Jl Sudamala. The string of small Muslim warung near the bemo terminus serve very cheap Javanese standards including grilled chicken, sate, *bakso* and *nasi goreng*.

Nightlife and entertainment

There are plenty of pleasant **bar-restaurants** along Sanur's beachfront, particularly between *La Taverna* and Jalan Sindhu, and between Jalan Kesumasari and Jalan Duyung; most stay reasonably lively till around 1am. The few **clubs** in the resort are rather formal places compared to Kuta's nightspots.

You can see **Balinese dancing** in or around Sanur on any day of the week, either at one of the hotels or restaurants, or by making a trip to dance stages in nearby Denpasar. The exuberant lion dance, the **barong**, is performed every morning (9.30–10.30am) at the Catur Eka Budhi on Jalan Waribang in the Kesiman district of Denpasar (see p.532), 3km by taxi from Sanur's Jalan Hang Tuah. The spectacular "monkey dance", or **kecak**, is performed nightly (6.30–7.30pm) at the Stage Uma Dewi, also on Jalan Waribang, about 300m south of the barong dance stage. All Sanur tour agencies offer trips to these for about $10–15 including return transport, but it's usually cheaper to take a taxi there and buy the fixed-price Rp50,000 tickets at the door. Balinese dance performances are staged free for diners at some restaurants on Jalan Danau Tamblingan, with times and details advertised on boards outside: these include *Penjor*, *Swastika Garden 2*, next to *Bali Wirasana* hotel, and *Lotus Pond*, opposite *Bali Moon*. The *Grand Bali Beach* (ⓣ0361/288511) hosts a **cultural evening** which includes traditional dances and a buffet dinner (Mon, Wed & Fri from 7pm; $15). Most other top hotels stage similar events.

Bars and clubs

Bali Janger Jl Danau Tamblingan 21. Flashy, cavernous disco with glitter balls but not much character. Midnight–5am.

Banjar Beachfront end of Jl Duyung. Shoreside bar and restaurant, with occasional club-nights fronted by local and international DJs.

Jazz Bar & Grille Beside *KFC* at the Jl Ngurah Rai Bypass/Jl Hang Tuah crossroads. In the downstairs bar, some of Bali's best jazz and blues bands play live sets every night from about 9.30pm, attracting a friendly mix of locals, expats and the occasional tourist. There's a pool table too. Daily 8am–1am.

Made's Pub Opposite *Gazebo* hotel on Jl Danau Tamblingan. Lively streetside drinking spot that sometimes hosts live music. Closes about 1am.

Mango Bar and Restaurant Beachfront end of Jl Sindhu. Beachfront bar and restaurant which features live reggae (Mon & Fri 9pm), a local band (Wed 8pm) and children's traditional *legong* dance (Mon & Fri 8pm).

Matahari Beach Bar Beachfront end of Jl Sindhu. Breezy beachfront bar and restaurant with a pool table and a well-stocked bar. Stages live music and dance performances from 7pm five nights a week. Closes around 1am.

The Trophy In the *Trophy Pub Centre* at Jl Danau Tamblingan 49. Typical expat pub with a darts board, pool table, satellite TV and live music (Wed & Sat).

Shopping

Jalan Danau Tamblingan is the main **shopping** area. The best-value outlets for cheap cotton clothes and souvenirs are the **art markets** alongside the beachfront walkway in north-central Sanur: there's one behind the *Desa Segara* hotel and another near the *Bonsai Café*. Nogo Ikat at Jalan Danau Tamblingan 100 sells expensive, good quality **ikat** by the metre and made into furnishings; Sinar Bagus Kites on Jl Danau Tamblingan has a great selection of hand-made **kites**. There are small **bookstores** in the *Gazebo* hotel piazza, and inside the *Grand Bali Beach* and *Sanur Beach* hotels; the supermarket on the corner of Jalan Duyung also stocks a reasonable selection. Alas Alarum **supermarket** on Jl Danau Tamblingan (daily 9am–11pm) sells everything from groceries and pharmacy items to handicrafts, groceries, sandals and motorbike helmets.

Listings

Airline offices Garuda flights and city check-in (Mon–Fri 9am–3pm, Sat, Sun & hols 9am–noon; 24hr phoneline ⓣ0361/270535) inside the *Sanur Beach Hotel* (ⓣ0361/287915) or at the *Bali Hyatt* (ⓣ0361/288011).

American Express Room 1111 inside the *Grand Bali Beach* (Mon–Fri 8.30am–4.30pm, Sat 8.30am–1pm; ⓣ0361/288449; toll-free number for lost cards and cheques ⓣ001-803-61005). Travellers' cheque refunds and help with lost cards, plus a poste restante service for Amex card and cheque holders (Poste Restante, c/o American Express, Room 1111, Grand Bali Beach Hotel, Sanur, Bali). Post is kept for one month. For poste restante faxes use the hotel fax number (ⓕ0361/287917) and state clearly that it's for the Amex office. Amex also acts as a Moneygram agent, but the money must be sent from an Amex agent.

Banks and currency exchange There are ATMs for Cirrus, MasterCard and Visa dotted all over the resort. The best rates are from the exchange counters and booths across the resort.

Hospitals and clinics The tourist-oriented Legian Clinic 2, near the *Hotel Santai* on central Jl Danau Tamblingan ⓣ0361/287446 is open 24 hours, will respond to emergency call-outs, and charges Rp100,000 per consultation. A similar service is operated by Sanur Clinic at Jl Danau Tamblingan 27, central Sanur ⓣ0361/282678. SOS Sanur, c/o *Hotel Santai*, Jl Danau Tamblingan 148

☎0361/287314, operates a 24-hour emergency call-out service. All the major hotels provide 24hr medical service; if yours doesn't, try the doctor at the *Grand Bali Beach* (☎0361/288511) or the *Bali Hyatt* (☎0361/288271). The nearest hospitals are all in Denpasar; see p.532.

Internet access There are email centres every few hundred metres in central Sanur, most of which charge Rp300–500/min and open daily 8am–11pm. The most efficient places include Ocha, opposite *Besakih* hotel at Jl Danau Tamblingan 84; the Environmental Information Centre (PIL) in the lobby of the *Hotel Santai*, Jl Danau Tamblingan 148; and the nearby UFO, near Legian Clinic 2.

Pharmacies Several on Jl Danau Tamblingan, as well as one inside the Alas Alarum supermarket.

Phones There are plenty of private wartels in central Sanur, and Direct Dial public phones in the basement shopping arcade of the *Grand Bali Beach* in north Sanur.

Police The police station is on the Ngurah Rai Bypass in north Sanur, just south of the *Radisson* hotel.

Post office Sanur's main post office is on Jl Danau Buyan, north-central Sanur. There are numerous small postal agents throughout the resort, including at the wartel next to *Diwangkara* hotel on Jl Hang Tuah in north Sanur; opposite *Respati* hotel at Jl Danau Tamblingan 66 in central Sanur; and inside the Trophy Centre at the southern end of the same road. You can receive poste restante c/o Agen Pos, Jl Danau Tamblingan 66, Sanur 80228 (Mon–Fri 8.30am–5.30pm, Sat 8.30am–1pm).

Travel agents International and domestic flights, plus organized tours, from Satriavi Tours (also the local Garuda agent), Jl Danau Tamblingan 27, south Sanur ☎0361/287074; Sumanindo Tour, Jl Danau Tamblingan 22, north-central Sanur ☎0361/288570, ⓔsumandps@indosat.net.id; JBA, inside the compound of the *Diwangkara Hotel*, Jl Hang Tuah 54 in north Sanur ☎0361/286501, ⓔjbadwkbl@denpasar.wasantara.net.id; and Nagasari Tours, Jl Danau Tamblingan 102, central Sanur ☎0361/288096, ⓔnagasari@mega.net.id. Domestic flights and day-trips from Tunas Tour, next to *Resto Ming*, Jl Danau Tamblingan 102, south-central Sanur ☎0361/288581, ⓔtunas@denpasar.wasantara.net.id.

Benoa Harbour (Pelabuhan Benoa)

BENOA HARBOUR (Pelabuhan Benoa) is located off the end of a long causeway that juts out into the sea 5km southwest of southern Sanur, and is the arrival and departure point for most of Bali's public and tourist **boat services,** including the Bounty Cruise boat from Gili Meno and Lombok, the Mabua Express and *Osiana 3* from Lombok, all Pelni and Barito ships from elsewhere in Indonesia, plus cruise liners and seaplanes.

Despite the shared name, there's just over a kilometre of sea between the harbour and the northern tip of the Tanjung Benoa peninsula (see p.551), and the journey between the two has to be done the long way round, by land. The easiest way to reach Benoa Harbour is by **metered taxi**; it's a short ride of about Rp20,000 from Sanur, or about Rp26,000 from Kuta, plus the Rp1000 toll. Occasional public **bemos** also run here from near Denpasar's Sanglah hospital, and there is also a sporadic return service.

Tickets for **Pelni** boats to other islands must be bought in advance (booking opens three days before departure), either through travel agents or at the Pelni offices in Benoa Harbour (Mon–Fri 8am–4pm, Sat 8am–12.30pm; ☎0361/723689) or Kuta (see p.563). For more on Pelni, see p.42.

All non-Pelni boats can be booked through tour agents in the main tourist resorts, but you usually need to arrange your own transport to the port: with **Bounty Cruise**, express to Gili Meno and Lombok ($35); with **Mabua**, express to Lombok ($30); on ***Osiania 3*** to Lombok, via Padang Bai (Rp129,000); and with **Barito**, express to Surabaya on Java (Rp170,000), Bima on Sumbawa (Rp200,000), Maumere on Flores (Rp200,000), Waingapu on Sumba (Rp300,000), and Kupang on Timor (Rp425,000). For journey times and frequencies, see p.665.

Ubud and around

The inland village of **Ubud** and its surrounding area form Bali's cultural heartland, home to a huge proliferation of temples, museums and art galleries, where Balinese dance shows are staged nightly and a wealth of arts and crafts studios provide the most absorbing shopping on the island. It's also set within a stunning physical environment – a lush landscape watered by hundreds of streams, with archetypal terraced paddy vistas at every turn – all of which gives plenty of scope for leisurely hikes and bicycle rides.

North of Denpasar

The stretch of road running 13km **north of Denpasar** to Ubud has become something of a sightseeing attraction in itself due to the almost unbroken string of **arts- and crafts-producing villages** that line its course. Despite the obvious commercialization, these villages all have genuine histories as centres of refined artistic activity and are still renowned for their specialist crafts.

Batubulan

Barely distinguishable from the northeastern suburbs of Denpasar, **BATUBULAN** acts as the capital's public transport interchange for all bemos heading east and northeast, but it's also an important village in its own right, home of the most famous *barong* dance troupes, and respected across the island for its superb stonecarvers. The village is a long ribbon strung out over 2.5km along the main road, defined by the bemo station in the south and the huge Barong statue at the Singapadu/Celuk junction in the north. The northern stretch of the village, known as **Tegaltamu**, is the most interesting, and it's here that you'll find the shops selling Batubulan's finest **stonecarvings**. Local sculptors specialize in freestanding images made either from the rough grey lava stone known as *paras*, or from smooth grey, yellow or pink sandstone.

As you'd expect in a village so renowned for its fine carvings, the main temple is exuberantly decorated. The main gateway to **Pura Puseh**, 200m east off the main road in the north of the village (follow the signs for the *barong* dance held next door) is graced by a grimacing Bhoma head and, to the right, Siwa stands ankle-deep in skulls and wears a string of them around his neck. The plot adjacent to Pura Puseh has been given over to a purpose-built stage,

Batubulan public transport

Batubulan's **bemo station** is at the southern end of the village and is the main terminal for transport to east and northeast Bali. Chocolate-brown bemos run **to Ubud** (50min; last departure 5.30pm) via Sukawati and Mas; dark-blue and fawn-coloured bemos run through Gianyar, Klungkung, **Padang Bai** and **Candi Dasa** on their way to **Amlapura** (last departure 5.30pm); and other bemos cross **Denpasar** to the Kereneng or Ubung terminals (see plan on p.528). **Buses** also travel from Batubulan bemo station to Amlapura, as well as to **Kintamani** via Tegalalang (last departure 2pm), and to **Singaraja** (last departure 2pm). White Damri buses also run to **Nusa Dua**, via the western edge of Sanur and the eastern outskirts of Kuta.

where, every morning of the year, the **barong** is performed (daily 9.30–10.30am; Rp50,000). It's quite feasible to get here by public bemo (see box opposite) and buy tickets on the door, but most spectators come on tours arranged through agents in Kuta or Sanur ($10–15 including return transport). Batubulan dancers also perform the **kecak dance** in a double bill with the **fire dance** (daily 6.30–7.30pm; Rp50,000) at the Barong Sahadewa stage, signed off the main Denpasar road about 500m south of the Pura Puseh junction.

Both the Bali Bird Park and the Bali Reptile Park (not to be confused with the vastly inferior reptile park in Mengwi) are fun places for children and fairly interesting for adults. The **Bali Bird Park** (**Taman Burung**; daily 8am–6pm; $7.50, kids $3.80; joint ticket for both parks $14/$7) is beautifully laid out with ponds, pavilions and plenty of flowers – and has an impressive array of birds, all of them identified with English-language labels. Highlights include various birds of paradise (most from Irian Jaya), as well as a couple of fluffy white **Bali starlings**, Bali's only endemic bird and a severely endangered species (see p.1075). The creatures at the **Bali Reptile Park** (**Rimba Reptil**; same hours and prices) are also informatively labelled: look out for the eight-metre-long reticulated python, thought to be the largest python in captivity in the world. The parks are right next door to each other, about 500m beyond the Barong statue at the Singapadu/Celuk intersection, or 3km northwest of Batubulan bemo terminal. All bemos between Batubulan and Ubud or Gianyar can drop you at the intersection.

Sukawati and Batuan

The lively market town of **SUKAWATI**, about 6km east of Batubulan, is famous for its **art market** (Pasar Seni), at the heart of the village, which trades every day from dawn till dusk inside a traditional covered two-storey building. Here you'll find a tantalizing array of artefacts, paintings, fabrics, sarongs and basketware, piled high on stalls that are crammed together so tightly you can barely walk between them. All Batubulan–Ubud bemos stop right in front of the marketplace.

Sukawati is also famous for its *wayang kulit* **shadow-puppet makers** and performers. I Wayan Nartha (Ⓣ0361/299080) has a shop on Jalan Padma (the road that runs east off the main Ubud road, one block south of the Pasar Seni); and I Wayan Mardika (Ⓣ0361/299646) sells from inside his home, which is on the road that runs parallel to the east of the main road, reached by walking east down Jalan Ciung Wanara (opposite the Pasar Seni) and then turning left after about 100m. Both workshops are in the *banjar* of Babakan and are signed off the main road.

Northern Sukawati merges into southern **BATUAN**, which was the original home of the Batuan style of painting (see box on p.577) and is now dominated by large **galleries** exhibiting pictures in all the main Balinese art styles. At the northern limit of Batuan, a plump stone statue of a Buddha (sometimes referred to as the Fat Baby Statue) marks the Sakah turn-off to Blahbatuh and points east, while the main road continues north.

Mas

The woodcarvers of **MAS** gained great inspiration from the local Pita Maha arts movement during the 1930s, which encouraged the carving of secular subjects as well as the more traditional masks and religious images. Today, the range of

woodcarvings on display in Mas is enormous, and it's a rewarding place both to browse and to buy, but as it stretches 5km from end to end you'll need plenty of time or your own transport to do it justice. At its northern end, Mas runs into the village of Peliatan, on the outskirts of Ubud, and all Batubulan–Ubud **bemos** pass through the village. The only **place to stay** is the charming *Taman Harum Cottages,* behind Tantra Gallery at the southern end of the village (Ⓣ0361/975567, Ⓕ975149, Ⓦwww.tamanharumcottages.com; ❻–❽).

Ubud

Ever since the German artist Walter Spies arrived here in 1928, **UBUD** has been a magnet for any tourist with the slightest curiosity about Balinese arts, and the traditional village of dancers and craftspeople is still apparent – the people of Ubud and adjacent villages really do still paint, carve, dance and make music, and religious practices here are so rigorously observed that hardly a day goes by without there being some kind of festival in the area. However, although it's fashionable to characterize Ubud as the "real" Bali, especially in contrast with Kuta, it actually bears little resemblance to a typical Balinese village. Cappuccino cafés, riverside losmen and chic boutiques crowd its central marketplace and, during peak season, foreigners seem to far outnumber local residents. There is major development along the central **Monkey Forest Road** (now officially renamed Jalan Wanara Wana), and the village has expanded to take in the neighbouring hamlets of Campuhan, Penestanan, Sanggingan, Nyuhkuning, Padang Tegal, Pengosekan and Peliatan.

Arrival and information

Perama runs several daily **shuttle bus** services to Ubud from all the major tourist centres on Bali and Lombok. Their Ubud terminus is inconveniently located at the southern end of Jalan Hanoman in Padang Tegal, about 750m from the southern end of Monkey Forest Road and 2.5km from the central marketplace. As there's no local bemo or taxi service from here, you'll have to deal with the touts offering free transport to whichever losmen they are promoting. Other shuttle bus operators are more likely to make drops either on Monkey Forest Road or near the central market.

Arriving by public **bemo**, you'll be dropped at the central market, on the junction of Jalan Raya and Monkey Forest Road (signed as "Jalan Wanara Wana"), from where it's an easy few minutes' walk to the main accommodation centres. Any bemo coming from Batubulan (Denpasar) or Kintamani can drop you in Peliatan if asked. See below for public transport to Campuhan/Sanggingan and Sayan; for Nyuhkuning, you'll either have to walk or negotiate a ride with a transport tout.

Ubud's **tourist office** (daily 10am–7.30pm; Ⓣ0361/973285) is located just west of the Jalan Raya/Monkey Forest Road intersection, right at the heart of central Ubud, and has noticeboards giving weekly dance-performance schedules, news on special events and a directory of emergency numbers. If you're planning to do any serious walking in the area, you should buy the **map** entitled Travel Treasure Maps' *Indonesia VI – Ubud Surroundings*, available in all the Ubud bookstores.

Transport and tours

The most enjoyable way of seeing Ubud and its immediate environs is on foot or by **bicycle** (available from most losmen and some tour agencies for Rp20,000/day). The transport touts and rental agencies along Monkey Forest Road all rent out **motorbikes, jeeps** and **jimneys**, and many can also supply a driver. Two local freelance **drivers** who have been recommended by readers are Nyoman Swastika (Ⓣ0361/980027, evenings only) and Nyoman Dan (Ⓣ0361/978320).

There are no metered taxis in Ubud, but it's easy enough to negotiate rides with the omnipresent **transport touts**. Typically, you can expect to pay around Rp10,000 for a ride from the Neka Art Museum north of the centre in Campuhan to *Café Wayan* halfway down Monkey Forest Road. Some of the outlying losmen and most midrange and expensive hotels provide free transport in and out of central Ubud. It's also possible to use the public **bemos** for certain short hops: to get to the Neka Art Museum, for example, flag down any bemo heading west (such as the turquoise ones going to Payangan), or ask at the terminal near the central market; tourists are generally charged Rp2000 for the ten-minute ride from the market. You can get to Pengosekan or Peliatan on a brown Batubulan-bound bemo, or to Petulu either on an orange Pujung-bound bemo or on a brown bemo going to Tegalalang and Kintamani. These local rides should cost about Rp2000, and they all go via Ubud's central market and/or tourist office.

Organized tours and outdoor activities

Ubud is well stocked with **tour agencies**, most of them located along Monkey Forest Road. The itineraries and prices of their organized **day-trips** vary little: most run daily, use air-conditioned minibuses seating eight to ten people and cost Rp65,000–110,000 per person.

One of Ubud's more unusual attractions is its regular **Bali bird walks**, organized by Victor Mason, landlord of the *Beggar's Bush* pub in Campuhan (Ⓣ0361/975009 from 8am–5pm; mobile Ⓣ0812/391 3801 after 5pm). The walks (Tues, Fri, Sat & Sun 9am) cost $33, or more if you book through an agent, including lunch and the use of shared binoculars. Keep Walking Tours, alongside Tegun Galeri, Jl Hanoman 44 (Ⓣ0361/973361), has an interesting programme of guided **cultural and ecological walks** (minimum two people; from Rp45,000), and offers **sunrise treks** up Gunung Batur ($55). Bali Sunrise 2001, Jl Raya Sanggingan 88, Campuhan/Sanggingan (mobile Ⓣ0818/552669, Ⓦwww.balisunrise2001.com), with another office in Toya Bungkah (see p.630), also runs sunrise treks up Gunung Batur (pick-up from Ubud hotels at 3am; $55 per person, minimum two participants; see p.631) and Gunung Agung (pick-up at 10pm; $100; see p.599).

Bali Budaya Tours on Jalan Raya Pengosekan (Ⓣ0361/975557) and Ary's Business and Travel Service on Jalan Raya, central Ubud (Ⓣ0361/973130, Ⓔary_s2000@yahoo.com) both run **guided mountain-bike rides** (Rp360,000 including lunch) down minor village roads from Gunung Batur. The stretch of Sungai Ayung just west of Ubud is the island's centre for **white-water rafting** and **kayaking**, and several companies run white-water excursions along its course; any Ubud tour agent can book you on.

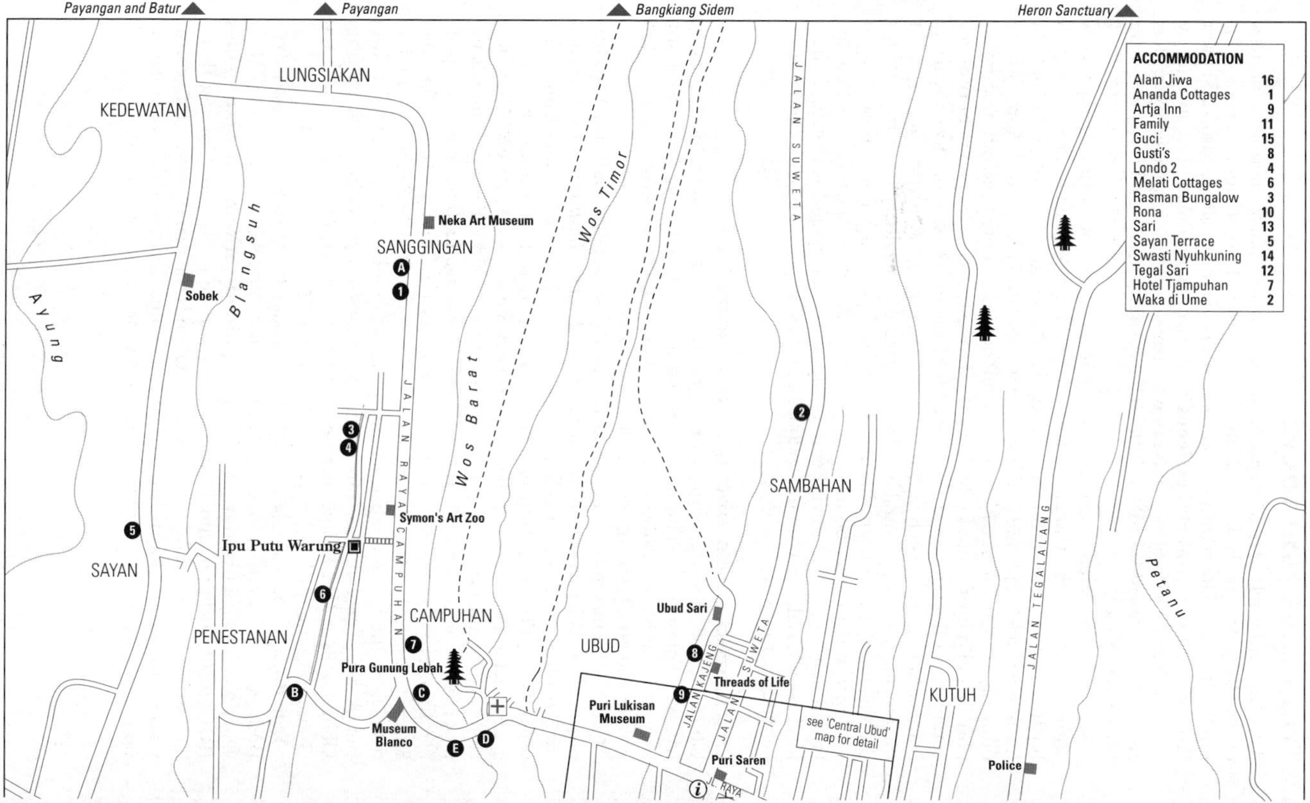

Payangan and Batur
Payangan
Bangkiang Sidem
Heron Sanctuary

ACCOMMODATION

Alam Jiwa	16
Ananda Cottages	1
Artja Inn	9
Family	11
Guci	15
Gusti's	8
Londo 2	4
Melati Cottages	6
Rasman Bungalow	3
Rona	10
Sari	13
Sayan Terrace	5
Swasti Nyuhkuning	14
Tegal Sari	12
Hotel Tjampuhan	7
Waka di Ume	2

LUNGSIAKAN
KEDEWATAN
Neka Art Museum
SANGGINGAN
Sobek
Blangsuh
Ayung
Wos Timor
Wos Barat
JALAN SUWETA
JALAN RAYA CAMPUHAN
SAMBAHAN
Symon's Art Zoo
Ipu Putu Warung
SAYAN
CAMPUHAN
PENESTANAN
Pura Gunung Lebah
Museum Blanco
UBUD
Ubud Sari
Threads of Life
JALAN KAJENG
JALAN SUWETA
Puri Lukisan Museum
see 'Central Ubud' map for detail
Puri Saren
JL. RAYA
KUTUH
JALAN TEGALALANG
Petanu
Police

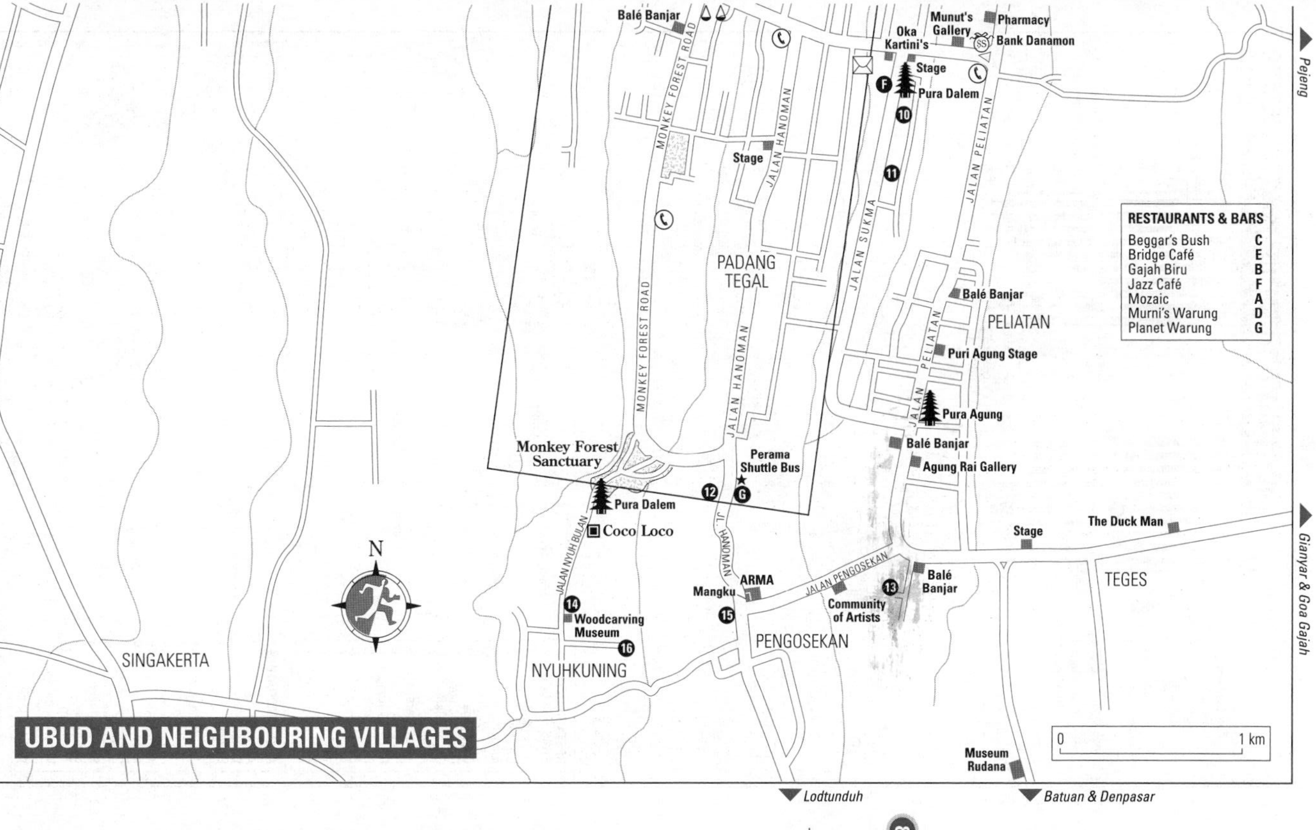
UBUD AND NEIGHBOURING VILLAGES
RESTAURANTS & BARS
Beggar's Bush C
Bridge Café E
Gajah Biru B
Jazz Café F
Mozaic A
Murni's Warung D
Planet Warung G
Pejeng
Gianyar & Goa Gajah
Lodtunduh
Batuan & Denpasar
Balé Banjar
Munut's Gallery
Pharmacy
Bank Danamon
Oka Kartini's
Stage
Pura Dalem
MONKEY FOREST ROAD
JALAN HANOMAN
JALAN SUKMA
JALAN PELIATAN
PADANG TEGAL
PELIATAN
Puri Agung Stage
Pura Agung
Agung Rai Gallery
Monkey Forest Sanctuary
Perama Shuttle Bus
Coco Loco
JL. HANOMAN
JALAN NYUH BULAN
JALAN PENGOSEKAN
ARMA
Mangku
Community of Artists
The Duck Man
TEGES
PENGOSEKAN
Woodcarving Museum
NYUHKUNING
SINGAKERTA
Museum Rudana
N
0
1 km

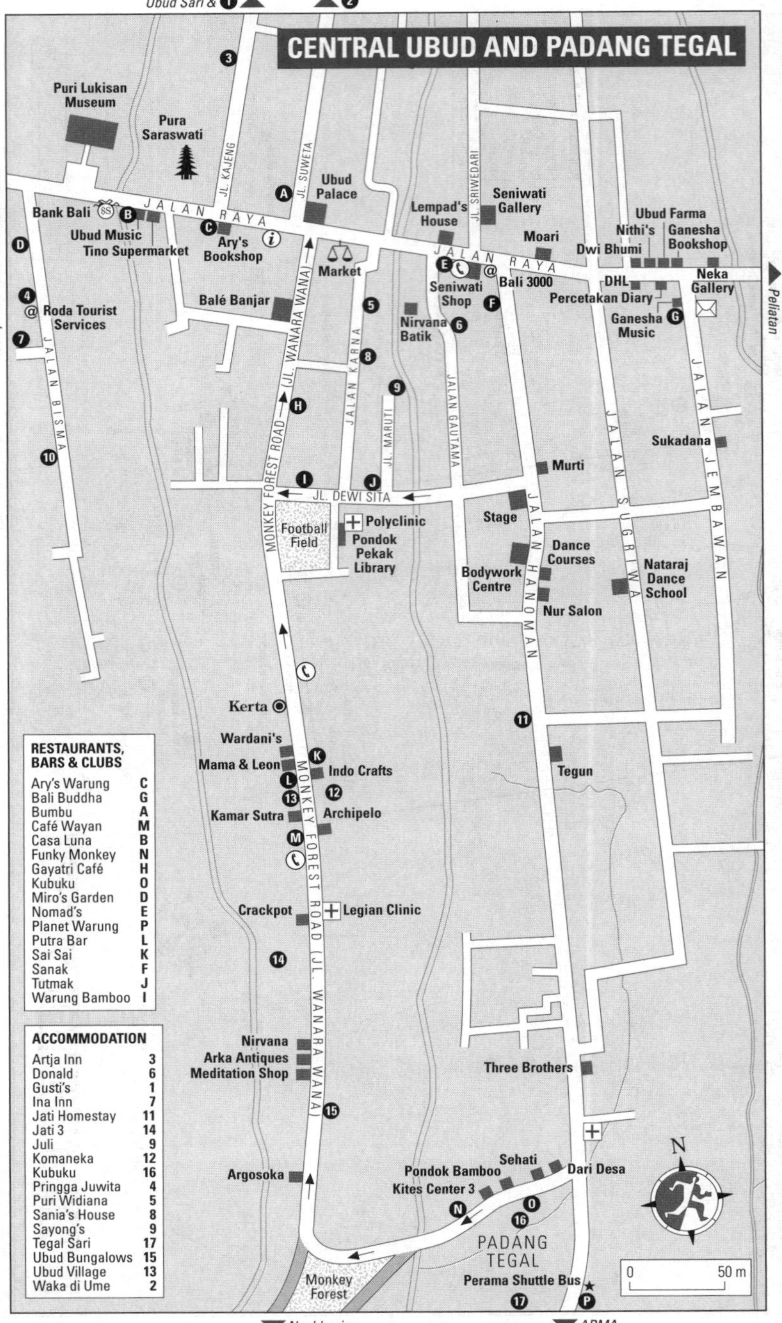
CENTRAL UBUD AND PADANG TEGAL
Ubud Sari & 1
2
Campuhan & Neka Museum
Peliatan
Nyuhkuning
ARMA
Puri Lukisan Museum
Pura Saraswati
JL. KAJENG
JL. SUWETA
Ubud Palace
JALAN RAYA
Bank Bali
Ubud Music
Tino Supermarket
Ary's Bookshop
Market
Balé Banjar
Roda Tourist Services
JALAN BISMA
JALAN KARNA
(JL. WANARA WANA)
MONKEY FOREST ROAD
JL. MARUTI
JALAN GAUTAMA
JL. SRIWEDARI
Lempad's House
Seniwati Gallery
Moari
Seniwati Shop
Bali 3000
Nirvana Batik
Ubud Farma
Nithi's
Ganesha Bookshop
Dwi Bhumi
DHL
Percetakan Diary
Neka Gallery
Ganesha Music
JALAN SUGRIWA
JALAN JEMBAWAN
Sukadana
Murti
JL. DEWI SITA
Football Field
Polyclinic
Pondok Pekak Library
Stage
JALAN HANOMAN
Dance Courses
Bodywork Centre
Nur Salon
Nataraj Dance School
Kerta
Wardani's
Mama & Leon
Indo Crafts
Kamar Sutra
Archipelo
Tegun
MONKEY FOREST ROAD (JL. WANARA WANA)
Crackpot
Legian Clinic
Nirvana
Arka Antiques
Meditation Shop
Three Brothers
Argosoka
Sehati
Pondok Bamboo
Dari Desa
Kites Center 3
PADANG TEGAL
Perama Shuttle Bus
Monkey Forest
N
0
50 m
RESTAURANTS, BARS & CLUBS
Ary's Warung C
Bali Buddha G
Bumbu A
Café Wayan M
Casa Luna B
Funky Monkey N
Gayatri Café H
Kubuku O
Miro's Garden D
Nomad's E
Planet Warung P
Putra Bar L
Sai Sai K
Sanak F
Tutmak J
Warung Bamboo I
ACCOMMODATION
Artja Inn 3
Donald 6
Gusti's 1
Ina Inn 7
Jati Homestay 11
Jati 3 14
Juli 9
Komaneka 12
Kubuku 16
Pringga Juwita 4
Puri Widiana 5
Sania's House 8
Sayong's 9
Tegal Sari 17
Ubud Bungalows 15
Ubud Village 13
Waka di Ume 2

Moving on from Ubud

By bemo

All **bemos** depart at least half-hourly until around 2pm, then at least hourly until about 5pm. They all leave from near the central crossroads on Jalan Raya; the east- and southbound bemos leave from the central marketplace, and the north- and westbound ones from in front of the tourist office. The **Ubud–Tegalalang–Pujung–Kintamani** route is usually served by brown bemos, while the **Ubud–Campuhan–Kedewatan–Payangan–Kintamani** bemos are generally either brown or bright blue. Frequent turquoise or orange bemos go to **Gianyar** (via Goa Gajah), where you can make connections to **Padang Bai** (for Lombok), **Candi Dasa**, **Singaraja** and **Lovina**. Any journey south, to Kuta or Sanur, involves an initial bemo ride to Denpasar's **Batubulan** station plus at least one cross-city connection, unless you take the Batubulan–Nusa Dua bus which makes drops on the western fringe of Sanur and at the eastern edge of Kuta. To reach western Bali and Java by bemo, you'll need to take a convoluted route via Batubulan.

By shuttle bus

Bali's ubiquitous **shuttle bus** operator, Perama, has pretty much cornered the market from Ubud and most tour operators sell Perama tickets. **Perama**'s head office is in Padang Tegal at the far southern end of Jalan Hanoman (Ⓣ0361/973316, Ⓔperama_tour@hotmail.com), but the buses do pick-ups from their tour operator agents in the centre. Perama buses run to most of the major tourist destinations on Bali, as well as to Lombok and Sumbawa (all prices include the boat transfer where relevant); see Travel Details on p.662 for a full list. Perama also sell inclusive tickets for public buses to Java. Sample prices include Rp10,000 to **Sanur**; Rp15,000 to **Kuta**, the **airport**, **Padang Bai** or **Candi Dasa**; and Rp45,000 to **Senggigi** on Lombok. There are no direct shuttle buses to Pemuteran, Gilimanuk and other parts of **northwest Bali**, but it's straightforward enough to take a shuttle bus to **Lovina** and then change onto a westbound bemo for the coastal stretch.

Accommodation

Anywhere in Ubud, you're almost certain to find that your **accommodation** is set in gorgeously lush surroundings. The further away from Monkey Forest Road you look, the better the views, and the more traditional the losmen, though restaurant and entertainment options will be limited.

Ubud's accommodation explosion has played havoc with its address system, particularly along Monkey Forest Road, where hardly a single losmen has an official road number. Every place we've listed is marked on a **map** – either the Central Ubud and Padang Tegal map (opposite) or the Neighbouring Villages map (p.568). For accommodation in Mas, see p.566.

Central Ubud and Padang Tegal

Monkey Forest Road is the most **central**, but also the most congested and expensive, part of town. Accommodation on most of the tiny adjacent roads, such as Jalan Karna, Jalan Kajeng, Jalan Bisma and Jalan Gautama, tends to be simpler and better value. **Padang Tegal** is about fifteen minutes' walk from Monkey Forest Road and much quieter, but has its own shops and restaurants.

Inexpensive

Artja Inn Jl Kajeng Ⓣ0361/974425. Six simple but pleasant bamboo-walled cottages with open-roofed, cold-water mandi. Set in a nice garden away from the road. ❷

Donald Jl Gautama 9 Ⓣ0361/977156. Tiny but

well-run and friendly homestay offering four exceptionally cheap, sparsely furnished bungalows in a secluded garden compound. ❷

Jati Homestay Jl Hanoman, Padang Tegal ⓣ0361/977701. Ten comfortable bungalows facing the rice paddies. All have hot water and peaceful views. Run by a family of painters. ❸

Jati 3 Down a *gang* off south-central Monkey Forest Rd ⓣ & ⓕ0361/973249. Five standard losmen bungalows plus four gorgeous split-level bungalows overlooking a river. ❸–❺

Juli Jl Bisma 102 ⓣ0361/97714. Good-value place on a quiet road, offering six well-maintained rooms overlooking the paddies, all with hot showers. ❸

Kubuku Off the southeastern end of Monkey Forest Rd, Padang Tegal ⓣ0361/974742, ⓕ971552. Seven bungalow rooms marooned in the rice-fields near one of Ubud's most prettily set cafés. ❺

Puri Widiana Jl Karna 5 ⓣ0361/973406. Very inexpensive, good-value basic rooms in a small family compound that's central but peaceful. ❷

Sania's House Jl Karna ⓣ0361/975535, ⓔinengah_merta@hotmail.com. Lots of clean, well-furnished bungalows in a compact but central compound with a small swimming pool. Some hot water. ❸–❹

Sayong's Bungalows Jl Maruti ⓣ0361/973305. Simple bungalow rooms in a variety of sizes, all with hot water. Swimming pool across the lane. ❸–❹

Mid-range and expensive

Gusti's Garden Bungalows Jl Kajeng 27 ⓣ0361/973311, ⓕ972159. Fifteen above-average losmen rooms, all with hot water, set around a swimming pool in a peaceful spot. ❹

Ina Inn Jl Bisma ⓣ0361/973317, ⓕ973282, ⓔinainn@eudoramail.com. Nicely furnished cottages in a panoramic spot surrounded by rice-fields; some have huge glass windows, and there's a rooftop pool. ❺

Komaneka Resort Central Monkey Forest Rd ⓣ0361/976090, ⓕ977140, ⓦwww.komaneka.com. Upmarket, elegantly designed air-con bungalows overlooking the paddy fields, a beautiful pool and a spa. ❽

Pringga Juwita Water Garden Cottages Jl Bisma ⓣ & ⓕ0361/975734, ⓦwww.thefibra.com/pringga.htm. Characterful bungalows (some air-con) featuring antique furniture and garden bathrooms. Surrounded by lotus ponds and has a pool. ❼

Tegal Sari Jl Hanoman, Padang Tegal ⓣ & ⓕ0361/973318, ⓦwww.travelideas.net/bali.hotels/hanoman-ubud.html. Exceptionally good-value fan and air-con rooms overlooking the paddyfields. Across the road from the Perama shuttle bus depot, but quite a hike from central Ubud (free local transport). Pool. ❹–❺

Ubud Bungalows Central Monkey Forest Rd ⓣ0361/971298, ⓕ975537, ⓔw_widnyana@hotmail.com. Good-value, comfortable, detached fan-cooled bungalows and some expensive air-con ones. Pool. ❺–❻

Ubud Village Hotel Central Monkey Forest Rd ⓣ0361/975571, ⓕ975069, ⓦwww.indo.com/hotels/ubud_village. Stylish, good-value upmarket hotel where each air-con room has its own little courtyard garden. Has a large pool and is very central. ❼–❽

The outskirts: Peliatan, Nyuhkuning, Campuhan, Penestanan and Sayan

Staying in **Peliatan** will be more of a village experience than central Ubud, while **Nyuhkuning** is a good in-between option, only a ten-minute walk through the forest from southern Monkey Forest Road (not ideal after dark) and with fine paddyfield views. West of central Ubud, **Campuhan** and **Sanggingan** hotels can only be reached via the busy main road, which is not a particularly pleasant walk, but public bemos run this way. Some **Penestanan** losmen overlook Campuhan and offer fine views, though for unsurpassed panoramas you should opt for one of the riverside hotels in **Sayan**, ten minutes' drive further west.

Alam Jiwa Nyuhkuning ⓣ & ⓕ0361/977463, ⓔalambali@indosat.net.id. Ten large, secluded, very smart bungalows, with great views. There's a pool and free transport into Ubud. ❼

Ananda Cottages Jl Raya, Sanggingan/Campuhan ⓣ0361/975376, ⓕ975375 ⓔanandaubud@denpasar.wasantara.net.id. Characterful cottages (some air-con) with garden bathrooms and verandahs, surrounded by rice-paddies; there's a pool and restaurant. 30min walk from central Ubud, but you can rent bicycles, motorbikes and cars. ❻–❼

Family Guest House Jl Sukma 39, Peliatan ⓣ0361/974054, ⓕ978292. Friendly place offering well-designed bungalows with large verandahs. Some hot water. 15min walk from central Ubud. ❸–❺

Londo 2 On the track that runs east from the top of the Penestanan steps ⓣ0361/976764. Three large, four-person cottages with kitchen, and stunning views over the paddies. Run by one of the original "Young Artists", I Nyoman Londo. ❸

Melati Cottages Penestanan ⓣ0361/974650, ⓕ975088, ⓔmelaticottages@hotmail.com. Large, traditional-style fan rooms with huge picture windows in a lovely rice-paddy setting. There's a pool too. ❻

Rasman Bungalow Penestenan ⓣ0361/975497. Simple, spartan two-storey four-person bungalows, similar to the nearby *Londo 2* (see above for access). Great views; friendly and quiet. ❸

Rona Jl Sukma 23, Peliatan ⓣ & ⓕ0361/973229. Good-value terraced bungalows (some hot water), with comfortable bamboo beds and armchairs. Deservedly popular. ❸–❹

Sari Bungalows Off the southern end of Jl Peliatan, Peliatan ⓣ0361/975541. Basic bungalows fronted by verandahs which afford superb paddy views. Some of the cheapest rooms in Ubud. ❷

Sayan Terrace Sayan ⓣ0361/974384, ⓕ975384, ⓦwww.geocities.com/sayanterrace. Awesome location overlooking Sungai Ayung. Some good-value, mid-priced cottages, plus a few exceptionally elegant ones. Swimming pool; some air-con. ❻–❽

Swasti Nyuhkuning Hideaway Nyuhkuning ⓣ0361/974079. Large, spacious and comfortably furnished rooms, all with hot water and rice-field views. Pool. Good value. ❺

Hotel Tjampuhan Jl Raya, Campuhan ⓣ0361/975368, ⓕ975137, ⓦwww.tjampuhan.com. Prettily positioned cottages (some air-con) set in steep terraced gardens that drop right down to the river, built on the site of the artist Walter Spies' former home. Two pools and a spa. 15min walk from central Ubud. Reservations essential. ❼–❽

Waka di Ume About 1.8km north along Jl Suweta from Ubud market, in the hamlet of Sambahan ⓣ0361/973178, ⓕ973179, ⓦwww.wakaexperience.com. Delightfully chic bungalows with picture-perfect rice-paddy views. Two pools, a spa and free transport into central Ubud. ❽

Central Ubud

Covering the area between Jalan Raya in the north and the Monkey Forest in the south, and between Campuhan bridge to the west and the GPO to the east, **central Ubud**'s chief attractions are its restaurants and shops, but it does hold a few worthwhile sights.

Although billed as central Ubud's major art museum, the **Puri Lukisan** on Jalan Raya (daily 8am–4pm; Rp10,000) has a less impressive collection than the far superior Neka Art Museum, 2km west in Sanggingan (see p.575). Set amongst lotus-filled ponds and shady arbours, Puri Lukisan (Palace of Paintings) was founded in 1956 by the Ubud *punggawa*, **Cokorda Gede Agung Sukawati** (whose descendants are still involved with the museum) and the Dutch artist **Rudolf Bonnet**. Both men had amassed a significant collection of work by local artists and almost the whole of the **First Pavilion**, located at the top of the garden, is given over to these works. Some of these are wayang-style canvases, but most are early Ubud-style, depicting local scenes (for some background on Balinese painting styles, see the box on p.576). A handful of finely crafted woodcarving pieces from the 1930s, 1940s and 1950s are also scattered about this gallery. The **Second Pavilion**, to the left of the First Pavilion, contains a fairly extensive showcase of works in the Young Artists style, though it's not very well lit. The **Third Pavilion**, to the right of the First Pavilion, houses temporary exhibitions.

At the end of the nineteenth century, the famously versatile artist I Gusti Nyoman Lempad arrived in Ubud from the court of Blahbatuh and was employed as chief stonecarver and architect to the Sukawati royal family; **Pura Saraswati** was one of his many commissions. He set the whole temple complex in a delightful water garden, landscaped around a huge lotus pond, and dedicated it to Saraswati, the name of both a sacred Hindu river and the

A rice-paddy walk through Ubud Kaja

A classic, almost circular **rice-paddy walk** begins and ends in the northern part of Ubud known as Ubud Kaja (*kaja* literally means "upstream, towards the mountains"); the walk takes two-and-a-half hours, is flat and not at all strenuous. There's no shade for the first hour, though, so you'll need a hat, sunblock and some water. Most of the route (with one deviation) is suitable for mountain bikes too.

The walk begins from the western end of Ubud's **Jalan Raya**, between the Casa Lina shop and the overhead aqueduct, where a track leads up to the *Abangan Hotel* on the north side of the road. Head up the slope and, at the top, follow the track which bends to the left before straightening out and heading north. Continue along the track for about 3km as it slices through gently terraced rice-fields fringed with coconut palms; you'll see scores of dragonflies en route, and plenty of **birdlife**, including, possibly, iridescent-blue Javanese kingfishers. After about 1hr 10min, the track comes to an end at a sealed road. Turn right here to cross the river, then look for the **southbound track** that starts almost immediately after the bridge and runs east of the river. (If you're on a bike, you should follow the road east of the bridge, and then head back to Ubud via Sakti on the road that merges into central Ubud's Jalan Suweta.) The southbound track becomes indistinct in places, so follow the narrow paths along the top of the rice-field dykes and keep the river in view on your right. Get back on the proper track as soon as you see it emerging from the woods alongside the river, and this will take you back down to Ubud, finishing at the far northern end of Ubud's Jalan Kajeng.

goddess of water and learning. A restaurant, *Café Lotus*, now capitalizes on the garden view. To get to the temple, either take the gateway that opens onto Jalan Raya, or go through the restaurant. A forest of metre-high lotus plants leads you right up to the red-brick entrance gate, through which you'll find a pavilion housing the two huge *barong* costumes used for exorcizing rituals: the lion-like Barong Ket and the wild boar Barong Bangkal.

The **Threads of Life Textile Arts Center and Gallery**, next to *Rumah Roda* restaurant at Jl Kajeng 24 (Mon–Sat 10am–6pm), aims to introduce visitors to the complex art of traditional weaving in Bali, Sumba, Flores, Lembata and Sulawesi; on all of these islands, certain weaving designs and techniques are in danger of being lost forever. The Threads of Life foundation commissions modern-day weavers to re-create the ritual textiles of their grandmothers, using traditional methods, and these pieces are displayed here, alongside exhibitions on their ritual use and cultural context.

Balinese women feature prominently in the paintings displayed in both the Neka Art Museum and Puri Lukisan, but there is barely a handful of works by women artists in either collection. To redress this imbalance, British-born artist Mary Northmore founded the **Seniwati Gallery of Art by Women** on Jalan Sriwedari (daily 9am–5pm; free), which is committed to the promotion, display and sale of work by women artists. The Seniwati organization currently represents about forty local and expatriate women, many of whom have pictures on show in the gallery's small but charming permanent collection. The collection covers all mainstream Balinese art styles, and the works are supported by excellent information sheets.

Campuhan, Sanggingan and Penestanan

Sited at the confluence of the rivers Wos Barat and Wos Timor, the hamlet of **CAMPUHAN** officially extends west from Ubud only as far as the *Hotel*

Tjampuhan, and is famous as the home of several of Bali's most charismatic expatriate painters. North up the Campuhan hill from this knot of artistic abodes, Campuhan turns into **SANGGINGAN** (though few people bother to distinguish it from its neighbour), and it's here that you'll find Bali's best art gallery, the **Neka Art Museum**. If you don't fancy walking or cycling along the busy main road that tears through its heart, you can take any westbound **bemo** from in front of the tourist information office on Jalan Raya. The neighbouring and still rather traditional hamlet of **Penestanan** is famous as the home of the original band of so-called Young Artists.

The Neka Art Museum

Boasting the most comprehensive collection of traditional and modern Balinese paintings on the island, the **Neka Art Museum** (daily 9am–5pm; Rp10,000) is housed in a series of purpose-built pavilions set high on a hill overlooking the Wos Barat river valley, alongside the main Campuhan/ Sanggingan road.

The first pavilion, the **Balinese Painting Hall**, gives an overview of the three major schools of Balinese painting from the seventeenth century to the present day (for an introduction to all of them, see p.576) It opens with some examples of the earliest known "school", the flat **wayang-style** works from Kamasan, here represented by a couple of typical nineteenth-century pictures, as well as by modern *wayang*-style pictures from the contemporary artist Ketut Kobot. One of the finest **Ubud-style** paintings in this pavilion is *The Bumblebee Dance* by Anak Agung Gede Sobrat, which shows a traditional flirtation dance, the *oleg tambulilingan*. I Wayan Bendi's *Busy Bali* is also a classic – a typically modern **Batuan-style** work that takes a wry look at the effects of tourism on the island.

The **Arie Smit Pavilion** is devoted to the hugely influential Dutch expatriate artist who has been based in Bali since 1956, and to works by the group of painters with which he was associated, who came to be known as the Young Artists. You enter the pavilion via the upstairs gallery, which is filled with pictures by Smit; the ground-floor hall exhibits naive, expressionistic works in the Young Artists style. The **Photography Archive Center** houses a very interesting archive of black-and-white photographs from Bali in the 1930s and 1940s, all of them taken by the remarkable American expat **Robert Koke**, who founded the first hotel in Kuta in 1936. His photographic record includes some stunning shots of village scenes, dances and cremations.

The small **Lempad Pavilion** is dedicated to the works of the multi-talented artist and architect I Gusti Nyoman Lempad, who lived in Ubud until his death, at about 116 years old, in 1978. Among his most famous works are cartoon-like line drawings inspired by religious mythology and secular folklore, including a series on Men and Pan Brayut, a humorous reworking of the well-known folk story about a poor couple and their eighteen children.

The **Contemporary Indonesian Art Hall** focuses on works by artists from other parts of Indonesia, whose style is sometimes labelled "Academic". Outstanding works displayed here include *Three Masked Dancers* and *Divine Union*, both by Javanese-born Anton H. Works by Indonesian artists spill over into the ground-floor galleries of the **East–West Art Annex**, where you'll find the Javanese artist Affandi's bold expressionist portrait of fighting cocks, *Fight to the Finish*. The upstairs galleries feature the paintings of foreign artists who lived and worked in Bali, including the *Temptation of Arjuna* by the influential Dutch painter Rudolf Bonnet.

Balinese painting

Up until the early twentieth century, Balinese painters, sculptors and woodcarvers dedicated themselves to honouring their gods and rajahs with splendid temples and palaces. Though highly skilled, these artists were not paid for their work, and earned their living as farmers or traders. By the 1930s, however, the rajahs had lost much of their power to the Dutch colonials, and foreign tourists were taking their place as **patrons of the arts** – and paying for the work. Gradually, artists began to paint secular subjects, to express themselves as individuals and to sign their own pictures. Painting and carving became full-time and relatively lucrative occupations, and the **arts and crafts industry** is now one of the most profitable on Bali.

In the last few decades, art historians have grouped **Balinese painting** into broad schools, most of them named after the village where a style originated. Inevitably the categories are over-generalized, but Balinese painters, like artists working in other media, are not shy about copying good ideas or even reproducing successful work, so it's not difficult to pinpoint representative features and techniques. Some of the finest Balinese paintings are displayed in Ubud's big art museums.

Wayang or Kamasan style

The earliest Balinese painters drew their inspiration from the *wayang kulit* shadow plays, re-creating puppet-like figures on their canvases and depicting episodes from the same religious and historical epics that were played out on the stage. Variously known as the **wayang style**, the **classical style** or the **Kamasan style** (after the village most noted for its *wayang*-style art), and still popular today, the pictures are packed full of people painted in three-quarter profile (both eyes visible), with caricature-like features and angular, puppet-like poses. Traditional *wayang* artists use only five different colours – red, blue, yellow, black and white – creating the characteristic muted effect.

In the seventeenth century, *wayang*-style art appeared mainly on the banners that were used to decorate temples, but the oldest surviving pictures are those that cover the ceilings of the old palace of **Klungkung** (see p.594), and these are less than two hundred years old. Most modern *wayang*-style artists are still based in the village of Kamasan near Klungkung, including the renowned **I Nyoman Mandra**.

Ubud style

In the 1930s, Balinese painters in the village of Ubud started to experiment with more realistic techniques such as perspective and the use of light and shadow, and began painting episodes from real life, including market and temple scenes. The **Ubud style** is now characterized by an overwhelming sense of activity, with each character engaged in some transaction, chore or conversation, and any intervening space taken up with tiny details such as images of offerings, insects or animals. The two expatriate artists most commonly associated with the emergence of the Ubud style are the German **Walter Spies** and the Dutchman **Rudolph Bonnet**, both of whom lived in the Ubud area in the 1930s and helped found the locally influential Pita Maha arts group.

Pengosekan style

During the 1960s, a group of young painters working in the Ubud style and living in the village of Pengosekan on the outskirts of Ubud came up with a new approach,

Symon's studio and Museum Blanco

Descending the Campuhan hill, in the direction of Ubud, you'll pass a few hotels and restaurants before reaching the ebullient studio-gallery of American-born artist **Symon**, 100m west of the Campuhan bridge. With its assortment of vivacious paintings and weird artefacts suspended around the subsequently known as the **Pengosekan style**. From the Ubud-style pictures, the Pengosekan school isolated just a few components, specifically the **birds**, **butterflies**, **insects** and **flowering plants** that featured, in miniature, in so many of them, and magnified these elements to fill a whole canvas. The best Pengosekan paintings look delicate and lifelike, generally depicted in soothing pastels of pinks, blues, creams, browns and greens, and slightly reminiscent of classical Japanese flower and bird pictures.

Batuan style

In contrast to the slightly romanticized visions of village events being painted by the Ubud-style artists in the 1930s, a group of painters in the nearby village of Batuan were coming up with more thought-provoking interpretations of Balinese life. Like the Ubud artists, **Batuan-style** painters filled their works with scores of people, but on a much more frantic and wide-ranging scale. A single Batuan-style picture might contain a dozen apparently unrelated scenes – a temple dance, a rice harvest, a fishing expedition, an exorcism, and a couple of tourists taking snapshots – all depicted in fine detail that strikes a balance between the naturalistic and the stylized. By clever juxtaposition, the best Batuan artists, like **I Wayan Bendi**, **I Made Budi** and **Ni Wayan Warti,** can turn their pictures into amusing and astute comments on Balinese society. Works by their precursors, the original Batuan artists, **Ida Bagus Made Togog** and **Ida Bagus Made Wija**, focused more on the darker side of village life and on the supernatural beings that hung around the temples and forests.

Young Artists

A second flush of artistic innovation hit the Ubud area in the 1960s, when a group of teenage boys from the hamlet of **Penestanan** started producing unusually expressionistic works, painting everyday scenes in vibrant, non-realistic colours. They soon became known as the **Young Artists**, a tag now used to describe work by anyone in that same style. The inspiration for the boys' experiments is generally attributed to the interest of Dutch artist **Arie Smit**, who settled in Penestanan in the 1960s. The style is indisputably childlike, even naive, the detailed observations of daily life crudely drawn with minimal attention to perspective, outlined in black like a child's colouring book, and often washed over in weird shades of pinks, purples and blues. All the major museums have works by some of the original Young Artists from the 1960s, including **I Ketut Tagen**, **I Wayan Pugur**, **I Nyoman Mundik** and **I Nyoman Mujung**. The Neka Art Museum in Ubud devotes a whole gallery to pictures by Arie Smit.

Academic (modern) style

Any modern artist whose work doesn't fit easily into the other major schools of Balinese painting usually gets labelled as **Academic** – meaning that they have studied and been influenced by Western techniques. The best-known Academic painters tend to be men and women from other parts of Indonesia, who have settled in Bali and painted Balinese subjects in a non-traditional style. Both the Neka and ARMA devote a whole gallery to these artists, and names to look out for there include **Affandi**, **Anton H** and **Abdul Aziz**, all from Java, the Sumatran-born **Rusli**, and from Bali, **I Nyoman Tusan** and **Nyoman Guarsa**.

steps leading up to the entrance, it's hard to ignore, and inside, the gallery houses similarly unconventional displays of Symon's paintings, sculptures and other creations, as well as a working atelier. His energetic take on Balinese life makes a refreshing change from the more sedate traditional views so popular in Ubud, and his pictures are well priced (from around $400).

A short distance further down the main road into Ubud from Symon's Studio, an ostentatious gateway leads you into the **Museum Blanco** (daily 10am–5pm; Rp10,000), former home of the flamboyant Catalan expatriate Antonio Blanco, who specialized in erotic paintings and drawings, particularly portraits of Balinese women in varying states of undress. Whatever you think of the man's artistic achievements, it's hard not to enjoy the sheer panache of this ultimate self-publicist and his undeniably camp museum, complete with gilded pillars and sweeping Spanish balustrades.

Penestanan

Just west of the Campuhan bridge, but invisible from the main road, the hamlet of **PENESTANAN** is more traditional than its neighbour, and makes a good focus for a pleasant two-hour circular walk. It's accessible from a side road that turns off beside Museum Blanco, but the most dramatic approach is via the steep **flight of steps** a few hundred metres further north along the Campuhan road, just before Symon's Studio. The steps lead up the hillside past arterial paths leading to some very panoramic accommodation (see p.573), before dropping down through rice-fields into the next valley, across Sungai Blangsuh and through a small wooded area, before coming to a crossroads with Penestanan's main street. This street connects Campuhan to the east with Sayan to the west; go straight on if you're heading for Sayan, or left for a walk through the village and then back down to Museum Blanco in Campuhan.

Penestanan's main claim to fame is as the original home of the **Young Artists** (see p.577). The Dutch painter Arie Smit settled here in the 1960s, and set about encouraging village youngsters to paint pictures dictated by their own instinct rather than sticking to the styles and themes passed down by their fathers. The boys came up with pictures that were bright, bold and expressionist, a style that is still followed by many painters in Penestanan today. The village now holds about a dozen art **galleries**, and is also the centre for the finest beadwork on Bali, including jewellery, belts, caps and handbags.

The Monkey Forest and Nyuhkuning

Ubud's best-known tourist attraction is its **Monkey Forest Sanctuary** (daylight hours; Rp10,000, kids Rp5000), which occupies the land between the southern end of Monkey Forest Road and the northern edge of the woodcarvers' hamlet of Nyuhkuning. The focus of numerous day-trips because of its resident troupe of malevolent but photogenic monkeys, the forest itself is actually small and disappointing, traversed by a concrete pathway. The only way to see the Monkey Forest is on foot, but it's hardly a strenuous hike: the entrance is a fifteen-minute walk south from Ubud's central market, and a stroll around the forest and its temple combines well with a walk around neighbouring Nyuhkuning.

Five minutes into the forest, you'll come to **Pura Dalem Agung Padang Tegal** (donation requested for compulsory sarong and sash), the temple of the dead for the *banjar* of Padang Tegal. *Pura dalem* are traditionally places of extremely strong magical power and the preserve of *leyak* (evil spirits); in this temple you'll find half a dozen stonecarved images of the witch-widow **Rangda** flanking the main stairway, immediately recognizable by her hideous fanged face, unkempt hair, lolling metre-long tongue and pendulous breasts. Two of the Rangda statues are depicted in the process of devouring children – a favourite occupation of hers. Casual visitors are not allowed to enter the inner sanctuary, but in the outer courtyard you can see the ornate *kulkul* **drum tower**, built in red brick and decorated with carvings of Bhoma heads and *garuda*.

Continuing south from the Pura Dalem Agung Padang Tegal, the track enters the tiny settlement of **NYUHKUNING**, whose villagers are renowned for their **woodcarvings**, particularly their elfin figurines and weeping Buddhas, most of them sculpted from coconut, hibiscus and "crocodile" wood. Prices are reasonable and the whole commercial process is much more low-key than in Mas. A number of the best local carvings have been preserved in the **Widya Kusuma Woodcarving Museum**, a tiny makeshift gallery about ten minutes south of the temple of the dead that keeps random hours. Scattered in amongst the woodcarving shops are several beautifully sited small **hotels**, each one offering uninterrupted rice-paddy views; see p.572 for details.

Pengosekan and Petulu

The villages of **Pengosekan** and **Petulu** lie to the east of central Ubud, and can be reached fairly easily on foot in an hour or less from the main market.

Pengosekan and ARMA

Located at the southern end of Jalan Hanoman, **PENGOSEKAN** is known locally as the centre of the Pengosekan Community of Artists, a co-operative that was founded in 1969. The co-operative was so successful that most of the original members have now established their own galleries, but the spirit of the collective lives on in the **Pengosekan Community of Artists showroom**, which stands just east of the river on the main Pengosekan road (daily 9am–6pm). As with other local communities of artists, the Pengosekan painters developed a distinct style, specializing in large canvases of birds, flowers, insects and frogs, painted in gentle pastels and depicted in magnified detail; most of the work here is for sale but the selection is a bit dull.

For a good selection of much meatier Balinese art, you should go instead to the **Agung Rai Museum of Art**, usually referred to as **ARMA** (daily 9am–6pm; Rp10,000), which is a few hundred metres west of the river and has entrances next to the *Kokokan Club* restaurant on Jalan Pengosekan as well as on Jalan Hanoman. ARMA also houses an excellent library and an open-air dance stage.

The upstairs gallery of ARMA's large **Balé Daja** pavilion gives a brief survey of the development of Balinese art (see box p.576) and includes some **wayang-style** canvases, hung high on the walls overlooking the central well, as well as a few good examples of I Gusti Nyoman Lempad's pen and ink cartoons. Two of the finest works up here, however, are Anak A Sobrat's *Baris Dance*, a typical example of **Ubud-style** art, and the popular, contemporary **Batuan-style** piece by I Wayan Bendi, *Life in Bali*, which is crammed with typical Balinese scenes – including a temple procession, a dance performance and a cockfight – and laced with satirical comments, notably in the figures of long-nosed tourists who pop up in almost every scene. The downstairs gallery houses temporary exhibitions.

Across the garden, the middle gallery of the **Balé Dauh** reads like a directory of Bali's most famous expats, featuring works by Adrien Jean Le Mayeur, Rudolf Bonnet, Antonio Blanco and Arie Smit (see opposite). The highlight is *Calonarang* by the German artist Walter Spies, a dark portrait of a demonic apparition being watched by a bunch of petrified villagers.

Petulu and the white heron sanctuary

Every evening at around 6pm, hundreds of thousands of white herons fly in from kilometres around to roost in certain trees in the village of **PETULU**, immediately to the northeast of Ubud – and it makes quite an astonishing spectacle. No one knows why the herons have chosen to make their home in Petulu, though one local story claims that the birds are reincarnations of the tens of thousands of men and women who died in the civil war that raged through Bali in 1966. Many of the victims were buried near here, and the birds are said to have started coming here only after a big ceremony was held in the village in memory of the dead. To find the so-called **white heron sanctuary**, follow the main Tegalalang–Pujung road north from the T-junction at the eastern edge of Ubud for about 1500m, then take the left-hand (signed) fork for a further 1500m. You may be asked to give a donation just before reaching the roosting area. Lots of public bemos ply the main Pujung road, but you'll have to walk the last 1500m from the fork.

Eating

With some 250 **restaurants** to choose from, eating in Ubud is a major pleasure. The quality of the food is high, and the emphasis is on wholesome ingredients. A mandatory ten percent local government tax is added to all restaurant bills.

Ary's Warung Jl Raya, central Ubud. Elegant Ubud institution whose expensive menu includes wonderful crab fishcakes, slowly roasted duck and white cheesecake. Closes about 1am.

Bali Buddha Jl Jembawan, opposite the GPO. Floor cushions, organic juices, filled bagels, chocolate mud pie, and brown-bread. Also a notice board with yoga and language course information.

Bumbu Jl Suweta 1, central Ubud. Delicious, mid-priced Indian, Balinese and vegetarian fare such as banana and coconut curry and chilli-fried fish, in a pleasant water-garden setting.

Café Wayan Monkey Forest Rd. Scrumptious but rather pricey breads and cakes plus a fairly good menu of Thai, Indonesian and European dishes served in *bale* furnished with cushions and low tables.

Casa Luna Jl Raya, central Ubud. Stylish riverside place specializing in mouthwatering breads and cakes, but also offering great salads, Indonesian, Indian and veggie fare. Nightly videos in a separate room.

Gajah Biru Jl Raya Penestanan ⓣ0361/979085. Fairly pricey, high-class Indian fare served in dining pavilions that look out onto a candlelit water garden.

Gayatri Café 67 Monkey Forest Rd. Cheap, popular place with a varied menu ranging from chilli (vegetarian or meat), red bean soup and pizza to salads and *nasi campur*.

Kubuku Off south end of Monkey Forest Rd, Padang Tegal. Ubud's most laid-back café stands on the edge of the rice-fields and serves a limited but delicious mid-priced veggie menu that includes home-baked bread.

Miro's Garden Jl Bisma, central Ubud. Lovely candlelit garden terrace, serving moderately priced international and Balinese dishes, including good nasi campur and *babi guling*.

Mozaic Jl Raya Sanggingan ⓣ0361/975768; open for lunch and dinner. Expensive, slightly formal restaurant serving a French- and Asian-inspired menu that includes salmon sashimi, steamed oysters and Bedugul rabbit.

Murni's Warung Jl Raya, Campuhan. High-class, mid-priced curries, thick home-made soups and Indonesian specialities in a multi-tiered restaurant built into the side of the Wos river valley.

Sanak Rumah Makan Padang Jl Hanoman, central Ubud. Inexpensive and authentic Sumatran fare, including fried chicken, baked eggs, potato cakes and fish curry.

Tutmak Jl Dewi Sita, central Ubud. Large, interestingly varied, mid-priced menu that includes meat, fish and vegetarian *nasi campur* and delicious breads and cakes. Board games, newspapers and lots of cushions.

Warung Bamboo Jl Dewi Sita, central Ubud. Inexpensive and tasty authentic Indonesian dishes, with recommended seafood and some interesting veggie options.

Nightlife and entertainment

Ubud is hardly a hotbed of hedonistic **nightlife**: most tourists spend the early part of the evening at a Balinese dance performance before catching last orders at a restaurant at around 9pm. But there are some bars and a few live music venues. Some restaurants show videos, including *Casa Luna* on Jalan Raya and *Bridge Café* in Campuhan.

△ Pura Ulun Danu Bratan, Bali

Traditional Balinese dance-dramas

Most Balinese **dance-dramas** have evolved from sacred rituals, and are still regularly performed at religious events and village festivals, with full attention given to the devotional aspects. They are nearly always accompanied by a Balinese gamelan orchestra (see p.1063). Most tourists, however, only get the chance to see commercial shows, but these are generally very good, as they're performed by expert local troupes in the traditional settings of temple courtyards, and always comprise a medley of highlights. There are few professional **dancers** in Bali; most performers don costumes and make-up only at festival times or for the tourist shows. Personal expression has no place in the Balinese theatre, but the skilful execution of traditional moves is always much admired, and trained dancers enjoy a high status within the village. They express themselves through a vocabulary of controlled angular movements of the arms, wrists, fingers, neck and, most beguilingly, eyes. Each gesture derives from a movement observed in the natural rather than the human world. Thus a certain flutter of the hand may be a bird in flight; a vigorous rotation of the forearms, the shaking of water from an animal's coat.

Baris

The **baris** or **warrior dance** can be performed either as a solo or in a group of five or more, and either by a young woman or, more commonly, a young man. Strutting on stage with knees and feet turned out, his centre of gravity kept low, the *baris* cuts an impressive figure in a gilded brocade cloak of ribboned pennants which fly out dramatically at every turn. In his performance, he enacts a young warrior's preparation for battle, goading himself into courageous mood, trying out his martial skills, showing pride at his calling and then expressing a whole series of emotions – ferocity, passion, tenderness, rage – much of it through the arresting movements of his eyes. In its original sacred form, this was a devotional dance in which soldiers dedicated themselves and their weapons to the gods.

Barong–Rangda dramas

Featuring the most spectacular costumes of all the Balinese dances, the Barong–Rangda dramas are also among the most sacred and most important. The mythical widow-witch character of **Rangda** represents the forces of evil, and her costume and mask present a duly frightening spectacle. The **Barong Ket** cuts a much more lovable figure, a shaggy-haired, bug-eyed creature, like a cross between a pantomime horse and a Chinese dragon. Barong–Rangda dramas can be self-contained as in the *calonarang*, or they can appear as just one symbolic episode in the middle of a well-known story like the *Mahabharata*. Whatever the occasion, Rangda is always summoned by a character who wants to cause harm to someone. When the opposition calls in the Barong (the defender of the good), Rangda appears, fingernails first, flashing her white magic cloth and stalking the Barong at every turn. When the Barong looks to be on his last legs, a group of village men rush in to his rescue, but are entranced by Rangda's magic and stab themselves instead of her. A priest quickly enters before any real injury is inflicted. The series of confrontations continues, and the drama ends in stalemate: good and evil remain as vital as ever, ready to clash again in the next bout.

Kecak

Sometimes called the **monkey dance** after the animals represented by the chorus, the **kecak** gets its Balinese name from the hypnotic chattering sounds made by the *a cappella* choir. Chanting nothing more than "cak cak cak cak", the chorus of fifty or more men uses seven different rhythms to create the astonishing music that accompanies the drama. Bare-chested, and wearing black-and-white checked cloth around their waists and a single red hibiscus behind the ear, the men sit cross-legged in tight concentric circles, occasionally swaying and clapping their hands in unison. The **narrative** is taken from a core episode of the *Ramayana*, centring around the kidnap of Sita by the demon king Rawana, and is acted out in the middle of the chorus circle, with one or two narrators speaking for all the characters. The *kecak* was invented in 1931 by the dancer I Wayan Limbak, who adapted the chants from the *sanghyang* trance dances (see below) and created the choreography.

Legong

Undoubtedly the most refined of all the temple dances, the **legong** is renowned for its elegantly restrained choreography. The dance is always performed by three pre-pubescent girls, who are bound tightly in sarongs and chest cloths of opulent green or pink, with gilded crowns filled with frangipani blossoms on their heads. The dance itself has evolved from a highly sacred *sanghyang* trance dance (see below) and generally tells the **story** of King Laksem, who has captured a princess and is about to go to war to prevent her being rescued. As he leaves, he is attacked by a raven, an extremely bad omen, after which he duly loses the battle and is killed. The performance begins with a solo dance by a court lady (*condong*) dressed in pink and gold. She then welcomes the two *legong* (literally "dancers") with a pair of fans. Dressed identically in bright green and gold, the two *legong* enact the story, adopting and swapping characters apparently at random. At the climax, the *condong* always returns as the raven, with pink wings attached to her costume.

Sanghyang: trance dances

The state of **trance** lies at the heart of traditional Balinese dance. In order to maintain the health of the village, the gods are periodically invited down into the temple arena to help in the exorcism of evil. When the deities descend, they possess certain people, and incite them into performing dances or astonishing physical feats. One of the most common trance dances is the *sanghyang dedari* (angel deity), in which the deities possess two young girls who perform a complicated duet with their eyes closed and, in part, while seated on the shoulders of two male villagers. Although they have never learnt the steps, the duo almost invariably performs its movements in tandem and sometimes continues for up to four hours. When they finally drop to the floor in exhaustion, the priest wakes them gently by sprinkling holy water over them. In the **sanghyang jaran** (horse deity), one or more men are put into a trance state while the temple floor is littered with burning coconut husks. As they enter the trance, the men grab hold of wooden hobbyhorse sticks and then gallop frantically back and forth across the red-hot embers as if they were on real horses.

Topeng: mask dances

Balinese masks are extremely sacred, carved and painted with great reverence to the spirits, and in the **topeng** or **mask dance** the performer is possessed by the spirit of the mask. The storylines of most *topeng* centre around folk tales or well-known episodes from history, and every character wears a mask. One of the most popular is the **topeng tua**, a portrayal of a shaky-limbed old man, whose mask is shrouded in straggly white hair and beard. Another classic tourist *topeng* is the **frog dance** which tells how a frog turns into a prince. In the **jauk**, a solo dancer portrays a terrifying demon-king. His red or white mask has huge bulging eyes, and a thick black moustache, and his hands are crowned with 30-centimetre-long fingernails. To the clashing strains of the gamelan, the *jauk* leaps mischievously about the stage as if darting through a forest and pouncing on villagers.

Wayang kulit

On an island where cinema screens and TVs haven't yet percolated through to the smallest villages, a **wayang kulit** performance, or **shadow-puppet drama**, still draws in huge crowds, and is often staged at weddings, cremations and temple festivals. The stories are familiar to all, and often come from the *Mahabharata*, but the eloquence and wit of a good puppeteer means the show is as likely to break news, spread gossip and pass on vital information as it is to entertain.

The Ubud region boasts dozens of outstanding dance and music groups, and there are up to five different **dance shows** performed every night in the area; the tourist office gives details of the regular weekly schedule and also arranges free transport to outlying venues. Tickets cost around Rp50,000 and can be bought either from touts or at the door. Performances start between 7pm and 8pm; arrive early for the best seats. If you have only one evening to catch a show, then go for whatever is playing at the **Ubud Palace** (Puri Saren Agung), opposite the market in central Ubud. The setting of this former rajah's home (now a hotel) is breathtaking, with the torchlit courtyard gateways furnishing the perfect backdrop. For an introduction to Balinese dance-dramas, see the box on p.582.

Bars and music venues

Beggar's Bush Jl Raya, Campuhan. Long-running British-style pub and restaurant with a good range of beers and a dart board.

Funky Monkey (Kafe Kera Lucu) Off the southern end of Monkey Forest Rd, Padang Tegal. Tiny, urban-style disco-bar that's currently Ubud's main gay venue, though it attracts a mixed crowd. Shuts about 1am. Closed Mon.

Jazz Café Jl Sukma 2, Peliatan. Lively bar-restaurant that stages quality live jazz every night from about 7.30pm; check the board for details. Free transport from the Archipelo shop on Monkey Forest Rd.

Planet Warung Opposite *Tegal Sari* hotel at the southern end of Jl Hanoman, Padang Tegal. Bar-restaurant staging live music twice a week – rock (Wed) and reggae (Sat) – and occasional video shows on other nights.

Putra Bar Central stretch of Monkey Forest Rd. Very lively bar-restaurant that runs frequent reggae evenings, with live music. There's a dance floor, live international sports on the TV, and a faintly Kuta-ish atmosphere.

Sai Sai Central stretch of Monkey Forest Rd. Restaurant-bar that serves beer till late and has live bands playing most nights from around 8pm.

Shopping

Most Ubud **shops** open daily, many not closing until 8 or 9pm. Tino Supermarket on Jalan Raya stocks all major essentials, from suntan lotion to beer.

Books and music

Ary's Bookshop Jl Raya, central Ubud. Decent stock of books on Bali and Indonesia.

Cinta Bookshop Jl Dewi Sita. Great range of secondhand books for sale and rent.

Ganesha Bookshop Jl Raya, central Ubud. The best bookshop in Bali, with a huge stock of new books on all things Balinese, plus numerous secondhand books. Also sells maps and Balinese cartoon postcards. Their Jl Jembawan branch opposite the GPO sells CDs of Indonesian music.

Moari Music Jl Raya, central Ubud. Specializes in traditional Balinese musical instruments.

Pondok Bamboo Off the far southern end of Monkey Forest Rd, Padang Tegal. Balinese instruments made from bamboo, including *genggong*, wind chimes and bamboo gamelan.

Rona Bookshop Jl Sukma 23, Peliatan. Secondhand bookstore and library.

Ubud Music Jl Raya, central Ubud. Inexpensive CDs.

Crafts, textiles and homewares

Archipelo Southern end of Monkey Forest Rd. Quality handicrafts and home accessories.

Arka Antiques Art Monkey Forest Rd, central Ubud. Massive collection of wooden masks.

Duck Man of Bali About 1500m east along the road to Goa Gajah, southeast of central Ubud. Phenomenal gallery of wooden ducks in all sizes, stances and permutations.

Indo Crafts Monkey Forest Rd, central Ubud. *Ikat* hangings and bedspreads from Sumba and Flores.

Kites Center 3 Off the far southern end of Monkey Forest Rd, Padang Tegal. Charismatic traditional kites.

Mangku Made Gina Beside ARMA at the southern end of Jl Hanoman in Padang Tegal/Pengosekan. Unrivalled collection of exquisite palm-leaf baskets made by a family of Pengosekan basket-weavers.

Murti Jl Hanoman 19, Padang Tegal, junction Jl

Dewi Sita. Distinctive ceramics from Pejaten in west Bali.

Pasar Seni Jl Raya, central Ubud. Two-storey art market selling sarongs, clothes and trinkets.

Tegun Jl Hanoman 44, Padang Tegal. Exceptionally fine crafts and unusual artefacts.

Wardani's Opposite *Sai Sai* on central Monkey Forest Rd. The best fabric shop in Ubud.

Courses and workshops

You'll find plenty of opportunities to take **courses** and **workshops** in Ubud, even if you're only in the area for a few days. Many places welcome younger participants, and most kids enjoy creating their own batik T-shirts and paintings, which they can do at the batik centres. Ganesha Bookshop welcomes all over-10s to its music workshops.

Batik, textiles and crafts

ARMA Jl Pengosekan, Pengosekan Ⓣ0361/976659, Ⓕ975332, Ⓔkokokan@dps.mega.net.id. Classes in Balinese painting, woodcarving, and batik. $15–50 per person, depending on subject and class size.

Crackpot Batik Monkey Forest Rd. Design your own batik fabrics, paintings and T-shirts.

Dwi Bhumi Art and Cultural Workshops Jl Raya, central Ubud Ⓣ & Ⓕ0361/974153, Ⓦwww.dwibhumi.com. Woodcarving, beadwork, kite-, mask- and puppet-making. From Rp65,000 (discounts for kids); book ahead.

Nirvana Batik Course Jl Gautama 10, Padang Tegal Ⓣ & Ⓕ0361/975415, Ⓔrodanet@denpasar.wasantara.net.id. Courses in batik painting by renowned artist I Nyoman Suradnya ($35 per day for one-day courses and $25 per day for four-and five-day courses).

Studio Perak North end of Jl Gautama, mobile Ⓣ0812/361 1785. Silversmithing courses, from Rp100,000.

Threads of Life Jl Kajeng 24, central Ubud Ⓣ0361/972187, Ⓕ976582, Ⓦwww.threadsoflife.com. Classes on the textiles of Bali (Tues morning; Rp50,000) and Indonesia (most Thurs mornings; Rp70,000). Phone ahead.

Cookery

Bumbu restaurant Jl Suweta 1, central Ubud Ⓣ0361/974217, Ⓔwizbali@indosat.net.id. One-day workshops in Balinese cooking (Rp120,000). Reserve ahead.

Casa Luna restaurant Jl Raya. Ⓣ0361/973282, Ⓔcasaluna@bali-paradise.com. Balinese cooking workshops (Mon, Tues & Wed morning; Rp150,000; minimum five people). Advance booking essential.

Sua Bali Kemenuh. Residential Indonesian language and cookery courses in Kemenuh, 7km east of Ubud.

Language

Dwi Bhumi Art and Cultural Workshops Jl Raya, central Ubud Ⓣ & Ⓕ0361/974153, Ⓦwww.dwibhumi.com. Private Indonesian language lessons (evenings only); Rp45,000 per person per hour, minimum two people.

Pondok Pekak Jl Dewi Sita, central Ubud Ⓣ0361/976194, Ⓔpondok@indo.net.id. Indonesian language courses (24hr; Rp540,000), usually spread over four weeks but can be changed to suit.

Sua Bali Kemenuh. Residential Indonesian language and cookery courses in Kemenuh, 7km east of Ubud.

Sukadana, Jl Jembawan Padang Tegal Ⓣ0361/974131. Classes and courses in Balinese and Indonesian.

Meditation, yoga and alternative therapies

Meditation Shop Monkey Forest Rd. Regular meditation sessions and talks.

Nur Salon Jl Hanoman 28, Padang Tegal Ⓣ0361/975352, Ⓔnursalon@yahoo.net. Traditional massage and beauty salon offering famous inexpensive *mandi lulur* exfoliation treatments.

Ubud Sari Health Resort Jl Kajeng 35, central Ubud Ⓣ0361/974393, Ⓦwww.ubudsari.com. Aromatherapy, reflexology, shiatsu, reiki, massages, wraps and scrubs.

Music, dance and culture

ARMA Jl Pengosekan, Pengosekan Ⓣ0361/976659, Ⓕ975332, Ⓔkokokan@dps.mega.net.id. Gamelan, dance, Balinese architecture, traditional healing, trance, and making offerings. $15–50 per person.

Dwi Bhumi Art and Cultural Workshops Jl Raya, central Ubud Ⓣ & Ⓕ0361/974153, Ⓦwww.dwibhumi.com. Gamelan, dance, kecak singing and making offerings. Rp50,000 (discount for under-11s); book ahead.

Ganesha Bookshop Jl Raya, central Ubud Ⓣ0361/976339, Ⓕ973359, Ⓦwww.ganeshabooksbali.com. Group workshops in traditional Balinese music (Tues 6–7.30pm; Rp45,000), for anyone over the age of 10.

Nataraja Dance School Jl Sugriwa 20, Padang Tegal. Informal dance and gamelan lessons.
Pondok Pekak Resource Centre Jalan Dewi Sita, central Ubud (☎0361/970194, ⓔpondok@denpasar.wasantara.net.id). Multilingual children's classes in gamelan and dance (for over-6s).
Sehati Southeast off the far southern end of Monkey Forest Rd, central Ubud. Lessons in traditional music and dance for Rp45,000/hr.

Listings

Banks and exchange Several Visa, MasterCard and Cirrus ATMs on Jalan Raya and Monkey Forest Rd. Numerous tour agents (daily 8am–6pm) offer exchange services. Visa and MasterCard cash advances (Mon–Fri 8am–1pm) from Bank Bali opposite Puri Lukisan Museum on Jalan Raya, and from Bank Danamon at the eastern end of Ubud's Jalan Raya. The Ubud GPO is an agent for Western Union money transfers.
Hospitals and clinics For minor casualties, go to the Legian Medical Clinic 5, Monkey Forest Rd ☎0361/976457, or to the Ubud Clinic near the Pura Gunung Lebah on Jl Raya Campuhan ☎0361/974911. Both are open 24 hours, are staffed by English-speakers, and will respond to emergency call-outs. A consultation should cost Rp100,000. The nearest hospitals are in Denpasar (p.532).
Internet access Average price is Rp4000 for 15min: Bali 3000 on Jl Raya (daily 9am–11pm); Roda Tourist Services, Jl Bisma 3 (daily 9am–9pm); Ary's Business and Travel Service, Jl Raya, central Ubud (daily 8am–10pm). The GPO has internet terminals.
Libraries The Pondok Pekak Library and Resource Centre on the east side of the football field (Mon–Sat 9am–9pm, Sun 10am–1pm) stocks books about Bali, Asia travel guides and English-language novels and has a multilingual kids' library. ARMA (see p.585) has the island's best library about Bali.
Pharmacies The two central Ubud branches of Ubud Farma on Jl Raya and Monkey Forest Rd (daily 8am–9pm) are staffed by helpful English-speaking pharmacists.
Phone and fax The government Kantor Telcom is out on the eastern end of Ubud's Jl Raya, but there are IDD direct-dial phones at the GPO on Jl Jembawan (daily 8am–6pm) as well as at several more central private wartels that charge almost the same rates, including: Ary's Business and Travel Service just west of the market on Jl Raya (daily 8am–10pm); Nomad Wartel, above *Nomad* restaurant on Jl Raya (daily 8am–10.30pm); Roda Tourist Services, Jl Bisma 3 (daily 9am–9pm); and Wartel Pertiwi on central Monkey Forest Rd (daily 8.15am–8.45pm). There's a Home Direct public telephone at the Kantor Telcom, and outside the GPO. Phone cards are available at the Kantor Telcom, and at most minimarkets. You can also send and receive faxes at any of the internet bureaus listed opposite.
Police The main police station is on the eastern edge of town, on Jl Tegalalang. There's a more central police booth beside the market at the Jl Raya/Monkey Forest Rd crossroads.
Post offices There are plenty of postal agents where you can buy stamps and send mail and parcels. The Ubud GPO on Jl Jembawan (daily 8am–6pm) keeps poste restante, and there's a parcel packing service next door.

East of Ubud

Slicing through the region immediately to the **east of Ubud**, the sacred Petanu and Pakrisan rivers flow down from the Batur crater rim in parallel, framing a narrow strip of land imbued with great spiritual and historical importance. This fifteen-kilometre-long sliver has been settled since the Balinese Bronze Age, around 300 BC, and now boasts the biggest concentration of antiquities on Bali.

Goa Gajah

Thought to have been a hermitage for eleventh-century Hindu priests, **Goa Gajah**, also known as the Elephant Cave (daylight hours; Rp3100, children

Rp1600, including sarong and sash rental), has now become a major tourist attraction, owing more to its proximity to the main Ubud–Gianyar road than to any remarkable atmosphere or ancient features. To get there, either walk or drive the 3km east from Ubud's Jalan Peliatan, take an Ubud–Gianyar **bemo**, which goes right past the entrance gate, or walk from Yeh Pulu (see below).

Descending the steep flight of steps from the back of the car park, you get a good view of the rectangular **bathing pool**, whose elegant sunken contours dominate the courtyard below. Local men and women would have bathed here in the segregated male (right-hand) and female (left-hand) sections before making offerings or prayers at the holy cave. The **carvings** that trumpet the entranceway to the cave are certainly impressive, if a little hard to distinguish. The doorway is a huge gaping mouth, framed by the upper jaw of a monstrous rock-carved head that's thought to represent either the earth god Bhoma, or the widow-witch Rangda, or a hybrid of the two. Early visitors thought it looked like an elephant's head, hence the cave's modern name. The T-shaped **cave** was hewn by hand from the rocky hillside to serve as meditation cells, or possibly living quarters, for priests or ascetics, and now contains a few Hindu statues.

Yeh Pulu

The rock-cut panels at **YEH PULU** (same hours and prices) are delightfully engaging, and the site is often empty. This is partly due to Yeh Pulu's relative inaccessibility: get off the Ubud–Gianyar bemo at the Yeh Pulu signs just east of Goa Gajah or west of the Bedulu crossroads, and then walk the kilometre south through the hamlet of **Batulumbang** to Yeh Pulu. If you're driving, follow the same signs to where the road peters out, a few hundred metres above the stonecarvings. The prettiest approach is on foot through the rice-fields from Goa Gajah, but you'll need to hire a guide (Rp50,000). *Made's Café*, beside the Yeh Pulu entrance, serves **food**, and you can **stay** at the nearby *Pondok Wisata Lantur* (Ⓣ0361/942399; ❷).

Chipped away from the sheer rock face, the 25-metre-long series of Yeh Pulu **carvings** are said to date back to the fourteenth or fifteenth century. They are thought to depict a five-part story and, while the meaning of this story has been lost, it's still possible to make out some recurring characters. One early scene shows a man carrying two water jars suspended from a shoulder pole, and another series depicts three stages of a boar hunt. The name of the site – *yeh* ("holy spring"), *pulu* ("stone vessel") – refers to the holy spring that rises from near the Ganesh statue at the far end of the carved sequence.

Pejeng

PEJENG'S three main temples all lie within a few hundred metres of each other on the Bedulu–Tampaksiring Road. To get to them from Ubud, take a Gianyar-bound bemo to the Bedulu crossroads and then either wait for a Tampaksiring-bound one, or walk the 1km to the temples. The alternative route from Ubud is the fairly scenic five-kilometre **back road** that heads east from the Jalan Raya/Jalan Peliatan junction at the eastern edge of Ubud. Wearing a sarong and sash is cumpulsory at all the temples, but these can be borrowed on site; entry is by donation.

Balinese people believe **Pura Penataran Sasih** to be a particularly sacred temple, because this is the home of the so-called Moon of Pejeng – hence the English epithet, **Moon Temple**. The moon in question is a large bronze gong, shaped almost like an hourglass, suspended so high up in its special tower that you can hardly see the decorations scratched onto its surface. It probably dates from the Balinese Bronze Age, from some time during the third century BC, and at almost 2m long is thought to be the largest such kettledrum ever cast. Etched into its green patina are a chain of striking heart-shaped faces punctured by huge round eyes. Legend tells how the gong was once the wheel of a chariot that transported the moon through the skies. The wheel shone just as brightly as the moon itself and, when it fell out of the sky and got stuck in a tree in Pejeng, a local thief became so incensed by its incriminating light that he tried to extinguish it by urinating over it. The wheel exploded, killing the thief, and then dropped to the ground. Ever since, the Balinese have treated the Moon of Pejeng as a sacred object.

Pura Pusering Jagat, literally translated as the "Temple of the Navel of the World", stands 100m south down the main road from Pura Penataran Sasih. Its most interesting feature is a metre-high, elaborately carved vessel for storing holy water, said to date from the fourteenth century. The vessel's exterior is sculpted with a detailed relief thought to depict the Hindu myth "The Churning of the Sea of Milk", whereby the gods and the demons vie with each other to extract and distil the elixir of eternal life.

The chief attraction at **Pura Kebo Edan**, 200m south of Pura Pusering Jagat, is a massive lifelike phallus, attached to the huge stone statue of a man, nicknamed the Pejeng Giant. In fact, this giant, nearly 4m tall, is said to possess six penises in all; aside from the one swinging out for all to see, one is supposed to have dropped to the ground during his very vigorous dancing, and four more are said to be hidden inside him. His principal penis is pierced from front to back with a huge bolt-like pin, probably a realistic reference to an age-old Southeast Asian practice designed to increase women's sexual pleasure.

As the main treasure house of such a historically significant region, the government-run archeological museum, **Gedung Koleksi Kepurbakalan**, 500m south of Pura Penataran Sasih (Mon–Fri 7.30am–2.30pm; free), makes unsatisfactory viewing, mainly because the objects are poorly labelled. Its four tiny pavilions house an eclectic assortment of artefacts found in the Pejeng area, ranging from Paleolithic chopping tools to bronze bracelets and Chinese plates, but the most interesting exhibits are the dozen sarcophagi at the back of the museum compound. These massive coffins fashioned from two fitted sections of hollowed-out stone probably date back to around 300 BC and range in length from 1m to nearly 3m.

North of Ubud: routes to Gunung Batur

All three major roads north out of Ubud lead eventually to the towering Gunung Batur and its huge crater. Whether you go via **Payangan** to the west, **Tegalalang** directly to the north, or **Tampaksiring** to the east, the village and rice-field scenery along the way makes it a pleasant drive. Distances along these three routes are comparable, about 40km to Batur, but the most significant tourist sights are located along the most easterly route, around the Tampaksiring area. Though there's little of concrete interest on the westerly route, which takes you via Campuhan (see p.574) and Payangan to Pura Ulun Danu Batur (see p.629), this is the prettiest and quietest of the three. The most frequent and reliable **bemo** service running north from Ubud is the brown fleet that covers the central route via Tegalalang and Pujung; there are frequent turquoise bemos along the first section of the westerly route, as far as Payangan, but only some of them continue to Kintamani. For the easterly route via Tampaksiring, you need to change bemos at the Bedulu crossroads.

Tegalalang, Pujung and the Elephant Safari Park

The **central route** up to Gunung Batur begins at the eastern edge of Ubud, from the point where Jalan Raya intersects with Jalan Peliatan. Turning left (north) to pass through the village of Petulu (see p.579), the road passes through the woodcarving village of **TEGALALANG** after about 7km, a strip that's lined with carvings of brightly painted birds, fish and fruit trees, most of which are snapped up for export. The views get increasingly spectacular as you continue through Tegalalang, with Bali's greatest mountains looming majestically ahead: Gunung Batur (to the north) and Gunung Agung (to the east). The sculpted rice-fields round here are also particularly eye-catching, and there's a signposted roadside **viewpoint** 3km out of Tegalalang.

The northern end of Tegalalang merges into southern **PUJUNG KELOD**, another woodcarving village, whose speciality is garudas. If you continue north along the main road for another 16km, you'll reach the Batur crater rim; alternatively, a right turn about 2km beyond Pujung Kelod takes you to Tampaksiring (for Tirta Empul and Gunung Kawi; see below).

Turning left off the main road a couple of kilometres beyond Pujung Kelod, a signposted little road leads you 6km west to the **Elephant Safari Park** (daily 9am–5pm; $7.50, kids $3.75, family discounts available), where you can pet and ride the resident troupe of Sumatran elephants. Most people visit the park as part of a tour arranged by Bali Adventure Tours (Ⓣ0361/721480, Ⓦwww.baliadventuretours.com).

Gunung Kawi and Tirta Empul

The most **easterly route** up to the mountains takes you along the Bedulu-Penelokan road, passing through Pejeng (see p.587), before reaching **TAMPAKSIRING**, 11km further on, the access point for Gunung Kawi and Tirta Empul. The Gianyar–Bedulu–Tampaksiring **bemos** terminate in the centre of the long settlement.

A few hundred metres north of Tampaksiring's bemo terminus, a sign points east off the main road to **Gunung Kawi** (daylight hours; Rp3100, kids Rp1600, including sarong and sash rental), the site of a series of eleventh-century tombs hewn from the rock face. It's an impressive spot, completely enclosed in the lush valley of the sacred Sungai Pakrisan and rarely visited by large groups. To reach it, walk past the souvenir stalls and down the steep flight of three hundred steps, through a massive rock-hewn archway, to the river. There are lots of theories about the origins and function of the Gunung Kawi tombs or *candi*, the most likely being that they were erected as memorials to a king – possibly the eleventh-century Anak Wungsu – and his queens. Before crossing the river, turn sharp left for the Queens' Tombs, a series of four huge, square-tiered reliefs, chiselled from the riverside cliff face to resemble temple facades. Originally, the surface of these *candi* would have been decorated with plaster carvings, but only the outlines of the false doors remain. Crossing Sungai Pakrisan you enter the Gunung Kawi temple complex, which contains an unusual cloister, complete with courtyard, rooms and cells, entirely cut from the ravine rock wall. This was probably built for the holy men who looked after the five Royal Tombs at the back of the temple complex. The Royal Tombs are in better condition than the Queens' Tombs, and you can see the false doors and facades quite clearly.

Balinese from every corner of the island make pilgrimages to **Tirta Empul** (same hours and prices), signposted off the main Tampaksiring–Kintamani road about 500m north of the turn-off to Gunung Kawi. They come seeking to cleanse themselves spiritually and to cure their physical ailments by bathing in the holy springs, which have been considered the most sacred in Bali ever since the tenth century, if not longer. The shallow red-brick bathing pools are sunk into the ground of the outer courtyard of a temple, fed by water from the springs in the inner sanctuary. Men, women and priests each have their own segregated sections in which to immerse themselves, though most modern devotees just splash their faces and smile for the camera.

East Bali

East Bali is dominated both physically and spiritually by the towering volcano **Gunung Agung** and the **Besakih** temple complex high on its slopes. The landscape ranges from sweeping rice terraces, to the dry, rocky expanses of the north coast and the far east. Formerly divided into a multitude of ancient Balinese kingdoms, evidence of these ancient courts remains in the Taman Gili in **Klungkung** and the Puri Agung in **Amlapura**. These small relics of past glory are now surrounded by everyday modern life.

Most visitors come to the east for the coast: **Candi Dasa**, **Padang Bai**, **Tulamben** and **Amed** offer some of the best diving and snorkelling in Bali. Off the south coast lie three islands: **Nusa Lembongan** with its excellent white-sand beaches, tiny **Nusa Ceningan** and little-visited **Nusa Penida**, whose south coast consists of towering limestone cliffs. Only Nusa Lembongan, with easy access from Sanur, has a developed tourist trade.

Inland, aside from the major draws of Gunung Agung and Besakih, there are peaks and impressive **temples** where you can escape the crowds, especially Pura Kehen in Bangli, Pura Lempuyang Luhur in the far east and Pura Pasar Agung above Selat. **Tenganan**, close to Candi Dasa, is the most welcoming of the traditional Bali Aga villages on the island, home to descendants of the early inhabitants of Bali, and now a centre for textiles and crafts.

The east is easily accessible by public **transport** from Kuta and Ubud and it's possible to explore the area on day-trips. The ideal bases are Candi Dasa; Padang Bai, the port for the Lombok ferries; Tirtagangga, surrounded by attractive rice terraces; or Amed on the far east coast.

Gianyar public transport

Gianyar is a local administrative capital 13km southeast of Ubud. Something of a travel hub for the region, it's hard to avoid but there's no need to stay long. Heading east **from Denpasar** (Batubulan terminal), most public transport follows the route to Gianyar via Sakah, Kemenuh, Blahbatuh, Kutri and Bitera. Coming **from Ubud**, get a bemo down to the large junction at Sakah and then change onto another bemo heading east to Gianyar via Kemenuh, Blahbatuh and Bona.

From Gianyar, bemos head east to Klungkung and Amlapura, as well as north to Bangli. For more, see p.571.

Rangda

The image of the Queen of the Witches, **Rangda**, is everywhere in Bali. You'll see her in dance-dramas and on masks, temple carvings, paintings and batiks. Although there's some variation in the way she's portrayed, several features are standard and all contribute to her grotesque appearance. She has a long mane of hair, with flames protruding from her head. Her face is fierce and hideous with bulging eyes, a gaping mouth, huge teeth or tusks and a long tongue often reaching to her knees. Her fingernails are long and curled, and she has enormous, pendulous breasts. She wears a striped shirt and pants, with a white cloth around her waist, an important instrument of her evil magic.

Several versions of the Rangda story are enacted across the island, the most common being the **barong** and **calonarang** (see p.582 for more), but she always speaks in the ancient Javanese Kawi language and alternates between high whining tones, loud grunts and cackles. To the Balinese, Rangda represents the **forces of evil**, death and destruction, and she's often associated with the Hindu goddess Durga.

Rangda may have been based on a real woman, **Mahendratta**, a princess from Java who married the Balinese Prince Udayana and bore him a son, Erlangga, in 1001 AD. According to legend, the king later banished Mahendratta to the forest for practising witchcraft. When Udayana died, Mahendratta, now a *rangda* (widow), continued to build up grudges against her powerful and unrelenting son. Eventually, she used her powers to call down a **plague** upon Erlangga's kingdom, nearly destroying it. Erlangga, learning the source of the pestilence, dispatched a troop of soldiers who stabbed Rangda in the heart; she survived, however, and killed the soldiers. In desperation, the king sent for a holy man, **Empu Bharadah**, whose assistant stole Rangda's book of magic with which he was able to restore Rangda's victims to life, and eventually destroy the witch by turning her own magic on herself.

Even in performances of the story, the figure of Rangda is believed to have remarkable powers, and offerings are made and prayers said before each show to protect the actors from the evil forces they are invoking. Village performances of the drama are often a means of pacifying Rangda's anger so that she will not turn her destructive forces against them.

Bangli

Situated between Gianyar and the massive volcanic formations of the Batur area, the peaceful market town of **BANGLI** is high enough in the hills to be cool yet low enough not to be cold. It's a pretty spot; every temple in the area seems to shower forth bold and exuberant carving. It fits in well on any itinerary to or from Batur, but don't be fooled by its proximity to Besakih: there are no public bemos on the Bangli–Rendang road.

The main reason to visit is to see the ancient and much revered **Pura Kehen** (daily 8am–5pm; Rp2600, car Rp1000, motorbike Rp500), 1500m north of the town, rising up steeply from the road in terraces lined with religious statues. Sporting several remarkably fierce Bhoma leering above fabulously carved doors, the great entrance leads into the **outer courtyard** containing a massive banyan tree with a *kulkul* tower built among the branches. A small compound, guarded by *naga* under a frangipani tree, contains a stone that is supposed to have glowed with fire when the site of the temple was decided. Steps lead up to the middle courtyard, from where you can look into the **inner courtyard**, with its eleven-roofed *meru* dedicated to Siwa.

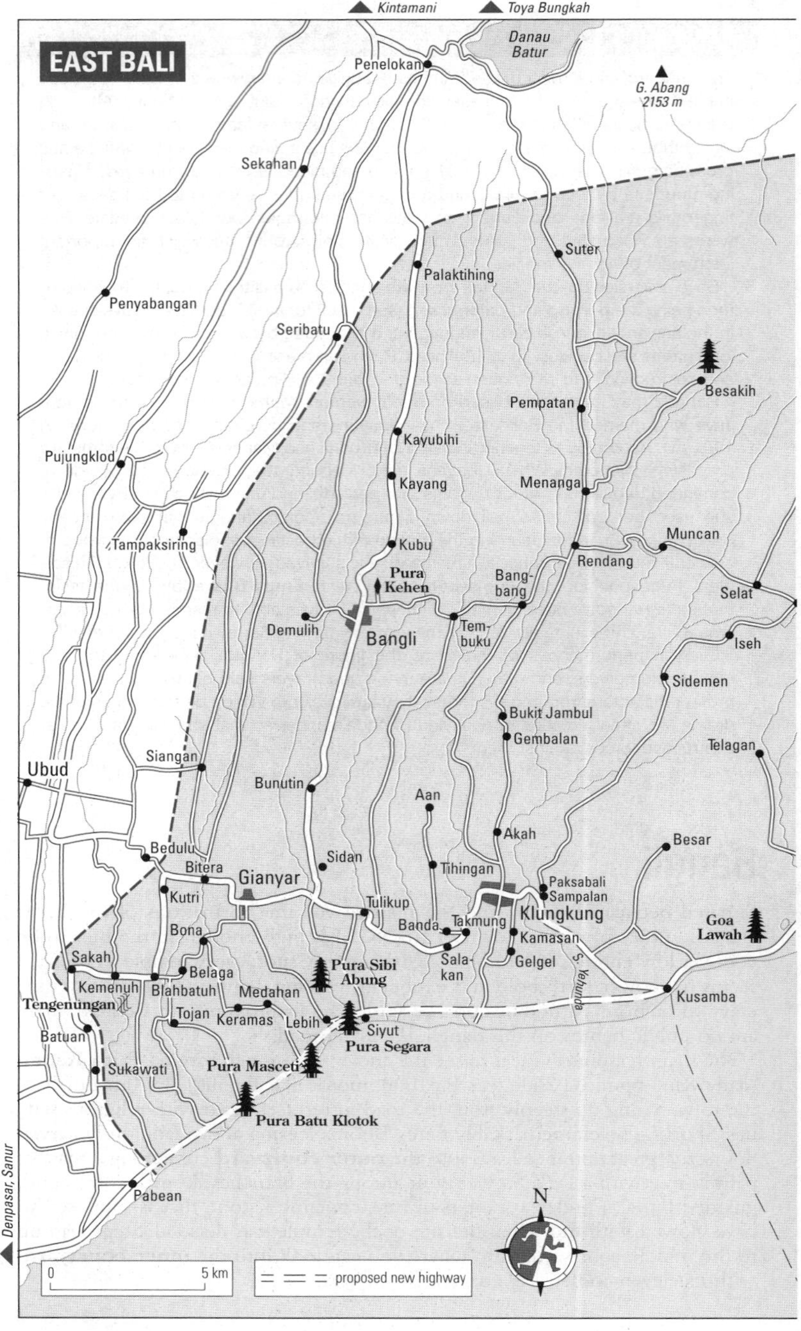
EAST BALI
Kintamani
Toya Bungkah
Danau Batur
Penelokan
G. Abang 2153 m
Sekahan
Suter
Palaktihing
Penyabangan
Seribatu
Besakih
Pempatan
Kayubihi
Pujungklod
Kayang
Menanga
Tampaksiring
Kubu
Muncan
Rendang
Pura Kehen
Bang-bang
Selat
Demulih
Bangli
Tem-buku
Iseh
Sidemen
Bukit Jambul
Gembalan
Telagan
Siangan
Ubud
Bunutin
Aan
Akah
Besar
Bedulu
Bitera
Sidan
Tihingan
Gianyar
Paksabali
Sampalan
Kutri
Tulikup
Klungkung
Goa Lawah
Bona
Banda
Takmung
Kamasan
Sakah
Belaga
Pura Sibi Abung
Salakan
Gelgel
S. Yehunda
Kemenuh
Blahbatuh
Medahan
Kusamba
Tengenungan
Tojan
Keramas
Lebih
Siyut
Batuan
Pura Segara
Sukawati
Pura Masceti
Pura Batu Klotok
Pabean
Denpasar, Sanur
N
0
5 km
proposed new highway

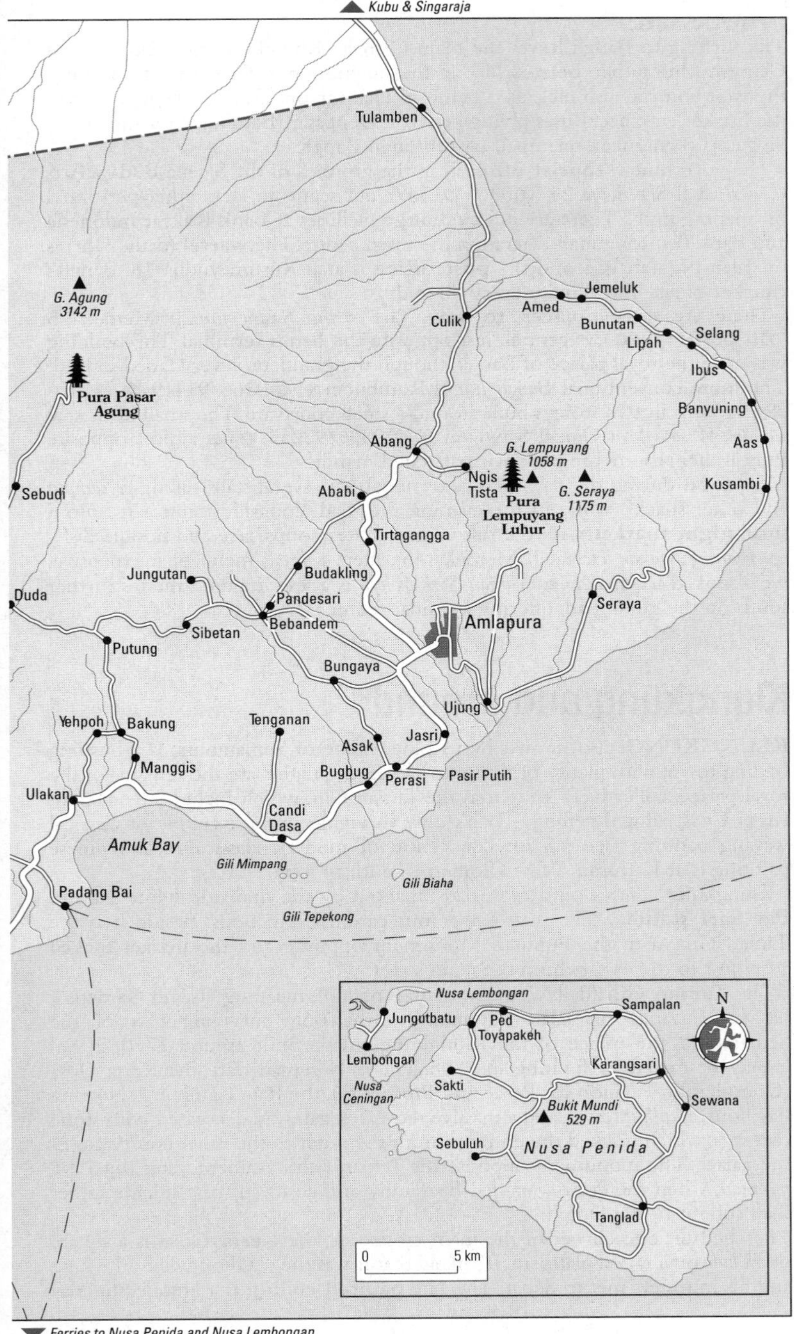
Kubu & Singaraja
Tulamben
G. Agung
3142 m
Pura Pasar Agung
Culik
Amed
Jemeluk
Bunutan
Lipah
Selang
Ibus
Banyuning
Aas
Kusambi
Abang
G. Lempuyang
1058 m
Ngis
Tista
Pura Lempuyang Luhur
G. Seraya
1175 m
Sebudi
Ababi
Tirtagangga
Budakling
Jungutan
Duda
Pandesari
Bebandem
Sibetan
Putung
Amlapura
Seraya
Bungaya
Ujung
Yehpoh
Bakung
Tenganan
Jasri
Asak
Manggis
Bugbug
Perasi
Pasir Putih
Ulakan
Candi
Dasa
Amuk Bay
Gili Mimpang
Gili Biaha
Padang Bai
Gili Tepekong
Ferries to Lembar (Lombok)
Nusa Lembongan
Jungutbatu
Lembongan
Ped
Toyapakeh
Sampalan
Karangsari
Sakti
Nusa
Ceningan
Sewana
Bukit Mundi
529 m
Sebuluh
Nusa Penida
Tanglad
0
5 km
N
Ferries to Nusa Penida and Nusa Lembongan

Practicalities

The turning to Bangli leaves the main Gianyar–Klungkung road 2km east of Gianyar. Blue public **bemos** lurk at the junction, but if you're coming from the west you can also pick up a bemo in Gianyar, on Jalan Berata, just outside the market entrance. Buses plying between Denpasar (Batubulan terminal) and Singaraja (Penarukan terminal) pass through Bangli.

The government **tourist office** is in the grounds of the Sasana Budaya Arts Centre at Jl Sriwijaya 23 (☎0366/91539), but seems to lack either personnel or opening times. There are full **exchange** facilities at Bank Rakyat Indonesia and Bank Pembangunan Daerah in the town centre. The **wartel** (daily 24hr) is on Jalan Ngurah Rai, and the **post office** is at Jl Kusumayudha 18. Bangli's **market** bursts into activity every three days.

There are several **places to stay**. The *Artha Sastra Inn*, Jl Merdeka 5 (☎0366/91179; ❶), is central, just opposite the bemo terminal. The building was once the royal palace of Bangli, though the grandeur is very faded indeed. The more conventional *Bangli Inn*, Jl Rambutan 1 (☎0366/91419; ❸–❹) has clean rooms in two storeys built around a small courtyard. The small homestay *Pondok Wisata Jaya Giri*, Jl Sriwijaya 6 (☎0366/92255; ❷) is almost opposite Pura Kehen; rooms are basic with attached mandi.

For **food** during the day, the bus terminal has several stalls selling *es campur* and other snacks, while in the evening the road alongside transforms into a small **night market** with the full range of sates, soups, rice and noodle dishes. *Warung Makan Hobby*, Jl Merdeka 45, offers a small menu of inexpensive, well-cooked food. *Warung Makan Sari Wahyu* is a few hundred metres further south on the same road, offering a similar menu.

Klungkung and around

KLUNGKUNG, also known by its older name of Semarapura, is a bustling trading town, with plenty of things to see. Its highlights are the remains of the royal palace, collectively known as the Taman Gili, which include the ancient Kerta Gosa painted ceiling – Bali's only surviving *in situ* example of classical wayang painting (see p.576). The centre of modern classical-style Balinese painting is at Kamasan, a few kilometres south of town.

Klungkung centres on a crossroads, marked by the dramatic white **Kanda Pat Sari statue** which guards the four cardinal directions. Beside it is the Taman Gili, with the Puputan Monument opposite and the market tucked away just to the east, behind the main street.

The **Taman Gili** (daily 7am–5.30pm; Rp5000), meaning "Island Gardens", has its entrance on Jalan Puputan. It's the only surviving part of the Semarapura, the palace of the Klungkung rulers. Built around 1710, it was largely destroyed by fighting in 1908. The only remains are the Kerta Gosa (Consultation Pavilion for Peace and Prosperity), the Bale Kambung (Floating Pavilion), a *kulkul* tower, and a massive red-brick gateway, decorated with stone carvings, which marked the entrance from the outer to the inner courtyards of the palace. The monument opposite the Taman Gili commemorates the 1908 *puputan*, when the *dewa agung* led his family and court in mass suicide rather than submit to the Dutch.

Perched on one corner of the main crossroads, the **Kerta Gosa** is a square open *bale* on a raised platform. It's likely that it was the pavilion where the king and his ministers met to debate law. The **painted ceiling** is a unique, superlative and intricate example of the Kamasan style of classical painting, often referred to as the wayang style because the figures are essentially the same as the characters in the wayang puppet theatre. There are nine levels of paintings. **Level one**, nearest the floor, shows scenes from the Tantri stories, an Indonesian version of the *Thousand and One Nights*, in which the girl, Tantri, weaves tales night after night. **Levels two** and **three** illustrate the Bhima Swarga story (part of the *Mahabharata* epic), and the suffering of souls in the afterlife as their sins are punished. **Level four** shows the Sang Garuda, the story of the Garuda's search for *amerta*, the water of life. **Level five** is the *palalindon*, predicting the effects of earthquakes on life and agriculture, while **levels six** and **seven** are a continuation of the Bhima Swarga story. **Level eight** is the Swarga Roh, which shows the rewards that the godly will receive in heaven; unfortunately, it's so far above your head that it's hard to see whether good behaviour is worth it. **Level nine**, the *lokapala*, right at the top of the ceiling, shows a lotus surrounded by four doves symbolizing good luck, enlightenment and salvation.

The **Bale Kambung**, almost beside the Kerta Gosa and surrounded by a moat, was the venue for royal tooth-filing ceremonies. Six levels of paintings cover Balinese astrology, the tales of Pan Brayut and, closest to the top, the adventures of Satusoma, whose adventures consist of a series of battles and selfless acts through which he defeats evil and brings peace to the world.

Practicalities

The main **bus** and **bemo terminal**, Terminal Kelod, is about 1km south of the centre; most public transport stops or passes through. In addition, a small terminal lies just north of the main crossroads, hidden away off Jalan Gunung Rinjani, where you can pick up bemos for Rendang and Besakih (which don't stop at Kelod). Bemos for Padang Bai and minibuses for Amlapura also pass through here heading east.

The government **tourist office** is in the same building as the Museum Daerah Semarapura in the Taman Gili grounds, Jl Untung Surapati 3 (Mon–Thurs 7.30am–3.30pm, Fri 7am–1.15pm; Ⓣ0366/21448). Across the road from the Kerta Gosa is the **wartel** (daily 24hr), while the **post office** is just west on Jalan Untung Surapati. Several banks along Jalan Diponegoro to the east of the main crossroads **change money**, and there's a Bank of Central Asia ATM in the main street.

Most people visit Klungkung as a day-trip from Candi Dasa. The best **accommodation** is at the *Loji Ramayana* in the eastern part of town (Ⓣ0366/21044; ❸), which has simple rooms set back from the road in a courtyard with a small restaurant. For inexpensive **food** head to Jalan Nakula; *Bali Indah* at no. 1, and *Sumba Rasa* at no. 5, are both used to foreign diners.

Around Klungkung

South of Klungkung, 500m beyond the Kelod bemo terminal, is the turning to **KAMASAN**, a tiny village packed with artists' houses, studios and small shops, and renowned on Bali as the historical and present-day centre of **classical wayang painting** (see p.576). Wayang style traditionally depicts religious subjects, astrological charts and calendars, and you'll be struck immediately by the uniform colours used: muted reds, ochres, blues, greens and blacks. While the artists obviously want to make sales, the atmosphere is pleasant and relaxed – although you should shop around and still bargain hard. **I Nyoman Mandra**, in particular, has a very good reputation and his work will give you a basis for comparison. **Ni Made Suciarmi** is one of very few women artists working in what is very much a male preserve (her work is also displayed in the Seniwati Women's Art Gallery in Ubud; see p.574). You can **stay** at Kamasan Art Centre (Ⓣ & Ⓕ0361/462611, Ⓔg_legong@hotmail.com; ❹–❺), in small, neat bungalows around a courtyard. There's usually an artist working here and they can arrange programmes involving local walks and visits to artists' studios.

Besakih and Gunung Agung

The **Besakih** temple complex, the most venerated site in Bali, is situated on the slopes of **Gunung Agung**, the holiest and highest mountain on the island. It's an irresistible combination, and inevitably attracts swarms of attendant hustlers, hassling the daily crowds of visitors (around a quarter of a million a year). Bus tours start arriving around 10.30am, after which the sheer volume of tourists, traders and self-styled guardians of the temple make the place pretty unbearable: it's well worth arriving early to get the best of the atmosphere.

The two sides of Besakih's personality rarely intersect. On the one hand it's the holiest spot on the island for Balinese Hindus, who don their finery and bring elaborate offerings for the gods. On the other hand Besakih is a jumble of buildings, unremarkable in many ways, around which has evolved the habit of separating foreign tourists from their money in as short a time as possible. Balinese worshippers pay little or no heed to the hundreds of camera-toting visitors milling around them as they pray, and tourists search in vain for any sacred aura around the place as they seek to evade local guides and struggle to take photographs that don't include the *Hard Rock Café*-sponsored rubbish bins.

Even the stark grandeur of Besakih's location is often shrouded in mist, leaving Gunung Agung in all-enveloping cloud. However the scale of Besakih is impressive and on a clear day, with ceremonies in full swing, before the hordes arrive, it's a wonderful place.

Arrival and information

Without your own transport, the easiest but least desirable way of getting to Besakih is to take an **organized tour**. If you decide to do this, check how much time you'll have to look around; anything less than an hour is hardly worth it. By **public transport**, one way is to approach from Klungkung: bemos leave from the small terminal just north of the main road in the town centre, although you may have to change at Rendang or Menanga, the turn-off for Besakih. Green bemos also run from Amlapura to Rendang via Selat and Muncan, with some going on to Menanga and Besakih. Plenty depart in the morning, but they dry up in both directions on both routes in the afternoon: after 1 or 2pm, you'll have trouble getting back. There are no public bemos north of Menanga to Penelokan, or between Rendang and Bangli.

The **tourist office** (daily 8.30am–3.30pm) is on the corner of the car park beside the road at Besakih. In the car park you'll also find a wartel and a small post office. Moneychangers – offering very poor rates – line the road up to the temple.

Besakih

The **Besakih complex** (daily 8am–5pm; Rp3100, camera Rp1100, parking Rp500) consists of 22 separate temples, each with its own name, spread over a site stretching for more than 3km. The central temple – largest on the island – is **Pura Penataran Agung**, with the other temples ranged around it. There's a **map** mounted on a noticeboard situated just at the top of the road leading from the car park to the temples.

Unless you're praying or making offerings, you are **forbidden to enter** any of the temples in the complex (unless you've paid for the services of a local "guide"; see box below); most temples remain locked unless there's a ceremony in progress. However a lot is visible through the gateways and over walls. A sarong and scarf are not strictly necessary, but you'll need them if you're in skimpy clothing; **sarong rental** is available, with negotiable prices from Rp2000. It's much easier to take your own.

Accommodation is very limited. The *Lembah Arca* hotel (ⓣ0366/23076; ❹–❺) on the road between Menanga and Besakih, 2km before the temple complex, has two neat, tiled bungalows in an attractive garden, but the altitude means it gets chilly at night. There are also a few unsigned and unauthorized lodgings (❸) behind the shops and stalls lining the road from the car park up to the temple, all very simple; ask at the tourist office for details. Several **restaurants** cater for the tour-bus trade, though you'll find more reasonably priced food at the *Lembah Arca* hotel and at the *Warung Mawar* in Menanga, on the left as you turn off to Besakih. There are a few basic warung on the walk up to Besakih from the car park.

The temples

Most of the tourist crowds tend to stick to the immediate area around Pura Penataran Agung; to get the best out of Besakih, it's a good idea to see this central temple first, and then wander at will.

The Great Temple of State, or **Pura Penataran Agung**, is built on seven ascending terraces, and altogether there are more than fifty structures including *bale*, shrines and stone thrones; about half are dedicated to specific gods, while the others have various ceremonial functions. A giant stairway, lined by seven levels of **carved figures**, leads to the first courtyard. The pavilion just inside the gateway is in two parts with a small walkway between. As worshippers process through here they symbolically sever their connection with the everyday world before proceeding into the second courtyard – the most important in the temple. The courtyards ascend consecutively in terraces which are visible from the path that skirts the entire perimeter wall. If you're hoping to see religious ceremonies, the second courtyard is the one to watch (the best views are from the west side). It's the largest courtyard in the temple

Unofficial guides at Besakih

There are many **unofficial guides** hanging around Besakih, adept at attaching themselves to tourists and then demanding large sums in payment for their services. They now resist the label of guides and have styled themselves "**guardians**" or "**keepers**" of the temple. With more than two hundred local men earning their living like this, you'll be approached whenever you arrive. There's no reason why you need a guide – although with one you'll be allowed to go through the two outer courtyards of Pura Penataran Agung. Always establish the **fee** beforehand; Rp10,000–20,000 is the going rate.

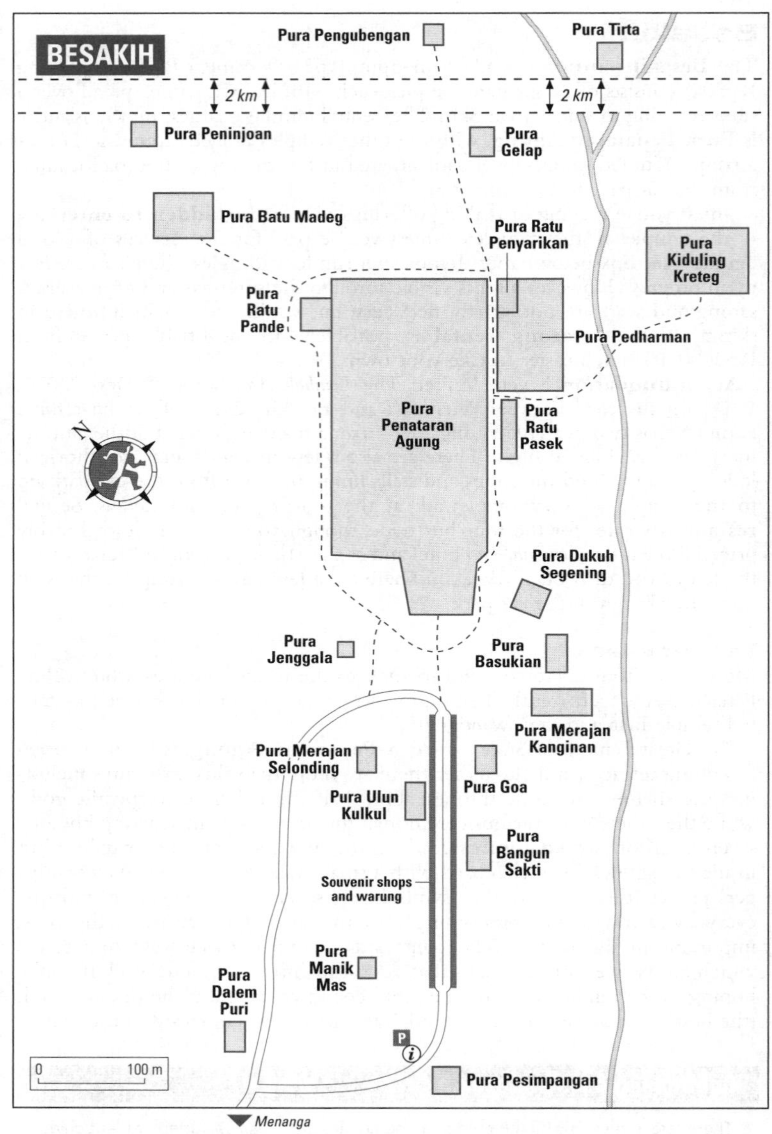

and contains the **padmatiga**, the three-seated lotus throne dedicated to Brahma, Siwa and Wisnu, where all pilgrims pray.

Elsewhere, the *meru* of **Pura Batu Madeg**, rising among the trees in the north of the complex, are particularly enticing, while the most far-flung of the temples, **Pura Pengubengan**, is a good 2km through the forest.

1963

The year **1963** is recalled in Bali as a time of disaster, in which the gods were displeased and took their revenge in dramatic fashion. Ancient texts prescribe that an immense ceremony, **Eka Dasa Rudra** – the greatest ritual in Balinese Hinduism – should be held every hundred years for the spiritual purification of the island. In the early 1960s, religious leaders believed that the trials of World War II and the ensuing fight for independence were indicators that the ritual was once again needed, and these beliefs were confirmed by a **plague of rats** that overran the entire island in 1962. Preparations began on October 10, 1962, with the climax of the festival scheduled for March 8, 1963. However on February 18, **Gunung Agung**, which had been dormant for centuries, started rumbling; the glow of the fire became visible within the crater and ash began to coat the area. Initially, this was interpreted as a good omen sent by the gods to purify Besakih, but soon doubts crept in. Some argued that the wrong date had been chosen for the event and wanted to call it off. However, by this time it was too late to cancel; President Sukarno was due to attend, together with an international conference of travel representatives who were meeting in Jakarta.

By March 8, black smoke, rocks and ash were billowing from the mountain, but the ceremony went ahead, albeit in a decidedly tense atmosphere. Eventually, on March 17, Agung **erupted** with such force that the top 100m of the mountain was ripped apart. The whole of eastern Bali was threatened by the poisonous gas and molten lava that poured from the volcano, villages were engulfed, and between 1000 and 2000 people are thought to have died, while the homes of another 100,000 were destroyed. Roads were wiped out, some towns were isolated for weeks and the ash ruined vast amounts of crops, causing serious food shortages for months afterwards. The lava tracks are still clearly visible on the north coast around Tianyar and Kubu. The east of Bali took many years to recover; hundreds of homeless people joined Indonesia's *transmigrasi* programme (see p.1041) and moved to the outer islands.

Despite the force of the eruption and the position of the Besakih complex high on the mountain slopes, a surprisingly small amount of damage occurred within the temples themselves, and the **closing rites** of Eka Dasa Rudra took place in Pura Penataran Agung on April 20. Subsequently, many Balinese felt that the mountain's eruption at the time of such a momentous ceremony was an omen of the civil strife that engulfed Bali in 1965 (see p.1046). In 1979, the year actually specified by the ancient texts, Eka Dasa Rudra was held again and this time passed off without incident.

Gunung Agung

According to legend, **Gunung Agung** was created by the god Pasupati when he split Mount Mahmeru (the centre of the Hindu universe), forming both Gunung Agung and Gunung Batur. At 3014m, the conical-shaped Agung is the highest Balinese peak and an awe-inspiring sight. The spiritual centre of the Balinese universe, it is believed to host the spirits of the ancestors of the Balinese people. Villages and house compounds are laid out in relation to the mountain, and many Balinese people prefer to sleep with their heads towards it.

Two **routes** lead up Gunung Agung, both involving a long, hard climb – one from Besakih, the other from Pura Pasar Agung on the southern slope near Selat (described on p.620). You'll need to set out very early in the morning if you want to see the spectacular **sunrise** from the summit around 7am. It's essential to take a **guide**, as the lower slopes are densely forested and it's easy to get lost. You'll also need strong footwear, a good flashlight, water and snacks to keep you going.

While it's not possible to climb at certain times of the year because of the weather, it's also not permitted at other times because of religious festivals: March and April are generally impossible from Besakih because of ceremonies. You'll also have to make offerings at temples at the start and on the way. **Weather**-wise, the dry season (April to mid-Oct) is the best time; don't contemplate it during January and February, the wettest months. At other times during the rainy season you may get a few dry days, but bear in mind that the weather up on the mountain can be very different from what it is on the beach.

From Pura Pasar Agung, it's at least a three-hour climb with an ascent of almost 2000m, so you'll need to set out at 3am or earlier. The path doesn't go to the summit, but ends at a point on the rim which is about 100m lower. From here you'll be able to see Rinjani, the south of Bali and Gunung Batukau and look down into the 500-metre crater.

From Besakih, the climb is longer (5–6hr); you'll need to leave between midnight and 2am. This path starts from Pura Pengubengan, the most distant of the temples in the Besakih complex, and takes you up to the summit of Agung with views in all directions. The descent is particularly taxing from this side, too (allow 4–5hr).

Practicalities

There are established **guiding** operations around the mountain and new ones are appearing all the time; you can also arrange climbs from several other areas. Bear in mind that this is a serious trek: satisfy yourself that potential guides have the necessary experience and knowledge.

To climb **from Pura Pasar Agung**, you'll find guides at both Muncan, 4km east of Rendang, and at Selat (see p.620 for more on the road east of Rendang). I Ketut Uriada, a part-time teacher and guide, is one of the most experienced guides; he has trained several assistants as well. His house is marked by a blue sign advertising his services, on the left as you enter the village of Muncan from the east. He'll help you arrange a bemo charter between Muncan and Pura Pasar Agung (about $10). Prices include simple accommodation in his house. To climb the mountain, expect to pay around $30 for one person, $40 for two, $50 for three. Larger groups may need more than one guide. You're expected to provide food for them. Alternative accommodation is at *Pondok Wisata Puri Agung* (☎0366/23037; 3–4) in Selat, 4km east of Muncan on the Amlapura road. They can also provide a guide for the climb, quoting Rp150,000 per person for a minimum of two people. This does not include accommodation or transport to and from Pura Pasar Agung (about Rp60,000 from Selat).

From Besakih, guides can be arranged at the tourist office; they can also help with nearby lodgings. The going rate from this side is $50 per guide, each of whom will lead up to five people.

Inevitably, prices are higher if you arrange the trek from further afield. Nyoman Budiarsa at **Tirtagangga** (see p.618) arranges climbs of Agung; his small shop is on the right as you head north through the town. The *Pondok Lembah Dukuh* and *Geria Semalung* losmen in the nearby village of Ababi (see p.619) also arrange Agung climbs. The guiding operations in **Toya Bungkah** in the area of Gunung Batur (see p.631) charge $75–95 per person (minimum numbers apply). Bali Sunrise 2001 in **Ubud** (☎0361/980470, mobile ☎0818/552669, Ⓦwww.balisunrise2001.com) will arrange pick-ups from various parts of **southern Bali** or **Lovina** for the trek, charging $100–110 per person. The Perama bus company also organizes the trip (from $45 per person); enquire at any of their offices.

Nusa Lembongan, Nusa Ceningan and Nusa Penida

Southeast of Bali, across the deep and treacherous Badung Strait, the islands of Nusa Lembongan, Nusa Ceningan and Nusa Penida rise alluringly out of the ocean swell. The nearest to the mainland is **Nusa Lembongan**, which is less than two hours by boat from Sanur and encircled by a mixture of white-sand **beaches** and mangrove. Seaweed farming is the major occupation, while the island's other main source of income is the tourist facilities in Mushroom Bay (Tanjung Sanghyang), Chelegimbai and Jungutbatu which grew up after the **surf** breaks off the northwest coast brought the first visitors to the island. Tourist facilities are just beginning to develop on tiny **Nusa Ceningan**, beyond which is **Nusa Penida**, roughly 20km long, dominated by a high, limestone plateau with a harsh, dry landscape reminiscent of the Bukit. The island is crisscrossed by miles of small lanes ripe for exploring, and its south coast has some spectacular scenery.

Nusa Lembongan

A small island, 4km long and less than 3km at its widest part, **Nusa Lembongan** is sheltered by offshore coral reefs which provide excellent snorkelling and create the perfect conditions for seaweed farming. You can **walk** around the whole island in three to four hours, and there are **bikes** (Rp10,000/hr, discounts for longer times) and **motorbikes** (Rp25,000–30,000/hr) for rent in Jungutbatu. A bridge, sturdy enough for motorbikes, spans the narrow strait to Nusa Ceningan.

All the accommodation is in **Jungutbatu** on the west coast and around **Chelegimbai** and **Mushroom Bay** (Tanjung Sanghyang), informally named after the mushroom coral in the offshore reef, where most of the upmarket places are situated. There's no post office and electricity is produced by an unreliable generator from 4pm to 9am only, which some individual guest-houses supplement with their own generators.

Jungutbatu

Spread out for well over 1km, the attractive village of **JUNGUTBATU** is a low-key place. You can **change money** at the moneychanger (daily 7am–7pm) behind *Mainski Inn*, or at Bank Pembangunan Daerah Bali (Mon–Fri 10am–1pm), but expect poor rates. There are **wartels** attached to *Bunga Lembongan* and *Mainski Inn*, open when there's electricity. The Perama office (daily 7am–6pm) is situated between *Pondok Baruna* and *Nusa Indah* bungalows and also gives **tourist information**. You can book tickets here to all the main destinations on Bali and Lombok and on to Sumbawa. The ticket office for **public boats** is at the southern end of the beach; boats leave at 8am. You can also **charter** a local boat: it'll cost about Rp300,000 to Padang Bai.

Most of the **accommodation** is just behind the beach. There are traditional thatch, wood and bamboo two-storey buildings, some older concrete losmen rooms and newer brick and tiled places. Rooms with sea views are more expensive than those behind, and upstairs rooms are pricier than downstairs. All the places below offer en-suite cold-water bathrooms.

All the places to stay have **restaurants** attached, most of them right on the beachfront, offering a good range of Indo-Chinese favourites and the usual travellers' fare plus local seafood. *Ketut's Warung* is rather hidden away behind

Boats and trips to the islands

From Benoa to Nusa Lembongan (Jungutbatu). US$25 economy fare, $30 executive; takes 1hr. On the *Bounty* catamaran, which makes 4 trips weekly (Sun, Tues, Thurs & Sat), returning same day. Book in advance (on Bali ⓣ0361/733333 or 726666, ⓦwww.balibountygroup.com).
From Gili Meno (Lombok) to Nusa Lembongan (Jungutbatu). US$25 economy fare, $30 executive; takes 2hr 30min. On the *Bounty* catamaran, which makes 4 trips weekly (Sun, Tues, Thurs & Sat), returning same day. Book in advance (on Lombok ⓣ0370/693666, or on Gili Meno ⓣ0370/649090, ⓦwww.balibountygroup.com).
From Kusamba to Nusa Penida (Toyapakeh and Sampalan), and Nusa Lembongan (Jungutbatu). Rp25,000; takes 1–2hr. Boats leave when (very) full, most heading out early in the morning. These are local *prahu* used mostly for cargo, and are not for the faint-hearted. For return times enquire in the villages or, from Jungutbatu, ask at Perama.
From Padang Bai to Nusa Penida (Sampalan). Rp10,000; takes 1hr. Boats leave when full, starting around 7am.
From Sanur to Nusa Lembongan (Jungutbatu). Rp30,000; takes 1hr 30min. Boats leave at 8am and 10am, returning at 8am. Buy tickets from the office near the *Ananda Hotel* beachfront in Sanur, and from the beachfront office in Jungutbatu. Perama operates a daily tourist shuttle boat (Rp40,000) at 10.30am from Sanur to Nusa Lembongan (Jungutbatu), returning at 8.30am; book one day in advance.
From Senggigi (Lombok) to Nusa Lembongan (Jungutbatu). US$35 economy fare, $40 executive; takes 2hr. On the *Bounty* catamaran, which makes 4 trips weekly (Sun, Tues, Thurs & Sat), returning same day. Book in advance (on Lombok ⓣ0370/693666, ⓦwww.balibountygroup.com).

Luxury trips

Sold by tour operators in the southern mainland resorts. A day-trip out to the **luxury resorts** in the Mushroom Bay area or to a pontoon moored just offshore at Toyahpakeh is a pleasant, if pricey, way to visit Nusa Lembongan or Nusa Penida in some style. Prices vary considerably (US$39–89) so it pays to shop around.
Bali Hai ⓣ0361/720331, ⓕ720334, ⓦwww.balihaicruises.com.
Island Explorer ⓣ0361/728088, ⓕ728089, ⓦwww.baliabc.com/explorer.html.
Lembongan Island Discovery Day ⓣ & ⓕ0361/287431, ⓦwww.lembongan-discovery.com.
Quicksilver ⓣ0361/729564, ⓕ729503, ⓦwww.quicksilver-bali.com.
Sail Sensations ⓣ0361/725864, ⓕ725866, ⓦwww.bali-sailsensations.com.
Waka Louka ⓣ0361/723629, ⓕ722077, ⓦwww.wakaexperience.com.

Nusa Lembongan Bungalows but is well worth searching out for well-cooked, cheap local food – it's always packed. To escape the beach for a more intimate meal, head for *Sukanusa 2003* on the road through the village. Tables are set in pleasant open *bale*, furnishings are stylish and music is soothing.

Accommodation

Agung ⓣ0811/386986, ⓔagungs_lembongan@mailcity.com. Some rooms in a concrete building, but the two-storey bamboo, wood and thatch places have most character; ones at the front have the best views and there's a good sunbathing area just above the beach. ❷–❸
Bungalow No. 7 ⓣ0812/380 1537. Popular, extremely good-value, clean, simple rooms at the far southern end of the beach, all with balconies or verandahs. *Bunga Lembongan* ⓣ0361/415184 is next door offering similar quality at a similar price. ❷
Ketut ⓣ082/361 4895. Well-built, well-furnished attractive accommodation, some of it with excellent sea views, set in pleasant grounds. The two-storey places at the front have good sea views, the better-built places are behind. ❺

Linda Bungalows ⓣ0812/394 3988. Rooms are in two-storey buildings which all face seawards but they don't all have sea views. They are well-built with good quality furnishings. ❸

Mainski Inn ⓣ & ⓕ082/361 1153. A long-standing favourite with a wide choice of accommodation. Some upstairs rooms have hot water. There are plenty of hammocks for relaxing in the garden. ❷–❸

Mandara Beach Bungalows ⓣ0812/391 4908. Clean, tiled bungalows set in a garden next to and behind the Perama office, so a short walk to the busier area to the north. ❷–❸

Nusa Lembongan Bungalows No phone. Accommodation at this popular place is in two-storey bamboo and thatch buildings with upstairs balconies set in a spacious compound. The ones at the front have especially good sea views. ❸–❹

Pondok Baruna ⓣ0812/390 0686, ⓕ0361/288500, ⓦwww.world-diving.com. A few hundred metres south of the main accommodation area, this small, quiet place has clean tiled rooms looking straight onto the beach. World Diving Lembongan is based here. ❸

Puri Nusa ⓣ & ⓕ0361/298613. Well-built, comfortably furnished rooms in two-storey buildings with good verandahs or balconies in an attractive garden. One of the most northerly places. Next door, Tarci ⓣ0812/390 6300 is similar. ❷–❹

Two Thousand Bungalows ⓣ0812/394 1273. Simple but adequate rooms in two-storey buildings set back behind the attached café. ❸

Diving, snorkelling and surfing

The area around the islands is popular for **diving** although the sea can be cold and difficult, so care is needed. There are plenty of sites; Toyapakeh, SD Point and Mangrove are the most reliable, predictable and frequently dived, and can get quite busy. The area hosts varied fish life, with reef sharks, manta rays and the occasional oceanic sunfish.

The only **dive operator** based on the islands is the very experienced World Diving Lembongan (ⓣ0812/390 0686, ⓕ0361/288500, ⓦwww.world-diving.com), based next to *Pondok Baruna* in Jungutbatu. They offer dives for certified divers (US$30 each, including equipment, for the first two; less for more dives) plus a full range of PADI courses up to Divemaster level. They know the area extremely well and dive less frequented sites that they have explored. They have an absolute ban on dropping anchor on the reefs, using fixed moorings instead.

You can charter boats from Nusa Lembongan to take you to **snorkelling** spots (ask at your losmen); one of the best is off **Mushroom Bay** with others at **Mangrove Corner** (also known as **Jet Point**) to the north, and **Sunfish** nearby. Boats will also take you to Nusa Penida where **Crystal Bay** is renowned for its crystal-clear waters; **Gamat**, off the coast near Sakti, and the reef off the coast at **Ped** are also popular. Prices depend on distance; start negotiating at around Rp100,000/hr for a boat holding up to four people, including equipment.

Surfing off Nusa Lembongan

The best **surfing** off Nusa Lembongan – easily accessible from Sanur, and much less crowded than Kuta – is from June to September, although full moons during other months are worth a try. Bring your own board, repair and first aid kits.

The breaks are mostly offshore from Jungutbatu. Just off the beach are **Lacerations** (to the south) and **Surgery** (to the north). **Playgrounds** is a gentle short left-hander on a small swell. The most famous break is **Shipwreck**, a powerful right-hander that breaks off the remains of a shipwreck on the reef, a 300m paddle from the beach. About 1km west of Jungutbatu, **Tanjung Sanghyang** has both a left and a right. **Ceningan**, in the channel between the two islands, is another popular left-hander.

Several places advertise **surf safaris** from Nusa Lembongan, the most obvious being Purnama Indah (mobile ⓣ0811/398553, in Sanur ⓣ0361/289213, ⓦwww.purnamaindah.com). They take in the main breaks along the southern coast of Lombok and Sumbawa; prices vary.

Chelegimbai and Mushroom Bay

About 1km around the coast southwest of Jungutbatu, the tiny white-sand bay of **Chelegimbai** has a few accommodation choices. **Mushroom Bay**, a fabulous white-sand cove, has long been a favourite snorkelling spot and destination for day-trippers from the mainland, but has now developed facilities for visitors who want to stay longer. Don't expect peace down on the beach once the day-trippers arrive – but it's a beautiful, idyllic spot before and after.

You can **charter a boat** to Mushroom Bay from Jungutbatu (expect to pay Rp50,000 per boat). **On foot**, the most attractive route is to walk around the coast. Climb the steps that lead up from the extreme southern end of the beach at Jungutbatu to a path which leads along the hillside past *Coconuts Resort* to Coconut Bay, then up the far side of the bay to *Morin Lembongan* and *Villa Wayan* and on to Chelegimbai beach. Another path leads up from the far southern end of Chelegimbai and passes above a couple of tiny bays before descending to the Mushroom Bay accommodation. A daily **boat** heads direct from Mushroom Bay back to Sanur on the mainland; check times locally. The Perama boat from Jungutbatu will call at Chelegimbai on its way back to Sanur so long as you book in advance.

The **accommodation** around this part of the coast is generally more upmarket than in Jungutbatu, although there's one notable budget option. It's worth repeating that several of the luxury places are best booked as an add-on to the day cruises that operate to the island (see p.602). Doing this will get you the best rates as well as a luxurious trip to and from the mainland.

All the places to stay have attached **restaurants**, with ambience, decor and price in direct relation to the luxury and cost of the accommodation. The cheapest place to eat is *Warung Adi* attached to *Adi Bungalows*, offering a small menu of inexpensive breakfasts and Indonesian main meals. A reasonable alternative is *Winda Sari Warung*, in a prime spot on the beach next to *Hai Tide Huts*, with good views and a large menu of Indonesian and Western food at moderate prices.

Accommodation

Adi Bungalows ⓣ081/735 3587. The cheapest option on this part of the island. Clean, tiled, well-furnished bungalows of brick and thatch set in a pretty garden a few hundred metres inland from Mushroom Beach; follow the track between *Hai Tide Huts* and *Waka Nusa*. There's a small restaurant attached. ❸–❹

Coconuts Beach Resort ⓣ0361/728088, ⓕ728089, ⓦwww.bali.activities.com. Book as an add-on to an *Island Explorer Cruise*. Accommodation is in circular, thatched bungalows (with fans or air-con) ranged up the hillside. The bungalows higher up have glorious views. There are two pools, and it's a short walk to the nearest beach. ❻–❼

Hai Tide Huts ⓣ0361/720331, ⓕ720334, ⓦwww.balihaicruises.com. A large set-up with accommodation in attractive, two-storey brick and thatch huts; the ones on the beachfront have stunning views. Bathrooms are not attached to each hut but a planned expansion will include huts with en-suite facilities. The terrific pool even has a small island in the middle. Book as part of a package with a *Bali Hai* cruise. ❼

Morin Lembongan Contact in Sanur ⓣ & ⓕ0361/288993. The three lovely bungalows here have the best views on the island. They are way up on the cliffside and are light, airy and comfortable with cold-water attached bathrooms. Features a tiny restaurant. It's a short walk to Cheligimbai Beach. ❻–❼

Mushroom Beach Bungalows/Tanjung Sanghyang Bungalows ⓣ082/361 2161. Well-built simple rooms with attached cold-water bathrooms, in a brilliant location on a small headland at the northern end of Mushroom Bay with a small, deserted cove down the other side. There's a small attached restaurant. Bungalows are over-priced for the facilities but you're paying for the location. ❺

Villa Wayan ⓣ & ⓕ0361/287431, ⓦwww.lembongan.discovery.com. There are several accommodation options here, with some bungalows ranged up the hillside and other rooms in imposing houses just behind Cheligimbai Beach. There's no pool but the beach is close and the restaurant has splendid views. ❺–❻

Waka Nusa Resort ⓣ0361/723629, ⓕ722077, ⓦwww.wakaexperience.com. Accommodation is in very comfortable fan-cooled, thatched bungalows with plenty of natural fabrics and attractive decor that are the hallmark of the Waka group – although this one does lack the wow factor enjoyed by many of the others. Located just behind the beach, there's a small pool. Book as an add-on to a *Waka Louka* cruise. ❻

Around Nusa Lembongan

For a trip **around Nusa Lembongan,** it's best to walk or cycle in a clockwise direction, avoiding a lengthy, painful climb up out of Jungutbatu to the south. Allow three to four hours to walk around the island, two hours to cycle, less than an hour by motorbike.

The road north along the coast passes **Pura Sakenan**, recognizable by a highly decorated central shrine, to the dead end at the northernmost tip of the island; the mangrove is very thick and there are few views of anything. Taking a right fork a few hundred metres south of Pura Sakenan leads to **Pura Empuaji**, with its highly carved doorway, the island's most venerated temple (take a sarong if you want to visit). The road around the island continues south from here for four almost uninhabited kilometres. At the point where the channel between Nusa Lembongan and Nusa Ceningan is narrowest, matching temples face each other across the water and a bold new **bridge** has been built to link the islands: you can walk, cycle or ride a motorbike across. The waters here are crystal clear over white sand almost completely filled with frames for seaweed farming. A steep hill climbs up into **LEMBONGAN**, the largest town on the island, 3km south of Jungutbatu. Here is the **Underground House** (open on request; Rp10,000), dug by a traditional healer or *dukun* named Made Biasa. All roads leading uphill through the village eventually join to become the main road up past the school and over the hill to Jungutbatu, with some fine views.

Nusa Ceningan

The tiny island of **Nusa Ceningan**, 4km long by 1km wide, is essentially a hill sticking out of the water, located picturesquely between Nusa Lembongan and Nusa Penida. With around 400 inhabitants, it's a sleepy place. The only **accommodation** is at *The Bungalows* (ⓣ0361/750550, ⓕ754749, ⓦwww.surftravelonline.com; ❼) on the southeast coast – six fan-cooled, grass-roofed bungalows with hot water, situated above a pure white-sand beach.

Nusa Penida

Tell a Balinese person you're heading to **Nusa Penida** and you won't get a positive reaction. The island is renowned as the home of the legendary evil figure **I Macaling** and was also formerly a place of banishment for the kingdom of Klungkung. It's still regarded as *angker*, a place of evil spirits and ill fortune, and many Balinese make the pilgrimage to the island expressly to ward off bad luck by making offerings at Pura Dalem Penataran Ped, home of the dreaded I Macaling. Nusa Penida is too dry to cultivate rice, and while you'll see maize, cassava, beans and tobacco in the fields during the rainy season, there's nothing at all in the dry season. The island can sustain a small population and many have already left to work on the mainland or as part of the government's *transmigrasi* programme. There are no dive operators based here, but those on the mainland and the one on Nusa Lembongan offer trips to the island's north and west coasts; see p.603 for more.

SAMPALAN is Nusa Penida's largest town, and has a shady street of shops, a bemo terminal, a market and the only post office, hospital and phone office on the island. The town is spread out along the beach, and its highlight, the **Pura Dalem**, close to the cemetery near the football field, has a six-metre-tall gateway adorned with five leering Bhoma and a pendulous-breasted Rangda. There are several **warung** in the main street, serving rice and noodles. *Losmen Made* (Ⓣ0818/345204; ❷), on Jalan Segara, 100m west of the bemo terminal, is small and friendly and has four **rooms** with attached mandi and squat toilet set in nice gardens 200m from the beach.

Some 9km from Sampalan on the northeast coast, the fishing town of **TOYAPAKEH** is separated from Nusa Ceningan by a channel less than 1km wide. With its lovely white **beach** and peaceful atmosphere, it's the island's best place to stay. There's a small daily **market** and a tiny mosque. The only **accommodation** is at *Losmen Trang* (Ⓣ082/361 4868; ❷), which has five basic rooms right next to the beach with attached mandi and squat toilet, and also serves simple meals.

Pura Dalem Penataran Ped, dedicated to I Macaling and built from volcanic sandstone and local limestone, lies 5km east of Toyapakeh on the Sampalan road. I Macaling, also known as Jero Gede Macaling, is feared throughout Bali and is believed to be responsible for disease and floods which he brings across to the mainland from Nusa Penida. The size of the courtyards and the grand entrances are impressive, emphasizing the prestige of the temple. The *odalan* festival here is well attended by pilgrims hoping to stave off sickness and ill fortune.

Around the island

The best way to see Nusa Penida is by **motorbike** – ask at your guesthouse for rental details – although you shouldn't drive unless you are confident on steep terrain. The island is a maze of country lanes and signposts are few, so make sure you start early and have plenty of fuel. A full circuit is only about 70km but, allowing time to visit the major attractions, it takes most of a day. The road between Toyapakeh and Sampalan is the busiest on the island and roughly follows the coast; traffic elsewhere is much lighter.

Sights worth aiming for include the limestone cave of **Goa Karangsari**, about 10km south of Sampalan. The tiny entrance is about 100m above the road and opens up into a large, impressive cavern which emerges after 300m onto a ledge with fine views looking out across a quiet mango grove, surrounded by hills on all sides. The real highlights are along the **south coast**. One of several access points is from **SEBULUH**. From the end of the road, a couple of hundred metres beyond the village green, a path leads to the left between high stone walls and heads out to the coast (45min to walk). The coast here is similar to the coastline at the south end of the Bukit, with dramatic limestone cliffs rising sheer out of the ocean and views that are utterly spellbinding. There are also two **temples**, one out on a promontory linked to the mainland by an exposed ridge, and the other, somewhat amazingly, sited at the bottom of an extremely narrow, incredibly exposed path that winds down the face of the cliff to a freshwater spring at the bottom. This type of scenery is typical of the whole southern coast of the island; there are waterfalls in places and several spots where hairy descents to the sea are possible – ask locally.

Candi Dasa and Amuk Bay

CANDI DASA is a laid-back holiday resort at the eastern end of **Amuk Bay**, a good centre for snorkelling and diving with a wide choice of accommodation and restaurants to suit every taste and every pocket. It's also a pleasant base from which to explore the east of Bali, with easy road access to many of the main sights. However, development has not been without its costs: throughout the 1980s Candi's offshore **reef** was systematically crushed to produce lime for cement. The beach was left so exposed that it simply washed away. Large sea walls now protect the land and jetties protrude into the sea in the hope, largely justified, that the **beach** will build up behind them: there are many little pockets of pretty, white sand nestling here and there. However, one of the best deserted stretches in the area lies just to the east of the resort: go straight on at the crossroads at the end of Forest Road; don't take the right turn down to *Puri Bagus Candidasa*, but take the road up onto the headland where it follows the top of the cliffs for a few hundred metres but eventually descends onto a glistening black-sand beach on the other side.

The village grew around its attractive lagoon, but the tourist developments have now spread west around the bay, through the villages of **Senkidu**, **Mendira**, **Buitan** and **Manggis**, where the beach is still a respectable size. Further west, just around the headland, the tiny cove of **Padang Bai** is home to the bustling access port for Lombok, and also has a small tourist infrastructure. The entire coastal area is well served by **public transport**, both long-distance buses and minibuses from Denpasar (Batubulan terminal) to Amlapura, and local bemos on shorter runs. You can expect a ride every five to ten minutes for short hops early in the day, diminishing to every half-hour or so by the end of the afternoon.

Candi Dasa is an ancient settlement, with its **temple**, just opposite the lagoon, believed to have been founded in the eleventh century. The statue of the fertility goddess Hariti in the lower section of the temple, surrounded by numerous children, is still a popular focus for pilgrims (the name Candi Dasa originally derives from *cilidasa*, meaning "ten children").

Arrival, information and accommodation

Hotel development now extends about 8km west of Candi Dasa into neighbouring villages, just to the south of the main Denpasar–Amlapura road; it's easy to get **bemo** drivers to drop you off where you want. **Shuttle buses** from the main tourist destinations serve Candi Dasa, and Perama has an office (see Travel Details on p.663 for more details). Fixed-price taxis serve Candi Dasa from Ngurah Rai airport (Rp199,000; takes up to 2hr). There's a centrally located **tourist office** in the main street close to the lagoon which has somewhat erratic opening hours.

There's a vast choice of **accommodation** spread about 1km along the main road running just behind the beach at Candi Dasa; beware of road noise. East of here, Forest Road offers a number of quiet guesthouses and hotels dotted among coconut palms. About 1km west of Candi Dasa is the village of Senkidu, slightly detached and quiet, and adjacent Mendira. If you decide to stay any further west towards Buitan you'll need your own transport to enjoy Candi's nightlife, as public transport stops at dusk. Further west, most of Manggis village is spread inland, but it does offer luxury accommodation. All the places listed below are keyed on the map.

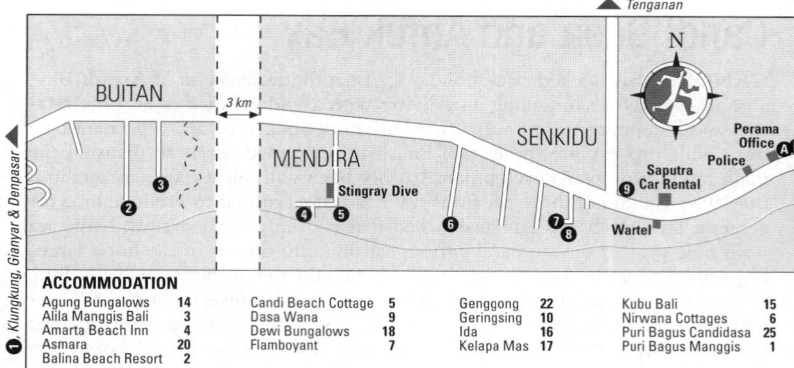

Candi Dasa

Agung Bungalows ⓣ0363/41535. Well-finished seafront bungalows with good-sized verandahs, fans and hot and cold water located in a lush garden complete with ponds. ❸

Asmara ⓣ & ⓕ0363/41929, ⓦwww.asmarabali.com, ⓔyosbali@indosat.net.id. New boutique dive resort and spa with stylish Balinese minimalist bungalows. There's a beach-side restaurant, swimming pool, and *Yos Marine Adventures* have a dive-shop here. ❻–❼

Dasa Wana ⓣ0363/41444, ⓕ0361/242993. Air-con rooms and villas with hot water in landscaped grounds across the road from the sea. Good value in this price bracket. ❺

Dewi Bungalows ⓣ0363/41166, ⓕ41177. Set in a spacious garden close to the lagoon and the sea, the best bungalows overlook the lagoon. Hot water is available in more expensive ones. ❸

Geringsing ⓣ0363/41084. Budget bamboo and thatch bungalows set in a small central compound next to the sea, offering excellent value. ❷

Ida ⓣ & ⓕ0363/41096. Six large, wood and thatch cottages all with fan, attached cold-water bathrooms and mosquito nets, in the centre of Candi, with huge verandahs, set in a lovely garden stretching down to the sea. ❸

Kelapa Mas ⓣ0363/41369, ⓕ41947, ⓦwww.welcome.to/kelapamas. Justifiably popular and centrally located, offering a range of clean bungalows set in a large well-maintained garden on the seafront. Most expensive options have hot water. ❹–❺

Kubu Bali ⓣ0363/41532, ⓕ41531. Excellent, well-furnished bungalows with deep and shady verandahs, fan, air-con and hot water are set in a glorious garden that ranges up the hillside, There's a great swimming pool at the top of the garden. Service is friendly yet efficient. ❻–❼

Rama ⓣ0363/41778. An excellent location between the sea and lagoon, with accommodation in two-storey buildings with fan and cold-water in a small garden. ❷

Segara Wangi ⓣ0363/41159. Excellent-value clean bungalows with attached cold-water mandi set in a pretty garden. Central and with great verandahs. Seafront places are best. ❸

Temple Seaside Cottages ⓣ & ⓕ0363/41629. Small, central place that offers several standards of fan-cooled accommodation from basic bungalows to ones on the seafront with picture windows and hot water. ❷–❺

The Watergarden/Hotel Taman Air ⓣ0363/41540, ⓕ41164, ⓦwww.watergardenhotel.com. Superb, characterful hotel in central Candi Dasa. Accommodation is in excellently furnished bungalows set in an atmospheric, lush garden. There's a pretty, secluded swimming pool. Service is excellent. ❼

Forest Road

Genggong ⓣ0363/41105. Bungalows plus rooms in a two-storey block. The big plus is the lovely garden and picturesque stretch of white-sand beach just over the wall. ❸–❺

Puri Bagus Candidasa ⓣ0363/41131, ⓕ41290, ⓦwww.bagus-discovery.com. In an excellent location at the far eastern end of Forest Road, this hotel offers top-quality accommodation. For a more rural location consider the sister operation, *Puri Bagus Manggis* (see below). Published prices start at US$115. ❽

Puri Pudak ⓣ0363/41978. Bungalows, all with hot water and fan, overlooking the beach. There's a good sunbathing area. ❸

Sekar Anggrek ⓣ0363/41086, ⓕ41977. The

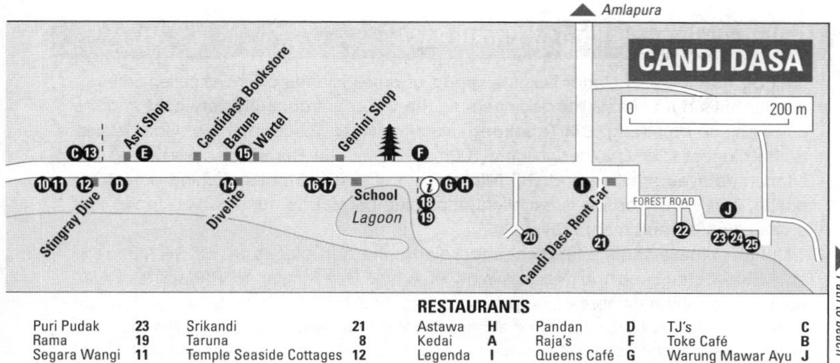

best value on Forest Road, with seven good-quality bungalows, all with fan and hot water, in a quiet seafront garden. ❸

Srikandi ⓣ0363/41972. A neat row of simple, good-value bungalows in an attractive garden by the sea, just at the start of Forest Road, so convenient for the centre of town as well. ❸

Senkidu and Mendira

Amarta Beach Inn ⓣ0363/41230. Large, tiled bungalows, all with fan and attached cold-water bathrooms, set in a pretty garden facing the ocean at Mendira. Plenty of space for sun-bathing and a beachside restaurant. ❸

Flamboyant ⓣ & ⓕ0363/41886, ⓦwww.flamboyant-bali.com. Spotless bungalows in a gorgeous, quiet garden beside the sea at Senkidu. There's a restaurant, a *lesehan* in the garden above the fish ponds and you can refill mineral water bottles here. ❸–❹

Nirwana Cottages ⓣ0363/41136, ⓕ41543, ⓔnirwanacot@denpasar.wasantara.net.id. A small establishment with well-furnished rooms and bungalows in a lush garden with an excellent pool and beachside restaurant. Bottom-end rooms with fan and hot-water are not brilliant value but the bungalows, especially those with a sea view are excellent. Very popular, so booking is recommended. ❻

Taruna ⓣ0363/41823, ⓕ41886, ⓔtaruna_bungalows@hotmail.com. A neat row of good-value bungalows in a pretty garden with a small seaside bar, in a quiet location next to *Flamboyant*. ❸

Buitan and Manggis

Alila Manggis Bali ⓣ0363/41011, ⓕ41015, ⓦwww.alilahotels.com. One of the most impressive hotels in eastern Bali is situated in a grand coconut grove beside the sea with rooms ranged around a gorgeous pool. Stylish, modern minimalist chic characterizes the decor, service is superb and there's a Mandara Spa attached to the hotel. The hotel is developing an international reputation for its two-day (US$220) and five-day ($550) residential cooking schools. Accommodation starts at $155. ❽

Balina Beach Resort Buitan ⓣ0363/41002, ⓕ41001. Offering a variety of bungalows in pretty gardens with an attractive pool almost on the beach; Spice Dive have a desk here. From the main road, look out for the turning signed "Royal Bali Beach Club". ❻–❼

Puri Bagus Manggis ⓣ0363/41304, ⓕ41305, ⓦwww.bagus-discovery.com. Part of the small Puri Bagus stable of hotels, with just seven beautifully furnished rooms set in a wonderfully rural setting in Manggis – the only accommodation in the village. There's a small swimming pool and orchid garden in the paddy fields just across the road, a temple in the gardens and free transport to the sister operation in Candi Dasa where guests can use their beachside facilities. A one- or two-day cooking school runs for guests who are interested (from US$35). Accommodation starts at US$115. ❽

Diving and snorkelling at Candi Dasa

Just off the coast of Candi Dasa, a group of small islands offers excellent **diving**, although it's not suitable for beginners as the water is frequently very cold and the currents can be strong. **Gili Tepekong** (also known as Gili Kambing or Goat Island) is the biggest island, although only 100m by 50m; **Gili Biaha** (also known as Gili Likman) is even smaller; and **Gili Mimpang** is just three rocks sticking out of the ocean. The variety of fish is excellent, including barracuda, tuna, white-tipped reef sharks, sunfish and manta rays.

Not all of these spots offer great **snorkelling**: the best places are off Gili Mimpang and Blue Lagoon on the western side of Amuk Bay, closer to Padang Bai (see p.614). Local boat owners will approach you to fix up snorkelling trips; the going rate is around Rp50,000/hr for a boat including equipment. Many dive shops take snorkellers along on dive trips; prices vary ($25–39). Always be clear whether or not equipment is included.

As well as the local sites, Candi Dasa is an ideal base from which to arrange **diving trips** to Padang Bai, Nusa Penida, Nusa Lembongan, Amed, Gili Selang and Tulamben. Candi Dasa is also a good place to take a course, as hotel swimming pools are available for initial tuition. A PADI Open Water course costs $300–360; the two-day advanced option around $250; the two- to three-day rescue diver $300; and divemaster courses can also be arranged. On trips for experienced divers prices are about $50–60 for the Candi Dasa, Padang Bai, Tulamben and Amed areas, $70–75 for Nusa Lembongan and Nusa Penida (see p.605) and $80 for Menjangan Island (see p.660).

Dive operators

Baruna Has a counter in town ⓣ0363/41185, and one at *Puri Bagus Candidasa* hotel ⓣ0363/41217. These are the Candi Dasa offices for this large Bali-wide operator, offering the full range of trips and courses.

Divelite ⓣ0363/41660, ⓕ41661, ⓦwww.divelite.com. A full range of PADI and SSI courses plus trips for experienced divers. They offer tuition in Japanese and English.

Pineapple Divers At *Candi Beach Cottage,* Senkidu ⓣ0363/41760. This small company offers dives and courses and two- and three-day package tours of the dive sites around the island, including accommodation.

Spice Dive At *Balina Beach Resort* ⓣ0363/41725, ⓕ41001, ⓦwww.damai.com/spicedive. The only southern office of this extremely well-regarded north-coast operator, offering trips for certified divers and courses.

Stingray Dive Centre Senkidu ⓣ0363/41268, ⓕ41062, and an office in central Candi Dasa ⓣ0363/41063. Features the usual range of trips plus courses.

Yos Marine Adventures At *Asmara* hotel ⓣ & ⓕ0363/41929, ⓔyosbali@indosat.net.id. This well-respected southern Bali operator has now branched out into Candi Dasa, offering a range of dives and courses.

Eating, drinking and nightlife

Candi Dasa offers a great variety of **places to eat** and the quality of the food, especially seafood, is generally excellent. Several places have good-value set meals and others feature Balinese dancing, mostly *legong*, to accompany your meal – look out for local adverts. Unless otherwise stated, all the places listed below offer inexpensive to moderately priced food and lie on or near the main road through the resort – which can be rather noisy.

Nightlife is low-key: apart from a few late-opening restaurants, things are pretty quiet by 11pm. There's no disco scene and live music comes and goes – check out *Legenda* and *Queen's Café*. Events are advertised with flyers nailed to trees around town. Videos are the main entertainment at *Raja's* and the *Candi Bagus Pub* next door, but viewing, or rather listening, can be frustrating as heavy traffic whizzes past.

Alila Restaurant ⓣ0363/41011. Probably the premier dining experience in eastern Bali which is expensive but worth every rupiah for real foodlovers. The huge gourmet menu of Indonesian and Pacific-Asian fusion dishes with interesting touches of Bali includes lamb, beef and kangaroo among a great deal of seafood, and changes daily. The cooking is extremely intricate and the surroundings stylish.

Astawa The most popular of a clutch of places at the eastern end of the main road, offering highly competitive prices for a large menu of well-cooked and attractively presented Western, Indo-Chinese and travellers' fare. Was undergoing renovation at the time of writing.

Kedai ⓣ0363/42020, ⓦwww.dekco.com. This offshoot of *Ary's Warung* in Ubud is a tasteful addition to refined dining in Candi Dasa and the soaring circular bale is a symphony in wood, bamboo and soft, creamy stone. The food is pricey but there are innovative, imaginative Western and Indonesian options. There's a big choice of cocktails and wines.

Kubu Bali The large dramatic kitchen in the restaurant at the front of the hotel in central Candi Dasa specializes in seafood, but also offers moderately priced Western, Chinese and Indonesian food. Better tables are tucked away from the road near the fish ponds.

Legenda Situated close to the junction of the Forest Rd with the main road, this is one of the few venues in Candi Dasa for live music. They also have a wide-ranging, inexpensive menu with plenty of Western dishes, including spaghetti, pizza and steak, alongside Indonesian food.

Pandan Ignore the breakwater in the foreground and this is a pretty fair spot for a sunset drink in central Candi Dasa. There's a big, moderately priced menu including some good seafood, and a twice-weekly Indonesian/Western buffet.

Raja's Lots of people come here, almost opposite the lagoon in central Candi Dasa, for the nightly videos, but there's also a vast drinks list and plenty of moderately priced Indonesian and Western dishes. Visa and MasterCard accepted.

Queens Café There's a good buzz here. Diners get a free welcome drink and popcorn and there is often live music. Set menus are good value although the choices aren't vast, the food is cheap and cheerful.

TJ's At the *Watergarden* hotel in the middle of Candi Dasa. There's a broad menu of Indonesian, Thai, Indian and Western dishes together with an enormous drinks list including cocktails and wine. Breakfast croissants are excellent as are the desserts.

Toke Café This long-term Candi Dasa favourite at the western end of central Candi Dasa offers a vast menu of moderately priced seafood, pasta, pizza, chicken, pork and steak. Set menus are real feasts.

Warung Mawar Ayu A friendly, family-run place on Forest Rd. It's a quiet spot for a meal, with an inexpensive menu of Indonesian food and plenty of local fish.

Shopping

While nobody would head to Candi Dasa for the **shopping** alone, there's now an enticing range of stores. Asri Shop (daily 8am–10pm) is central, sells everything for everyday as well as souvenir needs and has fixed prices which are a good guide for your bargaining elsewhere. There's a dense stretch of **clothing** shops along the main road just east of the Perama office which sell the usual range of tourist sarongs, trousers, skirts, shirts and T-shirts. Gogos, near the Perama office, and Putra, just along from the Asri Shop, sell a good range of **silver** items. Nusantara Archipelago, just east of the lagoon, has an excellent selection of **paper**, **wood** and **metal** items and, slightly further east, Surya Gana sells lovely cotton and silk **batik**. Also at this end of town, Balinese Ceramic, opposite *Queen's Café*, offers pretty **ceramic** items large and small. Further west, the Geringsing Shop is a treasure trove of the old and not-so-old and an extensive range of **textiles** from across Indonesia. Lenia sells great baskets, textiles and statues from throughout Indonesia, and the shop at *The Watergarden* stocks some of the most tasteful and unusual items in town including clothes, textiles, **jewellery**, wood and paper crafts. At the top end of the price range, *Kedai* has a small selection of gorgeous modern, well-designed and beautifully executed items. If you're seriously into shopping, there's a great choice of textiles and other crafts in the village of Tenganan (see opposite).

Listings

Bike rental Enquire at your losmen or at the places in the main street, and expect to pay Rp30,000/day. *Temple Café* in the main street has a selection.
Books *Candidasa Bookstore* has the largest selection.
Car and motorbike rental You'll be offered transport every few yards along the main road, or else enquire at your accommodation. There are also plenty of rental companies around the resort, with prices comparable to Kuta/Sanur (Rp70,000–75,000 for a Suzuki Jimney for one day, Rp100,000–120,000 for a Kijang). The going rate for a driver is Rp50,000/day. A motorbike costs Rp35,000–40,000. Well-established companies are Saputra ⓣ0363/41083, close to the police post; Safari ⓣ0363/41707 and Amarta ⓣ0363/41260 in the centre of town; and Candidasa Rent Car ⓣ0363/41225, just at the start of Forest Rd. The insurance included varies considerably.
Charter transport Putting together your own day-trip costs Rp200,000–300,000/day for vehicle, driver and petrol, depending on your itinerary. Negotiate with the guys along the main street, ask at your accommodation or approach the car rental companies. One-way drops to destinations throughout Bali are a convenient and – if you're in a group – a reasonable way of moving on.
Doctor Contact staff at your hotel initially if you need medical attention. Dr I Wayan Artana ⓣ0363/41321 (mobile ⓣ0812/390 0447) offers a 24-hour service at Candidasa Clinik on the track from the main road to *Flamboyant Bungalows* and *Taruna* in Sengkidu. The nearest hospitals are at Amlapura, Klungkung or Denpasar.
Exchange You'll find moneychangers every few metres along the main street.
Internet access Available at several spots including Safari Rent Car and Kelapa Mas, both on the main street. Prices are Rp300–400/min. Phone lines are unreliable and access can be suspended for a day or so every now and again.
Massage You'll be approached throughout the resort and on the beach. The going rate is Rp30,000/hr – more if you arrange it through your hotel.
Phones The wartel (daily 8am–11pm) is next to the *Kubu Bali Restaurant*.
Postal agents Several postal agents along the main street sell stamps. Asri Shop provides a poste restante service: mail should be addressed to you, c/o Asri Shop, Candi Dasa, PO Box 135, Karangasem, Bali.
Tourist shuttle buses Plenty of places offer shuttle buses from Candi Dasa to destinations throughout Bali and Lombok and further east to Bima and Sape. Perama ⓣ0363/41114 (daily 8am–9pm) is the most established operator. See Travel Details on p.663 for destinations and frequencies.

Around Candi Dasa

The cove of **Pasir Putih**, 6km northeast of Candi, has a 500-metre pure-white beach sheltered by rocky headlands with good views of Gili Biaha. Take a bemo as far as Perasi, from where the small Jalan Segara Madu with a little shop on the corner leads past paddy-fields to the coast. Two or three kilometres along the track, you reach a small temple where the path forks. The left fork leads to two black-sand beaches; the right descends through coconut groves to Pasir Putih. There are no facilities here at present, but the beach is rumoured to be earmarked for a big resort development.

From **Manggis**, 6km west of Candi, a very poorly surfaced road – check the condition before setting off in a vehicle – heads up into the hills. It's a lovely eight-kilometre walk up the steep, quiet lane, with stunning views of the entire coastal area, to Pesangkan (see p.620) on the Amlapura–Rendang road, where you can have lunch at *Pondok Bukit Putung*. For the return journey, bemos connect Pesangkan with Amlapura, where you can change for Candi Dasa.

Tenganan

The village of **TENGANAN** (admission by donation), is unique among the Bali Aga communities of the island in its strong adherence to traditional ways. Rejecting the Javanization of their land, the caste system and the religious reforms that followed the Majapahit conquest of the island in 1343, the **Bali Aga** or Bali Mula, meaning "original Balinese", withdrew to their village enclaves to live a life based around ritual and ceremony. Today, Tenganan is extremely wealthy, and the only place in Indonesia that produces the celebrated gringsing cloth. The road up to Tenganan is an easy **walk** from the centre of Candi Dasa but **ojek** (Rp2000) wait at the bottom to transport you the 3km

Ikat

Traditional textiles still have a **ritual purpose** on Bali – worn, given or hung at important rites of passage ceremonies such as first hair-cutting and toothfiling. The indigenous textile industry has always focused on the **ikat** technique, particularly the weft *ikat* or *endek* of Gianyar and the double *ikat* or *gringsing* of Tenganan. It's possible to see weavers at work in both these places, as well as at the smaller weaving factories of Singaraja; their fabrics are worn and sold all over the island. Easily recognized by the fuzzy-edged motifs it produces, the *ikat* weaving technique is common throughout Indonesia, woven either on back-strap, foot-pedal or semi-automatic looms from either silk, cotton or rayon. The distinctive feature of *ikat* is, however, not so much the weaving process as the dyeing technique – a sophisticated tie-dye process which has three variations.

In **warp-ikat**, the warp yarn (the threads that run lengthwise through the material) is first threaded onto a loom frame, and then tied with dye-resistant twine into the desired pattern before being dipped into a dye vat. The binding and dyeing processes are then repeated with different colours until the final effect is achieved, after which single-coloured weft threads are woven into the patterned warp. Warp-*ikat* is the most widely practised technique in almost every Indonesian island other than Bali. The warp-*ikat* of east Sumba are particularly distinctive, and very popular in the shops of Bali, woven with bold humanoid motifs and images of real and mythological creatures such as horses, lizards, birds, monkeys, phoenixes and lions. They are usually dyed in combinations of indigo and deep red and often take the form of *hinggi* or fringed shawls.

In **weft-ikat**, the warp threads are left plain and the weft yarn (the threads running across the fabric) is dyed to the finished design. Nearly all the *ikat* woven in Bali is weft-*ikat*, also known as **endek**, recognizable by its predominantly geometric and abstract motifs. The art of embroidered *ikat*, or supplementary weft-weaving, is also practised to fine effect in Bali, where it's known as **songket**. *Songket* fabric uses threads of gold and silver metallic yarn to add decorative tapestry-like motifs of birds, butterflies and flowers; *songket* sarongs are worn by the wealthiest Balinese at major ceremonial occasions. The brocaded sashes worn by performers of traditional Balinese dance are always made from *songket*, often so heavy with gold thread that you can hardly see the silk background.

The technique of **double ikat**, or **gringsing**, involves the dyeing of both the warp and the weft threads into their final designs before they're woven together; a double-*ikat* sarong can take five years to complete. There are just three areas in the world where this highly refined weaving method is practised: India, Japan, and the Bali Aga village of **Tenganan**. Not surprisingly, *gringsing* is exceedingly expensive to purchase. It's prized throughout Bali, as it's thought to provide protection against evil; many ceremonies require the use of the cloth. The origins of the technique remain shrouded in mystery and it is uncertain whether it's evidence of an outside influence or whether it was created within the village.

up to the village. It's a major stop on the tour-bus circuit: avoid the 11am–2pm rush if you can.

Tenganan's land is owned communally; the villagers do not work it, but have sharecropping agreements with other local people, leaving them free to pursue a complex round of **rituals** and **ceremonies**. The rituals are laid down in ancient texts and their observance is believed to prevent the wrath of the gods destroying the village. Most of the daily rituals observed by the villagers are not open to the public, but there are so many **festival** days that the *Calendar of Events* printed by the Bali government tourist office has an entire section devoted to events in Tenganan. The month-long Usaba Sambah festival, generally in May and June, is one of the most colourful.

Tenganan's most famous product is **gringsing** or double *ikat* (see p.613), a highly valued brown, deep-red, blue-black and tan cloth – so important that the village, officially Tenganan Pergringsingan, takes its name from the cloth. In recent years **basketwork** and **traditional calligraphy** have started to be produced more commercially within the village. You can see all of these crafts in the village. There are numerous weaving shops, plenty of people producing calligraphy work at tables outside their homes, and basketwork. A good place to visit is I Nyoman Uking's Ata Shop (☎0363/41167) up towards the top of the village over in the right-hand section; there's a small sign outside, you're welcome to take photographs, and Nyoman speaks English.

Padang Bai

Deriving from two languages – *padang* is Balinese for grass and *bai* is Dutch for bay – **PADANG BAI**, the port for Lombok, nestles in a small cove with a white-sand beach lined with fishing boats. Fast and slow boats run regularly to Lembar on **Lombok**; the jetty, ferry offices and car park are all at the western end of the bay, from where everything is within easy walking distance.

Bemos arrive at, and depart from, the port entrance; orange bemos from Amlapura via Candi Dasa, blue or white bemos from Klungkung (also known as Semarapura). Plenty of counters along the seafront offer tourist information, but these are commercial set-ups; the nearest government tourist office is in Candi Dasa (see p.607). The ticket office for **Nusa Penida** (marked on the map) is a little way east of the port; from 7am onwards, boats leave from the beach when they're full for Sampalan (Rp10,000). Perama **tourist shuttle buses** operate from their office (daily 7am–7pm; ☎0363/41419) near the jetty; see Travel Details on p.663 for more. If you're heading to southern Bali and can't bear the congested roads, try the boat *Osiania 3* (daily; 1hr; Rp54,000), which calls daily at Padang Bai on its way back from Lombok and goes on to dock at Benoa; book at Wannen (☎0363/41780) on the seafront.

Moving on to Lombok

The following operate from Padang Bai to **Lembar** on Lombok. See p.663 for information on other routes to Lombok.

Slow ferry Every 1hr 30min; takes 4hr–4hr 30min. Tickets cost Rp16,500 for VIP (air-con lounge with soft seats and TV), or Rp9000 for *ekonomi* (hard seats and TV). An extra charge is made for bicycles (Rp10,000), motorbikes (Rp25,000), and cars (from Rp175,000). See p.44 for information on taking rental vehicles between the islands.

Fast boat (the *Osiania 3*). Daily; takes 1hr 30min; Rp75,000. Book in Padang Bai at Wannen ☎0363/41780.

Tourist shuttle Tickets to destinations throughout Lombok are available at Perama; other operators advertise throughout the resort.

There's a **post office** near the port entrance and a **wartel** on the seafront (daily 7am–midnight) with another in the main road near the port (daily 6am–midnight). **Internet** services are springing up in many places, *Made* and *Ozone* to name just two; access (Rp350/min) can be rather erratic because of problems with the phone lines. Many seafront restaurants **change money**, while **car rental** (Rp80,000–90,000/day for a Suzuki Jimney, Rp150,000 for a Kijang) and **motorbike rental** (Rp40,000/day) are widely available.

If you find the main beach too busy, follow the road past the post office and, just as it begins to climb, take the track to the left which leads to the smaller, quieter bay of **Biastugal** (also known as Pantai Kecil), to the west. It has a few tiny warung that organize occasional beach parties in high season. There are rumours that this area is lined up for the development of a luxury resort, with uncertain implications for public access to the beach. Alternatively, head over the headland in the other direction and take the path from Pura Silayukti to another small cove named **Blue Lagoon** after the snorkelling and diving site located just offshore.

Accommodation

There's a wide choice of **accommodation** both in the village and along the road behind the beach; expect more to be added and others to be renovated any time soon. The beach places benefit from a sea breeze and are generally bigger and airier, but the ones in the village, especially up on the hill, have some excellent upstairs rooms.

Bagus Inn ⓣ0363/41398. An excellent budget choice with small rooms with attached bathroom in a friendly family compound. ❷

Darma ⓣ0363/41394. A small family set-up in the village; the downstairs rooms are dark but upstairs ones are bigger and have good sitting areas outside. ❷–❸

Kembar Inn ⓣ & ⓕ0363/41364. Clean, pleasant

Snorkelling and diving at Padang Bai

Several places in Padang Bai rent **snorkelling** equipment (Rp15,000/day); the best snorkelling is at Blue Lagoon. You can snorkel off the beach there, but you'll see more if you charter a boat (about Rp150,000 for 2hr for two people); you'll be approached on the beach about this, or ask at *Celagi* restaurant or your guesthouse. The most established **dive** operation is Geko Dive (ⓣ0363/41516, ⓕ41790, ⓦwww.gekodive.com), a large set-up on the seafront with a lot of experience. They offer the full range of PADI courses and dives for experienced divers. Diving Groove (ⓣ0812/398 9746, ⓦwww.divinggroove.com) offer both English and German, and pride themselves on their fish briefing prior to diving. Other operators are Bali Moon Divers, Jl Silayukti 15 (ⓣ0363/41727), Equator (ⓣ0363/41509) on the seafront, and Water Worxx, in the *Padang Bai Beach Inn* compound. Expect to pay $45 (including equipment rental) for two dives locally, $55 for two dives in Amed, Tulamben or Candi Dasa, and $70–75 for two dives at Nusa Lembongan, Nusa Penida, Pulau Menjangan or Gili Selang. The Discover Scuba day is approximately $75, and the PADI Open Water course $280–300. The local reef is **Tanjung Sari**, around and beyond the headland to the east of the bay, where you can reliably spot hawksbill and green turtles. The animal life is remarkable and includes several varieties of sharks, rays, scorpionfish, stargazers and plenty of species that you won't spot elsewhere in Bali.

tiled place in the village. There are many options and there's also a nice sitting area upstairs. ❹–❺

Kerti Beach Inn ⓣ0363/41391. Near the beach; some accommodation is in bungalows, some in two-storey *lumbung*-style barns. ❸

Made Homestay ⓣ0363/41441. Clean, tiled rooms with fan and attached cold-water bathrooms in a two-storey block convenient for both the beach and the village. ❸

Padang Bai Beach Homestay ⓣ0812/360 7946. A set of attractive well-built, clean bungalows on the seafront in a garden. ❸–❹

Padang Bai Beach Inns 1, 2, 3 & 4 With a large, attractive location near the beach, there are four places in a row offering bungalows and two-storey *lumbung*-style barns. Some accommodation faces seawards and some has a less attractive outlook. ❸

Pantai Ayu ⓣ0363/41396. Long-established place in the village up on the hill with good views, a pleasant breeze and a small attached restaurant. The better, pricier rooms are upstairs. All are extremely clean. ❷–❸

Parta ⓣ0363/41475. Pleasant, clean village place with rooms upstairs and down, some with hot water. There's a great sitting area on the top floor and the real gem is the room perched way up here. *Tirta Yoga* is across the alleyway here and also worth a look. ❷–❸

Pondok Wisata Serangan ⓣ0363/41425. Newly renovated rooms in a small compound in the village; upstairs rooms are lighter and better but the downstairs ones are much cheaper. ❷

Puri Rai ⓣ0363/41385, ⓕ41386. Large, clean, tiled rooms and bungalows with hot water and fan or air-con; try to get a room at the back which doesn't overlook the car park. The only place in town with a swimming pool. ❺

Serangan Inn ⓣ0363/41425. Spotless place built high up with some great views. Catches the breeze and boasts good rooms, all with fan and attached cold-water bathroom. ❸–❹

Eating, drinking and nightlife

Seafood is the speciality in Padang Bai **restaurants**, with marlin, barracuda, snapper and prawns on offer, depending on the catch. You'll also find regular tourist menus as well as rice and noodle dishes. The small places on the beach side of the road are unbeatable value, offering the perfect setting for that first cool drink of the evening. All are in the inexpensive to moderate price range and have Happy Hours, but tend to stop serving around 10pm.

Padang Bai doesn't have much **nightlife**. An exception is *Kledate*, an open-air reggae bar towards the eastern end of the beach, which has live music most evenings, getting going around 10pm; they keep open while there are customers.

Café Papa John A relaxed atmosphere, soothing music and an enormous menu of all the favourites. You can refill mineral water bottles here.

Kendedes A two-storey building up on the hill – an excellent spot from which to catch the breeze and watch the port. Food is good-quality and good-value.

Marina Last in line on the beach – a very popular place with great views. If this doesn't suit, try the nearby *Manalagi*, *Kasandra*, *Celagi* or *Dharma*.

Ozone Conveniently located near the accommodation in the village offering good food in slightly wacky surroundings. The menu is a long and entertaining read offering the usual travellers' fare plus some Balinese specialities. Specials are advertised on the blackboards; the spare ribs get good reports.

Pantai Ayu Two places share this name and the same menu, both in prime locations. One is at the top of the village, in the homestay of the same name, and the other in the row of tiny warung on the seafront. Both serve good, inexpensive food and a variety of drinks.

East of Candi Dasa

The far east of Bali, **east of Candi Dasa**, offers lush rice terraces just a few kilometres from parched landscapes where cultivation is all but impossible. The central volcanic mass of the island, most apparent in the overpowering bulk of Gunung Agung, extends right through to the smaller, forest-covered slopes at the far eastern end of the island where Gunung Lempuyang and Seraya are not as tall as Agung but rugged and imposing nonetheless. The main road beyond Candi Dasa cuts inland, passing close to the sleepy market town of **Amlapura** before crossing the hills to the north coast and continuing on the long coastal strip right round to Singaraja (see p.636). You can follow this route by public transport, but if you want to get further off the beaten track and explore the far eastern end of the island, with its remote beach hideaways around **Amed** or the fabulous scenery of the **Iseh** and **Sidemen** areas, you'll need your own transport.

Amlapura

Formerly known as Karangasem, **AMLAPURA**, 40km east of Klungkung, was renamed after the 1963 eruption of Gunung Agung, when much of the outskirts of the town were flattened by the lava flow. (Balinese people will sometimes change their name after a serious illness, believing that a name change will bring about a change of fortune.) Its relaxed atmosphere makes it a pleasant place to spend a few hours.

Built around a hundred years ago by Anak Agung Gede Jelantik, **Puri Agung** (daily 8am–6pm; Rp3000), also known as Puri Kaningan, is the only one of the Amlapura royal palaces open to the public, an unremarkable example of very faded grandeur. Within the compound, the highlight is the Maskerdam building with its intricately carved doors and furniture donated by Queen Wilhelmina of the Netherlands arranged in several rooms, which you can admire only through the windows. The verandah is decorated with photographs and paintings, explained in the English-language guide to the palace, and includes a picture of the last king of Karangasem, who died in 1966.

Public transport completes a massive circle around the top end of town, passing the **wartel** (open 24hr) on the way up, and Puri Agung on the way down to the terminal. The **post office** is at Jl Jend Gatot Subroto 25. **Exchange** facilities are at Bank Dannamon and BRI on Jalan Gajah Made, and BNI on Jalan Kesatrian near the bus/bemo terminal. You'd do best to travel early in the day. **Bemos** from the terminal serve Candi Dasa and Padang Bai (orange);

some of those to Selat and Muncan (green) go on to Besakih. Bemos for Ujung and Seraya (blue) leave from the southern end of Jalan Gajah Made not far from the terminal. There are also **buses** north to Singaraja, with some on to Gilimanuk (not after 3.30pm), and around the south to Batubulan (final departure 4pm). Bemos to Culik and Tianyar via Tirtagangga leave from the turnoff on the outskirts of town, as do dark-red minibuses to Singaraja. This turning is marked by a huge black and white pinnacle, a monument to the fight for independence, which is adorned with a *garuda*. The quiet **tourist office** is on Jalan Diponegoro (Mon–Thurs 7am–3pm, Fri 7am–noon; ⓣ0363/21196).

Villa Amlapura on Jalan Gajah Made (ⓣ0363/23246; ❷–❸) has neat, pleasant **rooms** in a small compound just south of Puri Agung. The attached *Café Lima* has a small, inexpensive **food** menu, while *Sumber Rasa* further south on Jalan Gajah Made offers a similar selection of soups, sate, steak, spaghetti, noodles and rice.

Tirtagangga and around

Some 6km northwest of Amlapura, **TIRTAGANGGA** is surrounded by beautiful paddy-fields offering pleasant walks, but its main draw is the lovely **Water Palace** (daily 7am–6pm; Rp3100, Rp1000 for camera, Rp2500 for video camera; ⓦwww.tirtagangga.nl), built in 1946 by Anak Agung Anglurah, the last raja of Karangasem, as testament to his obsession with pools, moats and fountains. It is being well restored and is an impressive terraced area featuring numerous pools, water channels and fountains set in a well-maintained garden. Check the website for historic photographs and information, plus up-to-the-minute details of the restoration efforts. You can swim in an upper, deeper pool (Rp4000) or a lower, shallower pool (Rp2000). Paddle-boats cost Rp10,000 for fifteen minutes.

Tirtagangga is served by **minibuses** and **buses** plying between Amlapura and Singaraja, and by Perama tourist shuttle buses (see Travel Details p.663 for frequency and journey durations). There are several **moneychangers** and a postal agent on the track to the Water Palace from the main road. **Internet** access is at *Purnama Restaurant* (daily 7am–9pm), also on the track to the Palace from the main road. It's worth checking out Nyoman Budiarsa's small shop (ⓣ0363/22436), next to *Genta Bali Warung* on the main road: he sells a printed **map** of walks to local villages and temples (Rp2500), more useful as a guide to the possibilities than a map to follow on the ground. He can also arrange **guides** for walking trips (Rp15,000/hr per person) plus longer trips involving transport in one or both directions and climbs up Gunung Agung (see p.599).

Accommodation

All the **accommodation** listed below is in or near Tirtagangga and accessed by road from the village or from Temega, slightly to the south. It's also worth considering the accommodation around the village of **Ababi** (see below): most is around 2km from Tirtagangga by road, but there are short footpaths that lead down to Tirtagangga in twenty minutes or less.

Cabé Bali ⓣ0363/22045, ⓦwww.cabebali.com. The most luxurious accommodation in the area, offering superb, tasteful bungalows, all with hot water, in lovely gardens with a swimming pool surrounded by rice fields with excellent views. Accessed from Temega; about 1500m south of Tirtagangga look out for the sign opposite the market. There's also a café with a small menu of snacks and meals, open to non-residents. ❻

Good Karma ⓣ0363/22445. Tiled, clean, simple rooms set in a small garden in the paddy-fields. Take the track on the left of the main road above *Good Karma* restaurant that follows the water-channel, then take the first path to the left. ❸

Kusumajaya Inn ⓣ0363/21250. About 300m north of the centre of Tirtagangga, on a hill; you'll see the bungalows perched high on the hill if you approach from the south. All have verandahs that make the most of the splendid views south across the fields. ❸

Puri Prima ⓣ0363/21316. About 500m north of the *Kusumajaya Inn*, with quite basic rooms offering great views of Gunung Lempuyang. The bigger, newer ones have huge picture windows. ❸–❹

Puri Sawah ⓣ0363/21847. Just 100m beyond the Water Palace, on a track heading left from a sharp turn in the main road. There are four well-furnished rooms with verandahs in a small, peaceful garden. More expensive ones have hot water and there's a family room sleeping 4 to 6. ❸–❺

Rijasa ⓣ0363/21873. Across the main road from the track leading to the Water Palace, this is a good-value, centrally located place with a neat row of bungalows in an attractive garden. The more expensive rooms are further from the main road and have hot water. ❸

Ababi

Heading north from Tirtagangga, the road climbs through the small village of **ABABI**, which is gradually developing a number of **accommodation** options, all of which are reached along a left-hand turn signed from the main road just over 1km from Tirtagangga. About 700m along this road, another left onto a track leads 200m to the hidden *Geria Semalung* (ⓣ & ⓕ0363/22116; ❺), with four clean, tiled, attractive bungalows in a pretty garden and stunning views. There's a small restaurant attached. Staff here can arrange a **guide** for local treks and climbs and it's about thirty minutes' walk from here along local footpaths to Tirtagangga. Another 500m further along the road is another track to the left, leading to two more accommodation options. Taking the left fork when the track divides brings you to *Pondok Batur Indah* (ⓣ0363/22342, ⓔpbaturindah@netscape.net; ❸), which offers simple rooms in a small family compound with fine views to Gunung Lempuyang. Walking down to Tirtagangga from here takes fifteen minutes or so. Taking the right fork in the track brings you to *Pondok Lembah Dukuh* (no phone; ❷), with three similarly simple rooms, cold-water bathrooms and fine views, just ten minutes' walk from Tirtagangga. Staff can arrange trekking both locally or further afield to Gunung Agung (Rp400,000 for two people including transport).

Eating

Tirtagangga caters primarily for passing tourists; the **warung** on the track to the palace offer the usual rice and noodle options. The **restaurants** at the *Kusumajaya* and the *Prima Bamboo* have good views and serve similar inexpensive Indo-Chinese dishes. The *Rice Terrace Coffee Shop* attached to *Puri Sawah* is one of the quietest spots in the village and has really excellent food. Above the car park, the *Good Karma* restaurant offers comfortable seating, a relaxed atmosphere and a cheap tourist menu, while across the main road *Genta Bali Warung* is also worth a try. After a twenty-minute walk from the main part of the village through the local paddy fields, the restaurant at *Cabé Bali* offers a small menu of moderately priced snacks, main courses and desserts in a pretty garden in a totally rural setting.

Pura Lempuyang Luhur

From Ababi the road continues to climb gradually to the village of **ABANG**, where a large sign points the way east to the important temple of **Pura Lempuyang Luhur**, on the upper slopes of Gunung Lempuyang, 8km off the main road and impressively visible, gleaming white on the hillside against the verdant greens of the surrounding forest. Festival days are the busiest time to visit, when the 1700 steps up to the temple swarm with worshippers, and extra public bemos run almost all the way to the temple. On other days, bemos only run from Abang to **NGIS TISTA**, about 2km of the way. However, in return for the difficulties of getting here, you'll be rewarded with one of the most staggering **views** in Bali. It's a two-hour climb up the staircase through the forest to the temple, which is believed to be the dwelling place of the god Genijaya (Victorious Fire) and has recently been renovated – but it's the view of Gunung Agung, perfectly framed in the *candi bentar*, that makes it all worthwhile. From the temple, a 90-minute climb up another staircase brings you to the **summit** of Gunung Lempuyang, where there's another small temple and even more spectacular views.

The Amlapura–Rendang road

From Amlapura, a **picturesque road** heads about 32km west through Sibetan and Muncan, joining the main Klungkung–Penelokan road 14km north of Klungkung at Rendang. Public **bemos** ply the Amlapura–Rendang route, but they're not very frequent, and without **private transport** the highlights of this area – Pura Pasar Agung above Selat and the rice paddies around Iseh and Sidemen – are very difficult to get to.

Around 18km west of Amlapura, the small village of **SELAT** has accommodation in pleasant, tiled, well-furnished rooms set in a nice garden at *Pondok Wisata Puri Agung* (Ⓣ0366/23037; ❹–❺), on the east side of the village just after the post office. They also offer rice-field **trekking** (Rp75,000 per person for 2hr 30min) and **climbing** up Gunung Agung (Rp150,000 per person, minimum two people, not including transport). Selat also marks the turn-off to **Pura Pasar Agung** (Temple of Agung Market). The road to the temple climbs steeply 10km through bamboo stands and a few salak and acacia forests. From the car park, five hundred concrete steps lead up to the temple. Rising in three terraces to the inner courtyard, it's an impressive and dramatic place, perched at about 1200m on the slopes of Gunung Agung, and is the starting-point for one of the routes up the mountain (see p.599). Even if you're not climbing Agung, this is a lovely spot with fabulous views.

From **Duda**, just east of Selat, a beautiful route leaves the Amlapura–Rendang road, heading south through Iseh and Sidemen to Klungkung. The views of the rice fields along this road are among the most lovely in Bali, rising into terraces on the hills behind. Artists Walter Spies and Theo Meier both lived in **ISEH** for some time, and Anna Mathews wrote her wonderfully evocative *Night of Purnama* about her life in the village before and during the 1963 eruption of Gunung Agung. A couple of kilometres south, at **SIDEMEN**, there are plenty of tracks through the fields for strolls: the village is an attractive base to experience a Bali that seems a million miles away from the bustle of the south. You can watch *endek*-weaving on foot looms at the Pelangi workshop, and, in the middle of the village, a signed turning leads to **accommodation** out in the rice fields. After a few hundred metres the road forks. A short distance along the right-hand turn is *Pondok Wisata Lihat Sawah* (Ⓣ0366/24183; ❺), clean, tiled bungalows with fine rice-field views. Several kilometres further along this road is *Sacred Mountain Sanctuary* (Ⓣ0366/24330, Ⓕ23456, Ⓦwww.sacredmountainbali.com; ❼–❽), a top-quality place with several standards of accommodation in well-designed wood, bamboo and thatch bungalows in lush gardens with a huge swimming pool. The left fork in the road from Sidemen brings you after 1500m to the *Nirarta Centre for Living Awareness* (Ⓣ0366/24122, Ⓕ21444, Ⓦwww.awareness-bali.com; ❺–❻); visit the website to read more about "The Way of Unfolding", the philosophical and spiritual base of the centre. The attached **restaurant** is semi-vegetarian (serving chicken and fish).

Amed

The stretch of coast in the **far east of Bali** from Culik to Aas has acquired the name of "**Amed**" in traveller-speak, although Amed is just one small village in a wonderful area offering peaceful bays, calm and clear waters, stunning coastal views and attractive inland scenery. The area is developing fast but it's an ideal spot for a quiet few days (or more). An increasing number of accommodation options cater for all tastes and budgets; all rent out snorkelling gear and are able to arrange dive trips.

Don't expect a post office out here and, although there are several moneychangers, rates are terrible so bring plenty of cash. At the time of writing there are still very few phones, although lines are currently being erected. You'll notice that much of the accommodation has the same fax number: they all use an agency in Amlapura, so be sure to write the name of the hotel you're communicating with very prominently and don't expect a speedy response.

The coastal route from **CULIK**, on the Singaraja road 10km northeast of Tirtagangga, around to Amlapura is only 42km, but if you do decide to do it all, allow yourself the best part of a day to negotiate the road and enjoy the scenery. Transport is slim. From Culik, **bemos** ply via Amed to Aas in the morning. After that you'll need to charter one or use an ojek. Staff at your accommodation will help arrange transport for your return. For the part of the coastline from Aas south to Seraya you'll need your own vehicle. It's a lovely trip but, at the time of writing, the road was appalling and only passable by skilled motorcyclists with plenty of time and patience. This situation may change, so check before setting off from either direction.

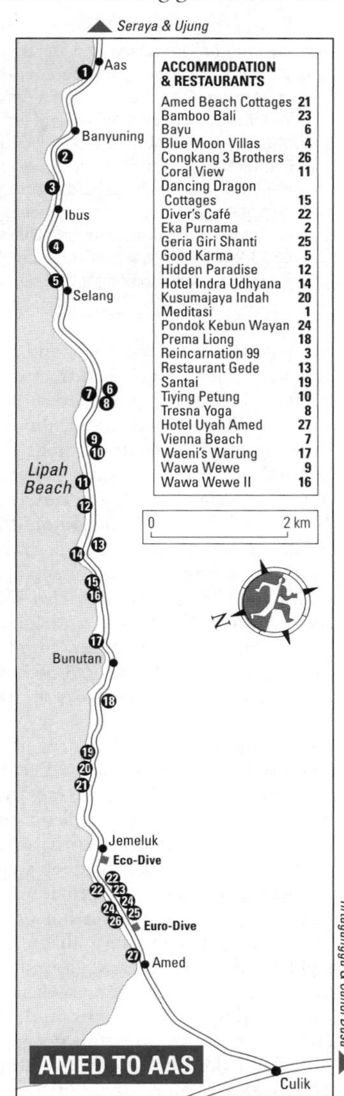

Amed and Jemeluk

From Culik, it's 3km east to the picturesque, sleepy fishing village of **AMED**. The following **accommodation** and **eating** options are described in order, as you come across them heading east. Just beyond Amed village, *Hotel Uyah Amed* (ⓣ0363/23462, ⓕ0361/285416, ⓦwww.naturebali.com/AMED_ECO_HOTEL_BALI.htm) has well-furnished bungalows with air conditioning and solar-powered hot water

Diving at Amed and Jemeluk

The main **diving area** is around the rocky headland to the east of the parking area at Jemeluk: a massive sloping terrace of coral, both hard and soft, leads to a wall dropping to a depth of more than 40m. The density of fish on the wall is extremely high – gorgonians, fans, basket sponges and table coral are especially good, sharks, wrasses and parrotfish have been spotted in the outer parts, and the current is generally slow.

There are several **dive operators** along this stretch. About 2km beyond Amed, just above the road, English and Dutch-speaking **Euro-Dive** (no phone, ⓕ0363/22958, ⓦwww.eurodivebali.com) offers all PADI courses up to Divemaster level, an introductory dive for new divers and a pool for the early stages of training. Dives for experienced divers are also available. Further east, **Stingray Dive** (ⓣ086812/163639) is at the *Divers Café* just before Jemeluk and they also have an office in Candi Dasa (see p.610). East again, **Eco-Dive** in Jemeluk (ⓣ0363/23482, ⓦwww.ecodivebali.com) is well-established in the area and arranges local dives and snorkelling trips as well as diving at Candi Dasa and Menjangan. They teach PADI Open Water courses and offer instruction in English, French, Dutch and German. **Mega Dive** (ⓣ0361/754165, ⓕ0363/21911 ⓦwww.megadive.com), at *Amed Beach Cottages* in Jemeluk, offers introductory dives, dives for certified divers and PADI courses.

nestling between the road and the beach clustered around the pool. The attached *Café Garam* is an attractive *bale* with a large menu of moderately priced Western and Indonesian food.

About 2km beyond Amed, almost next door to Euro-Dive, *Geria Giri Shanti* (no phone; ❸) has large, tiled, good-value bungalows just above the road. Almost opposite, *Congkang 3 Brothers* (ⓣ0363/23472; ❹) offers clean, tiled bungalows right beside the beach facing seawards in a lush, well-kept garden. Next door, *Pondok Kebun Wayan* (ⓣ0363/23473; ❸–❺) has an inexpensive-to-moderate beachside restaurant and sunbathing area, plus good-quality accommodation across the road and ranged up the hillside with a small pool. Some 300m further east, *Bamboo Bali* (ⓣ0363/23478; ❸) is a good budget choice seconds from the beach, with clean, tiled, fan-cooled bungalows in a pretty garden on the hillside. A few hundred metres further on, just before the village of Jemeluk, *Diver's Café* (ⓣ0363/23479; ❸) has a few bungalows, some with hot water, in a garden across the road from the beach and is very convenient for divers and snorkellers.

A couple of hundred metres further brings you to **JEMELUK**, the diving focus of the area. Just behind Eco-Dive's restaurant are very basic bamboo and thatch rooms (ⓣ0363/23482; ❷) with attached bathroom. About 1km further on, over an imposing headland and into the next bay, *Amed Beach Cottages* (ⓣ0363/23503; ❸–❺) are situated in a pretty garden between the road and the beach. There's a small but deep swimming pool just by the beach. Just beyond is a **wartel** (7am–10pm) providing expensive satellite communication with the outside world. Slightly further east, *Kusumajaya Indah* (ⓣ0363/23488; ❺) has attractive bungalows in a shady garden that slopes down to their restaurant right by the beach. Next door, the delightful *Santai* (previously *Gubuk Kita*; ⓣ & ⓕ0363/23487, ⓦwww.santaibali.com; ❻–❼) remains the **best hotel** in the area despite increased competition. Accommodation is in lovely wooden and thatch bungalows with gorgeous decor; all have air conditioning and hot water and the pool is terrific. A large restaurant serves excellent, moderately priced food. Some 700m further around the coast *Prema Liong* (no phone, ⓕ0363/23489, ⓦwww.bali-amed.com; ❺) comprises two-storey bungalows topped by thatch up on the hillside away from the road, with stunning views, fans and cold-water bathrooms.

Bunutan and Lipah Beach

The next bay to the east is the location of the small, peaceful village of **BUNUTAN**, about 8km from Culik. On the climb up out of the village look out for tiny *Waeni's Warung* (Ⓣ0363/23515; ❸) on the cliff side of the road. Their simple bungalows have excellent views west to Gunung Agung, Gunung Batur and beyond. Down the other side of the headland, about 500m further on, *Wawa Wewe II* (Ⓣ0363/23522, Ⓕ0363/22074, Ⓔwawawewe@hotmail.com; ❹–❺) are bungalows set down from the road overlooking the coast, plus a couple of large family villas each with two bedrooms. Next door, *Dancing Dragon Cottages* (Ⓣ & Ⓕ0363/23521, Ⓦwww.dancingdragoncottages.com; ❼) is designed using Balinese and feng shui principles; it has a pretty swimming pool. About 1km beyond, perched on a headland, is the top-quality *Hotel Indra Udhyana* (Ⓣ0361/241107, Ⓕ234907, Ⓦwww.indo.com/hotels/indra_udhyana; ❽), which boasts superb rooms and a great pool set in fine grounds stretching down to the coast. Published prices start at US$140. Just around the bend as the road begins to descend, the **restaurant** *Gede* is on the hill above the road. Their ambition must be admired – they have more than 250 items on the menu – and the cheap to moderately priced food is well-cooked, the place is attractively furnished and it gets a good breeze.

LIPAH BEACH is the most developed beach in the area (although still very peaceful), located around 10km from Culik. There's **accommodation** at *Hidden Paradise* (Ⓣ0363/23514, Ⓕ0363/22958, Ⓦwww.hiddenparadise-bali.com; ❻) and, slightly beyond this, *Coral View* (same contact details; ❻). Both offer large bungalows in lush gardens with pools beside the beach. A couple of **restaurants** are located nearby both with attached accommodation: *Tiying Petung* (Ⓣ0363/23508; ❸) has simple tiled rooms with attached bathroom, while next door *Wawa Wewe* (Ⓣ0363/23506, Ⓕ0363/22074, Ⓔwawawewe@hotmail.com; ❸) has slightly better verandahs in front of the rooms. Both have similar inexpensive to moderately priced menus offering the usual Indonesian and Western travellers' choices. There's reasonable **snorkelling** just off the coast here and, for **divers**, Lipah Bay is the site of the wreck of a small freighter at 6–12m depth, which is now covered with coral, gorgonians and sponges. The reef nearby is also rich and diverse.

Into the next bay, accommodation at *Vienna Beach* (Ⓣ0363/23494, Ⓕ0363/21883, Ⓦwww.bali-amed.com; ❺–❻) is ranged along the seafront in a small compound. The room price includes an evening meal. Across the road, away from the beach, *Tresna Yoga* (no phone; ❹) is perched high on the hillside; its bungalows are attractive and tiled with attached cold-water bathrooms. Next door *Bayu* (Ⓣ0363/23595, Ⓕ0363/21044; ❹) offers similar accommodation. The beach is a short walk across the road from both these places.

Selang and Ibus

Another 1500m past the headland is the bay at **SELANG**, almost 12km from Culik, where the long-standing, ever-popular *Good Karma* (no phone; ❹–❺) is located right on the beach. Various standards of accommodation are on offer, all set in a gorgeous garden. There are plans to upgrade the accommodation with hot water and air-con. About 500m further on are *Blue Moon Villas* (Ⓣ0812/362 2597, Ⓕ0363/21044, Ⓦwww.bluemoonvilla.com; ❻–❼), up on the headland as you climb out of Selang bay. They have top-quality bungalows, giving superb views. The attached café has an extensive menu of moderately priced food and drinks and there's a wonderfully relaxed atmosphere. Some 700m further, in the village of **IBUS**, *Reincarnation 99* (no phone; ❹–❺) has five good-quality bungalows just above the coast. The restaurant is up high near the road with views down onto the coast. Just 300m further along, on the way down into Banyuning, the popular *Eka Purnama* (no phone; Ⓕ0363/21044, Ⓔgeocowan@yahoo.com; ❺) has bungalows perched on the hillside above the road. There's a Japanese wreck not far off the coast here, which is visible to snorkellers. From here the road descends to the long bay of **Banyuning** where the beach is lined with colourful *jukung* and the inland hills slope steeply and impressively upwards.

Aas and beyond

The village of **AAS** is 2km beyond *Eka Purnama*, almost 15km from Culik. *Meditasi* (no phone, Ⓕ0363/22166; ❹–❺) is situated just behind a sandy beach here, offering three bamboo bungalows with entire walls that slide open to reveal a fine seaward view for the sunrise or an inland view towards Gunung Seraya. The attached *Kick Back Café* can arrange local treks, including climbing Gunung Seraya.

Around the coast from Aas is dry, barren country east of the mountains where the local farmers have a tough time scratching a living from the soil. The road leaves the coast at **KUSAMBI**, marked by a massive beacon. This is the most easterly point on Bali: on clear days you'll be able to see Lombok, 35km across the strait. Further on, the small market town of **SERAYA** features a grand temple, dominated by the looming Gunung Seraya. At **UJUNG**, 5km south of Amlapura, you'll spot a jumble of ruins down in a dip on the right – the third of the water palaces built by the last rajah of Karangasem, Anak Agung Anglurah, in 1921.

Tulamben

Heading north from Culik, you move into an entirely different landscape: from lush and green, the land becomes parched and dry. Rice fields give way to scrub and cactus and the landscape is comprised of boulder-strewn folds and channels, relics of the lava flow from the 1963 eruption of Gunung Agung (see p.599). The small, rather unattractive village of **TULAMBEN**, about 10km northwest of Culik, has little to draw you here unless you are into **diving** or **snorkelling**. This is the site of the most famous and most popular dive in Bali, the **Liberty wreck**, which sank during World War II and now attracts thousands of visitors every year. Up to a hundred divers a day visit the site, so it's worth avoiding the rush hours (11.30am–4pm). Night dives here are especially exciting.

Tulamben is easily accessible from either Singaraja or Amlapura by public minibus or bus. There's a Perama office (daily 8am–10pm) in the *Ganda Mayu* hotel (see Travel Details p.663 for more). Several **restaurants** offer the usual range of rice, noodles and pasta, and the area has seen a recent building boom, with accommodation options on the increase.

Accommodation

Bali Coral Bungalows Ⓣ & Ⓕ0363/22909. On the track leading to *Tauch Terminal Resort*. Set in a small garden, rooms have fan and cold-water bathrooms. ❹–❺

Di Riboet No phone. Basic but clean rooms just above the road just opposite *Matahari Tulamben Resort*. Fine if you're not worried about frills or being near the beach. ❷

Ganda Mayu Ⓣ0363/22912. A clean place (with the Perama office attached) offering tiled bungalows with fans and cold-water bathrooms just above the main road: a reasonable budget choice. ❷

Diving and snorkelling at Tulamben

Most divers come to Tulamben on day-trips from elsewhere. However, there are **dive operations** attached to most of the accommodation places: check out *Tauch Terminal Resort*, *Mimpi Resort* and *Dive Paradise Tulamben* at *Paradise Palm Beach Bungalows* as well as the places along the main road, which all arrange local dives for certified divers and run courses. Expect to pay around $50 for two dives at Tulamben, $55 for two dives at Amed or Jemeluk and $340–400 for a PADI Open Water course. **Snorkelling** gear is also available for rent. Operators arrange dives to other parts of Bali such as Menjangan (see p.660), Gili Tepekong and Gili Mimpang and Nusa Penida (see p.605), while *Tauch Terminal* offers all-in **dive safaris** incorporating several dive destinations in Bali and Lombok (from $300 for 3 days and 2 nights on Gili Air) and **liveaboard safaris** to further-flung locations from $1500 per person. They also offer dive and accommodation packages, with unlimited diving in Tulamben including equipment rental.

The **Liberty wreck** is encrusted with soft **coral**, gorgonians and hydrozoans plus a few hard corals, providing a wonderful habitat for around three hundred species of reef fish that live on the wreck and over a hundred species which visit from deeper water. Parts of the stern are only about 2m below the surface, making this a good snorkelling site too. The **Tulamben Drop-off**, sometimes called "The Wall", off the eastern end of the beach, comprises several underwater fingers of volcanic rock, which are home to an enormous variety of fish, including unusual species such as comets. Many divers rate this area at least as highly as the wreck itself. **Batu Kelebit** lies further east again and nurtures a somewhat different but equally rewarding sea-life; it's possibly the best local site for the bigger creatures such as sharks, barracuda, mantas, molas and tuna. Back in the bay, the site known as **The River** or **The Slope** is actually a bowl lined with sand and rocks and is possibly the best place in the whole of Bali to see rare, although perhaps not large or dramatic, species.

Matahari Tulamben Resort Ⓣ0363/22907, Ⓕ22908. On a track that runs from *Café Tulamben* to the coast at the eastern end of the village. There are two standards of rooms: clean, tiled fan rooms with cold-water bathroms or well-furnished cottages with air-con and hot water. ④–⑥

Paradise Palm Beach Bungalows Ⓣ0363/22910, Ⓕ22917. Long-established bungalows with several standards of accommodation in the cosy compound and a small restaurant overlooking the sea. ③–⑤

Puri Madha Ⓣ0363/22921. The most westerly place, about 300m beyond the village and the beach, very near the *Liberty* wreck. Rooms are simple and this is a good place from which to watch the daily diving activity. There's a pleasant beachside restaurant. ③

Tauch Terminal Resort Ⓣ0363/22911, or contact in Kuta Ⓣ0361/730200, Ⓕ0361/730201, Ⓦwww.tauch-terminal.com. Huge, gleaming establishment that fronts a long section of the coast. Features large landscaped gardens, an attractive little pool and a very busy dive centre. The more expensive rooms are the best in the area. ⑤–⑦

North Bali and the central volcanoes

Heading into **north Bali** from the crowded southern plains and foothills, you enter another world, with a slower pace, cooler climate and hugely varied countryside. The centre of the island is occupied by the awesome volcanic masses of the **Batur** and **Bedugul** areas, where dramatic mountain ranges shelter crater lakes and small, peaceful villages line their shores. With few peaks rising above 2000m, the mountains don't rival Gunung Agung in stature, but their accessibility and beauty are unbeatable. Most people come to the Batur area either on a day-trip to gaze at the crater panorama, or to stay down by the lake and trek up **Gunung Batur**, the most climbed peak in Bali. The Bedugul area offers more lakes, mountains and forests, but on a smaller scale, and is regularly besieged by tour groups swarming to the stunning lakeside temple of **Pura Ulun Danu**.

The dry northern coast is harsh and rugged, the mountains dropping steeply to the coastal plain. Many visitors head straight for the resort of **Lovina** which, despite its black sand, has grown rapidly so that it's now the largest resort outside the Kuta–Legian–Seminyak conurbation – although, it retains a laid-back air. A few kilometres east, **Singaraja** is a bustling, modern city and, being a transport hub, is impossible to avoid. The exuberant and distinctive temple carvings and sculptures of the north can be enjoyed in the best-known temples of the area – **Kubutambahan**, **Jagaraga** and **Sangsit** while further east again, a small resort has grown up around the cold springs of **Air Sanih**.

With good **bus** links from Java, Denpasar and Amlapura and **bemo** connections within the area, most of the sights are fairly easy to get to on public transport, although with your own vehicle you'll be able to explore the maze of quiet inland roads and reach some of the less popular places such as Danau Tamblingan and Munduk.

Gunung Batur and Danau Batur

The **Batur** area was formed thirty thousand years ago by the eruption of a gigantic volcano. Confusingly, the entire area is sometimes referred to as **Kintamani**, although this is the name of just one of several villages dotted along the rim of the ancient crater. Another group of villages is situated around **Danau Batur** at the bottom of the crater: **Toya Bungkah** is the start of the main route up Gunung Batur and the chief accommodation centre, although **Kedisan** offers a couple of options, and is the access point for boat trips across the lake to the Bali Aga village of **Trunyan**. Around on the southern shore of the lake, **Buahan** is the quietest spot of all. The highest points on the rim are **Gunung Abang** (2153m) on the eastern side, the third highest mountain in Bali, and **Gunung Penulisan** (1745m) on the northwest corner, with Pura Puncak Penulisan perched on its summit. Rising from the floor of the main crater, **Gunung Batur** (1717m) is an active volcano with four craters of its own.

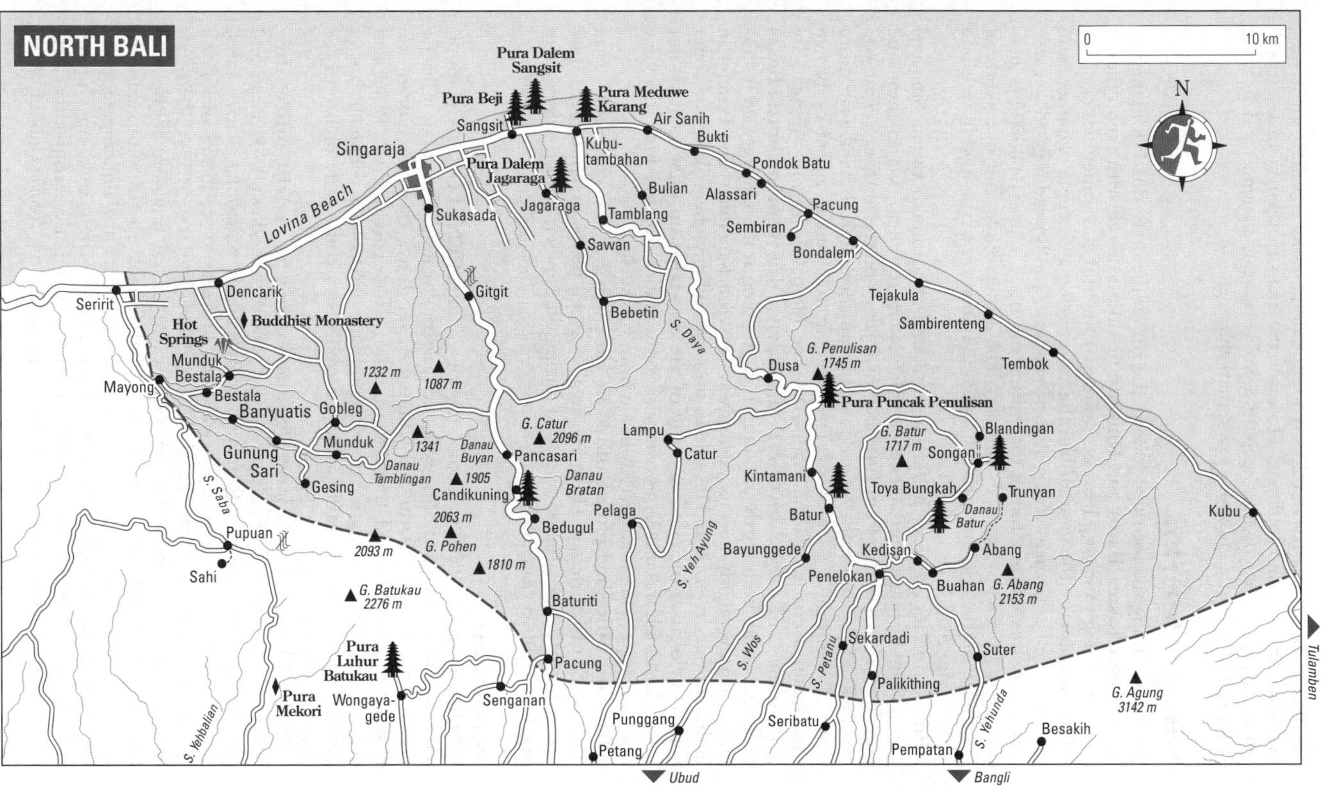
NORTH BALI
0
10 km
N
Pura Dalem Sangsit
Pura Beji
Pura Meduwe Karang
Sangsit
Air Sanih
Bukti
Singaraja
Kubu-tambahan
Pura Dalem Jagaraga
Pondok Batu
Alassari
Bulian
Lovina Beach
Jagaraga
Pacung
Sukasada
Tamblang
Sembiran
Sawan
Bondalem
Gilimanuk
Dencarik
Gitgit
Tejakula
Seririt
Buddhist Monastery
Bebetin
Hot Springs
S. Daya
Sambirenteng
Munduk Bestala
G. Penulisan 1745 m
Mayong
Bestala
1232 m
1087 m
Dusa
Tembok
Banyuatis
Gobleg
Pura Puncak Penulisan
G. Catur 2096 m
Lampu
G. Batur 1717 m
Blandingan
Munduk
1341
Gunung Sari
Danau Buyan
Pancasari
Catur
Songan
Danau Tamblingan
Kintamani
Gesing
1905
Danau Bratan
Toya Bungkah
Trunyan
Candikuning
S. Saba
2063 m
Pelaga
Batur
Danau Batur
Kubu
Pupuan
Bedugul
2093 m
G. Pohen
S. Yeh Ayung
Bayunggede
Kedisan
Abang
Sahi
1810 m
Penelokan
Buahan
G. Abang 2153 m
G. Batukau 2276 m
Baturiti
S. Wos
Sekardadi
Suter
Tulamben
Pura Luhur Batukau
Pacung
S. Petanu
Pura Mekori
Wongaya-gede
Senganan
Palikithing
G. Agung 3142 m
S. Yehbalian
Punggang
Seribatu
S. Yehunda
Besakih
Petang
Pempatan
Ubud
Bangli

Sadly, the Batur area has developed a reputation among travellers for hassles, over-charging and unfriendliness. However, the dramatic scenery makes it well worth taking a deep breath, keeping a hold on your patience and heading upwards for at least a glimpse of its remarkable scenery.

The crater rim

Spread out along the road that follows the rim of the crater for 11km, the villages of **Penelokan**, **Batur** and **Kintamani** almost merge with each other. If you're planning to stay up here, be aware that the mist and sometimes rain that roll in and obscure the view in late afternoon bring a creeping dampness, and the nights are extremely chilly; at the very least, you'll need a good sweater. There's an **admission charge** for visiting the crater area – Rp4000 per person (Rp1000 for a car or motorbike). The ticket offices are just south of Penelokan on the road from Bangli and at the junction of the road from Ubud and the rim road.

Buses run about every half-hour until mid-afternoon between Singaraja (Penarukan terminal) and Denpasar (Batubulan terminal), via Gianyar and Bangli. If you're coming from Tulamben or Tejakula on the northeast coast, you can pick up the bus from Singaraja at the junction at Kubutambahan, from where Kintamani is 40km away. The route from Ubud is served by brown (Kintamani) **bemos**, and the roads via Suter, Tampaksiring and Payangan are good-quality and easy to drive on. Perama operate daily **tourist shuttle buses** to the area from both north and south Bali, stopping at the *Gunung Sari* restaurant – inconveniently positioned midway between Kintamani and Penelokan (although the driver should be able to drop you off anywhere along the crater rim). Penelokan is included in many of the **day-trips** on offer at the major resorts, although this usually encompasses only a quick stop to admire the view from the crater rim amid serious hassle from hawkers.

The **post office** and **phone office** are close together just off the main road 2km north of Penelokan. There are usually several places to **change money** along the road, but rates are poor and during times when tourist numbers are low they tend to cease trading.

Penelokan

Literally meaning "Place to Look", the views from **PENELOKAN** (1450m) are excellent, a panorama of unexpected scale and majesty. Danau Batur lies far below, while Gunung Batur and Gunung Abang tower on either side of the lake. Over four thousand tourists are estimated to pass through Penelokan every day in high season, attracting an entourage of **hawkers** selling all sorts of goods. The only way to really avoid the circus is to come early or late in the day, or stay overnight.

Yayasan Bintang Danu, a local organization, runs the **tourist office** (daily 9am–3pm; ⓣ0366/51730), almost opposite the turning down to Kedisan, and has noticeboards giving information about accommodation, charter rates, routes up the volcano and leaflets and maps on what to see in the area. For a **place to stay**, go for the *Lakeview Hotel* (ⓣ0366/51394, ⓕ51464, ⓦwww.indo.com/hotels/lakeview; ❺), located at the junction of the road from the south and the crater rim: it has comfortable rooms with verandahs perched right on the crater's rim (they're constructing a new building, so prices may rise in the future). They also arrange early-morning treks up Gunung Batur to see the sunrise. The crater rim is packed with plush **restaurants** catering for the daytime crowd. For something cheaper try *Ramana*, about 300m

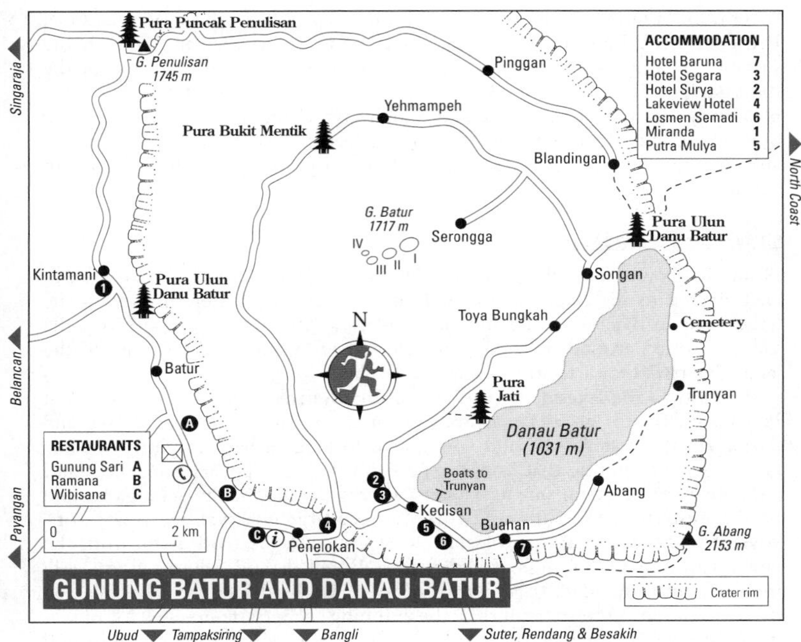

towards Kintamani from Penelokan, which is right on the crater's rim with glorious views. Closer to Penelokan, on the opposite side of the road, *Wibisana* is also good value.

Pura Ulun Danu Batur

About 4km north of Penelokan, **Pura Ulun Danu Batur** is the second most important temple on the island after the Besakih complex. It's a fascinating place to visit at any time as there are usually pilgrims making offerings or praying here; the mist that frequently shrouds the area adds to the atmosphere, with grand structures looming out of the cloud. The eleven-day *odalan* festival is particularly spectacular and attended by people from all over the island. The temple is overwhelming for most visitors, simply because of the sheer number of shrines. Most significant is the **eleven-roofed meru** in the inner courtyard, dedicated both to Dewi Danu, the goddess of the lake, and to the god of Gunung Agung.

Kintamani and around

Consisting almost entirely of concrete buildings with rusty corrugated iron roofs, **KINTAMANI**, 2km north of Pura Ulun Danu, isn't particularly appealing, and is too far north along the rim of the crater for the best views of Danau Batur. It's famous for its breed of furry dogs, and the huge outdoor **market** held every three days. Kintamani has the only budget **accommodation** on the rim – *Miranda* (☎0366/52022; ❷), about 100m north of the market on the left; all bemos and pick-ups plying between Kintamani and Penelokan pass the door. The owner, Made Senter, also works as a **tour guide** up Gunung Batur, Gunung Abang and Gunung Agung (see p.599).

About 5km north on the road towards Singaraja, in the village of Sukawana, **Pura Puncak Penulisan**, also known as Pura Tegeh Koripan, built on the summit of Gunung Penulisan, is the highest temple on Bali and one of the most ancient. It's a climb of 333 concrete steps from the road to the top temple, **Pura Panarajon**, dedicated to Sanghyang Grinatha, a manifestation of Siwa, and god of the mountains. On this top terrace, *bale* shelter various shrines and an array of ancient *lingga* and worn statues from the eleventh to thirteenth centuries.

Danau Batur

Home to Dewi Danu, the goddess of the crater lake, **Danau Batur** is especially sacred to the Balinese. Situated 500m below the crater rim, this is the largest lake in Bali, 8km long and 3km wide, and one of the most glorious: the villages dotted around its shores are referred to as *bintang danu* (stars of the lake). See p.629 for a **map** of the area.

The road to the lakeside, served by **public bemos**, leaves the crater rim at Penelokan. Bemos go as far as Songan on the western side of the lake and Abang on the eastern side and you'll have to bargain hard to get reasonable fares. It's worth noting that however peaceful the lake appears from the crater rim, once you're down on the western shores, peace is sadly lacking. Around on the western side of Gunung Batur there is a large quarry; huge, **noisy** convoys of trucks ferrying the volcanic stone *paras* use the road down from the crater rim and on through Kedisan, Toya Bungkah and Songan from early morning until nightfall. In addition to noise, the hassles of the lake area can make a visit far more stressful than the stunning scenery deserves. A lot of visitors have negative experiences and, in some cases, suffer **intimidation** and extortion. Most people stay the minimum amount of time needed to complete their trek. If you **arrive by car**, there's huge pressure on you to pay someone to "look after" your vehicle while you climb – sometimes followed up by threats of damage to the car if you decline. The best advice is to leave vehicles in the care of staff at a hotel you've stayed at or restaurant where you've eaten.

Kedisan

At the bottom of the steep descent, 3km from Penelokan, the road splits in the southernmost lakeside village of **KEDISAN**: the right fork leads to the jetty for boats to Trunyan and continues on to the villages of Buahan and Abang; the left fork leads to Toya Bungkah and Songan. In Kedisan there are a couple of **losmen**. A few hundred metres from the junction, towards Toya Bungkah, *Hotel Segara* (Ⓣ0366/51136, Ⓕ51212; ❸) has a variety of accommodation; phone in advance to check on their offer of a half-price pick-up from tourist centres. Next door, *Hotel Surya* (Ⓣ0366/51378; ❸) also has a variety of rooms, many with balconies offering lovely views; again, check on their offer of a free or discounted pick-up service. Turning right at the bottom of the road from Penelokan brings you to the quietest part of the lake; some 300m from the junction is *Putra Mulya* (Ⓣ0366/51754; ❷) and 200m further on is the small *Losmen Semadi* (Ⓣ0366/51819; ❷), both with simple rooms.

Toya Bungkah and around

TOYA BUNGKAH, 8km from Penelokan, is the accommodation centre of the lakeside area and the main starting-point for climbs up Gunung Batur. The stylish **hot springs** Tirta Sanjiwani (daily 8am–5pm) look extremely good, with a cold-water swimming pool and smaller hot-water pools ($5 for both) and private jacuzzis ($20), but the prices mean they've moved beyond the reach

Climbing Gunung Batur

With a choice of four main craters and a variety of access points, there are several ways to approach **climbing Gunung Batur**. The most common **route** up to Batur I, the largest and highest crater, for those without their own transport – and who are reasonably fit – is from either Toya Bungkah or Pura Jati, 4km to the south. From Toya Bungkah, numerous paths head up through the forest (one starts just south of the car park near *Arlina's*); after about an hour you'll come out onto the bare slope of the mountain, from where you can follow the paths that head up to the tiny warung perched way up on the crater rim. Allow two to three hours to get to the top from Toya Bungkah or Pura Jati, and about half that time to get back down. A **medium-length trek** involves climbing to Batur I, walking around the rim and then descending by another route. The **long-trek** option (about 8hr in total) involves climbing up to Batur I, descending to the rim of crater II and then to the rim of crater III. From here, the descent is to Toya Bungkah or Yehmampeh.

Practicalities

Climbing Batur is best done in the **dry season** (April–Oct). In **daylight**, you don't need a guide to find the way if you're just intending to climb up to Batur I from Toya Bungkah or Pura Jati. For the longer treks or the less well-trodden paths, you do need a guide: routes are trickier and harder to find – and it's important to stay away from the most active parts of the volcano. Most climb **in the dark** to reach the top for dawn: the view over the lake as the sun rises behind Gunung Abang and Gunung Rinjani on Lombok is definitely worth the effort. You'll need to leave early (by 4–5am), and a guide is a very good idea as it's easy to get lost in the forest in the dark. Anyone who wants to climb Batur is under intense pressure to engage a local guide. These are now organized into the **Association of Mount Batur Trekking Guides** (Ⓣ0366/52362, Ⓔvolcanotrekk@hotmail.com), known locally as "the Organization", which has one office in Toya Bungkah and another on the road nearby at Pura Jati. The price for the short climb up Batur to see the sunrise is fixed at a rather steep Rp300,000 per guide for a maximum of four people, with higher prices for the longer climbs. Despite recent assurances that prices have been cut by government order, nothing seems to have changed on the ground.

Trekking and tour agencies

If you prefer not to deal directly with the Association of Mount Batur Trekking Guides, or if you just want to check out the details you've had from them, you can get **information** about the Gunung Batur area and **organized trekking services** from three companies in Toya Bungkah: Roijaya Wisata (Ⓣ0366/51249, Ⓕ51250, Ⓦwww.balitrekking.com), which has an office at *Lakeside Cottages* and another at the start of Toya Bungkah; Bali Sunrise 2001, at the *Volcano Breeze Café* (Ⓣ0366/51824, Ⓦwww.balisunrise2001.com); and Arlina's (Ⓣ0366/51165). They use guides from the Association of Mount Batur Trekking Guides, but are more used to working with tourists (which can sometimes make the whole process easier) – although you do end up paying more than if you went through the Association. Bali Sunrise 2001 can also arrange pick-ups for Batur treks in Nusa Dua, Kuta, Sanur, Ubud, Candi Dasa or Lovina but transport costs are high: you'll pay $45–70 for the sunrise trek, depending on where you start.

In addition, all can arrange various treks in the area; prices vary, so it pays to shop around. There are climbs up **Gunung Abang** ($50 per person) and **Agung** ($75–95 per person). Arlina's has **canoes** for rental and they rent out **fishing** gear. Roijaya Wisata and Bali Sunrise 2001 offer treks in the **Bedugul** area (May–Nov; $85 per person including one night's accommodation), and Roijaya Wisata arranges **jungle trekking** (May–Nov; one day $100 per person, two days $200). Enquire at any of the trekking agencies about **shuttle bus** tickets and charter transport.

of many of the backpackers who are the mainstay of the local economy. You can **change money** and travellers' cheques at several places in the village, although rates aren't great. There's a 24-hour **wartel** at the start of Toya Bungkah, and Joy **internet** café is nearby.

There are plenty of **accommodation** options lining the road in Toya Bungkah, with a few more down by the lakeside. Given the perpetual daytime noise from the trucks try to get away from the road. Many losmen have inexpensive **restaurants** serving a good range of Western and Indo-Chinese options and freshwater fish from the lake. *Arlina's* is good-value (main courses Rp5000–15,000) and offers a wide choice and the liveliest surroundings, while the *Volcano Breeze Café* on the track down to the lake is a quiet spot.

Accommodation

Arlina's ⓣ0366/51165. A friendly, popular set-up at the southern end of town, with clean rooms, small verandahs and some rooms with hot water. ❺

Awangga No phone. A newer, quiet place on the road down to the lake with simple accommodation, all with good verandahs. ❷

Laguna ⓣ0366/51297. Simple, good-quality place set back from the road in the middle of the village. ❸

Lakeside Cottages ⓣ0366/51249, ⓕ51250. Aptly named place, with three standards of room, from large cottages with good verandahs, lake view, hot water and TV, to cheaper, cold-water rooms further from the lake. ❹–❺

Nyoman Mawar *(Under the Volcano)* ⓣ0366/51166. Located in the village, with clean, good-value rooms. Cold-water bathrooms only. ❷

Nyoman Mawar II *(Under the Volcano II)* ⓣ0366/52508. Some bungalows close to the lake with great views and some in a small garden further away; all are simple and adequate, with cold water only. ❷

Pualam ⓣ0366/52024. Quiet losmen, close to the hot springs, with clean, good-quality rooms set around a pleasant garden. ❷

Tirta Yatra No phone. A small establishment with extremely cheap, basic rooms and unenticing bathrooms. The position right down on the lakeside is excellent. ❷

Buahan and Abang

The most attractive section of road in the crater follows the eastern shore of the lake beyond Kedisan (see p.630), offering great views across the lake. A couple of hundred metres beyond the village of **BUAHAN**, 2.5km from the junction with the Penelokan road at Kedisan, *Hotel Baruna* (ⓣ0366/51221; ❷–❸) is one of the quietest places to stay near the lake. It has basic rooms plus a perfect view. From here the road edges between the lake and the cliffs, which rise up into the mass of Gunung Abang, and finally ends at the tiny village of **ABANG**, where a couple of shops sell soft drinks. From Abang, there's a lakeside footpath to Trunyan (4km).

Trunyan

The best-known Bali Aga village in Bali, inhabited by the original people of Bali who rejected the changes brought about by the Majapahit invasion in 1343 (see p.521), the village of **TRUNYAN** and its nearby cemetery at Kuban are a well-established tourist attraction. Situated in a dramatic position right beside Danau Batur with Gunung Abang rising up sheer behind, there are two main routes to the village: by boat from Kedisan or by footpath from Abang village. The **boat trip** is beautiful but chilly and takes less than an hour. Boats leave from the pier at Kedisan and complete a circuit from the pier to Trunyan village, on to the cemetery, then Toya Bungkah and back to Kedisan.

The village keeps many of the ancient **Bali Aga customs**, the most notorious being the traditional way of disposing of the dead, which involves neither burial nor cremation. Bodies are placed in open pits covered only by a cloth and a rough bamboo roof and left to decompose in the air. Trunyan's tiny

cemetery is at Kuban, just north of the village, and is accessible only by boat. All you're likely to see are a few artfully arranged bones and skulls and the covered graves. The village's main source of income is from tourists, and although the boat fee is supposed to include **donations** you'll be asked for more. While it's easy to suggest you stand firm on these demands, Trunyan can feel rather isolated and forbidding; you'd do well to make sure you have plenty of small notes to give away.

The Bedugul region

Neither as big nor as dramatic as the Batur region, the Danau Bratan area, sometimes just known as **Bedugul**, has impressive mountains, beautiful lakes, quiet walks and attractive and important temples. In many ways, the area is an Indonesian destination rather than one favoured by foreign tourists. Farmers make offerings to Dewi Danu, the goddess of the crater lake, at **Pura Ulun Danu Bratan** on the shores of **Danau Bratan**, while lowland dwellers come to the **Bali Botanical Gardens** in Candikuning on weekend picnics, and to the **Taman Rekreasi** (Leisure Park) on the shores of Danau Bratan, where a vast array of water sports are available. The entire area is frequently referred to as Bedugul or Bratan, but it's actually very spread out and it's sensible to know where you are aiming for. Danau Bratan nestles in the lee of Gunung Catur, on the main Denpasar–Mengwi–Singaraja road 53km north of Denpasar and 30km south of Singaraja. The smaller, quieter **Danau Buyan** and **Danau Tamblingan** lie about 6km northwest of Danau Bratan. All the lakes have superbly situated shoreside temples and the area is dotted with attractive villages. The main road is well served by frequent north–south bemos and buses, but having your own transport means you can enjoy the glorious roads in the region.

Candikuning and Danau Bratan

The small village of **CANDIKUNING** is situated above the southern shores of Danau Bratan. Its daily **market**, Bukit Mungsu, is small but extremely diverse and colourful; it offers a vast range of fruit, spices and plants, including orchids. A short walk south from the Bukit Mungsu market area, along a small side road by the giant corn-on-the-cob, are the **Bali Botanical Gardens** (Kebun Raya Eka Karya Bali; daily 8am–4pm; Rp2000; parking for cars Rp1000, for motorbikes Rp500; entry for cars Rp5000; motorbikes prohibited). The gardens range across the slopes of Gunung Pohon (Tree Mountain) and there are more than 650 different species of tree and over four hundred species of orchids. The gardens are also a rich area for bird-watching.

Danau Bratan

Situated at 1200m above sea level and thought to be 35m deep in places, **Danau Bratan** lies in the bottom of a once-gigantic, but now almost imperceptible, volcanic crater. Surrounded by rolling forested hills, with the bulk of Gunung Catur rising sheer behind, the lake becomes the scene of rampant water sports on holidays and at weekends. Revered by Balinese farmers as the source of freshwater springs across a wide area of the island, the lake (and its goddess) are worshipped in the immensely attractive temple of **Pura Ulun Danu Bratan** (daily 7am–5pm; Rp3300, cars Rp1000), one of the most photographed temples in Bali. Set in well-maintained grounds, the temple consists of several shrines, some spread along the shore and others dramatically situated on small islands.

The **Taman Rekreasi Bedugul** (Bedugul Leisure Park; daily 8am–5pm; Rp3300, cars Rp1500, motorbikes Rp600), on the southern shores of the lake, is signed "Bedugul" from the main road. You can indulge in waterskiing, parasailing and jet-skiing (expect to pay US$10 for 15min for these) or rent a speedboat (Rp65,000 for once round the lake) or rowing boat (Rp70,000 per hour). A vast number of private boat operators can be found around the lake, both near the Taman Rekreasi and the *Ashram Guesthouse*; with a bit of hard bargaining you should be able to get a boat for about Rp50,000 per hour.

Practicalities

There's a **wartel** (daily 8am–9.30pm) in the market and another next to the *As Siddiq* restaurant near Pura Ulun Danu Bratan. You can **change money** at the moneychangers in the car park at Pura Ulun Danu Bratan or in Bukit Mungsu market but rates are poor compared with lowland areas. For **tourist shuttle bus** tickets (see p.663 for journey details), the Perama office (ⓣ0368/21011) is at the *Sari Artha* losmen, just below the market on the main road in Candikuning. It's also possible to arrange charter transport in the area, for example at the *Ashram Guesthouse*. Most **accommodation** is in or near Candikuning village, although there are a few options slightly further afield.

Most **restaurants** in the area cater for the passing lunchtime trade. For simpler, better-value food, a row of stalls lines the lakeside road south of Pura Ulun Danu. In addition, several inexpensive places, including *Depot Mekar Sari*, line the road to the Botanical Gardens; *As Siddiq*, about 100m north of the car park on the opposite side of the road, is a good-value place serving Taliwang and Sasak food. The inexpensive-to-moderate *Warung Makan Bedugul* just above the *Ashram Guesthouse* has views of the lake as well as decent food. Most places tend to close around 8pm; in Candikuning, *Ananda* and *Anda* just across the road from the turning to the Botanical Gardens are both a good evening bet, as is *Warung Surya* on the opposite corner; all offer a range of inexpensive Indonesian and Chinese food.

Accommodation

Ashram Guesthouse ⓣ0368/21450, ⓕ21101. Situated in a good position in attractive grounds on the lakeside, this is a large establishment, offering a range of options. ❷–❹

Cempaka ⓣ0368/21402. Clean, quiet place just behind *Permata Firdaus* off the road to the Botanical Gardens. Accommodation is in a two-storey block. ❷–❸

Citera Ayu No phone. On the road to the Botanical Gardens; rooms are simple and set in a small, quiet compound. ❷

Lila Graha Bungalows ⓣ0368/21446, ⓕ21710. Located almost opposite the *Ashram Guesthouse*, 100m back towards Candikuning. Bungalows overlook the lake, although they're across the road. You can also arrange local treks from here. ❸–❹

Pacung Mountain Resort ⓣ0368/21038, ⓕ21043, ⓦwww.bali-pacung.com. This is a luxurious resort with a little swimming pool and splendid views offering the most comfortable accommodation in the area. ❽

Permata Firdaus ⓣ0368/21531. Just off the road to the Botanical Gardens, this place has clean good-value rooms in a quiet location. ❷

Rion Homestay ⓣ & ⓕ0368/21184, ⓔdheinze@indosat.net.id. A cosy homestay with an Australian–Balinese family on the road to the Botanical Gardens. A popular place – it's advisable to book. ❺

Sari Artha Inn ⓣ0368/21011. Situated north of the market, there's a choice of rooms set in a pretty garden. The Perama office is here. ❷–❸

Danau Buyan

Less frequently visited than Danau Bratan, the smaller lakes of Buyan and Tamblingan are accessible either with your own transport or by a combination of bemos and walking. The best way to explore **Danau Buyan**, 6km northwest of Bedugul, is on foot, although you can drive on the good, motorable side road that heads west just to the north of the Pancasari bemo terminal, between the terminal and a *kulkul* tower. This is lined with houses with beautifully carved household shrines, and leads directly to the village of **YEHMAS**. After about 3km, you pass the last house and the road turns rapidly into a dirt path which is no longer motorable. It follows close to the southern shores of the lake, mostly in the forest. After another 2km you'll come out onto the shores of the lake; if you look carefully, you'll spot the *meru* of Pura Tahun in the trees at the western end. Continue on the path as it heads up to the ridge and along to the temple. An eleven-roofed *meru* dominates the **temple** and there's a small *bale* to sit in and another for offerings. A short track leads west from here over to Danau Tamblingan across a raised shoulder of land, but it's extremely difficult to find and it's easy to lose your sense of direction in the densely forested terrain.

Danau Tamblingan and beyond

To reach **Danau Tamblingan**, you need to take the road west from **WANAGIRI**, 2km north of Pancasari – this is signed "scenic route" and runs along the ridge a couple of hundred metres above the northern shore of Danau Buyan. About 5km from Wanagiri, *Bukit Kembar* (Ⓣ082/836 1386; ❺) has a small row of simple rooms and extremely fine views from the sitting area just across the road. About 1500m beyond, the road divides. Take the left fork and it's another 3km down to the lakeside and the small village of **MUNDUK TAMBLINGAN**, where people make their living from growing vegetables, fishing for carp and rearing cattle on the *tunjung* (lotus) that grows on the lake. On the shore just in front of the village, **Pura Gubug** is dedicated to Dewi Danu. Farmers come here frequently on pilgrimages to the three lakeside temples of Batur, Bratan and Tamblingan to worship the lake goddess and pray for good harvests. Across the lake, in the trees, you can just see **Pura Dalem Tamblingan**, the temple of the dead. The area is particularly renowned for bird-watching, as the forest is relatively undisturbed, and you may spot babblers, woodpeckers, ground thrushes and malkohas.

The scenic route to the north coast

The road from Wanagiri turns away from the lakes as it continues west and descends through coffee fields and roads lined with clove trees. It continues to Munduk and on down to the coast. **Munduk waterfall** is signed off the main road to the south of Munduk. The falls are high, powerful and far more impressive than the falls at the more famous Gitgit (see p.638) on the road north to Singaraja; this is a quiet, peaceful and pleasantly landscaped spot, only one of several waterfalls on this river – anyone staying at *Puri Lumbung Cottages* (see below) can arrange a trek to visit the other falls as well. The village of **MUNDUK** is an excellent base for exploration either on foot or with your own transport. Munduk's most established **place to stay** is *Puri Lumbung Cottages* (Ⓣ0362/92810, Ⓕ92514, Ⓦwww.travelideas.net/bali.hotels/lumbung.html; ❻–❼), where accommodation is in replicas of traditional *lumbung* (rice storage barns) that used to stand on the site. *Puri Lumbung* also has some bungalows nearby (❻) and administers several local **homestays** (❺) in Munduk village. These aren't luxurious places, nor are they especially cheap, but all have hot water and breakfast included. A huge number of **activities** can be arranged at *Puri Lumbung Cottages:* local trekking, massage, Balinese Yoga Meditation, cooking classes, weaving, woodcarving, dancing and musical instrument classes. The enormous variety of

treks on offer take in waterfalls, springs, villages, coffee and clove plantations, rivers, *subak*, lakes and temples. An equally diverse variety of **sightseeing** trips is available, as is **horse-riding**. Just above *Puri Lumbung Cottages* a newer place, *Lumbung Bali Cottages* (Ⓣ & Ⓕ0362/92818, Ⓔlumbungbali@hotmail.com; ❻) offers comfortable bungalows set in attractive gardens. There are several warung in the village where you can eat as an alternative to eating at the hotels. The road from Munduk passes north through the small, pretty villages of Tabog, Gunung Sari and Banyuatis before reaching **MAYONG** where you can turn north to **Seririt** on the north coast.

Singaraja and around

The second-largest Balinese city after Denpasar, **SINGARAJA** has broad avenues, impressive monuments and colonial bungalows set in attractive gardens. With a population of over 100,000, it's home to an interesting religious mix of Hindus, Muslims and Buddhists. Behind the old harbour you can still see the shophouses and narrow streets of the original trading area; Jalan Hasanuddin is known locally as Kampong Bugis and Jalan Imam Bonjol as Kampong Arab after the Muslim Bugis settlers from Sulawesi whose descendants still live in the area.

The city's best-known attraction is somewhat esoteric, but surprisingly interesting. A couple of kilometres south of the town centre is **Gedong Kirtya**, Jl Veteran 20 (Mon–Thurs 7am–2.30pm, Fri 7am–noon, Sat 7am–1pm; contribution expected), the only library of lontar manuscripts in the world. This is an establishment for scholars, but visitors are welcome; a member of the library staff will show you around. There's also a small exhibition of manuscripts from India and Burma as well as illustrated ones showing the Tantri tales. Just behind Gedong Kirtya, **Puri Sinar Nadi Putri** (daily 8am–4pm) is a small **weaving factory**, where exquisite weft *ikat* cloth is produced, mostly from silk and cotton (see p.613 for more on this craft). A better bet if you're interested in superb textiles is **Berdikari**, Jl Dewi Sartika 42 (daily 7am–7pm), where they produce top-quality silk and cotton *ikat*. Some of the patterns are reproduced from traditional materials and their work is highly regarded nationally. There's a smaller workshop at *Berdikari Cottages* (see p.639), east of Singaraja. North along Jalan Pramuka, and over the intersection with Jalan Jen Achmad Yani, alleys run down to **Pasar Anyar**, a two-storey maze of stalls and tiny shops selling pretty much everything needed for everyday life. Continue north and you'll reach Singaraja's **waterfront**, site of the ancient harbour of Buleleng. A quiet spot, it's hard to imagine the days when this was the most important and busiest port on Bali. The local **Chinese temple**, Ling Gwan Kiong, is also along here.

Practicalities

Singaraja has three bus and bemo terminals: **Sukasada** (locally called Sangket) to the south of the town, serving Git Git, Bedugul and Denpasar (Ubung terminal); **Banyuasri** on the western edge of town serving the west, including Lovina, Seririt and Gilimanuk; and **Penarukan** in the east, for services eastwards along the coast via Tulamben to Amlapura and inland along the road to Kintamani, Penelokan (for the Batur area) and on to Denpasar via Bangli. Small bemos ply main routes around town linking two of the terminals. There are no metered taxis, although you'll see a few dokar; negotiate the destination and price before you get in.

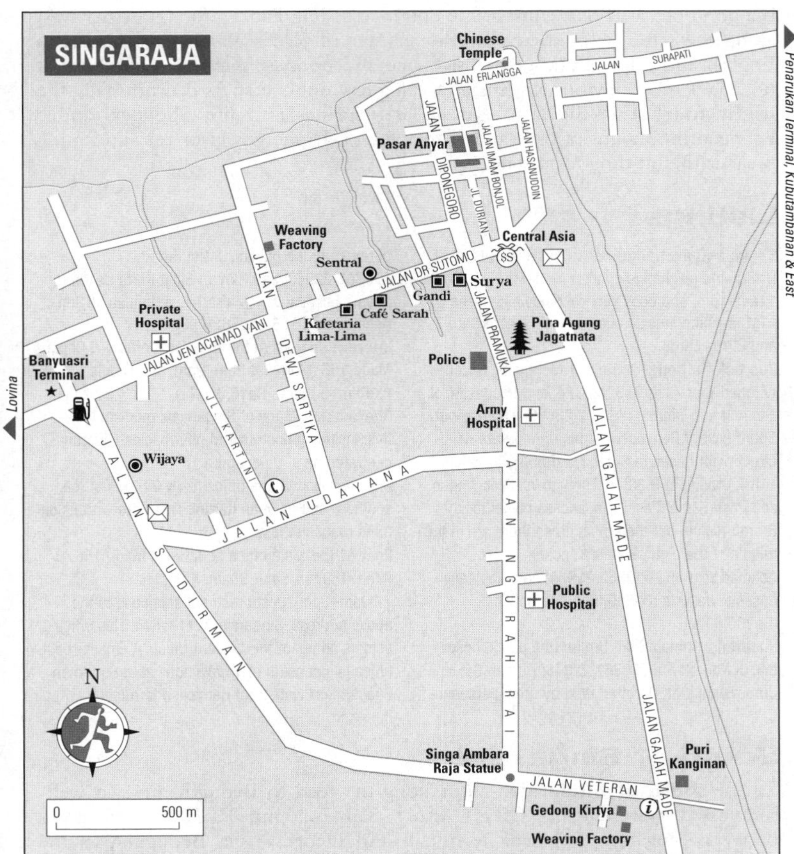

Spread out along the coast and stretching inland for several kilometres, Singaraja can be quite confusing initially. The main thoroughfare of **Jalan Jen Achmad Yani / Jalan Dr Sutomo** is oriented east–west and will eventually take you out onto the road to Lovina, while **Jalan Gajah Made** is oriented north–south and heads, via Sukasada, inland to the Bedugul area. The **tourist office** is south of the town centre at Jl Veteran 23 (Mon–Thurs 8.30am–2pm, Fri & Sat 8.30am–1pm; ⓣ0362/25141). Bemos heading to Sukasada terminal pass the eastern end of Jalan Veteran, 100m from the office.

The **hotels** don't really cater for tourists: with Lovina so close, very few people stay. One reasonable option is *Sentral*, Jl Jen Achmad Yani 48 (ⓣ0362/21896; ❷–❸) which offers fan or air-con rooms with an attached cold-water mandi. The most professional set-up is *Wijaya*, Jl Sudirman 74 (ⓣ0362/21915, ⓕ25817; ❷–❹), which has the widest range of rooms and is conveniently close to Banyuasri terminal.

The largest concentration of **restaurants** is at Jl Jen Achmad Yani 25, in a small square set slightly back from the road; the Chinese restaurant here, *Gandi*, is a good bet, as is *Surya*, just at the entrance, selling Padang food. Further west along the same street there's another cluster of places which have menus in English and offer good, inexpensive rice and noodles; *Kafetaria Lima-Lima* at no. 55a is most obvious, with *Café Sarah* a few doors east. As darkness falls, the **night market** in the Jalan Durian area springs into life. Shoppers amble between mountains of fruit and vegetables, exchange gossip or eat an evening meal at the bustling food stalls.

Listings

Banks and exchange Bank Central Asia is on Jl Dr Sutomo (exchange counter Mon–Fri 11am–1pm) and does Visa cash advances. The ATM machine outside accepts Visa, MasterCard and Cirrus cards.

Bus tickets (long-distance) Menggala, Jl Jen Achmad Yani 76 ⓣ0362/24374, and Puspasari, Jl Jen Achmad Yani 90 ⓣ0362/23062 – both about 300m east of Banyuasri terminal – operate daily direct night buses to Surabaya (Rp55,000; takes 11hr), leaving at 6.30pm. They go via Probolinggo and Pasuruan in East Java, access points for the Bromo region, but the arrival times there are in the middle of the night. Pahala Kencana, Jl Jen Achmad Yani 95a ⓣ0362/29945, operates daily buses to Jakarta (Rp200,000) and Bogor (Rp205,000).

Hospitals Rumah Sakit Umum (the public hospital), Jl Ngurah Rai ⓣ0362/22046; Rumah Sakit Umum Angkatan Darat (staffed by army personnel, but open to the public), Jl Ngurah Rai ⓣ0362/22543; and Rumah Sakit Kerta Usada (a private hospital which also has a dentist), Jl Jen Achmad Yani 108 ⓣ0362/22396.

Internet access At the main post office, Jl Gajah Made 156 (Mon–Sat 9am–9pm, Sun & hols 8.30am–5.30pm; Rp10,000/hr).

Pharmacies Many of Singaraja's medical facilities, including doctors and pharmacies, are concentrated on Jl Diponegoro.

Phones Main phone office (daily 24hr) is at the southern end of Jalan Kartini. There are wartels on main roads in the city.

Post office Main office at Jl Gajah Made 156 (Mon–Thurs & Sat 7.30am–4pm, Fri 7.30am–3pm). Poste restante service is to the above address, Singaraja 81113, Bali. This office acts as an agent for Western Union. A smaller post office is just south of *Wijaya* hotel at Jl Sudirman 68a, a short walk from Banyuasri terminal.

South of Singaraja

To the **south of Singaraja**, 10km along the road to Bedugul, are two well-signposted waterfalls at **Gitgit** (daily 8am–5.30pm; Rp3000). All buses between Singaraja (Sukasada terminal) and Denpasar via Bedugul pass the place. A multi-tiered upper fall descends in fairly unimpressive steps and, 2km further north, is a forty-metre single drop, 500m from the road along a concrete path lined with textile and souvenir stalls. A local belief has it that if you come to Gitgit with your partner you will eventually separate.

East of Singaraja

Many of the villages and the wealth of carved temples to the **east of Singaraja** can be visited on a day-trip from Singaraja or Lovina. The main sights are fairly close together and all lie on regular bemo routes.

Some 8km east of Singaraja, a small road north takes you 200m to the pink sandstone **Pura Beji** of **SANGSIT**, highly unusual in an area where every other temple is built of grey volcanic *paras*. Dedicated to Dewi Sri, the rice goddess, it's justly famous for the sheer exuberance of its carvings. About 400m to the northeast across the fields, you'll be able to spot the red roofs of **Pura Dalem**. The front wall of the temple shows the rewards that await the godly in heaven and the punishments awaiting the evil in hell. There's a preponderance of soft pornography here, and it isn't certain which of this is supposed to be hell and which heaven. The village of Sangsit straggles 500m north from here to a black-sand working beach with a few fishing boats, shops and warung.

Back on the main road, 500m east of the Sangsit turning, you come to the road heading 4km inland to **JAGARAGA**. The famous temple here is **Pura Dalem Jagaraga**, renowned for the pictorial carving on its front walls. Those on the left show a variety of village activities representing community life before the Dutch invasion. Next to these are the Dutch arriving in cars, boats, planes and on bicycles, destroying the community. On the right-hand side is a much-photographed carving of two Dutch men driving a Model T Ford, being held up by bandits. The only **place to stay** is back on the main road, about 200m east of the Jagaraga turning: *Hotel Berdikari* (Ⓣ0362/25195; ❷–❺) comprises attractive bungalows set in glorious gardens, far enough back from the main road to escape the noise. This is also a good place to **eat** a moderately priced lunch, with a good range of Indo-Chinese options. There's a small weaving workshop here (open for viewing 7.30am–4pm), owned by the highly regarded Berdikari company that has a larger workshop in Singaraja (see p.636).

Pura Meduwe Karang

The most spectacular of the many fine temples in the area is **Pura Meduwe Karang** at **KUBUTAMBAHAN**, 11km east of Singaraja and 300m west of the junction with the Kintamani road. Its lively and whimsical carvings have a human quality somehow missing in the other temples; if you only make it to one temple in the north, this is the one to go for. It is decorated with **carvings** of Balinese folk, including elderly people and mothers with babies and toddlers and it includes one of the most famous carvings on Bali: a cyclist, wearing floral shorts, with a rat about to go under the back wheel, apparently being chased by a dog. It's possible that this depicts the Dutch artist W.O.J. Nieuwenkamp, who first visited Bali in 1904 and explored the island by bicycle.

Air Sanih and around

Further east, 6km from Kubutambahan, **AIR SANIH**, also known as Yeh Sanih, is a small, quiet beach resort that has grown up around the freshwater springs on the coast, although the accommodation is spread out along the coast between Air Sanih and the small village of **BUKTI** 3km to the east. Public transport between Singaraja and Amlapura all passes through Air Sanih, as do Perama tourist shuttle buses (see Travel Details on p.663 for details). There's no Perama office in the village but you can either make arrangements to be picked up when you get dropped off or call one of the offices in Lovina (see p.648). The freezing cold **springs**, widely believed to originate in Danau Bratan, are set in attractive gardens with changing rooms (daily 7am–7pm; Rp2000).

Accommodation

Cilik's Beach Garden Ⓣ & Ⓕ0362/26561, Ⓦwww.ciliksbeachgarden.com. About 400m east of the springs, and the real gem in the area, with four lovely choices for accommodation: two superbly furnished bungalows, one villa and one *lumbung*-style two-storey place. All are set in great gardens overlooking the coast – a magical hideaway. ❻–❼

Puri Rahayu Ⓣ0362/26565. Just over 400m east of Air Sanih's springs, and across the road from the beach, with good-value bungalows in a small compound and a restaurant attached. ❸

Puri Rena Ⓣ & Ⓕ0362/26581, Ⓔpurirena@yahoo.com. Across the road from the springs, with simple rooms with fan and cold water plus a couple of larger suite rooms with a small private pool, again with fan and cold water. Rooms ❷ Suites ❺

Hotel Puri Sanih Ⓣ0362/26563. The most convenient place to stay, next to the beach and springs, with cheaper rooms and better-value, better-positioned bungalows all set in fine spacious grounds. ❸

Hotel Tara ⓣ0362/26575. Right on the coast 200m east of *Puri Rahayu*, 600m east of the springs, with a row of simple tiled bungalows, all facing seawards with nice verandahs. An excellent budget choice with a small attached restaurant. ❸

Wira Bali Arsanih ⓣ0361/262812. Around 2km east of Air Sanih, offering a range of rooms, a small oceanside swimming pool and there's an attached restaurant. A good-value choice. ❺–❻

Lovina and around

LOVINA stretches along 8km of black-sand beach, the largest resort in Bali outside the Kuta–Legian–Seminyak conurbation. Beginning 6km west of Singaraja, the resort encompasses six villages: from east to west, **Pemaron**, **Tukad Mungga**, **Anturan**, **Kalibukbuk**, **Kaliasem** and **Temukus**. Kalibukbuk is generally accepted as the centre of Lovina and it's here that you'll find most tourist facilities, the greatest concentration of accommodation and restaurants, and the little nightlife there is in the resort. While the peak season (June–Aug & Dec) is busy, Lovina remains far less frantic than the southern resorts and you can easily have a quiet and relaxing time. The main Singaraja–Gilimanuk road passes right through Lovina, and while some of the accommodation and tourist facilities line this road most of the accommodation is along side roads leading from the main road to the beach. Activity centres mainly on the beach, with **snorkelling**, **diving** and **dolphin-watching** as diversions. There are waterfalls, hot springs and a Buddhist temple nearby, and Singaraja and points east are easily accessible by bemo. The volcanic Bedugul and Batur areas (see p.626 and p.633 respectively) are also well within reach.

Arrival, information and transport

Getting to Lovina is easy: inter-island **buses** from Java to Singaraja pass through, as do Gilimanuk–Singaraja and Amlapura–Gilimanuk services, and all local buses and **bemos** from the west of the island. From Denpasar and the east of Bali, you'll come via Singaraja, from whose Banyuasri terminal it's a short bemo ride (Rp1000). **Tourist shuttle buses** also serve the resort from other parts of Bali and Lombok; however, Perama drop off only at their office in Anturan – inconvenient if you want to stay elsewhere in the resort. Check with other shuttle bus operators whether they will drop you off more centrally (as the resort is so spread out, it's well worth pinning down where you want to be dropped off, especially if you arrive late in the evening as many of the inter-island buses do).

Buffalo races

Lovina stages regular **buffalo races** (*sapi gerumbungan*), held in the late afternoon in a field in Kaliasem (Rp40,000) – twice weekly in the main tourist seasons and weekly at other times. Cooking, rice-pounding and martial arts displays supplement the races, turning the whole thing into a lovely, good-natured event. The buffalo are dolled up in ornate yokes and headdresses to prance along a set course, hampered somewhat by a huge bell around their neck, their jockeys perching on a painfully narrow seat. Spectators are encouraged to have a go themselves – and this is just as entertaining, especially the funny walks that result from bumpy contact with the aforementioned seat. A much grander, more serious event takes place annually on Independence Day (Aug 17).

Lovina's **tourist office** (Mon–Sat 8am–8pm) is on the main road at Kalibukbuk next to the police post. Getting around the resort on **public transport** is no problem during the day as you can pick up the frequent bemos and minibuses that zip through between Singaraja and Seririt, although the service can be erratic in the early morning and effectively dies after dark. At these times, you'll need to negotiate with the transport touts, unless your hotel or restaurant offers transport. A huge number of places offer **vehicles for rent** or charter (see Listings, p.648) and charges are competitive, on a par with the resorts in the south. There are also **bicycles** for rent, but the Singaraja–Seririt road is very busy, traffic is fast, and the heat doesn't make this a very pleasant option.

Accommodation

Despite its reputation as a backpackers' resort, Lovina has attracted big money and plenty of upmarket hotels, although there are still many inexpensive and moderately priced **accommodation** options, all of which is marked on the map on pp.642–643.

Most of the accommodation in the quiet area of **Pemaron** and **Tukad Mungga** (also known as Pantai Happy), at the eastern edge of the resort, is along side roads leading down to the beach; upmarket places have their own drives from the main road. The tiny fishing village of **Anturan** is developing rapidly: many of its basic homestays have moved upmarket, there are plenty of people around and you'll share the local beach with the villagers. The **Banyualit** side road marks the beginning of the developed part of Lovina, about 1500m east of Kalibukbuk: it's a self-contained little enclave with plenty of accommodation, restaurants and some shops. **Kalibukbuk**, centred around two side roads, Jalan Mawar (also known as Jalan Ketapang or Jalan Rambutan) and Jalan Bina Ria, has a huge number of places to stay and to eat, plus some nightlife and shops, moneychangers, dive shops, travel agents and car rental outlets. The narrow entrance to Jalan Mawar is easy to miss; look out for *Khi Khi Restaurant* on the opposite side of the road and The Lovina Wellness Spa and Healing Centre on the corner. As you head west from Kalibukbuk, passing through the villages of **Kaliasem** and **Temukus**, the main road runs much closer to the coast, and is lined with restaurants and accommodation.

Pemaron and Tukad Mungga

Baruna Beach Cottages ⓣ0362/41252, ⓕ41745, ⓦwww.indo.com/hotels/baruna. Comfortable, quiet accommodation set in attractive gardens, with a good-sized swimming pool by the beach at the far eastern end of Lovina. ❺

Happy Beach Inn *(Bahagia)* ⓣ0362/41017. Basic, cheap rooms with attached cold-water bathrooms close to Pantai Happy beach. ❷

Hepi ⓣ0362/41020, ⓕ41910, ⓦwww.balibackpacker.com. Good-quality fan and air-con rooms, all with cold water, in a quiet garden setting with a small pool, a short walk from the beach. ❸

Hotel Permai ⓣ0362/41224. There are two neighbouring places with this name near Pantai Happy. This one is closer to the sea, has no pool and no attached dive centre. ❸

Hotel Permai ⓣ0362/41471. The other place with this name near Pantai Happy – larger, with a good-sized pool. Permai dive centre is based here. A choice of rooms is available. A grand new restaurant and pool bar are under construction. ❸–❹

Puri Bagus Lovina ⓣ0362/21430, ⓕ22627, ⓦwww.bagus-discovery.com. This is one of the loveliest, most luxurious places in Lovina, offering large, airy, well-furnished villas located in superb grounds towards the far eastern end of Lovina. There's a lovely pool, a library and excellent restaurant. Service is friendly but efficient. Published prices start at US$125. ❽

Puri Bedahulu ⓣ0362/41731. Right next to the beach at Pantai Happy with a pretty garden. Bungalows are elegantly carved and comfortable. ❸–❹

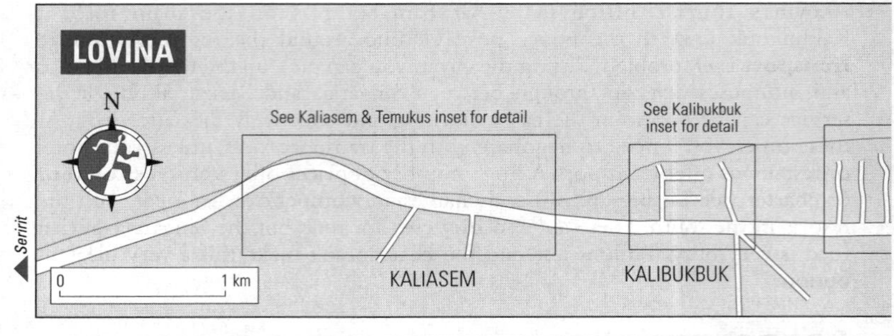

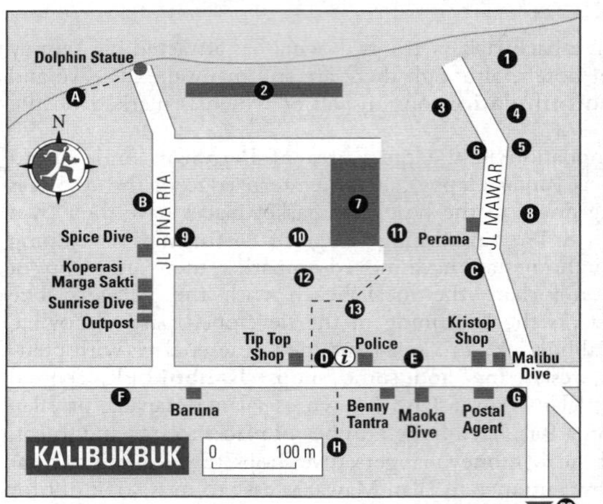

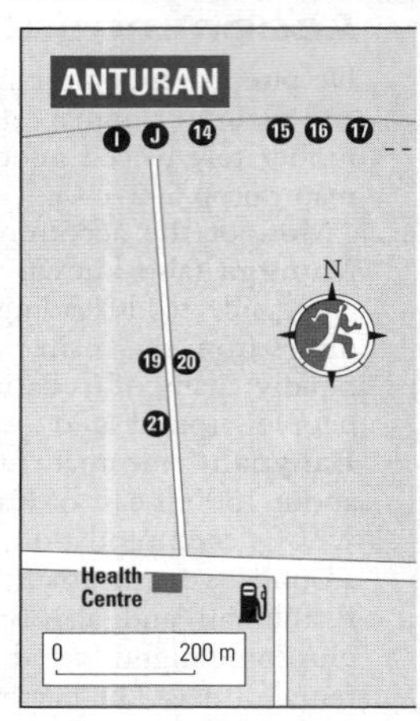

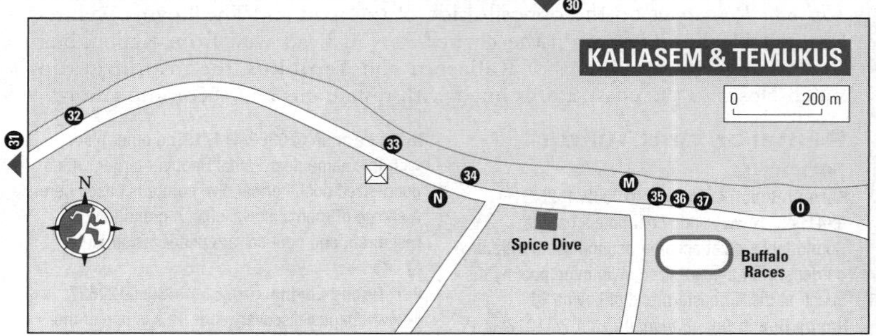

ACCOMMODATION

Agus Homestay	32	Billibo	33	Hotel Kalibukbuk	39	Padang Lovina	12
Angsoka	7	Hotel Celuk Agung	50	Made Janur	45	Parma	34
Astina	3	Damai Lovina Villas	30	Mandhara Chico	16	Hotel Permai	26
Awangga	48	Gede Homestay	14	Mari	15	Hotel Permai	28
Bagus Homestay	31	Happy Beach Inn	22	Mas	47	Pondok Elsa	10
Hotel Banyualit	43	Harris Homestay	11	Melka	46	Pulestis	9
Baruna Beach	24	Hepi	27	Mutiara	36	Puri Bagus Lovina	25
Bayu Kartika	1	Indra Pura	49	Nirwana Seaside	2	Puri Bali	5
Bayu Mantra	19	Juni Arta	40				

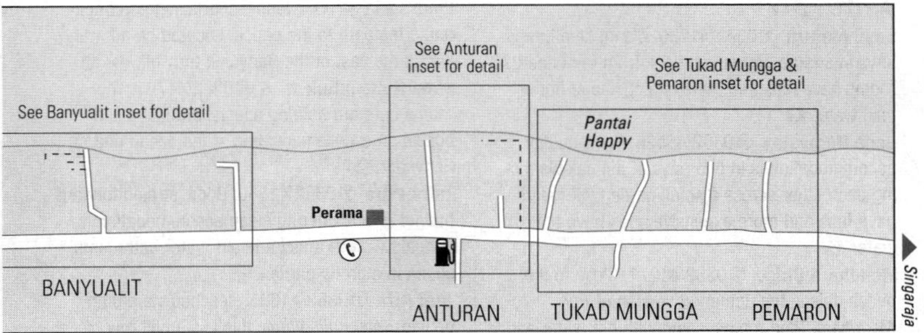

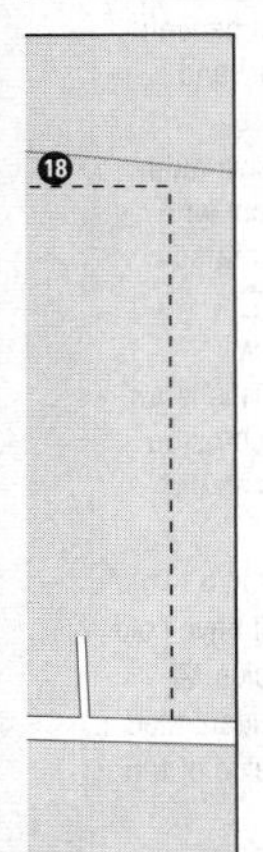

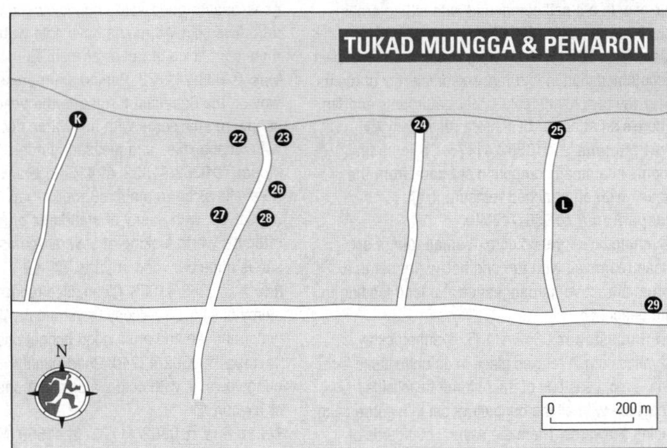

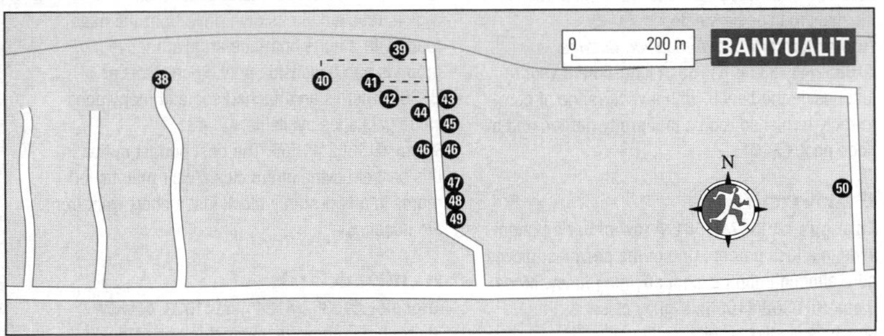

Puri Bedahulu	23	Ray 2	44
Puri Mandhara	20	Rini	4
Puri Manggala	37	Sartaya	42
Puri Manik Sari	13	Sol Lovina	38
Puri Tasik Madu	35	Sri Homestay	18
Puspa Rama	21	Suma	41
Putri Sari	29	Taman Lily's	6
Rambutan	8	Yudha	17

RESTAURANTS

Barakuda	C	Kubu Lalang	K
Biyu-Nasak	O	Malibu	E
Bu Warung	D	Planet Lovina	F
Café Spice	M	Sea Breeze	A
Café 3	H	Warung Bambu	L
Djani's	N	Warung Nyoman	J
Khi Khi	G	Warung Rasta	I
Kopi Bali	B		

Anturan

Bayu Mantra ⓣ0362/41930. Clean, tiled bungalows in a large garden set back from the beach. All rooms have fans and there is a choice of hot or cold water. ❸

Gede Homestay ⓣ0362/41526. Good-quality accommodation is in two rows of bungalows facing each other across a small garden. All rooms have fans and more expensive ones have hot water. ❷

Mandhara Chico ⓣ0362/41271. Close to the beach, this is the upmarket version of *Puri Mandhara*. Tiled rooms, some with hot water and air-con, in a small compound with sitting areas close to the beach. ❸–❹

Mari ⓣ0362/41882. Offering some of the cheapest accommodation in Anturan: one small row of rooms near the beach with cold-water bathrooms and fan. There's an attached beachside restaurant. ❷

Puri Mandhara ⓣ0362/41476. Basic budget rooms in a small compound set back from the beach with an attached restaurant. ❷

Puspa Rama ⓣ0362/42070, ⓔagungdayu@yahoo.com. A small row of six, clean rooms all with fan and hot-water set in a large, attractive garden just off the lane leading to the beach. ❸

Sri Homestay ⓣ0362/41135, ⓔsrihomestay@yahoo.com. A relaxed place in an unbeatable location – most easterly of the Anturan beachside options – with all the bungalows set in a garden and facing seawards. There are several standards of accommodation. You can reach here via a track from the main road or via the beach. ❷–❹

Yudha (formerly *Simon Seaside Cottage*) ⓣ0362/41183, ⓕ41160. A long-time favourite just beside the beach, with a wide range of comfortably furnished rooms in a pretty garden and a good pool. ❸–❹

Banyualit

Awangga ⓣ0362/41561. A row of basic bungalows in a lush garden. One of the cheapest places here although don't expect anything fancy. *Made Janur* (ⓣ0362/41056), slightly closer to the beach, is similar in price and quality. ❷

Hotel Banyualit ⓣ0362/41789, ⓕ41563, ⓦwww.banyualit.com. This long-standing Lovina landmark has several standards of well-furnished bungalows in a lush garden wilderness with an attractive pool. ❹–❼

Hotel Celuk Agung ⓣ0362/41039, ⓕ41379, ⓔcelukabc@singaraja.wasantara.net.id. Good-quality option in this price range, often with significant discounts. All rooms have hot water and air-con, the grounds are extensive and attractive and there's a large pool, tennis courts, jogging track and a footpath to the beach. Located on a turning just to the east of the Banyualit turn-off. ❻–❼

Hotel Kalibukbuk ⓣ & ⓕ0362/41701. The rooms here are nothing special but this place boasts an excellent location at the ocean end of Banyualit. ❸

Indra Pura ⓣ0362/41560. Good, straightforward budget choice offering clean accommodation in bungalows with attached cold-water bathrooms, all set in a pretty garden. ❷

Juni Arta ⓣ0362/41885. Reached via a path behind *Hotel Kalibukbuk*, this is a small row of good-quality, good-value bungalows in a peaceful, attractive spot. All rooms have cold water and there's a choice of fan or air-con. ❸

Mas ⓣ0362/41773. Behind an impressive gateway on the Banyualit turning to the beach, with simple rooms, some with hot water, decorated with local textiles in a pleasant garden. ❸

Melka ⓣ0362/41552, ⓕ41543, ⓦwww.freeyellow.com/members8/melka-bali. This is a big set-up, with plenty of standards of rooms on offer. It's worth looking at several rooms as the site is quite crowded in parts. ❸–❺

Ray 2 ⓣ0362/41088. Clean, tiled rooms in a two-storey block with balcony or verandah. All have cold water and fan and are a good budget choice. ❷

Sartaya ⓣ0362/42240. Good-quality. clean, tiled bungalows all with cold water and a choice of fan or air-con. ❸

Sol Lovina ⓣ0362/41775, ⓕ41659, ⓦwww.solmelia.com. One of the largest hotels in the region, reached via its own drive from the main road, with a huge entrance area, attractive grounds and beachside pool. Prices start at US$90. There's an attached spa and many good-value packages available. ❼–❽

Suma ⓣ0362/41566. The best budget option in this part of Lovina offers clean, well-maintained rooms in a two-storey block just a short walk from the beach. ❷

Kalibukbuk

Angsoka ⓣ0362/41841, ⓕ41023, ⓦwww.baliweb.net/angsoka. A variety of good-quality accommodation options in a large compound conveniently located off Jalan Bina Ria. Pleasant swimming pool (Rp20,000 for non-guests). ❸–❺

Astina ⓣ0362/41187. Plenty of standards of accommodation in this long-time budget favourite with a large garden compound in a quiet spot at the end of Jalan Mawar. ❷–❺

Bayu Kartika ⓣ0362/41055, ⓕ41219. Boasts one of the best positions in Lovina, on the coast at the end of Jalan Mawar. There is a good range of bungalows some with brilliant views of the sea. The pool is huge. ❺–❻

Damai Lovina Villas ⓣ0362/41008, ⓕ41009, ⓦwww.damai.com. Located in the village of Kayuputih, 4km inland from Kalibukbuk in a beautiful, cool location surrounded by paddy fields up in the hills. Accommodation, service and ambience are all elegantly luxurious and among the best in Lovina. There's a wonderful pool, spa treatments are available and the restaurant is one of the delights of northern Bali. Prices start at US$190; diving and golf packages available. ❽

Harris Homestay ⓣ0362/41152. A popular little gem tucked away in the back streets off Jalan Bina Ria – worth searching out for its good-value, good-quality rooms. ❷

Nirwana Seaside Cottages ⓣ0362/41288, ⓕ41090, ⓔnirwana@singaraja.wasantara.net.id. A large, well-organized development with a huge choice of comfortable accommodation, all with hot water. Has a lovely position in well-maintained gardens near the beach at the end of Jalan Bina Ria, with a pool. ❹–❺

Padang Lovina ⓣ0362/41302, ⓔpadanglovina@yahoo.com. Simple accommodation in a two-storey block just off Jalan Bina Ria. All rooms have good balconies or verandahs. Guests here can use the pool at *Pulestis*. ❹

Pondok Elsa ⓣ0362/41186) Just off Jalan Bina Ria, this place is newer than the others nearby. There's good-quality accommodation in bungalows set in a cosy compound. ❸–❹

Pulestis ⓣ0362/41035, ⓔpulestis@hotmail.com. Reached through a grand entrance on Jalan Bina Ria, the small compound has comfortable rooms and a pleasant pool. Excellent value. ❸–❹

Puri Bali ⓣ0362/41485. A variety of rooms in an attractive garden with a good-sized pool. Enjoys a quiet location on Jalan Mawar, not far from the beach. ❸–❹

Puri Manik Sari ⓣ0362/41089. Accessible from the main road and Jalan Bina Ria, there are a variety of bungalows in a pretty garden complete with pools and statues. ❷–❺

Rambutan ⓣ0362/41388, ⓕ41057, ⓦwww.rambutan.org. Halfway down Jalan Mawar with well-furnished, clean bungalows set well apart in a beautiful garden. Five standards of rooms to choose from, two pools, an attractive restaurant and some larger family villas also available. ❺–❻

Rini ⓣ & ⓕ0362/41386. Several choices of accommodation in an attractive garden location on Jalan Mawar just a short walk to the beach. There's a pool with a poolside restaurant. ❹–❺

Taman Lily's ⓣ0362/41307, ⓕ26653. A small row of attractive, spotless, tiled bungalows in a large and well-maintained garden on Jalan Mawar. Excellent value. ❸

Kaliasem and Temukus

Agus Homestay ⓣ & ⓕ0362/41202. A small place, close to the sea at the far western end of the main Lovina development. Clean, tiled rooms, with verandahs that face the ocean. ❸–❹

Bagus Homestay ⓣ0362/93407, ⓕ93406. Situated about 1km west of its sister operation, *Agus Homestay*, so quite separate from the main Lovina development. Six spotless bungalows in a lovely garden setting right beside a pleasant beach. ❺

Billibo ⓣ & ⓕ0362/41355. These tiled bungalows at Kaliasem are close to the beachfront in an attractive garden and there's a choice of fan or air-con and hot- or cold-water bathrooms. ❸–❺

Mutiara ⓣ0362/41132. Friendly, family-run place offering simple rooms in a two-storey building. Airier rooms are upstairs. It's just a short walk to the beach. ❷

Parma ⓣ0362/41555. The best budget option at the western end of Lovina. Simple fan rooms in a good quiet location in a pretty garden near the sea. ❷

Puri Manggala ⓣ0362/41371. Clean, simple rooms in a family compound tucked between the nearby beach and the road to the west of Kalibukbuk. ❸–❹

Puri Tasik Madu ⓣ0362/41376. Situated right next to the beach at Kaliasem, this budget cheapie offers basic rooms with attached bathrooms. ❷

The resort

Lovina's long **black-sand beach** stretches into the distance where, on clear days, the imposing peaks of East Java look surprisingly close. Fringed by palm trees, the widest stretch of beach is at Kalibukbuk, but there's at least some beach all along the resort. Swimming is generally calm and safe, although there are no lifeguards on duty. There's not a great deal to do other than enjoy the beach and the resort life that has built up behind it, although many people consider Lovina's early-morning **dolphin trips** (see box overleaf) to be the highlight of their stay.

Dolphin trips

Lovina has become famous (or infamous) for dawn trips to see the school of **dolphins** that frolics just off the coast: opinions are fairly evenly split between those who think it's grossly overrated and those who consider it one of the best things on Bali. Boats head out to sea at dawn, in a flotilla of thirty or more boats. The ensuing scenario is mildly comic, as one skipper spots a dolphin and chases after it, to be followed by the rest of the fleet, by which time, of course, the dolphin is long gone. Most people end up with more pictures of other boats than of dolphins, but if you can see the funny side, it's a good trip. Very, very occasionally **whales** have been spotted. Expect to **pay** Rp30,000 per person for the two-hour trip; you can book directly with the skippers on the beach or hotel or losmen staff may know particularly good skippers. Captains are banned from working for a week if they're discovered to have given discounts or allowed more than four passengers per boat.

Lovina is a good place to base yourself for **diving**, situated between the main diving areas on the north coast of Bali – Menjangan or Deer Island to the west (see p.660) and Tulamben (see p.624) and Amed (see p.621) to the east – although the reef here was decimated by anchoring of boats, fish-bombing, harpoon fishing and damage from snorkellers; it's beginning to rejuvenate through local efforts which have seen tyres, an old car, and a small wrecked boat placed on it to encourage coral growth. There's still an excellent range of fish. Plenty of **operators** work in the resort, all offering trips for qualified and experienced divers and some featuring introductory dives. For two-dive trips to Menjangan Island, Tulamben or Amed, the going rate is US$40–60; two dives in the Lovina area cost $35–40. Price wars break out from time to time, but maintaining dive equipment properly isn't cheap; if prices fall too low there's a risk that companies will cut costs, so don't be unduly swayed by the price. A four-day PADI Open Water course costs $250–350. Your losmen can also arrange **snorkelling trips** for you, or you can approach the boat skippers on the beach; expect to pay about Rp30,000 for a trip of one-and-a-half or two hours to the local reef. Most of the dive shops will take snorkellers along on dive trips further afield; this is more expensive ($20–39) but offers more variety. The *Kubu Lalang* restaurant (Ⓣ0362/42207) offers **night snorkelling** trips (Rp100,000 per person).

Dive operators

Aquatropic Ⓣ0362/42038. Has several counters on the main roads in Lovina, offering the usual dive trips for experienced divers plus courses.

Baruna On the main road in Kalibukbuk Ⓣ0362/41084, and at *Puri Bagus Hotel* Ⓣ0362/25542, Ⓦwww.comcen.com.au/~baruna. A branch of the main office near Denpasar, offering diving trips and courses.

Malibu Dive Next to *Malibu* restaurant Ⓣ & Ⓕ0362/41225, Ⓔmalibu@singaraja.wasantara.net.id. Also on Jalan Bina Ria Ⓣ0362/41061, and with counters all over the resort. A PADI dive centre operating a full range of dives for certified divers as well as PADI courses.

Permai At *Hotel Permai*, Pantai Happy Ⓣ0362/41471. Offers dives for certified divers, as well as PADI courses and introductory dives. The early stages of beginners' courses are in the *Permai* swimming pool.

Spice Dive Kaliasem Ⓣ0362/41305, Ⓕ41171, Ⓦwww.damai.com/spicedive. Also has shops on Jalan Bina Ria and Jalan Mawar. Established in Lovina for many years, and the resort's only PADI five-star dive centre, offering courses up to Assistant Instructor level, a range of trips and introductory dives. Also offer a two-day "Rainbow Tour" (US$150 per person) to Baluran National Park in Java.

Sunrise Dive Jalan Bina Ria Ⓣ0362/411820 and office Ⓣ & Ⓕ0362/42083. Offering local dives, dive trips further afield and courses.

Eating, drinking and nightlife

There's a high turnover of **restaurants**, and a healthy level of competition ensures plenty of good "Happy Hour" deals. The quality of food is generally reasonable, with seafood the local speciality. The places recommended below are all marked on the map on pp.642–643.

After a day relaxing on the beach, most people eat a leisurely dinner and head off to bed. *Malibu* is the liveliest **nightlife** spot and has the biggest video screen and most popular **live music**; *Café 3*, just off the main road in Kalibukbuk, offers something similar, and *Planet Lovina* on the main road in Kalibukbuk also has regular live music. Regular **Balinese dance shows** feature at several restaurants to accompany your dinner: look out for the flyers around town or check out the *Rambutan* bungalows. Friday-night **parties** at *Café Spice* last until the early hours, sometimes with live music.

Barakuda In a quiet spot on Jalan Mawar, this place doesn't look much from the outside but they specialize in superbly cooked, extremely good-value seafood. Your choice is served with one of eleven sauces and the chef will come and help you choose. There are plenty of vegetarian, pork and chicken options as well.

Biyu-Nasak On the main road in Kalibukbuk. The moderately-priced menu is vegetarian and seafood, with lots of imaginative and appetizing choices.

Bu Warung Probably the best-value food in Kalibukbuk, this tiny place on the main road has a small menu of around a dozen inexpensive main courses of rice, vegetables, noodles, chicken, pork and tuna dishes. The food is extremely well-cooked and you'll not notice the noise from the nearby road.

Café Spice ⓣ0362/41969. As the base of the Spice Beach water sports setup, this attractive café is located in a great spot beside the beach at Kaliasem. The menu includes seafood, Western and Indo-Chinese meals plus plenty of snacks, shakes and juices all at moderate prices. Phone for a free pick-up in the Lovina area. There are weekly parties on a Friday night, sometimes with live music, running until 3 or 4am. Open 8am–10pm.

Damai ⓣ0362/41008. The restaurant attached to the luxury *Damai Lovina Villas* offers the most exquisite gourmet dining experience in northern Bali, if not the entire island. The menu is expensive but highly imaginative, innovative, well-cooked and fabulously presented. The $38 five-course gastronomic treat is a feast beyond words.

Kopi Bali Popular place at the ocean end of Jalan Bina Ria. Features a big, inexpensive menu of pizza, seafood and Indo-Chinese dishes, lots of specials, plenty of breakfasts and everyone gets a free welcome drink and snack with dinner.

Kubu Lalang ⓣ0362/42207. On the coast at the eastern end of Lovina, with a free boat transfer for lunch or dinner for a minimum of two people from elsewhere in the resort (two hours' notice required). The moderately priced menu is huge, including plenty of vegetarian choices and slightly unusual, imaginative dishes. Closed Tues.

Malibu Centre of Lovina nightlife, this large restaurant is on the main road in Kalibukbuk, screens nightly videos, stages regular live music and is open until about 2am. It has a big range of moderately priced Western food, seafood and Indo-Chinese options and a huge drinks list.

Sea Breeze Superbly located on the beach at Kalibukbuk, this is the spot for a sunset drink, with an excellent menu of soups, salad, sandwiches and main meals and an equally fine selection of cakes and desserts all at moderate prices.

Warung Bambu ⓣ0362/27080 or 31455. On the road down to *Puri Bagus Lovina* at the eastern end of Lovina; serves only Balinese and Indonesian food. There's an excellent range of soups and starters, main courses plus a *rijsttaffel* and "Romantic Buffet" available for as few as two diners. Balinese dancing accompanies dinner twice a week (Wed & Sun) and gets very good reviews. Free transport in the Lovina area.

Warung Nyoman On the seafront just east of *Rasta* and the road to the beach at Anturan. Seafood beach barbecues are their speciality.

Warung Rasta At the end of the road in Anturan overlooking the beach, the location is the reason for a visit to this tiny place, which has a standard menu and reggae music. Food is inexpensive and there are plenty of vegetarian choices.

Listings

Banks and exchange Moneychangers can be found every few metres along the main road, Jalan Bina Ria and Jalan Mawar. There's a BCA ATM (Visa, MasterCard and Cirrus) on the main road in Kalibukbuk, and another on Jalan Bina Ria.

Car, bike and motorbike rental Available throughout the resort both from established firms and as charters from people who'll approach you on the street. Expect to pay around Rp85,000 a day for a Suzuki Jimney, Rp100,000 for a Kijang and Rp110,000 for a larger four-wheel drive or a people-carrier, plus Rp50,000 per day for a driver. Insurance deals vary and are only available with established companies. Motorbikes are also widely available (Rp30,000–40,000/day), as are bicycles (Rp15,000–25,000/day). Established companies include Koperasi Marga Sakti (Ⓣ0362/41061), on Jl Bina Ria; Damar (Ⓣ0362/42154, Ⓕ41999, Ⓔluhwiriadi@yahoo.com) on the main road in Kalibukbuk; or Yuli Transport, at Yuli Shop (Ⓣ0362/41184), opposite *Rambutan* on Jalan Mawar where Made Wijana (Ⓔmadewijana @hotmail.com) is a safe, reliable and recommended driver. It's also possible to charter transport one-way to destinations throughout Bali.

Cookery courses At *Djani's* restaurant (Ⓣ0362/41913), on the main road in Kaliasem, and *Barakuda* restaurant (Ⓔrestaurant_barakuda @hotmail.com) on Jalan Mawar.

Doctor Lovina Clinic (Ⓣ0362/41106), on the main road in Kalibukbuk, 200m east of Jalan Mawar, has a 24-hour call-out service for doctors. The tourist office can recommend doctors in Singaraja. The closest hospitals are in Singaraja (see p.638), although for anything serious you'll have to go to Denpasar.

Internet access Offered by many places (Rp350–400/min, often with discounts for long periods). *Outpost* and *Spice Dive* on Jalan Bina Ria are both good; *Planet Lovina* on the main road in Kalibukbuk and *Bali Bintang* on Jalan Bina Ria both have restaurants attached. In Anturan, head for Perama or *Sri Homestay*, and there's another place on the main road just west of the Banyualit turning.

Massage and treatments As well as the ladies on the beach offering massages, a couple of places have opened up offering a broader range. Indiana Massage (daily 10am–sunset, other times by appointment; Ⓣ0362/41570, Ⓔindiana@telkom.net) has a great location on the beach next to *Café Spice*. They offer massages in a lovely open-sided pavilion and also have open yoga classes. Lovina Wellness Spa and Healing Centre (Ⓣ0362/27297, Ⓔbalicenter@aol.com), on the corner of Jalan Mawar and the main road, offers several massages, spa treatments, therapeutic body work, Vipassana meditation classes and bodywork classes in Indonesian and English, intended for local people but open to all.

Phone Wartels are dotted throughout the resort. Wartel Lovina (daily 8am–11pm) is one of the most convenient, on the main road just west of Jalan Bina Ria; Mit Surya (daily 8am–11pm) is also central, on the main road in Kalibukbuk between Jalan Bina Ria and Jalan Mawar. There's one on the main road in Anturan (daily 7.30am–10.30pm) and one on the road to Pantai Happy (daily 8am–10.30pm). Prices vary.

Police Located in the same building as the tourist office; they'll also try to help you with information if the tourist office is closed.

Post office The post office (Mon–Thurs 7.30am–2.30pm, Fri 8am–noon, Sat 7.30am–1pm) is about 1km west of Kalibukbuk. For poste restante, have mail addressed to you at the Post Office, Jalan Raya Singaraja, Lovina, Singaraja 81152, Bali. Several postal agents in Kalibukbuk sell stamps.

Tours Available throughout the resort. The main ones on offer include Singaraja (Pura Beji, Jagaraga, Sawan, Kubutambahan, Pondok Batu and Hot Springs), Kintamani (Pura Beji, Kubutambahan, Penulisan, Penelokan and Toya Bungkah), Eastern Bali (Pura Beji, Kubutambahan, Penulisan, Besakih and Tenganan, Candi Dasa and Tirtaganggan), Sunset (Gigit, Danau Bratan, Taman Ayu and Tanah Lot), and Trekking (Singsing waterfall, Banjar Hot Springs and Buddhist temple, Pulaki and Bali Barat National Park).

Travel agents/shuttle buses Perama has two offices in the area – at Anturan (daily 8am–9pm; Ⓣ0362/41161) and on Jalan Mawar (daily 7am–10pm; Ⓣ0362/41161) – offering the full range of travel services, including shuttle buses on Bali and Lombok. Perama also book buses to other parts of Indonesia, including Jakarta and Yogyakarta. Mit Surya wartel are also agents for Pahala Kencana, offering tickets to Jakarta and Bogor.

Around Lovina

There are plenty of local attractions around Lovina. Several are accessible on public transport, while others in the area inland from Seririt are better explored with your own transport. A kilometre beyond the western limits of Lovina, Jalan Singsing leads 1km south to the **Singsing (Daybreak) waterfalls**, only really worth a look in the rainy season and not nearly as dramatic as other falls in the region.

Bali's only **Buddhist monastery** lies 10km southwest of Lovina and can be combined with a visit to the hot springs at Banjar, which are on a parallel road slightly further west. Catch any westbound bemo to **DENCARIK**, where a sign points inland to the monastery and ojek wait to take you the last steep 5km. The **Brahmavihara Arama** was consecrated in 1972. The temple complex enjoys a wonderful hillside setting: brilliant orange-tiled roofs stand over an entrance gate guarded by two fine *naga*, with a *kulkul* tower in the courtyard, a lower temple with a gold Buddha from Thailand as the centrepiece, carved stone plaques showing scenes from Buddha's life on all the main temples, and a colourful Buddhist grotto to the left of the top temple. From the temple you can walk to the **hot springs** (daily 8am–6pm; Rp3000, parking Rp1000). Head back downhill and take the first major left turn. After a few hundred metres – with fine views of the mountains of East Java in the distance – you'll reach a major crossroads and marketplace at the village of **BANJAR TEGA**. Turn left and a highly decorated *kulkul* tower will now be on your right. After about 200m you'll see a sign for the "Air Panas Holy Hot Springs" pointing you to a left turn. From here, it's a pleasant one-kilometre walk to the springs where there are three pools - it's a lovely spot. From the springs you can walk the 3km back down to the main road, or you should be able to find an ojek back in the market.

West Bali

Sparsely populated, mountainous, and in places extremely rugged, **west Bali** stretches from the northwestern outskirts of Denpasar across 128km to Gilimanuk at the island's westernmost tip. Once connected to East Java by a tract of land (now submerged beneath the Bali Strait), the region has always had a distinct Javanese character and now boasts a significant Muslim population. Apart from making the statutory visits to **Pura Tanah Lot** and **Sangeh Monkey Forest**, few tourists linger long, choosing instead to rush through on their way to or from Java, pausing only to board the ferry in the port town of **Gilimanuk**. Yet the southwest coast holds some fine black-sand beaches, and some good surf at **Medewi**, while the cream of Bali's coral reefs lie off the northwest coast between **Pulau Menjangan** (**Deer Island**) and **Pemuteran**. Over seventy percent of the land area in the west is preserved as **Bali Barat national park**, home to the endangered Bali starling.

Ubung public transport

All west- and north-bound buses and bemos from south Bali start from **Ubung**, a suburb on Denpasar's northwest fringes. Getting to Ubung from Sanur involves first taking a bemo to Denpasar's Kereneng terminal, then changing on to the Ubung-bound service (see p.528). From Kuta, take a bemo to Denpasar's Tegal terminal and then change to a bemo for Ubung.

Routes out of Ubung

Where there's a choice of transport, buses are faster and more comfortable than bemos, but up to fifty percent more expensive.

Buses and bemos (dark green) Ubung–Kediri–Pesiapan (west Tabanan)–Lalang Linggah–Medewi–Negara–Cekik–Gilimanuk.

Bemos (bright blue) Ubung–Mengwi–Baturiti–Pancasari–Singaraja (Sukasada terminal).

Bemos Ubung–Mengwi–Bedugul–Munduk–Seririt.

Large buses Ubung–Gilimanuk–Java (Surabaya, Yogyakarta & Jakarta).

Also occasional buses to Padang Bai in east Bali.

Mengwi

About 18km northwest of Denpasar, the small village of **MENGWI** has a glittering history as the capital of a powerful seventeenth-century kingdom and is the site of an important temple from that era. However, although **Pura Taman Ayun** (daily during daylight hours; Rp3100, kids Rp1600, includes sarong and sash rental) now features on numerous organized tours, lauded as a magnificent "garden temple", it looks far more impressive in aerial photographs than from the ground and doesn't merit a special trip. Probably built in 1634, it was designed as a series of garden terraces with each courtyard on a different level, and the whole complex was surrounded by a moat – now picturesquely choked with weeds and lilies – to symbolize the mythological home of the gods, Mount Meru, floating in the milky sea of eternity. Several **bemos** from Ubung travel via Mengwi; coming from Gilimanuk, take an Ubung-bound bemo to Tabanan's Pesiapan terminal, then change on to one for Taman Ayun.

Sangeh Monkey Forest

Monkeys have a special status in Hindu religion, and a number of temples in Bali boast a resident monkey population, respected by devotees and fed and photographed by tourists. The **Monkey Forest** (Bukit Sari; donation requested) in the village of **SANGEH** is probably the most visited of these on Bali, its inhabitants the self-appointed guardians of the slightly eerie **Pura Bukit Sari**. The temple was built here during the seventeenth century, in a forest of sacred nutmeg trees that tower to heights of 40m, and is best appreciated in late afternoon after the tour buses have left. During peak hours, the place can seem disappointing, but seen in waning light with only the monkeys for company the forest and the temple take on a memorably ghostly aspect. Sangeh is on a minor road that connects Denpasar, 21km south, with the mountainside village of Pelaga. The only way of getting to the Monkey Forest by public transport is by **bemo**, direct to Sangeh from the small Wangaya bemo terminal in central Denpasar. With your own vehicle, Sangeh is an easy drive from Mengwi, 15km southwest, or a pleasant forty-minute ride west from Ubud, via Sayan. Alternatively, you could join one of the numerous **organized tours** from any of the resorts, which usually combine Sangeh with visits to Mengwi, Tanah Lot and sometimes Bedugul.

Pura Tanah Lot

Dramatically marooned on a craggy wave-lashed rock sitting just off the south-west coast, **Pura Tanah Lot** (daily during daylight hours, Rp3300; plus Rp1500 per car) really does deserve its reputation as one of Bali's top sights. Fringed by frothing white surf and glistening black sand, its elegant multi-tiered shrines have become the unofficial symbol of Bali, appearing on a vast range of tourist souvenirs. Unsurprisingly, the temple attracts huge crowds every day, particularly around sunset. Even bigger crowds amass here at the time of Pura Tanah Lot's **odalan** festival. Be warned however that until at least the middle part of 2003, nearly all panoramas of Tanah Lot will be ruined by the presence of a long and unsightly temporary jetty that's been erected for anti-erosion construction work on the temple rock.

The temple is said to have been founded by the wandering Hindu priest **Nirartha**, who was drawn to Tanah Lot by a light that shone from a holy spring here. He began to preach to the local people of Beraban, but this angered the incumbent priest, who demanded that the rival holy man should leave. In response, Nirartha meditated so hard that he pushed the rock he was sitting on out into the sea; this became the Tanah Lot "island". He then dedicated his new retreat to the god of the sea and transformed his scarf into poisonous snakes to protect the place. Ever since then, Pura Tanah Lot has been one of the most holy places on Bali, closely associated with several other important temples along this coast, including Pura Rambut Siwi and Pura Luhur Uluwatu.

Because of its sacred status, only bona fide devotees are allowed to climb the temple stairway carved out of the rock face and enter the compounds; everyone else is confined to the patch of grey sand around the base of the rock, which is under water at high tide. When the waters are low enough, you can take a sip of **holy water** (*air suci*) from the spring that rises beneath the temple rock (donation requested) or stroke the docile holy **coral snakes** that are kept in nests behind the cliff face.

Construction work notwithstanding, if you follow the signed **clifftop path** to the southwest (right) of the temple rock you can admire the panorama and drop down to any number of tiny bays below, though the grey sandy beaches are prone to strong waves and aren't that inviting for swimming. After about 1km, the path veers inland, through a tiny hamlet; follow it round to the right of the village temple to get back to the Tanah Lot car park, or veer left to rejoin the coastal path which leads to the beach at Yeh Gangga, about an hour and a half's walk away (see p.652).

Practicalities

Though there are occasional bright-blue **bemos** from Denpasar's Ubung terminal direct to Tanah Lot, you'll probably end up having to go via **Kediri**, 12km east of the temple complex on the main Denpasar–Tabanan road. All Ubung (Denpasar)–Gilimanuk **bemos** drop passengers at Kediri bemo station (30min), where you should change on to a Kediri–Tanah Lot bemo (more frequent in the morning; 25min). Alternatively, join one of the numerous **tours** to Tanah Lot. The coastal path overlooking the temple complex is packed with pricey **restaurants**; the less expensive ones are further back, near the car park. The best-value **accommodation** is at *Pondok Wisata Atiti Graha* (Ⓣ0361/812955; ❸), a simple but spotless losmen set 500m back along the access road and surrounded by rice fields. The attractive *Dewi Sinta Cottages* (Ⓣ0361/812933, Ⓕ813956, Ⓦwww.balinetwork.com/dewisinta.html; ❺–❻) are more upmarket and just a few metres from the temple entrance, while the most luxurious place of all is the five-star *Le Méridien Nirwana Golf and Spa Resort* (Ⓣ0361/815900, Ⓕ815901, Ⓦwww.lemeridien-bali.com; ❽), whose construction close to such a holy temple caused a great deal of local upset.

Tabanan and around

Despite being the former capital of the ancient kingdom of Tabanan and the administrative centre of one of Bali's biggest rice-producing districts, **TABANAN** itself is only a medium-sized town with little to encourage a protracted stop. All Ubung (Denpasar)–Gilimanuk **bemos** bypass the town centre, dropping passengers at the **Pesiapan terminal** on the northwest edge of the town, from where bright-yellow city bemos ferry people into town. There are lots of regional bemo services from Pesiapan, including to Yeh Gangga, Kediri (for Tanah Lot) and Taman Ayun (Mengwi). The best **accommodation** is the clean and good value *Kuskus Indah Hotel*, Jl Pulau Batam 32 (Ⓣ0361/815373; ❸), located just a few metres west of the Pesiapan bemo station; alternatively, head for nearby Yeh Gangga beach (see opposite) or for Lalang Linggah (Balian Beach; p.655).

Tabanan's one worthwhile sight is the **Subak Museum** (Mon–Fri 8am–5pm; open at weekends if you ask the security guard; donation requested), which celebrates the role of the rice farmers' collectives, the *subak*, by describing traditional farming practices and exhibiting typical agricultural implements (for more on the *subak*, see p.522). One of its most interesting displays explains the highly complex and yet completely unmechanized irrigation system used by every *subak* on the island – a network of underground tunnels, small channels and tiny wooden dams that's known to have been in operation on Bali as early as 600 AD. Less than 100m from the Subak Museum, the **Traditional Balinese House** (daily during daylight hours; free) was built to give visitors an idea of the typical layout of a village home, comprising a series of thatched *bale* (pavilions) in a walled compound. Each *bale* has a specific function and must be located in a particular spot within the compound, specified by the sacred Balinese direction *kaja* and its counterpoint *kelod*; see p.522 for more.

The Subak Museum is signposted off the main Tabanan road in **BANJAR SENGGULAN**, 2km east of Tabanan town centre and about 4km west of the Kediri T-junction. Coming from Ubung, change on to a Tabanan city **bemo** at Kediri or to a town-centre bemo at Tabanan's Pesiapan terminal. Get out as soon as you see the prominent sign of the *Taman Bersaudara* restaurant on the south side of the road. The museum is 400m up the hillside road opposite, flagged by a tiny sign for "Mandala Mathika Subak". The Traditional House is signed from the museum.

Taman Kupu Kupu Butterfly Park

About 5km north of Tabanan, in the village of **WANASARI** on the road to Gunung Batukau, the **Taman Kupu Kupu Butterfly Park** (daily 8am–5pm; Rp30,000, kids Rp15,000) houses butterfly species from all over Indonesia in its small landscaped garden. Several are rare enough to feature on the CITES list of protected species, including the spectacular green and black *ornithoptera priamus*, which comes from Irian Jaya and has a wingspan of at least 10cm. All Tabanan–Penebel **bemos** pass the park, departing from the Tawakilang terminal, 2km north of Tabanan town centre on the Penebel road and accessed by a town-centre bemo from central Tabanan or Pesiapan terminal.

Yeh Gangga beach and Tibubiyu

Heading west out of Tabanan, nearly every minor road leads straight to the coast, an as yet undeveloped stretch of black sand notable for its strong currents and weird offshore rock formations. One of the most appealing sections is at **YEH GANGGA**, 10km southwest of Tabanan, where *Bali Wisata Bungalows* (ⓣ0361/261354, ⓕ812744, ⓦwww.baliwisatabungalows.com; ❺) make a good base from which to explore the area if you have your own transport. The access road to Yeh Gangga is signposted off the main road about 2km west of Tabanan town centre, and Yeh Gangga **bemos** depart Tabanan's Pesiapan terminal regularly throughout the morning and early afternoon (takes 45min). *Bali Wisata* is set in a wild shorefront garden and comprises half-a-dozen spacious bungalows (some with kitchen facilities), a small pool and a restaurant. The sea itself gets pretty rough and is punctuated by huge eroded rocks, but the **beach** stretches for kilometres in both directions. Heading southeast along the coast you can walk to Tanah Lot (see p.651) in about an hour and a half. About 1km northwest along the coast from *Bali Wisata* is *Waka Gangga* (ⓣ0361/416256, ⓕ416353, ⓦwww.wakaexperience.com; ❽), ten exquisite, circular bungalows scattered across terraced rice paddies offering panoramic ocean views; there's a pool and spa here too.

Occupying a similarly splendid spot in the village of **TIBUBIYU**, 12km southwest of Tabanan and a few kilometres west of Yeh Gangga, *Bibi's* (no phone, ⓕ0361/812744; ❸–❹), has five pretty rice-barn-style bungalows surrounded by paddy-fields with sea views from the upstairs bedrooms. The black-sand beach is ten minutes' walk away and you can borrow bicycles. To get to Tibubiyu, you'll need to go via the village of **Krambitan**, 4km north of *Bibi's*. Frequent turquoise **bemos** connect Krambitan with Tabanan's Pesiapan terminal (30min); the drivers can usually be persuaded to continue to Tibubiyu.

North to Gunung Batukau

Much of inland southwest Bali lies in the shadow of the massive **Gunung Batukau** (sometimes spelled "Bautukaru"; 2276m), the second-highest mountain on the island (after Gunung Agung) and one of the holiest. All west Bali temples have a shrine dedicated to the spirit of Gunung Batukau, and on the lower slopes of the holy mountain itself stands Pura Luhur Batukau, Bali's directional temple (*kayangan jagat*) for the west, and the focus of many pilgrimages. The dense tropical forest that clothes the uppermost slopes of Gunung Batukau has now been designated as a nature reserve, and is a particularly rewarding area for birdwatching.

From Tabanan, with your own transport, you have a choice of two very pretty routes to Batukau, 21km northwest. The following account describes a **circular route** to Pura Luhur Batukau and back, going up via Penatahan and Wongayagede and returning via Jatiluwih, Senganan and Penebel; it's equally viable in reverse. It's currently impossible to get to Pura Luhur Batukau by public **bemo**, though there is a service to Jatiluwih, via Penebel, and you may be able to charter the same bemo on to Pura Luhur. The Tabanan–Penebel–Jatiluwih bemos leave from the bemo station at Tawakilang, 2km north of Tabanan's town centre – approximately hourly in the mornings, less frequently after noon. Most tour operators sell sightseeing **tours** to Pura Luhur Batukau as well as guided mountain-bike trips down the lower slopes of Gunung Batukau or organized hikes through the Batukau rainforests.

Tabanan to Wongayagede (via Penatahan)

The main **Tabanan–Wongayagede route** follows a well-maintained road all the way from Tabanan town centre: simply keep a lookout for signs to Pura Luhur Batukau. Beyond Tabanan the road passes through some lovely shrub-lined villages, past the Butterfly Park in Wanasari (see p.652) and on through archetypal Balinese scenes of rice terraces before reaching a junction at **BURUAN**. The right-hand fork will take you up to Gunung Batukau via Penebel, Senganan and Jatiluwih, and is described in reverse below.

Soon after taking the left-hand fork you pass through the village of **PENATAHAN** and on to Wongayagede. If you're planning to climb Gunung Batukau (see box for details), you'll need to spend at least one night in **WONGAYAGEDE**, the remote and extremely scenic village nearest to the trailhead, about 2km south of the temple car park. You can **stay** at the very stylish *Prana Dewi* (Ⓣ & Ⓕ0361/732032, Ⓦwww.balipranaresort.com; ❻), signed west off the main road through the village (north of the side road to Jatiluwih), which occupies an idyllic spot literally surrounded by rice fields, serves home-grown red rice, organic vegetables and brown bread, hires out **guides** for the Batukau trek, and runs yoga courses. Accommodation at *Warung Kaja* (Ⓣ0811/398052, Ⓔpkaler@dps.centrin.net.id; ❹), which is set at the top of a steep flight of steps about 750m east along the Wongayagede–Jatiluwih road, is simpler but even more panoramic, and staff offer an extensive programme of **guided walks, cycle rides** and **treks** up Gunung Batukau (best arranged in advance).

Pura Luhur Batukau

Usually silent except for its resident orchestra of cicadas and frogs, **Pura Luhur Batukau** (Rp5000 donation requested; sarong and sash available to rent) does full justice to the epithet "the garden temple". The grassy courtyards are planted with flowering hibiscus, Javanese ixora and cempaka, forest surrounds the temple on three sides, and the monuments are encrusted with moist green moss. Batukau's **bird** population finds plenty to feed on here, so you're likely to see lots of barbets, scarlet minivets and flycatchers at least. Thought to have become a holy site in the eleventh century, Pura Luhur Batukau has been

Climbing Gunung Batukau

Few people **climb** the sacred slopes of Gunung Batukau, and during the rainy season (Nov–March), not even the most sure-footed Balinese would attempt it. If you do decide to climb, you'll definitely need a **guide**. Constant shade and low-lying cloud make the atmosphere damp and the paths quite slippery, so bring warm clothes, rainwear, and decent shoes. The usual guided climb takes four to six hours to reach the summit, and three to five hours to return to ground level. To complete the climb and descent in one day you'll need to start at sunrise, having spent the night in Wongayagede 2km down the road; some people prefer to camp near the top.

The best place to organize a **guided hike** is *Warung Kaja* in Wongayagede (see p.654); if possible you should contact them ahead of time so they can arrange permits and guides. Prices depend on the number of trekkers and whether you require an English-speaking guide as well as a porter and path-finder. Approximate per-person prices for the trek with/without an English-speaking guide are US$55/37.50 for one person, $32.50/25 for two people or $22.50/20 for three or four people. It's also possible to arrange guides through *Prana Dewi* in Wongayagede. The guys who hang around at Pura Luhur Batukau guide tourists up the mountain for Rp500,000 per group, excluding food and water (bring your own sleeping bag and tent if planning a night on the top).

rebuilt several times, most recently in 1959. Its most important shrine is the unusual seven-tiered pagoda which is dedicated to Mahadewa, the god of Gunung Batukau. To the east of the main temple compound, a large square **pond** has been dug to represent and honour the gods of nearby Danau Tamblingan (see p.653), which lies immediately to the north of Gunung Batukau. Members of local *subak* groups come here to draw holy water for use in agricultural ceremonies, and at the annual *Galungan* festivities truckloads of devotees make offerings here.

Wongayagede to Tabanan (via Jatiluwih)

The road to Jatiluwih branches east from Wongayagede about 2.5km south of Pura Luhur, and then proceeds to take you through some of the most famous rice-paddy vistas on Bali, offering expansive panoramas over the gently sloping terraces sculpted from the south-facing hillsides. A short distance along the road, you pass *Warung Kaja* (described above), the first of several stunningly located **restaurants**. Next up is the more commercial *Paddy Venture* (Ⓣ0361/289748, Ⓦwww.bali-adventures.com), which as well as serving food also runs **tours** through the rice paddies on foot, bicycle, quad-bikes and Land Rovers ($39–69). A couple of kilometres further east, the road begins to wend through the **JATILUWIH** district and its ever-more lush landscapes, dense with banana trees, *kopi bali* coffee plantations, fields of chilli peppers and tomato plants, ferns and *dadap* trees – a genuine garden of the gods. After about 14km in total from Wongayagede, the road arrives at the **SENGANAN** road junction. From here, the quickest route to the north or south coasts is the northeast (left) fork, a good, fast 7.5-kilometre road that feeds into the main Denpasar–Bedugul–Singaraja artery at **PACUNG**, 6km south of Bedugul and 25km north of Mengwi. For the slower, more scenic route to Buruan and Tabanan take the southbound (right) fork which runs via the market town of **PENEBEL** to **BURUAN** junction, a little way north of Tabanan.

Lalang Linggah and Balian beach

The main west coast road divides 16km west of Tabanan at the village of **ANTOSARI**, splitting the westbound Gilimanuk and Java traffic from the vehicles heading up to Seririt and the north coast. About 10km west of Antosari, the Gilimanuk road zips through **LALANG LINGGAH**, the village closest to **Balian beach**, a pleasant and peaceful place to base yourself for a few days. The grey-black sand beach here is popular with surfers, but the vicious current makes it far too dangerous for casual swimmers; there have been several fatalities in the last few years. There's a number of interesting local **walks**, including north along the course of Sungai Balian; local hotels can advise you on the best routes. Lalang Linggah has three **accommodation** possibilities, beautifully set on either side of Sungai Balian estuary, about ten minutes' walk from the shore. The friendly and informal *Balian Beach Bungalows* (Ⓣ & Ⓕ0361/814997, Ⓔbobbali@denpasar.wasantara.net.id; ❸–❹) attracts surfers and family groups and offers a range of rooms and bungalows plus a pool. Across the river, 300m west along the Gilimanuk road, the *Sacred River Retreat* (also signed as *Sungai Suci*; Ⓣ0361/814993, Ⓕ730904, Ⓦwww.sacred-river.com; ❻) has been set up as an alternative resort where the emphasis is on spiritual activities, including meditation and yoga, as well as Balinese painting and dancing. Its bungalows are simple but stylish, and there's a pool and vegetarian restaurant. About 400m west in Suraberata, *Gajah Mina* (Ⓣ0812/381 1630, Ⓕ0361/731174, Ⓦwww.gajahminaresort.com; ❼) has eight chic, Mediterranean-style air-conditioned bungalows and a pool.

All Ubung (Denpasar)–Gilimanuk **bemos** and buses pass through Lalang Linggah (1hr 15min from Ubung or 30min from Medewi). Coming from the north coast, take any Seririt–Pulukan or Singaraja–Seririt–Antosari bemo, then change onto the Ubung–Gilimanuk service.

Medewi beach

MEDEWI village sits on the main road 25km west of Lalang Linggah, and consists of little more than a mosque and a string of houses among coconut groves and paddy-fields. The beach is primarily a fishing beach, but there's a small enclave of shorefront bungalows and the black sand is fine, the current light, and the waves ideal for amateur **surfers**. The best **accommodation** is at the beachfront *Hotel Tin Jaya* (Ⓣ0365/42945; ❷), which has comfortable rice-barn-style cottages, as well as simpler losmen quarters. The four unsignposted rice-barn bungalows 100m further east along the road (next to the flashy *Hotel Pantai Medewi*) call themselves *Homestay Gede* (no phone; ❷), and are family-run and good value. Far larger, but soulless, the neighbouring *Hotel Pantai Medewi,* also known as *Medewi Beach Cottages* (Ⓣ0365/40029, Ⓕ41555, Ⓔbaliwest@indo.net.id; ❻), overcharges for its cheapest rooms, but has appealing air-con cottages and a pool. All three places have good restaurants attached.

Pura Rambut Siwi

Sixteen kilometres west of Medewi, **Pura Rambut Siwi** (donation requested) is another spectacularly sited coastal temple whose history is linked to the sixteenth-century Hindu priest Nirartha. Now the most important temple in Jembrana district, it contains a lock of Nirartha's hair, and its name translates as "the temple for worshipping the hair". The holy hair is enshrined, along with some of Nirartha's clothing, in a sandalwood box buried deep inside the central three-tiered *meru*. Descending the rock-cut steps from the temple gateway to the charcoal-black sand beach, you'll find a string of small shrines tucked into the cliff face to the left of the stairway. The first, a cave temple known as **Pura Tirta**, houses a holy freshwater spring and is guarded by a statue of Nirartha. A series of dank and bat-infested caves links Pura Tirta to **Goa Mayan Sati** (Cave of the Holy Tiger), 50m further east, but the underground complex is out of bounds to visitors, as all new priests of Pura Rambut Siwi meditate here before becoming fully ordained. All Ubung (Denpasar)–Gilimanuk **bemos** pass the turn-off for Pura Rambut Siwi: get out when you see the sign for the temple and a cluster of roadside warung, then walk 750m down the sideroad to the temple.

Gilimanuk

Situated on the westernmost tip of Bali, less than 3km from East Java, the small, ribbon-like town of **GILIMANUK** is used by visitors mainly as a transit point for journeys to and from Java. A 24-hour ferry service crosses the Bali Strait, so few travellers bother to linger in the town. All **bemos** and buses terminate at the bemo station in the town centre, ten minutes' walk from the ferry terminal or a short *dokar* ride. From **Denpasar** (128km southwest) and the southern beaches, take the dark-green bemos from Ubung or a Gilimanuk-bound bus. From **Singaraja** (88km northeast), dark-red bemos run regularly via **Lovina**, as do a few buses. It's also possible to get buses here from **Padang Bai** and **Amlapura** on the east coast. You can change money at the bank opposite the bemo terminal.

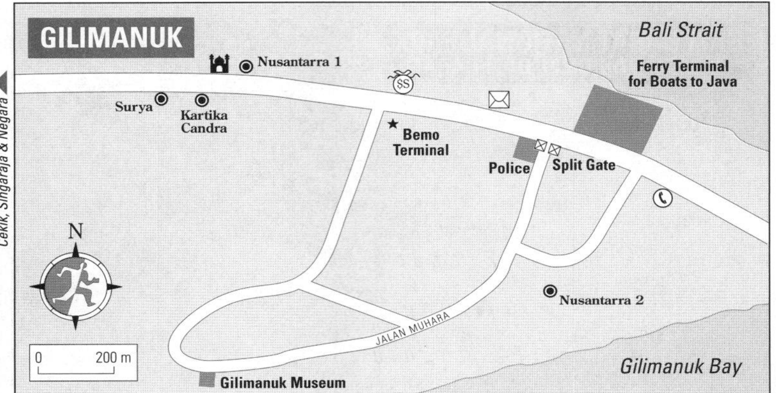

Accommodation in central Gilimanuk is poor and not at all tourist-orientated; your best option is *Nusantarra 2* (no phone; ❷), which offers very basic losmen-style rooms about five minutes' walk from the ferry terminal. If that's full, try *Kartika Candra* (❷) or *Surya* (❷), on the main road about fifteen minutes' walk south of the ferry terminal, and less than five minutes from the bemo station. There are a couple of better options about 2km south of the port along the road to Cekik, roughly 1500m north of the Bali Barat National Park headquarters: *Pondok Wisata Lestari* (ⓣ0365/61504; ❷–❸) has simple fan rooms and decent air-con ones, and *Sari* (ⓣ0365/61264, ⓕ61265; ❸) has more comfortable accommodation.

Bali Barat National Park

Nearly the whole of west Bali's mountain ridge is protected as **Bali Barat National Park** (Taman Nasional Bali Barat), a 760-square kilometre area of savannah, rainforest, monsoon forest, mangrove swamp and coastal flats, which

Crossing to Java

Crossing the Bali Strait between Bali and Java is easy: there are no formalities, and onward transport from both ports is frequent and efficient. If you're travelling quite a way into Java, to Probolinggo (for Mount Bromo) for example, or to Surabaya, Yogya or Jakarta, the easiest option is to get an all-inclusive ticket from your starting point in Bali. The cheapest **long-distance buses** travel out of Denpasar's Ubung bemo station (see p.528), with pick-up points in Tabanan and sometimes Gilimanuk, but there are also more expensive tourist shuttle buses and bus-and-train combinations operating from major tourist centres across Bali. Ticket prices always include the ferry crossing.

Ferries shuttle between Gilimanuk and **Ketapang** (East Java; see p.302) and back again 24 hours a day (every 20min; takes 30min including loading and docking). **Tickets** must be bought before boarding: foot-passengers buy them from the "Loket Penumpang" counter in the terminal building (Rp2000, kids Rp1300). Vehicle owners pay as they enter the compound, and the ticket price includes all passengers: bicycles cost Rp3000, motorbikes Rp5000, cars Rp25,000. Note that most car rental agencies on Bali prohibit tourists from taking their vehicles to other islands (see p.44 for more).

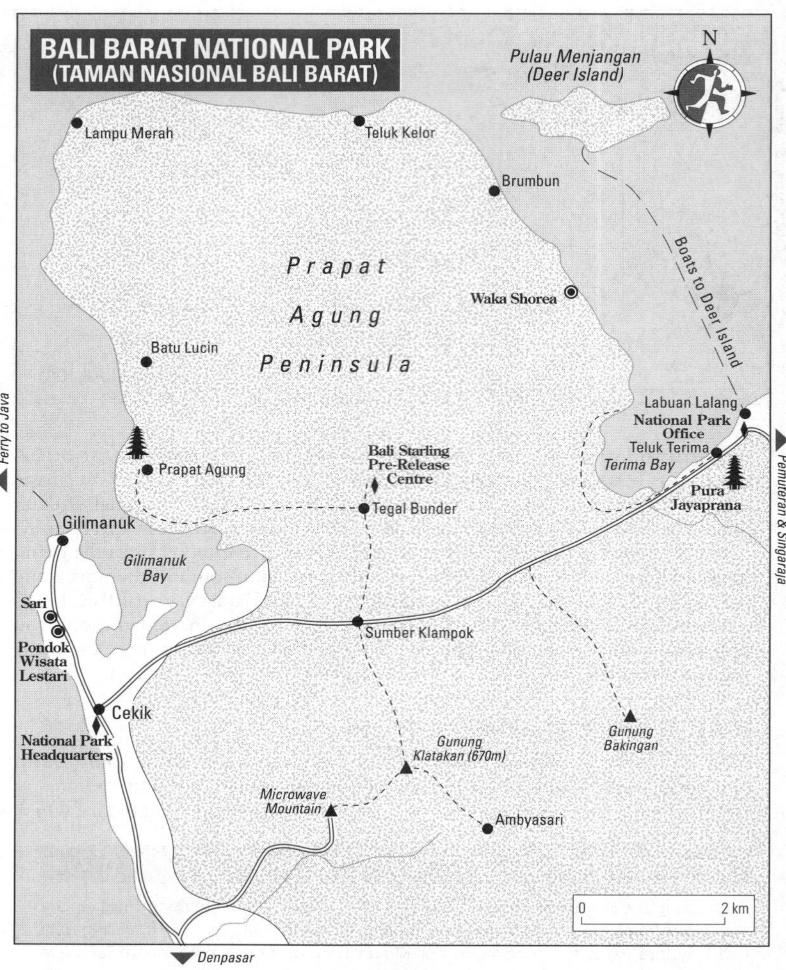

is home to a range of small animals and approximately 160 species of bird – including the elusive and endangered **Bali starling**, Bali's one true endemic creature. However, over ninety percent of the parkland is out of bounds to visitors, with only a few trails open to the public. All dark-green Ubung (Denpasar)–Gilimanuk **bemos** pass the national park headquarters at Cekik, as do all dark-red Singaraja–Gilimanuk bemos. These bemo routes also make access to trail heads a bit easier: the Gilimanuk–Denpasar road skirts the southern edge of the park, while the Gilimanuk–Singaraja road zips between the Prapat Agung peninsula in the northwest and the mountainous ridge to the east.

Anyone who enters the park has to be accompanied by an official park guide and must also be in possession of a permit. Both can be arranged through either the **National Park Headquarters** (daily 7am–5pm), conveniently located at **CEKIK** beside the Denpasar–Gilimanuk–Singaraja T-junction 3km south of Gilimanuk, or at the branch office at the Labuan Lalang jetty (see p.660). Most of the **guides** are English-speaking and they don't necessarily need to be booked in advance. The basic fee is Rp120,000 for a two-hour hike for up to two people (plus an extra Rp30,000 for every two extra people), then Rp20,000–40,000 per extra hour, depending on the route and total duration. If you don't have your own transport you'll also be expected to pay for bemo or boat charters to get to the trailhead. Having arranged a guide, you'll be granted a **permit**, which currently costs Rp2500 per person, though there are rumours of a possible price-hike to Rp20,000. Permits are good for only one day, unless you make other arrangements at the headquarters.

You can ask the rangers' permission to **camp** in the park, but you'll need your own tent, and should expect to pay Rp300,000 per person for the whole day and overnight experience. For Rp10,000, you may also pitch your own tent at the Cekik national park headquarters, though there are few facilities. Otherwise you'll have to stay in a **hotel** some distance from the trailheads. The best options are *Pondok Wisata Lestari* and *Sari* guest houses, about 1500m north of the park headquarters on the road into Gilimanuk (see p.656 for details). Alternatively, make for the appealing accommodation at Pemuteran (see p.661), 28km along the road towards Singaraja. It's possible to join a one-day or overnight **tour** of the park, arranged through tour agencies in major resorts. Hotels in Pemuteran also do day-trips.

Apart from a *bakso* and noodle cart that sets up outside the Cekik park headquarters everyday, there are no warung or **food** hawkers inside the park, so you'll need to take your own supplies for the hikes. The nearest restaurant is at *Pondok Wisata Lestari*.

The Tegal Bunder trail

If your main interest is birdspotting, you should opt for the **Tegal Bunder trek** (1–2hr; best in the early morning), a 25-minute drive from Cekik. The focus of this trek is the monsoon forest around the Bali Starling Pre-Release Centre near Sumber Klampok, which harbours a large **bird population**, including yellow-vented bulbuls, black-naped orioles, spotted doves, black drongos and olive-backed sunbirds. With its silky snow-white feathers, black wing and tail tips and delicate soft crest, the **Bali starling** or Rothschild's Myna (*leucopsar Rothschildi*) is an astonishingly beautiful bird and is the provincial symbol of Bali. It is Bali's only remaining endemic creature and lives only in the northwestern peninsula of Bali Barat national park. However, due to poaching and habitat destruction, it's estimated that there may now be just six Bali starlings left in the wild, so all known haunts are out of bounds to casual observers. At the Bali Starling Pre-Release Centre, the young birds are trained for new lives in the wild and then encouraged to settle nearby.

Gilimanuk Bay boat trip

The Tegal Bunder trail combines nicely with a boat trip round **Gilimanuk Bay**, which takes you through the mangrove forests that line most of the shore. Boats cost Rp70,000 for two people for two hours and should be arranged through the national park guides. **Mangroves** are best seen at low tide, when their aerial roots are fully exposed to form gnarled archways above the muddy banks, and boats should be able to get close enough for you to see some of the most common creatures who live in the swamps. These include fiddler crabs and mudskippers, as well as crab-eating or long-tailed macaques, who hang out along the shore. You might also spot some pacific reef egrets. The current off this shore is dangerously strong so it's not advisable to swim here, plus the beaches seem to end up covered with debris washed in from Java and the Bali Strait.

The Gunung Klatakan trail

The climb up **Gunung Klatakan** (5–6hr round-trip) is the most popular and most strenuous of the Bali Barat hikes, most of it passing through moderately interesting rainforest. The trail starts at the Sumber Klampok ranger post and for the most part follows a steep incline, via the occasional sheer descent, through **tropical rainforest** that's thick with ferns, vines and pandanus. Rattan and strangling fig abound too, as do all sorts of **orchids**, including the elegant long-stemmed white-sepalled madavellia orchid. You're unlikely to spot much wildlife on this trail, but you should certainly hear the black monkeys and might stumble across a wild boar or two. You could also encounter hornbills, pythons, green snakes and even flying foxes, but don't count on it.

Pulau Menjangan (Deer Island)

By far the most popular part of Bali Barat is **Pulau Menjangan** (**Deer Island**), a tiny uninhabited island just 8km off the north coast, whose shoreline is encircled by some of the most spectacular **coral reefs** in Bali. The sparkling azure-tinged water is incredibly calm, protected from excessive winds and strong currents by the Prapat Agung peninsula. As you near the island, the reefs form a band 100–150m around the coastline, and this is where you'll find the best **snorkelling** and **diving**, with drop-offs ranging from 40m to 60m, first-class wall dives with plenty of crevices and grottoes, and superb visibility from 15m to 50m. There's also an old shipwreck – the *Anker* – lying 7m deep off the western tip of the island, which is frequented by sharks and rays. Recent reports suggest that in some areas around Menjangan the reefs are showing signs of damage, and for once it's not the tourist trade that's the only culprit, but also El Niño and the dreaded coral-munching crown-of-thorns starfish. The current consensus seems to be that if your dive operator picks their spots well (and they probably will), you won't even know there's been any damage.

The departure point for Pulau Menjangan is **LABUAN LALANG**, just east of Teluk Terima, 13km from Cekik, and accessible by frequent bemos from Lovina (2hr) and Pemuteran (30min). There's a small national park office here (daily except national holidays 7.30am–3pm), as well as several warung. **Boats to Menjangan** can be hired at any time of day up to about 3pm; they hold up to ten people and prices are fixed at Rp200,000 for a round trip lasting a maximum of four hours, which includes the half-hour journey time each way. In addition you must pay Rp60,000 for one national park guide per boat, plus Rp2500 per person for the national park entry fee (the entry fee is slated to rise soon, perhaps to as much as Rp20,000). The boat can be hired for as many extra hours as you like for Rp15,000 per hour, and you can rent mask, fins and snorkel from the warung by the jetty for Rp30,000 a set. There have been recent reports of **thefts** from the boats while snorkellers are underwater, so leave your valuables elsewhere and if possible keep money with you in a waterproof pouch.

There are no accommodation facilities on Menjangan, and most divers and snorkellers come on organized **tours**, either from the north-coast resorts of Lovina and Pemuteran, or on longer excursions from Kuta, Sanur and Ubud; prices start at US$65 for two dives in one day (snorkellers $25). Unless you have your own diving equipment, tours are the only way for divers to explore the reefs. However, for snorkellers it can often work out cheaper to turn up at

Labuan Lalang and club together with other tourists to hire a boat. As the island comes under the jurisdiction of the national park, you have to go with a guide, but you can arrange both the guide and boat transport at the jetty in Labuan Lalang without first checking in at the Cekik headquarters.

Pemuteran

As the road heads east from Labuan Lalang, the scenery gets more and more arresting, with the great craggy folds of Bali Barat's north-facing ridges rising almost perpendicular from the roadside. In the foreground of this amazing setting sits the small fishing village of **PEMUTERAN**, 28km east of Cekik, the location of some lovely, if rather pricey, accommodation, and a good place to base yourself for diving and snorkelling. Just beyond the eastern edge of Pemuteran, the stark charcoal-grey stone of the sixteenth-century temple **Pura Agung Pulaki** peers down from a weatherworn cliff face, making a good viewpoint over the northwest coast. All dark-red Gilimanuk–Singaraja **bemos** pass through Pemuteran and will drop you in front of your chosen hotel (30min from Labuan Lalang, or 1hr 20min from Lovina). If coming from Ubud or the south coast resorts, your fastest option is to take a Perama shuttle bus to Lovina and then hop onto a bemo. The Bhakti Yoga Clinic on the main road about 1km west of *Pondok Sari* gives **medical** attention 24 hours (ⓣ082/361 1679).

During high season, all Pemuteran's **hotels** get booked up by diving tours, so you're strongly advised to reserve ahead. Note however that phone lines in this area are extremely unreliable and none of the hotels has on-site email (nearest internet access is in Lovina). The cheapest and best-value central option is *Pondok Sari* (ⓣ & ⓕ0361/92337, ⓦwww.bali-hotels.co.uk/pondok.html; ❺–❻), whose large, stylish fan and air-con cottages are set in a tropical garden that runs down to the black-sand beach. The adjacent *Taman Sari* (ⓣ0362/93264, ⓕ0361/286879, ⓦwww.balitamansari.com; ❻–❼) offers appealingly spacious and comfortable deluxe air-conditioned bungalows, some less good-value fan rooms, plus a pool and a good Thai restaurant. East of *Pondok Sari*, tiny, chic *Taman Selini* (ⓣ & ⓕ0362/93449, ⓦwww.tamanselini.com; ❼) is another fine place to stay, with just a few prettily furnished rooms, a pool and a Greek restaurant. About 3km east of *Taman Selini* in Banyupoh, *Segara Bukit Seaside Cottages* (ⓣ0828/365231, ⓕ0362/22471; ❸–❺) is the cheapest place to stay in the area, with decent fan and air-con rooms and a pool in a small seaside garden, not far from a fish farm.

Snorkelling, diving and other activities

All the hotels organize day-trips to local sights, including hikes through Bali Barat National Park, but the chief attraction here is the **snorkelling** and **diving**. Although there are some reasonable reefs within easy reach of Pemuteran's shore, most divers agree that these are nothing compared to nearby Pulau Menjangan (see opposite), and snorkellers will definitely be better rewarded there. Pemuteran's three main **dive centres** all run diving and snorkelling trips to local reefs as well as to Menjangan, and all are located beside the beach in front of the hotels: Reef Seen Aquatics (ⓣ & ⓕ0362/92339, ⓔreefseen@denpasar.wasantara.net.id) is beside *Taman Selini*; Yos Marine Adventures (ⓣ & ⓕ0362/92337, ⓦwww.yosdive.com) is in front of *Pondok Sari*; and Arkipelago Selam (ⓣ & ⓕ0828/365296, ⓦwww.archipelagodive.com) is based at *Taman Sari*. For boat-trips to the Pemuteran reefs, expect to pay about US$30 per diver or $6 per snorkeller; for Pulau Menjangan, the average is $65 per diver and $25 per snorkeller, but unaccompanied snorkellers will find it cheaper to go direct to Labuan Lalang, as described on p.660. All the Pemuteran dive operators also offer **dive courses** ($310 for the four-day open water) and diving excursions to Tulamben ($75 for two dives, or $25 for snorkellers; see p.624). Reef Seen dive centre runs **fishing trips** and sunrise cruises for **dolphin-watching** (both $6 per person for 2hr) – but don't count on seeing dolphins here. You can also take **horse rides** ($30 for 2hr), and horse-riding lessons ($30 for 1hr). Reef Seen also runs a **turtle-hatching** project at its dive centre.

Seririt and the road south

The town of **SERIRIT** is chiefly of interest to travellers as a junction. The main north-coast road slices through the town centre, travelled by frequent dark-red Gilimanuk–Singaraja bemos; this is also the departure point for the scenic back road to Munduk, Danau Bratan and Bedugul (see p.633). Most importantly, though, Seririt stands at the head of the most westerly route between the north and south coasts, a narrow and nerve-wrackingly twisty road which commands some breathtakingly lovely views as it crosses through the mountains, rice-growing valleys and hilltop villages that lie just beyond the eastern limits of Bali Barat National Park. The road divides at the village of **PUPUAN**, 25km south of Seririt, from where the more westerly route takes you via the pretty ridgetop settlement of **TISTA** (where you can veer off east, via Ceking and Bangal, down a road that ends just west of Balian beach; see p.655) and then through clove plantations and along the course of Sungai Pulukan to the village of **ASAHDUREN**. A few kilometres south of Asahduren, the road comes to a T-junction at **PEKUTATAN** on the main Tabanan–Gilimanuk road, 2km east of Medewi beach (see p.656).

The easterly branch of the road from Pupuan drops down through similarly eye-catching mountainscapes, passing dozens of **coffee plantations** (the *robusta* variety, known and drunk locally as *kopi bali*). About 40km south of Seririt, in the village of **BELIMBING**, sits the delightful little award-winning **hotel** *Cempaka Belimbing* (Ⓣ & Ⓕ 0361/754897, Ⓦ www.indo.com/hotels/cempaka_belimbing, Ⓔ purwa@denpasar.wasantara.net.id; ❼–❽), whose valley-view villas enjoy a breathtaking panorama of palm groves, paddy fields and the peaks of Gunung Batukau. About 10km south of Belimbing, the road meets the Denpasar–Gilimanuk highway at **Antosari** (see p.655), 16km west of Tabanan on the Tabanan–Gilimanuk road.

Travel details

Bemos and public buses

It's almost impossible to give the frequency with which bemos and public buses run, as they only depart when they have enough passengers to make the journey worthwhile. However, on the most popular routes, you should be able to count on getting a ride within half-an-hour if you travel before noon; things quieten down in the afternoon and come to a standstill by around 5pm. Journey times also vary a great deal: the times given below are the minimum you can expect. Only direct bemo and bus routes are listed below; for other journeys, you'll have to change at one or more of the island's major transport hubs – Denpasar, Gianyar or Singaraja.

Air Sanih to: Amlapura (2hr); Culik (1hr 30min); Gilimanuk (3hr); Lovina 1hr); Singaraja (Penarukan terminal; 30min); Tirtagangga (2hr); Tulamben (1hr).

Amlapura to: Air Sanih (2hr); Batubulan (2hr); Candi Dasa (20min); Culik (45min); Gianyar (1hr 20min); Gilimanuk (4–5hr); Klungkung (1hr); Lovina (3hr 30min); Seraya (40min); Singaraja (Penarukan terminal; 3hr); Tirtagangga (20min); Tulamben (1hr); Ujung (20min).
Bangli to: Denpasar (Batubulan terminal; 1hr 30min); Gianyar (20min); Singaraja (Penarukan terminal; 2hr 15min).
Bedugul to: Denpasar (Ubung terminal; 1hr 30min); Singaraja (Sukasada terminal; 1hr 30min).
Candi Dasa to: Amlapura (20min); Denpasar (Batubulan terminal; 2hr); Gianyar (1hr); Klungkung (40min); Padang Bai (20min).
Culik to: Aas (1hr 30min); Air Sanih (1hr 30min); Amed (20min); Amlapura (45min); Bunutan (45min); Jemeluk (30min); Lipah Beach (1hr); Lovina (2hr 30min); Selang (1hr 15min); Singaraja (Penarukan terminal; 2hr 30min).
Denpasar (Batubulan terminal) to: Amlapura (2hr 30min); Candi Dasa (2hr); Gianyar (1hr); Kintamani (1hr 30min); Klungkung (1hr 20min); Mas (35min); Nusa Dua (1hr); Padang Bai (for Lombok; 1hr 40min); Singaraja (Penarukan terminal; 3hr); Sukawati (20min); Tegalalang (1hr 15min); Ubud (50min).
Denpasar (Kereneng terminal) to: Sanur (15–25min).
Denpasar (Tegal terminal) to: Jimbaran (40min); Kuta (25min); Ngurah Rai Airport (35min); Nusa Dua (35min); Sanur (25min).
Denpasar (Ubung terminal) to: Bedugul (1hr 30min); Cekik (3hr); Gilimanuk (3hr 15min); Jakarta (Java; 24hr); Kediri (for Tanah Lot; 30min); Lalang Linggah (for Balian Beach; 1hr 15min); Medewi (1hr 30min); Mengwi (30min); Singaraja (Sukasada terminal; 3hr); Solo (Java; 15hr); Surabaya (Java; 10hr); Tabanan (35min); Yogyakarta (Java; 15hr).
Denpasar (Wangaya terminal) to: Sangeh Monkey Forest (45min).
Gianyar to: Amlapura (1hr 20min); Bangli (20min); Batur (40min); Blahbatuh (30min); Candi Dasa (1hr); Denpasar (Batubulan terminal; 1hr); Klungkung (20min); Ubud (20min).
Gilimanuk to: Cekik (10min); Denpasar (Ubung terminal; 3hr 15min); Kediri (for Tanah Lot; 2hr 45min); Medewi (1hr 45min); Labuan Lalang (for Menjangan; 25min); Lalang Linggah (for Balian beach; 2hr 15min); Pemuteran (1hr); Lovina (2hr 15min); Seririt (1hr 30min); Singaraja (Banyuasri terminal; 2hr 30min); Tabanan (2hr 30min).
Kintamani to: Singaraja (Penarukan terminal; 1hr 30min); Ubud (40min).
Klungkung to: Amlapura (1hr); Besakih (45min); Candi Dasa (40min); Denpasar (Batubulan terminal; 1hr 20min); Gianyar (20min); Rendang (30min).
Kuta to: Bualu (20min); Denpasar (Tegal terminal; 25min); Jimbaran (15min); Ngurah Rai Airport (10min).
Lovina to: Amlapura (3hr 30min); Gilimanuk (2hr 30min); Jakarta (24hr); Probolingo (for Bromo; 7hr); Seririt (20min); Singaraja (Banyuasri terminal; 20min); Surabaya (10–12hr).
Ngurah Rai Airport to: Bualu (20min); Denpasar (Tegal terminal; 35min); Kuta (10min); Jimbaran (10min).
Padang Bai to: Amlapura (40min); Candi Dasa (20min); Gilimanuk (3–4hr); Klungkung (20min).
Pemuteran to: Cekik (50min); Gilimanuk (1hr); Labuan Lalang (for Menjangan; 30min); Lovina (1hr 15min); Seririt (45min); Singaraja (1hr 30min).
Penelokan to: Bangli (45min); Buahan (30min); Denpasar (Batubulan terminal; 1hr 30min); Gianyar (50min); Singaraja (Penarukan terminal; 1hr 30min); Songan (45min); Toya Bungkah (30min).
Sanur to: Denpasar (Kereneng terminal; 15–25min); Denpasar (Tegal terminal; 25min).
Singaraja (Banyuasri terminal) to: Gilimanuk (2hr 30min); Lovina (20min); Seririt (40min); Surabaya (10–12hr); Yogyakarta (21hr).
Singaraja (Penarukan terminal) to: Amlapura (3hr); Culik (2hr 30min); Denpasar (Batubulan terminal; 3hr); Gianyar (2hr 20min); Penelokan (1hr 30min); Kubutambahan (20min); Sawan (30min); Tirtagangga (2hr 30min); Tulamben (1hr).
Singaraja (Sukasada terminal) to: Bedugul (1hr 30min); Denpasar (Ubung terminal; 3hr); Gitgit (30min).
Tirtagangga to: Air Sanih (2hr); Culik (30min); Amlapura (20min); Lovina (3hr); Singaraja (2hr 30min); Tulamben (1hr).
Tulamben to: Air Sanih (1hr); Culik (30min); Amlapura (1hr); Lovina (2hr 30min); Singaraja (2hr); Tulamben (1hr).
Ubud to: Campuhan/Sanggingan (5–10min); Denpasar (Batubulan terminal; 50min); Gianyar (20min); Goa Gajah (10min); Kedewatan (10min); Kintamani (1hr); Mas (15min); Pujung (25min); Sukawati (30min).

Perama shuttle buses

STO = overnight stopover is sometimes needed
Air Sanih to: Bangsal (daily; STO); Bedugul (daily; STO); Candi Dasa (daily; 2hr–2hr 30min); Kintamani (daily; STO); Kuta/Ngurah Rai airport (daily; 5hr 30min); Kuta, Lombok (daily; STO); Lovina (daily; 1hr); Mataram (daily; 7–8hr); Padang Bai (daily; 2hr 30min–3hr); Sanur (daily; 4hr 30min–5hr); Sengiggi (daily; 7–8hr); Tetebatu

(daily; STO); Tirtagangga (daily; 2hr); Ubud (daily; 3hr 30min–4hr).

Bedugul to: Air Sanih (daily; STO); Bangsal (daily; STO); Candi Dasa (daily; STO); Kintamani (daily; STO); Kuta/Ngurah Rai airport (daily; 2hr 30min–3hr); Kuta, Lombok (daily; STO); Lovina (daily; 1hr 30min); Mataram (daily; STO); Padang Bai (daily; STO); Sanur (daily; 2hr–2hr 30min); Sengiggi (daily; STO); Tetebatu (daily; STO); Tirtagangga (daily; STO); Tulamben (daily; STO); Ubud (daily; 1hr 30min).

Candi Dasa to: Air Sanih (daily; 2hr–2hr 30min); Bangsal (daily; 6hr–6hr 30min); Bedugul (2 daily; STO); Kintamani (daily; 3hr 15min); Kuta/Ngurah Rai airport (3 daily; 3hr); Kuta, Lombok (2 daily; STO); Lovina (2 daily; 3hr–3hr 30min); Mataram (2 daily; 5hr–5hr 30min); Nusa Lembongan (2 daily; STO); Padang Bai (3 daily; 30min); Sanur (3 daily; 2hr–2hr 30min); Sengiggi (2 daily; 5hr 30min–6hr); Tetebatu (2 daily; STO); Tirtagangga (daily; 30min); Tulamben (daily; 1hr 30min); Ubud (3 daily; 1hr 30min–2hr).

Kintamani to: Air Sanih (daily; STO); Bangsal (daily; STO); Bedugul (daily; STO); Candi Dasa (daily; 3hr 15min); Kuta/Ngurah Rai airport (daily; 2hr 30min–3hr); Kuta, Lombok (daily; 2hr 45min); Lovina (daily; 2hr); Mataram (daily; STO); Padang Bai (daily; 2hr 45min); Sanur (daily; 2hr 15min); Sengiggi (daily; STO); Tetebatu (daily; STO); Tirtagangga (daily; STO); Tulamben (daily; STO); Ubud (daily; 1hr 15min).

Kuta to: Air Sanih (1 daily; 5hr 30min); Bangsal (1 daily; 9hr 30min); Bedugul (1 daily; 2hr 30min–3hr); Bima (2 daily; STO); Candi Dasa (3 daily; 3hr); Jakarta (1 daily; 25–26hr); Kintamani (1 daily; 2hr 45min); Mataram (2 daily; 8hr 30min); Ngurah Rai Airport (6 daily; 30min): Kuta, Lombok (1 daily; STO); Lovina (2 daily; 3hr); Malang (1 daily; 16–17hr); Nusa Lembongan (1 daily; 2hr 30min); Padang Bai (3 daily; 2hr 30min); Sanur (7 daily; 30min); Sape (2 daily; STO); Senggigi (2 daily; 9hr); Surabaya (1 daily; 12–13hr), Tetebatu (1 daily; STO); Tirtagangga (1 daily; 4hr), Tulamben (1 daily; 5hr); Ubud (7 daily; 1hr–1hr 30min); Yogyakarta (1 daily; 16–17hr).

Lovina to: Air Sanih (daily; 1hr); Bangsal (daily; STO); Bedugul (daily; 1hr 30min); Candi Dasa (2 daily; 3hr–3hr 30min)); Kintamani (daily; 2hr); Kuta/Ngurah Rai airport (daily; 3hr); Kuta, Lombok (daily; STO); Mataram (daily; 7–8hr); Padang Bai (daily; 2hr 45min); Sanur (daily; 2hr 30min–3hr); Sengiggi (daily; 7hr 30min–8hr 30min); Tetebatu (daily; STO); Tirtagangga (daily; 2hr 30min); Tulamben (daily; 1hr 30min); Ubud (daily; 3hr 30min–4hr).

Nusa Lembongan to: Air Sanih (daily; 6hr–6hr 30min); Bangsal (daily; STO); Bedugul (daily; STO); Candi Dasa (daily; 3hr); Kintamani (daily; 4hr); Kuta/Ngurah Rai airport (daily; 2hr 30min–3hr); Kuta, Lombok (daily; STO); Lovina (daily; 5hr); Mataram (daily; 9hr); Padang Bai (daily; 3hr 30min); Senggigi (daily; 9hr); Tetebatu (daily; STO); Tirtagangga (1 daily; 5hr), Tulamben (daily; 5hr 30min–6hr).

Padang Bai to: Air Sanih (daily; 2hr 30min–3hr); Bangsal (daily; 5hr 30min–6hr); Bedugul (2 daily; STO); Candi Dasa (3 daily; 30min); Kintamani (daily; 2hr 45min); Kuta/Ngurah Rai airport (3 daily; 2hr 30min); Kuta, Lombok (2 daily; STO); Lovina (2 daily; 2hr 30min–3hr); Mataram (2 daily; 4hr 30min–5hr); Nusa Lembongan (2 daily; STO); Sanur (3 daily; 1hr 30min–2hr); Sengiggi (2 daily; 5hr–5hr 30min); Tetebatu (2 daily; STO); Tirtagangga (daily; 1hr); Tulamben (daily; 2hr); Ubud (3 daily; 1hr–1hr 30min).

Sanur to: Air Sanih (1 daily; 4hr 30min–5hr); Bangsal (1 daily; 9hr); Bedugul (1 daily; 2hr–2hr 30min); Bima (2 daily; STO); Candi Dasa (3 daily; 2hr–2hr 30min); Jakarta (1 daily; 25–26hr); Kintamani (1 daily; 2hr 15min); Kuta/Ngurah Rai airport (6 daily; 30min–1hr): Kuta, Lombok (2 daily; STO); Lovina (2 daily; 2hr 30min–3hr); Malang (1 daily; 16–17hr); Mataram (2 daily; 8hr); Padang Bai (3 daily; 1hr 30min–2hr); Sape (2 daily; STO); Senggigi (2 daily; 8hr 30min); Surabaya (1 daily; 12–13hr); Tetebatu (2 daily; STO); Tirtagangga (1 daily; 3hr 30min); Tulamben (1 daily; 4hr–4hr 30min); Ubud (7 daily; 30min–1hr); Yogyakarta (1 daily; 16–17hr).

Tirtagangga to: Air Sanih (daily; 2hr); Bangsal (daily; STO); Bedugul (daily; STO); Candi Dasa (daily; 30min); Kintamani (daily; STO); Kuta/Ngurah Rai airport (daily; 4hr); Kuta, Lombok (daily; STO); Lovina (daily; 2hr 30min); Mataram (daily; 6hr–6hr 30min); Padang Bai (daily; 2hr); Sanur (daily; 4hr–4hr 30min); Sengiggi (daily; 7hr 30min–8hr 30min); Tetebatu (daily; STO); Tulamben (daily; 1hr); Ubud (daily; 2hr 30min).

Tulamben to: Air Sanih (daily; 1hr); Bangsal (daily; STO); Bedugul (daily; STO); Candi Dasa (daily; 1hr 30min); Kintamani (daily; STO); Kuta/Ngurah Rai airport (daily; 5hr); Kuta, Lombok (daily; STO); Lovina (daily; 1hr 30min); Mataram (daily; 7–8hr); Padang Bai (daily; 2hr); Sanur (daily; 4hr–4hr 30min); Sengiggi (daily; 7–8hr); Tetebatu (daily; STO); Tirtagangga (daily; 1hr); Ubud (daily; 3hr–3hr 30min).

Ubud to: Air Sanih (1 daily; 3hr 30min–4hr); Bangsal (1 daily; 8hr); Bedugul (1 daily; 1hr 30min); Bima (2 daily; STO); Candi Dasa (3 daily; 1hr 30min–2hr); Jakarta (1 daily; 25–26hr); Kintamani (1 daily; 1hr 15min); Kuta/airport (6 daily; 1hr–1hr 30min); Kuta, Lombok (3 daily; STO); Lovina (2 daily; 1hr 30min–2hr); Malang (1 daily; 16–17hr); Mataram (2 daily; 7hr); Nusa Lembongan (1 daily; 2hr 30min); Padang Bai (3 daily; 1hr–1hr 30min); Sanur (6 daily; 30min–1hr); Sape (2 daily; STO); Senggigi (2 daily; 7hr 30min); Surabaya (1 daily; 12–13hr), Tetebatu (2 daily; STO); Tirtagangga (1 daily; 2hr 30min), Tulamben (1 daily; 3hr–3hr 30min); Yogyakarta (1 daily; 16–17hr).

Pelni ferries

For a chart of Pelni routes, see p.42.

Denpasar (Benoa Harbour) Except where indicated, fortnightly services to: Badas (16hr); Balikpapan (3 days); Bima (twice a fortnight; 31hr); Bitung (twice a fortnight; 4 days); Ende (2 days); Gorontalo (4–5 days); Jayapura (5 days); Kupang (3 times a fortnight; 26hr); Labuhanbajo (twice a fortnight; 2 days); Larantuka (36hr); Makassar (3 times a fortnight; 2 days); Maumere (3 days); Pantoloan (3 days); Surabaya (twice a fortnight; 15hr); Tanjung Priok (39hr); Waingapu (26hr).

Other ferries

Benoa Harbour to: Bima (Sumbawa; 1–2 weekly by Barito express; 7hr); Gili Meno (daily by Bounty Cruise; 2hr 30min); Kupang (Timor; 1 weekly by Barito express; 20hr); Lembar (Lombok; 1 direct boat daily on Mabua Express; 2hr; also 1 daily via Padang Bai on *Osiania 3*; 3hr 15min); Maumere (Flores; 1 weekly by Barito express; 12hr); Surabaya (Java; 1 weekly by Barito express; 7hr); Teluk Nara/Senggigi (Lombok; daily by Bounty Cruise; 3hr) and Waingapu (Sumba; 1 weekly by Barito express; 13hr).

Gilimanuk to: Ketapang (East Java; every 20min; 30min).

Jungutbatu (Nusa Lembongan) to: Benoa (4 weekly; 1hr); Gili Meno (4 weekly; 2hr 30min); Kusamba (daily; 1–2hr); Sanur (daily; 1–2hr); Senggigi (4 weekly; 2hr); Toyapakeh (daily; 45min).

Kusamba to: Nusa Lembongan (daily; 1–2hr); Nusa Penida (daily; 1–2hr).

Padang Bai to: Benoa (daily; 1hr); Lembar (Lombok; slow ferry, every 1hr 30min; 4–5hr; fast boat, daily; 1hr 30min); Nusa Penida (daily; 1hr).

Sampalan (Nusa Penida) to: Kusamba (daily; 1–2hr); Padang Bai (daily; 1hr).

Sanur to: Jungutbatu (Nusa Lembongan; 3 daily; 1hr 30min).

Toyapakeh (Nusa Penida) to: Jungutbatu (daily; 45min); Kusamba (daily; 1–2hr).

Domestic flights

Denpasar (Ngurah Rai Airport) to: Bima (6 weekly; 1hr 15min); Dili (2 daily; 1hr 50min); Jakarta (6 daily; 1hr 40min); Kupang (2–3 daily; 1hr 35min); Labuhanbajo (5 weekly; 1hr 45min–2hr 20min); Makassar (2–3 daily; 1hr 15min); Mataram (6 daily; 30min); Maumere (daily; 2hr 20min); Sumbawa (2 weekly; 1hr 40min); Surabaya (4–5 daily; 50min); Waingapu (3 weekly; 1hr 50min); Yogyakarta (3 daily; 1hr 10min).

Nusa Tenggara

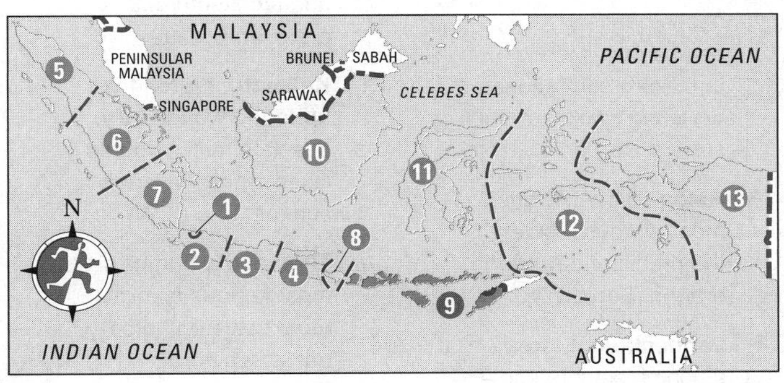

CHAPTER 9

Highlights

* **Gili Islands** Three perfect tropical islands off Lombok, each very different from its neighbours. See p.690
* **Gunung Rinjani** Highest mountain on Lombok, offering adventurous trekking. See p.701
* **South-coast beaches, Lombok** Hidden coves nestle between rocky headlands all along Lombok's south coast, while big swells attract surfers. See p.712
* **Rinca** Visit the island's most famous resident, the prehistoric Komodo dragon. See p.732
* **Labuanbajo, Flores** A stunning setting, some rewarding snorkelling, and dinner at the *Gardena* to round it off. See p.734
* **Traditional houses** From the conical houses of the Manggarai to Sumba's lofty witches' hats, Nusa Tenggara is a dream for those with a nose for anthropology and architecture. See p.737 and p.792
* **Kelimutu, Flores** Hike up to the wonderfully desolate multicoloured lakes at the volcano's summit. See p.749
* **The pasola** Sumba's most famous festival, a ritual battle on horseback. See p.797

9

Nusa Tenggara

Nusa Tenggara is the group of islands to the east of Bali, stretching like stepping stones towards New Guinea. While it comprises a spectacular and exotic diversity of landscapes, cultures, languages and peoples, it's regarded by most Indonesians as an obscure, sparsely populated and uncivilized region – characteristics which may indeed appeal to many travellers.

The two provinces of Nusa Tenggara – West and East Nusa Tenggara – occupy most of the **Lesser Sunda Islands**. A volcanic northern arc runs from Lombok, through Sumbawa and the Banda Islands to Alor. The southern arc runs from Raijua off Savu through Roti and Timor; these islands have no volcanoes, consisting mainly of raised coral reef. **Lombok** island is now the most popular destination in Nusa Tenggara, with tourists arriving to climb Gunung Rinjani, one of the highest peaks in Indonesia, and to enjoy the beaches and thriving cultures to be found here. A short hop east of Lombok lies **Sumbawa** island, fast becoming another big draw for surfers. The majority of travellers, however, just nip through here en route to the **Komodo national park**, a stark group of islands inhabited by the world's largest lizards, Komodo dragons.

Flores stretches east from Komodo towards the north tip of Timor. Its lush, dramatic landscape is peppered with smouldering **volcanoes**, of which Kelimutu, with its three coloured crater lakes, is the most unique and spectacular. Further east lies the **Alor and Solor archipelago**, the highlight of which is **Lembata**, where the local people hunt whales from frail wooden sailing boats.

The exposed, parched islands of **Savu** and **Roti** have become havens for die-hard surfers and also anthropologists – animist traditions still flourish here. In **East Sumba**, fine **ikat fabrics** are made and sold, while **West Sumba** offers the exciting spectacle of the **pasola** (a ritual war fought on horseback) and grandiose **funeral ceremonies** rivalled only by those of the Toraja of Sulawesi. **West Timor** is perhaps the most interesting and diverse of all the territories, though unfortunately at the time of writing it is still an unsettled province, and Western travellers are currently staying away (see box on p.771). The few who do manage to come here are often doing so en route to the newly independent East Timor, where it is possible to renew your Indonesian visa.

The majority of visitors to Nusa Tenggara follow obvious **linear routes** through the islands, typically travelling east from Bali and flying back from Flores. To make a full tour of Nusa Tenggara – from Lombok to Alor, south to West Timor (but see the warning on p.771 about safety in West Timor), looping round Roti, Savu and Sumba, and then back to civilization with a flight to Bima, Mataram or Denpasar – would take up all of your two-month visa.

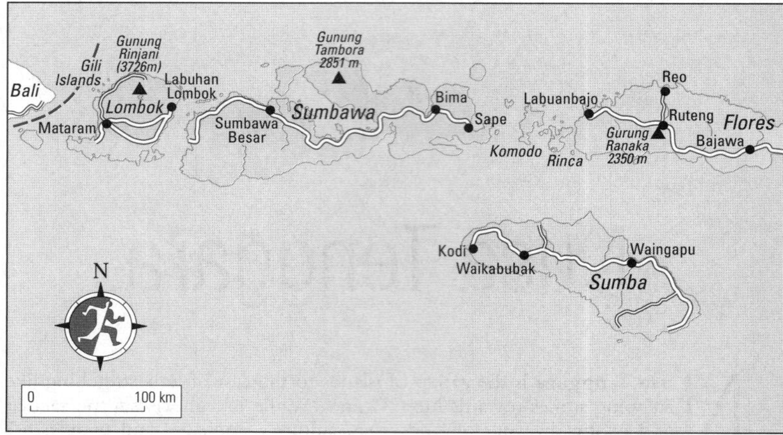

However, more selective island-hopping is possible, with Pelni, the new ASDP fast ferries and other vessels linking the islands. Although **transport** has improved beyond recognition on Lombok, Sumbawa, Flores and most of West Timor, it's still extremely primitive compared to Java and Bali. Navigating the appalling roads of the outer islands can be a major challenge, while the local boats look like salvaged shipwrecks, most services are delayed or cancelled and all journeys require determination.

Certain parts of Nusa Tenggara are difficult to negotiate during the **rainy season**, particularly Flores and the Alor and Solor archipelago. Note too that at this time a lot of the old public ferries simply stop running due to rough seas, so you'll have to rely on the Pelni, the fast ferries or flying to get around during this time. The rainy season lasts from about October to March, except in the more southerly islands, where it is much shorter. The dry season is also more pronounced here, with fierce mid-year temperatures in Roti, Savu and West Timor.

Some history

The first incursions into Nusa Tenggara by outside powers were made by Chinese traders as early as the sixth century, and later by the Makassarese and Bugis peoples of Sulawesi. Traders were mainly attracted by the **sandalwood** stands of Timor, and the convenient position of ports such as Bima on the sea route between Java and the abundant Spice Islands. The primary commodities of spices and timber were supplemented by slaves, horses from Sumba and Timor, and myriad oddities such as birds' nests, sharks' fins, and sulphur from around the archipelago. Much of Nusa Tenggara is presumed to have been under the control the East Javanese **Majapahit empire**, founded in the thirteenth century.

In 1504, **Ferdinand Magellan** (see p.1036) sailed along the coast of Flores on his way to Timor. Later in the sixteenth century, his **Portuguese** countrymen built forts in the east at Ende and on nearby Solor, to avoid having to stay on the inhospitable malarial coast of Timor. The colonizers plundered the sandalwood forests, and brought Christianity, along with smallpox and venereal diseases. In 1859, the Portuguese sold most of their remaining territiories in Nusa Tenggara

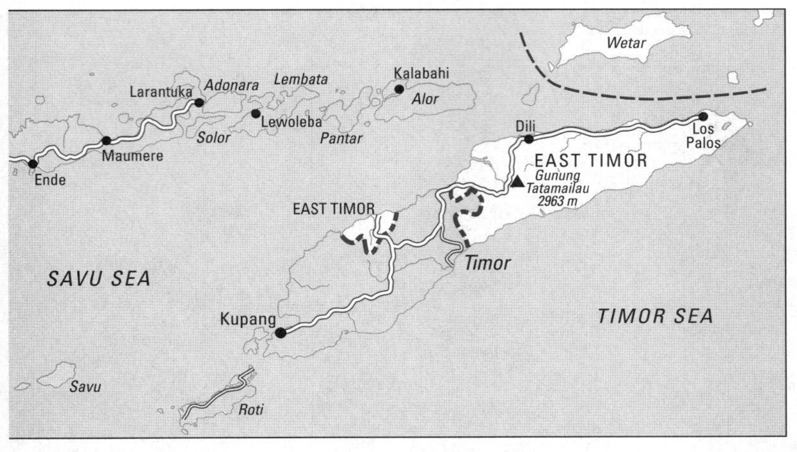

to the rapacious Dutch East Indies Company. Subsequently, in 1894 the Dutch invaded Balinese-controlled Lombok, leaving the tiny province of East Timor as the only territory remaining under Portuguese control. Sumba and Timor were both briefly held by the Japanese during World War II, but upon Independence in 1945 all of Nusa Tenggara became part of Indonesia, with the exception of **East Timor**, which remained in Portuguese hands until 1974. The following year Indonesia invaded its tiny eastern neighbour, incorporating its newly won territory into the province of Nusa Tenggara Timur. Over the next two decades all attempts by the Timorese to win back their sovereignty were brutally suppressed. The East Timorese finally won their Independence in 1999; for more details on their struggle, see the box on pp.772–773.

Lombok and the Gili Islands

Lying 35km east of Bali at its closest point, Lombok is inevitably compared with its better-known western neighbour, although the two differ physically, culturally, linguistically and historically. Lombok also has less widespread tourist facilities, sparser public transport and simpler accommodation, although things are changing pretty rapidly. Approximately ten percent of the island's 2.5 million inhabitants are Balinese, and it's very easy – especially if you arrive in the west where most Balinese are settled, surrounded by their distinctive temples and household architecture – to perceive Lombok simply as an extension of Bali, although the majority of the population are the indigenous Muslim **Sasak** people.

Lombok measures 80km by 70km and divides conveniently into three geographical regions. The mountainous **north** is dominated by the awesome bulk

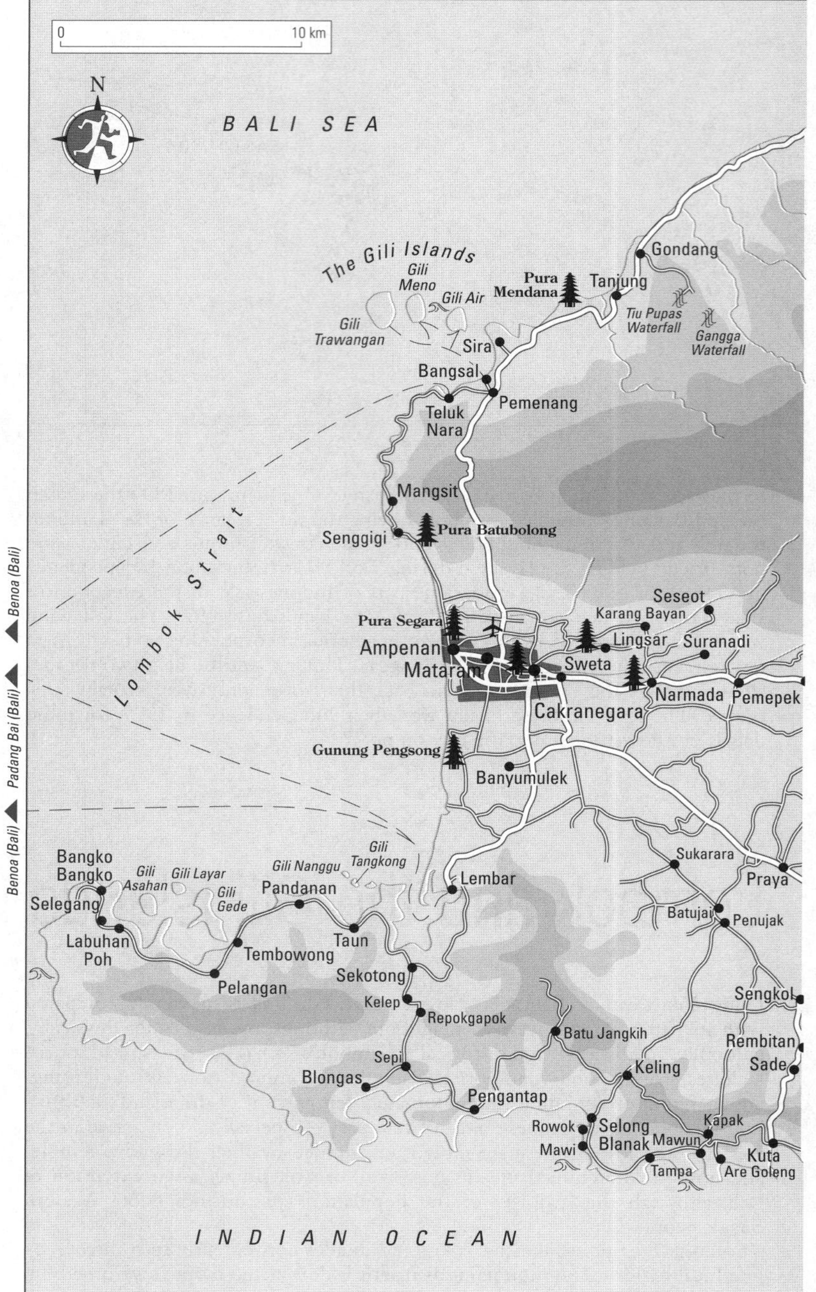
0
10 km
N
BALI SEA
The Gili Islands
Gili Meno
Gili Air
Gili Trawangan
Pura Mendana
Tanjung
Gondang
Tiu Pupas Waterfall
Gangga Waterfall
Sira
Bangsal
Pemenang
Teluk Nara
Mangsit
Senggigi
Pura Batubolong
Lombok Strait
Benoa (Bali)
Padang Bai (Bali)
Benoa (Bali)
Seseot
Karang Bayan
Pura Segara
Lingsar
Suranadi
Ampenan
Mataram
Sweta
Narmada
Pemepek
Cakranegara
Gunung Pengsong
Banyumulek
Gili Tangkong
Gili Nanggu
Bangko Bangko
Gili Asahan
Gili Layar
Gili Gede
Pandanan
Lembar
Sukarara
Praya
Selegang
Batujai
Penujak
Labuhan Poh
Tembowong
Taun
Pelangan
Sekotong
Sengkol
Kelep
Repokgapok
Batu Jangkih
Rembitan
Sepi
Sade
Blongas
Keling
Pengantap
Rowok
Selong Blanak
Kapak
Mawi
Mawun
Tampa
Kuta
Are Goleng
INDIAN OCEAN

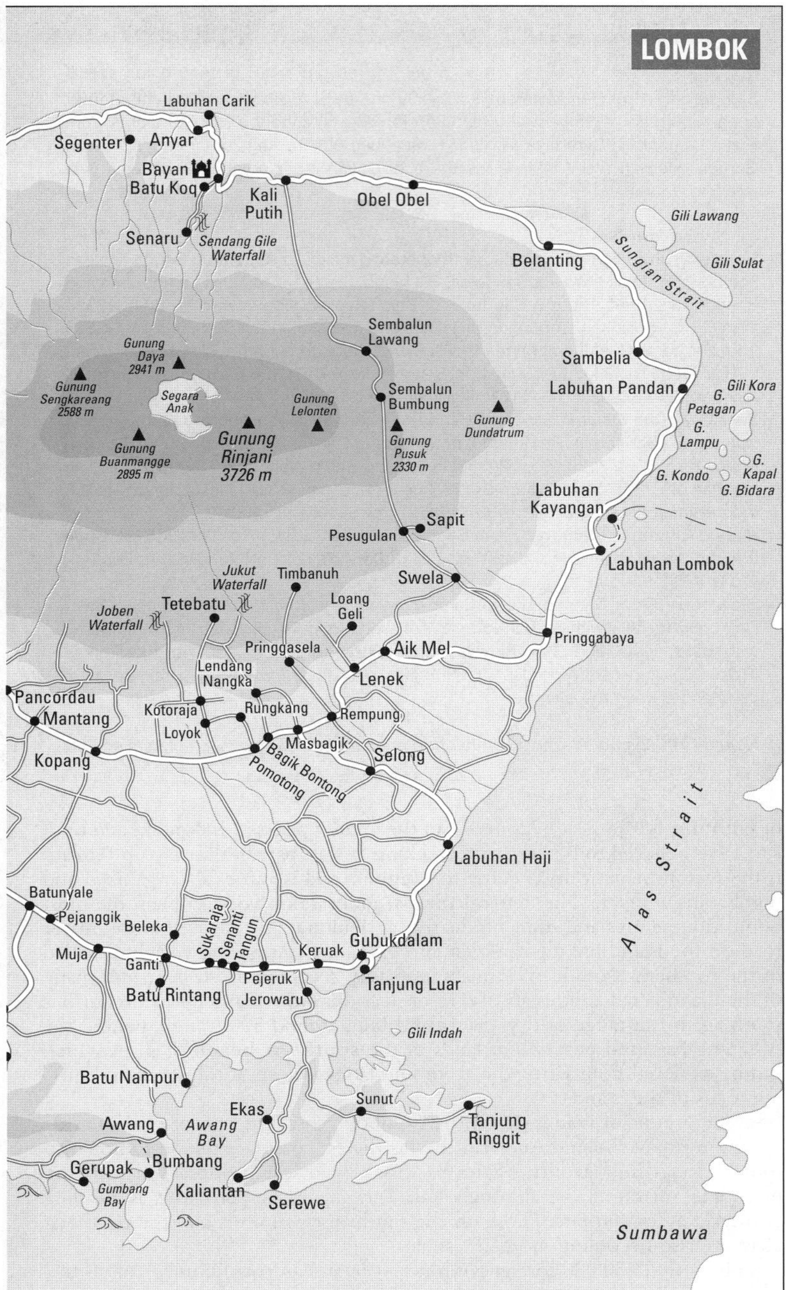
LOMBOK
Labuhan Carik
Segenter
Anyar
Bayan
Batu Koq
Kali Putih
Obel Obel
Senaru
Sendang Gile Waterfall
Gili Lawang
Sungian Strait
Gili Sulat
Belanting
Sembalun Lawang
Sambelia
Gunung Daya 2941 m
Gunung Sengkareang 2588 m
Segara Anak
Gunung Lelonten
Sembalun Bumbung
Labuhan Pandan
Gili Kora
G. Petagan
G. Lampu
Gunung Dundatrum
Gunung Buanmangge 2895 m
Gunung Rinjani 3726 m
Gunung Pusuk 2330 m
G. Kondo
G. Kapal
G. Bidara
Labuhan Kayangan
Sapit
Pesugulan
Labuhan Lombok
Poto Tano (Sumbawa)
Jukut Waterfall
Timbanuh
Swela
Joben Waterfall
Tetebatu
Loang Geli
Pringgabaya
Pringgasela
Aik Mel
Lendang Nangka
Lenek
Pancordau
Mantang
Kotoraja
Rungkang
Rempung
Loyok
Masbagik
Kopang
Bagik Bontong
Pomotong
Selong
Alas Strait
Labuhan Haji
Batunyale
Pejanggik
Beleka
Sukaraja
Senanti
Tangun
Gubukdalam
Muja
Keruak
Ganti
Pejeruk
Tanjung Luar
Batu Rintang
Jerowaru
Gili Indah
Batu Nampur
Sunut
Ekas
Tanjung Ringgit
Awang
Awang Bay
Bumbang
Gerupak
Gumbang Bay
Kaliantan
Serewe
Sumbawa

Getting to Lombok

By plane

Selaparang Airport in Mataram is the only one on Lombok. Its only direct international flights serve Singapore (see p.805 for details) although Merpati flights from Kuala Lumpur via Surabaya also arrive here (see p.805). Regular internal flights on Garuda, Merpati and Air Mark link the airport with other points in Indonesia (see p.805 for more).

By boat from Bali

Bounty Cruise High-speed catamaran operating a circular route from Benoa to Nusa Lembongan, Teluk Nara (for Senggigi), Gili Meno, then back to Nusa Lembongan and Benoa (Sun, Tues, Thurs & Sat; takes 2–3hr; Ⓦwww.balibountygroup.com). US$25 from Benoa or Nusa Lembongan to Teluk Nara (free shuttle bus to Senggigi); US$35 from Benoa or Nusa Lembongan to Gili Meno. Book through travel agents or direct in Bali Ⓣ0361/733333, Ⓕ730404; in Senggigi Ⓣ0370/693666, Ⓕ693678; or in Gili Meno Ⓣ0370/649090, Ⓕ641177, Ⓔgilimeno@indo.net.id.

Fast boat (the *Osiania 3*) From Benoa to Padang Bai, and on to Lembar. (daily; from Benoa 3hr 15min, Rp129,000; from Padang Bai 1hr 30min, Rp75,000). Book in Benoa on Ⓣ0361/723577 or 723353; in Padang Bai at Wannen on Ⓣ0363/41780; in Lembar on Ⓣ0370/644051 or 641268 or 644757 or 631034; in Mataram at P.T. Indonesia, Jl Airlangga 40A1 Ⓣ0370/645974 or 644051, Ⓕ632849.

Mabua Express catamaran From Benoa to Lembar (daily; takes 2hr; US$25). Book through travel agents or direct in Bali Ⓣ0361/721212, Ⓕ723615; in Lombok Ⓣ0370/681195, Ⓕ681124.

Slow ferry From Padang Bai to Lembar (every 1hr 30min; takes 4hr–4hr 30min; Rp16,500 for VIP, with air-con lounge, soft seats and TV, or Rp9000 for ekonomi, with hard seats and TV). Bicycles cost extra (Rp10,000), as do motorbikes (Rp25,000) and cars (from Rp175,000). See p.44 for information on taking rental vehicles between the islands.

Note that the bemo drivers at Lembar port are hard bargainers: most tourists end up

of **Gunung Rinjani**, at 3726m one of the highest peaks in Indonesia, and until late 1994 believed to be dormant. Trekking at least part of the way up Rinjani is the reason many tourists come to Lombok, and it's an easily organized and highly satisfying trip. The **central plains**, about 25km wide, contain the most population centres and most productive agricultural areas as well as the major road on the island linking the west and east coasts. Attractive villages perched in the southern foothills of Rinjani are easily accessible from here, and many of the island's craft centres are also in or near this cross-island corridor. Further south again is a range of dry, low inland hills, around 500m high, behind the sweeping bays and pure white sands of the **southern beaches**, all of which can be explored from **Kuta**, the accommodation centre of the south and surfing focus of the island.

Several groups of islands lie off the Lombok coast. The trio of **Gili Islands** – Trawangan, Meno and Air – off the northwest coast, are the best known to tourists, long-time favourites with backpackers in search of sea, sun and sand in simple surroundings, although Gili Trawangan, in particular, is heading upmarket at a rapid rate. Those off the southwest peninsula and the northeast coast are also becoming more accessible.

With around 250,000 foreign visitors a year, and an equal number of visitors *paying far more to get to Bertais/Mandalika terminal in Sweta than the correct price of about Rp2500. These hassles are one good reason to book through to Mataram or Senggigi with Perama or another tourist shuttle company; if you haven't booked in advance, you could try negotiating directly with the driver/conductor on the bus. A typical fare in a pale blue metered taxi from Lembar is Rp30,000 to Cakranegara, or Rp45,000–50,000 to Sengiggi. From 10am to 7pm taxis are obvious in the ferry port car park; at other times they wait on the road outside.*

By boat from Sumbawa and other islands

Ferry From Poto Tano (Sumbawa) to Kayangan, Labuhan Lombok (every 45min; takes 2hr; Rp5000). Bicycles cost extra (Rp6950), as do motorbikes (Rp12,500) and cars (from Rp85,000).

The Indonesian passenger line Pelni, operates services throughout the archipelago; see p.42 for full details of routes. Booking offices are in Jakarta, at Jl Gajah Mada 14 ⓣ021/384 3307, ⓕ384 4342 or 385 4130 (the ticket office is at Jl Angkasa 18 ⓣ021/421 1921); in Bali, on Jl Pelabuhan in Benoa Harbour ⓣ0361/723689, and at Jl Raya Tuban 299 in Kuta ⓣ0361/763963; and on Lombok at Jl Majapahit 2, Ampenan ⓣ0370/637212, ⓕ631604.

By bus

To Sweta (Bertais/Mandalika terminal) Several services daily from Java, Bali, Sumbawa and Flores, including from Denpasar (takes 6–8hr; Rp50,000); from Surabaya (20hr; Rp105,000); from Sumbawa Besar (6hr; Rp44,000); from Bima (12hr; Rp60,000); from Domphu (10hr; Rp42,000); from Sape (14hr; Rp51,000); from Labuhan Bajo (24hr; Rp70,000); from Ruteng (36hr; Rp80,000). Other fares include from Jakarta (32hr; Rp200,000 for air-con and reclining seats); from Yogyakarta (22hr; Rp165,000), from Medan on Sumatra (about 85hr; Rp500,000).

Tourist shuttle buses From Bali to Mataram, Senggigi, Bangsal for the Gili Islands, Tete Batu and Kuta. Perama are the most established company with offices in all major tourist areas.

from other parts of Indonesia, the **tourist** presence on Lombok is nowhere near as pervasive as in Bali. Most visitors stick to a relatively well-beaten track, meaning that it's easy to find less popular routes, remote villages, unspoilt coastline and village people still living traditional lives. Generally, **accommodation** is more limited and slightly more expensive than on Bali, concentrated in the west-coast resorts and the capital, Mataram. Elsewhere, simple accommodation is now being supplemented by luxury five-star resorts such as the *Oberoi* on the northwest coast and *Coralia Lombok Novotel* in the south.

Ampenan–Mataram–Cakranegara–Sweta and around

The conurbation of **AMPENAN–MATARAM–CAKRANEGARA–SWETA**, with a population of around 250,000, comprises four towns, the boundaries of which are all but indistinguishable to the casual visitor. At first sight rather overwhelming, the whole area measures over 8km from west to east, but a relatively straightforward local transport system allows you to get

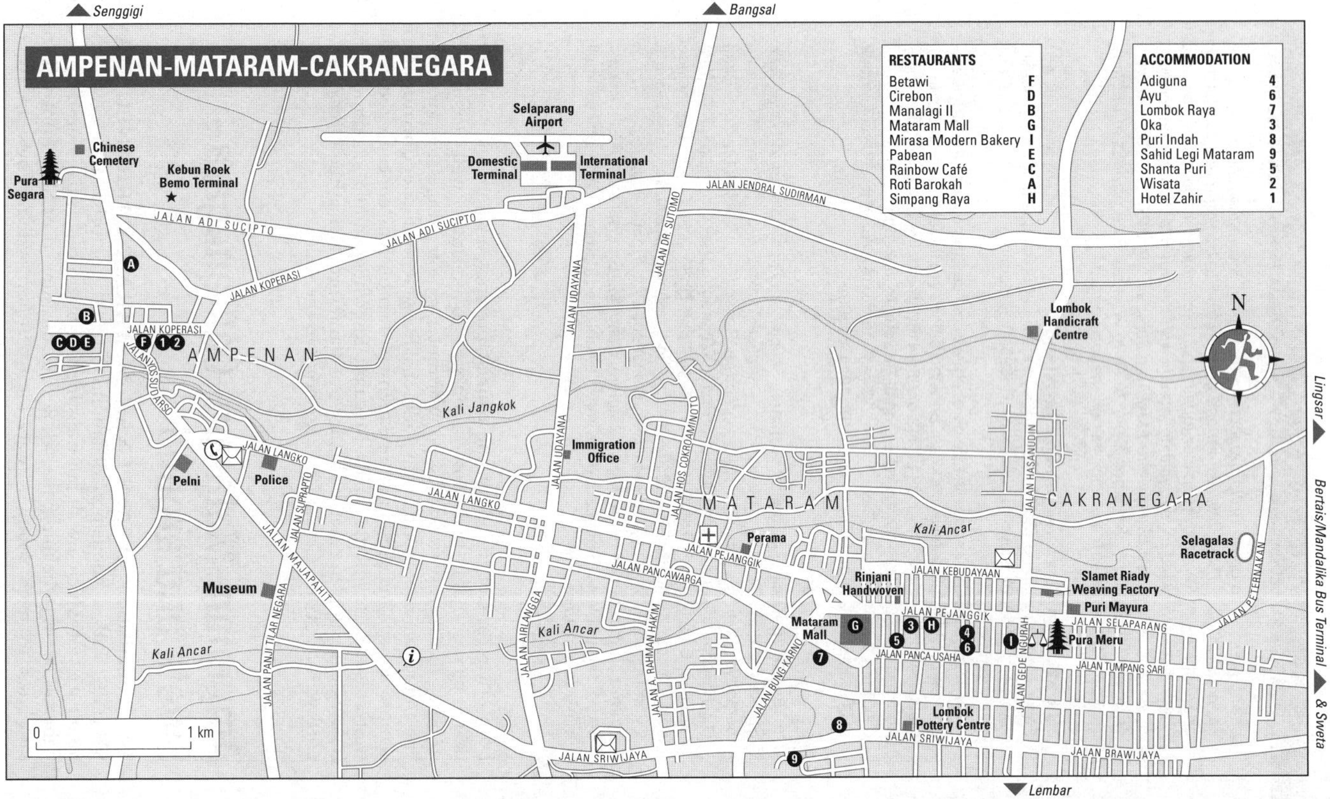

AMPENAN-MATARAM-CAKRANEGARA

RESTAURANTS	
Betawi	F
Cirebon	D
Manalagi II	B
Mataram Mall	G
Mirasa Modern Bakery	I
Pabean	E
Rainbow Café	C
Roti Barokah	A
Simpang Raya	H

ACCOMMODATION	
Adiguna	4
Ayu	6
Lombok Raya	7
Oka	3
Puri Indah	8
Sahid Legi Mataram	9
Shanta Puri	5
Wisata	2
Hotel Zahir	1

Senggigi
Bangsal
Lingsar
Bertais/Mandalika Bus Terminal & Sweta
Lembar
N
Selaparang Airport
Domestic Terminal
International Terminal
Pura Segara
Chinese Cemetery
Kebun Roek Bemo Terminal
JALAN ADI SUCIPTO
JALAN JENDRAL SUDIRMAN
JALAN DR. SUTOMO
JALAN UDAYANA
JALAN KOPERASI
AMPENAN
Kali Jangkok
JALAN YOS SUDARSO
JALAN LANGKO
Pelni
Police
Immigration Office
JALAN HOS COKROAMINOTO
MATARAM
Lombok Handicraft Centre
JALAN HASANUDIN
CAKRANEGARA
Kali Ancar
Perama
Selagalas Racetrack
JALAN PETERNAKAN
JALAN PEJANGGIK
JALAN PANCAWARGA
JALAN KEBUDAYAAN
Rinjani Handwoven
Slamet Riady Weaving Factory
Puri Mayura
Mataram Mall
JALAN SELAPARANG
Pura Meru
JALAN PANCA USAHA
JALAN TUMPANG SARI
JALAN GEDE NGURAH
JALAN SUPRAPTO
JALAN MAJAPAHIT
Museum
JALAN PANJI TILAR NEGARA
JALAN AIRLANGGA
JALAN A. RAHMAN HAKIM
JALAN BUNG KARNO
Lombok Pottery Centre
JALAN SRIWIJAYA
JALAN BRAWIJAYA
0 1 km

around easily. Most visitors pass through fairly quickly. The conurbation is laid out around three parallel roads, which stretch from **Ampenan** on the coast through **Mataram** and **Cakranegara** to **Sweta** on the eastern edge. The roads change their names several times along their length, the most northerly being Jalan Langko–Jalan Pejanggik–Jalan Selaparang, which allows travel only in a west–east direction. Its counterpart running parallel to the south, Jalan Tumpang Sari–Jalan Panca Usaha–Jalan Pancawarga–Jalan Pendidikan, allows only east–west travel. The third major route, Jalan Brawijaya–Jalan Sriwijaya–Jalan Majapahit, two-way for most of its length, skirts to the south of these, and is useful as the site of the central post office and tourist office.

Arrival, information and transport

Selaparang Airport is on Jalan Adi Sucipto at Rembiga, only a few kilometres north of Mataram and Ampenan. There's an exchange counter, open for all international arrivals, and a **taxi** counter with fixed-price fares. All the major luxury hotels have booking counters here (discounts vary from day to day) and there's a **wartel** (daily 7am–9pm). A few black **bemos** plying to Kebun Roek terminal in Ampenan (heading to the right) pass along the road in front of the airport. See p.690 for public transport details from the airport to Bangsal (for the Gili Islands).

If you're arriving in the city from east Lombok, from Lembar in the south (see p.683 for details of transport from Lembar), or from the airport, you'll come into the **bus station** on the eastern edge of the conurbation, known variously as **Bertais**, **Mandalika** or **Sweta**. This is the main bus terminal on the island: most public transport from the north arrives here as well as do the long-distance buses which ply as far as Flores, Java and Sumatra. Just across the road, a maze of stalls lining tiny alleyways sell produce, household items and crafts. Arriving **from Senggigi**, and on some of the bemos from Pemenang, you'll come into the **Kebun Roek** terminal in Ampenan. Both bus terminals are linked by the frequent yellow bemos that zip around the city.

The most helpful **tourist office** is the Provincial Tourist Service for West Nusa Tenggara, which is rather out of the way off Jalan Majapahit in the south of the city, at Jl Singosari 2 (Mon–Thurs 7am–2pm, Fri 7–11am, Sat 7am–1pm; ⓣ0370/634800, ⓕ637233). There are shorter opening hours during Ramadan (see p.58). They offer leaflets, a map of Lombok and advice about travel in Lombok and Sumbawa. Yellow bemos heading via "Kekalik" pass the end of Jalan Singosari as they go along Jalan Majapahit between Bertais terminal and Kebun Roek terminal.

City transport

All **bemo** trips within the four-cities area are a flat rate, and yellow bemos constantly ply between Kebun Roek terminal in Ampenan and Bertais/Mandalika terminal in Sweta from early morning until late evening. Most follow the Jalan Langko–Jalan Pejanggik–Jalan Selaparang route heading west to east, and Jalan Tumpang Sari–Jalan Panca Usaha–Jalan Pancawarga–Jalan Pendidikan heading east to west, although there are plenty of less frequently served variations. The horse-drawn carts here, unlike the ones on Bali, have small pneumatic tyres and are called **cidomo**; they aren't allowed on the main streets, covering instead the back routes that bemos don't work, and are generally used for carrying heavy loads. Always negotiate a price first. There are plenty of pale blue, easily identifiable official metered **taxis** in the street, or they can be ordered by phone (ⓣ0370/627000).

Accommodation

The range of **accommodation** is huge, although relatively few tourists stay here since Senggigi is only a few kilometres up the road. **Ampenan** is known for its budget backpackers' lodges, which are now looking decidedly frayed around the edges, but there's a good clutch of losmen in **Cakranegara** offering cleaner and better-value accommodation.

Ampenan

Wisata Jl Koperasi 19 ⓣ0370/626971, ⓕ621781. Tiled, reasonable-quality rooms; the expensive ones have air-con. ❷–❸

Hotel Zahir Jl Koperasi 9 ⓣ0370/634248. A good-value budget cheapie close to the centre of Ampenan, offering basic rooms around a tiny garden. ❷

Cakranegara

Adiguna Jl Nursiwan 9 ⓣ0370/625946. An excellent budget choice, situated in a quiet, convenient street near the bemo routes, and featuring reasonable rooms in a small garden. ❷

Ayu Jl Nursiwan 20 ⓣ0370/621761. This clean losmen has buildings on both sides of the road, and is popular with businesspeople, Indonesian families and foreign tourists. ❷–❸

Lombok Raya Jl Panca Usaha 11 ⓣ0370/632305, ⓕ636478, ⓔlora@mataram.wasantara.net.id. Yellow bemos from Bertais/Mandalika terminal in Sweta pass the door of this upmarket place. It has good rooms and an attractive pool. Discounts are often available. ❻

Oka Jl Repatmaja 5 ⓣ0370/622406. Fan rooms with attached mandi and good verandahs set in a convenient and quiet location. ❷

Puri Indah Jl Sriwijaya 132 ⓣ0370/637633, ⓕ637669. A bit out of the way, but excellent value and very popular. There's a pool and small restaurant. Prices are due to rise soon. ❷–❸

Sahid Legi Mataram Jl Sriwijaya 81 ⓣ0370/636282, ⓕ636281, ⓔsahid@mataram.wasantara.net.id. Comfortably furnished, elegant hotel with lovely gardens, good rooms and an excellent pool. Large discounts usually available. ❺–❻

Shanta Puri Jl Maktal 15 ⓣ0370/632649. The most popular travellers' place in Cakranegara, offering a wide range of rooms. There's an attached restaurant. They can arrange tours and shuttle buses and book long-distance bus tickets. ❷–❸

The City and around

In the far west of the city, the old port town of **AMPENAN** is situated around the mouth of the Jangkok River. It's the liveliest part of the city, with bustling narrow streets, a flourishing **market** and an atmosphere of business and enterprise that some of the enormous tree-lined roads further east lack. It's also the jumping-off point to the tourist resort of Senggigi a few kilometres up the coast, and has a selection of **restaurants** and antique, pearl and art **shops** (see p.680). The most interesting sight in the four towns is the peaceful **West Nusa Tenggara Provincial Museum**, Jl Panji Tilar Negara 6 (Mon–Thurs 7am–2pm, Fri 7–11am, Sat 7am–1pm; Rp750). The exhibits, with only a few labelled in English, range from displays about the geological formation of Indonesia and the various cultural groups of Nusa Tenggara to household and religious items. The museum's highlight is its collection of kris, elongated daggers which are objects of reverence, treasured as family heirlooms and symbols of manhood.

Merging into Ampenan to the east, **MATARAM** is the capital of West Nusa Tenggara province as well as of the district of Lombok Barat (West Lombok). It's full of offices and imposing government buildings, many set in spacious grounds on broad, tree-lined avenues, but there's little of interest. East again, **CAKRANEGARA**, usually known as Cakra (pronounced *chakra*), is the commercial capital of Lombok, with shops, markets, workshops and hotels. The main **market** centres on Jalan A.A. Gede Ngurah just south of the crossroads with Jalan Pejanggik and Jalan Selaparang; explore the alleyways here for a taste of pretty much everything that Lombok has to offer. Built in 1744 during the rule of the Balinese in West Lombok, the **Puri Mayura** (Mayura Water Palace), on Jalan Selaparang (daily 7am–4.30pm; Rp1000), is set in well-maintained grounds which get busy at weekends. It's pleasant if you're looking for a bit of relaxation in the city, although the grounds at nearby Narmada (see p.706) are more attractive. Across the main road, **Pura Meru**, also known as Pura Mayura, is the largest Balinese temple on the island. The *candi bentar* displaying scenes from the *Ramayana* is the highlight of the temple, which bustles and brims with activity on festival days but for the rest of the time is rather empty and cheerless.

Labuapi and Banyumulek

About 7km south of the city, on the main road that leads to Lembar, the small village of **LABUAPI** is lined with several workshops and small showrooms selling crafts. They specialize in woodcarving, including small wooden bowls, some with painted decoration, others inlaid with shells. The village of **BANYUMULEK**, 2km south of Labuapi, is one of the three main **pottery** centres on the island, stretching west of the main road to Lembar. It's an easy one-kilometre walk from the junction, marked by traffic lights and a monument composed of a tower of large pots, to the place where the pottery workshops and showrooms begin. The full variety of earthenware goods is on offer and the quality is high: come in the morning if you want to see the potters working.

Eating and drinking

There's a wide range of **places to eat**, with an excellent choice of cuisines. Great value is offered by the city's **Chinese** restaurants, and **Padang** and **Taliwang** food is also available – as is fast food should you get the urge. If you're really watching the rupiah, head for the food stalls in the Kebun Roek terminal, which sell very cheap local food. It's worth noting that although Lombok is predominantly Muslim, visiting here **during Ramadan** does not mean long hours during the day without sustenance. Most of the places below remain open during the day at this time, although a curtain at the window discreetly hides the eating tourists, as well as the resident Balinese and local Muslims who are not fasting.

Betawi Jl Yos Sudarso 152, Ampenan. Upstairs on the corner of Jalan Koperasi. A wide range of well-prepared, well-presented and moderately priced Western and Indonesian dishes including seafood, soups, salads and a two-person *rijsttafel*. The big plus is the balcony, where you can catch the breeze and watch life in the streets below. Mon–Sat 8am–10pm.

Mataram Mall Jl Pejanggik, Cakranegara. The gleaming shopping centre is impossible to miss as you travel into Cakranegara from the west. There's a *McDonald's* on the ground floor but the top-floor food court is more interesting with plenty of small stalls selling cheap, well-cooked local food.

Mirasa Modern Bakery Jl A.A. Gede Ngurah, Cakranegara. Takeaway only. A huge selection of excellent, moderately priced savouries, pastries, sweet breads and cakes.

Pabean Jl Yos Sudarso 111, Ampenan. Small Chinese restaurant with large servings of well-cooked inexpensive food. There are several other good options in this street if it's full; the closest is *Cirebon* next door, or *Manalagi II* is across the street at no. 128.

Rainbow Café Jl Yos Sudarso, Ampenan. This small travellers' place has a good, welcoming atmosphere and a small, inexpensive menu.

Shanta Puri Jl Maktal 15, Cakranegara. The restaurant attached to the popular losmen serves a range of travellers' fare and basic Indo-Chinese options all at cheap to moderate prices.

Simpang Raya Jl Pejangik 107, Cakranegara. Conveniently located for the Cakranegara losmen, selling a large range of well-cooked inexpensive Padang food.

Shopping

Ampenan has a clutch of art and antique shops selling **crafts** from Lombok and the islands further east. They're good fun to browse in, although you need to take the definition of "antique" with a pinch of salt. Most places close for two or three hours in the middle of the day and often on Friday afternoons too. Shops are concentrated in **Jalan Saleh Sungkar**, starting with Yufi Art Shop at no. 26, about 200m south of the turning to the bemo terminal, and in the area around **Jalan Yos Sudarso**, north of the bridge across the Jangkok River (check out Freti at Gang Sunda 15, towards the bridge). An excellent one-stop shopping spot is the **Lombok Handicraft Centre**, just beyond the Jangkok River about 2km north of Cakranegara along Jalan Hasanudin at Rungkang Jangkok, Sayang Sayang. It has numerous small shops selling every type of craftwork imaginable, although not many textiles. You can see some of them, including palm-leaf boxes, being made. A couple of local factories producing **ikat** cloth are worth a look; both have shops attached. Rinjani Handwoven (daily 9am–9pm) is at Jl Pejanggik 44–46 in Cakranegara; and Slamet Riady is at Jl Tanun 10, just off Jalan Hasanudin in Cakranegara, with a small sign just north of *Pusaka* hotel. The process is the same as that used in Bali (see p.613). The Cakranegara **market** (mentioned above) has some crafts scattered amongst the vegetables, fish, meat and plastic household goods, and the market near the bus terminal at Bertais is also worth a look (if you're interested in buying take a flashlight with you, as details are very hard to see in the gloom).

Lombok **pottery** is developing an international reputation for style and beauty, and it's possible to get a good idea of the range and quality of the products without venturing as far as the producer villages. **Lombok Pottery Centre**, Jl Sriwijaya 111a, Ampenan (ⓣ0370/640351, ⓕ640350, ⓔlpc_ami@mataram.wasantara.net.id) stocks some of the best-quality products of the three main pottery centres on the island – Banyumulek (see p.679), Penakak (in Masbagik Timur, where there are several pottery-making hamlets east of Masbagik) and Penujak (see p.710). There's also a showroom in Senggigi. The work of other artisans, including handweaving and wooden items, is also on sale. The largest pottery company on Lombok, also operating shops in several hotels, is **Sasak Pottery**, Jl Koperasi 102, Ampenan (ⓣ0370/631687, ⓕ642588, ⓦwww.sasak-pottery.com), located five minutes from the airport – phone for a free pick-up in the city or Senggigi area. This is the biggest earthenware showroom in Indonesia and staff can advise on good workshops to visit in the villages.

Another increasingly popular souvenir is a string of **pearls**. There are several pearl farms dotted around the coastline and many of the pearls find their way into the shops in Ampenan. They're sold by weight and come in a variety of sizes and shapes as well as colour. Shop around on Jalan Saleh Sungkar: check out Aneka Mutiara at no. 15, Surya Mutiara Indah at no. 51 and Central Mutiara at no. 58. For **gold** and **silver jewellery**, head for Kurmasan (see map p.676), north of Mataram. Small workshops are dotted around the area to the east of Jalan Hos Cokroaminoto.

Listings

Airlines All the domestic airlines have ticket counters at the airport, and some have offices in the city area. Air Mark, Selaparang Airport ⓣ0370/643564 or 646847, and at *Hotel Selaparang*, opposite Mataram Mall, Jl Pejanggik 42–44, Mataram ⓣ0370/633235; Merpati, Selaparang Airport ⓣ0370/633691, and at Jl Pejanggik 69, Mataram ⓣ0370/632226; Garuda,

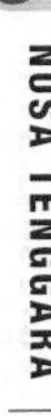

△ Carved tombstone, Sumba

Selaparang Airport Ⓣ0370/622987 ext 246, and at *Hotel Lombok Raya*, Jl Panca Usaha 11, Cakranegara Ⓣ0370/637950. Silk Air – the only international airline with offices on Lombok – is at Selaparang Airport Ⓣ0370/636924, and at *Hotel Lombok Raya*, Jl Panca Usaha 11, Cakranegara Ⓣ0370/628254.

Banks and exchange All the large Mataram and Cakra banks change money and travellers' cheques. The most convenient in Cakra is the Bank of Central Asia, Jl Pejanggik 67 (also with a Visa, MasterCard and Cirrus ATM). The BCA also has a convenient ATM on Jalan Sandu Jaya, about 500m west of the Bertais/Mandalika bus terminal in Sweta. The main branch of Bank Internasional Indonesia (BII), Jl Gede Ngurah 46b, Mataram Ⓣ0370/35027, and the main post office (see below) are both Western Union agents.

Boats Pelni, Jl Majapahit 2, Ampenan (Mon–Fri 8.30am–3.30pm, Sat 8.30am–1pm; Ⓣ0370/637212, Ⓕ631604).

Buses If you don't want to go out to Bertais/Mandalika terminal, you can buy long-distance bus tickets in Mataram from Karya Jaya, Jl Pejanggik 115d Ⓣ0370/636065; Langsung Indah, Jl Pejanggik 56b Ⓣ0370/634669; Perama, Jl Pejanggik 66 Ⓣ0370/635928; Simpatik, Jl Pejanggik 115 Ⓣ0370/634808; Vivon Sayang, Jl Langko 86.

Car rental Toyota Car Rental, Jl Adi Sucipto 5, Mataram Ⓣ0370/626363, Ⓕ627071, Ⓦwww.trac.astra.co.id; Rinjani Rent Car, Jl Panca Usaha 7b Ⓣ0370/632259. There's a better choice in Senggigi.

Dentist Dr Fjahja Hendrawan at Apotik Masyarakat III, Jl Sriwijaya, Mataram Ⓣ0370/638363.

Departure tax Leaving Lombok by air: Rp8000 (domestic), Rp70,000 (international).

Hospitals Catholic Hospital, Jl Koperasi, Ampenan Ⓣ0370/621397; Muslim Hospital, Jalan Pancawarga, Mataram Ⓣ0370/623498. At the public hospital (Rumah Sakit Umum, Jl Pejanggik 6, Mataram Ⓣ0370/621354) there's a Poly Klinik (Mon–Sat 8–11am) with specialists for most problems, an English-speaking "tourist doctor", Dr Felix, and a 24hr pharmacy (Ⓣ0370/637326). Pediatrician: Dr Djelantik, Jalan A.A. Gede Ngurah, Cakranegara (phone for appointment; Mon–Sat 5–7pm; Ⓣ0370/632169).

Immigration office *Kantor Imigrasi*, Jl Udayana 2, Mataram Ⓣ0370/622520.

Internet access Most convenient area is Jalan Cilinaya, down the side of Mataram Mall, where Global Internet (daily 9am–11pm; Rp6000/hr) is as good as any.

Motorbike rental The main rental place is at the roadside at Jl Gelantik 21, Cakranegara, 200m west of the *Srikandi* losmen on Jl Kebudayaan; you should be confident with bikes and not worried about insurance. See p.44 for general advice.

Phones The main phone office is at Jl Langko 23, Ampenan (daily 24hr). Also plenty of wartels in town, including Jl Panca Usaha 22b, Cakranegara (daily 8am–midnight); Jl Saleh Sungkar 2g, Ampenan (daily 7.30am–midnight); Jl Langko 88, Ampenan (daily 24hr); and Jl Pejanggik 105, Mataram (daily 6.30am–11pm).

Police Jalan Langko, Ampenan Ⓣ0370/631225.

Post office Lombok's main office is at Jl Sriwijaya 21, Mataram (Mon–Sat 8am–7pm, Sun 8am–noon). Offices at Jl Langko 21, Ampenan (Mon–Sat 8am–7pm) and on Jalan Kebudayaan in Cakranegara (same hours) are more accessible. For poste restante, the Senggigi post office is more used to dealing with tourists.

Supermarkets In the Mataram Mall, Mataram Plaza and the Cakra Plaza, all on Jl Pejanggik in Cakranegara (daily 10am–9pm).

Taxi Lombok Taxis Ⓣ0370/627000.

Lembar and the southwest peninsula

With several enticing offshore islands, some wonderful beaches and bays and a totally rural atmosphere, the **southwest peninsula** is a million miles away from the bustle of the port at **Lembar** or the frenetic activity of the city area. **Bangko Bangko** at the tip of the peninsula is legendary among surfers as the location of the Desert Point break, recently voted best in the world by readers of an Australian surf magazine. Even if you follow only part of the road to Bangko Bangko, you'll get a feel for this arid and harsh land.

Lembar

LEMBAR, the gateway to the peninsula and the port for Bali, is 22km south of Mataram. Approaching by boat from Bali, the entrance to the rugged harbour is spectacular, but the village itself is insignificant. There's little **accommodation** here; *Tidar* (no phone; ❷) is a new orange-and-red place where the road to the port meets the main road; and the *Sri Wahyu* losmen, Jl Pusri 1, Serumbung (Ⓣ0370/681048; ❷), is signposted from the main road about 1500m north of the port, with basic bungalows set in a garden. **Bemos** run between Sweta's Bertais/Mandalika terminal and the port at Lembar, connecting with the **ferry** and **catamaran** services to Bali (for details of which, see p.674). Public bemos from Lembar to the southwest peninsula leave from the large terminal 500m north of the port, at the junction of the main road and the turning to Bangko Bangko via Sekotong (this turn is clearly marked with hotel signs, including notices for *Hotel Bola Bola Paradis* and *Hotel Sekotong Indah*). Bemos operate from Lembar all the way to Selegang during the hours of daylight, although you may need to change on the way. Metered taxis will also do the run out to the villages here.

The southwest peninsula

As the crow flies it's around 23km from Lembar to Bangko Bangko, at the far western end of the peninsula. However, the journey by road is 57km, twisting around the bays and inlets. The scenery is great: many of the **beaches** are glorious and there are enticing offshore **islands** with pure white-sand beaches.

Out of Lembar, the road – often inland – traces the outline of the massive harbour. Much of the shore is black sand lined with mangroves. The small village of **SEKOTONG**, 19km from Lembar, marks the junction of the Bangko Bangko road with an alluring road that heads south to Sepi and Blongas on the south coast (see p.714). Past Sekotong, the scenery improves as you pass salt pans and lobster farms, eventually reaching the village of **TAUN**, 28km from Lembar. This is an especially lovely, broad, white-sand bay. Boats cost Rp40,000 each way for the trip to **Gili Nanggu** (takes 20min); the boat captains rent out **snorkelling** gear and are open to negotiation for trips to other islands. The only accommodation on the islands off Taun is at *Hotel Gili Nanggu* (Ⓣ0370/623783; ❷–❻), ranging from simple losmen rooms up to much more luxurious ones with air conditioning; it also has a small restaurant. Just 2km around the coast from Taun, in the village of **LABU**, *Hotel Sekotong Indah* (Ⓣ0818/362326; ❸) has bungalows in a pleasant garden across the road from the beach and a small restaurant.

Moving further west you'll see construction of new hotels at **PANDANAN**, 4km beyond Taun, and at **PEMALIK**, another 5km west. At the village of **TEMBOWONG**, 11km from Taun, *Putri Duyung Homestay* (Ⓣ0812/375 2459; ❸) is a little family-run place with simple rooms owned by Pak Gede Patra. This is an ideal base from which to explore **Gili Gede**, the largest offshore island, and the surrounding smaller islands; the family rent out a **boat**. A further 2km west, **PELANGAN** is the largest village in the area. *Hotel Bola Bola Paradis* (Ⓣ086812/104250, Ⓔbatuapi99@hotmail.com; ❹) boasts a great coastal location 2km beyond Pelangan. Boat trips are available.

From here, the coast road – lined with mangrove – turns inland before arriving at another picturesque bay at **SIUNG**, 7km from Pelangan. It follows the shore for another 3km to **LABUHAN POH**, where the bay appears almost circular, enclosed by hills, headlands and offshore islands, all fringed with startling and brilliantly white sand. About 3km west, the blacktop ends at **SELEGANG**, a small hamlet. A rutted dirt road, impassable in the rains, winds for another 3km to a white-sand bay lined with fishermen's huts and colourful sailing boats. This is **BANGKO BANGKO**, which from mid-May to September, and again in December, draws hundreds of **surfers** from as far afield as Brazil and Hawaii in search of the elusive, ultimate wave that is **Desert Point** just offshore here. The track continues around the bay to look down on the next hamlet of **PANDANA**, from where the surfers also rent boats to get out to the breaks. The place buzzes when the surfers hit town but it's otherwise as remote and isolated spot as you'll see in Lombok.

Senggigi and the northwest coast

SENGGIGI, covering a huge stretch of coastline, with sweeping bays separated by towering headlands, has a reputation for having been spoilt by big money and big hotels. It's a pleasant surprise, then, to find that it's in fact an attractive and laid-back beach resort, offering a wide range of accommodation and restaurants and low-key nightlife. It's perfectly possible to have an inexpensive and relaxing stay here, and proximity to the airport makes it an ideal first- or last-night destination.

Life centres on the **beach** or swimming pool during the day, with some low-key shopping also a possibility, and visits to the restaurants and bars in the evening. Senggigi's a good base for exploring further afield, although there are few sights very close; the only local place really worth visiting is **Batu Bolong Temple**, 1km south of the centre. The main part of the temple is built over an archway in the rock, a hole through which virgins were once supposedly sacrificed to appease the gods.

Arrival and orientation

Easily accessible by public transport, Senggigi is served by **bemos** from Ampenan throughout the day (every 15–20min). Pick them up on Jalan Saleh Sungkar just north of the turnoff to the bemo terminal in Ampenan, where they start their run. From the **airport**, fixed-price taxis operate to all parts of

Trips to Sumbawa, Komodo and Flores

Various travel agencies on Lombok and the Gili Islands run trips via **Sumbawa** and **Komodo** to **Flores**, with the highlight being a visit to see the feeding of the Komodo dragons. The fastest and most expensive trips involve **flying** at least part of the way, while the longer, slower journeys are completed by **boat** and **overland**, and include several **snorkelling** stops, usually some **trekking**, a **beach party** and sometimes some **camping**. Prices vary enormously, starting at about Rp400,000 per person for a four-day/four-night boat-and-overland trip in one direction; you can pay up to several million rupiah for longer trips including some flights (air transport out of Labuhanbajo can be difficult to arrange, so allow plenty of time if you book a one-way journey). The following all organize trips: Perama (contact any office); P.T. Wannen Wisata, Senggigi ⓣ0370/693165; Kotasi, Senggigi ⓣ0370/693435; Coconut Cottages, Gili Air ⓣ0370/635365, ⓦwww.coconuts-giliair.com; Lombok Mandiri, Senggigi ⓣ0370/693477; and Kencana Fun Sun Sea trips (available through agents in all the main resorts).

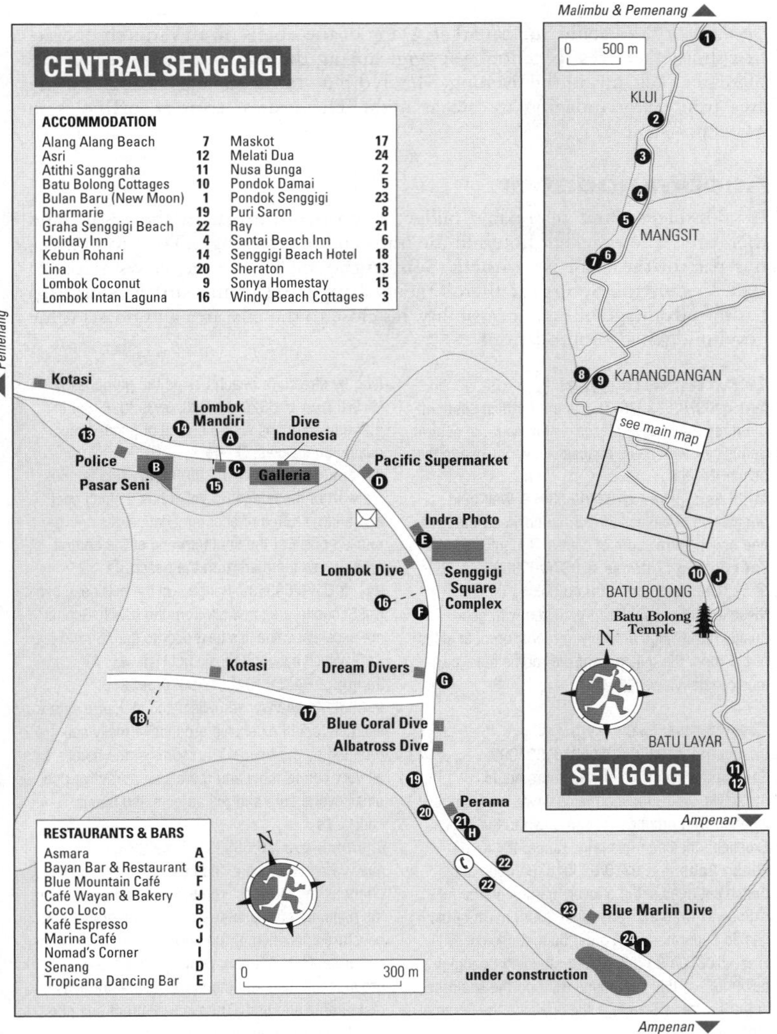

the resort. Perama **tourist shuttle buses** operate to Senggigi from all the main Bali and Lombok tourist destinations; see Travel Details on p.802 for more information. The *Bounty* catamaran (see p.674) docks four times weekly at **Teluk Nara**, north of Senggigi; free buses shuttle passengers into the centre.

The southern end of Senggigi is just 5km north of Ampenan, and a few places are spread out along the next 4km until the main concentration of hotels, which stretches for roughly 1km from the *Pondok Senggigi* to the *Sheraton*. Low-density development continues for another 7km to the most northerly development, *Bulan Baru* at Lendang Luar. **Bemos** ply the coast as far as here, but they aren't especially frequent and many terminate at the

Sheraton or the Pacific Supermarket. Many of the hotels on this stretch operate free shuttle services to central Senggigi during the day, and many restaurants offer free pick-ups in the evening. Metered blue **taxis** operate throughout the area from early morning to late at night. The nearest **tourist office** is in Mataram (see p.677).

Accommodation

It's possible to find reasonable budget **accommodation** in the resort, and there are some excellent hotels in the mid- and luxury ranges. The most attractive part of the coast is in **north Senggigi**, which has great views across to Bali. In **central Senggigi** there's plenty happening, while **south Senggigi** has the advantage of easy accessibility: it's close to the city area and boasts some good budget accommodation.

South Senggigi

Asri ⓣ0370/693075. This is the furthest south of the three Batu Layar places – 4km south of central Senggigi – with basic bungalows, very close to the beach. ❷–❸

Atithi Sanggraha ⓣ0370/693070. Well-built bungalows in a pleasant garden between the road and beach, 4km south of central Senggigi. ❷–❸

Batu Bolong Cottages ⓣ0370/693065, ⓕ693198. Just north of Batu Bolong temple, these are attractive, clean cottages with good-quality furnishings in lovely gardens, on both sides of the road; the deluxe seafront rooms have fabulous coastal views. ❸–❺

Central Senggigi

Dharmarie ⓣ0370/693050, ⓕ693099, ⓔdharmarie@mataram.wasantara.net.id. Attractive, well-furnished bungalows in a central location with grounds that go down to the beach. Excellent choice in this price range. ❺

Kebun Rohani ⓣ0370/693018. Bamboo and thatch cottages set in a lovely garden on the hillside away from the sea, about 200m north of the Pacific Supermarket. A great budget choice. ❷

Lina ⓣ0370/693237. A long-standing Senggigi favourite – a tiny compound right on the seafront in the centre of Senggigi just opposite the Perama office. ❸–❹

Lombok Intan Laguna ⓣ0370/693090, ⓕ693185, ⓦwww.intanhotels.com. Part of an international chain. Accommodation, which is comfortable without being plush, is in the heart of the central area and available in rooms, bungalows and cottages set in extensive grounds. The pool is reputedly the largest in Lombok and just behind the beach. There are several bars and restaurants. ❼

Maskot ⓣ0370/693365, ⓕ693236. Good-value, central, quiet place with pleasant grounds but no pool. Located on the road that runs from the main road to the *Senggigi Beach Hotel* – there's a lengthy stretch of beach beside the gardens. ❻

Melati Dua ⓣ0370/693288, ⓕ693028. Set in attractive gardens with a choice of good-value, quality bungalows. ❸–❹

Pondok Senggigi ⓣ0370/693277. This famous stalwart of the budget traveller has a small pool and a large range of accommodation. It's a large, relaxed place at the southern end of the central area across the road from the beach. ❸–❹

Ray ⓣ0370/693439. Ranged up the hillside in central Senggigi, a short walk from the beach. Rooms are excellent value. It's next door to the *Marina Café*, which has loud music until late. ❷–❸

Senggigi Beach Hotel ⓣ0370/693210, ⓕ693200, ⓦwww.aerowisata.co.id. Large establishment set in extensive grounds virtually surrounded by the beach. The rooms in the hotel are all very comfortable and there's an attractive pool plus several bars and restaurants and tennis courts. ❼

Sheraton ⓣ0370/693333, ⓕ693140, ⓦwww.sheraton.com The best hotel in Senggigi offers all the facilities, comfort and service that are the hallmark of this international hotel group. In a beachfront location at the northern end of the central area, the swimming pool is brilliant, the grounds are lush and there are several top-class restaurants and bars. There's a seafront spa plus health centre, shopping area and hair spa. Published prices start at US$170. ❽

Sonya Homestay ⓣ0370/693447. Basic budget rooms in a centrally located, cosy compound, tucked away behind the main road just north of the Galleria shopping complex. ❷

North Senggigi

Alang Alang Beach Resort ⓣ0370/693518, ⓕ693194. A lovely, atmospheric choice in this price bracket, located about 1km north of central Senggigi. The gardens are glorious, there's a beachside restaurant, the pool is good and on clear days there's a great view across to Bali. ❼

Bulan Baru (New Moon Hotel) ⓣ0370/693785, 693786, ⓔbulanbaru@hotmail.com. Situated at Lendang Luar, 7km north of central Senggigi. There are 12 spotless bungalows situated in a pretty garden with a lovely pool. It has a "no children" policy. It's a short walk to nearby Setangi beach, over a kilometre long and there's an excellent restaurant attached. ❹

Holiday Inn ⓣ0370/693444, ⓕ693092, ⓦwww.holiday-inn.com/lombok. Some 5km north of central Senggigi, this place is upmarket with a huge compound, comfortable rooms and good facilities. There's a giant swimming pool, a range of activities to entertain guests and a regular shuttle bus to central Senggigi. Also several bars and restaurants. ❽

Lombok Coconut ⓣ0370/693195, ⓕ693593, ⓔcoconuthotel@compuserve.com. Ranged up the hillside about 2km north of central Senggigi, these are good-value attractively decorated bungalows and there's also a pretty little pool. ❸–❺

Nusa Bunga Klui ⓣ0370/693034, ⓕ693036, ⓦwww.nusabunga.com. Over 5km north of the centre, this is a fabulous place to stay, with thatch-roofed brick cottages situated in their own small bay and a small swimming pool in an attractive garden. ❻

Pondok Damai ⓣ & ⓕ0370/693019. On the coast at Mangsit, 4km north of central Senggigi, this is a quiet spot with good-value accommodation in bamboo and thatch bungalows built on a tiled base. Beachside restaurant. ❸

Puri Saron ⓣ0370/693424, ⓕ693266, ⓔp_saron@mataram.indo.net.id. Good-quality accommodation 2km north of central Senggigi, close to the beachside pool and with an attached restaurant. A good choice in this price range. ❼

Santai Beach Inn ⓣ & ⓕ0370/693038, ⓦwww.santaibeachinn.com. Right on the coast at Mangsit, these popular thatched bungalows are set in a wonderfully overgrown garden. Vegetarian or vegan meals can be provided and are eaten communally in a *bale* lit by oil lamps in the evening; nobody objects if carnivorous guests want to dine outside. ❸–❹

Windy Beach Cottages ⓣ0370/693191, ⓕ693193, ⓔlidya@mataram.wasantara.net.id. Comfortable bungalows 5km north of central Senggigi, right on the coast at Mangsit. You can book shuttle bus tickets and tours of the island here, and rent snorkelling equipment. ❸–❹

Diving and snorkelling

There are quite a few **dive** operators, many with offices in the Gili Islands. If you're a qualified diver expect to pay around US$45 for two dives, including the boat trip from Senggigi and lunch; check whether equipment rental is included in the price, and see p.62 for some general guidelines. PADI courses, Scuba Reviews and Discover Scuba days are also widely available. Most operators run **snorkelling** trips to the Gili Islands; you go along with the divers and have to be fairly self-reliant in the water. Expect to pay $15–25, including equipment and lunch. All dive operators are marked on the map on p.685.

Albatross ⓣ0370/693399, ⓕ693388, ⓦwww.albatrossdive.com. Offers PADI courses up to Assistant Instructor level as well as dives for experienced divers, Discover Scuba, Scuba Review and snorkelling trips.

Blue Coral ⓣ0370/693441, ⓕ634765, ⓔbluecoral@mataram.wasantara.net.id Daily dive and snorkelling trips and they run PADI courses. They're linked to Oceanic Diving (ⓣ0385/41009), based in Labuhanbajo, Flores, so can help with information about diving there.

Blue Marlin ⓣ0370/692003, ⓕ641609, ⓦwww.diveindo.com. Senggigi counter of this well-established Gili Islands operator. See p.694 for more details of all their activities. They offer the full range of trips and courses from Senggigi.

Dive Indonesia ⓣ0370/693367, ⓕ693864, ⓔdeepblue@mataram.wasantara.net.id. Senggigi office, in the Galleria shopping area, of the Gili Trawangan operator offering all the usual dive trips and courses.

Divetastic ⓣ0370/692004, ⓦwww.divetastic.com. Live-aboard diving trips using *Felidae*, a traditional sailing yacht. Prices are much more affordable than the usual live-aboards.

Dream Divers ⓣ0370/692047, ⓕ693738, ⓦwww.dreamdivers.com. Well-established German company with offices also in Gili Air and Gili Trawangan. They offer training on the PADI Instructor Development Course and also Nitrox courses.

Lombok Dive ⓣ0370/693002, ⓔgrahampilgrim@hotmail.com. Offers diving trips, sometimes involving a beach barbecue on the way home. In addition they offer trips, both live-aboards and overland, to Moyo island off the north coast of Sumbawa.

Eating, drinking and nightlife

A wide range of **restaurants** offer international cuisines, mostly at inexpensive or moderate prices and generally of a high quality. They open daily, some in time for breakfast, closing around 10pm or 11pm. Small street carts selling local food congregate on the main stretch not far from the Pacific Supermarket after dark, and there's a row of sate sellers along the beach at the end of the road leading to the *Senggigi Beach Hotel*. These are the only places that shut during the hours of daylight fasting during the month of Ramadan: all tourist places remain open.

The **nightlife** in Senggigi, and indeed everywhere on Lombok, is very low-key, in keeping with the sensibilities of the local Muslim population. Venues are limited: *Marina Café*, close to the Perama office, and *Tropicana Dancing Bar* at the front of the Senggigi Square Complex are pretty much all there is. They have nightly live music but the atmosphere and closing time depends very much on how busy they are.

Asmara ⓣ0370/693619. Set back from the main road in central Senggigi, this tastefully furnished and relaxed restaurant serves excellent Western, Indonesian and seafood dishes at moderate to expensive prices. Free pick-up throughout Senggigi.

Bawang Putih At *Sheraton* hotel ⓣ0370/693333. The most dramatic and romantic of the *Sheraton* restaurants, and Senggigi's most upmarket dining experience – you eat beside the fabulous, superbly lit swimming pool under vaulted white umbrellas.

Bayan Bar and Restaurant Imposing place on the main street in central Senggigi. There's a massive drinks list, including pricey cocktails. You can eat fairly cheaply with simple Indonesian food or enjoy more costly steak or seafood. Live music nightly.

Blue Mountain Café One of a row of places in central Senggigi selling cheap and cheerful food with live music. There are plenty of Sasak, Indonesian and Chinese options and excellent Happy Hour offers. *Paradise*, *Trully* and *Honey Bunny* are nearby and in the same mould.

Bulan Baru (New Moon Hotel) At Lendang Luar, 7km north of central Senggigi. Well-cooked, nicely presented Indonesian and Western food, all described on the menu in mouth-watering detail; moderately priced and a big drinks list including Australian wines by the glass. A good spot for lunch, with Setangi Beach a short walk away.

Café Wayan & Bakery An offshoot of the Ubud setup, about 1km south of central Senggigi. Excellent Indonesian dishes, seafood, pizza and pasta and salads plus plenty of vegetarian choices at moderate to expensive prices. Fresh bread, croissants and cakes are a highlight.

Coco Loco Best of several shaded seafront places in Pasar Seni in central Senggigi, with Indonesian, Sasak and Western options plus barbecued fish. All are excellent value and moderately priced. You'll dine within sight and sound of the lapping waves – and the local beach hawkers.

Kafé Espresso Clean, friendly place towards the north of the central area serving up an enormous range of coffees and cakes and brownies to go with them. There are plenty of excellent soups, salads, burgers, sandwiches as well as Western and Indonesian favourites with everything at moderate prices.

Lina Large, popular restaurant attached to the cottages of the same name, just opposite the Perama office in central Senggigi. There's a big menu of soups, fish, chicken and Indo-Chinese options all at cheap to moderate prices. The tables on the terrace overlooking the beach are the place to watch the sunset.

Nomad's Corner A relaxed, sociable spot with satellite TV for sports and films, a pool table and coffee machine. The good-value menu includes breakfasts, salads, soup, pasta and seafood all inexpensively to moderately priced.

Senang Next to the Pacific Supermarket in central Senggigi. With a small Indonesian menu featuring simple rice, noodle and soup options, everything is good, plentiful and cheap.

Shopping

Senggigi's main road is lined with shops selling all varieties of Lombok **crafts** including textiles, jewellery, basketware and items from across the archipelago, as well as Western clothes and bags aimed at the tourist market. **Pasar Seni** is a collection of tiny stalls selling a variety of stuff. The nearby **Galleria** has more upmarket shops, including an outlet of the Lombok Pottery Centre. Asmara Art Shop sells an excellent range of extremely good-quality fixed-price items, with some lovely smaller pieces among less portable items of furniture. Pamour Art Gallery, opposite the post office, features a similarly wide choice. The road south, between Senggigi and Ampenan, is gradually filling up with an eclectic variety of art and crafts shops; very many of them sell stone carvings, furniture and other non-packable items but there's some smaller stuff as well.

Listings

Airlines See p.674 for details of airlines which serve Lombok.

Banks and exchange BCA and BNI banks both have central ATMs for Visa, MasterCard and Cirrus. There are exchange counters (daily 8.30am–7.30pm) every few yards on the main street.

Boats Perama (Ⓣ0370/693007, Ⓕ693009) operate a daily boat to Gili Trawangan (1hr 30min; Rp30,000). Bounty Cruises has an office in town (daily 8am–5pm; Ⓣ0370/693666, Ⓕ693678), from where free shuttle buses operate to Teluk Nara, where the *Bounty* docks. Kotasi (Ⓣ0370/693435) is the local co-operative for boat skippers as well as vehicle owners, so if you're interested in chartering a boat to the Gili Islands or for local fishing it's worth contacting them; charters cost Rp170,000–190,000 one-way, Rp300,000–340,000 return per ten-person boat, depending on destination. Taun (see p.683) is the nearest place from where to explore the islands off the southwest peninsula – Gili Nanggu, Gili Genting and Gili Tangkong: boat trips are advertised from Senggigi, but it takes at least 2hr by sea just to reach the islands.

Buses Lombok Mandiri (Ⓣ0370/693477) and Perama (Ⓣ0370/693007, Ⓕ693009) are among the companies that offer tourist shuttles to destinations on Bali and Lombok; they advertise all along the main street. See p.663 for details of Perama services.

Car and bike rental Plenty of places rent vehicles with and without drivers. Kotasi (Ⓣ0370/693435) is the local transport co-operative and has three counters, all marked on the map on p.685. Car rental includes insurance (the maximum you'll pay in case of an accident is US$100); check the deal at the time of renting. They have Suzuki Jimneys (Rp100,000/day), Kijangs (Rp150,000), motorbikes (Rp30,000–35,000 without insurance) and bicycles (Rp15,000); remember that the road north of Senggigi is extremely steep. Expect to pay around Rp50,000/day for a driver. It's worth shopping around at other travel agents. Chartering a vehicle, driver and fuel (from Kotasi, travel agents or street touts) costs Rp200,000–300,000/day all-in, depending on where you want to go.

Doctor Some of the luxury hotels have in-house doctors, including *Holiday Inn* Ⓣ0370/693444, *Sheraton* Ⓣ0370/693333 and *Senggigi Beach* Ⓣ0370/693210. There's also a clinic (Ⓣ0370/693210, Ⓕ693200) near *Senggigi Beach Hotel* that operates a 24hr call-out service.

Internet access Several internet cafés along the main street (daily 8am–10pm; Rp300/min).

Phones A couple of wartels are in the centre; the one above Indah Photo is as good as any (daily 8am–11.30pm).

Post office In the centre of Senggigi (Mon–Thurs 8am–7.30pm, Fri & Sat 8am–7pm). Poste restante is available here (address: Post Office, Senggigi, Lombok 83355, West Nusa Tenggara).

Supermarkets Several in the centre. Pacific (daily 8.30am–9.30pm) has the biggest selection, but tends to be pricier than the others. Most sell basic food, drink, toiletries and stationery as well as postcards, souvenirs and a selection of books about Indonesia. The English-language *Jakarta Post* usually arrives in the afternoon.

Tour companies There's a huge range of Lombok tours on offer. The upmarket hotels usually have tour desks on the premises and operators all have offices in town; check out a few as prices vary considerably, and make sure you know the exact itinerary and whether you're being quoted for the vehicle or per person.

The Gili Islands

Prized as unspoilt paradise islands by travellers in the 1980s, the **Gili Islands** – Gili Trawangan, Gili Meno and Gili Air – just off the northwest coast of Lombok, have developed rapidly to cope with crowds of visitors. Strikingly beautiful, with glorious white-sand beaches lapped by warm, brilliant blue waters and circled by coral reefs hosting myriad species of fish, each of the islands has developed its own character. Of the three, **Gili Trawangan** best fits the image of "party island". With its large number of places to stay, wide range of excellent restaurants and regular nightlife, it attracts the liveliest visitors, although it's still fairly low-key. If you want to get away from it all, head for the smallest of the islands, **Gili Meno**, which has absolutely no nightlife and not much accommodation. Closest to the mainland, **Gili Air** offers a choice, with plenty of facilities in the south, and more peace and quiet the further round the coast you go. All the beaches are public. The local people are probably more used to seeing scantily clad Western women than in any other part of Lombok, but you should definitely cover up when you move away from the beach.

Prices vary dramatically depending on the season and are probably more fluid than anywhere else on Bali or Lombok, being totally dependent on what the market will bear. A traditional bungalow costing Rp50,000 in February can cost Rp100,000 or more in July and August, hovering somewhere in between if the crowds arrive early or leave late in the year. In the peak season (July, Aug & Dec), prices can double throughout the islands.

Pemenang and Bangsal

The access port for the Gili Islands is **BANGSAL**, 25km north of Senggigi. Sadly Bangsal has developed a reputation as a place full of aggravation and **hassle** for tourists; there have even been punch-ups. Keep your cool: the Gilis are worth it. Bangsal is a short cidomo ride or a shadeless 1500m walk from **PEMENANG**, 26km beyond the Ampenan–Mataram–Cakranegara–Sweta area. Pemanang is served by **bemos** or **buses** from Bertais/Mandalika terminal in Sweta. (All transport between Sweta and points around the north coast passes through Pemenang.) **From the airport**, turn left on the road at the front of the terminal, head straight on across the roundabout and 500m further on, at traffic lights on a crossroads, turn left and catch a public bus marked "Tanjung", which will drop you at Pemenang. **From Senggigi**, there's no public bemo service along the coastal road north to Pemenang; see below for details of the boat service from Senggigi direct to the islands.

A gate at Bangsal stops all vehicles 500m from the harbour itself, so prepare to **walk** the final bit or bargain very hard with the drivers of the few cidomo that do ply up and down. Bangsal has a few **restaurants**, some moneychangers, several travel agents and the losmen *Taman Sari* (no phone; ❷), just by the gate where vehicles stop on the way to the harbour. They have clean **accommodation** opening onto a small, quiet garden, and all rooms have fan and an attached cold-water bathroom. There's an **internet** café next door (daily 6am–11pm; Rp300/min).

The **ticket office** for all boats to the islands is right on the seafront at the end of the road; it's all pretty organized, and there's a printed price-list covering public boats, shuttles and charters. You should go directly there and buy your ticket, since there's no advantage in buying from the numerous touts along the road. It's also useful to know that, despite anything you might be told, everything on sale in Bangsal is also on sale on the Gili Islands. Ideally, you should travel light enough to get your own bag onto and off the boats; if you cannot manage this, you should negotiate with the porters before you let them touch the bags – and be clear whether you're talking about rupiah, dollars, for one bag or for the whole lot.

Boats to and from the Gili Islands

From Bangsal

Public boats leave Bangsal throughout the day, when full (7.30am–4.30pm; journey time 20–45min). **Shuttle boats** depart at 10am and 4.30pm. You can also **charter** a boat, for a maximum of ten people. Day return trips are possible, as are trips taking in more than one island; enquire at the ticket office.

	To Gili Air	To Gili Meno	To Gili Trawangan
Public boat	Rp2800	Rp2800	Rp3000
Shuttle boat	Rp7000	Rp7500	Rp8000
Charter	Rp45,000	Rp55,000	Rp58,000

From Senggigi and elsewhere

From Senggigi, you can take the twice-daily Perama shuttle boat (Rp30,000; takes 1hr 30min). It's also possible to charter a boat to the Gili Islands from the Kotasi co-operative in Senggigi (see p.689): it's a great trip up the coast but the boats are small – you won't be able to travel if the winds and tides make the sea too rough. At both ends of all trips you'll get your feet wet, as the boats anchor in the shallows and you have to wade to and fro.

From Benoa or **Nusa Lembongan** you can reach Gili Meno on the *Bounty* high-speed catamaran, which follows a circular route from Benoa to Nusa Lembongan, Teluk Nara (for Senggigi), Gili Meno, then back to Nusa Lembongan and Benoa (Sun, Tues, Thurs & Sat; takes 2–3hr; US$35 from Benoa or Nusa Lembongan to Gili Meno; Ⓦwww.balibountygroup.com). Book through travel agents or direct in Bali on Ⓣ0361/733333, Ⓕ730404. Due to current agreements with the Gili Island boat-owners co-operative, you can't use the *Bounty* for the short hop between Senggigi and Gili Meno.

Perama sells **tourist shuttle bus** tickets for the Gili Islands from all main tourist destinations on Lombok and Bali.

Returning to Lombok or Bali

The times, frequencies and fares on the **public boats** are the same for the return journey as for the outward-bound trip. **Shuttle boats** leave Gili Meno and Gili Trawangan at 8.15am and Gili Air at 8.30am; note there is only one departure a day. Several operators on the islands offer shuttle tickets direct to Lombok or Bali destinations; whichever operator you use, you'll have to walk from the port at Bangsal to the *Taman Sari* losmen near the gate on the main road, where you'll be collected by the tour operator. The Perama counter on Gili Trawangan (see p.696) has full details. It's worth noting that even if you're returning to Senggigi, there is no direct boat: you must go to Bangsal and proceed overland. The **Bounty** (see above) is a speedy, if pricey, way of getting back to Nusa Lembongan or Benoa; note that you can't use it to move from Gili Meno back to Senggigi. Several agents on Gili Trawangan can book tickets on the *Bounty*, *Mabua Express* or *Osiania* (for route details, see p.674); prices usually include transfer to the relevant departure port (Lembar or Gili Meno).

From Bangsal, you can get **shuttle bus** tickets from any of the travel agents lining the road to all main Bali and Lombok destinations. There's also a fixed-price **taxi** service (to Mataram, Senggigi or the airport Rp50,000; Lembar Rp90,000; Senaru Rp100,000; Tetebatu Rp150,000; Kuta Rp170,000; Labuhan Lombok Rp200,000) – but you'll almost certainly get a better deal if you head for Pemenang and negotiate directly with the drivers to charter a bemo from there.

Island practicalities

Once on the islands, prices are fixed if you wish to **charter** a boat: they're clearly posted at the ticket offices on each of the islands. None of the islands has a particular **crime** problem, although there have been reports of attacks on women during and after the parties on Gili Trawangan. Do take reasonable precautions. Many of the sturdier bungalows feature locking drawers or cupboards for your valuables while you're on the beach. There are **no police** on the islands: it's the role of the kepala desa, the head man who looks after Gili Air (where he lives) and Gili Meno, and the *kepala kampung* on Gili Trawangan, to deal with any situation – although it seems that when problems do arise they are sometimes dealt with rather poorly. You should be taken to make a report to police on the mainland (at Tanjung or Ampenan).

The **snorkelling** and **diving** around the Gili Islands is some of the best and most accessible in Lombok. All the islands are fringed by **coral reefs** which slope down to a sandy bottom at around 25m, although there are some coral walls. Visibility is generally around 15m. Despite a lot of visitors, the reefs remain in fair condition. The **fish** life is the main attraction and includes white-tip and black-tip reef sharks, sea turtles, cuttlefish, moray eels, lobster, manta rays, Napoleon wrasse and bumphead parrotfish. There are good snorkelling spots just off the beaches of all the islands; most of the best dive sites involve short boat trips, for which operators will usually also take snorkellers. There are **dive operations** on all the islands. In theory there's a price agreement, with operators charging identical rates; however, operators vary quite a lot and you should choose one carefully. If you're a qualified diver, expect to pay US$25 for one dive, and then $20 for further dives. "Discover Scuba" (the PADI introductory course), "Scuba Review" and a full range of PADI courses are widely available. Check at the time of booking whether the price includes equipment rental. Dive operators on Gili Trawangan have established the Gili Eco Trust, funded by all divers paying a one-off fee of Rp20,000. The aim is to extend this to the other islands and use the money to safeguard the local marine environment. It's sensible to be especially careful over **safety precautions** out here: the nearest hospital is in Mataram and the nearest decompression chamber in Denpasar on Bali. Note, too, that **offshore currents** around the islands are strong and can be hazardous. Dive operators are aware of this and on the alert. However, if you're snorkelling or swimming off the beach you're potentially at risk: it's easy to lose an awareness of your distance from shore, get carried out further than you intend and then be unable to get back. There has been at least one fatality in recent years, when a snorkeller drowned.

"Hopping island" boat service

The "**hopping island**" boat service between all three Gili Islands is extremely handy. It does one circuit, Air–Meno–Trawangan–Meno–Air, in the morning, and another in the afternoon. It's fast and conveniently timetabled, and so makes taking a day-trip to another island a feasible option. The **fare** for any one leg of the route is Rp7000; for a two-leg journey (Air–Trawangan), it's Rp8000.

Gili Air to Gili Meno Departs 8.30am & 3pm.
Gili Meno to Gili Trawangan Departs 8.45am & 3.15pm.
Gili Trawangan to Gili Meno Departs 9.30am & 3.30pm.
Gili Meno to Gili Air Departs 9.45am & 4.15pm.

Gili Trawangan

GILI TRAWANGAN, the furthest island from the mainland and the largest, with a local population of 700, attracts the greatest number of visitors and has moved upmarket at meteoric speed. The southeast of the island is virtually wall-to-wall bungalows, restaurants and dive shops, although it still manages to be pretty low-key and relaxing. For quieter, less refined and less prettified surroundings, head to the laid-back northeast, northwest or southwest coasts. The island generator provides 24-hour electricity. Island **transport** is by cidomo. Ask about renting bicycles at your guesthouse or the stall near the jetty; prices vary from Rp10,000 per hour to Rp10,000 per day – but so does the quality of the bike. Only a tiny section of road in the island's southeast corner is paved so be prepared for some sandy cycling. A **walk** around the island, less than 3km long by 2km at the widest part, takes four hours or less. There's not much to

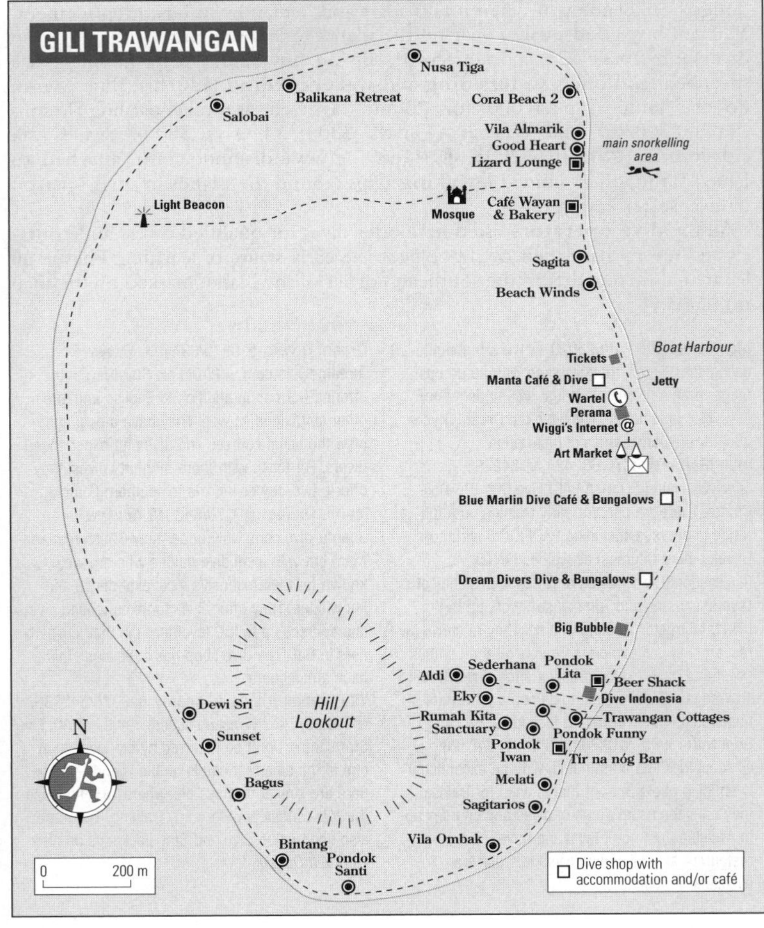

see on the west side other than seaweed in the shallows, the occasional monitor lizard and the giant cacti, ixorea, eucalyptus and palms which survive throughout the dry season. Whether you're cycling or walking, take plenty of water; there's a stretch of coast (about 45min on foot) between *Salobai* in the north and *Dewi Sri* in the southwest where there's nowhere at all to get a drink. Inland, the 100-metre **hill** is the compulsory expedition at sunset – follow any of the tracks from the southern end of the island for views of Agung, Abang and Batur on Bali with the sky blazing behind.

Diving, snorkelling and water sports

The northern end of the east coast is very popular for **snorkelling**: most people hang out here during the day, ambling a few metres inland to the warung behind the beach when it gets too hot. Enquire at the dive shops if you want to go out with one of the dive boats and snorkel further afield; it'll cost about US$10. Snorkel gear is available pretty much everywhere at around Rp10,000 per day; however, some of the more unscrupulous owners rent out extremely dodgy gear, blame you when it falls apart and demand you buy a replacement. You can buy good-quality gear on the island, for example in the Blue Marlin dive shop (mask $25, snorkel $5–10, slip-on fins $28). Manta Diving has a speedboat and offers **waterskiing** and **wakeboarding** ($40/hr); Blue Marlin do the same (Rp200,000 for 20min), as well as wakeboarding lessons (Rp400,000/hr) and courses (4 days $300; 14 days $800). Sea Kayak Adventures (Ⓣ0370/692003, Ⓕ641609, Ⓦwww.diveindo.com), attached to Blue Marlin, offers guided **kayaking** trips around the islands in single-person or two-seater kayaks ($45).

All the **dive operators** listed here offer dives for qualified divers and courses, and several have their own pools for the early stages of learning. They're all located close together in the southeast corner of the island, marked on the map on p.693.

Big Bubble Ⓣ0370/625020, Ⓦwww.bigbubblediving.com. Small, friendly place with no groups bigger than four and often just two students per instructor on courses. They use the Dream Divers pool for the early stages of instruction.

Blue Marlin Ⓣ0370/632424, Ⓕ642286, Ⓦwww.diveindo.com. A PADI Five Star IDC Dive Centre. There's a pool for early training on a full range of courses, including PADI IDC (Instructor Development Courses) as well as IANTD (International Association of Nitrox and Technical Divers) courses and Trimix instruction, up to the IANTD Instructor Training Course. They're currently researching and exploring wrecks off the Lombok coast and have explored newer sites closer to Gili Trawangan. They're soon to launch a 48m traditional boat with live-aboard facitilities.

Dive Indonesia Ⓣ0370/642289, Ⓕ642328, Ⓔdeepblue@mataram.net.id. With an exceptionally enticing pool out front that is used for training, they offer the usual range of dives and courses up to Assistant Instructor level and have a busy restaurant as well, which gives this place an excellent atmosphere.

Dream Divers Ⓣ0370/634496, Ⓦwww.dreamdivers.com. A PADI Five Star IDC centre offering German in addition to English and often other languages as well. They have a pool and offer the usual courses and dives for experienced divers. For those with more than fifty dives, they offer a two-day diving trip to southern Lombok.

Manta Diving Ⓣ0370/643649, Ⓦwww.manta-dive.com. Now under new British management but with local dive guides who are well known for their extensive local experience and knowledge. They offer dives for experienced divers and courses up to IDC level through their co-partners in Bali. The dive shop has a pleasant, laid-back atmosphere.

Vila Ombak Diving Academy Ⓣ0370/642336, Ⓕ642337, Ⓦwww.scubali.com. Another PADI Five Star centre. Don't be deterred by the location in one of the smartest hotels on the island – prices here are similar to those elsewhere, and they use the *Vila Ombak* pool for early training. There are also good-value Dive and Stay packages on offer with *Vila Ombak*.

Accommodation

Traditional **accommodation** is in bamboo and thatch bungalows on stilts, with simple furnishings, mosquito nets, a verandah and a concrete bathroom at the back with squat toilet and mandi. There are plenty of newer, bigger concrete-and-tile bungalows, more comfortably furnished, with fans and attached bathrooms (possibly including a Western-style toilet). The most upmarket places have hot water and air-conditioning. *Vila Almarik*, *Vila Ombak* and *Salobai* provide the real hotel options; everything else is much simpler. The north end of the island is relatively quiet while the bungalows at the southern end are livelier and closer to the restaurants and discos, though many lack views and sea breezes. A few simple, good-value places are springing up behind the warung on the northeast coast and in the village behind. Bright, gleaming new places very soon fade into dust, dirt and eventually squalor unless they're vigilantly maintained; it's worth keeping a keen eye out for new places, whether or not they're listed here, since they're likely to be a good, clean bet.

Beach Winds ⓣ0812/376 4347. Best-quality bungalows on the northeast coast. Rooms are clean and tiled with fans, in a good location near the main snorkelling spots and five minutes' walk from the main restaurant area. ❹

Coral Beach 2 ⓣ0812/376 8534. A fair option in the northeast with simple, straightforward fan bungalows just behind the beach. ❸

Dewi Sri No phone, ⓔsliehchelet@hotmail.com. Isolated place on the west coast, thirty minutes' walk from the main restaurant area. Some accommodation is in basic wood, bamboo and thatch bungalows but the newer, tiled rooms are the best ones in the area. Nearby *Sunset* is quite basic but also worth a look. ❷–❸

Good Heart ⓣ0812/377 1842. Three very simple tiled rooms set back from the beach in the northeast. *Creative 2*, *Impian* and *Matahari* are nearby and of similar quality and style. ❸

Melati ⓣ0370/642352. Decent, simple bungalows very close to the main restaurant area in the southeast. ❸–❹

Nusa Tiga ⓣ0370/643249. On the peaceful north coast, with traditional thatch and bamboo bungalows and more substantial concrete ones – all have seen better days. ❷–❸

Pondok Lita No phone. An excellent budget choice – a small family-run place, well tucked away in the village, about five minutes' walk from the beach (follow the track between Dive Indonesia and *Trawangan Cottages*). Rooms have fan and cold-water attached bathroom, set around a small garden. *Pondok Funny*, *Pondok Iwan* and *Aldi* are all close by, in the same vein. ❸

Pondok Santi No phone. Well-built traditional bungalows in a shaded location in a coconut grove near the sea in the south. A popular option as the bungalows have large verandahs and it's only a short walk (5min) to the main restaurant area. ❸

Rumah Kita Sanctuary No phone, ⓔrumahkita99@hotmail.com. Three bamboo and thatch bungalows in the village. They have fans and attached cold-water bathrooms, plus a pretty garden. ❸

Sagita ⓣ0812/376 9580. Small family homestay with just three rooms with attached bathrooms (squat toilets), close to the snorkelling and a short walk to the main restaurant area. ❸

Sagitarios ⓣ0370/642407. Bamboo and thatch rooms and bungalows, all with squat toilets in the attached bathrooms, in a huge garden at the southern end of the main restaurant area. The bungalows face seawards, which is rare for this part of the island. ❷–❸

Sederhana No phone. Another good village place; follow the track between Dive Indonesia and *Trawangan Cottages*. This is a row of four tiled cottages all with fan and attached cold-water bathroom. *Eky* (ⓣ0370/623582) is just nearby with similar rooms. ❸

Sirwa Homestay One of several new places behind the warung on the northeast coast. This is a row of four concrete rooms, each with attached bathroom and a small verandah. ❷

Trawangan Cottages ⓣ0370/637840. Two rows of clean, tiled good-quality cottages in the southeast corner. One set is further away from the beach along a track. All are a short walk to the beach. ❺

Vila Almarik ⓣ & ⓕ0370/638520, ⓦwww.almarik.com. A hotel in the quiet northeast corner offering the best rooms on the island, set in an attractive garden with air conditioning, hot water and stylish furnishings. The swimming pool is pretty. ❻–❼

Vila Ombak ⓣ0370/642336, ⓕ642337, ⓦwww.hotelombak.com. Centrally located, stylishly designed place with some accommodation in two-storey *lumbung*-style places and some in bungalows. The garden is well laid out, the pool comes complete with waterfall and there's an attached spa. ❼

Eating, drinking and nightlife

The east coast is pretty much lined with **restaurants** and **warung**. Wherever you eat, the quality and variety of the food is very good and prices are reasonable, with seafood the best option; many places have the raw material laid out on ice at the front. Many restaurants show videos (advertised daily); others have a strict no-video policy. The prices in all the places below are cheap to moderate. Gili Trawangan has long been renowned for its nightly **parties**, which last from roughly 11pm until 2 or 3am. Each night's venue is advertised on flyers; *Tír Na Nóg*, though, doesn't close until around 2am anyway, and has largely taken over as the late-night venue of choice. The Monday-night parties at *Blue Marlin* – featuring well-known European DJs – regularly attract hundreds of people from the islands and the mainland. Please note that, for reasons of **personal safety**, women should not leave these parties alone, even to go to the bathroom.

Beer Shack Attached to Dive Indonesia. Located right on the beachfront, with an excellent breakfast menu including croissants, Danish pastries, muffins and doughnuts. There are also plenty of meals on offer later in the day. The *Sweet Shack* and *Seafood Shack* are nearby.

Blue Marlin Café Attached to the Blue Marlin dive shop. Either dine near the pool at the front or up in the two-storey building behind. The menu is large and food well cooked and presented. All the usual favourites are there plus a selection of Thai food, hot plates, baked potatoes, all-day breakfasts and weekly Indonesian buffets.

Café Wayan and Bakery An island offshoot of the Ubud favourite – worth a visit for the bread, croissants, cinnamon rolls and other highly calorific but divine baked goods. Inexpensive to Moderate.

Tír Na Nóg An extremely popular Irish bar with good beer, darts, daily movies and CNN news. There's an ambitious menu with plenty of barbecued seafood and Indonesian and Western food including steaks, lasagne, Irish stew and shepherd's pie plus all-day breakfasts. The drinks list is equally large and includes Guinness in cans, draught Bintang and Carlsberg, and Irish whiskey. Outdoor *bale* all have individual TV screens and the sound system is good and loud.

Vila Ombak The island's most upmarket dining experience, with some tables on the outdoor terrace near the beach and some upstairs in the main building. The menu includes Asian and Western food and there are also plenty of delightful desserts. The wine list is extensive.

Listings

Boat and bus tickets The Perama office (daily 7am–9pm) is close to the jetty.

Exchange Moneychangers all along the main strip change cash and travellers' cheques; expect about ten percent less than on the mainland. As a last resort, the Blue Marlin dive centre can give a cash advance on a Visa card, but they charge ten-percent commission plus the standard four-percent Visa charge.

Internet Several places offer access (about Rp500/min; minimum 5min), including the wartel, which has the advantage of air conditioning, and Wiggi's Internet next to the harbour. Long-stay regular users could try negotiating a discount.

Phones The wartel is open 24hr.

Post There's a postal agent in the art market.

Shopping Several shops sell and exchange secondhand books in European languages and there's a small, centrally located art market plus shops and stalls where you can buy everyday necessities.

Gili Meno

GILI MENO is only about 2km long and just over 1km wide. It's the most tranquil of the three islands, with a local population of just 350. It takes a couple of hours to stroll around the island, which has a picturesque salt lake in the centre, surrounded by a few sets of salt-making paraphernalia. The **Gili Meno Bird Park** (daily 9am–5pm; Rp30,000; Ⓦwww.balipvbgroup.com) is rather incongruously grand in the middle of the island; it has a huge aviary containing hornbills, parakeets, cockatoos, parrots, pelicans, flamingoes and ibis, and there are tame deer and kangaroos to feed. All boats arrive at the **harbour** on

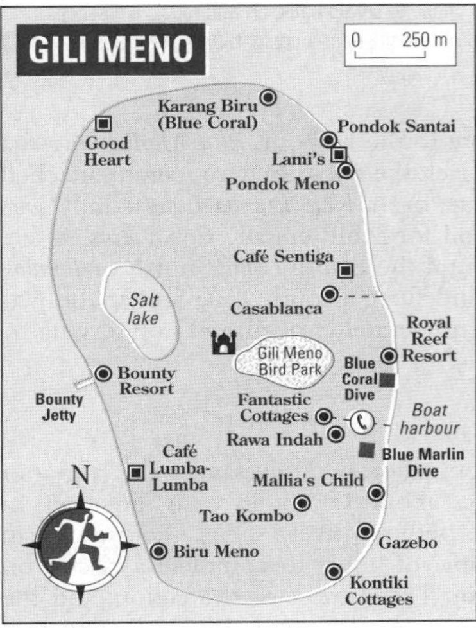

the east coast, apart from the *Bounty* cruise, which sails from Bali four times weekly (see p.674) and docks at the jetty in the west. You can **change money** at *Gazebo* and *Casablanca*. There's a **wartel** (daily 7.30am–10pm) near the harbour, with **internet** access too (Rp750/min, minimum 5min), but phone lines aren't totally reliable. The wartel and ticket office at the harbour sells tickets for shuttle buses to destinations on Lombok and Bali. The **snorkelling** is good all along the east coast. For **diving**, consult *Blue Marlin Dive and Café* – an offshoot of the Gili Trawangan set-up – or Blue Coral (☎0370/632823), who also have a dive shop in Senggigi.

Accommodation

The range of **accommodation** is pretty wide, with several mid-range choices - most is spread along the east coast over a fairly small area. Most bungalows have their own generator for electricity, except one or two at the northern end, which is where you'll get the best budget value.

Karang Biru (Blue Coral) No phone. Quiet accommodation in an isolated location at the peaceful north end of the island. *Good Heart* is ten minutes' walk further around to the west, offering similar accommodation and equal isolation. ❸

Biru Meno No phone. In a great location at the southern end of the island, ten minutes' walk from the harbour, with good-quality bamboo and thatch bungalows on a tile base. Electricity 7pm–midnight. ❸

Cafe Lumba-Lumba No phone; book through *Casablanca*. Three well-maintained, tiled bungalows on the isolated west coast, with the two at the front having excellent views to the sea. This is a great spot for the sunset. Electricity 5.30pm–midnight. ❸

Casablanca ☎0370/633847, Ⓕ642334, Ⓔlidyblanca@mataram.wasantara.net.id. Offering four standards of room set about 100m back from the beach with a pretty garden. There's a tiny pool and a pleasant restaurant. ❹–❻

Fantastic Cottages No phone. Two wood, thatch and bamboo bungalows with attached mandi with a squat toilet set back from the beach near the harbour. *Rawa Indah* is nearby and similar. ❸

Gazebo ☎0370/635795. Ten attractive and comfortable bungalows set in a coconut grove, with air-con. ❻

Kontiki ☎0370/632824. Close to a good beach. Cheaper bungalows are bamboo and thatch, the more expensive ones better quality and tiled, with fans. Electricity all night. ❸–❹

Mallia's Child ☎0370/622007. Bamboo and thatch bungalows with attached bathroom in a good location near a fine beach. ❸

Pondok Meno ☎0370/643676. Traditional, very basic bungalows without electricity, widely spaced in a shady garden, set slightly back from the beach towards the north of the island. ❷

Pondok Santai No phone. Traditional wood, thatch and bamboo bungalows facing seawards in a garden at the northern end of the island. The attached mandis have squat toilets. No electricity. ❷

Royal Reef Resort ☎0370/ 642340. Very close to the harbour, these wood, bamboo and thatch bungalows, set in a large garden, have good verandahs to enjoy the sea views. Electricity in the evening. ❸

Tao' Kombo' ☎0812/360 6859, Ⓔtao_kombo@yahoo.com. Set in a shady spot about 200m behind the beach in the south, with a large bar. Bungalows have excellent furnishings, attached bathroom, fan and a freshwater shower and there are also *brugak* (open-sided sleeping platforms) with lockable cupboards, mattress, screen, mosquito net and shared bathrooms. In the future they hope to set up batik, art and music workshops. Electricity 6pm–midnight. *Brugak* ❷ Bungalows ❸

Eating and drinking

There are plenty of **places to eat**. Close to the harbour, *Blue Marlin Dive and Café* offers Western and Indonesian choices; the two-storey restaurant attached to *Mallia's Child* boasts an excellent pizza oven. *Kafe Lumba-Lumba* and *Good Heart*, both on the west coast, have good food and equally fine views. A few beachside warung are springing up around the island: *Lami's*, north of *Pondok Meno* has great views across the water; and, further south, *Cafe Sentiga* also gets excellent breezes. All are inexpensive to moderately priced, and stop serving by about 9.30pm.

Gili Air

Closest to the mainland, with a local population of a thousand – the largest of the three islands – **GILI AIR** stretches about 1500m in each direction. In terms of atmosphere, it sits somewhere between lively, social Gili Trawangan and peaceful Gili Meno. It takes a couple of hours to complete a circuit on foot. The southeast corner is where you'll find most of the action, and the **beach** here is the most popular, with good **snorkelling**. Reefseekers (ⓣ0370/641008, ⓕ641005, ⓦwww.reefseekers.net) is a highly regarded local

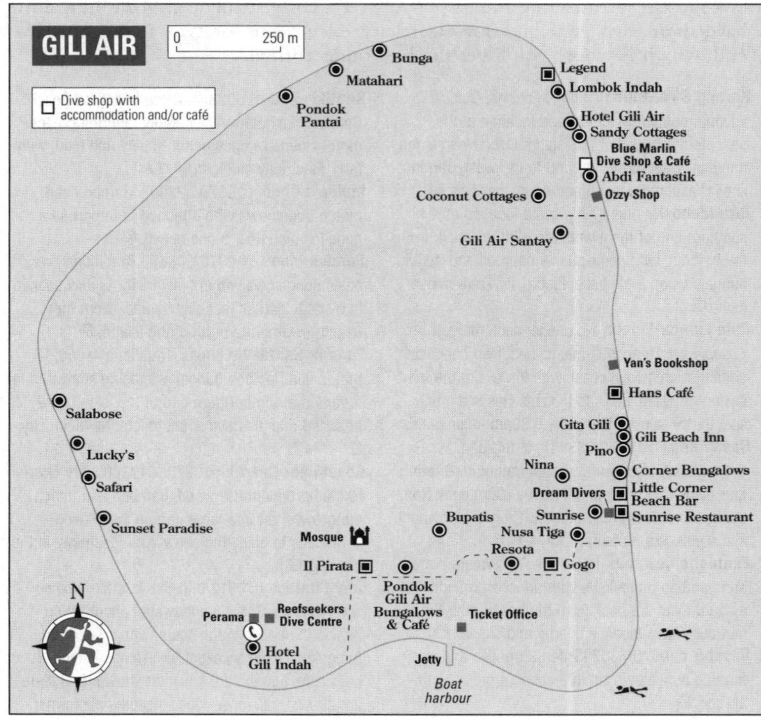

diving company, offering trips for experienced divers, a range of PADI courses up to IDC level and information for snorkellers. Reefseekers have established a small **turtle hatchery** for eggs they rescue from local markets, hatching them and then returning the turtles to the sea. It's a fascinating place and there's no admission charge (although donations to help with feeding costs are always welcome). Reefseekers also operates in Flores and can provide information on diving there (ⓦwww.angelisleflores.com). Other operators on Gili Air include Dream Divers (ⓣ0370/634547, ⓦwww.dreamdivers.com) and Blue Marlin (ⓣ0370/634387, ⓕ643928, ⓦwww.diveindo.com), both well established on Gili Trawangan. Yan's Bookshop on the east coast rents **bicycles** (Rp15,000 for 24 hours) and arranges **glass-bottomed boat trips** for Rp35,000 per person from 9.30am to 3pm for a minimum of four people. There are plenty of **moneychangers** around the island. The **wartel** (daily 8am–10pm) is behind *Hotel Gili Indah* together with the Perama office (same hours; ⓣ0370/637816), where tourist shuttle tickets to destinations throughout Bali and Lombok can be booked. Postcards and stamps are available from the shops; mail gets taken to the mainland regularly by Perama. **Internet access** is at the wartel, St@rnet, and *Coconut Cottages* (Rp500–650/min).

Accommodation

You'll find a selection of good-value **accommodation**, with the quietest spots on the north and west coasts. It makes sense to engage a horse cart to reach the more far-flung spots when you arrive with your bags. The island-wide electricity isn't very reliable so places with their own generators have an advantage when the cuts occur.

Abdi Fantastik No phone. In a great location looking seawards on the east coast; the wood and thatch bungalows are simple but well-built. ❸

Coconut Cottages ⓣ0370/635365, ⓦwww.coconuts-giliair.com. Widely spaced bungalows in a great garden set back from the east coast, about 25min walk from the harbour. The bungalows are attractive and well maintained and there are several standards of room. There's internet service and tours can be arranged. ❸–❹

Gili Air Santay ⓣ0370/641022. Popular, good-quality cottages in a fine location, set slightly back from the east coast in a shady garden behind a coconut grove. The best ones face the sea. ❸

Gili Beach Inn No phone. Traditional bungalows face the view and get a pleasant breeze on this part of the coast. Bungalows are simple and basic but there are *bale* for sitting and relaxing. ❷

Gita Gili No phone. In a good location near the coast and convenient for the harbour, with thatch, wood and bamboo bungalows. ❸

Hotel Gili Air ⓣ & ⓕ0370/634435. The most upmarket option on the island. The swimming pool is fabulous. Negotiate large discounts when it's quiet. ❻

Hotel Gili Indah ⓣ & ⓕ0370/637328, ⓦ202.159.75.163/gili. With a big compound near the harbour, and several standards of bungalows. ❺

Legend ⓣ0812/376 4552. Relaxed, popular spot on the northeast coast with simple bungalows. The attached warung holds weekly parties. ❸

Lombok Indah No phone. A good choice among the budget places on the mostly quiet northeast coast, set in a very pretty spot just behind the beach (be aware that the nearby *Legend* has weekly parties). *Sandy Cottages* are just down the coast and are similar. ❷–❸

Lucky's ⓣ0812/376 8239. A good choice over on this side of the island (5–10min walk from the harbour). Rooms are simple but OK. ❸

Matahari No phone. Probably the best choice on the far northwest coast. The bungalows are slightly better quality than the ones nearby – but things can change. Nearby options are *Pondok Pantai* and *Bunga*. ❷–❸

Nina No phone. Justifiably popular cottages reached by walking through *Corner Bungalows* in the southeast of the island. Bungalows are simple but good quality. ❸

Nusa Tiga No phone. Traditionally built bungalows in the southeast corner. A reasonable budget choice in this area. ❷

Pino No phone. Good bamboo, thatch and wood cottages in a neat garden just on the edge of the southeast corner. ❸

Pondok Gili Air Bungalows ⓣ0370/641014, ⓔsasaksavage@angelfire.com. Simple, pleasantly furnished bamboo, thatch and wood bungalows in the southeast corner of the island. *Bupatis* and *Resota*, nearby, are of similar style, quality and price. ❸

Safari No phone. Bungalows in a lovely spot over on the west coast (5–10min walk from the harbour). Great views to Bali one way and the Lombok coast the other. ❸

Sunrise ⓣ0370/642370. Located behind Dream Divers on the southeast corner of the island. Accommodation is in two-storey *lumbung* barns with sitting areas upstairs and down. The ones at the front have excellent sea views. ❸–❹

Eating, drinking and nightlife

There's a good range of **restaurants**, many of them attached to the accommodation. Most offer a range of Indonesian and Western food at inexpensive to moderate prices; plenty of places lay on Indonesian buffets – look for the flyers around the island. The most popular places to hang out in the day are along the southeast coast, where all the restaurants have small *bale* on the beach. *Sunrise Restaurant* is as fine as any, *Little Corner Beach Bar* is next door and just as acceptable while *Hans Café*, further north, is similar. *Pondok Gili Air Café* has mostly vegetarian food (and you can refill mineral water bottles). The most upmarket, imaginative dining experience is at *Coconut Cottages*, with seating in the main restaurant or in *bale* in the garden. It has appetizing and well-presented Western and local cuisine and seafood. **Sasak buffets** can be organized for a minimum of ten people. At the time of writing, **parties** were permitted three times a week, alternating between *Hans Café* on Tuesday, *Legend Warung* on Wednesday and *Gogo* on Saturday (9 or 10pm until 2am). Enquire at your guesthouse about the current situation.

The north coast road

From Pemenang (see p.690), the main coast road heads north. About 2km beyond the village, you'll reach a small road opposite the local school signed to Pantai Wisata Sira and *Lombok Golf Kosaido Country Club*. This leads a couple of kilometres to **SIRA**, the longest white-sand **beach** on Lombok. Glaringly beautiful, with palm trees swaying in the breeze and views across to Bangsal and the Gili Islands, it's still pretty much deserted, with no tourist facilities of any kind – at the moment. The entire area is slated for luxury hotel development, and just before you reach the beach a left turn brings you to Lombok Golf Kosaido Country Club (ⓣ0370/640137, ⓕ640135, ⓔsiregolf@mataram.wasantara.net.id), where incongruously smooth, verdant fairways and greens gleam between the coconut palms (green fees are US$80, excluding cart, shoe and club rental). Just over 4km from Pemenang, a small asphalted road leads to **The Oberoi** (ⓣ0370/638444, ⓕ632496, ⓦwww.oberoihotels.com; ❽), Lombok's most luxurious hotel and winner of several prestigious awards. All the accommodation is gorgeous; published prices start at US$240. The hotel also offers **diving** excursions and PADI courses in its Beach Club, and has a Banyan Tree **spa**. Several **restaurants** provide top-class, imaginative Western and Indonesian cuisine in wonderful surroundings. About 500m before you reach the hotel is *Medana Resort* (ⓣ0370/628000, ⓕ628100, ⓦwww.lombokmedana.com; ❼), with well-furnished villas in an attractive garden, plus a pretty pool and sunbathing area. The beach is a few minutes' walk away along a path.

Tanjung and around

Back on the main road, 4km further east, **TANJUNG** is the largest settlement around the north coast. It's a pleasant, attractive market town with stalls overflowing with local produce, including blocks of local tobacco. The mountains of coconut husks everywhere are the remnants of coconut-oil extraction in the small processing machines that dot the area. About 7km beyond, in the small village of **GONDANG**, *Suhadi Homestay* (☎0812/376 6668; ❷) comprises five rooms in a family house in an attractive spot. It's 300m from the main road but you'll only spot the small sign if you're coming from the west; turn seawards along the side of the huge, silver-domed mosque in the centre of the village. The homestay is in a small stand of trees on the right-hand side of the road, the beach about 400m further on. About 5km past Gondang in a hamlet called **MONTONG FAL**, *Montong Fal Homestay and Restaurant* (no phone; ❷) is up a steep path signed clearly from the road with fine coastal views. A few hundred metres further east the road turns inland; here, *Pondok Nusa Tiga* (no phone; ❷), comprises four rooms in a two-storey building with bathrooms just outside. The owners can point you in the direction of the local waterfalls and walks. It's a twisty, hot 28km from here to Anyar.

Segenter, Anyar and around

Almost at the northern tip of the island, 4km west of Anyar, the traditional village of **SEGENTER** is signed 2km inland. Park just outside the gate of the fenced village and a guide will meet you; along with Senaru (see below), this is Lombok's most welcoming and interesting traditional village. You'll be taken inside one of the bamboo and thatch houses to see the eating platform, stone hearth and the *inan bale*, a small house-within-a-house where newlyweds spend their first night. At the end of the visit you'll be expected to make a **donation** to the village and sign the visitors' book.

Much of the road from here to **ANYAR** passes inland through cashew orchards with great views across the lower slopes of Gunung Rinjani. Buses from Bertais/Mandalika terminal in Sweta terminate at Anyar, from where **bemos** regularly ply to Ancak, Bayan and on to Batu Koq and Senaru. There are a few buses (morning only) that travel further east via Kalih Putih to Labuhan Lombok, or you may have to travel by bemo to **ANCAK**, about 3km inland, to pick one up.

The small village of **BAYAN**, 5km south of Anyar, is generally accepted as the site of the **oldest mosque** on Lombok. You can't enter the mosque, but even from outside it's very striking: a traditional bamboo and thatch building atop a stone and concrete circular citadel rising up in tiers. East of Bayan, the main road winds laboriously through the rolling foothills of Rinjani but the extensive rice fields of the Bayan area soon give way to a much drier, dusty terrain that continues almost 10km to the small junction at **KALI PUTIH**. From here, minibuses run to Sembalun Lawang, an alternative access-point for treks up Rinjani, and the main road continues for about 10km to Obel Obel and the east coast (see p.709).

Gunung Rinjani and around

Most of Lombok has been heavily deforested, but an extensive area of forest does remain on the slopes of the huge volcano **Gunung Rinjani** (3726m), one of the highest peaks in Indonesia, and stretches for over 65km across the north of the island. From a distance, Rinjani – visible from Bali – appears to rise in solitary glory from the plains, but in fact the entire area is a throng of bare and soaring summits, wreathed in dense forest. Invisible from below, the

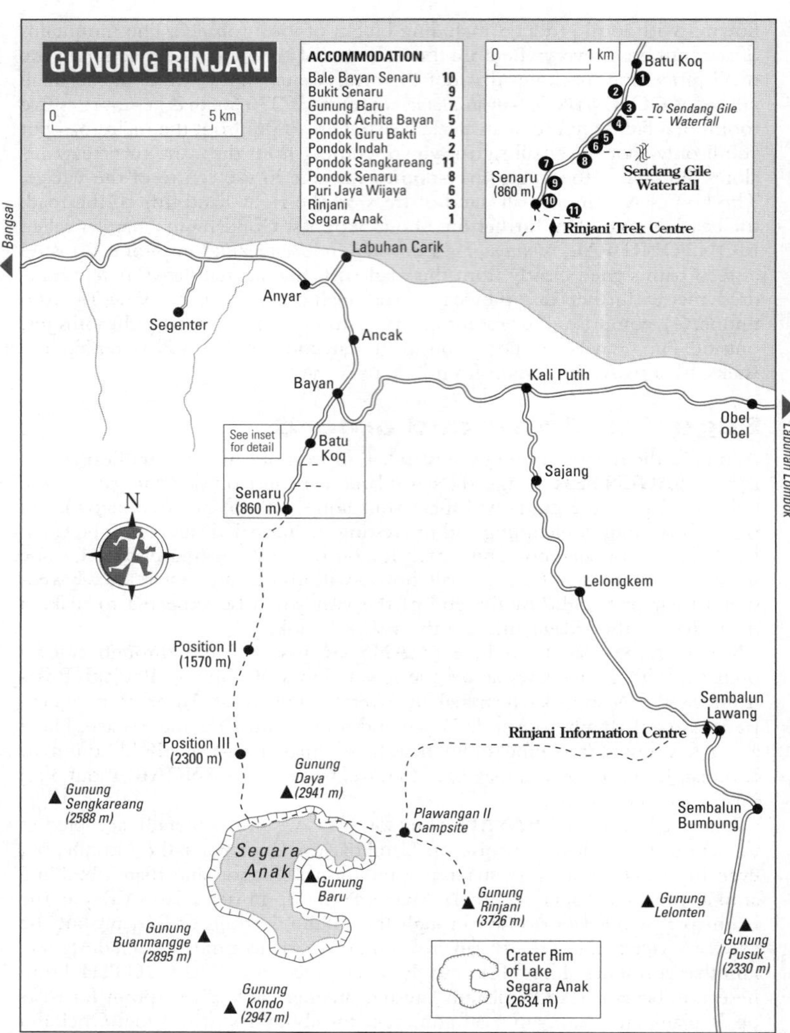

most breathtaking feature of the area is **Segara Anak**, the magnificent crater lake, measuring 8km by 6km. The **climb** up Rinjani is the most energetic the most rewarding trek on either Bali or Lombok. You can ascend from either **Senaru** or **Sembalun Lawang** independently or as part of a tour (see box p.705).

Batu Koq and Senaru

The small villages of **BATU KOQ** and **SENARU** are easily reached by bemo or ojek from Anyar, a few kilometres to the north: Rp5000–6000 is a fair price for an ojek. Just south of *Pondok Senaru*, a small path heads east to the river and **Sindang Gile waterfall**. This is a lovely spot where you can bathe, although the water is pretty chilly. **Tiu Kelep** is another waterfall a further hour's scramble beyond the first. You can also swim here and the effort of the trek may be worth it: local belief is that you become a year younger every time you swim behind the main falls here. It's worth visiting the **traditional village** at Senaru, a fenced compound with houses of bamboo and thatch set out in rows, next to *Bale Bayan Senaru*. Someone will appear to show you around and you'll be expected to make a donation and sign the visitors' book. You can arrange at the Rinjani Trek Centre (in the far south of the village, just at the start of the track up Gunung Rinjani) to go on the **Senaru Panorama Walk** through the immediate area, guided by local women (8am–noon; Rp45,000 per person; minimum two people).

Accommodation

Both Batu Koq and Senaru have **accommodation** spread for several kilometres along the road. Don't expect phones or luxury in any of these places, but they all have attached cold-water bathrooms. Breakfast is usually included in the price. Places on the east of the road generally have the best views towards the mountain. Most will store your stuff while you climb, and many have small **restaurants** attached, serving simple Indonesian and Sasak meals (food and drink prices tend to be higher than in more accessible areas).

Bale Bayan Senaru No phone. At the top of the road, close to the mountain; basic bungalows in a small garden. ❷

Bukit Senaru No phone. Bungalows well spaced in a charming garden with good verandahs. They're bigger and better than many in the area. ❷–❸

Gunung Baru No phone. Small setup, not far from the start of the trail. ❷

Pondok Achita Bayan No phone. Good bungalows with verandahs both back and front for mountain and garden views. ❷

Pondok Guru Bakti No phone. Three bungalows in a row set in a pretty garden, with great views of the waterfall from the verandahs. ❷

Pondok Indah No phone. Good bungalows and fine north-coast views. ❷

Pondok Sangkareang No phone. A small row of rooms, as close to the start of the trail as it's possible to get, located in a small garden just above the Rinjani Trek Centre. ❷

Pondok Senaru ⓣ086812/104141. The biggest setup, with a huge restaurant, offering a choice of good-quality accommodation, all with great verandahs, set in a pretty garden. ❸

Puri Jaya Wijaya No phone. Small place with verandahs overlooking the garden, rather than the great views behind. ❷

Rinjani No phone. Doesn't take advantage of the views, but the bungalows are adequate; ongoing renovation may improve things. ❷

Segara Anak No phone. The first place on the road from Bayan. There are stunning panoramas from the verandahs of the more expensive bungalows. There are two restaurants. ❷

Sembalun Lawang and Sembalun Bumbung

A steep, poorly surfaced road twists and turns 16km south from Kali Putih through several tiny villages to **SEMBALUN LAWANG**, set in countryside that is unique in Lombok – a high, flat-bottomed mountain valley virtually surrounded by hills. It's Lombok's **garlic** capital: during the harvest in September and October the smell pervades the entire area. There has recently been a renaissance of **handweaving** in the village; textiles are on show at the Rinjani Information Centre. They can give you directions to the weaver's homes to see work in progress (or you can look out for signs in the centre of the village). There's only one **place to stay** – *Pondok Sembalun* (no phone; ❷), which has simple rooms in a small garden just off the main road, marked by a large gate at the start of the Rinjani trail next to the Rinjani Information Centre.

South of the village is a vast, fertile plain ahead of which the valley closes in, the mountain walls rising steeply on all sides. Some 4km south of Sembalun Lawang is **SEMBALUN BUMBUNG**, an attractive village in the shadows of the surrounding mountains. At the far southern end of the village, *Paer Doe* (no phone; ❷) is a tiny **homestay** with basic rooms. They can help you arrange your Rinjani trek (Rp800,000 for two people for the three-day/two-night trip to the summit). From Sembalun Bumbung, the mountain road winds for 15km across Gunung Pusuk to Pesugulan, and on to Sapit (see p.708). This road is prone to closure due to landslips; you should check on its status before heading out. There's daily **public transport** (although rather infrequent) from Kali Putih to the valley, and daily buses north from Aik Mel via Sapit, depending on road conditions.

Climbing Gunung Rinjani

The **summit of Rinjani**, the highest point of the region's volcanic mountainous mass, is reached by relatively few trekkers; the majority are satisfied with a shorter, less arduous trip to the **crater rim** – from where you can see the beautiful turquoise lake, **Segara Anak** (Child of the Sea) inside the massive crater, and the small perfect cone of **Gunung Baru** (New Mountain) rising on the far side. The mountain should be treated with respect: the weather here is notoriously unpredictable and the volcano is dormant rather than extinct. **Trekking** on the mountain is not for the frail or unfit and shouldn't be attempted without adequate food and water. Although not all the treks need a porter or guide, you should definitely let somebody know where you're going and when you'll be back; you can report to the Rinjani Trek Centres at Senaru and Sembalun Lawang when you set off.

Routes

The shortest trek is **from Senaru**, climbing to the **crater rim**. At the Rinjani Trek Centre, at the start of the track, you pay Rp25,000 for **admission** to the national park, and register. The route takes you from the start of the trek at the top of the village at 600m (marked on some maps as **Position I**), up through the forest to further rest positions (*plawangan*) with small *bale*. **Position II** is at 1550m and **Position III** at 1950m; you then leave the forest for the steep slog up to the rim at 2600m. Most people take six to seven hours (or more), not allowing for rests, to get to the rim from Senaru: unless you're extremely fit and fast, you won't be able to get to the rim and back in a day. A tent is preferable to sleeping in the *bale*, and is vital if you plan to sleep on the crater rim.

A further possibility after climbing to the rim is to descend into the crater to **the lake**, at 2050m. The path into the crater (1hr 30min) is very steep and rather frightening at the top, but gets better further down. Most people get down to the lake in one day from Senaru, spend the night by the shore and return the same way the following day. From the lake it's possible to climb out on a different path to a site called **Plawangan II** at 2900m, and from there up to the **summit** of Rinjani. This is at least a seven-hour trek in total, for which you'll need a guide. You should try to get to the summit for sunrise.

A shorter route to Plawangan II and then to the summit is to climb **from Sembalun Lawang** on the east side of the mountain starting under a large

Rinjani practicalities

If you're climbing from Senaru to the rim or down to the lake you don't need a **guide**, although a **porter** is a great advantage. The path leaves to the left just beyond *Bale Bayan Senaru* in Senaru. From Sembalun Lawang the route is straightforward up to Plawangan II, but you should check in the village about conditions. To climb to the **summit**, you'll need a guide and – unless you're terribly fit – a porter to carry your gear, cook your food and pitch your tent. There is spring **water** at Positions II and III from the Senaru side during and just after the rainy season but you should check on this locally before setting out. It's vital to carry adequate food and water.

Typically, there are four options on offer: **one-night/two-day trips** to the crater rim; **two-night/three-day trips** to the rim and the lake, or to the summit (to and from Sembalun Lawang); and **three-night/four-day trips** to the summit (up from Sembalun Lawang, down to the lake and ending at Senaru). Prices are fixed and clearly displayed at the **Rinjani Trek Centre** in Senaru and **Rinjani Information Centre** in Sembalun Lawang (both daily 7am–5pm), which should be your first port of call in arranging a trek. Prices depend on the trek you want to do and the number of people in the group, and include equipment, transport to and from Sembalun Lawang (if necessary), porters and food. In addition there's a new radio communication system in operation; it costs Rp10,000 to rent radio equipment for one trek.

Trip	Alone	Per person in a group of 5
Rim (2-day)	Rp600,000	Rp250,000
Lake (3-day)	Rp700,000	Rp300,000
Summit (3-day)	Rp800,000	Rp400,000
Summit (4-day)	Rp950,000	Rp500,000

All-inclusive Rinjani trips

Although it's easy to go to Senaru or Batu Koq and arrange your own climb up Rinjani from there, many companies on Lombok arrange **inclusive trips** to climb the mountain – useful if time is short, but pricey. Prices include transport in both directions, guides, porters, accommodation, food and equipment, but costs vary according to the size of your group: the more people you have, the cheaper it becomes. It pays to shop around between operators.

Coconut Cottages Gili Air ⓣ0370/635365, ⓦwww.coconuts-giliair.com.
Kotasi Senggigi ⓣ0370/693435.
Lombok Mandiri Opposite *Asmara Restaurant*, Senggigi ⓣ0370/693477.
Lotus Asia Tours Jl Raya Senggigi 1G, Ampenan ⓣ0370/636781, ⓕ622344, ⓦwww.lotusasiatours.com.
Mahligai Senggigi Square B.09, Senggigi ⓣ & ⓕ0370/693139.
Nominasi Senggigi ⓣ0370/693690.

archway in the village next to the Rinjani Information Centre and passing *Pondok Sembalun*. This takes around seven hours to Plawangan II (where you'll overnight) and then another three hours plus to get to the summit the next morning.

The most complete exploration of the mountain involves a **round trip**, ascending from either Senaru or Sembalun Lawang, taking in the summit and the lake, and descending to the other. The Rinjani Information Centre and the Rinjani Trek Centre in Senaru provide all the information and help you need.

Central Lombok

Stretching for 74km from Ampenan–Mataram–Cakranegara–Sweta to Labuhan Lombok, the main road across the island is the nearest thing to a highway that you'll find, and passes close to many of the most attractive destinations in **central Lombok**. Small-scale tourist facilities have developed in the hills: the accommodation in the small village of **Tetebatu** and, to a lesser extent, in **Sapit**, is becoming increasingly popular. Down on the plains, **Lendang Nangka** has become something of a pilgrimage for travellers seeking the "real" village experience. The culturally minded make stops at Hindu sites at **Narmada**, **Pura Lingsar** and **Suranadi**. Reasonably well served by bemos and buses, much of the area is accessible without your own transport. Note that there are very few moneychangers east of Sweta.

Narmada and around

Built in 1805, the pretty gardens of **Taman Narmada** (daily 7am–6.30pm; Rp1000, swimming Rp1000), served by frequent bemos from Bertais/Mandalika terminal in Sweta (just 10km west) lie on the south side of the main road in **NARMADA**, opposite the bemo terminal and daily market (well worth a look if you're there early in the day). This is a good place to laze around, especially if you go early before the tour groups descend. The terraces and the lake are extensive and well maintained, and there's a swimming pool as well as paddle boats for rent.

A few kilometres north of Narmada, and easily reached by bemo from there, is **Pura Lingsar** (daily 7am–6pm; admission by donation). This temple is a focus of worship for the Hindu religion and a place of worship for followers of Islam – including the Wetu Telu adherents on the island. The furthest north, and highest, courtyard is the Hindu one guarded by fierce monsters at the *candi bentar*, while the Wetu Telu area has a pond overlooked by a vivid statue of Wisnu, home to some well-fed eels which emerge for hard-boiled eggs brought by devotees. This is a rural spot and not many tourists stay, but there is **accommodation**. About 1km west of the turning to the temple on the back road from Narmada to Cakranegara is *Puri Lingsar Homestay* (Ⓣ0370/671652; ❷), a small row of bungalows set back from the road in a pretty garden. Some 500m beyond the turning to the temple, *Losmen Ida* (Ⓣ0812/375 2083; ❷) is newer and has clean, tiled rooms set quite close to the road with attached mandi and squat toilet.

Situated about 300m above sea level, **SURANADI** is 7km north of Narmada at the site of a freshwater spring. The temple here, **Pura Suranadi**, is a holy pilgrimage site for Hindus: the Hindu saint Nirartha is believed to have located the springs while in a trance.

Tetebatu

TETEBATU is situated on the southern slopes of Gunung Rinjani, 50km from Sweta (11km north of the main cross-island road), and surrounded by some of the most picturesque scenery in Lombok. At an altitude of 400m, the area is cool relief from the heat of the plains, but not unpleasantly cold. It's an excellent base from which to explore the centre of the island or simply relax for a few days – quiet, but developing rapidly as a tourist centre. On public transport, get off the **bemo** or **bus** at Pomotong on the main road and either take an ojek straight up to Tetebatu or a bemo to Kotaraja and then a cidomo on to Tetebatu. Alternatively, you can reach Tetebatu by Perama tourist shuttle bus from many places on Bali and Lombok; see Travel Details on p.802 for details, but be aware that stopovers are needed on several journeys. From Tetebatu, you can explore nearby waterfalls and craft villages: the *Green Orry* (see below) rents motorcycles (Rp35,000–40,000/day), and can arrange a guide for a trek through the fields to a local waterfall (Rp75,000 for 5hr). They can also supply **charter transport** to other Lombok destinations. The village has a **moneychanger**, a Perama agent (requiring one-day advance bookings), transport rental and a **wartel**, just above the *Salabuse* restaurant on the road up to *Wisma Soedjono*.

Accommodation and eating

Accommodation is mostly on the main road leading up to the *Wisma Soedjono* from Kotoraja and the road off to the east, Waterfall Street, but there are now some further-flung options. All have **restaurants** attached and there are a few simple restaurants in the area. All serve inexpensive to moderately priced Indo-Chinese and travellers' fare, plus some Sasak options. *Warung Harmony* and *Salabuse*, on the main road are both worth a try. At the time of writing phones were being installed in the area; some but not all of the accommodation had them.

Cendrawasih ⓣ0376/22783. Accommodation here, in two-storey traditional *lumbung*-style barns, is some of the most attractive in the area; it's set in a great garden on Waterfall Street, and has a thatched restaurant. ②

Tetebatu Homestay No phone. Around 2km from the Kotoraja–Tetebatu road in the hamlet of Penyonggok; the turning is signed a few hundred metres south of the junction with Waterfall Street. Just a couple of small rooms in a family compound. ②

Green Orry ⓣ0376/22782, ⓕ23233. Traditional and modern tiled bungalows in a pleasant compound, plus a restaurant on Waterfall Street. Rooms are clean and well maintained. Plans to introduce hot water will increase prices. Guests receive a map of the local area to help exploration. This place also serves as the local Perama agent, has motorbikes for rent and can arrange a guide for local treks. ②–③

Hakiki No phone. Set in the middle of paddy-fields at the eastern end of Waterfall Street, accommodation is in two-storey traditional barns. There's a great view of Gunung Rinjani from here. ②

Mekarsari No phone. In a pleasant location in the fields behind *Pondok Tetebatu*, this is a small place with accommodation in brick bungalows. ②

Nirwana Cottages and Restaurant No phone. About 200m off Waterfall Street: brick and thatch cottages which have verandahs facing brilliant views of Rinjani. ②

Pondok Bulan ⓣ0376/22781. Located on Waterfall Street, close to the rice fields with good views south, there are traditional bamboo and thatch bungalows as well as bigger, more expensive family rooms. ②–③

Pondok Tetebatu No phone. Tiled rooms on the main road leading up to the *Wisma Soedjono*, with good verandahs looking onto a lovely garden and a restaurant with fine views. ②–③

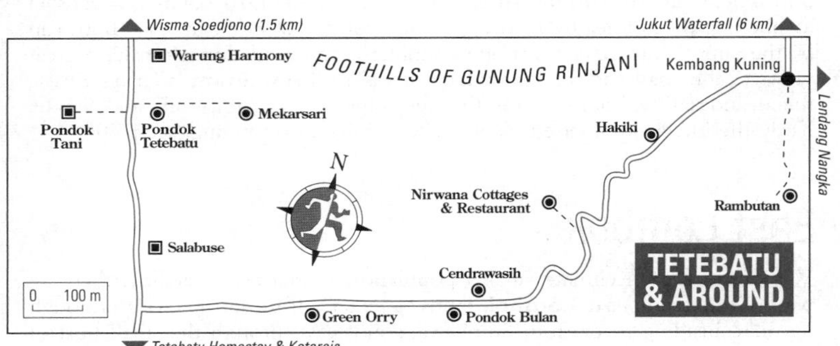

Rambutan No phone. The ultimate getaway – 400m along a rough but passable track in Kembang Kuning, with traditional bungalows in the middle of a rambutan orchard. It's best to check it's still open before hauling a lot of gear out here. ❷

Wisma Soedjono ⓣ0818/544265, ⓕ0376/22522. This old house used to be the home of Dr Soedjono, the first doctor in eastern Lombok, and is still owned by his family. It offers a range of accommodation set in great grounds at the far north end of the village and is the most upmarket option in the area. There's a moderately priced restaurant and a swimming pool. ❷–❸

Lendang Nangka

Developed single-handedly as a tourist destination by local teacher Haji Radiah, **LENDANG NANGKA** is a small farming community of about two thousand people, 2km north of the main cross-island road, and served by cidomo and ojek from Bagik Bontong. Although the scenery is not as dramatic or picturesque as Tetebatu, the atmosphere in the village is more welcoming and friendly. This is a great place to see what Lombok life is all about and to practise your Indonesian or Sasak. There's a wealth of **walks** through the rice fields around the village, and the local people are well used to strangers wandering around. Established in 1983, *Radiah's Homestay* (❷; includes three meals and tea or coffee), the original **accommodation** in the area, is a homestay in the real sense of the word. It's right in the middle of the village, but tucked away behind the school, so ask for directions. Many visitors enjoy an afternoon walk in the area with Radiah. Sannah, Radiah's wife, cooks traditional Sasak food and she's used to visitors in the kitchen learning recipes. You get a map with plenty of suggestions for local excursions and Radiah's nephew is also a Perama agent; you must book with him the day before you want to travel. An alternative is *Pondok Bambu* (❷; includes three meals), 500m north of Lendang Nangka and signed from the road that leads to Kembang Kuning. It may be a bit hard to find but the local ojek drivers know it. Its simple accommodation is in a family compound with a quiet, pleasant garden setting surrounded by fields.

Sapit

Situated high in the hills, 1400m up on the southern slopes of Gunung Pusuk, the small mountain village of **SAPIT** is a quiet retreat with wonderful views. It's 15km from Sembalun Lawang (2–3hr by daily bus, as long as the road is open), and the same distance from the cross-island road, either via Aik Mel or Pringgabaya (there's more public transport from the latter). Sapit is becoming increasingly popular, although it's very far from crowded. The road north is very steep and twisting and prone to being washed away – check in the Sembalun valley or Sapit on the current condition before setting off in your own transport. There's **accommodation** at *Hati Suci* (ⓣ & ⓕ0370/636545, ⓔhatisuci@inbox.as; ❸) and nearby *Balelangga* (same contact; ❷–❸), which are both run by the same family: *Balelangga* offers simpler accommodation. Both have great views to the coast and Sumbawa. Each has a small **restaurant** offering a basic menu, and staff will point you in the right direction for local walks and, for the hardy, the fifteen-kilometre trek across to Sembalun Bumbung (see p.704).

East Lombok

With a much drier climate, smaller population and far fewer facilities than the west of the island, **east Lombok** tends to be left off most itineraries, although if you're heading to or from Sumbawa, you'll pass through the small port of

Labuhan Lombok. To the north of Labuhan Lombok, the land is dramatically arid, giving striking views inland to the mountains, and the accommodation at **Labuhan Pandan** gives you the chance to organize a trip to the uninhabited islands just off the coast.

Labuhan Lombok and around

LABUHAN LOMBOK, 74km east of Mataram, is probably the least interesting town in Lombok, although its near-circular bay enclosed by a small curving promontory is very attractive. Boats to Sumbawa depart from the **ferry terminal**, Labuhan Kayangan, at the far end of the promontory, a three-kilometre shadeless walk along the new road around the south side of the bay; take a local bemo if you can (Rp1000). Buses run regularly along the cross-island road to the ferry terminal from the Bertais/Mandalika terminal at Sweta (if you're heading for Praya or Kuta from the ferry, follow this route and change at Kopang), and from Obel Obel and Bayan on the north coast via Sambelia (the best way to go, in reverse, if you're heading for Gunung Rinjani). The best **place to stay** is *Lima Tiga*, Jl Kayangan 14 (Ⓣ0376/23316; ❷), about 150m from the town centre on the road to the ferry terminal. The rooms are adequate, although bathrooms, with mandi and squat toilet, are shared. Several **warung**, fine for basic Indonesian food, line the same road; *Warung Kelayu* is very popular. There's a **wartel** along here, and if you head to the main road and turn left, the **post office** is 100m along on the right. If and when their Land-Sea Adventures to Sumbawa and Flores get started again, Perama will have an office (Ⓣ0376/21817) at Jalan Rajawali, a side street off Jalan Kayangan on the other side of the road from the *Lima Tiga*.

North of Labuhan Lombok

Travelling north from Labuhan Lombok, you're soon out into the countryside, though the scenery quickly becomes parched and villages are few and far between. About 7km north, in the village of **AIK MANIS**, is the great little *Aik Manis* (no phone, Ⓕ0376/218877; ❷), owned by an Indonesian–New Zealand couple. They have a set of wood, bamboo and thatch bungalows in a neat garden just behind an excellent beach, plus a small restaurant with great views. They can help you organize snorkelling and camping trips to the off-shore islands in local boats.

In the area north of **LABUHAN PANDAN**, 16km north of Labuhan Lombok and 9km from *Aik Manis*, there are two fine accommodation options in an excellent get-away-from-it-all spot. *Siola Cottages* (no phone; ❷) has wood, thatch and bamboo bungalows set well apart in a large garden behind a black-sand beach. There are fine views on a clear day. Just next door, *Matahari* (Ⓣ086812/104168, ❸) has a choice of bungalows on the seafront or larger rooms set further back in a two-storey block. All are clean and tiled and the

Moving on to Sumbawa

The **ferry to Sumbawa** departs Labuhan Lombok around the clock (every 45min; Rp5000; bicycle Rp6900, motorbike Rp12,500, 4WDs from Rp85,000). It goes to Poto Tano (see p.717) on Sumbawa's northwest coast, a few kilometres from the main road across the island. Buses meet the ferries bound for Taliwang (30km south) and Alas (22km east), plus Sumbawa Besar and, occasionally, Bima. Alternatively, you can book a **long-distance bus** ticket in Mataram (see p.682) – or with Perama – through to destinations on Sumbawa.

garden is excellent. There is an attached **restaurant**. There is **snorkelling** off the beach here; both accommodation places rent snorkelling gear. *Ma Jena's* is a simple but appealing warung by the roadside a few hundred metres south.

There are two groups of islands off the northeast Lombok coast. The most southerly are **Gili Petangan** and its satellites, Gili Lampu and Gili Pasaran, which have beaches as well as coral walls and attract many varieties of fish; further north are the larger islands **Gili Sulat** and **Gili Lawang**, surrounded by coastal mangrove, without any beaches but with a large array of offshore coral. All are uninhabited. You can arrange **snorkelling** and **fishing** expeditions to the islands from both *Matahari* and *Siola Cottages*. Overnight **camping** trips are also possible. Operators from Bali bring occasional dive groups here, but there's no local operator (although this may change soon; enquire at *Matahari*).

South Lombok

The largely undeveloped **south coast** of Lombok is extraordinarily beautiful, with mile upon mile of picturesque curving bays of pure white sand separated by rocky headlands and backed by sparsely inhabited dry hills. Known to surfers for several years, **Kuta** is a low-key development with fewer than a dozen places to stay – pretty much the only accommodation in the area. From here you can explore out to the west, where bay after bay lines the coast, and to the east, though access is not so easy. If you're restricted to public transport, you can still reach the inland villages specializing in pottery, weaving, basketware and carving, such as **Beleka**, **Sukarara**, **Penujak** and **Sukaraja**, and the traditional villages of **Sade** and **Rembitan**. Several years ago the south coast was targeted for massive tourist development. The coastal roads were improved dramatically and the *Coralia Lombok Novotel* opened near Kuta – and, so far, that has been that. It remains to be seen what the future holds, but for the moment the area is still pristine.

Praya and the craft villages

The busy market town and transport hub of **PRAYA**, 22km southeast of Sweta, is the capital of Central Lombok (Lombok Tengah), although it lies well to the south of the island. It's a pleasant place, easily accessible by **bus** or **bemo** from Bertais/Mandalika terminal in Sweta; there's a market on Saturdays. You should note that Praya is in a devout Muslim area and the town is officially "dry": no strong alcohol is available, although beer is sold. The only **accommodation** is the functional *Hotel Dienda Hayu*, Jl Untung Surapati 26 (☎0370/654319; ❷) with a small **restaurant** attached. To find it, turn right onto the main road at the bus terminal and turn left after 200m at the traffic lights; the hotel is up on the right. The **tourist office** is at Jl Gajah Made 125 (☎0370/653766), about 500m west of the bus terminal on the main road. There are BNI and BCA **bank** ATM machines for Visa, MasterCard and Cirrus on the main road between the bus terminal and the turning to *Dienda Hayu*, and several **wartels** on the main road. Most visitors change in Praya for local transport to Sengkol and Kuta (see opposite) without stopping.

PENUNJAK, 6km southwest of Praya, is one of the three main pottery villages on the island. Most workshops are on or near the main road and this is a good place to watch the potters at work if you come early in the day. Directly west of Praya (although the route is via Puyung or Batujai), the weaving village of **SUKARARA** is firmly on the tour-bus circuit and has some enormous showrooms offering the widest range of textiles that you'll find on Lombok. The weavers produce *ikat* and *songket* cloth using backstrap looms; the latter tends to be more aggressively colourful than the former, whose subtle shades are produced by vegetable dyes from indigo, betel nut, pineapple and bay leaves. Look out for the traditional *lumbung* barn designs as well as the "primitive" figures. There are plenty of shops in the village and you need to shop around.

East of Praya, the road to Gubukdalem is the main road across the south of the island. To reach **BELEKA**, known for the production of rattan basketware, turn north at Ganti, about 100m east of the Batu Nampar turning; it's a busy junction, with cidomo waiting to take you the 3km. There are a large number of shops and workshops here and the local specialities are wares made from grass, rattan and bamboo in a huge range of shapes and sizes. Known for its canoe-making, the village of **KERUAK**, 7km east of Sukaraja, has a few workshops east of the village in the hamlet of Batu Rimpang, to the right of the main road to Tanjung Luar. You can watch work in progress as simple hand tools are used to create dugout canoes from vast tree trunks. On completion, the boats are taken by road to **TANJUNG LUAR**, 5km east on the coast. This is a vibrant fishing village with typical Bugis houses built on high stilts.

Kuta and around

The only village with any degree of tourist development on Lombok's south coast is **KUTA**, 54km from Mataram and 32km from Praya, a tiny fishing village situated just behind the west end of the wide, white-sand – although fairly shadeless – Putri Nyale beach. It's rapidly becoming the favourite choice of travellers to Lombok seeking a few days by the sea, although some visitors find the hawkers and children especially persistent. The coast around the village is lovely: **Seger** and **Tanjung Aan** beaches are within walking or cycling distance. Apart from Sunday when the lively **market** takes place, the area is the ultimate in peace and quiet. The big swell here makes the sea good for **surfing** (see box p.712), but there's no diving or snorkelling; a seafront surf shop, Ocean Blue (Ⓣ0370/653911), repairs and rents boards. Coming from the west, **buses** and **bemos** run to Praya from Bertais/Mandalika terminal in Sweta. From Praya, bemos ply either to Sengkol, where you can change, or right through to Kuta. From the east of Lombok, bemos run to Praya via Kopang on the main cross-island road. Perama also offers **tourist shuttles** to Kuta from all destinations on Bali and Lombok; see p.713 for details.

Accommodation and eating

Kuta's **accommodation** is mostly simple losmen-style, although there are a couple of more upmarket options and the luxury end of the market is serviced by the *Coralia Lombok Novotel*. In Kuta itself the road runs about 50m inland from the beach; accommodation is spread out along the coast for about 500m on the far side, so don't expect cottages on the beach.

All Kuta's losmen have **restaurants** attached, offering inexpensive or moderately priced food; seafood is the speciality. *Segare Anak* has the biggest menu, *Anda* also has good-quality food and *Warung Ilalang* at the east end of the beach has the finest spot from which to admire the ocean. *Warung Mandalika*, attached to *Putri Mandalika* in the village, is worth a look as well. There are nightly **videos**; keep an eye out for notices.

Anda ⓣ0370/654836. Several standards of very basic bungalows in a shady garden setting on the road along the beach. ❷

Coralia Lombok Novotel ⓣ0370/653333, ⓕ653555, ⓦwww.novotel-lombok.com. Stunningly located 2km east of Kuta on the fabulous Seger beach, this is the only luxury development along this coast. Accommodation, all furnished in attractive, tasteful natural materials, is set in lovely grounds. Prices start at US$130 (plus 21-percent tax and service). It's a fairly isolated spot but there are several bars and restaurants, a pretty pool, plenty of organized activities and water sports and a wonderful on-site spa. ❽

Kuta Indah ⓣ0370/653781, ⓕ654628, ⓔkutaindah@indo.net.id. This is one of the newest places, located at the western end of the bay. They have a good garden and clean bungalows ranged around a pool. It's a short walk to the beach and there are free transfers to Tanjung Aan and Mawun beaches. Visa and MasterCard accepted. ❸–❺

Lamancha Homestay ⓣ0370/655186. Nice little place in the village, a short walk from the beach just inland from the police post, comprising a few bungalows and rooms. There are plenty of sitting areas and a pleasant atmosphere. ❷

Matahari Inn ⓣ0370/655000, ⓕ654909, ⓦwww.mataharіinn.com. Situated in the village, just west of the main road from Praya, this is an atmospheric place set in a lush garden. There's a swimming pool and free transport to Tanjung Aan beach. ❺

Putri Mandalika ⓣ0370/655342. Five well-kept rooms in a small, friendly family compound in the village. There's a small, attached restaurant. ❷

Rinjani Agung ⓣ0370/654849, ⓕ654852. Stretching back a long way from the road, this place has a huge range of accommodation on offer, the most expensive with air conditioning. ❷–❸

Segare Anak ⓣ0370/654834, ⓕ654835, ⓔkomangsin@yahoo.com. Set in the middle of the accommodation strip along the beach road, this long-standing favourite has more expensive, newer rooms and older, smaller rooms all set in a good garden behind the restaurant. ❷

Sekar Kuning ⓣ0370/654856. A variety of basic but adequate rooms in a garden setting on the road that runs along behind the beach. It remains in better condition than some of the competition. ❷

Surfing on Lombok

Generally, the quality of the **surf** breaks is not as good on Lombok as on Bali – with the exception of the world-class but elusive Desert Point. The great bonus for surfers on Lombok is fewer crowds and the wonderful south-coast scenery. Most of the well-known breaks are off the **south coast**, with Kuta the ideal base for them. The resort's own breaks are **Kuta Left**, in front of the village, and **Kuta Right**, at the eastern end towards Aan. There's also surf off the glorious **Aan** beach (see p.714), a left-hander at the western edge and a left- and a right-hander in the centre.

West of Kuta, most of the bays are worth a look, although they vary in accessibility and the surf is erratic. Around the headland, at **Selong Blanak** (see opposite), there's a good left-hander, best in the dry season. Further west, **Blongas** is less accessible, but has three good breaks, a left-hander in the east, a right in the west and another left in the centre. You'll need to charter a boat from the village to get here; it's a good spot to anchor overnight on a live-aboard. Check the local situation as the area is reported to be a shark breeding-ground.

East of Kuta the best but most inaccessible breaks are off the coast of the southeast peninsula near **Serewe**. There are two good right-handers about a mile to the west, but you'll have to come by boat. There are more breaks just inside the southern headland of **Awang Bay**, as well as further into the bay. You can charter boats from Awang (see p.714) on the west side of the bay to get out to the right-hander on the reef just south of the village. **Gumbang Bay**, which some people call Grupuk Bay, a short drive from Kuta, has the potential for big waves at its shallow mouth, plus smaller ones in the middle and to the east of the bay.

The world-famous break on Lombok is **Desert Point** off Bangko Bangko (see p.684), a fast but elusive left-hander with tubes that is best from June to September. The area is accessible by road and facilities are developing. Elsewhere around the island, **Gili Air**'s Pertama is a renowned though erratic right-hander and **Senggigi** offers a couple of breaks.

Listings

Changing money There are several moneychangers near the losmen (*Anda*, *Kuta Indah* and *Segare Anak* bungalows also change money), but expect about ten percent less for your money than you'd get in Mataram.

Charter transport Ask at your accommodation or at Perama. It costs around Rp250,000/day for a car (including driver and fuel); Rp35,000 per half-day to rent a motorbike; Rp15,000/day for a bicycle.

Internet access Available at several places including the wartel (Rp500/min; minimum 5min).

Phones There's a wartel in the village (daily 8am–10.30pm).

Post *Segare Anak* is a postal agent and you can use them for poste restante; get mail addressed to you at *Segare Anak*, Kuta Beach, Lombok Tengah, Nusa Tenggara Barat 8357. The nearest post office is in Sengkol.

Shuttle bus tickets To book, head to the Perama office (daily 7am–10pm), attached to *Segare Anak* and opposite the wartel; they have daily departures to destinations on Bali and Lombok, although some require a stopover.

West of Kuta

Along the coast **west of Kuta** you can explore half a dozen or so of the prettiest beaches on the island, backed by attractive, rolling coastal hills and widely dispersed rural communities. You'll need your own transport, but there are few signs and not many landmarks.

The road out of Kuta, past *Kuta Indah*, climbs up steeply for a couple of kilometres. The view from the top of the hill back across the entire Kuta area is one of the most dramatic in southern Lombok. A restaurant is planned up here; even without a drink at the top, the scenery is worth the sweaty walk. Some 5km out of Kuta you'll pass the "MTR 64" road marker (indicating 64km to Mataram). Just under 1km west of this, look out for a dirt-track heading off to the coast. After 2km it reaches the coastal village of **ARE GOLENG**. The beach here is about 400m long and the seaweed beds in the shallows are clearly visible. A tiny island, **Gili Nungsa**, sits out in the bay. Wend your way east through the coconut grove for a few hundred metres to find a more secluded part of the bay. The next beach west is **Mawun**, 8km from Kuta and reached by a 500-metre-long sealed road a few hundred metres beyond the "MTR 66" marker. The bay is almost semicircular, enclosed on both sides by rocky headlands with the water fading from turquoise to a deep, vibrant blue. About 3km further west, the main road reaches the coast and runs a few hundred metres inland from the gently curving **Tampa** beach. The area is not terribly attractive – the beach is backed by flat scrub and there isn't much shade – but it's pretty deserted. Access to the beach at **Mawi**, about 4km west of Tampa, isn't easy. Take the next sealed road branching off seaward (if you reach "MTR 75" you've gone too far). After 1500m it degenerates into a track before ending in a stand of banana, coconut and kapok trees with a couple of houses. It's a few hundred metres' walk to the lovely white-sand beach, separated from nearby **Rowok** by a rocky outcrop. From here, there are great views, plus the impressive sight of Gili Lawang – three pinnacles sticking almost sheer out of the ocean.

Back on the road, you soon reach **SELONG BLANAK**, 18km from Kuta, also accessible via Penujak from Praya (24km). The bay here has a long curving beach with rocky headlands at each end and the striking island of **Gili Lawang** just offshore. The only **accommodation** west of Kuta is here, at *Selong Blanak Cottages* (no phone; ❸), 2km inland from the beach; free transport to the beach is provided. The cottages are set in a lush garden and there's a moderately priced **restaurant** attached. A five-star resort is planned for the area. From Selong Blanak there are two roads west to Pengantap. Access to the shorter, coastal road depends on the road bridge across the river at Selong

Blanak. The longer road, curving 20km inland is a bit of an adventure via the tiny village of **KELING** where it splits. The right fork leads north to Penunjak (see p.710) while the left fork continues on westwards through tiny hamlets to the village of **PENGANGTAP**, a row of thatched houses just behind the beach. The village is served by bemos from Sekotong, 17km to the north. Some 8km beyond Pengangtap, the road splits at the tiny fishing village of **SEPI**. You can continue 1km west to **BLONGAS**, the end of the road, where there's good snorkelling, diving and surfing but no accommodation. Alternatively, follow the road directly north from Sepi and after 11km you reach Sekotong (see p.683) where you can turn west to Bangko Bangko or north to Lembar.

East of Kuta

The glorious beaches of **Seger** and **Tanjung Aan** are easily accessible from Kuta and, at a push, walkable if you have no transport (bicycles are a good idea). Seger is closest to Kuta (1km) and is now the location of the luxury *Coralia Lombok Novotel* development. To reach Tanjung Aan (5km from Kuta), follow the road east out of the resort and take the first sealed turning to the right. There are two perfect white-sand beaches here, **Aan** to the west and **Pedau** to the east, separated by a rocky outcrop, Batu Kotak. As their popularity has grown, the beaches now see a few hawkers and there are also some drinks stalls, but no other facilities.

Past Aan, the small fishing village of **GERUPAK**, just under 8km from Kuta, perches on the western shores of Gumbang Bay. **Lobster** is one of the local specialities and buyers come here from all the big hotels on Lombok and sometimes from Bali. *Kelapa Bungalows* (no phone; ❷) are on the road in from Kuta, about 300m before the beach. They're pretty basic but are set in a large garden; there's a small restaurant attached. Bungalows here seem to come and go; check in Kuta whether they're open. The thriving fishing village of **AWANG**, 16km east of Kuta, is well worth the trip for the views of **Awang Bay**, a massive inlet. As the road descends into the village, you'll be able to spot the tiny settlement of Ekas across on the southeast peninsula and see all the way south to the open sea. You can charter boats from Awang across to Ekas, a much easier option than tackling the rough roads. In Ekas *Laut Surga Cottages* (no phone), offers some of the hardest-to-reach **accommodation** in Lombok. They may have succumbed to their isolation and closed down by the time you read this: check at Kuta or Awang or try the surf websites on p.63 for up-to-date information as there's no way of contacting them directly.

Sumbawa, Komodo and Rinca

East of Lombok, the island of **Sumbawa** is scorched, rough and mountainous, consisting of two sparsely populated regions. On the **west coast** are deserted paradise **beaches**, with turtle-spawning grounds and crashing surf from

Sumbawan festivals

Although the widespread influence of Islam and wholesale migration from the congested Javan landmass has diluted Sumbawa's indigenous culture, it is far from dead. With a little luck, spectacular **festivals** such as bone-jarring bare-fist boxing, and horse and water-buffalo racing can be seen. The **buffalo racing** takes place before the rice is planted at the end of the rainy season: the animals drag a light plough (which usually disintegrates during the race), and are ridden by tenacious male competitors, goading them into charging down the rice paddies, before attempting to grab a coloured flag from a stick at the end of the fields. It's an exhilirating spectacle, with great, lumbering buffalo charging through knee-deep mud, their riders clinging on for dear life.

Berempuk, **bare-fist boxing**, can be seen at some of the festivals surrounding harvesting and planting. During these bloodthirsty contests, young men seek to appease the spirits while draining their aggression.

Jereweh to **Lunyuk**. **Sumbawa Besar**, the western capital, is home to the fine sultan's palace, as well as being the jumping-off point for **Pulau Moyo** to the north, declared a national park for its spectacular coral reefs and wealth of wild animals. **Bima** province in the east has become legendary amongst surfers for the exceptional reef breaks at **Hu'u**, which now also lures non-surfers with its relaxed reputation. The entire island is spanned by the Trans-Sumbawa Highway, one of the very few roads in Nusa Tenggara whose surface merits its lofty title.

Sumbawa is usually regarded by tourists as an inconvenient but necessary bridge between the popular destinations of Lombok and Komodo. This is a shame, as there is plenty to see here. Most places outside the regency capitals of Bima and Sumbawa Besar are relatively untravelled, and offer unique cultural experiences for the adventurous. Sumbawa is a strictly **Muslim** enclave, so all the usual rules of visiting Islamic communities should be observed here. Both male and female travellers should dress conservatively; looking scruffy or the wearing of shorts and vests will not win you friends.

Off the east coast of Sumbawa lies the **Komodo national park**, a group of parched but majestic islands famed as the home of the **Komodo dragon**, a living reminder of our prehistoric past. The south coast of the largest island, Komodo, is lined with impressive (mostly dormant) volcanoes, while the north is characterized by dusty plains, irrigated to create rice paddies around the major settlements. Tiny rocky **Rinca** also features dragons and, thanks to a convenient location close to the Flores harbour of Labuanbajo, now sees just as many visitors.

The majority of travellers coming to Sumbawa arrive by **ferry** from Lombok (90min) to the west, or from Flores (7–8hr) in the east. These ferries connect with buses that traverse the Trans-Sumbawa Highway.

Some history

Historically, West Sumbawa was perceived as a vassal state to more powerful **Bima**. The two sides of the island were subject to vastly different influences, which remain evident today. The Sumbawan people were influenced from the west, by the Balinese and the Sasaks of Lombok; the Bimans, however, owe more to the Makassarese of Sulawesi and the peoples of Flores and Sumba, showing linguistic and cultural similarities.

Most of Sumbawa is thought to have been nominally under the control of the East Javanese **Majapahit empire**. The poet Prapança, who chronicled the affairs of the dynasty, mentioned an expedition into Sumbawa, probably when

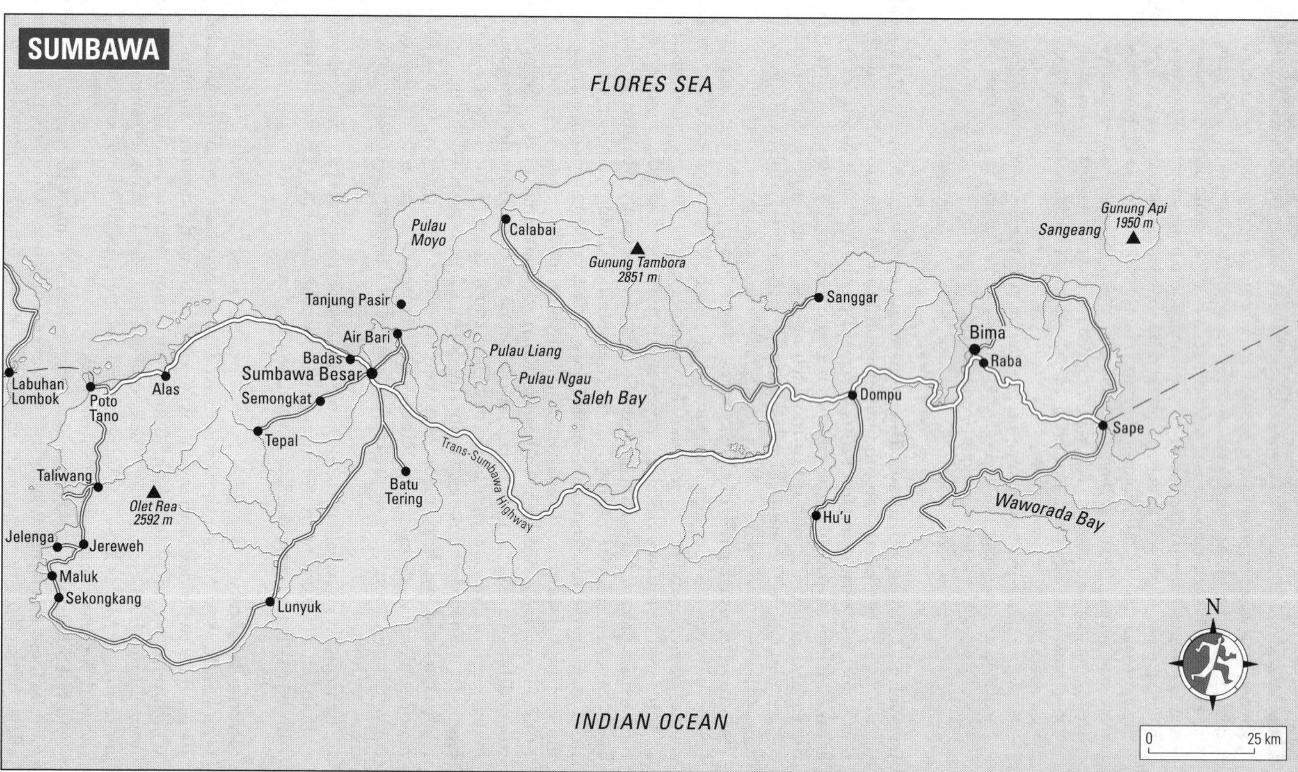
SUMBAWA
FLORES SEA
INDIAN OCEAN
Flores
Labuhan Lombok
Poto Tano
Alas
Taliwang
Olet Rea 2592 m
Jelenga
Jereweh
Maluk
Sekongkang
Lunyuk
Tepal
Semongkat
Sumbawa Besar
Badas
Air Bari
Tanjung Pasir
Pulau Moyo
Batu Tering
Trans-Sumbawa Highway
Pulau Liang
Pulau Ngau
Saleh Bay
Calabai
Gunung Tambora 2851 m
Sanggar
Dompu
Hu'u
Bima
Raba
Sape
Waworada Bay
Sangeang
Gunung Api 1950 m
N
0
25 km

the Majapahit was at the height of its powers in the early fourteenth century. Trade was based around timber and slaves, and Bima, with its well-protected bay, became the most important port in this part of Nusa Tenggara. The position of the island, on the **trade routes** between Java and both the sandalwood producers lying to the east and the Spice Islands to the north, helped to elevate the islands to a position of considerable strategic importance, and the kingdom of Bima expanded to claim the majority of Nusa Tenggara. From the middle of the fourteenth century until the end of the sixteenth century, Bima region was ostensibly ruled by a succession of **Hindu rajas** of Javanese origin.

When the Makassarese of Sulawesi took control in the early seventeenth century, they converted the people from their animist religion to Islam. Christian missionaries, on the other hand, had little success in their attempts to find new converts, and even the **Dutch East India Company** had only a limited stay here. The Dutch only had real control of the area at the beginning of the twentieth century, and were later ousted by the **Japanese** in World War II, whose rule constituted a bitter period in the island's history. After the Japanese defeat, Sumbawa became part of the modern republic of Indonesia. Although the original sultans were not recognized by the central government, some of their ancestors maintain prestige as well as palaces in the two main sultanates of Bima and Sumbawa Besar.

Today, the region's glory days are numbered. **Transmigration** and the wholesale reaping of the remaining sappanwood and sandalwood forests have put huge pressure on the little land that is useable. **Over-logging** has resulted in Bima's once illustrious bay filling with silt, which has poured unabated into the waters around the port until big ships can no longer call here.

West Sumbawa

Noticeably drier and less fertile than nearby Lombok, **West Sumbawa** has a stark landscape of craggy hills and charred volcanoes, with dark plains of mud fields in which rice is cultivated. However, the west-coast **beaches** are probably the most worthwhile attraction in the whole island. **Pulau Moyo** to the north is a plentifully stocked nature reserve offering good trekking and snorkelling, and some interesting historical sites can be found south of the capital, **Sumbawa Besar**. The town itself has little to offer, though it is a better place to stop than Bima if you have a choice, having a couple of reasonable places to eat and clean and spacious streets.

The coast

The west coast of Sumbawa offers surf, sand and solitude. You need time and patience to endure its appalling roads and public transport – although the situation with both has improved dramatically, thanks to the opening of an American mining operation. At the extreme western end of Sumbawa lies **Poto Tano**, the ferry terminal for boats from Lombok; buses meet all incoming ferries and run south from the harbour to **Taliwang** (1hr; Rp3000), and north to **Alas** (45min; Rp2500), **Sumbawa Besar** (2hr; Rp5000) and sometimes all the way to Bima (9hr; Rp20,000).

Taliwang

An hour's drive south of Poto Tano lies the small town of **TALIWANG**, a charming if somewhat ramshackle place, a necessary stop if you intend to visit the west coast. It rarely sees Western visitors, but treats the few that arrive here with great hospitality. Horse-drawn **dokar** are a more common sight than motorized vehicles, and, despite the call to prayer from the numerous mosques, it's a tranquil place to visit. In the backstreets, brightly painted houses are raised up to 3m off the ground on stilts; the space beneath is home to buffalo, pigs and chickens, and half-buried urns containing live eels and shrimp.

Taliwang's **bus station** lies on the street parallel to Jalan Sudirman, although buses can drop you off at the door of where you're staying. For **accommodation**, the best choice in town is the excellent-value *Taliwang Indah* (❶) on Jalan Sudirman, which offers clean, spacious rooms, balcony views, and a reasonable restaurant downstairs. The best meals in town are served either at their restaurant, or at the *Rasate Dua Rumah Makan* across the street. Both serve standard local fare and the nasi campur ayam is especially good, with a spicy piece of Taliwang's famous fried chicken.

A short bemo ride (Rp750) out of town and off the Poto Tano road is **Danau Taliwang**, also known as **Lebok Lebo**, a large lake covered in lotus flowers which has fantastic birdlife, with various birds of prey and elegant herons.

Jereweh and the south

JEREWEH, an hour south of Taliwang by bemo (Rp2000), is the largest town in the remote southwestern corner of Sumbawa. It's little more than a tiny market and a few government offices, with a good white-sand beach and passable **surf** 5km away to the west at **JELENGA**. The *Jelenga Beach Bungalows* and *Scar Surf Bungalows*, both right on the shore here, offer simple full-board accommodation (❷) and are a good hangout for committed surfers; the accommodation itself is nothing special, but the food is tasty.

Seventeen kilometres further on lies the village of **MALUK**, sitting by a huge arc of **stunning beach** flanked by cliffs, with a slightly erratic reef break that can be magnificent about 500m offshore. You could either paddle out, or ask one of the fishermen who sometimes sit on the beach mending their nets to give you a ride. The *Rumah Makan Cassanova* is the only place in the village to get a cold drink and good food; it's also a haven for workers from the nearby American-owned Newmont gold mine (the second largest in Indonesia). You can stay at the *Surya* or *Iwan Beach Bungalows* (❶) which are both down near the seafront. Both sets of accommodation have some rooms with en-suite mandi, but neither has mosquito nets, which are really a necessity on the coast.

SEKONGKANG, a 45-minute bemo ride (Rp3000) further down south from Maluk, has an even better beach, with more shade and huge waves. The beach itself is almost always deserted, but offers great snorkelling and large numbers of **turtles**, both in the sea and coming ashore to lay their eggs. The kepala desa (headman) has had fifteen simple beach bungalows (❶) built for tourists and surfers. From here, it's a gruelling three-hour truck trip to **Tongo** (Rp7500); the beach is wonderful – clean and almost always deserted –and you can stay at the kepala desa's house (❶). The road to **Lunyuk** (see p.724) is still under construction, and at the moment it can only be reached by heading south from Sumbawa Besar.

Alas and Pulau Bungin

Two hours' drive to the north of Poto Tano, the quiet old port of **ALAS** is the hopping-off point for nearby **Pulau Bungin**, apparently the most densely populated place in Indonesia. The seafaring Buginese, who started to settle on the island in the early nineteenth century, built their homes on a reef no more than a metre or so above sea level, in order to protect themselves from marauding mainlanders. When the island was full, they merely dug up lumps of coral and rock and dumped them into the sea to expand the developable land. Nowadays, when a man wants to marry and build his own home, he must first create the land to accommodate it. Today, Bungin is dotted with TV antennas and spanned by electricity cables, but traditional ways are strong and it remains an intriguing place to visit.

If you are planning a trip to Bungin, you'll probably need to spend a night in Alas before or afterwards – there's nowhere to stay on the island itself. The *Losmen Anda* (❷) near the Telkom office is the pick of the places to stay. To get to Bungin, take a dokar to the harbour for Rp1000, then a motorboat (Rp5000).

Sumbawa Besar

SUMBAWA BESAR, the old sultanate capital of Sumbawa, was in theory always subservient to the superior power of Bima, but is now the largest town on the island, and visitors looking to break up the bus-run across the island could do worse than stop here. Its open streets are lined with crumbling white plaster buildings, with bright blue wooden doors adorning its many shop fronts. It's a sprawling place, with no particular centre; apart from a small cluster of losmen on Jalan Hasanuddin near the river, accommodation is also spread from one end of town to the other.

Dalam Loka, the **Sultan's Palace**, is the only real sight of interest in town. This barn-like wooden structure, raised on great pillars, was built in 1885 by Sultan Jalashuddin. It was partially restored in the 1980s, after the government promised to revitalize the building and turn it into a museum of Nusa Tenggaran artefacts – although this grand plan has yet to materialize. Nearby, some of the sultan's descendants live in the appropriately named **Balai Kuning** (the yellow house) on Jalan Wahidin. Of passing interest are **Pura Agung Girinatha**, a Balinese-style temple near the post office, and the nondescript **New Sultan's Palace** on Jalan Merdaka, a few blocks away from the genuine article.

Practicalities

Buses arriving from the west usually arrive at **Brang Barat bus terminal** on the east side of town, a fifteen-minute walk south from the Sultan's Palace. Alternatively, they may drop you at the more central old bus station on Jalan Yos Sudarso. The **airport** is a five-minute dokar ride into town. Sumbawa Besar boasts the newest fleet of **bemos** in Nusa Tenggara and a wealth of horse-drawn dokar (known locally as *benhur*). The yellow bemos, *bemo kota*, do round-trips of the town; they can either be flagged down on the street, or picked up at the **Seketeng market terminal** on Jalan Setiabudi. *Bemo kota* will drop you off pretty much anywhere, charging a flat rate of Rp1000.

The regional **tourist office** (Mon–Thurs 8am–2pm, Fri 8–11am, Sat 8am–1pm; ⓣ0371/23714) is about the best you'll find in Nusa Tenggara. It lies 2km west of the town centre past the airport at Jl Bungur 1. To get there, take a west-bound yellow bemo from Jalan Hasanuddin. Some of the staff speak good English, and they can provide useful information about attractions in the surrounding area; the office is stocked with brochures about local festivals such as buffalo racing (see box p.715). The **PHPA parks office** – the Kantor Sub-Seksi Konservasi Sumber Daya Alam, to give it its full title – lies in the village of Nijang, about 4km southeast of the town centre (Mon–Sat 8am–3pm; ⓣ0371/23941); an ojek – which you can pick up from the corner by the *Hotel Tambora*, or by one of the markets – there should cost no more than Rp3000. They can provide information about Pulau Moyo, though not actual tours.

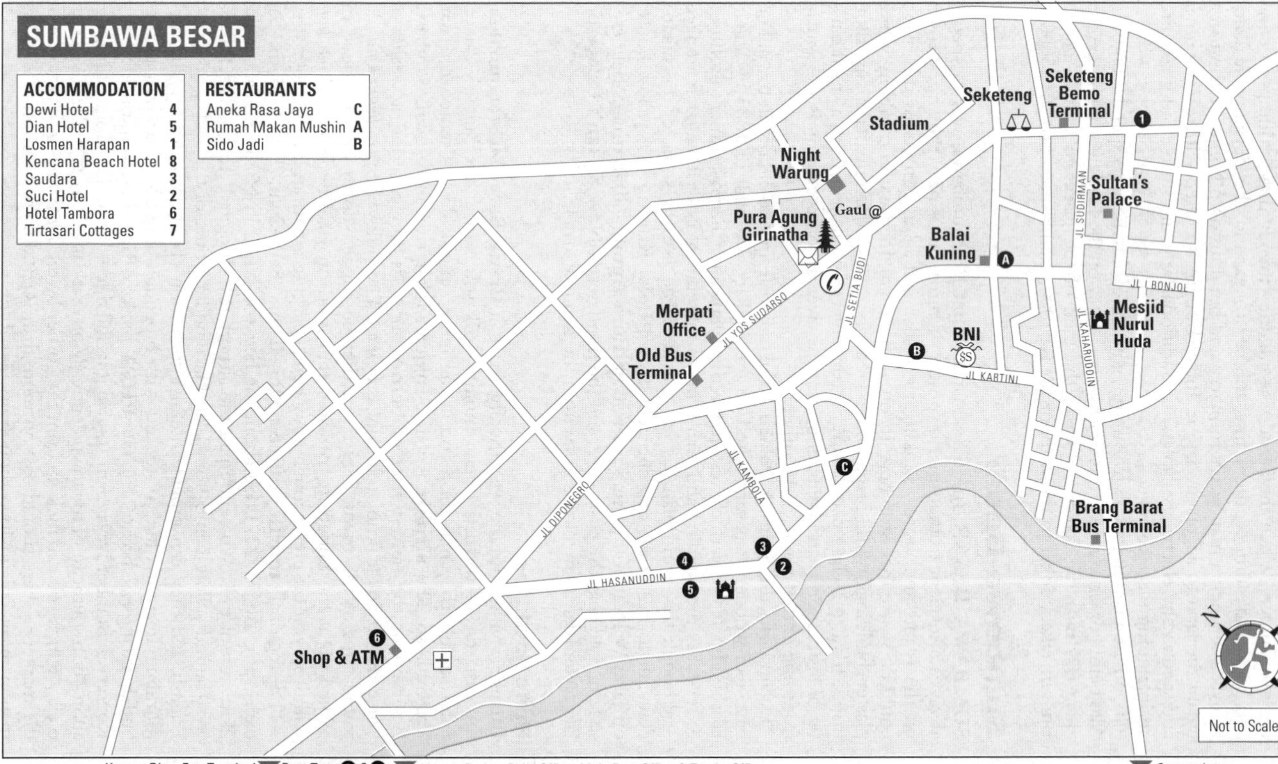
SUMBAWA BESAR
ACCOMMODATION
Dewi Hotel 4
Dian Hotel 5
Losmen Harapan 1
Kencana Beach Hotel 8
Saudara 3
Suci Hotel 2
Hotel Tambora 6
Tirtasari Cottages 7
RESTAURANTS
Aneka Rasa Jaya C
Rumah Makan Mushin A
Sido Jadi B
Air Bari & Moyo Island
Bima
Seketeng
Seketeng Bemo Terminal
Stadium
Night Warung
Gaul @
Pura Agung Girinatha
Sultan's Palace
Balai Kuning
JL SUDIRMAN
JL BONJOL
Mesjid Nurul Huda
JL KAHARUDDIN
BNI
JL KARTINI
JL SETIA BUDI
JL YOS SUDARSO
Merpati Office
Old Bus Terminal
JL KAMBOLA
JL DIPONEGRO
JL HASANUDDIN
Brang Barat Bus Terminal
Shop & ATM
Not to Scale
Karang Dima Bus Terminal, Poto Tano, 7 & 8
Airport, Badas, Pelni Office, Main Post Office & Tourist Office
Semongkat

Moving on from Sumbawa Besar

Buses going **east** to Bima and beyond leave from the Barang Barat bus terminal from 5.30am until 3.30pm to Dompu (4hr 30min; Rp15,000), Bima (7hr; Rp25,000) and Sape (8hr 30min; Rp30,000). For Taliwang and **night buses** running both east and west, use the Karang Dima terminal 6km northwest of town, reachable by bemo from the town centre. Alternatively, save yourself a trip by booking with one of the **bus agents** in town, such as PO Tiara Mas (ⓣ0371/21241) on Jalan Yos Sudarso, who have morning and night buses to Mataram (6hr; Rp40,000), Denpasar (24hr; Rp135,000), Surabaya (2 days; Rp121,500) and Jakarta (3 days; Rp225,000).

Merpati, Jl Yos Sudarso 16 (ⓣ0371/22002), have **flights** twice weekly to Denpasar via Lombok, from where you can connect with onward flights to Java.

The **Pelni** office is 3km out of town at the eastern end of Jalan Garuda. To get there, catch any westbound yellow or blue bemo from Jalan Hasanuddin (Rp1000). Pelni's *KM Wilis* calls in once a fortnight on its way east to Labuanbajo, Sumba and Kupang, and once a fortnight on its way west to Surabaya. The *KM Tatamailau* stops twice a month on its way either to Denpasar and east Java or to Makassar.

For changing foreign currency, the **BNI bank** on Jalan Kartini offers the best rates from here to Kupang. If you're heading east and have currency other than US dollars, then change enough here to see you through, though there are a couple of ATMs on Flores. The bank also has an **ATM**, and a second one outside the *Hotel Tambora* (see below). The **post office** is located on Jalan Yos Sudarso, and the **Telkom** opposite has international telephone, telex, telegram and fax facilities. One hundred metres to the east, Gaul **internet café** is the fastest in town (Rp10,000 for 1hr).

Accommodation

Quite a few places not mentioned here double as brothels, and one or two of them are renowned for being bug-ridden and really grotty. It's worth looking over your room carefully before checking in.

Dewi Hotel Jl Hasanuddin 60 ⓣ0371/21170. Thirty clean rooms ranging from cheap ekonomi to plush VIP suites with TV and bath, including breakfast. Not over-friendly, but still very good value. ❶–❸

Dian Hotel Jl Hasanuddin 69 ⓣ0371/21708. A clean and friendly hotel (actually more of a losmen), with fan-cooled or air-con rooms, all ensuite. ❷–❸

Losmen Harapan Jl Dr. Cipto 7 ⓣ0371/21629. A cheap and pleasant old timber-framed house, with friendly management offering fan-only rooms. ❷

Kencana Beach Hotel 11km west of town, on the coast, just off the Trans-Sumbawa Highway ⓣ0371/22555. Transport can be arranged by the *Tambora* (see next column). Comparatively expensive, but a quiet, relaxing, upmarket place, with Sumbawan-style wooden cottages near the seafront, as well as a swimming pool. ❺

Saudara Jl Hasanuddin 10 ⓣ0371/21528. Clean, quiet and inexpensive, with friendly owners; all rooms have en-suite mandi. ❶

Suci Hotel Jl Hasanuddin 57 ⓣ0371/21589. A sprawling place with a variety of rooms, from the fan-cooled cheapies round the courtyard by reception, to a new block with air-con, perfectly positioned to catch the full dawn blast from the mosque next door. ❷–❸

Hotel Tambora Jl Kebayan ⓣ0371/21555. The only hotel in town genuinely geared towards tourists, offering a range of accommodation from ekonomi rooms right through to luxurious suites with amazing bathrooms, complete with your own personal waterfall and goldfish. The pricey restaurant does a wonderful breakfast and some good Western and Chinese food. ❷–❹

Tirtasari Cottages. About 5km west of town at Seliperate, right on the beach ⓣ0371/21987. The best option if you don't mind being out of town, with a variety of rooms to suit most budgets, including hot water and air-con in the VIP bungalows. Buses and bemos run from Sekateng market. ❶–❸

Eating and drinking

While the majority of **eating places** in Sumbawa Besar are the usual local warung serving goat stews and sate, there are a couple of decent Chinese places. The larger hotels all have restaurants serving a few Western dishes plus Chinese and Indonesian food; the *Hotel Tambora*'s restaurant is pretty good, but a little overpriced.

Aneka Rasa Jaya Jl Hasanuddin 14. Chinese place serving huge portions of the best food in, and the beer is cheap and cold.

Rumah Makan Mushin Jalan Wahidin. A simple little place serving some of the best Taliwang chicken outside of Taliwang.

Sido Jadi Jl Wahidin 7. A mid-priced Chinese place with excellent seafood, catering mainly for businesspeople but very welcoming to travellers.

Around Sumbawa Besar

Apart from **Pulau Moyo**, which receives a steady trickle of nature lovers and wealthy tourists, the sights around Sumbawa Besar tend to be the preserve of domestic tourists. Moyo is probably the most rewarding destination in Sumbawa, surrounded by beautiful coral reefs and overrun with deer, monkeys and wild pigs. Lesser-known sights south of Sumbawa Besar include troglodyte caves and megaliths in the **Batu Tering** area, the Dutch hill resort of **Semongkat** and the tribal villages at **Tepal**. All of these are well worth a visit, and remain practically tourist-free all year round.

Serious castaways should head for **Pulau Liang** and **Pulau Dangar** in Saleh Bay. They have extraordinary fishing, snorkelling and beaches, but are mostly uninhabited and have no facilities, so bring everything you need from Sumbawa Besar. You can charter boats from Air Bari (see opposite) or Tanjung Pasir (see opposite).

Pulau Moyo

A few kilometres off the north coast of Sumbawa, sitting in the mouth of Saleh Bay, lies the national park of **Pulau Moyo**. It's a naturalist's dream, with an abundance of animals: wild pigs, snakes, monitor lizards, 21 species of bat, huge herds of native deer and hordes of crab-eating macaques, as well as plentiful birdlife, including sulphur-crested cockatoos, orioles and megapode birds. In 1902, an Australian cattle boat was shipwrecked on the island and now cows roam free, particularly over the central grass plains. Offshore, the pristine coral gardens are well stocked with fish. The best time to visit Moyo is in June and July, though the seas are clear and quiet from April.

Unless you bring your own camping equipment, trekking possibilities are limited by the lack of accommodation on the island, though you may be able to stay in one of the small coastal fishing villages that dot Moyo's shore. To hire a trekking guide from the PHPA posts costs Rp30,000 per day. Renting a fishing boat from Tanjung Pasir and going east to **Stama reef** is a terrific way to spend time around the island. It's only about fifteen minutes offshore, and the **snorkelling** here is marvellous, with lots of sharks and turtles. There's nowhere on Moyo to rent masks and snorkels, so it is best to bring your own, and fins are also advisable, due to the strong currents.

A large part of Moyo has been taken over by by the *Amanwana Resort* (Ⓣ0371/22330; US$750), situated on the west coast. This is one of the flashiest, most exclusive retreats in Asia: a nice option if you can afford US$750 a night. The accommodation is in spectacular tented suites, the idea being that you "rough it" under canvas with incredible luxuries at your disposal. The staff can arrange hunting safaris for those who would rather kill animals than watch them. Nearby is the gorgeous **Mata Jitu air terjun**, renamed the **Lady Di Waterfall** after the late princess stayed here in 1995.

For a donation of about Rp20,000, you can stay at one of the PHPA posts on the island. The basic **accommodation** consists of wooden cells with a mattress and threadbare mosquito net. None of the four posts can provide food, and it's best to check with the PHPA in Sumbawa Besar (see p.719) as to which are currently open. The only post that has anything even approaching permanent guesthouse status is that at **Tanjung Pasir** on the south coast facing Air Bari, where most boats from the mainland arrive. Private rooms with outside toilet and bathing facilities are available here.

Getting to Pulau Moyo

To get to Moyo, take a bemo from beside Seketang Market in Sumbawa Besar to **Air Bari**, a small port settlement northeast of Sumbawa Besar. Bemos run until 1pm and cost Rp5000. From Air Bari, ask around for Pak Lahi, who seems to do most of the boat organizing. A speedboat taking just ten minutes to Tanjung Pasir will set you back a ridiculous Rp50,000 for the boat. Prahu charter will cost a much more reasonable Rp30,000 for the forty-minute trip.

Another option is to take a regular bemo to **Labuhan Sumbawa**, the small port that serves the town and lies about 10km to the west. From Labuhan Sumbawa (reachable by bemo – Rp1000 – from Seketeng Market), charter a boat for the four-hour trip to Tanjung Pasir; while it takes considerably longer than going from Air Bari, there are far more boats to charter. Should all of this seem like too much effort, visit the **PHPA office** in Nijang, 4km out of Sumbawa Besar (see p.719), and you may be able to join one of their rangers heading out to the island for a small consideration.

Semongkat, Tepal and Roplang

Seventeen kilometres from Sumbawa Besar, high above the coastal plain and with wonderful views, lies the once grand hill resort of **SEMONGKAT**. The old **Dutch Palace** (Rp500) here has recently been restored and as a result, unfortunately, has lost a lot of its charm, but the surroundings are still glorious and there are some refreshing freshwater **springs** and a swimming pool. Public buses run fairly frequently from Seketeng market in Sumbawa Besar (90min; 2hr).

About 20km west of Semongkat, near the summit of **Batu Lanteh mountain**, lie the villages of **TEPAL** and **ROPLANG**. The people here still practise pre-Islamic animism and ancestor worship; if you stay here a while you may be lucky enough to witness one of their traditional festivals. It's a long walk up here – between six and eight hours – heading west from **Batu Dulang**, where the motorized transport from Sumbawa Besar terminates. You can hire a guide for the trek either in Sumbawa Besar or at Batu Dulang, and stay with the kepala desa in Tepal, but bring provisions, particularly fruit and tinned foods.

Batu Tering, Airnung and Lunyuk

About 25km southeast of Sumbawa Besar, near **BATU TERING** village, are a number of impressive **megaliths**, some of which possibly date from Neolithic times. Close to the Lunyuk road at **Liang Petang**, 36km south of Sumbawa Besar and 2km from Batu Tering, are a series of caves, which were once inhabited; a few beds, an old spinning wheel and some items of clothing still remain inside amongst the stalagmites and stalactites. Sometimes, particularly at weekends, there are guides (Rp5000) waiting outside with paraffin lamps, which are brighter and better than the average torch for exploring the caves (though you can explore independently). If nobody's around, ask in the houses nearby. Also near Batu Tering, the area around **AIRNUNG** village, is littered with carved sarcophagi of varying quality.

To get to all of these places, catch the daily bus to **LUNYUK** and ask to be let off at Batu Tering (1hr; Rp3000); to go all the way to Lunyuk will take a good three hours. Lunyuk itself is an excellent site for **turtle-watching**, with at least three species coming ashore at night to lay their eggs. The main laying season is from December to February, but can continue until June. As in most of Asia, locals consider turtle eggs a delicacy. They locate nests by following the turtle's trails (which resemble miniature tank tracks) up the beach to the buried nest. If you're lucky enough to see a turtle laying, erasing her tracks will give her offspring an extra chance. You can stay with the kepala desa at Lunyuk.

Gunung Tambora

On April 5, 1815 a monumental explosion took place at the **Tambora volcano**, lying on the bulbous northern penisula halfway between Bima and Sumbawa Besar. The two 4000-metre peaks had been smoking for several years, but the ferocity of the eruption took everyone by surprise. Most of the force was spent within eight days, but not before a shroud of ash as much as 1m deep had been spread over a vast area of farmland, and 20,000 people had lost their lives. The explosion was heard several thousand kilometres away; in Surabaya, Sir Stamford Raffles thought it was the sound of cannon fire and mobilized troops to defend the city. The death toll in Sumbawa and the nearby islands rose to an estimated 96,000 as the thick covering of ash choked crops, and outbreaks of cholera, dysentery and smallpox set in. Drought and famine occurred, the misery compounded by plagues of mice, which devastated food supplies.

Today, Gungung Tambora is an imposing cauldron with a brightly coloured crater lake, offering stunning views as far as Lombok and Komodo. The best base for the tough **trek** up the mountain is the **Pancasila Copee Plantation**, on the lower slopes of the volcano; it's a day's truck ride from Dompu bus terminal to the plantation, via the small logging town of **Calabai**, which lies on the coast of Saleh Bay. You can also reach Calabai by chartering a boat from Air Bari or Labuhan Sumbawa (see p.723), the two ports close to Sumbawa Besar. Stay overnight at the logger's guesthouse (❷) in Calabai, which provides basic but acceptable accommodation and meals. From Calabai, you can arrange a **guide** for between Rp30,000 and Rp50,000 a day; be sure to bring all your **supplies** from Bima or Sumbawa Besar. Alternatively, the large hotels in either town can set you up with an English-speaking guide; while you should be prepared to pay at least double if booking through a hotel, at least you'll have some comeback through your hotel should anything go wrong. Long trousers, walking boots and a vigilant eye for leeches and ticks are all essential, and it's best to check in with the police at Calabai.

Ascending the mountain requires an arduous **hike** up to the rim, first through dense rainforest and then over treacherous volcanic rock. Once at the summit you can go down to the lake – this trip takes about three days altogether from Sumbawa Besar, whereas only going to the rim and back can be done in two days.

△ Traditional house

East Sumbawa

The majority of the fine coastline of **East Sumbawa** is lined with photogenic fishing villages on stilts, a reminder of the Bajo, Buginese and Makassarese seafaring peoples who have long traded with the area. Centred on its capital town of **Bima**, eastern Sumbawa has little to recommend it, except for the surfing areas around **Hu'u** on the south coast. Travellers also head to the port town of **Sape**, where the ferries to Flores depart.

Bima

The slightly shabby port town of **BIMA** has little remaining of its former glories. The streets are coated with horse dung from its many dilapidated dokar (the horse-drawn carriages known locally as *benhur*) and the buildings are characterless and dull. The port remains fairly busy, with battered wooden schooners and the occasional rusting iron cargo ship, though it was once the most important port in Nusa Tenggara. In the fifteenth and sixteenth centuries, the kingdom of Bima claimed the majority of Nusa Tenggara, although this control probably manifested itself in nothing more than occasional slave raids on the surrounding islands and the administration of trade. Until the end of the sixteenth century, Bima was ruled by a succession of Hindu rajas with Javanese origins, but the region converted to Islam when the Makassarese of Sulawesi took control in the early seventeenth century.

The town has nothing to lure the prospective visitor, but it's a useful place to break up the otherwise arduous overland trip to Komodo and beyond. Bima's only attraction is the 1920s **Sultan's Palace** (a donation of around Rp5000 is extracted by the caretaker). This large white building with black beams could be anything from a school to a set of government offices, with its distinct lack of any external aesthetic appeal. The exhibits are pretty drab – a few gaudy reconstructions of costumes that the sultan might have worn and dusty glass cases full of unmarked, unfathomable junk.

Practicalities

Most travellers arrive in Bima at the long-distance **bus terminal**, a short dokar ride (Rp3000) south of town. The **airport** lies 20km away on the road to Sumbawa Besar; buses stop outside the airport and run all the way to the bus terminal. **Ferries** arrive at the harbour, 2km west of Bima, and dokar run from here to the town centre.

The town is centred around the market on Jalan Flores, and most of the losmen lie to the west of the Sultan's Palace. On Jalan Sukarno Hatta, but 2km out of town, is the **Telkom office**, for international telephone and fax as well as the best **internet connection** in town (Rp12,000 per hour). The **tourist office** (Ⓣ0374/44331) lies just 50m further on on the other side of the road. A yellow bemo (Rp750) drives along Jalan Sukarno Hatta from the market. The **BRI bank** (Mon–Fri 8am–2.30pm, Sat 8am–11.30pm) by the sports field is the best place to change money, while the BNI on Jalan Hasanuddin has the only ATM in town that will accept foreign cards. The main **post office**, if you need poste restante, is a little out of town on Jalan Gajah Mada, with a smaller branch on Jalan Hasanuddin, about 400m east of the *Taliwang Perdana* restaurant.

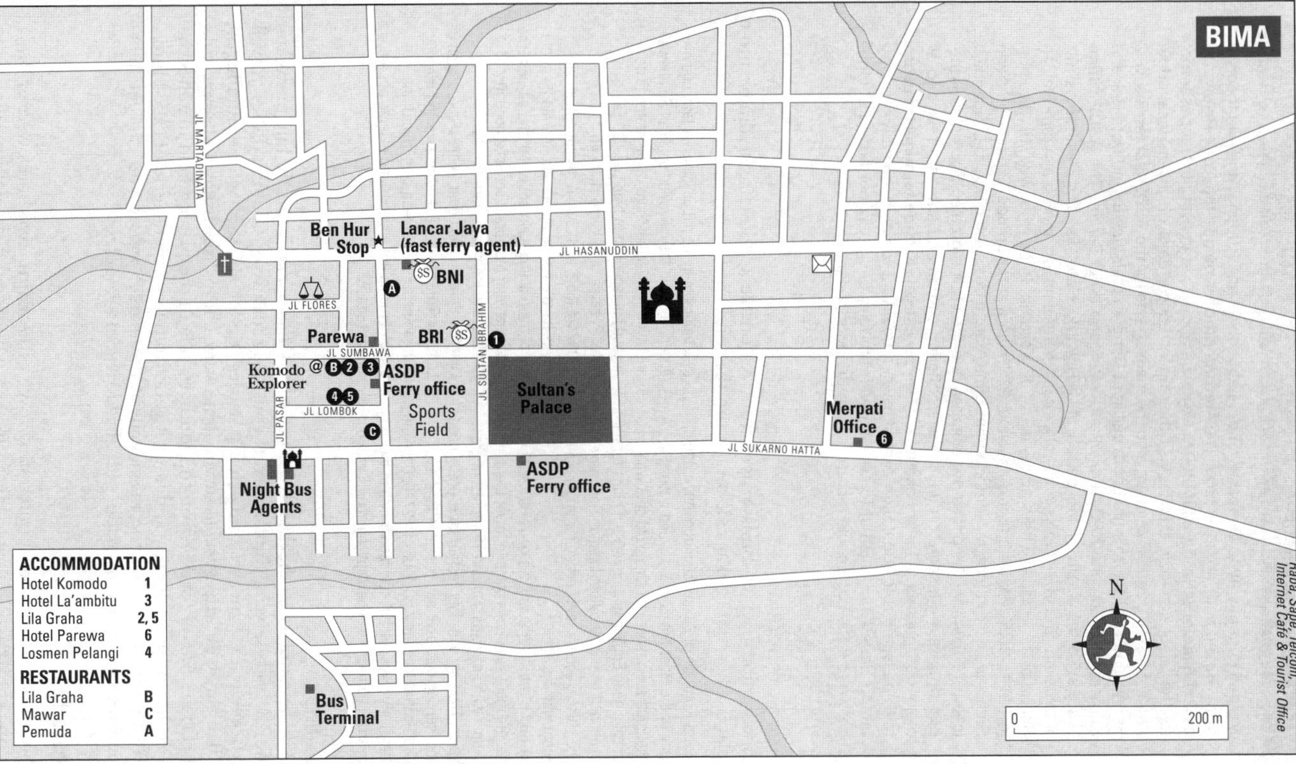
BIMA
Port & Pelni Office
Main Post Office
Kumbe Terminal, Merpati Office, Raba, Sape, Telcom, Internet Café & Tourist Office
Airport, Dompu & Sumbawa Besar
JL MARTADINATA
JL HASANUDDIN
JL FLORES
JL SUMBAWA
JL LOMBOK
JL PASAR
JL SULTAN IBRAHIM
JL SUKARNO HATTA
Ben Hur Stop
Lancar Jaya (fast ferry agent)
BNI
BRI
Parewa
Komodo Explorer
ASDP Ferry office
Sports Field
Sultan's Palace
Merpati Office
ASDP Ferry office
Night Bus Agents
Bus Terminal
N
0
200 m
ACCOMMODATION
Hotel Komodo 1
Hotel La'ambitu 3
Lila Graha 2, 5
Hotel Parewa 6
Losmen Pelangi 4
RESTAURANTS
Lila Graha B
Mawar C
Pemuda A

Moving on from Bima

Merpati currently **fly** to Denpasar, Ende, Labuanbajo and Kupang, and – in theory – fly to Ruteng and Tambolaka too. The **Merpati office** is next to the *Hotel Parewa* on Jalan Sukarno Hatta (Ⓣ0374/42897). Pelita are about to start flying to Denpasar too; for the latest schedule details, visit their agent Lancar Jaya on Jalan Hasanuddin (Ⓣ0374/43737). Lancar Jaya are also the main agents for the ASDP fast **ferries** *KFC Serayu* and *KFC Barito* which both call in at Bima on their way to and from Bali and Kupang via Maumere (*KFC Serayu*) and Waingapu (*KFC Barito*). The **ASDP office** lies just to the south of the palace at Jl Sukarno Hatta 5a. The Pelni ships *KM Tatamailau* and *KM Tilongkabila* also call in at Bima on their way from Bali to Sulawesi or Papua. Their office is at Jl Kesatria 2 on the way to the port (Ⓣ0374/42625). While agencies such as PT Pawera and Komodo Explorer on Jalan Sumbawa do run trips to Komodo from Bima, you're better off going to Labuanbajo (see p.734), where the prices are cheaper, and the choice greater. Scores of **night-bus agents** are located on Jalan Pasar, offering air-con and standard buses to all major destinations as far as Jakarta, a three-day journey. **Kumbe terminal** for buses to Sape is in Raba, about 5km east of town. If you want to catch the early-morning bus to Sape (2hr; Rp5000) to connect with the ferry east, tell your hotel the night before and the bus should pick you up at the door at 4am.

Accommodation

Accommodation in Bima ranges from reasonable to downright dingy; most places are a short dokar ride away from the southern bus terminal.

Hotel Komodo Jl Sultan Ibrahim Ⓣ0374/42070. One of the older hotels in town, and it looks it, though the manager is a kindly old soul who speaks good English and he has big plans for renovation. It has an excellent location right next to the palace, and it's fairly priced for an en-suite room with fan. ❷

Hotel La'mbitu Jl Sumbawa Ⓣ0374/42222. By far the most salubrious place in town: the standard rooms with hot water, fan and TV represent great value. Their second-floor restaurant is pretty good too, serving cold beer and passable food. ❷

Lila Graha Jl Lombok 20 Ⓣ0374/42740. Once the travellers' favourite, but now a poor rival to the nearby *La'mbitu*. The unexceptional rooms with outside bathroom in the old building are tatty and overpriced. Those in the new wing on Jalan Sumbawa are much smarter, but there rarely seems to be anybody at reception to help you. ❷–❸

Hotel Parewa Jl Sukarno Hatta 40 Ⓣ0374/42652, Ⓕ42304. A decent option: all rooms have en-suite mandi, and the rooms at the top of the building have hot water and air-con. The accompanying restaurant serves a good mix of Chinese and Indonesian fare. ❷–❸

Losmen Pelangi Next door to the *Lila Graha* on Jl Lombok Ⓣ0374/42878. Inexpensive and friendly, with rooms centred around a courtyard; the upstairs rooms are cheaper and quieter, but are not en suite. ❷

Eating

The restaurants at the hotels *La'mbitu* and *Lila Graha* are OK but unexceptional, both serving similar menus consisting mainly of Chinese dishes as well as omelettes, pancakes and fried potatoes. Better are the two restaurants on Jalan Sulawesi: the *Pemuda* serves some very cheap fish dishes and great cold beer; the *Mawar* (or *Rose*) on the southern side of the playing field matches the *Pemuda* for price, variety and taste; it's also home to a menagerie of caged birds. Also worth trying are the night stalls at the market, where you can get inexpensive sate, *soto ayam*, gado-gado, fried rice and noodles.

Hu'u

South of the large but uninteresting town of **Dompu**, two hours west of Bima along the Trans-Sumbawa Highway, on a white-sand coast with swaying palm trees is the **surfing** paradise of **HU'U**. The waves are not for the faint-hearted or inexperienced, breaking over razor-sharp finger coral; bring a helmet and a first-aid kit. Generally, surfing is best here between May and August, with June and July as the optimum months. It's practically impossible to get a bed at this time, so bringing a tent is a good idea.

To get to Hu'u, take a bus to Dompu from Sumbawa Besar or Bima (2hr; Rp5000), from where it's a one-hour trip south (Rp3000). One bus a day goes to Hu'u directly from Bima, leaving at around 7.30am. Alternatively, a charter bemo from Bima will cost about Rp75,000 per person (minimum four people. As you come into Hu'u from Bima or Dompu, the first place you'll pass through is the small fishing settlement of Hu'u village. Hu'u's **accommodation** lies in a cluster on the seafront about 3km from Hu'u village. The longest established of these is the *Mona Lisa Bungalows*, on the beach (❷). They have decent economy rooms in the main building through to pleasant bamboo-and-wood bungalows, with or without en-suite facilities; the restaurant, with good Western and Indonesian cuisine at reasonable prices, is very popular. Next door, the new *Hotel Amangati* (❷) has clean bungalows with en-suite mandi. The *Prima Donna Lakey Cottages* (Ⓣ0373/21168; ❷) have recently been renovated, and are, along with *Mona Lisa*, the current pick of the bunch, with the nicest, most spacious rooms; they also have the advantage of taking bookings in advance during high season. All of these losmen are convenient for the famous Lakey Peak and Lakey Pipe breaks. Just over 1km down the beach back towards Hu'u village and by the break of the same name is *Periscopes* (❷), a friendly surf camp with the wave on their doorstep.

Sape and on to Flores

More and more travellers are choosing to break their cross-island journey at the port town of **SAPE**. The town itself is no better or worse than Bima, and staying there has the advantage of allowing you a full night's sleep before catching the ferry to Flores (daily; 8am). Nearby **Gili Banta** is a good day-trip should you get stuck in Sape, with nice beaches and a burgeoning turtle population; ask around Sape and its harbour about boat charter (approximately Rp100,000 for a day).

Accommodation in Sape is not great – many places are dirty, infested with bedbugs and mosquitoes and many double as brothels. The better options are probably the *Friendship* and *Mutiara* losmen (both ❷), which are situated along the single main street that leads down to the port. *Mutiara* is right by the entrance to the port and *Friendship* is a couple of kilometres further inland, near the post office. They have genial staff and are reasonably clean, with some en-suite rooms. Apart from a few local warung, the **restaurant** near the *Mutiara* is the only option for reasonable food.

The daily ferry to **Labuanbajo** on Flores no longer calls at Komodo, so most travellers now head straight to Labuanbajo and organize their dragon-spotting trip to Komodo or Rinca from there; the fare to Labuanbajo is Rp16,500, with an extra Rp3000 if you want to sleep in "tourist class", though the extra comfort provided by the padded seats is offset by the lack of ventilation; tickets can be bought up to about an hour before from the harbour. The trip from Sape, through the tempestuous **Sape strait** which separates Sape from Komodo, is the part that is most subject to problems, and takes around four hours. Thereafter, the rest of the journey to Labuanbajo takes two or three hours through the cetacean-rich, sheltered calm of the **Lintah strait**.

Komodo and Rinca

Komodo island is a dry, hostile wilderness, with towering cliffs forming a forbidding skyline as you approach. Starkly beautiful as it is, the island's lack of water would deter tourists as it has deterred settlers, were it not for a quirk of nature that has left it the home of one of the world's most fascinating creatures. The **Komodo dragon**, or *ora* as it is known locally, is perhaps the most tangible legacy of our Jurassic predecessors, a modern dinosaur that lives only on Komodo and a few neighbouring islands.

Rinca island, to the east of Komodo, was for years the best-kept secret in the park. Its starkly beautiful, prehistoric landscape saw few visitors, even though the island contains almost as many dragons as its larger neighbour. With the curtailment of the public ferry to Komodo, Rinca currently receives at least as many visitors as Komodo, thanks to its proximity to Labuanbajo (just two hours by small boat). Nearby, tiny **Motong** and **Padar** have still eluded tourism almost completely – visitors on organized tours occasionally stop here for walks, but they rarely stay.

Komodo

Komodo used to receive in excess of 40,000 visitors a year, and with tourism in Indonesia slowly getting back on its feet again, both locals and park rangers hope that similar numbers will return. All visitors offload at the tiny **PHPA camp** at **LOH LIANG** at the east of the island, where at least one fully grown dragon is a regular scavenger. The camp is actually a series of smart and spacious wooden huts by the beach that serve as offices for the rangers, as well as housing a café, guest rooms and a few hungry, scavenging lizards. In the high season, when cruise ships dump tourists here by the hundred, it can seem a bit

Komodo dragons

Varanus komodoensis, the **Komodo dragon**, is the largest lizard in the world. Although remains of comparable size to the modern dragon have been excavated in Java and Timor, they date from the Pleistocene period, and there's no evidence that such creatures existed anywhere other than the Komodo area for well over a million years. Unlike many rare species around the globe, the dragon is actually steadily increasing in numbers.

The dragon is of the genus *varanid*, the largest species of monitor lizard, so called because in popular folklore the lizards "monitored" crocodiles, following them to feast on the scraps they left behind. The **largest recorded specimen** of a Komodo dragon was well in excess of 3m long and weighed a mammoth 150kg. The majority of fully grown adults are a more manageable 2m, weighing around 60kg, with the average female two-thirds the size of the males.

The dragon usually hunts by waiting hidden beside well-worn game paths, striking down its prey with its immensely powerful tail or slicing the tendons in its legs with scalpel-sharp fangs. Once the prey has been incapacitated, the dragon eviscerates it, feeding on its intestines while it slowly dies. Contrary to popular belief, the dragon has neither poisonous breath nor bite, but bitten creatures rapidly become infected and, weakened, put up little resistance when the dragon finally moves in for the kill. Nor are humans safe from the dragons. In 2001 a local tourist was bitten as he dozed on the verandah of his hut on Rinca. Though he was rushed to hospital and treated quickly, doctors were unable to prevent infection from setting in; in January of the following year the man died, a full two months after he had been attacked. Don't, therefore, be tempted to get too close to the lizards, and obey the orders of your guide.

like an adventure theme park. During the rainy season, however, you can easily find yourself practically alone on an island full of flesh-eating predators. The *ora* are in plentiful supply, and the vast majority of tourists see at least one of the monsters. However, there are no guarantees: the majority of this huge inhospitable island remains untrammelled, and one of the dragon's most effective defences is its ability to camouflage itself.

The PHPA charge Rp20,000 for **entry** to the park (which includes Rinca, and is valid for three days); in addition, there are guide fees (Rp5000 per person if there are more than three of you, Rp6000 otherwise), insurance (Rp5000 per group) and dock fees (Rp2000 for small boats, up to Rp10,000 for larger ones) to pay as well. On all excursions around the island, a guide is essential – they have sharp eyes and excellent knowledge of the area. Note that these fees are rarely included in the price negotiated with the boat owner/travel agent, so make sure you bring enough money (especially in small denominations, as change is difficult to come by on the islands). The stilted wooden cabins that comprise the **accommodation** (❷) on both islands are pretty rough-and-ready – the coffin-sized rooms come with a selection of bugs and an active rodent population. If the cabins are full, you'll have to camp out on the floor of the restaurant (❶). While the food in the **restaurants** has improved dramatically over the last few years, don't expect luxury: basic fried noodles, omelettes and banana pancakes are usually the best they can manage.

Treks and excursions on Komodo

The full day's walk from the PHPA camp to the top of **Gunung Ara** (826m), the highest point on the island, doesn't promise dragon sightings, but is absolutely extraordinary. It's an arduous, excruciatingly hot march to begin with, followed by a scorching scramble at the very top, but you'll see scores of unusual plants, animals and birdlife, such as sulphur-crested cockatoos, brush turkeys, and the megapode bird, which builds huge ground nests where its eggs are incubated in warm dung – easy plunder for dragons. The mountain walk culminates in a spectacular 360-degree panorama that takes the pain away in grand style. Don't forget to bring water and decent walking boots, and set out early. The ranger's fee is about Rp50,000 per group.

There are also regular walks from the PHPA camp, daily at 11am and 2pm, to **Banunggulung**, the riverbed where the dragons used to be fed fresh goats daily, for the benefit of tourists. This practice has been discontinued, as dragons were just hanging around here and not bothering to hunt, an artificial situation that was having an adverse effect on their development as predators. A few especially lazy *ora* still mope around here, though, anticipating their now weekly goat sacrifice, so the forty-minute walk will usually be rewarded with a sighting or two. The guided walk costs Rp5000 per person.

The seas around Komodo, though home to spectacular coral reefs and an abundance of fish, are a far cry from the Gili Islands or Bali. The giant saltwater crocodiles that haunted estuaries in this area as little as a decade ago have all been hunted out, but riptides, whirlpools, sea snakes, sea-wasp jellyfish and a healthy shark population make these waters potentially dangerous, so stick to recommended **snorkelling** locations such as the excellent **Pantai Merah**, across the bay from Kampung Komodo (see below). A day's boat trip to Pantai Merah can be bargained down to around Rp20,000–40,000 a day per person if you have a group of six or more people; the staff in the restaurant at the PHPA camp in Loh Liang can usually put you in touch with a boat owner if there are no boats waiting at the pier. You can take in some of the magnificent snorkelling locations around Padar and Rinca: both the hard and soft corals are pristine in

Tours to Komodo

Package **tours or cruises** that take passengers from one port to Komodo and Rinca before dropping them off at a second are currently the most popular way of visiting the islands. Agents in Lombok offer tours leaving from Lembar, Senggigi and the Gili Islands, from Bima on Sumbawa and from Labuanbajo on Flores, all subject to passenger availability. These tours typically call in at Komodo, Rinca and a couple of snorkelling stops on the way.

Tour boats **from Lombok to Labuanbajo** (four days and three nights, including a stop at beautiful Pulau Moyo on Sumbawa) can be very crowded; more than sixteen people on a fifteen-man boat is common. **From Labuanbajo**, the reverse is true, and you may have to wait a few days in order to find enough people to join you. The price is currently a set Rp500,000 per person, with a minimum of seven people. Alternatively, a two-day trip around Komodo, Rinca and the nearby islands, starting and finishing in Labuanbajo will set you back around Rp500,000 per boat, or around Rp400,000 if you arrange it yourself by approaching one of the boatmen down at the harbour. Organizing a tour **from Bima** is more expensive, and you'll have to charter your own boat (typically, more than a million rupiah for the two- to three-day trip).

With all these tours, ask to see the boat before handing over any money. Remember to enquire too about the number of passengers who will be joining you, where exactly you will be stopping, the number and type of meals included, and whether fin and snorkel hire is included in the price. Once on the boat, make sure the captain sticks to the itinerary.

most locations, and inhabited by a host of sea creatures including neon-blue spotted rays, parrotfish and lobster. The itinerary for these trips is negotiable and can be supplemented with onshore stops for treks or time on the beach.

Kampung Komodo

The only permanent settlement on the island is **KAMPUNG KOMODO**, on the coast 5km south of the PHPA camp. Once a prison colony for criminals from Sumbawa and Flores, the settlement here is now a poverty-stricken fishing village on stilts, clinging tenuously to survival in the most inhospitable of locations. There are still a couple of basic and rather dingy losmen here (❶), though with the public ferry no longer stopping at Komodo, the place sees very few visitors.

Rinca

Very similar in appearance to Komodo, **Rinca** consists mostly of steep rocky slopes covered in parched brown grasses, with drought-resistant lontar palms and hardy shrubs providing the only real vegetation. Your chances of seeing dragons is greater here than on Komodo; there is a greater concentration of numbers here, and there's less cover for them.

The **PHPA camp** at **LOH BUAYA** on the northwest coast is just as basic as that on Komodo (see p.730): the few rooms here (❷) are threadbare and bug-ridden, and they don't provide meals. However, by staying here and rising early the next day, your chances of seeing *ora* in the wild are greatly increased. There are two main walks around the island, one lasting two hours, the other three; both provide visitors with a reasonable chance of seeing dragons, as well as pigs, buffaloes, monkeys and wild horses. There are no regular boats to Rinca, so you'll need to **charter** one from Labuanbajo (see p.734); expect to pay Rp200,000 per boat (up to around eight people) for a half-day trip, including one stop at a nearby island for snorkelling.

Flores

A fertile, mountainous barrier separating the Savu and Flores seas, **Flores** offers one of the most alluring landscapes in the archipelago. When the Portuguese first encountered this dramatic island in the early sixteenth century they named it "Cabo das Flores" (Cape of Flowers). While it's neither a cape nor especially famed for its blooms today, it is undoubtedly endowed with a magnificent, untamed beauty that more than justifies the hyperbole. The volcanic spine of the island soars to 2500m, while torrential wet seasons have created a lushness that sets Flores apart from its scorched neighbours. Thanks to the recent influx of tourists flooding into the hotspots of **Labuanbajo**, **Bajawa** and **Moni**, facilities on the island are improving dramatically.

Despite being a mere 370km long and in some places as narrow as 12km, only Java and Sumatra have a greater number of **active volcanoes** than Flores. At the extreme western end of the island, Labuanbajo is cashing in on its position as the jumping-off point for Komodo and fast becoming a booming **beach resort**. The islands in the bay around the port hold some fine **coral gardens**, hotels and losmen springing up to accommodate Western beachcombers. Towards the west of the island, **Ruteng** is home to **Gunung Ranaka**, the island's highest peak, and has a cool climate and wonderfully lush scenery, as does **Bajawa**, another hill town near to Flores' newest volcano, **Wawo Muda**. Bajawa also has some fascinating surrounding villages, famed for their traditional lifestyle and **megaliths**, while the nearby **hot springs** at **Soa** are becoming a popular place to soak away the aches after a long hike. North from Bajawa, and just offshore from the quiet fishing village of Riung, the seas around the **Tujuhbelas Islands** offer the best snorkelling on Flores, while the islands themselves have their own giant lizards, a relative of the more famous dragons of Komodo. However, the most spectacular natural sight in Flores – and possibly in all of Nusa Tenggara – is magnificent **Kelimutu**, a unique volcano near **Moni**, northeast of **Ende**. The three craters of this extinct peak each contain a lake of gradually changing colours. Finally, in the east of Flores, high-quality **ikat weaving** is still a thriving concern in Sikka district and its capital, **Maumere**.

Some history

It's likely that as early as the twelfth century, the first Chinese traders – followed by the Makassarese and Bugis peoples – made incursions here on their **trade routes** to Timor and Maluku. In the process they started the slave trade in the region, raiding the coastal towns of Flores while restocking provisions for the long journey to Bima or Java. The people of Flores were subjected to unwelcome visits by the slave traders until the late nineteenth century, which explains why so many settlements are found inland. Soon after the Chinese came the Bugis and Makassarese, who began small-scale trading out of Larantuka on the eastern tip of the island.

In the sixteenth century, the **Portuguese** built forts in the east at Ende and on nearby Pulau Solor, to avoid having to stay on the inhospitable malarial coast of Timor, also taking advantage of the local materials of volcanic sulphur and cotton.

On December 12, 1992, a huge **earthquake**, with its epicentre off the north coast, killed over 3000 people and almost totally razed the town of Maumere,

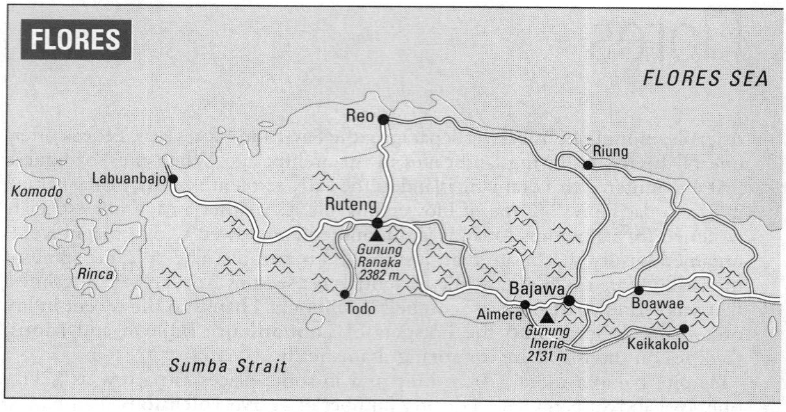

capital of the Sikka district. The quake measured 7.2 on the Richter scale, with the worst damage on nearby Pulau Babi, where the resultant *tsunami* (tidal wave) were said to have killed almost all of the thousand inhabitants. Only a month after the quake, a cyclone caused even more damage to buildings and crops; with many people left destitute, widespread starvation followed. Though much progress has been made, the rebuilding process, particularly in Maumere, is still some way from being complete.

Labuanbajo and around

The gateway to Flores and the Komodo islands is the sleepy little port town of **LABUANBAJO**. The boat journey to Labuanbajo from Sumbawa and all points west is an absolute delight, passing tiny green islands surrounded by colourful trimarans and often with schools of exuberant dolphins leaping alongside the ferry. *Labuanbajo* is short for Pelabuhan Bajo (Bajau harbour), named after its Muslim Bajau fishermen; indeed, your first sight of predominantly Catholic Flores will be the shiny metallic mosque right by the harbour.

No longer merely a transit zone, the town is waking up to the possibilities offered by tourists, who travel vast distances to see the dragons on nearby Komodo and Rinca and enjoy the splendours of the nearby **deserted beaches**. Hills at the north and south ends of the town offer fantastic sunset views of the harbour and surrounding bay, while the surrounding islands offer deserted beaches of white sands and waters teeming with an endless variety of marine life.

Practicalities

The harbour of Labuanbajo lies close to northern end of the main street, on which almost all of the losmen and restaurants are situated. **Ferries** from Sumbawa arrive late in the afternoon; touts and boats wait to take you to the losmen of your choosing. The **airport** is about 2km out of town and you'll probably have to charter a bemo to get there. Coming into town from the airport, taxis meet every incoming flight.

To book flights and buy tickets, head to the **Merpati office**, a fifteen-minute uphill hike to the east of town, or the newly opened **Pelita** office nearby on

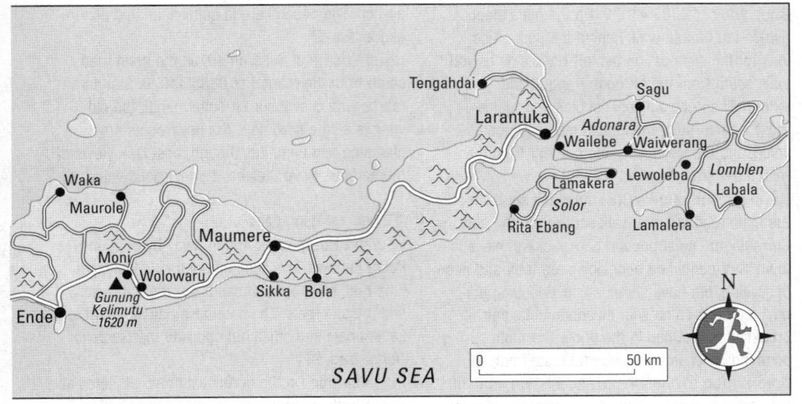

Jalan Ro WZ Yohanes (☎0385/41332). If you need to change money, head to the **BRI** at the south end of town; they will only accept prime-condition bills, and offer lousy rates for anything except dollars, but they do usually accept most brands of travellers' cheques, after a little persuasion, providing they are in US dollars. The **post office** (Mon–Thurs 7.30am–3pm, Fri & Sat 7.30–11am) is convenient, being close to the *Bajo Beach Hotel*, but the **PHPA** and **Telkom** offices are a one-kilometre hike out of town on the way to the airport: to get to them, walk south from the harbour, passing most of the hotels, and take the second left up the hill past the **market**. For most phone calls, the **wartels** in town are just as useful.

Moving on from Labuanbajo, the first **bus** heading east to **Ruteng** (4hr) leaves around 7am, and tickets can be bought from all the hotels for Rp15,000. A second one leaves at noon, though you can also join the Bajawa bus (6.30am; Rp30,000), which can take over eight hours in total. Buses meet the ferry from Sumbawa for the fourteen-hour trip to **Ende** (Rp45,000). The **ferry** west to Sumbawa leaves daily at 8am, and you can get tickets right up to departure. There are also ferries to **Sumba** on Mondays and Thursdays.

Accommodation

Most of Labuanbajo's **accommodation** is located along the main street that runs parallel to the sea. Some of the **beach hotels** sit on islands off the coast within an hour's boat trip from the town. If you are going to be in the Labuanbajo area for more than one night it's an excellent option as a quiet getaway with unspoilt beaches and decent snorkelling. Most places on the islands have only irregular electricity and running water, and none have phones. However, all have restaurants, include at least breakfast in their price, and offer regular free boats or bemos to and from the harbour. The first transport in the morning is guaranteed to connect with the ferries west or the second bus to Ruteng.

The Town

Bajo Beach Jl Sukarno Hatta ☎0385/41009. Popular with tour groups, *Bajo Beach* offers clean rooms around a pseudo-tropical garden a little way to the south of the *Gardena*. The rooms here are better than the *Gardena*'s, though they lack the latter's verandahs and views. ❷

Cendana A 30min drive south down the coast. Reasonable rooms; the more expensive ones boast air-con, en-suite mandi and shower. ❷–❸

Chez Felix ☎0385/41032. Up the hill a steep five-to-ten minute walk behind the post office; look for the signpost on the left-hand side as you walk south from the harbour. Tranquil and extremely spruce singles, doubles and triples, most with en-suite mandi and fan. Very good value, and the views over the harbour from the restaurant are wonderful. ❷
Gardena Bungalows On a small hill set back off the main road, a 3min walk south from the port. Currently the most popular backpackers' place in town. Self-contained bungalows are tatty and need upgrading, but have verandahs overlooking the bay; the beds come with mosquito nets, and breakfast is included in the price. The main selling point, however, is the wonderful restaurant. ❷
Golo Hilltop ☎0385/41337. About 1km north of the harbour; simply follow the coastal track round. Dutch-owned, new, and highly recommended, with very smartly furnished rooms – some with air-con – overlooking the bay. The restaurant serves great food and can arrange trips to the nearby islands. ❸
Mutiara ☎0385/41383. A little further south down the main street from the entrance to the *Gardena*, but on the seaward side of the street. Rooms are basic, ranging from simple singles (the cheapest in town, though, with no fan, you'd have to be pretty desperate to stay in one) to one triple with air-con and mandi. ❶–❷
New Bajo Beach ☎0385/41047.On the coast south of town, a 15–20min drive away. It has some basic, dingy but en-suite rooms while the more expensive rooms come with hot water and air-con. The beach here is quite clean and picturesque. ❷–❸
Hotel Wisata Jl Sukarno 40, on the main road south from the market ☎0385/41020. Standard rooms with or without en-suite mandi; the old wing is a little tired now, the new rooms are gleaming and beautiful, though most lack views of the harbour. Nevertheless, it's very good value. ❷

The islands

Kawana Hotel About 45min away by boat on Pulau Kanawa. The accommodation is looking a little tired now, but can still boast a great beach and pristine reefs. The hotel also has an agent in Labuanbajo in a small hut opposite the *Gardena Bungalows*. ❸
Puri Komodo On the northwestern tip of Flores at Batu Gosok, a 20min speedboat ride north of Labuanbajo, with an agent in town (☎0385/41319) near the post office. Top of the range, though facilities are less luxurious than the price would suggest. Smart en-suite bungalows, with some great snorkelling offshore. US$80 per bungalow, plus US$10 for lunch and US$12 for dinner; US$20 airport transfer by speedboat to the island. ❼
Seraya Bungalows A 30min boat ride north of Labuanbajo and named after the island on which it stands, this is the best-value accommodation on the islands. Neat and tidy en-suite bungalows with fan and mosquito nets, some great food served up in the restaurant, and the snorkelling offshore is fantastic. The price includes three meals. Contact the *Gardena* to book your bungalow and free transfer. ❷

Eating

Labuanbajo town has a handful of good **eating** options. If you're staying at a beach hotel, you'll be limited to its own restaurant, where fresh seafood is the norm. Many of Labuanbajo's hotels also have restaurants; in particular, the *Gardena* has a good reputation for the quality of its food – the snapper hotplates there are an absolute treat.

Borobodur Next to *Gardena Bungalows*. A little expensive and not always up to standard, but occasionally the *Borobodur* gets it just right and the food is excellent. They have great fresh seafood, including lobster, as well as steaks and good ice cream. A grilled barracuda or tuna steak costs about Rp20,000.
Dewata Next door to the *Borobudur*. More basic than its neighbour, but still worth a try for its seafood, particularly crab and prawns and various inexpensive Indonesian dishes.

Around Labuanbajo

Most of the hotels organize tours to nearby islands for **snorkelling** and sunbathing, depending on whether they can muster enough people to make it worthwhile. Trips to **Pulau Bidari**, an hour's sail west of town, run to about Rp40,000–50,000 for up to eight people. The coral here is mildly diverting, and the place is swarming with audacious monkeys. A full-day trip to **Pulau**

Sabolo, further north, is recommended as the coral is much better. Coral clusters can be found in just a couple of metres of water here, so it's perfect for inexperienced snorkellers, plus there's a swim through some caves for the more experienced, and a decent chance of seeing turtles and harmless small black-tip reef sharks.

Good **scuba diving** is an option in this area, with tours organized by Dive Komodo and many others along the waterfront. With enough people and money they can also arrange three- to four-day trips around Komodo, Rinca and Motong, where the diving is world-class. In the strong currents of the cold, plankton-rich seas around these three islands, you stand an excellent chance of seeing pelagic species, including whale sharks, manta rays and cetaceans, but diving here is for the experienced only. A few of the dive operators here also run live-aboard tours to the largely unexplored waters around Alor, to the east of Flores (see p.763).

Ruteng and the Manggarai district

The nearest large town to Labuanbajo is **RUTENG**, 140km to the east. Surrounded by stark, forested volcanic hills, studding rolling rice-paddy plains, it's an archetypal **hill town**. The streets are spacious and spotless, adorned with beautifully manicured gardens, and the town's altitude makes it a cool and relaxing place to stroll around. The **market** on Jalan Kartini is flooded with good-quality vegetables, fine tobacco, coffee and all the constituent ingredients of *cirih pinang* (betel nut). The market is the central meeting point for the local Manggarai people (see box below).

Manggarai culture

Traditions remain strong in **Manggarai**; all the stages of life and the calendar year are marked by festivals and traditional sacrifice, and visitors to an unknown place still occasionally take the precaution of licking the ground in order to make resident spirits aware of their presence.

In the area's legends, the first child on earth had no anus and suffered intensely as he could not defecate. He was killed by his father, cut up into little pieces and sprinkled on the ground. Magically, the earth suddenly became fertile and crops began to spring up everywhere, his blood making food for all humans. The spilling and drinking of blood in a ritual context is therefore guaranteed to bring fertility, and most festivals involve bloodletting of some sort.

The most spectacular festivals in Manggarai district involve ferocious **whip fighting** (*caci*). One combatant, often wearing a hideous mask, carries a baton and a shield, while the other wields an evil-looking bullwhip made from buffalo skin. The fights usually take place at **weddings**, but are also held regularly in August and at New Year, right in the centre of Ruteng town.

The traditional structures of the Manggarai tend to take a circular form. The local villages have conical houses arranged in concentric circles around a circular arena, in the centre of which is a sacrificial altar and totemic tree, surrounded by flat rocks. Even the rice paddies are round, divided up like spider's webs or a dartboard, with each clan receiving a slice. Though this unusual style of land division is rarely used nowadays, a good example can still be seen at **Golo Curu**, a three-kilometre walk uphill from the *Wisma Agung* in Ruteng town, with wonderful views of the surrounding countryside all the way to the top.

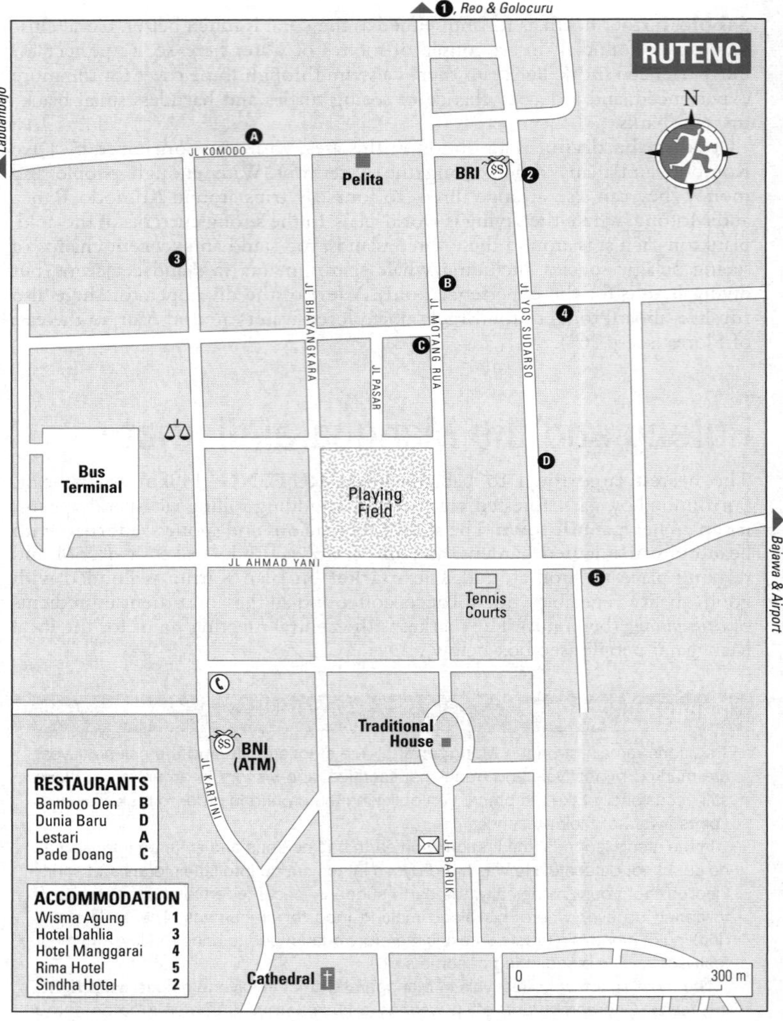

Manggarai district, of which Ruteng is the district capital, is the largest in Flores, comprising the western third of the island. The Manggarai people speak their own language; their distinctive culture is most in evidence in **Todo**, **Pongkor** and several villages on the south coast. Catholic missionaries have been in the area since the 1920s, but rarely, if ever, get to villages outside of Ruteng.

Practicalities

Most buses arriving in Ruteng can drop you off at a hotel if you ask. Otherwise, the **bus terminal** is relatively central and it's not much of a walk from there to most of the losmen. The airport lies about 2km east of town, from where most hotels offer free buses as long as you call ahead. The **BRI** (Mon–Thurs 7.30am–3.45pm, Fri 7.30–11.45am & 1.30–3.45pm, Sat 7.30am–noon) is on Jalan Yos Sudarso near the *Sindha* hotel; the BNI on Jalan Kartini has the only **ATM** between Labuanbajo and Ende. You'll find the **post office** at Jl Baruk 6 (Mon–Thurs 9am–3pm, Fri 9–11.30am, Sat 9am–1pm, Sun 9am–noon). For international telephone and fax, the new **Yantel office** is open 24hr.

Buses to Bajawa, Reo and Labuanbajo start from 7am and continue until early afternoon. Buses to Bajawa (4–5hr; Rp15,000) leave regularly, while Reo buses are far less frequent (2hr; Rp3000). Officially, **Merpati** still fly out of Ruteng once a week to Ende and Kupang, though this flight is often cancelled; their office is a little way out of town on the road leading to the airport. **Pelita** have also opened an office in the centre of town at Jl Pemuda 2, the continuation of Jalan Komodo (☎0385/21337); while they don't as yet fly out of Ruteng, they offer flights from Labuanbajo and Maumere.

Accommodation

Ruteng has no top-quality hotels, but the moderate places are all perfectly adequate.

Wisma Agung I Jl Waeces 10 ☎0385/21080. On the road out towards Reo, about a 15min walk from town. Set in a lovely location among the rice paddies, and with pleasant, clean rooms, most en suite and with good views over the town. ❷

Hotel Dahlia Jl Bhayangkari ☎0385/21377. Located a little way north of the market in the centre of town, the huge *Dahlia* is getting even bigger, so you're unlikely to have trouble getting a room. They have sit-down toilets and sporadic hot water in the better rooms, but little else to shout about in the rest. ❷

Hotel Manggarai Jl Adi Sucipto 6 ☎0385/21008. A slightly grim place with a central meeting area (with accompanying late-night noise of TV and loud locals). Rooms are shabby and basic but OK for a night if the better places are full. ❶

Rima Hotel Jl A. Yani 14 ☎0385/22196 or 22195. A sparkling-clean place. Most of the rooms come with en-suite mandi and the terrific staff are kind and attentive. Great value for money; there's also a reasonable restaurant showing DVDs nightly. ❶

Sindha Hotel Jl Yos Sudarso 26 ☎0385/21197. Fairly popular, with a good range of rooms, from budget singles and doubles to luxury rooms with en-suite shower and hot water. The manager is friendly and helpful. ❶–❷

Eating

Only a few places in town offer reasonable **food**. The *Rumah Makan Pade Doang* is just off the corner of Jalan Motong Rua and Jalan Lalamentik. They have cold beer and specials that include fairly fresh seafood, a rarity this far from the coast, though the *Lestari* on Jalan Komodo specializes in the stuff. The *Bamboo Den* nearby on Jalan Motong Rua is quite appealing and has a fair selection of Indonesian food including cold sate and soto ayam. The *Dunia Baru* on Jalan Yos Sudarso has a huge menu of standard Indonesian, Chinese and Western fare, much of it no more than passable. A number of places around the bus terminal serve standard Padang food, the quality of which can be assessed from their window displays. The *Hotel Sindah* and *Hotel Rima* both offer cold drinks and basic meals such as fried noodles and nasi campur.

Around Ruteng

TODO is a **traditional village** and seat of the (now defunct) raja, lying about 40km south of Ruteng, and well worth a visit. An irregular public bus leaving at about 8am from the main terminal in Ruteng will take you all the way (1hr; Rp5000). Although **megaliths** and Manggarai houses pepper the village, the main attraction here is a **mystical drum**, made from the belly-skin of a Bimanese slave. To actually see the drum is free, though there is a catch: for it to be replaced in its rooftop resting place the people have to perform a sacred dance and sacrifice a chicken, for which you'll pay about Rp50,000.

WAE RENO village, right on the south coast and a three-hour trip from Ruteng, features Flores's oldest *rumah adat* (traditional house). Apparently it was originally constructed in 1718, though how much of the original structure remains is unknown. The nearby beaches also provide great **snorkelling**, as does **Pulau Mulus**, a twenty-minute boat ride with one of the local fishermen (Rp5000 or so) from the shore. **Migrating whales** often pass very close to the shore here, and dolphins can be seen regularly all year round, especially in the early mornings. You can stay here with the kepala desa, or you can make it a day-trip from Ruteng; the bus journey (3hr) costs Rp10,000.

Gunung Ranaka, the highest peak in Flores, lies 15km southeast of Ruteng. Take a bus to **Robo** (Rp2000) and then walk the steep 5–6km to the smoking summit; there's a road running almost to the top, so you shouldn't need a guide. At **Liangbua**, north of Ruteng off the road to **Reo**, there is a rock quartz or mica **cave**. It's larger and less littered than Labuanbajo's Batu Cermin; the cavern has a tiny entrance but inside is huge, glassy and, with a powerful torch, quite impressive. The bemo ride takes an hour (Rp3000); alternatively, you can take the bus to Reo and ask the driver to stop at Liangbua Gua.

Beside the road from Ruteng to Bajawa sits **Danau Ranamese**, a stunning turquoise-blue lake surrounded by forest. The locals sometimes refer to it as Little Kelimutu, and the lake's brilliant colour and the magnificent view of surrounding highlands falling to the sea is certainly reminiscent of its more distinguished cousin (see p.749). The elevated lookout point beside the road is often used as a lavatory stop for the passengers of buses heading from Ruteng to Bajawa, so you will probably get to see it without making the effort to take a bemo or bus for the twenty-kilometre jaunt out here.

Near the north coast of the Manggarai district lies the port town of **REO**. The views on the bus ride from Ruteng (2–3hr; Rp10,000) are really beautiful, with endless terraced rice fields (*sawah*) set amongst the hills. The whole town seems to have been constructed for the benefit of the mission here; as they don't get many visitors, you can expect lots of stares. There are some nice beaches out of town, and boats sail to Labuanbajo – but be warned, it's a long trip. The better of Reo's two **losmen** is the *Nisang Nai* (❷), a little way out of town to the north opposite the police station, with both en-suite and shared-facility rooms.

Bajawa and the Ngada district

Surrounded by lush slopes and striking volcanoes, the hill town of **BAJAWA** (1100m), 120km to the east of Ruteng, is one of the most popular destinations for tourists in Flores. Not quite at the altitude of Ruteng, it still has a cool climate. Bajawa is the largest town in the **Ngada district**, an area that maintains its status as the spiritual heartland of Flores. Here, despite the growing encroachment of curious travellers, indigenous animist religions flourish and the villages are characterized by fascinating houses, megalithic stones and totemic structures. Up to 60,000 people in the Ngada district speak the distinct Ngada language; many of the older generation speak nothing else, and don't understand even basic Bahasa Indonesian.

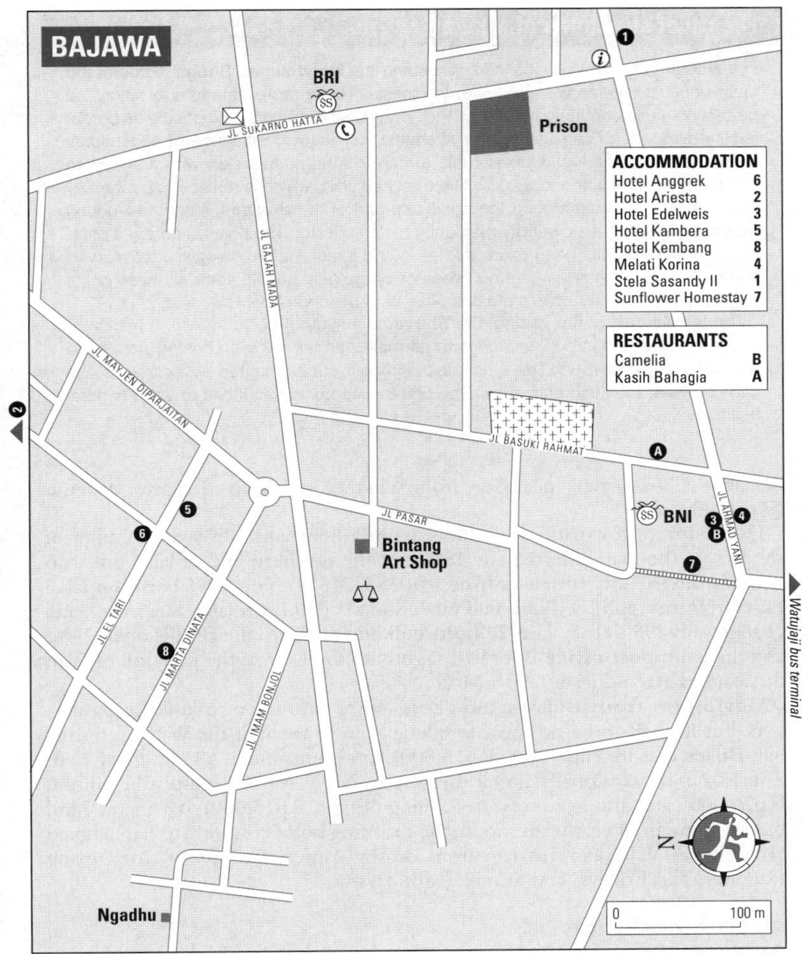

Gunung Inerie is just one of the active volcanoes near Bajawa: it's an arduous but rewarding hike, and on a clear day you can see all the way to Sumba from the summit. Not for the faint-hearted are the local specialities of *moke*, a type of wine that tastes like methylated spirits and *raerate*, dog meat marinated in coconut milk and then boiled in its own blood. Another popular attraction is Indonesia's newest volcano, **Wawo Muda**, which erupted and formed in 2001.

Practicalities

The **bus terminal**, 2km out of town at **Watujaji**, services all long-distance routes. Regular bemos from town to the terminal cost Rp1000. The **airport**

The ritual structures of Ngada

In the centre of many villages in Ngada stand the **Ngadhu** and **Bhaga**, some of the most unusual ceremonial edifices in Indonesia. These representations of ancestral protection – and continuing presence – of long-dead forebears also double as potent fertility symbols. Encapsulating the strength and ongoing influence of exceptional male ancestors, the Ngadhu resemble a man in a huge hula skirt with a shrunken head, carrying a spear and a knife. The thatched skirt, which is replaced about every four years, is wrapped around the significant part of the structure, a carved wooden pole imbued with the power of a particular male ancestor. The pole is actually a phallic tree trunk that has been excavated alive and intact, before being crudely carved and replanted in the village. In the village of **Wogo** (see p.744), some of these posts are said to be over 500 years old and have become completely petrified.

The female part of the pairing, the **Bhaga**, is a symbol of the womb; a miniature house constructed in conjunction with its male partner, always situated parallel to the Ngadhu in neat rows. The symbolic coupling is supplemented by a carved stake called a **Peo**, to which animals will be tied before being sacrificed at various ritual festivals.

lies almost 30km away near Soa, from where you'll have to charter a bemo (Rp50,000).

The centre of town still bears the scars of a fire that destroyed a number of shops near the market in the late 1990s. At the southern end of Jalan Sukarno Hatta is the friendly **tourist office** (☎0383/21554). The **BNI bank** on Jalan Hayam Wuruk, and the Bank Rakyat Indonesia (BRI) on Jalan Sukarno Hatta change only US dollars. The **Telkom** building opposite the BRI is open 24hr, and the main **post office** is located slightly to the west, at the junction of Jalan Sukarno Hatta and Jalan Gajah Mada.

Moving on from Bajawa, most buses come into town to look for passengers, but it's best to be on the safe side and go to them at the Watujaji terminal. **Buses** east to Ende (4hr; Rp15,000) run pretty much all day from 7am. Tourist buses occasionally go all the way to Moni for Kelimutu (5hr 30min; Rp20,000), and also head west to Ruteng (4–5hr; Rp15,000), starting at 7am, but stopping in the early afternoon; the morning buses continue to Labuanbajo (10hr; Rp20,000). **Ferries** run from nearby Aimere (see p.744) to Kupang (Tuesdays and Fridays) and Sumba (Mondays).

Accommodation

Accommodation in Bajawa is pretty basic – no hotels offer hot water – but there are a few decent options. There are two main hotel centres at either end of town, one gathered around the *Restaurant Camellia*, the other to the north of the market. Single rooms are a rarity, and unless it's low season, you'll be expected to pay the full double-room price.

Hotel Anggrek Jl Letjend Haryono 9 ☎0383/21172. Cleanish rooms, most of which have en-suite mandi and toilet. ❷

Hotel Ariesta Jl Diponegoro ☎0383/21292. Deservedly popular, a quiet and cosy family-run option, a little out of town to the north of the stadium. ❷

Hotel Edelweis Jl Yani 76 ☎0383/21345. Next to the *Restaurant Camellia*, a good choice with smart rooms that have thus far avoided the damp stains that afflict almost every other place in town. The staff are friendly, though they seem reluctant to put tourists in anything except their more expensive rooms. ❷

Hotel Kambera Jl El Tari, north of the market ☎0383/21166. The rooms here are decent and cheap, though are let down by their thriving cockroach population. ❶

Hotel Kembang Jl Marta Dinata ☎0383/21072. To the northwest of the market, the *Kembang* is a sizeable hotel built around a carefully manicured courtyard. It's also the best in town, not only because of the quality of its rooms but also because of the wonderfully kind and friendly staff. ❸

Melati Korina Jl Ahmad Yani 81 ☎0383/21162. One of the first places you come to on the road in from the bus terminal, almost opposite the *Restaurant Camellia*. It has clean single, double and triple rooms around a spacious central lounge, though much of the building is currently undergoing extensive renovation; the rooms still open are quite smart. ❷

Stela Sasandy II Down an alley running off Jl Sukarno Hatta ☎0383/21198. A homely, family-run little place with just three rooms, all en suite, clean and bright. Recommended for those who wish to avoid the tourist hordes. ❷

Sunflower Homestay ☎0383/21236. As the road from Watujaji bus terminal reaches the outskirts of the town, it splits at a T-junction and becomes Jl Ahmad Yani, where a small path leads up to the *Sunflower*. This was once the most popular place in town, though the travellers have moved on, and the place now seems in terminal decline, although the outward-facing rooms have nice views of the valley. ❷

Eating

The revamped *Restaurant Camellia*, opposite the *Korina* losmen on Jalan Ahmad Yani, serves reasonable guacamole and chips and some of the best *lumpiah* (spring rolls) around, although the rest of the food is distinctly average. Nearby, just round the corner on Jalan Basuki Rahmat, the overall slightly better *Kasih Bahagia* offers a similar menu. Cheaper and far more convenient for those staying at the northern end of town, the restaurant at the *Hotel Anggrek* is very reasonably priced, and acceptable enough if you don't expect *cordon bleu*. Near the mosque by the market, a few padang places and stalls sell snack food; nothing very substantial, but they're the cheapest places to eat in town.

The Ngada villages

The most popular attractions in the Ngada region are the villages themselves, still built and maintained to a traditional plan and style. While people can visit them independently and public transport runs to nearly all of them, a knowledgeable guide (see box below) will be able to explain in greater detail the significance of the village's layout. Note, too, that a couple of the better ones now charge an entrance fee of a few thousand rupiah.

From Bajawa, the most accessible Ngada village is **LANGA**, 6km away to the south. Lying under the dramatic shadow of **Gunung Inerie**, Langa is a good – though not the best or prettiest – example of a typical Ngada village, with two rows of thatched-roof houses separated by a central space in which you'll

Hiring guides

The influx of tourists to the Ngada region in the early 1990s has led to a booming **guide** industry in Bajawa. There used to be a standard fixed charge per person per day, though with the current decline in tourist numbers, this has vanished. These days, most guides will ask for around Rp75,000 per day for their services, including chartered transport, a driver, entrance to all the villages and often an excellent meal of traditional Bajawan food at the guide's home village. You need a minimum of four people for a day-tour that generally includes Langa, Bena, Bela or Luba, which are close by, as well as Wogo and the **hot springs** at Soa or the new volcano at Wawo Muda. It's impossible to do this all in one day on your own, so a tour represents excellent value for money if you get a decent guide. It's worth taking time to chat to them beforehand; most speak good English and are enthusiastic and knowledgeable, but a few are impatient and dour. Itineraries are negotiable, and you can easily arrange extended tours, mountain climbs or off-the-beaten-track adventures. Most guides can be found hanging around the *Restaurant Camellia* (see above).

find the *ngadhu* and *bhaga*. Tourists pass through here every day, and you'll be asked to sign a visitors' book and pay a minimum of Rp2000 to take photographs. You can stay here at the *Serleon Langa Homestay* (❶), a basic but clean and comfortable place. It's a good idea to overnight in Langa if you plan to scale Gunung Inerie; with an early-morning start from here, you can make the three- to four-hour climb to the smoking summit before the clouds roll in. The trek to the summit is actually closer from nearby Bena – but if you stay there, it's more likely to be on the kepala desa's floor, and a good night's sleep makes the climb seem much easier. You can usually persuade a villager to **guide** you to the summit for around Rp20,000.

Another 10km further south from Langa, mostly downhill, is **BENA**, another Ngada village popular with tourists. You'll have to walk there, unless you're lucky enough to catch a ride in the occasional passing truck or car, or charter a vehicle. Bena has nine different clans living in a village with nine levels and nine Ngadhu/Bhaga couplings (see box on p.742). It's the central village for the local area's religions and traditions, and a good place to observe **festivals**; the guides in Bajawa are the best source of information about forthcoming weddings, planting and harvest celebrations.

If you want a real sense of local life in this area, and would like to go to villages where few visit, you'll probably need to hire a guide from Bajawa. A two-day walking excursion passing through **Nage**, **Wajo** and **Gurasina** is recommended. The village of **NAGE** is a two- or three-hour walk south of Bena, the path offering views down to the coast and the Savu sea. The village itself sits on a green plateau with fine views of the surrounding volcanoes, and has some interesting megaliths and fine traditional structures. A white ghost is said to come out of the village's megaliths every Friday evening, trying to break into the houses. The very pretty village of **WAJO** lies just a short walk away from here and offers three Ngadhu/Bhaga pairings and great views of the surrounding countryside. From here, it takes up to two hours to walk to **GURASINA**, the biggest village in the area. The village is arranged on eight levels, and with a richly active ritual life. This is the best place to stay the night, probably sleeping on the floor of the kepala desa's house. Few tourists get to Gurasina and the welcome here is wonderful – expect to be the centre of attention for as long as you stay.

Some of the finest **megaliths** and Ngadhu can be found at the twin villages of **WOGO**, where tin-roofed houses are springing up and kids will ask you for pens and *gula gula* (candy). To get here, take one of the regular bemos from Bajawa to **Mataloko** (30min; Rp1000). From Mataloko, walk south along the road for about 1km and you'll come to Wogo Baru. The people moved here from Wogo Tua about thirty years ago because the old site had no freshwater source. What it does have is some distinctly eerie megaliths set in a clearing about 200m further down the road; local kids will lead you down to them. Mataloko has a decent **market** on Saturdays, with local sarongs, fruit and vegetables, and Bajawan knives which resemble kris.

Currently, the most popular destination near Bajawa is the **hot springs** at **SOA**, set in magnificent surroundings. The springs themselves are an absolute joy, especially at night or in the late afternoon, when Bajawa can get quite chilly. The hot-spring pool runs down into a river so you can happily spend all day alternating between hot and cold baths. To get here, a bus or bemo to Soa village costs Rp1000 from the bemo station in Bajawa, taking about an hour. From the village, it's a two-kilometre walk along a clear path to the springs.

AIMERE is a largish town near the south coast to the west of Bajawa; at the bustling markets on Thursday and Friday you can buy the *moke* wine (made

Wawo Muda – Indonesia's newest volcano

In early 2001, a new volcano erupted above the small village of **Ngoranale**, about 10km to the north of Bajawa. What had previously been just one of many large hills covered with pasture suddenly burst its top, incinerating the vegetation in the newly formed crater and turning the trees into spindly blackened sticks. According to locals who visited the crater over the next few days, the five lakes that had formed in the bottom of the crater were each of a different colour, and even today insist the sight is more spectacular than Kelimutu. Whilst it's difficult to agree entirely with the locals' boasts – the lakes are all now the same uniform red colour – there's no denying that Wawo Muda is worth a visit. The walk up to the summit through wonderful rural scenery is a delight, and the crater itself has an eerie and strange beauty.

To get there from Bajawa, catch a bemo to Ngoranale from the market or the main road to the west of the *Hotel Anggrek*; then ask a villager to show you the start of the wide and easy-to-follow trail, which takes about an hour to meander up to the summit. Alternatively, for Rp5000–10,000 or so, somebody from the village will show you the shortcut leading from behind the village. The trip can be completed in a morning; try to set off as early as possible to avoid the heat of the day, and bring drinking water.

from palm) and Bajawan *arak* (made from rice) that the town is renowned for and on any day see the fermentation process; *arak* is the more more palatable, especially if you add a little honey and orange juice. You can stay here with the kepala desa, but the other locals will clamour to have you stay with them, and are generally more welcoming. To get to Aimere, take a bus from Watujaji bus terminal in Bajawa (2hr; Rp5000). For details of ferries from Aimere, see p.804.

Near the town of **Boawae**, 40km to the east of Bajawa on the road to Ende (catch one of the through buses to Ende and jump off at Boawae; Rp3500), is **Gunung Ebulobo**, a hostile and decidedly active volcano, one of the most imposing in Flores. Adrenaline-seekers can climb Ebulobo, though conditions underfoot on the mountain can be a little treacherous, particularly after rain, and a guide from Boawae village (around Rp50,000 per day) is recommended. A good and convenient base is the friendly *Hotel Sao Wisata* (❷), who can also help you organize a guide. Even getting to the hotel involves a 1.5km hike, however, taking the rough road branching off by the inferior *Wisma Nusa Bunga* from the highway towards the church. From the hotel the climb to the top takes around four hours.

Riung and the Tujuhbelas Islands

The small town of **RIUNG** sits on Flores's lush north coast, about 60km north of Bajawa. It began as a string of seafront Bajau and Bugis fishing villages, all its houses perched precariously on fragile-looking stilts; today, its a tiny community whose sole focus is the sea. Most travellers get here on one of the daily northbound buses from Bajawa or Ende, which arrive right in the centre of town. Although of little particular interest in itself, Riung is the mainland route to the best beaches and snorkelling in central Flores, those of the verdant **Tujuhbelas Islands**, which lie scattered across the bay north of town.

Riung's small size makes it very easy to work your way around. Limited tourist information can be obtained from the **parks office** near the church on the eastern side of town; they also rent out some pretty decrepit snorkelling equipment (Rp10,000 a day). Although there are some white-sand beaches along this coast, if you've made it this far, it's definitely worth the effort of chartering a boat out to Pulau Tujuhbelas (Seventeen Islands), which lie out in the bay north of Riung. There are actually 24 islands, but the government decided to overlook seven of them, so that the name could tie in with Independence day – August 17. **Pulau Ontoloe** has an enormous colony of fruit bats, **Pulau Rutung** has startling varieties of pristine coral, and there are six or seven other uninhabited islands that are perfect places for castaways. A day-long **boat charter** to three islands with five snorkelling stops runs to around Rp200,000, and you will be approached by willing **guides** and boatmen in town.

Practicalities

All accommodation in Riung is full board. The missionary-run *Pondok SVD* (❸) is the best option, situated on the road as you come into town. All the rooms have Western toilets and showers, and the place is highly recommended. The *Florida Hotel* (❸) is nice enough, with spacious rooms, but it's rather inconveniently situated a couple of kilometres from the harbour on the road to Ende; alternatively, both the *Liberty Losmen* and *Madonna Homestay* (both ❷) are fairly central.

A daily bus from Bajawa goes all the way to Riung, leaving in the early morning (3hr; Rp10,000). You can also get there on the daily bus from Ende's Ndao terminal, which leaves at 6am and takes four hours (Rp12,000).

Ende and around

ENDE is the largest town and most important port on Flores, providing access for Kelimutu and Moni. It's situated on a narrow peninsula with flat-topped **Gunung Meja** and the active **Gunung Ipi** at the sea end; to the west lies another volcanic peak, **Gunung Ebolobo**, and black-sand beaches stretch down both east and west coasts. Ende suffered severe damage in the 1992 earthquake that razed Maumere and killed several hundred people here. The town still seems shaken by the whole experience – ramshackle, battered and with little to attract tourists other than banks and **ferries** to other destinations.

Both the Portuguese and Dutch based themselves here in the past, but they have left no buildings of note, apart from the shell of a Dutch house near the village of **Nuabosi**, 10km off the highway to Bajawa. Three or four bemos a day from the Ndao terminal make this trip, and there are fantastic views of the peninsula from up here. Ende's claim to fame is that President Sukarno was exiled here back in 1933: his house, **Situs Bung Karno**, lies on Jalan Parewa, 200m northeast of the harbour. It's now a museum of sorts (free), with some of the original furniture and a few dull photos, unlikely to captivate the casual visitor. Nearby on Jalan Hatta, by the football pitch is a second museum, the **Museum Bahari** or Maritime Museum (daily 7am–8pm; Rp750), though it's also rather unexciting; the rumah adat nearby, with its stone altar and mock-up of a village compound, is rather more interesting. The tumbledown **market** near the waterfront is worth a look; apart from the usual sarongs, fruit and vegetables, you can also find some amazing fish on offer, including huge tuna, sharks, rays and even dolphins. The **night market** lies out of the centre on Jalan Kelimutu, running daily from late afternoon until 9pm or 10pm. They have similar produce to the day market, supplemented by food stalls and lit by candles.

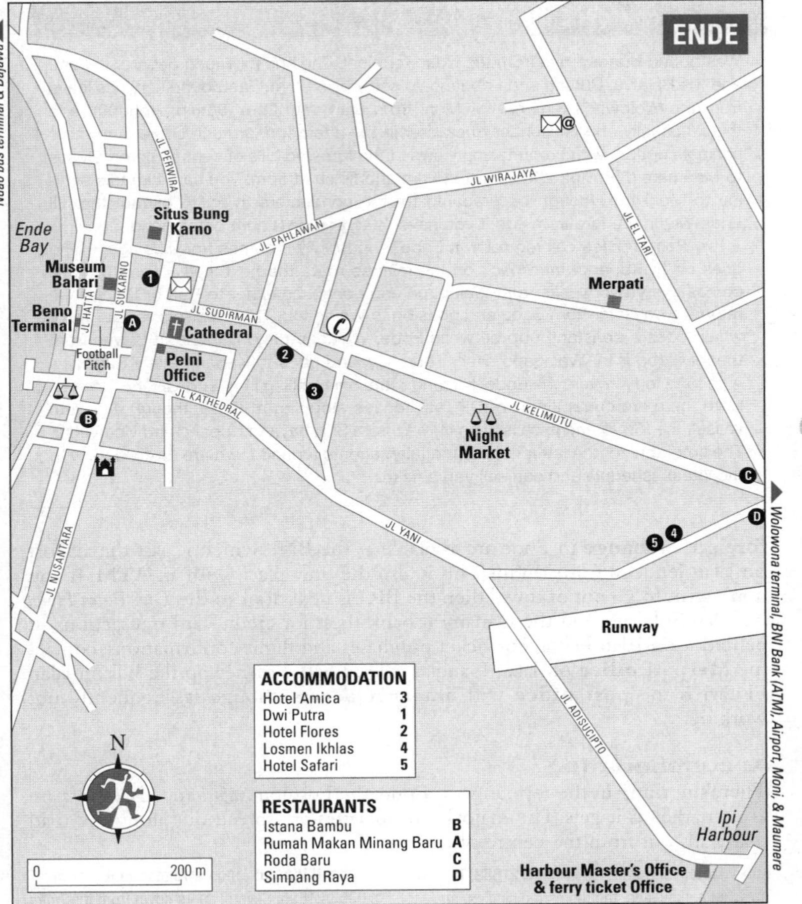

Practicalities

The **airport** at Ende is in town, slightly north of Ipi harbour on Jalan Jenderal Ahmad Yani; any bemo will take you into town (Rp1000). Travellers coming from Bajawa, Ruteng and beyond will arrive at the **Ndao bus terminal**, which is on the beach, about 2km west of the town centre. Bemos meet every bus and will take you to your destination of choice. Travellers coming from Moni, Maumere and Larantuka will arrive in the **Wolowana** terminal, situated at the extreme east of town and a five-kilometre bemo ride (Rp2500) from central Ende. On the southeastern coast of the peninsula, Ipi harbour is used for all long-distance **boats**: the ferry's and harbour master's offices are at the lower end of Jalan Adisucipto, the road leading down to the harbour.

The losmen, banks and accommodation are widely dispersed, so you'll probably end up using the **bemo kota** (town bemos; Rp1000). The best rates for

Moving on from Ende

Westbound **buses** leave from the Ndao terminal. The bus for Riung departs at 6am, and the Bajawa, Ruteng and Labuanbajo services at 7am. Eastbound services leave from the Wolowana terminal for Moni from 6am until 2pm (90min; Rp5000), and there's usually one passenger truck later in the afternoon, a much cooler and more sociable option, with breathtaking views of the forested hills of central Flores. Buses to Maumere (6hr; Rp20,000) start at 8am and finish at 5pm; you can take this service to Moni too, though be prepared for the conducters to try to extract the full Ende–Maumere fare from you if you haven't agreed on a sum beforehand.

Two **Pelni ferries** call regularly at Ende. The *KM Awu* comes from Waingapu and goes on to Kupang, then back on the reverse route the next week. The *KM Wilis* comes every two weeks from Waingapu and continues either to Roti or Savu, then returns a day later from Sabu and goes on to Waingapu. There's also a regular **ferry** which does a constant loop between Ende, Waingapu and Kupang. It leaves from the Ipi harbour for Waingapu every Thursday, and goes to Kupang every Saturday. A second ferry covers the Ende–Kupang route only, calling in at Ende every Tuesday. Note there are currently no ASDP **fast ferries** stopping at Ende, though a private vessel, the *KM Kirana II*, calls in on its way from Surabaya to Kupang and vice versa. The timetable for the latter is fairly irregular; agents around town are up-to-date with the latest schedule and can sell you a ticket.

foreign exchange in Ende are available at the BNI, which is past the airport on Jalan Jenderal Ahmad Yani. This is also the only place with an **ATM**. If you don't want to go out of town, then the BRI is next door to the *Dwi Putra Hotel* on Jalan Sukarno, and the Danamon bank (best for credit-card transactions) is behind it on Jalan Hatta. For ticket purchases and flight confirmations, contact the **Merpati office** on Jalan Nangka (closed Sat). Further up the hill on Jalan El Tari is the **post office** with **internet access**, though it's frequently not working.

Accommodation

There's nothing in the top range in Ende: the Losmen *Safari* and *Dwi Putra* are as upmarket as it gets. The majority of **losmen** are spread out along the road that leads out from the centre of town to the airport.

Hotel Amica Jl Garuda 39 ⓣ0383/21683. Tucked away on a leafy lane, the rooms (no singles) are cheap enough but without fans – a big disadvantage in sweaty Ende. ❷

Dwi Putra Jl Sudarso, next door to the BRI bank ⓣ0383/21685. Has a choice of cheap basic rooms with external toilet and mandi, or swanky luxury ones with en-suite facilities. The sea-facing rooms have huge windows overlooking the bay, and the first-floor restaurant serves reasonable Chinese and Indonesian food. Popular with tour groups. ❷–❹

Hotel Flores Jl Sudirman 28 ⓣ0383/21075. Near to the centre of town, scruffy and a touch overpriced, with noisy air-con, but well equipped with en-suite facilities and friendly enough. ❷

Losmen Ikhlas Jl Jenderal Ahmad Yani ⓣ0383/21695. Several doors down from the *Hotel* Safari, on the way to the airport. The original, and still the best as far as travellers are concerned. All the latest travel information is posted on the restaurant walls and the English-speaking owner can fill in any gaps for you. They have dirt-cheap, box-like en-suite rooms through to reasonable doubles with lounge area. ❶–❷

Hotel Safari Jl Jenderal Ahmad Yani 65 ⓣ0383/21997. A little east of the junction with Jalan Adi Sucipto and almost next door to the *Ikhlas*, a clean, plush place offering good value, with mandi in all the rooms and some rooms with air-con. ❷–❸

Eating

There's really nothing to shout about in Ende when it comes to **food**. The best option is the *Istana Bambu* at Jl Kemakmuran 30a, serving mid-priced Chinese food, fresh fish and fruit juices. *Rumah Makan Minang Baru* on Jalan Sukarno near Ende harbour serves simple Padang food, though the menu is pretty limited, considering the size of the restaurant. Better are the two Padang places, *Roda Baru* and *Simpang Raya*, on the roundabout to the east of *Ikhlas*. Both the markets provide decent enough food, serving standard sate *murtabak* and nasi campur, while the *Ikhlas* serves travellers' favourites such as banana pancakes, cold drinks, juices and milk shakes. Around the waterfront market are a few basic warung offering goat curry, sate and nasi dishes.

Beaches and weaving villages

Ende can be stiflingly hot, lying at sea level and sheltered from strong sea winds by its surrounding volcanoes. If you fancy a dip to cool off, there are reasonable black-sand **beaches** out of town in either direction. The Bajawa road runs right along the seafront; just catch a bemo out to Ndao bus terminal, and the beach begins right in front of the terminal.

The town is an ideal starting point for exploring some of the villages in the surrounding area, whose main source of income is derived from the weaving of **ikat** fabrics. **NGELLA** is the best and most popular weaving village near the coast, about 30km east from Wolowaru terminal in Ende; a bemo or truck there costs Rp3000. Ngella's *ikat* is generally good quality, made from handspun thread with natural dyes, though it's also expensive and the women are hard bargainers. Another weaving village only 7km from town is **WOLOTOPO**, which sees fewer tourists than Ngella and thus, in theory at least, has the better bargains; bemos go directly there from Wolowana terminal (Rp1000). From there you can walk about 3km along the seafront to the village of **NGALUPOLO**: few tourists get here and as well as weavings they have a few megaliths and traditional houses. You can stay here with the kepala desa, thus giving yourself the chance to explore more of the region around here, including other little-visited weaving villages nearby.

Kelimutu and Moni

Stunning **Kelimutu** volcano, with its three strangely coloured crater lakes, is one of the most startling natural phenomena in Indonesia. The nearby village of **Moni**, 40km northeast of Ende, sits close to the mountain's slopes, and is the base for people hiking on the volcano. Moni has a lazy charm, nestling among scores of lush rice paddies and flanked by green slopes. The main Ende–Maumere road that runs right through the centre of town sees surprisingly little traffic and often all you can hear is water babbling through the rice paddies and children splashing around in the roadside streams.

Kelimutu

The summit of **Kelimutu** (1620m) is a startling lunar landscape with, to the east, two vast pools separated by a narrow ridge. The waters of one are currently a luminescent green that seems to be heading for bright yellow, the other was a vibrant turquoise until a few years ago, but is now deep reddish brown. A few hundred metres to the west, in a deep depression, is the third lake, also

Walking on Kelimutu

Every morning at around 4am, an open-sided truck packed with bleary-eyed travellers runs from Moni up to **Kelimutu**. The 30min truck ride to the car park at the foot of the final climb to the summit costs Rp15,000, with an extra Rp1000 charged at the **PHPA post** on the way up to enter the volcano area. The truck heads back down to Moni at 7am sharp.

If you're bringing a camera, bear in mind that it's impossible to photograph the three crater lakes at once. The best possible view is from the south crater rim, looking north over the two sister lakes. The trails that run around other rims are extremely dangerous. According to losmen owners in Moni, two Dutch tourists disappeared on a trek around the craters; divers dragged the lakes, but their bodies were never found.

A much nicer alternative to returning with the truck is to **walk** back down to Moni, taking one of the paths that lead off the main road. The walks are enjoyable in themselves, enabling travellers to spend longer at the crater, observing the lakes change colour and mood as the sun rises higher in the sky. The first small path leading off the road, just five minutes below the car park, leads through fields to the village of Pemo, from where you can head around the lower slopes back to Moni. It's not a shortcut – it takes about four hours in total to reach Moni – but it's a beautiful trip. For something a little quicker, head further down the main road to a small gap in the hedge on the right side of the road by the 9km marker. It takes you past villages where young girls weave at backstrap looms. If you come down on a Sunday morning you may be invited into Mass, where all the women dress in fine *ikat* sarongs, and you can hear some beautiful choral singing. Entrepreneurs have set up stalls selling fruit and drinks all along this route – a godsend when the day starts to heat up.

The next short cut off the main road down from the summit is further down by the PHPA post and cuts off a good 4km from the road route. All three paths take you past the **waterfall** (*air terjun*), less than 1km from central Moni, which is a great spot for a cooling dip after what can be a very hot walk. There is also a small hot spring near the falls. The walk takes about three hours, with alpine scenery, rolling grassy meadows flanking extinct volcanic hills, and views all the way to the sea. Practically the whole walk is downhill, but always bring water and wear good walking boots. Wrap up warm for the sunrise at the summit, but make sure you can peel off layers for the descent.

a reddish-brown hue; clouds often hang in wisps about the water's surface, creating the illusion of a witch's cauldron.

The colours of the lakes are caused by the levels of certain **minerals** dissolving in them. As the waters gradually erode the caldera they lie in, they uncover bands of different compounds; as the levels of these compounds are in constant flux, so are the colours. In the 1960s, the lakes were red, white and blue, and locals predict that within years they will have returned to these hues.

In the dialect of the region, *keli* means "mountain" and *mutu* is the spirit of the lakes. Until Christian missionaries managed to dissuade locals from the practice in the middle of the twentieth century, sacrificial animals and food offerings were regularly thrown into the waters to pacify the powerful *mutu*, who, it was believed, had the power to destroy the harvest. The people of the surrounding villages also believe that these waters are the soul's resting place: youthful souls are taken by the brown lake to the east, the elderly repose in the yellow-green lake, while thieves and murderers languish for eternity in the lake to the west.

Moni

The village of **MONI** lies 52km from Ende on the road running northeast to Maumere. The road enters the north side of the village and after two sharp turns within the village heads east towards Maumere. Nowadays, the village consists almost entirely of losmen and restaurants, but it's still a quiet, relaxed place to spend a few days, with great walking in the surrounding hills. The **market** in Moni takes place on Monday mornings; though small, it attracts villagers from miles around, who come here to sell *ikat*, fruit and vegetables. Behind the *Amina Moe* losmen and opposite the market is a **rumah adat**, where occasional evening dance performances are held (Rp5000–10,000), and traders hang around trying to sell *ikat*.

There's no bank, post office or Telkom in Moni, though there are plans to open a wartel soon – expect it to be expensive, and make sure you bring enough cash from Ende or Maumere to see you through your time here.

Moving on, buses between Ende (90min; Rp5000) and Maumere (5hr; Rp15,000) stop at Moni about three times a day, the first one around 11am and the last at about 3pm. All the losmen owners know the approximate departure times.

Accommodation

All the accommodation is laid out along the main Ende–Maumere road. At the top of town are a number of newer, smarter places with cottages; the older homestays are found towards the lower end of town, opposite the market.

Amina Moe Opposite the market, this was once the favourite of travellers, who now tend to avoid its dingy rooms, despite the temptation of its once-legendary all-you-can-eat evening buffet. ❶

Flores Hotel A 500m walk out of the village, on the main road heading towards Maumere. This hotel always seems to be undergoing some sort of renovation, though sadly not enough to improve its tatty charmless facade. A real blot on the landscape, though the restaurant's reasonable and the rooms are some of the smartest in Moni. ❷

Homestay Daniel Just down from and next door to the *Amina Moe*, this is the last of the main bunch in the village. It's basic with dusty rooms and a choice of en-suite mandi or outside facilities, but with friendly staff. ❶

Hidayah Bungalows The first place you see coming from Ende, on the right-hand side on a bend. Rickety bamboo huts, though the host is very friendly, and the banana-pancake and fruit-salad breakfast is superb. ❷

Pondok Wisata Arwanty A couple of hundred metres down from the *Hidayah* heading towards Maumere. Following a recent upgrade, the rooms are now the smartest in Moni itself, spacious and clean, though curiously with no mosquito nets. Doubles/triples only. ❸

Saoria Wisata Bungalows Right by the Kelimutu turn-off, above the town on the way to Ende. The most upmarket option around Moni. Comparatively expensive and a long way from the village, but clean, and most rooms have en-suite mandi and TV. ❸

Watagona Bungalows Off the road to the right after *Arwanty*, just before the second bend if coming from Ende. Just one row of solid and clean rooms with mosquito nets. The manager is friendly, the price is good, though unfortunately it has become something of a meeting place for Moni's very own version of the Kuta cowboys. ❶

Eating

For such a small isolated village, the cuisine in Moni is fairly impressive. The *Mountain View*, opposite *Watagona*, specializes in very filling potato and vegetable balls which they call "Moni cakes", while their rivals and neighbours the *Bintang* do much the same, though call theirs "croquettes". Both have good views down the slopes and cold beer. Further up the hill, opposite the turn-off to the waterfall, is the friendly *Sarty Restaurant*, serving large portions of Indonesian staple dishes. In the other direction are a couple of small places with all-you-can-eat offers in the evening, the best by far being the *Nusa Bunga* opposite the market and its huge buffet; warn them in advance if you plan on eating there.

Maumere and Sikka

On the north coast of Flores, roughly equidistant between Ende and Larantuka, **MAUMERE** was once the visitor centre and best diving resort in Flores. However, the town achieved notoriety in the terrible earthquake that struck in December 1992, which, along with the resulting tsunami, killed thousands and razed the town. But though it's taken a while to get back on its feet, with plenty of rubble and unrepaired buildings still around, Maumere is starting to look like its old self again. With its better transport connections, communications, restaurants and other advantages, Maumere rivals Ende as the pre-eminent town in Flores.

Before the quake, Maumere featured on many tourist itineraries; in particular, **scuba divers** were enticed by the possibility of seeing pelagic creatures such as manta rays, sharks, and schools of dog-tooth and skipjack tuna, as well as the occasional dugong (sea cow). Though the majority of the dive sites were obliterated, there's still an outside chance of seeing these huge beasts, and a number of dive centres have set up, offering the chance to see coral emerging from the suffocating blanket of silt under which they were engulfed.

Maumere is the capital of **Sikka district**, which stretches all the way to the east coast. It's especially renowned for its **weaving**, which characteristically has maroon, white and blue geometric patterns, in horizontal rows on a black or dark-blue background. Usually these are woven into hooped sarong, the more attractive female version being the one that receives most commercial attention. The male sarong is usually a black sheet interwoven with bright, shop-bought blue threads.

Catholic priests from a variety of sects have been in the region for over four hundred years, and missionaries have made a concerted effort to educate and convert the majority of people here. As a result, the entire eastern end of Flores, and particularly the two main towns of Maumere and Larantuka, is the most devoutly Catholic in Flores and possibly all of Indonesia.

Practicalities

Maumere has a square and a market at its centre, and much of the town is very close to the seafront without the water actually being visible. There are two **bus terminals**, both of which are notorious for pickpockets and con artists, so watch your pack. Buses coming from Ende and Moni arrive at **Terminal Madawat** or **Ende terminal** on the southwest outskirts of town, though buses usually drop passengers off at their chosen destination in the centre of town first. Buses from Larantuka will stop at the **Terminal Lokaria**, which is 3km east of the centre.

Two **banks** change foreign currency: the BRI is on Jalan Raja Centis, but you can usually get better rates at the BNI on Sukarno Hatta (Mon–Fri 7.30am–2.30pm, Sat 7.30am–11am); they also have an ATM, the last one between here and Kupang. The **post office** is on Jalan Jenderal Ahmad Yani (Mon–Thurs 7.30am–3pm, Fri 7.30–11.30am, Sat 7.30am–1pm), and has internet facilities (usually non-functioning). The best **art and weaving store** in Flores is Toko Harapan Jaya on Jalan Moa Toda, with piles of dusty blankets and sarongs as well as some carvings and jewellery; if you have a good delve, you may find an occasional antique *ikat* cloth.

Moving on, Terminal Barat serves all areas to the west and Terminal Lokaria is used for eastbound buses. Both of these are a Rp1000 bemo ride out of town but most long-distance buses will circle town four or five times before leaving,

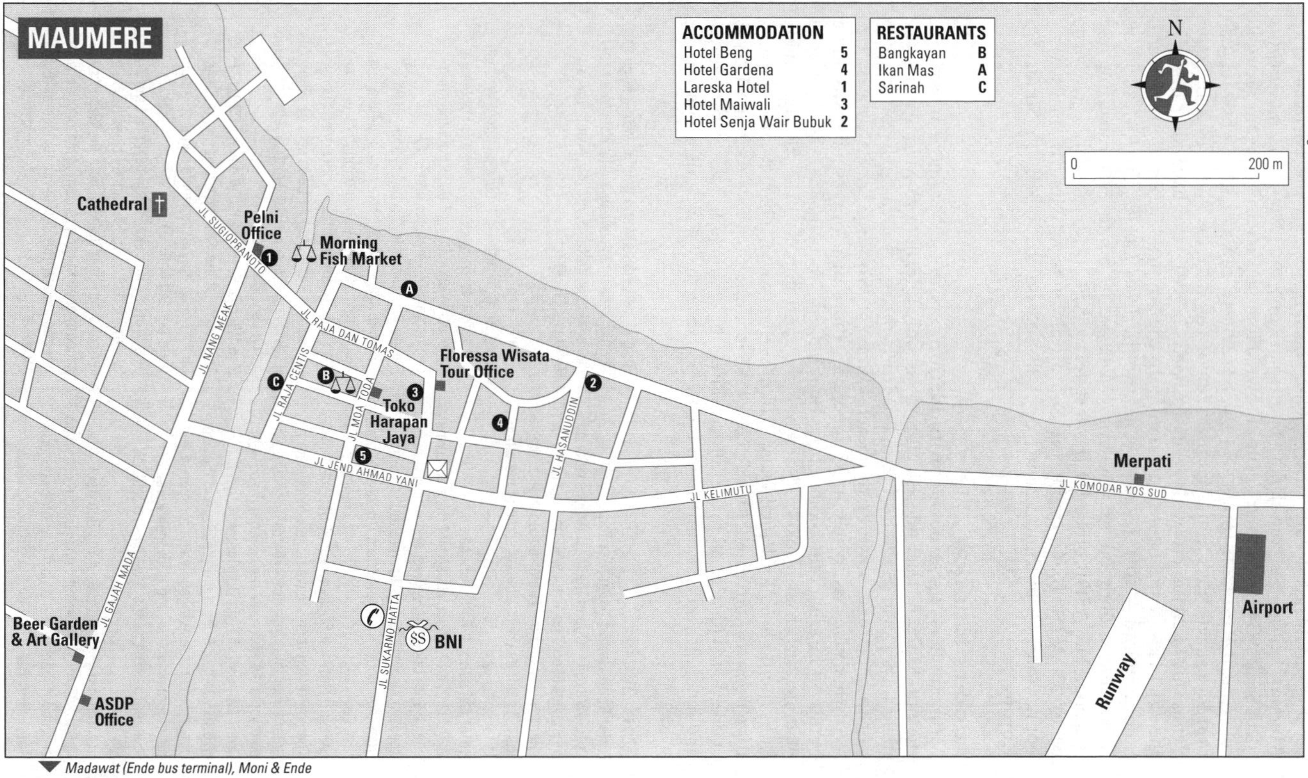

MAUMERE
ACCOMMODATION
Hotel Beng 5
Hotel Gardena 4
Lareska Hotel 1
Hotel Maiwali 3
Hotel Senja Wair Bubuk 2
RESTAURANTS
Bangkayan B
Ikan Mas A
Sarinah C
N
0
200 m
Wodong Beach Accommodation, Lokaria Bus Terminal & Laruntuka
Cathedral
Pelni Office
Morning Fish Market
JL SUGIOPRANOTO
JL NANG MEAK
JL RAJA DAN TOMAS
JL RAJA CENTIS
JL MOA TODA
Floressa Wisata Tour Office
Toko Harapan Jaya
JL JEND AHMAD YANI
JL HASANUDDIN
JL KELIMUTU
JL KOMODAR YOS SUD
Merpati
Airport
Runway
JL SUKARNO HATTA
BNI
JL GAJAH MADA
Beer Garden & Art Gallery
ASDP Office
Madawat (Ende bus terminal), Moni & Ende

so you should ask locals' advice before heading out to the terminals. The **Merpati** office is on Jalan Sudirman on the way to the airport (☎0383/21924), with their agent in town, Floressa Wisata, occupying their old offices at Jl Raja Don Tomas 18 (☎0383/22281). Merpati have a bad reputation for cancellations from Maumere, and if you have the choice, you're better flying out of Maumere with Pelita (☎0383/22994), who have their office in the *Beng Goan I* and offer free a transfer to the airport. The **Pelni** office is at Jl Sugiyopranoto 4 (☎0382/21013), next to the *Hotel Lareska*; the *KM Awu* calls in twice a month on its way from Makassar to Sumba via Kalabashi and Kupang. The ASDP office for the **fast ferry** *KFC Serayu* is at Jl Gajah Mada 61 (☎0382/21400). Currently the *Serayu* calls in every Monday on its westbound journey to Bima, Benoa on Bali and Surabaya, and on Sunday to Kupang.

Accommodation

Most travellers bypass the **accommodation** on offer in Maumere in favour of the out-of-town beachside establishments, only returning to Maumere for the night if they plan to catch a bus or boat early the next morning. If you're going east to Larantuka, however, the beach losmen at **Wodong** are on your way.

Anyone who has to stay in Maumere for more than one evening would be better off heading out to one of the **beach** areas. Wodong, 28km to the east of Maumere, with its black-sand beach, is the most popular place, though diving buffs should head for Pantai Waiara 10km west of town, where Maumere's only **dive** operators are based. Diving costs US$35 at the *Sea World Club* and US$45 at the *Sao Wisata Hotel* for a full day. These prices include two or three dives and lunch. If you arrive the night before you dive, they'll include a room in the price.

The Town

Hotel Beng Goan I Jalan Moa Toda ☎0382/21041. One of the least expensive and most central options – but with no fans in the dirt-cheap rooms and the higher-priced rooms slightly tatty, it's not as good value as some of the others in town. ❶–❷

Hotel Gardena Jl Patty Rangga 28 ☎0382/22644. Clean, cheap and the most popular choice with budget travellers, and run by a manager who is switched on to what tourists want from their hotel. Rates include a reasonable breakfast. ❷

Lareska Hotel Jl Sugiopranoto 4 ☎0382/21137. The sea-facing rooms have huge windows and great panoramas, are sparkling clean and reasonable value. Most rooms have shared mandi. ❷

Hotel Maiwali Jl Raja Don Tomas 6 ☎0382/21220. Quite a plush place and the economy rooms represent good value for money, but beware midnight wailing from their karaoke lounge. The best rooms have air-con and TV. ❷–❺

Hotel Senja Wair Bubuk Jl Yos Sudarso ☎0382/21498. Large but rather bare rooms with or without mandi, with amazingly kitsch decor. ❷

Hotel Wini Rai II Jl Sutomo ☎0382/21362. Central, very friendly and helpful, with a large variety of rooms which, while a little dark, are spacious and comfortable. A close rival to the *Gardena*. ❷–❸

The beach

Ankermi Bungalows On the beach at Wodong, and a rival to *Froggies*, with a choice of bungalows, some en suite, set back from the sand behind some freshwater ponds. ❶

Flores Froggies On the beach just outside Wodong village, on the road to Larantuka, about 28km from Maumere. Has a much nicer beach than the accommodation further east. The oldest place here, there are just three sets of simple bungalows and a dorm, all of which smell a bit damp and musty. ❷

Sao Wisata Hotel Pantai Waiara ☎0382/21555. The rooms at the *Sao Wisata* are not quite as upmarket as the prices would suggest, though all have fan and bath. ❻

Sea World Club aka **Pondok Dunia Laut** Pantai Waiara ☎0382/21570. Slightly cleaner and in better condition than its neighbour the *Sao Wisata*: accommodation ranges from clean bungalows with fan and shower through to rooms with air-con and TV. ❹–❻

Eating

Maumere has a number of decent seafood restaurants and the usual profusion of cheap **warung**. The best-value restaurant is the unpretentious *Sarinah* on Jalan Raja Centis, with scruffy decor, a lackadaisical approach to customer service – and often extraordinarily good food. Try the *ikan kukus*, a huge slab of tuna fish garnished with chicken, pork or garlic – excellent value at Rp20,000. Another good place is the *Ikan Mas* on Jalan Hasanuddin by the waterfront, serving fish and crustaceans fresh from tanks around the restaurant; a single portion of lobster costs around Rp40,000. Non-fish lovers seeking simpler fare should head to the basic but clean Padang-style *Bangkayan* on Jalan Mangga. There's also a beer garden-cum-art gallery on the way to the western bus terminal on Jalan Gajah Mada. The art is nothing to talk about, but they serve a wonderful ginger tea. The food at the *Ankermi Bungalows* is far and away the best of the Wodong bunch, with regular, fresh barbecued seafood. Both the *Sao Wisata Hotel* and *Sea World Club* serve excellent buffet meals three times a day; breakfast is US$5, lunch US$8 and dinner US$12.

Around Maumere

Twenty kilometres from Maumere on the road back to Ende is **LADALERO** village, based around a Catholic seminary; a bemo from the Ende terminal in Maumere costs Rp2000. The village's interesting but jumbled **museum** is maintained by the priests; the collection includes rare *ikat* from all over Flores, excellent picture books (in Indonesian) on the subject, plus a profusion of weapons, pottery, ivory, coins and other bric-a-brac and a number of small megaliths. There is no admission price, but they ask for a donation.

SIKKA, on the opposite coast from Maumere nearly 30km south and slightly east, is the most-visited weaving village in the area. As soon as you walk in, the cry "turis" goes up and women drape *ikat* over every fence and bush for your appraisal. Until you walk down onto the beautiful shaded beach, the village seems to be devoid of men, who are relegated to sitting on the sand under the palm trees, repairing their nets and smoking. The vast majority of weaving here is of poor quality, but it's possible to discover the occasional gem. Regular bemos here cost Rp2000, and it's about 30km from Ende terminal in Maumere.

One of the most picturesque villages in the region is **WATUBLAPI**, an *ikat* weaving village 20km southeast from Maumere. It offers magnificent panoramas of both coasts and the mountains stretching away to Larantuka and the west; a bus or bemo from Maumere's Lokaria terminal costs Rp2000.

About 12km west of Maumere on the coast is **WURING**, a stilted Bugis fishing village, which has recovered remarkably from the earthquake devastation of 1992. As with most of these villages, it's a photographer's dream, with mountainous **Pulau Besar** looming in the background. Again, buses leave from Maumere's Ende terminal (Rp2000).

Larantuka

A four-hour bus ride from Maumere, the port of **LARANTUKA** serves the Solor and Alor archipelagos and Timor. It's an inoffensive but slightly dull place to spend a night, as you will inevitably have to do if you're heading to the Alor or Solor archipelagos. The drive east from Maumere takes you through some of the most perfect scenery in Flores: tropical forests, punctuated by countless volcanoes and glimpses of the sea. The town itself has an attractive setting, at the foot of the Ile Mandiri volcano, with the bare, green, mountainous islands of Solor and Adonara nestling close by in the bay.

The area from Larantuka out to Pulau Lembata shares a distinct language, Lamaholot, which sounds remarkably like Indonesian spoken with a strong Italian accent. Communities here were once firmly ritual-based, yet Larantuka today is one of the most fervently Catholic areas in Indonesia, renowned for its processions at Easter and Christmas. This is largely due to the huge Portuguese presence here that began in the 1500s, when Larantuka was used as a stopover for traders en route to and from Timor and the Spice Islands.

Larantuka's Portuguese-style **cathedral**, two blocks back from the port, and the Holy Mary **chapel**, stand just to the southwest of the *Hotel Tresna*, and are fairly unimpressive in themselves, but on Sundays are worth a visit for the uplifting singing. **Weri beach**, 6km north of town, gets busy at the weekends but is a nice place for a dip and a little cleaner than other beaches nearer town. A little way south of Weri, the coastline runs so close to Pulau Adonara it seems you could almost swim across.

Practicalities

The main part of Larantuka is centred alongside the road that runs parallel to the coast. The **harbour** lies roughly in the centre of the town, with a small market around the entrance. The harbour master's office, on the left as you enter the jetty, provides some information on the ferry services, though your best bet is to ask at your hotel. All ferries leave from this harbour, except the car ferries, which leave from the pier about 5km south of town. To get there ask for a bemo to Labuhan Besar (Big Harbour).

The BNI **bank** is on the unnamed second road back from and parallel to the sea, heading towards Maumere; it seems willing to change at least dollars and sterling, both cash and travellers' cheques. Alternatively, the brand-new BRI on Jalan Piere Tandean, around the corner from their more prominent but disused old building and a short walk southeast of the harbour, has reasonable rates, but

Moving on from Larantuka

The **Pelni** ships *KM Tatamailau*, *KM Sirimau* and *KM Kelimutu* all call in at Larantuka's central harbour on their fortnightly (*KM Sirimau*) or monthly (*KM Kelimutu* and *KM Tatamailau*) circuits, coming from Kupang and going on to Ujung Padang on Sulawesi. Their office is at Jl Yohakim BL De Rosari 166 (☎0383/21155); take the road running behind the *Virgo Café* and a right at the top; it's about 30m from the junction. Motorboats depart twice daily for **Lewoleba** on Lembata (4hr; Rp7500), leaving at 8am and 2pm, going via **Waiwerang** on Adonara. There are regular boats to **Lamakera** and **Rita Ebang** on Solor, and **Waiwodan** on the northern side of Adonara, leaving daily at 8am. Once a week on Friday mornings at around 8am a boat goes direct to the whaling village of **Lamalera** on Lembata via Waiwerang, taking eight hours (Rp20,000). From the Pelabuhan Besar to the south of Larantuka, car ferries to **Kupang** leave on Mondays (noon) and Wednesdays (2pm), taking 12–15 hours, while boats to **Kalabahi** on Alor depart every Monday, Wednesday, Friday and Saturday morning from the same harbour; this journey takes at least a day and a night, and the Pelni ferry *KM Awu* is a much better option, being more comfortable, faster (10hr) and safer. There are no **fast ferries** running to and from Larantuka as yet, though the privately owned *Andhika Express* is rumoured to start a service soon between here and Kupang.

for cash dollars only (Mon–Fri 8am–2.30pm, Sat 8am–noon). Don't count on being able to change currency anywhere east of here except Kupang.

The best **place to stay** in Larantuka is *Hotel Rulies* (Ⓣ0383/21198; ❷), southeast of the pier; if you're arriving from the west, ask your bus to drop you off here. It's clean and friendly enough, with shared facilities. The *Hotel Tresna* (Ⓣ0383/21072; ❷) next door might take you if *Rulies* is full, and is not a bad alternative, though it lacks the charm of *Rulies*, which is built around an old Dutch-era wooden house. Several average Padang **warung** line the main road, but by far the best place to eat is the relatively inexpensive *Nirwana*, a couple of hundred metres north of the harbour, on the coastal road, Jalan Niaga. It's virtually the only place in town with cold drinks, and the asparagus soup here is delicious. Two blocks further north on the same street is the tiny and slightly bizarre *Virgo Café and Hair Salon*, a tiny little place run by a local guy who speaks English with an Australian accent and who, in between running the barber's shop, serves a decent portion of fish and chips with cold beer.

The Alor and Solor archipelago

Clustered at the eastern end of Flores, the five main islands of the **Alor and Solor archipelago** are some of the least-visited places in Indonesia – yet often prove the favourite destination of those travellers who do take the time and effort to come here. The closest islands to Flores are Adonara and Solor, where the harsh, rocky terrain is largely deforested and there is no tourist infrastructure. They are also commonly perceived to be less interesting than the spectacular islands further to the east. The island of **Lembata** receives most visitors, and for good reason. Its volcanoes, forests and beautiful coastline are supplemented by fascinating indigenous cultures, particularly the unique subsistence **whaling village** of Lamalera on the south coast. Lembata's capital and largest port, Lewoleba, also offers a fine **market**, while the volcano of **Ile Api** smoulders impressively over the bay.

Next in the chain heading east from Lembata, but closer in proximity and culture to Alor, is the remote island of **Pantar**; there are still places here that have never seen foreigner visitors, despite its boundless natural beauty, volcanoes, beaches and spectacular coral gardens.

Alor is as far east as you can go in the Alor Solor archipelago, and is home to extraordinary animist cultures. Along with Pantar, it has an unexplained proliferation of bronze *moko* drums in the style of the Vietnamese Dongson era, which ended around 300 AD. The islands also have many remote traditional villages, fantastic walking opportunities, and some of the best **scuba diving** and snorkelling in Indonesia.

All these islands are undeveloped and unaccustomed to westerners. There's no Western-standard accommodation in the whole archipelego, and travel is hard

– be prepared for long, hot journeys, nonexistent timetables and poor food. Very little English is spoken, and in some places people barely speak Bahasa Indonesian. The prevalent language in the east is Lamaholot, which has a bouncing inflection with accompanying animated facial and physical expressions. On Pantar and Alor, seclusion and conflict over the centuries has led to the evolution of fifteen different languages and innumerable dialects, some spoken by no more than a few hundred people.

The recorded **history** of the archipelago is sparse. Chinese traders, ubiquitous in the history of most of eastern Indonesia, only started trading around the coast of Alor at the end of the nineteenth century. The only historical site of real significance is the **Portuguese fort** on Solor, built with local slave labour under the watchful eye of Portuguese master masons: the structure's strength much impressed the Dutch when they overran it in 1613 after a lengthy siege.

Most people enter the archipelago by **ferry** or **motorboat** from **Larantuka** on the east coast of Flores. From Larantuka, you can reach Lembata, Solor and Adonara on relatively short motorboat trips. Getting to Alor is more difficult, although there are weekly ferries from Kupang or Atambua in West Timor, and weekly flights from Kupang and Larantuka to Kalabahi in Alor. The only way to reach Pantar is by boat from Kalabahi or Lembata.

Solor and Adonara

Though accessible by daily motorboats from Larantuka, **Solor** and **Adonara**, the two islands closest to Flores, are difficult to explore, with poor communications and accommodation. However, they do offer plenty of scope for off-the-beaten-track adventure.

Solor

Solor was once the strategic site of a **Portuguese stone fort**, built as a stop-off for trading ships to and from Timor. The remains of the fort can be seen in the north near **Lohajong** village, 16km from Solor's main port of **Rita Ebang** on the west coast, only a short motorboat trip from Larantuka. The fort walls at least were built to last, and the view is excellent. The place of greatest interest on the island is the whaling village of **Lamakera**, on the northeastern tip of Solor, and connected to Rita Ebang by the only real road on the island. A boat is supposed to connect Lamakera with the mainland every day, though in reality it only travels about three times a week; ask around the village for current departure times. The village has less charm than Lamalera on Lembata (see p.762), as it's extremely poor and the few people that do still hunt whales do so out of motorboats, much less romantic than the wooden sailing boats of Lembata. You can stay in Lamakera with the kepala desa and go out in the boats if the seas are right. There's a good chance of seeing dolphins, but much less chance of seeing whales.

Adonara

Adonara, dominated by the Ile Boleng volcano, is reputedly home to some of the most violent people in Indonesia. In Lamaholot, the local language, *Adonara* means "brother's blood", apparently because of an endless series of feuds and vendettas that have resulted in countless murders and tribal wars on the island throughout its history. Although Islam and Christianity are the official norm, many villages still have sacred rocks and totems, and ritual life still thrives. The main town here is **WAIWERANG**, which has a wealth of shiny new mosques and a market on Mondays and Thursdays. The *Ile Boleng Homestay* (❷), the only decent **accommodation** in town, is reasonably clean and offers good views looking out towards Solor; it's about 200m left out of the harbour. You can also get a sizeable (if not especially tasty) meal here; alternatively, a **warung** near to the harbour sells cheap but poor-quality Padang food.

All **ferries** between Larantuka and Lembata call in at Waiwerang (2hr) on the way, docking either at the jetty in the centre of town or, if the tide is out, at the car harbour 1km to the west. Occasional ferries from eastern Solor (in particular Lamakera) also visit Waiwerang. There is very little in the way of public transport around the island.

Lembata

Many people come to **Lembata** (also known as Lomblen) on a flying visit and end up missing other parts of their trip to stay longer. It's a captivating place, frustrating to travel around but full of friendly people, beautiful landscapes and intriguing culture. Most visitors arrive at the largest town of **Lewoleba** on the west coast, from where there's a twice-weekly boat or a less-reliable daily bemo to the unmissable primitive whaling village of **Lamalera** on the south coast. Alternatively, you can catch the weekly (Friday) ferry from Larantuka directly to Lamalera.

The island is also the home of one of the most renowned **weaving** traditions in Indonesia. The best cloths are fashioned in the remote villages on the northern coastal slopes of **Ile Ape** (Fire Mountain), the volcano that looms over Lewoleba. The cloths are an essential part of the "bride price" used by a young man to secure his partner's hand. Another dowry essential is an elephant tusk – an incredible amount of ivory exists around these few islands – many of which were brought here from Africa hundreds of years ago.

Lewoleba

Despite being the main settlement on Lembata, **LEWOLEBA** is a sleepy little place. It's extremely picturesque, sitting on a palm-lined bay under the shadow of the smoking volcano Ile Ape. The town comes alive once a week for the Monday **market**; people used to come from as far away as Timor to sell their goods here, and even now they still travel from Flores and the surrounding

Lembata's ikat

Most of Lembata's legendary *ikat* **cloths** are made from rough, hand-spun thread that becomes softer with age. Generally, the designs run horizontally across the base colours of dark brown or strong magenta. Although some of the *ikat* features characters and figures such as whales, horses and elephants, these figures are not as intricate as those from Sumba, and diametric patterns are more common. Traditionally, *ikat* sarongs are a requisite part of dowries, and the prime cloths are passed down through generations, constantly spiralling in value. Genuine antique cloths, which very rarely come to market, might sell for up to US$5000, but usually they are not even shown to westerners, being of important social significance and irreplaceable.

Moving on from Lembata

The fleet of ferries running in this part of the archipelago were retired here after full service on the busy routes around Java and Sumatra rendered them too old and unreliable for more arduous use. It's almost impossible to find out **schedules**; they change constantly, and nobody seems able to give you a straight, reliable answer as to when your boat will leave, so keep checking the details of departures with as many people of authority as you can, particularly during the rainy season.

Both **ferries to Alor** are currently out of action. If and when they start running again, the usual schedule is to depart on Monday and Friday evenings, stopping at Belauring in the northeast of Lembata for the night, before going on to Wairiang, at the extreme eastern tip, and Baranusa on Pantar. It takes six hours from Lewoleba to Belauring and then ten hours to Alor. The total trip takes about 20hr if you're lucky. The more comfortable and direct *Diana Express* is a smaller boat that departs once a week on the same trip, usually leaving Belauring at 6.30am on Wednesday. A much better option is to find out when the *Diana Express* is coming in, and take a bus to Belauring (2hr; Rp5000), stay there the night and catch the ferry the next morning. In Belauring, stay at the *Losmen Telaga Jan* (❶); it's a grotty place with fish swimming in the mandi and a cornucopia of insects, but they serve incredible Indonesian food.

Other destinations from Lewoleba include **Kupang**, with boats leaving every Monday at 4pm (15hr), and at least two boats daily to **Larantuka**; these smaller wooden boats are faster (4hr) and cheaper (Rp15,000) than the big iron ferries that leave on Mondays and Fridays (6hr; Rp17,500).

islands. This weekly event has lost a little of its edge – it used to be a regular party, with trading, drinking and games starting early in the morning and going on until the following morning, but now tends to peter out around midnight.

The centre of town is set a little way back from the bay, with the market as its focal point. On the seafront is a beautiful stilted **Bajo fishing village** and a small **fish market**.

Practicalities

All boats in and out of Lewoleba call at the harbour, 1km west of town. The harbour master's office opposite the port is usually shut, and of little use when it's open. The bemo and bus terminal is in the centre of town, behind the *Losmen Rejeki* (see below). The **bank** in Lewoleba will not change money in any form, though the Chinese-run shop, Toko Flores Jaya, on the south side of the market, will change US dollars at appalling rates. The **post office** (closes at 2pm) opposite is usually crowded, but efficient, and the **Telkom office** about 1km west of the market is open 24hr, though they don't accept collect calls. The *Rejeki* losmen is the agent for **Merpati**, though currently all flights have been suspended due to lack of demand. It's only a short bemo ride to the airport, but they're rather infrequent, so you're better off chartering one for yourself (around Rp20,000).

Accommodation and eating

The losmen *Lile Ile* (❷) – also known to locals as *Mister Jim's* – is a real gem, lying exactly halfway between the harbour and the market on the bay side of the road. Although its cottages are slightly tatty now, they come with mosquito nets and the communal verandah provides sensational views of Ile Ape and the nearby Bajo village. They also have an extensive video collection (Rp5000 a time), and serve simple but tasty meals. You couldn't ask for better hosts than the Dutchman and his family who run the place. The *Losmen Rejeki* (❷) is on the first corner of the market on the road to the harbour. It's the old standby, a decent place that does terrific food: try the *spesial dengan rusa* ("deer meat special"), which for Rp15,000 could easily feed two. The *kentang goreng* is pretty tasty too, and *Rejeki* is about the only place in town with cold beer.

Around Lewoleba

Heading west from Lewoleba on the path that hugs the coast, a black-sand **beach** is about 1km from the harbour, although a better white-sand one lies 6km further on. To get to them, you'll have to walk, as there's no real road. Near **Lerahinga** village, about 18km northeast of town, you'll find excellent **snorkelling**. It's one of the few places on Lembata that has not been destroyed by fish-bombing, lava flows or coral gathering (the locals burn coral to make lime); the best coral is a little west of the village. To get to Lerahinga from Lewoleba, ask for the bemo north to **Hadakewa**, which should go all the way to Lerahinga.

Ile Ape

While the **Ile Ape** volcano hasn't erupted on a violent scale for several decades, it always has at least a puff of smoke lingering around its summit. It seems a strange place to build upon, but is surrounded by **villages**, famed for their *ikat* weaving, but also worth visiting for the beauty of their situation and the warmth of their welcome. Make sure you bring lots of water and food as there are no warung and only a couple of kiosks all the way around the volcano.

There are two ways to tackle the mountain. If you're short of time, consider taking a bemo to Waipukang (30min) – although make sure you set off before 7.30am, to give yourself enough time to get back the same day. From Waipukang, walk for an hour (around 6km) northeast to **Jontona**, where you can ask the kepala desa for a guide; from Jontona, it's another hour's walk to **Kampung Lama** (Old Kampung), a ceremonial village left derelict all year except during the *Pesta Kacang* (Bean Festival) which takes place here in October. From there, it's about another four hours to the summit. The crater itself is dramatic, the walls having fallen away on one side in ancient lava flows that extend right down into the sea, and the upper slopes are a steaming, yellow, sulphurous wilderness.

A better option, however, is to tackle Ile Ape as a three-day trip out of Lewoleba, staying overnight in one of the villages at the foot of the mountain both the night before and after. The normal way to tackle the mountain is to climb to the summit at night in order to be at the top for sunrise, so do remember a torch. First, take the daily bemo to Atawatun (90min), a pretty little fishing village that appears almost Mediterranean. Here, you should enquire with the kepala desa about the possibilities of staying overnight. At around midnight, having hired a guide from the village, begin to climb to the summit, a slog of about 4–5 hours that, all being well, should mean you arrive in time to enjoy the sunrise. On your return from the summit, it's worth visiting Lamagate, the old kampung of Atawatun to the north of the volcano where, if you take some time to meet and speak with the locals, they may show you antique *ikat* cloths worth hundreds of dollars. If you're too late to catch the bemo back to Lewoleba (around 2pm), other than staying another night the only option is to embark on the fourteen-kilometre walk round the volcano to **Waipukang**, where transport is slighty more frequent. This walk takes you through little-visited and beautiful villages, where the children will stream out of their classrooms screaming with delight, and whole villages will empty to follow you.

Lamalera

Even if it wasn't for the spectacular occupation of its menfolk, the whale-hunting village of **LAMALERA**, on the south coast of Lembata, would be well worth a visit. The people are extremely friendly, the surrounding scenery is a stunning sweep of forests and mountains, and to sit in the small shaded square listening to the church choir practise is a remarkably pleasant way to spend time. On most afternoons, the entire village turns out for a volleyball match on the beach: join in and you'll be an instant hero.

The whales of Lamalera

A visit to Lembata can be combined with a hunt for **whales**. Nature-lovers should be warned, though, that this is not a whale-watching pleasure cruise: the people of Lembata are here to kill these magnificent beasts, an event which can be extremely harrowing to watch. Large whales take at least fifteen minutes to die, some much longer, and have been known to tow boats, attached to their harpoons, as far as Timor. Whaling takes place mainly from May to October – but never on Sundays, as the people are devout Christians.

Joining the hunt can be an exciting and unique experience. You'll be expected to take up a paddle and pull your weight as the whalers try to overhaul their quarry. The harpooner balances precariously on a flimsy platform at the front of the boat until you're within striking distance. Then he hurls the lance, leaping in after it irrespective of which creature he has speared, hoping to put his weight behind the spear and pull off as quick and painless a kill as possible. If the whale has survived the first strike, it will reel off a couple of bundles of rope (woven from palm fronds) and drag the boat as the harpooner struggles aboard. Then they will attempt to spear it again, playing it like a game fish until it is too exhausted to fight.

The **outrigger prahus** used to hunt the whale are truly extraordinary vessels. Varying from 10 to 12m long and a mere 2m across, the boats are constructed in accordance with ancient statutes. The entire length of the hull is constructed without nails – instead, wooden pegs are used, and the beams are sealed with pitch. The sails are made from palm fronds, woven into squares and then sewn together into a large rectangular sheet. Before the boats push out at the end of the rainy season, they are blessed by the Catholic priest. The prahus are generally manned by middle-aged men because the village youth shun the profession; it seems certain that the traditions will die out with the men that now follow them.

As with certain Inuit peoples, whaling at Lamalera purely serves for the needs of a small community. Lamalera has therefore been declared a protected, subsistence whaling village and is not subject to international whaling charters or limitations.The Worldwide Fund for Nature has carried out numerous surveys in the village and decided that their occupation has no effect on world whale stocks, or those of other endangered species such as turtles. In the peak year of 1969, the Lamalerans took only 56 sperm whales as well as a few manta rays, turtles, dolphins and other rare sea beasts.

Every part of a killed whale is used by the villagers. Its meat and blubber are shared out amongst the village people according to rights and ancient lore, the boat-builder and sailmaker both receiving a share. The parts of the whale that cannot be eaten are also used. The spermaceti is burnt as fuel, the bones are used to provide searing-hot fires to forge harpoon heads, and the teeth are carved into rings and necklaces. The only part of the animal that they ever get material compensation for is the penis, sold to Japanese traders who come by every few months to buy them for use in traditional medicines.

However pleasant Lamalera is, it's not the reason travellers arrive here – they come because the villagers maintain the same dangerous, barely profitable struggle with nature that they have pursued for over two centuries. The people of Lamalera hunt **whales**, not with radar and explosive harpoons, but with ten-metre wooden outriggers and bamboo-shafted spears (see box opposite).

Practicalities

There are three **accommodation** options in Lamalera, all of similar quality and all providing three meals a day. The most popular is the *Guru Ben Homestay* (❷). It's on top of the promontory that looms over the bay to the west; take the path that leads to your left coming up from the beach and follow it up about 200m. The views of the village and the morning preparations for hunting are superb, though the accommodation is otherwise very basic and mosquitoes are a problem. Due to the comparable outlook from their lavatory, *Guru Ben*'s has also been affectionately renamed "the poo with a view". The owner speaks fluent English and can tell you anything you could ever need to know about Lamalera. If you want to go out on a **whaling expedition**, Ben can arrange it; it's Rp30,000 a day if no whales are sighted, or Rp70,000 if you witness a kill (and more if you wish to film it); alternatively, you can hire Ben's boat for Rp100,000 per day.

If you come into the village by boat, the nearest accommodation to the beach where you land is the *White House* (❷). This is the villa-like house with a balcony that overhangs the beach at the eastern end. It has huge beds in three private rooms and good food, but it lies in close proximity to the part of the beach where fish are dried. The well-kept *Adel Beding* homestay (❷) is in the centre of the village, by the shaded square. Wherever you stay in Lamalera, make sure you bring plenty of **mosquito repellent**.

Getting to Lamalera can be a real pain. Every Sunday and Tuesday night a boat destined for the village leaves from the harbour in **Lewoleba**, returning at 9am on Saturday and Monday mornings. This trip takes four hours (Rp8000) and the boat can be seriously crowded. On Tuesday this boat then goes on to **Larantuka**, returning to Lamalera from there on Friday. The only other option from Lewoleba is to take one of the irregular bemos (4hr), though they're subject to frequent breakdowns. If you're lucky enough to find a truck going the same route, it's infinitely preferable; a daily truck leaves Lewoleba at 7am (4hr).

Alor and Pantar

Previously only a destination for a trickle of travellers, **Alor** and **Pantar** are gradually being discovered, sought after not only for their fine landscapes and traditional lifestyles, but also because of the phenomenal richness of the surrounding seas. It's practically impossible to spend a day on the water between the two islands without sighting whales or dolphins, and beneath the surface are some exceptional reefs, walls and slopes. Alor has become much easier to travel in over the last few years but, outside of the main few villages, it's still virtually untouched by the tourist invasion. Most areas of the islands are so isolated by their rugged surroundings that at least thirteen independent tribes maintain their own distinct languages. Head-hunting and cannibalism were only officially stopped here in the late 1950s, though some areas are so remote that vestiges of the violent past remained long after.

Moko

One of the most distinctive things about Alor and Pantar is the mysterious cache of bronze **Dongson-style drums** discovered here. *Moko,* or *nakara* as they are known locally, are a fascinating anomaly for which no satisfactory explanation has ever been found. Thousands have been dug up from shallow graves in the hard soil, some of them up to 2m in circumference and nearly 1.5m high. They're often beautifully moulded, sometimes with exquisite etchings. The style of the drums is reminiscent of the pre-Christian Dongson culture of North Vietnam. How they got here in such numbers without getting left in similar numbers at sites on the way from Vietnam is a mystery – Alor has never been an especially well-known trading post or stopover for colonial soldiers and missionaries, mainly due to the violent reputation of the islanders.

The drums now have particular significance in the bridal dowry: a suitor must provide the family of his intended with a good enough *moko* if he wants to secure her hand in marriage – the drums are sometimes described in terms of how many women they would buy. Good examples can fetch up to Rp50,000,000; probably the best surviving *moko* now resides in the East Nusa Tenggara Museum in Kupang (see p.774). Be warned that *moko* are now restricted items under cultural protection by the Indonesian government, and you need permission from the Ministry of the Interior to buy one and take it out of the country.

Kalabahi

The only large town in the entire island group, **KALABAHI** has a very mellow, friendly atmosphere. It has little in the way of tourist facilities, but can still be quite a bewitching place: the bay, with its scores of lush islands, is beautiful. Pearl divers make their homes on flimsy bamboo catamarans, huge shoals of fish turn the surface of the waters into regular maelstroms, and swarms of luminous jellyfish fill the dusk tides in ghostly invasions. Kalabahi itself is the only place on Pulau Alor with losmen, hotels and places to eat and, being the transport hub, is the best place to base yourself if you want to visit the sites of interest around the island.

Practicalities

The town is quite spread out, with the main harbour being fairly central and a good landmark to start from. The town stretches east and inland from here to the market and bus terminal: to the west is the ferry harbour. The **airport** is at Mali about 10km northeast of town, linked by regular buses and taxis with the town.

If you need to change money, the **BNI bank** is the only possible option in the whole Alor/Solor archipelago. They can usually be persuaded to change US dollars cash, but you'll have trouble with anything else. The bank is situated on Jalan Sukarno, on the side of a small green as you head northwest from the main harbour. From there, if you head inland (north) for 150m, the **post office** is about 200m away on your right (Mon–Sat 7am–4pm). Another 400m up this road, the red-and-white pylon of the **Telkom** office dominates the skyline; the office is open 24hr a day but there are often big queues. The main **bus terminal** and the Pasar Inpres **market** lie about 500m east of town. The market offers a decent variety of fruit and vegetables as well as woven baskets, mats and betel-nut holders.

Most buses heading east towards Alor Besar will come through town anyway so there's no point going out to the terminal – just stand by the *Hotel Adi*

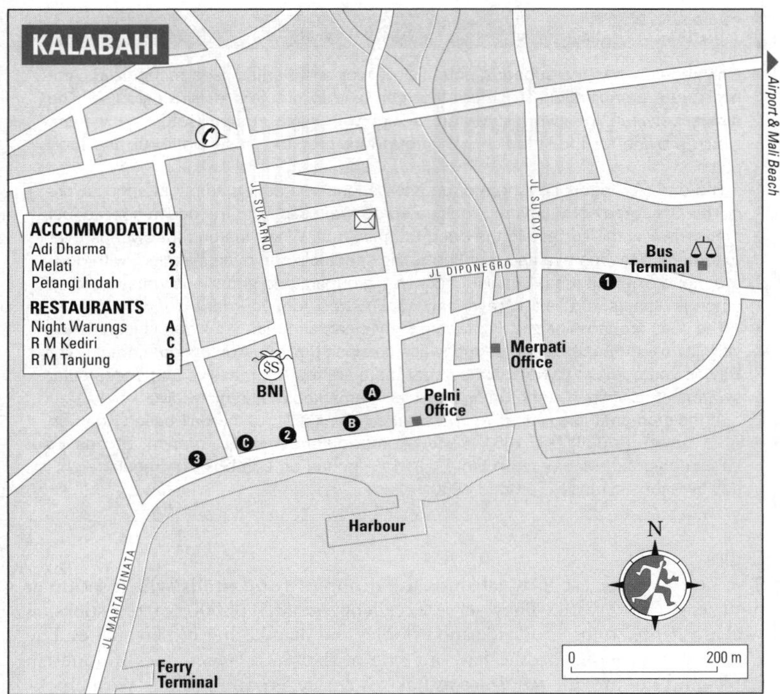

Dharma or the playing field north of the harbour and they should pass. Heading to other destinations, you're best to go to the terminal; a bemo from town costs Rp300, or it's a fifteen-minute walk.

Accommodation

While not actually in town, the most popular **accommodation** option near Kalabahi is the French-run *La Petite Kepa*, on tiny Pulau Kepa, 500m off Alor's west coast on the way to Pantar (❷). The homestay consists of beautiful, traditionally built bungalows; the very reasonable price includes three meals, tea and coffee and transfers to and from the mainland. Snorkelling in the sea around these parts is incredible; to reach the island, take a bus or bemo from Pasar Inpres and jump off at Alor Kecil, 15km from Kalabahi; the owners of the homestay will pick you up from there.

Hotel Adi Dharma Jl Martadinata 12/26 ☎0386/21280. On the harbourfront, a 100m walk west of the main harbour gates. The most popular place in town, mainly because the owner speaks good English and is a great source of information about the area. There's a choice of singles, doubles and triples all with fan and mandi. Rooms are very clean but some of the mandi have a flourishing cockroach population. ❷

Hotel Melati Between the *Adi Dharma* and the harbour ☎0386/21073. Recently refurbished, this is a nice clean place with reasonable prices and a choice of fan or air-con. ❷

Hotel Pelangi Indah Jl Diponegoro 100 ☎0386/21251. One of the few places in town with some air-con rooms, as well as cheaper rooms with shared mandi and no fan. Whatever room you opt for, make sure the facilities you are paying for actually work. ❶–❸

Underwater Alor

Only recently has the subaqua potential of Alor and Pantar been recognized. Alor has a rare combination of factors that combine to create a diver's paradise. The straits between the two islands are swept with cold, nutrient-saturated waters, which provide for the little fish who are in turn prey for those higher up the food chain.

The one site that is earning Alor an international reputation amongst sport divers is **The Dream**, a coral-covered rocky outcrop that rises from the ocean floor to just metres below the surface in the deep Pantar Strait. When the current sweeps over this site at between two and four knots, the spectacle can overwhelming, with dogtooth and skipjack tuna, Spanish mackerel, groupers and enormous wrasse gliding amongst sharks, turtles and rays, only centimetres from your face.

The seas around Alor and Pantar are fairly clear: although you'll rarely experience visibility over 20m, there are so many fish so close that you don't need more. In Alor Bay as you come in to Kalabahi by boat there are regular, massive and spectacular swarms of jellyfish, a sight that is especially remarkable on a night dive.

At the moment there is no dive operation on Alor itself, but the Bali-based Komodo Alor Safari (Ⓣ0361/287166, Ⓦwww.komodoalordive.com; branch offices in Labuanbajo and Maumere on Flores, and Ampenan on Lombok) run regular eight-day live-aboard trips for around $950.

Eating

The best place to eat in Kalabahi is the group of **food stalls** which set up at night east of the bank. They serve excellent sate at Rp5000 for ten sticks, as well as various soups, fried rice and noodles and many other old favourites. The *Rumah Makan Kediri* on the harbour side of the *Adi Dharma* does Indonesian staples and can provide *nasi bungkus* (takeaway rice; Rp3000), along with chicken, eggs and pretty much anything else you want. The only place in town for quality food is the *Rumah Makan Tanjung*, opposite the food stalls. They serve cold beer and a few lame Indonesian dishes as well as fried potatoes. However, if you give them a day's notice, they can serve up grilled fish, lobster, chicken or whatever else you fancy. They are only open after 6pm so you might have to order the night before.

Around Alor

Twelve kilometres from Kalabahi is the village of **TAKPALA**, which has maintained its traditional houses and practices, mainly it seems because of the cruise-ship tour groups who come here to see dancing and singing. These free performances usually take place on Monday mornings; to get there, ask for a bemo (Rp1000) to Takpala from Kalabahi's Inpres market, and you'll have to walk about 1km from where they drop you to get to the village. Another village that is just a bemo ride away from Kalabahi and has thatched-roof houses is **MONBANG**, about 3km east of town. *Monbang* means "snake village" – legend has it that a huge foreigner-eating serpent lives here. From Monbang you could walk the extra 1km north to **Otvai**, which is also close to Kalabahi and has staggering views over the bay, as well as many traditional houses.

East of Kalabahi and on the northern coast lies **Mali beach**. It has a good stretch of white sand and is very picturesque, but the coral here does not live up to its reputation. It's a ten-kilometre bus ride from Kalabahi bus terminal (Rp1000). If snorkelling is your sport of choice, you'd be better off heading around the northern coast of Kalabahi Bay. The first place of note on this road is **ALOR KECIL**, which has a rather poor showcase traditional house (with a big sign saying "traditional house" outside) and a couple of exceptional *moko* drums. The *kepala sekola* (schoolmaster) has a collection of five or six small drums, but the best are kept in a clearing inland; to see these amazing objects, you'll need to speak to the kepala desa and pay him about Rp5000–10,000. The beach in front of the village is covered with sharp stones and broken coral and is not recommended. However, if you take a boat to **PULAU KEPA** directly across the bay (around Rp1000, but bargain hard), the **snorkelling** is fantastic. Visibility is excellent, and there are lots of big fish out by the northward cape and off a cove on the western side. The waters here are well known for running so cold that they occasionally stun fish, bringing them floating to the surface; be wary of the strong currents. For details of the homestay on Kepa, see p.765.

Continuing round the coast, the next settlement is **ALOR BESAR**. The village is also very picturesque, and the kepala desa keeps a good collection of drums; betel nut or cigarettes are a good exchange for a look. The snorkelling off the coast here is also good, but even better at **SEBANJAR**, another 3–4km north. About 100m off shore is a drop-off running parallel to the beach for about 1km. The currents are strong, so if you enter the water from the end of the beach furthest from Alor Besar, then you can just drift down the reef's entire length. The coral is spectacular and there are large numbers of beautiful coloured fish. Although buses run all the way round to Sebanjar from Kalabahi, on the way back they become very irregular in the afternoon, stopping at about 3pm.

If you fancy a **trek** – with the knowledge that you'll have somewhere to stay at the end – take the long walk inland to **ATIMELANG**, the village that hosted one of the first Western anthropologists on Alor. Cora Dubois's *The People of Alor* was based on her experiences here in the 1930s, and much of the village is still recognizable from her descriptions. The village is an arduous but rewarding uphill hike, which takes about five hours from Takpala. If you speak good Indonesian, you can make the trip alone, asking for directions on the way. Otherwise, it's worth asking at the *Adi Dharma* losmen in Kalabahi to see if they can put you in touch with a guide. Once in Atimelang, the friendly kepala desa has a reasonably comfortable room where you can stay and eat.

The best place to see Alor's own brand of **ikat** being made is on the islands of **TERNATE** and **BUAYA**, situated just outside Kalabahi Bay. The *ikat* made on these two islands is actually quite similar to the more famous stuff being made on Lembata, but is much cheaper. There's also good snorkelling around

Moving on from Alor

The schedules for all modes of transport from Alor are subject to sudden and unreasonable changes. **Ferries** out of Alor depart from the western jetty, and other boats from the main harbour in the middle of town, heading to **Kupang** on West Timor, **Atapupu** in West Timor and **Larantuka**; currently just the *Diana Express* sails to **Belauring** on Lembata, with the two wooden ferries, which also stop at **Baranusa** on Pantar, at least temporarily out of service. The faster and more comfortable Pelni ferry *KM Awu* leaves from Kalabahi once a week (currently Thursday or Friday), travelling alternately to Kupang and **Maumere**; the Pelni office lies at Jl Cokroaminto 6 (☎0386/21195).

There's also one Merpati **flight** weekly to Kupang; a bemo to the airport costs Rp10,000.

these two islands, and it's best to charter a motorboat for a whole day in Kalabahi: a charter will cost around US$60. Buaya, which means "crocodile" in Indonesian, was once populated with a large number of fearsome saltwater crocodiles, who have been known to wander into Kalabahi and stroll into the market. However, during World War II the Japanese had a base on Buaya and ate the creatures.

Pantar

Pantar lies between Alor and Lembata, and remains one of the least-visited paradises in Indonesia – but only because it is difficult to get to and is such an unknown quantity, definitely not because it lacks interest. There are areas on Pantar where TV, electricity and foreigners are still unknown, and where traditional life has continued unaltered for centuries. Although currently out of action, the two **ferries** that plied the route from Kalabahi to Belauring on Lembata used to call in at Pantar on their way (every 2 days; 4hr; Rp10,000) and will hopefully do so again soon.

The main docking point in Pantar is **BARANUSA**, a small village in a cove at the centre of the north-facing coast. It's a good place to base yourself: the kepala desa has a four-room homestay (❷), and can provide you with basic meals; you'll definitely be the centre of attention. From February to April there are wedding and harvest festivals in the village, with dancing, feasting and music made with *moko* drums, gongs and bells.

If you fancy climbing an active volcano, take one of the daily trucks from Baranusa to **KAKAMAUTA**, about 15km inland and situated on the slopes of **Gunung Situng**. The kepala desa here rents out a room and can provide food but, as with everywhere in Pantar, it's always best to bring your own water; they may have some boiled water, but you can't count on it. The village sits at nearly 1000m, and you'll be glad of your sleeping bag. From Kakamauta, it takes just over an hour to climb to the rim, and the view of the colossal crater is spectacular. Try and get here early, as the clouds may soon roll in and obscure the view. Local kids will gladly get up early to guide you, for a few thousand rupiah. The truck heading back to Baranusa generally passes through Kakamauta mid-afternoon.

Another fascinating trip from Baranusa is to the south coast. A track runs across the island through Latuna to **Puntaru**, where the beach is covered in multicoloured sand and pebbles: trucks run the entire distance every day. At **KABIR** on the northwest coast, Pantar's largest village and district capital, hot springs burst up from beneath the seabed. Here you can enjoy the unusual experience of snorkelling in hot water, and the beach and coral gardens are pretty extensive and relatively pristine. If you are looking for a real **snorkelling** extravaganza, rent one of the sampans dotted around the harbours of Baranusa and Kabir for a safari, and head out around the coast or to the islands offshore: figure on between Rp40,000 and Rp60,000 per sampan a day. You will, of course, need your own snorkelling equipment.

West Timor

West Timor occupies the western half of the island of Timor, with the other half occupied by the newly independent East Timor. The violence and brutality that surrounded East Timor's struggle for independence was typical of this island, no stranger to upheaval and bloodshed. Though things have calmed down a lot since the late 1990s, the foreign offices of most Western nations still advise their citizens against visiting. That said, a number of travellers are beginning to return to Timor's shores, mainly in order to carry out a visa-run to Dili. For details on this visa-run, please see the box on p.783, while for advice on travelling safely in Timor, see the box on p.771.

West Timor sits at the extreme eastern end of the **Sunda Islands**, a chain beginning in Pulau Weh off the north coast of Sumatra and terminating just above East Timor. Unlike the vast majority of islands in this sequence, Timor is not volcanic; even so, the backbone of the island is extremely mountainous. Timor's biggest natural asset was (and to a much lesser extent still is) **sandalwood**, a richly fragrant timber much prized by Asian and European traders for centuries. The overfelling of sandalwood trees has led to minor ecological disasters, with wholesale topsoil erosion of land that was already poor, without the compensating enrichment of volcanic ash, leaving great swaths of the landscape barren.

The main city of West Timor is **Kupang**, a sweaty, noisy maelstrom with everything that's unpalatable in Asian cities – alongside the best restaurants and hotels for hundreds of kilometres. West Timor has vast areas where Western visitors are still a rarity. While the landscapes here are desolate, they can also be starkly beautiful, especially in the mountains around Soe and Kefamenanu. Isolated tribal kingdoms in the centre of the island have maintained unique houses, costumes, festivals and lifestyles, fascinating for anthropologists, photographers and travellers alike. From Kupang, the few travellers still willing to risk a tour around this troubled island head north to **Camplong** and then **Soe**, both hill towns with cool climates, fine *ikat* weavings and a few springs and waterfalls. Close to Soe is the tiny kingdom of **Boti**, a place that maintains ancient traditions and the distinctive "beehive"-style houses of the area. From either of the two towns, you can make numerous other day-trips to colourful markets, secluded tribal villages and scenic areas high in the mountains. Further north is **Kefamenanu**, also a centre of *ikat* weaving and the base for another excursion into tribal Timor in the village of **Tamkessi**.

The main highway running from Kupang to the border town of Atambua and on to Dili in the newly independent state of East Timor is an excellent sealed road, traversed by regular, well-maintained buses. However, the rest of the island is crisscrossed with poor, disintegrating tracks that can be impassable after heavy rain and are susceptible to subsidence and landslides. Public transport is poor, with irregular services and tatty buses.

The **climate** in West Timor differs dramatically from nearby islands such as Flores. In the most intense part of the dry season between June and October, the land is swept by monsoon winds blowing off the deserts of Australia and becomes unbearably hot and dusty. Along with Roti and Savu, Timor not only suffers oppressively arid periods, but is far enough south to risk tropical cyclones.

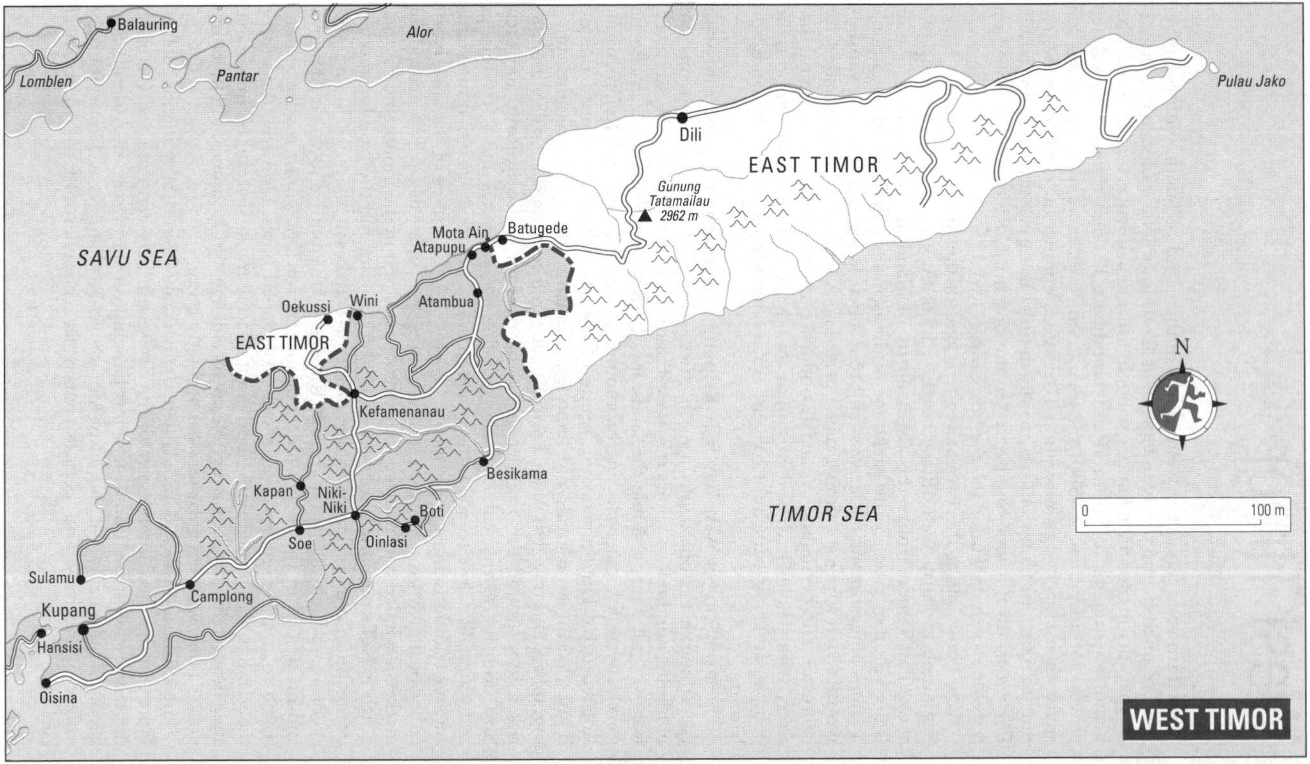

WEST TIMOR

Balauring
Alor
Lomblen
Pantar
Pulau Jako
Dili
EAST TIMOR
Gunung Tatamailau 2962 m
SAVU SEA
Mota Ain
Batugede
Atapupu
Atambua
Oekussi
Wini
EAST TIMOR
Kefamenanau
Besikama
Kapan
Niki-Niki
Boti
Soe
Oinlasi
TIMOR SEA
N
0
100 m
Sulamu
Camplong
Kupang
Hansisi
Oisina

West Timor travel advice

Since September 1999, when three UN workers were brutally murdered in the West Timor border town of Atambua, most countries have advised their citizens against travelling in Timor; and except for the occasional foreigner on his way to Dili to pick up a new visa, most travellers have heeded this advice. Kupang, the one place in West Timor which, thanks to its excellent travel connections with the rest of Nusa Tenggara, does still see tourists regularly, is safe at the time of writing, and the anti-Western (in particular, anti-Australian) resentment that occurred in the town immediately following the UN intervention in East Timor has largely dissipated now. During the research of this book we also visited Soe, Kefamenanu and Atambua, again without any problems, though some travellers have reported being on the receiving end of verbal abuse in Atambua, where there is still a rather uneasy atmosphere. While the situation seems to be improving, contact your foreign office (or look at the foreign office websites – see p.26), and follow their advice.

Some history

The indigenous inhabitants of Timor can trace their ancestry back nearly fourteen thousand years, to when a people perhaps related to the modern Atoni tribes roamed the island. The Atoni now live mainly in the mountains of West Timor and comprise nearly half its population. The other major ethnic group in Timor are the Tetum, who originated from migrant peoples from Sulawesi and Flores and probably started to squeeze the Atoni out of their lands from the fourteenth century onwards. Now the Tetum mainly inhabit areas of East Timor, being the most significant ethnic group there.

The majority of early visitors to Timor were lured by the sandalwood that once covered Timor's mountainsides. The **Chinese** arrived as early as the sixth or seventh century, and set the tone for future visitors by supplementing their cargoes with Timorese slaves. Europeans didn't arrive until the early sixteenth century, when the **Portuguese** used their garrisons on Flores and Solor to base expeditions into Timor, bringing with them smallpox and venereal diseases. The **Dutch** also made tentative forays into the interior in search of the wood and slaves, finally setting up a large garrison in Kupang in the mid-seventeenth century. The Portuguese never acceded their interests in the area, and in 1702 declared Timor a Portuguese colony under the control of Goa, though this declaration had little real effect on the rule of ascendant native kingdoms. By the mid-eighteenth century, the Portuguese had been pushed east, where they controlled East Timor, including the small province of Oekussi.

While European influence in terms of religion and language took effect in some areas, the Timorese had earned their reputation as brave and aggressive warriors who didn't succumb to pressure easily. The central areas of the island remained independent of colonialism, some of them only succumbing to foreign rule in the early part of the twentieth century. While the western part of Timor became part of Indonesia upon Independence in 1945, the east remained under Portugal's control until 1974.

For details of East Timor's troubled modern history, see pp.772–773.

Kupang and around

The dusty and chaotic streets of **KUPANG**, the biggest city in east Nusa Tenggara, are a mixture of torment and relief for the average traveller. Most would praise the city's facilities and food compared to those of neighbouring islands, but the pace, noise and grime can be trying; your seat on a typical

Kupang bemo, for example, is likely to be an immense speaker with the bass turned up to full volume. Furthermore, East Timor's painful split from its western neighbour, and the part that Western UN troops played in helping the separation, has helped to foster resentment against westerners in general: indeed,

East Timor: the birth of a nation

The modern history of East Timor began in 1904, when the Portuguese and Dutch divided Timor into provinces and East Timor was annexed from the rest of the island. **Portuguese control** continued until the advent of World War II, when the Japanese landed here in great numbers. The allies, fearing for the safety of nearby Australia, sent thousands of ANZAC troops into the hinterlands, where they waged a successful guerrilla war against the Japanese. The Timorese harboured the Australians and many fought with them against the Japanese. Retaliation was savage: an estimated 60,000 East Timorese were killed during the Japanese occupation, about thirteen percent of the population. When the Japanese ceded the land to Portugal at the end of the war, slave labour was reinstated, and only ten percent of the population were educated to basic literacy. There was no electricity or running water anywhere, and malaria was rife. In 1974, following the overthrow of the fascist Caetano regime, the incoming government declared that many of the colonial states were illegally occupied. East Timor was left to face its future alone, without external rule for the first time in nearly three hundred years.

Three parties formed, aspiring to lead the new country. In 1975, the first free general elections in East Timor's history resulted in a landslide victory for the **Fretilin** party, who wanted independence for East Timor, confident that they could at least rely on the support of their wartime ally Australia. They formed a transitional government, while the other two parties formed a coalition opposition. This coalition branded Fretilin as communists, and a small **civil war** followed, from which Fretilin comfortably emerged as victors, claiming independence for the new Democratic Republic of East Timor.

The Indonesian invasion

On December 7, 1975, Indonesian president Suharto held talks with US President Ford and Henry Kissinger. Just hours after the talks were completed, **Indonesia invaded** East Timor. In the first year of the conflict, eighty percent of Dili's male population were killed. The UN general assembly and Security Council passed ten resolutions calling on Indonesia to withdraw their troops: all were ignored. The savagery of the invading regime drove the Fretilin members into the highlands, where they fought a protracted guerrilla war. The Indonesian army stifled the independence movement with political executions, imprisonments and kidnappings; Amnesty International reports estimate that, between 1976 and 1986, 200,000 people out of a population of 700,000 were killed.

The **Western world** was far from blameless in what has come to be described as the attempted genocide of the East Timorese. The Australian Prime Minister Gough Whitlam told Suharto in 1974 that the dissolution of East Timor was "inevitable", and Australia's largest oil companies were duly given contracts to drill for oil and gas in the Timor strait. Over a ten-year period, America and Britain provided over a billion dollars' worth of **arms** to Indonesia. On November 12, 1991, the East Timor problem was brought to world attention when a massacre at a funeral in Dili's **Santa Cruz cemetery** was captured on film and relayed to the world's press. Around 5000 people had gathered to commemorate Sebastien Gomes, who had been shot by Indonesian troops two weeks earlier. Indonesian troops entered the cemetery and, without provocation, opened fire, killing an estimated 528 people.

The **Indonesian people** had no reports of the 1991 massacre, and were generally there's even a few West Timorese who have decided to drop the traditional "Hello Mister" in favour of something altogether less friendly, the "hello" replaced by something rather less welcoming. The vast majority of Kupang's population remain very welcoming, however, and although it can

told by their media that East Timor was a troublesome, irrelevant little province. However, the 1997 **Nobel peace prize** was awarded to Bishop Carlos Felipe Ximenes Belo and Jose Ramos Horta, the two loudest voices of the East Timorese in their fight for freedom. In another positive move, the jailed East Timorese resistance leader **Jose Alexandre "Xanana" Gusmao** was released from high-security prison in Jakarta and placed under house arrest, in order for him to play a role in bringing peace to the territory.

Independence

In January 1999, President Habibie promised to grant the province independence if his offer of autonomy was rejected. In the poll that followed later that same year, the Timorese, despite intimidation from pro-Indonesian militia and soldiers, voted overwhelmingly to sever all ties with Indonesia. This led to yet further violence as the pro-Jakarta militias ran rampage throughout the province, creating a wave of unprecedented bloodletting that the Indonesian military did little to stem. The UN were finally forced to step in, with an 8000-strong multinational force charged with the task of restoring the peace. The Indonesian army withdrew in shame the following month, and peace slowly returned to the region.

In October 1999, the United Nations Transitional Administration in East Timor (UNTAET) officially took control of the territory, with a mandate to help the Timorese rebuild their territory, enforce law and order, and help the establishment of a effective democratic government. In one of the first major steps towards this, in August 2001 an 88-seat Constituent Assembly, charged with drawing up East Timor's constitution, was elected. Full presidential elections were held on April 14, 2002, and were won by the charismatic **Xanana Gusmao** who, despite earlier protestations that he had no ambitions to be president (in one interview he stated that he'd rather stay at home on his farm and grow pumpkins), was forced by popular demand to stand. On May 19, 2002, the state of East Timor was officially declared to be independent.

The future

That is unlikely to be the end of East Timor's troubles, however. Almost every family in the state lost at least one member during the struggle for independence and the post-election bloodbath. Many of the survivors are still traumatized, and it is perhaps little wonder that East Timor is currently said to have the highest levels of domestic violence in the world. Unemployment is also an incredible ninety percent in some areas, and other than coffee growing, East Timor has few profitable industries. Tourism is a possibility for the future, with some wonderful beaches, superb diving and the occasional Portuguese building as possible attractions, though with the Timorese keen to adopt the US dollar as their permanent currency, the country is in danger of being seen as nothing but a more expensive, smaller, poorer and less colourful version of Bali. Whispers of a US naval base being established on the island is one possible source of much-needed foreign currency, but perhaps their greatest hope lies in the newly discovered oil and gas fields in the Timor Strait. In an agreement signed in 2001 with Indonesia and Australia, Timor is to get ninety percent of the revenue, which should amount to billions of dollars over the next twenty years. It will be sometime before either of these prospects becomes reality, however: until then, the world's newest state faces a difficult time.

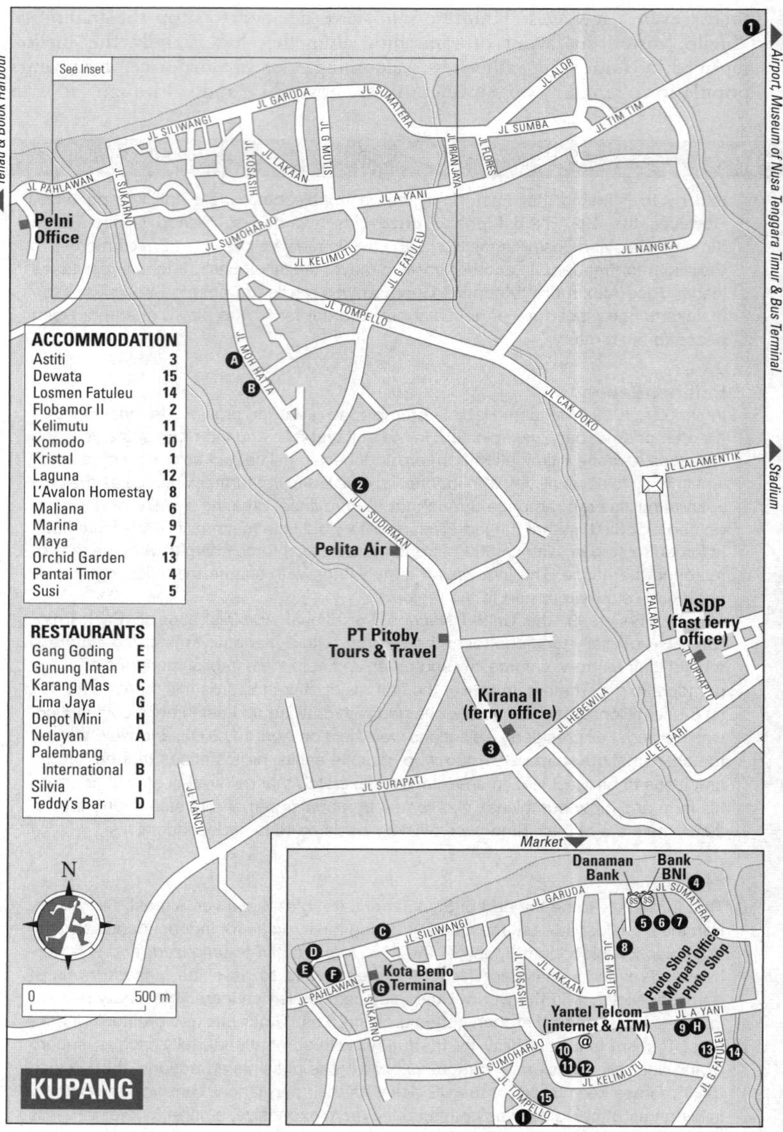

come as a relief to leave the smog and the noise of Kupang behind, you will in time probably miss the good food, cold beers and excellent facilities this town has to offer.

One of the few real sights in town is the **Museum of Nusa Tenggara Timur** (daily 8am–4pm; donation), about 300m from the bus terminal. It has an excellent collection of *ikat* from the area and a few other artefacts such as a *moko* drum from Alor and drawings of all the area's traditional houses and megaliths. An easy escape from the city itself is the **natural swimming pool** 1km south of town. There used to be some losmen nearby, and if tourists ever return to Timor, you can expect these to reopen.

Kupang's recorded history dates back to the seventeenth and eighteenth centuries, when the Dutch East India Company were active in the area. Their interest petered out once the stands of sandalwood around the city had been felled, and Kupang was all but deserted until the beginning of the twentieth century, when missionaries began to use it as a base for expeditions into central Timor. Kupang has an additional footnote in history as the place where a haggard Captain Bligh finally came ashore in 1789, having sailed nearly 6000km in an open boat, following the legendary mutiny on *HMS Bounty*.

Practicalities

The **Oebolo bus terminal**, about 6km east of town in **Walikota**, services all major destinations outside of Kupang. Swarms of bemos wait here to ferry passengers to the centre of town at the **Terminal Kota**, a bemo stand/square surrounded by shops right by the waterfront, at the heart of Kupang city. The **El Tari Airport** is another 10km from Oebolo to the east; the most convenient way to get into town from here is by one of the many taxis waiting outside (Rp25,000). Alternatively, walk out to the main road and flag down a passing bemo (Rp2500). There are two ports serving Kupang: all Pelni and fast ferries dock at **Tenau harbour** 13km west of town, while the smaller **Bolok harbour** lies 10km to the west of Kupang and serves all the local/car ferries; unnumbered bemos run to both ports.

Kupang is a fairly large city, and getting around involves frequent use of **bemos** (Rp1000 around town). It's best to ask a local which bemo you need, as the system can be a little complex and the numbers change constantly.

Leaving Timor

Most hotels have the latest schedules for the **slow (car) ferries** that use Bolok harbour, though you may want to double-check at the ticket office at the harbour to find out the exact departure time. Currently, there are services to Larantuka (Tues, Thurs & Sun), Waingapu via Aimere (Thurs & Sun), Ende (Fri), Alor (Tues & Sat), Sabu (Wed) and Roti (daily at 8am). For these ferries, you buy your ticket at the harbour before boarding the ship.

All Pelni and fast ferry boats leave from **Tenau harbour** (bemo #12 from Terminal Kota). The **Pelni office** (Mon–Fri 8.30am–noon & 1–2pm, Sat 8.30–11am; ⓣ0380/833804) is set slightly back from the road at Jl Pahlawan 3; from the Terminal Kota, head over the river bridge and up the hill, and it's on your left-hand side. The Pelni vessels *KM Dorolonda*, *KM Dobonsolo*, *Awu*, *KM Wilis*, *KM Sirimau*, *KM Tatamailau* and *KM Kelimutu* all call in at this harbour, as do the ASDP fast ferries *KM Barito* (to Waingapu, Bima and Benoa on Bali) and *KM Serayu* (Maumere, Bima, Benoa and Surabaya). The **ASDP** office for fast ferry tickets is at Jl Suprapto 2 (ⓣ0380/838830). The office for the car ferry *KM Kirana II* (leaving every Friday to Ende and Surabaya) lies opposite the *Hotel Astiti* on Jalan Sudirman.

Alternatively, the main agent in town for both Pelni and the fast ferries is the efficient **travel agent** Pitoby Tours and Travel Services at Jl Sudirman 140 (ⓣ0380/832700); they are also the agents for all the airlines flying out of Kupang. **Pelita** are back down the hill at Jl Sudirman 82 (ⓣ0380/827111); they have four flights weekly to Denpasar, and on to Surabaya, Yogyakarta and Jakarta. **Merpati**, with daily flights to Surabaya via Denpasar and less frequent flights to many destinations within Nusa Tenggara, are at Jl A Yani 6 (ⓣ0380/833833).

Useful ones include #2 to the Oebolo bus terminal and #3 or #8 to the Tabun bemo terminal (for local destinations to the east of Kupang). Many out-of-town bemos now display destination names rather than numbers.

Of the **banks**, the Danamon and BNI on the seafront near the hotels are your best bet for changing travellers' cheques, though nearly all of them accept US dollars cash. The BNI also has an **ATM** that accepts Visa and Maestro/Cirrus cards; another ATM is located at the *Hotel Astiti*, along Jalan Sudirman by the Telkom office.

The main **post office** lies 3km out of town, on Jalan Palapa (Mon–Sat 7am–4pm); take a #5 bemo from Terminal Kota. The Yantel **telephone office** is far more central on Jalan Yani. Both the post office and the Yantel have **internet facilities**; those at the latter are particularly fast and efficient. If you've just come from East Timor and want to try to change your visa from thirty to sixty days (see p.783), the **immigration office** is 4km out of town on Jalan Thamrin (ⓣ0380/831840).

Kutang is one of the few places where you can buy slide films, and there are two good **photo shops**, Studio Pro and Roda Baru, on Jalan Yani near the Merpati office. A couple of **souvenir shops** are also recommended, if only because they sell goods from all over Nusa Tenggara: Sinar Baru Foto at Jl Siliwangi 94, opposite the bemo terminal, and Loka Binkra by the main intersection opposite the large Bank Mandiri.

Accommodation

Kupang is unique on Timor for the amount and variety of **accommodation** available – although the current slump in the numbers of tourists visiting has led to the closure of many of the backpacker options.

Astiti Jl Sudirman 146 ⓣ0380/821810. Rather inconveniently situated at the top end of the hill, this is nevertheless a fine place. All rooms come with TV, air-con and en-suite mandi and rates include breakfast; the hotel also has an ATM machine and Merpati agent. ❹

Hotel Dewata Jl Tompello 17 ⓣ0380/821409. Perched neatly on the hill, a sprawling place with a wide range of rooms, from cheapies with outside bathroom to rooms with air-con and TV. ❷–❸

Losmen Fatuleu Jl Gunung Fatuleu 1 ⓣ0380/824518. Opposite the *Orchid Garden*; a bit dark and basic, but inexpensive, friendly and acceptable. ❷

Hotel Flobamor II Jl Sudirman 21 ⓣ0380/833476. Houses a dive centre (currently closed) and a small Merpati agent. All rooms have air-con, hot water, a minibar, ice machine and TV, though the rooms themselves have seen better days. Singles and doubles are the same price. ❸

Hotel Kelimutu Jl Kelimutu 38 ⓣ0380/831179. A friendly enough place, almost identical to its neighbour the *Komodo*, and charging the same prices; it can also offer lots of information about ferry and flight schedules. Rooms come with fan or air-con. ❸

Hotel Komodo Jl Kelimutu 40 ⓣ0380/822638. One of three hotels on a small road behind the telephone office, with room rates and facilities identical to its neighbour the *Kelimutu*. ❸

Hotel Kristal Jl Tim Tim 59 ⓣ0380/825100, ⓕ825104. This is the most expensive hotel around, but they offer discounts during the off-season. The luxuries include a large swimming pool, TV and air-con. ❼

Hotel Laguna Jl Kelimutu 36 ⓣ0380/833559. Perhaps the best of the three in this neighbourhood, set back from the road, its ekonomi singles with shared mandi and fan are the cheapest in town. More salubrious rooms come with en-suite bathroom and its best rooms have air-con and TV. ❶–❸

L'Avalon Homestay 30m down an alleyway off Jl Sumatera near the Danamon bank, on the right hand side as you head away from the sea ⓣ0380/832278. Closed due to lack of custom, but if backpackers ever return it's hard to see the irrepressible owner, Edwin Lerrick, resisting the temptation to reopen. He's a mine of information and the best person to speak to about the visa-run to East Timor. The rooms are currently in a parlous state, but it's nothing that a spring clean won't cure. If it does reopen, expect it to be both cheap and busy.

Hotel Maliana Jl Sumatera 35 ⓣ0380/821879 Simple and clean, though it suffers in comparison to the better-value *Maya* next door. The more expensive rooms are reasonable, however, with air-con and en-suite mandi. ❸

Hotel Marina Jl Jenderal Ahmad Yani 79 ☎0380/822566. Lovely and clean with delightful staff, the airy and sizeable best rooms are especially good value. Some have fan and shared mandi, while the more expensive rooms have air-con and TV. ❷–❸

Hotel Maya Jl Sumatera 31 ☎0380/832169. Quite plush for the price, with a good restaurant, and all the rooms feature air-con, TV, phone and bathtubs; the most expensive rooms also have hot water. ❸

Hotel Orchid Garden Jl Gunung Fateleu 2 ☎0380/833707, Ⓕ833707. The most upmarket place in town, with prices to match, and popular with tour groups. It has beautiful cottages around a sculpted pool, with a tame deer that wanders into your bedroom. Nonresidents can use the pool for a fee that varies, depending on who's running reception. ❹

Pantai Timor Jl Sumatera ☎0380/831651. A bit of a letdown: it looks great from the outside, but the rooms smell a little musty, though they do all come with air-con, which makes the cheapest ones good value. It also has a restaurant with great views overlooking the sea, though the food is distinctly average. ❷

Hotel Susi Jl Sumatera 37 ☎0380/822172. A pleasant place, clean and quiet with large communal areas, and the economy rooms are currently the cheapest on the seafront, though they're pretty grim; the more expensive rooms have air-con and TV. Has a steakhouse attached (see below). ❶–❷

Eating and drinking

Kupang is one of the few places east of Lombok offering a real diversity of food. Plenty of **night warung** are scattered throughout the city, the largest concentration being around Terminal Kota.

Depot Mini Jl Yani. Decent and reasonably priced Chinese grub and cold beers, reasonably convenient for the seafront hotels.

Gang Goding Next to *Teddy's Bar* at the western end of Jalan Siliwangi. Closed at the time of writing, and locals are uncertain whether it will reopen or not. If it does, expect cold beer and reasonably priced food served by a garrulous Australian.

Gunung Intan Jl Ikan Paus 14A. A bakery with a mixture of sweet bread, savoury snacks, strangely coloured cakes and unusual pastries.

Karang Mas Jl Siliwangi 88. Seafood and basic Indonesian dishes – perhaps a touch more expensive than you'll be used to paying, but the seafront balcony is a plus.

Lima Jaya Jl Sukarno 15. Chinese and Indonesian food, popular with locals for the nightclub upstairs.

Nelayan Jl Mohammed Hatta. On the right-hand side of the road heading south from the centre of town. Not as crowded as its better-known neighbour the *Palembang International*, but the meals are just as good, with an endless variety of seafood. Expect to pay around Rp40,000 for a full meal, with several different dishes for your main course.

Palembang International Jl Mohammed Hatta 54. A terrific option: the king prawns in chilli are excellent; the lobster and grilled fish superb. At night, everything is cooked in woks and barbecues right out by the pavement, the frantic bustle and flames of the open kitchen giving the place a frenetic and informal feel.

Silvia Jl Beringin. A good place to eat, more for the calm atmosphere, soft music, well-made furniture and pleasant staff as for the Western-style food on the menu, which is OK but not extraordinary.

Susi Steakhouse In the hotel of the same name. The cheaper meals are often either unavailable or unexceptional, but their steak sizzlers or fish from the day's catch (Rp27,500) are a treat.

Teddy's Bar On the seafront at the western end of Jl Siliwangi. This is the expat hangout of Kupang, serving burgers, pizzas and other Western fare. It's overpriced, but a reasonable spot for a cold beer, with lots of expensive imported brews.

Around Kupang

There are several reasonable **beaches** around Kupang. **Tablalong** lies 15km west of town; it's clean, and a better place for a swim than the closer and more popular **Lasiana beach**. To get to Tablalong, take bemo #3 (Rp1000) to the Tabun terminal and then Bemo Tablalong (Rp2000). Both beaches are busy at the weekends. The best beaches are on the islands just off Timor's western shore. **Monkey Island** has some excellent snorkelling and pristine beaches, but you'll have to charter a boat to get there, which, at around US$60 for a day, should at least assure that you have the beach to yourself. **Pulau Semauo**, on the other hand, is serviced by regular public boats departing daily: they leave whenever there are enough passengers from Tenau harbour and cost Rp8000 per person. There are decent beaches and a delightful **natural spring** on the island – and no cars or blaring bemos.

There is a beautiful **waterfall** 15km from Kupang at **Oenesu**, with two steps; one of about 15m, the other of about 7m. Reasonable Tarzan impressions can be achieved jumping from the top, but beware of the slippery banks when climbing up. It's a great place to escape the Kupang sweat: take bemo #3 to the Tabun terminal and then Bemo Oenesu. Depending on where the bemo driver stops, you may have to walk the last 2km or so from the main road. Out by Bolok Harbour, where the ferries arrive, 10km west of town, is an **underground cavern** with crystal-clear freshwater springs. It can be a little creepy swimming in the pitch darkness, so it's worth bringing a torch. To get there, take the Bolok bemo and get off as it makes the final right turn down towards the port. Local kids always seem to be waiting to guide you down to the caves for a few hundred rupiah.

Finally, there are a few "recreation spots" near to Kupang. One popular site used to be the village of **Bone**, south of Kupang, which has a few *rumah adat*. From the village, ask for a guide to take you the 5km to a waterfall, which is good for swimming. **Desa Oebelo**, about 20km east of Kupang, is the home of a cottage industry, where the Rotinese *sasando* and *Ti'i Langga* are made (see box below): the instrument is beautiful, the sound it makes is divine, and it would make the perfect souvenir if it wasn't so fragile.

Soe and around

Once a Dutch hill station, **SOE**, 110km north of Kupang, is now a thriving town with many attractive villages in the surrounding hills. The town was taken over by the Dutch during a brutal campaign of "pacification" at the turn of the last century. Hundreds of people come from miles around to the **market**, to sell everything from *ikat* to betel-nut and herbal medicines. The most distinctive feature of the villages around Soe district is the beehive-style **traditional houses** or *lopo*. Most of these also have another structure without walls in front

Timorese crafts

The best place for buying West Timorese **crafts** is in the central regions of Soe and Kefamenanu, where **weaving** and **carving** traditions are still thriving. Macabre **masks** and other primitive carvings are made from rosewood, sandalwood and mahogany. Some of the tribal peoples still hunt with blowpipes and boomerangs – rarely decorative, but still good souvenirs. The most impressive of Timorese crafts are the **ikat** fabrics produced in the central highlands; these cloths are unusually bright, notable for the vibrant reds used as background colour.

The *sasando* is a many-stringed **musical instrument**, most often associated with Roti but also found on Timor. Some have as many as 34 strings, and the body is generally woven from firm *lontar* palm leaves; you can see a rather bad drawing of one on the back of the old Rp5000 note. Another oddity that originates on Roti is the *Ti'i langga*, a bizarre cowboy-style **hat**, also woven from *lontar* leaves, and usually adorned with a pinnacle that points heavenwards; this allows the celestial spirits a direct route to the brain, a kind of divine antenna. They're often ornamented with plastic flowers and coloured ribbons, which can look rather incongruous on a gnarled Rotinese labourer.

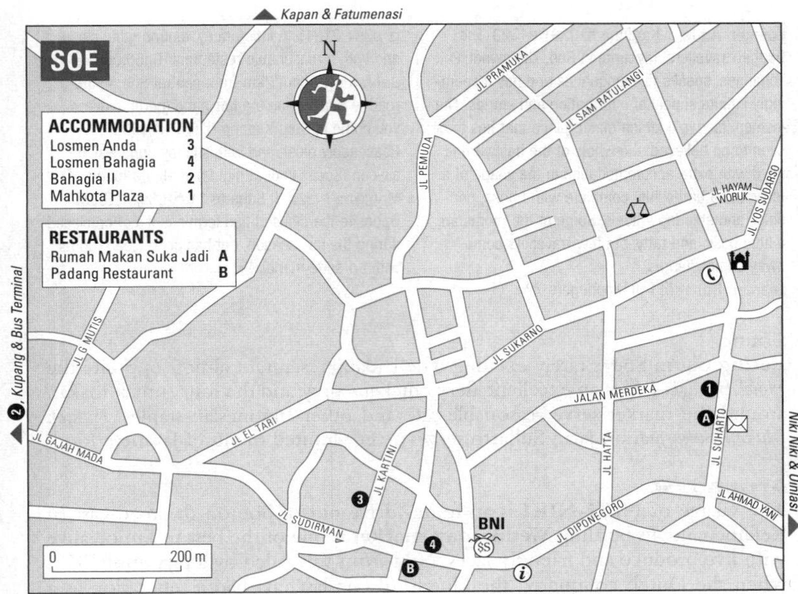

of the main house, its thatched roof supported on carved pillars; these serve as a meeting place and somewhere for the women of the family to do their day-time chores, shaded from the sun but with the benefit of the breeze. The Indonesian government actually banned *lopo* houses, considering them unhealthy, and, certainly if you ever have the chance to go inside one, the acrid, smoky interior feels decidedly noxious. The people of Soe, however, prefer them to their new cold, concrete abodes, and generally still build *lopo* – ostensibly for use as stores.

If you're intending to visit these villages, the best way to get around outside of town is by motorbike: ask around at any of the losmen or hotels.

Practicalities

The **town** itself is fairly compact. The main street is Jalan Diponegoro, which features a Western-style supermarket, three souvenir shops, a wartel, and tourist office that opens whenever they feel like it. Soe's **bemo** system is very efficient, most bemos doing a round-trip to the market and then to the out-of-town **bus station**, which lies to the west of town.

Be warned that the **BNI bank** on Jalan Diponegoro will only change US dollars cash, though rumour has it an **ATM** is about to open here. The **souvenir shop** next door to the *Bahagia I* has some excellent *ikat* and some of the few genuine antique masks found in Timor. Starting prices are very high, but if you are prepared for lengthy bargaining, it's possible to get the asking price halved.

Accommodation

Most buses into Soe will drop you off on Jalan Diponegoro, within walking distance of the majority of **accommodation** places.

Losmen Anda Jl Kartini 5 ⓣ0391/21323. The budget-travellers' favourite in Soe. The owner, Pak Yohannes, speaks five languages and has a seemingly infinite supply of information and stories. The losmen itself is a kitsch masterpiece that has to be seen to be believed: the whole of the backyard is filled with extra accommodation in the shape of a ferry and a battleship, complete with bunks, portholes and steering wheels. Some of the rooms are a little basic and tatty, but few travellers come away complaining. ❷

Losmen Bahagia I Jl Diponegoro 72 ⓣ0391/21015. A little pricey, though quite clean and with a reasonable restaurant. Rp60,000. ❷

Bahagia II About 2km from central Soe on the road to Kupang, on the left-hand (north) side as you come in from Kupang ⓣ0391/21095. Reasonably plush and with slightly unnecessary air-con (Soe is cool at nights) in all the rooms. ❸

Mahkota Plaza Jl Suharto 11 ⓣ0391/21068. Opposite the disused bus terminal. It's often closed during the low season, but has good clean rooms with en-suite mandi. ❷

Eating

Eating out in Soe is rarely exciting. The Padang restaurant almost opposite the *Hotel Bahagia I* does an excellent, fiery chicken curry, and the four rumah makan around the market serve reasonable sate and other Indonesian staples. *Rumah Makan Suka Jadi* on Jalan Suharto serves a very limited menu of Javanese food.

Around Soe

The village of **NIKI-NIKI** is an hour's drive out of Soe on the road east to Kefamenanu; its bustling **Wednesday market** is one of the best in Timor, alive with live produce and friendly faces. Niki-Niki was ruled by a raja until 1912, when the Dutch conquered the kingdom. The last raja had a reputation as a brutal tyrant who used to butcher his enemies publicly and display parts of their bodies on poles around the village. The **royal graves** are behind the old raja's house and worth a look. There are a couple of reasonable **warung** in Niki-Niki, but no losmen.

About 8km north of Soe, **Oehala** is the site of a set of **waterfalls**, well shaded and with many pools that you can bathe (but not quite swim) in. It's a nice spot, popular with locals at the weekends, when there are direct bemos all the way down to the falls. At other times, you'll have to catch a bus or bemo from Soe market to Kapan, asking the driver to drop you off at the Oehala turn-off. From here, it's a downhill stroll of about 3km (45min) to the falls.

Twenty kilometres north of Soe, **KAPAN** is another of the many towns in this area whose greatest asset is its **market**. The market here is on a Thursday, when the place really comes alive with colourful cloths, carved betel-nut holders and the usual selection of fruit and vegetables being sold. The drive up here is also very scenic, along one of the few asphalt roads in Timor off the main highway. A ninety-minute walk past Kapan is the fascinating village of **TUNUA**: head towards Fatumenasi from Kapan and then take the right turn by the first settlement you come to. Near to Tunua is a huge **obelisk**, split neatly down the middle, covered with plants and topped with magical musical stones. There are several important **ritual sites** in the area, which are difficult to visit on your own. An English-speaking guide might be able to help you get to them, but few of the locals even speak Indonesian, so some travellers who particularly want to see this area in depth bring one of the young guides all the way from Kupang.

The countryside from Kapan north to the village of **FATUMENASI** is dramatic; in particular, the road there offers spectacular views of **Gunung Mutis**, which towers to 2470m. Although the area is quite green by Timor's standards, there's little or no water, settlements are few and far between, and it gets ferociously hot. Fatumenasi is set among the most inhospitable of mountains, and gets few visitors, though it's cool at nights, and remains a quiet friendly place to see how the majority of Timorese people live. You can stay here with the kepala desa but there are no losmen or warung.

Boti

Lying 45km to the southeast of Soe, the kingdom of **BOTI** has become the most popular destination in the area. Boti has remained independent of external influence, due to its raja, a proud man who doesn't want to see the traditions of old Timor disappear. Boti now sees a steady influx of curious visitors and – ironically – the place now feels like a mock-up of a traditional village. Here you can visit a weaving co-operative, a small thatched workshop that women will suddenly and miraculously inhabit as soon as your presence is verified (work ceases immediately you have seen enough), a souvenir shop and big painted direction signs so you don't get lost. It's also one of the few places in Timor where the men are still forbidden from cutting their hair after they marry. The raja refuses to speak Indonesian (though he seems to understand it pretty well) and requires all guests to come with a guide from Soe (Rp50,000 normally, though with the current lack of tourists you can probably get one for Rp30,000). He particularly likes Marsellinus Besa, who is contactable through the *Losmen Anda*, as he speaks the local language and knows all the customs. It is essential to bring a bag of **betel nut** and the raja charges Rp15,000 per person to enter, eat with him and stay overnight in his purpose-built four-bedroom homestay. Note that he's not very keen on people wandering around Boti independently, and may forbid you to go anywhere without him. As he's well into his seventies and has trouble getting out onto the porch sometimes, this can be somewhat restrictive.

Getting to Boti is only straightforward if you have a **motorbike** (try negotiating with a bike owner in Soe, and expect to pay around US$10 per day), though you'll probably have to do some pushing and walking. If you want to go by public transport, catch a bus to **Oinlassi** (Rp7500) and then it's a three-hour walk (12km), and that's including the shortcut recommended by your guide. It's definitely not worth walking to Boti unless you plan on overnighting there.

Kefamenanu

KEFAMENANU, usually shortened to "Kefa", is a pleasant but anonymous little town northeast of Soe and nearly 100km north of Kupang. It's a good stop on the trans-island journey, both to break up long bus rides and as a base for excursions to the surrounding countryside – but always check with locals on the current situation before embarking on any trip out of town.

The town is centred around the marketplace, with the **post office** and supermarket both nearby. The **bus station** is about 2km south of town, but all the buses run through town, so you shouldn't need to go out there. There are several **losmen**: the *Soko Windu* (☎0391/31122; ❶) on Jalan Kartini is the cheapest place, with reasonable rooms, shared mandi and satellite TV for those pining for CNN, though at the time of writing all but one of the rooms is being used by families of refugees. The *Cendana* (☎0391/31168; ❷) is 1.5km out of town on Jalan Sonbai: you'll need to take a bemo (Rp1000) to get there – it's basic, with very small rooms and outside mandi. *Ariesta Losmen* (☎0391/31007; ❷) on Jalan Basuki Rachmat offers a choice of rooms with or without en-suite mandi. The *Ariesta Losmen*'s restaurant is about the only place in Kefa with **food** to tempt the average tourist, though in and around the market you'll find plenty of stalls and a few dodgy warung. You could also try the *Rumah Makan Padang* or the *Lumayan Sami Jaya*, also near the market.

Buses heading north to Atambua and beyond start leaving at about 7am, but there are usually only a few in the afternoon. Buses south to Kupang run almost all day.

Tamkessi

Visitors looking for a genuine insight into Timor's animist heritage are nowadays bypassing Boti and heading 50km east of Kefamenanu to the village of **TAMKESSI**. As many travellers go no further north than Soe, Tamkessi receives fewer visitors. The houses are nearly all of traditional design, and the village is built entirely on rock. Good-quality *ikat* cloths are made here, the men still hunt with blowpipes, and there are even a few boomerangs kicking about, though it's unlikely that you'll see them in use unless you ask specifically. The village is dominated by two large rocks which you can climb for fine views of the surrounding countryside, but make sure to ask permission from the kepala desa first.

To get there from Kefamenanu, take one of the regular buses east to **Manufui**; from there, it's a two-hour walk to the north. If you speak good Indonesian, you'll be able to ask directions in Manufui and probably won't need a guide, otherwise you'll have to obtain a guide in Soe, as nobody seems to be offering guide services in Kefa.

Atambua and Atapupu

ATAMBUA is the capital city of Belu Regency, which borders East Timor. The town has been open to tourists since 1989, when the authorities considered the danger of Fretilin guerrillas spilling over the border had diminished. Supposedly it's safe now, but caution is still advised if you're thinking of going off the beaten track: always check in with the police, and listen to local advice. Some travellers have reported verbal abuse from the locals here; true, there's some resentment against foreigners, though on the whole the people, while more reticent, are just as friendly as elsewhere in the archipelago. Nevertheless, it probably pays to arrive in Atambua before dark.

Atambua is a large but rather dull town; there's nothing of note to see, but you'll find plenty of losmen and Padang restaurants, and it's OK for one night. The **bus terminal** lies in the centre of town, but all buses come through town looking for custom anyway. Near the market and the bus terminal, the **hotels** *Nusantara Satu* (❷) and its plusher sister the *Nusantara Dua* (❸) are both open and accept foreigners, even if the latter goes to some length to make it clear that they don't actually welcome them. Just outside of town on a hill overlooking Atambua at **Ro'okfau** is a ruined Tetum settlement. Take a bemo to **Fatuketi**, then ask local kids if they can guide you for the short (1.5km) but strenuous walk to the deserted village. Close by is a vast cave complex, where swallow's nests are collected to make bird's-nest soup.

ATAPUPU is the port 25km to the north of Atambua. You might be able to pick up unscheduled boats from here to interesting places around the archipelago, but the main reason to come here is for the **weekly ferry** to **Kalabahi** on Alor, which leaves at 10am every Monday and takes seven hours. You can easily get from Atambua to the ferry in the morning, and there's no need to try and stay the night before in Atapupu. Bemos also run along the main road to the border with East Timor at Mota Ain (1hr; Rp25,000), and to the bus station in Atambua (30min; Rp1500).

The visa-run to Dili

Currently the main reason travellers are visiting Timor in these uncertain times is to cross the border into East Timor to pick up a **new visa**. Be warned that the situation is likely to change over the next few months, and much of the information given in this box may become obsolete, so always check first before attempting the crossing.

Currently you can leave Indonesia at this border with just a regular sixty-day tourist "short-stay" visa, though these tourist visas are not available at the border for those entering the country. Instead, you have to go to Dili to buy a new visa, which will either be for thirty or, if you plead hard enough and are lucky, sixty days. Given that these visas take two working days to process, and that the border is closed at weekends and public holidays, it's probably better to make the trip at the beginning of the working week if you are hoping to return to Indonesia as quickly as possible.

From Kupang, the first step is to buy a bus ticket for **Atambua** (Rp20,000; 7–8hr), where if you're relying on public transport you'll have to spend the night; the *Nusantara Dua* is a smart and clean option that's handy for the bemo and bus terminal. From Atambua bemos depart from outside the bus station (1hr; Rp3000) for the border crossing at **Mota Ain**. Having had your bags searched both by the Indonesian police and, after passing through Indonesian immigration and customs, by the officers on the East Timorese side (currently UN soldiers), you can catch a bus to Dili from the border for US$3. (Note that East Timor is currently using **US dollars**, and though this may change now they are independant; you can exchange your rupiah for dollars at a reasonable rate from the moneychangers at the border, though exercise extreme caution if you do so.)

In Dili there are any number of mid-range to luxury places to stay, costing US$30 upwards; expect prices to tumble dramatically when the UN pulls out. For backpackers, the *Dili Guest House* (☎0407/364974; ❶), just south of the roundabout by the bemo terminal, has become a bit of a legend over the last few years, though has sadly declined rapidly since the departure of the helpful Australian boss. Cheaper (no phone; ❶) and better is the unnamed losmen opposite the western end of Jalan Kaikoli (the road running west from the roundabout past the bemo terminal); look for the standard road-sign for a hotel (a black bed inside a blue border) and a building with "café" in fading letters painted on it.

The **Indonesian consulate** is in the Pertamina complex to the west of town; a taxi from the centre costs US$0.50 after bargaining. One photo is required, and a **fee of US$35** cash is demanded for both thirty- and sixty-day visas. To give yourself a greater chance of getting sixty days, speak to one of the officials there, and maybe even attach a note to your application form demanding sixty days. Applications are handed in in the morning between 9am and midday, and visas are collected two days later between 3 and 4pm.

Roti and Savu

The island of **Roti**, a four-hour ferry trip southwest of Kupang, is becoming a regular tourist destination. The vast majority of visitors are Australian surfers in search of waves at **Nemberala beach** on the west coast; the rest of the island remains all but unvisited. Roti is relatively flat and exceptionally dry, and the main crop is a drought-resistant palm called the **lontar**, which supplies vitamin-rich syrup as well as the fibres that Rotinese use for everything from house-building to cutlery. These spindly trees with their spiky crowns are ubiquitous on the island, their silhouettes against the sunset providing many photo opportunities.

Savu is about equidistant from Timor, Flores and Sumba and is extremely isolated. During the rainy season, ferries rarely make it here, and the island can go months at a time without seeing tourists. Even so, Savu is a place of gorgeous beaches and thriving animist cultures and it remains one of the most rewarding off-the-beaten-track destinations in all of Indonesia.

Roti

The main town on Roti is the small port of **Ba'a**, about halfway along the north-facing coast of the island. Pelni boats dock offshore here, but ferries to and from Kupang stop at the harbour in **Olafulihaa**, situated in a bay at the north of the island. The majority of surfing destinations, including highly rated Nembrala beach, are found on the southwest coast, have the best accommodation and beaches and are fantastic places to chill out, even if you're not seeking waves.

The villages in the area around **Boni** still maintain traditional ways, adhere to the *lontar* economy and hold a spectacular festival in late June/early July. Triggered by the full moon, this *hu'us* festival involves animal sacrifices, horse races and dancing – basically, two weeks of pagan knees-up.

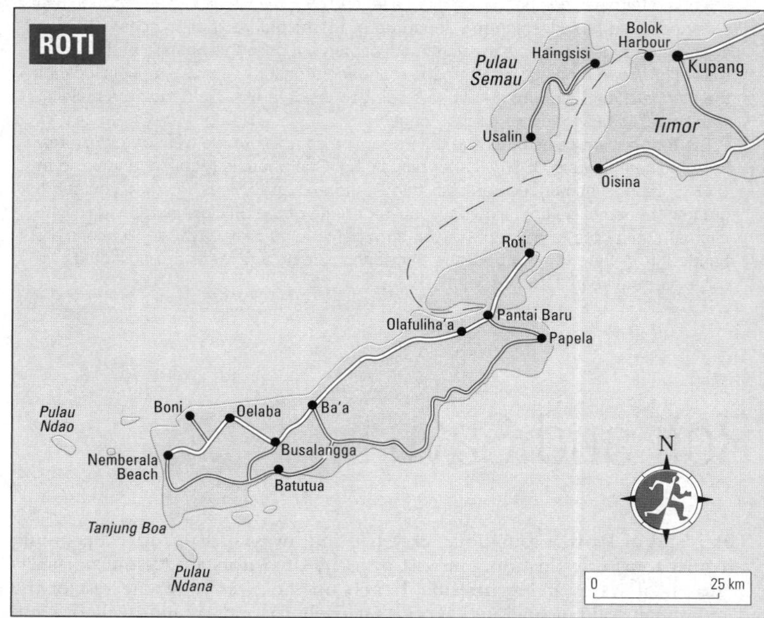

Roti has its place in **history** as one of the success stories of the Dutch East India Company. On their arrival in Roti, the colonizers met with little resistance, and quickly allied themselves with local factions. At first, the Dutch influence seemed to be taking effect gradually and progressively, but then a powerful and brutal VOC campaign established their position by force, quelling opposition and strengthening the position of their allies. Roti became a supply base for Kupang, and slaves became a regular export. In 1729, the Rotinese raja became a Christian, and more conversions followed swiftly, the locals realizing that embracing Christianity, adopting European education systems and aiding the colonists would bring them power and advancement. Today, the island still has a reputation for producing a high proportion of the nation's high-ranking officials and diplomats.

Most travellers **arrive** in Roti at the northern port of Pantai Baru on the daily ferry from Kupang. It gets in at about 11am, and there's always a crowd of buses waiting to whisk passengers away to Nemberala (Rp10,000; 4hr). The same buses will drop you off at Ba'a (Rp7500), which is about halfway between the port and Nemberala. The **airport** is near to Ba'a town: from here, your best bet is to catch one of the waiting taxis into Ba'a and, if you want to go on to Nembrala, try to flag down a bus as it heads down the main street. Ferries returning to Kupang leave daily at noon and buses leave from Nembrala every morning from 6.30am to 8am to reach the port in time. The Pelni ferry *KM Wilis* for Waingapu, Ende, Savu and Kupang leaves from Ba'a – check schedules in a large town before coming to Roti and then double-check at the Pelni office in Ba'a.

Ba'a and Boni

BA'A may be the largest town on Roti, but it's a small, sleepy place with little to recommend it to visitors: it's dusty, decrepit and has no shops or good places to eat. If you're planning a trip to the traditional area of Boni, or heading out on a Pelni boat to Sumba, Flores, Timor or Savu, then you might have to stop here. There's only one losmen open at the present time, though it's a good one: the *Hotel Ricki* on Jalan Gereja (Ⓣ0380/871045; ❷), offering clean rooms with en-suite mandi and fans. Every eating place in Ba'a is dire, the least awful being the *Dewi* on Jalan Hatta, which does a fair *mie bakso*, and the Padang restaurant on Jalan Pabean, the seafront road to the east of Jalan Gereja, which also has a few traditional *ti'i langga* hats for sale. Right on the junction is the **Pelni office**, while if the **Kendari Expres** to Kupang and Flores ever sails again you'll be able to buy tickets from the agent just a few metres further east on Jalan Pabean; further east still on the same street is the **Merpati office**. The bank does not change money and the post office is on the other side of the green at the western end of town.

To get to **BONI**, it's best to hire a guide and motorbike in town (or at least an ojek and driver, which is probably all you'll be able to find in Ba'a). You could try this from Nemberala, but it's a longer trip. Boni lies west of Ba'a and slightly off the main road, and is one of the few places left on Roti that maintains the distinctive houses with high sloping roofs and exposed scimitar-shaped, carved ridgepoles. Traditional dress is the norm: women wear only a simple sarong, and the men sport the Rotinese *ti'i langga*, a woven cowboy hat with a pole pointing heavenwards. Boni's **hu'us festival** is well worth heading for if you are on Roti in June or July. At any time, though, the village is worth a visit, giving a fine insight into the island's agrarian, animist past.

Nemberala beach

Nemberala beach is a terrific **surfing** destination. The main break is called T' land, on the reef that runs offshore: it's a long rideable left that's best from April to September. At **Boa**, about an eight-kilometre bike ride from Nemberala, is a right-hander that's worth trying in the morning before the wind picks up. The wave is never as busy as the main breaks in the high season. The **wildlife** is notable for its dwindling stocks of turtles. These giants come ashore to lay their eggs and are often rolled over by villagers, hacked up and eaten alive – a harrowing sight.

There are presently four **places to stay** and eat in Nemberala, all on the front: *Losmen Anugurah* (❷) is the best, offering en-suite rooms with attached mandi; three enormous helpings of food are included in the price, and you'll also find the coldest beer in town here. They now have a satellite phone, and show DVDs in the evening. *Homestay Thomas* (❷) and *Losmen Ti Rosa* (❷) offer similar deals, but are less popular. *Nemberala Beach Hotel* (Ⓣ0380/823973; ❸) is an overpriced set of bungalows in a good location on the beach that seems to survive on the occasional surfing tour group that drops in.

Just offshore are two islands worth a trip: **Ndao** is famous for producing the finest filigree silver and gold in Nusa Tenggara, while **Ndana** is an uninhabited island which swarms with wildlife – thousands of deer, pelicans, herons, monkeys and wild boar, all seemingly indifferent to humans. Turtles are a common sight in the seas around Ndana and the beaches are egg-laying sites. For either of these islands you will need to **charter** a boat from Nemberala.

Savu

The stunning island of **Savu** (also known as Sabu or Sawu) is an arid yet beautifully rugged paradise sitting in the Savu Sea between Timor and Sumba. It's an exposed, flat and isolated lump of rock, where, somehow, human life manages to thrive with more success than on the fertile lands of Flores and Sumba. The annual rainfall on Savu is pitiful, the ground is stony and barren, yet due to the *lontar* palm economy, the Savunese are some of the healthiest-looking people in the region, and, along with the Rotinese, have a disproportionate representation in Indonesian public life.

For several hundred years, Savu repelled colonial powers with remarkable ease. A Portuguese war expedition that stopped in search of slaves in 1676 was decimated, and the Portuguese and Dutch kept their distance thereafter. For westerners, the biggest milestone in the history of Savu was the visit in 1770 of **Captain Cook**, who visited several villages around the island and wrote on Savu's *lontar* plant economy. Savu remained virtually isolated from the outside world until 1860, when Christian missionaries landed here, also bringing smallpox to the island; it's estimated that up to half of the population died of the disease. Unlike on Roti, converts to Christianity received few favours, and were for the most part shunned by the other Savunese; often they migrated to Sumba and Timor, a move encouraged by the missionaries, who hoped to stem the spread of Islam there.

Today, Savu is divided into eastern and western districts, with its largest town, **Seba**, lying in the middle of the northwest coast. **Ferries** leaving for Kupang depart every Wednesday at 2pm (10hr; Rp12,000); the ferry to Waingapu leaves on Sundays at the same time (16hr; Rp14,000). Ferry schedules can be unpredictable, though, and they often don't run in the rainy season. There are also

The festivals

The main **festival** on Savu, the **pedoa**, takes place between April and June; as a spectacle, it's second in Nusa Tenggara only to Sumba's *pasola*. The *pedoa* is a thanksgiving after the planting season; it's also a special chance for young people to find a partner. The three-month ceremonies include dancing, horse races, ritual wars and stone-throwing battles.

Another notable festival is the **pehere jara** or "horse dancing" held in February. In folklore, it was decreed that the stampeding sound of constantly dancing horses' hooves would drive off a plague of locusts. Now, before the sorghum is planted, young men mount their horses bareback and race endlessly around a field near Namata throwing betel nuts, which the onlookers have to try and rescue from beneath the flailing hooves. If many people fall from their horses, then seeds will also fall from the sky and the harvest will be good; the riding, therefore, is exhilaratingly reckless.

smaller passenger boats to Roti, though they as yet do not follow any set timetable; ask in Seba for the latest details.

The island is circumnavigated by a single track, the only other road of note neatly bisecting it. To the west of Savu lies tiny **Pulau Raijua**, considered by the Savunese as their place of origin and spiritual home: it is reputedly the driest place in all of Indonesia. While most people on Savu now claim to be Christians, the island is actually the site of the most fervent **animism** in Indonesia. Village compounds, sacred buildings, festivals and rites are loaded with significance, so that a guide from Seba is essential when touring Savu; otherwise, you may inadvertently offend people. In addition, always bring enough betel nut to share around and offer your hosts as an offering when you visit villages.

The only craft of note on Savu is their **ikat weaving**, rated by experts as amongst the finest in Indonesia. They tend to use chemical dyes rather than those made from plants, but the colours appear far more natural than on Roti, and are still very appealing to the Western buyer.

Surfing on Savu can be exceptionally good: in November and December, strong winds come from the southwest, bringing great surf from **Uba Ae** beach on the south coast right round to Seba.

Seba

The main town and port of **SEBA** lies on the west coast of Savu. It features a wide sweep of perfect beach, strewn with coloured pebbles; fisherman stand waist-deep in the surf with throw nets, while the shores are thick with gangly-topped *lontar* palms.

While there are three **losmen** in Seba, the best by far is the *Ongka Dai Homestay* (❶). Just walk up the street from the jetty and it's on your right. The rooms have en-suite mandi, the staff are fun and friendly, and you get three huge meals a day included in the price.

The best **guide** on Savu is Pak Junas Tacoy, Seba's English teacher. Junas is extremely helpful, speaks very good English, and has boundless knowledge of the area. If you're staying at the *Ongka Dai Homestay*, then he'll probably find you. For a seat on the back of his motorbike and his guiding abilities you should expect to pay US$20–30 a day, which sounds steep but is well worth it.

The **Raja's Palace** (Teni Hawu) sits slightly southwest of the port. It's a grand name for the crumbling edifice, but the late raja's wife can tell you a bit about Savu's royalty and might show you around some of the ramshackle buildings.

Around the island

The villages around Savu have a number of striking traditional structures and distinctive stone **megaliths**; they are all difficult to get to by public transport and unless you intend staying a while in any of the villages, then renting a motorbike is recommended (your losmen should be able to give details).

The closest village to Seba is **NAMATA**. Off the main road, heading clockwise around the island, Namata has a host of Savunese houses, shaped like upturned boats as a symbol of the people's seafaring ancestry. Those whose roofs reach the ground are sacred houses for storing ritual objects and mixing magic, and are strictly taboo. Never photograph, touch or (under any circumstances) look into these houses. Namata also has some of the finest examples of Savunese megaliths, oval boulders apparently rolled up to their hill-top position from the bottom of the sea and then set in brick cradles in neat groups. The village is a good place to see **ikat weaving**, and also the famous stone plaque that may have been carved and presented by Captain Cook. It's a fascinating place, and only a three-kilometre walk northeast from town.

In the far east of Savu, **KUDJIRATU** is the centre of the island's animism and the starting point for the *pedoa* (see p.787). You need to speak to people outside before you enter through the narrow slit in the spectacular black-rock walls of the kampung. At the time of writing, the kampung had just been reconstructed and was vulnerable to outside magic; visitors had to be exorcized by the *kepala adat* before being allowed inside. In the far south, **MISARA** is another fascinating traditional kampung. With three sets of megaliths and complex ritual structures, it is bounded by taboos, so tread carefully. A rock here is apparently guaranteed to make you fertile. When a priest dies in Misara, a new acolyte must drink a potion of the old priest's blood mixed with the venom from a highly poisonous fish. Those who survive this ordeal are ordained; this ritual last took place in 1997. A more regular ritual called the **holai** takes place here in April or May, when live animals and food are pushed out to sea bound up in *lontar* palm boats, wrapped in *ikat* as an offering to the gods. Puppies and goat kids whose eyes are as yet unopened are particularly valued offerings, as they represent helpless victims who will suffer the punishment of the gods in place of the villagers. You can stay here with the friendly *kepala sekola* (schoolmaster), who lives just outside the main kampung.

Pulau Raijua lies to the west of Savu and is the driest place in Indonesia. Even the *lontar* palm will not grow here and the locals have to live on sorghum and imported food. The Savunese believe their ancestors passed through Raijua on the way from India, so the place has great significance in their ritual affairs. A handful of hardy surfers make the arduous hike across the island to **surf** the promising reef on the south coast, camping on the beach there – but note that there are reputed to be hordes of tiger sharks in the Raijua Straits. Boats run to **Ledeunu** on Raijua's north coast three times a week from Seba (Rp3000, 90min); there are no boats from December to February.

Sumba

Christened by the national tourist board "The Island of Spirits", **Sumba** has a reputation in Indonesia for the excesses of its funerals, the wealth of its *ikat* fabrics and the thrill of the **pasola**, a ritual war fought on horseback. While the *pasola* is still the main reason people visit Sumba, local customs, distinctive villages and fine coastline are enough to make a trip to Sumba worthwhile at any time of year.

The east of the island is rocky, parched and fairly undulating, and has to ship most of its food from the west. In contrast, the west is green and fertile, with rolling hills and a rainy season that seems to last twice as long as that in the east. Unlike Alor and Timor, where the rugged, impenetrable landscape has led to the evolution of many completely different languages in relatively small areas, the many dialects of Sumba all have a single root. Significantly, Sumba is the only island in the archipelago whose animist **religion** is officially recognized by the Indonesian government.

East Sumba, with its capital at **Waingapu**, is well-known for producing the finest *ikat* in the whole of Indonesia; in the vicinity of Waingapu are several villages where you can see the weaving process and buy finished cloths. Many of the traditional houses no longer keep their colossal roofs clad in thatch, preferring practical but miserable-looking corrugated iron. Southeast from Waingapu, at the villages of **Rende** and **Melolo** you can find stone tombs with bizarre carvings, while other villages right out on the east coast offer the chance to see quality weaving and traditional structures near to some deserted beaches. On the south coast, **Tarimbang** is an up-and-coming surfers' Mecca with a few waterfalls inland.

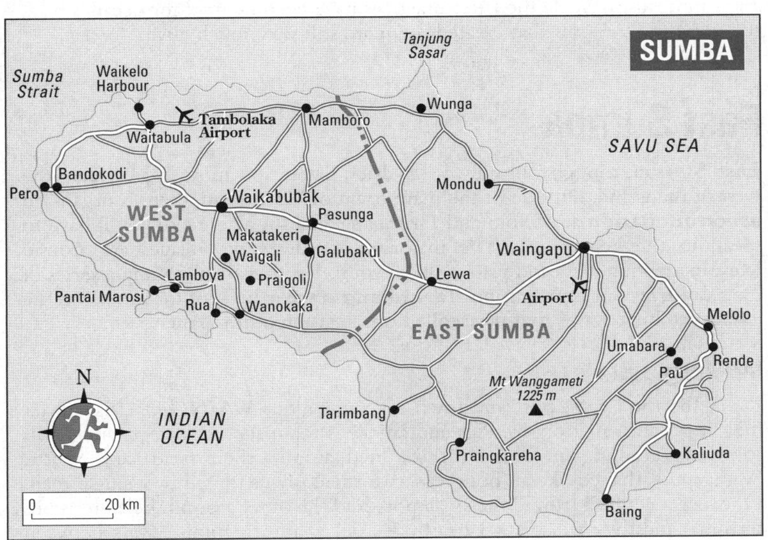

West Sumba's main town is **Waikabubak**, where characteristic houses with thatched roofs soar to an apex over 15m above the ground. In this top part of the roof, the family's heirlooms and objects of ceremonial significance are kept, so that they can be closer to the heavens. West Sumba is especially remarkable for its stunning rituals; as well as the *pasola*, the funerals of the district are also noteworthy; they involve the sacrifice of many animals and are preceded by stone-dragging, dancing and singing.

Some history

It seems unlikely that the Javanese Majapahit empire (which claimed to control Sumba until the fifteenth century) actually had any real hold here. Later, in the sixteenth and seventeenth centuries, Sumba is listed in official records as a vassal state of Bima on Sumbawa, and it's possible that the Makassarese (who were allied with Bima) had small-scale trade with Sumba, for slaves, sandalwood and the sturdy **ponies** that were shipped as far as India and South Africa. The island is marked on early maps as "Sandalwood Island", the wood largely being exported for use as incense in temples and shrines all over the east. These trades are all long dead, though Sumba still has a good supply of powerful but diminutive ponies, most obviously in evidence during the *pasola*.

Incursions by colonial powers onto Sumba's shores were inevitably brief and bloody due to the Sumbanese tribes' ferocious hostility towards invaders. The Dutch finally set up a garrison here in 1906, collecting taxes, trading in horses and enforcing their presence with violent military "pacification". This reign lasted for forty years until the Japanese took nominal control for a brief period during World War II. None of these invaders managed any notable degree of religious conversion amongst the Sumbanese, while Christian missionaries had little more luck, and the majority of the island's inhabitants remain committed to animist beliefs. As well as the missionaries, Sumba in the twentieth century began to receive a slow trickle of **anthropologists**, attracted by tales of grandiose ceremonies, head-hunting and rituals involving human sacrifice and cannibalism. While the latter practices have been defunct for decades now, the ideas and customs that created them are still very much alive.

East Sumba

East Sumba, though still hilly, is far drier, flatter and more barren than the west of the island. Outside of the main town of **Waingapu**, there is organized **accommodation** at Melolo and Tarimbang, but anywhere else you'll have to speak to the kepala desa. The majority of interesting villages are around **Melolo**, making it a good place to base yourself rather than making a series of long day-trips out of Waingapu. **Tarimbang** is the main spot for surfers on the island, catching waves that have rolled uninterrupted from Antarctica.

Waingapu

It may be the largest port and town on Sumba, but **WAINGAPU** is still far from a modern metropolis. Pigs and chickens roam the backstreets and locals still walk around barefoot, with *ikat* tied around their heads and waists. Waingapu is shaped like an hourglass, two small towns joined by a single road. One half is centred around the small port, and the other around the eastern bus terminal and the main market nearby. It's only a fifteen-minute walk between

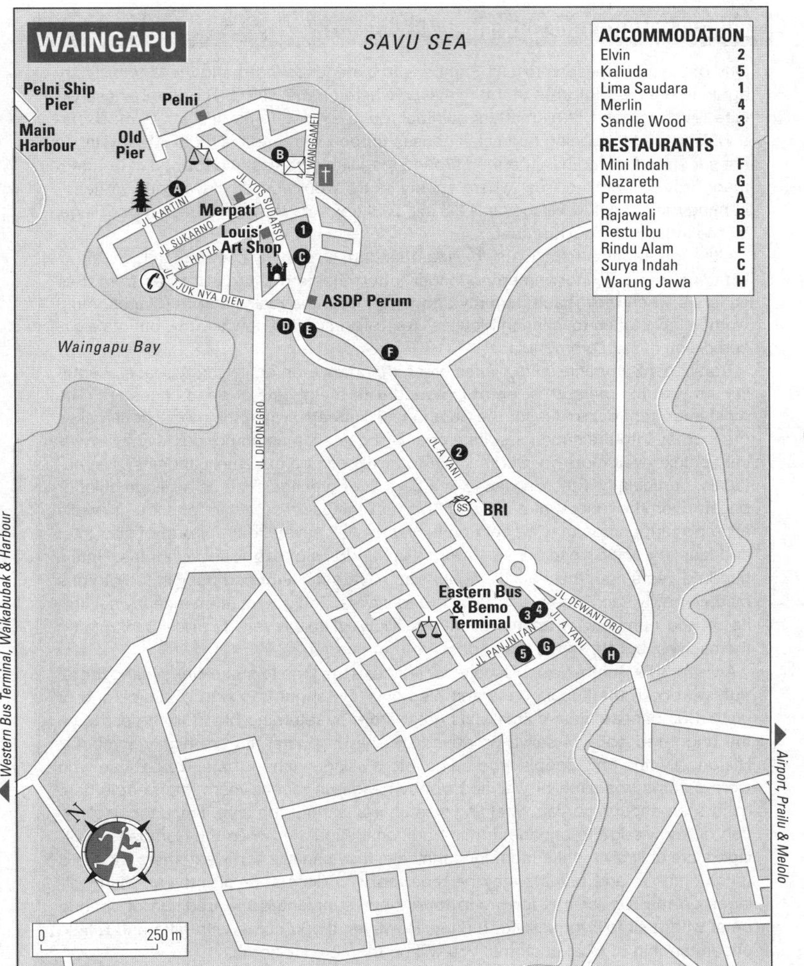

the two, but an endless army of bemos make the circular trip and will generally drop you off exactly where you want to go (Rp1000). The bay to the west of town has a harbour at the extreme northern point of either shore: all ASDP, Pelni and the car ferries dock at the **western harbour**, requiring an eight-kilometre journey all around the bay to town (Rp1000 by bemo).

There's little in the town for tourists, but if there's something you need and you can't find it in Waingapu, you certainly won't find it anywhere else on Sumba. A couple of shops at the market end of town on Jalan Yani sell photographic film, but be sure to check the sell-by date and don't expect a great choice. There's a reasonable **pharmacy** on the linking road, and two **markets**. The market by the eastern bus terminal is grubby and full of pushy *ikat* traders,

Village culture and tourism

One of the main reasons to visit Sumba is to experience first-hand the extraordinary agrarian **animist cultures** that thrive everywhere on the island. The Sumbanese village is at the heart of all matters spiritual, quite striking in its design, its most distinguishing feature being huge clan houses topped with hat-like roofs. Most villages are set upon fortified hills, centred around megalithic graves and topped by a totem made from a petrified tree, where enemy skulls would be displayed after a head-hunting raid. Very few villages still exhibit skull trees, as they have been made illegal by the Indonesian government.

Although tradition here is still thriving, there are also many customs that are slowly fading away. Young women no longer tattoo their arms and cut holes from their earlobes when they reach maturity and, apart from the really remote villages, most women have taken to wearing blouses. Teeth-filing is also now a rarity, but male circumcision is still commonplace.

Traditional Sumbanese life places great importance on achieving a peaceful equilibrium with the *merapu*, or **spirits** imbued with the ghosts of dead ancestors. The most important part of life for the Sumbanese is **death**, when the mortal soul makes the journey into the superior spirit world. Dying is seen as an honour, dying in a ritual context even more so. Sumbanese **funerals** can be extremely impressive spectacles, particularly if the deceased is a person of prestige such as a village chief or priest. Even the funeral of a child will warrant the sacrifice of five or six pigs, while an important person may be sent on their way with several days' worth of slaughter and feasting, the corpse buried wrapped in hundreds of exquisite *ikat* cloths. Until a hundred years ago, the wealthy would also have been kept company in their tombs by their newly sacrificed wives, horses and slaves. The government recently set limits on the numbers of animal sacrifices allowed, to prevent families bankrupting themselves, but these are rarely observed.

A visitor to a Sumbanese village must first take the time to share *cirih pinang* (**betel nut**) with both the kepala desa and his hosts. Betel nut is a sign of peace and of unity; Sumbanese ritual culture sets great store by returning blood to the earth, so the bright-red gobs of saliva produced by chewing betel nut are highly symbolic. Historically, the only people who came into a village without betel were those who were coming in search of war and trophy heads. In recent years, the people here have seen enough camera-wielding westerners without the time, language, inclination or knowledge to engage in this traditional etiquette; while the Sumbanese villagers are unlikely to take them for cannibals, they can still find westerners rude and unfathomable, and tourists may be received with distrust or disinterest. Many villages on the regular trail for group tours have supplanted the tradition of sharing betel with a simple request for money. However, if you come with gifts and a little understanding of local customs, you will be far more welcome.

but sells fantastic fruits and vegetables imported from the west. The market towards the port is just grubby. A small **Hindu temple** near the *Restaurant Permata* often has Balinese music playing and if you ask nicely, they may let you in for a closer inspection.

Practicalities

Most visitors to Sumba arrive in Waingapu by sea. All passenger ferries these days arrive at the western end of the bay about 8km away from town, and packed **bemos** will meet you and drop you off at the hotel of your choice (Rp1000). The **airport** is about 10km to the southeast on the road to Rende, with flights on Pelita and Merpati to Kupang, Bali, Lombok and Flores. Representatives from the main hotels are usually on hand to ferry tourists into town – as long as you agree to look at their hotel first; if they're not there, head out to the main road and flag down a bus (Rp3000) or take a taxi (Rp10,000).

Waingapu has two bus terminals. **Buses to Waikabubak** and all points west leave from the terminal 5km to the west of town; bemos drive around the town before heading out to there (Rp1000) – the main market by the bemo terminal is your best place to hail one. Buses serving Sumba Timur use the old or eastern bus terminal in the centre of town near the main market. The office for **Pelni** ships is down at the bottom of the hill near the east pier; the **ASDP** office is up the hill by the main junction at Jl Wanggameti 33 (☎0387/61533). You can buy tickets for the car ferries here, but for the fast ferry **KM Barito**, you need to go to the efficient travel agent PT Andrew Jonathan at Jalan Yani 81 (☎0387/61363); they are also the agents for **Pelita**. The **Merpati office** is on Jalan Sukarno (☎0387/61232) near to the main square. Opposite PT Andrew Jonathan is the BRI, the only **bank** in town that will change travellers' cheques, and which can also arrange cash advances on credit cards (there are as yet no ATMs that accept foreign credit or debit cards in the whole of Sumba). The main **post office** (Mon–Thurs 8am–3pm, Fri 8am–noon, Sat 8am–1pm) is at Jl Sutomo 21 at the northern end of town. No sooner had the **internet café** Warnet Elshacom opened here than it ran into bureaucratic problems and was forced to close again; hopefully, by the time you read this the problems will have been resolved. The 24hr **Telkom** is on Jalan Cut Nyak Dien. For souvenirs, most of the hotels have some *ikat* for sale – the *Merlin*'s collection is the largest in town – and there are always street sellers milling around outside the hotels waiting to pounce. Down at the other end of town, Louis' Art Shop on Jalan Sudirman has a dusty collection of *ikat* and woodcarvings.

Leaving Waingapu, Merpati currently operate three flights per week, one to Denpasar (Wed) and two to Kupang (Tues & Sat), with the Tuesday service continuing on to Maumere. Pelita fly on Thursday and Sunday to Denpasar and on to Surabaya (the latter going via Labuanbajo, the former continuing on from Surabaya to Yogyakarta). Pelni's *KM Awu* and *KM Wilis* both dock every fortnight in Waingapu on their way to and from Flores, Sumbawa and Kupang, with the latter going via both Roti and Sabu as well. ASDP's fast **ferry** *KFC Barito* calls in to Waingapu's Pelni dock (the western harbour) twice weekly on its way to and from Kupang and Denpasar/Surabaya via Bima. There are also three car ferries weekly (although they often stop altogether in the rainy season due to rough seas). Currently, they sail on Monday to Aimere, on Wednesday to Kupang via Sabu, and on Friday to Kupang via Ende.

Accommodation

The majority of **places to stay** are at the market end of town, with only one near the port. The hotels all offer rental cars with driver.

Hotel Elvin Jl Ahmad Yani 73 ☎0387/62097. The staff are attentive, friendly and helpful, although the rooms are a little spartan, some with fan, others with air-con. This place is popular with visiting Indonesian businessmen. ❸

Losmen Kaliuda Jl Lalamentik 3 ☎0387/61264. Close to the market and bemo terminal at the southern end of town, this is a good place – quite quiet, friendly, clean and with the option of shared or en-suite mandi. ❷

Hotel Lima Saudara Jl Wanggameti 2 ☎0387/61083. The town's cheapest, and the only option at the northern end of town. The rooms are a little grim, but all are en suite and bearable for a night or two, and rates include free tea and coffee. ❷

Hotel Merlin Jl Panjaitan ☎0387/61300. By far the plushest place in Waingapu, not as expensive as you might expect with the current lack of tourists in Sumba. The sparkling rooms have air-con and en-suite bathrooms, and come with free mineral water and breakfast, and the top-floor restaurant is a great place for a meal (though see below about ordering in advance). Also on the top gallery next to the restaurant is a good but expensive art shop. ❸

Hotel Sandle Wood Jl Panjaitan 23 ☎0387/61887. Near the bemo terminal and market, this place retains some tired charm. There's a back room which serves as an art shop, stuffed full of piles of dusty *ikat* blankets; ask the manager if you want a look. Single, double and triple rooms range from basic with mandi outside through to full air-con, TV and en-suite bathrooms. ❷–❹

Eating

There's a limited choice of **restaurants** in Waingapu, and many close between lunch and dinner. A number of warung and food carts are dotted about town, but the food is generally of a lower standard than other comparable places around Nusa Tenggara.

Hotel Merlin Jl Panjaitan. On the fourth floor at the top of a Himalayan staircase with fine views of the town, the food is good but perhaps the most expensive on Sumba: around Rp45,000 for a full Chinese meal with several courses. If you plan to eat here in the quiet season (which is all year round, with the current lack of tourists), warn them ahead of time that you're coming and tell them roughly what you want so they can buy the ingredients from the market.

Mini Indah Jl A Yani 21A. Standard Indonesian warung, unremarkable except for the fact that it stays open all day.

Nazareth Jl Lalamentik. Opposite the *Hotel Kaliuda*, some great Chinese food and cold beers make this one of the better options in town, and one of the few places that stays open all day too.

Permata Jl Kartini. Formerly the owner of the main backpackers' homestay in Sumba, the helpful Pak Ali, now a local senator, has given up on hotel management altogether and instead built this huge and beautiful restaurant overlooking the two harbours. The food is fine, the beers are cold and, if you can put up with the interminable karaoke, this place is highly recommended.

Restaurant Rajawali Right by the post office on Jalan Hasanuddin. Unexceptional food and unfriendly owners, but one of the few places to cater specifically for tourists with an English-language menu.

Restu Ibu Jl Juanda 1. Unpretentious, cheap and tourist-friendly restaurant serving Indonesian staple dishes (nasi goreng etc), situated at the northern end of town opposite the flashier *Rindu Alam*. The *ikan bakar* is reasonable.

Rindu Alam Jl Juanda. Probably the finest restaurant in town, with pleasant outdoor seating, specializing in great *ikan bakar* served with some wonderful sambal sauces.

Surya Indah Jl Sudirman. An unassuming little place opposite the Al-Jihad Mosque with good coffee and cakes.

Warung Jawa Jl A Yani. One of the most popular places in town, serving large portions of Indonesian staples at rock-bottom prices.

Around Waingapu

Few people come to East Sumba without checking out its prime attraction, the *ikat*-weaving villages, several of which are in the immediate vicinity of Waingapu and can be reached easily. **PRAILU** is the most visited, just a ten-minute, 2km bemo hop away (Rp1000). After signing in at the large traditional house, and paying Rp2000 or so, you can inspect weavings that weren't good enough to be bought by the traders. **Lamba Napu** lies about 6km south off the main road from Prailu and receives slightly fewer visitors than the other two. If you really want to buy some *ikat* in east Sumba, it's wise to take a few days to get some experience about the stuff, and going to these villages to see the weaving processes is a good start.

PRAINATANG, northwest of Waingapu and on the road to **Maru**, is probably the finest example of a traditional village in East Sumba, beautifully set on a hilltop above a fertile plain. Not many travellers get up here; only one bus a day goes from Waingapu, leaving at 7am (3–5hr). If this has left, you'll have to catch a bus to **Mondu** and walk the final 5km from there.

For the really adventurous, it's possible to continue from Mondu up to the northern cape of Sumba at **TANJUNG SASAR** which lies 40km northeast of Prainatang. Here the people are relatively untouched by the modern world, still wear clothes made from tree bark, and live in strict accordance with animist dictates.

The Sumbanese ikat tradition

The **ikat** blankets of East Sumba are ablaze with dragons, animals, gods, and images of head-hunting. Each creature is associated with certain qualities: the turtle, for example, is identified with the feminine and is the wisest and most dignified of creatures; the crocodile represents the masculine. Other characters such as the Chinese dragon and the Dutch lion are obvious imports, generally designed to appeal to foreign traders. The *patola rato*, a motif which originated in India, has become very highly prized; only rajas were allowed to make and wear cloths with this flower-like pattern. Other popular images include *andung*, or head-hunting symbols, the skull tree, and *anatau* (corpses in their pre-burial state).

The cloth worn by men is called the **hinggi**, and is made from two identical panels sewn together into a symmetrical blanket; one is worn around the waist and the other draped across one shoulder. These are the most popular cloths for souvenir seekers, as they make great wall-hangings. The cloth worn by women is called the **lau** and takes the form of a cylindrical skirt.

The process of making *ikat* in East Sumba is especially laborious. The cotton is generally harvested in July and **spinning** continues until October. Patterns are then tied onto the vertical warp threads of the cloth, with dye-resistant string. These strings serve much the same function as wax in batik; when the cloth is dyed, the covered parts will not take up the colour and the design will be represented on them in negative. After the rains in April and May, the indigo and *kombu* (rust) dye baths are prepared and the threads are soaked. The baths are taboo, and must be obscured from men's eyes: they also smell of rotting corpses. The dyeing is repeated to intensify the colours, and threads are retied so that the design can incorporate many different colours and shades. Finally, weaving begins in August, a year after the process was begun.

Ikat is one of the most traded fabrics in Indonesia, and methods to make it cheaper and easier to produce, while maintaining the high asking price, are commonplace. Most pieces retailing at under US$100 are made with a *campur* (mix) of traditional vegetable dyes and manufactured chemical dyes, while many cloths under US$50 use only chemical dye. Whilst most cloths use hand-spun cotton for the vertical threads, black, commercially produced threads are usually used for the horizontal weft. Bright and vibrant colours are achieved on the best cloths by repeated dippings in the dye baths, on lesser cloths with chemicals; often it's difficult to tell the difference. The attractive fading that denotes an **antique cloth** can be hastened by simple sun-bleaching or washing in rice water.

The signs of a good piece include a tight weave, clean precise motifs and sharp edges between different colours. Dealers in the towns will often charge you less than those in the villages; generally, the villagers have guaranteed sales for all their work, with a steady supply of Japanese and Balinese traders ready to pay big money for work fresh off the loom.

The east Sumban villages

The villages of eastern Sumba have made small concessions to modernity, now sporting rusty metal roofs on their houses and using concrete to build their tombs. Most of these villages are used to visitors and will request around Rp2000 as a "signing-in fee", even if you bring betel nut to offer on arrival.

East of Waingapu and 4km to the southwest of the larger town of Melolo, are **PAU** and **UMBARA**. Pau, though tiny, is actually an independent kingdom with its own raja, an interesting character who is very knowledgeable about Sumba and its traditions. Umbara has a few thatched-roof houses and some tombs; to see them you will be expected to pay Rp2000. Buses from Waingapu to Melolo (90min; Rp3000) run until the late afternoon and you can ask the driver to stop at Pau or Umbara.

MELOLO, 62km southeast from Waingapu, has three high-roofed houses and a few crudely carved tombs as well as a clean and friendly **losmen** (❷), which makes a good base if you intend to do a fairly extended tour of the area. The next major settlement as you head east is **RENDE**. Here the house roofs are all made from tin, but are nevertheless spectacular, and doorways are adorned with huge buffalo horns. Rende is also the site of the finest **tombs** in East Sumba, huge flat slabs topped by animal carvings. There are buses every couple of hours direct to Rende from Waingapu (2hr), and occasional trucks; otherwise, catch a bus to Melolo and one of the regular bemos from there. There are also regular buses and trucks from Melolo.

South of Rende on the east coast, **KALIUDA** is a small, fairly traditional village with a justified reputation for producing the best *ikat* on the island. However, the villagers have no interest in selling individual pieces and, unless you're lucky enough to arrive at a fallow time, you won't get a good price for a cloth here. The final destination for buses from Waingapu is at the end of the road at the southern coastal village of **BAING**, where the surf is reasonable in the middle of the year.

About 40km out of Waingapu on the road west to Waikabubak, a turn-off leads down to **TARIMBANG** on the south coast. Buses leave Waingapu for Tarimbang daily at around 8am (4hr). Here you'll find the *Martin Homestay* (❸ full-board), with its rooms fashioned to resemble Sumbanese clan houses which cater for surfers and those looking for quiet beaches and relaxation. The surf can be outstanding and it's a nice place to hang out for a while. From here, the road curves round to the east to **PRAINGKAREHA**. It's not much of a village, but there's a wonderful waterfall about a four-kilometre walk from the road, with a pool at the bottom where you can swim. Several kilometres further down the Praingkareha road is another waterfall near **LUMBUNG**. This one is about a quarter of the height, but during the rainy season it has a huge volume of water cascading over it and is also a great place to cool down; it's about a two-kilometre walk from the main road. For both falls you will need to ask directions or even ask someone in Praingkareha to direct you to the *air terjun* (waterfall); if they offer to guide you, a few thousand rupiah would be a suitable recompense.

West Sumba

Western Sumba has attracted eager **anthropologists** for over a hundred years. It's one of the few places left in Indonesia with true commitment to its animist, spiritual past, which manifests itself in spectacular **rituals** and vibrant **festivals**, offering unforgettable experiences to its visitors. The largest town in the west is **Waikabubak**, which contains several enclosed kampung where life proceeds according to the laws of the spirits.

The extreme western districts are fast becoming the most popular destination for travellers. The **Pero** district, for example, offers some wonderful beaches and excellent surf, combined with perfect examples of Sumbanese traditional villages; those near **Kodi** have the highest roofs in Sumba. **Wanokaka** and **Lamboya** districts, south of the western capital, host annual *pasola* festivals (see box opposite) and have a wealth of villages dotting the countryside atop fortified hills as the land gently slopes down to the coast. There are embryonic

The pasola

By far the best known and most dazzling festival in Nusa Tenggara, the **pasola** is one of those rare spectacles that actually surpasses all expectations. This brilliant pageant of several hundred colourfully attired, spear-wielding horsemen in a frenetic and lethal pitched battle is truly unforgettable. Unfortunately for the visitor, it's difficult to predict when the event will take place; it occurs four times within the first two moons of the year, and is set off by the mass appearance of the **nyale**, a type of sea worm. *Pasola* comes from the local word *sola*, which means "throwing spear". The event is a rite to balance the upper sphere of the heavens and the lower sphere of the seas, a duality reflected by West Sumbanese settlements, which have an upper village in the hills and a lower village down towards the seashore. The *pasola* places the men of each village as two teams in direct opposition; the spilling of their blood placates the spirits and restores balance between the two spheres. The proceedings begin several weeks before the main event, with villagers hurling abuse and insults at their neighbours in order to get the blood up. As the day approaches, all prospective combatants must bring a chicken to their village *ratu* (priest), who sacrifices it and examines the spirit messages in its intestines to determine the bearer's suitability for the conflict. If the signs revealed by this process are inauspicious, the owner will be forbidden from taking part.

During the full-moon period in the first or second lunar month of the year, priests keep watch on the coastlines each morning for the coming of the **nyale**. *Nyale* is the name of the goddess of the oceans, and is also given to the sea worm *Eunis viridis*, whose annual procreation sets off festivals all over the archipelago. For two days a year, the shores are turned into a maelstrom of luminous red, yellow and blue as the cavorting worms wash into the shallows to be eagerly harvested by the locals. In the month preceding this time, fishing, bathing and even surfing is strictly forbidden off the *pasola* beaches. When ashore, the worms are a rather dull-brown or dark-green and black colour, and have a flavour and consistency somewhere between seaweed and oysters. For best results, they should be consumed raw and wriggling, but can be boiled, fried or baked, and are highly prized for their aphrodisiac qualities.

When the *nyale* arrive, the sample specimens are examined by the high priests, their quality relating to the success of the ensuing harvest. Then the **fighting** commences – actually on the beaches. After a few tentative exchanges, the two teams move to the special *pasola* fields – large flat areas of grass near the village – where the battle has taken place for centuries. The teams surge towards each other, usually led by a single warrior, who will attempt to isolate one of the opposition for a "kill". Spears fill the air, and many of the combatants are startlingly accurate with their missiles. Injuries are numerous, and riders are often trampled underfoot; fatalities are now relatively rare – the Indonesian government has ruled that spears with sharpened tips must not be carried – but it's still a potentially lethal event. This is not a circus show arranged for tourists: be aware that your safety is irrelevant to the participants, so always stay behind the guide ropes and keep at a safe distance if there aren't any barriers.

The *pasola* takes place four times throughout the year, twice in February and twice in March, the venues being Lamboya, Kodi, Wanokaka and Gaura. Trying to find out the exact date and location can be tricky. The best plan is as follows: first, phone one of the Waikabubak hotels (*Artha*, *Manandang* and *Aloha* are all good bets) to find out approximate details. By mid-January, they should know the approximate dates for the February *pasola*, and by mid-February, they should know the rough dates for March. Once you know the date of the event, try to be in Waikabubak a few days before; this will allow for the unpredictable nature of this festival. It will also give you the opportunity to watch the preliminaries such as the **pajura**, a nocturnal boxing match usually held two nights before the *pasola*. During the *pajura*, two teams of seven or so youths line up to beat the hell out of each other, their fists wrapped with pandanus grass.

beach resorts at **Rua** and **Marosi**, with pristine coastlines where foreigners still bewilder the locals by either baking in the sun or by riding the waves all day on a plastic plank. East of Waikabubak, in the **Anakalang** district are the most photographed **tombs** in Sumba.

The **ikat** of West Sumba may suffer in comparison with its eastern cousin, but there are many attractive cloths made here. More compact motifs with fewer colours are used, along with stylized symbols that often only suggest the eyes or the tail of a creature. Another important West Sumban symbol is the **mamuli**, an omega shape often seen in earrings or pendants and traditionally worn only by the *ratu*, the high priests of the Merapu religion. The shape represents the female vagina and uterus, enclosed by a male exterior. Also peculiar to this part of the island are **swords** with carved bone or wood handles, and grotesque masks and statues, complete with animal hair and teeth.

Waikabubak

WAIKABUBAK is a small town surrounded by lush green meadows and forested hills. One of the most striking facets of the town is that several enclosed **kampung** with slanting thatched roofs and megalithic **stone graves** nestle among the concrete and satellite dishes of more modern buildings. The western capital bears little relation to Waingapu in the east; whereas the east spends the majority of the year on the brink of drought, Waikabubak enjoys an extended rainy season that lasts way into May, when the countryside can be drenched by daily downpours. Due to Waikabubak's slight elevation, it can get a bit chilly at night in the rainy season.

One of the most important ritual sites in Sumba is to be found right in the town itself. **Tarung** kampung, on a hilltop just west of the main street, has some excellent megalithic graves and is regarded as one of the most significant spiritual centres on the island. The *ratu* of Tarung are responsible for the annual **wula padu** ceremony, which lasts for a month at the beginning of the Merapu new year in November. The ceremony commemorates the visiting spirits of important ancestors, who are honoured with the sacrifice of many animals and entertained by singing and dancing. The *ratu* enforce a month of repose before the festive final day, during which even mourning is forbidden in Tarung.

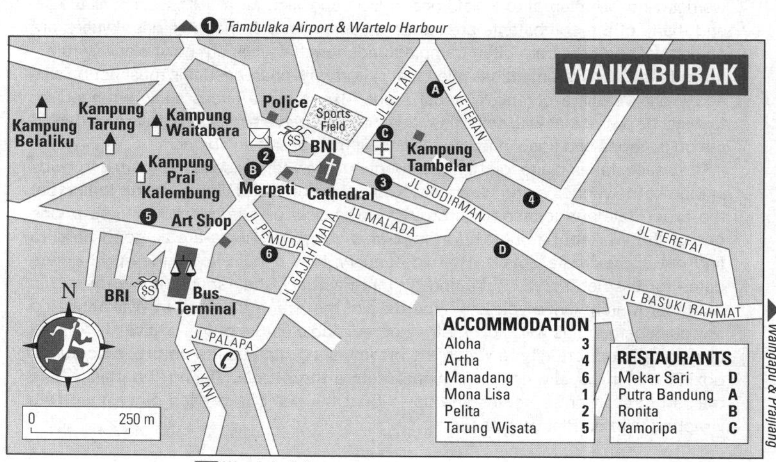

There are plenty of other kampung worth seeing in and around Waikabubak. **Kampung Praijiang**, a five-tiered village on a hilltop surrounded by rice paddies, is a particularly good example several kilometres east of town. You can catch a bemo to the bottom of the hill and will be asked for Rp2000 or so to look around and take photographs.

Practicalities

Most people **arrive** in Waikabubak at the **bus terminal** in the southwestern quarter of the town, though the driver may well be prepared to drop you off at your hotel if it is on the way. Otherwise, bemos run from the terminal to the hotels (Rp1000). Tambolaka **airport** is a good ninety-minute drive to the north of town; buses and taxis meet arriving planes and bring passengers to Waikabubak.

Most things you might need in Waikabubak lie either on the main street of Jalan Ahmad Yani, or within several minutes' walk of it. At the southern end, the market and bus terminal are sandwiched together, with the 24hr **Telkom office** a few hundred metres further southeast; there are rumours of an **internet café** opening here soon. A little to the north along Jalan Yani is the Fatsal Art shop, the best souvenir emporium in town, full of old carvings and a few pieces of jewellery and *ikat*. The **market**, though dirty and full of flies is well worth a stroll. People come from all over west Sumba to buy and sell, sporting colourful *ikat* sarongs and with their mouths stained black by betel nut. The men can sometimes be seen with a distinctive headdress of two scarves, usually a white one around the ears and a red one wound under the chin and up over the crown of the head to make two horns.

The new **BNI bank**, a few hundred metres north of the bus terminal, at the junction of Jalan Yani and Jalan Sudirman, will change US dollars and sterling travellers' cheques. On the opposite corner lies the **post office** (Mon–Thurs 8am–2pm, Fri 8am–noon, Sat 8am–1pm).

Moving on, the bus station services all areas of western Sumba, and trucks and bemos also stop here. All of these services run far too erratically to make a route listing worthwhile. You will find it difficult to get a bus anywhere after late morning, apart from buses to Waingapu, which continue until about 3pm. Agents for Waingapu buses such as Sumba Mas and Romantis can be found on Jalan Yani. The **Merpati office**, which is often closed, is on the eastern side of Jalan Yani on the second floor of a dusty store (Ⓣ0387/21051). Buses leave daily for Tambolaka airport in the early mornings, and will pick you up at your hotel in plenty of time to get there. If you miss this, catch a bus to Waitabula and take a taxi from there. Be warned that flights out of Tambolaka airport have a very bad reputation for cancellations or severe delays, especially in the rainy season. If you have to leave Sumba at a precise time, then go by ferry from Waingapu. In *pasola* season, flights are more reliable and used to be full in the halcyon days when tourists regularly came to Sumba; should they return again, be prepared to book your seat months in advance. Currently, there is supposed to be one flight per week to Denpasar (Sun) and one to Kupang (Sat). **Waikelo harbour** is near the airport. At present, there are two slow ferries per week to Sape on Sumbawa (Tues & Fri) and one to Aimere on Flores (Tues).

Accommodation

Accommodation in and around Waikabubak is by and large better value than that of Waingapu.

Hotel Aloha Jl Sudirman 26 Ⓣ0387/21245. Curiously, when this place was grotty and the bathrooms were full of mosquito larvae, it was the backpackers' favourite. Now the rooms are sparklingly clean, all en suite and come with fan, the place is empty. A touch overpriced, but nevertheless very pleasant, and the attached restaurant's not bad either. ❷

Hotel Artha Jl Veteran ⓣ0387/21112. Just off the road in from Waingapu; very clean, very friendly, and with a reasonable variety of rooms around a flower-filled central garden. Highly recommended. ❸

Hotel Manandang Jl Permuda 4 ⓣ0387/21297, ⓕ21634. The most luxurious option in the town itself, a clean and comfortable place with a giant satellite TV. It boasts a wide range of rooms, from overpriced ekonomi with shared bathroom to ones with shower, fan and TV. ❷–❹

Mona Lisa Cottages Jl Adhyaksa ⓣ0387/21364, ⓕ21042. Quite upmarket, with a number of semi-detached or individual bungalows set on a hillside about 2km from town amongst the rice paddies. Some of the cheaper ones are a little grotty and very dark, but the top ones are really lovely. ❷–❸

Hotel Pelita Jl Ahmad Yani 2 ⓣ0387/21104. Currently undergoing some extensive renovations, this centrally located hotel has some grotty en-suite economy rooms at the front and a couple of sparklingly clean and pleasant en-suite ones towards the back. ❷

Tarung Wisata Jl Pisang 26 ⓣ0387/21332. Dirt-cheap and very friendly losmen near the market below Kampung Tarung. The most expensive rooms lack natural light, the cheaper ones are brighter but a little bare. Come here if money is truly tight. ❶

Eating

There's not a lot of choice in Waikabubak. There are some very unsanitary **warung** around the market; you may well find the proprietor putting a severed buffalo head next to your meal and starting to hack off the least palatable bits for the pot. Otherwise, you're pretty much confined to the options listed below.

Hotel Manandang Jl Pemuda 4. The flashiest restaurant in Waikabubak, twice the price of something similar on the street. It is, however, by far the most hygienic option, and their fried *tempe* is excellent.

Mekar Sari Jl Sudirman. One of the cleaner places in town, and highly recommended too. The menu is limited most nights to fried chicken or nasi goreng, but they're well presented and the fried chicken contains (unusually for Indonesia) far more meat than bone and gristle. They also serve cold beer.

Putra Bandung Jl Veteran. A no-nonsense, one-table warung that's popular with the locals; the menu is limited to whatever is in the tiny display cabinet, but it always tastes good and the portions are large.

Ronita Jl Yani. Nothing special, just simple Indonesian fare plonked on your table by surly staff, but it's one of the cleaner places near the bus station, and very popular.

Yamoripa Jl El Tari. Simple warung in the grounds of the hospital specializing in *mie bakso* (Rp2500), and one of the few to stay open throughout the day.

Anakalang district

Anakalang district, to the east of Waikabubak, is the site of the most impressive **tomb** in Sumba, which is found beside the main road at **Kampung Pasunga**, about 20km east of Waikabubak (served by regular buses until 1pm, or catch any Waingapu-bound bus and ask to be dropped off at Kampung Pasunga; Rp3000). An exquisitely carved upright slab fronts the table-shaped grave, its fascia adorned with a male and female figure standing side by side and its sides carved with smaller figures. The kampung is quite striking, consisting of two rows of towering parallel buildings, topped by tin roofs.

Opposite Pasunga, a side road leads about 1km down to the village of **Matakakeri**, home to the single largest tomb in Sumba. Unless you encounter one of the irregular bemos that head this way, you'll have to walk. On the way, you pass through a market, which has a part-time warung providing noodles and eggs. When you reach the village, you'll be directed to the large traditional house at the end of the kampung, where you pay Rp2000 to look around. They do a roaring trade in *kelapa muda* (young coconut) at around Rp500 a time. The tomb itself is pretty much uncarved and not particularly interesting.

From the tomb, walk around the back of the huts and follow the path for the ten-minute walk up to **Lai Tarung**, a hill-top kampung offering fine views of the surrounding countryside, with its verdant fields, hedgerows and forested hills. There are actually several different kampung on different levels, and the name "Lai Tarung" only refers to one at the summit. There's a ritual structure here, with a thatched roof resting on several carved, petrified columns – a resting place for the dead. If you share betel nut with the family who live in the one serviceable house and ask nicely, they may show you inside to see their drum, which they claim is made from human belly skin.

Galubakul, the next kampung down the main road from Pasunga, also has a few huge tombs, which you'll have to pay to see (Rp2000). Beyond here is the eastern part of the **Wanokaka** area, most of which lies south of Waikabubak. A few trucks infrequently venture down this way; otherwise, you'll have to walk.

Wanokaka

Travelling in **Wanokaka district** is very rewarding, as all the villages are built to traditional patterns and it's far from touristy. However, it is one of the poorest areas in Sumba; malnutrition and disease are commonplace, so bring your own supplies (including plenty of cigarettes to share around), and try to share as much as you can. Most villages will gladly take you in, but don't expect comfort. **Bemos** between villages are fairly regular, but stop about 1pm – a bit of a pity, as the area is worth a whole day. For this reason it's probably better to hire a motorbike (US$10 per day) or car (US$25) in Waikabubak; speak to your hotel or the *Hotel Artha*, who'll be able to arrange this.

The usual route into the Wanokaka area is to go due south out of Waikabubak. Most tourists take the left fork after 7km that heads another 7km to **WAIGALI** village, popular as the site of some excellent stone **tombs**. The inauguration ceremonies for the area's *pasola* take place in January in the *pusat* or navel at the highest point of this village, an important religious site. From here there is a great 360-degree panorama of the surrounding countryside, and the large sacrificial altars are often caked with blood from recent ceremonies. Heading south you'll pass through several settlements. **Laihuruk** has a Saturday market when, with a little luck and determination, you may well be able to catch a truck to some very remote villages. **Praigoli** is another comparatively often-visited hamlet to the south of here, famous for its large and beautifully sculpted tomb. From here, you can get all the way down to the **beach**, a stunning two-kilometre walk.

The alternate fork in the road before Waigali heading south eventually reaches **Rua** beach, about 28km from Waikabubak. You might be lucky enough to pick up transport in town or on the road near Waigali, but the wonderful views make walking or cycling a real joy, a fantastic panorama of cornfields dotted with palm trees and hill-top kampung, rolling down to the sea. On Wednesdays, a market is held in nearby **Padedewatu**, 7km before Rua, and you may be able to get a truck all the way to Rua. The beaches here are sensational, long stretches of empty sands with dramatic crashing surf, with forest and palm trees right down to the beachfront; it's a little too rough for safe swimming. Rua village has one budget **losmen** catering mainly for surfers: the *Ahong* homestay is basic but friendly, and provides three large meals a day (full-board ❷).

Instead of following the road from Waikabubak directly south all the way to the coast, some travellers choose to take the second major turning off towards

Lamboya. Buses from Waikabubak will usually stop here and then it's an enjoyable five-kilometre downhill walk to **Pantai Marosi**. A budget homestay on the way provides full board – the *Matebelu* (❷), which is in Watukarere, about 2km from a paradisal coastline where *nyale* are gathered before the *pasola* (see p.797). The views from here are magnificent, and if you walk around the surrounding countryside you'll pass some quite isolated settlements. The surf can be excellent, though you'll have to carry your board all the way down to the beach every day. One bus a day, the *Nusa Cendana*, leaves Waikabubak at 7am heading into this area: ask beforehand if it will go all the way to Marosi.

Kodi and Pero

In the extreme west of Sumba lie the increasingly popular areas of Kodi and Pero. The Kodi district, with its centre in the village of **BANDOKODI**, 60km from Waikabubak, is particularly well known for the towering roofs that top the traditional houses. There is one bus direct a day from Waikabubak to Bandokodi; otherwise you'll have to take a bus to **Waitabula** in the north and then wait for a bus to fill up for the trip around the coast.

This bus will usually take you all the way to **PERO**, just a couple of kilometres further on, a seaside village with one losmen. The village is not constructed in traditional Sumbanese style, but its rough cobbled street flanked by colourful wooden houses has a certain charm. Numerous kampung with teetering high roofs and mossy stone **tombs** dot the surrounding countryside, only a short walk away. The *Homestay Story* (full-board ❸) is quite clean and provides huge meals, but come prepared for the mosquitoes. To get to the beach, walk down the path outside the losmen and then either head left across the river (local kids will charge exorbitant fees to ferry you across when the tide is high) or right, down to the part of the beach with the most regular offshore surf breaks. The beach to the left is very sheltered with a narrow stretch of fine yellow sand, whereas the other is far more exposed. Whichever one you choose it'll become immediately evident that the currents here are not for beginners – the undertow can be ferocious, and even with a surfboard you're not necessarily safe.

If instead you've crossed the river to the south, you could carry on around the coast to the villages of **Ratenggaro**, **Paranobaro** and **Wainyapu**, 6km away. Their houses are the skyscrapers of Nusa Tenggara, with roofs towering to nearly 20m, and their coastline settings are perfect. It can be quite infuriating trying to find the villages: their roofs are visible from several kilometres away, but it's often impossible to find the right path unaided. Local kids will be glad to guide you – offer a few pens as a thank-you.

Travel details

Buses and bemos

It's almost impossible to give the **frequency** with which bemos and buses run, as they only depart when they have enough passengers to make the journey worthwhile. However, on the most popular routes you should be able to count on getting a ride within thirty minutes if you travel before noon; things quieten down in the afternoon and come to a standstill by around 5pm. **Journey times** also vary a great deal. The times given below are the minimum you can expect the journeys to take.

Ampenan to: Senggigi (20min).

Bajawa to: Ende (4hr); Labuanbajo (10hr); Moni (5hr 30min); Ruteng (4–5hr).

Bima to: Mataram (Bima terminal 11hr); Sape (Kumbe terminal; 2hr); Sumbawa Besar (Bima terminal; 7hr).

Ende to: Bajawa (Ndao terminal; 4hr); Maumere (Wolowana terminal; 6hr); Moni (Wolowana terminal; 90min); Riung (Ndao terminal; 4hr).
Kupang to: Camplang (1hr); Soe (3–4hr); Atambua (8hr).
Labuhan Lombok to: Bayan (2hr); Konpang (for Praya; 1hr); Sembalun Lawang (2hr 30min); Sweta (Mandalika terminal; 90min).
Labuanbajo to: Bajawa (8hr); Ende (14hr); Ruteng (4–5hr).
Larantuka to: Maumere (4hr).
Lembar to: Sweta (Mandalika terminal; 30min).
Maumere to: Ende (Terminal Barat; 6hr); Larantuka (Terminal Lokaria; 4hr); Moni (Terminal Barat; 3hr 30min); Wodong (Terminal Lokaria; 1hr).
Poto Tano to: Alas (45min); Bima (9hr); Sumbawa Besar (2hr); Taliwang (1hr).
Praya to: Gubukdalem (1hr 30min); Kuta (1hr); Mandalika terminal, Sweta (30min).
Ruteng to: Bajawa (4–5hr); Ende (14hr); Ruteng (4–5hr).
Soe to: Kupang (3–4hr); Niki-Niki (1hr).
Sumbawa Besar to: Bima (7hr); Dompu (4hr 30min); Sape (8hr 30min).
Sweta (Mandalika terminal) to: Bayan (for Rinjani; 2hr 30min); Bima (Sumbawa; 12hr); Dompu (Sumbawa; 10hr); Jakarta (Java; 48hr); Labuhan Lombok (2hr); Labuanbajo (Flores; 24hr); Lembar (30min); Pemenang (50min); Pomotong (for Tetebatu; 1hr 15min); Praya (for Kuta; 30min); Ruteng (Flores; 36hr); Sape (Flores; 14hr); Sumbawa Besar (Sumbawa; 6hr); Surabaya (20hr); Yogyakarta (26hr).
Waingapu to: Melolo (1hr 30min); Rende (3hr); Waikabubak (4hr 30min).
Waikabubak to: Tambolaka (1hr 30min); Waingapu (4hr 30min).

Pelni ferries

For a chart of the Pelni routes, see p.42. There are no longer any services running to and from Dili in East Timor.
Badas (Sumbawa Besar) to: Banyuwangi (*KM Tatamailau*, monthly; 19hr); Denpasar (*KM Tatamailau*, monthly; 11hr); Ende (*KM Wilis*, 2 monthly; 32hr); Fak Fak (*KM Tatamailau*, monthly; 4 days); Kupang (*KM Wilis*, 2 monthly; 54hr); Labuanbajo (*KM Wilis*, 2 monthly; 13hr); Makassar (*KM Tatamailau*, monthly; 20hr); Roti *KM Wilis*, 2 monthly; 49hr); Sabu (*KM Wilis*, 2 monthly; 41hr); Surabaya (*KM Wilis*, 2 monthly; 21hr); Waingapu (*KM Wilis*, 2 monthly; 22hr).
Bima to: Banyuwangi (*KM Tatamailau*, monthly; 26hr); Denpasar (*KM Tatamailau*, monthly; 19hr/*KM Tilongkabila*, monthly; 18hr); Fak Fak (*KM Tatamailau*, monthly; 4 days); Larantuka (*KM Tatamailau*, monthly; 22hr); Lembar (*KM Tilongkabila*, monthly; 14hr); Makassar (*KM Tilongkabila*, monthly; 7hr); Saumlaki (*KM Tatamailau*, monthly; 38hr); Surabaya (*KM Tilongkabila*, monthly; 42hr); Tual (*KM Tatamailau*, monthly; 7hr).
Ende to: Badas (*KM Wilis*, 2 monthly; 32hr); Denpasar (*KM Awu*, 2 monthly; 40hr); Kalabahi (*KM Awu*, 2 monthly; 24hr); Kupang (*KM Awu*, 2 monthly; 11hr/*KM Wilis*, 2 monthly; 21hr); Labuanbajo (*KM Wilis*, 2 monthly; 18hr); Lembar (*KM Awu*, 2 monthly; 33hr); Makassar (*KM Awu*, 2 monthly; 62hr); Maumere (*KM Awu*, 2 monthly; 38hr); Rote (*KM Wilis*, 2 monthly; 16hr); Savu (*KM Wilis*, 2 monthly; 8hr); Surabaya (*KM Wilis*, 2 monthly; 53hr); Waingapu (*KM Awu*, 2 monthly; 8hr/*KM Wilis*, 2 monthly; 8hr).
Kalabahi to: Kupang (*KM Sirimau*, 2 monthly; 11hr/*KM Awu*, 2 monthly; 10hr); Larantuka (*KM Sirimau*, 2 monthly; 24hr); Makassar (*KM Sirimau*, 2 monthly; 2 days/*KM Awu*, 2 monthly; 36hr); Maumere (*KM Awu*, 2 monthly; 12hr).
Kupang to: Ambon (*KM Dobonsolo*, 2 monthly; 27hr/*KM Doro Londa*, monthly; 20hr); Badas (*KM Wilis*, 2 monthly; 52hr); Batulicin, 5hr from Banjarmasin (*KM Sirimau*, 2 monthly; 58hr); Denpasar (*KM Dobonsolo*, 2 monthly; 27hr/*KM Awu*, 2 monthly; 55hr); Dobo (*KM Kelimutu*, monthly; 59hr); Ende (*KM Awu*, 2 monthly; 10hr/*KM Wilis*, 2 monthly; 19hr); Fak Fak (*KM Doro Londa*, monthly; 37hr); Jayapura (*KM Dobonsolo*, 2 monthly; 3–4 days/*KM Doro Londa*, monthly; 3–4 days); Kalabahi (*KM Awu*, 2 monthly; 21hr); Labuanbajo (*KM Wilis*, 2 monthly; 38hr); Larantuka (*KM Sirimau*, 2 monthly; 9hr); Lembar (*KM Awu*, 2 monthly; 11hr); Makassar (*KM Sirimau*, 2 monthly; 35hr/*KM Awu*, 2 monthly; 48hr/*KM Doro Londa*, monthly; 23hr); Maumere (*KM Awu*, 2 monthly; 24hr); Merauke (*KM Kelimutu*, monthly; 4–5 days); Saumlaki (*KM Kelimutu*, monthly; 41hr); Savu (*KM Wilis*, 2 monthly; 8hr); Sorong (*KM Dobonsolo*, 2 monthly; 2 days); Surabaya (*KM Dobonsolo*, 2 monthly; 44hr/*KM Doro Londa*, monthly; 2 days/*KM Wilis*, 2 monthly; 73hr); Tanjung Priok, Jakarta (*KM Doro Londa*, monthly; 3 days); Timika (*KM Kelimutu*, monthly; 52hr); Waingapu (*KM Awu*, 2 monthly; 19hr/*KM Wilis*, 2 monthly; 28hr).
Labuanbajo to: Badas, Sumbawa Besar (*KM Wilis*, 2 monthly; 13hr); Bima (*KM Tatamailau*, monthly; 6hr); Denpasar (*KM Tatamailau*, monthly; 26hr); Ende (*KM Wilis*, 2 monthly; 18hr); Kupang (*KM Kelimutu*, monthly; 22hr/*KM Wilis*, 2 monthly; 36hr); Larantuka (*KM Kelimutu*, monthly; 16hr); Lembar (*KM Kelimutu*, monthly; 19hr/*KM Tatamailau*, monthly; 22hr); Makassar (*KM*

Kelimutu, monthly; 4 days/*KM Tatamailau*, monthly; 14hr); Rote (*KM Wilis*, 2 monthly; 35hr); Savu (*KM Wilis*, 2 monthly; 27hr); Surabaya (*KM Kelimutu*, monthly; 39hr/*KM Tatamailau*, monthly; 49hr/*KM Wilis*, 2 monthly; 34hr); Timika (*KM Kelimutu*, monthly; 4–5 days); Waingapu (*KM Wilis*, 2 monthly; 8hr).

Larantuka to: Banyuwangi (*KM Tatamailau*, monthly; 48hr); Batulicin, Banjarmasin (*KM Sirimau*, 2 monthly; 2 days); Bima (*KM Tatamailau*, monthly; 20hr); Denpasar (*KM Tatamailau*, monthly; 42hr); Kalabahi (*KM Sirimau*, 2 monthly; 7hr); Kupang (*KM Sirimau*, 2 monthly; 19hr/*KM Kelimutu*, monthly; 9hr); Labuanbajo (*KM Kelimutu*, monthly; 17hr); Lembar (*KM Kelimutu*, monthly; 37hr); Makassar (*KM Sirimau*, 2 monthly; 24hr); Saumlaki (*KM Tatamailau*, monthly; 38hr); Surabaya (*KM Kelimutu*, monthly; 57hr); Timika (*KM Kelimutu*, monthly; 3–4 days); Tual (*KM Tatamailau*, monthly; 53hr).

Lembar to: Bau Bau (*KM Tilongkabila*, monthly; 3 days); Bima (*KM Tilongkabila*, monthly; 24hr); Bitung (*KM Tilongkabila*, monthly; 5 days); Denpasar (*KM Tilongkabila*, monthly; 4hr); Gorontalo (*KM Tilongkabila*, monthly; 4 days); Kendari (*KM Tilongkabila*, monthly; 3 days); Kolonedale (*KM Tilongkabila*, monthly; 3 days); Labuanbajo (*KM Tilongkabila*, monthly; 31hr); Lirung (*KM Tilongkabila*, monthly; 6 days); Luwuk (*KM Tilongkabila*, monthly; 4 days); Makassar (*KM Tilongkabila*, monthly; 48hr); Raha (*KM Tilongkabila*, monthly; 3 days); Tahuna (*KM Tilongkabila*, monthly; 8 days).

Maumere to: Ende (*KM Awu*, 2 monthly; 37hr); Kalabahi (*KM Awu*, 2 monthly; 13hr); Kupang (*KM Awu*, 2 monthly; 24hr); Makassar (*KM Awu*, 2 monthly; 20hr); Waingapu (*KM Awu*, 2 monthly; 46hr).

Roti to: Ende (*KM Wilis*, 2 monthly; 24hr); Kupang (*KM Wilis*, 2 monthly; 4hr).

Savu to: Ende (*KM Wilis*, 2 monthly; 8hr); Kupang (*KM Wilis*, 2 monthly; 11hr); Labuanbajo (*KM Wilis*, 2 monthly; 27hr); Roti (*KM Wilis*, 2 monthly; 6hr); Waingapu (*KM Wilis*, 2 monthly; 19hr).

Waingapu to: Badas, for Sumbawa Besar (*KM Wilis*, 2 monthly; 17hr); Denpasar (*KM Awu*, 2 monthly; 31hr); Ende (*KM Awu*, 2 monthly; 7hr/*KM Wilis*, 2 monthly; 9hr); Kalabahi (*KM Awu*, 2 monthly; 34hr); Kupang (*KM Awu*, 2 monthly; 20hr/*KM Wilis*, 2 monthly; 32hr); Labuanbajo (*KM Wilis*, 2 monthly; 8hr); Lembar (*KM Awu*, 2 monthly; 24hr); Makassar (*KM Awu*, 2 monthly; 3 days); Maumere (*KM Awu*, 2 monthly; 2 days); Roti (*KM Wilis*, 2 monthly; 25hr); Savu (*KM Wilis*, 2 monthly; 17hr); Surabaya (*KM Wilis*, 2 monthly; 2 days).

ASDP fast ferries

There are two ASDP fast ferries currently servicing Nusa Tenggara. Both travel from Surabaya via Benoa on Bali, Bima on Sumbawa, and on to Kupang, with the *KFC Serayu* travelling from Bima via Maumere to Kupang, and the *KFC Barito* from Bima via Waingapu to Kupang. Both ships then follow their same respective routes on their return.

Bima to: Benoa, Bali (*KFC Serayu*, weekly; 7hr; *KFC Barito*, weekly; 7hr); Maumere (*KFC Serayu*, weekly; 5hr); Surabaya (*KFC Serayu*, weekly; 17hr; *KFC Barito*, weekly; 17hr); Waingapu (*KFC Barito*, weekly; 7hr).

Kupang to: Benoa, Bali (*KFC Serayu*, weekly; 21hr; *KFC Barito*, weekly; 21hr); Bima (*KFC Serayu*, weekly; 14hr); Maumere (*KFC Serayu*, weekly; 7hr); Surabaya (*KFC Serayu*, weekly; 29hr); Waingapu (*KFC Barito*, weekly; 7hr).

Maumere to: Benoa, Bali (*KFC Serayu*, weekly; 16hr); Bima (*KFC Serayu*, weekly; 7hr); Kupang (*KFC Serayu*, weekly; 20hr); Surabaya (*KFC Serayu*, weekly; 24hr).

Waingapu to: Benoa, Bali (*KFC Barito*, weekly; 14hr); Bima (*KFC Barito*, weekly; 7hr); Kupang (*KFC Barito*, weekly; 6hr); Surabaya (*KFC Barito*, weekly; 22hr).

Other ferries

Aimere to: Kupang (2 weekly; 20hr); Waingapu (weekly; 8hr).

Bangsal to: Gili Islands (several times daily; 20–45min).

Ende to: Kupang (2 weekly; 16hr); Waingapu (weekly; 10hr).

Kalabahi to: Kupang (3 weekly; 16hr); Atapupu (weekly; 7hr); Larantuka (3 weekly; 24hr).

Kupang to: Aimere (2 weekly; 20hr); Ende (weekly; 16hr/ *KM Kirana II*, weekly; 12hr); Kalabahi (2 weekly; 16hr); Larantuka (3 weekly; 14hr); Roti (daily; 4hr); Sabu (weekly; 15hr); Surabaya (*KM Kirana II*, weekly; 48hr); Waingapu (2 weekly; 48hr).

Labuanbajo to: Sape (daily; 7hr); Waingapu (2 weekly; 14hr)

Labuhan Lombok to: Poto Tano (Sumbawa; hourly; 2hr).

Larantuka to: Kalabahi (4 weekly, 36hr); Kupang (2 weekly; 14hr); Lamelera, Lembata (weekly; 7–8hr); Lewoleba, Lembata (two daily; 4hr); Waiwerang, Adonara (2 daily; 2hr).

Lembar to: Benoa Harbour (Bali; 2 daily; 2hr); Padang Bai (Bali; daily every 2hr; 4hr–4hr 30min).

Lembata to: Kalabahi (from Belauring; *Dian*

Expres, 2 weekly, 20hr); Lamalera (2 weekly; 4hr); Larantuka (at least 2 daily; 4hr).
Sape to: Labuanbajo (daily; 7–8hr).
Senggigi to: Gili Trawangan: (daily; 1hr 30min).
Waingapu: to Aimere (weekly; 8hr) Ende (weekly; 10hr); Kupang (3 weekly; 48hr); Savu (weekly; 9hr).

Flights

All flights are with Merpati unless otherwise stated.
Bima to: Denpasar (4 weekly; 1hr 15min); Ende (3 weekly; 1hr 30min); Kupang (2 weekly; 2hr 10min); Labuanbajo (4 weekly; 55min); Mataram (2 weekly; 1hr 10min); Ruteng (weekly; 1hr 10min); Surabaya (4 weekly; 2hr 20min).
Ende to: Bima (2 weekly; 1hr 30min); Kupang (3 weekly; 1hr 10min).
Kupang to: Denpasar (Merpati, 10 weekly/Pelita, 4 weekly; 1hr 35min); Jakarta (Merpati, daily/Pelita, 4 weekly; 3hr 25min); Labuanbajo (4 weekly; 2hr 45min); Larantuka (weekly; 1hr 5min); Maumere (4 weekly; 55min); Ruteng (weekly; 1hr 45min); Savu (weekly; 1hr 35min); Surabaya (Merpati, daily/Pelita, 4 weekly; 2hr 5min); Tambolaka (weekly; 1hr 50min); Waingapu (weekly; 1hr 35min).
Labuanbajo to: Bima (3 weekly; 45min); Denpasar (Pelita, 2 weekly; 1hr 40min); Maumere (Pelita, weekly; 1hr).
Mataram to: Bima (daily; 45min); Denpasar (connecting to Jakarta; 9 daily; 30min); Kupang (daily; 5hr); Maumere (3 weekly; 3hr 30min); Singapore (daily; 2hr 30min); Sumbawa (daily; 40min); Surabaya (connecting to Jakarta; 3 daily; 45min); Waingapu (4 weekly; 3hr).
Maumere to: Denpasar (Merpati, 4 weekly/Pelita, 3 weekly; 2hr 10min; Kupang (4 weekly; 55min).
Sumbawa Besar to: Denpasar (2 weekly; 1hr 55min); Mataram (2 weekly; 45min).
Waikabubak to: Bima (weekly; 1hr 15min); Denpasar (weekly; 2hr); Kupang (weekly; 40min); Waingapu (weekly; 1hr 40min).
Waingapu to: Denpasar (Merpati, weekly/Pelita, 2 weekly; 1hr 40min); Kupang (2 weekly; 1hr 20min); Labuanbajo (weekly; 40min).

10

Kalimantan

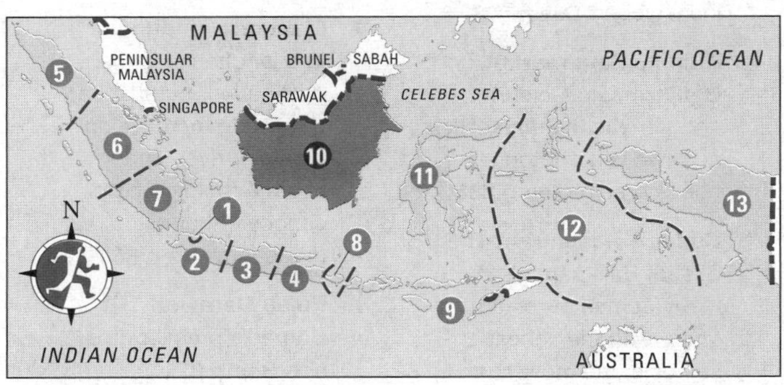

CHAPTER 10

Highlights

* **Sungai Kapuas** Indonesia's longest river offers a five-day river trip from Pontianak into Kalimantan's remote interior. **See p.821**

* **Tanjung Puting Orang-utan Rehabilitation Centre** Watch the orang-utans being fed, then meet Berry, the park's resident gibbon. **See p.828**

* **Kuin floating market, Banjarmasin** Colourful and frenetic,the market at dawn is a photographer's dream. **See p.838**

* **Bondy's Restaurant** The best of Balikpapan's many upmarket restaurants, with the fieriest sambals, the most succulent fish and the coldest beers. **See p.851**

* **Sungai Mahakam** Experience one of the world's great river journeys, drifting down the Mahakam on a public ferry, investigating the culture and crafts of the traditional Dayak villages on the way. **See p.857**

* **Mancong longhouse** The longhouse is the destination, but it's the dawn ride there – along a narrow river, underneath a monkey-filled canopy – that is the real attraction. **See p.863**

* **Pulau Derawan** Borneo's premier dive site. **See p.874**

Kalimantan

Cupped in the palm of an island arc stretching between the Malay peninsula and Sulawesi, **Kalimantan** comprises the southern, Indonesian two-thirds of the vast island of **Borneo** (the northern reaches of which are split between the independent sultanate of Brunei and the Malaysian states of Sabah and Sarawak). Borneo has conjured up sensational images in the outside world ever since Europeans first visited

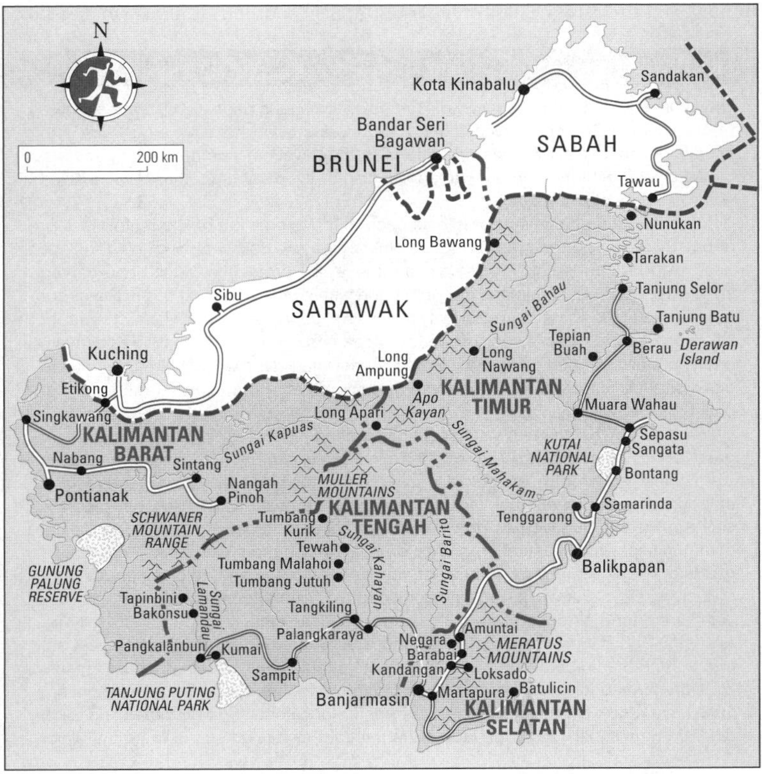

Kota Kinabalu
Sandakan
Bandar Seri Bagawan
BRUNEI
SABAH
0 200 km
Tawau
Nunukan
Long Bawang
Tarakan
Tanjung Selor
Sibu
SARAWAK
Sungai Bahau
Tanjung Batu
Tepian Buah
Berau
Derawan Island
Kuching
Long Ampung
Long Nawang
Etikong
Apo Kayan
KALIMANTAN TIMUR
Singkawang
Long Apari
Muara Wahau
KALIMANTAN BARAT
Sungai Kapuas
Sungai Mahakam
Sepasu
Sangata
Nabang
Sintang
KUTAI NATIONAL PARK
Bontang
Pontianak
Nangah Pinoh
MULLER MOUNTAINS
Samarinda
SCHWANER MOUNTAIN RANGE
Tumbang Kurik
KALIMANTAN TENGAH
Tenggarong
Tewah
Balikpapan
GUNUNG PALUNG RESERVE
Tumbang Malahoi
Tumbang Jutuh
Sungai Kahayan
Sungai Barito
Tapinbini
Bakonsu
Sungai Lamandau
Tangkiling
Amuntai
Pangkalanbun
Kumai
Palangkaraya
Negara
Barabai
MERATUS MOUNTAINS
Sampit
Kandangan
Loksado
TANJUNG PUTING NATIONAL PARK
Banjarmasin
Martapura
Batulicin
KALIMANTAN SELATAN

in the sixteenth century. The first Europeans here found coastal city-states governed by wealthy sultans, whose income derived from trading trinkets and salt with inland tribes for resins, gold and gemstones – Kalimantan means "river of gems". Explorers who later managed to return alive from the interior confirmed rumours of a land cut by innumerable rivers and cloaked in a dense green jungle, inhabited by bizarre beasts and fierce Dayak headhunters. Until recently, the situation had changed very little: Kalimantan only emerged briefly into the limelight as the stage for Japanese–Allied conflict in the latter stages of World War II, and during Indonesia's Konfrontasi with Malaysia over that country's federation in 1963.

Modern Kalimantan has a tough time living up to its romantic tradition, however. Part of the problem is that, in all Kalimantan's 500,000-square-kilometre spread, there are few obvious destinations, and even the best of these often take second place to the lure of adventurous travel for its own sake. Administratively split into four unequally sized provinces, Kalimantan divides more simply into an **undeveloped interior**, with a largely Dayak population, and a Muslim **coastal fringe** with a large ethnic Malay presence, where you'll find all of the major cities. Stripped of their former status as regencies and with little obvious heritage, even the provincial capitals – Pontianak in Kalimantan Barat, Palangkaraya in Kalimantan Tengah, Banjarmasin in Kalimantan Selatan, and Samarinda in Kalimantan Timur – rarely offer much aside from their services. Get beyond them, however, and things improve: despite increasingly rapacious logging and mining, and the recent catastrophic forest fires in southern Kalimantan (see box

The Dayak

Dayak is an umbrella name for all of Borneo's indigenous peoples, who arrived here from mainland Southeast Asia around 2500 years ago and have since split into scores of interrelated groups. Traditionally, they lived in communal longhouses, raised on three-metre stumps, home for a clan or even a village; these also offered some defence against attack.

Dayak **religions** trace worldly events back to the interaction of spirits. Evil is kept at bay by attracting the presence of helpful spirits, and courting the goodwill of the dead with lavish funerals – or else scared away by protective tattoos and carved spirit posts (*patong*). Shamans also intercede with spirits on behalf of the living, but for centuries the most powerful way to ensure good luck was by **headhunting**, which forced the victim's soul into the service of its captor. Headhunting raids were often carefully planned campaigns led by warrior-magicians who invoked demons to possess their followers, granting them ferocity in battle but allowing them no rest until they had killed.

Condoned by Kalimantan's sultans, headhunting disgusted the Dutch, who made great efforts to stamp it out during the nineteenth century. Otherwise, the Dayak were highly regarded by the colonial government: their honesty was legendary, and ethnographers admired their **social systems**, some of which defined separate classes. Wealth, acquired as dowries or by trading in forest products with coastal communities, was measured in bronze drums (looking more like gongs), decorative beads and Chinese dragon jars, all of which today command colossal prices from collectors. Dayak **artwork**, too, is much sought after, and some groups are particularly famed for their decorative designs and woodcarvings.

Most Dayak still use a system of **ladang agriculture**, in which areas of forest are cleared and the timber burnt to ash in order to supplement the mineral-poor topsoil; plots are farmed for a few years, then left to return to their former state. For hunting, guns have widely replaced traditional two-metre-long ironwood **blowpipes** and darts dipped in the lethal sap of the *ipoh* or *upas* tree. Fresh *upas* sap is white and fluid, on p.820), sizeable tracts of the interior remain forested and carry echoes of earlier times. Get out to remoter Dayak settlements, and you could well find yourself more deeply involved than you planned, sharing a room in a traditional house, or caught up in the middle of a festival or shamanistic ritual.

With few roads, Kalimantan's abundant **rivers** become the interior's highways. The two biggest are the Kapuas in the west (Indonesia's longest river), and the eastern Mahakam, which between them total over 1100 navigable kilometres and virtually bisect the island. There are scores of smaller waterways, travelled by everything from bamboo rafts to large ferries. When even the rivers become too small or treacherous for boats, those who have come properly prepared can reach further into Kalimantan's heart by **hiking**, which allows unparalleled contact with the people, wildlife and places of the interior – serious adventurers can even make a month-long trek across Kalimantan. Everywhere, you'll get the most rewarding experience by being flexible and making the most of chance encounters.

Kalimantan is well connected to the outside world, with **flights** from Brunei to eastern Balikpapan, and **boats** from Tewah in Sabah to northeastern Pulau Nunukan. From elsewhere in Indonesia, there are direct flights from Java, with a half-dozen Pelni vessels stopping off in Kalimantan on their Java–Sulawesi–Maluku runs. Once here, small aircraft link Kalimantan's bigger cities with the interior, cutting days off boat travel to the same destinations – if you can get a seat. Kalimantan has few major **roads**; in ideal conditions, you can travel for 1500km around the coast from the island's southwestern corner

drying as a brown, crumbly resin rendered liquid by warming – you can sometimes find older trees deeply scarred from frequent milking. The **mandau**, a lightweight machete, is still ubiquitous as a general-purpose bush knife, and was formerly the primary weapon in battle (a thinner blade attached to the back of the scabbard was used for removing heads). The best blades are made from locally forged steel, though everyday versions are likely to have started life as part of a truck's suspension.

Today, traditional Dayak culture can seem to have become almost an academic issue. Most, if not all, Dayak converted to **Christianity** or, in the case of some Iban in Pontianak, Islam, especially in the wake of the anti-Communist bloodbath in the late 1960s, for fear that their animism would be taken for atheism, a sure sign in the eyes of Suharto's New Order of hardened Leftist sympathies. Even after slogging out to remote areas, visitors searching for a glimpse of the old Dayak lifestyle find instead ostensibly Christian communities, whose inhabitants dress in shorts and T-shirts; the dances performed at more accessible villages are shows geared towards entertaining tourists, and the formerly inspired crafts are now churned out as souvenirs. City dwellers are also prone to portray Dayak as wild animals, while governments and powerful companies habitually appropriate their lands for mining, timber and resettlement projects. Even so, on their own territory, the Dayak are still feared for their jungle skills, abilities with magic, and the way they violently take the law into their own hands if provoked – such as in 1997 and 2000, when West Kalimantan's Dayak and Malay communities exacted a fearsome revenge against Madurese transmigrants (see p.813). The violence of recent years has abated but the Madurese driven away have yet to return.

Recent years have seen a resurgence in the more acceptable side of Dayak tradition. Communal houses, once banned by the government, are being restored, and public festivals like the hugely social funerals or the annual **Erau Festival**, a massive assembly of Kalimantan's eastern Dayak groups on Sungai Mahakam, provide an assurance that Dayak culture is still very much alive, if being redefined.

right up towards the northeastern border with Sabah, and the mass of disconnected tracks probing inland from this trail are often accessible only to motorbikes. Reliable all-weather roads, however, currently extend only between Pontianak and Sintang in Kalimantan Barat, and from Banjarmasin to Bontang in eastern Kalimantan. The already famous **Trans-Borneo highway** across the island has actually yet to eventuate, though in 1996 a convoy of 4WD vehicles made it from Samarinda to Pontianak by following logging trails through the interior.

Crossed by the equator, Kalimantan has no real **seasons**. April through to September is the optimum time for a visit: at the height of the rains (Jan–March), you'll find towns isolated by flooding, with normally calm stretches of water turned to raging torrents, and planes grounded for weeks on end, while the driest months (Aug–Oct) see boats stranded by low river levels. Dayak festivals often occur during slacker agricultural periods, when people have enough spare time to participate.

With only fragmentary infrastructure, **costs** in Kalimantan are higher than in most of the rest of the country, especially for transport in remote areas – fuel can be incredibly expensive. Accommodation is pricey, too: even simple country losmen charge US$2–3 a night, and it's rare in cities to find anything under US$3–4. Note that West and Central Kalimantan operate on Western time, while the south and eastern provinces run on Eastern time.

Kalimantan Barat

Kalbar (short for "Kalimantan Barat"), or **West Kalimantan**, is Kalimantan's most densely populated province, with nearly four million inhabitants spread over 146,800 square kilometres. Unsurprisingly, given the province's relative proximity to southern China, it also has the highest ethnic **Chinese population** in Indonesia: a third of the inhabitants of the capital, Pontianak, and over two-thirds of Kalbar's second biggest town, Singkawang, are of Chinese origin. Many of the Chinese are very poor, and there is a steady flow of ethnic Chinese suitors from Taiwan and Hong Kong through here looking for brides. Of the rest of the population, nearly half are **Malay**, with most of the rest belonging to one of the indigenous **Dayak** tribes, of which the Iban are the most numerous in the province.

The capital of Kalbar, **Pontianak**, stands in the delta of the Kapuas, which at 1243km is Indonesia's longest river. Early settlers and missionaries regarded the Kapuas as a causeway to the interior of Borneo; as a result, the small Dayak towns that line the banks of the Kapuas, such as Sintang and Putussibau, were some of the first in Borneo to receive foreign visitors, and have a more cosmopolitan feel than many other inland settlements. The sultanate of Pontianak, now a tired reflection of its earlier glory, was Arab in origin, the family being al-Kadri. The Kapuas remains an extremely busy and photogenic waterway, with passenger ferries, fishing boats, *toko teapung* (the traditional floating shops of the Kapuas) and rusty little barges tugging huge loads of timber still cruising up and down the river today.

Timber remains Kalbar's number-one industry; although the forests around the Kapuas have been seriously degraded, the more remote corners of the province remain relatively untouched. The two national parks, **Gunung Palung Reserve** in the south and the nascent **Bentuang Karimun** on the border with Sarawak, form the cornerstone of Kalbar's tiny tourist industry, and contain vast tracts of primary rainforest; however, in early 2002, *The Jakarta Post* claimed Gunung Palung has in fact suffered severe degradation by loggers. Be warned that there have been reports of chloroquine-resistant **malaria** (see p.32) in these remoter outreaches of the province.

Kalbar's **transport network** is improving all the time; however, away from the coast and the Pontianak–Putussibau highway, the roads are not sealed and often prove impassable in the rainy season, and public transport is unreliable all year round. Passenger ferries continue to sail up and down the Kapuas, except in the dry season, when the water level is too low.

Social conditions have been greatly altered by the policies of the New Order regime, particularly transmigration. In the first two months of 1997, the Dayak of the Kalimantan Barat undertook a campaign against the ethnic Madurese of the province, which took a startling and violent form. Eyewitnesses said that Dayak followed traditional pre-battle rituals, performing the *tertu* ceremony, where warriors enter a trance-like state and the spirits of their ancestors are invoked. The practice of headhunting was also revived during the fighting. Five thousand Dayak, armed with machetes and *mandau* (traditional swords) stormed the villages of Sanggau Ledo, Jerak and Kampung Jawa. The army, called in to quell the unrest, was helpless in the face of such numbers, and the slaughter went unchecked: estimates of the number of deaths range from 300 to 2000. Underlying tension in the region remains; the Madurese often complain of being overlooked for jobs and promotion by their Dayak bosses, while the Dayak regularly complain about Madurese gangs who, they insist, are responsible for many of the crimes in the province. In October 2000, there were several days of further violence between the Madurese and the Malays in Pontianak, but this seems to have been mainly a gangland turf war over street levies. Unlike in other parts of Indonesia, however, the Chinese have not yet been targets.

Pontianak and around

The capital of Kalimantan Barat, **PONTIANAK**, is a sprawling, grey industrial city of 400,000 lying right on the equator on the confluence of the Landak and Kapuas Kecil rivers. The city is at its best in the evenings, when the local kids fly their kites above the roofs, swifts flock in their thousands to find a suitable roosting spot for the night, and the sky slowly melts into a delicious golden orange hue. During the day, however, Pontianak is hot, noisy, and holds little of interest for the average sightseer.

Pontianak was founded in 1770 by an Arabian pirate-cum-trader **Abdul Rahman**. The name of the city translates roughly as "the ghost of a woman who died in childbirth", a reference to the ghostly howl heard by early visitors to these shores. Believing that this noise was the work of local spirits, Abdul Rahman used cannon fire to frighten them away before he landed. Initially, his town was just one of the many private fiefdoms on the coast; however, the discovery of **gold deposits** just a few kilometres to the north led to Pontianak's rapid expansion.

The city's provincial museum is one of the best of its kind in Indonesia, and Sultan Abdul Rahman's Kadriyah Palace and the adjoining mosque are mildly diverting. You may be lucky enough to meet an old member of the al-Kadri family, who will give you a brief tour of this faded palace. Nevertheless, most travellers stay for only a day or so in Pontianak – just long enough to stock up on supplies and enjoy the comforts and conveniences of a big city – before heading up the Kapuas or straight on to Kuching.

Orientation, arrival and information

Pontianak is bisected by the north–south flowing Sungai Kapuas Kecil. On the southern side of the river, you'll find the **Chinese quarter**, the commercial heart of the city where most of the hotels, restaurants and travel agents are located. In the centre of this quarter, right on the water's edge, is the Kapuas Indah **bemo terminal**, which is connected to a second bemo and bus terminal in Siantan, on the eastern side of the river, by a regular passenger ferry. Pontianak's Supadio **airport** lies 20km south of the city centre; taxis (Rp25,000) can take you into town.

The **ferry port** lies a few hundred metres to the northwest of the Kapuas Indah bemo station near the very centre of town. By contrast, the Batu Layang **bus terminal** is inconveniently located 6km north of Siantan. Regular white bemos (Rp500) run from Batu Layang to the Siantan bemo terminal, from where you can catch a ferry (Rp150) to the western side. Note that when leaving Pontianak, there's no need to travel all the way to the Batu Layang bus terminal; all the bus companies have agents in the centre of town on the western side of the river, and buses depart from these offices.

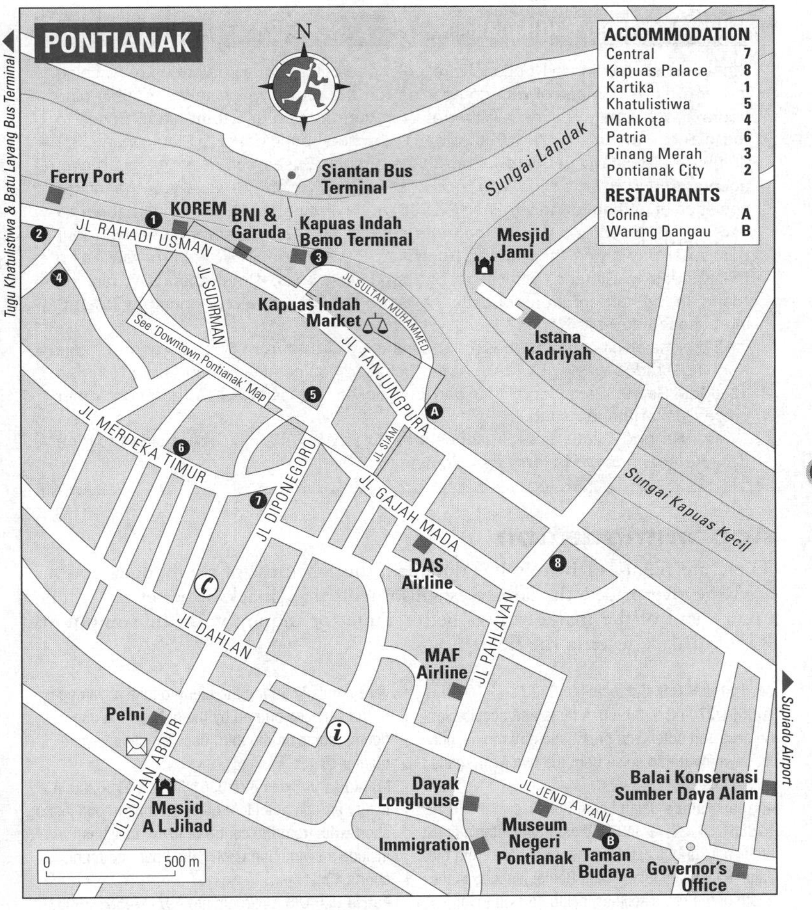

Pontianak's regional **tourist office** (Mon–Thurs & Sat 8am–2pm, Fri 8–11am; ⓣ0561/36712) lies tucked away in the quiet suburbs to the west of Jalan Jend A. Yani at Jl Ahmad Sood 25. It's really not worth the hassle to get here, unless you wish to pick up a couple of useless glossy brochures and swap a few pleasantries with the friendly but unhelpful non-English-speaking staff. For information on Kalbar's national parks, or to pick up a free two-week visitor permit for them, visit the **Balai Konservasi Sumber Daya Alam** at Jl Rahman Saleh 33 (Mon–Thurs & Sat 7am–2pm, Fri 7am–noon). Again, no English is spoken here.

Note that addresses in Pontianak can be confusing. Streets often go by two different names (for example, Jalan H.O.S. Cokroaminto is also known as Jalan Merdeka Timur, and Jalan Diponegoro is also known as Jalan Sisingamangaraja), and address numbers do not run in sequence. However, most of the locals will be able to point you in the right direction.

Moving on from Pontianak

Many tourists arriving in Pontianak are looking to catch a **bus** straight up to Kuching in Sarawak. A number of bus companies run the route, which takes roughly nine hours; most departures leave either early in the morning or late at night. Buses to the interior – to Sintang (7hr), Putussibau (12hr) and up the coast to Singkawang (3hr 30min) – also leave frequently from these agents. Buses call in at the bus-ticket agents around town en route to their destinations, which will save you the inconvenience of getting to the terminal. PT SJS (Setia Jiwana Sakti), Jl Sisingamangaraja 155 (ⓣ0561/34626), is one of the more popular and reliable companies, with four buses per day plying the route to Kuching, Sibu and Miri. They also run buses up the Kapuas to Sintang, with a couple continuing on to Putussibau. CV Tanjung Niang, in the harbour area opposite the bemo station, is the only company operating buses (3 daily) to Nanga Pinoh.

All the major cities in Indonesia are served by **flights** from Supadio airport, as is Kuching – thrice-weekly by MAS. At the Pelni ferry office at Jl Sultan Abdur Rahman 12 (Mon–Sat 9.30am–noon) you can buy tickets for services to, amongst other places, Jakarta and Kijang.

Mitra Kalindo Samudera, Jl Diponegoro 39 (ⓣ0561/49751), sells tickets for the daily *Ketapang Express* **ferry** to Ketapang (6hr).

Accommodation

There are plenty of **hotels** in Pontianak, though most of the budget options are large, overpriced, threadbare establishments that smack of better times. The luxury end of the market offers better value for money, with the sumptuous Kapuas Palace leading the field.

Central Jl H.O.S. Cokroaminto 232 ⓣ0561/37444, ⓕ34993. A huge and hospitable Chinese-run hotel with bright and airy rooms, only let down by traffic noise from the two main roads outside. ❹

Kapuas Palace Jalan Imam Bonjol ⓣ0561/36122, ⓕ34374. West Kalimantan's finest hotel, a luxurious establishment set back from the Jalan Pahlawan/Jalan Imam Bonjol junction in the south of the city. Facilities include a swimming pool, bars, restaurants and coffee shops; every room has satellite TV and a bath or shower. ❼

Kartika Jalan Rahadi Usman ⓣ0561/34401, ⓕ38457. A pleasant riverside hotel (most of the foundations are actually in the water), suffering, for no apparent reason, from a lack of custom. Facilities include a restaurant, tennis courts, parking, laundry and a gift shop. It may be worth trying to haggle for a cheaper rate. ❺

Khatulistiwa Jl Diponegoro 56 ⓣ0561/36793, ⓕ34930. A huge, shabby hotel built around a central courtyard. The rooms (all doubles with attached bathrooms) are reasonably comfortable, though your sleep could well be disturbed by the long-distance lorry drivers who pull into the courtyard regularly during the night to take advantage of the services offered by the girls on the upper floors; rooms on the third floor are cheaper and quieter. ❸

Mahkota Jl Sidas 8 ⓣ0561/36022, ⓕ36200. A luxury air-con hotel in a quiet neighbourhood just a short walk from the centre of town; facilities include a swimming pool, coffee bar and tennis courts. ❻

Patria Jl H.O.S. Cokroaminto 497 ⓣ0561/36063. This sprawling establishment is the best of the budget bunch, despite a far-from-central location. The rooms all come with a bathroom, though watch out for the rats late at night. ❹

Pinang Merah Jl Kapten Marsan 51–53 ⓣ0561/32547, ⓕ39032. The best of the two options in the tawdry port area. The manager speaks English and offers a variety of rooms, mostly fairly tatty, but with TV, air-con and mandi. ❸

Pontianak City Jl Pak Kasih 44 ⓣ0561/32495, ⓕ33781. An excellent-value hotel a 2min walk to the right of the harbour, with friendly staff and well-appointed rooms that come with TV, air-con and telephone. ❹

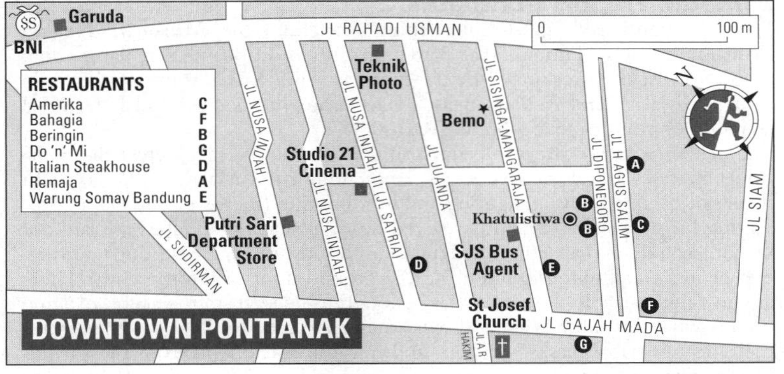

The City

Though Pontianak lacks any truly compelling tourist attractions, the **royal palace** and **mosque** of Abdul Rahman and the **Museum Negeri** (State Museum) offer enjoyable ways to spend an afternoon. If you've still got time to kill after these sights, sit on the water's edge and watch the photogenic river life go by, or have a look around the Kapuas Indah market, where you'll find a couple of small **Taoist Buddhist temples** (watch your belongings, however, as pickpockets operate in the area). The truly restless can head up to the Tugu Khatulistiwa, Pontianak's "equator monument".

Ateng Tours, Jl Gajah Mada 201 (☎0561/32683), offer a one-day **tour** of Pontianak, including the museum and palace for US$25.

The Mesjid Jami and Istana Kadriyah

These two eye-catching buildings stand near each other on the eastern side of the Kapuas Kecil, just to the south of the confluence with the Landak. This area, known as the Kampung Baris, is the site of Abdul Rahman's original settlement and both the Mesjid Jami (mosque) and the Istana Kadriyah (palace) are his creations. Small passenger boats with a driver/rower can be rented from the eastern end of Jalan Mahakam II, in the Kapuas Indah market.

The **Mesjid Jami**, also known as the Mesjid Abdurrakhman (an Indonesian corruption of Abdul Rahman), stands right by the water's edge where the boats dock, its traditional Javanese four-tiered roof towering above the low-slung kampung that surrounds it. Indeed, the yellow exterior (both the palace and the mosque are painted yellow, the traditional colour of royalty amongst the Malays) is somewhat more impressive than the rather creaky green interior, which contains little of note.

Two hundred metres to the southwest is the ironwood **Istana Kadriyah**, built by Abdul Rahman in 1771. The descendants of Abdul still own the istana today, and the son of the seventh sultan lives in one of the wings. There don't seem to be any set opening times, and for long periods it remains closed to the public altogether. When it does open, visitors are treated to a rather odd collection of items, from the bust of a Dutch woman who married into the family to a large collection of mirrors, thrones, tables and other gilt furniture. It's all a little surreal, especially when one considers that this ostentatious wealth stands right in the heart of one of Pontianak's poorer districts.

Museum Negeri Pontianak

Probably Pontianak's most entertaining attraction, the **Museum Negeri Pontianak** (Mon–Thurs & Sat 8am–1pm, Fri 8–11.30am, Sun 9am–noon; Rp500) is usually overlooked by travellers, as it lies 1.5km south of the town centre on Jalan Jend A. Yani; bemos leave from the Kapuas Indah terminal (Rp500) or you can take a becak (Rp1000).

A series of kitsch **concrete reliefs** on the museum's facade depict the traditional lifestyles of Kalbar's two largest ethnic minorities, Malay and Dayak, with scenes of fishing, hunting, fighting and headhunting (there's even a Dayak presenting his wife with a recently severed head). Inside, the exhibits are laid out by subject rather than ethnic origin (significantly, the Chinese don't feature, except in a small pottery section on the ground floor of the museum). There are no English labels, though it's easy enough to guess from the accompanying photos what the exhibits are and what they were used for. The comprehensive collection of tribal masks, weapons and musical instruments from the various Dayak tribes of the interior are probably the highlight. There are also some fine examples of woven baskets, used by the Dayak for fishing, and a small selection of carved wooden blocks that were used as templates for tattoos.

Just round the corner from the museum, on Jalan Sutoyo, is an impressive but empty replica of a **Dayak longhouse**, over 50m long and 15m high, where you're free to wander around.

Equator monument

Pontianak's **equator monument**, built in 1928 and one of the few remnants of Dutch architecture in the city, stands on its own little patch of grass by the side of Jalan Khatulistiwa, about 2km from town, on the way to the Batu Layang bus terminal. For some reason, the locals are inordinately proud of the rather squat-looking, twelve-metre obelisk; every March and September equinox, when the monument casts no shadow, they flock in their thousands to witness this phenomenon, before heading back to town for a party. To get there, catch any bemo to the bus terminal from the Siantan bemo terminal.

Eating

Pontianak has the usual oversupply of cheap, grubby **warung** serving basic Indonesian snacks, particularly around Jalan Pasar Indah. Care should be exercised in these places: hygiene standards are often lower in Pontianak than in other parts of Indonesia, particularly in the dry season, when the public water supply is rationed and warung owners are forced to find their own sources. Street stalls congregate every night on the KOREM Place, a small concrete square by the river named after the Komando Regimen Militer building that stands behind it. Locally grown coffee is Pontianak's speciality, and all over town *warung kopi* (coffee houses) serve glasses of this dark, thick brew.

Amerika Jl H. Agus Salim 114. A popular mid-priced young hangout that specializes in frying up every edible part of a chicken. Try the liver, gizzard or, for something more substantial, the entire bird. Not cheap, but tasty.

Bahagia Jl H. Agus Salim 182. One of the very few vegetarian cafés in town, serving unexceptional budget fare that's fine for a lunchtime snack.

Beringin Jl Diponegoro 113 & 149. Two mid-priced, hygienic Padang food restaurants under one name, standing within 40m of each other on the same side of Jalan Diponegoro.

Corina Jl Tanjungpura 124. A clean and quiet budget restaurant serving Chinese and Indonesian food, including a particularly tasty crab omelette.

Do 'n' Mi Jalan Patimura. A neon-lit local hangout where green-clad staff serve well-to-do Pontianak citizens with cakes, ice creams and a few hot meals. The prices are reasonable, the food is delicious, but portions are small.

Italian Steakhouse Jl Satria 109–111. A friendly and clean restaurant, with a sizeable Japanese menu as well as a wide range of Western fast food standards. Overall not bad at all, though a little expensive.

Remaja Jl H. Agus Salim 92. Fast food, Kalbar-style. A fried-chicken outlet that's very popular in the early evenings with Pontianak's young professionals, even though the chicken can be a little stringy and the portions on the small side.

Warung Dangau Jalan Jend A. Yani. A highly recommended and flashy little mid-priced restaurant, tucked away in the Taman Budaya. Lovingly prepared Indonesian food is served with a twist (their nasi goreng, for example, is embellished with prawn crackers and sate sticks).

Warung Somay Bandung Jl Sisingamangaraja 132. Possibly the city's best warung, this no-fuss eating place serves six or seven basic meals that cost no more than Rp5000, and also provides free drinking water.

Listings

Airline offices Bouraq, Jl Pahlawan Blok D no. 3 ⓣ0561/37261; DAS, Jl Gajah Mada 67 ⓣ0561/32313; Garuda, Jl Rahadi Usman 8a ⓣ0561/78111; MAF, Jl Supranto 50a ⓣ0561/30271; MAS, Jl Sidas 8 ⓣ0561/30069; Merpati, Jl Gajah Mada 210 ⓣ0561/36568.

Banks and exchange BNI, Jalan Rahadi Usman; PT Safari moneychangers, Jl Nusa Indah III 45.

Cinema Studio 21 on Jalan Nusa Indah III has four screens showing recent Hollywood films.

Consulates Malaysian consulate, Jl Jend A. Yani 42.

Internet access Warposnet at the GPO; Mon–Thurs, Sat & Sun 8am–2pm, Fri 8–11am.

Ferries The Pelni office is at Jl Sultan Abdur Rahman 12; Mon–Sat 9.30am–noon.

Post office Jl Sultan Abdur Rahman 49 (daily 8am–9pm). The poste restante, at the back of the building, closes at 2pm.

Telephone and fax Telkom, Jl Teuku Umar 15, has IDD, fax and reverse-charge facilities; open 24hr.

South of Pontianak

Transport connections between Pontianak and the neighbouring towns on the west coast are poor. The northern Pontianak–Sambas road peters out at the village of Supadio, just 10km south of Pontianak; to travel any further, you'll need to take a boat.

This dire transport situation can be annoying, especially if you're trying to reach the remote **Gunung Palung Reserve**, a pretty little national park 90km south of Pontianak. The park features a wide variety of flora, from thick low-lying mangrove forest to the sparse, mountain vegetation of Gunung Palung (1116m) itself, as well as a large troop of proboscis monkeys and macaques. Unfortunately, the park was ravaged by the 1997 fires (see box on p.820), and large tracts of it now lie charred and desolate; much is accessible only by boat, and with the cost of benzene so high on Borneo, the total cost of the trip can be fairly exorbitant.

Getting to the park is also extremely time-consuming. Having picked up your permit from the parks office in Pontianak (see p.815), the next step is to catch the Ketapang Express ferry to Ketapang (8am, 6hr). From Ketapang, it's four hours to **Sukadana** by bus (Rp2000), 30km north back along the coast; this small town has a small KSDA office where you can hire off-duty park officials as guides. **Telok Melano**, a thirty-minute bemo ride away, is the last village before the park entrance; there is a small, anonymous *penginapan* (❶) and a couple of warung here. From Telok Melano, you can hire one of the boatmen to ferry you to the park itself. Officially, you aren't allowed into the park without a guide, nor are you allowed to camp there – but neither of these rules seem to be rigidly adhered to. Guides can be hired at the park entrance, or in Telok Melano (about Rp30,000 per day).

Forests and fires

During the mid-1980s, a series of disastrous fires cleared thousands of square kilometres of Kalimantan's native forests. Sadly, these were only a prelude to events of a decade later. May 1997 saw the first flames of a conflagration which was to last over a year and reduce huge swaths of Kalimantan to charcoal. By August, smoke from the fires covered an area stretching from Thailand to West Papua, and north to the Philippines; visibility in cities in southern Kalimantan was reduced to tens of metres, and ineffective surgeons' masks were all that local people were offered against inhaling the fumes. Kuala Lumpur and Singapore were also covered in a smog-like haze, which at its worst closed airports in those cities, while expats and wealthier citizens queued to fly to cleaner climes. As President Suharto, in an unprecedented move, apologized to neighbouring nations, the September 1997 crash of a Garuda airliner in Sumatra, along with numerous regional shipping collisions and the impossibility of flying relief supplies to famine-struck regions of West Papua, were all blamed on the smoke.

While human attention focused on the effects of the smoke, the fires themselves were devouring sixty thousand square kilometres of national parks. One of the worst affected was Kutai (see p.871), north of Samarinda in eastern Kalimantan, which had already been seriously degraded by the 1980s fires, along with government-approved logging and transmigrant settlements within the park. Kutai's few remaining areas of forest were destroyed, along with over one hundred resident orang-utans. It's been estimated that, across Kalimantan, fires have either killed or destroyed the habitat of seven thousand of these apes, a third of the entire world population.

Traditional slash-and-burn agriculture was initially blamed as the cause of the fires, but as this has been practised for thousands of years in Kalimantan without causing such widespread devastation, it can't be entirely responsible. Most likely, the 1997 fires were started by plantation companies, who, despite a ban of the practice in 1995, use burning off as an inexpensive way to prepare areas for planting oil palms or commercial timber. The effects of this would have been compounded by logging, which clears areas of damp, fire-resistant forest and leaves highly flammable debris in its wake. Logged areas are also initially recolonized by grassland, which withers during the dry season, becoming highly combustible. Another major factor in the extent of the 1997 fires is that much of Kalimantan's soils are peat, a material which, once ignited, is capable of burning underground and so is almost impossible to extinguish.

Though the Indonesian government came under criticism for its ineffectual handling of the fires – Jakarta was south of the smoke haze, and it has been suggested that if the capital had been worse affected, the response would have been speedier – the truth is that there simply weren't enough resources available in Indonesia to deal with such a disaster. The heavy wet-season rains, which naturally would have done so, failed almost completely between 1996 and 1998 when the *El Niño* climate phenomenon was at its strongest and, with the causes of the fires still to be dealt with, it seems inevitable that the situation will occur again.

North of Pontianak and on to the border

Kalbar's second biggest town, **SINGKAWANG**, lies 145km north of Pontianak. It was originally founded as a mining settlement by the Hakka Chinese, who maintain an overwhelming presence in the town today. Crisscrossed by wide, tidy streets flanked by covered walkways, Singkawang is an attractive, easy-going town with some decent hotels and a number of excellent-value Chinese restaurants. There's little to see, though the town has a unique atmosphere, being neither absolutely Chinese nor Indonesian, and it's a useful base for exploring Kalbar's northern shores. Adventurous travellers may like to check out the possibility of hiring boats out to the offshore islands.

Of the **hotels**, the best of the budget options is the *Khatuliwista Plaza I*, situated at the heart of the action at Jl Selamat Karman 17 (ⓣ0562/31697; ❶). Clean rooms and a pleasant TV lounge on every floor make this one of the best-value places on the west coast. Its only serious rival is the *Wisata Hotel*, Jl Diponegoro 59 (ⓣ0562/31082, ⓕ32563; ❶), which has a similar standard of rooms, though it's let down a little by its location, 2km south of the town centre. In the mid-price bracket, the *Hotel Kalbar* at Jl Kepol Machmud 1 (ⓣ0561/31460; ❷) is very friendly, has some smart rooms and is probably the best value. Even if you don't plan to stay in Singkawang, don't miss out on the opportunity of tasting some excellent **Chinese food**: the *Rumah Makan Selera*, at Jl Diponegoro 106, has some superb Chinese noodle dishes, especially the *kue tiaw* (flat noodles with seafood), and *Aquarin*, Jl Sejahtera 70, provides the *Selera* with some healthy competition. If Chinese food doesn't appeal, try the Padang specialists *Restoran Roda Beringin*, at the northern end of Jalan Diponegoro.

The coastline around Singkawang is crammed with **beaches**. **Pasir Panjang**, a two-kilometre stretch of golden sand luxuriating just 13km south of town, is the best of these, particularly during the week, when it's deserted. Bemos leave regularly from Singkawang's central terminal on Jalan Stasiun, one block south of the *Hotel Kalbar*. There's a small picnic area at the beach's northern end, and a rather shabby hotel, the *Palapa* (ⓣ0562/33367; ❷). The accommodation on offer is nothing special, though the hotel redeems itself somewhat by organizing trips to the nearby uninhabited island of **Pulau Randayan**, a haven of peace and isolation.

Another day-trip from Singkawang, **SAMBAS** is a two-hour bemo ride north along the coast. The town acquired a degree of fame earlier last century when archeologists discovered Indian coins and Hindu statuary that proved that the Sriwijaya empire (see p.1034), based in Sumatra during the seventh and eighth centuries, once extended at least as far as this remote corner of West Kalimantan. Today, the town is one of the west coast's most picturesque, with most of the inhabitants living in the riverside kampungs that stand on stilts in the water of the Sungai Sambas basin. At the northern end of Sambas, just over the small bridge, is the muted yellow **kraton** of the Malay sultan who still rules over the town. The palace itself was built in 1812, during Sir Stamford Raffles' period in office; the mosque next door was built in 1890, and is currently closed to the public.

The border: Etikong

Indonesia's only authorized open land crossing – pending normalization of relations with East Timor – is at **ETIKONG**, on the Pontianak–Kuching highway, some seven hours by bus from Pontianak.

The interior

With its headwaters in the Muller Mountain Range of central Borneo and its mouth on Kalimantan's western shore, **Sungai Kapuas** is, at 1243km, Indonesia's longest river by far. It is reasonably picturesque, though hardly spectacular, with sawmills and timber stations rapidly replacing traditional Dayak villages along the riverbank. Most of the settlements along the Kapuas are tiny, though there are a couple of fairly sizeable towns en route, such as **Sintang** and **Putussibau**, both of which were founded during the Dutch era. Many of the people who now inhabit these towns and villages are non-native, having arrived in Kalbar as part of the government's transmigration programme during the 1980s and early 1990s (see p.1041). The Madurese, in particular, make up a considerable percentage of the population, though their presence is not always welcomed by the locals. For a glimpse of traditional Dayak settlements you need to travel beyond Putussibau, the last major settlement in West Kalimantan, to the longhouses further upstream.

Passenger ferries still travel between Pontianak and Putussibau, at least during the rainy season; in the dry season, the waters are too shallow for all but the smallest vessels. The meandering double-decker *bandung* are the most traditional and common passenger ferries on the Kapuas, and are extremely slow, taking up to five days to travel the 870km between Pontianak and Putussibau. However, the journey between Pontianak and Sintang takes only two days, and is far less arduous. The conditions on board these ferries are extremely basic.

With improvements in the condition and maintenance of the **Trans-Kalbar Highway**, buses have now superseded boats as the most popular and convenient mode of transport into the interior. The highway begins at Mandor, 40km north of Pontianak, and only joins the Kapuas at Sanggau, 256km east of Pontianak, though it roughly follows the course of the river thereafter. Buses tend to leave in the early evening, boats in the early morning.

Sintang

SINTANG, 325km east of Pontianak, is built on the confluence of the Kapuas and Melawai rivers, and makes an ideal overnight stop for those wishing to break the journey between Pontianak and Putussibau. It seems almost surreal to find such a bustling town in the middle of Kalbar's untamed landscape, yet it has a population of over 20,000, many of whom migrated from Java and Sumatra to work in the timber and construction industries. The town, by Kalbar's standards at least, also has a long and well-documented history, having been one of the first Dutch towns in the interior of Borneo, and one that could also boast its own local royal family. Though the royal line died out at the beginning of the twentieth century, the **palace** still stands on the northern side of the Kapuas, where it's been converted into a small **museum**, housing a few Dayak artefacts and some faded photos of the raja and his family. The museum doesn't charge an entrance fee, though it's often locked and you'll have to ask one of the neighbours to fetch you the key. Just down from the palace is the local mosque, the Mesjid Jamik, a charming little place faced almost entirely with wooden planks.

Sintang is lively, friendly and easy to get around; the bus and bemo stations, as well as a tidy selection of hotels and restaurants, are all within walking distance of each other, on the southern side of the Kapuas to the west of the Melawai. The **accommodation** is clean and, for Kalbar, fairly inexpensive. The best-value hotels are on the waterfront, 150m due north of the bus station. The *Sesean*, at Jl Brigjen Katamso 1 (Ⓣ0565/21011; ❶), is a cheerful and reasonably smart hotel popular with both travellers and swifts, which nest in the eaves and make a terrible din at night; the rooms on the ground floor are quieter. Just behind the *Sesean* is the *Setian*, Jl Brigjen Katamso 78 (Ⓣ0565/21611; ❶), one of the cheapest in town. You don't get a fan at this price, however, which in this sticky climate is a major drawback. Of better value is the *Safary*, just a little further south on Jalan Kol Sugiano (Ⓣ0565/21776; ❶), where doubles come with a fan and TV.

Putussibau and around

A further 412km east of Sintang, the ramshackle little frontier town of **PUTUSSIBAU** was the easternmost outpost of the Dutch during the latter half of the nineteenth century. Situated at the point where the Sungai Sibau empties into the Kapuas (Putussibau translates as "Break in the Sibau River"), the town fairly buzzes in the morning when the riverside market is in full swing, but slowly winds down thereafter, until nearly all activity has ceased by sunset. There's little to do in Putussibau itself, though the town serves as an important base for exploration of the interior.

Much of Putussibau, including most of the market, stands on stilts on the riverbank. There are a couple of **hotels** here, near the large *bupati*'s house (Putussibau's *bupati*, or village head, is the most important of the six in Kalbar, and presides over Kalbar's *bupatis'* annual conference), which was once the home of the Dutch governor. The cheapest is the *Gautama* floating hotel (❶). These floating hotels, known locally as *penginapan terapung*, can be found throughout Kalbar, though this is one of the very few that accepts foreigners. Don't expect much comfort, privacy or space, but if you don't mind roughing it you'll gain an interesting insight into the daily life of the itinerant market traders, fishermen and prostitutes. Overlooking the *Gautama* is the *Aman Sentosa* on Jalan Diponegoro (Ⓣ0567/21533; ❷), which offers more conventional and comfortable accommodation.

There are also a couple of **longhouses** just a few kilometres upriver from Putussibau that still manage to retain a fairly traditional farming and fishing lifestyle, though they have been receiving tourists for years. The *Melapi I* longhouse and the *Sayut* are arguably the most impressive. Boat owners will approach you offering a guided tour of four or five longhouses: don't forget to bring presents, and see the box below for more details on longhouse etiquette.

Iban culture and longhouses

The Iban have a reputation as a very egalitarian people, and it's true that the longhouse *tuai*, or village chief, is more of a figurehead than somebody who wields actual power. Traditionally, the men are the **hunters** in the community, while the women are famous for their **weaving** prowess. The beautiful *pua kumba*, a ritual cloth of intricate design, can be found in Pontianak's souvenir shops, and is typical of the Iban style and flamboyant use of colour.

The Iban love a good party, the highlight of their calendar being the *gawai* (harvest festival), celebrated in May or June when the rice harvest has been gathered in. Visitors are welcome to join in the celebrations, providing they come bearing gifts. Western clothes, children's toys, cassettes and cigarettes are all appreciated. It's also important that you socialize with the chief's family first, and give him gifts to distribute amongst the villagers. Iban **etiquette** dictates that you should only enter the longhouse when invited, and should shake any proffered hands – though don't touch any other part of their body (particularly the head, even of small children). The Iban will doubtless feed you to bursting point – it's part of their tradition of hospitality. If you're invited for a swim in the local river, don't miss out – though don't wear revealing clothes, which may embarrass your hosts.

Bentuang Karimun national park

West of Putussibau, the fledgling **Bentuang Karimun national park**, covering over two hundred square kilometres, has the potential to be one of the greatest in Southeast Asia, particularly if, as is hoped, it links up with the neighbouring reserves in Sarawak to form a transnational sanctuary for Borneo's endangered wildlife. At the moment, however, there is no tourist infrastructure in the park and visitors have to organize their own guides and transport. Most of the time, you'll be travelling the park by motorboat. All visitors to the park must also have a free permit, issued by the KSDA office in Pontianak at Jl Yos Sudarso 129.

Southern Kalimantan

Dropping down from Kalimantan's central highlands and out to the Java Sea, **southern Kalimantan** splits into two very different parts. Until 1957 this was a single province governed by an Islamic majority settled around the southeastern city of **Banjarmasin**, but that year saw the region's Dayak population – after a brief armed struggle – granted autonomy. With the tiny river port of **Palangkaraya** as its capital, the western three-quarters of the region became the thinly populated, Dayak-controlled Kalimantan Tengah, or **Kalteng**. The Muslim southeast continued as Kalimantan Selatan, or **Kalsel**, Kalimantan's smallest, most densely settled province. Though the process won a huge territory for the Dayak, it wasn't such a good move financially: despite its smaller size, Kalsel commands the regional economy, with Banjarmasin's port fronting one of the busiest cities in the whole of Borneo. In contrast, Kalteng remains an undeveloped backwater, whose tiny urban centres appear distinctly downmarket and with the main regional asset – timber – rapidly being stripped. However, the independence movement was also about state recognition of Dayak identity, and this was certainly achieved, with the government even approving the local religion, **Kaharingan**.

Down near the southwestern town of **Pangkalanbun**, **Tanjung Puting national park** is one of Kalimantan's biggest draws, whose primates – which include rambunctious **orang-utans** and the peculiar **proboscis monkey** – alone justify the journey here. Over in the southeast, **Banjarmasin** is another obvious destination, a city stamped with its own assertive culture, and with the attraction of **gem mines** nearby at **Martapura**. Inland, about half of Kalteng's Dayak remain devotees of the Kaharingan faith, with villages upstream from Pangkalanbun and Palangkaraya still featuring old **longhouses**, memorials to the dead, and occasional large-scale **festivals**. More easily reached, Kalsel's **Meratus mountains** make for good hiking into the domain of the **Bukit** people.

Provincial divisions are very apparent once you start moving around the region. Kalteng's sole **transport artery** is the partially sealed, four-hundred-kilometre "highway" joining Pangkalanbun to Palangkaraya, traversed in dry conditions by daily buses. There are no airstrips and few roads inland, so transport here is usually by river; a general principle is that even scheduled public vessels (often desperately overcrowded *sped*, outboard-propelled speedboats) depart when they fill up. For its part, Kalsel has more roads and public transport than any other province in Kalimantan, with the 500-kilometre Banjarmasin–Balikpapan highway skirting the west side of Kalsel's mountains and running northeast out of the region.

Pangkalanbun, Kumai and around

Stuck way down in the region's isolated southwestern corner, **Pangkalanbun**'s government offices and satellite port 25km away at **Kumai** conveniently plug an administrative and supply gap in Kalimantan's coastline. A dusty town unencumbered by sights, you'll have to stop briefly in Pangkalanbun to sort out paperwork for visiting the more engaging **Tanjung Puting national park**, reached through Kumai, or to make preparations for heading inland to **Dayak villages**.

Pangkalanbun

The downtown area of **PANGKALANBUN** is a cluster of marketplaces and shops on the eastern bank of the modest **Sungai Arut**, though the river itself is obscured by buildings along the waterfront. A plywood plant and the huge numbers of diesel pumps for sale, used in working gold deposits, point to local industries, though Pangkalanbun is also romantically known as a source of *kecubung*, **amethysts**. The best stones – mined 60km west at **Sukarma** – are very dark, said to be a sign of age; polished and lustrous, they sell in lucky sets of five. There are a few gem stalls at Pangkalanbun's markets – try **Pasar Baru**, about 500m east of the BNI bank along Jalan Antasari – and a bigger selection at Kecubung Antik on Jalan Santrek, which also stocks brightly coloured Dayak mementoes. Those heading **to Tanjung Puting national park** must first register with Pangkalanbun's **police** at their headquarters, 1km south of the centre on Jalan Diponegoro (daily 7am–5pm; catch a bemo from the Jalan Kasamayuda–Jalan Santrek intersection). It costs nothing to do this, but you'll need your passport and copies of both the photo page and the visa page; the nearest photocopier is at a small kiosk 300m up the road. The whole registration process takes about ten minutes, and leaves you with a registration certificate to be handed to the conservation office (PHPA). Following a disagreement in early 2000 with some locals – the park authorities seized and destroyed some timber that had been cut from the park, and in revenge the PHPA offices in Kumai were ransacked and all the equipment destroyed – the PHPA are now operating from a rented house on Jalan Maligo in Pangkalanbun (Ⓣ0532/22340; Mon–Thurs 7.30am–2pm, Fri 7–11am, Sat 7.30am–1pm). By the time you read this, however, they may well have moved again, this time to their new offices on Jalan H.M. Rafi'i, near the main roundabout that you pass on the way into Pangkalanbun. Wherever they are, it is to them that you pay the park entrance fee of Rp2000 per person per day, with another Rp2000 per boat per day.

Practicalities

Following the river's southern bank, Jalan Antasari is Pangkalanbun's main street. Orientate yourself by finding the intersection with Jalan Rangga Santrek – the BNI **bank** here (foreign exchange Mon–Thurs 8am–3pm, Fri 8–11am) is a useful landmark – which runs 70m or so south to where Jalan Kasamayuda parallels Jalan Antasari. **Arrival points** are scattered; the **airport** is 5km out to the southeast, and you'll need to charter a bemo to your destination at a flat rate of Rp15,000. **Long-distance buses** stop at their respective out-of-town head offices, with the most popular, Bis Yessoe, at Jl Kawitan 68; from there, it's an Rp2000 ojek ride down to the town centre, and Lina Tama in the centre of town at the junctions of Jalan Santrek and Jalan Kasamayuda. **Boats** from Java and elsewhere in Kalimantan dock at Kumai (see p.827). Though the town is

Moving on from Pangkalanbun

The **bus agents** Yessoe and Lina Tama can be found at the junction of Jalan Pra Kesuma Yudha and Jalan Rangga Santrek. Both operate twice-daily departures to Palangkaraya (10hr, Rp50,000), and on to Banjarmasin (Rp78,000). Both also make airline bookings to Palangkaraya, Pontianak or Java and Pelni ferry bookings out of Kumai to Java, though the main **Pelni** office is at Jl Diponegoro 71 (Ⓣ0532/24420), a couple of hundred metres above the police station on the opposite side of the road. **Merpati**, with flights to Semarang, are at Jl Hasanuddin 11 (Ⓣ0532/21478), with the DAS offices nearby, also on Jalan Hasanuddin. If available, **water taxis** inland leave from the **jetty** behind, and to the west of, the BNI bank. An ojek **to Kumai** costs Rp15,000 or, before about 3pm, you can catch a bemo (Rp4000) from the bus lot at the top of the hill at the eastern end of Jalan Pra Kesuma Yudha.

small, Pangkalanbun's yellow **bemos** are a cheap way to get around (Rp1000), or negotiate fares with ojeks.

Few of Pangkalanbun's cheaper **lodgings** want foreign custom. Next to the waterboat jetty off Jalan Antasari, the *Selecta*, (Ⓣ0532/21526; ❷) does, but you'll get more for your money at the basic but friendly *Rahayu*, Jl Pra Kesuma Yudha 73 (Ⓣ0532/21135; ❷), 150m down from the bus offices. Slightly more upmarket, the *Hotel Abadi*, virtually opposite the BNI bank at Jl Antasari 150 (Ⓣ0532/21021, Ⓕ22800; ❷–❸), has rooms with fans or air-con, though it's often full, especially when the Pelni ship calls in at Kumai. On the hill above Jalan Kasamayuda, the *Blue Kecubung* (Ⓣ0532/21211, Ⓕ21513; ❺) is helpful but overpriced, and it takes bookings for *Rimba Lodge* in Tanjung Puting national park (see p.829). Most hotels serve **meals**, otherwise the usual range of inexpensive staples at stalls around the markets is supplemented by pricey Chinese fare at the *Phoenix* and a good Padang selection at *Beringin Padang*, both on Jalan Antasari.

There is an **internet** café, Artha Warnet (Rp10,000 per hour), on Jalan Pasana, a few kilometres out of the town centre in the same area as the PHPA office, while the **post office** is by the junction of Jalan Pra Kesuma Yudha and Jalan Rangga Santrek.

North to Tapinbini

Indonesian speakers on an ethnological quest will find it worthwhile exploring the headwaters of **Sungai Lamandau**, which originates 160km north of Pangkalanbun on the provincial border. The main attractions here are the villages of **Bakonsu**, some 90km upstream, and **Tapinbini** 20km further north, both draped in the trappings of the Kaharingan religion. There are no facilities for travellers, but it's possible to stay and eat in longhouses; for more on Kaharingan village etiquette, see p.833.

Transport here can be tricky. **By river**, a four-seat speedboat charter to Tapinbini will get you there in five hours, but at a cost of Rp600,000. More realistically, there's a daily water taxi to **Kotawaringin Lama** (Rp10,000), a small town about 35km up the Lamandau. From here, irregular services continue 30km upstream to **Kujan**, from where it's possible to find an ojek to take you overland to Tapinbini (Rp20,000–30,000). You can also reach Kujan on the weekly **bus** from Pangkalanbun's long-distance depot. The bike track from Kujan is frightful at the best of times, but then so are the boulder-ridden rapids above Bakonsu, while Tapinbini itself marks the start of a fierce stretch of cataracts. Once here, **BAKONSU** has several longhouses and, as a result of a massive funeral ceremony in June 1997, a host of traditional mausoleums and memorials to the dead; for its part, **TAPINBINI** has forests and more longhouses, two of which are reputedly three hundred years old, and the chance to organize a guide for hiking through surrounding limestone hills to weird monoliths known as **Batu Batongkat**, the Stone Sticks.

Kumai and park preparations

Connected to Pangkalanbun by a deteriorating road, **KUMAI**'s small port, shipyard and couple of streets face across broad **Sungai Kumai** to where a fringe of mangroves and nipa palms frame the border of Tanjung Puting national park. Transport from Pangkalanbun passes by the **market** on the three-kilometre-long strip of Jalan Idris; the last bemo back leaves around 3pm (Rp4000).

The new **losmen** *Edyson* (☎0532/61229; ❶) on Jalan Idris, 2km north of the market, has its own generator – useful for the regular power cuts. The rooms are simple, the walls a bit flimsy and the whole building creaks, but it is more welcoming than similarly priced accommodation in Pangkalanbun, and the best value. The *Aloha*, near the port at the junction with Jalan Gerliya, has similar rooms (❶–❷), though you need to haggle here. Kumai's only air-con rooms are at the *Garuda*, Jl Gerliya 377 (☎0532/61145; ❷), though their economy rooms, both in the *Garuda* and over the road at the *Losmen Kumara*, are fanless, overpriced and to be avoided. The best **restaurant** in town is the *Depot Asri* on Jalan Gerliya, though ignore the menu: it's quicker to ask what they have got than what they haven't.

The **Pelni** office is opposite the market on Jalan Idris, though there are plenty of agents around town, and the travel agent Anggun Jaya across the road from the *Aloha* on Jalan Gerliya can issue Pelni tickets for the *Binaya*, *Lawit*, *Tilongkabila* and *Leuser*, all of which call in on their way to Surabaya and Semarang (with the latter then continuing up to Pontianak – useful for those who are trying to explore Kalimantan in its entirety). The *KM Dharma Kencana* and *KM Senopati* also ply the route to Java's north coast; details can be found at Anggun Jaya, who can also issue **bus tickets** from Pangkalanbun to Palangkaraya (8–10hr) and Banjarmasin (12hr).

Having sorted out the paperwork for the national park in Pangkalanbun, (Rp20,000 by ojek or Rp4000 by bemo from outside the *Aloha*), the next stage is to organize a **boat into Tanjung Puting** – access is by water only. Public speedboats (Rp10,000 per person) leave when full to Tanjung Harapan, 10km up the Sungai Sekonyer, from opposite the market in Kumai. However, many visitors want to explore further upriver than that, which means hiring yourself a boat in Kumai. **Speedboats** are expensive, scare wildlife, mangle turtles and crocodiles, and should be avoided. Slower, quieter **klotok** are six-metre-long hulls powered by an inboard engine, with enclosed mandi, open sides, a wooden roof which makes a fine vantage point, and room for three or four people plus two crew members. Rates are around Rp200,000–250,000 per day plus food, though hard haggling occasionally brings the price down. Sleeping aboard sidesteps the park's often pricey accommodation and, stocked with supplies from Kumai's market, the crew will cook for you. A number of *klotoks* have received recommendations from visitors, in particular the *Satria*, whose owner, the hard-working Yono, is a great cook and a friendly and reliable captain; he lives north of the port at Jl Idris 600 (☎0532/61240). Other recommendations include the Baso family's fleet of *Garuda* klotoks; track them and their owners down at Kumai's port. Finally, before setting off ensure that you pack walking shoes, sunscreen, a hat, a torch, drinking water and anything else you might need, as there are no shops inside the park.

Safety in the park

On January 19, 2002, villagers from the settlement of **Tanjung Harapan** stormed the nearby ranger post (see p.829), and threatened to move north and invade the second station at **Pondok Tanggui**. At the heart of the villagers' grievances is the lack of compensation they received for giving up a lot of their land to the park when it was founded, way back in 1971. Unable to protest throughout the suppressive Suharto era, the villagers are now taking advantage of the new freedoms to voice their complaints. Unfortunately, the situation since January has worsened, and on May 10 the villagers, unhappy that talks between themselves and the government had failed to produce any concrete resolution, occupied the second park station at Pondok Tanggui.

At the time of going to press, tourists were still safely visiting the park, though naturally their schedules have been affected. Hopefully by the time you read this a peaceful settlement will have been found, and both the rangers' posts will be functioning as normal, though before agreeing to hire a *klodok* – or even before you arrive in Kalten – it would be wise check on the latest situation, either by calling the local PHPA conservation office, or visiting Ⓦwww.orangutan.com.

Tanjung Puting national park

A wild and beautiful expanse of riverine forest, coastal swamp and peat bogs bursting with wildlife, **TANJUNG PUTING NATIONAL PARK** is Kalimantan at its best. The park's fame rests on the efforts of **Dr Birute Galdikas**, who in 1971 founded **Camp Leakey** here as an **orang-utan rehabilitation centre** for animals that had been orphaned or sold as pets. As incapable of forest survival as a human baby, young orang-utans need to be taught how to forage by park staff or foster mothers, a process that takes several years, making the work here very long-term. A downside to the park's popularity is that visitors only increase the orang-utans' exposure to humanity, and many youngsters prefer to hang around ranger stations to take advantage of the twice-daily feedings. However, none of this should stop you from visiting: few people leave Tanjung Puting with any complaints about the experience of such an easy, close contact with these animals.

Aside from the thousand-plus orang-utans in Tanjung Puting, the park is home to 28 other mammal species, including *owa-owa*, the vocal, long-armed **gibbon**, and very visible troops of Borneo's indigenous, big-nosed *bukantan*, or **proboscis monkey**, a fantastic sight as they hurl themselves through the trees with upstretched arms. Habitat reduction through logging and fires have seen proboscis monkey numbers decline throughout Kalimantan since the 1980s, but they are still common enough here. Along the rivers, look for monitor lizards and **false ghavials**, a narrow-nosed crocodile which grows to about 3m, plus scores of birds; on land, **sun bears** are thrilling, if unpredictably tempered animals to encounter, while hikers need to be aware of potentially dangerous **snakes**.

Practicalities

Tanjung Puting national park covers 4000 square kilometres south of Sungai Sekonyer, though public access is confined to just four areas along 25km of the Sekonyer and its tributaries: **ranger posts** at Tanjung Harapan and Pondok Tanggui, and **research stations** at Natai Lengkuas and Camp Leakey. There are no roads in the park, so **getting around** is primarily by boat. From Kumai, a klotok takes about two hours to reach Tanjung Harapan, three hours to Pondok Tanggui, and between four and five hours to reach either Natai Lengkuas or Camp Leakey. Bear in mind that craft are prohibited from travelling after dark. **On arrival** at each stopover, you must report with your permit to park staff. Heed their **warnings**, especially about getting too close to the immensely strong adult orang-utans – adult males, or females with children, should be given a wide berth – and don't carry food, as orang-utans will rip bags apart to find it. Each area has fairly easy **paths** to explore, the longest of which are at Camp Leakey, while the five-day forest trail through chest-deep swamps between here and Tanjung Harapan should only be attempted by fully equipped, experienced hikers, accompanied by a ranger.

You need at least two full days in the park. If you don't sleep aboard your klotok, there are three **places to stay**, all in the vicinity of Tanjung Harapan. The ranger post here has basic **cabins** (❷), rented out to visitors by previous arrangement through the park office at Pangkalanbun. The alternatives are sparsely furnished but very comfortable rooms across the river at the *Ecolodge* (ⓣ0532/24559; ❻), and, five minutes upstream, the much better-value, full-blown "safari camp" at *Rimba Lodge* (ⓣ0532/21513 for bookings, or contact the *Blue Kecubung* in Pangkalanbun; ❻). Both lodges have good restaurants, which are the only **places to eat** in the park, and can arrange **guides**, canoes and klotoks for rental. Staff at the two ranger posts and Camp Leakey also offer their services as guides at around Rp20,000 per hour, though this is very negotiable.

The park

Having crossed from Kumai (see p.827), you enter the mouth of small **Sungai Sekonyer**, where an avenue of trunkless **nipa palms** gradually recede to a riverside tangle of vines and patchy forest at **Tanjung Harapan ranger post**. An information hut here has a good rundown on the park's ecology, the odd crocodile skull and stuffed birds – the door is kept locked to keep out inquisitive apes, but the ranger here can open it up. A few orang-utans move in for feeding at 8am and 3pm, but not in the numbers that you'll find them elsewhere in the park; if you don't mind getting muddy, there's a five-kilometre circuit track into surrounding thickets. Just upstream, past the park's two **lodges**, is the village of **TANJUNG HARAPAN**, most of whose residents have given up trying to farm the area's poor soils and now work at the nearby **Asapai Gold Fields**, where mud churned up in the mining process has turned the Sekonyer's previously clean waters into their current soupy state.

The jungle closes in after Tanjung Harapan; lining the banks are giant lilies, pandanus (which look like a pineapple tuft growing straight out of the water on a slender trunk), and gardenia bushes with yellow flowers and bright-orange seeds. Behind them grow dense stands of tall, thin-trunked trees with buttressed roots, providing perches for vines, orchids and ferns. The next stop, 7km on, is **Pondok Tanggui**, whose long, solid wooden jetty is a good place to moor for the night and watch family groups of proboscis monkeys settle into the trees on the opposite bank. A friendly gibbon called Berry will probably greet you on the jetty, and then hug your shin all the way to the ranger's office. A two-kilometre track from here ends in woodland at an **orang-utan feeding area**, where eight or so apes receive handouts of sweetened milk and bananas at 8am; the surrounding treetops have been stripped by the orang-utans to make beds, which is where they head when the food runs out. Cynical comparisons between this and feeding time at the zoo are compensated for by the sight of the orang-utans' coarse red fur seen against green leaves in the morning, or watching youngsters involved in power plays over choice bits of fruit.

Past Pondok Tanggui, you veer east off the Sekonyer up **Leakey Creek**. The water immediately turns tea-coloured and deep; the trees almost meet overhead in the early stages, before opening up on the south bank into grassy marshland – with the triangular heads of false ghavials just breaking the water. Soon after the junction on the left is **Pondok Ambung**, a proboscis monkey research station that's currently closed to the public. The land around **Camp Leakey** is a mix of primary forest and open heathland; orang-utans waiting on the jetty for new arrivals give you an idea of what to expect from the local population, which includes two mature males whose overgrown cheek pouches and sheer size are impressive – one weighs 100kg. An education centre here details the work of the research centre, and there's another feeding area, with the orang-utans currently being fed at 3pm. If you have the time, ask the camp's rangers to take you on a short hike into the forest proper for a small fee (about Rp10,000).

Palangkaraya and around

Set inland at the upper margin of southern Kalimantan's extensive marshes, the city of **PALANGKARAYA** sprang into being in 1957, grafted onto the village of **Pahandut** as capital of the new province of Kalteng. Though the remote location seems a poor choice for what is in effect a symbol of Dayak autonomy, everything about Palangkaraya reflects the circumstances of its foundation. Laid out 100km up the convoluted **Sungai Kahayan**, the city is both accessible to the predominantly traditional lands upstream, yet also pragmatically close enough to Banjarmasin not to be too isolated from its economic benefits – it's only a few hours away by speedboat. Palangkaraya is a compromise between big-scale urban planning and small-town intimacy, and most people only pass through it in transit between Pangkalanbun and Banjarmasin. However, those who linger will find that Palangkaraya offers good food, interesting markets and the best starting point for a broader investigation of Kalteng's Dayak people.

The City

Palangkaraya is characterized largely by organized blocks of government offices expanding westwards into the countryside, the buildings separated by neat borders of black and white kerbing. The most interesting part of town, however, is the dock area around Jalan Dharmosugondo, where, in a pastiche of Dayak iconography, a brightly painted *sandung* and heroic bronze tableau are overshadowed by a **clock tower**, bizarrely emerging out of a dragon jar mounted on hornbill heads. Immediately to the west, Palangkaraya's **markets** operate two shifts: early morning is the best time to mingle with crowds buying fresh meat, fruit and vegetables, while youngsters arrive later to hang around booths selling sunglasses, cassettes, shoes, belts, toys and trinkets, which set up in the late afternoon, completely blocking the streets. Any remaining gaps are filled by night-time food stalls. It's a good place to pick up locally made **bamboo and rattan ware**, attractively patterned in purple, green and red; rain hats sell for about Rp2500, baskets and large floormats for Rp5000. **Souvenir shops** along Jalan Madura stock old porcelain, rubbery models of Dayak funeral boats, gems, carved shields and dangerous-looking sets of bows and arrows. Further west, a ten-minute walk brings you to the steps leading north off Jalan Yani into **Flamboyan**, an area of wooden stalls and seedy hostels built high out over the river on boardwalks, which terminate 500m along at **Flamboyan Pier**. Back on Jalan Yani, bemo "A" runs 5km out to the **Provincial Museum** (Tues–Thurs, Sat & Sun, 8am–noon & 4–6pm, Fri 8–11am; free) on Jalan Cilik Riwut, though it's hardly worth the journey to see the few dragon jars and bronze drums sitting forlornly in oversized halls.

Practicalities

Most of Palangkaraya's services are up in the northeastern end of town off Jalan Yani. **Cilik Riwut airport** is a kilometre further east again, with a taxi to the accommodation in town Rp10,000. With the completion of the bridges between here and Banjarmasin, there is sadly no longer a regular speedboat service to the city from Rambang Pier, with everybody now making the journey by road. **Buses** pull in at their respective offices, most of which are on or near Jalan Yani, though some end their journey 2km from town at the terminal on Jalan Yos Sudarso. Palangkaraya's **bemos** are lettered and run fixed routes for a flat rate of Rp1000; the terminus is at the eastern end of Jalan Yani, at the junction with Jalan Dharmosugondo, while ojeks wait around the major junctions during daylight hours.

Moving on **to Banjarmasin**, buses (Rp25,000) leave from their offices until mid-afternoon, while Kijangs (Rp40,000) circle around town looking for passengers: Rambang pier and Jalan Dharmosugondo are good places to hail one. Buses **to Pangkalanbun** (Rp50,000) are best booked a day in advance. Yessoe, the biggest of the bus companies, ply both routes, and are at Jl Banda 7, just off Jalan Dharmosugondo, while their main rivals Lina Tama are west of the *Hotel Dian Wisata* on Jalan Yani. If you're **heading upstream** from Palangkaraya, see p.833 for transit points.

Sort out **money** at the BNI on Jalan Dharmosugondo (Mon–Thurs 9am–2pm, Fri 9–11am), which handles foreign currency and also has an ATM that accepts Cirrus/Maestro cards. There are plenty of **wartels** dotted around town; ICC, west along Jalan Yani near the *Hotel Dian Wisata*, has **internet access** (Rp120 per minute), and there are a number of other internet places down Jalan Yos Soedarso near the *Hotel Dandang Tingang*. **Merpati** (for flights to Jakarta and Surabaya) are at Jl Yani 69a (ⓣ0536/21411), while further west at no. 86, the travel agents Adi Angkasa Travel (ⓣ0536/21480) can make bookings with other airlines. **Information** on upriver festivals and villages (and also guides to the region) can be obtained from Pak Ariel Adrianus Ahut, manager of the *Pasah Asi Hotel*, or at the Provincial Tourist Office, 5km west of town along Jalan Cilik Riwut (Mon–Sat 9am–noon; ⓣ0536/21416, ⓕ31007). To get to the tourist office, take bemo "A" from Jalan Yani to Kantor Dinas Parawisata.

Accommodation

Most of Palangkaraya's budget **accommodation** lies around Rambang Pier, but it's generally difficult for foreigners to get a room here. If you don't have any luck, you'll have to look instead along the main street, Jalan A Yani, where a number of different hotels and losmen lie spaced out all along its length. Watch out, too, for the twenty-percent tax which most hotels add on to the bill.

Dandang Tingang Jl Yos Soedarso 13, 3–4km west of the town centre ⓣ0536/21805, ⓕ21254. A little distant from transit points – bemo "C" from Jalan Yani will get you there – but it's a pleasant place which tries hard to please, and the rooms are spacious, with air-con doubles and private units. ❸

Dian Wisata Jl Yani 68 ⓣ0536/21241. Just over 1km west of the town centre on the main road, this hotel has very tidy VIP and standard rooms, but avoid the damp and musty economy rooms in the basement. ❷

Mina Jl Nias 17, just by Rambung Pier ⓣ0536/22182. The nicest of the local budget options around the pier, with friendly and efficient staff and clean rooms. Welcomes foreigners, but is often genuinely full. ❷

Pasah Asi Jl Galaxi 96 ⓣ0536/30111, ⓕ27058. A smart and excellent-value hotel, whose manager is one of the best sources of local information and can arrange guides to Kaharingam areas. Unfortunately, it's located some way from the town centre, off Jalan Yos Soedarso. Bemo "C" will drop you fairly nearby. ❷

Sakura Jl Yani 87 ⓣ0536/22355. A smart new hotel with spacious rooms (all en-suite and with air-con), polite, helpful staff and a top-floor pub/karaoke bar. Rp160,000–200,000.

Yanti Jl Yani 82 ⓣ0536/21634. Spotless, though some rooms are quite small and a little overpriced. Rp55,000–85,000.

Eating

Palangkaraya offers a number of good **places to eat**. Stalls at the night markets near Rambang Pier sell cheap soups, sates and fry-ups, but it's hard not to be tempted by the smoky grills outside the area's open-fronted **fish restaurants**, where thick fish steaks and fillets are cooked to your order. *Sampurna*, on Jalan Jawa, is always busy, as are the *Senggol* on Jalan Madura and *Almuminun* on Jalan Dharmosugondo; all three serve juicy river prawns, *pipih* – which looks like a cross between a trout and a flounder – and fatty *patin* (reputedly toxic in large amounts). Failing this, *Sing Kar Wang* is a first-rate Chinese restaurant two minutes' distant at Jl Bangka 87, with pricey but large portions of crispy fish, sweet and sour pork, and greens in oyster sauce.

Upriver from Palangkaraya: Kaharingan country

The region upstream from Palangkaraya remains a stronghold for adherents to Kalteng's indigenous **Kaharingan faith**, and makes for an absorbing few days' excursion. The best time to visit is during **reburial ceremonies** (see box opposite), which are open to all and most frequently occur between June and August. Even if you miss the ceremonies themselves, the Dayak villages here generally welcome guests at any time, and retain not only impressively decorated memorials to the dead, but also some old traditional longhouses, or **betang**.

There are two ways into the region from Palangkaraya. With a week or more to spare, you'll get the best returns from following the Sungai Kahayan 175km up into **Ot Danum** territory around **Tumbang Kurik**, although the river's more accessible stretches below the town of **Tewah** are really not that interesting. A quicker and reliable alternative is to make a three-day return trip 130km up the **Sungai Rungan** to **Tumbang Jutuh** (*tumbang* means "the junction of two rivers"), which is within easy reach of **Ngaju** villages, where tradition coexists comfortably with Christianity. If you allow an extra couple of days, it's also possible to circuit the area by **hiking** through the forests between here and Tumbang Kurik. The quickest, most expensive way to travel is by chartered speedboat (the small wooden docks to the north of Jalan Yani are good places to look for these), but you can cut costs by avoiding public transport and asking around for others heading your way on slower longboats, or *alkons*. Ot Danum and Ngaju cultures are superficially similar, with the Ngaju language widely understood across the region – in remoter corners, you'll sometimes draw a blank with Indonesian. **Guides** from Palangkaraya are best arranged through the *Pasah Asi Hotel*, or the Provincial Tourist Office.

Kaharingan and funeral rites

A **Dayak** faith practised across interior Kalimantan, **Kaharingan** became an approved state religion in 1980. Though the religion revolves around ancient rituals and ancestor worship, adherents were able to persuade the government that it was an offshoot of Balinese Hinduism – a religion to which it bears no resemblance – and thus avoid the suppression of animist faiths in the mid-twentieth century (see p.1055). Kaharingan exists in several forms, but one unifying characteristic is a multi-staged funeral, when the spirit is sent into the afterlife feeling satisfied and respected. This usually involves a **reburial ceremony**, the most elaborate of these being the **kwangkei** performed by Benuaq Dayak in Kaltim, and the **tiwah** of Kalteng. By whatever name, these ceremonies are fantastic events which last a whole month and may take years to organize – distant relatives must be invited, and the expense of hiring musicians, and buying food and animals to sacrifice, runs into millions of rupiah. Communities often collaborate, saving up their dead for a single big festival during which dozens or even hundreds of individuals are reburied.

Overseen by *basir*, the Kaharingan priesthood, the ceremony begins with a ritual purification, when the bones are dug up from their first grave and placed in a wooden coffin. Other important stages include **dances** to ancestral spirits, whose help is needed in the proceedings, and the **sacrifice** (formerly a slave, but now a buffalo) for each person being reburied. The animal is tied to a *patong sapundu*, a wooden post carved with a human face with the tongue lolling out, before having its throat cut; buffalo heads are later stacked in an open wooden framework. Finally, the purified bones are permanently housed in a **sandung**, an ornate hardwood mausoleum often raised off the ground like a miniature rice barn and flanked by carved and painted wooden figures, servants to the dead in the afterlife. Having spent the period between death and reburial at a sort of halfway stop between the real world and the afterlife, the deceased's spirit, buoyed along by the goodwill of the mourners, navigates through a cloud of demons and reaches heaven aboard a *melambong*, a **funeral boat** guided by a hornbill and protected from evil by a tiger. At the end of the event, **pantar** (tall, thin poles topped by a hornbill) are raised in honour of the dead, as are similar spiky **sanggaran**, usually further embellished by having valuable Chinese jars speared on them. Long pauses – sometimes lasting for days – between separate stages of the ceremonies are filled by sociable bouts of eating, drinking and gambling at cards, dice, cock-fighting (a relatively recent introduction) and *tongko*, a Dayak version of roulette.

Palangkaraya to Tewah and Tumbang Kurik

If they fill up, speedboats (5hr; Rp80,000) and *alkon* (12hr; Rp30,000) leave Palangkaraya's Flamboyan Pier every morning at around 6am for the gold-mining town of **TEWAH**, 130km up the Kahayan. This is virtually the limit of public transport on the river (although if the conditions are right the occasional speedboat makes it all the way up to Tumbang Miri), with a couple of inexpensive **losmen** – the *Batu Mas* and adjacent *Tewah* (❷) – and some overgrown *sandung* (mausoleums) to check out while you search for other passengers to share the costs of a vessel onwards. Tewah marks the southern boundary of the Ot Danum Dayak, and it is possible to walk the 10km or so upstream to **Upun Batu**, which has some fine *sandung* and limestone scenery. Better yet is the village of **TUMBANG KURIK**, 45km northwest of Tewah on a small tributary of the Kahayan, which has more *sandung* and a splendid, run-down *betang* – you should be able to get here for Rp60,000 if you share, though a speedboat charter can cost six times as much. There's a homestay at Tumbang Kurik; visit the kepala desa on arrival to introduce yourself and make arrangements.

Up the Rungan to Tumbang Jutuh and beyond

From Palangkaraya, the trip **up the Rungan** starts by catching bemo "A" from Jalan Yani to Terminal Tangkiling, 8km north of town, from where regular minibuses make the 30km run to Tangkiling township – allow Rp3000 and at least ninety minutes for the whole ride. **TANGKILING** is simply a dock on the Rungan, where you should immediately sign up for the single daily public **speedboat to Tumbang Jutuh** (Rp80,000), which leaves any time before 11am if enough passengers arrive (and returns the following day, customers permitting).

The journey upstream follows steadily narrowing, ever shallower channels fringed by thin forest, arriving four hours later at **TUMBANG JUTUH**'s tall, almost vertical jetty steps. A small trading post, Jutuh is split between Muslim merchants and Christian Ngaju Dayak; there's a **ticket office** for the return journey at the docks, a single 100-metre-long cobbled street lined with clothes and hardware shops, and the unexpectedly spacious and clean **losmen** *Tiga Dara* (❷), off to the right. **Meals** at the losmen are expensive, but there are several simple warung to choose from – the one by the dock is good, with a pet gibbon as an added attraction.

The main reason for coming to Tumbang Jutuh is to reach the village of **TUMBANG MALAHOI**, 13km away; it's an easy walk, or you could charter an ojek for the day from the dock area (Rp30,000 return). There's little forest along the way, but the countryside is pleasant, with a broad stretch of rapids about 2km upstream and you'll pass plenty of villages, some with *sandung*. Tumbang Malahoi is an attractive place, with a large **church** from the 1930s, excellent *sandung* and *pantar* decorated with Chinese plates and jars, and a superbly restored, fifty-metre **betang**, whose massive supporting ironwood posts were sunk in 1817 – guests are invited to try to encircle them with their arms. At the time it was built, the Dayak here were headhunters, and construction of this *betang* would have required a slave to be buried under the central post. Check out the eaves above the doorway, which have some elderly painted panels, including a hunter with a rifle, patterns representing the sun and moon and mythical animals. Most impressive are the two-centuries-old, skilfully carved *patong* flanking the longhouse steps, depicting figures standing upright with **tigers** atop them – strength and night vision make cats prime guardian creatures in Dayak lore. You might stay here with the kepala desa's permission, and delve deeper into local history, or organize a guide for the full-day walk east to Tumbang Kurik. Bring all supplies, as there are no stores in the village.

Banjarmasin and around

Set down in Kalimantan's southeastern corner on the closest part of the island to Java, **BANJARMASIN** occupies flat country east of the **Sungai Barito**, where the last couple of kilometres of the smaller **Sungai Martapura** break up into numerous channels and streams. The city has a deep, strong sense of its own identity; over ninety percent of it is Muslim, and the streets tick in time with calls to prayer. It's easy to spend a day soaking up the atmosphere of Banjarmasin's markets, where boats remain a major form of transport, and wooden houses, built on piles as protection against daily tides, still line the canals and rivers. Hiring your own vessel is a fine way to experience the ebb and flow of life here, and will also take you down the Barito to a couple of monkey-infested islands. Not far to the east, **Martapura**'s gem mines make for an interesting day-trip, or as first stop on the way into the rest of the province.

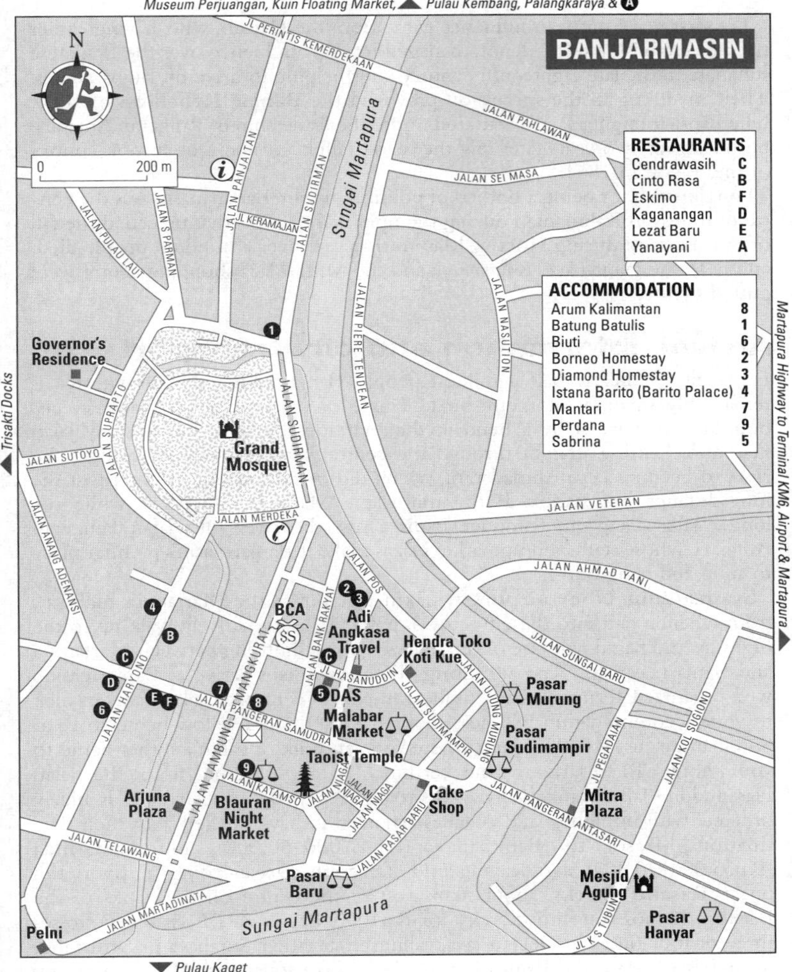

Some history

Banjarmasin's history reaches back to when Indian traders founded the Hindu **Negara Kingdom** north of here during the thirteenth century. Within seventy years, its rulers were marrying into the powerful Majapahit empire, but the fall of the Majapahit in the late 1470s saw Negara disintegrate into smaller city-states. These were reunified fifty years later after a local prince, **Samudera**, enlisted military assistance from a recently Islamicized Java and conquered the region, converting to **Islam** and shifting his capital south to near the lower **Barito River** at Banjarmasin. Abundant supplies of spices and timber from upstream soon brought the city wealth and a place in regional trade, though sixteenth-century Portuguese missionaries and British merchants found Banjarmasin and its rulers squalid and dangerous.

The first real European influence came from the **Dutch**, who, having earlier tried to establish a VOC depot, managed to exert influence over the Banjarese sultanate in the late eighteenth century, after helping to drive off Bugis pirates. Their meddling in the succession provoked the **Banjar Rebellion** of 1860, when anti-foreigner factions united under the leadership of Pangeran Antasari, but his death two years later saw the revolt falter, and the Dutch took control of the region in 1864.

Long known for being a hotbed of political dissent, Banjarmasin was the centre of unrest in Kalimantan during the upheaval of 1997 that preceded the fall of Suharto, and during **riots** of May in that year over a hundred people died, and both the giant *Hotel Kalimantan* and the Mitra Plaza shopping centre were gutted by fire.

Arrival, information and city transport

For a city of nearly half a million people, Banjarmasin's downtown area is remarkably small, a kilometre-broad tangle of markets, services and streets, bounded to the east by a bend in the Martapura, and to the west by Jalan Haryono. Cutting straight through the centre, Jalan Hasanuddin bridges the river to become Jalan Ahmad Yani, which dips southeast out of town past the long-distance bus station as the multi-lane Martapura highway, while the longer Jalan Pangeran Samudera runs across the river into Jalan Pengeran Antasari, whose stalls, and upmarket plazas make it Banjarmasin's premier place to shop and hang out.

Syamsuddin Noor airport is 25km east down the Martapura highway, from where a taxi into the city costs Rp30,000 – alternatively, walk up to the highway and flag down one of the orange bemos shuttling between Martapura and Banjarmasin for Rp3000. **Long-distance buses** arrive at Banjarmasin's well-organized Terminal Km6, 6km southeast of centre on Jalan Yani; an ojek to your accommodation will cost about Rp5000, and a yellow bemo to Pasar Sudimampir just Rp1000, from where you can walk or catch another bemo to your hotel. To return to the terminal, catch a bemo from the Jalan Hasanuddin–Jalan Bank Rakyat crossroads (Rp1000). The terminal is nicely ordered, with minibuses and coaches arranged in bays labelled with their destinations. Buses to Balikpapan (Rp47,000–60,000) and Samarinda (Rp55,000–70,000) start leaving mid-afternoon. Ocean-going transport ties up at **Trisakti Docks**, about 5km west of the centre on the banks of the Barito – bemos run into the city for Rp1000. Pelni's *KM Egon* **ferry** crosses three or four times a week to Java, calling in at either Surabaya or Semarang, from Trisakti Port; the Pelni office is about 1km southwest of the centre by Sungai Martapura on Jalan Martadinata.

Ojek and becak operators hang around markets or arrival points, though it's usually easier to board a **yellow bemo** (Rp1000 flat fare). Because of one-way traffic flows through the centre, Jalan Hasanuddin is the place to catch a bemo straight down Jalan Yani to the long-distance bus station, while Pasar Hanyar (near the site of the old Pasar Antasari) or the western end of the Jalan Antasari bridge are the places to find bemos to anywhere else. The ideal way to see the city is by canal boat, or **klotok**, which can carry six or more people and be rented out for Rp15,000 an hour from the vicinity of the Jalan Hasanuddin Bridge. A motorized canoe is slightly cheaper at Rp10,000. For trips further afield, **taxis** charging Rp30,000 an hour wait in Jalan Bank Rakyat, directly behind the *Hotel Kalimantan*.

For impartial and generally sound **information**, the Government Tourist Office (Kantor Dinas Parawisata) is north of the town centre at Jl Panjaitan 34

(Mon–Thurs 8am–2pm, Fri 8–11am, Sat 8am–noon; ⓣ0511/52982). Otherwise, staff at *Borneo Homestay* can offer good local information (see below).

Accommodation

All of Banjarmasin's **accommodation** places are central, offer at least breakfast, and can make travel bookings.

Arum Kalimantan Jalan Lambung Mangkurat ⓣ0511/66818, ⓕ67345. Banjarmasin's plushest, now all spruced up following a lengthy renovation. Rooms come with satellite TV and air-con as standard, but watch out for the hefty 21-percent tax they whack onto the bill. ❻

Batung Batulis Jl Sudirman 1 ⓣ0511/66269, ⓕ66270. A pleasantly sunny mid-range hotel to the north of the mosque. All rooms are furnished with a minibar, TV and air-con. ❺

Biuti Jl Haryono 21 ⓣ0511/54493. Good budget option with the best-value economy rooms in town, neat, clean, en suite and with a fan, as well as superior rooms with TV and soft mattresses. ❷–❸

Borneo Homestay Jl Simpang Hasanuddin I no. 33 ⓣ0511/66545, ⓕ57515. Along with the *Diamond*, the only accommodation in Kalimantan solely geared to foreign backpackers, with a travel and tour office specializing in Loksado trekking (see p.843). The owner, Johan Yasin, is very clued up about what foreigners want and how much they're prepared to pay. ❷

Diamond Homestay Jl Simpang Hasanuddin II ⓣ0511/66100. Very friendly place, competing with the *Borneo* for the backpacker market; the range of rooms is smaller here, but these (and their tours) are somewhat cheaper. ❷

Istana Barito (Barito Palace) Jl Haryono 16–20 ⓣ0511/67300, ⓕ52240. The next best thing in town to the *Arum Kalimantan*, but not as smart, and its age is starting to show. It boasts Japanese, European and Korean restaurants. ❻

Mentari Jl Lambung Mangkurat 32 ⓣ0511/68944, ⓕ53350. Directly opposite – and in direct opposition to – the *Arum Kalimantan*, the *Mentari* has comfortable but rather plain rooms, and the hotel seems to be slipping slowly into some kind of torpor as customers flock to the newly renovated *Arum*. ❺

Perdana Jalan Brigjen Katamso ⓣ0511/53276, ⓕ67988. Columns lend a colonial air to the exterior, contradicted by a traditionally Banjarese high roof. The pricier rooms are spacious and fair value. ❸

Sabrina Jl Bank Rakyat 5 ⓣ0511/54442. A pleasantly dingy place, clean and not too stuffy. The air-con rooms are more expensive, and offer poorer value than those with fan. ❸

The City

As befits the capital city of a culture dominated by Islam, Banjarmasin's focus is the marble-and-bronze exterior of **Mesjid Raya Sabilal Muhtadin**, the **Grand Mosque**, which sits in parkland overlooking the west bank of Sungai Martapura, just above the city centre. Built in 1981, and one of the country's largest mosques, Masjid Raya's interior impresses by its sense of space, rather than any gaudy furnishings; you can look around outside the main prayer times, provided you dress conservatively, with legs and arms fully covered. From here, you can walk to the river and flag down a water taxi heading 3km north to **Museum Perjuangan** (Tues–Thurs 8.30am–2.30pm, Fri 8.30–11am, Sat & Sun 8.30am–1.30pm; free), a single tall building whose best feature is its **Banjar design**, with high-pitched roof – the display inside is an uninspired collection of weapons used against the Dutch during the Independence struggle.

Following the riverbank south of the Grand Mosque, central Banjarmasin is a mosaic of **markets**, each specializing in specific merchandise. Along Jalan Ujung Murung, **Pasar Murung** has a small bird market, and marks the entrance to a wooden riverside quarter, a notoriously fire-prone labyrinth of undercover boardwalks, homes and tea kiosks. Emerging into the open again to the south, by the Jalan Antasari bridge amongst **Pasar Sudimampir**'s porcelain sellers, you'll find gem stalls west of here off Jalan Sudimampir at **Pasar Malabar**, while crossing south over Jalan Samudera takes you down into the clothing wholesalers of **Pasar Baru**. There's a small **Taoist temple** nearby on Jalan Niaga, whose caretakers tell rambling tales about wartime bombings and the stuffed tiger next to the altar, and on adjoining Jalan Katamso the Blauran **night market** sets up at about 4pm. At any one of these markets, incidentally, you may find **street performers**, refugees from the old and now sadly defunct Pasar Antasari. With that market now cleared to make way for a new plaza, these entertainers, including musclemen who break coconuts with their heads, chew glass and hammer nails up their noses, and quacks who advertise their snake-oils by wrestling with crocodiles to prove their virility, are now forced to ply their peculiar trade elsewhere.

Around Kuin floating market and Pulau Kaget

You haven't seen Banjarmasin until you've travelled the city's waterways in a klotok or motorized canoe. Despite a gradual clearing of riverside homes around the centre, half of Banjarmasin's population spend their days on wooden porches overlooking the water. Normal conventions regarding clothing are dropped as whole streets wash and socialize in public, women in sarongs, men wearing just underpants. While a specific tour past homes in the "back-street" canals smacks of voyeurism, there are a couple of less intrusive trips, the best being an excursion to one of Banjarmasin's famous *pasar terapang*, or **floating markets**. The largest is at **Kuin**, where one of the Martapura's side-branches joins Sungai Barito about 4km northeast of the centre, starting daily at dawn and effectively over by 9am. It takes about half an hour to get here from the Jalan Yani bridge; try to arrange a motorized canal boat (*klotok*) the night before by hailing one from the riverbank near the Jalan Hasanuddin Bridge (about Rp15,000 per hour), as they can be hard to come by in the early morning, and aim to be at the market by 6.30am. As you approach the market, the canals open into the kilometre-wide Barito, and you suddenly find yourself bumping around in the middle of a jam of small boats, full of shoppers who have hired a klotok between them, and dugouts paddled by old women, their bows weighed down with bunches of bananas. Vendors, some moored in midstream waiting for customers, others hunting for business by following bigger craft, sell everything: medicines, huge bricks of fermented prawn *trasi*, salted and fresh fish, and piles of pineapples, beans or watermelons. There are even **floating warung**, where you can have a breakfast of coffee and cakes by tying up alongside and hooking your choice of pastry by means of a pole-and-nail arrangement.

After visiting the market, you can observe some of the contradictions of Banjarese traditions a short way downstream at lightly wooded **Pulau Kembang** (Flower Island), where both Chinese and Muslims pray for success in personal or business ventures at a small, unpretentious **shrine** to a monkey god derived from Hanuman, a Hindu deity. Criticism of the practice by Banjarmasin's imams seems to have had little effect, and the island gets packed out at weekends, when long-tailed macaque monkeys pester visitors for handouts of peanuts.

A separate trip takes you past Banjarmasin's floating suburbs and industrial wharves out to **Pulau Kaget**, 12km down the Barito. Once the most accessible place in Kalimantan to spot **proboscis monkeys**, this island has now been cleared almost totally to allow rice cultivation, and the leaf-eating monkeys have virtually abandoned it. Still, the journey down Sungai Martapura and out to the mouth of the Barito is interesting enough, passing Banjarmasin's **shipyards**, which turned out beautiful Bugis schooners with exaggerated, curved prows until the ironwood forests upstream were logged out in the early 1990s. Plenty of schooners still dock here to load up with timber, however, and the shipyards are still kept busy refitting modern ocean tugs and tankers.

Eating and entertainment

Banjarese food has characteristic sweet flavours accompanied by unusually hot sambals. Fish and sates are particularly good, coming together as *katupat kandangan*, a local treat consisting of catfish sate and duck eggs covered in a spicy coconut sauce. Other Banjar dishes include the similar *ikan kipus*, *papuyu baubar* (grilled fish and pumpkin), *saluang* (crispy-fried sprats) and *soto Banjar* (a thick soup of rice, chicken, egg, carrot, fried onion and glass noodles). Sweet **cakes**, *kue*, are another Banjarese tradition, popular as a mid-afternoon snack, when men congregate around backstreet kiosks to munch on them, drink tea and chat. For cheap **warung**, try Jalan Niaga in the Pasar Baru area, and the area around Pasar Antasari; Mitra Plaza has some good-value **ice cream** and sanitized food outlets on the top floor. The streets are usually where you'll find the most authentic Banjar fare, as most of the city's **restaurants** are Chinese, but in addition to those listed below, there are a couple of inexpensive Banjarese places around Pasar Antasari.

For organized entertainment, there are a couple of **discos** in the Mitra Plaza, or try *Tara's* in the *Hotel Mentari*; otherwise after-dark action means mingling with the crowds and people-watching.

Restaurants and warung

There are several takeaway **cake** shops along Jalan Sudimampir, but the best selection is at *Menseng Utarid*, on the corner of Jalan Samudera and Jalan Pasar Baru. *Toko Roti Kue Hendra* on Jalan Sudimampir offer a similar selection, and are more convenient for the cheap hostels. Packed rooftop warung overlooking the river and the Jalan Antasari bridge above Pasar Sudimampir serve tea and Banjar pancakes, two-centimetre-thick discs coated in sugar and syrup; you have to sit on the floor and eat off low tables elbow-to-back with other patrons. For Western food, there's a *KFC* below the post office, and the *Rama Steakhouse* in the Arjuna Plaza.

Cinto Rasa Diagonally across from the *Istana Barito* on Jalan Haryono. Clean and cheap Padang food.

Eskimo At the western end of Jalan Samudera. Small but spacious place with Chinese-Indonesian menu; it's modestly priced and serves decent-sized portions, but the service is incredibly slow.

Kaganangan and **Cendrawasih** Opposite each other at the western end of Jalan Samudera. Banjarese restaurants serving a Padang-style assortment of prawns and fish dishes, washed down with vegetable soup, tea or fluorescent pink *es dewet*; everything is good, but avoid the sharp spines of black-skinned *pupuyu* fish.

Lezat Baru At the western end of Jalan Samudera. The best Chinese restaurant in town, with an extensive menu including frog and pigeon, but with appallingly slow service.

Yanayani Jalan Sungai Jingah. Serves the best *soto Banjar* in the city; take a water taxi (Rp600) or ocek (Rp3000) and ask to be dropped off at Jalan Sungai Jingah.

Listings

Airline offices Office hours are Mon–Thurs 8am–5pm, Fri 8–11am & 2–5pm, Sat & Sun 9am–1pm. Bouraq, Jl Yani 343 ⓣ0511/252445; DAS, Jl Hasanuddin 6 ⓣ0511/52902; Garuda at the *Istana Barito* hotel ⓣ0511/59064, ⓕ59064; Mandala, Jl A Yani Km3.5 ⓣ0511/266737; Merpati, Jl A Yani 147D, Km3.5 ⓣ0511/268833, ⓕ268461.

Banks and exchange BCA on Jalan Lambung Mangkurat (Mon–Fri 8am–3.30pm, Sat 8–11am) change cash and travellers' cheques. Adi Angkasa Travel (see p.840) will change money and travellers' cheques outside banking hours, but their rates are poor.

Bookshops Gramedia Books, on the top floor of the Mitra Plaza, has a selection of standard city and provincial maps, a tiny, random assortment of books in English, and a few postcards.

Hospital Banjarmasin's General Hospital is about 1.5km east of the centre on Jalan Yani.

Internet access The post office has internet facilities on the ground floor, though the connection here can be terribly slow. Daissy, to the north of the *Istana Barito*, is slightly quicker, or if you're heading out to Martapura or the museum, you'll find that the internet cafés in Banjarbaru are much better.

Pharmacies Apotik Kasio is diagonally across from the Istana Barito on Jalan Haryono; a well-stocked pharmacy and clinic, with doctors on call from 4pm to 6pm.

Police Police headquarters are 2.5km out of town along Jalan Yani.

Post office Jalan Lambung Mangkurat, at the junction with Jalan Samudera. There are separate buildings for letters and parcels; the staff are helpful, but give the impression they've never had to send anything overseas before.

Souvenirs Shops on Jalan Sudimampir II stock a full range of Dayak crafts and weapons, plus a few pieces of porcelain and gems. Banjarmasin also manufactures its own strongly coloured tie-dyed batik, *sasirangan*, whose patterns hark back to shamanistic rituals. The best selection is at Toko Citra, some 3km east of town down Jalan Yani, though you might track some down at Pasar Baru – Martapura's markets also stock them, if you're heading that way. Prices depend on the quality of the cloth.

Telephone and fax There is a wartel open 24hr a day at the mosque end of Jalan Lambung Mangkurat; the bigger hotels also have international call facilities.

Tours The main tours offered by agents in Banjarmasin are a short cruise of local waterways; an early-morning trip to Kuin floating market and Pulau Kembang; an afternoon proboscis monkey-spotting at Pulau Kaget; a day-tour to Martapura and Cempaka; and three to five days' hiking and rafting around Loksado. The cruises and Cempaka tours are easy enough – and cheaper – to organize yourself, though an English-speaking guide makes them that much more interesting, and is definitely recommended if you speak little Indonesian and are heading to Loksado. Whether or not you stay there, the cheapest and most experienced tour agents in town are the *Borneo Homestay* and *Diamond Homestay* (see p.837; US$100–150 for 2–5 days in Loksado), with a similarly competent Adi Angkasa Travel (see below) charging far more for the same packages.

Travel agents If your accommodation can't help, Adi Angkasa Travel, Jl Hasanuddin 27 (☎0511/53131), can make all accommodation, plane, bus and boat bookings.

Martapura, Banjarbaru and Cempaka

A busy country town 40km east of Banjarmasin, **Martapura** became famous in the 1660s when **Sheik Muhammad Arsyad al-Banjari** founded the blue-domed **mosque** here on his return from a forty-year sojourn at Mecca. He then settled down to spend the rest of his 102 years teaching Islamic law and compiling two enduringly famous **books**: *Sabilal Muhtadin*, the guide to daily morals which lent its name to Banjarmasin's Grand Mosque; and the *Khiltab Barincung*, a religious commentary. Since his time, Martapura has also become famous for **gems**, especially *berlian* (diamonds), mined nearby at the village of **Cempaka**, and it's the chance to see the mining operations and maybe pick up a bargain stone that draws most visitors today. Orange bemos leave Banjarmasin's Terminal Km6 throughout the day whenever full (Rp3000), and take about ninety minutes to reach Martapura; the mines are closed on Fridays, Martapura's main market day.

MARTAPURA itself is basically a **marketplace** next to the mosque on Sungai Martapura. Bemos from Banjarmasin terminate in the forecourt of a white-tiled **plaza** housing gemstone and clothing stores – you can buy *sasirangan* **batik** here – behind which a camp of low canvas awnings abutting the mosque walls lends the produce and hardware markets the flavour of an Arabian bazaar. Hawkers around the plaza latch on to foreigners, often sneaking you off to one side before unravelling a twist of paper with a diamond inside, or furtively pulling a piece of agate out of an inner pocket; don't deal with them, unless you're sure you can tell coloured glass from the real thing.

The area's religious connotations make Martapura's gems intrinsically valuable to locals, and features that would elsewhere diminish a stone's worth can here increase it – internal flaws resembling stars or Arabic script, for instance.

△ Woodcarving outside longhouse, Mancong

Even if you have no intention of buying, it's fascinating to look around the trays of precious stones: there are diamonds, turquoise, honey-coloured tiger's-eye, pale-blue topaz, amethysts, citrines, smoky quartz crystals, and unusual *kelulud*, or **tektites**. These black pebbles of opaque volcanic glass derive from a prehistoric meteorite impact and, for some reason, lie alongside gems at the Cempaka fields, earning them the local tag "friend of the diamond" – the two stones are often mounted together on rings.

Once you've looked around the plaza, head over to the edge of the adjoining grassy park, where **showrooms** geared to tour groups and serious buyers offer a more reliable place to shop, with the chance to see **diamond polishing** at the Kayu Tangi factory (closed Fri) two blocks back on Jalan Sukaramai. Plenty of **food** stalls will keep you fed, while Martapura's single *penginapan*, the *Mutiara* (ⓣ0511/721762; ❸), is a surprisingly quaint and characterful old place on Jalan Sukaramai overlooking over the market, though you'll need to pay an extra Rp10,000 for a fan in your room. The market houses a number of cheap eateries.

Some 5km short of Martapura, you could call in at **Banjarbaru** for an interesting hour's browse around Hindu relics and Banjar ceremonial artefacts at **Museum Lambung** (Mon–Thurs & Sun 8.30am–2.30pm, Fri 8.30–11am, Sat 8.30am–1.30pm; Rp750).

Green minibuses labelled "*Mart-Cemp*" depart regularly from Martapura's plaza for the fifteen-minute ride (Rp1000) south to **Cempaka**, a village which lent its name to the local **gem fields**. Drivers will leave you at the point where a muddy, two-kilometre track leads off from the roadside, past a concrete diamond monument and paddy-fields, and out to the diggings. Gems of all kinds are found here, though Cempaka is famous for its **diamonds** – most are yellow and tiny, but the largest ever found here was the impressive 167-carat **Trisakti**, unearthed in 1965. The bigger, open excavations form flooded bowls where people flounder around in the water with diesel suction pumps, drawing the gravel up to ground level and dumping it in huge heaps, later to be panned for anything valuable. Most of the excavations are far smaller, however, and worked entirely by hand: a hole in the ground marks a shaft with a human chain reaching down into the water 10m below. Panning is done by putting a handful of gravel in a conical wooden vessel and swilling it around so that the heavier gems collect in the middle, and it can be an interesting process to watch when a valuable stone is found – the automatic, well-rehearsed movement of the panners giving way to sudden excitement as they examine the swill.

The Meratus mountains

Kalsel province is shaped around the 200-kilometre-long spine of the partially forested **Meratus mountains**, home of the **Bukit**, one of the most approachable of Dayak groups. Said to have been driven into these hills by the power struggles preceding Banjarmasin's foundation, the Bukit are traditionally animistic and, though few ceremonies are now performed and little is known about their original beliefs, they still enjoy a reputation for powerful magic amongst Kalsel's Muslims. Visitors to the region still have a chance to stay in square Bukit communal houses, or **balai**, bamboo-and-beam apartments which range in size from small huts to vast barns, covering twenty square metres or more. All social activities take place inside, where a sunken area in the middle, filled by a bamboo-and-palm frond shrine, acts as a stage during **festivals**. The biggest of these is the **harvest celebration** in late July or early August, whose week-long festivities kick off with twelve hours of ever-accelerating drumming, dancing and drinking. Guests – who should bring a gift – are welcome except on the penultimate day, when they are thought to bring bad luck with them.

Around 150km northeast of Banjarmasin on the Balikpapan highway, the country town of **Kandangan** is the jumping-off point for trips to the Meratus around **Loksado**, 30km east at the foot of the mountains. A pleasant place to hang out for a day or two, Loksado also offers **bamboo rafting**, and **hikes** into the hills of anything from a few hours to several days' duration. You definitely need **guides** for longer trails; unless you speak good Indonesian, **tours** from Banjarmasin or Barabai are the best option (if expensive, at US$100 or more for a five-day trek), though you could always just hire an interpreter, or find Indonesian-speaking guides on site for a fraction of this sum.

Kandangan and Loksado

Hourly bemos throughout the day (4hr) are the most convenient way to reach **KANDANGAN** from Banjarmasin; buses from Balikpapan tend to pass through at night. If you get stuck here, recommended **places to stay** include the comfortable *Hotel Bankau* (Ⓣ0517/21455; ❷) or similar *Losmen Loksado* (❷), both close to each other on Jalan Suprato, where you'll also find a good, cheap **restaurant**; otherwise, get the first vehicle for the hour-long run to Loksado (Rp5000). About 10km into the journey, you have to get out to register with the police at **Padang Batung**, so bring photocopies of relevant passport pages. Six kilometres short of Loksado, the few houses along the road marking **Tanhui** are a useful orientation point for later exploring the area.

LOKSADO marks the end of the road, a small collection of buildings grouped either side of the twenty-metre-wide **Sungai Amandit**. Not a traditional village by any means – a mosque and a church are found down the street – Loksado is nonetheless a nice base, which rouses itself for its **Wednesday market**, when entire Bukit villages from the back of beyond come to town to sell goods; market day is also a good time to look for a Dayak guide. From the

Rafting the Amandit

While Loksado provides a market for villagers from the hills, locals shop in Kandangan. Until the road was sealed in the mid-1990s, the only way to get there was on the Amandit, and, as the rapids along the way don't allow for big craft, people used **bamboo rafts** instead. Eight-metre-long bamboo stems, tied together at their tips and then lashed along their length to create a long, narrow, triangular vessel, these rafts are easy to make and can be broken up and sold at the journey's end. The road has made them redundant, but the rafts are still used by tourists willing to pay for the experience. It's a long twelve hours to Kandangan, however, and most people find that the three-hour stretch to the main road at Tanhui is quite enough. If you take anything with you, make sure it's securely waterproofed (tough plastic wraps are sold in Loksado) – the rafts can't sink, but passengers and goods can fall off, water pours over you almost continually, and you'll arrive soaking wet. With the river high, it's an exciting trip: long, calm stretches overhung with trees are separated by violent rapids and cascades, the raft bouncing off boulders as the boatmen, straining every muscle, use poles to guide you through. You'll certainly be approached if you stay at Loksado; otherwise ask at the guesthouse for details about arranging the trip.

bus stop, a fine suspension bridge crosses the river into town, where early-closing warung and a dozen shops line the single street. Loksado's only **accommodation** is the row of riverside cabins comprising a guesthouse (❶). Stay on the same side as the bus stop, and a sealed motorbike track heads off along the bank towards the mountains, past the **police post** and the open square at **Kayu Manis marketplace**.

Around Loksado

Rising steeply around Loksado through a covering of grassland, tangled undergrowth and highland forest, the Meratus mountains offer some excellent hiking. While you might see a little wildlife along the way, including birds, deer, squirrels, pigs and monkeys, it's the Bukit which are the main attraction, and there are over fifty *balai* to visit, some easily reached on day-trips, others requiring more time and stamina to hike out to. **Day-trips** don't require any special preparation, though it's a good idea to bring snacks, an umbrella for the frequently inclement weather and a few packets of cigarettes to share around. **Hikers** should come properly prepared, but with a minimum of gear; gifts for your hosts and just two sets of clothes – shorts and a T-shirt for hiking, long pants and another shirt for the evenings – are enough. All but the shorter trails require a **guide**; the paths are clear enough, but the trick is knowing which one to follow.

Melaris and Manatui

Despite electricity, satellite TV and motorbikes, **MELARIS** is a good place to start exploring Bukit life. Just forty minutes from Loksado, take the bike track past Pasar Kayu Manis, over another suspension bridge, and then turn left and follow the power lines. Melaris is the biggest *balai* of all, with 34 families and 200 people; the village head is the *damank* (ceremonial and cultural leader) of the entire Meratus region. You could **stay** the night here instead of at Loksado (pay about Rp10,000), though the TV means that people don't sit around and talk much after dark.

Ten minutes away, **Barajang** is the smaller of two **waterfalls** in the area, but it's often clogged up with garbage. For a slightly more authentic feel, the second largest *balai* is thirty minutes from Melaris at **MANATUI**, or you could head back towards Loksado and then take the path uphill for ninety minutes to **Manikili** (see opposite).

The Niwak loop

With moderate fitness and at least three days – five is better – the **circuit from Loksado** up into the mountains via the village of **Niwak** offers some excellent scenery, and overnight stops in at least two *balai*. Start 6km down the road from Loksado at **Tanhui**, from where it's an easy three-hour walk, past five villages, across seven increasingly rickety suspension bridges and through bamboo-grove scenery, to **BUMBIAN**, a large settlement whose kepala desa can sort out a bed. The next morning, the path enters rubber groves and then real forest, becoming ever steeper, muddier and tougher – look for parakeets and star-shaped red flowers of stemless ginger growing out of the ground like fungus. A very stiff burst levels out on a high ridge, with a view of limestone cliffs and adjacent peaks rising out of forest. Descending the far side, you pass a couple of small *balai*, and from here the path is very slippery, passing onto cleared slopes sectioned into *ladang* plots planted with cassava, long beans, peanuts, sweet potato and rice.

Eight hours from Bumbian should see you to **NIWAK**, a single, large *balai* housing eighteen families, built in 1990 at the upper end of a kilometre-high valley. It's a lovely place to spend a couple of days, set beside a stream with tall peaks rising behind, and the people are tolerant of foreign faces. The only modern appliance here is a generator used to power a rice-husking apparatus, but it's used sparingly – eight people take two days to carry a fuel drum here from Loksado – and you're more likely to be kept awake at night by pigs, chickens and dogs snuffling about under the floor. Check out the huge tree across the stream, deliberately left unfelled because it attracts honeybees, and ask someone to guide you for the forty-minute walk to **Mandin Malapan waterfall**, which drops 30m off a cliff into a shallow swimming hole, encircled by walls of greenery.

It takes another six hours to cross the ridges behind Niwak, initially ascending along a network of logs which replace paths on the slopes above the five-person *balai* of **Panggung**. There's some remaining rainforest inhabited by gibbons at the very top, but the steep, cleared slopes on the far side make for plenty of "mud-skiing" through tall, sharp-edged grass. On the way down, a little earth mound covered in coins and shrouded in yellow silk marks the 400-year-old **grave of Ratu Mona**; local lore holds that she ruled southern Kalimantan, but committed suicide after her husband and son were killed in battle. Not far from here, the view opens up over the Amandit valley, with Loksado and the sea off in the distance, but the first stop is an hour later at **MANIKILI**, where eleven families share a slightly run-down, cramped *balai*. It's another pleasant spot, but Manikili's inhabitants are far less laid-back than Niwak's, and foreigners – especially women – can expect to be the centre of attention during their stay. If it all gets too much, another ninety minutes brings you down to the sealed Loksado–Melaris road, with either settlement only a short walk away.

The Negara wetlands

Thirty kilometres north of Kandagan, the towns of **Barabai**, **Amuntai** and **Negara** enclose the green reed-beds of the waterlogged **Negara wetlands**, site of the province's original kingdom. With the purple ridges of the mountains behind, these lowlands form a pleasant landscape of rivers and marsh, banana palms and rice fields, rubber plantations and patches of forest; an almost continuous band of villages and towns along the highway adds the glitter of aluminium-domed mosques, buses forever slowing down to negotiate road-blocks set by villagers soliciting mosque rebuilding funds. Though hardly somewhere you'd cross Kalimantan to see, the wetlands are nonetheless a relaxing place to spend a day; you can catch **bemos** here from Kandangan, or get dropped off by Banjarmasin–Balikpapan traffic.

Barabai and around

The starting point for forays into the Negara wetlands, **BARABAI** sits on a river of the same name. Buses stop at the huge, open **terminal** on the north side of town; walk 100m down past the **market** and you'll end up on Jalan Brigjen Hasan Basri, which runs along the riverbank. Turn right and it's a two-minute walk along Jalan Brigjen Hasan Basri to **accommodation** under the traditionally pitched Banjar roof of *Hotel Fusfa* (☎0517/41136; ❸); the rooms have fan or air-con, and the hotel can arrange meals, and has English-speaking (but wearingly overenthusiastic) **guides**. Barabai's backstreets have plenty of old Dutch town houses, but there's not much excitement in this rather serious, conservative town. Many older people here speak only the rapid Banjar dialect, not Indonesian, and there's a strong Muslim feel to the place, with a huge mosque overlooking the river and a resident pocket of ethnic Arabs. **Moving on**, buses from Banjarmasin to Balikpapan and Samarinda start arriving at the bus terminal around 6pm, bemos to Amuntai and Kandangan run all day, and the last minibus back to Banjarmasin leaves in the mid-afternoon.

Amuntai, Alabio and Negara

AMUNTAI lies an hour away to Barabai's northwest, where, 1.5km from the centre at **Paliwara**, a few grassy mounds and disjointed stonework are all that remain of a thirteenth-century Negaran palace, **Candi Agung**. From Amuntai, you can catch a bemo 7km southwest to **ALABIO**, where a huge Wednesday **market** alongside **Sungai Negara** is crammed with shoppers and stalls hawking rattan crafts, dried fish, buckets of river snails and, most famously, live **ducks**. A klotok, rented from below the bridge here (try for Rp15,000 an hour), can take you downstream to Negara town in about two hours, through a rustic version of Banjarmasin's canals – stilt homes, outhouses, duck pens and graceful suspension bridges. If the water level is high enough, you can detour through the fields and shallow channels before Negara, where you'll see plenty of birdlife, and people fishing with cast nets and wicker fish-traps.

Busy though it is, complete with a small shipyard, timber mills and the inevitable market, it's impossible to imagine that today's **NEGARA**, a kilometre-long street beside the river, was once the pivot of all Kalsel. Resounding to the chink of tiny hammers, the **Sungai Pinang** area of town is renowned for recycling metals; during World War II, gun barrels were forged here for guerrilla use against the Japanese, but the industry has since turned to producing handmade drill bits, kitchen utensils and silverware. People work in little shacks outside their houses, bellows pumped by foot; knock on front doors, and ask to see the process. Down past the market, start back towards Barabai by catching a bemo 10km down the Kandangan road to **Bangkau**, a village at the southern edge of **Danau Bangkau**. Settlements around the lakeshore are the best place to see the local practice of penning **water buffalo** in *kerbau kalan*, raised ironwood enclosures that resemble islands – during the day, the animals swim around and wallow, grazing. From here, there's bemos and buses to Kandangan and Barabai until late afternoon.

Kalimantan Timur

Kalimantan Timur, or **Kaltim**, is Kalimantan's biggest and, in places, most developed and affluent region. Nowhere is this more obvious than in the coastal centres of **Balikpapan** and **Samarinda**, the only cities in Kalimantan which could be described as conspicuously wealthy. Though more accessible areas of Kaltim have been permanently scarred by decades of logging, parts of the mountainous interior remain very wild, and you could spend months here, whatever your interests. Samarinda itself is the terminus for cruising up the

Mahakam on one of the world's great river journeys, while the northeast counts among its attractions prime scuba diving on beautiful **Pulau Derawan**. Head to the interior, to the upper Mahakam or isolated **Apo Kayan** region around the border with Malaysia, and there's the chance to meet the Dayak on their home ground – a guaranteed adventure, however you attempt it.

Scattered relics are all that remain of Kaltim's early **Hindu kingdoms**, which were established in the Mahakam basin as early as the fourth century AD and expanded a millennium later by political refugees from Java. Their demise came with the spread of Islam, and by the seventeenth century Kaltim was divided into rival **Muslim sultanates**, the most influential of which was based on the lower reaches of the Mahakam in the **Kutai** region. Rich, yet far from omnipotent – their capitals were occasionally the target of pirate raids, and their rule was always nominal in the interior – the sultans held onto power throughout the colonial era, though they lost all effective control when **Japan invaded** from Sarawak in 1942 and began exploiting Kaltim's oilfields to power their Pacific campaigns. After the war, Independence saw the sultans formally stripped of their status, and their regencies merged to form Kaltim province, though their names – and some former **palaces** – survive as administrative districts.

Samarinda is Kaltim's **transport** terminus, with regular road traffic south into Kalsel, north along the coast, and inland to towns on the Mahakam's lower reaches; this is also where public **river ferries** depart up the Mahakam, and where most of Kaltim's internal **flights** originate. Balikpapan handles domestic and international flights, while both Samarinda and Balikpapan are major seaports; elsewhere, private and public craft come in handy for exploring Kaltim's lesser-known rivers. There are endless possibilities for **hiking** too, but, despite the lengthy border with Malaysian Borneo, the only official overland crossing is into Sabah via **Pulau Nunukan** and nearby Tarakan to Tewau (see p.875).

Balikpapan

Staked out over Kalimantan's richest petroleum deposits, **BALIKPAPAN** has always been a company town. The Dutch founded Balikpapan's mass of purpose-built services and housing in 1897, and two years later the city's first **oil refinery** was up and running. Occupied by the Japanese during World War II, and the scene of heavy fighting when Allied troops drove them out in 1945, the city's fortunes have otherwise waxed and waned along with international fuel prices: business has boomed since the Gulf War ended years of stagnation in 1991. Balikpapan's 350,000 residents currently enjoy a tidy and busy city, with plenty of traffic, a few high-rises, and large numbers of expatriate oil workers from the US and Australia. Arriving by air from Brunei for your first look at Indonesia, however, you may wonder why you bothered – with its Western ambience, Balikpapan is probably best experienced after a long sojourn in Kalimantan's interior, when its above-average facilities can be properly appreciated.

Orientation, arrival and city transport

Occupying a ten-square-kilometre corner of land bordered by the Makasar Strait to the south and Balikpapan Bay to the west, Balikpapan's commercial district surrounds three-kilometre-long Jalan Yani, with the nearest thing to a downtown hub at its southern intersection with Jalan Sudirman. **Sepinggan airport** lies 8km east of the city (15min by taxi; Rp22,000). Alternatively, walk

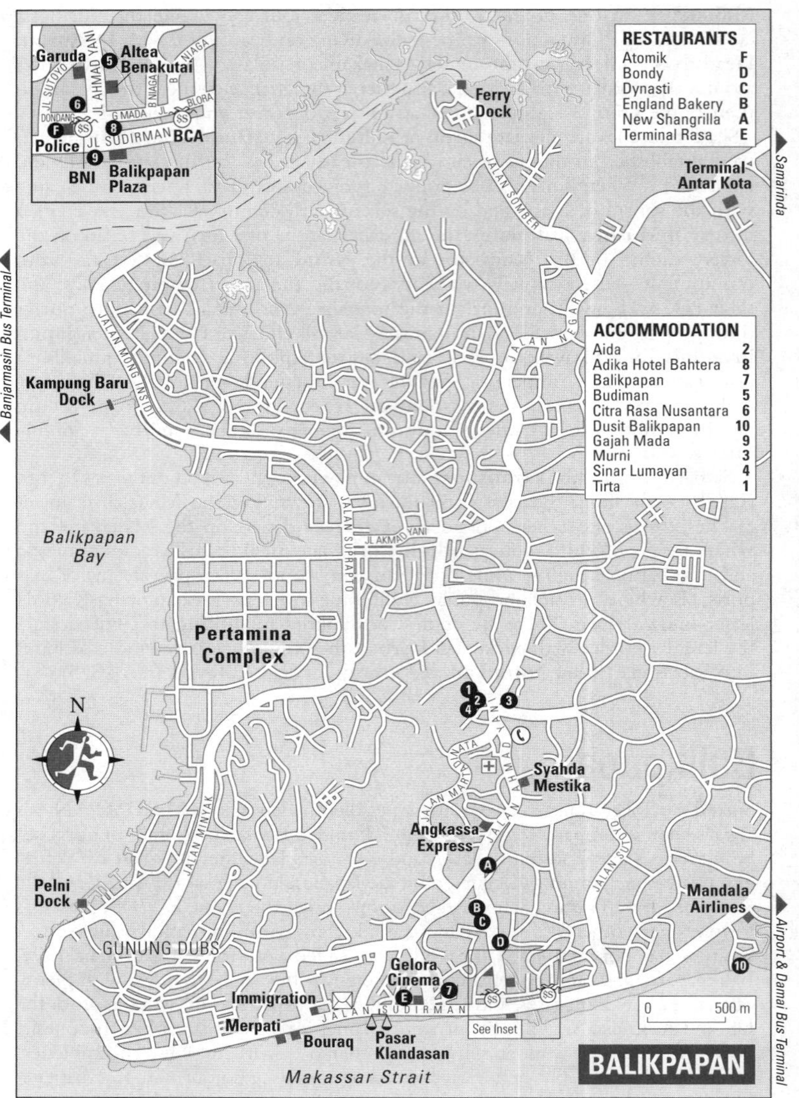

to the airport gates, flag down a green #7 bemo to terminal Damai, then a second into town (for the cluster of cheap hotels on Jalan Yani, jump onto yellow bemo #5). Arriving by air from Singapore or Brunei in northern Borneo, sixty-day tourist visas are issued with no problems. The **Banjarmasin bus terminal** is on the west side of Balikpapan Bay, opposite the city at the hamlet of **Penajam** and connected to it by an hourly ferry to the **Kampung Baru dock** on Jalan Mong Insidi (daily 8am–3pm, Rp2500, or Rp5000 by speedboat). Buses from Banjarmasin continuing to Samarinda, however, cross the bay to the dock at the top of Jalan Somber, then drop off passengers at their offices on Jalan Negara, about 2.5km north of the centre. **Samarinda buses** (Rp8000, 10,000 for air-con) use **Terminal Antar Kota** (the Inter-city Bus Terminal), some 6km out of town along Jalan Soekarno-Hatta in the Batu Ampar district, linked to the centre by blue bemo #3 (though not all the bemos go that far, so make sure you state your destination first before boarding). Vessels running regular services from Java, Sumatra and Sulawesi berth at the **Pelni docks**, 2.5km west of the centre on Jalan Sudirman. Incidentally, when trying to locate an address, don't rely on house numbers, which follow no logical order whatsoever.

City transport consists of numbered **bemos**, which are also often distinguishable by their colour and are called, rather confusingly, *taksis*. They follow reasonably fixed routes (though state your destination before entering the *taksi* to ensure that it is going your way) for Rp1000 a ride (or Rp1500 to the bus and ferry teminals). Three useful ones are the dark blue #6, which starts at the Kampung Baru ferry dock and runs all along the coast on Jalan Minyak and Jalan Sudirman towards the airport, terminating eventually at the Damai *taksi* stop; the lighter blue #3, which runs south from Terminal Antar Kota down Jalan Negara and Jalan Yani past the cheaper hostels, before turning west along Jalan Sudirman to terminate at the Pelni docks; and yellow #5, which runs from the Kampung Baru ferry dock inland down Jalan Negara and Jalan Yani (again past the cluster of cheap hotels and losmen), before turning left at the junction onto Jalan Sudirman, finishing at terminal Damai as well. All of these then reverse their routes. **Taxis** can be arranged through your accommodation.

Moving on from Balikpapan

Six **Pelni ferries** now call in at Balikpapan, including the monthly *KM Doro Londa* and fortnightly *KM Sinabung* to West Papua and Jakarta; the weekly *KM Agoa Mas* to Sulawesi and Nunukan; the *KM Kerinci* and *KM Umsini* to Java and Sulawesi; and the *KM Fudi* to Java and Makassar. Tickets and timetables are available through their offices on Jalan Minyak, opposite the harbour, or from tour agents such as Borneo Mitra Wisata (☎0542/733103) at Jl Sudirman 147, 300m east of *Adika Hotel Bahtera*. Apart from Pelni, there are **other ferries** plying the Balikpapan–Surabaya run, most going via Batulicin (6hr east of Banjarmasin). Currently, the fast *KFC Serayu* sails every Friday afternoon at 2pm and the *KFC Ambulu* sails every Monday at the same time (16hr; Rp310,000 for the cheapest *Bisnis II* class), while the slower *Kirama* departs every Wednesday at 5pm, taking two nights to cover the same journey (Rp168,000). These ferry companies come and go regularly, and the timetable changes frequently as a result, so for the latest information, call in at the Borneo Mitra Wisata (see above) or the helpful PT Sadena Supermarket Tiket (☎0542/394349) on Jalan Sudirman opposite the *Dusit Balikpapan*. For non-Pelni ferries north to Berau and Tarakan, you'll have to go to Samarinda.

Buses to Banjarmasin (Rp67,000) leave through the day from the far side of Balikpapan Bay; catch a ferry there (Rp2500) or a speedboat for (Rp5000) from the Kampung Baru dock on Jalan Mong Insidi. Alternatively, you can make things easier for yourself by booking with PO Pulau Indah (☎0542/420289). They have seven buses per day (Rp47,000, or Rp60,000 with air-con), leaving from their offices at Km3 Jalan Soekarno Hatta (on the way to the Antar Kota bus terminal; catch bemo #3 from Jalan Yani). Buses for Samarinda (Rp8000–9500) depart hourly from morning to late afternoon from Terminal Antar Kota, 6km north of the centre on Jalan Negara. Tickets can be bought at departure points, and there should be no trouble getting on the next departure on either route.

Accommodation

Adika Hotel Bahtera Jalan Sudirman, PO Box 490, Balikpapan ⓣ0542/422563, ⓕ731889. Centrally located, and with plenty of marble in the lobby, but the rooms are ordinary for the price. ❻

Balikpapan Jl Garuda 2 ⓣ0542/421490, ⓕ446058. Hill-top location with plain, neat air-con rooms, a bar, coffee shop, friendly staff and week-end discounts. ❹–❺

Budiman Jl Yani 18 ⓣ0542/736030. Quiet and gloomy, but reasonably priced, and all rooms have air-con. ❸

Citra Rasa Nusantara Jl Gajah Mada 76 ⓣ0542/425366, ⓕ410311. Friendly guesthouse and warung hidden down a side street off Jalan Yani. There are tiny rooms with fan and shared mandi, and pricier ones with air-con and en-suite mandi. ❸

Dusit Balikpapan Jalan Sudirman ⓣ0542/420155, ⓕ420150. Balikpapan's finest, located a few kilometres east of the town centre with its own private beach. All the rooms come with air-con, TV, phone and minibar. ❽

Gajah Mada Jl Sudirman 14 ⓣ0542/734634, ⓕ34636. In a good location and fairly priced, with clean, spacious rooms with mandi on the top floor facing out to sea. Book in advance; otherwise, they always insist they're full, regardless of vacancies. ❸

Murni Jalan Yani ⓣ0542/425920. One of a cluster of losmen by a busy road junction, and the best value of the bunch. Painted sky blue inside and out, the rooms are a little noisy (try to get one as far away from the road as possible), but clean. ❷

Sinar Lumayan Jl Yani 49 ⓣ0542/736092. Hidden away opposite the *Murni*, a decent, friendly alternative if the latter is full. The rooms are less than clean, but they all come with bathroom and fan. ❷

Tirta Jl Yani 8 ⓣ0542/422772, ⓕ422132. With cheaper rooms in the main building, and pricier self-contained bungalows set around a pool. ❹

The City

For a peek at what makes Balikpapan tick, head down to the junction of Jalan Yani and Jalan Sudirman, where **Balikpapan Plaza** (10am–late) is three storeys of duty-free-style boutiques selling designer clothes, music and hi-fi systems and fast food. If nothing else, the air-con makes this an excellent place to hang out. By day, the ground-floor **supermarket** is packed with shopping expats; at night, the balconies throng with the city's middle-class youth, who gather to people-watch and make the most of the funfair and disco at the back. West down Jalan Sudirman, the morning produce market at **Pasar Klandasan** is the place to stock up on fresh fruit, dried fish and general necessities, while the clothing stalls here sell inexpensive sarongs and shirts. Further along, past government offices decked out with Dayak carvings and rooftop motifs, undeveloped seafront blocks provide views of distant oil platforms and tankers lining up offshore, then the road bends around to the **Pelni dock** on **Balikpapan Bay**'s broad inlet. The hill above is **Gunung Dubs**, one of the wealthier of Balikpapan's suburbs, whose winding lanes and groves of banana and cunjevoi pleasantly complement the mildewed colonial houses. From here, you can look down on the gargantuan **Pertamina oil complex** to the north, whose countless kilometres of rounded silver piping assume organic qualities at night, lit up by sporadic breaths of orange flame spouting from the refinery, all reflected in the dark waters of the bay.

Eating and entertainment

There's a decent range of **food** in town, including some stylish, good-value restaurants. Entertainment is largely limited to **nightclubs** patronized by Westerners at the foreign-orientated hotels, and a **cinema**, the Gelora, down towards the GPO on Jalan Sudirman, with daily screenings of the latest Hollywood pictures.

Restaurants

For Western fare, try the hotel menu at the *Altea Benakutai*. There are also a string of cheap **warung** opposite Cinema Antasari on Jalan Sutoyo. *Terminal Rasa*, near the Gelora cinema on Jalan Sudirman, is a huge, airy canteen with various stalls offering all the usual staples.

Atomik Jalan Wiluyo. A long-running Chinese favourite, with frog, pigeon and snails pepping up a mid-priced menu of standard stir-fries.
Bondy Jalan Yani. An unexceptional exterior conceals a wonderful split-level, open-air courtyard out the back, where you can eat superbly grilled seafood in real comfort. It may not be the cheapest place in town, but it may be the best US$4–5 you spend in Balikpapan.
Dynasti Jalan Yani. A Chinese-Indonesian restaurant serving unimaginative but filling fare, including a decent *kue tiaw goreng*
England Bakery Jalan Yani. Bakery, café and restaurant, with steak, cakes, doughnuts and cheerfully named ice-cream sundaes.
New Shangrilla Jl Yani 29. A popular Chinese restaurant with check tablecloths and excellent crab, fried prawn balls and spicy tofu.

Listings

Airline offices Bouraq, Jalan Sudirman ⓣ0542/731475; DAS, at the airport ⓣ0542/766886; Garuda, Jl Yani 19 ⓣ0542/422300, ⓕ735194 (to Jakarta, Batam and various points in Sumatra); KAL Star/Tragana Air, Jl Jend Sudirman 86a, ⓣ0542/731350 (to Samarinda, Tarakan, Tanjung Selor and Berau); Mandala, Kompleks Balikpapan Permai, Blok H1 Kav 4, by the *Dusit Balikpapan Hotel* ⓣ0542/412017; Merpati, Jl Sudirman 22 ⓣ0542/424452; Royal Brunei, at the *Hotel Bahtera* ⓣ0542/426011; Silkair, at the *Hotel Altea Benakutai* ⓣ0542/419444 (to Singapore); Star Air, in the *Hotel Altea Benakutai* complex ⓣ0542/737222 (to Surabaya and Jakarta).
Banks The BCA, Jalan Sudirman, 200m east of *Hotel Bahtera*, has good rates but only accepts Visa travellers' cheques; otherwise, use the BNI, also on Jalan Sudirman, opposite the *Hotel Gadjah Mada*. ATMs outside the Balikpapan Plaza take Cirrus/Maestro cards.
Bookshops Gramedia, 2nd floor, Balikpapan Plaza, is Kalimantan's best-stocked bookshop; English titles include a few coffee-table volumes, guides, an assortment of writings on Borneo and standard city and provincial maps for Kalimantan and Indonesia. English-language magazines and newspapers are sold at the *Hotel Altea Benakutai*.
Hospital Public Hospital (Rumah Sakit Umum) is halfway up Jalan Yani ⓣ0542/434181.
Internet access There's a good internet café in the basement of the BNI building on Jalan Sudirman (Rp9000), a very good one at the post office (Rp6000 per hr), and a reasonable one in the *Hotel Budiman* (Rp8000). Other smaller places are dotted around town.
Pharmacies Pharmacies and evening consultations at Apotik Vita Farma, at the junction of Jalan Yani and Jalan Martadinata, and Apotik Kimia Farma, further down Jalan Yani at number 95. The supermarket at Balikpapan Plaza stocks aspirin, cough medicines, plasters, and so on.
Police Jalan Wiluyo ⓣ0542/421110.
Post Big hotels will hold mail for you if you have a reservation; the GPO with poste restante, parcel post and EMS counters is at Jl Sudirman 31.
Souvenirs For a broad range of local rattanwork, Banjar and Samarinda batik, Dutch coins, Dayak crafts from all over Kalimantan, Chinese porcelain, gemstones and even fossils, head to Syahda Mestika, Jl Yani 2. With the decline in the tourist trade, the Syahda Mestika seems to be concentrating more on producing furniture now, which they make on the pavement outside the shop, (and with the sign well-hidden, it's the only way to find the place), but you can still find some interesting items here. Most items are made for the tourist trade, but collectors might look out for old decorative Kenyah wooden baby-carriers, strings of ceramic beads once used as currency among Dayak groups, and green-glazed celadon crockery. Toko Borneo Antik, further south at Jl Yani 34, is a more conventional souvenir outlet, though it still has some interesting curios.
Telephone and fax The main Telkom office is on Jalan Yani; wartels are scattered all over town.
Tours and guides All but the cheapest hotels can make transport bookings. For this and hiking expeditions, Sungai Mahakam cruises, diving at Pulau Derawan, or private guides, try Angkasa Express at Jl Yani 12 (ⓣ0542/735363, ⓕ35124); they take most credit cards, but offer a ten-percent discount for cash payments on air fares.

Samarinda

Some 120km north of Balikpapan, **SAMARINDA** sprang to life during the eighteenth century after a raiding party of Bugis pirates from Sulawesi founded a settlement on the lower reaches of the **Sungai Mahakam**. Positioned 50km upstream from the sea, where the Mahakam is 1km wide and deep enough to be navigable by ocean-going cargo ships, Samarinda has become increasingly prosperous since large-scale **logging** of Kaltim's interior began in the 1970s, its western riverfront abuzz with mills turning the huge log rafts floated downstream into plywood and planking. The city has also long provided jobs, markets and amenities for communities along the Mahakam, benefits that new air links have recently brought within reach of more isolated regions across the province. There's not much to see here, but as the place to get Sungai Mahakam ferries and flights to Dayak strongholds on the Upper Mahakam and Apo Kayan, Samarinda makes a good place to stock up for trips into Kalimantan's wilds – or to recover on your return.

Arrival, information and city transport

Hemmed in by hills, the bulk of Samarinda occupies the north bank of the Mahakam. The centre is a three-square-kilometre mesh of broad streets and alleys running back from waterfront **Jalan Gajah Mada**, bordered initially by Jalan Awang Long to the west and Jalan Sangaji to the east. Most services are near to the river in the vicinity of **Pasar Pagi**, along **Jalan Khalid** and **Jalan Panglima Batur**. South of the river, semi-rural suburbs are connected to the centre by ferries from near Pasar Pagi – the only **bridge** across the Mahakam is 5km to the west.

Samarinda's **airport** is 2km north of the centre, surrounded by suburbs. Taxis into town charge Rp8000, ojeks Rp3000. **Buses** from the north terminate 5km northeast of the city at Terminal Bontang, from where you catch a brown bemo to the centre. If you come on a bus from Banjarmasin or Tenggarong, you'll arrive on the south bank of the Mahakam at Terminal Banjarmasin; cross over the road to the pier, and catch a boat directly across to Pasar Pagi (Rp1000). Buses direct from Balikpapan or Kota Bangun, however, end up beyond the bridge north of the river, 5km west of the city at Terminal Sungai Kunjang – as do **Mahakam river ferries**, which stop at the nearby docks. At either, green 'A' bemos await to take you downtown. All **ocean-going vessels** use the docks immediately east of the centre along Jalan Sudarso.

For **information**, Dinas Pariwisata (Provincial Tourist Office) is at Jl Sudirman 22, opposite the big Bank BPPD building (Ⓣ0541/736866). On a good day, they're thoroughly informed about costs, transport and accommodation throughout the province. For basic city and more detailed provincial **maps**, try the bookshops at the corner of Jalan Panglima Batur and Jalan Sulawesi. You'll need to find a **guide** in Samarinda if your Indonesian is poor and you're heading further upstream than Long Bagun on the Mahakam, or into the Apo Kayan. Choosing an experienced, bilingual guide is vital, and the best are accredited by the Dinas Pariwisata – test them by discussing your intended route in detail before committing yourself. Some work through hotel tour companies, such as that at the *Mesra*, but most are freelance, and you'll save money by tracking them down yourself. The *Hotel Pirus* is a good place to find one, or if you walk around town for long enough you may well be approached by one on the street; seek out Andi Subagio at the *Pirus*, or the experienced and knowledgeable Sarkani Gambi – ask at the *Mesra* for his

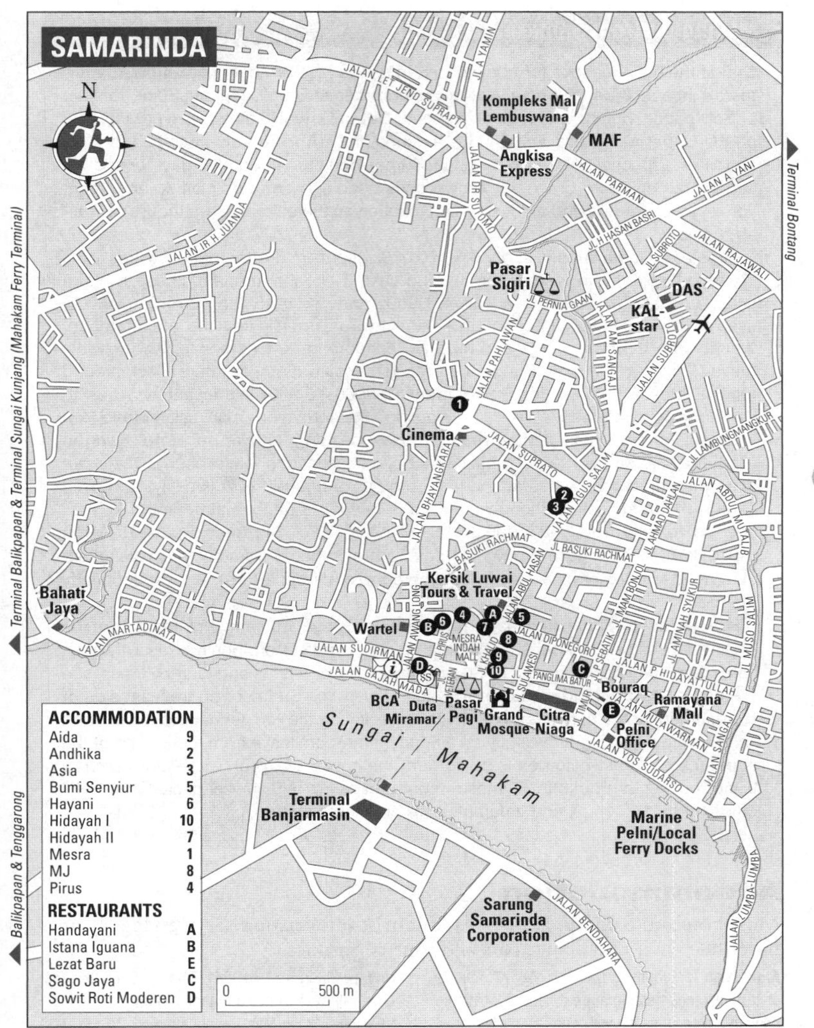

whereabouts. Expect to pay Rp60,000 a day, plus food and lodgings, or Rp100,000 a day all-inclusive.

Samarinda's colour-coded **bemos** cost Rp1000 within town, or up to Rp1500 out to the terminals, and run between particular areas rather than following strict routes – tell the driver your destination as you embark. Jalan Awang Long is a good place to find one heading north, while either side of Pasar Pagi on Jalan Sudirman or Jalan Gajah Mada is where to hail westbound traffic. **Ojeks** wait around Pasar Pagi and the Mesra Plaza; **taxis** can be found west of Pasar Pagi on Jalan Veteran, or at the rank on Jalan Panglima Batur.

Moving on from Samarinda

One of the main reasons for coming to Samarinda is to arrange a ticket out. **By air**, there's little problem getting a seat on major routes to Berau, Tanjung Selor, Tarakan or Balikpapan, but it's vital to book flights to **Datah Dawai** (3 times weekly with DAS) on the Upper Mahakam, and various airstrips in the **Apo Kayan** – handled by DAS and MAF respectively – well in advance. Bemos don't run to Samarinda's Temindung airport, but stopping orange or brown ones heading north up Jalan Awang Long, you might eventually find a driver willing to take you there for an extra thousand rupiah or two.

Buses to Banjarmasin (around Rp70,000) depart mid-afternoon onwards from Terminal Banjarmasin, across the river on Jalan Bendahara, and it's best to buy a ticket at least a few hours in advance. **Buses and taksis to Tenggarong** (Rp5000) used to leave all the time from outside Terminal Banjarmasin until the late afternoon, though with the new bridge and road to Tenggarong now complete, it's probable they will start at the main Sungai Kanjung terminal in the near future – ask around for the latest situation. For **Balikpapan** (Rp8000–10,000), either catch a bus to Banjarmasin, or a green 'A' bemo from outside Pasar Pagi on Jalan Gajah Mada 5km west to Terminal Balikpapan, where buses heading upriver to **Kota Bangun** (Rp8000–10,000) also depart; buses to both destinations leave hourly. There are even the occasional buses all the way through to **Melak** (twice weekly) and even **Tanjung Issuy** (weekly), though the road is in such a parlous state you'd be well advised to take a ferry this far up the Mahakam. For **Bontang** (Rp8500), Berau (Rp75,000) and **Sangata** (Rp13,000), take a brown bemo from Jalan Bhayangkara 5km northeast to Terminal Lempake, where there are departures at least until early afternoon.

Sungai Mahakam ferries leave from Terminal Sungai Kunjang, upstream from the city past Terminal Balikpapan – catch a green 'A' bemo from behind Pasar Pagi on Jalan Gajah Mada. For details of Sungai Mahakam ferry fares and journey times, see the box on p.859. **Marine docks** are along Jalan Yos Sudarso, on the east side of town. Independent services to Berau (four weekly on the *KM Teratai*, Rp86,000) and Tarakan (2 weekly, both currently on a Friday afternoon) leave from the far end of the street (catch a rust-coloured B bemo from the centre of town), with Pelni's *Binaiya* using the western dock four times a month on its Java–Sulawesi circuit. The Pelni office (Ⓣ0541/741402) and timetables are on Jalan Sudarso.

Accommodation

Most hotels in Samarinda offer basic tourist information services; bigger ones have their own restaurants, bars and tour companies.

Aida Jalan Temenggung Ⓣ0541/742572. A budget-to-mid-range hotel in a great central location; book in advance, as it's very popular, particularly with local businessmen. The rooms have fan or air-con. ❷

Andhika Jl Agus Salim 37 Ⓣ0541/742358, Ⓕ747389. An occasionally rowdy Muslim establishment, but clean and generally sound. ❷

Asia Jl Agus Salim 33 Ⓣ0541/736665. A fine budget hotel, with friendly staff and small but acceptable rooms. ❷

Bumi Senyiur Jl Diponegoro 17–19 Ⓣ0541/735101, Ⓕ738014. An opulent hotel for international tour groups; standard rooms and suites. ❼–❽

Hayani Jl Pirus 31 Ⓣ0541/742653. Cool, tidy and quiet; all rooms have a mandi. ❷–❸

Hidayah I Jalan Mas Temenggung Ⓣ0541/731408. With a nice central location, offering decent rooms with fan or air-con, but a little overpriced and the staff can be rude. ❷

Hidayah II Jl Khalid 25 Ⓣ0541/741712. One of the cheapest places in town, but certainly not the best value. The cheaper rooms have clanking ceiling fans, water stains down the walls and dirty red cloth over the windows, while the more expensive ones come with attached mandi. ❷–❸

Mesra Jl Pahlawan 1 Ⓣ0541/732772, Ⓦwww.mesra.com. The most prestigious accommodation in Kalimantan, with acres of parkland, its own radio transmitter, medical facilities, golf course and tennis court. The economy rooms and pricier cottages are not bad value, considering. 6–7

MJ Jl KH Khalid 1 ⓣ0541/747689, ⓕ747690. A smart, modern air-con hotel on the main drag, with friendly staff and an internet café. The rates include breakfast but not tax, and offer reasonable value. 4

Pirus Jl Pirus 30 ⓣ0541/741873, ⓕ735890. Banjarmasin's best-value accommodation, ranging from basic (slightly dirty) rooms with fans and shared mandi, to self-contained, air-con comfort. 

The City

Full of bustle, slightly ramshackle and lined with open sewers and low-roofed shops, Samarinda's streets exude the atmosphere of a typical tropical port. Despite the city's origins, most residents are of Banjar descent, mixing with an ever-changing transient population: upcountry workers and transmigrant villagers here to party or shop, sailors and merchants from Sulawesi and Java, and students from all over eastern Kalimantan.

For an insight into what Samarinda once looked like, head north to **Pasar Sigiri** and Jalan Pernia Gaan, where the canal behind the market remains crowded with rickety wooden housing, boats pulled up on the muddy banks, washing hung out to dry and children playing in the water. Further south, the green dome and untiled concrete spires of Samarinda's own **Grand Mosque** dominate the riverfront view along Jalan Gajah Mada, though nearby **markets** are far busier and more interesting. **Pasar Pagi** is the standard Indonesian maze of overflowing stalls and tight spaces, with a choice range of just about everything you could ever need for daily living; shops nearby are strangely divided between gold stores and chandlers with rudders, bells and *ketingting* props hung up outside. Just up the road on Jalan Khalid, **Mesra Plaza** shopping centre is not as attractive as Balikpapan's, but it's still somewhere to see and be seen. East between Jalan Gajah Mada and Jalan Panglima Batur, **Citra Niaga** is a purpose-built bazaar, whose layout of cheap clothing and souvenir stalls and shops around a central open-air plaza won an architectural award; the plaza sometimes hosts evening song-and-dance sessions, featuring modern pop as well as traditional Banjar and Bugis pieces.

Catching a ferry (Rp1000) from the dock behind Pasar Pagi carries you across the Mahakam to **Seberang** district, a string of small country villages grown together and totally different in feel to downtown Samarinda. Landing opposite the mosque at the main jetty, walk up to Terminal Banjarmasin and then turn east down Jalan Bendahara, where wooden houses are built on poles over the water. A short way along, you pass a small grove of carved wooden posts marking a cemetery, then look for a small sign on the right advertising the presence of the **Sarung Samarinda Corporation** about 500m further on, which produces silk sarongs hand-woven in Bugis "tartan" styles. Further east again, the road runs past what appears to be a dilapidated Dayak longhouse, before fizzling out 1km later in a Muslim kampung.

Eating and entertainment

The bigger **hotels** all have Indonesian and Western restaurants; *Bumi Senyiur* also has a café with excellent pastries, while the *Mesra*'s 24-hour coffee bar sells sandwiches, burgers and Western breakfasts. There are cheap **warung** on Jalan Sulawesi, Jalan Jamrud north of Pasar Pagi and Jalan Khalid, opposite Mesra Plaza, with another row on Jalan Awang Long. There's also a small, sanitized café on Jalan Mutiara selling a limited range of juices, rice and soto, and rooftop warung at the Mesra Plaza offering chicken soup and gado-gado with views out over Samarinda's rusting iron rooftops to the Mahakam. For Western fare, there's a *KFC* at the mall at the eastern end of Jalan Mulawarman (with a *Pizza Hut* rumoured to be moving into the Ramayana in the near future), and various Indonesian derivatives of American fast-food chains dotted around, including an *AFC* at the Mall Lembuswana, a *Texas Chicken* at the Mesra Indah Mall and a *Hanking Donats* on the opposite side of the road. A good stop for breakfast if you're staying nearby is the take-out only *Suwit Roti Moderen* on Jalan Sudirman, with cream cakes and rolls galore.

Rumah Makan Handayani Jalan Abul Hasan, opposite Jalan Diponegoro. A cheap, filling, hygienic and friendly restaurant with a huge menu: heartily recommended, though strangely often empty.

Istana Iguana Jl Awang Long 22. This Chinese-run place with nice open-plan bamboo decor specializes in seafood; some dishes are a bit bland, but *cha udang kacang ment* (prawns cooked with chillies, peanuts and mint) is the highlight, when available.

Lezat Baru Jl Mulawarman 56. The best Chinese food in town, with a long list of favourites. Unfortunately, it lacks atmosphere unless you go in a group, and portions can be on the small side.

Sajo Jaya Jalan Panglima Batur. A noisy and popular Padang restaurant, crowded after dark.

Entertainment

Samarinda's **nightlife** runs to disco-bar pick-up joints, the least sleazy being the *Mitra* bar opposite the new Ramayana shopping mall on Jalan Irian, the bar and live music venue upstairs at the huge *Golden* restaurant on Jalan Subroto, on the way to the airport, and the slightly seedy *Zona* club, on Jalan Hasan by the side entrance to the *Bumi Senyiur*. The multi-screen **cinema** across from the *Hotel Mesra* on Jalan Bhayangkara shows the usual Western and Hong Kong action movies.

Listings

Airline offices Bouraq, Jl Mulawarman 24 (Ⓣ0541/741105) with a second office at Jl Gatot Subroto 32 (Ⓣ0541/738666); DAS, Jl Gatot Subroto 92 (Ⓣ0541/735250), with a second office in the Lembuswana Mall at Blok D, no. 8 (Ⓣ0541/736989); KAL Star-Trigana Air, Jl Gatot Subroto 80 (Ⓣ0541/742110), to Tarakan, Balikpapan, Berau and Tanjung Selor; MAF, Jalan Ruhui Rahayu, 2km northwest of the airport off Jalan Let Jend Parman Ⓣ0541/743628, 203930.

Exchange The BCA on Jalan Sudirman has fair rates, while ATMs are ubiquitous.

Internet access Kaltimnet on the ground floor of the *MJ Hotel* is the most efficient in town, and stays open until midnight (Rp10,000 per hour).

Pharmacies Supermarkets at the Mesra Plaza and Apotik Tanjung Batu, just north of Ankassa Travel on Jalan Abul Hasan, stock various brand-name remedies; Rumah Sakit Bhakti Nugraha on Jalan Basuki Rachmat (Ⓣ0541/741363) comes recommended for anything more serious.

Police Jalan Bhayangkara, about 200m south of the cinema Ⓣ0541/741516.

Post office On the corner of Jalan Gajah Mada and Jalan Awang Long.

Shopping The souvenir shop near the BCA on Jalan Sudirman sells silk sarongs made across the river at the Samarinda Sarung Corporation. For Dayak carvings, beads, blowpipes and baby carriers, try the row of run-down shops 1.5km out from the centre along Jalan Martadinata. Most of the stuff here is made for the tourist trade, and sometimes not even by Dayak; arrive unexpectedly, and you may catch staff assembling beadwork themselves. Bahati Jaya, at Jl Martadinata 16, is better than most, with a range of tribal artefacts and Chinese ceramics.

Telephone and fax 24hr wartel on Jalan Awang Long, across from the *Istana Iguana* restaurant, and down next to the post office, with a smaller office in the Citra Niaga plaza (8am–midnight).

Travel agents, tours and guides Borneo Kersik Lluwai Tour & Travel, Jl Hasan 3 (Ⓣ0541/41486, Ⓕ36728) are helpful, and can arrange most airline (including Royal Brunei, but not MAF) and Pelni tickets, private Mahakam cruises, and trips to Pulau Derawan. Also good are Duta Miramar, Jl Sudirman 20 (Ⓣ0541/743385), though they don't deal with MAF or DAS, and Angkasa Express in the Kompleks Mal Lembuswana, Blok D, no. 3 Ⓣ0541/200280.

Sungai Mahakam

Borneo's second longest river, the **Mahakam**, winds southeast for over 900km from its source far inside the central ranges on the border between Kaltim, Kalbar and Malaysia, before emptying its muddy waters into the Makassar Straits through a complex, multi-channelled delta. Upstream from Samarinda, the river gradually evolves through distinct lower, middle and upper reaches, cutting through a tableau which describes Kalimantan's entire history. In its first half, the **Lower Mahakam** loops over a broad region of marshes, where forests have long since ceded to disjointed woods and farmland, and towns along the bank stand in memory of defunct kingdoms. Beyond the marshes, the transitional **Middle Mahakam** is under increasing pressure from mining and logging operations, but still with some wild corners echoing to the cries of the hornbill. Continuing west, mountains begin to rise up, and entry into the **Upper Mahakam** is through a series of formidable **rapids**, a barrier which has preserved much of the region's forests and, to some extent, ethnic traditions intact.

Against this constantly changing background, it's the Mahakam's **people** that make the journey upstream so worthwhile. Pushed to its fringes by more recent settlers – almost all settlements downstream from Long Iram are Muslim – the Mahakam nonetheless remains a stronghold for **Bahau**, **Benuaq** and **Kayan** Dayak, alongside **Kenyah**, more recently arrived from their Apo Kayan homelands. It's best not to have too romantic a notion of what you'll see, but there are endless opportunities to get acquainted with Dayak culture here, not least during festivals, or by staying in *lamin*, communal **longhouses**. Closest to Samarinda, the Lower Mahakam is the most touristy area, and there's an established three-day circuit taking in the historic town of **Tenggarong** and Benuaq Dayak settlements at **Tanjung Issuy** and adjacent **Mancong**. With a week to spare, scanty forest and less sanitized communities inland from the Middle Mahakam townships of **Melak** and **Long Iram** are within range; ten days is enough to include a host of Kenyah and Benuaq villages between Long Iram and **Long Bagun**, where the Upper Mahakam begins. Getting beyond Long Bagun can be difficult, if you even make it at all: it takes at least two days to run the rapids as far as the Upper Mahakam at **Long Lunuk** – though you could cheat and **fly** directly here from Samarinda – and another day or more to reach the Kayan village of **Long Apari**, the last settlement on the river, some 90km short of the Mahakam's source. Long Apari marks the start of an **overland trek** west into Kalbar and the headwaters of the Kapuas, but even if you don't get this far, there are plenty of other hiking trails from the river's lower and middle sections out of the Mahakam basin and into adjacent regions, not to mention over a dozen major **tributaries** to investigate.

Practicalities

Bring as little as possible with you. A change of clothes, wet-weather gear, and essentials such as a torch and first-aid kit are all you should need for the Lower and Middle Mahakam, as there's accommodation, places to eat and well-supplied stores at towns along the way. Self-sufficiency is required in the Upper Mahakam and other remoter areas, especially with food (even if you end up giving it away as gifts to your hosts), though you'll generally find room and board with locals. Don't bother with a tent or cooking gear unless you're planning to trek out of the region, but decent footwear is vital for even short walks; a sleeping bag also comes in handy for the cool heights of the Upper

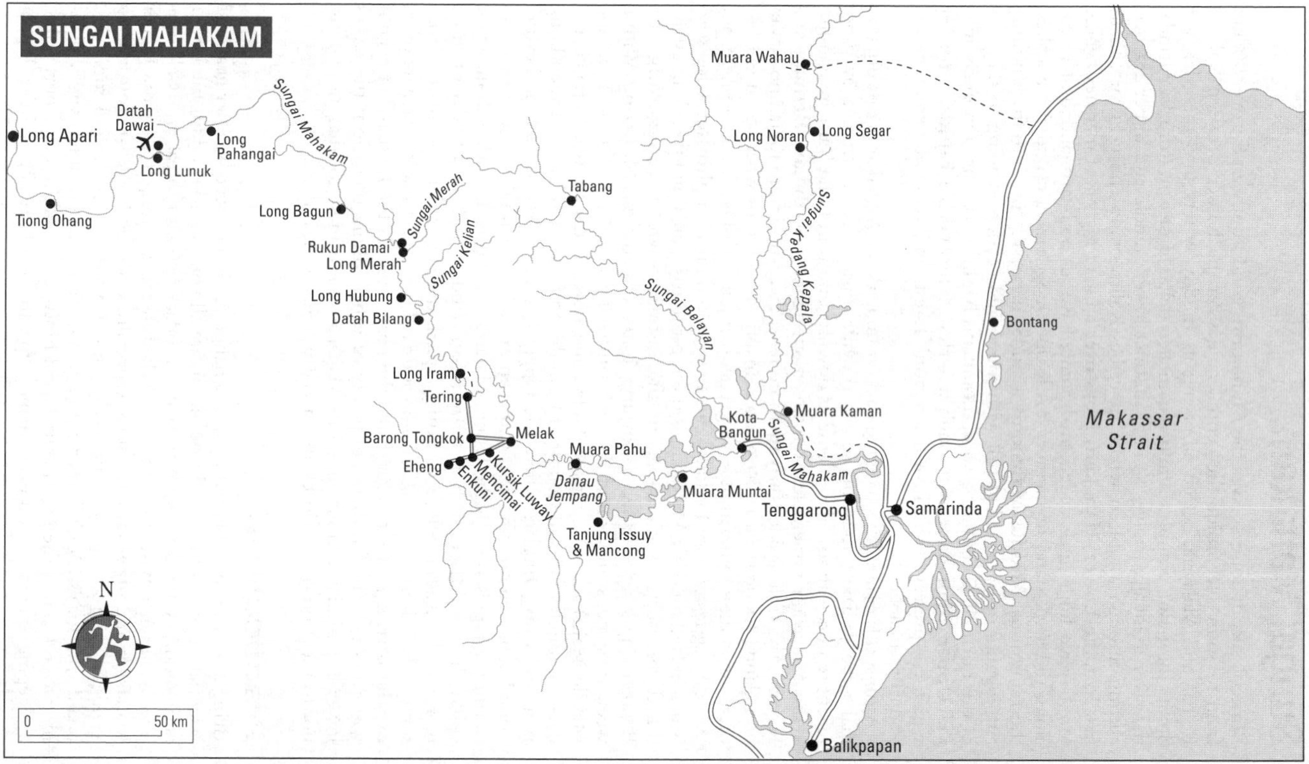

SUNGAI MAHAKAM

Long Apari
Datah Dawai
Long Lunuk
Long Pahangai
Tiong Ohang
Sungai Mahakam
Long Bagun
Sungai Merah
Rukun Damai
Long Merah
Sungai Kelian
Long Hubung
Datah Bilang
Long Iram
Tering
Barong Tongkok
Melak
Eheng
Enkuni
Mencimai
Kursik Luway
Tabang
Sungai Belayan
Muara Pahu
Danau Jempang
Tanjung Issuy & Mancong
Muara Muntai
Kota Bangun
Sungai Mahakam
Muara Kaman
Tenggarong
Samarinda
Muara Wahau
Long Noran
Long Segar
Sungai Kedang Kepala
Bontang
Makassar Strait
Balikpapan
N
0 50 km

Mahakam. After Tenggarong, there are **no banks** on the Mahakam capable of changing money. Assuming that you have a rudimentary grasp of Indonesian, **guides** are not essential for the Lower and Middle reaches, but they certainly are if you're going beyond Long Bagun and can't speak the language, or if you're planning serious hiking at any stage. Samarinda is a good place to hire a guide (see p.856), though there are a few opportunities to pick one up along the way.

Note that, while overall the Mahakam flows southeast, the extreme twisting and looping of its course means that you'll often find that boats travel in almost every direction. **Place names** can also be confusing, with the common prefixes *Muara* and *Long* both indicating a river junction. December through to March is the wettest period of the year, with fabulous electrical storms against heavy skies, while July through to October is the driest.

Mahakam transport

From public ferries to private speedboats and meandering luxury tourist houseboats, there are plenty of craft travelling up and down the Mahakam. **Public ferries** (often called *taksis*) are the cheapest way to tackle the lower and middle reaches of the Mahakam, their crowded decks forcing you into contact with fellow travellers. Broad, flat-bottomed and about 20m long, they are roofed over but open at their sides; passengers sit on the floor, though night services provide a bedroll (and sometimes even TV) on an enclosed upper level. Toilets are a simple bucket-and-hole affair at the back; some ferries also serve hot drinks and basic snacks, though hawkers and dockside warung at stops along the way are the main source of food.

Ferries leave Samarinda's Terminal Sungai Kunjang every morning for towns as far upstream as Long Iram and, when the water is high enough, Long Bagun. All services pause for half an hour or so at Tenggarong, making this a good alternative starting point. Typically, there are two ferries daily to Long Iram, one or two that go on to Long Bagun, and one a day that turns off at Muara Muntai to go to Tanjung Issuy. In addition to these, others terminate at points in between such as Melak or Kota Bangun. As all ferries depart at roughly the same time, if you get off at any stage, you'll have to stop over for 24 hours until the next batch arrive.

To catch a ferry from smaller settlements, stand on the jetty and hail passing traffic; locals know roughly at what time the regular services pass, though the further you get from Samarinda, the less accurate any schedules are. When you board, take your shoes off and put them in the overhead rack, squeeze yourself into a space on the deck (away from the exhaust, if you have any choice), and

Ferry fares and journey times from Samarinda

The following **schedule** from Samarinda is a guide only. Fares vary depending on the facilities of individual ferries, and journey times are affected by the size of the motor, the number of stops along the way, and how much rain there has been – with the river in full spate, it can take five days to reach Long Bagun. Conversely, returning with the current from Long Bagun to Samarinda can shorten the trip to just 24hr. The following fares are typical for the upper-deck "A" class fares; lower deck "B" class fares are around Rp5000–10,000 lower.

Tenggarong 3hr; Rp7500
Melak 24hr; Rp45,000
Kota Bangun 10hr; Rp11,000
Long Iram 30hr; Rp60,000
Muara Muntai 14hr; Rp15,000
Long Bagun 40hr; Rp90,000

wait for someone to collect your fare. If you plan to disembark before the boat's ultimate destination, make sure that the pilot, not the ticket collector, knows where you want to get off.

A more luxurious option for seeing the Mahakam is **private houseboats**, which can be rented for upwards of US$150 a day (with discounts of up to fifty percent in the low season) through agencies in Samarinda and Balikpapan (see p.856 and p.851), and come complete with guides, cooks and private cabins.

For village-hopping and detours off the Mahakam, you'll need assistance from smaller **ces** or **ketingting**, ubiquitous narrow-hulled speedboats capable of seating about four people. They're rented out by the day and, as the price of fuel increases as you head away from the coast, so does the cost of rental. Check the condition of your *ces* before hiring it, and never travel in one after dark, as logging debris – including whole rafts of felled timber – makes deadly obstacles. Rougher stretches of the Mahakam are covered by ten-seater **longboats** powered by up to three outboard engines.

Away from the water, **buses** link Samarinda to Tenggarong and Kota Bangun, and are a useful short cut for heading upstream, or if you run out of patience with the ferries on your way back to civilization. To head straight into the heart of Dayak territory, however, you can **fly** directly from **Samarinda to Datah Dawai** on the Upper Mahakam; though bad weather often causes delays, this is actually cheaper than taking a ferry to Long Bagun and then battling through the rapids in a longboat. DAS in Samarinda charge just Rp70,300, a subsidized fare which needs to be booked a month in advance – though paying double will find you a seat on the next flight.

Tenggarong

As the ferry leaves Samarinda early in the morning, you settle into your deck space surrounded by upriver villagers returning home. The river here is broad, slow and smooth, sawmills and villages pepper the banks, and *ces* zip past at twice the speed of ferries, their passengers holding umbrellas against the spray and sun. Groves of coconut and spindly kapok trees punctuate the regular sprinkle of villages and sudden cleared spaces filled by shipyards or the hulking machinery of timber and coal operations. Rooflines rise to satellite dishes and mosque domes, low wooden stilt buildings backing onto the water, each with a flight of stairs – or notched palm-trunk – descending to a private outhouse at river level, where people wash themselves and their clothes.

TENGGARONG, 45km and three hours upstream from Samarinda – or just an hour by bus – is an extremely prosperous town built around a canal running off the Mahakam. This wealth is reflected both in the Tengarrong's healthy collection of large houses and gleaming new mosques, with the enormous Mesjid Agung on the northern side of the river as the definite showpiece. Tenggarong has a deserved reputation as one of the tidiest and most orderly towns in the country, with the curious "hand" monument in the centre a celebration of just one of the many awards it has won for its efforts in this field. For visitors, Tenggarong is a cheaper and far more relaxed place to stay than Samarinda.

Tenggarong has also played its part in the history of the region; until 1959, it was the seat of the **Kutai Sultanate**, whose territory encompassed the entire Mahakam basin and adjacent coastline. Originally known as **Kartanegara**, the sultanate was founded downstream in the fifteenth century, when Muslim raiders annexed the older Hindu **Mulawarman Kingdom**; Tenggarong itself was established three hundred years later, after Bugis pirates forced the sultan to shift his capital further inland. The former palace and contents are on display just up from the docks at the **Museum Negeri Mulawarman** (Tues–Thurs & Sun 9am-4pm, Fri 9–11am; Rp1000) on Jalan Diponegoro. The original wooden structure burnt down in 1935, and was replaced by this angular Dutch-designed building. The front door is guarded by a statue of the strange **Lambu Suana**, a griffin with a scaly body and elephant's head; inside, the collection begins with Art Deco tile portraits of sultans in the entrance hall, and a bedroom assembly – including an over-the-top bridal bed trimmed in silver, red velvet and brass – off to the right. Further on, the Mahakam's Hindu period is illustrated by statuary from the basin's northern fringes, and replicas of fourth-century conical stone *yupa* found upstream near Muara Kaman, whose cursive inscriptions are Indonesia's oldest written records. Dayak pieces include explanations of Benuaq weaving, and some examples of Kenyah beadwork and grotesque *hudoq* masks used by the Bahau. Outside, all nineteen of Kutai's sultans are buried in the adjacent **cemetery**, while the forecourt often hosts **Dayak dancing** on Sundays.

If you're in Tenggarong in late September, try and catch the **Erau Festival**, when Dayak groups from all over the province descend for a week-long performance at the showgrounds outside of town, a fantastic display of traditional costumes, dances and ceremonies.

Practicalities

The **docks** are at the downstream end of town on Jalan Sudirman, which runs 250m north along the river, over a small canal, and continues as Jalan Diponegoro past **Seni Tepian Pandan marketplace** and the museum. There are **ATMs** at the Lippobank on Jalan Sudirman, north of the docks, and the BNI by the canal on Jalan Parman. Tenggarong's **tourist information centre** is at the back of the marketplace, and can advise on all aspects of the Mahakam.

Accommodation includes the clean and welcoming *Penginapan Anda II*, near the canal at Jl Sudirman 63 (Ⓣ0541/661409; ❷), offering simple rooms with shared mandi and self-contained, air-con units. Nearer the docks is the friendly but rather down-at-heel *Penginapan Diana* (Ⓣ0541/661160; ❷). Additional comforts such as TV and hot water are available at *Timbau Indah*, 250m south of the docks towards Samarinda at Jl Muksin 15 (Ⓣ0541/661367; ❸). For **places to eat**, the *Rumah Makan Tepian Pandan* overlooking the river almost opposite the museum is a great place to tuck into Chinese and Indonesian food; there are also several good Banjar warung between the docks and canal on Jalan Sudirman.

Moving on, **taksis** to Samarinda leave from the **bus station**, 5km south of town beyond the huge new bridge. For buses to Kota Bangun (Rp9000), you'll need to wait by the junction beyond the bus station at the southern end of town, but be warned: all buses to Kota Bangun start in Samarinda and are usually full by the time they reach Tenggarong, so you may have a very long wait. **Ferries** heading upstream leave all day from the docks (Rp15,000 to Muara Muntai), though check departure times and destinations the day before.

Muara Kaman, Kota Bangun and detours

About four hours from Tenggarong, the handful of dirt lanes which comprise the township of **MUARA KAMAN** were once the focus of the powerful Hindu **Mulawarman Kingdom**, though, aside from the name and a few enigmatic stone relics off in the scrub 2km inland, almost nothing is known about them. The only reason to stop here – in which case, seek **accommodation** at the basic *Penginapan Martapura* (❶) – would be to detour north to

Dayak communities along **Sungai Kedang Kepala** (Severed Head), where you'll find the recently settled Kenyah villages of **Long Noran** and **Long Segar**, and where you can sleep in a *lamin* (longhouse) for Rp10,000. Beyond here, the town of **Muara Wahau** has overland connections back to Samarinda, or further north up the coast. Seasonal ferries run from Muara Kaman to Muara Wahau for around Rp15,000; otherwise you'll have to rent a *ces* for about ten times this price.

Back on the Mahakam, the river narrows perceptibly as it continues to **KOTA BANGUN**, a large, well-supplied town, four hours from Samarinda by **bus** (Rp9000). Ferries dock on the north bank, where you'll find 500m of sealed road, and **places to stay** and eat, either off to the left at *Penginapan Mukjizat* (❷), or ten minutes' walk along to the right at the surprisingly comfortable *Sri Bangun Lodge* (❸). Kota Bangun offers further detours off the Mahakam, this time 120km northwest along **Sungai Belayan** to **TABANG**; *ces* are the only way there, but Kota Bangun is big enough that you should eventually be able to find others to share costs. Tabang itself is another Kenyah community, and offers the possibility of trekking westwards through densely forested **Punan** territory to the upper **Sungai Merah**, which enters the Mahakam way upstream near Rukun Damai (see p.868). Nomadic hunters, the Punan are the least known of all Kalimantan's Dayak; they are wary of strangers, and if you plan to hike west from Tabang, it's essential that you take a Punan guide to smooth the way.

Muara Muntai and around

The Mahakam continues to narrow beyond Kota Bangun, and there's a definite thickening of the forest along the banks as the river enters the flat, marshy regions of the basin's lakelands. This is the first place that you're likely to see **hornbills**, big black birds with outsized curved beaks, honking, flapping and coasting across the treetops in the late afternoon light. Symbolic of the Dayak as a people, one species, the helmeted hornbill, has a solid beak once much in demand in China as ivory for carvings.

Around four hours from Kota Bangun and fourteen from Samarinda, **MUARA MUNTAI** sits northeast of **Danau Jempang**. The town is raised over the surrounding swamps on piles, with a very impressive network of interconnected wooden **boardwalks** which serve as streets complete with motorbikes rattling along them. Turn left from the dock and *Penginapan Nita Wardana* (Rp10,000 per person) is about 50m along on the right, with *Sri Muntai Indah* (Rp10,000 per person) just a bit further down. Fans and essential mosquito nets are supplied in the cell-like rooms of both, though the *Nita* is probably slightly superior, thanks to the amiable elderly manager. Incredibly hot and sticky during the day, not much happens in town until ferries start arriving after dark – even the couple of warung don't seem to want business – and there's nothing to distract from negotiating a visit to **Benuaq** settlements on the far side of the lake with *ces* operators at the dock (Rp75,000).

Danau Jempang, Tanjung Issuy and Mancong

Assuming there are enough passengers, a *taksi* leaves Muara Muntai every morning at about 8am for Tanjung Issuy (Rp15,000 per person). Right out from Muara Muntai, watch for the slate-grey backs and tiny dorsal fin of **pesut**, freshwater dolphins; woods lining the channels leading from the river to the lake are home to **proboscis monkeys** (see p.1074). Once through these channels, Jempang's hundreds of square kilometres of reed beds open up, and it takes about an hour to reach **TANJUNG ISSUY**, a small township of gravel lanes, timber houses and fruit trees built on a slope overlooking the water. Turn right off the jetty, past a couple of lumber yards, stores and workshops, and follow the street for around 300m to *Losmen Wisata*, a restored Dayak **lamin** maintained as tourist accommodation (❶). It's not exactly authentic, with the adjacent building given over to souvenir sellers, but the place is surrounded by carved wooden *patong* posts; also, Benuaq **dances** are performed for tour groups, which provide excellent photo opportunities as well as drawing crowds of local spectators. Out the back is a six-tier **mausoleum** where Tanjung Issuy's founder was laid to rest in 1984, decorated with carvings of dragons, hornbills and scenes from the **kwangkei reburial ceremonies** (see box on p.833). The losmen offers coffee and tea, and the unnamed one-table rumah makan down the boardwalk by the side of the dock does a reasonable fish curry. There's also an unrestored *lamin* with bigger *patong* to check out near Tanjung Issuy's mosque. You can also spend the day at **MANCONG**, a pretty Benuaq village built on boardwalks like Muara Muntai, whose own two-storey *lamin* can house 200 people. You can walk to Mancong in a couple of hours from Tanjung Issuy, though it's a hot and unpleasant tramp along a wide road through farmland, while ojeks (Rp15,000 one-way, Rp25,000 return) usually drive like maniacs, so your best option is to charter a *ces* (Rp60,000–80,000 return). Though much of the local forest has been decimated by the logging companies, and the remainder largely burnt down in the fires of the late 1990s (see p.820), there are also some **forest walks** that can be done from nearby villages. Pak Teng at Lempunah village, 12km from Tanjung Issuy (30min by ojek, or catch a boat/*ces* up the Ohong River), arranges overnight treks through a nearby forest filled with over 170 species of birdlife, as well as monkeys, civets and muntjac deer, with the possiblity of staying overnight in a simple *pondok* (shelter). The cost for this is just Rp60,000 for a group of up to four people, plus Rp10,000 for the upkeep of the *pondok*. A simpler alternative is the short day-walk from the village of Muara Tae, one hour from Tanjung Issuy, where Pak Asuy and Pak Aguy run standard three-hour hikes (Rp50,000) through forests said to conceal the rare argus pheasant.

Heading on **up the Mahakam** from Tanjung Issuy, you could either return to Muara Muntai (there's a *taksi* every morning; Rp15,000), or hire a *ces* to take you across the forested northwest corner of Danau Jempang and back to the Mahakam west at **Muara Pahu** (1hr, 100,000; 3hr to Melak, Rp175,000).

The Middle Mahakam: Melak and around

The Mahakam's middle reaches are defined by a steady rising of the landscape as the river begins to edge into the first outrunners of central Borneo's granite and limestone plateaux. Initially, this isn't very obvious, though a few hills rise around **MELAK**, a small Muslim town about ten hours by ferry beyond Muara Muntai, servicing **gold mines** in the vicinity. A convenient jumping-off point for exploring the surrounding forest and villages, Melak comprises two surfaced roads, one running along the riverbank, and the other heading inland from the docks. A knot of stores and services surround their intersection: down Piere Tendean, the clean *Penginapan Rahamat Abadi* (Ⓣ0545/41007; ❷) and the new *Salsabila* (Ⓣ0545/41444; ❷) provide simple **accommodation**, with cheap **padang restaurants** strung out along the front; for more upmarket fare, the *Rumah Makan Anda* down Piere Tendean does a good spread, though watch the bill here. Villages and townships further inland from Melak also have accommodation, with a network of dirt roads running through the region and on to the upstream Mahakam port of **Tering** (see opposite).

Transport out to local sights includes ojeks from the docks, or minibuses, which wait for passengers at the **market square** about 50m downstream. To Barong Tongkok (Rp5000) and Tering (Rp10,000) there are *taksi* bemos or Kijangs every morning, but to Kersik Luway, Eheng and other inland destinations (see below) there is no regular public transport. An ojek charter to Eheng via Kersik Luway costs around Rp60,000–80,000 return. Alternatively, if there are enough of you to split the cost (Rp120,000 one-way) and you plan to continue upstream towards Tering, it may be more sensible to charter a Kijang or minibus to Kersik Luway, Eheng (via the museum at Mencimai (see below) and the *lamin* at Enkuni), and on to Barong Tongkok, halfway between Melak and Tering, where there is a tourist-class hotel. Returning to Kota Bangun, there are a number of *taksis* daily, or you can hire a speedboat to whisk you there in much less than half the time (Rp450,000–750,000, depending on the number of passengers).

Inland to Kersik Luway Forest Reserve, Barong Tongkok and Eheng

It's a bumpy motorbike ride on dirt roads 19km southwest of Melak to hot, sandy heathland at **Kersik Luway Forest Reserve**, where, surrounded by former forests destroyed in the fires of the late 1990s, shady "islands" of dense vegetation conceal spongy mosses, trailing vines of carnivorous **pitcher plants**, and over sixty species of **orchid**. Most famous is the lightly scented *anggrek hitam* or **black orchid**, which unfurls a pale-green flower with a mottled black centre between January and April. Guides are on hand to show you around – a few thousand rupiah repays their help.

Eighteen kilometres west from Melak, **Benuaq villages** surround the transmigrant settlement of **BARONG TONGKOK**, making it a good place to stay for a few days. The 250-metre-long main road comes in from Melak, passes Barong Tongkok's **market** and **minibus compound**, and forks as it runs uphill and out of town. A lane down the side of the compound leads to the surprisingly smart *Puteri Tunjung*, offering rooms with fans or air-con (❷); the *Green Garden Café* there looks great, but never seems to actually have any food, making the Padang warung at the bus compound the only **place to eat**. A **Catholic church** on the far side of the playing field identifies a Dayak quarter, with two brightly painted and wonderfully lively *patong* of former Dutch priests at the church gates. Following the road past the playing field brings you to the tiny Benuaq village of **Lei**, where reburials are characterized by days of dancing and gambling, and the carving of a dragon *patong* and wooden mausoleum for a late village head. **Moving on**, minibuses can run you back to Melak (Rp5000), 35km north to Tering and the Mahakam (Rp7500), or out to other Benuaq villages.

The best of these villages lie southwest of Barong Tongkok. A surprising **museum** (open daily except Fri; ask for the key from the talkative old gentleman in the house next door) lies 7km down the road at **MENCIMAI**, a tiny hut by the roadside concealing some fine Benuaq artefacts and a detailed rundown of agricultural practices and scale models of various animal traps, while a further 8km brings you to **ENKUNI**'s tidy *lamin*. Another 10km due west of Enkuni, **EHENG** has a **cemetery** with more mausoleums, and also one of the most authentic *lamin* in the region, a 75-metre-long structure of hardwood, rattan and bamboo, raised 3m off the ground and reached by a traditional ladder made from a notched pole. Inside, an open gallery runs the length of the building, where people sit during the day; the living quarters for each of the *lamin*'s thirteen families are partitioned off behind a wall. Residents have become used to visitors breezing quickly in and out of Eheng, and offer a variety of tourist trinkets; to get more out of the place, ask the kepala desa if you can stay overnight (offer about Rp10,000–15,000).

Tering

TERING, five hours upstream from Melak by ferry or just ninety minutes by road (1hr; Rp7500 by Kijang), is doing very well supplying the nearby **Kelian Equator Mining** (better known as P.T. KEM pronounced "Petakem") gold mine. The town is bisected by the Mahakam, with river ferries and roads winding up on the south bank at **Tering Sebarang**, where you'll find muddy streets, a Muslim population, and a hugely busy Saturday market. A *ces* from the dock here can whisk you straight across the river to **Tering Lama** (Rp1000), a quieter **Bahau Dayak** village, where a Catholic mission has been based since the 1920s. Considered a downriver offshoot of the Kayan, the Bahau are best known for their **rice-planting festivals**, in which performers dressed in palm fronds and wearing huge-nosed **hudoq masks** dance to snare the goodwill of the agricultural goddess Hunai. Tering Lama's large green, red, black and white meeting house, which used to sit just above the landing stage, is currently undergoing extensive restorations and has been largely dismantled, though there are still dozens of human *patong* around the place, including a two-metre-high figure with mirror eyes, supporting a satellite dish. Tering Lama is the first place you're likely to see older Dayak with **tattoos and stretched earlobes**, decorations seldom seen nowadays. Foreigners are often grabbed and taken to see a collection of antique pieces stored in a private house here: *hudoq* masks, posts which once supported Tering's defunct *lamin*, and ceremonial costumes.

A *ces* from Tering Sebarang can run you upstream to **Long Iram** in about forty minutes (negotiate for Rp30,000, including a visit to Tering Lama), or you can **walk** there through overgrown *ladang* and open woodland in an easy three hours: turn left from above Tering Lama's landing stage and walk 50m upstream through the village, then follow the footpath and power lines heading north into the countryside.

Long Iram

Marking the furthest point on the Mahakam that passenger ferries can reach year-round, **LONG IRAM** has been a government post since colonial times, and retains government offices and a small military barracks. A sleepy, Muslim place on the surface, the town borders Benuaq and Bahau lands; make local connections here, and you can find yourself witnessing some unusual events (see box on pp.866–867). If you've got this far, you may also want to spend a day or two arranging transport and guides to escort you around Dayak villages upstream.

Long Iram's main street is a sealed road running for several kilometres along the north bank of the Mahakam, though the stores which make up the tiny town centre surround the ferry dock. The track from Tering Lama joins the main street about 500m upstream from the docks near Long Iram's **police station**. Arriving by river, climb the tall steps to the road and turn right (downstream), where you'll find all **accommodation** within a two-minute walk. Nearest is the spartan *Losmen Susanti* (❶), while further along you'll find spacious rooms at *Losmen Wahyu* (Rp15,000 per person, or Rp25,000 including a filling breakfast). The floating rumah makan right on the harbour is the only place in town with cold drinks from the fridge. If you're after a **guide** for the

A visit to the exorcist

The girl was sick – did we want to see a *basir*, a Dayak shaman, cure her? Having immediately agreed hours before, we now felt awkward standing outside a stranger's home after dark on the edge of Long Iram, the master of the house listening to our introductions before politely inviting us in. We sat down in a front room while the girl's brothers came and checked us out, proffering cigarettes and glaring at these tourists invading a family affair – at least, that's how we felt, though perhaps everyone was just nervous. Something was out of place; surely this was a Muslim family, with lines from the Koran written in gold above the door? Yes, but the girl was ill because someone unknown, probably motivated by jealousy, had paid a *basir* to evoke the spirit causing her sickness. Only another *basir* could send this spirit back to plague whoever had originally sponsored the curse.

Ushered into the plain room where the ceremony would take place, we sat cross-legged on the bare wooden floor in what little space wasn't taken up by other spectators, a bed and the *basir*'s paraphernalia. In one corner of the room, a dozen plates of cooked rice, meat and vegetables were neatly arranged on banana leaves in a split bamboo tray, the whole assembly scattered with flowers and decorations made from shaved wood. A heavy black drape the size of a curtain hung down all the way from the ceiling to just above the floor, while a man in military fatigues tied a long piece of rattan cable diagonally across the room, so that it stretched about a metre off the ground like a tightrope. Through a doorway into the kitchen, the parents and brothers could be seen talking with two men, one short, muscular and dark, the other tall, wiry and moustached. The *basir* and his assistant, said someone – another anomaly, as it was obvious that neither were local Bahau or Benuaq Dayak, who are pale-skinned. No, they were Muslim Banjarese from 500km south in Kalsel, but were descended from the Bukit Dayak of that province. It didn't matter; their principles were the same.

Wailing suddenly came from the kitchen, then the father came in, carrying the girl in his arms. Nobody had been too specific about her illness, and, having expected to see someone perhaps pathetically sick with fever, her appearance was shocking: she was in her mid-teens, dressed in a shirt and trousers and, as it became immediately clear, was completely deranged. Placed on the bed, she squatted on her haunches, hands and arms horribly twisted up at her sides, and crowed harshly at everyone. A whisper from next to me: the spirits which cause this type of illness always adopt the form of an animal – this was a chicken. The *basir* would try to dislodge the spirit from

area, ask around the village for Rudi Yanto; he's a Muslim, but genuinely interested in the Dayak, and can wrangle fair *ces* rates. With time to kill, some big trees, hornbills and giant red squirrels lurk in a patch of woodland 1km or so downstream from Long Iram's docks, while a couple of **lakes** about 3km down the Tering track are home to monkeys and kingfishers. Leaving Long Iram, there are currently two ferries daily back to Samarinda, at around 8am and 1pm.

Upriver to Long Bagun

Beyond Long Iram, the Mahakam squeezes between forested hills and cliffs. In drier months (July–Nov), the water is too shallow for ferries, while heavy rains see the river swell rapidly and race past town, making Long Bagun anything between ten hours and two days away, depending on the current. Even if passenger services are running, it's better to cover this stretch by *ces* (Rp250,000), stopping off to explore **villages** along the banks; it's polite to introduce yourself to the kepala desa, who can sort out accommodation or simply assist your investigations.

the girl, then take it on himself and overpower it, frightening it away.

A sudden uproar came from the bed, as the girl started to bash her head against the wall. Her brothers leapt up with pillows, trying to restrain her, but she screamed and butted them off, then calmed abruptly as the *basir* entered the room holding a freshly killed fowl by the feet. Its throat had been cut, and, his back to the bed, he sprinkled blood over the plates, turned around, and invited her over to inspect the food. Still squatting and holding her hands like folded wings, she jumped down and sniffed around the plates, but soon lost interest and returned to the bed, where she rocked back and forth, crooning quietly. The *basir* seemed satisfied; this was clearly the way things should proceed. Picking up a glass jar from the edge of the room, he removed a twist of paper from it, which he placed in a crucible and lit before sitting on the floor under the black drape and drawing the cloth about him.

Nothing happened for a while, then the assistant unwound the cloth to reveal the *basir* sitting in a trance; face screwed up, he rose slowly to his feet and started making senseless, chicken-like noises to the girl. She responded, and their exchange went on until the girl again lost interest, though the *basir* continued long after she stopped responding and seemed completely oblivious to his surroundings. A lull followed, while both the *basir* and his assistant went into a huddle under the cloth. Then things suddenly got violent; the girl started screaming and bashing her head again, and the *basir* rocketed up, grabbed the drape, and began swinging wildly around on it, crashing into the spectators. As we scattered to the sides of the room, the girl became more and more hysterical, lashing out at everyone; while the *basir* still oscillated above, his assistant dragged her roughly off the bed, held her down and sucked grotesquely at her midriff. Suddenly he sat up and spat out a stone – the spirit's physical form, dislodged from her belly – and, with a shriek, she stopped thrashing and lay still on the floor. The assistant, eyes closed, crawled over to the rattan cable and, in a seemingly impossible balancing act, stretched out along its length and stayed there for the next hour.

Things went quiet; now unconscious, the girl was laid out on the bed, while the *basir* had returned to earth and was sitting on the floor, muttering softly, gradually bringing himself back to the present. We sat and watched for a long time while both men recovered, then the girl sat up, got off the bed and walked out of the room – the first time she had stood upright in six weeks.

David Leffman

Sungai Kelian and Datah Bilang

An hour upstream from Long Iram, detouring along **Sungai Kelian** takes you past a half-dozen shantytowns, where private enterprises are busy excavating huge muddy quarries, unearthing alluvial deposits for **gold**. Pumps suck up the watery slush, which is then cascaded down a stepped trough lined with **carpet**. Being heavier than anything else, grains of gold settle into the pile and are trapped, while most mud washes out – independent panners sit downstream from the quarries' outflows, picking up missed bits and pieces. Weekly treatment of the carpets' trapped sludge with mercury and cyanide removes the gold, but has also killed off all of the Kelian's fish life.

Back on the Mahakam, lumber camps have yet to strip all of the forest, and more extreme slopes above the river are covered in huge trees, ferns and vines, rock ledges and small waterfalls breaking through the canopy. Another hour brings you to flatter country around **DATAH BILANG**, a **Kenyah** village settled between 1972 and 1975 by migrants from a (then) economically isolated Apo Kayan (see p.870).

Like all Dayak villages along this stretch, Datah Bilang is extremely tidy and, though people here are Catholic and live in ordinary houses instead of *lamin*, traditional ways are still followed. The Kenyah have a stratified society, with aristocrats still held in considerable respect by lower classes. Once considered amongst the fiercest of headhunters, today they are best known for their **artistry**, evident in their architecture, weaving, carving and decorative beadwork. Government attention has made Datah Bilang a good place to catch official ceremonies: dressed in full war regalia, men weave a strange, slow-motion **sword dance** performed in a half-crouch, encircled by a gently swaying ring of women holding fans of hornbill feathers. The two large wooden **meeting halls** here are supported by posts carved into faces and spirit figures; check out the **murals** inside, one of which details the story of the migration from the Apo Kayan, and the rafters, where festival masks and carvings are stashed. There are also a couple of tall *patong* of dragons and warriors in the village, one outside the upstream meeting hall, the other on the edge of the playing fields – a monument to Suharto's visit here during the 1970s. Stretched miniature roofs across the river mark a **cemetery** (Dayak spirits are unable to cross water). Datah Bilang's sole **losmen** is the *Cahaya Sidenreng* (Rp10,000 per person), whose manager has a collection of Dayak curios, and there are a couple of **warung** at the docks, whose basic repertoires occasionally stretch to deer curry.

Long Hubung, Long Merah and Rukun Damai

LONG HUBUNG is the next good place to stop, a Bahau village an hour beyond Datah Bilang, with two suspension bridges and the extremely basic *Losmen Benitha* (❶). Autumnal rice-planting **festivities** are performed here, *hudoq* masks and all, and the kepala desa can tell you if any other rituals are imminent. The same distance upstream again, you pass **Sungai Merah** on the north bank, just past which is **LONG MERAH**, whose meeting hall is a riot of wildly ornate **Bahau carving** – the supporting posts inside and out are alive with animal and human figures, some implausibly sexual. Long Merah is one end of a cross-country hike up the Merah and over to **Tabang** (see p.862); April is a good time to look for a Punan guide here, as they come downstream to trade after the rains. Further on from Long Merah, **RUKUN DAMAI** is essentially a Kenyah settlement with two *lamin*, whose long-lobed, tattooed residents will proudly show you their ceremonial finery and dragon-jar dowries while children stare on. From here on, the forest comes and goes, but below Long Bagun a spectacular hundred-metre-high **limestone cliff** rears up on the north bank, streaked in yellow, white and grey.

Long Bagun

A messy trading post 583km upstream from Samarinda, **LONG BAGUN**'s appeal stems from its position right on the edge of the Mahakam's wilds. It's divided into **Long Bagun Ilir** downstream and **Long Bagun Ulu** upstream. Ulu is where you'll find **stores** offering a scanty display of essential supplies, and a **mattress** on the floor at *Penginipan Artomorow* (❶); the only warung is down at the docks. Across the Mahakam, a small wooden enclosure above the river at the Sumalindo Timber Company houses a surprising relic of the Mulawarman Kingdom in a **stone cow sculpture**, a metre-long carving of the Hindu god Nandi. Locals say that it was originally found a short way northwest at **Batu Majang**, and can predict floods by turning its head upstream.

If Long Bagun is as far as you're going, ferries or *ces* take only about five hours back to Long Iram. Otherwise, you'll have to ask around for longboats heading on through the rapids **into the Upper Mahakam**; Rp60,000–80,000 is the usual price for a seat on the 140-kilometre, two- to four-day ride through to the next large settlement at Long Pahangai, though you'd have to pay ten times this to charter an entire longboat yourself. Days can be spent in Long Bagun waiting to set off, with April through to July the best time to travel. **Overland treks** from Long Bagun include a ten-day, moderately hard trail running southwest through thick forest and **Ot Danum** villages to **Puruk Cahu** on **Sungai Barito**, from where you can find ferries south to Banjarmasin in Kalsel Province. **Guides** can be arranged through Kosmos Trekking in Long Bagun Ulu.

The Upper Mahakam

It's an exciting and exhausting run through the rock-strewn rapids above Long Bagun, as, with the jungle closing in around you, twin-engined longboats capable of travelling 50km an hour on calm water are brought nearly to a standstill by the force of the river. Don't underestimate the **dangers** involved in the journey: this violent stretch claims twenty lives a year, and pilots often deposit passengers on the banks while they negotiate the worst sections, or may enlist your help in hauling the longboat through the foam. If your boat **capsizes** in rapids with you aboard, try to hang onto the hull until the current carries you down to a calmer stretch, then swim to shore. Once through, all of the Upper Mahakam's villages are Dayak. On arrival you should announce yourself to the kepala desa and, if necessary, the police too – either of whom can be invaluable in helping to find transport and accommodation.

Long Pahangai to Long Apari and Kalbar province

Interspersed with calm stretches, the rapids continue all the way to **LONG PAHANGAI**, an administrative centre where the Norwegian ethnographer **Carl Lumholz** based himself for a time during World War I while studying the Upper Mahakam's tribes. Long Pahangai's population comprises various **Kayan** groups, who settled here after fleeing roving Kenyah, who had themselves been forced south by Sarawak's fierce Ibn Dayak. There's a run-down *lamin* at Long Pahangai, and a Catholic mission who might be able to organize a bed if asked politely.

Half a day upstream, **Long Lunuk** is ordinary in itself, but services the Upper Mahakam's **airstrip** nearby at **Datah Dawai**. Flying in from Samarinda, confirm your return flight at the airstrip and ask around to see if anyone is heading your way and might share longboat costs. Another half-day from Long Lunuk takes you past the Kayan village of **Long Bluu** to **Tiong Ohang**, where there are more *lamin* and a final day's ride on the river to **LONG APARI**, the Mahakam's last village. There's an excellent *lamin* here and a century-old, four-metre-high dragon *patong*, plus surrounding forests and hills to explore, and locals may act as guides for trips out of Kaltim Province. It's a two- to four-day trek west across a 1900-metre range **into Kalbar province** at **Tanjung Longkong** on a tributary of the **Sungai Kapuas**, from where it's possible to continue downstream by foot and boat to Pontianak.

Interior Kaltim: the Apo Kayan

While the coastal fringes become ever more tamed, Kaltim's **interior** seems initially to be everything that Borneo's reputation promises. Though scarred by logging roads, forests extend to the horizon as a dark-green haze, interrupted where the occasional bare grey ridge pokes skywards and convoluted brown rivers reflect the sun as they run towards the sea. Dayak communities exist here as they have done for centuries, hunting, farming and performing traditional rites. This is the last expanse of wilderness in Kalimantan, and if you've come looking for Borneo's traditional heart, you'll find it 300km northwest of Samarinda in the highlands of the **Apo Kayan**, so isolated from the rest of the province that it can take four months to reach here overland by following rivers and tracks from the coast.

Even ardent trekkers, however, find that it's better to **fly** from Samarinda into the Apo Kayan on **missionary aircraft**, and burn up energy after arrival. The two operators are **Dirgantara Air Service** (DAS) and **Missionary Air Fellowship** (MAF) – see p.876. Both run fairly regular schedules, yet travel on a specific day is by no means guaranteed – planes are small, and **cancellations** (most often due to bad weather) are frequent. Furthermore, MAF, who are at pains to point out that they are not a passenger service, are becoming less and less inclined to accept tourists on their flights, even if there are seats available, and you may receive short shrift from their offices in Samarinda and Balikpapan.

After arrival in Apo Kayan, there are various ways to **get around**. Trails link many villages; Dayak almost always build near rivers, so **canoes** and **ces** are another common mode of travel. Some people will show you around for free, but you should plan to pay about Rp40,000 a day for a **guide**, on top of transport costs. **Accommodation** is with officials or local families, for which you should also either pay or give about Rp10,000 worth of goods. Without overloading yourself, bring everything you'll need for the trip along from the coast – supplies here are limited and very expensive. It's always **wet** in the Apo Kayan, and, with the highlands here rising to around 2000m, often cool at night.

The Apo Kayan

Based around the headwaters of Sungai Kayan, the **Apo Kayan** was originally inhabited by Kayan Dayak, who were mostly displaced south during the nineteenth century by Sarawak's aggressive Iban and neighbouring Kenyah groups. In the 1890s, the Dutch founded a **garrison** on the Apo Kayan at **Long Nawang**, in a move to counter what they saw as British expansionism from Sarawak; **missionaries** followed, engineering a peace treaty between the Apo Kayan's still-warring tribes in 1924. Stability lasted until the **Japanese** took Long Nawang eighteen years later; the garrison was later revived during the 1960s Konfrontasi with Malaysia and ensuing "communist" insurgency within Indonesia, when the army held tight rein over the whole area. By this time, population pressures had caused a huge **migration** of Kenyah from the Apo Kayan to government-sponsored settlements in the Mahakam basin.

Despite all this, even a few days here offers a fascinating insight into a way of life which, on this scale at least, has all but vanished elsewhere in Kalimantan. **Flights** arrive in the Apo Kayan several times a week from Samarinda and Tarakan; the most used airstrip (served by DAS) is a half-day journey from Long Bawang at **Long Ampung**, though MAF fly on a regular basis to Long Nawang and a handful of other locations.

Long Ampung, Long Nawang and around

The ninety-minute flight from bustling Samarinda leaves you unprepared for arrival at peaceful, isolated **LONG AMPUNG**, a fair-sized settlement on the banks of **Sungai Boh**. The two well-constructed **meeting houses** here are covered in elaborately curling roof decorations, and are typical of Kenyah designs – a couple of tigers and a hornbill (both guardian figures in Dayak lore) are among the less abstract motifs. A wide, shadeless track runs west along the river from here to **LONG NAWANG**, a hot five-hour walk away. Still the seat of the Apo Kayan's administration, Long Nawang is the Apo Kayan's biggest settlement, and boasts a couple of stores, a school and police and army barracks; you should introduce yourself to the district *camat* (chief) here, who can help with guides and canoe rental. You'll need a boat to reach **LONG BETOAH**, a pretty village to settle down in for a few days (ask the *camat* for accommodation), six hours or so to the northwest of Long Nawang, though rapids along the way make this a doubtful trip in drier weather. Much closer in, **NAWANG BARU** is just a short walk south of Long Nawang, with brightly decorated rice barns, a Dayak cemetery, and two *lamin* to check out.

The northeast

Kaltim's **northeast**, comprising the 500-kilometre coastal strip between Samarinda and Kalimantan's open border with Malaysian Sabah, is an area of fragmentary forests, islands, river deltas and mountains, administered by self-contained towns, which seem to have sprung up out of nothing. Daily **buses** follow a good road for 145km north from Samarinda's Terminal Bontang past **Bontang**'s refineries to **Muara Wahau**. Beyond here, the road becomes an unreliable, dry-weather-only track, and you'll probably have to **fly** or travel by **boat** to reach further destinations: there's **Berau**, springboard for underwater realms surrounding **Pulau Derawan**, and **Tanjung Selor** and **Tarakan**, last stops on the way out of the country into Malaysia.

Bontang, Sangata and Kutai National Park

Two twisting hours by road from Samarinda, **BONTANG** is a sprawling township built around Badak NGL's huge liquid gas refinery and Pupuk Kaltim's fertilizer plant. Along with the neighbouring town of **SANGATA**, Bontang used to be a staging post for trips east into **Kutai national park**, one of the easiest places in the world to see genuinely wild orang-utans. Unfortunately, about ninety percent of the park was affected to some degree by the appalling 1997–98 forest fires (see p.820), with 140 apes left homeless and likely to end their days as pets. Furthermore, the building of the road from Bontang to Sangata – which bisects the park – opened up the area to farmers looking for fertile land to settle on, leading to a sharp increase in logging, burning and clearing. Over 24,000 hectares of rainforest have been replaced by banana trees since the road was built in the 1990s. There are, however, still vast pockets of forest that have thus far survived both the fires and the chainsaw, where you can still easily see many of Borneo's endemic and endangered wildlife.

A trip to the park begins in Botang with collecting a Rp3000 **permit** (valid for 3 days) from the national park office (Balai Taman Nasional Kutai; Mon–Thurs 7.30am–4pm, Fri 8–11am; ⓣ0548/27218) on Jalan Awang Long, close to the mayor's office. You will need to take a photocopy of your passport. The office will help you arrange your trip and the staff can act as guides for around Rp50,000 per day. There are no shops or restaurants in the park itself, so you should also stock up on supplies here. If you need to spend the night at Bontang, **accommodation** includes the new and recommended *Cahaya Bone (CB) Hotel* (①0548 22798; ❷), which has rooms with fans or air-con. It's on the right-hand side of the road into town (Jalan Parman Km6), near the Bontang Plaza shopping mall, and only minutes from the bus terminal using the small public transport vans which locals call *takxi* (Rp1100 flat fare). About a ten-minute taxi ride further along the main road into town, on the right (Jalan P. Diponegoro), the *Roadah Hotel* has rooms with fan and air-con (❸). **Heading on** from Bontang, buses run back to Samarinda (2hr; Rp10,000) and through the former boundaries of the national park to Sangata (2hr; Rp12,000) until mid-afternoon, and there are daily Kijang from the bus station, 3km out of town, north to Berau (12–14hr; Rp40,000). These buses can drop you off at the park entry points listed below, though make sure the driver is aware of your destination.

There are currently three main areas in the national park, and all three have basic guesthouses (❸). The first is the **Camp Kakap international orang-utan research centre**, reached by taking a boat from Kabo Jaya (also known as Papa Charlie; 25min; Rp50,000 return), on the edge of Sangata. Unlike other orang-utan spotting centres such as Tanjung Puting in Kalimantan Tengah (see p.828) or Bukit Lawang in Sumatra (see p.356), the apes here are wild; there are no feeding stations or rangers providing regular handouts of fruit here. Nevertheless, your chances of spotting apes are high, particularly now a guesthouse has been built at the centre allowing you to stay overnight in the park and explore the forest at dawn. There are trails around the centre, and you'll need a guide to help you locate the orang-utans; you're also likely to encounter monkeys, gibbons and hornbills.

The second area is **Sangkima** on the Bontang–Sangata road (ask the bus driver to drop you off at Pos Sangkima), where a four-kilometre adventure trail has been set up, which includes a series of swinging bridges. There are also other non-adventure trails, including a 1.5-kilometre boardwalk through the rainforest. Guides are not really necessary for this section.

The third destination is **Teluk Kaba**, which can be reached by sea or by taking the turn-off from the Bontang-Sangata road. The mangroves here are still in excellent condition, and at their best in the early morning or late afternoon. A boardwalk runs through them; if you're lucky, you may see proboscis monkeys and a wide range of birds. Besides these three destinations, with enough notice the guides can take adventurous types to camp deeper into the forest (for a minimum of 2 days). To get the latest information, visit the park office's website (Ⓦwww.tn-kutai.or.id) or call the office.

Over the Sambaliung mountains: Muara Wahau

The journey between Bontang and Berau is spectacular, circling the north-eastern edge of the Mahakam river basin before entering a huge spread of rain-forest where the **Sambaliung mountains**, karst formations weathered into incredible, shark-toothed escarpments, rise 1300m out of the canopy. Thirty kilometres of sealed road north of Sangata, **Sepasu** marks where the route to Berau diverges west for 100km to **MUARA WAHAU**, from where you can catch ferries down past Dayak settlements to Muara Kaman on Sungai Mahakam (see p.857). Outside of Muara Wahau, Hindu sculptures have been found at the **Kongbeng Caves**, whose stalactites and stalagmites are under threat from cement companies mining the hills for limestone. From here the road follows Sungai Wahau northeast, then crosses between the pinnacles of the

Sankulirang Forest Reserve to the Dayak villages of **Muara Lasan**, **Merasak** and **Tumbit**, and on up the Sungai Kelai valley to Berau.

Berau

Three hundred kilometres north of Samarinda, **BERAU** (also known as **Tanjung Redeb**) occupies a prong of land where two minor rivers converge to form **Sungai Berau**. Although 50km from the sea, Berau has long been a trading port, and is also the site of a now declining wood-pulping industry. You'll need to stop off here in order to catch marine traffic heading on up the coast to Pulau Derawan and Tarakan. The town was also once the seat of **two sultanates**, visited in the late 1880s by **Joseph Conrad**, then mate on the trading vessel *SS Vidar*, whose experiences here formed the basis for his novels *Almayer's Folly* and *An Outcast of the Islands*.

Berau's languid pace picks up after dark with open-air stalls and a party atmosphere along the Jalan Yani riverfront. From the east end of Jalan Yani, catch a *ces* across to the old **sultan's palaces**, now private buildings, which face each other and the town across the waters. To the north, there's a small display of period pieces at **Keraton Gunung Tabur**, rebuilt after Allied bombs destroyed the building during the Japanese occupation in World War II, and a sacred cannon south at **Keraton Sambaliung**, which apparently protected this palace from a similar fate.

Practicalities

Berau's central core is a small grid of streets running back from the wharves and stores, fronted by 150-metre-long, riverbank Jalan Yani. Larger boats use the **port** at Jalan Yani's western end, where you'll also find the **Pelni office**; smaller vessels tie up further east along the waterfront. **Buses** from Bontang and Sangata terminate about 1km across town in the Jalan Guna market, while the **airport** is a ten-minute bemo or ojek ride to the south. Running back from the Samarinda docks off Jalan Yani's western end, Jalan Antasari is where you'll find Berau's **accommodation**: right behind the docks, *Losmen Sederhana* (Ⓣ0554/21353; ❺) is fine, the *Kartika* is a dive, but cheap (❷), and Berau's best-value rooms are found at the *Hotel Citra Indah* (Ⓣ0554/21171; ❷). **Places to eat** can be scarce during the day, but the *Citra Indah* has a reasonable restaurant and there are plenty of evening warung along Jalan Yani.

Heading on, Pelni's *Awu* runs twice-monthly from the port to **Nunukan** and **Tarakan**, as part of a huge Sulawesi–Flores–Timor loop. Other boats to Tarakan or Samarinda leave several times a week from the Jalan Yani waterfront, where owners post departure times on trees alongside their vessels; fast craft to Tarakan charge Rp80,000 (5hr), while slower boats cost Rp32,500 (10hr). **For Pulau Derawan**, catch a Tarakan boat to the halfway point of Tanjung Batu and proceed from there (see p.874), or charter a **speedboat** direct to the island for Rp300,000. If they're running, **buses to Tanjung Selor** or Bontang leave early in the morning from the Jalan Guna market; buy tickets at the stop (3hr 30min; Rp55,000 either way). Kijangs also ply the two routes and leave later. Berau–Tarakan vessels don't stop off at Tanjung Selor, so if you can't get there by bus, you'll have to go to Tarakan first and take a ferry from there (see p.876). For **flights** from Berau, DAS are at the *Penginapan Sutomo* (Ⓣ0554/21221) on Jalan Durian, and KAL Star-Trigana are at Jl Maulana 17 (Ⓣ0554/21151); both operate to Balikpapan, Samarinda and Tarakan, with the latter also going daily to Tanjung Selor.

Pulau Derawan

The shallow seas and reefs surrounding islands 40km east of the mouth of the Sungai Berau have gained a well-deserved reputation in **scuba-diving** circles recently. However, you don't have to be a dedicated diver to enjoy the islands' sand, coral and palm trees. **Pulau Derawan** is the easiest place to base yourself, with access from here to other islands in the group.

Speedboats from Berau get to Derawan in a couple of hours, but it's far cheaper to catch a Tarakan-bound ferry to the mainland fishing village of **TANJUNG BATU**, which looks over to where the islands lie temptingly on the skyline; there's accommodation and food at the simple *Losmen Famili* (❷). Low-key touts at Tanjung Batu's dock can run you over to the island of your choice for about Rp25,000, though it's also possible to arrange a ride with fishermen here, who ask far less.

Pulau Derawan, Sangalaki and around

A tiny rise of coarse white sand and coral rubble stabilized by coconut trees, **PULAU DERAWAN** is a delightful place. The village here features a mosque, the nearby losmen *Ilham* (full board ❷) and the **Derawan Dive Resort** (bookings through the *Hotel Benakutai* in Balikpapan; resort phone ⓣ0551/23275, ⓕ23274, ⓔderawan@bpp.mega.net.id; full-board ❻; all-inclusive dive packages ❽). Non-guests can arrange **scuba** or snorkelling through the resort (around US$50 for two tanks); Derawan's waters are especially good for seahorses, nudibranchs and other invertebrates, as well as small reef sharks, barracuda and hulking Maori wrasse.

Southeast of Derawan, **PULAU SANGALAKI** is similar to Derawan but uninhabited except for its own wooden cabin **dive resort**, run by Borneo Divers in Sabah (bookings through Borneo Divers, Rooms 401–412, Floor 4, Wisma Sabah, Kota Kinabalu; ⓣ60-88/222226, ⓕ221550; all-inclusive packages ❽). Coral outcrops near Sangalaki's **lighthouse** attract cuttlefish and **green turtles**, whose local population is one of the biggest in the world, coming ashore year-round to lay their eggs in the sand. Across a channel from Sangalaki, **KAKABAN** is an extinct volcano with good wall diving, where you are likely to encounter big schools of pelagic fish, and an internal **lake** with some strange, stingless jellyfish. Northeast of Kakaban, **MARATUA** is the biggest island of all, thin and curved, with some tiny settlements ashore and exceptional drop-offs into the deeps, patrolled by barracuda, sharks and manta rays.

Tanjung Selor

With forests edging down from upstream and little more to the town than blocks of government buildings, **TANJUNG SELOR** is the backwater to end them all, marking where Kalimantan's roads finally give up the ghost, having run – on a good day – all the way from Pangkalanbun, 1500km away in southwestern Kalteng province. There's no reason to visit Tanjung Selor unless you want to try and arrange a trip upstream to remote Kenyah and Punan settlements.

Practicalities

Tanjung Selor sits on the western bank of the Kayan, with the mid-point of a two-kilometre-long road – Jalan Katamso – along the river marked by a pillar topped with a hornbill. Jalan Pasar runs inland from here, curving left past a mosque, a couple of **restaurants**, and out to the **airstrip**. Problems with weather and the road from Berau makes arrival via speedboat from Tarakan more likely; vessels running between Berau and Tarakan do not stop here. The **speedboat docks** and **ticket office** are south along the waterfront (the 14-daily services to Tarakan take 1–2hr and leave until 4.30pm; Rp31,500). The **bus stop** is on Jalan Skip; if the road is passable, there are normally two buses per day (2hr), the last one leaving at 10am; after that, Kijangs ply the route for Rp40,000 per person. For **flights** to Samarinda and Tarakan, the DAS office (☎0552/21215) is at Jl Langsat 116, while KAL Star-Trigana Air are at Jl Jeruk 40 (☎0552/221723). The Merpati agents can be found in the *Hotel Banjar Indah* (☎0552/21050; ❷–❸), north past the Chinese temple at Jl Tendean 4, who also provide some of the better-value **accommodation** in Tanjung Selor. The cheapest place in town is the *Losmen Keluarga* (Rp15,000 per person), though its location on the waterfront 3km north of the pillar is a bit of a hike out of town.

Heading **upstream to Long Alango** takes between three days and a week; with luck, you might be able to catch public **boats** all the way to Long Alango, but otherwise you'll have to **fly** in with MAF – arrange this through their offices in Tarakan, or you can charter a speedboat from one of the operators by the hornbill pillar.

Tarakan, Nunukan and border crossings

A 24-kilometre spread of low hills just off the coast northeast of Tanjung Selor, **Pulau Tarakan** floats above extensive **oil** reserves: offshore rigs dot the horizon, while the west-coast town of **TARAKAN** is surrounded by smaller-scale "nodding donkey" pumps, patiently drawing oil out of wells and piping it into storage tanks above the harbour. With plenty of money passing through town, Tarakan is a surprisingly busy and prosperous place, just a stone's throw (4–6hr) from **Pulau Nunukan** and the open **border with Malaysia**.

Practicalities

Tarakan has just two main roads, set at right angles to each other. Paralleling the coast, Jalan Sudarso runs north from the port area for a couple of kilometres, where it's crossed by Jalan Sudirman, which runs east for a similar distance into the suburbs. Their **intersection** serves as a town centre, though services are quite widely scattered. The **airport** is 2km north of town (taxis charge Rp10,000 to accommodation), while all marine traffic docks at the southern end of Jalan Sudarso: ferries from Berau and Tanjung Selor at the Tengkayu **jetty** about 1.5km south of the intersection, Pelni ships and ferries to Tewau in Malaysia at the main Mulundung **port**, 500m further down near the end of the road, where you'll also find the **Pelni office**. Bemos around town are plentiful and cost Rp1000 a ride.

Though there are numerous **places to stay**, mostly east down Jalan Sudirman within 150m of the centre, you get very little for your money in Tarakan. If you're arriving by one of the Pelni ships, it's essential that you reserve a room before you arrive; if you forget, the grotty but friendly *Hotel Wisata*, Jl Sudirman 46 (☎0551/21245; ❷–❸) is the place most likely to have rooms. The best value is the likeable *Hotel Jakarta*, about 600m from the roundabout at Jalan Sudirman (❷). Behind the plaza, the *Depot* is a fine and popular Chinese **restaurant** with *lesehan* seating upstairs, serving large portions. For **supplies**, there's a huge produce market at the Jalan Sudirman–Jalan Sudarso intersection, and a supermarket opposite the *Orchid* hotel on Jalan Sudirman. Good exchange rates and ATMs can be found at the BNI **bank** south of the intersection and across from the **police station** on Jalan Sudarso.

Crossing into Malaysia

The visa-free border crossing between Indonesia and the Malaysian town of Tewau in Sabah is open daily except Sunday. From Tarakan, the *Indomaya Express* fast ferry departs Mulundung harbour daily except Sunday at 7.30am, taking three hours to reach Tewau (Rp150,000), leaving for the return journey at 11am. Their main agents in Tarakan are Tanjung Harapan Mulia (☎0551/21572), or you can usually pick up a ticket at the harbour an hour before departure. Border formalities are completed without fuss at both the Mulundung and Tewau harbours. Return tickets to Indonesia can be bought at *Indomaya*'s office at the harbour (☎089/762583).

A slightly cheaper – if more complicated – option is to travel via **NUNUKAN**, a busy, sleazy town on an island of the same name, 100km north of Tarakan, right up against Malaysian **Sabah**. Crossing is straightforward: Nunukan's **Immigration Department**, Kantor Imigrasi, is about 200m from the port on the main road into town, and opens at 8am; it can take a little while to sort out the paperwork, so if you get stuck overnight, catch a bemo to the downmarket *Losmen Nunukan* (❷) on the central square or, slightly better, the *Monaco* (❷), just five minutes on foot from the port. Once exit formalities are complete, *Saturia I* and *Saturia Utama* leave Nunukan in the morning and potter along the coast for a couple of hours to **TEWAU** in Sabah. Return tickets can once again be bought at the harbour (RM20), with the boats back to Indonesia leaving at 2 and 4pm.

Moving on, Wisma Murni Travel at the *Hotel Wisata* (☎0551/21697) can book **flights** to Samarinda, Nunukan and Balikpapan. KAL Star-Trigana Air, Jl Sudirman 9 (☎0551/25840), fly direct from Tarakan to Berau and Tanjung Selor, and from there on to Balikpapan and Samarinda, while DAS are next to the police station on Jalan Sudarso (☎0551/21248); both DAS and MAF are the people to contact for flights to the interior Apo Kayan or Long Alango regions. At the Tengkayu jetty, you'll find tickets and **ferries** for Tanjung Selor (about 14 daily; Rp32,000), Berau (3 weekly; Rp60,000) and Nunukan (about 4 daily, 15,000). Pelni ferries Kerinci, Tidar, Awu, Leuser and Binaya, which service the routes to Samarinda, Balikpapan, Berau, Nunukan, Sulawesi and Java, also dock at Mulundung. For details of ferries heading to Malaysia, see the box above.

Travel details

Buses

Balikpapan to: Banjarmasin (10 daily; 12–14hr); Samarinda (10 daily; 2hr 30min).
Banjarmasin to: Balikpapan (10 daily; 12–14hr); Barabai (frequent; 4hr); Kandangan (frequent; 3hr 30min); Martapura (frequent; 1hr 30min); Palangkaraya (several daily; 5hr); Samarinda (10 daily; 14–16hr).
Kumai to: Pangkalanbun (many bemos daily; 30min).
Palangkaraya to: Banjarmasin (several daily; 5hr); Pangkalanbun (8 daily; 12hr).
Pangkalanbun to: Kumai (many daily; 30min); Palangkaraya (8 daily; 10hr).
Pontianak to: Putussibau (early morning & evening; 12hr); Kuching (Sarawak; 7 daily; 12hr); Singkawang (every 30min; 3hr 30min); Sintang (8 daily; 8hr).
Putussibau to: Lanjak (daily 8am; 5hr 30min); Nanga Badau (daily 8am; 7hr); Pontianak (8 daily; 12hr); Sintang (8 daily; 6hr).
Samarinda to: Balikpapan (10 daily; 2hr 30min); Banjarmasin (10 daily; 14–16hr); Berau (2 daily; 12hr); Bontang (several daily; 2hr); Kota Bangun (several daily; 4hr); Sanggata (several daily; 4hr); Tenggarong (many daily; 1hr).
Semitau to: Pontianak (3 daily; 11hr); Putussibau (2 daily; 5hr); Sintang (3 daily; 3hr 30min).
Sintang to: Nanga Pinoh (hourly; 90min); Pontianak (8 daily; 8hr); Putussibau (daily 6am; 6hr); Semitau (3 daily; 3hr 30min).

Pelni ferries

For a chart of the Pelni routes, see p.42.

Balikpapan to: Biak (*KM Doro Londa*, monthly; 4 days); Bitung (*KM Umsini*, 2 monthly; 40hr/*KM Sinabung*, 2 monthly; 31hr/*KM Doro Londa*, monthly; 37hr); Jayapura (*KM Sinabung*, 2 monthly; 5 days/*KM Doro Londa,* monthly; 5 days); Kwandang (*KM Sinabung*, 2 monthly; 21hr/*KM Doro Londa,* monthly; 26hr); Makassar (*KM Umsini*, 2 monthly; 17hr/*KM Sinabung*, 2 monthly; 14hr/*KM Fudi*, 2 monthly; 20hr/*KM Agoa Mas*, weekly; 21hr); Manokwari (*KM Sinabung*, 2 monthly; 70hr/*KM Doro Londa*, monthly; 70hr); Nunukan (*KM Kerinci*, 2 monthly; 44hr); Pantoloan (*KM Kerinci*, 2 monthly; 11hr/*KM Umsini*, 2 monthly; 11hr/*KM Doro Londa*, monthly; 9hr); Pare Pare (*KM Kerinci*, 2 monthly; 14hr); Sorong (*KM Sinabung*, 2 monthly; 57hr/*KM Doro Londa*, monthly; 57hr); Surabaya (*KM Kerinci*, 2 monthly; 42hr/*KM Sinabung*, 2 monthly; 37hr/*KM Umsini*, 2 monthly; 45hr/*KM Tidar*, 2 monthly; 24hr/*KM Doro Londa*, monthly; 24hr); Tanjung Priok, Jakarta (*KM Kerinci*, 2 monthly; 3 days/*KM Doro Londa*, monthly; 2 days/*KM Umsini*, 2 monthly; 3 days/*KM Fudi*, weekly, 3–4 days); Tarakan (*KM Kerinci*, 2 monthly; 36hr/*KM Tidar*, 2 monthly; 21hr); Ternate (*KM Kerinci*, 2 monthly; 36hr/*KM SInabung*, 2 monthly; 45hr/*KM Doro Londa*, monthly; 48hr); Toli-Toli (*KM Umsini*, 2 monthly; 24hr/*KM Kerinci*, 2 monthly; 22hr).

Banjarmasin to: Semarang (*KM Egon* 1–2 weekly; 24hr); Surabaya (*KM Egon* 1–2 weekly; 24hr).

Batulicin to: Kupang (*KM SIrimau*, 2 monthly; 69hr); Larantuka (*KM SIrimau*, 2 monthly; 46hr); Makassar (*KM SIrimau*, 2 monthly; 19hr); Pare Pare (*KM Binaiya*, 2 monthly; 19hr); Semarang (*KM SIrimau*, 2 monthly; 30hr); Tanjung Priok, Jakarta (*KM SIrimau*, 2 monthly; 51hr); Surabaya (*KM Binaiya*, 2 monthly; 21hr).

Berau to: Nunukan (*KM Awu*, 2 monthly; 22hr); Tarakan (*KM Awu*, 2 monthly; 12hr).

Kumai to: Pontianak (*KM Lawit*, 2 monthly; 57hr); Semarang (*KM Lawit*, 2 monthly; 21hr/*KM Leuser*, monthly; 20hr; *KM Binaiya*, 2 monthly; 19hr); Surabaya (*KM Tilongkabila*, monthly; 21hr/*KM Binaiya*, 2 monthly; 21hr).

Nunukan to: Balikpapan (*KM Tidar*, 2 monthly; 28hr); Makassar (*KM Awu*, 2 monthly; 47hr); Maumere (*KM Awu*, 2 monthly; 74hr); Pantoloan (*KM Kerinci*, 2 monthly; 25hr); Pare Pare (*KM Agoa Mas*, weekly; 38hr/*KM Tidar*, 2 monthly; 44hr); Surabaya (*KM Tidar*, 2 monthly; 71hr); Tarakan (*KM Tidar*, 2 monthly; 5hr); Toli Toli (*KM Kerinci*, 2 monthly; 14hr).

Pontianak to: Natuna (*KM Bukit Raya*, 2 monthly; 31hr); Semarang (*KM Tatamailau*, 2 monthly; 34hr/*KM Lawit*, 2 monthly; 32hr); Serasan (*KM Bukit Raya*, 2 monthly; 20hr); Tanjung Priok, Jakarta (*KM Ambulu*, every 3 days; 11hr/*KM Lawit*, weekly; 33hr); Tarempa (*KM Bukit Raya*, 2 monthly; 40hr).

Samarinda to: Belang Belang, Sulawesi (*KM Binaiya*, 2 monthly; 13hr); Pare Pare (*KM Binaiya*, 2 monthly; 24hr).

Sampit to: Semarang (*KM Binaiya*, 2 monthly; 23hr/*KM Tilongkabila*, 2 monthly; 20hr/*KM Wilis*, 2 monthly; 25hr); Surabaya (*KM Leuser*, 2 monthly; 22hr/*KM Binaiya*, 2 monthly; 21hr/*KM Tilongkabila*, monthly; 22hr/*KM Bukit Raya*, 2 monthly; 20hr).

Tarakan to: Balikpapan (*KM Tidar*, 2 monthly; 20hr); Makassar (*KM Tidar*, 2 monthly; 35hr/*KM Awu*, 2 monthly; 60hr); Nunukan (*KM Awu*, 2 monthly; 8hr/*KM Kerinci*, 2 monthly; 5hr); Pantoloan (*KM Tidar*, 2 monthly; 15hr/*KM Kerinci*, 2 monthly; 33hr); Toli Toli (*KM Kerinci*, 2 monthly; 22hr).

Other ferries

Berau to: Tanjung Batu (for Pulau Derawan; 2–3 weekly; 4hr); Tarakan (3 weekly; 10hr).

Lanjak to: Semitau (daily 8am; 8hr).

Palangkaraya to: Tewah (daily; 8hr); Tumbang Jutuh (from Tangkiling, daily; 4hr).

Pontianak to: Jakarta (*Kapuas Expres*, twice weekly; 19hr); Ketapang (*Ketapang Expres*, daily 8am; 6hr); Putussibau (*Kapal Bandung*, weekly; 5 days); Sintang (*Kapal Bandung*, weekly; 3 days).

Putussibau to: Pontianak (*Kapal Bandung*, weekly; 4 days); Sintang (*Kapal Bandung*, weekly; 36hr).

Samarinda to: Berau (several weekly; 24hr); Kota Bangun (several daily; 10hr); Long Bagun (seasonally, 2 daily; 40hr–4 days); Long Iram (1–2 daily; 30hr); Melak (several daily; 24hr); Muara Kaman (several daily; 6hr); Muara Muntai (several daily; 14hr); Tanjung Issuy (daily; 16hr); Tenggarong (several daily; 3hr).

Semitau to: Lanjak (speedboat, daily; 3hr 30min; passenger ferry, daily; 8hr).

Sintang to: Putussibau (*Kapal Bandung*, weekly; 2 days/*Bunut Utama* speedboat, 3–4 weekly; 6hr).

Tanjung Selor to: Tarakan (14 daily; 1–2hr).

Tarakan to: Berau (3 weekly; 10hr); Nunukan (4 daily; 6–12hr); Tanjung Selor (14 daily; 1–2hr); Tewau, Malaysia (*Indomaya Expres*, daily except Sunday; 3hr).

Flights

Balikpapan to: Banjarmasin (3 weekly with Merpati, weekly with DAS; 40min); Berau (daily

with KAL Star, daily except Sunday with DAS; 2hr); Brunei (2 weekly with Royal Air Brunei; 2hr); Jakarta (2 daily with Bouraq and Garuda, daily with Mandala; 2hr); Makassar (3 weekly with Merpati; 1hr 10min); Palu (daily with Bouraq; 45min); Pontianak (4 weekly with Merpati; 1hr 25min); Singapore (2 daily with Garuda, 4 weekly with Silk Air; 2hr 15min); Surabaya (2 daily with Bouraq, daily with Merpati and Mandala; 1hr 25min); Tanjung Selor (daily with KAL Star; 2hr 30min); Tarakan (daily with KAL Star, daily except Sunday with DAS; 2hr).
Banjarmasin to: Balikpapan (3 weekly with Merpati, weekly with DAS; 40min); Jakarta (2 daily with Garuda, daily with Bouraq; 1hr 45min); Pangkalanbun (5 weekly with DAS; 35min); Pontianak (5 weekly with DAS; 1hr 25min); Surabaya (2 daily with Mandala, 2 daily with Bouraq; 1hr 10min).
Berau/Tanjung Redeb to: Balikpapan (daily with KAL Star, daily except Sunday with DAS; 1hr 25min); Samarinda (2 daily with KAL Star, 2 daily except Sunday with DAS; 1hr 30min); Tanjung Selor (daily with KAL Star; 15min); Tarakan (2 daily with KAL Star, daily except Sunday with DAS; 40min).
Palangkaraya to: Surabaya (4 weekly; 1hr 10min).
Pangkalanbun to: Banjarmasin (5 weekly with DAS; 2hr); Pontianak (5 weekly with DAS, 2 weekly with Merpati; 1hr 30min); Semarang (5 weekly with Merpati; 1hr 40min).
Pontianak to: Balikpapan (4 weekly; 2hr 35min); Ketapang (3 daily; 1hr); Kuching (3 weekly; 1hr 45min); Medan (3 weekly; 3hr 35min); Pekanbaru (3 weekly; 2hr 50min); Putussibau (5 weekly; 1hr 25min).
Samarinda to: Balikpapan (daily with KAL Star; 40min); Berau (2 daily except Sunday with DAS, 2 daily with KAL Star; 50min–1hr 30min); Datah Dawai (3 weekly with DAS; 1hr 35min); Long Ampung (5 weekly with DAS; 1hr 50min); Tanjung Selor (daily with KAL Star, daily except Sunday with DAS; 2hr); Tarakan (2 daily with KAL Star, daily except Sunday with DAS; 2hr).
Tarakan to: Balikpapan (daily except Sunday with DAS, daily with KAL Star via Berau; 2hr 40min); Berau (2 daily with KAL Star, daily except Sunday with DAS; 25min); Long Bawan, Apo Kayan (2 weekly; 2hr); Nunukan (4 weekly with DAS; 30min); Samarinda (2 daily with KAL Star via Berau, daily except Sunday with DAS; 2hr); Tanjung Selor (daily except Sunday with DAS, daily with KAL Star; 15min).

Sulawesi

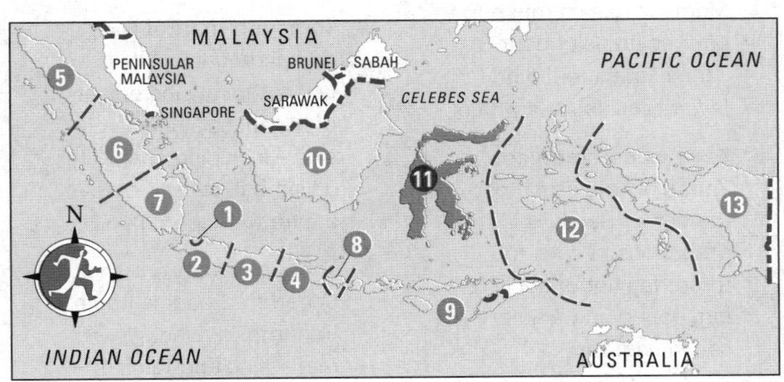
MALAYSIA
PENINSULAR MALAYSIA
SINGAPORE
BRUNEI
SABAH
SARAWAK
CELEBES SEA
PACIFIC OCEAN
N
INDIAN OCEAN
AUSTRALIA
1
2
3
4
5
6
7
8
9
10
11
12
13

CHAPTER 11

Highlights

* **Street food, Makassar** Take an evening stroll along the waterfront to sample some of the cheapest and tastiest food to be found on the streets of any Indonesian city. See p.885
* **Mamasa** Wonderful hiking, superlative scenery and fascinating culture, Mamasa has as much to offer as its neighbour Tanah Toraja, but with far fewer tourists. See p.906
* **Funeral ceremonies, Tanah Toraja** The most famous of Sulawesi's attractions, a two- to three-day riot of socializing, eating and animal sacrificing. See pp.918–919
* **Pulau Togian** A pristine tropical hideaway with beautiful white-sand beaches and magnificent coral walls plunging deep into the blue ocean. See p.940
* **Bunaken Marine Reserve** Indonesia's official scuba centre, with 200m-plus reef walls, sharks, dolphins and turtles. See p.956
* **Tomohon market** Lively and photogenic, this is where the raw ingredients of Minahasa's unique cuisine – including chargrilled bat, rat and dog – are traded. See p.960
* **Tangkoko reserve** This underrated park is home to hornbills, black macaques and tarsiers – and most people see all of these in just one day. See p.962

Sulawesi

Sulawesi sprawls in the centre of the Indonesian archipelago, its bizarre outline a foretaste of the many peculiarities that make this one of the country's most compelling regions. Occupying a marine corridor where the influences of Java, the Philippines and Papuan Maluku overlap, the island is saved from being an untidy mixture of these neighbours by its shape, a 1000-kilometre letter "K" with the upright arm swept eastwards. Formed by tectonic shuffles uplifting and rotating two long, parallel landmasses together to create four separate peninsulas, nowhere in Sulawesi is much more than 100km from the sea, though an almost complete covering of mountains not only isolated these peninsulas from one another, but also made them difficult to penetrate individually. Invaders were hard pushed to colonize beyond the coast and, despite echoes of external forces, a unique blend of cultures and habitats developed.

Even now, Sulawesi's division into three parts – the south, centre and north – is very apparent. **Southern Sulawesi**, comprising the two peninsula provinces of **Sulawesi Selatan** and **Sulawesi Tenggara**, is geographically the least extreme region, its lower reaches comprising conveniently flat coastal fringes and relatively small-scale limestone hills. The most settled part of the island, the south is home to most of Sulawesi's fifteen million inhabitants, and the obvious location of its capital, the energetic port of **Makassar**. Rich in history, the southern plains rise to the mountain fastness of **Tanah Toraja**, the attractively fertile home of one of Indonesia's most securely self-aware ethnic groups.

Beyond here lies **Sulawesi Tengah**, Central Sulawesi Province, whose crumpled interior provides for some quality **trekking**. While parts of the province are currently off-limits due to a bloody civil battle being waged around the lake and city of Poso (see box on p.884), the province's most popular destination, the **Togian Islands**, remains untouched by events on the mainland and continues to attract those looking to soak up the sun.

Safety in Sulawesi

During the past couple of years, violent unrest between Christians and Muslims around the town and lake of Poso has claimed over a thousand lives. While at the time of writing it's still possible to travel through Sulawesi – and indeed plenty of people are still doing so – you should contact your foreign office for up-to-date advice before arrival (see p.26). For details of the situation in Poso at the time of going to press, see p.929, while for details on how this affects travelling in Sulawesi, see the box on p.884.

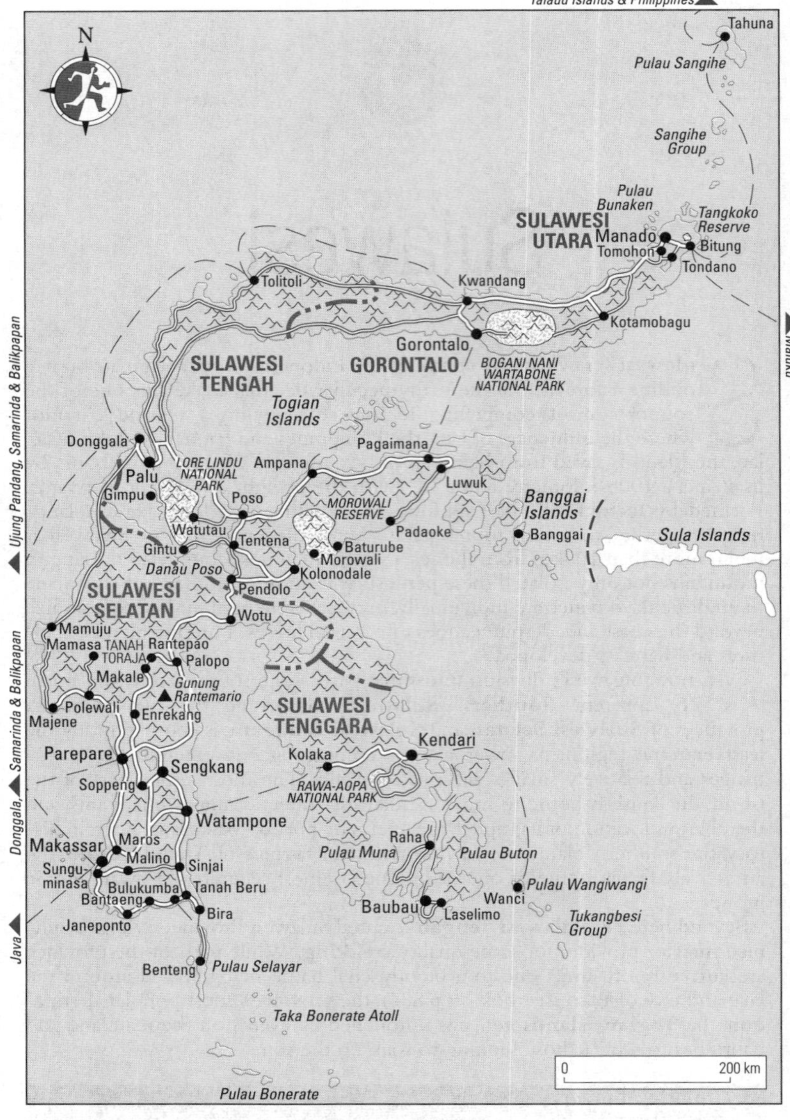

Sulawesi's final third, made up of **Sulawesi Utara** (North Sulawesi Province) and the newly created province of **Gorontalo**, is a volcanic tail of land covered in coconut plantations and thick rainforest, the peninsula topped by the unique people and still-smoking cones of the **Minahasa highlands**. Offshore, each region also has its own archipelagos, strewn with everything from unlikely evidence of contact with distant empires to simply beautiful beaches. Here you'll find excellent **scuba diving**; new sites are being pioneered continually, but the most popular place is still **Pulau Bunaken**, out from the northern city of **Manado**. Sulawesi also sits on the western side of **Wallacea** (see box on p.1073) and is spotted with some exceptional **wildlife reserves**, where you can spend days on humid jungle tracks looking for unusual creatures.

Formerly focused on Tanah Toraja, **tourism** has discovered the rest of Sulawesi over the past decade, and though this has brought certain irritations – such as rising **costs** and a tendency to be quickly pigeonholed by locals – the infrastructure has improved greatly, especially with regard to **getting around**. The southern peninsula's **highways** reach up into Sulawesi Tengah, though north of Parepare there's hardly a straight stretch anywhere, and travel involves endless, nausea-inducing slaloms. Nor can the southeastern peninsula or Sulawesi Utara be reached easily overland, though roads elsewhere are well covered by public transport – freelance Kijang and minibuses are often faster and cheaper than scheduled buses. Where these fail, you'll find **ferries**, even if services are unreliable. Tanah Toraja and all outlying provincial capitals (**Kendari** in Sulawesi Tenggara, **Palu** in Sulawesi Tenggah, Manado and Gorontalo) are also connected by direct **flights** to Makassar or neighbouring cities. Crossed by the equator, Sulawesi shares its **weather** patterns with western Indonesia, with August through to November the driest time of year, and December to April the wettest. Tourism peaks with the European summer holidays (June–Sept) and Christmas, so April is the best time to see things at their greenest and least crowded.

Some history

Thirty-thousand-year-old remains from caves near the southern town of Maros provide the earliest evidence of human occupation in Sulawesi, but it's likely that the peoples here today are descended from the bronzeworking cultures which arrived in Indonesia from the Asian mainland after 3000 BC. By the time the **Portuguese** first marked Sulawesi as the "**Celebes**" – an name with endless possible origins – on their maps during the sixteenth century, the island was ethnically divided much as it is today, with the south split between the highland **Torajans** and the lowland **Bugis**, various isolated tribes in the central highlands, and the Filipino-descended **Minahasans** in the far north. Both Minahasans and Bugis had contacts with the rest of the Indonesian region through their ports, the north coming under the influence of the sultan of Ternate, while the south was part of the decaying Hindu Majapahit empire. They were also the first to be affected by European contact, as the next few centuries saw the Portuguese and their **Dutch** successors build forts, meddle in local politics and introduce **Christianity** to the north of the island, just as **Islam** swept the south and coastal communities elsewhere. But for a long while the Dutch considered Sulawesi only inasmuch as its involvement in maritime trade affected their concerns elsewhere; it wasn't until the late nineteenth century that they decided to bring the whole island under their thumb.

By this time, the north had already proved compliant to the European presence, but southern Sulawesi was not so malleable. The Dutch had achieved a loose hold over the Bugis states in 1825, but an attempt in 1905 to make Sulawesi's kingdoms sign a declaration of obedience to Holland sparked furious resistance, and the south took two years of bloody warfare to subjugate. Not surprisingly, the **Japanese** were welcomed as liberators on arrival in 1942, and the south rose again when the Dutch returned in 1946. This time, even north Sulawesi joined in the revolution before coming to terms with colonial powers, who needed their support – or at least didn't want them at their backs

Travelling across Sulawesi: the current situation

With the violence around Poso continuing, and the ferries to the Togians in some disarray following the demise of the regular Ampana–Togian–Gorontalo and Poso–Gorontalo boats, the overland route previously favoured by many travellers through Sulawesi is now almost impossible. At the moment, it's still possible to travel overland from Makassar to Manado. However, if you are planning to do so, it's vital to ask as many people as possible about the current situation; tourist offices and hotels are often the best source, though don't take every piece of information you hear as gospel.

There are **two main overland routes** through Sulawesi Tengah that avoid Lake Poso, which at the time of writing is off-limits to travellers. With the road from Mamuju now extending all the way to Palu, you can bypass the Poso region by travelling along the west coast. Note, however, that the gruelling stretch from Polewali to Palu alone can take more than 36 hours. Once in Palu, however, you can either continue north on the Trans-Sulawesi highway to Gorontalo or, with the army now a highly visible presence on the Palu to Luwuk highway, you can also travel via Poso itself to Ampana, the port for the Togian Islands. Having visited the Togians, you can then return to Ampana, catch a bus to Pagaimana, and from there take the nightly boat to Gorontalo. (If Poso is closed once again, however, then in order to visit the Togians from Palu, you will have to continue on the Trans-Sulawesi highway to Gorontalo, then catch the boat to Pagaimana and a bus to Ampana from there – a much longer journey).

The second option is to travel across Sulawesi's southeastern arm. From Makassar, the route follows the Trans-Sulawesi Highway to Pendolo, at the southern tip of Lake Poso, before turning east via Palopo to Kolonodale, from where overnight boats leave for Baturube. From Baturube, buses to Luwuk take five hours, and from there Ampana is an eight-hour bus ride away. This route does have the advantage of bringing you right to the doorstep of the wonderful Morowali National Park at Baurube. However, it also assumes that Pendolo is safe and open to visitors, which at times during the conflict has not always been the case. Given these choices, you may decide, as most travellers are currently doing, that flying between the north and south is currently the best option.

– for what became an exceptionally brutal campaign against the Bugis. Independence in 1950 wasn't the end of trouble, either: economic discontent led to widespread guerrilla action, which snowballed during the next decade under the pro-Muslim-state **Darul Islam** banner, and then the **Permesta** movement – the word being a telescoping of the Indonesian for "United Struggle". Support for Permesta focused in the north, where it formed dangerous ties with Sumatran rebel groups before being finished off by a full-scale military campaign in the early 1960s.

Southern Sulawesi

Southern Sulawesi descends from the island's highest mountain, **Gunung Rantemario**, out to some of its remotest islands. The **south peninsula** is thoroughly infused with the outgoing character of its famously quarrelsome **Bugis** population, whose squabbling split the region into competing states and left Sulawesi's modern capital, **Makassar**, surrounded by the ghosts of former kingdoms, where you'll still find traditional shipbuilding communities and palaces occupied by royal descendants. As Muslims, the Bugis also had confrontations with their pagan neighbours, especially the **Torajans**, whose inaccessible homeland in the region's mountainous north allowed them to resist conversion, and where beautiful scenery coupled with unusual architecture and festivals today make **Mamasa** and **Tanah Toraja** some of the most rewarding parts of the country to delve into indigenous culture. Off to the southeast, only the lower third of **Sulawesi Tenggara** province is really accessible and, broken up into a group of islands as it is, you'll need some time to cover the attractions here, which include cave art and a scattering of remote coral reefs.

Transport is as plentiful as anywhere in Sulawesi, with good roads around Makassar, the south peninsula, and Mamasa and Tanah Toraja. Very much more isolated, Sulawesi Tenggara has to be reached by air from Makassar or ferry from the eastern town of Watampone, though once there you'll find roads out to the sights and regular ferries connecting the main islands.

Makassar and around

Set down at Sulawesi's southwestern corner and facing Java and Kalimantan, **MAKASSAR** is an animated, determinedly unpretentious port city geared up as a transit point and business centre. It's also dauntingly large, hot and crowded, but, in terms of specific attractions, it has more than the average provincial hub. There's good food and a visibly lively history to investigate and, with Makassar's docks and airport forming an increasingly vital bridge between eastern and western Indonesia, a growing number of visitors are spending time in town. More than anything, Makassar offers an introduction to Sulawesi's largest ethnic group, the **Bugis**, seafarers whose twanging pronunciation fills in the spaces between the city's traffic noise. Apt to turn to piracy if the need arose, the Bugis are considered headstrong and short-tempered by other Indonesians, and continue to export their goods and presence well beyond Sulawesi in **prahu**, distinctive vessels with steep, upcurved prows.

The city traces its history back five hundred years or more to the rise of **Makassar**, a grouping of western Bugis states whose central position on the Indonesian maritime trade routes won it a huge amount of trade. To protect their harbours, these states constructed a string of coastal defences, most notably **Ujung Pandang fort** and the nearby fortified town of **Somba Opu**. By the mid-seventeenth century, the accumulated wealth and military skills of its Muslim ruler, **Sultan Hasanuddin**, had brought the Makassan state of **Gowa** (whose capital was just south of Makassar) to the ascendancy right across southern Sulawesi. This also made them direct rivals with the Dutch, who wanted all regional trade to funnel through their base at Malacca, a Malaysian holding recently acquired from the Portuguese. Trying to destabilize Gowa, the Dutch found an ally in the rival eastern Bugis kingdom of Bone; they helped the kingdom to defeat Gowan forces in 1667. The subsequent **Bungaya Treaty** ceded Ujung Pandang fort to the Dutch (which they renamed **Fort Rotterdam**), closed Makassan ports to foreign merchants, and exiled the Gowan royalty to Somba Opu – until fears over that town's defences prompted the Dutch into razing it two years later, dismembering the Makassan empire.

Initially a garrisoned outpost with a mandate to suppress commerce and enforce the Dutch presence, Fort Rotterdam eventually became the core of the new **city of Makassar**, and by the 1830s, Makassan ports were again at the centre of a broad trading network – something which the Dutch, now beneficiaries, did nothing to discourage. The city was made capital of the whole of eastern Indonesia a century later, retaining the position through the Japanese wartime occupation and on until Independence. The next decade was a difficult one, however, as growing demands in outlying regions of the country for greater autonomy, and a watering down of PKI influence in the government, triggered the Permesta revolt of 1957, led initially from Makassar by **Lieutenant Colonel Sumual**. Government forces and judicious political appointments calmed the south within a year, but the aftermath saw Sulawesi's administration restructured, Makassar's name reverting to **Ujung Pandang**, and its sphere of influence apparently dwindling to no more than that of a provincial capital. Today, however, the city is booming, and its million-strong population live in the largest, fastest-growing, and most economically important metropolis east of Java. What's more, as an indication that the city is regaining its typically brash Bugis self-confidence and loosening itself from Jakarta's apron strings once again, in 2000 the local authorities reverted once again to the name of Makassar, the original title of the Bugis states that founded the port. It's not a restful place, but if the city's in-your-face attitude proves too much to bear, nearby islands and hill scenery provide surprisingly complete escapes.

Arrival, information and city transport

Contained elsewhere by the sea, Makassar is expanding south and east, drawing previously well-separated towns within its suburbs. The centre is quite a manageable couple of square kilometres, pivoting around where roads into the city converge on **Medan Karebosi** (Karebosi Square). North of here across Jalan Ahmad Yani are various harbours, a tangle of grubby back lanes making up the Chinese quarter, and the downtown shopping and business district of **Pasar Sentral**, also known as Sentral or Makassar Mall. West of Karebosi, Fort Rotterdam overlooks the seafront on Jalan Ujung Pandang, while to the south and east a concentration of tourist services and hotels cedes to official residences and government offices along Jalan Jendral Sudirman.

Arrival points are mostly scattered around Makassar's fringes. **Hasanuddin Airport** is 25km northeast of the city, near the town of Maros. Taxis from the airport charge a stiff Rp35,000 fixed fare for the forty-minute ride into the city – pay at the booth on the left of the exit hall. Between about 6.30am and 6.30pm you can also opt for a pete-pete (Rp750–1000) or bus (Rp2000) from just beyond the terminal car park to Pasar Sentral. Depending on your route, you may pass the mighty **Mesjid al Markaz al Islami** on Jalan Mesjid Raya, eastern Indonesia's largest mosque and Islamic school, an angular, grey-stone edifice built during the 1990s. Returning to the airport, catch the thrice-hourly Maros bus (6am–6pm) from Jalan Cokroaminoto on the west side of Pasar Sentral and tell the driver you want to be dropped at the airport (Rp2000); at other times, you'll have to take a taxi.

Makassar's two main **bus stations** are both about 5km and a Rp750–1000 pete-pete ride from the centre. Coming in from Rantepao or the north you'll arrive east at **Terminal Panaikang**, on the Maros road; from the south, you're most likely to end up at **Terminal Tamalate** on Jalan Gowa Raya (an extension of Jalan Sudirman). Some vehicles from the south coast might favour

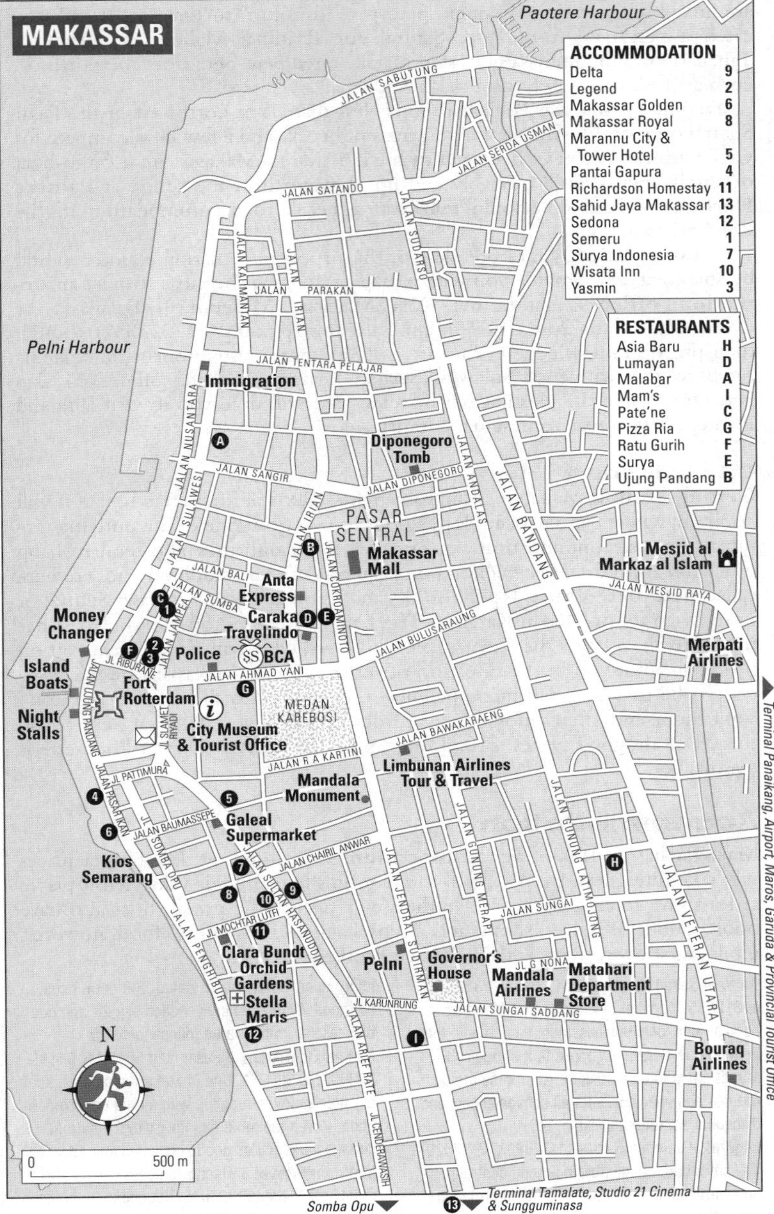
MAKASSAR
ACCOMMODATION
Delta 9
Legend 2
Makassar Golden 6
Makassar Royal 8
Marannu City & Tower Hotel 5
Pantai Gapura 4
Richardson Homestay 11
Sahid Jaya Makassar 13
Sedona 12
Semeru 1
Surya Indonesia 7
Wisata Inn 10
Yasmin 3
RESTAURANTS
Asia Baru H
Lumayan D
Malabar A
Mam's I
Pate'ne C
Pizza Ria G
Ratu Gurih F
Surya E
Ujung Pandang B
Paotere Harbour
Pelni Harbour
Immigration
Diponegoro Tomb
PASAR SENTRAL
Makassar Mall
Mesjid al Markaz al Islam
Anta Express
Caraka Travelindo
Money Changer
Police
BCA
Island Boats
Fort Rotterdam
Night Stalls
City Museum & Tourist Office
MEDAN KAREBOSI
Merpati Airlines
Limbunan Airlines Tour & Travel
Mandala Monument
Galeal Supermarket
Kios Semarang
Clara Bundt Orchid Gardens
Stella Maris
Pelni
Governor's House
Mandala Airlines
Matahari Department Store
Bouraq Airlines
JALAN SABUTUNG
JALAN SERDA USMAN
JALAN SATANDO
JALAN SUDARSO
JALAN KALIMANTAN
JALAN IRIAN
JALAN PARAKAN
JALAN TENTARA PELAJAR
JALAN NUSANTARA
JALAN SANGIR
JALAN DIPONEGORO
JALAN ANDALAS
JALAN BANDANG
JALAN SULAWESI
JALAN IRIAN
JALAN COKROAMINOTO
JALAN BALI
JALAN SUMBA
JALAN JAMPEA
JALAN MESJID RAYA
JALAN BULUSARAUNG
JL RIBURANE
JALAN AHMAD YANI
JALAN UJUNG PANDANG
JL SLAMET RIYADI
JALAN BAWAKARAENG
JALAN R A KARTINI
JL PATTIMURA
JALAN PASAR IKAN
JALAN BAUMASSEPE
JL SOMBA OPU
JALAN CHAIRIL ANWAR
JALAN SULTAN HASANUDDIN
JALAN JENDRAL SUDIRMAN
JALAN GUNUNG MERAPI
JALAN GUNUNG LATIMOJONG
JALAN VETERAN UTARA
JALAN SUNGAI
JL MOCHTAR LUTFI
JALAN PENGHIBUR
JL G NONA
JL KARUNRUNG
JALAN SUNGAI SADDANG
JALAN ARIEF RATE
JL CENDERAWASIH
N
0
500 m
Terminal Panaikang, Airport, Maros, Garuda & Provincial Tourist Office
Somba Opu
Terminal Tamalate, Studio 21 Cinema & Sungguminasa

smaller depots such as **Terminal Mallengkeri**, 7km from the centre, also on Jalan Gowa Raya, or 10km southeast of Makassar at **Sungguminasa** – both are linked to the city by frequent pete-pete. To return to Terminal Panaikang, catch a pete-pete from Pasar Sentral; for Terminal Mallengkeri, Terminal Tamalate or Sunguminasa's bus station, take a red pete-pete from the northeast corner of Medan Karebosi on Jalan Sudirman.

Arriving **by sea**, the Pelni harbour is less than 1km northwest of the Pasar Sentral on Jalan Nusantara, where a mass of becaks and a few taxis compete for your business. If you've managed to hitch a ride to Makassar on a cargo boat or Bugis prahu, you'll probably end up 3km north of the centre at **Paotere Harbour** – Rp3000 should rent you a becak to accommodation in the Karebosi area.

For **information**, your hotel desk or the airport information counter should be able to at least provide you with a map of the city. The city's **tourist information office** is inside the Kota Makassar Museum, Jl Balaikota 11 (Mon–Thurs 7am–2pm, Fri 7–11am, Sat 7am–1pm; ⓣ0411/333357), though their practical knowledge of the city is slight; there's also a tourist office dedicated to the whole of Sulawesi Selatan near the Garuda office on Jalan Pettarani, where the pleasant but hopeless staff will urge you to visit Bira and Rantepao whatever your actual enquiry.

City transport

Getting around Makassar is unproblematic. **Taxis** are metered: Rp5000 will cover anywhere central, or it's Rp13,000–15,000 from one of the outlying terminals. Your accommodation can organize them, and they also tend to hang out across from the *Marannu* hotel on Jalan Sultan Hasanuddin. Bemos are here called **pete-pete**, charge Rp750–1000, and terminate either at Pasar Sentral or in the vicinity of Medan Karebosi. The best way to find one to your destination is to shout it or the street name at drivers, who will either wave you on board or point you in the direction of other vehicles. Makassar's **becak** drivers can be irritating and incompetent – they're hard to shake off if you don't want them, and often ignorant of your destination if you do. Pasar Sentral and the GPO are good places to find one, and a fare of Rp1500 per kilometre is reasonable.

Accommodation

Makassar has no lack of **accommodation**, though few of the cheaper places will take foreigners. Even so, mid-range rooms here are fair value. Most places at least give travel advice or have their own agents; the pricier ones also have pools, laundry services, shops, and discos/karaoke halls. Hotel food, however, tends to be overpriced, and you're better off eating out.

Delta Jl Sultan Hasanuddin 43 ⓣ0411/312711, ⓕ312655. Pleasant blue-glass-and-tile affair, popular with local businessmen, though with the better-value *Wisata Inn* opposite it struggles to attract much foreign custom. The rooms are comfortable and spacious, with all conveniences, and discounts are often available. ❺

Legend Jl Jampea 5 ⓣ0411/328203, ⓕ328204. The city's budget standby, in a good central position with helpful staff and heaps of information about the rest of Sulawesi – though with the lack of travellers currently coming through, most of that information is now rather dated. The dorm beds are good value, the flimsy-walled singles and doubles less so, with shared mandis only. ❶

Makassar Golden Jl Pasar Ikan 50–52 ⓣ0411/333000, ⓕ320951. One of Makassar's oldest luxury hotels, now struggling with all the new competition – even though it has finer views, seafront cottages and just as good service as any. ❻

Makassar Royal Jl Daeng Tompo 8 ⓣ0411/328488, ⓕ328045. Not cheap, but quiet, good-value rooms with air-con, bathroom, TV and breakfast. ❸

Marannu City and Tower Hotel Jl Sultan Hasanuddin 3–5 ⓣ0411/315087, ⓕ321821. Large, gloomy, charmless but central landmark, worth a mention because part of the hotel is undergoing renovations, so big discounts are currently available in the other part. Merpati stick their delay victims here. ❼

Pantai Gapura Jl Pasar Ikan 10 ⓣ0411/325791, ⓕ316303. Four-star hotel for those staying in Makassar, but who wish they weren't: cottage accommodation hidden away from the city and overlooking the sea, with a restaurant on a traditional Pinisi boat. ❺

Richardson Homestay Jl Mochtar Lufti 21 ⓣ0411/320348. Homely little place next to the Orchid Garden, run by an elderly lady and with very clean, noiseless fan or air-con rooms. Highly recommended. ❷

Sahid Jaya Makassar Jl Ratulangi 33 ⓣ0411/875757, ⓕ875858. Part of an Indonesian chain and yet another high-rise four-star hotel in Makassar, this time away from the seafront near the Ratu Indah shopping mall. Facilities include swimming pool and gym, and Korean/Japanese restaurant. ❹

Sedona Jl Somba Opu 297 ⓣ0411/870555, ⓕ870222. Two hundred and thirty deluxe air-con rooms right on the seafront with swimming pool, Tex-Mex bar and cyber-business centre. One of the smartest in the city, yet actually quite reasonably priced. ❼

Semeru Jl Jampea 27 ⓣ0411/318113, ⓕ332239. New and incredibly good-value losmen with air-con doubles. The annexe opposite (ⓣ0411/310410) has larger rooms. ❷

Surya Indonesia Jl Dg Tompu 3 ⓣ0411/327568, ⓕ311498. Tiled, pleasant place; all rooms with air-con, hot water, fridge and TV. ❸

Wisata Inn Jl Sultan Hasanuddin 36–38 ⓣ0411/324344, ⓕ312783. A nicely placed, welcoming and well-run hotel. The older rooms have fans, while the doubles in the new wing have air-con. ❸

Yasmin Jl Jampea 5 ⓣ0411/320424, ⓕ328283. A friendly business venue with good new facilities and free airport pick-up. ❻

The City

A monument to Sulawesi's colonial era, **Fort Rotterdam** on Jalan Ujung Pandang (Tues–Sun 7.30am–6pm; free – ignore the guard asking for "donations") would be worth a look even if it wasn't also the quietest spot in the city centre. The site has been a defensive position since 1545, when the tenth Gowan king, Tunipa Langa, first raised a fort here with Portuguese assistance and named it **Jum Pandan** (from which the name "Ujung Pandang" derives), after pandanus trees growing in the vicinity. Enlarged a century later, in 1667 the fort become Dutch property following the Bungaya Treaty, under the command of **Cornelius Speelman**, who rechristened the complex Fort Rotterdam in memory of his home town. A rebuilding of the walls in stone was followed by the addition of solid barracks, residences and a church, and the fort remained the regional Dutch military and governmental headquarters until the 1930s. During World War II, the Japanese used it as a college, after which it fell into disrepair, until it was restored in the 1970s. The renovated eighteenth-century buildings now house new government offices and a **museum** (Tues–Thurs 8am–2pm, Fri 8–10.30am, Sat 8am–1pm; Rp750).

Forming a protective square with drawn-out corners, Rotterdam's high **walls** are perhaps the most impressive part of the entire fort; orientate yourself by climbing them and promenading along the top, where you'll get a fine view of the tall, white buildings inside, their steep roofs tiled in grey slate. On the northwest side, **Speelman's House** – actually dating from after his death in 1686 – is the oldest surviving building, and now houses one half of **La Galigo museum** (Rp750). Named after a Bugis prince featured in a lengthy romantic poem, the museum is worth seeing, but brief captions make it hard to put exhibits into context: the most absorbing items are some prehistoric megaliths from Watampone. South across a courtyard, where the **church** stands alone, the other part of the museum illustrates local skills in silk weaving, agriculture and boatbuilding, with some fine scale models of different types of prahu.

South of Fort Rotterdam

South of Fort Rotterdam, Jalan Ujung Pandang runs down along the seafront as Jalan Penghibur, a picturesque place to watch the sunset over the Makassar Strait and one which the city's hotels have taken full advantage of. This esplanade — also known as **Pantai Losari** — is famous for its **evening food stalls**, which stretch way down south and are more romantic places to eat than the upmarket bars and restaurants which overlook them. Parallel and just east of Jalan Penghibur, **Jalan Somba Opu** is known across Indonesia for its **gold shops**; other stalls sell silk from Sengkang, intricate silver filigree in the Kendari style, and potentially antique Chinese porcelain, all priced at about three times what you'd pay elsewhere. The street's southern end is crossed by Jalan Mochtar Lufti, down which you'll find the **Clara Bundt Orchid Gardens** at no. 15a. A privately owned nursery rather than a public space, visitors are allowed in to inspect row upon row of planter pots and orchids held in bamboo frames. The type and quantity of flowers depends on the season, but look for purple hybrids, golden "dancing ladies" and long-petalled spider orchids. It's free to enter, though one gets the feeling that the place is getting tired of tourists traipsing through their home, and the welcome is underwhelming.

Medan Karebosi and beyond

Medan Karebosi is a scruffy, spacious patch of green surrounded by trees, the venue for daytime football matches or military parades, and the source of much local gossip concerning the activities of its transvestite prostitutes. The shaded fringes along Jalan Ahmad Yani also attract street performers and panacea-sellers with megaphones. About 200m to the south, down Jalan Sudirman you'll encounter the **Mandala Monument**, whose thirty-metre tower rising out of a colonial-style building flanked by flaming bamboo is a weird concoction even by Indonesian standards. Continuing along Jalan Sudirman, the grounds of the **Governor's House**, about a ten-minute walk beyond the Mandala Monument on the corner of Jalan Sungai Saddang, sports a small aviary built around a fig tree, the grass kept short by a herd of deer, while a lonely cassowary stalks the tennis court. Jalan Sungai Saddang itself is becoming a popular middle-class shopping district, with a string of cosmetically neat businesses and plazas centred around the glossy new Matahari Department Store further east.

Five hundred metres **west of Medan Karebosi**, and one block east of the post office, is the **Museum Kota Makassar** (Tues–Thurs 8am–2pm, Fri 8–11am, Sat 9am–2pm; free) a run-through of the history of the city with a number of mildly diverting old photos, maps and official documents. The area **north of Medan Karebosi** is a mix of down-to-earth commercial districts and twisting alleys, once the heart of eighteenth-century Makassar. Northwest of Karebosi, and bordered by north-orientated Jalan Nusantara and Jalan Irian (the latter also labelled Jalan Sudirohusodo on street signs), the **Chinese quarter** is worth a look for its half-dozen **temples**, decked in dragons and brightly coloured decor, which cluster along the lower reaches of Jalan Sulawesi. Cross east over Jalan Irian and you'll find circling pete-petes, crowds, and hawkers selling leather belts, wallets and fruit, which make up the chaotic melange surrounding **Pasar Sentral**. In the middle of it all, **Makassar Mall** is a crowded, multistorey firetrap of a fabric warehouse full of beggars and pickpockets, where cheap cotton, silk and synthetics are sold by the metre. Push northeast through this onto Jalan Diponegoro, where **Makam Pengeran Diponegoro** marks the final resting place of Prince Diponegoro of Yogyakarta. Exiled to Sulawesi by the Dutch after instigating the five-year Javan

War of 1825, he was imprisoned at Fort Rotterdam in 1845 and died there a decade later. He and his wife are buried side by side in a large but plain multi-tiered **tomb** up against the western side of this small Islamic cemetery.

From Pasar Sentral you can also catch a pete-pete heading 3km north up Jalan Sudarso to where **Bugis prahu** from all over Indonesia unload and embark cargo at **Paotere harbour** (Rp350 admission). Though the smell and lack of sanitation can be unpleasant on a hot day, it's quite a spectacle when the harbour is crowded, the red, white and green prahu lined up along the dock wall with much shifting of bales, boxes, barrels and jerry cans on backs and carts. The adjoining streets are one of the most attractively squalid parts of the city: tattooed sailors on shore leave roam around blearily, vendors display fresh and grilled fish on banana leaves, and shops sell huge mats of spongy tree bark, spices, and cloth from all four corners of the archipelago.

Eating

Eating out in Makassar involves plenty of **seafood**; other specialities such as *soto makassar* – a soup made from buffalo offal – may not appeal to everyone. For unequalled atmosphere and the lowest prices, try the after-dark alfresco stalls opposite Fort Rotterdam on Jalan Ujung Pandang where, lit by hissing pressure lamps and protected from the elements by a tarpaulin, you share benches with other diners while cats scavenge around your ankles. Rice, tea, and a big plate of either prawns, duck, squid or fish, grilled or fried to your order, will set you back Rp7000. Another fine evening spot is the sea wall above Pantai Losari along Jalan Penghibur, whose kilometre-long string of mobile food carts sell more seafood, fried rice, noodles, bananas and cakes than you could ever hope to eat, with the sunset as a backdrop. **Restaurants** are pricey compared with the rest of Sulawesi, though portions are healthy; the biggest drawback is that most have similar Chinese-style menus, leading to monotony if you're in town for any length of time. **Western food** at the bigger hotels is not recommended, though there are plenty of fast-food places, including *KFC* and *McDonald's*, usually located in the bigger malls.

Restaurants

Asia Baru Jl Gunung Salahutu 2. Inexpensive fish restaurant, whose menu classes items according to size and quantity of bones; very busy at weekends.

Lumayan Jalan Samalona. Bugis-run restaurant offering well-priced servings of staples such as sate, excellent grilled fish, and nasi campur.

Malabar Jl Sulawesi 290. Indian restaurant with functional decor and no vegetable, let alone vegetarian, courses. Otherwise, a short but very tasty menu offering crisp, light *martabak* (meat-stuffed roti), aromatic sate and curries, and chicken korma or *kebuly* rice specials served noon to midnight on Friday. Fractionally more expensive than the average rumah makan.

Mam's Jl Layaligo 31, off Jl Ratulangi. Western-style mid-price fare, including exquisite Black Forest gateaux and some quintessentially European dishes ranging from bruschetta to fish and chips.

Pate'ne Jalan Sulawesi. Though full of Bugis patrons and describing itself as an east Javanese establishment, the menu betrays this restaurant's Chinese ownership. Big, noisy, enjoyable atmosphere, cheap and filling fish, soup and noodle staples, and often open during the day when other places are closed – though they should really give their floor a wash occasionally.

Pizza Ria Jalan A Yani and other locations around town. Formerly part of the Pizza Hut chain, a Western-style pizza joint that is overpriced, but you pay for the hygiene and air-con.

Ratu Gurih Jl Sulawesi 38/46. The best-value restaurant near Jalan Jampea. You choose the fish from one of the ice boxes outside, and ten minutes later it lands on your plate, still sizzling from the barbecue, with peanut and chilli sauces as optional extras. Highly recommended.

Surya Jl Nusakambangan 16. Nothing but shellfish and rice here; great crab and mid-range prices.

Ujung Pandang Jl Irian 42. Pricey seafood restaurant with comfortable furnishings; chargrilled fish or giant prawns are best, but staff can get pushy if they don't think you've ordered enough.

Entertainment

Makassar's after-dark **entertainment** is Western-orientated, with popular sessions at the *Makassar Golden* hotel's *Zig-Zag Disco* (daily from 8pm; Rp 5000) – the hotel also sometimes has live bands at the weekend. There's also a salsa evening every Saturday at the *Hotel Sedona*, extremely popular with expats at least. To see what locals do with their time off, spend a few hours one weekend out at Pulau Kayangan (see p.895). One **bar** worth patronizing for sunset views and evening atmosphere is the *Taman Safari*, on the corner of Jalan Penghibur and Jalan Haji Bau, south of the Stella Maris hospital; the *Kios Semarang*, also on the waterfront, one block south of the *Makassar Golden*, has a good cheap bar on its top floor and an equally inexpensive restaurant underneath. The most comfortable **cinema** is Studio 21, just north of the *Hotel Sahid* on Jalan Ratulangi, with daily screenings of recent Hollywood and Hong Kong releases, and weekend late-night specials.

Listings

Airline offices Hasanuddin airport is the busiest in eastern Indonesia, with flights to Maluku, West Papua, Nusa Tenggara, Java, Kalimantan, and beyond Indonesia. Most airline offices open Mon–Fri 8.30am–5.30pm, Sat 8.30am–12.30pm. Bouraq, Jl Veteran Selatan 1 (Ⓣ0411/452506), to Palu and Surabaya; Garuda, Jl Pettarani 18b–c (Ⓣ0411/437676), to Biak, Denpasar, Jakarta and Manado; Kartika, agent in town Limbunan Tour and Travel (Ⓣ0411/333555), for Surabaya and Jakarta; Lion Air, *Makassar Golden* hotel, (Ⓣ0411/322211), to Manado and Jakarta; Mandala, Komplex Latanette Plaza, Jalan Sungai Saddang (Ⓣ0411/325592), to Jakarta, Manado and Surabaya; Merpati, Jl Gunung Bawakareang 109, near *Ramayan Satrya* hotel (Ⓣ0411/442474, Ⓕ442480), to all destinations in Sulawesi, Biak, Denpasar, Jakarta, Surabaya; Pelita Air, *Makassar Golden* hotel (Ⓣ0411/319222), to Java, Kendari and Sorong; Silk Air, 2nd Floor, *Hotel Sahid Jaya*, Jalan Sam Ratalungi (Ⓣ0411/834348), to Singapore.

Banks and exchange Main branches of most banks are along the northern side of Medan Karebosi; all have ATMs, but give very variable rates of exchange for cash and travellers' cheques. BCA have good rates; the BNI, bad. The best moneychanger in town is Haji La Tunrung, in the building by the seafront at the southern end of Jalan Nusantara; the rates aren't wonderful, but they're open when most places aren't.

Bookshops There's a good range of English-language novels, maps and guidebooks at Promedia, on the top floor of the Matahari Department Store on Jalan Sungai Saddang.

Diving Marlin Dive Centre, Jl Bangkau 14 (Ⓣ0411/858762, Ⓕ831003, Ⓦwww.marlindive.com), is a Belgian operation that specializes in dives around the Speermonde Archipelago and Bira. Rates start at US$45 for two dives, including weights, tank, boat, dive guide and food. There's a two-person minimum, but solo divers can join in if a group is going already. Lack of large fish is compensated by stretches of good fringing coral, plus deep walls at distant Pulau Kapoposang and a couple of World War II wrecks.

Ferries The Pelni office is at Jl Sudirman 38 Ⓣ0411/331401, Ⓕ331411. Tickets (Mon–Fri 8am–4pm) on ground floor; top floor for timetables. Connections here to ports all over Sulawesi, plus Java, Sumatra, Kalimantan, Bali, Nusa Tenggara, Maluku and West Papua. Alternatively, a number of travel agents – including Caraka Travelindo (see below) – have signs outside their offices advertising online access to Pelni, thereby saving you the hassle of fighting through the masses at the Pelni office; they charge a small premium, but most people think this is money well spent. There are a couple of other passenger ferries running to Surabaya, including the *KM Kimana* and the *KM Titian Nusantara*. The timetable for these ferries changes frequently; check with the agents opposite the harbour entrance for the latest details.

Hospitals Stella Maris, Jalan Penghibur Ⓣ0411/854341. Your best chance in southern Sulawesi for correct diagnosis and treatment by English-speaking staff.

Immigration Jl Tentara Pelajar 2 Ⓣ0411/831531. Officials here can be obstructive, and it's not the easiest place in Indonesia to get a visa extended.

Internet access By far the most pleasant and efficient of Makassar's many internet places is the Surf@Cybercafé, above the *Pizza Ria* on Jalan Yani (Rp6000 per hour).

Pharmacies Apotik Kimia Firma, Jalan Ahmad

Yani, and Apotik Via Farma, south of Galael supermarket on Jalan Sultan Hasanuddin, are large establishments open 24hr.

Police Main office is on Jalan Ahmad Yani.

Post office Jalan Slamet Riyadi, southeast of Fort Rotterdam (Mon–Sat 8am–8pm, Sun 9am–3pm). Stalls outside sell postcards, envelopes and an occasional copy of the *Jakarta Post*. The parcel office is one block south at Jl Balaikota 5.

Shopping Matahari Department Store, Jalan Sungai Saddang, is the city's premier source of Western-style clothing, home appliances, stationery and groceries. Another good supermarket is Galael, across from the *Marannu* hotel on Jalan Sultan Hasanuddin.

Souvenirs There are a string of souvenir shops along Jalan Pattimura, just south of the post office, including the large Kanebo store and Nostalgia Art's Gallery, Jl Pattimura 8. The Indonesian Handicraft Centre, Jl Somba Opu 28, and Toko Mas Benteng, Jl Somba Opu 86, both have a good general stock, or try Asdar Art, Jl Somba Opu 207, and Toko Subur, Jl Somba Opu 114, for porcelain and ethnic artefacts.

Telephone and fax Aside from bigger hotels, there are international wartel booths on the western side of Medan Karebosi on Jalan Kajaolaliddo, at the post office, and also on Jalan Bali, west of Pasar Sentral.

Travel agents All tour and transport bookings from Anta Express, Jl Irian 34a ⓣ0411/318648, ⓕ313910; or Sena, Jl Jampea 1a ⓣ0411/318373, ⓕ323906. Caraka Travelindo, Jl Samalona 12 (ⓣ0411/318877, ⓕ318889), are splendid, with English-speakers and unbiased advice on Hoga Island (see p.926). They also organize upmarket, four- to eight-day tours to Tanah Toraja and southern Sulawesi, the Bada Valley, and Minahasa. Limbunan Tour and Travel (ⓣ0411/333555) on Jalan Bawakaraeng are particularly good for flight tickets, and are the agent for PT Kartika.

Around Makassar

Few Indonesian cities can boast extensive archeological remains, tropical islands and forests within 40km of their centres, so it's worth spending a day or two exploring Makassar's suburbs and surrounding areas. A short ride south of town are the well-displayed foundations of the old Gowan port **Somba Opu**, along with royal remnants at **Gowa Tua** and **Sungguminasa**. Offshore, the sandbars and reefs of the **Speermonde archipelago** offer fairgrounds and fragmentary coral, while inland is a steep-sided, 150-kilometre-long plateau extending from Bantaeng on the peninsula's south coast to Parepare in the northwest. Surrounded by dry plains, these eroded limestone hills – ancient coral reefs, now quarried for cement – hide some unexpectedly lush pockets of scenery east of the city at **Malino** and northeast at **Bantimurung** via the town of **Maros**, also the jumping-off point for exploring Sulawesi's prehistory at **Leang-Leang**.

Somba Opu

Somba Opu is a former trading settlement which grew up 7km south of Makassar at the mouth of **Sungai Jenberang** as part of the Makassan coastal defences. To get there, catch a pete-pete labelled either "Cenderawasih" or "C/Wasih" from Jalan Ahmad Yani down Jalan Cenderawasih to the **Abdul Kadir** terminus (Rp1000). This leaves you by a wooden bridge spanning a river, where you can either rent a waiting becak or stroll across and ask directions for the one-kilometre walk.

At the peak of Gowa's power in the early seventeenth century, Somba Opu was the largest Makassan port, a well-fortified town of several square kilometres, with warehouses stocked by traders from all over Asia and royal residences protected by walls 7m high. Siltation has since moved the site more than 1km inland, but it was Dutch determination to break the Bugis trading empire that brought Somba Opu down in 1669, after fierce fighting. Now surrounded by vegetable plots and grazing buffalo, ongoing excavations have restored a 150-metre stretch of Somba Opu's western **ramparts**, where you can see the rammed-earth and red-brick construction and climb the reinforced corners which once supported watchtowers. Supplementing the remains, the area also incorporates full-scale **wooden replicas** of south Sulawesi architecture: a thirty-metre-long Mandar dwelling from the northwest coast stands out, raised high off the ground on posts. There's a **museum** here, too (open if the caretaker sees you; donation), identifiable by its grey-blue walls and the cannon outside. The exhibits include an ingeniously displayed aerial view of Somba Opu in its heyday, bricks decorated with animal tracks and incised patterns, Dutch musket balls from their 1669 attack, and a Gowanese spear-blade of similar vintage.

Gowa Tua and Sungguminasa

Red pete-petes from the northeast corner of Medan Karebosi on Jalan Sudirman take forty minutes to cover the ten-kilometre highway running southeast to the town of **Sungguminasa** (Rp750–1000), passing more royal relics along the way – tell the driver where you want to go and get dropped off nearby. Some 8km towards Sungguminasa, a small signpost labelled "Hasanuddin Tomb" points east off the highway into the vanished bounds of **Gowa Tua**, Old Gowa, once the Makassan state's spiritual core. Dodging down the semi-rural lanes, you pass first the stocky, grey **Syeh Yussuf Mosque**, named after a seventeenth-century Islamic mystic whose whitewashed pyramidal tomb lies in the adjacent graveyard; bearing right after this brings you in about fifteen minutes to **Tamalate cemetery**, planted with frangipani trees and reserved for the Gowan royalty. The biggest mausoleum here belongs to the ill-fated **Sultan Hasanuddin** who died in 1670, one year after the fall of Somba Opu marked the close of Gowa's fortunes. Just east of here on a rise is **Batu Pelantikan**, the stone where Gowan royalty were crowned, while off to the southwest is **Tempat Tomanurung**, the point where the goddess Tomanurung arrived on earth to found the Gowan royal line. Conspicuously unheralded, a separate alley from the Sungguminasa road leads to a further cemetery and the tomb of **Arung Palakka**, the king of Bone (see p.900), who colluded with the Dutch to overthrow Gowa. As Hasanuddin's nemesis, Arung Palakka is understandably unpopular in Makassar, and it's something of a mystery why he was buried here, though east in Watampone – the only place where Palakka is considered a hero – they say that it was so that he could continue his fight with Hasanuddin in the afterlife.

Arrival at **SUNGGUMINASA** itself is signalled by the statue of a Bugis horseman, but otherwise there's nothing to separate this town from the rest of the suburbs that have flanked the highway from Makassar. Pete-petes terminate at Sungguminasa's bus station, from where it's a couple of minutes' walk to **Balla Lompoa**, the former **Sultan of Gowa's Palace** and now a museum (daily 8am–1pm; free). Deprived of all real power, the Gowan state actually survived into recent times, and the last king was crowned in 1947. Built of wood in the traditional style, Balla Lompoa is only some sixty years old, but its curators take great pride in their exhibits. Antique ceremonial clothing almost crumbles under your stare, and there are documents written in angular **Makassarese writing**, said to have been invented in 1538 by Gowa's harbour master, Daeng Panatte. **Bugis script**, on which Makassarese is based, originated a century earlier; the 23 bent and curved characters represent sounds such as *ka*, *ga*, *nga*, *nka*, with attached dots, circles and "elbows" modifying pronunciation. A **map** shows the Gowan view of their empire in 1660, enclosing West Papua, Lombok, north Australia, and half of Kalimantan, while a **royal family tree** illustrates the tangled relationships binding the different Bugis states.

Photos of the Gowan regalia – stored safely elsewhere – include a 1.7-kilogram, solid-gold crown, while a token from 1814 provides a memento of Britain's brief occupation of Sulawesi, given by the British to Raja Lambang Parang "in friendship and esteem and in testimony of his attachment and faithful services".

The Speermonde archipelago

While Makassar's offshore ecology labours under city garbage and the widespread practice of bombing for fish, the hundred or more islands and reefs of the **Speermonde archipelago** still have much to offer. Spread northwest of the city for 80km, there's fair snorkelling around the further islands, and **divers** should try to reach remote **Kapoposang**, where there are sharks, shallow coral in reasonable condition, and deep walls – see p.892 for dive operators. The islands are best reached by giving in to the touts and **chartering a boat** at about Rp60,000–80,000 for a half-day from the harbour opposite Fort Rotterdam on Jalan Ujung Pandang. Cheaper public ferries – except weekend services to Kayangan (Rp8000 return) – are unreliable, and can leave you stranded overnight.

The two easiest islands to reach are **Lae-lae** (15min) and **Kayangan** (45min), but there are drawbacks: Kayangan sets the scene, with a tacky day-resort whose cabins are rented by the hour, loudspeakers blaring pop music, and vast throngs at weekends. Far better is **Samalona** (1hr), also popular but less tourist-orientated, despite the Rp2000 landing charge. The island itself is a bit dowdy, but the beaches are clean, and during the week you can sunbathe in peace or snorkel over patchy reef outcrops. If you'd like to spend the night, *Wisma Pulau Samalona* (❺) has reasonable cottages and houseboats. **Barang Lompo** (30min) is a partly vegetated sand islet covered with houses belonging to a fishing village; there's not much coral left, but it is anyway more interesting to have a look around this self-supporting community. The domain of local fishermen, **Kodingareng** and **Barang Caddi** have far fewer facilities but better reefs, and are both about an hour away – take food and water.

Malino

Set about halfway to the top of 2560-metre Gunung Bawa Karaeng amongst a refreshing landscape of pine trees and rice fields, **MALINO** is one of the nicer legacies of Dutch rule in Sulawesi. Originally a haunt of the Gowan aristocracy, it was the Dutch who developed the town as a popular retreat from the baking lowlands. There's early-morning transport from Terminal Tamalate or Sunguminasa (Rp3000), and the seventy-kilometre, two-hour journey from Makassar means that it's possible to make a return trip in one day, but Malino is really somewhere to unwind and spend at least a night. The weekend is best, as there's a big Sunday-morning **market** here where Malino's excellent fruit gets an airing. Most **accommodation** and eating options are basic, though the *Celebes* on Jalan Hasanuddin (ⓣ0417/21183; ❹) offers comfortable bungalows. Malino can get decidedly nippy at night, and is often very damp, so come prepared. An easy four-kilometre walk east of town takes you to the **Takapala waterfall**, a narrow band of water dropping 50m or so into the side of a paddy-field; for something more adventurous, try the four-hour hike to the peak of Bawa Karaeng from **Appiang**, a village about 10km east of Malino. It's not a difficult trail, but it's a good idea to take a guide (Rp15,000–20,000) from Malino – ask at your accommodation place – to prevent you from losing the way between Appiang and the summit.

Maros, Leang-Leang and Bantimurung

The market town of **MAROS**, its stalls crowded with mangoes and bananas, lies about 30km northeast of Makassar, an air-con ride in the "Patas" **buses** which depart three times an hour between 6am and 6pm from Pasar Sentral on Jalan Cokroaminoto – the **last bus** back to Makassar leaves Maros around 7pm. There's nothing to keep you in Maros itself, but the road to Watampone runs east across the hills from here, with turn-offs along the way to prehistoric remains at Leang-Leang, 15km distant, and waterfalls at Bantimurung (11km). The bus from Makassar leaves you near Maros's **pete-pete terminal**, where there are frequent departures to Bantimurung and far less regular services **to Leang-Leang**, both for around Rp750. If you're in a hurry to reach the latter, either charter a vehicle (at Rp30,000 an hour), or take a Bantimurung-bound pete-pete to the Leang-Leang junction and walk the rest of the way – but be aware that this involves a five-kilometre hike in the blazing sun.

LEANG-LEANG – the name means simply "caves" – is a handful of houses and a tile factory at the northern end of a valley, the flat plain planted with rice and backed by looming limestone walls. Just before the village, **Taman Purbakala Leang-Leang**, the Caves' Archeology Park (Rp500) encloses an area where thousands of years ago humans occupied a natural network of tunnels hollowed into the hillside. The first is **Pettae cave**, a small cleft decorated with red ochre hand stencils and pictures of long-since extinct wildlife; further back and reached up a ladder is the larger, bat-ridden **Pettakere cave**, whose low passage walls include more stencils and some recent graffiti – bring good shoes and a torch. Stone blades known as **maros points** found here indicate 2500 BC as a minimum date of occupation of these caves.

Back on the Maros–Watampone road, 5km past the Leang-Leang turn-off, a giant concrete monkey marks the entrance to **Bantimurung**, a lovely little area of woodland and waterfalls where you can unwind in peace during the week or join sociable crowds eating ice creams and cooling off at weekends. The park is immediately damp, green and shady, with marked paths winding off along minor gorges. **Goa Mimpi** is a kilometre-long, electrically lit cavern (Rp1000; take a torch in case of power failures) right through a hillside, but the best part of the park is **Bantimurung waterfall**; steps up the side follow the river upstream to another cascade – beware of undertows if you go swimming. Aside from plentiful **butterflies**, look for kingfishers, birds of prey and dark-grey **flying lizards** (see p.946), most likely sunbathing with wings fanned out on tall trunks.

The south coast and Pulau Selayar

Along Sulawesi's agriculturally starved **south coast** people turned to the sea for their livelihood and became Indonesia's foremost sailors and shipwrights, industries still enthusiastically pursued around the village of **Tanah Beru**, with good beaches at the nearby resort of **Bira**, and peaceful, little-visited **Pulau Selayar** only a short ferry ride away. From Makassar, **buses** to Bira (5hr; Rp17,500) and other south-coast destinations leave early in the morning from Terminal Tamalate, and also from Sungguminasa's bus station. If you can't find anything heading further than Bulukumba, go there first and then hop on local Kijang to your destination. Terminal Tamalate is also where to find morning buses all the way to **Benteng** on Pulau Selayar (about 11hr). Bina Bakti and Nusamukti Lestari are good bus companies; note that the ferries themselves cross from either Bulukumba or Bira, depending on seasonal winds. There are **no banks** capable of exchanging foreign currency in the region.

Tanah Beru

A pretty hamlet stretching for a couple of kilometres along the beach, **TANAH BERU's** status as Indonesia's foremost traditional shipbuilding centre seems at first rather unlikely, but a wander soon uncovers front yards piled with sawdust, boats of all sizes lying on the sand and in the water in various stages of completion, and much carving, sawing and assembling going on underneath the palms. **Prahu** come in various **styles**, such as bulky **pelari**, used for heavy cargo, and more graceful, mid-sized **pinisi**, the form most commonly seen in southern Sulawesi. Both share unique oar-shaped and seemingly awkward side-mounted rudders, though some features have been absorbed from other cultures over the years: the *pelari*'s broad stern is modelled on sixteenth-century Portuguese vessels, and the *pinisi* shape owes quite a bit to turn-of-the-twentieth-century European schooners. While still equipped with at least one mast, prahu also no longer rely solely on sails, and carry powerful engines. Until recently, vessels from southern Sulawesi used the prevailing winds to spend the year ranging east to Aru and west to Singapore; today, the main trade route has constricted to a Sulawesi–Java–Kalimantan circuit. **Construction** of a prahu is a prolonged process, the building involving no plans, only basic tools, and a great deal of superstition and ritual – including the sacrifice of a goat, whose forelegs are strung up on the stern of newly floated ships. Preferred timbers, such as the ironwood *kayu ulin*, are now in very short supply in Indonesia, let alone locally, and Tanah Beru's materials come from the Palopo district, 250km to the north.

Tanah Beru is a fascinating place to spend half a day, but if you fancy stopping over, the Bulukumba–Bira road passes through as Jalan Sultan Alauddin, with an intersection grouped with warung and stores partway along defining the village centre. Local Kijang circle here, with simple **accommodation** at the *Losmen Anda* (❶) and a backstreet market that sometimes sells dolphin along with fish of all descriptions.

Bira and around

About 15km east of Tanah Beru, **BIRA** is an unassuming group of wooden homes painted green and blue and raised on stumps. Shipbuilding is here a thing of the past and, though the village retains a reputation for woven cloth, there's nothing to see as such and visitors generally continue to the powdery sand at **Paloppalakaya Bay** (also known as **Bira beach**), 4km south. Between the two is **Panrang Luhuk**, the tiny port for seasonal **ferries to Pulau Selayar**, which cross to the north tip of the island in the early afternoon (5hr). A few Kijangs and minibuses orbit a Bulukumba–Bira–Paloppalakaya Bay route throughout the day.

The **beach** at Paloppalakaya Bay is a narrow strip of blindingly white sand below which a dry headland overburdened with tourist accommodation overlooks the Selayar Strait and tiny Pulau Lihukan. Shallow water off the beach is safe for swimming, ending in a coral wall dropping into the depths about 150m from shore. Snorkellers can see turtles and graceful, three-metre-wide manta rays here, with exciting diving deeper down featuring strong currents, cold water and big sharks. All accommodation rents out snorkels and fins, and *Anda Bungalows* has scuba gear and packages for qualified divers starting at US$60. Another way to spend some time is to rent a boat and visit Lihukan, or buy a hand line in the store up the road and go fishing for small fry – trying to catch tuna or sharks on a hand line is exhilarating, but definitely not a relaxing day out.

Orientation is simple: the road from Bira runs past the port and straight down to the headland, with what few services there are clustered at its end above Paloppalakaya Bay. The pick of the cheaper **places to stay** includes *Riswan Guest House* (❷), a nice traditional Bugis house on a breezy hilltop with all meals included; and cabins at *Riswan Bungalows* (Ⓣ0413/82127; ❷), on the right-hand side as you enter town, and nearby *Anda Bungalows* (Ⓣ0413/82125; ❷). More upmarket are the chic cabins with sea views at *Bira Beach Hotel* (Ⓣ0413/81515; ❸), with a travel agent and the only public **telephone** in the area; and the bungalows at *Bira View Inn* (Ⓣ0413/82043; ❹). As there's virtually no fertile soil around Bira, **food** is straightforward, but cooks try hard to vary the fish-and-rice standby or make it interesting; the clean *Melati* is the sole alternative to hotel kitchens. From Makassar's Terminal Mallengkeri, **Kijangs** to Bulukumba (5hr; Rp15,000) leave early in the morning, from where you can catch a bemo to Bira (1hr; Rp5000); although you may have to travel from Bulukumba via Tanah Beru (Rp2500 to Tanah Beru; Rp2000 to Bira). There are also a few direct buses that leave in the morning to Bira (5hr; Rp17,500).

Pulau Selayar and beyond

A hundred-kilometre ridge pointing south towards Flores, **Pulau Selayar** has great esoteric appeal. Planted with pomegranates, the north of the island is a stony continuation of the mainland, but there are waterfalls and patchy tropical woodlands in the south, the latter thick enough to shelter cuscus and deer. There are some good beaches too, empty aside from long walls of bamboo fish traps, and the island is ringed by coconut plantations and small villages, with the only settlement of any size, Benteng, halfway down Selayar's west coast. Little is known about the island's early history, though the **Layolo**, now found mainly in the south and interior, are said to be the oldest of Selayar's five ethnic groups. Bugis traders from Makassar introduced Islam in 1605, naming the island **Tanah Doang**, the Land of Prayer. Selayar's kingdoms paid tribute to Gowa before its fall, when the island became a vassal state of the sultan of Ternate in distant Maluku; the Dutch chased the Maluccans out a century later, set up a government post at Benteng, and tried to offset Selayar's declining cotton industry with **copra**, still the primary – not very profitable – source of income.

Whether you cross directly from Bulukumba, or land at the north of the island from Bira and bus down the west coast, all traffic winds up at **BENTENG**, an informal, tropical town with a scattering of colonial-era buildings and sandy backstreets. As you'd expect, the **market** between Jalan Haji Hayung and Jalan Sukarno-Hatta overflows with seafood, with catches unloaded on the beach behind in the morning: giant cuttlefish, emperor trout and spider shells accompany vegetables and very little fruit. Indonesian speakers can arrange with boat owners for beach-and-snorkelling excursions a couple of kilometres offshore to the northern end of **Pulau Pasi**, or there are a couple of trips to be made by pete-pete or foot **around Benteng**. A half-day walk east from town takes you to **Gantarang**, a fortified village whose ancient stone walls are still maintained; the mosque here is of antique design, and is thought to date back to the early seventeenth century.

Benteng's main square faces east out to sea over a stone jetty, with most

A back door to Flores

Around 300km of sea separate Pulau Selayar from the north coast of Flores (see pp.773–757), and it's feasible to travel the distance on local vessels, though you'll need to be patient and very flexible with both timetables and destinations. If it's simply the chance to see somewhere remote that interests you, there's marginally more traffic to **Taka Bonerate**, Indonesia's largest coral atoll. Also known as the **Macan Islands**, Taka Bonerate is about 90km due east of Selayar's southern tip, and shouldn't be confused with Pulau Bonerate, 150km southeast. Taka's main islands are **Latombu**, **Tarupa** (both with homestay accommodation) and **Rajuni**. People here make a living from collecting *trepang* (sea slugs) to sell to the Chinese. Getting to Taka Bonerate or Flores from Selayar involves waiting at Benteng until transport turns up, though there may soon be regular dive expeditions to Taka Bonerate operating from Bira and Selayar – ask at *Anda Bungalows* in Bira or Pak Arafin in Benteng for the latest details.

essentials on three parallel roads running north from here: Jalan Sukarno-Hatta along the seafront; Jalan Haji Hayung, 50m back; and Jalan Sudirman. The seldom-staffed **tourist office** is in the old Dutch controller's house, on the eastern side of the square, but a better source of **information** is Pak Arafin, at Jl Haji Hayung 102 (Ⓣ0414/21388, Ⓕ21813). A retired teacher who speaks English, he acts as an interpreter and organizes trips to forests, caves and waterfalls, as well as sleepovers in villages, and excursions to nearby islets for Rp50,000 a day. **Accommodation** is limited to the clean *Hotel Berlian* at Jl Sudirman 45 (Ⓣ0414/21129; ❷), offering plain doubles with mandi and aircon rooms. The *Berlian* can provide **meals**, but *Rumah Makan Crystal* on Jalan Haji Hayung is better, and there are also coffee houses nearby, whose patrons will be most amused to find a Westerner joining them for breakfast. Before discussing you, they'll ask if you understand *bahasa Selayar* – you could reply *"Soh'dhi"* ("a little"). **Transport** around the island is by pete-pete from behind the market on Jalan Sukarno-Hatta, with **buses** back to Makassar leaving in the morning from their agencies on Jalan Haji Hayung – there is no bus depot.

Matalalang

A relic of old Selayar lies 3km south of Benteng at **MATALALANG** (Rp2000 by ojek), half a dozen buildings and a glassed-in pavilion containing a metre-high, narrow-waisted **bronze drum**. This is **Gong Nekara**, a beautiful example of Bronze Age artistry: four frogs sit up on the rim of the tympanum, while the sides are finely chased in friezes of peacocks, elephants, palm trees, birds, fish, and highly stylized human figures, with plumed headdresses, in a boat. Of a form typical to southwestern China two thousand years ago, when they were a symbol of aristocratic power, Gong Nekara's presence on Selayar is a mystery. Locals say that the drum was an heirloom of the local **Putabangun kingdom**, brought to the island by the kingdom's founder **Wi Tenri Dio**, a Palopo prince whose mother was Chinese. Used in rainmaking ceremonies, the drum was lost after being buried in the seventeenth century to protect it from Maluccan raiders; rediscovered in 1868, it was acquired by the sultan of **Bontobangun**, whose decaying palace is next door. The drum is plainly visible from outside the pavilion, though for a closer look keys (Rp3000) are kept at the adjacent government office, whose three staff are masters of bureaucratic delay.

The central kingdoms

The centre of Sulawesi's two-hundred-kilometre southern peninsula is the heart of the Bugis' world. Long split into **feuding kingdoms**, the seventeenth century saw the state of **Bone** (based around the modern city of **Watampone**) brought to supremacy with Dutch military aid, following which princes from the rival states felt a lack of opportunity at home and left Sulawesi to earn the Bugis a piratical reputation abroad as they sought plunder across the region's seas. Holland put these insurgents down with difficulty, only to see their holdings in Indonesia taken by the British during the Napoleonic wars, and then endured yet another uprising – led this time by their former ally, Bone – when they resumed ownership of Sulawesi in 1817. It took another ninety years, and the systematic routing of Sulawesi's rebel kingdoms, for the Dutch position to become secure, if only briefly. A few Bugis rulers reinstated during the 1930s became figureheads for **Independence movements**, first under the Japanese during World War II, then against the return of the Dutch, relinquishing their power to the Indonesian government as recently as 1955.

It's easy to soak up some of this past, even if you're just in transit through the region. While a network of Dutch-inspired irrigation canals hover in the background, the foremost targets are the historically proud towns of Watampone, from where ferries depart to Sulawesi Tenggara, and **Sengkang**, the latter set on the shores of a gradually shrinking system of **freshwater lakes**. Everywhere, you'll find local **architecture** – whether simple homes, or one of the several surviving **sultans' palaces** – is a record of the Bugis **class system**, buildings identifying their owner's status in the construction of their triangular end gables: royals' gables were divided into five sections, nobles' into four, and so on down to commoners and slaves. Roofs are also typically decorated with two upright wooden prongs known as **tandung tedong**, buffalo horns, denoting strength, calmness and patience.

From Makassar's Terminal Panaikang, it's about 150km to either Sengkang (6hr) or Watampone (5hr), both routes covered by buses throughout the day. Watampone can also be reached by Kijang from Bulukumba on the south coast, via Sinjai.

Watampone

Once the capital of **Bone**, southern Sulawesi's strongest state, **WATAMPONE** owed its days of glory to an alliance with the Dutch that destroyed the rival Makassarese empire – though from the Bone perspective the move was justifiable. Having been unwillingly absorbed by Gowa in the early seventeenth century, Bone triumphed twenty years later under its larger-than-life leader **Arung Palakka**, 2m tall and one of the most vivid characters in Sulawesi's history. Palace politics saw Palakka forced into exile in his youth, though after returning in the 1660s he spent the rest of his life expanding Bone's empire, accumulating titles – Arung Palakka just means "Lord Palakka", the most common abbreviation of his lengthy full name – and wearing out his twenty wives in the quest for an heir. Bone remained the dominant power in southern Sulawesi for a century after Palakka's death in 1696 and, though the Dutch finally muscled in around 1905, their puppet raja sponsored a rebellion.

Now a faded but prosperous and tidy town, Watampone's main appeal is its history, amply illustrated in sites surrounding a small **public square** up in the old quarter. On the north side, **Museum Lapalawoi** (open daily, no set times; donation of around Rp5000 expected; English-speaking guides sometimes on

△ Tanah Toraja house

hand) on Jalan Thamrin is maintained by **Andi Mappassissi**, grandson of the last Bone king. Amongst more mundane silver *sireh* sets and dinner services, look for Bone's sacred sword and shield, gold wedding ornaments, a magical kris, and a document in Dutch outlining the terms of the alliance between Bone and Holland, accompanied by two interlocked iron rings symbolically representing the strength of the deal. Contemporary portraits of a long-haired, muscular and half-naked Arung Palakka are the basis of a wild **statue** outside; Palakka's five-kilogram **gold chain** is kept locked away at the **Bupati's residence** across on the west side of the square, outside of which you might see **transvestite priests** – formerly palace officials known as *waria* or *bissu* in Indonesian – teaching children traditional dance steps.

About ten minutes' walk south down Jalan Sudirman and west along Jalan Sukawati, **Bola Soba** (Audience Hall) and **Saoraja Petta Ponggawae** (Palace of the King's Army Commanders) are two lifeless, well-maintained antique ironwood buildings; much more entertaining, and proving that there's more to Watampone than nostalgia, is a wander around the town's excellent **market** on the edge of town, about 1km southwest of the public square. It's a real Arabian-style bazaar; vendors call you over to their booths and lean-to stalls to inspect Muslim prayer rugs, vegetables, piles of scented, dried spices, and cones of palm sugar. A **goldsmiths' quarter** sits at the market's core, where you can see artisans making fine bracelets – and deepening the colour of poor-quality items with nitric acid.

Practicalities

Watampone's **bus station** is about 3km west of town. Becaks and ojeks are plentiful and not too hard to bargain with, though the town centre is compact and, apart from the terminal, nowhere is too far to walk. **Accommodation** includes the relatively expensive *Wisma Wisata* at Jl Sudirman 14, 1km south of the square (ⓣ0481/21362; ❹), but there are two better-value options nearer the square: the characterful *Wisma Bola Ridie*, Jl Merdeka 6, to the east of the square (ⓣ0481/21412; ❷), is an airy Dutch house from the 1930s with original furnishings and tiled floor; the people are lovely and the house is beautiful, but some of the rooms are starting to show their age. Off the southwest corner of the square at Jl Yani 2A, *Wisma Amrach* (ⓣ0481/21589; ❷) is smart, new and spotless. Many people have also recommended the *Rio Rita*, a tidy, sunny place just off Jalan Sudirman at Jalan Karewang 4 (ⓣ0481/21053; ❷). Running north off the northwestern corner of the square, short Jalan Mesjid offers several **stores** and **places to eat**, the best of which are good Chinese-Indonesian menus at the *Ramayan* or the *Victoria*, while the *Dynasty* cake shop is the place for a snack breakfast. There's also a **post office** near the Museum Lapolowoi on Jalan Thamrin, and a wartel on the east side of the square.

Heading on, buses and Kijang run direct to Bulukumba (4hr), Makassar (5hr), Sengkang (2hr 30min) and Parepare (5hr), though station touts expect Westerners to be heading south and herd you towards Bulukumba-bound vehicles. There are also **minibus agencies** in town to save you traipsing to the terminal to book your ticket, including Padaidi, Jl Andalas 47 (ⓣ0418/22860), a five-minute walk north from the market. **For Sulawesi Tenggara**, catch a pete-pete heading 7km east from outside Museum Lapawawoi to the port of **Bajoe** (Rp750), where you'll find a **ticket office** and a long, warped stone jetty. Three ferries daily make the eight-hour crossing to Kolaka, departing at 5pm, 8pm and 11pm, though these times are very variable. Tickets are around Rp25,000, and are usually still available about ninety minutes before departure.

Goa Mampu, Sengkang and Danau Tempe

Halfway along the sixty-kilometre road between Watampone and Sengkang, the township of **Uloe** marks the turning west to **Goa Mampu**, the largest limestone caverns in southern Sulawesi. Lured by tales of the fossilized remains of a lost kingdom, **James Brooke** – later Rajah Brooke of Sarawak – investigated the caves in 1840, only to find that the statues he was hoping for were stalagmites. Split into upper and lower galleries, the encrusted rock formations are impressive in their own right, however, and you'll only need to extend your journey by an hour for a quick examination. Pete-pete or ojek make the five-kilometre run from Uloe to the caves in ten minutes, where guides (around Rp2000) with torches await your custom.

Sengkang

SENGKANG is a pretty town on the shores of **Danau Tempe**, a shallow, seasonally fluctuating lake with floating villages and a healthy bird population. Once the seat of the **Wajo kingdom**, the town is a pleasant stop on the road north, with the lake and an emerging **silk industry** to investigate, and a number of Western expats working in the gas industry stationed here. Sengkang itself is fairly functional and shouldn't take up much of your time: the kilometre-long town centre is on the east side of **Sungai Walanae** (though the river isn't visible from the main streets), which flows north into Danau Tempe. The main road zigzags south through the centre under various names, with the **bus station** on Jalan Kartini, within a short walk of all amenities.

For **accommodation**, *Pondok Eka*, Jl Maluku 12 (☎0485/21296; ❷), is friendly, but cheaper rooms come with unwanted vermin; *Hotel Alsalam Dua*, Jl Emy Saelan 8 (☎0485/21278; ❷), is cleaner and nicer; while higher prices and a longer walk to the *Hotel Apada*, Jl Durian 9 (☎0485/21053; ❹), are compensated by spacious grounds and aristocratic Bugis owners. Accommodation can organize **tour guides** for lake trips (something Indonesian-speakers can arrange for a fraction of the cost by going to boatmen and bargaining) and tours of the silk industry – impossible alone – for a steep Rp40,000.

Sengkang's silk

Sengkang's flourishing **silk industry** was established in the last decade with help from local officials and support from Thailand. Set up in the airy space under traditional Bugis houses, it's fascinating to follow the entire process from caterpillar to glossy sarong, but as each stage is handled by independent home industries scattered all over the town and surrounding kampung, you need a couple of hours and a guide to show you around.

In the first stage, pale-green caterpillars spend three weeks chomping their way through piles of mulberry leaves, before spinning a silk cocoon. When complete, the cocoon is boiled to kill the caterpillar and dissolve the glue binding it together, then the single strand – over 1km long – is ingeniously unravelled using aubergine leaves and wound onto a spool. Spun into thread, the raw silk is tied into lengths, then dyed; in the case of *ikat* designs, the colours are painted by women dyers who work cross-legged on the floor, their brush hands permanently stained. They pass on their finished work to weavers, who might take a week just to set up an *ikat* loom, and another actually to produce a bolt of the brightly coloured tartan or chevron patterns favoured by the Bugis. The final stage is the selling, with a quality *ikat* going for Rp30,000 per metre – not cheap, but half the price you'd pay in Makassar. Unless you know how to check quality by the way threads fray, ask your accommodation to point you towards reputable dealers, as some stores in town sell silk–rayon mixes as the real thing.

For **places to eat**, the *Apada* has a fine, costly restaurant; otherwise, *Rumah Makan Sulawesi*, on Jalan Latain Rilai, is where to head if you arrive late looking for a beer and generous helpings of grilled fish and chicken sate. Down the hill on Jalan Mesjid Raya, *Warung Sengkang* has cheaper portions of fried chicken, plus fossils and local memorabilia in the glass case at the back. For the best *soto makassar*, try the dirty, enormously busy place next to *Warung Marodadi*, across the road from the bus station. There's a **wartel** and BNI **bank** which accepts travellers' cheques on central Jalan Sudirman.

Moving on, Parepare is two or more hours away by bus, alternative roads circuiting Danau Tempe to the north via **Pangkajene**, or to the south via the attractive, bat-ridden town of **Soppeng** – after the late September harvest, look for troops of brightly outfitted ponies carrying heavy white bags of husked rice back to villages along the roadside.

Danau Tempe

Danau Tempe and smaller lakes nearby are the diminishing remains of a gulf which once cut the southern peninsula in two. Fed by Sungai Wallanae, the lake level is capricious, sometimes flooding violently, or drying up completely, as it did in October 1997, beaching whole communities and their **floating houses**. If the water level is high enough (the lowest period is September through to the December rains), taking a brightly painted *lopi* – a dugout with an outboard – from the riverbank on Jalan Sudirman is a great way to spend a morning (Rp15,000 per hour). Passing castnet fishermen and Bugis homes with filigree flared roof adornments and tall stilts along the river, the lake unfolds suddenly in front of the boat, a vast, open space. This is where you'll start to see Tempe's renowned **birdlife**: terns, white egrets, long-legged stilts, black ibis, spoonbills and herons all hunt food in their own fashion, some using the bamboo walls of **fish farms** as perches. These farms are Danau Tempe's equivalent of fields, the villagers first gathering huge mats of floating aquatic grasses, which attract fish with shade and food. The mats are initially contained in loose-sided bamboo pens, which are tightened up after a week or two to prevent fish escaping; trapped fish are then left to grow fat on the grasses before harvesting.

In amongst all this is the floating village of **Salo Tengah**, a group of some dozen bamboo, rattan and thatch homes built on buoyant platforms of bamboo, the houses tethered as protection from shifting winds, though the whole village might move in the face of a storm or floods. These dangers are averted by **flags** on the roof, with yellow offering protection from flooding, white from storms, and red from fire. Tours (see p.903) will usually include a visit to a home at Salo Tengah, something you should not otherwise do without an invitation.

Parepare to Mamuju

With abrupt limestone escarpments in the background, the fine road heading north of Makassar and Maros runs inexorably up towards the Torajan highlands in the north of the province. Routes diverge some 150km along at **Parepare**, southern Sulawesi's second largest port, the point at which most people continue northeast to Rantepao and Tanah Toraja; continue northwest along the coast, however, and you'll find transport ascending from **Polewali** to the less-travelled side of the highlands at Mamasa (see p.906), and some unspoilt coastal scenery before the road terminates at **Mamuju**, a Mandar fishing town. **Buses** to Parepare and Polewali depart from Makassar's Terminal Panaikang at least until early afternoon, or you can also reach Parepare on local transport from Sengkang.

Parepare

Somewhat earthquake-prone, **PAREPARE** inevitably invites comparisons with its sister city Makassar, five hours to the south. Sharing similar locations on west-facing harbours, in fact the two couldn't differ more in character, and Parepare's lack of both sights and the manic atmosphere of Makassar make it a far friendlier spot to spend an evening mingling with the crowds. This quiet pace is slightly at odds with Parepare's position as a bottleneck for highway traffic from all over Sulawesi, and belies the importance of the city's **port**, which connects Parepare to multiple destinations in Java and Kalimantan.

Overlooked by dry hills and with the sea immediately west, central Parepare is a small grid of narrow streets and mildewed colonial buildings with cartwheel rims sunk into the plasterwork forming decorative motifs. Jalan Panggir Laut and Jalan Andi Cammi both follow the shore, with Jalan Hasanuddin and Jalan Baumassepe parallel and further inland. Jalan Baumassepe runs south past a broad **sports field**, out of the centre, and down to the Makassar highway, while Jalan Hasanuddin bypasses the very Islamic-looking **Mesjid Raya** before becoming northern Jalan Baso Patompo.

Buses from Rantepao and Makassar arrive 2km south of town at the **Terminal Induk** (known locally as Terminal Lumpue); catch a "Balai Kota" pete-pete to the centre. Transport from Sengkang or Polewali uses the eastern **Mapade** and northern **Kilometre Dua** terminals respectively. The **port** and **Pelni office** are obligingly more central on Jalan Andi Cammi, with ticket agents and blackboard schedules for alternative maritime services on Jalan Baso Patompo.

Parepare's **accommodation** includes the *Hotel Gandaria*, Jl Baumassepe 395 (Ⓣ0421/21093; ❷), which is friendly though nothing special, offering rooms with fan or air-con; they have now opened a second branch at Jl Samparaja 4 (Ⓣ0421/22971) which is smarter, quieter and charges the same prices. Less appealing, despite an elegant colonial exterior, *Hotel Siswa*, Jl Baso Patompo 3 (Ⓣ0421/21374; ❷), has nice staff and some air-con rooms, but the budget rooms with fans are very grubby.

The breezy seafront and harbour are picturesque in the late afternoon, with plenty of prahu and the occasional bigger passenger ferry or cargo ship in dock. Further out are huge **fishing platforms** built of giant bamboo poles, and three-pole frames with nets underneath and their owners patiently waiting above to haul in the catch. A prahu **shipyard** – mostly dealing in repairs – hides off the northern end of Jalan Panggir Laut, where there's also a popular **night market** with stocks of shoes, fruit, toys, cakes and seafood – check out tuna, shining like muscular torpedoes, and multi-hued dorado. Karaoke nightclubs and cheap **warung** dot the area, with excellent chargrilled fish and giant prawns at the black-glassed *Restaurant Asia*, and the less formal, open-fronted *Warung Sedap*, next to each other and opposite the *Hotel Siswa* on Jalan Baso Patompo. Sort out **money** at the BNI (with a Cirrus/Maestro ATM) on Jalan Veteran, north of the sports field; rates at the moneychanger on Jalan Hasanuddin aren't especially good, but they're open late, closing briefly for evening prayers. Your accommodation can advise on **onward transport**; as an alternative to slogging out to the terminals, some services can be hailed as they pass through the centre, and night buses to Makassar and Tanah Toraja accumulate around the *Hotel Siswa* in the afternoon.

Polewali, Majene and Mamuju

Northwest of Parepare, the coastal road and buses continue for 250km via Polewali and Majene to Palu in Sulawesi Tengah; there are plans to stretch the bitumen all the way through too, though currently the road remains extremely rough along most of its length. Two hours from Parepare, **POLEWALI** is the administrative capital and springboard for the **Mamasa region** (see below); the town's amenities cluster in two separate satellites, though all essentials are in the southern section, where the highway runs through as Jalan Ahmad Yani. Here you'll find warung and the delightful *Hotel Melati* (Ⓣ0428/21075; ❷), 500m along the main road from where transport departs for Mamasa.

Pinched between steep mountain sides and the sea, the coastal road beyond Polewali traverses the beautiful homeland of the **Mandar**, who, like the more outgoing Bugis, are famed shipbuilders and fishermen. They have a capital of sorts in the small town of **MAJENE**, whose sea wall and attached boatyards are worth a wander, with pre-Islamic **graves** sporting unusual headstones in the nearby village of **Cillallang**, and beds at *Wisma Cahaya* (Ⓣ0422/21105; ❷) on Jalan Rahman. Beyond Majene, the seascapes continue to where the best part of the road evaporates at **MAMUJU**, though few find the scenery an adequate reason to make the long haul to this hot, disappointing backwater town.

Mamasa and around

Cocooned in a cool, isolated valley 1200m up in the mountains above Polewali, the **Mamasa region** – also known as **Western Toraja** – comes as a pleasant surprise. A landscape of terraced hills and rice terraces make for fairly easy hiking along narrow paths to a huge number of traditional villages, most of which feature extraordinary architecture and noticeably friendly people. Though culturally similar to their eastern neighbours in Tanah Toraja (see p.910), Mamasa is a far poorer district and its heritage is much lower-key; consequently, the hordes of foreigners are absent, and the area is welcoming without catering overly to mass tourism.

The only settlement of any size in the valley is **Mamasa**, reached either along a two- to four-day hiking trail from Tanah Toraja (see p.910) or **by road** from the coast via Polewali, covered by buses from Makassar and Rantepao. Vehicles also originate in Polewali itself, leaving whenever full; opt for a bus if possible, as minibuses are very cramped, and mechanically on their last legs. The 95-kilometre road is steep and sometimes closed by landslides but otherwise fine, and the trip from the coast takes five hours on a good day.

Mamasa

MAMASA is a spacious village of wooden houses beside Sungai Mamasa, where electricity and telephones are still recent arrivals. The **marketplace** and most amenities are along Jalan Ahmad Yani, with everything else – homes bordered by roses and hibiscus, a few stores selling bananas, soap powder and chillies, and a coffee-roasting plant – scattered around the perimeter of a large and unkempt **football field** where dogs and stunted horses sport in the morning. A **mosque** sits in the shadows between the market and river, but Mamasa is predominantly Christian, and a white stone **church** dominates the slope above town; from up here Mamasa's few-score buildings sit on the edge of a sprawl of paddy-fields and bamboo thickets. The twice-weekly **market** on Thursday and Sunday is Mamasa's sole organized entertainment, but it's a good one, with people from distant hamlets often dragging their wares – including the heavy, boldly coloured **sambu blankets**, for which Mamasa is famed – into town on horseback. Locals know what Westerners will pay and seldom haggle, even if you hike out to the villages where the blankets are made. To see some older pieces – including cloth from India, once regularly imported by coastal Bugis and believed to have influenced some local designs – visit the rather empty **museum of antiquities** (ask around for the caretaker with the key if it's not open; free), housed in the ostentatiously traditional house up the hill above town. On the way there you'll pass both the **tourist office** (Mon–Fri 8.30–11am) at Jl Sudirman 22, and the **post office** nearby at no. 33. There's an efficient if expensive **wartel** around the corner from the *Mantana Lodge*, and another at the end of Jalan Yani.

As if by decree, all **accommodation** in town charges Rp25,000 for a room, with only the slightly upmarket *Mantana Lodge* (☎0411/23558), around the corner from the market on Jalan Emy Salean, bending this rule slightly by offering its most expensive rooms (those with hot water) for Rp65,000. Clean, friendly and with the finest restaurant in Mamasa, this is currently the best value in town. For those who prefer a more homely option, the *Losmen Mini* offers cosy rooms in an old wooden house near the market on Jalan Ahmad Yani, while the scruffier *Guest House Toraja Mamasa Church*, at the top end of town on the road to Rantepao, is now rapidly going downhill. The former travellers' favourite, the *Losmen Marapan*, is currently closed for business; whether it will reopen, and in what form, is unknown.

For **food**, both *Mantana* and *Mini* serve Indonesian meals as good as any in town; *Rumah Makan Pada Idi*, opposite the bank on Jalan Yani, has coconut chicken or sates of low cost and unpredictable quality (it's sometimes excellent), while two warung dealing in coffee and cakes complete Mamasa's gastronomic possibilities. **Leaving**, there are two or three bemos back to Polewali every day (with the last one departing at around 2.30pm), a daily service to Makassar, and a thrice-weekly service straight to Rantepao (12hr; contact the Heryanto agency in Mamasa for details). Your accommodation can find out departure times and arrange a pick-up, or organize **horses** and **guides** for the trail to Tanah Toraja (see p.910).

Mamasa trails

Mamasa is surrounded by **walking trails**, allowing for hikes of anything between a couple of hours and three days or more. Most are a little demanding in places, as villages are set on isolated hillocks surrounded by terraced fields, all linked by muddy footpaths. Scenery aside, one of the big attractions here is **traditional houses**, similarly covered in carvings and adorned with buffalo horns like those in Tanah Toraja. Lacking the extreme roof angles and bamboo tiles typical of buildings further east, a few are large and clearly very old, adding immense character to the villages they adorn.

Home-made **maps** available from your accommodation in Mamasa are useful indicators of paths between villages, but they don't distinguish between easily discernible tracks and those completely invisible without local knowledge. Some trails return to Mamasa, others terminate south of town at various points along the Polewali road, such as the neglected open-air **hot springs** 3km south of town at **Mese Kada** – looking like a grubby swimming pool, but somewhere to relax with locals after a hard day out. Bemos run in both directions along the Polewali road (not all go as far as Polewali) at least until mid-afternoon, though you may have to wait a while. For day-trips you'll need footwear with a good grip, a torch, something to keep the rain off, food and drink, and a packet of cigarettes to share around; biros are good gifts for children, though they always ask for money or sweets. There are a few **campsites** if you plan to stay out overnight – in which case you'll need a pullover to keep out the chill – though it's more interesting to negotiate accommodation with locals.

The Loko circuit

There's a great four-hour **circuit from Mamasa** via **Loko**, involving much cross-country tracking. From Mamasa, cross the river to **Tusan**, a cluster of traditional thatched houses about fifteen minutes from Mamasa's market. A shed on the far side of the village provides panoramas south down the valley, distant mountains looming black and grey, peaks fringed in forestry plantations. Past here are some newish graves and two churches, 500m before **TONDOK BAKARU**, whose wobbly houses are said to be the oldest in the valley. The most interesting is towards the far end of village, a much-patched and restructured home under a twenty-metre roof covered in ironwood shingles – a sign of status – with elaborate, weather-worn carved panels of buffalo, geometric patterns, and birds.

Bearing left into a creaking bamboo grove after Tondok Bakaru, follow a path downhill, across a covered bridge, then uphill again to **Rantebonko**. At this point the Loko trail simply vanishes into the fields, and you'll need continual help to know which of the very narrow tracks to follow. But it's worth the effort: **LOKO** perches like an island on a hilltop, with fields descending straight off the eastern side into the valley, sacrificial stones fronting its heavily carved houses, buffalo horns adorning their front posts. Just outside Loko, a trail leads 8km west from the village to where **Mambulillin waterfall** tumbles off the hillside. Alternatively, continue south from Loko to Taupe, but the track is in no way clear and has some exhausting, if short, gradients. **TAUPE** itself is not that engrossing, though there's a huge meeting hall and a good lookout point. From here, there's a further 5km of weaving across paddy-fields to the Polewali road via **Osango**, situated on the main road 2km south of Mamasa, or a direct trail back to Mamasa which fizzles out midway, leaving you to choose your own path down the river, over an extremely basic bamboo bridge, and into town behind the market.

Around Rante Balla Kalua

Mamasa's most celebrated *sambu* weavers live southwest of town around the village of Rante Balla Kalua. Start by taking a bemo 9km down the Polewali road to **RANTE SEPANG**, where you'll see women working away on looms under the houses; cross Sungai Mamasa over a good suspension bridge and follow the path uphill for ten minutes to simply ornamented homes at **Sumua**. A kilometre further on, past **Tumangke**, eight **house graves** face west towards the hills – simple open wooden frames with aluminium roofs covering burial mounds, and strewn with offerings of cigarettes, betel nuts and bottles. Though these graves are traditional in style, one with carved images of the deceased, others display crucifixes. At this point the path bears right (ignore the left fork) to **RANTE BALLA KALUA**, a large village of fifty or more homes surrounded by tall trees at the upper end of a small valley; among thatched dwellings of split rattan and bamboo is a row of three fine old houses and accompanying rice barns adorned with buffalo horns, pig-jaws stacks, and drums. Weavers or their agents will find you, invite you to sit down and start bargaining, but are easy enough to refuse if you're not interested. A short walk downhill leads to the similar village of **BATARIRAK**, where you can stay in one impressive old building with dozens of ancestor carvings and horns. At this point, there are two alternatives to backtracking simply to Rante Sepang: either spending around ninety minutes – if you don't become thoroughly lost – following the usual obscure rice-field course northeast to **Lumbatu**, where a further hour will take you across to the Polewali road at Osango; or a similar length of time for a nice trail southeast of Batarirak, via more graves and buffalo-horn-bedecked houses at **Buntu Balla**, and back to the Polewali road some 14km from Mamasa at **Pena**.

Rambu Saratu and on to Tanah Toraja

Mamasa's easiest trek follows the vehicle road for 3km north from town to alternative accommodation and a splendid traditional house at Rambu Saratu, past postcard-pretty scenery of vivid green fields and mountain slopes receding into blues and greys. After about half an hour you'll see a turning west across the river to **KOLE** and the valley's best **accommodation** at *Mamasa Cottages* (❺), whose **hot springs** are technically guests-only. Another ten minutes and you're at **RAMBU SARATU** (also known as **Rante Buda**), a name meaning something like "a hundred possibilities", referring to the number of interconnected families in this village. The main building here is magnificent, easily the finest traditional house in the whole Mamasa district: the body is 25m long and the roof – supported by a huge pole where it stretches out over the forecourt – extends this considerably, with every possible space on the front wall intricately carved. The interior is partitioned into a small front room for greeting guests (look up and you'll see some odd antiques stashed in the rafters) opening into sleeping quarters and kitchen. Visitors are often encouraged to spend the night here by the caretaker and his wife, who speak some English.

Beyond Rambu Saratu, there's a **hiking trail** 70km east **to Bittuang** in **Tanah Toraja**, feasible either on foot or using ponies (Rp80,000 per day) to help carry your gear. The walk spreads comfortably over three days, with regularly spaced kampung along the way growing used to the trickle of foreign faces, the homestays charging around Rp25,000 for room and board. Following the road north past Rambu Saratu to **Timbaan** (27km from Mamasa), most of the first day is spent climbing steadily through pleasant rural scenes against a backdrop of low terraced hills, though the last 8km after **Pakassasan** features a pass through the range with patches of forest. The next day follows the trail across two rivers (with a good swimming spot 12km along at the second) before a steep stretch to **PONDING** (40km), a possible first-day destination for the very fit. If you decide to end your trek here you can stay at *Ponding Peningapan* (❷), then catch the 8am 4WD (Rp10,000) to Bittuang. If you decide to walk on, 8km above Ponding lies **Paku** (48km), with more accommodation, while the final day enters pine plantations east of Paku, crosses another pass, then descends to the trailhead at **BITTUANG** (66km). Here you'll find more basic accommodation, a further two-day hiking track north to **Panggala** (see p.921), or a daily bemo (Rp10,000) for the forty-kilometre run to **Makale** (p.912).

Tanah Toraja

Some 250km north of Makassar, a steep wall of mountains marks the limits of Bugis territory and the entrance into the highlands of **Tanah Toraja**, a gorgeous spread of hills and valleys where fat buffalo wallow beside lush green paddy-fields and where the people enjoy one of Indonesia's most confident and vivid cultures. Ostensibly Christian, trappings of the old religion are still an integral part of Torajan life: everywhere you'll see extraordinary **tongkonan** and **alang**, traditional houses and rice barns, while the Torajan social calendar remains ringed with exuberant **ceremonies** involving pig and buffalo sacrifice. All this is easy to explore, even on a brief visit, as Torajans are masters at promoting their culture, and encourage outsiders to experience their way of life. With straightforward access, Tanah Toraja is planted firmly on the agenda of every visitor to Sulawesi, though tour groups tend to concentrate on key sites, and it's not difficult to find more secluded corners and spend an afternoon chatting, or day hiking, in places that see far fewer Western faces.

Tanah Toraja's main towns are the district capital of **Makale**, and larger **Rantepao**, 18km further north along the Sungai Sadan valley. Rantepao's range of services make it the favoured base for tourists, the bulk of whom descend for the major **festival season** between July and September, though the only really quiet time is from February to perhaps May. Expect hot days

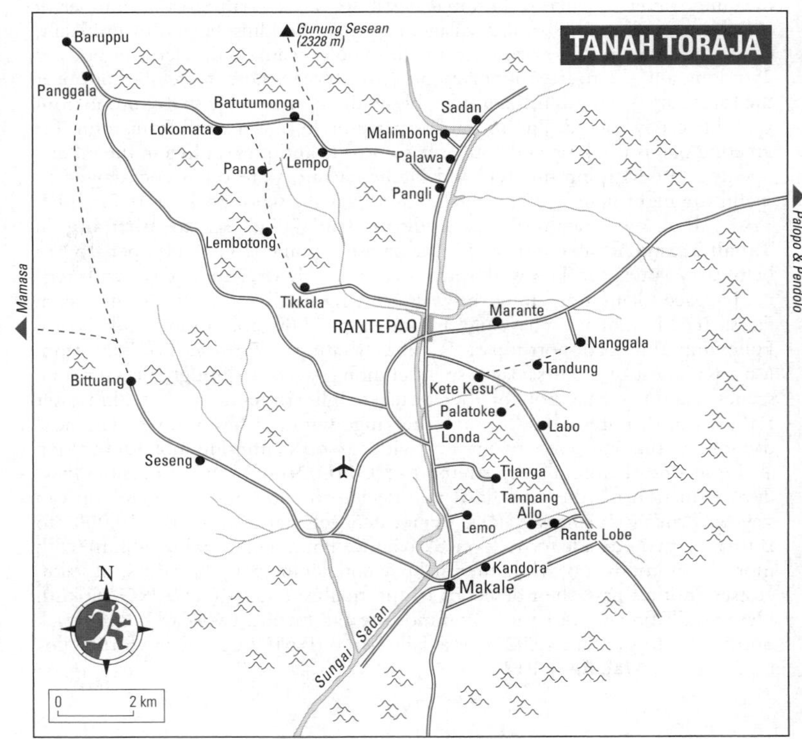

The Torajans

Anthropologists place Torajan origins as part of the Bronze Age exodus from Vietnam. However, Torajans themselves claim their ancestors descended from heaven by way of a stone staircase, which was later angrily smashed by the creator **Puang Matua** after his laws were broken. These laws became the root of **aluk todolo**, the way of the ancestors, which at its most basic divides the world into **opposites** associated with **directions**: north for gods, south for humanity, east for life, and west for death. Rather than an overall Torajan state, each kampung had its own hereditary leaders (**class** remains markedly important in Torajan society), and achieved fame through the ferocity of its blowpipe-toting warriors. Fortified villages were positioned on hilltops as protection against **raiding parties** seeking heads and captives – the latter kept as slaves or sacrificed at funerals.

Not entirely isolated from the outside world – the need for coffee and slaves fuelled lasting trade, intermarriage and warfare between the Torajans and Bugis – Tanah Toraja managed to avoid contact with Europeans until the twentieth century. In 1905 the Dutch ordered Sulawesi's leaders to recognize Holland as their sovereign state, treating any refusals as a declaration of war. Torajans were amongst the many dissenters, the warlord **Pong Tiku** of Baruppu holding out for two years before being captured and executed. The new rulers introduced Christianity, which has proved increasingly popular since the 1970s, though if you've just spent the day visiting freshly built tongkonan or at a funeral watching buffalo being sacrificed, it seems at first that *aluk* still underpins Torajan life. In fact, only a fraction of Torajans now follow the old religion, the strict practice of which was prohibited after headhunting and raunchy life-rites proved unacceptable to colonial and nationalist administrations. Though **to minaa** – the Torajan priesthood – still set the agricultural calendar and officiate at ceremonies, festivals have been largely stripped of their religious meanings to become social events, a chance to display wealth and status and reinforce secular rather than spiritual ties.

and cool nights; there is a "dry" season between April and October, but this is relative only to the amount of rain at other times, so bring non-slip walking boots and a waterproof jacket or umbrella. **Moving around**, there are endless opportunities for hiking between villages, and a range of roads and vehicles spanning out across the hills above Makale and Rantepao, though surfaces tend to be rough and travel's rather slow.

Getting to Tanah Toraja

Tanah Toraja is known as **Tator** in the local idiom, and you should look for this on transport timetables. At the time of writing there are no **flights** to Makale, and the surest way to Tanah Toraja is by **bus**, with Makale and Rantepao connected to points all over Sulawesi. From Makassar, buses leave day and night from Terminal Panaikang, the good road and range of coaches making the eight-hour journey fairly comfortable. First following the lowland plains, the road starts climbing about 70km north of Parepare at aptly named **ENREKANG** (Place to Ascend): not only does Sulawesi's highest peak, **Bulu Rantemario**, rise 3455m to the east, but this is also the site of the mythical celestial stairway linking the earth to the heavens – the remains are now known as "Porn Mountain" from the shape of its rock formations. Sixty kilometres further on, the road levels out at Makale before heading up along the Sadan valley for the final 18km to Rantepao.

Makale and around

MAKALE is a small town studded with churches and administrative offices set around a large pond and public square. Jalan Merdeka enters from the south into the square, while Jalan Pong Tiku exits north from the pond towards Rantepao; a sprinkling of monuments include a model of the Eiffel Tower welcoming the ubiquitous French package groups to Tanah Toraja, and an equine statue of Pong Tiku. Every six days, Makale's large **market** fires up after about 9am, drawing people from all over southern Tanah Toraja to buy pigs, jerry cans of palm wine and other necessities. Long-distance traffic continues to Rantepao, and there's little reason to stop overnight here, but if you fancy a change or simply miss the last bemo onwards at some point, Makale's **accommodation** includes the inexpensive *Losmen Litha* (ⓣ0423/22009; ❷), right on the square at Jl Pelita 97 (also the agent for buses back south), and the better-value *Wisma Bungin* (❷) at Jalan Nusantara 35. Up near the mosque, the nasi campur-orientated *Idaman* is the cleanest **place to eat**. Moving on, **bemos** to Rantepao and other destinations – including **Bittuang**, the trailhead for the three-day walk west to Mamasa – leave the square whenever full between dawn and dusk.

Villages along an eight-kilometre road **east of Makale** offer a quick introduction to Tanah Toraja, and are far less visited than better-known sites between here and Rantepao. A couple of kilometres from Makale, look for **hanging graves** and the remains of a hillfort of doubtful vintage on cliffs at **KANDORA**, while a track leading north after some 5km leads to some oddly shaped **megaliths** at **RANTE LOBE**, and more hanging graves with **tau-tau** (statues of the dead) at **TAMPANG ALLO**. For more about these features, see pp.918–919.

For those who really want to get away from it all, or who are looking for a rural base for their trekking, 6km south along the road from Makale to Makassar, a turn-off left leads along a stony track for about an hour to the *Kandora Mountain Lodge* (ⓣ0811/464228, ⓦwww.toraja.net/walda; ❶). Built by European NGOs and with some of the income generated benefiting the local community, the accommodation is good value; the cheapest rooms come with a simple mat, blanket and pillow, and meals are also available. Bookings must be made before arriving.

Rantepao

RANTEPAO is a prosperous market town on the rocky banks of **Sungai Sadan**, home to both the Sadan Toraja and, for half the year, swarms of foreigners. However unfavourably you view this, Rantepao has excellent facilities and local contacts, while a couple of sites within walking distance will keep you interested for as long as it takes to orientate yourself and decide in which direction to head off into the countryside. While you're doing this, the town offers intrinsically Torajan scenes: chilly mornings with men wrapped in blankets and shivering, smoking furiously; smartly dressed women with Bibles tucked under their arms off to church on Sunday; teenagers gathering in single-sex groups under streetlamps in the evening, watching each other furtively.

Arrival, orientation and information

Rantepao stretches for 1km along the eastern bank of the Sadan, just where the river bends sharply in from the east to flow south down the valley. The central **crossroads** is marked by a miniature tongkonan on a pedestal: north from here, Jalan Mapanyukki is a short run of souvenir shops, bus agents and restau-

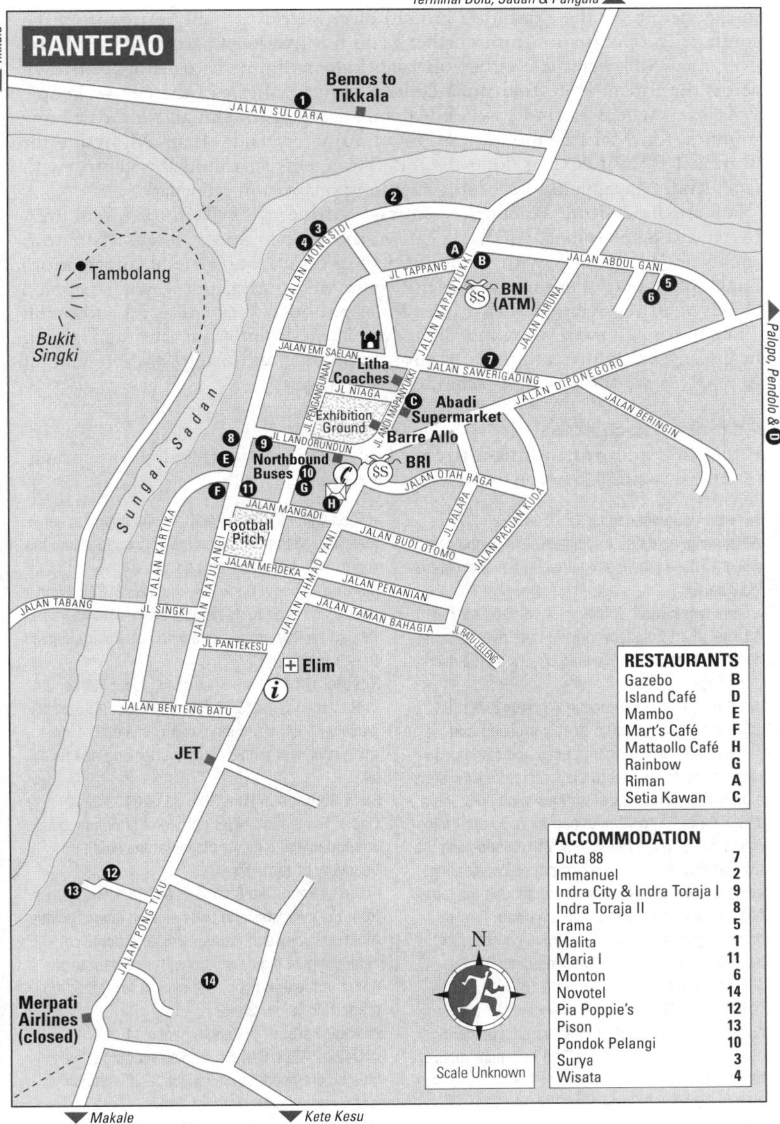

rants; Jalan Ahmad Yani points south towards Makale past more of the same to become Jalan Pong Tiku; east is Jalan Diponegoro and the Palopo road; while westerly Jalan Landorundun heads over to the riverside along the bottom edge of a large **exhibition ground**, covered in forlorn-looking ceremonial platforms.

Arriving, long-distance buses will either drop you off at accommodation, or in the vicinity of the exhibition ground or crossroads, as will **bemos** from the south or Palopo. Bemos from northern and northwestern parts of Toraja, however, may well terminate either on Jalan Suloara, immediately north of town across the Sadan, or at **Terminal Bolu**, 2.5km northeast of the centre. People walk everywhere around town, but bemos leave Jalan Ahmad Yani every few minutes for Makale, and just as often from riverside Jalan Mongsidi for Terminal Bolu. **Leaving**, long-distance bus agents surround the centre, with Jalan Andi Mapanyukki becoming one long bus station after dark.

For **information**, Rantepao's **tourist office** is at Jl Ahmad Yani 62A (Mon–Fri 8am–4pm; ⓣ0423/21277), on the Makale side of town. Many tour agents and restaurants with guide services also give out general information, but don't expect them to divulge the venue of a festival unless you've agreed to buy their services. Travel Treasure Maps put out a very colourful and useful "Tanah Toraja" **map**, showing distances, villages, important sites and giving heaps of local information; the Abadi supermarket and *Setia Kawan* restaurant (see p.916) are the cheapest places to buy a copy.

Accommodation

Rantepao's **accommodation** is varied, plentiful, and scattered all over town, often down side lanes you'd otherwise overlook.

Duta 88 Jl Sawerigading 12 ⓣ0423/23477. Welcoming, beautiful traditional-style bungalows, albeit a little squashed together, in an ideal central location. ❸

Wisma Immanuel Jl Mongsidi 16 ⓣ0423/21416. A large smart house overlooking the river, offering decent rooms with hot water, but it's a little overpriced. ❸

Hotel Indra Jl Londurundun 63 ⓣ0423/21583, ⓕ21547. Chain of three closely grouped mid-range hotels, whose room prices and standards rise the closer you get to the river. *Indra City* offers a good deal (❸) but the staff are a bit cold; *Indra Toraja I* (❹–❺) next door and *Indra Toraja II* (also called *Indra Toraja River View*, ❺), overlooking the river across the road, are overpriced considering what this will get you elsewhere, though the latter has nice riverside rooms and a garden, Torajan dance nights, and a treasure trove collection of paperback novels in various languages.

Wisma Irama Jalan Abdul Gani 16 ⓣ0423/21371. A big, tiled, blancmange-pink palace, clean and with a huge garden, bordering budget to mid-range prices. The first-floor rooms have hot water. ❷

Wisma Malita Jl Suloara 110 ⓣ0423/21011. Extremely tidy, well-run wisma, deserving more custom than it actually receives. The upstairs rooms have hot water, and the price includes breakfast. ❷

Maria I Jl Sam Ratulangi 23 ⓣ0423/21165. Quiet, medium-sized hotel with pretensions of grandeur built around a central courtyard and furnished with cupboards stuffed with antiques and junk. The ekonomi singles are very good value; the rooms with hot water less so. ❷–❸

Monton Jl Abdul Gani 14A, ⓣ0423/21675. Similar in size and style to its neighbour the *Wisma Irama*, though slightly prettier and with hot water supplied to every room. ❸

Novotel Off the Kete Kesu road, about 3km south of Rantepao ⓣ0423/27000, ⓕ21666. A luxurious place with full-sized tongkonan "chalets", swimming pool, and tennis court overlooking rice fields. ❼

Pia's Poppies Jl Pong Tiku 27 ⓣ0423/21121. One of Rantepao's older upmarket offerings: quiet, comfortable and nicely placed at the southern boundary of town. ❸

Pison Jl Pong Tiku 8 ⓣ & ⓕ0423/21344. Across from *Pia's Poppies* and fairly similar, though a little more spacious and formal; ordinary rooms set behind a nice big courtyard with rice barn to sit under in the afternoon. The singles for Rp25,000 are terrific value. ❷–❸

Pondok Pelangi Jl Pengangunan 11 ⓣ0423/21753. Central, backstreet homestay; a little bit cramped, but fair value, and with hot water and a fine restaurant. ❸

Surya Jl Mongsidi 36 ⓣ0423/21312. Next door to the more popular *Wisma Wisata* and, though a good place, now faring badly by comparison, being more expensive and in need of refurbishment. ❷

Wisma Wisata Jl Mongsidi 40 ⓣ423/21746. The cheapest place in town, with smart rooms overlooking the river. ❶

The Town

Away from the couple of main streets, west of the exhibition ground, **stalls** supply locals' day-to-day needs – heavy stone rice mortars, plastic chairs, noodles, fish (couriered up from the coast by motorbike every morning), fresh noodles and tempeh, and chillies, with a warung or two for fried bananas and coffee. Further south, there's a **football pitch** off Jalan Mederka, and games seem to have taken up where warfare left off – weekend matches draw huge crowds, whose victory roars and cheers of encouragement can be heard miles away. Rantepao's main **market** – the biggest in Tanah Toraja and located 2.5km northeast of the centre at Terminal Bolu – is a must, even if they usually bore you; where else could you pick up a bargain buffalo then celebrate your purchase with a litre or two of palm wine? As at Makale, it operates on a six-day cycle, and an entry fee of Rp6000 is demanded of foreigners – you could argue the point that you're there to buy, not sightsee. Around the edge of the market are various woodcarvers and carpenters, also worth a look; one specializes in ornamental buffalo heads, another in parts of rice barns.

An easy hour's **walk from Rantepao** follows Jalan Singki west across the river, and then bears right into the fields along the Sadan's west bank. Across the paddy, hamlets such as **Pa'bontang** are marked by stately tongkonan, but look for where a white mausoleum at **TAMBOLANG** stands below a cliff-side niche sporting rows of tau-tau and coffins. It's all a bit neglected, but perhaps more authentic than other sites which have been smartened up for tourists. A path leads briefly south from here and then climbs through woodland to the summit of **Bukit Singki** and a view over Rantepao; the top – the remains of a lookout post of Pong Tiku vintage – is terraced in dangerously loose stones, and planted with cassava and papaya.

Eating, drinking and entertainment

Rantepao spoils you for **food**, with everything from market snacks – try *soko* for breakfast, rice steamed in banana leaf, shredded coconut and *sambal* – to warung and restaurants serving reasonable Western fare. Most places along Jalan Ahmad Yani and Jalan Andi Mapanyukki cater exclusively to tourists, stay open late, and can produce Torajan specialities such as *papiong* (meat grilled in bamboo tubes), *mengrawang* (sate) and *bale tongkonan* (fish cooked in banana leaves), with a couple of hours' warning. Torajans have two favourite beverages: locally grown arabica **coffee**, and **balok** palm wine, both a vital part of the daily routine. *Balok* is traditionally sold frothing in bamboo tubes, though the festival season sees markets stocked with five-litre jerry cans to keep up with demand, and its flavour – somewhere between lager and Alka-Seltzer – is actually quite pleasant.

Eating aside, Rantepao offers little **nightlife**. The *Cancer* nightclub-cum-karaoke bar on Jalan Andi Mappanyukki is very seldom open, and is usually empty when it is, while Rantepao's cinema closed down years ago and they're still awaiting a replacement.

Restaurants

Gazebo Jl Andi Mappanyukki 96. One of the finest places in town, with a broad and reasonably priced menu and some pleasant outdoor seating. A fruit dessert is usually given free at the end of your meal.

Island Café 3km north of Rantepao past Tallunglipu ("Pangli" bemo). A riverside open-air restaurant, with a mix of Indonesian and pricey Western dishes.

Mambo Jalan Sam Ratulangi. Currently the most popular place in town and the centre of Rantepao's expat community (the local Hash House Harriers meet here regularly), with good food, a huge Western/Chinese/Indonesian menu to choose from, and beer in frosted glasses.

Mart's Café Jl Sam Ratulangi 44a. You can mock the pretensions of the chef at this mid-range restaurant, who arranges all the chips on your plate like petals on a flower, but you can't knock the Indonesian/Chinese/Western menu or the food itself.

Mattaollo Café Jl A Yani 87. Reasonably priced place serving Torajan staples and a delicious toffee caramel.

Rainbow At *Pondok Pelangi*, Jl Pengangunan 11. Slow service, but a fine kitchen, if a little over-priced; try the garlic beans and chewy buffalo sate.

Riman Jl Andi Mapanyukki 113. Low-priced Indonesian and Torajan menu, with friendly staff (though don't show any interest in hiring a guide or you'll never get rid of them); their chicken with lime sauce is excellent.

Setia Kawan Jl Andi Mapanyukki 32. Slightly pricey Indonesian-Chinese place, but the roomy, cool setting makes it a favourite spot for Westerners to sit for an hour over a coffee or cold drinks and peruse the newspapers.

Listings

Banks and exchange The BRI and BNI on Jalan Ahmad Yani offer good exchange on currency and travellers' cheques (but ignore their seldom-updated display boards), and the latter also now has an ATM installed. Most tour agencies and larger hotels can change money too, though Rantepao's official moneychangers are not reliable, often renegotiating rates or revealing substantial service fees after you've signed your travellers' cheques.

Buses For Parepare and Makassar, use Litha, across from the Abadi supermarket on Jalan Andi Mapanyukki, who run basic, comfortable and luxury buses (daily 7.30am–9pm). Departures north to Pendolo, Tentena, Poso and Palu are handled by a small depot just west along Jalan Landorundun. Mamasa buses come and go with demand, though currently there are three per week. There is no vehicle road directly between Rantepao and Mamasa, and Tator–Mamasa buses travel via Parepare and Polewali.

Ferries Agents along Jalan Andi Mappanyukki sell Pelni ferry tickets for ferries from all ports in Sulawesi, though at a huge mark-up.

Internet access There are a couple of places on the main drag now offering an internet service, including Tomindo (Jl A Yani 75), but at the moment all services are connected via Makassar and thus are expensive (Rp2400 per minute).

Hospital The best doctors are at Elim Hospital, Jalan Ahmad Yani.

Massage Perfect after a long trek, Manaman Spa at Wisma Tana Bua (Jl Palopo 43) offers a variety of massages, including a 2hr massage with "traditional lulur body scrub" for Rp120,000.

Pharmacies Rantepao's pharmacies, on Jalan Andi Mapanyukki, have very old stock.

Post office Jl Ahmad Yani 111. Daily 7am–6pm.

Souvenirs Shops on the eastern side of exhibition grounds along Jalan Andi Mapanyukki offer carefully aged items clearly made for the tourist market – model tongkonan, bamboo flutes, local necklaces and headbands in orange, black and white beads, plenty of porcelain and coins, plus *ikat* and sarongs from Flores and Bali. Barre Allo has locally made knives with fine wooden scabbards and hilts, and also the best carvings, including panels salvaged from old buildings. Also recommended are Todi, an ikat weaving centre and shop at Jl A Yani 117, and the R.Bugis Gallery on Jalan Abdul Gani, named after an artist whose work is sometimes exhibited in the *Novotel* hotel.

Telephone and fax Rantepao's exchange on Jalan Ahmad Yani opens 8am–late. Toraja Permai Tours and Travel, next to the Abadi supermarket on Jalan Andi Mapanyukki, are useless as a tour agent but have good phone rates for local and international calls.

Tour agents Best of the many available operators is JET, Jl Pong Tiku 31 ⓣ0423/21145, ⓕ23227.

Touring Tanah Toraja

There's a morbid attraction to many of Tanah Toraja's sights, which feature ceremonial animal slaughter, decaying coffins and dank mausoleums spilling bones. Fortunately, the people and landscape are very much alive, and there's nothing depressing about spending time here, nor are these key sights obligatory viewing. There's a good deal to be said for just picking somewhere on the edge of the map and hiking off into the distance. Torajaland's sixty-odd villages make it impossible to give a comprehensive rundown on the area, though almost all have tongkonan and rice barns, and you might find yourself at any number of otherwise insignificant places if a funeral is in progress. View those listed below simply as a starting point, and note that **entry fees** of around

Rp6000 are becoming common at sites around Rantepao. If you overdose on landscape and culture, try a two-day **white-water** excursion through the 1500-metre-deep Sadan Gorge with Sobek Tour (Torango Buya, Jalan Pongtiku, Rantepao; ⓣ0423/21336, ⓔtoranggo@indosat.net.id; US$155 inclusive), or on the more placid Maulu (US$45 for half a day). Indo Sella, Jalan Suloara (ⓣ0423/25210) offer a one-day version.

One of the decisions in Tanah Toraja is whether you'll need a **guide**. If you speak a little Indonesian, they are seldom necessary for hiking or visiting villages – though outsiders should really have an **invitation** to visit a ceremony, which guides with connections can provide. As more participants means greater honour, however, it's also possible to turn up at an event and hang around the sidelines until somebody takes it upon themselves to act as your host. Guides can add considerable depth to the sights, but they vary in quality, and most speak passable English; almost all, however knowledgeable, are pushy for gifts for themselves, and can churn out a mash of semi-anthropological interpretations. If nobody else you meet offers their services, accommodation, tour agents and some restaurants in Rantepao can all organize guides from around Rp60,000 a day. With luck, however, you'll meet people during your stay who will offer to show you around as a friend.

Bemos to just about everywhere originate at Rantepao's Terminal Bolu, though those heading south can be hailed on Jalan Ahmad Yani. While it's possible to flag down a constant stream of bemos on the Makale road, you may find only one a day heading to remote corners such as Baruppu, so the further you're going, the earlier you should start looking for transport. Accommodation and tour agents also rent out **bicycles** (Rp30,000 a day), **motorbikes** (Rp60,000), or **minibus and drivers** (Rp150,000) if you don't want to rely on public transport. **Hikers** heading off to villages should carry cigarettes, if only to initiate conversations along the way. Many places are close enough for day-trips, or at least to catch a bemo out to and hike back, though you'll also find a few homestays around the countryside, or you may be offered private accommodation – in which case, it's polite to offer further small gifts.

Rantepao to Makale

Tanah Toraja's most famous sites lie off the eighteen-kilometre Rantepao–Makale road, worthy attractions despite the flow of tourists. Just south of Rantepao, a concrete statue of a pied buffalo marks the four-kilometre road east to four much-restored tongkonans at **KETE KESU** (Rp5000). The central one is said to be the oldest in the district, and it's a fine spot to get a first close look at the structure and decoration of tongkonan and alang, built facing each other as "husband" and "wife". An adjacent rante ground sports a dozen megaliths, the tallest about 3m high, with a path leading up the hill past hanging and no-longer-hanging coffins mortised into the side of the truncated peak. Some coffins are shaped as animals, with fallen skulls and bones artfully arranged, and tau-tau of various vintages are protected by a grille in a suitable overhang. Less-visited sites beyond Kete Kesu include views from the clifftop village of **PALATOKE** (9km from Rantepao), whose hanging graves are said to have been positioned by a race whose gecko-like hands allowed them to climb up here without ladders.

Back on the Makale road, a signpost at 5km prompts you east towards **LONDA**, a fifteen-minute walk from the highway. A shaded green well underneath tall cliffs, overhung with a few coffins and a fantastic collection of very lifelike tau-tau, Londa boasts two **caves** whose entrances are piled high with more coffins and bones, all strewn with offerings of tobacco and booze.

Ceremonial rites and wrongs

Witnessing a traditional ceremony is what draws most visitors to Tanah Toraja, particularly during the "peak festival season" in the agriculturally quiet period from June to September. The atmosphere at these events is very sociable, and Torajans are tolerant of crowds of Westerners invading proceedings with long lenses poking all over the place, but there are some things to bear in mind. Take a **gift** for your hosts – a carton of cigarettes, or a jerry can of *balok* – and hand it over when they invite you to sit down with them. Gift-giving is an integral part of Torajan ceremonies, an expression of the reciprocal obligations binding families and friends, and close relations of the hosts may contribute a brace of buffalo or pigs. Do not sit down uninvited, or take photos without asking (though permission is invariably given); dress modestly, and wear **dark clothing** for funerals – a black T-shirt with blue jeans is perfectly acceptable, as are thong sandals. Most importantly, spend **time** at any ceremony you attend, as too many tourists just breeze in and out, bored by the long lulls in the proceedings. Instead, use them to play cards, drink coffee and *balok*, and just gossip with your hosts as *papiong* pop in the background. In this regard, small affairs are more intimate and rewarding, though large funerals are certainly splendid.

Ceremonies are divided into *rambu tuka*, or **smoke ascending** (associated with the east and life), and *rambu solo*, **smoke descending** (west and death). All *rambu tuka* events begin in the morning, while the sun is rising, and *rambu solo* start after noon, when the sun is falling westwards. A typical *rambu tuka* ceremony is the **dedication of a new tongkonan** (family house). Tongkonan design is credited to Puang Matua, the upcurving roof symbolizing the shape of the sky – though, as an example of how modern Torajans have reinterpreted their beliefs in the light of anthropology, some say that roof shape derives from when ancestral Torajans used their overturned boats as shelter when they first arrived in Sulawesi. It would be hard to overstate the tongkonan's symbolic importance: for example, they face north, so the front door is a gate between human and divine worlds, and are aligned north–south, defining a borderline between life and death. **Carved panels** of patterns, cockerels, buffalo, horses and birds all have their own meanings, as do the red, black, white and yellow **colours** used. And, if nothing else, a traditionally built tongkonan is a sure sign of wealth – even the simplest costs upwards of thirty million rupiah – and the lavishness of its dedication is a further indication of its owner's prestige: the ceremony is called **mangrara banua** if just pigs are sacrificed, and **merok** if buffalo are involved. Lasting a single day and not a huge event compared with a funeral, the dedication of a noble's house nonetheless draws a big slaughter and crowds.

The biggest of all Torajan ceremonies are **funerals**, the epitome of a *rambu solo* occasion. Known as **aluk to mate**, funerals are performed to send the spirit (which remains near the body after death) to **Puya**, the Torajan afterlife. The scale of the event is determined by the deceased's class, and – what with financing the event

Guides with pressure lamps (Rp7500) are a necessity for venturing inside the bat-ridden labyrinth, where tunnels slippery with guano weave off into the earth.

At around 7km from Rantepao, a trail heads up to a **swimming hole** in the forest at **Tilanga**, a refreshing target on a hot day. Around halfway to Makale, another road runs 1km east to **LEMO**, past a church curiously designed in the shape of a boat. Lemo is famous for the sheer number of its much-photographed tau-tau, set 30m up on a flat cliff-face; they're not as sophisticated as those at Londa, but are more expressive, staring mutely over the fields with arms outstretched. There are also several dozen square-doored mausoleums bored straight into the rock face, a type of burial site more common further north, and said to be a comparatively recent innovation.

and the need to assemble relatives from afar – invariably takes place long after death. Spread over several days, the ceremony is held in a special field, with purpose-built spectator accommodation erected around the perimeter, and two platforms or towers facing each other at either end, all decorated in gold, red and yellow trim. The funeral starts with the moving of the oval coffin from the south room of the deceased's house – where it will have lain since death – and parading it with much jostling and shouting to the platform, where photos of the dead are displayed. Pigs and **buffalo** provided by close family are trotted out too, and later dispatched to feed guests. Torajans measure their wealth in buffalo, spend hours every day grooming and washing their animals, and might save for years to buy a really fine one – much-coveted piebalds cost eight million rupiah or more. At the end of the first afternoon you'll see **buffalo fights**, *mapasi laga tedong*, where, amid much discreet betting, the buffalo are led up to face each other, heads raised and turned aside as if in scorn. Then they charge suddenly, spectators going wild and running in as close as possible before the loser turns tail and gallops off to whoops and jeers, scattering the crowd. Northeast of Rantepao, buffalo fights are followed by the all-male pursuit of **sisemba**, Torajan kick boxing, where pairs hold hands, using each other as pivots to execute cartwheeling kicks and belt the living daylights out of their opponents. Kicking the fallen is forbidden, but otherwise there are no "illegal" moves, and injuries are common.

The following day – or days, if it's a big funeral – is spent **welcoming guests**, who troop village by village into the ceremonial field, led by a noblewoman dressed in orange and gold, bearing gifts of *balok*, pigs trussed on poles, and buffalo. Formal introductions make everyone – including the tax inspectors at the gate – aware of how many people have come and what they've brought, thereby increasing the respect being paid to the deceased. **Ma'badong singing** starts up at some point, with a group in black forming a ring, and chanting a soulful song as they sway and move in a slow rotation, the ring growing as other mourners join in. The day after all the guests have arrived, the **major sacrifice** takes place: slaves can get away with just one buffalo, but the nobility must sacrifice at least 24, with 100 needed to see a high-ranking chieftain on his way. With their horns decorated with gold braid and ribbons, the buffalo are tied one by one to a post and their throats slit, the blood caught in bamboo tubes and used in cooking. Dogs prowl and flies swarm as the heads are stacked up and the meat hacked into chunks and distributed to guests, the *to minaa* calling out names and throwing pieces down from the second platform. Finally, the coffin is laid to rest in a west-orientated house-grave or rockface mausoleum, with a **tau-tau**, a life-sized wooden effigy of the deceased, positioned in a nearby gallery facing outwards, and – for the highest-ranking nobles only – a megalith raised in the village **rante ground** (ceremonial ground).

East to Nanggala, and north to Sadan

If you're pushed for time, you can see almost all the main features of Torajaland at **MARANTE**, a spread-out village 6km east from Rantepao on the Palopo road. Close to the road are a fine row of tongkonan, one with a monumentally carved dragon's head out the front; behind, a path leads to where tau-tau and weathered coffins face out over a river – some of the coffins are large and very old, adorned with dragon and buffalo motifs. **NANGGALA**, about 11km along the Palopo road and then 2km south, is a stately village whose dozen brilliantly finished tongkonan are a splendid sight. There's a very pleasant five-hour walk due west to Kete Kesu from here, via **Tandung** village, patches of pine forest and a couple of small lakes.

For something a bit different, spend a day making the slow haul from

Rantepao's bemo terminal **north to Sadan**. Seven kilometres along the way you pass **PANGLI**, famed for its *balok* and home village to the great nineteenth-century Torajan chief, **Pong Massangka**. Not much further, a rante ground with thirty upright stones marks the short track to **PALAWA**, a well-presented village whose tongkonan are embellished with scores of buffalo horns stacked up their tall front posts, while in the hills beyond the village are **babies' graves**, wooden platforms in the trees. Five kilometres more brings you to a fork in the road: east is **SADAN** itself, with another market every six days; west is riverside **MALIMBONG**, famous for its **ikat**, which you can watch being made.

Northwest to Batutumonga, Pangala and beyond

The area northwest of Rantepao surrounding **Gunung Sesean**, the region's highest peak, is quite accessible but not overly explored, and different in feel to the Torajan lowlands. There's a smattering of morning traffic about 17km to Lempo; the road climbs through semi-cultivated forest out onto hill terraces scattered with coffee bushes and house-sized boulders, some hollowed into mausoleums with heavily carved stonework around the doors. **LEMPO** has a great series of moss-ridden tongkonan; there are views off the three-kilometre road between here and Batutumonga, with **accommodation** in the area providing the perfect rural base. Before Batutumonga, a sign on the roadside points to basic bamboo rooms with meals included in the price at friendly *Mama Siska's* (❷); *Mentirotiku* (❸), a little further along and right on the road, is a smart, pretentious affair with an expensive restaurant overlooking the valley, and cosy accommodation in tongkonan or cabins. Around the corner is **BATUTUMONGA** itself, comprising a school, a church with tongkonan-like roof, a football pitch, village stores, and comfortable cabin/tongkonan **homestays** at *Londurundun* (❷), or the excellent-value *Betania's* (also known as *Mama Rina's*; ❷), where the price includes breakfast and dinner.

Gunung Sesean's 2328-metre **summit** can be reached in a couple of hours from Batutumonga; your accommodation place can point you to the nearest trails, which lead sharply up through a smudge of forest and onto open heath. All tracks converge at a south-facing ridge overlooking the Sadan valley and Rantepao far below, then continue climbing through the heath before plunging into thickets. The first peak brings you suddenly into the open again and is a splendid spot to stop, with swifts wheeling above your head and the main peak on your left usually tufted in cloud. It's another steep half-hour from here to the summit, with more vistas and a cliff dropping vertically away at your feet.

Another fine walk from Batutumonga can take you **back to Rantepao** in under four hours; take the road through Batutumonga until you see a sign to your right pointing down a broad stone trail to **PANA**. Towards the end of the village, concrete steps to the left of the path lead up the site of some very old **graves** set into the side of a huge rock, with baby graves located in a nearby tree; back on the main track, the next left after the graves brings you to a rante ground with four-metre-high **megaliths**. From here, the track continues; you may even find a bemo to Rantepao, but it's worth walking at least as far as **LEMBOTONG**, a kampung famed for its **blacksmiths**, with roadside forges ringing with hammering, the finished products hung up for sale out front. The remainder of the walk down to the flat fields below is less interesting, and you end up at **TIKKALA**, a nondescript spread of homes where you'll find bemos for the seven-kilometre ride back to Rantepao's Jalan Suloara.

The rest of the road northwest of Batutumonga is harder to cover. Six kilometres from Batutumonga, a massive boulder along the roadside at **LOKO-MATA** has become an apartment building for the dead, with about sixty mausoleums. It's another 15km from here to **PANGGALA**, the last place you could reach on scheduled public transport from Rantepao (about 3hr). A nice mountain village, there's well-organized **accommodation** and information available at *Wisma Sandro* (❷), with a two-day hiking track south to Bittuang on the Mamasa trail (see p.909). Ask for directions to Pong Tiku's **tomb**, rumoured to be nearby; his last stand against the Dutch was at the end of the road at **BARUPPU**, where remains of his fort can still be seen. The Dutch brought in cannon, which made short work of the Torajan defenders, who had only spears and tubes full of crushed chillies to spray into the faces of anyone scaling the walls. One story says that Pong Tiku escaped from Baruppu, but was later ambushed by the Dutch while attending his mother's funeral. He was executed in Rantepao in 1907 – shot while bathing, according to one tale, the only time he was without his magically bulletproof clothing.

Sulawesi Tenggara

The province of **Sulawesi Tenggara** is joined to the rest of Sulawesi by a crumpled mountain range that makes overland access impossible. South of the mountains, the flatter end of the peninsula breaks up into some sizeable islands, the largest being **Muna** and **Buton**. Muslim since the early seventeenth century, much of the region was governed by the powerful **Sultan of Wolio**, whose formidably defended royal complex survives at **Baubau** on Pulau Buton. Elsewhere, you'll find an undercurrent of pre-Islamic belief, which becomes tangible in rural areas such as **Mabolo** on Pulau Muna, where expressive **cave paintings** illustrate pagan times. There's also some scenery and an undervisited wetlands national park to soak up in passing, but for **scuba divers**, Sulawesi Tenggara's ultimate destination lies southeast of Pulau Buton, where the land fragments further into the Banda Sea as the **Tukangbesi group**, whose reefs are amongst the best in Indonesia.

The province's only **airport** is at its capital, **Kendari**, with two or three flights daily with Pelita and Merpati from Makassar. For around a tenth of the air fare, it seems sensible to travel by **ferry** from Bajoe (Watampone) to Sulawesi Tenggara's western port at **KOLAKA**, and then catch a Kijang for the 120-kilometre ride to Kendari – about a twelve-hour journey in all. But though the ferry crossing is none too bad, landing at Kolaka in the early hours of the morning to be loaded into the back of a suicidally driven Kijang for a five-hour ride is an experience to avoid. As alternatives, Kendari, **Raha** (on Pulau Muna) and Baubau are viable ports, with regular Pelni and freighter traffic to Makassar and up Sulawesi's eastern coast. **Getting around**, there's surprisingly good access throughout the province on local Kijang and bemos, with a daily air-con speedboat moving both ways between Kendari, Raha and Baubau. Food and accommodation are generally more **expensive** here than elsewhere in Sulawesi, and **currency exchange** is only possible in Kendari and Baubau, where it's a prolonged process – try and bring enough to see you through.

Kendari and around

Five hours by road from Kolaka on the eastern side of the mainland, **KENDARI** is Sulawesi Tenggara's largest settlement, though there's little of substance here. The city stretches along **Kendari Bay** with its two centres – western **Pasar Mandonga** and eastern **Kota** – linked by a seven-kilometre main road, which changes its name at every opportunity. Pasar Mandonga consists of a market, a cluster of businesses and a bemo terminal south of a large main-road **roundabout** along Jalan Silondae; Kota comprises a kilometre or two of the main road, with key services and another market, culminating at Kendari's **port**. If you don't arrive here, the **airport** is forty minutes southwest of Pasar Mandonga, and waiting taxis charge about Rp10,000 to anywhere in Kendari. **Kijangs from Kolaka** drop off about 8km west of Pasar Mandonga at **Puwutu** (Terminal Kolaka), where bemos frequently depart to town. Fixed-fare bemos run continually between Pasar Mandonga and Kota through the day, though the absence of clear orientation points along the main road makes finding destinations confusing at first – tell bemo drivers exactly where you want to go.

Accommodation places are spread all over Kendari. In Kota, the pick of the town's accommodation is *Hotel Cenderawasih*, where terrace units overlook the bay at (main road) Jl Diponegoro 42 (☎0401/321932; ❷). On the way to the airport, the *Hotel Aden* at Jl Yani 54 (☎ & ⓕ0401/390177; ❹) is new, smart but overpriced. West of Kota on the main road, *Kendari Beach Hotel*, Jl Hasanuddin 44 (☎0401/321988; ❸), offers cavernous, quietly mouldering, characterless air-con rooms, but its very reasonably priced **restaurant** and terrace bar are fine places to while away a sultry evening. Set back from Pasar Mandonga's traffic circle, *Wisma Duta*, Jl Silondae 1 (☎0401/321053; ❷–❸), has bungalow-style air-con rooms with a small garden. For somewhere **to eat** in Kota, try the *Ayam Goreng* on the main road, Jalan Sukarno; it's a typical, open-fronted Chinese place whose manager spends most of his time at his desk playing with a mountain of cashew nuts. Pasar Mandonga's options include the *Aden* on Jalan Silondae, for sit-down coffee and cream cakes, sponges, and sticky Bugis treats such as *lempar* (a mix of sago, palm sugar and coconut), and the *Marannu*, a flash and reasonably pricey Chinese restaurant also on Jalan Silondae at no. 24. For **entertainment**, the Hollywood Sineplex next to the *CFC* on Jalan Saranani, south of Jalan S Parman, shows mainly American movies with Indonesian subtitles, while the *Shooter* karaoke bar opposite the *Hotel Aden* is packed most nights.

Most of Kendari's **services** are in the Kota end of town; on Jalan Hatta you'll find the Telkom office, BNI **bank** with a Cirrus/Maestro ATM (a branch of the BII, with ATM, lies just south of the main roundabout at Madonga), and local cashew nuts, pearls and hand-woven cloth at Citra Permai, diagonally across the road from Telkom. For more of this, as well as the gold and the silver **filigree jewellery** for which Kendari is famed, visit Toko Diamond Kendari, opposite the market on Jalan Silondae at Mandonga. Helping out with advice on less well-known locations, the **provincial tourist office**, Dinas Parawista, is 2km south of Pasar Mandonga, just off Jalan Ahmad Yani at Jl Tepau Ningu 2 (Mon–Thurs 7am–2pm, Fri 7–11am; ☎0401/326634). For **internet access**, Kend@rinet at Jl S. Parman 115 is currently the best place to surf the net.

Leaving Kendari, tickets for Pelni **ferries** are available at numerous agents near the dock, where you'll also find the Super Jet office which currently runs three speedboats daily to Raha (7.30am, 1pm & 2pm; Rp33,000); the first two continue on to Baubau (Rp44,500). There's also a thrice-weekly **ferry to Wangiwangi** (currently Mon, Wed & Sat; 12hr; Rp40,000) in the Tukangbesi group (p.926). The Merpati office (☎0401/321896) is currently at Jl Soekarno 85, though there are plans to move near the *Hotel Aden* at Jl Yani 80; they can organize a shared taxi (around Rp25,000) to the airport. They supposedly fly nine times a week to Makassar and once a week to Sorong, though the schedule is rather unreliable. Pelita Air (daily flights to Makassar) are in the *Hotel Aden* (☎0401/394222). Cahaya Ujung on Jalan Sukarno have three daily **buses** to Watampone and on to Makassar, with the last one leaving at around 2pm; though for Watampone you're probably better off taking a quicker Kijang from the Puwatu terminal.

Around Kendari

Kendari may not require much of your time, but with a spare day it's worth making the tedious journey 65km southeast of town to the delightful **Air Terjun Moramo**, where a river cascades from a small plateau over a series of limestone terraces, each forming natural swimming pools surrounded by teak forest. A couple of shelter sheds and weekend stalls are the only artificial intrusions; get there by taking a bemo from Pasar Mandongo 3km south to Pasar Baru, change vehicles for **Lapuko**, and there rent a bemo or ojek for the last 15km to Moramo. An hour offshore from Kendari, **Pulau Hari** – the Island of Sun – has a fine beach and splintered reef, the best place to check out local marine life; boats can be chartered by the day from the wharf 100m west of Kendari's port, and are not bad value for two or more people (Rp90,000).

Requiring far more advance planning and determination to visit, those with a yen for the great outdoors should consider exploring the peat swamps and forest at **Rawa-Aopa national park**, roughly 70km west of Kendari by road. This is the only place in southern Sulawesi you can see anoa (dwarf buffalo), though crocodiles, snakes, monkeys and birds are more likely to cross your path. You need at least three days, must be prepared to travel by foot and canoe through the park, and to pay for a **guide** (Rp30,000 per day) and **permit** (Rp2500) from Sulawesi Tenggara's forestry department – Kendari's tourist office can make all the arrangements.

Pulau Muna: Raha and around

It takes about three hours to make the crossing by speedboat from Kendari to **RAHA** on **Pulau Muna**, the boat travelling due south between steep, thinly vegetated headlands as it follows the deep blue channel. First impressions of Raha are of the sun blazing down on a shadeless **jetty**, and a small town with half the animation of a Mexican border post during siesta; nor is there much to experience here once everybody has said "hello mister" to you a dozen times. From the jetty, Jalan Sudirman and a cluster of shops are immediately south, while Jalan Ahmad Yani runs 1km north along the seafront, past a couple of colonial-era buildings and a **post office**, to Raha's market and **bemo terminal**; look here for vehicles to sites around Raha. Raha's **accommodation** is fair value, but check first on screens and nets in your room as mosquitoes are a problem, and be warned that places are often full – or at least claim they are. *Hotel Alia*, Jl Sudirman 5 (☎0403/21218; ❷), with its back garden just a few metres from the jetty, is the best option, with friendly staff and big rooms, though the economy rooms are a little dingy. *Hotel Ihlam* (☎0403/21070; ❷), up the hill from the wartel at Jl Jati 16, is nice but overpriced for economy rooms, and the noise of vermin running across the tin roof does little to encourage a good night's sleep. Raha's choice of **restaurants**, never very tantalizing, is now downright dire with the closure of a couple of the more attractive places. The three-table *Rumah Makan Nikmat* is currently the best option on Jalan Sudirman; its take-it-or-leave-it menu, however, is actually rather good. The *Hotel Alia* has a small restaurant, and there are a number of night warung around the harbour and near the bemo terminal. **Speedboat tickets** to Baubau and Kendari aboard the Super Jet and tickets for Pelni boats are available from kiosks at the harbour.

Lagoons and caves

Fortunately, Raha's surroundings compensate for the town. Sunday is the big day for families to picnic and teenagers to get drunk 15km south of Raha at the exquisite **Nappabale and Motonunu lagoons**. Encircled by forest, swimming is safe here and canoes can be rented by the hour (Rp10,000) to paddle over the water into a low-ceilinged **tunnel** connecting the two lagoons. It's a fine day out, but for a glimpse under the everyday skin of Sulawesi Tenggara, trek out to **Liang-liang Mabolu** (Mabolo Caves), a pleasant two-hour walk beginning at the kampung of **MABOLO**, a half-hour bemo ride west of Raha. Bemos go this way fairly regularly, but make it clear if you don't want to charter a vehicle because drivers at the terminal will assume you do. At Mabolo, take your pick of the trails behind the houses on the south (left) side of the road; the paths themselves are clear, but there are many to choose from, so keep asking directions or hunt around for guides. You can walk through a Muslim **cemetery** – note the stalactite headstones – and then off under the shade of sprawling groves of **cashew trees** (*menta*), whose nuts are hidden under a swollen, purple-green, cyanide-laden husk. You emerge into an open countryside of scrub and dry-stone walls separating the brown fields between villages, an abundantly poor area whose porous soil makes water a critical concern during the dry season, when children spend their days staggering out to public tanks on the main road with jerry cans.

Soon the path weaves between an increasing number of ever-larger, rough-sided limestone hillocks; look for the first **primitive paintings** on a hillside on your right, a clear group of **horses** with one human figure, perhaps holding a sword. Horses were a vital part of life in pagan times on Muna, and ritual horse-fighting is still performed in villages around Raha. Press on from here to the minuscule whitewashed mosque at **Kampung Liang Kabori**, where elderly Pak Lahadha waits in ambush to escort foreigners to the caves. The first of these, **Liang Toko**, is perhaps 20m deep and 15m high, floored in boulders covered with green algae, and has some large ochre paintings of three more horses, fat and clearly male, being ridden by small human figures. Around the other walls are more people, ships, and what look like sun symbols, with these themes repeated around the corner at **Liang Kabori** – look for two human figures with taloned hands and feet. A couple of **shrines** at the caves point to a religious significance which has survived Islam.

Pulau Buton

At over 150km long, **Pulau Buton** is the largest island in all Sulawesi. Its northern end is heavily forested, and there are villages steeped in animist tradition, where children run screaming at the sight of foreigners, but a lack of roads effectively limits exploration to the vicinity of the southern city of **BAUBAU**. Especially if you've worked your way down through Kendari and Raha, Baubau's size, order and sense of purpose is unexpected. This was once the seat of the **Wolio Sultanate**, whose founder, Wakaka, was a grandson of Kublai Khan. Here, as on the mainland, the seventeenth century was portentous: Islam arrived; an invading army led by the Dutch East Indies governor general, **Antony van Dieman**, was beaten off; and Arung Palakka of Bone sought sanctuary on Buton while fleeing the wrath of Gowa's Sultan

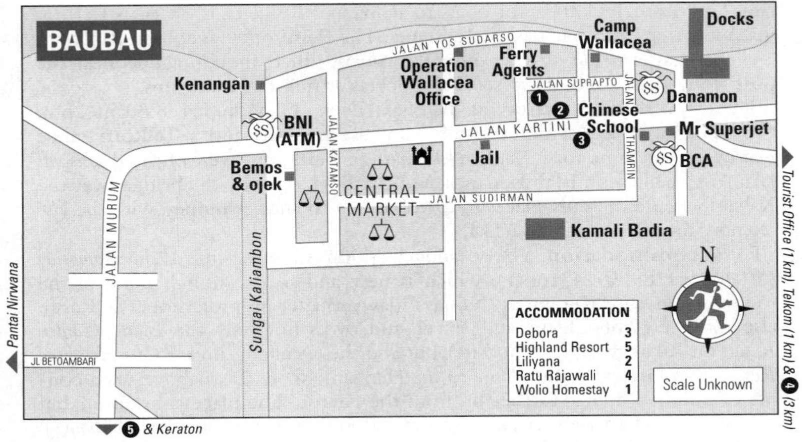

Hasanuddin, whose forces were defeated here by the Dutch in 1667. The Wolio line proved resilient: although Baubau became the seat of a Dutch controller in the nineteenth century, the sultanate survived until 1960.

Baubau's centre, a busy dockside area, makes for a good wander past the few century-old European-style buildings along Jalan Kartini, where the solid **jail** and more refined shutters and arched windows of the former Chinese school at the corner of Jalan Kenanga stand out. Back off Jalan Sudirman, **Kamali Badia** is a wooden three-tiered Bugis palace dating back to the 1920s, and would have been impressive in its day, though it's now run-down. About 500m further west off the end of Jalan Sudirman, Baubau's **central market** is all you'd expect given the city's position on trade routes between Java and Maluku: a tight square of busy stalls selling imported fruit and vegetables, spices from the Spice Islands, gold, silk, ships' chandlery, and locally cast **brassware**.

You can catch a bemo or ojek from the market 2km south to Baubau's **Kraton**, the largest and most impressive pre-Dutch construction in Sulawesi. This was Wolio's stronghold, an entire hill-top citadel ringed by 3km of stone walls, now fully restored, where the sultan, his wives, family and servants all lived. You'll need a good hour to circuit the walls, past rusting cannon (some stamped with the VOC logo), and to check out the various royal tombs and dwellings, which include **Benteng Wolio**, the last sultan's home and now a museum (a donation of around Rp5000 is expected by the family who live there and will show you around), with period furniture, heavy wooden decor, and family portraits by the score. The most obvious landmark up here is a lichen-covered "flagpole" of unknown provenance, though it looks like the mast and crow's-nest of an eighteenth-century European vessel. Next to this is a square-sided, blue-and-white stone **mosque** dating back to 1712, the oldest unrestored example in Sulawesi; while opposite is the neat, two-storey port controller's house. **Out of town**, the most popular place to unwind, sunbathe and snorkel (though the reef is a long way offshore) is the sandy **Pantai Nirwana**, about 11km west – again, catch an ojek or charter a bemo from the market.

Baubau practicalities

The Kendari–Raha ferry and Pelni vessels stop at Baubau's north-facing **docks**, with the town centre immediately west. Ojek and becak meet all ferries. The **Superjet** office, for boats to Raha and Kendari, is on Jalan Kartini, just a few steps from the harbour entrance. The **Pelni** office is at Jalan Pahlawan 1 on the eastern side of town near the tourist office, though agents near the port along Jalan Yos Sudarso sell Pelni tickets at minimal mark-ups.

There's a **tourist office** at Jl Njak Dien 1 (Mon–Fri 8.30am–2pm; ⓣ0402/23588), a ten-minute walk from the harbour, and a **Telkom** office nearby on the same road. Baubau's Danamon **bank**, just west of the docks off Jalan Yos Sudarso on Jalan Kenanga, and the BNI, right by the bridge over the Kaliambon, are the only places in town willing to change money, with the latter now furnished with an ATM.

For **accommodation**, a good budget option is Pak Kasim's *Wolio Homestay* (ⓣ0402/21189, ⓕ24316; ❷), which is new and smart, though none of the rooms are en suite. Known as "Notaris" (lawyer) after his profession, Pak Kasim also manages Wolio Tours and Travel, and owns not only the *Island Garden Resort* on Tukangbesi (see opposite), but also the excellent three-room *Highland Resort* (also known as the *House on the Hill*; same ⓣ & ⓕ as above; ❹) a couple of hundred metres further on from the Kraton. The place is beautiful, but the food is overpriced. Back near the harbour, the air-con *Hotel Debora*, Jl Kartini 15 (ⓣ0402/21203; ❷) and the *Hotel Liliyana*, Jl Kartini 18 (ⓣ0402/21197; ❷–❸), which has rooms with fan or air-con, are cool and welcoming, and both a short walk from the dock. The best place in town is the *Ratu Rajawali* at Jl Sultan Hasanuddin 69 (ⓣ0402/22162; ❹–❺), 2km east of the tourist office – it's the only hotel in this part of Sulawesi Tenggara that can boast a swimming pool. **Places to eat** include the many fish stalls near the harbour; for something more comfortable, try the smart *Sri Solo*, just a little further west along Jalan Sudarso, and the overpriced but decent *Kenangan*, at the far end of Sudarso just before the market.

The Tukangbesi group: Wangiwangi, Kaledupa and Hoga

The **Tukangbesi group** is a hundred-kilometre string east of Buton comprising the four major islands of **Wangiwangi**, **Kaledupa**, **Tomea** and **Binongko** – the four being sometimes abbreviated to Wakatobi after their initial letters – all of which are hilly and inhabited. Extensive **coral reefs**, which include fringing formations around each island, as well as an isolated complex to the south, have been the subject of ongoing research since the early 1990s, and the Tukangbesi group have recently been drawing a steady trickle of scuba enthusiasts willing to put up with simple living and prolonged travel in order to pioneer diving in this largely unexplored area. There's an Rp10,000 **entrance fee** into the **Wakatobi national marine park**, home to coral reefs teeming with small fish as well as larger predators such as tuna, sharks, dolphins and turtles; your accommodation in Wakatobi should be able to arrange this for you, or you can visit the park's head office in Baubau at Jl Murhum 47 (ⓣ0402/21826).

From Baubau, there's a daily 4am bus (picks up from accommodation; Rp15,000) to the port 70km east at **Laselimo**, where a ferry (Rp15,000) takes ninety minutes to reach Wanci on Pulau Wangiwangi. **WANCI** is a large fishing village with the distinctly average *Losmen Samudra* (❷), but you should arrive in time to catch a smaller barge onwards to **Pulau Kaledupa** (3–4hr; Rp10,000), where you'll find a few toko (shops) and homestay accommodation. From here, ask at the docks for an outboard-driven "johnston" (Rp10,000) to run you across to **Pulau Hoga**, about five square kilometres of sand, scrub and coconut trees ten minutes east of Kaledupa. Alternatively, there are four ferries a week sailing direct from Baubau to Kaledupa (12–14hr; Rp30,000); there is no set timetable, so ask around in Baubau for when the next boat leaves. It's worth bearing in mind that the return journey from Hoga to the mainland takes two days, with a night in Wanci, as the Wanci–Baubau ferry leaves first thing in the morning, before you arrive from Kaledupa. The direct Wanci–Kendari ferry runs twice a week, but the crossing can be very rough, so it's better to travel the long way round via Baubau.

On Hoga there are plenty of **places to stay**, though do try to arrange your accommodation before you arrive. Furthermore, be warned that the food on Hoga is usually mediocre at best, and there's a distinct lack of vegetables; bring fruit and vegetables from Baubau before setting off. Two recommended homestays are Pak Kasim's *Island Garden Resort* (contact details in the Baubau section opposite; ❸), which is, like his places on Baubau, smart and pretty but a little overpriced, particularly the food; and the Dutch-run *Hoga Cottages* (❸), which includes three meals in the price. To book the latter, contact the Caraka Travelindo travel agency in Makassar (see p.893). Alternatively, **Operation Wallacea**, a British-based volunteer organization surveying the seas around this part of Indonesia, have self-contained bungalows scattered over Pulau Hoga; while tourists are forbidden from using them (the volunteers are recruited from the UK), in the past it has been known for tourists to stay at the bungalows if there are no volunteers around. Contact the Wallacea camp office on the seafront in Baubau to find out the latest situation, or visit their website (Ⓦwwww.opwall.co.uk) to find out more about their work, forthcoming schedules and fees. All of the accommodation places on Hoga rent equipment, allowing you to snorkel and dive the nearby reefs, and you can also visit the **Bajau fishing village** of **Sampela** (around Rp20,000 on a tour), raised over the sea on stilts between Kaledupa and Hoga.

Of the other islands, the *Wakatobi Dive Resort* on **Pulau Tomea** is by far the plushest place in southeast Sulawesi. Charging between US$1500 and US$2000 for a seven- to fourteen-day stay, the price includes a return flight from Bali, accommodation in exquisite beachfront cottages or traditional longhouse rooms, and the only decent food in Wakatobi. To arrange a stay, contact their offices in Sanur, Bali (Ⓣ0361/284227, Ⓕ270313) or visit Ⓦwww.wakatobi.com.

Sulawesi Tengah

Though the peaks are of no great height, **Sulawesi Tengah** – the island's second largest province, and one which includes Sulawesi's physical centre as well as parts of the northern, and all of the eastern, peninsula – is almost completely covered in mountains, terrain made all the more impenetrable by what survives of its forests. Over the last few years, a large part of the province has suffered a horrific, internecine **religious war** that, despite extensive government and military intervention, shows no sign of abating. While it is still possible to visit large areas of the province, crossing it is sometimes a little tricky, and travellers are advised to seek out the latest news and information before attempting to visit; see the box on pp.928–929 for details.

As the influence of Portugal, Holland and Ternate waxed and waned down on the coast, Sulawesi Tengah's highlands remained more remote than those of Toraja or Minahasa, whose inhabitants were at least aware of the outside world; the **Mire** people of the eastern peninsula had their first contact with foreigners in 1992, when a mission aircraft spotted huts in the jungle. Even the road from southern Sulawesi is barely a decade old, and local infrastructure remains minimal. Nonetheless, there's superlative **hiking** through two wilderness reserves: **Lore Lindu**, where you'll encounter the remains of a vanished megalithic culture, and **Morowali**, domain of the nomadic Wana. Stay on the main roads, and you'll experience little of the highlands beyond the backdrop surrounding **Danau Poso**; instead, your view of this otherwise landlocked region will be confined to the coast, where a five-hundred-kilometre road follows the southern line of **Tomini Bay** between the easterly provincial capital, **Palu**, the

The Poso conflict

According to reports, the trouble started on Christmas Day 1998, which happened to fall in the holy Muslim month of Ramadan. A local Christian, apparently drunk, got into a fierce quarrel with a Muslim from a neighbouring village, and in the ensuing scuffle was stabbed several times. During the hours that followed, Muslim youths rampaged through the streets of Poso, looting shops that had been selling alcohol throughout Ramadan, setting fire to a nightclub and damaging four others. What happened that Christmas Day set in motion a chain of events that has led, thus far, to the deaths of over a thousand people. A bloody **inter-religious war** has since been fought in the villages around Poso (although the town itself has thus far managed to avoid the worst of the fighting, and with the exception of a couple of churches and a few houses razed by fire, has been relatively unaffected).

Quite why it should be Poso that has become the focus of all this turbulence remains unclear: it's a quiet, unassuming town of thirty thousand people, with little previous history of inter-religious rivalry. Rumours of **conspiracies** are therefore numerous, with some blaming agitators sent from Java to stir up inter-religious trouble and bring about the foundation of a purely Islamic nation. The Java-based Islamic organization Laskar Jihad, whose website has "Onwards to Poso" as its title banner and who have been involved in so much of the fighting in Maluku, has admitted sending guerrillas to the region; they in turn blame the local Christian priests, whom they accuse of organizing attacks on Muslim villages.

A second theory suggests that supporters of former president Suharto and his army cronies – many of whom were arrested following the events of 1998 – may be behind the attacks, and point to the fact that many of the weapons seized by the authorities in Poso are standard issue in the Indonesan forces, and that so far no attempt has been made to stop suspected troublemakers such as Laskar Jihad members from travelling to the region.

After a lull of several months, in December 2001, tension began once again to rise in the area. Seven more villagers were killed in clashes at the beginning of the month, and the largely Christian lakeside town of Tentena – once a popular stopover point for travellers – was surrounded by Muslim fighters. In response, Chief Security Minister Bambang Yudhoyono visited the region and committed another 2600 troops to the region, bolstering the rather ineffectual force of 1500 already stationed there. A six-month **peace plan** was also outlined, the first two months of which were to concentrate on ending the violence, and the following four to monitor reconciliation between the warring sides.

By the end of 2002 the situation seemed a lot calmer, but the discovery in December of a stash of ammonium nitrate – the explosive used in the Bali bombing transport hub of **Poso town**, and the western port of **Luwuk**. None of these should slow you down for long, though out in the bay itself the **Togian Islands**' seascapes lull almost everyone into extending their stay, besides providing a stepping stone into northern Sulawesi.

There are daily **flights** from Makassar and Manado to Palu, and plenty of public transport into the province from Makassar or Rantepao via the coastal towns of Palopo and Wotu. Arriving from the north, you will most likely land at either Poso – if the boats have restarted – or on the eastern peninsula at **Pagaimana**, both terminals for ferries from Gorontalo. In theory, it's also possible to travel by road down the north peninsula from Gorontalo to Palu or Poso, though even in ideal conditions this is at least a two-day ordeal. Once here, you'll find that long-distance buses seldom stop except at main towns, and between these points it's always easier to make use of short-range minibuses and Kijangs.

– at a house in Palu would seem to suggest that it is too early to talk of a complete end to hostilities in the region.

Travelling in the Poso region

Though tourists have not been specifically targeted by either side, there is always the risk of being caught in the crossfire, and as such the town of **Poso** and **Lake Poso**, including the lakeside resorts of Pendolo and Tentena, are effectively **out-of-bounds** (though the situation changes frequently, so it is always worth asking around to find out the latest situation). Those places in Sulawesi Tengah that *are* currently open to tourists include, to the west of Poso, the regional capital Palu, the nearby dive resort of Donggala and the Lore Lindu national park – though many of the walks in the park that used to end at Lake Poso are for the time being impossible. To the east of Poso, the Togian Islands, Ampana, Pagaimana, Luwuk and the Morowali Reserve are also currently open to tourists.

Transport to and around the region has also been badly affected. The boats to and from Poso via the Togian Islands to Gorontalo are no longer running. Most inconveniently of all, however, the Trans-Sulawesi highway through the province is currently closed around Lake Poso and north to Poso. This means that those who wish to travel overland across Sulawesi Tengah now have to travel along the very rough west-coast road from Palu to Mamuju and Polewali. Given the appalling state of both the roads and buses plying this route, it is not uncommon for the journey from Palu to Polewali to last for more than two days.

Whilst the situation in Poso makes for pretty bleak reading, it's worth noting here that, at times over the past few years, there have been prolonged lulls in the fighting when the villages around Lake Poso, including both Tentena and Pendolo, have **reopened to tourists** once more. Furthermore, the very centre of Poso town seems to have emerged relatively unscathed from the battles; indeed, the hotels *Aluguro* and *Beringin* were at the time of writing both still open for business, though buses were not stopping in the town and their main source of custom was from visiting officials and army personnel. It's therefore worth contacting your **foreign office** about the current state of affairs before setting off, and to ask locals for their advice when you arrive in Sulawesi. With all this in mind, and in the hope that a permanent solution to the troubles can be found soon, accounts of Poso, Tentena, Pendolo and the lake have been left in from the previous edition. Please note, however, that they have **not been updated** since the last visit by a Rough Guide author, in 2000.

The Poso Valley: Pendolo and Danau Poso

The highway from southern Sulawesi winds up into the ranges at **Mangkutana**, buses taking a couple of hours to reach a sign welcoming you to Sulawesi Tengah before the road starts a downhill run into the hundred-kilometre-long **Poso Valley**. Domain of the **Pomona**, a Christianized offshoot of the Torajans, the valley's flooded upper reaches form **Danau Poso**, drained by a river that flows out of the top end of the lake past **Tentena** and follows the valley north to the coast at **Poso town**.

Set on the lake's sandy southern shore and pretty well bang in the centre of Sulawesi, the village of **PENDOLO** is a convenient place to break your journey. The pleasant village comprises just a few houses, a market, and a large church where the highway kinks around the lake, with a scattering of low-profile **accommodation** stretching a kilometre or two to the east. The best places to stay in Pendolo itself are *Pondok Wisata Victory* (❶) and *Pondok Masamba* (❶), which both enjoy beachside locations on Jalan Pelabuhan; further east, *Pendolo Cottages* (❶) has nicer wooden cabins with balconies facing north over the water. All supply filling meals and advice on boat rental and hiking around the lake. **Moving on**, minibuses leave early for Mangkutana (where you can find more of the same to Palopo), or Tentena (3hr; Rp10,000) – trying to flag down long-distance buses heading beyond these points is a waste of time. The road north is tortuous, however, and unless the weather is rough you're better off catching a morning **ferry** across the lake to Tentena in three hours (Rp20,000). Seasonal water levels dictate which of Pendolo's two **jetties** are in use; one is in the town, the other 2km east near *Pendolo Cottages*.

Some 35km long, **Danau Poso** fills a 450-metre-deep rift between two mountain ranges with clear-blue water, the shoreline a mixture of steep rock faces, and sandy bays backed by forest. There are rough trails along both sides of the lake, though the main Pendolo–Tentena road stays well clear of the eastern shore, and you'll need to venture out onto the water to appreciate the scenery fully. Some accommodation has basic snorkelling gear for you to goggle at crabs, eels and fish, and is also where to ask about renting a boat for broader explorations. A good trip to the western shore takes in **Bancea reserve**, famed for the quantity and variety of its **orchids**; there's a fifteen-kilometre, five-hour hike back to Pendolo from here, or you could continue across the lake to **TOLAMBO**, a fishing village with nearby caves, a waterfall, and beaches patrolled by wading birds.

Tentena and around

Surrounded by clove, cocoa and coffee plantations, **TENTENA** sits right where the lake empties into Sungai Poso through a V-shaped barrage of eel traps. A scruffy Christian town, which perks up for three days of dancing and boat races during the annual **Danau Poso festival** in late August, Tentena's character is salvaged by its location and services, besides being a necessary staging post for transport west to **Gintu** at the southern end of Lore Lindu national park. As at Pendolo, exploring the lake is the main pastime, but make sure you also spend half a day at **air terjun Salopa** (Rp1000), an enchanting **waterfall** up against the hills 15km west of town. If you don't want to rent a minibus through your accommodation place – often not a bad deal if you can get a group together – catch a bemo from the far side of the bridge for the twenty-minute haul to **Tonusu**, then walk the last 4km through fields and groves of fruit trees festooned with the zigzag climbing stems of vanilla orchids. Entry into the forest is sudden;

there's a caretaker here who takes your admission fee and gravely requests that you sign his book before pointing you along the path to the falls. Alive with butterflies and birds, these tumble for over 4km down the mountain range, the pale-blue, lime-rich waters glazing rocks and sculpting pools. Unofficially you can spend the night here, sheltering in a tent or using one of the tumbledown wooden huts at the base of the falls; come prepared for damp conditions and bring a fuel stove rather than counting on finding firewood.

Everything you'll need in Tentena is in a close grid of streets on the eastern side of covered, well-maintained **Pomona Bridge**. Next to the bridge you'll find a **post office**, market and shops, with most **places to stay** south of here off Jalan Yos Sudarso. Inexpensive options in the vicinity include basic but clean beds at *Sinar Abadi*, at Jl Sudarso 2 (ⓣ0458/21031; ❷), and *Moro Seneng*, just around the corner on Jalan Diponegoro (ⓣ0458/21165; ❷). Helpful management and airy rooms make *Hotel Victory*, Jl Diponegoro 18 (ⓣ0458/21392; ❷), one of the best choices in town, while *Natural Cottages*, at the junction with Jalan Yani and Yos Sudarso (ⓣ0458/21311; ❶–❷), has unobstructed views over the lake. *Hotel Victory*'s **restaurant** has the most hygienic kitchen, but spicy Padang fare at *Moro Seneng* (the warung is on Jalan Sudarso) tastes better and is far cheaper; *R.M. Danau Poso*, immediately on the western side of the bridge, seldom has food, but the riverside balcony makes it ideal for a coffee. The Ebony Visitor Information, two streets behind *Pondok Remaja* on Jalan Setia Budi, is where to find advice, transport and **guides** for trekking around the regional reserves, with alternatives offered by *Natural Cottages* and *Hotel Victory*.

Leaving, in normal times, the good road to Poso during daylight hours has a continual stream of minibuses from Tentena's **bus terminal**, 2km north of town. There are also departures at least daily to Pendolo, and to **Kolonodale** for access to Morowali, but for anywhere beyond Poso, or direct services to Rantepao or Makassar, go first to Poso and look for further transport there. The **ferry to Pendolo** leaves around 4pm from the shore off Jalan Yos Sudarso, arriving at 7pm, and the spray-soaked crossing is cool enough for a shirt.

Sturdy Toyota **4WDs** for the eighty-kilometre, four-wheel-drive-only track west from Tentena to Bomba and Gintu in **Lore Lindu national park** (see p.936) can be arranged through Tentena's information services, or more cheaply by approaching the drivers of these badly battered vehicles in town and negotiating directly. 4WDs make a couple of runs a week in dry weather, when the journey takes at least seven hours; after heavy rain, convoys have been known to spend a week on the trail. You can also **walk** from Tentena to Gintu in three days, for which you'll need a tent, warm clothing and all supplies, as there are no settlements or shelters along the way.

Poso

POSO is an orderly administrative centre on the south side of **Tomini Bay**, a vast expanse of water encircled by Sulawesi's eastern and northern peninsulas. Its port, and its location at the junction of Sulawesi Tengah's main roads, used to be a real transport hub before the fighting started; now very few vehicles come this way. Poso offers no distractions, and once you've sorted your next move there's no reason to hang around.

The town covers a couple of square kilometres either side of **Sungai Poso**, which flows west into the bay. On the northern side you'll find the **port** at the end of Jalan Sudarso, which runs south for 500m to a riverside **roundabout**. Minibuses from Tentena, and some services from the eastern peninsula, terminate at the **bus depot** about 2km east of here, while Jalan Kalimantan crosses the river into the southern side of town. About 200m down Jalan Kalimantan,

Jalan Sumatra branches west for 1km, passing a knot of services before heading out of town past bus company offices and the **main market** – you might get dropped off here if you're coming in from Palu. **Bemos** run between the eastern bus depot and market all through the day (Rp350), as do ojeks.

Poso's **post office** is also north of the river on Jalan Tadulako, as are the **Telkom** office, round the corner on Jalan Urip Sumoharjo, and moneychanging facilities at Bank Dagang Negara, Jl Hasanuddin 13. Information is on hand at the **tourist office** at the junction of Jalan Sumatra and Jalan Kalimantan (Ⓣ0452/21211).

The most handy **accommodation** is south of the river: *Hotel Alugoro* at Jl Sumatra 20 (Ⓣ0452/23736; ❶) has rooms with fans and mandi and is great value and almost always full, its overflow handled by the slightly less salubrious *Beringin* (Ⓣ0452/21851; ❶) opposite. North of the river on Jalan Agus Salim, *Hotel Kalimantan* (Ⓣ0452/21420; ❶) and *Hotel Bambu Jaya* (Ⓣ0452/21570; ❷–❸) are a little run-down but comfortable, though the *Kalimantan* sits opposite a huge and busy mosque. **Eating** out, try the *Pemuda*, next to the cinema on Jalan Sumatra, for fine nasi goreng and sweet-and-sour prawns; *R.M. Lelanga Jaya*, just outside the dock gates on Jalan Sudarso, has expensive Chinese meals, cold beer and good seascapes, or try the *Pangkep*, on the roundabout on Jalan Sudarso, with excellent chargrilled seafood.

On from Poso

Bemos to Tentena, and **buses** for the east peninsula towns of Ampana, Pagaimana and Luwuk, and all points south to Makassar, leave Poso from the eastern bus depot. For Palu, use one of the bus companies on Jalan Sumatra. Before the trouble in Poso, a daily Kijang service (90km; 6hr) ran west from Poso to **Watutau** in the **Napu Valley** (p.939), useful for those heading to the **Lore Lindu national park**; assuming the situation is once more peaceful, it might be worth enquiring at the offices of the tour agents Lore Indah, Jl Enggano 23, in the Kaya Manya district of town to see if they are once again running – ojeks, or Dinas Parawisata (see above), can get you there in time to sign up for the mid-morning departure.

Western Sulawesi Tengah

Western Sulawesi Tengah is very different from the green and central Poso Valley, the mountain range in the background capturing the clouds and rendering the **Palu Valley** beyond one of the driest areas in Indonesia. Here you'll find the capital city of **Palu** surrounded by fields of bleached brown grass and prickly-pear cactus, though the coast at **Donggala** is more attractive, with good beaches and clean water. In contrast, the mountains that receive all the rain are perennially verdant, rich in wildlife, forests and enigmatic **megaliths**, which sprout along a series of stepped valleys in the **Lore Lindu national park**. Lore Lindu used to be the main reason for tourists coming to this part of Sulawesi, but with the current unrest in Poso, more and more people are passing through Palu to use the coastal road connecting the city with Polewali – the only overland crossing between the province and neighbouring Sulawesi Selatan.

For advice on safety in the Suluwesi Tengah region, see p.929.

Palu

At the base of the northern peninsula and the mouth of the Palu Valley, there has been a town on the site of **PALU** for centuries, but the city only gained its current importance during World War II, developed by the Japanese as a supply centre. Trade is still keeping the city ticking over, and a moderate pace and pleasant people – including a noticeable Christian **Kaili** minority, the valley's original inhabitants – make Palu an easy place to pass a day.

Arrival, orientation and information

Palu is set on **Sungai Palu**, which cuts the city in two as it flows north into the bay. The city covers a fair few square kilometres, but the **centre** is a small area on the eastern bank around the junction of Jalan Sudirman and Jalan Hasanuddin, which crosses west over the river into a commercial district along Jalan Gajah Mada and Jalan Bonjol. **Arrivals** on Pelni vessels from Makassar, Bitung, Kalimantan or Java land 24km north of town at **Pantoloan harbour**, while **Mutiara Airport** is 7km southeast – microlets or taxis will be waiting. Long-distance buses and vehicles from Gimpu generally wind up at **Terminal Masomba**, 2km southeast of the centre, though some companies disembark passengers at their various offices around the suburbs. You can reach anywhere within the city boundaries by waving down **microlets** (bemos) already heading in the required direction; fares are fixed at Rp1000, but, as drivers adapt their routes to fit the passengers' needs, rides often involve lengthy tours of the city.

Reasonably good **information** from English-, German- and French-speaking staff is on hand at Palu's **tourist office**, inconveniently located to the south

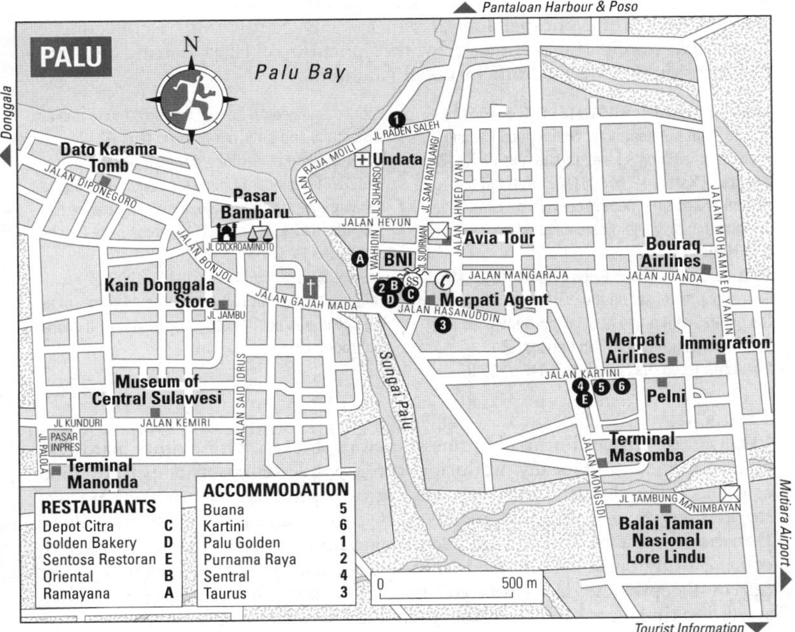

Moving on from Palu

Terminal Manonda, on the southwest side of town, is where to find **bemos** for Donggala. **Buses** to all destinations between Manado and Makassar depart from **Terminal Masomba**, southeast of the centre. Before the trouble in Poso, very few visitors would travel the 500km road north from Palu to Gorontalo and Sulawesi Utara, a rough, two-day excursion in the back of a bus along the inner curve of Tomini bay, as the experience was rendered unnecessary by less excruciating bus-and-ferry connections from the eastern peninsula; with that route occasionally cut off, however, you may find you now have no choice. If you're heading to Lore Lindu national park, there are at least two buses each morning to Gimpu, 100km south of Palu at the start of the walking trail to the Bada Valley, and there's also less regular transport to Wuasa in the eastern Napu Valley with Napu Star – ask at the tourist office (see below) for details. The **Pelni office** is at Jl Kartini 96 (Mon–Thurs 8am–noon, Fri & Sat 8–11am; ⓣ0451/421696). **Taxis** congregate at the junction of Jalan Sudirman and Jalan Hasanuddin Dua.

of town at Jl Dewi Sartika 91 (Mon–Thurs & Sat 7.15am–2pm, Fri 7.15–11.30am; ⓣ & ⓕ0451/483941), where you can also arrange PHPA permits for Morowali or Lore Lindu (Rp2500). Unfortunately, some of them are a little too keen to promote their (expensive) guided tours to Lore Lindu, so for unbiased advice on this topic visit the **Balai Taman Nasional Lore Lindu** (ⓣ0451/423439) at Jl Tambung Manimbayam 144, a government-run office dealing specifically with the park.

Accommodation

Palu has basically two concentrations of **places to stay**, geared to specific budgets: you'll find cheaper lodgings in the city centre, with a collection of mid-range hotels 1km southeast by the junction of Jalan Kartini and Jalan Monginsidi, not too far from Terminal Masomba.

Buana Jl Kartini 8 ⓣ0451/421475, ⓕ454133. Nondescript but neat hotel with a good Padang restaurant; all rooms have air-con and TV. ❷–❸

Kartini Jl Kartini 12 ⓣ0451/421964. Old but decent rooms off a central courtyard; some have fan and mandi, while others have air-con, shower and TV. ❷–❸

Palu Golden Jl Raden Saleh 1 ⓣ0451/421126. Tour-group hotel set on the waterfront due north of the centre, with a fine pool, all conveniences and international pretensions and prices. ❺

Purnama Raya Jl Wahidin 4 ⓣ0451/23646. Popular and central budget standby; the rooms are a bit stuffy and tatty, but all have fans. ❷

Hotel Sentral Jl Kartini 6 ⓣ0451/422789, ⓕ428288. Standard Chinese-owned hotel with a booking agent, coffee shop, top-floor karaoke hall and attached supermarket. All rooms have air-con, mandi and TV. ❸

Taurus Jl Hasanuddin 36 ⓣ0451/422902. Friendly, simple but poorly maintained place, offering cheap and central economy rooms with shared bathroom. ❷

The City

Palu's centre thrives on small businesses: shops stocked with clothes, hardware, electrical goods and locally produced pottery, while stalls outside private houses offer chillies, bananas or other home-grown produce. The markets are well stocked but pretty functional, and dismally divided into concrete booths; **Pasar Bambaru**, west of the river on Jalan Cokroaminoto, is the busiest, with piles of *rono*, a tiny dried fish crushed and used as a garnish, and excellent October durian. Deep in the dry season you have to wonder that anything grows here at all; looking upstream from the Jalan Hasanuddin bridge, men scrub their bikes and cattle in the toe-deep river while behind them the valley is squeezed dry between the mountains, their heights blued by distance and dust. Across the river, a fifteen-minute walk takes you past a large Catholic **church** on Jalan Gajah Mada to a **mosque** on Jalan Cokroaminoto, which claims to be amongst the oldest in Sulawesi, founded in the sixteenth century by the Javanese Imam **Dato Karama**, whose **tomb** is a further 2km west off Jalan Diponegoro.

For an insight into the region, catch a microlet southwest of the centre to the **Museum of Central Sulawesi** on Jalan Kemiri (Mon–Thurs 8am–2pm, Fri 8–11am, Sat 8am–1pm; Rp750), whose front lawn has full-sized concrete copies of Lore Lindu's megaliths. Inside, a selection of stuffed fauna mounted in a forest diorama share space with ceramics, clothing of *kulit kayu*, soft and not very sturdy **bark cloth**, and some beautiful **silks** (*kain Donggala*), woven in the local fashion and featuring animals, plants and an unusual "chessboard" *ikat* pattern. Other designs incorporate cottons and gold thread; this cottage industry is enjoying a small boom in villages around Donggala, having been banned by the Japanese during World War II. There are also wooden coffins and clay burial jars from the Poso Valley's **Pamona** population, while archeological odds and ends in a separate hall illustrate fragments of Donggala's past: the best are some peculiar jewellery and whips cast in bronze, as well as tiny cult figurines with hideous faces and rampant genitals.

Eating

Palu has some good food, including **local dishes** such as *utakelo* (vegetables with coconut milk) and *Palu mara* (fish with turmeric, tomatoes and chilli). For snacking, the chocolate and cream **cakes** at the *Golden Bakery* on Jalan Wahidin can't be beaten. To eat with locals it's worth tracking down the nocturnal **grilled-fish stalls** near the cinema on Jalan Heyun and overlooking the bay on Jalan Moili.

Depot Citra Jalan Hasanuddin Dua. A big, noisy, sociable canteen serving *cap cay*, nasi goreng, sate, grilled prawns, great barbecued fish and iced fruit drinks.

Sentosa Restoran Jalan Kartini, above and behind the supermarket. Functional café with unexciting Indonesian standards and occasional live music; one of the few places to stay open during the day throughout Ramadan.

Oriental Jalan Hasanuddin Dua. Authentic Chinese menu with fish stomach, shark fin and *trepang* soups amongst expensive exotics, but also less pricey tofu and crab dishes.

Ramayana Jalan Wahidin. Very good Chinese-Indonesian fare, including a chicken in chilli sauce which leaves your lips buzzing.

Listings

Airlines Offices open Mon–Fri 8am–4pm, Sat & Sun 8am–2pm. Bouraq, Jl Juanda 83 (☎0451/422995), to Makassar, Manado and Balikpapan; Merpati at Jl Kartini 33 (☎0451/453821), to Makassar.

Banks and exchange Good rates for travellers' cheques at BNI on Jalan Sudirman. Nearly all the bank offices have ATMs, and there are BII and BCA cash machines at the Sentosa supermarket.

Internet access The wartel by the Telkom building has by far the fastest internet connection in Palu, while the Geonet Café near the *Kartini Hotel* on Jalan Kartini is reasonably efficient.

Hospital Hospital Undata, Jl Suharso 33 ☎0451/421370.

Immigration Jl Kartini 53 ☎0451/421433.

Post office The most central branch is at Jl Sudirman 17 (Mon–Sat 7am–6pm); the GPO itself is several kilometres southeast of the centre on Jalan Mohammed Yamin.

Shopping If you can't find what you need at the markets or shops around the centre, Sentosa supermarket, on the corner of Jalan Mongsidi and Jalan Kartini, has a host of imported chocolates, kitchenware and stationery. For local flavour, *kain Donggala* is sold at Rp250,000 a piece from a small, anonymous store west of the river on Jalan Jambu, though from the outside the shop seems to stock only medicinal honey-and-egg drinks – the

tourist office can help locate the store.
Telephone and fax International phone and fax services at the Telkom office on Jalan Dahlan are supposedly available around the clock.

Travel agents and tours Avia Tour, Jl Moh Hatta 4 (☎0451/422895), and Siga Tours and Travel, Jl Hasanuddin 36 (☎0451/422902), for all airlines and Pelni bookings.

Donggala and around

The sleepy port of **DONGGALA**, 40km north of Palu at the mouth of the bay, was once the busiest town in the region, for centuries a regular stop on the trading routes between Sulawesi, Kalimantan and India. Elevated to the status of local capital under the Dutch, a siltation-prone harbour and Japanese influence saw Donggala lose the title to Palu, and its wharves finally closed to passenger shipping during the 1980s. A peaceful town, with the gentle hills nearby planted with coconut trees and the streets reeking of drying copra and cloves, it's the perfect place to unwind for a few days, checking out the shallow-draught Bugis schooners in the harbour, or enjoying the shallow seas hereabouts. **Shared taxis** (Rp4000) take under an hour to get here from Palu's Terminal Manonda, dropping you at the bus terminal just short of Donggala, where an ojek (Rp3000) can take you to Donggala's accommodation, about 3km north of town at **Tanjung Karang**, a rocky headland with some gorgeous beaches. If you want to **scuba dive**, *Prince John Dive Resort* (☎0457/71710; ❺ full board, plus US$27 per person per dive) has all the facilities and its bungalows overlook the reef; otherwise, there are decent cheaper options nearby at *Natural Cottages* (❹ full board; price negotiable), overlooking the sea; and the ridiculously cheap *Sandy Cottages* (❸ full board).

Lore Lindu national park

Southeast of Palu, the land rises to a forested plateau, 2500 square kilometres of which is given over to **Lore Lindu national park**, itself based around 2355-metre **Gunung Nokilolaki** and the catchment areas of the Palu and Lariang rivers. Much of the park is thinly settled, the most accessible regions being the southern **Bada Valley**, central **Besoa Valley**, and the eastern **Napu Valley**, each rising higher than the other and linked by trails. Natural attractions aside, the valleys also feature impressively physical **megaliths**, including male and female stone **statues** of anything between 50cm and 4.5m in height, and **kalamba**, large, cylindrical stone basins. Probably raised a millennium ago, these *megalitik* predate Lore Lindu's current inhabitants, and nothing definite is known about their purpose. Christianity now predominates, and the village churches all have clock towers, with the hands painted on at the time of Sunday service.

The most popular route through the park, taking in some good forest, river crossings and many statues, starts south of Palu at the village of **Gimpu**, and then follows the Lariang south and east to the Bada Valley settlements of **Gintu** and **Bomba**, exiting the region – when the situation in Poso allows – via a rough vehicle road over the mountains to Tentena. In ideal conditions, Palu to Bomba takes four days, but allowing six is more realistic, giving you enough time to have a good look around. One drawback to this trail is that it actually skirts around the park; for a closer look at Lore Lindu's interior you should consider extending your trip north from the Bada Valley, through to **Doda** in the Besoa Valley, and then over to the Napu Valley and the villages of **Watutau** and **Wuasa**, from where there's regular traffic on to Poso or back to Palu – about an extra four days in all. Note that the walks described below are included on the assumption that Tentena is open to tourists. If this is not the case, trekkers will have to return to Palu, usually by retracing their steps.

Practicalities

The first step is to visit the Lore Lindu national park office in Palu (see p.934). Assuming you speak rudimentary Indonesian and are prepared to reach Lore Lindu on foot or by local transport, you'll find **guides** and tours from Palu and – should they reopen to tourists again – Poso and Tentena are unnecessarily expensive, especially along the well-defined and serviced Palu–Bada Valley–Tentena trail. You do need guides for locating megaliths, and for the tracks to Doda from either Gimpu or Bomba, but these are far cheaper to engage on site – about Rp50,000 a day. (There are rumours that the authorities are trying to introduce a fixed fee of Rp100,000 per day, though this has yet to be enforced). There are a few formal **lodgings** within the park, but you can also call on village hospitality where these are lacking by presenting yourself to the village head, who will probably put you up himself for a fee. The only time that you're likely to end up **camping out** is if you decide to walk between Bomba and Tentena, for which you'll need a tent, stove and food. **Meals** usually come with accommodation and there are very few places to eat in the area, though food is very plain – even if you're not camping, you won't regret bringing some goodies with you. Boiled **water** in villages is safe to drink, but any collected along trails needs to be purified; carry a decent-sized water bottle, as the valleys can be exposed and very hot, especially in the July–October dry season. Conversely, nights are cool, even chilly enough for a heavy shirt in the Besoa and Napu valleys, while heavy rain – possible at any time – swells streams and turns the fields and tracks into quagmires, making hiking between villages or out to megaliths a much more difficult and lengthy operation. All this means that **distances** and **walking times** are unpredictable, and most of those given below are minimum estimates.

Palu to Tentena: the Bada Valley

Note that the following route is currently **impossible** due to the closure of Tentena to tourists (see p.929), and those who wish to follow it are currently having to turn back before their destination and return to Gimpu on foot the way they came. The following account assumes that Tentena has reopened, but be prepared to alter your itinerary if the town remains closed to tourists.

Buses from Palu's Masomba terminal take about five hours to reach trailheads at **GIMPU**, a tidy collection of homes and stores at the end of the bitumen 100km south of Palu, whose inhabitants subsist by collecting rattan and planting cocoa. There's homestay accommodation here, and transport back to Palu in the morning. The Bada Valley trail starts with an eight-hour walk southeast along the Lariang to **MOA**, a pretty village whose friendly homestay and surrounding dry forest of solid, grey-barked **eucalyptus trees** and big butterflies might encourage you to hang around for a day. From here, in another full day's walk east you'll ford the river to **Tuare**, and then climb over the ridges and down into the Bada Valley at Gintu.

Orientated east–west right on the southern tip of the national park, the **Bada Valley** is a broad, fifteen-kilometre-long oval basin surrounding Sungai Lariang, its shallow slopes given over to rice and slash-and-burn cultivation. South of the Lariang, Gintu is pretty central to the valley, with another half-dozen kampung and a score of megalithic statues scattered on both sides of the river in the 7km east of here to the village of Bomba. Either settlement makes a good base: **GINTU** has two fine losmen (❷ full board), and a bitumen road along the south side of the river to **BOMBA**, a slightly nicer prospect with coconut trees, a couple of small stores, and a one-kilometre walk north to tiny twin rooms with mandi, breakfast and dinner at *Losmen Ningsi* (❷). As always, your accommodation can produce guides and also arrange a seat in a jeep to Tentena (Rp40,000 for the 4WD), though this town is currently closed due to the war being waged around there (see p.929).

To explore Bada **north of the river**, start by backtracking over the Lariang 1km from Gintu to **Lengkeka** village, where there are **hot springs** five minutes' walk uphill. Four statues lie off the path in the 3km east between Lengkeka and kampung **Sepe**; the most interesting are **Oba**, a tiny, dumpy figure, and the reclining **Mpeime**. Southeast of Sepe is **Palindo**, at 4.5m high, the biggest megalith in all Lore Lindu – even so, it's impossible to find on your own – whose clearly carved, stylized face betrays nothing concerning the cause of a startling erection. From Sepe it's forty minutes further east to a waterfall at **Kolori**, where trails diverge east to the Besoa Valley, and a twenty-minute walk south over the Lariang to Bomba across a deathtrap of a suspension bridge – one hundred scary metres of missing planks, broken cables and no handrails. **South of the river**, you'll find easily the small statues at Gintu itself and 3km east at **Bewa**, though there are four more hidden in the scrub along a track which loops 7.5km south between the two villages; one of these, known as **Dula Boe**, is unique in having the body of a buffalo. In a grove fifteen minutes' walk east of Bomba, another carving worth seeing is two-metre-high **Lanke Bulawa**, a rare female statue.

Whether you walk in three days, or spend at least eight hours bucking around on a plank across the back of a 4WD, the road **from Bomba to Tentena** – assuming it's open – is quite an adventure. The first stage ascends into the mountains along very steep, muddy and rutted tracks, where every ridge scaled means a hair-raising plunge on the far side to a gully spanned by tree trunks or branches, though a couple of solid bridges cross bigger creeks. A highland scrub of bushes, pitcher plants and stunted trees right on top of the range marks the halfway point. Once past this, the gradient levels out somewhat as the road follows crests through cloud forest, the trees draped with wisps of old man's beard. Look for **knobbed hornbills**, with their heavy yellow beaks, and long-tailed, deep-blue **bearded bee-eaters** – both common enough here, but found only on Sulawesi. The last third of the journey winds down the western side of the Poso Valley on a wide road, gaps in the canopy allowing occasional views over Danau Poso. Once you hit the bitumen at the base of the range, it's another twenty minutes or so to Tentena.

Bomba to Doda and the Besoa Valley

The thirty-kilometre trail between Bomba and Doda is harder than anything the Bada Valley has to offer; mostly uphill, with plenty of gullies and narrow paths with crumbly edges to negotiate. You'll need at least ten hours, and come prepared to camp out. From Bomba, cross the river to Kolori, then turn east over a stream into marshy fields beyond **Lelio** and start climbing into woodland above the Lariang, where the river cuts a steep gorge between the hills, especially impressive after the level flow through the valley. At first the walk is only semi-shaded and hot, but you reach the forest proper by the mid-point **waterfall**, a good spot to cool off and have lunch. There's jungle most of the way from here to Bomba, with huge mountain pandanus, silvery trunks climbing out of a mass of supporting roots, long-stemmed heliconia growing like ginger alongside the path, and a couple of big fig trees. The last hour is spent descending a low saddle through the Besoa Valley's paddy-fields and streams, and then down a broad track to Doda.

Set at a 1200-metre altitude, the **Besoa Valley** runs north along a tributary of the Lariang, a much greener and somehow tidier bowl than Bada, with a huge number of *kalamba* basins found here. A large public-square-cum-playing-field surrounded by houses, **DODA** is at the southeast side of valley, with the path from Bomba entering the square near the kepala desa's house. Both the latter and the nearby losmen provide **board and lodging** (❶). Negotiate guiding services for the valley with either the kepala desa, or Doda's English-speaking schoolteacher, and check out the **museum** next to the kepala desa's home, where a traditional bamboo rice barn and wooden, A-frame **tambi** house sit on thick supporting posts.

There are three megalithic sites in the valley: **Pokekea** is the biggest single grouping of megaliths in the park, with two figures and a dozen or more *kalamba*, but it's 7km west and you can see just as much closer to Doda. At **Tadulakoh**, a twenty-minute walk over muddy fields, a half-dozen *kalamba* stand exposed on a slope, accurately sculpted cylinders 1.5m across and similarly deep with slightly bulging sides, some grooved in wide bands. A few **lids** lie beside the basins, carved with flat central "nipples" and probably weighing a tonne or more, with a sole two-metre-high male statue overlooking the site. The third location is 3km southeast of Doda near **LEMPE**, whose kepala desa will arrange for somebody to show you to the megaliths, which are spookily surrounded by forest on the hills behind the village. The first is a recently propped-up statue with a moss-covered body and very distinct face, set in a tiny clearing from where trails lead deeper into the vegetation to two lidless *kalamba*, filled with water, the guide bounding along barefoot, casually pointing out passion-fruit vines and tunnels made through the undergrowth by anoa.

The Napu Valley

There's a decent 31-kilometre mud road from Doda to Watutau in the **Napu Valley**, and, though Doda's kepala desa may recommend that you charter a 4WD (Rp150,000) or at least hire a guide, it's an easy eight-hour walk along an obvious track. Trekkers should check on the current situation in Poso before setting off for this part of the park. If it's open, follow the road out of Doda and bear sharply right at the fork about 3km further on; flat fields cede to a steep road under a light forest canopy. Over the top, the road quickly drops into the Napu Valley, where you'll need to ask directions at every village you pass through in order to stay on track for Watutau. The indescribably warped and twisted covered wooden bridges along the way are another good reason to make this journey on foot.

Lying north–south along the headwaters of the Lariang, only the western side of the twenty-kilometre long Napu Valley is actually inside the national park, and it's all thoroughly farmed and settled. **WATUTAU** lies across the river at the southern end, a single sandy street; the kepala desa is a serious man who offers bed and breakfast for a donation. A satellite dish outside his home is the first in the village and at night the entire household gathers to watch the soaps, sprawled amongst a sea of cobs from the year's maize harvest. There are more **hot springs** and five **megaliths** in the valley, including a 1.5-metre example outside the kepala desa's house, and one with prominent ears off across the fields; try and get out early in the morning, when a thick mist covers everything.

From Watutau, a twenty-kilometre sealed road runs flat **to Wuasa** at the northern end of the valley, past another megalith right by the roadside at **Wangga**, a metre-high male with a broad smile. **WUASA** is a large settlement by local standards: a grid of gravel streets, a big church and a couple of tiny mosques, a few toko selling fuel and essentials, **accommodation** (❷) at

Losmen Mes Penda or *Losmen Citra*, three **places to eat**, and daily **buses** out on the *Napu Star* for Palu (6hr). If you're heading over the range to Poso, ask the driver to stop on the lower slopes of the valley at **Batu Nonkoh**, an atypical roughly shaped *kalamba* with eyes and nose carved into its side, and also on the hillsides above, where there are grand views back over Napu – villages dotting brilliant-green fields.

The eastern peninsula and islands

Most of the 300-kilometre-long eastern peninsula is exceptionally rugged, the majority of peaks topping 2000m. While the adventurous can see something of this by hiking into the undeveloped **Morowali Reserve**, most of the area's attractions lie offshore. The main road from Poso skirts along the north coast to the ports of **Ampana**, springboard for the maritime pleasures surrounding the **Togian Islands**, and **Pagaimana**, departure point for the crossing to Gorontalo and Sulawesi Utara. South across the peninsula's thin neck from Pagaimana, **Luwuk** is a staging post into the Morowali Reserve, and also out to the seldom-visited **Banggai Islands**. There are no **banks** at all in the region, so change money first in Poso or Gorontalo.

For advice on safety in the Suluwesi Tengah region, see p.929.

Ampana

Five hours east of Poso along a road crossed by a handful of flood-prone rivers, **AMPANA** is a dusty little hole whose bus station, market and Pertamina fuel storage tanks are the focus of a tumbledown **port area** from where most Togian traffic departs. The bus station is about 500m east of the town centre, where you'll find the port, market and the best of the accommodation. The most popular **place to stay**, and deservedly so, is the *Oasis Hotel* (ⓣ0464/21058; ❷) just back from the seafront at Jl Kartini 5. The extremely smart fan-cooled rooms here are good value, though the dormitory beds are less reasonable, and budget travellers should instead consider heading 100m up the road to the *Losmen Irama* (ⓣ0464/21055; ❷), which offers doubles with mandi and breakfast. A third option lies just around the corner at Jalan Mohammed Hatta 37 at the *Family Hotel* (ⓣ0464/21034; ❷). For **food**, the huge and beautiful *Green Garden Café* on the seafront, attached to the *Oasis Hotel*, is the perfect place to catch the sea breeze and watch the sun go down while sipping a cold Bintang; the curries are pretty good here too. Ask at the port about **ferry schedules** – there's transport to Wakai and Bomba most days from here – though some boats leave from an anonymous beach about 3km east of town, best reached by dokar or ojek. Ampana isn't really the sort of place to hang around in unnecessarily, but with a spare half-day it's worth hiring a longboat from the docks for the short ride east to **Tanjung Api**, the Fire Cape, where there are a couple of interesting beaches to picnic at, and blue-burning **volcanic gases** seeping up through the sands.

The Togian Islands

The **Togian Islands** form a fragmented, 120-kilometre-long crescent across the shallow blue waters of Tomini Bay, their steep grey sides undercut by tides and weathered into sharp ridges capped by coconut palms and hardwoods. The soil is poor, so people make a living from the sea, fishing from vessels ranging from eight-metre catamarans with little off-centre huts and sails on each hull, to smaller craft outrigged with thigh-thick bamboo – some opportunists even spear fish with home-made goggles and guns made from wood, rubber and glass. Not all the Togians are inhabited, and **fauna** on remoter islands includes monkeys, the weird babirusa, and huge coconut crabs, *kedang kenari*, though their popularity as a novelty cuisine with visitors has made them rare. Offshore, the ubiquitous yellow buoys of Japanese and Australian pearl farms are testament to the bay's pristine waters, and the exceptional **snorkelling** and **diving** around the islands features excellent visibility, turtles, sharks, octopus, garden eels, and a mixed bag of reef and pelagic fish species. On the down side, there are also nine depots in the Togians dealing in the live export of seafood to restaurants in Asia; many of these operations employ cyanide sprays, which stun large fish but kill everything else, including coral.

From west to east, **Batu Daka**, **Togian** and **Talata Koh** are the Togian's three main islands, together forming a tightly grouped, sixty-kilometre-long chain, each island separated from its neighbour by a narrow channel. The main settlements here are **Bomba** and **Wakai** on Batu Daka, and **Katupat** on Pulau

Togian transport

The lack of information about **inter-island transport** in the Togians is only partly due to deliberate fudging by private operators, who want your custom for themselves. The truth is that even scheduled public services are notoriously unreliable, either through a lack of customers on any particular day, the incessant mechanical failures on the large passenger vessels, or the reluctance of the owners of smaller craft to put to sea in anything but perfect conditions.

Transport to the islands

The only **public ferry services** to the islands at present are the 10am ferries from Ampana to Wakai (daily except Fri; 4hr 30min; Rp14,000) from the central harbour, and to Bomba (daily except Fri; 2hr; Rp8000) from the second harbour 3km out of town – both depending on the weather and the size of the swell. Coming from Gorontalo, you can either catch the nightly ferry to Pagaimana, and from there a bus to Ampana, or you can charter a boat from Marisa, three hours to the west of Gorontalo (Rp600,000 after bargaining). The Black Marlin office in Gorontalo has details of the latest ferry schedules (see p.947), and also rents out its own boat from Marisa to Pulau Kadidiri (Rp1,000,000).

Transport around the islands

On the Togians themselves, the following services seem to be operating reasonably regularly:

- Wakai–Bomba/Bomba–Wakai (daily; 4hr; Rp16,000).
- Wakai–Katupat/Katupat–Wakai (3 or more weekly; 2hr).
- Wakai–Kadidiri/Kadidiri–Wakai (all three cottages on Kadidiri transfer guests free of charge from Wakai; if you don't plan to stay with them, however, expect to pay Rp20,000; 1hr). The boats meet the ferry from Ampana.
- Wakai–Malenge/Malenge–Wakai (1–2 weekly; 3hr).

Elsewhere, there's bound to be something along eventually if you can afford to wait, or you can **charter** a motorized outrigger at about Rp125,000 an hour – you'll probably get soaked, but it's not necessarily expensive if you can find others to share costs.

Togian is something of a regional hub, with transport out to smaller islands such as **Kadidiri**, off Togian, and **Malenge**, due north off Talata Koh. Further east of this main trinity are another two large islands, **Walea Kodi** and **Walea Bahi**, with the main town of **Dolong** on Walea Kodi. There are no vehicle roads or widespread electricity in the Togians and, with all travel by boat, you'll find it pays not to be on too tight a schedule. With little time or money, it's a good idea to confine yourself to one area, and make use of various day-trips or shared transfers offered by your accommodation. Tourism in the islands is budget-orientated, though lodgings are often surprisingly good; **meals** are usually included in room price. Be conservative with **water**, which has to be shipped in to many places. July through to September are the coolest months, when winds often interrupt ferries and make for poor diving; at other times, Tomini is rated as the calmest bay on earth, its waters often glassy-smooth.

Batu Daka

Three hours from Ampana and at the western end of Batu Daka, **BOMBA** comprises two dozen houses and a mosque facing north across a pleasant bay. There's a long **beach** 5km west of town, but it's the sea which warrants a visit here, with the Togians' best **snorkelling** an hour distant at **Catherine reef**. The coast here is interesting, too, with the possibility of seeing **crocodiles** in remote inlets, and some islets east of Bomba completely covered by villages, their sides reinforced with hand-cut coral ramparts. In Bomba itself, dockside *Losmen Poya Lisa* (❷ full board) is a fine **place to stay**; but just a little way to the south of Bomba, the American-run *Island Retreat* (❹ full board) is a fair bit smarter and just that little bit better. They also run a diving operation (US$55 for two dives); contact the *Island Café* in Rantepao (☎0423/23502; see p.915) for bookings. Entrepreneurs at the dock can run you across to the place of your choice, and your accommodation will arrange boat trips to suit guests' needs. Ferries back to Ampana leave Bomba most mornings as long as the swell is not too great, and assuming they don't run aground on the reef just out from the jetty.

At the eastern end of Batu Daka, about five hours from Ampana and two from Bomba, **WAKAI** is similar to the dock area at Ampana, though with far better accommodation at the white timber *Togian Islands Hotel* (❹). Slow and expensive, the restaurant here is Wakai's best; there are also a few warung and well-stocked stores around the dock.

Kadidiri

Half an hour by motorized outrigger from Wakai, **Kadidiri** is one of the nicest of the islands, 3km long and with fine beaches and ample lodgings. The highest-profile accommodation on the Togians is provided both by the *Kadidiri Paradise Bungalows* (❷) and the hillside *Kadidiri Wakai Cottages* (☎0435/824026; ❸), with the English-run Black Marlin dive school attached. Safety-conscious **scuba** teams at both places charge a flat US$25 per dive for all-inclusive trips to nearby reefs such as **Taipi Wall**, with additional transport costs if you want to visit the submerged wreck of a B-24 fighter plane or volcanic **Pulau Una-Una**. The third place on Kadidiri, *Lestari Homestay* (❷), is more relaxed and unpretentious, serves gargantuan portions of food and is deservedly hugely popular with travellers. Just offshore, there are secluded cabins on **Pulau Taipi** (❷), run by the same people who own *Paradise* on Kadidiri. Shallow coral around Taipi makes for good skin-diving, and, if you want some solitude, tracks through undergrowth lead across to Kadidiri's isolated southern beaches.

Togian

On Pulau Togian's central northern coast, **KATUPAT** village was a tourist core before Kadidiri got going, but few visitors make it here now – a Friday market means that you're most likely to find transport heading this way on Thursday morning. A sleepy hundred metres of coral-rubble streets strewn with goats and drying copra runs east into mangroves and a coconut plantation, with the couple of stores at the jetty specializing in soap, tobacco and tins of sardines. A good four hours northeast of Katupat off the top of Talata Koh – but probably more reliably reached directly from Wakai – ten-kilometre-long **Malenge**'s primary forests make it one of the best spots in the Togians to hunt for wildlife. *Losmen Malenge Indah* (❷) and *Lestari* (❷), both near the jetty, are recommended **places to stay** and organize hiking and snorkelling.

Walea Kodi and Walea Bahi

Until the demise of the weekly Ampana–Gorontalo ferry, visitors could have made **Dolong** on **Walea Kodi** their point of entry into the Togians. This village is somewhere to experience Togian life beyond tourism; you can rent boats to local reefs, but to get treated like a celebrity you should walk 4km west across the island to the remote village of **Tutung**, where foreign faces are an extremely rare sight. There are no losmen in Dolong, so you'll need to locate and make arrangements with Umrah, the hospitable kepala desa. A few kilometres further east again, **Walea Bahi** is right off any regular transport routes, though the *Walea Dive Resort* (❸) has opened up at **Tanjung Kramat**, on the forested southeastern tip. The **dive operation** here concentrates on some exceptional reef walls off **Pulau Dondoia**, a square of white coral sand topped by a single tree.

Pagaimana, Luwuk and beyond

Five hours east of Ampana, **PAGAIMANA** is a small Bajau town with a dense collection of houses built over the water next to a busy port for the overnight **ferry to Gorontalo** (see p.947), which departs every day. Leaving, the cheapest option for the crossing is to buy an ekonomi fare (Rp19,500) at the harbour, and then rent a mattress for Rp3000; turn up early to book your space on the floor. The crossing takes about twelve hours and is not too bad. If you've just arrived from Gorontalo, you'll be grabbed and ushered towards a host of minibuses heading to Luwuk, Ampana and Poso; take your pick.

Three hours from Pagaimana and thirteen from Poso, **LUWUK**, the east peninsula's largest town, looks south across the Seleng Straits to the **Banggai Islands**. A relaxed place to spend the evening in transit, there are good rooms and food at *Hotel Ramayana*, Jalan Anau Lindu (☎0461/21073; ❷), and cheaper beds at the *City* (❶) on Jalan Gunung Mulia. Moving on, morning **buses** head all the way back west to Palu, and along the southern coast to trailheads for the Morowali Reserve. From the **port**, Pelni stop here on their east-coast run, and there's also a nightly **ferry** for the nine-hour run southeast past large **Pulau Peleng** to **BANGGAI**, the main town on the island of the same name. Only about a dozen tourists visit Banggai each year and facilities are rudimentary, but there's losmen and hotel accommodation, supposedly good snorkelling, the high-set former **palace** of the sultan of Banggai, and the possibility of hitching a ride on cargo vessels and fishing boats heading east to Maluku.

Morowali Reserve

On one of Sulawesi's wildest corners, the boundaries of the **Morowali Reserve**, 100km southwest of Luwuk at the base of the eastern peninsula, enclose every terrain from coastal swamp to mountainous heathland. Home to butterflies, birds and a broad slice of Sulawesi's endemic mammals, Morowali is also the haunt of several thousand **Wana**, nomads who use blowpipes and poison darts for hunting, and have so far resisted government attempts to settle them. Unless you arrange a tour into Morowali with operators in Tentena, Poso or Palu, you need to be able to speak Indonesian and come fully equipped for hard hiking and minimal comforts.

There are various ways to tackle Morowali. The most common **entry point** is via **KOLONODALE**, a small town of stilt houses and shops clustered around a port on the southwestern shore of **Tomori Bay**, whose blue waters are studded with rocky islands. Kolonodale is also a stop for Pelni ferries heading up the east coast between Baubau and Bitung. The Sahabat Morowali (Friends of Morowali; ☎0465/21124) can provide all sorts of information about the reserve, and arrange permits and tours; they can be contacted through the *Penginapan Sederhana* (❷), at Jl Jend A Yani 154, the best-value of the **accommodation** options, though better facilities can be found at either *Penginapan Lestari* (❷ full board), five minutes' walk away along Jalan Sudarso, or *Penginapan Rejeki Jaya* (❷ full board), the same distance down Jalan Hasanuddin. Before entering the park you will need to have a **permit** (Rp2500), available either from the **PHPA office** at Jl Prof Yamin 17 (Mon–Thurs 8.30am–2pm, Fri 8.30–11am), or at the parks office in Palu (see p.934). Ask in the PHPA office about guides, or at the *Sederhana*, who can also organize a boat across to the reserve.

The Morowali Reserve can also be approached from the eastern side of the park. Do check on the regulations regarding permits however, and if possible pick one up in Palu or Kolonodale before attempting to enter the park from this side, for there are rumours that permits are no longer available in Baturube. **From Luwuk** a daily bus runs to **Padaoke** (also known as Donggi), where you can catch a public boat or, if the road is open, another bus, to **BATURUBE**, just outside the eastern edge of the reserve. Baturube has two losmen and a bimonthly **market** attended by Wana drifting in from the wilds; hikers should stock up here with presents – **salt** and rough-smoking *leta* or *adidie* **tobacco** (sold in bamboo tubes at about Rp1000 a slice) are much appreciated in the interior. Baturube's kepala desa can help to find essential **guides** for the reserve at Rp35,000 a day, or try to track down Nasip Njee or Yonathon, both highly experienced escorts and sources of information.

From Baturube, there's a tough ten-day trek north through virgin forests **to Tobamawu** on Sungai Bongka, with transport on from here to **Tamponompo** on the Ampana–Poso road; almost all of this is actually outside the reserve, but it's the best area to find wildlife and groups of Wana. A shorter option, which takes you **into the reserve** itself, heads west along a vehicle track from Baturube to the village of **Tokala Atas**, from where you can hike or catch a ride on an ojek to **Tarongo**. It's a long day's hike from here to **KAYUPOLI**, a relatively modernized Wana village at the centre of the reserve where you can base yourself for day-trips south to **Ranu lakes**, strangely still, twinned pools surrounded by forest. Another day south of Kayupoli, villagers in kampung around the mouth of the Morowali estuary can organize transport across the bay to **Kolonodale** and the road to Tentena – ask for Pak Nawir.

Sulawesi Utara and Gorontalo

A narrow trail of active volcanic ranges continuing out across the Celebes Sea as a scattered group of islands, isolation from the south and close contacts with outside powers has always marked **Sulawesi Utara** and the newly created province of **Gorontalo** apart from the rest of the island. Not that the two provinces are particularly similar: **Gorontalo Province**, comprising the city and the former **Bolaang-Mongondow** regency, is Islamic, while at the peninsula's tip, around the provincial capital of **Manado**, the ancestors of the **Minahasans** island-hopped down from the Philippines, converting to Christianity during the nineteenth century. What both provinces share is a strong legacy of Dutch influence, which became so entrenched that the region was nicknamed "Holland's Twelfth Province", its people even widely supporting Dutch attempts to resume control of Indonesia after World War II. A sense of being different continued beyond Independence, when in 1958 the north became the last stand of the **Permesta revolt**, the military-backed uprising against increasing Javan influence in regional affairs which had started the year before in Makassar. But within a matter of months, and before Permesta's support of similar groups in Java and Sumatra could lead to unified opposition against his rule, Sukarno had **bombed** the revolution into submission, though Permesta guerrillas (with covert aid from the US) continued sporadic resistance until 1961.

Northern Sulawesi abounds with natural attractions; if you've just arrived from the drier southern peninsula, it's striking just how fertile the north's volcanic soils are – one of the most lasting impressions of the lowlands here is of millions of mature **coconut trees**, and much of what isn't given over to palm plantations or rice is covered in **rainforest**. The provinces' two most accessible reserves, **Dumoga-Bone** east of Gorontalo, and **Tangkoko** near Manado, are the easiest places in Sulawesi to find wildlife, with sightings of the island's unusual mammals and birds almost guaranteed. For their part, the gently cultivated **Minahasan highlands** south of Manado have live **volcanoes** to climb and, as the heart of Minahasan culture, offer a different picture from the coast. Offshore, the waters and vertical coral walls around **Pulau Bunaken** have been attracting scuba divers for the last decade, and are in themselves enough reason for any enthusiast to spend a week or more up here. Far less well known are the **Sangihe and Talaud Islands** between Manado and the Philippines, though with time they are easy enough to reach either as part of a round-trip, or as a last stop on the way out of Indonesia.

Roads onto the northern peninsula are poor, but this part of Sulawesi is otherwise well connected to other parts of Sulawesi and Indonesia, as well as Singapore and the Philippines, with two airports and six major harbours servicing Pelni and local passenger ferries. Transport within and between the provinces is reliable, with a 400-kilometre **highway** between Gorontalo and Manado and plenty of sealed roads elsewhere.

Sulawesi's forest fauna

Sulawesi's forests support a healthy diversity of **wildlife**, some of it unique to the island and much becoming increasingly rare, requiring dedication and luck to track down. The largest endemic mammal is the sheep-sized **anoa** or dwarf buffalo, a sharp-horned inhabitant of thick forest which, despite its small stature, is extremely fierce and greatly feared for its habit of attacking unprovoked – take care if you cross paths with one. The less aggressive **babirusa** (deer-pig) is an extraordinary beast, a thinly haired hog with two sets of upcurving tusks, one pair spreading out from the lips and the other forming what looks like a double horn growing up through its forehead. Sadly, the babirusa's liking for villagers' crops, and the fact that Christians consider it good eating, has made it scarce, likely to be spotted only in remote areas. The tailless **black macaque** (*monyet hitam* in Indonesian) is more widespread; with a stretched face, bright-orange eyes and a cheerful upright tuft on top of it's head, it's an entertaining resident of northern Sulawesi's national parks.

Native birds include parrots, pigeons the **knobbed hornbill** (whose large black body is offset by a curved yellow beak and blue wattle), and the chicken-sized **maleo**, a pied, plump fowl with a curious lumpy "helmet". The maleo is a **megapode**, a family of birds found in Asia and Australasia who build mound nests where their eggs incubate in the heat of decaying leaves; male birds (whose mouths are natural thermometers) tend the nests, adding or removing compost as necessary to keep the eggs at the right temperature. Maleos are widespread, but have become endangered as their eggs are greatly valued for food.

Other animals worth looking out for, though found elsewhere in Asia, include **cuscus** and **lorises** (*kukang*), both resembling small, slow-moving bears and difficult to see in the forest canopy, and the enchanting **tarsier** (*bangka*), a mug-sized primate with a squat body, feathery tail, long fingers with padded tips, enormous ears and eyes, and a round head that it can turn through 180 degrees. Common in lowland forest margins, tarsiers spend the day dozing in bamboo clumps, and at night spring around in shrubs chasing insects. Often ignored, **flying lizards** (*cecak trebang*, or *bunglon*) are at first sight dull-grey, bony little lizards, which habitually sit immobile on tree trunks in open woodland. Catch them at the right moment, however, and you'll see them suddenly flick out a little white "banner" from their chin, and spread their **wings** (extensions of the lizard's ribs) for sunbathing, as a territorial display or to glide from tree to tree like a paper dart.

Gorontalo and Bolaang-Mongondow

Arriving in **Gorontalo** from either the south or from Sulawesi Utara, you'll find a couple of surrounding historic and scenic sights, but it's the wilds of Bogani Nani Wartabone **national park** that really warrant a stop. A small area of the western side of the park (formerly known as Dumoga Bone national park) can be explored easily from Gorontalo, with greater access to the less-frequented eastern end of the park through the village of **Doloduo** in the **Bolaang-Mongondow district**, reached off the Gorontalo–Manado road via the town of **Kotamobagu**.

Gorontalo and around

GORONTALO is a pleasant Muslim city and, since 12 May 2000, capital of the newly created 32nd province of Indonesia. Its centre is a set piece of whitewashed, verandahed and wooden-shuttered Dutch bungalows, and colonial associations run deep here; many older people in Gorontalo speak perfect Dutch and English, and the statue of pro-Independence guerrilla **Nani Wartabone** stands ignored on the southern side of town, more of a necessary patriotic nod to the government than a heartfelt memorial. The place exudes a sleepy charm; by late morning shutters are pulled tight against the heat and everything closes down until about 4pm. With dokars clip-clopping around and the streets littered with broken horseshoes, you can almost step back fifty years amongst Gorontalo's lanes.

Sited just east of unimpressive **Sungai Bolango**, Gorontalo's **city centre** is a standard net of a dozen or so streets more or less centred on **Mesjid Baitur Rahim**, a multiple-domed mosque and tall, smoothly tiled minaret set at a wide crossroads. Be warned that many streets are in the process of being renamed, but since most locals still use the old name, we have continued to use the old names in the following account.

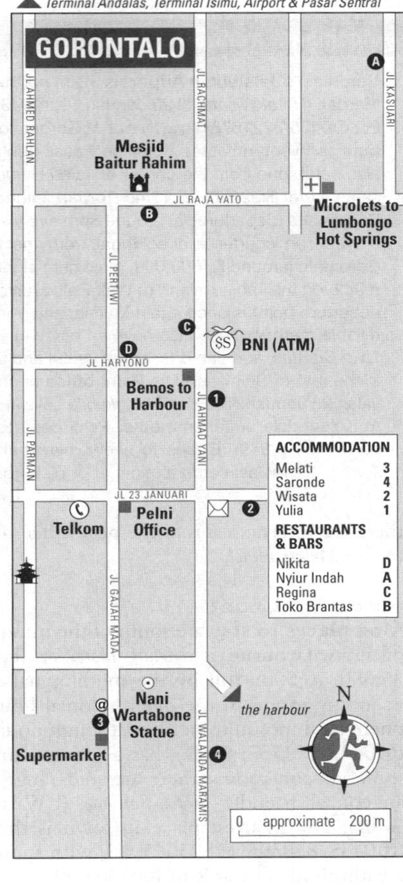

Practicalities

Ferries from Pagaimana – and, if they're running again, from Poso and Ampana – in Sulawesi Tenggara dock 7km southeast of the centre at Gorontalo's **port**, and long-distance **buses** wind up 3km north of the centre at **Terminal Andalas** or, if you're coming from Manado or Kotamobagu, and are unlucky, at **Terminal Isimu**, where the Trans-Sulawesi highway meets the main road into Gorontalo, a full 30km from the town centre (microlet into town Rp3000). Gorontalo's **Jalaluddin Airport** is nearby. Kijangs, microlets and ojeks from all these points end up at the city's **microlet terminal**, 1km north of the centre at **Pasar Sentral** on Jalan Sam Ratulangi, a busy acre of covered stalls selling fresh produce, coconut shredders, betel nut and cakes. **Dokar** (Rp500–1000 depending on distance) can be rented all around downtown Gorontalo, although the area is so small there's no need to look for one unless you're impossibly encumbered with luggage.

All **banks** are on Jalan Ahmad Yani; the BNI offers bad rates, but has an ATM and is the only place in town accepting American Express travellers' cheques. The **post office** is on the corner of Jalan Ahmad Yani and Jalan 23 Januari, while the Telkom office is a block west of here on Jalan 23 Januari;

Moving on from Gorontalo

Gorontalo's **Jalaluddin Airport** is 32km northwest of town near Terminal Isimu. Both Merpati (*Hotel Wisata*, Jl 23 Januari 19, ⓣ0435/821736) and Bouraq (Jl Jend A Yani 26, ⓣ0435/8221678) now fly out of Gorontalo to destinations in Sulawesi. The **harbour** is twenty minutes from the Pasar Sentral microlet terminal, though you can also catch one from the corner of Jalan Haryono and Jalan A Yani, which takes the same time (Rp2000). For the **Togian islands**, you can either take the ferry to Pagaimana (departures at around 8pm every evening) and then a bus up to Ampana, or you can charter a direct boat from the town of Marisa, three hours west of Gorontalo (around Rp600,000, maximum eight pasengers). The *Wakai Cottages* (see p.942) on the Togian island of Wakai also run a boat for its guests (Rp1,000,000); the departure point is once again Marisa, and you may find this a more convenient and reliable method. They also have an office in Gorantalo above the surf shop next to *Toko Brantas*, and can offer some useful and up-to-date information about travelling in the rest of Sulawesi. The **Pelni office** is on the corner of Jalan Gajah Mada and Jalan 23 Januari. The *KM Tilongkabila* calls in to Gorontalo twice a month on its way to Kolonodale or Tahuna; other Pelni departures use Kwandang, two hours to the north (see p.949). **Buses** to everywhere between Palu and Makassar leave from Terminal Andalas; catch a microlet or ojek from Pasar Sentral.

there are internet cafés at the post office, above the *Regina* restaurant and next to the *Melati Hotel*.

Accommodation

Most **places to stay** are south of the mosque and within easy walking distance of it. A favourite is *Melati Hotel* at Jl Gajah Mada 33 (ⓣ0435/822934; 35,000–70,000), run by the mutlilingual and irrepressible Alex. The cheaper economy rooms in the older colonial house next door have far more atmosphere (and mosquito nets too, though no fans). *Hotel Wisata*, at Jl 23 Januari 19 (ⓣ0435/821737; ❷–❸), has a gloomy interior but is quiet and clean, with some air-con rooms; there are mid-range comforts with rooms with fans or air-con at friendly *Hotel Saronde*, Jl Walanda Maramis 17 (ⓣ0435/821735; ❷–❸). The smartest place in town is the *Yulia Hotel* on Jl Ahmad Yani 26 (ⓣ0435/828395, ⓕ823063; ❹), with spotless rooms, air-con, satellite TV and a bathtub for upwards of Rp130,000.

Eating, drinking and entertainment

For **places to eat**, night stalls south off Jalan Hasanuddin on Jalan Pertiwi have endless assortments of buns, jackfruit soup, rice and noodle dishes. *Toko Brantas*, opposite the mosque on Jalan Raja Eyato, is Gorontalo's best cake shop and always sells out early, and the attached restaurant is also good for cheap local and Chinese food. Offering similar fare, but a bit more convenient to most hotels, is *Regina*, opposite the BNI at Jl Ahmad Yani 23. For something better, head north behind the hospital to the *Nyiur Indah*, Jl Kasuari 35, a Chinese establishment with cold beer, juicy grilled fish and sweet chicken with pineapple and chillies, and full-on karaoke. Finally, check out the *Nikita*, upstairs at the corner of Jalan Pertiwi and Jalan Haryono, a lively and popular – if slightly sleazy – **disco-bar**.

Danau Limboto and Lumbongo hot springs

A twenty-minute microlet ride west from Pasar Sentral takes you to the shores of shallow, gradually contracting **Danau Limboto**. There are excellent views over the 56-square-kilometre basin from **Benteng Otanaha**, a series of three circular stone **forts** arranged on a stony, dry hilltop at the eastern edge of the lake, possibly built in the sixteenth century by the Portuguese and later used by local warlords. Microlets to the village of **Dembe** (Rp750) leave you where stairs climb to the turret-like walls, whose blocks are held together by a mixture of cement laced with maleo eggs. The lake sprawls below into the hazy distance, its marshy fringes a patchwork of fish farms, aluminium village roofs, and the soft, dark green of palm tops.

In the other direction, **Lumbongo hot springs** lie 17km east of Gorontalo at the edge of Dumoga-Bone national park, crowded at weekends (when transport is plentiful) and otherwise deserted. Microlets in this direction leave at irregular intervals from outside Gorontalo's hospital on Jalan Sultan Botutihe, and you'll have to bargain down ridiculous asking prices for the thirty-minute journey – the springs are about 1km off the main road, and drivers charge extra to take you right to the gates. Entry to the springs – which fill a couple of swimming pools at the foot of a steep, wooded mountain range – is Rp1000, but those intending to hike 3km beyond them to a series of **waterfalls** inside the national park are supposed to call in first at the **ranger station** (just before the entrance) for a **permit** (Rp2500). This is also valid for entry into Dumoga-Bone's eastern end, if you're heading that way, and the ranger himself is happy to chat about wildlife and the possibility of five-day traverses of the park. The path to the waterfall is rocky and easy to follow, crossing nine streams and taking you through some respectable forest; clearings with pools along the way allow a view of the treetops, and are good spots to look for butterflies, reptiles, birds and monkeys. The last microlet **back to Gorontalo** passes along the main road at about 6pm, but is often full – don't leave things this late.

Kwandang, Kotamobagu and Bogani Nani Wartabone national park

Two hours north from Gorontalo, the Manado road crosses the peninsula to the far coast at **KWANDANG**, where it's a short microlet hop from the tiny centre to Kwandang's **Pelni harbour**, port of call for a monthly service to Palu, Makassar, Kalimantan and Java. There are also two more **forts** of Portuguese stamp just south of town, though neither are worth a special visit; **Ota Mas Udangan** is a pile of rubble, with renovations fleshing out the remains of **Benteng Oranje**.

The highway continues 300km east from Kwandang and on up to Manado, but about halfway along a secondary road cuts inland at **Inobonto** to **KOTAMOBAGU**, one-time capital of the Bolaang-Mongondow sultanate, a hideout for Permesta rebels, and now a friendly market town. Eight hours from Gorontalo, buses pull in to Terminal Bonawang (also called Terminal Mongkonai after the village in which it's located) at the northern edge of town, where microlets will ferry you to the mosque, market, stores and active, scruffy streets that make up Kotamobagu's centre. Coming from Manado, if you miss the early morning direct bus to Kotamobagu you'll have to catch a bemo to Inobonto (3hr), and change for a second bemo from there. The pick of the **accommodation** here lies on the approach road to the centre: the clean, spacious and comfy *Hotel Tenteram*, at Jl Adampe Dolot 38, (☎0434/21183; ❷), and the slightly fading former favourite *Hotel Ramayana*, just 50m down the road at no. 50 (☎0434/23110; ❷), with brighter upstairs rooms. **Places to eat** include warung near the mosque and a couple of Padang and Indonesian canteens on Jalan Ahmad Yani – try the *Nasional* or *Surya*, or, better still, *La Rose*

Bakery and Restoran, just down and across the road from the *Hotel Ramayana*. For **banks**, BNI on Jalan A Yani has an ATM and can change money, and there are a couple of tiny internet places here too.

Set aside a day in Kotamobagu and catch a minibus 25km east via **Modayang** to **Modoinding** village on the western side of **Danau Mooat**, a flooded volcano crater ringed by forest. Trails from behind Modoinding's church lead west up 1780-metre-high **Gunung Ambang** – check with locals to make sure of the track. A couple of hours should see you at the apparent summit; thick vegetation means no views, but steaming, sulphurous vents and the jungle compensate. **Leaving Kotamobagu**, buses to Gorontalo or Manado depart from Terminal Bonawang in the morning, mid-afternoon and evening, with shared Kijang to Doloduo and Dumoga-Bone (best organized early on in the day) leaving from the Serasi bemo terminus on Jalan Borian. Tickets on the Paris Expres buses to Gorontalo and Manado can be bought from the Paris Supermarket at the top of Jalan Adampe Dolot.

Doloduo and Bogani Nani Wartabone national park

The paddy-field colours along the fifty-kilometre, well-watered **Dumoga Valley** southwest of Kotamobagu terminate with the drier, darker tones of **Bogani Nani Wartabone national park**, a 1900-square-kilometre reserve created as much to protect water-catchment areas as to provide a safe haven for Sulawesi's dwindling populations of endemic fauna. The first step to visiting the park is to call in at the **park's headquarters** (Mon–Thurs 8.30am–2pm, Fri 8.30–11am; ⓣ0434/22548) in Kotamobagu, where they have reams of information, including some useful maps showing the major trails, and where you can also buy a permit (Rp3000). About two-thirds of the way to the park from Kotamobagu, and just past **Dumoga**, the village of **IMANDI** marks a detour 7km south to a **maleo nesting ground**, the best place in the region to encounter this elusive bird – though reports suggest that sightings are rare even here. You might be able to arrange for a Kijang from Kotamobagu to take you to the site, or hunt around for an ojek at Imandi.

All transport, including the convenient microlets, terminates at **DOLODUO**, a dusty T-intersection on **Sungai Kasingolan**, from where vehicles back to Kotamobagu and Manado leave in the morning. Ask around in Doluduo for inexpensive **homestay** accommodation at the *Niko Guest House*. They can arrange an obligatory **guide** into Bagani Nani Wartabone for a flat Rp30,000, irrespective of whether you spend forty minutes or four hours in the jungle (bear in mind that unless a group comprises "family members", each person has to pay).

Fortunately, Bagani Nani Wartabone's interior is impressively wild, with circuit tracks fording shallow **Sungai Kasingolan** into a margin of vines and bamboo clumps, which gradually merge with a mix of mature fan palms and mighty rainforest trees, fig trunks reaching 40m skywards while their buttress roots form complex tangles at ground level. Steamy heat and crunchy leaf litter make for tiring stalking, and abundant rattan means boots, legs and arms can take a scratching. **Wildlife** is best seen at dawn; birds find the break in the canopy over the river a convenient highway between the trees, and you can spot native pigeons, racquet-tail parrots and hornbills within a minute's walk of the park entrance. Further into the forest, you might catch tarsiers nestling down for the day, get checked out by an inquisitive black macaque or two, or glimpse snakes and jungle fowl (wild chickens) tearing off into the undergrowth at your approach.

Manado, Minahasa and beyond

Mainland Sulawesi's final 120km descends north off the volcanic plateau of the **Minahasan highlands** and out over a string of sand-and-coral islands, which start immediately offshore inside **Bunaken Marine Reserve** and reach right on up to the **Sangihe-Talaud group** towards the Philippines. On the western shore, **Manado** is the north's largest city, well positioned for trips up into the hills, out to sea, or across the peninsula to more mountains, forests, and the port of **Bitung**.

Manado

Capital of Sulawesi Utara, **MANADO** is a cosmopolitan place, its blended population of islanders, Minahasans, Chinese, Indonesians and Westerners reflecting a long history of absorbed influences. Facing west over **Manado Bay**, there was already a settlement called **Wenang** here before the Portuguese and Spanish introduced Catholicism in the sixteenth century, but the city's current name seems to have been in vogue by the time that the VOC evicted the Iberians and built the now-defunct **Fort Amsterdam** against Ternate's claims on the area a hundred years later. Today Manado projects a prosperous, self-respecting air, managing to be modern without having fallen victim to the cheap concrete constructions that overwhelm so many of Indonesia's cities, and you don't have to look hard to find backstreets with neat houses and gardens.

Arrival and information

Downtown Manado is a couple of blocks of markets, squares, roundabouts and intersections on the north side of the city immediately below a shallow, silted **harbour**, with other businesses and services south of here along the first kilometre or so of Jalan Sam Ratulangi, which runs parallel with seafront Jala Pierre Tendean. **Sam Ratulangi airport**, with a moneychanger and ATM, is 12km northeast, where taxis (Rp22,000) and touts for accommodation and

Dive resorts

If you're in Manado to **dive**, and are prepared to spend a little in order to do it with any comfort and safety, you can find accommodation-and-scuba packages with the following resorts. All are on the coast 5–10km either side of Manado; packages include airport transfers, or catch a taxi from the centre to the place of your choice. **Prices** below are per person per day, for double/twin-share rooms, two dives, boat and guide, weight belt and all meals. For gear rental rates, plus the cost of dive trips from the mainland without accommodation, see "Diving" in the Manado Listings on p.955.

Manado Seagarden PO Box 1535, Manado ⓣ & ⓕ0431/861100. Clean, motel-like rooms 5km south of Manado at Malalayang; well-maintained dive gear and a knowledgeable Italian instructor.

Manado Underwater Explorations (**Murex**) Jalan Raya Trans Sulawesi ⓣ0431/826091, ⓕ826092, ⓦwww.murexdive.com. Small, friendly and relaxed resort 7km south at Desa Kelasay, with helpful staff, fine food and great live-aboard packages; the dive gear is in good condition, but dated.

Nusantara Dive Centre (**NDC**) PO Box 1015, Manado ⓣ0431/863988, ⓕ860368, ⓦwww.ndc-manado.com. 5km north at Molas Beach, big grounds and fine facilities make NDC the most established dive resort in Manado, but not really suitable for beginners. Some rental equipment is a bit worse for wear, but the dive guides are excellent – ask for Daeng.

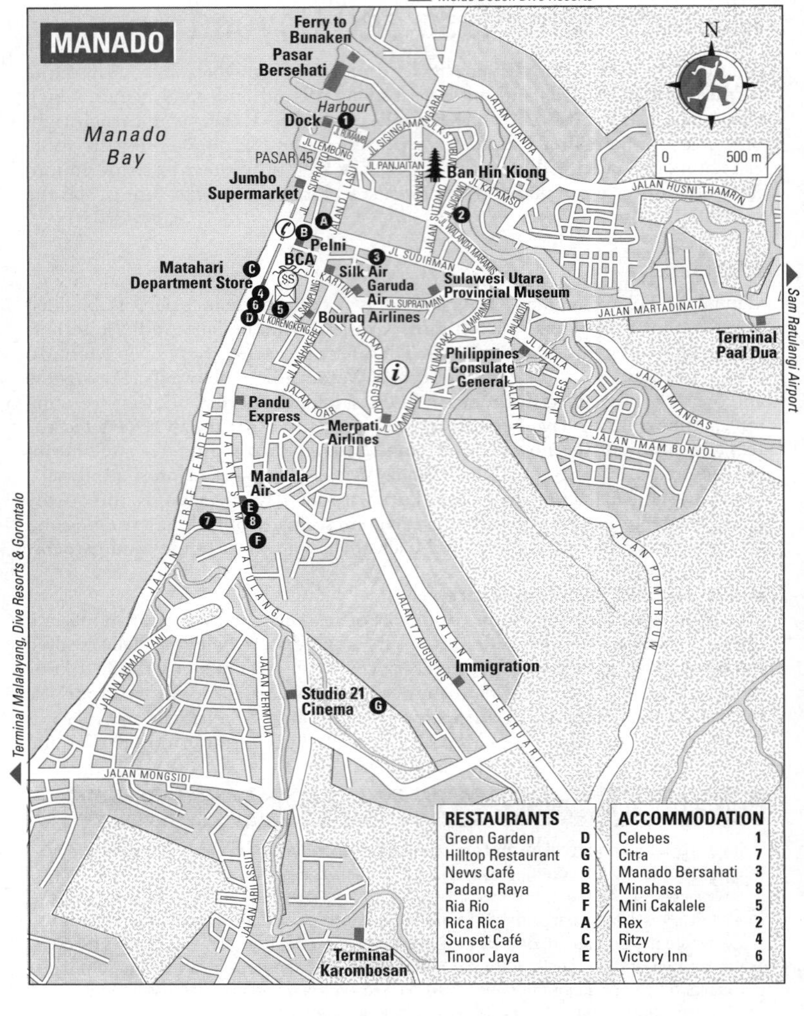

dive operations meet new arrivals. Long-distance **buses** stop on Manado's southern outskirts at **Terminal Malalayang**; minibuses from the Minahasa highlands arrive southeast at **Terminal Karombasan**; those from Bitung (the regional Pelni port) wind up east at **Terminal Paal Dua**; microlets to the centre of town run from all of these stations. Manado has no becaks, but an inordinate quantity of numbered and labelled **microlets** converge downtown at the top of Jalan Sam Ratulangi at **Pasar 45** ("Pasar Empat Lima"), an area of back-lane stalls, supermarkets and ferry agents next to the **dock**. Their destinations are usually displayed in the windscreen, and fares are a standard Rp750. Otherwise, **taxis** are on hand outside the Matahari and Golden department stores about 500m south of Pasar 45 on Jalan Ratulangi.

Seek **information** at your accommodation or one of the helpful travel agencies in town. The nearest thing to a tourist office in Manado is the Tourism Department on Jalan Diponegoro (Mon–Thurs 8.30am–2pm, Fri 8.30–11am; ⓣ0431/851723), which hands out brochures but offers no practical advice.

Accommodation

Manado has plenty of central, fair-value lodgings, nearly all with restaurants, which can provide at least basic information about the city and surroundings. There are also a handful of **dive resorts** outside the city offering good deals for divers – see box on p.951. Breakfast is included in the room charge for all the hotels listed below.

Hotel Celebes Jl Rumambi 8 ⓣ0431/870425, ⓕ859068. A new place, backing onto the harbour, within 100m of Pasar 45. The tiled, four-storey building has ekonomi singles on the top floor smaller than a monastic cell, and better air-con doubles with TV and mandi. ❷

Hotel Citra Jl Sam Ratulangi XVIII/12 ⓣ0431/863812. Family-run, friendly and quiet (except for the marauding kids) hotel down a gang off Jalan Ratulangi, close to *Hotel Minahasa*. All rooms come with bathroom attached; some have fans, others air-con and TV. ❷–❸

Hotel Manado Bersahati Jl Sudirman 20 ⓣ0431/855022, ⓕ857238. "Traditional" wooden exterior with balcony; the interior is a little confined but spotless and one of the best budget deals in town, offering bicycle rental and good local information. Small singles (the cheapest in town) and doubles, plus bigger rooms with air-con and mandi. ❷

Hotel Minahasa Jl Sam Ratulangi 199 ⓣ0431/862059, ⓕ854041. South of Pasar 45 on microlet #1, #2, #3 and #4 route. Unusually atmospheric, older hotel with attentive staff and peaceful grounds. ❸

Hotel Mini Cakalele Jl Korengkeng 40 ⓣ0431/852942, ⓕ866948. Old, tidy and friendly, with quieter rooms out the back facing onto the garden. Cheaper, fan-cooled rooms on the second floor; the rest have air-con, and all rooms come with mandi. ❷

Hotel Rex Jl Sugiono 3 ⓣ0431/851136, ⓕ867706. Very clean and fairly priced, if somewhat cramped. The cheaper rooms include breakfast in the price, but come with no fan or inside bathroom; the better rooms have fans or air-con. ❷

Ritzy Jalan Piere Tendean Blvd ⓣ0431/855555, ⓕ868888, ⓦwww.ritzymanado.20m.com. Formerly the *Novotel*, the *Ritzy* is Manado's finest, with everything you'd expect for the price (US$115) including a wonderful rooftop swimming pool looking over the bay. ❽

Victory Inn Jl Sam Ratulangi 58 ⓣ0431/863422, ⓕ862214. The new travellers' centre, following the demise of the *Smiling Hostel*, with smart but dark and often windowless rooms and helpful staff. ❸

The City

Start a tour of Manado on the north side of the harbour at the city's most active market, **Pasar Bersehati**, where a blaring loudspeaker is, for once, not calling the faithful to prayer but announcing **fish prices** as boats unload their catches on the beach behind. In 1997, the contents of one vessel returning from a deep-water trawl around Manado Tua sent shock waves through the icthyological world when a **coelacanth** – an exceptionally rare "living fossil" fish only known previously from the Comoro islands off East Africa – was offered for sale. At least one more has been netted since, adding new importance to the preservation of Manado's marine habitat.

Though you're unlikely to see such wonders, the **market** presents a squalid, bustling scene, the angles of the three-storey building swamped under a mass of humanity; blue shoals of microlets circle in the forecourt, spangled street magicians balance heavy rocks on bottle necks or perform sword tricks while shifty urchins eye spectators, and men parade with fighting cockerels tucked under their arms. The **harbour** itself is rimmed by a sea wall, the water a shambles of floating and semi-submerged boats, island ferries and outrigger canoes. Heading south towards the centre from here takes you through **Pasar Ikan**

Tua, the old fish market, a scrap of wasteland covered in shacks selling hardware; bear east and you'll soon arrive at the yellow walls and red trim of the **Ban Hin Kiong temple** (free) on the corner of Jalan Panjaitan and Jalan Sutomo. An indication of Manado's wealthy Chinese population, this recently restored, nineteenth-century Taoist complex with fairy lights and elegant dragons crawling along the rooftop is the focus for lunar new year festivities, usually in February.

Weaving past the markets and shops southwest of the temple, and the gold shops along Jalan Walanda Maramis, the top end of Jalan Sam Ratulangi is marked by a complex traffic flow around **Victory monument**, a tableau of seven concrete soldiers painted garish green and yellow. Southwest again, Jalan Piere Tendean is Manado's wide boulevard, whose northern end seems to have been earmarked as the site of future upmarket tourist development. It's a bit barren at present, though Manado's poor have taken advantage of the situation and built corrugated-iron shanties in vacant blocks facing the sea, pulling their boats up the steep sea walls on bamboo slipways. Further down, a few bars and mobile warung open up in the afternoon, and there are always a handful of people in the vicinity soaking up the fine views of the sunset and nearby islands. A thirty-minute walk east of here past a half-dozen **churches**, or about the same time in a microlet from Pasar 45, the dusty halls of the **Sulawesi Utara Provincial Museum** on Jalan Supratman (Mon–Fri 8am–3pm; Rp750 or Rp500 for a guide) might appeal to history buffs, but the contents are otherwise of minor interest – a coral diorama and *waruga* mausoleums from the Airmadidi region are amongst the few topical items here.

Eating and entertainment

Minahasan cooking features **dog** (*rintek wuuk* in Minahasan, usually shortened to *rw*, or "airway"), **rat** (*tikkus*) and **fruit bat** (*paniki*), generally unceremoniously stewed with blistering quantities of chillies – though deep-fried bat wings make an interesting side dish. Wash it down with *tuak*, palm wine, or a distilled tipple known as **sopi** and marketed under the Cap Tikkus (Rat Brand) label. Most of Manado's restaurants serve more familiar Indonesian fare, though there is one Minahasan place in town, and others range along the road to Tomohon (p.959). **Cheap warung** are legion around Pasar 45 and Jalan Sudirman. Try the markets for *tuak*, *sopi* and fresh fruit – salak, mangoes and huge pawpaws – with groceries also on hand at the Matahari, Golden and Jumbo **supermarkets**, all south of Pasar 45 on Jalan Sam Ratulangi.

The two most popular **discos** in town are *Boulevard Bar* (free), conveniently located on Jalan Piere Tendean behind the *News Café*, and the heaving, sweaty club under the *Hotel Gran Puri*, 3km south of Matahari (taxi Rp10,000; Rp40,000 entrance fee before 2am, free afterwards), both of which host live bands most nights. The Studio 21 **cinema** at the southern end of Jalan Sam Ratulangi shows mainly Western releases.

Restaurants

Green Garden Jl Sam Ratulangi 52. Extremely busy, airy, open-sided Chinese establishment with moderate prices, good soups, seafood and *sayur lohan* (monks' vegetables).

Hilltop Restaurant Off Jalan 17 Augustus; turn off west opposite the governor's offices. Moderately priced Chinese restaurant with a menu that is, in typical Manado fashion, intriguing, including frogs and pigeons, sharks and cuttlefish. But even more delicious than the food is the view encompassing the whole of the bay.

News Café Jl Sam Ratulangi 50. Classy American-owned, Western-style eatery and the centre of Manado's large expat community, serving the best burgers and salads in the city, with English-language newspapers to accompany the meal and the fastest internet café in town attached.

Padang Raya Jalan Sam Ratulangi, across from

Yantel. Above-average Padang meals; some dishes are extremely hot.
Ria Rio Jl Sudirman 3. Cheap, fresh, tasty seafood, simple decor and noisy patrons.
Rica Rica Jalan Ratulangi. Trendy local hangout serving mainly Indonesian staples and a few of the less exotic Minahasan dishes to the sound of MTV.
Sunset Café Jalan Piere Tendean, opposite *Ritzy Hotel*. Pleasant, breezy pizza and burger joint and, as the name suggests, the best place to watch the sun dip beyond the sea.
Tinoor Jaya Jl Sam Ratulangi 169. Check tablecloths and a breezy upstairs setting for consuming Minahasan specialities; the fruit bat here looks as if the animal was hit by a grenade – fragments of bone, skin and chunky black meat – but is very tasty.

Listings

Airlines Some accommodation, but no airlines, run minibuses to the airport; otherwise take a microlet from Terminal Paal Dua, or a taxi. Airline offices generally open Mon–Fri 8am–4pm, Sat & Sun 9am–1pm. Bouraq, Jl Sarapung 29 (ⓣ0431/862757), to Davao, Palu and Surabaya; Garuda, Jl Diponegoro 15 (ⓣ0431/864535, ⓕ851390), to Makassar; Lion Air (ⓣ0431/814196), to Makassar; Mandala, Jl Sam Ratulangi 175 (ⓣ0431/859333, ⓕ851779), to Makassar; Merpati, Jl Diponegoro 119 (ⓣ0431/841126, ⓕ851525), to destinations in Sulawesi including Luwuk, Palu, Gorontalo and Melangguane, as well as Ternate and Sorong; Silk Air, Jalan Lasut (ⓣ0431/863744, ⓕ853841), to Singapore.
Banks and exchange BCA, Jalan Sam Ratulangi, across from Matahari store (Mon–Fri 8am–2pm, Sat 8am–noon), is fast and efficient, with fair exchange rates and cash advances on Visa or Mastercard. The American Express agents are Pola Tours (ⓣ0431/852231), tucked away by the driveway to the *Ritzy Hotel*. There are ATMs all over town, including at the Matahari supermarket, the bakery at the Galean mall, the post office and the offices of nearly all the major banks.
Buses Long-distance buses to Kotamobagu, Doloduo, Gorontalo and beyond depart from Terminal Malalayang; Paris Expres have air-con and Marina have older buses. Services to Minahasan highlands depart from Terminal Karombasan through the day, as do those for Airmadidi, Girian and Bitung from Terminal Paal Dua.
Consulates Philippines Consulate General, Jl Tikala Ares 12 (Mon–Fri 8–11.30am; ⓣ0431/862181).
Diving Day-trips from the mainland with two dives, boat, dive guide, weight belt, air and lunch cost from US$65. Hiring a suit, gauges, BCD, and mask, snorkel and fins will set you back a further US$30; certification courses and night dives can also be arranged. Aside from Manado's dive resorts (p.951), a recommended option is Blue Banter, on the seafront by the *Sunset Café* on Jl Piere Tendean (ⓣ0431/863302, ⓕ862135), with good equipment, facilities and dive crew; a full day's diving on Bunaken (including two dives) starts at US$65. Diving costs on Pulau Bunaken are far lower than Manado, but first read the account on p.956.
Ferries Pelni, opposite the Yantel on Jalan Sam Ratulangi is a busy office with – unusually – copies of the entire Pelni schedule, and can sell tickets for ferries out of Bitung. For tickets and schedules for boats from Manado to Tahuna on the Sangihe Islands, Lirung on Pulau Talaud, and Ambon, try agents in the streets between Pasar 45 and the dock.
Hospital Public hospital 6km south of the city beside Terminal Melalayang ⓣ0431/853191; take microlet #1–4 from Pasar 45. However, there's a better hospital in the hills at Tomohon (see p.960).
Immigration office Jalan 17 Augustus ⓣ0431/863491.
Internet access The post office's cyber net café (daily 8am–9pm; Rp6000 per hour) is one of the more efficient in town. For something a little more upmarket, visit the *News Café* (see opposite); at Rp150 per minute it's more expensive than most, but the charge does include a glass of water and a cold towel upon arrival.
Post office Jl Sam Ratulangi 21.
Shopping Golden, Matahari and Jumbo supermarkets have all supplies; there's also a top-floor bookshop with a few maps at the Matahari. For cheap bags, shoes, clothes, watches and hats try Pasar 45. You can also get specially designed "Dive Manado" T-shirts from Toko Karawang, Jalan Walanda Maramis.
Swimming pool The pool at the *Hotel Kawanua Sahid* is open for nonresidents (Rp7000).
Telephone and fax Yantel, Jl Sam Ratulangi 4, has a fax service and international phones.
Travel and tour agents Wherever possible, it's easier to go direct to airlines or Pelni, but you can also make bookings through: Maya Express, Jl Sudirman 15 ⓣ0431/870111, ⓕ870603; Dian Sakatho Tours and Travel, Jalan Sam Ratulangi ⓣ0431/860003; and Pandu Express, Jl Sam Ratulangi 91 ⓣ0431/851188, ⓕ861487.

Bunaken Marine Reserve

Eight kilometres northwest of Manado, a 75-square-kilometre patch of sea is sectioned off as **Bunaken Marine Reserve**, where **coral reefs** around the reserve's four major islands drop to a forty-metre shelf before falling into depths of 200m and more, creating stupendous reef **walls** abounding with marine life. Blue-green Napoleon (Maori) wrasse and coral-crunching hump-headed parrotfish are two of the largest fish here, usually encountered over deep water; barracuda materialize disconcertingly for a closer look, while divers are frequently buzzed by schools of trevally and tuna, and the odd shark. Turtles, manta rays, whales and dolphin put in an appearance, too, though pods of the latter are more often seen from boats around the islands than met underwater. Smaller creatures include gaping morays; at shallower depths look for vividly coloured nudibranchs, camouflaged scorpionfish, mantis shrimps with razor-sharp forelegs, and black-and-silver banded sea snakes, which remain totally indifferent to your following them around as they forage in crevices for fry. Set aside concerns about snakes and sharks and avoid instead the metre-long Titan triggerfish, sharp-beaked and notoriously pugnacious when guarding its nest; and small, fluorescent-red anemone fish, which are prone to giving divers a painful nip in defence of their territory.

Promoted as Indonesia's official scuba centre, loosely enforced management plans and the soaring popularity of the marine reserve are starting to take its toll on conditions here, particularly around **Pulau Bunaken**, whose prime sites receive the most attention from visitors and tend to eclipse the potential of nearby **Siladen**, **Manado Tua** and **Montehage** islands. Indeed, from November to February Bunaken's popular reserve, Liang Beach, is little more than a 500m-long rubbish tip as litter from the sea is swept ashore by the seasonal winds, and while the beaches of Pangalisang, on the island's eastern coast, tend to escape most of this debris, even they get inundated from time to time. To combat this and other environmental problems, in 2001 a national park fee was introduced to help finance various conservation projects, including – hopefully – the introduction of full-time beach cleaners to clear away the rubbish. With luck, Bunaken will start to show signs of improvements as a result of these initiatives in the near future.

Visiting and diving the reserve

The **entrance fee** for the national park is currently Rp75,000, though there are plans to increase it to Rp150,000 in the near future. This is paid either to your divemaster, your homestay or directly to one of two national park offices on Bunaken (at Liang Beach and in the village). In return you'll receive a tag, valid for the rest of the calendar year, that you are supposed to wear at all times.

Organizing a trip to Bunaken Marine Reserve is complicated by a good deal of mudslinging about the quality of specific operations. Much depends on your budget and personal expectations, but basically you can visit the reserve in two ways, both of which allow for snorkelling and diving: either on **day-trips** from Manado, which can be arranged privately or through dive operations (see "Listings" on p.955), or by staying at **budget accommodation** within the reserve on Bunaken or Siladen islands. As regards what type of **dive operation** to use, if you need any training or qualified assistance you might be better off opting for one of the pricier, professional operators in Manado itself, or with one of the larger operators – Froggies or Two Fish on Bunaken (see opposite for details). If you are already certified, however, you'll save money by shopping around on the island, though you must check the **reliability** of rental gear and **air quality**, the two biggest causes for concern here.

The best **weather conditions** are between June and November, with light breezes, calm seas and visibility underwater averaging 25m and peaking beyond 50m. Try to avoid the westerly storms between December and February – though on calm days, you'll see a fair amount even then, and fewer visitors means that it's a good time to push for deals – and less severe, easterly winds from March until June, which make for cold water and reduced visibility.

Pulau Bunaken and around

About an hour by ferry out from Manado, **Pulau Bunaken** is a low-backed, five-kilometre-long comma covered in coconut trees and ringed by sand and mangroves. You will doubtless be approached in Manado – either by your hotel or by touts on the street – about booking accommodation on Bunaken. If you do book in advance, Bunaken's homestays usually arrange free transport to and from the island for their guests. If you decide not to, however, then you will have to rely on public transport to get you there: there's a **public ferry** (Rp15,000) from the dock behind Manado's Pasar Bersehati daily at 2pm (get there 30min early; return 7.30am; 1hr), and plenty of private boat owners (Rp50,000). Either way, you end up at **Bunaken village** on the island's south-eastern tip.

The homestays listed below draw generally good press and are clustered in two groups within a couple of kilometres of the village, providing rooms with shared mandi, and cottages with own mandi and all meals. On the east coast, **Pangalisang beach** is quiet and, though the sand is sometimes compromised by too many mangrove trees, the coral wall is close to hand and adventurous skin-divers can test their lungs on some fine drop-offs. Places to stay include *Lorenzo Beach Garden Resort* (Ⓣ0812/4406705; ❷), a very friendly place with fine food and a convivial atmosphere; *Daniels* (Ⓣ0812/4404882; ❸), with a reputation for being the party-place on the island; *Sea Breeze* (Ⓣ0431/859379, Ⓕ859368; ❸), with beautiful cottages often occupied by German holidaymakers (they have a deal with a German travel agent); and the new, serene *MC Cottages* (❸), just to the north of the village, with a great little beach and some of the island's best snorkelling just offshore. Western **Liang beach** is the most popular spot – a little too popular at weekends when daytripping city-dwellers pop over – with fewer trees and perhaps Bunaken's best coral 100m offshore. *Froggies* (Ⓣ0812/4301356, Ⓦwww.divefroggies.com; ❸–❹) is the most established place here – clean, smart, with great food and efficiently run by the extremely gregarious and helpful Christine, a half-French half-Italian expat – though some stiff competition is now being provided by three other places: the huge *Bastiano's* (Ⓣ0812/853566; ❹) whose communal area is exceptionally vast and airy, though there have been some problems recently with the plumbing in some of the rooms; *Panorama* (Ⓣ0812/863023; ❷), nestling on the cliffs above the beach (a good thing when the rubbish is at its worst) and with the nicest views; and, at the northwestern end of the beach, the pleasant and underrated *Nelson's* (❷).

Currently, the two most popular and reliable **dive operators** are Froggies (see above) on Liang Beach, and Two Fish Divers (Ⓣ0811/432805, Ⓦwww.twofishdivers.com), run by English couple Nigel and Tina, who can be found at *Lorenzo's Beach Garden Resort* on Pangalisang. Two dives typically start from US$50 all-inclusive (Froggies $75), though most operators now offer bulk deals, typically eleven dives for the price of ten.

Off the west beach between Bunaken village and Liang beach, **Lekuan** 1, 2 and 3 are exceptionally steep, deep walls, and the place to find everything from gobies and eels to deep-water sharks. Further around on the far western end of the island, there are giant clams and stingrays at **Fukui**, while **Mandolin** is good for turtles, occasional mantas and even marlin, and **Mike's Point** attracts more sharks and sea snakes. On shore, there are a few seafood restaurants on Liang beach, with women selling fruit and shells outside – collected elsewhere, they say, should you ask – and tracks over the middle of the island, which you can follow to a couple of isolated little sandy coves on the north shore.

The reserve's **other islands** can be reached by chartering a boat from Manado or Bunaken, though there are also occasional public ferries from Manado to Siladen too (departures at 2pm from the dock behind Pasar Bersehati; Rp15,000). Just east of Bunaken, tiny **Siladen** has better beaches, fewer visitors, and a few places to stay, including the relaxed and amiable *Tantamata* homestay (❸ full board), and the newer and slightly smarter *Onong Balrekobong* (❸ full board), with wooden Minahasan-style cottages a feature here. To the west, **Manado Tua** features a prominent, steep-sided cone, with a tiring trail to the top. Seven kilometres north of Bunaken, **Montehage** is the biggest island in the reserve, with a Bajau village on its north end. There's also a potentially good dive site here, known as **Barracuda Point** for the numbers of these fierce-looking fish often seen hanging motionless in the current, but if the barracuda don't show there's nothing else to see.

The Minahasan highlands

Fertile, forested and home to two towering volcanoes and a lake teeming with fish, the **Minahasan highlands**, rising 20km south of Manado, offer more than just an escape from the heat of the coast. These chilly highlands are home to the **Minahasans**, a people who colonized this corner of Sulawesi from the Philippines some two millennia ago. Minahasan legends, however, name the goddess **Lumimuut** and her husband (and son) **Toar** as the ancestors of **seven clans**, which, though they co-operated in many ways through the ages – the word *Minahasa* derives from a term meaning "unity" – never had an overall ruler. The success of **Protestantism** since its nineteenth-century introduction to the highlands means that little survives of traditional Minahasan life, though head-hunting was practised and the dead were buried in stone mausoleums called **waruga**. First contacts with the West came when the Spanish tried to foist a puppet king on the highlands during the seventeenth century, but the Minahasans allied with the Dutch and kicked them out, and were subsequently left much to their own devices until Holland itself subjugated the north with the abrupt **Tondano War** of 1809. The new rulers introduced coffee cultivation and schooling, simultaneously finding this remote land useful as a quarantine for **political troublemakers** from elsewhere in the archipelago – Javan War instigator Prince Diponegoro and his general Kyai Modjo were exiled here, as was their fellow countryman Imam Bonjol. **Japanese occupation** during the 1940s was a low point, the population put to forced labour digging caves and tunnels against Allied air raids, but things have picked up since Independence, particularly during the **clove** boom of the 1970s, when Minahasa had the highest per-capita income of any rural district in Southeast Asia. There's been a fall in prices since then, but the highlands remain a refreshingly confident place, whose people make the most of any excuse to enjoy themselves; get out to the smaller villages up here for one of the countless minor festivals through the year, and soak up the local style of music, dancing and drink.

Minibuses from Manado's Terminal Karombasan climb the winding range road to the **western highlands** at **Tomohon** (1hr), from where there's trans-

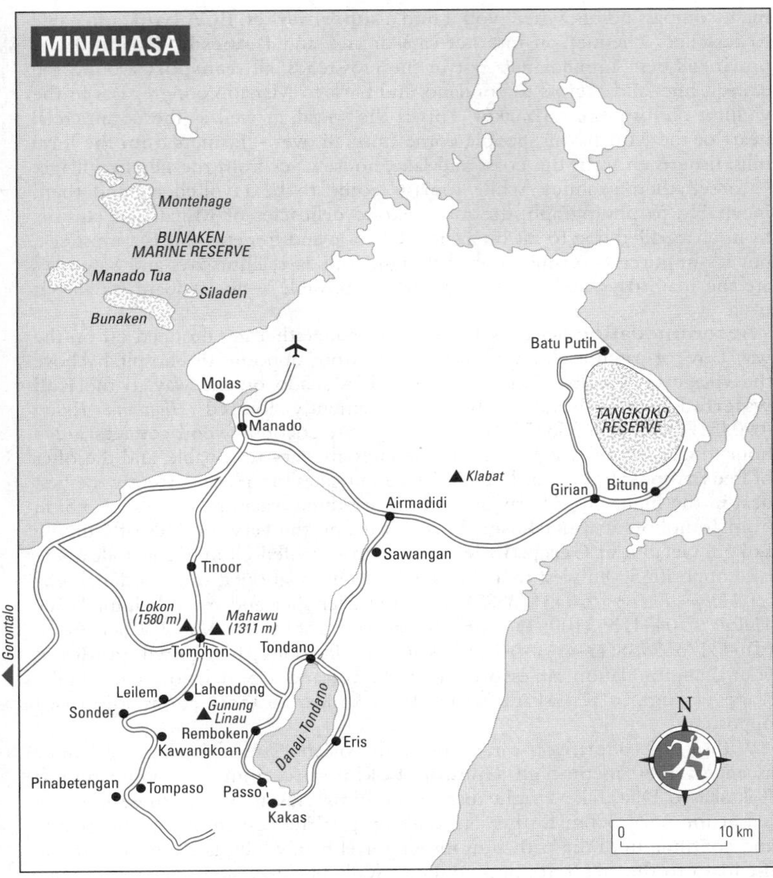

port to everywhere else in Minahasa. On the way, stop at **Tinoor** for a Minahasan meal at one of the **restaurants** built looking out down the hillside to the coast; try the *Tinoor Indah*, for some of the best views and tastiest grilled pig – not to mention rat – that the region has to offer. There's also a route running up **from Airmadidi**, on the Manado–Bitung road, to the **eastern highlands**, which focus around **Tondano** town and its adjoining **lake**. Microlets cover all but the smallest roads, where dokar take over; come dressed for cool nights, morning mists and hot days.

Tomohon and volcanoes

The approach to **TOMOHON**, 30km from Manado and the highland's second town, is through 5km of flower nurseries between the rumbling, highly active cones of **Gunung Lokon**, abode of the Minahasan deity Pinondoan, and the slightly shorter **Gunung Mahawu**. A busy, friendly, strongly Christian place, the town clusters about a **crossroads** whose four streets align with main compass points, where you'll find a **supermarket**, BCA **bank** amenable to travellers' cheques, an internet café or two and **Bethesda Hospital**, the province's best. Immediately east of the crossroads, all **transport** around the eastern highlands, across to Tondano, and back to Manado congregates in the vicinity of Tomohon's **market**. This is the social, as well as the commercial heart of the Minahasans; people come from all over – farmers from the local hills, fishermen from the coast and lake, housewives from the nearby villages – to sell their produce, while tourists come to be revolted by, and then, inevitably, to photograph, the more exotic delicacies of Minahasan cuisine, from chargrilled dog to rat on a stick. Chaotic and frenetic, this is a must-see, but it's important to time your visit right: Tuesdays, Thursdays and Saturdays are the main days, and get here as early as possible – by 10.30am it's all but over.

Accommodation lies back towards Manado; either get dropped off on the way here, or catch a blue microlet or **taxi** from opposite the hospital. Above the village of Kinolow, 3km back towards Manado on the way to the **Kali waterfall** is the beautiful but inconveniently located *Highland Resort* (Ⓣ0431/353888, Ⓕ353777; ❹), with exquisite coconut-wood cottages, a 24-hour restaurant and a video room. The rates are very reasonable, and the offer of free transport from your hotel in Manado makes this place currently the best deal in the highlands. Alternatively there are three places to stay about 3.5km from Tomohon at **Kakaskasen Dua** village, on the very foothills of Gunung Lokon. Get out at **Gereja Pniel**, a large, iron-roofed church, and follow the lane opposite 500m west to a choice of accommodation at the wooden, high-set *Happy Flower* (Ⓣ0431/352787; ❷), the friendlier and more helpful *Lokon Valley* (Ⓣ0431/353100; ❷), or the smarter cabins at *New Volcano Resort* (Ⓣ0431/352988; ❷–❸) – all prices include breakfast. If required, **guides** at your accommodation can escort you up the volcanoes, or help locate five bulky stone **waruga** in Kakaskasen's back lanes, similar to those at Sawangan (see opposite).

With a little effort, you can climb both volcanoes in a day. The two-hour ascent of 1580-metre-high **Gunung Lokon** starts from accommodation at Kakaskasen Dua. Take a right turn at the crossroads above the three hotels, a left at the next, 500m further on, walk up past the cemetery and the quarry and continue until the path runs into a gravel bed, which leads up over solidified lava to the crater. It's not a difficult walk, but very slow-going after rain. The crater is a 500-metre-broad steaming pit stinking of sulphur, covered in brown ash and edged in obsidian boulders; poisonous fumes make climbing inside a dangerous undertaking. Lokon's south rim rises steeply to the mountain's summit, scaled by a tiring track of loose scree, and views from the grassy top encompass Manado Tua and Tomohon.

For an easier climb, and with better views at the summit, **Gunung Mahawu** is well worth the effort. Catch a microlet (Rp1350) from Tomohon's market towards Rurukan and ask to be dropped off at the start of the hour-long path to the top (*"Tolong turunkan saya di jalan ke Mahawu"*). Thin woodlands along the way open up to a 1311-metre summit covered in fire-prone grasslands. The crater is sheer-sided and deep, and winds, cloud and crumbly edges make the entire trail around the rim very hazardous – a slip here would be fatal. The views encompass Bunaken and Manado Tua, Lake Tondano and Lokon's crater.

The western highlands

The road south from Tomohon heads down through the **western highlands**, with more vulcanism some 7km along at **Gunung Linau**, in Minahasan lore the first of all volcanoes to be created. A sealed, kilometre-long road uphill from the church at **Lahendong** passes a rim-side restaurant (with cold drinks) and views into the semi-cultivated interior and bright blue-green disc of **Danau Linau**, the broad crater lake. The mountain is dormant but still ticking, with **hot springs** on its southern slopes, just down the road before **LEILEM** village; a cracked footpath leads through a hostile terrain of bubbling mud and desolate grey rubble streaked with yellow, the ground covered in a crunchy crystallized crust with steam oozing out of the soil.

Five kilometres past Leilem and at the centre of Minahasan **clove** production, **SONDER** is a wealthy little retreat of wooden houses in the chalet-like Minahasan style. The same distance south again brings you to **KAWANGKOAN**, where **caves** (more like large tunnels) built to store ammunition under Japanese orders during World War II, and now standing empty, can be explored with a torch. Push on from here for a final 10km past **Tompaso** to **PINABETENGAN**, from where it's a forty-minute walk uphill to **Watu Pinabetengan**, a large, oblong slab of rock said to have been hurled here by an eruption of Gunung Linau, and a site of immense importance to Minahasans. It was at Watu Pinabetengan that the goddess Lumimuut divided up the highlands between Minahasa's seven clans, and the stone became a rallying point through the ages where leaders met to reject formally the idea of kings and to present a united front against invaders. Associations and the walk make the journey worthwhile, as the rock itself is covered with concrete, recent graffiti and an ugly pavilion, and the faint archaic symbols carved on one side are almost invisible.

The eastern highlands: Tondano and the lake

Ringed by hills, Minahasa's **eastern highlands** form a flat, green, grassy basin around fifty-square-kilometre **Danau Tondano**, with **TONDANO** town on its northern tip. A small high street with a market at one end and a minibus terminal at the other, and smelling – as does everywhere up here – of cloves and horses, Tondano is prettier but less active than Tomohon; there's **accommodation** here at the tidy *Asri Baru* (❸), a couple of warung along the high street, and **memorials** to local heroes Sam Ratulangi, a pro-Independence fighter who governed Sulawesi briefly before his death in 1949, and Sarapung and Korengkeng, Minahasan leaders during the 1809 anti-Dutch Tondano war, which was fought around the lake.

Starting in town, you can travel down both sides of Danau Tondano by microlet, though the south end is infrequently serviced and it's best to allow most of a day to get right around the perimeter; out on the lake is an ever-changing scenery of fish farms, pole houses reached along rickety bamboo bridges, and dark-blue water whipped with white crests raised by the afternoon winds. Halfway down the west shore is the pottery centre of **REMBOKEN** and **Obyek Wisata Sumaru Endo** (Rp1000), a tourist complex with pedal boats, naturally heated hot spas and excellent fresh *ikan mas* served in the restaurant, all very popular at the weekends. There are more thermal pools south of Remboken at **Passo**, whose fields are strung with plastic bags to keep birds away, then the road leaves the lakeside for **Kakas** before heading up the eastern side to **ERIS**, a quiet town opposite Remboken where it's possible to rent a boat out to **Likri islet**, a speck of rock out in the middle of the water.

Sawangan

North of Tondano, it takes around ninety minutes for minibuses to follow the twenty-kilometre twisting road down the range to Airmadidi on the Manado–Bitung highway. About 5km from Airmadidi is **SAWANGAN** village, where a short lane off the road ends at **Taman Purbakala Waruga-Waruga**, a cemetery with a difference. Here stand over a hundred *waruga*, Minahasan sarcophagi, gathered from across the region during the 1970s and all predating an 1828 Dutch ban on their use; two-metre upright stone boxes with spreading, roof-shaped lids, arranged in rows like fossilized mushrooms. Most of the boxes are plain, but the lids are heavily carved with male and female figures, some naked, others seemingly attired in Western-style clothing; other motifs include birds, cattle and dragons. Pieces of porcelain, spiky (and improbably heavy) bronze armbands, iron axes and even a few bone fragments which looters missed are on show at a small **museum** nearby, whose caretaker laboriously produces keys and a donation box when foreigners arrive.

The northern tip: Airmadidi, the Tangkoko Reserve and Bitung

The fifty-kilometre highway running east across the peninsula from Manado to Bitung is covered by frequent minibuses from Terminal Paal Dua. About halfway along, **AIRMADIDI** is where to look for traffic heading south into the highlands at Tondano, but the town also sits below the province's highest peak, **Gunung Klabat**. Minahasan lore has it that Klabat was once Gunung Lokon's summit until villagers, feeling that Lokon was too tall, sliced the top off and carried it here. It's a solid six-hour climb on a sometimes dodgy path from Airmadidi's police station to Klabat's 1995-metre-high apex (guide required); start at midnight to catch the sunrise over Minahasa.

Past Airmadidi and forty minutes from Manado, **Girian** is the jumping-off point for the mix of dry woodlands and full-blown rainforest of **Tangkoko-Batuangus-Dua-Saudara Reserve**, named after the three mountains around which the park is formed and usually abbreviated to just Tangkoko. A battered bus (Rp5000) leaves Girian late morning (with a second occasionally leaving later in the day) along the one-hour, twenty-kilometre potholed track to **BATU PUTIH** village, which faces the sea at the northern edge of the reserve. If you miss the bus, there are pick-ups that charge much the same amount, or you can charter one from Girian for Rp50,000. Get out 500m short of Batu Putih at Tangkoko's **entrance**, where there are three **homestays**: the popular *Mama Roos*, with shabby rooms, intermittent electricity and plentiful food (❷), the rowdier and less pleasant *Tangkoko Ranger* (❷), and the smart but quiet *Tarsius Homestay* (❷). All three include meals in the price. Alternatively, you could opt for the secluded *Benteng Resort*, an hour's walk northwest along the coast with its own white-sand beach. Traditional cottages look great on the outside, though the interiors are rather disappointing. Contact their office in Girian (Ⓣ0438/30556) for reservations and free transport.

At the homestays you'll often be approached by **guides** offering their services in the park. The **entrance fee** is Rp750, plus Rp35,000 for a guide (Rp25,000 if two or more people). These fees must be paid every time you enter the park, which for most visitors is twice a day: once at dawn for the black macaques and hornbills which are Tangkoko's pride, and again at dusk to track down the tiny tarsiers. You're pretty certain of encountering all these creatures, as the guides know where to look and tear off through the undergrowth, so bring plenty of film. Particularly memorable are close encounters with families of **black macaques**, which stay up in the branches until the chunky lead male has nerved himself up to climb down; then you're suddenly surrounded by twenty or more animals, youngsters romping and adults foraging and clouting them to order. Look too for **flying lizards**, which display around the bunkhouses in the early morning, and keep your fingers crossed for glimpses of maleos scratching up leaf litter – though sightings usually turn out to be the related and similar-looking scrub fowl. One thing to protect against are **mites**, *gonone*, whose burrowing causes an infuriating rash; insect repellent or Tiger balm kills them and lessens the irritation. Buses return **to Girian** between 7am and 8am, or pick-ups leave throughout the day.

To the Sangihe-Talaud Islands and the Philippines

The 500-kilometre straits separating mainland north Sulawesi and the Philippines is dotted with the seventy-odd **islands** of the **Sangihe-Talaud group**, whose Filipino people were subjected to the shifting spheres of sultanate and Western influences since the sixteenth century. Though there are regular boat connections with both Indonesia and the Philippines, the islands are remote in feel, planted with cash crops such as coconut and cloves, and with all but the biggest settlements being basic fishing villages; you need to speak Indonesian and have plenty of time, but you'll find friendly people, white beaches and good coral, plus the chance of continuing your journey beyond Indonesia. There are two main groups: southernmost are the loosely scattered **Sangihe Islands**, with the capital of **Tahuna**. Accommodation in Tahuna is provided by the *Veronica Hotel* or the *Hotel Nasional* (both ❷) on Pulau Sangihe itself, within a two-hour bemo ride of waterfalls and jungle at **Tamako** (where you can stay at the *Rainbow*; ❷).

On the nearby **Toade Islands**, to the north of Sangihe, is Salise Beach Village, home to sixteen families including Pak Guru Manorek and Ellen, who provide simple but homely accommodation (Rp60,000 per person full-board). To reach here, take a bus to Petta (45min), walk to the seafront and track down Pak Guru.

Further north and east of Sangihe, within about 150km of the Philippines, the **Talaud Islands** are a compact little group, with the main settlement of **LIRUNG** on central **Pulau Salibau**. Lirung's accommodation options include *Penginepan Sederhana* or the *Chindy* (both ❷); you can also rent small craft for a fifteen-minute run out to the tiny, uninhabited **Sara Islands** for a day in paradise.

There used to be three passenger boats a week each way between Manado and Tahuna and one a week between Manado and Lirung. Unfortunately, a fire in November 2001 on one of the ferries plying this route spread to the two other ships which were docked next to it in the port of Manado. For this reason, the islands have been all but cut off from the mainland, their only connection now being the monthly **Pelni ferries** *KM Tilongkabila* and *KM Sangiang* to and from Bitung that call in to Tahuna and Lirung, and the two weekly **flights** with Merpati to Melangguane, near Lirung in the Tahaud group, and to Naha near Tahuna (this second flight then also flies on to Melangguane), with both these flights departing Manado on a Monday morning. Some sort of ferry service will probably have resumed by the time you read this, though precisely what this will be is impossible to predict.

To the Philippines

At the time of writing there were no passenger ferries leaving for the Philippines, though an occasional (approximately monthly) **cargo ferry** runs between Bitung and **General Santos**, a few hours south of Davao, and will often take passengers for around US$30 (US$40 return); the journey takes two days. It's an incredibly rough ride; bring a sleeping mat, a tent (if you have one) and plenty of comfort food. Ask at the *Victory Inn* in Manado (see p.953) for details. Filipino immigration board the boats on arrival in General Santos and generally hand out three-week visas on the spot to Davao. The only other alternative used to be the twice-weekly Bouraq **flight** from Manado to Davao, though this too has been suspended due to lack of interest; it may be worth enquiring at the Bouraq office in Manado (see p.955) to see if they have resumed flights on this route.

Back on the main road, minibuses from Manado wind up at **Terminal Tangkoko**, from where a microlet will carry you the final 5km into **BITUNG**. A hot grid of a town servicing the port, the only reason to come here is for onward connections. The **Pelni port** is along Jalan Jakarta, with departures down Sulawesi's east coast to the Philippines, Makassar and Kadidiri, and further afield to Java, Kalimantan, Maluku and West Papua; organize tickets and timetables in Manado, or try the Pandu Express office here at Jl Sukarno 5 (ⓣ0438/30480).

There are a handful of places to **eat** along Jalan Sudarso – the *Remaja Jaya* is a pricey Chinese place serving big portions – but Bitung's accommodation is pretty dire, and new arrivals should catch a microlet from Jalan Sukarno to Terminal Tangkoko, where minibuses to Tondano and Manado await. Alternatively, head up the coast to Likupang, the northernmost point of Sulawesi and the home of the comfortable *Pulisan Jungle Beach Resort* (ⓣ0438/856902; ❺ full-board), from where you can explore the unusual marine life of the **Lembeh Strait**; be warned, however, that cold waters and strong currents make this an option for seasoned divers only.

Travel details

Buses

Note that this section was researched against a backdrop of continued upheaval in Poso, when many of the regular bus services were suspended, or, if buses were actually running, journey times were often greatly extended. Where the following bus timetables contain two schedules separated by a "/", the first time given indicates now long the journey used to take before the Poso conflict started, while the second time is an estimate of how long the journey takes now, with much of the Trans-Sulawesi highway around Poso and the lake off-limits to buses.

Ampana to: Luwuk (daily; 8hr); Makassar (daily; 26hr/no service); Pagaimana (daily; 5hr); Palu (daily; 15hr); Poso (daily; 5hr/no service).

Gorontalo to: Kotamobagu (1 daily; 8hr); Manado (daily; 12hr); Makassar (daily; 2–4 days/no service).

Manado to: Gorontalo (daily; 12hr); Kotamobagu (daily at around 9am; 4hr); Makassar (daily; 2–4 days/no service); Tomohon (daily; 1hr).

Palu to: Ampana (daily; 13hr); Luwuk (daily; 18hr); Makassar (daily; 29hr/3days); Pagaimana (daily; 20hr); Poso (daily; 5hr/no service).

Parepare to: Makassar (daily; 5hr); Polewali (daily; 2hr/no service); Rantepao (daily; 4hr); Sengkang (daily; 2hr 30min); Watampone (daily; 5hr).

Poso (note all services currently suspended) to: Ampana (daily; 5hr); Luwuk (daily; 12hr); Makassar (daily; 21hr); Pagaimana (daily; 10hr); Palu (daily; 10hr); Pendolo (daily; 5hr); Rantepao (daily; 13hr); Tentena (daily; 2hr).

Rantepao to: Makassar (daily; 8hr); Mamasa via Parepare (3 weekly; 11hr); Palu (daily; 21hr/no service); Parepare (daily; 4hr); Pendolo (daily; 8hr/no service); Poso (daily; 13hr/no service); Tentena (daily; 11hr/no service).

Sengkang to: Makassar (daily; 6hr); Parepare (daily; 2hr 30min); Watampone (daily; 2hr 30min).

Makassar to: Ampana (daily; 26hr/no service); Benteng (daily; 11hr); Bira (daily; 5hr); Bulukumba (daily; 5hr); Gorontalo (daily; 2–4 days/no service); Mamasa (most days; 15hr); Manado (daily; 2–4 days/no service); Palu (daily; 29hr/3 days); Parepare (daily; 5hr); Pendolo (daily; 16hr/no service); Polewali (daily; 7hr); Poso (daily; 21hr/no service); Rantepao (daily; 8hr); Sengkang (daily; 6hr); Tentena (daily; 19hr/no service); Watampone (daily; 5hr).

Watampone to: Bulukumba (daily; 4hr); Makassar (daily; 5hr); Parepare (daily; 5hr); Sengkang (daily; 2hr 30min).

Pelni ferries

For a chart of the Pelni routes, see p.42.

Baubau to: Ambon (*KM Rinjani,* 2 monthly; 22hr/*KM Bukit Siguntang*, 2 monthly; 21hr/*KM Lambelu*, 2 monthly; 21hr); Banda (*KM Bukit Siguntang*, 2 monthly; 21hr/*KM Rinjani*, 2 monthly; 22hr); Badas (*KM Tatamailau*, monthly; 43hr); Banggai (*KM Ciremai*, 2 monthly; 12hr); Bitung (*KM Ciremai*, 2 monthly; 25hr/*KM Lambelu*, 2 monthly; 45hr/*KM Tilongkabila*, monthly; 4 days); Bima (*KM Kelimutu*, 2 monthly; 38hr); Denpasar (*KM Tatamailau*, monthly; 53hr/*KM Tilongkabila*, monthly; 65hr); Fak Fak (*KM*

Tatamailau, monthly; 53hr/*KM Rinjani*, 2 monthly; 53hr/*KM Kelimutu*, 2 monthly; 58hr); Gorontalo (*KM Tilongkabila*, monthly; 46hr); Jayapura (*KM Ciremai*, 2 monthly; 4 days); Kolonodale (*KM Tilongkabila*, monthly; 24hr); Lirung (*KM Tilongkabila*, monthly; 3 days); Luwuk (*KM Tilongkabila*, monthly; 33hr); Makassar (*KM Bukit Siguntang*, 2 monthly; 12hr/*KM Lambelu*, 2 monthly; 12hr/*KM Rinjani*, 2 monthly; 14hr/*KM Tatamailau*, monthly; 18hr/*KM Ciremai*, 2 monthly; 14hr/*KM Tilongkabila*, monthly; 16hr); Manokwari (*KM Rinjani*, 2 monthly; 3 days/*KM Ciremai*, 2 monthly; 3 days); Raha (*KM Tilongkabila*, monthly; 3hr); Sorong (*KM Rinjani*, 2 monthly; 3 days/*KM Ciremai*, 2 monthly; 56hr); Surabaya (*KM Rinjani*, 2 monthly; 42hr/*KM Bukit Siguntang*, 2 monthly; 38hr/*KM Lambelu*, 2 monthly; 38hr); Tahuna (*KM Tilongkabila*, monthly; 3 days); Tanjung Priok (*KM Ciremai*, 2 monthly; 62hr/*KM Bukit Siguntang*, 2 monthly; 62hr/*KM Lambelu*, 2 monthly; 62hr); Ternate (*KM Ciremai*, 2 monthly; 39hr/*KM Lambelu*, 2 monthly; 2 days); Wanci (*KM Tatamailau*, monthly; 7hr).

Bitung to: Agats (*KM Sangiang*, 2 monthly; 4–5 days); Balikpapan (*KM Sinabung*, monthly; 30hr/*KM Doro Londa*, monthly; 37hr/*KM Umsini*, 2 monthly; 46hr); Banggai (*KM Ciremai*, 2 monthly; 11hr); Baubau (*KM Ciremai*, 2 monthly; 28hr); Biak (*KM Doro Londa*, monthly; 49hr/*KM Ciremai*, 2 monthly; 52hr); Fak Fak (*KM Sangiang*, 2 monthly; 46hr); Gorontalo (*KM Tilongkabila*, monthly; 12hr); Jayapura (*KM Doro Londa*, monthly; 67hr/*KM Ciremai*, 2 monthly; 70hr); Kendari (*KM Tilongkabila*, monthly; 2 days); Kolonodale (*KM Tilongkabila*, monthly; 33hr); Kwandang (*KM Sinabung*, 2 monthly; 10hr/*KM Doro Londa*, monthly; 9hr); Labuanbajo (*KM Tilongkabila*, monthly; 4 days); Lirung (*KM Tilongkabila*, monthly; 13hr/*KM Sangiang*, 2 monthly; 45hr); Luwuk (*KM Tilongkabila*, monthly; 22hr); Makassar (*KM Ciremai*, 2 monthly; 42hr/*KM Sinabung*, 2 monthly; 47hr/*KM Umsini*, 2 monthly; 67hr/*KM Tilongkabila*, monthly; 76hr); Manokwari (*KM SInabung*, 2 monthly; 40hr/*KM Ciremai*, monthly; 43hr/*KM Doro Londa*, monthly; 44hr); Padang (*KM Umsini*, 2 monthly; 6 days); Pantoloan/Palu (*KM Umsini*, 2 monthly; 28hr/*KM Doro Londa*, monthly; 26hr); Raha (*KM Tilongkabila*, monthly; 54hr); Serui (*KM Sinabung*, 2 monthly; 56hr); Sorong (*KM SInabung*, 2 monthly; 23hr/*KM Doro Londa*, monthly; 26hr/*KM Ciremai*, 2 monthly; 27hr/*KM Sangiang*, 2 monthly; 52hr); Surabaya (*KM Doro Londa*, monthly: 65hr); *KM Sinabung*, 2 monthly; 70hr/*KM Umsini*, 2 monthly; 80hr); Tahuna (*KM Tilongkabila*, monthly; 24hr/*KM Sangiang*, 2 monthly; 36hr); Tanjung Priok (*KM Doro Londa*, monthly; 4 days; *KM Umsini*, 2 monthly; 4–5 days); Ternate (*KM Doro Londa*, monthly; 8hr/*KM Sinabung*, monthly; 8hr/*KM Ciremai*, 2 monthly; 9hr); Toli Toli (*KM Umsini*, 2 monthly; 18hr); Tual (*KM Sangiang*, 2 monthly; 3 days).

Gorontalo to: Baubau (*KM Tilongkabila*, monthly; 2 days); Bitung (*KM Tilongkabila*, monthly; 13hr); Denpasar (*KM Tilongkabila*, monthly; 4–5 days); Kendari (*KM Tilongkabila*, monthly; 34hr); Kolonodale (*KM Tilongkabila*, monthly; 21hr); Lirung (*KM Tilongkabila*, monthly; 29hr); Luwuk (*KM Tilongkabila*, monthly; 9hr); Makassar (*KM Tilongkabila*, monthly; 63hr); Raha (*KM Tilongkabila*, monthly; 41hr); Tahuna (*KM Tilongkabila*, monthly; 40hr).

Kendari to: Baubau (*KM Tilongkabila*, monthly; 10hr); Bitung (*KM Tilongkabila*, monthly; 2 days); Denpasar (*KM Tilongkabila*, monthly; 3 days); Gorontalo (*KM Tilongkabila*, monthly; 34hr); Kolonodale (*KM Tilongkabila*, monthly; 13hr); Luwuk (*KM Tilongkabila*, monthly; 20hr); Makassar (*KM Tilongkabila*, monthly; 27hr); Raha (*KM Tilongkabila*, monthly; 5hr).

Kwandang to: Balikpapan (*KM Sinabung*, 2 monthly; 20hr/*KM Doro Londa*, monthly; 24hr); Biak (*KM Doro Londa*, monthly; 62hr); Bitung (*KM Sinabung*, 2 monthly; 9hr/*KM Doro Londa*, monthly; 9hr); Makassar (*KM Sinabung*, 2 monthly; 37hr); Manokwari (*KM Sinabung*, 2 monthly; 2 days/*KM Doro Londa*, monthly; 53hr); Nabire (*KM Sinabung*, 2 monthly; 58hr); Pantoloan (*KM Doro Londa*, monthly; 14hr); Sorong (*KM Sinabung*, 2 monthly; 35hr/*KM Doro Londa*, monthly; 35hr); Surabaya (*KM Doro Londa*, monthly; 53hr/*KM Sinabung*, 2 monthly; 60hr); Tanjung Priok (*KM Doro Londa*, monthly; 3 days/*KM Sinabung*, 2 monthly; 85hr); Ternate (*KM Sinabung*, 2 monthly; 20hr/*KM Doro Londa*, monthly; 21hr).

Lirung to: Bitung (*KM Sangiang*, 2 monthly; 21hr/*KM Tilongkabila*, monthly; 21hr); Tahuna (*KM Sangiang*, 2 monthly; 7hr/*KM Tilongkabila*, monthly; 7hr).

Luwuk to: Baubau (*KM Tilongkabila*, monthly; 35hr); Bitung (*KM Tilongkabila*, monthly; 24hr); Gorontalo (*KM Tilongkabila*, monthly; 10hr); Kendari (*KM Tilongkabila*, monthly; 23hr); Kolonodale (*KM Tilongkabila*, monthly; 9hr); Makassar (*KM Tilongkabila*, monthly; 27hr); Raha (*KM Tilongkabila*, monthly; 30hr).

Makassar to: Amahai (*KM Kelimutu*, 2 monthly; 55hr); Ambon (*KM Rinjani*, 2 monthly; 37hr/*KM Bukit Siguntang*, 2 monthly; 36hr/*KM Lambelu*, 2 monthly; 36hr/*KM Doro Londa*, monthly; 45hr); Badas (*KM Tatamailau*, monthly; 19hr); Balikpapan (*KM Sinabung*, 2 monthly; 15hr/*KM Umsini*, 2 monthly; 16hr/*KM Tidar*, 2 monthly; 16hr/*KM Fudi*, 2 monthly; 20hr); Banda (*KM Rinjani*, 2 monthly;

46hr/*KM Bukit Siguntang*, 2 monthly; 2 days/*KM Rinjani*, 2 monthly; 2 days); Batulicin (*KM Sirimau*, 2 monthly; 42hr); Baubau (*KM Rinjani*, 2 monthly; 13hr/*KM Tatamailau*, monthly; 18hr/*KM Ciremai*, 2 monthly; 13hr/*KM Bukit Siguntang*, 2 monthly; 13hr/*KM Lambelu*, 2 monthly; 12hr/*KM Kelimutu*, 2 monthly; 18hr); Berau (*KM Awu*, 2 monthly; 41hr); Biak (*KM Ciremai*, monthly; 4 days); Bima (*KM Tilongkabila*, monthly; 22hr/*KM Kelimutu*, 2 monthly; 15hr/*KM Tatamailau*, monthly; 56hr); Bitung (*KM Umsini*, 2 monthly; 58hr/*KM Ciremai*, 2 monthly; 39hr); Denpasar (*KM Tilongkabila*, monthly; 42hr/*KM Tatamailau*, monthly; 31hr); Fak Fak (*KM Tatamailau*, monthly; 3 days/*KM Kelimutu*, 2 monthly; 74hr/*KM Doro Londa*, monthly; 67hr/*KM Rinjani*, 2 monthly; 69hr); Gorontalo (*KM Tilongkabila*, monthly; 67hr); Jayapura (*KM Rinjani*, 2 monthly; 5–6 days/*KM Ciremai*, 2 monthly; 4–5 days/*KM Doro Londa*, monthly; 6 days); Kalabahi (*KM Sirimau*, 2 monthly; 33hr/*KM Awu*, 2 monthly; 38hr); Kupang (*KM Awu*, 2 monthly; 2 days/*KM Sirimau*, 2 monthly; 48hr/*KM Doro Londa*, monthly; 23hr); Kwandang (*KM Sinabung*, 2 monthly; 43hr); Labuanbajo (*KM Tilongkabila*, monthly; 15hr); Larantuka (*KM Tatamailau*, monthly; 3–4 days/*KM Sirimau*, 2 monthly; 24hr); Lembar (*KM Tilongkabila*, monthly; 40hr); Manokwari (*KM Ciremai*, 2 monthly; 4 days/*KM Rinjani*, 2 monthly; 4 days); Maumere (*KM Awu*, monthly; 23hr); Nias (*KM Umsini*, 2 monthly; 4 days); Nunukan (*KM Agoa Mas*, weekly; 59hr/*KM Awu*, 2 monthly; 60hr); Padang (*KM Umsini*, 2 monthly; 3–4 days); Parepare (*KM Awu*, 2 monthly; 60hr/*KM Agoa Mas*, weekly; 8hr); Semarang (*KM Tilongkabila*, monthly; 26hr); Sorong (*KM Ciremai*, 2 monthly; 3 days/*KM Rinjani*, 2 monthly; 3–4 days); Surabaya (*KM Rinjani*, 2 monthly; 24hr/*KM Umsini*, 2 monthly; 24hr/*KM Tidar*, 2 monthly; 24hr/*KM Bukit Siguntang*, 2 monthly; 24hr/*KM Lambelu*, 2 monthly; 24hr/*KM Fudi*, 2 monthly; 30hr/*KM Doro Londa*, monthly; 22hr/*KM Ganda Dewata*, weekly; 24hr/*KM Sinabung*, 2 monthly; 20hr); Tanjung Priok (*KM Ciremai*, 2 monthly; 40hr/*KM Bukit Siguntang*, 2 monthly; 48hr/*KM Lambelu*, 2 monthly; 48hr/*KM Tilongkabila*, monthly; 47hr/*KM Umsini*, 2 monthly; 48hr/*KM Sinabung*, 2 monthly; 43hr/*KM Doro Londa*, monthly; 47hr/*KM Fudi*, 2 monthly; 52hr/*KM Ganda Dewata*, weekly; 46hr); Tarakan (*KM Awu*, 2 monthly; 54hr/*KM Tidar*, 2 monthly; 40hr); Ternate (*KM Umsini*, 2 monthly; 38hr/*KM Ciremai*, 2 monthly; 52hr); Tual (*KM Rinjani*, 2 monthly; 2–3 days/*KM Bukit Siguntang*, 2 monthly; 2–3 days); Wanci (*KM Tatamailau*, monthly; 26hr).

Pantoloan/Palu to: Balikpapan (*KM Doro Londa*, monthly; 9hr/*KM Umsini*, 2 monthly; 10hr/*KM Kerinci*, 2 monthly; 11hr/*KM Tidar*, 2 monthly; 2 days); Bitung (*KM Doro Londa*, monthly; 25hr/*KM Umsini*, 2 monthly; 28hr); Kwandang (*KM Doro Londa*, monthly; 14hr); Makassar (*KM Tidar*, 2 monthly; 14hr/*KM Agoa Mas*, weekly; 23hr/*KM Umsini*, 2 monthly; 31hr); Nunukan (*KM Tidar*, 2 monthly; 18hr; *KM Kerinci*, 2 monthly; 31hr); Parepare via Kalimantan (*KM Tidar*, 2 monthly; 3 days); Surabaya (*KM Doro Londa*, monthly; 37hr/*KM Kerinci*, 2 monthly; 56hr/*KM Kambuna*, 2 monthly; 56hr/*KM Tidar*, 2 monthly; 43hr); Tarakan (*KM Kerinci*, 2 monthly; 23hr/*KM Tidar*, 2 monthly; 26hr); Ternate (*KM Doro Londa*, monthly; 37hr).

Parepare to: Balikpapan (*KM Agoa Mas*, weekly; 17hr/*KM Kerinci*, 2 monthly; 14hr/*KM Tidar*, 2 monthly; 65hr); Batulicin (*KM Binaiya*, 2 monthly; 18hr); Belang Belang (*KM Binaiya*, 2 monthly; 10hr); Berau (*KM Awu*, 2 monthly; 30hr); Makassar (*KM Tidar*, 2 monthly; 50hr); Nunukan (*KM Tidar*, 2 monthly; 35hr/*KM Agoa Mas*, weekly; 38hr/*KM Awu*, 2 monthly; 55hr); Pantoloan (*KM Agoa Mas*, weekly; 14hr/*KM Tidar*, 4 monthly; 14hr–3days/*KM Kerinci*, 2 monthly; 30hr); Surabaya (*KM Kerinci*, 2 monthly; 26hr/*KM Tidar*, 2 monthly; 24hr/*KM Binaiya*, 2 monthly; 41hr); Samarinda (*KM Binaiya*, 2 monthly; 24hr); Tarakan (*KM Tidar*, 2 monthly; 43hr/*KM Awu*, 2 monthly; 43hr); Tanjung Priok (*KM Kerinci*, 2 monthly; 53hr).

Raha to: Baubau (*KM Tilongkabila*, monthly; 4hr); Bitung (*KM Tilongkabila*, monthly; 55hr); Gorontalo (*KM Tilongkabila*, monthly; 42hr); Kolonodale (*KM Tilongkabila*, monthly; 21hr); Labuanbajo, (*KM Tilongkabila*, monthly; 37hr); Luwuk (*KM Tilongkabila*, monthly; 28hr); Makassar (*KM Tilongkabila*, monthly; 21hr).

Tahuna to: Bitung (*KM Tilongkabila*, monthly; 10hr/*KM Sangiang*, 2 monthly; 12hr); Lirung (*KM Sangiang*, 2 monthly; 7hr).

Wanci to: Amahai (*KM Tatamailau*, monthly; 27hr); Badas (*KM Tatamailau*, monthly; 50hr); Baubau (*KM Tatamailau*, monthly; 7hr); Denpasar (*KM Tatamailau*, monthly; 62hr); Fak Fak (*KM Tatamailau*, monthly; 53hr); Makassar (*KM Tatamailau*, monthly; 27hr).

Other ferries

Ampana to: Bomba (daily; 3hr); Dolong (1 weekly; 12hr); Katupat (1 weekly; 8hr); Wakai (daily; 3hr).

Baubau to: Kendari (daily; 5hr); Raha (2 daily; 2hr).

Gorontalo to: Pagaimana (daily; 10–12hr).

Kendari to: Baubau (2 daily; 5hr); Raha (3 daily; 3hr); Wangiwangi (3 weekly; 12hr).

Makassar to: Surabaya (2–3 weekly; 24hr).

Manado to: Bunaken (daily; 1hr); Lirung (1 week-

ly; 20hr – see note on p.963); Tahuna (3 weekly; 12hr – though see note on p.963).
Raha to: Baubau (2 daily; 1hr 30min); Kendari (3 daily; 3hr).

Flights

Gorontalo to: Manado (5 weekly with Merpati; 1hr 15min)
Kendari to: Makassar (2–3 daily with Merpati and Pelita; 1hr).
Luwuk to: Makassar (3 weekly; 4hr 20min); Manado (3 weekly, 1hr 40min); Palu (4 weekly; 1hr 30min).
Makassar to: Ambon (9 weekly with Merpati; 2hr 45min); Balikpapan (3 weekly with Merpati; 1hr 10min); Biak (4 weekly with Garuda and 4 weekly with Merpati; 2hr 50min); Denpasar (daily with Garuda, 2 weekly with Merpati; 1hr 20min); Jakarta (3–4 daily with Garuda, 2 daily with Merpati, 1 daily with Mandala and Lion Air, 5 weekly with Pelita Air; 2hr 10min); Kendari (daily with Pelita Air and Merpati; 45min); Manado (daily with Garuda, Mandala and Lion Air; 1hr 35min); Palu (5 weekly with Bouraq, 6 weekly with Merpati; 55min); Singapore (3 weekly with Silk Air; 2hr 45min); Sorong (5 weekly with Pelita Air; 3hr 15min); Surabaya (2 daily with Merpati, daily with Bouraq, Pelita Air and Mandala; 1hr 20min); Timika (6 weekly with Merpati, 2hr 50min).
Manado to: Gorontalo (6 weekly with Merpati; 1hr 15min); Luwuk (3 weekly with Merpati; 1hr 40min); Makassar (1 daily with Garuda, Mandala and Lion Air; 1hr 35min); Palu (2 weekly with Bouraq; 1hr 20min); Singapore (3 weekly with Silk Air; 3hr 30min); Sorong (1 weekly with Merpati; 1hr 25min); Surabaya (daily with Bouraq, 1hr 35min); Ternate (1–2 daily with Merpati; 1hr 20min).
Palu to: Balikpapan (1 daily with Bouraq; 40min); Luwuk (4 weekly with Merpati; 1hr 30min); Makassar (6 weekly with Merpati; 2hr 30min); Manado (2 weekly with Bouraq; 1hr 10min).

Maluku

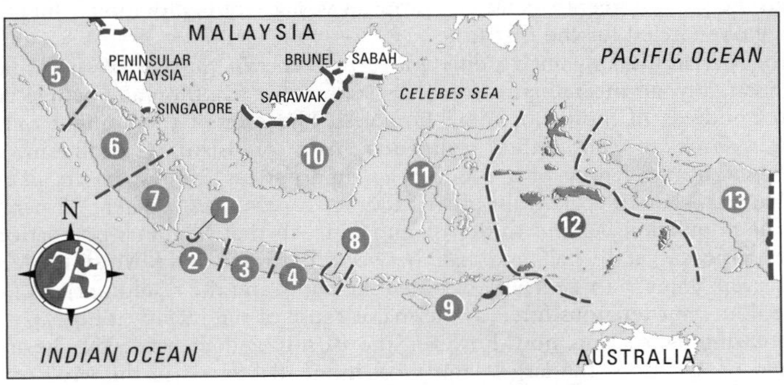

MALAYSIA
PENINSULAR MALAYSIA
SINGAPORE
BRUNEI
SABAH
SARAWAK
CELEBES SEA
PACIFIC OCEAN
INDIAN OCEAN
AUSTRALIA
N

Maluku

Scattered over the ample space separating Sulawesi from West Papua, the thousand or more islands comprising the province of **Maluku** seem at first rather insignificant, many too small to feature noticeably on maps of the region. Yet the Moluccas (or Maluku in Indonesian) have been known to the outside world for longer than anywhere else in Indonesia: these were the fabled Spice Islands, whose produce was in demand everywhere between here and Europe two thousand years ago, and the search for which fired the great sixteenth-century European voyages of exploration which saw the globe circled for the first time.

Today, Maluku has gained a different sort of renown. Since 1999, it has been devastated by an **internecine war** that has left over five thousand people dead and hundreds of thousands more homeless. The root of the conflict can be traced back to the islands' **religious mix** of Islam, Catholicism and Protestantism, a legacy of the European superpowers' interest in the islands. What sets Maluku apart from other Indonesian provinces – where 85 percent of the population belongs to the Islamic faith – is that Maluku's population is split almost exactly half and half between Christians and Muslims. Many observers point to this equality between the faiths, and the resulting lack of any one dominant religious force, as the major cause of the recent troubles.

Amazing as it seems now, however, the islands, and in particular the main island of Ambon – the largest and most influential island in the Moluccas – were, up until the end of the 1990s, famed throughout the country for their religious tolerance. Under a system known as **Pela Gandung**, where villages of different faiths formed alliances and pacts that knitted their whole society together, the Ambonese lived in religious harmony with their neighbours for centuries.

Maluku travel advice

Maluku remains an extremely tense and, in parts, **dangerous** place to travel around. As this book was being researched, a few travellers were making their way to the Banda Islands, which were safe at the time of writing, and some were even heading further afield, to central and northern Maluku, including Halmahera, most of which was reported to be returning to some sort of normality. For the time being, however, the authorities insist that the greater part of Maluku remains off-limits to tourists. If you really, positively, have to visit, listen to the latest news reports, ask your foreign office for their advice (see p.000), canvass as many locals and other travellers as you can about the situation before you get there, and heed any advice given to you.

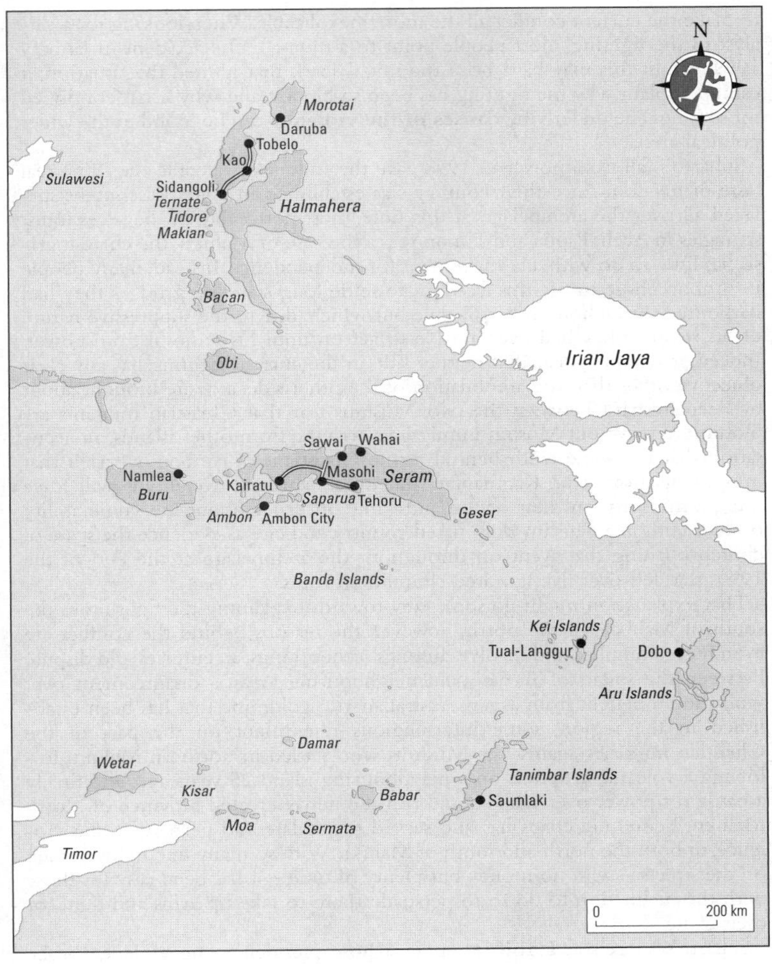

Instead, it was purely secular battles that blighted the islands' history during most of the twentieth century. Heavily influenced by the Dutch, who had maintained a strong hold over the islands for centuries, the Ambonese willingly fought on the Dutch side against the Javanese-dominated **independence movement** in Indonesia during the late 1940s. Defeated, the Ambonese believed that the Indonesians would be unwilling to keep the disloyal Maluku within its borders, and looked forward to forming their own independent state. However, it wasn't to be: the Indonesian army crushed all attempts to form a republic, and thousands of Ambonese fled to Holland to escape retribution for the part they had played in supporting the Dutch.

For the next fifty years Maluku, though unhappy at being neglected by the powers-that-be in Jakarta, meandered on peacefully enough – which only goes to make the current conflict all the more inexplicable. When looking for a catalyst to the fighting, most people point to a minor traffic accident in January 1999. Whilst this may have been the initial spark that ignited the situation, it cannot explain why the fighting has been so bloody, and why it has continued for so long. The underlying **causes of the violence** can be found in the wider political arena.

Suharto's fall from power in 1998 gave the Indonesian people their first real taste of freedom since their country was established in 1949. Discontent surfaced all over the archipelago at this time, most noticeably in the secessionist struggles in Aceh, Papua and Timor. Yet in the case of Maluku, the current crisis has little to do with any movement for independence. Instead, many people in Ambon chose to use this freedom to settle long-standing grudges they had harboured throughout Suharto's rule but which, due to the suppressive nature of his regime, they had been unable to act on until his removal from power. Indeed, it would appear that neither side in the current fighting has any clear objective other than the annihilation of the other side, a desire brought about by deep mistrust between the two. Muslims fear that Christian militants are plotting to drive out Muslim immigrants arriving from other islands, an accusation that has some truth behind it: the Christians of Ambon, worried that immigrants from Java, Kalimantan and other Muslim strongholds will leave them a minority on their own islands, are concerned about the vulnerability of their faith in a Muslim-dominated country, and cite as evidence the spate of church-burning that went on throughout the archipelago at the end of the 1990s that left over five hundred churches in ruins.

That explanation might go some way towards explaining the fighting in the south of Maluku. In the north, however, the reasons behind the conflict are even more complex, and involve, amongst other things, a centuries' old dispute between the sultan of Ternate and neighbouring areas, a disagreement over who should benefit from a new Australian-run goldmine that has been established in the region, some interreligious resentment on the part of the Christian minority against the Muslims who settled in northern Maluku following a volcanic eruption on a neighbouring island 25 years ago, and finally a battle for power over who should run the newly created province of North Maluku. Economic chaos has also served to escalate and perpetuate the violence, in both the north and south of Maluku. With so many unemployed men on the streets – with no money but plenty of time – it has been easy for those with the inclination to do so to persuade them to take up arms and fight for their cause.

Suharto's successor, **Habibie**, under whose presidency the violence broke out, failed to stamp it out during his short time in power; indeed, it was his inability to resolve the regional discontent erupting around the country that led to his downfall. His replacement, Abdurrahman Wahid (known as **Gus Dur**) – though more altruistic and less self-serving than his predecessors – also achieved very little during his rather chaotic term in office, preoccupied as he was with the myriad of other problems facing his government. Though the military presence deployed in Maluku increased manifold under Gus Dur, the army did little to contain the violence and, worryingly, many soldiers even became involved in the conflict, some supplying weapons to their chosen faction, others deserting the army altogether to take up arms with their Christian or Muslim brethren. Indeed, one news bulletin in 2000 reported the strange sight of soldiers fighting policemen on the streets of Ambon.

The military also proved to be totally ineffectual when trying to prevent the arrival of thousands of **Laskar Jihad** members in the summer of 2000. Based and trained in the small village of Munjul near Bogor in West Java, the Laskar Jihad – disciplined and well-armed with modern automatic weapons – claimed the intention of fighting a holy war against the Christians. Some assert that the organization's leaders had a more sinister agenda, and point to the group's close ties with former president Suharto. By stirring up trouble in the provinces, so the theory goes, the Laskar Jihad made Gus Dur's administration seem increasingly incompetent, thus theoretically paving the way for the return of Suharto to power (in fact the beleaguered Gus Dur was replaced by his vice-president, Megawati, in July 2001). As evidence they point to the fact that nobody stopped the Laskar from travelling to Maluku, suggesting connections with some political elite. Whatever their motives, the movement's presence in Maluku led inevitably to an escalation in the violence, and several raids on Christian communities in the north of Maluku – in which the assailants used speedboats and military-issue weapons – left over 200 Christians dead.

One ray of hope in the midst of all this gloom was the signing of a **peace agreement** between Muslims and Christians in neutral Sulawesi on February 12, 2002. Seasoned observers of this war, however, put little faith in this latest initiative. For one thing, one of the main antagonists, the Laskar Jihad, were not represented at the meetings; and while the agreement calls on groups from outside Maluku to surrender their weapons and return home, representatives of Laskar Jihad have already stated that they have no intention of leaving. Then, just two days after the peace agreement was signed, on February 14, four **bombs** went off in the no-man's land that divides Christian and Muslim Ambon. Though nobody was hurt, it was evident that not everybody was happy with the peace deal. Even a rally for peace, held in Ambon a few days later on February 20, during which Christians and Muslims were to be seen walking hand in hand and chatting, was not without controversy, with opponents of the peace deal dismissing it as nothing more than a publicity stunt staged by the government, using coerced students and hired hands to boost numbers. Another bomb blast in Ambon, in September 2002, that left three women dead, provides further evidence that this troubled corner of the Indonesian archipelago, while a lot calmer than it has been for some time, still falls some way short of normality.

13

West Papua (Irian Jaya)

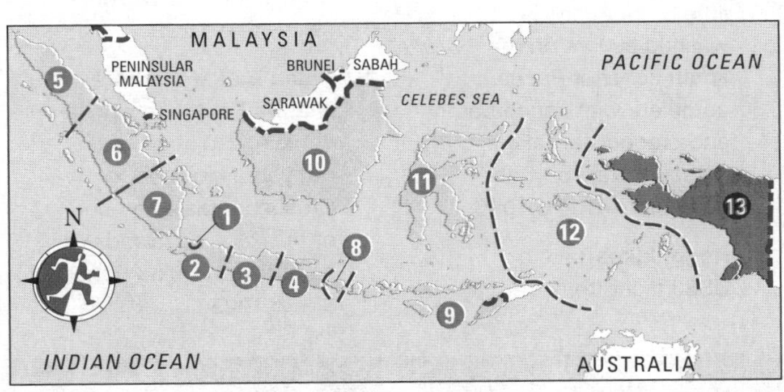

13 WEST PAPUA (IRIAN JAYA)

CHAPTER 13 **Highlights**

* **The Baliem Valley** Wonderful scenery, superb trekking, traditional villages and locals wearing penis gourds – Indonesia doesn't get any more exotic. **See p.993**

* **The Asmat region** Remote and unexplored – the ultimate goal for latter-day adventurers. **See p.1004**

* **Wasur national park** A little bit of Australia washed ashore on the south coast of Papua, complete with kangaroos and crocodiles. Take a horse for transport and go explore. **See p.1006**

* **Anggi lakes** Take a US$3 flight from Manokwari to these two gorgeous lakes – then spend the next two days walking back down to Ransiki and the coast. **See p.1020**

* **Cenderawasih Bay** Hundreds of kilometres of untouched coral reefs, all of them so difficult and expensive to explore that, if you do get this far, you'll almost certainly have them all to yourself. **See p.1021**

* **Pulau Biak's offshore islands** For those who thrive on isolation, act out your Robinson Crusoe fantasies on one of the Padaido islands or coral-ringed Pulau Rani. **See p.1023**

13

West Papua (Irian Jaya)

West Papua is one of the world's last great wildernesses: maps of the area still show stretches as wide as 300km without any relief data at all. In 1996, emissaries from two unknown tribes emerged from the Asmat jungle. One tribe began its first tentative steps towards communication with the outside world, the other slipped back into the jungle and has not been heard of since. From the towering glacial highlands of its spine to the sweaty mangrove swamps of the coast, West Papua is a tantalizing place for explorers.

The island of **New Guinea**, the second largest in the world, is neatly bisected down its north–south axis, the eastern portion comprising independent Papua New Guinea and the western half, **West Papua** (formerly Irian Jaya, a name that is still used by every Indonesian who doesn't live in Papua), belonging to Indonesia. It is surrounded by thousands of other smaller islands that pepper the southwestern corner of the Pacific. The whole area is known as Melanesia which means "Black Islands", either a reference to the dark skin of the inhabitants, or to the distinctive volcanic black ash that makes up much of its soil. Melanesians comprise one percent of the world's population, but speak twenty-five percent of its languages; in West Papua alone there are between 250 and 300 different languages, some spoken by only a few hundred people. This is due to extreme isolation, the harshness of the terrain and the ceaselessly warlike nature of the tribes, all of which have combined to maintain small, fiercely insular communities.

The majority of visitors will arrive, after a night flight from Java, in the capital city **Jayapura**, or on **Biak**, with its fabulous birdlife and fascinating coral reefs: travelling around West Papua takes a lot of planning (see box on p.980), and these are the best places to do it from. From Jayapura there are daily flights to the **Baliem Valley**, the highland plain that is home to the Dani tribes, and which features the most dramatic scenery imaginable. The jungles of the **south** are also a draw for travellers, as is the **Asmat region**, with its wonderful primitive art. On the **Bird's Head peninsula**, there are stunning ancient cave paintings near **Fak Fak**, gorgeous lakes near **Manokwari** and **Nabire**, and the untouched coral reefs of the **Cenderawasih national park**.

The **climate** of the region varies greatly, some parts of the island receiving heavy rainfall every day of the year. On the highest mountains, such as 5030-

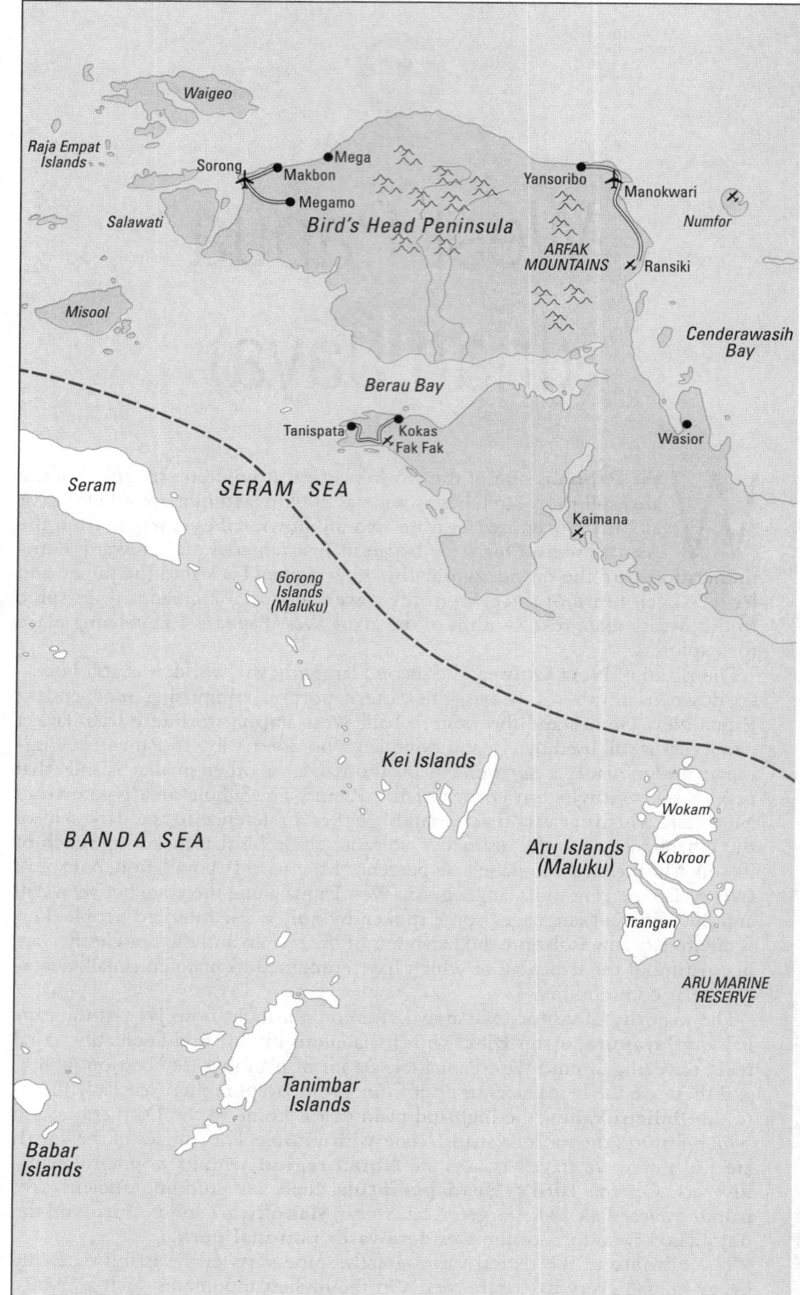
Waigeo
Raja Empat Islands
Sorong
Makbon
Mega
Megamo
Salawati
Bird's Head Peninsula
Yansoribo
Manokwari
Numfor
ARFAK MOUNTAINS
Ransiki
Misool
Cenderawasih Bay
Berau Bay
Tanispata
Kokas
Fak Fak
Wasior
Seram
SERAM SEA
Kaimana
Gorong Islands (Maluku)
Kei Islands
Wokam
BANDA SEA
Aru Islands (Maluku)
Kobroor
Trangan
ARU MARINE RESERVE
Tanimbar Islands
Babar Islands

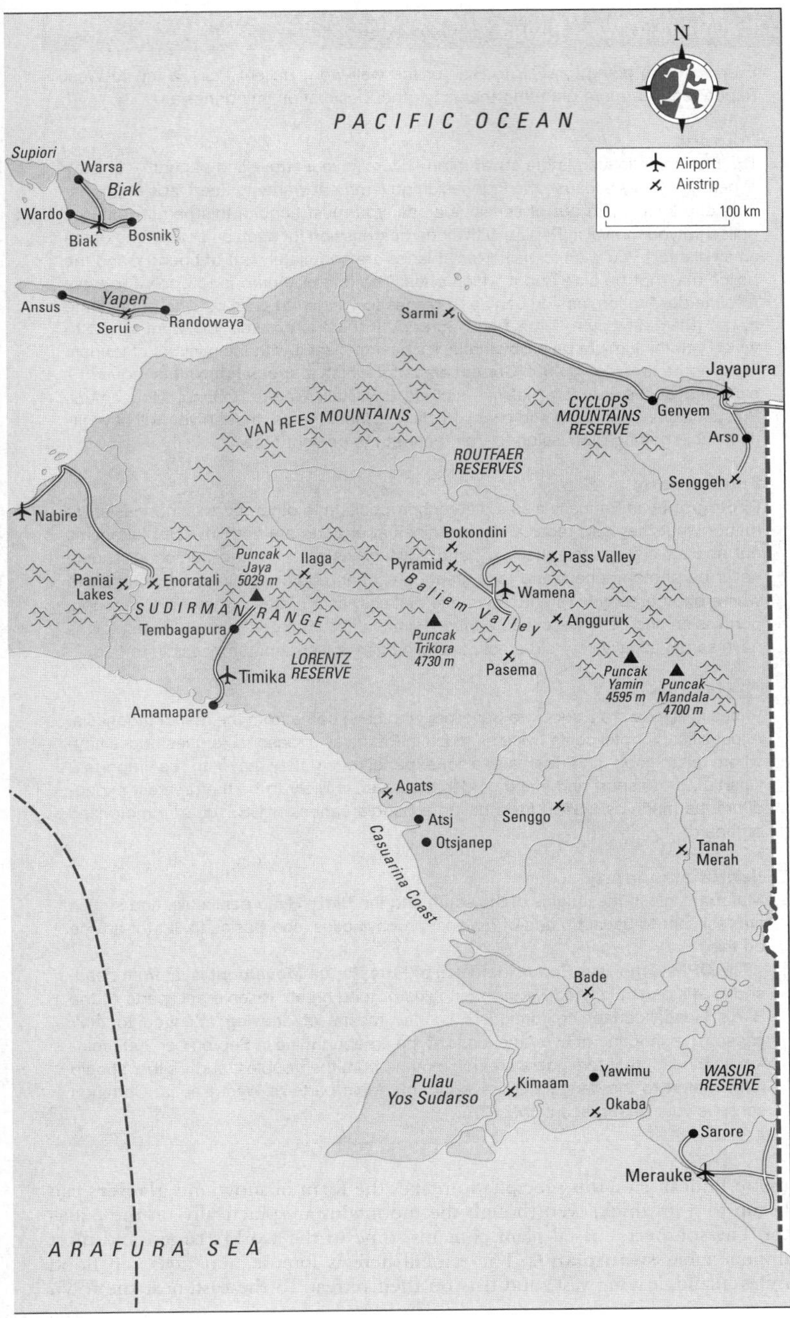
PACIFIC OCEAN
Airport
Airstrip
0
100 km
Supiori
Warsa
Biak
Wardo
Biak
Bosnik
Yapen
Ansus
Serui
Randowaya
Sarmi
Jayapura
Genyem
CYCLOPS MOUNTAINS RESERVE
Arso
Senggeh
VAN REES MOUNTAINS
ROUTFAER RESERVES
Nabire
Bokondini
Pyramid
Pass Valley
Wamena
Paniai Lakes
Enoratali
Puncak Jaya 5029 m
Ilaga
Baliem Valley
Angguruk
SUDIRMAN RANGE
Tembagapura
Puncak Trikora 4730 m
Pasema
Puncak Yamin 4595 m
Puncak Mandala 4700 m
Timika
LORENTZ RESERVE
Amamapare
Agats
Atsj
Otsjanep
Senggo
Tanah Merah
Casuarina Coast
Bade
Pulau Yos Sudarso
Kimaam
Yawimu
Okaba
WASUR RESERVE
Sarore
Merauke
ARAFURA SEA

Travelling in West Papua

Even if you're going to stick to Biak or the well-worn Baliem trails, a trip to West Papua requires more **planning** than any other destination in Indonesia.

Permits

The first complication is the **surat jalan** – literally your "travelling papers" – or travel permit. Mainly because the Indonesian government wants to keep tabs on all visitors and keep them out of sensitive areas, you must acquire this permit from the police on your arrival in Papua, with signed permission for each and every one of the small districts you wish to visit. Many places are completely out of bounds, and the police may not be sure about which ones. The rule of thumb is to apply for every feasible destination, as you can't add places to your *surat jalan* outside of the large towns (Biak, Jayapura, Timika and Sorong). If there is an area you want to get to which you think might be problematic, it's best to clear it with the minister of tourism in Jayapura first (see p.990). Current areas for which a **special permit** is required – over and above the *surat jalan* – include Enarotali, Wagite, Obano, Mounamuni, Puncak Jaya, Sepanjang and even, officially at least, Agats, though you will have little trouble getting permission to visit there at the present time.

Photography

Photography in Papua is also a different proposition to other parts of Indonesia. No matter what they say, most X-ray machines at airports are not film safe; take films out and have them searched by hand. Military installations and personnel should never be photographed, and take great care when photographing people; in areas where photography is rare it can cause distress, and in areas where it is common, permission and cash are expected first. Film is difficult to get hold of; the big towns have some, usually very old stock, and slide film is just about impossible to find.

Costs

Prices in Papua are a shock to travellers who have come from the rest of Indonesia. A lousy fleapit hotel costs twice as much in Papua as a reasonable guesthouse anywhere else; food and fuel are also **expensive** as they have to be imported. Chartering transport and hiring guides, however, is likely to be the greatest expenditure, as much as US$50 for a day in a paddle canoe, or US$100 in a motorized outboard.

Health and safety

Malaria is rife in the jungles of the south and the Bird's Head peninsula, and strains are resistant to usual brands of malarial prophylactics; see Basics (p.32) for advice on this.

The **OPM** (Organisas Papua Merdeka) or **Free Papua Movement** is far from dead, and is still particularly active in the jungles of the Lorentz reserve and parts of the Bird's Head; kidnapping foreigners is their means of drawing attention to their cause. The shooting of two Americans at the Freeport mine in September 2002 reinforces the fact that foreigners are not immune from the troubles, and visitors should remain alert to the dangers of travelling in certain parts of West Papua. Common sense is your best precaution.

metre Puncak Jaya, this precipitation takes the form of snow, and **glaciers** can be up to 40m thick, even though the mountains are practically on the equator. The southern coastal plain contains some of the world's largest and most impenetrable **swamplands**. The rainfall here is intense, and tides can flood miles inland, leaving vast mud flats on their retreat. To the east, near the town of Merauke, the land is much like that in the Northern Territory of Australia, with eucalyptus trees clinging to harsh, red soil. Several hundred miles inland are tropical **rainforests** of gigantic buttress-rooted trees, the tallest tropical trees in the world, cut through with myriad streams, rivers and waterfalls. As the tropical rainforest climbs to become **cloud forest**, the fauna becomes more alpine, with ferns, shrubs, grasses and mosses.

Some history

Despite numerous attempts by Western explorers to tame Papua, the colossal island all but repelled them right up until the latter part of the twentieth century. The extraordinary remoteness and hostility of its landscape combined with reports of vicious cannibals to deter even the most committed of adventurers. It seemed to early pioneers that the island had no prospect of mineral deposits – coconuts and timber were too difficult to farm profitably and trade in bird of paradise feathers and crocodile skins was far too arduous.

Papua's early history is of a succession of budding landing parties meeting intense opposition. The Dutch came first in 1597: Willem Janz landed and lost six of his men; Carstenz tried in 1623 and his party was decimated; and Captain Cook barely set foot at the Casuarina coast in 1770 before being forced to withdraw. Finally, in 1714, the Dutch East India Company took over the island with a decree from the sultan of Tidore, but mainly ignored the place.

On Indonesian **Independence**, it seemed logical that West Papua should itself become independent. After all, it was a world away from Java: the capitals of Jakarta and Jayapura are as far apart as London and Baghdad. However, there was no way the Indonesians were going to let such a vast, mostly empty landmass with potential natural resources be meekly ceded to tribal rule. So, while the Dutch prepared the island for union with Papua New Guinea, the Indonesians, with the collusion of the US, planned to ensure that every part of the old Dutch East Indies would become Indonesian.

Eventually, on November 19, 1969, the UN passed a resolution to endorse an **Indonesian occupation** of West Papua, on the understanding that a Vote of Free Choice would be held within six years. When this vote took place, it was stage-managed by the Indonesians, who selected, then bribed or threatened every one of the 1025 tribal delegates, and West Papua was ceded entirely to the Indonesians, to be renamed Irian Jaya, or "Victorious Irian".

Resentment amongst Papuan people continued to escalate. Initially, programmes to clothe and house the "natives" in Indonesian-style homes and clothing were begun benignly, but when the results were slow, tribal villages were bombed and napalmed, and local leaders were tortured, executed or dropped out of helicopters to their death. The cleansing, or pacification of native people in Papua, paved the way for the largest **transmigration** scheme the world has ever seen. The people who took up the government's offer of a plot of soil and a plane ticket to Papua found themselves ditched on infertile land, or crammed into bitterly depressing townships. The empty, colossal bulk of Papua that had seen no external influence or noticeable population increase in thousands of years, was suddenly inundated with four million new inhabitants in little over a decade. In places where they mixed with the natives, the Javanese took over Papuan enterprises and lands, while elsewhere, the government shunted the Papuan people off their land to make way for mining and timber interests. As towns started to expand around the plunder of Papua's resources, people from Maluku and Sulawesi started the trek east and to populate towns like Sorong and Jayapura, further disinheriting the native population. It has been estimated that up to one sixth of the native Papuan population – 300,000 people – have lost their lives to the Indonesian tyranny, with at least 15,000 refugees in New Guinea and thousands more displaced and homeless.

The fall of Suharto brought a change of policy towards Irian Jaya: where Suharto's attitude towards his easternmost province was characterized by brutality and coercion, Gus Dur's treatment of Papua relied instead on atonement and appeasement. On January 1, 2000, his government admitted to past errors in their treatment of the province, and on a trip to the region later that year the president apologized for human rights abuses perpetrated by the Indonesian army. On the same trip, however, he rejected – in no uncertain terms – calls for independence. His successor, Megawati Sukarnopuri, did likewise one year later in August 2001.

Neither of these declarations, however, did anything to dampen the enthusiasm of the **Free Papua Movement** (usually known by its Indonesian acronym of **OPM**), founded in 1964 soon after the Indonesian invasion. On June 2, 2000, at the end of a week-long conference in Jayapura attended by 2500 delegates representing 250 different tribal groups, the Papua Presidium Council – consisting of the leaders of various pro-independence groups – declared the province to be independent.The chairman of the proceedings was **Theys Eluay**, a colourful 64-year-old. One year later, in November 2001, his

Papua's wildlife

West Papua's **wildlife** differs widely from that found in the rest of Indonesia, with a dazzling variety of species and some spectacular oddities.

Papua's **marsupials** include cuscus, feather-tail possums and bandicoots. The echidna or spiny anteater is a burrowing, toothless creature with a great, long snout that it uses to suck up ants and earthworms: it is practically blind, and black with protruding white spines. Many marsupials live on plant sap, nectar or insects, but the **quoll** is a particularly vicious little predator that feeds on birds, reptiles and small mammals. About the size of a domestic cat and with big dark eyes, its cute appearance hides a ferocious predatory instinct. The mbaiso **tree kangaroo** is a black-and-white tree-living creature which emits a characteristic whistle, measures about 1.5m long and weighs 15kg. It was discovered in 1994 by Dr Tim Flannery, making it the largest new mammal to be found in recent times. Papua is also the possible home of the Tasmanian Tiger, the "most frequently seen extinct species" in the world, which also happens to be the world's largest carnivorous marsupial.

Papua's **birds** are fabulously attractive. In the dense shadow of the forest, they have developed extravagant showy plumage to ensure they attract a mate. Due to the lack of sizeable carnivores, several birds have evolved as ground dwellers. The **maleo fowl**, or megapode bird, a turkey-like creature with big powerful feet for burrowing, incubates its eggs by means of a giant rotting compost heap. The megapode bird and crowned pigeon (the largest and probably most beautiful pigeon extant) can laboriously fly short distances if threatened, but the island's largest inhabitant (other than humans), is an entirely ground-bound bird, the **cassowary**. It stands over 1.5m tall and possesses immensely powerful claws; its head is iridescent electric blue with a solid bony protuberance on the crown and a turkey-like, wattled red neck. Its spray of stringy black feathers are used to adorn the hats of the highlanders, and jungle dwellers pierce their noses with single feathers which curl upwards like antennae. The cassowary's eggs are laid in shallow nests on the forest floor and look like giant shiny avocados; the males guard the eggs and then the offspring for several months after hatching. The world's only known poisonous bird is found here: the **New Guinea Pitohi**, whose feathers and flesh contain one of the most powerful toxins around, poached from berries and used to deter predators.

body was found in his car on a quiet stretch of road near the Papuan border. A popular figure amongst both Papuans and the local (mainly Javanese) police force – on the night he disappeared he had been having dinner with a number of officers in the Indonesian army – it was later announced that he had been suffocated. His driver fled the scene of the crime and went into hiding. In a phone call to his family, however, he declared that Eluay had been abducted by non-Papuans. The suspicious circumstances in which Eluay had died, and the alleged incompetence of the subsequent investigation by Indonesian police provoked anger amongst the Papuans. In his hometown of Sentani mourners went on the rampage, and over the next few hours burnt down a number of Javanese-owned buildings.

The events of November 10, 2001 were a significant blow to Megawati Sukarnoputri's efforts to restore harmony in the restive province. Just one month prior to Eluay's murder, in an unsubtle but generous attempt to buy peace, Megawati had offered the Papuans **autonomy** within Indonesia, and complete control in everything except defence, foreign and monetary affairs, the police and law courts. Included in the autonomy package was a series of **concessions**, including one that allowed the provincial flag to fly alongside the red and white of the Indonesian flag (though pertinently, the provincial flag still had to be at a lower level). Furthermore, Megawati sanctioned a **change of name** for the province, from the unpopular Irian Jaya to the locally preferred Papua. While these measures were little more than symbolic gestures, Megawati also announced that the Papuan provincial government would now be allowed to keep seventy percent of revenue from oil and gas production and eighty percent from other mineral and forestry activity. Given the enormous unexploited natural resources remaining on Papua, that concession alone should be worth billions of dollars a year. The **trial** of seven special forces soldiers for the murder of Eluay, scheduled for early 2003, is further evidence of Jakarta's willingness to be seen to act honourably in its dealings with the rebels. Whether it will be enough to appease the OPM and their allies, however, remains to be seen.

Sentani and Jayapura

The vast majority of visitors to Papua will first arrive at **Sentani**'s airport, which also services Papua's capital town of **Jayapura**. Sentani is 30km away from Jayapura and it takes about ninety minutes to reach the city by public transport from the airport. Sentani is a smaller and quieter place to stay, but travellers will have to call at the capital to arrange a **surat jalan** (see the box on p.980). Jayapura is also the central point for visiting travel agents, exchanging foreign currencies and getting visas for Papua New Guinea, but it's usually possible to arrange **flights** around Papua from Sentani.

Although Jayapura is the biggest settlement in Papua, its entire municipality, taking up most of the north coast, boasts a population of only 168,000. There is almost no industry here and everything but a few foodstuffs is imported at great expense by boat or plane from other areas of Indonesia. Travelling essentials such as medicines and camera film should all be brought with you. The north coast is not quite as malarial and steamy as the south, but is extremely hot; the rainy season lasts from December to March and the average temperature is just under 30°C.

Sentani and around

Around 15km inland from the northern coast and 30km west of Jayapura, **SENTANI** is the central transport hub of Papua, with the largest and busiest airport. As planes circle to begin their descent into Sentani, they afford a breathtaking view of one of the north's most impressive features, **Danau Sentani**. Unfortunately, the lake is not actually visible from any part of Sentani town, which is not much more than an airport with a few buildings thrown up around it. The undulating hills that slope sharply down to the town's perimeters are totally deforested, but just beyond these are peaks as dramatic as knife points, covered with thick forest. It's possible to get to some good **beaches** from Sentani, two hours' drive northwest around **Depapre**. The lake is also well worth a visit, though there are no organized tours and you will have to arrange a motorized canoe yourself.

Sentani has in the past been viewed by most tourists as a relaxing and popular stopover, and an ideal alternative base to Jayapura. However, in November 2001, following the funeral of murdered independence leader Theys Eluay, several buildings were burnt to the ground or looted, including the main shopping centre and a number of "immigrant"-owned hotels and businesses. An air of suspicion and mistrust lingered on in the months that followed, and many tourists opted to stay in Jayapura instead. While locals insist, and are probably right in doing so, that tourists are safe, it remains to be seen at the time of writing whether normality, and tourists, will return to Sentani.

Practicalities

The **airport** is located in the south of the town and most facilities and hotels are within easy walking distance; the **minibus** (here known as *taksi*) **terminal** lies 1500m to the west. Garuda and Merpati have offices at the airport, and though they'll probably insist that you go to Jayapura to buy your ticket, you can check on availability, reserve a seat and find out about cancellations here. There is an **information office**, though it's rarely open. The police station is at the main entrance to the airport, but at the time of writing you could not get a **surat jalan** here.

If you plan to head straight **to Jayapura** on arrival at Sentani airport, then the easiest way is just to hop in a taxi outside the terminal (35min; Rp80,000). If you want to take public transport or are not in a hurry, then you can walk out to Jalan Sentani Kimeri (500m to the north) and flag down a *taksi* heading east. This will terminate at Abepura terminal (30min; Rp2000), but if you tell the driver you are going to Jayapura he'll drop you off just before, from where you can catch another *taksi* on to Jayapura's Terminal Entrop (20min; Rp1200). From there you'll need to take a final *taksi* into the centre of town (15min; Rp1000).

The **Telkom** (Yantel) office in Sentani is on the way north from the airport to the main road and is easily located by its red-and-white communications mast. It is open 24hr and is relatively efficient, though prices are subject to sudden and unexplained fluctuations. The **post office** (Mon–Sat 8am–5pm) is on the main road to Jayapura, Jalan Sentani Kimeri. The only **ATM** in town is often locked; it lies at the western end of Jalan Kimeri next to the Multi supermarket and a small **internet café** which manages the impressive feat of having a connection even slower than the one in Jayapura. Take a torch if you're walking around Sentani after dark: the street lighting is unreliable and there are plenty of drainage ditches and sewers awaiting the unwary.

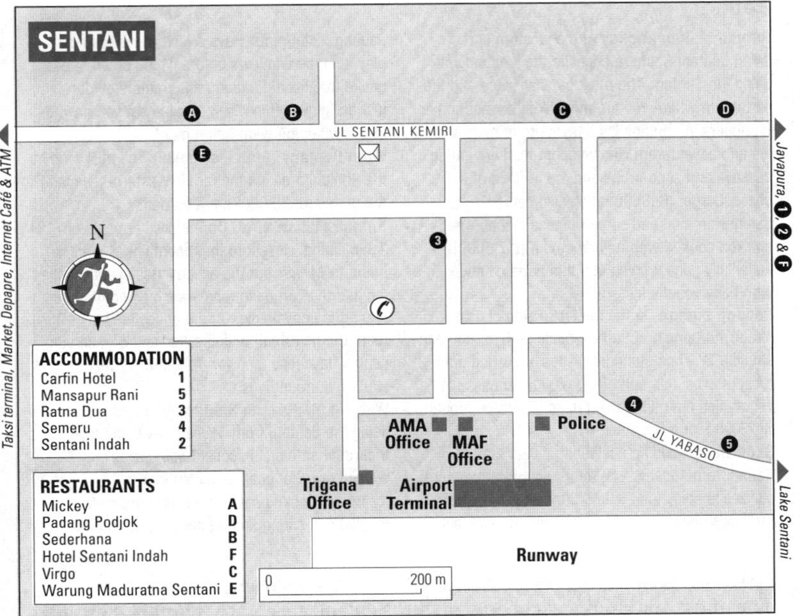

Accommodation

Most **hotels** in Sentani are pretty close to the airport and will send staff to wait at the terminal to greet incoming flights and ferry passengers to their hotels. Places here are generally quieter but more expensive than those in Jayapura, and with the recent immolation of several of the cheaper options, budget places are hard to find.

Carfin Hotel Jalan Flafon ⓣ0967/591478. Next door to the Onomi Christian Church at the eastern end of Jalan Sentani Kimeri. Prices here include full board; it's a clean place with lots of shiny glass and ceramic tiles. Each room has a TV and air-con and the restaurant features karaoke. ❸

Mansapur Rani Jl Yabaso 113 ⓣ0967/591219. Close to the airport: turn right out of the terminal gates and it's a 5min walk. The owner proudly boasts that his is the only Papuan-owned hotel in town, and thus the safest too. The economy rooms are spacious and en-suite, though the mandis are grotty and the rooms, like everywhere in Sentani, are overpriced. The VIP air-con rooms at the bottom of the pretty garden are much more comfortable but at Rp200,000, way too expensive. ❸–❺

Hotel Ratna Dua Jalan Penerangan ⓣ0967/592277 or 592496, ⓕ591200. Features beautiful, sizeable air-con rooms with gleaming white-tiled floors around a central restaurant. The price includes a breakfast of tea, coffee, fruit and sweetmeats. Out the back is an aviary, where birds are kept before export to private collectors around Asia. It's a bleak, dung-spattered chicken-wire affair, but usually full of startling lorries, parrots, parakeets and a few mambruk and raja cockatoos. ❹

Hotel Semeru Jalan Yabaso ⓣ0967/591447. Perhaps the best value in Sentani now – though that's not saying much – and the closest place to the airport, just a 3min walk east of the gates. Decent, clean rooms with (noisy) air-con and en-suite mandi cost Rp60,000. Try to phone ahead as it's often full. ❸

Hotel Sentani Indah Jalan Raya Hawaii ⓣ0967/591900. From the road this three-star joint looks more like an airport terminal, but inside it's a different story, with all the rooms arranged around a large swimming pool with a sunken bar. All rooms have satellite TV, hot water and fridge and there is an additional ten-percent tax charged on everything. ❻

Eating

Rumah Makan Mickey At the western end of Jalan Sentani Chimera opposite the junction with Jalan Pln Sentani. The most popular place and the restaurant where you are most likely to meet other foreigners in Sentani: it's a favourite of missionaries and adventurers who've spent too long eating cassava and sago grubs and are in need of a cheeseburger (Rp8500); they also serve Indonesian food and some Chinese dishes. The chicken cooked with mushrooms (Rp17,500) is especially good, served in a thin tomato sauce with baby vegetables.

Padang Podjok On the mountain side of Jalan Flafon. An upmarket Padang place with air-con and satellite TV. Their standard dishes of curried potatoes, prawns, fish and chicken with varieties of vegetables are a little overpriced; figure on around Rp25,000 for a full meal.

Sederhana Heading east along Jalan Sentani Kemiri from *Mickey*. A Padang restaurant that specializes in spicy food. About 50m further east of the *Sederhana*, are the *Tanjung* and *Mutiara*, also Padang restaurants. Have a look at the food displayed in the windows before sitting down to eat; unlike traditional Padang restaurants they don't just bring everything to your table but you have to select what you want beforehand.

Hotel Sentani Indah (see p.985). The best food in the Sentani area. All the fare is Western-style, and the pizzas (Rp25,000) are a bargain.

Rumah Makan Virgo On the northern side of Jalan Flafon, closest to the mountains. A similar menu to *Mickey* but the execution is slightly lacking and the European food – such as hamburgers – is often unavailable. On the opposite side of the road are the rumah makans *Sari* and *Lily*, serving central Javanese food for Rp10,000 in basic warung surroundings.

Warung Maduratna Sentani About 20m down Jalan Pln Sentani from *Mickey*. Javanese food; their deer sate and excellent *ikan bakar* are cooked over hot coals outside the front door. Ask for freshly cooked sate rather than the stuff they've had sitting around out back for hours.

Danau Sentani, Waena and the beaches

The most rewarding excursion in the Sentani area is to **Danau Sentani**. Standing 75m above sea level and covering over fifteen square kilometres, the lake is an exceedingly beautiful expanse of island-studded azure and cobalt blue, teeming with catfish and gurami and framed by the looming green lower slopes of the Cyclops mountains. The best way to see the lake is to take a *taksi* from Sentani down to **Yahim harbour** and then try and find someone with a motorized dugout canoe – no more than a hacked-out tree trunk with an outboard nailed to the back. The usual rate for an hour's charter of one of these boats is about $10, though you would need a little longer than an hour to get out to a few islands and take a swim. A good island to head for is **Apayo**, one of the few places in the Sentani area where the people still practise sculpture and distinctive paintings on bark canvases. The paintings are characterized by stylized geckos and snakes painted in natural pigments, and resemble Australian aboriginal art.

Six kilometres or so southwest of Sentani and on the lakeside is **DOYO LAMA** village, renowned for a nearby black boulder, covered with faint, ancient carvings and believed to have magical powers. It's possible to get to the village by *taksi* from Sentani. The lakeside *Yougga Cottage* (Ⓣ0967/571570; Rp115,000), about 23km from downtown Jayapura and accessible by *taksi* from Abepura, is a **restaurant** and small **guesthouse** on the shores of the lake. All rooms come with breakfast and en-suite mandi and the restaurant has reasonable Indonesian and Chinese food.

To see the lake from a distance, the best lookout is at the **MacArthur Monument**, 325m up Gunung Ifar. The plaque on the monument cites this spot as the headquarters of General Douglas MacArthur's "Reckless task force" during the Pacific War. The monument is about 6km from Sentani and, at the weekends, *taksis* will run right up to it. At all other times you'll probably have to charter a *taksi*: take care to check in with the guard on the way up to the monument, who may want to see your passport or *surat jalan* if you have one.

△ Asats (fish on jetty), West Papua

The village of **WAENA**, a twenty-minute *taksi* ride east of Sentani, has a couple of worthwhile attractions. The **Taman Budaya** (Cultural Park) has some mock-ups of traditional Papuan houses; they're rather exaggerated replicas and not a particularly good representation of the buildings you'll see around Papua, but it's free to get in. The **Museum Negeri** next door (daily 8am–4pm; Rp750) is much better: a large map shows where every one of West Papua's 250 languages are spoken and others depict the geology and history of Papua (mostly in Indonesian). There are several *bisj* poles and decorated skulls from the Asmat region, some fine Baliem Valley stone axe-heads and several ammonites and mammoth shark's teeth. Other relics document Papua's more recent past, with samurai swords, bayonets and shells from American servicemen, and pistols and cannons left behind by the VOC. To get there, take a *taksi* from Sentani to Abepura and ask the driver to stop at the Museum Negeri.

To the northwest of Sentani there are a few good **beaches** in Depapre district, most notably **Pantai Amai**. It's no more than 15km from Sentani, but takes over an hour to reach in a crammed *taksi*. You will be dropped off at the harbour in Depapre, from where the usual course is to hire a boat over to Amai. It costs around $10 for a boat that can seat about fifteen, and at the weekend you may be able to share a boat with locals also heading over to the lovely white-sand beach.

Jayapura and around

Huddled in a narrow valley between jungle-covered hills, **JAYAPURA** is West Papua's capital city and major port town. If you're arranging a serious tour around Papua, you will probably have to take advantage of the city's poor amenities. Outside the city you'll find a few reasonable beaches, as well as sites associated with World War II.

The Jayapura area was first surveyed by the Dutch steamship *Etna* on a voyage of exploration in 1858. They docked near the present city's site, naming it **Humbold Bay**. The Dutch eventually decided to construct a city here to keep watch over the border with German-occupied New Guinea, which lies only 20km or so away. This city, which they declared capital of the Netherlands New Guinea province on March 17, 1910, and named **Hollandia**, was overtaken swiftly by the Japanese in World War II, who also made their base here. The Japanese ascendancy was to be relatively short-lived, with MacArthur's troops retaking the area in an amphibious assault at **Hamadi beach**. Nowadays, Jayapura is quite a thriving town, very obviously populated and run by migrant Indonesians from Java, Sulawesi and Maluku. Very few shop or hotel owners are native Papuans, and Papuans in government office are as rare a sight as the birds of paradise.

The **University of Cenderawasih Museum** (Tues–Sat 8am–4pm) between Jayapura and Abepura, has an excellent and well-organized collection of artefacts from around Papua, with a good deal of *bisj* poles and other carvings from the Asmat region. There are also a few older objects here that were presented to the museum by Michael Rockefeller (see p.1012) after his expeditions in the south. A good souvenir stall is located near the entrance.

Practicalities

Jayapura is probably about as compact a capital as you will ever find, the main reason being that there's very little here. The two main streets of Jalan Ahmad Yani and Jalan Percetakan run parallel to each other and at right angles to the seafront. Coming by public transport from Sentani, you'll end up at **Terminal Entrop**, 5km east of town; regular bemos drive along the seafront to the cen-

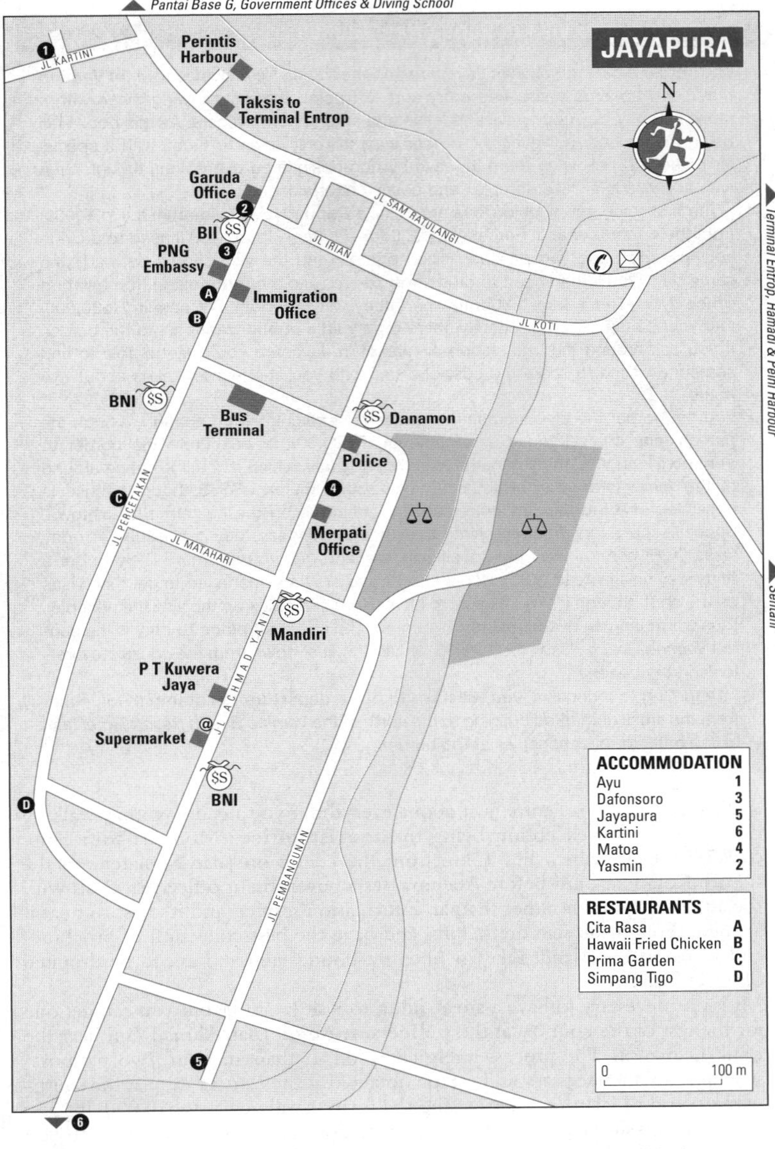

tre of town. The **Pelni port** is 2km east of town; an ojek should charge no more than Rp2000 to take you to your hotel, which is a far quicker option than waiting for the *taksis* which, though they fill up quickly, often get stuck in the heavy traffic that's inevitable when the Pelni boats arrive. Currently the *KM Ciremai*, *KM Rinjani*, *KM Sinabung*, *KM Dobonsolo* and *KM Doro Londa* all call in at Jayapura at the end of their journey through Indonesia's eastern islands; see p.1028 for details.

Renewing your visa in Papua New Guinea

The border crossing between Jayapura and the Papua New Guinea town of **Vamino** may soon become a visa-free entry and exit point, thereby allowing those with a standard sixty-day (tourist) visa to leave and enter Indonesia here. As this book was being researched, however, the border was still only open to those with a special visa (see p.23) allowing them to leave by non-designated exit points, though even with this visa it is still a complex and costly undertaking.

The first thing you should do is apply for a **Papua New Guinea visa** (Rp30,000) from the **consulate** at Jl Percetakan 28 (Mon–Fri 9am–4pm); you'll need to provide your passport and two passport-sized photos, and the visa should be ready the same day. You'll then need to cross over the road to the **Indonesian immigration office** (Mon–Thurs 8am–2.30pm), where they will stamp an exit permit (Rp30,000) into your passport. Unfortunately, there is very little **public transport** to the border. If you ask around the bus station or market in Jayapura you may be able to find someone willing to share the cost of a taxi with you; the journey takes about two hours.

At the border the bureaucratic formalities are straightforward enough, though the guards may charge you a small amount (Rp20,000 or so). From the border to **Vamino** it's another thirty minutes to an hour by taxi, which sometimes hang around by the border (around 180 Papuan Kina, or approximately US$55, though hitching is possible). The **Indonesian consulate** in Vamino is on the eastern side of town, opposite the *Sandaun Hotel*. Note that though they say they can issue sixty-day visas (K30) here, unless you specifically demand one you are more likely to get a thirty-day visa instead (K30). Some lucky travellers have managed to get their visas on the spot, though it's more usual to have to wait and pick up the visa the next day, thus warranting an overnight stay in Vamino. The cheapest **place to stay** is the central *Vamino Beach Resort Hotel* (K83, or US$25), just down from the consulate overlooking the beach.

Returning to Indonesia, you will need to buy a **departure tax stamp** (K15), either from the small unmarked building to the north of the *Vamino Beach Resort Hotel* (ask at the hotel for directions), or at the border.

Once in the town centre, just about everything you need is within walking distance, the one exception being the **tourist office** (Mon–Fri 8am–5pm; ⓣ967/534871), which lies 12km from the centre on Jalan Sumatera, in the suburb Kota Raja, just before Abepura. It's a government office that deals with the affairs of tourism rather than an information service, and it's best to treat it as such, though the staff are helpful and have the best collection of brochures and maps on the island. Take an Abepura-bound *taksi* and ask to be dropped off at Otonom.

It is not necessary to have a **surat jalan** to visit Jayapura, but you can get one for the rest of the country at the **police station** on Jalan Ahmad Yani near the Bank Danamon. The process rarely takes longer than an hour. Two passport-sized photos are necessary and can be obtained at the camera shop at the south-western end of Jalan Yani. Processing the form usually costs Rp10,000. It's best to plan this visit well in advance, and write down every single destination you could conceivably want to visit in Papua. If asked for your profession, it's least contentious to say you are a student. It's essential once the form is processed to photocopy it several times (several nearby shops have copiers); it's much easier to leave photocopies at the many regional police stations who will want to keep a copy, than to risk leaving the original.

The main **post office** with **internet facilities** (Rp10,000) can be found on the waterfront on Jalan Sam Ratulangi, and the 24-hour **Telkom** is located right next door. Other, slightly cheaper but equally slow internet places have opened up along Jalan Yani and Jalan Percetakan. There are several **banks** in Jayapura; if in doubt about whether you will have enough money later on, change it now as there are no banks for exchange in the Baliem Valley or Asmat region. The Bank BII on Jalan Percetakan and the Bank BNI on Jalan A Yani both have **ATMs**; the former is also the best bank for credit card transactions and dollar exchange, while the latter is one of the only banks in mainland West Papua that will even look at travellers' cheques in currencies other than US dollars. In case of emergency, the **hospital** is located 3km east of town; catch a *taksi* heading northeast around the bay and ask for the *rumah sakit umum*.

Garuda (Mon–Thurs 8am–noon & 1–5pm, Fri 8am–noon & 2–5pm, Sat 8am–2pm, Sun 10am–2pm; ⓣ967/536218) are at Jl Percetakan 4–6 next to the *Hotel Yasmin*, and the **Merpati office** is at Jl Ahmad Yani 15 (Mon–Sat 8am–5pm, Sun 10am–3pm; ⓣ967/533111); the Merpati office will only take bookings on their flights departing from Jayapura, and neither office has facilities for paying by credit card. For credit card bookings, head for one of Jayapura's several **travel agents**, of which PT Kuwera Jaya, Jl Ahmad Yani 39 (ⓣ967/531583, ⓕ532236) is the longest established and most efficient. They sell all tickets for Garuda, Kartini and Merpati, can arrange diving, rafting on the Baliem river and numerous walking and bird-watching tours around Papua, and are far better for **Pelni** tickets and information than the out-of-town Pelni office on Jalan Argapura (ⓣ0967/536931). However, they – along with all the other agents in Jayapura – do not deal with the "pioneer" airlines, the small companies which mainly transport cargo around the region; for these you'll have to go to Sentani airport and ask there.

The **Papua New Guinea consulate** is at Jl Percetakan 28 (Mon–Fri 9am–4pm), by the *Hotel Dafonsoro*; see the box opposite for details of crossing into Papua.

Accommodation

With one exception, Jayapura doesn't have much in the way of good-value **accommodation**, and quite a few of the smaller hotels can be real fleapits. Even in the larger, smarter hotels it's essential to check your room before you agree to check in.

Hotel Ayu Jl Tugu II 1 ⓣ0967/534263. The best option for budget travellers; the cheaper rooms are cramped but clean, the staff are friendly, and the rates include a light breakfast and some welcome little touches such as a towel and soap. ❸

Hotel Dafonsoro Jl Percetakan 20 ⓣ0967/531695 or 531696, ⓕ534055. All the rooms here have hot water, TV, breakfast and air-con, though some smell very musty. ❺

Hotel Jayapura Jl Olahraga 4 ⓣ0967/533216. The cheapest hotel in town, with tiny windowless rooms, some en suite: it's a bit like sleeping in a Turkish bath, particularly as the rooms come without fan, an essential piece of furniture in Jayapura. ❷

Hotel Kartini Jl Perintis 2 ⓣ0967/531557. A good and well-established alternative to the *Ayu*, and often full, located just by the river in the southern part of town. The staff are friendly, the rooms – some with attached bathroom – kept very clean, and it's one of the few places with natural light in the rooms. ❷

Hotel Matoa Jl Ahmad Yani 14 ⓣ0967/531633. The best in town, though now feeling very dated with a very 1970s beige and brown decor. All of the rooms here have air-con and hot-water baths, though curiously there are no "standard" doubles, the cheapest room for two people costing a whopping Rp400,500. ❻

Hotel Yasmin Jl Percetakan 8 ⓣ0967/533222, ⓕ536027. Newest, shiniest and most modern of the upper-bracket hotels, still way overpriced at US$45 for a standard (the cheapest) room, though these do come with air-con, TV and a shower. Quibble about the price and they should let you pay in rupiah, for which the rates are curiously almost fifty percent cheaper. ❻–❼

Eating

Night warung along Jalan Irian, at the waterfront and at the northern end of both Jalan Ahmad Yani and Jalan Percetakan sell the usual Indonesian snacks, as well as *ikan bakar*, sate and various soups and stews. There are a number of good **bakeries** downtown selling cream cakes as well as samosas and vegetable snacks, including *Roti Mawar* near the Bank BNI on Jalan Yani (good and cheap, though the noise from the nearby karaoke market stalls may drive you away), the more genteel *Prima Garden* (see below) and the slightly more upmarket *SSW* at the northern end of Jalan Percetakan.

Cita Rasa Jl Percetakan 66. Slightly expensive but still good-value Indonesian and Chinese restaurant, with an excellent choice of fish dishes; busy at lunchtimes, but often deserted in the evenings.
Hawaii Fried Chicken Jalan Percetakan. Standard Indonesian rip-off of a Western fast-food joint, though the fried chicken, it must be said, is good here. Upstairs they serve traditional Indonesian and Chinese dishes to a soundtrack of wailing Indonesian businessmen singing karaoke.
Fantasi Restoran In *Hotel Dafonsoro*, Jl Percetakan 20. Indonesian-style beef, pork and seafood dishes for around Rp15,000. A small, cold Bintang beer is Rp10,000.
Matoa In *Hotel Matoa*, Jl Yani 14. Stocks a good variety of well-prepared Indonesian foods at reasonable prices, as well as a number of Western dishes: homegrown rump steak comes in at Rp27,500, the imported New Zealand variety costs double.
Prima Garden Opposite the *Hotel Matoa*. A bakery serving excellent coffee, cold drinks and a variety of cakes, puddings and sandwiches.
Simpang Tigo Jalan Percetakan. Standard Padang restaurant serving healthy portions of the usual curries and dried fish; extremely popular at lunchtimes with locals.

Around Jayapura

Most of the attractions in the Jayapura area are coastal, with a few decent beaches and some pleasant seaside villages. Nearby **HAMADI** was the scene of MacArthur's historic World War II landings, but is now a lazy seaside suburb of Jayapura. The market here is well worth a look: it's a busy bric-a-brac affair, flooded with souvenirs. The beach is a short walk away and is no great shakes, with littered sands and murky water, but it's a quick and easy escape from Jayapura. A few rusting hulks of old tanks and a commemorative statue lie nearby. Across Yotefa bay from Hamadi is **ENGROS**, a picturesque fishing village with houses perched on precarious stilts. The road that runs round the bay to this village continues east into New Guinea. Hamadi is about 5km from Jayapura and *taksis* run here every few minutes. On the road between Hamadi and Jayapura are a couple of **hotels** – the *Pacific* (Ⓣ0967/534005; ❸) and the *99* (Ⓣ0967/535689; ❸) – both overlooking the sea and with reasonable air-con rooms with en-suite mandi. In Hamadi itself, the *Hotel Asia* (Ⓣ0967/535478; ❸–❹) has basic rooms with fan or air-con, while the upmarket *Hotel Mahkota* (Ⓣ0967/532997; ❹) is wildly overpriced for rooms with air-con and TV but no hot water. The *Mahkota*'s restaurant has sea views and a mix of European and Indonesian foods; figure on about $7 for a full meal.

A far better and cleaner beach then Hamadi's can be found at **Tanjung Ria**, otherwise known as Pantai Base G: it's about 4km north of Jayapura and can get very crowded over the weekends. Public transport only goes there at the weekends, so at other times you'll have to charter a *taksi* or get as close as possible and then walk. The beach itself has no coral, but about ten minutes' boat-ride offshore is a fantastic reef that starts at a depth of around 5m and plunges down to about 30m. It's festooned with hard corals and plenty of exotic sea creatures dart about: blue spotted rays, bumphead parrot fish, clown fish and the odd white-tip reef shark. Further north at **Pasir Lima** is another good slope, with barracuda, rays, surgeonfish and triggerfish. To get to these reefs you will need to find a knowledgeable local boat-owner, for there are currently no dive operators in Jayapura.

The Baliem Valley

Today's visitors to the **Baliem Valley** will have their first glimpse of it from the plane, as the undulating jungle-covered mountains abruptly plunge into an unexpected and remarkable landscape. All of a sudden, from flying over a vast wilderness of uncharted forests, harsh cliff-faces fall away to a cultivated plain: a chess board of terraced fields, divided by rattan fences to keep the pigs out and the crops segregated. Sprinkled over the valley floor are jumbled assemblies of thatched *honai* huts. Occasional crude, dusty roads and snaking streams carve up the plains, and Sungai Baliem slowly meanders across it before falling into fierce rapids in the southeastern **Baliem Gorge**.

Nowadays the majority of visitors to **Jayawijaya regency**, as it is known, come here to encounter the inhabitants of the valley, the **Dani**. These proud people have managed, in the face of continued government and missionary pressure, to maintain a culture of incredible depth and beauty. Whilst the warlike nature of the Dani lives on only symbolically in dance and festival, for the most part they still live by the same methods as have existed in the valley for thousands of years. They mostly shun Western clothes, the men dressing solely in a penis gourd (*horim*), with pig teeth pushed through their noses and their bodies decorated in clay-and-grease warpaint.

Some history

In 1938, the millionaire Richard Archbold was on a reconnaissance mission for the American Museum of Natural History when he first saw the Baliem Valley from his seaplane. He returned and landed on Danau Habbema some months later, with porters, soldiers and tonnes of equipment, and set to walk across the valley. Their reception by the natives varied from almost frenzied welcomes to showers of spears and arrows, but Archbold's party found the inhabitants to be at a remarkable stage of agricultural development, with stone-and-wood terracing making steep valley walls into viable fields, and crop rotation and irrigation in use. Though the Archbold expedition was a tremendous success, it was not until after World War II that another entered the valley, and not until the 1960s that the missionaries and Indonesian officials started to trickle in.

In 1969 and 1977, the Dani people revolted against Indonesian rule: the government was trying to force them to adopt Western clothes and discard their cultural practices. The Indonesians also began huge logging commissions in Dani areas, which have now almost entirely cleared the Baliem Valley of forests. The Dani **uprising** was brutally suppressed, with many people killed, villages bombed, and tribal leaders publicly tortured and executed.

The summer of 1997 saw the beginning of one of the harshest periods in the memory of the peoples of the central highlands. The El Niño weather system was blamed for the terrible destruction all over the island, with Papua New Guinea having to receive supply drops from Australia and much of West Papua's normally drenched forests drying up. **Fires** started by slash-and-burn farmers raged out of control, a situation exacerbated by locals starting more fires in the belief that the smoke in the sky would become cloud and cause rain. Such a vast amount of smoke poured into the air that for months the haze blocked out the sun, and visibility in Wamena was down to a few hundred metres. Merpati

The tribes of the Baliem

The people of Jayawijaya regency can be subdivided into many different groups, but the three broadest tribes are the Dani, Western Dani or Lani, and the Yali. **Dani people** are instantly recognizable, because they use the thin end of a gourd for their *horim*: the length of the gourd encloses the penis and points it upwards in a permanent erection. Dani headdresses are made of cockerel feathers in a fetching circular crown, often with longer, more elaborate feathers falling down to frame the face. Once these were made from the furs of the cuscus, but now the more vibrantly coloured cuscus are all but extinct.

Dani **women** wear knee-length skirts, traditionally made of grass, and usually go bare-chested. All women are considered to be witches in the highlands, with powerful magic that increases with age. Aged women, it is believed, can put curses on men, causing them to become infertile and die horrible deaths.

The **Yali**, who come from the east of the Baliem, have a different kind of *horim*. They use the thick end of the gourd but it points straight out at right angles to the body from beneath a rattan skirt, which appears to be made of strung-together hula hoops whose size ascends towards the ground. The **Lani** cover their heads in a palm tree-like spray of cassowary feathers, which spills out over the head and hair. Their *horim* are also made from the thick end of the gourd but are secured around the waist by a wide, brightly coloured sash. Often the top of their gourd is used as a pouch for keeping money or tobacco in.

Even during freezing cold evenings, valley peoples remain practically naked, hugging themselves with folded arms and coating their bodies with insulating pig fat to keep warm. Pigs themselves are central to the highlanders culture, and very much a part of the family they are owned by. Pigs sleep in the *honai* with their owners and, if a sow dies, it's customary for the piglets to be suckled by a woman of the household.

The traditional **weapon** of the valley is the bow and arrow. A four-pronged arrow is for shooting birds, three prongs are used to shoot fish, a single bamboo is used on pigs, and a single shaft of wood or bone is for people. Around the Baliem Valley, the highlanders have a very distinctive diet, dominated by sweet potato but supplemented by fruits such as pandanus and *buah merah*. The latter is a large spiky pod, the insides of which are crushed and boiled; it tastes a bit like dark chocolate.

didn't fly into Wamena for many weeks at a time, and missionary mercy flights were also grounded, completely stranding unfortunate travellers. By the end of 1997, after four rainless months in the usually lush valley, over 500 people had starved to death in the immediate area of Wamena. While this situation was certainly intensified by El Niño, summer smoke haze and its knock-on effects have become quite regular over recent years. Whilst the thickest smoke has been in Kalimantan and northern Sumatra, it's much more of a problem for travellers in Papua, as almost all travel is by air. It may soon be the case that July to September become months when travellers should steer well clear of travel in Papua.

Wamena and around

At first sight, the town of **WAMENA** appears to be the only blot on the wonderful rural landscape of the Baliem Valley, with characterless tin-roofed buildings, clapped out old mini-van taxis and deep slurry-filled drainage trenches along its streets. However, the streets themselves are spacious, as the valley people, used to living in small isolated communities, are loath to live crammed together. Missionary houses lie on manicured lawns behind white picket

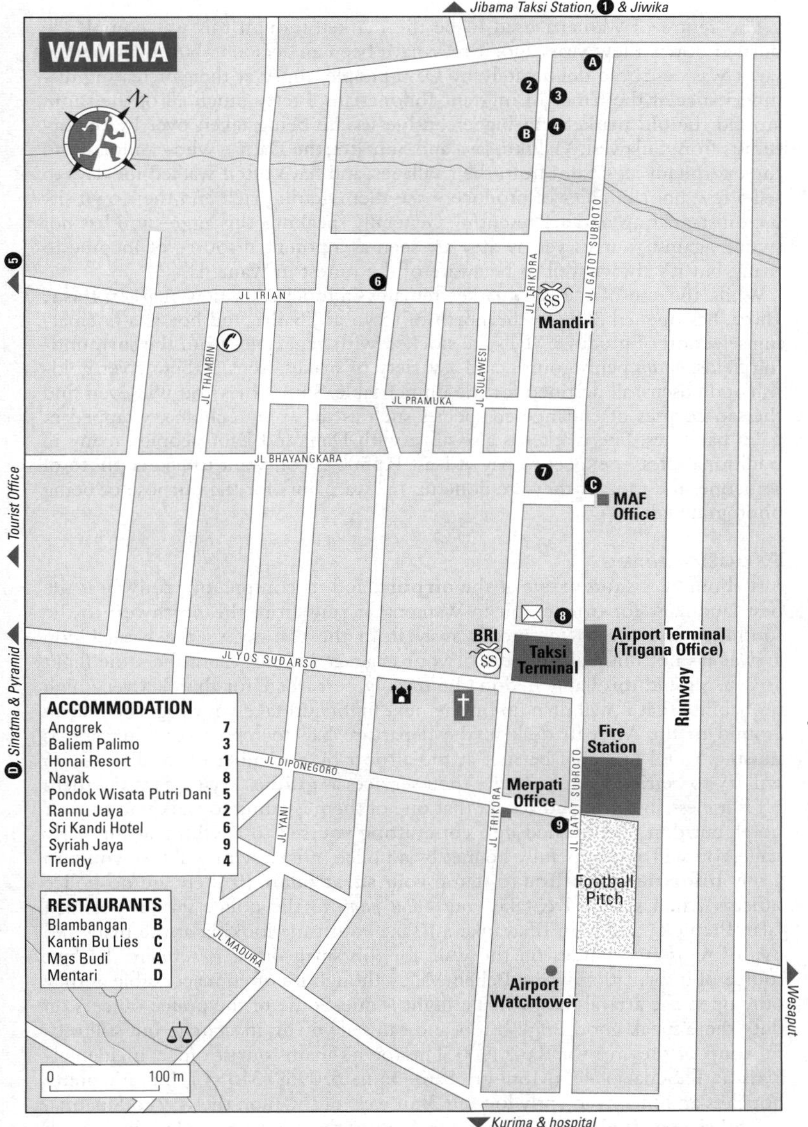

fences, amongst the strolling, naked Dani and their ubiquitous pigs. The town's **climate** is excellent, cold enough so you need a blanket at night and rarely suffering the daytime swelter of sea-level towns such as Jayapura. An additional bonus for walkers is the heavy, refreshing wind that rushes into the valley in the afternoons. Several of the **villages** around Wamena, such as Jiwika, give an insight into the agrarian way of life of the valley people.

The centre of Wamena used to be the market, though this was completely burned down a few years ago; it may have been an accident, but many people say it was destroyed deliberately by Dani people, angry at their increasing disinheritance at the hands of migrant Indonesians. Pretty much all of the shops around the old market and bigger businesses are being taken over by opportunists from Sulawesi, Maluku, Java and Sumatra; the Dani – who cannot afford the exorbitant *taksi* fares from their villages, and have often walked for days to sell a few, poor bundles of produce – see them getting rich and their own situation stagnating, and are resentful. Generally speaking, this aggression has not swung against tourists yet, as they are seen as a potential source of income to many, but it's always well to be aware of the unrest in Wamena.

While the site of the old market remains untouched, a new market, **Pasar Baru**, has opened 3km to the north of town at Jibama, and boasts a fascinating selection of produce. Stalls are stocked with vegetables from the surrounding fields, *horim* penis gourds, and a variety of snakes, frogs, Baliem river goldfish and cuscus, all destined for the dinner table. Sometimes you will even find the sad corpses of endangered species such as the spiny echidna, wrapped in palm packages. The market is also alive with Dani and Lani peoples, many in traditional dress – expect to pay at least Rp500 if you want to take a photo of someone, and more if they are done up in "warpaint" for the purpose of being photographed.

Practicalities

Just about all visitors arrive at the **airport**, and its conspicuous runway is the best landmark for orientation in Wamena: it runs from the northwest to the southeast, and the town spreads away from the runway to the west. Upon arrival, it's not unusual to find that your baggage did not catch the same flight as you. Should this happen, don't be unduly perturbed, for there's a very high probability that it will turn up on the next flight; just take your baggage receipt around to the Merpati desk in the departure hall to report your luggage as missing. You'll probably be met at the airport by a number of local lads who will try to befriend you and offer their services as **guides**. Trying to shake them off is useless; just grin and accept that one of them is going to walk you to your hotel, but don't get pushed into committing yourself to anything at this early stage. You will also hopefully be met by a police officer, who will take you into a tiny **information office** to stamp your **surat jalan**. (If there are no police officers when you arrive, take your *surat jalan* to the police station between Jalan Pramuka and Jalan Bhayankara.) Take your time looking at the maps and lists of registered guides on the wall, for this small office is actually the best source of information in the Baliem Valley, though it's often inaccessible as they only open the arrivals hall when a flight is due. Some of the police officers on duty there speak good English too, and can sell you an inaccurate but still useful **map** of the area for Rp20,000. The town's main tourist office, incidentally, is at Jl Sudarso 47 (Mon–Fri 8am–3pm; ☎0969/31365;), but it's pretty hopeless and inconveniently located 3km west of town on the way to Sinatma.

A **taksi terminal** is situated right in front of the main airport buildings, with a second (serving mainly northern destinations) 3km to the north at Pasar Baru in Jibama. The **post office** is next to the airport on Jalan Timor (Mon–Thurs & Sat 8am–2pm, Fri 8–11am), though it's not tremendously reliable; they have no scales and just guess how much letters weigh and cost. A fair stroll away on Jalan Thamrin is the Yantel **Telkom** office, supposedly open 24hr but often nonoperational. Near to the huge, sparkling new church is the BRI **bank** on the corner of Jalan Yos Sudarso and Jalan Timor, while Bank Mandiri is

Moving on from Wamena

To Sentani

Curiously, it costs less to fly from Wamena back **to Sentani** than it does to fly in the other direction (Rp305,000 as opposed to Rp405,000). Merpati, towards the southern end of Jalan Trikora (☎0969/31488), currently make the trip twice daily in the mornings (1 daily Tues & Wed), while Trigana Air (☎0969/31611) in the airport have as many as four flights a day depending on demand. If you're arriving in the high season be sure to book your return flight to Sentani as soon as you arrive, or you could end up spending a lot longer in the Baliem than you planned. In low season, however, it's a very different story, with flights often cancelled due to lack of demand; if you need to leave on a certain day book the first flight out, so if it's cancelled you have the option of taking a later flight.

Around the Baliem Valley

Battered **minibuses** and **4WD taksis** (that have to be flown in from Jayapura), depart from the *taksi* terminal by the airport or, for destinations to the north, from the Pasar Baru market in Jibama, 3km north of town (Rp3000 by slow becak from the town centre, or Rp1000 by *taksi* from the terminal opposite the airport), leaving when they are crammed full to bursting. Especially long journeys such as those to end-of-the-road destinations such as Bokondini (5hr; Rp20,000), Pit River (6hr; Rp70,000) and Pondok Yabbagaima for Danau Habbema (4hr; Rp40,000), leave on most days early in the morning if there are enough passengers, and must be booked a day in advance. The *taksis* should pick you up from your hotel; ask around the terminal for information. *Taksis* to destinations like Yetni for Kurima (40min; Rp3500), Kurulu for Jiwika (Rp3500) and Kimbim (Rp5000) leave almost every hour. Those to nearby Wesaput and Sinatma leave regularly when full.

Since the valley opened up to tourists, the most popular way of getting around has been to walk out to a destination with an airfield and then catch a mission **flight** back. This method is, however, becoming less and less viable. The pioneer and missionary airlines are generally far too busy to take commercial passengers, and are for the most part pretty sick of tourists using their mercy flights as holiday transport. Plane schedules are already overstressed – even the workers themselves need to book flights several weeks in advance – and if you can get a flight to the area you want to go to, at the time you want to go, then you'll be extremely lucky. However, if you're desperate, the missionary airlines, and Pioneers Airfas, Trigana and Manunngal, all have offices in or around Wamena's terminal, and it may be worth asking if they can help you out.

opposite the end of Jalan Irian; both change US dollars cash for a lousy rate (currently twenty percent less than in Jayapura, with the Bank Mandiri offering slightly better rates than the BRI) and will break large rupiah notes down into denominations more practical for use when trekking. **Transport** around town is either by foot or by pedal-powered **becak**. These are easily hailed and charge Rp1000 for most town journeys, Rp2000 or so out to the tourist office and Rp3000 round to Wesaput.

Accommodation

Because of Wamena's altitude, it can get cold at night, and luxuries such as hot water and heaters are important. **Accommodation** options in town are limited, which at present, with the lack of foreign visitors, is not a great problem. However, should tourism begin to pick up again, and during large festivals in the area, accommodation should be booked well in advance. An alternative to staying in town is the losmen at **Wesaput** (see p.999) across the runway, which is cheap, quiet and well designed.

Hotel Anggrek Jalan Ambon ⓣ0969/31242. Conveniently close to the airport, sparklingly clean and with friendly management, this eight-roomed hotel is one of the few places in Wamena that comes close to justifying its price tag. All rooms are en suite (with hot water) and breakfast is included. ❹

Baliem Palimo Jalan Trikora ⓣ0969/31043 or 32359, ⓕ31798. Probably the nicest place to stay in Wamena: the staff are friendly and some speak English. Standard rooms don't have hot water, but the more expensive rooms do, along with satellite TV and their own little private garden and minibar. Bathrooms come with a private rainforest, complete with waterfall, flowers and trees, the roof open to the stars. ❹–❺

Baliem Valley Resort Reservations c/o Jl Thamrin 16, Wamena ⓣ0969/32240. Situated 25km out of Wamena near the tiny village of Sipkosi, this German-owned hotel is the last word in luxury in the Baliem. The traditional-style *honai* huts are beautiful inside and out, and come with hot water and electricity – no mean feat for a hotel this remote. Transfer to and from the airport is included. ❻

Honai Resort Jalan Pikhe ⓣ0969/31515 or 31516, ⓕ31513. Currently the smartest address in Wamena (though it's actually in Desa Hibukoshi, 3km north of town), situated 500m from the *taksi* station, and popular with tour groups. Smart thatched rooms with hot water, but otherwise this place is nothing special. ❼–❽

Hotel Nayak Jl Gatut Sabroto 67 ⓣ0969/31067, ⓕ32641. The manager here is Javanese and speaks fluent Dutch. Suite rooms have TV and bath, but no hot water; standard rooms are relatively clean and well kept but are only a few hundred yards away from the runway, with all its daytime racket of planes and *taksis*. The central areas of the hotel are all charming – the restaurant has a high roof and is hung with Asmat carvings, although food is erratic: it may be possible to eat here if the hotel is full. ❹

Pondok Wisata Putri Dani Jl Irian 40 ⓣ0969/31223. Small homely place slightly out of town, with seven identical double rooms, all with hot water and attached mandi. Pleasantly cosy, but again, way overpriced. ❺

Rannu Jaya Jl Trikora 109 ⓣ0969/31257. Standard rooms all have dark and grimy mandi. Economy rooms are almost identical but you save Rp20,000 by foregoing the pleasures of Indonesian television. ❸

Sri Kandi Hotel Jl Irian 16 ⓣ0969/31367. The owners here are friendly and speak a little English, and rooms are reasonable although a little lacking in natural light. Still, it's currently the best value in Wamena – though if you're after a quiet night's sleep, make sure the café is not holding one of its occasional karaoke/disco nights before checking in. ❸

Hotel Syriah Jaya Jalan Gatut Subroto ⓣ0969/31306. A 200m walk south of the airport. The economy rooms are the cheapest in town, but are dark and musty with paper-thin walls. Standard rooms are made of concrete and overpriced. ❷–❸

Hotel Trendy Jl Trikora 91 ⓣ0969/313264. Hidden behind a restaurant next to the *Baliem Pilamo*, there's nothing particularly striking about this place: it has average rooms with en-suite mandi and, though the owner is friendly, the rooms are ridiculously overpriced, even by Wamena's standards. ❸

Eating

The **rumah makan** in Wamena serve almost identical food, the choice obviously being limited to what the valley can produce, but wonderful prawns, goldfish and crayfish are plucked daily from Sungai Baliem, and the speciality hot lemon/orange juice is a joy on cold valley evenings. For the cheapest food in town, the stalls along Jalan Irian dish up *murtabak*, *bakso* and *soto ayam*, and there are a number of cheap Padang places there too.

Blambangan Jalan Trikora. Perhaps the best-value place within easy walking distance of the town centre, with large portions of standard Indonesian food served in clean surroundings.

Baliem Palimo Jalan Trikora. Within the hotel of the same name, this restaurant comes complete with its own indoor waterfall and serves tasty soups: the macaroni and the chicken and corn are particularly good. It's also the only place in town where you can enjoy a beer (Rp30,000) without having to endure karaoke at the same time.

Kantin Bu Lies Next to the airport. Serves decent but expensive Padang food. Their fried chicken is tasty and the prawns are also good. In the evenings, there's a barbecue out front, serving superb goat sate.

Mas Budi. Around the corner from the *Hotel Baliem Pilamo*. The most popular place in town for foreigners, missionaries and wealthier locals, though it's often closed in the low season due to lack of custom. Their speciality is prawns and crayfish, and they also serve a variety of Indonesian and Chinese food.

Mentari Jl Yos Sudarso 46. About 2km out of town out by the tourist office. Easily the best restaurant in the Baliem Valley, it's sparklingly clean and constructed of wood from floor to ceiling, with gingham tablecloths and not a scrap of Formica or lino in sight. Succulent shrimp sate fresh from Sungai Baliem costs Rp25,000, and goldfish costs from Rp30,000.

Around Wamena

JIWIKA lies 20km northwest of Wamena and is serviced by regular *taksis* from the Pasar Baru market (40min; Rp3000): it's a *kecamatan* (administrative capital), which attracts tourists to its nearby showcase villages and strange blackened mummies. Jiwika has one losmen, the *La'uk Inn* (❷), a beautifully kept little place with nice gardens and a charming Javanese manager who speaks a little English. They can arrange food with a little notice and have rooms both with and without en-suite mandi. About 250m further up the road from the losmen and on the right-hand side, is a signpost, pointing up a dirt track to the "momi". In the traditional kampung at the end of this track, an **ancient mummified corpse** is kept, its knees hunched up to its chest and its taut flesh sooty black. The village is a real tourist trap, and it costs about Rp10,000 after bargaining to bring the mummy outside or Rp7000 for you to enter the *honai* and see it inside. Don't believe the guest book, which shows other guests have paid tens or hundreds of thousands to see it; they add extra noughts after you leave.

From behind the market in Jiwika, a path heads up the mountainside to **Iluemainma**, a brine spring 1800m above sea level and just over an hour's hike out of the village. Here the women harvest salt by soaking banana stems in the water. These are later burned and the salty ash used to flavour food. If you continue on the main road towards the crossroads town of Uwosilimo, you come to the **Kontitlola Caves**, near the village of **Waga Waga**: the tunnel-like cavern is adorned with stalactites and stalagmites and has a river flowing through it. On the way back to Wamena, the main road passes close to **Akima** village, which also has a mummy, incongruously stuck together with sticky tape.

Wesaput

On the eastern side of Wamena, the other side of the runway from the town, lies **WESAPUT** village, the turn-off marked by an orange clock tower – without a clock. There are a few traditional *honai* houses by the end of the road and some of the locals still dress traditionally in *horim* and grass skirts, but they're very camera conscious. Just show that you've got a camera and you could be assaulted by locals, chanting "seribu, seribu, seribu" (Rp1000, 1000, 1000). On a more pleasant note, Wesaput is the home of the only **museum** in the valley, the **Pilamo Adat** (Rp1000 donation). It's a beautifully laid-out building, built to resemble a *honai*, but it rarely sees visitors these days; you'll have to scrape the dust off the display cabinets to peer at the variety of Baliem curiosities inside, including weapons and traditional clothing — most of which you can see for much less bother in the souvenir shops in Wamena. The caretaker/curator speaks only Indonesian but if you have a trekking guide, it's normal for him to accompany you here and translate.

Behind the Pilamo Adat is a **suspension bridge** – a good spot for a swim if you can brave Sungai Baliem, as the water is slow-moving and deep here. Beyond the bridge, a good flat path leads to **Pugima** village; the forty-minute walk is far from taxing, and though the scenery isn't as magnificent as in the mountains, it's a good way to view the Dani's agrarian lifestyle. Just off this path is a large cave, fairly musty smelling and damp but satisfyingly spooky.

Taksis come all the way to Wesaput from Wamena, circumnavigating the northwestern end of the runway, and cost Rp1000. It's often quicker to walk right across the middle of the runway on the path that starts at the fire station than to wait for a *taksi* to fill up; the start of the road to Wesaput on the other side of the runway is marked by a curious two-metre-high concrete tree-stump. If you hear the klaxon which warns of a plane's arrival, do like the locals and run. You can also cut across the fields at the northwestern end of the runway, and then walk down the road to the tree stump. Before you reach Wesaput you'll come across the *Wiosilimo Losmen* (❸). It's not signposted, but look for the most garishly decorated house in the Baliem, 300m along on the right-hand side of the road. They have several rooms in slightly kitsch reproductions of *honai*, the walls decorated with mosaic animal murals made from bits of dried plant. It's a nice quiet place to stay, all the rooms have their own mandi and patio and the owners will give you transport to and from town in the evenings to the restaurant of your choice (though you will probably have to help push-start their truck).

Trekking in the valley

The Baliem Valley is changing fast, and although Wamena and the nearby villages are still vastly different to anywhere else in Indonesia, you won't experience the really extraordinary aspects of Dani life and culture unless you get off the beaten track. Due to the paucity of roads and the expense and infrequency of flights, this means a lot of **walking** and significant **planning**: see the box opposite. For information on transport around the area, see the box on p.997, and Travel Details on p.1028.

Northern Baliem

To the north of the valley, standing 4750m above sea level, **Gunung Trikora** is West Papua's second-highest mountain after Puncak Jaya. Nestling in its northern shadow, **Danau Habbema** is about the most beautiful and mysterious expanse of water in the highlands, mirror smooth, deep and icy cold, and usually framed by perfect blue skies and rocky hills. The air is thin and pure up here, the pleasant warmth of the day changing the instant the sun dips below the horizon to chill nights, with bright stars above. Due to the movements of the OPM (see p.980), this area is sometimes closed to tourists, though travel companies can usually get you a special permit. Danau Habbema is not worth visiting in June and July, when it generally dries up.

Danau Archbold is another exciting and beautiful area to head for, particularly noted for its bird and animal life and named after the first white man to see the valley from the air. It's situated at a lower altitude than Habbema, and has dense forests in its environs, stocked with cuscus, cassowaries and birds of paradise. The best way to visit this little-known and stunningly beautiful area is to fly to **Kelila** or **Bokondini**, both situated in the northwest of the Baliem Valley, and then trek northeast for several days to the lake.

Eastern Baliem

The areas to the east of the valley, home to the **Yali people**, are becoming increasingly popular for those with the time and money for adventure tours. The Yali are renowned for fierce adherence to custom, bizarre traditional dress and ritual war festivals. Some of the tribes here were cannibals right up until

Planning a trek

Apart from a few treks in the Baliem Gorge and along other well-forged trails that can be done alone, a **guide** and **porter** are necessary. Most nights will be spent in tribal villages where nobody speaks Indonesian, let alone English, or you may need to bed down in a rough shelter hacked out of the jungle, which most guides are expert at constructing. To be comfortable you will need more food and water for the trip than you can carry for yourself, and if this doesn't convince you to take a guide, bear in mind that main trails are crisscrossed by side tracks that could take you off into the middle of nowhere.

Finding a guide is not a problem: as soon as you land in Wamena you'll be under siege from guides all looking to take you off on treks. It's a little more difficult to find a good guide. All those who are registered with the police and speak foreign languages are listed in the police office in the airport terminal (see p.996), so that's a good place to start. Generally speaking, a guide should **cost** $5–10 a day, though they may charge more for longer treks, and will expect all food and transport to be paid for. Porters and cooks will usually be found by the guide and will cost about $3 a day.

If you go to one of the many **travel companies** in Wamena or Jayapura and arrange a tour through them, you're likely to get a good guide, but prices are significantly higher. Desa Tours and Travel (☎0969/31107) are one of the more established companies.

Long treks of a week or more in the Jayawijaya area require even more planning. After the terrible droughts and famine of 1997–98, you cannot count on being able to buy food in the villages, though the situation has improved over the past few years. The market next to Wamena's main *taksi* station at Jibama is a reasonable place to purchase food, although (as long as you do not get charged for excess luggage) it is much, much cheaper to bring supplies from Jayapura. For trekking, the best food is packet noodles, rice and canned sardines in tomato sauce. You can usually buy a few vegetables along the way, and fish, eggs, chicken, snakes or frogs to spice it up.

Other **necessities** will depend on your destination. Anywhere in the valley or around the valley walls you'll need a sleeping bag, fleece, long trousers and, preferably, a woolly hat. If you intend to take a serious trek out of the valley and into the lowlands, then a mosquito net is an absolute must: you can buy them for Rp30,000 in Jayapura's market. A **water-purifier** (see p.30) is a real bonus, as is a bottle of flavoured cordial to hide the taste of boiled or iodine-tinged water. Insect repellent with a high percentage of deet, applied all over, will deter fleas, ticks and bed bugs. Though the jungle shelters most guides will construct are excellent, you can improve their water resistance (and keep yourself and your pack dry while walking) with a poncho. Shaking out your boots each morning is essential; they're more likely to be inhabited by cockroaches than scorpions and snakes but it's best to be cautious.

the 1970s, having reputedly eaten two of the highest-profile missionaries in the area. The Yali are now the only people who still build wooden towers to keep watch over surrounding territory and warn of advancing enemy tribes. Yali villages are the favourites of many photographers' as spectacular festivals and mock battles can be arranged here (for a price).

The Yali region is only accessible by plane and by foot, the usual arrival point being the largest village of **Angguruk**. The village has a mission station, and one of the more frequently used runways in the central highlands: the people here are quite used to Western faces and you will probably be led hand-in-hand by delighted local schoolchildren to the house of the *kepala sekola* who has a room put aside for unexpected tourist guests.

From Angguruk, you'll have to walk out to the surrounding villages, and, if a flight can't be arranged, you'll have to walk all the way from Wamena: a minimum of five days.

Western Baliem

The western Baliem Valley is home to the **Lani people**, and is notable as the place where Sungai Baliem drops underground into a cavern system, to reappear by the town of **Tiom**. According to guides in Wamena, this stretch of subterranean tunnel was surveyed in 1996 by an American team, who lowered themselves down the raging Baliem on dinghies attached to ropes. However, it is difficult to see how, as the 100-metre-wide Baliem seems to vanish in a whirlpool up against a limestone wall.

This area boasts some of the most spectacular **scenery** in Jayawijaya, forested cliffs plunging down to the valley floor, and gullies thick with jungle carving up the hillsides to form razor-edged ridges. The road is passable by *taksi* through **Pyramid**, where there is a large Protestant missionary set-up, a church and a weekly market held on Saturdays, to Pit River and on to Tiom where the road ends. From Tiom there are two "major" walking paths that skirt the valley edges and head right up to Bokondini and Kelila in the north. Any walk that attempts to bridge these two areas will take weeks rather than days.

Southern Baliem

South of the Baliem Valley lies the magnificent scenery of the **Baliem Gorge**. Here, tumultuous Sungai Baliem leaves the broad flat plain it has flowed across for some 60km, and tears violently into the steep gorge, with waterfalls and scree-covered rock-faces, and villages precariously perched on cliffside promontories. The area is relatively regularly visited, but still retains a raw, natural appeal, especially when you venture beyond the canyon walls.

The people who live here are **Dani**, the most prevalent of the peoples in the central highlands and possibly the most welcoming. Spending nights in a thatched *honai* to a lullaby of gently grunting pigs may not be especially comfortable, but is certainly an experience you will not easily forget. Most of the internal Baliem Valley in the south has been deforested with slash-and-burn techniques, and is not as enjoyable to trek through. However, the route into the gorge and surrounding mountains is stunning.

Kurima and around

The road from Wamena runs south to **Yetni**, and is paved the entire way except for a 200-metre section which was covered by a landslide in the late 1990s. Yetni is the venue for the annual Baliem festival, the biggest in the West Papuan year, a celebration of the various cultures of the Baliem including spectacular displays of traditional dancing and music, and *taksis* run here from 7am until the early evening (1hr; Rp3500). From Yetni it's about an hour's walk to the administrative centre of **KURIMA**, where the gorge begins. Here, an **airstrip** and **mission** have been cut into a precipitous rockface, 300m above the valley floor. The simple *Huak Cottages* (❷), overlooking the river at the far end of the village, 500m on from the market, can provide **accommodation**, though you'll need to bring your own food (which you can buy at the market).

Back on the main road, an hour's walk north of Yetni lies **Sugokmo**, from where you can take a trek uphill and west to **Wulik** village. It's a tough three-hour trek for which you'll be rewarded with a magnificent panorama of the valley and a nearby waterfall. From here you can trek round to **Tangma**, a six-hour walk, mostly through dense forest, for which a guide is a must: the scramble down is extremely steep and difficult. Tangma is arranged around a rarely used airfield where the houses are more modern than the *honai* of nearby settlements. It's wise to stay here with the *kepala sekola*, whose house is at the bottom of the runway. Alternatively, you could push on through **Wamarek** village to areas where several waterfalls tumble down the steep gorge sides. Raging Sungai Baliem is crossed here on a safe, but nonetheless heartstopping **suspension bridge**, ninety minutes' walk from Tangma. During the height of the rains, when the river is in full force, the waters actually lap about the boards as each step causes the slats to lunge downwards. Next to the bridge are the remnants of the old bridge that collapsed a few years back, just to add a touch of apprehension.

From here it's another two to three hours' trek to **Wusurem**, a smaller and more traditional kampung, where you can stay the night, again with the *kepala sekola*. If you speak a bit of Indonesian it's perfectly feasible to do this trek without a guide. Another option is to hire someone in each village as a guide/porter to take you on to the next place, which will be infinitely cheaper than getting a guide from Wamena, and a good way of distributing your money to people who would not normally benefit from tourism. However, if you intend to go on any further than Wusurem, you'll probably have to carry too much food to make this method, or going solo, practical.

From Wusurem, the usual route is to continue on to Wet, and then **Passema** or **Soba**. The scenery along this route is dramatic: great ravaged cliff faces torn by landslides, earthquakes and waterfalls. Scree-covered slopes tumble down to the Baliem and its tributaries, with dark-green vegetation clinging to any plausible holds. It's possible to make Passema in a day from Wusurem, but Soba will take two days, overnighting in **Werima** village. Both Passema and Soba are set at altitude in stunning scenery, but suffered greatly in the famine and are desperately poor. The airstrips and missions here were set up in the 1960s, and both villages are centred around the airstrips, built more like Swiss log cottages than Baliem *honai*. The dark, planked walls are surrounded by flowerbeds, their windows and gables edged in gay purple and blue paint. It's quite an experience to land at one of these "airstrips", which are little more than small, grassy football pitches.

If you don't fancy backtracking from Wusurem, you can **return to Kurima** on the eastern side of the river. It's a solid day's hike, with the first part through stunning gorge scenery. The latter part however is a little desolate, as the forests are being cleared, presumably for agriculture, with the dreaded slash-and-burn techniques. When you stop to rest, the silence will be cut by the methodical thud of axes coming down on the few remaining trees in this area of the valley. Occasionally a loud crack and then a wrenching creak will be followed by the workmen's whooping chorus.

Yali country and beyond

Another exciting alternative, an extensive undertaking but one of the most rewarding treks south of the Baliem Valley, is to head right over the rim of the valley into **Yali country**. Trails from Wusurem and Kurima head over the top of stunning 3600-metre **Gunung Elit**, and then descend for four tough days through wild palm-tree forests to Angguruk, the capital of the Yali tribes (see p.994). Other possibilities include following the 60km route east described by Benedict Allen in *Into the Crocodile's Nest*, which took him through the mission stations of Ninia, Lolat, Korupun and Sela.

Several tour companies now arrange nearly month-long treks which continue south from Soba to Holowun, Sumo and Dekai, before taking to canoes and heading into the **Korowai** and **Kombai regions** north of Senggo. These are amongst the most exciting places to visit anywhere in the world and this trip, though extremely expensive and demanding, is a holy grail for explorers. If you arrange the trek independently it will cost upwards of $50 a day per person for everything, and then you will have to arrange your own transport out of Senggo. Travel companies charge about $80 a day.

Asmat and the south

The **south** of West Papua features vast areas of inhospitable, untrammelled wilderness. It's possible to fly for hours over the **Asmat region** and see nothing but lightly undulating oceans of jungle and alluvial swamps cut through with vast, meandering brown rivers, with not so much as a glimmer of life. At ground level however, it's a completely different story. Nervous crocodiles duck beneath the water's surface at a canoe's approach, and fabulous birds and reptiles provide flashes of iridescent colour amongst the mossy boughs. The area is known for the **woodcarving** of its few indigenous inhabitants, the **Asmat people**, who construct huge communal **longhouses**, living on sago and animals hunted from the surrounding jungles.

Transport in the Asmat region

Most travellers enter the Asmat region on the unreliable twice-weekly flight from Merauke to Senggo, and hire longboats from there out into the jungle or down to Agats. At the time of writing, the Merpati office in Merauke (see p.1006) ran **flights** from there to Jayapura (Wed), Tanah Merah (Fri), Senggo (Mon & Wed), Bade (Mon & Thurs) and Kimam (Mon). Apart from the Jayapura flight, which uses a large aircraft, you cannot rely on any of these. If they do by some miracle go on the right day, it won't be until many hours after departure time, and the smaller planes' susceptibility to bad weather means a very high proportion either get turned back before landing or just don't take off at all.

The flight into Ewer airstrip, which lies very close to **Agats** and is wonderfully convenient, has not been used commercially for many years. Charter and missionary planes still land here, as well as the occasional flying boat and a couple of Merpati flights during the Asmat festival in August, but for the average traveller, Ewer airport is not an option.

Senggo is probably the most frustrating and expensive place to leave in the whole archipelago. The Javanese merchants who control Benzine and oil sales for the longboats that provide the only practical method of transport here, also control the prices through intimidation: the local Papuans are too scared to talk to you and prices are ludicrous. Even if a boat is already heading to your destination, they would rather go empty than take you along for less than a full charter price. Sample prices include: to the Basman area (7hr in a 15hp boat; 5hr in a 40hp boat; $230–280), to Atsj (6–9hr; $195–290), to Agats (4–8hr; $215–345). For any trip that crosses a seaward river mouth, a 15hp boat is not recommended as they really struggle against the current.

If you are going upriver from Senggo, a **daiyung** (paddle canoe) is far less noisy and gives you some peace to enjoy the incredible sights and sounds of the jungle. It does, however, take an eternity to get anywhere and it's difficult to find people to take you on an extended trip. To get to Basman for the Korowai region takes four days and three nights, and you'll have to sleep rough for at least one of those nights. Coming back, it's much easier to find a boat and takes three days if you paddle hard.

There are two large towns on the south coast of Papua: **Merauke** to the east of the Asmat jungle, and **Timika** to the west. Merauke is quite a decent destination, with Australasian landscapes and wildlife, while Timika is an unpleasant town which has sprung up around **Tembagapura**, the Freeport company's gold-and-copper mine. Generally speaking, if you want to explore this region, you'll need to spend some time in one or both of these places. Between the two lie miles of forests, punctuated by occasional tiny villages and a few fair-sized settlements. **Agats** is the focus for visitors to the Asmat, right between the two main towns, an amazing riverside village raised entirely on stilts above the mud and the centre for the culture and art of the area.

However romantic a trip into **the jungle** of the Asmat region may seem, it should not be undertaken lightly. It bears no resemblance to travel in any other part of Indonesia: there's no tourist infrastructure, transport is dangerous and exorbitantly expensive, and unless you invest substantial time and money, you'll see nothing much at all. However, if you have the patience and cash, you can access one of the world's few genuine frontiers. In the backwoods are peoples who probably still practise cannibalism, wonderfully exotic birds and vast stands of jungle. Access to the Asmat area is generally either by plane into Senggo (inland in the east), or by boat into Agats, Otsjanep or Atsj (all on the south coast).

Merauke and the Wasur national park

MERAUKE is a dusty dry settlement that's somewhere between a typical Indonesian outpost and an Australian outback town. Its main street is lined with wire-mesh-fronted stores and blue wooden houses with shaded verandahs, alongside Padang restaurants. The town is at the southernmost point in West Papua, as far east as you can go in Indonesia, and is surrounded by wide expanses of flat, grassy savannah, fading to great stretches of tidal sand and mudflats. Beyond this, innumerable rivers crisscross thick rainforest which covers flat land, rarely raising more than a few metres above sea level. This area comprises the near 690 square kilometres of the **Taman Wasur national park**, protected by the WWF for its exceptional birdlife and Australasian animals.

Merauke was set up by the Dutch in 1902, because the English in New Guinea were complaining about cross-border head-hunting raids by the Marindanim tribes who inhabit the areas to the north. The pious Dutch duly "pacified" and then attempted to convert these tribes, and Merauke became what it is today: the easternmost outpost of the Indonesian archipelago.

Practicalities

The vast majority of visitors to Merauke will arrive at **Mopah airport**, about 3km east of town, generally by the once-weekly morning flight from Jayapura. From here, charter a minibus taxi from the terminal (Rp20,000), or walk out to the main road and flag down one of the blue minibuses heading west. This road is Jalan Raya Mandala, which becomes the main street of Merauke town, where most of the hotels, restaurants and other sites of interest are situated.

The sandy streets are traversed by a surfeit of new **minibuses**, so short of custom that they'll take passengers to the door anywhere in town for Rp1000. If your **surat jalan** is checked on your arrival at the airport, you don't need to report to a police station in Merauke. However, if you arrive by boat it might be advisable to report to the main police station on Jalan Raya Mandala. **Tourist information** is handled at the Kantor Dinas Parawisata, Jalan Ahmad Yani 1 (Ⓣ0971/322588). Nobody here speaks English, though the staff are very friendly and may even give you a tour around town on the back of a motorbike. This is a good place to organize trips around the national park, and to get information about the Asmat region.

The **post office** can be found on Jalan Brawijaya (Mon–Fri 8am–4pm) and there is a branch of the **BRI** on Jalan Raya Mandala which will change dollars cash only. There are two good **art shops** in Merauke, the Ude Atsj on Jl Parakomando 42, being easily the best. Their speciality is Asmat woodcarvings, shields, figures and spears, though they also sell pricey Baliem curios. **Moving on**, the **Merpati office** in Merauke is at Jl Raya Mandala 226 (Ⓣ0971/321242), on the way into town from the airport, and the manager, Pak Ronny, will do anything humanly possible to make sure that you get on a flight if there is one.

Accommodation

Due to Merauke's temperature, a fan at least is a necessity and air-con is very welcome. Few people arrive here direct from other parts of Indonesia without having passed through Jayapura, so the poor value and standard of the **accommodation** shouldn't come as much of a surprise.

Akat Hotel Jl Prajurit 111 Ⓣ0971/322944. Exceedingly friendly and helpful staff; their central lounge area has satellite TV and all rooms have en-suite mandi. Cheaper rooms have fans, the others air-con. ❸

Asmat Hotel Jl Trikora 3 Ⓣ0971/321065. This hotel offers the most reasonable rates in Merauke, but is often full with parties of government officials. ❸

Marina Hotel Jl Biak 73 Ⓣ0971/321375. The cheaper rooms here are an absolute rip-off: filthy and fanless. However, the top rooms, which come with air-con and TV, and the central lounge area are well laid out and pleasant, and all rooms have en-suite mandi. ❹

Megaria Hotel Jl Raya Mandala 166 Ⓣ0971/321932. All rooms here have air-con, hot water and TV, and the bathrooms are decked out in pristine dark-blue tiles, with bath and shower. ❹

Nirmala Hotel Jl Raya Mandala 66 Ⓣ0971/321932. Has a choice of rooms, with or without air-con, hot water and en-suite mandi: the price includes a simple breakfast. ❺

Eating

The **food** in Merauke is really not all that special, but if you've just spent a few days in the jungle, it'll seem like paradise. Venison and kangaroo meat sometimes turn up in the restaurants, as does a reasonable variety of seafood.

Merapi Jaya Jl Raya Mandala 69. A standard, slightly overpriced Padang restaurant. As is usual, all the food is available for you to look at in the outside window before you commit to entering.

Nusantara Jl Raya Mandala 189. If you're desperately in need of fried rice or an omelette, this is the place to stock up. They generally serve the average Indonesian staples.

Serumpun Indah Jalan Raya Mandala. Right next door to the *Megaria Hotel*, this serves terrific Padang food – excellent curry sauces with chicken, beef, squid, prawns, crab. A full meal costs between Rp5000 and Rp15,000 a head.

The Wasur national park

The **Wasur national park** is particularly enticing to bird-lovers, with an estimated 419 species, 74 of which are found nowhere else. The park straddles the southern part of the border between Papua New Guinea and West Papua, and is a world away from the lush, dark caverns of the island's vast jungles. The plain that encompasses Wasur is more reminiscent of the Australian outback; it was only separated from the Australian landmass 8000 years ago, when the Torres Strait was engulfed by rising sea levels. Because Australia and New Guinea were so recently connected, the species are almost identical where climate and habitat allow. Wasur has herds of **wallabies** and **kangaroos**, kookaburras, huge bustards, cranes and flocks of pelicans that coast low, over the plains and swarm about the lakes. In addition, a monotreme (egg-laying mammal) echidna related to the duck-billed platypus flourishes here, feeding on the inhabitants of Wasur's omnipresent towering red termite mounds with its powerful claws and thirty-centimetre tongue. The **world's longest lizard**, Salvatori's monitor, is also a resident. The Komodo dragon is much heftier than Salvatori's, but the latter is far longer, growing up to 5m from tail to flickering tongue; it is mainly arboreal, living in the woods that border the grasslands. Of these trees, acacias, gum trees and eucalyptus are the most common, and the scrub beneath them bristles with Australian snakes such as the deadly taipan.

Wasur is best explored on **horseback** or **motorcycle**; horses can be hired in the villages of Wasur, Ndalir or Yanggandur on the outskirts of the park. There are park offices at Ndalir and Wasur, where you will have to register and **pay** Rp5000. You'll probably have to charter a **taksi** from Merauke to get to these places. Alternatively, visit the tourist information and WWF offices at the junction of Jalan Biak and Jalan Missi in Merauke (ⓣ0971/21397); both can help to set you up with a motorbike, and the guides may even offer to take you themselves on the back of a bike, though this is very uncomfortable, over dreadful roads. **Accommodation** is either under canvas of your own providing, or in small villages along the main trails.

Senggo

Lying well northeast of Merauke, **SENGGO** is the next stepping-stone to the Asmat region: it's a bleak place, so far inland as to be utterly remote, but with enough deforestation to lack the charm of a jungle village. It sprawls between two kampung, one clustered around the grass airstrip and the other at the river harbour, with a few houses and kiosks along the footpath that joins them. The airstrip part of town is slightly higher than the harbour, and contains the missionary buildings and hospital – Australian homestead-style wooden buildings among pristine lawns, landscaped with palm trees and flowers.

The *Kasim Homestay* (❸) is also near the airstrip, offering very basic rooms. From here, a path leads downwards about 2km to the river. Just before reaching the wooden harbour, Senggo's other **homestay** is on the left-hand side: it's unnamed but obvious, as it's the only building more than a single storey high. They have two double rooms here, at Rp50,000 full board or Rp30,000 without food. The owner cooks up rice, noodles, fish and meat, which is a considerable improvement on the fare of the town's only warung. There have been several reports of thefts from both of these losmen, so bring your own lock for the rooms and keep your valuables with you at all times.

Kombai and Korowai

A visit to the tree-living peoples of the **Kombai** and **Korowai** regions, which lie west and north of Senggo respectively, is a unique experience. Beyond the "pacification line", no more than 20km to the west of the mission village of Yaniruma, lie the "Stone Korowai", tribes of warlike tree-inhabitants who have had no real contact with the outside world and attack anyone who ventures towards their territory with poisoned arrows and spears. To the east of here, between the Dairam Hitam and Eilanden rivers, are a score of tiny settlements, where the natives live as much as 20m up in the jungle canopy, naked except for the cassowary feathers protruding like whiskers from piercings in their noses, and greet visitors with suspicion and wonder.

Villages such as **Yaniruma** and **Wanggemalo** were built by missionaries and government agencies to attempt to lure the Kombai and Korowai people out of the trees. Such places are completely alien to the natives, who are used to living in territories that have belonged to their clan for generations. Inside these territories the people live in households of patrilineal descent in groups of tree houses that may number as few as two or three. The people are traditionally polygamous and exogamous, that is they take many wives, all of whom are from external villages. Marriage is a massive undertaking, involving elaborate transactions and bride prices. Korowai people are all primitive horticulturists, tending sago and banana groves near their tree houses. The women raise domestic pigs, while the men hunt for wild pigs, cassowaries, snakes and anything else that adds protein to their poor diet. In areas close to main waterways, a kind of pidgin Papuan-Indonesian is spoken, which is sufficient to maintain contact with traders.

Depending on how far the river is navigable at the time of year you arrive, the best course of action is to head for the mission villages of **Binerbis**, **Basman** or Yaniruma on the central Dairum Kabur river, or **Sepanape** or **Sirape** on the northern Eilanden river. From Basman, it's a six-hour walk to Muh, which is right on the boundary of Korowai. Kurfa, Ferma and Yapupla villages are all sensational examples of Korowai life. It's wise to approach the area with great **caution** and common sense. As recently as 1999, missionaries reported that head-hunters had killed fifteen men, women and children in a single raid on a village in the Stone Korowai region. The same missionaries were certain that cannibalistic practices still exist in these areas.

Agats and around

At the mouth of the Aswetsj river on Papua's south coast, **AGATS** is a peculiar mixture of rustic romance and outright squalor, depending on the whim of the tides. Its rickety kiosks tower either above litter-strewn mud or murky lapping waves, perched on precipitous thick stilts. The pavements are precarious plankways, that range from sturdy ironwood boardwalks to creaking death-traps. However, somehow it manages to have much more charm than apparently similar Asmat towns such as Atsj and Otsjanep. There's only electricity for a few hours at night, so fans and cold drinks are unfortunately hard to come by.

The **Asmat festival** is based here at the beginning of October, and is one of the few times when you won't be the only foreigner in Agats. The festival involves canoe racing, dancing and a carving competition. All accommodation in Agats will be booked up months in advance, but you'll always be able to find families willing to let you stay, or you could camp. It's also one of the few times in a year that commercial **flights** from Timika and Merauke will come here, arriving five minutes away by boat at Ewer, seaplanes landing on the river right in front of town.

The Town

Agat's major draw is its **museum**, about 300m to the southeast of the helipad. Similar *bisj* poles and shields can be seen at local art shops, but the huge **rattan masks** and **trophy skulls** are fascinating. The most appealing part of the museum is the collection of modern carvings that have won commendation in the annual competition held during the Asmat festival. These are derived from the old forms, but are generally infinitely more appealing to the Western eye, with cleaner, less crude work and remarkable subjects. Some illustrate local stories, others show macabre images from the days of cannibalism, often with darkly humorous caricatures.

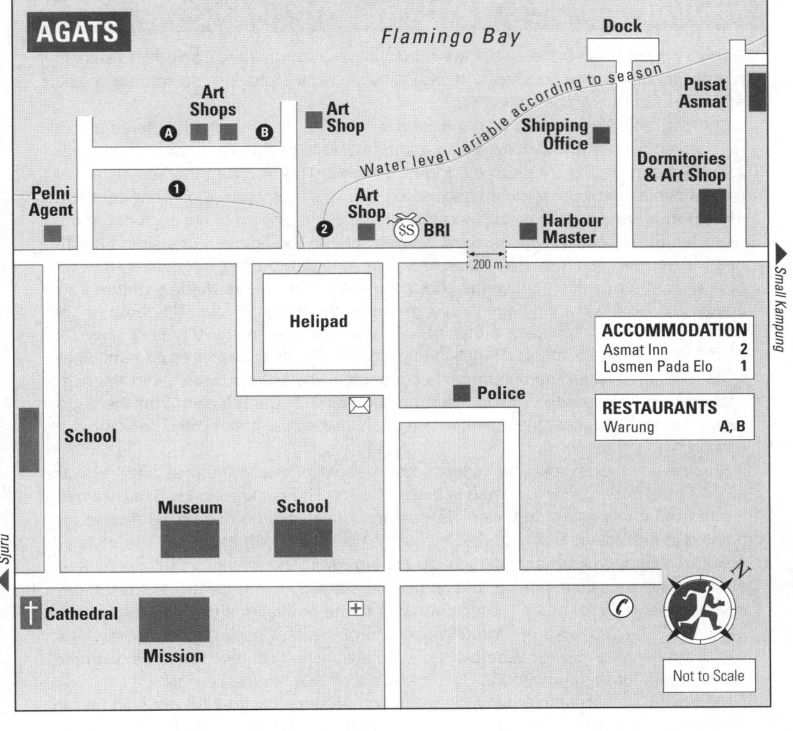

Next to the BRI bank is an **art shop** which sells high-quality carvings to American and Japanese bulk buyers. Their prices are very high, but they are willing to bargain. Opposite the *Losmen Pada Elo* are two more art shops: the one on the left sells poor-quality work, while the other sells a good variety of shields and figures at reasonable prices. From here, if you walk towards the helipad and then take the first left, there is another shop right by the river – the friendly owner will take time to help you find exactly what you want from his mounds of pieces, and his prices are good. Another shop can be found by the dormitories before the Pusat Asmat, which is located down the second left turning out of town, and after the new dock.

The **Pusat Asmat** (literally navel, or centre of the Asmat) was set up by missionaries to assist **artists**, providing a space where they can live and work in comparatively comfortable circumstances. The central building is a tatty but charming wooden hall, adorned with friezes and *bisj* poles. Most of the year it's almost empty, but during the festival the place throngs with people, cooking around open hearths while they whittle away at wonderful carvings; it becomes a magical place to spend a few hours, chatting and watching the artists work.

Practicalities

Everyone arrives in Agats by **boat**, most of which pull up at the foot of the stilts that hold up the main street. From here it's a matter of metres to either of

Asmat art

Asmat art takes several forms, mostly mangrove and ironwood carved into shields, drums, spears, canoe paddles and prows, "soul ships", ancestor sculptures, masks and a kind of totem pole called *bisj*.

The **bisj** pole is the most regarded of the Asmat art forms, and is often over 5m tall, carved from a whole, fully grown mangrove. One heavy plank root is left intact, to form a sort of flag shape at the top of the pole. This is called the *tjemen*, which means penis, and is an intricate fretworked phallic shape protruding from the figure at the top of the pole. The main length of the pole is made up of carvings of famous head-hunter ancestors (whose spirit is invested into the figures), one sitting on the head of another. Many of these poles have canoes at the base, suggesting that the pole is itself a development of the soul ship. Several poles are made together for a special *bisj* ceremony, a pledge to avenge these ancestors' deaths. No death for the Asmat is by natural causes: either people are killed by enemy tribes, or they die because of the black magic of malignant neighbours, so all deaths must traditionally be avenged. When the ceremony is completed, the pole is thrown into the sago orchards, where it decomposes, allowing the spirits to be released into the sago. When the sago is eaten, the power of the dead ancestor is transported back into the person who consumes it.

Shields are made from the buttress plank roots of the mangrove, and, as with other Asmat carvings, are painted in three colours. The background is usually white, made from chalk mixed in water. Tattoos and bones on the decorative figures are painted in red, mixed from the soil; hair is stained black with charcoal. The **stylized creatures** depicted are connected with cannibalism. The praying mantis is revered as it actually eats its own kind, but as trees are analogous to people in Asmat lore, any animals that eat the fruit (which equates to the brains) of a tree, are also potent symbols. The raja cockatoo, flying fox and hornbill are all used liberally in carvings, and warriors dress up to resemble these animals when on revenge raids, with red eye-patches for the cockatoo and feathers in their hair for the hornbill.

Masks are less common than many of the other forms, as they are not sold for the tourist market. Really more of a full body-suit, they consist of a bodice made from cord or rattan basketry, painted red-and-white and with a suitably dramatic face. After a villager dies, a dancer will come out of the forest in a mask, to dance one last time in the place of the deceased. He is then chased into the longhouse, to begin the symbolic journey to the spirit world. This journey is then continued by the soul ship, a small bottomless canoe carving filled with carved figures, which is left outside the door of the longhouse to ferry the deceased to the afterlife.

Under the guidance of the missions, and to cater to the tastes of those who come to buy carvings for export to souvenir stalls in Bali and Java, certain very modern interpretations of these traditional forms have evolved. Most popular is a three-dimensional melee of climbing figures that has developed from the *bisj* pole. Canoe prows and flat paddle-handle carvings have been extended to form beautiful flat friezes, generally in symmetrical shapes, and ancestor sculptures are now being made to last, rather than to rot in the sago groves.

the two losmen. The boardwalks run parallel to the river, and head off 1km southwest to the village of **Sjuru** and northeast to the **new dock**, which has a shipping office nearby that can be handy for information about boats in and out of Agats.

Heading away from the river and the main street, you'll come to a large flat wooden platform. This is used as a **helipad** and for dances during the festival. The **post office** is at the corner furthest away from the main street. Don't be lulled by the fact that there is a branch of the BRI near to the helipad; it has

Moving on from Agats

Moving on is likely to be more of a problem than arriving in town. The Pelni **ferry** *KM Sangiang* calls in monthly at Agats, depending on the tides, as it travels along the southern and western coasts of West Papua to Tahuna and Lirung (see p.963) and the northern Sulawesi port of Bitung. Infrequent cargo boats may take you on to Timika or Merauke, but don't hold your breath. There is also one boat that monthly plies the route from Merauke to Senggo, stopping off at several villages en route, but it runs to an unpredictable schedule, is often out of service, and is squalid and dangerous on high seas. The missionaries may be able to help you out and it is worth checking with their office near the museum to see if they have any **flights**, otherwise you may have to **charter** a plane or boat. Bear in mind that to charter a **motorboat** to Timika (the most common escape for those who are really stuck), may cost 1.5 million rupiah.

no foreign exchange or credit card advance. If you're anywhere in the 600-kilometre stretch between Merauke and Timika, you'll be living on the rupiah you bring in with you. About 500m to the east of the helipad is the **Telkom building** for domestic and international phone calls. Their service is quite reliable but, as you would expect, very expensive.

Accommodation and eating

There are two **losmen** in Agats, with total room for about 35 guests. You should have no problems getting a room, except during October, when the festival means most rooms will be pre-booked. Along with all the residential properties in Agats, the losmen have real problems with water. Their only supply is run off from their roofs, which, given the almost continual rainfall here, is usually more than enough. However, just a few dry days mean that all water has to be carted along the boardwalks in barrels from a small tributary. The *Asmat Inn* (❸) is the best losmen in town, clean and relatively cool, decked out in dark wood and with artworks dotted around the foyer. Their basic rooms come with choice of mandi in or outside. The slightly cheaper *Losmen Pada Elo* (❸) is right on the main boardwalk and can get a bit noisy. Each room has only two beds and a bit of tatty lino, and no mandi or fan.

Both losmen provide breakfast and can get basic **meals** for you. Opposite the *Pada Elo* is a small **warung** selling rice with fish, chicken and vegetables for between Rp3000 and Rp8000. Around the corner and opposite the art shop is a similar place. Strictly speaking Agats is a "dry" town and alcohol is frowned on; some of the stores will sell you whisky but at high prices.

Nearby villages

Only 1km down the boardwalks southwest of Agats is **SJURU** village, really more like a suburb of Agats. The village has a single *jeu* (longhouse), which you can enter and take photos of for a donation of around Rp5000. Sjuru is probably the best place to go to rent *daiyung* (paddle canoes), great for a day's paddle in the jungle (around $30 a day).

Southeast of here, **YEPEM** is just about reachable in a day by paddle canoe, or it's ninety minutes by Jonson (motorized canoe). Yepem is an attractive village where locals fish, and net prawns, crabs and other river fare. At low tide, village boys play on the steep mud banks, sledding down them in tiny dugout canoes and splashing around in the slime. There is also some quality carving done here.

A full day's paddle south of Yepem, or an hour in a Jonson, **PER** village is

Michael Clark Rockefeller

The son of the then governor of New York, **Michael Clark Rockefeller**, first visited West Papua in 1961, as a photographer and sound technician for the Harvard-Peabody expedition studying the lives of the Ndani peoples of the central highlands. After his work was completed, he and a friend headed south into the Asmat swamps and were immediately captivated by the astounding primitive art they found there. Twenty-three-year-old Michael decided to return later that year, to study and collect some of this art for the New York Museum of Primitive Art. Two months into this trip, on November 18, 1961, Rockefeller's flimsy canoe capsized at the mouth of the Betsj river. The two Asmat guides swam for shore, leaving Michael and his companion, Rene Wassing, clinging to the upturned hull overnight. The next morning, Michael struck out for shore, with an empty petrol can for flotation, and was never seen again.

Governor Rockefeller himself flew out to Agats to oversee a mammoth search of the area, but it was utterly fruitless. The world's media revelled in the story of a millionaire's son eaten by cannibals, but it's equally likely that strong tides, sharks or crocodiles were responsible. However the cooking-pot theory has many adherents. Lorne Blair visited the Asmat area in the early 1980s to research part of his wonderful book *Ring Of Fire*, and was pretty much obsessed with the theory that Michael Rockefeller had been eaten by cannibals, coming to the conclusion that the villagers of Otsjanep (see below) were responsible. His reasoning was that it was revenge for "pacification raids" by white Dutch soldiers, who had massacred all of Otsjanep's tribal leaders only a few years earlier, in an attempt to stamp out cannibalism. Like many adventurers who come here, Blair seemed keen to believe in this more dramatic version of the tale, a story of rare theatre from the dying days of exploration.

renowned for the quality of its friezes and *bisj* style climbing figures. From here, many travellers go on to **Owus**, about 10km upriver, where they make fantastic *bisj* poles and have a new losmen, and **Beriten** which has a perfect *jeu*. Up the Betsj river from here is **ATSJ**, the biggest and one of the least pleasant villages in the Asmat area. Much like Agats, the whole town is raised up on stilts with tin-roof shacks rather than wooden *jeu*. However it is surrounded by sawmills and deforested mud swamps, and its boardwalks are covered with rusting oil barrels and broken engines.

Continuing south from Atsj, you come into the area known as the **Casuarina Coast**, where the people wear only traditional clothes and are far less often contacted. The area was named for its huge casuarina trees, which are unfortunately being rapidly logged and are disappearing. You'll definitely need a 40hp Jonson boat to visit the area; it'll take five hours from Agats to **OTSJANEP**, the nearest large village. Otsjanep itself is not much to look at, very much a mission station with some grass lawns, very unusual in this part of Asmat, and a modern church. It's amazing how much Otsjanep must have changed since the Blair brothers stopped here researching *The Ring Of Fire* (see box above); they walked in on a tribal war.

Timika and around

Although **TIMIKA** is older than the Freeport mines, it feels now much like an overspill town for the rich "copper city" **Tembagapura**, located some 70km away in the mountains. The immediate surrounding countryside is a fairly bleak sandy flood plain that gets dusty and dry during the middle of the year. The town itself is pretty sleazy and unfriendly, and there are several bars and less salubrious hotels with extortionate prices which are best avoided. Timika is, however, a place you'll find difficult to avoid if you're visiting the south of

Papua, and it's a possible gateway to West Papua from the rest of Indonesia.

If you're coming from the Asmat region, then Timika's saving grace is its restaurants and the incredible and incongruous *Sheraton Hotel*, which offers five-star luxury. The **mines** themselves contain the world's largest reserves of gold and copper, and create a total daily profit of well over US$1,000,000. Until recently the mine was the subject of continued misery among indigenous peoples: a tiny proportion of the employees of copper city are Papuan, most being imported from other parts of Indonesia. Furthermore, tribal lands were claimed by the Indonesian government with barbaric stringency and widespread slaughter, and the waste from the site continues to pollute the surrounding land. As a result, Timika became the site of numerous protests and riots, some of which resulted in armed response from the Indonesian army. In 1997 for example, fifteen protesters armed with bows and arrows were gunned down by the military. Megawati's announcement at the end of 2001 that eighty percent of profits will now go to the local community should go some way to redressing the injustices. Until that money starts to trickle through, however, Timika remains a place to be vigilant.

Practicalities

Most visitors arrive in Timika at the **airport**, located about 4km to the northeast of town; Garuda, Kartika and Merpati flights between Sentani and the major cities in Indonesia all route via Timika. Occasionally, minibus *taksis* head into town, otherwise motorbike taxis (ojeks) will take you for about Rp3000, though they'll ask outrageous prices at first. Boats arrive at **Amamapare port**, about 15km southeast of Timika – regular *taksis* connect the port and town, or you can hire a motorbike taxi. The **Pelni ferries** *KM Tatamailau*, *KM Kelimutu* and *KM Sangiang* all stop in Timika en route from Fak Fak to Merauke.

At the centre of Timika town is the **market**, which has a few Padang-style restaurants but doesn't sell much of interest. The main street that runs alongside is Jalan Yos Sudarso, where at no. 17 you'll find the **post office**, the most reliable in the south of Papua, with an efficient internet office too (Rp12,000 per hour). Branching west off Yos Sudarso is Jalan Cenderawasih, home to both **Garuda** (Ⓣ0901/323767) and, at no. 28, **Merpati** (Ⓣ0901/323362). One block down towards the market is Jalan Belibis and the **Yantel** office. **Travel agents** near the market and on Jalan Yos Sudarso – including the Timika branch of the Jayapura-based Kuwera Jaya (Ⓣ0901/322409), opposite the *Hotel Serayu* – sell flight tickets and are more convenient than Merpati or Garuda; the **Kartika** agent (Ⓣ0901/321909) is currently in the lobby of the *Hotel Serayu* on Jalan Yos Sudarso. The Freeport mines are off limits, except to those with a professional interest and a **permit** for visiting the area, which can only be obtained in Jakarta.

Accommodation

There are no budget **hotels** in Timika: a couple of hotel/brothels will give you a bed full of lice where you may be robbed, but the price will be little less than those of the decent hotels listed.

GSBJ Komoro Tame Jl Cenderawasih 2 Ⓣ0901/321962. A super-plush place with a large pool; rooms (US$170) come with hot water, spring beds, parabola TV, breakfast and laundry. Tends to fill up at the weekends with mine-workers. ❽

Guest House 0089 Jl Trikora 37 Ⓣ0901/321777. A new and welcome addition to Timika's meagre hotel scene, a spotlessly clean hotel run by young, eager-to-please staff. All rooms are en suite and come with fan. ❸

Lawamena Jalan A. Yani Ⓣ0901/321138. One of the better options in town. The rooms are basic and fail to match the hotel's rather sumptuous exterior and reception area, but they're clean, have fan or air-con and en-suite mandi, and by Timika's standards they're cheap too. ❸–❹

Hotel Serayu Jl Yos Sudarso 10 ⓣ0901/321777, ⓕ321004. Central, large but rather tired-looking hotel, way overpriced, though the rooms are all en suite and air-conditioned, and the rates do include three meals. ❺

Sheraton Hotel On the outskirts of town near the airport ⓣ0901/394949, ⓕ394950. Has everything you would expect from a Sheraton: tennis courts, a pool, health centre, several bars and restaurants. In addition, it's a beautifully designed and grandly decorated building. Rooms cost US$250. ❽

Eating

Timika is close to the sea, and **seafood** is definitely the best buy here. Chicken and beef are extortionately expensive, but many places cook reasonably priced prawns, crab and squid on coals out in front of their shop.

Golden Dragon Jalan Yos Sudarso. Plush Chinese-Indonesian restaurant with some excellent soups (Rp10,000), though the noodle dishes can sometimes taste as if they've been sitting around for a while.

Kebun Sirih Jalan Ahmad Yani. Squid and fish are this restaurant's speciality, shipped in from Jayapura and cooked out front on the griddle for a pricey Rp35,000. Fresh, very tasty and a good place for a slap-up meal.

Kharisma Jl Bhangkara 98. Speciality of the house is *garo rica ayam*, a hearty piece of chicken, fried in a very hot and spicy sauce – delicious, but expensive at Rp25,000.

Phoenix Jalan Yos Sudarso. The *Golden Dragon*'s main rival, located just across the road and dishing up a similar menu, though a little cheaper. Staff can be moody, but the food's fine.

Seafood Lestari Jl Yos Sudarso 14. Serves reasonable *ikan bakar* and standard Indonesian dishes. Next door, the *Jakarta 99* is an identical place.

Warung Bangkalan Jl Komp Pasar 105. Serving barbecued fish and Padang food; there are several similar places around the market but this is the best.

Puncak Jaya, the Lorentz reserve and the Paniai lakes

The most potent attraction near Timika is **Puncak Jaya**, the highest peak in Southeast Asia (5030m) and one of only three snow-capped equatorial mountains in the world. Unfortunately, although it's a tantalizingly short distance away, it's very difficult to access Puncak Jaya from here, as it would mean crossing Freeport mine property, which is politically very sensitive. The usual starting point for an ascent is Illaga village to the east, usually reached by plane from Wamena. A climb of Puncak Jaya, sometimes known as Carstenz peak, takes eight days each way, and you won't get a **permit** unless you go with an established tour company: Chandra Nusantara Travel and Tours, formerly of the Baliem Valley, are due to open an office in Timika very soon (it should be open by the time you read this) and may be your best bet for a permit.

To the east of Timika is the massive **Lorentz reserve**, one of the best-protected, most remote stretches of rainforest remaining in the world; it comprises an amazing 34 different ecosystems, from mangrove swamp to banks of snow. The area stretches over some 15,000 square kilometres, and is the largest conservation area in Indonesia. Over half of all West Papua's birds and mammals live here: 639 species of birds and 123 species of mammals, including tree kangaroos and possums. It's accessible by longboat from Timika's port, but it should be noted that it was while studying in the northeastern highland section of Lorentz that Dan Start and his colleagues were kidnapped and frogmarched through the jungle for four months in 1996 by the OPM (they were eventually released unharmed). An expedition into this area will need to be planned extensively in advance; with enough notice and money, tour companies in Jayapura can plan tours for you. The WWF office in Timika at Jl Pendidikan 169 (ⓣ0901/321746) is helpful but has little in the way of practical information.

To the northeast of Timika and near **Enoratali** is the beautiful area of the **Paniai lakes**. The valley around these lakes is much like a smaller version of the Baliem, with pygmy peoples living Stone Age agrarian lifestyles. A nearby mountain reserve features abundant mammal- and birdlife. This area suffered greatly from Indonesian pacification in the 1970s, and was additionally decimated when imported Javanese pigs (gifts from the Indonesian government supposedly to placate the locals) were found to be riddled with a type of tapeworm completely alien to Papua. These imported gifts spread disease through the entire populace causing widespread deaths. Paniai was, at the time of writing, off limits to westerners; when it opens again it may be easier to reach from Nabire (see p.1021).

The Bird's Head Peninsula

The **Bird's Head Peninsula** (Vogelkop in Dutch, Kepala Burung in Indonesian) contains some of the least explored areas in the world, with mountain ranges, lakes and forests leading down to swamps in the south. It's a very difficult area to visit, much of it being subject to continual conflict between Indonesian forces and the Pemka wing of the OPM, based around Manokwari. Trying to get a **surat jalan** to most of the peninsula's regencies is a constant headache, and outside of the main towns you'll find no transport or tourist infrastructure at all.

The largest town in the Bird's Head is **Sorong**, a settlement with few redeeming features, based around harvesting oil and timber. However, you'll have to stop here if you wish to visit the **Raja Empat Islands** or **Pulau Waigeo**, which feature intact stands of forests, home to the marvellous birds of paradise. **Manokwari** is the second biggest town in the Bird's Head, and the location most favoured by missionaries. There are some beautiful tropical islands in the vicinity, with white-sand beaches and teeming coral reefs, but probably the biggest attraction is the **Anggi lakes**, which lie to the south in the **Arfak mountains**. The scenery of the lakes, which sit in valleys high above sea level, is utterly spectacular, and the surrounding forests are renowned as the home of some exquisite butterflies. If you plan to visit **Cenderawasih Bay**, then you'll probably have to base yourself in **Nabire**, a small, quiet coastal town with excursions to beaches, waterfalls, deserted islands and one of West Papua's few hot springs. Cenderawasih Bay is a fine bird-watching site, and the diving is terrific. However, don't expect any dive schools to facilitate things for you: if you want to dive here, then you're going to have to sort the whole thing out yourself.

The **Bomberai peninsula** lies at the throat of the Bird's Head, a south-western chunk of mountains and forest below massive Bintuni Bay. **Fak Fak** and **Kaimana** are the two towns of note in the peninsula, both unusually pleasant for largish Papuan towns, and notable for nearby cave paintings, similar to those produced by Australian aborigines. Unless you're **flying** around the region, getting between any of these towns will either take a very long time or will be horrifyingly expensive, most probably both. The Pelni **ferry** *KM Tatamailau* calls into Fak Fak three times a month (and Kaimana twice a month) from southern Papua and the small islands of Amahai and Tual, while the *KM Ciremai*, *KM Sinabung*, *KM Doro Londa* and *KM Dobonsolo* ply routes along the north coast fortnightly. The *KM Kelimutu* also links Amahai with Fak Fak, while the *KM Sangiang* links Fak Fak and Kaimana with southern Papua. The **Pelni office** is on Jalan Panjaitan in Fak Fak (☎0956/23230). In addition, there are occasional smaller boats and cargo ships, all of which will redefine your idea of discomfort.

Sorong and around

SORONG is nobody's idea of a seaside resort town, a glum stretch of tin-roofed shacks fronted by littered shores, which melts away into glummer transmigration settlements. The second largest city in Papua after Jayapura, Sorong, which was located on nearby Doom Island until 1965, became something of a boom town after Dutch Shell started drilling for oil nearby in 1932. Other industries such as logging followed, and have now taken over as the oil stocks diminish. Now pearl farming is one of the biggest businesses in the area, with numerous Japanese pearl farms, including that at **Pulau Kabra**, which is the largest in New Guinea.

Practicalities

Most visitors will arrive by air, at the **airfield** on Pulau Jeffman, which is a set Rp25,000 speedboat trip from Sorong town. From the pier you can walk to most places in town, but there are also plenty of *taksis* available: the dock for **Pelni ferries** and the Pelni office (ⓣ0951/321716) is a short walk west of here. A **surat jalan** is not strictly necessary for Sorong town, but if you intend to visit anywhere else around the area you'll need one. Check in upon arrival at the **police station**, on Jalan Basuki Rahmat. The Bumi Daya bank on Jalan Ahmad Yani will change money, but as yet has no facilities for credit card advances. The **post office** is also on Jalan Ahmad Yani, situated slightly closer to the port. **Merpati**'s offices can be found at Jl Raya Ampat 105 (ⓣ0951/321402), while **Pelita** are at Jl Gunung Tamrau 6 (ⓣ0951/333222).

Accommodation

Sorong has a variety of **hotels**, some as close to budget as you will find in Papua.

Cenderawasih Hotel Jl Sam Ratulangi 54 ⓣ0951/321966. Quite a plush establishment; all rooms have air-con and bath, plus there's a large restaurant with occasional karaoke. ❹

Hotel Indah Jl Yos Sudarso 4 ⓣ0951/321514. The closest place to the port, with some very reasonably priced rooms – probably the best deal in Papua. Good views from the sea-facing rooms in the upper storeys. ❷

Hotel Manise Jalan Jend Sudirman ⓣ0951/321456. The town's one real budget hotel. It's not especially well kept and the rooms are tiny, but it's OK for a night. ❸

Sahid Mariad Hotel Jalan Ahmad Yani ⓣ0951/323535. The last word in luxury in the Bird's Head. All rooms (US$130) come with hot water, satellite TV, and air-con. Expect to meet all the town's expats in the restaurant at night. ❽

Eating

Night **warung** near the port serve sate and *ikan bakar* over barbecues outside the shops; there are also places serving nasi campur and fried noodles around here. The major hotels have expensive **restaurants** with limited European and Chinese food, often in air-con rooms with hostesses and karaoke.

Dafior Jl Misol 84. Has great sea views and a good selection of Chinese food at reasonable prices.

Irian beach Jalan Yos Sudarso. Specializes in baked fish, squid and prawns. All dishes can be served sweet and sour, or barbecued. A whole fish costs around Rp12,000.

Marino Jl Sam Ratulangi 26. A good selection of Indonesian and Chinese food, including crab and prawn dishes at around Rp20,000.

Miami Lido Jalan Yos Sudarso. Standard inexpensive mix of Indonesian staples and Chinese favourites such as *fu yung hai*.

Nearby beaches and islands

Cassowary Point, 8km to the north of town, has the best accessible beach on the mainland, with a reasonably intact coral reef. You'll need to charter a *taksi* for around Rp40,000, except at the weekends when locals pour down there to

Birds of paradise

In 1522, Magellan landed in Seville with several **birds of paradise** skins he had purchased in Maluku. The birds' legs had been removed by trappers, and Europeans immediately seized on the idea that they were actually built this way, and were born in the air, spending their entire lives aloft and supping on dew. This myth was not properly dispelled until 1824, when Rene Lesson became the first westerner to see the birds alive. Shortly after, in 1884, when German rule commenced in northeast New Guinea, 50,000 bird of paradise pelts were shipped to Europe to adorn women's hats. This trade continued right up until 1924, when legislation was passed to protect the birds, which by then were almost extinct.

There are 43 species of birds of paradise in the world, and New Guinea has 38 of them. Most of these species are notable for the male's extravagant tail plumage that can be well over double the length of the body: the King Of Saxony bird of paradise has similar feathers, but they cascade from behind its head, while others have huge chest pouches or coloured linings to their mouths. The purpose of these outlandish accoutrements is to attract a female of the same species in the darkness of the forest canopy, and is usually complemented by a courtship dance and song. Some, such as the raggiana, hang upside-down from branches like bats, others clear a hole in the leaves above to create a brilliant shaft of sunlight to dance in. The male birds gather together at special courtship trees called leks, and drab females cluster around to choose the most handsome mate. Normally hard to detect in the jungle's half-light, they return habitually to show off on the same stage and are thus easy prey for vigilant poachers.

picnic and there's plenty of public transport. Better beaches can be found twenty minutes away at **Pulau Matan** and ten minutes away at **Pulau Buaya** (Crocodile Island). The former is the best bet, with beautifully clear water and clean, white-sand beaches lined by thick forests.

The village of **Klayili**, 5km west from Sorong or ten minutes by *taksi*, has a nearby hot spring surrounded by forest. The water is said to have healing properties, and, altogether, it's a lovely spot for a dip. At **Sansapur**, a five-hour speedboat trip north around the coast, is a stunning **beach** which has a reputation as a turtle-breeding and egg-laying ground. The surrounding countryside is also alive with birds and jungle.

The **Raja Empat islands** to the east of the Bird's Head Peninsula – Batanta, Waigeo, Salawati and Misool – are all sanctuaries for birds of paradise (see box above), but they aren't accessible by public transport, so you'll have to charter a boat from Sorong harbour. The nearest spot on Batanta takes about four hours by speedboat from Sorong, while some of the further islands will take several days. In addition, bird-watchers can feast their eyes on exotic species such as terek sandpipers, hooded pittas, singing starlings, various honeyeaters, and puff-backed meliphagas: the red and Wilson's bird of paradise are also endemic to Waigeo and Batanta.

Manokwari and around

Surrounded by dark-green hills and deep-blue sea, **MANOKWARI**, at the eastern edge of the peninsula, has more to maintain a visitor's attention than most towns of comparable size in Papua. Its surrounding islands, beaches, mountains and lakes provide some very enjoyable **excursions**, and the facilities that have sprung up to cater for Manokwari's burgeoning missionary population make it a good place to base yourself. The town first received the Word

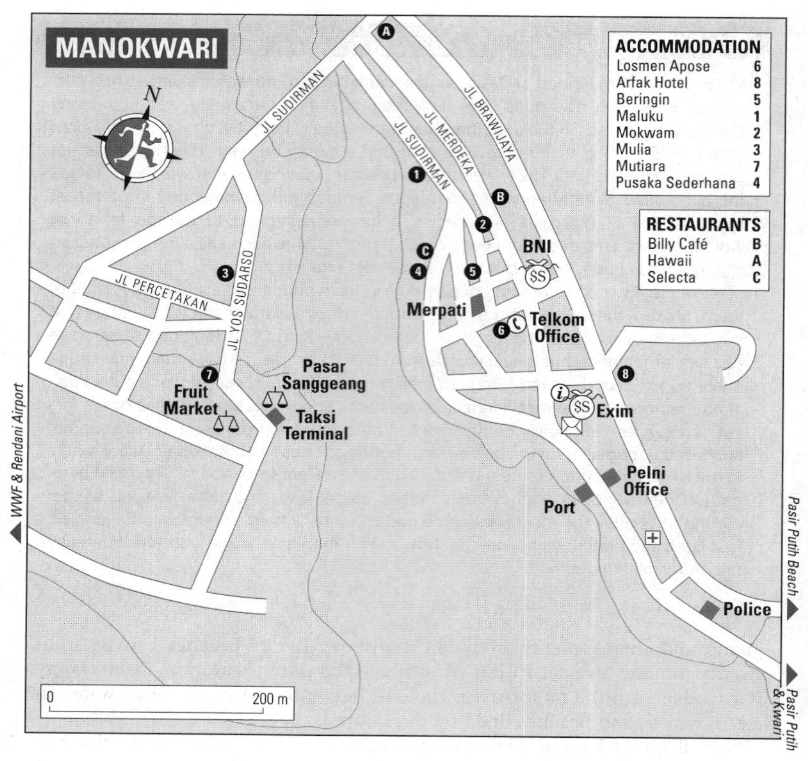

from Ottow and Geisler, two Protestant priests from Germany who set up a mission here in 1855 and, despite their low conversion rate, the town has been a hub for pioneer pastors ever since. Alfred Russell Wallace (see p.1073) also had a brief stay here, studying birds in the 1850s. During World War II, the highlanders who lived in the mountains south of here were air-dropped rifles by the Allies in the hope that they would fight off the Japanese, who had made several bases here and lived in many cave encampments around Manokwari. Legend has it that, not satisfied with just shooting the enemy, the tribes decided to eat their corpses, terrifying the invaders, who soon withdrew.

Practicalities

Most visitors will either arrive at the **Rendani Airport**, ten minutes out of town, or at the **Pelni dock**, which is about as central as it is possible to get, within walking distance of most hotels. From the airport you can either take a taxi (Rp10,000) or an ojek (Rp5000); alternatively, walk out to the main road and flag down a minibus *taksi* heading into town (Rp1000), though bear in mind that most of these terminate at **Terminal Wosi**, from where you'll probably have to catch a second *taksi* to **Pasar Sanggeang**, and then a third if you wish to stay on the eastern side of the bay.

It's best to report to the local **police** at Jalan Bhayangkara, about 600m east of the port, before heading off into the wilderness, as they'll want to check your **surat jalan**. Information about the area can be gleaned from the **tourist office** on Jalan Merdeka (Mon–Thurs 7.30am–2.30pm, Fri 7.30am–noon; ⓣ0986/212030), where the staff have a bundle of leaflets and are always delighted to see foreigners. There are several **banks** in Manokwari, but the BNI on Jalan Merdeka is the only one that has an ATM. The 24-hour **Telkom office** can be found on Jalan Kota Baru, and there are several wartels around town. The **post office**, now with **internet** facilities, is located on Jalan Siliwangi. There are a few souvenir and **arts and crafts** places, the best known and most established being the Cinta Alam, above the market on Jalan Pasar Sanggeang. They sell Asmat carvings, lots of old porcelain and occasional pinned dead butterflies.

If you're planning to trek in the reserves of the **Arfak mountains**, it's best to call in first at the **WWF office** on Jalan Trikora Wosi (ⓣ0986/211497) on the way to the airport. You'll probably need a permit from them before you go, but even if you don't they are still the best source of information about the area and can furnish you with a guide; Matias Rumbruren is a reliable guide who often hangs out there, and his English and knowledge of the local fauna is excellent. The tourist office can also help to arrange trips, as can the several **tour operators** in town: Cahaya Alam Agung Tours are at Jl Kota Baru 39, next to Merpati (ⓣ0986/211153).

Accommodation

Most of the **hotels** are in Kota, the part of Manokwari town that hugs the eastern shore of Doreri Bay. Most accommodation is mid-range, but some are unusually good value for Papua.

Losmen Apose Jalan Kota Baru ⓣ0962/211369). One of the cheapest and friendliest places in town, with a choice of private or shared mandi. All rooms come with fan. ❷

Arfak Hotel Jl Brawijaya 8 ⓣ0962/213079. Once a resort for Dutch officials, the *Arfak* retains a certain colonial presence, and has the added advantage of views over Dorerei Bay. The huge rooms are tatty but clean and fairly priced, some with air-con and TV. ❸

Hotel Beringin Jl Sudirman 17A ⓣ0962/211909. Small, central, slightly overpriced but friendly hotel above a row of shops, with choice of air-con or Melati rooms. ❸

Hotel Maluku Jalan Jend Sudirman ⓣ0962/211948. Has a choice of passably clean rooms, from those with shared bath and fan to ones with TV and air-con. ❷–❸

Hotel Mokwam Jl Merdeka 49 ⓣ0962/211891. Once very smart, now rather tired but clinging gamely to its original standards with uniformed (and efficient) staff. Rooms, however, are now distinctly overpriced, though they do all come with TV and air-con. ❹

Hotel Mulia Jalan Yos Sudarso ⓣ0962/211320. Tired and scruffy hotel, on western side of the bay, which could do with a spring clean and happier staff. Some rooms have air-con. ❸

Hotel Mutiara Jalan Yos Sudarso ⓣ0962/211777. The most luxurious place in town, with air-con, TV, hot water and breakfast included. ❹

Pusaka Sederhana Jl Bandung 154 ⓣ0962/211263. One of the better deals in Manokwari, the *Pusaka Sederhana* has rooms with attached mandi, fan and two snacks per day for just Rp33,000. The air-con room on the other hand is overpriced, especially as the TV doesn't work. ❷

Eating

The best-value **food** is to be found at night stalls that set up near the market on Jalan Pasar Sangeang and along Jalan Sudirman. Here you can get excellent *ikan bakar* and sate for a few thousand rupiah. Beer is hard to come by outside of a few local shops and the *Dynasti* karaoke bar on the west side of the bay.

Billy Café Jalan Merdeka. God-awful hamburgers and other Western fare, though the Indonesian dishes are fine and even the karaoke is a touch more tasteful than the norm.

Hawaii Jalan Sudirman. Serves Indonesian and Chinese food, with some seafood. The crab and corn soup is excellent at Rp10,000.

Hotel Mutiara Jalan Yos Sudarso. Not surprisingly the best place in town, with air-con and music some evenings. Mainly Chinese food, though there are also a few Western dishes, and it's all quite reasonably priced.

Selecta Jalan Sudirman. Standard Indonesian fare served in hygienic and friendly restaurant; cheap.

Around Manokwari

The most popular destination in the immediate vicinity of Manokwari is **Pasir Putih** beach, 3km to the east of town; regular *taksis* from the terminal in town will take you there. The water is quite clear and the sands are lined by thick forest. **Taman Gunung Meja** (Table Mountain Park), the flat-topped hill that provides the backdrop to the eastern half of Manokwari, offers a pleasant two-hour walk through a forest of tall trees filled with birds and butterflies. From the *Hotel Arfak*, Jalan Diponegoro leads uphill to the start of the walk; at the top of the road follow the path as it bends left, and take a second left where the path forks fifteen minutes later. The path flattens out soon after this and the **Monument Jepang**, commemorating the first Japanese landings in the area, lies ten minutes further along, 50m to the left of the path overlooking the bay. The path eventually finishes on the main road to Amban, from where you can catch a *taksi* back to town.

Other excursions include the nearby islands of **Mansinam** and **Leman**, which, with their coral gardens and gorgeous beaches, are the archetype of a tropical paradise. The former is the site of the first missionary landing in the Manokwari area, and has a monument to the two unfortunate priests who perished here having converted nobody. If you're anywhere near Manokwari at the beginning of February, try to catch the annual festival that commemmorates their arrival, held on Mansinam on the 5th of that month and celebrated by people from all over northern West Papua and even Sulawesi. Off the west coast of Mansinam is a submerged **Japanese wreck** which makes for sensational snorkelling if your lungs are powerful and the waters clear.

Further afield (perhaps too far to warrant a journey in itself), is **Danau Kabori**, 25km from Manokwari on the road to the transmigration settlement of **Ransiki**, and serviced rarely by public transport. It's a good spot for fishermen and there's some good walking in the area.

The Anggi lakes

The most dominant and impressive sight around Manokwari are the **Arfak mountains** which lie to the south, and, in the valley they enclose, the **Anggi lakes**. The valley contains many groups of traditional peoples, and is a particularly fine place to trek, with a cool, breezy climate and stunning panoramas. The forests along the lower mountainsides feature some fantastic butterflies, huge multicoloured creatures of fantastic beauty. The birdlife too is extravagant, with mountain firetails, honeyeaters and lorries flocking out to feed at dawn.

Before travelling to the lakes, check with the police in Manokwari whether you need an additional entry on your **surat jalan** for the Arfak mountain area. The lakes are at altitude, so bring a sleeping bag and some warm clothing: as soon as the sun goes down the temperature falls, usually to around 4°C at night. Bring plenty of food too: other than one small kiosk at Irai by the airstrip, there are few places to buy provisions. The small **airstrip** at **Irai** near **Sureri village**, the largest in the area, services the highland area. Upon arrival, you'll need to register with the police: bring a photocopy of your passport. The police will let tourists stay in one of their empty units for a small consideration (Rp20,000). The flight is itself fabulously exciting: you skirt over the rim of near-3000-metre mountain ridges in a twin Otter, plunging down to the lakeshore. Merpati make the trip from Manokwari twice weekly, weather permitting (Wed & Fri), the subsidized fare costing just US$3.

Once you've arrived, a climb up **Kobrei Hill** affords wonderful views of both lakes, and you can stay the night at the kepala desa's house in Trikora village at the foot of the hill. From there, the next day you can climb **Gunung Trikora** for more glorious views of the two Anggi lakes. From the top of Gunung Trikora you can see the road leading down to Ransiki. Though not quite finished yet, irregular public transport is beginning to ply the route between Ransiki and the end of the road, about ten kilometres before the lakes. Alternatively, you can walk down in one very long day. If you run out of daylight on the walk down, **Senebuai** village, just before Ransiki, should be able to put you up. At Ransiki itself there's one small losmen near the Telkom office. From Ransiki there's a *taksi* every hour or so (2hr; Rp20,000) back to Manokwari.

Nabire and Cenderawasih Bay

The mellow, seaside town of **NABIRE** at the extreme south of Cenderawasih Bay, with its friendly locals and fine coastline, is one of the more charming towns in Papua. It's the capital town of Paniai district that includes the Paniai lakes and most of **Cenderawasih Bay**, an area that has the potential to be one of Asia's great scuba-diving locations, with hundreds of kilometres of fringing reefs, though it's still utterly without provision for casual visitors. At the moment, most visitors who want to explore the Cenderawasih **national reserve**, for bird-watching or trekking, have to do so by taking expensive organized tours out of Manokwari or Jayapura.

Some of the major islands in the reserve are **Anggromeos**, which has fine beaches and coral reefs as well as substantial indigenous birdlife, **Rumberpon** which offers more of the same and scores of giant sea turtles which come to the protected areas to breed and lay their eggs, and **Wairondi**. To get anywhere in the reserve or Cenderawasih Bay as a whole, you'll need to charter a boat; the best places for this are Ransiki, Nabire and **Wasior**, a small village on the east coast of the Bird's Head. Wasior has a small airstrip serviced weekly by Merpati and occasionally by MAF. There are also boats here from Ransiki. Nabire is accessible by daily Merpati flights from Biak and Jayapura, and the Pelni ferries *KM Tatamailau* and *KM Sinabung* as well as, occasionally, the Perentis boat *Ilosangi*. The Pelni office in Nabire is on Jalan Frans Kasiepo (Ⓣ0984/22850). There is organized **accommodation** in Nabire, but in Wasior and Ransiki you will have to improvise.

The Bomberai Peninsula

For those with a lot of money, time and patience, the **Bomberai Peninsula**, the throat of the Bird's Head, is a rewarding destination. The coastal scenery is astounding, with stark white-and-grey limestone cliff-faces and islands cloaked with tangled vegetation, the soft rock cut dramatically by wind and tides. The pretty towns of **Fak Fak** to the northwest and **Kaimana** to the southeast are quiet little settlements that see few foreign faces. From these towns the most usual excursions are by boat or foot, to see the **painted cliff-faces** that have fascinated explorers since their discovery three centuries ago. Much like some of the aboriginal art of Australia, these astounding paintings show human and animal figures, boomerangs and abstract designs, but the most frequent image is that of a human hand, created by blowing pigment over the hand like a stencil. Most of the paintings can be found in caverns on offshore islands or on sea-facing cliffs, though some of the finest examples are inland. All of them take some getting to.

This region was the first to be **colonized** by the Dutch in all of Papua, who made their base at Fak Fak in the late seventeenth century. Because of its proximity to Maluku, the Bomberai Peninsula was under the sway of the sultan of Tidore for many centuries. Thus it has had more influence from Islam than Christianity, and the towns have mosques and a higher proportion of practising Muslims than any other place in Papua.

Fak Fak

The town of **FAK FAK** is extremely charming, with a strong colonial Dutch feel; it's situated on a hillside leading down to **Tambaruni Bay**, and is surrounded by limestone hills, dotted with rivers and caves. It also has one of the world's most terrifying **runways**, a tiny airstrip that's been hacked into a precipitous rocky ridge, with gut churning drops to either side. On the northern coast of the peninsula is **Kokas**, a smaller village close to many of the rock art sites. A road from Fak Fak is nearing completion, but if you can't take a minibus you'll need a Jonson dugout and a guide – you should be able to find someone through one of the losmen – to find all of these places; the best rock art site is several days' walk away in the Fak Fak mountains. Another good trip from Fak Fak is to **Maredred waterfall**, a beautiful twenty-metre cataract tumbling into an icy pool. It can be reached in about fifteen minutes by boat from town.

Practicalities

On arrival, you should register your **surat jalan** with the **police** at their offices on Jalan Tambaruni. The **tourist office** is up on the hillside, at Jalan Diponegoro, and though they speak no English, the staff can be quite useful in helping you to set up a **tour** to see surrounding areas. The **post office** is also on a steep hill, at Jalan Letjen Haryono, with the 24-hour **Telkom** on Jalan Cenderawasih. The Merpati agent is on the main coastal street of the town, Jalan Izak Telusa (Ⓣ0956/71275).

There's some good-value **accommodation** available in Fak Fak, and there are so few visitors that you shouldn't have any trouble finding a bed. The *Hotel Marco Polo*, just off Jalan Izak Telusa, is probably the best place to stay (Ⓣ0956/22537; ❸); they have quite basic rooms with fan and decent views, and a few with air-con. The *Tembagapura* at Jl Izak Telusa 16 (Ⓣ0956/22136; ❸) is another option, featuring a choice of rooms with air-con or fan, all with en-suite mandi. The only other place here is the cheap and cheerful *Sulinah*, near the police station at Jl Tambaruni 93 (Ⓣ0956/22447; ❸); their rooms are reasonable and well kept and they offer full board for a decent price. The *Marco Polo* and *Tembagapura* both have good **seafood restaurants** and the *Amanda* at Jalan Izak Telusa serves Indonesian and Chinese meals to the accompaniment of karaoke.

Kaimana

KAIMANA may be tiny and remote, but it's a minor legend in Indonesia, as a well-known popular song tells of the town's magical sunsets, said to be the most beautiful in the world. It's another Muslim settlement, serviced by **Utarom airstrip** and with more fantastic side trips possible, to see cave paintings, coral reefs, beaches, orchid groves and forests filled with birds and butterflies. Merpati has regular flights into Kaimana from Biak, Timika, Sorong, Nabire and Fak Fak, and the Pelni **ferries** *KM Tatamailau*, *KM Sangiang* and

KM Kelimutu are scheduled to stop here monthly, though in reality they often just sail straight past; the Pelni office is at the harbour (☎0957/21009). There are two reasonable **hotels** here: the *Selatan Indah* on Jalan Brawijaya (☎0957/21230; ❹), and the *Diana* on Jalan Trikora (☎0957/21053; ❸).

Pulau Biak

Pulau Biak is about the only place in Papua whose charms are easily savoured. It's the first stop for most planes from Java and the rest of Indonesia, and its beaches, coral reefs and waterfalls are only hours away from the main airport. By contrast, adjoining **Supiori** and the surrounding islands such as **Yapen** and **Numfor** are much more difficult to visit, with no tourist infrastructure and little transport, and so their lagoons and forests, filled with brilliantly coloured fish and birds, remain practically undiscovered by tourists. Less than a degree south of the equator, Biak is hot and sticky, and during the rainy season of January to June it rains practically every day, though this actually provides some relief from the humid swelter.

Biak had great strategic significance during **World War II**, when the Japanese occupied the island. The Americans invaded in 1944, and the Japanese retreated to massive cave systems which they had turned into functioning subterranean towns. They launched raids on the US forces from the cover of the caverns, the Americans responding by pumping gas into the tunnels and igniting it, blowing most of the occupants away. Many of the remaining Japanese committed hara-kiri, realizing they were about to be defeated. There are still reminders of the war in many places in these islands: decrepit tank shells, sunken wrecks and caves filled with oily wartime debris.

The island group's main town is **Kota Biak**, located on the south coast of Pulau Biak. There are no other large towns here, though there are a scattering of smaller settlements, most of which are also coastal. The highlights of a journey to Biak are generally beaches, reefs and waterfalls, of which the islands have an abundance. The **Padaido Islands** off Biak's southeastern coast feature great snorkelling and diving, and the northern part of Pulau Biak and Supiori have several stunning **waterfalls** such as **Warsa** and **Wardo**, cascading out of thick tropical jungle. In addition, in the vicinity of Biak and Bosnik towns are an excellent **bird and orchid park**, a huge **crocodile farm** and some of the World War II **caves**.

Kota Biak

At the centre of the south coast of Biak lies **KOTA BIAK**, the only sizeable settlement in this entire island group. Though it is not of much interest in itself, it's an excellent base for exploring the islands. It's also worth considering as an alternative base to Jayapura if you're intending forays into the northern part of Papua: the airport services most of the mainland towns and you can get a **surat jalan** here. The island's main attractions aren't far away and it's a fairly relaxed port town, with some good restaurants and hotels.

Practicalities

Arriving at the Frans Kasiepo **airport**, just walk out to the road and flag down any bemos – known here as *taksis* – heading west (to your right as you leave the airport); the town is only a couple of kilometres away (Rp1000). The **main road** which comes into town from the airport starts as Jalan Mohammed

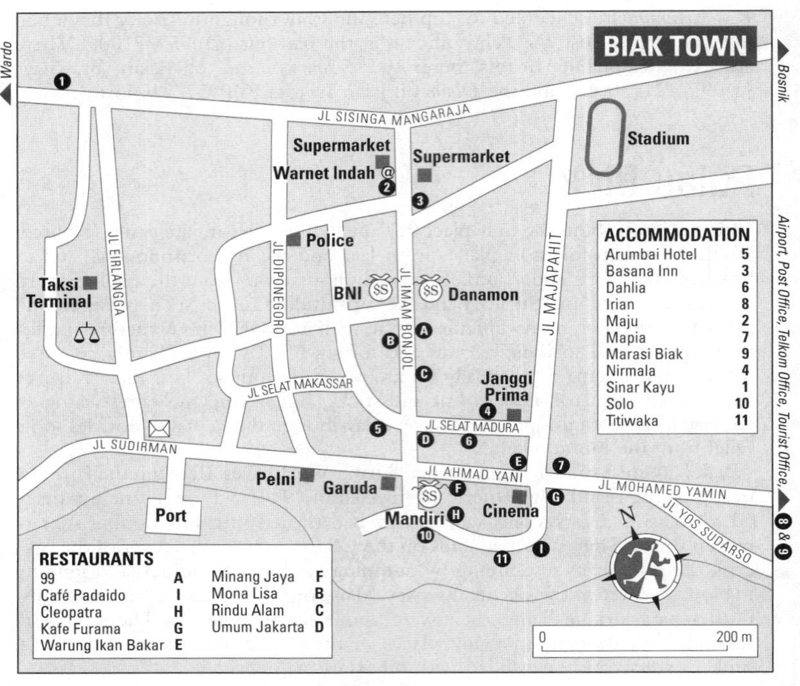

Yamin, then becomes Jalan Ahmad Yani and finally turns into Jalan Sudirman. The road is parallel to and only a stone's throw away from the sea, and pretty much everything you'll need is along either it or the side road, Jalan Imam Bonjol.

For a **surat jalan** allowing travel around all of Papua, head to the **police office** on Jalan Diponegoro: take two photographs and a copy of your passport (Rp10,000). Note that most shops and private enterprises, including many restaurants, close for a siesta from noon to 4pm. The **tourist office** (Mon–Fri 8am–3pm; ⓣ0961/21663) is about halfway between the airport and town on Jalan Mohammed Yamin 58, and is accessible by *taksis* joining the two; staff here are very friendly and helpful, but have limited resources. Opposite is the main **post office** (Mon–Thurs 8am–3pm, Fri 8am–noon, Sat 8am–1pm), incorporating a poste restante service and an **internet** office, though there's a cheaper (Rp7500 per hr) and more central internet place, the Warnet Indah, squeezed between the *Hotel Maju* and the supermarket on Jalan Imam Bonjol. The modern 24-hour **Telkom** building can be found on Jalan Yos Sudarso, about a ten-minute walk east of **Bank Mandiri**. This bank is the most prominent in Biak, and you can change US dollars cash and travellers' cheques here; the Bank Danamon and Bank BNI, opposite each other on Jalan Imam Bonjol (both Mon–Fri 8am–4pm, Sat 8am–noon), also change money, and the latter has an **ATM** that accepts Cirrus/Maestro and Visa. There are a couple of **tour agents** in town that may be your best bet for visiting and diving around some of the Padaido islands: Biak Paradise are in the *Arumbai Hotel* (ⓣ0961/23196), and

Janggi Prima are at the eastern end of Jalan Selat Madura (ⓣ0961/22973). For buying air tickets and reserving flights, the **Merpati** office (Mon–Fri 8am–5pm, Sat & Sun 9am–2pm; ⓣ0961/21251) is opposite the airport between the two hotels there, and the **Garuda** office is downtown at Jl Sudirman 3 (Mon–Fri 7.30am–9pm, Sat & Sun 8am–noon, 5–9pm; ⓣ0961/25737). The latter has friendly English-speaking staff who will do whatever they can to help you out.

Accommodation

On the whole, the quality of accommodation in Biak is excellent when compared with the rest of Papua, but still more expensive than the rest of Indonesia. Most hotel rates include a small breakfast snack.

Arumbai Hotel Jl Selat Makassar 3 ⓣ0961/22745, ⓕ22501. Sparklingly clean, black-and-white tiled hotel built round a swimming pool; the standard rooms, with attached mandi and air-con, are reasonable value, the top rooms exceedingly plush and priced accordingly, with satellite TV, air-con, hot water. ❹–❻

Basana Inn Jl Imam Bonjol 46a ⓣ0961/22281. One of the better mid-range options; all rooms come with attached mandi and air-con, and all except the economy rooms have TV too. But beware of the receptionist's attempts to extract as much money as possible (Rp20,000 for the tourist office's free city map, for example). ❹

Hotel Dahlia Jl Selat Madura 6 ⓣ0961/21851. Scruffy, slightly damp but friendly hotel with a wide variety of rooms, from shared mandi cheapies to a reasonable value air-con "showroom". ❷–❸

Hotel Irian Jalan Mohammed Yamin, PO Box 137 ⓣ0961/21939, ⓕ21458. Right opposite the airport if you need somewhere to collapse after the cross-archipelago flight. Has a good bar and a lovely sea-view garden; standard rooms and above come with air-con and TV and are fairly priced; economy rooms are surprisingly cheap and come with en-suite mandi and fan. ❸–❺

Hotel Maju Jl Imam Bonjol 45 ⓣ0961/21841. Even the basic rooms here have attached mandi and are good value. Air-con rooms all have TV with satellite and bilingual option, but at the price are a little drab and scuffed. ❷

Hotel Mapia Jl A. Yani 23 ⓣ0961/21383. All the rooms here have attached mandi, though the cheapest are not much of a deal as they have no fan, a necessity in sweaty Biak. Luxury rooms have air-con and are pretty cavernous. The hotel bar is sculpted like a hollowed-out pumpkin, and is a nice if rather expensive place for a cold beer. ❷

Hotel Marasi Biak Jalan Yamin ⓣ0961/22345, ⓕ21496. The other hotel near the airport, friendly enough but lacking the style of the *Irian*. Still, a good enough fallback option if you need somewhere smart to crash between flights. Cheaper rooms have fan, more expensive ones come with TV and air-con; all are a little overpriced. ❸–❹

Hotel Nirmala Jl Selat Madura 13 ⓣ0961/22005, ⓕ24660. Amongst the swishest in the town centre. Rates include all meals, and considering every room is furnished with air-con, mandi and water heater, this is good value. ❺

Losmen Sinar Kayu Jl Selayar 1 ⓣ0961/21933. The economy rooms with outside mandi are amongst the cheapest in town: well kept, clean, and set around very well-crafted – if flimsy – wood-beamed halls. The air-con rooms with TV are pretty decent value too. Economy rooms with en-suite mandi, on the other hand, are rather threadbare and musty. ❷

Losmen Solo Jl Wolter Monginsidi 4 ⓣ0961/21397. The cheapest place in town, with inexpensive rooms with fan but shared mandi. The best, quietest rooms are the ones nearest the sea overlooking the fish market and boatyard. ❷

Hotel Titiwaka Jalan Monginsidi ⓣ0961/21891) Two different tariffs here: bed and breakfast (Rp169,000 double), or the better-value room-and-full-board option (with three big meals a day; Rp217,000 double); transport to and from the airport is also included. All rooms have hot water, air-con and satellite TV with bilingual function. They arrange a variety of trips around the island and rent masks and snorkels by the day. ❺

Eating

The **food** in Biak is the best in West Papua, with some fantastic Padang places and lots of Chinese restaurants serving up excellent seafood. Beer here is also much more affordable than on mainland Papua.

99 Jalan Imam Bonjol. Full air-con and darkened windows, rated by the locals as the best Chinese and Indonesian place in town.
Café Padaido Jalan Monginsidi. This often looks closed from the street, but behind the house there's a very pleasant outdoor seating area overlooking the sea and the local boatyard. Great place to relax with a cold drink during the afternoon siesta.
Cleopatra Jalan Monginsidi. Open evenings only, a popular and hygenic restaurant serving Indonesian and Chinese dishes, with ayam goreng a speciality.
Kafe Furama Opposite the *Hotel Mapia* on Jalan Yani. Restaurant serving great (if overpriced) food, blighted by the karaoke machines that play non-stop throughout the day.
Warung Ikan Bakar Opposite the *Hotel Mapia* on Jalan Majapahit. A very basic warung that sells excellent fresh seafood, barbecued out front.
Minang Jaya In the arcade on Jalan A. Yani. Serves quality Padang food: the *ayam bakar* is exceptional.
Mona Lisa Jalan Imam Bonjol. Opposite the *99*, this place has karaoke and air-con, and serves Chinese food at average prices.
Rindu Alam Jl Imam Bonjol 22. A good Padang place with several different curry sauces: hygienic and swish.
Umum Jakarta Jl Imam Bonjol 10. A well-cooled Chinese-run place with immaculate white-tile floors, and both Chinese and Indonesian cuisine. Prices are high but the food is tasty. The fried beef in oyster sauce and fried chicken in *cai sim* are especially recommended.

Around the island

The only other settlement of any size on Biak is **Bosnik**, not much more than a sprawling fishing village. Twenty kilometres or so further round the coast, however, in the village of **Manau**, is the *Biak Hotel*, once the last word in luxury but now closed due to lack of custom. While not worth a special trip in itself, it's actually quite interesting walking around the overgrown building and its gardens, once perfectly manicured, but now covered with creepers and vines. Some of the best spots for **snorkelling** are also near here, including **Saba beach**, right in front of the hotel, and **Barito village**, about 5km further east. At Barito, there's a fantastic drop-off with schools of lionfish, barracuda and occasional Napoleon wrasse and sharks.

Some of the best coral can be found off **Pulau Rani**, reachable by daily afternoon boat from **Wardo**, 35km northwest of Kota Biak. Accommodation on Pulau Rani is with the kepala desa (expect to pay around Rp35,000 including three meals); you'll have to stay at least one night on the island, as the boat back to Biak leaves in the morning only – though the few visitors who make it here find themselves spending much longer here than they anticipated anyway. There's more snorkelling to the southeast of Bosnik around the **Padaido islands**, though the coral off many of the islands has been rather degraded by bombing. All but the nearest of the Padaido islands, **Pulau Owi**, can be very difficult to access; the best time to travel is Wednesday or Saturday, when there's a market in Bosnik and boats are plentiful – you should be able to get a boat at least to Owi (Rp5000) or **Pulau Pakaspi** (Rp20,000), the largest of the islands. On other days you could try to charter a boat (Rp200,000) or hitch a lift. From Pulau Pakaspi it's possible to charter a boat to some of the smaller islands nearby, including **Pulau Dawi**, which has accommodation and is said to be home to a few of the arboreal, slow moving cuscus. **Pulau Wundi** is regarded as having some of the best coral in the regency, though the islands of Pakreki, Mansurbabur, Mapia, Rurbon and Patodui also have excellent reputations for their reefs and fishlife.

Back on Biak, 12km to the west of Biak Kota is the small settlement of **Sorido**, where a **falconry centre** is in the process of being established. At the time of writing they have yet to decide on entrance fees and opening hours, so it is probably best if you phone the Belgian owner, Phillipe, in advance

(☎0961/25988) to let him know you're coming. An ojek to the site will cost about Rp7000. There are a few more attractions en route to Bosnik; catch a minibus to Bosnik (30min; Rp2000) and ask to be let off at the relevant site. Six kilometres east of Biak town is **Gua Jepang**, one of the caves that the Japanese hid in to evade American detection, leading ultimately to their incineration. It's best visited at dusk, when no other visitors are around, and the bats, monitor lizards and snakes that inhabit it all come out to feed. The caves are filled with rusting oil drums nestling amongst bulbous limestone outcrops, intertwined with tree roots that hang down in ropes from the cavern roof high above. Pay Rp5000 at the house and museum opposite the entrance, and walk through the graveyard of old bomb shells, plane propellers and destroyed jeeps and down a flight of steep slippery steps into the cave. The **Japanese War Memorial** is a couple of kilometres away from the caves at the seafront, and consists of a large concrete bowl with several memorial plaques and picnic tables alongside a beautiful palm-lined stretch of sand with the skeleton of a beached shipwreck. To one side is a tunnel where the remains of several Japanese victims are kept inside steel boxes, adorned with flowers and photos of the dead. Bones and fragments of clothing are clearly and macabrely visible inside the lidless boxes. At Km 12, the **Taman Burung dan Anggrek** (opening hours dependent on the whim of the keepers) is an excellent bird park, with a fully grown cassowary and its mate roaming free around the park, alongside birds of paradise, mambruk and assorted birds of prey.

Other destinations around Biak have far less reliable public transport, and will generally involve long waits for battered minibuses to take you over deeply rutted roads. However, the far corners of Biak are not often visited and offer some rewarding destinations. Probably the best excursion is to **Wardo** in the northwest of Biak. The road splits just before the village: take the left fork in the road and carry on down to Wardo village. Here the river flows into the sea in a beautiful estuary, and a bridge high above the river makes a sensational diving board. From Wardo village you can hire a motorboat or paddled outboard to take you upriver through the jungle to the Wardo **waterfall**. Prices are high, but it's a great trip (2hr; Rp50,000), with snakes and lizards on the boughs and brilliant birdlife.

Pulau Yapem

Only a quick flight or day's boat ride from Biak, **Pulau Yapem** remains extremely untouristy, seeing few westerners. The only town of any size here is **SERUI**. There's a daily Merpati flight from Biak to Serui, and the Pelni ships *KM Sinabung* and *KM Rinjani* go from Jayapura to Serui and then on to Nabire twice a month. Upon arrival in Serui, report with your **surat jalan** to the police station on Jalan Bhayangkara. There are three **hotels** here, the cheapest being the *Bersaudara* on Jalan Jend Sudirman (☎0981/31420; ❸). They have decent rooms with choice of en-suite or shared mandi and fan. Of the several **restaurants** in Serui, the *Banuwa Beach* at Jalan Pantai Banawagoro is probably the best, serving Chinese, Indonesian and even a few European dishes. Their speciality is baked fish, which costs around Rp9500 for a whole fair-sized specimen.

The island is renowned for its birdlife, and has huge stands of orchid-filled tropical forests and coastal mangrove swamps. Some of the attractions around the island include **Haribi Waterfall**, some 20km from Serui, and stunning **Danau Sarwandori**, 5km from the town.

Travel details

Getting to Papua from Indonesia's capital city of Jakarta, will take you across two time zones and take a minimum of eight hours flying; the only realistic way to get to the region is by **plane**. There are no roads to speak of in West Papua (though the Jayapura–Wamena highway is theoretically nearing completion), apart from a few in the Baliem Valley and around the major towns, meaning that you can only get around by plane, boat or foot.

Pelni ferries

For a chart of the Pelni ferries, see p.42.

Agats to: Bitung (*KM Sangiang*, 2 monthly; 80hr); Fak Fak (*KM Sangiang*, 2 monthly; 51hr); Kaimana (*KM Sangiang*, 2 monthly; 42hr); Merauke (*KM Sangiang*, 2 monthly; 29hr); Timika (*KM Sangiang*, 2 monthly; 9hr); Tual (*KM Sangiang*, 2 monthly; 32hr).

Biak to: Ambon (*KM Dobonsolo*, 2 monthly; 40hr); Balikpapan (*KM Doro Londa*, monthly; 4 days); Bitung (*KM Ciremai*, 2 monthly; 52hr/*KM Doro Londa*, monthly; 50hr); Denpasar (*KM Dobonsolo*, 2 monthly; 4 days); Jayapura (*KM Ciremai*, 2 monthly; 16hr/*KM Dobonsolo*, 2 monthly; 16hr/*KM Doro Londa*, monthly; 15hr); Kupang (*KM Dobonsolo*, 2 monthly; 67hr); Makassar (*KM Ciremai*, 2 monthly; 4 days); Manokwari (*KM Ciremai*, 2 monthly; 7hr/*KM Dobonsolo*, 2 monthly; 7hr/*KM Doro Londa*, 2 monthly; 6hr); Sorong (*KM Ciremai*, 2 monthly; 20hr/*KM Dobonsolo*, 2 monthly; 20hr/*KM Doro Londa*, 2 monthly; 20hr); Surabaya (*KM Dobonsolo*, 2 monthly; 5 days); Ternate (*KM Ciremai*, 2 monthly; 40hr/*KM Doro Londa*, monthly; 39hr).

Fak Fak to: Ambon (*KM Rinjani*, 2 monthly; 30hr/*KM Doro Londa*, monthly; 13hr); Biak (*KM Doro Londa*, monthly; 31hr); Bitung (*KM Sangiang*, monthly; 23hr); Jayapura (*KM Doro Londa*, monthly; 2 days/*KM Rinjani*, 2 monthly; 2–3days); Kaimana (*KM Kelimutu*, monthly; 12hr/*KM Tatamailau*, monthly; 11hr/*KM Sangiang*, 2 monthly; 11hr); Kupang (*KM Doro Londa*, monthly; 38hr/*KM Tatamailau*, monthly; 4–5days); Makassar (*KM Doro Londa*, monthly; 64hr/*KM Tatamailau*, monthly; 3 days/*KM Kelimutu*, monthly; 3 days); Manokwari (*KM Rinjani*, 2 monthly; 26hr/*KM Doro Londa*, monthly; 23hr); Sorong (*KM Rinjani*, 2 monthly; 12hr/*KM Doro Londa*, monthly; 10hr/*KM Sangiang*, 2 monthly; 13hr); Timika (*KM Tatamailau*, 2 monthly; 25hr/*KM Kelimutu*, monthly; 29hr/*KM Sangiang*, 2 monthly; 44hr); Tual (*KM Rinjani*, 2 monthly; 9hr/*KM Tatamailau*, monthly; 54hr/*KM Sangiang*, 2 monthly; 23hr).

Jayapura to: Ambon (*KM Rinjani*, 2 monthly; 4 days/*KM Dobonsolo*, 2 monthly; 58hr/*KM Doro Londa*, monthly; 67hr); Biak (*KM Doro Londa*, monthly; 16hr/*KM Ciremai*, 2 monthly; 13hr/*KM Dobonsolo*, 2 monthly; 16hr); Bitung (*KM Ciremai*, 2 monthly; 70hr/*KM Doro Londa*, monthly; 68hr/*KM Sinabung*, 2 monthly; 66hr); Fak Fak (*KM Doro Londa*, monthly; 52hr/*KM Rinjani*, 2 monthly; 2–3 days); Kupang (*KM Doro Londa*, monthly; 92hr/*KM Dobonsolo*, 2 monthly; 3–4 days); Makassar (*KM Rinjani*, 2 monthly; 5-6 days/*KM Sinabung*, 2 monthly; 5 days/*KM Doro Londa*, monthly; 5 days/*KM Ciremai*, 2 monthly; 4–5 days); Manokwari (*KM Dobonsolo*, 2 monthly; 25hr/*KM Ciremai*, 2 monthly; 25hr/*KM Rinjani*, 2 monthly; 36hr/*KM Sinabung*, 2 monthly; 31hr/*KM Doro Londa*, monthly; 24hr); Nabire (*KM Rinjani*, 2 monthly; 24hr/*KM Sinabung*, 2 monthly; 21hr); Serui (*KM Rinjani*, 2 monthly; 16hr/*KM Sinabung*, 2 monthly; 14hr); Sorong (*KM Rinjani*, 2 monthly; 51hr/*KM Sinabung*, 2 monthly; 42hr/*KM Ciremai*, 2 monthly; 38hr/*KM Dobonsolo*, 2 monthly; 38hr/*KM Doro Londa*, monthly; 45hr); Ternate (*KM Ciremai*, 2 monthly; 58hr/*KM Sinabung*, 2 monthly; 58hr/*KM Doro Londa*, monthly; 57hr).

Kaimana to: Agats (*KM Sangiang*, 2 monthly; 42hr); Fak Fak (*KM Tatamailau*, monthly; 11hr//*KM Sangiang*, 2 monthly; 11hr/*KM Kelimutu*, monthly; 41hr); Merauke (*KM Tatamailau*, monthly; 55hr); Timika (*KM Tatamailau*, monthly; 16hr/*KM Kelimutu*, monthly; 15hr/*KM Sangiang*, 2 monthly; 31hr).

Manokwari to: Biak (*KM Ciremai*, 2 monthly; 7hr/*KM Dobonsolo*, 2 monthly; 7hr/*KM Doro Londa*, monthly; 6hr); Jayapura (*KM Rinjani*, 2 monthly; 36hr/*KM Dobonsolo*, 2 monthly; 25hr/*KM Doro Londa*, monthly; 24hr/*KM Ciremai*, 2 monthly; 25hr); Nabire (*KM Rinjani*, 2 monthly; 10hr/*KM Sinabung*, 2 monthly; 9hr); Serui (*KM Rinjani*, 2 monthly; 17hr/*KM Sinabung*, 2 monthly; 15hr); Sorong (*KM Ciremai*, 2 monthly; 11hr/*KM Rinjani*, 2 monthly; 12hr/*KM Doro Londa*, 2 monthly; 11hr/*KM Dobonsolo*, 2 monthly; 11hr/*KM Sinabung*, 2 monthly; 11hr).

Merauke to: Agats (*KM Sangiang*, 2 monthly; 39hr); Fak Fak (*KM Tatamailau*, monthly; 4 days/*KM Tatamailau*, monthly; 64hr); Timiika (*KM Kelimutu*, monthly; 32hr/*KM Sangiang*, 2 monthly; 50hr/*KM Tatamailau*, monthly; 30hr).

Nabire to: Fak Fak (*KM Rinjani*, 2 monthly; 39hr); Jayapura (*KM Rinjani*, 2 monthly; 24hr); Manokwari (*KM Rinjani*, 2 monthly; 10hr/*KM Sinabung*, 2 monthly; 9hr); Serui (*KM Rinjani*, 2 monthly; 5hr); Sorong (*KM Rinjani*, 2 monthly; 25hr/*KM Sinabung*, 2 monthly; 21hr).
Serui to: Jayapura (*KM Rinjani*, 2 monthly; 17hr/*KM Sinabung*, 2 monthly; 21hr); Manokwari (*KM Rinjani*, 2 monthly; 18hr/*KM Sinabung*, 2 monthly; 15hr); Nabire (*KM Rinjani*, 2 monthly; 6hr/*KM Sinabung*, 2 monthly; 5hr).
Sorong to: Ambon (*KM Dobonsolo*, 2 monthly; 17hr/*KM Rinjani*, 2 monthly; 44hr/*KM Doro Londa*, monthly; 25hr); Biak (*KM Ciremai*, 2 monthly; 21hr/*KM Dobonsolo*, 2 monthly; 20hr/*KM Doro Londa*, monthly; 19hr); Fak Fak (*KM Rinjani*, 2 monthly; 12hr/*KM Sangiang*, 2 monthly; 12hr/*KM Doro Londa*, monthly; 10hr); Jayapura (*KM Rinjani*, 2 monthly; 50hr/*KM Doro Londa*, monthly; 38hr/*KM Dobonsolo*, 2 monthly; 50hr/*KM Ciremai*, 2 monthly; 39hr); Kupang (*KM Doro Londa*, monthly; 50hr); Makassar (*KM Rinjani*, 2 monthly; 81hr/*KM Sinabung*, 2 monthly; 3 days/*KM Ciremai*, 2 monthly; 3 days/*KM Doro Londa*, monthly; 76hr); Manokwari (*KM Dobonsolo*, 2 monthly; 11hr/*KM Doro Londa*, monthly; 10hr/*KM Rinjani*, 2 monthly; 12hr/*KM Ciremai*, 2 monthly; 12hr); Nabire (*KM Rinjani*, 2 monthly; 24hr); Ternate (*KM Ciremai*, 2 monthly; 16hr/*KM Sinabung*, 2 monthly; 14hr).
Timika to: Agats (*KM Sangiang*, 2 monthly; 9hr); Fak Fak (*KM Sangiang*, 2 monthly; 44hr/*KM Tatamailau*, monthly; 28hr/*KM Kelimutu*, monthly; 24hr); Kaimana (*KM Tatamailau*, monthly; 16hr); Merauke (*KM Tatamailau*, monthly; 35hr/*KM Sangiang*, 2 monthly; 40hr/*KM Kelimutu*, monthly; 33hr).

Flights

Kartika, Merpati, Pelita and Garuda have flights into Papua from Java and Bali. These flights originate in Denpasar or Jakarta, and often stop in Makassar before flying onto Sorong, Timika or Biak, and terminating at Jayapura. The following are with Merpati unless otherwise stated.
Biak to: Fak Fak (2 weekly; 2hr); Jakarta (4 weekly with Garuda; 6hr 30min); Jayapura (4 weekly with Merpati, 4 weekly with Garuda; 1hr); Kaimana (weekly; 1hr 45min); Makassar (3 weekly with Kartika, 4 weekly with Merpati, 4 weekly with Garuda; 3hr 45min); Manokwari (4 weekly; 1hr 10min); Nabire (5 weekly; 1hr 15min); Numfor (weekly; 50min); Serui (4 weekly; 35min); Sorong (4 weekly via Timika with Merpati; 1hr 10min); Timika (4 weekly; 1hr 5min).
Jayapura to: Biak (3 weekly via Timika with Kartika, 4 weekly with Garuda, 3 weekly with Merpati; 1hr); Manokwari (4 weekly via Biak; 2hr 10min); Denpasar (3 weekly with Garuda via Timika; 8hr 15min); Merauke (weekly; 1hr 10min); Nabire (2 weekly; 1hr 50min); Serui (weekly; 2hr); Sorong (weekly via Timika; 4hr 20min); Tanah Merah (weekly; 1hr 40min); Timika (6 weekly with Merpati, 3 weekly with Garuda, 3 weekly with Kartika; 1hr); Wamena (2 daily with Merpati, 3-4 daily with Trigana; 1hr).
Kaimana to: Fak Fak (2 weekly; 1hr); Nabire (2 weekly; 1hr).
Manokwari to: Anggi (2 weekly; 35min); Biak (4 weekly; 1hr 10min); Wasior (weekly; 1hr 5min).
Merauke to: Bade (2 weekly; 55min); Kepi (weekly; 1hr 25min); Kimam (weekly; 1hr 10min); Senggo (2 weekly; 1hr 40min); Tanah Merah (weekly; 1hr 15min); Timika (weekly; 2hr 30min).
Nabire to: Biak (7 weekly; 1hr 15min); Enarotali (3 weekly; 45min); Fak Fak (3 weekly; 2hr 30min); Illaga (weekly; 1hr 10min); Kaimana (2 weekly; 1hr).
Sorong to: Fak Fak (2 weekly; 1hr 5min); Jakarta (5 weekly with Pelita, 3 weekly with Merpati; 5hr 15min) Kaimana (2 weekly; 2hr 30min); Makassar (5 weekly with Pelita, 3 weekly with Merpati; 3hr 15min); Nabire (2 weekly; 4hr); Timika (4 weekly; 3hr 30min); Surabaya (5 weekly with Pelita, 3 weekly with Merpati; 4hr 25min); Yogyakarta (5 weekly with Pelita; 5hr 55min).
Timika to: Biak (3 weekly with Kartika, 3 weekly with Merpati; 55min); Denpasar (3 weekly with Garuda; 4hr 30min); Jakarta (3 weekly with Garuda, 3 weekly with Merpati, 3 weekly with Kartika); Jayapura (6 weekly with Merpati, 3 weekly with Garuda, 3 weekly with Kartika; 1hr); Kaimana (weekly; 1hr 30min); Makassar (6 weekly with Merpati, 3 weekly with Kartika; 2hr); Sorong (4 weekly with Merpati; 1hr 30min).
Wamena to: Bokondini (weekly; 45min); Jayapura (2 daily with Merpati, 3–4 daily with Trigana; 1hr); Karubaga (weekly; 45min).

Contexts

Contexts

History

Prior to the colonial era, the story of Indonesia is the aggregation of separate histories. The country is a modern invention: until the Dutch subsumed most of the islands under the title the "Dutch East Indies" towards the end of the nineteenth century, the Indonesian archipelago was little more than a series of unrelated kingdoms, sultanates and private fiefdoms whose histories remained distinct, though they overlapped occasionally. A further problem for historians is the lack of reliable records and other evidence. Few contemporary accounts were written, fewer still have survived, and almost all early buildings, being made of wood, have either burnt down or rotted away.

The guide chapters have more information on the specific histories of each island, and the following account merely describes generic trends – the first inhabitants, the arrival of Islam, the beginning of sea trade and so on – that affected most or all of the archipelago.

Beginnings

Hominids first arrived in Indonesia about eight hundred thousand years ago. Excavations in 1890 by the Dutch-born paleontologist Eugene Dubois uncovered parts of the skull of *Pithecanthropus erectus*, since renamed *Homo erectus* – or **Java Man** as he's now more popularly known – in the tiny village of Sangiran near Solo.

Homo sapiens first made an appearance in about 40,000 BC, having crossed over to the Indonesian archipelago from the northern parts of Southeast Asia – the Philippines, Thailand and Burma – using land bridges exposed during the Ice Ages that temporarily connected the archipelago with the mainland. Later migrants brought with them specialized knowledge of rice irrigation and animal husbandry, sea navigation and weaving techniques. From the seventh or eighth century BC, the **Bronze Age** began to spread south from Southern China. Important centres for Bronze Age skills arose in Annam and Tonkin in what is now northern Vietnam, famed for their bronze casting, particularly of drums, decorated with animal, human and geometric patterns. The drums have been found throughout Indonesia, as have the stone moulds used in their production.

Early traders and kingdoms

One of the methods of rice cultivation brought by the early migrants was the **sawah**, or wet-field cultivation, which suited the volcanic soil of Java and Bali. This method of cultivation, however, was extremely labour-intensive, requiring co-operation between early Indonesian villages in order for it to succeed. This inter-village co-operation necessitated a degree of organization and leadership and, inevitably, an established hierarchy emerged between the villages. These tiny first-century AD village federations gradually evolved into the first **kingdoms** in the archipelago.

Trade with other islands – and, later, with India, China and the rest of Southeast Asia – also began at this time. Some historians believe that these merchants arriving from India were the first to bring Hinduism to the archipelago. The new religion quickly took root; early Hindu inscriptions from around the third century AD have been found in places as far apart as Sulawesi and Sumatra, and early Indonesian rulers were usually portrayed as incarnations of Shiva or Vishnu. By the fifth century, a myriad of small Hindu kingdoms, such as the fifth-century **Tarumanegara** kingdom in west Java, peppered the archipelago.

The Sriwijaya, Saliendra and Sanjaya kingdoms

The **Sriwijaya** kingdom, based in Palembang in south Sumatra, was the most successful of the early Indonesian kingdoms. For approximately four hundred years, beginning in around the seventh century AD, it enjoyed unrivalled power, controlling the Melaka Straits – and the accompanying lucrative trade in spices, wood, camphor, tortoise shell and precious stones – and extending its empire as far north as Thailand and as far east as west Borneo. Sriwijaya also enjoyed a reputation as a seat of learning and religion, with over a thousand Buddhist monks living within the city, studying Sanskrit and Buddhist scriptures.

Despite this power, the town of Sriwijaya itself was little more than a strip of houses stretching for a kilometre or so along the banks of Sungai Musi. Influence was confined to the region's coastal ports; as the basis of the Sriwijayans' wealth and power was the trade that passed through the straits, they had little incentive to head inland and subjugate the people of the interior.

Thus, whilst the Sriwijayans enjoyed supremacy around the coasts of Indonesia, small kingdoms began to flourish inland. In particular, the rival **Saliendra** and **Sanjaya** (the latter sometimes known as Mataram) kingdoms began to wield considerable influence in their homeland on the volcanic plains of central Java. Unlike Sriwijayas', these two rival kingdoms could boast huge populations, which they mobilized to build monumental structures such as the magnificent temple at **Borobudur**, built by the Buddhist Saliendras, and the Sanjaya's Hindu temples of **Prambanan**.

While the Sriwijaya Empire enjoyed by far the greatest wealth and influence of any of these dynasties, and its territories extended much further, the coastal location left it vulnerable to attack from overseas. Its hold over the more remote outposts was extremely tenuous too: apart from paying a regular tribute to the Sriwijayans, the rulers of the more remote corners of the empire were allowed to rule without interference. The Sriwijaya Empire was thus little more than a collection of small kingdoms and, as a result, following a devastating attack perpetrated by the **Cholas** of southern India in the twelfth century, it broke up completely into its component parts. The Saliendrans and Sanjayans too, after engaging in internecine fighting for centuries, found their control diminishing as new empires emerged in the east of Java.

The Majapahit Empire

The **Majapahit Empire** enjoyed unrivalled success for almost a hundred years, from its foundation in 1292 to the death in 1389 of its greatest king, **Hayam Wuruk**. Based in Trowulan in east Java, the Majapahit (whose name means Bitter Gourd) were a Hindu people who enjoyed their greatest successes under the guidance of their charismatic prime minister and general, **Gajah**

Mada, a former royal guard who rose to power after putting down an anti-royalist revolt in 1323. During his lifetime, the Majapahit enjoyed at least partial control over a vast area covering Java, Bali, Sumatra, Borneo, Sulawesi, Lombok and Timor – the first time the major islands of the Indonesian archipelago had been united, however loosely, under one command.

The Majapahit Empire is usually referred to as Indonesia's **golden age**, and during Gajah Made's term of office, the empire wielded considerable influence over much of East Asia, conducting mutually beneficial relations with the courts of China, Vietnam, Cambodia and Siam. As well as economic prosperity, the Majapahit empire also saw the first flowering of Indonesian culture. The *Nagarakertagama*, an ancient historical text from central Java, was written at this time, and though little is known about the lifestyle and political organization of the Majapahit royal house, it is believed that the courtly traditions still found in Indonesia derive from it. The success was continued by Hayam Wuruk, who ascended to the throne in 1350, while Gajah Made was still serving as prime minister, and reigned for 39 years.

Hayam's death, however, precipitated the slow collapse of the empire. The arrival of Islam on Java and a massive revolt in the north of the island soon after Hayam's demise left the empire weak and in disarray, and although it managed to survive for more than another hundred years on its new home in Bali, it was never to regain its former power.

The arrival of Islam

Islam first gained a toehold in the archipelago as early as the eighth century AD, during the rule of the Buddhist Sriwijaya Empire. Merchants from **Gujarat** in India who called in at Aceh in northern Sumatra were the first to bring the message of Mohammed, followed soon after by traders from Arabia, who went on to found small settlements on the east coast of Sumatra.

From Sumatra, Islam spread eastwards, first along the coast and then into the interior of Java and the rest of Indonesia (Bali, Flores and West Papua excepted), where it syncretized with the Hindu, Buddhist and animist faiths already practised throughout the archipelago. The faith also spread to **Melaka**, which had become the pre-eminent port in the region.

The first Islamic kingdoms in the archipelago emerged not on Sumatra, however, but on neighbouring Java. Small coastal sultanates grew in the vacuum left by the Majapahit; the **sultanates** of **Demak**, **Cirebon**, **Jepara** and finally **Banten** (in west Java near Jakarta) took it in turns to control the north coast. This was also the period of the **Wali Songo**, nine holy men, who, from their bases on the north coast, spread the word of Islam throughout Java and beyond.

The Portuguese and the spice trade

The first Europeans to exploit Indonesia's abundant natural resources arrived in the sixteenth century. This proved impeccable timing; a united Indonesia, which almost emerged under the Majapahit Empire less than a hundred years before, would probably have been able to repel any attempts by European traders to capitalize on the lucrative **spice trade**. As it was, the Majapahit, severely weakened by attacks from the nascent Islamic states emerging on the north coast of Java, could offer no resistance, and though these Islamic states, and the **Gowa** and **Makassar** kingdoms of southern Sulawesi – the first Indonesian power to trade regularly with Aborigines from Australia and Papua New Guinea – flourished briefly towards the end of the sixteenth century, none of them were sufficiently powerful to offer any real opposition to the Europeans.

The **Portuguese** were the first Europeans to arrive. Portuguese ships, following in the wake of **Vasco da Gama's** trailblazing journey around the South African cape in 1498, began appearing in the seas around Indonesia in the early sixteenth century. As with the Dutch who followed eighty years later, the Portuguese weren't in the Indonesian archipelago for the glory of the empire, but simply to get rich as quickly and expeditiously as possible. What drew them to Indonesia were its immense natural resources and, in particular, the unique produce of the **Moluccas (Maluku)**, which soon became known as the **Spice Islands**. Pepper, nutmeg, cloves, mace, ginger and cinnamon were all produced on the Moluccas. They were the ideal cargo, being light and compact and with a long shelf life; above all, they fetched enormous prices in sixteenth-century Europe, where they were used to preserve meat and hide the taste of semi-decayed food, as well as being a vital ingredient in early medicine.

To ensure a smooth passage through the archipelago, and to provide an ideal springboard for an invasion of the Moluccas, the Portuguese, under **Alfonso d'Albuquerque**, attacked and took control of the once-invincible port of Melaka in 1511. The Moluccas fell to **Ferdinand Magellan**, Albuquerque's compatriot, the following year. From then on the Portuguese operated a virtual monopoly over the spice trade that lasted until the latter part of the sixteenth century.

Despite this, most of the Indonesian islands were unaffected by the Portuguese presence, and life outside of the Spice Islands continued as before. But the Portuguese had left the door open to other European powers to explore the Indonesian archipelago. Portugal's traditional enemy, the **Spanish**, with the help of Magellan (who, having quarrelled with the Portuguese king following his return from the Moluccas, defected to Spain in 1512) established themselves to the north in the Philippines in 1521, from where they fought a ferocious and long-running battle with the Portuguese over the ownership of the Spice Islands. (Incidentally, one of Magellan's ships, the *Vittoria*, which visited the Moluccas on its return to Spain, was the first ship to circumnavigate the globe). The Portuguese and Spanish finally signed a peace accord in which the Spanish were pronounced rulers over the Philippines, while Portugal kept the Moluccas.

The Dutch conquest of Indonesia

In 1580, Portugal was annexed by Spain, and their iron grip on the spice trade relaxed. The Spanish themselves were defeated by the English a few years later with the destruction of the Armada in 1588, opening the way for the **Dutch**, themselves part of the Spanish Empire at this time, to explore the Indonesian archipelago. Their forays began in 1595, when **Cornelius de Houtman** led an ill-starred expedition of four ships to Java. When they returned two years later, only 89 of the original 249 crew were left; most had fallen victim to scurvy. They had had to burn one of their ships for want of crew, and while in west Java they had also managed to upset the local Bantenese, killing one of their princes. Nevertheless, the expedition had brought back a small profit for its investors, and a second expedition the following year proved much more successful, reaping four times the amount invested. Soon Dutch fleets were rounding the southern capes of South America and Africa, each bent on exploiting the seemingly endless trading possibilities that the archipelago offered.

Rivalry with the English at this time was intense. By 1600, the Dutch, by now the supreme European trading power in the region, felt it necessary to amalgamate the various Dutch fleets operating in the archipelago into a monopoly organization, to prevent the local sultanates from trading directly with the Chinese and English. Thus in 1602, the **United Dutch East India Company (VOC)**, was founded, with monopoly control over trade with the Moluccas. To further consolidate their control over the spice trade, the Dutch invaded and occupied the Banda Islands, part of the Moluccas, in 1603. It was the first overtly aggressive act by the Dutch against their Indonesian hosts. Two years later, the VOC successfully chased the Portuguese from their remaining strongholds on Tidore and Ambon, and the Dutch annexation of Indonesia began in earnest. Trading vessels were now being replaced by warships, and the battle for the archipelago commenced.

The VOC and the Mataram Empire

By the end of the first decade of the seventeenth century, the VOC had begun to build, almost by accident, a loose but lucrative empire. Although their motives remained purely financial, and their influence over much of the archipelago was still small, they were given considerable responsibility by the Dutch government, who authorized them to be their official representatives in the archipelago. As John Crawfurd, the British resident in Java from 1811 to 1816, wrote of the early VOC: "The first Dutch adventurers to the East were a set of rapacious traders, who found themselves unexpectedly called upon to exercise the functions of politicians and sovereigns."

At the helm of the VOC at this time was the ruthless **Jan Pieterzoon Coen**, an aggressive leader who once stated that there could never be trade without war, nor war without trade. Indeed, it appeared that his one goal was to prove this maxim. Having already wiped out two-thirds of the Bandanese during the invasion in 1603, Coen set about raising the prices of nutmeg and cloves artificially high by destroying vast plantations on the island, thus devastating the livelihood of Banda's already decimated population.

Coen then turned his attention to Java, and in particular **Jayakarta** (now Jakarta), which he decided would be the ideal location for the capital of the ever-expanding VOC territories. Having been granted permission to build a warehouse at Jayakarta by the local sultan, Fathillah, the Dutch converted it into a fortress. Besieged by both an angry Bantenese population and the British, the Dutch retaliated, razing the city and renaming it **Batavia**. Further strategically important territories were acquired soon after, including **Melaka**, the last Portuguese stronghold in the region, in 1641, and **Makassar**, one of the last remaining British territories, in 1667.

Unlike previous trading powers, however, the VOC were not content with control over the sea trade, and turned their sights inland. Java by this time was in the grip of the small but highly influential Islamic **Mataram Empire**, the last of the great home-grown empires of Indonesia (and different from the Mataram, or Sanjaya, empire, which was Hindu). Though the Mataram's territories extended little further than the plains of central Java and the northern shores, its rulers, beginning with **Sultan Agung**, who ruled between 1613 and 1646, were treated almost as deities by their subjects. However, the royal house of Mataram was often riven with internal squabbling. During the early years of the eighteenth century the region was paralysed by **Three Wars of Succession**, as different members of the royal house struggled for supremacy. The last of these (1746–57) brought about the division of the empire into three separate sultanates, two at Solo and one at Yogyakarta. The only winners of these hugely destructive wars were the Dutch, who, by playing off one rival against the other, had successfully divided the Mataram's power base, making it easier for them to subjugate the entire territory.

Though they were now the first rulers of a united Java, by the end of the eighteenth century, things had taken a turn for the worse for the VOC. The Treaty of Paris (1780) permitted free trade in the East, and the VOC's fortunes dwindled as a result in the face of huge competition from the British and French. In addition, the expense of running an empire, financing battles for further territorial gains and maintaining law and order over their dominions was proving prohibitive. In 1795, the Dutch government, investigating the affairs of the company that for 99 years had represented their interests in the Far East, found mismanagement and corruption on a grand scale. The VOC company was **bankrupt** – indeed, it had last been solvent way back in 1724. The Dutch government decided to pull the plug on the VOC there and then; the company struggled on as a purely private concern for another four years, eventually expiring in 1799 with debts of 134,000,000 guilders. The Netherlands government took possession of all VOC territories, and thus all of the islands we regard as Indonesia today formally became part of the **Dutch colonial empire**.

Governor Daendals and the arrival of the British

In 1795, the French, under Napoleon, invaded and occupied Holland. Amongst the French battalions was a small legion of patriotic Dutchmen who believed that they were liberating their country from the hands of despotism into which it had fallen. One of their number was **Herman Willem Daendels**. To thank him for his part in the success of the invasion, Napoleon's brother, Louis, the new king of Holland, sent Daendels to act as governor-general of the East Indies.

Known for his ferociousness and contempt for local Indonesian aristocracy, Daendals ruled over the archipelago for just three years, during which time he built all sorts of fortifications to fend off attacks by the British who, under the leadership of **Sir Thomas Stamford Raffles**, were showing a renewed interest in the islands. Troops were recruited from Ambon, Madura, Bali and Makassar to help with the defence, and fortresses were built along the Javanese coast – but all to no avail. With diminishing supplies and a lack of reinforcements from either France or Holland, the British found they were able to pick off the islands one by one, and duly landed at Batavia in August 1811 with a fresh fleet of up to 10,000 men.

Raffles' tenure in the archipelago lasted for just five years before he was forced to hand back the territories under a new peace deal signed with the Dutch. His time in the archipelago, however, left a lasting impact. Raffles was one of the first Europeans to take an interest in the ancient monuments that littered the island, among them Borobudur and Prambanan; he also ordered surveys of every historical building, and conducted extensive research into the country's fascinating flora and fauna.

The British also unwittingly sowed the seeds of revolution during their stay. By passing over the valid claims of **Prince Diponegoro** to the throne of the sultanate of Yogyakarta, in favour of his pro-British younger brother, they not only upset the royal households of Java, who disliked outsiders meddling in their affairs, but also, in the disaffected Diponegoro, created a charismatic leader for the anti-colonial cause.

The return of the Dutch

The Dutch returned to Indonesia in 1816 and were soon embroiled in a couple of bloody disputes against opponents of their rule. One of the most serious of these was the **Paderi War** in Sumatra. Led by three Islamic holy men who had been inspired by a recent pilgrimage to Mecca, the Paderi movement started out as a crusade against lax morals amongst the Sumatran people, and had nothing to do with the Dutch. By the time the Dutch arrived to retake control of the archipelago, however, the Paderi had already moved across the centre of the island from their base in Padang, converting the southernmost Batak tribes to their ultra-orthodox (by Indonesian standards) brand of Islam, where alcohol, gambling, cockfighting and smoking were forbidden. With the arrival of the Dutch in southern Sumatra in 1819, war between these two forces was inevitable; just two years later the Dutch and Paderi engaged in a ferocious seventeen-year struggle for central and southern Sumatra, with the Dutch finally winning a decisive victory at Daludalu in 1838.

The Dutch probably would have won sooner had they not had to concentrate most of their efforts on a second war, centring around Yogyakarta in central Java. Led by Prince Diponegoro, the local Indonesian aristocracy, including fifteen out of central Java's 29 princes and 41 out of 88 senior courtiers, had united with the peasants to launch guerrilla attacks against Dutch strongholds. The Dutch suffered some serious defeats during the five-year **Javanese War** (1825–1830), and only by tricking Diponegoro into peace negotiations in Magelang – where he was unsportingly arrested and sent in exile to Makassar – were they able to resume control over Java. The war had cost the lives of over two hundred thousand Javanese, mainly through starvation, and eight thousand Dutch troops.

Expansion and exploitation

Having finally regained control over their old colonies, the rest of the nineteenth century and the beginning of the twentieth saw the Dutch attempting to expand into previously independent territories. Their early efforts met with limited success: the **Balinese** only surrendered in 1906, a full sixty years after the Dutch had first invaded, whilst the war in Aceh, which the Dutch had first tried to annex in 1873, dragged on until 1908, costing thousands of lives on both sides. By 1910, however, following the fall of **Banjarmasin** in 1864, **Lombok** in 1894 and **Sulawesi** in 1905, the Dutch had conquered nearly all of what we today call Indonesia; the only major exception, **West Papua**, finally accepted colonial rule in 1920.

This expansionism coincided with renewed Dutch attempts to increase the exploitation of their Indonesian territories – policies which provoked more anti-colonial sentiment in Indonesia and outrage back in Holland. Following the debilitating battles in Java and Sumatra, the Dutch in Indonesia faced bankruptcy and needed an instant return on their investments in the archipelago. Unfortunately, the policies they implemented to try and achieve this were ineffectual at best, and at worst downright cruel.

The first of these policies was the so-called **Cultural System**, implemented in 1830 following the war with Diponegoro. Under this scheme, local farmers in Java had to give up a portion of their land – usually two-fifths, though sometimes as much as half was appropriated – to grow lucrative cash crops that could then be sold back in Europe for a huge profit. This system replaced land rent, though the farmers were still liable to the land tax on all of their land.

The Cultural System was not implemented everywhere, and in some districts farmers were unaffected; in other areas, however, farmers starved as the land used for cash crops was too great, and the remaining land too small to grow enough rice and other staple foodstuffs to subsist on. The primary aim of the Dutch was achieved: the islands staved off bankruptcy and Indonesia became a major world exporter of indigo, coffee and sugar. Unfortunately, their profits were reaped at the expense of the indigenous farmers, some of whom starved to death. In effect, Java had become one giant plantation.

The **Liberal System** (1870–1900) was a reaction to the exploitation of these farmers and a response to the new laissez-faire school of economic thought. Under this system, only local farmers could own land, although foreigners could lease it from the government for up to 75 years. The aim of these reforms was to open the islands up to private enterprise and the free market and to end the exploitation of the local population, while at the same time increasing local demand (by improving the purchasing power of the new farmers), thus maintaining the profits accruing to the Dutch.

Unfortunately, the liberal period coincided with some pretty devastating natural and economic disasters. **Coffee-leaf disease** began to spread in the 1870s, and a **sugar blight** in 1882 hit Cirebon and moved east throughout Java. Sugar beet from the West Indies and Africa flooded the European market at this time, lowering prices and leading to economic depression throughout the islands. Even without this bad luck, however, it is still doubtful whether the Liberal System would have achieved all of its goals. Policies moved very slowly, and, by maintaining the monopoly on coffee production – the most profitable crop – the Dutch prevented local farmers from enjoying the kind of windfalls they had been expecting. The farmers were still being exploited, and, as the Dutch made further territorial gains in the archipelago, farmers from neighbouring islands outside Java began to be exploited too.

As the harsh realities of the Liberal System continued, a vocal, altruistic minority in the Dutch parliament began pressing for more drastic policies to end the injustices in Indonesia. Their motives were admirable, but unfortunately their ideas on how to change the system were both patronizing and misguided. The policies, implemented during the first few years of the twentieth century, gave rise to what is now called the **Ethical Period**. During this time, radical irrigation, health care, drainage and flood control programmes were started, and **transmigration** policies, from Java to the outlying islands, were introduced. But transmigration, as is still seen today, while temporarily alleviating overpopulation on Java, brought its own set of problems, with the displaced often ending up as the victims of ethnic violence in their new homelands. The irrigation programme, although fairly successful in increasing arable land, also had the consequence of ensuring that Indonesia remained an agrarian country, unable to reap the massive profits that were accruing to industrialized nations. Though the ideas behind the Ethical Period were laudable, at the end of the day the Indonesians were still treated as inferiors by the Dutch, and progress was slow.

The Independence movement

Though widely seen as a failure, the Ethical Period, and in particular its emphasis on education, did have far-reaching and unforeseen consequences. Though education amongst Indonesians was still the preserve of a rich minority, it was from this minority that the leaders of the **Independence movement** would emerge in the generations to come. Educated Indonesians were not only better at pinpointing the injustices of colonial rule, but were more able to articulate their grievances to their Dutch masters.

The **Islamic Association**, or **Sarekat Islam**, founded in 1909, was the first of these nationalist movements. Originally formed by an educated elite to protect Indonesians against Chinese dealers, the group received a lot of popular support among the peasant population. Out of the Sarekat Islam came the **Indonesian Communist Party**, or **PKI** (Perserikatan Kommunist Indonesia), which shared many of Sarekat's goals. Following a series of PKI-organized strikes and civil disruptions a few years later, however, the PKI leaders were arrested, and the organization was to play little part in the revolution that followed.

A third party, the **Partai Nasional Indonesia** (PNI), founded a few years later in 1927 by **Achmed Sukarno**, grew to become the biggest of the independence organizations. With a huge following amongst the uneducated masses, the PNI aimed to achieve independence through nonco-operation and mass action, and quickly became a major threat to Dutch domination, so much so that the Dutch outlawed the party four years after its foundation, throwing its leaders, Sukarno included, into prison.

After 1927, and with the Dutch cracking down hard on any anti-colonial organizations, the independence movement gained little momentum: new nationalist parties came and went (including one, the **PNI Baru** – new PNI – which was led by former PKI member **Muhammed Hatta**); Sukarno was released from prison in 1933, then promptly rearrested in the same year and exiled to Flores, while Hatta was apprehended in 1934 and exiled to Boven Digul. Without their natural leaders, the movement faltered and grew fractious. In an attempt to move forward once more, another Independence party, the **Partai Indonesia Raya**, changed tack, opting to win independence through co-operation with the Dutch rather than the disruption and dissent which had so far met with little success. It was felt that the Dutch, under threat both in Europe and the Far East from the rising tide of fascism, would be more amenable to the idea of independence if, in return, they were guaranteed the support of the Indonesians against the Japanese army. The Dutch, however, continued stubbornly to refuse all Indonesian offers, and the independence movement was thwarted once more. On May 10, 1940, Hitler invaded Holland and the Dutch government fled to London. The issue of Indonesia's independence was now on ice.

The Japanese invasion

The **Japanese** made no secret of their intention to "liberate" Indonesia. Indonesia's seemingly inexhaustible supply of oil, rubber and bauxite had always been vital to the Japanese economy, and Japanese traders had a good working relationship with their Indonesian counterparts. Indeed, when the Japanese did finally invade, in January 1942, most Indonesians saw the Japanese army as liberators, rather than just another occupying force. This welcome ensured the success of the invasion, and less than two months later, on March 8, 1942, the Dutch on Java surrendered.

The three-and-a-half-year **occupation** was a mixed blessing for Indonesians. While the Japanese were every bit as ruthless as the Dutch whom they had replaced, this had the effect of politicizing the masses, adding more fuel to the fires of independence. The Japanese also encouraged the independence movement – particularly towards the end of World War II, when defeat at the hands of the Allies became a foregone conclusion – helping to train and prepare the indigenous population for the inevitable struggle ahead. One man in particular, a Japanese vice admiral and fervent pro-nationalist called **Maeda Tadashi**, conspicuously sided with the independence movement, and diverted money from the Japanese navy to fund lectures and rallies given by the recently freed Sukarno and Hatta.

By 1945, dozens of **youth movements** (revolutionary groups dedicated to the country's independence), had sprouted up throughout Java. The Japanese, meanwhile, began manoeuvring the old guard – Sukarno, Hatta *et al* – to the forefront of the nationalist movement, no doubt feeling that they would find it easier to negotiate with the old campaigners rather than the hot-headed youth groups. The "Investigating Body for Preparatory Work for Indonesian Independence", a committee that included most of the established nationalist leaders, was founded by the Japanese in 1945. It was from these meetings that Sukarno came up with his doctrine of **Pancasila**, the "five principles" by which an independent Indonesia would be governed: belief in God, nationalism, democracy, social justice and humanitarianism. From this, the committee was able to draw up the country's first constitution.

Despite these preparations, when the Japanese finally surrendered to the Allied forces, on August 15, 1945, there was a short hiatus. Maeda was keen to transfer the power to the Indonesian people, with Sukarno at their head, as quickly as possible, before either the Allies returned to Indonesia or the youth groups took it upon themselves to assume control. That night, Sukarno and Hatta were kidnapped by one of these youth groups, **Menteng 31 Asrama**, in an attempt to force them to declare Independence outside of the orderly arrangements laid down by the Japanese. Maeda, however, managed to persuade the group to return both of the hostages, and that night all three – Sukarno, Hatta and Maeda – were safely ensconced in Maeda's house, where they drafted a Declaration of Independence. Menteng 31 Asrama hoped for a fiery declaration full of inflammatory phrases and revolutionary sentiments, but on August 17, 1945, Sukarno read a simple, unemotional declaration to a small group of people outside his house in Menteng. The Republic of Indonesia was born, with Achmed Sukarno as its first president and Muhammed Hatta as vice president.

The revolution

Announcing that they were now an independent republic was one thing; ensuring that it stayed that way was quite another. Under the terms of the surrender agreed with the Allies, the Japanese had no right to hand over Indonesia to the Indonesian people. **Lord Louis Mountbatten** arrived in mid-1945 with several thousand British troops to accept the surrender of the Japanese occupying force. Their presence only added to an already tense situation, and skirmishes between the British troops and the Indonesians were frequent. The Japanese, realizing that they had obligations to the Allies in the terms of surrender, tried to retake towns that they'd previously handed over to the local people. The situation was getting out of hand. Some intense, short-lived battles occurred between Japanese and Indonesian forces, and later between Indonesian and British, including a particularly horrific ten-day fight for **Surabaya**. Throughout this time the British tried to remain neutral, planning to withdraw only when the Dutch were in a position to resume control and sort the mess out for themselves. By November 1946, 55,000 Dutch troops had arrived and the British finally left the archipelago.

The war with the Dutch, however, continued for the next three years. It was a curious affair, with diplomacy giving way to all-out war and vice versa. The situation looked to be heading rapidly towards stalemate, until pressure from outside the archipelago exerted itself on the Dutch. The world was turning against their campaign in Indonesia, finding their attempts to re-establish a colonial empire anachronistic in the twentieth century. The US was particularly strong in its criticism, threatening the Dutch with economic sanctions unless they pulled out of the war. The Dutch finally withdrew in December 1949, and sovereignty was handed over to the new Republic of Indonesia.

While it's fair to say that the Indonesians had won a great victory, it would be wrong to think that the revolution was fought by a totally united Indonesian people against imperialist oppressors. The islands, while more united than ever before, had poor communications, and some islands, particularly those ruled by leaders who had grown wealthy under the Dutch regime, viewed the declaration of Independence with something akin to disappointment. Even within the revolutionary vanguard, there was little consensus on how the republic should be run or what form it should take. When Independence was finally won, these differences – strategic, ideological and religious – rose quickly to the surface to dog the first steps of the republic.

1957–65: guided democracy and the last years of Sukarno

According to Sukarno, **guided democracy** was an attempt to create a wholly Indonesian political system based on the traditional, hierarchical organization of Indonesian villages. Sukarno considered the Western form of democracy as divisive, a system that led to too much political infighting and rarely to a universally acceptable outcome. In Sukarno's idealized view of traditional village life, however, decisions were made with the consent of everyone, and not simply the majority – though this unanimous agreement was only to be found with the considerable help and influence of the village elders. In guided democracy, the various political factions would still have their say, though Sukarno would now play the part of village chief, with all the power that entailed.

To many, the term guided democracy was a euphemism: despite the name, democracy featured little in Sukarno's new political system, and the measures introduced under guided democracy can be seen as the first step on the road to **authoritarian rule**, removing power from the elected cabinet and investing it instead with the presidency. These measures included the establishment of the **Kabinet Karya** (Business Cabinet), made up of a selection of nonelected representatives of all the main parties (including the PNI, the NU, the army and, a few years later as their influence grew, the PKI), to replace the existing, democratically elected cabinet that was dissolved in 1960, and the founding of the Supreme Advisory Committee, another nonelected body, with Sukarno as the self-appointed chairman, that made decisions on national policy.

Sukarno adorned his new political system with a smattering of newly coined terms to describe the ideas behind guided democracy, chief amongst which was **Nas-A-Kom**, made up of the three essential parties of his co-operative government – *nasionalisme*, *agaman* and *komunisme*, or nationalism, religion and communism, representing the major parties (the nationalist PNI, Islamic NU party and communist PKI) which formed his new government. Sukarno would bandy terms such as Nasakom about, promising in his speeches to "Nasakom the armed forces" and, in the long run, even Nasakom every public body in the country.

Unsurprisingly, many people, both within and outside government, were suspicious of Sukarno's real motives in introducing guided democracy, and lengthy protests in Sulawesi (where the first of two attempts on the president's life took place in 1960) and Sumatra marred the early years of guided democracy. For a short time, a breakaway parliament, the **PRRI**, founded by disgruntled former politicians who had had their authority diminished under guided democracy, emerged in the Sumatran city of Bukittingi.

The rise of the communists

It was around this time that Sukarno began to forge strong ties with the **Soviet Union**. The Soviets appreciated Sukarno's Marxist leanings and his aggressively anti-Western foreign policy, and began pouring money into the country to finance the Konfrontasi (see opposite) against the neocolonial state of Malaysia. The increasing Soviet influence also had far-reaching consequences for Indonesian politics. Sukarno still relied on maintaining a delicate balance between the various factions in his cabinet to maintain control. Even before the period of guided democracy, the communist PKI could boast the support of almost a third of the electorate; the influence that Soviet doctrine had over Sukarno made the president more sympathetic towards the communists' views, and further swelled their support at ground level.

Perversely, the rise in power of the **Indonesian army**, the communists' natural enemy, also increased the PKI's power. Thanks to a law allowing them to confiscate the last few Dutch interests that remained on the archipelago – such as the Royal Mail Steam Packet Company which controlled much of the inter-island shipping – the army had grown wealthy. This increasing prosperity, combined with their successful annihilation of the rebel PRRI government in 1958, had done much to increase the army's standing in society. Indeed, by the 1960s, Sukarno had begun to look upon the army's Chief of Staff, **Colonel A.H. Nasution**, as a challenge to his authority and a serious rival for his role as president. Inevitably, therefore, Sukarno and the PKI began siding with each other against the army. This in turn led to the polarization of the entire parliament, with different factions forming temporary allegiances in an attempt to defeat a mutual enemy, with Sukarno and the communists on one side, and the army and its unlikely allies – including the NU and PNI – on the other.

This fractious situation continued throughout the first half of the 1960s. The political fighting in parliament was mirrored by pitched battles between the various factions on the streets of the capital, and law and order began to break down. Nevertheless, if it hadn't been for the drive, political acumen and impassioned speeches of President Sukarno, many believe that democracy in any form would never have got off the ground in Indonesia.

Konfrontasi

Sukarno made no secret of his desire to wreak revenge for all the humiliations and poverty Southeast Asia had suffered at the hands of Western imperialists. To this end, and to distract his people from the economic crisis his wayward financial policies had engendered, he began a crusade to rid the region of the last vestiges of Western colonialism. After both diplomatic and military effort, the Dutch were ousted from their last remaining Indonesian territory – West Papua – in 1963, and in the same year Sukarno launched the bruising **Konfrontasi** ("Confrontation") against Malaysia, who he saw as a mere puppet state of their erstwhile British rulers. At stake in the Konfrontasi were the northern Borneo states of Sabah, Sarawak and Brunei, which had initially been reluctant to join Peninsular Malaysia and Singapore in the newly-formed Malaysian federation. However, Sukarno was unwilling to commit too many troops to fight battles in the jungles of Kalimantan when, thanks to a failing economy and inter-party friction, there was increasing unrest on Java and other islands. As a result, their ambition to bring Sabah, Sarawak and Brunei into the Indonesian republic failed, and the Indonesians under new president Suharto finally gave up the Konfrontasi (they never dignified the struggle by calling it a war) in 1965.

In hindsight, the decision to take up arms in an ultimately fruitless battle against his country's northern neighbours was one of Sukarno's gravest mistakes. The Konfrontasi weighed heavily on Indonesia's fledgling economy, and, as funds were diverted to the cause, subsidies were withdrawn from several areas of the public sector, leading to annual **hyperinflation** of at least one hundred percent throughout the early 1960s. The Konfrontasi also alienated the West at a time when the country needed it – or at least its cash – most of all. This only forced the Indonesians further into the arms of the Soviets until, less than twenty years after throwing off the yoke of Dutch imperialist rule, the Indonesians found themselves financially dependent on another foreign power.

1965: the communist coup

By mid-1965, Sukarno's health began to fail and his grip on power weakened, leading to a flurry of activity from each of the various factions in the cabinet as they jockeyed for position, ready to take advantage should the ailing president finally step down. Sukarno's eventual demise, however, was accelerated by the events of late September, events which not only precipitated his fall from power, but saw the rise to prominence of the man who would eventually replace him: General Suharto.

Nobody is really sure what happened on the night of September 30, 1965. What is known for certain is that, at about midnight, a number of leading generals were taken from their homes at gunpoint to Halim airport. Those who refused to co-operate, such as General A. Yani, were shot immediately. Those who went to Halim Airport suffered the same fate; their bodies were later discovered down a nearby well. Their abductors were a group of communist-inspired renegade army divisions and other leftist sympathizers. These **revolutionaries** were later to claim that they were only preventing an army-led coup that was due to occur later that same night – a claim that has never been substantiated. Of more significance, however, was the presence of President Sukarno at Halim. Although the rebels claimed that he was only taken there as a precaution, ready to fly out at the first sign of army insurrection, it was hard not to feel that Sukarno was somehow in cahoots with the communists, and that the idea of an army coup was a complete fabrication, invented by Sukarno and the PKI as an excuse for their extermination of senior figures in the armed forces.

The rebels managed to occupy Medan Merdeka in the middle of Jakarta, and thus controlled the telecommunications centre and the presidential palace situated nearby. Their success was shortlived, however. **General Suharto**, a veteran of the West Papua campaign and a senior member of the Indonesian army, rounded up those generals who weren't kidnapped and began to plan a countermove to retake Jakarta and quash the coup. In the event, this proved surprisingly easy. Suharto managed to persuade many of those holding Medan Merdeka to retreat back to their base at Halim Airport, and, as he gained further support, more of the coup participants fled, until Medan Merdeka was under his control completely.

The **failure of the coup** had disastrous consequences for both the communist PKI and Sukarno. Over the next five years, the communists became the victims of a massive Suharto-led purge. It was also the beginning of the end of Sukarno's rule. Though he lived until 1970, his grip on power had almost completely slipped by the end of 1965, and for the remaining year of his presidency he ruled in name only, as General Suharto manoeuvred himself to the top of the political ladder.

1965–67: Suharto takes control

In the months immediately following September 1965, Sukarno must have felt that his grip on power was still pretty secure. Some of his keenest rivals in the armed forces had been murdered, and his part, if any, in the events of that night had not been discovered. Unfortunately for Sukarno, he underestimated the political guile of his new rival, **General Suharto**. While Sukarno sought to prove that the coup was just another turbulent moment in the ongoing revolution that was his rule, Suharto, using the powers granted to him by Sukarno to restore order, began a campaign against the communist PKI party and their sympathizers, rounding up the ringleaders of the coup, anybody connected with the PKI and, eventually, anybody whose political ideology leaned more to the left than right. As more communists were arrested and killed, so violence and anti-PKI demonstrations filled the streets of the capital and elsewhere, allowing Suharto to remain in effective control of the country until they subsided.

The slaughter of communist sympathizers continued until the early months of March 1966. It was the **bloodiest episode** in Indonesia's history: most experts today reckon that at least 500,000 people lost their lives, although the official figure was a more modest 160,000. A similar number were thrown into jail where, up to a decade later, at least 100,000 languished without ever having been convicted or even charged. It was just as Suharto wanted. He had enjoyed a few months in power, had totally crushed the anti-army PKI and, as the main beneficiary of PKI support, Sukarno's grip on power had been severely weakened. The army was now the dominant force in Indonesian society and politics.

Sukarno, on returning to power, tried desperately to save his beloved guided democracy, reshuffling the cabinet in an attempt to weaken the power of the armed forces. In response, Suharto encouraged a **renewed outbreak of violence**, compelling Sukarno to hand over the controls to Suharto once again, just as he had in the aftermath of the initial communist uprising of September of the previous year, in order to quell these latest disturbances.

It was a simple tactic, but it worked. On March 11, 1966, Sukarno was informed that unidentified troops (positioned there, so it turned out, by Suharto himself) were surrounding his palace, and in panic the president fled to Bogor. Once there, Sukarno was persuaded to sign a document giving Suharto full authority to restore order and protect the president by whatever means necessary. It was just the invitation Suharto required.

The next day, anti-Suharto members of the cabinet were arrested. The following year, the MPRS (the People's Consultative Assembly, Indonesia's parliament), was purged of any pro-Sukarno elements and the man himself was asked to explain the mismanagement and corruption of his rule. Pro-Suharto Adam Malik was made minister for foreign affairs, and quickly set about restoring relations with the West and loosening existing ties with communist China. The debilitating Konfrontasi, the last obstacle to renewing relations with the West, ended in May 1966, with a peace treaty signed in December of that year, and soon aid from the West began pouring back into Indonesia, rescuing the ailing economy and providing essential relief to thousands of the poorest in Indonesian society. Suharto now had popular support to go with his burgeoning political power, and, in the new bourgeoisie that emerged as the economy improved, he found a powerful and secure foundation for his regime. The final *coup de grâce* to Sukarno's 21-year reign occurred on March 12, 1967, when the MPRS stripped Sukarno of all his powers and named Suharto **acting president**.

Indonesia has never had a more charismatic leader than Sukarno, and there were times during his rule when his popularity reached unprecedented levels. He embodied the conflicts and contradictions inherent in Indonesian society. A devout Muslim who nevertheless clung to the timeworn superstitions of traditional Javanese religion, whose fondness for alcohol and extramarital affairs are the stuff of legend, and whose political allegiances gravitated, throughout his career, towards the secular tenets of Marxism – the anomalies in Sukarno's personality mirrored the contradictions of the country he governed.

Unfortunately, policy decisions, most of which were of national importance, were seldom granted the same level of care and attention to detail that he lavished on his public image. It was typical of Sukarno that, while the country struggled to clamber out of the economic trough of the 1960s, he frittered away millions building colossal monuments in his beloved Jakarta: the Monumen Nasional in the centre of Medan Merdeka, the Free Irian Monument in Lapangan Benteng and the Mesjid Istiqlal – the largest mosque in Southeast Asia – were all built during his rule and still stand testimony to his wastefulness.

Ultimately, Sukarno was at heart a revolutionary. In order to rule effectively, he required Indonesia to be in a state of permanent revolution: fighting wars on all fronts, undertaking radical changes of government, and even entire political systems. His ideas, beliefs and speeches were that of the zealous revolutionary – perfectly suited for the turbulent years of 1945–46, but of limited use in the years that followed when stability and order were required.

The New Order

Suharto's first few years in power were seen as a brave new dawn, and there seems no doubt that he did bring some benefits to Indonesia. Suharto dubbed his new regime the **New Order**, to distinguish it from the chaos of the "Old Order" of Sukarno's presidency. It was an apt choice of words: after the turbulent years of Sukarno's rule, Suharto managed to restore a measure of order to society unseen since the Dutch era. The **economy** improved beyond all recognition: even inflation, which had dogged almost every year of Sukarno's rule, was brought under control. The new links forged with the West also brought significant benefits, both financially and politically. Furthermore, Suharto managed to create a **pluralistic society** where religious intolerance had no place; providing people belonged to one of the five main faiths, their religious beliefs were respected. (This tolerance, however, did not stretch to those who held traditional animist beliefs, for they worshipped more than one god. Nor did it stretch to atheism, which in Suharto's eyes equated with communism. During the late 1960s there was a rush of conversions to Islam and Christianity by people frightened of being labelled communists.)

There was a price to pay for the blessings of the Suharto era. The religious tolerance Suharto promoted in society was not matched by any political tolerance on his part. Instead, his people were forced to live under a suffocating **dictatorial regime** and take part in the charade of the so-called "festivals of democracy", the "elections" that took place every five years. With the restrictions placed on the opposition parties, the re-election of Suharto was a foregone conclusion.

Throughout his term in office, Suharto promised to bring about greater political freedoms, but these never materialized. Critics of Suharto's New Order found themselves languishing in jails alongside those arrested in the aftermath of the September 1965 coup – jails where torture was the rule rather than the exception. Improvements in the country's economy too, while significant, tended to benefit only the privileged minority, while a huge underclass developed in rural areas and in slum districts on the outskirts of large cities. There was also widespread **corruption** throughout society, from the president down. The scale of Suharto's nepotism, bestowing privilege, power and lucrative monopolies on his children and cronies, was breathtaking.

Throughout the late 1960s, Suharto continued his persecution of all things communist, tracking down existing PKI units in jungle hideouts in West Kalimantan. He also consolidated his position within parliament by simplifying the political system: where beforehand there had been a multitude of political parties, Suharto reduced them to just three – the **PPP** (United Development Party) made up of the old Islamic parties; the **PDI** (Indonesian Democratic Party) made up largely of the old nationalist party, the PNI; and the government's own political vehicle, **Golkar**. Political expression and criticism of Suharto's heavy-handed techniques were suppressed. Opposition parties were impotent, and participation in the government-controlled five-yearly elections gave Suharto a veneer of democratic legitimacy he clearly didn't deserve.

The 1970s and 1980s

Suharto, encircled by a close and trusted band of loyal followers, now had complete control over the country, which had expanded its boundaries during the mid-1970s. **East Timor**, independent since a revolution in Portugal had emancipated the tiny former colony in 1974, collapsed into civil war the following year as various factions failed to agree on whether the territory should become part of Indonesia. In the event, the decision was taken out of their hands by the Indonesians themselves, who invaded on Suharto's orders in December 1975. Despite strong condemnation from the United Nations, and regular Amnesty International reports of human rights abuses in East Timor, the US and Europe were unwilling to upset their new Southeast Asian ally. East Timor was incorporated into the Republic of Indonesia the following year.

The oil crisis of the 1970s raised the price of oil, then Indonesia's most lucrative export, significantly. This windfall lasted until the oil price collapsed in 1983, allowing the government to use the **oil revenue** to create a sound industrial base founded on steel and natural gas production, oil refining and aluminium industries. Welfare measures were introduced, with 100,000 new schools built. With breakthroughs in pesticides and improved farming methods, the 1980s also saw an increase of fifty percent in agricultural production, avoiding the food shortages many had predicted for the country following the post-war population explosion.

Yet these were minor triumphs in the face of the country's overwhelming poverty. The beneficiaries of Suharto's economic miracle were a small but wealthy minority who lived in air-conditioned luxury in the big cities, while the majority continued to struggle, eking out a meagre existence in the rural areas of the country. The people who belonged in this disaffected underclass, though numerous, lacked the organization and influence necessary to change matters, and Suharto knew it. As long as the middle and upper classes continued to support his regime, his position was safe.

Suharto's downfall

For over three decades, Suharto had managed to concentrate power almost exclusively in his own hands. This political stability had raised confidence among foreign investors, enabling the economy to grow steadily throughout his tenure. But even such suffocating control and economic prosperity could not mask the growing disapproval of Suharto's government. The previously supportive middle classes were tiring of his brazen **nepotism** and the unbridled corruption of his government, and, although there was never any direct challenge to his authority, resentment against the regime grew throughout the 1990s.

Nevertheless, Suharto would probably have survived for a few more years if it wasn't for the **currency crisis** that hit the region in the latter part of 1997, a crisis triggered by a run on the Thai baht. In a few dramatic months, the rupiah slipped in value from Rp2500 to the US dollar to nearly Rp9000. Prices of even the most basic of goods such as fuel and food rose five hundred percent.

Suharto recognized the seriousness of the situation and contacted the IMF for aid. The IMF, however, promised to help only after certain conditions had been met. Suharto had been backed into a corner. If he refused to comply, his country faced ruin. If he agreed to the IMF's terms – which included removing his family and friends from a number of senior and lucrative posts – his hold on the country would be seriously undermined. Suharto eventually decided to comply with the IMF's demands, but then committed political suicide by appointing a cabinet full of his own cronies – including his old golfing partner – following the last "festival of democracy" in May 1998. Foreign investors lost all confidence in Suharto, and the rupiah went into freefall. Pressure on Suharto was also growing from his own people, as many took to the streets to protest against his incompetence and demand greater political freedom. These demonstrations, initially fairly peaceful, grew more violent as the people's frustration increased, until a state of lawlessness ensued. For over a week, riots took place in all the main cities, buildings were set on fire and shops looted. The **Chinese community**, long resented in Indonesia for their domination of the economy and success in business, were targeted by the rioters for special persecution. Over 1200 people died in the mayhem that followed the May elections, until, on May 21, 1998, Suharto stepped down and his vice-president, B.J. Habibie, took over.

The rise and fall of Gus Dur

Though Suharto's resignation quelled the riots in the short term, few believed that the appointment of **Habibie**, a close friend of Suharto for many years, would end the public's dissatisfaction with the political situation. Despite promises to introduce sweeping reforms, many believed Habibie was dragging his feet over a number of issues, and, in early November 1998, more **rioting** occurred. The rioters – largely students – wanted to see a number of measures taken instantly, including the removal of the army from parliament, an end to corruption within government, the bringing to trial of Suharto on charges of mismanagement and corruption, and a return to democracy. In the days leading up to a special session of parliament convened by Habibie to address these issues, fifteen protesters were shot dead in the capital by the army. Further protests took place in a number of other cities, but still Habibie failed to deliver. The cry for **Reformasi**, first heard in May, grew more voluble by the day.

Nobody expected Indonesia's transition to democracy to be an easy one after so many years of totalitarian rule, and for the first few years, the country was gripped by a mixture of fear, intrigue and hope. Occasionally this manifested itself in the form of **religious intolerance**: a number of churches were burnt down and Christians killed in a series of attacks, prompting revenge killings by Christian gangs. Adding to the tension was the phenomenon of the so-called "Ninja murders". In 1998–99, almost two hundred Muslim clerics were brutally killed. To this day, nobody knows who was behind the slaughter – dubbed the Ninja murders because of the assailants' black costumes and face masks. The murders prompted a spate of revenge killings, and for a while the entire archipelago seemed to teeter on the brink of holy war.

Despite the widespread mistrust of Habibie, he did lay the ground for the first **free and democratic elections** ever to be held in Indonesia, keeping a promise that he made during his first few days in power. In the elections, held on June 7, 1999, the Indonesian Democratic Party of Struggle, led by **Megawati Sukarnoputri**, the daughter of the country's first president, Sukarno, scored an easy victory. However, Indonesia's parliament, the People's Consultative Assembly, decided she couldn't be trusted to lead, a decision that resulted, once again, in widespread rioting on the streets of Jakarta. In the vote that followed, parliament chose **Abdurrahman Wahid** (known affectionately as **Gus Dur**) – the leader of the Islamic National Awakening Party, which came third in the elections – to be the country's first democratically elected president. To placate the rioters, Megawati was installed as vice president.

A president impeached

At the beginning of his presidency, **Gus Dur** joked that while Sukarno was crazy about women, Suharto was crazy about money and Habibie was just crazy, in his own case, it was the ones who voted for him who were crazy. It was a typical Gus Dur statement: self-mocking, off-the-cuff and humorous. By the end of his term of office, however, just 21 months into his four-year mandate, most Indonesians were agreeing with him.

But while his administration was riddled with controversy and his final fall from power almost farcical, Gus Dur's **achievements** should not be overlooked. Perhaps the most important of these was the removal of army officers from his cabinet, and therefore from political power. The army's role in politics had traditionally been enshrined in the constitutional concept of *dwifungsi*, or dual function, which gave it the right to engage in politics while also fulfilling its more traditional role of defending the country. Unfortunately, the army had become preoccupied with its civilian role and, to the alarm of many people, had become an important political force in Indonesia. In his first cabinet, Gus Dur did indeed give the army's powerful chief-of-staff, General Wiranto, a ministerial post. But by giving him the role of security minister rather than defence minister, the wily president succeeded in removing Wiranto from directly controlling the army. Soon after, the president threatened to sack anyone found to be culpable of the murder and **human rights abuses** in East

Timor; when the results of an investigation into the atrocities were released, General Wiranto was implicated, along with five other generals. Ignoring Gus Dur's call for him to resign, Wiranto was eventually sacked by his president. To further weaken the army's political influence, Gus Dur replaced many of the army's higher echelon with moderate reformers, promoted navy and air force officers to his cabinet ahead of the army, and insisted that all military men who joined his cabinet must resign first from their military positions.

Gus Dur also did much to **reform the political process** in Indonesia, nurturing the country's newly won democracy and making the government far more accountable – to his own cost, as he would later find out. The **press** were also allowed greater freedom, to the extent that they are now one of the most unfettered in Southeast Asia.

However, Gus Dur's rather erratic way of ruling began to exasperate his cabinet and colleagues. It was not unusual for him to make a policy statement one day, then retract it the next, while his inability to make an impact on the problems – of poverty, civil unrest and an economy in turmoil – that beset Indonesia soon lost him the support of his people. In particular, it was his failure to stem the rising tide of **regional conflict** that secured his downfall. With East Timor showing the way in 1999, other far-flung Indonesian provinces began to become more vocal – and violent – in their own struggle for sovereignty; in particular, West Papua (formerly Irian Jaya) and the north Sumatran province of Aceh both embarked on their own fight to break free from Indonesia. Gus Dur tried to placate them with offers of greater autonomy within the country, but independence leaders rejected these advances, and the unrest continues to this day. In Poso, central Sulawesi, Christians and Muslims began a protracted internecine battle that, by 2002, had already cost over four thousand lives (see p.928). The holy war in the Maluku islands (see p.969), which started in 1999 under the reign of Habibie, rumbled on under his successor, with the total number of casualties by March 2002 numbering well over five thousand. And in Kalimantan in early 2001, the local Dayak tribes embarked on a spree of wholesale slaughter against the Madurese transmigrants whom they had long resented, killing three thousand and maiming thousands of others.

Exactly why Gus Dur's term in office should have been so beset by these regional battles is unclear. Most observers suggest that the potential for conflict in these areas had existed for a long time, but under Suharto's authoritarian regime, any signs of trouble had been quickly and brutally suppressed. Others suggest that most of these battles were started, or at least encouraged, by pro-Suharto supporters and army personnel seeking to discredit Gus Dur's government. Whatever the truth, by continuing to embark on his foreign jaunts in his vain quest to find foreign investors, Gus Dur earned himself a reputation as a leader who holidayed while his country burned. Also working against him was his failure to bring Suharto to account for the massive corruption and human rights abuses that took place during the latter's rule. While Gus Dur could not be directly blamed for the 32-member panel of doctors' decision that Suharto was unfit to stand trial, this outcome was seen as a personal defeat of Gus Dur's administration.

By late 2000, with the economy still moribund and showing little tangible signs of recovering from the collapse of 1998, dissatisfaction with the president's ineffectiveness was already being voiced. In October of that year, **Amien Rais**, chairman of the Upper House, one of the most influential men in Indonesian politics and the man regarded by many as the country's "kingmaker", made an apology "to the whole of the Indonesian people for having proposed [Wahid] for president at the 1999 MPR session. It is because we are human and can all make mistakes." Amien Rais also suggested that Gus Dur's days in power were numbered, and that if he was to remain in power for another year, the country would be in danger of disintegrating.

Yet it was to be another nine months before Gus Dur was forced out of office – a delay that has led many to call for a change in the state constitution. When it happened, Gus's exit from the political stage was ignominious. Embroiled in two **corruption scandals** – "Bulogate", in which his masseur was believed to have walked off with some US$4 million embezzzled from the State Logistics Agency, and "Bruneigate", in which US$2 million of funds donated by the sultan of Brunei for humanitarian purposes went missing – Gus Dur, the man many Indonesians believed was incorruptible, suffered the humiliation of being censured by parliament on February 1, 2001 for his alleged part in these affairs, and again on April 30. He was finally impeached in July of the same year, even though the corruption charges against him were dropped at the end of May.

A few low-key protests followed, but Gus Dur's refusal to mobilize the militias from his homeland of East Java, who had vowed to fight on his side, won him commendation from observers worldwide. However, his **unwillingness to step down** and leave the palace following his impeachment smacked of childish petulance, and did little to increase his standing either at home or abroad. Furthermore, his declaration on July 23 of a state of emergency (which parliament quickly rejected) and his plea to the army to support him against his impeachment, almost undid his good work by bringing the armed forces back into the political arena.

Megawati and the future

While Gus Dur remained in the palace, his vice president, **Megawati Sukarnoputri**, wasted little time in setting up her own administration. At the time of writing, with her government only a couple of years old, it is still too early to judge her progress; her critics, however, are quick to suggest that her impact has been less than remarkable. In her favour, Megawati can count on a huge groundswell of support, from both the average citizen and the Indonesian parliament. But this support is probably due more to affection for her charismatic father than a belief that she can succeed where Gus failed. Indeed, as Gus Dur's vice president, Megawati must accept some responsibility for the failings of that administration. During that time, she was renowned most for her reluctance to speak out – leading some Indonesians to joke that she was the dumb leading the blind (in the form of the partially sighted Gus Dur).

Whatever the debate surrounding Megawati's abilities as leader, one thing is certain: her administration faces serious problems. As well as an economy that refuses to emerge from the crisis precipitated by the Asian stock-market crash of 1998, Megawati will also have to deal with rising **Islamic fundamentalism**, particularly since the attack on the World Trade Centre on September 11, 2001. The growing antipathy towards foreigners from certain parts of Indonesian society came to a head on October 12, 2002, when a huge bomb exploded in a nightclub in the tourist hotspot of Kuta on Bali. Over two hundred people, many tourists from Australia and Europe, were killed in the blast, shattering Bali's well-earned reputation as a safe haven in a turbulent archipelago. Though Megawati has been at pains to show the outside world that her government is doing all that it can to eliminate fundamentalism from Indonesia

– and a number of suspects were quickly arrested in the wake of the blast – there are those observers who believe that her country has become something of a refuge for terror networks, with rumours circulating of terrorist training camps being established in the remoter parts of the archipelago. As a result, Indonesia's reputation as a safe country, where attacks on tourists were rare, has been damaged, and it will take a lot of time and effort to try and restore it.

Then there is the problem of how to deal with Indonesia's often murky past; Megawati's response to dealing with central figures from the Suharto regime will show how much she is willing to press ahead with **anti-corruption reforms**. Early indications are mixed. Though Suharto himself may have escaped, his son **Tommy Suharto** is now serving fifteen years for murdering the judge who sentenced him in September 2000 to 18 months' imprisonment on corruption charges – a sentence he initially evaded by going into hiding for a year. While some observers felt the punishment was too lenient – a life sentence or even the death penalty could have been handed down by the judge – the result at least appeared to show that the days of avoiding justice with large pay-offs are at an end. Weighing against this positive move forward, however, is Megawati's reluctance to press charges against her generals over the **East Timor slaughter**. While the UN tribunal was sentencing 10 militia members to jail terms of up to 33 years for their part in the atrocities, Megawati has thus far refused to extradite anybody said to have been involved in the massacres. Instead, and only after increasing pressure from Western leaders who refused to resume full economic and military ties until the main culprits were brought to justice, Jakarta agreed to convene their own human rights trial, which after lengthy delays finally got under way at the beginning of 2002. Scepticism surrounding the trial remains high, however, for not only have a number of Indonesia's top military brass – including the armed forces commander at the time, General Wiranto – managed to evade prosecution due to lack of evidence, but there are also those that fear that the trial will do little except whitewash the conduct of the army.

Finally, there is the continuing spectre of **regional conflict** that threatens to tear the country apart. As vice president, Megawati has signally failed to make any major breakthroughs in preventing the conflict. Her father is perhaps best remembered for his ability to unite the disparate tribes and peoples of the country under one flag and one administration. As Indonesia progresses through the 21st century, Megawati will need to pull off much the same sort of trick if the country is to remain unified, and face the many problems that beset it.

Religion

Every citizen in Indonesia professes, officially at least, one of five major faiths: Islam, Buddhism, Hinduism, Catholicism and Protestantism. Yet the Islam you'll find in Indonesia is very different from the Islam you'll find in west Asia or the Indian subcontinent, and likewise the other major faiths in the archipelago bear striking differences to their counterparts in other parts of the world.

Religion in Indonesia is dynamic, not dogmatic; by gaining a foothold in the archipelago, each of the major faiths has undergone major changes. These changes may have been introduced deliberately – to make the new religion more attractive to the local population and thus ensure its long-term survival – or they may just be the natural result of introducing a new faith into a region that already has very deep-rooted beliefs of its own. For example, Hinduism in Indonesia, brought over to the archipelago in the first few centuries AD, has significant elements of **indigenous animism** (once the predominant faith in the archipelago) grafted onto the more orthodox faith that you'll find in India. Thus converts to the new religion need not forsake their old animist beliefs entirely, but instead can continue to adhere to them, within the framework of Hinduism. Similarly, Islam, brought over a few centuries later by merchants from Gujarat in India, has aspects of Hinduism, Buddhism and animism – the three major faiths that had preceded it in the archipelago – incorporated within its rituals and beliefs.

These changes to the major religions still continue to this day, though nowadays the alterations usually arise through political pressure, rather than from a desire to appeal to potential converts as before. For example, as part of its code of national law (Pancasila), the Jakarta administration also requires that all Indonesian faiths be **monotheistic** – a proviso that doesn't sit easily with either **Hindu** or animist tenets. By emphasizing the role of their supreme deity, Sanghyang Widi Wasa (who manifests himself as the Hindu trinity of Brahma, Siwa and Wisnu), the Hindu Council of Bali (which, uniquely in Indonesia, is 93 percent Hindu) convinced the Ministry of Religion that Bali was essentially monotheistic, and in 1962 Balinese Hinduism was formally recognized by Jakarta. As a result, a host of new Balinese temples were dedicated to a unifying force – Jagatnata or "Lord of the World".

Outside of Bali, Indonesia has a predominantly **Muslim** population, though with significant **Buddhist** (the Chinese populations in the large cities and in West Kalimantan), Hindu and animist minorities (in West Papua, Sumatra, Kalimantan and other remote outposts). **Christianity** is not particularly widespread in Indonesia. The Batak of North Sumatra, the Ambonese, Florinese and a few tribes in West Papua and Kalimantan are the only pockets of Christianity, despite three hundred years of Dutch rule. Nevertheless, the Christian minority is a powerful one; those who converted under the Dutch were offered the opportunity to receive a European education, and this has ensured that the Christians form a disproportionate presence in the elite of the army, government and business.

Animism

Animism is the belief that all living things – including plants and trees – and some non-living natural features such as rocks and waterfalls, have **spirits**. **Ancestor worship** – the practice of paying tribute to the spirits of deceased relatives – is also common throughout the archipelago. As with Hinduism, the animistic faiths teach the necessity of living in harmony with these spirits; disturb this harmonious balance, by upsetting a spirit for example, and you risk bringing misfortune upon yourself, your household or your village. For this reason, animists consult, or at least consider the spirits before almost everything they do, and you'll often see small offerings of flowers or food left by a tree or river to appease the spirits that live within. Spirits can also be called upon for favours: to cure sickness, for example, or to bring rain or guarantee a fine harvest. As such, the witch doctors, or **dukun** in Indonesian, who traditionally act as the medium between the temporal and spirit world, rank high in the village hierarchy.

Animism is still the predominant faith in some of the villages of the outlying islands, particularly Sumatra, Kalimantan and West Papua. The rituals and beliefs vary significantly between each of these islands. Many of these ancient animist beliefs permeate each of the five major religions, and many Indonesian people, no matter what faith they profess, still perform animist rituals. Indeed, it was widely reported that President Sukarno, during the revolution of 1946, spent an entire day praying to his ceremonial kris to gain courage and fortitude.

Islam

Indonesia is the largest **Islamic nation** in the world. Initially brought over to **Aceh** by traders from Gujarat in the eighth century, the religion slowly filtered down to the rest of the archipelago in the centuries that followed. Its progress is reflected in the religious make-up of the islands today: the northernmost province of Aceh, which received Islam directly from India, is still the most orthodox area, whereas Muslims in the rest of the archipelago follow a style of Islam that has been syncretized with other, older religions, such as animism, Buddhism and Hinduism. Indeed, so different is the Indonesian version of Islam compared to the orthodox faith as followed in Arabia, that a follower of the latter would probably find the former idolatrous, or even blasphemous.

The youngest of all the major religions, the beginnings of Islam are fairly well documented. Born in 570 AD, **Mohammed**, an illiterate semi-recluse from Mecca in Arabia, began, at the age of forty, to receive messages from **Allah** (God) via the Archangel Gabriel. On these revelations Mohammed began to build a new religion: Islam or "Submission", as the faith required people to submit to God's will.

His early proselytizing met with limited success in his home town, and in 622 AD, Mohammed, accompanied by his followers, the **Muslims**, or "Surrendered Men" (as they had surrendered themselves to God's will), abandoned Mecca for Medina. There he built up a massive following, and returned in triumph to Mecca in 630 AD.

Soon after Mohammed's death in 632 AD, the religion he had founded split into two over an argument over succession, with the **Sunni** Muslims preferring an elected leader, and the **Shi'ites** preferring the caliphate to be hereditary. Since that initial split, the two factions have drifted further apart in matters of dogma and ritual, to a point of irreconcilability.

To many Westerners, it comes as something of a surprise to find how close the Islamic faith is to Christianity: the ideas of heaven and hell and the creation story are much the same, and many of the prophets – Abraham, Noah, Moses – appear in both faiths. Indeed, Jesus is an Islamic prophet too, although Muslims believe that Mohammed is the only true prophet, to whom everything was revealed.

The Islamic religion is founded on the **Five Pillars**, the essential tenets revealed by Allah to Mohammed and collected in the **Koran**, the holy book which Mohammed dictated before he died. Essentially, Mohammed preached that all Muslims should base their lives on these five rules. The first is that one should profess one's faith in Allah with the phrase "There is no God but Allah and Mohammed is his prophet". It is this sentence that is intoned by the muezzin five times a day when calling the faithful to prayer. The act of praying is the second pillar. According to Mohammed's teachings, praying can be done anywhere, and not just in a mosque, though the same ritual should always be performed: Muslims should always face Mecca when praying, the head must also be covered, and a ritual set of ablutions, including the washing of feet and hands, should be carried out before starting. The third pillar demands that the faithful should always give a percentage of their income to charity, whilst the fourth states that all Muslims must observe the fasting month (Ramadan; see p.58). The fifth pillar demands that every Muslim should make a pilgrimage to Mecca at least once in their lifetime. Those who do are known as *haji* (*haja* for women) and are accorded great respect in Indonesia.

Islam in Indonesia

Nearly all Indonesian Muslims are followers of the **Sunni** sect. Indeed, in Indonesia the argument is not between Sunni and Shi'ite, but between those who practise a more orthodox form of the religion, the **Santri Muslims**, and those who follow a mystical, homegrown form of Islam which combines elements of Hinduism and animism, and which has more in common with the spiritual Sufi faith of eastern Turkey and Iran. A good example of the latter can be found in Central Java, where the sultans of Yogyakarta and Solo, though they will insist they practise a fairly orthodox brand of Islam, put on puppet festivals where tales are performed from the Hindu classics the *Ramayana* and *Mahabarata*. Traditionally, the sultan of Solo is also believed to have close ties with the Goddess of the South Seas, Loro Kidul, and every year the sultan visits the goddess's home at Parangtritis where he prays to the goddess and leaves offerings. Indeed, according to popular legend, the Islamic faith was initially spread throughout Java by the **Wali Songo** (Nine Saints), nine holy men who were supposedly blessed with supernatural powers.

There are other differences between the Indonesian-style Islam and that practised by the rest of the Islamic world. Indonesian women tend to be accorded far more respect, with veils and women in full purdah a rare sight. Indonesian men are only allowed two wives, as opposed to four in Arabian countries, though just one wife is the norm. Islam in Indonesia is also far **less political** than in many other parts of the Islamic world – the country is, after all, a secular state – though this may be about to change. Suharto, for all his faults, did at least try to keep Indonesia faithful to its pluralistic concepts as laid down in the Pancasila. Despite growing pressure from Islamic groups, the archipelago remained a pluralist state throughout his lengthy term of office. President Habibie, however, was seen as an aggressive defender of "the faith", and was once president of the Association of Muslim Intellectuals. Currently, the status quo from Suharto's reign has been preserved, but a more Islamic form of governance may well be adopted in the future.

The mosque

The mosque, or **mesjid** as it's known in Indonesia, is simply a prayer hall. Most towns have at least two mosques: one for Friday prayers, the *jami mesjid*, and the *musalla*, which is used every day except Friday. In addition, you'll find rooms set aside for praying in hotels, airports and in train and bus stations. Visitors are nearly always allowed to tour around the mosque, though obviously not during prayer times.

Different parts of Indonesia have developed their own idiosyncratic mosque design. The multitiered, or *joglo* roofs of the older Javanese mosques (which, it is believed, grew out of the Hindu Meru shrines of Bali) are a classic example. However, each conforms to the same basic layout that you'll find in mosques all over the Islamic world. Stand by the gateway to any mosque and you'll notice the same features: a **courtyard** at the front, often with a **fountain** or washroom to one side where worshippers can perform their ritual ablutions before proceeding into the mosque to pray; the mosque itself, which is normally just one large room or hall; and a **minaret**, or *menara*, from where the muezzin used to call the faithful to prayer five times a day. More often than not these days, the muezzin doesn't actually climb the minaret, but calls the faithful via loudspeakers attached to the top of the minaret; in many cases, there's no muezzin at all, the call to prayer being performed by a prerecorded cassette.

The interior of the mosque is usually very simple. The congregation sit or kneel on the carpeted floor when praying, so there is usually very little furniture within the mosque, save, perhaps, for the **mimbar** – the pulpit, from where the Friday sermon is delivered. The direction of Mecca, which the faithful must pray towards, is indicated by a small niche, or **mihrab**, in what is known as the **qibla** wall (usually the wall nearest the mimbar). The decor of the mosques adheres to the strict iconoclastic rules of Islam, with no images of any living creatures inside a mosque. Nevertheless, the walls are occasionally enlivened – sometimes, particularly in Banda Aceh and Medan, beautifully so – by elaborate geometric patterns or verses from the Koran.

Hinduism

Despite certain obvious similarities, Balinese Hinduism, or **Agama Hinduism** as it's usually termed, differs dramatically from Indian and Nepalese Hinduism. At the root of Agama Hinduism lies the fundamental understanding that the world – both natural and supernatural – is composed of **opposing forces**. These can be defined as good and evil, positive and negative, pure and impure, order and disorder, gods and demons, or as a mixture of all these things – but the crucial fact is that the forces need to be balanced. Positive forces, or **dharma**, are represented by the gods (*Dewa* and *Bhatara*), and need to be cultivated, entertained and honoured – with offerings of food, water and flowers, with dances, beautiful paintings and sculptures, fine earthly abodes (temples) and ministrations from ceremonially clad devotees. The malevolent forces, **adhar-**

ma, which manifest themselves as earth demons (*bhuta*, *kala* and *leyak*) and cause sickness, death and volcanic eruptions, need to be neutralized with elaborate rituals and special offerings.

To ensure that malevolent forces never take the upper hand, elaborate **purification** rituals are undertaken for the exorcism of spirits. Crucial to this is the notion of **ritual uncleanliness** (*sebel*), a state which can affect an individual (during a women's period for example, or after a serious illness), a family (after the death of a close relative, or if twins are born), or even a whole community (a plague of rats in the rice fields, or a fire in village buildings). The focus of every purification ritual is the ministering of **holy water** – such an essential part of the religion that Agama Hinduism is sometimes known as *agama tirta*, the religion of holy water. As the main sources of these life-giving waters, Bali's three great mountains are also worshipped. Ever since the Stone Age, the Balinese have regarded their **mountains** as being the realm of the deities, the sea as the abode of demons and giants, and the valleys in between as the natural province of the human world. From this concept comes the Balinese sense of direction and spatial orientation, whereby all things, such as temples, houses and villages, are aligned in relation to the mountains and the sea.

Finally, there are the notions of **karma**, reincarnation, and the attaining of **enlightenment**. The aim of every Hindu is to attain enlightenment (*moksa*), which brings with it the union of the individual and the divine, and liberation from the endless painful cycle of death and rebirth. *Moksa* is only attainable by pure souls, and this can take hundreds of lifetimes to attain. Hindus believe that everybody is reincarnated according to their karma, a kind of account book which registers all the good and bad deeds performed in the past lives of a soul. Karma is closely bound up with caste, and the notion that an individual should accept rather than challenge their destiny.

Gods and demons

All Balinese gods are manifestations of the supreme being, **Sanghyang Widi Wasa**, a deity only ever alluded to in abstract form by an empty throne-shrine, the *padmasana*, that stands in the holiest corner of every temple. Sanghyang Widi Wasa's three main aspects manifest themselves as the Hindu trinity: **Brahma**, **Wisnu** and **Siwa**. Each of these three gods has different roles and is associated with specific colours and animals. Brahma is the Creator, represented by the colour red and often depicted riding on a bull. His consort is the goddess of learning, **Saraswati**, who rides a white goose. As the Preserver, Wisnu is associated with life-giving waters; he rides the **garuda** (half-man, half-bird) and is honoured by the colour black. Wisnu also has several avatars, including Buddha – a neat way of incorporating Buddhist elements into the Hindu faith. Siwa, the Destroyer or, more accurately, the Dissolver, is associated with death and rebirth, with the temples of the dead and with the colour white. He is sometimes represented as a phallic pillar or lingam, and sometimes in the manifestation of Surya, the sun god. Siwa's consort is the terrifying goddess **Durga**, whose Balinese personality is the gruesome widow-witch Rangda, queen of the demons. The son of Siwa and Durga is the elephant-headed deity **Ganesh**, generally worshipped as the remover of obstacles.

Brahma, Wisnu and Siwa all have associated lesser deities or **dewi** (**dewa** if male), many of them gods of the elements and of the physical world. The most famous of these, and certainly the most widely worshipped, is **Dewi Sri**, the goddess of rice.

The forces of evil are personified by a cast of **bhuta** and **kala**, invisible goblins and ghosts who inhabit eerie, desolate places like the temples of the dead, cemeteries, moonless seashores and dark forests. Various strategies are used to repel, confuse and banish the *bhuta* and *kala*. Most entrance gates to temples and households are guarded by fierce-looking statues and demonic images designed to be so ugly as to frighten off even the boldest demon. Many gateways are also blocked by a low brick wall, an *aling-aling*, as demons can only walk in straight lines, and so won't be able to negotiate the necessary zigzag to get around the wall. These demons can also be appeased and placated with offerings just as the gods can – the difference being that the offerings for the demons consist mainly of dirty, unpleasant, unattractive and mouldy things, which are thrown down on the ground, not placed respectfully on ledges and altars.

In addition to the unseen *bhuta* and *kala*, there are the equally fearful **leyak**, or witches, who take highly visible and creepy forms, transforming themselves into such horrors as headless chickens and riderless motorbikes. *Leyak* can transform themselves effortlessly from one form to another, and most assume the human form during the daytime. Even in their human form, *leyak* cannot be killed with knives or poisons, but they can be controlled and disempowered by harnessing white magic, as practised by **shamanic balian** (traditional healers), or by priests.

The temples

The focus of every community's spiritual activity is the **temple** or *pura* – a specially designed temporary abode for the gods to inhabit whenever they so desire, open and unroofed so as to invite easy access between heaven and earth. Every *banjar* or small village is obliged to build at least three temples, each one serving a specific role within the community. At the top of the village stands the **pura puseh**, the temple of origin, which is dedicated to the founders of the community. For everyday spiritual activities, villagers worship at the **pura desa**, the village temple, which always lies at the heart of the village. The essential triumvirate is completed by the **pura dalem**, or temple of the dead, at the *kelod* (unclean) end of the village, which is usually dedicated either to Siwa, or to the widow-witch Rangda.

Bali also has nine directional temples, or *kayangan jagat*, which are regarded as extremely sacred by all islanders as they protect the island as a whole and all its people. The *kayangan jagat* are located at strategic points across the island, especially on high mountain slopes, rugged cliff-faces and lakeside shores.

Nearly all Balinese temples are designed around three courtyards, each section divided from the next by a low wall punctuated by a huge, and usually ornate, gateway. The outer courtyard or **jaba**, holds the secular world at bay. The middle courtyard, the **jaba tengah**, acts as a transition zone between the human and the divine world, and generally contains pavilions for the preparation of offerings and the storing of temple paraphernalia. The extremely sacred inner courtyard, or **jeroan**, houses all the shrines, and is the focus of all temple rituals. All offerings are brought here, prayers are held in front of the shrines, and the most sacred dances are performed within its confines. The *jeroan* is quite often out of bounds to the lay community and opened only during festivals.

Every *pura* contains a whole collection of small structures, each one devoted to a specific purpose. *Gedong* is the generic term for the squat, often cube-shaped shrines that are generally made of brick, with thatched roofs. Each *gedong* is dedicated to a particular deity or ancestor, and sometimes contains a symbolic image. The elegant pagoda-style shrines that tower over every temple wall are known as *meru*, after the sacred Hindu peak **Mount Meru**, home of the gods. There is always an odd number of roofs (three, five, seven, nine or eleven), the number indicating the status of the god to whom the temple is dedicated.

Temple festivals

Aside from the daily propitiation of the household spirits, Agama Hinduism requires no regular act of collective worship from its devotees. The temple's **anniversary celebration**, or *odalan*, is a three-day devotional extravaganza held at every temple either once every 210 days (every Balinese calendar year), or once every 365 days (the *saka* year). The purpose is always the same: to invite the gods down to earth so that they can be entertained and pampered by as many displays of devotion and gratitude as the community can afford. In the days before the *odalan*, the *pemangku* (priest) dresses the temple statues in holy cloths, either the spiritually charged black and white *kain poleng*, or a length of plain cloth in the colour symbolic of that temple's deity. Meanwhile, the women of the community begin to construct their offering towers, or *banten*, and to cook ceremonial food.

Odalan celebrations start in the afternoon, with a procession of women carrying their offerings to the temple. At the *pura*, the offerings are taken into the inner sanctum where the *pemangku* receives them and then blesses the devotees with holy water. Sometimes the gods will temporarily inhabit the body of one of the worshippers, sending him or her into a trance and conveying its message through gestures or words. Elsewhere in the temple compound, there's generally some performance going on: the local gamelan orchestra play, and often sacred dances are performed as well, particularly the *pendet* or offertory dance and perhaps a *barong* as well. After dark, a shadow play, wayang kulit, is often staged.

Music

The shimmering sounds of the gamelan have fascinated and delighted Western visitors to Indonesia for half a millennium. Sir Francis Drake, who visited Java in 1580, described music "of a very strange kind, pleasant and delightful" – which sums up most people's reaction. The structural complexity of the music alongside its sonorous and ethereal sound gives it a lasting fascination. From the beginning of the twentieth century, composers as diverse as Debussy, Messiaen, Britten and John Cage were inspired by the music and, in recent years, there's been an enthusiastic growth of gamelan ensembles in Britain and the US. Javanese gamelan is predominantly slow and refined, whereas Balinese is fast and quixotic – and there are many other types besides. The popular music scene in Indonesia is one of the most robust and exciting in Southeast Asia, from the bewildering range of folk and popular styles throughout the islands, to the world of *kroncong*, *dangdut*, *jaipongan* and more.

Gamelan

A **gamelan** has been described as "one instrument played by many people". It's an ensemble of tuned percussion, consisting mainly of gongs, metallophones and drums. Gamelan **instruments** may be made of bronze, iron, brass, wood or bamboo, with wooden frames, which are often intricately carved and painted. The term "gamelan" covers a wide variety of ensembles ranging from the bronze court gamelans of Central Java to the bamboo village orchestras in Bali.

Central Java

The largest **bronze gamelans** in Indonesia are found in **Central Java**. A complete Javanese gamelan is made up of two sets of instruments, one in each of two scales – the five-note *laras slendro* and the seven-note *laras pelog*. The two sets are laid out with the corresponding instruments at right angles to each other. No two gamelans are tuned exactly alike, and a Javanese musician will often prefer the sound and feeling of a piece played on one gamelan to another. Larger bronze gamelans are traditionally given a name, such as "The Venerable Rain of Love".

All the instruments in the gamelan have a clear role to play, and this is reflected in the **layout** of the ensemble. Various hanging and mounted gongs are arranged at the back of the gamelan and provide the structure and form of the music. In the middle, the metallophones play the central melody. At the front are the more complex instruments, which lead and elaborate the melody. These include metallophones, a wooden xylophone, spike fiddle, bamboo flute and zither. The full ensemble also includes vocalists – a male chorus and female solo singers – and is led by the drummer in the centre of the gamelan.

The large **gong** (*gong ageng*) at the back of the gamelan is the most important instrument in the ensemble, and it's believed that the spirit of the gamelan resides within it. A large gong can be over 1m in diameter, and is made from a single piece of bronze. The skilled gongsmiths of Central Java are highly respected, and receive orders from the whole of Java and Bali.

Although a large gamelan may be played by as many as thirty musicians, there is neither a conductor nor any visual cues, as the players all sit facing the same way. Musical notation, although now used extensively in teaching, is never used in performance. Gamelan musicians learn all the instruments and so develop a deep understanding of the music, combined with great sensitivity and flexibility in ensemble playing. During an all-night **wayang kulit**, you may see musicians changing places, and special guests are sometimes invited to play. Gamelan is a communal form of music-making – there are no soloists or virtuosos – and although the female singers tend to use microphones, they are not considered soloists in the Western sense.

Some of the finest gamelans in Java are housed in the courts, including a number of **ceremonial gamelans**; some of the ceremonial gamelans are believed to be magically charged. The gongs are the most sacred instruments, and are given offerings of flowers and incense before performances. The largest and loudest, known as **Gamelan Sekaten**, are still played once a year in the palace mosques of Solo and Yogya. These large gamelans were built in the early days of Islam in Java to draw people into the mosques. To this day a pair of Gamelan Sekaten are played almost continuously for a week during the **sekaten festival**, to commemorate the birth and death of the prophet Mohammed. The powerful sound of these gamelans attracts huge crowds into the mosques, where calls to prayer mingle with gamelan music, incense, offerings, and the hubbub of the fair outside.

However, gamelan music is played by a wide range of people in Central Java. Most village halls and neighbourhoods in major towns have a gamelan for use by the local community. The majority of schoolchildren learn basic gamelan pieces and can continue their studies in conservatories and academies of performing arts in the major towns of Solo and Yogyakarta. Gamelan music accompanies many types of dance and theatre, ranging from lively village **ketoprak** performances to the refined palace **srimpi** dance. The radio station RRI (Radio Republik Indonesia) employs professional studio musicians and broadcasts a wide range of gamelan music.

Bali

Most villages in **Bali** boast several gamelans owned by the local music club. The club members meet in the evenings to rehearse, after earning their living as farmers, craftsmen or civil servants. Gamelan playing is traditionally considered a part of every man's education, as important as the art of rice growing or cooking ceremonial food. Children also play, and learn by sitting in their father's laps as they rehearse.

The **village gamelan** is kept in a public place, and rehearsals usually draw an interested audience of onlookers who offer comments and suggestions. Many villages have a distinctive style or speciality: Peliatan is known for the refinement of its courtly *legong* dance and music, Sukawati for the complexity and brilliance of its *gender* playing. It's said that people can find their way around the island in the dark by recognizing the distinctive tones of the local gamelans shimmering across the rice fields.

When the Dutch took control of Bali in the early twentieth century, the island's courts all but disappeared, with an enormous impact on the musical life of the island. The court gamelans had no function outside the palace walls and were sold or taken to the villages where they were melted down to make new gamelans for the latest style that was taking Bali by storm: **kebyar**. The word literally means "like the bursting open of a flower". *Kebyar* originated in north

Bali and replaced the slow, stately court pieces with fast, dynamic music, full of dramatic contrasts, changes of tempo and sudden outbursts. It was not long before Bali's most famous dancer, **I Mario**, choreographed the first *kebyar* dance, in which the intricate and beautiful movements of the dancer's eyes, head and hands mirror the dazzling display of the music. It is this dynamic new virtuoso style that makes much Balinese gamelan music today sound so different from the Javanese form.

Kebyar has influenced other ensembles in Bali: the most stunning example being the all-bamboo **joged bumbung**, Even the "gong" is made from bamboo. *Joged bumbung* is very popular in West Bali, where it developed in the 1950s from a small bamboo ensemble used to accompany lively village dances.

Where Javanese music is quiet, contemplative and restrained, Balinese is loud, sparkling and extrovert. It is, after all, outdoor music. Like the elaborate temple carvings and paintings, the music is intricately detailed. Just as the harmony of village life depends on the delicate balance of opposing forces, so in the gamelan the instruments appear in pairs, even the drums, which are called male and female.

The rhythmic vitality of Balinese music comes from lively interlocking patterns played on various pairs of instruments. These patterns, called **kotekan**, are played on the bronze *gangsas* (similar to the Javanese *gender* but struck with hard wooden mallets), a pair of drums and the *reong* (a row of small kettle-gongs in a frame, played by four people).

Apart from the rhythm, there's another kind of beat in Balinese gamelan music. The various pairs of instruments are tuned slightly "out" with each other, so that when two instruments are played together, there is a "harmonic beating". This gives the sound of the Balinese gamelan its characteristic shimmering quality.

West Java (Sunda)

The island of Java is inhabited by several ethnic groups, each producing their own musical style. The Sundanese, for example, live mainly in West Java – the so-called Sunda region – and their **degung** is arguably the most accessible of all gamelan music to Western ears. Its musical structures are clear and well-defined, and the timbres of the instruments blend delicately with one another without losing any of their integrity or individuality. The ensemble is small, consisting only of a few instruments, but includes the usual range of gongs and metallophones found in all gamelan. However, the very special character of *degung*, which uses its own five-note version of the *pelog* scale found in the rest of Java, owes much to the additional presence of the **suling** and is regarded as something of a signature for Sundanese music. In fact, no other instrument more perfectly exemplifies the musical heart of Sunda or better conjures up the traditional picture of gentle, picturesque paddy-fields and restful, idyllic village life.

Degung is unique to Sunda, and was developed during the last century. Deriving from a court tradition, it has a more exalted place among the performing arts than gamelan *salendro* – although the best musicians frequent the circles of both – and is now mainly used in concert form for wedding receptions and other social events. Nevertheless, examples of *degung* for *tari topeng* (masked dances) exist, and, more recently, augmented forms of the ensemble have been used to accompany performances of wayang golek. In addition, it has made inroads into popular culture through **"pop Sunda"** (using Western pop instruments) which achieved immense popularity during the 1980s through the hands of composers such as **Nano S.** (see p.1069).

East Java

Heading through East Java, the prevailing musical style becomes marked by increasing dynamism and aggressiveness. Whilst it is true to say that groups performing in the province's capital city of Surabaya often play pieces in a mixture of styles, those from rural areas, particularly from around the town of Malang, are usually more genuinely **East Javanese** in expression.

Perhaps the most dramatic element of East Javanese gamelan music, and certainly one not found outside the region, is that of the **gamyak drum**. Larger than the Central Javanese equivalent, its drumheads are made from buffalo rather than goat skin, and the piercing sound produced is immediately recognizable. It is especially associated with the *ngremo* dance – the drumming for which is considered some of the most technically demanding anywhere in Java – and various forms of *tari topeng* (masked dance) popular around Malang. In addition, *tayuban* – dances where male spectators may request pieces from the gamelan and, for a small gratuity, dance with one of the *tandhak* (female dancers) present – have helped steer the popular gamelan repertoire away from the classical refinement associated with Central Java. Once common throughout Java, these are rowdy affairs and only continue to exist in areas where Islam has a limited influence on daily life. As a consequence it is still popular in the Tengger region, where the prevailing religion synthesizes elements of Hinduism with pre-Hindu beliefs.

By Jenny Heaton and Simon Steptoe

Gamelan discography

Bali

Bali: A Suite of Tropical Music and Sound (World Network, Germany). Volume 35 in WN's ambitious global survey. The ideal introduction to the varied sounds of Balinese music, beginning with frogs and cicadas. Includes many of the lesser-known gamelan styles – *gambuh, selunding, jegog, joged bumbung* and *kecak*. The only thing missing is the straight *kebyar* sound, but there's plenty of that to be found elsewhere.

Gamelan Semar Pegulingan Saih Pitu: The Heavenly Orchestra of Bali (CMP, Germany). The "love gamelan", the ethereal, tinkling sound of this sort of ensemble, accompanied the king while he slept with the queen. Gamelan, flutes and drums in a lovely clear recording of a 29-strong ensemble from Kamasan, eastern Bali. The best Semar Pegulingan recording, with good sleeve notes.

Gamelan Semar Pegulingan (II) (JVC, Japan). The Semar Pegulingan group from Peliatan village. Another exquisite recording without the bamboo flutes but with atmospheric insects in the background. Poor notes in English.

Jegog of Nagara (King, Japan). The best *jegog* disc around. Thunderous sound, lots of atmosphere and the competing of two groups from West Bali; turn it up loud and enjoy the thrill.

Music for the Gods (Rykodisc, US). Recordings made (mostly in Bali) in 1941 by Bruce and Sheridan Fahnestock, weeks before World War II and later tourism changed the island forever. These unique recordings include Semar Pegulingan, *kebyar*, a *gender* quartet for wayang and *kecak*, plus three tracks of fascinating material from the island of Madura.

Java

Gamelan of the Kraton, Yogyakarta (Celestial Harmonies, US). The most atmospheric and beautifully recorded of Javanese gamelan discs. Here the court musicians play grandiose ceremonial pieces, elegant dance repertoire and the extraordinary music, peculiar to the Yogya kraton, of the *bedhaya* dance with added snare drums and brass. Excellent.

Gamelan of Surakarta (JVC, Japan). The best introduction available to the Surakarta style of Javanese gamelan. Three pieces played by the Surakarta School of Indonesian Arts (STSI), from serene music with choral singing to dynamic and varied instrumental playing, co-ordinated by the virtuoso drumming of Rahayu Supanggah, the composer. The final piece, intended to accompany traditional dance drama, reveals gamelan as a living, developing tradition.

West Java

Flutes and Gamelan Music of West Java (Topic Records, UK). A rare glimpse of gamelan music from Cirebon, as well as a selection of *kecapi suling*. It features Sulaeman, a player of the Sundanese *suling* with a recording career stretching back to the days of 78s.

Java – Pays Sunda, 2: L'art du Gamelan Degung (Ocora, France). One of the definitive recordings of gamelan *degung* currently available in the West, with a fine representation of pieces from the classical repertoire as well as new compositions, Featuring the bamboo flute playing of Ono Sukarna.

Tembang Sunda (Nimbus, UK). Mellow performances from male and female vocalists, Imas Permas and Asep Kosasih, accompanied by zither and flute; a refined classical repertoire plus more easy-going love songs. Translations included.

Other

Banyumas Bamboo Gamelan (Nimbus, UK). The only widely available recording of Banyumas *calung* music, the Javanese bamboo gamelan. Traditional dance pieces with vocals and some more contemporary styles drawing on *jaipongan* and *dangdut*. Great frog imitations on track no. 3.

Lombok, Kalimantan, Banyumas: Little-Known Forms of Gamelan and Wayang (Smithsonian Folkways, US). Part fourteen of SF's extensive survey of Indonesian music features *wayang sasak* from Lombok, a theatrical form related to Balinese *gambuh*; masked and shadow theatre music from South Kalimantan; and *jemblung* from Banyumas which comprises amazing vocal imitations of gamelan.

New Gamelan music

Asmat Dream (Lyrichord, US). More for gamelan or new music specialists perhaps, but ample illustration of the radical experiments under way with gamelan and other traditional instruments. Includes music by four Sundanese composers, including Nano S.

Music of K.R.T. Wasitodiningrat (CMP, Germany). *Rebab* player and composer Wasitodiningrat was associated with the Paku Alaman court gamelan of Yogyakarta. The eight compositions on this disc are within the traditional framework of Central Javanese gamelan.

Thanks to Penny King and Maria Mendonça for help with the discography.

Pop

There are any number of rock groups, rappers, boy groups and pop singers and a growing dance scene for which the name "house" has been co-opted. It seems that every region has its own house music – Bali House, Java House, Batak House from Sumatra and so on. But this is not to discount the ongoing popularity of the more identifiably home-grown **pop music**: *kroncong, dangdut, jaipongan, degung, pop-Sunda, mandarin, pop-batak* and *qasidah*.

Kroncong

Kroncong (pronounced ker-ong-chong), can trace its roots back several centuries to when the Portuguese were establishing trade links with Africa and South Asia. The arrival of European instruments laid the basis for what later became the first major urban-folk style. By the early 1900s, *kroncong* was mainly associated with the lowlife of the cities, but began gaining national popularity in the 1930s through its use by the new Indonesian film industry. During the independence struggle, many inspirational patriotic songs were set to *kroncong* music.

At that time, a typical ensemble consisted of two *kroncong* (three-string ukuleles), guitar, violin, flute, percussion and, variously, a cello played pizzicato or a double bass accompanying a singer, usually female. The distinctive *kroncong* rhythm is set up by the two ukuleles – one known as the *cik*, the other as the *cuk* – playing alternate strokes of the beat. The medium-pace tempo, the diatonic melodies and the languid, crooning singing style invite comparison with east African Taarab music and even Portuguese Fado. The most celebrated *kroncong* number, *Bengawan Solo*, was written by composer and singer Gesang in 1943. It's about the beauty of the river in Solo and is probably the most famous and most covered of Indonesian pop songs. In and around Solo, there's also a regional style of *kroncong* called **langgam jawa**, an enchanting and sentimental sound in which the *pelog* (seven-note) scale and textures of gamelan music are imitated by the *kroncong* ensemble.

Gambang Kromong

Gambang kromong developed out of the type of *kroncong* music featured in an urban folk-theatre form called *komedi stambul*, popular in the early decades of the twentieth century. If you travel to the town of Tangerang, about two hour's drive from Jakarta, you may be able to catch the modern-day equivalent called *lenong*, or get yourself invited to a wedding. In either case the music will be *gambang kromong* played on a bewildering array of Chinese, Indonesian and Western instruments. A typical ensemble can bring together two-string fiddle, bamboo flute (*suling*), xylophone (*gambang*), pot-gongs, drums and percussion from the Javanese gamelan, plus one or more Western instruments such as trumpet, keyboards, electric bass guitar, clarinet or Hawaiian guitar. Melodies weave in and out and against the *loping* percussive backdrop, sounding at times like a Dixieland jazz band jamming with a gamelan.

Dangdut

Dang-dut-dang-dut-dang-dut-dang-dut. You can't mistake it and you'll hear it everywhere you go. **Dangdut**, Indonesia's equivalent of danceable Latin music, has been thriving since the mid-1970s. It grew out of *kroncong* and *orkes Melayu* (Malay) – the sort of music typified by Malaysia's P. Ramlee – but its most obvious influence is that of Indian film song. As with many Indonesian musical terms, *dangdut* is an onomatopoeic word derived from the rhythm, usually played on the *gendang* (a pair of bongo-like drums tuned to sound like *tabla*). So that you know your dang from your dut, count in fours and hear the low dang note struck on the fourth beat and the high dut note struck on the first beat of the following bar. Alongside the *gendang*, a typical group consists of electric guitar, bass, mandolin, drum kit and keyboards. But the real stars, of course, are the singers: glamorous men and women singing of love found, lost and wanted or of moral issues, family matters – the everyday and fantasy life of the *dangdut* audience.

Following on from the *orkes Melayu* crooners like Munif and Ellya Agus, came the first superstars of *dangdut*. **Rhoma Irama** and **Elvy Sukaesih** are still known today as the king and queen of *dangdut*. They made many successful recordings as a duo in the early 1970s, and both have many million-selling albums to their credit. Rhoma Irama has always been identified as a "working class hero"; starting out as a long-haired rebel, he found his true artistic direction only after his *haj* to Mecca. He went on to star in several films and still tours regularly with his Soneta group, putting his inspirational messages over with all the paraphernalia of a full-blown rock-show.

Jaipongan

Just occasionally in the *dangdut* dancehalls, the drum machines and bendy guitars may be interrupted by a percussion-based style with an unpredictable tempo. This will be **jaipongan**, a style that has no detectable Western influence, using only instruments from the Sundanese gamelan tradition.

The *rebab* (a two-stringed bowed fiddle) plays the introduction, as the *khendang* (a large two-headed barrel drum) improvises in free time underneath; then, with whooping cries, the rest of the orchestra enters. The *khendang* sets to building and releasing tension through a cyclical pattern marked by a single stroke on a large gong, while a smaller gong, a *kempul*, beats out one-note basslines. The mellow sounds of the *bonang rincik* and the *panerus* (sets of pot-shaped gongs) play stately cyclical melodies as the *saron* (a row of seven bronze keys set over a resonating box) hammers out faster arpeggios. The *rebab* anticipates, accompanies and answers the singer (*pesindhen*) as she floats like a butterfly through tales of love, money and agriculture, while throughout, various members of the orchestra indulge in more whooping, wailing and rhythmic grunting known as *senggak*.

It was in Bandung that *jaipongan* first appeared in the mid-1960s. By the end of the decade, it had become a national dance-craze, and all without an electric guitar in sight. *Jaipongan* is still popular today, and in recent years, the distinctive drumming style has been co-opted by several *dangdut* artists.

Degung, Kecapi Suling and Pop-Sunda

Wistful, melancholic, meditative, the sound of **degung** embodies the feeling Indonesians describe as "Sakit Hati". The literal English translation is "sick liver", but, of course, that is losing some of the romantic inference. In Bahasa Indonesia, the poetic organ of affection is the liver rather than the heart, and "Sakit Hati" describes a feeling of longing and sadness.

Gamelan degung developed as a court music deemed the most suitable for playing while guests were arriving at social occasions, and modern *degung* music performs a similar function today. It has found a whole new audience, particularly among tourists in Bali, where *degung* cassettes provide the ambience in many cafés and restaurants. It is peaceful, harmonious background music, characterized by gentle percussion, delicate improvising on the *suling* and soft arpeggios played on the *bonang* and *saron*, and underpinned by the warm tones of the hanging gongs which give the music its name.

Kecapi Suling is an instrumental form developed from another court tradition of sung entertainment music called *tembang Sunda*. A typical ensemble consists of a *suling* accompanied by two or three *kecapi* – a zither or koto-like instrument of varying sizes and number of strings. Each string has a separate bridge to facilitate tuning between various modes. *Kecapi Suling* utilizes the pentatonic scales known as *pelog* and *sorog*. When singing is included, the haunting melodies carry poetic and sometimes mysterious images sung in Sundanese.

A mark of quality to look out for is the name of **Nano S.** on the cassette cover. This amazingly prolific composer is also responsible for some of the best examples of the **pop-Sunda** style, where *degung* meets modern technology. Sequenced drum and bass patterns accompany the traditional-style melodies, and often all the Sundanese instruments are replaced by synthesized sounds.

Qasidah Modern

Qasidah is a classical Arabic word for epic religious poetry, traditionally performed by a storyteller-singer, accompanied by percussion and chanting. Indonesian Muslims practise their own versions of this, improvising lyrics in local languages that address contemporary concerns and moral issues.

Qasidah modern places this in a pop-song form, adding electric guitars, mandolin, keyboards, violins and flutes. Rhythms and melodies from *dangdut* and Arabic pop are used, while the lyrics frequently offer moral advice to young lovers, extolling a virtuous life and warning against corruption and other temptations. Sometimes the lyrics even tackle environmental issues such as pollution, nuclear power and cigarette smoking.

The pioneers of *qasidah modern* are **Nasida Ria**, a nine-woman orchestra from Semarang who have released over 25 albums and have twice toured Germany. One of their albums is available on the Berlin-based Piranha label. At home they perform chiefly at Muslim weddings throughout Java or occasionally at open-air rallies sponsored by religious groups, where the proceedings are opened by a sermon or two before the orchestra takes the stage. In their colourful headscarves and close-fitting dresses covering them from head to foot, they manage to look simultaneously alluring and modest, and the occasional heavy-metal posturing of the guitarists is also conducted with great decorum.

If the strong Arabic influence of this music is to your taste then you might want to plan a trip along the north coast of Java to **Surabaya**, home of Gambus music.

Gambus

Gambus is the Indonesian word for the Arabic lute, the *oud*, but it is now used to denote both a style of music and the orchestra that plays it. The *oud* was brought to Indonesia along with Islam, and much of the music and dances associated with it were introduced by settlers from the Yemen. In the Arab quarter in Surabaya, you may hear the voice of **Oum Kalthoum** wafting out of one of the shops in the bazaar, or it could be Surabaya's own diva, **Soraya**. You may also hear what sounds like a typical modern pop production from Saudi or Kuwait, but it is more likely to be one of the local stars of the *gambus* modern scene – **Muhdar Alatas** or **Ali Alatas** (no relation).

Many *gambus* songs are lifted straight from imported Arabic cassettes and given a local stamp. Some retain the Arabic texts, many are rewritten in Bahasa Indonesia. All the hallmarks of great Arabic pop are there: rolling rhythms on the *derbuka* and the *oud*, sinuous melody lines on flute and violins and, regardless of the language, much silky ornamentation of the vocal lines from the singer. Although loved by millions, *gambus* is hardly known outside Indonesia, and there are still no recordings available internationally.

By Colin Bass

Pop music discography

Kroncong and dangdut

Music of Indonesia Vol 2: Kroncong, Dangdut and Langgam Jawa (Smithsonian Folkways, US). Part of Philip Yampolsky's ambitious series, and certainly the most approachable for newcomers. Beautiful *kroncong* tracks, with good *dangdut* selections from the Soneta Group with Rhoma Irama, Elvy Sukaesih and others. Excellent sleeve notes.

Street Music of Java (Original Music, US). Wonderful recordings made in the late 1970s of more homespun versions of *kroncong* and *dangdut*, plus *ronggeng* dances and zither music.

Hetty Koes Endang *Keroncong Asli* (Musica, Indonesia). Currently available only in Indonesia, recorded in the early 1980s, but still sounding fresh. This is high-quality *kroncong* by the most versatile of popular singers, accompanied by the greatest orchestra of the time, Orkes Kroncong Bintang Jakarta.

Rhoma Irama *Begadang 1975–1980* (Meta, Japan). A good introduction to the rock-influenced style of the man still known as the king of *dangdut*. Featuring some of his most famous songs including the great *Santai* ("*Relax*").

Elvy Sukaesih *Raja dan Ratu* (Rice Records, Japan).Featuring Rhoma Irama and Elvy Sukaesih, these are sparkling pop gems from the early 1970s from the king and queen (*raja* and *ratu*) of *dangdut*.

Jaipongan and Pop-Sunda

Hetty Koes Endang *The Best of Sundanese Pop Songs* (Musica, Indonesia).Only available in Indonesia, but an essential buy if you're there. Sweet, haunting melodies with pop arrangements, including the multi-million selling hit *Cinta*.

Jugala Orchestra *The Sound of Sunda* (GlobeStyle, UK).A cross section of modern *degung* and other popular music. To be played "after 6pm in a peaceful environment, while your guests are arriving for dinner, or when your love-object has left you". Strongly recommended.

Detty Kurnia *Coyor Panon* (Wave, Japan; Flame Tree, UK). Detty Kurnia, the daughter of a famous Sundanese gamelan player, is pop-Sunda's brightest star, singing both pop and traditional styles. A first-class collection of songs betraying the influence of *degung*, *jaipongan*, *calung* and more. Highly recommended, although currently unavailable.

Yayah Ratnasari & Karawang Group *Break Pong* (Meta Co, Japan). This female vocalist and band are one of the best current *jaipongan* outfits, based in the Sundanese town of Karawang. An unusual recording; they obviously had lots of fun adding a drum machine to their traditional percussion setup.

Traditional

Sing Sing So: Songs of the Batak People (JVC, Japan). The Batak are famed for the beauty of their folk songs, justifiably so, on the strength of these performances. The tunes are rather European in character with a strongly lyrical line but Southeast Asian warmth. Solo songs are accompanied by Western-style guitar, while wonderful instrumental tracks of wooden gamelan and flute and choral numbers sound distinctly evangelical. Very approachable.

Contemporary

Djaduk Ferianto & Kua Etnika *Nang Ning Nong Orkes Sumpeg* (Galang Comm, Indonesia). Djaduk Ferianto and his group use instruments from all over the archipelago to create their own "world music". So far only available in Indonesia, this is an exciting new direction from Yogyakarta; traditional violins, flutes, percussion and metallophones interact with modern keyboard sounds and global rhythms. Recommended.

Moluccan Moods Orchestra *Wakoi* (Piranha, Germany). A band of expatriates based in Holland, led by guitarist Eddy Lekransy until his death in 1988. Moluccan songs are given a contemporary jazz-funk treatment, with guitar, keyboards, sax, flutes and percussion, plus wonderful harmony singing from the three female vocalists.

Sabah Habas Mustapha *Denpasar Moon* (Wave, Japan; Piranha, Germany). A wonderful disc from 1994. *Dangdut* and Sundanese styles performed with musicians in Jakarta with global rhythms and English lyrics. Great for reminiscing about those fleeting holiday romances and strongly recommended even if you've never set foot there.

Nasida Ria *Keadilan* (Piranha, Germany). The leading exponents of *qasidah modern*. Hugely successful nine-member, all-female band from Central Java with a moralistic message. An enjoyable, bouncy mix of Arabic and *dangdut* styles, sung with plenty of synthesizer plus flute and violin.

Environment and wildlife

Indonesia's environment and wildlife reflect the country's unique position as a series of island stepping stones between the Southeast Asian mainland and Australia, comprising some of the last great expanses of prime tropical wilderness on earth. While it's possible to visit areas which have hardly changed since they were first seen by Europeans in the mid-nineteenth century, it's also true that Indonesia's natural history – in common with that of Asia, Africa and South America – is also under severe threat from the modern world.

Habitats and inhabitants

Although all of Indonesia is equatorial, resulting in locally stable temperatures and rainfall, varied geology has created a huge range of habitats. Most famous, perhaps, is the country's position on the "Ring of Fire", a tectonic fault line responsible for creating much of the archipelago, and centring the world's greatest concentration of active **volcanoes** in Java and Bali. Elsewhere, older ranges have eroded to form the **alluvial lowlands** of Sumatra, Kalimantan and West Papua. Southern Kalimantan's **peat beds** are compressed ancient forests, while uplifted fossil reefs are the basis of the porous **limestone** hills of southern Sulawesi and southeastern Maluku. And, as Indonesia's thousands of islands encompass terrain ranging from sandy beaches to snow-clad mountains, you'll also find a broad slice of the world's environments represented within this single country: montane heathland, temperate, tropical and even deciduous forests, savannah and semi-arid grassland, and coastal sand flats fringed by swamps.

Indonesia's flora and fauna can be split into three **biological zones**. The western section, from Sumatra to Bali, was once connected to the Asian mainland during lower ice-age sea levels, which allowed **Oriental** species to cross and colonize. Over in the east, West Papua and parts of Maluku were similarly once joined to Australia, and so are home to mainly **Australasian** species. The region in between, which contains a mixture of Oriental, Australasian and unique species, is known as **Wallacea** after the naturalist who first recognized the division – see the box opposite. In addition, the abrupt volcanic formation of many islands results in typically steep **underwater** drop-offs, encouraging abundant coral reefs with a staggering range of marine life.

Flora

Indonesia has the most extensive coastal **mangrove swamps** in tropical Asia, concentrated in West Papua and Kalimantan. Though not the prettiest of trees, mangroves are specially adapted to living in salt water, many species having distinctively arched and buttressed roots, and they aerate the typically thick, sticky mud that they live in. Another salt-tolerant tree, the **nipa palm**, has a trunk which grows almost completely underwater in brackish estuaries, with just the tall fronds showing. Indonesia has a palm tree for almost every situation: cultivated coconuts; thorny rattan, which look like vines but are actually a climbing palm and are used all over the country in furniture, houses and household goods; sago from Maluku, the pith of which is turned into tapioca; tall, elegant

Wallace and Wallacea

Born in 1823, **Alfred Russell Wallace** was a largely self-educated naturalist who spent his early professional life hunting wildlife in Europe and the Amazon for museum collections. In 1854, he began what was to become a 22,000-kilometre, eight-year expedition to Indonesia (engagingly recounted in his book *The Malay Archipelago*), amassing 125,000 specimens and discovering countless new creatures for science.

During his travels in Indonesia, Wallace noticed how similar animals varied between islands, and began to wonder if isolated environments might allow identical forms to **evolve** over time into completely different species. This prompted his 1858 thesis, *On the Tendency of Varieties to Depart Indefinitely from the Original Type*, which he sent from his north Maluku base to the foremost biologist of the day, **Charles Darwin**. Unknown to Wallace, Darwin had formulated a similar theory 25 years earlier whilst in the Galapagos islands; fearing the negative reception such a notion would receive in creationist Victorian England, however, he had kept his conclusions private. The two now made a joint public announcement, but, with Wallace still in distant Indonesia, it was Darwin whose name became fixed in the public mind as the inventor of evolutionary theory following publication in 1859 of his classic *On the Origin of Species by Means of Natural Selection*.

Not begrudging Darwin his fame – he even dedicated his book *The Malay Archipelago* to him – Wallace spent the rest of his ninety years refining his views on **biogeography**, the factors affecting the distribution of species throughout the world. Most importantly, he identified Indonesia as a crossover point between Oriental and Australasian fauna, and drew a definite line running north through the region between Bali and Lombok, and Borneo and Sulawesi, either side of which species were predominantly either Oriental or Australasian. A straightforward idea in itself, **Wallace's Line** became the subject of a complicated set of revisions, clarified in the 1920s by the creation of **Wallacea**, a region which sidesteps definite boundaries by encapsulating Sulawesi, Nusa Tenggara and Maluku as a biological **transition zone** between Asia and Australasia. With wildlife and plants from both regions to draw upon, as well as a huge number of species found nowhere else – over 240 endemic types of bird, for example – Wallacea remains one of the richest hunting grounds on earth for anyone interested in natural history.

arecas, source of the stimulating betel nut; and lontar fan palms, a hardy species equally at home in Maluku's swampy lowland forest and drier parts of Sulawesi and Nusa Tenggara, where trees stand widely spaced across the grasslands.

Indonesia's rainforests range from steamy, swampy lowland jungle thick with bamboo, vines, gingers, ferns and lianas, to high-altitude cloud forests where trees are whiskered in **orchids**, carnivorous pitcher plants, patches of moss and strands of old man's beard. Western Indonesian forests are dominated by dipterocarps, a family of trees found from Asia through to Africa which includes teak and meranti, both valuable timbers. Of no commercial use, **rafflesia** is a rainforest parasite found mainly on Java and Sumatra, whose family includes the largest, tallest, and smelliest fruiting bodies of any plants. Further east, forest giants are more likely to be **quandongs**, whose spherical blue seeds litter the ground in Aru and parts of West Papua, or figs, some of which start life as a seedling at the top of another tree before encircling and strangling the host. The myrtle family is also well represented in Wallacea and the east: there are some massive gum trees as far west as central Sulawesi, while both cloves and aromatic ti-tree oil (once famous as Makassar oil) are derived from myrtle trees native to Maluku. Right over in southeastern West Papua, the country becomes downright Australian, an open savannah peppered with wattles and sclerophyl.

Fauna

The populations of **large mammals** found in western Indonesia dwindle rapidly as you move east through the archipelago. Along with five kinds of deer, the forests of Java and Sumatra are the last place you've a chance to see wild tigers, rhino or elephants in Southeast Asia. There's also a range of primates here, including chunky macaques, long-armed gibbons and the orange-furred orang-utan of Kalimantan and Sumatra, while Kalimantan's riverine forests are home to the big-nosed proboscis monkey, a vegetarian ape which enjoys swimming.

Deer are still found in parts of Wallacea, along with a few monkeys such as Sulawesi's black macaque, but are overshadowed by some unusual animals such as Nusa Tenggara's giant **Komodo dragon**, a three-metre-long monitor lizard, and Sulawesi's mysterious **babirusa**, a horned pig-like beast with no known relatives. This region is also renowned for its **birdlife**, including endemic hornbills, parrots, pigeons and megapodes, grouse-sized birds which incubate their eggs in a specially constructed mound of rotting leaves and soil. You'll also start to encounter a trickle of distinctly Australian creatures in Wallacea – cockatoos for instance – which become prolific further east in West Papua. The most distinctive are the **marsupials**, or pouched mammals, who give birth to a partially formed embryo which is nurtured in a special pouch. Indonesian examples include forest-dwelling, slow-moving cuscus possums, found as far west as Sulawesi, with grassland-loving wallabies and kangaroos, along with arboreal **tree kangaroos**, confined to West Papua and nearby islands. Looking like a long-nosed porcupine or hedgehog, West Papua's ant-eating **echidnas** are even stranger, one of only two egg-laying mammals (the other is eastern Australia's platypus). Lowland vine forests in West Papua and eastern Maluku are also home to the ostrich-like cassowary, while full-blown West Papuan rainforest hides over twenty species of **birds of paradise**, unquestionably the most spectacularly adorned of all birds – if also some of the hardest to actually see.

The environment and conservation

The biggest threats to Indonesia's environment are modern economic and human pressures. Worst hit are those areas which, until now, have been by their very natures the least touched: primary rainforest and the marine environment.

Forests across the archipelago are rapidly retreating, cleared either to create new farmland, or to provide commercial timber. The problem here is not so much the logging itself, but rather the methods employed, which tend to strip forests back to bedrock either by dragging chains or simply setting **fire** to the trees. The latter method was almost certainly to blame for igniting the massive 1997–98 conflagrations in Kalimantan's forests (see p.820), which had been degraded to a lesser extent during the 1980s. In the short term, burning enriches the soil for cultivation – a method traditionally used on a far smaller scale by Kalimantan's Dayaks – but the nutrients are soon exhausted and, unless left to grow wild again, are not replaced. A side effect of logging is that it opens up new areas to **mining**, which, whether on a small or large scale, is an industry notorious for not clearing up after itself – witness the heavy-metal-laden Sungai Sekonyer in Kalimantan's southwest.

Once their habitat has gone, there's little chance for wildlife. Obvious species such as tigers or elephants may survive in zoos, but this ignores the demise of smaller, less appealing animals. Extinction in the wild may be permanent, even if the animal itself thrives in captivity and suitable reserves are later established. Young orang-utan, for example, need a lengthy education to teach them how to live in the wild; unless raised there, it's unlikely that they can be reintroduced at a later stage. Other factors affect successful reintroduction: the **Bali starling** is a common-enough cage bird, but attempts to re-establish a viable population in western Bali have been stymied by **collectors**. The demand for cage birds in Southeast Asia is a major drain on many species, particularly in Maluku and West Papua – populations of endemic parrots have declined rapidly in recent years.

While Indonesia's **seas** themselves remain clean, encouraging a healthy pearl industry, fishing practices are beginning to have a serious impact. The popularity of **reef bombing** is fading in the face of government pressure, but **drift-netting** seems to be on the increase, a method which – like bombing – catches everything, whether commercially useful or not. Unlike bombing, however, a good deal of commercial fishing in Indonesia is run by Japanese, Korean, Chinese, Singaporean and Taiwanese companies, who have no interest in preserving local fish stocks. The acute demand for shark's fin has seen populations almost wiped out in southeastern Maluku, and an increasing number of Indonesian vessels are being caught fishing in Australian waters as a result.

Conservation and the future

Indonesia has an impressive number of **national parks** and **reserves** covering every imaginable habitat. While these areas are not inviolate, they provide an excellent basis for preserving the archipelago's range of environments. The problem lies with ensuring that protection within these reserves is enforced – a difficult task, considering that many are remote from major population centres and effective policing is therefore almost impossible. Remoteness, and the practical difficulties involved in simply tracking down and seeing wildlife – even common species – in thick undergrowth, has also limited the commercial potential of **eco-tourism**. This means that most Indonesian reserves are not financially viable, and that government protection is altruistic – and so vulnerable to other pressures.

It's likely that the effect of Indonesia's economic downturn on its natural heritage will be two-sided. Development projects, such as the construction of new roads to, or through, wilderness areas, will slow down; at the same time, there will be an ever-growing need to earn export income from mining and timber resources. As Indonesia faces the twenty-first century, it remains to be seen how far its commitment to its environment is compromised by the country's uncertain economic future.

Books

While much has been written on the culture, temples and arts and crafts of Bali, there has been relatively little coverage of the rest of Indonesia. Early visitors produced a clutch of fascinating first-hand accounts of a now vanished world, and many of these are available through the OUP Asia imprint. Periplus is a specialist on the region, and produces a range of excellently written and photographed works about Indonesia, including a six-volume ecology series, cookbooks, a host of travel guides, and adventure guides on the best places to go diving, birding and surfing. Many of these books are published by Indonesian publishers – you may be able to order them from bookshops in your own country, but most are available in Indonesia. In the following reviews, o/p indicates the book is currently out of print; titles marked ★ are particularly recommended.

Travel

Benedict Allen *Into the Crocodile's Nest.* Allen treks alone through West Papua's forests in search of a certain tribe, fails dismally and has to add Papua New Guinea to his trip in order to fill a book.

David Attenborough *Zoo Quest for a Dragon* (o/p). A youthful Attenborough's erratic travels through the archipelago during the 1950s as a wildlife collector and filmmaker, peaking with the capture of a Komodo dragon.

Nigel Barley *Not a Hazardous Sport.* A humourous, double-sided culture-shock tale, as the anthropologist author visits Indonesia for the first time and persuades craftsmen from Sulawesi to return to London with him in order to build a traditional Torajan rice barn in the Museum of Mankind.

Vicki Baum *A Tale from Bali.* Sometimes moving, and always interesting, a semi-factual historical novel based on the events leading up to the 1906 *puputan* in Denpasar. It was written from the notes bequeathed to the author in 1937 by a Dutch doctor who had lived and worked in Sanur for several decades.

★ **Lawrence and Lorne Blair** *Ring of Fire.* Possibly the definitive account of a tour around the Indonesian archipelago. The photos are great, the tales are occasionally tall, but certainly not lacking in drama, atmosphere and a genuine passion for the country.

Carl Bock *Head Hunters of Borneo.* Taken with a pinch of salt, Bock's account of his trek into the unknown wilds of Kalimantan during the 1870s is an excellent read, though he gets carried away by the gorier side of Dayak tradition.

Peter Carey and G. Carter Bentley (eds) *East Timor at the*

Online travel bookstores

Abe Books (ⓦ www.abebooks.com) is a worthwhile site that lets you search for your title in new and secondhand bookshops worldwide, while Amazon (ⓦ www.amazon.co.uk and ⓦ www.amazon.com) is the world's biggest online bookstore. Ganesha Bookshop (ⓦ www.ganeshabooksbali.com) is Bali's best bookshop; located in Ubud, it stocks a good range of specialist books and offers an online ordering service.

Crossroads. A mixture of scholarly essays and personal accounts of the East Timor problem. The material is – as you might expect – mostly seen from the East Timorese perspective, but it remains an excellent, non-sensationalist document.

Anna Forbes *Unbeaten Tracks in Islands of the Far East*. Island life in remote corners of Maluku and Nusa Tenggara as observed by the resourceful wife of nineteenth-century naturalist Henry Forbes, as she battles rough living, bouts of malaria, and the attempted murder of her husband.

William Ingram *A Little Bit One O'Clock: Living with a Balinese Family* (Ersania Books, Ubud, Bali). A warm, funny and affectionate portrait of the author's life with an Ubud family in the 1990s. The warts-and-all approach makes a nice change from more impersonal sociological studies, yet you still learn a lot about the daily rituals and concerns of a modern Balinese community. Both the author and his adoptive family still live in Ubud.

Louise G. Koke *Our Hotel in Bali* (Pepper, Singapore). The engaging story of two young Americans who arrived in Bali in 1936 and decided almost immediately to build a hotel on Kuta beach, the first of its kind. The book describes a Bali that was just beginning to attract tourists, and also includes some great black-and-white photos from the time, some of which are displayed in the Neka Art Museum in Ubud (see p.575).

Carl Lumholtz *Through Central Borneo*. A dry cultural sketch of Kalimantan's Dayak tribes in the early twentieth century by this seasoned anthropologist.

Anna Matthews *Night of Purnama* (o/p). An evocative, moving and affectionate description of village life and characters of the early 1960s, focusing on events in Iseh and the surrounding villages, from the first eruption of Gunung Agung until the Matthews left in 1963.

George Monbiot *Poisoned Arrows: An Investigative Journey Through Indonesia*. The author travels through some of the less-well-known areas of West Papua, researching the effects of the Indonesian government's transmigration policy, and uncovers startling poverty and, in some places, deep hatred of the central government. Monbiot paints a grim picture of the new settlements to contrast sharply with the rural idyll of life before interference.

Hickman Powell *The Last Paradise*. Highly readable reflection of an American traveller's experiences in Bali in the late 1920s. Interesting accounts of village customs and temple festivals, plus a few spicy anecdotes.

Tim Severin *The Spice Island Voyage*. Rather downbeat account of Severin's travels around Maluku in the 1990s, following Wallace's trail in a traditional boat and finding Indonesia's wildlife and people on the brink of collapse.

Mark Shand *Skullduggery!* By the man best known for travelling across India on an elephant, with Goldie Hawn in tow. *Skullduggery!* is a 1990s *Boys Own*-style adventure, as Shand and a group of bored British dilettantes go to the Asmat region of West Papua looking for head-hunting trophies – and nearly leave their own behind.

Neville Shulman *Zen Explorations in Remotest New Guinea: Adventures in the Jungles and Mountains of Irian Jaya*. Even if you find Shulman's determination to find the zen in everything irritating, you can't escape his genuine delight and enthusiasm for his journey and his surroundings.

John Joseph Stockdale *Island of Java*. A travelogue describing the author's journey through Java during the first year of British rule in 1811. The book includes some interesting anecdotes regarding the tribulations of travel in the nineteenth century; overall, however, this tome is of more interest to students and fans of Indonesian history.

★ **K'tut Tantri** *Revolt in Paradise* (o/p). The extraordinary story of an extraordinary woman. British-born artist and adventurer Muriel Pearson – known in Bali as K'tut Tantri and in Java as Surabaya Sue – tells the astonishing tale of her fifteen years in Bali and Java. First living in close association with the raja of Bangli, then building one of the first hotels on Kuta beach, K'tut Tantri finally became an active member of the Indonesian Independence movement, for which she suffered two years' imprisonment and torture at the hands of the Japanese invaders.

Adrian Vickers (ed.) *Travelling to Bali: Four Hundred Years of Journeys*. Thought-provoking anthology which includes accounts by early Dutch, Thai and British adventurers, as well as excerpts from writings by the expat community in the 1930s, and the musings of late-twentieth-century visitors. The editor's extensive introductions to the pieces make interesting reading, but the extracts themselves merely whet the appetite.

Harry Wilcox *Six Moons in Sulawesi*. Immediately after World War II, a battle-weary Wilcox spent six months recuperating in Sulawesi's Tanah Toraja highlands, and wrote this warmly affectionate, sometimes gushy, portrait of the people he found there.

History

Nigel Barley *In the Footsteps of Stamford Raffles*. Barley follows Raffles' career through Indonesia and Malaysia, using the historical figure to compare the past with the present.

Charles Corn *The Scents of Eden: A Narrative of the Spice Trade*. Well-written historical account of the European power struggle to gain control of the lucrative spice trade in the East Indies.

Edwin M. Loeb *Sumatra, its History and People* (o/p). A classic 1935 account, and one of the few in-depth studies of the island. Perhaps too detailed for the average reader, and parts of the analysis have even been proved wrong since the book was published. Worth reading, however, if only because the book's introduction remains the best overview of Sumatra in existence.

★ **M.C. Ricklefs** *A History of Modern Indonesia Since c.1300*. Acknowledged as the most thorough study of Indonesian history, Ricklef's 300-page account is written in a rather dry and scholarly style, and with its comprehensive index is probably best used as a textbook to dip into rather than as a work to be read from start to finish.

John G. Taylor *Indonesia's Forgotten War: The Hidden History of East Timor*. Clear and incisive account of the disastrous events in East Timor, from the fifteenth century up to the present day, with the final chapter looking at possible future scenarios.

Culture and society

A.J. Bernet Kempers *Monumental Bali: Introduction to Balinese Archaeology and Guide to the Monuments*. A fairly highbrow analysis of Bali's temples and ruins, written by a Dutch ethnology and archeology professor. Worth reading if you have a serious interest in the historical sites.

Jean Couteau *Bali Today: Real Balinese Stories; Vol 1* (Spektra Communications, Bali). A fascinating little anthology of the author's newspaper columns written for the *Bali Post*. Much of the book reads like a juicy conversation with a well-informed gossip – topics range from the use of sexual innuendo in the Balinese language, to true tales of cross-cultural romance and observations on the impact of tourism.

Miguel Covurrubias *Island of Bali*. The Mexican artist and amateur anthropologist describes all aspects of life in Bali in the 1930s, from the daily routines of his adopted village household to the religious and philosophical meanings behind the island's arts, dramas and music. An early classic (first published in 1937) that's still as relevant and readable today.

Dr A.A.M. Djelantik *The Birthmark: Memoirs of a Balinese Prince*. This engaging autobiography tells the fascinating life story of the son of the last raja of Karangsamen. Djelantik, who was born in East Bali in 1919, became Bali's most respected and influential doctor, and still lives on the island today.

★ **Fred B. Eisemann Jr** *Bali: Sekala and Niskala Vols 1 and 2*. The fascinating and admirably wide-ranging cultural and anthropological essays of a contemporary American, thirty years resident in Bali. His pieces encompass everything from the esoteric rituals of Balinese Hinduism to musings on the popularity of the clove cigarette. Essential background reading for any interested visitor.

David J. Fox *Once a Century: Pura Besakih and the Eka Dasa Rudra Festival* (Penerbit Sinar Harapan, Citra, Indonesia). Fabulous colour pictures, and an erudite but readable text, make this the best introduction to Besakih both ancient and modern. It also includes careful and sympathetic accounts of the 1963 Eka Dasa Rudra festival and the eruption of Gunung Agung.

Gregor Krause *Bali 1912* (January Books, New Zealand). A reprinted edition of the original black-and-white photographs that inspired the first generation of arty expats to visit Bali. The pictures were taken by a young German doctor, and give unrivalled insight into Balinese life in the early twentieth century.

Hugh Mabbett *The Balinese* (Pepper, Singapore). An accessible collection of short anecdotal essays on various aspects of contemporary Balinese life, from the role of Bali's women to a discussion on the impact of tourism.

Scott Merrillees *Batavia*. Over 200 rare photos of nineteenth-century Batavia (Jakarta), mostly topographical, providing a fascinating portrait of the city's colourful past.

V.S. Naipaul *Beyond Belief – Islamic Conversions Among the Converted Peoples*. An account of Naipaul's travels to four Islamic nations, the first chapter of which deals with his time in Indonesia where he meets, among others, Abdurrahman Wahid, leader of the Islamic Nahdatul Ulama Party and the man who would become Indonesia's first democratic president. Overall, a worthwhile and absorbing investigation into the current state of Islam that also touches on the political and socioeconomic situation of the country.

Graham Saunders *The Simple Guide to Indonesia: Customs and Etiquette*. A succinct guide to avoiding offensive gaffes with plenty of interesting cultural insights.

Adrian Vickers *Bali: A Paradise Created*. Detailed, intelligent and highly readable account of the outside world's perception of Bali, the development of tourism and how events inside and outside the country have shaped the Balinese view of themselves as well as outsiders' view of them.

Natural history

Cubitt & Whitten *Wild Indonesia*. Plenty of good pictures and text in this overview of Indonesia's natural history, including coverage of main island groups and national parks.

Fred and Margaret Eisemann *Flowers of Bali*. A slim, fully illustrated handbook describing fifty of the most common flowers growing in Bali, with Latin, English, Indonesian and Balinese names given where possible.

★ **Paul Jepson and Rosie Ounsted** *Birding Indonesia: A Bird-watcher's Guide to the World's Largest Archipelago*. An excellent introduction to the subject, with plenty of good photographs, clear descriptions and practical detail. Suitable for beginners and experts alike.

John MacKinnon *Field Guide to the Birds of Java and Bali*. The most comprehensive field guide of its kind, with full-colour plates, useful pointers for amateur spotters, and detailed descriptions of the 820 species found on the four islands.

Victor Mason *Bali Bird Walks* (o/p). A delightful, highly personal offbeat guidebook to the Ubud area, focusing on the neighbourhood's flora and fauna, particularly the birds. The book describes over a dozen walks of varying lengths and difficulty. Available from Ubud bookshops or from the author's bar and restaurant, *The Beggar's Bush* in Campuhan, west Ubud.

Mary Nightingale *New Guinea, An Island Apart*. Excellent photographs and analysis of the unique and extraordinary Papuan flora and fauna, including generous sections on West Papua.

David Quammen *The Song of the Dodo*. The author retraces many of Alfred Wallace's footsteps in Maluku as he updates Wallace's notions of biogeography. Very accessible, and a heartfelt tribute to Wallace.

Wendy Veevers-Carter *Riches of the Rain Forest*. A user-friendly introduction to both common and unusual rainforest flora, including figs, rattans, durian and the extraordinary rafflesia.

★ **Alfred Russell Wallace** *The Malay Archipelago* (o/p). A thoroughly readable account of the eight years that Wallace – whose independent discovery of the theory of evolution by natural selection prompted Charles Darwin to publish his more famous *Origin of Species* – spent in Indonesia studying wildlife during the mid-nineteenth century.

Fiction

★ **Joseph Conrad** *Almayer's Folly*, *An Outcast of the Islands*, and *Victory*. In his time as a sailor, Conrad visited Indonesia several times and later set some of his novels there. These – the first two set in Kalimantan, the third in Surabaya and the remote island of Sam – are atmospheric pieces revolving around self-destructive characters forced into each others' company by circumstance.

Vern Cook (ed) *Bali Behind the Scenes: Recent Fiction from Bali* (Darma Printing, Australia). An interesting and insightful collection of short stories by contemporary Balinese and Javanese writers. Many of the stories explore the ways in which Bali is changing, highlighting the tensions between the generations and their different outlooks on traditions, families and westernization.

Odyle Knight *Bali Moon: A Spiritual Odyssey* (Sandstone Publishing, NSW, Australia). Riveting tale of an Australian woman's deepening involvement with the Balinese spirit world as her romance with a young Balinese priest draws her onto disturbing ground. Apparently based on true events.

Putu Oka Sukanta *The Sweat of Pearls: Short Stories about Women of Bali* (Darma Printing, NSW, Australia). All the stories in this slim volume were written by a man, which somewhat detracts from their authenticity, but the vignettes of village life and traditions are enlightening, and the author is a respected writer who spent many years in jail because of his political beliefs.

Arts, crafts and architecture

★ **Philip Cornwel-Smith** *Property of the Artist: Symon* (PT Sang Yang Seni, Ubud, Bali). A lively and hugely enjoyable monograph of the expat Ubud artist Symon (see p.576), which artfully interweaves the musings and bons mots of the painter with insights from his friends, models, collaborators and collectors.

Jacques Dumarcay *Borobudur*. Concentrates specifically on Indonesia's most famous monument. Its sister publication, *The Temples of Java*, is a slim but entertaining rundown of all the major historical temple complexes in Java, beginning with the earliest temples (on the Dieng Plateau) and continuing in chronological order through to Ceto and Sukuh.

Gianni Francione and Luca Invernizzi Tetoni *Bali Modern: The Art of Tropical Living*. A celebration of modern Balinese architecture, with sumptuous and tasteful reinventions of traditional themes; it also gives space over to the modern exuberance of Waterbom Park, the *Hard Rock Hotel* and even the Kuta strip.

Edward Frey *The Kris: Mystic Weapon of the Malay World*. A small but well-illustrated book outlining the history and making of the kris, along with some of the myths associated with this magical weapon.

John Gillow and Barry Dawson *Traditional Indonesian Textiles*. A beautifully photographed and accessible introduction to the *ikat* and batik fabrics of the archipelago, whether you are thinking of buying or just enjoying them in museums.

Brigitta Hauser-Schaüblin, Marie-Louise Nabholz-Kartaschoff and Urs Ramseyer *Balinese Textiles*. A thorough and gloriously photographed survey of

Balinese textiles and their role within contemporary society. Includes sections on the more common fabrics such as *endek*, *songket* and *kain poleng*, as well as introductions to some of the much rarer weaves including the *geringsing* of Tenganan.

Rio Helmi and Barbara Walker *Bali Style*. A sumptuously photographed glossy volume celebrating all things Balinese, from the humblest bamboo craftwork to some of the most fabulous buildings on the island. A good souvenir and an inspiration for potential visitors.

Garret Kam *Perceptions of Paradise: Images of Bali in the Arts* (Yayasan Dharma Seni Neka Museum, Bali). Ostensibly a guide to the paintings displayed in Ubud's Neka Art Museum, this is actually one of the best introductions to Balinese art so far published. Plenty of full-colour plates and wider references as well.

Idanna Pucci *Bhima Swarga: The Balinese Journey of the Soul*. Fabulously produced guide to the *Mahabharata* legends depicted on the ceiling of Klungkung's Kerta Gosa, illustrated with large, glossy colour photographs and a panel-by-panel description of the stories.

Hans Rhodius and John Darling *Walter Spies and Balinese Art* (Tropical Museum, Amsterdam, distributed in Britain by IBD Ltd). The biography of the German expat artist and musician Walter Spies, which discusses, in brief, his early life and influences and then takes up the controversial debate over the extent of Spies' influence on modern Balinese art, asking whether the received view is actually a colonialist view of art history.

Anne Richter *Arts and Crafts of Indonesia*. A general guide to the fabrics, carvings, jewellery and other folk arts of the archipelago, with some background on the practices involved.

★ **Haryati Soebadio and John Miksic (eds)** *Art of Indonesia*. A huge coffee-table book packed with gorgeous photographs of the collection at the National Museum in Jakarta. An excellent (though pricey) introduction to the archipelago and its varied cultures.

Tara Sosrowardoyo, Peter Schoppert and Soedarmadji Damais *Java Style*. A sumptuous volume in this glossy series, brilliantly and evocatively photographed, with illuminating descriptions of buildings and design all across the island, from ancient to modern.

Michael Tenzer *Balinese Music*. A well-pitched introduction to the delights and complexities of the gamelan, by an American composer who did a six-month stint at Batubulan's KOKAR high school of music and dance. It contains sections on theory, practice and history, as well as interesting anecdotes from expert Balinese musicians.

William Warren and Luca Invernizzi Tetoni *Balinese Gardens*. This gorgeously photographed, large-format coffee-table book concentrates mostly on modern gardens, but has fascinating and informative sections on Balinese flora, offerings, the role of plants and gardens in Balinese culture and classical gardens across the island.

Diving

Guy Buckles *Dive Sites of Indonesia*. An exhaustively researched, attractive and up-to-date guide for potential divers with good sections on Bali and Lombok. Especially strong on the practical details.

★ **Kal Muller et al** *Diving Indonesia*. This is the handbook for anybody wanting to dive in Indonesia. Written by experts, it's also exquisitely photographed and supplemented with clear, useful maps.

David Pickell and Wally Siagian *Diving Bali: The Underwater Jewel of Southeast Asia*. A beautifully photographed and detailed account of everything you'll ever need to know about diving in Bali. Full of anecdote, humour, advice and practical knowledge, as well as plenty of detailed maps.

Food and cookery

Heinz von Holzen and Lother Arsana *The Food of Bali*. Sumptuously illustrated paperback on all aspects of Balinese cuisine, including the religious and cultural background. The bulk of the book comprises recipes for local specialities – everything from snail soup to unripe-jackfruit curry.

★ **Wendy Hutton (ed)** *The Food of Indonesia: Authentic Recipes from the Spice Islands*. Excellent series with helpful preparation advice, stunning photography and carefully chosen recipes.

Sri Owen *Indonesian Regional Cooking*. Relatively few recipes, but an otherwise excellent book with plenty of theory, techniques and background to Indonesian cuisine.

★ **Jacqueline Piper** *Fruits of South-East Asia: Fact and Folklore* (o/p). Although only 94 pages long, this is an exhaustive, well-illustrated book, introducing all the fruits of the region, together with the influence they have had on the arts and crafts and the part they have played in religious and cultural practices.

Language

Language

Language

The national language of Indonesia is Bahasa Indonesia, although there are also over 250 native languages and dialects spoken throughout the archipelago. Until the 1920s, the lingua franca of government and commerce was Dutch, but the emerging independence movement adopted a form of Bahasa Malay as a more suitable revolutionary medium; by the 1950s this had crystallized into Bahasa Indonesia. Now taught in every school and widely understood across Indonesia, Bahasa Indonesia was a crucial means of unifying the new nation. The indigenous languages of Bali (see p.1090) and Lombok (see p.1091), are still spoken in the islands' villages.

Bahasa Indonesia is written in Roman script, has no tones and uses a fairly straightforward grammar – all of which makes it relatively easy for the visitor to get to grips with. The pocket-sized *Indonesian: A Rough Guide Phrasebook* makes a handy, comprehensive travelling companion, and includes an exhaustive dictionary of useful words as well as pronunciation details, some cultural hints, and information on grammar. Otherwise, try the *Berlitz Indonesian Phrase Book and Dictionary*, which can be supplemented by a ninety-minute cassette tape. Of the numerous teach yourself options, Sutanto Atmosumarto's *Colloquial Indonesian: A Comprehensive Language Course* (Routledge), including two 60-minute tapes, makes the best investment – an easy to follow step-by-step guide, complete with listening comprehension, written exercises and situational dialogues. Once you're in Indonesia, you might want to get hold of the portable – though definitely not pocket-sized – dictionary *Kamus Lengkap Inggeris–Indonesia, Indonesia–Ingerris* (Hasta Penerbit).

Grammar

Bahasa Indonesia uses the same subject-verb-object **word order** as in English. The easiest way to make a **question** is simply to add a question mark and use a rising intonation. **Nouns** have no gender and don't require an article. To make a noun **plural** you usually just say the noun twice, eg: *anak* (child), *anak-anak* (children). **Adjectives** always follow the noun, while **verbs** have no tenses. To indicate the past, prefix the verb with *sudah* (already) or *belum* (not yet); for the future, prefix the verb with *akan* (will). For example, *saya sudah makan* means "I have already eaten", *saya belum makan* "I haven't eaten yet", and *saya akan makan* "I will eat".

Pronunciation

Vowels and dipthongs

a as in a cross between f**a**ther and c**u**p

e sometimes as in **a**long; or as in p**ay**; or as in g**e**t; or sometimes omitted (*selamat* pronounced "slamat")

i either as in bout**i**que; or as in p**i**t

o either as in h**o**t; or as in c**o**ld

u as in b**oo**t

ai as in f**i**ne

au as in h**ow**

Consonants

Most are pronounced as in English, with the following exceptions:
c as in cheap
g always hard as in girl
k hard, as in English, except at the end of the word, when you should stop just short of pronouncing it. In written form, this is often indicated by an apostrophe, for example, *beso'* for *besok*.

Conversation

Selamat is the all-purpose greeting derived from Arabic, which communicates general goodwill. If addressing a married woman, it's polite to use the respectful term *Ibu* or *Nyonya*; if addressing a married man use *Bapak*.

Mau ke mana? (literally "want to where") is the usual opening gambit in any conversation, and means "where are you going?" The proper reply is *mau ke* (want to go to) followed by your intended destination. Other good answers are *saya jalan jalan* (I'm just walking) or *saya makan angin* (literally "I'm eating the wind"). The next question will be *darimana?* (from where), and relates to your nationality. Other keywords to listen out for in questions about nationality are *negera* (country) and *asal* (native). The response should be *dari Amerika/Ingerris/Ferancis* and so on.

You will probably also be asked about your **marital status**: *sudah kawin?* (already married?) *sudah ada isteri* or *suami?* (already have wife/husband?). The proper response is either *ja* ("yes") or *belum* ("not yet"); marriage is a natural goal for all Indonesians so a straight no is too blunt. From here, you'll be asked if you have children: *sudah ada anak?* If the answer is "yes", they'll want to know how many and how old – the suffix for years is *tahun*. When asking your age, people will use one of the "you" pronouns, with *berapa tahun?* ("how many years?"). To answer, say: *saya duapuluh tahun* ("I am twenty"). Another concern of Indonesians is your **religion**; listen out for questions with the word *agama* (religion) in them, such as *Agamamana?* The response might be: *Agama Catholik*. Whatever you do, don't try and tell anyone you have no religion – in Indonesia, this equates with communism, which is still utterly derided.

You may be asked if you can **speak Indonesian**: *bisa berbicara bahasa Indonesia?* The usual response is *saya belum lanca* ("I'm not yet fluent") or *sedikit sedikit* ("just a little"); the less confident should go for *ma'af tidak bisa* ("sorry, not at all").

Bahasa Indonesia words and phrases

Greetings and basic phrases

Good morning (5–11am) - **Selamat pagi**
Good day (11am–3pm) - **Selamat siang**
Good afternoon (3–7pm) - **Selamat sore**
Good evening (after 7pm) - **Selamat malam**
Good night - **Selamat tidur**
Goodbye - **Selamat tinggal**
See you later - **Sampai jumpa lagi**
Have a good trip - **Selamat jalan**
Welcome - **Selamat datang**
Enjoy your meal - **Selamat makan**
Cheers/Enjoy your drink - **Selamat minum**
How are you? - **Apa kabar?**
I'm fine - **Bagus/Kabar baik**
Please (requesting) - **Tolong**
Please (offering) - **Silakan**
Thank you (very much) - **Terima kasih (banyak)**
You're welcome - **Sama sama**

Sorry/Excuse me - **Ma'af**
No worries/Never mind - **Tidak apa apa**
Yes - **Ya**
No (with noun) - **Bukan**
Not (with verb) - **Tidak (sometimes pronounced tak)**
What is your name? - **Siapa nama anda?**
My name is - **Nama saya**
Where are you from? - **Dari mana?**
I come from - **Saya dari**
Do you speak English? - **Bisa bicara bahasa Inggris?**
I don't understand - **Saya tidak mengerti**
Do you have? - **Ada?**
I want/would like - **Saya mau**
I don't want it/No thanks - **Tidak mau**
What is this/that? - **Apa ini/itu?**
What? - **Apa?**
When? - **Kapan?**
Where? - **Dimana?**
Why? - **Mengapa?**
Who? - **Siapa?**
How? - **Berapa?**
Boyfriend or girlfriend - **Pacar**
Foreigner - **Turis**
Friend - **Teman**
Men/women - **Laki-laki/perempuan or wanita**
Another - **Satu lagi**
Beautiful - **Cantik**
Big/small - **Besar/kecil**
Clean/dirty - **Bersih/kotor**
Cold - **Dingin**
Expensive/inexpensive - **Mahal/murah**
Fast/slow - **Cepat/lambat**
Good/bad - **Bagus/buruk**
Hot (water/weather) - **Panas**
Hot (spicy) - **Pedas**
Hungry/thirsty - **Lapar/haus**
Ill/sick - **Sakit**
Married/single - **Kawin/bujang**
Open/closed - **Buka/tutup**
Tired - **Lelah**
Very much/a lot - **Banyak**

Pronouns

When addressing people, two multipurpose respectful tags you cannot overuse are *bu/ibu* (for women) and *pak/bapak* (for men). In Java, use *Mas* instead for men.

You (the most neutral and safest) - **anda**
You (familiar) - **engkau and kamu**
You (superpolite) - **tuan (sir), bu or pak**
You (to a young child) - **adik**
I - **saya**
He/she - **Ia/dia**
We/us/our - **kita**
We (but not the person you're addressing) - **kami**
They/them/their - **mereka**
This/these - **ini**
That/those - **itu**

Getting around

Where is the? - **dimana?**
I would like to go to the - **Saya mau pergi ke**
- airport - **lapangan terbang**
- bank - **bank**
- beach - **pantai**
- bemo/bus station - **terminal**
- city/downtown - **kota**
- hospital - **sakit**
- hotel - **losmen**
- market - **pasar**
- pharmacy - **apotik**
- police station - **kantor polisi**
- post office - **kantor pos**
- restaurant - **restoran/rumah makan/warung**
- shop - **toko**
- telephone office - **wartel/kantor telkom**
- tourist office - **kantor turis**
- village - **desa**

Bicycle - **Sepeda**
Bus - **Bis**
Car - **Mobil**
Entrance/exit - **Masuk/keluar**
Ferry - **Ferry**
Fuel (petrol) - **Bensin**
Horse cart - **Dokar/cidomo**
Motorbike - **Sepeda motor**
Motorbike taxi - **Ojek**
Taxi - **Taksi**
Ticket - **Karcis**

To drive - **Mengendarai**
To walk - **Jalan kaki**
To come/go - **Datang/pergi**
How far? - **Berapa kilometre?**
How long? - **Berapa jam?**
How much is the fare to? - **Berapa harga karcis ke?**
Where is this bemo going? - **Kemana bemo pergi?**
When will the bemo/ bus leave? - **Bila bemo/bis berangkut?**
Where is this? - **Dimana ini?**
Stop! - **Estop!**
Here - **Disini**
Right - **Kanan**
Left - **Kiri**
Straight on - **Terus**
Near - **Dekat**
Far - **Jauh**

Balinese

The Balinese language, **Bahasa Bali**, has three main **forms** (and dozens of less widespread variations) – High (*Ida*), Middle or Polite (*Ipun*), and Low (*la*). The speaker decides which form to use, depending on the caste of the person he or she is addressing and on the context. If speaking to family or friends, or to a low-caste (Sudra) Balinese, you use **Low Balinese**; if you are addressing a superior or a stranger, you use **Middle** or **Polite Balinese**; if talking to someone from a high caste (Brahman, Satriya or Wesya), or discussing religious affairs, you use **High Balinese.** If the caste is not immediately apparent, then the speaker will traditionally open the conversation with the euphemistic question "Where do you sit?", in order to elicit an indication of caste. However, in the last couple of decades there has been a move to popularize the use of the polite Middle Balinese form, and to disregard the caste factor wherever possible. Despite its numerous forms, Bahasa Bali is essentially a **spoken language**, with few official rules of grammar or syntax and hardly any textbooks or dictionaries. However, there is a useful if rather basic **primer** for any interested English-speaker, called *Bali Pocket Dictionary* by N Shadeg (Yayasan Dharma Bhakti Pertiwi), available from some bookshops on the island. All phrases and questions given below are shown in the Middle or Polite form.

Useful phrases

What is your name? - **Sira pesengan ragane?**
Where are you going? - **Lunga kija?**
Where have you been? - **Kija busan?**
How are you? - **Kenken kebara?**
How are things? - **Napa orti?**
I'm/things are fine - **Becik**
I am sick - **Tiang gele**
What is that? - **Napi punika?**
Yes - **Inggih, patut**
No - **Tan, nente**
Child - **Putra, putri**
Family - **Panyaman, pasa metonan**
Food - **Ajeng-ajengan, tetedan**
Friend - **Switra**
House- **Jeroan**
Husband - **Rabi**
Rice - **Pantu, beras, ajengan**
Wife - **Timpal, isteri**
Bad - **Corah**
Big - **Ageng**
Delicious - **Jaen**
Good - **Becik**
Small - **Alit**
To come - **Rauh, dateng**
To eat - **Ngajeng, nunas**
To go - **Lunga**
To sleep - **Sirep sare**
One - **Siki, diri**
Two - **Kalih**
Three - **Tiga**
Four - **Pat**
Five - **Lima**
Six - **Nem, enem**
Seven - **Pitu**
Eight - **Kutus**
Nine - **Sia**
Ten - **Dasa**
To come - **Rauh, dateng**
To eat - **Ngajeng, nunas**
To go - **Lunga**
To sleep - **Sirep sare**

Sasak

The language of Lombok is **Sasak**, a purely oral language which varies from one part of the island to another. Realistically, Bahasa Indonesia is more practical for travellers, but even a few words of Sasak are likely to be greeted with delight. The following – transcribed for the English-speaker – should get you started.

There's no Sasak equivalent to the Indonesian **greetings** *selamat pagi* and the like. If you meet someone walking along the road, the enquiry *Ojok um bay?* ("Where are you going?") serves this purpose, even if the answer is blatantly obvious.

Useful phrases

Where are you going? - **Ojok um bay?**
Just walking around - **Lampat-lampat**
I am going to Rinjani - **Rinjani wah mo ojok um bay**
Where is? - **Um bay tao?**
How are you? - **Berem bay khabar?**
I'm fine- **Bagus/solah**
I'm tired - **telah**
I'm thirsty - **goro**
I'm hungry - **lapar**
I'm hot - **beneng**
And you? - **Berem bay seeda?**
What are you doing? - **Upa gowey de?**
Nothing - **Ndarak**
See you (I'm going) - **Yak la low**
No problem - **Nday kambay kambay**
Go away! - **Nyeri too!**
Today - **Djelo sine**
Tomorrow - **Djema**
Yesterday - **Sirutsin**
Big/small - **Belek/kodek**
Dark/light - **Peteng/tenang**
Delicious - **Maik**
Fast/slow - **Betjat/adeng-adeng**
Heavy/light - **Berat/ringan**
Brother/sister - **Semeton mama/ semeton nine**
Child/grandchild - **Kanak/bai**
Daughter/son - **Kanak nine/kanak mame**
Friend - **Kantje**
Husband/wife - **Semame/senine**
How many children do you have? - **Pira kanak de?**
None - **Ndarak**
One - **Skek**
Two - **Dua**
Three - **Telu**
Four - **Empat**
Five - **Lima**
Six - **Enam**
Seven - **Pitook**
Eight - **Baluk**
Nine - **Siwak**
Ten - **Sepulu**

Accommodation and shopping

How much is? - **Berapa harga?**
single room - **kamar untuk satu orang**
double room - **kamar untuk dua orang**
Do you have a cheaper room? - **Ada kamar yang lebih murah?**
Can I look at the room? - **Boleh saya lihat kamar?**
To sleep - **Tidur**
To buy/sell - **Membeli/menjual**
Money - **Uang**
Is there? - **Apakah ada?**
air-conditioning - **AC**
bathroom - **kamar mandi**
breakfast - **makan pagi**
fan - **kipas**
hot water - **air panas**
mosquito net - **kelambu nyamuk**
swimming pool - **kolam renang**
toilet - **kamar kecil/wc** (pronounced **way say**)

Numbers

Zero - **Nol**
One - **Satu**
Two - **Dua**
Three - **Tiga**
Four - **Empat**
Five - **Lima**
Six - **Enam**
Seven - **Tujuh**
Eight - **Delapan**
Nine - **Sembilan**
Ten - **Sepuluh**
Eleven - **Sebelas**
Twelve - **Duabelas**
Thirteen - **Tigabelas**
Twenty - **Duapuluh**
Twenty-one - **Duapuluh satu**
Twenty-two - **Duapuluh dua**
Thirty - **Tigapuluh**

Forty - **Empatpuluh**
One hundred - **Seratus**
Two hundred - **Duaratus**
Three hundred - **Tigaratus**
One thousand - **Seribu**
Two thousand - **Duaribu**
Three thousand - **Tigaribu**
Ten thousand - **Sepuluhribu**
One hundred thousand - **Seratusribu**
One million - **Sejuta**
Two million - **Dua juta**

Time and days of the week

What time is it? - **Jam berapa?**
When does it open/close? - **Kapan dia buka/tutup?**
It's three o'clock - **jam tiga**
It's ten past four - **jam empat lewat sepuluh**
It's quarter to five - **jam lima kurang seperempat**
It's six-thirty - **jam setengah tujuh (literally "half to seven")**
in the morning - **pagi**
in the afternoon - **sore**
pm/in the evening - **malam**
Minute/hour - **Menit/jam**
Day - **Hari**
Week - **Minggu**
Month - **Bulan**
Year - **Tahun**
Today/tomorrow - **Hari ini/besok**
Yesterday - **Kemarin**
Now - **Sekarang**
Not yet - **Belum**
Never - **Tidak pernah**
Already - **Sudah**
Monday - **Hari Senin**
Tuesday - **Hari Selasa**
Wednesday - **Hari Rabu**
Thursday - **Hari Kamis**
Friday - **Hari Jumaat**
Saturday - **Hari Sabtu**
Sunday - **Hari Minggu**

A food glossary

General terms

Asam manis - Sweet and sour
Daftar makanan - Menu
Dingin - Cold
Enak - Delicious
Garpu - Fork
Gelas - Glass
Goreng - Fried
Makan - To eat
Makan malam - Dinner
Makan pagi - Breakfast
Makan siang - Lunch
Minum - Drink
Panas - Hot (temperature)
Pedas - Hot (spicy)
Piring - Plate
Pisau - Knife
Saya injin bayar - I want to pay
Saya seorang vegetaris - I am vegetarian
Saya tidak makan daging - I don't eat meat
Sendok - Spoon

Meat, fish and basic foods

Anjing - Dog
Ayam - Chicken
Babi - Pork
Bakmi - Noodles
Buah - Fruit
Es - Ice
Garam - Salt
Gula - Sugar
Ikan - Fish
Itik - Duck
Jaja - Rice cakes
Kambing - Goat
Kare - Curry
Kecap asam - Sour soy sauce
Kecap manis - Sweet soy sauce
Kepiting - Crab
Nasi - Rice
Paniki - Fruit bat
Petis - Fish paste
Sambal - Hot chilli sauce
Sapi - Beef
Soto - Soup
Tikkus - Rat
Telur - Egg
Udang - Prawn
Udang karang - Lobster

Everyday dishes

Ayam bakar - Fried chicken
Ayam goreng - Grilled chicken
Babi gulin - Balinese pork
Bakmi goreng - Fried noodles mixed with vegetables and meat
Bakso - Soup containing meatballs
Botok daging sapi - Spicy minced beef with tofu, tempeh and coconut milk
Cap cay - Mixed fried vegetables
Es campur - Fruit salad and shredded ice
Fu yung hai - Seafood omelette
Gado-gado - Steamed vegetables served with a spicy peanut sauce
Ikan bakar - Grilled fish
Ikan mas - Carp
Kangkung - Water convolvulus
Krupuk - Rice or cassava crackers, usually flavoured with prawn
Kue tiaw - Singaporean stir-fry of flat rice noodles and meat
Lalapan - Raw vegetables and sambal
Lawar - Balinese raw meat paste; also refers to a sea worm eaten in parts of Maluku
Lontong - Steamed rice in a banana-leaf packet
Lumpia - Spring rolls
Murtabak - Thick, dough pancake, often filled with meat
Nasi ayam - Boiled rice with chicken
Nasi campur - Boiled rice served with small amounts of vegetable, meat, fish and sometimes egg
Nasi goreng - Fried rice
Nasi gudeg - Rice with jackfruit and coconut milk curry
Nasi putih - Plain boiled rice
Nasi rames - Rice with vegetable and meat side dishes
Nasi rawon - Rice with soya-braised meat
Nasi soto ayam - Chicken-and-rice soup
Pisang goreng - Fried bananas
Rendang - Dry-fried beef and coconut-milk curry
Rijstaffel - Dutch/Indonesian dish made up of six to ten different meat, fish and vegetable dishes with rice
Rujak - Hot spiced fruit salad
Rujak petis - Vegetable and fruit in spicy peanut and shrimp sauce
Tahu goreng telur - Tofu omelette
Sate - Meat or fish kebabs served with a spicy peanut sauce
Soto ayam - Chicken soup
Soto daging - Beef soup
Soto makassar - Buffalo offal soup
Sayur bening - Soup with spinach and corn
Sayur lodeh - Vegetable and coconut-milk soup
Urap-urap/urap timum - Vegetables with coconut and chilli

Fruit

Apel - Apple
Belimbing - Starfruit
Buah anggur - Grapes
Jeruk manis - Orange
Jeruk nipis - Lemon
Kelapa - Coconut
Mangga - Mango
Manggis - Mangosteen
Nanas - Pineapple
Nangka - Jackfruit
Pisang - Banana
Salak - Snakefruit
Semangkha air - Watermelon
Sirsak - Soursop

Drinks

Air jeruk - Orange juice
Air jeruk nipis - Lemon juice
Air minum - Drinking water
Arak - Palm or rice spirit
Bir - Beer
Brem - Local rice beer
Kopi - Coffee
Kopi susu - White coffee
Sopi - Palm spirit
Susu - Milk
Teh - Tea
Tolong tanpa es - Without ice, please
Tolong tanpa gula - Without sugar, please
Tuak - Palm wine

Glossary

Adat Traditional law and custom.
Air terjun Waterfall.
Alkon Type of longboat.
Alun-alun Town square.
Andong Horse-drawn carriage.
Angkuta Minibus transport that plies routes inside a town's limits.
Anklung Musical instrument from Bali and Java, made from suspended bamboo tubes.
Arak Palm liquor.
Arjuna The most famous of the five Pandawa brothers, stars of the *Mahabharata*.
Baileu Meeting hall.
Bajaj Motorized rickshaw.
Balai Dayak meeting hall.
Bale Open-sided pavilion found in temples, family compounds and on roadsides, usually used as a resting place or shelter.
Balian (or *dukun*) Traditional faith healer, herbalist or witch doctor.
Balok Palm wine.
Banteng Wild cattle.
Bapak Father, also with its shortened form "pak", the usual address for an adult male.
Basir Dayak shaman.
Batik Cloth made by covering designs with wax, dying the whole cloth, melting off the wax (which has been protected from the dye) then reapplying the wax and redying.
Batu tulis Inscriptions in rock.
Becak Three-wheeled bicycle taxi.
Bemo Minibus.
Benhur Horse-drawn carriage (after the Charlton Heston epic).
Bensin Petrol.
Benteng Fortress.
Bhaga Traditional structure built to commemorate female ancestors.
Bhoma (or **Boma**) The son of the earth, who repels evil spirits and is most commonly represented as a huge open-mouthed face above temple gateways.
Bis Bus.
Bisj Totem pole.
Bissu Transvestite priests.
Brem Rice wine.
Bukit Hill.
Bunga Flower.
Bupati Village head.
Camat District head.
Cidomo Horse-drawn cart used as a taxi on Lombok.
Cirih (pinang) Betel nut, a mild narcotic originally of ritual significance, chewed by many women (and some men) up and down the archipelago, which stains the mouth and teeth bright red.
Dalang Storyteller/shaman, the operator of Javanese wayang kulit.
Danau Lake.
Dayak Indonesian term for the indigenous peoples of Kalimantan.
Debus player Self-mutilating Sundanese performer.
Desa Village.
Dokar Horse-drawn carts.
Doktor gigi Dentist.
Dongson Ancient bronze drums of Chinese origin.
Dukun Traditional healer.
Ekonomi Inexpensive option.
Endek (or **ikat**) Cloth in which the weft threads are dyed to the final pattern before being woven.
Galungan The most important Bali-wide holiday, held for ten days every 210 days in celebration of the triumph of good over evil.
Gamelan Indonesian orchestra.
Ganesh Hindu elephant-headed deity, remover of obstacles and god of knowledge.
Garuda Mythical Hindu creature – half-man and half-bird – and the favoured vehicle of the god Wisnu; featured in numerous sculptures and temple reliefs and as a character in several dance-dramas.
Gereja Church.
Gili Small island or atoll.
Gorengan Street vendor selling deep-fried snack food.
Gua Cave.
Gunung Mountain.

Hajj Pilgrimage to Mecca.

Hinggi Cloth shawl or sarong.

Ibu (bu) Mother, usual address for any adult woman.

Ikat Distinctive and complex weaving style.

Jaipongan West Javan dance originally practised by prostitutes and incorporating elements of Pencak Silat.

Jalan Street.

Java man *Homo erectus*; prehistoric inhabitant of Java, the fossilized remains of which have greatly influenced international theories of evolution.

Jimbeh Type of drum.

Kain Type of cloth.

Kamar kecil/way say Toilet.

Kampung Village.

Kantor Office, as in *kantor telkom* (telecom office) and *kantor pos* (post office).

Kebun Gardens.

Kepala desa/Kepala kampung Village head man.

Kepala sekola Schoolmaster.

Konfrontasi Sukarno's 1960s campaign against the West and Malaysia.

Kraton Walled royal residence.

Kretek Clove cigarettes.

Kris Traditional dagger, with scalloped blade edges, of great symbolic and spiritual significance.

Kulit kayu Cloth made out of beaten tree bark.

Kuningan The culminating day of the important ten-day *Galungan* festivities.

Legong Classical Balinese dance, performed by two or three pre-pubescent girls.

Lontar Spindly palm tree whose nectar is gathered by certain peoples of the east for sustenance, and whose dried leaves have been used for manuscripts for centuries.

Lopi Dugout canoe.

Lopo Beehive-shaped houses of West Timor.

Losmen Simple accommodation, usually family-run.

Lumbung Traditional Lombok barns.

Mahabharata Lengthy Hindu epic describing the battles between representatives of good and evil, and focusing on the exploits of the Pandawa brothers – the inspiration for a huge number of dance-dramas, paintings and sculptures.

Mandi Traditional scoop-and-slosh method of showering, often in open-roofed or "garden" bathrooms.

Meru Multi-tiered Hindu shrine with an odd number of thatched roofs (from one to eleven), which symbolizes the cosmic mountain Mahameru.

Mesjid Mosque.

Microlet Form of public transport, similar to a bemo.

Moko Dongson-style drums found in Alor.

Ngadhu Male equivalent of *Bhaga*.

Odalan Individual temple festival held to mark the anniversary of the founding of every temple on Bali.

Ojek Motorbike taxi.

Ora Komodo dragon.

Padmatiga Throne.

Pancasila The five principles of the Indonesian constitution: belief in one supreme god; the unity of the Indonesian nation; democracy; social justice; and humanitarianism. Symbolized by an eagle bearing a five-part crest.

Pasar baru New market.

Pasar senggkol Night market.

Pasar seni Literally art market, usually selling fabrics and sometimes artefacts and souvenirs.

Pasola Sumbanese ritual war.

Patola Ikat motif of regular stylized patterns, often used on cloths for regal persons.

Pelni National ferry company.

Pemangku Village priests.

Pencak silat Indonesia's martial art.

Penginapan Accommodation, sometimes a little less plush than a losmen.

Perada Type of textile.

Pete-pete Bus.

Pinisi High-masted wooden Bugis or Makassar schooner.

Pondok Guest house.

Prahu Traditional wooden fishing boat.

Pulau Island.

Puputan Ritual fight.

Rafflesia The world's largest bloom, pollinated by flies and with a strong smell.

Raja King or person of highest stature.

Ramayana Hugely influential Hindu epic, essentially a morality tale of the battles between good and evil – the source material for numerous dance-dramas, paintings and sculptures.

Rangda Legendary widow-witch who personifies evil and is most commonly depicted with huge fangs, a massive lolling tongue and pendulous breasts; features in carvings and in Balinese dance performances.

Raya Main or principal, as in Jalan Raya Ubud – the main Ubud road.

Rumah adat Traditional house.

Rumah makan Restaurant.

Rumah sakit Hospital.

Sandung Mausoleum.

Sanghyang Trance dance.

Sarong The anglicized generic term for any length of material wrapped around the lower body and worn by men and women.

Sasak Native of Lombok.

Sawah Terraced rice field.

Selat Strait.

Shophouse Shuttered building with living space upstairs and shop space on ground floor.

Songket Silk brocade often woven with real gold thread.

Sungai River.

Tau-Tau Torajan death carving.

Teluk Bay.

Toko Shop.

Topeng Wooden masks, and dances that use them.

Transmigration The controversial government policy of relocating people from overcrowded Java to other parts of the country.

Tsunami Japanese word meaning "pressure wave", usually related to earth tremors and volcanic eruptions.

Tuak Palm wine.

Wallacea The area to the east of the archipelago studied by Alfred Russell Wallace, marking the transition between Asian and Australasian flora and fauna.

Waria Transvestite priests.

Warpostel Private postal service.

Wartel Private telecom office.

Waruga Sarcophagus, Sulawesi.

Warung Foodstall or tiny street-side restaurant.

Warung kopi Coffee house.

Wisma Guesthouse.

Index

and small print

Index

map entries are in **colour**

C

D

E

F

G

H

I

J

K

INDEX

L

M

INDEX

P

Q

R

S

INDEX

U

V

W

Y

Twenty Years of Rough Guides

In the summer of 1981, Mark Ellingham, Rough Guides' founder, knocked out the first guide on a typewriter, with a group of friends. Mark had been travelling in Greece after university, and couldn't find a guidebook that really answered his needs.There were heavyweight cultural guides on the one hand – good on museums and classical sites but not on beaches and tavernas – and on the other hand student manuals that were so caught up with how to save money that they lost sight of the country's significance beyond its role as a place for a cool vacation. None of the guides began to address Greece as a country, with its natural and human environment, its politics and its contemporary life.

Having no urgent reason to return home, Mark decided to write his own guide. It was a guide to Greece that tried to combine some erudition and insight with a thoroughly practical approach to travellers' needs. Scrupulously researched listings of places to stay, eat and drink were matched by careful attention to detail on everything from Homer to Greek music, from classical sites to national parks and from nude beaches to monasteries. Back in London, Mark and his friends got their Rough Guide accepted by a farsighted commissioning editor at the publisher Routledge and it came out in 1982.

The Rough Guide to Greece was a student scheme that became a publishing phenomenon. The immediate success of the book – shortlisted for the Thomas Cook award – spawned a series that rapidly covered dozens of countries. The Rough Guides found a ready market among backpackers and budget travellers, but soon acquired a much broader readership that included older and less impecunious visitors. Readers relished the guides' wit and inquisitiveness as much as the enthusiastic, critical approach that acknowledges everyone wants value for money – but not at any price.

Rough Guides soon began supplementing the "rougher" information – the hostel and low-budget listings – with the kind of detail that independent-minded travellers on any budget might expect. These days, the guides – distributed worldwide by the Penguin Group – include recommendations spanning the range from shoestring to luxury, and cover more than 200 destinations around the globe. Our growing team of authors, many of whom come to Rough Guides initially as outstandingly good letter-writers telling us about their travels, are spread all over the world, particularly in Europe, the USA and Australia. As well as the travel guides, Rough Guides publishes a series of dictionary phrasebooks covering two dozen major languages, an acclaimed series of music guides running the gamut from Classical to World Music, a series of music CDs in association with World Music Network, and a range of reference books on topics as diverse as the Internet, Pregnancy and Unexplained Phenomena. Visit **www.roughguides.com** to see what's cooking.

Rough Guide Credits

Text editor: Fran Sandham & Claire Saunders
Series editor: Mark Ellingham
Editorial: Martin Dunford, Jonathan Buckley, Kate Berens, Ann-Marie Shaw, Helena Smith, Olivia Swift, Ruth Blackmore, Geoff Howard, Gavin Thomas, Alexander Mark Rogers, Polly Thomas, Joe Staines, Richard Lim, Duncan Clark, Peter Buckley, Lucy Ratcliffe, Clifton Wilkinson, Alison Murchie, Matthew Teller, Andrew Dickson, Sally Schafer (UK); Andrew Rosenberg, Yuki Takagaki, Richard Koss, Hunter Slaton (US)
Production: Susanne Hillen, Andy Hilliard, Link Hall, Helen Prior, Julia Bovis, Michelle Draycott, Katie Pringle, Zoë Nobes, Rachel Holmes, Andy Turner, Dan May
Cartography: Maxine Repath, Melissa Baker, Ed Wright, Katie Lloyd-Jones
Cover art direction: Louise Boulton
Picture research: Sharon Martins, Mark Thomas
Online: Kelly Martinez, Anja Mutic-Blessing, Jennifer Gold, Audra Epstein, Suzanne Welles, Cree Lawson (US)
Finance: John Fisher, Gary Singh, Edward Downey, Mark Hall, Tim Bill
Marketing & Publicity: Richard Trillo, Niki Smith, David Wearn, Chloë Roberts, Demelza Dallow, Claire Southern (UK); Simon Carloss, David Wechsler, Megan Kennedy (US)
Administration: Julie Sanderson, Karoline Densley

Publishing Information

This second edition published April 2003 by
Rough Guides Ltd,
80 Strand, London WC2R 0RL
345 Hudson St, 4th Floor,
New York, NY 10014, USA
Distributed by the Penguin Group
Penguin Books Ltd,
80 Strand, London WC2R 0RL
Penguin Putnam, Inc.
375 Hudson Street, NY 10014, USA
Penguin Books Australia Ltd,
487 Maroondah Highway, PO Box 257,
Ringwood, Victoria 3134, Australia
Penguin Books Canada Ltd,
10 Alcorn Avenue, Toronto, Ontario,
Canada M4V 1E4
Penguin Books (NZ) Ltd,
182–190 Wairau Road, Auckland 10,
New Zealand
Typeset in Bembo and Helvetica to an original design by Henry Iles.

Printed in Italy by LegoPrint S.p.A

1136pp includes index
A catalogue record for this book is available from the British Library

ISBN 1-85828-991-2

Help us update

We've gone to a lot of effort to ensure that the second edition of **The Rough Guide to Indonesia** is accurate and up to date. However, things change – places get "discovered", opening hours are notoriously fickle, restaurants and rooms raise prices or lower standards. If you feel we've got it wrong or left something out, we'd like to know, and if you can remember the address, the price, the time, the phone number, so much the better.

We'll credit all contributions, and send a copy of the next edition (or any other Rough Guide if you prefer) for the best letters. Everyone who writes to us and isn't already a subscriber will receive a copy of our full-colour thrice-yearly newsletter. Please mark letters: "**Rough Guide Indonesia Update**" and send to: Rough Guides, 80 Strand, London WC2R 0RL, or Rough Guides, 4th Floor, 345 Hudson St, New York, NY 10014. Or send an email to **mail@roughguides.com**

Have your questions answered and tell others about your trip at **www.roughguides.atinfopop.com**

Acknowledgements

Lesley Reader: I Nengah Parni, Made Wijana and Man for their endless patience, good driving; Jude Armstrong for the usual Candi Welcome; Elaine and Kath on Gili Air; Mark and Shirley for invaluable details; and everyone along the way who made it so pleasant. In the US, special thanks as always to Barbara Unger and Yau Sang Man.

Henry Stedman: Thanks to Erwin Posma (The Netherlands), Christiane Muller (Bunaken), Tommy Massie, Siddharta (Manado), Tina Melson and Nigel Thomas (Bunaken), Ben Farrar (Bau Bau), Kasim and Fiah (Bau Bau), Herry Carascallao (Makassar), Bradford M Sanders (Samarinda), Simon (UK), Ziggy (The Netherlands) and Paul (UK) for advice in Makassar, Graham Usher (Australia), Juliette Chan, Mattheus Rumbawar (Biak), Yuseman Usemahu (Wamena), Suyono and Gilang Albanjari (Kumai), Yoab Syatfle, Matias Runbruren (Manokwari), Wiwin Aryanti (Banjarmasin), Steve McLean (Canada), Mariska van Vreumingen (The Netherlands), Emily Fripp (UK), Stefan Merklein (Germany), Jean-Claude and Rauni Billaud (France), and Carol Findlay and Fergus (UK).

Arnold Barkhordarian: Thanks to all the staff at Bandar Lampung tourist info.

David Jardine: Thanks to Al, Jalan Jaksa character, for his help with Jakarta listings; Ina, my Dayak sweetheart from Pontianak, for her help with Pontianak maps; the expat crowd, in particular David Merrells (UK), Joel Friedman (US), Peter Sanders (Canada), John Miller (US), Hank Tegtmeiher (US), and Geoff McKell (Australia), for their encouragement.

Lucy Ridout: Thanks to Wayan Artana, Wayan Patrum in Sanur, Yos in Tanjung Benoa, and Bambang Supeno.

Graeme Steel: Many thanks to my parents for their support, to Peter Mudd, Ken Burns and Philip Krone for their encouragement, to Samsul Arifin for chasing up information that was hard to find, to Sumarno for keeping the home fires burning, to Jo, Fran and Helena at Rough Guides for their guidance, to all the wonderful people in Java who helped me, and to my trusty Jeep for taking me safely over thousands of kilometres of often difficult terrain.

Thanks from the editors to Rachel Holmes for picture layout and typesetting, Mark Thomas for picture research, Louise Boulton for the cover, Maxine Repath, Ed Wright and The Map Studio, Romsey, Hants for cartography, and David Price for proofreading.

SMALL PRINT

Readers' letters

Thanks to all the readers who took the trouble to write in with their comments and suggestions (and apologies to anyone whose name we've misspelt or omitted):

Roy and Audrey Bradford, Kristina Brodrick, Matt Dines, Richard Draycott, Mark Erdmann, L Goodhart, Angus GW, Kevin Heyne, Catherine Jenkins, Katy Jenkyns, Michael Kwek, Richard Lindsay, Odette, Mark Ogilvie, Whitney O'Neill, WA Osmond, Beata Pal, Natali Pride, Kathryn Sharpe, Rachel and Justin Small, Nettert Smit, Phillipa Stevens, Joe Stern.

Photo Credits

Cover Credits

Main front image Nusa Tenggara © Stone
Front top small image Borobudur © Stone
Front lower image Orang-utan © Stone
Back top photo Volcano, Java © Stone
Back lower picture Shadow puppets, Yogyakarta © Robert Harding

Colour introduction

Borobudur, Central Java © C. Bowman
Diver, Maluku © Louise Murray/Robert Harding
Raksasa decoration, Yogyakarta © Henry Stedman
Fruit juice vendor, Jakarta © P. Aithie/Ffotograff
Martapura Market, Kalimantan © CC/Trip
Wooden puppets © Patrick Lucero
Jakarta © Paul Van Riel/Robert Harding
Borobudur, Central Java © Mikihiko Ohta/Axiom
Abuolo tribe woman © Joe Beynon/Axiom
Match of the day, Kuta Beach © Chris Humphrey
Java © RH Productions/Robert Harding

Things not to miss

01 Gamelan music © Adina Tovy/Robert Harding
02 Prigi, East Java © Graeme Steel
03 Orang-utang © Henry Stedman
04 Bukittiuggi © Lesley Reader
05 Pura Luhur Batukau © Lesley Reader
06 Traditional house with kids and pig © Henry Stedman
07 Morning market © J Garrett/Trip
08 Tarsier © Patrick Lucero
09 Initiation leap, Pulau Nias © Macintyre/Hutchison Library
10 Floating market, Banjarmasin © Henry Stedman
11 View of Gunung Rinjani © Lesley Reader
12 Dani tribesman © George Wright/Axiom
13 Borobudur temple carving © Jacobs/Robert Harding
14 Gili Islands © Sang Man
15 Ramayana dance © C. Bowman/Robert Harding
16 Sunda Kelapa © C. Bowman/Axiom
17 Gunung Agung © Jim Holmes/Axiom
18 Cloth at market, Yogyakarta © Robert Francis/Robert Harding
19 Ubud © Sylvain Grandadam/Robert Harding
20 Bali fishing boat © G. Hellier/Robert Harding
21 Krakatau erupting © R. Belbin/Trip
22. Pasola festival © Henry Stedman
23 Surfing at "G-Land" © John Helper
24 Komodo dragon © Henry Stedman
25 Funeral ceremony © Jane Sweeney/Robert Harding
26 Bogor Botanical Gardens © Robert Francis/Hutchison Library
27 Padang Bai © Jake Fitzjones/Travel Ink
28 Pulau Belitung, South Sumatra © Lesley Reader
29 Snorkelling © Patrick Lucero
30 Gunung Bromo © C. Gray/Trip

Black and white photos

Sunda Kelapa © R. Nichols (p.84)
Al-Azhar mosque © Patricia Aithie/Ffotograff (p.97)
Fishermen, Pananjung Bay © J. Pugh/Trip (p.128)
Shadow puppets © Michael Macintyre/Hutchison Library (p.175)
Prambanan © C. Bowman/Robert Harding (p.186)
Borobudur © Mikihiko Ohta/Axiom (p.199)
Gotang puppets © J. Greenberg/Trip (p.245)
Gunung Bromo © P. Mercea/Trip (p.276)
Sulphur miner, Kawah Ijen © Giles Calidicott/Axiom (p.301)
Orang-utan sanctuary © Henry Stedman (p.342)
Entrance to mosque, Medan © Henry Stedman (p.367)
Minang roofs © Lesley Reader (p.392)
Bukittinggi © Lesley Reader (p.425)
Danau Ranau © Lesley Reader (p.468)
Bengkulu © Lesley Reader (p.479)
Pura Meduwe Karang © Lesley Reader (p.518)
Washing the salt off, Kuta beach, Bali © Jim Holmes/Axiom (p.537)
Pura Ulun Danu Bratan © Jim Holmes/Axiom (p.581)
Buffalo racing, Sumbawa © C. Marshall/Travel Ink (p.668)
Carved tombstone, Sumba © Stephen Backshall (p.681)
Traditional house © J. Sweeney/Trip (p.725)
Floating market at Banjarmasin © Henry Stedman (p.808)
Woodcarving outside longhouse, Mancong © Henry Stedman (p.841)
Snorkelling – © Henry Stedman (p.880)
Tanah Toraja house – © T. Bognar (p.901)
Yali men © W. Irian/Robert Harding (p.976)
Asats (fish on jetty), West Papua © G. Wright/Axiom (p.987)

Rough Guide computing & internet series

Plain speaking pocket guides to help you get the most out of your computer and the world wide web

£6.00/US$9.95. *Website Directory only available in the UK £3.99